HO

IN TRAINING 2013

123rd YEAR OF PUBLICATION

Raceform

INDEX TO GENERAL CONTENTS

Editor	Richard Lowther; Raceform Ltd., Compton, Newbury, RG20 6NL. Fax: 01635 578101 E-mail: richard.lowther@racingpost.com
Assistant Editor	Simon Turner
Production Editor	Adrian Gowling; Bloodstock Services, Weatherbys
Production Assistants	Weatherbys Bloodstock Services Department and Lucy Brown
Typesetting	Maggie Elvie; Printing Services, Weatherbys, Sanders Road, Wellingborough, NN8 4BX.
Orders	Raceform Ltd., Sanders Road, Wellingborough, Northants NN8 4BX. Tel: 01933 304858 www.racingpost.com/bookshop Fax: 01933 270300 E-mail: Shop@racingpost.com
Advertisements	Julian Brown; Raceform Ltd., Compton, Newbury, RG20 6NL. Tel: 01635 577603 E-mail: julian.brown@racingpost.com
ISBN	978-1-908216-83-0

Printed and bound by MPG PRINTGROUP, UK

© Raceform Ltd 2013

INDEX TO ADVERTISERS

2013

RACING FIXTURES

AND SALE DATES

(SUBJECT TO ALTERATION)

Flat fixtures are in **Black Type**; Jump in Light Type; Irish in *Italic*;
asterisk (☆) indicates an evening or Twilight meeting;
† indicates an All Weather meeting. Sale dates are at foot of fixtures

MARCH

Sun	Mon	Tues	Wed	Thur	Fri	Sat
31 *Cork* *Fairyhouse* **Musselburgh** Plumpton Towcester					**1** Doncaster *Dundalk*†☆ **Lingfield Park**† Newbury **Wolverhampton**†☆	**2** Doncaster Kelso **Lingfield Park**† *Navan* Newbury
3 Huntingdon *Leopardstown* Sedgefield	**4** Ffos Las **Kempton Park**† Southwell	**5** Exeter Newcastle **Southwell**†	**6** Catterick Bridge *Downpatrick* Fontwell Park **Kempton Park**†☆ **Lingfield Park**†	**7** Carlisle *Clonmel* **Southwell**† Wincanton **Wolverhampton**†☆	**8** Ayr *Dundalk*†☆ Leicester Sandown Park **Wolverhampton**†☆	**9** Ayr Chepstow *Gowran Park* Sandown Park **Wolverhampton**†
10 Market Rasen *Naas* Warwick	**11** Plumpton Stratford-on-Avon Taunton	**12** Cheltenham Sedgefield **Southwell**† **Wolverhampton**†☆	**13** Cheltenham Huntingdon **Kempton Park**†☆ **Southwell**†	**14** Cheltenham Hexham Towcester **Wolverhampton**†☆	**15** Cheltenham *Dundalk*☆ Fakenham **Lingfield Park**† **Wolverhampton**†☆	**16** *Down Royal* Ffos Las Kempton Park *Limerick* **Lingfield Park**† Uttoxeter **Wolverhampton**†☆
17 Carlisle *Limerick* **Lingfield Park**† Wexford	**18** **Kempton Park**† *Navan* Southwell **Wolverhampton**†	**19** Exeter **Southwell**†† **Wolverhampton**†	**20** Haydock Park **Kempton Park**†☆ Newcastle Warwick	**21** Chepstow *Cork*☆ Huntingdon **Kempton Park**†☆ **Wolverhampton**†	**22** **Doncaster** *Dundalk*†☆ Newbury Sedgefield **Wolverhampton**†☆	**23** Bangor-on-Dee **Doncaster** *Gowran Park* Kelso Newbury Stratford-on-Avon Doncaster (Newbury) Sale
24 *Curragh* *Downpatrick* **Lingfield Park**† Wincanton	**25** **Lingfield Park**† Taunton Towcester Fasig-Tipton Sale	**26** Fontwell Park **Lingfield Park**† **Southwell**††	**27** *Leopardstown*☆ **Lingfield Park**† **Southwell**†† Wetherby **Wolverhampton**†☆ Goffs (Kempton) Sale	**28** *Clonmel*☆ Ffos Las Ludlow **Wolverhampton**†	**29**	**30** Carlisle *Cork* Haydock Park **Kempton Park**† **Musselburgh** Newton Abbot

APRIL

Sun	Mon	Tues	Wed	Thur	Fri	Sat
	1	**2**	**3**	**4**	**5**	**6**
	Cork Fairyhouse Fakenham Huntingdon Newcastle Plumpton **Redcar Warwick Yarmouth**	Exeter Fairyhouse **Kempton Park**† **Southwell**†	*Dundalk*☆ **Kempton Park**†☆ **Lingfield Park**† **Southwell**† Wetherby	Aintree **Lingfield Park**† Taunton *Thurles*☆ **Wolverhampton**†☆	Aintree *Dundalk*☆ **Leicester** Sedgefield **Wolverhampton**†☆	Aintree Chepstow **Lingfield Park**† *Navan* **Newcastle** **Wolverhampton**†☆
			Fasig-Tipton Sale			
7	**8**	**9**	**10**	**11**	**12**	**13**
Ascot *Curragh* Hexham *Limerick*	Kelso **Kempton Park**† **Wolverhampton**†	Carlisle *Gowran Park*☆ **Pontefract Southwell**†	**Catterick Bridge** **Kempton Park**†☆ **Lingfield Park**† **Nottingham**	Fontwell Park **Kempton Park**†☆ *Limerick*☆ Ludlow Wincanton	Chepstow **Lingfield Park**† Wetherby **Wolverhampton**†☆	**Doncaster** **Kempton Park**† Stratford-On-Avon *Tramore* Uttoxeter
Keeneland Sale	*Keeneland Sale*					
14	**15**	**16**	**17**	**18**	**19**	**20**
Ffos Las *Leopardstown* Market Rasen *Tramore*	**Newcastle Redcar Windsor**	Exeter Fairyhouse Kempton Park **Southwell**†	**Beverley** Cheltenham **Kempton Park**†☆ Newmarket	Cheltenham **Newmarket Ripon** *Tipperary*☆ **Wolverhampton**†☆	Ayr **Bath**☆ Fontwell Park **Newbury** *Southwell*☆ *Wexford*☆	Ayr Bangor-On-Dee *Naas* **Newbury** *Nottingham*☆ **Thirsk** **Wolverhampton**†☆
		Tattersalls Sale	*Tattersalls Sale* *Cheltenham Sale*	*Tattersalls Sale*		
21	**22**	**23**	**24**	**25**	**26**	**27**
Navan Stratford-on-Avon Wincanton	*Cork*☆ Hexham **Kempton Park**† **Pontefract** **Windsor**☆ **Wolverhampton**†☆	Ffos Las Newton Abbot *Punchestown*☆ Towcester☆ **Wolverhampton**† *Yarmouth*☆	**Catterick Bridge** **Epsom Downs** Perth *Punchestown*☆ Sedgefield☆ Taunton☆	**Beverley** **Brighton**☆ **Newcastle**☆ Perth *Punchestown*☆ **Wolverhampton**†	*Chepstow*☆ **Doncaster** Perth Plumpton☆ *Punchestown*☆ **Sandown Park**	*Doncaster*☆ *Haydock Park*☆ **Leicester** Market Rasen *Punchestown* **Ripon** Sandown (mixed)
Tattersalls (IRE) Sale Doncaster Sale	*Doncaster Sale Ascot Sale*	*Doncaster Sale*		*Goffs Sale*		
28	**29**	**30**				
Gowran Park Ludlow Wetherby	Kelso **Lingfield Park**†☆ Towcester **Windsor**☆ **Wolverhampton**†	*Ballinrobe*☆ **Bath** Exeter☆ **Lingfield Park**† Worcester☆ **Yarmouth**				

MAY

Sun	Mon	Tues	Wed	Thur	Fri	Sat
			1 Ascot Cheltenham☆ **Kempton Park**☆ **Pontefract** Southwell Ascot Sale	**2** Brighton☆ **Lingfield Park**† **Redcar** Sedgefield Taunton☆ *Tipperary*☆ Tattersalls Sale	**3** Bangor-On-Dee☆ **Chepstow** *Dundalk*☆ Fontwell Park☆ *Kilbeggan*☆ **Lingfield Park**† **Musselburgh** Tattersalls Sale	**4** Doncaster☆ **Goodwood** Hexham☆ *Limerick* **Newmarket** Thirsk Uttoxeter
5 Hamilton Park *Limerick* **Newmarket** Salisbury *Sligo*	**6** Bath **Beverley** *Curragh* *Down Royal* Flos Las **Kempton Park**† **Warwick** Windsor	**7** Ayr **Brighton** **Catterick Bridge**☆ Exeter☆ Fakenham	**8** Chester *Gowran Park*☆ Kelso **Kempton Park**†☆ **Newcastle**☆ **Southwell**† Cheltenham Sale	**9** Chester *Clonmel*☆ **Goodwood** Newton Abbot **Southwell**☆ Wincanton☆	**10** Ascot☆ **Chester** *Cork*☆ *Downpatrick*☆ **Hamilton Park**☆ **Lingfield Park** Market Rasen **Nottingham**☆ Ripon☆ Baden-Baden Sale	**11** Ascot **Haydock (Mixed)** Hexham **Lingfield Park** **Nottingham** *Punchestown* **Thirsk**☆ **Warwick**☆ Arqana Sale
12 *Killarney* *Leopardstown* Plumpton Worcester	**13** **Doncaster** *Killarney*☆ **Musselburgh** Towcester☆ **Windsor**☆ **Wolverhampton**† Doncaster Sale	**14** **Beverley** **Chepstow**☆ *Killarney*☆ Sedgefield **Southwell**☆ Wincanton Doncaster Sale	**15** Bath☆ Fontwell Park Naas☆ Perth☆ Uttoxeter **York** Doncaster Sale	**16** Fontwell Park☆ Ludlow☆ **Newmarket**☆ Perth **Salisbury** *Tipperary*☆ **York** Doncaster Sale	**17** Aintree☆ **Hamilton Park**☆ *Kilbeggan*☆ Newbury Newmarket **York** Doncaster Sale	**18** Bangor-on-Dee **Doncaster**☆ Newbury **Newmarket** Thirsk Uttoxeter☆ *Wexford*
19 *Limerick* Market Rasen *Navan* **Ripon** Stratford-On-Avon	**20** Leicester☆ Newton Abbot **Redcar** *Roscommon*☆ **Southwell**† **Windsor**☆ Fasig-Tipton Sale	**21** **Brighton** **Newcastle** **Nottingham** **Pontefract**☆ Towcester☆ Fasig-Tipton Sale	**22** Huntingdon **Kempton Park**†☆ **Lingfield Park** *Sligo*☆ **Southwell**† Worcester☆	**23** *Clonmel*☆ **Goodwood** **Haydock Park** **Salisbury**☆ **Sandown Park**☆ Wetherby Goresbridge Sale	**24** **Catterick Bridge**☆ *Cork*☆ **Goodwood** **Haydock Park** **Musselburgh**☆ Towcester☆ **Yarmouth** Goresbridge Sale	**25** Cartmel☆ **Chester** *Curragh* Flos Las☆ **Goodwood** **Haydock Park** **York**
26 *Curragh* Fontwell Park Kelso Uttoxeter	**27** *Ballinrobe*☆ **Carlisle** Cartmel **Leicester** **Redcar** Windsor	**28** *Ballinrobe*☆ **Leicester** **Lingfield Park**☆ Newton Abbot **Redcar** **Yarmouth**☆	**29** **Beverley** Cartmel Fontwell Park **Kempton Park**†☆ **Nottingham** *Punchestown*☆	**30** *Gowran Park* **Hamilton Park** **Lingfield Park** **Sandown Park**☆ Wetherby☆ **Wolverhampton**†	**31** Bath☆ **Catterick Bridge** *Down Royal*☆ **Epsom Downs** **Goodwood**☆ Market Rasen *Tramore*☆ Cheltenham Sale	

JUNE

Sun	Mon	Tues	Wed	Thur	Fri	Sat
30						**1**
Curragh **Salisbury** Uttoxeter **Windsor**						Doncaster **Epsom Downs** Hexham **Lingfield Park**☆ **Musselburgh** **Newcastle**☆ *Tramore* Worcester
2	**3**	**4**	**5**	**6**	**7**	**8**
Fakenham *Kilbeggan* *Listowel* Southwell	**Carlisle**☆ **Chepstow** **Leicester** *Listowel* *Naas* **Windsor**☆	Hexham☆ **Lingfield Park**† **Ripon** **Yarmouth**☆	Ayr *Fairyhouse*☆ **Kempton Park**†☆ Newton Abbot **Ripon**☆ **Southwell**†	Ayr **Brighton** Ftos Las **Sandown Park**☆ *Tipperary*☆ Worcester☆	Bath *Downpatrick*☆ **Haydock Park**☆ *Leopardstown*☆ **Lingfield Park** **Newmarket** **Pontefract**☆ Stratford-on-Avon☆	Beverley **Catterick Bridge** **Chester** **Haydock Park** *Navan* **Newbury**☆ **Newmarket** Stratford-on-Avon☆
					Ascot Sale	
9	**10**	**11**	**12**	**13**	**14**	**15**
Curragh **Nottingham** *Perth*	**Brighton** Newton Abbot *Roscommon*☆ Southwell☆ **Windsor**☆	Fontwell Park **Lingfield Park**☆ *Roscommon*☆ **Salisbury** Worcester☆	**Beverley** *Fairyhouse*☆ **Hamilton Park**☆ **Haydock Park** **Kempton Park**☆ **Yarmouth**	Haydock Park☆ *Leopardstown*☆ **Newbury** **Nottingham** Uttoxeter☆ **Yarmouth**	Aintree☆ **Chepstow** *Clonmel*☆ **Goodwood**☆ **Musselburgh** *Navan*☆ **Sandown Park** **York**	Bath Hexham **Leicester**☆ *Limerick*☆ **Lingfield Park**☆ **Musselburgh** **Sandown Park** **York**
			Goffs Sale	Goffs Sale		
16	**17**	**18**	**19**	**20**	**21**	**22**
Cork Doncaster **Salisbury**	**Carlisle** **Kempton Park**† **Warwick**☆ **Windsor**☆	**Ascot** **Brighton**☆ **Kempton Park**†☆ *Sligo*☆ Stratford-On-Avon **Thirsk**	**Ascot** **Hamilton Park** **Kempton Park**† **Ripon**☆ Uttoxeter *Wexford*☆	**Ascot** Ftos Las☆ **Leicester**☆ *Leopardstown*☆ **Lingfield Park**†☆ **Ripon** **Warwick**	**Ascot** *Down Royal*☆ **Goodwood**☆ *Limerick*☆ Market Rasen **Newmarket**☆ Redcar	**Ascot** Ayr *Down Royal* **Haydock Park**☆ **Lingfield Park**☆ **Newmarket** Redcar
23	**24**	**25**	**26**	**27**	**28**	**29**
Gowran Park Hexham **Pontefract** Worcester	**Chepstow** *Kilbeggan*☆ **Thirsk**☆ **Windsor**☆ **Wolverhampton**†	*Ballinrobe*☆ **Beverley** **Brighton** **Newbury**☆ Newton Abbot☆	Bath☆ **Carlisle** **Kempton Park**†☆ *Naas*☆ **Salisbury** Worcester	Hamilton Park☆ **Leicester**☆ Newcastle *Tipperary*☆ **Warwick** **Yarmouth**	Chester☆ *Curragh*☆ Doncaster **Musselburgh** Newcastle☆ **Newmarket**☆ **Yarmouth**	Chester *Curragh* Doncaster☆ **Lingfield Park**☆ Newcastle **Newmarket** Windsor
				Tattersalls (IRE) Sale	Tattersalls (IRE) Sale	

JULY

Sun	Mon	Tues	Wed	Thur	Fri	Sat
	1	**2**	**3**	**4**	**5**	**6**
	Ffos Las☆ Pontefract Windsor☆ Wolverhampton†	Bath☆ Brighton *Gowran Park*☆ **Hamilton Park** Stratford-On-Avon☆	Catterick Bridge Chepstow☆ *Fairyhouse*☆ Kempton Park†☆ Perth Worcester	Epsom Downs☆ Haydock Park *Leopardstown*☆ Newbury☆ Perth Yarmouth	*Bellewstown*☆ **Beverley**☆ **Doncaster** **Haydock Park**☆ Sandown Park Warwick *Wexford*☆	*Bellewstown*☆ **Beverley**☆ Carlisle☆ **Haydock Park** Leicester Nottingham☆ **Sandown Park**
		Arqana Sale	*Arqana Sale*	*Arqana Sale*		
7	**8**	**9**	**10**	**11**	**12**	**13**
Ayr *Bellewstown* Limerick Market Rasen	Ayr Newton Abbot **Ripon**☆ *Roscommon*☆ **Windsor**☆	Pontefract *Roscommon*☆ **Southwell**†☆ Uttoxeter☆ **Wolverhampton**†	Catterick Bridge Kempton Park†☆ Lingfield Park *Naas*☆ Worcester☆ **Yarmouth**	Bath☆ **Doncaster** Epsom Downs☆ *Leopardstown*☆ **Newmarket** **Warwick**	Ascot Chepstow☆ Chester☆ *Cork*☆ *Dundalk*† **Newmarket** York	Ascot Chester *Downpatrick* Hamilton Park☆ **Newmarket** Salisbury☆ *Tipperary* York
		Tattersalls Sale	*Tattersalls Sale* *Goresbridge Sale*	*Tattersalls Sale* *Goresbridge Sale*	*Tattersalls Sale*	
14	**15**	**16**	**17**	**18**	**19**	**20**
Fairyhouse Perth *Sligo* Southwell Stratford-On-Avon	Ayr *Killarney*☆ **Newton Abbot** **Windsor**☆ **Wolverhampton**†☆	Bath **Beverley** Kempton Park†☆ *Killarney*☆ **Yarmouth**☆	Catterick Bridge *Killarney*☆ **Lingfield Park** **Sandown Park**☆ Uttoxeter Worcester	Brighton **Doncaster**☆ Epsom Downs☆ Hamilton Park *Killarney* **Leicester** *Leopardstown*☆	Hamilton Park☆ **Haydock Park** *Kilbeggan*☆ Newbury **Newmarket**☆ Nottingham Pontefract☆	Cartmel *Curragh* **Haydock Park**☆ **Lingfield Park**☆ Market Rasen Newbury **Newmarket** Ripon
	Fasig-Tipton Sale	*Ascot Sale*				
21	**22**	**23**	**24**	**25**	**26**	**27**
Curragh Newton Abbot **Redcar** Stratford-On-Avon *Tipperary*	Ayr *Ballinrobe*☆ **Beverley**☆ Cartmel **Windsor**☆	*Ballinrobe*☆ Bangor-On-Dee☆ Ffos Las☆ **Musselburgh** Southwell	Catterick Bridge **Leicester**☆ **Lingfield Park**† *Naas*☆ **Sandown Park**☆ Worcester	Bath Brighton☆ **Doncaster**☆ Epsom Downs☆ *Leopardstown*☆ *Limerick*☆ **Sandown Park** Yarmouth	Ascot Chepstow☆ *Down Royal*☆ Newmarket☆ Thirsk Uttoxeter *Wexford*☆ York☆	Ascot **Lingfield Park**☆ Newcastle Newmarket Salisbury☆ *Wexford* York
28	**29**	**30**	**31**			
Ascot Carlisle Pontefract	Ayr *Galway*☆ Uttoxeter☆ **Windsor**☆ **Wolverhampton**†	Beverley *Galway*☆ **Goodwood** Perth☆ Worcester☆ **Yarmouth**	*Galway*☆ **Goodwood** **Leicester**☆ Perth **Redcar** **Sandown Park**☆			

AUGUST

Sun	Mon	Tues	Wed	Thur	Fri	Sat
				1	**2**	**3**
				Epsom Downs☆ Ffos Las☆ *Galway* Goodwood Nottingham *Stratford-On-Avon*	Bangor-On-Dee Bath☆ *Galway*☆ Goodwood Musselburgh☆ Newmarket☆ Thirsk	Doncaster *Galway* Goodwood Hamilton Park☆ Lingfield Park☆ Newmarket *Newton Abbot* Thirsk
4	**5**	**6**	**7**	**8**	**9**	**10**
Chester *Galway* Market Rasen Newbury	Carlisle☆ *Cork* *Naas* Ripon Windsor☆ Wolverhampton† *Doncaster Sale* *Fasig-Tipton Sale*	Catterick Bridge *Cork*☆ Ffos Las Kempton Park†☆ Ripon☆ *Roscommon*☆ *Doncaster Sale* *Fasig-Tipton Sale*	Brighton Kempton Park†☆ Newcastle Pontefract *Sligo*☆ Yarmouth☆ *Doncaster Sale*	Brighton☆ Chepstow☆ Haydock Park *Leopardstown*☆ Sandown Park☆ *Sligo*☆ Southwell†☆ Yarmouth *Tattersalls (IRE) Sale*	Brighton Haydock Park☆ Lingfield Park† Musselburgh Newmarket☆ *Tipperary*☆ *Tattersalls (IRE) Sale*	Ascot *Ayr*☆ Haydock Park *Kilbeggan*☆ Lingfield Park☆ Newmarket Redcar *Fasig-Tipton Sale*
11	**12**	**13**	**14**	**15**	**16**	**17**
Curragh *Downpatrick* Leicester Windsor *Fasig-Tipton Sale*	Ayr *Ballinrobe*☆ Thirsk☆ Windsor☆ Wolverhampton† *Arqana Sale*	Carlisle Nottingham☆ *Stratford-On-Avon*☆ Worcester	Beverley Ffos Las *Gowran Park*☆ Kempton Park†☆ Salisbury Yarmouth☆	Beverley Chepstow☆ *Fontwell Park*☆ *Leopardstown*☆ Newmarket Salisbury *Tramore*☆	Catterick Bridge☆ Newbury Newcastle Newmarket☆ Nottingham *Tramore*☆	Chester Doncaster Lingfield Park☆ Market Rasen☆ Newbury Newmarket Perth Ripon *Tramore*☆ *Arqana Sale*
18	**19**	**20**	**21**	**22**	**23**	**24**
Dundalk† Pontefract Southwell *Tramore* *Arqana Sale*	*Roscommon*☆ Thirsk Windsor☆ Wolverhampton†☆ Worcester *Arqana Sale*	Brighton Leicester☆ *Sligo*☆ Worcester☆ Yarmouth *Arqana Sale*	*Bellewstown*☆ Lingfield Park Musselburgh *Newton Abbot*☆ Warwick☆ York	Bath *Bellewstown*☆ Ffos Las *Newton Abbot* *Tipperary*☆ Wolverhampton†☆ York	Ffos Las (Mixed) Goodwood☆ Hamilton Park☆ *Kilbeggan*☆ Newcastle☆ Newmarket *Wexford*☆ York	Cartmel *Curragh* Goodwood Newmarket Redcar☆ Windsor☆ York
25	**26**	**27**	**28**	**29**	**30**	**31**
Beverley *Cork* Goodwood Yarmouth	Bangor-On-Dee Cartmel Chepstow *Downpatrick* Epsom Downs Huntingdon Newcastle Ripon Warwick *Fasig-Tipton Sale*	*Ballinrobe*☆ Epsom Downs Ripon Sedgefield☆ Southwell†☆ *Ascot Sale*	Carlisle Catterick Bridge Kempton Park†☆ *Killarney*☆ Southwell†☆ Worcester *Doncaster Sale*	*Fontwell Park* Hamilton Park Kempton Park†☆ *Killarney*☆ Lingfield Park☆ *Stratford-On-Avon* *Doncaster Sale*	Chester *Down Royal*☆ *Killarney*☆ Salisbury☆ Sandown Park Thirsk Wolverhampton†☆ *Baden-Baden Sale*	Bath☆ Beverley Chester *Killarney* Market Rasen☆ *Newton Abbot* Sandown Park *Baden-Baden Sale*

SEPTEMBER

Sun	Mon	Tues	Wed	Thur	Fri	Sat
1 **Brighton** *Curragh* Newton Abbot	**2** **Brighton** **Ffos Las** **Hamilton Park** *Roscommon☆*	**3** **Goodwood** *Laytown☆* **Leicester** **Musselburgh**	**4** **Bath** *Gowran Park☆* **Kempton Park†☆** **Lingfield Park** Southwell	**5** *Clonmel☆* **Haydock Park** **Kempton Park†☆** **Salisbury** Sedgefield	**6** **Chepstow** **Haydock Park** **Kempton Park†☆** *Kilbeggan☆* **Newcastle**	**7** **Ascot** **Haydock Park** **Kempton Park†** Leopardstown Stratford-On-Avon **Thirsk** **Wolverhampton†☆**
8 *Dundalk†* Fontwell Park **York**	**9** **Brighton** *Galway☆* Huntingdon Perth Keeneland Sale	**10** *Galway☆* **Leicester** **Redcar** Worcester Keeneland Sale	**11** **Carlisle** **Doncaster** *Galway☆* **Kempton Park†☆** Uttoxeter Keeneland Sale	**12** **Chepstow** **Doncaster** **Epsom Downs** **Wolverhampton†☆** Doncaster Sale Keeneland Sale	**13** Bangor-On-Dee **Doncaster** *Down Royal☆* **Sandown Park** **Wolverhampton†☆** Doncaster Sale Keeneland Sale	**14** **Bath** **Chester** *Curragh* **Doncaster** **Kempton Park†☆** **Lingfield Park** Keeneland Sale
15 **Bath** *Curragh* **Ffos Las** *Listowel* Keeneland Sale	**16** **Brighton** *Listowel* **Musselburgh** **Wolverhampton†** Keeneland Sale	**17** **Chepstow** *Listowel* **Thirsk** **Yarmouth** Keeneland Sale	**18** **Beverley** **Kempton Park†☆** *Listowel* **Sandown Park** **Yarmouth** Keeneland Sale	**19** **Ayr** **Kempton Park†☆** *Listowel* **Pontefract** **Yarmouth** Keeneland Sale	**20** **Ayr** *Listowel* **Newbury** **Newcastle** **Wolverhampton†☆** SGA Sale Keeneland Sale	**21** **Ayr** **Catterick Bridge** *Listowel* **Newbury** **Newmarket** **Wolverhampton†☆** SGA Sale Keeneland Sale
22 *Gowran Park* **Hamilton Park** Plumpton Uttoxeter Keeneland Sale	**23** *Fairyhouse* **Hamilton Park** **Kempton Park†** **Leicester** Tattersalls (IRE) Sale	**24** *Ballinrobe* **Beverley** **Lingfield Park†** Newton Abbot Tattersalls (IRE) Sale	**25** **Goodwood** **Kempton Park†☆** Perth **Redcar**	**26** **Newmarket** Perth **Pontefract** **Wolverhampton†☆**	**27** *Downpatrick* *Dundalk†☆* **Haydock Park** **Newmarket** **Wolverhampton†☆** Worcester	**28** **Chester** **Haydock Park** Market Rasen *Navan* **Newmarket** **Ripon** **Wolverhampton†☆**
29 *Curragh* **Epsom Downs** **Musselburgh**	**30** **Bath** **Hamilton Park** Newton Abbot *Roscommon☆* Fasig-Tipton Sale					

IT'S SHOWTIME

BONUS WINNERS
TAKE A BOW

OCTOBER

Sun	Mon	Tues	Wed	Thur	Fri	Sat
		1 **Ayr** Chepstow Sedgefield Goffs Sale	**2** **Kempton Park**†☆ **Newcastle** **Nottingham** **Salisbury** *Sligo* Goffs Sale	**3** Bangor-On-Dee *Clonmel* **Southwell**† **Warwick** **Wolverhampton**†☆ Goffs Sale	**4** *Ascot* *Dundalk*†☆ Fontwell Park Gowran Park Hexham **Wolverhampton**†☆ Goffs Sale	**5** **Ascot** Fontwell Park *Gowran Park* **Newmarket** **Redcar** **Wolverhampton**†☆ Arqana Sale
6 Huntingdon Kelso *Tipperary* Uttoxeter	**7** **Pontefract** Windsor **Wolverhampton**† Fasig-Tipton Sale	**8** **Brighton** **Catterick Bridge** **Leicester** *Tipperary* Tattersalls Sale Ascot Sale	**9** **Kempton Park**†☆ Ludlow *Navan* **Nottingham** Towcester Tattersalls Sale	**10** **Ayr** Exeter **Kempton Park**☆ *Tramore* Worcester Tattersalls Sale	**11** Carlisle *Dundalk*†☆ Newton Abbot **Wolverhampton**†☆ **York** Tattersalls Sale	**12** Chepstow *Fairyhouse* Hexham **Newmarket** **Wolverhampton**†☆ **York**
13 *Curragh* *Flos Las* **Goodwood** *Limerick*	**14** **Musselburgh** **Salisbury** Windsor Tattersalls Sale	**15** Huntingdon **Leicester** **Newcastle** Tattersalls Sale Goresbridge Sale	**16** **Kempton Park**†☆ **Lingfield Park**† **Nottingham** *Punchestown* Wetherby Tattersalls Sale Goresbridge Sale	**17** **Brighton** **Kempton Park**☆ *Punchestown* Uttoxeter Wincanton Tattersalls Sale Baden-Baden Sale	**18** Cheltenham *Downpatrick* *Dundalk*†☆ **Haydock Park** **Redcar** **Wolverhampton**†☆ Baden-Baden Sale	**19** **Ascot** **Catterick Bridge** Cheltenham *Cork* Kelso **Wolverhampton**†☆ Baden-Baden Sale
20 **Bath** *Cork* Kempton Park *Naas*	**21** Plumpton **Pontefract** Windsor Arqana Sale Fasig-Tipton Sale	**22** Exeter **Lingfield Park**† Yarmouth Arqana Sale Fasig-Tipton Sale	**23** Fontwell Park **Kempton Park**†☆ *Navan* **Newmarket** Worcester Arqana Sale Fasig-Tipton Sale	**24** Carlisle Ludlow Southwell *Thurles* **Wolverhampton**†☆ Goffs Sale	**25** **Doncaster** *Dundalk*†☆ Fakenham **Newbury** **Wolverhampton**†☆ Goffs Sale	**26** Aintree Chepstow **Doncaster** *Leopardstown* **Newbury** Stratford-On-Avon *Wexford* **Wolverhampton**†☆
27 Aintree *Galway* *Wexford* Wincanton	**28** Bangor-On-Dee *Galway* **Leicester** *Naas* **Redcar** Tattersalls Sale	**29** **Catterick Bridge** *Flos Las* Yarmouth Tattersalls Sale	**30** **Ayr** Haydock Park **Kempton Park**†☆ **Nottingham** *Punchestown* Tattersalls Sale	**31** *Clonmel* **Kempton Park**†☆ **Lingfield Park**† Sedgefield Stratford-On-Avon Tattersalls Sale		

NOVEMBER

Sun	Mon	Tues	Wed	Thur	Fri	Sat
					1	**2**
					Down Royal *Dundalk†☆* **Newmarket** Uttoxeter Wetherby **Wolverhampton†☆**	Ascot Ayr *Down Royal* **Newmarket** Wetherby
					Tattersalls Sale	
3	**4**	**5**	**6**	**7**	**8**	**9**
Carlisle *Cork* Huntingdon *Leopardstown*	Kempton Park Plumpton **Wolverhampton†**	Exeter **Redcar** Southwell†	Chepstow *Fairyhouse* **Kempton Park†☆** **Nottingham** Warwick	**Lingfield Park†** Musselburgh *Thurles* Towcester **Wolverhampton†☆**	*Dundalk†☆* Fontwell Park Hexham Musselburgh **Wolverhampton†☆**	**Doncaster** Kelso *Naas* Sandown Park Wincanton
	Doncaster Sale Keeneland Sale					
Keeneland Sale	Fasig-Tipton Sale	Doncaster Sale *Keeneland Sale*	Doncaster Sale *Keeneland Sale*	Ascot Sale *Keeneland Sale*	*Keeneland Sale*	*Keeneland Sale*
10	**11**	**12**	**13**	**14**	**15**	**16**
Ftos Las *Limerick* Market Rasen *Navan*	Carlisle **Kempton Park†** Southwell	Huntingdon Lingfield Park Sedgefield	Bangor-On-Dee *Dundalk†☆* Exeter **Kempton Park†☆** **Lingfield Park†**	*Clonmel* **Kempton Park†☆** Ludlow **Southwell†** Taunton	Cheltenham *Dundalk†☆* **Lingfield Park†** Newcastle **Wolverhampton†☆**	Cheltenham **Lingfield Park†** *Punchestown* Uttoxeter Wetherby **Wolverhampton†☆**
					Tattersalls (IRE) Sale *Cheltenham Sale*	
Tattersalls (IRE) Sale *Keeneland Sale*	*Tattersalls (IRE) Sale* *Keeneland Sale*	*Tattersalls (IRE) Sale* *Keeneland Sale*	*Tattersalls (IRE) Sale* *Keeneland Sale*	*Tattersalls (IRE) Sale* *Keeneland Sale*	*Keeneland Sale* *SGA Sale*	*Tattersalls (IRE) Sale* *Keeneland Sale* *SGA Sale*
17	**18**	**19**	**20**	**21**	**22**	**23**
Cheltenham *Cork* Fontwell Park *Punchestown*	Leicester Plumpton **Wolverhampton†**	Fakenham Lingfield Park **Southwell†** *Wexford*	*Fairyhouse* Hexham **Kempton Park†☆** **Lingfield Park†** Warwick	Chepstow **Kempton Park†☆** Market Rasen *Thurles* Wincanton	Ascot *Dundalk†☆* Ftos Las Haydock Park **Wolverhampton†☆**	Ascot Gowran Park Haydock Park Huntingdon **Lingfield Park†** **Wolverhampton†☆**
Tattersalls (IRE) Sale	Goffs Sale *Arqana Sale*	Goffs Sale *Arqana Sale*	Goffs Sale	Goffs Sale	Goffs Sale	Goffs Sale
24	**25**	**26**	**27**	**28**	**29**	**30**
Exeter *Navan* Towcester	Kempton Park Ludlow **Wolverhampton†**	Lingfield Park Sedgefield **Southwell†**	*Dundalk†☆* Fontwell Park **Kempton Park†☆** **Lingfield Park†** Wetherby	**Kempton Park†☆** Newbury Taunton *Thurles* Uttoxeter	Doncaster *Dundalk†☆* Musselburgh Newbury **Wolverhampton†☆**	Bangor-On-Dee *Fairyhouse* Newbury Newcastle Towcester **Wolverhampton†☆**
						Tattersalls Sale Doncaster *(Newbury) Sale*
Goffs Sale	Tattersalls Sale		Tattersalls Sale	Tattersalls Sale	Tattersalls Sale	

DECEMBER

Sun	Mon	Tues	Wed	Thur	Fri	Sat
1 Carlisle *Fairyhouse* Leicester	**2** **Kempton Park†** Plumpton **Wolverhampton†**	**3** Sedgefield Southwell **Wolverhampton†**	**4** Catterick Bridge **Kempton Park†☆** **Lingfield Park†** Ludlow	**5** *Clonmel* Leicester Market Rasen Wincanton **Wolverhampton†☆**	**6** *Dundalk†☆* Exeter **Lingfield Park†** Sandown Park **Wolverhampton†☆**	**7** Aintree Chepstow *Navan* Sandown Park Wetherby **Wolverhampton†☆**
	Tattersalls Sale Fasig-Tipton Sale	Tattersalls Sale	Tattersalls Sale	Tattersalls Sale	Tattersalls Sale	Arqana Sale
8 *Cork* Kelso *Punchestown* Warwick	**9** **Lingfield Park†** Musselburgh **Wolverhampton†**	**10** Fontwell Park **Southwell†** Uttoxeter	**11** *Dundalk†☆* Hexham **Kempton Park†☆** Leicester **Lingfield Park†**	**12** Huntingdon **Kempton Park†☆** Newcastle Taunton *Tramore*	**13** Bangor-On-Dee Cheltenham *Downpatrick* *Dundalk†☆* **Southwell†** **Wolverhampton†☆**	**14** Cheltenham Doncaster *Fairyhouse* Lingfield Park **Southwell†** **Wolverhampton†☆**
Arqana Sale	Fasig-Tipton Sale Arqana Sale	Ascot Sale Arqana Sale	Doncaster Sale		Cheltenham Sale	
15 Carlisle *Navan* Southwell	**16** Ffos Las Plumpton **Wolverhampton†**	**17** Catterick Bridge Fakenham **Southwell†**	**18** **Kempton Park†☆** **Lingfield Park†** Ludlow Newbury	**19** Exeter **Kempton Park†☆** **Southwell†** Towcester	**20** Ascot *Dundalk†☆* **Southwell†** Uttoxeter **Wolverhampton†☆**	**21** Ascot Haydock Park **Lingfield Park†** *Navan* Newcastle
		Goffs Sale				
22 Bangor-On-Dee Lingfield Park *Thurles*	**23**	**24**	**25**	**26** *Down Royal* Ffos Las Fontwell Park Huntingdon Kempton Park *Leopardstown* *Limerick* Market Rasen Sedgefield Towcester	**27** Kempton Park Leicester *Leopardstown* *Limerick* **Southwell†** Wetherby **Wolverhampton†☆** Wetherby Wincanton **Wolverhampton†**	**28** Catterick Bridge Chepstow *Leopardstown* *Limerick* **Lingfield Park†** Newbury
29 Doncaster Kelso *Leopardstown* *Limerick* **Southwell†**	**30** Haydock Park **Lingfield Park†** Taunton	**31** **Lingfield Park†** *Punchestown* Uttoxeter Warwick				

DATES OF PRINCIPAL RACES
(SUBJECT TO ALTERATION)

JANUARY

Dipper Novices' Steeple Chase (Cheltenham)..1st
victorchandler.com Steeple Chase (Handicap) (Cheltenham)..1st
E. B. F. "High Sheriff of Gloucestershire's" "Junior" Standard Open National Hunt Flat Race (Cheltenham)..............1st
Holden Plant Chase (Tramore)...1st
Phil Sweeney Chase (Thurles)...3rd
32Red Novices' Hurdle Race (Registered As The Tolworth Hurdle Race) (Sandown Park)..5th
32Red Mares Hurdle Race (Sandown Park)..5th
Slaney Novices' Hurdle (Naas)..6th
The William Hill Lanzarote Hurdle Race (Handicap) (Kempton Park)...12th
Neptune Investment Management Leamington Novices' Hurdle Race (Warwick)...12th
Betfred Classic Steeple Chase (A Handicap) (Class 1) (Warwick)...12th
Juvenile Hurdle (Punchestown)...12th
Foxrock Handicap Chase (Navan)...13th
Coolmore E.B.F. Mares Novices' Chase (Thurles)...17th
Kinloch Brae Chase (Thurles)..17th
Victor Chandler Steeple Chase (Registered As The Clarence House Steeple Chase) (Ascot)...................................19th
1942 Was A Vintage Year Mares' Hurdle Race (Registered As The Warfield Mares' Hurdle Race) (Ascot)................19th
Bet With Your Mobile At victorchandler.com Holloway's Hurdle Race (A Limited Handicap) (Ascot).........................19th
williamhill.com Supreme Novice Hurdle Trial (Registered As The Rossington Main Novices' Hurdle)(Haydock Park).....19th
stanjames.com Champion Hurdle Trial (Haydock Park)..19th
Altcar Novices' Steeple Chase (Haydock Park)..19th
Peter Marsh Steeple Chase (A Limited Handicap) (Haydock Park)...19th
Limestone Lad Hurdle (Naas)..19th
Woodlands Novices' Chase (Naas)...19th
Dan Moore Memorial Handicap Steeple Chase (Fairyhouse)..20th
Mares Novices' Hurdle (Fairyhouse)...20th
Galmoy Hurdle (Gowran Park)..24th
Goffs Theyestes Handicap Chase (Gowran Park)...24th
Neptune Investment Management Novices' Hurdle Race (Registered As The Classic Novices' Hurdle Race) (Cheltenham).....26th
Cleeve Hurdle Race (Cheltenham)..26th
Argento Steeple Chase (Registered As The Cotswold Steeple Chase) (Cheltenham)..26th
JCB Triumph Hurdle Trial (Registered As The Finesse Juvenile Hurdle Race) (Cheltenham)...................................26th
Murphy Group Steeple Chase (A Handicap) (Cheltenham)...26th
The Sky Bet Chase (A Handicap) (formerly The Great Yorkshire Chase)...26th
Lightning Novices' Steeple Chase (Doncaster)..26th
Albert Bartlett Novices' Hurdle Race (Registered As The River Don) (Doncaster)..26th
OLBG Doncaster Mares' Hurdle Race (Doncaster)...26th
Boylesports Handicap Hurdle (Leopardstown)...26th
boylesports.com Killiney Novices' Chase (Leopardstown)..26th
Leopardstown Chase (Leopardstown)...26th
BHP Irish Champion Hurdle (Leopardstown)...27th
Frank Ward Solicitors Arkle Novices' Chase (Leopardstown)...27th
Synergy Security Solutions Golden Cygnet Novices' Hurdle (Leopardstown)..27th

FEBRUARY

William Hill Welsh Champion Hurdle Race (Ffos Las)..2nd
Betfred "Double Delight" Contenders Hurdle Race (Sandown Park)...2nd
Betfred "Goals Galore" Challengers Novices' Steeple Chase (Registered As The Scilly Isles Novices' Steeple Chase)
(Sandown Park)..2nd
Betfred Heroes Handicap Hurdle Race (Sandown Park)..2nd
Totepool Towton Novices' Steeple Chase (Wetherby)..2nd
Grand National Trial Handicap Chase (Punchestown)...3rd
boylesports.com Tied Cottage Chase (Punchestown)...3rd
Moscow Flyer Novices' Hurdle (Punchestown)..3rd
Powerstown Novice Hurdle (Clonmel)...7th
Betfair Denman Steeple Chase (Newbury)...9th
Betfair Super Saturday Game Spirit Steeple Chase (Newbury)..9th
Betfair Mobile For Best Prices Bumper (A Standard Open National Hunt Flat Race) (Newbury)................................9th
Betfair Hurdle Race (Handicap) (Newbury)..9th
Warwick Kingmaker Novices' Steeple Chase (Warwick)...9th
Deloitte Novices' Hurdle (Leopardstown)...9th
Dr P J Moriarty Novices' Chase (Leopardstown)..9th
Spring 4yo Hurdle (Leopardstown)..9th
Hennessy Gold Cup (Leopardstown)...9th
Bathwick Tyres Taunton Novices Hurdle Race (Exeter)...10th
Jane Seymour Mares' Novices' Hurdle (Sandown Park)...15th
Betfair Ascot Steeple Chase (Ascot)..16th

Weatherbys Bloodstock Insurance Steeple Chase 16th
Sodexo Prestige Reynoldstown Novices' Steeple Chase (Ascot) 16th
Albert Bartlett Novices' Hurdle Race (Registered As The Prestige Novices' Hurdle Race) (Haydock Park) 16th
Betfred Hurdle Race (Registered As The Rendlesham Hurdle Race) (Haydock Park) 16th
Betfred Grand National Trial (A Handicap Steeple Chase) (Haydock Park) 16th
Bathwick Tyres Kingwell Hurdle Race (Wincanton) 16th
Red Mills Trial Hurdle (Gowran Park) 16th
Red Mills Chase (Gowran Park) 16th
Ten Up Novices' Chase (Navan) 17th
Flyingbolt Novices' Chase (Navan) 17th
Ladbrokes Boyne Hurdle (Navan) 17th
Sidney Banks Memorial Novices' Hurdle (Huntingdon) 21st
bluesquare.com Cleves Stakes (Lingfield Park) 23rd
Get Your Bet On At bluesquare.com Winter Derby Trial Stakes (Lingfield Park) 23rd
Betfred Eider Steeplechase (Newcastle) 23rd
williamhill.com Supreme Novice Hurdle Trial (Kempton Park) 23rd
Adonis Juvenile Hurdle Race (Kempton Park) 23rd
Pendil Novices' Steeple Chase (Kempton Park) 23rd
Racing Plus Steeple Chase (Handicap) (Kempton Park) 23rd
Winning Fair Juvenile Hurdle (Fairyhouse) 23rd
At The Races Bobbyjo Chase (Fairyhouse) 23rd
National Spirit Hurdle Race (Fontwell Park) 24th
Paddy Power Johnstown Novices' Hurdle (Naas) 24th
Paddy Power Nas na Riogh Novices' Chase (Naas) 24th
Paddy Power Newlands Chase (Naas) 24th
Michael Purcell Novices' Hurdle (Thurles) 28th

MARCH

Doncaster Mares' Novices' Hurdle Race (Doncaster) 2nd
William Hill Grimthorpe Chase (A Handicap Steeplechase) (Doncaster) 2nd
Totepool Premier Kelso Novices' Hurdle Race (Kelso) 2nd
Greatwood Gold Cup Handicap Steeple Chase (Newbury) 2nd
Carrickmines Handicap Chase (Leopardstown) 3rd
European Breeders' Fund paddypower.com 'National Hunt' Novices' Handicap Hurdle Final (Sandown Park) 9th
Paddy Power Imperial Cup Handicap Hurdle Race (Sandown Park) 9th
E.B.F. / DBS Mares' Standard Open National Hunt Flat Race (Sandown Park) 9th
The New William Hill Iphone App Lady Wulfruna Stakes (Wolverhampton) 9th
William Hill Lincoln Trial Handicap Stakes (Wolverhampton) 9th
Shamrock Handicap Chase (Gowran Park) 9th
Leinster National (Naas) 10th
Directors Plate Novices' Chase (Naas) 10th
Kingsfurze Novices' Hurdle (Naas) 10th
William Hill Supreme Novices' Hurdle Race (Cheltenham) 12th
Racing Post Arkle Challenge Trophy Novices' Steeple Chase (Cheltenham) 12th
The Stan James Champion Hurdle Challenge Trophy (Cheltenham) 12th
OLBG Mares Hurdle Race (Registered As David Nicholson Mares' Hurdle Race) (Cheltenham) 12th
Jardine Lloyd Thompson Specialty Handicap Steeple Chase (Cheltenham) 12th
Pulteney Land Investments Novices' Handicap Steeple Chase (Cheltenham) 12th
Glenfarclas Handicap Steeplechase (A Cross Country Steeple Chase) (Cheltenham) 12th
Neptune Investment Management Novices' Hurdle Race (Registered As The Baring Bingham Novices' Hurdle Race)
(Cheltenham) 13th
RSA Novices' Steeple Chase (Cheltenham) 13th
John Oaksey 143rd National Hunt Steeple Chase (Amateur Riders' Novices' Steeple Chase) (Cheltenham) 13th
sportingbet.com Queen Mother Champion Steeple Chase (Cheltenham) 13th
Weatherbys Champion Bumper (A Standard Open National Hunt Flat Race) (Cheltenham) 13th
Fred Winter Juvenile Novices' Handicap Hurdle Race (Cheltenham) 13th
Coral Cup (A Handicap Hurdle Race) (Cheltenham) 13th
Ladbrokes World Hurdle (Cheltenham) 14th
Ryanair Steeple Chase (Registered As The Festival Trophy Steeple Chase) (Cheltenham) 14th
Jewson Novices' Steeple Chase (Registered As The Golden Miller Novices' Steeple Chase) (Cheltenham) 14th
Byrne Group Plate (A Handicap Steeple Chase) (Cheltenham) 14th
Pertemps Final (Handicap) Hurdle Race 14th
Fulke Walwyn Kim Muir Challenge Cup Handicap Steeple Chase (Cheltenham) 14th
Albert Bartlett Novices' Hurdle Race (Registered As The Spa Novices' Hurdle Race) (Cheltenham) 15th
JCB Triumph Hurdle Race (Cheltenham) 15th
Betfred Cheltenham Gold Cup Steeple Chase (Cheltenham) 15th
Johnny Henderson Grand Annual Steeple Chase Challenge Cup (Handicap) (Cheltenham) 15th
Foxhunter Steeple Chase Challenge Cup (Cheltenham) 15th
Martin Pipe Conditional Jockeys Handicap Hurdle (Cheltenham) 15th
Vincent O'Brien County Handicap Hurdle Race (Cheltenham) 15th
Blue Square Winter Derby (Lingfield Park) 16th
Bluesquare.com Spring Cup (Lingfield Park) 16th
Get Your Bet On At Blue Square Hever Sprint Stakes (Lingfield Park) 16th
Betfred Midlands Grand National Steeple Chase (A Handicap) (Uttoxeter) 16th
Shannon Spray E.B.F. Mares Novices' Hurdle (Limerick) 17th

Dawn Run E.B.F. Mares Novices' Chase (Limerick) 17th
William Hill Lincoln (Heritage Handicap) (Doncaster) 23rd
William Hill Spring Mile (Handicap) (Doncaster) 23rd
The New William Hill Iphone App Cammidge Trophy (Doncaster) 23rd
European Breeders' Fund / Thoroughbred Breeders' Association Mares Novices' Steeple Chase Finale (A Handicap) (Newbury) . 23rd
E.B.F. Ultima Business Solutions Mares' 'National Hunt' Novices' Hurdle Race Finale (A Handicap) (Newbury) 23rd
E.B.F. Park Express Stakes (Curragh) 24th
William Hill App-Download Today! Magnolia Stakes (Kempton Park) 30th
Cork Sprint Stakes (Cork) 30th
Easter Handicap Hurdle (Cork) 31st
Imperial Call Chase (Cork) 31st
Power Gold Cup (Fairyhouse) 31st
INHSO Final Novices' Handicap Hurdle (Fairyhouse) 31st
E.B.F. Mares Novices' Hurdle Final (Fairyhouse) 31st
Coolmore NH Sires Festival Novices' Hurdle (Fairyhouse) 31st

APRIL

Rathbarry Novices' Hurdle (Fairyhouse) 1st
Keelings Hurdle (Fairyhouse) 1st
Arkle Bar Novice Handicap Chase (Fairyhouse) 1st
Ladbrokes Irish Grand National (Handicap Chase) (Fairyhouse) 1st
thetote.ie Handicap Hurdle (Fairyhouse) 1st
Weatherbys 4yo Hurdle (Fairyhouse) 2nd
John Fowler Memorial Mares Chase (Fairyhouse) 2nd
Normans Grove Chase (Fairyhouse) 2nd
Matalan Anniversary 4-Y-O Juvenile Hurdle Race (Aintree) 4th
Silver Cross Handicap Hurdle (Aintree) 4th
John Smith's Fox Hunters Steeple Chase (Aintree) 4th
BGC Partners Liverpool Hurdle Race (Aintree) 4th
Betfred Bowl Steeple Chase (Aintree) 4th
Betfred Manifesto Novices' Steeple Chase (Aintree) 4th
matalan.co.uk Red Rum Handicap Steeple Chase (Aintree) 4th
John Smith's Sefton Novices' Hurdle Race (Aintree) 5th
John Smith's Melling Steeple Chase (Aintree) 5th
John Smith's Mildmay Novices' Steeple Chase (Aintree) 5th
John Smith's Top Novices' Hurdle Race (Aintree) 5th
John Smith's Handicap Hurdle Race (Aintree) 5th
John Smith's Mares' Standard Open National Hunt Flat Race (Aintree) 5th
John Smith's Topham Steeple Chase (Handicap) (Aintree) 5th
John Smith's Maghull Novices' Steeple Chase (Aintree) 5th
John Smith's Aintree Hurdle (Aintree) 6th
John Smith's Champion Standard Open National Hunt Flat Race (Aintree) 6th
John Smith's Mersey Novices' Hurdle Race (Aintree) 6th
John Smith's Grand National Steeple Chase (Aintree) 6th
John Smith's Handicap Steeple Chase (Aintree) 6th
Free Grand National Bets At FreeBetting.co.uk International Trial Stakes (Lingfield Park) 6th
An Uaimh Chase (Navan) 6th
Alleged Stakes (Curragh) 7th
Big Bad Bob Gladness Stakes (Curragh) 7th
Loughbrown Stakes (Curragh) 7th
Hugh McMahon Memorial Novices' Chase (Limerick) 7th
Kevin McManus Bumper (Limerick) 7th
Betfred Barry Hills 'Further Flight' Stakes (Nottingham) 10th
Best Odds Guaranteed At williamhill.com Doncaster Mile Stakes (Doncaster) 13th
Betfred Mobile Sports Snowdrop Fillies' Stakes (Kempton Park) 13th
2000 Guineas Trial (Leopardstown) 14th
1000 Guineas Trial (Leopardstown) 14th
Heritage Stakes (Leopardstown) 14th
Ballysax Stakes (Leopardstown) 14th
Ceres Estates Silver Trophy Steeple Chase (A Handicap) (Cheltenham) 17th
Lanwades Stud Nell Gwyn Stakes (Newmarket) 17th
Bet at bluesquare.com European Free Handicap (Newmarket) 17th
Blue Square Feilden Stakes (Newmarket) 17th
£100,000 Tattersalls Millions 3-y-o Sprint Stakes (Newmarket) 17th
Novae Bloodstock Insurance Craven Stakes (Newmarket) 18th
Weatherbys Earl Of Sefton Stakes (Newmarket) 18th
Connaught Access Flooring Abernant Stakes (Newmarket) 18th
£200,000 Tattersalls Millions 3-y-o Trophy (Newmarket) 18th
OLBG.com Mares' Handicap Hurdle Race (Cheltenham) 18th
The Thoroughbred Breeders' Association Mares' Novices' Hurdle (Cheltenham) 18th
E.B.F. and Whitsbury Manor Stud Lansdown Fillies' Stakes (Bath) 19th
Arcadia Consulting William Dickie & Mary Robertson Future Champion Novices Steeple Chase (Ayr) 20th
Isle Of Skye Blended Whisky Scottish Champion Hurdle Race (A Limited Handicap) (Ayr) 20th
Coral Scottish Grand National Handicap Steeple Chase (Ayr) 20th
The Scotty Brand Handicap Steeple Chase (Ayr) 20th

Aon Greenham Stakes (Newbury) 20th
Dubai Duty Free Stakes (Registered As The Fred Darling Stakes) (Newbury) 20th
Dubai Duty Free Finest Surprise Stakes (Registered As The John Porter Stakes) (Newbury) 20th
Woodlands Stakes (Naas) 20th
Salsabil Stakes (Navan) 21st
Evening Herald Champion Novices' Hurdle (Punchestown) 23rd
Growise Novices' Chase (Punchestown) 23rd
Boylesports Champion Chase (Punchestown) 23rd
Boylesports Handicap Hurdle (Punchestown) 23rd
Irish Daily Mirror War of Attrition Novices' Hurdle (Punchestown) 24th
Guinness Handicap Chase (Punchestown) 24th
betchronicle Champion Bumper (Punchestown) 24th
thetote.com Punchestown Gold Cup (Punchestown) 24th
Ladbrokes World Series Hurdle (Punchestown) 25th
Ryanair Novices' Chase (Punchestown) 25th
Bet365 Mile (Sandown Park) 26th
Aon Novice Handicap Chase (Punchestown) 26th
Rabobank Punchestown Champion Hurdle (Punchestown) 26th
Cathal Ryan Memorial Champion Novice Hurdle (Punchestown) 26th
totetentofollow.co.uk Leicestershire Stakes (Leicester) 27th
Bet365 Classic Trial (Sandown Park) 27th
bet365.com Celebration Steeple Chase (Sandown Park) 27th
Bet365 Gold Cup Steeple Chase (Handicap) (Sandown Park) 27th
Bet365 Gordon Richards Stakes (Sandown Park) 27th
ITBA Mares Hurdle (Punchestown) 27th
3' Pat Taafe Handicap Chase (Punchestown) 27th
Aes Champion 4yo Hurdle (Punchestown) 27th
www.thetote.com Handicap Hurdle (Punchestown) 27th
Victor McCalmont Stakes (Gowran Park) 28th

MAY

Sagaro Stakes (Ascot) 1st
Battersea Dogs and Cats Home Paradise Stakes (Ascot) 1st
Redstone Pavilion Stakes (Ascot) 1st
Qipco 2000 Guineas Stakes (British Champions Series) (Newmarket) 4th
Qipco Jockey Club Stakes (Newmarket) 4th
Pearl Bloodstock Palace House Stakes (Newmarket) 4th
Qatar Racing Newmarket Stakes (Newmarket) 4th
The Mobile Casino British Stallion Studs E.B.F. Conqueror Stakes (Goodwood) 4th
Betfred The Bonus King E.B.F. Daisy Warwick Stakes (Goodwood) 4th
Qipco 1000 Guineas Stakes (British Champions Series) (Newmarket) 5th
Qatar Bloodstock Dahlia Stakes (Newmarket) 5th
Tweenhills Pretty Polly Stakes (Newmarket) 5th
Coolmore E.B.F. Tetrarch Stakes (Curragh) 6th
Coolmore E.B.F. Athasi Stakes (Curragh) 6th
Coolmore E.B.F. Mooresbridge Stakes (Curragh) 8th
stanjames.com Chester Cup (Heritage Handicap) (Chester) 8th
Weatherbys Bank Cheshire Oaks (Chester) 8th
Mbna Chester Vase (Chester) 9th
Betfair Huxley Stakes (For The Tradesman's Cup) (Chester) 9th
Stobart Barristers Dee Stakes (Chester) 10th
Boodles Diamond Ormonde Stakes (Chester) 10th
Betfred Victoria Cup (Heritage Handicap) (Ascot) 11th
John Doyle Buckhounds Stakes (Ascot) 11th
Pertemps Network Handicap Hurdle (Registered As The Swinton Hurdle) (Haydock Park) 11th
The Network Group Spring Trophy Stakes (Haydock Park) 11th
Betfred 0800 221 221 Chartwell Fillies' Stakes (Lingfield Park) 11th
Betfair Derby Trial Stakes (Lingfield Park) 11th
Betfred 'The Bonus King' Oaks Trial Stakes (Lingfield Park) 11th
Weatherbys Bloodstock Insurance Kilvington Fillies' Stakes (Nottingham) 11th
Poule d'Essai des Poulains (Longchamp) 12th
Poule d'Essai des Pouliches (Longchamp) 12th
Ladbrokes Handicap Hurdle (Killarney) 12th
Derrinstown 1000 Guineas Trial (Leopardstown) 12th
Derrinstown Derby Trial (Leopardstown) 12th
Amethyst Stakes (Leopardstown) 12th
The Sky Bet Stakes (Windsor) 13th
Duke Of York Stakes (York) 15th
Tattersalls Musidora Stakes (York) 15th
Blue Wind Stakes (Naas) 15th
Betfred Dante Stakes (York) 16th
Betfred Middleton Stakes (York) 16th
Betfred Hambleton Stakes (York) 16th
Yorkshire Cup (British Champions Series) (York) 17th
The EquinIty Powered by Garmin Fillies' Stakes (York) 17th

The Langley Solicitors LLP E.B.F. Marygate Fillies' Stakes (York)..17th
William Hill Braveheart Stakes (Handicap) (Hamilton Park)..17th
Swettenham Stud Fillies' Trial Stakes (Newbury)..17th
Bathwick Tyres Carnarvon Stakes (Newbury)..17th
JLT Lockinge Stakes (British Champions Series) (Newbury)..18th
JLT Aston Park Stakes (Newbury)..18th
The poptelecom.co.uk King Charles II Stakes (Newmarket)..18th
The poptelecom.co.uk Fairway Stakes (Newmarket)..18th
Vintage Crop Stakes (Navan)..19th
Height Of Fashion Stakes (Goodwood)..23rd
Casco Cocked Hat Stakes (Goodwood)..24th
Betfred.com Temple Stakes (British Champions Series) (Haydock Park)..25th
Betfred Silver Bowl (Heritage Handicap) (Haydock Park)..25th
Abu Dhabi Irish 2000 Guineas (Curragh)..25th
Marble Hill Stakes (Curragh)..25th
TRI Equestrian Ridgewood Pearl Stakes (Curragh)..25th
Weatherbys Ireland Greenlands Stakes (Curragh)..25th
32Red Festival Stakes (Goodwood)..25th
Southern Daily Echo Tapster Stakes (Goodwood)..25th
Stowe Family Law LLP Grand Cup (York)..25th
Prix d'Ispahan (Longchamp)..26th
Prix Saint Alary (Longchamp)..26th
Etihad Airways Irish 1000 Guineas (Curragh)..26th
Tattersalls Gold Cup (Curragh)..26th
Airlie Stud Gallinule Stakes (Curragh)..26th
Betfair Henry II Stakes (Sandown Park)..30th
Betfair Brigadier Gerard Stakes (Sandown Park)..30th
Betfair Heron Stakes (Sandown Park)..30th
Betfair Funds the PJA Doctor National Stakes (Sandown Park)..30th
Investec Coronation Cup (British Champions Series) (Epsom Downs)..31st
Investec Oaks (British Champions Series) (Epsom Downs)..31st
Investec Diomed Stakes (Epsom Downs)..31st
Princess Elizabeth Stakes (Sponsored By Investec) (Epsom Downs)..31st
Investec Surrey Stakes (Epsom Downs)..31st

JUNE

Investec Derby (British Champions Series) (Epsom Downs) 1st
Investec Entrepreneurial Class 'Dash' (Heritage Handicap) (Epsom Downs)..1st
Investec Woodcote Stakes (Epsom Downs) 1st
Edinburgh Cup (Heritage Handicap) (Musselburgh) 1st
Prix du Jockey Club (Chantilly)..2nd
The davisbakerycaribbean.com Leisure Stakes (Windsor)..3rd
Coolmore Stud Juvenile Fillies Stakes (Naas) 3rd
Rochestown Stakes (Naas)..3rd
Whitehead Memorial Stakes (Naas)..3rd
Savel Beg Stakes (Leopardstown) 7th
Nijinsky Stakes (Leopardstown) 7th
Multiplex Achilles Stakes (Haydock Park)..7th
Timeform Jury Stakes (Registered As The John Of Gaunt Stakes) (Haydock Park)..8th
Grosvenor Casinos Pinnacle Stakes (Haydock Park)..8th
E.B.F. Play Poker With Grosvenor Casinos Stakes (Haydock Park)..8th
Blue Square Sandy Lane Stakes (Haydock Park)..8th
Silver Stakes (Curragh) 9th
Lord Weinstock Memorial Stakes (Newbury)..13th
Ballycorus Stakes (Leopardstown) 13th
Ballyogan Stakes (Leopardstown) 13th
Bond Tyres Trophy (Heritage Handicap) (York)..13th
The Ian and Kate Hall Macmillan Ganton Stakes (York)..15th
Novae Bloodstock Insurance Scurry Stakes (Sandown Park)..15th
Martin Molony Stakes (Limerick) 15th
Bathwick Tyres Cathedral Stakes (Salisbury)..15th
Kerry Group Noblesse Stakes (Cork)..16th
Midsummer Sprint Stakes (Cork)..16th
Voute Sales Warwickshire Oaks Stakes (Warwick)..17th
Prix de Diane (Chantilly)..17th
King's Stand Stakes (British Champions Series & Global Sprint Challenge) (Royal Ascot)......................................18th
Queen Anne Stakes (British Champions Series) (Royal Ascot)..18th
St James's Palace Stakes (British Champions Series) (Royal Ascot)..18th
Coventry Stakes (Royal Ascot)..18th
Windsor Castle Stakes (Royal Ascot)..18th
Prince Of Wales's Stakes (British Champions Series) (Royal Ascot)..19th
Queen Mary Stakes (Royal Ascot) 19th
Windsor Forest Stakes (Royal Ascot)..19th
Jersey Stakes (Royal Ascot) 19th
Royal Hunt Cup (Heritage Handicap) (Royal Ascot) 19th

Sandringham Handicap Stakes (Royal Ascot) 19th
Gold Cup (British Champions Series) (Royal Ascot) 20th
Norfolk Stakes (Royal Ascot) 20th
Ribblesdale Stakes (Royal Ascot) 20th
Britannia Stakes (Heritage Handicap) (Royal Ascot) 20th
Glencairn Stakes (Leopardstown) 21st
Coronation Stakes (British Champions Series) (Royal Ascot) 21st
King Edward VII Stakes (Royal Ascot) 21st
Albany Stakes (Royal Ascot) 21st
Queen's Vase (Royal Ascot) 21st
Wolferton Handicap Stakes (Royal Ascot) 22nd
Diamond Jubilee Stakes (British Champions Series & Global Sprint Challenge) (Royal Ascot) 22nd
Hardwicke Stakes (Royal Ascot) 22nd
Wokingham Stakes (Heritage Handicap)(Royal Ascot) 22nd
Chesham Stakes (Royal Ascot) 22nd
Scottish Sun / E.B.F. Land O'Burns Fillies' Stakes (Ayr) 23rd
totepool Pontefract Castle Stakes (Pontefract) 23rd
Grand Prix de Saint-Cloud (Saint-Cloud) 26th
Naas Oaks Trial (Naas) 27th
Weatherbys Bloodstock Insurance Eternal Stakes (Warwick) 28th
Betfred / British Stallion Studs E.B.F. Hoppings Stakes (Newcastle) 29th
Betfred.Com Chipchase Stakes (Newcastle) 29th
John Smith's Northumberland Plate (Heritage Handicap) (Newcastle) 29th
Bet365 Criterion Stakes (Newmarket) 29th
Betfair Supports The Animal Health Trust Fred Archer Stakes (Newmarket) 29th
ACD Projects Supporting The Animal Health Trust Empress Stakes (Newmarket) 29th
Betfred The Bonus King Stakes (Windsor) 29th
Dubai Duty Free Irish Derby Stakes (Curragh) 29th
Dubai Duty Free Railway Stakes (Curragh) 29th
Woodies DIY Sapphire Stakes (Curragh) 29th
Dubai Duty Free Celebration Stakes (Curragh) 29th
Prix Jean Prat (Chantilly) 30th
International Stakes (Curragh) 30th
Pretty Polly Stakes (Curragh) 30th
At The Races Curragh Cup (Curragh) 30th
Grangecon Stud Balanchine Stakes (Curragh) 30th
The John Smith's Summer Cup (A Handicap Steeple Chase) (Uttoxeter) 30th

JULY

Brownstown Stakes (Fairyhouse) 3rd
Ambant Gala Stakes (Sandown Park) 5th
Mobile Betting At coral.co.uk Dragon Stakes (Sandown Park) 5th
Bet365 Lancashire Oaks (Haydock Park) 6th
Bet365 Old Newton Cup (Heritage Handicap) (Haydock Park) 6th
Coral-Eclipse (British Champions Series) (Sandown Park) 6th
Coral Charge (Registered As The Sprint Stakes) (Sandown Park) 6th
Coral Distaff (Sandown Park) 6th
Coral Marathon (Sandown Park) 6th
Coral Challenge (Heritage Handicap) (Sandown Park) 6th
Lenebane Stakes (Roscommon) 8th
Arkle Finance Pipalong Stakes (Pontefract) 9th
Princess Wales's Goldsmith Stakes (Newmarket) 11th
TNT July Stakes (Newmarket) 11th
Bahrain Trophy (Newmarket) 11th
Betfred 'The Bonus King' Heritage Handicap (Newmarket) 12th
Etihad Airways Falmouth Stakes (British Champions Series) (Newmarket) 12th
Irish Thoroughbred Marketing Cherry Hinton Stakes (Newmarket) 12th
Tyregiant.com Summer Stakes (York) 13th
Transformers & Rectifiers Summer Mile Stakes (Ascot) 13th
Darley July Cup (British Champions Series & Global Sprint Challenge) (Newmarket) 13th
32Red.com Superlative Stakes (Newmarket) 13th
32Red Bunbury Cup Handicap (Heritage Handicap) (Newmarket) 13th
chesterBET City Plate (Chester) 13th
John Smith's Cup (Heritage Handicap) (York) 13th
John Smith's City Walls Stakes (York) 13th
John Smith's Silver Cup Stakes (Handicap) 13th
Grand Prix de Paris (Longchamp) 13th
Tipperary Stakes (Tipperary) 13th
Belgrave Stakes (Fairyhouse) 14th
Glasgow Stakes (Hamilton Park) 18th
Silver Flash Stakes (Leopardstown) 18th
Challenge Stakes (Leopardstown) 18th
Rose Bowl Stakes - Sponsored by Compton Beauchamp Estates Ltd (Newbury) 19th
Newbury Stakes (Registered As The Hackwood Stakes) (Newbury) 20th
Calico Cat at chrisbeekracing.com Stakes (Newbury) 20th

Newsells Park Stud Stakes (Newmarket) 20th
Jebel Ali Racecourse & Stables Anglesey Stakes (Curragh) 20th
Kilboy Estate Stakes (Curragh) 20th
Darley Irish Oaks (Curragh) 20th
The Betfred Summer Plate (A Handicap) Steeple Chase (Market Rasen) 20th
The Betfred 'The Bonus King' Summer Hurdle Race (A Handicap) (Market Rasen) 20th
Minstrel Stakes (Curragh) 20th
Grimes Hurdle (Tipperary) 21st
Sweet Mimosa Stakes (Naas) 21st
Weatherbys VAT Services Star Stakes (Sandown Park) 24th
Tyros Stakes (Leopardstown) 25th
Meld Stakes (Leopardstown) 25th
Woodcote Stud E.B.F. Valiant Stakes (Ascot) 25th
E.B.F. Stobart PJA Testimonial Lyric Fillies' Stakes (York) 26th
King George VI And Queen Elizabeth Stakes (Sponsored By Betfair) (British Champions Series) (Ascot) .. 27th
Carraig Insurance Winkfield Stakes (Ascot) 27th
Betfair Summer Double First Leg International Stakes (Heritage Handicap) (Ascot) 27th
Princess Margaret Juddmonte Stakes (Ascot) 27th
Sky Bet York Stakes (York) 27th
Skybet Supporting The Yorkshire Racing Summer Festival (Pontefract) 28th
Prix Rothschild (Deauville) 28th
Bet365 Lennox Stakes (Goodwood) 30th
Neptune Gordon Stakes (Goodwood) 30th
Bet365 Molecomb Stakes (Goodwood) 30th
Qipco Sussex Stakes (British Champions Series) (Goodwood) 31st
Veuve Clicquot Vintage Stakes (Goodwood) 31st
thetote.com Galway Plate (Handicap Chase) (Galway) 31st

AUGUST

Artemis Goodwood Cup (British Champions' Series) (Goodwood) 1st
I-Shares Fillies' Stakes (Registered As The Lillie Langtry Stakes) (Goodwood) 1st
Guinness Galway Hurdle (Handicap) (Galway) 1st
Corrib EBF Fillies Stakes (Galway) 1st
Gordon's King George Stakes (Goodwood) 1st
Audi Richmond Stakes (Goodwood) 2nd
Coutts Glorious Stakes (Goodwood) 2nd
Oak Tree Stakes (Goodwood) 2nd
Betfred Mile (Heritage Handicap) (Formerly Known As The Golden Mile) (Goodwood) 2nd
Thoroughbred Stakes (Goodwood) 2nd
Markel Insurance Nassau Stakes (British Champions Series) (Goodwood) 2nd
Blue Square Stewards' Cup (Heritage Handicap) (Goodwood) 3rd
Mervue Handicap Hurdle (Galway) 3rd
M & S Bank Queensferry Stakes (Chester) 4th
British Stallion Studs E.B.F. Chalice Stakes (Newbury) 4th
Prix Maurice de Gheest (Deauville) 4th
Platinum Stakes (Cork) 6th
Give Thanks Stakes (Cork) 6th
Ballyroan Stakes (Leopardstown) 8th
El Gran Senor Stakes (Tipperary) 9th
Abergwaun Stakes (Tipperary) 9th
Rose Of Lancaster Stakes (Haydock Park) 10th
British Stallion Studs Dick Hern E.B.F. Fillies' Stakes (Haydock Park) 10th
Watch Races Live At Racinguk.Com Handicap Stakes (Heritage Handicap) (Haydock Park) 10th
German-Thoroughbred.Com Sweet Solera Stakes (Newmarket) 10th
Phoenix Sprint Stakes (Curragh) 11th
Royal Whip Stakes (Curragh) 11th
Keeneland Phoenix Stakes (Curragh) 11th
Debutante Stakes (Curragh) 11th
Prix Jacques Le Marois (Deauville) 11th
Hurry Harriet Stakes (Gowran Park) 14th
European Breeders' Fund Upavon Fillies' Stakes (Salisbury) 14th
Totepool.com Sovereign Stakes (Salisbury) 15th
Desmond Stakes (Leopardstown) 15th
Bathwick Tyres St Hugh's Stakes (Newbury) 16th
Betfred Hungerford Stakes (Newbury) 17th
Betfred 'The Bonus King' Geoffrey Freer Stakes (Newbury) 17th
Denford Stud Stakes (Newbury) 17th
William Hill Great St Wilfrid Stakes (Heritage Handicap) (Ripon) 17th
British Stallion Studs E.B.F. Flying Fillies' Stakes (Pontefract) 18th
Prix Morny (Deauville) 18th
Prix Jean Romanet (Deauville) 18th
Juddmonte International Stakes (British Champions Series) (York) 21st
Neptune Investment Management Great Voltigeur Stakes (York) 21st
Pinsent Masons Llp Acomb Stakes (York) 21st
Darley Yorkshire Oaks (British Champions Series) (York) 22nd

Irish Thoroughbred Marketing Gimcrack Stakes (York) 22nd
Jaguar Cars Lowther Stakes (York) 22nd
British Stallion Studs Supporting British Racing E.B.F. Galtres Stakes (York) 22nd
Fairy Bridge Stakes (Tipperary) 22nd
Coolmore Nunthorpe Stakes (British Champions Series) (York) 23rd
Sky Bet Strensall Stakes (York) 23rd
Betfair Celebration Mile (Goodwood) 24th
Prestige Stakes (Goodwood) 24th
Windflower March Stakes (Goodwood) 24th
Betfair Summer Double Second Leg Stakes (Heritage Handicap) (Goodwood) 24th
Betfred Winter Hill Stakes (Windsor) 24th
Weatherbys Insurance Lonsdale Cup (British Champions Series) (York) 24th
Betfred Ebor (Heritage Handicap) (York) 24th
Chris Blackwell Memorial Hopeful Stakes (Newmarket) 24th
totepool August Stakes (Windsor) 24th
Julia Graves Roses Stakes (York) 24th
Betfred City Of York Stakes (York) 24th
Curragh Stakes (Curragh) 24th
Galileo EBF Futurity Stakes (Curragh) 24th
Ballycullen Stakes (Curragh) 24th
Dance Design Stakes (Curragh) 24th
Supreme Stakes (Goodwood) 25th
Ripon Champion Two Years Old Trophy (Ripon) 26th
Ruby Stakes (Curragh) 28th
Weatherbys Bloodstock Insurance Stonehenge Stakes (Salisbury) 30th
Logh Leane Handicap Chase (Killarney) 30th
Betfred Beverley Bullet Sprint Stakes (Beverley) 31st
Golden Square Shopping Centre Warrington Chester Stakes (Chester) 31st
Solario Stakes (Sandown Park) 31st
Atalanta Stakes (Sandown Park) 31st
Brandon Handicap Hurdle (Killarney) 31st
The Lord Mildmay Memorial Handicap Steeple Chase (Newton Abbot) 31st

SEPTEMBER

Flying Five Stakes (Curragh) 1st
Round Tower Stakes (Curragh) 1st
Moyglare Stud Stakes (Curragh) 1st
Peter Willett Stakes (Goodwood) 3rd
Country Gentlemen's Association E.B.F. Dick Poole Fillies' Stakes (Salisbury) 5th
Betfred Sprint Cup (British Champions Series) (Haydock Park) 7th
Betfred Bundles Old Borough Cup (Heritage Handicap) (Haydock Park) 7th
Betfred "Still Treble Odds On Lucky 15's" Stakes (Haydock Park) 7th
The Celebrating 45 Years of Betfred Superior Mile (Haydock Park) 7th
Betfred September Stakes (Kempton Park) 7th
Betfred Bonus King Sirenia Stakes (Kempton Park) 7th
Red Mills Irish Champion Stakes (Leopardstown) 7th
Coolmore Matron Stakes (Leopardstown) 7th
KPMG Enterprise Kilternan Stakes (Leopardstown) 7th
Icon Breeders' Cup Juvenile Trial (Golden Fleece) Stakes (Leopardstown) 7th
Oyster Stakes (Galway) 7th
Celebrating 45 years of Betfred Garrowby Stakes (York) 8th
Scarbrough Stakes (Doncaster) 11th
Park Hill Stakes (Doncaster) 12th
Barrett Steel May Hill Stakes (Doncaster) 13th
Doncaster Cup (British Champions Series) (Doncaster) 13th
Flying Childers Stakes (Doncaster) 13th
Ladbrokes St Leger Stakes (British Champions Series) (Doncaster) 14th
OLBG Park Stakes (Doncaster) 14th
Champagne Stakes (Doncaster) 14th
Ladbrokes Portland (Heritage Handicap) (Doncaster) 14th
Minstrell Recruitment Stand Cup (Chester) 14th
Gain Irish St Leger Stakes (Curragh) 14th
Goffs Vincent O'Brien National Stakes (Curragh) 14th
Flame Of Tara Stakes (Curragh) 14th
Blandford Stakes (Curragh) 15th
Solonoway Stakes (Curragh) 15th
Renaissance Stakes (Curragh) 15th
Prix du Moulin de Longchamp (Longchamp) 15th
Prix Vermeille (Longchamp) 15th
Latrigue 4yo Handicap Hurdle (Listowel) 17th
John Dunlop Fortune Stakes (Sandown Park) 18th
E.B.F. At The Races John Musker Fillies' Stakes (Yarmouth) 18th
Guinness Kerry National (Handicap Chase) (Listowel) 18th
Listowel Stakes (Listowel) 18th
Guinness Handicap Hurdle (Listowel) 19th

OCTOBER

NOVEMBER

Rewards4Racing Handicap Steeple Chase (Cheltenham)..16th
Ultima Business Solutions Handicap Hurdle Race (Cheltenham)..16th
Neptune Investment Management Novices' Hurdle Race (Registered As The Hyde Novices' Hurdle Race) (Cheltenham)............17th
November Novices' Steeple Chase (Registered As The November Novices' Steeple Chase) (Cheltenham).................17th
Racing Post Hurdle Race (Cheltenham)..17th
Cheltenham Standard Open National Hunt Flat Race (Cheltenham)..17th
Blackwater Handicap Hurdle (Cork)...17th
Florida Pearl Novices' Chase (Punchestown)..17th
Dobbins & Madigans Morgiana Hurdle (Punchestown)...17th
Craddockstown Novices' Chase (Punchestown)...17th
Betdaq Mobile Apps Hyde Stakes (Kempton Park)..17th
Read Nicholls & McCain Exclusively on Betfair Novices' Hurdle Race (Registered as The Newton Novices' Hurdle)
(Haydock Park)..20th
Amlin 1965 Steeple Chase (Ascot)..22nd
Coral Hurdle Race (Registered As The Ascot Hurdle Race) (Ascot)..23rd
Betfair Steeple Chase (Registered As The Lancashire Chase) (Haydock Park)..................................23rd
betfair.com "Fixed Brush" Handicap Hurdle Race (Haydock Park)...23rd
Monksfield Novices' Hurdle (Navan)..23rd
Ladbrokes Troytown Handicap Chase (Navan)...24th
Mares Bumper (Navan)..24th
The OLBG Mares' Hurdle Race (Kempton Park)...24th
Betdaq Casino Games Wild Flower Stakes (Kempton Park)..25th
GPG Novices' Steeple Chase (Registered As The Worcester Novices' Steeple Chase) (Newbury)...........27th
Sportingbet Intermediate Hurdle Race (Newbury)..28th
Fuller's London Pride Novices' Steeple Chase (Registered As The Berkshire Novices' Steeple Chase) (Newbury)..........28th
Sportingbet Long Distance Hurdle Race (Newbury)..29th
Hennessy Gold Cup Steeple Chase (Handicap) (Newbury)..30th
The Thoroughbred Breeders' Association Mares' Novices' Hurdle (Newbury).....................................30th
Stanjames.com Fighting Fifth Hurdle Race (Newcastle)...30th
At The Races Rehearsal Steeple Chase (A Handicap) (Newcastle)...30th
Ballyhack Handicap Chase (Fairyhouse)...30th
New Stand Handicap Hurdle (Fairyhouse)...30th

DECEMBER

Bar One Royal Bond Novices' Hurdle (Fairyhouse)...1st
Bar One Hattons Grace Hurdle (Fairyhouse)..1st
Porterstown Handicap Chase (Fairyhouse)..1st
Bar One Drinmore Novices' Chase (Fairyhouse)...1st
Winter Festival Juvenile Hurdle (Fairyhouse)..1st
Neptune Investment Management Novices' Hurdle Race (Registered As The Winter Novices' Hurdle Race) (Sandown Park)........6th
The Sportingbet Future Stars Steeple Chase (Sandown Park)..6th
Sportingbet Tingle Creek Steeple Chase (Sandown Park)...6th
Henry VIII Novices' Steeple Chase (Sandown Park)..7th
Sportingbet Handicap Hurdle Race (Sandown Park)..7th
Betfred Becher Handicap Steeple Chase (Aintree)...7th
Betfred Treble Odds On Lucky 15's Steeple Chase (Aintree)..7th
Betfred 'The Bonus King' Fillies' Juvenile Hurdle Race (Aintree)...7th
Proudstown Handicap Hurdle (Navan)...7th
Lombardstown Mares Novices' Chase (Cork)...7th
Hilly Way Chase (Cork)...8th
Cork Stayers Novices' Hurdle (Cork)...8th
John Durkan Memorial Chase (Punchestown)...8th
EBF Novices Hurdle (Punchestown)..8th
Betfred Peterborough Steeple Chase (Huntingdon)..8th
Majordomo Hospitality Handicap Steeple Chase (Cheltenham)..12th
Albert Bartlett Novices' Hurdle Race (Registered As The Bristol Novices' Hurdle Race) (Cheltenham).......13th
stanjames.com International Hurdle Race (Cheltenham)...14th
Unicoin Homes Relkeel Hurdle Race (Cheltenham)...14th
December Gold Cup (A Handicap Steeple Chase) (Cheltenham)..14th
Summit Juvenile Hurdle Race (Doncaster)..14th
December Novices' Steeple Chase (Lingfield Park)..14th
Future Champions Bumper (Navan)...14th
Navan Novices' Hurdle (Navan)..15th
Tara Hurdle (Navan)...15th
Betfred Novices' Steeple Chase (Registered As The Noel Novices' Steeple Chase) (Ascot)...................20th
Mitie Kennel Gate Novices' Hurdle Race (Ascot)..20th
Ascot Championship Standard Open National Hunt Flat Race (Ascot)..20th
Quebec Stakes (Lingfield Park)...21st
Long Walk Hurdle Race (Ascot)..21st
Ascot Racecourse Silver Cup Handicap Steeple Chase (Ascot)..21st
The Ladbroke (A Handicap Hurdle Race) (Ascot)...21st
The Bet At bluesq.com Mares' Novices' Hurdle Race (Haydock Park)..21st
Horse and Jockey Hurdle (Thurles)..22nd
Kauto Star Feltham Novices' Steeple Chase (In Memory Of Nigel Clark) (Kempton Park)....................26th
williamhill.com Christmas Hurdle Race (Kempton Park)...26th

William Hill King George VI Steeple Chase (Kempton Park)..26th
Rowland Meyrick Handicap Steeple Chase (Wetherby) 26th
Racing Post Novices' Chase (Leopardstown) 26th
Leopardstown Juvenile Hurdle (Leopardstown) 26th
Greenmount Park Novices' Chase (Limerick) 26th
williamhill.com Desert Orchid Steeple Chase (Kempton Park)..27th
williamhill.com Novices' Steeple Chase (Registered As The Wayward Lad Novices' Steeple Chase) (Kempton Park)..................27th
Betfred Challow Novices' Hurdle Race (Newbury)..27th
Paddy Power Handicap Chase (Leopardstown) 27th
Paddy Power Future Champions Novices' Hurdle (Leopardstown) 27th
Paddy Power Dial A Bet Chase (Leopardstown) 27th
Tim Duggan Memorial Handicap Chase (Limerick) 27th
Coral Future Champions Finale Juvenile Hurdle Race (Chepstow) 28th
Coral Welsh National (A Handicap Steeple Chase) (Chepstow) 28th
Lexus Chase (Leopardstown) 28th
Woodies DIY Christmas Hurdle (Leopardstown) 28th
Topaz Fort Leney Novices' Chase (Leopardstown) 28th
Dorans Pride Novices' Hurdle (Limerick) 28th
Istabraq December Hurdle (Leopardstown) 29th
EBF Mares Hurdle (Leopardstown)..29th
The totepool.com Mares' Novices' Hurdle Race (Taunton) 30th

The list of Principal Races has been supplied by the BHA and is provisional. In all cases, the dates, venues and names of sponsors are correct at the time of going to press, but also subject to possible alteration.

INDEX TO TRAINERS

†denotes Permit to train under N.H. Rules only

Name	Team No.
BRAVERY, MR GILES	061
BRENNAN, MR BARRY	062
†BREWER, MISS ALI	063
†BREWIS, MISS RHONA	064
BRIDGER, MR JOHN	065
BRIDGWATER, MR DAVID	066
BRISBOURNE, MR MARK	067
BRITTAIN, MR CLIVE	068
BRITTAIN, MR MEL	069
†BROOKE, LADY	070
BROOKS, MRS ANNA	071
BROOKS, MR CHARLIE	072
BROTHERTON, MR ROY	073
BROWN, MR ALAN	074
BROWN, MR DAVID	075
BROWN, MR GARY	076
†BROWN, MR IAN	077
†BROWN, MR REGINALD	078
†BRYANT, MISS MICHELLE	079
†BUCKETT, MRS KATE	080
BUCKLER, MR BOB	081
BUCKLEY, MR MARK	082
BURCHELL, MR DAI	083
BURGOYNE, MR PAUL	084
BURKE, MRS E. M.	085
BURKE, MR KEIRAN	086
†BURNS, MR HUGH	087
BUTLER, MR GERARD	088
BUTLER, MR JOHN	089
BUTLER, MR PADDY	090
†BUTTERWORTH, MRS BARBARA	091
BYCROFT, MR NEVILLE	092

C

Name	Team No.
CAMACHO, MISS JULIE	093
CAMPION, MR MARK	094
CANDLISH, MS JENNIE	095
CANDY, MR HENRY	096
CANN, MR GRANT	097
CANTILLON, MR DON	098
†CARR, MR DAVID	099

Name	Team No.
CARR, MRS RUTH	100
CARROLL, MR DECLAN	101
CARROLL, MR TONY	102
CARSON, MR TONY	103
CARTER, MR LEE	104
CASE, MR BEN	105
CECIL, SIR HENRY	106
CHAMINGS, MR PATRICK	107
CHANCE, MR NOEL	108
CHANNON, MR MICK	109
CHAPMAN, MR MICHAEL	110
CHAPPLE-HYAM, MS JANE	111
CHAPPLE-HYAM, MR PETER	112
CHARLTON, MR GEORGE	113
CHARLTON, MR ROGER	114
CHISMAN, MR HARRY	115
†CLARKE, MRS ANGELA	116
CLEMENT, MR NICOLAS	117
CLEMENT, MR TERRY	118
CLINTON, MR PATRICK	119
CLUTTERBUCK, MR K. F.	120
COAKLEY, MR DENIS J.	121
†COBB, MRS HEATHER	122
COLE, MR PAUL	123
COLES, MR TOBIAS B. P.	124
COLTHERD, MR STUART	125
†CONNELL, LADY ANNE	126
COOGAN, MR ALAN	127
COOMBE, MR JOHN	128
†CORBETT, MRS SUSAN	129
CORCORAN, MR LIAM	130
CORNWALL, MR JOHN	131
COWELL, MR ROBERT	132
COWLEY, MR PAUL	133
COX, MR CLIVE	134
COYLE, MR TONY	135
CRAGGS, MR RAY	136
CRATE, MR PETER	137
CROOK, MR ANDREW	138
CROWLEY, MISS JO	139
CUMANI, MR LUCA	140

Name	Team No.
CUNDELL, MR PETER	141
CUNNINGHAM, MR MICHAEL	142
CURRAN, MR SEAN	143
CURTIS, MISS REBECCA	144
CURTIS, MR ROGER	145
CUTHBERT, MR TOM	146

D

Name	Team No.
D'ARCY, MR PAUL	147
DACE, MR LUKE	148
DALGLEISH, MR KEITH	149
†DALTON, MR NEALE	150
DALY, MR HENRY	151
DANDO, MR PHILIP	152
DARTNALL, MR VICTOR	153
DASCOMBE, MR TOM	154
DAVIES, MR JOHN	155
†DAVIES, MR PAUL	156
DAVIES, MISS SARAH-JAYNE	157
DAVIS, MISS JOANNA	158
DAVISON, MISS ZOE	159
†DAY, MR ANTHONY	160
†DAY, MISS LISA	161
DE GILES, MR ED	162
DE GILES, MR JONATHEN	163
DE HAAN, MR BEN	164
DEACON, MR GEOFFREY	165
†DENNIS, MR TIM	166
DICKIN, MR ROBIN	167
†DIXON, MR JOHN	168
DIXON, MR SCOTT	169
†DIXON, MR STEVEN	170
DOBBIN, MRS ROSE	171
†DODGSON, MR ASHLEY	172
DODS, MR MICHAEL	173
DORE, MR CONOR	174
DOUMEN, MR FRANCOIS	175
DOW, MR SIMON	176
DOWN, MR CHRIS	177
†DOWNIE, MISS AMY	178
DREW, MR CLIVE	179

Name	Team No.
DU PLESSIS, MISS JACKIE	180
DUFFIELD, MRS ANN	181
DUKE, MR BRENDAN W.	182
DUNCAN, MR IAN	183
†DUNGER, MR NIGEL	184
DUNLOP, MR ED	185
DUNLOP, MR HARRY	186
†DUNN, MRS ALEXANDRA	187
DUNNETT, MRS CHRISTINE	188
DURACK, MR SEAMUS	189
DUTFIELD, MRS NERYS	190
DWYER, MR CHRIS	191
DYSON, MISS CLAIRE	192

E

Name	Team No.
EARLE, MR SIMON	193
EASTERBY, MR MICHAEL	194
EASTERBY, MR TIM	195
†ECKLEY, MR BRIAN	196
EDDERY, MR PAT	197
EDDERY, MR ROBERT	198
†EDWARDS, MR GORDON	199
EGERTON, MR CHARLES	200
ELLISON, MR BRIAN	201
ELSWORTH, MR DAVID	202
ENRIGHT, MR GERRY	203
ETHERINGTON, MR TIM	204
EUSTACE, MR JAMES	205
EVANS, MR DAVID	206
EVANS, MR JAMES	207
†EVANS, MRS MARY	208
EVANS, MRS NIKKI	209
EWART, MR JAMES	210

F

Name	Team No.
FAHEY, MR RICHARD	211
FAIRHURST, MR CHRIS	212
FANSHAWE, MR JAMES	213
FEILDEN, MISS JULIA	214
FENTON, MR PHILIP	215

Name	Team No.
FERGUSON, MR JOHN	216
FFRENCH DAVIS, MR DOMINIC	217
FIERRO, MR GIUSEPPE	218
FIFE, MRS MARJORIE	219
FITZGERALD, MR TIM	220
FITZSIMONS, MR PAUL	221
FLINT, MR JOHN	222
FORD, MRS PAM	223
FORD, MR RICHARD	224
†FORD, MRS RICHENDA	225
FORSEY, MR BRIAN	226
FORSTER, MISS SANDY	227
FOSTER, MISS JOANNE	228
FOX, MR JIMMY	229
FRANCE, MISS SUZZANNE	230
†FRANKLAND, MR DEREK	231
FROST, MR JAMES	232
FRY, MR HARRY	233
FRYER, MISS CAROLINE	234

G

Name	Team No.
GALLAGHER, MR JOHN	235
GANSERA-LEVEQUE, MRS ILKA	236
GARDNER, MRS SUSAN	237
GASK, MR JEREMY	238
†GASSON, MRS ROSEMARY	239
†GATES, MR MICHAEL	240
GEAKE, MR JONATHAN	241
GEORGE, MISS KAREN	242
GEORGE, MR TOM	243
†GIBSON, MRS THERESA	244
GIFFORD, MR NICK	245
GILLARD, MR MARK	246
GILLIGAN, MR PATRICK	247
GIVEN, MR JAMES	248
GOLDIE, MR JIM	249
†GOLDIE, MR ROBERT	250
GOLDSWORTHY, MR KEITH	251
GOLLINGS, MR STEVE	252
GORDON, MR CHRIS	253
GORMAN, MR J T	254

Name	Team No.
GOSDEN, MR JOHN	255
GRAHAM, MRS HARRIET	256
GRANT, MR CHRIS	257
GRASSICK, MR LIAM	258
GRASSICK, MR M. C.	259
GRAY, MR CARROLL	260
GRAYSON, MR PETER	261
GREATREX, MR WARREN	262
GREEN, MR PAUL	263
GRETTON, MR TOM	264
GRIFFIN, MR PATRICK	265
GRIFFITHS, MR DAVID C.	266
GRIFFITHS, MR SIMON	267
†GRIFFITHS, MR SIRRELL	268
GRISSELL, MRS DIANA	269
GROUCOTT, MR JOHN BRYAN	270
GUBBY, MR BRIAN	271
GUEST, MR RAE	272
GUEST, MR RICHARD	273
GUNDRY, MISS POLLY	274

H

Name	Team No.
HAGGAS, MR WILLIAM	275
HALES, MR ALEX	276
HALFORD, MR MICHAEL	277
HALL, MISS SALLY	278
HAMBRO, MRS MARY	279
HAMER, MRS DEBRA	280
†HAMILTON, MRS ALISON	281
HAMILTON, MRS ANN	282
HAMILTON, MR B. R.	283
†HAMILTON, MRS CATHY	284
HAMMOND, MR MICKY	285
HAMMOND, MR MIKE	286
HANNON, MR RICHARD	287
HARKER, MR GEOFFREY	288
†HARPER, MR RICHARD	289
HARRINGTON, MRS JESSICA	290
HARRIS, MR RONALD	291
HARRIS, MR SHAUN	292
HARRISON, MISS LISA	293

Name	Team No.
HASLAM, MR BEN	294
HASSETT, MR P. J.	295
HAWES, MRS FLEUR	296
HAWKE, MR NIGEL	297
HAWKER, MR RICHARD	298
HAYDN JONES, MR DEREK	299
†HAYNES, MR JONATHAN	300
HAYNES, MR TED	301
HEAD-MAAREK, MRS C.	302
HEARD, MR COLIN	303
HEDGER, MR PETER	304
HENDERSON, MR NICKY	305
HENDERSON, MR PAUL	306
HERRIES, LADY	307
HERRINGTON, MR MICHAEL	308
HIATT, MR PETER	309
HILL, MRS LAWNEY	310
HILL, MR MARTIN	311
HILLS, MR CHARLES	312
HILLS, MR J. W.	313
HOAD, MR MARK	314
HOBBS, MR ANDY	315
HOBBS, MR PHILIP	316
HODGES, MR RON	317
HODGSON, MR SIMON	318
†HOGARTH, MR HENRY	319
HOLLINGSWORTH, MR ALAN	320
HOLLINSHEAD, MR REG	321
HOLMES, MR PATRICK	322
HOLT, MR JOHN	323
HONEYBALL, MR ANTHONY	324
HOURIGAN, MR MICHAEL	325
HOWE, MR STUART	326
HOWLING, MR PAUL	327
HUGHES, MR D. T.	328
†HUGHES, MR J. S.	329
HUGHES, MRS JO	330
†HUGHES, MR STEPHEN	331
HUGO, MS N. M.	332
HUMPHREY, MRS SARAH	333
†HUNTER, MR KEVIN	334

Name	Team No.
†THURLEY, MISS LAURA	335
HUTCHINSON, MISS ALISON	336

I

Name	Team No.
INGRAM, MR ROGER	337
IVORY, MR DEAN	338

J

Name	Team No.
JACKSON, MISS TINA	339
†JACKSON, MRS VALERIE	340
JAMES, MR LEE	341
JARDINE, MR IAIN	342
JARVIS, MR ALAN	343
JARVIS, MR WILLIAM	344
JEFFERSON, MR MALCOLM	345
JENKINS, MR J. R.	346
†JESSOP, MR ALAN	347
JEWELL, MRS LINDA	348
JOHNSON, MR BRETT	349
JOHNSON HOUGHTON, MISS EVE.	350
JOHNSON, MR ROBERT	351
†JOHNSON, MRS SUSAN	352
JOHNSTON, MR M. S.	353
JONES, MR ALAN	354
JONES, MR GEORGE	355
JONES, MS LUCY	356
JORDAN, MRS VIOLET M.	357

K

Name	Team No.
KEDDY, MR TOM	358
KEEVIL, MRS CAROLINE	359
KEIGHLEY, MR MARTIN	360
KELLETT, MR CHRISTOPHER	361
KELLEWAY, MISS GAY	362
KELLY, MR G. P.	363
†KENDALL, MISS LYNSEY	364
KENT, MR NICK	365
†KERSWELL, MISS SARAH	366
KING, MR ALAN	367
KING, MR NEIL	368

Name	Team No.
MOORE, MR J. S.	446
MORGAN, MR KEVIN	447
MORRIS, MR DAVE	448
MORRIS, MR M. F.	449
MORRIS, MR PAT	450
MORRISON, MR HUGHIE	451
MOSS, MR GARRY	452
MUIR, MR WILLIAM	453
MULHALL, MR CLIVE	454
MULHOLLAND, MR NEIL	455
MULLANEY, MR LAWRENCE	456
MULLINEAUX, MR MICHAEL	457
MULLINS, MR SEAMUS	458
MULLINS, MR WILLIAM P.	459
MURPHY, MRS ANABEL	460
MURPHY, MR COLM	461
MURPHY, MR FERDY	462
MURPHY, MR M. P. F.	463
MURPHY, MR MIKE	464
MURPHY, MR PAT	465
MURTAGH, MR BARRY	466
MUSSON, MR WILLIE	467

N

Name	Team No.
NAGLE, MR DAVID	468
NAYLOR, DR JEREMY	469
†NEEDHAM, MR JOHN	470
NELMES, MRS HELEN	471
†NENADICH, MR CHRIS	472
NEWCOMBE, MR TONY	473
NEWLAND, DR RICHARD	474
NEWTON-SMITH, MISS ANNA	475
NICHOLLS, MR DAVID	476
NICHOLLS, MR PAUL	477
NIVEN, MR PETER	478
†NIXON, MR RAYSON	479
†NOCK, MRS SUSAN	480
NOLAN, MR S. T.	481
NORMILE, MRS LUCY	482
NORTON, MR JOHN	483
NOSEDA, MR JEREMY	484

O

Name	Team No.
O'BRIEN, MR A. P.	485
O'BRIEN, MR DANIEL	486
O'BRIEN, MR FERGAL	487
O'KEEFFE, MR JEDD	488
O'MEARA, MR DAVID	489
†O'NEILL, MR JOHN	490
O'NEILL, MR JONJO	491
O'SHEA, MR JOHN	492
OLD, MR JIM	493
OLDROYD, MR GEOFFREY	494
OSBORNE, MR JAMIE	495
OXX, MR JOHN M.	496

P

Name	Team No.
PALLING, MR BRYN	497
PALMER, MR HUGO	498
PANVERT, MR JOHN	499
†PARROTT, MRS HILARY	500
†PAYNE, MR JAMES	501
PEACOCK, MR RAY	502
PEARCE, MRS LYDIA	503
PEARS, MR OLLIE	504
†PEARSON, MR DAVID	505
PERRATT, MISS LINDA	506
PERRETT, MRS AMANDA	507
PHELAN, MR PAT	508
PHILLIPS, MR RICHARD	509
PIPE, MR DAVID	510
PITT, MR TIM	511
POGSON, MR CHARLES	512
POMFRET, MR NICHOLAS	513
PORTMAN, MR JONATHAN	514
POULTON, MR JAMIE	515
POWELL, MR BRENDAN	516
POWELL, MR TED	517
PRESCOTT BT, SIR MARK	518
PRICE, MR ANDREW	519
†PRICE, MR JOHN	520
PRICE, MR RICHARD	521
PRITCHARD, MR PETER	522

Name	Team No.
PURDY, MR PETER	523

Q

Name	Team No.
QUINLAN, MR NOEL	524
QUINN, MR JOHN	525
QUINN, MR MICHAEL	526

R

Name	Team No.
†RATCLIFFE, MR C. I.	527
†REED, MR WILLIAM	528
REES, MR DAVID	529
†REES, MRS HELEN	530
REGAN, MR SEAN	531
REID, MR ANDREW	532
†RETTER, MRS JACQUELINE	533
REVELEY, MR KEITH	534
RICH, MR PAUL	535
†RICHARDS, MR DAVID	536
RICHARDS, MRS LYDIA	537
RICHARDS, MR NICKY	538
RIMELL, MR MARK	539
RIMMER, MR MARK	540
†ROBERTS, MISS BETH	541
ROBESON, MRS RENEE	542
ROBINSON, MISS SARAH	543
ROBSON, MISS PAULINE	544
ROHAUT, MR FRANCOIS	545
†ROSS, MISS JOSIE	546
ROTHWELL, MR BRIAN	547
ROTHWELL, MR P. J.	548
ROUGET, MR J. C.	549
ROWE, MR RICHARD	550
ROWLAND, MISS MANDY	551
ROYER-DUPRE, MR A. DE	552
RUSSELL, MS LUCINDA	553
RYALL, MR JOHN	554
RYAN, MR JOHN	555
RYAN, MR KEVIN	556

S

Name	Team No.
SADIK, MR AYTACH	557
SALAMAN, MR MATTHEW	558
SALMON, MR PETER	559
†SANDERSON, MRS MARY	560
SAUNDERS, MR MALCOLM	561
SAYER, MRS DIANNE	562
SCARGILL, DR JON	563
†SCOTT, MR DERRICK	564
†SCOTT, MRS ELIZABETH	565
SCOTT, MR JEREMY	566
SCUDAMORE, MR MICHAEL	567
SHAW, MR DEREK	568
†SHAW, MRS PATRICIA	569
SHEPPARD, MR MATT	570
SHERIDAN, MR FRANK	571
SHERWOOD, MR OLIVER	572
SHIRLEY-BEAVAN, MR SIMON	573
SIDDALL, MISS LYNN	574
SIMCOCK, MR DAVID	575
†SLACK, MRS EVELYN	576
SLY, MRS PAM	577
SMAGA, MR DAVID	578
SMART, MR BRYAN	579
SMITH, MR CHARLES	580
SMITH, MR JULIAN	581
SMITH, MR MICHAEL	582
SMITH, MR RALPH	583
SMITH, MR ROBERT	584
SMITH, MRS SUE	585
SMITH, MISS SUZY	586
SMYLY, MR GILES	587
SNOWDEN, MR JAMIE	588
SOWERSBY, MR MIKE	589
SPEARING, MR JOHN	590
SQUANCE, MR MICHAEL	591
STACK, MR TOMMY	592
†STEELE, MR DANIEL	593
†STEPHEN, MRS JACKIE	594
STEVENS, MR OLLY	595
STIMPSON, MR JOHN	596

Name	Team No.
STOKELL, MISS ANN	597
STONE, MR WILLIAM	598
STOREY, MR BRIAN	599
STOREY, MR WILF	600
STOUTE, SIR MICHAEL	601
STUBBS, MISS KRISTIN	602
SUMMERS, MR ROB	603
SUPPLE, MR JOHN A.	604
SWINBANK, MR ALAN	605
SYMONDS, MR TOM	606

T

Name	Team No.
TALLIS, MR PATRICK	607
TATE, MR JAMES	608
TATE, MR TOM	609
†TAYLOR, MRS SUSAN	610
TEAGUE, MR COLIN	611
TEAL, MR ROGER	612
†THOMAS, MRS D.	613
THOMPSON, MR DAVID	614
†THOMPSON, MR VICTOR	615
THOMSON, MR SANDY	616
TIERNEY, MR RUAIDHRI J.	617
TINKLER, MR NIGEL	618
TIZZARD, MR COLIN	619
TODHUNTER, MR MARTIN	620
TOLLER, MR JAMES	621
TOMPKINS, MR MARK	622
TORK, MR KEVIN	623
TUER, MR EDWIN	624
TUITE, MR JOSEPH	625
TURNELL, MR ANDREW	626
TURNER, MR BILL	627
TURNER, MR JAMES	628
TUTTY, MRS KAREN	629
TWISTON-DAVIES, MR NIGEL	630

U

Name	Team No.
UNETT, MR JAMES	631
UPSON, MR JOHN	632

Name	Team No.
USHER, MR MARK	633

V

Name	Team No.
VARIAN, MR ROGER	634
VAUGHAN, MR ED	635
VAUGHAN, MR TIM	636
VON DER RECKE, MR CHRISTIAN	637

W

Name	Team No.
WADE, MR JOHN	638
WADHAM, MRS LUCY	639
WAGGOTT, MISS TRACY	640
WAINWRIGHT, MR JOHN	641
†WALEY-COHEN, MR ROBERT	642
WALFORD, MR ROBERT	643
WALFORD, MR TIM	644
WALKER, MR ED	645
WALL, MR CHRIS	646
†WALL, MRS SARAH	647
WALL, MR TREVOR	648
†WALTON, MR JAMES	649
WALTON, MRS JANE	650
WALTON, MRS SHEENA	651
WARD, MR JASON	652
WATSON, MR FREDERICK	653
WATT, MRS SHARON	654
WAUGH, MR SIMON	655
WEAVER, MISS AMY	656
WEBBER, MR PAUL	657
WELD, MR D. K.	658
†WELLICOME, MR DEREK	659
WEST, MISS SHEENA	660
WEST, MR SIMON	661
†WESTON, MR MARTIN	662
†WESTWOOD, MISS JESSICA	663
WEYMES, MR JOHN	664
WHEELER, MR ERIC	665
WHILLANS, MR ALISTAIR	666
WHILLANS, MR DONALD	667
WHITAKER, MR RICHARD	668

PROPERTY OF HER MAJESTY

The Queen

Colours: Purple, gold braid, scarlet sleeves, black velvet cap with gold fringe

Trained by **Sir Michael Stoute**, Newmarket

  1 ESTIMATE (IRE), 4, b f Monsun (GER) - Ebaziya (IRE)

THREE-YEAR-OLDS

  2 BERKELEY STREET (USA), b g Street Cry (IRE) - Dream Ticket (USA)
  3 BOLD SNIPER, b c New Approach (IRE) - Daring Aim
  4 CIRCUS TURN (USA), b g Street Cry (IRE) - Showlady (USA)

Trained by **Richard Hannon**, Marlborough

THREE-YEAR-OLDS

  5 PRINCE'S TRUST, b g Invincible Spirit (IRE) - Lost In Wonder (USA)
  6 SEA SHANTY (USA), b g Elusive Quality (USA) - Medley
  7 SWEET AS HONEY, b f Duke of Marmalade (IRE) - Tempting Prospect

TWO-YEAR-OLDS

  8 BOLD SPIRIT, b c 9/3 Invincible Spirit (IRE) - Far Shores (USA) (Distant View (USA))
  9 KINLOSS, ch f 6/2 Kheleyf (USA) - Celtic Cross (Selkirk (USA))
  10 MUSICAL COMEDY, b c 3/3 Royal Applause - Spinning Top (Alzao (USA))

Trained by **Roger Charlton**, Beckhampton

  11 BORDER LEGEND, 4, ch g Selkirk (USA) - Bonnie Doon (IRE)

THREE-YEAR-OLDS

  12 CANDOLUMINESCENCE, br f Dansili - Flash of Gold
  13 INAUGURAL, b g Invincible Spirit (IRE) - Anasazi (IRE)

Trained by **Michael Bell**, Newmarket

  14 SIGN MANUAL, 4, b g Motivator - New Assembly (IRE)

THREE-YEAR-OLDS

  15 DALLIEFOUR (IRE), b f Cape Cross (IRE) - Daliyana (IRE)
  16 GAMBLE, ch f Galileo (IRE) - Pretty Face
  17 HANDIWORK, ch g Motivator - Spinning Top
  18 SOUVENIR, b f Cape Cross (IRE) - Trianon

PROPERTY OF HER MAJESTY

The Queen

Trained by **Andrew Balding**, Kingsclere

THREE-YEAR-OLDS
19 WHITE MONTH, b g Tiger Hill (IRE) - Purple Heather (USA)

TWO-YEAR-OLDS
20 MICRAS, b f 20/2 Medicean - Purple Heather (USA) (Rahy (USA))

Trained by **Mrs Gai Waterhouse**, Sydney, Australia

21 CARLTON HOUSE (USA), 5, b h Street Cry (IRE) - Talented

Trained by **Nicky Henderson**, Lambourn

22 CLOSE TOUCH, 5, ch g Generous (IRE) - Romantic Dream
23 KILLIECRANKIE, 5, b g Kayf Tara - Bella Macrae
24 OPEN HEARTED, 6, b g Generous (IRE) - Romantic Dream
25 SIDE STEP, 4, b f Norse Dancer (IRE) - Magic Score
26 SPECIAL AGENT, 4, b g Invincible Spirit (IRE) - Flight of Fancy

To be allocated

TWO-YEAR-OLDS
27 DALMATIA (IRE), gr f 20/3 Cape Cross (IRE) - Dalataya (IRE) (Sadler's Wells (USA))
28 DUMFRIES HOUSE, b c 8/3 New Approach (IRE) - Bonnie Doon (IRE) (Grand Lodge (USA))
29 ENLIVEN, b f 9/5 Dansili - Aurore (IRE) (Fasliyev (USA))
30 B f 18/2 Street Cry (IRE) - Enticement (Montjeu (IRE))
31 FIERY SUNSET, b f 23/3 Galileo (IRE) - Five Fields (USA) (Chester House (USA))
32 GOOD HOPE, b f 13/2 Cape Cross (IRE) - Fairy Godmother (Fairy King (USA))
33 PURPLE SPECTRUM, gr c 17/2 Verglas (IRE) - Rainbow's Edge (Rainbow Quest (USA))
34 QUEEN'S PRIZE, b f 27/1 Dansili - Daring Aim (Daylami (IRE))
35 RAVENOUS, b c 6/2 Raven's Pass (USA) - Supereva (IRE) (Sadler's Wells (USA))
36 SHAMA (IRE), b f 28/4 Danehill Dancer (IRE) - Shamadara (IRE) (Kahyasi)
37 SHARP LOOKOUT, b c 23/3 Shamardal (USA) - Tempting Prospect (Shirley Heights)
38 SILVER MIRAGE, b f 9/3 Oasis Dream - Phantom Gold (Machiavellian (USA))
39 TREPIDATION, ch c 12/2 Danehill Dancer (IRE) - Trianon (Nayef (USA))

1 MR HANS ADIELSSON, Kingston Lisle
Postal: **Compton Beauchamp Estates Ltd (Racing), Manor Farm Stables,
Kingston Lisle Business Centre, Kingston Lisle, Oxfordshire, OX12 9QX**
Contacts: **PHONE Office (01367) 820690 FAX (01367) 820690 MOBILE (07500) 044748**
E-MAIL manorstables@btconnect.com

1 **BEAUCHAMP XERXES**, 7, ch g Compton Admiral—Compton Astoria (USA) **Mr Erik Penser**
2 **BUCKLAND (IRE)**, 5, b g Oratorio (IRE)—Dollar Bird (IRE) **Mr P. S. McNally**
3 **COMPTON BABY**, 4, b f Proud Citizen (USA)—Baby Victory (BRZ) **Mr Erik Penser**
4 **COMPTON BIRD**, 4, b f Motivator—Noble Peregrine **Mr Erik Penser**
5 **COMPTON CROFTER**, 4, ch g Sleeping Indian—Crofters Ceilidh **Mr Erik Penser**
6 **HURRICANE SPIRIT (IRE)**, 9, b g Invincible Spirit (IRE)—Gale Warning (IRE) **Hans Adielsson A.B.**
7 **KARATE (IRE)**, 5, ch g Exceed And Excel (AUS)—La Belle Katherine (USA) **Mr Erik Penser**

THREE-YEAR-OLDS
8 **BEAUCHAMP ASTRA**, b f Observatory (USA)—Ashford Castle (USA) **Mr Erik Penser**
9 **BEAUCHAMP BELLA**, b f Manduro (GER)—Baharah (USA) **Mr Erik Penser**
10 **BEAUCHAMP SUNSET**, b g Tiger Hill (IRE)—Orange Sunset (IRE) **Mr Erik Penser**
11 **CATCH THE CIDER**, b g Medicean—Zanna (FR) **P & D Bronsman**
12 **COMPTON SILVER**, ch g Haafhd—Anna Oleanda (IRE) **Mr Erik Penser**
13 **LARS KRISTER (IRE)**, b g Clodovil (IRE)—Ann's Annie (IRE) **Hans Adielsson A.B.**

TWO-YEAR-OLDS
14 **BEAUCHAMP AMBER**, b f 8/4 Compton Admiral—Aquarelle (Kenmare (FR)) **Mr Erik Penser**
15 **BEAUCHAMP GEM**, ch f 24/5 Compton Admiral—Baharah (USA) (Elusive Quality (USA)) **Mr Erik Penser**
16 **BEAUCHAMP KITE**, b c 7/4 Compton Admiral—Orange Sunset (IRE) (Roanoke (USA)) **Mr Erik Penser**
17 **BEAUCHAMP MELBA**, b f 23/4 Compton Admiral—Ashford Castle (USA) (Bates Motel (USA)) **Mr Erik Penser**
18 **BEAUCHAMP ROCK**, b c 9/5 Proclamation (IRE)—Beauchamp Utopia (Compton Admiral) **Mr Erik Penser**
19 **COMPTON REX**, br g 24/2 Mount Nelson—Jane Austen (Galileo (IRE)) (15000) **Mr Erik Penser**

Apprentice: Nicole Nordblad.

2 MR MAHMOOD AL ZAROONI, Newmarket
Postal: **Godolphin Management Co Ltd, Godolphin Stables, Snailwell Road, Newmarket,
Suffolk, CB8 7YE**

The following list has not been supplied by the trainer and is as accurate as possible at the time of going
to press. Some horses listed may not return to Britain from Dubai. Only 2yos entered in the 2014 Derby
are shown. **For the latest information please visit www.godolphin.com**

1 **AHTOUG**, 5, b h Byron—Cherokee Rose (IRE)
2 **AICHI (AUS)**, 8, b g Strategic—Nagoya (AUS)
3 **ALDGATE (USA)**, 4, ch g Street Cry (IRE)—Adonesque (IRE)
4 **ANATOLIAN**, 5, ch g Pivotal—Poseidon's Bride (USA)
5 **ANOMALY**, 4, ch c Pivotal—Anna Palariva (IRE)
6 **ARTHUR'S TALE (USA)**, 5, b h Bernardini (USA)—Owsley (USA)
7 **BANK MERGER (USA)**, 6, ch h Consolidator (USA)—Lucrative (USA)
8 **BANNOCK (IRE)**, 4, b c Bertolini (USA)—Laoub (USA)
9 **CALVADOS BLUES (FR)**, 7, ch h Lando (GER)—Persian Belle
10 **CAPPONI (IRE)**, 6, ch h Medicean—Nawaiet (USA)
11 **CITY STYLE (USA)**, 7, ch g City Zip (USA)—Brattothecore (CAN)
12 **COUNTERGLOW (IRE)**, 4, b g Echo of Light—Quintellina
13 **DOUBLE DEALER**, 5, b g Dubawi (IRE)—Infiel
14 **ENCKE (USA)**, 4, b c Kingmambo (USA)—Shawanda (IRE)
15 **ENERGIZER (GER)**, 4, b c Monsun (GER)—Erytheis (USA)
16 **FALLS OF LORA (IRE)**, 4, b f Street Cry (IRE)—Firth of Lorne (IRE)
17 **FIREBEAM**, 5, b g Cadeaux Genereux—Firebelly
18 **FRENCH NAVY**, 5, b h Shamardal (USA)—First Fleet (USA)
19 **FULBRIGHT**, 4, b c Exceed And Excel (AUS)—Lindfield Belle (USA)
20 **GENIUS BEAST (USA)**, 5, b h Kingmambo (USA)—Shawanda (IRE)
21 **GENIUS STEP (IRE)**, 4, b c Dubawi (IRE)—Kathy College (IRE)
22 **GOLD RALLY (USA)**, 4, gr g Medaglia d'oro (USA)—Beright (USA)
23 **GREEK WAR (IRE)**, 4, ch g Monsun (GER)—Gonfilia (GER)

MR MAHMOOD AL ZAROONI - Continued

24 **INLER (IRE)**, 6, br g Red Ransom (USA)—Wedding Gift (FR)
25 **KINGLET (USA)**, 4, b br c Kingmambo (USA)—Karen's Caper (USA)
26 **LAAJOOJ (IRE)**, 5, b h Azamour (IRE)—Flanders (IRE)
27 **MANDAEAN**, 4, b c Manduro (GER)—Summertime Legacy
28 **MARINER'S CROSS (IRE)**, 4, b c Dubawi (IRE)—Trilemma
29 **MARSHGATE LANE (USA)**, 4, b c Medaglia d'oro (USA)—Louvain (IRE)
30 **MASTERSTROKE (USA)**, 4, B C Monsun (GER)—Melikah (IRE)
31 **MAYWOOD**, 5, b g Cape Cross (IRE)—Murrieta
32 **MEASURING TIME**, 5, b g Dubai Destination (USA)—Inchberry
33 **MENTAL (AUS)**, 5, b g Lonhro (AUS)—Intrigues (AUS)
34 **MIGHTY AMBITION (USA)**, 4, b c Street Cry (IRE)—New Morning (IRE)
35 **MODERN HISTORY (IRE)**, 5, b g Shamardal (USA)—Fatefully (USA)
36 **MONTEROSSO**, 6, b h Dubawi (IRE)—Porto Roca (AUS)
37 **MOONWALK IN PARIS (FR)**, 5, b g Oratorio (IRE)—Shining Glory
38 **NAQSHABBAN (USA)**, 5, b g Street Cry (IRE)—Reem Three
39 **NOVELTY SEEKER (USA)**, 4, B C Street Sense (USA)—Nawaiet (USA)
40 **OCEAN WAR**, 5, gr g Dalakhani (IRE)—Atlantic Destiny (IRE)
41 **OPINION POLL (IRE)**, 7, b h Halling (USA)—Ahead
42 **PARLOUR GAMES**, 5, ch h Monsun (GER)—Petrushka (IRE)
43 **POLICE FORCE (USA)**, 4, b g Street Sense (USA)—Land of Dreams
44 **PRINCE OF ORANGE (IRE)**, 4, b c Shamardal (USA)—Cox Orange (USA)
45 **PRUSSIAN**, 4, b f Dubai Destination (USA)—Russian Snows (IRE)
46 **RED GULCH**, 6, b g Kyllachy—Enrapture (USA)
47 **ROSTRUM (FR)**, 6, b g Shamardal (USA)—En Public (FR)
48 **RUBAN (IRE)**, 4, ch c Dubawi (IRE)—Piece Unique
49 **RUWAIYAN (USA)**, 4, b br c Cape Cross (IRE)—Maskunah (IRE)
50 **SADEEK'S SONG (USA)**, 5, ch h Kingmambo (USA)—New Morning (IRE)
51 **SAINT BAUDOLINO (IRE)**, 4, B C Pivotal—Alessandria
52 **SAMBA KING**, 4, b g Dubai Destination (USA)—Dance of Leaves
53 **SAMURAI SWORD**, 5, b h Motivator—Japanese Whisper (UAE)
54 **SHIMRAAN (FR)**, 6, b g Rainbow Quest (USA)—Shemriyna (IRE)
55 **SPLASH POINT**, 5, b h Street Cry (IRE)—Dianehill (IRE)
56 **SWEDISH SAILOR**, 4, b c Monsun (GER)—Epitome (IRE)
57 **TAHITIAN WARRIOR (USA)**, 6, gr ro g Maria's Mon (USA)—Chatique (USA)
58 **TAYLOR SAID (CAN)**, 5, b br g Stephanotis (CAN)—Fleet Amyanne (CAN)
59 **TENENBAUM**, 4, b g Authorized (IRE)—Al Hasnaa
60 **TIME PRISONER (USA)**, 6, gr ro h Elusive Quality (USA)—Zelanda (IRE)
61 **VAN ELLIS**, 4, b c Shamardal (USA)—Jalousie (IRE)
62 **ZAEEM**, 4, b c Echo of Light—Across (ARG)
63 **ZIP TOP (IRE)**, 4, b c Smart Strike (CAN)—Zofzig (USA)

THREE-YEAR-OLDS

64 **ALTRUISM (IRE)**, b c Authorized (IRE)—Bold Assumption
65 **ARTIGIANO (USA)**, ch c Distorted Humor (USA)—Angel Craft (USA)
66 **AUTHORSHIP (IRE)**, b c Authorized (IRE)—Desert Frolic (IRE)
67 **BATHRAT AMAL (JPN)**, ch f New Approach (IRE)—Zameyla (IRE)
68 **BOURBON (IRE)**, b c Raven's Pass (USA)—Traou Mad (IRE)
69 **CAP O'RUSHES**, b c New Approach (IRE)—Valley of Gold (FR)
70 **CAT O'MOUNTAIN (USA)**, b br c Street Cry (IRE)—Thunder Kitten (USA)
71 **CERTIFY (USA)**, b f Elusive Quality (USA)—Please Sign In (USA)
72 **CHESTERFIELD (IRE)**, ch c Pivotal—Antique (IRE)
73 **DESERT BLOSSOM (IRE)**, ch f Shamardal (USA)—Elshamms
74 **DESERT WINGS (IRE)**, ch c Raven's Pass (USA)—Rise and Fall (USA)
75 **DOLDRUMS (USA)**, b f Bernardini (USA)—Appealing Storm (USA)
76 **ENNISTOWN**, b c Authorized (IRE)—Saoirse Abu (USA)
77 **ENNOBLED FRIEND (USA)**, b c Malibu Moon (USA)—Seek To Soar (USA)
78 **EXPLORATORY (USA)**, ch c New Approach (IRE)—Arlette (IRE)
79 **FAULKNER**, ch c Pivotal—Fibou (USA)
80 **FILFIL (USA)**, b c Hard Spun (USA)—Dixietwostepper (USA)
81 **FOR POSTERITY**, b c Shamardal (USA)—Past The Post (USA)
82 **GHANAIAN (FR)**, b f Shamardal (USA)—Ghanaj
83 **GHOSTFLOWER (IRE)**, b f Dansili—Silkwood
84 **GOLDEN LEAVES (USA)**, b f Tiznow (USA)—Desert Gold (USA)
85 **GREAT TIMING (USA)**, ch f Raven's Pass (USA)—Rumors Are Flying (USA)
86 **IMPROVISATION (IRE)**, b c Teofilo (IRE)—Dance Troupe

MR MAHMOOD AL ZAROONI - Continued

87 KALISPELL (IRE), b f Singspiel (IRE)—Genovefa (USA)
88 KOSIKA (USA), b f Hard Spun (USA)—Song of Africa (USA)
89 LAWMANS THUNDER, b c Lawman (FR)—Rhapsodize
90 LAYL (USA), b br c Street Cry (IRE)—Cymbal (IRE)
91 LIFE PARTNER (IRE), b c Cape Cross (IRE)—Miss Intimate (USA)
92 LILAC TREE, b c Dubawi (IRE)—Kalidasa (USA)
93 LORD PROVOST (IRE), b c Teofilo (IRE)—Mayoress
94 LOUD, ch g Dutch Art—Applauding (IRE)
95 LOVELY PASS (IRE), b f Raven's Pass (USA)—Macadamia (IRE)
96 MONDLICHT (USA), b c Malibu Moon (USA)—Moonlight Cruise (USA)
97 MRS BANNOCK (IRE), b f Shamardal (USA)—Laoub (USA)
98 MUSIC CHART (USA), b f Exchange Rate (USA)—Conchita (USA)
99 NATIONAL POET (IRE), ch c Nayef (USA)—Reve d'iman (FR)
100 NEWSREADER (USA), b c New Approach (IRE)—Headline
101 NIGHTSTER (IRE), ch c Raven's Pass (USA)—Ama (USA)
102 NOW SPUN (USA), b c Hard Spun (USA)—Campionessa (USA)
103 PERSONABLE, b c Cape Cross (IRE)—Likeable
104 POWER OF LIGHT (IRE), b f Echo of Light—Dubai Power
105 PRESS ROOM (USA), b c Street Cry (IRE)—Causeway Lass (AUS)
106 PUPPET THEATRE (IRE), ch f Pivotal—Eilean Ban (USA)
107 QUINTILIAN (IRE), b g Cape Cross (IRE)—Athenian Way (IRE)
108 REEHAN (USA), b f Bernardini (USA)—Remember (USA)
109 REQUESTED, b c Dubawi (IRE)—Dream Quest
110 RESTRAINT OF TRADE (IRE), br c Authorized (IRE)—Zivania (IRE)
111 ROLE PLAYER, ch c Exceed And Excel (AUS)—Dresden Doll (USA)
112 SNOW ROSE (USA), b f Elusive Quality (USA)—Ascutney (USA)
113 SNOWBOARDER (USA), ch c Raven's Pass (USA)—Gaudete (USA)
114 SPECKLED (USA), b br f Street Cry (IRE)—Painted Lady (USA)
115 STAMFORD, b c Dubawi (IRE)—Pure
116 SUGAR HOUSE (USA), ch f Distorted Humor (USA)—Malibu Mint (USA)
117 SWEET ROSE, ch f New Approach (IRE)—White Rose (GER)
118 THATCHMASTER (USA), b br c Street Cry (IRE)—Michita (USA)
119 TIMONEER (USA), b br c Elusive Quality (USA)—Gentle Gale (USA)
120 TOP JOKER, b c Raven's Pass (USA)—French Bid (AUS)
121 TRAVEL (USA), ch f Street Cry (IRE)—Away (USA)
122 TUMBLEDOWN (USA), b f Bernardini (USA)—Freeroll (USA)
123 VALLEY OF QUEENS (IRE), ch f Raven's Pass (USA)—Sweet Folly (IRE)
124 WAVERUNNER, ch f Raven's Pass (USA)—Danuta (USA)
125 WILLOWING (USA), b f Hard Spun (USA)—Sweet Arizona (USA)
126 WINTERLUDE (IRE), b c Street Cry (IRE)—New Morning (IRE)
127 ZURBRIGGEN, ch c Raven's Pass (USA)—Zanzibar (IRE)

TWO-YEAR-OLDS

128 B c 28/2 Sea The Stars (IRE)—Argentina (IRE) (Sadler's Wells (USA))
129 B c 11/3 Dubawi (IRE)—Assabiyya (IRE) (Cape Cross (IRE))
130 B c 11/4 Dubawi (IRE)—Calando (USA) (Storm Cat (USA))
131 B c 19/4 Shamardal (USA)—Cape Verdi (IRE) (Caerleon (USA))
132 B c 27/3 Shamardal (USA)—Chaquiras (USA) (Seeking The Gold (USA))
133 B br c 15/4 Medaglia d'oro (USA)—Criticism (USA) (Machiavellian (USA))
134 CRY JOY (USA), b c 5/5 Street Cry (IRE)—Blushing Ogygian (USA) (Ogygian (USA)) (245775)
135 Ch c 18/2 Raven's Pass (USA)—Damiana (IRE) (Thatching)
136 Ch c 10/4 Dubawi (IRE)—Danella (FR) (Highest Honor (FR))
137 B c 11/2 Cape Cross (IRE)—Dove (IRE) (Sadler's Wells (USA))
138 Ch c 27/1 New Approach (IRE)—Dubai Surprise (IRE) (King's Best (USA)) (280000)
139 B c 3/2 New Approach (IRE)—Firth of Lorne (IRE) (Danehill (USA))
140 Ch c 26/4 Teofilo (IRE)—Goldthroat (IRE) (Zafonic (USA)) (222221)
141 B c 17/3 Shamardal (USA)—Inchmahome (Galileo (IRE)) (57142)
142 B c 3/3 Teofilo (IRE)—Innclassic (IRE) (Stravinsky (USA))
143 B c 27/2 Dubawi (IRE)—Lion Forest (USA) (Forestry (USA)) (260000)
144 B c 23/2 Teofilo (IRE)—Mialuna (Zafonic (USA))
145 B c 10/4 Shamardal (USA)—Miracolia (IRE) (Montjeu (IRE)) (150000)
146 B c 9/2 Dubawi (IRE)—Miss Delila (USA) (Malibu Moon (USA)) (320000)
147 B c 28/3 Teofilo (IRE)—Most Charming (FR) (Darshaan)
148 B c 12/3 Monsun (GER)—Pongee (Barathea (IRE)) (400000)
149 B c 12/3 Teofilo (IRE)—Rachelle (IRE) (Mark of Esteem (IRE))

MR MAHMOOD AL ZAROONI - Continued

150 Gr c 22/2 Dubawi (IRE)—Ronaldsay (Kirkwall) (171428)
151 Ch c 13/1 New Approach (IRE)—Sentimental Value (USA) (Diesis)
152 B c 25/1 Street Cry (IRE)—Serenading (USA) (A P Indy (USA)) (737327)
153 B c 13/4 Dansili—Short Skirt (Diktat)
154 B c 23/3 Dansili—Snow Ballerina (Sadler's Wells (USA))
155 B c 31/1 New Approach (IRE)—Speirbhean (IRE) (Danehill (USA))
156 B c 20/2 Dubawi (IRE)—Tender Is Thenight (IRE) (Barathea (IRE))
157 B c 13/4 Sea The Stars (IRE)—Time On (Sadler's Wells (USA)) (125000)
158 B c 24/5 Sea The Stars (IRE)—Virtuosity (Pivotal) (125000)
159 B br c 4/3 Smart Strike (CAN)—Wile Cat (USA) (Storm Cat (USA)) (307219)

---

3 MR N. W. ALEXANDER, Kinneston
Postal: **Kinneston, Leslie, Glenrothes, Fife, KY6 3JJ**
Contacts: PHONE **(01592) 840774** MOBILE **(07831) 488210**
E-MAIL nicholasalexander@kinneston.com WEBSITE www.kinneston.com

1 ACADEMY (IRE), 5, br g Montjeu (IRE)—Rock The Casbah (FR) **Al Partners**
2 BACK ON THE ROAD (IRE), 11, br g Broken Hearted—Special Trix (IRE) **J. F. Alexander**
3 BERTIE MILAN (IRE), 8, b g Milan—Miss Bertaine (IRE) **Turcan Barber Douglas Miller Dunning**
4 BUFFALO BALLET, 7, b g Kayf Tara—Minora (IRE) **H W Turcan E MacGregor Sir Simon Dunning**
5 CAPITAL VENTURE (IRE), 7, b g Moscow Society (USA)—
                                    Benrue Adventure (IRE) **Mrs Ray Calder & Mrs Jan Scott**
6 CAUGHT IN THE ACT (IRE), 6, br g Overbury (IRE)—Catch Those Kisses **Turcan Barber Fletcher Dunning**
7 COMMERCIAL EXPRESS (IRE), 12, b g Oscar (IRE)—Biddy Earley (IRE) **N. W. Alexander**
8 DAASIJ (IRE), 8, b g Dalakhani (IRE)—Alyakkh (IRE) **Liddle Philipps Stanistreet Robinson**
9 ELMAATIGRA, 6, b g Elmaamul (USA)—Noble Tiger (IRE) **Macdonald, Fleming & Bradburne**
10 FLAMING THISTLE (IRE), 9, b g Flemensfirth (USA)—Native Thistle **N. W. Alexander**
11 FLEET FOX, 6, b g Alflora (IRE)—Minora (IRE) **Hardie & Robb**
12 FORCEFIELD, 7, b g Kalanisi (IRE)—Force of Nature (USA) **Kinneston Racing**
13 FRANKIE'S PROMISE (IRE), 5, ch g Fruits of Love (USA)—According To Molly (IRE) **Mr B. C. Castle**
14 GOLDTREK (USA), 6, b m Medallist (USA)—Traipse (USA) **J & S Dudgeon G & S Irwin W Alexander**
15 HERE'S TO HARRY, 6, b g Helissio (FR)—Harrietfield **Mrs R. C. Calder**
16 ISLA PATRIOT, 7, b g Silver Patriarch (IRE)—Salem Beach **Mrs P. M. Gammell**
17 ISLA PEARL FISHER, 10, br g Supreme Sound—Salem Beach **Mrs P. M. Gammell**
18 ISSABELLA GEM (IRE), 6, b m Marju (IRE)—Robin **Mrs M Stemp & Mrs P Robinson**
19 JET MASTER (IRE), 7, b g Brian Boru—Whats The Reason (IRE) **Mr H W Turcan & Sir Simon Dunning**
20 KING BREX (DEN), 10, b g Primatico (USA)—Moon Shine (DEN) **Alexander Family**
21 LITTLE GLENSHEE (IRE), 7, gr m Terimon—Harrietfield **Kinneston Racing**
22 MAKHZOON (USA), 9, b br g Dynaformer (USA)—Boubskaia **The Ladies Who**
23 MILANO MAGIC (IRE), 7, b g Milan—Magical Mist (IRE) **Mr A. Cochrane**
24 NATIVE COLL, 13, ch g Primitive Rising (USA)—Harrietfield **Alexander Family**
25 NORTHERN ACRES, 7, b g Mtoto—Bunting **C. Lysaght Media, Quandt & Cochrane**
26 NORTHERN FLAME (IRE), 8, b g Luso—Gails Gift (IRE) **The Peglegs**
27 OR DE GRUGY (FR), 11, b g April Night (FR)—Girlish (FR) **Lord Cochrane & Partners**
28 PAPAMOA, 8, gr g Terimon—Larksmore **The Papamoans**
29 ROSSINI'S DANCER, 8, b g Rossini (USA)—Bint Alhabib **Turcan Barber Fletcher Dunning**
30 SPINNING AWAY, 5, ch m Alflora (IRE)—Minora (IRE) **Alexander Family**
31 TIPSY DARA (IRE), 9, gr m Dushyantor (USA)—Tara The Grey (IRE) **Mr M. R. D. Fleming**

Other Owners: Mr Nicholas Alexander, Mr Jamie Alexander, Mr James Barber, Miss Emma Barlow, Mr John Bradburne, Mrs Ray Calder, The Hon Thomas Cochrane, Lord Cochrane of Cults, Mrs J. Douglas Miller, Mr John Dudgeon, Sir Simon Dunning, Mr Mark Fleming, Miss F. M. Fletcher, Mr Timothy Hardie, Mrs Margaret M. Henderson, Mrs S. Irwin, Mr Cornelius Lysaght, Miss E. G. Macgregor, Mr Dan Macdonald, Miss S. Quandt, Mrs L. Robb, Mrs Peter Robinson, Mrs Jan Scott, Mr D. Stanistreet, Mr H. W. Turcan.

Conditional: Lucy Alexander. **Apprentice:** Lucy Alexander. **Amateur:** Mr Kit Alexander, Mr Blair Campbell.

4 **MR JIM ALLEN, Tiverton**
Postal: **West Steart Farm, Stoodleigh, Tiverton, Devon, EX16 9QA**

1 BEACH RHYTHM (USA), 6, ch g Footstepsinthesand—Queen's Music (USA) **J. P. Allen**

THREE-YEAR-OLDS
2 INCANTARE, gr f Proclamation (IRE)—Mythical Charm **J. P. Allen**

---

5 **MR ERIC ALSTON, Preston**
Postal: **Edges Farm Stables, Chapel Lane, Longton, Preston, Lancashire, PR4 5NA**
Contacts: PHONE (01772) 612120 FAX (01772) 619600 MOBILE (07879) 641660
E-MAIL eric1943@supanet.com

1 BALLARINA, 7, b m Compton Place—Miss Uluwatu (IRE) **Mrs P. O. Morris**
2 BARKSTON ASH, 5, b g Kyllachy—Ae Kae Ae (USA) **The Selebians**
3 CHESTER ARISTOCRAT, 4, ch g Sakhee (USA)—New Light **Paul Buist & John Thompson**
4 DIMAN WATERS (IRE), 6, br g Namid—Phantom Waters **Paul Buist & John Thompson**
5 KING OF EDEN (IRE), 7, b g Royal Applause—Moonlight Paradise (USA) **The Grumpy Old Geezers**
6 KING OF PARADISE (IRE), 4, b g Hurricane Run (IRE)—Silly Game (IRE) **P. G. Buist**
7 LORD FRANKLIN, 4, ch g Iceman—Zell (IRE) **Liam & Tony Ferguson**
8 RED BARON (IRE), 4, b c Moss Vale (IRE)—Twinberry (IRE) **J. W. Stephenson**
9 SALLY'S SWANSONG, 7, b m Mind Games—Sister Sal **Miss F. D. Fenley**
10 SPAVENTO (IRE), 7, gr m Verglas—Lanasara **Whitehills Racing Syndicate**
11 TENHOO, 7, b g Reset (AUS)—Bella Bambina **Edges Farm Racing Stables Ltd**

THREE-YEAR-OLDS
12 CANTARA, b f Piccolo—Damalis (IRE) **Liam & Tony Ferguson**
13 LITTLE ELI, b g Green Desert (USA)—Princess Ellis **Whittle Racing Partnership**
14 SPIRIT OF PARKES, gr g Fair Mix (IRE)—Lucky Parkes **J. Heler**

TWO-YEAR-OLDS
15 BLITHE SPIRIT, b f 15/3 Byron—Damalis (IRE) (Mukaddamah (USA)) **Liam & Tony Ferguson**
16 MIGUELA MCGUIRE, b f 14/3 Sir Percy—Miss McGuire (Averti (IRE)) (6000) **J. W. Stephenson**
17 SPRING WILLOW (IRE), b c 11/4 Camacho—Twinberry (IRE) (Tagula (IRE)) (20952) **J. W. Stephenson**

Other Owners: Mrs J. E. Buist, M. L. Ferguson, Mr C. A. Ferguson, J. E. Jackson, M. S. Kelly, Mr R. Ormisher, J. Thompson.

Assistant Trainer: Mrs Sue Alston

Jockey (flat): David Allan.

---

6 **MR WILLIAM AMOS, Hawick**
Postal: **Broadhaugh Farm, Newmill on Teviot, Hawick, Roxburghshire, TD9 0JX**
Contacts: PHONE (01450) 850323 MOBILE (07810) 738149

1 ALL FOR A BUZZ, 8, ch m Alflora (IRE)—G'ime A Buzz **Aitchison Amos Hall Stenhouse**
2 APOLSKAPART (IRE), 5, b g Red Ransom (USA)—Polska (USA) **J. W. Stephenson**
3 ARC WARRIOR (FR), 9, b g Even Top (IRE)—What The Hell (FR) **J. J. Paterson**
4 BALLET D'ANGES (FR), 7, b br g Ange Gabriel (FR)—Balm (FR) **Mr I. A. Gauld**
5 BILLSGREY (IRE), 11, gr g Pistolet Bleu (IRE)—Grouse-N-Heather **John & Mary Stenhouse**
6 BOB'S DREAM (IRE), 11, b g Bob's Return (IRE)—Back In Kansas (IRE) **Kyle, Elliott & Crook**
7 BRIERYHILL BOY, 6, gr g Terimon—Bella Mary **Mr & Mrs D. S. Byers**
8 BURGUNDY BEAU, 7, br g Grape Tree Road—Chantilly Rose **Miss R. G. Brewis**
9 CYRUS DARIUS, 4, b g Overbury (IRE)—Barton Belle **J. W. Stephenson**
10 ISAACSTOWN LAD (IRE), 6, b g Milan—Friends of Friends (IRE) **J. W. Stephenson**
11 JAN JANDURA (IRE), 8, b g Flemensfirth (USA)—Friends of Friends (IRE) **S. Bonney**
12 JULIA TOO, 6, b m King's Theatre (IRE)—Candello **J. L. Gledson**
13 LOCHORE (IRE), 7, b g Morozov (USA)--Fulgina (FR) **Mr I. A. Gauld**
14 NEVILLE WOODS, 6, b g Alflora (IRE)—Angie Marinie **J. L. Gledson**
15 OIL BURNER, 8, b g Sir Harry Lewis (USA)—Quick Quote **Mr J. W. Clark**

MR WILLIAM AMOS - Continued

16 **PRINCE BLACKTHORN (IRE)**, 7, b g Desert Prince (IRE)—Notable Dear (ITY) **Abbadis Racing Club**
17 **RAVENSBILL (IRE)**, 11, b g Sea Raven (IRE)—Two Hills Folly (IRE) **John & Mary Stenhouse**
18 **SILVA SAMOURAI**, 4, gr g Proclamation (IRE)—Ladykirk **Mr I. A. Gauld**
19 **WHAT A DREAM**, 7, ch g Supreme Sound—Ben Roseler (IRE) **R. J. Kyle, D. & J. Byers**
20 **WILLIE HALL**, 9, b g Alflora (IRE)—G'ime A Buzz **R. H. Hall**

Other Owners: W. M. Aitchison, W. Amos, D. S. Byers, Mrs M. J. Byers, Mr J. R. Crook, K. R. Elliott, Mr J. H. Gibson, R. E. Jackson, R. J. Kyle, Mr J. M. Stenhouse, Mrs M. Stenhouse.

7	**MR MICHAEL APPLEBY, Newark**

Postal: **Stubby Nook Lodge Bungalow, Danethorpe Lane, Danethorpe, Newark, Nottinghamshire, NG24 2PD**
Contacts: **MOBILE (07884) 366421**
E-MAIL appleby477@aol.com

1 **ANGEL CAKE (IRE)**, 4, b f Dark Angel (IRE)—Royal Jelly **Mr W. J. Sewell**
2 **ARABIAN FLIGHT**, 4, b f Exceed And Excel (AUS)—Emirates First (IRE) **Dallas Racing**
3 **ART SCHOLAR (IRE)**, 6, b g Pyrus (USA)—Marigold (FR) **Mrs J. Scrivens**
4 **BANCNUANAHEIREANN (IRE)**, 6, b g Chevalier (IRE)—Alamanta (IRE) **Dallas Racing & Stephen Almond**
5 **BEYEH (IRE)**, 5, b m King's Best (USA)—Cradle Rock (IRE) **T. R. Pryke**
6 **BITAPHON (IRE)**, 4, br g Acclamation—Pitrizzia **Dallas Racing**
7 **CHESSETTS WOOD**, 7, b m Karinga Bay—La Bella Villa **K. D. Pugh**
8 **DEWALA**, 4, b f Deportivo—Fuwala **Goldform Racing**
9 **DUBAI RYTHM**, 4, b g Echo of Light—Slave To The Rythm (IRE) **M. Appleby**
10 **ELEGANT MUSE**, 5, b m Fraam—Georgianna (IRE) **T. R. Pryke**
11 **EXPOSE**, 5, ch g Compton Place—Show Off **The Giggle Factor Partnership**
12 **FALCON'S REIGN (FR)**, 4, ch g Haahhd—Al Badeya (IRE) **T. R. Pearson**
13 **FAVORITE GIRL (GER)**, 5, b m Shirocco (GER)—Favorite (GER) **T. R. Pryke**
14 **FIRST GLANCE**, 4, br g Passing Glance—Lady Santana (IRE) **Sarnian Racing**
15 **FLEETING FASHION**, 4, b f Alhaarth (IRE)—Sempre Sorriso **P. J. & Mrs J. P. Haycock**
16 **GENES QUEST**, 6, b m Rainbow High—Polly Tino **Mr A. Jordan**
17 **HARDWICK BAY**, 7, ch m Karinga Bay—Silver Madam **P. G. Hepworth**
18 **HELL HATH NO FURY**, 4, b f Oratorio (IRE)—Sagamartha **M. Appleby**
19 **HONOURED (IRE)**, 6, ch g Mark of Esteem (IRE)—Traou Mad (IRE) **Dallas Racing**
20 **HOT SUGAR (USA)**, 4, b g Lemon Drop Kid (USA)—Plaisir Des Yeux (FR) **M. Appleby**
21 **IRISH JUGGER (USA)**, 6, ch g Johannesburg (USA)—Jinny's Gold (USA) **Dallas Racing**
22 **JIMMY SEWELL (IRE)**, 4, b g Catcher In The Rye (IRE)—Starway To Heaven (ITY) **Mr W. J. Sewell**
23 **JONNY RYE (IRE)**, 9, ch g Anshan—Claudia Electric (IRE) **M. Appleby**
24 **LAPWORTH (IRE)**, 6, b g Alflora (IRE)—La Bella Villa **K. D. Pugh**
25 **LAYLA'S DANCER**, 6, b g Danehill Dancer (IRE)—Crumpetsfortea (IRE) **Dallas Racing**
26 **LIEUTENANT DAN (IRE)**, 6, b g Danroad (AUS)—Dakhira **Dallas Racing**
27 **LOCKANTANKS**, 6, ch g Compton Place—Locharia **Dallas Racing**
28 **MAGGIE PINK**, 4, b f Beat All (USA)—Top Notch **Mr A. W. Bult**
29 **MATA HARI BLUE**, 7, ch m Monsieur Bond (IRE)—Feeling Blue **Mr M. Golding**
30 **MEREVALE**, 4, b g Selkirk (USA)—A Thousand Smiles (IRE) **Dallas Racing & Stephen Almond**
31 **MINSKY MINE (IRE)**, 6, b g Montjeu (IRE)—Summer Trysting (USA) **T. R. Pryke**
32 **MISTRESS SHY**, 6, b m Zafeen (FR)—Nicholas Mistress **P. G. Hepworth**
33 **NO DIAMOND**, 6, b g Helissio (FR)—Diamond Swan **Mrs V. Kinder**
34 **OUR IVOR**, 4, gr g Cape Town (IRE)—Caprice **J & G Bacciochi, A Taylor, Bruce W Wyatt**
35 **RAAFA'S JIGSAW**, 4, ch f Araafa (IRE)—Puzzling **Dallas Racing**
36 **REACTION**, 7, ch g Alhaarth (IRE)—Hawas **The Giggle Factor Partnership**
37 **ROYAL PECULIAR**, 5, b h Galileo (IRE)—Distinctive Look (IRE) **T. R. Pryke**
38 **SERJEANT BUZFUZ**, 4, b g Halling (USA)—Anastasia Storm **M. Appleby**
39 **SQUIRE TRELAWNEY**, 7, b g Domedriver (IRE)—Crockadore (USA) **P. J. Haycock**
40 **STELLAR EXPRESS (IRE)**, 4, b f Royal Applause—Aitch (IRE) **Mr & Mrs James Sumsion**
41 **TAMASOU (IRE)**, 8, b g Tamarisk (IRE)—Soubresaut (IRE) **Brooklands Racing**
42 **THE LOCK MASTER (IRE)**, 6, b g Key of Luck (USA)—Pitrizza (IRE) **Kenneth George Kitchen**
43 **THEREABOUTS (USA)**, 4, b g Singspiel (IRE)—Around **Mr M. C. Elvin**
44 **TYSOE LAD**, 5, br g Zafeen (FR)—Nicholas Mistress **P. G. Hepworth**
45 **WHITE DIAMOND**, 6, b m Bertolini (USA)—Diamond White **T. R. Pryke**

MR MICHAEL APPLEBY - Continued

THREE-YEAR-OLDS

46 HIDDEN ASSET, ch c Sakhee's Secret—Petite Epaulette **T. R. Pryke**
47 IVY PORT, b f Deportivo—Ivy Bridge (IRE) **Goldform Racing**
48 MIAKO (USA), ch g Speightstown (USA)—Bond Queen (USA) **Rod In Pickle Partnership**
49 NO WIN NO FEE, b g Firebreak—Milliscent **Dallas Racing**
50 PETRA, b f Arkadian Hero (USA)—Moody Style (IRE) **Mrs J. Scrivens**
51 SHIRLEY'S PRIDE, b f Byron—Feeling Blue **Mr M. Golding**

TWO-YEAR-OLDS

52 B f 14/2 Piccolo—Tanning (Atraf) **M. Appleby**

Other Owners: Mr S. Almond, J. T. Bacciochi, Mr S. A. Ballard, M. H. Bates, Mr H. Birah, J. Branson, Mr C. Dixon, Mr M. A. Glassett, Mrs J. P. Haycock, Mr R. Hoiles, Mr J. R. Holt, Mr A. W. Le Page, Mr C. Le Page, D. S. Lovatt, Mrs A. M. Mercs, N. P. Sennett, Mr J. Soiza, Mr J. Sumsion, Mrs B. Sumsion, B. W. Wyatt.

Assistant Trainer: Mr Jonathan Clayton **Head Lad:** Jason Parkhouse

Jockey (flat): Neil Chalmers, Luke Morris, Robbie Fitzpatrick, Liam Jones. **Jockey (NH):** Will Kennedy, Rhys Flint, Richie Killoran. **Apprentice:** Jack Duern. **Amateur:** Miss Leanne Masterton.

MR DAVID ARBUTHNOT, Dorking
Postal: Henfold House Cottage, Henfold Lane, Beare Green, Dorking, Surrey, RH5 4RW
Contacts: PHONE (01306) 631529 FAX (01306) 631529 MOBILE (07836) 276464
E-MAIL dwparbuthnot@hotmail.com WEBSITE www.henfoldracing.co.uk

1 AATHER (IRE), 8, b g Key of Luck (USA)—Alkaffeyeh (IRE) **A. T. A. Wates**
2 BEDARRA BOY, 7, ch g Needwood Blade—Roonah Quay (IRE) **Mr P. M. Claydon**
3 DON POOLEONI (IRE), 8, b g Catcher In The Rye (IRE)—Liss Rua (IRE) **The Dons**
4 FEEL THE FORCE (IRE), 9, br g Presenting—Shipping News (USA) **A. T. A. Wates**
5 FIREITFROMYE (IRE), 8, b g Milan—Sweet Merenda (IRE) **Mr J G M Wates & Mr A T A Wates**
6 GANDALFE (FR), 8, b br g Laveron—Goldville (FR) **A. T. A. Wates**
7 LEELU, 7, b m Largesse—Strat's Quest **P. Banfield**
8 MAX MILAN (IRE), 4, b g Milan—Sunset Leader (IRE) **Mr P. M. Claydon**
9 PREUTY BOY (FR), 8, b g Saint Preuil (FR)—Titian Queen **A. T. A. Wates**
10 ROCKY ELSOM (USA), 6, b g Rock of Gibraltar (IRE)—Bowstring (IRE) **Mr J G M Wates & Mr A T A Wates**
11 SHUIL ROYALE (IRE), 8, b g King's Theatre (IRE)—Shuil Na Lee (IRE) **R. P. Fry**
12 SNOWBALL (IRE), 6, gr g Alderbrook—Rosafi (IRE) **Mr P Fry & Mr P Claydon**
13 STARLUCK (IRE), 8, gr g Key of Luck (USA)—Sarifa (IRE) **A. T. A. Wates**
14 STROLLAWAYNOW (IRE), 6, b g Oscar (IRE)—Rose of Salome (IRE) **A. T. A. Wates**
15 THE RINKY DINK, 5, b m Gold Well—Rose Revolution (IRE) **J. G. M. Wates**
16 TINGO IN THE TALE (IRE), 4, b g Oratorio (IRE)—Sunlit Skies **G. S. Thompson**
17 TOPOLSKI (IRE), 7, b g Peintre Celebre (USA)—Witching Hour (IRE) **Mr P. M. Claydon**
18 URCALIN (FR), 5, b g Network (GER)—Caline So (FR) **Mr A T A Wates & Mrs S Wates**
19 WESTAWAY (IRE), 6, b br g Westerner—I'llaway (IRE) **Mr P. M. Claydon**
20 WHENINDOUBTDOIT (IRE), 6, ch g Shantou (USA)—Warning Cry (IRE) **A. T. A. Wates**

Other Owners: Mr C. Blackburn, Mr R. F. Magrath, Mrs S. M. Wates.

Jockey (NH): Daryl Jacob. **Conditional:** Ross Wishart, Tom Cannon.

MR PETER ATKINSON, Northallerton
Postal: Yafforth Hill Farm, Yafforth, Northallerton, North Yorkshire, DL7 0LT
Contacts: PHONE (01609) 772598 MOBILE (07751) 131215

1 CROCO BAY (IRE), 6, b g Croco Rouge (IRE)—April Thistle (IRE) **Mr P. G. Atkinson**
2 SPARKLING HAND, 7, b m Lend A Hand—Sparkling Yasmin **Mr P. G. Atkinson**

10 MR MICHAEL ATTWATER, Epsom

Postal: **Tattenham Corner Stables, Tattenham Corner Road, Epsom Downs, Surrey, KT18 5PP**
Contacts: **PHONE** (01737) 360066 **MOBILE** (07725) 423633
E-MAIL Attwaterracing@hotmail.co.uk WEBSITE www.attwaterracing.com

1 BEAT ROUTE, 6, ch g Beat Hollow—Steppin Out **Canisbay Bloodstock**
2 BOWSTAR, 4, b f Oasis Dream—Bold Empress (USA) **Canisbay Bloodstock**
3 BRAVO ECHO, 7, b g Oasis Dream—Bold Empress (USA) **Canisbay Bloodstock**
4 BRONZE PRINCE, 6, b g Oasis Dream—Sweet Pea **Canisbay Bloodstock**
5 CUTHBERT (IRE), 6, ch g Bertolini (USA)—Tequise (IRE) **Canisbay Bloodstock**
6 GEORGE GURU, 6, b g Ishiguru (USA)—Waraqa (USA) **T. M. Jones**
7 HOWLIN MOON, 5, ch m Zamindar (USA)—Steppin Out **Canisbay Bloodstock**
8 KINDIA (IRE), 5, b m Cape Cross (IRE)—Susu **Canisbay Bloodstock**
9 L'HIRONDELLE (IRE), 9, b g Anabaa (USA)—Auratum (USA) **Canisbay Bloodstock**
10 LION'S MAID, 4, b f Iceman—Steppin Out **Canisbay Bloodstock**
11 5, B m Royal Applause—Mo Stopher **Canisbay Bloodstock**
12 PARSONS GREEN, 4, b f Sakhee (USA)—Anastasia Venture **Canisbay Bloodstock**
13 PERFECT SHOT (IRE), 7, b g High Chaparral (IRE)—Zoom Lens (IRE) **Mrs C. Kerr**
14 PRINCE OF THEBES (IRE), 12, b g Desert Prince (IRE)—Persian Walk (FR) **Canisbay Bloodstock**
15 QUEENIE'S STAR (IRE), 6, b m Arakan (USA)—Starway To Heaven (ITY) **The Attwater Partnership**
16 ROLLIN 'N TUMBLIN, 9, ch g Zaha (CAN)—Steppin Out **Canisbay Bloodstock**
17 SALIENT, 9, b g Fasliyev (USA)—Savannah Belle **Canisbay Bloodstock**
18 SHE WONT TELL, 4, b f Doyen (IRE)—Who Goes There **T. M. Jones**
19 SUHAILAH, 7, ch m Sulamani (USA)—Vrennan **Canisbay Bloodstock**
20 TROVE (IRE), 4, b g Rock of Gibraltar (IRE)—Cache Creek (IRE)

THREE-YEAR-OLDS

21 ASK THE GURU, b c Ishiguru (USA)—Tharwa (IRE) **Canisbay Bloodstock**

TWO-YEAR-OLDS

22 B f 13/2 Sleeping Indian—Miss Uluwatu (IRE) (Night Shift (USA)) (1904) **The Attwater Partnership**
23 Ch c 4/3 Three Valleys (USA)—Sorara (Aragon) (2857) **The Attwater Partnership**

Other Owners: Mr B. M. Attwater, Mr M. J. Attwater, R. F. Kilby, Miss M. E. Stopher.

Assistant Trainer: K. F. Latchford

Jockey (flat): Mark Coumbe. Apprentice: Aaron Chave.

11 MR NICK AYLIFFE, Minehead

Postal: **Glebe Stables, Little Ham, Winsford, Minehead, Somerset, TA24 7JH**
Contacts: **PHONE** (01643) 851265 **MOBILE** (07975) 657839

1 FREDDY'S STAR (IRE), 11, ch g Kris—Kutaisi (IRE) **F. A. Clegg**
2 HOLDEN CAULFIELD (IRE), 8, b g Catcher In The Rye (IRE)—God Speed Her **R. Allatt**
3 SI BIEN (FR), 8, b g Solon (GER)—Secret Gold (GER) **Barrett, Young & Brown**
4 SPARKLING HERO, 5, gr g Arkadian Hero (USA)—Sparkling Lass **Mrs M. A. Barrett**
5 TRANSVESTITE (IRE), 11, b g Trans Island—Christoph's Girl **Mrs M. A. Barrett**
6 VALONA STAR, 5, b m Man Among Men (IRE)—Valona Valley (IRE) **Mrs M. A. Barrett**

Other Owners: Mrs M. A. Barrett, Mrs K. Brown, Mrs J. J. Young.

Assistant Trainer: Miss N. French

12 MR ALAN BAILEY, Newmarket

Postal: **Cavendish Stables, Hamilton Road, Newmarket, Suffolk, CB8 7JQ**
Contacts: **PHONE** (01638) 664546 **FAX** (01638) 664546 **MOBILE** (07808) 734223
WEBSITE www.alanbaileyracing.co.uk

1 BARBICAN, 5, b g Hurricane Run (IRE)—The Faraway Tree **Mr J. F. Stocker**
2 BUBBLY BALLERINA, 4, ch f Footstepsinthesand—Pain Perdu (IRE) **The Champagne Club**
3 BUBBLY BOUNTY, 4, b f Bahamian Bounty—Eljariha **The Champagne Club**
4 CONNISHKA, 4, gr f Verglas (IRE)—Profit Alert (IRE) **Mr R. J. H. West**
5 DAZZLING VALENTINE, 5, b m Oratorio (IRE)—Bedazzling (IRE) **The Glenbuccaneers**

MR ALAN BAILEY - Continued

6 **IMPRIMIS TAGULA (IRE)**, 9, b g Tagula (IRE)—Strelitzia (IRE) **Middleham Park Racing XLI & Alan Bailey**
7 **MAZ**, 5, ch m Needwood Blade—Lady Mytton **AB Racing Limited**
8 **OUTPOST (IRE)**, 5, ch g Giant's Causeway (USA)—Southern Migration (USA) **Rathordan Partnership**
9 **ROY THE BOY (USA)**, 5, b g Pomeroy (USA)—Mrs M (USA) **Cakey Bundles 2**
10 **SMART AFFAIR**, 4, b f Trade Fair—Che Chic (IRE) **Mr R. J. Jeffrey**
11 **SON VIDA (IRE)**, 5, b g Titus Livius (FR)—Sombreffe **A. J. H.**
12 **ST IGNATIUS**, 6, b g Ishiguru (USA)—Branston Berry (IRE) **A. J. H.**
13 **STRICTLY SILVER (IRE)**, 4, gr c Dalakhani (IRE)—Miss Chaussini (IRE) **A. J. H.**
14 **TURJUMAN (USA)**, 8, ch g Swain (IRE)—Hachiyah (IRE) **AB Racing Limited**

THREE-YEAR-OLDS

15 **BADDILINI**, b g Bertolini (USA)—Baddi Heights (FR) **Mrs A Shone & Mrs V Hubbard**
16 **BUBBLY BAILEY**, b g Byron—Night Gypsy **The Champagne Club**
17 **COINCIDENTLY**, b f Acclamation—Miss Chaussini (IRE) **Tom Mohan & A. J. H.**
18 **EQUITANIA**, b f Pastoral Pursuits—Clarice Orsini **Mr J. F. Stocker**
19 **GO FAR**, b c Dutch Art—Carranita (IRE) **Mr M. Turner**
20 **HAWSIES DREAM**, ch f Dubawi (IRE)—Petong's Pet **Mr J. F. Stocker**
21 **KING GEORGE RIVER (IRE)**, b c Danehill Dancer (IRE)—Butterfly Blue (IRE) **Mr J. F. Stocker**
22 **LA BRAVA**, ch f Kheleyf (USA)—La Belga (ARG) **Danron Syndicate**
23 **LA DANZA**, b f Country Reel (USA)—Freedom Song **Danron Syndicate**
24 **SERAPHIMA**, b f Fusaichi Pegasus (USA)—Millestan (IRE) **Danron Syndicate**
25 **SIXTIES QUEEN**, b f Sixties Icon—Lily of Tagula (IRE) **Tregarth Racing & Partner**

TWO-YEAR-OLDS

26 B f 5/3 Dark Angel (IRE)—Known Class (USA) (Known Fact (USA)) (14285) **Dr Simon Hargreaves**
27 **MIMI LUKE (USA)**, b f 9/3 U S Ranger (USA)—
　　　　　　Hard As Nails (USA) (Holy Bull (USA)) (28571) **Dr Simon Hargreaves**

Other Owners: Mr A. Bailey, Mr Robert Beach, Mr G. C. Clifford, Mr D. J. Connolly, Mr M. Heffernan, Mr H. Herne, Mrs Valerie Hubbard, Mr Allan McNamee, Mr T. Mohan, Mr P. M. Murphy, Mr T. S. Palin, Mr M. Prince, Mr M. Quirke, Mrs A. Shone, Mr R. Spence, Mr Ron Tan, Mr Danny Wong.

Assistant Trainer: Mrs J. P. Bailey

Apprentice: Natasha Eaton.

---

13 **MRS CAROLINE BAILEY, Northampton**
Postal: **37 Eastfield Road, Brixworth, Northampton, Northamptonshire, NN6 9ED**
Contacts: **PHONE** (01604) 883729 **(Home)** (01604) 770234 **(Yard) FAX** (01604) 770423
MOBILE (07831) 373340
E-MAIL caroline.bailey4@btinternet.com **WEBSITE** www.carolinebaileyracing.co.uk

1 **ALDIVA**, 7, b g Alflora (IRE)—Diva **Mrs Joy Fenton & Partners**
2 **BRASSBOUND (USA)**, 5, b g Redoute's Choice (AUS)—In A Bound (AUS) **C. W. Booth**
3 **DENALI HIGHWAY (IRE)**, 6, ch g Governor Brown (USA)—Amaretto Flame (IRE) **Ian Payne & Kim Franklin**
4 **DERMATOLOGISTE**, 10, b m Kayf Tara—Poor Skin (IRE) **Mrs L. C. Taylor**
5 **GALWAY JACK (IRE)**, 8, b g Witness Box (USA)—Cooldalus (USA) **Mrs M. E. Moody**
6 **GLOBAL DOMINATION**, 5, b g Alflora (IRE)—Lucia Forte **Mrs S. Carsberg**
7 **GLOBAL FLYER**, 9, b g Sir Harry Lewis (USA)—Flicker **Mrs S. Carsberg**
8 **MALAPIE (IRE)**, 5, b g Westerner—Victorian Lady **Mr & Mrs D. Bailey**
9 **MORNING MOMENT**, 11, b g Killer Instinct—Golf World (IRE) **C Flinton R Lloyd G Bailey**
10 **NOBLE LEGEND**, 6, b g Midnight Legend—Elmside Katie **Mr P. Dixon Smith**
11 **PRINCE DES MARAIS (FR)**, 10, b br g Network (GER)—Djeba Royale (FR) **C. W. Booth**
12 **QUEEN OLIVIA**, 5, b m King's Theatre (IRE)—Queen's Leader **Mr R. Hunnisett**
13 **QUINSMAN**, 7, b g Singspiel (IRE)—Penny Cross **C. W. Booth**
14 **REFUSAL**, 5, b g Teofilo (IRE)—Frankie Fair **Varley, Lloyd & Bailey**
15 **SEE YOU JACK**, 8, b g Dolpour—Layston Pinzal **Mr C. Flinton & Mr A. Hurn**
16 **THREE CHORDS (IRE)**, 9, b g Winged Love (IRE)—Crystal Chord (IRE) **Mrs C. Aldridge & Mr R. Juleff**
17 **WHERRIMON**, 9, gr g Terimon—Swazi Princess (IRE) **Mr A. & Mrs P. Hurn**

Other Owners: Mrs C. M. Aldridge, G. T. H. Bailey, Mrs D. A. Bailey, Mr D. C. Bailey, Mrs I. J. Fenton, C. Flinton, Miss K. M. Franklin, A. Hurn, The Hon Mrs A. Hurn, Mr R. Juleff, Mr R. B. Lloyd, Mr I. T. Payne, R. J. Preston, Mr M. Varley, B. Winfield, J. Wright.

Jockey (NH): Tom Messenger, Adam Pogson, Andrew Thornton. **Amateur:** Mr Jonathan Bailey.

14 MR KIM BAILEY, Cheltenham

Postal: **Thorndale Farm, Withington Road, Andoversford, Cheltenham, Gloucestershire, GL54 4LL**
Contacts: **PHONE (01242) 890241 FAX (01242) 890193 MOBILE (07831) 416859**
E-MAIL info@kimbaileyracing.com WEBSITE www.kimbaileyracing.com

1 **A SHADE OF BAY**, 5, b m Midnight Legend—Pulling Strings (IRE) **Mrs S. J. Steer-Fowler**
2 **ABLE DEPUTY**, 6, b g Lomitas—Island Colony (USA) **W. J. Ives**
3 **AGENT FEDORA**, 5, b m Kayf Tara—Flora Poste **Mrs S. F. Dibben**
4 **ALFIE WILLS**, 6, b g Alflora (IRE)—Inesse **P. J. H. Wills**
5 **ALL FOR CASH**, 8, b g Alflora (IRE)—Mrs Moneypenny **Mrs P. A. Perriss**
6 **AMAZING D'AZY (IRE)**, 5, br m Presenting—Shuil Mavourneen (IRE) **Mrs E. Ellis**
7 **ARGENTIA**, 8, b m Silver Patriarch (IRE)—Ludoviciana **Mrs G. Leigh & Mr G. W. Paul**
8 **BALLYWATT (IRE)**, 7, b g Kayf Tara—Lady Arpel (IRE) **Mrs V. W. H. Johnson**
9 **BASODA**, 10, b g Karinga Bay—Another Wag **Angie & Michael Storey**
10 **BISHOPHILL JACK (IRE)**, 7, b g Tikkanen (USA)—Kerrys Cross (IRE) **The On The Bridle Partnership**
11 **BUFFALO BOB (IRE)**, 10, b g Bob's Return (IRE)—Back In Kansas (IRE) **The GFH Partnership**
12 **BUFFY THE BEATLE**, 5, b g Beat All (USA)—Wishy (IRE) **Racing For Research (Kidney Research UK)**
13 **DANCE TEMPO**, 6, b g Dansili—Musical Twist **A. N. Solomons**
14 **DARNA**, 7, b g Alflora (IRE)—Dutch Dyane **Mrs Julie Martin & David R. Martin**
15 **FINMERELLO**, 7, b m Definite Article—Belle Magello (FR) **K. Marsden & J. P. Lim**
16 **GRACE AND GLAMOUR**, 4, b f Grape Tree Road—Jolika (FR) **Jeanette & Janine Campbell**
17 **HANDSOME HARRY (IRE)**, 7, b g Broadway Flyer (USA)—Whistful Suzie (IRE) **Mrs E. A. Kellar**
18 **HARRY TOPPER**, 6, b g Sir Harry Lewis (USA)—Indeed To Goodness (IRE) **A. N. Solomons**
19 **JACALOU**, 8, b m Exit To Nowhere (USA)—Dalticia (USA) **Kim Bailey Racing Partnership III**
20 **KAFFIE**, 8, b m Kayf Tara—Galix (FR) **D. H. Morgan**
21 **LORD TOMNODDY**, 11, b g Tragic Role (USA)—Rosemoss **M. D. C. Jenks**
22 **LUCETTE**, 5, b m Overbury (IRE)—Winnow **Have Fun Racing Partnership**
23 **MAGIC MONEY**, 5, b m Midnight Legend—Sticky Money **M. D. C. Jenks**
24 **MARK TWAIN (IRE)**, 6, b g Rock of Gibraltar (IRE)—Lady Windermere (IRE) **Mrs V. W. H. Johnson**
25 **MIDNIGHT HAZE**, 11, b g Midnight Legend—Gypsy Haze **Kim Bailey Racing Partnership**
26 **MIDNIGHT OSCAR (IRE)**, 6, br g Oscar (IRE)—Midnight Light (IRE) **The Oscar Partnership**
27 **MILORD (GER)**, 4, br c Monsun (GER)—Montserrat (GER) **Kim Bailey Racing Partnership VII**
28 **MOLLY'S A DIVA**, 6, ch m Midnight Legend—Smokey Diva (IRE) **J. F. Perriss**
29 **MRS PEACHEY (IRE)**, 6, b m Brian Boru—Maracana (IRE) **The Boom Syndicate**
30 **MULDOON'S PICNIC (IRE)**, 7, b g King's Theatre (IRE)—Going My Way **Mr C. A. Washbourn**
31 **OSCAR'S SECRET (IRE)**, 6, b g Oscar (IRE)—Black Flora (IRE) **Mrs J. Shipp**
32 **POINTS OF VIEW**, 8, b g Galileo (IRE)—On Point **W. J. Ives**
33 **QUIET WHISPER (IRE)**, 7, b g Quiet American (USA)—Relish (IRE) **W. J. Ives**
34 **REGAL APPROACH (IRE)**, 10, b g Bob Back (USA)—Crash Approach **P. J. Vogt**
35 **RUBY CROWN**, 11, b m Rakaposhi King—Suilven **I. F. W. Buchan**
36 **SANCTUARY**, 7, ch g Dr Fong (USA)—Wondrous Maid (GER) **Mrs Julie Martin & David R. Martin**
37 **SAVANT BLEU (FR)**, 7, ch g Agent Bleu (FR)—Avane Iii (FR) **Kim Bailey Racing Partnership III**
38 **SET IN HER WAYS (IRE)**, 7, b m Old Vic—Yes Your Honour **Have Fun Racing Partnership**
39 **SILVER EAGLE (IRE)**, 5, gr g Presenting—Lady Lincon (IRE) **Kim Bailey Racing Partnership IV**
40 **SIRIUS CHESNUT**, 5, ch g Domedriver (IRE)—Heart **Have Fun Racing Partnership**
41 **SMOKEY GEORGE**, 8, ch g Kadastrof (FR)—Smokey Diva (IRE) **Mrs P. A. Perriss**
42 **SOUTH STACK**, 8, b g Alflora (IRE)—Mandy Chat (IRE) **Mrs Julie Martin & David R. Martin**
43 **SPARVILLE (IRE)**, 7, ch g Docksider (USA)—
                          Play The Queen (IRE) **Racing For Research (Kidney Research UK)**
44 **SUCH A LEGEND**, 5, ch g Midnight Legend—Mrs Fizziwig **Mrs S. J. Steer-Fowler**
45 **SUPREME PRESENT**, 5, b m Presenting—Deep Sunset (IRE) **Lucky Bin Racing & Little Lodge Farm**
46 **THE RAINBOW HUNTER**, 9, b g Rainbow High—Sobranie **May We Never Be Found Out Partnership**
47 **TRUMIX**, 5, b g Fair Mix (IRE)—Indeed To Goodness (IRE) **Kim Bailey Racing Partnership II**
48 **TWELVE ROSES**, 5, ch g Midnight Legend—Miniature Rose **Jones Broughtons Wilson Weaver**
49 **UP FOR AN OSCAR (IRE)**, 6, b g Oscar (IRE)—Queen of Harts (IRE) **The Hon Mrs A. M. Cookson**
50 **WEDGER PARDY (IRE)**, 12, b g Zaffaran (USA)—Raise The Bells **Lord Leigh**
51 **WENLOCKS BOXER**, 4, b g Kayf Tara—Black Collar **W. J. Ives**

Other Owners: Mr K. C. Bailey, Mrs Kim Bailey, Mr Oliver Bell, Sir Martin Broughton, Mr Stephen Broughton, Mr Michael J. Campbell, Miss Janine Campbell, Mrs Jeanette Campbell, Mr Stephen Cannon, Mr R. D. Chugg, Mrs Robert Chugg, Mr Kevin T. Clancy, Mr Dermot M. Clancy, Mr J. De Lisle Wells, Mr Gordon Farr, Mr Chris Guy, Mr N. R. Jennings, Mrs Nicholas Jones, Mr P. S. Kerr, Mr D. J. Keyte, Mr Henry Kimbell, Mrs G. Leigh, Mr J-P Lim, Mr K. Marsden, Mrs Julie Martin, Mr David R. Martin, Mr G. W. Paul, Mr B. Robbins, Mr Richard Sheppard, Miss C. Shipp, Mr Michael Storey, Mrs Angela Storey, Mr G. D. W. Swire, Mrs C. A. T. Swire, Mrs Nicky Van Dijk, Mrs Giles Weaver, Mr J. Webber, Mr Tom Wilson.

MR KIM BAILEY - Continued

Assistant Trainer: Mathew Nicholls
Jockey (NH): Charles Greene. **Conditional:** Ed Cookson.

---

15 **MISS EMMA BAKER, Cheltenham**
Postal: Brockhill, Naunton, Cheltenham, Gloucestershire, GL54 3BA
Contacts: PHONE (01451) 850714 (Home) FAX (01451) 850199 MOBILE (07887) 845970
E-MAIL emmajbakerracing@hotmail.co.uk WEBSITE www.emmabakerracing.com

1 BACK BY MIDNIGHT, 4, ch g Midnight Legend—Roberta Back (IRE) **Mrs J. Arnold**
2 BAJARDO (IRE), 5, b g Jammaal—Bit of Peace (IRE) **Mrs J. Arnold**
3 CRACKERJACK, 6, ch g Lahib (USA)—Tidesong **Mrs J. Arnold**
4 FEN FARM, 8, b g Luso—Regan (USA) **Mrs J. Arnold**
5 MASTER CARDOR VISA (IRE), 8, br g Alderbrook—Princess Moodyshoe **Mrs J. Arnold**
6 MIDNIGHT CHARMER, 7, b g Midnight Legend—Dickies Girl **Mrs J. Arnold**
7 PADDLEYOUROWNCANOE (IRE), 12, b g Saddlers' Hall (IRE)—
Little Paddle (IRE) **Miss E. J. Baker & Mrs M. J. Arnold**
8 PETRARCHICK (USA), 6, b m Arch (USA)—Tustin (USA) **Mr P. G. Horrocks**
9 SOCIAL OVERDRIVE (IRE), 7, b g Alderbrook—La Grande Duchesse (IRE) **The Socialites**
10 SUBTLE APPROACH (IRE), 8, b g Subtle Power (IRE)—Rotoruasprings (IRE) **Mrs J. Arnold**
11 TIGNELLO (IRE), 8, b g Kendor (FR)—La Genereuse **Mrs J. Arnold**

Other Owners: Mrs David Bedford, Mr John Perriss, Mrs M. J. Arnold, Miss E. J. Baker.

---

16 **MR GEORGE BAKER, Marlborough**
Postal: Barton Yard, Manton Estate, Marlborough, Wiltshire, SN8 4HB
Contacts: PHONE OFFICE: (01672) 515493 (01672) 516234 FAX (01672) 514938
MOBILE (07889) 514881
E-MAIL gbakerracing@gmail.com WEBSITE www.georgebakerracing.com

1 ABIGAIL LYNCH (IRE), 5, b m Oscar (IRE)—Tanit Lady (IRE) **Rose Tinted Racing**
2 ANCIENT GREECE, 6, b g Pivotal—Classicism (USA) **Inkin, Inkin, Byng, Baker & Partners**
3 AQUA ARDENS (GER), 5, b g Nayef (USA)—Arduinna (GER) **M Khan X2**
4 BELGIAN BILL, 5, b h Exceed And Excel (AUS)—Gay Romance **PJL, Cooper & Baker**
5 BELLE DE FONTENAY (FR), 8, b m Spadoun (FR)—Friendly Hostess **George Baker & Partners**
6 BILLYRAYVALENTINE (CAN), 4, b g Elusive Quality (USA)—
Sweet and Careless (USA) **Russell, Wheeler, Vail Partnership**
7 BUGSY'S BOY, 9, b g Double Trigger (IRE)—Bugsy's Sister **Seaton Partnership**
8 CHARLES TYRWHITT, 4, b g Iffraaj—Riverside Dancer (USA) **Wheeler, Russell, Vail, Meadon & Hippychick**
9 CONTRADIKTIVE (IRE), 7, b g Diktat—Additive (USA) **M Khan X2**
10 DANA'S PRESENT, 4, ch g Osorio (GER)—Euro Empire (USA) **Whitsbury Racing Club**
11 DOUBLE DASH, 9, b g Sir Harry Lewis (USA)—Dashing Executive (IRE) **Mrs P. A. Scott-Dunn**
12 FOUR NATIONS (USA), 5, ch g Langfuhr (CAN)—Kiswahili **The Transatlantic Syndicate**
13 GEORGE BAKER (IRE), 6, b g Camacho—Petite Maxine **Popbitch Racing Club**
14 HUMIDOR (IRE), 6, b g Camacho—Miss Indigo **M Khan X2**
15 I'M FRAAM GOVAN, 5, ch g Fraam—Urban Dancer (IRE) **Sir A. Ferguson**
16 I'M HARRY, 4, b g Haafhd—First Approval **Keith Jones & Family**
17 IF I HAD HIM (IRE), 9, b g City Honours (USA)—Our Valentine (IRE) **Sir A. Ferguson**
18 JACK'S REVENGE (IRE), 5, br g Footstepsinthesand—Spirit of Age (IRE) **PJL Racing**
19 JAKE'S DESTINY (IRE), 4, b g Desert Style (IRE)—
Skehana (IRE) **Delancey Real Estate Asset Management Limited**
20 NOT SO SURE DICK (IRE), 8, b g Flemensfirth (USA)—
The Peckaloo (IRE) **Peter Earl, Lin Baker & Irene Paterson**
21 PANDY, 4, b f Sakhee (USA)—Ceiriog Valley **R. J. McAlpine**
22 PERCYTHEPINTO (IRE), 4, b g Tiger Hill (IRE)—Tullawadgeen (IRE) **Seaton Partnership**
23 PIERS GAVESTON (IRE), 4, b g Amadeus Wolf—Dancing Tempo **Marcus Edwards-Jones & Friends**
24 PLACE IN MY HEART, 4, ch f Compton Place—Lonely Heart **Turf Club 2012**
25 REFRESHESTHEPARTS (USA), 4, ch f Proud Citizen (USA)—
St Francis Wood (USA) **Mr M. R. De Carvalho De Vaz Neneken**
26 RELENTLESS HARRY (IRE), 4, gr g Excellent Art—Les Alizes (IRE) **PJL Racing**
27 SINBAD THE SAILOR, 8, b g Cape Cross (IRE)—Sinead (USA) **Sir A. Ferguson**

MR GEORGE BAKER - Continued

THREE-YEAR-OLDS

28 **ALL ON RED (IRE)**, b f Red Clubs (IRE)—Champion Tipster **PJL Racing**
29 **AUSSIE LYRICS (FR)**, gr c Aussie Rules (USA)—Operam **Michael Watt, J. A. McGrath, The Anzacs**
30 **BOOMSHACKERLACKER (IRE)**, gr c Dark Angel (IRE)—Allegrina (IRE) **PJL Racing**
31 **BOUNTYBEAMADAM**, b f Bahamian Bounty—Madamoiselle Jones **Whitsbury Hopefuls**
32 **BUGSY'S BABE**, ch f Tobougg (IRE)—Oak Tree Miss (USA) **Seaton Partnership**
33 **CHATTANOOGA LINE**, b f Rail Link—Gay Romance **George Baker & Wickfield Stud**
34 **DEE AITCH DOVE**, gr f Sakhee's Secret—Fluttering Rose **Lady Cobham & Mr G. Irwin**
35 **ETON RAMBLER (USA)**, b br c Hard Spun (USA)—Brightbraveandgood (USA) **The Eton Ramblers**
36 **JOEY'S DESTINY (IRE)**, ch g Kheleyf (USA)—
                     Maid of Ailsa (USA) **Delancey Real Estate Asset Management Limited**
37 **JOLLIFICATION (IRE)**, b f Acclamation—Improvise **Mr & Mrs J Pittam**
38 **LUCKY BLACK STAR (IRE)**, b g Lawman (FR)—Silver Bandana (USA) **Black Star Limited & Andy Luckhurst**
39 **MISTER CARROT**, b g Elusive City (USA)—It's Twilight Time **Mr Ed Seyfried, Mr A Nicolls, Mr T Stockdale**
40 **NENGE MBOKO**, b g Compton Place—Floppie (FR) **Russell Conrad Vail Wheeler Hippychick**
41 **PETITE GEORGIA (IRE)**, b f Camacho—Petite Maxine **D Wain G Baker & Partners**
42 **RED FOUR**, ch f Singspiel (IRE)—Protectorate **Lady Cobham & Mr G. Irwin**
43 **RUTHERGLEN**, b c Tiger Hill (IRE)—Hanella (IRE) **F. Brady**
44 **SUTTON SID**, ch g Dutch Art—Drastic Measure **Mr P. Bowden**
45 **UGANDA GLORY (USA)**, b br f Hat Trick (JPN)—Febrile (USA) **Mr R. Bauer**
46 **YUL FINEGOLD (IRE)**, b c Invincible Spirit (IRE)—Mascara **Mrs V. Finegold**

TWO-YEAR-OLDS

47 B c 5/4 Bushranger (IRE)—Bronze Baby (USA) (Silver Charm (USA)) (28000) **Mr G. Baker**
48 B f 9/3 High Chaparral (IRE)—Chervil (Dansili) (39000) **Mr & Mrs T. Pittam & Partners**
49 **FIFTY SHADES OF GREY (IRE)**, gr c 24/1 Verglas (IRE)—Vasilia (Dansili) (50000) **Team Fifty**
50 Ch c 6/5 Art Connoisseur (IRE)—Kafayef (USA) (Secreto (USA)) (15872) **Mr G. Baker**
51 **LOVING YOUR WORK**, b c 29/1 Royal Applause—
                     Time Crystal (IRE) (Sadler's Wells (USA)) (44000) **The Traditionalists**
52 **MISTER MAYDAY (IRE)**, b c 21/4 Kheleyf (USA)—
                     Soxy Doxy (IRE) (Hawk Wing (USA)) (24761) **Miss Emily Asprey, Mr T. Kane, Mr S. Thomas**
53 B f 15/4 Kheleyf (USA)—Mistle Thrush (Storm Bird (CAN)) (10000) **Mr G. Baker**
54 **SLEEPING VENUS (IRE)**, ch f 22/2 Excellent Art—
                     Sun Moon And Stars (IRE) (Galileo (IRE)) (12000) **Equi ex Incertis Partners**

Other Owners: Mrs C. E. S. Baker, Mrs L. Baker, Mr George Baker, Mrs V. P. Baker, Mr David Barrie, Blackstar (Europe) Limited, Mr P Bowden, Earl of Brecknock, Mr I. Briggs, Mr & Mrs Hank Brockman, Mr V. W. Chandler, Mr A. S. Conrad, Mr R. Cooper, Mr P. H. Earl, Mrs R. S. Evans, Mr Richard Evans, Mr Campbell Fleming, Mr A. Flintoff, Miss Lucy Gemmill, Hippychick Limited, Miss L. Hurley, Mr P A. D. Inkin, Erika James, Mr K. Jones, Mrs L. Jones, Mr Tim Keaney, Mr Diarmid Kelly, Mr Mustafa Khan, Mr. M. Khan, Mr A. Luckhurst, Mr E. Lugg, Mr T. Macleod, Sir I. Magee, Mr J. A. McGrath, Mr D. I. N. McKenzie, Mr Mike Mellor, Congressman Toby Moffett, Mr N. Patsiledes & Partners, Mrs Annie Penny, Popbitch Racing Club, Mr W. A. B. Russell, Mr D. I. Russell, Mr Ned Sangster, Mr Tim Slade, Earl Spencer, Mr Ed Spurrier, Mr Dudley Thorp, Dominic Vail, Mr D. Wain, M. H. Watt, Mr N. Wheeler, Mr M. Wilson, Ms Camilla Wright, Yeomanstown Stud.

Assistant Trainers: Patrick Murphy, Valerie Murphy

Jockey (NH): Andrew Tinkler. **Conditional:** Trevor Whelan. **Apprentice:** Aaron Jones. **Amateur:** Mr J. Goss.

---

17 MR ANDREW BALDING, Kingsclere
Postal: **Park House Stables, Kingsclere, Newbury, Berkshire, RG20 5PY**
Contacts: **PHONE** (01635) 298210 **FAX** (01635) 298305 **MOBILE** (07774) 633791
E-MAIL admin@kingsclere.com **WEBSITE** www.kingsclere.com

1 **A BOY NAMED SUZI**, 5, b g Medecis—Classic Coral (USA) **Qatar Racing Limited**
2 **ANGELIC UPSTART (IRE)**, 5, b g Singspiel (IRE)—Rada (IRE) **Mr B. Burdett**
3 **BANA WU**, 4, ch f Shirocco (GER)—My Way (IRE) **G. B. Russell**
4 **BENZANNO (IRE)**, 4, b g Refuse To Bend (IRE)—Crossanza (IRE) **Martin & Valerie Slade & Partner**
5 **BERNIE THE BOLT (IRE)**, 7, br g Milan—Chaparral Lady (IRE) **Mr B. P. McGuire**
6 **BEYOND CONCEIT (IRE)**, 4, b g Galileo (IRE)—Baraka (IRE) **Mrs F. H. Hay**
7 **BONFIRE**, 4, b g Manduro (GER)—Night Frolic **Kingsclere Thoroughbred Racing - Pocahontas**
8 **CAPE CROSSING (IRE)**, 4, br f Cape Cross (IRE)—Dame Hester (IRE) **Mildmay Racing & D. H. Caslon**
9 **CHIBERTA KING**, 7, b g King's Best (USA)—Glam Rock **The Pink Hat Racing Partnership**
10 **COMMUNICATOR**, 5, b g Motivator—Goodie Twosues **Lady S. Davis**
11 **DANDY (GER)**, 4, b c Nayef (USA)—Diacada (GER) **Mr R. E. Tillett**

MR ANDREW BALDING - Continued

12 **DUNGANNON**, 6, b g Monsieur Bond (IRE)—May Light **Dr E. Harris**
13 **FORTROSE ACADEMY (IRE)**, 4, b g Iceman—Auspicious **Mr E.M. Sutherland**
14 **HALLINGS COMET**, 4, ch g Halling (USA)—Landinium (ITY) **Lord J. Blyth**
15 **HIGHLAND COLORI (IRE)**, 5, b g Le Vie Dei Colori—Emma's Star (ITY) **Mr E.M. Sutherland**
16 **HIGHLAND KNIGHT (IRE)**, 6, b g Night Shift (USA)—Highland Shot **J. C. Smith**
17 **INTRANSIGENT**, 4, b g Trans Island—Mara River **Kingsclere Racing Club**
18 **JOHN BISCUIT (IRE)**, 5, ch g Hawk Wing (USA)—Princess Magdalena **Dr P. J. Brown**
19 **MAGMA**, 4, b f Singspiel (IRE)—Rakata (USA) **A. H. Robinson**
20 **MEGAN'S MOTIVATOR**, 5, ch g Motivator—Top Sauce **Mr E.M. Sutherland**
21 **MISS CAP ESTEL**, 4, b f Hernando (FR)—Miss Cap Ferrat **J. L. C. Pearce**
22 **MYSTERIOUS MAN (IRE)**, 4, b g Manduro (GER)—Edabiya (IRE) **Mr & Mrs R. Gorell/Mr & Mrs P. Pausewang**
23 **NORTHERN OUTLOOK**, 4, b g Selkirk (USA)—Casual Glance **Kingsclere Racing Club**
24 **OMAR KHAYYAM**, 4, b c Pivotal—Kithanga (USA) **J. L. C. Pearce**
25 **OPEN WATER (FR)**, 4, b g Orpen (USA)—So Stream (ITY) **Thurloe Thoroughbreds XXVI**
26 **PERFECT MISSION**, 5, b g Bertolini (USA)—Sharp Secret (IRE) **Mildmay Racing & D. H. Caslon**
27 **QUEEN'S STAR**, 4, ch f With Approval (CAN)—Memsahib **Sir Gordon Brunton**
28 **RAHY'S PROMISE (USA)**, 4, ch g Rahy (USA)—Promise Me This **Mr E.M. Sutherland**
29 **RAWAKI (IRE)**, 5, b g Phoenix Reach (IRE)—Averami **Kingsclere Racing Club**
30 **RESTAURATEUR (IRE)**, 4, b g Excellent Art—Velvet Appeal (IRE) **Brook Farm Bloodstock**
31 **ROSERROW**, 4, ch g Beat Hollow—Sabah **Sir Roger Buckley, Mr Gerald Oury**
32 **SEA SOLDIER (IRE)**, 5, b g Red Ransom (USA)—Placement **Mrs M. E. Wates**
33 **SIDE GLANCE**, 6, b c g Passing Glance—Averami **Pearl Bloodstock Limited**
34 **SILVER SAMBA**, 4, gr f Dalakhani (IRE)—Fancy Dance **BA Racing**
35 **SPIRITUAL STAR (IRE)**, 4, b g Soviet Star (USA)—Million Spirits (IRE) **Mr M. B. Lee**
36 **STIRRING BALLAD**, 4, ch f Compton Place—Balnaha **G. Strawbridge**
37 **SWAN SONG**, 4, br f Green Desert (USA)—Lochsong **J. C. Smith**
38 **TAGLIETELLE**, 4, b g Tagula (IRE)—Averami **Kingsclere Racing Club**
39 **TOP COP**, 4, b g Acclamation—Speed Cop **J. C. Smith**
40 **TULLIUS (IRE)**, 5, ch g Le Vie Dei Colori—Whipped Queen (USA) **Kennet Valley Thoroughbreds VI**
41 **WHIPLASH WILLIE**, 5, ch g Phoenix Reach (IRE)—Santa Isobel **J. C. & S. R. Hitchins**

THREE-YEAR-OLDS

42 **ABSOLUTELY SO (IRE)**, b c Acclamation—Week End **Jackie & George Smith**
43 **BALLINDERRY BOY**, b g Kayf Tara—Spring Dream (IRE) **Rainbow Racing**
44 **BLUE TWISTER**, ch c Pivotal—Blue Siren **J. C. Smith**
45 **BRICK RISING**, ch g Phoenix Reach (IRE)—Comtesse Noire (CAN) **Brick Racing**
46 **BUTTERFLY MCQUEEN (USA)**, b f Curlin (USA)—Distant Roar (CAN) **A. Ferguson, G. Mason & P. Done**
47 **DAYLIGHT**, ch g Firebreak—Dayville (USA) **Kennet Valley Thoroughbreds V**
48 **DEBDEBDEB**, b f Teofilo (IRE)—Windmill
49 **DESERT COMMAND**, b g Oasis Dream—Speed Cop **J. C. Smith**
50 **DESERT DONKEY**, b g Acclamation—Honky Tonk Sally **G. A. D. Partnership**
51 **FLORIDA BEAT**, br g Passing Glance—Florida Heart **Kingsclere Racing Club**
52 **FONSECA (IRE)**, b br f Red Clubs (IRE)—Guajira (FR) **Kennet Valley Thoroughbreds IV**
53 **HALLING'S TREASURE**, ch c Halling (USA)—Perfect Treasure (IRE) **D. H. Caslon & Mildmay Racing**
54 **HAVANA BEAT (IRE)**, b c Teofilo (IRE)—Sweet Home Alabama (IRE) **Mick and Janice Mariscotti**
55 **HAVANA MOON (IRE)**, b f Teofilo (IRE)—Island Destiny **The C H F Partnership**
56 **HERE COMES WHEN (IRE)**, b c Danehill Dancer (IRE)—Quad's Melody (IRE) **Mrs F. H. Hay**
57 **HOT SECRET**, b f Sakhee's Secret—Harryana **Hot To Trot Racing Club 1**
58 **IMPERIAL GLANCE**, br c Passing Glance—Juno Mint **Mrs J. S. Newton**
59 **INTERNATIONAL LOVE**, ch f Manduro (GER)—Marika **Mr & Mrs R. Gorell/Mr & Mrs P. Pausewang**
60 **KING MURO**, b g Halling (USA)—Ushindi (IRE) **Mr P. Brend & Mr J. Dwyer**
61 **LADY OF THE VINE**, b f Master Command (USA)—
                                         Silverbulletlover (USA) **A. Ferguson, G. Mason & P. Done**
62 **LIGHT CATCHER**, b f Sakhee (USA)—Exorcet (FR) **J. C. Smith**
63 **LIZZIE TUDOR**, ch f Tamayuz—Silca Destination **Ms K. Gough**
64 **MARISHI TEN (IRE)**, b g f Invincible Spirit (IRE)—Scripture (IRE) **Dr P. J. Brown**
65 **MARTIAL ART (IRE)**, ch g Compton Place—Brush Strokes **Jackie & George Smith**
66 **MELVIN THE GRATE (IRE)**, b c Danehill Dancer (IRE)—Hawala (IRE) **Mrs F. H. Hay**
67 **MISS MITIGATE**, b f Sir Percy—Oblige **Birkdale Racing Syndicate**
68 **MR FITZROY (IRE)**, b g Kyllachy—Reputable **Dr P. J. Brown**
69 **MUSIKHANI**, b f Dalakhani (IRE)—Musicanna **Mrs K. Holmes**
70 **NEAR TIME**, ch f New Approach (IRE)—Time Away (IRE) **R. Barnett**
71 **NELLIE FORBUSH**, b f Phoenix Reach (IRE)—Santa Isobel **J. C. & S. R. Hitchins**
72 **NEW FFOREST**, b f Oasis Dream—Ffestiniog (IRE) **Elite Racing Club**
73 **NINGARA**, b c Singspiel (IRE)—Garanciere (FR) **G. B. Russell**

MR ANDREW BALDING - Continued

74 **OASIS SPIRIT**, b f Oasis Dream—Fearless Spirit (USA) **G. Strawbridge**
75 **OPERATION CHARIOT (IRE)**, b g Refuse To Bend (IRE)—Dona Royale (IRE) **Mr P. Brend & Mr J. Dwyer**
76 **PEARL CASTLE (IRE)**, b c Montjeu (IRE)—Ghurra (USA) **Pearl Bloodstock Limited**
77 **PERFECT SPELL**, ch c Singspiel (IRE)—Flamjica (USA) **The Cadagan Partnership**
78 **POEM (IRE)**, ch f Dylan Thomas (IRE)—Almarai (USA) **Mr R. J. C. Wilmot-Smith**
79 **POWDER HOUND**, b c Lucarno (USA)—Balnaha **G. Strawbridge**
80 **PRAIRIE RANGER**, b c Montjeu (IRE)—No Frills (IRE) **Dr P. J. Brown**
81 **PURCELL (IRE)**, b g Acclamation—Lyca Ballerina **Highclere Thoroughbred Racing - John Porter**
82 **RACE AND STATUS (IRE)**, b c Raven's Pass (USA)—Love Excelling (FR) **Jackie & George Smith**
83 **RANCHO MONTOYA (IRE)**, b f High Chaparral (IRE)—Congress (IRE) **Racegoers Club Owners Group**
84 **REFECTORY (IRE)**, b c Danehill Dancer (IRE)—Akuna Bay (USA) **Brook Farm Bloodstock**
85 **ROCKY RIDE (IRE)**, b f Rock of Gibraltar (IRE)—Sidecar (USA) **Kingsclere Racing Club**
86 **SIGNATURE DISH (IRE)**, b f Galileo (IRE)—Magic Carpet (IRE) **Brook Farm Bloodstock**
87 **SIMPLE JOYS**, b f Singspiel (IRE)—Chance Dance (IRE) **Mr R. J. C. Wilmot-Smith**
88 **SOVIET ROCK (IRE)**, b g Rock of Gibraltar (IRE)—Anna Karenina (USA) **Jackie & George Smith**
89 **STORMING (IRE)**, b g Stormy Atlantic (USA)—French Lady (NZ) **CJJR Partnership**
90 **TARARA**, b f Royal Applause—Anneliina **Russell's**
91 **THE WIZARD OF AUS (IRE)**, b g Aussie Rules (USA)—Dyness (USA) **The Pink Star Racing Partnership**
92 **THISTLEANDTWOROSES (USA)**, ch c Lion Heart (USA)—Country Again (USA)
93 **TRANSLUSCENT (IRE)**, b g Trans Island—Little Miss Diva (IRE) **Mrs E. A. M. Balding**
94 **VAN PERCY**, b g Sir Percy—Enforce (USA) **Mrs L. E. Ramsden & Richard Morecombe**
95 **VICKSBURG**, b f Cape Cross (IRE)—Totality **Mr R. J. C. Wilmot-Smith**
96 **WHITE MONTH (IRE)**, b g Tiger Hill (IRE)—Purple Heather (USA) **Her Majesty The Queen**
97 **WINTER MUSIC (IRE)**, b g Oratorio (IRE)—Alpine Park (IRE) **Kingsclere Racing Club**
98 **YOU DA ONE (IRE)**, br g Footstepsinthesand—Shenkara (IRE) **Mr & Mrs R. Gorell/Mr & Mrs P. Pausewang**
99 **ZANETTO**, b c Medicean—Play Bouzouki **Mick and Janice Mariscotti**

TWO-YEAR-OLDS

100 Ro c 8/4 Mastercraftsman (IRE)—Agnetha (GER) (Big Shuffle (USA)) (20000) **James/Michaelson/Greenwood 1**
101 B c 8/2 Champs Elysees—Aswaaq (IRE) (Peintre Celebre (USA)) (20000) **Thurloe Thoroughbreds 31**
102 Br c 5/3 Passing Glance—Averami (Averti (IRE)) **Kingsclere Racing Club**
103 **BELFILO (IRE)**, ch c 27/4 Teofilo (IRE)—Belsay (Belmez (USA)) (100000) **Mrs F. H. Hay**
104 B f 23/4 Excellent Art—Bint Zamayem (IRE) (Rainbow Quest (USA)) (22000)
105 **BISHOP OF RUSCOMBE**, b c 23/4 Mount Nelson—Pain Perdu (IRE) (Waajib (USA)) (55000) **D. E. Brownlow**
106 **BORN IN BOMBAY**, b c 28/5 Shamardal (USA)—Pearl Dance (USA) (Nureyev (USA)) **G. Strawbridge**
107 B f 16/4 Haafhd—Casual Glance (Sinndar (IRE)) **Kingsclere Racing Club**
108 **CATRIONA'S BOY**, ch c 18/4 Exceed And Excel (AUS)—
                                          Miss Chaussini (IRE) (Rossini (USA)) (130000) **Mrs F. H. Hay**
109 **CHINOTTO (IRE)**, b c 18/3 Duke of Marmalade (IRE)—
                                          Muskoka Dawn (USA) (Miswaki (USA)) (80000) **Mick and Janice Mariscotti**
110 **COLLABORATION**, b c 25/2 Halling (USA)—Red Shareef (Marju (IRE)) (57000) **Another Bottle Racing**
111 **COMANCHERO (IRE)**, b c 16/3 Camacho—Trempjane (Lujain (USA)) (45000) **Kennet Valley Thoroughbreds VII**
112 B c 5/4 Champs Elysees—Cross Your Fingers (USA) (Woodman (USA)) **Dr P. Brown**
113 **DARTING**, b f 30/4 Shamardal (USA)—Dararita (IRE) (Halo (USA)) **Birdcage/Lady Lloyd-Webber**
114 **DEE BEES GIFT**, gr c 23/2 Firebreak—Josie May (USA) (Aljabr (USA)) **Mrs A. Lane**
115 B c 24/4 Jeremy (USA)—Double Vie (IRE) (Tagula (IRE)) (20000) **Mr N. Botica & Mrs Wendy Gorell**
116 Ch f 14/4 Bahamian Bounty—Duena (Grand Lodge (USA)) (3500) **Mr M. E. Wates**
117 **END OF LINE**, b c 2/3 Pastoral Pursuits—Just Devine (IRE) (Montjeu (IRE)) (50000) **Qatar Racing Limited**
118 B c 8/3 Norse Dancer (IRE)—Flamjica (USA) (Real Quiet (USA)) **Cadagan Partnership**
119 B c 10/2 Passing Glance—Floriana (Selkirk (USA)) **Kingsclere Racing Club**
120 **FROM FROST**, b c 20/4 Nayef (USA)—Salutare (IRE) (Sadler's Wells (USA)) **G. Strawbridge**
121 **GIVE HIM A GLANCE**, bl gr c 20/3 Passing Glance—Giving (Generous (IRE)) **Mr & Mrs D. Holmes**
122 **GRACE AND FAVOUR**, b f 3/5 Montjeu (IRE)—Gryada (Shirley Heights) **N. Jones**
123 **HIGHLAND ACCLAIM (IRE)**, b c 2/2 Acclamation—Emma's Star (ITY) (Darshaan) (80000) **Mr E.M. Sutherland**
124 B f 15/2 High Chaparral (IRE)—Highland Shot (Selkirk (USA)) **J. C. Smith**
125 **IF (GER)**, b c 3/5 Rock of Gibraltar (IRE)—Ianapourna (GER) (Dai Jin) (20634) **Mr N. Botica & Mrs Wendy Gorell**
126 B g 31/3 Amadeus Wolf—Imelda (USA) (Manila (USA)) (9523) **M & V Slade/KTS**
127 **IMPULSIVE MOMENT (IRE)**, ce 30/1 Galileo (IRE)—Luas Line (IRE) (Danehill (USA)) **Brook Farm Bloodstock**
128 B c 17/2 Kheleyf (USA)—Inhibition (Nayef (USA)) **Kingsclere Racing Club**
129 **KNOCKROON**, b c 15/4 Royal Applause—Spring Touch (USA) (Elusive Quality (USA)) (63491) **D. E. Brownlow**
130 **KOKOVOKO (IRE)**, br c 15/3 Trans Island—Khazaria (FR) (Sinndar (IRE)) (13888) **Mrs T. Miller**
131 B c 22/3 Sirocco (GER)—Lady Brora (Dashing Blade) **Kingsclere Racing Club**
132 **LIBECCIO (FR)**, b c 22/3 Shirocco (GER)—Francais (Mark of Esteem (IRE)) (40000) **Mick and Janice Mariscotti**
133 **MAN OF HARLECH**, b c 14/4 Dansili—Ffestiniog (IRE) (Efisio) **Elite Racing**
134 Ch c 28/4 Firebreak—Manderina (Mind Games) (16666)

MR ANDREW BALDING - Continued

135 B c 15/4 Tagula (IRE)—Marajuana (Robellino (USA)) **Kingsclere Racing Club**
136 MERRY ME (IRE), b f 9/4 Invincible Spirit (IRE)—Thought Is Free (Cadeaux Genereux) **Mrs F. H. Hay**
137 MICRAS, b f 20/2 Medicean—Purple Heather (USA) (Rahy (USA)) **Her Majesty The Queen**
138 MIME DANCE, b c 22/1 Notnowcato—Encore My Love (Royal Applause) (32000) **D. E. Brownlow**
139 Ch f 19/4 Teofilo (IRE)—Mimisel (Selkirk (USA)) (28000) **Sky Sports News**
140 Br c 25/4 Bushranger (IRE)—Miss Assertive (Zafonic (USA)) (46000) **Dr P. Brown**
141 MUIR LODGE (GER), b c 1/4 Monsun (GER)—Sqillo (IRE) (Bachelor Duke (USA)) (158729) **Mrs F. H. Hay**
142 MYMATECHRIS (IRE), b c 24/4 High Chaparral (IRE)—
　　　　　　　　　　　　　　　　Splendour (FR) (Desert King (IRE)) (53967) **D. E. Brownlow**
143 NABATEAN (IRE), b c 18/4 Rock of Gibraltar (IRE)—Landinium (ITY) (Lando (GER)) **Lord Blyth**
144 B f 10/5 Authorized (IRE)—No Frills (IRE) (Darshaan) **Dr P. Brown**
145 OBSTINATE (IRE), b c 5/4 Fastnet Rock (AUS)—Sangita (Royal Academy (USA)) (206348) **Mrs F. H. Hay**
146 OPERA DUKE (IRE), ch c 5/3 Duke of Marmalade (IRE)—Opera Glass (Barathea (IRE)) **J. C. Smith**
147 PEARL SPECTRE (USA), ch c 9/3 Street Cry (IRE)—
　　　　　　　　　　　　　　　　Dark Sky (USA) (Storm Cat (USA)) (368663) **Pearl Bloodstock Limited**
148 PICARDY (IRE), ch f 3/4 Notnowcato—Sabah (Nashwan (USA)) **Sir Roger Buckley**
149 POOL HOUSE, b c 21/1 Sakhee's Secret—Gitane (FR) (Grand Lodge (USA)) (20952) **D. E. Brownlow**
150 B c 30/4 Rock of Gibraltar (IRE)—Portentous (Selkirk (USA)) (70000) **Mr N. Botica & Mrs Wendy Gorell**
151 ROSKILLY (IRE), ch c 10/2 Hurricane Run (IRE)—
　　　　　　　　　　　　　　　　Party Feet (IRE) (Noverre (USA)) (50000) **Mick and Janice Mariscotti**
152 Ch f 13/3 Sir Percy—Royal Patron (Royal Academy (USA)) **Sir Gordon Brunton**
153 ROYAL PRESERVE, ch c 12/3 Duke of Marmalade (IRE)—
　　　　　　　　　　　　　　　　Castaway Queen (IRE) (Selkirk (USA)) (45000) **Mick and Janice Mariscotti**
154 SCOPPIO DEL CARRO, b c 8/4 Medicean—
　　　　　　　　　　　　　　　　Sadie Thompson (IRE) (King's Best (USA)) (20000) **M & V Slade/ KTS**
155 B f 8/2 Phoenix Reach (IRE)—Seaflower Reef (IRE) (Robellino (USA)) **Kingsclere Racing Club**
156 SECRET HINT, b f 29/1 Oasis Dream—Teeky (Daylami (IRE)) **G. Strawbridge**
157 SIGNAL, b c 10/2 Cape Cross (IRE)—
　　　　　　　　　　　　　　　　Moon Sister (IRE) (Cadeaux Genereux) (115000) **Highclere Thoroughbred Racing - Conquest**
158 SILENT SERVICE (USA), b br c 11/3 Arch (USA)—
　　　　　　　　　　　　　　　　Seeking Silence (USA) (Seeking The Gold (USA)) (230414) **Qatar Racing Limited**
159 SMILING STRANGER (IRE), b c 13/3 Nayef (USA)—
　　　　　　　　　　　　　　　　Carraigoona (IRE) (Rock of Gibraltar (IRE)) (22221) **N. M. Watts**
160 STORM FORCE TEN, b c 31/3 Shirocco (GER)—Stravinsky Dance (Stravinsky (USA)) **R. Waley-Cohen**
161 STYBBA, b f 30/4 Medicean—Time Saved (Green Desert (USA)) (240000) **Qatar Racing Limited**
162 B f 28/4 Royal Applause—Succinct (Hector Protector (USA)) (52000) **Dr P. Brown**
163 B c 6/3 Firebreak—Sukuma (IRE) (Highest Honor (FR)) (7619)
164 TELEGRAPH (IRE), b c 4/2 Bushranger (IRE)—
　　　　　　　　　　　　　　　　Vampire Queen (IRE) (General Monash (USA)) (65000) **Highclere Thoroughbred Racing - Alcove**
165 Gr c 28/1 Danehill Dancer (IRE)—Tiffany Diamond (IRE) (Sadler's Wells (USA)) **J. C. Smith**
166 B f 27/3 Pivotal—Time Away (IRE) (Darshaan) **R. Barnett**
167 TRADING PROFIT, br c 2/3 Kheleyf (USA)—Avessia (Averti (IRE)) (38000) **Another Bottle Racing**
168 VECHEKA (IRE), b c 24/4 Lawman (FR)—Lidanski (IRE) (Soviet Star (USA)) (75000) **Mick and Janice Mariscotti**
169 B f 5/3 Mount Nelson—Victoria Montoya (High Chaparral (IRE)) **Kingsclere Racing Club**
170 B c 19/3 Shirocco (GER)—Wakytara (GER) (Danehill (USA)) (38888) **Mr N. Botica & Mrs Wendy Gorell**
171 B f 23/1 Authorized (IRE)—Welsh Diva (Selkirk (USA)) (180000) **Jackie & George Smith**
172 B c 3/5 Konigstiger (GER)—Wurfspiel (GER) (Lomitas) (30158) **Mr N. Botica & Mrs Wendy Gorell**
173 WYLYE, gr f 26/1 Dalakhani (IRE)—Tavy (Pivotal) **Mrs A. Wigan**

Other Owners: Mr I. A. Balding, Mrs I. A. Balding, Mr P. Blaydon, Mr Peter Box, Mr P. A. Brend, Mr John Bridgman, Mr J. S. Bromfield, Sir Roger Buckley, Mr D. H. Caslon, Mr P. M. Claydon, Mr P. Coates, Mr C. Conroy, Mr P. E. Done, Dr Bridget Drew, Mr N. R. R. Drew, Miss G. B. Drew, Mr John Drew, Mr J. Dwyer, Mr P. A. Elson, Mr P. E. Felton, Sir A. Ferguson, Mr K. H. Fischer, Mr C. H. Fischer, Mr J. K. Gale, Mr J. Glasgow, Mr R. M. Gorell, Mrs W. E. Gorell, Mr P. Green, Mr P. W. Haddock, Mr S. J. Harding, Mr C. J. Harper, Mr N. G. R. Harris, The Hon H. M. Herbert, Highclere Thoroughbred Racing Ltd, Mr S. Hill, Mr Michael Hill, Mr Tony Hill, Mr J. C. Hitchins, Mr S. R. Hitchins, Mr J. R. Hitchins, Mr R. S. Hoskins, G. R. Ireland, Ms S. J. Johnson, Mr R. C. Knight, Mr C. E. Lewis, Mr Luke Lillingston, Mr D. I. Lubert, Mrs R. Lyon, Mr M. G. Mariscotti, Mrs J. M. Mariscotti, Mr G. A. Mason, Mr R. H. W. Morecombe, Mr J. A. Newman, Miss M. Noden, Mr Gerald Oury, Mr P. Pausewang, Mrs D. M. Pausewang, Mr O. J. W. Pawle, Mr E. C. Powell, Mrs L. E. Ramsden, Mr N. J. F. Robinson, Mr J. Rodosthenous, Mr G. Shepherd, Mr D. M. Slade, Mrs V. J. M. Slade, Mr G. A. E. Smith, Mrs G. A. E. Smith, Mr J. A. B. Stafford, Mr R. Starczewski, Mr B. G. Swallow, Mr A. J. Thomas, Mr S. R. Thomas, Mrs C. S. Whitaker.

Assistant Trainer: C. Bonner

Jockey (flat): Liam Keniry, David Probert, Neil Chalmers, Jimmy Fortune. **Apprentice:** Thomas Brown, Daniel Muscutt, Jonathan Willetts. **Amateur:** Mr A. Rawlinson.

18 | MR JOHN BALDING, Doncaster
Postal: **Mayflower Stables, Saracens Lane, Scrooby, Doncaster, South Yorkshire, DN10 6AS**
Contacts: **HOME (01302) 710096 FAX (01302) 710096 MOBILE (07816) 612631**
E-MAIL **j.balding@btconnect.com**

1 IMAGINARY WORLD (IRE), 5, b m Exceed And Excel (AUS)—Plutonia **Hairy Gorrilaz**
2 POINT NORTH (IRE), 6, b g Danehill Dancer (USA)—Briolette (IRE) **Mr W. Herring**
3 SLEEPY BLUE OCEAN, 7, b g Oasis Dream—Esteemed Lady (IRE) **Tykes & Terriers Racing Club**
4 THIS ONES FOR EDDY, 8, b g Kyllachy—Skirt Around **Mr W. Herring**

Other Owners: Mr K. Ackroyd, Mr P. Birley, M. V. Firth, Mr A. J. Sharp, Mr B. Topliss.

Assistant Trainer: Claire Edmunds, Jason Edmunds

Apprentice: Andrew Smith.

19 | MR MICHAEL BANKS, Sandy
Postal: **Manor Farm, Manor Farm Road, Waresley, Sandy, Bedfordshire, SG19 3BX**
Contacts: **PHONE (01767) 650563 FAX (01767) 652988 MOBILE (07860) 627370**
E-MAIL **waresleyfarms@btconnect.com**

1 CLERK'S CHOICE (IRE), 7, b g Bachelor Duke (USA)—Credit Crunch (IRE) **M. C. Banks**
2 LOMBARDY BOY (IRE), 8, b g Milan—Horner Water (IRE) **M. C. Banks**
3 MAX LAURIE (FR), 8, bl g Ungaro (GER)—Laurie Mercurialle (FR) **Mrs M. C. Banks**
4 ROGUE DANCER (FR), 8, b g Dark Moondancer—Esperanza IV (FR) **M. C. Banks**

20 | MR MARC BARBER, Amroth
Postal: **Amroth Farm, Amroth, Narberth, Dyfed, SA67 8NJ**

1 CORNERHOUSE SAM (IRE), 8, b g Norwich—She Nogan (IRE) **Mr A. D. Quinn**
2 DEREKS RED RUBY, 5, br m Kayf Tara—Scarlet Dawn (IRE) **Mr G. J. Barber**
3 KENALECK (GER), 9, ch g Urban Ocean (FR)—Kengar (FR) **Mr G. M. Barber**
4 KIMORA (IRE), 7, b m Bach (IRE)—Blue Gale (IRE) **Mr G. J. Barber**
5 ODD ONE OUT (IRE), 8, b br m Luso—Tawny Owl (IRE) **Mr G. M. Barber**

21 | MRS TRACEY BARFOOT-SAUNT, Wotton-under-Edge
Postal: **Cosy Farm, Huntingford, Charfield, Wotton-under-Edge, Gloucestershire, GL12 8EY**
Contacts: **PHONE (01453) 520312 FAX (01453) 520312 MOBILE (07976) 360626**

1 BARRY THE BARBER (IRE), 7, b g Flemensfirth (USA)—Dining Hall (IRE) **Six Of The Very Best**
2 LOUGHMORE VIC (IRE), 8, ch g Old Vic—Princess Lizzie (IRE) **A Good Days Racing**
3 PRESENTING DR T (IRE), 7, b g Luso—Halfway Home **T. Jewitt**

Other Owners: Mrs T. M. Barfoot-Saunt, Mr G. C. Barfoot-Saunt.

Jockey (NH): Henry Oliver. **Amateur:** Mr Geoff Barfoot-Saunt.

22 | MR MAURICE BARNES, Brampton
Postal: **Tarnside, Farlam, Brampton, Cumbria, CA8 1LA**
Contacts: **PHONE/FAX (01697) 746675 MOBILE (07760) 433191**
E-MAIL **anne.barnes1@btinternet.com**

1 ABOUT THYNE (IRE), 8, ch g Anshan—Down The Garden (IRE) **The Wizards**
2 ACROSS THE TWEED (IRE), 7, b br g Alderbrook—Cash Chase (IRE) **The Last Chancers**
3 ATTYCRAN (IRE), 8, b g Snurge—Baltimore Lass (IRE) **Miss A. P. Lee**
4 6, B m Tamure (IRE)—Bob Back's Lady (IRE) **Mr J. Wills**
5 CARRIGDHOUN (IRE), 8, gr g Goldmark (USA)—Pet Tomjammar (IRE) **M. A. Barnes**
6 DORSET DORA, 5, b m Exit To Nowhere (USA)—Pems Gift **Mr S. J. Baird & M. A. Barnes**
7 FA'SIDE CASTLE (IRE), 4, b g Dylan Thomas (IRE)—Keyaki (IRE) **M. A. Barnes**

MR MAURICE BARNES - Continued

8 **FLAYBAY**, 5, b m Grape Tree Road—I'll Skin Them (IRE) **Miss A. P. Lee**
9 **GARLETON (IRE)**, 12, b g Anshan—Another Grouse **East-West Partnership**
10 **GEORGE ALMIGHTY**, 5, b g Denounce—Etching (USA) **M. D. Townson**
11 **HOWIZEE**, 7, gr g Baryshnikov (AUS)—Sendai **Mr G. Baird**
12 **I'LL BE FRANK**, 8, b g Fraam—Miss Opulence (IRE) **M. D. Townson**
13 **L'EMINENCE GRISE (IRE)**, 6, gr g Kahyasi—Belle Innocence (FR) **Mr C. Davidson**
14 4, B f Fantastic View (USA)—Little Cascade **M. A. Barnes**
15 **MY IDEA**, 7, b g Golan (IRE)—Ghana (GER) **The Whisperers**
16 **ODDSMAKER (IRE)**, 12, b g Barathea (IRE)—Archipova (IRE) **M. A. Barnes**
17 5, B h Rainbow High—On The Bay **Mr M. Townson**
18 **OVERPRICED**, 7, b m Chocolat de Meguro (USA)—One Stop **M. A. Barnes**
19 **PAS TROP TARD (FR)**, 6, b g Caballo Raptor (CAN)—This Melody (FR) **Mr C. Davidson**
20 **SOFT SPOKEN GUY (IRE)**, 10, b g Saddlers' Hall (IRE)—Pisa (IRE) **Mr S. Lowther & Mr M. Barnes**
21 6, B m Exit To Nowhere (USA)—Sparkling Jess **M. A. Barnes**
22 **STORMONT BRIDGE**, 5, b g Avonbridge—Stormont Castle (USA) **M. A. Barnes**
23 **TOLEDO GOLD (IRE)**, 7, ch g Needwood Blade—Eman's Joy **Mr M. Barnes, Mr Scott Lowther**
24 **WATCHMEGO**, 5, b m Supreme Sound—One Stop **M. A. Barnes**
25 **WEETFROMTHECHAFF**, 8, gr g Weet-A-Minute (IRE)—Weet Ees Girl (IRE) **J. M. Carlyle**

TWO-YEAR-OLDS

26 B c 21/2 Captain Gerrard (IRE)—Little Cascade (Forzando) **M. A. Barnes**
27 B f 13/4 Byron—Skiddaw Wolf (Wolfhound (USA)) **Mr J. Willis**

Other Owners: Mr M. Barnes, Mr R. H. Briggs, Mrs F. H. Crone, Mr C. Davidson, Mr David Gillespie, Mr J. G. Graham, Mr D. Graves, Mr Keith Greenwell, Mr Neil Haughan, Mr S. G. Johnston, Mr Scott Lowther, Mr William Muir.

Jockey (NH): Michael McAlister. **Conditional:** Stephen Mulqueen.

23　**MR BRIAN BARR, Sherborne**
Postal: **Tall Trees Stud, Longburton, Sherborne, Dorset, DT9 5PH**
Contacts: **PHONE (01963) 210173 MOBILE (07826) 867881**

1 **CASTLEMORRIS KING**, 5, br g And Beyond (IRE)—Brookshield Baby (IRE) **Miss D. Hitchins**
2 **DON'T LOOK BACH (IRE)**, 8, b g Bach (IRE)—Buckalong (IRE)
3 **FORGOTTEN PROMISE**, 6, b m Revoque (IRE)—Ivory's Promise **Miss D. Hitchins**
4 **OUR JOSEPH (IRE)**, 7, ch g Alderbrook—Witchy Native (IRE)
5 **PA MURPHY (IRE)**, 6, b br g Wizard King—Katie Stobling (IRE)
6 **SALEAL**, 4, b g Gentleman's Deal (IRE)—Sales Flow **Miss D. Hitchins**
7 **SWIFT LORD (IRE)**, 8, b g Spectrum—Ediyrna (IRE)
8 **TUFFSTUFF**, 5, b g Generous (IRE)—Life Line **Miss D. Hitchins**
9 **VACARIO (GER)**, 9, br g Acatenango (GER)—Vaillance (GER) **Miss D. Hitchins**
10 **VILLAGE SECRET**, 7, ch g Pasternak—Daphne Odora

Assistant Trainer: Daisy Hitchins

Conditional: Gavin Sheehan.

24　**MR RON BARR, Middlesbrough**
Postal: **Carr House Farm, Seamer, Stokesley, Middlesbrough, Cleveland, TS9 5LL**
Contacts: **PHONE (01642) 710687 MOBILE (07711) 895309**
E-MAIL christinebarr1@aol.com

1 **AL FURAT (USA)**, 5, b g El Prado (IRE)—No Frills (IRE) **R. E. Barr**
2 **BAYBSHAMBLES (IRE)**, 9, b g Compton Admiral—Payvashooz **Miss S. Haykin**
3 **FOREIGN RHYTHM (IRE)**, 8, ch m Distant Music (USA)—Happy Talk (IRE) **R. E. Barr**
4 **GRACEFUL ACT**, 5, b m Royal Applause—Minnina (IRE) **Mrs C. Barr**
5 **ISLE OF ELLIS (IRE)**, 6, b g Statue of Liberty (USA)—Fable **R. E. Barr**
6 **KARATE QUEEN**, 8, b m King's Best (USA)—Black Belt Shopper (IRE) **Mrs C. Barr**
7 **KYZER DREAM**, 8, b g Rouvres (FR)—Payvashooz **R. E. Barr**
8 **SCARLET ROCKS (IRE)**, 5, b m Chineur (FR)—Alexander Duchess (IRE) **Balios Racing**
9 **SILLY GILLY (IRE)**, 9, b m Mull of Kintyre (USA)—Richly Deserved (IRE) **D. Thomson**
10 **TOFFEE NOSE**, 6, b g Ishiguro (USA)—The Synergist **Mrs C. Barr**
11 **TROPICAL DUKE (IRE)**, 7, ch g Bachelor Duke (USA)—Tropical Dance (USA) **R. E. Barr**

MR RON BARR - Continued

THREE-YEAR-OLDS

12 **MIDNIGHT WARRIOR**, b g Teofilo (IRE)—Mauri Moon **Mr K. Trimble**

TWO-YEAR-OLDS

13 B f 21/4 Josr Algarhoud (IRE)—Pay Time (Timeless Times (USA)) **R. E. Barr**

Other Owners: Mr R. E. Barr, Mr J. Darby, Mrs S. M. Darby.

Assistant Trainer: Mrs C. Barr

Amateur: Miss V. Barr.

---

25 **MR DAVID BARRON, Thirsk**
Postal: **Maunby House, Maunby, Thirsk, North Yorkshire, YO7 4HD**
Contacts: **PHONE (01845) 587435 FAX (01845) 587331**
E-MAIL **david@harrowgate.wanadoo.co.uk**

1 **AMAZING AMORAY (IRE)**, 5, b g Tagula (IRE)—Amistad (GER) **R. C. Miquel**
2 **ANNIE BEACH (IRE)**, 4, ch f Redback—Kiva **Mrs S. C. Barron**
3 **BERTIEWHITTLE**, 5, ch g Bahamian Bounty—Minette **JKB Johnson & Norton Common Farm Racing II**
4 **BIG JOHNNY D (IRE)**, 4, ch g Alhaarth (IRE)—Bakiya (USA) **Mr C. A. Washbourn**
5 **BOSUN BREESE**, 8, b g Bahamian Bounty—Nellie Melba **Harrowgate Bloodstock Ltd**
6 **CLON BRULEE (IRE)**, 4, ch g Modigliani (USA)—Cloneden (IRE) **Ms Colette Twomey**
7 **COLONEL MAK**, 6, br g Makbul—Colonel's Daughter **Norton Common Farm Racing, O'Kane, Murphy**
8 **FIELDGUNNER KIRKUP (GER)**, 5, b g Acclamation—Fire Finch **K. Kirkup**
9 **FREE SPIN (IRE)**, 4, ch c Iffraaj—Romea **L. G. O'Kane**
10 **GOTTCHER**, 5, b g Fasliyev (USA)—Danalia (IRE) **Twinacre Nurseries Ltd**
11 **HEROIC ENDEAVOUR (IRE)**, 4, b g Ishiguru (USA)—Enchantment **Lady J. Brookeborough**
12 **HITCHENS (IRE)**, 8, b g Acclamation—Royal Fizz (IRE) **Mr Laurence O'Kane & Mr Paul Murphy**
13 **LEWIS**, 4, b g Kayf Tara—Island of Memories (IRE) **A. J. Duffield**
14 **LONG AWAITED (IRE)**, 5, b g Pivotal—Desertion (IRE) **Peter Jones**
15 **LUPIN POOTER**, 4, b g Bertolini (USA)—Carrie Pooter **Liam & Dermot Kelly**
16 **MAGICAL MACEY (USA)**, 6, ch g Rossini (USA)—Spring's Glory (USA) **Harrowgate Bloodstock Ltd**
17 **MISSISSIPPI**, 4, b g Exceed And Excel (AUS)—Ruby Rocket (IRE) **L. G. O'Kane**
18 **MUFFIN MCLEAY (IRE)**, 5, b g Hawk Wing—Youngus (USA) **Harrowgate Bloodstock Ltd**
19 **NOVA SAM (FR)**, 5, ch g Black Sam Bellamy (IRE)—Elasili (FR) **The Depot Boys**
20 **PEARL ICE**, 5, b g Iffraaj—Jezebel **Mr Laurence O'Kane & Mr Paul Murphy**
21 **PEARL SECRET**, 4, ch c Compton Place—Our Little Secret (IRE) **Pearl Bloodstock Limited**
22 **PROFILE STAR (IRE)**, 4, b g Kodiac—Fingal Nights (IRE) **Profile Storage Ltd**
23 **PTOLEMY**, 4, b g Royal Applause—Rydal Mount (IRE) **R. S. E. Gifford**
24 **SHESASTAR**, 5, b m Bahamian Bounty—Celestial Welcome **Star Alliance 4 - Lancs 2 Lincs**
25 **SIRVINO (IRE)**, 8, b g Vettori (IRE)—Zenita (IRE) **Mr Theo Williams & Mr Charles Mocatta**
26 **SOHCAHTOA (IRE)**, 7, b g Val Royal (FR)—Stroke of Six (IRE) **Douglas Pryde Jim Beaumont**
27 **SPES NOSTRA**, 5, b g Ad Valorem (USA)—Millagros (IRE) **Mr J. Cringan & Mr D. Pryde**
28 **SUITS ME**, 10, ch g Bertolini (USA)—Fancier Bit **D. E. Cook**
29 **TRES CORONAS (IRE)**, 6, b g Key of Luck (USA)—Almansa (IRE) **Mr D. Pryde & Mr J. Cringan**
30 **VITAL CALLING**, 4, b g Vital Equine (IRE)—Crosby Millie **J. E. Raper**
31 **WAFFLE (IRE)**, 7, ch g Kheleyf (USA)—Saphire **Mr Laurence O'Kane & Mr Paul Murphy**

THREE-YEAR-OLDS

32 **A J COOK (IRE)**, b g Mujadil (USA)—Undertone (IRE) **Norton Common Farm Racing Ltd**
33 **AHERN**, ch c Dutch Art—Petra Nova **Qatar Racing Limited**
34 **ANTONIO GRAMSCI (IRE)**, b g Misu Bond (IRE)—La Corujera **Norton Common Farm Racing Ltd**
35 **BIG JOHN CANNON (IRE)**, b g High Chaparral (IRE)—Bakiya (USA) **Mr C. A. Washbourn**
36 **COSMIC CHATTER**, b g Paris House—Paradise Eve **Highclere T'Bred Racing & David Barron**
37 **ESTEAMING**, b c Sir Percy—Night Over Day **D. E. Cook**
38 **FIRST SERVE (IRE)**, b f Bachelor Duke (USA)—Mauresmo (IRE) **Oghill House Stud**
39 **LA SYLPHE**, b f Refuse To Bend (IRE)—Naayla (IRE) **Mr M. R. Dalby**
40 **MARCUS CAESAR (IRE)**, b g Antonius Pius (USA)—Skyscape **Mr G. Fawcett**
41 **NEWSTEAD ABBEY**, b g Byron—Oatcake **Let's Be Lucky Partnership**
42 **NEXT DOOR (IRE)**, b f Elusive City (USA)—Lamh Eile (IRE) **Oghill House Stud & Partner**
43 **ROBOT BOY (IRE)**, ch c Shamardal (USA)—Pivotal's Princess (IRE) **Qatar Racing Limited**
44 **ROYAL STYLE (IRE)**, ch f Windsor Knot (IRE)—Christeningpresent (IRE) **Wensleydale Bacon Limited**
45 **SLEEPY HAVEN (IRE)**, b g Indian Haven—High Society Girl (IRE) **T. D. Barron**

MR DAVID BARRON - Continued

46 **TRANQUILITY COVE (USA)**, b br f Rock Hard Ten (USA)—South Bay Cove (CAN) **Mrs J. M. Dwyer**
47 **WISHING GATE (IRE)**, b c Kyllachy—Rydal Mount (IRE) **R. S. E. Gifford**

TWO-YEAR-OLDS

48 **AMOUR NOIR (IRE)**, br c 19/2 Footstepsinthesand—
                    Announcing Peace (Danehill (USA)) (119047) **Qatar Racing Limited**
49 **ANOTHER LINCOLNDAY**, ch c 2/4 Desideratum—Another Paris (Paris House)
50 B c 18/3 Intikhab (USA)—Autumn Star (IRE) (Mujadil (USA)) (7619) **Twinacre Nurseries Ltd**
51 **CAVALLO BELLA**, gr f 3/2 Bertolini (USA)—Crosby Millie (Linamix (FR)) **J. E. Raper**
52 Ch f 3/4 Thousand Words—Consensus (IRE) (Common Grounds) (8729) **Norton Common Farm Racing Ltd**
53 **DECKARD (IRE)**, b c 31/3 Amadeus Wolf—Victory Peak (Shirley Heights) (7619) **A. J. Duffield**
54 B g 1/2 Haafhd—Deira Dubai (Green Desert (USA)) (9523) **D. G. Pryde, Jim Beaumont & James Callow**
55 B f 3/4 Camacho—Evelyn One (Alhaarth (IRE)) (1983) **Leods Contracts Limited**
56 Ch c 3/4 Sir Percy—Fantasy Princess (USA) (Johannesburg (USA)) (6348) **Norton Common Farm Racing Ltd**
57 B br c 24/4 War Front (USA)—Judy's Magic (USA) (Wavering Monarch (USA)) (202764) **Qatar Racing Limited**
58 **KASHSTAREE**, b f 12/3 Sakhee (USA)—Celestial Welcome (Most Welcome) **Star Alliance 5**
59 Gr f 22/4 Verglas (IRE)—Khayrat (IRE) (Polar Falcon (USA)) (11904) **Leods Contracts Limited**
60 **LA FERRUJA (IRE)**, b f 10/3 Camacho—Lorena (IRE) (Bishop of Cashel) (1428) **J. G. Brown**
61 B c 27/4 Kodiac—Mildmay (USA) (Elusive Quality (USA)) **Mr R. G. Toes**
62 **MISS SOPHISTICATED**, b f 25/2 Bahamian Bounty—
                    Miss Sophisticat (Alhaarth (IRE)) (12500) **Wensleydale Bacon Limited**
63 **PRECARIOUSLY GOOD**, b f 21/2 Oasis Dream—
                    Danceabout (Shareef Dancer (USA)) (87301) **Qatar Racing Limited**
64 B br f 28/2 Dixie Union (USA)—Shriek (USA) (Street Cry (IRE)) (98310) **Qatar Racing Limited**
65 **TIASTA (IRE)**, ch f 10/4 Footstepsinthesand—La Stravaganza (USA) (Rainbow Quest (USA)) (2380) **Mr J. Sagar**
66 B c 27/4 Oratorio (IRE)—Velvet Appeal (IRE) (Petorius) (24761) **Twinacre Nurseries Ltd**
67 **VIVA VERGLAS (IRE)**, gr c 26/3 Verglas (IRE)—Yellow Trumpet (Petong) (52380) **R. C. Miquel**

Other Owners: Mr J. R. Barr, J. J. Beaumont, J. R. Callow, Mr A. R. C. Cox, J. A. Cringan, J. A. Evans, Mr R. A. Gorrie, Mr S. T. Gorrie, The Hon H. M. Herbert, Highclere Thoroughbred Racing Ltd, Mr P. Hyland, Mr H. D. Hyland, Mr L. Kelly, Mr D. Kelly, Mr C. T. Mocatta, Mr P. A. Murphy, D. G. Pryde, Mr G. S. Slater, T. Williams, Mr A. Worrall.

Assistant Trainer: Nicola-Jo Barron

Apprentice: Luke McNiff.

---

26   MR P. BARY, Chantilly
Postal: **5 Chemin des Aigles, 60500 Chantilly, France**
Contacts: **PHONE (0033) 3445 71403 FAX (0033) 3446 72015 MOBILE (0033) 6075 80241**
E-MAIL p-bary@wanadoo.fr

1 **ALAMARIE (FR)**, 4, b f Acclamation—Marie Rheinberg (GER) **Mr & Mrs R. Woolcott**
2 **ANATOLIA (MOR)**, 4, b f Country Reel (USA)—Byzanz (GER) **Jalobey Stud**
3 **ATOMIC WAVES**, 4, ch c Hernando (FR)—Atlantic Blue (USA) **Skymarc Farm Inc.**
4 **DAWNING (USA)**, 4, b f War Chant (USA)—Sun Is Up (JPN) **Niarchos Family**
5 **HASNA (FR)**, 4, ch f American Post—Harriet (FR) **G. Sandor**
6 **LA MUTINE (IRE)**, 4, b f Muhtathir—Petit Calva (FR) **E. de Waldner**
7 **MAINSAIL (FR)**, 4, b c Oasis Dream—Docklands (USA) **K. Abdulla**
8 **MENARDAIS (FR)**, 4, b c Canyon Creek—Madeleine's Blush **G. Sandor**
9 **MORTGA (FR)**, 4, b c Anabaa—Cornelia (FR) **Saeed Nasser Al Romaithi**
10 **POUPEE FLASH (USA)**, 4, b f Elusive Quality (USA)—Modesty Blaise (USA) **Niarchos Family**
11 **RED HURRICANE (IRE)**, 4, b c Hurricane Run (IRE)—Red Blossom (USA) **J-M Hegesippe**
12 **SMOKING SUN (USA)**, 4, b br c Smart Strike (CAN)—Burning Sunset **Niarchos Family**
13 **STELWAY (FR)**, 4, ch c Gold Away (IRE)—Hill Tiger (IRE) **D. Jacob**
14 **UNNEFER (FR)**, 8, b h Danehill Dancer (IRE)—Mimalia (USA) **Niarchos Family**

THREE-YEAR-OLDS

15 **ACHERNAR (USA)**, ch c Lemon Drop Kid (USA)—Ikat (IRE) **Niarchos Family**
16 **ALAMEIRA (FR)**, b f Layman (USA)—Annee de La Femme (IRE) **M. Ohana**
17 **ALBARELLA (FR)**, ch f Green Tune (USA)—Angeluccia (USA) **Razza Dormello Olgiata**
18 **ALBARES (FR)**, b c Lando (GER)—Aspolina (IRE) **M. Randelli**
19 **ART COMTEMPORAIN (USA)**, gr c Smart Strike (CAN)—Super Lina (FR) **Ecurie J. L. Bouchard**
20 **AVIDLY**, b f Beat Hollow—Balmy **K. Abdulla**
21 **BARSAM (FR)**, b c Tomorrows Cat (USA)—Belga Wood (USA) **G. Sandor**

MR P. BARY - Continued

22 **CASSELLS ROCK (IRE)**, br c Rock of Gibraltar (IRE)—Se La Vie (FR) **Saeed Nasser Al Romaithi**
23 **CHEYENNE HOME (USA)**, b c Empire Maker (USA)—Cheyenne Dream **K. Abdulla**
24 **CONDOR QUEST**, b c Oasis Dream—Condition **K. Abdulla**
25 **CORYCIAN (IRE)**, b c Dansili—Colza (USA) **Niarchos Family**
26 **CUCUMA (FR)**, b f Invincible Spirit (IRE)—Cumin (USA) **M. Randelli**
27 **DAIVIKA (USA)**, b f Dynaformer (USA)—Divine Proportions (USA) **Niarchos Family**
28 **ELITISTE (IRE)**, b f Danehill Dancer (IRE)—Alpha Lupi (IRE) **Ecurie La Boetie**
29 **FISCAL UNION**, b c Three Valleys (USA)—Mooring **K. Abdulla**
30 **FREQUENTLY**, b f Dansili—Freedonia **Niarchos Family**
31 **FREUD (FR)**, b g Dalakhani (IRE)—Ailette **Ecurie La Boetie**
32 **HER STAR (USA)**, b f Harlan's Holiday (USA)—Silver Comic (USA) **Niarchos Family**
33 **HIPPOLYTO (IRE)**, b c Galileo (IRE)—Fountain of Peace (USA) **Ecurie J. L. Bouchard**
34 **IMPATIENTE (FR)**, b f Gold Away (IRE)—Good To Dance (IRE) **Haras du Mezeray**
35 **KISS ME GOODBYE**, b f Raven's Pass (USA)—Khumba Mela (IRE) **Ecurie des Monceaux**
36 **LADY JANE (FR)**, b f Peintre Celebre (USA)—Anassa (GER) **P. Lazare**
37 **LEGITIMITE (FR)**, b f Lando (GER)—Alcidiana (FR) **M. Ohana**
38 **MARKET SHARE**, b c Zamindar (USA)—Winter Solstice **K. Abdulla**
39 **MISRAI (IRE)**, gr c Dalakhani (IRE)—Altruiste (USA) **Ecurie J. L. Bouchard**
40 **MODESTY'S WAY (USA)**, b f Giant's Causeway (USA)—Modesty Blaise (USA) **Niarchos Family**
41 **MONSOON (IRE)**, b f Cape Cross (IRE)—Mirina (FR) **Lady O'Reilly**
42 **NAME DROPPING (IRE)**, b c Dalakhani (IRE)—Naissance Royale (IRE) **Ecurie des Monceaux**
43 **NERVI (FR)**, b c Orpen (USA)—O' Keefe (IRE) **L. Dassault**
44 **NOLENE (FR)**, ch f Layman—Noemie **G. Sandor**
45 **NOTAIRE (IRE)**, b c Nayef (USA)—Aiglonne (USA) **Skymarc Farm Inc.**
46 **PARLE MOI (IRE)**, b f Montjeu (IRE)—Di Moi Oui **Grundy Bloodstock Ltd**
47 **PASSIONABLE**, ch f New Approach (IRE)—Raisonnable **Niarchos Family**
48 **PREEMPT**, b c Dansili—Perfect Hand **K. Abdulla**
49 **SAINT THOMAS (FR)**, b c Dalakhani (IRE)—Metisse (USA) **Ecurie La Boetie**
50 **SHARED ACCOUNT**, br f Dansili—Imbabala **K. Abdulla**
51 **SLOPE**, gr f Acclamation—Bandanna **J. R. Treptow**
52 **SPHERE OF GRACE (FR)**, b f High Chaparral (IRE)—Misty Heights **Niarchos Family**
53 **SPINACRE (IRE)**, gr f Verglas (IRE)—Spinamix **Ecurie La Boetie**
54 **SPIRITJIM (FR)**, b c Galileo (IRE)—Hidden Silver **J-M. Hegesippe**
55 **STRIX**, ch c Muhtathir—Serandine (IRE) **Laghi France**
56 **SYNCHRONIC (IRE)**, b f Dansili—Platonic **Niarchos Family**
57 **TANTRIS (FR)**, ch c Turtle Bowl—Tianshan **G. Sandor**
58 **TEMPS LIBRE (USA)**, b g Medaglia d'oro (USA)—Orellana (USA) **Haras du Mezeray**
59 **TRIUMVIRATE**, b f Rail Link—Strike Lightly **K. Abdulla**
60 **TRY OUT**, b c Rail Link—Morzine **K. Abdulla**
61 **US LAW (IRE)**, gr c Lawman (FR)—Dookus (IRE) **Ecurie J. L. Bouchard**
62 **VENTEUSE**, b f Beat Hollow—Summer Breeze **K. Abdulla**
63 **YOGA (IRE)**, ch f Monsun (GER)—Remote Romance (USA) **Niarchos Family**
64 **ZHIYI (USA)**, b c Henrythenavigator (USA)—Burning Sunset **Niarchos Family**

TWO-YEAR-OLDS

65 Gr f 12/4 Dalakhani (IRE)—Amonita (Anabaa (USA)) **Haras du Mezeray**
66 B f 9/5 Falco (USA)—Angeluccia (USA) (Grand Slam (USA)) **Razza Dormello Olgiata**
67 **AUBAGNE (FR)**, gr f 4/5 Elusive City (USA)—Aliyeska (IRE) (Fasliyev (USA)) (46031) **Ecurie J. L. Bouchard**
68 Ch f 24/1 Naaqoos—Aviane (GER) (Winged Love (IRE)) (45238) **R. Dabdoub**
69 **AZARIANE (FR)**, b f 26/3 Sageburg (IRE)—
　　　　　　　　　　　　　　　　Peace Talk (FR) (Sadler's Wells (USA)) (134920) **Ecurie J. L. Bouchard**
70 **BUSHIDO (FR)**, ro ch c 1/4 Bernebeau (FR)—Belga Wood (USA) (Woodman (USA)) **G. Sandor**
71 **CASTAGNOU (IRE)**, b c 23/3 Lawman (FR)—
　　　　　　　　　　　　　　Around Me (IRE) (Johannesburg (USA)) (71428) **Ecurie J. L. Bouchard**
72 B c 21/5 Empire Maker (USA)—Conference Call (Anabaa (USA)) **K. Abdulla**
73 **CONQUETE (FR)**, ch f 3/3 Kyllachy—Chesnut Bird (Storm Bird (CAN)) (10317) **G. Sandor**
74 **CORIANDA (FR)**, b f 8/4 Danehill Dancer (IRE)—Cumin (USA) (Fusaichi Pegasus (USA)) (55555) **M. Randelli**
75 **DEEP SHADOW (IRE)**, b c 23/2 Manduro (GER)—Ossun (FR) (Anabaa (USA)) (57142) **Ecurie J. L. Bouchard**
76 Br f 8/1 High Chaparral (IRE)—Dream Day (Oasis Dream) (87301) **Ecurie des Monceaux**
77 **DUKE AGAIN (IRE)**, ch c 19/3 Duke of Marmalade (IRE)—
　　　　　　　　　　　　　　　Thanks Again (IRE) (Anabaa Blue) (51587) **Laghi France**
78 **DURANO (FR)**, gr c 1/5 Verglas (USA)—Darasa (FR) (Barathea (IRE)) (51587) **Ecurie J. L. Bouchard**
79 **ENZINA**, ch f 2/4 New Approach (IRE)—Kyniska (IRE) (Choisir (AUS)) (71428) **Ecurie J. L. Bouchard**
80 **FAUFILER (IRE)**, b f 8/5 Galileo (IRE)—Six Perfections (FR) (Celtic Swing) **Niarchos Family**
81 **FINGLASS (IRE)**, b f 18/3 Elusive City (USA)—Samya (Invincible Spirit (IRE)) **Laghi France**

MR P. BARY - Continued

82 B f 19/5 Deep Impact (JPN)—Forest Rain (FR) (Caerleon (USA)) **Niarchos Family**
83 B f 24/4 Nayef (USA)—Half Glance (Danehill (USA)) **K. Abdulla**
84 B f 13/2 Empire Maker (USA)—Helstra (USA) (Nureyev (USA)) **K. Abdulla**
85 **LAKA (IRE),** b f 23/3 Oasis Dream—Mimalia (USA) (Silver Hawk (USA)) **Niarchos Family**
86 B c 10/5 Cape Cross (IRE)—Lumiere Astrale (FR) (Trempolino (USA)) **Haras du Mezeray**
87 Ch c 21/2 Medicean—Lumiere Noire (FR) (Dashing Blade) **Haras du Mezeray**
88 **MISTERDAD (IRE),** b c 11/3 Cape Cross (IRE)—Flaming Cliffs (USA) (Kingmambo (USA)) **Niarchos Family**
89 **MONOCEROS (USA),** b c 26/4 Giant's Causeway (USA)—
                                      Divine Proportions (USA) (Kingmambo (USA)) **Niarchos Family**
90 **OSAGE (FR),** b c 8/2 Green Tune (USA)—Belle Chasse (Kyllachy) (7936) **G. Algranti**
91 B f 30/3 Sir Percy—Pink Topaz (USA) (Tiznow (USA)) **Niarchos Family**
92 B c 19/3 Oasis Dream—Pretty Face (Rainbow Quest (USA)) **K. Abdulla**
93 B f 9/3 Champs Elysees—Revealing (Halling (USA)) **K. Abdulla**
94 Bl f 6/4 Neo Universe (JPN)—Second Happiness (USA) (Storm Cat (USA)) **Niarchos Family**
95 **ST OLAVS GATE (FR),** b f 8/4 Sageburg (IRE)—Final Whistle (IRE) (Rossini (USA)) (37301) **M. Ohana**
96 **STELLA RIVER (FR),** b f 2/5 Stormy River (FR)—Montagne Magique (IRE) (King's Best (USA)) (35714) **D. Jacob**
97 **STEPHILL (FR),** ch c 25/2 Footstepsinthesand—Magic Hill (FR) (Danehill Dancer (IRE)) (24603) **Laghi France**
98 **SURFACE OF EARTH (USA),** b f 24/2 Empire Maker (USA)—Wild Planet (USA) (Nureyev (USA)) **Niarchos Family**
99 **TATOOINE (FR),** ch c 15/2 Galileo (IRE)—Three Mysteries (FR) (Linamix (FR)) **Niarchos Family**
100 **TOP OF THE MOON (IRE),** b f 14/4 Rock of Gibraltar (IRE)—
                                 Trip To The Moon (Fasliyev (USA)) (75396) **Ecurie J. L. Bouchard**
101 B f 20/2 Rock Hard Ten (USA)—Tsar's Pride (Sadler's Wells (USA)) **K. Abdulla**
102 B c 14/4 Three Valleys (USA)—West Dakota (USA) (Gone West (USA)) **K. Abdulla**
103 **WHAT MATTERS NOW (USA),** b c 27/3 Medaglia d'oro (USA)—Glia (USA) (A P Indy (USA)) **Niarchos Family**
104 B c 23/4 Shamardal (USA)—Winter Solstice (Unfuwain (USA)) **K. Abdulla**

Assistant Trainer: Miss Charlotte De Roualle

 27

MR ROBIN BASTIMAN, Wetherby
Postal: **Goosemoor Farm, Warfield Lane, Cowthorpe, Wetherby, West Yorkshire, LS22 5EU**
Contacts: **PHONE (01423) 359397 MOBILE (07976) 282976**
WEBSITE www.rbastimanracing.com

1 **COPPER TO GOLD,** 4, ch f Avonbridge—Faithful Beauty (IRE) **Mrs C. Steel**
2 **GREEN HOWARD,** 5, ch g Bahamian Bounty—Dash of Lime **Ms M. Austerfield**
3 **JACK BARKER,** 4, b g Danbird (AUS)—Smiddy Hill **I. B. Barker**
4 **KYLLACHYKOV (IRE),** 5, ch g Kyllachy—Dance On **Ms M. Austerfield**
5 **LIZZY'S DREAM,** 5, ch g Choisir (AUS)—Flyingit (USA) **Mrs P. Bastiman**
6 **MISS BLINK,** 6, ch m Compton Place—Tawny Way **J. A. Reed**
7 **MONSIEUR PONTAVEN,** 6, b g Avonbridge—Take Heart **Ms M. Austerfield**
8 **NOVALIST,** 5, ch g Avonbridge—Malelane (IRE) **Ms M. Austerfield**
9 **SECRET CITY (IRE),** 7, b g City On A Hill (USA)—Secret Combe (IRE) **Ms M. Austerfield**
10 **SEE VERMONT,** 5, b g Kyllachy—Orange Lily **Mr J. Smith**
11 **SINGEUR (IRE),** 6, b g Chineur (FR)—Singitta **Ms M. Austerfield**

THREE-YEAR-OLDS
12 **FAOLAN (IRE),** b c Amadeus Wolf—Sudden Interest (FR) **Ms M. Austerfield**
13 **HELLOLINI,** b f Bertolini (USA)—Smiddy Hill **I. B. Barker**
14 **MASAI KING (IRE),** b c Kheleyf (USA)—Masai Queen (IRE) **Ms M. Austerfield**
15 **TROY BOY,** b c Choisir (AUS)—Love Thing **Ms M. Austerfield**

TWO-YEAR-OLDS
16 **SHIKARI,** ch c 13/2 Sakhee's Secret—Hickleton Lady (IRE) (Kala Shikari) (24761) **Ms M. Austerfield**

Other Owners: Mr E. N. Barber, Mrs P. Bastiman, Mr Robin Bastiman, Mr David Dickson.

Assistant Trainers: H. Bastiman & Miss R. Bastiman

Jockey (flat): Robert Winston, Daniel Tudhope. **Amateur:** Miss R. Bastiman.

28 MRS ALISON BATCHELOR, Petworth
Postal: **Down View Farm, Burton Park Road, Petworth, West Sussex, GU28 0JT**
Contacts: **PHONE (01798) 343090 FAX (01798) 343090**
E-MAIL alison@alisonbatchelorracing.com WEBSITE www.alisonbatchelorracing.com

1 BOLLYWOOD (IRE), 10, ch g Indian Rocket—La Fille de Cirque **Mrs A. M. Batchelor**
2 BORDER STATION (IRE), 7, b g Shantou (USA)—Telemania (IRE) **Mrs A. M. Batchelor**
3 CONFIRMED, 4, b g Authorized (IRE)—Vas Y Carla (USA) **Mr R. Cooper**
4 DO MORE BUSINESS (IRE), 6, b g Dubai Destination (USA)—Tokyo Song (USA) **Mrs A. M. Batchelor**
5 GOLAN GUY (IRE), 8, b g Golan (IRE)—Countess Marengo (IRE) **Mrs A. M. Batchelor**
6 HIGHTOWN (IRE), 6, b g King's Theatre (IRE)—Faucon **Mrs A. M. Batchelor**
7 MICHKA D'ALBEN (FR), 5, gr g Passing Sale (FR)—Tibesti Mail (FR) **Mrs A. M. Batchelor**
8 SEVENTH HUSSAR, 7, b g Alflora (IRE)—Shuil Do (IRE) **Mrs A. M. Batchelor**
9 TRY CATCH ME (IRE), 8, b g Commander Collins (USA)—Misty River (IRE) **Mrs A. M. Batchelor**

Assistant Trainer: Jose Dos Santos

Amateur: Mr S. Hanson.

29 MR BRIAN BAUGH, Stoke on Trent
Postal: **Brooklands Farm, Park Lane, Audley, Stoke on Trent**
Contacts: **HOME (01782) 723144 MOBILE (07771) 693666**

1 ACTON JENSON, 4, gr g Proclamation (IRE)—Crystal Attraction **Magnate Racing**
2 AVONLINI, 7, b m Bertolini (USA)—Avondale Girl (IRE) **J. H. Chrimes**
3 BENTLEY, 9, b g Piccolo—April Lee **Mr B. P. J. Baugh**
4 BRET MAVERICK (IRE), 9, b g Josr Algarhoud (IRE)—
  Shady Street (USA) **Mr J.H. Chrimes & Mr & Mrs G.W. Hannam**
5 COMPTONSPIRIT, 9, ch m Compton Place—Croeso Cynnes **Mr G. B. Hignett**
6 CONSISTANT, 5, b g Reel Buddy (USA)—Compact Disc (IRE) **Miss J. A. Price**
7 DARING DAMSEL (IRE), 4, b f Van Nistelrooy (USA)—Serengeti Day (USA) **Mr S. Holmes**
8 DEAR BEN, 4, b g Echo of Light—Miss Up N Go **C. Turner**
9 GOLDSTORM, 5, ch m Storming Home—Antonia Bertolini **Magnate Racing**
10 JOHN POTTS, 8, b g Josr Algarhoud (IRE)—Crown City (USA) **Miss S. M. Potts**
11 JULY DAYS (IRE), 7, b m Exceed And Excel (AUS)—Tocade (IRE) **Mr S. Holmes**
12 KIELTY'S FOLLY, 9, gr g Newt-A-Minute (IRE)—Three Sweeties **Saddle Up Racing**
13 KYLE OF BUTE, 7, ch g Kyllachy—Blinding Mission (IRE) **Mr J.H. Chrimes & Mr & Mrs G.W. Hannam**
14 LOVE CLUB, 5, ch g Kheleyf (USA)—Avondale Girl (IRE) **Mr J.H. Chrimes & Mr & Mrs G.W. Hannam**
15 MASTER OF DISGUISE, 7, b g Kyllachy—St James's Antigua (IRE) **21C Telecom.co.uk**
16 PEARL NATION (USA), 4, b g Speightstown (USA)—Happy Nation (USA) **Mr C. Iddon**
17 PICCOLO EXPRESS, 7, b g Piccolo—Ashfield **Mr G. B. Hignett**
18 SCAMPERDALE, 11, br g Compton Place—Miss Up N Go **Saddle Up Racing**
19 SUPASTARQUEEN, 5, b br m El Corredor (USA)—Supamova (USA) **Mr G. B. Hignett**
20 TANFORAN, 11, b g Mujahid (USA)—Florentynna Bay **Miss S. M. Potts**
21 TYFOS, 8, b g Bertolini (USA)—Warminghamsharpish **Mr J. Tomlinson/ Mr G. Williams**

THREE-YEAR-OLDS

22 LOULOU VUITTON, ch f Needwood Blade—Shepherds Warning (IRE) **Mr G. B. Hignett**

Other Owners: W. G. Hannam, Mrs C. Hannam, Mr R. A. Hunt, Mrs N. Hunt, Mr G. Ratcliffe, Mrs M. Robinson, Mr K. V. Robinson, J. Tomlinson, Mrs L. E. Tomlinson, Mr D. G. Williams.

Assistant Trainer: S Potts

30 MR CHRIS BEALBY, Grantham
Postal: **North Lodge, Barrowby, Grantham, Lincolnshire, NG32 1DH**
Contacts: **OFFICE (01476) 564568 FAX (01476) 572391 MOBILE (07831) 538689**
E-MAIL chris@northlodgeracing.co.uk WEBSITE www.northlodgeracing.co.uk

1 APPLAUDE, 8, b g Royal Applause—Flossy **Miss F. Harper**
2 AWAREINESS (IRE), 7, b g Flemensfirth (USA)—Special Case (IRE) **R. A. Jenkinson**
3 BLACK SAMBUCA, 6, b g Samraan (USA)—Derring Floss **R. P. Kernohan**
4 CHAC DU CADRAN (FR), 7, b g Passing Sale (FR)—L'indienne (FR) **Bingley, Williams & Pepperdine**

MR CHRIS BEALBY - Continued

5 **COUNTESS COMET (IRE)**, 6, b m Medicean—Countess Sybil (IRE) **Payplan Partnership II**
6 **FLORA SKY**, 6, b m Alflora (IRE)—Portia Sky (FR)
7 **GENERAL SAMARSKI**, 5, b g Samraan (USA)—Misty Cay (IRE) **R. P. Kernohan**
8 **GERS BENEFIT (IRE)**, 9, b m Beneficial—Sara's Pinkie (IRE) **Mr Timothy Rogers**
9 **IFONLYALFIE**, 8, b g Alflora (IRE)—Ifni du Luc (FR) **Triumph In Mind**
10 **INTENT (IRE)**, 4, b f Jeremy (USA)—Cant Hurry Love **Payplan Partnership II**
11 **L'ELDORADO (FR)**, 8, b g Urban Ocean (FR)—Little Warden **Mrs C. M. Radford**
12 **LEGENDARY HOP**, 7, b m Midnight Legend—Hopping Mad **Messrs Duke, Umpleby, Holmes & Bealby**
13 **MR FEZZIWIG**, 6, b g Erhaab (USA)—Mrs Fizziwig **C. C. Bealby**
14 **OLIVER JAMES**, 6, b g Kayf Tara—Shuil Tsarina (IRE) **C. C. Bealby**
15 **OVERRULE (USA)**, 9, b g Diesis—Her Own Way (USA) **Miss F. Harper**
16 **RAKTIMAN (IRE)**, 6, ch g Rakti—Wish List (IRE) **Michael Hill**
17 **REARRANGE**, 4, b f Rail Link—New Order **Payplan Partnership II**
18 **ROCKY REBEL**, 5, b g Norse Dancer (IRE)—Gulchina (USA) **R. A. Jenkinson**
19 **ROI DE GARDE (FR)**, 7, b g Kapgarde (FR)—Belle du Roi (FR) **Michael Hill**
20 **TANGO IN THE NIGHT**, 6, b g Fleetwood (IRE)—Secret Dance **C. C. Bealby**
21 **THE PURCHASER (IRE)**, 5, b g Definite Article—Cash Customer (IRE) **C. C. Bealby**
22 **TWEET ALL**, 5, b g Beat All (USA)—Lambrini (IRE) **C. C. Bealby**
23 **TWIST DE L'ISLE (FR)**, 6, b g Dark Moondancer—Gratiene de L'isle (FR) **C. C. Bealby**
24 **VINTAGE RED**, 5, ch g Grape Tree Road—Simply Stunning **C. C. Bealby**
25 **WHY ALWAYS ME (IRE)**, 5, b g Milan—Cool Supreme (IRE) **Mrs Robert Bingley & Mrs Bryan Spooner**

Other Owners: Mrs E. A. Bingley, Mr D. M. Cook, B. G. Duke, F. M. Holmes, Mrs M. J. Pepperdine, Mr G. P. D. Rann, Mrs L. E. Rann, Mrs B. M. Spooner, Mr P. Umpleby, Mr T. Wendels, Mrs A. M. Williams, R. F. Wright.

Jockey (flat): Dane O'Neill. **Jockey (NH):** Tom Messenger, Noel Fehily. **Conditional:** Adam Wedge. **Amateur:** Mr Olly Murphy.

---

31 MR RALPH BECKETT, Andover
Postal: **Kimpton Down Stables, Kimpton Down, Andover, Hampshire, SP11 8QQ**
Contacts: **PHONE (01264) 772278 FAX (01264) 771221 MOBILE (07802) 219022**
E-MAIL trainer@rbeckett.com WEBSITE www.rbeckett.com

1 **ALBERT BRIDGE**, 5, gr g Hernando (FR)—Alvarita **The Cheyne Walkers**
2 **ASTRA HALL**, 4, ch f Halling (USA)—Star Precision **G. B. Balding**
3 **COLIMA (IRE)**, 4, b f Authorized (IRE)—Coyote **Mr & Mrs David Aykroyd**
4 **CUBANITA**, 4, ch f Selkirk (USA)—Caribana **Miss K. Rausing**
5 **FINESSE**, 4, ch f Shamardal (USA)—Clare Hills (IRE) **P. K. Gardner T/A Springcombe Park Stud**
6 **FLEUR DE LA VIE (IRE)**, 4, ch f Primary (USA)—Francophilia **Prime Of Life 3**
7 **HAAF A SIXPENCE**, 4, b g Haafhd—Melody Maker **Melody Racing**
8 **HURRY UP GEORGE**, 4, b g Intikhab (USA)—Digamist Girl (IRE) **A. E. Frost**
9 **JOLAINE**, 4, b f Medicean—Fancy Rose **Mrs E. Kennedy**
10 **MAVERIK**, 5, ch g Iceman—Nouvelle Lune **Athos, Cooper, Quinn, EPL**
11 **MOONSTONE MAGIC**, 4, b f Trade Fair—Woodcock Moon **Tullpark Limited**
12 **NICEOFYOUTOTELLME**, 4, b g Hernando (FR)—Swain's Gold (USA) **Mr R. J. Roberts**
13 **PEARL MIX (IRE)**, 4, gr c Oratorio (IRE)—Rosamixa (FR) **Pearl Bloodstock Limited**
14 **RADIOACTIVE**, 4, b f Haafhd—Toxique (IRE) **P. K. Gardner T/A Springcombe Park Stud**
15 **RHAGORI**, 4, b f Exceed And Excel (AUS)—Cresta Gold **Landmark Racing Limited**
16 **RIOT OF COLOUR**, 4, b f Excellent Art—Riotous Applause **The Eclipse Partnership**
17 **SEASIDE SIZZLER**, 6, ch g Rahy (USA)—Via Borghese (USA) **I. J. Heseltine**
18 **SHEA**, 4, b f Dubai Destination (USA)—Shasta **Larksborough Stud Limited**
19 **STEREOTYPICAL**, 4, ch g Notnowcato—Delightful Rhythm (USA) **The Anagram Partnership**

THREE-YEAR-OLDS

20 **ALDBOROUGH (IRE)**, b c Danehill Dancer (IRE)—Kitty O'shea **Mr & Mrs David Aykroyd**
21 **ANNA'S PEARL**, ch c Pivotal—Mi Anna (GER) **Pearl Bloodstock Limited**
22 **ARE YOU MINE (IRE)**, b f Nayef (USA)—Celtic Slipper (IRE) **P. D. Savill**
23 **AT A CLIP**, b f Green Desert (USA)—First Bloom (USA) **Lady N. F. Cobham**
24 **AUTUMN DRAW**, b g Marju (IRE)—Shallow Ground (IRE) **Brook House**
25 **BLAZING KNIGHT (IRE)**, b c Red Clubs (IRE)—Johar Jamal (IRE) **Circuit Racing**
26 **CAPERINA (IRE)**, b f Cape Cross (IRE)—Catherine Palace **J. H. Richmond-Watson**
27 **CITY GIRL (IRE)**, b f Elusive City (USA)—Lochridge **J. C. Smith**
28 **CROSS YOUR FINGERS (IRE)**, b c Monsun (GER)—Capestar (IRE) **D & J Newell**
29 **DAY IN DAY OUT**, b g Notnowcato—Cockatrice **P. Hickey**

MR RALPH BECKETT - Continued

30 **EXOTIC ISLE**, ch f Exceed And Excel (AUS)—Paradise Isle **Pearl Bloodstock Ltd & Mr N. H. Wrigley**
31 **FORTINBRASS (IRE)**, b c Baltic King—Greta d'argent (IRE) **Hillier, Lawrence, Turney & Goddard**
32 **FOXTROT JUBILEE (IRE)**, b g Captain Marvelous (IRE)—Cool Cousin (IRE) **Foxtrot Racing Partnership IV**
33 **HELLO SAILOR**, b g Mount Nelson—Fairy Queen (IRE) **Racing Club UK LLP**
34 **HIDDEN BELIEF (IRE)**, b f Holy Roman Emperor (IRE)—Crossanza (IRE) **Clipper Group Holdings Ltd**
35 **HIPSTER**, b g Kingsalsa (USA)—Hip **Mr R. J. Roberts**
36 **HOLD ON TIGHT (IRE)**, ch f Hernando (FR)—Wait It Out (USA) **The Eclipse Partnership**
37 **INGOT OF GOLD**, b f Dubawi (IRE)—Cresta Gold **Landmark Racing Limited**
38 **INKA SURPRISE (IRE)**, b g Intikhab (USA)—Sweet Surprise (IRE) **McDonagh Murphy & Nixon**
39 **JAN DE HEEM**, ch g Dutch Art—Shasta **Larksborough Stud Limited**
40 **LADY VERMEER**, b f Dutch Art—Classic Vision **W. E. A. Fox**
41 **LADY WHO**, b f Sir Percy—Herminoe **Dulverton Equine**
42 **LEMON PEARL**, ch f Singspiel (IRE)—Basemah (FR) **Pearl Bloodstock Ltd & Mr N. H. Wrigley**
43 **LEWISHAM**, b g Sleeping Indian—Almunia (IRE) **R. C. Tooth**
44 **LUNETTE (IRE)**, b f Teofilo (IRE)—Princess Luna (GER) **Mr Mr T D Rootes & Mr O F Waller**
45 **MME SANS GENE**, gr f Verglas (IRE)—Diablerette **Miss K. Rausing**
46 **MOMBASA**, b c Dubawi (IRE)—Limuru **Wis Green Partners**
47 **MOTION LASS**, b f Motivator—Tarneem (USA) **R. C. Tooth**
48 **PEARL BRIDGE**, b g Avonbridge—Our Little Secret (USA) **Pearl Bloodstock Limited**
49 **PERFECT BEAT**, b f Beat Hollow—Paradise Dancer (IRE) **The Perfect Partnership**
50 **PERFECT HAVEN**, gr f Singspiel (IRE)—Night Haven **Hants & Herts**
51 **POMPEIA**, ch f Singspiel (IRE)—Caesarea (GER) **J. L. Rowsell**
52 **PROSPERA (IRE)**, b f Cape Cross (IRE)—Opera **The Millennium Madness Partnership**
53 **QUINTET (IRE)**, ch f Pivotal—Possessed **Highclere Thoroughbred Racing - Party**
54 **RIO'S PEARL**, b f Captain Rio—Agony Aunt **Pearl Bloodstock Limited**
55 **ROYAL PRIZE**, ch g Nayef (USA)—Spot Prize (USA) **J. C. Smith**
56 **SECRET ART (IRE)**, ch g Excellent Art—Ivy Queen (IRE) **Circuit Racing**
57 **SECRET BEAU**, gr c Sakhee's Secret—Belle Reine **Mrs H. I. Slade**
58 **SECRET GESTURE**, b f Galileo (IRE)—Shastye (IRE) **Newsells Park Stud Limited**
59 **SIZZLER**, ch g Hernando (FR)—Gino's Spirits **Heseltine, Henley & Jones**
60 **SQUEEZE MY BRAIN (IRE)**, b f Lawman (FR)—Arctic Hunt (IRE) **Qatar Racing Limited**
61 **TALENT**, ch f New Approach (IRE)—Prowess (IRE) **Mr J L Rowsell & Mr M H Dixon**
62 **THORPE (IRE)**, b g Danehill Dancer (IRE)—Minkova (IRE) **Mr & Mrs David Aykroyd**
63 **THWART**, ch f Refuse To Bend (IRE)—Jump Ship **M. H. Dixon**
64 **WATERWAY RUN (USA)**, b f Arch (USA)—Princess Consort (USA) **Thurloe T'Breds XX & Martin S Schwartz**

TWO-YEAR-OLDS

65 B c 14/4 High Chaparral (IRE)—Al Ihsas (IRE) (Danehill (USA)) (75000) **Cheyne Walkers II**
66 **AMANDA'S DREAM (IRE)**, b c 19/4 Intikhab (USA)—Catatonic (Zafonic (USA)) (25396) **I. J. Heseltine**
67 B f 18/2 Halling (USA)—Bassinet (USA) (Stravinsky (USA)) **Mildmay Racing**
68 Ch c 12/3 Compton Place—Belle des Airs (IRE) (Dr Fong (USA)) (35000) **Mrs H. I. Slade**
69 **BELROG**, ch c 23/4 New Approach (IRE)—Millennium Dash (Nashwan (USA)) (110000) **Qatar Racing Limited**
70 **BOLD JACK DONAHUE (IRE)**, b br c 14/4 Bushranger (IRE)—
                                               Mother's Hope (IRE) (Idris (IRE)) (30000) **The Outlaws**
71 B f 19/4 Bushranger (IRE)—Boston Ivy (USA) (Mark of Esteem (IRE)) (19000) **McCalmont and Drew**
72 Ch f 30/4 Champs Elysees—Capistrano Day (USA) (Diesis) (35000) **R. Barnett**
73 **CASINO DANCER**, b f 22/4 Danehill Dancer (IRE)—
                                          Minkova (Sadler's Wells (USA)) **Mr & Mrs David Aykroyd**
74 Ch f 4/2 Galileo (IRE)—Castara Beach (IRE) (Danehill (USA)) (200000) **Mrs John Magnier**
75 **CINNILLA**, b f 2/5 Authorized (IRE)—Caesarea (GER) (Generous (IRE)) **J. L. Rowsell**
76 **CRYSTAL LAKE (IRE)**, gr c 16/4 Verglas (IRE)—
                                          Entail (USA) (Riverman (USA)) (19047) **The Pickford Hill Partnership**
77 **DARK REALITY (IRE)**, b f 2/3 Intikhab (IRE)—Sunny Slope (Mujtahid (USA)) (48000) **Qatar Racing Limited**
78 B f 30/4 Clodovil (IRE)—Desert Alchemy (IRE) (Green Desert (USA)) (11904) **Mildmay Racing**
79 **DINNERATMIDNIGHT**, b c 27/2 Kyllachy—
                                          The Terrier (Foxhound (USA)) (33333) **Mr N. Patsalides & Mr M. Patel**
80 **DUDLEY QUEEN (IRE)**, ch f 1/4 Excellent Art—
                                          Royal Bounty (IRE) (Generous (IRE)) (47619) **Qatar Racing Limited**
81 Ch f 4/2 Pivotal—Entente Cordiale (IRE) (Ela-Mana-Mou) (110000) **Newsells Park Stud Limited**
82 B f 1/3 Intikhab (USA)—Esteraad (IRE) (Cadeaux Genereux) (7000) **McDonagh Murphy & Nixon**
83 **FREE REIN**, b f 8/4 Dansili—Sant Elena (Efisio) **The Eclipse Partnership**
84 **GOT TO DANCE**, b f 20/2 Selkirk (USA)—Mullein (Oasis Dream) **Landmark Racing Limited**
85 Gr f 1/4 Mastercraftsman (IRE)—Grain of Gold (Mr Prospector (USA)) **R. Barnett**
86 **HONOR BOUND**, b f 24/4 Authorized (IRE)—Honorine (IRE) (Mark of Esteem (IRE)) **Ashley House Stud**
87 B c 9/2 Sir Percy—La Peinture (GER) (Peintre Celebre (USA)) (50000) **Ballymore English Syndicate**

MR RALPH BECKETT - Continued

88 **LIGHTNING SPEAR**, ch c 5/4 Pivotal—
　　　　　　　　　　　Atlantic Destiny (IRE) (Royal Academy (USA)) (260000) **Qatar Racing Limited**
89 B c 12/3 Oratorio (IRE)—Lochridge (Indian Ridge) **J. C. Smith**
90 **LUNAR SPIRIT**, b f 4/5 Invincible Spirit (IRE)—Kitty O'shea (Sadler's Wells (USA)) **Mr & Mrs David Aykroyd**
91 B c 5/5 Lawman (FR)—Make Me Blush (USA) (Blushing John (USA)) (3967) **Mr A. R. Adams**
92 **MELROSE ABBEY (IRE)**, ch f 10/3 Selkirk (USA)—Villa Carlotta (Rainbow Quest (USA)) **J. H. Richmond-Watson**
93 **MONTAIGNE**, b c 26/1 Exceed And Excel (AUS)—Autumn Pearl (Orpen (USA)) **Mr K. Watts**
94 **NORSE LIGHT**, ch c 12/2 Norse Dancer (IRE)—Dimelight (Fantastic Light (USA)) **J. C. Smith**
95 **PORTA PORTESE**, ch f 5/3 Zamindar (USA)—
　　　　　　　　　　　Agata Laguna (IRE) (Elnadim (USA)) (15000) **Scuderia Archi Romani**
96 B c 24/3 Oratorio (IRE)—Primissima (GER) (Second Set (IRE)) (47619) **Thurloe Thoroughbreds**
97 B f 17/2 Whipper (USA)—Priory Rock (IRE) (Rock of Gibraltar (IRE)) **Mrs I. M. Beckett**
98 **RAGING BOB (IRE)**, br c 18/4 Big Bad Bob (IRE)—Lanasara (Generous (IRE)) (19047) **A.W.A. Partnership**
99 **REGARDEZ**, b f 3/5 Champs Elysees—Look So (Efisio) **J. H. Richmond-Watson**
100 **SEA HERE**, ch c 2/4 Sea The Stars (IRE)—Look Here (Hernando (FR)) **J. H. Richmond-Watson**
101 B c 29/3 Holy Roman Emperor (IRE)—Spangle (Galileo (IRE)) (20000) **Mr R. J. Roberts**
102 Br c 28/2 Proud Citizen (USA)—Spring Tale (USA) (Stravinsky (USA)) (23000) **Anagram Partnership**
103 **STARLIGHT SERENADE**, ch f 27/2 Three Valleys (USA)—Melody Maker (Diktat) **Melody Racing**
104 **TAQUKA (IRE)**, b c 14/3 Kodiac—
　　　　　　　　　　　Dubai Princess (IRE) (Dubai Destination (USA)) (15000) **The Pickford Hill Partnership**
105 **VENUS GRACE**, b f 5/3 Royal Applause—Basque Beauty (Nayef (USA)) **Lady Coventry & Partners**
106 **WEISSE SOCKEN (IRE)**, b f 20/4 Acclamation—Playful (Piccolo) (40000) **Mrs E. Kennedy**
107 **WILDE INSPIRATION (IRE)**, ch c 23/4 Dandy Man (IRE)—
　　　　　　　　　　　Wishing Chair (USA) (Giant's Causeway (USA)) (29000) **Mrs E. Kennedy**

Other Owners: Mr D. Abraham, Mrs L. M. Aykroyd, D. P Aykroyd, Countess R. Coventry, P A. Deal, D. W. Dennis, Dr S. B. Drew, J. R. Drew, N. J. Forman Hardy, R. Frisby, Mr M. P Gibbens, Mr P Gregg, Mrs M. R. Gregory, M. G. H. Heald, Mr A. M. H. Heald, The Hon H. M. Herbert, Highclere Thoroughbred Racing Ltd, Mr S. Hill, Mr J. Hillier, Mr R. W. Lane, Mr K. Lawrence, Mr O. C. S. Lazenby, Mr E. A. M. Leatham, Mrs S. E. Leatham, Mr J. Makin, Mr P G. Murphy, D. J. M. Newell, Mrs J. Newell, Mr B. O'Brien, R. L. Page, Mr M. Patel, Mr N. Patsalides, O. J. W. Pawle, G. R. Pooley, Mr J. W. Randall, Mr J. A. Randall, T. D. Rootes, M. S. Schwartz, Mrs H. L. Smyly, Mr B. P. J. Spiers, Mr J. A. B. Stafford, Mr R. W. Stirling, O. F. Waller, Mr R. Weston, Miss C. J. Wills, N. F. J. Wood, N. H. T. Wrigley.

Assistant Trainer: Charlie Duckworth

Jockey (flat): Jim Crowley.

---

32 | **MR MICHAEL BELL, Newmarket**
Postal: Fitzroy House, Newmarket, Suffolk, CB8 0JT
Contacts: **PHONE** (01638) 666567 **FAX** (01638) 668000 **MOBILE** (07802) 264514
E-MAIL office@fitzroyhouse.co.uk **WEBSITE** www.michaelbellracing.co.uk

1 **ALLIED POWERS (IRE)**, 8, b g Invincible Spirit (IRE)—Always Friendly **Mr David Fish & Mr Edward Ware**
2 **BITE OF THE CHERRY**, 4, ro f Dalakhani (IRE)—Bianca Nera **Mr R. L. W. Frisby**
3 **BORN TO SURPRISE**, 4, b c Exceed And Excel (AUS)—Dubai Surprise (IRE) **Dr A. Ridha**
4 **BRIDGEHAMPTON**, 4, b g Lando (GER)—Gaze **M. B. Hawtin**
5 **CANDYCAKES (IRE)**, 4, b f Cape Cross (IRE)—Charita (IRE) **Mr J. Acheson**
6 **CREME ANGLAISE**, 5, b m Motivator—Reading Habit (USA) **Mrs G. E. Rowland-Clark**
7 **EXCEEDEXPECTATIONS (IRE)**, 4, b g Intikhab (USA)—Jazan (IRE) **Mr M. Caine**
8 **EXTREMELY ALERT**, 4, ch g Nayef (USA)—Megdale (USA) **Mr L. J. Inman**
9 **FORTIETH AND FIFTH (IRE)**, 4, b g Lemon Drop Kid (USA)—Maugusta (USA) **C. Bryce**
10 **KING OF JAZZ (IRE)**, 5, b g Acclamation—Grand Slam Maria (FR) **Mr R. Upshall**
11 **ONE KOOL DUDE**, 4, ch g Iceman—Hiraeth
12 **PICCADILLY LINE**, 4, b g Lawman (FR)—Crystal (IRE) **M. L. W. Bell Racing Ltd**
13 **REFRACTOR (IRE)**, 5, ch g Refuse To Bend (IRE)—Fancy Intense **Mr Alex Elliott**
14 **SIGN MANUAL**, 4, b g Motivator—New Assembly (IRE) **Her Majesty The Queen**
15 **SOVEREIGN DEBT (IRE)**, 4, br c Dark Angel (IRE)—Kelsey Rose **Mr L. J. Inman**
16 **SURAJ**, 4, ch c Galileo (IRE)—Maid of Killeen (IRE) **Lady Bamford**
17 **TAHLIA REE (IRE)**, 4, b f Acclamation—Dora Carrington (IRE) **P. E. Barrett**
18 **THE BETCHWORTH KID**, 8, b g Tobougg (IRE)—Runelia **Mr W. H. Ponsonby**
19 **UNEX MODIGLIANI (IRE)**, 4, ch g Hurricane Run (IRE)—Chronicle **W. J. Gredley**
20 **WIGMORE HALL (IRE)**, 6, b g High Chaparral (IRE)—Love And Laughter (IRE) **M. B. Hawtin**

MR MICHAEL BELL - Continued

THREE-YEAR-OLDS

21 **ALGORITHMIC (IRE),** b c Danehill Dancer (IRE)—Tanami Desert **Mr L. J. Inman**
22 **AZRUR (IRE),** b c Sir Percy—Tiger Spice **Saleh Al Homaizi & Imad Al Sagar**
23 **BILL OF RIGHTS,** b f Kyllachy—Bijou A Moi **Mr R. L. W. Frisby**
24 **BOUYRIN (IRE),** b f Invincible Spirit (IRE)—Needles And Pins (IRE) **Saleh Al Homaizi & Imad Al Sagar**
25 **CAPELLA'S SONG (IRE),** b f Oratorio (IRE)—Bright Bank (IRE) **P. A. Philipps & C. E. L. Philipps**
26 **CARLARAJAH,** ch g Sleeping Indian—Carla (FR) **Thurloe Thoroughbreds XXX**
27 **CHEBIKA,** b f Oasis Dream—Dancing Abbie (USA) **Sheikh Marwan Al Maktoum**
28 **COMMON COURTESY,** b f Motivator—Crystal Swan (IRE) **Saleh Al Homaizi & Imad Al Sagar**
29 **DALLIEFOUR (IRE),** b f Cape Cross (IRE)—Daliyana (IRE) **Her Majesty The Queen**
30 **DEFICIT (IRE),** gr c Dalakhani (IRE)—Venturi **Mr L. J. Inman**
31 **DIVERGENCE (IRE),** b f Teofilo (IRE)—Min Alhawa (USA) **Mr L. J. Inman**
32 **EMPOWERMENTOFWOMEN (IRE),** b f Manduro (GER)—Miss Brown To You (IRE) **W. J. Gredley**
33 **FANNY SQUEERS,** b f New Approach (IRE)—Whazzat **W. J. Gredley**
34 **FASHION LINE (IRE),** b f Cape Cross (IRE)—Shadow Roll (IRE) **Sheikh Marwan Al Maktoum**
35 **FILS ANGES (IRE),** gr c Dark Angel (IRE)—La Piaf (FR) **Mr D. Hanafin**
36 **FORCED FAMILY FUN,** b g Refuse To Bend (IRE)—Juniper Girl (IRE) **M. B. Hawtin**
37 **GAMBLE,** ch f Galileo (IRE)—Pretty Face **Her Majesty The Queen**
38 **GEORGE CINQ,** b c Pastoral Pursuits—Fairnilee **Tamdown Group Limited**
39 **HANDIWORK,** ch g Motivator—Spinning Top **Her Majesty The Queen**
40 **HARTWRIGHT,** b g Exceed And Excel (AUS)—All For Laura **Mrs L. J. Garton**
41 **HISPANIA (IRE),** b f Teofilo (IRE)—Badalona **Marwan Al Maktoum**
42 **HOT MUSTARD,** b g Pastoral Pursuits—Lihou Island **Mrs G. E. Rowland-Clark**
43 **HOYAM,** b f Royal Applause—Christmas Tart (IRE) **A. Al Shaikh**
44 **HUNTSMANS CLOSE,** b c Elusive Quality (USA)—Badminton **Marwan Al Maktoum**
45 **JADESNUMBERONE (IRE),** b f Authorized (IRE)—Gabriella **Sir Alex Ferguson & Mr Mike Dawson**
46 **KENSINGTON GARDENS,** b f Oasis Dream—Wendylina (IRE) **Mrs Julia Scott & Mr J F Dean**
47 **KIMBERELLA,** b g Kyllachy—Gleam of Light (IRE) **Mr K. J. P. Gundlach**
48 **LOVESOME,** b f Kheleyf—Heavenly Bay (USA) **Marwan Al Maktoum**
49 **MADAME DEFARGE (IRE),** b f Motivator—Friendlier **W. J. Gredley**
50 **MESSAGEINABOTTLE (USA),** b br f Grand Slam (USA)—
Devine (USA) **C Wright, Miss C Wright & Miss H Wright**
51 **MOVES LIKE JAGGER (IRE),** b c Danehill Dancer (IRE)—Lucky Spin **Mr K. J. P. Gundlach**
52 **MRS MICAWBER,** gr f Nayef (USA)—Under The Rainbow **W. J. Gredley**
53 **OILINDA,** b f Nayef (USA)—Loyal Love (USA) **Karmaa Racing Limited**
54 **POINT OF CONTROL,** b f Pivotal—Finlaggan **Mr L. J. Inman**
55 **PRINCESS PATSKY (USA),** b br f Mr Greeley—Kamarinskaya (USA) **My Meadowview LLC**
56 **RISKIT FORA BISKIT (IRE),** b f Kodiac—Miss Brief (IRE) **Mr C. Wright & The Hon Mrs J.M.Corbett**
57 **SANTO PRINCE (USA),** b br g Henrythenavigator (USA)—Sally Wood (CAN) **Mr L. Caine**
58 **SEEMENOMORE,** b g Bahamian Bounty—Rise **Mr K. J. P. Gundlach**
59 **SHANTI,** b c Dansili—Maycocks Bay **Lady Bamford**
60 **SHREWD,** b f Street Sense (USA)—Cala (FR) **Marwan Al Maktoum**
61 **SOUVENIR,** b f Cape Cross (IRE)—Trianon **Her Majesty The Queen**
62 **SPIRIT OF SUCCESS,** b f Invincible Spirit (IRE)—Isabella Glyn (IRE) **Dr A. Ridha**
63 **SPIRITUAL GIRL,** gr f Invincible Spirit (IRE)—Clizia (IRE) **TSEGA Horses Company Ltd**
64 **STAR OF ROHM,** ch g Exceed And Excel (AUS)—Noble Desert (FR) **Mrs Louise Whitehead & Mr Chris Lomas**
65 **SUGAR COATED (IRE),** b f Duke of Marmalade (IRE)—
Crystal Curling (IRE) **Mr D Smith, Mrs J Magnier & Mr M Tabor**
66 **SWORD OF THE LORD,** b c Kheleyf (USA)—Blue Echo **Saleh Al Homaizi & Imad Al Sagar**
67 **THE LARK,** ch f Pivotal—Gull Wing (IRE) **Lady Bamford**
68 **THE MANX MISSILE,** ch g Sakhee's Secret—Careless Freedom **P. J. Ransley**
69 **WE ARE CITY,** b f Elusive City (USA)—Musique Magique (IRE) **Middleham Park Racing VI & Partner**
70 **WILDCRAFTING,** ch f Exceed And Excel (AUS)—Local Spirit (USA) **Marwan Al Maktoum**
71 **WINSLOW ARIZONA (IRE),** b g Danehill Dancer (IRE)—Buffalo Berry (IRE) **Rathordan Partnership**
72 **ZERO GAME (IRE),** b f High Chaparral (IRE)—Freezing Love (USA) **E. J. Ware**

TWO-YEAR-OLDS

73 **AL KHAWANEEJ STAR (USA),** b br c 17/2 Arch (USA)—
Frolic Away (USA) (Pentelicus (USA)) (67588) **A. Al Shaikh**
74 B f 12/2 Kheleyf (USA)—Ballantrae (IRE) (Diktat) **Sheikh Marwan Al Maktoum**
75 B f 10/4 Nayef (USA)—Bedara (Barathea (IRE)) (33000)
76 **BORN TO REIGN,** b c 11/2 Sir Percy—Oat Cuisine (Mujahid (USA)) **Mrs G. Rowland-Clark**
77 B c 8/4 Fastnet Rock (AUS)—Bowstring (IRE) (Sadler's Wells (USA)) (82000) **Mr K. J. P. Gundlach**
78 Ch f 15/3 Manduro (GER)—Cape Marien (IRE) (Cape Cross (IRE)) (48000) **S. Ali**
79 Gr c 5/2 Authorized (IRE)—Cozy Maria (USA) (Cozzene (USA)) (70000) **Saleh Al Homaizi & Imad Al Sagar**

MR MICHAEL BELL - Continued

80 B c 28/3 Dansili—Dancing Abbie (USA) (Theatrical) **Sheikh Marwan Al Maktoum**
81 B c 20/2 Exceed And Excel (AUS)—Extreme Beauty (Rahy (USA)) (80000) **Dr A. Ridha**
82 B c 26/2 Exceed And Excel (AUS)—Finnmark (Halling (USA)) **S. Ali**
83 B f 18/3 Holy Roman Emperor (IRE)—Friendlier (Zafonic (USA)) **W. J. Gredley**
84 **FUTOON,** b f 14/3 Royal Applause—Cefira (USA) (Distant View (USA)) (52000) **A. Al Shaikh**
85 B f 18/2 Invincible Spirit (IRE)—Galistic (IRE) (Galileo (IRE)) (30000) **S. Ali**
86 Ch gr c 1/4 Aqlaam—Good Enough (FR) (Mukaddamah (USA)) (22000) **R. N. Frosell**
87 B f 25/2 Acclamation—Have Faith (IRE) (Machiavellian (USA)) (130000) **Saleh Al Homaizi & Imad Al Sagar**
88 **INVOKE (IRE),** b f 25/1 Kodiac—
        Tides (Bahamian Bounty) (34285) **Highclere Thoroughbred Racing - Herbert Jones**
89 B c 31/3 Rock of Gibraltar (IRE)—Inya Lake (Whittingham (IRE)) (50000) **Karmaa Racing Limited**
90 B c 27/2 Peintre Celebre (USA)—Kotdiji (Mtoto) (62000) **Mr K. J. P. Gundlach**
91 B c 18/2 Rock of Gibraltar (IRE)—Leonica (Lion Cavern (USA)) (50000) **Mr Malcolm Caine**
92 **MARWEENA (IRE),** b f 26/3 Cape Cross (IRE)—Dunes Queen (USA) (Elusive Quality (USA)) **J. Abdullah**
93 B c 4/3 Art Connoisseur (IRE)—Narmeen (Royal Applause) (40000) **Saleh Al Homaizi & Imad Al Sagar**
94 PIAZON, br c 9/4 Striking Ambition—Colonel's Daughter (Colonel Collins (USA)) (23809) **R. P. B. Michaelson**
95 **RHONDA (IRE),** b f 7/2 Fastnet Rock (AUS)—
        Regal Darcey (IRE) (Darshaan) (75000) **The Royal Ascot Racing Club**
96 Ch f 22/4 Galileo (IRE)—Saturn Girl (IRE) (Danehill Dancer (IRE)) **Mr D. Smith, Mrs J. Magnier & Mr M. Tabor**
97 B c 11/3 Street Cry (IRE)—Say No Now (IRE) (Refuse To Bend (IRE)) **Saif Ali & Saeed H. Altayer**
98 Ch c 9/5 Teofilo (IRE)—Shadow Roll (IRE) (Mark of Esteem (IRE)) **Sheikh Marwan Al Maktoum**
99 B f 3/4 Artie Schiller (USA)—Siempre Asi (USA) (Silver Hawk (USA)) (87000) **Mr Christopher Wright**
100 **SPEEDY APPROACH,** ch c 1/4 New Approach (IRE)—Height of Vanity (IRE) (Erhaab (USA)) **J. Abdullah**
101 **SPIRITOFTHEUNION,** b f 17/3 Authorized (IRE)—Kahlua Kiss (Mister Baileys) (50000) **A. Al Shaikh**
102 **SUGAR RUSH,** ch c 24/2 Pastoral Pursuits—Panic Stations (Singspiel (IRE)) (476) **D. W. & L. Y. Payne**
103 **SUNNINGDALE ROSE (IRE),** b f 16/2 Art Connoisseur (IRE)—
        Eloquent Rose (IRE) (Elnadim (USA)) (19047) **Mrs Susan Roy**
104 **THATCHEREEN (IRE),** b f 3/3 Mastercraftsman (IRE)—
        Roof Fiddle (USA) (Cat Thief (USA)) (42857) **Mr T Redman & Mr P Philipps**
105 **WADI ALAMARDI,** ch c 2/3 Lucky Story (USA)—Thicket (Wolfhound (USA)) (28571) **A. Al Shaikh**
106 Gr c 21/2 Mastercraftsman (IRE)—Wait It Out (USA) (Swain (IRE)) (58000) **M. Tabor**

Other Owners: Mr Imad Al-Sagar, S. H. Altayer, The Hon Mrs C. Corbett, Mr Mike Dawson, J. F. Dean, Sir Alex Ferguson, D. T. Fish, Mr M. Heffernan, The Hon H. M. Herbert, Highclere Thoroughbred Racing Ltd, Mr Saleh Al Homaizi, Mr C. Lomas, Mrs John Magnier, Mr T. S. Palin, Mr O. J. W. Pawle, Mr D. W. Payne, Mrs L. Y. Payne, M. E. Perlman, P. A. Philipps, Mr C. E. L. Philipps, Mr M. Prince, Mr M. Quirke, T. S. Redman, Mr J. M. M. Scott, Mr Derrick Smith, Mr J. A. B. Stafford, Mrs L. Whitehead, W. J. Williams, Mrs M. Williams, Miss Holly Wright, Ms Chloe Wright.

Assistant Trainer: Richard Spencer

Jockey (flat): Hayley Turner, Jamie Spencer. **Apprentice:** Thomas Hemsley, Ian Burns.

---

33 **MR JAMES BENNETT, Wantage**
Postal: **2 Filley Alley, Letcombe Bassett, Wantage, Oxfordshire, OX12 9LT**
Contacts: PHONE **(01235) 762163** FAX **(01235) 762163** MOBILE **(07771) 523076**
E-MAIL **jabennett@tiscali.co.uk**

1 **PRINCESSE KATIE (IRE),** 7, b m Presenting—Another Shot (IRE) **Miss J. C. Blackwell**

Assistant Trainer: Miss J. Blackwell

Conditional: Matthew Stanley.

---

34 **MR ALAN BERRY, Cockerham**
Postal: **Moss Side Racing Stables, Crimbles Lane, Cockerham, Lancashire, LA2 0ES**
Contacts: PHONE **(01524) 791179** FAX **(01524) 791958** MOBILE **(07880) 553515**
E-MAIL **mosssideracing@tiscali.co.uk** WEBSITE **www.alanberryracing.co.uk**

1 **ANDRASTA,** 8, b m Bertolini (USA)—Real Popcorn (IRE) **A. Berry**
2 **BUSY BIMBO (IRE),** 4, b f Red Clubs (IRE)—Unfortunate A. **Berry**
3 **COME TO MIND,** 4, b g Mind Games—Hillside Heather (IRE) **Hillside Racing**
4 **CRIMSON KNOT (IRE),** 5, b m Red Ransom (USA)—Green Minstrel (FR) **W. Burns**
5 **ECONOMIC CRISIS (IRE),** 4, ch f Excellent Art—Try The Air (IRE) **Mr & Mrs T. Blane**
6 **FACE EAST (USA),** 5, b g Orientate (USA)—Yes Honey (USA) **W. Burns**

MR ALAN BERRY - Continued

7 **GRETHEL (IRE)**, 9, b m Fruits of Love (USA)—Stay Sharpe (USA) **Mr J. P. Smith**
8 **JORDAURA**, 7, br g Primo Valentino (IRE)—Christina's Dream **A. B. Parr**
9 **KAY GEE BE (IRE)**, 9, b g Fasliyev (USA)—Pursuit of Truth (USA) **A. Berry**
10 **LADY BENTINCK (IRE)**, 4, b f Mujadil (USA)—Lady Graigie (IRE)
11 **MYSTIFIED (IRE)**, 10, b g Raise A Grand (IRE)—Sunrise (IRE) **A. Willoughby**
12 **PRO VALOUR (IRE)**, 5, b g Elusive City (USA)—Red Vale (IRE) **A. K. Collins**
13 **RARE COINCIDENCE**, 12, ch g Atraf—Green Seed (IRE) **A. Willoughby**
14 **RED ROAR (IRE)**, 6, ch m Chineur (FR)—Unfortunate **Sporting Kings**
15 **SCRIPT**, 4, b f Firebreak—Signs And Wonders **A. Berry**
16 **SPREAD BOY (IRE)**, 6, b g Tagula (IRE)—Marinka **A. Berry**
17 **TINZO (IRE)**, 5, b g Auction House (USA)—Costa Verde **A. R. White**
18 **WICKED WILMA (IRE)**, 9, b m Tagula (IRE)—Wicked **Mrs L. White**

THREE-YEAR-OLDS

19 **BIX (IRE)**, b c Holy Roman Emperor (IRE)—Belle Rebelle (IRE) **A. B. Parr**
20 **DARK MARVEL (IRE)**, b f Captain Marvelous (IRE)—Starisa (IRE) **Happy Elders**
21 **LADY CALANTHA**, b f Byron—Brooklyn's Sky **A. B. Parr**
22 **PARTNER'S GOLD (IRE)**, b c Red Clubs (IRE)—Unfortunate **Partner's Brewery**

Other Owners: Mr S. J. Allen, Mrs J. M. Berry, J. Berry, T. W. Blane, Mrs S. Blane, H. J. Cook, Mrs S. E. Cook, Mr I. Griffiths, Ms A. Hartley, Mr I. D. Johnson, Mr N. Sharp.

Jockey (flat): Franny Norton. Apprentice: Billy Cray. Amateur: Miss Sarah Richardson, Mr Ryan Lynam.

---

35   **MR J. A. BERRY, Blackwater**
Postal: Ballyroe, Blackwater, Enniscorthy, Co. Wexford, Ireland
Contacts: PHONE (00353) 53 9127205 MOBILE (00353) 53 8625 57537

1 **ACRIVEEN (IRE)**, 11, ch g Accordion—Raheen River (IRE) **J. A. Berry**
2 **BALLYROE RAMBLER (IRE)**, 6, br g Lahib (USA)—Victoria's Rose (IRE) **Fire & Ice Syndicate**
3 **CALL ME EMMA (IRE)**, 5, b m Beneficial—Clody Girl (IRE) **Not For Friends Syndicate**
4 **CARA VIC (IRE)**, 6, ch m Old Vic—Sonnerschien (IRE) **B. Bourke**
5 **CIVENA (IRE)**, 7, b m Oscar (IRE)—The Village Merc (IRE) **Go For It Syndicate**
6 **COOTAMUNDRA (IRE)**, 10, ch g Broken Hearted—Sigginstown **Turbine Syndicate**
7 **DEEP INSPIRATION (IRE)**, 5, b g Heron Island (IRE)—The Wrens Nest (IRE) **Mrs A. Berry**
8 **FAMOUS BALLERINA (IRE)**, 5, b m Golan (IRE)—World of Ballet (IRE) **J. Berry**
9 **GIVE US A HAND (IRE)**, 11, br g Anshan—Desperado Dawn (IRE) **Mrs J. Berry**
10 **ON THE RADAR (IRE)**, 5, b m Classic Cliche—Spread Your Wings (IRE) **B. Parnell**
11 **PRETTY HAPPY (IRE)**, 11, b m Shernazar—Cash It In (IRE) **Mrs J. Berry**
12 **SEE IT AS IT IS (IRE)**, 6, b g Shantou (USA)—Opus One **Fire & Ice Syndicate**
13 **SHINGLE BAY**, 7, b g Karinga Bay—Riva La Belle **P. M. Berry**
14 **SILVER CAVALIER (IRE)**, 7, gr g Sonus (IRE)—Benaughlin (IRE) **J. A. Berry**
15 **SWEET MARIA (IRE)**, 7, b m Luso—Over The Sands (IRE) **J. A. Berry**
16 **THE BOOSHY MAN (IRE)**, 7, b g Luso—Hallaniya (IRE) **Not For Friends Syndicate**
17 **TOMPATPEG (IRE)**, 6, b g Luso—River Grove (IRE) **M. I. Cloney**
18 **VILLAGE WHISPERS (IRE)**, 6, b g Classic Cliche—Raheen River (IRE) **M. Devine**
19 **WHAT ABOUT THAT (IRE)**, 5, b g Spartacus (IRE)—Cajo (IRE) **Not For Friends Syndicate**
20 **WHATS ON THE MENU (IRE)**, 9, ch g Anshan—Leading Dream (IRE) **Mrs J. Berry**

Assistant Trainer: Blain Parnell

Conditional: A. F. O'Neill.

---

36   **MR JOHN BERRY, Newmarket**
Postal: Beverley House Stables, Exeter Road, Newmarket, Suffolk, CB8 8LR
Contacts: PHONE (01638) 660663
WEBSITE www.beverleyhousestables.com

1 **ALCALDE**, 7, b g Hernando (FR)—Alexandrine (IRE) **The Alhambra Partnership**
2 **DOUCHKIRK (FR)**, 6, b g Prince Kirk (FR)—Douchka (FR) **The Beverley Hillbillies**
3 **ETHICS GIRL (IRE)**, 7, b m Hernando (FR)—Palinisa (FR) **The 1997 Partnership**
4 **GIFT OF SILENCE**, 4, gr f Cadeaux Genereux—Not A Word **Mr John Berry**
5 **GRAND LIAISON**, 4, b f Sir Percy—Dancinginthedark (IRE) **Barrie Catchpole & Michael Meaney**

MR JOHN BERRY - Continued

6 **OSCAR BERNADOTTE**, 5, b g Sulamani (IRE)—Desiree (IRE) **Mrs Emma Berry**
7 **SILKEN THOUGHTS**, 5, b m Tobougg (IRE)—The Jotter **The Renewal Partnership**
8 **WASABI (IRE)**, 4, b f Tiger Hill (IRE)—Quinzey (JPN) **Mr A. W. Fordham**
9 **ZAROSA (IRE)**, 4, b f Barathea (IRE)—Shantalla Peak (IRE) **Mr R. G. Vicarage**

THREE-YEAR-OLDS

10 **JACK IRISH**, b g Bertolini (USA)—Desiree (IRE) **Mrs Emma Berry**
11 **MAGIC ICE**, b f Royal Applause—Winter Ice **The Acorn Partnership**
12 **MANY LEVELS**, br g Nayef (USA)—Polygueza (FR) **The Acorn Partnership**
13 **ORLA'S RAINBOW (IRE)**, b c Oratorio (IRE)—Red Ray **The Alhambra Partnership**
14 **PLATINUM PROOF (USA)**, b br c Smart Strike (CAN)—Keeper Hill (USA) **The Golden Years Partnership**
15 **PURRFECT**, b f Tiger Hill (IRE)—B Beautiful (IRE)
16 **ROY ROCKET (FR)**, gr g Layman (USA)—Minnie's Mystery (FR) **Mr John Berry**
17 B g Shamardal (USA)—Twiggy's Sister (IRE)

TWO-YEAR-OLDS

18 Ch f 7/3 Sleeping Indian—Forever Loved (Deploy) (3000)

Other Owners: Mr W. F. Benter, Mr C. Berry, Mr J. Bond, Mrs J. Braithwaite, Mr A. Brannon, Mr S. Brodie, Mr R. Fleck, Mr Ken Gibbs, Mr Gerry Grimstone, Mr Jason Hathorn, Mrs Fiona Hathorn, Mr P. Holden, Mr D. J. Huelin, Mr Richard Jones, Mr S. Jones, Mr L. Kingston, Mr S. Lee, Mr Kevan Leggett, Miss L. I. McCarthy, Mrs I. McCarthy, Mr S. McCormick, Mrs M. L. Parry, Mr P. Steele-Mortimer, Mr L. Stratton, Mr P. Temple, Mr T. Trounce, Mr C. Vautier, Mr L. C. Wadey, Ms Sarah Louise Williams.

Assistant Trainer: Hugh Fraser

Jockey (NH): Will Kennedy.

---

37 MR JIM BEST, Lewes
Postal: **Grandstand Stables, The Old Racecourse, Lewes, East Sussex, BN7 1UR**
Contacts: **PHONE (01435) 882073 (01273) 480249 FAX (01435) 882073 MOBILE (07968) 743272**
E-MAIL jimandtombest@btinternet.com WEBSITE www.jimandtombestracing.co.uk

1 **ACE FIGHTER PILOT**, 7, b g Silver Patriarch (IRE)—Vedra (IRE) **Odds On Racing**
2 **BEGGAR'S OPERA (IRE)**, 6, b g Singspiel (IRE)—Hannda (IRE) **David & Jane George**
3 **BOLLIN JUDITH**, 7, br m Bollin Eric—Bollin Nellie **Mr J. J. Callaghan**
4 **BOOGIE DANCER**, 9, b m Tobougg (IRE)—Bolero **Mr D. Stockdale**
5 **BUGSY'S GIRL (IRE)**, 5, ch m Desert King (IRE)—Icydora (FR) **Mrs S. C. Head**
6 **BURNT AGAIN (IRE)**, 9, b m Moscow Society (USA)—Divebomb **Mr R. Grice**
7 **CASTLE MYTH (USA)**, 7, b br g Johannesburg (USA)—Castlemania (CAN) **Fruits Incorporated**
8 **GENEROUS JUNE (IRE)**, 5, ch m Generous (IRE)—Outo'theblue (IRE) **Mr J. J. Callaghan**
9 **HEAD HUNTED**, 6, b g Dubai Destination (USA)—Tropical Breeze (IRE) **Mrs S. C. Head**
10 **LYSSIO (GER)**, 6, b g Motivator—Lysuna (GER) **Mr J. J. Callaghan**
11 **MISSILE MAN (IRE)**, 4, b c Winged Love (IRE)—Miss Ondee (FR) **Jack Callaghan & Christopher Dillon**
12 **MONEY MONEY MONEY**, 7, b m Generous (IRE)—Shi Shi **Flowerbud Partnership**
13 **NORTHERN LAD (IRE)**, 11, ch g Lord of Appeal—Deep Green **J. D. Sells**
14 **ON THE FEATHER**, 7, br m Josr Algarhoud (IRE)—Fotheringhay **Sills Racing**
15 **PLANETOID (IRE)**, 5, b g Galileo (IRE)—Palmeraie (USA) **Mr J. J. Callaghan**
16 **RENAGISHA (IRE)**, 7, b m Luso—Slaney Rose (IRE) **Mr B. Reilly**
17 **ROCKY RYAN (IRE)**, 10, b g Even Top (IRE)—The Dara Queen **Mr & Mrs F. W. Golding**
18 **ROYAL TROOPER (IRE)**, 7, b g Hawk Wing (USA)—Strawberry Roan (IRE) **Sills Racing**
19 **SCHOOL FOR SCANDAL (IRE)**, 5, b g Pivotal—Sensation **Goodwood Starlight Partnership**
20 **SHARAKTI (IRE)**, 6, b g Rakti—Easter Parade **Silverton Racing Inc**
21 **SLANEY STAR (IRE)**, 5, b h Cloudings (IRE)—Slaney Rose (IRE) **Fruits Incorporated**
22 **SPEAR THISTLE**, 11, ch g Selkirk (USA)—Ardisia (USA) **Mrs S. C. Head**
23 **SUDDEN LIGHT (IRE)**, 7, b m Presenting—Coolshamrock (IRE) **M&R Refurbishments Ltd**
24 **SUGAR HICCUP (IRE)**, 5, b m Refuse To Bend (IRE)—Raysiza (IRE) **Jack Callaghan & Christopher Dillon**
25 **WAYWARD GLANCE**, 5, b g Sadler's Wells (USA)—Daring Aim **Mr J. J. Callaghan**
26 **WESTERN HIGH**, 8, b g Rainbow High—Western Ploy **Fruits Incorporated**

Other Owners: Mr A. Achilleos, Mr C. Attrell, L. Best, Mr J. Cumber, Mr J. Cumber, Mr C. J. Dillon, Mr P. E. Gardener, Mr P. J. Gardner, Mr D. W. George, Mrs J. George, Mrs M. J. Golding, Mr F. W. Golding, Mr T. J. Good, Mr P. W. Goodfellow, S. P. Graham, Mr G. C. Sales, N. J. Sillett.

MR JIM BEST - Continued

Assistant Trainer: Mr T. Best
Jockey (NH): Marc Goldstein, A. P. McCoy.

---

38 MR JOHN BEST, Maidstone
Postal: **Scragged Oak Farm, Scragged Oak Road, Hucking, Maidstone, Kent, ME17 1QU**
Contacts: **PHONE (01622) 880276 FAX (01622) 880525 MOBILE (07889) 362154**
E-MAIL john.best@johnbestracing.com WEBSITE www.johnbestracing.com

1 **BAHRI SHEEN (IRE)**, 5, b g Bahri (USA)—Kama's Wheel **Kingsgate Racing 2**
2 **BAYLEYF (IRE)**, 4, b g Kheleyf (USA)—Hi Katriona (IRE) **Graham Jones & Partners**
3 **BORIS THE BOLD**, 4, b g Librettist (USA)—Santiburi Girl **Folkestone Racecourse Owners Group II**
4 **CASUAL MOVER (IRE)**, 5, b g Diamond Green (FR)—Baileys On Line **Brian Goodyear & Rhonda Wilson**
5 **EL CALAFATE (USA)**, 4, ch g Mr Greeley (USA)—Jive Talk (USA) **Mr S. D. Malcolm**
6 **GUNG HO JACK**, 4, b g Moss Vale (IRE)—Bijan (IRE) **Mr J. Fletcher**
7 **RED RAMESSES (IRE)**, 4, br g Red Clubs (IRE)—Marasem **H. J. Jarvis**
8 **SAFFRON PARK**, 4, ch g Compton Place—Beacon Silver **Kingsgate Racing 3**
9 **SOWETO STAR (IRE)**, 5, ch g Johannesburg (USA)—Lady of Talent (USA) **Part Two Partnership**
10 **STREWTH (IRE)**, 5, ch g Encosta de Lago (AUS)—Alpine Park (IRE) **Mr S. Malcolm & Mr J. Foulger**
11 **VALE OF LINGFIELD (IRE)**, 4, b g Moss Vale (IRE)—Celtic Guest (IRE) **Lingfield Park Owners Club II**
12 **YALDING DANCER**, 4, b f Zafeen (FR)—Daughters World **Mrs Bennett & Mr Schabacker**

THREE-YEAR-OLDS
13 **AZABITMOUR (FR)**, b c Azamour (IRE)—Brixa (FR) **Mr G Jones & Mr B Malt**
14 **BIG MOZA**, b f Pastoral Pursuits—Zaynah (IRE) **Watson & Malyon**
15 **BIRDIE KING**, b g Dutch Art—Daughters World **The Golf Partnership**
16 **BOLD ASSERTION**, ch c Assertive—Fanciful Dancer **Hucking Horses V**
17 **ELOUNTA**, b f Dubawi (IRE)—Santiburi Girl **Laura Malcolm & Bob Malt**
18 **FEARLESS LAD (IRE)**, b c Excellent Art—Souffle **Mrs J. O. Jones**
19 **FIT FOR A KING (IRE)**, b g Royal Applause—Sancia (IRE) **Malt, Howland, Sharp & Partners**
20 **HALLING'S WISH**, br g Halling (USA)—Fair View (GER) **WBC Partnership**
21 **HATS OFF**, b g Royal Applause—Miriam **Malt, Longman, Curtis & Hemmens**
22 **LE DELUGE (FR)**, b c Oratorio (IRE)—Princess Sofia (UAE) **Longman & Malt**
23 **MAD ABOUT HARRY (IRE)**, b c Mujadil (USA)—Caro Mio (IRE) **H. J. Jarvis**
24 **MASTERED (IRE)**, ch c Refuse To Bend (IRE)—Woodmaven (USA) **Miss H. J. Williams**
25 **MOSSGO (IRE)**, b g Moss Vale (IRE)—Perovskia (USA) **Hucking Horses V**
26 **OTTO THE FIRST**, b g Holy Roman Emperor (IRE)—Paquita (IRE) **Longman, Malt & Fuller**
27 **OUR SWEET ART**, ch f Dutch Art—Break of Dawn (USA) **Mr S. Malcolm & Mr J. Foulger**
28 **PASTORAL SYMPHONY**, br f Pastoral Pursuits—Hucking Harmony (IRE) **Five In Harmony**
29 **SABRE ROCK**, b c Dubawi (IRE)—Retainage (USA) **Mark Curtis & Rob Hemmens**
30 **ZHUBA (IRE)**, b c Elusive Quality (USA)—Lilium Malcolm (USA) **Fuller, Demarco & Perkins**

TWO-YEAR-OLDS
31 B c 15/2 Bahri (USA)—Band of Colour (IRE) (Spectrum (IRE))
32 Ch f 5/3 Major Cadeaux—Cheap N Chic (Primo Valentino (IRE)) (2095)
33 B c 13/4 Champs Elysees—Fancy Rose (USA) (Joyeux Danseur (USA)) (26000)
34 B c 13/3 Champs Elysees—First Approval (Royal Applause) (13000)
35 B c 30/1 Oratorio (IRE)—Fleeting Mirage (USA) (Afleet Alex (USA)) (14285)
36 B f 3/5 Virtual—Hucking Harmony (IRE) (Spartacus (IRE)) (3047) **Five In Harmony**
37 **LINGFIELD SKYFALL (IRE)**, b c 24/3 Amadeus Wolf—
                              Clytha (Mark of Esteem (IRE)) (9523) **Lingfield Park Owners Group**
38 B f 12/4 Three Valleys (USA)—Loquacity (Diktat) (7619)
39 B c 27/4 Pastoral Pursuits—Miriam (Forzando) (11428)
40 B c 2/5 Duke of Marmalade (IRE)—My Dream Castles (USA) (Woodman (USA)) (3174) **M. J. Ward**
41 B f 16/4 Amadeus Wolf—Pilda (IRE) (Princely Heir (USA)) (3967)
42 B c 28/4 Myboycharlie (IRE)—Retainage (USA) (Polish Numbers (USA)) (2857) **Mr J. R. Best**
43 B f 29/3 Virtual—Santiburi Girl (Casteddu) (2476) **Mrs Jackie Jones & Mr John Best**
44 Ch f 4/4 Elnadim (USA)—Saralea (FR) (Sillery (USA)) (17142)
45 **TRIPLE O SEVEN (IRE)**, b c 10/2 Kodiac—
                              Triple Zero (IRE) (Raise A Grand (IRE)) (24761) **Lingfield Park Owners Group**
46 B c 6/2 Baltic King—Zafaraya (IRE) (Ashkalani (IRE)) (14000) **The Golf Partnership**

MR JOHN BEST - Continued

Other Owners: Mrs J. A. Bennett, Mr A. R. Brightwell, Mr M. J. Coles, Mr M. B. Curtis, Mr J. Foulger, C. B. Goodyear, Mr R. E. Hemmens, Mr G. R. Jones, A. Longman, Mrs L. C. G. Malcolm, Mr R. C. Malt, A. J. Perkins, Mr P. Schabacker, Mr A. Watson, Mr M. J. Wellbelove, Mr S. Wellbelove, Ms R. L. Wilson, Mr S. Wishart.

Assistant Trainer: David Menuisier

---

39 **MRS LOUISE BEST, Maidstone**
Postal: **Northdown Croft, Broad Street Hill, Hollingbourne, Maidstone, Kent, ME17 1QY**
Contacts: **PHONE (01622) 880456 MOBILE (07712) 588188**
E-MAIL louise@louisebestracing.com WEBSITE www.louisebestracing.com

1 AWESOME ROCK (IRE), 4, ch g Rock of Gibraltar (IRE)—Dangerous Diva (IRE) **Rock On Racing Partnership**
2 JUSTBOOKIES DOTNET, 4, b g Kheleyf (USA)—Moly **Louise Best Racing & Martyn Cruse**

THREE-YEAR-OLDS

3 SALLY BRUCE, b f Byron—Show Trial (IRE) **Ripple Racing**

Other Owners: Mrs L. A. Best, Mr M. F. Cruse, Miss K. M. Ferguson, Mrs Janys Ferguson.

---

40 **MR JAMES BETHELL, Middleham**
Postal: **Thorngill, Coverham, Middleham, North Yorkshire, DL8 4TJ**
Contacts: **PHONE (01969) 640360 FAX (01969) 640360 MOBILE (07831) 683528**
E-MAIL james@jamesbethell.co.uk WEBSITE www.jamesbethell.com

1 CHARLCOT, 5, ch g Monsieur Bond (IRE)—Miss Apricot **Clarendon Thoroughbred Racing**
2 HARTFORTH, 5, ch g Haafhd—St Edith (IRE) **Clarendon Thoroughbred Racing**
3 MISTER BOB (GER), 4, ch g Black Sam Bellamy (IRE)—Mosquera (GER) **R. F. Gibbons**
4 RICH AGAIN (IRE), 4, b g Amadeus Wolf—Fully Fashioned (IRE) **R. T. Vickers**
5 TRUE PLEASURE (IRE), 6, b m Choisir (AUS)—Absolute Pleasure **Clarendon Thoroughbred Racing**

Other Owners: J. D. Bethell, Mrs S. Bethell.

---

41 **MR EDWARD BEVAN, Hereford**
Postal: **Pullen Farm, Ullingswick, Herefordshire, HR1 3JQ**
Contacts: **PHONE/FAX (01432) 820370 MOBILE (07970) 650347**

1 BOLD CROSS (IRE), 10, b g Cape Cross (IRE)—Machikane Akaiito (IRE) **E. G. Bevan**
2 BOLD DUKE, 5, b g Sulamani (IRE)—Dominant Duchess **E. G. Bevan**
3 LEGAL PURSUIT, 4, b g Proclamation (IRE)—Trysting Grove (IRE) **E. G. Bevan**
4 REINETTE O'BRY, 7, b m Sulamani (IRE)—Dominant Duchess **E. G. Bevan**

Assistant Trainer: I Pickard

---

42 **MR GEORGE BEWLEY, Hawick**
Postal: **South Dean Farm, Bonchester Bridge, Hawick, Roxburghshire, TD9 8TP**
Contacts: **PHONE (01450) 860651 MOBILE (07704) 924783**
E-MAIL southdean.farm@btconnect.com

1 BRAE ON (IRE), 5, ch g Presenting—Raphuca (IRE) **West Coast Racing Partnership & Bewley**
2 CUMBRIAN FARMER, 6, ch g Alflora—Quark Top (FR) **G. T. Bewley**
3 EASEMENT, 10, b g Kayf Tara—Raspberry Sauce **Southdean Racing Club**
4 HUNTERS BELT (IRE), 9, b g Intikhab (USA)—Three Stars **Mr R A Fisher & Mr John Blair**
5 INOOGOO (IRE), 8, b g Great Palm (USA)—Ballindante (IRE) **EBB Racing**
6 JAMADDJI, 6, b m Needwood Blade—Tintera (IRE) **West Coast Racing Partnership**
7 OUR JOEY (IRE), 5, b g Wareed (IRE)—Put On Hold (IRE) **John Gibson, Kevin Twentyman & Bewley**
8 SOUTH LEINSTER (IRE), 8, b g Chevalier (IRE)—Easy To Please **WEB Racing & K Twentyman**
9 TEERIE EXPRESS, 12, b g Sir Harry Lewis (USA)—Trecento **G. T. Bewley**

MR GEORGE BEWLEY - Continued

Other Owners: Mrs L. Bewley, Mr J. J. Blair, Mr R. H. Brown, H. A. Brydon, Mr Gary Etheridge, Mr R. A. Fisher, Mr J. H. Gibson, Mr D. Kerr, Mr J. R. Kerr, Mr K. Twentyman.

Conditional: Jonathon Bewley.

---

43 MR JOSEPH BEWLEY, Jedburgh
Postal: **Newhouse Cottage, Camptown, Jedburgh, Roxburghshire, TD8 6RW**
Contacts: **PHONE (01835) 840273 MOBILE (07758) 783910**
E-MAIL bewley18@tiscali.co.uk

1 4, B g Exit To Nowhere (USA)—Aberdare **J. R. Bewley**
2 4, B g Indian Danehill (IRE)—Native Novel (IRE) **J. R. Bewley**
3 TOPO GIGIO (FR), 9, b g Even Top (IRE)—Chateau Lina (IRE) **J. R. Bewley**

Assistant Trainer: Mrs K Bewley

Jockey (NH): Ryan Mania. **Amateur:** Mr Callum Bewley.

---

44 MR SAEED BIN SUROOR, Newmarket
Postal: **Godolphin Office, Snailwell Road, Newmarket, Suffolk, CB8 7YE**

> The following list has not been supplied by the trainer and is as accurate as possible at the time of going to press. Some horses listed may not return to Britain from Dubai. Only 2yos entered in the 2014 Derby are shown. **For the latest information please visit www.godolphin.com**

1 **ADROITLY (AUS)**, 6, br g Octagonal (NZ)—Easy Out (AUS)
2 **AFRICAN STORY**, 6, ch h Pivotal—Blixen (USA)
3 **AHZEEMAH (IRE)**, 4, b g Dubawi (IRE)—Swiss Roll (IRE)
4 **AL SAHAM**, 4, b c Authorized (IRE)—Local Spirit (USA)
5 **ALBASHARAH (USA)**, 4, b f Arch (USA)—Desert Gold (USA)
6 **ALKIMOS (IRE)**, 5, b g High Chaparral (IRE)—Bali Breeze (IRE)
7 **ALMAAS (USA)**, 4, ch g Hard Spun (USA)—Summer Dream Girl (USA)
8 **ANJAZ (USA)**, 4, b f Street Cry (IRE)—Playful Act (IRE)
9 **ASATIR (USA)**, 4, b c Elusive Quality (USA)—Valid Warning (USA)
10 **BIG AUDIO (IRE)**, 6, b g Oratorio (IRE)—Tarbela (IRE)
11 **BURJ HATTA (USA)**, 5, b br g Kingmambo (USA)—Vadahilla (FR)
12 **CAVALRYMAN**, 7, b h Halling (USA)—Silversword (FR)
13 **CAYMANS (AUS)**, 8, b g Secret Savings (USA)—Easy Out (AUS)
14 **CLUB OCEANIC**, 5, b g Cape Cross (IRE)—My Lass
15 **COLOUR VISION (FR)**, 5, gr g Rainbow Quest (USA)—Give Me Five (GER)
16 **CON ARTIST (IRE)**, 6, b h Invincible Spirit (IRE)—Hoodwink (IRE)
17 **DESERT LAW (IRE)**, 5, b g Oasis Dream—Speed Cop
18 **DO IT ALL (USA)**, 6, b br h Distorted Humor (USA)—Stupendous Miss (USA)
19 **EHTEDAAM (USA)**, 4, b c Arch (USA)—Bow River Gold
20 **EXPERT FIGHTER (USA)**, 4, ch c Dubai Destination (USA)—Porto Roca (AUS)
21 **FAMOUS POET (IRE)**, 4, b c Exceed And Excel (AUS)—Asfurah (USA)
22 **FARHH**, 5, b h Pivotal—Gonbarda (GER)
23 **FLAG OFFICER**, 5, b g Dubai Destination (USA)—Dusty Answer
24 **FREE WHEELING (AUS)**, 5, b h Ad Valorem (USA)—Miss Carefree (AUS)
25 **GLOBAL CITY (IRE)**, 7, b h Exceed And Excel (AUS)—Victory Peak
26 **GOLD CITY (IRE)**, 4, b g Pivotal—Storm Lily (USA)
27 **HANDSOME MAN (IRE)**, 4, ch c Nayef (USA)—Danceabout
28 **HUNTER'S LIGHT (IRE)**, 5, ch h Dubawi (IRE)—Portmanteau
29 **IBTAHAJ**, 4, b c Invincible Spirit (IRE)—Maroussies Wings (IRE)
30 **INDUNA (AUS)**, 5, b g Elusive Quality (USA)—Camarena (NZ)
31 **INTHAR (USA)**, 4, ch c Medicean—Mont Etoile (IRE)
32 **INVISIBLE HUNTER (USA)**, 4, ch c Rahy (USA)—Madeline P (USA)
33 **INVISIBLE MAN**, 7, ch g Elusive Quality (USA)—Eternal Reve (USA)
34 **KASSIANO (GER)**, 4, b g Soldier Hollow—Kastila (GER)
35 **LAATAFREET (IRE)**, 5, ch h Singspiel (USA)—Cerulean Sky (IRE)
36 **LANDAMAN (IRE)**, 5, br g Cape Cross (IRE)—Mayoress
37 **LAST FIGHTER (IRE)**, 4, b g Cape Cross (IRE)—Launch Time (USA)
38 **LAYALI DUBAI (USA)**, 4, b f Street Sense (USA)—Make My Heart Sing (USA)

MR SAEED BIN SUROOR - Continued

39 **LES TROYENS**, 5, b h Librettist (USA)—Native Blue
40 **LEY HUNTER (USA)**, 6, b h Kingmambo (USA)—Lailani
41 **LOST IN THE MOMENT (IRE)**, 6, b h Danehill Dancer (IRF)—Streetcar (IRE)
42 **MAN OF ACTION (USA)**, 6, ch g Elusive Quality (USA)—Dixie Melody (USA)
43 **MASTEROFTHEROLLS (IRE)**, 5, b h Refuse To Bend (IRE)—Miss Sally (IRE)
44 **MAWHUB**, 4, b g Singspiel (IRE)—Native Blue
45 **MENDIP (USA)**, 6, b br h Harlan's Holiday (USA)—Well Spring (USA)
46 **MODUN (IRE)**, 6, br g King's Best (USA)—Olympienne (IRE)
47 **MUNTASIR (IRE)**, 4, b c Distorted Humor (USA)—Mansfield Park
48 **MY FREEDOM (IRE)**, 5, b g Invincible Spirit (IRE)—Priere
49 **MYSTICISM (USA)**, 5, b g A P Warrior (USA)—Wild Catseye (USA)
50 **OUT OF BOUNDS (USA)**, 4, ch c Discreet Cat (USA)—Unbridled Elaine (USA)
51 **PIED A TERRE (AUS)**, 5, b g Ad Valorem (USA)—Masonette (AUS)
52 **PISCO SOUR (USA)**, 5, b br g Lemon Drop Kid (USA)—Lynnwood Chase (USA)
53 **PRINCE BISHOP (IRE)**, 6, ch g Dubawi (IRE)—North East Bay (USA)
54 **QUICK WIT**, 6, b h Oasis Dream—Roo
55 **RAINBOW PEAK (IRE)**, 7, b g Hernando (FR)—Celtic Fling
56 **RASSAM (IRE)**, 4, b br g Dansili—Vantive (USA)
57 **RETRIEVE (AUS)**, 6, b h Rahy (USA)—Hold To Ransom (USA)
58 **ROAYH (USA)**, 5, ch g Speightstown (USA)—Most Remarkable (USA)
59 **ROYAL EMPIRE (IRE)**, 4, b c Teofilo (IRE)—Zeiting (IRE)
60 **SAAMIDD**, 5, b h Street Cry (IRE)—Aryaamm (IRE)
61 **SAJJHAA**, 6, b m King's Best (USA)—Anaamil (IRE)
62 **SANDAGIYR (FR)**, 5, b h Dr Fong (USA)—Sanariya (IRE)
63 **SAYTARA (IRE)**, 4, b f Nayef (USA)—Celtic Silhouette (FR)
64 **SCARF (AUS)**, 6, gr g Lonhro (AUS)—Muffle (AUS)
65 **SHARESTAN (IRE)**, 5, b h Shamardal (USA)—Sharesha (IRE)
66 **SONGCRAFT (IRE)**, 5, b g Singspiel (IRE)—Baya (AUS)
67 **SOUL (AUS)**, 6, b g Commands (AUS)—Marvilha (AUS)
68 **SPRING OF FAME (USA)**, 7, b g Grand Slam (USA)—Bloomy (USA)
69 **START RIGHT**, 6, b g Footstepsinthesand—Time Crystal (IRE)
70 **SURPRISE MOMENT (IRE)**, 4, b f Authorized (IRE)—Criquette
71 **TAHAAMAH**, 5, ch h King's Best (USA)—Russian Snows (IRE)
72 **TERDAAD (IRE)**, 5, ch g Shamardal (USA)—Akrmina
73 **USTURA (USA)**, 4, b c Nayef (USA)—Calando (USA)
74 **VOLCANIC WIND (USA)**, 4, b g Distorted Humor (USA)—Sundrop (JPN)
75 **WILLING FOE (USA)**, 6, b br g Dynaformer (USA)—Thunder Kitten (USA)
76 **YAA WAYL (IRE)**, 6, b g Whipper (USA)—Lidanna

THREE-YEAR-OLDS

77 **AL JAMAL**, b f Authorized (IRE)—Kydd Gloves (USA)
78 **AL MANAAL**, b f Echo of Light—Mall Queen (USA)
79 **ARABIAN SKIES (IRE)**, b c Authorized (IRE)—Chaturanga
80 **DAAREE (IRE)**, b c Teofilo (IRE)—Mawaakeb (USA)
81 **ELNADWA (USA)**, b f Daaher (CAN)—Magical Allure (USA)
82 **EXCELLENT RESULT (IRE)**, b c Shamardal (USA)—Line Ahead (IRE)
83 **FUTURE REFERENCE (IRE)**, ch c Raven's Pass (USA)—Mike's Wildcat (USA)
84 **GOLD HUNTER (IRE)**, b c Invincible Spirit (IRE)—Goldthroat (IRE)
85 **HOODNA (IRE)**, b f Invincible Spirit (IRE)—Heaven's Cause (USA)
86 **I'M BACK (IRE)**, b c Exceed And Excel (AUS)—Paracel (USA)
87 **IKHTISAS (USA)**, b c Street Sense (USA)—Any For Love (ARG)
88 **INAAD (IRE)**, b c New Approach (IRE)—Athreyaa
89 **INTIBA (USA)**, b f Street Cry (IRE)—Danelagh (AUS)
90 **MANSOREEN**, ch c Monsun (GER)—Mandellicht (IRE)
91 **MAR MAR (IRE)**, b f Invincible Spirit (IRE)—Queen of Tara (IRE)
92 **MUHARRIB (IRE)**, b c Oasis Dream—Manhattan Dream (USA)
93 **MUHTARIS (IRE)**, b c Teofilo (IRE)—Fann (IRE)
94 **MUKHABARAT (IRE)**, b c Exceed And Excel (AUS)—Counterclaim
95 **MUTHABIR (IRE)**, b c Nayef (USA)—Northern Melody (IRE)
96 **MY DIRECTION**, ch c Singspiel (IRE)—Ejlaal (IRE)
97 **MY TRUST (IRE)**, b f Exceed And Excel (AUS)—Alizes (NZ)
98 **OSTAAD (IRE)**, b c Marju (IRE)—Almansoora (USA)
99 **SADIQ**, b c Invincible Spirit (IRE)—Miss Particular (IRE)
100 **SECRET NUMBER**, b c Raven's Pass (USA)—Mysterial (USA)
101 **SHURUQ (USA)**, b f Elusive Quality (USA)—Miss Lucifer (FR)

MR SAEED BIN SUROOR - Continued

102 **SPOKESWOMAN (IRE)**, b f Invincible Spirit (IRE)—Devil's Imp (IRE)
103 **TAKAATHUR (USA)**, ch c Hard Spun (USA)—Vague (USA)
104 **TAMARKUZ (USA)**, ch c Speightstown (USA)—Without You Babe (USA)
105 **TARIKHI (USA)**, b c Bernardini—Caffe Latte (IRE)
106 **TAWHID**, gr c Invincible Spirit (IRE)—Snowdrops
107 **THA'IR (IRE)**, b c New Approach (IRE)—Flashing Green
108 **THIQA (IRE)**, b f New Approach (IRE)—Sunray Superstar
109 **THOUWRA (IRE)**, b c Pivotal—Cape Verdi (IRE)
110 **WADI AL HATTAWI (IRE)**, b c Dalakhani (IRE)—Carisolo
111 **WINTER SNOW (IRE)**, b f Raven's Pass (USA)—Gonfilia (GER)
112 **ZA'HARA (IRE)**, b br f Raven's Pass (USA)—Opera Comique (FR)

TWO-YEAR-OLDS

113 **ALMERZEM (USA)**, b br c 15/4 Medaglia d'oro (USA)—Tashawak (IRE) (Night Shift (USA))
114 B c 3/5 Monsun (GER)—Ameerat (Mark of Esteem (IRE))
115 Ch c 14/4 New Approach (IRE)—Call Later (USA) (Gone West (USA))
116 B c 3/4 Lawman (FR)—Coconut Show (Linamix (FR)) (182539)
117 B c 17/1 New Approach (IRE)—Danuta (USA) (Sunday Silence (USA))
118 **ELJADDAAF (IRE)**, b c 14/2 Shamardal (USA)—Almansoora (USA) (Bahri (USA))
119 B c 4/1 Dalakhani (IRE)—Emmy Award (IRE) (Sadler's Wells (USA))
120 B c 8/1 New Approach (IRE)—Evil Empire (Acatenango (GER))
121 Ch c 8/5 Dubawi (IRE)—Fantastic Flame (IRE) (Generous (IRE))
122 B c 17/4 Pivotal—Gonbarda (GER) (Lando (GER))
123 Ch c 27/4 Shamardal (USA)—Hi Dubai (Rahy (USA))
124 **ISTIMRAAR (IRE)**, b c 2/4 Dansili—Manayer (IRE) (Sadler's Wells (USA))
125 **KAABER (USA)**, b c 5/3 Daaher (CAN)—Taseel (USA) (Danzig (USA))
126 B br c 23/1 New Approach (IRE)—Kazzia (GER) (Zinaad)
127 Ch c 31/1 Pivotal—Local Spirit (Lion Cavern (USA))
128 B c 1/4 New Approach (IRE)—Mannington (AUS) (Danehill (USA))
129 Ch gr c 8/4 Dalakhani (IRE)—Mont Etoile (IRE) (Montjeu (IRE))
130 B c 1/2 Shamardal (USA)—Moonshadow (Diesis)
131 **MUJAAHER (IRE)**, ch c 12/2 Nayef (USA)—Raaya (USA) (Giant's Causeway (USA))
132 B c 14/3 Cape Cross (IRE)—Northern Melody (IRE) (Singspiel (IRE))
133 Ch c 9/3 King's Best (USA)—Pictavia (IRE) (Sinndar (IRE))
134 B c 2/3 Cape Cross (IRE)—Reunite (IRE) (Kingmambo (USA))
135 B c 16/3 Dubawi (IRE)—River Pearl (IRE) (Turfkonig (GER))
136 **ROSE AUTHOR**, b c 3/5 Authorized (IRE)—Rosenreihe (IRE) (Catcher In The Rye (IRE)) (43650)
137 B c 5/4 Teofilo (IRE)—Rosia (IRE) (Mr Prospector (USA))
138 B c 15/2 Dubawi (USA)—Russian Society (Darshaan)
139 Ch ro c 15/4 New Approach (IRE)—Summer Sonnet (Baillamont (USA))
140 **TABJEEL**, b c 17/3 Sakhee (USA)—Intishaar (IRE) (Dubai Millennium)
141 B c 6/3 Manduro (GER)—Tanzania (USA) (Darshaan)
142 B c 6/3 Halling (USA)—White Star (IRE) (Darshaan)
143 B c 2/4 Authorized (IRE)—Wood Vine (USA) (Woodman (USA))

45	**MR KEVIN BISHOP, Bridgwater**

Postal: **Barford Park Stables, Spaxton, Bridgwater, Somerset, TA5 1AF**
Contacts: **PHONE/FAX (01278) 671437 MOBILE (07816) 837610**
E-MAIL hevbishop@hotmail.com

1 **BATHWICK BRAVE (IRE)**, 6, b g Westerner—Dorans Grove **H. M. W. Clifford**
2 **BERNARD**, 13, b g Nashwan (USA)—Tabyan (USA) **K. Bishop**
3 **CRUISE IN LUXURY (IRE)**, 8, ch m Definite Article—Galvina (FR) **K. Bishop**
4 **CRUISE IN STYLE (IRE)**, 7, b m Definite Article—Henrietta Street (IRE) **K. Bishop**
5 **FRED THE SHRED (IRE)**, 7, b g Flemensfirth—Smiling Away (IRE) **W. Davies**
6 **JUST SPOT**, 6, ch m Baryshnikov (AUS)—Just Jasmine **K. Bishop**
7 **PERFECT TIMING**, 5, b g Shantou (USA)—Winnetka Gal (IRE) **P. M. Tosh**
8 **QUEENS GROVE**, 7, gr m Baryshnikov (AUS)—Just Jasmine **Mrs E. K. Ellis**
9 **SUMDANCER (NZ)**, 11, b g Summer Suspicion (JPN)—Epic Dancer (NZ) **Mr D. Plowright**
10 **SWAINS MEADOW**, 8, ch m First Trump—Level Headed **Mr S. G. Atkinson**
11 **TARA TAVEY (IRE)**, 8, gr m Kayf Tara—Slieve League (IRE) **K. Bishop**
12 **TARABELA**, 10, b m Kayf Tara—Rocky Revival **G2 Recruitment Solutions Ltd**
13 **TREGONY BRIDGE**, 6, b g Avonbridge—Serotina (IRE) **H. J. W. Davies**

MR KEVIN BISHOP - Continued

14 **WILD GROUND (IRE)**, 12, ch m Simply Great (FR)—Rapid Ground **Jim Kilduff & Ken Jones**
15 **WITHY MILLS**, 8, gr m Baryshnikov (AUS)—Gipsy Rose **Slabs & Lucan**

Other Owners: Mr K. Jones, Mr K. J. Kilduff, C. J. Macey, C. H. Roberts.

Assistant Trainer: Heather Bishop

Conditional: James Best. **Amateur:** Mr Jo Park.

| 46 | **MISS LINDA BLACKFORD, Tiverton**
Postal: **Shortlane Stables, Rackenford, Tiverton, Devon, EX16 8EH**
Contacts: **PHONE (01884) 881589 MOBILE (07887) 947832**
E-MAIL overthelast@talktalk.net WEBSITE www.overthelast.com |

1 **CHANCE ENCOUNTER (IRE)**, 7, b g Anshan—Glittering Grit (IRE) **The Profile Partnership**
2 **FLYING QUEST**, 4, b g Rainbow High—Dinkies Quest **D. J. Cocks**
3 **MOUNTAIN OF MOURNE (IRE)**, 4, ch g Mountain High (IRE)—Katies Native (IRE) **Over De Last Racing**
4 4, B g Mountain High (IRE)—Rachel's Choice (IRE) **Over De Last Racing**
5 **ROMANY QUEST**, 6, b g Nomadic Way (USA)—Dinkies Quest **18 Red Lions Partnership**
6 **ROOFTOP RAINBOW (IRE)**, 9, b g Lord Americo—Rulleena (IRE) **Mrs N. M. Sellman**
7 **SHADES OF AUTUMN (IRE)**, 8, ch g Anshan—Be Right (IRE) **The Profile Partnership**

Other Owners: Miss L. A. Blackford, Mrs Sarah Child, Mr David Cocks, Mr Rob Pitcher, Mr M. J. Vanstone, Mr Terry Wheatley.

Assistant Trainer: M J Vanstone

Jockey (NH): Nick Scholfield, Andrew Glassonbury. **Conditional:** Micheal Nolan. **Amateur:** Mr Joshua Guerriero, Miss L. Tickle.

| 47 | **MR ALAN BLACKMORE, Hertford**
Postal: **'Chasers', Stockings Lane, Little Berkhamsted, Hertford, SG13 8LW**
Contacts: **PHONE (01707) 875060 MOBILE (07803) 711453** |

1 **COOL CHIEF**, 4, b g Sleeping Indian—Be Bop Aloha **A. G. Blackmore**
2 **MONROE PARK (IRE)**, 8, b g Spectrum (IRE)—Paloma Bay (IRE) **A. G. Blackmore**
3 **OCCASIONALLY YOURS (IRE)**, 9, b g Moscow Society (USA)—Kristina's Lady (IRE) **A. G. Blackmore**

Assistant Trainer: Mrs P. M. Blackmore

Jockey (NH): Marc Goldstein. **Amateur:** Miss Emily Crossman.

| 48 | **MR MICHAEL BLAKE, Trowbridge**
Postal: **Staverton Farm, Trowbridge, Wiltshire, BA14 6PE**
Contacts: **PHONE (01225) 782327 MOBILE (07971) 675180**
E-MAIL mblakestavertonfarm@btinternet.com |

1 **ANNELKO**, 6, b g Sulamani (IRE)—Creeking **Mr D. Prosser**
2 **BASLE**, 6, b m Trade Fair—Gibaltarik (IRE) **West Wilts Hockey Lads**
3 **BATHWICK JUNIOR**, 6, b m Reset (AUS)—Bathwick Babe (IRE) **H. M. W. Clifford**
4 **DUNE SHINE**, 8, b g Karinga Bay—Caipirinha (IRE) **Mark Holder Racing Limited**
5 **ELLVISS (IRE)**, 6, ch g Presenting—Bathwick Annie **H. M. W. Clifford**
6 **FIRST MORNING (IRE)**, 8, b g Tamayaz (CAN)—Emily's Pride **Mark Holder Racing Limited**
7 **GORMANSTOWN CUCKOO**, 9, b g King's Theatre—Cloud Cuckoo **Mrs V. A. Butcher**
8 **HASSADIN**, 7, ch g Reset (AUS)—Crocolat **H. M. W. Clifford**
9 **LAMPS**, 6, b g Dynaformer (USA)—Conspiring (USA) **Mrs V. A. Butcher**
10 **MIDNIGHT SEQUEL**, 4, b f Midnight Legend—Silver Sequel **Dajam Ltd**
11 **PACHA D'OUDAIRIES (FR)**, 10, b g Ungaro (GER)—Forlane V (FR) **Mrs J. M. Haines**
12 **ROYAL CHATELIER (FR)**, 8, b g Video Rock (FR)—Attualita (FR) **Mrs V. A. Butcher**
13 **SOVEREIGN SPIRIT (IRE)**, 11, b g Desert Prince (IRE)—Sheer Spirit (IRE) **Mark Holder Racing Limited**

MR MICHAEL BLAKE - Continued

14 **SPORTING BOY (IRE)**, 5, b g Barathea (IRE)—Sportsticketing (IRE) **H. M. W. Clifford**
15 **TORRENTIAL RAINE**, 5, b g Storming Home—La Riveraine (USA) **H. M. W. Clifford**
16 **UMUSTBEJOKING (FR)**, 5, b m Lavirco (GER)—Arika (FR) **Mrs V. A. Butcher**

Other Owners: M. J. Blake, Mrs S. E. Blake.

---

49   MR MICHAEL BLANSHARD, Upper Lambourn
Postal: **Lethornes Stables, Upper Lambourn, Hungerford, Berkshire, RG17 8QP**
Contacts: **PHONE (01488) 71091 FAX (01488) 73497 MOBILE (07785) 370093**
E-MAIL blanshard.racing@btconnect.com WEBSITE www.michaelblanshard.co.uk

1 **BAJAN BEAR**, 5, ch g Compton Place—Bajan Rose **C. McKenna**
2 **BAJAN STORY**, 4, b g Lucky Story (USA)—Bajan Rose
3 **CAROLINGIAN (USA)**, 4, b c Empire Maker (USA)—Shoogle (USA) **Lady E. Mays-Smith**
4 **DISHY GURU**, 4, ch g Ishiguru (USA)—Pick A Nice Name **Clifton Partners**
5 **DOC HILL**, 4, ch g Dr Fong (USA)—Cultural Role **S. Hinton**
6 **MAE CIGAN (FR)**, 10, gr g Medaaly—Concert **A. D. Jones**
7 **PETERSBODEN**, 4, b g Iceman—Bowden Rose **N. C. D. Hall**
8 **POETRY WRITER**, 4, ch g Byron—Away To Me **J. Finch**
9 **SAINT IRENE**, 4, ch f Halling (USA)—Santorini (USA) **The Breeze-in Partnership**
10 **THE COMPOSER**, 11, b g Royal Applause—Superspring **A. D. Jones**

THREE-YEAR-OLDS

11 **FAIR COMMENT**, b f Tamayuz—Cliche (IRE) **J. Oliver & Partners**
12 **IVANHOE**, b c Haafhd—Marysienka **The Lansdowners & N. Price**
13 **KATY SPIRIT (IRE)**, b f Invincible Spirit (IRE)—Katy Guest (IRE) **A. D. Jones**
14 **SPREADING**, b f Ad Valorem (USA)—Churn Dat Butter (USA) **M. T. W. Blanshard**

TWO-YEAR-OLDS

15 Gr f 18/3 Verglas (IRE)—Indaba (IRE) (Indian Ridge) (14000)
16 B f 7/4 Refuse To Bend (IRE)—Island Rapture (Royal Applause) **D. Poole**
17 **KHLOE**, gr f 29/4 Clodovil (IRE)—Owdbetts (IRE) (High Estate) (16000) **J K Racing**
18 B f 13/2 Tiger Hill (IRE)—Lacandona (USA) (Septieme Ciel (USA)) (2500)
19 B c 15/4 Kodiac—River Style (IRE) (Desert Style (IRE)) (5000)
20 B f 7/4 Duke of Marmalade (IRE)—Sandtime (IRE) (Green Desert (USA)) (10000)
21 Gr f 25/4 Sakhee's Secret—Snowing (Tate Gallery (USA)) (3200)
22 **STELLARTA**, b f 7/4 Sakhee's Secret—Torgau (IRE) (Zieten (USA)) (5000) **V. Ward**

Other Owners: Mr J. F. Baldwin, Mr D. Cannings, Mr Philip Chakko, Mr John K. Gale, Mr Brian Mitchell, Mr J. A. Oliver, Mr M. J. Prescott, Mr Nick Price, Mr C. D. Pritchard, Dr Mike Webley, Mr R. T. Wilkins.

---

50   MR J. S. BOLGER, Carlow
Postal: **Glebe House, Coolcullen, Carlow, Ireland**
Contacts: **PHONE (00353) 56 4443150 FAX (00353) 56 4443256**
E-MAIL racing@jsb.ie

1 **AURIFODINA (IRE)**, 4, ch c Dylan Thomas (IRE)—Ovazione **Mrs J S Bolger**
2 **FIONNUAR (IRE)**, 4, b f Teofilo (IRE)—Six Nations (USA) **Mrs J S Bolger**
3 **HEAVY WEIGHT (IRE)**, 4, b c Teofilo (IRE)—Sister Angelina (USA) **Mrs J S Bolger**
4 **LIGHT HEAVY (IRE)**, 4, ch c Teofilo (IRE)—Siamsa (USA) **Mrs J S Bolger**
5 **LONRACH (IRE)**, 4, b f Holy Roman Emperor (IRE)—Luminous One (IRE) **Mrs J S Bolger**
6 **MIRACLE CURE (IRE)**, 4, b c Whipper (USA)—Bring Back Matron (IRE) **Mrs J S Bolger**
7 **MISS EKATERINA (IRE)**, 4, b f Teofilo (IRE)—Najmati **Mrs J S Bolger**
8 **MISS FORDE (IRE)**, 4, gr f Clodovil (IRE)—Right Ted (IRE) **Mrs J S Bolger**
9 **PAENE MAGNUS (IRE)**, 4, ch c Teofilo (IRE)—Luminaria (IRE) **Mrs J S Bolger**
10 **PARISH HALL (IRE)**, 4, b c Teofilo (IRE)—Halla Siamsa (IRE) **Mrs J S Bolger**
11 **SIANSA (IRE)**, 4, b f Teofilo (IRE)—Arjooch (IRE) **Mrs J S Bolger**
12 **SOMETHING GRACEFUL**, 4, ch f Galileo (IRE)—Que Puntual (ARG) **Mrs June Judd**
13 **TIGER AT HEART (IRE)**, 4, ch c Teofilo (IRE)—Julie Girl (USA) **Mrs June Judd**
14 **TWIN FOCUS (IRE)**, 4, b c Galileo (IRE)—Twin Sails (USA) **Mrs J S Bolger**

MR J. S. BOLGER - Continued

THREE-YEAR-OLDS

15 **ALPINIST**, b c New Approach (IRE)—Alouette **Mrs J S Bolger**
16 **BEDECKED (IRE)**, b f Holy Roman Emperor (IRE)—Fainne (IRE) **Mrs J S Bolger**
17 **BEYOND THANKFUL (IRE)**, b c Whipper (USA)—Beyond Compare (IRE) **Mrs J S Bolger**
18 **BUNAIRGEAD (IRE)**, b f New Approach (IRE)—Montecito (USA) **Mrs J S Bolger**
19 **BUNREACHT (USA)**, gr c Mr Greeley (USA)—Unbridled Treasure (USA) **Mrs J S Bolger**
20 **CAESARIA (IRE)**, br c Hannouma (IRE)—Sweet Shop **Sylvian Benillouche**
21 **CHANCE TO DANCE (IRE)**, b c Teofilo (IRE)—Crystal Ballet (USA) **Mrs J S Bolger**
22 **DAWN APPROACH (IRE)**, ch c New Approach (IRE)—
                     Hymn of The Dawn (USA) **Godolphin Management Company Ltd**
23 **DIAMOND SKY (IRE)**, gr f Montjeu (IRE)—Danaskaya (IRE) **Ballylinch Stud**
24 **ERE YESTERDAY (IRE)**, b f Invincible Spirit (IRE)—Heir Today (IRE) **Mrs J S Bolger**
25 **FEILE BRIDE (IRE)**, b f Dylan Thomas (IRE)—Teacht An Earraig (USA) **Mrs J S Bolger**
26 **FEILE NA MBAN (IRE)**, b f New Approach (IRE)—Ard Fheis (IRE) **Mrs J S Bolger**
27 **GLOBAL REACH (IRE)**, ch f Galileo (IRE)—Luminaria (IRE) **Mrs J S Bolger**
28 **GLOVE SMITH (IRE)**, ch c Teofilo (IRE)—Sukeena (IRE) **Mrs J S Bolger**
29 **GOLD BAND (IRE)**, ch c Teofilo (IRE)—Gold Bust **Mrs J S Bolger**
30 **HALLA NA SAOIRE (IRE)**, ch f Teofilo (IRE)—Siamsa (USA) **Mrs J S Bolger**
31 **HUDSON'S BAY (IRE)**, b c Teofilo (IRE)—Cache Creek (IRE) **Sheikh Mohammed**
32 **LEGS ON DISPLAY (IRE)**, b c Duke of Marmalade (IRE)—Elida (IRE) **Mrs J S Bolger**
33 **LEITIR MOR (IRE)**, b f Holy Roman Emperor (IRE)—Christmas Letter (IRE) **Mrs J S Bolger**
34 **LOCH GARMAN (IRE)**, b c Teofilo (IRE)—Irish Question (IRE) **Mrs J S Bolger**
35 **MAC LIR (USA)**, ch c Majestic Warrior (USA)—Saintly Hertfield (USA) **Mrs J S Bolger**
36 **MONTFERRAT (IRE)**, b c Invincible Spirit (IRE)—Alessandria **Sheikh Mohammed**
37 **MORGA (IRE)**, b f Whipper (USA)—Langfuhrina (USA) **Mrs J S Bolger**
38 **MORNING WITH IVAN (IRE)**, b f Ivan Denisovich (IRE)—Grinneas (IRE) **Mrs J S Bolger**
39 **MOVE TO STRIKE (IRE)**, b c Lawman (FR)—Alamanta (IRE) **Mrs J S Bolger**
40 **NEOPHILIA (IRE)**, b f Teofilo (IRE)—Tiffed (USA) **Mrs J S Bolger**
41 **NEW REGALIA (IRE)**, b f New Approach (IRE)—Simonetta (IRE) **Mrs J S Bolger**
42 **NEWS AT SIX (IRE)**, ch c New Approach (IRE)—Dublin Six (USA) **Mrs J Judd**
43 **PACK THE PUNCH (IRE)**, b c Teofilo (IRE)—Zavaleta (IRE) **Mrs J S Bolger**
44 **PERFUME DAYS (IRE)**, b f New Approach (IRE)—Marionnaud (IRE) **Mrs J S Bolger**
45 **RAPID APPROACH (IRE)**, b c New Approach (IRE)—Blas Ceoil (USA) **Mrs J S Bolger**
46 **REHN'S NEST (IRE)**, b f Authorized (IRE)—Solas Na Greine (IRE) **Mrs J S Bolger**
47 **RING CRAFT (IRE)**, b c Teofilo (IRE)—Masnada (IRE) **Mrs J S Bolger**
48 **SCINTILLULA (IRE)**, b f Galileo (IRE)—Scribonia (IRE) **Kirsten Rausing**
49 **SOLAR OUTBURST (IRE)**, ch f Galileo (IRE)—Twin Sails (USA) **Mrs J S Bolger**
50 **SOPHISTICATED HEIR (IRE)**, b c New Approach (IRE)—My Girl Sophie (USA) **Mrs June Judd**
51 **STARLAND (IRE)**, b f Galileo (IRE)—Key To Coolcullen (IRE) **Mrs J S Bolger**
52 **STRAPLESS (IRE)**, b f Whipper (USA)—Bring Back Matron (IRE) **Mrs J S Bolger**
53 **SUN ON THE RUN (IRE)**, b c Whipper (USA)—Gaisce (USA) **Patrick Bolger**
54 **TEOCHRIOS (IRE)**, b f Teofilo (IRE)—Tamra Delight (USA) **Mrs J S Bolger**
55 **TEOIRICIUIL (IRE)**, b f Teofilo (IRE)—National Swagger (IRE) **Mrs J S Bolger**
56 **TEORAINN (IRE)**, b f Teofilo (IRE)—Six Nations (USA) **Mrs J S Bolger**
57 **TEORANTA (IRE)**, b f Teofilo (IRE)—Arjooch (IRE) **Mrs J S Bolger**
58 **TOBANN (IRE)**, b f Teofilo (IRE)—Precipitous (IRE) **Mrs J S Bolger**
59 **TONABROCKY (IRE)**, ch c Pivotal—Abigail Pett **Mrs June Judd**
60 **TRADING LEATHER (IRE)**, b c Teofilo (IRE)—Night Visit **Mrs J S Bolger**
61 **WE'LL GO WALKING (IRE)**, b f Authorized (IRE)—Senora Galilei (IRE) **Mrs J S Bolger**
62 **WEXFORD OPERA (IRE)**, b br c New Approach (IRE)—Sister Angelina (USA) **Mrs J S Bolger**
63 **ZELIE MARTIN (IRE)**, b f Invincible Spirit (IRE)—Saor Sinn (IRE) **Mrs J S Bolger**

TWO-YEAR-OLDS

64 **AERIALIST (IRE)**, ch c 31/1 Sea The Stars (IRE)—Maoineach (USA) (Congaree (USA)) (317460) **Mrs J S Bolger**
65 **AG FOCUS (IRE)**, ch c 4/5 Intense Focus (USA)—Machinale (USA) (Kingmambo (USA)) **Mrs J S Bolger**
66 **AIRGEAD NUA (IRE)**, ch f 3/4 Leroidesanimaux (BRZ)—Azarina (IRE) (Kenmare (FR)) **Mrs J S Bolger**
67 **AMBER GRAIN (IRE)**, b f 11/3 Hurricane Run (IRE)—Star Port (Observatory (USA)) (31745) **Mrs J S Bolger**
68 **ARDMORE (IRE)**, b c 18/3 Whipper (USA)—Ard Fheis (IRE) (Lil's Boy (USA)) **Mrs J S Bolger**
69 **AUSTERE APPROACH (IRE)**, ch c 6/3 New Approach (IRE)—Ovazione (Seeking The Gold (USA)) **Mrs J S Bolger**
70 **BEYOND INTENSITY (IRE)**, ch f 27/3 Intense Focus (USA)—
                     Beyond Compare (IRE) (Galileo (IRE)) **Mrs J S Bolger**
71 **BRU MOR (IRE)**, ch f 14/4 Intense Focus (USA)—Aeraiocht (IRE) (Tenby) (4364) **Mrs J S Bolger**
72 **CEISTEACH (IRE)**, ch f 20/1 New Approach (IRE)—Ceist Eile (IRE) (Noverre (USA)) **Mrs J S Bolger**
73 **CENTRE OF INTEREST (USA)**, ch c 29/4 Leroidesanimaux (BRZ)—
                     Saintly Hertfield (USA) (Saint Ballado (CAN)) **Mrs J S Bolger**

MR J. S. BOLGER - Continued

74 **CEOL COIS TINE (IRE)**, b f 8/4 Teofilo (IRE)—Arjooch (IRE) (Marju (IRE)) **Mrs J S Bolger**
75 **CLUB WEXFORD (IRE)**, b c 23/5 Lawman (FR)—Masnada (IRE) (Erins Isle) **Mrs J S Bolger**
76 **CORRECT APPROACH (IRE)**, ch c 17/1 New Approach (IRE)—
                              Gleigeal (USA) (Mr Greeley (USA)) (95238) **Mrs J S Bolger**
77 **COUNTY WEXFORD (IRE)**, b c 3/2 Teofilo (IRE)—Tiffed (USA) (Seattle Slew (USA)) (59523) **Mrs J S Bolger**
78 **CRAIC AGUS SPRAOI (IRE)**, b f 9/5 Intense Focus (USA)—
                              Halla Siamsa (IRE) (Montjeu (IRE)) (238095) **Mrs J S Bolger**
79 **CROI NA FEILE (USA)**, b f 17/3 Perfect Soul (IRE)—Regally Bred (USA) (A P Indy (USA)) (6144) **Mrs J S Bolger**
80 **DOUBLE FOCUS (IRE)**, ch f 7/2 Intense Focus (USA)—Grinneas (IRE) (Barathea (IRE)) **Mrs J S Bolger**
81 B c 27/2 Authorized (IRE)—Dublino (USA) (Lear Fan (USA)) **Sheikh Mohammed**
82 **DUSHLAN (IRE)**, ch f 12/1 New Approach (IRE)—Duaisbhanna (IRE) (Rock of Gibraltar (IRE)) **Mrs J S Bolger**
83 **EVASON**, b c 21/3 Galileo (IRE)—Soneva (USA) (Cherokee Run (USA)) (238095) **Claudia Jungo**
84 **FISCAL FOCUS (IRE)**, b c 16/5 Intense Focus (USA)—Elida (IRE) (Royal Academy (USA)) **Mrs J S Bolger**
85 **FOCAS MOR (IRE)**, ch f 13/4 Intense Focus (USA)—
                              Intriguing Humor (CAN) (Distorted Humor (USA)) **Mrs J S Bolger**
86 **FOCUS ON VENICE (IRE)**, b c 1/2 Intense Focus (USA)—Marina of Venice (IRE) (Galileo (IRE)) **Mrs June Judd**
87 **FOCUSSED (IRE)**, b c 4/5 Intense Focus (USA)—Tus Maith (IRE) (Entrepreneur) (8729) **Mrs J S Bolger**
88 **FREEDOM SQUARE (IRE)**, b c 30/3 Lawman (FR)—Manger Square (IRE) (Danehill (USA)) **Mrs J S Bolger**
89 **FURASTA (USA)**, b f 6/4 Leroidesanimaux (BRZ)—Easy Now (USA) (Danzig (USA)) **Mrs J S Bolger**
90 **GOLD FOCUS (IRE)**, ch f 21/4 Intense Focus (USA)—Gold Bust (Nashwan (USA)) **Mrs J S Bolger**
91 **GREANTA (IRE)**, b f 3/2 Intense Focus (USA)—
                              Greannmhar (USA) (Distorted Humor (USA)) (7142) **Mrs J S Bolger**
92 **HEART FOCUS (IRE)**, b f 12/2 Intense Focus (USA)—
                              Have A Heart (IRE) (Daggers Drawn (USA)) (23809) **Mrs J S Bolger**
93 **HIGH FOCUS (IRE)**, b f 30/5 Intense Focus (USA)—High Stool Lady (USA) (Distant View (USA)) **Mrs J S Bolger**
94 **HOME SCHOOL (IRE)**, b c 6/3 Intense Focus (USA)—Lavender Blue (Galileo (IRE)) **Mrs J S Bolger**
95 **INTENSE DEBATE (IRE)**, b f 5/5 Intense Focus (USA)—Bronntanas (IRE) (Spectrum (IRE)) **Mrs J S Bolger**
96 **INTENSE LIGHT (IRE)**, ch f 30/3 Intense Focus (USA)—Tintreach (CAN) (Vindication (USA)) **Mrs J S Bolger**
97 **INTENSICAL (IRE)**, b c 19/2 Intense Focus (USA)—Christmas Letter (IRE) (Galileo (IRE)) (43650) **Mrs J S Bolger**
98 **INTENSIFIED (IRE)**, b br c 16/1 Intense Focus (USA)—
                              Sway Me Now (USA) (Speightstown (USA)) **Mrs J S Bolger**
99 **IONSAI NUA (IRE)**, b c 25/1 New Approach (IRE)—
                              Toirneach (USA) (Thunder Gulch (USA)) (63491) **Mrs J S Bolger**
100 **LE CHEILE (IRE)**, b f 25/4 Intense Focus (USA)—Faoileoir (USA) (Dehere (USA)) **Mrs J S Bolger**
101 **LEAFY SUBURB (IRE)**, ch f 25/4 Intense Focus (USA)—Dublin Six (USA) (Kingmambo (USA)) **Mrs June Judd**
102 B c 12/3 Intense Focus (USA)—Luminous One (IRE) (Galileo (IRE)) **Mrs J S Bolger**
103 **MAN OF CONQUEST (IRE)**, b c 17/5 Teofilo (IRE)—My Girl Sophie (USA) (Danzig (USA)) **Mrs June Judd**
104 **MANDATARIO**, b c 29/4 Manduro (GER)—Crystal Mountain (USA) (Monashee Mountain (USA)) **Mrs June Judd**
105 B c 15/4 New Approach (IRE)—Marion (IRE) (Doyoun) (83333) **Mrs J S Bolger**
106 Ch c 16/3 New Approach (IRE)—Miss Marvellous (USA) (Diesis) (110000) **Sheikh Mohammed**
107 **MUILEATA (IRE)**, b f 13/4 Diamond Green (FR)—Buiochas Mor (USA) (Mr Greeley (USA)) **Mrs J S Bolger**
108 **MUININ (IRE)**, ch f 10/5 Teofilo (IRE)—Vasanta (IRE) (Indian Ridge) **Mrs J S Bolger**
109 **NEWS FOCUS (IRE)**, b c 22/3 Intense Focus (USA)—Derpat (IRE) (Invincible Spirit (IRE)) **Mrs J S Bolger**
110 **NOVEL APPROACH (IRE)**, b f 9/2 New Approach (IRE)—Altarejos (IRE) (Vettori (IRE)) **Mrs J S Bolger**
111 **PLAMAS (IRE)**, b f 27/3 Teofilo (IRE)—Danemarque (AUS) (Danehill (USA)) **Mrs J S Bolger**
112 **PRINTHA (IRE)**, ch f 25/4 New Approach (IRE)—Scarpetta (USA) (Seattle Dancer (USA)) **Mrs J S Bolger**
113 **PRUDENT APPROACH (IRE)**, b f 1/5 New Approach (IRE)—
                              Hymn of The Dawn (USA) (Phone Trick (USA)) (615079) **Mr Paddy Spain**
114 **PUNCH BAG (IRE)**, ch c 14/5 Teofilo (IRE)—Heir Today (USA) (Princely Heir (IRE)) **Mrs J S Bolger**
115 Ch c 30/4 Teofilo (IRE)—Raghida (IRE) (Nordico (USA)) **James Hanly**
116 **RING CHIEF (IRE)**, ch c 26/3 Teofilo (IRE)—Tamra Delight (USA) (Diesis) **Mrs J S Bolger**
117 **RING SPEED (IRE)**, b c 18/3 Teofilo (IRE)—Julie Girl (USA) (Jules (USA)) **Mrs J S Bolger**
118 **ROCK FOCUS (IRE)**, br c 15/3 Intense Focus (USA)—
                              Nancy Rock (IRE) (Rock of Gibraltar (IRE)) (12698) **Mrs J S Bolger**
119 **ROYAL FOCUS (IRE)**, b c 30/4 Intense Focus (USA)—
                              Groves Royal (USA) (Royal Academy (USA)) **Mrs J S Bolger**
120 **SAR OICHE (IRE)**, b f 21/4 Teofilo (IRE)—Zavaleta (IRE) (Kahyasi) **Mrs J S Bolger**
121 B c 24/1 Cape Cross (IRE)—Scatina (USA) (Samum (GER)) **Sheikh Mohammed**
122 **SOILSE AN LAE (USA)**, b f 16/3 Leroidesanimaux (BRZ)—Wild Heaven (IRE) (Darshaan) **Mrs J S Bolger**
123 **SOLAR FOCUS (IRE)**, b c 15/5 Intense Focus (USA)—Saor Sinn (IRE) (Galileo (IRE)) **Mrs J S Bolger**
124 B c 3/5 Intense Focus (USA)—Solas Na Greine (IRE) (Galileo (IRE)) **Mrs J S Bolger**
125 **SPARANAI (USA)**, ch f 14/3 Leroidesanimaux (BRZ)—
                              Unbridled Treasure (USA) (Unbridled's Song (USA)) **Mrs J S Bolger**
126 **SPRING FOCUS (IRE)**, b c 22/4 Intense Focus (USA)—Teacht An Earraig (USA) (Galileo (IRE)) **Mrs J S Bolger**
127 **STIRABOUT (USA)**, b c 1/5 Leroidesanimaux (BRZ)—Fardus (IRE) (Danehill (USA)) **Mrs J S Bolger**

MR J. S. BOLGER - Continued

128 **SUNDARA (IRE)**, b c 25/4 Galileo (IRE)—Saoire (Pivotal) **Mrs Marguerite Joyce**
129 **TEOLEENA (IRE)**, b f 30/5 Teofilo (IRE)—Darina (IRE) (Danehill (USA)) **Mrs J S Bolger**
130 **THEOPHILUS (IRE)**, b c 22/4 Teofilo (IRE)—Simonetta (IRE) (Lil's Boy (USA)) **Mrs J S Bolger**
131 B c 8/2 Montjeu (IRE)—Thinking Positive (Rainbow Quest (USA)) (240000) **Mrs J S Bolger**
132 **TIRGHRA (IRE)**, b f 25/5 Teofilo (IRE)—National Swagger (IRE) (Giant's Causeway (USA)) **Mrs J S Bolger**
133 **UPPER SILESIAN (IRE)**, b f 19/3 Lawman (FR)—Silesian (IRE) (Singspiel (IRE)) (23809) **Mrs J S Bolger**
134 **VERY INTENSE (IRE)**, b c 9/4 Intense Focus (USA)—Astralai (IRE) (Galileo (IRE)) **Mrs J S Bolger**
135 B f 1/4 Intense Focus (USA)—Voronova (IRE) (Sadler's Wells (USA)) **Mrs J S Bolger**
136 **WEXFORD TOWN (IRE)**, b c 27/3 Teofilo (IRE)—Night Visit (Sinndar (IRE)) **Mrs J S Bolger**

Other Owners: Mr John Corcoran, Ms Kirsten Rausing.

Jockey (flat): R. P. Cleary, K.J. Manning. **Apprentice:** Ben Dawson, Killian Hennessy, Daniel Redmond, Dylan Robinson,
R P Whelan.

---

51 MRS MYRIAM BOLLACK-BADEL, Lamorlaye
Postal: **20 Rue Blanche, 60260 Lamorlaye, France**
Contacts: **(0033) 9774 89044 FAX (0033) 3442 13367 MOBILE (0033) 6108 09347**
E-MAIL myriam.bollack@gmail.com WEBSITE www.myriam-bollack.com

1 **ABSENT MINDED**, 4, b f Medicean—Divergence (USA) **Mrs Niederhauser**
2 **AVIATOR (FR)**, 4, b c Motivator—Summer Wave (IRE) **Mr Forgeard**
3 **HESIONE (FR)**, 4, gr f Aussie Rules (USA)—Hortanse (FR) **Mr Cecil Motschmann**
4 **KANOTIER (FR)**, 5, b h Daliapour (IRE)—Knout (FR) **Mrs Francoise de Chatelperron**
5 **KATHERINE DEUX (FR)**, 4, b f Poliglote—Knout (FR) **Mrs Francoise de Chatelperron**
6 **LONG JOHN SILVER (FR)**, 8, b g Marchand de Sable (USA)—Lune Et L'autre **Mme Myriam Bollack-Badel**
7 **NORSE KING (FR)**, 4, ch c Norse Dancer (IRE)—Angel Wing **Mr J. C. Smith**
8 **OH OH (FR)**, 6, b m Vettori (IRE)—Anna Francesca (FR) **Mrs Francoise de Chatelperron**
9 **ZEMIRO (FR)**, 5, b h Daliapour (IRE)—Zython (FR) **Scuderia Mirabella**
10 **ZIMRI (FR)**, 9, b g Take Risks (FR)—Zayine (IRE) **Mme Myriam Bollack-Badel**

THREE-YEAR-OLDS

11 **CANDY BUBBLE (FR)**, b f American Post—Hay Amor (ARG) **Scuderia Mirabella**
12 **CINDER'S POST (FR)**, b f American Post—Cinders' Prize **Mr J. C. Smith**
13 **KUKURUN (FR)**, b c Kouroun (FR)—Knout (FR) **Mrs Francoise de Chatelperron**
14 **SEMPRE MEDICI (FR)**, b c Medicean—Sambala (IRE) **Mr Forgeard**
15 **SINNDERELLE (FR)**, b f Sinndar (IRE)—Summer Wave (IRE) **Mr Gilibert**
16 **SLICE OF LIFE (FR)**, b f Nombre Premier—Cortiguera **Mr A. Pinot**
17 **SOLE REIGN (FR)**, b f Desert Style (IRE)—Hokey Pokey (FR) **Mr Cecil Motschmann**
18 **WINGLAND (FR)**, b f Lando (GER)—Angel Wing **Mr J. C. Smith**
19 **ZAAFRAN (FR)**, b f Medecis—Zython (FR) **Scuderia Mirabella**

TWO-YEAR-OLDS

20 **ANGELIC NEWS (FR)**, b f 6/3 American Post—Angel Wing (Barathea (IRE)) **Mr J. C. Smith**
21 **GREEN SPEED (FR)**, ch f 9/2 Green Tune (USA)—Speed of Sound (Zafonic (USA)) **Mr J. C. Smith**
22 **HARLOW (FR)**, b c 2/4 Lando (GER)—Hokey Pokey (FR) (Lead On Time (USA)) **Mr Cecil Motschmann**
23 B f 16/4 Manduro (GER)—King's Folly (FR) (King's Best (USA)) **Mr Cecil Motschmann**
24 B c 1/4 Aussie Rules (USA)—Mary Linda (Grand Lodge (USA)) **Mr J. C. Smith**
25 **MON ADJUDANT (FR)**, b c 30/4 My Risk (FR)—Adjuvence (FR) (Kahyasi) **Scuderia Mirabella**
26 **MOREL FORENTINO (FR)**, ch c 14/4 Vespone (IRE)—
                                  Hay Amor (ARG) (Candy Stripes (USA)) **Scuderia Mirabella**
27 **MY VALLEY (FR)**, b f 30/3 My Risk (FR)—Squadra Valley (FR) (Orpen (USA)) **Henri D'Aillieres**
28 **NORSE PRIZE (FR)**, ch c 21/2 Norse Dancer (IRE)—Cinders' Prize (Sinndar (IRE)) **Mr J. C. Smith**
29 **NORSE WAVE (FR)**, b f 24/2 Norse Dancer (IRE)—Wave Goodbye (Linamix (FR)) **Mr J. C. Smith**
30 **OWLAM**, b f 7/4 Astronomer Royal (USA)—
                                  October Winds (USA) (Irish River (FR)) (15873) **Mme Myriam Bollack-Badel**
31 **ZYGMUNT (FR)**, ch c 19/4 Vespone (IRE)—Zython (FR) (Kabool) **Mme Myriam Bollack-Badel**

Assistant Trainer: Alain Badel

52 MR MARTIN BOSLEY, Chalfont St Giles

Postal: **Bowstridge Farm, Bowstridge Lane, Chalfont St. Giles, Buckinghamshire, HP8 4RF**
Contacts: **PHONE (01494) 875533 FAX (01494) 875533 MOBILE (07778) 938040**
E-MAIL martin@martinbosley.com WEBSITE www.martinbosleyracing.com

1 ALFRESCO, 9, b g Mtoto—Maureena (IRE) **Mrs A. M. Riney**
2 ARACHNOPHOBIA (IRE), 7, b g Redback—La Mata (IRE)
3 BELLINDA, 4, b f Aussie Rules (USA)—Bonnie Belle **Mrs E. Morris**
4 BOB'S LEGEND (IRE), 7, b g Bob's Return (IRE)—Pepsi Starlet (IRE) **K. Quinn/ C. Benham/ I. Saunders**
5 BURNT CREAM, 6, b m Exceed And Excel (AUS)—Basbousate Nadia **Mrs P. M. Brown**
6 CAROBELLO (IRE), 6, b g Luso—Vic's Queen (IRE)
7 DRUSSELL (IRE), 7, b g Orpen (USA)—Cahermee Queen (USA) **Walid & Paula Marzouk**
8 GILES DREAM (IRE), 6, ch g Fahris (IRE)—Kit Kat Kate (IRE) **J. Carey**
9 LISSELTON CROSS, 5, ch g Compton Place—Sweet Myrtle (USA) **Mrs J. M. O'Connor**
10 LITTLE OSCAR (IRE), 6, b m Oscar (IRE)—Legendsofthefall (IRE) **J. Carey**
11 MASTER MYLO (IRE), 6, ch g Bertolini (USA)—Sheboygan (IRE) **K. Quinn/ C. Benham/ I. Saunders**
12 NOTNOWIVORHEADACHE, 4, b f Notnowcato—Inchcoonan **The Attwood-Coggon-Edwards-Neville**
13 ROMAN SENATE (IRE), 4, b g Holy Roman Emperor (IRE)—Indian Fun **Solario Racing (Chalfont)**
14 SPACEMAN, 10, b g In The Wings—Souk (IRE) **J. Carey**
15 THOMAS THE RHYMER (IRE), 5, b g City Honours (USA)—African Keys (IRE)
16 TOPTHORN, 7, gr g Silver Patriarch (IRE)—Miss Traxdata **Stephenson - Vollaro - Clark - Bosley**

THREE-YEAR-OLDS

17 CHILTERN SECRET, ch f Sakhee's Secret—Regal Curtsy **Solario Racing (Latimer)**
18 GUNNING FOR GLORY, b g Indesatchel (IRE)—Today's The Day **Solario Racing (Amersham)**

TWO-YEAR-OLDS

19 B f 8/4 Amadeus Wolf—Divine Quest (Kris) (5714)

Other Owners: Mr T. Attwood, Mr C. F. Benham, G. F. Clark, Mr S. J. Coggon, Mr S. K. I. Double, Mr M. G. Edwards, Mr I. Herbert, Mr W. Marzouk, Mrs P. Marzouk, Mr J. R. Neville, K. J. Quinn, Mr I. N. Saunders, I. H. Stephenson, Ms Lucy Vollaro.

Jockey (flat): George Baker, Martin Lane, Luke Morris. **Amateur:** Mr Zac Baker.

53 MR MARCO BOTTI, Newmarket

Postal: **Prestige Place, Snailwell Road, Newmarket, Suffolk, CB8**
Contacts: **PHONE (01638) 662416 FAX (01638) 662417 MOBILE (07775) 803007**
E-MAIL office@marcobotti.co.uk WEBSITE www.marcobotti.co.uk

1 BE PERFECT (USA), 4, b c Street Cry (IRE)—Binya (GER) **Sheikh Mohammed Bin Khalifa Al Maktoum**
2 CALIFORNIA ENGLISH (IRE), 4, b g Oasis Dream—Muwali (USA) **California English Partnership**
3 CANARY WHARF (IRE), 4, b c Danehill Dancer (IRE)—Wedding Morn (IRE) **Mr G. Manfredini & Mr J. Allison**
4 CEREMONIAL JADE (UAE), 10, b g Jade Robbery (USA)—Talah **G. Manfredini**
5 CRACKERJACK KING (IRE), 5, gr ro h Shamardal (USA)—
                                     Claba di San Jore (IRE) **Effevi & Australian T'Bred Bloodstock**
6 DE RIGUEUR, 5, b g Montjeu (IRE)—Exclusive **Mr K. J. P. Gundlach**
7 FANUNALTER, 7, b g Falbrav (IRE)—Step Danzer (IRE) **Mr A. Al Kathiri**
8 FATTSOTA, 5, b g Oasis Dream—Gift of The Night (USA) **Scuderia Rencati Srl**
9 FOUR LEAVES (IRE), 4, ch f Singspiel (IRE)—
                                     My Heart's Deelite (USA) **HE Sheikh Sultan Bin Khalifa Al Nahyan**
10 GOLDEN SHARE (USA), 4, b br c Medaglia d'oro (USA)—Siempre Asi (USA) **Cuderia Africa**
11 GREY MIRAGE, 4, b g Oasis Dream—Grey Way (USA) **Scuderia Vittadini SRL 1**
12 GUEST OF HONOUR (IRE), 4, b c Cape Cross (IRE)—Risera (IRE) **Mr G. Manfredini**
13 HAFTOHAF, 4, b c Haafhd—Piper's Ash (USA) **Miss C. Loder**
14 JAKKALBERRY (IRE), 7, b h Storming Home—Claba di San Jore (IRE) **ATB Jakkalberry Sy, Porter & Duke**
15 KINGSDESIRE (IRE), 4, b g King's Best (USA)—Lucky Clio (IRE) **G. Manfredini**
16 MEZZOTINT (IRE), 4, b c Diamond Green (FR)—Aquatint **Mrs L. Botti**
17 PLANTEUR (IRE), 6, b h Danehill Dancer (IRE)—Plante Rare (IRE) **Mr M. A. M. Albousi Alghufli**
18 SOLAR DEITY (IRE), 4, b c Exceed And Excel (AUS)—Dawn Raid (IRE) **Mr G. Manfredini & Mr A. Tinkler**
19 SPANISH WEDDING, 4, ch g Hernando (FR)—I Do **K. A. Dasmal**
20 SPIFER (IRE), 5, gr g Motivator—Zarawa (IRE) **Op Center One**
21 SUEGIOO (FR), 4, ch c Manduro (GER)—Mantesera (IRE) **Scuderia Rencati Srl**

MR MARCO BOTTI - Continued

22 **THEREABOUTS (USA)**, 4, b g Singspiel (IRE)—Around **G. Manfredini**
23 **WHAILEYY (IRE)**, 5, b g Holy Roman Emperor (IRE)—Alshoowg (USA) **Saleh Al Homaizi & Imad Al Sagar**

THREE-YEAR-OLDS

24 **AL EMIRATI (IRE)**, b c Tamayuz—Corrine (IRE) **Mr A. A. Al Shaikh**
25 **AL GHARRAFA**, b f Dutch Art—Smart Ass (IRE) **Mr A. N. Mubarak**
26 **ARAMAM**, ch f Kyllachy—Triple Sharp **Saleh Al Homaizi & Imad Al Sagar**
27 **AUTRISK (IRE)**, b c Authorized (IRE)—Maid To Order (IRE) **G. Manfredini**
28 **AUTSPREAD**, b c Authorized (IRE)—Ridotto **G. Manfredini**
29 **AVATAR STAR (IRE)**, b c Peintre Celebre (USA)—Homegrown (IRE) **Mr K. J. P. Gundlach**
30 **BELLITUDO (IRE)**, ch f Shamardal (USA)—Night Life (IRE) **Mr M. A. M. Albousi Alghufli**
31 **BRAVO YOUMZAIN (IRE)**, b c Invincible Spirit (IRE)—Grizel **J. Abdullah**
32 **CAMACHOICE (IRE)**, b c Camacho—Nouvelle Reve (GER) **G. Manfredini**
33 **CHEEKTOCHEEK (IRE)**, b g Chineur (FR)—Diamond Soles (IRE) **G. Manfredini**
34 **FATHER AND SON (IRE)**, b c Duke of Marmalade (IRE)—Slap Shot (USA) **Op Center One**
35 **FIRST SARGEANT**, gr c Dutch Art—Princess Raya **Rothmere Racing Limited**
36 **GIOIA DI VITA**, b c Sakhee (USA)—Dhuyoof (IRE) **Mrs L. Botti**
37 **GLORY CITY (IRE)**, b c Azamour (IRE)—Zara's Birthday (IRE) **Mr F. L. Li**
38 **GRENDISAR (IRE)**, b c Invincible Spirit (IRE)—Remarkable Story **Mr M. A. M. Albousi Alghufli**
39 **GROOVE ON (IRE)**, ch c Iffraaj—Dance On **Mrs L. Botti**
40 **HASOPOP (IRE)**, b c Haatef (USA)—Convenience (IRE) **G. Manfredini**
41 **HOLY WARRIOR (IRE)**, b c Holy Roman Emperor (IRE)—
                                         If Dubai (USA) **Mr Clive Washbourn & Mr Chris McHale**
42 **KATTAF (IRE)**, ch c Hernando (FR)—Decision Maid (USA) **Mr A. N. Mubarak**
43 **MAGIC TREND (IRE)**, b f Henrythenavigator (USA)—Leopoldine **Mr J. Allison & Mr R. Grossman**
44 **MAGICAL KINGDOM (IRE)**, b c Danehill Dancer (IRE)—
                                         Al Saqiya (USA) **Mr M. Tabor, Mrs J. Magnier & Mr D. Smith**
45 **MAGIKA**, b f Dubawi (IRE)—Aline's Wings (ITY) **Marco & Sara Moretti & Partner**
46 **MAKIN (IRE)**, b c Shirocco (GER)—Cuca Vela (USA) **Mr A. N. Mubarak**
47 **MAXIMITO**, b c Motivator—Lorien Hill (IRE) **Mr M. A. M. Albousi Alghufli**
48 **MESMERIZED (IRE)**, b f Duke of Marmalade (IRE)—Margot **Immobiliare Casa Paola SRL**
49 **MOOHAAJIM (IRE)**, b c Cape Cross (IRE)—Thiella (USA) **Sheikh Mohammed Bin Khalifa Al Maktoum**
50 **OPUS CACTUS (USA)**, b f Johannesburg (USA)—Momix **Scuderia Vittadini SRL**
51 **REDBATTLE (IRE)**, b c Redback—Florida City (IRE) **G. Manfredini**
52 **REVISE (IRE)**, b c Dansili—Niner's Home (USA) **HE Sheikh Sultan Bin Khalifa Al Nahyan**
53 **RHYOLITE (IRE)**, b c Rock of Gibraltar (IRE)—Ghenwah (FR) **HE Sheikh Sultan Bin Khalifa Al Nahyan**
54 **SALFORD EXCEL**, b f Exceed And Excel (AUS)—Steeple **A. J. Thompson**
55 **SAND GROUSE**, b f Mr Greeley (USA)—Gentle On My Mind (IRE) **Prince A. A. Faisal**
56 **SECRET SESSION (USA)**, b c Mizzen Mast (USA)—Lynnwood Chase (USA) **Mr K. J. P. Gundlach**
57 **SEDENOO**, b g Cape Cross (IRE)—Eternity Ring **Scuderia Rencati Srl**
58 **SEMAI (IRE)**, gr c Exceed And Excel (AUS)—Mango Lady **Scuderia Rencati Srl**
59 **SHALWA**, ch f Galileo (IRE)—Kite Mark **Sheikh Mohammed Bin Khalifa Al Maktoum**
60 **SHOCKINGDANCER (IRE)**, b c Danehill Dancer (IRE)—Jalys (IRE) **La Tesa SPA**
61 **SPEED BOOGIE**, b c Oasis Dream—Wickwing **La Tesa SPA**
62 **SPICY (IRE)**, ch f Footstepsinthesand—Shivaree **Miss Y. M. G. Jacques**
63 **SUMMER DREAM (IRE)**, b f Oasis Dream—Star On Stage **Niarchos Family**
64 **SURENESS (IRE)**, ch f Hurricane Run (IRE)—Silk Dress (IRE) **Mr A. M. Cati**
65 **SWEET FORCE (IRE)**, b c Beat Hollow—Sweet Power **Dachel Stud**
66 **TEOPHILIP (IRE)**, b br c Teofilo (IRE)—Triomphale (USA) **G. Manfredini**
67 **TIGER DAY**, b c Tiger Hill (IRE)—Diamond Day
68 **TOP SET (IRE)**, ch c Tamayuz—Pray (IRE) **K. A. Dasmal**
69 **WAKEUP LITTLE SUZY (IRE)**, ch f Peintre Celebre (USA)—Maramba (USA) **P. Newton**
70 **WHIPPY CREAM (IRE)**, b f Dansili—Diavla (USA) **La Tesa SPA**
71 **YELLOW MOUNTAIN (IRE)**, b c Danehill Dancer (IRE)—
                                         Singing Diva (IRE) **Mrs J. Magnier, Mr D. Smith & Mr M. Tabor**

TWO-YEAR-OLDS

72 **ABSOLUTE (IRE)**, b c 30/1 Danehill Dancer (IRE)—
                Beyond Belief (IRE) (Sadler's Wells (USA)) (59523) **Highclere Thoroughbred Racing - Brunel**
73 **AL ZAMAN THAMAN (FR)**, b c 5/2 Nayef (USA)—Angie Eria (FR) (Galileo (IRE)) **Jaber Abdullah**
74 **ALEXANOR (IRE)**, b c 1/5 Pivotal—Butterfly Cove (USA) (Storm Cat (USA)) (45000) **Op Centre**
75 B f 26/3 Cape Cross—Anna Pallida (Sadler's Wells (USA)) **Sheikh Mohammed Bin Khalifa Al Maktoum**
76 B c 7/2 Oasis Dream—
                Beach Bunny (IRE) (High Chaparral (IRE)) (425000) **Sheikh Mohammed Bin Khalifa Al Maktoum**
77 **BURSTINGROCK (IRE)**, ch g 27/2 Rock of Gibraltar (IRE)—Second Burst (IRE) (Sadler's Wells (USA)) (11000)

MR MARCO BOTTI - Continued

78 B c 23/3 Exceed And Excel (AUS)—Emirates Hills (Dubawi (IRE)) (34920)
79 B br c 26/4 Soldier of Fortune (IRE)—Far Across (Common Grounds) (4761) **Niarchos Family**
80 Ch f 15/2 Shamardal (USA)—Fragrancy (IRE) (Singspiel (IRE)) (52000)
81 B c 8/1 Azamour (IRE)—Ghenwah (FR) (Selkirk (USA)) **Sheikh Mohammed Bin Khalifa Al Maktoum**
82 LATIN CHARM (IRE), b c 31/3 Cape Cross (IRE)—Di Moi Oui (Warning) (47619) **Grundy Bloodstock**
83 LIGHTNING SHOWER (USA), b c 15/4 Mr Greeley (USA)—
                                            Lightning Show (USA) (Storm Cat (USA)) (19000) **Mr J. Allison**
84 NABATEO, ch c 27/2 Sea The Stars (IRE)—
                                            Rosa Del Dubai (Dubai Destination (USA)) (198412) **Scuderia Rencati Srl**
85 ROSE KAZAN (IRE), ch f 23/3 Teofilo (IRE)—Zahour Al Yasmeen (Cadeaux Genereux) **Jaber Abdullah**
86 B f 8/3 New Approach (IRE)—
                                            Rouge Noir (USA) (Saint Ballado (CAN)) (126983) **Sheikh Mohammed Bin Khalifa Al Maktoum**
87 SAYED YOUMZAIN, b c 10/4 Dalakhani (IRE)—Silver Touch (IRE) (Dansili) **Jaber Abdullah**
88 B c 7/2 Amadeus Wolf—Secret Justice (USA) (Lit de Justice (USA)) (20000) **Sultan Ali**
89 Br c 27/5 Sea The Stars (IRE)—
                                            Silent Heir (USA) (Sunday Silence (USA)) **Sheikh Mohammed Bin Khalifa Al Maktoum**
90 SMAGETA, b f 3/3 Shirocco (GER)—Sensibility (Halling (USA)) (28571) **Scuderia Rencati Srl**
91 Gr ro c 7/4 Mastercraftsman (IRE)—Sparkle of Stones (FR) (Sadler's Wells (USA)) (87300) **Coolmore**
92 SUFRANEL (IRE), b c 1/5 Galileo (IRE)—Noelani (Indian Ridge) (95000) **Scuderia Rencati Srl**
93 B c 7/4 Cape Cross (IRE)—Trick Or Treat (Lomitas) (100000) **Sheikh Mohammed Bin Khalifa Al Maktoum**

Other Owners: Mr Imad Al-Sagar, Mr K. Albahou, Mr Jonny Allison, Mr Joseph Barton, Mr L. Biffi, Mrs Lucie Botti, Mr E. Bulgheroni, Mr D. P. Dance, Mr Sean Edward Duke, Effevi Snc Di Villa Felice & Co, Mr S. Gereaux, Mr G. Gereaux, Mr Richard Grossman, Mr Saleh Al Homaizi, Mr Mick Johnston, Mr Khalid Khalifa Al Nabooda, Mr O. H. Kingsley, Mrs John Magnier, Mr Giuliano Manfredini, Mr Chris McHale, Mr I. Montone, Mr Marco Moretti, Mrs S. P. E. Moretti, Mrs Rosalynd Norman, Mr Tim Porter, Scuderia Vittadini SRL, Mrs F. Shaw, Mr Derrick Smith, Mr M. Stein, Mr M. Tabor, Mr Andrew Tinkler, Mr Patrizio Urbanelli, Mr Clive Washbourn.

Assistant Trainer: Lucie Botti

Apprentice: Toby Atkinson.

---

54 | **MR PETER BOWEN, Haverfordwest**
Postal: Yet-Y-Rhug, Letterston, Haverfordwest, Pembrokeshire, SA62 5TB
Contacts: PHONE (01348) 840486 FAX (01348) 840486 MOBILE (07811) 111234
E-MAIL info@peterbowenracing.com WEBSITE www.peterbowenracing.com

1 ALWAYS WAINING (IRE), 12, b g Unfuwain (USA)—Glenarff (USA) **Mr & Mrs P. J. Douglas**
2 AWAYWITHTHEGREYS (IRE), 6, gr g Whipper (USA)—Silver Sash (USA) **W. Bryan**
3 BALLYBOUGH GORTA (IRE), 6, b g Indian Danehill (IRE)—Eyelet (IRE) **Yeh Man Partnership**
4 BALLYVESEY (IRE), 8, ch g Anshan—Bridgequarter Lady (IRE) **Roddy Owen & Paul Fullagar**
5 BEREA COURT (IRE), 6, ch g Pierre—Tournore Court (IRE) **Mr A. J. R. Hart**
6 BIG TIME BILLY (IRE), 7, b m Definite Article—Zaratu (IRE) **Miss R. L. Bryan**
7 BUACHAILL ALAINN (IRE), 6, b g Oscar—Bottle A Knock (IRE) **Roddy Owen & Paul Fullagar**
8 CATCH THE FIRE, 5, b g Motivator—Salinova (FR) **Roddy Owen & Paul Fullagar**
9 CORSO PALLADIO (IRE), 11, b g Montjeu (IRE)—Falafil (FR) **F. Lloyd**
10 DARE TO ENDEAVOUR, 6, b g Alflora (IRE)—Miss Chinchilla **Nationwide Acquisitions PLC**
11 DERWEN PRYDE, 9, b m Hazaaf (USA)—Landsker Pryde **V. T. Beynon**
12 DINEUR (FR), 7, ch g Discover d'auteuil (FR)—Sky Rocket (IRE) **G. J. Morris**
13 DIPITY DOO DAH, 9, b m Slip Anchor—Lyra **C. G. R. Booth**
14 FOREVER MY FRIEND (IRE), 6, b g King's Theatre (IRE)—Kazan Lady (IRE) **Mrs K. Bowen**
15 GULLIBLE GORDON (IRE), 10, ch g Anshan—Cronohill (IRE) **Yeh Man Partnership**
16 GWILI SPAR, 5, ch g Generosity—Lady of Mine **R. Morgans**
17 HANDMAID, 4, b f King's Theatre (IRE)—Hand Inn Glove **Patrick Burling Developments Ltd**
18 HAROUET (FR), 8, ch g Vertical Speed (FR)—Lairna (FR) **Mrs K. Bowen**
19 HENRI PARRY MORGAN, 5, b g Brian Boru—Queen of Thedaises **Ednyfed & Elizabeth Morgan**
20 HODGSON (IRE), 8, gr g Oscar (IRE)—Gairha Grey (IRE) **Roddy Owen & Paul Fullagar**
21 ITS A MISTAKE (IRE), 6, b g Aboo Hom—Creative Princess (IRE) **West Coast Haulage Limited**
22 LUCKY TO BE ALIVE (IRE), 6, b b g Presenting—Praisethepreacher (IRE) **L. Mulryan**
23 MARKET MAKER (IRE), 5, ch g Trade Fair—Papier Mache (IRE) **Mr D. Rodney**
24 MISS KALIFA (IRE), 6, b m Catcher In The Rye (IRE)—Verbena (IRE) **R. D. J. Swinburne**
25 MUMBLES BAY (IRE), 7, b g Oscar (IRE)—Klipperstreet (IRE) **Ms J. Day**
26 MUMBLES HEAD (IRE), 12, ch g Flemensfirth (USA)—Extra Mile **Mrs K. Bowen**
27 MUMBLES PIER (IRE), 8, b g Definite Article—Golden Jorden (IRE) **G. J. Morris**
28 PENSION PLAN, 9, b g Alflora (IRE)—Dalbeattie **The Loppington Five**

MR PETER BOWEN - Continued

29 **PLINY (IRE)**, 9, b br g Accordion—American Chick (IRE) **Ron and Tania Stepney**
30 **PURE FAITH (IRE)**, 9, b g Anshan—Bolaney Girl (IRE) **P. Bowling, S. Scott, R. Harvey & K. Bowen**
31 **REGAL DIAMOND (IRE)**, 5, b h Vinnie Roe (IRE)—Paper Money (IRE) **D. A. Smith**
32 **RIO GAEL (IRE)**, 7, br g Captain Rio—Palavera (FR) **Mrs K. Bowen**
33 **SAINTLY LADY (IRE)**, 8, b m Old Vic—Ban Ri Ciara (IRE) **The Hedonists**
34 **SERTAO (FR)**, 7, b g Passing Sale (FR)—Etoile Bleu (FR) **West Coast Haulage Limited**
35 **SIGN PRO (IRE)**, 5, b g Noverre (USA)—Sadalsud (IRE) **Mrs K. Bowen**
36 **SIZING SANTIAGO (IRE)**, 7, br g Accordion—Denys Daughter (IRE) **Yeh Man Partnership**
37 **STRUMBLE HEAD (IRE)**, 8, b g Anshan—Milan Moss **Mr J. A. Martin**
38 **THE ROAD AHEAD**, 6, b m Grape Tree Road—Althrey Flame (IRE) **F. Lloyd**
39 **VINNIE MY BOY (IRE)**, 5, ch g Vinnie Roe (IRE)—Copper Magic (IRE) **R. D. J. Swinburne**

Other Owners: Mr A. W. Barker, Mrs Karen Bowen, Mr Peter Bowling, Mr W. Bryan, Mr R. Burden, Mr Peter J. Douglas, Mrs L. Douglas, Mr P. Fullagar, Mrs Rachael Harvey, Mr E. O. Morgan, Mrs Elizabeth Morgan, Miss S. Munrowd, Mr Roddy Owen, Mr B. S. Port, Mr S. D. Reeve, Mr Simon Scott, Mr Ron Stepney, Mrs Tania Stepney.

Assistant Trainer: K Bowen

Jockey (NH): Jamie Moore, Tom O'Brien. **Conditional:** Donal Devereux. **Amateur:** Mr Alan Johns.

---

55 | MR ROY BOWRING, Edwinstowe
Postal: **Fir Tree Farm, Edwinstowe, Mansfield, Nottinghamshire, NG21 9JG**
Contacts: **PHONE (01623) 822451 MOBILE (07973) 712942**
E-MAIL bowrings@btconnect.com

1 **ACE MASTER**, 5, ch g Ballet Master (USA)—Ace Maite **S. R. Bowring**
2 **CLUBLAND (IRE)**, 4, b g Red Clubs (IRE)—Racjilanemm **S. R. Bowring**
3 **DANCING MAITE**, 8, ch g Ballet Master (USA)—Ace Maite **S. R. Bowring**
4 **DIVERTIMENTI (IRE)**, 9, b g Green Desert (USA)—Ballet Shoes (IRE) **K. Nicholls**
5 **FLYING APPLAUSE**, 8, b g Royal Applause—Mrs Gray **K. Nicholls**
6 **HIGH FIVE SOCIETY**, 9, b g Compton Admiral—Sarah Madeline **S. R. Bowring**
7 **MAAKIRR (IRE)**, 4, b g Street Cry (IRE)—Zayn Zen **K. Nicholls**
8 **MARINA BALLERINA**, 5, br m Ballet Master (USA)—Marinaite **S. R. Bowring**
9 **MARINA'S OCEAN**, 9, b m Beat All (USA)—Ocean Song **S. R. Bowring**
10 **MASTER OF SONG**, 6, ch g Ballet Master (USA)—Ocean Song **S. R. Bowring**
11 **SEAWOOD**, 7, b g Needwood Blade—Ocean Song **S. R. Bowring**
12 **SOFIAS NUMBER ONE (USA)**, 5, b br g Silver Deputy (CAN)—Storidawn (USA) **S. R. Bowring**
13 **SOLARMAITE**, 4, b f Needwood Blade—Marinaite **S. R. Bowring**
14 **WEST END LAD**, 10, b g Tomba—Cliburnel News (IRE) **K. Nicholls**
15 **XPRES MAITE**, 10, b g Komaite (USA)—Antonias Melody **Charterhouse Holdings Plc**

TWO-YEAR-OLDS

16 B f 18/3 Misu Bond (IRE)—Magical Flute (Piccolo) **S. R. Bowring**
17 B f 27/3 Milk It Mick—Marinaite (Komaite (USA)) **S. R. Bowring**

Jockey (flat): Mark Coumbe. **Apprentice:** Lee Topliss.

---

56 | MR JIM BOYLE, Epsom
Postal: **South Hatch Stables, Burgh Heath Road, Epsom, Surrey, KT17 4LX**
Contacts: **PHONE (01372) 748800 FAX (01372) 739410 MOBILE (07719) 554147**
E-MAIL info@jamesboyle.co.uk & jimboylesec@hotmail.co.uk **(Secretary)**
WEBSITE www.jamesboyle.co.uk

1 **DIVINE PAMINA (IRE)**, 4, br f Dark Angel (IRE)—Greek Symphony (IRE) **Sir D. J. Prosser**
2 **FINAL DELIVERY**, 4, b g Three Valleys (USA)—Bowled Out (GER) **M Khan X2**
3 **MARCUS ANTONIUS**, 6, b g Mark of Esteem (IRE)—Star of The Course (USA) **The Grosvenor Club**
4 **PALOMA'S PRINCE (IRE)**, 4, ch g Nayef (USA)—Ma Paloma (FR) **Serendipity Syndicate 2006**
5 **PERFECT PASTIME**, 5, ch g Pastoral Pursuits—Puritanical (IRE) **Country Friends**
6 **REE'S RASCAL (IRE)**, 5, gr g Verglas (IRE)—Night Scent (IRE) **Mr W. J. Hayford**

THREE-YEAR-OLDS

7 B f Sakhee (USA)—Sweet Pickle **M Khan X2**

MR JIM BOYLE - Continued

Other Owners: Mr M. P. Chitty, Mrs H. Colraine, Mr N. Higham, M. Khan, M. Khan, Mr K. J. Mackie, Mr S. D. O'Connell, Miss V. J. Palmer.

Apprentice: Nathan Alison, Daniel Cremin.

---

57 **MR RICHARD BRABAZON, Co. Kildare**
Postal: **Rangers Lodge, The Curragh, Co. Kildare, Ireland**
Contacts: **PHONE 00353 (0) 45 441259 FAX 00353 (0) 45 441906 MOBILE 00353 (0) 87 2515626**
E-MAIL richardbrabazon@eircom.net WEBSITE www.richardbrabazon.ie

1 CUL NA SHEE (IRE), 7, ch g Lomitas—Puppet Play (IRE) **Mrs F. D. McAuley**
2 KORBOUS (IRE), 4, ch g Choisir (AUS)—Puppet Play (IRE) **Mrs F. D. McAuley**
3 LIGHTENING STRICKS (IRE), 6, b g King's Best (USA)—Opera Comique (FR) **Mrs Alice Perry**
4 PLACERE (IRE), 5, ch m Noverre (USA)—Puppet Play (IRE) **Mrs F. D. McAuley**
5 TORETTO (IRE), 5, ch g Peintre Celebre (USA)—Petite-D-Argent **R. Brabazon**

THREE-YEAR-OLDS
6 FLOWING AIR (IRE), b f Authorized (IRE)—Al Kamah (USA) **R. Brabazon**

Assistant Trainer: Michelle Cox

---

58 **MR DAVID BRACE, Bridgend**
Postal: **Llanmihangel Farm, Pyle, Bridgend, Mid-Glamorgan, CF33 6RL**
Contacts: **PHONE (01656) 742313**

1 AFRICAN SWAN, 5, b m Loup Sauvage (USA)—Coolvawn Lady (IRE) **D. Brace**
2 BAJAN BLU, 5, b g Generous (IRE)—Bajan Girl (FR) **D. Brace**
3 BASEBALL TED (IRE), 11, b g Beneficial—Lishpower **D. Brace**
4 BRINGINTHEBRANSTON, 5, ch g Generous (IRE)—Branston Lily **D. Brace**
5 DOCTOR TOM (IRE), 10, b g Dr Massini (IRE)—Frolicsome (IRE) **D. Brace**
6 INDIAN RIFLE, 4, b f Needle Gun (IRE)—Commanche Token (IRE) **D. Brace**
7 KNIGHT BLAZE, 6, b m Bach (IRE)—Braceys Girl (IRE) **D. Brace**
8 LENNIE DA LION, 5, b g Tamure (IRE)—Lynoso **D. Brace**
9 MOON STREAM, 6, b g Kayf Tara—Moon Catcher **D. Brace**
10 MYSTICAL ROSE (IRE), 7, b m Overbury (IRE)—Never Dawned (IRE) **D. Brace**
11 NURSE BRACE, 4, b f Milan—Bajan Girl (FR) **D. Brace**
12 OH SUZANNAH, 5, b m Generous (IRE)—La Lambertine (FR) **D. Brace**
13 RESPECTUEUX (FR), 7, b g Robin des Pres (FR)—Rouge Folie (FR) **D. Brace**
14 SILVER TOKEN, 8, gr g Silver Patriarch (IRE)—Commanche Token (IRE) **D. Brace**
15 SON OF SWALLOW (IRE), 7, b g Swallow Flight (IRE)—Heresheis **D. Brace**
16 SPIRIT OF BARBADOS (IRE), 7, b g Oscar (IRE)—Finnisk Dream (IRE) **D. Brace**

Assistant Trainer: Miss Jessica Roberts

---

59 **MR MILTON BRADLEY, Chepstow**
Postal: **Meads Farm, Sedbury Park, Chepstow, Gwent, NP16 7HN**
Contacts: **PHONE (01291) 622486 FAX (01291) 626939**

1 ATLANTIC BEACH, 8, ch g Kyllachy—Amused **E. A. Hayward**
2 COLOURBEARER (IRE), 6, ch g Pivotal—Centifolia (FR) **E. A. Hayward**
3 COMPTON PRINCE, 4, ch g Compton Place—Malelane (IRE) **E. A. Hayward**
4 COMPTON TARGET (IRE), 4, b g Strategic Prince—Tarakana (USA) **J. M. Bradley**
5 COURAGEOUS (IRE), 7, ch g Refuse To Bend (IRE)—Bella Bella (IRE) **T. Reffell**
6 DANCING WELCOME, 7, b m Kyllachy—Highland Gait **J. M. Bradley**
7 DEVEZE (IRE), 5, b m Kyllachy—La Caprice (USA) **Mr D. Hudson-Wood**
8 DIVINE CALL, 6, b g Pivotal—Pious **E. A. Hayward**
9 EFFECTSMENONE, 7, br g Beat All (USA)—Rulou (IRE) **Mr C. R. Miles**
10 EMIRATESDOTCOM, 7, b g Pivotal—Teggiano (IRE) **Ms S. A. Howell**
11 FALASTEEN (IRE), 6, ch g Titus Livius (FR)—Law Review (IRE) **T. Reffell**
12 FLAXEN LAKE, 6, b g Sampower Star—Cloudy Reef **Asterix Partnership**

MR MILTON BRADLEY - Continued

13 **FLEETWOODSANDS (IRE)**, 6, b g Footstepsinthesand—Litchfield Hills (USA) **E. R. Griffiths**
14 **FROG HOLLOW**, 4, gr g Intikhab (USA)—The Manx Touch (IRE) **Dab Hand Racing**
15 **HAMIS AL BIN (IRE)**, 4, b g Acclamation—Paimpolaise (IRE) **J. M Bradley**
16 **HEIRGOLD**, 6, b h Son And Heir (IRE)—Seagold **Evenco Gold Racing Limited**
17 **HIGH FIVE PRINCE (IRE)**, 4, br g Strategic Prince—Lady Georgina **T. Reffell**
18 **ISLAND LEGEND (IRE)**, 7, b g Trans Island—Legand of Tara (USA) **J. M. Bradley**
19 **JARROW (IRE)**, 6, ch g Shamardal (USA)—Wolf Cleugh (IRE) **E. A. Hayward**
20 **LOYAL ROYAL (IRE)**, 10, b g King Charlemagne (USA)—Supportive (IRE) **Mr D. Hudson-Wood**
21 **NASRI**, 7, b g Kyllachy—Triple Sharp **E. A. Hayward**
22 **NEW DECADE**, 4, ch g Pivotal—Irresistible **Mr D. Hudson-Wood**
23 **PETRARCHAN**, 5, ch g Pivotal—Summer Sonnet **E. A. Hayward**
24 **REGAL PARADE**, 9, ch g Pivotal—Model Queen (USA) **Dab Hand Racing**
25 **REITERATE**, 4, b f Three Valleys (USA)—Rive (USA) **E. A. Hayward**
26 **SOLE DANSER (IRE)**, 5, b g Dansili—Plymsole (USA) **E. A. Hayward**
27 **SOLEMN**, 8, b g Pivotal—Pious **E. A. Hayward**
28 **SPIRIT OF GONDREE (IRE)**, 5, b g Invincible Spirit (IRE)—
                                          Kristal's Paradise (IRE) **Paul & Ann de Weck & Partner**
29 **TEMPLE ROAD (IRE)**, 5, b g Street Cry (IRE)—Sugarhoneybaby (IRE) **Mr D. Hudson-Wood**
30 **THE GREY ONE (IRE)**, 10, gr g Dansili—Marie Dora (FR) **Mr R. Miles Mr T. Stamp**
31 **TRIPLE DREAM**, 8, ch g Vision of Night—Triple Joy **J. M. Bradley**
32 **VOLCANIC DUST (IRE)**, 5, b m Ivan Denisovich (IRE)—Top of The Form (IRE) **Miss D. Hill**

THREE-YEAR-OLDS

33 **INDIAN AFFAIR**, b c Sleeping Indian—Rare Fling (USA) **J. M. Bradley**
34 **SHAKEN NOT STIRRED**, b f Monsieur Bond (IRE)—Kanisfluh **E. R. Griffiths**
35 **TELAMON (IRE)**, b g Rock of Gibraltar (IRE)—Laureldean Express **Dab Hand Racing**

TWO-YEAR-OLDS

36 B c 1/5 Myboycharlie (IRE)—Read Federica (Fusaichi Pegasus (USA)) (3500) **J. M. Bradley**
37 Ch f 26/3 Zahran (IRE)—Royal Supremacy (IRE) (Desert Prince (IRE)) (380) **J. M. Bradley**
38 **SLEEPING ANGEL**, ch f 5/3 Sleeping Indian—Ellopassoff (Librate) (666) **E. R. Griffiths**
39 Ch f 2/4 Notnowcato—Tuppenny (Salse (USA)) (2500) **J. M. Bradley**

Other Owners: Mr Philip Banfield, Mr J. M. Bradley, Mrs A. De Weck, Mr T. A. Godbert, C. M. Hunt, S. McAvoy, R. Miles, D. Pearson, A. D. Pirie, Mr Tony Stamp, P. L. de Weck.

Assistant Trainer: Miss Hayley Davies

Jockey (flat): Robert Winston, Graham Lee, Richard Kingscote. **Jockey (NH):** Richard Johnson. **Conditional:** Chris Davies, Charlie Wallis.

MR MARK BRADSTOCK, Wantage
Postal: **The Old Manor Stables, Letcombe Bassett, Wantage, Oxfordshire, OX12 9NB**
Contacts: PHONE (01235) 760780 MOBILE (07887) 686697
E-MAIL mark.bradstock@btconnect.com WEBSITE www.markbradstockracing.co.uk

1 **BUSINESS MOVER (IRE)**, 5, ch g Shantou (USA)—Bit of A Chance **Business Moves Group Ltd**
2 **CARRUTHERS**, 10, b g Kayf Tara—Plaid Maid (IRE) **The Oaksey Partnership**
3 **CHOUROMANESCO (FR)**, 10, ch g Maresca Sorrento (FR)—Fleur de Chou (FR) **The Poker Face Partnership**
4 **CONEYGREE**, 6, b g Karinga Bay—Plaid Maid (IRE) **The Max Partnership**
5 **DAHTESTE**, 5, b m Overbury (IRE)—Sunday News'n'echo (USA) **The Elgram Club**
6 4, Ch g Stowaway—Fiddlers Pal (IRE) **M. S. Tamburro**
7 **MAID OF OAKSEY**, 5, br m Overbury (IRE)—Plaid Maid (IRE) **The Plaid Maid Partnership**
8 **MEGASTYLE**, 6, b g Kayf Tara—Shoptillyoudrop **Happy Valley Racing (2009)**
9 **MIDNIGHT PEARL (USA)**, 10, b br m Woodman (USA)—Elegant Ridge (IRE) **Mrs J. Hall**
10 4, B g Kayf Tara—Plaid Maid (IRE)
11 **STAR RIDE**, 4, b g Kayf Tara—Star Diva (IRE) **C. A. Vernon**
12 **SUPER VILLAN**, 8, ch g Alflora (IRE)—Country House **M. S. Tamburro**

Other Owners: Mr Martyn Butler, Mr C. Elgram, Mrs D. Elgram, Mr Duncan King, Miss Amy Marshall, Mrs H. Marshall, Rachel Lady Oaksey, Mr Alan Waller.

Assistant Trainer: Sara Bradstock

Jockey (NH): Mattie Batchelor.

61 MR GILES BRAVERY, Newmarket
Postal: 2 Charnwood Stables, Hamilton Road, Newmarket, Suffolk, CB8 7JQ
Contacts: PHONE (01638) 454044 MOBILE (07711) 112345
E-MAIL Braverygc@aol.com

1 CANTOR, 5, b g Iceman—Choir Mistress **Mr J. F. Tew**
2 JEMIMAVILLE (IRE), 6, b m Fasliyev (USA)—Sparkling Isle **Midbras Group Holdings Ltd**
3 SCHOOLMASTER, 5, b g Motivator—Londonnetdotcom (IRE) **Penny Farm**
4 SUBTLE KNIFE, 4, ch f Needwood Blade—Northern Bows **D. B. Clark & Russel Grant**

THREE-YEAR-OLDS

5 AMBER SPYGLASS, ch c Act One—Northern Bows **Hyphen Racing & Mrs F. E. Bravery**
6 BISON GRASS, b c Halling (USA)—Secret Blend **Mr J. P. Carrington**
7 Ch f Notnowcato—La Gazzetta (IRE) **D. B. Clark & Russel Grant**
8 TRACKS OF MY TEARS, b f Rail Link—Policy Setter (USA) **D. B. Clark**

TWO-YEAR-OLDS

9 LITTLE MISS BECKY, b f 21/2 Piccolo—Boojum (Mujtahid (USA)) (4500) **Mark James**

Other Owners: Mrs F. E. Bravery, Mr D. B. Clark, Mr R. C. Grant, Mr Ed Peate, Mrs Tanya Peate, Mr John Peter-Hoblyn, Mrs Isabel Peter-Hoblyn.

62 MR BARRY BRENNAN, Upper Lambourn
Postal: Flemington Stables (Small Barn), Upper Lambourn, Hungerford, Berkshire, RG17 8QH
Contacts: MOBILE (07907) 529780
E-MAIL barrybrennan2@hotmail.co.uk WEBSITE barrybrennanracing.co.uk

1 BATHCOUNTY (IRE), 6, ch g Tobougg (IRE)—Seasons Estates **Kedgeree Racing Club**
2 BIN END, 7, b g King's Best (USA)—Overboard (IRE) **D. R. T. Gibbons**
3 CLOWANCE HOUSE, 7, ch g Galileo (IRE)—Corsican Sunset (USA) **Seasons Holidays**
4 DUNKELLY CASTLE (IRE), 9, ch g Old Vic—Nanna's Joy (IRE) **Vetlab Supplies Ltd**
5 ESTRELA, 4, b f Authorized (IRE)—Wannabe Grand (IRE) **Seasons Holidays**
6 HOBACK JUNCTION (IRE), 9, b g Heron Island (IRE)—Lizzie Simms (IRE) **T. E. Ford**
7 KALUCCI (IRE), 4, b g Kalanisi (IRE)—Anno Luce **D. R. T. Gibbons**
8 LET'S BE FAMOUS (IRE), 6, b g Indian Danehill (IRE)—Mulligans Fool (IRE) **Mrs M. B. Rowley**
9 LUCKY VIC (IRE), 7, b g Old Vic—Graphic Lady (IRE) **Mr K. Brennan**
10 MANGER HANAGMENT (IRE), 8, br g Heron Island (IRE)—Island Religion (IRE) **Mr K. Brennan**
11 NUMEN (IRE), 9, b g Fath (USA)—Hawala (IRE) **F. J. Brennan**
12 RUDINERO (IRE), 11, gr g Rudimentary (USA)—Cash Chase (IRE) **D. R. T. Gibbons**
13 SAINT GURU, 6, b g Ishiguru (USA)—St James's Antigua (IRE) **J. Pennington**
14 SOUTHFORK, 4, ch g Nayef (USA)—New Choice (IRE) **Equity Racing**

Other Owners: Ms J. Alli, Mr C. K. Bunting, Dr I. A. Cragg, Mr J. Hewish.

Amateur: Mr M. Ennis.

63 MISS ALI BREWER, Eastbury
Postal: Castle Piece Racing Stables, Eastbury, Hungerford, Berkshire, RG17 7JR
Contacts: PHONE (01488) 72818 MOBILE (07779) 285205
E-MAIL info@castlepiecestables.com WEBSITE www.castlepiecestables.com

1 HERMINELLA, 5, b m Lucky Story (USA)—Herminoe **Miss A. J. Brewer**
2 PROUD TIMES (USA), 7, b br g Proud Citizen (USA)—Laura's Pistolette (USA) **Miss A. J. Brewer**
3 SIR TYTO (IRE), 5, b g Fruits of Love—Sophie May **Mr W. H. Simpson**
4 VICO (IRE), 9, b g Old Vic—Over The Glen (IRE) **Mrs V. Verdin**

Other Owners: Miss Ali Brewer.

Assistant Trainer: Sam Stronge

64 **MISS RHONA BREWIS, Belford**
Postal: **Chester Hill, Belford, Northumberland, NE70 7EF**
Contacts: **PHONE (01668) 213239/213281**

1 COROLYNN, 4, b f Grape Tree Road—Conchita **Mrs G. E. Brewis**
2 JACARANDA STAR, 5, b g Grape Tree Road—Chantilly Rose **Miss Rhona Brewis**

65 **MR JOHN BRIDGER, Liphook**
Postal: **Upper Hatch Farm, Liphook, Hampshire, GU30 7EL**
Contacts: **PHONE (01428) 722528 MOBILE (07785) 716614**
E-MAIL jbridger@btconnect.com

1 BYRD IN HAND (IRE), 6, b g Fasliyev (USA)—Military Tune (IRE) **Marshall Brooks Bridger**
2 CHORAL FESTIVAL, 7, b m Pivotal—Choirgirl **Mrs E. Gardner**
3 COMMANDINGPRESENCE (USA), 7, b br m Thunder Gulch (USA)—Sehra (USA) **Mrs E. Gardner**
4 FAIRY MIST (IRE), 6, b g Oratorio (IRE)—Prealpina (IRE) **Mr J. J. Bridger**
5 FLYING KITTY, 4, b f One Cool Cat (USA)—Flying Millie (IRE) **Mr J. J. Bridger**
6 GOWER RULES (IRE), 5, gr g Aussie Rules (USA)—Holy Norma **Mrs E. Gardner**
7 LE KING BEAU (USA), 4, b g Leroidesanimaux (BRZ)—Berine (IRE) **P. Cook**
8 LILY EDGE, 4, b f Byron—Flaming Spirt **Allsorts**
9 PHAROH JAKE, 5, ch g Piccolo—Rose Amber **The Hair & Haberdasher Partnership**
10 SILVEE, 6, gr m Avonbridge—Silver Louie (IRE) **Mr & Mrs K. Finch**
11 SURREY DREAM (IRE), 4, b g Oasis Dream—Trois Graces (USA) **P. Cook**
12 WELSH INLET (IRE), 5, br m Kheleyf (USA)—Ervedya (IRE) **Mr K. J. Walls**

THREE-YEAR-OLDS

13 DARK RUMOUR (IRE), b f Azamour (IRE)—Adjisa (IRE)

TWO-YEAR-OLDS

14 DESERT ISLAND DUSK, b c 30/3 Superior Premium—Desert Island Disc (Turtle Island (IRE)) **W. A. Wood**
15 MOVIE MAGIC, b f 12/4 Multiplex—Alucica (Celtic Swing) **Mr & Mrs K. Finch**
16 SPIRITED SILVER, gr f 6/4 Proclamation (IRE)—Real Emotion (USA) (El Prado (IRE)) **Mr & Mrs K. Finch**

Other Owners: Mrs K. Bicknell, Mr B. P. Brooks, K. Finch, Mrs J. E. Lunn, C. Marshall, Mr A. P. Prockter, Mrs J. M. Stamp.

Assistant Trainer: Rachel Cook

66 **MR DAVID BRIDGWATER, Stow-on-the-Wold**
Postal: **Wyck Hill Farm, Wyck Hill, Stow-on-the-Wold, Cheltenham, Gloucestershire, GL54 1HT**
Contacts: **PHONE (01451) 830349 FAX (01451) 830349 MOBILE (07831) 635817**
E-MAIL sales@bridgwaterracing.co.uk WEBSITE www.bridgwaterracing.co.uk

1 ALL FOR FREE (IRE), 7, b g Atraf—Milain (IRE) **The Jesters**
2 BAWDEN ROCKS, 4, b g Anabaa (USA)—Late Night (GER) **Mr S. Hunt**
3 BIG TALK, 6, b g Selkirk (USA)—Common Request (USA) **Deauville Daze Partnership**
4 DEE AYES DELIGHT, 6, gr g Beat All (USA)—Copper Castle **Mrs J. Frieze**
5 DIRTY BERTIE (FR), 7, ch g Dream Well (FR)—Ma Reilly (FR) **Mr Paul Russell**
6 DONT DO MONDAYS (IRE), 6, b g Rashar (USA)—Bit of A Chance **F. W. K. Griffin**
7 DOUBLE CHOCOLATE, 10, b g Doubletour (USA)—Matching Green **Red & Black Racing**
8 EDGEWORTH (IRE), 7, b g Pyrus (USA)—Credibility **J. Star**
9 ELECTRIC TIGER (GER), 6, b g Konigstiger (GER)—Elle Plate (GER) **Mr D. J. Smith**
10 ENGAI (GER), 7, b g Noroit (GER)—Enigma (GER) **Building Bridgies**
11 ESCARDO (GER), 10, b g Silvano (GER)—Epik (GER) **J. Star**
12 GANNAWAY BAY, 6, ch g Denounce—Bay Maid **Gannaway Racing Club**
13 NINFEA (IRE), 5, b m Le Vie Dei Colori—Attymon Lill (IRE) **Mr G. White**
14 NOTHING TO HIDE (IRE), 5, ch g Barathea (IRE)—Fine Detail (IRE) **Mr G. White**
15 PRESENT TO YOU (IRE), 8, ch g Presenting—Charm of Toulon (IRE) **Deauville Daze Partnership**
16 REG'S RUBY, 7, b m Pursuit of Love—Sweets (IRE) **Mrs M. A. Bridgwater**
17 REGAL ONE (IRE), 5, b g Antonius Pius (USA)—Regal Dancer (IRE) **Terry & Sarah Amos**
18 RIGHT ON ROSE, 5, b m Alflora (IRE)—One Wild Night **Mr Richard Bailey**
19 RUNSHAN (IRE), 13, ch g Anshan—Whitebarn Run **Terry & Sarah Amos**
20 SAFFRON LORD, 8, b g Alflora (IRE)—Jan's Dream (IRE) **Mrs J. A. Chenery**

MR DAVID BRIDGWATER - Continued

21 **SAFFRON PRINCE,** 5, b g Kayf Tara—Jan's Dream (IRE) **Mrs J. A. Chenery**
22 **SAWPIT SAMBA (IRE),** 8, b g Orpen (USA)—Kymin (IRE) **D. A. Hunt**
23 **SAWPIT SUPREME,** 11, b m Cloudings (IRE)—Dara's Course (IRE) **D. A. Hunt**
24 **SHUH SHUH GAH (IRE),** 6, ch g Accordion—Hannigan's Lodger (IRE) **Dean Bostock & Raymond Bostock**
25 **SNOWFLAKE FLO,** 5, ch m Bold Edge—Trumpington **Mr Paul Russell**
26 **SPEEDY BRUERE (FR),** 7, gr g Turgeon (USA)—Divine Bruere (FR) **Terry & Sarah Amos**
27 **SWINCOMBE ROCK,** 8, ch g Double Trigger (IRE)—Soloism **Mills & Mason Partnership**
28 **THE GIANT BOLSTER,** 8, b g Black Sam Bellamy (IRE)—Divisa (GER) **Mr S. Hunt**
29 **VINEMAN,** 6, b g Grape Tree Road—Great Ovation (FR) **Mr A. A. Wright**
30 **WAH WAH TAYSEE (IRE),** 6, b g Saddlers' Hall (IRE)—Slieve Bernagh (IRE) **Dean Bostock & Raymond Bostock**
31 **WYCK HILL (IRE),** 9, b g Pierre—Willow Rose (IRE) **SAB Partnership**

Other Owners: Mr T. P. Amos, Mrs S. P. Amos, Mr Robert Aplin, Mr R. Bailey, Mr J. R. Bostock, Mr Dean Graham Bostock, Mr R. J. Brennan, Mr Russell Bridgeman, Mr R. J. Chenery, Mr Steve Corcoran, Mr J. Follows, Mrs C. A. Follows, Mr R. W. Frost, Mr M. V. Hill, Mrs E. A. Huckle, Mr J. Huckle, Mr A. J. Kincaid, Mr J. K. Llewellyn, Mr David Mason, Mr F. J. Mills, Mr W. R. Mills, Mr Tim Payton, Mr S. J. Raybould, Mr David J. Smith.

Jockey (NH): Robert Thornton, Tommy Phelan, Tom Scudamore. **Conditional:** Jake Hodson.

---

67   MR MARK BRISBOURNE, Nesscliffe
Postal: **Ness Strange Stables, Great Ness, Shrewsbury, Shropshire, SY4 2LE**
Contacts: **PHONE (01743) 741536/741360 FAX (01743) 741285 MOBILE (07803) 019651**

1 **AMANA (USA),** 9, b m Diesis—Ma-Arif (IRE) **Mr G. Coleman**
2 **BRANDY SNAPPING,** 4, ch f Needwood Blade—Sunisa (IRE) **Mr G Greaves & Mickley Stud**
3 **CRUCIS ABBEY (IRE),** 5, b g Acclamation—Golden Ribes (USA) **Abbey Racing Team**
4 **DANCING PRIMO,** 7, b m Primo Valentino—Tycoon's Last **Mr Les Owen**
5 **HARRYS YER MAN,** 9, b g Nomadic Way (USA)—Barden Lady **D. G. Blagden**
6 5, Gr m Silver Patriarch (IRE)—Hill Farm Dancer **W. M. Brisbourne**
7 **JOIN UP,** 7, b g Green Desert (USA)—Rise **P. R. Kirk**
8 **LADY TYCOON,** 4, b f Indesatchel (IRE)—Tycoon's Last **Mr Les Owen**
9 **MARKET PUZZLE (IRE),** 6, ch g Bahamian Bounty—Trempjane **W. M. Brisbourne**
10 **MULTIPOWER,** 4, b g Multiplex—River Ensign **Mrs Mary Brisbourne**
11 **MUTTLEY,** 5, gr g Iceman—Amarella (FR) **Mr Phil Evans**
12 **PENDLE LADY (IRE),** 4, b f Chineur (FR)—Rose of Battle **Mr P. L. Mort**
13 **PRINCESS GAIL,** 5, b m Ad Valorem (USA)—First Musical **W. M. Brisbourne**
14 **QEETHAARA (USA),** 9, gr m Aljabr (USA)—Aghsaan (USA) **Mrs Anne Broughton**
15 **ROWAN SPIRIT (IRE),** 5, gr g Captain Rio—Secret Justice (USA) **The Bourne Connection**
16 **SHELOVESTOBOUGGIE,** 5, b m Tobougg (IRE)—Bowled Out (GER) **Mr S. Singh**
17 **SILVAS ROMANA (IRE),** 4, b f Holy Roman Emperor (IRE)—Triple Wood (USA) **The Bourne Connection**
18 **STORM LIGHTNING,** 4, b g Exceed And Excel (AUS)—All For Laura **Law Abiding Citizens**
19 **TAKAJAN (IRE),** 6, b g Barathea (IRE)—Takaliya (IRE) **Mr Stephen Jones**
20 **TARO TYWOD (IRE),** 4, br f Footstepsinthesand—Run To Jane (IRE) **Rasio Cymru Racing I**
21 **THE KICKING LORD,** 4, b g Avonbridge—Lady Killer (IRE) **Mr T. H. Heckingbottom**
22 **VERY FIRST BLADE,** 4, b g Needwood Blade—Dispol Verity **Mr Les Owen**
23 **WHIPPHOUND,** 5, b g Whipper (USA)—Golden Symbol **Mr W. M. Clare**

THREE-YEAR-OLDS

24 B g Dutch Art—Celeb Style (IRE) **The Celeb Partnership**
25 **ELLA MOTIVA (IRE),** b f Motivator—Stormy View (USA) **Mr P. L. Mort**
26 **ELLE REBELLE,** b f Cockney Rebel (IRE)—Lille Ida **The Bourne Connection**
27 **HONEY HAVEN (IRE),** b f Indian Haven—Condilessa (IRE) **Crewe & Nantwich Racing Club**
28 **WINDSOR ROSE (IRE),** ch f Windsor Knot (IRE)—Rose of Battle **Mr P. L. Mort**

TWO-YEAR-OLDS

29 B f 5/2 Multiplex—Kyllachy Magic (Kyllachy) **Mr Stephen Jones**
30 B f 31/3 Multiplex—Musical Maze (Distant Music (USA)) **Mark Brisbourne & Marshall Barnett**
31 **SARLAT,** b f 17/3 Champs Elysees—Midnight Sky (Desert Prince (IRE)) (10000) **The Bourne Connection**

Other Owners: Mrs M. Ashbrooke, A. J. Banton, Mrs Ann Broughton, Mr J. M. Davies, Mr Derek Dean, Mrs Marie Dean, Mr Bryan Edwards, Mr A. W. Ellis, Mrs C. M. Gibson, G. A. Greaves, Mr R. W. Jones, Mr A. Jones, R. Kent, Mr Mike Murray, Mrs C. A. Naylor, Mr J. Owen, Mr J. D. Pierce, A. Pitt, Mr J. D. Ranson, N. Ridgway, Mr David Robey, Mr David Slingsby, Twenty Four Seven Recruitment, M. G. West, Mrs P. H. Williams.

MR MARK BRISBOURNE - Continued

Assistant Trainer: Antony Brisbourne

Jockey (flat): Liam Jones, Tom McLaughlin, Eddie Ahern, Shane Kelly. **Jockey (NH):** Liam Treadwell. **Apprentice:** Ryan Clark, Jack Duern, Racheal Kneller. **Amateur:** Miss Becky Brisbourne.

MR CLIVE BRITTAIN, Newmarket

Postal: 'Carlburg', 49 Bury Road, Newmarket, Suffolk, CB8 7BY
Contacts: OFFICE (01638) 664347 HOME (01638) 663739 FAX (01638) 661744
MOBILE (07785) 302121
E-MAIL carlburgst@aol.com

1 **AFKAR (IRE)**, 5, b g Invincible Spirit (IRE)—Indienne (IRE) **C. E. Brittain**
2 **AMTHAL (IRE)**, 4, b f Dalakhani (IRE)—Al Ithithar (IRE) **A. M. A. Al Shorafa**
3 **ATMANNA**, 4, br f Manduro (GER)—Samdaniya **S. Manana**
4 **CAPE ALEX**, 4, b f Cape Cross (IRE)—Alexander Three D (IRE) **S. Manana**
5 **DAGHASH**, 4, b c Tiger Hill (IRE)—Zibet **M. Al Nabouda**
6 **HADAJ**, 4, b g Green Desert (USA)—My Amalie (IRE) **S. Manana**
7 **MANOMINE**, 4, b g Manduro (GER)—Fascinating Hill (FR) **Mrs C. E. Brittain**
8 **MIBLISH**, 4, b c Teofilo (IRE)—Triton Dance (IRE) **S. Manana**
9 **MUDHISH (IRE)**, 8, b g Lujain (USA)—Silver Satire **C. E. Brittain**
10 **MUZHIL (IRE)**, 4, b f Manduro (GER)—Mazuna (IRE) **S. Manana**
11 **QUIXOTE**, 4, ch g Singspiel (IRE)—Rainbow Queen (FR) **C. E. Brittain**
12 **RED AGGRESSOR (IRE)**, 4, b g Red Clubs (IRE)—Snap Crackle Pop (IRE) **C. E. Brittain**
13 **RUBBAMAA**, 4, b f Singspiel (IRE)—Lady Hen **S. Manana**
14 **SEMAYYEL (IRE)**, 4, b f Green Desert (USA)—Lii Najma **S. Manana**

THREE-YEAR-OLDS

15 **ARJAWAN**, b c Byron—Al Hawa (USA) **S. Manana**
16 **ASEELA (IRE)**, b f Teofilo (IRE)—Valse Mystique (IRE) **S. Manana**
17 **BOOKTHEBAND (IRE)**, ch c Dubawi (IRE)—Songbook **C. E. Brittain**
18 B f Manduro (GER)—Bunting **M. Al Nabouda**
19 **HADEEYA**, b f Oratorio (IRE)—Pivotting **S. Manana**
20 **HASANAN**, b f Rail Link—Dance Solo **S. Manana**
21 **JATHABAH (IRE)**, b f Singspiel (IRE)—Zibet **M. Al Nabouda**
22 **MASARAH (IRE)**, b f Cape Cross (IRE)—Fragrancy (IRE) **M. Al Nabouda**
23 **RITAACH (IRE)**, b f Compton Place—Golubitsa (IRE) **S. Manana**
24 **SADFIG**, b c Notnowcato—Coconut Queen (FR) **S. Manana**
25 **SADIIGAH**, b f Medicean—Regal Riband **S. Manana**
26 **SHAFAANI**, b f Green Desert (USA)—Amalie (IRE) **S. Manana**
27 **SINAADI (IRE)**, b f Kyllachy—Quantum (IRE) **S. Manana**
28 B br c Kheleyf (USA)—Snap Crackle Pop (IRE) **Sheikh J. Al Dalmook Maktoum**
29 **TAHAF (IRE)**, b c Authorized (IRE)—Lady Zonda **M. Al Nabouda**
30 **TUFFAN (USA)**, b c Bernardini (USA)—Love of Dubai (USA) **Mr M. Al Shafar**

TWO-YEAR-OLDS

31 **BAHAMIAN HEIGHTS**, b c 15/4 Bahamian Bounty—
Tahirah (Green Desert (USA)) (50000) **Sheikh J. Al Dalmook Maktoum**
32 B c 28/2 New Approach (IRE)—Bush Cat (USA) (Kingmambo (USA)) (70000) **S. Manana**
33 **CADEAUX POWER**, b f 22/2 Major Cadeaux—
Right Answer (Lujain (USA)) (20000) **Sheikh J. Al Dalmook Maktoum**
34 Ch f 2/3 New Approach (IRE)—Calakanga (Dalakhani (IRE)) (35000) **S. Manana**
35 B c 6/3 Teofilo (IRE)—Clear Voice (USA) (Cryptoclearance (USA)) (28000) **S. Manana**
36 B f 3/4 Lawman (FR)—Dance of Light (USA) (Sadler's Wells (USA)) (40000) **S. Manana**
37 B f 5/3 Authorized (IRE)—Dancing Fire (USA) (Dayjur (USA)) (22000) **S. Manana**
38 B f 7/4 Aqlaam—Dream Vision (USA) (Distant View (USA)) (40000) **S. Manana**
39 B f 15/2 Cape Cross (IRE)—Fann (USA) (Diesis) (80000) **S. Manana**
40 B f 28/4 Bushranger (IRE)—Firecross (IRE) (Pivotal) (7500) **C. E. Brittain**
41 Ch c 1/2 Piccolo—Fleeting Moon (Fleetwood (IRE)) (11000) **S. Manana**
42 B c 28/2 Cape Cross (IRE)—Guarantia (Selkirk (USA)) (20000) **S. Manana**
43 B f 15/4 Acclamation—Hovering (IRE) (In The Wings) (30000) **S. Manana**
44 B f 6/5 Cape Cross (IRE)—Kaabari (USA) (Seeking The Gold (USA)) **S. Manana**
45 B f 10/4 Medaglia d'oro (USA)—Love of Dubai (USA) (More Than Ready (USA)) **Mr M. Al Shafar**
46 B c 27/1 Dalakhani (IRE)—Lunda (IRE) (Soviet Star (USA)) **S. Manana**

MR CLIVE BRITTAIN - Continued

47 B c 15/4 Street Cry (IRE)—Maskunah (IRE) (Sadler's Wells (USA)) **S. Manana**
48 B c 16/4 Dandy Man (IRE)—Miss Demure (Shy Groom (USA)) (20952) **S. Ali**
49 B c 2/2 Exceed And Excel (AUS)—O Fourlunda (Halling (USA)) (27000) **S. Manana**
50 Ch c 7/4 Halling (USA)—Pachanga (Inchinor) (11000) **C. E. Brittain**
51 B c 15/4 Bushranger (IRE)—Poetry Aloud (IRE) (Kheleyf (USA)) (14000) **S. Manana**
52 Ch f 19/3 Iffraaj—Poyle Caitlin (IRE) (Bachir (IRE)) (10000) **S. Manana**
53 B f 22/1 Kyllachy—Precious Secret (IRE) (Fusaichi Pegasus (USA)) (14000) **S. Manana**
54 B f 14/3 Medicean—Qui Moi (CAN) (Swain (IRE)) (20000) **S. Manana**
55 B f 4/3 Major Cadeaux—Quiz Show (Primo Dominie) (22000) **S. Manana**
56 B c 1/5 Medaglia d'oro (USA)—Rajeem (Diktat) **S. Manana**
57 B c 8/3 Authorized (IRE)—Red Blooded Woman (USA) (Red Ransom (USA)) (17000) **S. Manana**
58 Ch c 31/1 Virtual—Rosabee (IRE) (No Excuse Needed) (10000) **S. Manana**
59 B f 21/2 Cape Cross (IRE)—Roslea Lady (IRE) (Alhaarth (IRE)) (40000) **S. Manana**
60 B c 5/4 Teofilo (IRE)—Samdaniya (Machiavellian (USA)) (20000) **S. Manana**
61 B c 14/4 Dubawi (IRE)—Scotch Bonnet (IRE) (Montjeu (IRE)) (70000) **S. Manana**
62 B f 14/2 Bushranger (IRE)—Scottendale (Zilzal (USA)) (30000) **S. Manana**
63 B f 20/3 Royal Applause—Senta's Dream (Danehill) (USA) (45000) **S. Manana**
64 B f 24/3 Iffraaj—Serena's Storm (IRE) (Statue of Liberty (USA)) (50000) **Sheikh R. D. Al Maktoum**
65 Gr c 24/3 Clodovil (IRE)—Shambodia (IRE) (Petardia) (80000) **S. Manana**
66 B c 18/4 New Approach (IRE)—Shimna (Mr Prospector (USA)) (85000) **S. Manana**
67 B c 5/5 Aqlaam—Sirena (GER) (Tejano (USA)) (10000) **S. Manana**
68 **SLEEPING PRINCESS (IRE)**, ch f 13/2 Dalakhani (IRE)—Savignano (Polish Precedent (USA)) (21428) **S. Ali**
69 B f 1/3 Royal Applause—Tarbiyah (Singspiel (IRE)) (25000) **S. Manana**
70 B f 8/4 Halling (USA)—Tithcar (Cadeaux Genereux) (37000) **S. Manana**
71 B f 30/3 Bushranger (IRE)—Trim (IRE) (Ela-Mana-Mou) (15000) **S. Manana**
72 B f 24/1 Acclamation—Week End (Selkirk (USA)) (28000) **S. Manana**
73 B f 26/3 Invincible Spirit (IRE)—Wing Stealth (IRE) (Hawk Wing (USA)) (50000) **S. Manana**
74 B f 15/2 Pastoral Pursuits—Witness (Efisio) (16000) **S. Manana**
75 B f 26/3 Manduro (GER)—Yukon Hope (USA) (Forty Niner (USA)) (20000) **S. Manana**
76 B f 13/2 Cape Cross (IRE)—Zamhrear (Singspiel (IRE)) (30000) **S. Manana**
77 Ch f 7/4 Halling (USA)—Zarara (USA) (Manila (USA)) (50000) **S. Manana**
78 B c 26/2 Intikhab (USA)—Zither (Zafonic (USA)) (32000) **S. Manana**

Assistant Trainer: Mrs C. E. Brittain

---

69 **MR MEL BRITTAIN, Warthill**
Postal: **Northgate Lodge, Warthill, York, YO19 5XR**
Contacts: **PHONE (01759) 371472 FAX (01759) 372915**
E-MAIL email@melbrittain.co.uk WEBSITE www.melbrittain.co.uk

1 **AD VITAM (IRE)**, 5, ch g Ad Valorem (USA)—Love Sonnet **Mr C. J. Bennett**
2 **BROCKFIELD**, 7, ch g Falbrav (IRE)—Irish Light (USA) **M. A. Brittain**
3 **CARRAGOLD**, 7, b g Diktat—Shadow Roll (IRE) **M. A. Brittain**
4 **COTTAM STELLA**, 5, br m Diktat—Flower Breeze (USA) **P. Easterby**
5 **DEFENCE COUNCIL (IRE)**, 5, b g Kheleyf (USA)—Miss Gally (IRE) **R. J. Mustill**
6 **DUNNINGTON**, 4, b g Gentleman's Deal (IRE)—First Harmony **M. A. Brittain**
7 4, B f Doyen (IRE)—Flower Breeze (USA) **P. Easterby**
8 **GENEROUS DREAM**, 5, ch m Generous (USA)—First Harmony **M. A. Brittain**
9 4, B f Doyen (IRE)—Northern Bird **P. Easterby**
10 4, B f Generous (USA)—Seems So Easy (USA) **M. Swallow**
11 **SELDOM (IRE)**, 7, b g Sesaro (USA)—Daisy Dancer (IRE) **M. A. Brittain**
12 **STEEL STOCKHOLDER**, 7, b g Mark of Esteem (IRE)—Pompey Blue **M. A. Brittain**
13 **TOBRATA**, 7, ch g Tobougg (IRE)—Sabrata (IRE) **M. A. Brittain**
14 **TRADE SECRET**, 6, b g Trade Fair—Kastaway **M. A. Brittain**

THREE-YEAR-OLDS

15 **BALINKA**, b f Bahamian Bounty—Eurolinka (IRE) **Northgate Grey**
16 **DREAM SCENARIO**, b f Araafa (IRE)—Notjustaprettyface (USA) **Northgate Black**
17 **GREY DESTINY**, gr g Desideratum—Mother Corrigan (IRE) **M. A. Brittain**
18 **LUCKY LODGE**, b g Lucky Story (USA)—Melandre **M. A. Brittain**
19 **LUCKY PRIZE**, b f Lucky Story (USA)—Mana Pools (IRE) **M. A. Brittain**
20 **MARABOUT (IRE)**, b g Haafhd—Nirvana (IRE) **Koo's Racing Club**
21 **MAYFIELD GIRL (IRE)**, br f One Cool Cat (USA)—Rose of Mooncoin (IRE) **M. A. Brittain**

MR MEL BRITTAIN - Continued

22 MISTER MARCASITE, gr g Verglas (IRE)—No Rehearsal (FR) **S. J. Box**
23 B f One Cool Cat (USA)—Musicology (USA) **M. A. Brittain**
24 SANDERIANA, b f Lucky Story (USA)—Guadaloup **Northgate White**
25 Ch f Indian Haven—Spartan Girl (IRE)

TWO-YEAR-OLDS

26 Ch c 30/3 Sleeping Indian—Clancassie (Clantime) (2857)
27 B f 10/4 Lucky Story (USA)—Cockatrice (Petong) (2857)
28 Bl c 16/4 Naaqoos—Dream Day (FR) (Spectrum (IRE)) (3200)
29 B f 11/2 Virtual—Entrap (USA) (Phone Trick (USA)) (4200)
30 B c 25/3 Rainbow High—Lord Conyers (IRE) (Inzar (USA)) **Partnership**
31 Ch gr f 18/4 Paris House—Melandre (Lujain (USA)) (1142) **M. A. Brittain**
32 B f 31/3 Virtual—My Golly (Mozart (IRE)) (8000) **The How Rude Partnership**
33 Ch g 6/3 Three Valleys (USA)—Niseem (USA) (Hennessy (USA)) (761)
34 B f 10/4 Avonbridge—Out Like Magic (Magic Ring (IRE)) (4761) **Northgate Partnership**
35 B f 11/4 Araafa (IRE)—Racina (Bluebird (USA)) (6500) **Northgate Partnership**
36 B f 12/5 Iffraaj—Seven Sing (USA) (Machiavellian (USA)) (2800)
37 Ch f 31/3 Sleeping Indian—Silver Purse (Interrex (CAN)) (9000)
38 Ch f 18/3 Iffraaj—Taalluf (USA) (Hansel (USA)) (4000)

Other Owners: Mr R. T. Adams, Mr J. Allan, Mr L. Chambers, Mr Paul Chambers, Mr & Mrs N. Dobbs, Mr & Mrs M. Foster, Mrs F. Godson, Mr J. Gunn, Mr S. Imeson, Mr J. Jarvis, Mr M. Laws, Mr G. Pritchard, Mr D. C. Rayment, Mr H. Redhead, Mr C. Sim, Mr Kristian Strangeway, Mr S. Taylor, Mr Donald B. White, Mr G. Wilson, Mr N. Wilson.

Assistant Trainer: Paul Sedgwick, **Head Lad:** Neil Jordan

Apprentice: Robert Dodsworth, Kenny Corbett.

---

70 **LADY BROOKE, Llandrindod Wells**
Postal: **Tyn-y-Berth Farm, Dolau, Llandrindod Wells, Powys, LD1 5TW**
Contacts: **PHONE (01597) 851190 MOBILE (07977) 114834**

1 AHCOMERETOME (IRE), 8, ch g Oscar Schindler (IRE)—Call Me Over (IRE) **Lady Brooke**
2 ALPHA WAY (GER), 9, b g Kendor (FR)—Alpha City **Lady Brooke**
3 NO RECEPTION (IRE), 12, b br g Mister Mat (FR)—The Lar (FR) **Lady Brooke**
4 RADIUS BLEU (FR), 8, gr g Dadarissime (FR)—Regence Bleue (FR) **Lady Brooke**

Assistant Trainer: Lorna Brooke

Amateur: Miss Lorna Brooke.

---

71 **MRS ANNA BROOKS, Towcester**
Postal: **Horton House, Alderton, Towcester, Northamptonshire, NN12 7LN**
Contacts: **PHONE (01327) 811354 FAX (01327) 811496 MOBILE (07802) 541294**
E-MAIL onespotracing@hotmail.com

1 ALLUSIVE POWER (IRE), 4, gr f Verglas (IRE)—Fernanda **T. B. Brown**
2 DUKE OF ORMOND (IRE), 10, ch g Flemensfirth (USA)—Supreme Alannah (IRE) **Brooks & Robinson**
3 EVERKINGLY, 7, b g Bollin Eric—Pink Mosaic **Brooks, Haley, Masterson & Wain**
4 MIDNIGHT MAISIE, 6, ch m Midnight Legend—Persian Silk (IRE) **Lloyd & Linda**
5 6, B m Kayf Tara—Pink Mosaic
6 ROSSBRIN (IRE), 8, b g Flemensfirth (USA)—Mustard Mor (IRE) **Mr J. H. Moorhouse**

Other Owners: T. L. Brooks, Mrs A. E. Brooks, Mrs L. M. Pestell, Mr J. L. Robinson.

---

72 **MR CHARLIE BROOKS, Chipping Norton**
Postal: **Castle Barn Farm, Churchill, Chipping Norton, Oxfordshire, OX7 6RA**
Contacts: **MOBILE (07778) 476759**

1 CESTUS (IRE), 5, bl g High Chaparral (IRE)—Monte Solaro (IRE) **Pudlicote Partnership**

Other Owners: Mr C. P. E. Brooks, Mr T. F. Lacey.

73   MR ROY BROTHERTON, Pershore
Postal: **Mill End Racing Stables, Netherton Road, Elmley Castle, Pershore, Worcestershire, WR10 3JF**
Contacts: **PHONE/FAX (01386) 710772 MOBILE (07973) 877280**

1 AUGUSTUS JOHN (IRE), 10, gr g Danehill (USA)—Rizerie (FR) **Mr A. T. L. Clayton**
2 CAPE OF STORMS, 10, b g Cape Cross (IRE)—Lloc **Mr A. T. L. Clayton**
3 CAPE SKY, 6, gr m Cape Town (IRE)—Herecomespapin (IRE) **M. D. Coulson**
4 CRIMSON QUEEN, 6, ch m Red Ransom (USA)—Rainbow Queen **Mr A. T. L. Clayton**
5 FANTASTIC INDIAN, 4, b f Sleeping Indian—Quite Fantastic (IRE) **Mr A. T. L. Clayton**
6 LADYDOLLY, 5, b m Kyllachy—Lady Pekan **P. S. J. Croft**
7 MAXDELAS (FR), 7, ch g Sabrehill (USA)—Quendora (FR) **Mrs C. A. Newman**
8 POYLE TODREAM, 5, b g Oasis Dream—Lost In Lucca **Cecil & Miss Alison Wiggins**
9 PRINCE FREDDIE, 5, b g Red Ransom (USA)—Pitcroy **Mrs T. J. Byrne**
10 SILVER THREEPENCE, 5, ch m Trade Fair—Silver Gyre (IRE) **Mr A. T. L. Clayton**
11 TAWSEEF (IRE), 5, b g Monsun (GER)—Sahool **Millend Racing Club**
12 TREVOSE (IRE), 4, b g Barathea (IRE)—Cape Jasmine (IRE) **R. Brotherton**

Other Owners: Mr Roy Brotherton, Mr T. L Martin.

Assistant Trainer: Justin Brotherton

Jockey (flat): Tom Eaves. **Amateur:** Mr Sam Drinkwater, Mr Chris Martin.

74   MR ALAN BROWN, Malton
Postal: **Lilac Farm, Yedingham, Malton, North Yorkshire, YO17 8SS**
Contacts: **PHONE (01944) 728090 FAX (01944) 728071 MOBILE (07970) 672845**
E-MAIL ad.brownn@globaluk.net

1 BLUE SEA OF IBROX (IRE), 5, gr m Subtle Power (IRE)—Jerpoint Rose (IRE) **Rangers Racing**
2 CHARLIE CRAB, 10, b g Tamure (IRE)—Minigale **Mr D. J. Sturdy**
3 JASANI, 5, b g Gentleman's Deal (IRE)—Bred For Pleasure **A. Brown**
4 O CROTAIGH (IRE), 9, b g Beneficial—Jerpoint Rose (IRE) **Mr D. J. Sturdy**
5 OUR GOLDEN BOY (IRE), 7, b g Milan—Just Little **The Golden Boys Partnership**
6 RED SHADOW, 4, b f Royal Applause—Just A Glimmer **S. E. Pedersen**

Other Owners: Mr M. Lovett, Mr M. White, Mr J. T. Winter.

75   MR DAVID BROWN, Averham
Postal: **The Old Stables, Averham Park, Newark, Nottinghamshire, NG23 5RU**
Contacts: **PHONE (01636) 613793 MOBILE (07889) 132931**
E-MAIL david@davidbrownracing.com

1 DAMIKA (IRE), 10, ch g Namid—Emly Express (IRE) **Miss E. Bullock**
2 DUBAWI SOUND, 5, b g Dubawi (IRE)—Hannah's Music **Pearl Bloodstock Limited**
3 GUISING, 4, ch c Manduro (GER)—Trick Or Treat **Mr P. Onslow & Mr I. Henderson**
4 ONELADYOWNER, 5, b h Auction House (USA)—Inya Lake **Oneladyowner Partnership**
5 TEMPLE MEADS, 5, ch h Avonbridge—Harryana **J. C. Fretwell**

THREE-YEAR-OLDS

6 BEACH CLUB, b c Footstepsinthesand—Dunya **J. C. Fretwell**
7 BURNING DAWN (USA), b f Bernstein (USA)—Winter Morning (USA) **Qatar Racing Limited**
8 CLEAN BLOW (USA), b br f Street Boss (USA)—Strike Hard (IRE) **J. C. Fretwell**
9 FIDGET, ch f Bertolini (USA)—Record Time **P. Onslow**
10 FIRE EYES, b c Exceed And Excel (AUS)—Wunders Dream (IRE) **Qatar Racing Limited**
11 HIDDEN TALENT, b c Kyllachy—Creative Mind (IRE) **Mr & Mrs Archer**
12 HOLLOWINA, ch f Beat Hollow—Trick Or Treat **P. Onslow**
13 ORDER OF SERVICE, ch c Medicean—Choir Gallery **J. C. Fretwell**
14 PEARL SEA (IRE), b f Elusive City (USA)—Catch The Sea (IRE) **Pearl Bloodstock Limited**
15 SATSUMA, ch f Compton Place—Jodrell Bank (IRE) **John Kilbride, Adam Watson, James Hughes**
16 SIXTY MINUTES, b c Compton Place—Passing Hour (USA) **J. C. Fretwell**
17 SO VAIN (IRE), b g Elusive City (USA)—Vanitycase (IRE) **Mr D. H. Brown**
18 YORKSHIREMAN (IRE), b c Red Clubs (IRE)—Ossiana (IRE) **Yorkshireman Partnership**

MR DAVID BROWN - Continued

TWO-YEAR-OLDS

19 B c 2/3 Sir Percy—Barawin (IRE) (Hawk Wing (USA)) (40000) **Mr D. H. Brown / Mr R. Hull / Mr C. Watson**
20 CAPTAIN MIDNIGHT (IRE), b c 5/3 Bushranger (IRE)—Beverley Macca (Piccolo) (11428) **D. A. West**
21 B c 24/3 Footstepsinthesand—Clear Vision (Observatory (USA)) (16000) **J. C. Fretwell**
22 B f 20/3 Elusive City (USA)—Coachhouse Lady (Rahy (USA)) (28571) **J. C. Fretwell**
23 Ch f 1/3 Pastoral Pursuits—Creative Mind (IRE) (Danehill Dancer (IRE)) **Mr & Mrs Archer**
24 B c 28/1 Hard Spun (USA)—Divorce Settlement (USA) (Stormin Fever (USA)) (129032) **Qatar Racing Limited**
25 HUMOROUS LADY (USA), b f 5/3 Distorted Humor (USA)—
A P Dream (USA) (A P Indy (USA)) (58371) **Qatar Racing Limited**
26 ILLUMINATING DREAM (IRE), b f 30/4 High Chaparral (IRE)—
Massada (Most Welcome) (39681) **Qatar Racing Limited**
27 B c 17/3 Pastoral Pursuits—Markova's Dance (Mark of Esteem (IRE)) (25714) **J. C. Fretwell**
28 Ro c 26/1 Mastercraftsman (IRE)—Prairie Moon (Halling (USA)) (95238) **Qatar Racing Limited**

Other Owners: Mr Steve Bolland, Mr D. H. Brown, Mr Ian Henderson, Mr James Hughes, Mr J. Kilbride, Mr Peter Onslow, Mr Clive Watson, Mr A. R. Watson.

Assistant Trainer: Dushyant Dooyea

Jockey (flat): Philip Makin, Robert Winston, Jamie Spencer.

---

76 MR GARY BROWN, Lambourn
Postal: **50 Child Street, Lambourn, Hungerford, Berkshire, RG17 8NZ**
Contacts: **MOBILE (07545) 915253**
E-MAIL gbrownracing@hotmail.co.uk

1 HILALI (IRE), 4, b g Sakhee (USA)—Mufradat (IRE) **J. P. McManus**
2 O'GORMAN, 4, b g Sleeping Indian—Harryana **We Haven't Told The Wives Syndicate**
3 ROSSLYN CASTLE, 4, ch g Selkirk (USA)—Margarula (IRE) **Chanelle Medical Group**

Other Owners: Mr P. Curtin, Mr P. J. Fahy, Mr Ollie Hynes.

Jockey (flat): Liam Keniry. **Jockey (NH):** A P McCoy, Jamie Moore. **Conditional:** Joshua Moore.

---

77 MR IAN BROWN, Nawton
Postal: **Pasture House Farm, Nawton, York, YO62 7TU**
Contacts: **YARD/HOME (01439) 771250 MOBILE (07840) 842281**

1 ANDY VIC (IRE), 10, b g Old Vic—Garranard Ros (IRE) **I. A. Brown**

Amateur: Mrs Joanne Brown.

---

78 MR REGINALD BROWN, Abergavenny
Postal: **The Firs, Grosmont, Abergavenny, Gwent, NP7 8LY**
Contacts: **PHONE (01873) 821278**

1 UMORISTIC (FR), 5, gr g Baroud d'honneur (FR)—Canlastou (FR) **R. L. Brown**

---

79 MISS MICHELLE BRYANT, Lewes
Postal: **Bevern Bridge Farm Cottage, South Chailey, Lewes, East Sussex, BN8 4QH**
Contacts: **PHONE/FAX (01273) 400638 MOBILE (07976) 217542**

1 CORLOUGH MOUNTAIN, 9, ch g Inchinor—Two Step **Miss M. P. Bryant**
2 HAWK GOLD (IRE), 9, ch g Tendulkar (USA)—Heiress of Meath (IRE) **Miss M. P. Bryant**
3 NIGHT GROOVE (IRE), 10, b g Night Shift (USA)—Taysala (IRE) **Miss M. P. Bryant**

Amateur: Miss M. P. Bryant.

80 MRS KATE BUCKETT, Bishops Waltham
Postal: **Woodlocks Down Farm, Upham, Bishops Waltham, Hampshire, SO32 1JN**
Contacts: **PHONE (01962) 777557**

1 **BACKHOMEINDERRY (IRE)**, 8, b g Oscar (IRE)—Foyle Wanderer (IRE) **Mrs K. A. Buckett**
2 **BELLOSGUARDO**, 10, ch g Medicean—Barsham **Mrs K. A. Buckett**
3 **JOIN THE NAVY**, 8, b g Sea Freedom—Join The Parade **Mrs K. A. Buckett**
4 **UPHAM ATOM**, 10, b g Silver Patriarch (IRE)—Upham Lady **Mrs K. A. Buckett**

Jockey (NH): Mark Grant, Liam Treadwell. **Amateur:** Miss Chloe Boxall.

81 MR BOB BUCKLER, Crewkerne
Postal: **Higher Peckmoor, Henley, Crewkerne, Somerset, TA18 8PQ**
Contacts: **PHONE (01460) 75922 FAX (01460) 74851 MOBILE (07785) 773957**
E-MAIL rbuckler@btconnect.com WEBSITE www.robertbucklerracing.co.uk

1 **BALLYEGAN (IRE)**, 8, b g Saddlers' Hall (IRE)—Knapping Princess (IRE) **Ballyegan Partnership**
2 **DIFFERENT TRADES (IRE)**, 9, b g Oscar (IRE)—Gale Tan (IRE) **R. H. Buckler**
3 **DIGGER'S MATE**, 5, b g General Gambul—Miss Diskin (IRE) **M. J. Forrester**
4 **DORA CANINA**, 5, b m Doyen (IRE)—Rosa Canina **R. H. Buckler**
5 **DOUBLE DIZZY**, 12, b g Double Trigger (IRE)—Miss Diskin (IRE) **M. J. Forrester**
6 **DOUBLE OR QUITZ**, 8, b g Relief Pitcher—Straight Courage **Strictly Come Racing**
7 **GLENWOOD PRESENT (IRE)**, 6, ch g Presenting—Chancy Lass (IRE) **N. Elliott**
8 **HEARTENING**, 5, b m Wace (USA)—Heartleys Quest (IRE) **Mr P. M. Phillips**
9 **MALIN HEAD (IRE)**, 8, b g Presenting—Dedham Gale (IRE) **Strictly Come Racing**
10 **MISTER MATT (IRE)**, 10, b g Alflora (IRE)—Swing Quartet (IRE) **Strictly Come Racing**
11 **NEVER SAYS NEVER**, 5, b g Tamure (IRE)—Quick Exit **Mr R. Hall**
12 **SOMERSET LIAS (IRE)**, 5, b g Golan (IRE)—Presenting Gayle (IRE) **P. L. Hart**
13 **SULPIUS (GER)**, 8, b g Tertullian (USA)—Suva (GER) **Mrs J. M. Gregson**
14 **THE HAPPY WARRIOR**, 5, b g Luso—Martomick **N. Elliott**
15 **THE SAWYER (BEL)**, 13, ch g Fleetwood (IRE)—Green Land (BEL) **D. R. Fear**

Other Owners: Mr R. H. Buckler, Mr D. R. Fear, Mrs Clare Lewis, Mr Nick Robinson, Mrs H. E. Shane.

Head Lad: Giles Scott

Jockey (NH): Andrew Glassonbury, Will Kennedy. **Conditional:** Giles Hawkins.

82 MR MARK BUCKLEY, Stamford
Postal: **Potters Hill Stables, Morkery Lane, Castle Bytham, Stamford, Lincolnshire, NG33 4SP**
Contacts: **OFFICE (01780) 411158 MOBILE (07808) 360488**
E-MAIL markbuckley215@btinternet.com

1 **ELECTRICKERY**, 4, b f Excellent Art—Exultate Jubilate (USA) **C. C. Buckley**
2 **LIBERTY SHIP**, 8, b g Statue of Liberty (USA)—Flag **David Lockwood & Fred Lockwood**
3 **STEELCUT**, 9, b g Iron Mask (USA)—Apple Sauce **Potters Hill Racing**

Other Owners: M. A. Buckley, D. J. Lockwood, Mr F. M. Lockwood.

Assistant Trainer: Kim Buckley

83 MR DAI BURCHELL, Ebbw Vale
Postal: **Drysiog Farm, Briery Hill, Ebbw Vale, Gwent, NP23 6BU**
Contacts: **PHONE (01495) 302551 MOBILE (07980) 482860**

1 **ACAPULCO BAY**, 9, b g Pursuit of Love—Lapu-Lapu **J. Parfitt**
2 **ANRHEG**, 5, b m Diktat—Dim Ots **Mrs D. J. Hughes**
3 **COMMERCE**, 6, b m Trade Fair—Well Away (IRE) **B. J. Williams**
4 **CRUCHAIN (IRE)**, 10, ch g Shernazar—Mack Tack (IRE) **Mr & Mrs A. J. Mutch**
5 **FEELING (IRE)**, 9, b g Sadler's Wells (USA)—La Pitie (USA) **W. D. Burchell**
6 **FLYING PHOENIX**, 5, b m Phoenix Reach (IRE)—Rasmalai **B. J. Williams**
7 **GOING FRENCH (IRE)**, 6, ch g Frenchmans Bay (FR)—Easy Going **Mr A. P. Shinton**
8 **KING OF THE MOORS (USA)**, 10, b g King of Kings (IRE)—Araza (USA) **J. L. Spearing**

MR DAI BURCHELL - Continued

9 **NOTABOTHERONME (IRE)**, 11, b br g Religiously (USA)—Kylogue's Delight **J. E. Mutch**
10 **OLD PEG**, 8, b m Mujahid (USA)—Giggleswick Girl
11 **REBECCAS CHOICE (IRE)**, 10, b g Religiously (USA)—Carolin Lass (IRE) **J. E. Mutch**
12 **SPINNING WATERS**, 7, b g Vettori (IRE)—Secret Waters **B. M. G. Group**
13 **SYMPHONY OF STARS**, 4, b f Primo Valentino (IRE)—Echostar **T. R. Pearson**

THREE-YEAR-OLDS

14 **SYMPHONY OF DREAMS**, b f Primo Valentino (IRE)—Flying Lion **T. R. Pearson**

TWO-YEAR-OLDS

15 **SYMPHONY OF PEARLS**, b f 6/3 Lucarno (USA)—Echostar (Observatory (USA)) **T. R. Pearson**

Other Owners: Mr W. R. A. Davies, Mrs S. Mutch, Mr A. J. Mutch, Mr D. H. Protheroe.

Assistant Trainer: Ruth Burchell

Jockey (flat): Kelly Harrison, Sam Hitchcott. **Jockey (NH):** Robert Dunne, Donal Fahy, Charlie Wallis, Christian Williams. **Conditional:** Robert Williams. **Amateur:** Mr Nick Williams, Mrs Alex Dunn, Mr Frank Windsor Clive.

---

84 | **MR PAUL BURGOYNE, Wincanton**
Postal: **Knowle Rock, Shepton Montague, Wincanton, Somerset, BA9 8JA**
Contacts: **PHONE (01963) 32138 MOBILE (07894) 081008**
E-MAIL **knowlerockracing@hotmail.co.uk**

1 **DARK AGES (IRE)**, 4, ro f Dark Angel (IRE)—Prosaic Star (IRE) **Mrs Helen Adams**
2 **IRENE KENNET**, 6, b m Kayf Tara—Evaporate **Richard Floyd**
3 **METROPOLITAN CHIEF**, 9, b g Compton Place—Miss Up N Go **Mrs C. E. E. Turner**
4 **TEEN AGER (FR)**, 9, b g Invincible Spirit (IRE)—Tarwiza (IRE) **Mrs C. E. E. Turner**
5 **WEST LEAKE (IRE)**, 7, b g Acclamation—Kilshanny **Dave Tibbetts**

Other Owners: Mr Mark Burgoyne, Mr Simon Burgoyne, Mr Dave Tibbetts.

Assistant Trainer: Mrs Corinna Leigh-Turner

---

85 | **MRS E. M. BURKE, Leyburn**
Postal: **Spigot Lodge, Middleham, Leyburn, North Yorkshire, DL8 4TL**
Contacts: **PHONE (01969) 625088 FAX (01969) 625099 MOBILE (07778) 458777**
E-MAIL **karl@karlburke.co.uk** WEBSITE **www.karlburke.co.uk**

1 **AQUILIFER (IRE)**, 5, b g Holy Roman Emperor (IRE)—Sassy Bird (USA) **J. Kelsey-Fry**
2 **BOLD MARC (IRE)**, 11, b g Bold Fact (USA)—Zara's Birthday (IRE) **Market Avenue Racing Club Ltd**
3 **BOOTS AND SPURS**, 4, b g Oasis Dream—Arctic Char **C. Bryce**
4 **BUZZ LAW (IRE)**, 5, b g Fasliyev (USA)—Buzz Two (IRE) **Mr Mark James & Mrs Elaine Burke**
5 **DANCHEUR (IRE)**, 4, ch f Chineur (FR)—Daneville (IRE) **Mr Mark James & Mrs Elaine Burke**
6 **FAIR LOCH**, 5, gr g Fair Mix (IRE)—Ardentinny
7 **FRONTLINE PHANTOM (IRE)**, 6, b g Noverre (USA)—Daisy Hill **Ontoawinner & Mrs E Burke**
8 **GANGSTERBANKSTERS (FR)**, 4, b g High Chaparral (IRE)—Pantelleria (GER) **Mr W Chow & Mrs E Burke**
9 **HAWAIIAN STORM**, 4, b f Jeremy (USA)—Malahini (UAE) **The Storm Partnership**
10 **LISIERE (IRE)**, 4, b f Excellent Art—Sahara Sky (IRE) **David & Yvonne Blunt**
11 **MEDIA HYPE**, 6, b h Tiger Hill (IRE)—Hyperspectra **Light Valley Stud & Mrs E Burke**
12 **MIAMI GATOR (IRE)**, 6, ch g Titus Livius (FR)—Lovere **Ontoawinner & Mrs E Burke**
13 **NOW MY SUN**, 4, ch g Notnowcato—Sienna Sunset (IRE) **R. Bailey**
14 **PARADISE SPECTRE**, 6, b g Firebreak—Amber's Bluff **The Paradise Partnership**
15 **PRIESTLEY'S REWARD (IRE)**, 4, b g Whipper (USA)—Prima Figlia (IRE) **Mr P Dean & Mrs E Burke**
16 **ROSSELLI (IRE)**, 4, b g Iffraaj—Special Ellie (FR) **W. P. Richards**
17 **SPYKES BAY (USA)**, 4, ch g Speightstown (USA)—She's a Rich Girl (USA) **Mr M. T. Gittins**
18 **SUNNYBRIDGE BOY (IRE)**, 4, br g Strategic Prince—Reem One (IRE) **Keep Racing**
19 **TEPMOKEA (IRE)**, 7, ch g Noverre (USA)—Eroica (GER) **C. V. Wentworth**
20 **YEEOOW (IRE)**, 4, b g Holy Roman Emperor (IRE)—Taraya (IRE) **Mr R. Lee & Mrs E. Burke**

THREE-YEAR-OLDS

21 **ANGELS CALLING**, b f Multiplex—Angel Voices (IRE) **Ontoawinner & Mrs E Burke**
22 **ANGUS OG**, b g Pastoral Pursuits—Winter Moon **Mr D Simpson & Mrs E Burke**

MRS E. M. BURKE - Continued

23 **BARON RUN**, ch g Bertolini (USA)—Bhima **The Sidney Club**
24 **BOLD PREDICTION (IRE)**, b c Kodiac—Alexander Eliott (IRE) **Clipper Group Holdings Ltd**
25 **CEEKAY'S GIRL**, ch f Medicean—Duena **Mr S Marley & Mrs E Burke**
26 **CLOCK OPERA (IRE)**, b f Excellent Art—Moving Diamonds **Clipper Group Holdings Ltd**
27 **EXACTEMENT (IRE)**, ch f Speightstown (USA)—Rakiza (IRE) **Mr M. T. Gittins**
28 **FIZZY PINK**, b f Singspiel (IRE)—Lady Hen **O C Racing**
29 **GEORGIAN BAY (IRE)**, b c Oratorio (IRE)—Jazzie (FR) **Mr P. J. O'Grady**
30 **HAY DUDE**, ch c Dubawi (IRE)—Inaminute (IRE) **R. Bailey**
31 **HIGH LIGHTNING**, b f High Chaparral (IRE)—Kyle Akin **The Lightning Partnership**
32 **ISHIGUNNAEATIT**, b f Ishiguru (USA)—It's Toast (IRE) **Mr D Redvers & Mrs E Burke**
33 **KRUPSKAYA (FR)**, b f Dubai Destination (USA)—Willows World **Norton Common Farm & Mrs E Burke**
34 B f Ishiguru (USA)—Lady-Love **Mrs E. M. Burke**
35 **LIBERTARIAN**, b c New Approach (IRE)—Intrum Morshaan (IRE) **Mr H. J. Strecker**
36 **LOKI'S STRIKE**, ch g Firebreak—Citron **The Mount Racing Club, J O'Shea & S Hunt**
37 **LONDON CITIZEN (USA)**, ch c Proud Citizen (USA)—Sally Bowles (SAF) **Mr H Strecker & Mrs E Burke**
38 **MOLLYVATOR (IRE)**, ch f Motivator—Gazebo **David & Yvonne Blunt**
39 **ODELIZ (IRE)**, ch f Falco (USA)—Acatama (USA) **McMahon Thoroughbreds Ltd & Mrs E Burke**
40 **RECONSIDER BABY (IRE)**, ch f Refuse To Bend (IRE)—Rockahoolababy (IRE) **M. Nelmes-Crocker**
41 **RIVELLINO**, b c Invincible Spirit (IRE)—Brazilian Bride (IRE) **Mrs M. Bryce**
42 **SNAP CRACKLE (IRE)**, b f Whipper (USA)—Glasheen (USA)
43 **STEPPING AHEAD (FR)**, ch g Footstepsinthesand—Zghorta (USA) **Mr Mark James & Mrs Elaine Burke**
44 Ch f Kyllachy—Tara's Force (IRE)
45 **VISIT COPENHAGEN (USA)**, ch f Speightstown (USA)—Nomistakeaboutit (CAN) **Kentaur A/S**
46 **YOURARTISONFIRE**, ch c Dutch Art—Queens Jubilee **Mr J O'Shea, Mr W Rooney & Ontoawinner**

TWO-YEAR-OLDS

47 B f 5/3 Stormy River (FR)—Aaliyah (GER) (Anabaa (USA)) (8730) **Mrs E Burke**
48 B c 1/5 Excellent Art—Amou Daria (FR) (Kendor (FR)) (15079) **Mrs E Burke**
49 **ARAN SKY (IRE)**, b c 15/4 Arakan (USA)—Fayr Sky (IRE) (Fayruz) (4364) **Mr E. J. Hughes**
50 **BALTIC FIRE (IRE)**, b c 9/3 Baltic King—Teutonic (IRE) (Revoque (IRE)) (9523) **McKeown & Wotherspoon**
51 **BETTY BERE (FR)**, b f 10/2 Peer Gynt (JPN)—Monatora (FR) (Hector Protector (USA)) (39682) **Mrs E Burke**
52 B f 5/4 Majestic Missile (IRE)—College of Arms (Lujain (USA)) (7936) **The Mount Racing Club & Mrs E Burke**
53 **DALMARELLA DANCER**, b f 15/4 Mastercraftsman (IRE)—
    Ting A Greeley (Mr Greeley (USA)) (11500) **Dr M. Glaze & Mr I. McInnes**
54 B f 12/3 Baltic King—Danccalli (IRE) (Traditionally (USA)) (4000) **Mr M Hulin & Ontoawinner**
55 B f 5/5 Falco (USA)—Diamond Life (FR) (Montjeu (IRE)) (9523) **Mrs E Burke**
56 B c 29/4 Diamond Green (FR)—Five Sisters (Mujahid (USA)) (4000) **Mrs E Burke**
57 **JAEGER TRAIN (IRE)**, b c 11/4 Captain Rio—
    Marigold (FR) (Marju (IRE)) (19840) **Market Avenue Racing Club Ltd**
58 B f 23/2 Intikhab (USA)—Lady McBeth (IRE) (Avonbridge) (4761) **Mrs M. Bryce**
59 B c 29/4 Authorized (IRE)—Magic Music (IRE) (Magic Ring (IRE)) **Mr R. Bailey**
60 B f 28/3 Whipper (USA)—Maryqueenofscots (IRE) (Fantastic Light (USA)) **Mrs M. Bryce**
61 B c 26/2 Shirocco (GER)—Moon Tree (FR) (Groom Dancer (USA)) (21428) **Mrs E Burke**
62 B f 15/4 Art Connoisseur (IRE)—Nilassiba (Daylami (IRE)) **Mrs E. M. Burke**
63 **STYLENA (FR)**, b f 29/3 Desert Style (IRE)—Serfalya (FR) (Fasliyev (USA)) (12698) **Mrs E Burke**
64 B br f 8/3 Mujadil (USA)—Tucum (IRE) (Diktat) **Mrs E Burke**
65 **TWO SMART (IRE)**, b f 24/1 Cape Cross (IRE)—
    Smartest (IRE) (Exceed And Excel (AUS)) (75000) **David & Yvonne Blunt**

Other Owners: Mr D. Blunt, Mrs Y. Blunt, Mrs V. Brazier, Miss J. P Buxton, Mr W. W. K. Chow, Mr B. Dahl, Mrs A. Dahl, P. Dean, A. J. Duke, Mr A. N. Eaton, Mr G. W. Holden, Mr S. Hunt, Mr M. J. James, Mrs S. Kelsey-Fry, Mr R. Lee, S. P. Marley, Mr R. C. McKeown, McMahon Thoroughbreds Ltd, Mr D. P. Meagher, Norton Common Farm Racing Ltd, N. J. O'Brien, Mr R. P. O'Donnell, Mr J. O'Shea, Mr J. Parker, Mr D. Redvers, Mr W. Rooney, D. Simpson, Mr A. Watson, Mr J. W. Wotherspoon.

Assistant Trainer: Mr Karl Burke

Jockey (flat): Martin Harley. **Conditional:** Alexander Voy. **Apprentice:** Michael Metcalfe, Conor Harrison.

---

86   MR KEIRAN BURKE, Martock
Postal: Lavenoak Racing Stables, Burrough Street, Ash, Martock, Somerset, TA12 6NZ
Contacts: PHONE (01935) 823459

1 **BIG CASINO**, 7, b g Court Cave (IRE)—Migsy Malone **R. N. Jukes**

MR KEIRAN BURKE - Continued

  2 **BUSINESSMONEY JIVE**, 6, b m Kayf Tara—Cloverjay **Business Money Promotions Limited**
  3 **FORTIFICATION (USA)**, 10, gr g With Approval (CAN)—Palisade (USA) **Mr C. P. Rudd**
  4 **HELL'S BAY (FR)**, 11, b g Supreme Leader—Queen's Flagship (IRE) **A. G. Fear & A. J. Norman**
  5 **HUNT BALL (IRE)**, 8, b g Winged Love (IRE)—La Fandango (IRE) **A. C. W. Knott**
  6 **JUST A WHISPER**, 7, b m Talkin Man (CAN)—T'be Sure (IRE) **R. N. Jukes**
  7 5, B m Lucky Story (USA)—Kasamba
  8 **NOWWEARESEVEN**, 6, b m Court Cave (IRE)—Migsy Malone **R. N. Jukes**
  9 **RED JADE**, 8, ch g Dubai Destination (USA)—Red Slippers (USA) **Keiranwho Partnership**
10 **TRUQ CHOUET (FR)**, 6, ch g Valanour (IRE)—Tulipp D'avril (IRE) **Graham, Kate & Paul Darby**
11 **VIN CHAUD**, 5, b m Fair Mix (IRE)—Bayrouge (IRE) **A. C. W. Knott**
12 **WHISPERING JACK**, 8, b g Beat All (USA)—Ski Shot **Prestige Cars and Couriers**

Other Owners: Mr N. Bagwell, Mrs S. L. Bender, Mr R. J. Bender, Mr G. A. Darby, Mrs K. A. Darby, Mr P. Darby, A. G. Fear, A. J. Norman, Mr J. Palmer.

---

87   **MR HUGH BURNS, Alnwick**
Postal: Rose Cottage, Hedgeley Hall, Powburn, Alnwick, Northumberland, NE66 4HZ

  1 **BUN OIR (USA)**, 6, b br g Seeking The Gold (USA)—Fraulein **Mr H. Burns**
  2 **BUSINESS TIME**, 7, b g Definite Article—Blue Shannon (IRE) **Mr H. Burns**
  3 **GARTH MOUNTAIN**, 6, b g Rock of Gibraltar (IRE)—One of The Family **Mr H. Burns**
  4 **NORTHERN WARRIOR**, 5, b g Tamure (IRE)—Rail Cat **Mr H. Burns**
  5 **OVERPRESENTLY**, 5, b m Overbury (IRE)—Coole Presence (IRE) **Mr H. Burns**
  6 **ROUGH TIMES (IRE)**, 8, br g Bishop of Cashel—Lady Arpel (IRE) **Mr H. Burns**
  7 **SOLIS**, 7, b g Josr Algarhoud (IRE)—Passiflora **Mr H. Burns**

---

88   **MR GERARD BUTLER, Newmarket**

Trainer did not wish details of his string to appear.

---

89   **MR JOHN BUTLER, Newmarket**
Postal: **The Bungalow, Charnwood Stables, Hamilton Road, Newmarket, Suffolk, CB8 7JQ**
Contacts: **MOBILE (07764) 999743**

  1 **ATACAMA SUNRISE**, 7, b m Desert Sun—Top of The Morning **Mr J. Butler**
  2 **BELLE NOVERRE (IRE)**, 9, b m Noverre (USA)—Belle Etoile (FR) **Mr J. Butler**
  3 **FASHION FLOW**, 6, ch m Danehill Dancer (IRE)—Verasina (USA) **Mr J. Butler**
  4 **FINAL DRIVE (IRE)**, 7, b g Viking Ruler (AUS)—Forest Delight (IRE) **Par 4 Racing**
  5 **FLORALYS (USA)**, 4, b f Flower Alley (USA)—Search Mission (USA) **Mr J. Butler**
  6 **LOW KEY (IRE)**, 6, b h Pentire—La Capilla **Mr J. Butler**
  7 **PIPERS PIPING (IRE)**, 7, b g Noverre (USA)—Monarchy (IRE) **Mr J. Butler**
  8 **PROHIBITION (IRE)**, 7, b g Danehill Dancer (IRE)—Crumpetsfortea (IRE) **Mr J. Butler**
  9 **RAISE THE RAFTERS (IRE)**, 8, ch g Monashee Mountain (USA)—Zolube (IRE) **Mr J. Butler**
10 **STAND GUARD**, 9, b g Danehill (USA)—Protectress **Mr J. Butler**
11 **TRIP SWITCH**, 7, b g Reset (AUS)—Caribbean Star **Mr J. Butler**
12 **VITZNAU (IRE)**, 9, b g Val Royal (FR)—Neat Dish (CAN) **Mr J. Butler**

THREE-YEAR-OLDS

13 **MISLEADING PROMISE (IRE)**, b g Refuse To Bend (IRE)—Farthing (IRE) **Mr J. Butler**

Other Owners: Mr P. A. Cafferty, Mr M. J. Gavin.

90 MR PADDY BUTLER, Lewes
Postal: **Homewood Gate Racing Stables, Novington Lane, East Chiltington, Lewes, East Sussex, BN7 3AU**
Contacts: **PHONE/FAX (01273) 890124 MOBILE (07973) 873846**
E-MAIL homewoodgate@aol.com

1 **BENANDONNER (USA)**, 10, ch g Giant's Causeway (USA)—
                      Cape Verdi (IRE) **Miss M P Bryant, David & Eileen Bryant**
2 **BRAVO BELLE (IRE)**, 6, b m Bertolini (USA)—Dazilyn Lady (USA) **C. W. Wilson**
3 **CARLTON SCROOP (FR)**, 10, ch g Priolo (USA)—Elms Schooldays **Miss M. P. Bryant**
4 **CURRAGH DANCER (FR)**, 10, ch g Grand Lodge (USA)—Native Twine **Miss M. P. Bryant**
5 **GUILDED WARRIOR**, 10, b g Mujahid (USA)—Pearly River **Miss M. P. Bryant**
6 **HEADING TO FIRST**, 6, b g Sulamani (IRE)—Bahirah **Homewoodgate Racing Club**
7 **LOVE PEGASUS (USA)**, 7, b br g Fusaichi Pegasus (USA)—Take Charge Lady (USA) **Mrs E. Lucey-Butler**
8 **PROPHET IN A DREAM**, 5, b g Fath (USA)—Princess Dariyba (IRE) **C. W. Wilson**
9 **QUERIDO (GER)**, 9, b g Acatenango (GER)—Quest of Fire (FR) **Homewoodgate Racing Club**
10 **USQUAEBACH**, 6, b m Trade Fair—Mashmoom **Miss M. P. Bryant**
11 **WHAT'S FOR TEA**, 8, b m Beat All (USA)—Come To Tea (IRE) **Mrs E. Lucey-Butler**

THREE-YEAR-OLDS
12 **SWEET PICCOLO**, ch g Piccolo—Quality Street **Mr D. M. Whatmough**

Other Owners: Mr D. Bryant, Mrs E. Bryant, Mr P. J. Charman, Mrs A. Horrell.

Assistant Trainer: Mrs E Lucey-Butler

Jockey (flat): Robert L. Butler. Amateur: Miss M. Bryant, Miss Zoe Lilly.

91 MRS BARBARA BUTTERWORTH, Appleby
Postal: **Bolton Mill, Bolton, Appleby-in-Westmorland, Cumbria, CA16 6AL**
Contacts: **PHONE (01768) 361363 MOBILE (07778) 104118**

1 **FRED BOJANGALS (IRE)**, 11, b g Scribano—Southern Princess **Miss E. Butterworth**
2 **KNIGHT VALLIANT**, 10, gr g Dansili—Aristocratique **Mrs B. Butterworth**
3 **WESTERN BOUND (IRE)**, 12, ch g Presenting—Mid West Girl (IRE) **Miss E. Butterworth**

Assistant Trainer: Miss Elizabeth Butterworth

Amateur: Miss Elizabeth Butterworth.

92 MR NEVILLE BYCROFT, Malton
Postal: **Cotman Rise, Brandsby, York, YO61 4RN**
Contacts: **PHONE (01347) 888641 MOBILE (07802) 763227**

1 **ADIATOR**, 5, b m Needwood Blade—Retaliator **N. Bycroft**
2 **AUTO MAC**, 5, b g Auction House (USA)—Charlottevalentina (IRE) **Mrs C. M. Whatley**
3 **DUAL MAC**, 6, bl g Paris House—Carol Again **Mrs C. M. Whatley**
4 **EENY MAC (IRE)**, 6, ch g Redback—Sally Green (IRE) **Mrs J. Dickinson**
5 **FAMA MAC**, 6, b g Fraam—Umbrian Gold (IRE) **Mrs C. M. Whatley**

Assistant Trainer: Seb Spencer

Jockey (flat): Jimmy Quinn, Franny Norton.

93 MISS JULIE CAMACHO, Malton
Postal: **Star Cottage, Welham Road, Norton, Malton, North Yorkshire, YO17 9QE**
Contacts: **PHONE (01653) 696205 FAX (01653) 696205 MOBILE (07779) 318135 / (07950) 356440**
E-MAIL julie@jacracing.co.uk WEBSITE www.juliecamacho.com

1 **BELINSKY (IRE)**, 6, b g Compton Place—Westwood (FR) **Wentdale Limited**
2 **DANDARRELL**, 6, b g Makbul—Dress Design (IRE) **Mr J. S. De W. Waller**
3 **DIESCENTRIC (USA)**, 6, b g Diesis—Hawzah **Axom (XVIII)**
4 **DUBAI CELEBRATION**, 5, b g Dubai Destination (USA)—Pretty Poppy **L Bolingbroke, N Gravett & J Camacho**

MISS JULIE CAMACHO - Continued

5 **JUSTINE TIME (IRE)**, 4, b f Kodiac—Sinn Time (IRE) **Mr N. Gravett**
6 **MY SINGLE MALT (IRE)**, 5, b g Danehill Dancer (IRE)—Slip Dance (IRE) **Mr N. Gravett**
7 **NOWDORO**, 4, ch g Notnowcato—Salydora (FR) **Wentdale Limited**
8 **SIR NOD**, 11, b g Tagula (IRE)—Nordan Raider **Miss J. A. Camacho**
9 **SPANISH LEGACY**, 4, b f Dr Fong (USA)—Spanish Lace **Miss J. A. Camacho**
10 **TOM SAWYER**, 5, b g Dansili—Cayman Sunset (IRE) **Bolingbroke J Howard FAO MerseyR & Ptns**
11 **WEBBOW (IRE)**, 11, b g Dr Devious (IRE)—Ower (IRE) **Wentdale Limited**
12 **ZAKATAL**, 7, gr g Kalanisi (IRE)—Zankara (FR) **David Furman & John Sugarman**

THREE-YEAR-OLDS
13 **REX WHISTLER (IRE)**, b g Tamayuz—Dangle (IRE) **Axom XXXVIII**

TWO-YEAR-OLDS
14 B c 20/4 Captain Gerrard (IRE)—Cumbrian Concerto (Petong) (5714) **Axom XLIV**

Other Owners: Axom, Mr Lee Bolingbroke, Mr Tony Bruce, Mr S. Burrows, Miss Julie Camacho, Mr Dan Downie, Mr Nigel Gravett, Mr Brian Hankey, Mr Tony Hill, Mr Graeme Howard, Ms S. M. Jamieson, Mrs Faith O'Connor, Mr J. E. Townend.

Assistant Trainer: Mr S. Brown

Jockey (flat): Tom Eaves, Barry McHugh.

---

94 MR MARK CAMPION, Malton
Postal: **Whitewell House Stables, Whitewall, Malton, North Yorkshire, YO17 9EH**
Contacts: **PHONE (01653) 692729 FAX (01653) 600066 MOBILE (07973) 178311**
E-MAIL **info@markcampion-racing.com** WEBSITE **www.markcampion-racing.com**

1 **ALISTORM**, 7, b m Bob Back (USA)—Storm In Front (IRE) **Medbourne Racing Club**
2 **CHARMING GRACE (IRE)**, 7, b m Flemensfirth (USA)—Lady Laureate **The Saddlers' Flyers**
3 **DESERT NOVA (IRE)**, 11, ch g Desert King (IRE)—Assafiyah (IRE) **Whitewall Racing**
4 5, B g Holy Roman Emperor (IRE)—Ghita (IRE) **Mrs C. Rattray**
5 **MINKIE MOON (IRE)**, 4, b g Danehill Dancer (IRE)—Minkova (IRE) **Faulkner West & Co Ltd**
6 **PANASHKA (IRE)**, 8, ch m Ashkalani (IRE)—Dressed In Style (IRE) **Pan's People**
7 **SADDLERS' SECRET (IRE)**, 8, b m Saddlers' Hall (IRE)—Birdless Bush (IRE) **The Saddlers' Flyers**

Other Owners: Mrs J. Bautell, Mrs L. Beale, Mr A. C. Brett, Mr A. M. Campion, Mr Barrie Coleman, Mr D. Hern, Mr Glenn Nurse, Mr I. T. Stevens.

Assistant Trainer: Mrs F. Campion

---

95 MS JENNIE CANDLISH, Leek
Postal: **Basford Grange Racing Stables, Basford, Leek, Staffordshire, ST13 7ET**
Contacts: **PHONE (01538) 360324 (07779) 047826 FAX (01538) 360324 MOBILE (07889) 413639**
E-MAIL **jenniecandlish@yahoo.co.uk** WEBSITE **www.jenniecandlishracing.co.uk**

1 **AMROTH BAY**, 9, b g Alflora (IRE)—La Bella Villa **West Mercia Fork Trucks Ltd**
2 **BARAFUNDLE (IRE)**, 9, ch g Flemensfirth (USA)—Different Dee (IRE) **Mrs J. M. Ratcliff**
3 **BASFORD BEN**, 5, b g Trade Fair—Moly (FR) **Alan Baxter & Anthony Bloor**
4 **BEAUBOREEN (IRE)**, 6, b g Revoque (IRE)—Roseboreen (IRE) **Mr & Mrs R. N. C. Hall**
5 **BEST EXCUSE**, 6, b g Lucky Owners (NZ)—Zambia (IRE) **Mr D. J. Critchley**
6 **BOB'S WORLD**, 4, b g Multiplex—Vocation (IRE) **Mr R. J. Cant**
7 **CHESTERTERN**, 6, ch g Karinga Bay—My Tern (IRE) **Mr P. C. Dutton**
8 **CRESCENT BEACH (IRE)**, 6, b g Presenting—Angelas Choice (IRE) **Mr P. & Mrs G. A. Clarke**
9 **CROSS KENNON (IRE)**, 9, b g Craigsteel—Gaelic Million (IRE) **Mr P. & Mrs G. A. Clarke**
10 **DECENT LORD (IRE)**, 9, b g Lord of Appeal—Otorum (IRE) **Ms J. Candlish**
11 **DETOUR AHEAD**, 5, ch m Needwood Blade—My Tern (IRE) **Mr P. C. Dutton**
12 **DONT TELL SAILOR (IRE)**, 7, b g Saddlers' Hall (IRE)—Pharlen's Dream (IRE) **Mr P. & Mrs G. A. Clarke**
13 **EBONY RIVER (IRE)**, 7, b g Alderbrook—Dishy (IRE) **Mr & Mrs R. Hall & Mrs W. Glazebrook**
14 **FAIRWEATHER FRIEND**, 4, gr f Fair Mix (IRE)—Lucylou (IRE) **Mr P. & Mrs G. A. Clarke**
15 **FIENDISH FLAME (IRE)**, 9, ch g Beneficial—Deenish (IRE) **Mr & Mrs R. N. C. Hall**
16 **FLAME OF DIXIE (IRE)**, 7, b m Beneficial—Deenish (IRE) **Mr & Mrs R. N. C. Hall**
17 **FRENCH TIES (IRE)**, 11, ch g John French—No Ties (IRE) **A. J. Baxter**

MS JENNIE CANDLISH - Continued

18 GRANVILLE ISLAND (IRE), 6, b g Flemensfirth (USA)—Fox Glen **Mr P. & Mrs G. A. Clarke**
19 HIGHLAND RAIN, 5, ch g Sir Harry Lewis (USA)—Scottish Clover **Mr P. & Mrs G. A. Clarke**
20 LUCKY LUKEY, 7, gr g Cape Town (IRE)—Imprevue (IRE) **John Pointon & Sons**
21 LUKEYS LUCK, 7, b g Cape Town (IRE)—Vitelucy **John Pointon & Sons**
22 MAOI CHINN TIRE (IRE), 6, b g Mull of Kintyre (USA)—Primrose And Rose **A. J. Baxter**
23 MECOX BAY (IRE), 6, b g Noverre (USA)—Birdsong (IRE) **The Can't Do Ten Stone Anymore Partnership**
24 MISTYBOREEN (IRE), 5, gr m Great Palm (USA)—Roseboreen (IRE) **Mr & Mrs R. N. C. Hall**
25 PARTY ROCK (IRE), 6, b g Vinnie Roe (IRE)—Garryduff Eile (IRE) **J. Candlish**
26 PRIME CONTENDER, 11, b g Efisio—Gecko Rouge **Mrs F. M. Draper**
27 PYRACANTHA, 8, b g Muhtarram (USA)—Forsythia **A. J. Baxter**
28 SCHEHERAZADESDREAM, 6, ch m Stage Pass—Ambitious Annie **Mrs F. M. Draper**
29 SNOWED IN (IRE), 4, gr g Dark Angel (IRE)—Spinning Gold **Alan Baxter & David Cheetham**
30 TERNTHEOTHERCHEEK, 4, b f Multiplex—My Tern (IRE) **Mr P. C. Dutton**
31 WAKE YOUR DREAMS (IRE), 5, b g Oscar (IRE)—Rose Karanja **Mrs P. M. Beardmore**

THREE-YEAR-OLDS

32 LE DUDE, b g Lateral—Vocation (IRE) **Mr R. J. Cant**

Other Owners: Mr Alan Baxter, Mr Anthony Bloor, Mr David Cheetham, Mr Peter Clarke, Mrs Gwenda Ann Clarke, Mrs Sara Glazebrook, Mr R. N. C. Hall, Mrs R. N. C. Hall.

Assistant Trainer: Alan O'Keeffe

Jockey (flat): Joe Fanning, Paul Hanagan, Sean Quinlan. **Jockey (NH):** Alan O'Keeffe, Sean Quinlan.

96	**MR HENRY CANDY, Wantage** Postal: Kingston Warren, Wantage, Oxfordshire, OX12 9QF Contacts: **PHONE (01367) 820276 / 820514 FAX (01367) 820500 MOBILE (07836) 211264** E-MAIL henrycandy@btconnect.com

1 AMBER HEIGHTS, 5, b m Kyllachy—Jumairah Sun (IRE) **Ms L. Burns**
2 DINKUM DIAMOND (IRE), 5, b h Aussie Rules (USA)—Moving Diamonds **Eight Star Syndicate**
3 DREAM CATCHER (FR), 5, gr g Della Francesca (USA)—Gallopade (FR) **Miss N. M. Haine**
4 JAVA ROSE, 4, b f Ishiguru (USA)—Mighty Splash **Mrs M. D. Low**
5 JOCASTA DAWN, 4, b f Kyllachy—Jubilee Dawn **Mrs David Blackburn & Mr M. Blackburn**
6 L'AMI LOUIS (IRE), 5, b g Elusive City (USA)—Princess Electra (IRE) **First Of Many Partnership**
7 PICABO (IRE), 5, b m Elusive City (USA)—Gi La High **Mr Tom Ford**
8 SELKIE'S FRIEND, 4, b g Elnadim (USA)—T G's Girl **Henry D. N. B. Candy**
9 THE CONFESSOR, 6, b g Piccolo—Twilight Mistress **Six Too Many**
10 WOOLSTON FERRY (IRE), 7, b g Fath (USA)—Cathy Garcia (IRE) **Ms L. Burns**
11 ZHIGGY'S STARDUST, 4, b g Zafeen (FR)—Lady Natilda **Ian Higginson/ H. Candy**

THREE-YEAR-OLDS

12 Br f Clodovil (IRE)—Alenushka **Mrs Fiona Gordon**
13 ANNAWI, b f Dubawi (IRE)—Anna of Brunswick **Major M. G. Wyatt**
14 ANNINA (IRE), b f Singspiel (IRE)—Lysandra (IRE) **The Earl Cadogan KBE**
15 APRICOT SKY, ch g Pastoral Pursuits—Miss Apricot **Simon Broke & Partners III**
16 BENONI, b c Bertolini (USA)—Ladykirk **Clayton, Frost, Kebell & Candy**
17 BOOKMAKER, b g Byron—Cankara (IRE) **Giles, McCarthy, Stephens & Newton**
18 CAPE PERON, b g Beat Hollow—Free Offer **The Earl Cadogan KBE**
19 CODE OF HONOR, b c Zafeen (FR)—Verbal Intrigue (USA) **Mr D B Clark / Mr J J Byrne**
20 GREY'S ELEGY, gr g Ishiguru (USA)—Christmas Rose **Henry D. N. B. Candy**
21 JUST CHARLIE, b g Piccolo—Siryena **Mrs A. D. Bourne/ Mr H. Candy**
22 LADY PIMPERNEL, ch f Sir Percy—Angelano **Henry Candy & Partners II**
23 MEDISKA, b f Medicean—Silca Boo **Mr & Mrs R. Scott**
24 MUSIC MASTER, b c Piccolo—Twilight Mistress **Mr Godfrey Wilson**
25 MUSKAT LINK, b g Rail Link—Muskat Rose (IRE) **The Muskateers**
26 PEARL STREET (USA), b f Street Sense (USA)—Pretty Meadow (USA) **Pearl Bloodstock Limited**
27 PEDRO SERRANO (IRE), b c Footstepsinthesand—Shaiyadima (IRE) **Six Too Many**
28 SECRETLY, ch f Sakhee's Secret—The Cat's Whiskers (NZ) **Bloomsbury Stud**
29 SILK ROUTE, ch f Dubai Destination (USA)—Crinolette (IRE) **D. B. Clark**
30 SPEEDY WRITER, b g Byron—Merch Rhyd-Y-Grug **Henry D. N. B. Candy**
31 TIGHT FIT, ch f Assertive—Bikini **W. M. Lidsey & H. Candy**
32 VIENNESE VERSE, b g Byron—Teller (ARG) **The Chevaliers**

MR HENRY CANDY - Continued

TWO-YEAR-OLDS

33 CHARLES MOLSON, b c 30/3 Monsieur Bond (IRE)—Arculinge (Paris House) (26666) **Simon Broke & Partners**
34 B f 2/3 Mount Nelson—Cinnas Ransom (Red Ransom (USA)) (3500) **The Port & Brandy Syndicate**
35 CORNISH PATH, b f 30/3 Champs Elysees—Quintrell (Royal Applause) (4000) **Mrs D. Blackburn/ Mr H. Candy**
36 DALASI (IRE), b f 20/2 Dalakhani (IRE)—Holly's Kid (USA) (Pulpit (USA)) (40000) **Major M. G. Wyatt**
37 Ch f 5/3 Three Valleys (USA)—Descriptive (IRE) (Desert King (IRE)) (5500) **Henry D. N. B. Candy**
38 B f 11/2 Assertive—Ela Paparouna (Vettori (IRE)) **Lady Whent**
39 Ch c 29/3 Nayef (USA)—Emily Blake (IRE) (Lend A Hand) **Mr & Mrs R. Scott**
40 FAURE ISLAND, b c 3/2 Myboycharlie (IRE)—Free Offer (Generous (IRE)) **The Earl Cadogan KBE**
41 GREENSIDE, b c 10/4 Dubawi (IRE)—Katrina (IRE) (Ela-Mana-Mou) (38000) **T. Barr**
42 HALLBECK, ch f 20/2 Halling (USA)—Goslar (In The Wings) **Major M. G. Wyatt**
43 JETHOU ISLAND, ch f 3/4 Virtual—Lihou Island (Beveled (USA)) (7500) **Mrs F. A. Veasey**
44 LACOCK, b c 19/4 Compton Place—Puya (Kris) **Girsonfield Ltd**
45 B f 2/4 Champs Elysees—Luanas Pearl (Bahri (USA)) (22000) **Mr P. A. Deal/ Mr H. Candy**
46 MARYDALE, ch f 10/2 Aqlaam—Mary Goodnight (King's Best (USA)) (50000) **Major M. G. Wyatt**
47 MICROWAVE (IRE), b f 22/1 Fastnet Rock (AUS)—
Chrisalice (GR) (Lujain (USA)) (103174) **Qatar Bloodstock Ltd**
48 MIND, b c 11/4 Zamindar (USA)—Danae (Dansili) **Girsonfield Ltd**
49 ROSITA, b f 24/2 Firebreak—Muskat Rose (IRE) (One Cool Cat (USA)) (1714) **The Muskat Rose Syndicate**
50 ROYAL FFANCI, b f 17/4 Royal Applause—Madamoiselle Jones (Emperor Jones (USA)) (27000) **Hunscote Stud**
51 SCARLET SASH, b f 23/2 Sir Percy—Scarlet Buttons (IRE) (Marju (IRE)) (6190) **Henry Candy & Partners III**
52 Ch f 27/4 Bertolini (USA)—Sheesha (USA) (Shadeed (USA)) **Mr J. Porteous/ Mr H. Candy**
53 TRIPLE DIPPER, b f 12/1 Dubai Destination (USA)—Rumbled (Halling (USA)) **The Rumble Racing Club**
54 B f 29/3 Assertive—Twilight Mistress (Bin Ajwaad (IRE)) (14285) **Six Too Many/T. A. Frost/G. Wilson**
55 VEILED INTRIGUE, b f 12/5 Pastoral Pursuits—Verbal Intrigue (USA) (Dahar (USA)) **Mr D B Clark / Mr J J Byrne**
56 WARRENDALE, b f 9/3 Three Valleys (USA)—
Swynford Pleasure (Reprimand) (15238) **Mrs D Blackburn/Lady Morrison/H. Candy/A L Smith-Maxwell**
57 WHITE RUSSIAN, ch f 7/3 Sir Percy—Danse Russe (Pivotal) (5000) **Six Too Many**

Other Owners: Mr Alexander Acloque, Mrs David Blackburn, Mr Mark Blackburn, Mrs A. D. Bourne, Mr Simon Broke, Mr C. J. Burley, Mr J. J. Byrne, Mr D. B. Clark, Mr S. Clayton, Mr W. R. Collins, Mr T. A. Daniels, Mr P. A. Deal, Mr A. L. Deal, Mrs Amanda Dixon, Mr D. J. Erwin, Mr Alexander Frost, Mr T. A. F. Frost, Mrs F. Gordon, Mr T. Gould, Mr K. J. P. Gundlach, Mrs Charlotte Harris, Mr I. Higginson, Mr Tony Hirschfeld, Mr John Inverdale, Mr J. Kebell, Mr W. M. Lidsey, Mr H. McNeill, Mrs Jonathan Moore, Mr D. Norris, Mrs Angela Pinder, Mrs C. M. Poland, Mr Robert Scott, Mrs P. M. Scott, Mrs Jo Slogrove, Mr S. M. Smith, Mrs L. A. Smith, Mrs Jenny Snowball, Mr Martin Thompson, Mrs F. A. Veasey, Mrs C. S. Whitaker.

Assistant Trainer: David Pinder

---

97 | **MR GRANT CANN, Cullompton**
Postal: **Newlands Farm, Cullompton, Devon, EX15 1QQ**
Contacts: **PHONE (01884) 32284 MOBILE (07968) 271118**

1 ARCTIC WATCH, 8, gr g Accondy (IRE)—Watcha (USA) **P. J. Cave**
2 BROGEEN BOY (IRE), 5, br g Golan (IRE)—Brogeen Lady (IRE) **T. J. Whitley**
3 HOW'S MY FRIEND, 8, b g Karinga Bay—Friendly Lady **J. G. Cann**
4 I'M NOT TELLING (IRE), 5, ch g Definite Article—Incognito (FR) **J. G. Cann**

---

98 | **MR DON CANTILLON, Newmarket**
Postal: **10 Rous Road, Newmarket, Suffolk, CB8 8DL**
Contacts: **PHONE (01638) 668507 MOBILE (07709) 377601**

1 ALPINE BREEZE (IRE), 7, b m King's Theatre (IRE)—Alpine Gale (IRE) **D. E. Cantillon**
2 AS I AM (IRE), 5, b m Old Vic—Faucon **D. E. Cantillon**
3 4, B g Westerner—Faucon **D. E. Cantillon**
4 GREEN TO GOLD (IRE), 8, gr g Daylami (IRE)—Alonsa (IRE) **Sir Alex Ferguson & Sotirios Hassiakos**
5 4, B g Flying Legend (USA)—Jennylee (IRE) **D. E. Cantillon**
6 LA ESTRELLA (USA), 10, b g Theatrical—Princess Ellen (USA) **D. E. Cantillon**
7 ODIN (IRE), 5, b g Norse Dancer (IRE)—Dimelight **Mrs C. Reed**
8 OSCARS WAY (IRE), 5, b g Oscar (IRE)—Derrigra Sublime (IRE) **D. E. Cantillon**

MR DON CANTILLON - Continued

THREE-YEAR-OLDS

9 B f One Cool Cat (USA)—Good Thought (IRE) **D. E. Cantillon**

TWO-YEAR-OLDS

10 B f 29/1 Holy Roman Emperor (IRE)—Etaaq (IRE) (Sadler's Wells (USA)) **Mrs C. Reed**

Other Owners: Sir A. Ferguson, S. Hassiakos.

---

99 **MR DAVID CARR, Hexham**
Postal: Clancy House, Shaws Farm, Hexham, Northumberland, NE46 3AS
Contacts: **PHONE (01434) 603725 (01434) 603710 MOBILE (07717) 443780**

1 **ARDNACLANCY (IRE)**, 10, br g Darnay—Ardnataggle (IRE) **D. Carr**
2 **COASTLEY (IRE)**, 11, b g Lord Americo—Cosima (IRE) **D. Carr**
3 **COOL STAR (IRE)**, 7, b g One Cool Cat (USA)—Pack Ice (USA) **D. Carr**
4 **WINCES WELL (IRE)**, 6, b g Helissio (FR)—Cardinal Press **D. Carr**

---

100 **MRS RUTH CARR, Stillington**
Postal: Mowbray House Farm, Easingwold Road, Stillington, York, North Yorkshire, YO61 1LT
Contacts: PHONE (01347) 823776 (home) (01347) 821683 (yard) MOBILE (07721) 926772
E-MAIL ruth@ruthcarrracing.co.uk WEBSITE www.ruthcarrracing.co.uk

1 **AL MUHEER (IRE)**, 8, b g Diktat—Dominion Rose (USA) **Antigua Cavaliers & Mrs R Carr**
2 **AMAZING BLUE SKY**, 7, b g Barathea (IRE)—Azure Lake (USA) **G Scruton, D Williamson & R Carr**
3 **BECKERMET (IRE)**, 11, b g Second Empire (IRE)—Razida (IRE) **Mrs M. Chapman**
4 **CHOSEN ONE (IRE)**, 8, ch g Choisir (AUS)—Copious (IRE) **Bridget Houlston, Chris Jeffery & Co**
5 **CHUNKY DIAMOND (IRE)**, 4, b g Diamond Green (FR)—Balance The Books **The Bottom Liners & Mrs R. Carr**
6 **CONO ZUR (FR)**, 6, b g Anabaa (USA)—Alaskan Idol (USA) **Ruth Carr Racing**
7 **DHHAMAAN (IRE)**, 8, b g Dilshaan—Safe Care (IRE) **S. B. Clark**
8 **DUBAI DYNAMO**, 8, b g Kyllachy—Miss Mercy (IRE) **The Bottom Liners**
9 **ELLAAL**, 4, b g Oasis Dream—Capistrano Day (USA) **Paul Saxton & The Bottom Liners**
10 **GLORIAM (USA)**, 4, b g War Chant (USA)—Amandas Bandit (USA) **Mrs R. A. Carr**
11 **GRAN MAESTRO (USA)**, 4, ch g Medicean—Red Slippers (USA) **Paul Saxton & The Bottom Liners**
12 **HAB REEH**, 5, gr g Diktat—Asian Love **Mrs B Taylor, Mr A Dickman, Mrs R Carr**
13 **HEAD SPACE (IRE)**, 5, b g Invincible Spirit (IRE)—Danzelline **The Bottom Liners & Mrs R. Carr**
14 **IMPERIAL DJAY (IRE)**, 8, b g Dilshaan—Slayjay (IRE) **Hollinbridge Partnership**
15 **KLYNCH**, 7, b g Kyllachy—Inchcoonan **Mr Douglas Renton**
16 **LIGHT THE CITY (IRE)**, 6, b g Fantastic Light (USA)—Marine City (JPN) **Atkins Legal Services & Mrs. R. Carr**
17 **MARINE COMMANDO**, 5, b g Pastoral Pursuits—Carollan (IRE) **Mr M. Wynne**
18 **MUTAFAAKIR (IRE)**, 4, b g Oasis Dream—Moon's Whisper (USA) **Mr Michael Hill**
19 **NONAYNEVER**, 5, ch g Nayef (USA)—Qirmazi (USA) **Mrs Sally Doyle**
20 **NORTH CENTRAL (USA)**, 6, b br g Forest Camp (USA)—Brittan Lee (USA) **Grange Park Racing**
21 **ORPSIE BOY (IRE)**, 10, b g Orpen (USA)—Nordicolini (IRE) **Miss V. Church**
22 **RED CAPE (FR)**, 10, b g Cape Cross (IRE)—Muirfield (FR) **Middleham Park Racing LVI**
23 **RUBY GLASS (IRE)**, 4, b g Red Clubs (IRE)—Gold Bar (IRE) **Mrs Ruth A. Carr**
24 **VICTOIRE DE LYPHAR (IRE)**, 6, b g Bertolini (USA)—Victory Peak **Middleham Park Racing XVIII**

THREE-YEAR-OLDS

25 **GOLD ROLL (IRE)**, b g Intikhab (USA)—Sopran Marida (IRE) **Reach For The Moon & Mrs R Carr**
26 **LOOK ON BY**, gr g Byron—Where's Carol **Mr J. A. Swinburne**
27 **MULTISURE**, b g Multiplex—Sharoura **Mrs Ruth A. Carr**
28 **OUT OF THE BLOCKS**, b g Firebreak—Suzie Fong **Mr Michael Hill**

Other Owners: Mr Toby Brereton, Mrs Ruth A. Carr, Mrs Marion Chapman, Mr S. B. Clark, Mr Alan D. Crombie, Mr Andrew Dickman, Mr J. P. Hames, Mr Andy Harris, Mr T. S. Palin, R J H Limited, Mr A. Riaz, Mr P. A. Saxton, Mrs B. Taylor.

Jockey (flat): P J McDonald, James Sullivan.

101 MR DECLAN CARROLL, Sledmere

Postal: **Sledmere House Stables, Sledmere, Driffield, East Yorkshire, YO25 3XG**
Contacts: **PHONE** (01377) 236161 **FAX** (01377) 236161 **MOBILE** (07801) 553779
E-MAIL sledmereracing@hotmail.co.uk

1 BAILE ATHA CLIATH (IRE), 4, b g Barathea (IRE)—Danielli (IRE) **Dreams**
2 BOUCHER GARCON (IRE), 5, b g Spartacus (IRE)—Valamander (IRE) **M. Cunningham**
3 COME HERE YEW (IRE), 5, ch g Refuse To Bend (IRE)—Red Zinger (USA) **K. Mackay & L. Ibbotson**
4 GREEN PARK (IRE), 10, b g Shinko Forest (IRE)—Danccini (IRE) **G. A. Fixings Ltd**
5 ILLUSTRIOUS PRINCE (IRE), 6, b g Acclamation—Sacred Love (IRE) **R. J. Flegg**
6 INVINCIBLE HERO (IRE), 6, b g Invincible Spirit (IRE)—Bridelina (FR) **Mrs S. A. Bryan**
7 MICK SLATES (IRE), 4, b g Moss Vale (IRE)—Sonic Night (IRE) **Ormskirk**
8 MY DESTINATION (IRE), 4, b g Dubai Destination (USA)—Gossamer **Mrs S. A. Bryan**
9 PRESIDENT LINCOLN (USA), 5, b br g First Samurai (USA)—Preach (USA) **Mr M. Stewart**
10 PROPHESY (IRE), 4, ch g Excellent Art—Race The Wild Wind (USA) **Mr M. Stewart**
11 PULL THE PIN (IRE), 4, b g Kheleyf (USA)—Inscribed (IRE) **Mr C. J. Harding**
12 REGAL ACCLAIM (IRE), 4, b g Acclamation—Certain Charm (USA) **Mrs Margaret Woolfitt, Mrs Angela Sellers**
13 4, B f Doyen (IRE)—Rock Concert **Mr Steve Ryan**
14 SAVE THE BEES, 5, b g Royal Applause—Rock Concert **Mr S. P. Ryan**
15 SIR RYAN, 4, b g Multiplex—Mrs Oh (IRE) **Mr Steve Sankey**
16 SWIFTLY DONE (IRE), 6, b g Whipper (USA)—Ziffany **Mr D Watts, Miss C King, J Syme & M Syme**
17 WATTS UP SON, 5, b g Diktat—Local Fancy **L. Ibbotson, D. Watts & J. Syme**
18 WHOZTHECAT (IRE), 6, b g One Cool Cat (USA)—Intaglia (GER) **Ninerus**

THREE-YEAR-OLDS

19 BIG JOE SENIOR (IRE), b c Oratorio (IRE)—Kalambara (IRE) **Patsy Melvin**
20 DEEPEST BLUE, b g Sakhee's Secret—Midnight Sky **Mr & Mrs I. H. Bendelow**
21 DUKE OF YORKSHIRE, b g Duke of Marmalade (IRE)—Dame Edith (IRE) **Mr M. Stewart**
22 JOMARI (IRE), ch g Ad Valorem (USA)—Love Valentine (IRE) **The Lucky Three**
23 LASTCHANCELUCAS, b g Ishiguru (USA)—Light of Aragon **C. H. Stephenson & Partners**
24 Gr g Verglas (IRE)—Mis St Tropez **Dreams**
25 SANTRY, ch g Ishiguru (USA)—Mis Chicat (IRE) **Dreams**
26 TWO PANCAKES, b g Compton Place—Fancy Rose (USA) **Mr K. McConnell**

TWO-YEAR-OLDS

27 B f 10/3 Amadeus Wolf—America Lontana (FR) (King's Theatre (IRE)) (4761) **Miss A. Muir, Mr K. McConnell**
28 BOUSFIELD, b c 31/3 Duke of Marmalade (IRE)—Exodia (Dr Fong (USA)) (6000) **R. J. Flegg**
29 FARANG BER SONG, b c 21/4 Selkirk (USA)—Dazzle (Gone West (USA)) (16000) **Lee Ibbotson**
30 Ch f 1/4 Rock of Gibraltar (IRE)—Princesse Sonia (FR) (Ashkalani (IRE)) (9000) **Mr & Mrs J. G. Johnson**
31 PULL THE PLUG (IRE), b f 12/4 Sleeping Indian—Babylonian (Shamardal (USA)) (4285) **Mr C. J. Harding**

Apprentice: Neil Farley, Jason Hart, Michael Kenny, Luke Leadbitter.

102 MR TONY CARROLL, Cropthorne

Postal: **The Cropthorne Stud, Field Barn Lane, Cropthorne, Pershore, Worcestershire, WR10 3LY**
Contacts: **PHONE** (01386) 861020 **FAX** (01386) 861628 **MOBILE** (07770) 472431
E-MAIL a.w.carroll@btconnect.com **WEBSITE** www.awcarroll.co.uk

1 ARCTIC WINGS (IRE), 9, b g In The Wings—Arctic Hunt (IRE) **Jojopepadao**
2 ARTE DEL CALCIO, 4, b g Manduro (GER)—Movie Queen **K. F. Coleman**
3 BET NOIR (IRE), 8, b m King's Best (USA)—Ivowen (USA) **A. W. Carroll**
4 BOSTON BLUE, 6, b g Halling (USA)—City of Gold (IRE) **Mr B. J. Millen**
5 CANE CAT (IRE), 6, b br m One Cool Cat (USA)—Seven Wonders (USA) **J. W. Egan**
6 4, B c Shantou (USA)—Close To Shore (IRE)
7 CRAZY BOLD (GER), 10, ch g Erminius (GER)—Crazy Love (GER) **Mrs S. R. Keable**
8 DIRTY DEAL, 9, ch m Karinga Bay—Lady Confess **Mr J. Tucker**
9 EASYDOESIT (IRE), 5, b g Iffraaj—Fawaayid (USA) **T. R. Pearson**
10 FAST SAMURAI (USA), 5, ch h First Samurai (USA)—Lady Blockbuster (USA) **Mr S. N. A. Alromaithi**
11 FIRST REBELLION, 4, ch g Cockney Rebel (IRE)—First Dawn **Let's Give It A Go Racing & J Dewhurst**
12 GOURANGA, 10, b m Robellino (USA)—Hymne d'amour (USA) **G1 Racing Club Ltd**
13 GRACCHUS (USA), 7, b g Black Minnaloushe (USA)—Montessa (USA) **R H Harris & Mr Alan Prestwich**
14 JAKE THE SNAKE (IRE), 12, ch g Intikhab (USA)—Tilbrook (IRE) **Mr T. P. Ramsden**
15 JOLI SOLEIL, 4, b g Kyllachy—Jolie (IRE) **Mrs C. S. Baylis**
16 KICKS MILAN (IRE), 6, b m Milan—Honor Kicks (FR) **Mr C. D. Rogers**

MR TONY CARROLL - Continued

17 **KING OLAV (UAE)**, 8, ch g Halling (USA)—Karamzin (USA) **Cover Point Racing**
18 **KINKEEL (IRE)**, 14, b g Hubbly Bubbly (USA)—Bubbly Beau **G1 Racing Club Ltd**
19 **LAUGHING JACK**, 5, b g Beat Hollow—Bronzewing **Mr P. A. Downing**
20 **LE BACARDY (FR)**, 7, b h Bahhare (USA)—La Balagna **Mr C. Hodgson**
21 **LUGGERS HALL (IRE)**, 5, b g Cape Cross (IRE)—Saabga (USA) **Mr M. S. Cooke**
22 **LYTHAM (IRE)**, 12, b g Spectrum (IRE)—Nousaiyra (IRE) **Mr Morgan, Clarke & Parris**
23 **MALANOS (IRE)**, 5, b br g Lord of England (GER)—Majorata (GER) **Mr B. J. Millen**
24 **MAYAN FLIGHT (IRE)**, 5, b g Hawk Wing (USA)—Balimaya (IRE) **Burns, Carroll, Miles & Ward**
25 **MISSIONAIRE (USA)**, 6, b br g El Corredor (USA)—Fapindy (USA) **Mr B. J. Millen**
26 **MR LANDO**, 4, b g Shirocco (GER)—Capitana (GER) **Mr G. Attwood**
27 **MR ROBINSON (FR)**, 6, b g Robin des Pres (FR)—Alberade (FR) **Neville Statham & Family**
28 **MUJAMEAD**, 9, b g Mujahid (USA)—Island Mead **Six Pack**
29 **OCEAN LEGEND (IRE)**, 8, b g Night Shift (USA)—Rose of Mooncoin (IRE) **Mr W. McLuskey**
30 **OPERETTIST**, 4, b f Singspiel (IRE)—Demi Voix **Longview Stud & Bloodstock Ltd**
31 **OSCAR FLYER (IRE)**, 6, b g Oscar (IRE)—Cointosser (IRE) **West Coast Haulage Limited**
32 **PAHENTE**, 5, br gr g Silver Patriarch (IRE)—Miss Tehente (FR) **Mayden Stud**
33 **RIGID**, 6, ch g Refuse To Bend (IRE)—Supersonic **Mr & Mrs J. B. Bacciochi**
34 **ROSA LOCKWOOD**, 4, b f Needwood Blade—Star of Flanders **Mr D Lowe & Mr J Loftus**
35 **ROSE GARNET (IRE)**, 5, b m Invincible Spirit (IRE)—Chanterelle (IRE) **Nicholls Family**
36 **ROSEINI (IRE)**, 7, b m Dr Massini (IRE)—Deise Rose (IRE) **Bella Statham & Family**
37 **SEAQUEL**, 7, b m Kyllachy—Broughton Singer (IRE) **Mr M. P. Webb**
38 **SECRET MILLIONAIRE (IRE)**, 6, b g Kyllachy—Mithl Al Hawa **Mr T. P. Ramsden**
39 **SHALAMBAR (IRE)**, 7, gr g Dalakhani (IRE)—Shalama (IRE) **Mr B. J. Millen**
40 **SHARE OPTION**, 11, b g Polish Precedent (USA)—Quota **Last Day Racing Partnership**
41 **SHELFORD (IRE)**, 4, b g Galileo (IRE)—Lyrical **Mr C. Hodgson**
42 **SMART CATCH (IRE)**, 7, b g Pivotal—Zafaraniya (IRE) **Cover Point Racing**
43 **SUN DREAM**, 6, b m Desert Sun—I Have A Dream (SWE) **Mayden Stud**
44 **SUPA SEEKER (USA)**, 7, b br g Petionville (USA)—Supamova (USA) **A. W. Carroll**
45 **TAROUM (IRE)**, 6, b g Refuse To Bend (IRE)—Taraza (IRE) **Mr J. Tucker**
46 **THE YANK**, 4, b g Trade Fair—Silver Gyre (IRE) **Mr G. Attwood**
47 **TIDAL'S BABY**, 4, b g Dutch Art—Tidal **Mrs B. Quinn**
48 **TIME MEDICEAN**, 7, gr g Medicean—Ribbons And Bows (IRE) **A. W. Carroll**
49 **TIME SQUARE (FR)**, 6, b g Westerner—Sainte Parfaite (FR) **Mr M. S. Cooke**
50 **TRAVELLING**, 4, b f Dubai Destination (USA)—Attune **Longview Stud & Bloodstock Ltd**
51 **TROUBLETIMESTWO (FR)**, 7, gr g Linamix (FR)—Time of Trouble (FR) **Mill House Racing Syndicate**
52 **UNLIMITED**, 11, b g Bold Edge—Cabcharge Blue **A. W. Carroll**
53 **VALKOV**, 6, b m Val Royal (FR)—Petrikov (IRE) **Mayden Stud**
54 **VERTUEUX (FR)**, 8, gr g Verglas (IRE)—Shahrazad (FR) **Mr J. Rutter**
55 **WALDEN PRINCE (IRE)**, 6, b g Saffron Walden (FR)—Kahyasi Princess (IRE) **Mr G. Attwood**
56 **WAVING**, 4, b g High Chaparral (IRE)—Pretty Davis (USA) **Mr C. Hodgson**
57 **YOUM JAMIL (USA)**, 6, gr ro g Mizzen Mast (USA)—Millie's Choice (IRE) **Tom & Neville Statham**
58 **ZAFARABAN (IRE)**, 6, gr g Dalakhani (IRE)—Zafaraniya (IRE) **Mr P. A. Downing**
59 **ZAFRANAGAR (IRE)**, 8, b g Cape Cross (IRE)—Zafaraniya (IRE) **Mr P. A. Downing**

THREE-YEAR-OLDS

60 **ADMIRABLE ART (IRE)**, b g Excellent Art—Demi Voix **Longview Stud & Bloodstock Ltd**
61 **CHORAL RHYTHM (IRE)**, b f Oratorio (IRE)—Sierra **Longview Stud & Bloodstock Ltd**
62 **EXIT CLAUSE**, b c Manipulator (IRE)—Claws **Orbit Performance**
63 **MOONVALE (IRE)**, gr f Verglas (IRE)—Artistry **Longview Stud & Bloodstock Ltd**
64 **SHEARIAN**, b g Royal Applause—Regal Asset (USA) **A. W. Carroll**
65 **WOODLAND FLEUR**, b f Astronomer Royal (USA)—Ultimate Court (USA) **A. W. Carroll**

Other Owners: Mr J. Babb, J. T. Bacciochi, Mrs J. M. Bacciochi, Mr R. Buckland, Mr P. W. Burns, Mrs C. J. Chamberlain, Mr M. B. Clarke, Mr J. R. Daniell, Mr M. S. Day, J. A. Dewhurst, Mrs D. S. Dewhurst, Mr L. Garside-Beattie, R. H. Harris, Ms N. C. Heath, Mr J. Loftus, D. J. Lowe, Mr P. G. McDonald, Mr S. Miles, R. J. Millen, Mr D. S. G. Morgan, Mr M. Nichol, Mr R. Nicholls, Mrs E. Nicholls, Mr K. J. Parris, Mr A. F. Prestwich, Mr D. A. D. Rogers, D. T. Shorthouse, Mr N. J. Statham, Mr T. W. A. Statham, Mrs P. Statham, Mrs I. Whitehead.

Jockey (NH): Lee Edwards. **Conditional:** Josh Hamer. **Apprentice:** George Downing. **Amateur:** Mr Mark J. J. Smith, Mr Charles Carroll.

103 MR TONY CARSON, Newmarket
Postal: **5 Churchill Avenue, Newmarket, Suffolk, CB8 0BZ**
Contacts: **PHONE (01638) 660947 MOBILE (07837) 601867**
E-MAIL topcatcarson@ymail.com

1 AMIS REUNIS, 4, b f Bahamian Bounty—Spring Clean (FR) **Peter Alderson & Willie Carson**
2 BRIMSTONE HILL (IRE), 4, b c Royal Applause—Right As Rain **G Houghton, S Ebanks-Blake & K P Foley**
3 DASHWOOD, 6, b g Pivotal—Most Charming (FR) **Macattack, William Lea Screed & Form IT**
4 DIVEA, 4, b f Dylan Thomas (IRE)—Cumin (USA) **Willie Carson**
5 GEEAITCH, 4, ch g Cockney Rebel (IRE)—Grand Rebecca (IRE) **G. Houghton**
6 HAIL PROMENADER (IRE), 7, b g Acclamation—Tribal Rite **Athos Racing**
7 PARANDIH (USA), 4, b g Dubai Destination (USA)—Princess Nada **Willie Carson**
8 PEACE IN OUR TIME, 4, b g Echo of Light—Deira (USA) **Neville Chamberlain Syndicate 1**
9 PEACE SEEKER, 5, b g Oasis Dream—Mina **Neville Chamberlain Syndicate**
10 STATUS SYMBOL (IRE), 8, ch g Polish Precedent (USA)—Desired **Willie Carson**
11 TETH, 4, br f Dansili—Beta **Christopher Wright & Minster Stud**

THREE-YEAR-OLDS
12 KASBHOM, b g Refuse To Bend (IRE)—Summerstrand (IRE) **Macattack, William Lea Screed & Form IT**
13 MADE IT (IRE), b f Oratorio (IRE)—Theebah **Mr S Ebanks-Blake & Mr K P Foley**
14 Ch f Three Valleys (USA)—Tanasie **Willie Carson**
15 B f Dubai Destination (USA)—Trounce **Willie Carson**

TWO-YEAR-OLDS
16 Ch c 5/3 Selkirk (USA)—Culture Queen (King's Best (USA)) (10000) **Willie Carson**
17 B c 21/3 High Chaparral (IRE)—Kasakiya (IRE) (Zafonic (USA)) (7000) **Willie Carson**
18 B c 16/2 Medicean—Love Me Tender (Green Desert (USA)) **Willie Carson**
19 PIEMAN'S GIRL, b f 12/3 Henrythenavigator (USA)—Aromatherapy (Oasis Dream) (25000) **Willie Carson**

Other Owners: Mr Peter Alderson, Mr Howard Burdett, Mrs E. Carson, Mr W. H. Carson, Mr S. Ebanks-Blake, Mr K. P. Foley, Mr M. P. Gibbens, Mr George Houghton, Mr David Hudd, Mr William Lea, Mr T. J. McLoughlin, Mr Chris O'Donnell, Mr J. S. Wills, Mr Christopher Wright, Mrs Chris Wright.

Assistant Trainer: Graham Carson

Jockey (flat): William Carson. **Amateur:** Mr Graham Carson.

104 MR LEE CARTER, Epsom
Postal: **The Old Yard, Clear Height Stables, Epsom, Surrey, KT18 5LB**
Contacts: **PHONE (01372) 740878 FAX (01372) 740898 MOBILE (07540) 877259**
E-MAIL akehurstracing@btconnect.com WEBSITE www.akehurstracing.com

1 BLUE DEER (IRE), 5, b g Bahamian Bounty—Jaywick (UAE) **Mrs I. Marshall**
2 HALLING DANCER, 4, b g Halling (USA)—Ballet Ballon (USA) **Tattenham Corner Racing IV**
3 IRONS ON FIRE (USA), 5, ch g Tale of The Cat (USA)—One and Twenty (USA) **BPL Partnership**
4 KING'S FUTURE, 4, b g King's Best (USA)—Las Beatas **P. A. Allard**
5 LOWTHER, 8, b g Beat All (USA)—Ever So Lonely **Mr P. G. Marsh**
6 MARY'S PET, 6, b m Where Or When (IRE)—Contrary Mary **Mrs I. Marshall**
7 MIDNIGHT FEAST, 5, b g Ishiguro (USA)—Prince's Feather (IRE) **One More Bid Partnership**
8 REIGN SILVER (IRE), 5, gr m Cloudings (IRE)—Charlies Rising (USA) **The Green Pastures Partnership II**
9 TAKEITFROMALADY (IRE), 4, b g Intikhab (USA)—Pinheiros (IRE) **Only One Bid Partnership**

THREE-YEAR-OLDS
10 MANY ELEMENTS, b g Multiplex—Park's Girl **Mr P. G. Marsh**

Other Owners: Mr P. A. Allard, Mr Colin Ballantyne, Mr Neville Boyce, Mrs K. T. Carter, Mr Gus Gordon, Mr B. Laxton.

105 MR BEN CASE, Banbury
Postal: **Wardington Gate Farm, Edgcote, Banbury, Oxfordshire, OX17 1AG**
Contacts: **PHONE (01295) 750959 FAX (01295) 758840 MOBILE (07808) 061223**
E-MAIL info@bencaseracing.com WEBSITE www.bencaseracing.com

1 BEBINN (IRE), 6, b m Brian Boru—Windmill Star (IRE) **Fly Like The Wind Partnership**

MR BEN CASE - Continued

2 **BRASS TAX (IRE)**, 7, b g Morozov (USA)—Cry Before Dawn (IRE) **Mrs C. Kendrick**
3 **CALL A TRUCE (IRE)**, 5, b g Court Cave (IRE)—No More Trouble (IRE) **Lady Jane Grosvenor**
4 **DANCE ISLAND (IRE)**, 10, b g Turtle Island (IRE)—Inse Na Rince (IRE) **Lady Jane Grosvenor**
5 **DEEP TROUBLE (IRE)**, 6, b g Shantou (USA)—Out of Trouble (IRE) **Lady Jane Grosvenor**
6 **GINGER FIZZ**, 6, ch m Haafhd—Valagalore **Itchen Valley Stud**
7 4, B g Midnight Legend—Half Inch **Mrs M. Howlett**
8 **HANDTHEPRIZEOVER**, 8, b g Exit To Nowhere (USA)—Main Dans La Main (FR) **D. C. R. Allen**
9 **ISLAND WHISPER (IRE)**, 6, b m Turtle Island (IRE)—Whistles Dream (IRE) **Mrs S. Case**
10 **KERNEL VICTOR**, 5, b g Old Vic—Noisetine (FR) **D. C. R. Allen**
11 **MARK THE BOOK (IRE)**, 12, b g Mister Lord (USA)—Boardroom Belle (IRE) **D. C. R. Allen**
12 4, B g Definite Article—Mazuma (IRE) **Lady Jane Grosvenor**
13 **MOSS ON THE MILL**, 5, b g Overbury (IRE)—Mimis Bonnet (FR) **S. D. Hemstock**
14 **MY NOSY ROSY**, 5, b m Alflora (IRE)—Quiz Night **Mr I. A. Low & Mr J. S. English**
15 4, B g Shantou (USA)—Nut Touluze (IRE)
16 **ORANGEADAY**, 6, b g Kayf Tara—One of Those Days **D. C. R. Allen**
17 **PERCY'S REFLECTION**, 6, b g Lord Americo—Bewitch **Mrs S. R. Bailey**
18 **PHARE ISLE (IRE)**, 8, b g Turtle Island (IRE)—Pharenna (IRE) **Nicholson Family Moore Moore & Kendrick**
19 **TEMPEST RIVER (IRE)**, 7, b m Old Vic—Dee-One-O-One **Fly Like The Wind Partnership**
20 **THORESBY (IRE)**, 7, b g Milan—I Remember It Well **D. C. R. Allen**
21 **TOP DANCER (FR)**, 6, b g Dark Moondancer—Latitude (FR) **Case Racing Partnership**
22 **UN ACE (FR)**, 5, b g Voix du Nord (FR)—First Ball (FR) **Case Racing Partnership**
23 **USSEE (FR)**, 5, gr m Vangelis (USA)—Duchesse Pierji (FR) **J. Wright**

THREE-YEAR-OLDS

24 **MY RENAISSANCE**, b br g Medicean—Lebenstanz **N. S. Hutley**

Other Owners: Mr & Mrs D. Baines, Mrs A. D. Bourne, Mr T. Boylan, Mrs S. Case, Mr A. Case, Mrs A. Charlton, Mr C. K. Crossley Cooke, Mr & Mrs Derbyshire, Mr J. S. English, Mr & Mrs J. Grindlay, Roger Hagen, Mrs S. Harrison, Mrs M. Howlett, Joyce Hulse, Charles Illsley, Mrs Carolyn Kendrick, Mrs C. Lawrence, Helen Loggin, Lynda Lovell, Mr I. A. Low, Mr & Mrs P. Lush, Miss A. Lush, Mrs Wendy Moore, Mr T. W. Moore, Mr Grahame Nicholson, Mr & Mrs C. Nixey, Mr J. Nowell-Smith, Mr & Mrs G. Payne, Mrs K. Perrem, Mrs C. Wallace, Mrs P. Williams.

---

106 SIR HENRY CECIL, Newmarket
Postal: **Warren Place, Newmarket, Suffolk, CB8 8QQ**
Contacts: **OFFICE (01638) 662192 FAX (01638) 669005**
E-MAIL henry@henrycecil.co.uk WEBSITE www.henrycecil.com

1 **ACE OF VALHALLA**, 4, b c Authorized (IRE)—Trick of Ace (USA) **Mr I. Wilson**
2 **BEAUTY PARLOUR**, 4, b f Deep Impact (JPN)—Bastet (IRE) **Wildenstein Stables Limited**
3 **CHIGUN**, 4, b f Oasis Dream—Stormy Weather **Mr V. I. Araci**
4 **CONTINUUM**, 4, b br c Dansili—Clepsydra **K. Abdulla**
5 **CRYSTAL MONARCH (IRE)**, 4, b g Dalakhani (IRE)—Top Crystal (IRE) **M. D. Poland**
6 **DR YES (FR)**, 4, b c Dansili—Light Shift (USA) **Niarchos Family**
7 **FIRST MOHICAN**, 5, ch g Tobougg (IRE)—Mohican Girl **W. H. Ponsonby**
8 **FRAGONARD**, 4, ch f Teofilo (IRE)—Delicieuse Lady **Sir R. Ogden C.B.E., LLD**
9 **MALEKOV (IRE)**, 4, b c Dansili—Young and Daring (USA) **Al Asayl**
10 **NOBLE MISSION**, 4, b c Galileo (IRE)—Kind (IRE) **K. Abdulla**
11 **REGENCY (GER)**, 4, ch c Galileo (IRE)—Reem Dubai (IRE) **Gestut Etzean**
12 **RUNNING DEER (IRE)**, 4, b f Hurricane Run (IRE)—Sweet Sioux **W. H. Ponsonby**
13 **SONGBIRD**, 4, ch f Danehill Dancer (IRE)—Mine Excavation (IRE) **Sir R. Ogden C.B.E., LLD**
14 **SPIRITOFTOMINTOUL**, 4, gr c Authorized (USA)—Diamond Line (FR) **Angus Dundee Distillers Plc**
15 **STIPULATE**, 4, b g Dansili—Indication **K. Abdulla**
16 **THOMAS CHIPPENDALE (IRE)**, 4, b r c Dansili—All My Loving (IRE) **Sir R. Ogden C.B.E., LLD**
17 **TICKLED PINK (IRE)**, 4, gr f Invincible Spirit (IRE)—Cassandra Go (IRE) **T. C. Stewart**
18 **TIGER CLIFF (IRE)**, 4, b g Tiger Hill (IRE)—Verbania (GER) **W. H. Ponsonby**
19 **TORUK MACTO (IRE)**, 4, b c Authorized (USA)—Mythical Girl (USA) **Mr V. I. Araci**
20 **WILD COCO (GER)**, 5, ch m Shirocco (GER)—Wild Side (GER) **K I Farm Corporation**
21 **WORLD DOMINATION (USA)**, 5, b h Empire Maker (USA)—Reams of Verse (USA) **K. Abdulla**
22 **ZEYRAN**, 4, ch f Galileo (IRE)—Chervil **Miss Z. Araci**

THREE-YEAR-OLDS

23 **AL ARISH (IRE)**, b g Iffraaj—Flash And Dazzle (IRE) **Mr A. N. Mubarak**
24 **AL DEEBLE (IRE)**, b c Lawman (FR)—Green Lassy (FR) **Mr A. N. Mubarak**

SIR HENRY CECIL - Continued

25 **AL GUWAIR (IRE)**, b c Shirocco (GER)—Katariya (IRE) **Mr A. N. Mubarak**
26 **AL RAYYAN (IRE)**, ch c Pivotal—Kirkinola **Mr A. N. Mubarak**
27 **AL WAAB (IRE)**, ch c Danehill Dancer (IRE)—Aunt Julia **Mr A. N. Mubarak**
28 **AL WUKIR (IRE)**, b c Jeremy (USA)—Collada (IRE) **Mr A. N. Mubarak**
29 **ALEGRA**, gr f Galileo (IRE)—Altitude **Sir R. Ogden C.B.E., LLD**
30 B f Haafhd—All Glory **Andrew Bull**
31 **AMELIORATE (IRE)**, b f Galileo (IRE)—Arkadina (IRE) **Merry Fox Stud Limited**
32 **ANEW**, b f Oasis Dream—Kid Gloves **K. Abdulla**
33 **ARCHIVE**, b f Dansili—Modesta (IRE) **K. Abdulla**
34 **ATARAXIS (FR)**, b c Nayef (USA)—Seven Magicians (USA) **Niarchos Family**
35 **ATLANTIC ISLE (GER)**, b f Tamayuz—All Time Great **Ammerland Verwaltung GmbH & Co.KG**
36 **AUTUN (USA)**, b c Empire Maker (USA)—Sense of Joy **K. Abdulla**
37 **BEJEWELED (IRE)**, br f Rock of Gibraltar (IRE)—Gems of Araby **Mr V. I. Araci**
38 **BLIGHTY (IRE)**, ch c Beat Hollow—Brisk Breeze (GER) **Ennismore Racing I**
39 **BUCHANAN**, b c Dansili—Because (IRE) **T. Barr**
40 B f Dalakhani (IRE)—Camaret (IRE) **Andrew Bull**
41 **CONSERVE (IRE)**, b f Duke of Marmalade (IRE)—Minor Point **Highclere Thoroughbred Racing-Lord Mayor**
42 **COSMIC CURIOUS (GER)**, gr c Rock of Gibraltar (IRE)—Cosmic Fire (FR) **Niarchos Family**
43 **COURT PASTORAL**, b f Mount Nelson—Teggiano (IRE) **J. Shack**
44 **DARIA (GER)**, ch f Rock of Gibraltar (IRE)—Desabina (GER) **Gestut Rottgen**
45 **DEMONIC**, b c Dansili—Bionic **K. Abdulla**
46 **DISCLAIMER**, b g Dansili—Novellara **K. Abdulla**
47 **ELEKTRA MARINO**, b f Mount Nelson—Entente Cordiale (IRE) **Newsells Park Stud**
48 **EMPERICAL**, b c Oasis Dream—Kalima **K. Abdulla**
49 **ETOILE DE LUNE**, ch f Zamindar (USA)—Jolie Etoile (USA) **K. Abdulla**
50 **FAFA O O (IRE)**, b f Galileo (IRE)—Witch of Fife (USA) **Sir R. Ogden C.B.E., LLD**
51 **FINGER POPPIN**, b f Haafhd—Quest For Freedom **Mr J. A. Coleman**
52 **FLOW (USA)**, b br c Medaglia d'oro (USA)—Enthused (USA) **Niarchos Family**
53 **GERTRUDE GRAY (IRE)**, b f Hurricane Run (IRE)—Canterbury Lace (USA) **Lady Bamford**
54 **GHOST RUNNER (IRE)**, b c Tagula (IRE)—Ball Cat (FR) **Middleham Park Racing L**
55 **GRASPED**, ch f Zamindar (USA)—Imroz (USA) **K. Abdulla**
56 **HALUL**, b c Dutch Art—Bella Bertolini **Mr A. N. Mubarak**
57 **HAMELIN (IRE)**, b c Cape Cross (IRE)—Love Divine **Lordship Stud**
58 **HOT SNAP**, ch f Pivotal—Midsummer **K. Abdulla**
59 **IBERIS**, b f Nayef (USA)—Isis (USA) **Dr C. M. H. Wills**
60 **JUST ONE KISS**, b f Cape Cross (IRE)—Kissing **Lordship Stud**
61 **KORANTAM (IRE)**, b c Galileo (IRE)—Miss Beatrix (IRE) **Mr V. I. Araci**
62 **KYLLACHY RISE**, b c Kyllachy—Up And About **Mr A. C. Waney**
63 **MAGIC OF REALITY (FR)**, ch f Galileo (IRE)—Breathe (FR) **Niarchos Family**
64 **MAJESTY (IRE)**, gr c Shamardal (USA)—Princess Serena (USA) **Highclere Thoroughbred Racing - Archer**
65 **MIGHTY YAR (IRE)**, gr c Teofilo (IRE)—Karaliyfa (USA) **R. A. H. Evans**
66 **MISFER**, ch c Byron—Diliza **Mr A. N. Mubarak**
67 **MISSED CALL (IRE)**, b f Authorized (IRE)—Incoming Call (USA) **M. C. Denmark**
68 **MORPHEUS**, b c Oasis Dream—Kind (IRE) **K. Abdulla**
69 **OPTICAL**, ch f Observatory (USA)—Blueberry (USA) **K. Abdulla**
70 **ORIGINATE**, b f Oasis Dream—Sandglass **K. Abdulla**
71 **PARALLAX (IRE)**, b c Galileo (IRE)—Moonlight's Box (USA) **Niarchos Family**
72 **PASSING PARADE**, b f Cape Cross (IRE)—Model Queen (USA) **Merry Fox Stud Limited**
73 **PERFECT SUMMER (IRE)**, b f High Chaparral (IRE)—Power of Future (GER) **Mr G. Schoeningh**
74 **PHAENOMENA (IRE)**, ch f Galileo (IRE)—Caumshinaun (IRE) **Niarchos Family**
75 **PHOSPHORESCENCE (IRE)**, b c Sakhee (USA)—Eccentricity (USA) **Niarchos Family**
76 **RAJARATNA (IRE)**, b f Galileo (IRE)—Coup de Genie (USA) **Niarchos Family**
77 **REASON TO SMILE**, b c Teofilo (IRE)—Easy To Love (USA) **Maze Rattan Limited**
78 **RETIREMENT PLAN**, b br c Monsun (GER)—Passage of Time **K. Abdulla**
79 **RIDGEWAY STORM (IRE)**, b c Hurricane Run (IRE)—Hesperia **W. H. Ponsonby**
80 **RIPOSTE**, b f Dansili—Rainbow Lake **K. Abdulla**
81 **ROME**, b c Holy Roman Emperor (IRE)—Magical Cliche (USA) **John Penny**
82 **SAGUA LA GRANDE (IRE)**, b c Teofilo (IRE)—Water Fountain **Lady Jane Cecil**
83 **SEA MEETS SKY (FR)**, b f Dansili—Sacred Song (USA) **Niarchos Family**
84 **SQUIRE OSBALDESTON (IRE)**, b c Mr Greeley (USA)—Kushnarenkovo **P. Hickman**
85 **STANLOW**, b c Invincible Spirit (IRE)—Ghazal (USA) **Ms A. Quinn**
86 **TOMINTOUL MAGIC (IRE)**, b f Holy Roman Emperor (IRE)—Trois Graces (USA) **Angus Dundee Distillers Plc**
87 **VENUE**, b c Beat Hollow—Shirley Valentine **K. Abdulla**
88 B g Zamindar (USA)—Zarannda (IRE) **M. C. Denmark**

SIR HENRY CECIL - Continued

TWO-YEAR-OLDS

89 B c 9/2 Oasis Dream—Bionic (Zafonic (USA)) **K. Abdulla**
90 B f 23/3 Dansili—Blend (Zafonic (USA)) **K. Abdulla**
91 Gr ro c 5/2 Mizzen Mast (USA)—Brief Look (Sadler's Wells (USA)) **K. Abdulla**
92 B f 9/4 High Chaparral (IRE)—Brisk Breeze (GER) (Monsun (GER)) **Ennismore Racing I**
93 BRYCE CANYON (IRE), b f 3/5 Galileo (IRE)—Bright Sky (IRE) (Wolfhound (USA)) **Wildenstein Stables Limited**
94 CHANTREA (IRE), br f 21/2 Dansili—Celestial Lagoon (JPN) (Sunday Silence (USA)) **Niarchos Family**
95 B f 31/1 Dansili—Emplane (USA) (Irish River (FR)) **K. Abdulla**
96 B f 3/4 Invincible Spirit (IRE)—Entre Nous (IRE) (Sadler's Wells (USA)) (150000) **Mr V. I. Araci**
97 C b 6/4 Fastnet Rock (AUS)—Holly Blue (Bluebird (USA)) (55555) **P. Hickman**
98 B c 13/1 Dansili—Honest Quality (USA) (Elusive Quality (USA)) **K. Abdulla**
99 HOOP OF COLOUR (USA), b f 19/4 Distorted Humor (USA)—Surya (USA) (Unbridled (USA)) **Niarchos Family**
100 B c 31/1 Galileo (IRE)—Hveger (AUS) (Danehill (USA)) (450000) **P. Hickman**
101 B f 12/2 Dansili—Ithaca (USA) (Distant View (USA)) **K. Abdulla**
102 B f 22/4 Galileo (IRE)—Jessica's Dream (IRE) (Desert Style (IRE)) (400000) **Mr V. I. Araci**
103 B f 10/4 Oasis Dream—Kind (IRE) (Danehill (USA)) **K. Abdulla**
104 Br c 1/4 Sea The Stars (IRE)—Love Divine (Diesis) (200000) **Lordship Stud**
105 B f 25/4 Danehill Dancer (IRE)—Mail The Desert (IRE) (Desert Prince (IRE)) (140000) **Lady Bamford**
106 METEOROID (USA), b br c 23/3 Dynaformer (USA)—Enthused (USA) (Seeking The Gold (USA)) **Niarchos Family**
107 B f 27/4 Oasis Dream—Midsummer (Kingmambo (USA)) **K. Abdulla**
108 B f 1/4 Oasis Dream—Modesta (IRE) (Sadler's Wells (USA)) **K. Abdulla**
109 MORNING WATCH (IRE), b c 26/3 Azamour (IRE)—
           Lady of Kildare (IRE) (Mujadil (USA)) (62000) **Lord De La Warr**
110 NICTATE (IRE), br f 31/3 Teofilo (IRE)—Woodmaven (USA) (Woodman (USA)) (240000) **Niarchos Family**
111 B br f 15/2 Oasis Dream—Passage of Time (Dansili) **K. Abdulla**
112 B c 25/4 Danehill Dancer (IRE)—
           Perihelion (IRE) (Galileo (IRE)) (91269) **Highclere Thoroughbred Racing- Distinction**
113 B c 4/3 Montjeu (IRE)—Piste Noire (IRE) (Diesis) **Sir R. Ogden C.B.E., LLD**
114 Ch c 22/4 Pivotal—Portodora (USA) (Kingmambo (USA)) **K. Abdulla**
115 B c 18/3 Rail Link—Quota (Rainbow Quest (USA)) **K. Abdulla**
116 B c 19/2 Invincible Spirit (IRE)—Red Feather (IRE) (Marju (IRE)) **Highclere Thoroughbred Racing -Harbinger**
117 RIVER GLASS (IRE), gr c 28/3 Verglas (IRE)—Spartan Girl (IRE) (Ela-Mana-Mou) (22857) **W. H. Ponsonby**
118 B f 20/2 Rock of Gibraltar (IRE)—Sevenna (FR) (Galileo (IRE)) **Ammerland Verwaltung GmbH & Co.KG**
119 SHE'S GORGEOUS (IRE), b f 16/2 Acclamation—Acquiesced (IRE) (Refuse To Bend (IRE)) **John Johnstone**
120 Gr c 20/4 Galileo (IRE)—St Roch (IRE) (Danehill (USA)) (186507) **P. Hickman**
121 STERLING RUN (IRE), b c 30/3 Oasis Dream—
           Sarabande (USA) (Woodman (USA)) **Wildenstein Stables Limited**
122 SYNAESTHESIA (FR), b br f 27/1 High Chaparral (IRE)—I'm Sensational (Selkirk (USA)) **Niarchos Family**
123 TACTICUS (USA), b c 24/3 A P Indy (USA)—Visions of Clarity (IRE) (Sadler's Wells (USA)) **Niarchos Family**
124 B f 30/3 Shamardal (USA)—Tudor Court (IRE) (Cape Cross (IRE)) (57000) **Lady Bamford**
125 B f 9/2 Zamindar (USA)—Wemyss Bay (Sadler's Wells (USA)) **K. Abdulla**

Other Owners: Mr Ray Antell, Ms Caroline Bailey, Mrs Denise Casey-McCarthy, Mr Joe Chester, J. L. Clarke, Mr J. B. Cohen, R. Cressey, Mr David Crossley, Mr J. M. O. Evans, Mr R. W. Guy, T. F. Harris, Mrs E. A. Harris, Mr R. Hellaby, The Hon H. M. Herbert, Mr P. J. Hickman, Highclere Thoroughbred Racing Ltd, Mr G. C. Johns, Mr J. Johnson, Mr J. W. Johnstone, Mrs Zara Johnstone, Mrs A. M. Johnstone, K I Farm Corporation, Miss E. A. Lake, Mrs S. M. Maine, J. R. Penny, Miss E. Penny, Mrs J. Penny, Mr G. Schoeningh, Mr J. A. Tabet, Ms Miranda Thomas, Mr J. Turner, Mr D. Underwood, Mr T. N. White, Mr T. Withers.

Assistant Trainer: Michael Marshall

Jockey (flat): Tom Queally, Ian Mongan. **Apprentice:** Amelia Green.

---

107 | **MR PATRICK CHAMINGS, Tadley**
Postal: **Inhurst Farm Stables, Baughurst, Tadley, Hampshire, RG26 5JS**
Contacts: **PHONE (01189) 814494 FAX (01189) 820454 MOBILE (07831) 360970**
E-MAIL chamingsracing@talk21.com

1 AYE AYE DIGBY (IRE), 8, b g Captain Rio—Jane Digby (IRE) **Trolley Action**
2 BOLACHOIR (IRE), 11, b g Hubbly Bubbly (USA)—Boolindrum Lady (IRE) **R. V. Shaw**
3 CAPE BRETON, 7, b g Cape Cross (IRE)—Red Bouquet **Mrs A. J. Chandris**
4 COMMANCHE, 4, ch g Sleeping Indian—Happy Memories (IRE) **K. W. Tyrrell**
5 DIRECTORSHIP, 7, br g Diktat—Away To Me **Mrs R Lyon,Mrs P Hayton,Mr P R Chamings**
6 EAGER TO BOW (IRE), 7, b g Acclamation—Tullawadgeen (IRE) **Mrs J. E. L. Wright**

MR PATRICK CHAMINGS - Continued

7 **ELSIE'S ORPHAN,** 6, br m Pastoral Pursuits—Elsie Plunkett **Mrs J. E. L. Wright**
8 **FLAVIUS VICTOR (IRE),** 4, b g Holy Roman Emperor (IRE)—Teslemi (USA) **P R Chamings F T Lee**
9 **FOXHAVEN,** 11, ch g Unfuwain (USA)—Dancing Mirage (IRE) **The Foxford House Partnership**
10 **JUST WHEN,** 4, b g Dalakhani (IRE)—Cape Grace (IRE) **Inhurst Players**
11 **MY SILVER ROSE,** 7, gr m Silver Patriarch (IRE)—Clifton Match **Mr S. D. Whiting**
12 **RONDEAU (GR),** 8, ch g Harmonic Way—Areti (GR) **The Foxford House Partnership**
13 **SCOTTISH GLEN,** 7, ch g Kyllachy—Dance For Fun **The Foxford House Partnership**
14 **TAKE A NOTE,** 4, b g Singspiel (IRE)—Ela Paparouna **The Foxford House Partnership**
15 **TREASURE ACT,** 5, ch m Act One—Benjarong **Mrs J. E. L. Wright**
16 **UNCLE FRED,** 8, b g Royal Applause—Karla June **The Foxford House Partnership**
17 **WOODCOTE PLACE,** 10, b g Lujain (USA)—Giant Nipper **The Foxford House Partnership**

THREE-YEAR-OLDS

18 **HAIL TO PRINCESS,** ch f Dr Fong (USA)—Bob's Princess **P. R. Chamings**
19 **PRETTY DANCER,** b f Byron—Pretty Miss **Mrs J. E. L. Wright**

TWO-YEAR-OLDS

20 Gr c 11/3 High Chaparral (IRE)—Alambic (Cozzene (USA)) (41269)
21 Ch c 26/4 Iffraaj—Astuti (IRE) (Waajib)
22 B c 13/2 Archipenko (USA)—Maria di Scozia (Selkirk (USA)) (31745)
23 **POETIC PRINCE,** b c 6/4 Byron—Bob's Princess (Bob's Return (IRE)) (2857) **Mrs J. E. L. Wright**
24 B f 20/2 Clodovil (IRE)—Pulau Pinang (FR) (Dolphin Street (FR)) (5000)
25 Ch c 10/5 Tobougg (IRE)—Tamise (USA) (Time For A Change (USA)) (10000)
26 **TOO BEND,** b c 29/4 Tobougg (IRE)—Benjarong (Sharpo) (2857) **Mrs J. E. L. Wright**

Other Owners: Mrs P. L. Hayton, F. T. Lee, Mrs R. Lyon, Mr I. J. Matthews, Mr M. R. Stewart.

Assistant Trainer: Phillippa Chamings

---

108 **MR NOEL CHANCE, Lambourn**
Postal: Bottom Yard, Delamere House Stables, Baydon Road, Lambourn, Hungerford, Berkshire, RG17 7LE
Contacts: OFFICE (01488) 73974 MOBILE (07785) 300168
E-MAIL info@noelchanceracing.com WEBSITE www.noelchanceracing.com

1 **ATHWAAB,** 6, b m Cadeaux Genereux—Ahdaaf (USA) **Mr N. P. Horsfall**
2 **BRACKLOON HIGH (IRE),** 8, b g Bob Back (USA)—
　　　　　　　　　　　Homebird (IRE) **Mr T. Conway, Mrs Conway & Mr T. G. Warren**
3 **EXOTIC FRIEND (IRE),** 5, ch g Croco Rouge (IRE)—Prima Nox **Mrs M. Chance**
4 **FABULOUS FRED (IRE),** 9, b g Beneficial—Roseabel (IRE) **T. F. C. Partnership**
5 **GORES ISLAND (IRE),** 7, b g Beneficial—Just Leader (IRE) **Collins, Horsfall, Michael & O'Sullivan**
6 **I'M A COLLEGE BOY (IRE),** 7, b g Winged Love (IRE)—Hatherley **Mr Conway & Mrs Conway & Mr T G Warren**
7 **I'M SO SPECIAL (IRE),** 7, b m Milan—Hudson Hope (IRE) **Mrs M. Chance**
8 **ICANSEECLEARLYNOW,** 5, ch g Bold Edge—Helens Last (IRE) **Mrs M. C. Sweeney**
9 **TALLEVU (IRE),** 4, ch g Stormy River (FR)—Pascarina (FR) **K. P. Trowbridge**
10 **WAVES AND WIND (IRE),** 6, b g Old Vic—Water Stratford (IRE) **J. P. McManus**

THREE-YEAR-OLDS

11 **TODOISTODARE,** b f Tobougg (IRE)—Misrepresented (IRE) **T. G. Warren**

Other Owners: Mr J. A. Collins, Mr T. Conway, Mrs Thomas Conway, Mr J. P. Craughwell, Mr R. J. Fairlie, Mr Steve Michael, Mr K. P. Trowbridge, Mr T. G. Warren.

Assistant Trainer: Eimear Chance

Jockey (flat): George Baker. **Jockey (NH):** Richard Johnson, Will Kennedy. **Conditional:** Kodie Aubrey, Jeremiah McGrath.

109 MR MICK CHANNON, West Ilsley

Postal: West Ilsley Stables, West Ilsley, Newbury, Berkshire, RG20 7AE
Contacts: PHONE (01635) 281166 FAX (01635) 281177
E-MAIL mick@mick-channon.co.uk/susan@mick-channon.co.uk WEBSITE www.mickchannon.tv

1 ALTONA (IRE), 4, b f Redback—Flawless **Mr R. W. Bastian**
2 ARNOLD LANE (IRE), 4, b c Footstepsinthesand—Capriole **Nick & Olga Dhandsa & John & Zoe Webster**
3 ATLANTIC SPORT (USA), 8, b h Machiavellian—Shy Lady (FR) **M. R. Channon**
4 BALBRIGGAN (IRE), 6, gr g King's Theatre (IRE)—Halfway Home **Mrs C. M. Radford**
5 BALLYLIFEN (IRE), 6, b g Brian Boru—Line Jade **T. Cole**
6 BALLYPATRICK (IRE), 7, b br g Presenting—Jewell For A King (IRE) **Martin, Jocelyn & Steve Broughton**
7 BATELEUR, 9, b g Fraam—Search Party **Dave & Gill Hedley**
8 CALGARY BAY (IRE), 10, b g Taipan (IRE)—Dante's Thatch (IRE) **Mrs C. M. Radford**
9 CTAPPERS, 4, b g Imperial Dancer—Stride Home **P. Taplin**
10 DEVINE GUEST (IRE), 4, b f Holy Roman Emperor (IRE)—Mandavilla (IRE) **John Guest Racing Ltd**
11 ESSELL, 4, ch f Singspiel (IRE)—Londonnetdotcom (IRE) **Mr & Mrs D. D. Clee**
12 FOSTER'S ROAD, 4, b g Imperial Dancer—Search Party **Dave & Gill Hedley**
13 GOOD OF LUCK, 4, b g Authorized (IRE)—Oops Pettie **Mr & Mrs Bernard Panton**
14 HANDLES FOR FORKS (IRE), 5, b m Hawk Wing (USA)—Wood Sprite **M. R. Channon**
15 HIGHLIFE DANCER, 5, br g Imperial Dancer—Wrong Bride **The Highlife Racing Club**
16 I'M SO GLAD, 4, b f Clodovil (IRE)—Dilag (IRE) **Mr C. Wright & The Hon Mrs J.M.Corbett**
17 INFFIRAAJ (IRE), 4, b f Iffraaj—Incense **Mr W. G. Parish**
18 JAARYAH (IRE), 5, ch m Halling (USA)—Albahja **Mrs T. Burns**
19 KNOCK HOUSE (IRE), 4, ch g Old Vic—Lady's Gesture (IRE) **Mrs C. M. Radford**
20 LOCH BA (IRE), 7, b g Craigsteel—Lenmore Lisa (IRE) **Mrs C. M. Radford**
21 MONTAFF, 7, b g Montjeu (IRE)—Meshhed (USA) **Barry Walters Catering**
22 NEW YOUMZAIN (FR), 4, b g Sinndar (IRE)—Luna Sacra (FR) **J. Abdullah**
23 PETALUMA, 4, b f Teofilo (IRE)—Poppo's Song (CAN) **Jon & Julia Aisbitt**
24 SAVANNA DAYS (IRE), 4, ch f Danehill Dancer (IRE)—Dominante (GER) **Jon & Julia Aisbitt**
25 SELINDA, 4, b f Piccolo—Evanesce **Dave & Gill Hedley**
26 SGT RECKLESS, 6, b g Imperial Dancer—Lakaam **Mrs C. M. Radford**
27 SHAMROCKED (IRE), 4, b g Rock of Gibraltar (IRE)—Hallowed Park (IRE) **Mr W. G. Parish**
28 SOMERSBY (IRE), 9, b g Second Empire (IRE)—Back To Roost (IRE) **Mrs C. M. Radford**
29 SPANISH FORK (IRE), 4, br g Trans Island—Wings Awarded **Mr R. W. Bastian**
30 TIDAL RUN, 5, b m Hurricane Run (IRE)—Tidie France (USA) **M. R. Channon**
31 TIDENTIME (USA), 4, b br g Speightstown (USA)—Casting Call (USA) **Jon & Julia Aisbitt**
32 TYCOONS REFLECTION (IRE), 8, b g Definite Article—Tudor Thyne (IRE) **Mrs S. R. Bailey**
33 VERY GOOD DAY (FR), 6, b g Sinndar (IRE)—Picture Princess **Dr M. B. Q. S. Koukash**
34 VIVA STEVE (IRE), 5, b g Flemensfirth (USA)—Eluna **Mrs C. M. Radford**
35 WARDEN HILL (IRE), 5, br g Presenting—Moon Storm (IRE) **Mrs C. M. Radford**
36 WASEEM FARIS (IRE), 4, b g Exceed And Excel (AUS)—Kissing Time **Lease Terminated**
37 YOJIMBO (IRE), 5, gr g Aussie Rules (USA)—Mythie (FR) **Jon & Julia Aisbitt**

THREE-YEAR-OLDS

38 AMRALAH (IRE), b c Teofilo (IRE)—Sharp Mode (USA) **Prince A. A. Faisal**
39 ANTROBUS (IRE), br g Dalakhani (IRE)—Ask Annie (IRE) **M. R. Channon**
40 AYAAR (IRE), b br c Rock of Gibraltar (IRE)—Teide Lady **Sheikh M. B. K. Al Maktoum**
41 BEAUTIFUL STORY (IRE), gr f Verglas (IRE)—To The Skies (USA) **J. Abdullah**
42 BEE JAY KAY, ch f Sixties Icon—Straight Sets (IRE) **M. R. Channon**
43 BUNGLE INTHEJUNGLE, b c Exceed And Excel (AUS)—
Licence To Thrill **Christopher Wright & Miss Emily Asprey**
44 B c Sixties Icon—Canadian Capers **P. Taplin**
45 CHILWORTH DIVA, b f Sixties Icon—Cibenze **7RUS**
46 CHILWORTH ICON, b c Sixties Icon—Tamara Moon (IRE) **7RUS**
47 CRUCK REALTA, b f Sixties Icon—Wansdyke Lass **Anne & Steve Fisher**
48 DALAWAY (IRE), gr f Dalakhani (IRE)—In The Limelight (IRE) **Jon & Julia Aisbitt**
49 B g Footstepsinthesand—Danehill Kikin (IRE)
50 DUKE OF ORANGE (IRE), br c Duke of Marmalade (IRE)—High Society (IRE) **Mr D. M. FitzGerald**
51 EFFIE B, ch f Sixties Icon—Blakeshall Rose **Mr R. W. Bastian**
52 ELIDOR, br c Cape Cross (IRE)—Honorine (IRE) **Jon & Julia Aisbitt**
53 ENAITCH (IRE), gr f New Approach (IRE)—Hotelgenie Dot Com **Mr & Mrs D. D. Clee**
54 EPIC CHARM, b c Kodiac—Gayala (IRE) **Mr P. A. Bowles**
55 GOLDEN LULU, b f Indesatchel (IRE)—Its Another Gift **J. Abdullah**
56 GRAPHIC GUEST, ch f Dutch Art—Makara **John Guest Racing Ltd**
57 GREY GAZELLE, gr f Verglas (IRE)—Hampton Lucy (IRE) **M. R. Channon**

MR MICK CHANNON - Continued

58 HATTIE JACQUES, b f Sixties Icon—Funny Girl (IRE) **Norman Court Stud**
59 HAYYONA, b f Multiplex—Shemriya (IRE) **Prince A. A. Faisal**
60 IMPERIAL SPIRIT, b g Imperial Dancer—Country Spirit **Tytherley Partnership**
61 JILLNEXTDOOR (IRE), b f Henrythenavigator (USA)—
Royal Shyness **Nick & Olga Dhandsa & John & Zoe Webster**
62 JONTLEMAN (IRE), b g Whipper (USA)—Gandia (IRE) **Mr P. D. Corbett**
63 JULLUNDAR (IRE), b c Refuse To Bend (IRE)—Announcing Peace **Nick & Olga Dhandsa & John & Zoe Webster**
64 LADY MARMELO (IRE), b f Duke of Marmalade (IRE)—Mooretown Lady (IRE) **The Three Amigos Partnership**
65 LAMBERT PEN (USA), ch c Johannesburg (USA)—Whiletheiron'shot (USA) **M. R. Channon**
66 LIGHTNING LAUNCH (IRE), b g Kheleyf (USA)—Launch Time (USA) **J. Abdullah**
67 LUHAIF, b c Cape Cross (IRE)—Hot And Spicy **Sheikh M. B. K. Al Maktoum**
68 NICE STORY (IRE), ch f Suave (USA)—Royal Aly (USA) **J. Abdullah**
69 NINE IRON (IRE), gr g Verglas (IRE)—Sevi's Choice (USA) **The Hon Mrs J. M. Corbett & Mr C. Wright**
70 OLLIE OLGA (USA), b br f Stormy Atlantic (USA)—Card Shop (USA) **N. Bizakov**
71 ORPHA, b f New Approach (IRE)—Garah **Prince A. A. Faisal**
72 PAY FREEZE (IRE), b c Baltic King—Banco Solo **Qatar Racing Limited**
73 B f Bahamian Bounty—Perfect Partner **Miss G M Richardson & M R Channon**
74 B f Authorized (IRE)— Purple Vision **Barry Walters Catering**
75 SANDREAMER (IRE), b f Oasis Dream—Alsharq (IRE) **Jon & Julia Alsbitt**
76 SANJURO (IRE), br g Manduro (GER)—Kind Regards (IRE) **Jon & Julia Aisbitt**
77 SHORE STEP (IRE), br g Footstepsinthesand—Chatham Islands (USA) **Jon & Julia Aisbitt**
78 SHRIMPTON, b f Cadeaux Genereux—Feather Boa (IRE) **Mr W. G. Parish**
79 SILCA'S DREAM, b g Oasis Dream—Silca-Cisa **Aldridge Racing Partnership**
80 SOJOUM, b f Sixties Icon—Natalie Jay **Mr F. T. Adams**
81 SOL DIVA, b f Sixties Icon—Solmorin **Lease Terminated**
82 SORELLA BELLA (IRE), ro f Clodovil (IRE)—Anazah (USA) **Mrs A. C. Black**
83 B c Bahamian Bounty—Stan's Smarty Girl (USA) **Mr S. D. Fisher**
84 STRICTLY SILCA, ch f Danehill Dancer (IRE)—Silca Chiave **Aldridge Racing Partnership**
85 STRONG CONVICTION, ch g Piccolo—Keeping The Faith (IRE) **Materna, Dunleavy, Barrett**
86 SYMBOLINE, b f Royal Applause—Ashes (IRE) **Insignia Racing (Emblem)**
87 TALQAA, b f Exceed And Excel (AUS)—Poppo's Song (CAN) **Sheikh M. B. K. Al Maktoum**
88 THE SCUTTLER (IRE), b c Rakti—Common Rumpus (IRE) **Lord Ilsley Racing (Hern Syndicate)**
89 THOUGHT AND MEMORY (IRE), ch c Raven's Pass (USA)—Sadinga (IRE) **Riverdee Stable**
90 B f Authorized (IRE)—Tidie France (USA) **Barry Walters Catering**
91 UNIDEXTER (IRE), br g Footstepsinthesand—Run To Jane (IRE) **M. R. Channon**
92 VALLARTA (IRE), b c Footstepsinthesand—Mexican Miss (IRE) **Tails & Bargate**
93 WARRANT OFFICER, gr g Misu Bond (IRE)—Kilmovee **Insignia Racing (Emblem)**
94 WHISKEYMACK, b g Mount Nelson—Dream Day **Nick & Olga Dhandsa & John & Zoe Webster**

TWO-YEAR-OLDS

95 Gr c 7/4 Clodovil (IRE)—Ajig Dancer (Niniski (USA)) (20634) **M. R. Channon**
96 AMBIANCE (IRE), b c 19/2 Camacho—Thawrah (IRE) (Green Desert (USA)) (66666) **Prince A. A. Faisal**
97 ARANTES, b c 21/3 Sixties Icon—Black Opal (Machiavellian (USA)) **M. R. Channon**
98 B f 13/4 Kheleyf (USA)—Atishoo (Revoque (IRE)) (87300) **John Guest Racing Ltd**
99 B f 23/2 Mujadil (USA)—Cant Hurry Love (Desert Prince (IRE)) (11507) **M. R. Channon**
100 B f 11/3 Rock of Gibraltar (IRE)—
Cartimandua (Medicean) (52000) **Miss Miss Emily Asprey & Christopher Wright**
101 CHARACTERISE, ch c 4/1 Winker Watson—Artistic License (IRE) (Chevalier (IRE)) **J. P. Repard**
102 CHESTURO (IRE), ch f 28/4 Manduro (GER)—Joyfullness (USA) (Dixieland Band (USA)) (20000) **J. Abdullah**
103 CRAZEE DIAMOND, b f 6/3 Rock of Gibraltar (IRE)—
Final Dynasty (Komaite (USA)) (41904) **Nick & Olga Dhandsa & John & Zoe Webster**
104 DEEDS NOT WORDS (IRE), b c 3/2 Royal Applause—Wars (IRE) (Green Desert (USA)) (60000) **G. D. P. Materna**
105 B c 28/4 Sixties Icon—Elegant Dance (Statoblest) **M. R. Channon**
106 GOOD MORNING LADY, b f 28/2 Compton Place—Baldemosa (FR) (Lead On Time (USA)) (10000) **J. Abdullah**
107 GREVILLEA (IRE), b f 4/5 Admiralofthefleet (USA)—Louve Heureuse (IRE) (Peintre Celebre (USA)) **N. J. Hitchins**
108 HEDY, ch f 10/4 Winker Watson—Jollyhockeysticks (Fantastic Light (USA)) **M. R. Channon**
109 HESKA (IRE), b c 15/4 Rock of Gibraltar (IRE)—Sweet Sioux (Halling (USA)) (38000) **Box 41**
110 HOMESTRETCH, b c 17/3 Holy Roman Emperor (IRE)—Sharp Mode (USA) (Diesis) **Prince A. A. Faisal**
111 ISABELLA BIRD, b f 12/2 Invincible Spirit (IRE)—Meetyouthere (IRE) (Sadler's Wells (USA)) **Jon & Julia Aisbitt**
112 JALLOTA, b c 15/3 Rock of Gibraltar (IRE)—
Lady Lahar (Fraam) (100000) **Nick & Olga Dhandsa & John & Zoe Webster**
113 KEEP CLOSE, b f 21/3 Cape Cross (IRE)—Kelucia (IRE) (Grand Lodge (USA)) (35000) **J. Abdullah**
114 Ch c 7/4 Compton Place—Kindallachan (Magic Ring (IRE)) (15238) **M. R. Channon**
115 KISANJI, b c 13/4 Teofilo (IRE)—Al Kamah (USA) (Kingmambo (USA)) (46000) **Box 41**
116 B c 2/4 Iffraaj—Luxie (IRE) (Acclamation) (103174) **Sheikh M. B. K. Al Maktoum**

MR MICK CHANNON - Continued

117 B f 11/5 Fastnet Rock (AUS)—Madaen (USA) (Nureyev (USA)) (55555) **Christopher Wright & Miss Emily Asprey**
118 MINI LIGHT, b f 26/3 Royal Applause—Kind of Light (Primo Dominie) (7000) **J. Abdullah**
119 MISS CAPE (IRE), b f 23/4 Cape Cross (IRE)—Miss Sally (IRE) (Danetime (IRE)) (51586) **Jon & Julia Aisbitt**
120 B f 7/2 Grand Slam (USA)—Miss Sea Oats (USA) (Langfuhr (CAN)) (52227) **Qatar Racing Limited**
121 NAKEETA, b c 2/3 Sixties Icon—Easy Red (IRE) (Hunting Lion (IRE)) **M. R. Channon**
122 NARBOROUGH, b c 25/4 Winker Watson—Solmorin (Fraam) **Mrs E. J. Maxted**
123 Ch f 14/3 Bahamian Bounty—One Giant Leap (IRE) (Pivotal) (40000) **Mrs A. C. Black**
124 PALERMA, b f 6/2 Shamardal (USA)—West Lorne (USA) (Gone West (USA)) (55000) **Jon & Julia Aisbitt**
125 B c 12/2 Teofilo (IRE)—Queen of Lyons (USA) (Dubai Destination (USA)) (134920) **Sheikh M. B. K. Al Maktoum**
126 RIVERBOAT SPRINGS (IRE), b c 15/3 Bushranger (IRE)—
              Mashie (Selkirk (USA)) (55000) **Mr C. Wright & The Hon Mrs J.M.Corbett**
127 ROSE GLORIA (IRE), ch f 30/4 Haatef (USA)—Western Sky (Barathea (IRE)) (32000) **J. Abdullah**
128 ROSSO CORSA, b c 24/3 Footstepsinthesand—Lady Scarlett (Woodman (USA)) **Box 41**
129 SARTORI, b c 12/4 Elnadim (USA)—Little Caroline (IRE) (Great Commotion (USA)) (20000) **Box 41**
130 Ch f 17/1 New Approach (IRE)—Shy Appeal (IRE) (Barathea (IRE)) **M. R. Channon**
131 SLEEPY JOE (IRE), b c 2/4 Jeremy (USA)—
              Rocking (Oasis Dream) (23809) **Nick & Olga Dhandsa & John & Zoe Webster**
132 B f 3/2 Winker Watson—Stephanie's Mind (Mind Games) **M. R. Channon**
133 TANOJIN (IRE), ch f 22/4 Thousand Words—
              Indianmie Moon (Fraam) (19840) **Nick & Olga Dhandsa & John & Zoe Webster**
134 THE SMART ONE (IRE), b c 3/4 Exceed And Excel (AUS)—Bareilly (USA) (Lyphard (USA)) **J. Abdullah**
135 B f 16/2 Authorized (IRE)—Umniya (IRE) (Bluebird (USA)) (45714) **Sheikh M. B. K. Al Maktoum**

Other Owners: J. R. Aisbitt, Mrs J. M. Aisbitt, E. Aldridge, Miss C. T. Aldridge, Miss E. Asprey, M. Barrett, Sir M. F. Broughton, S. W. Broughton, Mr S. Clancy, D. D. Clee, Mrs J. P. Clee, J. P Coggan, The Hon Mrs C. Corbett, Dr N. Dhandsa, Mr T. V. Drayton, Mr S. Dunleavy, Mrs A. P. Fisher, Mr M. Grier, Mrs G. H. Hedley, Insignia Racing Limited, Mrs A. M. Jones, Miss E. Lawlor, Mike Channon Bloodstock Ltd, Mr B. Panton, Mrs J. E. Panton, Miss G. M. Richardson, Mr M. Swallow, Simon Trant, Mrs T. G. Trant, Mr P. Trant, Mr J. Webster, J. A. Williams, C. N. Wright.

---

110 MR MICHAEL CHAPMAN, Market Rasen
Postal: **Woodlands Racing Stables, Woodlands Lane, Willingham Road, Market Rasen, Lincolnshire, LN8 3RE**
Contacts: **PHONE/FAX** (01673) 843663 **MOBILE** (07971) 940087
E-MAIL woodlands.stables@btconnect.com **WEBSITE** www.woodlandsracingstables.co.uk

1 EPEE CELESTE (FR), 7, ch m Spadoun (FR)—Juste Ciel (USA) **Mrs S. M. Richards**
2 FEELING PECKISH (USA), 9, ch g Point Given (USA)—Sunday Bazaar (USA) **J. E. Reed**
3 GALLEY SLAVE (IRE), 8, b g Spartacus (IRE)—Cimeterre (IRE) **Mrs M. M. Chapman**
4 HERESELLIE (IRE), 5, b m Clodovil (IRE)—Special Dissident **Mrs M. M. Chapman**
5 KATHINDI (IRE), 6, ch g Pearl of Love (IRE)—Turfcare Flight (IRE) **Mrs M. M. Chapman**
6 KHESKIANTO (IRE), 7, b m Kheleyf (USA)—Gently (IRE) **F. A. Dickinson**
7 LENDERKING (IRE), 5, b g Sleeping Indian—Roses From Ridey (IRE) **Mrs M. M. Chapman**
8 MAZOVIAN (USA), 5, b g E Dubai (USA)—Polish Style (USA) **Mrs M. M. Chapman**
9 MONZINO (USA), 5, b br g More Than Ready (USA)—Tasso's Magic Roo (USA) **Mrs M. M. Chapman**
10 ORPEN WIDE (IRE), 11, b g Orpen (USA)—Melba (IRE) **Mrs M. M. Chapman**
11 PEAK SEASONS (IRE), 10, ch g Raise A Grand (IRE)—Teresian Girl (IRE) **J. E. Reed**
12 SIMPLIFIED, 10, b m Lend A Hand—Houston Heiress (USA) **R. A. Gadd**
13 SOPHIE'S BEAU (USA), 6, b g Stormy Atlantic (USA)—Lady Buttercup (USA) **Mrs M. M. Chapman**
14 TAYARAT (IRE), 8, b g Noverre (USA)—Sincere (IRE) **Mrs M. M. Chapman**
15 TROPICAL SKY (IRE), 5, b g Librettist (USA)—Tropical Breeze (IRE) **Mrs M. M. Chapman**
16 VOGARTH, 9, ch g Arkadian Hero (USA)—Skara Brae **Mrs M. M. Chapman**
17 XENOPHON, 5, b g Phoenix Reach (IRE)—Comtesse Noire (CAN) **Mr Milson Robinson**

Assistant Trainer: Mr S. Petch

---

111 MS JANE CHAPPLE-HYAM, Newmarket
Postal: **Rose Cottage, The Street, Dalham, Newmarket, Suffolk, CB8 8TF**
Contacts: **PHONE** (01638) 500451 **FAX** (01638) 661335 **MOBILE** (07899) 000555
E-MAIL janechapplehyam@hotmail.co.uk

1 APACHE (IRE), 5, b g Galileo (IRE)—Charroux (IRE) **Invictus**
2 BIG BAY (USA), 7, b g Horse Chestnut (SAF)—Takipy (USA) **Jane Chapple-Hyam & Mrs B. J. Hirst**

MS JANE CHAPPLE-HYAM - Continued

3 **BIG KAHUNA**, 6, br g Trade Fair—Pistoia **Miss E. Foley**
4 **COACH MONTANA (IRE)**, 4, b g Proud Citizen (USA)—Market Day **Mr C. R. Moore**
5 **EXCELLENT JEM**, 4, b g Exceed And Excel (AUS)—Polar Jem **Norcroft Park Stud**
6 **FEVER FEW**, 4, b f Pastoral Pursuits—Prairie Oyster **Redgate Bloodstock & Mrs Zara Wise**
7 **FLYING TRADER (USA)**, 4, gr ro g Mizzen Mast (USA)—
Remediate (USA) **Peacock Hirst Fahy Mulshaw Chapple-Hyam**
8 **FROSTY SECRET**, 4, b f Echo of Light—Raze **Mr S. Brewster**
9 **JUNGLE BAY**, 6, b g Oasis Dream—Dominica **Mr S. Brewster**
10 **MFIFTYTHREE FORD (IRE)**, 4, b f Royal Applause—Maid For Romance **Mr M. Shirtliff & Mr B. Ressell**
11 **MULL OF KILLOUGH (IRE)**, 7, b g Mull of Kintyre (USA)—Sun Shower (IRE) **Invictus**
12 **SASKIA'S DREAM**, 5, b m Oasis Dream—Swynford Pleasure **Peter Bottomley & Jane Chapple-Hyam**
13 **SECRET ASSET (IRE)**, 8, gr g Clodovil (IRE)—Skerray **Simon & Jeanette Pierpoint & Paul Salisbury**
14 **STORM KING**, 4, b c Shamardal (USA)—Tarandot (IRE) **Norcroft Park Stud**

THREE-YEAR-OLDS

15 **CRESTA ONE**, gr f Act One—Collect **Miss C. Blockley**
16 **DAAR DAAR**, b f Dubai Destination (USA)—Effetto Ottico (IRE) **Miss R. Al Attiya**
17 **MASTER WIZARD**, b c Motivator—Enchanted **Norcroft Park Stud**
18 **PLANCHETTE**, b f Mount Nelson—Cruinn A Bhord **Mr Lee Jordan & Mr Judd O'Connor**
19 **SKATING OVER (USA)**, ch f Giant's Causeway (USA)—Annie Skates (USA) **R. H. W. Morecombe**
20 **TOMMY'S SECRET**, gr g Sakhee's Secret—La Gessa **Ms J. F. Chapple-Hyam**

TWO-YEAR-OLDS

21 B c 22/3 Rock of Gibraltar (IRE)—Hannah Frank (IRE) (High Chaparral (IRE)) (10000) **Norcroft Park Stud**
22 **INJUN SANDS**, b c 13/2 Halling (USA)—Serriera (FR) (Highest Honor (FR)) **Mrs M. D. Morriss**

Other Owners: Mr P. Bottomley, Mrs Jane Chapple-Hyam, Mr C. J. Fahy, Mrs J. Hirst, A. J. Hollis, Mr D. M. Hollis, Mr D. A. Mccormick, Mr W. P. Mulshaw, The Hon A. S. Peacock, Mr S. W. Pierpoint, Mr P. J. Salisbury, N. E. Sangster.

Assistant Trainer: Abigail Harrison

Apprentice: Ian Burns.

---

112 **MR PETER CHAPPLE-HYAM, Newmarket**
Postal: St Gatien Stables, All Saints Road, Newmarket, Suffolk, CB8 8HJ
Contacts: PHONE (01638) 560827 FAX (01638) 561908 MOBILE (07770) 472774
E-MAIL pchapplehyam@yahoo.com WEBSITE www.peterchapplehyam.com

1 **AUTHORA (IRE)**, 4, b f Authorized (IRE)—Danseuse du Soir (IRE) **Woodcote Stud Ltd**
2 **CARAVAN ROLLS ON**, 5, b h Hernando (FR)—Grain Only **Pearl Bloodstock Limited**
3 **KING'S WARRIOR (FR)**, 6, b g King's Best (USA)—Save Me The Waltz (FR) **Mr P. Hancock**
4 **MY PROPELLER (IRE)**, 4, b f Holy Roman Emperor (IRE)—Incise **J. Barton**
5 **NEVER PERFECT (IRE)**, 4, b g Galileo (IRE)—Dapprima (GER) **Mrs Fitri Hay**

THREE-YEAR-OLDS

6 **AGENT ALLISON**, b f Dutch Art—Loquacity **Mrs Fitri Hay**
7 **AL MUKHDAM**, b c Exceed And Excel (AUS)—Sakhya (IRE) **Mr Ziad A. Galadari**
8 **ARBEEL**, b f Royal Applause—Waafiah **Mr Ziad A. Galadari**
9 **BOITE (IRE)**, b c Authorized (IRE)—Albiatra (USA) **Eledy SRL**
10 **BUCKSTAY (IRE)**, b g Lawman (FR)—Stella Del Mattino (USA) **Mrs Fitri Hay**
11 **CAPE OF HOPE (IRE)**, b c Cape Cross (IRE)—Bright Hope (IRE) **Eledy SRL**
12 **DODINA (IRE)**, b f Acclamation—Etica (IRE) **Eledy SRL**
13 **FUNKY COLD MEDINA**, b f Cockney Rebel (IRE)—Monica Campbell **Mr Phil Cunningham**
14 **GRANULE**, b f Hernando (FR)—Grain Only **Miss K. Rausing**
15 **HASBAH (IRE)**, b f Cape Cross (IRE)—Gimasha **Mr Ziad A. Galadari**
16 **HERMOSA VAQUERA (IRE)**, b f High Chaparral (IRE)—Sundown **Mr Paul Hancock**
17 **INDIGO LADY**, b f Sir Percy—Seal Indigo (IRE) **Mr Paul Hancock**
18 **KING BERTIE (IRE)**, b g Clodovil (IRE)—Jouel (FR) **Mr Paul Hancock**
19 **MAXENTIUS (IRE)**, b g Holy Roman Emperor (IRE)—Guantanamera (IRE) **Mr Tony Elliott**
20 **MOCENIGO (IRE)**, ch c Refuse To Bend (IRE)—Doregan (IRE) **Eledy SRL**
21 **MY LUCKY VALENTINE (IRE)**, b f High Chaparral (IRE)—Lasso **Mr Paul Hancock**
22 **OSCILATE WILDLY (IRE)**, b f Mount Nelson—Marisa (GER) **Mr Joseph Barton**
23 **SARJINSKY (IRE)**, ch c Raven's Pass (USA)—Dinka Raja (USA) **Mr S. Rudolf**

MR PETER CHAPPLE-HYAM - Continued

24 **ST ELMO'S FIRE**, b c Bahamian Bounty—Firebelly **The Saints & Sinners Partnership**
25 **TIMELESS APPEAL (IRE)**, br f Kheleyf (USA)—Elegant Times (IRE) **Mr Allan Belshaw**

TWO-YEAR-OLDS

26 **ALPHABETIQUE**, b f 5/3 Zamindar (USA)—Almamia (Hernando (FR)) **Miss K. Rausing**
27 **AROD (IRE)**, b c 21/4 Teofilo (IRE)—My Personal Space (USA) (Rahy (USA)) (134920) **Qatar Racing Limited**
28 Ch f 5/2 New Approach (IRE)—Blue Rocket (IRE) (Rock of Gibraltar (IRE)) (100000) **Mr Joseph Barton**
29 **DINO MITE**, b f 15/4 Doctor Dino (FR)—Compose (Anabaa (USA)) **Mr P. Cunningham**
30 **DIRECT TIMES (IRE)**, b c 8/2 Acclamation—Elegant Times (Dansili) (20000) **Mr Allan Belshaw**
31 **DOGARESSA (IRE)**, ch f 4/5 Mastercraftsman (IRE)—Doregan (IRE) (Bahhare (USA)) **Eledy SRL**
32 **ETERNITYS GATE**, b c 28/2 Dutch Art—Regency Rose (Danehill (USA)) (190000) **Mrs Fitri Hay**
33 B f 23/3 Dubawi (IRE)—Everlasting Love (Pursuit of Love) **A. W. Black**
34 **FARQUHAR**, ch c 13/3 Archipenko (USA)—Pointed Arch (IRE) (Rock of Gibraltar (IRE)) **Mr Tony Elliott**
35 **FEMALE STRATEGY (IRE)**, b f 4/3 Holy Roman Emperor (IRE)—
                                     Strategy (Machiavellian (USA)) (38095) **Mrs Fitri Hay**
36 B f 4/2 Shamardal (USA)—Gimasha (Cadeaux Genereux) **Mr Ziad A. Galadari**
37 **HAY CHEWED (IRE)**, b f 8/4 Camacho—Titian Saga (IRE) (Titus Livius (FR)) (14285) **Mr John C. Davies**
38 B f 9/4 Pivotal—Heavenly Bay (USA) (Rahy (USA)) (57142) **Mrs Fitri Hay**
39 **HYDROGEN**, b c 12/3 Galileo (IRE)—Funsie (FR) (Saumarez) (2500000) **Qatar Racing Limited**
40 **INCHILA**, b f 6/4 Dylan Thomas (IRE)—Inchiri (Sadler's Wells (USA)) **Woodcote Stud Ltd**
41 **KATAWI**, b f 7/5 Dubawi (IRE)—Purring (USA) (Mountain Cat (USA)) **Moyns Park Estate and Stud Ltd**
42 B br f 22/4 Cape Cross (IRE)—Maramba (Rainbow Quest (USA)) **Five Horses Ltd**
43 **PINK DANCE**, b f 19/4 Dutch Art—Dance Away (Pivotal) (60000) **Mrs Fitri Hay**
44 **SEMARAL (IRE)**, b f 15/4 High Chaparral (IRE)—Semaphore (Zamindar (USA)) **Moyns Park Estate and Stud Ltd**
45 Gr c 2/4 Aussie Rules (USA)—Silk Meadow (IRE) (Barathea (IRE)) (14285) **Mr Paul Hancock**
46 **SONG OF ROWLAND (IRE)**, b c 27/2 Holy Roman Emperor (IRE)—
                                     Makarova (IRE) (Sadler's Wells (USA)) (47619) **Mrs Fitri Hay**
47 B c 19/2 Bushranger (IRE)—Tatora (Selkirk (USA)) (70000) **Mr Khalifa Dasmal & Mrs Clodagh McStay**
48 **VOICE OF A LEADER (IRE)**, b c 10/1 Danehill Dancer (IRE)—
                                     Thewaytosanjose (IRE) (Fasliyev (USA)) (210000) **Mrs Fitri Hay & Mrs John Magnier**

Other Owners: Mrs L. M. Shanahan, M. Tabor.

---

113 MR GEORGE CHARLTON, Stocksfield
Postal: Mickley Grange Farm, Stocksfield, Northumberland, NE43 7TB
Contacts: PHONE (01661) 843247 MOBILE (07808) 955029
E-MAIL gcharlton@fsmail.net

1 **BALLYMACDUFF (IRE)**, 9, b g Strategic Choice (USA)—Ashpark Rose (IRE) **G. A. G. Charlton**
2 **BALLYVOQUE (IRE)**, 7, b g Revoque (IRE)—Timissa (IRE) **J. I. A. Charlton**
3 **BOGSIDE (IRE)**, 9, ch g Commander Collins (IRE)—Miss Henrietta (IRE) **Mrs S. M. Wood**
4 **FREDDIE BROWN**, 9, b g Missed Flight—Some Shiela **J. R. Jeffreys**
5 **HEEZ A STEEL (IRE)**, 12, b g Naheez (USA)—Ari's Fashion **J. I. A. Charlton**
6 **KNOCKARA BEAU (IRE)**, 10, b g Leading Counsel—Clairabell (IRE) **W. F. Trueman**
7 **LORD USHER (IRE)**, 6, b g Lord Americo—Beet Five (IRE) **G. A. G. Charlton**
8 **MASTER BEAU**, 9, b g Beat All (USA)—Golden Aureole **J. I. A. Charlton**
9 **MONASHEE (IRE)**, 8, b br g Monashee Mountain (USA)—On The Bridle (IRE) **G. A. G. Charlton**
10 **SHERIFF HALL (IRE)**, 8, b g Saddlers' Hall (IRE)—Derravarra Breeze (IRE) **Mr & Mrs Raymond Anderson Green**
11 **WINSTONE (IRE)**, 8, b g Pierre—Cushenstown Best (IRE) **G. A. G. Charlton**

Other Owners: Mr Raymond Anderson Green, Mrs Anita Green.

Assistant Trainer: Mr J. I. A. Charlton

Jockey (NH): Alistair J. Findlay. **Conditional:** Lucy Alexander.

---

114 MR ROGER CHARLTON, Beckhampton
Postal: Beckhampton House, Marlborough, Wiltshire, SN8 1QR
Contacts: OFFICE (01672) 539533 HOME (01672) 539330 FAX (01672) 539456
MOBILE (07710) 784511
E-MAIL r.charlton@virgin.net WEBSITE www.rogercharlton.com

1 **AL KAZEEM**, 5, b h Dubawi (IRE)—Kazeem **D. J. Deer**

MR ROGER CHARLTON - Continued

2 **BISHOP ROKO**, 4, b g Rock of Gibraltar (IRE)—Kirk **Mr Michael Pescod**
3 **BORDER LEGEND**, 4, ch g Selkirk (USA)—Bonnie Doon (IRE) **Her Majesty The Queen**
4 **CACTUS VALLEY (IRE)**, 4, b g Lawman (FR)—Beech Gardens **H.R.H. Sultan Ahmad Shah**
5 **CAPTAIN CAT (IRE)**, 4, b br g Dylan Thomas (IRE)—Mother of Pearl (IRE) **Seasons Holidays**
6 **CITYSCAPE**, 7, ch h Selkirk (USA)—Tantina (USA) **K. Abdulla**
7 **CLOWANCE ESTATE (IRE)**, 4, b g Teofilo (IRE)—Whirly Bird **Seasons Holidays**
8 **CRY FURY**, 5, b g Beat Hollow—Cantanta **K. Abdulla**
9 **DEFINIGHTLY**, 7, b br g Diktat—Perfect Night **Mr S. Emmet & Miss R. Emmet**
10 **MAFETENG**, 5, b m Nayef (USA)—Marakabei **Mrs Jane Poulter**
11 **MARZANTE (USA)**, 5, gr ro g Maria's Mon (USA)—Danzante (USA) **K. Abdulla**
12 **MINCE**, 4, ch f Medicean—Strut **Lady Rothschild**
13 **SILVER LIME (USA)**, 4, b c Mizzen Mast (USA)—Red Dot (USA) **K. Abdulla**
14 **THISTLE BIRD**, 5, b m Selkirk (USA)—Dolma (FR) **Lady Rothschild**
15 **TIOMAN LEGEND**, 4, b g Kyllachy—Elegant Times (IRE) **H.R.H. Sultan Ahmad Shah**
16 **TOP OFFER**, 4, b g Dansili—Zante **K. Abdulla**
17 **TRADER JACK**, 4, b g Trade Fair—Azeema (IRE) **D. J. Deer**
18 **WATERCLOCK (IRE)**, 4, ch g Notnowcato—Waterfall One **Lady Rothschild**

THREE-YEAR-OLDS

19 **ABATED**, b f Dansili—Tantina (USA) **K. Abdulla**
20 **CANDOLUMINESCENCE**, br f Dansili—Flash of Gold **Her Majesty The Queen**
21 **DAWN OF EMPIRE (USA)**, b f Empire Maker (USA)—Didina **K. Abdulla**
22 **DEFIANT SPIRIT**, ch g Compton Place—Muffled (USA) **Mr D. Carter and Mr P. Inglett**
23 **DERWENT (USA)**, b g Mizzen Mast (USA)—Skiable (IRE) **K. Abdulla**
24 **DON MARCO**, b g Choisir (AUS)—Dolma (FR) **Lady Rothschild**
25 **DUNDONNELL (USA)**, b c First Defence (USA)—Family (USA) **K. Abdulla**
26 **FIRST SECRETARY**, b f Nayef (USA)—Spinning Queen **Lady Rothschild**
27 **GREENERY (IRE)**, b f Green Desert (USA)—Go Between **D. J. Deer**
28 **IMPASSE**, b f Dansili—Meetyouthere (IRE) **P. R. Mitchell**
29 **INAUGURAL**, b g Invincible Spirit (IRE)—Anasazi (IRE) **Her Majesty The Queen**
30 B c Royal Applause—Kazeem **D. J. Deer**
31 **LIBERTY JACK (IRE)**, b g Sakhee (USA)—Azeema (IRE) **D. J. Deer**
32 **MAGOG**, br g Dansili—Margarula (IRE) **Lady Rothschild**
33 **MAWSON**, b g Starcraft (NZ)—No Fear No Favour (AUS) **Mondial Racing**
34 B g Sakhee (USA)—Oystermouth **D. J. Deer**
35 **PATERNOSTER**, b g Teofilo (IRE)—Rosse **A. E. Oppenheimer**
36 **PYTHAGOREAN**, b g Oasis Dream—Hypoteneuse (IRE) **K. Abdulla**
37 **TOP FOR MORE (IRE)**, b c Teofilo (IRE)—No Quest (IRE) **H.R.H. Sultan Ahmad Shah**
38 **RAIL STAR**, b f Rail Link—Widescreen (USA) **K. Abdulla**
39 **RANDOM SUCCESS (IRE)**, b f Shamardal (USA)—Foreplay (IRE) **Mr P. Inglett**
40 **RUSSIAN LINK**, b f Rail Link—Zathonia **K. Abdulla**
41 **SECONDO (FR)**, b c Sakhee's Secret—Royal Jade **D. J. Deer**
42 **SERENITY SPA**, gr f Excellent Art—Molly Mello (GER) **Seasons Holidays**
43 **SEYMOUR PLACE**, b f Compton Place—Perfect Night **Mr S. Emmet & Miss R. Emmet**
44 **SIBAYA**, b f Exceed And Excel (AUS)—Abunai **A. E. Oppenheimer**
45 **SO BELOVED**, b c Dansili—Valencia **K. Abdulla**
46 **TARTARY (IRE)**, b c Oasis Dream—Tamso (USA) **Lady Rothschild**
47 **THE DARK WIZARD (IRE)**, gr g Dark Angel (IRE)—Knapton Hill **Mr P Inglett & Mr D Carter**
48 **TOP TRAIL (USA)**, b br f Exchange Rate (USA)—Trekking (USA) **K. Abdulla**
49 **UNDER MILK WOOD**, b f Montjeu (IRE)—Freni (GER) **Seasons Holidays**

TWO-YEAR-OLDS

50 B c 6/2 Rail Link—Affluent (Oasis Dream) **K. Abdulla**
51 Ch c 26/3 Medicean—Amber Queen (IRE) (Cadeaux Genereux) (105000) **H.R.H. Sultan Ahmad Shah**
52 **CANOVA (IRE)**, ch c 28/3 Art Connoisseur (IRE)—
Rain Dancer (IRE) (Sadler's Wells (USA)) (45000) **Royal Ascot Racing Club**
53 B c 16/4 Sir Percy—Cassique Lady (IRE) (Langfuhr (CAN)) (30000) **Beckhampton Stables Ltd**
54 **CATADUPA**, ch f 2/3 Selkirk (USA)—Caribana (Hernando (FR)) **Miss K. Rausing**
55 Ch c 16/2 Three Valleys (USA)—Chasing Stars (Observatory (USA)) **K. Abdulla**
56 B c 3/3 Authorized (IRE)—Corsican Sunset (USA) (Thunder Gulch (USA)) **Seasons Holidays**
57 **DARK LEOPARD**, b c 26/2 Dubawi (IRE)—Clouded Leopard (Danehill (USA)) **Lady Rothschild**
58 B c 22/3 Bahamian Bounty—Desert Royalty (IRE) (Alhaarth (IRE)) (35000) **The Hon. Philip Havers QC**
59 B f 27/3 First Defence (USA)—Didina (Nashwan (USA)) **K. Abdulla**
60 B c 6/5 Sir Percy—Enforce (USA) (Kalanisi (IRE)) (28000) **Beckhampton Stables Ltd**
61 B f 28/2 First Defence (USA)—Family (USA) (Danzig (USA)) **K. Abdulla**

MR ROGER CHARLTON - Continued

62 Ch f 9/5 Shirocco (GER)—Femme Fatale (Fairy King (USA)) (15000) **Mr A. Bengough**
63 FRANGIPANNI (IRE), b br f 19/4 Dansili—Frizzante (Efisio) **Lady Rothschild**
64 HIGH CHURCH (IRE), b c 8/5 High Chaparral (IRE)—Tamso (USA) (Seeking The Gold (USA)) **Lady Rothschild**
65 B br f 25/2 Smart Strike (CAN)—Intercontinental (Danehill (USA)) **K. Abdulla**
66 KIDDING APART (USA), ch c 18/3 Lemon Drop Kid (USA)—Oceans Apart (Desert Prince (IRE)) **Elite Racing**
67 B f 28/1 Cape Cross (IRE)—La Conquistadora (Pivotal) **Mr J. Stewart**
68 B f 7/4 Sixties Icon—Marathea (FR) (Marathon (USA)) **Mr C. Platel**
69 OLD GUARD, b c 22/2 Notnowcato—Dolma (FR) (Marchand de Sable (USA)) **Lady Rothschild**
70 Ch c 1/3 Medicean—Oshiponga (Barathea (IRE)) **Mr J. Stewart**
71 Gr ro c 16/2 Mizzen Mast (USA)—Palisade (USA) (Gone West (USA)) **K. Abdulla**
72 Ch c 27/2 Galileo (IRE)—Party (IRE) (Cadeaux Genereux) (200000) **Seasons Holidays**
73 Ch f 9/3 Bahamian Bounty—Procession (Zafonic (USA)) (21000) **AXOM**
74 SCARLET PLUM, b f 2/1 Pivotal—Scarlet Runner (Night Shift (USA)) **Nicholas Jones**
75 Gr f 28/2 Oasis Dream—Scuffle (Daylami (IRE)) **K. Abdulla**
76 B f 19/1 Champs Elysees—Short Dance (USA) (Hennessy (USA)) **K. Abdulla**
77 STOMP, b c 3/3 Nayef (USA)—Strut (Danehill Dancer (IRE)) **Lady Rothschild**
78 Ch f 13/3 Halling (USA)—Susun Kelapa (USA) (St Jovite (USA)) **Mr P. Hearson**
79 B c 3/2 Mastercraftsman (IRE)—Treacle (USA) (Seeking The Gold (USA)) (20000) **Beckhampton Stables Ltd**
80 B f 23/3 First Defence (USA)—Trekking (USA) (Gone West (USA)) **K. Abdulla**
81 VALLILA, b f 19/2 Dunkerque (FR)—Villabella (FR) (Hernando (FR)) **Norris Bloodstock**
82 B c 4/3 Empire Maker (USA)—Yashmak (USA) (Danzig (USA)) **K. Abdulla**

Other Owners: Mr K. Carter, Mr J. Chalk, Mr C. Curry, Mrs Susan Davis, Mr P. Dean, Miss C. A. Green, The Hon. Philip Havers QC, Mr D. Johns, Mr J. Osborne, Mrs V. Pakenham, Mr P. Roche, Mr S de Zoete.

Assistant Trainer: C. Finnegan

Jockey (flat): James Doyle.

---

115 | MR HARRY CHISMAN, Stow-on-the-Wold
Postal: **The Retreat Stables, Maugersbury, Stow-on-the-Wold, Gloucestershire, GL54 1HP**
Contacts: **PHONE (07787) 516723**

1 ALL RILED UP, 5, b m Dr Massini (IRE)—Martha Reilly (IRE) **Unregistered Partnership**
2 AUGHCARRA (IRE), 8, b g High Chaparral (IRE)—Pearly Brooks **Grabham Waggott Seal Baker Byrne Bell**
3 GAINSBOROUGH'S ART (IRE), 8, ch g Desert Prince (IRE)—
  Cathy Garcia (IRE) **Wood Appleyard Goodall Welsh Cooke Byrne**
4 JACK THEHATMCVITIE, 4, b c Midnight Legend—Top Gale (IRE) **Unregistered Partnership**

Other Owners: Mr H. J. Appleyard, Mr P. M. Baker, Mr Terry Bell, Mrs H. Byrne, Mr Harry Chisman, Mr V. R. Cooke, Mr M. J. Flowers, Mr Ray Goodall, Ms Shirley Grabham, Mr S. Kirkland, Mr M. Madden, Mr B. Seal, Mr J. W. Waggott, Mr D. Welch, Mr Duncan Wood.

Jockey (NH): Tom O'Brien, Sean Quinlan, Andrew Tinkler.

---

116 | MRS ANGELA CLARKE, Llangadog
Postal: **Marlands, Llangadog, Dyfed, SA19 9EW**

1 DIDDLE'EM, 12, b g Accondy (IRE)—Morepatience **Dr S. R. Clarke**
2 PANACHE, 8, b g King's Best (USA)—Exclusive **Dr S. R. Clarke**

---

117 | MR NICOLAS CLEMENT, Chantilly
Postal: **37, Avenue de Joinville, 60500 Chantilly, France**
Contacts: **PHONE (0033) 3445 75960 FAX (0033) 3445 77084 MOBILE (0033) 6072 34640**
E-MAIL clementoffice@wanadoo.fr WEBSITE www.nicolasclement.com

1 BECQUANIS (FR), 4, bl c Panis (USA)—Berangele (FR)
2 BENWAKI (FR), 4, ch c Sandwaki (USA)—Benghor (GER)
3 CORSAGE (USA), 4, b f Exchange Rate—Gingivere
4 DIEPPE (IRE), 4, gr g Dutch Art—Spinamix
5 FRENCH FIFTEEN (FR), 4, ch c Turtle Bowl (IRE)—Spring Morning (FR)

MR NICOLAS CLEMENT - Continued

  6 GRIMOD (FR), 4, ch g Vespone (IRE)—Metaline (FR)
  7 HI YA PAL (USA), 4, b c Pulpit (USA)—Cloon (USA)
  8 ISLET (IRE), 4, b f Manduro (GER)—Eilean Shona
  9 LADY ANA (FR), 4, b f Anabaa (USA)—The Wise Lady (FR)
10 NOW WE CAN, 4, b c Martillo (GER)—Notre Dame (GER)
11 SAGA BOREALE (USA), 4, b f Arch (USA)—Scarlett's Pride (FR)
12 SEA FIGHT (USA), 7, ch g Smart Strike (CAN)—Incredulous (FR)
13 SIBERIAN FREEZE (IRE), 4, b gr c Verglas (IRE)—Debbie's Next (USA)
14 SNAKESTONE, 4, b f Sakhee (USA)—Moidart
15 TABREED, 4, b f Sakhee (USA)—Za Aamah (USA)
16 YELLOW AND GREEN, 4, br f Monsun (GER)—Green Swallow (FR)

THREE-YEAR-OLDS

17 AS ROYAL (FR), ch g Royal Assault (USA)—Vetority
18 AYLIN (FR), ch f Gold Away (IRE)—Street Lightning (FR)
19 CAN TWIST AND RUN (FR), b g Turtle Bowl (IRE)—Cazorla (IRE)
20 CATNISS (USA), b f Tale of The Cat (USA)—A Party For Two (USA)
21 CESNY (FR), b f Green Tune (USA)—Croquet (USA)
22 CHAGARI (USA), ch f Giant's Causeway (USA)—Titian Time (USA)
23 CHAO PHRAYA (FR), b c Stormy River (FR)—Yes My Love (FR)
24 CORTOGNA (USA), b f Belong To Me (USA)—Gingivere (USA)
25 FANDEE (IRE), b c Oasis Dream—Priere
26 GALAXIE STAR (FR), b f Lawman (FR)—Margie Queen (GER)
27 GREEN MAN (FR), b c Green Desert (USA)—Give Me Five (GER)
28 HAUVILLE (FR), b f Hurricane Run (IRE)—Slyta (FR)
29 KYRIELLE, b f Medicean—Kyle Rhea
30 LAVA (FR), b g Rock of Gibraltar (IRE)—Forewarned (IRE)
31 LOWER LAKE (FR), b c Medecis—Black Dahlia
32 MA JOIE (IRE), b f Montjeu (IRE)—Hideaway (FR)
33 MANTICORE (IRE), gr c Dark Angel (IRE)—Bellacoola (GER)
34 MORNING GALE (FR), b f Stormy River (FR)—Matin de Tempete (FR)
35 MUSIC HALL (FR), gr c Stormy River (FR)—Aaliyah (USA)
36 QUEEN'S DAUGHTER (FR), b f American Post—Queen's Conquer
37 RIVER RUN (FR), b c Stormy River (FR)—Mixture
38 SEREZ (IRE), b c Shamardal (USA)—Afya
39 SHAREEL (FR), b f Country Reel—Shaking
40 SNOW BELL (FR), b f Kendargent (FR)—Makisarde (FR)
41 SO MUCH, b c Green Tune (USA)—Arbalette (IRE)
42 STORMY COAST (FR), b c Stormy River (FR)—Coastline
43 STORMY REEF (FR), b c Stormy River (FR)—Vipassana
44 STYLE VENDOME (FR), gr c Anabaa (USA)—Place Vendome (FR)
45 TELL THE TALE (FR), ch f Elnadim (USA)—Didn't I Tell You (IRE)
46 TIANJIN CITY (FR), gr g Holy Roman Emperor (IRE)—Tenepia (FR)
47 VER COQUIN (FR), gr g Verglas (IRE)—Afra Tsitsi (FR)
48 ZANTERO (GER), b c Doyen (IRE)—Zanana

TWO-YEAR-OLDS

49 B f 8/3 Cape Cross (IRE)—Alla Prima (IRE) (In The Wings) (50000)
50 B f 10/3 Teofilo (IRE)—Blue Fern (USA) (Woodman (USA)) (43650)
51 CAPE MAGIC (IRE), b f 2/2 Cape Cross (IRE)—Galley (Zamindar (USA))
52 B c 4/2 Caradak (IRE)—Famous Angel (FR) (In The Wings) (7936)
53 FUDGEIT (FR), ch c 5/2 Tertullian (USA)—Hot Fudge (SWE) (Lomitas)
54 B c 9/3 Hat Trick (JPN)—Furusato (USA) (Sendawar (IRE)) (11674)
55 HEAVEN'S SAKE, b f 12/2 Cape Cross (IRE)—Heaven's Cause (USA) (Giant's Causeway (USA)) (39682)
56 LAUGHING WATER (FR), b f 20/3 Duke of Marmalade (IRE)—Sosquaw (FR) (Numerous (USA)) (39682)
57 NOT GOLIATH (USA), b c 3/3 Henrythenavigator (USA)—Miss Shegaas (USA) (Medaglia d'oro (USA))
58 B f 18/2 Invincible Spirit (IRE)—Palace Weekend (USA) (Seattle Dancer (USA)) (99206)
59 Ch c 18/4 Rock of Gibraltar (IRE)—Perfidie (IRE) (Monsun (GER)) (35714)
60 Ch f 16/3 Teofilo (IRE)—Ponte Vechio (FR) (American Post) (65079)
61 B c 12/2 Authorized (IRE)—Red Begonia (Pivotal) (55614)
62 SAINT CLEMENT (FR), b c 16/3 Mount Nelson—Scarley Secret (IRE) (Royal Applause)
63 SAINT VIGOR (FR), b c 19/4 Le Havre (IRE)—Summer Melody (USA) (War Chant (USA))
64 Ch f 11/2 Mr Greeley (USA)—Shake The Moon (GER) (Loup Solitaire (USA)) (59523)
65 B f 22/4 Rock of Gibraltar (IRE)—Signella (Selkirk (USA)) (62000)

MR NICOLAS CLEMENT - Continued

66 Ch c 13/3 Pivotal—Trylko (USA) (Diesis) (115079)
67 **YOUR GRACE (FR),** b f 4/2 Duke of Marmalade (IRE)—The Wise Lady (FR) (Ganges (USA)) (61111)

---

118 MR TERRY CLEMENT, Newmarket
Postal: **Calder Park, Hamilton Road, Newmarket, Suffolk, CB8 0NY**
Contacts: **MOBILE (07885) 674474**

1 **BALTI'S SISTER (IRE),** 4, b f Tiger Hill (IRE)—Itsibitsi (IRE) **Mrs M. E. Smith**
2 **BATGIRL,** 6, ch m Mark of Esteem (IRE)—Serriera (FR) **Little Princess Racing**
3 **BELUGA BISCUIT,** 5, b m Needwood Blade—Nine To Five **Ms S. K. Jensen**
4 **BOBBYOW,** 5, b g Bertolini (USA)—Brooklyn's Sky **S. M. Jacobs**
5 **GIANTSTEPSAHEAD (IRE),** 4, br g Footstepsinthesand—Salty Air (IRE) **Mr K. R. Hills**
6 **SMOKY CLOUD (IRE),** 6, ch g Refuse To Bend (IRE)—Pirie (USA) **Mrs J. E. Lambert**

Other Owners: Mr M. P. B. Smith.

Apprentice: George Buckell.

---

119 MR PATRICK CLINTON, Doveridge
Postal: **Lordlea Farm, Marston Lane, Doveridge, Ashbourne, Derbyshire, DE6 5JS**
Contacts: **PHONE (01889) 566356 MOBILE (07815) 142642**

1 **IMPERIAL ROYALE (IRE),** 12, ch g Ali-Royal (IRE)—God Speed Her **In The Clear Racing**
2 **NEZAMI (IRE),** 8, b g Elnadim (USA)—Stands To Reason (USA) **In The Clear Racing**
3 8, B m Beat All (USA)—Salska **P. L. Clinton**
4 7, B g Beat All (USA)—Salska **In The Clear Racing**

Other Owners: G. Worrall.

Jockey (flat): Russ Kennemore.

---

120 MR K. F. CLUTTERBUCK, Newmarket
Postal: **Pond House Stables, Church Lane, Exning, Newmarket, Suffolk, CB8 7HF**
Contacts: **PHONE (01638) 577043 MOBILE (07868) 605995**

1 **BUCKLEY BOY,** 4, b g Araafa (IRE)—Waseyla (IRE) **K Clutterbuck & Mr P & Mrs A Pearce**
2 **ROLLWITHTHEPUNCHES,** 8, b g Hernando (FR)—Zarma (FR) **Four Winds Racing Partnership**
3 **RUM GINNEY,** 5, b m Carnival Dancer—Silent Gem **K. F. Clutterbuck**

Other Owners: S. J. Mear, Mrs E. A. Mear, Mr P. R. Pearce, Mrs A. E. Pearce.

Assistant Trainer: James Clutterbuck

---

121 MR DENIS J. COAKLEY, West Ilsley
Postal: **Keeper's Stables, West Ilsley, Newbury, Berkshire, RG20 7AH**
Contacts: **PHONE (01635) 281622 MOBILE (07768) 658056**
E-MAIL racing@deniscoakley.com WEBSITE www.deniscoakley.com

1 **FANNY MAY,** 5, b m Nayef (USA)—Sweet Wilhelmina **C. T. Van Hoorn**
2 **GABRIEL'S LAD (IRE),** 4, b g Dark Angel (IRE)—Catherine Wheel **Killoran Ennis Conway**
3 **HARDY PLUME,** 4, ch g Manduro (GER)—Macleya (GER) **Mrs B. Coakley**
4 **REBECCA ROMERO,** 6, b m Exceed And Excel (AUS)—Cloud Dancer **Keepers Racing II**
5 **ROCKFELLA,** 7, ch g Rock of Gibraltar (IRE)—Afreeta (USA) **Mr L. Raissi**
6 **ROYAL DUTCH,** 4, ch g Nayef (USA)—Shersha (IRE) **C. T. Van Hoorn**

THREE-YEAR-OLDS

7 **ALCANDO (IRE),** ch c Alhaarth (IRE)—Cantando (IRE) **The Good Mixers**
8 **BANREENAHREENKAH (IRE),** b f Steppe Dancer (IRE)—Carmencita **Mrs B. Coakley**
9 **INDIGO MOON,** b f Sleeping Indian—Ewenny **Count Calypso Racing**
10 **KASTINI,** b g Halling (USA)—Toucantini **West Ilsley Racing**

MR DENIS J. COAKLEY - Continued

11 **MISS MARJURIE (IRE)**, b f Marju (IRE)—Kazatzka **C. T. Van Hoorn**
12 **NORPHIN**, b c Norse Dancer (IRE)—Orphina (IRE) **Mr J. A. Mould**
13 **THOMASINA**, b f One Cool Cat (USA)—Jemiliah **N. J. Stafford**

TWO-YEAR-OLDS

14 **CASTAGNA GIRL**, ch f 14/3 Major Cadeaux—Ewenny (Warrshan (USA)) (7000) **Finders Keepers Partnership**
15 **KING CALYPSO**, ch c 24/4 Sir Percy—Rosa de Mi Corazon (USA) (Cozzene (USA)) (5000) **Count Calypso Racing**
16 **KUALA QUEEN (IRE)**, b f 19/4 Kodiac—See Nuala (IRE) (Kyllachy) (8095) **Keeper's 12**
17 **MON CIGAR (IRE)**, b c 25/4 Bushranger (IRE)—
Practicallyperfect (IRE) (King Charlemagne (USA)) (24761) **Mr L. Raissi**
18 **MONSIEUR BLANC (IRE)**, ch c 10/1 Kheleyf (USA)—Sley (FR) (Lomitas) (7619) **Mr L. Raissi**
19 **PRINCESS ALMALEK (IRE)**, ch f 24/3 Dylan Thomas (IRE)—Diamond Circle (Halling (USA)) (1000) **Mr L. Raissi**
20 **PRINCESS ALMAS**, b f 9/3 Medicean—Tereshkina (IRE) (Sadler's Wells (USA)) (7000) **Mr L. Raissi**
21 **PRINCESS HANANE (IRE)**, b gr f 25/1 Clodovil (IRE)—Golden Ora (ITY) (Nordance (USA)) (14285) **Mr L. Raissi**
22 **SKANDER**, b c 17/2 Archipenko (USA)—Midnight Allure (Aragon) (15238) **Mr L. Raissi**

Other Owners: Mr A. P. Bloor, R. J. Bolam, G. Callegari, P. M. Emery, J. T. Ennis, Mr E. P. L. Faulks, Mr T. A. Killoran, J. G. Ross, R. D. Whitehead.

---

122 | **MRS HEATHER COBB, Pulborough**
Postal: **Kilbrannan Stud Farm, Gay Street, Pulborough, West Sussex, RH20 2HJ**
Contacts: **PHONE (01798) 812541 FAX (01798) 817371 MOBILE (07764) 942854**
E-MAIL kilbrannanstud@aol.com

1 **CLASSIC PEARL**, 8, b m Spendent—Aun Ella **Mrs H. J. Cobb**
2 **GENEROUS SPENDER**, 7, b g Spendent—Molly Dreamer **Mrs H. J. Cobb**
3 **MASTER ALF (IRE)**, 13, ch g Anshan—The Little Bag **Miss G. Cobb**
4 **MONTYS CASH**, 7, b g Spendent—Satcotino (IRE) **Mrs H. J. Cobb**
5 **SAN JOSE (IRE)**, 10, b g Frimaire—Leinster Lady (IRE) **Miss G. Cobb**
6 **WINNIE WOOD**, 9, b m Spendent—Effie Wood **Mrs H. J. Cobb**

---

123 | **MR PAUL COLE, Whatcombe**
Postal: **Whatcombe Estate, Whatcombe, Wantage, Oxfordshire, OX12 9NW**
Contacts: **PHONE (01488) 638433 FAX (01488) 638609**
E-MAIL jenny@paulcole.co.uk WEBSITE www.paulcole.co.uk

1 **CIRCUMVENT**, 6, ch g Tobougg (IRE)—Seren Devious **The Fairy Story Partnership**
2 **DON LIBRE**, 4, b c Librettist (USA)—Darwinia (GER) **Mrs E. A. Bass**
3 **GIFTED GIRL (IRE)**, 4, b f Azamour (IRE)—Hoodwink (IRE) **A. D. Spence**
4 **KEY APPOINTMENT**, 4, b g Pivotal—Appointed One (USA) **Mrs F. H. Hay**
5 **SILVERHEELS (IRE)**, 4, gr g Verglas—Vasilia **P. F. I. Cole Ltd**
6 **STORMBOUND (IRE)**, 4, b g Galileo (IRE)—A Footstep Away (USA) **P. F. I. Cole Ltd**

THREE-YEAR-OLDS

7 **ANOTHER NAME (IRE)**, b c Red Clubs (IRE)—Pure Gold **PJL Racing**
8 **BLUEGRASS BLUES (IRE)**, gr c Dark Angel (IRE)—Dear Catch (IRE) **Mrs F. H. Hay**
9 **CALL ME MARILYN (USA)**, ch f Henny Hughes (USA)—Ball Gown (USA) **Mr Christopher Wright**
10 **CUT NO ICE (IRE)**, gr f Verglas (IRE)—Limpopo **Denford Stud**
11 **DANCE WITH DRAGONS (IRE)**, b c Namid—Duck Over **P. F. I. Cole Ltd**
12 **DENOTE**, b c Motivator—Darwinia (GER) **Mrs E. A. Bass**
13 **FALUKA (IRE)**, gr f Iffraaj—Tortue (IRE) **Denford Stud**
14 **INTERMIX (IRE)**, b g Intikhab (USA)—Bermuxa (FR) **P. F. I. Cole Ltd**
15 **KALICAMIX**, br c Bahamian Bounty—Heather Mix **P. F. I. Cole Ltd**
16 **KEEP THE DREAM**, b c Oasis Dream—Mimisel **Mrs F. H. Hay**
17 **KUANTAN ONE (IRE)**, b c Strategic Prince—Starfish **H.R.H. Sultan Ahmad Shah**
18 **LADY IN PINK (IRE)**, b f Duke of Marmalade (IRE)—Blessyourpinksox (IRE) **C. Shiacolas**
19 **MONETS SECRET**, ch g Excellent Art—Queen Isabella **Whatcombe Partnership**
20 **PUTERI NUR LAILA (IRE)**, br f Strategic Prince—Asian Lady **H.R.H. Sultan Ahmad Shah**
21 **SECRET SUCCESS**, b c Exceed And Excel (AUS)—Magic Music (IRE) **A. D. Spence**
22 **SERENATA (IRE)**, b f Oratorio (IRE)—Seren Devious **The Fairy Story Partnership**
23 **SOVEREIGN POWER**, b c Royal Applause—Tafiya **Jill Haines, Josephine Green, P. F. I. Cole Ltd**

MR PAUL COLE - Continued

24 **ST PAUL DE VENCE (IRE)**, b c Oratorio (IRE)—Ring The Relatives **Sir M Arbib, Mr C Wright & P. F. I. Cole Ltd**
25 **STANDING BEAR (IRE)**, b g Excellent Art—Sweet Sioux **W. H. Ponsonby**
26 **STRATEGIC STRIKE (IRE)**, b g Strategic Prince—Puteri Wentworth **H.R.H. Sultan Ahmad Shah**
27 **STRAWBERRY JAM**, b c Duke of Marmalade (IRE)—Farfala (FR) **M. Arbib**

TWO-YEAR-OLDS

28 **BERKSHIRE (IRE)**, b c 11/4 Mount Nelson—
Kinnaird (IRE) (Dr Devious (IRE)) (60000) **H.R.H. Sultan Ahmad Shah**
29 **CAFETIERE**, b f 14/3 Iffraaj—Coffee Cream (Common Grounds) **A. H. Robinson**
30 **CAPE ARROW**, b c 6/5 Cape Cross (IRE)—Aiming (Highest Honor (FR)) (48000) **C. Shiacolas**
31 **DARK DAYS**, b c 7/5 Black Sam Bellamy (IRE)—Darwinia (GER) (Acatenango (GER)) (50000) **Mrs E. A. Bass**
32 **DESERT FLUTE**, b c 28/4 Piccolo—Hawait Al Barr (Green Desert (USA)) (9000) **Mrs Jill Haines**
33 **GRECIAN (IRE)**, gr c 3/5 Dark Angel (IRE)—Law Review (IRE) (Case Law) (39681) **Mrs F. H. Hay**
34 **MERITOCRACY (IRE)**, b c 22/1 Kheleyf (USA)—Chiosina (IRE) (Danehill Dancer (IRE)) (38095) **Mrs F. H. Hay**
35 B c 4/5 Captain Rio—Molomo (Barathea) (21000)
36 **POLISH BALLET**, b c 1/3 Iffraaj—Madam Ninette (Mark of Esteem (IRE)) (48000) **Mrs F. H. Hay**
37 **RUSH**, ch f 19/2 Compton Place—Dorelia (IRE) (Elisio) **Denford Stud**
38 **SKATERS WALTZ (IRE)**, gr c 29/3 Verglas (IRE)—
Xarzee (IRE) (Xaar) (20000) **Sir G Meyrick & Sir Dunnington-Jefferson**
39 B c 28/3 Azamour (IRE)—Sweet Clover (Rainbow Quest (USA)) (27000)
40 **THRILLER (IRE)**, b c 11/3 Naaqoos—Burn The Breeze (IRE) (Beat Hollow) (9500) **Lane Racing Limited**
41 **TIOGA PASS**, b f 15/5 High Chaparral (IRE)—Seren Devious (Dr Devious (IRE)) **The Fairy Story Partnership**
42 **TREASURE CAY (IRE)**, ch c 5/4 Bahamian Bounty—
Expedience (USA) (With Approval (CAN)) (22000) **Jefferson, Meyrick, Wright & Cole**
43 B c 2/4 Champs Elysees—Trinkila (USA) (Cat Thief (USA)) (15000) **Mr D. S. Lee**
44 Ch c 20/3 Iffraaj—Up On Points (Royal Academy (USA)) (20000)
45 B c 5/4 Fastnet Rock (AUS)—Verbania (IRE) (In The Wings) (35000)

Other Owners: Sir Martyn Arbib, Mr George Baker, Mr T. M. Bird, Mr P. F. I. Cole, Mrs P. F. I. Cole, Sir Mervyn Dunnington-Jefferson, Mr E. R. Goodwin, Mrs Josephine Green, Mrs J. M. Haines, Mr L. Lugg, Sir George Meyrick, P.F. I. Cole Ltd, Miss C. S. Scott-Balls, Mr Christopher Wright.

Assistant Trainer: Oliver Cole

---

124 MR TOBIAS B. P. COLES, Newmarket
Postal: **The Cottage, Phantom House, Fordham Road, Newmaket, Suffolk, CB8 7AA**
Contacts: **MOBILE (07904) 779222**

1 **CAMELOPARDALIS**, 4, b f Tobougg (IRE)—Bonne Etoile
2 **DEAR MAURICE**, 9, b g Indian Ridge—Shamaiel (IRE)
3 **JOY FOR LIFE**, 4, b f Pivotal—Gallivant
4 **LYCIDAS (GER)**, 4, b c Zamindar (USA)—La Felicita
5 **PENINSULA**, 4, b f Rock of Gibraltar (IRE)—Kayah
6 **SKYBLUE**, 4, b f Royal Applause—Fiina

THREE-YEAR-OLDS

7 **CLUB ELECTRA (IRE)**, br f Red Clubs (IRE)—Princess Electra (IRE)
8 **HOLDING FAST (IRE)**, b g Balmont (USA)—Eschasse (USA)
9 **MASTER HAMILTON**, ch c Mount Nelson—Oomph
10 **NELSON'S MUSE**, b f Mount Nelson—French Quartet (IRE)
11 **SPEED DATE**, b f Sakhee's Secret—See You Later
12 **TIMELESS**, b f Tamayuz—Sandtime (IRE)

TWO-YEAR-OLDS

13 **APTITUDE**, ch f 14/2 With Approval (CAN)—Moi Aussi (USA) (Mt Livermore (USA))
14 B f 1/4 Champs Elysees—Bolsena (USA) (Red Ransom (USA))
15 B f 2/3 Rock of Gibraltar (IRE)—Cecily (Oasis Dream)
16 **EPSOM HILL (SWE)**, b c 3/4 Homme d'honneur (FR)—Energiya Sacc (SWE) (Exceller (USA)) (5796)
17 **LA GRASSETTA (GER)**, b f 12/2 Nayef (USA)—La Reine Noir (GER) (Rainbow Quest (USA))
18 **LEALTANZA (GER)**, b br f 20/1 Zamindar (USA)—La Martina (GER) (Seattle Dancer (USA))
19 **NABLUS (GER)**, b c 10/4 Dai Jin—Nouvelle Princesse (GER) (Bluebird (USA)) (7936)
20 B f 22/3 Lemon Drop Kid (USA)—Nafisah (IRE) (Lahib (USA)) (130000)
21 B f 18/3 Moss Vale (IRE)—Notley Park (Wolfhound (USA)) (18095)

MR TOBIAS B. P. COLES - Continued

22 Ch c 18/2 Hernando (FR)—Ryella (USA) (Cozzene (USA)) (29000)
23 Gr f 23/3 Aussie Rules (USA)—Unintentional (Dr Devious (IRE)) (9000)
24 B c 18/4 Intikhab (USA)—Winsa (Riverman (USA))

Owners: H H Sheikh Fahad Al Thani, H H Sheikh Hamad Al Thani, Andrew Black, Julian Broughton, Chris Budgett, Charlie Budgett, Miss Harriet Budgett, Tom Cahalan, Matt Coleman, Mrs R. Coles, Peter Deal, Dr Stephen Eversfield, Michael Fitzroy, Dot Fleming, Paul Foster, Terry Foster, Sarah Hamilton, Chris Harper, R. S. Hoskins, Lyndsey Hughes, Derek Iceton, Katarcha Jacobson, Mr & Mrs N. Newall, John Oakes, Kirsten Rausing, Julian Richmond-Watson, C. G. Rowles-Nicholson, Mr & Mrs M. Slade, Mark Tuckwell, Graf & Graffin Philipp Von Stauffenberg, Richard Williams.

---

125   MR STUART COLTHERD, Selkirk
Postal: **Clarilawmuir Farm, Selkirk, Selkirkshire, TD7 4QA**
Contacts: **PHONE (01750) 21251 FAX (01750) 21251 MOBILE (07801) 398199**
E-MAIL **wscoltherd@clarilawmuir.wanadoo.co.uk**

1 FOZY MOSS, 7, b g And Beyond (IRE)—Peggy Sioux (IRE) **J. Hogg**
2 MAN OF PRINCIPLES (IRE), 10, b br g Bob Back (USA)—Shuil Le Gaoth (IRE) **Coltherd, Jeffrey & Hall**
3 MIDLEM MOSS, 6, b m And Beyond (IRE)—Midlem Melody **W. S. Coltherd**
4 OVERLADY, 11, b br m Overbury (IRE)—Chief Lady Nicola **W. F. Jeffrey**
5 OVERLAW, 11, br g Overbury (IRE)—Reprieve **Mrs E. A. Fletcher**
6 SUPRISE VENDOR (IRE), 7, ch g Fath (USA)—Dispol Jazz **Mr A. Gunning**
7 TALKIN SENCE (IRE), 8, b g Heron Island (IRE)—Catatonia (IRE) **Gunning, Conchar, Hancock**
8 TARTAN SNOW, 13, b g Valseur (USA)—Whitemoss Leader (IRE) **R. V. Westwood**

Other Owners: Mr T. Conchar, Mr I. Hall, Mr N. Hancock, J. B. Jeffrey.

Jockey (NH): Richie McGrath, Paddy Aspell, Henry Brooke, Brian Harding. **Conditional:** Gary Rutherford.

---

126   LADY ANNE CONNELL, Brackley
Postal: **Steane Park, Brackley, Northamptonshire, NN13 6DP**
Contacts: **PHONE (01280) 705899 FAX (01280) 700873**

1 COURT AGAIN, 9, b g Alflora (IRE)—Southern Survivor (IRE) **Exors of the late Sir Michael Connell**
2 LEGAL LEGEND, 6, b g Midnight Legend—Calaminta **Exors of the late Sir Michael Connell**
3 MIDNIGHT MONKEY, 5, ch g Midnight Legend—Teeton Glaive **S. M. Connell**
4 NEEDS TIME (IRE), 12, gr g Lord Americo—Galice Du Soleil (FR) **Lady Connell**
5 NOBLE CRUSADER (USA), 10, b g Giant's Causeway (USA)—
          Suitably Discreet (USA) **Exors of the late Sir Michael Connell**

Assistant Trainer: Mr Christopher Henn

---

127   MR ALAN COOGAN, Ely
Postal: **31 Hasse Road, Soham, Ely, Cambridgeshire, CB7 5UW**
Contacts: **PHONE (01353) 721673 FAX (01353) 721117**

1 CAPE SCHANCK, 9, b g Observatory (USA)—Sally Gardens **A. B. Coogan**
2 SEVENTEEN SEVENTY, 4, b g Byron—Rolexa **A. B. Coogan**
3 SUNNY BANK, 4, b g Notnowcato—Sweet Mandolin **Mr G. R. D. Boughey**

THREE-YEAR-OLDS

4 ABANOAS (USA), b br f Proud Citizen (USA)—Alabaq (USA) **A. B. Coogan**

---

128   MR JOHN COOMBE, Weymouth
Postal: **Sea Barn Farm, Fleet, Weymouth, Dorset, DT3 4ED**
Contacts: **PHONE (01305) 761745 (0780) 3752831 FAX (01305) 775396 MOBILE (07796) 990760**
E-MAIL **wib@seabarnracing.com WEBSITE www.seabarnracing.com**

1 CHESIL BEACH BOY, 10, b g Commanche Run—Eatons **M. J. Coombe**
2 DAIS RETURN (IRE), 9, b g Lahib (USA)—Bayazida **J. D. Roberts**

MR JOHN COOMBE - Continued

3 **JUST WATCH OLLIE (IRE)**, 7, b g Indian Danehill (IRE)—Westgate Run **M. J. Coombe**
4 **PROPOSABLE (FR)**, 6, b g King's Best (USA)—Irika (USA) **M. J. Coombe**
5 **SAN MARINO (FR)**, 10, ch g Bering—Sienne (FR) **M. J. Coombe**
6 5, B m Arkadian Hero (USA)—Zambran Calypso

Assistant Trainer: Mr John Roberts

Amateur: Mrs M. Roberts.

---

129 **MRS SUSAN CORBETT, Otterburn**
Postal: **Girsonfield, Otterburn, Newcastle upon Tyne, Tyne and Wear, NE19 1NT**
Contacts: **PHONE (01830) 520771 FAX (01830) 520771 MOBILE (07713) 651215**
E-MAIL girsonfield@tiscali.co.uk WEBSITE www.girsonfield.co.uk

1 **BILLERICAY ALLSTAR**, 5, ch m Septieme Ciel (USA)—Magical Day **Mr W. F. Corbett**
2 **BLAKEMANS LAW**, 5, b g Ferrule (IRE)—Cogolie (FR) **Mr W. F. Corbett**
3 **CLARESBURN**, 9, b m Milieu—Make The Grade **Mr W. F. Corbett**
4 **DEFINITE APPEAL (IRE)**, 10, ch g Definite Article—Marian's Wish (IRE) **Mr W. F. Corbett**
5 **DUN TO PERFECTION**, 6, ch g Endoli (USA)—Dun To A Tern **Mr W. F. Corbett**
6 **JONSFELLA**, 5, gr g Silver Patriarch (IRE)—Piracy **Mr W. F. Corbett**
7 **SPIRITWALKER**, 4, b g Phoenix Reach (IRE)—Sevenminutesilence **Mr W. F. Corbett**
8 **SUMMER SOUL (IRE)**, 11, b g Danehill (USA)—Blend of Pace (IRE) **Mrs S. Corbett**

Amateur: Mr James Corbett.

---

130 **MR LIAM CORCORAN, Castle Cary**
Postal: **Lovington Racing Stables, Ashview Farm, Lovington, Castle Cary, Somerset, BA7 7PU**
Contacts: **MOBILE (07789) 368234**
E-MAIL corcoranracing@aol.co.uk

1 **BLITZED ECKIE (IRE)**, 7, b g Zagreb (USA)—Glasson Storm (IRE) **The A T P Racing Partnership**
2 **DESTINED FOR FAME (IRE)**, 7, b m Dubai Destination (USA)—Pantoufle **The Happy Days Partnership**
3 **DRUMADOON (IRE)**, 5, b g Hawk Wing (USA)—Lady Taufan (IRE) **GD Building & Roofing Contractors Ltd**
4 **FRANCIS DU MESNIL (FR)**, 11, b g Saint Preuil (FR)—Franciscaine (FR) **Mr R. Prince**
5 **IRON DUKE**, 7, gr g Refuse To Bend (IRE)—Arinaga **Mr N. A. Eggleton**
6 **JANUARY**, 10, gr g Daylami (IRE)—Noushkey **L. Gilbert**
7 **MOSSTOWN (IRE)**, 7, b g Dilshaan—Tavildara (IRE) **Miss C. L. Bowles**
8 **MURCAR**, 8, ch g Medicean—In Luck **Mr R. B. Antell**
9 **NENUPHAR COLLONGES (FR)**, 12, b g Video Rock (FR)—Diane Collonges (FR) **Mr R. Prince**
10 **PORT HILL**, 6, ch g Deportivo—Hill Farm Dancer **Mr N. A. Eggleton**
11 **STERLING GENT (IRE)**, 6, gr g Cloudings (IRE)—Company Credit (IRE) **Mr R. B. Antell**
12 **SULA TWO**, 6, b m Sulamani (IRE)—There's Two (IRE) **Mr R. Prince**
13 **THE GOSSMOOR YANK (IRE)**, 10, b g Shernazar—Nightngale Express (IRE) **Mr R. Prince**
14 **TINY TWISTER**, 4, b f Imperial Dancer—Colonial Lady **Mrs J. M. Thompson**
15 **VERING (FR)**, 7, b g Bering—Forcia (FR) **Michael & Will Potter**
16 **VOTE FOR DOODLE (IRE)**, 8, ch g Subtle Power (IRE)—Shuil Ash (IRE) **Mr R. Prince**

Other Owners: Mrs P. Elliot, A. J. McClafferty, T. A. Parker, Michael Potter, Mr W. E. Potter, Mr A. Shead.

Jockey (NH): Timmy Murphy.

---

131 **MR JOHN CORNWALL, Melton Mowbray**
Postal: **April Cottage, Pasture Lane, Hose, Melton Mowbray, Leicestershire, LE14 4LB**
Contacts: **PHONE (01664) 444453 FAX (01664) 444754 MOBILE (07939) 557091**

1 **EIGHTEEN CARAT (IRE)**, 9, b g Luso—Jemma's Gold (IRE) **J. R. Cornwall**
2 **FLICHITY (IRE)**, 8, br g Turtle Island (IRE)—Chancy Gal **J. R. Cornwall**
3 **GRENOLI (FR)**, 12, b g Garde Royale—Pietrosella (FR) **J. R. Cornwall**
4 **MAD PROFESSOR (IRE)**, 10, b g Mull of Kintyre (USA)—Fancy Theory (USA) **J. R. Cornwall**

MR JOHN CORNWALL - Continued

5 **PHOENIX DES MOTTES (FR)**, 10, b g Useful (FR)—Camille des Mottes (FR) **J. R. Cornwall**
6 **RADSOC DE SIVOLA (FR)**, 8, bl g Video Rock (FR)—Kerrana (FR) **J. R. Cornwall**
7 **THAT'S THE DEAL (IRE)**, 9, b br g Turtle Island (IRE)—Sister Swing **J. R. Cornwall**

Conditional: Joe Cornwall.

---

132 MR ROBERT COWELL, Newmarket

Postal: Bottisham Heath Stud, Six Mile Bottom, Newmarket, Suffolk, CB8 0TT
Contacts: **PHONE (01638) 570330 FAX (01638) 570330 MOBILE (07785) 512463**
E-MAIL robert@robertcowellracing.co.uk WEBSITE www.robertcowellracing.co.uk

1 **ARCTIC LYNX (IRE)**, 6, b g One Cool Cat (USA)—Baldemara (FR) **Heading For The Rocks Partnership**
2 **CARDINAL**, 8, ch h Pivotal—Fictitious **Mrs J. May**
3 **CATS EYES**, 4, b f Echo of Light—Desert Lynx (IRE) **Manor Farm Stud (Rutland)**
4 **CLERICAL (USA)**, 7, b g Yes It's True (USA)—Clerical Etoile (ARG) **Bottisham Heath Stud**
5 **COMPTON**, 4, ch g Compton Place—Look So **The Morley Family**
6 **FANTASY GLADIATOR**, 7, b g Ishiguru (USA)—Fancier Bit **The Fantasy Fellowship**
7 **FOUR WINDS**, 7, b g Red Ransom (USA)—Fairy Godmother **T. W. Morley**
8 **GOLDREAM**, 4, br g Oasis Dream—Clizia (IRE) **Mr J Sargeant & Mrs J Morley**
9 **INDIAN TINKER**, 4, b g Sleeping Indian—Breakfast Creek **Mr J. Sargeant**
10 **JIROFT (ITY)**, 6, b g Blu Air Force (IRE)—Dexia (ITY) **T. W. Morley**
11 **JWALA**, 4, b f Oasis Dream—Kangra Valley **Manor Farm Stud & Miss S. Hoare**
12 **KINGSGATE NATIVE (IRE)**, 8, b g Mujadil (USA)—Native Force (IRE) **Cheveley Park Stud Limited**
13 **LITTLE GARCON (USA)**, 6, b g Bernstein (USA)—Demure **J. Barton**
14 **MARMALADE MOON**, 4, ch f Shamardal (USA)—Frascati **Lord Crawshaw**
15 **MONSIEUR JOE (IRE)**, 6, b g Choisir (AUS)—Pascali **Mrs H. Checkley**
16 **PANDAR**, 4, b g Zamindar (USA)—Pagnottella (IRE) **The Morley Family**
17 **PROHIBIT**, 8, b g Oasis Dream—Well Warned **Dasmal, Rix, Barr, Morley, Mrs Penney**
18 **SILKEN EXPRESS (IRE)**, 4, ch f Speightstown (USA)—Laureldean Express **Malih L. Al Basti**
19 **SPIRIT QUARTZ (IRE)**, 5, b g Invincible Spirit (IRE)—Crystal Gaze (IRE) **Qatar Racing Limited**
20 **UBETTERBEGOOD (ARG)**, 5, b h Distorted Humor (USA)—Movie Star (BRZ) **Malih L. Al Basti**

THREE-YEAR-OLDS

21 **DARK DIAMOND (IRE)**, b c Dark Angel (IRE)—Moon Diamond **K. A. Dasmal**
22 **DIVA DELIGHT (IRE)**, b f Jeremy (USA)—Wattrey **K. Quinn/ C. Benham/ I. Saunders**
23 **HAND IN GLOVE**, ch f Kyllachy—Cape Trafalgar (IRE) **J. Barton**
24 **IMMEDIATELY**, b f Notnowcato—Two Step **Bullseye Partnership**
25 **LADY FARAH**, b f Exceed And Excel (AUS)—Bint Makbul **Malih L. Al Basti**
26 **NELINA**, b f Mount Nelson—Naralina (FR) **Newsells Park Stud & Mr A Rix**
27 **NORMAL EQUILIBRIUM**, b c Elnadim (USA)—Acicula (IRE) **Qatar Racing Limited**
28 **PEARL ACCLAIM (IRE)**, b c Acclamation—With Colour **Pearl Bloodstock Limited**
29 **PROM DRESS**, b f Mount Nelson—Dress Code (IRE) **Newsells Park Stud Limited**
30 **QUEEN AT HEART**, b f Exceed And Excel (AUS)—Royal Flame (IRE) **Malih L. Al Basti**
31 **ROYAL ACQUISITION**, b c Royal Applause—Flavian **Mr J. Sargeant**
32 **SATWA'S SISTER**, b f Elusive City (USA)—Black Tribal (IRE) **K. A. Dasmal**
33 **TARTAN BLUE**, b f Kyllachy—Poly Blue (IRE) **Mr Khalifa Dasmal & Bottisham Heath Stud**
34 **VIVA L'INGHILTERRA (IRE)**, b f Refuse To Bend (IRE)—Whipped Queen (USA) **Scuderia Archi Romani**

TWO-YEAR-OLDS

35 B f 18/4 Dutch Art—Action Girl (Act One) **Bottisham Heath Stud**
36 B br c 23/3 Henny Hughes (USA)—Cosmic Wing (USA) (Halo (USA)) (33794) **K. A. Dasmal**
37 Ch c 22/1 Haafhd—Elle Crystal (Mozart (IRE)) (11904) **A Partnership**
38 B c 11/2 Kyllachy—Fondled (Selkirk (USA)) (42000) **Malih L. Al Basti**
39 Gr ro f 16/3 Mizzen Mast (USA)—Hasheema (IRE) (Darshaan) (36866) **K. A. Dasmal**
40 Ch c 23/4 Teofilo (IRE)—Neat Shilling (IRE) (Bob Back (USA)) (68000) **Malih L. Al Basti**
41 Ch f 17/1 Langfuhr (CAN)—Tres Chaud (USA) (French Deputy (USA)) (20276) **Mr T W Morley & Partners**

Other Owners: P. Agostini, Mrs E. Agostini, Malih L. Al Basti, Mr J. C. Archer, Mr J. Archer, Mr Federico Barberini, Mr F. G. Barr, Mr J. Barton, Mr C. F. Benham, A. M. Blewitt, Bottisham Heath Stud, Mrs H. Checkley, Cheveley Park Stud, Mr Khalifa Dasmal, Mr J. Hay, Miss S. Hoare, Lord Crawshaw, Manor Farm Stud (Rutland), Mrs J. Morley, Mr T. W. Morley, Mr C. M. Newing, Newsells Park Stud, Pearl Bloodstock, Mrs J. M. Penney, Qatar Racing Limited, K. J. Quinn, Mr P. Quintale, A. J. Rix, Mr J. Sargeant, Mr I. N. Saunders, Mr S. J. Whelan, Richard R. Wright, Mr R. Wright.

MR ROBERT COWELL - Continued

Assistant Trainer: Mr Nikki Himsworth

Apprentice: Miss Hannah Nunn.

---

133 **MR PAUL COWLEY, Banbury**
Postal: **Lodge Farm Barn, Culworth, Banbury, Oxfordshire, OX17 2HL**
Contacts: **PHONE** (01295) 768998 **MOBILE** (07775) 943346
E-MAIL paulcowleyequine@yahoo.co.uk

1 **BILL THE LAD (IRE)**, 6, b g Classic Cliche (IRE)—Quilty's Rose Bud (IRE) **S. G. West**
2 **CUDDLE ME CLOSER**, 9, b m Alflora (IRE)—Cuddles Daughter **Mrs D. B. Cowley**
3 **SEAS OF GREEN**, 6, ch m Karinga Bay—Emerald Project (IRE) **Mrs R. M. Wilkinson**

---

134 **MR CLIVE COX, Hungerford**
Postal: **Beechdown Farm, Sheepdrove Road, Lambourn, Hungerford, Berkshire, RG17 7UN**
Contacts: **OFFICE** (01488) 73072 **FAX** (01488) 73500 **MOBILE** (07740) 630521
E-MAIL clive@clivecox.com **WEBSITE** www.clivecox.com

1 **ACCESSION (IRE)**, 4, b g Acclamation—Pivotal's Princess (IRE) **Brighthelm Racing**
2 **APOLLO D'NEGRO (IRE)**, 5, br g Fasliyev (USA)—Special One **Gwyn Powell & Peter Ridgers**
3 **DANCE EXPRESS (IRE)**, 4, b f Rail Link—Swingsky (IRE) **Mrs T. L. Cox**
4 **DREAM TUNE**, 4, b c Oasis Dream—Play Bouzouki **HE Sheikh Sultan Bin Khalifa Al Nahyan**
5 **EMMUSKA**, 4, b f Sir Percy—Tintac **Mr M. A. Collins**
6 **FABLED CITY (USA)**, 4, ch g Johannesburg (USA)—Fabulous Fairy (USA) **The Tenners**
7 **FOREST ROW**, 4, b g Cockney Rebel (IRE)—Forest Fire (SWE) **The Bodkins**
8 **GREYLAMI (IRE)**, 8, gr g Daylami (IRE)—Silent Crystal (USA) **Mr J Humphreys & Mr B Ecclestone**
9 **HASSLE (IRE)**, 4, b c Montjeu (IRE)—Canterbury Lace (USA) **A. D. Spence**
10 **HE'S NO ANGEL (IRE)**, 4, ch c Excellent Art—Gentle Night **Mr B Ecclestone & Mr J Humphreys**
11 **HIGHLAND DUKE (IRE)**, 4, b g Dansili—House In Wood (FR) **Highland Thoroughbred Ltd**
12 **JIMMY STYLES**, 9, ch g Inchinor—Inya Lake **Gwyn Powell & Peter Ridgers**
13 **LETHAL FORCE (IRE)**, 4, gr c Dark Angel (IRE)—Land Army (IRE) **A. G. Craddock**
14 **LUCKY HENRY**, 4, br g Lucky Story (USA)—Seldemosa **T. P. Bostwick**
15 **NARLA**, 4, b f Nayef (USA)—Polygueza (FR) **Mrs S. L. Richardson**
16 **PERFECT CRACKER**, 5, ch g Dubai Destination (USA)—Perfect Story (IRE) **Mildmay Racing**
17 **PERFECT DELIGHT**, 4, b f Dubai Destination (USA)—Perfect Spirit (IRE) **Mildmay Racing & D. H. Caslon**
18 **POET**, 8, b g Pivotal—Hyabella **Mrs T. L. Cox**
19 **POETIC DANCER**, 4, ch f Byron—Crozon **The Laureates**
20 **PRESENT DAY**, 4, gr f Cadeaux Genereux—Crackle **A. Parker**
21 **SAUCY BARON**, 7, gr g Karinga Bay—Grey Baroness **T. Y. Bissett**
22 **SEEKING MAGIC**, 5, b g Haafhd—Atnab (USA) **The Seekers**
23 **SHADES OF GREY**, 6, gr m Dr Fong (USA)—Twosixtythreewest (FR) **Dr & Mrs John Merrington**
24 **WINTER'S NIGHT (IRE)**, 5, b m Night Shift (USA)—Woodland Glade **Mr J. T. Thomas**

THREE-YEAR-OLDS

25 **ADDICTIVE NATURE (IRE)**, b g Acclamation—Movie Queen **Mr M. W. Goodall**
26 **ADUVEE**, b f Avonbridge—Emma Peel **Mrs Dee Barker**
27 **AINT GOT A SCOOBY (IRE)**, br c Red Clubs (IRE)—La Bataille (USA) **Exors of the Late Mr D. Shaw**
28 **COLOR SHADES**, ch f Galileo (IRE)—Red Yellow Blue (USA) **HE Sheikh Sultan Bin Khalifa Al Nahyan**
29 **ENTWINED (IRE)**, b f Elusive City (USA)—Corryvreckan (IRE) **Loose Connections**
30 **GOLD CHAIN (IRE)**, b f Authorized (IRE)—Mountain Chain (USA) **HE Sheikh Sultan Bin Khalifa Al Nahyan**
31 **GOLDEN SECRET**, ch f Sakhee's Secret—Tahara (IRE) **Wood Street Syndicate & Mr C. J. Harper**
32 **GRAND DENIAL (IRE)**, b g Thousand Words—The Oldladysays No (IRE) **A. G. Craddock**
33 **HAAFAGUINEA**, ch c Haafhd—Ha'penny Beacon **Exors of the Late Mr D. Shaw**
34 **ISHIAMBER**, ch f Ishiguru (USA)—Black And Amber **Mrs P. Scott-Dunn**
35 **JUBILANT QUEEN**, b f Kyllachy—Hector's Girl **Doreen Swinburn & Pierpont Scott**
36 **LITTLE CHOOSEY**, ch f Cadeaux Genereux—Little Nymph **Mr Trevor Fox**
37 **MALILLA (IRE)**, b f Red Clubs (IRE)—Maleha (IRE) **Mrs T. L. Cox**
38 **MELBOURNE MEMORIES**, b f Sleeping Indian—Three Decades (IRE) **M. P. Coleman & R. J. Coleman**
39 **MILLY'S GIFT**, b f Trade Fair—Milly's Lass **Ken Lock Racing**
40 **PERFECT MUSE**, b f Oasis Dream—Perfect Echo **Mr R. J. Vines**
41 **PERFECT VENTURE**, b f Bahamian Bounty—Perfect Cover (IRE) **Mildmay Racing**

MR CLIVE COX - Continued

42 **POLLY'S LOVE (IRE)**, b f Antonius Pius (USA)—Kotdiji **Wickham Stud**
43 **RECKLESS ABANDON**, b c Exchange Rate (USA)—Sant Elena **Miss J. Deadman & Mr S. Barrow**
44 **RED TO AMBER (IRE)**, b c Redback—Amber's Bluff **Exors of the Late Mr D. Shaw**
45 **ROANNE (USA)**, b f Lemon Drop Kid (USA)—Chalamont (IRE) **HE Sheikh Sultan Bin Khalifa Al Nahyan**
46 **SANDAURA (IRE)**, b f Footstepsinthesand—Stratospheric **Mrs T. L. Cox**
47 **SCENT OF ROSES (IRE)**, b f Invincible Spirit (IRE)—Moy Water (IRE) **S. R. Hope**
48 **VEGA DANCE (IRE)**, b f Danehill Dancer (IRE)—
                      Young and Daring (USA) **HE Sheikh Sultan Bin Khalifa Al Nahyan**
49 **WELL ACQUAINTED (IRE)**, b c Orientate (USA)—Stunning Rose (IRE) **The Orienteers**

TWO-YEAR-OLDS

50 B c 22/1 Cape Cross (IRE)—Ada River (Dansili) (120000) **Mr P. W. Harris**
51 Ch c 2/2 Nayef (USA)—Beatrix Potter (IRE) (Cadeaux Genereux) (55555) **P. N. Ridgers**
52 B f 29/4 Cockney Rebel (IRE)—Blaeberry (Kirkwall) **Lady Bland**
53 B c 24/3 Cape Cross (IRE)—Blue Parade (IRE) (Singspiel (IRE)) (50000) **Mr & Mrs P. Hargreaves**
54 **BRIGHT CECILY (IRE)**, b f 18/2 Excellent Art—Roman Love (IRE) (Perugino (USA)) (24761) **Old Peartree Stud**
55 B f 19/4 Holy Roman Emperor (IRE)—Catch Us (FR) (Selkirk (USA)) **HE Sheikh Sultan Bin Khalifa Al Nahyan**
56 Ch c 4/3 Kheleyf (USA)—Champion Place (Compton Place) (26666) **Kheleyf Colt Syndicate**
57 **DREAM SIKA (IRE)**, b c 23/2 Elnadim (USA)—
                   Enchantment (Compton Place) (23809) **Miss J. Deadman & Mr S. Barrow**
58 B f 17/3 Moss Vale (IRE)—Evening Promise (Aragon) (8000) **Mildmay Racing & D. H. Caslon**
59 B c 25/2 Amadeus Wolf—First Eclipse (IRE) (Fayruz) (9000) **Miss E. Foley**
60 Ch c 24/2 Dutch Art—Frivolity (Pivotal) **HE Sheikh Sultan Bin Khalifa Al Nahyan**
61 B c 12/1 Holy Roman Emperor (IRE)—Greek Easter (IRE) (Namid) (77000) **Mr P. W. Harris**
62 B f 11/3 Camacho—Hartstown House (IRE) (Primo Dominie) (8000)
63 **HIGHLAND STARDUST**, b f 22/3 Sakhee (USA)—
                 Highland Starlight (USA) (Dixieland Band (USA)) (6000) **Highland Thoroughbred Ltd**
64 B c 24/2 Haafet (USA)—Insaaf (Averti (IRE)) (12698) **Lakes Bathrooms Ltd**
65 B c 8/3 New Approach (IRE)—
                 Invincible Isle (IRE) (Invincible Spirit (IRE)) **HE Sheikh Sultan Bin Khalifa Al Nahyan**
66 **LE MAITRE CHAT (USA)**, b c 13/5 Tale of The Cat (USA)—Bedside Story (Mtoto) (27777) **Michael Watt**
67 B br c 16/4 Henrythenavigator (USA)—
                 Look Out Lorie (USA) (Orientate (USA)) (14285) **Henrythenavigator Colt Syndicate**
68 B c 2/3 Footstepsinthesand—Maybe I Will (IRE) (Hawk Wing (USA)) (19000) **Mr A. Le Herissier**
69 Br c 25/2 Monsun (GER)—Miracle Seeker (Rainbow Quest (USA)) (240000) **Whitley Stud**
70 B c 26/3 Amadeus Wolf—
                 Miss Shangri La (Rainbow Quest (USA)) (13491) **HE Sheikh Sultan Bin Khalifa Al Nahyan**
71 B f 23/4 Champs Elysees—
                 My Heart's Deelite (USA) (Afternoon Deelites (USA)) **HE Sheikh Sultan Bin Khalifa Al Nahyan**
72 Ch c 21/4 Dandy Man (IRE)—
                 Noble View (USA) (Distant View (USA)) (71428) **HE Sheikh Sultan Bin Khalifa Al Nahyan**
73 **PASSADOURO (IRE)**, gr f 28/1 Dark Angel (IRE)—
                 Passage To India (IRE) (Indian Ridge) (40000) **Wood Hall Stud Limited**
74 **PENDLEY LEGACY**, b f 7/4 Leporello (IRE)—Albavilla (Spectrum (IRE)) **Mr P. W. Harris**
75 Ch f 22/3 Compton Place—Perfect Treasure (IRE) (Night Shift (USA)) **Mildmay Racing**
76 B c 18/4 Teofilo (IRE)—Quite Elusive (IRE) (Elusive Quality (USA)) (72000) **A. D. Spence**
77 B c 17/1 Aqlaam—Rabeera (Beat Hollow) **HE Sheikh Sultan Bin Khalifa Al Nahyan**
78 **RAISE YOUR GAZE**, gr c 9/3 Mastercraftsman (IRE)—
                 Regal Magic (IRE) (Sadler's Wells (USA)) (45000) **Miss J. Deadman & Mr S. Barrow**
79 **ROSINA JAY (IRE)**, b f 7/4 Art Connoisseur (IRE)—Noora (IRE) (Bahhare (USA)) (19047) **P. G. Jacobs**
80 B c 28/4 Pivotal—Silver Kestrel (USA) (Silver Hawk (USA)) **Whitley Stud**
81 B f 3/2 Dansili—So Squally (GER) (Monsun (GER)) (130000) **Mr P. W. Harris**
82 **STRATEGIC FORCE (IRE)**, b c 3/4 Strategic Prince—
                 Mooching Along (IRE) (Mujahid) (27777) **P. N. Ridgers**
83 Gr c 27/4 Verglas (IRE)—Summer Spice (IRE) (Key of Luck (USA)) (26190) **Verglas Colt Syndicate**
84 B f 10/4 Bushranger (IRE)—Tara Gold (IRE) (Royal Academy (USA)) (31000) **Mr A. Le Herissier**
85 **TRILLIAN ASTRA (IRE)**, b f 28/2 Bahamian Bounty—
                 Ms Sophie Eleanor (USA) (Grand Slam (USA)) (25000) **Mr A. B. S. Webb**
86 **TUBEANIE (IRE)**, ch f 13/3 Intense Focus—Ryalahna (IRE) (High Chaparral (IRE)) (21428) **A. Butler**
87 B f 19/4 Acclamation—Unlock (IRE) (Key of Luck (USA)) (20634) **B. Allen, G. Hill & N. Wagland**
88 B f 4/3 Kyllachy—Windermere Island (Cadeaux Genereux) (20000) **Hot To Trot Racing Club**
89 B f 25/3 Kheleyf (USA)—Yxenery (IRE) (Sillery (USA)) (40000) **Mr John Drew & Mr Ian M. Brown**

MR CLIVE COX - Continued

Other Owners: S. W. Barrow, Mr S. R. Bullard, Mr D. H. Caslon, Mr C. G. Cox, Mrs T. L. Cox, Miss J. Deadman, Dr S. B. Drew, J. R. Drew, Mr B. C. Ecclestone, G. W. Elphick, Mr J. Hetherington, Mr S. Hill, J. Humphreys, Ms D. S. Jones, Mr A. McIver, Dr J. Merrington, Mrs U. Merrington, Mr J. H. Wilkinson.

Jockey (flat): Luke Morris, John Fahy, Jennifer Ferguson, Adam Kirby. **Apprentice:** Ryan Tate. **Amateur:** Miss Rachel King.

---

135 MR TONY COYLE, Norton
Postal: **Long Row Stables, Beverley Road, Norton, Malton, North Yorkshire, YO17 9PJ**
Contacts: **MOBILE (07976) 621425**
E-MAIL **tonycoyleracing@hotmail.co.uk**

1 **BILLY CUCKOO (IRE)**, 7, b g Alderbrook—First Battle (IRE) **Gap Personnel Franchises Limited**
2 **CRYSTAL ROCK (IRE)**, 8, br g Rock of Gibraltar (IRE)—State Crystal (IRE) **M. A. O'Donnell**
3 **DUBAIANSWER**, 5, b m Dubawi (IRE)—Answered Prayer **C. E. Whiteley**
4 **GALLANT LEADER (USA)**, 4, b g Zamindar (USA)—Real Trust (USA) **O. R. Dukes**
5 **KEEP IT DARK**, 4, b g Invincible Spirit (IRE)—Tarneem (USA) **N. Hetherton**
6 **LUCKY LANDING (IRE)**, 7, b br g Well Chosen—Melville Rose (IRE) **Gap Personnel Franchises Limited**
7 **NATARAJA**, 4, b g Norse Dancer (IRE)—Floral Rhapsody **Ms M. H. Matheson**
8 **PASTORAL**, 4, b f Rail Link—Cut Corn **B. Dunn**
9 **RIO'S GIRL**, 6, br m Captain Rio—African Breeze **W P S Johnson & Brian Kerr**
10 **RIVER DRAGON (IRE)**, 8, b g Sadler's Wells (USA)—Diarshana (GER) **Brian Kerr & Tony Coyle**
11 **SHARWAKOM (IRE)**, 5, b m Dansili—Candelabra **Mr B. Kerr**
12 **SILVER DRAGON**, 5, gr g Silver Patriarch (IRE)—Gotogeton **Mr B. Kerr**
13 **THE BULL HAYES (IRE)**, 7, b g Sadler's Wells (USA)—No Review (USA) **Mr J. Wholey**
14 **TY'N Y WERN**, 4, b g Dylan Thomas (IRE)—Silk (IRE) **Mr A. C. Coyle**
15 **VENTURE TO WAR (IRE)**, 7, ch m Wareed (IRE)—Wayward Venture (IRE)
16 **VOLCANIC JACK (IRE)**, 5, b g Kodiac—Rosaria Panatta (IRE) **V. Kelly**
17 **WEE GIANT (USA)**, 7, ch g Giant's Causeway (USA)—
Christmas In Aiken (USA) **Gap Personnel Franchises Limited**

THREE-YEAR-OLDS

18 **DUTCH DELIGHT**, ch f Dutch Art—Tetou (IRE) **Mr A. C. Coyle**
19 **HE'S A STRIKER (IRE)**, br bl g Footstepsinthesand—Aiming Upwards **B. Dunn**
20 **MAD JAZZ**, b f Sir Percy—Gwen John (USA) **Chris Green & Tony Coyle**
21 Ch c Primo Valentino (IRE)—Newgate Bubbles **W. P. S. Johnson**
22 **PRINCESS HOLLOW**, ch f Beat Hollow—Lothian Lass (IRE) **Mr A. C. Coyle**
23 **SHILLITO**, b g Kyllachy—Kiss Me Kate (IRE) **J. L. Marriott**
24 **STREET BATTLE (USA)**, b c Street Boss (USA)—J J's Kitty (USA) **B. Dunn**

TWO-YEAR-OLDS

25 Gr f 29/3 Phoenix Reach (IRE)—Arctic Queen (Linamix (FR)) **W. P. S. Johnson**
26 **BARBARA ELIZABETH**, b f 15/4 Sir Percy—Fair View (GER) (Dashing Blade) (2095) **M. A. O'Donnell**
27 B c 28/4 Three Valleys (USA)—Bollin Rita (Rambo Dancer (CAN)) (761)
28 Br f 23/2 Aussie Rules (USA)—Causeway Charm (USA) (Giant's Causeway (USA)) (8500) **C. E. Whiteley**
29 Ch c 27/2 Avonbridge—Dunloe (IRE) (Shaadi (USA)) (2500) **Mrs V. C. Sugden**
30 B f 6/3 Piccolo—Fizzy Treat (Efisio) (20000)
31 **NEVADA BLUE**, ch c 5/3 Pastoral Pursuits—Nevada Princess (IRE) (Desert Prince (IRE)) (23809) **B. Dunn**
32 B f 22/3 Myboycharlie (IRE)—Olindera (GER) (Lomitas) **W. P. Flynn**
33 B f 5/3 Shirocco (GER)—Pete's Passion (Rock of Gibraltar (IRE)) **P. D. Smith Holdings Ltd**

Other Owners: C. R. Green, M. Kelly, A. L. Marriott.

Assistant Trainer: Jaimie Kerr

Jockey (flat): Stephen Craine, Barry McHugh. **Conditional:** Brian Toomey. **Amateur:** Miss Harriet Dukes.

---

136 MR RAY CRAGGS, Sedgefield
Postal: **East Close Farm, Sedgefield, Stockton-On-Tees, Cleveland, TS21 3HW**
Contacts: **PHONE (01740) 620239 FAX (01740) 623476**

1 **BELLINGO**, 6, b m Danroad (AUS)—Rasin Luck **R. Craggs**

MR RAY CRAGGS - Continued

2 DOWNTOWN BOY (IRE), 5, br g Kheleyf (USA)—Uptown (IRE) **R. Craggs**
3 FLEURTILLE, 4, b f Tillerman—Miss Fleurie **R. Craggs**
4 NEEDWOOD PARK, 5, br g Needwood Blade—Waterpark **R. Craggs**
5 PARK HOUSE, 4, b g Tillerman—Rasin Luck **R. Craggs**
6 SHOWMEHOW, 5, b m Grape Tree Road—Rasin Luck **R. Craggs**

Assistant Trainer: Miss J N Craggs

---

137 **MR PETER CRATE, Newdigate**
Postal: Springfield Farm, Parkgate Road, Newdigate, Dorking, Surrey, RH5 5DZ
Contacts: **MOBILE (07775) 821560**

1 ELNA BRIGHT, 8, b g Elnadim (USA)—Acicula (IRE) **P. D. Crate**
2 PICANSORT, 6, b g Piccolo—Running Glimpse (IRE) **P. D. Crate**
3 SANDFRANKSKIPSGO, 4, ch g Piccolo—Alhufoof (USA) **P. D. Crate**
4 TAAJUB (IRE), 6, b g Exceed And Excel (AUS)—Purple Tiger (IRE) **P. D. Crate**

THREE-YEAR-OLDS

5 SAND AND DELIVER, b f Royal Applause—Alhufoof (USA) **P. D. Crate**

---

138 **MR ANDREW CROOK, Leyburn**
Postal: Ashgill Stables (Yard 2), Tupgill Park, Coverham, Middleham, North Yorkshire, DL8 4TJ
Contacts: **PHONE (01969) 640303 MOBILE (07764) 158899**
E-MAIL andycrookracing@fsmail.net **WEBSITE** www.andrewcrookracing.co.uk

1 AGESILAS (FR), 5, gr g Ultimately Lucky (IRE)—Aimessa du Berlais (FR) **R. P. E. Berry**
2 ALONG CAME ROSIE, 9, b m Alflora (IRE)—Seraphim (FR) **Friends Of Rosie & Select Racing Club**
3 BOCAMIX (FR), 7, gr g Linamix (FR)—Bocanegra (FR) **Mrs H. Sinclair**
4 CABAL, 6, br m Kyllachy—Secret Flame **Leeds Plywood & Doors Ltd**
5 CORNISH CASTLE (USA), 7, ch g Mizzen Mast (USA)—Rouwaki (USA) **Mrs D. S. Wilkinson**
6 DANSILI DUTCH (IRE), 4, gr f Dutch Art—Joyful Leap **Mrs C. Hopper**
7 ENJOY YOUR LIFE (IRE), 6, ch g Zafeen (FR)—Queen Chief (IRE) **S. Mason & R. Stipetic**
8 FAIRLIE DINKUM, 5, b m Tobougg (IRE)—Fairlie **Lucky Catch Partnership**
9 FORTYSECOND STREET (IRE), 9, ch g Flemensfirth (USA)—Miss Murtle (IRE) **Mr G. Heap**
10 GERONIMO CHIEF (IRE), 5, b g Sleeping Indian—Portorosa (USA) **Mrs S. Mason, Mr R. Stipetic**
11 JIMMIE BROWN (USA), 5, b g Street Cry (IRE)—Vid Kid (CAN) **The 100 Club**
12 MATMATA DE TENDRON (FR), 13, gr g Badolato (USA)—Cora des Tamarix (FR) **Lucky Catch Partnership**
13 PELICAN ROCK (IRE), 4, b g Amadeus Wolf—Darby Shaw (IRE) **Spence Ellerby Heightley Sowerby**
14 PHILCHEZSKI (IRE), 6, ch g Pilsudski (IRE)—Springfield Gilda (IRE) **R. Berry & Andrew Crook**
15 RANGEFINDER, 9, gr g Linamix (FR)—Risen Raven (USA) **Leeds Plywood & Doors Ltd**
16 REVERBERATE, 4, b f Echo of Light—Niseem (USA) **Lucky Catch Partnership**
17 RORY BOY (USA), 8, b g Aldebaran (USA)—Purr Pleasure (USA) **J. D. Gordon**
18 SAVILLE ROW (IRE), 8, b g Snurge—Designer Lady (IRE) **John Sinclair (Haulage) Ltd**
19 SEA CLIFF (IRE), 9, b g Golan (IRE)—Prosaic Star (IRE) **Mrs D. S. Wilkinson**
20 SHEILAS LADY, 5, b m Tamure (IRE)—Ladies From Leeds **Mr T. England & Mrs A. Young**
21 STRATHAIRD (IRE), 9, b g Medicean—Heed My Warning (IRE) **Mrs Kath Savage**
22 5, B m Tamure (IRE)—Two Dreamers **Mr R. Jones**
23 TWO OSCARS (IRE), 7, b g Oscar (IRE)—Coumeenoole Lady **Arc Racing Yorkshire I**
24 ZAZAMIX (FR), 8, b g Sagamix (FR)—Ombre Bleue (FR) **Mrs Christine Hopper**

THREE-YEAR-OLDS

25 LORD AVONBROOK, b g Avonbridge—Miss Brookie **Lucky Catch Partnership**

Other Owners: Mr A. Crook, Mr M. Ellerby, Mr G. Heap, Mr A. Heightley, Mrs Christine Hopper, Mr Michael Marsh, Mrs S. J. Mason, Mr Mike Palmer, Mr J. Saxby, www.Select-Racing-Club.co.uk, Mr A. Sowerby, Mr S. A. Spence, Mr R. A. Stipetic.

MR ANDREW CROOK - Continued

Jockey (flat): Robert Havlin, Franny Norton. **Jockey (NH):** Dougie Costello, Ryan Mania. **Conditional:** Johnny England. **Amateur:** Mr Darren Costello, Miss Rebecca Shepherd.

---

139 MISS JO CROWLEY, Whitcombe
Postal: **Whitcombe Monymusk Racing Stables, Whitcombe, Dorchester, Dorset, DT2 8NY**
Contacts: **PHONE (01305) 265300 FAX (01305) 265499 MOBILE (07918) 735219**
E-MAIL jocrowley61@hotmail.co.uk

1 COMADOIR (IRE), 7, ch g Medecis—Hymn of The Dawn (USA) **Mrs E. A. M. Nelson**
2 DEORAI (IRE), 5, ch g Choisir (AUS)—Tropical Lake (IRE) **Kilstone Ltd**
3 DESTINY OF DREAMS, 5, b m Dubai Destination (USA)—Valjarv (IRE) **Kilstone Ltd**
4 DRESSED IN LACE, 4, b f Dark Angel (IRE)—Pure Speculation **Mrs E. A. M. Nelson**
5 EBONY SONG (USA), 5, b br g Songandaprayer (USA)—Thiscatsforcaryl (USA) **Kilstone Ltd**
6 KALOKAGATHIA (IRE), 4, b c Kodiac—Seabound **Kilstone Ltd**
7 PATAVIUM PRINCE (IRE), 10, ch g Titus Livius (FR)—Hoyland Common (IRE) **Mrs E. A. M. Nelson**
8 PRINCESS ICICLE, 5, b m Iceman—Sarabah (IRE) **Kilstone Ltd**
9 RUNNING MATE (IRE), 6, b g Acclamation—It Takes Two (IRE) **Kilstone Ltd**
10 SAKHEE'S PEARL, 7, gr m Sakhee (USA)—Grey Pearl **The Peregrina Partnership**
11 SHAMIR, 6, b g Dubai Destination (USA)—Lake Nyasa (IRE) **Kilstone Ltd**
12 SONDRAY, 5, b m Diktat—Hoh Dancer **Kilstone Ltd**
13 THE HOLYMAN (IRE), 5, ch g Footstepsinthesand—Sunset (IRE) **Kilstone Ltd**
14 THRASOS (IRE), 4, b c Invincible Spirit (IRE)—Plymsole (USA) **Kilstone Ltd**
15 TICK TOCK LOVER, 5, gr g Tikkanen (USA)—Ivory's Promise **Kilstone Ltd**
16 WILFRED PICKLES (IRE), 7, ch g Cadeaux Genereux—Living Daylights (IRE) **Kilstone Ltd**

THREE-YEAR-OLDS
17 CAPTAIN STARLIGHT (IRE), b c Captain Marvelous (IRE)—Jewell In The Sky (IRE) **Kilstone Ltd**
18 EMPEROR JULIUS (IRE), b g Antonius Pius (USA)—Queen's Victory **Kilstone Ltd**
19 LADY TABITHA (IRE), b f Tamayuz—Kimola (USA) **Mrs E. A. M. Nelson**
20 MISS LEGAL EAGLE (IRE), b f Authorized (IRE)—Pride of My Heart **Mrs E. A. M. Nelson**
21 MYSTICAL SAPPHIRE, b f Sakhee's Secret—Nadyma (IRE) **Mrs E. A. M. Nelson**
22 SWEET MARWELL (IRE), b f Excellent Art—Bee Eater (IRE) **Mrs E. A. M. Nelson**

TWO-YEAR-OLDS
23 DREAM RULER, b g 31/3 Holy Roman Emperor (IRE)—
                                    Whatcameoverme (USA) (Aldebaran (USA)) **Mrs E. A. M. Nelson**
24 PERRYDOT (IRE), b f 16/3 Footstepsinthesand—Titoli di Coda (IRE) (Bertolini (USA)) **Mrs E. A. M. Nelson**
25 ROSARINA, ch f 6/4 Rock of Gibraltar (IRE)—Spring Fashion (IRE) (Galileo (IRE)) **Mrs E. A. M. Nelson**

Other Owners: Miss C. J. Davies, T. A. Edwards, Mrs L. Kellaway, Mr J. Luck, Mrs A. P. Wilkinson.

Assistant Trainer: Anthony Clark

Jockey (flat): Dane O'Neill, Ian Mongan, Fergus Sweeney.

---

140 MR LUCA CUMANI, Newmarket
Postal: **Bedford House Stables, Bury Road, Newmarket, Suffolk, CB8 7BX**
Contacts: **PHONE (01638) 665432 FAX (01638) 667160 MOBILE (07801) 225300**
E-MAIL luca@lucacumani.com WEBSITE www.lucacumani.com

1 AFSARE, 6, b g Dubawi (IRE)—Jumaireyah **Sheikh Mohammed Obaid Al Maktoum**
2 DANADANA (IRE), 5, b h Dubawi (IRE)—Zeeba (IRE) **Sheikh Mohammed Obaid Al Maktoum**
3 EMIRATES QUEEN, 4, b f Street Cry (IRE)—Zomaradah **Sheikh Mohammed Obaid Al Maktoum**
4 FRANCISCAN, 5, b g Medicean—Frangy **Dr M. B. Q. S. Koukash**
5 FURZANAH, 4, b f Dubawi (IRE)—Latent Lover (IRE) **Sheikh Mohammed Obaid Al Maktoum**
6 HIPPY HIPPY SHAKE, 4, b f Danehill Dancer (IRE)—Hyperspectra **Helena Springfield Ltd**
7 KHIONE, 4, b f Dalakhani (IRE)—Sularina (IRE) **Aston House Stud**
8 KIRTHILL (IRE), 5, b h Danehill Dancer (IRE)—Kirtle **L. Marinopoulos**
9 MANKINI (IRE), 4, b c Dansili—Fashion Statement **L. Marinopoulos**
10 MOBACO (FR), 4, b c Slickly (FR)—Lunaa (FR) **O.T.I. Racing**
11 MOLDOWNEY, 4, ch c Dalakhani (IRE)—Danehill's Dream (IRE) **O.T.I. Racing**
12 MOUNT ATHOS (IRE), 6, b g Montjeu (IRE)—Ionian Sea (IRE) **Dr M. B. Q. S. Koukash**

MR LUCA CUMANI - Continued

13 **OUT DO**, 4, ch g Exceed And Excel (AUS)—Ludynosa (USA) **L. Marinopoulos**
14 **ROCKALONG (IRE)**, 4, b c Rock of Gibraltar (IRE)—High Spot **Mr Nagy El Azar**
15 **SEMEEN**, 4, b c Dubawi (IRE)—Zeeba (IRE) **Sheikh Mohammed Obaid Al Maktoum**
16 **VALIDUS**, 4, b g Zamindar (USA)—Victoire Finale **Mr S. A. Stuckey**
17 **ZACYNTHUS (IRE)**, 5, ch g Iffraaj—Ziria (IRE) **Mrs J. Bownes**

THREE-YEAR-OLDS

18 **ABILENE**, ch f Samum (GER)—Altamira **Wildenstein Stables Limited**
19 **AJMAN BRIDGE**, ch c Dubawi (IRE)—Rice Mother (IRE) **Sheikh Mohammed Obaid Al Maktoum**
20 **AJMANY**, b c Kheleyf (USA)—Passarelle (USA) **Sheikh Mohammed Obaid Al Maktoum**
21 **BARTACK (IRE)**, b c Acclamation—Bentley's Bush (IRE) **B. Corman**
22 **BLACK ROLLER**, b c Kavafi (IRE)—Vallota **Mrs M. Marinopoulos**
23 **BONANZA CREEK (IRE)**, b f Anabaa (USA)—Bright Moon (USA) **Wildenstein Stables Limited**
24 **BOUCLIER (IRE)**, ch c Zamindar (USA)—Bastet (IRE) **Wildenstein Stables Limited**
25 **CANON LAW (IRE)**, b c Holy Roman Emperor (IRE)—Delisha **Mr S. A. Stuckey**
26 **DESERTED**, b f Oasis Dream—Tentpole (USA) **Fittocks Stud Limited**
27 **DIAMOND MINE**, br gr c Rock of Gibraltar (IRE)—Kassiyra (IRE) **Fittocks Stud Ltd**
28 **DON PADEJA**, b c Dansili—La Leuze (IRE) **TSEGA Horses Company Ltd**
29 **DUKE OF PERTH**, b g Danehill Dancer (IRE)—Frangy **Fittocks Stud Ltd**
30 **ELECTRA SPECTRA**, b f Dansili—Hyperspectra **Helena Springfield Ltd**
31 **ELHAAME (IRE)**, b c Acclamation—Gold Hush (USA) **Sheikh Mohammed Obaid Al Maktoum**
32 **ENDLESS CREDIT (IRE)**, b br c High Chaparral (IRE)—Pay The Bank **L. Marinopoulos**
33 **GREATWOOD**, b c Manduro (GER)—Gaze **Highclere Thoroughbred Racing - Archer**
34 **HAVANA COOLER (IRE)**, ch c Hurricane Run (IRE)—Unquenchable (USA) **L. Marinopoulos**
35 **JAZZ MASTER**, b c Singspiel (IRE)—Turn of A Century **Castle Down Racing**
36 **KIKONGA**, b f Danehill Dancer (IRE)—Kibara **Fittocks Stud Ltd**
37 **KINDU**, b f Pivotal—Kithanga (IRE) **Fittocks Stud Ltd**
38 **LIONHEART**, ch c Zamindar (USA)—Victoire Celebre (USA) **Fittocks Stud & Andrew Bengough**
39 **MAKAFEH**, br g Elusive Quality (USA)—Demisemiquaver **Sheikh Mohammed Obaid Al Maktoum**
40 **MALLORY HEIGHTS (IRE)**, b c Dalakhani (IRE)—My Dark Rosaleen **Merry Fox Stud Limited**
41 **MARKTTAG**, b c Manduro (GER)—Makhsusah (IRE) **Mr S. A. Stuckey**
42 **MOUNT MACEDON**, b c Hernando (FR)—White Palace **Mr S. A. Stuckey**
43 **NARGYS (IRE)**, b f Lawman (FR)—Spesialta **Sheikh Mohammed Obaid Al Maktoum**
44 **NELSON'S HILL**, b c Mount Nelson—Regal Step **L. Marinopoulos**
45 **NORWAY CROSS**, b f Cape Cross (IRE)—Queen of Norway (USA) **TSEGA Horses Company Ltd**
46 **PARADISE WATCH**, b g Royal Applause—Ocean View (USA) **L. Marinopoulos**
47 **PARKER RIDGE (FR)**, ch c Green Tune (USA)—Peinture Bleue (USA) **Wildenstein Stables Limited**
48 **PETRIFY**, b g Rock of Gibraltar (IRE)—Frigid **Fittocks Stud Ltd**
49 **PLEASURE BENT**, b c Dansili—Nitya (FR) **C. Bennett**
50 **QUANTIFY (USA)**, b f Giant's Causeway (USA)—Measure (USA) **Mr M Tabor, Mrs J Magnier & Mr D Smith**
51 **ROYAL BALLET**, ch c Pivotal—Dance A Dream **Singapore Thoroughbred Racing-Lord Mayor**
52 **SAIGON CITY**, b g Mount Nelson—Hoh Chi Min **L. Marinopoulos**
53 **SASKATCHEWAN**, ch c Peintre Celebre (USA)—Sarabande (USA) **Wildenstein Stables Limited**
54 **SHARAREH**, b f Sir Percy—You Too **Sheikh Mohammed Obaid Al Maktoum**
55 **SHARQAWIYAH**, b f Dubawi (IRE)—Pompey Girl **Sheikh Mohammed Obaid Al Maktoum**
56 **SILK SARI**, b f Dalakhani (IRE)—So Silk **Fittocks Stud & Andrew Bengough**
57 **SLEEPING GIANT (GER)**, gr c Dalakhani (IRE)—Special Delivery (IRE) **Wildenstein Stables Limited**
58 **SORYAH (IRE)**, b f Shamardal (USA)—Dirtybirdie **Sheikh Mohammed Obaid Al Maktoum**
59 **SPIETA (IRE)**, gr f Shirocco (GER)—Zarawa (IRE) **Wright**
60 **VELOX**, b g Zamindar (USA)—Victoire Finale **Mr S. A. Stuckey**
61 **VERMONT (IRE)**, b c Muhtathir—Venetian Beauty (USA) **Wildenstein Stables Limited**

TWO-YEAR-OLDS

62 **ALISIOS (GR)**, b c 28/2 Ialysos (GR)—Macanuda (IRE) (Slickly (FR)) **L. Marinopoulos**
63 **ALKETIOS (GR)**, b c 10/2 Kavafi (IRE)—Mazea (IRE) (Montjeu (IRE)) **L. Marinopoulos**
64 B c 4/5 New Approach (IRE)—Astorg (USA) (Lear Fan (USA)) (47619) **H.E. Sheikh J. B. H. B. K. Al Thani**
65 **BACK TO BUXTED (IRE)**, b c 19/3 Aqlaam—
                                    Incoming Call (USA) (Red Ransom (USA)) (72000) **Buxted Partnership**
66 **BLUE WALTZ**, b f 19/4 Pivotal—Blue Symphony (Darshaan) **Fittocks Stud Ltd**
67 **BRACKEN**, ro c 11/3 Dubawi (IRE)—
                                  Belle Reine (King of Kings (IRE)) (100000) **Sheikh Mohammed Obaid Al Maktoum**
68 B f 3/4 Pivotal—Brigitta (IRE) (Sadler's Wells (USA)) (180000) **Mr S. A. Stuckey**
69 **COMEDY KING (IRE)**, b br c 18/4 Dansili—
                                  Comic (IRE) (Be My Chief (USA)) (90000) **Sheikh Mohammed Obaid Al Maktoum**

MR LUCA CUMANI - Continued

70 **CONNECTICUT,** b c 1/2 New Approach (IRE)—
                                Craigmill (Slip Anchor) (110000) **Sheikh Mohammed Obaid Al Maktoum**
71 **CROSS COUNTRY (IRE),** b c 20/4 Cape Cross (IRE)—
                                Altruiste (USA) (Diesis) (253967) **Sheikh Mohammed Obaid Al Maktoum**
72 **DON'T,** b f 12/5 Invincible Spirit (IRE)—Frigid (Indian Ridge) **Fittocks Stud Ltd**
73 **FREDERIC,** b g 9/5 Zamindar (USA)—Frangy (Sadler's Wells (USA)) **Fittocks Stud Ltd**
74 B c 2/3 Montjeu (IRE)—High Reserve (Dr Fong (USA)) (80000) **Meon Valley Stud**
75 B c 24/2 New Approach (IRE)—Hyabella (Shirley Heights) **Meon Valley Stud**
76 **JOYS OF SPRING (IRE),** b f 13/3 Invincible Spirit (IRE)—
                                Sonachan (Darshaan) (320000) **Sheikh Mohammed Obaid Al Maktoum**
77 **KINSHASA,** b c 26/4 Pivotal—Kibara (Sadler's Wells (USA)) (85000) **Fittocks Stud Ltd**
78 **KLEO,** b f 10/4 Kavafi—Selfish (Bluebird (USA)) **L. Marinopoulos**
79 **LAWYER (IRE),** b c 27/3 Acclamation—
                              Charaig (Rainbow Quest) (110000) **Sheikh Mohammed Obaid Al Maktoum**
80 **MADAME CLOUSEAU (IRE),** b f 24/3 Galileo (IRE)—Healing Music (FR) (Bering) **Jon S. Kelly**
81 B f 2/4 Invincible Spirit (IRE)—Marika (Marju (IRE)) (90000) **Mr S. A. Stuckey**
82 B c 28/3 Galileo (IRE)—Moments of Joy (Darshaan) (275000) **Jon S. Kelly**
83 **MOUNT LOGAN (IRE),** ch c 30/4 New Approach (IRE)—
                              Vistaria (USA) (Distant View) (107142) **Sheikh Mohammed Obaid Al Maktoum**
84 B c 11/4 Sea The Stars (IRE)—Musical Treat (IRE) (Royal Academy (USA)) (500000) **Jon S. Kelly**
85 **PATTERNED,** b f 2/4 Dansili—Paisley (Pivotal) **Fittocks Stud Ltd**
86 **PETTICOAT LANE,** b f 17/3 High Chaparral (IRE)—Barter (Daylami (IRE)) **Fittocks Stud Ltd**
87 **PLEASANT VALLEY (IRE),** b f 6/5 Shamardal (USA)—
                              Poughkeepsie (IRE) (Sadler's Wells (USA)) **Wildenstein Stables Limited**
88 **POSTPONED,** b c 4/4 Dubawi (IRE)—
                              Ever Rigg (Dubai Destination (USA)) (360000) **Sheikh Mohammed Obaid Al Maktoum**
89 Ch f 14/3 Smart Strike (CAN)—Queen of The Night (Sadler's Wells (USA)) **Mrs S. Magnier**
90 B c 18/2 Dansili—Quelle Vitesse (Sadler's Wells (USA)) (320000) **Jon S. Kelly**
91 B c 10/3 Cape Cross (IRE)—Rambler (Selkirk (USA)) (70000) **Mr Nagy El Azar**
92 **ROSEBURG (IRE),** ch c 16/2 Tamayuz—
                              Raydraniya (IRE) (In The Wings) (38095) **Sheikh Mohammed Obaid Al Maktoum**
93 **SECOND STEP (IRE),** b c 21/3 Dalakhani (IRE)—My Dark Rosaleen (Sadler's Wells (USA)) **Merry Fox Stud**
94 B c 30/3 Danehill Dancer (IRE)—Sharplaw Star (Xaar) (160000) **Jon S. Kelly**
95 **TOLMIAS,** br c 1/1 Ialysos—Shitasta **L. Marinopoulos**
96 B br c 30/4 High Chaparral (IRE)—Trebles (IRE) (Kenmare (FR)) (52000) **Mr S. A. Stuckey**
97 B f 4/5 Mount Nelson—Victoire Finale (Peintre Celebre (USA)) **Mr S. A. Stuckey**
98 **VIRGIN ISLAND (GER),** b f 3/5 Peintre Celebre (USA)—
                              Venetian Beauty (USA) (Lear Fan (USA)) **Wildenstein Stables Limited**
99 **WILLOW VIEW (USA),** b f 12/1 Lemon Drop Kid (USA)—Time Control (Sadler's Wells (USA)) **Merry Fox Stud**
100 **WISTAR,** b c 20/4 Dubawi (IRE)—
                              Vallota (Polish Precedent (USA)) (260000) **Sheikh Mohammed Obaid Al Maktoum**
101 **ZOVIOS,** b c 1/1 Ialysos—Messini **L. Marinopoulos**

Other Owners: Mr A. N. C. Bengough, Mr Daniel Boorer, Mr P. Booth, Mrs Luca Cumani, Mr T. Henderson, The Hon H. Herbert, Prof John Hunter, Mrs John Magnier, Mr Paul Moulton, Mr S. O'Donnell, Mr Andrew Patey, Mr Paul Silver, Mr Derrick Smith, Mr M. Tabor, Mr M. Weinfeld, Mr Christopher Wright.

Assistant Trainer: Matthew Cumani

Jockey (flat): Kieren Fallon. **Apprentice:** Patrick Hills. **Amateur:** Miss F. Cumani.

---

141   MR PETER CUNDELL, Compton
Postal: **Roden House, Wallingford Road, Compton, Newbury, Berkshire, RG20 6QR**
Contacts: **PHONE** (01635) 578267 **FAX** (01635) 578267 **MOBILE** (07967) 227346
E-MAIL peter.cundell@googlemail.com

1 **ERNIE,** 6, ch g Reset (AUS)—Bonita Bee **P. D. Cundell**
2 **HAVING A BALL,** 9, b g Mark of Esteem (IRE)—All Smiles **P. D. Cundell**
3 **TAKITWO,** 10, b g Delta Dancer—Tiama (IRE) **P. D. Cundell**

Assistant Trainer: Miss L. E. Newberry

142   MR MICHAEL CUNNINGHAM, Navan
Postal: **Gormanstown Stables, Kildalkey, Navan, Co.Meath, Ireland**
Contacts: **PHONE (00353) 4694 31672 FAX (00353) 4694 31467 MOBILE (00353) 8625 93962**
E-MAIL **cunninghamstables@gmail.com**

1 CROWDED ROOM (IRE), 7, b g Oscar (IRE)—
           Leadamurraydance (IRE) **Mr T. A. Fitzpatrick & Mrs Michael Cunningham**
2 MARTIN CASH (IRE), 7, b g Oscar (IRE)—Native Singer (IRE) **Mr Herb M. Stanley & Mrs Michael Cunningham**
3 PARKERS MILL (IRE), 5, b g High Chaparral (IRE)—Celtic Wing **Mrs Paul Shanahan**

143   MR SEAN CURRAN, Upper Lambourn
Postal: **Frenchmans Lodge Stables, Upper Lambourn, Hungerford, Berkshire, RG17 8QT**
Contacts: **PHONE (01488) 72095 FAX (01488) 72095 MOBILE (07774) 146169**
E-MAIL **seancurran99@hotmail.co.uk**

1 CHARGEN (IRE), 10, b g Charente River (IRE)—Blasgan (IRE) **Mrs E. Madden**
2 EDGWARE ROAD, 5, ch g Selkirk (USA)—Bayswater **L. M. Power**
3 EPIC STORM (IRE), 5, b g Montjeu (IRE)—Jaya (USA) **L. M. Power**
4 LESLEY'S CHOICE, 7, b g Lucky Story (USA)—Wathbat Mtoto **L. M. Power**
5 LIKEAROLLINGSTONE (IRE), 8, ch g Definite Article—Bannow Girl (IRE) **L. M. Power**
6 LINDORO, 8, b g Marju (IRE)—Floppie (FR) **L. M. Power**
7 SAINGLEND, 8, b g Galileo (IRE)—Verbal Intrigue (USA) **L. M. Power**
8 WALDSEE (GER), 8, b g Xaar—Wurftaube (GER) **L M Power & Global Self Drive**
9 ZELOS DIKTATOR, 7, br g Diktat—Chanterelle (IRE) **A. J. White**

Other Owners: Mr L. M. Power, Mr Chris Webb.

144   MISS REBECCA CURTIS, Newport
Postal: **Fforest Farm, Newport, Pembrokeshire, SA42 0UG**
Contacts: **PHONE (01348) 811489 MOBILE (07970) 710690**
E-MAIL **rebcurtis@hotmail.com**

1 AMIFUNNYYET, 5, b g Helissio (FR)—Flying Form (IRE) **A. J. Mossop**
2 AT FISHERS CROSS (IRE), 6, b g Oscar (IRE)—Fermoy Supreme (IRE) **J. P. McManus**
3 BENHEIR (IRE), 7, b g Beneficial—Victford (IRE) **T43 Partners**
4 BOB FORD (IRE), 6, b g Vinnie Roe (IRE)—Polar Lamb (IRE) **G. Costelloe**
5 BOYFROMNOWHERE (IRE), 6, br g Old Vic—Eist Do Gale (IRE) **Mr A J Rhead & Mr G B Williams**
6 CASTLE BEACH (IRE), 4, b g Millenary—Don't Fall (IRE) **M Duthie, G Williams, H Scale**
7 CHEAT THE CHEATER (IRE), 6, b g Flemensfirth (USA)—Ballyclough Gale **G. Costelloe**
8 FISHOUTOFWATER (IRE), 9, ch g Old Vic—Frost Bound **J. P. McManus**
9 GOD OF THE KOP (IRE), 6, ch g Old Vic—Liss Rua (IRE) **J. P. McManus**
10 GUS MACRAE (IRE), 9, b g Accordion—Full of Surprises (IRE) **Quicksilver Racing Partnership**
11 HARE IN A ROUND (IRE), 5, b g Craigsteel—Killone Brae **Chris Trembath and Dave Owen**
12 IN THE POST (IRE), 8, b g Oscar (IRE)—Watch Your Step (IRE) **Mr T. Collery**
13 INTERNATIONALAPEAL (IRE), 5, ch g Saffron Walden (FR)—Just Native (IRE) **T43 Partners & Friends**
14 MEGANISI (IRE), 6, b g Galileo (IRE)—Cland di San Jore (IRE) **M. A. Sherwood**
15 MISTER W K (IRE), 5, b g Definite Article—Love The Lord (IRE) **J. P. McManus**
16 MONKEY KINGDOM, 5, b g King's Theatre (IRE)—Blast Freeze (IRE) **G. Costelloe**
17 MONTE CAVALLO (SAF), 8, b g Saumarez—Mufski (SAF) **Mrs L. E. Ramsden**
18 O'FAOLAINS BOY (IRE), 6, b g Oscar (IRE)—Lisa's Storm (IRE) **Mr C Trembath & Mr R Hyde**
19 ONE TERM (IRE), 6, b g Beneficial—One Edge (IRE) **Miss L Reid & Mr G Costelloe**
20 PECKHAMECHO (IRE), 7, b g Beneficial—Nolans Pride (IRE) **C. R. Trembath**
21 RENDL BEACH (IRE), 6, b g Milan—Erins Emblem (IRE) **The O'Connor Duffy Racing Partnership**
22 SALOMO (GER), 7, b g Monsun (GER)—Salka (GER) **Mr A J Rhead & Mr G B Williams**
23 SANDANSKI (IRE), 5, b g Definite Article—Castle Hope (IRE) **The O'Connor Duffy Racing Partnership**
24 SCOTER FONTAINE (FR), 7, b g Sleeping Car (FR)—Blanche Fontaine (FR) **J. P. McManus**
25 STOW, 8, ch g Selkirk (USA)—Spry **GSM Properties Ltd**
26 TEAFORTHREE (IRE), 7, b g Oscar (IRE)—Ethel's Bay (IRE) **T437**
27 THE BEAR TRAP (IRE), 6, b g Westerner—Calendula **J. P. McManus**
28 THE JUGOPOLIST (IRE), 6, b g Oscar (IRE)—Chance My Native (IRE) **C. R. Trembath**

MISS REBECCA CURTIS - Continued

29 **THE ROMFORD PELE (IRE)**, 6, b g Accordion—
　　　　　　　　　　Back And Fore (IRE) **C. Trembath, M. Hill, T. Outhart, N. Fletcher**
30 **WESTERN COMMANDER (IRE)**, 6, b g King's Theatre (IRE)—The Third Sister (IRE) **G. Costelloe**

Other Owners: Mr J. Conyers, D. P. Duffy, M. Duthie, Mr N. Fletcher, Mr C. J. Guyver, M. Hill, Mr R. Hyde, Mr E. M. O'Connor, Mr J. P. O'Reilly, A. J. Outhart, Mr D. V. Owen, Miss L. Reid, Mr A. J. Rhead, Mr N. M. Roddis, Mr W. B. H. Scale, Mr G. Sturgeon, Mr G. B. Williams, Mr G. Williams, D. C. Zeffman.

Assistant Trainer: Paul Sheldrake

---

145 **MR ROGER CURTIS, Lambourn**
Postal: Delamere Stables, Baydon Road, Lambourn, Hungerford, Berkshire, RG17 8NT
Contacts: **PHONE (01488) 73007 FAX (01488) 73909 MOBILE (07836) 320690**
E-MAIL rcurtislambourn@aol.com WEBSITE www.rogercurtis.com

1 **BALLY GUNNER**, 8, br g Needle Gun (IRE)—Rich Pickings **The Bally Gunners**
2 **BLUE PENCIL**, 4, b g Ishiguru (USA)—Gold And Blue (IRE) **The Racing 4 Fun Partnership**
3 **ELEGANT OLIVE**, 10, b m Alflora (IRE)—Strong Cloth (IRE) **Collective Dreamers**
4 **HIGH 'N DRY (IRE)**, 9, ch m Halling (USA)—Sisal (IRE) **The Cool Blue Partnership**
5 **JACK THE JOKER**, 4, b g Librettist (USA)—Sonda (IRE) **The Highgrove Garden Centre Partnership**
6 **KAYCEE (IRE)**, 8, ch g King Charlemagne (USA)—Bollicina (USA) **R. M. Carson**
7 **KILCOMMON PRIDE (IRE)**, 8, br g Catcher In The Rye (IRE)—Ballyhookeen Lass (IRE) **Healycoyle & Partners**
8 **MACCABEES**, 4, b g Motivator—Takarna (IRE) **Mrs F. J. Dean**
9 **PLAY THE BLUES (IRE)**, 6, gr m Refuse To Bend (IRE)—Paldouna (IRE) **The Cool Blue Partnership**
10 **RAINBOW RICHES (IRE)**, 4, b f Princely Heir (IRE)—Another Rainbow (IRE) **The Racing 4 Fun Partnership**
11 **ROMNEY MARSH**, 12, br m Glacial Storm (USA)—Mirador **The Romney Marsh Partnership**
12 **ROSE MADDER**, 4, b f Singspiel (IRE)—Crimson Year (USA) **The Racing 4 Fun Partnership**

Other Owners: M. A. Allen, Miss A. Atkin, Ms L. M. Barton, Mr T. N. Coyle, R. Curtis, Mr R. Dean, Mrs D. S. Gibbs, Mrs C. Lowman, Mrs P. McCluskey, B. Newman, Mr D. N. Thurlow, Dr P. G. Walker.

Assistant Trainer: Dawn Gibbs

Jockey (flat): Dane O'Neill, James Doyle. **Jockey (NH):** Dave Crosse, Hadden Frost. **Amateur:** Mr Jos Curtis, Mr Freddy Tett.

---

146 **MR TOM CUTHBERT, Brampton**
Postal: Woodlands, Cowranbridge, How Mill, Brampton, Cumbria, CA8 9LH
Contacts: **PHONE (01228) 560822 FAX (01228) 560822 MOBILE (07747) 843344**
E-MAIL cuthbertracing@fsmail.net

1 **EDAS**, 11, b g Celtic Swing—Eden (IRE) **Mrs J. Cuthbert**
2 **MOYNAHAN (USA)**, 8, ch g Johannesburg (USA)—Lakab (USA) **T. A. K. Cuthbert**
3 **SECOND REEF**, 11, b g Second Empire (IRE)—Vax Lady **Mrs J. Cuthbert**

Assistant Trainer: Helen Cuthbert

Amateur: Miss H. Cuthbert.

---

147 **MR PAUL D'ARCY, Newmarket**
Postal: Charnwood Stables, Hamilton Road, Newmarket, Suffolk, CB8 7JQ
Contacts: **PHONE (01638) 662000 FAX (01638) 661100 MOBILE (07768) 807653**
E-MAIL pauldarcy@fsmail.net WEBSITE www.pauldarcyracing.com

1 **COME ON BLUE CHIP (IRE)**, 4, b g Holy Roman Emperor (IRE)—Rapid Action (USA) **Blue Chip Feed Ltd**
2 **DARNATHEAN**, 4, b g Librettist (USA)—Meddle **Mr K. Snell**
3 **FAIRYINTHEWIND**, 4, ch f Indian Haven—Blue Daze **Spittinginthewind Partnership**
4 **FAST FINIAN (IRE)**, 4, gr g Clodovil (IRE)—Delphie Queen (IRE) **Mr J. W. Kennedy**
5 **MCBIRNEY (USA)**, 6, b g Danehill Dancer (IRE)—Dear Girl (IRE) **Mrs S. I. D'Arcy**
6 **TEIDE PEAK (IRE)**, 4, b g Cape Cross (IRE)—Teide Lady **C. M. Wilson**

MR PAUL D'ARCY - Continued

THREE-YEAR-OLDS
7 BLACKDOWN SPIRIT, b g Ishiguru (USA)—Shielaligh **Rowley Racing**
8 GLENREEF, ch f Three Valleys (USA)—Grand Coral **Mr J. N. Reus**
9 JD ROCKEFELLER, ch g Sakhee (USA)—Perle d'or (IRE) **The Perle d'Or Partnership**
10 LYRIC ACE (IRE), b g Thousand Words—Aces Dancing (GER) **Champion Bloodstock Limited**
11 MAGICAL ROSE (IRE), b f Elusive City (USA)—Xarzee (IRE) **Mr K. Snell**
12 PERPETUAL AMBITION, b g Avonbridge—Never Enough (GER) **Champion Bloodstock Limited**
13 SMART EIGHTEEN, b c Exceed And Excel (AUS)—Papabile (USA) **Champion Bloodstock Limited**
14 SPIRIT MAN, b c Manduro (GER)—World Spirit **Stapleford Racing Ltd**
15 TRUE SPIRIT, b c Shamardal (USA)—Petonellajill **Mr K. Snell**

TWO-YEAR-OLDS
16 BIKINI CLUB, br f 28/2 Pastoral Pursuits—Black Sea Pearl (Diktat) **Mrs J. Harris**
17 B c 16/4 Shirocco (GER)—World Spirit (Agnes World (USA)) **Stapleford Racing Ltd**

Other Owners: Mr K. Bradley, Mr A. J. T. D'Arcy, P. W. D'Arcy, Mr R. J. Delnevo, Mr M. J. Hyson, Mrs D. L. Smyth.

Assistant Trainer: Sue D'Arcy

---

148 **MR LUKE DACE, Billingshurst**
Postal: Copped Hall Farm, Okehurst Lane, Billingshurst, West Sussex, RH14 9HR
Contacts: **OFFICE (01403) 780889 FAX (01403) 780889 MOBILE (07949) 401085**
E-MAIL lukedace@yahoo.co.uk WEBSITE www.lukedace.co.uk

1 ALNOOMAS (IRE), 4, b g Oasis Dream—Remarkable Story **M. J. Benton**
2 AMERICAN SPIN, 9, ch g Groom Dancer (USA)—Sea Vixen **Mr G Collacott & Mr R Gadd**
3 BARACHIEL, 5, b g Pivotal—Coveted **Mr Peter Gray & Mr John Buchanan**
4 GHOSTWING, 6, gr g Kheleyf (USA)—Someone's Angel (USA) **M. J. Benton**
5 HIP HIP HOORAY, 7, ch m Monsieur Bond (IRE)—Birthday Belle **M. C. S. D. Racing Partnership**
6 LASCAUX, 4, ch f Pivotal—Tora Bora **M. J. Benton**
7 MY LORD, 5, br g Ishiguru (USA)—Lady Smith **M. J. Benton**
8 SERGEANT ABLETT (IRE), 5, b g Danehill Dancer (USA)—Dolydille (IRE) **M. J. Benton**
9 SHARED MOMENT (IRE), 7, ch m Tagula (IRE)—Good Thought (IRE) **M. J. Benton**
10 TARTAN TRIP, 6, b g Selkirk (USA)—Marajuana **M. J. Benton**
11 TRACK STAR (IRE), 8, b g Sadler's Wells (USA)—Angelica Tree (CAN) **Copped Hall Farm & Stud**
12 WELL SPRUNG (IRE), 7, b m Generous (IRE)—Cool Spring (IRE) **Copped Hall Farm & Stud**

THREE-YEAR-OLDS
13 FIANCE FIASCO, b f Motivator—Wise Little Girl **M. J. Benton**
14 LIMOGES, b f Bertolini (USA)—China Cherub **Angels Partnership**
15 MAJESTIC JESS (IRE), b c Majestic Missile—Ginger Not Blonde (USA) **M. J. Benton**

Other Owners: Mr J. C. Buchanan, Mr G. Collacott, L. A. Dace, Mrs L. J. Dace, R. A. Gadd, Mr P. J. Gray, Mrs S. E. Lakin, B. J. McClean, Mrs M. B. McClean, N. S. Scandrett, Mrs V. J. Thrower.

Assistant Trainer: Mrs L Dace

---

149 **MR KEITH DALGLEISH, Carluke**
Postal: Belstane Racing Stables, Carluke, Lanarkshire, ML8 5HN
Contacts: **PHONE (01555) 773335**

1 ACT YOUR SHOE SIZE, 4, b f Librettist (USA)—Howards Heroine (IRE) **G. McDowall**
2 ARAGORN ROUGE, 5, b g Aragorn (IRE)—Red Top (IRE) **Mr K. W. Dalgleish**
3 BASINGSTOKE (IRE), 4, b g Elusive City (USA)—Ryninch (IRE) **Straightline Construction Ltd**
4 BASSETT ROAD (IRE), 5, ch g Byron—Topiary (IRE) **Mr K. W. Dalgleish**
5 BLOWN IT (USA), 7, b br g More Than Ready (USA)—Short Shadow (USA) **D. G. Savala**
6 CADGERS BRIG, 5, ch g Halling (USA)—Burghmuir (IRE) **J. F. Allan**
7 CHOOKIE AVON, 6, ch g Avonbridge—Lady of Windsor (IRE) **Keith Dalgleish Racing Club**
8 CHOOKIE HAMILTON, 9, ch g Compton Place—Lady of Windsor (IRE) **Straightline Construction Ltd**
9 CHOOKIE ROYALE, 5, ch g Monsieur Bond (IRE)—Lady of Windsor (IRE) **Raeburn Brick Limited**
10 CIRCUITOUS, 5, b g Fasliyev (USA)—Seren Devious **A. R. M Galbraith**
11 FINDHORNBAY, 4, b f Ishiguru (USA)—Sweet Cando (IRE) **Mrs L. B. K. Bone**

MR KEITH DALGLEISH - Continued

12 **FLEETWOODMAXI (USA)**, 6, b br g Afleet Alex (USA)—Swain's Gold (USA) **Weldspec Glasgow Limited**
13 **FORT BELVEDERE**, 5, ch h King's Best (USA)—Sweet Folly (IRE) **Straightline Construction Ltd**
14 **FREQUENCY**, 6, br g Starcraft (NZ)—Soundwave **Mrs F. E. Mitchell**
15 **GOLDMADCHEN (GER)**, 5, b m Ivan Denisovich (IRE)—Goldkatze (GER) **G L S Partnership**
16 **JEANNIE GALLOWAY (IRE)**, 6, b m Bahamian Bounty—Housekeeper (IRE) **Mr D. Renwick**
17 **JOSHUA THE FIRST**, 4, br g Kheleyf (USA)—Newkeylets **Newkeylets**
18 **LADY OF EDGE**, 4, b f Librettist (USA)—Lady of Windsor (IRE) **Raeburn Brick Limited**
19 **LUCTOR EMERGO (IRE)**, 4, b g Amadeus Wolf—Batilde (IRE) **Straightline Construction Ltd**
20 **NADEMA ROSE (IRE)**, 4, b f Elnadim (USA)—Noctilucent (JPN) **Joseph Leckie & Sons Ltd**
21 **NORTH CENTRAL (USA)**, 6, b br g Forest Camp (USA)—Brittan Lee (USA) **Dogberry Racing**
22 **PARDOVEN (IRE)**, 4, b f Clodovil (IRE)—Dancing Prize (IRE) **J. Harrison**
23 **RAWAAFED (IRE)**, 4, b br g Invasor (ARG)—Holly's Kid (USA) **Straightline Construction Ltd**
24 **SANTEFISIO**, 7, b g Efisio—Impulsive Decision (IRE) **Weldspec Glasgow Limited**
25 **SOUND ADVICE**, 4, b g Echo of Light—Flylowflylong (IRE) **G L S Partnership**
26 **STONEFIELD FLYER**, 4, b c Kheleyf (USA)—Majestic Diva (IRE) **Mr G. R. Leckie**

THREE-YEAR-OLDS

27 **ARGAKI (IRE)**, ch c Strategic Prince—Amathusia **D. G. Savala**
28 **CORTON LAD**, b g Refuse To Bend (IRE)—Kelucia (IRE) **Mr J. J. Hutton**
29 **FAITHER**, b c Bertolini (USA)—Hawait Al Barr **Mac Asphalt Ltd**
30 **FOOLBYTHEPOOL**, b c Refuse To Bend (IRE)—Rapsgate (IRE) **J S Morrison & Raymond McNeill**
31 **HANALEI BAY (IRE)**, b c Tamayuz—Genial Jenny (IRE) **Mrs F. E. Mitchell**
32 **HELLO GORGEOUS**, b f Phoenix Reach (IRE)—Roman Fun (IRE) **Exchange Court Properties Ltd**
33 **LUCY BEE**, ch f Haafhd—Procession **Mrs L. B. K. Bone**
34 **NATURES LAW (IRE)**, b f Lawman (FR)—Misaayef (USA) **Mr K. W. Dalgleish**
35 **SALVATORE FURY (IRE)**, b g Strategic Prince—Nocturnal (FR) **Prestige Thoroughbred Racing**
36 **SECRET ADVICE**, ch f Sakhee's Secret—Flylowflylong (IRE) **G L S Partnership**
37 **STAR REQUEST**, b f Urgent Request (IRE)—Carahill (AUS) **Mr S. Aitken**
38 B c Medaglia d'oro (USA)—Viaduct (USA) **Weldspec Glasgow Limited**
39 **WINDSOR SECRET**, ch f Sakhee's Secret—Lady of Windsor (IRE) **Raeburn Brick Limited**

TWO-YEAR-OLDS

40 B c 30/4 Archipenko (USA)—Flylowflylong (IRE) (Danetime (IRE)) **G L S Partnership**
41 **FRANCESCADARIMINI**, ch f 23/2 Three Valleys (USA)—
                                Fountains Abbey (USA) (Giant's Causeway (USA)) **J. G. Thom**
42 B c 5/4 Diamond Green (FR)—Incendio (Siberian Express (USA)) (9523) **Middleham Park Racing III**
43 Ch c 19/4 Heliostatic (IRE)—Kimono (IRE) (Machiavellian (USA)) (19047)
44 Ch f 26/4 Compton Place—Lady of Windsor (IRE) (Woods of Windsor (USA)) **Raeburn Brick Limited**
45 B c 6/5 Iffraaj—Monarchy (IRE) (Common Grounds) (28571) **Weldspec Glasgow Limited**
46 B f 28/2 Captain Rio—Oceanico Dot Com (IRE) (Hernando (FR)) (4285) **Straightline Construction Ltd**
47 B c 26/4 Halling (USA)—Rapsgate (IRE) (Mozart (IRE)) **J. S. Morrison**
48 **ROBYNELLE**, b f 25/2 Royal Applause—Chicita Banana (Danehill Dancer (IRE)) (14285) **Mac Asphalt Ltd**
49 **SCOTS LAW (IRE)**, b f 10/4 Lawman (FR)—Misaayef (USA) (Swain (IRE))
50 Br f 6/2 Pastoral Pursuits—Twenty Seven (IRE) (Efisio) (2666) **KDR Ltd**
51 Ch c 5/4 Arakan (USA)—Vento Del Oreno (FR) (Lando (GER)) (4285) **Straightline Construction Ltd**

Other Owners: Mr G. Adams, Mr W. Brand, Mr William Burke, Mrs L. M. Burke, Mr Keith Dalgleish, Mr A. R. M. Galbraith, Mr A. Hamilton, Mr G. R. Leckie, Mr Raymond McNeill, Mr A. Moir, Mr J. S. Morrison, Mr T. S. Palin, Mr M. Prince, Mr D. G. Savala, Mr Colin Sinclair, Mr R. K. Walkinshaw.

Assistant Trainer: Kevin Dalgleish

---

150 **MR NEALE DALTON, Shifnal**
Postal: Sutton House Farm, Sutton Maddock, Shifnal, Shropshire, TF11 9NF
Contacts: PHONE (01952) 730656 FAX (01952) 730261 MOBILE (07831) 555351
E-MAIL neale.dalton@farming.co.uk

1 **CELTIC BALLAD (IRE)**, 7, br g Celtic Swing—Birdsong (IRE) **J. N. Dalton**
2 **GLIDEWELL**, 11, b g Gildoran—Throw In Your Hand **J. N. Dalton**
3 **KADUNA**, 8, b m Kadastrof (FR)—Mystic Legacy **J. N. Dalton**
4 **PLAYFUL GIRL (IRE)**, 5, b m Byron—Feminine Touch (IRE) **J. N. Dalton**
5 **PRIME DESIGN (IRE)**, 8, b m Blueprint (IRE)—Rare Vintage (IRE) **J. N. Dalton**

Other Owners: A. N. Dalton, Mrs C. A. Dalton.

151 MR HENRY DALY, Ludlow
Postal: **Downton Hall Stables, Ludlow, Shropshire, SY8 3DX**
Contacts: **OFFICE (01584) 873688 FAX (01584) 873525 MOBILE (07720) 074544**
E-MAIL henry@henrydaly.co.uk WEBSITE www.henrydaly.co.uk

1 ARCTIC BEN (IRE), 9, gr g Beneficial—Hurst Flyer **Mrs A. W. Timpson**
2 BEST DIRECTOR (IRE), 5, b g Oscar (IRE)—Taneys Leader (IRE) **R. M. Kirkland**
3 BRAVE BUCK, 5, b g Bollin Eric—Silken Pearls **P. E. Truscott**
4 BRIERY VIXEN, 7, ch m Alflora (IRE)—Briery Gale **Mrs H Plumbly J Trafford K Deane S Holme**
5 BRIGHT INTERVALS, 5, b m Flemensfirth (USA)—Sail By The Stars **T. F. F. Nixon**
6 CASTLE CONFLICT (IRE), 8, b g Close Conflict (USA)—Renty (IRE) **Strachan, Clarke, Gabb, Corbett & Salwey**
7 CROSTON (IRE), 5, ch g Presenting—Mistric **T. J. Hemmings**
8 CYRIEN STAR, 6, b g Bollin Eric—Sainte Etoile (FR) **Puteus Profundus**
9 FIDELOR (FR), 7, b g Sagacity (FR)—Fille Fidele (FR) **R. M. Kirkland**
10 GARTON KING, 9, b g Sovereign Water (FR)—Country Choice (IRE) **Trailer Resources Ltd**
11 GO WEST YOUNG MAN (IRE), 5, b g Westerner—Last of Her Line **T. F. F. Nixon**
12 GOOHAR (IRE), 4, b g Street Cry (IRE)—Reem Three **R. J. Brereton**
13 GROVE PRIDE, 8, b g Double Trigger (IRE)—Dara's Pride (IRE) **T. J. Hemmings**
14 HERONSHAW (IRE), 6, b g Heron Island (IRE)—
Cool Merenda (IRE) **Strachan, Stoddart, Griffith, Barlow & Harf'd**
15 KALI, 4, B f Multiplex—Hurtebise (FR) **Sir John Barlow**
16 KAYFLEUR, 4, b f Kayf Tara—Combe Florey **B. G. Hellyer & N. Statham**
17 KESHI PEARL, 5, b m Kayf Tara—Pearly-B (IRE) **The Wadeley Partnership**
18 KINGSMERE, 8, b g King's Theatre (IRE)—Lady Emily **Hamer & Hawkes**
19 KRIS SPIN (IRE), 5, br g Kris Kin (USA)—Auditing Empress (IRE) **Mrs D. J. Ralph**
20 LORD GRANTHAM (IRE), 6, b g Definite Article—Last of Her Line **T. F. F. Nixon**
21 MICKIE, 5, gr m Kayf Tara—Island Mist **Ludlow Racing Partnership**
22 NEOPOLIS (FR), 12, ch g Ragmar (FR)—Apside (FR) **The Earl Cadogan**
23 NO DUFFER, 6, ch g Karinga Bay—Dolly Duff **Mr D. C. Robey**
24 OYSTER SHELL, 6, br g Bollin Eric—Pearly-B (IRE) **The Glazeley Partnership 2**
25 PEARLYSTEPS, 10, ch g Alflora (IRE)—Pearly-B (IRE) **The Glazeley Partnership**
26 PICKAMUS (FR), 10, gr g April Night (FR)—Duchesse du Cochet (FR) **Neville Statham & Family**
27 POSSOL (FR), 10, b g Robin des Pres (FR)—Alberade (FR) **Neville Statham & Family**
28 QUENTIN COLLONGES (FR), 9, gr g Dom Alco (FR)—Grace Collonges (FR) **Neville Statham & Family**
29 ROCKITEER (IRE), 10, b g Rudimentary (USA)—Party Woman (IRE) **Michael O'Flynn & John Nesbitt**
30 SAFRAN DE COTTE (FR), 7, gr g Dom Alco (FR)—Vanille de Cotte (FR) **Mrs A. W. Timpson**
31 SANDYNOW (IRE), 8, ch g Old Vic—Kasterlee (FR) **The Hon Mrs M. J. Heber-Percy**
32 SURE THING (FR), 7, b g Ragmar (FR)—Harpe (FR) **H. D. J. Daly**
33 TARA MIST, 4, gr f Kayf Tara—Island Mist **Mrs E. Strachan**
34 THE FALKLANDER, 9, gr g Silver Patriarch (IRE)—Island Mist **J. B. Sumner**
35 TIMPO (FR), 10, ch g Baby Turk—Faensa (FR) **Mrs A. W. Timpson**
36 TOBY BELCH (IRE), 10, ch g Presenting—Peptic Lady (IRE) **Strachan, Griffith, Gabb, Lewis & Lawson**
37 TOOT SWEET (IRE), 6, b m Generous (IRE)—Cresswell Native (IRE) **A. J. Haden**
38 TOP TOTTI, 5, b m Sir Harry Lewis (USA)—Jannina (FR) **E. R. Hanbury**
39 TYGER PRYNT (IRE), 5, b m Presenting—Beauchamp Gigi (IRE) **Lord Daresbury**
40 UP TO THE MARK, 8, b g Mark of Esteem (IRE)—Villella **Strachan, Gabb, Griffith, Harford, Lewis & Graham**
41 UPBEAT COBBLER (FR), 5, gr m Brier Creek (USA)—Jade de Chalamont (FR) **Mrs A. W. Timpson**
42 VICE ET VERTU (FR), 4, b g Network (GER)—Duchesse du Cochet (FR) **Neville Statham & Family**
43 WESSEX KING (IRE), 9, b g Second Empire (IRE)—Winchester Queen (IRE) **Mrs D. P. G. Flory**
44 WILD CARD, 6, b g First Trump—Vanina II (FR) **E. R. Hanbury**
45 WINDS AND WAVES (IRE), 7, b g Alflora (IRE)—Sail By The Stars **T. F. F. Nixon**

Other Owners: Mrs Henry Daly, Mr Henry Daly, Mrs K. Deane, Mrs Roger Gabb, Mrs Douglas Graham, Mrs J. G. Griffith, Mr C. M. Hamer, Mr H. Harford, Mr M. Hawkes, Mrs J. Hearn, Mrs S. Holme, Mr Peter Holt, Mrs A. S. Lawson, Mrs David Lewis, Mr R. Mapp, Mr John Nesbitt, Mr Michael O'Flynn, Mrs Helen Plumbly, Mr Neville Statham, Mrs P. Statham, Mr M. Stoddart, Mrs Richard Strachan, Mrs Jane Trafford.

Assistant Trainer: Alastair Ralph

Jockey (NH): Richard Johnson, Andrew Tinkler. **Conditional:** Jake Greenall.

152 MR PHILIP DANDO, Peterston-Super-Ely
Postal: **Springfield Court, Peterston-Super-Ely, Cardiff, South Glamorgan, CF5 6LG**
Contacts: **PHONE (01446) 760012 MOBILE (07872) 965395**

1 AUTUMN HAZE, 8, b g Chaddleworth (IRE)—Kristal Haze **P. C. Dando**
2 ILLEGALE (IRE), 7, b m Poliglote—Pinkai (IRE) **Hanford's Chemist Ltd**
3 RAINBOW HAZE, 7, b g Rainbow High—Kristal Haze **Mr Phillip Dando & Dr Michael Armitage**
4 RUBY HAZE, 6, ch m Dreams End—Kristal Haze **Dreaming Of Cleeve**

Other Owners: Dr M. G. Armitage, Mr P. J. Cardosi.

Assistant Trainer: Miss Rebecca Dando

153 MR VICTOR DARTNALL, Barnstaple
Postal: **Higher Shutscombe Farm, Charles, Brayford, Barnstaple, Devon, EX32 7PU**
Contacts: **PHONE (01598) 710280 FAX (01598) 710708 MOBILE (07974) 374272**
E-MAIL victor@victordartnallracing.com WEBSITE www.victordartnallracing.com

1 ACE HIGH, 9, b g Kayf Tara—Celtic Native (IRE) **All The Aces**
2 AMBION WOOD (IRE), 7, b g Oscar (IRE)—Dorans Grove **Mr O. C. R. Wynne & Mrs S. J. Wynne**
3 EXMOOR RANGER (IRE), 11, ch g Grand Plaisir (IRE)—Slyguff Torus (IRE) **The Rangers Partnership**
4 GILES CROSS (IRE), 9, b g Saddlers' Hall (IRE)—Mystockings **Mrs K. Birchenhough**
5 GREAT GUSTO (IRE), 7, ch g Moscow Society (USA)—Warm Front **Mr D G Staddon, Mr M Bevan, Mr A Saye**
6 HENRY HOOK (IRE), 9, ch g Presenting—Swing The Lead (IRE) **Under The Radar**
7 HENRY KING (IRE), 9, gr g Great Palm (USA)—Presenting Shares (IRE) **Mrs C. M. Barber**
8 HONOURABLE ARTHUR (IRE), 10, br g Presenting—Ronkino (IRE) **Miss A. J. Woolley**
9 JEWELLERY (IRE), 6, b br m King's Best (USA)—Eilean Shona **M. J. Rowe**
10 KNOW MORE OATS (IRE), 5, b g Sanglamore (USA)—Greenacre Mandalay (IRE)
11 MIC'S DELIGHT (IRE), 9, b g Witness Box (USA)—Warrior Princess (IRE) **The Higos Hopefuls**
12 MIGHTY MONTY, 8, br g Overbury (IRE)—Ruby Star (IRE) **V. R. A. Dartnall**
13 MOLESKIN (IRE), 10, b g Saddlers' Hall (IRE)—Magic Gale (IRE) **Mrs C. M. Barber**
14 MR HOOPER, 7, b g Karinga Bay—Rempstone **Mrs J. E. Purdie**
15 MYSOCKS, 7, ch g Lahib (USA)—Mystockings **Mrs K. Birchenhough**
16 NICTO DE BEAUCHENE (FR), 12, b g Nashamaa—Chipie d'angron (FR) **Mrs S. De Wilde**
17 REGAL PRESENCE (IRE), 6, ch g Presenting—Lucy Lodge (IRE) **Fine Wine & Bubbly**
18 REQUIN (FR), 8, b br g Video Rock (FR)—Funkia (FR) **Mrs S. De Wilde**
19 RICHARD'S SUNDANCE (IRE), 11, b g Saddlers' Hall (IRE)—
                            Celestial Rose (IRE) **Elizabeth Masterman & Sara Vernon**
20 ROUDOUDOU VILLE (FR), 8, b br g Winning Smile (FR)—Jadoudy Ville (FR) **Mrs S. De Wilde**
21 SAMSON'S BAY (IRE), 5, b g Oscar (IRE)—Living A Dream (IRE) **The Hake & Northover Partnership**
22 SEEBRIGHT, 6, b g Milan—Aranga (IRE) **Mrs D. J. Fleming**
23 SHAMMICK BOY (IRE), 8, b g Craigsteel—Dulcet Music (IRE) **First Brayford Partnership**
24 SILVER COMMANDER, 6, gr g Silver Patriarch (IRE)—New Dawn **Exe Valley Racing**
25 SLEEPING CITY (FR), 6, b br g Sleeping Car (FR)—City Prospect (FR) **The Whacko Partnership**
26 STARSKY DES MOTTES (FR), 7, b g Useful (FR)—Camille des Mottes (FR) **V. R. A. Dartnall**
27 THREE OLD AMIGOS, 7, b g Karinga Bay—Quiet Confidence (IRE) **A. Hordle, V. Dartnall & G. Dartnall**
28 TOLKEINS TANGO (IRE), 5, ch g Beneficial—Aule (FR) **Mrs S. M. Hall**
29 TUROYAL (FR), 5, gr g Turgeon (USA)—Quelle Est Belle (FR) **O. J. W. Pawle**
30 TWYFORD, 6, b g Bach (IRE)—Commanche Token (IRE) **Under The Radar**
31 UN BLEU A L'AAM (FR), 5, b g Shaanmer (IRE)—Bleu Perle (FR) **F. R. Williamson**

Other Owners: Mr M. Bevan, Mr T. G. Cowell, Mrs Paula Cunliffe, Mr V. R. A. Dartnall, Mr G. A. Dartnall, Mr Jeffery Edelman, Mr Peter Emery, Mrs Jill Emery, Mrs Mary Fletcher, Mr. I. F. Gosden, Mr B. Greening, Mr G. D. Hake, Mr Bill Hinge, Mr A. Hordle, Mr G. Kennington, Mr G. Leatherbarrow, Mrs Elizabeth Masterman, Mrs L. M. Northover, Mr M. W. Richards, Mr P. A. Roberts, Mr Mike Rowe, Mr T. Saye, Mr John Searchfield, Mr D. G. Staddon, Mrs Sara Vernon, Mr R. Watts, Mr C. R. Wilde, Mr David Willis, Mrs S. J. Wynne, Mr O. C. R. Wynne.

Assistant Trainer: G A Dartnall

Jockey (NH): Andrew Glassonbury. **Amateur:** Mr Josh Guerriero.

154 MR TOM DASCOMBE, Malpas
Postal: **Manor House Stables, Malpas, Cheshire, SY14 8AD**
Contacts: **PHONE** (01948) 820485 **FAX** (01948) 820495 **MOBILE** (07973) 511664
E-MAIL tom@manorhousestables.com **WEBSITE** www.manorhousestables.com

1 **ADORABLE CHOICE (IRE)**, 5, b br m Choisir (AUS)—Burnin' Memories (USA) **Mr J. D. Brown**
2 **ANACONDA (FR)**, 4, b c Anabaa (USA)—Porretta (IRE) **The MHS 8X8 Partnership**
3 **ANTON CHIGURH**, 4, b g Oasis Dream—Barathiki **Panarea Racing**
4 **BALLISTA (IRE)**, 5, b g Majestic Missile (IRE)—Ancient Secret **Well Done Top Man Partnership**
5 **BEAR BEHIND (IRE)**, 4, b g Kodiac—Gerobies Girl (USA) **Bellman Black Marantelli Owen**
6 **BROCKWELL**, 4, b g Singspiel (IRE)—Noble Plum (IRE) **South Wind Racing 3**
7 **BROWN PANTHER**, 5, b h Shirocco (GER)—Treble Heights (IRE) **Mr A. Black & Owen Promotions Limited**
8 **CHOSEN CHARACTER (IRE)**, 5, b g Choisir (AUS)—Out of Thanks (IRE) **Aykroyd & Sons Limited**
9 **DECISION BY ONE**, 4, ch g Bahamian Bounty—Intellibet One **Manor House Racing Club**
10 **ELECTRIC QATAR**, 4, b g Pastoral Pursuits—Valandraud (IRE) **Mr A. Black & Owen Promotions Limited**
11 **EQUALIZER**, 4, b c Authorized (IRE)—Octaluna **L. A. Bellman**
12 **GAUL WOOD (IRE)**, 4, b g Amadeus Wolf—Emly Express (IRE) **Star Sports**
13 **KENNY POWERS**, 4, b g Vital Equine (IRE)—Alexander Ballet **First Manor**
14 **MENELIK (IRE)**, 4, b g Oasis Dream—Chica Roca (USA) **L. A. Bellman**

THREE-YEAR-OLDS

15 **APE ATTACK**, ch f Nayef (USA)—Patacake Patacake (USA) **A. W. Black**
16 **ARCHIE STEVENS**, b g Pastoral Pursuits—Miss Wells (IRE) **Mr L Bellman & Manor House Stables LLP**
17 **BARRACUDA BOY (IRE)**, b c Bahamian Bounty—Madame Boulangere **L. A. Bellman**
18 **BOMBER THORN**, b c Manduro (GER)—Treble Heights (IRE) **Owen Promotions Limited**
19 **BRAVE ACCLAIM (IRE)**, b c Acclamation—Indienne (IRE) **Mr G Lowe & Mrs A Whiteside**
20 **CAPO ROSSO (IRE)**, b g Red Clubs (IRE)—Satin Cape (IRE) **Deva Racing Red Clubs Partnership**
21 **COOL RUNNINGS (IRE)**, gr c Dalakhani (IRE)—Aguinaga (IRE) **Siwan & David Ward Jnr**
22 **DEAUVILLE PRINCE (FR)**, b c Holy Roman Emperor (IRE)—
               Queen of Deauville (FR) **N & S Mather, C Ledigo, L Basran**
23 **DOUBLE DISCOUNT (IRE)**, b g Invincible Spirit (IRE)—Bryanstown Girl (IRE) **L. A. Bellman**
24 **ELUSIVE BLEU (IRE)**, b c Elusive City (USA)—Jamrah (IRE) **Sharon Mather & Noel Martin**
25 **EVAN ELPUS (IRE)**, br g Footstepsinthesand—Birthday (IRE) **A. W. Black**
26 **FAT GARY**, ch g Dutch Art—Suzuki (IRE) **Manor House Stables LLP**
27 **GOOD EVANS**, ch c Mount Nelson—Alexia Reveuse (IRE) **Manor House Stables LLP**
28 **HURRY HOME POPPA (IRE)**, b c Holy Roman Emperor—My Renee (USA) **Mr D. Ward**
29 **ICE PIE**, b f Mount Nelson—Statua (IRE) **Mr A. Black & Owen Promotions Limited**
30 **LORD ASHLEY (IRE)**, ch g Iffraaj—Mrs Dalloway (IRE) **Mr D. R. Passant**
31 **MISS AVONBRIDGE (IRE)**, b f Avonbridge—Red Planet **Deva Racing Avonbridge Partnership**
32 **MONTJESS (IRE)**, b f Montjeu (IRE)—Wing Stealth (IRE) **The Tipperary Partners**
33 **MULLIT (IRE)**, b g Kodiac—Gouache (IRE) **Gary & Linnet Woodward**
34 **NOBLE BACCHUS (IRE)**, b g Acclamation—Vintage Tipple (IRE) **Lowe Silver Deal**
35 **NORTHERN STAR (IRE)**, b f Montjeu (IRE)—Slow Sand (USA) **Mr D. Ward**
36 **PIPPY**, b g Exceed And Excel (AUS)—Gandini **Mr & Mrs W. Rooney**
37 **SAGA LOUT**, b g Assertive—Intellibet One **L. A. Bellman**
38 **SPYMISTRESS**, ch f Sakhee's Secret—Martha (IRE) **Mr P. A. Deal & Mr A. Black**
39 **SWITCHAROONEY (IRE)**, b c Bahamian Bounty—Amazon Beauty (IRE) **Mr & Mrs W. Rooney**
40 **TAMALETTA (IRE)**, ch f Tamayuz—Annaletta **L. A. Bellman**
41 **THIS IS NICE (IRE)**, ch f Exceed And Excel (AUS)—Spanish Quest **L. A. Bellman**
42 **TRINITYELITEDOTCOM (IRE)**, b g Elusive City (USA)—Beal Ban (IRE) **Manor House Stables LLP**
43 **UNKNOWN VILLAIN (IRE)**, gr g Verglas (IRE)—Ragtime Blues (IRE) **Panarea Racing**
44 **WALL OF SOUND**, b f Singspiel (IRE)—Veiled Beauty (USA) **A. W. Black**
45 **ZARLA**, b f Zamindar (USA)—Ikhteyaar (USA) **K. P. Trowbridge**

TWO-YEAR-OLDS

46 B c 11/3 Royal Applause—Aegean Shadow (Sakhee (USA)) (40000) **Manor House Stables LLP**
47 B f 14/3 High Chaparral (IRE)—
               All Embracing (IRE) (Night Shift (USA)) (26190) **Laurence Bellman & David Lowe**
48 B f 12/2 Winker Watson—Baldovina (Tale of The Cat (USA)) **A. W. Black**
49 Gr f 3/3 Verglas (IRE)—Barathiki (Barathea (IRE)) (16666) **Manor House Stables LLP**
50 **BETTY THE THIEF (IRE)**, b f 24/3 Teofilo (IRE)—Siphon Melody (USA) (Siphon (BRZ)) (20000) **Mr D. Ward**
51 B c 24/3 Footstepsinthesand—
               Bright Bank (IRE) (Sadler's Wells (USA)) (67460) **L Bellman, D Lowe, K Trowbridge**
52 B c 14/4 Kodiac—Brizana (USA) (Diesis) (11110) **The MHS 2013 Partnership**
53 B f 10/1 Haatef (USA)—Cafe Creme (IRE) (Catrail (USA)) (15872) **The MHS 2013 Partnership**

MR TOM DASCOMBE - Continued

54 B c 12/3 Holy Roman Emperor (IRE)—
Calypso Dancer (FR) (Celtic Swing) (34285) **Attenborough Bellman Ingram Lowe**
55 B c 24/3 Invincible Spirit (IRE)—Chica Roca (USA) (Woodman (USA)) (75396) **Manor House Stables LLP**
56 Ro c 11/4 Invincible Spirit (IRE)—
Exclusive Approval (USA) (With Approval (CAN)) (85000) **Manor House Stables LLP**
57 GABBLE, ch f 20/2 Compton Place—Royal Manor (King's Best (USA)) (5238) **Owen Promotions Limited**
58 B c 1/3 Green Desert (USA)—Hawas (Mujtahid (USA)) (39681) **David Lowe & Laurence Bellman**
59 HICKSTER (IRE), br c 19/4 Intense Focus (USA)—
Surrender To Me (USA) (Royal Anthem (USA)) (7936) **Edwards Hughes Jenkins Roberts**
60 B f 7/3 Kodiac—Infinitely (Fantastic Light (USA)) (15873) **Edwards Hughes Jenkins Roberts**
61 B f 30/3 Amadeus Wolf—Italian Affair (Fumo di Londra (IRE)) (2857) **The MHS 2013 Partnership**
62 Ch c 28/4 Exceed And Excel (AUS)—Jeed (IRE) (Mujtahid (USA)) (60000) **Manor House Stables LLP**
63 B f 28/1 Aqlaam—Jinskys Gift (IRE) (Cadeaux Genereux) (14285) **De La Warr Racing**
64 B c 28/3 Myboycharlie (IRE)—Lady Raj (USA) (El Prado (IRE)) (49206) **Manor House Stables LLP**
65 B c 15/3 Bahamian Bounty—Lindesberg (Doyoun) (33333) **Manor House Stables LLP**
66 B f 30/3 Dubawi (IRE)—Logic (Slip Anchor) (48000) **Manor House Stables LLP**
67 B f 18/2 Art Connoisseur (IRE)—
Madame Boulangere (Royal Applause) (34126) **Laurence Bellman & Lyn Rutherford**
68 Ch f 3/2 Compton Place—Max One Two Three (IRE) (Princely Heir (IRE)) **A. W. Black**
69 B f 17/3 Whipper (USA)—May (Montjeu (IRE)) (21428) **The Whipper Partnership**
70 Ch f 5/5 Medicean—Nuit Sans Fin (FR) (Lead On Time (USA)) (15872) **Mr D. R. Passant**
71 B c 29/1 Bushranger (IRE)—Operissimo (Singspiel (IRE)) (60000) **Aykroyd & Sons Limited**
72 PASSIONATE AFFAIR (IRE), ch c 4/5 Broken Vow (USA)—
Charmgeer (USA) (Nureyev (USA)) (12698) **The Passionate Partnership**
73 Ch c 28/2 Dandy Man (IRE)—Pearly Brooks (Efisio) (28571) **Manor House Stables LLP**
74 B f 14/4 Compton Place—
Queen Bodicea (IRE) (Revoque (IRE)) (53174) **N & S Mather, Owen Promotions, I Flanagan**
75 Ch c 18/2 Compton Place—Raphaela (FR) (Octagonal (NZ)) (41904) **L. A. Bellman**
76 B f 2/2 Naqoos—Safqa (Singspiel (IRE)) (20952) **A. W. Black**
77 SHELLEY'S CHOICE (IRE), b f 27/1 Lawman (FR)—
Fantastic Opinion (IRE) (Fantastic Light (USA)) (22221) **O. P. Building Maintenance Services Ltd**
78 B c 3/5 High Chaparral (IRE)—Shine Like A Star (Fantastic Light (USA)) (70000) **Manor House Stables LLP**
79 Ch f 15/2 Rock of Gibraltar (IRE)—
Sightseer (USA) (Distant View (USA)) (25396) **Deva Racing Classic Partnership**
80 B br c 22/4 Kodiac—Teem (IRE) (Xaar) (15872) **Manor House Stables LLP**
81 B f 14/3 Tagula (IRE)—Teodora (IRE) (Fairy King (USA)) (28571) **Attenborough Bellman Ingram Lowe**
82 WHALEWEIGH STATION, b c 30/1 Zamindar (USA)—Looby Loo (Kyllachy) **A. W. Black**
83 B c 3/3 Bushranger (IRE)—Zaynaba (IRE) (Traditionally (USA)) (38095) **Manor House Stables LLP**

Other Owners: N. B. Attenborough, A. M. Basing, Mr L. S. Basran MBE, Mr S. Brewster, Mrs M. Coxon, Mrs S. A. E. Dascombe, B. Dascombe, T. G. Dascombe, Lord De La Warr, Countess De La Warr, P. A. Deal, Mr M. Edwards, Mr I. R. Flanagan, M. D. Foster, Mrs J. Foster, Mr D. J. Haddrell, Mr N. J. Hughes, Mrs C. L. Ingram, Mr B. Keith, Mr C. Ledigo, Mr E. N. Liddiard, Mr D. J. Lowe, G. A. Lowe, Mr D. I. Lubert, Mr B. Marantelli, Mr N. P. P. Martin, Mr N. P. Mather, Mrs S. E. Mather, Mr G. Nicholas, Mr D. O'Sullivan, Mrs R. O'Sullivan, Mr M. Owen, Mr C. D. Pritchard, Mr C. R. Pugh, Mrs B. M. Richmond, S. E. Roberts, Mr W. Rooney, L. M. Rutherford, Mr G. Shepherd, M. J. Silver, Stoneygate 48 Limited, Ms S. A. Ward, Mr D. A. Ward, Mrs B. A. Whiteside, G. Woodward, Mrs L. Woodward.

Assistant Trainer: Colin Gorman

Jockey (flat): Richard Kingscote

155	**MR JOHN DAVIES, Darlington** Postal: Denton Grange, Piercebridge, Darlington, Co. Durham, DL2 3TZ Contacts: **PHONE** (01325) 374366 **MOBILE** (07746) 292782 E-MAIL johndavieshorses@live.co.uk

1 DOYENTHEDECENTHING, 5, gr m Doyen (IRE)—Nearly Decent **Mr P. Taylor**
2 TAMARA BAY, 5, b m Selkirk (USA)—Tamalain (USA) **Mr & Mrs R. Scott**
3 THE OSTEOPATH (IRE), 10, ch g Danehill Dancer (IRE)—Miss Margate (IRE) **K. Kirkup**

THREE-YEAR-OLDS

4 MILLWOOD, b g Millkom—Wedgewood Star **K. Kirkup**
5 NOOSA SOUND, ch f Halling (USA)—Crimson Topaz **Mr P. Taylor**
6 TOCCOA, gr f Great Palm (USA)—Pleasant Dreams **Mr Christopher Davies**

MR JOHN DAVIES - Continued

TWO-YEAR-OLDS

7 B c 11/4 Avonbridge—Swift Baba (USA) (Deerhound (USA)) (3047) **Mr Christopher Davies**
8 B c 26/5 Ferrule (IRE)—Wedgwood Star (Bishop of Cashel) **Mr Kevin Kirkup**

Other Owners: Mr Robert Scott, Mrs P. M. Scott.

Jockey (flat): P. J. McDonald.

MR PAUL DAVIES, Bromyard
Postal: **20 Hatton Park, Bromyard, Herefordshire, HR7 4EY**

1 EMMA SODA, 8, b m Milan—Ms Trude (IRE) **Mr P. S. Davies**

157
MISS SARAH-JAYNE DAVIES, Leominster
Postal: **The Upper Withers, Hundred Lane, Kimbolton, Leominster, Herefordshire, HR6 0HZ**
Contacts: **PHONE (01584) 711780 MOBILE (07779) 797079**
E-MAIL sjdracing@live.co.uk

1 ACCESSALLAREAS (IRE), 8, ch g Swift Gulliver (IRE)—Arushofgold (IRE) **Mr D. R. Bevan**
2 DRESDEN (IRE), 5, b g Diamond Green (FR)—So Precious (IRE) **Miss S. J. Davies**
3 GRIMLEY GIRL, 7, b m Sir Harry Lewis (USA)—Grimley Gale (IRE) **R. M. Phillips**
4 MISS DIMPLES (IRE), 4, gr f Tikkanen (USA)—Scolboa House (IRE) **Ms H. Taylor**
5 NOBLE CHIC, 8, ch g Generous (IRE)—Chicodove **Miss S. J. Davies**
6 PEMBROKE HOUSE, 6, gr g Terimon—Bon Coeur **Mr A. Mortimer**
7 TWIN BARRELS, 6, ch g Double Trigger (IRE)—Caballe (USA) **K. E. Stait**

Other Owners: Mr Andrew Mortimer.

Assistant Trainer: Jeremy Mahot

Jockey (NH): Will Kennedy, Liam Treadwell. **Amateur:** Miss Sarah-Jayne Davies, Mr Jeremy Mahot.

158
MIISS JOANNA DAVIS, East Garston
Postal: **South Cottage, Pounds Farm, East Garston, Hungerford, Berkshire, RG17 7HU**
Contacts: **PHONE (01488) 649977 FAX (01488) 649977 MOBILE (07879) 811535**
E-MAIL davisjo_007@hotmail.com WEBSITE www.jodavisracing.com

1 CLOVER NOVA, 6, b m Exit To Nowhere (USA)—Catriona **Mr R. Plant**
2 ELIXIR DU LAC, 6, gr m Fair Mix (IRE)—Hutcel Loch **V. R. Bedley**
3 GO ANNIE, 5, gr m Proclamation (IRE)—Bright Spangle (IRE) **Lockstone Business Services Ltd**
4 HOLLIE, 5, ch m Bertolini (USA)—Musical Refrain (IRE) **Miss J. S. Davis**
5 INDIEFRONT, 4, b f Indesatchel (IRE)—Jonchee (FR) **Mr B. Hatton**
6 KINGSTON TIGER, 5, b g Tiger Hill (GER)—Gretna **D. Clayton**
7 LEEROAR (IRE), 5, b g Let The Lion Roar—Leane (IRE) **The Hard Hat Gang**
8 4, B br g Cape Cross (IRE)—Lilia **Mrs P. Brown**
9 LYMM GREY, 4, gr f Fair Mix (IRE)—Ellie Bee **D. Clayton**
10 NATAANI (IRE), 10, br g Presenting—Clahada Rose (IRE) **Mr A. G. Worth**
11 PASSATO (GER), 9, b g Lando (GER)—Passata (FR) **P. J. Ponting**
12 ROSE OF THE WORLD (IRE), 5, ch m Vinnie Roe (IRE)—Frankly Native (IRE) **Oakhedge Racing**
13 SWEET LIKE YOU, 5, b m Kayf Tara—Ginger Rogers **P. J. Ponting**
14 THE IRON MAIDEN, 4, gr ro f Proclamation (IRE)—Bright Spangle (IRE) **Lockstone Business Services Ltd**
15 WAS MY VALENTINE, 6, b m Best of The Bests (IRE)—Eleonor Sympson **Oakhedge Racing**

TWO-YEAR-OLDS

16 B f 7/4 Rainbow High—Bright Spangle (IRE) (General Monash (USA)) **Miss J. S. Davis**

Other Owners: Mr A. D. Hutchinson, Mrs J. P. Hutchinson, Mr M. Morgan, Mrs Mary Tobin.

159 MISS ZOE DAVISON, East Grinstead

Postal: **Shovelstrode Racing Stables, Shovelstrode Lane, Ashurstwood, East Grinstead, West Sussex, RH19 3PN**
Contacts: **FAX** (01342) 323153 **MOBILE** (07970) 839357 & (07812) 007554
E-MAIL andy01031976@yahoo.co.uk **WEBSITE** www.shovelstroderacing.co.uk

1 **AIREDALE LAD (IRE)**, 12, b g Charnwood Forest (IRE)—Tamarsiya (USA) **Mrs S. E. Colville**
2 **ASHMOLIAN (IRE)**, 10, b g Grand Lodge (USA)—Animatrice (USA) **The Secret Circle**
3 **CARBIS BAY**, 7, b g Deploy—Hi Lily **A. J. Irvine**
4 **DOLLY COLMAN**, 5, br gr m Diamond Green (FR)—Absolutely Cool (IRE) **Mr K. Corke**
5 **HIGHWAY JOE**, 6, b m Central Park (IRE)—Fringe Benefit (IRE) **Mr P. M. Mannion**
6 **HIGHWAY WARRIOR**, 4, b f Ishiguru (USA)—Blue Topaz (IRE) **Mr P. M. Mannion**
7 **HOMEWARD STRUT**, 4, ch g Needwood Blade—Piccante **Mr David J Bearman & Charlie's Starrs**
8 **INDIAN VIOLET (IRE)**, 7, b g Indian Ridge—Violet Spring (IRE) **Macable Partnership**
9 **JOHN'S GEM**, 8, ch g Silver Patriarch (IRE)—Hollow Legs **Golfguard Limited**
10 **JUMEIRAH LIBERTY**, 5, ch g Proclamation (IRE)—Gleam of Light (IRE) **The Lump O'Clock Syndicate**
11 **JUST BEWARE**, 11, b m Makbul—Bewails (IRE) **The Secret Circle**
12 **KELLYS EYE (IRE)**, 6, b g Noverre (USA)—Limit (IRE) **Macable Partnership**
13 **LINDSAY'S DREAM**, 7, b m Montjeu (IRE)—Lady Lindsay (IRE) **Mr D. P. O'Keeffe**
14 **MAC'S GREY (IRE)**, 6, gr g Great Palm (USA)—Gypsy Kelly (IRE) **Macable Partnership**
15 **NOBODY'S BUSINESS (IRE)**, 12, ch g Carroll House—Arctic Crush (IRE) **Shovelstrode Racing Club**
16 **NOZIC (FR)**, 12, b g Port Lyautey (FR)—Grizilh (FR) **The Lump O'Clock Syndicate**
17 **PIAZZA SAN PIETRO**, 7, ch g Compton Place—Rainbow Spectrum (FR) **Mr K. Corke**
18 **SHERJAWY (IRE)**, 9, b g Diktat—Arruhan (IRE) **Charlie's Starrs**
19 **SHROPSHIRELASS**, 10, b m Beat All (USA)—Emma-Lyne **The Secret Circle**
20 **SIMPSON MILLAR**, 4, b g Librettist (USA)—Scented Garden **CW Racing Club**
21 **STANDING STRONG (IRE)**, 5, b g Green Desert (USA)—Alexander Three D (IRE) **Mrs J. A. Irvine**
22 **TCHANG GOON (FR)**, 9, b g Marathon (USA)—Royal Hostess (IRE) **J. E. Belsey**
23 **THELORDBEWITHYOU (IRE)**, 9, b g Turtle Island (IRE)—Georgic **A. J. Irvine**
24 **WISHFORMORE (IRE)**, 6, b m Chevalier (IRE)—Terra Nova **Mr P. M. Mannion**

Other Owners: Mr S. W. Bain, Mr A. W. Bain, D. J. Bearman, S. J. Clare, Mr P. A. P. Clays, Miss Z. C. Davison, Mr S. Mackintosh, Mr F. W. Mackintosh, Mr D. Percival, A. N. Waters.

Assistant Trainer: A. Irvine

Jockey (flat): Sam Hitchcott. **Conditional:** Gemma Gracey-Davison.

160 MR ANTHONY DAY, Hinckley

Postal: **Wolvey Fields Farm, Coalpit Lane, Wolvey, Hinckley, Leicestershire, LE10 3HD**
Contacts: **PHONE** (01455) 220225 **MOBILE** (07842) 540137
E-MAIL kathy197@btinternet.com

1 **CHARMING LAD (IRE)**, 8, b g Dushyantor (USA)—Glens Lady (IRE) **Mrs K. D. Day**
2 **OHMS LAW**, 8, b g Overbury (IRE)—Polly Live Wire **Mrs K. D. Day**
3 **SHESLIKETHEWIND**, 5, b m Central Park (IRE)—Velvet Leaf **Mrs K. D. Day**

Assistant Trainer: Mrs K. D. Day (07546) 593485

Amateur: Mr Jon Day.

161 MISS LISA DAY, Pontypool

Postal: **Well Cottage, Penyhroel, Pontypool, Gwent, NP4 5XS**

1 **BABE HEFFRON (IRE)**, 12, ch g Topanoora—Yellow Ochre (IRE) **Miss L. Day**
2 **EDGEVINE**, 9, b m Grape Tree Road—Vieille Russie **W. J. Day**
3 **STRAND LINE (IRE)**, 13, b g Supreme Leader—Good Credentials **Miss L. Day**

162 MR ED DE GILES, Ledbury
Postal: **Lilly Hall Farm, Little Marcle, Ledbury, Herefordshire, HR8 2LD**
Contacts: **PHONE (01531) 637369 MOBILE (07811) 388345**

1 **A HEART BEATS ON (IRE)**, 7, b g Kaieteur (USA)—Helen's Sisters (IRE) **GLMM**
2 **AJZAL (IRE)**, 9, b g Alhaarth (IRE)—Alkaffeyeh (IRE) **John Manser & Claire de Giles**
3 **BREAK RANK (USA)**, 4, b c Broken Vow (USA)—Divert (USA) **T. Gould**
4 **CRAVAT**, 4, b c Dubai Destination (USA)—Crinolette (IRE) **T. Gould**
5 **CROQUEMBOUCHE (IRE)**, 4, b g Acclamation—Wedding Cake (IRE) **Mr P. J. Manser**
6 **DIAMONDHEAD (IRE)**, 4, b c Kyllachy—Hammrah **T. Gould**
7 **GENTLEMAN IS BACK (USA)**, 5, b br g Johannesburg (USA)—Torros Straits (USA) **T. Gould**
8 **GO NANI GO**, 7, b g Kyllachy—Go Between **T. Gould**
9 **GREEK ISLANDS (IRE)**, 5, b g Oasis Dream—Serisia (FR) **E. B. de Giles**
10 **JINKER NOBLE**, 4, b c Green Desert (USA)—Depressed **Mr A. P. Ridgers**
11 **KINGSGATE CHOICE (IRE)**, 6, b g Choisir (AUS)—Kenema (IRE) **T. Gould**
12 **LIVING IT LARGE (FR)**, 6, ch g Bertolini (USA)—Dilag (IRE) **T. Gould**
13 **LUCKY BREEZE (IRE)**, 6, b m Key of Luck (USA)—Lasting Chance (USA) **C. C. Shand Kydd**
14 **MAHADEE (IRE)**, 8, br g Cape Cross (IRE)—Rafiya **2 1/2 - 3 1/2 Club**
15 **MEN DON'T CRY (IRE)**, 4, b g Street Cry (IRE)—Naissance Royale (IRE) **Clarke, King & Lewis**
16 **MINGUN BELL (USA)**, 6, b g Mingun (USA)—Miss Tippins (USA) **Blackham & Gould Partnership**
17 **MUTANAKER**, 6, b g Cape Cross (IRE)—Purple Haze (IRE) **Mr D. J. Greenall**
18 **NAABEGHA**, 6, ch g Muhtathir—Hawafiz **Tight Lines Partnership**
19 **PRINCE OF DREAMS**, 6, b g Sadler's Wells (USA)—Questina (FR) **Jennifer & Alex Viall**
20 **RYE TANGLE (IRE)**, 5, br g Catcher In The Rye (IRE)—Kadarassa (IRE) **E. B. de Giles**
21 **SHES ROSIE**, 5, b m Trade Fair—Wintzig **S. G. Martin**
22 **SPRINGINMYSTEP (IRE)**, 4, b c Footstepsinthesand—Joyful (IRE) **T. Gould**
23 **TIJUCA (IRE)**, 4, b f Captain Rio—Some Forest (IRE) **E. B. de Giles**
24 **TWENTY ONE CHOICE (IRE)**, 4, ch g Choisir (AUS)—Midnight Lace **Penna Racing**

THREE-YEAR-OLDS
25 B f Ishiguru (USA)—Cute **E. B. de Giles**

TWO-YEAR-OLDS
26 B c 13/4 Bahamian Bounty—Brazilian Style (Exit To Nowhere (USA)) (12000) **E. B. de Giles**
27 Gr c 7/3 Medicean—Bunditten (IRE) (Soviet Star (USA)) (35000) **Mr S. Treacher**
28 Gr c 17/4 Verglas (IRE)—Cloudchaser (IRE) (Red Ransom (USA)) (5238) **Mrs S. Smith**
29 B c 30/4 Kodiac—Kris's Bank (Inchinor) (15872) **Mr S. Treacher**
30 Ch c 10/4 Captain Rio—Quizzical Lady (Mind Games) (18253) **Mr A. Mortazavi**
31 B c 12/4 Iffraaj—Royal Esteem (Mark of Esteem (IRE)) (19047) **Mr A. Mortazavi**
32 B c 23/3 Tiger Hill (IRE)—Sagamartha (Rainbow Quest (USA)) (13000) **E. B. de Giles**

Other Owners: Mr K. Blackham, Mr D. Clarke, Mr M. J. Gibbons, I. W. Gibson, C. J. King, Mrs E. V. Lewis, Mr C. Morris, Mr M. C. Penna, A. J. Viall, Mrs C. R. de Giles.

163 MR JONATHEN DE GILES, Highworth
Postal: **South Farm, Stanton Fitzwarren, Swindon, Wiltshire, SN6 7RZ**
Contacts: **PHONE (01793) 763094 FAX (01793) 763109**
E-MAIL jonathen.degiles@btinternet.com

1 **PRINCE NAMID**, 11, b g Namid—Fen Princess (IRE) **Mr J. A. T. de Giles**
2 **SECRET WORLD (IRE)**, 10, ch g Spinning World (USA)—Classic Park **Mr J. A. T. de Giles**
3 **THEAIMANS GIRL**, 7, b m Band On The Run—Panienka (POL) **The Milk Sheiks**

Other Owners: Mr S. M. P. Leahy, Mr K. D. Linsley.

164 MR BEN DE HAAN, Lambourn
Postal: **Fair View, Long Hedge, Lambourn, Newbury, Berkshire, RG17 8NA**
Contacts: **PHONE (01488) 72163 FAX (01488) 71306 MOBILE (07831) 104574**
E-MAIL bendehaanracing@aol.com WEBSITE www.bendehaanracing.com

1 **COOL HAND JAKE**, 7, b g Storming Home—Monawara (IRE) **Wedgewood Estates**
2 **DECIDING MOMENT (IRE)**, 7, b g Zagreb (USA)—Fontaine Jewel (IRE) **W. A. Tyrer**

MR BEN DE HAAN - Continued

3 **EDUCATED SON**, 5, br g Diktat—Spring Sunrise **Mrs D. Vaughan**
4 **GENERALYSE**, 4, b g Cadeaux Genereux—Dance To The Blues (IRE) **Mrs D. Vaughan**
5 **LONDON SILVER**, 4, b g Zafeen (FR)—Princess Londis **J. Simms**
6 **LOOKS LIKE SLIM**, 6, b g Passing Glance—Slims Lady **Mr M. Butler**
7 **MALIH**, 4, b g Echo of Light—Sultry Lass (USA) **Wedgewood Estates**
8 **NATIVE GALLERY (IRE)**, 8, gr g Portrait Gallery (IRE)—Native Bev (IRE) **W. A. Tyrer**
9 **NOM DE GUERRE (IRE)**, 11, b g Presenting—Asklynn (IRE) **Mr & Mrs Nicholas Tatman**
10 **OCULIST**, 5, b g Dr Fong (USA)—Eyes Wide Open **Mrs C. Walwyn**
11 **TENESSEE**, 6, b g Nayef (USA)—Shukran **Ms E. A. Judd**
12 **THE STOUT ITALIAN (IRE)**, 6, b g Milan—Clonogan (IRE) **Mr William A Tyrer & Mr Duncan Heath**

THREE-YEAR-OLDS

13 **ASSERTIVE AGENT**, b f Assertive—Agent Kensington **Wedgewood Estates**
14 **ICON DANCE**, b f Sixties Icon—Dance To The Blues (IRE) **Mrs D. Vaughan**
15 **ZETEAH**, b f Passing Glance—Ajeebah (IRE) **Ms E. A. Judd**

TWO-YEAR-OLDS

16 Ch f 23/4 Byron—Dance To The Blues (IRE) (Danehill Dancer (IRE)) **Mrs D. Vaughan**

Other Owners: B. D. Heath, N. A. Tatman, Mrs E. Tatman.

Jockey (flat): Adam Kirby. **Jockey (NH):** Noel Fehily, Daryl Jacob. **Apprentice:** Kirsten Smith.

---

165 MR GEOFFREY DEACON, Compton
Postal: **Hamilton Stables, Hockham Road, Compton, Newbury, Berkshire, RG20 6QJ**
Contacts: **MOBILE (07967) 626757**
E-MAIL geoffdeacon@aol.com WEBSITE www.geoffreydeacontraining.com

1 **AFFILIATE**, 5, ch m Nayef (USA)—Allied Cause **Woodhall, Nicol & Co**
2 **ARCTIC GUNNER**, 9, gr g Alflora (IRE)—Arctic Chick **D. Teevan**
3 **CONN MAN (IRE)**, 8, ch g Whitmore's Conn (USA)—Special Artist (IRE) **White Star Racing Syndicate**
4 **ESEEJ (USA)**, 8, ch g Aljabr (USA)—Jinaan (USA) **Miss S. J. Duckett**
5 **GLASTONBERRY**, 5, gr m Piccolo—Elderberry **Mr J. J. Kelly**
6 **PROPER VILLAN (IRE)**, 8, b br g Naheez (USA)—Nativa Negra (IRE) **Mr S. Darvall**
7 **STOCKADE**, 7, b g Alflora (IRE)—Norstock **The Stockade Partnership**
8 **VERMEYEN**, 4, b g Dutch Art—Madame Maxine (USA) **Miss S. J. Duckett**
9 **VICTORIAN NUMBER (FR)**, 5, ch g Numerous (USA)—Malaisia (FR) **Mr A. R. Pittman**

THREE-YEAR-OLDS

10 **BERTIE MOON**, b c Bertolini (USA)—Fleeting Moon **Mr J. J. Kelly**

Other Owners: Mr G. Deacon, Mrs A. Nicol, Mrs H. C. L. Woodhall, D. M. Woodhall.

Assistant Trainer: Sally Duckett

Jockey (flat): Sophie Doyle. **Jockey (NH):** Jimmy McCarthy. **Amateur:** Miss Emily MacMahon.

---

166 MR TIM DENNIS, Bude
Postal: **Thorne Farm, Bude, Cornwall, EX23 0LU**
Contacts: **PHONE (01288) 352849 MOBILE (07855) 785781**

1 **TANS HILL (IRE)**, 8, b g Revoque (IRE)—Lady Delight (IRE) **Mrs J. E. Dennis**
2 **WISHES AND STARS (IRE)**, 7, b m Old Vic—She's No Trouble (IRE) **Mrs J. E. Dennis**

167 **MR ROBIN DICKIN, Alcester**
Postal: **Hill Farm, Park Lane, Great Alne, Alcester, Warwickshire, B49 6HS**
Contacts: PHONE (01789) 488148 (01789) 488249 MOBILE (07979) 518593 / (07979) 518594
E-MAIL robin@robindickinracing.org.uk WEBSITE www.robindickinracing.org.uk

1 AMERICAN KISS (SWE), 4, b f American Post—Power Kiss (SWE) **Christer Svanholm AB**
2 ATHERSTONE HILL (IRE), 11, b g Presenting—Mystic Madam (IRE) **Colin & Co**
3 AUTUMM SPIRIT, 9, ch m Kadastrof (FR)—Dickies Girl **Mr Brian Wilson**
4 BADGERS COVE (IRE), 9, b g Witness Box (USA)—Celestial Rose (IRE) **E. R. C. Beech & B. Wilkinson**
5 BALLY LAGAN (IRE), 5, gr g Kalanisi (IRE)—Rose Palma (FR) **Park Lane Partnership**
6 BALLYHOOLEY BOY (IRE), 6, b g Oscar (IRE)—Nivalf **The Tricksters**
7 CORNISH ICE, 9, b g Dolpour—Icelandic Poppy **R. G. Whitehead**
8 DAN'S MARTHA, 5, b m Tagula (IRE)—Piedmont (UAE) **D. G. O. Partnership**
9 DANCE FOR LIVVY (IRE), 5, br m Kodiac—Dancing Steps **Mr M. J. James**
10 DANCING DAFFODIL, 8, ch m Kadastrof (FR)—Whistling Song **Mr Mr & Mrs Cooper and Mrs C Dickin**
11 5, B m Silver Patriarch (IRE)—Dickies Girl **Mr Brian Wilson**
12 ENTERTAIN ME, 9, b m Kadastrof (FR)—Just The Ticket (IRE) **Mrs A. L. Merry**
13 GRAYLYN AMBER, 8, b m Nomadic Way (USA)—State Lady (IRE) **Graham & Lynn Knight**
14 GRAYLYN RUBY (FR), 8, b g Limnos (JPN)—Nandi (FR) **Graham & Lynn Knight**
15 GRAYLYN VALENTINO, 4, b g Primo Valentino (IRE)—Rhuby River (IRE) **Graham & Lynn Knight**
16 GUNS OF LOVE (IRE), 11, b g Lord of Appeal—Golden Seekers **Whoops 72!**
17 KAWA (FR), 7, gr g Kouroun (FR)—Kulitch (FR) **P. R. Armour**
18 KITEGEN (IRE), 7, b g Milan—Keen Gale (IRE) **R. G. Whitehead**
19 LAIDBACK LEO, 5, ch g Golden Snake (USA)—Rockstine (IRE) **The Jameson & Elbro Partnership**
20 LAKE LEGEND, 9, b g Midnight Legend—Lac Marmot (FR) **J. Wright, P. Wilson, F. J. Allen & R. Preston**
21 MUSIC IN THE AIR, 9, ch m Kadastrof (FR)—Makin Whoopee (IRE) **Mrs A. L. Merry**
22 NICKS POWER (IRE), 7, b g Luso—Shii-Take's Girl **Mr J. F. R. Stainer**
23 PACCO (FR), 10, b g Assessor (IRE)—Uguette IV (FR) **Ray & Marian Elbro**
24 PIE POUDRE, 6, ch g Zafeen (FR)—Eglantine (IRE) **Bredon Hill Racing Club**
25 PLAYING WITH FIRE (IRE), 9, gr m Witness Box (USA)—Smokey Path (IRE) **Mrs A. L. Merry**
26 RESTLESS HARRY, 9, b g Sir Harry Lewis (USA)—Restless Native (IRE) **R. G. Whitehead**
27 RIPOFF, 8, b g Kadastrof (FR)—Just The Ticket (IRE) **Mrs A. L. Merry**
28 SCARLETT O'TARA, 7, b m Kayf Tara—Lynoso **Mr J. F. R. Stainer**
29 SIR DU BEARN (FR), 7, b br g Passing Sale (FR)—Girl du Bearn (FR) **Nic Allen & Carl Mason**
30 STORM QUEST, 6, ch m Storming Home—Rercherchee **Mr Andrew Bull**
31 THE ABSENT MARE, 5, gr m Fair Mix (IRE)—Precious Lucy (IRE) **Mr J. C. Clemmow**
32 THE DE THAIX (FR), 6, b g Polish Summer—Etoile de Thaix (FR) **John Priday**
33 THOMAS CRAPPER, 6, b g Tamure—Mollycarrs Gambul **Apis.uk.com**
34 TILT DU CHATELIER (FR), 6, ch g Arnaqueur (USA)—
Une Du Chatelier (FR) **Avante Leisure Group Holdings Limited**
35 TOM O'TARA, 9, b g Kayf Tara—Mrs May **G. Knight, D. Ward & C. Marriott**
36 TROYAN (IRE), 6, b g King's Theatre (IRE)—Talk The Talk **John Priday**
37 UNFORGETTABLE (IRE), 10, b g Norwich—Miss Lulu (IRE) **J. Rogers**
38 VALRENE, 7, b m Grape Tree Road—Across The Water **T. M. Mifflin**
39 WESTERLY BREEZE (IRE), 5, b g Westerner—Sup A Whiskey (IRE) **P. R. Armour**
40 YOUNG LOU, 4, b f Kadastrof (FR)—Wanna Shout **E. R. C. Beech & B. Wilkinson**

THREE-YEAR-OLDS

41 Gr g Kadastrof (FR)—My Beautiful Loser (IRE) **Mr John Clemmow**

Other Owners: N. J. Allen, E. R. C. Beech, Mr H. Brown, Mr D. J. Busby, Ms J. E. Clark, J. R. Cooper, Mrs M. A. Cooper, C. J. Dickin, Mrs C. M. Dickin, Mrs M. Elbro, Mr R. J. Elbro, Mrs J. Gibson, Mr B. M. R. Haslam, Mr Mark James, Mrs V. Jameson, Miss N. A. Jameson, Mr S. P. J. Kirby, G. Knight, Mrs L. C. Knight, Mr C. E. Mason, Mrs M. Payne, Mr Alan Varey, Mr P. Venvell, Mr A. M. Wadley, Mr R. G. Whitehead, B. Wilkinson, B. P. Wilson.

Assistant Trainer: Claire Dickin

Jockey (flat): Luke Morris, Martin Lane. **Jockey (NH):** Charlie Poste, Wayne Kavanagh. **Conditional:** Chris Ward, Arron Kennedy.

168 **MR JOHN DIXON, Carlisle**
Postal: **Moorend, Thursby, Carlisle, Cumbria, CA5 6QP**
Contacts: PHONE (01228) 711019

1 BALLELA ROAD (IRE), 11, b m Zaffaran (USA)—Ballela Girl (IRE) **Mrs S. F. Dixon**

MR JOHN DIXON - Continued

   2 **CROFTON ARCH**, 13, b g Jumbo Hirt (USA)—Joyful Imp **Mrs E. M. Dixon**
   3 **CROFTON LANE**, 7, b g And Beyond (IRE)—Joyful Imp **Mrs S. F. Dixon**
   4 **DANIEL'S DREAM**, 13, b g Prince Daniel (USA)—Amber Holly **Mrs E. M. Dixon**
   5 **JOYFUL BE**, 8, ch m And Beyond (IRE)—Joyful Imp **Mrs E. M. Dixon**

Amateur: Mr J. J. Dixon.

169	**MR SCOTT DIXON, Retford**

Postal: **Haygarth House Stud, Haygarth House, Babworth, Retford, Nottinghamshire, DN22 8ES**
Contacts: PHONE **(01777) 869079** FAX **(01777) 869326**
E-MAIL scottdixon1987@hotmail.com

   1 **ALPHA TAURI (USA)**, 7, b g Aldebaran (USA)—Seven Moons (JPN) **W. McKay**
   2 **ASKAUD (IRE)**, 5, b m Iffraaj—Tarabaya (IRE) **Paul J Dixon & Mrs Audrey Hobson**
   3 **BADA BING**, 4, ch f Beat Hollow—Trustthunder **Mr P J Dixon & Mr Phil Dixon**
   4 **BENGALINE**, 4, b g Bahamian Bounty—Indian Silk (IRE) **P. J. Dixon & The Nulli Secundus Friends**
   5 **BURNHOPE**, 4, b g Choisir (AUS)—Isengard (USA) **P. J. Dixon**
   6 **CADEAUX PEARL**, 5, b g Acclamation—Anneliina **P. J. Dixon**
   7 **CHOKIDAR (IRE)**, 5, b g Sleeping Indian—Lola Sapola (IRE) **Ontoawinner 4**
   8 **DOCOFTHEBAY (IRE)**, 9, ch g Docksider (USA)—Baize **P. J. Dixon**
   9 **EVEN STEVENS**, 5, br g Ishiguru (USA)—Promised (IRE) **P. J. Dixon**
  10 **GLAD EYE GLADYS**, 4, b f Milk It Mick—Thunderous Days **Paul J Dixon & Mrs Jayne Jackson**
  11 **MAN OF MY WORD**, 4, b g Milk It Mick—Promised (IRE) **P J Dixon & Partners**
  12 **MASKED DANCE (IRE)**, 6, gr g Captain Rio—Brooks Masquerade **Mrs S. Morcombe**
  13 **PICENO (IRE)**, 5, b g Camacho—Ascoli **Ontoawinner 4**
  14 **SCROOBY DOO**, 4, br f Kheleyf (USA)—Scrooby Baby **P. J. Dixon & The Nulli Secundus Friends**
  15 **SIR GEOFFREY (IRE)**, 7, b g Captain Rio—Disarm (IRE) **Dixon, Howlett & The Chrystal Maze Ptn**
  16 **SIX WIVES**, 6, b m Kingsalsa (USA)—Regina **Sexy Six Partnership**
  17 **SPOWARTICUS**, 4, ch g Shamardal (USA)—Helen Bradley (IRE) **P. J. Dixon**
  18 **STYLISTICKHILL (IRE)**, 5, gr m Desert Style (IRE)—Anemone **Paul Dixon & The Tickhill Racing Partnership**
  19 **THUNDERBALL**, 7, ch g Haafhd—Trustthunder **P. J. Dixon**
  20 **TOTALLY TRUSTED**, 5, b m Oasis Dream—Trustthunder **P. J. Dixon**

THREE-YEAR-OLDS

  21 **CON LECHE**, br c Milk It Mick—Capital Lass **Paul J Dixon & Mrs Jayne Jackson**
  22 **KING OF KUDOS (IRE)**, b c Acclamation—Perugina (FR) **P. J. Dixon**
  23 **LUCKY MOUNTAIN**, ch c Mount Nelson—Wild Clover **P. J. Dixon**
  24 **MICKSTATHETRICKSTA**, ch g Milk It Mick—Chrystal Venture (IRE) **Paul J Dixon & The Chrystal Maze Ptn**
  25 **PEARL NOIR**, b c Milk It Mick—Cora Pearl (IRE) **Dixon, Baker & Dixon**
  26 **ROBYN**, b f Byron—Discoed **P. J. Dixon**

TWO-YEAR-OLDS

  27 Ch f 22/3 Byron—Ginger Cookie (Bold Edge) (4761) **P. J. Dixon**
  28 B f 13/1 Sleeping Indian—Honesty Pays (Dr Fong (USA)) **P. J. Dixon**

Other Owners: Mr A. D. Baker, P. G. Dawson, P. J. Dixon, Mr S. Frobisher, Mrs M. A. Hobson, General Sir G. H. W. Howlett, Mrs J. Jackson, N. J. O'Brien, Mr S. W. Rowbotham, Mr A. C. Timms.

170	**MR STEVEN DIXON, Salisbury**

Postal: **West Paces Racing Stables, Apple Tree Barn, Livery Road, Winterslow, Nr Salisbury, Wiltshire, SP5 1RJ**
Contacts: PHONE **(01980) 862930** MOBILE **(07771) 963011**
E-MAIL sarahjdixon@hotmail.co.uk

   1 5, B m General Gambul—Pink Lady **Mr S. D. Dixon**
   2 **POWER MAN (IRE)**, 8, ch g Subtle Power (IRE)—Karinga Duff **Mr S. D. Dixon**
   3 **SPARROW HILLS (IRE)**, 9, b g Moscow Society (USA)—Glenstal Forest (IRE) **Mr S. D. Dixon**

MR STEVEN DIXON - Continued

4 SUN QUEST, 9, b g Groom Dancer (USA)—Icaressa **Mr S. D. Dixon**
5 WARSAW PACT (IRE), 10, b g Polish Precedent (USA)—Always Friendly **Mr S. D. Dixon**

Assistant Trainer: Mrs Sarah Dixon

Jockey (NH): Wayne Kavanagh.

---

171 MRS ROSE DOBBIN, Alnwick

Postal: **South Hazelrigg Farm, Chatton, Alnwick, Northumberland, NE66 5RZ**
Contacts: **PHONE (01668) 215395 (office) (01668) 215151 (house) FAX (01668) 215114**
MOBILE (07969) 993563
E-MAIL hazelriggracing1@btconnect.com WEBSITE www.rosedobbinracing.co.uk

1 EVERYLASTING (IRE), 6, b g Millenary—All French (IRE) **Miss C. L. Jones**
2 FLYING SQUAD (UAE), 9, b g Jade Robbery (USA)—Sandova (IRE) **Major-Gen C. A. Ramsay**
3 JURISDICTION, 9, b g Goldmark (USA)—Juris Prudence (IRE) **River Tweed Syndicate**
4 MARKEM (IRE), 6, ch g Beneficial—Dummy Run (IRE) **Mr & Mrs Duncan Davidson**
5 MARRAKECH TRADER (NZ), 6, ch g Pentire—Eastern Bazzaar (IRE) **Mr Tom Jenks**
6 MIRAGE DORE (FR), 10, b g Muhtathir—Rose Venitien (FR) **Mr & Mrs Duncan Davidson**
7 ONE MILLION, 4, b g Dubai Destination (USA)—Talwin (IRE) **The Friday Lions**
8 OSCAR STANLEY (IRE), 6, b g Oscar (IRE)—Mujavail (IRE) **Another Fine Mess Partnership**
9 POLITENESS (FR), 4, b g Poliglote—Martiniquaise (FR) **Mr & Mrs Duncan Davidson**
10 PURCELL'S BRIDGE (FR), 6, b g Trempolino (USA)—Theatrical Lady (USA) **Mr J. A. F. Filmer-Wilson**
11 PYJAMA GAME (IRE), 7, b g Hernando (FR)—Princess Claudia (IRE) **Mr & Mrs Duncan Davidson**
12 ROBIN'S COMMAND (IRE), 6, gr g Tikkanen (USA)—Marian's Wish (IRE) **M Hunter, J Matterson & R Jacobs**
13 ROCKING BLUES (FR), 8, b g Lavirco (GER)—Herbe de La Roque (FR) **Mr J Filmer-Wilson & Mrs D Davidson**
14 ROS CASTLE (IRE), 7, ch g Flemensfirth (USA)—Castlehaven (IRE) **Mr & Mrs Duncan Davidson**
15 SIERRA VICTOR (IRE), 10, b g Blueprint (IRE)—An Charraig Mhor (IRE) **M S Borders Racing Club**
16 SNOOKER (GER), 7, ch g Acambaro (GER)—Sheraton (IRE) **Mr & Mrs Duncan Davidson**
17 SPITZ (FR), 5, b g Enrique—Spezzia (FR) **Mr R. A. Jacobs**
18 STITCHED IN TIME (IRE), 6, b g Needle Gun (IRE)—Broken Pockets (IRE) **Mr & Mrs Duncan Davidson**
19 TWEEDO PARADISO (NZ), 6, br g Golan (IRE)—Buzz (NZ) **Mr J. L. Dickson**
20 VINNY GAMBINI (IRE), 6, b g Vinnie Roe (IRE)—Red Velvet **Mr & Mrs Duncan Davidson**

Other Owners: R. H. T. Barber, D. H. Davidson, Mrs S. K. Davidson, Mrs R. Dobbin, Mrs R. L. Elliot, R. A. Green, Mrs A. Green, A. N. Hamilton, M. S. Hunter, J. R. Jeffreys, Sir Chippendale Keswick, Mr J. H. Lovett, Miss J. G. K. Matterson, Mr M. T. Ord, The Duke Of Roxburghe.

Assistant Trainer: Tony Dobbin (07775) 680894

Jockey (NH): Wilson Renwick. **Amateur:** Mr Nick Orpwood, Miss Joanna Walton.

---

172 MR ASHLEY DODGSON, Thirsk

Postal: **Southerby House, Catton, Thirsk, North Yorkshire, YO7 4SQ**

1 CANDLEFORD, 8, b g Vettori (IRE)—Second Affair (IRE) **Mr A. C. Dodgson**
2 WITCH ONE, 10, b m Silver Patriarch (IRE)—Catton Lady **Mrs F. M. G. Dodgson**

---

173 MR MICHAEL DODS, Darlington

Postal: **Denton Hall Farm, Piercebridge, Darlington, Co. Durham, DL2 3TY**
Contacts: **PHONE (01325) 374270 FAX (01325) 374020**
MOBILE (07860) 411590/ (07773) 290830 C Dods
E-MAIL dods@michaeldodsracing.co.uk WEBSITE www.michaeldodsracing.co.uk

1 AMADEUS DENTON (IRE), 4, b g Amadeus Wolf—Wood Sorrel (IRE) **Denton Hall Racing Ltd**
2 BARNEY MCGREW (IRE), 10, b g Mark of Esteem (IRE)—Success Story **Mr W. A. Tinkler**
3 BONNIE ECHO, 6, b m Overbury (IRE)—Sunday News'n'echo (USA) **D. C. Batey**
4 CHEATING TIGER (IRE), 5, b g Tiger Hill (IRE)—Chita Rivera **D. C. Batey**
5 COMMANCHE RAIDER (IRE), 6, b g Tale of The Cat (USA)—Alsharq (IRE) **D. R. Graham**
6 DOS AMIGOS (IRE), 4, b g Clodovil (IRE)—Ide Say (IRE) **Doug Graham, Roger Stokell, Michael Dods**
7 ESCAPE TO GLORY (USA), 5, b g Bernstein (USA)—Escape To Victory **Pearson, Lamb, Wynn Williams**

MR MICHAEL DODS - Continued

8 FINE ALTOMIS, 4, b g Lomitas—Mi Anna (GER) **Steve Catchpole & Keith Hanson**
9 HAKUNA MATATA, 6, b g Dubai Destination (USA)—Green Song (FR) **Sekura Trade Frames Ltd**
10 HALF A BILLION (IRE), 4, b g Acclamation—Amankila (IRE) **I.Galletley, B.Stenson, S.Lowthian**
11 KIWI BAY, 8, b g Mujahid (USA)—Bay of Plenty (FR) **Kiwi Racing**
12 LADY CHAPARRAL, 6, b m High Chaparral (IRE)—La Sylphide **Mr & Mrs G. Turnbull**
13 LE CHAT D'OR, 5, b g One Cool Cat (USA)—Oh So Well (IRE) **Calum Stewart Anne Gillespie**
14 MASS RALLY (IRE), 6, b g Kheleyf (USA)—Reunion (IRE) **Business Development Consultants Limited**
15 MOHAWK RIDGE, 7, b g Storming Home—Ipsa Loquitur **D. R. Graham**
16 ODDYSEY (IRE), 4, b f Acclamation—Darling Smile (IRE) **Pearson & Lowthian**
17 ORBIT THE MOON (IRE), 5, b h Oratorio (IRE)—Catch The Moon (IRE) **Appleton - Davison - Spinks**
18 ROCKTHERUNWAY (IRE), 4, ch g Nayef (USA)—Femme Fatale **Sedgewick, Dods, Sunley Racing Partnership**
19 STAR CITY (IRE), 4, b g Elusive City (USA)—Teacher Preacher (IRE) **Appleton Davison Dods**
20 TIGER REIGNS, 7, b g Tiger Hill (IRE)—Showery **J. Buzzeo**
21 VIKING WARRIOR (IRE), 6, ch g Halling (USA)—Powder Paint **Transpennine Partnership**

THREE-YEAR-OLDS

22 AERONWYN BRYN (IRE), b f Dylan Thomas (IRE)—Hecuba **Mr W. A. Tinkler**
23 BEAT THE TIDE, b g Black Sam Bellamy (IRE)—Sablonne (USA) **J A Wynn-Williams & D Neale**
24 CRACKING CHOICE (IRE), ch c Choisir (AUS)—Champagne Cracker **Mr J. J. McLaren**
25 CURL (IRE), b f Duke of Marmalade (IRE)—Fringe **Mr W. A. Tinkler**
26 DENTON SKYLINE (IRE), b g Celtic Swing—Fayr Sky (IRE) **Denton Hall Racing Ltd**
27 ELLE WOODS (IRE), b f Lawman (FR)—Lady Livius (IRE) **Mr W. A. Tinkler**
28 LADY ARAAFA, ch f Araafa (IRE)—Locharia **Appleton Davison Dods**
29 LUCIES DIAMOND (IRE), ch f Iffraaj—Lucies Pride (IRE) **Business Development Consultants Limited**
30 MANDEVILLE (IRE), b f Kodiac—Olympia Theatre **Mr W. A. Tinkler**
31 MASH POTATO (IRE), b g Whipper (USA)—Salva **Bennett Potatoes & Banister**
32 MULTIFACT, b g Multiplex—Subtle Move (USA) **M. J. K. Dods**
33 PERFECT POSE (IRE), b f Amadeus Wolf—Interpose **Mr W. A. Tinkler**
34 ROCKY TWO (IRE), ch g Rock of Gibraltar (IRE)—Toorah Laura La (USA) **Mr & Mrs G. Turnbull**
35 Ch g Captain Rio—Walk In My Shadow (IRE) **K. Kirkup**

TWO-YEAR-OLDS

36 Ch c 3/4 Assertive—Bikini (Trans Island) (8729) **K. Kirkup**
37 BROOKES BOY (IRE), b c 28/4 Tagula (IRE)—Satan's Sister (Tout Ensemble) (8729) **Sekura Trade Frames Ltd**
38 CAMATINI (IRE), b f 18/4 Camacho—Trentini (IRE) (Singspiel (IRE)) (10500) **Mr G. C. Thompson**
39 Gr f 21/2 Dark Angel (IRE)—Folga (Atraf) (16000) **D. T. J. Metcalfe**
40 B c 24/3 Acclamation—Miss Cambridge (Dubawi (IRE)) (12000) **J A Wynn-Williams & D Neale**
41 B g 25/3 Amadeus Wolf—Monet's Lady (Daylami (IRE)) (7142) **M. J. K. Dods**
42 ONE BOY (IRE), ch g 14/3 Captain Gerrard (IRE)—
                              Paris Song (IRE) (Peintre Celebre (USA)) (9920) **Sekura Trade Frames Ltd**
43 SECRET APPLAUSE, b f 27/3 Sakhee's Secret—
                              Royal Pardon (Royal Applause) (4761) **Mr K Knox & Mr M Hutchinson**
44 Gr c 10/5 Kheleyf (USA)—Zamiyla (IRE) (Daylami (IRE)) (15000)

Other Owners: Mr P. Appleton, Mr C. Banister, Mr I. Bennett, Bennett Potatoes Ltd, Mr S. L. Catchpole, Mr J. Cockcroft, R. Davison, Mrs C. E. Dods, Mr I. Galletley, Dr A. J. F. Gillespie, Mr K. Hanson, M. Hutchinson, T. K. Knox, W. S. D. Lamb, S. R. Lowthian, D. Neale, Mr M. D. Pearson, Mr M. J. Sedgewick, V. J. Spinks, J. W. Stenson, Mr C. M. Stewart, R. Stokell, D. J. Stokell, Mr G. Turnbull, Mrs S. E. Turnbull, F. Watson, D. Watts, J. A. Wynn-Williams.

Assistant Trainers: C Dods, Steve Alderson (07533) 401887

Jockey (flat): Tom Eaves. **Apprentice:** Connor Beasley.

---

174   **MR CONOR DORE, Frampton Fen**
Postal: **Barford Farm, Swineshead Road, Frampton Fen, Boston, Lincolnshire, PE20 1SG**
Contacts: **PHONE (01775) 822747 MOBILE (07984) 609170**
E-MAIL dores@supanet.com

1 ACE OF SPIES (IRE), 8, br g Machiavellian (USA)—Nadia **Mrs L. J. Marsh**
2 CHJIMES (IRE), 9, b g Fath (USA)—Radiance (IRE) **Mrs L. J. Marsh**
3 DESERT STRIKE, 7, b g Bertolini (USA)—Mary Jane **A. N. Page**
4 EFISTORM, 12, b g Efisio—Abundance **Mrs J. R. Marsh**
5 ELHAMRI, 9, b br g Noverre (USA)—Seamstress **C. D. Marsh**
6 ELIJAH PEPPER (USA), 8, ch g Crafty Prospector (USA)—Dovie Dee (USA) **Mrs L. J. Marsh**

MR CONOR DORE - Continued

  7 HINTON ADMIRAL, 9, b g Spectrum (IRE)—Shawanni **C. J. McHugh**
  8 LASTKINGOFSCOTLAND (IRE), 7, b g Danehill Dancer (IRE)—Arcade **Mrs J. R. Marsh**
  9 PUNCHING, 9, b g Kyllachy—Candescent **L. Breslin**
10 SATWA LAIRD, 7, b g Johannesburg (USA)—Policy Setter (USA) **Mrs J. R. Marsh**
11 STANDPOINT, 7, b g Oasis Dream—Waki Music (USA) **Mrs J. R. Marsh**
12 THORPE BAY, 4, b g Piccolo—My Valentina **Mr M. Fitzsimons**

Other Owners: Mr C. T. Eliades, J. Gunnell.

MR FRANCOIS DOUMEN, Bouce
Postal: **Le Gue, 61570 Bouce, France**
Contacts: **PHONE (0033) 2 33 67 11 59 FAX (0033) 2 33 67 82 37 MOBILE (0033) 6 07 42 33 58
E-MAIL doumenecouves@orange.fr WEBSITE francoisdoumenracing.com**

  1 AUTORITAIRE (FR), 4, b f Authorized (IRE)—Castilly
  2 CABARETUNE (FR), 8, b h Green Tune (USA)—Cabaret Club (FR)
  3 CELTIC CELEB (IRE), 6, ch h Peintre Celebre (USA)—Gaelic Bird (FR)
  4 CHICHITEUSE (FR), 4, b f Chichicastenango (FR)—Gigawatt (FR)
  5 CROIX MADAME (FR), 6, ch m Forestier (FR)—She Runs (FR)
  6 DIABLE DE JIM (FR), 7, b g Diableneyev (USA)—Jolie Jim (FR)
  7 FAST FLIGHT (FR), 4, b g Anabaa (USA)—Flight Night
  8 GOLD SAVE THE KING (IRE), 6, ch g King's Best—Beringold
  9 GOLDIE JOLIE (FR), 4, b f Gold Away (IRE)—Jolie Jim (FR)
10 GREEN BANANAS (FR), 7, b m Green Tune (USA)—Anabaa Republic (FR)
11 JOLIE NOCE (FR), 5, b m Muhtathir—Jolie Jim (FR)
12 KASBAH BIS (FR), 4, b g Kahyasi—Marital Bliss (FR)
13 KASBAH BLISS (FR), 11, b g Kahyasi—Marital Bliss (FR)
14 KHASMA (IRE), 4, b f Rock of Gibraltar (IRE)—Kassana (IRE)
15 KISS ROYAL (IRE), 5, b m Exceed And Excel (AUS)—Kinnego (IRE)
16 PHIL MAN (IRE), 4, b c Manduro (GER)—Fureau (GER)
17 RAGEUR (FR), 5, b g Iffraaj—Ethelinda
18 STEED (FR), 11, b g Double Bed (FR)—River Tweed
19 TASTEVIN (FR), 6, ch g Dark Moondancer—Donitille (FR)
20 THORZIEN (FR), 4, ch g Muhtathir—Hertzienne (FR)
21 TIP TOE (FR), 6, b h Footstepsinthesand—Midnight Queen (GER)
22 TOP TRIP, 4, b c Dubai Destination (USA)—Topka (FR)
23 UMBRAGE (FR), 5, b m Astarabad (USA)—Ma'am (FR)
24 VOUS MEME (FR), 4, b g Le Fou (USA)—Ma'am (FR)
25 XPO UNIVERSEL (FR), 4, b g Poliglote—Xanadu Bliss (FR)

THREE-YEAR-OLDS

26 COQUERELLE'S BEST, b f Galileo (IRE)—Coquerelle (IRE)
27 DAUPHINE RUSSE (FR), b f Russian Blue (IRE)—Dauphine (SAF)
28 DERNIERE CARTE (FR), b f Sunday Break (JPN)—Carte Blanche (FR)
29 DYLAN PHILLY (FR), ch f Dylan Thomas (IRE)—Titillate (IRE)
30 FAST ESCAPE (IRE), b f King's Best (USA)—Runaway Top
31 FIERE (FR), b f Authorized (IRE)—Dan's Pride (USA)
32 FIRST TO RISE (FR), ch f Bedawin (FR)—Next Sunrise (FR)
33 KANSHE (IRE), gr f Dalakhani (IRE)—Karmifira (FR)
34 KAPSTADT (FR), b c Country Reel (USA)—King's Parody (IRE)
35 LIBRARY (FR), b c Librettist (USA)—Irunarri (FR)
36 QUATRE ARPENTS (FR), b c Bedawin (FR)—Queen Aida (FR)
37 QUEEN PHILLY (FR), b f King's Best (USA)—Bleu Kobalt (FR)
38 TOPZA (FR), b f Zamindar (USA)—Topka (FR)

TWO-YEAR-OLDS

39 B c 7/4 Shamardal (USA)—Bunting (USA) (Private Account (USA)) (63492)
40 CERAMICK (FR), b f 13/2 Slickly (FR)—Hertzienne (FR) (Hernando (FR))
41 CRAZY CAT (FR), b c 3/3 Hold That Tiger (USA)—Folle Dingue (FR) (Golan (IRE))
42 DAUPHINE DORÉE, b f 11/4 Archange d'or (IRE)—Dauphine (SAF) (Rich Man's Gold (USA))
43 ENERGIVORE (FR), b c 16/3 Layman (USA)—The Trollop (FR) (Double Bed (FR))
44 B f 17/3 Authorized (IRE)—Flamingo Flower (USA) (Diesis) (9523)
45 GREAT SILENCE (FR), gr c 8/4 Great Journey (JPN)—Henrietta (FR) (Hernando (FR))

MR FRANCOIS DOUMEN - Continued

46 B f 23/4 Creachadoir (IRE)—Margot Mine (IRE) (Choisir (AUS))
47 NANIA (FR), b f 3/3 Namid—Gigana (FR) (Anabaa Blue)
48 PRETZELLE (FR), b f 2/2 Zamindar (USA)—Pretty As Can Be (Giant's Causeway (USA)) (46031)
49 B f 29/3 Arch (USA)—Providanza (FR) (Okawango (USA)) (51587)
50 B f 23/2 Forestier—Quibble
51 B c 24/4 Elusive City (USA)—Topka (FR) (Kahyasi) (19841)
52 UNDER THE RADAR (FR), b c 16/3 Footstepsinthesand—Fast Lane Lili (Fasliyev (USA)) (37301)
53 VAMOSALAPLAYA (FR), ch c 29/3 Footstepsinthesand—Marital Bliss (FR) (Double Bed (FR))
54 XCELLENCE (FR), b f 12/3 Champs Elysees—Xanadu Bliss (FR) (Xaar)

Owners: Mr Dermot Cantillon, Mr Xavier Doumen, Gold and Blue Ltd, Haras D'Ecouves, Mr Robert Jeffcock, Marquise de Moratalla, Comte Henri de Pracomtal, Mr Eric Puerari, Mr Gerard Rollain, Mr Anthony Smurfit, Mr Michael Somerset-Leeke, Mr Joerg Vasicek, Mr Hans Peter Vogt.

Jockey (flat): Thomas Huet, Gerald Mosse.

---

176 MR SIMON DOW, Epsom
Postal: **Clear Height Stables, Derby Stables Road, Epsom, Surrey, KT18 5LB**
Contacts: **PHONE** (01372) 721490 **FAX** (01372) 748099 **MOBILE** (07860) 800109
E-MAIL simon@simondow.co.uk **Office:** mary@simondow.co.uk **WEBSITE** www.simondow.co.uk
Twitter: @SimonDowRacing

1 BROCKLEBANK (IRE), 4, b g Diamond Green (FR)—La Stellina (IRE) **C. G. J. Chua**
2 CHRISTOPHER CHUA (IRE), 4, gr g Clodovil (IRE)—Pearls of Wisdom **C. G. J. Chua**
3 CLAUDE MONET (BRZ), 4, ch g Vettori (IRE)—Femme Fatale (BRZ) **HoweSharp**
4 CLEAR PRAISE (USA), 6, b g Songandaprayer (USA)—Pretty Clear (USA) **Racing Clear Partnership**
5 DIAMOND CHARLIE (IRE), 5, br g Diamond Green (FR)—Rosy Lydgate **David & Stanley Adams**
6 FAIR VALUE (IRE), 5, b m Compton Place—Intriguing Glimpse **Don & Val Churston**
7 FORCEFUL APPEAL (USA), 5, b br g Successful Appeal (USA)—Kinetic Force (USA) **Mr S. A. Caunce**
8 GOLDEN DESERT (IRE), 9, b g Desert Prince (IRE)—Jules (IRE) **T. G. Parker**
9 JUHD (IRE), 5, gr g Nayef (USA)—Norfolk Lavender (CAN) **P. G. Jacobs**
10 KAYPEA, 4, br f Imperial Dancer—Cape Maya **Clear Height Racing**
11 KERFUFFLE (IRE), 4, b f Kheleyf (USA)—Chiosina (IRE) **J Taylor L Robinson & W J Taylor**
12 LiTMUS (USA), 4, ch f Latent Heat (USA)—Fairy Glade (USA) **T. G. Parker**
13 NOTABADGIRL, 4, ch f Denounce—Lady Jo **K. F. Butler**
14 RENOIR'S LADY, 5, b m Peintre Celebre (USA)—Marie de Blois (USA) **Malcolm & Alicia Aldis**
15 SPRING TONIC, 4, b g Fantastic View (USA)—Nukhbah (USA) **Robinson, Butler, Parker & Scandrett**
16 SQUAD, 7, ch g Choisir (AUS)—Widescreen (USA) **Sarah Snell & Anne Devine**
17 SUGAR LIPS, 4, b f Byron—Maria Bonita (IRE) **Star Pointe Ltd**

THREE-YEAR-OLDS

18 DAWN ROCK, b f Rock of Gibraltar (IRE)—Ommadawn (IRE) **Malcolm & Alicia Aldis**
19 FIDUCIA, b f Lawman (FR)—Silca Key **P. G. Jacobs**
20 MALAYSIAN BOLEH, ch c Compton Place—Orlena (USA) **JCG Chua & CK Ong**
21 MARJONG, b f Mount Nelson—Vermilliann (IRE) **Mr J. L. Marsden**
22 MIGHTY THOR, b c Norse Dancer (IRE)—Leyaaly **M. P. Merwood**
23 NOEL'S HOPE, b g Anabaa (USA)—Sourire **Mr M. McAllister**
24 PRESUMIDO (IRE), b c Iffraaj—Miss Megs (IRE) **R. Moss & J. Page**

Other Owners: Mr D. Adams, Mr S. J. Adams, Mrs A. Aldis, Mr M. S. Aldis, D. G. Churston, Mrs V. Churston, Mrs A. M. Devine, S. L. Dow, Mr R. I. Goalen, Mr M. R. Howe, Mr R. Moore, Mr R. J. Moss, Mr F. Ong, Mr J. W. Page, Ms E. Robinson, N. S. Scandrett, Mr J. Sharp, Ms S. A. Snell, Miss J. E. Taylor, Mr W. J. Taylor.

Assistant Trainer: Daniel Hutchison

---

177 MR CHRIS DOWN, Cullompton
Postal: **Upton, Cullompton, Devon, EX15 1RA**
Contacts: **PHONE** (01884) 33097 **FAX** (01884) 33097 **MOBILE** (07828) 021232
E-MAIL cjdownracing@gmail.com

1 BILLY DUTTON, 7, ch g Sir Harry Lewis (USA)—Tinoforty (FR) **W. A. Bromley**
2 5, B h Tikkanen (USA)—Copper Valley **Mrs G. H. Leeves**
3 CURLEW (IRE), 7, b g Cape Cross (IRE)—Billbill (USA) **F. G. Hollis**

MR CHRIS DOWN - Continued

4   5, B m Grape Tree Road—Dalticia (FR) **C. J. Down**
5   **DRAGON'S DEN (IRE)**, 6, b g Antonius Pius (USA)—Tallassee **G. R. Waterman**
6   **EXTREMELY SO**, 7, ch m Kyllachy—Antigua **Mrs M. Trueman**
7   **JAMBOBO**, 4, b g Acclamation—Hovering (IRE) **Mrs M. Trueman**
8   **KEY TO MILAN**, 7, b g Milan—Key West (FR) **M. R. Lavis & C. J. Down**
9   4, B g Volochine (IRE)—Key West (FR) **J. B. Radford**
10 **KINGS FLAGSHIP**, 8, b g Lahib (USA)—Queen's Flagship (IRE) **Mrs G. H. Leeves**
11 **LADIES DANCING**, 7, b g Royal Applause—Queen of Dance (IRE) **Upton Racing**
12 **LEGION D'HONNEUR (UAE)**, 8, b g Halling (USA)—
                                                 Renowned (IRE) **P. Holland, J. T. Measures, A. V. Price, V. Holland**
13 **LILY POTTS**, 4, gr f Proclamation (IRE)—Jucinda **Mr T. J. Pole**
14 **LOYAUTE (FR)**, 6, ch m Green Tune (USA)—Iles Marquises (IRE) **Upton Racing 2**
15 4, B f Oscar (IRE)—Made For A King **C. J. Down**
16 **MISTER SNOWBALL (FR)**, 6, ch g Ballingarry (IRE)—
                                                 No Coincidence (IRE) **P. Holland, J. T. Measures, A. V. Price, V. Holland**
17 **NEW CHRISTMAS (USA)**, 6, gr ro g Smoke Glacken (USA)—Occhi Verdi (IRE) **Dr M. J. Dixon**
18 **ORDENSRITTER (GER)**, 5, ch g Samum (GER)—Dramraire Mist **Red Baron Racing**
19 **REVEREND GREEN (IRE)**, 7, b g Tagula (IRE)—Red Letter **C. J. Down**
20 **RUSSIE WITH LOVE**, 7, b m Alflora (IRE)—Vieille Russie **Howzat Partnership**
21 **SERAPHIEL**, 4, b g Royal Applause—Angel Sprints **Ms V. Halloran**
22 **SOME SECRET**, 8, b m Fleetwood (IRE)—Secret Dance **Mrs G. H. Leeves**
23 **THEDEBOFTHEYEAR**, 9, b m Sir Harry Lewis (USA)—Juste Belle (FR) **Culm Valley Racing**
24 **UPTON OAKS**, 7, b g Sir Harry Lewis (USA)—Copper Valley **C. J. Down**
25 **UPTON WOOD**, 7, ch g Fleetwood (IRE)—Miss Counsel **C. J. Down**

THREE-YEAR-OLDS

26 **INCOGNITA**, ch f Sakhee's Secret—Angel Sprints **Ms V. M. Halloran**

Other Owners: Dr Mark Dixon, Mr C. J. Down, Mrs F. Down, Mr A. D. Hill, Mr P. Holland, Mrs V. Holland, Mr M. R. Lavis, Mr J. T. Measures, Mrs S. E. Norman, Mr J. A. G. Norman, Mrs A. V. Price, Mr Bruce Stevens, Mr K. W. Tyrrell.

Jockey (flat): Jemma Marshall. **Jockey (NH):** James Davies, Richard Johnson, Tom Scudamore. **Conditional:** Giles Hawkins.

---

178 ## MISS AMY DOWNIE, Chipping Sodbury
Postal: **Chescombe Farm, Dodington Road, Chipping Sodbury, Bristol, South Gloucestershire, BS37 6HY**
Contacts: **MOBILE (07766) 727869**
E-MAIL ahdracing@hotmail.co.uk

1   **CHESHIRE PRINCE**, 9, br g Desert Prince (IRE)—Bundle Up (USA) **Miss A. H. Downie**
2   **MASTERLEADERMAN (IRE)**, 5, b g Beneficial—Atagirl (IRE) **Miss A. H. Downie**

Conditional: Michael Byrne.

---

179 ## MR CLIVE DREW, Rampton
Postal: **Fox End Stables, 83 King Street, Rampton, Cambridgeshire, CB24 8QD**
Contacts: **PHONE/FAX (01954) 250772 MOBILE (07917) 718127**

1   **MAISON BRILLET (IRE)**, 6, b g Pyrus (USA)—Stormchaser (IRE) **C. Drew**
2   **MY SILVER LILLY**, 6, b m Silver Patriarch (IRE)—Myumi **Miss P. Drew**
3   **MYTARA**, 8, br m Kayf Tara—Myumi **M. Brown, J. Burt, C. Drew & J. Paull**
4   **SMILE FOR US**, 10, b g Whittingham (IRE)—Don't Smile **Miss P. Drew**

Other Owners: Mr D. Bird, Mrs Jacquie Bland, Mr M. M. Brown, Mrs J. K. Burt, Mr C. Drew, Mr J. D. Paull, Mr A. Plumb.

Assistant Trainer: Miss Polly Drew

180 MISS JACKIE DU PLESSIS, Saltash
Postal: Burell Farm, Longlands, Saltash, Cornwall, PL12 4QH
Contacts: PHONE (01752) 842362 MOBILE (07970) 871505
E-MAIL ziggerson@aol.com

1 ARMENIAN BOY (FR), 10, b g Simon du Desert (FR)—Jade d'eau (IRE) **Miss J. M. du Plessis**
2 COOL GEORGE, 5, b g Pastoral Pursuits—Magic Valentine **Mr R. J. Reip**
3 DIDDYPURPTOON, 7, b m Lucky Story (USA)—Dafne **Miss J. M. du Plessis**
4 FEAR GLIC (IRE), 7, b g Dr Massini (IRE)—Graineuaile (IRE) **Du Plessis Treleaven Martin Waterman**
5 FOR THE STAFF (IRE), 9, br g Tamayaz (CAN)—Shanes Bay (IRE) **Mrs E. M. Worth**
6 LANDULPH LASS, 6, b m Thank Heavens—Easter Again **Miss J. M. du Plessis**
7 LONG JOHN, 6, gr g Silver Patriarch (IRE)—Magic Valentine **Mr R. J. Reip**

Other Owners: Ms A. Argyrides, Mr T. J. G. Martin, Mrs A. A. Treleaven, G. R. Waterman.

181 MRS ANN DUFFIELD, Leyburn
Postal: Sun Hill Racing Stables, Sun Hill Farm, Constable Burton, Leyburn,
North Yorkshire, DL8 5RL
Contacts: PHONE (01677) 450303 FAX (01677) 450993 MOBILE (07802) 496332
E-MAIL ann@annduffield.co.uk WEBSITE www.annduffield.co.uk

1 DUBIOUS ESCAPADE (IRE), 4, b f Dubawi (IRE)—Brief Escapade (IRE) **Mr C. L. Stirling**
2 ELUSIVE ISLAND (USA), 4, b g Elusive Quality (USA)—Quiet Word (USA) **Mr Peter Odle & Mr James Pak**
3 FERNDALE, 4, b f Royal Applause—Carradale **The Duchess of Sutherland**
4 HEIDI'S DELIGHT (IRE), 4, b f Red Clubs (IRE)—Alexander Confranc (IRE) **David & Carole McMahon**
5 JESSIE'S SPIRIT (IRE), 4, gr f Clodovil—Alexander Anapolis (IRE) **David & Carole McMahon**
6 JUST LILLE (IRE), 10, b m Mull of Kintyre (USA)—Tamasriya (IRE) **MPR Warrender Baines Farrington Kay**
7 LADY BY RED (IRE), 5, ch m Redback—Antonia's Dream **Mr N. Saint**
8 4, B g Diamond Green (FR)—Pivotal Role
9 SOVEREIGN STREET, 5, ch m Compton Place—Mint Royale (IRE) **The Duchess of Sutherland**
10 SPRINGHEEL JAKE, 4, b g Lawman (FR)—Rye (IRE) **Mr J. A. Kay**
11 SWIFT ENCOUNTER (IRE), 4, b br g Antonius Pius (USA)—Eucalyptus Hill (USA) **Middleham Park Racing VII**
12 ZILZIE (IRE), 4, b f Intikhab (USA)—Novosibirsk (USA) **D. G. Iceton**

THREE-YEAR-OLDS
13 ALL BLACK ROSE, b f Vita Rosa (JPN)—All A Dream **Miss K. Rausing**
14 BY A WISKA, b g Kheleyf (USA)—Tropical Breeze (IRE) **Mr J. Gatenby**
15 CHANT (IRE), b g Oratorio (IRE)—Akarita (IRE) **Mrs Ann Starkie & Partners**
16 CHLOE'S DREAM (IRE), gr f Clodovil (IRE)—Extravagance (IRE) **Mr P. A. Bowles**
17 CINDERSLIPPER (IRE), b f Jeremy (USA)—Love City (IRE) **Mrs Ann Starkie & Partners**
18 DISTANT SUNRISE, b f Tobougg (IRE)—Prairie Sun (USA) **Middleham Park Racing XL**
19 HELTERSKELTER GIRL, b f Firebreak—Eloquent Isle (IRE) **Mrs D. Addison**
20 MELODY OF LOVE, b f Haafhd—Tamzin **Mrs P. Good**
21 RANGOONED, gr f Bahamian Bounty—Dansa Queen **Morecool Racing & David Redvers**
22 RED CHARMER (IRE), b g Red Clubs (IRE)—Golden Charm (IRE) **Mr I Farrington & Mr R Chapman**
23 RED HIGHLITES (IRE), br f Red Clubs (IRE)—High Lite **Middleham Park Racing XL**
24 RUST (IRE), b c Elnadim (USA)—Reddening **The Duchess of Sutherland**
25 SCARLET SPIRIT (IRE), b f Red Clubs (IRE)—Waroonga (IRE) **Mr B. G. Spittles**
26 SCENTPASTPARADISE, b f Pastoral Pursuits—Centenerola (USA) **Mr M. Curtis**
27 SPIRIT OF RIO (IRE), b c Footstepsinthesand—Batilde (IRE) **Billy & Debbie Glover**
28 VAL'S DIAMOND (IRE), b f Mujadil (USA)—More Respect (IRE) **D. K. Barker**
29 WILLIE THE WHIPPER, b c Whipper (USA)—Anna Simona (GER) **Qatar Racing Limited**

TWO-YEAR-OLDS
30 B c 29/4 Bertolini (USA)—Apple Sauce (Prince Sabo) (2857)
31 BOY RANGER (IRE), b c 7/3 Bushranger (IRE)—Nonsense (IRE) (Soviet Star (USA)) (12380) **Sandra Shewring**
32 B f 6/2 Pastoral Pursuits—Easy Mover (IRE) (Bluebird (USA)) (3333)
33 B f 10/5 Major Cadeaux—Eloquent Isle (Mull of Kintyre (USA)) (2857)
34 B f 31/3 Milk It Mick—Floral Spark (Forzando) (3333)
35 FOCUSOFOURTHOUGHTS (IRE), b c 25/4 Intense Focus (USA)—
                                          Inourthoughts (IRE) (Desert Style (IRE)) (8729) **Eshwin Racing**
36 GARFUNKEL (IRE), b c 12/3 Excellent Art—Intricate Dance (USA) (Aptitude (USA)) (12000) **Morecool Racing**
37 GREENBURY (IRE), b c 22/2 Jeremy (USA)—Truly Genuine (IRE) (Hernando (FR)) (9523) **David Barker**
38 B c 24/3 Whipper (USA)—Hedera (USA) (Woodman (USA)) (13491) **James Kay**

MRS ANN DUFFIELD - Continued

39 **HELLO BEAUTIFUL (IRE)**, ch f 23/3 Captain Rio—Tekhania (IRE) (Dalakhani (IRE)) (9523) **Nick Allenby**
40 **IN VINO VERITAS (IRE)**, b c 25/1 Art Connoisseur (IRE)—Robin (Slip Anchor) (11110) **James Kay**
41 B f 26/3 Myboycharlie (IRE)—Khafayif (USA) (Swain (IRE)) (7936) **Derek & Sandra Shewring**
42 **LADY JAMESWAY (IRE)**, b f 4/3 Acclamation—Baltic Dip (Benny The Dip (USA)) (25000) **James Pak**
43 **MASTER CLOCKMAKER (IRE)**, gr c 31/3 Mastercraftsman (IRE)—
                        Mairead Anne (USA) (Elusive Quality (USA)) (40000) **Mr & Mrs Thompson**
44 **MUSPELHEIM**, b c 25/3 Firebreak—Ticcatoo (IRE) (Dolphin Street (FR)) (7142) **Grange Park Racing**
45 **NAUGHTY BETTY**, b f 7/3 Myboycharlie (IRE)—Sweet Power (Pivotal) **Graeme & Vanessa Thompson**
46 **PETITE MADAME (IRE)**, b f 28/3 Champs Elysees—Seeking The Fun (USA) (Alhaarth (IRE)) (6745) **Nick Saint**
47 **SHESADANSER**, b f 4/5 Dutch Art—
                        Broughton Bounty (Bahamian Bounty) (3809) **Ian Hill (Bridge Extraction Systems)**
48 B c 29/1 Lucky Story (USA)—Toboggan Lady (Tobougg (IRE)) (7619) **David McMahon**
49 B f 21/4 Jeremy (USA)—Travel Tricks (IRE) (Presidium) (11110)

Other Owners: Mr Jimmy Kay, Mrs H. Baines, Mr S. Bland, Mr R. P. Chapman, Mrs Ann Duffield, Mr I. Farrington, Mr W. D. Glover, Mrs D. A. Glover, David Hibbert, Val Hubbard, Tony Livingston, Mrs C. A. McMahon, Mr D. McMahon, Mr P. J. Odle, Mr James Pak, Mr T. S. Palin, Mr John Preece, Mr M. Prince, Mr David Redvers, Shaun Slack, Mrs Ann Starkie, Mr M. Sykes, Mr James Warrender.

Assistant Trainer: G Duffield

Apprentice: Rowan Scott.

---

182 MR BRENDAN W. DUKE, The Curragh
Postal: **Fenway House, Pollardstown, The Curragh, Co. Kildare, Ireland**
Contacts: **PHONE (00353) 045 521104 MOBILE (00353) 85 8189724**
E-MAIL **brendanwduke@hotmail.com**

1 **BLACKTHORN STICK (IRE)**, 4, b g Elusive City (USA)—Hi Lyla (IRE) **Mr W. J. Dunphy**
2 **CIRCUS ACT**, 5, b g Cape Cross (IRE)—Carry On Katie (USA) **Mr Joseph Duke**
3 **HARBOUR MOON (IRE)**, 6, b g Refuse To Bend (IRE)—Decant **Monread Stud**
4 4, Ch f Trans Island—Hayward's Heath **Mrs Angela Duke**
5 **I'M SHEIKRA (IRE)**, 4, b f Captain Rio—Gentle Peace (IRE) **Near Buy Friends Syndicate**
6 **MAXIMUM FEAT (IRE)**, 4, b g Fruits of Love (USA)—Sheilas Joy (IRE) **Fenway Syndicate**
7 **MISTER BENEDICTINE**, 10, b g Mister Baileys—Cultural Role **Mr Joseph Duke**
8 **OLD PHOBIE (IRE)**, 6, b m Catcher In The Rye (IRE)—Blackchurch Mist (IRE) **Mr Patrick Brennan**
9 **QI JIGUANG (IRE)**, 4, b g Catcher In The Rye (IRE)—Rem Time (IRE) **Mr John Nelligan**
10 **SPIRIT OF SEVE (IRE)**, 5, b g Indian River (FR)—Queen of Catwalk (IRE) **Mr Mark McDonagh**
11 5, B g Chevalier (IRE)—Swallowtailed Kite (USA) **Mr Joseph Duke**
12 4, B g Tiger Hill (IRE)—Taca d'oli (FR) **Mrs Angela Duke**
13 **THE MASIE (IRE)**, 6, b m Sendawar (IRE)—Maeveen (IRE) **Monread Stud**
14 **WELSH NAYBER**, 4, ch g Nayef (USA)—Aberdovey **Mr Mark McDonagh**

THREE-YEAR-OLDS

15 **FRANK LLOYD WRIGHT (IRE)**, b c Ramonti (FR)—Hollow Haze (USA) **Mr Joseph Duke**
16 **MATILDA PLUM (IRE)**, b f Duke of Marmalade (IRE)—Moon Unit (IRE) **Mrs Paula Davidson**

TWO-YEAR-OLDS

17 B f 10/3 Diamond Green (FR)—Hi Lyla (IRE) (Lahib (USA)) **Mr W. J. Dunphy**

Jockey (flat): Shane Foley. **Jockey (NH):** David Crosse.

---

183 MR IAN DUNCAN, Coylton
Postal: **Sandhill Farm, Coylton, Ayr, Ayrshire, KA6 6HE**
Contacts: **PHONE (01292) 571118 FAX (01292) 571118 MOBILE (07731) 473668**

1 **DODGEY DREAM**, 11, ch g Zaffaran (USA)—Dinnys Dream (IRE) **Miss H. A. Cross**
2 **GOLDEN SPARKLE (IRE)**, 7, ch m Samraan (USA)—Bye For Now **Miss H. A. Cross**

Other Owners: Mr I. A. Duncan.

184 MR NIGEL DUNGER, Pulborough
Postal: **Generation House, Coombelands Stables, Pulborough, West Sussex, RH20 1BP**
Contacts: **PHONE (01798) 872194 MOBILE (07790) 631962**

1 4, B f Beat All (USA)—Kansas City (FR) **N. A. Dunger**
2 SNOW PATROL, 12, gr g Linamix (FR)—Overcast (IRE) **N. A. Dunger**
Assistant Trainer: Mrs D Dunger

185 MR ED DUNLOP, Newmarket
Postal: **La Grange Stables, Fordham Road, Newmarket, Suffolk, CB8 7AA**
Contacts: **PHONE (01638) 661998 FAX (01638) 667394 MOBILE (07785) 328537**
E-MAIL edunlop@eddunlopracing.co.uk WEBSITE www.eddunlop.com

1 AEGEAUS, 4, b g Monsun (GER)—Ouija Board **The Earl Of Derby**
2 BURWAAZ, 4, b c Exceed And Excel (AUS)—Nidhaal (IRE) **Hamdan Al Maktoum**
3 FORT BASTION (IRE), 4, b c Lawman (FR)—French Fern (IRE) **Sir Robert Ogden C.B.E., LLD**
4 GABRIAL'S STAR, 4, b c Hernando (FR)—Grain Only **Dr M. B. Q. S. Koukash**
5 HARLESTONE TIMES (IRE), 6, b g Olden Times—Harlestone Lady **J. L. Dunlop**
6 HOMERIC (IRE), 4, b g Montjeu (IRE)—Al Saqiya (USA) **Highclere Thoroughbred Racing - Jackson**
7 JOSHUA TREE (IRE), 6, b h Montjeu (IRE)—Madeira Mist (IRE) **Mr K. K. Al Nabooda & Mr K. Albahou**
8 LEXI'S HERO (IRE), 5, b g Invincible Spirit (IRE)—Christel Flame **Dr M. B. Q. S. Koukash**
9 LYRIC STREET (IRE), 5, b g Hurricane Run (IRE)—Elle Danzig (GER) **The Hon Earle I. Mack**
10 MAN OF PLENTY, 4, ch g Manduro (GER)—Credit-A-Plenty **Bluehills Racing Limited**
11 MUBARAZA (IRE), 4, ch c Dalakhani (IRE)—Mokaraba **Hamdan Al Maktoum**
12 RED CADEAUX, 7, ch g Cadeaux Genereux—Artisia (IRE) **R. J. Arculli**
13 ROMEO MONTAGUE, 5, b g Montjeu (IRE)—Issa **Mrs G. A. Rupert**
14 SNOW FAIRY (IRE), 6, b m Intikhab (USA)—Woodland Dream (IRE) **Anamoine Ltd**
15 TESTOSTERONE (IRE), 5, br m Dansili—Epopee (IRE) **Mr Nurlan Bizakov**
16 THE GREAT GABRIAL, 4, b g Oasis Dream—Quiff **Dr M. B. Q. S. Koukash**
17 THE TIGER, 5, b g Tiger Hill (IRE)—Rafiya **J. R. Weatherby**
18 TIMES UP, 7, b g Olden Times—Princess Genista **Mrs I. H. Stewart-Brown & Mr M. J. Meacock**
19 VOODOO PRINCE, 5, b g Kingmambo (USA)—Ouija Board **The Earl Of Derby**

THREE-YEAR-OLDS
20 ABRAQ, b c Danehill Dancer (IRE)—Nordhock (USA) **Royal Cavalry Oman**
21 AFICIONADO, ch g Halling (USA)—Prithee **Red Book Partnership**
22 AMAZONAS (IRE), b f Cape Cross (IRE)—Francesca d'gorgio (USA) **Sir Robert Ogden C.B.E., LLD**
23 AUCTION (IRE), b f Mr Greeley (USA)—Exhibit One (USA) **Highclere Thoroughbred Racing - Coventry**
24 BANTAM (IRE), b f Teofilo (IRE)—Firecrest (IRE) **Brooke Kelly Partnership**
25 BOLD CITIZEN (IRE), b c New Approach (IRE)—Claxon **Bluehills Racing Limited**
26 BOWLAND PRINCESS, b f Tiger Hill (IRE)—Kozmina (IRE) **Lowe Silver Deal**
27 CONCISE, b f Lemon Drop Kid (USA)—Cut Short (USA) **St Albans Bloodstock LLP & Cliveden Stud**
28 CONTRIBUTER (IRE), b c High Chaparral (IRE)—Serisia (FR) **Mr G. B. Bolton**
29 EGHNAA, b br f Cape Cross (IRE)—Alzaroof (USA) **Hamdan Al Maktoum**
30 EL CORDOBES (IRE), b c Montjeu (IRE)—Mayano Sophia (USA) **Sir Robert Ogden C.B.E., LLD**
31 ELHATHRAH (IRE), b f Nayef (USA)—Arch Swing (USA) **Hamdan Al Maktoum**
32 FILIA REGINA, b f Galileo (IRE)—Ouija Board **The Earl Of Derby**
33 FLYING TEMPO, b c Royal Applause—Bel Tempo **Mr R. Ng**
34 GWORN, b c Aussie Rules (USA)—Crochet (IRE) **Mr N. Martin**
35 HANZADA (USA), b br f Arch (USA)—Chocolate Mauk (USA) **Mr Nurlan Bizakov**
36 HIGH TROJA (IRE), b c High Chaparral (IRE)—Theben (GER) **Mr R. Ng**
37 HIGHLY GENTLE (FR), b g Gentlewave (IRE)—High Contrast (USA) **Mr Jon Haseler & OTI Racing**
38 IHTIKAR (USA), b g Invasor (ARG)—Ranin **Hamdan Al Maktoum**
39 INVINCIBLE CARA (IRE), b f Invincible Spirit (IRE)—Cara Fantasy (IRE) **Windflower Overseas Holdings Inc**
40 JABHAAT (USA), b f Hard Spun (USA)—Ishraak (USA) **Hamdan Al Maktoum**
41 JEERAAN (USA), b c Distorted Humor (USA)—Jaish (USA) **Hamdan Al Maktoum**
42 KAAHEN (USA), b br g Jazil (USA)—Khassah **Hamdan Al Maktoum**
43 LAMUSAWAMA, b c Acclamation—Intrepid Queen (USA) **Hamdan Al Maktoum**
44 LEXI'S DANCER, ch f Danehill Dancer (IRE)—Ravine **Dr M. B. Q. S. Koukash**
45 MANDY THE NAG (USA), b br f Proud Citizen (USA)—Storm to Glory (USA) **Dr M. B. Q. S. Koukash**
46 MANDY'S BOY (IRE), b g Kyllachy—African Queen (IRE) **Dr M. B. Q. S. Koukash**
47 MISTRAL WIND (IRE), b f Hurricane Run (IRE)—Grable (IRE) **Kean, Mitchell, O'Leary & ORS**
48 B f Dynaformer (USA)—Must Be a Lady (USA) **Dr M. B. Q. S. Koukash**

MR ED DUNLOP - Continued

49 **NAAZ (IRE)**, ch c Tamayuz—Naazeq **Mr R. Ng**
50 **NABAT SEIF (USA)**, b f Street Sense (USA)—Sierra Madre (FR) **Hamdan Al Maktoum**
51 **NARDIN**, b f Royal Applause—Third Party **Hamdan Al Maktoum**
52 **OF COURSE DARLING**, ch f Dalakhani (IRE)—Whazzis **Gredley, Hurley, ORS & Stanley**
53 **PAIRUMANI PRINCE (IRE)**, b c Choisir (AUS)—Pairumani Princess (IRE) **Anamoine Ltd**
54 **RED AVENGER (USA)**, b br c War Front (USA)—Emotional Rescue (USA) **R. J. Arculli**
55 **RED RUNAWAY**, ch c Medicean—Gretna **R. J. Arculli**
56 **SAXON SOLDIER**, br c Kyllachy—Gwyneth **H. Channon**
57 **SEJALAAT (IRE)**, br g Kheleyf (USA)—Laqataat (IRE) **Hamdan Al Maktoum**
58 **SINGERSONGWRITER**, ch f Raven's Pass (USA)—Independence **Cliveden Stud Ltd**
59 **SPECKLED HILL**, b g Oasis Dream—World's Heroine (IRE) **H. Channon**
60 **WAR HORSE (FR)**, b c Galileo (IRE)—Million Wishes **The Hon Earle I. Mack**

TWO-YEAR-OLDS

61 **ANIPA**, ch f 18/3 Sea The Stars (IRE)—Anna Amalia (IRE) (In The Wings) **Mr Nurlan Bizakov**
62 Br c 11/3 Sleeping Indian—Anytime Baby (Bairn (USA)) (20952) **Mrs S. M. Roy**
63 B br c 2/2 Henrythenavigator (USA)—Archstone (USA) (Arch (USA)) **Mrs Patricia Moseley**
64 **AURORA BOREALIS (IRE)**, b f 15/4 Montjeu (IRE)—Elaflaak (USA) (Gulch (USA)) **Sir Robert Ogden C.B.E., LLD**
65 **BIG BONED (USA)**, b f 24/4 Street Sense (USA)—
                        Lizzy Cool (USA) (Saint Ballado (CAN)) (58371) **Qatar Racing Limited**
66 B f 2/5 Dalakhani (IRE)—Brazilian Samba (IRE) (Sadler's Wells (USA)) (31745) **Dr M. B. Q. S. Koukash**
67 **CRADLE OF LIFE (IRE)**, ch f 14/3 Notnowcato—Pursuit of Life (Pursuit of Love) (55000) **A. W. Black**
68 **FIALKA**, b f 27/3 Cape Cross (IRE)—First (Highest Honor (FR)) **Mr Nurlan Bizakov**
69 Ch c 19/2 Pivotal—First Bloom (USA) (Fusaichi Pegasus (USA)) (47619) **Mrs S. M. Roy**
70 **FREDDIE KILROY**, b c 12/4 Pastoral Pursuits—Pretty Davis (USA) (Trempolino (USA)) (26000) **Mr C. R. Kilroy**
71 Ch gr f 18/3 Galileo (IRE)—Hotelgenie Dot Com (Selkirk (USA)) (210000) **St Albans Bloodstock LLP**
72 B c 1/4 Dalakhani (IRE)—Jamboretta (IRE) (Danehill (USA)) (90000) **Mr R. G. Arculli & Mr Robert Ng**
73 **KAAB (IRE)**, b c 18/3 Kheleyf (USA)—Ms Victoria (IRE) (Fasliyev (USA)) (42000) **Hamdan Al Maktoum**
74 **KINEMA (IRE)**, b c 14/3 Galileo (IRE)—Bon Nuit (IRE) (Night Shift (USA)) (198412) **Mr M. Keller**
75 B f 10/2 Galileo (IRE)—La Sylvia (IRE) (Oasis Dream) (570000) **Mrs G. A. Rupert**
76 B c 3/4 Oratorio (IRE)—Lucy Cavendish (USA) (Elusive Quality (USA)) (100000) **Mr R. G. Arculli & Mr Robert Ng**
77 **MAGHAANEM (IRE)**, b c 21/3 Acclamation—Shishangaan (IRE) (Mujadil (USA)) (123809) **Hamdan Al Maktoum**
78 Ch f 5/2 Galileo (IRE)—Mubkera (IRE) (Nashwan (USA)) (150000) **Mrs G. A. Rupert**
79 **MUSALAHA (IRE)**, b f 30/3 Nayef (USA)—Gilded (IRE) (Redback) (80000) **Hamdan Al Maktoum**
80 Ch c 21/4 Notnowcato—My American Beauty (Wolfhound (USA)) (10000) **Miltil Consortium**
81 B c 1/3 Galileo (IRE)—Night Woman (GER) (Monsun (GER)) (260000) **Mr M. Keller**
82 **OASIS FANTASY (IRE)**, br c 16/4 Oasis Dream—
        Cara Fantasy (IRE) (Sadler's Wells (USA)) **Windflower Overseas Holdings Inc & J. L. Dunlop**
83 Ch c 5/2 Tamayuz—Peace Summit (Cape Cross (IRE)) (60000) **Thurloe Thoroughbreds XXXI**
84 **PERYZAT (IRE)**, b f 21/3 Mastercraftsman (IRE)—Plethora (Sadler's Wells (USA)) **Mr Nurlan Bizakov**
85 **RAWOOF (IRE)**, b f 26/2 Nayef (USA)—Tanaghum (Darshaan) **Hamdan Al Maktoum**
86 **REHANAAT (USA)**, b f 16/3 Daaher (CAN)—Sultana (USA) (Storm Cat (USA)) **Hamdan Al Maktoum**
87 **ROXANNA**, b f 1/4 Myboycharlie (IRE)—Anagram (Efisio) (17142) **PLP Partnership**
88 **SHAF (IRE)**, b c 5/4 Medaglia d'oro (USA)—Jaish (USA) (Seeking The Gold (USA)) **Hamdan Al Maktoum**
89 **SHUSHU SUGARTOWN (IRE)**, b f 30/3 Invincible Spirit (IRE)—Landela (Alhaarth (IRE)) (39681) **Mr N. Martin**
90 B c 31/3 Sakhee's Secret—Sinduda (Anabaa (USA)) (75000) **Mr R. J. Arculli & Mr Robert Ng**
91 **TAQNEEN (IRE)**, b c 6/4 Cape Cross (IRE)—Badee'a (IRE) (Marju (IRE)) (240000) **Hamdan Al Maktoum**
92 **TASHBEEH (IRE)**, b c 1/2 Iffraaj—Kayak (Singspiel (IRE)) (58000) **Hamdan Al Maktoum**
93 **YAWAIL**, b br f 5/2 Medicean—Al Tamooh (IRE) (Dalakhani (IRE)) **Hamdan Al Maktoum**
94 **ZAAWIA (IRE)**, b f 21/3 Elnadim (USA)—Nidhaal (IRE) (Observatory (USA)) **Hamdan Al Maktoum**
95 **ZILBER (GER)**, b c 1/5 High Chaparral (IRE)—
                            Zephyrine (IRE) (Highest Honor (FR)) (35714) **Dr M. B. Q. S. Koukash**

Other Owners: Brigadier Abdulrazak Alshahwarzi, Mr A. A. Bamboye, Mr A. N. C. Bengough, Bloomsbury Stud, Sir Francis Brooke Bt., Mr P. A. Deal, Mr Nicholas Deterding, Caroline Dickens, Mr R. L. W. Frisby, Mrs W. J. Gredley, The Hon H. Herbert, Highclere Thoroughbred Racing Ltd, Mr Mark Horne, Mr A. D. P. Hurley, Mr Michael Kean, Mr Diarmaid Kelly, Alex Leonidas, Mr A. M. Mitchell, Mrs E. O'Leary, Mr Richard Pilkington, Sir Thomas Pilkington, Mr Anthony Rogers, The Hon. Peter Stanley.

Assistant Trainer: Mr George Peckham

186 MR HARRY DUNLOP, Lambourn

Postal: **Windsor House Stables, Crowle Road, Lambourn, Hungerford, Berkshire, RG17 8NR**
Contacts: **PHONE (01488) 73584 FAX (01488) 674172 MOBILE (07880) 791895**
E-MAIL info@harrydunlopracing.com WEBSITE www.harrydunlopracing.com

1 **RED SEVENTY**, 4, b g Sakhee (USA)—Dimakya (USA) **T. Neill**
2 **SAINT HELENA (IRE)**, 5, b m Holy Roman Emperor (IRE)—Tafseer (IRE) **W R B Racing 47**
3 **VIKING STORM**, 5, b g Hurricane Run (IRE)—Danehill's Dream (IRE) **Be Hopeful Partnership**

THREE-YEAR-OLDS

4 **ALPINE MYSTERIES (IRE)**, b f Elusive City (USA)—Alpine Gold (IRE) **Windflower Overseas Holdings Inc**
5 **BURLESQUE STAR (IRE)**, b f Thousand Words—Es Que **The Wigwam Partnership**
6 **CRYSTAL MIST**, br gr f Dalakhani (IRE)—Snow Crystal (IRE) **Mr K. A. Drake**
7 **DRAGON CITY**, b c Elusive City (USA)—Oulianovsk (IRE) **The Blue Bar Partnership**
8 **ENDURA**, b f Manduro (GER)—Special Moment (IRE) **Mrs M. Burrell & Partners**
9 **FENTON**, b f Tiger Hill (IRE)—Monteleone (IRE) **Cavendish Bloodstock Racing**
10 **LE GRANDE CHEVAL (IRE)**, b g Jeremy (USA)—Theory of Law **Mr D. A. Woodley**
11 **MISS TIGER LILY**, b f Tiger Hill (IRE)—Waitingonacloud **Mr & Mrs D. Hearson**
12 **NANDURA**, b f Motivator—Nando's Dream **P. G. Goulandris**
13 **OLYMPIC JULE**, b f Shamardal (USA)—Jules (IRE) **Mr M. Stewkesbury**
14 **PINK MISCHIEF**, gr f Holy Roman Emperor (IRE)—Feather (USA) **The Windsor House Stables Partnership**
15 **POITIN**, b f Kheleyf (USA)—Port Providence **David & Paul Hearson**
16 **RANCHER (IRE)**, b c High Chaparral (IRE)—Shot of Redemption **The Ranchers**
17 **ROZ**, b f Teofilo (IRE)—Debonnaire **Mrs M. Parker**
18 **SIR PATRICK MOORE (FR)**, gr c Astronomer Royal (USA)—America Nova (FR) **The Astronomers**
19 **TRISARA**, b f Exceed And Excel (AUS)—Hiddendale (IRE) **Mrs S. M. Roy**
20 **VELVETINA (IRE)**, b f Barathea (IRE)—Pershaan (IRE) **Windflower Overseas Holdings Inc**

TWO-YEAR-OLDS

21 **ARTWOLF (IRE)**, b c 30/4 Peintre Celebre (USA)—Steno (USA) (Devil's Bag (USA)) (6000) **The Hungry Wolves**
22 B c 24/4 Medicean—Black Belt Shopper (IRE) (Desert Prince (IRE)) (8000)
23 **CADMIUM**, b f 17/4 Major Cadeaux—Miss Mirasol (Sheikh Albadou) (6500) **Susan Abbott Racing**
24 **CINNAMON SPICE**, b br c 9/2 High Chaparral (IRE)—Hot And Spicy (Grand Lodge (USA)) (21000) **Be Hopeful (2)**
25 **EARLY MORNING (IRE)**, gr c 15/4 New Approach (IRE)—Summer's Eve (Singspiel (IRE)) (36000) **Early Risers**
26 **ENCORE ENCORE (FR)**, b f 30/3 Royal Applause—
    Angel Rose (IRE) (Definite Article) (3174) **Pam & Peter Deal & Jeni & David Sieff**
27 B f 14/2 Champs Elysees—Fairy Dance (IRE) (Zafonic (USA)) (13000) **Mr J. Hobby**
28 B f 7/2 Indesatchel (IRE)—Flying Highest (Spectrum (IRE)) (4761)
29 Ch f 26/2 Teofilo (IRE)—Future Flight (Polar Falcon (USA)) (40000) **Sir Eric Parker & Mary Anne Parker**
30 **GAMGOOM**, b c 19/3 Exceed And Excel (AUS)—Danidh Dubai (IRE) (Noverre (USA)) **J. Abdullah**
31 **GENEROUS HEART**, ch f 25/2 Sakhee's Secret—Lonely Heart (Midyan (USA)) **Harry Dunlop Racing Partnership**
32 **JANET'S LEGACY**, b c 15/1 Bahamian Bounty—Spunger (Fraam) (12380) **The Spungers**
33 B f 11/3 Mount Nelson—Mexican Hawk (USA) (Silver Hawk (USA)) **W R B Racing 53**
34 **PERSIAN CALIPH (IRE)**, ch g 26/1 Intikhab (USA)—
    Persian Memories (IRE) (Indian Ridge) **Windflower Overseas Holdings Inc**
35 Ch f 12/4 Dylan Thomas (IRE)—
    Portrait of A Lady (IRE) (Peintre Celebre (USA)) (18000) **Sir Eric Parker & Mary Anne Parker**
36 B c 4/4 Astronomer Royal (USA)—Rubber (IRE) (Namid) (35000) **S. F. Bloodstock**
37 B f 5/2 Astronomer Royal (USA)—Sasicha (IRE) (Montjeu (IRE)) (13492) **The Astronomers 2**
38 **SPACE WALKER (IRE)**, b c 23/2 Astronomer Royal (USA)—
    Hot Property (USA) (Thunder Gulch (USA)) (19047) **J. Abdullah**
39 **SPANISH ARTIST**, gr c 2/2 Archipenko (USA)—Alicante (Pivotal) (17000) **Bluehills Racing Limited**
40 B f 19/2 Pastoral Pursuits—Torcross (Vettori (IRE)) (5500)

Other Owners: Earl of Balfour, Mr A. W. A. Bates, Mr J. L. Dunlop, Mr D. Leach, Mr J. Mortonson, Mr C. M. Parker, Sir Eric Parker, Mr A. J. Struthers, Mrs S. A. K. Watson, Sir Philip Wroughton.

187 MRS ALEXANDRA DUNN, Wellington

Postal: **Georges Farm, Cutsey, Trull, Taunton, Somerset, TA3 7NY**
Contacts: **MOBILE (07738) 512924**
E-MAIL info@alexandradunnracing.co.uk WEBSITE www.alexandradunnracing.co.uk

1 **ARRAYAN**, 8, b g Catcher In The Rye (IRE)—Ganga (IRE) **Mr T. H. Dunn**
2 **DOUBLE MEAD**, 11, b m Double Trigger (IRE)—Normead Lass **Mrs K. R. Smith-Maxwell**

MRS ALEXANDRA DUNN - Continued

3 **LION ON THE PROWL (IRE)**, 9, b g Sadler's Wells (USA)—Ballerina (IRE) **Mrs K. R. Smith-Maxwell**
4 **NEXT TO NOWHERE (IRE)**, 8, ch g Exit To Nowhere (USA)—Zarote (IRE) **Mr T. H. Dunn**
5 **PICAROON**, 9, b g Jade Robbery (USA)—Anaam **Mrs K. R. Smith-Maxwell**
6 **RAINBOW TREE**, 13, b g Rainbows For Life (CAN)—Little Twig (IRE) **Mrs K. R. Smith-Maxwell**
7 **WINNING COUNSEL (IRE)**, 11, br m Leading Counsel (USA)—Dainty Daisy (IRE) **Mrs K. R. Smith-Maxwell**

---

188 MRS CHRISTINE DUNNETT, Norwich

Postal: **College Farm, Hingham, Norwich, Norfolk, NR9 4PP**
Contacts: **PHONE (01953) 850596 FAX (01953) 851364 MOBILE (07775) 793523**
E-MAIL christine@christinedunnett.com WEBSITE www.christinedunnett.com

1 **BARATHEA DANCER (IRE)**, 5, b m Barathea (IRE)—Showering **Mr P. D. West**
2 **COLLEGE DOLL**, 4, ch f Piccolo—Southwarknewsflash **P. D. West, A. S. Machin & C. A. Dunnett**
3 **DANZOE (IRE)**, 6, br g Kheleyf (USA)—Fiaba **One For All**
4 **FIDDLERS DREAM**, 7, gr g Karinga Bay—Roseta Pearl (IRE) **Mr T. M. Colk**
5 **GIVE US A BELLE (IRE)**, 4, b g Kheleyf (USA)—Bajan Belle (IRE) **Mr F. Butler & Mrs C. Dunnett**
6 **ITUM**, 6, ch g Bahamian Bounty—Petomi **Mrs Christine Dunnett**
7 **JESSICA'S GOLD**, 4, b f Iceman—Capstick (JPN) **Christine Dunnett Racing (Jessica's Gold)**
8 **LATER IN LIFE**, 4, ch f Notnowcato—Life's A Whirl **Life's a Whirl Partnership**
9 **MYSTICAL WITCH**, 4, b f Kyllachy—Shifty Night (IRE) **Mrs C. A. Dunnett & Mr P. D. West**
10 **NORCROFT**, 11, b g Fasliyev (USA)—Norcroft Joy **Mrs C. A. Dunnett**
11 **ONWARDS'N'UPWARDS**, 5, b g Diktat—Lunar Goddess **Mrs C. A. Dunnett & Mr P. D. West**
12 **SPEEDYFIX**, 6, b g Chineur (FR)—Zonnebeke **Annwell Inn Syndicate**

THREE-YEAR-OLDS

13 **MARVELOUS MISS (IRE)**, b f Captain Marvelous (IRE)—
Abbeyleix Lady (IRE) **Mrs C. A. Dunnett & Mr P. D. West**
14 **PERSEVERENT PETE (USA)**, b br c Johannesburg (USA)—Indian Halloween (USA) **Mr P. D. West**

TWO-YEAR-OLDS

15 Ch f 29/3 Phoenix Reach (IRE)—Bongoali (Fraam) **Mrs C. A. Dunnett**
16 **GIVE IT A WHIRL**, br f 4/3 Pastoral Pursuits—
Life's A Whirl (Machiavellian (USA)) **Mr A. Machin & Mrs C. Dunnett**
17 B c 17/4 Phoenix Reach (IRE)—Southwarknewsflash (Danetime (IRE)) **Mrs C. A. Dunnett**
18 Ch c 1/4 Dutch Art—Tata Naka (Nashwan (USA)) **Mrs C. A. Dunnett**

Other Owners: Mrs Mary Benjafield, Mr G. Bromley, Mr David Burt, Mr F. Butler, Mr M. L. Clements, Mrs Christine Dunnett, Miss Karen Everitt, Mr A. S. Machin, Mr M. Skellett, Mr Eamonn Sparkes, Mr P. D. West.

---

189 MR SEAMUS DURACK, Upper Lambourn

Postal: **16 Downsmead, Baydon, Marlborough, Wiltshire, SN8 2LQ**
Contacts: **PHONE (01488) 686581 MOBILE (07770) 537971**
E-MAIL sd111@btinternet.com

1 **BROKEN EAGLE (USA)**, 5, b g Broken Vow (USA)—Tricky Bird (USA) **Miss S. J. Beddoes**
2 **GRAND GOLD**, 4, b g Librettist (USA)—Night Symphonie **P. A. Deal**
3 **INVINCIBLE BEAUTY (IRE)**, 4, b f Invincible Spirit (IRE)—Beautiful Note (USA) **Mrs A. Cowley**
4 **LAKOTA GHOST (USA)**, 5, b g Rockport Harbor (USA)—Political Alert (USA) **Grandpa's**
5 **REYES MAGOS (IRE)**, 7, b g Indian Danehill (IRE)—Cincuenta (IRE) **Walters Plant Hire Ltd Egan Waste Ltd**
6 **SUGARFORMYHONEY**, 4, ch f Dutch Art—Sweetsformysweet (USA) **W. A. Harrison-Allan**
7 **WORDINESS**, 5, br h Dansili—Verbose (USA) **W. A. Harrison-Allan**

THREE-YEAR-OLDS

8 **SHAOLIN (IRE)**, b c Footstepsinthesand—Baboosh (IRE) **Miss S. J. Beddoes**

Other Owners: J. J. Blackshaw, Egan Waste Services Ltd, Walters Plant Hire Ltd.

190 MRS NERYS DUTFIELD, Seaton
Postal: **Crabhayne Farm, Axmouth, Seaton, Devon, EX12 4BW**
Contacts: **PHONE (01297) 553560 FAX (01297) 551185**
E-MAIL nerys.dutfield@tiscali.co.uk WEBSITE www.nerysdutfield.com

1 MAN OF LEISURE, 9, b g Karinga Bay—Girl of Pleasure (IRE) **Mrs P. N. Dutfield**
2 PRESENT ACCEPTED, 6, b g Presenting—Kwaheri **S. J. Dutfield**

191 MR CHRIS DWYER, Newmarket
Postal: **Brickfields Stud, Exning Road, Newmarket, Suffolk, CB8 7JH**
Contacts: **MOBILE (07831) 579844**
E-MAIL getadwyer@aol.com

1 DUBAI EMERALD (USA), 4, b br f Henny Hughes (USA)—Zanoubia (USA) **Mrs S. Dwyer**
2 ELLEMUJIE, 8, b g Mujahid (USA)—Jennelle **Mrs J. A. Cornwell**
3 MIA'S BOY, 9, b g Pivotal—Bint Zamayem (IRE) **Mrs S. Dwyer**
4 MISS POLLY PLUM, 6, b m Doyen (IRE)—Mrs Plum **Mrs J. Hughes & Miss C. Hughes**
5 PATRIOTIC (IRE), 5, b g Pivotal—Pescara (IRE) **M. M. Foulger**
6 4, B f Librettist (USA)—Primavera **Mrs I. L. Sneath**
7 RING FOR BAILEYS, 4, ch f Kyllachy—Ring of Love **Mr P. Venner**
8 TATTING, 4, ch g Street Cry (IRE)—Needlecraft (IRE) **Mrs I. L. Sneath**
9 TORNADO FORCE (IRE), 5, ch g Shamardal (USA)—Pharma West (USA) **M. M. Foulger**

THREE-YEAR-OLDS
10 BALATINA, ch f Byron—Primavera **Mrs I. L. Sneath**
11 BRYNFORD, b f Sir Percy—Bull's Crown (USA) **R. S. G. Jones**
12 HANNAHS TURN, b f Dubai Destination (USA)—Fontaine House **Mrs I. L. Sneath**
13 NOT NOW BLONDIE, ch f Notnowcato—Gretel **Not Now Partnership**
14 WHITFORD (IRE), b c Jeremy (USA)—Linette (GER) **R. S. G. Jones**

TWO-YEAR-OLDS
15 B c 6/4 Tiger Hill (IRE)—Canis Star (Wolfhound (USA)) (8000) **D. L. Bowkett**
16 B c 28/4 Tobougg (IRE)—Dolly Coughdrop (IRE) (Titus Livius (FR))
17 LUCARVEY, b f 16/3 Lucarno (USA)—Split Briefs (IRE) (Mull of Kintyre (USA)) **Mrs S. Dwyer**

Other Owners: Mr J. W. Farley, Mrs J. V. Hughes, Miss C. J. Hughes.

Assistant Trainer: Shelley Dwyer

Jockey (flat): Cathy Gannon, Andrea Atzeni. **Apprentice:** Josh Crane.

192 MISS CLAIRE DYSON, Evesham
Postal: **Froglands Stud Farm, Froglands Lane, Cleeve Prior, Evesham, Worcestershire, WR11 8LB**
Contacts: **PHONE (07803) 720183 (01789) 774000 FAX (01789) 774000**
E-MAIL cdyson@live.co.uk WEBSITE www.clairedysonracing.co.uk

1 BOOMTOWN, 8, b g Fantastic Light (USA)—Ville d'amore (USA) **Miss C. Dyson**
2 BURNTHILL (IRE), 8, b g Winged Love (IRE)—Kilcorig (IRE) **Miss C. Dyson**
3 CHADFORD, 5, b g Trade Fair—Quiz Time **B & S Vaughan, Lisa Rogers & Partner**
4 DR DREAMY (IRE), 6, b g Dr Massini (IRE)—Proud Aldi (IRE) **Guy Sainsbury & Partner**
5 DROMORE HILL (IRE), 9, b g Flemensfirth (USA)—Tree Oaks (IRE) **Mr Tim Wixted & Mr Tony Anderson**
6 DUDLEY LIGHT, 6, b g Needwood Blade—Dudleys Delight **FSF Racing**
7 GIVEITACHANCE (IRE), 6, b g Clerkenwell (USA)—Native Lisa (IRE) **FSF Racing**
8 HERON RUN (IRE), 7, b m Heron Island (IRE)—Deep Satisfaction **Ms I. Heritage**
9 ICANMOTOR, 6, b m Midnight Legend—Lochnagold **Mr K. Elvins**
10 KHAZIUM (IRE), 4, br g Kheleyf (USA)—Hazium (IRE) **Mr Tim Wixted & Mr Tony Anderson**
11 MR JAY DEE (IRE), 8, b g Lord Americo—Emmas Flyer (IRE) **B & S Vaughan & Partner**
12 MUSICAL WEDGE, 9, ch g Sir Harry Lewis (USA)—Wedge Musical **D. J. Dyson**
13 MYSULA, 6, b m Sulamani (IRE)—Air of Affection **Miss R. J. Rowland**
14 NELTARA, 9, b g Kayf Tara—Lucia Forte **D. J. Dyson**
15 OVER MY HEAD, 5, bl gr g Overbury (IRE)—Altesse de Sou (FR) **Ms I. Heritage**
16 QUALITEE, 8, b m Superior Premium—Coco Loco **C. R. Green**
17 QUAYSIDE COURT (IRE), 9, ch g Anshan—Rustic Court (IRE) **Guy Sainsbury & Carl Mason**

MISS CLAIRE DYSON - Continued

18 WHEELAVHER, 7, br m Fair Mix (IRE)—True Rose (IRE) **Miss S. J. Turner**
19 WHEELAVIM, 5, b g Beat All (USA)—Plus Tu Mets (FR) **D. J. Dyson**

THREE-YEAR-OLDS

20 Ch g Midnight Legend—Owlesbury Dream (IRE) **D. J. & C. Dyson**

Other Owners: Mr Tony Anderson, Mrs C. Dyson, Mr D. J. Dyson, Mr Carl Mason, Lisa Rogers, Mr Guy Sainsbury, Mr B. Vaughan, Mrs S. Vaughan, Mr Tim Wixted.

Assistant Trainer: John Dyson

Jockey (NH): Tom O'Brien, Nick Scholfield. **Conditional:** Ian Popham, Gerald Quinn.

---

193 **MR SIMON EARLE, Warminster**
Postal: **Little Croft, Tytherington, Warminster, Wiltshire, BA12 7AD**
Contacts: **PHONE (01985) 840450 FAX (01985) 840450 MOBILE (07850) 350116**
E-MAIL simon@simonearleracing.com WEBSITE www.simonearleracing.com

1 BENOZZO GOZZOLI, 7, ch g Medicean—Star Precision **Mr J. R. Powell**
2 FAIRWOOD DANTE (IRE), 9, b g Mr Combustible (IRE)—Lady de Hatton (IRE) **Mrs S. J. Symonds**
3 GET BACK TO ME (IRE), 6, br g Presenting—My Name's Not Bin (IRE) **R. L. Dacombe**
4 HEADLY'S BRIDGE (IRE), 7, b g Tillerman—Brockton Flame **Mrs P. L. Bridel**
5 HOMER RUN (IRE), 6, b g Classic Cliche (IRE)—Suir Native (IRE) **EPDS Racing Partnership 3**
6 LOXLEY MEZILE, 4, br f Strategic Prince—Haiti Dancer **EPDS Racing Partnership 2**
7 OUTSIDE THE BOX, 9, b g Karinga Bay—Maydoo (IRE) **Mrs B. O'Flynn**
8 RED NOT BLUE (IRE), 10, b g Blueprint (IRE)—Silent Valley **The Plum Merchants**
9 SHILPA (IRE), 8, b m Medicean—Nature Girl (USA) **EPDS Racing Partnership I**
10 SNOWY VALLEY, 4, ch g Three Valleys (USA)—Rasseem (IRE) **P & M Racing**
11 STARLIGHT SECRET, 4, b g Exceed And Excel (AUS)—Caribbean Star **P & M Racing**
12 VIC THE VIKING, 5, b g Norse Dancer (IRE)—Rasseem (IRE) **P & M Racing**
13 WATER RAIL, 4, b g Manipulator (IRE)—Madame Mozaik (USA) **Mr Simon Earle**

THREE-YEAR-OLDS

14 VICKY THE VIKING, ch f Norse Dancer (IRE)—Rasseem (IRE) **P & M Racing**

Other Owners: Mr M. G. Hancock, Mrs P. Hancock, Mr John Powell, Miss T. Sloan.

Jockey (flat): George Baker. **Jockey (NH):** Andrew Thornton, Gerard Tumelty. **Amateur:** Mr Luke Kilgarriff.

---

194 **MR MICHAEL EASTERBY, Sheriff Hutton**
Postal: **New House Farm, Sheriff Hutton, York, North Yorkshire, YO60 6TN**
Contacts: **PHONE (01347) 878368 FAX (01347) 878204 MOBILE (07831) 347481**
E-MAIL enquiries@mickeasterby-racing.co.uk WEBSITE www.mickeasterby-racing.co.uk

1 ABOVE STANDARD (IRE), 5, ch g Shamardal (USA)—Prealpina (IRE) **Mr A. Saha**
2 AERODYNAMIC (IRE), 6, b g Oratorio (IRE)—Willowbridge (IRE) **David Scott & Co (Pattern Makers) Ltd**
3 ALLURING STAR, 5, b m Gentleman's Deal (IRE)—Alustar **Jeff Hamer & Bernard Bargh**
4 ANCIENT CROSS, 9, b g Machiavellian (USA)—
    Magna Graecia (IRE) **Mr Pete Bown, Backup Technology & Steve Hull**
5 BARREN BROOK, 4, b g Beat Hollow—Carinthia (IRE) **Mr D. Scott, Mrs E. Wright & Mr J. Clark**
6 BLACK ANNIS BOWER, 5, gr m Proclamation (IRE)—Bow Bridge **Mrs A. Jarvis**
7 BORIS GRIGORIEV (IRE), 4, b br g Excellent Art—Strategy **Mrs L. M. Ward**
8 CITY GROUND (USA), 6, b br g Orientate (USA)—Magnet (USA) **S. Hull**
9 CROOKED ARROW (IRE), 5, b g Galileo (IRE)—Mythologie (FR) **D. Scott**
10 DAY OF THE EAGLE (IRE), 7, b g Danehill Dancer (IRE)—
    Puck's Castle **Mr S. Hull, Mr J. Bryan & Mr S. Hollings**
11 DESERT STING, 4, b g Scorpion (IRE)—Skipcarl (IRE) **Loud Daresbury & Steve Hull**
12 DESERT VISION, 9, b g Alhaarth (IRE)—Fragrant Oasis (USA) **A. Black, R Edmonds, J. Holdroyd, J. Quickfall**
13 FAME AGAIN, 5, b g Gentleman's Deal (IRE)—Ballet Fame (USA) **Mrs C. E. Mason**
14 FIGHTER BOY (IRE), 6, b g Rock of Gibraltar (IRE)—In My Life (IRE) **Mr A. G. Greenwood**
15 FRIDAYTHORPE (IRE), 8, b g Flemensfirth (USA)—Calm Waters (IRE) **N. H. T. Wrigley**
16 GINGER'S LAD, 9, ch g Elmaamul (USA)—Chadwick's Ginger **W. H. & Mrs J. A. Tinning**
17 HALLMARK HARRY, 7, b g Silver Patriarch (IRE)—Society Girl **N. W. A. Bannister**

MR MICHAEL EASTERBY - Continued

18 **HERNANDO TORRES**, 5, b g Iffraaj—Espana **M. W. Easterby**
19 **HOOF IT**, 6, b g Monsieur Bond (IRE)—Forever Bond **Mr A. Chandler & Mr L. Westwood**
20 **ICEBLAST**, 5, b g Iceman—Medici Princess **Mr B. Padgett**
21 **ITLAAQ**, 7, b g Alhaarth (USA)—Hathrah (IRE) **Mrs L. J. Turpin**
22 **IVESTAR (IRE)**, 8, b g Fraam—Hazardous **Mrs K. R. Brown**
23 **KALK BAY (IRE)**, 6, b g Hawk Wing (USA)—Politesse (USA) **Mrs L. J. Turpin**
24 **LIGHTENING ROD**, 8, b g Storming Home—Bolero **N. W. A. Bannister**
25 **MAJESTIC DREAM (IRE)**, 5, b g Exceed And Excel (AUS)—Tallassee **Mr A. Simpson, B. Hoggarth & S. Hull**
26 **MILLYMONKIN**, 4, b f Gentleman's Deal (IRE)—Royal Distant (USA) **Mr T. Dewhirst & Mr R. Moore**
27 **NAMEITWHATYOULIKE**, 4, b g Trade Fair—Emma Peel **Mr S. Bowett, Mr S. Hollings & Mr S. Hull**
28 **OIL STRIKE**, 6, b g Lucky Story (USA)—Willisa **Mr A. Saha**
29 **ON THE HOOF**, 4, gr g Monsieur Bond—Smart Hostess **Mr A. Chandler & Mr L. Westwood**
30 **ONE OF TWINS**, 5, b g Gentleman's Deal (IRE)—Miss Twiddles (IRE) **Clark Industrial Services Partnership**
31 **OUR CRUSADE**, 6, ch g Rainbow Quest (USA)—Angeleno (IRE) **Lord Daresbury**
32 **PERTEMPS NETWORKS**, 9, b g Golden Snake (USA)—Society Girl **E. A. Brook**
33 **POLITBUREAU**, 6, b g Red Ransom (USA)—Tereshkova (USA) **W. H. & Mrs J. A. Tinning**
34 **PRINCE JAMES**, 6, b g Danroad (AUS)—Lawless Bridget **Mr A. Saha**
35 **ROYAL DEAL**, 6, b g Gentleman's Deal (IRE)—
                                         Royal Distant (USA) **T. Dewhirst, R. Moore & Lucky 5 Partnership**
36 **SAINTS AND SINNERS (IRE)**, 5, b g Gold Well—How Provincial (IRE) **Mr P. Deal & Mr N. Wrigley**
37 **SHADOWS LENGTHEN**, 7, b g Dansili—Bay Shade (USA) **T. A. F. Frost**
38 **SHEEPCLOSE (IRE)**, 8, b g Beneficial—Returning **Lord Daresbury**
39 **SINGZAK**, 5, ch g Singspiel (IRE)—Zakuska **Clark Industrial Services Partnership**
40 **SPACE WAR**, 6, b g Elusive City (USA)—Princess Luna (GER) **M. W. Easterby**
41 **SPECIAL MIX**, 5, b g Proclamation (IRE)—Flaming Spirt **E. A. Brook**
42 **STRONG MAN**, 5, b g Gentleman's Deal (IRE)—Strong Hand **Mrs L. J. Turpin**
43 **TAPIS LIBRE**, 5, b g Librettist (USA)—Stella Manuela (FR) **M. W. Easterby**
44 **THIRTEEN SHIVERS**, 5, b g Iceman—Thirteen Tricks (USA) **Keith Wreglesworth & Andre Fordham**
45 **TOWBEE**, 4, b g Doyen (IRE)—Bow Bridge **Mrs A. Jarvis**
46 **UP TEN DOWN TWO (IRE)**, 4, b g Hurricane Run (IRE)—
                                      Darabela (IRE) **B. Delaney, A. Duke & Backup Technology**
47 **WE'LL DEAL AGAIN**, 6, b g Gentleman's Deal (IRE)—Emma Amour **K. Wreglesworth**

THREE-YEAR-OLDS

48 **AETNA**, b f Indesatchel (IRE)—On The Brink **Mr B. Padgett**
49 **CLOCK ON TOM**, b g Trade Fair—Night Owl **Mr A. G. Simpson**
50 **EL MOLINO BLANCO**, b f Royal Applause—Forest Prize **David Scott & Co (Pattern Makers) Ltd**
51 **HOOFALONG**, b g Pastoral Pursuits—Baymist **A. Chandler, L. Westwood, D. & Y. Blunt**
52 **MY BOY BILL**, b g Dutch Art—Pious **Mrs L. M. Ward**
53 **NETWORK STORY**, b f Pastoral Pursuits—Ballet Fame (USA) **Mr M. Cox**
54 **OLD MAN CLEGG**, b g Pastoral Pursuits—Stolen Melody **Irkroy Racing & Steve Hull**
55 **PERFECT PASTURE**, b g Pastoral Pursuits—Word Perfect **Mrs L. J. Turpin**
56 **ROCKY COULOIR**, ch g Rock of Gibraltar (IRE)—Framboise **David & Yvonne Blunt 1**

TWO-YEAR-OLDS

57 B c 25/4 Clodovil (IRE)—Accounting (Sillery (USA)) (19047) **Clark Industrial Services**
58 B f 17/5 Monsieur Bond (IRE)—Amalfi Storm (Slip Anchor) **Lucky 5 Partnership**
59 B c 19/4 Dutch Art—Ballet Fame (USA) (Quest For Fame) **Mrs Christine Mason**
60 Ch c 29/4 Captain Gerrard (IRE)—Bond Shakira (Daggers Drawn (USA))
61 Ch f 15/3 Captain Gerrard (IRE)—Danifah (IRE) (Perugino (USA)) (4761) **Mr E. Morgans**
62 **ELLE WEST**, ch f 20/2 Elnadim (USA)—Leominda (Lion Cavern (USA)) (7619) **Mr Mike Pollitt**
63 Ch f 15/5 Monsieur Bond (IRE)—Fujakka (IRE) (Vettori (IRE)) (3809)
64 **HOOF'S SO LUCKY**, ch f 27/2 Compton Place—Lucky Dip (Tirol) (20952) **Mr A. Chandler & Mr L. Westwood**
65 B c 5/2 Aqlaam—Hufflepuff (IRE) (Desert King (IRE)) (20000) **Mr Eric Brook**
66 B f 3/3 Sleeping Indian—Ma-Arif (IRE) (Alzao (USA)) (5714)
67 B f 20/3 Distant Peak (IRE)—Mount Hillaby (IRE) (Mujadil (USA))
68 **OH MY FLOW**, ch f 16/3 Avonbridge—Highland Cascade (Tipsy Creek (USA)) (3333) **Mr Peter Hunt**
69 B c 15/4 Champs Elysees—Rowan Flower (IRE) (Ashkalani (IRE)) (3000) **Mr Andrew Morse**
70 Ch f 20/4 Bahamian Bounty—Silca Key (Inchinor) (5714)
71 **SLICK INDIAN**, b c 17/3 Sleeping Indian—Jesting (Muhtarram (USA)) (15238) **Mr Mike Pollitt**
72 B c 7/4 Byron—Stolen Melody (Robellino (USA)) (4761)
73 B c 24/3 Tobougg (IRE)—Three Gifts (Cadeaux Genereux) (3809) **Mr David Standring**
74 **UNCLE BOBBY**, b c 22/4 Avonbridge—Aunt Hilda (Distant Relative) (3809) **Mrs Albertine Blanchard**
75 B c 10/4 Piccolo—Whitby (IRE) (Dubawi (IRE)) (7619)
76 Ch c 11/5 Distant Peak (IRE)—Word Perfect (Diktat) (7619)

MR MICHAEL EASTERBY - Continued

Other Owners: Mr Bernard Bargh, Mr Andy Barlow, Mr A. G. Black, Mr David Blunt, Mrs Y. Blunt, Mr S. Bowett, Mr P. J. Bown, Mr E. A. Brook, Mr John Bryan, Mr Andrew Chandler, Mr S. Chappell, Mr Jim Clark, Mr A. W. Clark, Lord Daresbury, Mr P. A. Davies, Mr Peter Davies, Mr P. A. Deal, Mr Bill Delaney, Mr T. C. Dewhirst, Mr A. Duke, Mr M. W. Easterby, Mr Ray Edmonds, Mr Ritchie Fiddes, Mr Andre Fordham, Mr Bernard Hoggarth, Mr John L. Holdroyd, Mrs S. A. Hollings, Mr Malcolm Hoyle, Mr Steve Hull, Mr O. H. Kingsley, Mr J. R. Moore, Mr A. Morse, Mrs Rosalynd Norman, Mr J. E. H. Quickfall, Mr David Scott, Mr Andrew Simpson, Stittenham Racing, Mrs J. A. Tinning, Mr W. H. Tinning, Mr K. Wreglesworth, Mrs E. Wright, Mrs A. M. Wright, Mr N. H. T. Wrigley.

Assistant Trainer: D. M. Easterby

Jockey (flat): Graham Gibbons, Paul Mulrennan, James Sullivan. **Conditional:** Jake Greenall. **Apprentice:** Matthew Hopkins. **Amateur:** Mr H. Bannister, Miss S. Brotherton, Miss J. Coward, Mr T. Greenall, Miss Anna Hesketh, Miss Joanna Mason.

195	**MR TIM EASTERBY, Malton**

Postal: **Habton Grange, Great Habton, Malton, North Yorkshire, YO17 6TY**
Contacts: **PHONE (01653) 668566 FAX (01653) 668621**

1 ABSOLUTE FUN (IRE), 4, b f Lawman (FR)—Jallaissine (IRE) **Mr M. O'Mahony**
2 ANOTHER CITIZEN (IRE), 5, b g Byron—Royal Rival (IRE) **Middleham Park Racing V & Partners**
3 ARC LIGHT (IRE), 5, b g Shamardal (USA)—Banakill (FR) **Habton Farms**
4 ART DZEKO, 4, b g Acclamation—Delitme (IRE) **Middleham Park Racing LIX & Partners**
5 AURA BORA (USA), 5, b g North Light (IRE)—A Rose for Chris (USA) **Habton Farms**
6 BALLYMARTIN KING (IRE), 7, b g King's Theatre (IRE)—Lady Sipash **Mrs J. E. Pallister**
7 BLUE SHOES (IRE), 4, b f Kodiac—Alexander Capetown (IRE) **C. H. Stevens**
8 BOLLIN FELIX, 9, br g Generous (IRE)—Bollin Magdalene **Mrs S. J. Easterby**
9 BOLLIN GRETA, 8, b br m Mtoto—Bollin Zola **Habton Farms**
10 CAPTAIN DUNNE (IRE), 8, b g Captain Rio—Queen Bodicea (IRE) **Middleham Park Racing XV & Partners**
11 CHEERS FOR THEA (IRE), 8, gr m Distant Music (USA)—Popiplu (USA) **R. A. George**
12 CHOISAN (IRE), 4, b g Choisir (AUS)—Attanagh (IRE) **Croft, Taylor & Hebdon**
13 CLOCKMAKER (IRE), 7, b g Danetime (IRE)—Lady Ingabelle (IRE) **Middleham Park Racing XI & Partners**
14 COCKTAIL CHARLIE, 5, b g Danbird (AUS)—Royal Punch **C. H. Stevens**
15 CONFESSIONAL, 6, b g Dubawi (IRE)—Golden Nun **Mr T. G. & Mrs M. E. Holdcroft**
16 CRACKENTORP, 8, b g Generous (IRE)—Raspberry Sauce **C. H. Stevens**
17 DARK DUNE (IRE), 5, b g Diamond Green (FR)—Panpipes (USA) **Miss B. C. Duxbury**
18 DAZZLIN BLUEBELL (IRE), 4, b f Strategic Prince—Sharamaine (IRE) **Mr C. Wilson**
19 DEAUVILLE FLYER, 7, b g Dubai Destination (USA)—Reaf **Mr & Mrs J. D. Cotton**
20 DEEPSAND (IRE), 4, br g Footstepsinthesand—Sinamay (USA) **T. J. Hemmings**
21 DUBAI DESTINY, 4, b g Dubai Destination (USA)—Ukraine (IRE) **Habton Farms**
22 ELEGANT GIRL (IRE), 4, b f Amadeus Wolf—Zuccini Wind (IRE) **P. C. J. Bourke**
23 FAST SHOT, 5, b g Fasliyev (USA)—Final Pursuit **Ontoawinner & Partners**
24 FAVOURS BRAVE, 7, b g Galileo (IRE)—Tuning **Mrs J. M. Bowser**
25 FAYR FALL (IRE), 4, b g Fayruz—Keshena Falls (IRE) **Reality Partnerships**
26 FIRST CLASS FAVOUR (IRE), 5, b m Exceed And Excel (AUS)—Lamh Eile (IRE) **S. A. Heley**
27 FISHERMAN'S FRIEND (IRE), 6, b g Heron Island (IRE)—Sabang **Habton Farms**
28 FORSTER STREET (IRE), 4, b g Acclamation—Easy To Thrill **L. Mulryan**
29 FOURJACKS, 8, b g Karinga Bay—Jack's The Girl (IRE) **T. J. Hemmings**
30 GETABUZZ, 5, b g Beat Hollow—Ailincala (IRE) **Langham Hall Stud Three**
31 GRISSOM (IRE), 7, b g Desert Prince—Misty Peak (IRE) **Jim & Helen Bowers**
32 HAMISH MCGONAGALL, 8, b g Namid—Anatase **Reality Partnerships I**
33 HAYEK, 6, b g Royal Applause—Salagama (IRE) **Numac Engineering Ltd**
34 HAZELRIGG (IRE), 8, b g Namid—Emma's Star (ITY) **The Senators**
35 HELLO STRANGER (IRE), 4, ch c Redback—Bobbydazzle **N. A. Jackson**
36 HOLY ANGEL (IRE), 4, b g Dark Angel (IRE)—Bakewell Tart (IRE) **Three Jolly Farmers**
37 IF YOU WISH (IRE), 5, ch g Zerpour (IRE)—Bu Hagab (IRE) **Mr P S Cook & Mr A Parker**
38 JONNY LESTERS HAIR (IRE), 8, b g Danetime (IRE)—Jupiter Inlet (IRE) **Reality Partnerships II**
39 JUST LIKE HEAVEN (IRE), 4, b g Kodiac—Night Beauty **D. B. Lamplough**
40 KING OF THE CELTS (IRE), 5, b g Celtic Swing—Flamands (IRE) **Mrs B. Oughtred**
41 LAST BID, 4, b f Vital Equine (IRE)—Manderina **C. H. Stevens**
42 LEASE LEND, 10, ch g Zilzal (USA)—Moogie **C. H. Stevens**
43 LITTLE JIMMY ODSOX (IRE), 5, b g Namid—September Tide (IRE) **Reality Partnerships III**
44 LOST IN PARIS (IRE), 7, b g Elusive City (USA)—Brazilia **W. H. Ponsonby**
45 LOUKOUMI, 5, b m Iffraaj—Odalisque (IRE) **Habton Farms**
46 MAPPIN TIME (IRE), 5, b g Orientate (USA)—Different Story (USA) **P. Baillie**

MR TIM EASTERBY - Continued

47 **MARIACHI MAN**, 5, b g Haafhd—Popocatepetl (FR) **A. J. J. Gompertz**
48 **MAVEN**, 5, b m Doyen (IRE)—Bollin Jeannie **Habton Farms**
49 **MAYBEAGREY**, 4, b f Shamardal (USA)—Grey Again **Habton Farms**
50 **MEDICI TIME**, 8, gr g Medicean—Pendulum **Mrs C. A. Hodgetts**
51 **MILITARY GREEN (FR)**, 4, b g Cadeaux Genereux—Dallaah **Lease Terminated**
52 **MOJOLIKA**, 5, ch g Motivator—Kalandika **Mr A. Brannon & Habton Farms**
53 **MONITA BONITA**, 4, b f King's Theatre (IRE)—Monita des Bois (FR) **Habton Farms**
54 **NEARLY A GIFT (IRE)**, 4, b f Tagula (IRE)—Chaukao (IRE) **A. H. Arton**
55 **NO POPPY (IRE)**, 5, b m Chineur (FR)—Capetown Girl **Exors of the Late Mrs P. M. Easterby**
56 **ONE FOR LUCK**, 6, b g Bollin Eric—One For Terry (IRE) **Ryedale Partners No 8**
57 **OSCAR ROMEO (IRE)**, 7, gr g Environment Friend—Oscar Leader (IRE) **C. H. Stevens**
58 **PONTY ACCLAIM (IRE)**, 4, b f Acclamation—Leopard Creek **Calvert, O'Neill & Partner**
59 **QUEENS REVENGE**, 4, b f Multiplex—Retaliator **W. H. Ponsonby**
60 **QUINTAIN (IRE)**, 5, b g Olden Times—Seek Supremacy (IRE) **Habton Farms**
61 **RENE LE ROI (FR)**, 4, b g King O' The Mana (IRE)—Madonna da Rossi **Habton Farms**
62 **ROYAL COMPOSER (IRE)**, 10, b g Mozart (IRE)—Susun Kelapa (USA) **Mrs B. Oughtred**
63 **RYEDANE (IRE)**, 11, b g Danetime—Miss Valediction (IRE) **Habton Farms**
64 **SEE CLEARLY**, 4, b f Bertolini (USA)—True Vision (IRE) **Ryedale Partners No 4**
65 **SILVERY MOON (IRE)**, 6, gr g Verglas—Starry Night **Mr R. J. Swinbourne**
66 **THE FUN CRUSHER**, 5, ch g Halling (USA)—South Rock **Mr J. C. McGrath**
67 **TIPTOEAWAY (IRE)**, 8, b g Insan (USA)—My Blackbird (IRE) **T. J. Hemmings**
68 **TRUST FUND BABE (IRE)**, 4, b f Captain Rio—Perfect Order (USA) **The Mutineers & Habton Farms**
69 **TRUSTAN TIMES (IRE)**, 7, b g Heron Island (IRE)—
                    Ballytrustan Maid (IRE) **Mrs M E Armitage & Mr Peter Armitage**
70 **VINTAGE TIMES (IRE)**, 6, b g Croco Rouge (IRE)—Rare Vintage (IRE) **T. J. Hemmings**
71 **WOOD NYMPH (IRE)**, 4, b f Acclamation—Forest Call **D. F. Powell**
72 **ZITENKA (IRE)**, 11, b g Beneficial—Volobollea (IRE) **Mrs J. E. Pallister**

THREE-YEAR-OLDS

73 **ANNIE GOGH**, b f Dutch Art—Spunger **Mrs J. P. Connew**
74 **ART MISTRESS (IRE)**, b f Excellent Art—Hammrah **D. A. West**
75 **ATTANSKY (IRE)**, b g Ivan Denisovich (IRE)—Attanagh (IRE) **R. Taylor & Mr P. Hebdon**
76 **BACHOTHEQUE (IRE)**, b g Chineur (FR)—Bacchanalia (IRE) **R. Taylor & Mr P. Hebdon**
77 **BANNOCKBURN BOY**, b c Motivator—Senta's Dream **Numac Engineering Ltd**
78 **BLUE LOTUS (IRE)**, b g Elnadim (USA)—Saffa Garden (IRE) **C. H. Stevens**
79 **BODY AND SOUL (IRE)**, b f Captain Rio—Goodwood March **C. H. Stevens**
80 **BOLLIN BILLY**, b g Lucky Story (USA)—Bollin Jeannie **Habton Farms**
81 **CUMBRIAN CRAIC**, b g Pastoral Pursuits—Bollin Janet **Mrs J. E. Pallister**
82 **DARK EROS (IRE)**, b f Dark Angel (IRE)—Capetown Girl **Habton Farms**
83 **DENNIS**, b c Mind Games—Hetti Lewis **Habton Farms**
84 **DREAM VALE (IRE)**, b f Moss Vale (IRE)—Dream State (IRE) **Middleham Park Racing LII & Partner**
85 **FAFFA**, ch g Araafa (IRE)—Forever Fine (USA) **Habton Farms**
86 **HAWK HIGH**, b g High Chaparral (IRE)—Septembers Hawk (IRE) **T. J. Hemmings**
87 **HAZARD WARNING (IRE)**, b c Haatef (USA)—Hazardous **Habton Farms**
88 **HIGH FLAME (IRE)**, b f High Chaparral (IRE)—Noble Flame (IRE) **Habton Farms**
89 **INOVATE (IRE)**, ch g Intikhab (USA)—Julianne (IRE) **Habton Farms**
90 **KAT MOON**, b f Cockney Rebel (IRE)—Damelza (IRE) **Ryedale Partners No 7**
91 **LILAC LACE (IRE)**, b f Captain Marvelous (IRE)—Lilac Mist **S. A. Heley**
92 **MARBLE SILVER**, gr f Notnowcato—Serena's Storm (IRE) **Miss B. C. Duxbury**
93 **MEDICI DANCER**, ch f Medicean—Dance Away **Ryedale Partners No 3**
94 **MISS CHUCKLES**, ch f Medicean—Heckle **The Hecklers**
95 **NONOTNOW**, ch g Notnowcato—Get Jealous (IRE) **Habton Farms**
96 **NOTIONAL DEMAND**, b g Multiplex—Bonsai (IRE) **Mr J. R. Beamson**
97 **OFF ART**, ch c Dutch Art—Off Camera **D. B. Lamplough**
98 **PENNY GARCIA**, b f Indesatchel (IRE)—Katie Boo (IRE) **Jim & Helen Bowers**
99 **RED COBRA (IRE)**, b g Redback—Queen Cobra (IRE) **J & P Baillie & C & G Baillie**
100 **RELIGHT MY FIRE**, ch g Firebreak—Making Music **J. Gill**
101 **ROYAL RASCAL**, b f Lucky Story (USA)—Royal Punch **C. H. Stevens**
102 **RYEDALE VALLEY**, b f Three Valleys (USA)—Phi Phi (IRE) **Ryedale Partners No 9**
103 **SHOWTIME GIRL (IRE)**, b f Tamayuz—Zuccini Wind (IRE) **P. C. J. Bourke**
104 **SHRIMPER ROO**, b g Byron—Piper's Ash (USA) **Reality Partnerships IV**
105 **STORMA NORMA**, b f Royal Applause—Icing **J. Musgrave**

MR TIM EASTERBY - Continued

106 SURROUND SOUND, b g Multiplex—Tintera (IRE) **Mr C. Wilson**
107 TAXUS, b g Indesatchel (IRE)—High Lady **Mrs M. Buckley**
108 TEAM CHALLENGE, b g Araafa (IRE)—Passionforfashion (IRE) **Mrs J. E. Pallister**
109 THE NIFTY BLAZE, ch g Firebreak—Nifty Alice **R. A. Peebles**
110 THREE GLASSES, br c Excellent Art—Sinamay (USA) **T. J. Hemmings**
111 TOBACCO, b g Manduro (GER)—Wonderful Desert **P. H. Milmo**
112 TWILIGHT PEARL, b f Pastoral Pursuits—Branston Gem **D. A. West**
113 WYNYARD BOY, ch g Pastoral Pursuits—Woodcock Moon **J. Musgrave**

TWO-YEAR-OLDS

114 B c 19/3 Observatory (USA)—Ailincala (IRE) (Pursuit of Love) (12000) **Langham Hall Stud Three**
115 ALPINE FLOWER (IRE), b f 2/2 Intense Focus (USA)—
                                         Wine House (IRE) (Sadler's Wells (USA)) (2857) **Miss B. C. Duxbury**
116 ANOTHER ROYAL, b f 4/3 Byron—Royal Punch (Royal Applause) **C. H. Stevens**
117 Ch c 2/2 Captain Gerrard (IRE)—Barley Bree (IRE) (Danehill Dancer (IRE)) (4761) **Habton Farms**
118 BOUNTY GIRL (IRE), b f 25/1 Bushranger (IRE)—Josphiel (IRE) (Okawango (USA)) (15872) **P. C. J. Bourke**
119 B f 9/4 Mastercraftsman (IRE)—Cape Jasmine (IRE) (Danehill (USA)) (19047) **Mr & Mrs J. D. Cotton**
120 Ch c 27/3 Dandy Man (IRE)—Changari (USA) (Gulch (USA)) (10476) **April Fools**
121 Ch c 8/3 Assertive—Cocabana (Captain Rio) (6666) **Habton Farms**
122 DANCARINA, b f 28/2 Multiplex—Sambarina (IRE) (Victory Note (USA)) (3809) **The Mutineers & Habton Farms**
123 ELECTION NIGHT, b f 4/4 Mount Nelson—Psychic (IRE) (Alhaarth (IRE)) (32000) **J. Shack**
124 B f 23/2 Captain Marvelous (IRE)—Hemasree (IRE) (Exceed And Excel (AUS)) (4602) **Habton Farms**
125 HEROIQUE (IRE), b f 23/3 Acclamation—Gay Heroine (Caerleon (USA)) (21000) **Mr K. Nicholson**
126 JESSIE K, ch f 18/1 Compton Place—Fairnilee (Selkirk (USA)) (3571)
127 Ch c 15/4 Captain Rio—Kelso Magic (USA) (Distant View (USA)) (17142) **Reality Partnerships V**
128 B f 12/2 Pastoral Pursuits—Kerry's Dream (Tobougg (IRE)) (20000) **Habton Farms**
129 MARGRETS GIFT, ch f 29/4 Major Cadeaux—Its Another Gift (Primo Dominie) (3619) **Margaret's Partnership**
130 MIDNIGHT MUSCIDA (IRE), b f 23/2 Kodiac—Nose One's Way (IRE) (Revoque (IRE)) (9523) **D. A. West**
131 B c 10/4 Halling (USA)—Murielle (Diktat) (4761)
132 Ch c 21/3 Dutch Art—Oasis Breeze (Oasis Dream) (59047) **Mr & Mrs J. D. Cotton**
133 PONTY PURSUIT, b f 5/2 Pastoral Pursuits—Spring Clean (FR) (Danehill (USA)) (10476) **Mr M. O'Neill**
134 B f 12/4 Sakhee's Secret—Rainbow Spectrum (FR) (Spectrum (IRE)) (8095) **Habton Farms**
135 REMEMBERANCE DAY, ch f 31/1 Major Cadeaux—
                                         Today's The Day (Alhaarth (IRE)) (11428) **Mr T. G. & Mrs M. E. Holdcroft**
136 ROOMIE, b f 21/4 Pastoral Pursuits—Pomponette (USA) (Rahy (USA)) (12380) **Mrs J. Boxcer**
137 SOUL BROTHER (IRE), b c 15/2 Captain Rio—Goodwood March (Foxhound (USA)) (36190) **C. H. Stevens**
138 STORYLINE (IRE), b f 25/4 Kodiac—Petite Histoire (IRE) (Desert Story (USA)) (14285) **Miss Y. M. G. Jacques**
139 THIANG (IRE), b f 7/2 Tamayuz—Bryanstown Girl (IRE) (Kalanisi (IRE)) (14285) **Mrs J. P. Connew**
140 Ch f 24/1 Intikhab (USA)—Tofana (IRE) (Bold Fact (USA)) (2857) **Ryedale Partners No 5**

Other Owners: Mrs M. E. Armitage, P. Armitage, Mr G. M. Baillie, Mr P. M. Baillie, Mr C. P. Barker, G. M. Barnard, P. J. W. Botham, J. F. Bowers, Mrs H. M. Bowers, Mr A. Brannon, Mr P. S. Cook, J. D. Cotton, Mrs B. Cotton, Mrs P. D. Croft, T. D. Easterby, M. H. Easterby, Mrs M. Forsyth, Mr P. M. Goldsmith, R. V. Harding, Mr P. F. Hebdon, Mrs M. E. Holdcroft, Mr R. A. Jacobs, Mr C. Jones, Miss E. A. Lake, Mr M. J. Lewendon, Mr J. Mounsey, Lady Nelson, Mr P. E. Nodding, N. J. O'Brien, T. S. Palin, Mr A. R. Parker, Mr M. Pearson, Mr D. Pearson, Mr J. Preston, M. Prince, A. H. Raby, Mr A. Reid, Mrs F. C. Saint Jean, Mr G. Sunley, B. G. Swallow, R. Taylor, Miss S. J. Turner, D. E. Wilsdon.

---

196 **MR BRIAN ECKLEY, Brecon**
Postal: **Closcedi Farm, Llanspyddid, Brecon, Powys, LD3 8NS**
Contacts: **PHONE (01874) 622422 MOBILE (07891) 445409**
E-MAIL brian.eckley@live.co.uk

1 BYRONSPRINCESS, 5, b m Byron—Sun Bonnet **B. J. Eckley**
2 4, B g Busy Flight—Jaunty Walk **B. J. Eckley**
3 LUCKY PRINCE, 6, b g Lucky Owners (NZ)—Sun Bonnet **B. J. Eckley**
4 LUCKY SUN, 7, b g Lucky Owners (NZ)—Sun Bonnet **B. J. Eckley**
5 4, B f Cloudings (IRE)—Poppy Smith **B. J. Eckley**
6 REVOCATION, 5, b g Revoque (IRE)—Fenella **B. J. Eckley**
7 TIMEFORAGIN, 6, b m Pasternak—Little Time **B. J. Eckley**

197 MR PAT EDDERY, Nether Winchendon

Postal: Musk Hill Stud, Nether Winchendon, Aylesbury, Buckinghamshire, HP18 0EB
Contacts: RACING OFFICE: (01844) 296153 FAX (01844) 290282 MOBILE (07718) 984799
E-MAIL info@patedderyracing.com WEBSITE www.patedderyracing.com

1 ASCALON, 9, ch h Galileo (IRE)—Leaping Flame (USA) **P. J. J. Eddery, Mrs John Magnier, M. Tabor**
2 BARNACLE, 4, b g Compton Place—Bombalarina (IRE) **P. J. J. Eddery**
3 DESERT RECLUSE (IRE), 6, ch g Redback—Desert Design **The Hill Top Partnership**
4 HOONOSE, 4, ch g Cadeaux Genereux—Roodeye **Miss E. L. Owen**
5 PASHAN GARH, 4, b g Anabaa (USA)—Mimisel **Miss E. L. Owen**
6 RAPID WATER, 7, b g Anabaa (USA)—Lochsong **Miss E. L. Owen**
7 WRENINGHAM, 8, br g Diktat—Slave To The Rythm (IRE) **Miss E. L. Owen**

THREE-YEAR-OLDS

8 APHRODITE SPIRIT (IRE), b f Key of Luck (USA)—Rosewater (GER) **Pat Eddery Racing (Key Of Luck)**
9 COOL AND CLEAR (IRE), b g One Cool Cat (USA)—Manon's Song (IRE) **P. J. J. Eddery**
10 GEORDIE MAN, b c Manduro (GER)—Opening Ceremony (USA) **Mr L. F. Daly**
11 B f Tiger Hill (IRE)—Grey Pearl **Pat Eddery Racing (Tiger Hill)**
12 B g Tiger Hill (IRE)—Guilty Secret (IRE) **P. J. J. Eddery**
13 INCORPORATE, ch c Beat Hollow—Five Fields (USA) **K. Abdulla**
14 MARVELINO, b c Captain Marvelous (IRE)—Aimee's Delight **The Marvelino Partnership**
15 MISTS OF TIME (IRE), b f Excellent Art—Capriole **Pat Eddery Racing (Excellent Art)**
16 SOMERTON STAR, b c Avonbridge—Leaping Flame (USA) **P. Dean**
17 WISHING BRIDGE, ch c Pastoral Pursuits—Dunloe (IRE) **P. J. J. Eddery**

TWO-YEAR-OLDS

18 B c 6/4 Empire Maker (USA)—Around (Danehill (USA)) **K. Abdulla**
19 Ch f 15/4 Manduro (GER)—Baltica (IRE) (Sadler's Wells (USA)) (45000) **Mr L. F. Daly**
20 B f 11/3 Pastoral Pursuits—Crochet (Mark of Esteem (IRE)) (380) **Miss E. L. Owen**
21 B f 11/4 Bertolini (USA)—Malvadilla (IRE) (Doyoun) (380) **P. J. J. Eddery**
22 B f 24/4 First Defence (USA)—Rougeur (USA) (Blushing Groom (FR)) **K. Abdulla**

Other Owners: Mr P. Burgoyne, Mr P. J. J. Eddery, Mr John Magnier, Mr D. J. Martin, Miss Emma L. Owen, Mr M. Tabor.

Assistant Trainer: Miss Emma L. Owen (07718984799)

Jockey (flat): Luke Morris, Cathy Gannon, Joe Fanning.

198 MR ROBERT EDDERY, Newmarket

Postal: Robert Eddery Racing, Heyward Place Stables, Hamilton Road, Newmarket,
Suffolk, CB8 7JQ
Contacts: PHONE (01638) 428001 MOBILE (07938) 898455
E-MAIL info@robertedderyracing.com WEBSITE www.robertedderyracing.com

1 VASILY, 5, b h Sadler's Wells (USA)—Red Bloom **Mr O. O'Brien & Mr D. Bannon**
2 WORLD HERITAGE, 7, b g Kahyasi—Imbabala **Mr E. Phillips & Giggles Partnership**

THREE-YEAR-OLDS

3 ADMIRALOFTHESEA (USA), b c Henrythenavigator (USA)—Duchess Royale (IRE) **Mrs P. Aitken & Ms T. Keane**
4 BEAU SELECT (IRE), b g Lucky Story (USA)—Practicallyperfect (IRE) **Ms T. Keane**
5 CARAMEL SUNDAE, b f Oratorio (IRE)—Sundae Girl (USA) **Mr O. D. Costello**
6 FORCEFUL FLAME, ch g Assertive—Noor El Houdah (IRE) **M. Moss, M. Rayment & E. Phillips**
7 FRONT PAGE NEWS, ch f Assertive—Branston Berry (IRE) **Mr C. Gurnett, Mrs J. Rayment & Mr I. Anderson**
8 HEYWARD BOY (IRE), ch g Intikhab (USA)—Kashoof **Mr E. Phillips**
9 QUADRIGA (IRE), b c Acclamation—Turning Light (GER) **Mr O. O'Brien**
10 SPESSARTINE (IRE), b c Duke of Marmalade (IRE)—Lasting Chance (USA) **Mr E. Phillips**

TWO-YEAR-OLDS

11 B f 24/4 Myboycharlie (IRE)—Alectrona (FR) (Invincible Spirit (IRE)) **Mr O. O'Brien**
12 Ch f 24/2 Avonbridge—All The Nines (IRE) (Elusive City (USA)) (4761) **Mr J. Mitchell**
13 B c 19/3 Jeremy (USA)—Blanchelande (IRE) (Subotica) (2777) **Mrs G. Fullerton**
14 CRAFTSMANSHIP (FR), ch c 9/3 Mastercraftsman (IRE)—
Jennie Jerome (IRE) (Pivotal) (9523) **Trisha Keane & Julia Rayment**
15 B c 8/2 American Post—Dansia (GER) (Lavirco (GER)) (17460) **Mr I. Anderson**

MR ROBERT EDDERY - Continued

16 B c 31/3 Captain Gerrard (IRE)—Goes A Treat (IRE) (Common Grounds) (8095) **Champion Bloodstock Limited**
17 **ISABELLA LIBERTY (FR),** b f 20/1 Soldier of Fortune (IRE)—
Samsa (FR) (Zafonic (USA)) (13492) **Mr E Phillips & Mrs M Matthews**
18 B c 27/4 Bushranger (IRE)—Lady Corduff (IRE) (Titus Livius (FR)) (25000) **Mr O. O'Brien**
19 **OLYMNIA,** b f 23/2 Teofilo (IRE)—Diotima (High Estate) (26984) **EDS Roofing Supplies Midlands Ltd**
20 B c 19/2 Captain Gerrard (IRE)—Sahara Silk (IRE) (Desert Style (IRE)) (10476) **Mr O. O'Brien & Mr D. Bannon**
21 Br c 29/3 Captain Marvelous (IRE)—Seasonal Style (IRE) (Generous (IRE)) (11507)
22 **SHREWD BOB (IRE),** b c 22/1 Whipper (USA)—Cheyenne Spirit (Indian Ridge) (15872) **Mr E. Phillips**

Other Owners: Mr Michael Moss, Mr Edwin S. Phillips, Mr Mark Rayment.

Jockey (flat): Andrea Atzeni.

---

199 **MR GORDON EDWARDS, Minehead**
Postal: **Summering, Wheddon Cross, Minehead, Somerset, TA24 7AT**
Contacts: **PHONE (01643) 831549 FAX (01643) 831549 MOBILE (07970) 059297**
E-MAIL dazjock001@hotmail.com

1 **BLAMETHEPOSTMAN (IRE),** 7, b br g Anshan—Slaney Queen **G. F. Edwards**
2 **BRIEFCASE (IRE),** 8, b g Witness Box (USA)—Another Tycoon (IRE) **G. F. Edwards**
3 **CONSULATE (IRE),** 9, b g Rock of Gibraltar (IRE)—Soha (USA) **G. F. Edwards**
4 **SHANANN STAR (IRE),** 7, br m Anshan—Baile An Droichid (IRE) **G. F. Edwards**

Amateur: Mr D. Edwards.

---

200 **MR CHARLES EGERTON, Upper Lambourn**
Postal: **Uplands, Upper Lambourn, Berkshire, RG17 8QH**
Contacts: **OFFICE (01488) 73164 FAX (01488) 73133 MOBILE (07795) 220630**
E-MAIL charles@charlesegerton.co.uk WEBSITE www.charlesegerton.co.uk

1 **AVOCA PROMISE (IRE),** 8, b g Oscar (IRE)—High Ace (IRE) **Bailey-Carvill Equine**
2 **CAPELLINI,** 6, b g Cape Cross (IRE)—Red Stella (FR) **Bruce Pomford & Malcolm Frost**
3 **CARRIBS LEAP (IRE),** 8, b g Old Vic—Majister Ludi (IRE) **Equis**
4 **DR LIVINGSTONE (IRE),** 8, b g Dr Fong (USA)—Radhwa (FR) **C. R. Egerton**
5 **EASY BEESY,** 5, b g Kalanisi (IRE)—Queen of The Bees (IRE) **Mrs S. A. Roe**
6 **GEE HI (IRE),** 7, b g Milan—Curzon Street **Equis**
7 **JOHN GULLY (IRE),** 6, b g High Chaparral (IRE)—Desperate Virgin (BEL) **Equis**
8 **JUST WALKING JACK,** 5, ch m Old Vic—Lady Llancillo (IRE) **R. F. Bailey**
9 **SEEDLING,** 4, b g Cockney Rebel (IRE)—Unseeded **Equis & Christopher Spence**
10 **SEEDSMAN,** 6, ch g Sulamani (USA)—Unseeded **Christopher Spence & Partners**

Other Owners: Mr Clive Bull, Mr R. K. Carvill, Mr J. Cavanagh, Mr Malcolm Davidson, Mr D. J. Erwin, Mr Tod Floyd, Mr Richard Glasspool, Mr Andrew Jones, Mr M. B. J. Kimmins, Mr Patrick Knapman, Mr Bill Parker, Mr Jamie Ritblat, Mr Johnno Spence, Mr John Strachan, Mr Chris Taylor, Mr Damian Thomas, Mr R. C. C. Villers.

Assistant Trainer: David Plunkett (07778) 379341

Jockey (NH): A. P. McCoy, Sam Twiston-Davies.

---

201 **MR BRIAN ELLISON, Malton**
Postal: **Spring Cottage Stables, Langton Road, Norton, Malton, North Yorkshire, YO17 9PY**
Contacts: **OFFICE (01653) 690004 FAX (01653) 690008 MOBILE (07785) 747426**
E-MAIL ellisonracing@aol.com WEBSITE www.brianellisonracing.co.uk

1 **AL FREEJ (IRE),** 4, b f Iffraaj—Why Now **Kevin Corcoran Aaron Pierce Chris Weare**
2 **ALASKAN BULLET (IRE),** 4, b g Kodiac—Czars Princess (IRE) **M Khan X2**
3 **AMTIRED,** 7, gr g Beauchamp King—Rising Talisker **Mr G. Smith**
4 **ANDREO BAMBALEO,** 9, ch g Silver Patriarch (IRE)—Time And A Place (IRE) **P. C. Andries**
5 **ARISDA,** 5, b m Exit To Nowhere (USA)—Clotted Cream (USA) **Sarah Faulks & Robin Cook**
6 **ARLEY HALL,** 4, ch f Excellent Art—Gee Kel (IRE) **M Khan X2**
7 **ARTISAN,** 5, ch g Medicean—Artisia (IRE) **Dan Gilbert & Kristian Strangeway**
8 **BANG TIDY (IRE),** 4, b g Moss Vale (IRE)—Bound To Glitter (USA) **Koo's Racing Club**

MR BRIAN ELLISON - Continued

9 **BECAUSEWECAN (USA)**, 7, b g Giant's Causeway (USA)—
Belle Sultane (USA) **D. Gilbert, M. Lawrence, A. Bruce**
10 **BEST TRIP (IRE)**, 6, b g Whipper (USA)—Tereed Elhawa **Koo's Racing Club**
11 **BISHOP'S CASTLE (USA)**, 4, b br c Distorted Humor (USA)—Miss Caerleona (FR) **Koo's Racing Club**
12 **BOCCIANI (GER)**, 8, b g Banyumanik (IRE)—Baila **J. D. Macgregor**
13 **BOTHY**, 7, ch g Pivotal—Villa Carlotta **Mr D. R. Gilbert**
14 **BRUSLINI (FR)**, 8, gr g Linamix (FR)—Brusca (USA) **Middleham Park Racing LXII & B. Ellison**
15 **CALAF**, 5, b g Dubai Destination (USA)—Tarandot (IRE) **Prism Bloodstock**
16 **CAPE EXPLORER**, 4, b g Cape Cross (IRE)—Eve **Mr M. Grayson & Mr I. P. O'Brien**
17 **CAPELLANUS (IRE)**, 7, b g Montjeu (IRE)—Secret Dream (IRE) **P. J. Wilmott**
18 **CHRISTMAS LIGHT**, 6, b m Zafeen (FR)—Arabian Dancer **Mrs L. Lumley**
19 **DIZZY RIVER (IRE)**, 8, ch g Flemensfirth—Dizzy Dealer **Mr D. R. Gilbert**
20 **DOLPHIN ROCK**, 6, b g Mark of Esteem (IRE)—Lark In The Park (IRE) **Mia Racing**
21 **DONTPAYTHEFERRYMAN (USA)**, 8, ch g Wiseman's Ferry (USA)—Expletive Deleted (USA) **Koo's Racing Club**
22 **DREAM RISK (FR)**, 7, b m Dream Well (FR)—Lovarisk (FR) **Mr L. S. Keys**
23 **DREAM WIN**, 7, b h Oasis Dream—Wince **Koo's Racing Club**
24 **DUSKY BOB (IRE)**, 8, br g Bob Back (USA)—Sunsets Girl (IRE) **Mr D. R. Gilbert**
25 **FEELING GOOD**, 4, b g Shamardal (USA)—Lady Golan (IRE) **Koo's Racing Club**
26 **FINE KINGDOM**, 4, b g King's Best (USA)—Eurolink Sundance **Mr S. L. Catchpole & Mr K. Hanson**
27 **FLEET DAWN**, 7, b g Polish Precedent (USA)—Wychnor Dawn (IRE) **Prism Bloodstock**
28 **GOURAY GIRL (IRE)**, 6, b m Redback—Brillano (FR) **Brian Ellison**
29 **GRAND SHIFT (IRE)**, 5, ch g Night Shift (USA)—Lady Hawk (GER) **Brian Ellison**
30 **IT'S A MANS WORLD**, 7, b g Kyllachy—Exhibitor (USA) **Brian Ellison**
31 **KERCHAK (IRE)**, 6, b g Royal Academy (USA)—Traude (USA) **J. D. Macgregor**
32 **KNIGHTLY ESCAPADE**, 5, ch g Sakhee (USA)—Queen of Iceni **P. J. Martin**
33 **KOO AND THE GANG (IRE)**, 6, b g Le Vie Dei Colori—Entertain **The Country Stayers**
34 **LAKEMAN (IRE)**, 7, b g Tillerman—Bishop's Lake **Koo's Racing Club**
35 **LIFETIME (IRE)**, 5, b g Shamardal (USA)—La Vita E Bella (IRE) **Koo's Racing Club**
36 **LOCAL PRESENT (IRE)**, 10, ch g Presenting—Local Issue (IRE) **Prism Bloodstock**
37 **LOOKS LIKE RAIN**, 4, ch f Medicean—Hippogator (USA) **Peter Alderson & Brian Ellison**
38 **MASHAARI (IRE)**, 6, b g Monsun (GER)—Thakafaat (IRE) **P. J. Martin**
39 **MISS TWIGGY**, 5, b m Alflora (IRE)—Gee Tee Supermodel **Antonio Marucci & Brian Ellison**
40 **MON BRAV**, 6, b g Sampower Star—Danehill Princess (IRE) **Koo's Racing Club**
41 **MUSNAD (USA)**, 5, ch g Mr Greeley (USA)—Jadarah (USA) **Mr D. R. Gilbert**
42 **NEPTUNE EQUESTER**, 10, b g Sovereign Water (FR)—All Things Nice **Koo's Racing Club**
43 **PELMANISM**, 6, b g Piccolo—Card Games **Koo's Racing Club**
44 **PENDRAGON (USA)**, 10, ch g Rahy (USA)—Turning Wheel (USA) **Dan Gilbert & Kristian Strangeway**
45 **PHASE SHIFT**, 5, b m Iceman—Silent Waters **Mr D. R. Gilbert**
46 **PORGY**, 8, b g Dansili—Light Ballet **A. R. Barnes**
47 **POWERFUL AMBITION (IRE)**, 7, b g Bob Back (USA)—Native Shore (IRE) **Koo's Racing Club**
48 **PRAVDA STREET**, 8, ch g Soviet Star (USA)—Sari **Koo's Racing Club**
49 **QUIET ROUTE (IRE)**, 4, b g Manduro (GER)—Step With Style (USA) **Brian Ellison**
50 **RANO PANO (USA)**, 4, b f Proud Citizen (USA)—Princess Aries (USA) **Mr D. R. Gilbert**
51 **RED INCA**, 5, ch g Pivotal—Magicalmysterykate (USA) **D. Gilbert, M. Lawrence, A. Bruce**
52 **ROYAL OPERA**, 5, b g Acclamation—Desert Gold (IRE) **Dan Gilbert & Kristian Strangeway**
53 **SAMDELLIN**, 5, b g Helissio (FR)—Pepper Star (IRE) **David Foster & Brian Ellison**
54 **SANS LOI (IRE)**, 4, b g Lawman (FR)—Lady Elysees (USA) **Mrs Z. Wentworth**
55 **SEATTLE DRIVE (IRE)**, 5, b g Motivator—Seattle Ribbon (USA) **J. C. Smith**
56 **SERENITY NOW (IRE)**, 5, b g Key of Luck (USA)—Imdina (IRE) **Mr J. M. Basquill**
57 **SIMONSIDE**, 10, b g Shahrastani (USA)—Only So Far **Racing Management & Training Ltd**
58 **SOOPACAL (IRE)**, 5, b g Captain Rio—Fiddes (IRE) **Lee Bolingbroke & Mrs C. L. Ellison**
59 **SPANISH DUKE (IRE)**, 6, b g Big Bad Bob (IRE)—Spanish Lady (IRE) **Dan Gilbert & Chris Weare**
60 **SPIN CAST**, 5, b g Marju (IRE)—Some Diva **W. A. Bethell**
61 **STAR KINGDOM (IRE)**, 4, b g Marju (IRE)—Appetina **Koo's Racing Club**
62 **STORMY WEATHER (FR)**, 7, gr g Highest Honor (FR)—
Stormy Moud (USA) **Mr S. L. Catchpole & Mr K. Hanson**
63 **TAPPANAPPA (IRE)**, 6, b g High Chaparral (IRE)—Itsibitsi (IRE) **Mr N. Ahmad**
64 **TEAATREIDS (IRE)**, 5, br m Royal Anthem (USA)—Orchard Lass **Racing Management & Training Ltd**
65 **THREE WHITE SOCKS (IRE)**, 6, b g Whipper (USA)—Halesia (USA) **Racing Management & Training Ltd**
66 **TOTALIZE**, 4, b g Authorized (USA)—You Too **D. Gilbert, M. Lawrence, A. Bruce**
67 **TRAVIS COUNTY (IRE)**, 4, b g Jeremy (USA)—Manchaca (FR) **D. Gilbert, M. Lawrence, A. Bruce**
68 **TWELVE STRINGS (IRE)**, 4, b g Iffraaj—Favoritely (USA) **M Khan X2**
69 **TY GWR**, 4, b g Echo of Light—House Maiden (IRE) **Mrs A. Simcock**
70 **ULTIMATE**, 7, b g Anabaa (USA)—Nirvana **Mr D. R. Gilbert**
71 **WYBORNE**, 4, ch g Halling (USA)—Coraline **Dan Gilbert & Brian Ellison**

MR BRIAN ELLISON - Continued

72 YESYOUCAN (IRE), 8, b g Beneficial—Except Alice (IRE) **Prism Bloodstock**

THREE-YEAR-OLDS
73 BIG STORM COMING, b g Indesatchel (IRE)—Amber Valley **Fishlake Commercial Motors Ltd**
74 NIKNAD, b f Zafeen (FR)—Eau Rouge **Market Avenue Racing Club Ltd**
75 RED GIFT (IRE), b g Chineur (FR)—Kiva **Brian Ellison**

Other Owners: Mr Peter Alderson, Mr Lee Bolingbroke, Mr S. L. Catchpole, Mr Robin Cook, Mr K. J. Corcoran, Mr Brian Ellison, Mrs Claire Ellison, Mrs Sarah Faulks, Mr David Foster, Mr Dan Gilbert, Mr M. Grayson, Mr K. Hanson, Mr B. Hickson, Mr M. Khan, Mr Mustafa Khan, Mr Mark Lawrence, Mr A. Marucci, Mr I. P O'Brien, Mr T. S. Palin, Mr A. Pierce, Mr M. Prince, Mr Kristian Strangeway, Mr M. A. Tickle, Mr A. Tickle, Mrs I. M. Tickle, Mr C. E. Weare.

Assistant Trainer: Mrs Claire Ellison, Mobile (07979) 570652

Jockey (flat): Tom Eaves, Paul Pickard, Dale Swift. **Jockey (NH):** Danny Cook. **Conditional:** Kyle James, Garry Lavery. **Apprentice:** Richard Oliver, Robbie Walsh. **Amateur:** Miss Harriet Bethell, Mr Declan Levey.

202	**MR DAVID ELSWORTH, Newmarket** Postal: **Kings Yard, Egerton House Stables, Cambridge Road, Newmarket, Suffolk, CB8 0TH** Contacts: **PHONE (01638) 665511 FAX (01638) 665310 MOBILE (07771) 804828** E-MAIL david.elsworth@virgin.net

1 COPLOW, 4, ch f Manduro (GER)—Anna Oleanda (IRE) **R. J. McCreery**
2 ELUSIVE FLAME, 4, b f Elusive City (USA)—Dimelight **J. C. Smith**
3 HANDSOME MOLLY, 4, b f Halling (USA)—However (IRE) **Mrs T. A. Foreman**
4 HIGHLAND CASTLE, 5, b g Halling (USA)—Reciprocal (IRE) **Mr J Wotherspoon & Mr W Harrison-Allan**
5 NORSE SONG, 4, b f Norse Dancer (IRE)—Blue Lullaby (IRE) **D and C Bloodstock**

THREE-YEAR-OLDS
6 BOLD AND FREE, b g Bertolini (USA)—Lady Broughton (IRE) **Ten Green Bottles I**
7 COCKTAIL QUEEN (IRE), b f Motivator—Premier Prize **J. C. Smith**
8 DASHING STAR, b c Teofilo (IRE)—Dashiba **J. C. Smith**
9 EMERGING, b c Mount Nelson—Pan Galactic (USA) **Mr B. C. M. Wong**
10 FRIENDSHIP IS LOVE, ch f Byron—Silver Sail **Mrs T. A. Foreman**
11 B f New Approach (IRE)—Gower Song **GB Partnership**
12 GREAT DEMEANOR (USA), b g Bernstein (USA)—Hangin Withmy Buds (USA) **Mr V. Wong**
13 LAST HOORAY, b f Royal Applause—Dodo (IRE) **Usk Valley Stud 1**
14 LLAREGYB (IRE), br c Dylan Thomas (IRE)—Tango Tonic (IRE) **Mrs A. M. Coughlan**
15 MAID A MILLION, b f Kyllachy—Poldhu **K. A. Dasmal**
16 ROCK UP (IRE), b g Kheleyf (USA)—Kissing Time **Lordship Stud 1**
17 SENATOR BONG, ch c Dutch Art—Sunley Gift **J. Dwyer**
18 SNOQUALMIE CHIEF, b c Montjeu (IRE)—Seattle Ribbon (USA) **J. C. Smith**
19 SONG LIGHT, b g Echo of Light—Blue Lullaby (IRE) **D and C Bloodstock**
20 UPAVON, b g Avonbridge—Blaina **McPabb Racing**
21 ZEUS MAGIC, b c Zamindar—Milly of The Vally **J. C. Smith**

TWO-YEAR-OLDS
22 B c 23/2 Jeremy (USA)—Certainly Brave (Indian Ridge) (18000) **D. R. C. Elsworth**
23 B c 4/2 Nayef (USA)—Dashiba (Dashing Blade) **J. C. Smith**
24 B f 28/1 Milk It Mick—Matilda Peace (Namaqualand (USA)) **Al Hodge & D. Elworth**
25 Ch f 6/3 Compton Place—Phoenix Rising (Dr Fong (USA)) **Al Hodge & D. Elworth**
26 B c 1/3 High Chaparral (IRE)—Premier Prize (Selkirk (USA)) **J. C. Smith**
27 Ch c 15/4 Ad Valorem (USA)—River Patrol (Rousillon (USA)) (30000) **J. C. Smith**

Other Owners: Mr John Adams, Mr M. D. Elliott, Mr T. F. Harris, Mrs E. A. Harris, Mr Alex Hoctor-Duncan, Mr K. J. Mercer, Mrs S. Mercer, Mr D. Morgan, Mr K. J. Parris, Miss Sarah Stoneham, Mr D. D. Sutherland, Mr E. B. C. Van Cutsem, Mr Charles Wilson.

Assistant Trainer: Mr Paul Holley

203 MR GERRY ENRIGHT, Lewes
Postal: **The Oaks, Old Lewes Racecourse, Lewes, East Sussex, BN7 1UR**
Contacts: **PHONE/FAX (01273) 479183 MOBILE (07922) 085875**
E-MAIL enright@btinternet.com

1 DOCTOR RIC (IRE), 8, b g Dr Massini (IRE)—Merric (IRE) **M. Forbes-Wood**
2 JIMMY THE BRAVE, 7, b g Josr Algarhoud (IRE)—Polly Minor **A. O. Ashford**
3 KEEP A WELCOME, 10, ch g Most Welcome—Celtic Chimes **Homebred Racing**
4 POLARITY, 7, b m Hamas (IRE)—Snowy Mantle **Homebred Racing**
5 REVERT (USA), 4, b f Rail Link—Chaminade (USA) **Macdonald, Gorringe, Ross**

THREE-YEAR-OLDS
6 Ch f Apple Tree (FR)—Carly Bay **A. O. Ashford**

Other Owners: Mr Edward Gorringe, Mr Graham MacDonald, Miss P. A. Ross, Mr Chris Wall, Mrs Sarah Wall.

Assistant Trainer: Mrs M Enright

Jockey (NH): Robert Thornton.

204 MR TIM ETHERINGTON, Malton
Postal: **Wold House Stables, Langton Road, Norton, Malton, North Yorkshire, YO17 9QG**
Contacts: **OFFICE (01653) 692842 HOME (01653) 693049**

1 ABSOLUTE BEARING (IRE), 4, b g Majestic Missile (IRE)—Garnock Academy (USA) **T. J. Etherington**
2 ARTILLERY TRAIN (IRE), 4, b g Amadeus Wolf—Another Valentine (FR) **Mr Chris Clark Mr Tim Etherington**
3 BAILADEIRA, 5, b br m Intikhab (USA)—Sainte Gig (FR) **World Wide Racing Partners**
4 BURNING THREAD (IRE), 6, b g Captain Rio—Desert Rose **T. J. Etherington**
5 ROYAL GIG, 4, br f Val Royal (FR)—Sainte Gig (FR) **World Wide Racing Partners**
6 TOUCHING HISTORY (IRE), 4, b g Titus Livius (FR)—Lady Naryana (IRE) **T. J. Etherington**

Other Owners: C. J. Clark, Mr P. N. Dowding, Mrs N. Dowding.

205 MR JAMES EUSTACE, Newmarket
Postal: **Park Lodge Stables, Park Lane, Newmarket, Suffolk, CB8 8AX**
Contacts: **PHONE (01638) 664277 FAX (01638) 664156 MOBILE (07802) 243764**
E-MAIL jameseustace@tiscali.co.uk WEBSITE www.jameseustace.com

1 BAAN (USA), 10, ch g Diesis—Madaen (USA) **Mrs G. R. Eustace**
2 FULNEY, 4, b f Dr Fong (USA)—Postage Stampe **Major M. G. Wyatt**
3 GO SET GO, 6, b g Reset (AUS)—Dragon Star **T. H. Barma**
4 HESTON SOUND, 4, ch g Nayef (USA)—Complimentary Pass **The MacDougall Two**
5 IRON BUTTERFLY, 4, b f Shirocco (GER)—Coh Sho No **H. D. Nass**
6 IRON CONDOR, 6, b g Tobougg (IRE)—Coh Sho No **H. D. Nass**
7 SCOTTISH STAR, 5, gr g Kirkwall—Child Star (FR) **J. C. Smith**
8 SEABOUGG, 5, ch g Tobougg (IRE)—Sea Jade (IRE) **T. H. Barma**
9 SPA'S DANCER (IRE), 6, b g Danehill Dancer (IRE)—Spa **The MacDougall Two**
10 TIGHT LIPPED (IRE), 4, gr g Dark Angel (IRE)—Kayoko (IRE) **Blue Peter Racing 11**
11 TORRAN SOUND, 6, b g Tobougg (IRE)—Velvet Waters **The MacDougall Two**
12 WILY FOX, 6, ch g Observatory (USA)—Kamkova (USA) **Blue Peter Racing 10**

THREE-YEAR-OLDS
13 GIFT OF MUSIC (IRE), b f Cadeaux Genereux—Loch Verdi **J. C. Smith**
14 HIMALAYAN PEAK, b g Tiger Hill (GER)—Rosy Outlook (USA) **J. C. Smith**
15 LONDON SKOLAR, b g Tobougg (IRE)—Coh Sho No **H. D. Nass**
16 PRECINCT, b f Refuse To Bend (IRE)—Preceder **Major M. G. Wyatt**

TWO-YEAR-OLDS
17 GREEN MUSIC, b f 13/3 Oratorio (IRE)—Loch Verdi (Green Desert (USA)) **J. C. Smith**
18 Ch f 14/2 Norse Dancer (IRE)—Indian Angel (Indian Ridge) **J. C. Smith**
19 MAJOR CRISPIES, b c 23/4 Pastoral Pursuits—Nellie Melba (Hurricane Sky (AUS)) (26000) **Mr Guy Carstairs**

MR JAMES EUSTACE - Continued

20 **NIMBLE KIMBLE**, ch f 6/3 Kirkwall—Lovely Lyca (Night Shift (USA)) (6500) **Mr Ian Rushby**
21 **POSTAL ORDER**, b f 2/2 Medicean—Postage Stampe (Singspiel (IRE)) **Major M. G. Wyatt**

Other Owners: Mr D. F. Ballheimer, C. Z. Curtis, Mr A. C. Frost, Mrs L. R. Lawson, Mrs K. A. McGladdery, Mr I. L. Rushby.

---

206 **MR DAVID EVANS**, Abergavenny
Postal: Ty Derlwyn Farm, Pandy, Abergavenny, Monmouthshire, NP7 8DR
Contacts: **PHONE (01873) 890837 (07834) 834775 E. Evans FAX (01873) 890837
MOBILE (07860) 668499**
E-MAIL pdevansracing@uwclub.net WEBSITE www.pdevansracing.co.uk

1 **AL'S MEMORY (IRE)**, 4, b g Red Clubs (IRE)—Consensus (IRE) **Mr W. R. J. Dawson**
2 **ANNALUNA (IRE)**, 4, b f Whipper (USA)—Annaletta **N. Shutts**
3 **AVISO (GER)**, 9, b g Tertullian (USA)—Akasma (GER) **M. Duthie**
4 **BATHWICK STREET**, 4, ch g Compton Place—Bahawir Pour (USA) **H. M. W. Clifford**
5 **BEAUTY PAGEANT (IRE)**, 6, ch m Bahamian Bounty—My American Beauty **Dukes Head Racing**
6 **BODEGA**, 5, b g Grape Tree Road—Gurleigh (IRE) **Mrs E. Evans**
7 **BUSSA**, 5, b g Iceman—Maid To Dance **N. Shutts**
8 **CAPTAIN KENDALL (IRE)**, 4, b g Clodovil (IRE)—Queen's Lace (IRE) **J. G. K. White**
9 **DANZIGER (IRE)**, 4, b f Modigliani (USA)—Star On A Hill (IRE) **Mrs E. Evans**
10 **DARK LANE**, 7, b g Namid—Corps de Ballet (IRE) **Mr J. Tucker**
11 **DELIGHTFUL SLEEP**, 5, b g Sulamani (IRE)—Naemi (GER) **Mrs E. Evans**
12 **DIXIE GWALIA**, 5, b m Tobougg (IRE)—Dixieanna **Mrs I. M. Folkes**
13 **ELUSIVE HAWK (IRE)**, 9, b g Noverre (USA)—Two Clubs **Mrs I. M. Folkes**
14 **ESHTYAAQ**, 6, b g Mark of Esteem—Fleet Hill (IRE) **T. H. Gallienne**
15 **ESTEEM**, 10, b g Mark of Esteem (IRE)—Please **N. Shutts**
16 **FOREST EDGE (IRE)**, 4, b g Amadeus Wolf—Compass Light (USA) **Mr P. B. Swinnerton**
17 **HAADEETH**, 6, b g Oasis Dream—Musical Key **Dukes Head Racing**
18 **HONEY OF A KITTEN (USA)**, 5, b g Kitten's Joy (USA)—Sweet Baby Jane (USA) **Mrs E. Evans**
19 **JACK MY BOY (IRE)**, 6, b g Tagula (IRE)—Bobanlyn (IRE) **Mr T Earle & Mr G Evans**
20 **JACK WHO'S HE (IRE)**, 4, b g Red Clubs (IRE)—Annus Iucundus (IRE) **Mr B. McCabe**
21 **JOHN REEL (FR)**, 4, b g Country Reel (USA)—John Quatz (FR) **Walters Plant Hire Ltd**
22 **MARSHALL ART**, 4, b g Lawman (FR)—Portrait of A Lady (IRE) **Mrs E. Evans**
23 **MOTHER JONES**, 5, b m Sleeping Indian—Bella Chica (IRE) **M. F. Nolan**
24 **MY OWN WAY HOME**, 5, b m Danbird (AUS)—Wenden Belle (IRE) **T. H. Gallienne**
25 **NEVERMINDAPETE**, 5, b g Mutamarkiz (USA)—Lavender Della (IRE) **M. N. Jenkins**
26 **NUMBERCRUNCHER (IRE)**, 7, b g Beneficial—Josie's Turn (IRE) **Walters Plant Hire Ltd**
27 **ONE WAY OR ANOTHER (AUS)**, 10, b g Carnegie (IRE)—True Blonde (AUS) **Mrs E. Evans**
28 **SCOTSBROOK CLOUD**, 8, gr g Cloudings (IRE)—Angie Marinie **Mrs E. Evans**
29 **SCRIBE (IRE)**, 5, b g Montjeu (IRE)—Crafty Example (USA) **Shropshire Wolves/John Wilcox**
30 **SOMMERSTURM (GER)**, 9, b g Tiger Hill (IRE)—Sommernacht (GER) **Ms S. A. Howell**
31 **SONARA (IRE)**, 9, b g Peintre Celebre (USA)—Fay (IRE) **Mrs E. Evans**
32 **SUDDEN WISH (IRE)**, 4, b f Jeremy (USA)—Fun Time **Mrs I. M. Folkes**
33 **TEMUCO (IRE)**, 4, b g Bachelor Duke (USA)—La Chinampina (FR) **Mrs S Howell & Mrs E Evans**
34 **THE MONGOOSE**, 5, b g Montjeu (IRE)—Angara **Mr G Evans & Mr P D Evans**
35 **THIRD OF THE THIRD**, 6, b br g Presenting—Gavotte du Cochet (FR) **Walters Plant Hire Ltd**
36 **VERSE OF LOVE**, 4, b g Byron—Lovellian **H. M. W. Clifford**
37 **ZING WING**, 5, ch m Hawk Wing (USA)—Zietory **Exors of the Late Mrs S. E. Edwards**

THREE-YEAR-OLDS

38 **BLACK DAVE (IRE)**, b c Excellent Art—Miss Latina (IRE) **Mrs E. Evans**
39 **HANDSOME STRANGER (IRE)**, ch g Tamayuz—Just Special **Mrs E. Evans**
40 **JAWINSKI (IRE)**, b g Jeremy (USA)—Karinski (USA) **Mr J. A. Wilcox**
41 **LAGER TIME (IRE)**, b g Tagula (IRE)—Polish Belle **Mrs E. Evans**
42 **MAYPOLE JOE (IRE)**, b g Iffraaj—Spanish Needle **Dukes Head Racing**
43 **QUEEN AGGIE (IRE)**, b f Elnadim (USA)—Catfoot Lane **Shropshire Wolves 4**
44 **RUN IT TWICE (IRE)**, b g Dark Angel (IRE)—Alinda (IRE) **Shropshire Wolves 4**
45 **STUDFARMER (IRE)**, b g Multiplex—Samadilla (IRE) **Mr W T Whittle & Mr R Kent**

TWO-YEAR-OLDS

46 B f 5/2 Kyllachy—Authoritative (Diktat) (20634) **T. H. Gallienne**
47 B c 12/4 Indian Haven—Cappuccino (IRE) (Mujadil (USA)) (15872) **P. D. Evans**

MR DAVID EVANS - Continued

48 Ch f 23/1 Kyllachy—Careless Freedom (Bertolini (USA)) (5200) **H. M. W. Clifford**
49 B f 27/4 Bushranger (IRE)—Daanaat (IRE) (Kheleyf (USA)) **P. D. Evans**
50 **JAZZY LADY (IRE),** b f 12/5 Intikhab (USA)—Lock's Heath (CAN) (Topsider (USA)) (6348) **Mr W. R. J. Dawson**
51 B f 7/3 Kalanisi (IRE)—Littleton Liberty (Royal Applause) (1269) **Mrs E. Evans**
52 B f 2/4 Azamour (IRE)—Miss Tango Hotel (Green Desert (USA)) (5555) **Exors of the Late Mrs S. E. Edwards**
53 B f 10/4 Bushranger (IRE)—Nice One Clare (IRE) (Mukaddamah (USA)) (12698) **Mr J. A. Wilcox**
54 Ch f 27/4 Captain Rio—North Cider Rose (IRE) (Goldmark (USA)) (634) **Mrs I. M. Folkes**
55 B f 16/4 Mujadil (USA)—Rorkes Drift (IRE) (Royal Abjar (USA)) (4364) **J. E. Abbey**
56 Ch c 10/4 Majestic Missile (IRE)—Stravinskaya (USA) (Stravinsky (USA)) (5714) **P. D. Evans**
57 B f 1/3 Amadeus Wolf—Sugars for Nanny (Brocco (USA)) (793) **Mrs I. M. Folkes**
58 B f 26/4 Kodiac—Summer Sunshine (Dubai Destination (USA)) (3174) **Mrs E. Evans**
59 B br f 24/2 Intense Focus (USA)—Titania (Fairy King (USA)) (952) **Mrs I. M. Folkes**
60 Br f 27/4 Kodiac—Zafine (Zafonic (USA)) (7936) **Exors of the Late Mrs S. E. Edwards**

Other Owners: Mr J. Babb, J. L. Collins, Mr P. G. Dalton, Miss R. Dorrell, Mr T. H. Earle, Mr G. G. Evans, R. Kent, R. Simpson, W. T. Whittle.

Assistant Trainer: Mrs Emma Evans

Jockey (flat): Cathy Gannon. **Conditional:** Peter Hatton. **Apprentice:** Richard Evans. **Amateur:** Mrs E. Evans.

---

207 | MR JAMES EVANS, Worcester
Postal: **Stone Farm, Broadwas, Worcester, Worcestershire, WR6 5NE**
Contacts: **PHONE (01886) 822054 FAX (01886) 821303 MOBILE (07813) 166430**
E-MAIL herbie_evans@hotmail.com WEBSITE www.hjamesevans.co.uk

1 **CALDERCRUIX (USA),** 6, ch g Rahy (USA)—Al Theraab (USA) **Mr D. C. Mantle**
2 **CARD LOVER,** 7, b m First Trump—American Pie **Mr R. J. Davis**
3 **CATCHING STARDUST,** 5, b m Umistim—Star Control (IRE) **Mrs J. Evans**
4 **DREAM PROSPECTOR,** 4, b g Oasis Dream—Prospectress (USA) **The Prince Of Darkness Partnership**
5 **ESTATES RECOVERY (IRE),** 8, b g Luso—Jendam (IRE) **Threemorelargeones**
6 **HEEZAGREY (IRE),** 10, gr g Naheez (USA)—Silver Belle (IRE) **Miss S. Troughton**
7 **MIDNIGHT CHOICE,** 8, b g Midnight Legend—Pearl's Choice (IRE) **Mrs O. H. Stewart**
8 **NEIGHBOURHOOD (USA),** 5, b br g Street Cry (IRE)—Miznah (IRE) **James Evans Racing**
9 **PHOENIX FLIGHT (IRE),** 8, b g Hawk Wing (USA)—Firecrest (IRE) **Mr D. T. Ross**
10 **PROPHETE DE GUYE (FR),** 10, b g Apple Tree (FR)—Kasibelle de Guye (FR) **Elegant Clutter Ltd**
11 **ROC DE GUYE (FR),** 8, b g Video Rock (FR)—Kasibelle de Guye (FR) **S. Crawley, T. Crawley**
12 **SHAKESPEARE DANCER,** 4, b f Norse Dancer (IRE)—Sharbasia (IRE) **Mrs Jane Evans & Shakespeare Racing**
13 **SUPERIOR KNIGHT,** 9, b g Superior Premium—American Pie **Mr R. J. Davis**
14 **TRACKMATE,** 7, b g Muhtarram (USA)—Cruz Santa **Mr B. W. Preece**

Other Owners: M. J. Benton, Mrs S. E. Crawley, Mr T. P. M. Crawley, Mr H. J. Evans, Mr M. S. Hamilton, Mr N. Higginson, Mr T. Lively, J. F. Long, B. J. McClean.

Assistant Trainer: Mrs Jane Evans

---

208 | MRS MARY EVANS, Haverfordwest
Postal: **Hengoed, Clarbeston Road, Haverfordwest, Pembrokeshire, SA63 4QL**
Contacts: **PHONE (01437) 731336**

1 **MAIZY MISSILE (IRE),** 11, b m Executive Perk—Landsker Missile **Mary & Billy Evans**
2 **VERUMONTANUM (IRE),** 8, b g Bach (IRE)—Emma O (IRE) **Mary & Billy Evans**

Other Owners: Mrs M. Evans, W. J. Evans.

Assistant Trainer: W J Evans

---

209 | MRS NIKKI EVANS, Abergavenny
Postal: **Penbiddle Farm, Penbidwal, Pandy, Abergavenny, Gwent, NP7 8EA**
Contacts: **(01873) 890957 FAX (01873) 890957 MOBILE (07977) 753437**
E-MAIL nikki@penbiddle.fsnet.co.uk WEBSITE www.nikki-evans-racing.co.uk

1 **AMORALIST,** 4, b g Tobougg (IRE)—Ellablue **Mrs S. M. Roy**

MRS NIKKI EVANS - Continued

2 BASHAMA, 5, ch m Dubai Destination (USA)—My Amalie (IRE) **Running Dragon Racing 2**
3 BUAITEOIR (FR), 7, b g Mineshaft (USA)—Witching Hour (FR) **Mr J. Berry**
4 DUNEEN DREAM (USA), 8, ch g Hennessy (USA)—T N T Red (USA) **Iwantaracehorse.Com**
5 HECTOR'S HOUSE, 7, b g Tobougg (IRE)—Thrasher **Iwantaracehorse.Com**
6 LOOK LEFT, 5, ch g Observatory (USA)—Stage Left **Mr J. Berry**
7 MINELLA BLISS (IRE), 8, gr g Old Vic—Carraigrose (IRE) **Running Dragon Racing 2**
8 STEEL RAIN, 5, b g Striking Ambition—Concentration (IRE) **Mr J. Berry**
9 TUNNEL VISION (IRE), 6, b br g Craigsteel—Mill Top Lady (IRE) **Mrs N. S. Evans**

THREE-YEAR-OLDS

10 ARABOUGG, b g Tobougg (IRE)—Arabellas Homer **Mr J. Berry**

Other Owners: Mrs D. J. Babbage, Mr M. Llewelyn, Mrs H. Llewelyn, Mr L. W. Merrick.

Assistant Trainer: Mr P. T. Evans

Conditional: Peter Hatton.

---

210 **MR JAMES EWART, Langholm**
Postal: James Ewart Racing Limited, Craig Farm, Westerkirk, Langholm, Dumfriesshire, DG13 0NZ
Contacts: PHONE (01387) 370707 FAX (01387) 370733 MOBILE (07786) 995073
E-MAIL office@jeracing.co.uk WEBSITE www.jamesewartracing.com

1 BELLGROVE (IRE), 5, b g Gold Well—Less Hassle (IRE) **M. Sawers**
2 BENEFICIAL REFORM (IRE), 8, ch g Beneficial—Miss Performance (IRE) **Mr M. J. Tedham**
3 BISHOPS HEIR, 8, b g Turbo Speed—Linns Heir **Reid, Humbert, Graham, Barrie, Scott**
4 CAPTAIN AMERICO (IRE), 11, b g Lord Americo—Excitable Lady **D Coppola J Ewart**
5 CIVIL UNREST (IRE), 7, ch g Blueprint (IRE)—Yore (IRE) **Carruthers, Halliday, Optimists & Ancrum**
6 CLASSIC CUT, 9, b g Classic Cliche (IRE)—Leading Line **J. D. Gordon**
7 FRONTIER BOY (IRE), 9, b g New Frontier (IRE)—Mary Bridie (IRE) **The Frontier Boys**
8 GILNOCKIE, 5, b g Kayf Tara—Eloquent Lawyer **N. M. L. Ewart**
9 HARRY THE LEMMON (IRE), 7, br g Milan—Na Habair Tada (IRE) **Boyce, Payne, Panther, Four Fat Bellies**
10 HERON'S MILL (IRE), 5, b g Heron Island (IRE)—Princess Vic (IRE) **Jump Racing Up North**
11 LETS GET SERIOUS (IRE), 7, b g Overbury (IRE)—Vendimia **Mr Murrills, Mr Graham, Longlands Racing**
12 LORD WISHES (IRE), 6, b g Milan—Strong Wishes (IRE) **Leeds Plywood & Doors Ltd**
13 MANDARIN SUNSET (IRE), 6, ch g Presenting—Danatello (FR) **The Sunsets**
14 , B g Kalanisi (IRE)—Marvellous Dream (FR)
15 ROCKAWANGO (FR), 7, b g Okawango (USA)—Janou La Belle (FR) **Mr M. J. Tedham**
16 SACRE TOI (FR), 7, b g Network (GER)—Magicielle (FR) **Miss A. Bramall**
17 SCORPIONS STING (IRE), 4, b g Scorpion (IRE)—Strong Wishes (IRE) **Dodd, Reid, Carruthers, Kesson**
18 SHARIVARRY (FR), 7, ch g Ballingarry (IRE)—Sharsala (IRE) **Leeds Plywood & Doors Ltd**
19 SLEEP IN FIRST (FR), 7, b br g Sleeping Car (FR)—First Union (FR) **Miss A. Bramall**
20 SNUKER, 6, b g Snurge—Briar Rose (IRE) **Mrs Percy, Mr Down & Mr Boyd**
21 TEO VIVO (FR), 6, gr g Great Pretender (IRE)—Ifranne (FR) **It's a Bargain Syndicate**
22 TOUCH OF STEEL (IRE), 4, b g Craigsteel—Tourmaline Girl (IRE) **Mrs Hugh Fraser**
23 TRESOR DE L'ISLE (FR), 6, br g Dark Moondancer—Ad Vitam Eternam (FR) **Miss A. Bramall**
24 UEUETEOTL (FR), 5, gr g Tikkanen (USA)—Azturk (FR) **Going Grey**
25 UN GUET APENS (FR), 5, b g Enrique—Belisama (FR) **Drew, Sperling, Graham, Carruthers**
26 UNEX CANALETTO, 4, b g Motivator—Logic **The Craig Farm Syndicate**
27 VOSGES (FR), 6, b g Turgeon (USA)—Vanilla Sky (FR) **Humbert, Drew, Sperling**
28 WILDE PASTURES (IRE), 8, gr g Oscar (IRE)—Kingsfield Clover **Border Pastures**
29 ZARU (FR), 7, b br g Laveron—Zianini (FR) **Mrs Humbert, Drew**

THREE-YEAR-OLDS

30 CA LE FERRA (FR), b g Turgeon (USA)—Branceilles (FR) **Maurice Friel & Southhayrigg Partnership**

TWO-YEAR-OLDS

31 FLIXX, b f 26/2 Multiplex—Playful Lady (Theatrical Charmer) **Mrs Hugh Fraser**

MR JAMES EWART - Continued

Other Owners: Mr J. D. Allen, Mr R. A. Barrie, Mrs D. Blythe, Mr J. Boyce, Mr R. M. Boyd, Mr R. Carruthers, Mr A. C. Cartner, Mr G. Chamberlain, B. Conneely, Mr D. J. Coppola, Mr M. T. Cowen, Mrs J. E. Dodd, Mr D. Down, Mrs L. J. Drew, J. Ewart, Mrs E. M. Fairbairn, Exors of the Late Mr G. B. Fairbairn, Mr M. Friel, Mrs L. R. Gander, W. Graham, Mr D. Graham, Mrs M. J. Hales, R. M. Halliday, Mrs A. G. Humbert, Dr C. M. Kesson, Mr J. D. Mason, Mr W. Murphy, Mr S. A. Murrills, Mrs K. Nairn, Mr P. M. Ogilvie, Dr R. A. Palmer, Panther Racing Limited, Mr J. Payne, Mrs J. D. Percy, Mr G. Reid, Capt T. W. Ritson, Mr B. Robinson, Mr R. E. Smith, Mr N. A. Sperling, Mrs J. Sperling, Mr G. Taitt, Mr G. Taylor, Ms H. K. Walker, Mr W. D. Weir, James Westoll, Mr S. B. White.

Jockey (NH): Brian Hughes. **Conditional:** Dale Irving. **Amateur:** Mr James Smith.

---

211 MR RICHARD FAHEY, Malton
Postal: **RF Racing Ltd, Mews House, Musley Bank, Malton, North Yorkshire, YO17 6TD**
Contacts: **PHONE (01653) 698915 FAX (01653) 699735 MOBILE (07713) 478079**
E-MAIL enquiries@richardfahey.com WEBSITE www.richardfahey.com

1 **ABOVE THE STARS**, 5, b m Piccolo—Swindling **Mrs K. R. Scaife**
2 **ALBEN STAR (IRE)**, 5, b g Clodovil (IRE)—Secret Circle **Mr J. K. Shannon & Mr M. A. Scaife**
3 **ALEJANDRO (IRE)**, 4, b g Dark Angel (IRE)—Carallia (IRE) **Frank Lenny Financial Services Limited**
4 **AQUARIAN SPIRIT**, 6, b g Fantastic Light (USA)—Notable Lady (IRE) **P. S. Cresswell & Mrs P. A. Morrison**
5 **ARCTIC FEELING (IRE)**, 5, ch g Camacho—Polar Lady **Percy / Green Racing 2**
6 **AREA FIFTY ONE**, 5, b g Green Desert (USA)—Secret History (USA) **Dr M. B. Q. S. Koukash**
7 **AVAILED SPEAKER (IRE)**, 4, ch g Iffraaj—Privileged Speech (USA) **R. A. Fahey**
8 **BACCARAT (IRE)**, 4, ch g Dutch Art—Zut Alors (IRE) **Sir R. Ogden C.B.E., LLD**
9 **BADEA**, 4, b g Cockney Rebel (IRE)—Gibraltar Bay (IRE) **Dr M. B. Q. S. Koukash**
10 **BALDEMAR**, 8, b g Namid—Keen Melody (USA) **A. Rhodes Haulage & Mr P. Timmins**
11 **BORDER REVIA (IRE)**, 4, b g Celtic Swing—Maraami **Mr J. Gaffney**
12 **BRIDLE BELLE**, 5, b m Dansili—River Belle **Mrs H. Steel**
13 **COLBYOR**, 4, ch g Orientor—College Maid (IRE) **E. Bruce**
14 **COSMIC HALO**, 4, ch f Halling (USA)—Cosmic Case **The Cosmic Cases**
15 **COSMIC MOON**, 5, b m Doyen (IRE)—Cosmic Case **The Cosmic Cases**
16 **COSMIC SUN**, 7, b g Helissio (FR)—Cosmic Case **The Cosmic Cases**
17 **CRACKING LASS (IRE)**, 6, b m Whipper (USA)—Lady From Limerick (IRE) **Mr Mel Roberts & Ms Nicola Meese**
18 **DAKOTA CANYON (IRE)**, 4, b g Rock of Gibraltar (IRE)—Dakota Sioux (IRE) **Mrs U. Towell**
19 **DOCS LEGACY (IRE)**, 4, b g Ad Valorem (USA)—Lunamixa (GER) **Mr D. A. Bardsley**
20 **DUTCH HERITAGE**, 4, b g Dutch Art—Starstone **P. Timmins & A. Rhodes Haulage**
21 **EASTERN DESTINY**, 4, gr f Dubai Destination (USA)—Night Haven **B. H. Farr**
22 **EL VIENTO (FR)**, 5, ch g Compton Place—Blue Sirocco **John Nicholls Ltd/David Kilburn**
23 **EXTRATERRESTRIAL**, 9, b g Mind Games—Expectation (IRE) **G. J. Paver**
24 **FLASHMAN**, 4, ch g Doyen (IRE)—Si Si Si **The G-Guck Group**
25 **GABRIAL (IRE)**, 4, b g Dark Angel (IRE)—Guajira (FR) **Dr M. B. Q. S. Koukash**
26 **GATEPOST (IRE)**, 4, br g Footstepsinthesand—Mandama (IRE) **Dr M. B. Q. S. Koukash**
27 **GLEN'S DIAMOND**, 5, b g Intikhab (USA)—Posta Vecchia (USA) **S & G Clayton**
28 **GOING GREY (IRE)**, 4, ro g Diamond Green (FR)—Incendio **Mrs H. Steel**
29 **HI THERE (IRE)**, 4, b g Dark Angel (IRE)—Ornellaia (IRE) **Market Avenue Racing Club Ltd**
30 **HIGH OFFICE**, 7, b g High Chaparral (IRE)—White House **J. C. Parsons**
31 **INGLEBY SPIRIT**, 6, b g Avonbridge—Encore du Cristal (USA) **Percy/Green Racing**
32 **JOHANNES (IRE)**, 10, b g Mozart (IRE)—Blue Sirocco **John Nicholls Ltd/David Kilburn**
33 **JUSTONEFORTHEROAD**, 7, b g Domedriver (IRE)—Lavinia's Grace (USA) **The Pontoon Partnership**
34 **KALDOUN KINGDOM (IRE)**, 8, b g King's Best (USA)—Bint Kaldoun (IRE) **P. D. Smith Holdings Ltd**
35 **LADY LOCH**, 4, b f Dutch Art—Locharia **D. W. Armstrong**
36 **LADYS FIRST**, 4, b f Dutch Art—Like A Dame **Mrs H. Steel**
37 **LAS VERGLAS STAR (IRE)**, 5, gr g Verglas (IRE)—Magnificent Bell (IRE) **CBWS Partnership**
38 **LEXINGTON BAY (IRE)**, 5, b g High Chaparral (IRE)—
　　　　　　　　　　　　　　　　Schust Madame (IRE) **Mr Keith Denham & Mr Tony Denham**
39 **LORD AERYN (IRE)**, 6, b g Antonius Pius (USA)—White Paper (IRE) **Mrs H. Steel**
40 **MAJESTIC MYLES (IRE)**, 5, b g Majestic Missile (IRE)—Gala Style (IRE) **Mr J. Gaffney**
41 **MICA MIKA (IRE)**, 5, ch g Needwood Blade—Happy Talk (IRE) **Mrs U. Towell**
42 **NEIL'S PRIDE**, 4, b f Dubai Destination (USA)—Collette's Choice **P. D. Smith Holdings Ltd**
43 **NEMUSHKA**, 4, ch f Sakhee (USA)—Dame de Noche **The G-Guck Group**
44 **POLAR KITE (IRE)**, 5, b g Marju (IRE)—Irina (IRE) **Mr & Mrs J. D. Coulson**
45 **SIR REGINALD**, 5, b g Compton Place—Clincher Club **Mr J. C. McGrath**
46 **SNOOKY**, 4, b g Exceed And Excel (AUS)—Quintrell **Mrs J. M. MacPherson**
47 **SPARKLING PORTRAIT**, 4, b c Excellent Art—Time Crystal (IRE) **M. F. Browne**
48 **STANLEY RIGBY**, 7, b g Dr Fong (USA)—Crystal (IRE) **Mr D. Hardman & Mrs S. Hardman**

MR RICHARD FAHEY - Continued

49 SUFFICE (IRE), 4, b g Iffraaj—Shallat (IRE) **R. A. Fahey**
50 SUNNY SIDE UP (IRE), 4, b f Refuse To Bend (IRE)—
    Feeling Wonderful (IRE) **Jim McGrath, Roger & Dianne Trevitt**
51 VALERY BORZOV (IRE), 9, b g Iron Mask (USA)—Fay's Song (IRE) **D. R. Kilburn/John Nicholls Trading**
52 VENTURA SANDS (IRE), 5, b g Footstepsinthesand—Beautiful Noise **Mr K. Denham**
53 VENTURA SPIRIT, 4, b g Royal Applause—Jalissa **Mr K. Denham**
54 VIVA RONALDO (IRE), 7, b g Xaar—Papaha (FR) **Aykroyd & Sons Limited**
55 WARCROWN (IRE), 4, b c Azamour (IRE)—Alikhlas **Mrs H. Steel**
56 YEOMANOFTHEGUARD, 4, b g Librettist (USA)—Red Blooded Woman (USA) **H. J. P. Farr**

THREE-YEAR-OLDS

57 ALLNECESSARYFORCE (FR), gr c Verglas (IRE)—Kosmic View (USA) **Mr P. F. O'Callaghan**
58 ANDERTON (IRE), b g Invincible Spirit (IRE)—Alarme Belle **D. W. Armstrong**
59 ANNALOVA, b f Araafa (IRE)—Danalova **Galaxy Racing**
60 ANOTHER CLARET, b g Avonbridge—Sylvan (IRE) **Hazel Tattersall & Mr G. Hyde**
61 AVEC ROSE, b f Tagula (IRE)—Rose Siog **The Mick Sweeney Syndicate**
62 BAHAMAMAY, ch g Bahamian Bounty—May West **Benatom Racing 1**
63 BAYAN KASIRGA (IRE), b f Aussie Rules (USA)—Gwyllion (USA) **Mr S. Humphreys**
64 BISPHAM GREEN, b c Green Desert (USA)—Royal Grace **D. W. Armstrong**
65 BROOKE'S BOUNTY, ch g Bahamian Bounty—Choysia **Mr J. Gaffney**
66 CASH IS KING, b g Bahamian Bounty—Age of Chivalry (IRE) **Penman Bond Partnership**
67 CLASSY TRICK (USA), b g Hat Trick (JPN)—Classiest Gem (CAN) **Dr M. B. Q. S. Koukash**
68 DOLPHIN VILLAGE (IRE), b g Cape Cross (IRE)—Reform Act (USA) **Mr Y. M. Nasib**
69 DUSKY QUEEN (IRE), b f Shamardal (USA)—Sanna Bay (IRE) **Mrs H. Steel**
70 ERIC THE GREY (IRE), gr g Verglas (IRE)—Queens Wharf (IRE) **The Clynes & Knaggs Partnership**
71 FLIGHTY CLARETS (IRE), ch f Bahamian Bounty—Flying Clarets (IRE) **The Matthewman One Partnership**
72 FLYMAN, b c Pastoral Pursuits—Satin Bell **G. Murray**
73 FORGING THE PATH (USA), b c Henrythenavigator (USA)—Atitudeofgratitude (IRE) **Mr P. F. O'Callaghan**
74 GABRIAL THE MASTER (IRE), ch g Strategic Prince—Kualke (IRE) **Dr M. B. Q. S. Koukash**
75 GABRIAL THE THUG (FR), b g Azamour (IRE)—Baliyna (USA) **Dr M. B. Q. S. Koukash**
76 GABRIAL'S KAKA (IRE), b g Jeremy (USA)—Love In May (IRE) **Dr M. B. Q. S. Koukash**
77 GABRIAL'S WAWA, b g Dubai Destination (USA)—Celestial Welcome **Dr M. B. Q. S. Koukash**
78 GARSWOOD, b c Dutch Art—Penchant **D. W. Armstrong**
79 GREY STREET, b gr f Royal Applause—Good Enough (FR) **Havelock Racing**
80 HEAVEN'S GUEST (IRE), b g Dark Angel (IRE)—Bakewell Tart (IRE) **Mr J. K. Shannon & Mr M. A. Scaife**
81 INGLEBY ROYALE, b f Royal Applause—Lay A Whisper **Percy Green Racing 4 & Partner**
82 INGLEBY SYMPHONY (IRE), b f Oratorio—Alizaya (IRE) **Percy Green Racing 4 & Partner**
83 JAMESBO'S GIRL, ch f Refuse To Bend (IRE)—Donna Anna **Hardisty Rolls**
84 JUBILEE GAMES, b g Pastoral Pursuits—Jane Jubilee (IRE) **Lets Go Racing 1**
85 KHELMAN (IRE), b g Kheleyf (USA)—Mandolin (IRE) **S & G Clayton**
86 LA LUZ DEL SOL, b f Misu Bond (IRE)—Villa Del Sol **R. A. Fahey**
87 LASARALEEN (IRE), b f Amadeus Wolf—Rosy Dudley (IRE)
88 LAUDATE DOMINUM (IRE), b f Oratorio (IRE)—Feeling Wonderful (IRE) **Inner Circle Thoroughbreds - Ab Ovo**
89 LEXINGTON PLACE, ch g Compton Place—Elidore **Middleham Park Racing XXXI**
90 LIGNUM VITAE, b g Vita Rosa (JPN)—Pat Or Else
91 LOCH MOY, b g Kyllachy—Dixielake (IRE) **Inner Circle Thoroughbreds - Carpe Diem**
92 MAJESTIC MOON (IRE), b g Majestic Missile (IRE)—Gala Style (IRE) **Mr J. Gaffney**
93 MAKINSON LANE (IRE), b c Acclamation—Subtle Affair (IRE) **D. W. Armstrong**
94 MANCHESTAR, b g Elusive City (USA)—Grande Terre (IRE) **Mr & Mrs G. Calder**
95 MARY'S DAUGHTER, b f Royal Applause—Aunty Mary **Mr & Mrs J. D. Cotton**
96 MYSTERY BET (IRE), b f Kheleyf (USA)—Dancing Prize (IRE) **Mrs H. Steel**
97 ORIONS HERO (IRE), b g Oasis Dream—La Reine Mambo (USA) **Mrs H. Steel**
98 OSTRALEGUS, b g Choisir (AUS)—Midnight Pearl (USA) **The Oystercatcher Racing Syndicate**
99 POLSKI MAX, b g Kyllachy—Quadrophenia **Market Avenue Racing & Tremouser**
100 RENE MATHIS (GER), ch g Monsieur Bond (IRE)—Remina (GER) **Dr M. B. Q. S. Koukash**
101 ROMANTIC SETTINGS, ch f Mount Nelson—Lacework **Mr Mel Roberts & Ms Nicola Meese 1**
102 SHE'S SOME GIRL (IRE), ch f Camacho—Tea Service (IRE) **Mr J. Gaffney**
103 SIMPLY SHINING (IRE), ch f Rock of Gibraltar (IRE)—Bright Smile (IRE) **Mrs H. Steel**
104 STRANGE MAGIC (IRE), b f Diamond Green (FR)—Blue Daze **Middleham Park Racing LX**
105 TANGHAN (IRE), b g Invincible Spirit (IRE)—Rose de France (IRE) **Mrs H. Steel**
106 TATLISU (IRE), b g Red Clubs (IRE)—Zwadi (IRE) **Middleham Park Racing LIV**
107 TIME AND PLACE, ch c Compton Place—Forthefirstime **Mr Mel Roberts & Ms Nicola Meese 1**
108 UNSINKABLE (IRE), gr c Verglas (IRE)—Heart's Desire **Penman Bond Partnership**
109 WHITE COPPICE, ch g Pivotal—Finchley **D. W. Armstrong**
110 WYLDFIRE (IRE), ch g Raven's Pass (USA)—Miss Sally (IRE) **Mrs H. Steel**

MR RICHARD FAHEY - Continued

TWO-YEAR-OLDS

Please see page 552

Other Owners: A. Rhodes Haulage Ltd, Mr D. Abraham, Mr S. G. Barnes, Mr Mike J. Beadle, Mr Peter J. Bond, Mr D. Bowen, Mr A. Brown, Mr Stuart Brown, Mr I. T. Buchanan, Mr G. Calder, Mrs J. Calder, Mr J. P. Carr, Mr M. Channon, Mr A. Clark, Mr Steven Clayton, Mrs G. A. Clayton, Mr Bill Clynes, Mrs Eileen Collier, Mr N. Collins, Mr Richard Connaughton, Mr A. E. Corbett, Mr S. C. Corbett, Mr J. D. Cotton, Mrs B. Cotton, Mr R. Cowie, Mr P. S. Cresswell, Mr Keith Denham, Mr Sam Ellis, Mr R. A. Fahey, Mr K. J. Farrer, Mr David M. Fulton, Mr Brian W. Goodall, Mr Jeff Goodall, Mrs Anne Marie Goodall, Mr J. D. Gordon, Mr David A. Green, Mr J. P. Hames, Mr Dean Hardman, Mrs Stella Hardman, Mr John Harris, Mrs E. A. Harris, Mr T. F. Harris, Mr P. L. Harrison, Mr Kevin Hart, Mr K. Hind, Mr Christopher A. Hood, Mr G. R. Hunnam, Mr G. Hyde, Inner Circle Thoroughbreds Limited, Mr R. H. Jennings, Mr D. R. John, John Nicholls (Trading) Ltd, Mr R. F. Johnson, Mr D. Kilburn, Mr D. M. Knaggs, Mrs Jackie Knaggs, Mrs Christine Lally, Mr Mark A. Leatham, Mr G. H. Leatham, Mrs J Malcolmson, Market Avenue Racing Club Ltd, Mr Bill Martin (Fife), Mr Jim McGrath, Mr D. J. P. McWilliams, Mr T. M. McKain, Ms Nicola Meese, Mrs P. A. Morrison, Mrs Margaret Nelson, Mr T. S. Palin, Mrs J. Penman, Mr M. Prince, Mr Mel Roberts, Mr P. Rolls, Mrs J. Rolls, Mr A. Scaife, Mr Dave Scott, Mr J. K. Shannon, Mr A. Shearer, Mr D. W. E. Sowden, Mr Michael Sweeney, Mr A. Tattersall, Mrs Hazel Tattersall, Mr D. M. Tempest, Mr Peter Timmins, Mr Roger Trevitt, Mrs Dianne Trevitt, Mr G. Weaver, Mr John Wicks, Mr David Wild.

Assistant Trainer: Robin O'Ryan

Jockey (flat): Tony Hamilton, Paul Hanagan, Frederik Tylicki, Barry McHugh. **Jockey (NH):** Brian Hughes. **Apprentice:** George Chaloner, Laura Barry, Lee Topliss. **Amateur:** Miss Alyson Deniel, Mr Jamie Hamilton.

---

212 **MR CHRIS FAIRHURST, Middleham**
Postal: **Glasgow House, Middleham, Leyburn, North Yorkshire, DL8 4QG**
Contacts: **PHONE/FAX (01969) 622039 MOBILE (07889) 410840**
E-MAIL **cfairhurst@tiscali.co.uk** WEBSITE **www.chrisfairhurstracing.com**

1 DISTRICT ATTORNEY (IRE), 4, b g Lawman (FR)—Mood Indigo (IRE) **The PQD Partnership**
2 FERNEY BOY, 7, b g Courteous—Jendorcet **Mrs P. J. Taylor-Garthwaite**
3 MOOTABAR (IRE), 6, gr g Verglas (IRE)—Melanzane **Mrs A. M. Leggett**
4 SHIRLS SON SAM, 5, b g Rambling Bear—Shirl **Mrs S. France**
5 SPRUZZO, 7, b g Emperor Fountain—Ryewater Dream **980 Racing**
6 THACKERAY, 6, b g Fasliyev (USA)—Chinon (IRE) **Mrs C. Arnold**
7 TIGERINO (IRE), 5, b g Tiger Hill (IRE)—Golden Shadow (IRE) **980 Racing**
8 WHO'S SHIRL, 7, b m Shinko Forest (IRE)—Shirl **Mrs S. France**

THREE-YEAR-OLDS

9 MEGALEKA, b f Misu Bond (IRE)—Peyto Princess **North Cheshire Trading & Storage Ltd**
10 POPPY BOND, b f Misu Bond (IRE)—Matilda Peace **North Cheshire Trading & Storage Ltd**

---

213 **MR JAMES FANSHAWE, Newmarket**
Postal: **Pegasus Stables, Snailwell Road, Newmarket, Suffolk, CB8 7DJ**
Contacts: **PHONE (01638) 664525 / 660153 FAX (01638) 664523**
E-MAIL **james@jamesfanshawe.com** WEBSITE **www.jamesfanshawe.com**

1 AQUA JETER (IRE), 4, b g Dansili—Silk And Scarlet **Dragon Gate**
2 DANDINO, 6, br h Dansili—Generous Diana **Elite Racing Club**
3 DEACON BLUES, 6, b g Compton Place—Persario **Jan & Peter Hopper & Michelle Morris**
4 EMILIO LARGO, 5, b g Cadeaux Genereux—Gloved Hand **Mr Malcolm C. Denmark**
5 ENTITLEMENT, 4, b f Authorized (IRE)—Applecross **Dr Catherine Wills**
6 HALLELUJAH, 5, b m Avonbridge—My Golly **CLS (Chippenham) Ltd**
7 HIGH JINX (IRE), 5, b h High Chaparral (IRE)—Leonara (GER) **Mr & Mrs W. J. Williams**
8 IF SO, 4, b f Iffraaj—Persario **Hopper, Grundy, Handscombe**
9 ISOLA VERDE, 4, b f Oasis Dream—Firenze **Jan & Peter Hopper**
10 LEVI DRAPER, 4, b g Rock of Gibraltar (IRE)—Splice **Andrew & Julia Turner**
11 LURCHER, 4, gr g With Approval (CAN)—Pitcroy **Dr Catherine Wills**
12 MISS DASHWOOD, 4, b f Dylan Thomas (IRE)—Dash To The Front **Helena Springfield Ltd**
13 NOVIRAK (IRE), 5, gr g Noverre (USA)—Manchaca (FR) **Mr Norman Brunskill**

MR JAMES FANSHAWE - Continued

14 **PRIMAEVAL**, 7, ch g Pivotal—Langoustine (AUS) **Mr Simon Gibson**
15 **SEAL OF APPROVAL**, 4, b f Authorized (IRE)—Hannda (IRE) **Mr T. R. G. Vestey**
16 **SOCIETY ROCK (IRE)**, 6, b h Rock of Gibraltar (IRE)—High Society (IRE) **Mr Simon Gibson**
17 **VILLORESI (IRE)**, 4, b g Clodovil—Villafranca (IRE) **Mr & Mrs W. J. Williams**

THREE-YEAR-OLDS

18 **AOMEN ROCK**, b g Rock of Gibraltar (IRE)—Siren Sound **Dragon Gate**
19 **ARAGOSTA**, ch f Pivotal—Langoustine (AUS) **Lord Vestey**
20 **ARDAAL**, ch c Singspiel (IRE)—Moonmaiden **Mr Saeed bel Obaida**
21 **BADR AL BADOOR (IRE)**, b f Acclamation—Dani Ridge (IRE) **Mr Mohamed Obaida**
22 **BOMBARDIER**, ch c Manduro (GER)—Lady Stardust **Mrs Martin Armstrong**
23 **COSSETED**, b f Pivotal—Fondled **Cheveley Park Stud**
24 **DELICIOUS POISON**, ch c Pivotal—Pediment **Mr Mohamed Obaida**
25 **DON'T STARE**, b g Zamindar (USA)—Joshua's Princess **Mr Guy A. A. C. Gredley**
26 **DRAHEM**, b f Teofilo (IRE)—Carinae (USA) **Mr Salem bel Obaida**
27 **GLANELY (IRE)**, b g Exceed And Excel (AUS)—Bon Ton Roulet **Mr Simon Gibson**
28 **GONE DUTCH**, ch g Dutch Art—Ice Palace **The Ice Syndicate**
29 **GREEN MONKEY**, b g Green Desert (USA)—Firenze **Mr & Mrs P. Hopper, Mr & Mrs M. Morris**
30 **KNIGHT OWL**, b g Rock of Gibraltar (IRE)—Miss Ivanhoe (IRE) **Miss Annabelle Condon**
31 **KOALA BEAR**, b f Oasis Dream—Birthday Suit (IRE) **Lady Halifax**
32 **LOVED ONE**, b f Medicean—Embraced **Cheveley Park Stud**
33 **MAC'S SUPERSTAR (FR)**, b g Elusive City (USA)—Diamond Light (USA) **Mr Michael McDonnell**
34 **MAGIC HURRICANE (IRE)**, b c Hurricane Run (IRE)—Close Regards (IRE) **Dragon Gate**
35 **NINJA LADY**, b f Nayef (USA)—Galaxy Highflyer **Helena Springfield Ltd**
36 **OKAVANGO**, ch f Nayef (USA)—Ivory Gala (FR) **Mr T. R. G. Vestey**
37 B g Tiger Hill (IRE)—Possessive Artiste **Rockwell Bloodstock**
38 **QUALITY ALLIANCE**, ch f Dubai Destination (USA)—Allied Cause **Helena Springfield Ltd**
39 **RABDAAN**, ch c Sakhee (USA)—Maghya (IRE) **Mr Mohamed Obaida**
40 **RED TULIP**, br f Kheleyf (USA)—Red Carnation (IRE) **Mrs Doreen M. Swinburn**
41 **RIBBONS**, ch f Manduro (GER)—Sister Act **Elite Racing Club**
42 **ROUBLE**, b f Royal Applause—Mycenae **Dr Catherine Wills**
43 **SHWAIMAN (IRE)**, br c Authorized (IRE)—Blue Lightning **Mr Mohamed Obaida**
44 **SORN (IRE)**, ch g Galileo (IRE)—Dame Again (AUS) **Mr Thomas Barr**
45 **VANVITELLI**, b c Shamardal (USA)—Treble Seven (USA) **Mrs C. C. Regalado-Gonzalez**
46 **WALL STREET BOSS (USA)**, b br g Street Boss (USA)—Pad The Wallet (USA) **Axom XXXIV**
47 **WEDDING SPEECH (IRE)**, b f Acclamation—Wedding Cake (IRE) **Mr G. & Mrs L. J. Marney**
48 **ZADOK**, b g Nayef (USA)—Panna **Lord Halifax**

TWO-YEAR-OLDS

49 **ANWAR DUBAI**, ch f 15/4 Aqlaam—Ha'penny Beacon (Erhaab (USA)) (32000) **Mr Mohamed Obaida**
50 **AQLAAM HUNT (IRE)**, ch f 17/3 Aqlaam—Leopard Hunt (USA) (Diesis) (55000) **Mr Mohamed Obaida**
51 **BARBARY (IRE)**, b c 3/3 Rock of Gibraltar (IRE)—
      Silver Cache (USA) (Silver Hawk (USA)) (58000) **Mr Simon Gibson**
52 **CAPTAIN GEORGE (IRE)**, b c 1/4 Bushranger (IRE)—
      High Society Girl (IRE) (Key of Luck (USA)) (47000) **Mr Peter Tarrant & Mr Robert Morton**
53 B c 24/2 Dubawi (IRE)—Caribbean Pearl (USA) (Silver Hawk (USA)) **Mr Mohamed Obaida**
54 B br f 13/3 Medaglia d'oro (USA)—Damaniyat Girl (USA) (Elusive Quality (USA)) **Mr Mohamed Obaida**
55 **DUBAI POST (IRE)**, b c 2/3 Dubawi (IRE)—Storming Sioux (Storming Home) **Mr Mohamed Obaida**
56 **DUBIAN TO (IRE)**, ch f 6/4 Sea The Stars (IRE)—Mrs Lindsay (USA) (Theatrical) (400000) **Mr Mohamed Obaida**
57 **ELIZONA**, b f 20/2 Pastoral Pursuits—Morning After (Emperor Jones (USA)) **Mrs Alice Cherry**
58 **ENCOUNTERING**, b c 13/4 Duke of Marmalade (IRE)—
      Naval Affair (IRE) (Last Tycoon) (90000) **Mr Ben C. M. Wong**
59 **ENSURING**, br c 2/2 New Approach (IRE)—Dynacam (USA) (Dynaformer (USA)) (110000) **Mr Ben C. M. Wong**
60 B c 28/4 Peintre Celebre (USA)—Flying Finish (FR) (Priolo (USA)) (50000) **Dragon Gate**
61 **FORFEIT (USA)**, b g 6/2 Langfuhr (CAN)—Intangible (USA) (Diesis) **Dr Catherine Wills**
62 B c 7/3 Compton Place—Garter Star (Mark of Esteem (IRE)) (37000) **Carivalis, Eady, Papworth & Swinburn**
63 B f 27/4 Shirocco (GER)—Hannda (IRE) (Dr Devious (IRE)) (15000) **Mr T. R. G. Vestey**
64 **HE'S MY BOY**, gr c 9/5 Dark Angel (IRE)—Rose of Battle (Averti (IRE)) (36000) **Mr P. S. Ryan**
65 **IBO HAIL (USA)**, b c 12/4 Invasor (ARG)—Sayyedati Symphony (USA) (Gone West (USA)) **Mr Mohamed Obaida**
66 **IT'S A YES FROM ME**, b c 3/4 Bahamian Bounty—Valjarv (IRE) (Bluebird (USA)) (42000) **The Foncey Syndicate**
67 B c 24/4 Invasor (ARG)—Lonely Ahead (USA) (Rahy (USA)) **Mr Mohamed Obaida**
68 B f 31/3 Shamardal (USA)—Lune Rose (High Chaparral (IRE)) (55555) **Dragon Gate**
69 Ch c 28/2 Mount Nelson—Maid For Winning (USA) (Gone West (USA)) (40000) **Mr Chris van Hoorn**
70 Ch c 27/3 Sleeping Indian—Neyraan (Lujain (USA)) **Mr Chris van Hoorn**

MR JAMES FANSHAWE - Continued

71 B f 22/3 Medicean—Panna (Polish Precedent (USA)) **Lord Halifax**
72 B f 18/2 Invasor (ARG)—Ras Shaikh (USA) (Sheikh Albadou) **Mr Mohamed Obaida**
73 B f 23/2 War Chant (USA)—Rosy Mantle (Daylami (IRE)) **Nigel & Carolyn Elwes**
74 **SPIRIT RAISER (IRE)**, b f 29/3 Invincible Spirit (IRE)—
                    Macadamia (IRE) (Classic Cliche (IRE)) **The Hon. William Vestey**
75 **SWORDBEARER**, ch c 18/4 Selkirk (USA)—Isis (USA) (Royal Academy (USA)) (16000) **Dr Catherine Wills**
76 **ZMAN AWAL (IRE)**, ch f 17/2 Dubawi (IRE)—Pivotal Lady (Pivotal) **Mr Mohamed Obaida**

Other Owners: Mr John E. Bodie, Mr S. Cowell, Mr D. Donnelly, Mrs H. S. Ellingsen, Mrs Olivia Hoare, Mr A. McPartlin, Mr J. H. Richmond-Watson, Mr M. Weinfeld, Mr B. York.

Assistant Trainer: Charlie Fellowes

---

214 MISS JULIA FEILDEN, Newmarket
Postal: **Harraton Stud, Laceys Lane, Exning, Newmarket, Suffolk, CB8 7HW**
Contacts: **PHONE (01638) 577470 FAX (01638) 578628 MOBILE (07974) 817694**
E-MAIL hoofbeatstours@aol.com WEBSITE www.juliafeildenracing.com

1 **AL REEFA (IRE)**, 5, b g Elusive City (USA)—Cameo Story **Mr J. C. Jakes**
2 **ATTAIN**, 4, b g Dansili—Achieve **Miss J. D. Feilden**
3 **AUTOMOTIVE**, 5, b g Beat Hollow—Bina Ridge **Stowstowquickquickstow Partnership**
4 **CHILLI GREEN**, 6, b m Desert Sun—Jade Pet **P. M. Crane**
5 4, B f Nayef (USA)—Elizabethan Age (FR) **Mr I. Marks**
6 **ENTRANCE**, 5, ch m Iceman—Enrapture (USA) **Hoofbeats Racing Club**
7 **EXOPUNTIA**, 7, b m Sure Blade (USA)—Opuntia **J. W. Ford**
8 **FARAWAY LAND (USA)**, 5, b m Empire Maker (USA)—Out of Reach **Miss J. D. Feilden**
9 **HANDHELD**, 6, ch g Observatory (USA)—Kid Gloves **Miss J. D. Feilden**
10 **KHAJAALY (IRE)**, 6, b g Kheleyf (USA)—Joyfullness (USA) **Geegeez.co.uk**
11 **LEA VALLEY**, 4, b f Araafa (IRE)—Guaranda **R. J. Creese**
12 **NO SUCH NUMBER**, 5, b g King's Best (USA)—Return (USA) **Good Company Partnership**
13 **OMEGA OMEGA**, 4, b f Halling (USA)—In Luck **Mr John W. Ford**
14 **SAIL HOME**, 6, b m Mizzen Mast (USA)—Bristol Channel **Mr P. Foster**
15 **SANCHO PANZA**, 6, b g Zafeen (FR)—Malvadilla (IRE) **Carol Bushnell & Partners**
16 **SILVER ALLIANCE**, 5, gr g Proclamation (IRE)—Aimee Vibert **In It To Win Partnership**
17 **SPIRIT OF SHARJAH (IRE)**, 8, b g Invincible Spirit (IRE)—Rathbawn Realm **Mr A. Dee**
18 **THE DUCKING STOOL**, 6, ch m Where Or When (IRE)—Dance Sequel **Mrs S. McGuiness**
19 **VASTLY (USA)**, 4, gr c Mizzen Mast (USA)—Valentine Band (USA) **Sultans of Speed Partnership**

THREE-YEAR-OLDS

20 **AMELIA GEORGE**, b f Avonbridge—Tamara **J. W. Ford**
21 **BELIEVE IN ME**, b f Bertolini (USA)—Zephrina **Hoofbeats Racing Club**
22 **HONEYMOON EXPRESS (IRE)**, br f Mujadil (USA)—Royal Jelly **Miss J. D. Feilden**
23 **SHEILA'S HEART**, ch c Dubai Destination (USA)—Sefemm **Mr P. Foster**
24 **TIGER'S HOME**, b f Tiger Hill (IRE)—Homeward (IRE) **Hoofbeats Racing Club**

TWO-YEAR-OLDS

25 B c 27/3 Araafa (IRE)—Air Maze (Dansili)
26 B c 9/3 Araafa (IRE)—Angel Kate (IRE) (Invincible Spirit (IRE))
27 **BUSHY GLADE (IRE)**, b f 15/2 Bushranger (IRE)—Cladantom (IRE) (High Estate) (6000) **R. J. Creese**
28 Ch c 20/4 Araafa (IRE)—Golden Flyer (FR) (Machiavellian (USA))
29 **OPUS TOO (IRE)**, b c 26/4 Lawman (FR)—
                    Jerez (IRE) (Lake Coniston (IRE)) (8000) **Mr A. Dee & Mr G. Smith Bernal**
30 B c 9/4 Araafa (IRE)—Saga River (FR) (Sagacity (FR))

Other Owners: Mr J. Birkett, Mr M. Bisogno, Miss J. Feilden, Mrs Jackie Olkowicz, Mr Chris Page, Miss Amanda Rawding, Mrs A. S. Styles, Mr R. Wright.

Assistant Trainer: John Birkett

Jockey (flat): Adam Beschizza. **Apprentice:** Shelley Birkett. **Amateur:** Mr R. Birkett.

215   MR PHILIP FENTON, Carrick-On-Suir

Postal: Glenbower Stables Ltd., Garryduff, South Lodge, Carrick-On-Suir, Co. Tipperary, Ireland
Contacts: PHONE (00 353) 51 647901 FAX (00 353) 51 647901 MOBILE (00 353) 87 2581048
E-MAIL glenbowerstables@gmail.com WEBSITE www.glenbowerstables.com

1 BAND OF BLOOD (IRE), 5, b g King's Theatre (IRE)—Cherry Falls (IRE) **Gigginstown House Stud**
2 BRIGHTON ROAD (IRE), 6, b g Milan—Grand Quest **Philip Fenton**
3 CAIM HILL (IRE), 10, b g Deploy—Glen's Gale (IRE) **M. Dempsey**
4 CASINO MARKETS (IRE), 5, br g Fruits of Love (USA)—Vals Dream (IRE) **Pan European Bloodstock**
5 CASTLE CONNELL (IRE), 5, b g Bienamado (USA)—Duneavey (IRE) **Kevin Fenton**
6 CASTLETOWN WARRIOR (IRE), 5, gr g Pierre—Nancymar (IRE) **M. McDonagh**
7 4, B g Fruits of Love (USA)—Ding Dong Belle **John Power**
8 DRIVE ON LOCKY (IRE), 6, b g Milan—Husyans Beauty (IRE) **Keep on Dreaming Syndicate**
9 DUNGUIB (IRE), 10, b g Presenting—Edermine Berry (IRE) **Mrs E. Lawlor**
10 FIVE POINT PLAN (IRE), 7, b g Rashar (USA)—Grangeway **James Moran**
11 4, B g Flemensfirth (USA)—Flaming Brandy (IRE) **Kevin Power**
12 GOLDEN ECLIPSE (IRE), 5, b br g Golan (IRE)—Pinkeen Lady (IRE) **M. Daly**
13 4, B g Fruits of Love (USA)—Haven Island (IRE) **Philip Fenton**
14 JUMPY (IRE), 5, b g Presenting—Shuil Again (IRE) **Woodhall Stud**
15 4, B g Vinnie Roe (IRE)—Kingsspice (IRE) **D. Gray**
16 LADY GERONIMO (IRE), 4, b br f Hawk Wing (USA)—Birthday (IRE) **M. Daly**
17 LAST INSTALMENT (IRE), 8, ch g Anshan—Final Instalment (IRE) **Gigginstown House Stud**
18 5, Br m Presenting—Loch Na Mona (IRE) **Philip Fenton**
19 LOWANBEHOLD (IRE), 6, gr g Cloudings (IRE)—Marble Quest (IRE) **T. O'Dwyer**
20 MAKING HEADLINES (IRE), 6, br g Presenting—Name For Fame (USA) **J. McDonald**
21 4, B g Kayf Tara—Miss Orchestra (IRE) **Mr Huglin**
22 5, B m Dr Massini (IRE)—Miss Toulon (IRE) **Mr Rice**
23 ON MY OWN (IRE), 9, b g Shernazar—Bloomfield (IRE) **John Sayers**
24 PASSING THROUGH, 9, b g Exit To Nowhere (USA)—Island Hopper **Border Macs Syndicate**
25 PATSIO (IRE), 5, b g Moscow Society (USA)—Supreme Favour (IRE) **Colm Herron**
26 PINEAU DE RE (FR), 10, b g Maresca Sorrento (FR)—Elfe du Perche (FR) **Barry Connell**
27 REAL STEEL (IRE), 5, br b g Old Vic—Grangeclare Dancer (IRE) **Gigginstown House Stud**
28 ROBBER BARON (IRE), 6, b g Goldmark (USA)—Geraldine's Girl (IRE) **E. Lyons**
29 SUPREME BOB (IRE), 7, b g Bob's Return (IRE)—Supremememories (IRE) **Coole Tavern Syndicate**
30 THE TULLOW TANK (IRE), 5, b g Oscar (IRE)—Bobbing Back (IRE) **Barry Connell**
31 VENTURE CAPITAL (IRE), 6, b g Presenting—Dare To Venture (IRE) **J. P. McManus**
32 VERMOUT FOUGERAY (FR), 4, b g Visionary (FR)—Ile Au Tresor (FR) **E. Burke**
33 VIRGILE DE GENE (FR), 4, b g Le Fou (IRE)—Dame de Gene (FR) **Philip Fenton**
34 VOLUPTUEUX (FR), 4, b g Enrique—Orphee de Vonnas (FR) **Voluptueux Syndicate**
35 VOLVALIEN (FR), 4, b g Network (GER)—Josvalie (FR) **Barry Connell**

Jockey (NH): Brian O'Connell. **Amateur:** Mr R. J. Kiely.

---

216   MR JOHN FERGUSON, Cowlinge

Postal: Bloomfields, Cowlinge, Newmarket, Suffolk, CB8 9HN
Contacts: PHONE (01638) 500423 FAX (01638) 500387

1 ALLOWED, 4, b g Authorized (IRE)—Japanese Whisper (UAE) **Bloomfields**
2 ASAID, 5, b g Singspiel (IRE)—Forum Floozie (NZ) **Bloomfields**
3 BAB AL SALAM (USA), 7, b g Seeking The Gold (USA)—Encandiladora (ARG) **Bloomfields**
4 BEAUJOLAIS (IRE), 5, ch g Moscow Society (USA)—Chirouble (IRE) **Bloomfields**
5 BIRDWATCHER (IRE), 5, ch g Cadeaux Genereux—Dancing Feather **Bloomfields**
6 BORDONI (USA), 4, b g Bernardini (USA)—Argentina (IRE) **Bloomfields**
7 BUTHELEZI (USA), 5, b br g Dynaformer (USA)—Ntombi (USA) **Bloomfields**
8 CAPE DUTCH (IRE), 6, b g Cape Cross (IRE)—Rosia (IRE) **Bloomfields**
9 CAYMAN ISLANDS, 5, b g Shirocco (GER)—Barbuda **Bloomfields**
10 CHABAL (IRE), 6, b g Galileo (IRE)—Vagary (IRE) **Bloomfields**
11 CHAT ROOM, 5, ch g Dubawi (IRE)—Contradictive (USA) **Bloomfields**
12 COTTON MILL, 6, b g Tiger Hill (IRE)—Mill Line **Bloomfields**
13 CREEKSIDE, 5, b g Dubai Destination (USA)—Khubza **Bloomfields**
14 CRY OF FREEDOM (USA), 7, b g Street Cry (IRE)—Tustarta (USA) **Bloomfields**
15 DUKESTOWN (USA), 5, ch g Street Cry (IRE)—Ascot Starre (CAN) **Bloomfields**
16 EARTH DREAM (IRE), 10, b g Old Vic—Barbaras Mews (IRE) **Bloomfields**
17 HALIFAX (IRE), 5, ch g Halling (USA)—Lady Zonda **Bloomfields**

MR JOHN FERGUSON - Continued

18 **HAYMARKET**, 4, b g Singspiel (IRE)—Quickstyx **Bloomfields**
19 **JAMEEL (USA)**, 5, b g Monsun (GER)—Maids Causeway (IRE) **Bloomfields**
20 **LIFE AND TIMES (USA)**, 5, b br g Medaglia d'oro (USA)—Sur Ma Vie (USA) **Bloomfields**
21 **MODERNISM**, 4, b g Monsun (GER)—La Nuit Rose (FR) **Bloomfields**
22 **MONARCH'S WAY**, 6, b g King's Best (USA)—La Bayadere **Bloomfields**
23 **NEW YEAR'S EVE**, 5, b g Motivator—Midnight Angel (GER) **Bloomfields**
24 **ONCE MORE DUBAI (USA)**, 8, b br g E Dubai (USA)—Go Again Girl (USA) **Bloomfields**
25 **PERE BLANC (IRE)**, 8, b g King's Theatre (IRE)—Sunset Leader (IRE) **Bloomfields**
26 **PERPETUALLY (IRE)**, 7, b g Singspiel (IRE)—Set In Motion (USA) **Bloomfields**
27 **PINE CREEK**, 5, b g Doyen (IRE)—Valley of Gold (FR) **Bloomfields**
28 **PLAIN SAILING (IRE)**, 4, b g Manduro (GER)—Ocean Silk (USA) **Bloomfields**
29 **POPULATION**, 6, ch g Noverre (USA)—Ville d'amore (USA) **Bloomfields**
30 **RED DEVIL BOYS (IRE)**, 6, b g Oscar (IRE)—Lohort Castle (IRE) **Bloomfields**
31 **RUACANA**, 4, b g Cape Cross (IRE)—Farrfesheena (USA) **Bloomfields**
32 **SEA LORD (IRE)**, 6, b g Cape Cross (IRE)—First Fleet (USA) **Bloomfields**
33 **THREE KINGDOMS (IRE)**, 4, ch g Street Cry (IRE)—Chan Tong (BRZ) **Bloomfields**
34 **WHISPERING GALLERY**, 7, b g Daylami (IRE)—Echoes In Eternity (IRE) **Bloomfields**

Other Owners: Mr John P. Ferguson, Mrs Fiona Ferguson.

---

217 **MR DOMINIC FFRENCH DAVIS, Lambourn**
Postal: **Upshire House Racing Stables, Hungerford Hill, Lambourn, Hungerford, Berkshire RG17 7LE**
Contacts: **YARD (01488) 73675 Home (01488) 72342 FAX (01488) 73675 MOBILE (07831) 118764**
E-MAIL ffrenchdavis@btinternet.com WEBSITE www.ffrenchdavis.com

1 **ADMIRABLE DUQUE (IRE)**, 7, b g Selkirk (USA)—Stunning (USA) **Mrs J. E. Taylor**
2 **ADVERSANE**, 9, ch g Alhaarth (IRE)—Cragreen
3 **ANTY WREN**, 11, gr g Tragic Role (USA)—Granny Nix
4 **BALADY (IRE)**, 4, b f Zamindar (USA)—Faydah (USA) **Marchwood Aggregates**
5 **BEDOUIN BLUE (IRE)**, 10, b g Desert Style (IRE)—Society Fair (FR)
6 **BRANDYWELL BOY (IRE)**, 10, b g Danetime (IRE)—Alexander Eliott (IRE) **D. J. S. Ffrench Davis**
7 **ENLIST**, 9, b g Beat Hollow—Dawna **B. G. Powell**
8 **GAELIC WIZARD (IRE)**, 5, b h Fasliyev (USA)—Fife (IRE) **D. J. S. Ffrench Davis**
9 **IF I WERE A BOY (IRE)**, 6, b m Invincible Spirit (IRE)—Attymon Lill (IRE) **Mr R. F. Haynes**
10 **JUSTCALLMEHANDSOME**, 11, ch g Handsome Ridge—Pearl Dawn (IRE) **Mrs J. E. Taylor**
11 **SURF IN SEPTEMBER (IRE)**, 4, b f September Storm (GER)—Juno Beach **Mr D. G. Cramm**

THREE-YEAR-OLDS

12 **CANDYMAN CAN (IRE)**, b g Holy Roman Emperor (IRE)—Palwina (FR) **Miss Alison Jones**
13 **FRANS HALS**, b g Dutch Art—Glory Oatway (IRE) **Gary Black, Miss A Jones, Mark Duthie**

TWO-YEAR-OLDS

14 B c 9/4 Rail Link—Breathing Space (USA) (Expelled (USA)) (8500) **Miss Alison Jones**

Other Owners: G. H. Black, M. Duthie.

Assistant Trainer: Avery Ffrench Davis

Jockey (flat): James Doyle. **Jockey (NH):** Mark Grant. **Apprentice:** Josh Baudains. **Amateur:** Mr Ben Ffrench Davis

---

218 **MR GIUSEPPE FIERRO, Hednesford**
Postal: **Bentley Brook House, Rawnsley Road, Hednesford, Cannock, Staffordshire, WS12 1RB**
Contacts: **HOME/YARD (01543) 879611 MOBILE (07976) 321468**

1 **FRANKIE FALCO**, 7, br h Bollin Eric—Marsh Marigold **G. Fierro**
2 **JUST LIKE BETH**, 5, b m Proclamation (IRE)—Just Beth **G. Fierro**
3 **LITTLE DOTTY**, 4, br f Erhaab (USA)—Marsh Marigold **G. Fierro**
4 **PEHERA BOY**, 6, b g Fleetwood (IRE)—Abbiejo (IRE) **G. Fierro**
5 **RED HOTT ROBBIE**, 4, b g Revoque (IRE)—Abbiejo (IRE) **G. Fierro**
6 **SUNDANCE BOY**, 4, gr g Proclamation (IRE)—Just Beth **G. Fierro**

Assistant Trainer: M Fierro

219 MRS MARJORIE FIFE, Stillington
Postal: White Thorn Farm, Stillington, Easingwold, York, YO61 1LT
Contacts: PHONE (01347) 822012 MOBILE (07890) 075217
E-MAIL wfife10416@aol.com

1 KING MAK, 11, gr g Makbul—Miss Nova **Mrs M. Turner**
2 PARAMYTHI (IRE), 4, ch g Peintre Celebre (USA)—The Spirit of Pace (IRE) **E. W. Lerigo**
3 ROYAL HOLIDAY (IRE), 6, ch g Captain Rio—Sunny Slope **Mrs M. Turner**
4 YORKSTERS PRINCE (IRE), 6, b g Beat Hollow—Odalisque (IRE) **R. W. Fife**

220 MR TIM FITZGERALD, Malton
Postal: Norton Grange, Norton, Malton, North Yorkshire, YO17 9EA
Contacts: OFFICE (01653) 692718 FAX (01653) 600214 MOBILE (07950) 356437
E-MAIL fitzgeraldracing@hotmail.com

1 ACRAI RUA (IRE), 10, ch g Rock Hopper—Dontbelieveaword (IRE) **T. J. Fitzgerald**
2 COMERAGH KING, 9, b g Kayf Tara—Velcro Girl (IRE) **T. J. Fitzgerald**
3 EMPEROR OF ROME (IRE), 5, b g Antonius Pius (USA)—Fire Flower **N. H. T. Wrigley**
4 KASTELA STARI, 6, b m Beat Hollow—Campaspe **Mr Paul Coulter & Mr T J Fitzgerald**
5 MR SYNTAX (IRE), 9, b g King's Theatre (IRE)—Smile Awhile (USA) **Regalmist Associates Ltd**

Other Owners: Mr P. Coulter.

221 MR PAUL FITZSIMONS, Upper Lambourn
Postal: Saxon Gate Stables, Malt Shovel Lane, Upper Lambourn, Berkshire, RG17 8QH
Contacts: PHONE (01488) 72712 FAX (01488) 72716 MOBILE (07795) 566359
E-MAIL paulfitzsimons@saxon-gate.com WEBSITE www.saxon-gate.com

1 CORRES (IRE), 6, b g Peintre Celebre (USA)—Kesh Kumay (IRE) **R. C. Tooth**
2 IVAN THE ENGINE, 5, b g Ivan Denisovich (IRE)—Silk Daisy **Lewis Caterers**
3 KYLEAKIN LASS, 4, b f Kyllachy—Local Fancy **C.R. Lambourne, M. Forbes, D. Losse**
4 PERFECT CH'I (IRE), 6, b m Choisir (AUS)—Agouti **P. E. Barrett**
5 QUASI CONGAREE (GER), 7, ch g Congaree (USA)—Queens Wild (USA) **Mr M. Forbes & Mr C. R. Lamborne**
6 SHELLING PEAS, 4, b f Val Royal (FR)—Meditation **P. E. Barrett**

THREE-YEAR-OLDS
7 INDIAN BILLIONAIRE (IRE), b g Red Clubs (IRE)—Tabrina (IRE) **Mr B. Sohal**
8 MISS MOCCA, b f Bahamian Bounty—Mocca (IRE) **C.R. Lambourne, M. Forbes, D. Losse**
9 B c Teofilo (IRE)—Red Bravo (USA) **R. C. Tooth**

TWO-YEAR-OLDS
10 MARO, b c 27/2 Royal Applause—Meditation (Inchinor) (952) **P. E. Barrett**
11 Ch c 8/3 Dutch Art—Photographie (USA) (Trempolino (USA) (42000)
12 B f 10/5 Pastoral Pursuits—Rosapenna (IRE) (Spectrum (IRE)) (11000) **C.R. Lambourne, M. Forbes, D. Losse**
13 B f 23/3 Royal Applause—Roseum (Lahib (USA)) (19000)

Other Owners: M. I. Forbes, Mr C. R. Lambourne, Mr D. R. Losse, Mrs L. J. Losse.

Assistant Trainer: Chris Martin

222 MR JOHN FLINT, Bridgend
Postal: Cherry Tree, 71 Woodlands Park, Kenfig Hill, Bridgend, Mid-Glamorgan, CF33 6EB
Contacts: PHONE (01656) 744347 FAX (01656) 744347 MOBILE (07581) 428173
E-MAIL johnl.flint@talktalk.net WEBSITE www.johnflintracing.com

1 ALL RIGHT BUT, 6, b g Beat All (USA)—Scottish Dance **Mr S. H. Owen**
2 BEN CYFELACH, 4, ch g Big John (IRE)—Proprioception (IRE) **J. L. Flint**
3 BERNISDALE, 5, ch m Bertolini—Carradale **Roderick James & Geraint Anstee**
4 BRACKEN HOUSE (IRE), 6, ch g Great Palm (USA)—Carraig Aille (IRE) **Ms S. A. Howell**
5 CAPTAIN SCARLETT (IRE), 7, b g Milan—Count My Blessings (IRE) **J. L. Flint**
6 CRISTALIYEV, 5, b g Fasliyev (USA)—Desert Cristal (IRE) **J. L. Flint**

MR JOHN FLINT - Continued

7 **DULCEMARA (IRE)**, 5, b m Bahri (USA)—Almnadia (IRE) **Mr J. Hennessy**
8 **FIRST BEAUTY (IRE)**, 9, b br m Norwich—Alleged Beauty (IRE) **Mr G. Cosgrave**
9 **GRAMS AND OUNCES**, 6, b g Royal Applause—Ashdown Princess (IRE) **Mr R. C. Williams**
10 **GROUCH ONTHE COUCH (IRE)**, 6, b m Old Vic—High Priestess (IRE) **J. L. Flint**
11 **GUILETTA (IRE)**, 4, gr f Dalakhani (IRE)—Guilia **Mr B. M. Jones**
12 **HEAVENSTOWN (IRE)**, 7, ch g Bienamado—Little Bliss (IRE) **Mr M. Page**
13 **KAPDOR (FR)**, 6, b g Kapgarde (FR)—La Vernantaise (FR) **J. L. Flint**
14 **LADY LECTRA**, 4, b f Multiplex—Coronation Queen **Mr R. Quinn**
15 **MARCHAND D'ARGENT (FR)**, 10, b g Marchand de Sable (USA)—Masslama (FR) **Mrs C. A. Y. Vaughan**
16 **MONTY FAY (IRE)**, 4, b br g Iffraaj—Blast (USA) **Mr R. Williams**
17 **ONE FOR JOULES (IRE)**, 6, b m Choisir (AUS)—Stuttgart **Mr S. H. Spence**
18 **PALIO SQUARE (USA)**, 6, b br g Harlan's Holiday (USA)—Teewee's Hope (CAN) **Mr E. Storan**
19 **PARHELION**, 6, b g Fantastic Light (USA)—Shamaiel (IRE) **Mr R. Williams**
20 **ROCK ME JOHN (IRE)**, 6, b g Zagreb (USA)—Boston Green (IRE) **Mr R. C. Williams**
21 **ROWLESTONE LAD**, 6, b g Sulamani (IRE)—Charmante Femme **Mr R. C. Williams**
22 **SILVA FLINT**, 5, gr m Generous (IRE)—Senna da Silva **J. L. Flint**
23 **STONY ROAD (IRE)**, 6, b g Hubbly Bubbly (USA)—Laur's Melody (IRE) **J. L. Flint**
24 **TOWERS LADY (IRE)**, 10, b m Bob Back (USA)—Festival Leader (IRE) **Mr W. G. Cleary**

TWO-YEAR-OLDS

25 B f 5/4 Dr Massini (IRE)—Senna da Silva (Prince of Birds (USA)) **J. L. Flint**

Other Owners: Mr Geraint Anstee, Mr Roderick James.

Assistant Trainer: Mrs Martine Louise Flint (07968) 044487

Jockey (NH): Rhys Flint. **Conditional:** Thomas Flint.

---

223 MRS PAM FORD, Hereford
Postal: **Stone House Stables, Preston Wynne, Hereford, Herefordshire, HR1 3PB**
Contacts: **HOME/FAX (01432) 820604 MOBILE (07733) 152051**
E-MAIL pam_ford@hotmail.co.uk

1 8, B gr m M'bebe—Candy Copper
2 6, B m Erhaab (USA)—Candy Copper
3 **CAPTAIN OATS (IRE)**, 10, b g Bahhare (USA)—Adarika **R. S. Herbert**
4 5, B g Tikkanen (USA)—Dara's Course (IRE)
5 **HIGHLAND CADETT**, 6, ch g Putra Sandhurst (IRE)—Highland Rossie (IRE) **R. S. Herbert**

Assistant Trainer: Mr K Ford

Jockey (flat): Hayley Turner, Royston Ffrench. **Jockey (NH):** J. Davies.

---

224 MR RICHARD FORD, Garstang
Postal: **Lancashire Racing Stables, The Paddocks, Strickens Lane, Barnacre, Garstang, Lancashire, PR3 1UD**
Contacts: **PHONE (01995) 605790 (07802) 764094 MOBILE (07976) 522768**
E-MAIL clarksonhorses@barnacre.fsbusiness.co.uk
WEBSITE www.lancashireracingstables.co.uk

1 **BILLY THISS**, 5, b g Beat All (USA)—Queens Stroller (IRE) **Mr D. R. Thistlethwaite**
2 **BLACKAMOOR HARRY**, 4, b g Indesatchel (IRE)—Libretta **F M Racing**
3 **BOWLANDS LEGACY**, 4, b f Grape Tree Road—Bowlands Madam **Brandsby Racing**
4 **CALCULAITE**, 12, b g Komaite (USA)—Miss Calculate **The Hexham Handicappers**
5 **CHEERY CAT (USA)**, 9, b br g Catienus (USA)—Olinka (USA) **The Cataractonium Racing Syndicate**
6 **CHORISTER GIRL**, 4, b f Acclamation—Hazelhurst (IRE) **Richard Ford**
7 4, B g And Beyond (IRE)—Cotton Easter **The Newcastle Racing Club**
8 **DANE COTTAGE**, 6, ch m Beat Hollow—Lady Soleas **The Carlisle Cavaliers**
9 **GOLDEN DREAM (IRE)**, 9, ch g Golden Tornado (IRE)—Orion Dream **The Cartmel Race Club**
10 **HUMUNGOSAUR**, 4, b c Red Ransom (USA)—Fabulously Fast (USA) **Mrs R. Farrington-Kirkham**
11 5, Ch m Alflora (IRE)—Island Hopper **Brandsby Racing**
12 **KAZBOW (IRE)**, 7, b g Rainbow Quest (USA)—Kasota (IRE) **The Most Wanted Partnership**
13 **KINGDOM OF MUNSTER (IRE)**, 6, b g Danehill Dancer (IRE)—Kitty O'shea **J. D. Clark & Partners**

MR RICHARD FORD - Continued

14 **MARK OF MEYDAN**, 8, ch g Mark of Esteem (IRE)—Rose Bounty **The Bounty Hunters**
15 **MEGLIO ANCORA**, 6, ch g Best of The Bests (IRE)—May Fox **The Most Wanted Partnership**
16 **MEYDAN STYLE (USA)**, 7, b g Essence of Dubai (USA)—Polish Ruby (USA) **The Style Council**
17 **MIDNIGHT RETURN (IRE)**, 7, b m Midnight Legend—By Return (IRE) **Harpers Brook Racing**
18 **MINISTEROFINTERIOR**, 8, b g Nayef (USA)—Maureen's Hope (USA) **Mrs R. Farrington-Kirkham**
19 **NANI JANI**, 4, ch f Halling (USA)—Betty's Pride **Betty's Brigade**
20 **PEACEBETHEJOURNEY**, 4, b f Crosspeace (IRE)—Royal Shepley **P B J Racing**
21 **REGGIE RABBIT**, 4, br g Iceman—School Days **Mr L. T. Finlayson**
22 **SEAMSTER**, 6, ch g Pivotal—Needles And Pins (IRE) **The Haydock Club**
23 **SHARP AND CHIC**, 6, b m Needwood Blade—Moreover (IRE) **Miss N. C. Taylor**
24 **SILVER STEEL (FR)**, 10, b g Robin des Pres (FR)—Oliver's Queen (FR) **Mrs Julie Gordon & Mr Keith Hesketh**
25 **STATE SENATOR (USA)**, 5, b br g Mr Greeley (USA)—Summer Night **The Four Aces**
26 **SWALEDALE LAD (IRE)**, 6, b g Arakan (USA)—Tadjnama (USA) **Mr D. Challoner**
27 4, Ch g Tobougg (IRE)—Synergie (IRE) **Mrs S. E. Barclay**
28 **YOU'RELIKEMEFRANK**, 7, ch g Bahamian Bounty—
　　　　　　　　　　　　　　　　　　Proudfoot (IRE) **Mrs K. E. Barrett, Mr P. Clarkson & Mr D. Clarkson**

THREE-YEAR-OLDS

29 **ALFRED THE GREAT**, ch g Proclamation (IRE)—Synergie (IRE) **Network Racing**
30 B f Proclamation (IRE)—Approved Quality (IRE) **The Foulrice Twenty**
31 B f Zafeen (FR)—Betty's Pride **Mrs S. E. Barclay**
32 B g Byron—Hasty Lady **The Haydock Hopefuls**
33 **JONNY WOMBAT**, b g Avonbridge—Moonlight Angel **Mr B. Hartley**
34 B f Kyllachy—Magic Peak (IRE) **The Haydock Badgeholders**
35 B f Zafeen (FR)—Monica Geller **Mrs S. E. Barclay**
36 B f Proclamation (IRE)—No Comebacks **Mrs S. E. Barclay**
37 B g Tiger Hill (IRE)—Rose Bounty **Mrs S. E. Barclay**

TWO-YEAR-OLDS

38 B f 14/2 Proclamation (IRE)—Betty's Pride (Lion Cavern (USA)) **Mrs S. E. Barclay**
39 B g 25/3 Proclamation (IRE)—Ishela (IRE) (Barathea (IRE)) **Mrs S. E. Barclay**
40 B g 29/4 Proclamation (IRE)—Monica Geller (Komaite (USA)) **Mrs S. E. Barclay**
41 Ch g 12/4 Proclamation (IRE)—Synergie (IRE) (Exit To Nowhere (USA)) **Mrs S. E. Barclay**

Other Owners: Mr Matt Watkinson, Mr A. Bell, Mrs Leslie Buckley, Mr J. Calderbank, Mr A. R. Calderbank, P. M. Clarkson, Mr David Clarkson, Mr Andrew Faulkner, Mr L. J. Fielding, Mr Linden Hacking, R. Hall, Mrs I. Hall, Mr R. J. Hewitt, H. Kirkham, Mr R. D. Mattinson, Mr Frank Nicholls, Mr T. R. Vaughan, Mr Paul Wrench.

Assistant Trainer: Stella Barclay

Jockey (flat): Frederik Tylicki, Graham Lee. **Conditional:** Harry Challoner, Lucy Alexander. **Apprentice:** Racheal Kneller. **Amateur:** Mr Thomas Greenwood.

---

225 MRS RICHENDA FORD, Dorchester
Postal: Cross Farm, Brockhampton, Buckland Newton, Dorchester, Dorset, DT2 7DJ

1 **ABAYAAN**, 7, gr g Sadler's Wells (USA)—Showdown **K. B. Snook**
2 **GARLANDS QUEST**, 4, b f Relief Pitcher—Coolers Quest **K. B. Snook**
3 **ROISINI BAY (IRE)**, 9, b g Saddlers' Hall (IRE)—Zuhal **K. B. Snook**
4 **SOMERBY (IRE)**, 10, b g Sadler's Wells (USA)—Oriental Mystique **K. B. Snook**
5 **STEEL GOLD (IRE)**, 7, b g Craigsteel—It Time To Run (IRE) **K. B. Snook**

---

226 MR BRIAN FORSEY, Taunton
Postal: Three Oaks, Ash Priors, Taunton, Somerset, TA4 3NQ
Contacts: PHONE (01823) 433914 MOBILE (07747) 392760
E-MAIL forsey2001@yahoo.com

1 **AUREATE**, 9, ch g Jade Robbery (USA)—Anne d'autriche (IRE) **Mr K. C. Jago**
2 **BARISTA (IRE)**, 5, b g Titus Livius (FR)—Cappuccino (IRE) **Mr K. C. Jago**
3 **FOLLOW THE MASTER**, 7, b g Alflora (IRE)—Daisy May **Mrs P. M. Bosley**

MR BRIAN FORSEY - Continued

4 **SIR LEXINGTON (IRE)**, 4, b g Desert Style (IRE)—Shulammite Woman (IRE)
5 **SOLITARY PALM (IRE)**, 10, gr ro g Great Palm (USA)—
　　　　　　　　　　　　　　　　Grande Solitaire (FR) **Mr A Stevens, Mr W McKibbin, Mr B Forsey**

Other Owners: B. Forsey, W. McKibbin, A. G. Stevens.

Assistant Trainer: Susan Forsey

---

227 **MISS SANDY FORSTER, Kelso**
Postal: **Halterburn Head, Yetholm, Kelso, Roxburghshire, TD5 8PP**
Contacts: **PHONE/FAX (01573) 420615 FAX (01573) 420615**
MOBILE (07880) 727877 or (07976) 587315
E-MAIL clivestorey@btinternet.com

1 **APPEAL DENIED (IRE)**, 11, ch g Lord of Appeal—Cothu Na Slaine (IRE) **Miss S. E. Forster**
2 **BARNEVELDER (IRE)**, 8, ch g Old Vic—Cluain-Ard (IRE) **Mr J. M. Crichton & Miss H. M. Crichton**
3 **BORDER PHOENIX**, 6, b g Karinga Bay—Dusky Dante (IRE) **Anne & Tony Howarth, Dave & Ann Skeldon**
4 **HIGH FAIR**, 7, b m Grape Tree Road—Miss Tango **D. Simpson**
5 **NISAAL (IRE)**, 8, b g Indian Ridge—Kahalah (IRE) **Anne & Tony Howarth**
6 **RUMOUR HAD IT (IRE)**, 6, b m Milan—Single Trigger (IRE) **C. Storey**
7 **SEE THE LEGEND**, 8, b m Midnight Legend—Amys Delight **The Border Racers**
8 **SOUL ANGEL**, 9, ch g Tipsy Creek (USA)—Over Keen **Soul Searchers**
9 **WELL OILED (IRE)**, 12, b g Supreme Leader—Mightyatom **Miss S. E. Forster**

Other Owners: Mr F. Berry, Mr J. M. Crichton, Miss Hazel Crichton, Miss Sandra Forster, Mr A. J. Howarth, Mr D. Skeldon, Mr M. Smith (Tyne & Wear), Mr C. Storey.

Assistant Trainer: C. Storey

Conditional: Gary Rutherford. **Amateur:** Mr C. Bewley.

---

228 **MISS JOANNE FOSTER, Ilkley**
Postal: **Brookleigh Farm, Burley Road, Menston, Ilkley, West Yorkshire, LS29 6NS**
Contacts: **PHONE (07980) 301808 MOBILE (07980) 301808**
E-MAIL info@jofosterracing.co.uk WEBSITE www.jofosterracing.co.uk

1 **GARRYOWEN OSCAR (IRE)**, 7, b g Oscar (IRE)—Austocon (IRE) **Miss J. E. Foster**
2 **KEEVERFIELD (IRE)**, 12, b g Lord Americo—Quayfield (IRE) **Mrs J. E. Drake**
3 **LEAC AN SCAIL (FR)**, 12, b g Lord Americo—Swings'n'things (USA) **Mrs J. E. Drake**
4 **MARINO PRINCE (IRE)**, 8, b g Dr Fong (USA)—Hula Queen (USA) **The Golden Syndicate**
5 **PEAKS OF FIRE (IRE)**, 6, b g High Chaparral (IRE)—Crimson Glory **The Wilde Boys**
6 **UMVERTI**, 8, b m Averti (IRE)—Umbrian Gold (IRE) **S Hollings & Partners**
7 **VARDAS SUPREME (IRE)**, 10, b g Beneficial—Mrs Supreme (IRE) **Mrs J. E. Drake**
8 **WINGED FARASI**, 9, b g Desert Style (IRE)—Clara Vale (IRE) **The Smash Block Partnership**

Other Owners: Mr P. J. Deakin, Miss J. E. Foster, Mr P. Foster, Mr S. A. Hollings, Mr J. Wildman.

Assistant Trainer: P. Foster

Conditional: Sam Drake.

---

229 **MR JIMMY FOX, Marlborough**
Postal: **Highlands Farm Stables, Herridge, Collingbourne Ducis, Marlborough, Wiltshire, SN8 3EG**
Contacts: **PHONE (01264) 850218 (07931) 724358 MOBILE (07702) 880010**
E-MAIL jcfoxtrainer@aol.com

1 **ANNES ROCKET (IRE)**, 8, b h Fasliyev (USA)—Aguilas Perla (IRE) **Claire Underwood, Fay Thomas & S-J Fox**
2 **BIG JAKE**, 7, b g Karinga Bay—Spellbinder (IRE) **G. B. Balding**
3 **COOL MAGIC**, 5, b g Kayf Tara—Spellbinder (IRE) **G. B. Balding**
4 **HENRY HURST (IRE)**, 7, b g Bob's Return (IRE)—Proper Primitive **G. B. Balding**
5 **MAYDREAM**, 6, b m Sea Freedom—Maedance **The Dancing Partners**
6 **ORPEN'ARRY (IRE)**, 5, b g Orpen (USA)—Closing Time (IRE) **Mrs B. A. Fuller**
7 **THE WEE CHIEF (IRE)**, 7, ch g King Charlemagne (USA)—La Belle Clare (IRE) **R. E. Kavanagh**

MR JIMMY FOX - Continued

THREE-YEAR-OLDS
8 **GRACIOUS GEORGE (IRE)**, b c Oratorio (IRE)—Little Miss Gracie **Mrs B. A. Fuller**
9 **NEWTOWN CROSS (IRE)**, ch c Kheleyf (USA)—Sacred Pearl (IRE) **Mrs A. M. Coughlan**

Other Owners: Mrs E. Estall, Mrs S. J. Fox, Miss F. L. Thomas, Mrs C. C. Underwood.

Assistant Trainer: Sarah-Jane Fox

Jockey (flat): Pat Dobbs.

---

230   **MISS SUZZANNE FRANCE, Norton on Derwent**
Postal: Newstart Racing, Cheesecake Hill House, Highfield, Beverley Road, Norton on Derwent, North Yorkshire, YO17 9PJ
Contacts: **PHONE** (01653) 691947 **FAX** (01653) 691947 **MOBILE** (07904) 117531
E-MAIL suzzannemunchie@talk21.com

1 **BACHELOR KNIGHT (IRE)**, 5, b g Bachelor Duke (USA)—Labetera **Newstart Partnership**
2 **BOND BLADE**, 5, ch g Needwood Blade—Bond Cat (IRE) **Newstart Partnership**
3 **STAMP DUTY (IRE)**, 5, b g Ad Valorem (USA)—Lothian Lass (IRE) **Newstart Partnership**

Other Owners: Mrs P. France, Mr P. R. France.

Amateur: Mr Aaron James.

---

231   **MR DEREK FRANKLAND, Brackley**
Postal: Springfields, Mixbury, Brackley, Northamptonshire, NN13 5RR
Contacts: **FAX** (01280) 847334 **MOBILE** (07763) 020406
E-MAIL dsfrankland@aol.com

1 **MULAAZEM**, 10, b g King's Best (USA)—Harayir (USA) **D. S. Frankland & D. J. Trott**
2 **ORIGINAL STAR**, 8, b g Rashar (USA)—Hogan Stand **D. S. Frankland & D. J. Trott**
3 **REBEL HIGH (IRE)**, 9, ch g Hymns On High—Celia's Fountain (IRE) **D. S. Frankland & D. J. Trott**

Other Owners: D. S. Frankland, Mr D. J. Trott.

Jockey (NH): David Bass, Harry Skelton, Liam Treadwell.

---

232   **MR JAMES FROST, Buckfastleigh**
Postal: Hawson Stables, Buckfastleigh, Devon, TQ11 0HP
Contacts: **YARD** (01364) 642267 **HOME** (01364) 642332 **FAX** (01364) 643182
MOBILE (07860) 220229

1 **ALL FOR EVE**, 7, ch g Alflora (IRE)—Evening Scent **P. M. Tosh**
2 **ANNIE MOON**, 6, b m Morpeth—Workamiracle **J. D. Frost**
3 **CHASE GATE**, 8, ch g Arkadian Hero (USA)—Carlingford Lass (IRE) **Mrs J. Bury**
4 **KILDERRY DEAN (IRE)**, 6, b g Croco Rouge (IRE)—Perkalette (IRE) **Miss M. D. Wheaton**
5 **MASTER WELLS (IRE)**, 12, b g Sadler's Wells (USA)—Eljazzi **J. D. Frost**
6 **NORTH LONDON**, 6, b m Morpeth—Miss Grace **Mr T. G. Russell**
7 **PERCIMON RIDGE (IRE)**, 6, b g Oscar (IRE)—Bally Robin (IRE) **J. D. Frost**
8 **PRUDENT GEORGE**, 7, b g Morpeth—Prudent Peggy **Mrs J. McCormack**
9 **ROLANTA (FR)**, 8, b m Maresca Sorrento (FR)—Gazelle de Sou (FR) **Mrs J. McCormack**
10 **SARENICE (FR)**, 7, gr g April Night (FR)—Delice du Soleil (FR) **Mrs J. Bury**
11 **STIR ON THE SEA (IRE)**, 7, b br m Turtle Island (IRE)—Ballyroe Flash (IRE) **Dr D. Edwards**
12 **TOP GREEN (FR)**, 6, b g Mad Tax (USA)—Suzana des Brosses (FR) **Mrs J. Bury**
13 **UNION SAINT (FR)**, 5, b g Saint des Saints (FR)—Us Et Coutumes (FR) **P. M. Tosh**
14 **WINNING NOTE (FR)**, 6, b m Voix du Nord (FR)—Moderato Cantabile (IRE) **Share My Dream**

Other Owners: Mr J. D. Frost, Mr M. Kay, Ms H. Vernon-Jones.

Assistant Trainer: G. Frost

Jockey (NH): Hadden Frost, Tom O'Connor.

233 MR HARRY FRY, Seaborough
Postal: **Flat 1, Manor Farm, Seaborough, Beaminster, Dorset, DT8 3QY**
Contacts: **PHONE (01308) 868192**
E-MAIL **info@harryfryracing.com** WEBSITE **www.harryfryracing.com**

1 ASSAM BLACK (IRE), 5, b g Oscar (IRE)—Contrasting Lady
2 BILLY MERRIOTT (IRE), 7, b g Dr Massini (IRE)—Hurricane Bella (IRE) **G. D. Taylor**
3 BOLD CHIEF (IRE), 8, br g Oscar (IRE)—Cottage Girl (IRE) **The Eyre Family**
4 CHEMISTRY MASTER, 5, b g Doyen (IRE)—Elemental **Trebles Holford Thoroughbreds**
5 DANCINGTILMIDNIGHT, 6, ch m Midnight Legend—Solo Dancer **Mrs S. J. Maltby**
6 FAIR DREAMER, 5, gr g Fair Mix (IRE)—Emma's Dream **J. P. Blakeney**
7 HENRYVILLE, 5, b g Generous (IRE)—Aquavita **R P B Michaelson & R A Fry**
8 HIGHLAND RETREAT, 6, b m Exit To Nowhere (USA)—St Kilda **R. Barber**
9 KARINGA DANCER, 7, b g Karinga Bay—Miss Flora **H. B. Geddes**
10 KING OF THE NIGHT (GER), 9, b g Lomitas—Kaiserlerche (GER) **Mr & Mrs G. Calder**
11 OPENING BATSMAN (IRE), 7, b g Morozov (USA)—Jolly Signal (IRE) **The Twelfth Man Partnership**
12 OSCAR ROCK (IRE), 5, b g Oscar (IRE)—Cash And New (IRE) **Mr & Mrs G. Calder**
13 OUR BOMBER HARRIS, 9, b g Saddlers' Hall (IRE)—Gaye Fame **R. P. Fry**
14 POLAMCO (IRE), 4, b g Old Vic—Shanesia (IRE) **Mr A. D. Polson**
15 PRESENTING ARMS (IRE), 6, b g Presenting—Banningham Blaze **Mr J. M. Dare**
16 REGAL COUNTY (IRE), 7, b g King's Theatre (IRE)—County Kerry (FR) **Mrs A. Tincknell**
17 ROCK ON RUBY (IRE), 8, b g Oscar (IRE)—Stony View (IRE) **The Festival Goers**
18 4, B g Midnight Legend—Severn Air
19 VEXILLUM (IRE), 4, br g Mujadil (USA)—Common Cause **Hazard Chase Racing**
20 VIOLIN DAVIS (FR), 7, b m Turgeon (USA)—Trumpet Davis (FR) **Mr A. D. Polson**

Other Owners: J. R. Barber, P. H. Boss, G. Calder, Mrs J. Calder, Mrs C. A. Eyre, Mr H. Eyre, Miss R. E. Eyre, Mr C. G. S. Eyre, R. A. Fry, R. P. B. Michaelson, Mr M. Powell, A. G. Sim, W. C. Tincknell, Mr J. P. G. Turner, Mr J. C. Whiting.

Assistant Trainer: Ciara O'Connor

Jockey (NH): Noel Fehily, Nick Scholfield, Harry Skelton. **Conditional:** Ryan Mahon. **Amateur:** Mr Jack Barber, Mr Martin Cooney, Mr Martin McIntyre.

234 MISS CAROLINE FRYER, Wymondham
Postal: **Browick Hall Cottage, Browick Road, Wymondham, Norfolk, NR18 9RB**
Contacts: **PHONE (01953) 601257 MOBILE (07768) 056076**
E-MAIL **caroline@carolinefryerracing.co.uk** WEBSITE **www.carolinefryerracing.co.uk**

1 COUNTY ZEN (FR), 10, b br g Lost World (IRE)—Fair County (FR) **Miss C. Fryer**
2 FESTIVAL BOUND (IRE), 7, b g Insan (USA)—Copper Hill (IRE) **C. J. Underwood**
3 IDE NO IDEA (IRE), 9, b g Anshan—Gales Wager **Mrs S. Fryer**
4 MERIDIEM, 9, b g Tamure (IRE)—Anatomic **Mr M. S. U. Hustler**
5 RIDDLESTOWN (IRE), 6, b g Cloudings (IRE)—Gandi's Dream (IRE) **Mr J. D. Ward**
6 RONNIE RONALDE (IRE), 8, b g Laveron—Carryonharriet (IRE) **Miss C. Fryer**
7 WORKING TITLE (IRE), 11, b g Oscar (IRE)—Dantes Term (IRE) **Miss C. Fryer**

235 MR JOHN GALLAGHER, Moreton-In-Marsh
Postal: **Grove Farm, Chastleton, Moreton-In-Marsh, Gloucestershire, GL56 0SZ**
Contacts: **PHONE/FAX (01608) 674492 MOBILE (07780) 972663**
E-MAIL **gallagherracing@phonecoop.coop** WEBSITE **www.gallagherracing.com**

1 ALPHA DELTA WHISKY, 5, ch g Intikhab (USA)—Chispa **Adweb Ltd**
2 CELESTIAL ISLAND, 6, gr m Silver Patriarch (IRE)—Celtic Island **Mr R. W. Brown**
3 DEVON DIVA, 7, b m Systematic—General Jane **Mrs J. S. Dorey**
4 HEARTSONG (IRE), 4, b f Kheleyf (USA)—Semiquaver (USA) **C. Rashbrook**
5 ORLA (IRE), 5, b m Hawk Wing (USA)—Irish Ensign (SAF) **Ms A. Clifford**
6 PETER ISLAND (FR), 10, b g Dansili—Catania (USA) **C. R. Marks (Banbury)**
7 SOUNDBYTE, 8, b g Beat All (USA)—Gloaming **John Gallagher**
8 THE PUNDIT, 6, gr g Silver Patriarch (IRE)—Native Thatch (IRE) **Mr R. W. Brown**
9 WILD DESERT (FR), 8, b br g Desert Prince (IRE)—Sallivera (IRE) **Whites of Coventry & Stephen Dunn**

MR JOHN GALLAGHER - Continued

THREE-YEAR-OLDS

10 **FINALEE**, b f Cockney Rebel (IRE)—Celtic Island **Mr R. W. Brown**
11 **FLETCHER CHRISTIAN**, b g Bahamian Bounty—Lady Dominatrix (IRE) **C. R. Marks (Banbury)**
12 **LADWEB**, ch g Bertolini (USA)—Adweb **Adweb Ltd**

TWO-YEAR-OLDS

13 B f 11/3 Multiplex—Border Ballet (IRE) (Noverre (USA)) **R. Biggs**
14 B f 20/2 Multiplex—Glitz (IRE) (Hawk Wing (USA)) **R. Biggs**
15 **ISEEMIST (IRE)**, gr f 15/3 Verglas (IRE)—
                        Krasivaya (IRE) (Soviet Star (USA)) (2857) **J-P Lim & Mr Keith Marsden**
16 **PRINCESS FLORENTIA**, b f 21/1 Misu Bond (IRE)—Medici Princess (Medicean) (4285) **Ms A. Clifford**
17 **PUSEY STREET VALE**, b f 1/3 Moss Vale (IRE)—Pusey Street Girl (Gildoran) (7619) **C. R. Marks (Banbury)**

Other Owners: Mr S. W. Dunn, Mr J. P. Lim, J. F. Long, Mrs B. A. Long, K. Marsden, Whites of Coventry Limited.

Assistant Trainer: Mrs R. Gallagher

Jockey (flat): Neil Callan, Jamie Spencer, Chris Catlin, Martin Lane.

---

236 **MRS ILKA GANSERA-LEVEQUE, Newmarket**
Postal: **4 The Maples, Snailwell Road, Newmarket, Suffolk, CB8 7DH**
Contacts: **PHONE (01638) 665504 MOBILE (07855) 532072**
E-MAIL ilkagansera@gmail.com WEBSITE www.gansera-leveque.com

1 **CRYSTAL HIGH**, 5, b m High Chaparral (IRE)—Park Crystal (IRE)

THREE-YEAR-OLDS

2 **BOBOLI GARDENS**, b c Medicean—Park Crystal (IRE)
3 **DUKE OF GRAZEON (IRE)**, b g Duke of Marmalade (IRE)—Rambler **J. R. Rowbottom**
4 **TOSCA (GER)**, b f Amadeus Wolf—Tamarita (GER) **Mrs I. Gansera-Leveque**

TWO-YEAR-OLDS

5 B f 12/4 Bushranger (IRE)—Interim Payment (USA) (Red Ransom (USA)) (44000)
6 **MR CONWAY**, b g 12/3 Byron—Lambeth Belle (USA) (Arazi (USA)) (761) **Mrs I. Gansera-Leveque**
7 **RAISED ON GRAZEON**, ch f 12/2 Lucky Story (USA)—Graze On And On (Elmaamul (USA)) **J. R. Rowbottom**

---

237 **MRS SUSAN GARDNER, Longdown**
Postal: **Woodhayes Farm, Longdown, Exeter, Devon, EX6 7SB**
Contacts: **PHONE/FAX (01392) 811213 MOBILE (07971) 097936**
E-MAIL woodhayesstudfarm@btinternet.com

1 **BREDON HILL LAD**, 6, ch g Kirkwall—Persian Clover **R. W. Mitchell**
2 **CALL ME SIR (IRE)**, 11, b g Lord Americo—Crash Call **D. V. Gardner**
3 **FLYING AWARD (IRE)**, 9, br g Oscar (IRE)—Kates Machine (IRE) **Mr & Mrs P. George & Mrs B. Russell**
4 **HIGHLAND PARK (IRE)**, 6, ch g Pivotal—Highland Gift (IRE) **D. V. Gardner**
5 **LOOK FOR LOVE**, 5, b g Pursuit of Love—Look Here's May **M & B Racing**
6 **MAJESTIC BULL (USA)**, 7, b br g Holy Bull (USA)—Croissant (USA) **Woodhayes Racing**
7 **ORION EXPRESS**, 12, b g Bahhare (USA)—Kaprisky (USA) **D. V. Gardner**
8 **QUICK BREW**, 5, b h Denounce—Darjeeling (IRE) **D. V. Gardner**
9 **SOUTHWAY STAR**, 8, b m Morpeth—Nearly A Score **T. R. Watts**
10 **STORM ALERT**, 6, ch g Karinga Bay—Rash-Gale (IRE) **D. V. Gardner**
11 **TREVAYLOR BOY (IRE)**, 6, b g Lahib (USA)—Blue Glass **G. N. Noye**

Other Owners: Mr D. V. Gardner, Mrs P. George, Mr P. George, Mr M. Hooper, Mrs Brenda Russell.

Assistant Trainer: D. V. Gardner

Jockey (NH): Aidan Coleman, Sam Thomas. **Conditional:** Micheal Nolan. **Amateur:** Miss L. Gardner.

238 MR JEREMY GASK, Warminster

Postal: The Beeches, Deverill Road, Sutton Veny, Warminster, Wiltshire, BA12 7BY
Contacts: PHONE (01985) 841166 FAX (01985) 840474 MOBILE (07507) 555303
E-MAIL info@horsesfirstracing.com WEBSITE www.horsesfirstracing.com

1 **BAHAMA SPIRIT (IRE)**, 4, b f Invincible Spirit (IRE)—Braziliz (USA) **Lease Terminated**
2 **BERBERANA (IRE)**, 5, b m Acclamation—Barbera (GER) **Berberana Partnership**
3 **CLOUDY LADY**, 5, gr m Afflora (IRE)—Cirrious **Carmel Stud**
4 **CREW CUT (IRE)**, 5, b gr g Acclamation—Carabine (USA) **Guy Carstairs & Horses First Racing**
5 **DESERT SPREE**, 4, ch f Byron—Babaraja **Gracelands Stud Partnership**
6 **DOMINIUM (USA)**, 5, b g E Dubai (USA)—Sudenlylastsummer (USA) **Horses First Racing Ltd**
7 **EXKALIBER**, 4, b g Exceed And Excel (AUS)—Kalindi **The Exkaliber Partnership**
8 **FOXTROT INDIA (IRE)**, 4, b g Tagula (IRE)—Mayfair **R. L. Page**
9 **GABBIANO**, 4, b g Zafeen (FR)—Hollybell **Mr A. G. Bloom**
10 **HIGH STANDING (USA)**, 8, b br g High Yield (USA)—Nena Maka **Mr A. G. Bloom**
11 **LA PASSIONATA**, 4, ch f Proclamation (IRE)—Miss Madame (IRE) **Mrs K. M. Young**
12 **LASER BLAZER**, 5, b g Zafeen (FR)—Sashay **Calne Engineering Ltd**
13 **LUCKY ROYALE**, 5, b m Lucky Story (USA)—Bella Bertolini **Rock & Rollers, Gracelands Stud & O A R**
14 **MEDICEAN MAN**, 7, ch g Medicean—Kalindi **Mr Stuart Dobb & Miss Kate Dobb**
15 **PRANA (USA)**, 5, b m Proud Citizen (USA)—Javana (USA) **The Prana Syndicate**
16 **PRECISION FIVE**, 4, b f Proclamation (IRE)—Sashay **Calne Engineering Ltd**
17 **PRINCE OF BURMA (IRE)**, 5, b h Mujadil (USA)—Spinning Ruby **The Nobles**
18 **SASHEEN**, 6, b m Zafeen (FR)—Sashay **Sasheen Partnership**
19 **STREET POWER (USA)**, 8, b br g Street Cry (IRE)—Javana (USA) **Horses First Racing & Ownaracehorse**
20 **SULIS MINERVA (IRE)**, 6, b m Arakan (USA)—Lacinia **R. L. Page**
21 **TITUS GENT**, 8, ch g Tumbleweed Ridge—Genteel (IRE) **Mr A. G. Bloom**
22 **TOGA TIGER (IRE)**, 6, b g Antonius Pius (USA)—Minerwa (GER) **For Sale**
23 **TRENDING (IRE)**, 4, gr g Dark Angel (IRE)—Call Later (USA) **The Twitterati**

THREE-YEAR-OLDS

24 B c Joe Bear (IRE)—Anytime Anywhere
25 **COMPTON ALBION (IRE)**, ch f Compton Place—Yomalo (IRE) **Mr A. G. Bloom**
26 **COPPER LEYF**, ch c Kheleyf (USA)—Silver Quest **Copper Leyf Partnership**
27 **GREEN MILLIONAIRE**, b c Green Desert (USA)—Millyant **Mr A. G. Bloom**
28 B f Barathea (IRE)—Kritzia **The Kathryn Stud Limited**
29 **LUCULLAN**, b g Lucarno (USA)—Towaahi (IRE) **Five Horses Ltd**
30 **MAP OF LOVE (IRE)**, b f Dylan Thomas (IRE)—Maramba **Five Horses Ltd**
31 **NELSON QUAY (IRE)**, b c Holy Roman Emperor (IRE)—Frippet (IRE) **S. T. Brankin**
32 **NEVER A QUARREL (IRE)**, b f Acclamation—Welsh Mist **Lease Terminated**
33 B c Oasis Dream—Pinacotheque (IRE) **R. G. & T. E. Levin**
34 **SAKHEE'S ENIGMA (IRE)**, b f Sakhee's Secret—Maramkova (IRE) **Five Horses Ltd**

TWO-YEAR-OLDS

35 **CAMINEL (IRE)**, b f 23/3 Kyllachy—Jalissa (Mister Baileys) (23809)

Other Owners: Mr M. J. Board, G. N. Carstairs, Miss K. M. Dobb, J. A. Knight, R. G. Levin, Mrs T. E. Levin, P H. Morgan, Mrs M. E. Morgan, Ownaracehorse Ltd, A. C. Pickford, E. Wilmott, Mrs O. J. Wilmott, Mr A. S. Wood, R. V. Young.

239 MRS ROSEMARY GASSON, Banbury

Postal: Alkerton Grounds, Balscote, Banbury, Oxfordshire, OX15 6JS
Contacts: PHONE (01295) 730248 MOBILE (07769) 798430
E-MAIL arb@aqf.myzen.co.uk

1 **ADIOS ALONSO (IRE)**, 7, b g Saffron Walden (FR)—Rosy Rockford (IRE) **Mrs R. Gasson**
2 **CROCO MISTER (IRE)**, 6, ch g Croco Rouge (IRE)—Nimrods Dream (IRE) **Mrs R. Gasson**
3 **ELITE BENEFICIAL (IRE)**, 8, ch g Beneficial—A Fine Romance (IRE) **Mrs R. Gasson**
4 **GENTLEMAN ANSHAN (IRE)**, 9, b g Anshan—Second Violin (IRE) **Mrs R. Gasson**
5 **JOLLY BOYS OUTING (IRE)**, 10, b g Glacial Storm (USA)—St Carol (IRE) **Mrs R. Gasson**
6 **KILCASCAN**, 9, b g Alflora (IRE)—Peasedown Tofana **Mrs R. Gasson**
7 **OFFICIALLY MODERN (IRE)**, 6, ch g Beneficial—Musical Millie (IRE) **Mrs R. Gasson**

Conditional: Ben Poste. **Amateur:** Miss Hannah Watson.

240 MR MICHAEL GATES, Stratford-on-Avon

Postal: **Comfort Park Stud, Campden Road, Clifford Chambers, Stratford-on-Avon, CV37 8LW**
Contacts: **MOBILE (07581) 246070**
E-MAIL comfortparkstud@hotmail.co.uk

1 CRACK AT DAWN (IRE), 12, b br g Insan (USA)—Ten Quid Short (IRE) **M. Gates**
2 FULL OV BEANS, 9, ch g Midnight Legend—Scarlet Baroness **M. Gates**
3 HANDSOME BUDDY (IRE), 6, br g Presenting—Moya's Magic (IRE) **M. Gates**
4 IMPERIAL LAIDY (IRE), 9, b br m Corrouge (USA)—Encalchoise (FR) **M. Gates**
5 MEZARAT (ITY), 8, ch g Dream Well (FR)—Dayara (GER) **M. Gates**
6 TOUGH COOKIE (IRE), 10, b g Rashar (USA)—Vam Cas (IRE) **M. Gates**
7 WATCH HOUSE (IRE), 8, ch g Deploy—Derby Affair **M. Gates**

241 MR JONATHAN GEAKE, Marlborough

Postal: **Harestone House, East Kennett, Marlborough, Wiltshire, SN8 4EY**
Contacts: **PHONE (01672) 861784 MOBILE (07768) 350738**
E-MAIL jageake@yahoo.co.uk

1 ABBEY DORE (IRE), 10, ch g Alderbrook—Bone of Contention (IRE) **Dr & Mrs Peter Leftley**
2 ACROSS THE STRAITS (FR), 9, b g Dansili—Skipnight **Mrs S. A. Geake**
3 BALLYMAN (IRE), 12, gr g Accordion—Sliabhin Rose **Dr & Mrs Peter Leftley**
4 BEWARE CHALK PIT (IRE), 9, b g Anshan—Rakiura (IRE) **Dr & Mrs Peter Leftley**
5 BONDI MIST (IRE), 4, gr f Aussie Rules (USA)—Akoya (IRE) **Double Kings Partnership**
6 DANCE WITH ME (IRE), 4, b g Danehill Dancer (IRE)—Perpetual Time **A. J. Geake & Partners**
7 MICQUUS (IRE), 4, b g High Chaparral (IRE)—My Potters (USA) **Dr & Mrs Peter Leftley**
8 RAMBRIDGE COPSE, 6, b g Terimon—Copper Rose Hill **H. M. F. McCall**
9 SHOT IN THE DARK (IRE), 4, ch g Dr Fong (USA)—Highland Shot **Mrs P. D. Gulliver**
10 SUNSET PLACE, 6, ch g Compton Place—Manhattan Sunset (USA) **Jag Racing 1**

TWO-YEAR-OLDS

11 A LASTING JOY, b f 23/2 Refuse to Bend (IRE)—Sir Kyffin's Folly (Dansili) **Dr & Mrs Peter Leftley**
12 THEA'S DANCE, b f 6/3 Delta Dancer—Tagula Song (IRE) (Tagula (IRE)) **Double Kings Partnership**

Other Owners: Dr Peter Leftley, Mrs Ann Leftley.

Assistant Trainer: Mrs S A Geake **Pupil Assistant:** Mr Sam Geake

Jockey (flat): Richard Thomas. **Jockey (NH):** Jimmy McCarthy, Andrew Thornton.

242 MISS KAREN GEORGE, Crediton

Postal: **Higher Eastington Stables, Lapford, Crediton, Devon, EX17 6NE**
Contacts: **PHONE (01363) 83154 FAX (01363) 83154 MOBILE (07917) 007892**
E-MAIL eastington1@yahoo.com WEBSITE www.eastingtonracing.co.uk

1 BOOMTOWN KAT, 9, b g Double Trigger (IRE)—Storm Kitten (IRE) **P. J. H. George**
2 CALL ME APRIL, 5, b m Generous (IRE)—Anyhow (IRE) **Mrs J. V. Wilkinson**
3 CASH INJECTION, 4, b g Halling (USA)—Cape Siren **Mr R. N. O'Carroll**
4 GIZZIT (IRE), 7, b g Son of Sharp Shot (IRE)—Suez Canal (FR) **Miss K. M. George**
5 JEZZA, 7, br g Pentire—Lara (GER) **Kilcash Bloodstock Limited**
6 SPIRIT OF LAKE (IRE), 11, b g Sheer Danzig (IRE)—Rosheen (IRE) **R. A. Bimson**

THREE-YEAR-OLDS

7 ICANBOOGIE, b g Tobougg (IRE)—Dubai Marina **Mr J. Lefevre**
8 MR BLUE NOSE, b g Tobougg (IRE)—Cape Siren **Miss K. M. George**

243 MR TOM GEORGE, Slad

Postal: **Down Farm, Slad, Stroud, Gloucestershire, GL6 7QE**
Contacts: **PHONE (01452) 814267 FAX (01452) 814246 MOBILE (07850) 793483**
E-MAIL tom@trgeorge.com WEBSITE www.tomgeorgeracing.co.uk

1 ABSOLUTE RETURN, 4, b g Kayf Tara—Kitty Wong (IRE) **Mr & Mrs R. E. R. Rumboll**

MR TOM GEORGE - Continued

2 ARTHUR'S PASS, 9, b g Midnight Legend—Bella Coola **Vicki Robinson & James Williams**
3 BABY MIX (FR), 5, gr g Al Namix (FR)—Douchka (FR) **GDM Partnership**
4 BACK BOB BACK (IRE), 8, b g Bob Back (USA)—Joyney **Power Panels Electrical Systems Ltd**
5 BALLINVARRIG (IRE), 6, b g Beneficial—Leos Holiday (IRE) **Lady Hilda Clarke & Simon W. Clarke**
6 BALLYALLIA MAN (IRE), 8, b g Flemensfirth (USA)—
Hatch Away (IRE) **H. S. Smith, R. & M. Gabbertas and Doone Hulse**
7 BE DEFINITE (IRE), 9, b g Definite Article—Etoile Margot (FR) **Simon W. Clarke & Vicki Robinson**
8 BIG FELLA THANKS, 11, b g Primitive Rising (USA)—Nunsdream **Crossed Fingers Partnership**
9 BIG SOCIETY (IRE), 7, b g Flemensfirth (USA)—Choice of Kings (IRE) **Simon Clarke & David Thorpe**
10 CELTIC INTRIGUE (IRE), 6, b g Celtic Swing—Macca Luna (IRE) **O'Donohoe, Nelson, Stratford & Barlow**
11 CHARTREUX (FR), 8, gr g Colonel Collins (USA)—Ruaha River (FR) **R. S. Brookhouse**
12 COEUR DE FOU (FR), 8, ch g Limnos (JPN)—Folly Lady (FR) **Lady H. J. Clarke**
13 CRACK AWAY JACK, 9, ch g Gold Away (IRE)—Jolly Harbour **GDM Partnership**
14 DEFINITELY BETTER (IRE), 5, ch m Definite Article—Chevet Girl (IRE) **Mrs E. A. Fletcher**
15 DESPERATE DEX (IRE), 13, b g Un Desperado (FR)—Too Sharp **Crossed Fingers Partnership**
16 EGYPT MILL SPIRIT (IRE), 7, b g Overbury (IRE)—Miss Tickill (IRE) **S. R. Webb**
17 FIVENINETYFOR (USA), 7, b g Giant's Causeway (USA)—Baraka (USA) **R. S. Brookhouse**
18 FLASH CRASH, 4, b g Val Royal (FR)—Tessara (GER) **Mr & Mrs R. Cornock**
19 FORGOTTEN GOLD (IRE), 7, b g Dr Massini (IRE)—Ardnataggle (IRE) **Mr & Mrs R. Cornock**
20 GOD'S OWN (IRE), 5, b g Oscar (IRE)—Dantes Term (IRE) **Crossed Fingers Partnership**
21 GOOD ORDER, 8, b g Alflora (IRE)—Twinnings Grove (IRE) **Sharon C. Nelson & Dermot O'Donohoe**
22 HALLEY (FR), 6, b g Loup Solitaire (USA)—Moon Glow (FR) **PJL Racing & Mr T. R. George**
23 HEEZ A CRACKER (FR), 7, b g Goldneyev (USA)—Jolly Harbour **GDM Partnership**
24 HIGH HO SHERIFF (IRE), 7, ch g Presenting—Miss Snapdragon (IRE) **Simon Clarke & David Thorpe**
25 HOARE ABBEY (IRE), 7, ch g Definite Article—Tourist Attraction (IRE) **Mr S. W. Clarke**
26 IN BY MIDNIGHT, 5, ch m Midnight Legend—Moyliscar **Silkword Racing**
27 IRONIC (FR), 5, b g Califet (FR)—Iron Lassie (USA) **St Albans Bloodstock LLP**
28 KAUTO SHINY (FR), 5, b m Priolo (USA)—Kauto Relstar (FR) **Mrs L. M. Kemble & P. Atkinson**
29 KELLYSTOWN LAD (IRE), 10, b g Old Vic—Kissangel (IRE) **Crossed Fingers Partnership**
30 LEXICON LAD (IRE), 8, ch g Presenting—Hazel's Glory (IRE) **C. B. Compton**
31 LORDOFTHEHOUSE (IRE), 5, ch g Danehill Dancer (IRE)—Bordighera (USA) **St Albans Bloodstock LLP**
32 MAIL DE BIEVRE (FR), 8, b g Cadoudal (FR)—Coyote Davis (IRE) **Mr P. E. Atkinson**
33 MAJALA (FR), 7, b g Lavirco (GER)—Majae (FR) **Sharon Nelson Jayne Taylor Darren Taylor**
34 MASTER CYNK, 6, ch g Diableneyev (USA)—Model View (USA) **Barlow, Nelson, O'Donohoe & Stratford**
35 MODULE (FR), 6, b g Panoramic—Before Royale (FR) **Mr S. W. Clarke**
36 MONSIEUR CADOU (FR), 8, b g Cadoudal (FR)—Dame De Trefles (FR) **T. George**
37 MOONLIGHT MAGGIE, 6, b m Pasternak—Moyliscar **Capt & Mrs J. A. George**
38 MORGAN'S BAY, 8, b g Karinga Bay—Dubai Dolly (IRE) **Mr S. W. Clarke**
39 MOSCOW CHANCER (IRE), 7, b g Moscow Society (USA)—I'll See You Again (IRE) **T. D. J. Syder**
40 MY INHERITANCE (IRE), 5, b g Araafa (IRE)—Glory Days (GER) **Miss J. A. Hoskins**
41 NACARAT (FR), 12, gr g Smadoun (FR)—Gerbora (FR) **Mr S. W. Clarke**
42 NODEBATEABOUTIT, 8, b g Alflora (IRE)—Mystere (IRE) **Sharon C. Nelson & Dermot O'Donohoe**
43 OLOFI (FR), 7, gr g Slickly (FR)—Dona Bella (FR) **McNeill Family Ltd**
44 ON THE CASE, 5, ch g Generous (IRE)—Tulipa (POL) **Mrs S. C. Nelson**
45 OVERNIGHT FAME (IRE), 9, b m Kayf Tara—Best of The Girls (IRE) **Mr & Mrs R. Cornock**
46 PARSNIP PETE, 7, b g Pasternak—Bella Coola **The Parsnips**
47 PRIEST ISLAND (IRE), 7, b g Heron Island (IRE)—Chapel Field (IRE) **Thoroughbred Ladies**
48 ROC D'APSIS (FR), 4, gr g Apsis—Rocapina (FR) **Mr M. N. Khan**
49 RODY (FR), 8, ch g Colonel Collins (USA)—Hamelie II (FR) **R. A. Dalton & J. C. E. Laing**
50 SAINDOR (FR), 9, b br g Saint des Saints (FR)—Fleche d'or (FR) **Mrs L. M. Kemble & P. Atkinson**
51 SEIGNEUR DES BOIS (FR), 7, b g Ballingarry (IRE)—Studieuse (FR) **Crossed Fingers Partnership**
52 SHOULD I STAY (FR), 5, b g Muhtathir—Dusky Royale (FR) **M. L. Bloodstock Ltd**
53 SIVOLA DE SIVOLA (FR), 7, gr g Martaline—Kerrana (FR) **D. O'Donohoe, S. & P. Nelson & D. Silvester**
54 SOPHONIE (FR), 7, b m Kapgarde (FR)—Kore des Obeaux (FR) **Crossed Fingers Partnership**
55 TERRE DU VENT (FR), 7, b m Kutub (IRE)—Phlizz (FR) **Mr S. W. Clarke**
56 TIRE LARIGOT (FR), 6, b g Muhtathir—Rhaetia (IRE) **Mr T. R. George**
57 TRIANGULAR (USA), 8, b g Diesis—Salchow (USA) **Mrs H. Charlet**
58 UNIK DE NOUGI (FR), 5, b g Califet (FR)—Gracieuse de Nouji (FR) **Deal, Lowe, Silver, St Quinton & Syder**
59 UNTIL WINNING (FR), 5, b g Kapgarde (FR)—Fripperie (FR) **Thoroughbred Ladies**
60 VIACOMETTI (FR), 4, gr g Alberto Giacometti (IRE)—L'epi (FR) **Sharon Nelson Jayne Taylor Darren Taylor**
61 WATLEDGE (FR), 6, b g Lando (GER)—Flower of Freedom (IRE) **Stratford, Nelson, O'Donohoe & Barlow**
62 WESTON LODGE (FR), 7, b g Aahsaylad—Slip Me Fippence **Miss G. I. G. McCormick**

Other Owners: Mr C. Levan, Mr G. Lowe, Mr M. J. Silver, Mr M. G. St Quinton, Mr Richard Woods.

Jockey (NH): Paddy Brennan, Liam Heard. **Conditional:** Gerald Quinn. **Amateur:** Mr Robert Hogg, Mr Freddie Tett.

244 MRS THERESA GIBSON, Hexham
Postal: **Embley, Steel, Hexham, Northumberland, NE47 0HW**
Contacts: PHONE (01434) 673334
E-MAIL theresagibson356@btinternet.com

1 **GOLD CYGNET (IRE)**, 8, b g Beneficial—Windy Bee (IRE) **Mrs T. M. Gibson**
2 **SUNSET SONG**, 9, b m Supreme Sound—Cudder Or Shudder (IRE) **Mrs T. M. Gibson**

245 MR NICK GIFFORD, Findon
Postal: **The Downs, Stable Lane, Findon, West Sussex, BN14 0RT**
Contacts: OFFICE (01903) 872226 FAX (01903) 877232 MOBILE (07940) 518077
E-MAIL downs.stables@btconnect.com WEBSITE www.nickgiffordracing.co.uk

1 **BALLYBACH (IRE)**, 9, b g Bach (IRE)—Croom River (IRE) **Mr M. K. O'Shea**
2 **CARIFLORA**, 6, b m Alflora (IRE)—Oso Special **Nick Gifford Racing Club**
3 **CATCHER STAR (IRE)**, 5, b g Catcher In The Rye (IRE)—Drumdeels Star (IRE) **P. A. Byrne**
4 **CHRISTOPHER WREN (USA)**, 6, ch g D'wildcat (USA)—Ashley's Coy (USA) **J. P. McManus**
5 **DIGGER GETS LUCKY (IRE)**, 11, b g Lord Americo—Exclusive View (IRE) **The Chanctonbury Ring**
6 **DOLLAR BILL**, 4, ch g Medicean—Jardin **Mrs C. L. Kyle**
7 **FAIRY RATH (IRE)**, 7, ch g Accordion—Killoughey Fairy (IRE) **Mrs C. L. Kyle**
8 **GENEROUS RANSOM (IRE)**, 5, ch g Generous (IRE)—Penneyrose Bay **Sir Christopher Wates**
9 6, Ch g Soviet Star (USA)—Jazzy Refrain (IRE) **Mrs C. J. Zetter-Wells**
10 5, B m Alflora (IRE)—Jazzy Refrain (IRE) **Mrs C. J. Zetter-Wells**
11 4, B g Alflora (IRE)—Jazzy Refrain (IRE) **Mrs C. J. Zetter-Wells**
12 **KUILSRIVER (IRE)**, 6, b g Cape Cross (IRE)—Ripple of Pride (IRE) **Mrs T. J. Stone-Brown**
13 **MONTE KAOLINO (IRE)**, 5, ch g Sandmason—Direct Pursuit (IRE) **Mrs T. J. Stone-Brown**
14 **MURPHY (IRE)**, 11, b g Lord Americo—Kyle Cailin **Mrs T. J. Stone-Brown**
15 **OLD DREAMS (IRE)**, 7, b m Old Vic—I Can Imagine (IRE) **Nick Gifford Racing Club**
16 **ON TREND (IRE)**, 7, b g Jammaal—Comrun (IRE) **Ham Manor Farms Ltd**
17 **OSCAR PAPA**, 8, ch g Presenting—Oso Special **Mrs C. J. Zetter-Wells**
18 5, B m Alflora (IRE)—Oso Special **Mrs C. J. Zetter-Wells**
19 4, Ch g Alflora (IRE)—Oso Special **Mrs C. J. Zetter-Wells**
20 **PARIGINO (FR)**, 5, b g Panis (USA)—Loretta Gianni (FR) **Bayonet Partners**
21 **PASCHA BERE (FR)**, 10, gr g Verglas (IRE)—Ephelide (FR) **Mr & Mrs Mark Tracey**
22 4, B f Oscar (IRE)—Penneyrose Bay
23 **ROYAL WEDDING**, 11, b g King's Best (USA)—Liaison (USA) **D. G. Trangmar**
24 **SILVER SOPHFIRE**, 7, gr m Silver Patriarch (IRE)—Princess Timon **Mrs C. J. Zetter-Wells**
25 **SPECIALAGENT ALFIE**, 7, b g Alflora (IRE)—Oso Special **Mr M. K. O'Shea**
26 **SPIRITOFCHARTWELL**, 5, ch g Clerkenwell (USA)—Rollin Rock **Unregistered Partnership**
27 **THEOPHRASTUS (IRE)**, 11, b g Overbury (IRE)—Over The Glen (IRE) **A. W. Black**
28 **TO LIVE (FR)**, 6, ch g Brier Creek (USA)—Obrigada (FR) **J. P. McManus**
29 **TULLAMORE DEW (IRE)**, 11, ch g Pistolet Bleu (IRE)—Heather Point **Give Every Man His Due**
30 **UTOPIAN (FR)**, 5, ch g Kapgarde (FR)—Djeti (FR) **Coldunell Limited**
31 **WHAT WILL YOU SAY**, 6, gr g Kayf Tara—Janiture (FR) **D. Dunsdon**

Other Owners: G. H. L. Bird, D. H. C. Boath, Mr A. Bradley, Mrs S. Cotty, Mr D. Ellis, Mrs R. E. Gifford, Mr L. Horvath, Mr M. J. Tracey, Mrs I. M. Tracey.

Jockey (NH): Denis O'Regan, Liam Treadwell. **Conditional:** Tom Cannon. **Amateur:** Mr D. H. Dunsdon.

246 MR MARK GILLARD, Sherborne
Postal: **Elm Tree Stud, Holwell, Sherborne, Dorset, DT9 5LL**
Contacts: PHONE (01963) 23026 FAX (01963) 23297 MOBILE (07970) 700605
E-MAIL Mark@thegillards.co.uk WEBSITE markgillardracing.com

1 **BLACK PHANTOM (IRE)**, 7, br g Alderbrook—Blenheim Blinder (IRE) **T. L. Morshead**
2 **BORDER LAD**, 9, b g Double Trigger (IRE)—Rosevear (IRE) **The Almost Hopefull Partnership**
3 **BRAVO BRAVO**, 6, b g Sadler's Wells (USA)—Top Table **Davies & Price**
4 **CALLERLILLY**, 9, ch m Double Trigger (IRE)—Callermine **Whitegate Stud & N. J. McMullan**
5 **CLOUDBUSTING**, 5, b m Midnight Legend—Minibelle **Pippa Grace**
6 **COMICAL RED**, 5, ch g Sulamani—Sellette (IRE) **N. J. McMullan**
7 **DONT CALL ME OSCAR (IRE)**, 6, b g Oscar (IRE)—Coolrua (IRE) **Davies & Price**
8 **ENCHANTING SMILE (FR)**, 6, b m Rakti—A Thousand Smiles (IRE) **Miss Kay Russell**

MR MARK GILLARD - Continued

9 **HARD HOUSE**, 6, ch g Trade Fair—Tuppenny Blue **Mr D. M. G. Fitch-Peyton**
10 **ICE 'N' EASY (IRE)**, 7, b g Dushyantor (USA)—Glacial Valley (IRE) **R. Jenner & J. Green**
11 **LADY BRIDGET**, 5, b m Hawk Wing (USA)—Change Partners (IRE) **Mr B. R. Rudman**
12 **LADY WILLA (IRE)**, 6, b m Footstepsinthesand—Change Partners (IRE) **T. J. C. Seegar**
13 **OH SO CHARMING**, 4, b g Kayf Tara—Charmatic (IRE) **T. L. Morshead**
14 **PETITO (IRE)**, 10, b g Imperial Ballet (IRE)—Fallacy **D. E. Hazzard**
15 **RED LAW (IRE)**, 9, b g Reprimand—Trouville Lass (IRE) **Mr T J C Seegar & Mrs T Connor**
16 **REVAADER**, 5, b m Revoque (IRE)—Wave Rider **Miss Kay Russell**
17 **TAHITI DANCER**, 5, b m Tamure (IRE)—Rosevear (IRE) **N. J. McMullan & S. H. Bryant**
18 **WAYLON**, 5, b g Pasternak—Soldier's Song **Pippa Grace**

THREE-YEAR-OLDS

19 **BUSTLING DARCEY**, ch f Assertive—Bint Baddi (FR) **M. C. Denning**
20 **KARL MARX (IRE)**, b g Red Clubs (IRE)—Brillano (FR) **D. E. Hazzard**

Other Owners: Mr Steve Bryant, Ms Tammy Conner, Mr R. A. Davies, Ms J. Henly, Mr N. J. McMullan, Mr A. G. Price, Mr T. J. C. Seegar.

Assistant Trainer: Ben Clarke

Jockey (flat): Eddie Ahern. **Jockey (NH):** Tommy Phelan.

---

247 MR PATRICK GILLIGAN, Newmarket
Postal: **Sackville House, Sackville Street, Newmarket, Suffolk, CB8 8DX**
Contacts: **PHONE (01638) 669151 MOBILE (07881) 796612**
E-MAIL gilliganmax@aol.com WEBSITE www.patrickgilligan.org

1 **BIG THING COMING**, 5, b g Kyllachy—Lady's Walk (IRE) **Miss C. L. Elbrow**
2 **REPLICATOR**, 8, b g Mujahid (USA)—Valldemosa **Mr L. J. Doolan**
3 **SHAHRAZAD (IRE)**, 4, b f Cape Cross (IRE)—Khulasah (IRE) **F. Brian Barnes**

TWO-YEAR-OLDS

4 B f 10/3 Footstepsinthesand—Zapping (IRE) (Lycius (USA)) (4000) **Mrs M. Roche**

Assistant Trainer: Jack Gilligan

---

248 MR JAMES GIVEN, Willoughton
Postal: **Mount House Stables, Long Lane, Willoughton, Gainsborough, Lincolnshire, DN21 5SQ**
Contacts: **PHONE (01427) 667618 FAX (01427) 667734 MOBILE (07801) 100496**
E-MAIL james@jamesgivenracing.com WEBSITE www.jamesgivenracing.com

1 **BUSTER BROWN (IRE)**, 4, ch c Singspiel (IRE)—Gold Dodger (USA) **Mrs L. P. Fish**
2 **CLUMBER PLACE**, 7, ch m Compton Place—Inquirendo (USA) **Catherine Stocks & Julie Walsh**
3 **DAY OF DESTINY (IRE)**, 8, gr g Clodovil (IRE)—El Corazon (IRE) **Suzanne & Nigel Williams**
4 **GLENRIDDING**, 9, b g Averti (IRE)—Appelone **Tremousser Partnership**
5 **KUNG HEI FAT CHOY (USA)**, 4, b g Elusive Quality (USA)—
                                                  Lady Succeed (JPN) **Danethorpe Racing Partnership**
6 **MALINDI**, 4, b f Compton Place—Mana Pools (IRE) **H. J. P. Farr**
7 **MY MATE JAKE (IRE)**, 5, ch g Captain Rio—Jam (IRE) **Mr A. Owen**
8 **NO DOMINION (IRE)**, 4, b g Dylan Thomas (IRE)—Boast **Mr J. A. Barson**
9 **ROYAL BAJAN (USA)**, 5, gr ro g Speightstown (USA)—Crown You (USA) **Danethorpe Racing Partnership**
10 **SLEWTOO**, 4, b f Three Valleys (USA)—Red Slew **Dachel Stud**
11 **TOYMAKER**, 6, b g Starcraft (NZ)—Eurolink Raindance (IRE) **Antoniades Family**

THREE-YEAR-OLDS

12 **AMANDA WOLF (IRE)**, b f Amadeus Wolf—Alexander Phantom (IRE) **Danethorpe Racing Partnership**
13 **ARTFUL PRINCE**, ch c Dutch Art—Royal Nashkova **Ingram Racing**
14 **CALON LAD (IRE)**, ch c Redback—Flames **Simply Racing Limited**
15 **CONSTANT DREAM**, br f Kheleyf (USA)—Pizzicato **Bolton Grange**
16 **CRYSTAL PEAKS**, b f Intikhab (USA)—Crozon **Danethorpe Racing Partnership**
17 **GIRL AT THE SANDS (IRE)**, gr f Clodovil (IRE)—Invincible Woman (IRE) **P. Swann**
18 **JADANNA (IRE)**, b f Mujadil (USA)—Savannah Poppy (IRE) **Danethorpe Racing Partnership**

MR JAMES GIVEN - Continued

19 **MIDNIGHT POET**, ch g Byron—Molly Pitcher (IRE) **Ingram Racing**
20 **SLEEPING BINDIAN**, b g Sleeping Indian—Binaa (IRE)
21 **THE POWER OF ONE (IRE)**, b c Duke of Marmalade (IRE)—Mustique Dream **Suzanne & Nigel Williams**
22 **THIRLESTANE**, b f Auction House (USA)—Island Colony (USA) **Mrs J. Bownes**
23 **WOODY BAY**, b g New Approach (IRE)—Dublino (USA) **Mr J. A. Barson**

TWO-YEAR-OLDS

24 **CHATSWORTH EXPRESS**, b c 5/5 Redoubtable (USA)—
Teo Torriate (IRE) (Daggers Drawn (USA)) **Unregistered Partnership**
25 B f 18/3 Compton Place—Cheeky Girl (College Chapel) (9523) **P. Swann**
26 B f 29/3 Lawman (FR)—Corryvreckan (IRE) (Night Shift (USA)) (3809) **P. Swann**
27 Ch f 23/3 Mount Nelson—Forever Fine (USA) (Sunshine Forever (USA)) (12000) **G. R. Bailey Ltd**
28 **FRANCISCA**, b f 10/3 Byron—Requiem (USA) (Royal Anthem (USA)) (1428) **R. C. Spore**
29 Ch f 12/3 Pastoral Pursuits—Glencal (Compton Place) (7000) **Danethorpe Racing Partnership**
30 **MASTER DAN**, b c 21/3 Mastercraftsman (IRE)—
Danella (IRE) (Platini (GER)) (24000) **Danethorpe Racing Partnership**
31 B f 29/4 Le Havre (IRE)—Miskina (Mark of Esteem (IRE)) (3047) **Mrs S. Oliver**
32 B f 22/3 Shamardal (USA)—Nolas Lolly (IRE) (Lomitas) (41269) **Danethorpe Racing Partnership**
33 **SHADES OF SILK**, b f 22/2 Bahamian Bounty—Terentia (Diktat) (32380) **Danethorpe Racing Partnership**
34 B f 28/1 Avonbridge—T G's Girl (Selkirk (USA)) (4761) **P. Swann**
35 B f 27/1 Galileo (IRE)—Thermopylae (Tenby) (140000)

Other Owners: Mrs Carolyn Antoniades, Miss E. C. Antoniades, A. Antoniades, Miss A. C. Antoniades, M. J. Beadle, J. A. Ellis, Mrs M. E. Ellis, Mr P. A. Horton, R. H. Jennings, O. H. Kingsley, Mrs R. J. Norman, Mrs C. H. Stocks, Mrs J. Walsh, Mrs B. E. Wilkinson, Mrs S. E. Williams, N. Williams, G. Wilson.

Jockey (flat): Paul Mulrennan.

---

249 MR JIM GOLDIE, Glasgow

Postal: Libo Hill Farm, Uplawmoor, Glasgow, Lanarkshire, G78 4BA
Contacts: PHONE (01505) 850212 MOBILE (07778) 241522
WEBSITE www.jimgoldieracingclub.co.uk

1 **A SOUTHSIDE BOY (GER)**, 5, b g Samum (GER)—Anthurium (GER) **Connor & Dunne**
2 **ARCTIC COURT (IRE)**, 9, b g Arctic Lord—Polls Joy **Mr & Mrs Raymond Anderson Green**
3 **BENE LAD (IRE)**, 11, b br g Beneficial—Sandwell Old Rose (IRE) **Mr & Mrs Raymond Anderson Green**
4 **CALEDONIA**, 6, b g Sulamani (IRE)—Vanessa Bell (IRE) **Lorimer Racing**
5 **CAPTAIN BALDWIN**, 4, b g Dubai Destination—Tripti (IRE) **The Reluctant Suitor's**
6 **CIRCUS CLOWN**, 8, b g Vettori (IRE)—Comic (IRE) **D. L. McKenzie**
7 **COMPTON HEIGHTS**, 4, ch g Compton Place—Harken Heights (IRE) **D. L. McKenzie**
8 **GRAND DIAMOND (IRE)**, 9, b g Grand Lodge (USA)—Winona (IRE) **Caledonia Racing**
9 **HAWDYERWHEESHT**, 5, b g Librettist (USA)—Rapsgate (IRE) **J. S. Morrison**
10 **HAWKEYETHENOO (IRE)**, 7, b g Hawk Wing (USA)—Stardance (USA) **Johnnie Delta Racing**
11 **HILLVIEW BOY (IRE)**, 9, b br g Bishop of Cashel—Arandora Star (USA) **Connor & Dunne**
12 **INNISCASTLE BOY**, 4, b g Sir Percy—Galapagar (USA) **Johnnie Delta Racing**
13 **JONNY DELTA**, 6, ch g Sulamani (IRE)—Send Me An Angel (IRE) **Johnnie Delta Racing**
14 **KAOLAK (USA)**, 7, b br h Action This Day (USA)—Cerita (USA) **Thomson & Fyffe Racing**
15 **LADY GARGOYLE**, 5, br m Lucky Story (USA)—Gargoyle Girl **The Reluctant Suitor's**
16 **LATIN REBEL (IRE)**, 6, b g Spartacus (IRE)—Dance To The Beat **Mr R. W. C. McLachlan**
17 **LAYBACK (IRE)**, 9, br g Bach (IRE)—River Breeze (IRE) **Alan & Barry Macdonald**
18 **LILLIOFTHEBALLET (IRE)**, 6, b m Rakti—Lillibits (USA) **The Dregs Of Humanity**
19 **LOS NADIS (GER)**, 9, ch g Hernando (FR)—La Estrella (USA) **I. G. M. Dalgleish**
20 **MISTER PAGAN**, 5, b g Sulamani (IRE)—Gunner Marc **R. Murray**
21 **MOLLY MILAN**, 5, b m Milan—Dolly Sparks (IRE) **Barraston Racing**
22 **MONEL**, 5, ch g Cadeaux Genereux—Kelucia (IRE) **Great Northern Partnership 1**
23 **MUSIC FESTIVAL (USA)**, 6, b g Storm Cat (USA)—Musical Chimes (USA) **Jim Goldie Racing Club**
24 **NANTON (USA)**, 11, gr ro g Spinning World (USA)—Grab The Green (USA) **J. S. Morrison**
25 **RONALD GEE (IRE)**, 6, ch g Garuda (IRE)—Panache Lady (IRE) **Mrs J. Perratt**
26 **SEVEN IS LUCKY (IRE)**, 11, b g Old Vic—Green Legend (IRE) **The Dregs Of Humanity**
27 **SOPRANO (GER)**, 11, b g Sendawar (USA)—Spirit Lake (GER) **Johnnie Delta Racing**
28 **SPIRIT OF A NATION (IRE)**, 8, b g Invincible Spirit (IRE)—Fabulous Pet **Mr & Mrs Gordon Grant**
29 **TITUS BOLT (IRE)**, 4, b g Titus Livius (FR)—Megan's Bay **I. G. M. Dalgleish**
30 **TOO COOL TO FOOL (IRE)**, 10, b g Bob Back (USA)—Mandysway (IRE) **J. S. Goldie**

MR JIM GOLDIE - Continued

31 WYSE HILL TEABAGS, 8, b g Theatrical Charmer—Mrs Tea **Mr & Mrs Philip C. Smith**
32 YOURLOOKINATHIM (IRE), 7, b g Flemensfirth (USA)—Christmas River (IRE) **J. S. Goldie**

THREE-YEAR-OLDS

33 HAYLEY, b f Halling (USA)—Gargoyle Girl **Jim Goldie Racing Club**
34 MOWHOOB, b g Medicean—Pappas Ruby (USA) **Johnnie Delta Racing**
35 SUGAR BLAZE, ch f Orientor—Harrken Heights (IRE) **Mrs V. C. Macdonald**

Other Owners: Mr G. Adams, R. M. S. Allison, Mrs S. Armstrong, Mr F. J. Connor, Mr H. G. Connor, Mrs M. Craig, Mr G. Dunne, Mr J. Fyffe, Mrs D. I. Goldie, Mr G. R. Grant, Mrs C. H. Grant, R. A. Green, Mrs A. Green, Mr A. L. Gregg, A. G. Guthrie, E. W. Hyslop, Mrs C. M. Hyslop, Mr B. N. MacDonald, Mr A. G. MacDonald, Mrs W. McGrandles, Mr G. P. O'Shea, Mr P. C. Smith, Mrs J. W. Smith, G. M. Thomson.

Assistant Trainers: James & George Goldie

Jockey (flat): D. Tudhope, G. Bartley. Jockey (NH): Henry Brooke, Ryan Mania, Denis O'Regan. Amateur: Mrs Carol Bartley, Mrs I. Goldie.

---

250 MR ROBERT GOLDIE, Kilmarnock
Postal: **Harpercroft, Old Loans Road, Dundonald, Kilmarnock, Ayrshire, KA2 9DD**
Contacts: **PHONE (01292) 317222 FAX (01292) 313585 MOBILE (07801) 922552**

1 ALEXANDER OATS, 10, b g Insan (USA)—Easter Oats **R. H. Goldie**
2 ALFRED OATS, 9, b g Alflora (IRE)—Easter Oats **R. H. Goldie**

Assistant Trainer: Mrs R H Goldie

---

251 MR KEITH GOLDSWORTHY, Kilgetty
Postal: **Grumbly Bush Farm, Yerbeston, Kilgetty, Pembrokeshire, SA68 0NS**
Contacts: **PHONE/FAX (01834) 891343 MOBILE (07796) 497733**
E-MAIL grumbly@supanet.com WEBSITE www.keithgoldsworthyracing.co.uk

1 CALDEY, 4, b f Overbury (IRE)—Barfleur (IRE) **S. F. Barlow**
2 CASPER'S SHADOW (IRE), 7, gr g Great Palm (USA)—Kambaya (IRE) **Mrs P. A. Gough**
3 COCK OF THE ROCK (IRE), 8, b g Pierre—Glynn View (IRE) **The Rooster Partnership**
4 PUTNEY BRIDGE, 11, b g Slip Anchor—Mayroni **K. Goldsworthy**
5 ROAD SHOW, 6, b g Sadler's Wells (USA)—Danilova (USA) **Racing Coast Ltd**
6 SIR BENFRO, 7, b g Runyon (IRE)—Dunrowan **Racing Coast Ltd**
7 STREET DANCE (IRE), 7, b g Beneficial—Zvezda (IRE) **Racing Coast Ltd**
8 TENBY JEWEL (IRE), 8, ch g Pilsudski (USA)—Supreme Delight (IRE) **Racing Coast Ltd**
9 THEWESTWALIAN (USA), 5, b br g Stormy Atlantic (USA)—
Skies Of Blue (USA) **Greenacre Racing Partnership Ltd**
10 WHITECHAPEL, 6, gr g Oasis Dream—Barathiki **Mr J. Boland**
11 WILLIAM HOGARTH, 8, b g High Chaparral (IRE)—Mountain Holly **ROL Plant Hire Ltd**

Other Owners: Mr E. A. P. Arkell, Mr R. J. Barrack, M. Duthie, Mrs F. V. Miller, G. Mills, Mr P. O'Leary, Mr M. Reidy, Mr M. J. Skidmore, Mr G. Williams, Mr J. H. Williams.

Assistant Trainer: Mrs L. A. Goldsworthy

Amateur: Miss Charlotte Evans, Miss Rebecca Bockhart.

---

252 MR STEVE GOLLINGS, Louth
Postal: **Highfield House, Scamblesby, Louth, Lincolnshire, LN11 9XT**
Contacts: **YARD (01507) 343204 HOME/FAX (01507) 343213 MOBILE (07860) 218910**
E-MAIL stevegollings@aol.com WEBSITE www.stevegollings.com

1 ALLIED ANSWER, 5, gr g Danehill Dancer (IRE)—Hotelgenie Dot Com **P. J. Martin**
2 BAR DE LIGNE (FR), 7, b g Martaline—Treekle Toffee (FR) **P. J. Martin**
3 BRUNSWICK GOLD (IRE), 8, ch g Moscow Society (USA)—Tranbu (IRE) **P. J. Martin**
4 CONQUISTO, 8, ch g Hernando (FR)—Seal Indigo (IRE) **P. J. Martin**

MR STEVE GOLLINGS - Continued

5 4, Br f Sakhee (USA)—Darariyna (IRE) **Mr P. S. Walter**
6 **DUNLUCE CASTLE (IRE)**, 5, br g Secret Singer (FR)—Royale Laguna (FR) **P. J. Martin**
7 **HONEST JOHN**, 9, b g Alzao (USA)—Tintera (IRE) **P. J. Martin**
8 **INTO WAIN (USA)**, 6, b g Eddington (USA)—Serene Nobility (USA) **P. J. Martin**
9 **JAMARJO (IRE)**, 6, b g Marju (IRE)—Athlumney Lady **Northern Bloodstock Racing**
10 **KYLLADDIE**, 6, ch g Kyllachy—Chance For Romance **Mr P. S. Walter**
11 **LANDESHERR (GER)**, 6, b g Black Sam Bellamy (IRE)—Lutte Marie (GER) **Richard Atterby & Christine Atterby**
12 **LATERLY (IRE)**, 8, b g Tiger Hill (IRE)—La Candela (GER) **P. J. Martin**
13 **LOCAL HERO (GER)**, 6, b g Lomitas—Lolli Pop (GER) **P. J. Martin**
14 **RELIC ROCK (IRE)**, 5, b g Bienamado (USA)—Nighty Bless (IRE) **P. J. Martin**
15 **ROCKWEILLER**, 6, b h Rock of Gibraltar (IRE)—Ballerina Suprema (IRE) **P. Whinham**
16 **RUSSIAN GEORGE (IRE)**, 7, ch g Sendawar (IRE)—Mannsara (IRE) **Mrs Jayne M. Gollings**
17 **SOUDAIN (FR)**, 7, ch g Dom Alco (FR)—Ebene d'avril (FR) **P. J. Martin**
18 5, B m Act One—Taqreem (IRE) **Mr P. S. Walter**
19 **THEOLOGY**, 6, b g Galileo (IRE)—Biographie **P. J. Martin**
20 **TROOPINGTHECOLOUR**, 7, b g Nayef (USA)—Hyperspectra **Northern Bloodstock Racing**
21 **WALKABOUT CREEK (IRE)**, 6, b g Alderbrook—La Mouette (USA) **P. J. Martin**

TWO-YEAR-OLDS

22 B c 8/2 Tiger Hill (IRE)—Lady Darayna (Polish Precedent (USA)) **Mr P. S. Walter**

Other Owners: Mr R. J. Atterby, Mrs C. A. Atterby, S. Gollings.

Assistant Trainer: Mrs J M Gollings

Jockey (flat): Darryll Holland, Ian Mongan, Jamie Spencer. **Jockey (NH):** Keith Mercer, Brian Hughes, Timmy Murphy, A. P. McCoy, Tom Scudamore. **Conditional:** Paul Bohan.

---

253 MR CHRIS GORDON, Winchester
Postal: **Morestead Farm Stables, Morestead, Winchester, Hampshire, SO21 1JD**
Contacts: **PHONE** (01962) 712774 **FAX** (01962) 712774 **MOBILE** (07713) 082392
E-MAIL chrisgordon68@hotmail.co.uk **WEBSITE** www.chrisgordonracing.com

1 **BALUSTRADE (IRE)**, 7, b g Barathea (IRE)—Haladiya (IRE) **Gordon Racing**
2 **BENNY THE SWINGER (IRE)**, 8, b g Beneficial—The Olde Swinger (IRE) **L. Gilbert**
3 **CHILWORTH SCREAMER**, 5, b m Imperial Dancer—The Screamer (IRE) **7RUS**
4 **ECO'S GAMEBIRD**, 8, b g Classic Cliche (IRE)—Ollie's Lady **S Wain & B Drozd**
5 **GILDED AGE**, 7, b g Cape Cross (IRE)—Sweet Folly (IRE) **Draper Edmonds Draper**
6 **KING EDMUND**, 10, b g Roi de Rome (USA)—Cadbury Castle **A. C. Ward-Thomas**
7 **MANGONEL**, 9, ch m Beckett (IRE)—Apachee Flower **Chris Gordon Racing Club**
8 **MARIE DEJA LA (FR)**, 7, b m Daliapour (IRE)—Comedie Divine (FR) **Chris Gordon Racing Club**
9 5, B g Overbury (IRE)—Materiality
10 **MY BOY GINGER**, 4, ch g Byron—Lady Chef **The Not Over Big Partnership**
11 **OSMOSIA (FR)**, 8, b m Mansonnien (FR)—Osmose (FR) **Mr J. Bone**
12 **OWNER OCCUPIER**, 8, ch g Foxhound (USA)—Miss Beverley **Mrs D. M. Lawes**
13 **PERAZZI GEORGE (IRE)**, 7, b g High Roller (IRE)—Kit Kat Kate (IRE) **Mrs K. Digweed**
14 **PRINCELY HERO (IRE)**, 9, b g Royal Applause—Dalu (IRE) **L. Gilbert**
15 **PROMISED WINGS (GER)**, 6, ch g Monsun (GER)—Panagia (USA) **Mr Roger Alwen Mrs Heather Alwen**
16 **SUPERCILIARY**, 4, b g Dansili—Supereva (IRE) **Mr D. F. Henery**
17 **SWEET BOY VIC (IRE)**, 5, b g Old Vic—Sweet Second (IRE)
18 **TAKEROC (FR)**, 10, gr g Take Risks (FR)—Rochambelle (FR) **Mrs K. Digweed**
19 **THE KINGS ASSASSIN (IRE)**, 5, b br g King's Theatre (IRE)—Assidua (IRE)
20 **THE MASTER REMOVER (IRE)**, 4, ch g Royal Anthem (USA)—Kit Kat Kate (IRE) **A. C. Ward-Thomas**
21 **YES CHEF**, 6, ch g Best of The Bests (IRE)—Lady Chef **Mr Roger Alwen Mrs Heather Alwen**
22 **ZA'LAN (USA)**, 4, b g Street Sense (USA)—Calista **Mrs K. Digweed**

Other Owners: Mr R. N. Alwen, Mrs H. J. Alwen, J. Draper, Mr M. J. Draper, Mr B. Drozd, T. W. Edmonds, C. E. Gordon, Mrs J. L. Gordon, P. J. H. Rowe, Mr M. Swallow, Simon Trant, R. M. Venn, Mr L. S. Wain.

Assistant Trainer: Jenny Gordon

Conditional: Tom Cannon. **Amateur:** Miss M. R. Trainor.

254   MR J. T. GORMAN, Curragh
Postal: Maddenstown Lodge Stables, Maddenstown, Curragh, Co. Kildare, Ireland
Contacts: PHONE (00353) 45 441404 MOBILE (00353) 872 599603
E-MAIL jtgorman1@hotmail.com

1 CONAN'S ROCK, 4, b g Shamardal (USA)—Reeling N' Rocking (IRE) **Mrs P. A. Foley**
2 CRYING ALOUD (USA), 8, b br m Street Cry (IRE)—Angelic Deed (USA) **Miss M. McWey**
3 ELUSIVE GENT (IRE), 6, b g Elusive City (USA)—Satin Cape (IRE) **Mrs P. A. Foley**
4 GABH MO LEITHSCEAL (IRE), 5, b g Aussie Rules (USA)—Lady Windermere (IRE) **Mrs J. Bolger**
5 GOLDEN SHOE (IRE), 5, br g Footstepsinthesand—Goldilocks (IRE) **Mrs P. A. Foley**
6 KINGDOMFORTHEBRIDE (IRE), 4, b f Titus Livius (FR)—Desert Bride (USA) **Miss M. McWey**
7 LIBERTY TO ROCK (IRE), 7, b g Statue of Liberty (USA)—Polynesian Goddess (IRE) **Mrs P. A. Foley**
8 LOVEINASANDDUNE, 5, b g Oasis Dream—Windy Gulch (USA) **Mrs P. A. Foley**
9 MR ROCKNROLL, 6, b g Monsieur Bond (IRE)—Stream **Mrs P. A. Foley**
10 PIERRE D'OR (IRE), 4, ch c Rock of Gibraltar (IRE)—Gilded Edge **Mrs P. A. Foley**
11 ROCK OF FIRE (IRE), 5, b g Statue of Liberty (USA)—Polynesian Goddess (IRE) **Mrs P. A. Foley**
12 ROCKIN N REELIN (USA), 6, b g Forest Camp (USA)—Dusti's Tune (USA) **Mrs P. A. Foley**
13 WATERHOUSE (IRE), 6, b g Key of Luck (USA)—Blue Mantle (IRE) **Miss M. McWey**
14 WREKIN ROCK (IRE), 5, br g Statue of Liberty (USA)—Orpendonna (IRE) **Mrs P. A. Foley**

THREE-YEAR-OLDS

15 APRICOT LIL (IRE), ch f Refuse To Bend (IRE)—Aspen Falls (IRE) **Miss M. McWey**
16 C'EST MA SOEUR (IRE), b f Oratorio (IRE)—Gilded Edge **Mrs P. A. Foley**
17 CEST NOTRE GRIS (IRE), gr c Verglas (IRE)—Alikhlas **Mrs P. A. Foley**
18 JUST MY STORY (IRE), ch f Footstepsinthesand—Tiddle About (IRE) **Miss M. McWey**
19 PAPER PETAL (IRE), b f Refuse To Bend (IRE)—Catwalk Dreamer (IRE) **Miss M. McWey**

TWO-YEAR-OLDS

20 LE TROISIEME GRIS (IRE), gr c 17/2 Verglas (IRE)—Suailce (IRE) (Singspiel (IRE)) (15872) **Mrs P. A. Foley**
21 UN AUTRE GRIS (IRE), gr c 6/5 Verglas (IRE)—Overlook (Generous (IRE)) (30158) **Mrs P. A. Foley**

Jockey (flat): Kevin Manning, C. D. Hayes, D. McCormack.

255   MR JOHN GOSDEN, Newmarket
Postal: Clarehaven, Bury Road, Newmarket, Suffolk, CB8 7BY
Contacts: PHONE (01638) 565400 FAX (01638) 565401
E-MAIL jhmg@johngosden.com

1 AIKEN, 5, b h Selkirk (USA)—Las Flores (IRE)
2 CAMBORNE, 5, b g Doyen (IRE)—Dumnoni
3 CAUCUS, 6, b g Cape Cross (IRE)—Maid To Perfection
4 COLOMBIAN (IRE), 5, b br h Azamour (IRE)—Clodora (FR)
5 ELUSIVE KATE (USA), 4, b f Elusive Quality (USA)—Gout de Terroir (USA)
6 ESHTIBAAK (IRE), 5, b h Dalakhani (IRE)—Nanabanana (IRE)
7 FENCING (USA), 4, ch g Street Cry (USA)—Latice (IRE)
8 GALLIPOT, 4, b f Galileo (IRE)—Spinning Queen
9 GREGORIAN (IRE), 4, gr c Clodovil (IRE)—Three Days In May
10 HANSEATIC, 4, b c Galileo (IRE)—Insinuate (USA)
11 HEPWORTH, 4, b f Singspiel (IRE)—Annalina (USA)
12 LAHAAG, 4, b g Marju (IRE)—Chater
13 PROOFREADER, 4, b g Authorized (IRE)—Blixen (USA)
14 QUESTIONING (IRE), 5, b h Elusive Quality (USA)—Am I (USA)
15 SHANTARAM, 4, b c Galileo (USA)—All's Forgotten (USA)
16 STARSCOPE, 4, ch f Selkirk (USA)—Moon Goddess
17 SWISS SPIRIT, 4, b c Invincible Spirit (IRE)—Swiss Lake (USA)
18 TEMPEST FUGIT (IRE), 4, b f High Chaparral (IRE)—Diary (IRE)
19 THE FUGUE, 4, b br f Dansili—Twyla Tharp (USA)
20 TRADE COMMISSIONER (IRE), 5, b g Montjeu (IRE)—Spinning Queen
21 WANNABE LOVED, 4, b f Pivotal—Wannabe Posh (IRE)
22 WILLOW BECK, 4, b f Shamardal (USA)—Woodbeck

MR JOHN GOSDEN - Continued

THREE-YEAR-OLDS

23 **AJZAA (USA)**, b g Dynaformer (USA)—Tabrir (IRE)
24 **ASHDAN**, b c Dansili—Bonash
25 **BLESSINGTON (IRE)**, b c Kheleyf (USA)—Madam Ninette
26 **BLUMEN (USA)**, b f Dynaformer (USA)—Merchant (USA)
27 **BRASS RING**, b c Rail Link—Moraine
28 **BREDEN (IRE)**, b c Shamardal (USA)—Perfect Touch (USA)
29 **BRIGHT STRIKE (USA)**, b c Smart Strike (CAN)—Seebe (USA)
30 **CAPE ELIZABETH (IRE)**, b f Invincible Spirit (IRE)—Maine Lobster (USA)
31 **CHAT (USA)**, b br f Dynaformer (USA)—Verbal (USA)
32 **CLOSE AT HAND**, b f Exceed And Excel (AUS)—Classic Remark (IRE)
33 **CORNROW**, ch c New Approach (IRE)—Needlecraft (IRE)
34 **CUSHION**, b f Galileo (IRE)—Attraction
35 **DEBORAH**, b f New Approach (IRE)—Danelissima (IRE)
36 **ETHEL**, b f Exceed And Excel (AUS)—Agnus (IRE)
37 **EXCESS KNOWLEDGE**, br c Monsun (GER)—Quenched
38 **FALSAFA**, b f Dansili—Hureya (USA)
39 **FEEL LIKE DANCING**, b c Galileo (IRE)—Maid of Killeen (IRE)
40 **FERJAAN**, b c Oasis Dream—Bahja (USA)
41 **FLEDGED**, b c Dansili—Innocent Air
42 **FLYING OFFICER (USA)**, b c Dynaformer (USA)—Vignette (USA)
43 **FREEDOM'S LIGHT**, b f Galileo (IRE)—Aricia (IRE)
44 **GHURAIR (USA)**, b br c Elusive Quality (USA)—Alta Moda
45 **HOARDING (USA)**, b c Elusive Quality (USA)—What A Treasure (IRE)
46 **HOME FRONT (IRE)**, b c Duke of Marmalade (IRE)—Overruled (IRE)
47 **KHOBARAA**, b br f Invincible Spirit (IRE)—Deyaar (USA)
48 **KHUDOUA**, b g Nayef (USA)—Danehill Dreamer (USA)
49 **MAGISTRAL**, b c Manduro (GER)—Tamalain (USA)
50 **MAXI DRESS (IRE)**, b f Shamardal (USA)—Fashion Trade
51 **MONZZA**, b f Montjeu (IRE)—Zee Zee Top
52 **MUMEYEZ**, ch g Motivator—Twelfth Night (IRE)
53 **MUNHAMER (IRE)**, ch c Iffraaj—Khibraat
54 **MUTANAWEB (IRE)**, b c Tamayuz—Diary (IRE)
55 **NARMIN (IRE)**, b f Pivotal—Ulfah (USA)
56 **NAUTILUS**, b c Medicean—Fickle
57 **NICHOLS CANYON**, b c Authorized (IRE)—Zam Zoom (IRE)
58 **NICKELS AND DIMES (IRE)**, b f Teofilo (IRE)—Neat Shilling (IRE)
59 **OBSTACLE**, ch c Observatory (USA)—Stage Left
60 **PHIZ (GER)**, b f Galileo (IRE)—Peace Time (GER)
61 **POMEROL**, ch c Kyllachy—Clinet (IRE)
62 **POMODORO**, ch c Pivotal—Foodbroker Fancy (IRE)
63 **POMOLOGY (USA)**, br f Arch (USA)—Sharp Apple (USA)
64 **PROMPT BEAUTY (USA)**, b f Dynaformer (USA)—Promptly (USA)
65 **RELENTLESS (IRE)**, b g Dylan Thomas (IRE)—Karamiyna (IRE)
66 **REMOTE**, b c Dansili—Zenda
67 **REQAABA**, b f Exceed And Excel (AUS)—Something Blue
68 **ROTTINGDEAN**, gr c Oasis Dream—Misk (FR)
69 **RUFFLED**, b f Harlan's Holiday (USA)—Mirabilis (USA)
70 **SCALLYWAG (IRE)**, ch f Raven's Pass (USA)—Brattothecore (CAN)
71 **SEEK AGAIN (USA)**, ch c Speightstown (USA)—Light Jig
72 **SHAMAL**, b g Exceed And Excel (AUS)—Miss Meltemi (IRE)
73 **SHARED EXPERIENCE**, ch f Raven's Pass (USA)—Felicity (IRE)
74 **SHE'S LATE**, ch c Pivotal—Courting
75 **SISTER TERRI (USA)**, ch f Mr Greeley (USA)—Nunnery (USA)
76 **SMOKE RING (IRE)**, gr ro f Dalakhani (IRE)—Desert Tigress (USA)
77 **SNOW KING (USA)**, ch c Elusive Quality (USA)—Cloudspin (USA)
78 **SNOW POWDER (IRE)**, ch f Raven's Pass (USA)—Multicolour Wave (IRE)
79 **SNOWBRIGHT**, b f Pivotal—Snow Gretel (IRE)
80 **SPACE SHIP**, ch c Galileo (IRE)—Angara
81 **STRESA**, b f Pivotal—Bay Tree (IRE)
82 **TAAYEL (IRE)**, b c Tamayuz—Sakhee's Song (IRE)
83 **THOMAS HOBSON**, b c Halling (USA)—La Spezia (IRE)
84 **TOAST OF THE TOWN (IRE)**, b f Duke of Marmalade (IRE)—Boast
85 **TRAPEZE**, ch f Pivotal—Miss Penton
86 **VANITY RULES**, b f New Approach (IRE)—Miss Pinkerton

MR JOHN GOSDEN - Continued

87 **WALLENBERG**, b c Rock of Gibraltar (IRE)—Waldmark (GER)
88 **WINSILI**, b f Dansili—Winter Sunrise
89 **WOODLAND ARIA**, b f Singspiel (IRE)—Magic Tree (UAE)

TWO-YEAR-OLDS

90 B c 29/3 Montjeu (IRE)—Reina Blanca (Darshaan)
91 B c 22/3 Medicean—Al Joudha (FR) (Green Desert (USA)) (49000)
92 B f 30/4 Oasis Dream—All For Laura (Cadeaux Genereux) (280000)
93 B c 5/3 Galileo (IRE)—All's Forgotten (USA) (Darshaan)
94 **ALLEGRIA (IRE)**, gr f 2/2 Dalakhani (IRE)—Drifting (IRE) (Sadler's Wells (USA))
95 B f 7/2 Oasis Dream—Arosa (IRE) (Sadler's Wells (USA))
96 B f 7/2 Oasis Dream—Arty Crafty (USA) (Arch (USA)) (450000)
97 B f 25/2 Galileo (IRE)—Ask For The Moon (FR) (Dr Fong (USA))
98 **BEYOND SMART (USA)**, b c 8/2 Smart Strike (CAN)—Beyond The Waves (USA) (Ocean Crest (USA))
99 B c 2/3 Teofilo (IRE)—Bezant (IRE) (Zamindar (USA)) (125000)
100 **BILLY BLUE (IRE)**, b c 12/4 High Chaparral (IRE)—Silk Dress (IRE) (Gulch (USA)) (28000)
101 B c 8/3 High Chaparral (IRE)—Blue Rhapsody (Cape Cross (IRE)) (50000)
102 B c 18/4 Bushranger (IRE)—Champion Tipster (Pursuit of Love) (110000)
103 B c 14/3 Cape Cross (IRE)—Cinnamon Rose (USA) (Trempolino (USA)) (80000)
104 **CLOUDSCAPE (IRE)**, b c 5/5 Dansili—Set The Scene (IRE) (Sadler's Wells (USA))
105 B c 31/3 Empire Maker (USA)—Costume (Danehill (USA))
106 **CRITERIA (IRE)**, b f 28/4 Galileo (IRE)—Aleagueoftheirown (IRE) (Danehill Dancer (IRE)) (535000)
107 B f 8/2 Invincible Spirit (IRE)—Crossmolina (IRE) (Halling (USA)) (200000)
108 **D'AVIGNON (USA)**, b br c 30/4 Smart Strike (CAN)—No Matter What (USA) (Nureyev (USA))
109 **DANJEU (IRE)**, b c 4/2 Montjeu (IRE)—Wanna (IRE) (Danehill Dancer (IRE)) (725000)
110 B c 17/3 Compton Place—Deora De (Night Shift (USA)) (55000)
111 B f 25/4 New Approach (IRE)—Doctrine (Barathea (IRE)) (60000)
112 **DREAM MELODY**, ch f 2/3 Selkirk (USA)—Dream Again (Medicean)
113 B br c 28/4 Kitten's Joy (USA)—Dynamia (USA) (Dynaformer (USA)) (184331)
114 B c 16/3 Cape Cross (IRE)—Elle Galante (GER) (Galileo (IRE))
115 **FASTNET RED**, b c 31/3 Fastnet Rock (AUS)—Gyroscope (Spinning World (USA))
116 Br c 20/1 Invincible Spirit (IRE)—Gemini Joan (Montjeu (IRE)) (105000)
117 **GEORGE HERBERT**, b c 20/2 Yeats (IRE)—Colorado Dawn (Fantastic Light (USA)) (100000)
118 **GM HOPKINS**, b c 23/4 Dubawi (IRE)—Varsity (Lomitas) (95238)
119 **GRANDEST**, b c 21/1 Dansili—Angara (Alzao (USA))
120 **HOLBERG SUITE**, b f 3/5 Azamour (IRE)—Humouresque (Pivotal)
121 B f 20/4 Intikhab (USA)—Indolente (IRE) (Diesis) (60000)
122 B c 30/1 Pivotal—Infamous Angel (Exceed And Excel (AUS)) (120000)
123 B f 25/3 Oasis Dream—Innocent Air (Galileo (IRE))
124 Gr ro f 7/4 Mizzen Mast (USA)—Light Jig (Danehill (USA))
125 **LIVELY SPIRIT**, b f 15/4 Dansili—Felicity (IRE) (Selkirk (USA))
126 B f 9/3 Dubawi (IRE)—Loch Jipp (USA) (Belong To Me (USA)) (100000)
127 **LONG CROSS**, b c 14/3 Cape Cross (IRE)—Majestic Roi (USA) (Street Cry (IRE))
128 Br c 1/3 Raven's Pass (USA)—Love The Rain (Rainbow Quest (USA))
129 B c 4/3 High Chaparral (IRE)—Lure of The Moon (USA) (Lure (USA)) (130000)
130 **MATALLEB (USA)**, b c 7/5 Elusive Quality (USA)—Our Rite of Spring (USA) (Stravinsky (USA)) (110599)
131 **MAVERICK WAVE (USA)**, ch c 20/2 Elusive Quality (USA)—Misty Ocean (USA) (Stormy Atlantic (USA)) (61443)
132 **MIHANY (IRE)**, b c 6/3 Teofilo (IRE)—Love Excelling (FR) (Polish Precedent (USA)) (600000)
133 B f 15/3 Oasis Dream—Mirabilis (USA) (Lear Fan (USA))
134 **MR SMITH**, gr c 11/2 Galileo (IRE)—Intrigued (Darshaan) (280000)
135 **MUCH PROMISE**, b f 19/2 Invincible Spirit (IRE)—Prowess (IRE) (Peintre Celebre (USA))
136 **MUNJAZ**, ch c 1/3 Sea The Stars (IRE)—Qurrah (IRE) (Zafonic (USA))
137 B f 6/3 E Dubai (USA)—Musicanti (USA) (Nijinsky (CAN))
138 **MUWAARY**, b br c 11/2 Oasis Dream—Wissal (USA) (Woodman (USA))
139 B f 1/2 Dansili—Neartica (FR) (Sadler's Wells (USA)) (550000)
140 Ch c 6/2 Shirocco (GER)—Pelagia (IRE) (Lycius (USA)) (100000)
141 B c 12/4 Oasis Dream—Phantom Wind (USA) (Storm Cat (USA))
142 B c 20/4 Medicean—Phillippa (IRE) (Galileo (IRE)) (55238)
143 **PRINCE OF STARS**, b c 15/4 Sea The Stars (IRE)—Queen's Logic (IRE) (Grand Lodge (USA))
144 **RECTITUDE**, b f 23/3 Virtual—Evasive Quality (FR) (Highest Honor (FR))
145 B c 23/1 Bushranger (IRE)—Sassy Gal (IRE) (King's Best (USA)) (60000)
146 **SEAGULL (IRE)**, b f 17/3 Sea The Stars (IRE)—Caumshinaun (IRE) (Indian Ridge)
147 **SEJEL (IRE)**, b f 29/3 Cape Cross (IRE)—Wajaha (IRE) (Haafhd)
148 **SEMBLANCE**, b f 7/2 Pivotal—Illusion (Anabaa (USA))
149 **SHAHEEN ZAIN (IRE)**, b f 17/2 Oasis Dream—Majestic Desert (Fraam)

MR JOHN GOSDEN - Continued

150 B f 9/3 Fastnet Rock (AUS)—Slow Sand (USA) (Dixieland Band (USA)) (130000)
151 **SOLAR MAGIC**, ch f 6/3 Pivotal—Moon Goddess (Rainbow Quest (USA))
152 **STAR CHART (IRE)**, b f 26/3 Dubawi (IRE)—Star Express (Sadler's Wells (USA)) (200000)
153 B c 11/2 Empire Maker (USA)—Summer Shower (Sadler's Wells (USA))
154 **SWISS KISS**, br f 15/2 Dansili—Swiss Lake (USA) (Indian Ridge)
155 **TAGHROODA**, b f 27/1 Sea The Stars (IRE)—Ezima (IRE) (Sadler's Wells (USA))
156 **TERHAAB (USA)**, b f 6/2 Elusive Quality (USA)—Star of Paris (USA) (Dayjur (USA)) (202764)
157 **THE THIRD MAN**, gr c 18/2 Dalakhani (IRE)—Spinning Queen (Spinning World (USA))
158 **THRONE ROOM**, b c 21/2 Oasis Dream—Magnificient Style (USA) (Silver Hawk (USA))
159 **TOO THE STARS (IRE)**, ch f 25/2 Sea The Stars (IRE)—Finsceal Beo (IRE) (Mr Greeley (USA))
160 **TRUST THE WIND**, b f 8/1 Dansili—Hypnology (USA) (Gone West (USA)) (195000)
161 **VALLAR (USA)**, b c 10/1 Lemon Drop Kid (USA)—Polaire (IRE) (Polish Patriot (USA))
162 Ch c 1/1 Giant's Causeway (USA)—Vignette (USA) (Diesis)
163 Ch f 14/2 New Approach (IRE)—Zam Zoom (IRE) (Dalakhani (IRE)) (52000)
164 B c 26/2 Invincible Spirit (USA)—Zenda (Zamindar (USA))
165 **ZERFAAL**, br c 9/4 Dubawi (IRE)—Dhelaal (Green Desert (USA))
166 B br f 25/2 Kheleyf (USA)—Zerky (USA) (Kingmambo (USA)) (150793)

Jockey (flat): William Buick, Robert Havlin, Nicky Mackay, Marc Halford, Saleem Golam.

---

256 **MRS HARRIET GRAHAM, Jedburgh**
Postal: **Brundeanlaws Cottage, Camptown, Jedburgh, Roxburghshire, TD8 6NW**
Contacts: **PHONE (01835) 840354 MOBILE (07843) 380401**
E-MAIL hgrahamracing@aol.com

1 **BALLYBROE (IRE)**, 6, b g Presenting—Mini Minor (IRE) **H G Racing**
2 **MACGILLYCUDDY**, 4, b g And Beyond (IRE)—Tofino Swell **H G Racing**
3 **PRINCE TAM**, 9, gr g Terimon—Princess Maxine (IRE) **Miss G. Joughin**
4 **SCOTSWELL**, 7, b g Endoli (USA)—Tofino Swell **H G Racing**
5 **SOUL MAGIC (IRE)**, 11, b g Flemensfirth (USA)—Indian Legend (IRE) **H G Racing**

Other Owners: Mrs H. O. Graham, Mr R. D. Graham.

Assistant Trainer: R D Graham

Jockey (NH): James Reveley. **Conditional:** Gary Rutherford.

---

257 **MR CHRIS GRANT, Billingham**
Postal: **Low Burntoft Farm, Wolviston, Billingham, Cleveland, TS22 5PD**
Contacts: **PHONE/FAX (01740) 644054 MOBILE (07860) 577998**
E-MAIL chrisgrantracing@gmail.com WEBSITE www.chrisgrantracing.co.uk

1 **ALAPLEE**, 5, b g Alflora (IRE)—Cloudy Pearl **Miss A. P. Lee**
2 **ALPHA ONE (IRE)**, 7, b g Fruits of Love (USA)—Dunedin Lass (IRE) **J. Wade**
3 **ASTEROID BELT (IRE)**, 4, ch g Heliostatic (IRE)—Affaire Royale (IRE) **Straightline Construction Ltd**
4 **BOB WILL (IRE)**, 8, b g Bob's Return (IRE)—Mini Moo Min **Mr D. Armstrong**
5 **CINNOMHOR**, 5, b m Grape Tree Road—Brass Buckle (IRE) **Miss A. P. Lee**
6 **DARK GLACIER (IRE)**, 8, b g Flemensfirth (USA)—Glacier Lilly (IRE) **T. J. Hemmings**
7 **EMIRATE ISLE**, 9, b g Cois Na Tine (IRE)—Emmajoun **Bell Bridge Racing**
8 **GLAISDALE**, 4, b f Hurricane Run (IRE)—Picacho (IRE) **Straightline Construction Ltd**
9 **GRAMMAR**, 4, b g Rail Link—Comma (USA) **Seneca Investments & Developments Ltd**
10 **GUMND (IRE)**, 6, b g Selkirk (USA)—Surval (IRE) **Elliott Brothers And Peacock**
11 **IFYOUTHINKSO**, 6, b g Hernando (FR)—Evriza (IRE) **Mr D. Armstrong**
12 **LEYLAND (IRE)**, 4, b g Peintre Celebre (USA)—Lasting Chance (USA) **Straightline Construction Ltd**
13 **LUCEMATIC**, 7, b m Systematic—Soldier's Song **Mrs P. C. Stirling**
14 **LYSINO (GER)**, 4, ch c Medicean—Lysuna (GER) **Straightline Construction Ltd**
15 **MICRO MISSION (IRE)**, 7, b m Flemensfirth (USA)—Micro Villa (IRE) **Mr D. Armstrong**
16 **MILANO SUPREMO (IRE)**, 8, b g Milan—Lucy Popp (IRE) **Mr D. Armstrong**
17 **MOLAISE LAD (IRE)**, 7, b g Morozov (USA)—Artic Annie (IRE) **Mr & Mrs G. E. Pickering**
18 **MONTOYA'S SON (IRE)**, 8, ch g Flemensfirth (USA)—Over The Grand (IRE) **Straightline Construction Ltd**
19 **NOTONEBUTTWO (IRE)**, 6, b g Dushyantor (USA)—Daiquiri (IRE) **Mr D. Armstrong**
20 5, B g Craigsteel—Old Cup (IRE) **Straightline Construction Ltd**
21 **OVERQUEST**, 11, b g Overbury (IRE)—Foleys Quest (IRE) **D. Mossop**

MR CHRIS GRANT - Continued

22 **OVERYOU**, 8, bl m Overbury (IRE)—Keep The Treasure (IRE) **D. Mossop**
23 **PHAR AWAY ISLAND (IRE)**, 5, br g Heron Island (IRE)—Phar From Men (IRE) **Straightline Construction Ltd**
24 **ROCK RELIEF (IRE)**, 7, gr g Daylami (IRE)—Sheer Bliss (IRE) **Mr D. Armstrong**
25 4, B g Brian Boru—Sister Anna **Straightline Construction Ltd**
26 5, B g Iktibas—Staggering (IRE)
27 **STOP ON**, 8, b g Fraam—Tourmalet **D. M. P. R. Racing**
28 **STORM TO PASS**, 5, b g Overbury (IRE)—Silver Peak (FR) **Straightline Construction Ltd**
29 **SUPREME GOLD**, 5, ch g Supreme Sound—Salem Beach **The Hon Mrs D. Faulkner**
30 **SWINGBRIDGE (IRE)**, 5, b g Milan—Creative Approach (IRE) **T. J. Hemmings**
31 **THATILDEE (IRE)**, 5, b g Heron Island (IRE)—Good Thyne Mary (IRE) **Peacock Boys Partnership**
32 **TOUGH TRADE**, 4, b g Trade Fair—Cesana (IRE) **David Armstrong & Nigel E M Jones**
33 **ULYSSE COLLONGES (FR)**, 5, b g Voix du Nord (FR)—Kapucine Collonges (FR) **Elliott Brothers And Peacock**
34 **WILLIAM MONEY (IRE)**, 6, b g Cloudings (IRE)—All of A Kind (IRE) **Mr D. Armstrong**

THREE-YEAR-OLDS

35 **BROADWAY BELLE**, b f Lucarno (USA)—Theatre Belle **Division Bell Partnership**

Other Owners: T. Cunningham, J. M. Elliott, C. R. Elliott, C. Grant, Mr J. Henderson, N. E. M. Jones, Mr D. A. Lofthouse, A. Meale, Mrs L. Monkhouse, Mr J. H. Monkhouse, Mrs M. Nicholas, Mrs P. Pickering, Mr G. E. Pickering, Mr R. Poole, A. D. Wright.

Assistant Trainer: Mrs S. Grant

Jockey (NH): Denis O'Regan, Wilson Renwick. **Conditional:** Diarmuid O'Regan.

---

258 | MR LIAM GRASSICK, Cheltenham
Postal: **Postlip Racing Stables, Winchcombe, Cheltenham, Gloucestershire, GL54 5AQ**
Contacts: **PHONE (01242) 603124 YARD (01242) 603919 MOBILE (07816) 930423**
E-MAIL mark.grassick@btopenworld.com

1 **CLEEVE CLOUD (IRE)**, 7, b g Noverre (USA)—La Galeisa (IRE) **Mrs T. A. Macey**
2 **COMMANCHE DREAM**, 10, b g Commanche Run—Busy Girl **Mr M J Dunn**
3 **LATE REG**, 14, br m Chaddleworth (IRE)—Prominent Princess **C. M. Rutledge**
4 **THE WALNUT TREE (IRE)**, 12, b g Mister Lord (USA)—Janet's Girl (IRE) **Mr M J Dunn**

Assistant Trainer: Mark Grassick

---

259 | MR M. C. GRASSICK, Curragh
Postal: **Fenpark Stables, Pollardstown, Curragh, Co. Kildare, Ireland**
Contacts: **PHONE (00353) 4543 4483 FAX (00353) 4543 7895 MOBILE (00353) 86 364 8829**
E-MAIL mcgrassick@hotmail.com WEBSITE www.michaelcgrassick.com

1 **ARGENTINIAN TANGO (IRE)**, 5, ch m Prince Arch (USA)—Tordasia (IRE) **Mrs Mary T. Crowley**
2 **CASIMIR ROAD (IRE)**, 5, b g High Chaparral (IRE)—Six Nations (USA) **P. McKeon**
3 **CURRENTIS (IRE)**, 4, b f Dylan Thomas (IRE)—Bounce (FR) **Joseph E. Keeling**
4 4, B g Vinnie Roe (IRE)—Dariyba (IRE) **M. C. Grassick**
5 **DORIAN BAY (IRE)**, 5, b g Oscar (IRE)—Silks Princess **J. Martin Smith**
6 **ELUSIVE IN PARIS (IRE)**, 4, b g Elusive City (USA)—Bradwell (USA) **Joseph E. Keeling**
7 **KING OF ARAN (IRE)**, 6, b br g Val Royal (FR)—Innishmore (IRE) **Dont Tell The Missus Syndicate**
8 **LAUREL CREEK (IRE)**, 8, b g Sakura Laurel (JPN)—Eastern Sky (AUS) **P. McKeon**
9 **ONLY EXCEPTION (IRE)**, 4, b f Jeremy (USA)—Misaayef (USA) **A. Goonan**
10 **TRIKIRK (IRE)**, 12, b g Selkirk (USA)—Shastri (USA) **M. C. Grassick**

THREE-YEAR-OLDS

11 **AMAZING GLORY (IRE)**, ch g Indian Haven—Porto Venere (IRE) **J. Kavanagh**
12 **BOULE DE NEIGE (IRE)**, gr f Verglas (IRE)—Poulkovo (IRE) **Matt Duffy**

TWO-YEAR-OLDS

13 B f 19/2 Bushranger (IRE)—Mythie (FR) (Octagonal (NZ)) (42000) **Joseph E. Keeling**
14 **RO ALAINN (IRE)**, b f 14/4 Westerner—Tordasia (IRE) (Dr Devious (IRE)) **M. C. Grassick**
15 B c 19/4 Rock of Gibraltar (IRE)—Vestavia (IRE) (Alhaarth (IRE)) **Joseph E. Keeling**
16 B f 30/4 High Chaparral (IRE)—Virgin Hawk (USA) (Silver Hawk (USA)) **J. Higgins**

MR M. C. GRASSICK - Continued

Assistant Trainer: Dave Flynn

Jockey (flat): N. G. McCullagh.

---

260 **MR CARROLL GRAY, Bridgwater**
Postal: **Horlake, Moorland, Bridgwater, Somerset, TA7 0AT**
Contacts: **HOME (01278) 691359 MOBILE (07989) 768163**

1 **BOVS CASTLE**, 4, gr f Proclamation (IRE)—Focosa (ITY) **S. C. Botham**
2 **GLEANNACREIM (IRE)**, 10, ch g Old Vic—Rosie Brook (IRE) **Riverdance Consortium 2**
3 **MON CHEVALIER (IRE)**, 10, b g Montjeu (IRE)—Kumta (IRE) **S. C. Botham**

Other Owners: Mr R. G. Botham, M. J. Colenutt, Mr R. Flenk.

Assistant Trainer: Mrs C M L Gray

Jockey (NH): Harry Skelton.

---

261 **MR PETER GRAYSON, Formby**
Postal: **Apartment 2, The Sandwarren, 21 Victoria Road, Formby, Merseyside, L37 7AQ**
Contacts: **PHONE (01704) 830668 FAX (01704) 830668**
E-MAIL info@pgr.uk.com WEBSITE www.pgr.uk.com

1 **AVONVALLEY**, 6, b m Avonbridge—Piper's Ash (USA) **R. S. Teatum**
2 4, B c Tiger Hill (IRE)—B Beautiful (IRE)
3 **DINGAAN (IRE)**, 10, b g Tagula (IRE)—Boughtbyphone **R. S. Teatum**
4 **EVENS AND ODDS (IRE)**, 9, ch g Johannesburg (USA)—Coeur de La Mer (IRE)
5 **FLOW CHART (IRE)**, 6, b g Acclamation—Free Flow **Mr E. Grayson**
6 **ISHETOO**, 9, b g Ishiguru (USA)—Ticcatoo (IRE) **R. S. Teatum**
7 4, B c Refuse To Bend (IRE)—Kaveri (USA)
8 4, B c Echo of Light—Legend of Aragon
9 **MID YORKSHIRE GOLF**, 4, b f Doyen (IRE)—Jodeeka **R. S. Teatum**
10 **RAJEH (IRE)**, 10, b g Key of Luck (USA)—Saramacca (IRE) **Mr E. Grayson**
11 **RIGHTCAR**, 6, b g Bertolini (USA)—Loblolly Bay **R. S. Teatum**
12 4, B f Araafa (IRE)—Sabina
13 4, B f Echo of Light—Seeking Utopia
14 **SONG OF PARKES**, 6, b m Fantastic Light (USA)—My Melody Parkes **Mr E. Grayson**
15 **STONEACRE HULL (IRE)**, 4, b f Bachelor Duke (USA)—Amount **R. S. Teatum**
16 **STONEACRE LAD (IRE)**, 10, b h Bluebird (USA)—Jay And-A (IRE) **R. S. Teatum**
17 **STONEACRE OSKAR**, 4, b f Echo of Light—Keidas (FR) **R. S. Teatum**
18 **STONEACRE THIRSK (IRE)**, 4, br f Red Clubs (IRE)—Alexander Eliott (IRE) **R. S. Teatum**
19 **VHUJON (IRE)**, 8, b g Mujadil (USA)—Livius Lady (IRE) **R. S. Teatum**
20 4, B f Echo of Light—Zagala

Assistant Trainer: Mrs S. Grayson

---

262 **MR WARREN GREATREX, Upper Lambourn**
Postal: **Uplands, Upper Lambourn, Hungerford, Berkshire, RG17 8QH**
Contacts: **PHONE (01488) 670279 FAX (01488) 670279 MOBILE (07920) 039114**
E-MAIL info@wgreatrexracing.com WEBSITE www.wgreatrexracing.com

1 **BARLOW (IRE)**, 6, br g Beneficial—Carrigeen Kerria (IRE) **GDM Partnership**
2 **BERKELEY AVENUE**, 4, ch g Needwood Blade—Dropitlikeit's Hot (IRE) **Mr W. J. Greatrex**
3 **BUNGLASHA LADY (IRE)**, 8, b m Snurge—Enchanted Valley (IRE) **Mrs T. J. Stone-Brown**
4 **CARPIES BOY**, 4, b g Dreams End—Bungar Belle (IRE) **Mr P. Turley & Partners**
5 **CHASE THE WIND (IRE)**, 4, ch g Spadoun (FR)—Asfreeasthewind (IRE) **Mrs Jill & Mr Robin Eynon**
6 **CITY PRESS (IRE)**, 7, b g Presenting—Phargara (IRE) **Lewis, Reid, Moss & Luck**
7 **DOLATULO (FR)**, 6, ch g Le Fou (IRE)—La Perspective (FR) **Chasemore Farm**
8 **DOUBLE CEE**, 4, ch g Haafhd—Razzle (IRE) **Tracy Stone-Brown & Judy England**
9 **EGRETTA ISLAND (IRE)**, 7, b m Heron Island (IRE)—Ring Mam (IRE) **Let's Live Racing**
10 **ELLNANDO QUEEN**, 5, b m Hernando (FR)—Queen of Spades (IRE) **Mrs R. I. Vaughan**

MR WARREN GREATREX - Continued

11 **FAIREY DELTA**, 6, b m Milan—Motcombe (IRE) **Lady N. F. Cobham**
12 **FEATHERINTHEATTIC (IRE)**, 8, b g Bahri (USA)—Silk Feather (USA) **Chasemore Farm**
13 **FIVE RIVERS (IRE)**, 7, ch g Accordion—Native Country (IRE) **Mrs Jill Eynon & Mr Robin Eynon**
14 **FLITE (IRE)**, 7, b m Flemensfirth (USA)—Lite 'n Easy (IRE) **M. Luck, Lady Clark, Pam Deal & A. Lambert**
15 **HAND ON BACH (IRE)**, 5, b g Bach (IRE)—Deise Blues (IRE) **Outdoor Five**
16 **HEAD RUSH**, 5, b g Exit To Nowhere (USA)—Petale de Rose (IRE) **Mrs T. J. Stone-Brown**
17 **HIGH KITE (IRE)**, 7, b br g High-Rise (IRE)—Sister Rose (IRE) **The High Kites**
18 **HOW'S BUSINESS**, 9, b m Josr Algarhoud (IRE)—Love And Kisses **Group Clean Ltd**
19 **JACK THE CRACKER**, 5, b g Grape Tree Road—Wild Happening (GER) **Mr W. J. Greatrex**
20 **MASQUERADE (IRE)**, 4, b g Fruits of Love (USA)—Beechill Dancer (IRE) **Mrs S. Griffiths**
21 **MIXOLOGIST**, 6, gr g Fair Mix (IRE)—Matchband Again (IRE) **Mrs T. J. Stone-Brown**
22 **MORANA (IRE)**, 6, b g Alhaarth (IRE)—Blushing Barada (USA) **A. W. Black**
23 **OSCAR PRAIRIE (IRE)**, 8, b g Oscar (IRE)—Silver Prairie (IRE) **Mr W. J. Greatrex**
24 **PAINT THE CLOUDS**, 8, b g Muhtarram (USA)—Preening **Peter Deal & Jill & Robin Eynon**
25 **PROFESSEUR EMERY (FR)**, 6, b g Officiel (FR)—Karmadeine (FR) **GDM Partnership**
26 **RANTHAMBORE**, 6, b g Kayf Tara—Lucia Forte **R. A. H. Perkins**
27 **STAGE KING**, 7, b g King's Theatre (IRE)—Blue Dante (IRE)
28 5, b m Kayf Tara—Tamergale (IRE) **Mrs R. I. Vaughan**
29 **TURBO DU RANCH (FR)**, 6, gr g Useful (FR)—Zoumba du Ranch (FR) **Mr W. J. Greatrex**
30 **UMADACHAR (FR)**, 5, gr m Turgeon (USA)—Intelectuelle (FR) **Mrs T. J. Stone-Brown**
31 **WESTWARD POINT**, 6, ch g Karinga Bay—Hottentot **Mr J. F. F. White**

Other Owners: Mr M. Ball, Mr Andrew Black, Mr Gregory Charlesworth, Mr Daniel Charlesworth, Lady Clark, Lady Cobham, Mr P. A. Deal, Judy England, Mrs J. M. Eynon, Mr R. A. F. Eynon, Mr Warren Greatrex, Mr M. W. Gregory, Mrs Annie Lambert, Mr Christopher Lewis, Mr James Luck, Mrs Clare Luck, Mrs M. L. Luck, Mr Justin Moss, Mr E. R. Newnham, Mr Bernard Panton, Mr Anthony Reid, Mr Michael Smith, Mrs R. I. Vaughan.

Head Lad: Graham Baines

Jockey (NH): Noel Fehily, Wayne Hutchinson. **Conditional:** Will Pettis.

---

263 MR PAUL GREEN, Lydiate
Postal: **Oak Lea, Southport Road, Lydiate, Liverpool, Merseyside, L31 4HH**
Contacts: **PHONE (0151) 526 0093 FAX (0151) 520 0299 MOBILE (07748) 630685**
E-MAIL paulgreen@mitchell-james.com

1 **BEAU MISTRAL (IRE)**, 4, ch f Windsor Knot (IRE)—Carpet Lover (IRE) **The Winsor Not Group**
2 **DUBARA REEF (IRE)**, 6, ch g Dubawi (IRE)—Mamara Reef **Oaklea Aces**
3 **FERDY (IRE)**, 4, b c Antonius Pius (USA)—Trinity Fair **Mr E. Sciarrillo**
4 **FOREVER JANEY**, 4, b f Indesatchel (IRE)—Nee Lemon Left **Mr A. Mills**
5 **INVINCIBLE FORCE (IRE)**, 9, b g Invincible Spirit (IRE)—Highly Respected (IRE) **P. Green**
6 **LEGAL EAGLE (IRE)**, 8, b g Invincible Spirit (IRE)—Lupulina (CAN) **I. P. Mason**
7 **LUCKY DAN (IRE)**, 7, b g Danetime (IRE)—Katherine Gorge (IRE) **P. Green**
8 **M J WOODWARD**, 4, b c Needwood Blade—Canina **Mr E. Sciarrillo**
9 **MY NEW ANGEL (IRE)**, 4, gr f Dark Angel (IRE)—Mynu Girl (IRE) **Mr C. J. Dingwall**
10 **RUSTY ROCKET (IRE)**, 4, ch c Majestic Missile (IRE)—Sweet Compliance **Seven Stars Racing**

THREE-YEAR-OLDS

11 **BALTIC PRINCE (IRE)**, b c Baltic King—Brunswick **Mr A. Mills**
12 **HOLLYDANFAYE**, b f Avonbridge—Canina **Mr I. Furlong**

TWO-YEAR-OLDS

13 Ch f 27/2 Windsor Knot (IRE)—Carpet Lover (IRE) (Fayruz) (7539) **P. Green**
14 B f 3/4 Elnadim (USA)—Daily Double (FR) (Unfuwain (USA)) (3174) **P. Green**
15 B f 10/5 Myboycharlie (IRE)—Jilly Why (IRE) (Mujadil (USA))
16 B c 2/5 Myboycharlie (IRE)—Sudden Impact (IRE) (Modigliani (USA))
17 B f 26/4 Captain Rio—Suddenly (Puissance) (6983) **P. Green**

Other Owners: Mr G. Barton.

Assistant Trainer: Fiona Ford

264 MR TOM GRETTON, Inkberrow
Postal: C/o Gretton & Co Ltd, Middle Bouts Farm, Bouts Lane, Inkberrow, Worcester, WR7 4HP
Contacts: PHONE (01386) 792240 FAX (01386) 792472 MOBILE (07866) 116928
E-MAIL tomgretton@hotmail.co.uk WEBSITE www.tomgrettonracing.com

1 AL SHABABIYA (IRE), 6, b m Dubawi (IRE)—Multaka (USA) **T. R. Gretton**
2 ARMEDANDDANGEROUS (IRE), 8, b g Kris Kin (USA)—Lucky Fountain (IRE) **The Beats Working Partnership**
3 4, B br f Definite Article—Blue Romance (IRE) **Mr E. M. O'Connor**
4 CLARA PEGGOTTY, 6, b m Beat All (USA)—Clair Valley **Geoffrey Price & Edward Gretton**
5 DE WAITING GAME (IRE), 7, b g Sesaro (USA)—Tansey Yearwood (IRE) **Ms A. S. Potze**
6 5, B m Oscar (IRE)—Grey Mistral **Mr J. R. Hynes**
7 4, B g Lavirco (GER)—Jaxelle (FR) **Mr & Mrs J. Dale, Mr M. Vivian**
8 LITTLE JIMMY, 6, br g Passing Glance—Sementina (USA) **The Archers Partnership**
9 PRIZE POINT, 7, ch g Bahamian Bounty—Golden Symbol **The Archers Partnership**
10 VICPOL (ITY), 7, b g Poliglote—Vehota Vic **Mr D. E. I. Horsley**
11 ZIPIT (IRE), 8, b g Zagreb (USA)—Pollys Rock (IRE) **Mrs S. Cartridge**

Other Owners: Mr T. R. Gretton, Mrs Laura Gretton, Mr E. P. Gretton, Mr J. Hynes, Mr Robert Pope, Mr G. H. E. Price.

Assistant Trainer: Laura Gretton (07789) 754806

Jockey (NH): Dougie Costello, Felix De Giles.

265 MR PATRICK GRIFFIN, Co Dublin
Postal: Killeen House, Oldtown, Co. Dublin, Ireland
Contacts: PHONE (00353) 18433128 FAX (00353) 18433128 MOBILE (00353) 871301719
E-MAIL pggriffin@live.ie

1 BENDIGO CREEK (USA), 8, b g Gone West (USA)—Relish The Thought (IRE) **Jackeve Syndicate**
2 DICA (FR), 7, ch g Kapgarde (FR)—Easy World (FR) **Mr M. Deren**
3 DRISHOGUE LAD (IRE), 9, ch g Naheez (USA)—Astronomer Lady (IRE) **Mr J. Lawless**
4 INCA KOLA, 5, gr g Verglas (IRE)—Palm Reef (USA) **Mr J. A. Griffin**
5 4, Br f Beneficial—Kigali (USA) **B. Griffin**
6 LISBON (IRE), 5, b g Cape Cross (IRE)—Caraiyma (IRE) **Mr M. Deren**
7 MAGGIO (FR), 8, b g Trempolino (USA)—La Musardiere (FR) **Mr M. Deren**
8 TWENTYPOUNDLUCK (IRE), 8, ch g Beneficial—Guitane Lady (IRE) **Mr M. Deren**
9 ZAMBEZI TIGER (IRE), 4, b g Tiger Hill (USA)—Johannesburg Cat (USA) **Mr M. Deren**

THREE-YEAR-OLDS
10 B g Poliglote—Place d'armes (IRE) **Mr M. Deren**
11 B f Balmont (USA)—Quay Moment (IRE) **P. Griffin**
12 SORROW (FR), b g Early March—Cochinchine (IRE) **Mr M. Deren**
13 Br g Arcadio (GER)—Soviet Princess (IRE) **Mrs F. Griffin**

Other Owners: Clarricien Syndicate, D. Dillon, J. Dillon, M. D. Fitzpatrick, R. T. Griffin, L. Heron, A. Hulme, S. Quirke, P. Scholes, C. White.

Assistant Trainer: James Griffin

Jockey (NH): James Reveley, B. Cash, Ryan Mania. Conditional: C. D. Maxwell, K. M. Donoghue.

266 MR DAVID C. GRIFFITHS, Bawtry
Postal: Martin Hall, Martin Common, Bawtry, Doncaster, South Yorkshire, DN10 6DA
Contacts: PHONE (01302) 714247 MOBILE (07816) 924621
E-MAIL davidgriffiths250@hotmail.com WEBSITE www.dcgracing.co.uk

1 ARABIAN STAR (IRE), 5, b g Green Desert (USA)—Kassiopeia (IRE) **Mr C. Buckingham**
2 BYPASS, 4, br f Passing Glance—Florida Heart **Mr C. Buckingham**
3 4, Ch f Doyen (IRE)—Cos I Do (IRE)
4 CYFLYMDER (IRE), 7, b g Mujadil (USA)—Nashwan Star (IRE) **Eros Bloodstock**
5 DUBAWI PHANTOM, 6, ch g Dubawi (IRE)—Anna Amalia (IRE) **Mr C. Buckingham**
6 GORGEOUS GOBLIN (IRE), 6, b m Lujain (USA)—Tama (IRE) **K Humphries & Sons Roofing Contractors Ltd**
7 LADY LIBBY LAMB, 5, bl m Statue of Liberty (USA)—
    Lady Caroline Lamb (IRE) **K Humphries & Sons Roofing Contractors Ltd**

MR DAVID C. GRIFFITHS - Continued

8 **LAYLA'S KING**, 5, b g Dubawi (IRE)—Top Jem **Norcroft Park Stud**
9 **TAKE COVER**, 6, b g Singspiel (IRE)—Enchanted **Norcroft Park Stud**
10 **WAKE UP SIOUX (IRE)**, 4, b f Sleeping Indian—Dubious **Eros Bloodstock**
11 **YUNGABURRA (IRE)**, 9, b g Fath (USA)—Nordic Living (IRE) **Mr D. W. Noble**

THREE-YEAR-OLDS

12 **FIRSTKISSOFLOVE**, br f Byron—Jolies Dee **Mr C. Buckingham**
13 **I'VE NO MONEY (IRE)**, b g Camacho—Inonder **R P B Michaelson, J Lumb, D & S Griffiths**
14 **SYLVIA PANKHURST (IRE)**, b f Antonius Pius (USA)—Spinning Gold **Norton Common Farm Racing Ltd**

TWO-YEAR-OLDS

15 **EMILY DAVISON (IRE)**, br gr f 3/2 Moss Vale (IRE)—
                        Carabina (USA) (Dehere (USA)) (2380) **Norton Common Farm Racing Ltd**
16 Ch f 25/2 Dutch Art—Golden Asha (Danehill Dancer (IRE)) **Norcroft Park Stud**
17 B f 28/4 Captain Gerrard (IRE)—Rebel County (IRE) (Maelstrom Lake) (1904) **Mickley Stud & D. C. Griffiths**
18 **RED BIBA (IRE)**, ch f 13/4 Intense Focus (USA)—
                        Vital Laser (USA) (Seeking The Gold (USA)) (2777) **Mr C. Buckingham**
19 **RED DAKOTA (IRE)**, gr f 14/3 Clodovil (IRE)—Dom Pennion (Dansili (8729) **Mr C. Buckingham**
20 **RED FONIC (IRE)**, b c 3/2 Captain Rio—Marefonic (Zafonic (USA)) (5238) **Mr C. Buckingham**
21 **RED HOUSE**, b c 15/3 Auction House (USA)—
                        Highest Dream (IRE) (Highest Honor (FR)) (2380) **Mr C. Buckingham**
22 **RED RECRUITER**, ch c 3/5 Captain Gerrard (IRE)—
                        Madame Jones (IRE) (Lycius (USA)) (5555) **Mr C. Buckingham**
23 **RED WIFEY (IRE)**, b f 27/3 High Chaparral (IRE)—
                        Raspberry Beret (IRE) (Danehill Dancer (IRE)) (7539) **Mr C. Buckingham**
24 **THISONESMINE (IRE)**, ch c 27/4 Haatef (USA)—
                        Jersey Lillie (IRE) (Hector Protector (USA)) (1983) **Norton Common Farm Racing Ltd**

Other Owners: Mr D. Clark, Mr D. Griffiths, Mrs S. Griffiths, Mr A. J. Hollis, Mr D. M. Hollis, Mrs Janet Lumb, Mr R. P B. Michaelson, Mrs S. Noble, Mr S. Young.

Assistant Trainer: Mrs S. E. Griffiths

Apprentice: Alistair Rawlinson.

267

MR SIMON GRIFFITHS, Easingwold
Postal: **Hazel Hill Farm, Blackwoods, Easingwold, York, North Yorkshire, YO61 3ER**
Contacts: **PHONE (01347) 823589 MOBILE (07967) 039208**
E-MAIL elizabeth.grant@grantsvets.co.uk

1 **CHARLES PARNELL (IRE)**, 10, b g Elnadim (USA)—Titania **Mr S. P. Griffiths**
2 **PHOENIX JOY**, 5, b m Presidium—Miss Ceylon **Mr S. P. Griffiths**
3 **TENDER CARE**, 5, b g Gentleman's Deal (IRE)—Intavac Girl **Mr S. P. Griffiths**

Assistant Trainer: Elizabeth Grant

268

MR SIRRELL GRIFFITHS, Carmarthen
Postal: **Rwyth Farm, Nantgaredig, Carmarthen, Dyfed, SA32 7LG**
Contacts: **PHONE (01267) 290321/290120**

1 **HARRY WESTON**, 8, b g Sir Harry Lewis (USA)—Fractious **S. G. Griffiths**
2 **MISTY SAILS**, 5, b m Overbury (IRE)—Tirikumba **S. G. Griffiths**

Assistant Trainer: Martyn Roger Griffiths

269

MRS DIANA GRISSELL, Brightling
Postal: **Brightling Park, Robertsbridge, East Sussex, TN32 5HH**
Contacts: **PHONE (01424) 838241 MOBILE (07950) 312610**
E-MAIL digrissell@aol.com WEBSITE www.grissellracing.co.uk

1 **ARBEO (IRE)**, 7, b g Brian Boru—Don't Waste It (IRE) **Nigel & Barbara Collison**

MRS DIANA GRISSELL - Continued

2 **BLUE BEAR (IRE)**, 4, b g Blueprint (IRE)—In For It (IRE) **Ms J. A. Lambert**
3 **BOY OF BORU (IRE)**, 6, b g Brian Boru—Don't Waste It (IRE) **The Wasteinit Partnership**
4 **DUNLOUGHIN (IRE)**, 7, ch g Definite Article—Mother Imelda (IRE) **Mrs P. A. Wilkins**
5 **OSCAR BABY (IRE)**, 7, b m Oscar (IRE)—Snowbaby (IRE) **Mr R. E. Halley**
6 **QUARTZ DU MONTCEAU (FR)**, 9, b g Robin des Champs (FR)—Emeraude (FR) **Mr E. S. Hicks**
7 **ROPARTA AVENUE**, 6, b g Nomadic Way (USA)—Miss Fizz **Mrs D. M. Grissell**
8 **SHARMON**, 10, b g Terimon—Sayshar **R. Thomson**
9 **SOLE AGENT (IRE)**, 11, b g Trans Island—Seattle Siren (USA) **Mrs S. M. Russell**

Other Owners: Mr N. Collison, Mrs B. Collison, Mr M. Cutler.

Jockey (NH): Marc Goldstein, Alex Merriam, Sam Thomas.

---

270 MR JOHN BRYAN GROUCOTT, Much Wenlock
Postal: **11 Bourton Cottages, Much Wenlock, Shropshire, TF13 6QF**
Contacts: **PHONE** (01746) 785603 **FAX** (01746) 785603 **MOBILE** (07866) 480830
E-MAIL lisajmwillis@aol.com

1 **ONE MORE DINAR**, 10, b g Kayf Tara—One More Dime (IRE) **Mrs A. V. Winwood**
2 **PRET A THOU (FR)**, 10, ch g Funny Baby (FR)—Va Thou Line (FR) **C. J. Tipton**
3 **WAYWOOD PRINCESS**, 8, b m Sir Harry Lewis (USA)—First Bee **Mr P Price & Mr P Williams**

Other Owners: Mr P. Price, P. J. D. Williams.

---

271 MR BRIAN GUBBY, Bagshot
Postal: **Dukes Wood, Bracknell Road, Bagshot, Surrey, GU19 5HX**
Contacts: **OFFICE** (01276) 850513 **FAX** (01276) 479859 **MOBILE** (07768) 867368

1 **AL AQABAH (IRE)**, 8, ch m Redback—Snow Eagle (IRE) **B. Gubby**
2 **AURENS (IRE)**, 4, b g One Cool Cat (USA)—Al Aqabah (IRE) **B. Gubby**
3 **KINGLAMI**, 4, b c Kingsalsa (USA)—Red Japonica **B. Gubby**

THREE-YEAR-OLDS
4 **PAL OF THE CAT**, ch g Choisir (AUS)—Evenstorm (USA) **B. Gubby**

Assistant Trainer: Larry Wilkins

---

272 MR RAE GUEST, Newmarket
Postal: **Chestnut Tree Stables, Hamilton Road, Newmarket, Suffolk, CB8 ONY**
Contacts: **PHONE** (01638) 661508 **FAX** (01638) 667317 **MOBILE** (07711) 301095
E-MAIL raeguest@raeguest.com **WEBSITE** www.raeguest.com

1 **ALICE ROSE (IRE)**, 4, ch f Manduro (GER)—Bold Assumption **O. T. Lury**
2 **BE MY ROCK**, 4, b f Rock of Gibraltar (IRE)—Supa Sal **Willis, Jennings & Carter**
3 **ED DE GAS**, 4, b g Peintre Celebre (USA)—Sambala (IRE) **Mr R. A. Pegum & Dr C. G. Lawler**
4 **EVER FORTUNE (USA)**, 4, ch g El Corredor (USA)—Beyond Price (USA) **Mr Fung Lok Li**
5 **FIRST CLASS**, 5, b g Oasis Dream—Break Point **Mr B. Cooper & Mrs E. Reffo**
6 **FLYNN'S BOY**, 5, ch g Tobougg (IRE)—Bukhoor (IRE) **Mr C. J. Murfitt**
7 **HEADLINE NEWS (IRE)**, 4, ch f Peintre Celebre (USA)—Donnelly's Hollow (IRE) **The Chestnuts**
8 **KICKINGTHELILLY**, 4, ch f Byron—Teller (ARG) **T. Hailstone, T. Hirschfeld, S. Piper, D. Scott**
9 **MACCHIARA**, 4, ch f Medicean—Castaway Queen (IRE) **Mrs Linda Fish**
10 **MIGHTY FINN**, 4, b g Shamardal (USA)—Daniella **Mr B. Cooper & Mrs E. Reffo**
11 **MILIIKA**, 4, b f Green Desert (USA)—Miss Anabaa **Bradmill Ltd**
12 **MILLION FACES**, 4, ch f Exceed And Excel (AUS)—Millyant **Mr Chris J. Mills**
13 **MINALISA**, 4, b f Oasis Dream—Mina **Mr Chris J. Mills**
14 **MINTY FOX**, 4, gr f Dalakhani (IRE)—Quantum (IRE) **The Hightailers**
15 **MIRZA**, 6, b g Oasis Dream—Millyant **Mr Chris J. Mills**
16 **MY COLLEEN (USA)**, 4, ch f Discreet Cat (USA)—Navasha (USA) **E. P. Duggan**
17 **POISSON D'OR**, 4, b f Cape Cross (IRE)—Lille Hammer **The Family Fish**
18 **PRINCESS OF ORANGE**, 4, ch f Dutch Art—Radiate **Mr Colin Joseph**

MR RAE GUEST - Continued

THREE-YEAR-OLDS

19 BACK ON THE TRAIL, b g Singspiel (IRE)—Boleyna (USA) **Mrs P. Smith**
20 CALM ATTITUDE (IRE), ch f Dutch Art—Turban Heights (IRE) **The Calm Again Syndicate**
21 CAMILLA DE ROSSI, b f Oratorio (IRE)—Supa Sal **Willis, Davies & Carter**
22 FLAMINGO BEAT, ch g Beat Hollow—Flamingo Flower (USA) **The Storm Again Syndicate**
23 GODS GIFT (IRE), ch c Dalakhani (IRE)—Guilia **The Hornets**
24 HESTER STREET, b f Kyllachy—Fascination Street (IRE) **R. Guest**
25 HOW'S LIFE, b f Layman (USA)—Get The Ring (FR) **Mr J. H. Metzger**
26 IT'S TIME TO DANCE (FR), b f Country Reel (USA)—Just Dance Me (FR) **Mr J. H. Metzger**
27 LET'S RHUMBA, b f Medicean—Rhumba Rage (USA) **The Calm Again Syndicate**
28 NINGBO EXPRESS (IRE), b f Jeremy (USA)—Sunlit Skies **Maze Rattan Ltd & R. Guest**
29 ROSIE FUTURE (IRE), b f Azamour (IRE)—Auspicious **E. P. Duggan**
30 ROSIE REBEL, ch f Cockney Rebel (IRE)—Meandering Rose (USA) **P. W. Saunders, R. Guest & O. Lury**
31 SECRET OF SUCCESS, ch f Johannesburg (USA)—Live Life (FR) **Mr J. H. Metzger**
32 TUMBLEWEED FINALE, ch f Tumbleweed Ridge—Poyle Kiera **Seven To One Partnership**
33 YOUTHINKYOU'REBUSY, b f Johannesburg (USA)—Big Day Today (FR) **Mr J. H. Metzger**

TWO-YEAR-OLDS

34 ARCHDUCHESS, b f 25/2 Archipenko (USA)—Eminencia (Sadler's Wells (USA)) **Miss K. Rausing**
35 CAPE FACTOR (IRE), b f 28/3 Oratorio (IRE)—Crossanza (IRE) (Cape Cross (IRE)) (7936) **Derek Willis**
36 CHESS VALLEY, b f 10/3 Shamardal (USA)—
    Grecian Air (FR) (King's Best (USA)) (28000) **The Boot Sarratt Partnership**
37 DANCE FOR YOU (FR), b f 29/1 Falco (USA)—Just Dance Me (FR) (Linamix (FR)) **Mr J. H. Metzger**
38 Ch f 30/3 Compton Place—Dayrose (Daylami (IRE)) (9500) **Sakal, Davies & Jennings**
39 B f 19/1 High Chaparral (IRE)—Distant Dreamer (USA) (Rahy (USA)) **Mrs Paula Smith & Mr Rae Guest**
40 Br f 11/4 Aqlaam—Fen Guest (Woodborough (USA)) (44000) **Mr C. J. Murfitt**
41 B c 15/3 Oratorio (IRE)—Guilia (Galileo (IRE)) **The Hornets**
42 Gr c 2/4 Virtual—Live Life (FR) (Linamix (FR)) **Mr J. H. Metzger**
43 B f 6/4 Tamayuz—Lolla's Spirit (IRE) (Montjeu (IRE)) (9000)
44 Ch g 3/4 Halling (USA)—Magdalene (Act One) **Mrs Paula Smith**
45 MISS BUCKSHOT (IRE), b f 6/3 Tamayuz—Miss Bellbird (IRE) (Danehill (USA)) (28571) **Mr Tony Hirschfeld**
46 POWER OF GOOD NEWS (FR), b f 1/4 Kyllachy—Big Day Today (FR) (Linamix (FR)) **Mr J. H. Metzger**
47 SOUND OF LIFE (IRE), b f 10/4 Cape Cross (IRE)—
    Stylist (IRE) (Sadler's Wells (USA)) (15000) **The Purple and Yellow Partnership**
48 B f 22/2 Dubawi (IRE)—Still Small Voice (Polish Precedent (USA)) **Mrs Melba Bryce**
49 STROLL ON (IRE), ch f 14/2 Exceed And Excel (AUS)—
    Violet (IRE) (Mukaddamah (USA)) (45000) **Mr Trevor Benton**
50 TOOGOODTOBEGOOD (FR), gr c 3/5 Virtual—Get The Ring (FR) (Linamix (FR)) **Mr J. H. Metzger**
51 B f 15/4 High Chaparral (IRE)—Twyla (AUS) (Danehill (USA)) (150000) **Mr John Cammileri**

Other Owners: Mr E. P. Duggan, Mr B. J. Flahive, Mr John Fullick, Mr R. T. Goodes, Mr Rae Guest, Mr Tim Hailstone, Mr Tony Hirschfeld, Mrs Marsha Holliman, Mr O. T. Lury, Mr C. J. Mills, Mr S. J. Piper, Mr D. G. Raffel, Mr P. W. Saunders, Mr D. I. Scott, Mrs Paula Smith, Mr Barry Stewart, Mrs H. M. A. Worboys, Mr J. R. Worboys, Mrs Alison Yorke.

Assistant Trainer: Nicholas McKee **Head Lad:** Steve Lodge

Jockey (flat): Chris Catlin.

---

273 MR RICHARD GUEST, Stainforth

Postal: **Future Racing (Notts) Limited, Haggswood Racing Stables, Stainforth, Doncaster, South Yorkshire, DN7 5PS**
Contacts: **PHONE** (07760) 755741 **MOBILE** (07760) 755742
E-MAIL future-racing@hotmail.com

1 AMBITIOUS ICARUS, 4, b g Striking Ambition—Nesting Box **We Know Partnership & Partner**
2 BARNET FAIR, 5, br g Iceman—Pavement Gates **Mr Donald Wheatley**
3 BE MY DEPUTY (IRE), 8, b g Oscar (IRE)—Have A Myth **Malcolm Penney & Miss Alison Ibbotson**
4 CAPTAIN SCOOBY, 7, b g Captain Rio—Scooby Dooby Do **Res Dev**
5 CATAWOLLOW, 6, b m Beat Hollow—Catalonia (IRE) **Miss C. Fordham**
6 DICKIE LE DAVOIR, 9, b g Kyllachy—Downeaster Alexa (USA) **Future Racing (Notts) Limited**
7 DIMASHQ, 11, b m Mtoto—Agwaas (IRE) **Mr A. Bell**
8 GEORGE FENTON, 4, ch g Piccolo—Mashmoum **Maze Rattan Limited**
9 GEORGEBERNARDSHAW (IRE), 8, b g Danehill Dancer (IRE)—Khamseh **Future Racing (Notts) Limited**
10 JOHNNY CAVAGIN, 4, b g Superior Premium—Beyond The Rainbow **Mr A. Bell**

MR RICHARD GUEST - Continued

11 **KAMES PARK (IRE)**, 11, b g Desert Sun—Persian Sally (IRE) **Future Racing (Notts) Limited**
12 **LORD BUFFHEAD**, 4, br g Iceman—Royal Pardon **Future Racing (Notts) Limited**
13 **MISERERE MEI (IRE)**, 4, b f Moss Vale (IRE)—Flying Clouds **Future Racing (Notts) Limited**
14 **NOLECCE**, 6, ch g Reset (AUS)—Ghassanah **Future Racing (Notts) Limited**
15 **NURSE DOMINATRIX (IRE)**, 4, br f Whipper (USA)—Medica Boba **Future Racing (Notts) Limited**
16 **OUTLAW TORN (IRE)**, 4, ch g Iffraaj—Touch And Love (IRE) **Mr James S. Kennerley**
17 **POBS TROPHY**, 6, b g Umistim—Admonish **Miss C. Fordham**
18 **QUALITY ART (USA)**, 5, ch g Elusive Quality (USA)—Katherine Seymour **Maze Rattan Limited**
19 **RYEDALE DANCER (IRE)**, 5, ch m Refuse To Bend (IRE)—Saik (USA) **Mr J. W. Wilkinson**
20 **RYLEE MOOCH**, 5, gr g Choisir (AUS)—Negligee **Katie Hughes, Sheila White, Julie Mccarlie**
21 **SLEEPY LUCY**, 4, b f Multiplex—Millie The Filly **Future Racing (Notts) Limited**
22 **TED'S BROTHER (IRE)**, 5, b g Fath (USA)—Estertide (IRE) **Maze Rattan Limited**
23 **THERE'S NO RULES**, 4, br g Authorized (IRE)—Excellent **Mrs Alison Guest**
24 **VELVET VIC (IRE)**, 7, b g Old Vic—Elleena Rose (IRE) **Res Dev**

THREE-YEAR-OLDS

25 **CHARLEMAGNE DIVA**, b f Holy Roman Emperor (IRE)—Opera Ridge (FR) **Mr Chris Penney**
26 **DUCHESS OF DREAMS**, br f Royal Applause—Wood Chorus **Dale & Katie Partnership**
27 **HAZZA THE JAZZA**, br g Jeremy (USA)—Zagaleta **Maze Rattan Limited**
28 **MODERN LADY**, b f Bertolini (USA)—Lady Natilda **Maze Rattan Limited**
29 **NORS THE PANIC**, ch g Bahamian Bounty—Creoso Bach **Future Racing (Notts) Limited**
30 **POLAR FOREST**, br g Kyllachy—Woodbeck **Maze Rattan Limited**
31 **PRECISION STRIKE**, b g Multiplex—Dockside Strike **Future Racing (Notts) Limited**
32 Gr f Aussie Rules (USA)—River Grand (IRE) **Future Racing (Notts) Limited**

TWO-YEAR-OLDS

33 B f 5/3 Sleeping Indian—Aimee's Delight (Robellino (USA))
34 Ch g 22/3 Captain Rio—Annals (Lujain (USA)) (4761)
35 B f 1/4 Byron—Ballet Princess (Muhtarram (USA))
36 Ch g 24/3 Camacho—Night Eyes (IRE) (Night Shift (USA)) (1190)
37 Ch f 5/5 Papal Bull—Skerries (IRE) (Dr Fong (USA)) (4761) **Miss C. Fordham**
38 Ch g 19/3 Sleeping Indian—St Edith (IRE) (Desert King (IRE)) (5238)
39 B f 27/4 Multiplex—Wonderful Island (GER) (Turtle Island (IRE)) (761)

Other Owners: Mr Anthony Bullock-Smith, Future Racing (Notts) Limited, Mrs Alison Guest, Miss Katie Hughes, Mr J. Paul Morris, Mr Malcolm Penney, Mr D. I. Perry, Mr M. Thompson, Mr Dale White, Mr Mick White, Mrs S. White.

Assistant Trainer: Mr Ronald Thompson

Jockey (flat): Robbie Fitzpatrick. **Apprentice:** Lisa Todd. **Amateur:** Mrs A. Guest.

 MISS POLLY GUNDRY, Ottery St Mary
Postal: Holcombe Brook, Holcombe Lane, Ottery St. Mary, Devon, EX11 1PH
Contacts: PHONE (01404) 811181 MOBILE (07932) 780621
E-MAIL polly.gundry@live.co.uk

1 **DALRYMPLE (IRE)**, 7, ch g Daylami (IRE)—Dallaah **G. N. Carstairs**
2 **DENTON (NZ)**, 10, b g Montjeu (IRE)—Melora (NZ) **G. N. Carstairs**
3 **GLADSTONE (IRE)**, 5, b g Dansili—Rockerlong **Miss P. Gundry**
4 5, B g Tikkanen (USA)—Maritsa-B **Miss P. Gundry**
5 **MR GARDNER (IRE)**, 10, b g Deploy—Lady Padivor (IRE) **Mr & Mrs R. G. Kelvin Hughes**
6 **SAMBA NIGHT (IRE)**, 4, b g Dark Angel (IRE)—Brazilia **G. N. Carstairs**
7 **TEENAGE KICKS (IRE)**, 8, ch g Giant's Causeway (USA)—Ruissec (USA) **G. N. Carstairs**

Other Owners: R. G. Kelvin-Hughes, Mrs E. A. Kelvin-Hughes.

Assistant Trainer: Edward Walker

Jockey (NH): Hadden Frost, Tom O'Brien. **Amateur:** Mr Ed Barrett, Mr Robbie Henderson.

275 MR WILLIAM HAGGAS, Newmarket

Postal: **Somerville Lodge, Fordham Road, Newmarket, Suffolk, CB8 7AA**
Contacts: PHONE (01638) 667013 FAX (01638) 660534 MOBILE (07860) 282281
E-MAIL william@somerville-lodge.co.uk

1 ARSAADI (IRE), 4, b f Dubawi (IRE)—Arsad (IRE) **Sultan Ali & Saeed Misleh**
2 CAPE CLASSIC (IRE), 5, b h Cape Cross (IRE)—Politesse (USA) **Mr B. Kantor**
3 DANCHAI, 4, gr g Authorized (IRE)—Scarlet Empire (IRE) **Saleh Al Homaizi & Imad Al Sagar**
4 FAST OR FREE, 4, ch g Notnowcato—Ewenny **Mr & Mrs Ian Beard**
5 FURY, 5, gr g Invincible Spirit (IRE)—Courting **Cheveley Park Stud Limited**
6 GRAPHIC (IRE), 4, ch c Excellent Art—Follow My Lead **The Royal Ascot Racing Club**
7 GUARANTEE, 4, b c Authorized (IRE)—Zuleika Dobson **Highclere Thoroughbred Racing**
8 HARRIS TWEED, 6, b g Hernando (FR)—Frog **Mr B. Haggas**
9 HEERAAT (IRE), 4, b c Dark Angel (IRE)—Thawrah (IRE) **Hamdan Al Maktoum**
10 MUKHADRAM, 4, b c Shamardal (USA)—Magic Tree (UAE) **Hamdan Al Maktoum**
11 NINE REALMS, 4, b c Green Desert (USA)—Bourbonella **Mr & Mrs D. Hearson**
12 SENTARIL, 4, b f Danehill Dancer (IRE)—Superstar Leo (IRE) **Lael Stable**
13 STENCIVE, 4, b c Dansili—Madeira Mist (IRE) **B. Kantor & M. Jooste**
14 SUN CENTRAL (IRE), 4, ch c Galileo (IRE)—Bordighera (USA) **Lael Stable**
15 VOW, 4, b f Motivator—Frog **Highclere Thoroughbred Racing - Pocahontas**
16 WELL PAINTED (IRE), 4, ch g Excellent Art—Aoife (IRE) **Options O Syndicate**
17 WESTWITHTHENIGHT (IRE), 4, b f Cape Cross (IRE)—Hidden Hope **A. E. Oppenheimer**

THREE-YEAR-OLDS

18 AKEED DUBAWI, b c Dubawi (IRE)—Anosti **J. Abdullah**
19 ANAMAR, b g Raven's Pass (USA)—Loulwa (IRE) **Saleh Al Homaizi & Imad Al Sagar**
20 ANEEDH, b g Lucky Story (USA)—Seed Al Maha (USA) **Mohammed Jaber**
21 ARAQELLA (IRE), b f Oasis Dream—Bourbonella **Mr & Mrs D. Hearson**
22 ASSEMBLY, ch c Kyllachy—Constitute (USA) **Highclere Thoroughbred Racing - Coventry**
23 AZIKI (IRE), ch c Duke of Marmalade (IRE)—Mubkera (IRE) **Saleh Al Homaizi & Imad Al Sagar**
24 BATTALION (IRE), b c Authorized (IRE)—Zigarra **Sheikh Juma Al Dalmook Maktoum**
25 BLOC, ch g Medicean—Macleya (GER) **Mr B. Haggas**
26 BOTTEEN (IRE), b g Invincible Spirit (IRE)—Dundel (IRE) **Sheikh Ahmed Al Maktoum**
27 CARA GINA, b f Bahamian Bounty—Princess Georgina **Mrs D. J. James**
28 CHOCOLATE BLOCK (IRE), br f Singspiel (IRE)—Pingus **Wood Hall Stud Limited**
29 CROSS MY HEART, b f Sakhee's Secret—Sacre Coeur **Hot To Trot Partnership**
30 CRY PEARL (USA), b f Street Cry (USA)—Onda Nova **Pearl Bloodstock Limited**
31 DANAT AL ATHEER, ch f Shamardal (USA)—Height of Vanity (IRE) **J. Abdullah**
32 DARE TO ACHIEVE, b c Galileo (IRE)—Mussoorie (FR) **B. Kantor & M. Jooste**
33 EKHTIZAAL (IRE), ch g Haafet (USA)—Bezant (IRE) **Hamdan Al Maktoum**
34 EMPRESS ADELAIDE, ch f Pivotal—Emperice (USA) **Cheveley Park Stud Limited**
35 ENFIJAAR (IRE), b f Invincible Spirit (IRE)—Harayir (USA) **Hamdan Al Maktoum**
36 ENVIOUS STAR, b f Shirocco (GER)—Star Express **Dr A. Ridha**
37 EPIC BATTLE (IRE), b c Acclamation—Wrong Key (IRE) **Saleh Al Homaizi & Imad Al Sagar**
38 ESTIQAAMA (USA), b f Nayef (USA)—Ethaara **Hamdan Al Maktoum**
39 FEHAYDI, b c Nayef (USA)—Red Camellia **Sheikh Ahmed Al Maktoum**
40 FERSAH (USA), b f Dynaformer (USA)—Jaleela (USA) **Hamdan Al Maktoum**
41 FLOATING ALONG (IRE), b f Oasis Dream—Politesse (USA) **Lael Stable**
42 GALEB WARRIOR, b c Duke of Marmalade (IRE)—Katrina (IRE) **Mr A. G. Bloom**
43 GALLENA, b f Invincible Spirit (IRE)—Emily Blake (IRE) **Mr & Mrs R. Scott**
44 GARDEN ROW (IRE), b gr f Invincible Spirit (IRE)—Gladstone Street (IRE) **Cheveley Park Stud Limited**
45 HAIRY ROCKET, b f Pivotal—Asaawir **Rockcliffe Stud**
46 HEROINE REQUIRED (FR), ch f Muhtathir—Tiger Mist (IRE) **M S Bloodstock Ltd**
47 I SAY (IRE), b f Oratorio (IRE)—Lisieux Orchid (IRE) **R. C. Tooth**
48 LADY NOUF, b f Teofilo (IRE)—Majestic Sakeena (IRE) **Saleh Al Homaizi & Imad Al Sagar**
49 LEITRIM PASS (USA), ch c Raven's Pass (USA)—Santolina (USA) **Gallagher Equine Ltd**
50 MARTIAN (IRE), b c Duke of Marmalade (IRE)—Starship (IRE) **Scott/Magnier/Piggott**
51 MATROOH (USA), b f Distorted Humor (USA)—Rockcide (USA) **Hamdan Al Maktoum**
52 MUNDAHESH (IRE), ch g Tamayuz—Kawn **Hamdan Al Maktoum**
53 MUTHAFAR (IRE), b c Tamayuz—Etizaaz (USA) **Hamdan Al Maktoum**
54 MUTHMIR (IRE), b c Invincible Spirit (IRE)—Fairy of The Night (IRE) **Hamdan Al Maktoum**
55 NOBLE DEED, ch g Kyllachy—Noble One **Cheveley Park Stud Limited**
56 ODOOJ (IRE), b g Pivotal—Shabiba (USA) **Hamdan Al Maktoum**
57 OUR OBSESSION (IRE), ch f Shamardal (USA)—Hidden Hope **A. E. Oppenheimer**
58 PALKIN, b f Singspiel (IRE)—Winds of Time (IRE) **Mr & Mrs R. Scott**

MR WILLIAM HAGGAS - Continued

59 **PARIS ROSE**, b f Cape Cross (IRE)—Samira Gold (FR) **J. Abdullah**
60 **PEMBROKE (IRE)**, b c Excellent Art—Mrs Marsh **Highclere Thoroughbred Racing -Wavertree**
61 **QUEENSBERRY RULES (IRE)**, b c Teofilo (IRE)—Fantastic Spring (USA) **Mr Liam Sheridan**
62 **RESPONSE**, ch c New Approach (IRE)—Spotlight **Highclere Thoroughbred Racing - Dalmeny**
63 **RHOMBUS (IRE)**, b g Authorized (IRE)—Mathool (IRE) **Sheikh Rashid Dalmook Al Maktoum**
64 **ROCK CHOIR**, b f Pivotal—Choir Mistress **Cheveley Park Stud Limited**
65 **ROSDHU QUEEN (IRE)**, b f Invincible Spirit (IRE)—Green Minstrel (FR) **Clipper Group Holdings Ltd**
66 **SACRED SQUARE (GER)**, ch c Peintre Celebre (USA)—Square The Circle **Mr A. G. Bloom**
67 **SKY GARDEN**, b f Acclamation—Superstar Leo (IRE) **Lael Stable**
68 **SULTANAH HEYAM**, br f Manduro (GER)—Royal Secrets (IRE) **Mohammed Jaber**
69 **TANAWAR (IRE)**, b g Elusive City (USA)—Parakopi (IRE) **Sheikh Ahmed Al Maktoum**
70 **TRIPLE CHOCOLATE**, b c Danehill Dancer (IRE)—Enticing (IRE) **Lael Stable**
71 **TWEED**, b f Sakhee (USA)—Frog **Mr B. Haggas**
72 **VALTINA (IRE)**, b f Teofilo (IRE)—Vassiana (FR) **M. J. & L. A. Taylor**
73 **VEERAYA**, b g Rail Link—Follow Flanders **Mr Reyaz Farook**
74 **YARN**, ch f Dutch Art—Spinneret **R. C. Tooth**
75 **ZUHD (IRE)**, b g Cape Cross (IRE)—Street Star (USA) **Hamdan Al Maktoum**

TWO-YEAR-OLDS

76 B c 27/2 Acclamation—Adorn (Kyllachy) (90000) **Sheikh Ahmed Al Maktoum**
77 **ALSHADHIA (IRE)**, b f 10/3 Marju (IRE)—Wijdan (USA) (Mr Prospector (USA)) **Hamdan Al Maktoum**
78 B f 7/3 Royal Applause—Amalie (IRE) (Fasliyev (USA)) (70000) **Sheikh Juma Al Dalmook Maktoum**
79 B f 11/2 Invincible Spirit (IRE)—Applauded (IRE) (Royal Applause) (180000) **St Albans Bloodstock Ltd**
80 Ch c 13/2 Teofilo (IRE)—Arctic Char (Polar Falcon (USA)) (85000) **Mr A. G. Bloom**
81 B c 11/2 Authorized (IRE)—Audaz (Oasis Dream) (75000) **Abdulla Al Mansoori**
82 B f 26/2 Cape Cross (IRE)—Avila (Ajdal (USA)) (85000) **Saeed Manana**
83 Ch f 25/4 Galileo (IRE)—Beauty Bright (IRE) (Danehill (USA)) (100000) **Mrs L. Sheridan**
84 **BEST TAMAYUZ**, ch c 5/3 Tamayuz—Pink Ivory (Sakhee (USA)) **J. Abdullah**
85 **BILIMBI (IRE)**, b c 19/3 Duke of Marmalade (IRE)—Starship (IRE) (Galileo (IRE)) **Scott/Magnier/Piggott**
86 B c 28/2 Dutch Art—Blithe (Pivotal) (120000) **Sheikh Ahmed Al Maktoum**
87 B c 30/5 New Approach (IRE)—Broken Peace (USA) (Devil's Bag (USA)) (60000) **Sultan Ali**
88 B f 11/3 Shamardal (USA)—Central Force (Pivotal) (50000) **Mohammed Jaber**
89 B c 19/1 Authorized (IRE)—Cross Current (Sakhee (USA)) (38000) **Sheikh Juma Al Dalmook Maktoum**
90 C c 21/2 Exceed And Excel (AUS)—Crystal Moments (Haafhd) (52000) **Mohammed Jaber**
91 **DANEHILL REVIVAL**, b f 7/3 Pivotal—Danehill Destiny (Danehill Dancer (USA)) **Cheveley Park Stud Limited**
92 Br c 18/3 Pastoral Pursuits—Dansa Queen (Dansili) (85000) **Sheikh Ahmed Al Maktoum**
93 B c 16/4 Sea The Stars (IRE)—Dash To The Top (Montjeu (IRE)) (190000) **Mr A. G. Bloom**
94 B c 24/2 Invincible Spirit (IRE)—
          Dream Valley (IRE) (Sadler's Wells (USA)) (38000) **Roberts/Green/Savidge/Whittal-Williams**
95 Ch f 16/2 Dalakhani (IRE)—Dress Uniform (USA) (Red Ransom (USA)) (55000) **Mr B. Haggas**
96 **DUTCH DAWN**, b f 20/4 Dutch Art—Shebaan (Compton Place) **Cheveley Park Stud Limited**
97 **EHTIFAAL (IRE)**, b c 29/1 Teofilo (IRE)—Kashoof (Green Desert (USA)) **Hamdan Al Maktoum**
98 B c 5/4 Oasis Dream—Enticing (IRE) (Pivotal) **Lael Stable**
99 **ERTIJAAL (IRE)**, b c 11/3 Oasis Dream—Shabiba (USA) (Seeking The Gold (USA)) **Hamdan Al Maktoum**
100 **ETAAB (USA)**, b f 1/1 Street Cry (IRE)—Ethaara (Green Desert (USA)) **Hamdan Al Maktoum**
101 **EXAMINER (IRE)**, ch c 30/4 Excellent Art—Therry Girl (Lahib (USA)) (25000) **Mr & Mrs Ian Beard**
102 **FELWAH**, ch f 20/2 Aqlaam—Efisio's Star (Efisio) **Hamdan Al Maktoum**
103 **GHANY (IRE)**, b f 28/4 Lawman (FR)—Broken Spectre (Rainbow Quest (USA)) **Hamdan Al Maktoum**
104 **GOLD APPROACH**, ch f 18/3 New Approach (IRE)—Samira Gold (FR) (Gold Away (IRE)) **J. Abdullah**
105 B f 2/3 Dubawi (IRE)—Grasshoppergreen (IRE) (Barathea (IRE)) (85000) **R. C. Tooth**
106 **KALASKADESEMILLEY**, b c 11/4 Mybycharlie (IRE)—
          Congressional (IRE) (Grand Lodge (USA)) (36000) **Sheikh Hamdan Bin Maktoum Al Maktoum**
107 **KHAAWY (USA)**, b f 1/1 Arch (USA)—Jaleela (USA) (Kingmambo (USA)) **Hamdan Al Maktoum**
108 Ch c 11/3 Intikhab (USA)—Klang (IRE) (Night Shift (USA)) (52000) **Sheikh Ahmed Al Maktoum**
109 **LADY IN BLUE (IRE)**, ch f 4/2 Iffraaj—Compton Girl (Compton Place) (20000) **The Duchess Syndicate**
110 **LILLY JUNIOR**, b f 15/2 Cape Cross (IRE)—Sweet Lilly (Tobougg (IRE)) **J. Abdullah**
111 B f 20/3 Lawman (FR)—Lisieux Orchid (IRE) (Sadler's Wells (USA)) (30000) **Sultan Ali**
112 B f 16/2 Shamardal (USA)—Loulwa (IRE) (Montjeu (IRE)) **Saleh Al Homaizi & Imad Al Sagar**
113 **LYRA**, b f 23/2 Mybycharlie (IRE)—
          Park Melody (IRE) (Refuse To Bend (IRE)) (70000) **Highclere Thoroughbred Racing - Conquest**
114 B c 23/2 Invincible Spirit (IRE)—Majestic Sakeena (IRE) (King's Best (USA)) **Saleh Al Homaizi & Imad Al Sagar**
115 B c 21/4 Camacho—Mama Angela (IRE) (Titus Livius (FR)) (22857) **Options O Syndicate**
116 **MANGE ALL**, b g 5/4 Zamindar (USA)—Blancmange (Montjeu (IRE)) **Mr B. Haggas**
117 **MEETING WATERS**, ch f 20/3 Aqlaam—Paradise Isle (Bahamian Bounty) (45000) **Mr L. Sheridan**
118 **MITRAAD (IRE)**, ch c 26/2 Aqlaam—Badweia (USA) (Kingmambo (USA)) **Hamdan Al Maktoum**

MR WILLIAM HAGGAS - Continued

119 Ch f 17/3 Pivotal—Moon Dazzle (USA) (Kingmambo (USA)) (110000) **Mr B. Kantor**
120 **MR MCLAREN**, b c 12/3 Royal Applause—
　　　　Mamma Morton (IRE) (Elnadim (USA)) (50000) **Sheikh Hamdan Bin Maktoum Al Maktoum**
121 **MUTAKAYYEF**, ch c 5/5 Sea The Stars (IRE)—Infallible (Pivotal) (260000) **Hamdan Al Maktoum**
122 **NOTEBOOK**, b c 23/3 Invincible Spirit (IRE)—
　　　　Love Everlasting (Pursuit of Love) (110000) **Highclere Thoroughbred Racing - Brunel**
123 **PERMITTED**, b f 13/4 Authorized (IRE)—Discerning (Darshaan) (8000) **Cheveley Park Stud Limited**
124 Ch f 11/3 Dutch Art—Petong's Pet (Petong) (104761) **Saleh Al Homaizi & Imad Al Sagar**
125 **PRINCESS ROSE**, b f 24/1 Royal Applause—Mystical Spirit (IRE) (Xaar) (30476) **Ian & Christine Beard**
126 **QAMAAT**, b f 24/4 Aqlaam—Martha (IRE) (Alhaarth (IRE)) **Hamdan Al Maktoum**
127 **QUEEN OF ICE**, b f 25/4 Selkirk (USA)—Ice Palace (Polar Falcon (USA)) **Cheveley Park Stud Limited**
128 **REDKIRK**, ch c 6/4 Notnowcato—Flag (Selkirk (USA)) (22000) **Scotney/Symonds/Fisher Partnership**
129 **RESOLUTE**, b c 19/2 Pivotal—Coy (IRE) (Danehill (USA)) (50000) **Cheveley Park Stud Limited**
130 B c 26/3 Royal Applause—Rice Mother (IRE) (Indian Ridge) (103174) **Sheikh Juma Al Dalmook Maktoum**
131 **ROSA BUD**, b f 21/3 Cape Cross (IRE)—Miss Rochester (IRE) (Montjeu (IRE)) **Cheveley Park Stud Limited**
132 B f 19/2 Champs Elysees—Sailing Days (Kris) (2000) **Mrs C. A. Cyzer**
133 **SCRUTINY**, b c 23/3 Aqlaam—
　　　　Aunty Mary (Common Grounds) (85000) **Highclere Thoroughbred Racing - Lake Coniston**
134 B c 16/3 Kodiac—Silk Fan (IRE) (Unfuwain (USA)) (30476) **Sheikh Juma Al Dalmook Maktoum**
135 **SPIRITUAL FLAME**, b f 25/4 Invincible Spirit (IRE)—
　　　　Secret Flame (Machiavellian (USA)) **Cheveley Park Stud Limited**
136 B f 11/3 Danehill Dancer (IRE)—Superstar Leo (IRE) (College Chapel) **Lael Stable**
137 **SURVIVED**, b f 28/2 Kyllachy—Regina (Green Desert (USA)) **Cheveley Park Stud Limited**
138 Ch c 24/2 Mastercraftsman (IRE)—Teddy Bears Picnic (Oasis Dream) (61904) **Saleh Al Homaizi & Imad Al Sagar**
139 B f 28/2 Elusive City (USA)—Tiger Mist (IRE) (Galileo (IRE)) **M S Bloodstock Ltd.**
140 B f 16/3 Dubawi (IRE)—Turning Leaf (IRE) (Last Tycoon) (65000) **Sultan Ali**
141 **WOJHA (IRE)**, ch f 13/3 Pivotal—Hureya (USA) (Woodman (USA)) **Hamdan Al Maktoum**
142 **WRANGLER**, b c 25/2 High Chaparral (IRE)—
　　　　Tipsy Me (Selkirk (USA)) (80000) **Highclere Thoroughbred Racing - Ashes**
143 Ch c 29/3 Champs Elysees—Zee Zee Gee (Galileo (IRE)) (75000) **Mr B. Kantor**

Other Owners: Mr Imad Al-Sagar, Mr J. Flannery, Mr B. Haggas, Mr D. Hearson, Mrs David Hearson, The Hon H. M. Herbert, Highclere Thoroughbred Racing Ltd, Mr Tony Hirschfeld, Saleh Al Homaizi, R. Jackson, Mrs G. S. Jackson, Mr M. J. Jooste, Mr Bernard Kantor, Mr Michael Kerr-Dineen, L. K. Piggott Ltd, Mrs John Magnier, Mr D. I. Scott, Somerville Lodge Limited, Mr Andrew Stone, Mrs M. F. Stone, Mr M. Tabor, Mr M. J. Taylor, Mr L. A. Taylor, Mr C. P. Watson, Mr Peter Watson, Mr S. G. Wignall.

Assistant Trainers: Archie Watson & Jason Favell

---

276 **MR ALEX HALES, Banbury**
Postal: **Trafford Bridge Stables, Edgcote, Banbury, OX17 1AG**
Contacts: **PHONE (01295) 660131 FAX (01295) 660128 MOBILE (07771) 511652**
E-MAIL alex@alexhalesracing.co.uk WEBSITE www.alexhalesracing.co.uk

1 **ANTONIUS CAESAR (FR)**, 10, b g Mansonnien (FR)—Kandania (FR) **A. M. Hales**
2 **BERABANI (FR)**, 4, gr c Lawman (FR)—Bernimixa (FR) **Mr S. A. Helaissi**
3 **BOBBISOX (IRE)**, 8, ch m Bob Back (USA)—Swift Approach (IRE) **Tony & Dee Lousada**
4 **CAUSEWAY KING (USA)**, 7, ch g Giant's Causeway—A P Petal (USA) **A. M. Hales**
5 **COOL STRIKE (UAE)**, 7, b g Halling (USA)—Velour **A. M. Hales**
6 **CRAFTY ROBERTO**, 5, ch g Intikhab (USA)—Mowazana (IRE) **Mr S. Brown & Mrs H. Steele**
7 **DUNDRUM DANCER (IRE)**, 6, b m Refuse To Bend (IRE)—Sincere (IRE) **Edging Ahead**
8 **FAREWELLATMIDNIGHT**, 7, b m Midnight Legend—Fond Farewell (IRE) **Mrs J. Way**
9 **GILZEAN (IRE)**, 7, b g Flemensfirth (USA)—Sheknowso **Edging Ahead**
10 **GUMBRILLS'S GEORGE**, 5, b g Revoque (IRE)—Chilly Squaw (IRE) **Gumbrills Racing Partnership**
11 **ICONOCLAST (IRE)**, 12, b br g Topanoora—La Cigale (IRE) **John & Lorraine Barlow**
12 **LILAC BELLE**, 7, b m Robellino (USA)—Lilac Dreams **The Of-Ten Racing Partnership**
13 **LORD KENNEDY (IRE)**, 8, b g Saddlers' Hall (IRE)—Minstrel Madame (IRE) **The Patient Partnership**
14 **MIDNIGHT CHORISTER**, 5, b g Midnight Legend—Royal Musical **Mrs J. Way**
15 **MINELLAFORLEISURE (IRE)**, 5, br g King's Theatre (IRE)—Dame Foraine (FR) **The Patient Partnership**
16 **RIF (FR)**, 8, b g Byzantium (FR)—Isabellita (FR) **The Patient Partnership**
17 **ROCK SALMON**, 10, ch g Silver Patriarch (IRE)—The Lady Scores (IRE) **Mr A. F. Lousada**
18 **ROSENEATH (IRE)**, 9, b g Saddlers' Hall (IRE)—Vital Approach (IRE) **The Strathclyders**
19 **ROYAUME BLEU (FR)**, 8, ch g Kapgarde (FR)—Dear Blue (FR) **The Royaume Bleu Racing Partnership**
20 **SALUT HONORE (FR)**, 7, b g Lost World (IRE)—Kadalkote (FR) **The Hexagon Racing Partnership**

MR ALEX HALES · Continued

THREE-YEAR-OLDS

21 **MUMBAI STAR (IRE),** ch g Choisir (AUS)—Wood White (UAE) **Mr R. Gough**
22 **RIO CATO,** ch f Notnowcato—Brazilian Terrace **La Grange Syndicate**

Other Owners: Mrs Lorraine Barlow, Mr John K. Barlow, Mr Steve Brown (Towcester), Miss Sally Burnell, Mr John Cleary, Mr E. A. L. Dunlop, Mrs Edward Dunlop, Mr John S. C. Fry, Mrs K. A. Fry, Mr A. M. Hales, Mr A. F. Lousada, Mrs D. Lousada, Mr R. E. Morris-Adams, Mrs H. Steele, Mrs Carolyn Taylor, Mrs J. Wood.

277

MR MICHAEL HALFORD, Kildare

Postal: **Copper Beech Stables, Doneaney, Kildangan Road, Kildare Town, Co. Kildare, Ireland**
Contacts: **PHONE (00 353) 45 526119 FAX (00 353) 45 526157 MOBILE (00 353) 87 2579204**
E-MAIL info@michaelhalford.com WEBSITE www.michaelhalford.com

1 **ALVAR (USA),** 5, ch g Forest Danger (USA)—Diameter (USA) **Mr Paul Rooney**
2 **BANNA BOIRCHE (IRE),** 7, b g Lucky Owners (NZ)—Ziet d'alsace (FR) **Mr Paul Rooney**
3 **BENSOON,** 4, b g Refuse To Bend (IRE)—Monsoon Wedding **Mrs G. McDonald**
4 **CASTLE GUEST (IRE),** 4, b g Rock of Gibraltar (IRE)—Castelletto **Mr Paul Rooney**
5 **CEBUANO,** 8, ch g Fraam—Ideal Figure **Mr P. McMahon**
6 **CERTERACH (IRE),** 5, b g Halling (USA)—Chartres (IRE) **Mr Paul Rooney**
7 **COACH BOMBAY (IRE),** 5, b g Ad Valorem (USA)—Molly-O (IRE) **Sean Dalton**
8 **DANZERINI (IRE),** 4, b g Bernardini (USA)—Lucifer's Stone (USA) **Barouche Stud**
9 **EASTERN RULES (IRE),** 5, b g Golden Snake (USA)—Eastern Ember **S. Hales**
10 **HUJAYLEA (IRE),** 10, b g Almutawakel—Red Eagle (IRE) **Mr G. M. O'Leary**
11 **INVINCIBLE ASH (IRE),** 8, b m Invincible Spirit (IRE)—Fully Fashioned (IRE) **Mr P J Condron**
12 **LILY OF KENMARE (IRE),** 5, b m Exceed And Excel (AUS)—Zoudie **Mr B. Gallivan**
13 **LONAN (IRE),** 4, b g Dubawi (IRE)—Chartres (IRE) **Mrs M. Halford**
14 **LORD KENMARE (USA),** 7, b g Hold That Tiger (USA)—The Fur Flew (USA) **Mr B. Gallivan**
15 5, B m Clodovil (IRE)—Manazil (IRE) **Mr John Dewberry/Mrs C. Hartery**
16 **MEA PARVITAS (IRE),** 4, b f Oasis Dream—Red Rita (IRE) **M. Halford**
17 **MOY DIAMOND (IRE),** 4, b g Diamond Green (FR)—Glamour Stock (USA) **Mr P. Madigan**
18 **ONDEAFEARS (IRE),** 6, b m Chineur (FR)—Irma La Douce (IRE) **Mrs C. Roper**
19 **PADDY THE CELEB (IRE),** 7, ch g Peintre Celebre (USA)—On The Razz (USA) **Mr P. McMahon**
20 **PIPERS CHOICE (IRE),** 5, b g Choisir (AUS)—Pipewell (IRE) **Sin A Bhfuil Syndicate**
21 **RED LASER (IRE),** 4, br g Red Clubs (IRE)—Prancing **Mr M. Phelan**
22 **REGULATION (IRE),** 4, br g Danehill Dancer (IRE)—Source of Life (IRE) **Barouche Stud**
23 **RIDAYEF (IRE),** 6, b g Dr Fong (USA)—Ridakiya (IRE) **Mr R. McNally**
24 **RUMMAGING (IRE),** 5, ch g Chineur (FR)—Roundabout Girl (IRE) **Mr P. E. I. Newell**
25 **RUSSIAN SOUL (IRE),** 5, b g Invincible Spirit (IRE)—Russian Hill **Mrs A. G. Kavanagh**
26 **SAINT BY DAY (IRE),** 7, b g Marju (IRE)—Spring To Light (USA) **Mr Paul Rooney**
27 **SHAIYZAR (IRE),** 4, b c Azamour (IRE)—Shaiyzima (IRE) **Mr P. Woods**
28 **SHARP AND SMART (IRE),** 4, b f Dark Angel (IRE)—Church Road (IRE) **J. Harley/R. Boland Partnership**
29 **SLIPPER ORCHID (IRE),** 4, gr f Verglas (IRE)—Lahiba (IRE) **Mrs C. Roper**
30 **VIA BALLYCROY (IRE),** 4, b f Lawman (FR)—Via Milano (FR) **Rollix Syndicate**

THREE-YEAR-OLDS

31 Br f Kalanisi (IRE)—Aladiyna (IRE) **M. F. Healy**
32 **BEHLAYAN (IRE),** b c Manduro (GER)—Behkiyra (IRE) **H. H. Aga Khan**
33 **BOSSTIME (IRE),** b c Clodovil (IRE)—Smoken Rosa (USA) **Mr J. Deuberry**
34 **CAPE GLORY (IRE),** b c Cape Cross (IRE)—Array of Stars (IRE) **Mrs W. O'Leary**
35 **DABADIYAN (IRE),** b c Zamindar (USA)—Dabista (IRE) **H. H. Aga Khan**
36 **DIBAYANI (IRE),** b c Shamardal (USA)—Dibiya (IRE) **H. H. Aga Khan**
37 **DRIFTING MIST (IRE),** gr f Muhtathir—Fenella's Link **Mrs A. G. Kavanagh**
38 **HARAZA (IRE),** b f Haafhd—Haratila (IRE) **H. H. Aga Khan**
39 **LA FEMME (IRE),** b f Cape Cross (IRE)—Nick's Nikita (IRE) **Mr N. Hartery**
40 **MAZANDARAN (IRE),** b c Tiger Hill (IRE)—Masiyma (IRE) **H. H. Aga Khan**
41 **MIZZAVA (IRE),** b br f Cape Cross (IRE)—Flamanda **Mr G. M. O'Leary**
42 **OPERA GLOVES (IRE),** b f Dalakhani (IRE)—Chan Tong (BRZ) **Sheikh Mohammed**
43 **PASTICHES,** ch f Street Cry (IRE)—Nadia **Sheikh Mohammed**
44 **ROSE IN WINTER (IRE),** b f Danehill Dancer (IRE)—Mount Klinovec (IRE) **Gigginstown House Stud**
45 **SARIYFA (IRE),** br f Zamindar (USA)—Saricana (IRE) **H. H. Aga Khan**
46 **SENYUMAN (IRE),** ch f Shirocco (GER)—Skerries (IRE) **M. Donohue**
47 **VICTOR'S BEACH (IRE),** b g Footstepsinthesand—Your Village (IRE) **Dr K. Swanick**
48 **WON DIAMOND,** b c Mount Nelson—Read Federica **Mr Paul Rooney**

MR MICHAEL HALFORD - Continued

49 ZADAWAN (IRE), b c Kheleyf (USA)—Zaziyra (IRE) **H. H. Aga Khan**
50 ZARKIYR (IRE), b c Acclamation—Zarkalia (IRE) **H. H. Aga Khan**
51 ZARMA (IRE), b f Rock of Gibraltar (IRE)—Zarwala (IRE) **H. H. Aga Khan**

TWO-YEAR-OLDS

52 Ch f 28/4 Manduro (GER)—Adelfia (IRE) (Sinndar (IRE)) **H. H. Aga Khan**
53 B c 30/1 Royal Applause—Air Biscuit (IRE) (Galileo (IRE)) (75396) **Sheikh Mohammed**
54 Gr f 28/4 Galileo (IRE)—Alabastrine (Green Desert (USA)) (269840) **Mr M. Enright**
55 B c 30/3 Bushranger (IRE)—Alexander Express (IRE) (Sri Pekan (USA)) **Mr F. Lynch**
56 AUSBURY BOSS (IRE), b br c 22/1 Dalakhani (IRE)—Nick's Nikita (IRE) (Pivotal) **Mr N. Hartery**
57 B f 22/4 Acclamation—Caherassdotcom (Compton Place) **Mr N. Hartery**
58 B c 4/4 Soviet Star (USA)—Crazy About You (IRE) (Montjeu (IRE)) (13491) **Mr G. Tae**
59 B f 20/4 Authorized (IRE)—Crystal House (CHI) (Golden Voyager (USA)) **Sheikh Mohammed**
60 B c 22/4 Rock of Gibraltar (IRE)—Dabista (IRE) (Highest Honor (FR)) **H. H. Aga Khan**
61 B c 21/3 Excellent Art—Daganya (IRE) (Danehill Dancer (IRE)) **Mr J. D. Cague**
62 HAZLEDOC (IRE), b f 2/4 Azamour (IRE)—Grand Oir (IRE) (Grand Slam (USA)) (42857) **Mr John Kennedy**
63 B c 18/4 Iffraaj—Journey's End (IRE) (In The Wings) (39681) **Sheikh Mohammed**
64 B br c 29/3 Arch (USA)—Lettre Spirituelle (Invincible Spirit (IRE)) (55000) **Corrib Partnership**
65 B f 2/4 Tiger Hill (IRE)—Neptune's Bride (USA) (Bering) **Sheikh Mohammed**
66 Ch f 22/1 Speightstown (USA)—Passified (Compton Place) (19047) **Mr M. Keaveney**
67 B 10/3 Manduro (GER)—Pearlitas Passion (IRE) (High Chaparral (IRE)) **Mr M. Enright**
68 B f 25/4 Clodovil (IRE)—Serious Delight (Lomond (USA)) **Mr N. Hartery**
69 B f 1/5 Clodovil (IRE)—Smoken Rosa (USA) (Smoke Glacken (USA)) **Mr John Dewberry**
70 Ch c 24/1 Peintre Celebre (USA)—Society Gal (IRE) (Galileo (IRE)) (20634) **Gigginstown House Stud**
71 B c 3/3 Rock of Gibraltar (IRE)—Velandia (IRE) (Sadler's Wells (USA)) **H. H. Aga Khan**
72 Br c 24/3 Sinndar (IRE)—Virana (IRE) (King's Best (USA)) **H. H. Aga Khan**
73 ZAIMAN (IRE), gr c 8/3 Oratorio (IRE)—Zaziyra (Dalakhani (IRE)) **H. H. Aga Khan**
74 ZAINDERA (IRE), b f 9/2 Acclamation—Zalaiyma (FR) (Rainbow Quest (USA)) **H. H. Aga Khan**
75 B c 31/1 Azamour (IRE)—Zariziyna (IRE) (Dalakhani (IRE)) **H. H. Aga Khan**

Assistant Trainer: Louise Halford

Jockey (flat): Shane Foley. **Apprentice:** Conor Hoban, Damien Melia, Peter Donnelly, Evan Lawlor, Marc Monaghan.
Amateur: Mr J. Heavey.

---

278 MISS SALLY HALL, Middleham
Postal: Brecongill, Coverham, Leyburn, North Yorkshire, DL8 4TJ
Contacts: **PHONE** (01969) 640223 **FAX** (0800) 066 4274
E-MAIL sally@brecongill.co.uk

1 DANCING LAMB, 4, gr f Norse Dancer (IRE)—Charlotte Lamb **Colin Platts**
2 MAGIC HAZE, 7, b g Makbul—Turn Back **Mrs J. Hodgson**
3 OAKWELL (IRE), 5, b g Antonius Pius (USA)—Cindy's Star (IRE) **Colin Platts**
4 ROCK A DOODLE DOO (IRE), 6, b g Oratorio (IRE)—Nousaiyra (IRE) **Colin Platts**

Other Owners: Miss S. E. Hall.

Assistant Trainer: Colin Platts

Jockey (NH): Richard Johnson. **Amateur:** Mrs D.S. Wilkinson.

---

279 MRS MARY HAMBRO, Cheltenham
Postal: Cotswold Stud, Sezincote, Moreton-In-Marsh, Gloucestershire, GL56 9TB
Contacts: **PHONE** (01386) 700700 **FAX** (01386) 700701 **MOBILE** (07860) 632990
E-MAIL maryhambro@mac.com

1 DOVER'S HILL, 11, b g Pistolet Bleu (IRE)—Classic Beauty (IRE) **Mrs M. C. Hambro**
2 HAZEL BROOK, 4, b f High Chaparral (IRE)—Didbrook **Mrs M. C. Hambro**
3 5, B m Sleeping Indian—Neptunalia **Mrs M. C. Hambro**
4 SQUIRREL WOOD (IRE), 5, b m Sadler's Wells (USA)—Didbrook **Mrs M. C. Hambro**

280 **MRS DEBRA HAMER, Carmarthen**
Postal: **Bryngors Uchaf Stables, Nantycaws, Carmarthen, Dyfed, SA32 8EY**
Contacts: HOME **(01267) 234585** MOBILE **(07980) 665274**
E-MAIL **hamerracing@hotmail.co.uk**

1 BENDANT, 8, b g Beat All (USA)—Rendita (IRE) **T. L. Cooper**
2 GROVEMERE (IRE), 8, b br g Beneficial—Holly Grove Lass **Davies & Price**
3 MICHIGAN ASSASSIN (IRE), 11, b g King's Theatre (IRE)—Shuil Ar Aghaidh **Mr C. A. Hanbury**
4 MY LAD PERCY, 5, b g Central Park (IRE)—Only Millie **Davies & Price**
5 PENNANT DANCER, 6, b g Grape Tree Road—Pennant Princess **Lost Souls Racing**
6 PRIME EDITION (IRE), 8, b g Publisher (USA)—Oneoftheclan (IRE) **Formula One Racing**
7 SIGNE D'ESTRUVAL (FR), 7, b g Lavirco (GER)—Balbeck (FR) **Hanford's Chemist Ltd**
8 WHO AM I, 7, b br g Tamayaz (CAN)—Short Fuse (IRE) **Mrs G. A. Davies**

Other Owners: Mr R. A. Davies, Mr David Harding, Mr A. G. Price, Mrs Joyce Taylor, Mr P. J. Woolley, Mr A. Yorke.

Assistant Trainer: Mr M P Hamer

281 **MRS ALISON HAMILTON, Denholm**
Postal: **The Dykes, Denholm, Roxburghshire, TD9 8TB**
Contacts: PHONE **(01450) 870323** MOBILE **(07885) 477349**
E-MAIL **Alisonhamilton53@yahoo.com**

1 BOW SCHOOL (IRE), 12, b g New Frontier (IRE)—Sallaghan (IRE) **J. P. G. Hamilton**
2 DAMASCUS STEEL (IRE), 5, gr g Definite Article—Diamarouna (FR) **J. P. G. Hamilton**
3 DANEHILLS WELL (IRE), 5, b g Indian Danehill (IRE)—Collatrim Choice (IRE) **J. P. G. Hamilton**
4 GRANARUID (IRE), 10, br g Alderbrook—Lady Lorraine (IRE) **J. P. G. Hamilton**
5 SOME LAD (IRE), 8, b g Beneficial—Some News (IRE) **J. P. G. Hamilton**
6 WHAT A NIGHT, 14, gr g Environment Friend—Misty Night **J. P. G. Hamilton**

Assistant Trainer: Mr G. Hamilton

282 **MRS ANN HAMILTON, Newcastle Upon Tyne**
Postal: **Claywalls Farm, Capheaton, Newcastle Upon Tyne, NE19 2BP**
Contacts: PHONE **(01830) 530219**
E-MAIL **annhamilton1952@hotmail.com**

1 DR FLYNN (IRE), 8, b g Tikkanen (USA)—Tallaquale (IRE) **I. Hamilton**
2 EDMUND (IRE), 6, b g Indian River (FR)—Awomansdream (IRE) **I. Hamilton**
3 FARM PIXIE (IRE), 7, b g Snurge—Blue Bobby (IRE) **I. Hamilton**
4 PROUD JACK (IRE), 9, b g Generous (IRE)—Miss Royello **I. Hamilton**
5 ROLECARR (IRE), 10, b g Tragic Role (USA)—Nuit d'ete (USA) **I. Hamilton**
6 TRUST THOMAS, 5, ch g Erhaab (USA)—Yota (FR) **I. Hamilton**

THREE-YEAR-OLDS

7 B f Great Palm (USA)—Miss Royello **I. Hamilton**

TWO-YEAR-OLDS

8 Gr g 9/5 Great Palm (USA)—Miss Royello (Royal Fountain) **I. Hamilton**

Other Owners: Mr Ian Hamilton.

Assistant Trainer: Ian Hamilton

283 **MR B. R. HAMILTON, Co. Down**
Postal: **100 Ballynoe Road, Downpatrick, Co. Down, Northern Ireland**
Contacts: PHONE **(004428) 44842843** MOBILE **(07779) 591970**
E-MAIL **brianhamilton70@yahoo.co.uk**

1 BOBBINA (IRE), 6, br m Bob Back (USA)—Twinkle Sunset **Mrs B. Cunningham**
2 CORDELIA BELLE (IRE), 6, b m Accordion—Unfaithful Thought **Johnnie Flanagan**
3 HONEY BACH (IRE), 6, b m Bach (IRE)—Lough Lein Leader (IRE) **Stick To The Cows Syndicate**

MR B. R. HAMILTON - Continued

    4 **JOHNNYOFCOURSE (IRE)**, 9, b g Saddlers' Hall (IRE)—Zafilly **Mr B. Turley**
    5 **MOSCOW MANNON (IRE)**, 7, b g Moscow Society (USA)—Unfaithful Thought **Johnnie Flanagan**
    6 **WARNE (IRE)**, 9, b g Bob Back (USA)—Dusky Diva (IRE) **Mrs C. Magill**

Assistant Trainer: B. A. Hamilton

Jockey (NH): D. Lavery. **Amateur:** Mr P. E. Turley.

284	**MRS CATHY HAMILTON, Gillingham**
	Postal: **New Town Farm, New Town, Kington Magna, Gillingham, Dorset, SP8 5EU**
	Contacts: **MOBILE (07875) 092134**

    1 **FOR SAHKEY MOONY (IRE)**, 8, b g Welsh Lion (IRE)—Dromhale Lady (IRE) **Mr M. W. Hoskins**
    2 **GUNSHIP (IRE)**, 12, b g Needle Gun (IRE)—Teejay's Future (IRE) **Mr M. W. Hoskins**
    3 **REALIGNMENT (IRE)**, 8, b g Celtic Swing—Sharera (IRE) **The Family Goes Racing**
    4 **SIR BATHWICK (IRE)**, 14, b g Oscar (IRE)—Karenda **The Family Goes Racing**

Other Owners: Mrs S. A. Gent, Mrs C. M. Hamilton.

Jockey (NH): Danny Cook, Mark Quinlan. **Conditional:** Tom Cannon. **Amateur:** Mr Lee Drowne, Miss Emma Hamilton, Mr James Ridley.

285	**MR MICKY HAMMOND, Middleham**
	Postal: **Oakwood Stables, East Witton Road, Middleham, Leyburn, North Yorkshire, DL8 4PT**
	Contacts: **PHONE (01969) 625223 MOBILE (07808) 572777**
	E-MAIL mdhammondracing@tiscali.co.uk WEBSITE www.mickyhammondracing.co.uk

    1 **AMIR PASHA (UAE)**, 8, br g Halling (USA)—Clarinda (IRE) **The Steven Kay Partnership**
    2 **CHERNIK (IRE)**, 12, b g Norwich—Sue Pickering (IRE) **Bendery Properties Holdings Ltd**
    3 **DANCEINTOTHELIGHT**, 6, gr g Dansili—Kali **The Family Of Roland Roper**
    4 **DARK CASTLE**, 4, b g Dark Angel (IRE)—True Magic **Mr J. Cox & Mr E. Tasker**
    5 **DAWN RIDE (IRE)**, 12, b g New Frontier (IRE)—Atlantic Dawn (IRE) **Belarus 2 Partnership**
    6 **EASTLANDS LAD (IRE)**, 4, b br c Strategic Prince—Uisce Tine (IRE) **Mr J. F. Wilson**
    7 **FALCUN**, 6, b g Danehill Dancer (IRE)—Fanofadiga (IRE) **Mr Joe Buzzeo**
    8 **FIVE FRANKS (USA)**, 4, b br g More Than Ready (USA)—Salchow (USA) **Mr Frank Hanson**
    9 **FRANK THE SLINK**, 7, b g Central Park (IRE)—Kadari **Mr Frank Hanson**
    10 **GONOW**, 5, b g Red Ransom (USA)—Isotta (GER) **Mike & Eileen Newbould**
    11 **HEART OF DUBAI (IRE)**, 8, b g Outofthebox (USA)—Diablo's Blend (USA) **M. D. Hammond**
    12 **HER NIBBS**, 4, b f Lucky Story (USA)—The Pen **Mrs L. Peacock**
    13 **HOLLINS**, 9, b g Lost Soldier (USA)—Cutting Reef (IRE) **Mrs H. E. Aitkin**
    14 **JUSTJOE (IRE)**, 7, b g Carroll House—Made of Marble (IRE) **Mr Joe Buzzeo**
    15 **KATHLATINO**, 6, b m Danbird (AUS)—Silver Rhythm **M. D. Hammond**
    16 **MA KELLYS (IRE)**, 4, ch g Compton Place—Western Sal **The Bay Horse Masham**
    17 **MAJOR DOMO (FR)**, 4, ch g Domedriver (IRE)—Raphaela (FR) **Mrs H. E. Aitkin**
    18 **MAKELLYS BLACKPOOL**, 4, b f Sir Harry Lewis (USA)—Pondimari (FR) **Miss Rachel Kelly**
    19 **MARGO CHANNING**, 4, ch f Three Valleys (USA)—Charlotte Vale **Mr Peter J. Davies & Mrs Gemma Hogg**
    20 **MEETINGS MAN (IRE)**, 6, gr g Footstepsinthesand—Missella (IRE) **Paul, Vicky, Gabby, Tom & Hattie Snook**
    21 **MERCHANT OF MEDICI**, 6, b g Medicean—Regal Rose **Mr J. F. Wilson**
    22 **MOTAFARRED (IRE)**, 11, ch g Machiavellian (USA)—Thurayya **M. D. Hammond**
    23 **MR CRYSTAL (FR)**, 9, ch g Trempolino—Iyrbila (FR) **Champagne Ascent Partnership**
    24 **MR PERCEPTIVE (IRE)**, 5, b g Iffraaj—Astuti (IRE) **M.H.O.G.**
    25 **ONLY ORSENFOOLSIES**, 4, b g Trade Fair—Desert Gold (IRE) **This Time Next Year Partnership**
    26 **PERTUIS (IRE)**, 7, gr g Verglas (IRE)—Lady Killeen (IRE) **M. D. Hammond**
    27 **RALEIGH QUAY (IRE)**, 6, b g Bachelor Duke (USA)—Speedbird (USA) **S. T. Brankin & J. Zuppinger**
    28 **RONNIE RHINO**, 5, b g Darsi (FR)—Pondimari (FR) **Mike & Eileen Newbould**
    29 **ROSAIRLIE (IRE)**, 5, ch m Halling (USA)—Mrs Mason (IRE) **The Bay Horse Masham**
    30 **STICKLEBACK**, 4, ch f Manduro (GER)—The Stick **Mr Nick Rust**
    31 **SWERVINIRVIN**, 5, b g Noverre (USA)—Saada One (IRE) **Mr Frank Hanson**
    32 **TERENZIUM (IRE)**, 11, br g Cape Cross (IRE)—Tatanka (ITY) **O'Sunburn Partnership**
    33 **TINY DANCER (IRE)**, 5, b g Darsi (FR)—Taipans Girl (IRE) **Mrs H. E. Aitkin**
    34 **XCLAIM**, 5, ch g Proclamation (IRE)—Tahara (IRE) **Mike & Eileen Newbould**
    35 **YORKIST (IRE)**, 5, ch g Urban Ocean (FR)—Kilbarry Demon (IRE) **Mike & Eileen Newbould**

MR MICKY HAMMOND - Continued

THREE-YEAR-OLDS
36 **DIDDY ERIC,** b c Oratorio (IRE)—Amber Queen (IRE) **M. D. Hammond**
37 **SPATS COLOMBO,** ch c Notnowcato—Charlotte Vale **P. J. Davies**

Other Owners: Mr P. H. Bell, Mr S. T. Brankin, Mr P. B. Finnegan, Mr Richard Green, Mr M. D. Hammond, Mr D. Hartley, Mr Nik. H. B. Ingham, Mr Steven Kay, Mrs H. Kitching, Mr A. Kitching, Mr S. Lorimer, Mr Mike Newbould, Mrs E. E. Newbould, Mr T. Rodney, Mr R. M. Roper, Mr R. S. Roper, Mr Nick Rust, Mr Paul Sellars, Mr Paul R. Snook, Mrs Victoria Snook, Mr K. Ward, Mr J. Zuppinger.

Assistant Trainer: Mrs. G. Hogg (07809) 428117

Conditional: Joe Colliver. **Apprentice:** Katie Dowson. **Amateur:** Miss R. Smith.

---

286 | **MR MIKE HAMMOND, Abberley**
Postal: Cherry Ash, Bank Lane, Abberley, Worcester, Worcestershire, WR6 6BQ
Contacts: PHONE (01299) 896057 MOBILE 07894 050183
E-MAIL mphatwellcottage@aol.com WEBSITE www.hammondracing.co.uk

1 **CHAPTER NINE (IRE),** 7, b g Expelled (USA)—Abbey Ever After **The General Asphalte Company Ltd**
2 **DOCTOR JOE (IRE),** 4, b g Dr Massini (IRE)—The Polecat (IRE)
3 4, B g Catcher In The Rye (IRE)—Footsteps (IRE) **D. P. Constable**
4 **GENERAL VILLEGAS (IRE),** 8, gr g Commander Collins (IRE)—Rongai (IRE) **Marksmen**
5 **THE FERBANE MAN (IRE),** 9, b g Dr Massini (IRE)—Hi Up There (IRE) **Mr M. P. Hammond**
6 **TURTLE TOO (IRE),** 4, b g Turtle Island (IRE)—Panaea (IRE)
7 4, B g Turtle Island (IRE)—Youwoudhavethat (IRE)

Other Owners: Mr M. McLornan, Mr K. Niththyananthan.

Assistant Trainer: Zoe Hammond

---

287 | **MR RICHARD HANNON, Marlborough**
Postal: East Everleigh Stables, Everleigh, Marlborough, Wiltshire, SN8 3EY
Contacts: PHONE (01264) 850 254 FAX (01264) 850076
E-MAIL richard.hannon@btopenworld.com WEBSITE www.richardhannonracing.co.uk

1 **ALDWICK BAY (IRE),** 5, b g Danehill Dancer (IRE)—Josie Doocey (IRE) **Mrs A. Williams**
2 **CAI SHEN (IRE),** 5, ch h Iffraaj—Collada (IRE) **Mrs J. Wood**
3 **CAPE JOY (IRE),** 4, b f Cape Cross (IRE)—Perils of Joy (IRE) **Mrs N. F. Lee**
4 **CRIUS (IRE),** 4, b c Heliostatic (IRE)—Fearless Flyer (IRE) **Titan Assets**
5 **DEMOCRETES,** 4, ch c Cadeaux Genereux—Petite Epaulette **The High Flyers**
6 **DUKE OF CLARENCE (IRE),** 4, gr c Verglas (IRE)—Special Lady (FR) **D Dixon J Stunt J Fiyaz**
7 **FORGIVE,** 4, b f Pivotal—Amira **Highclere Thoroughbred Racing -Spearmint**
8 **LIBRANNO,** 5, b h Librettist (USA)—Annabelle Ja (FR) **McDowell Racing Ltd**
9 **LORD OFTHE SHADOWS (IRE),** 4, ch c Kyllachy—Golden Shadow (IRE) **Richard Hitchcock Alan King**
10 **MAGIC CITY (IRE),** 4, b g Elusive City (USA)—
Annmarie's Magic (IRE) **Barker, Ferguson, Mason, Hassiakos, Done**
11 **NORTH STAR BOY (IRE),** 4, b g Acclamation—Isla Azul (IRE) **Mr R. W. Tyrrell**
12 **PILGRIMS REST (IRE),** 4, ch c Rock of Gibraltar (IRE)—Holly Blue **M. Jooste & B. Kantor**
13 **POETIC LORD,** 4, b g Byron—Jumairah Sun (IRE) **Mrs N. F. Lee**
14 **POOLE HARBOUR (IRE),** 4, b g Elusive City (USA)—Free Lance (IRE) **The Heffer Syndicate**
15 **PRODUCER,** 4, ch c Dutch Art—River Saint (USA) **J. Palmer-Brown**
16 **ROCK BAND,** 4, b g Rock of Gibraltar (IRE)—Decision Maid (USA) **Mrs J. Wood**
17 **SHAMAAL NIBRAS (USA),** 4, b c First Samurai (USA)—Sashay Away (USA) **S. H. Altayer**
18 **SILKEE SUPREME,** 4, b c Primo Valentino (IRE)—Sodelk **B. C. Oakley**
19 **STRINGER BELL,** 4, ch c Cockney Rebel (IRE)—Heckle **M. Pescod**
20 **TRUMPET MAJOR (IRE),** 4, b c Arakan (USA)—Ashford Cross **J. D. Manley**
21 **VIEWPOINT (IRE),** 4, b g Exceed And Excel (AUS)—Lady's View (USA) **The Heffer Syndicate**

THREE-YEAR-OLDS
22 **A LADIES MAN (IRE),** b c Kyllachy—Ego **Mrs J. Wood**
23 **ABSOLUTELY RIGHT (IRE),** b f Teofilo (IRE)—Dabawiyah (IRE) **Mr H. R. Bin Ghadayer**
24 **AGAINST THE TIDE (IRE),** ch f Teofilo (IRE)—Hundred Year Flood (USA) **S. Manana**
25 **AL ZEIN,** b c Notnowcato—Luminda (IRE) **S. H. Altayer**

MR RICHARD HANNON - Continued

26 **ALHEBAYEB (IRE)**, gr c Dark Angel (IRE)—Miss Indigo **Hamdan Al Maktoum**
27 **AMBERLEY HEIGHTS (IRE)**, b f Elnadim (USA)—Fawaayid (USA) **Elaine Chivers & Peter Reglar**
28 **ANNUNCIATION**, b c Proclamation (IRE)—Rockburst **Middleham Park Racing XXXIX & James Pak**
29 **ARCTIC ADMIRAL (IRE)**, gr c Verglas (IRE)—Fag End (IRE) **Mr P. D. Merritt**
30 **BALTIC KNIGHT (IRE)**, b c Baltic King—Night of Joy (IRE) **Thurloe Thoroughbreds XXX**
31 **BEAT OF THE DRUM (IRE)**, b f Duke of Marmalade (IRE)—
Square Pants (USA) **Mr M Tabor, Mrs J Magnier & Mr D Smith**
32 **BEEDEE**, b c Beat Hollow—Dawnus (IRE) **Mr & Mrs D. D. Clee**
33 **BRIGADE (IRE)**, b c Mujadil (USA)—Ela Tina (IRE) **Mr M. S. Al Shahi**
34 **BROADWAY DUCHESS (IRE)**, ch f New Approach (IRE)—Annee Lumiere (IRE) **M. Pescod**
35 **BROWNSEA BRINK**, b c Cadeaux Genereux—Valiantly **The Heffer Syndicate**
36 **BURSLEDON (IRE)**, b c Jeremy (USA)—Desert Drama (IRE) **Mrs J. Wood**
37 **CARAMACK**, ch g Danehill Dancer (IRE)—Oshiponga **Potensis Limited & Mr Chris Giles**
38 **CARRY ON SYDNEY**, ch c Notnowcato—River Fantasy (USA) **The Sydney Arms Partnership**
39 **CITY IMAGE (IRE)**, gr f Elusive City (USA)—Photophore (IRE) **P. A. Byrne**
40 **COLMAR KID (IRE)**, b c Choisir (AUS)—Roselyn **The Heffer Syndicate**
41 **DAMA DE LA NOCHE (IRE)**, b f Teofilo (IRE)—Alessia (GER) **Mr A. T. J. Russell**
42 **DANZ CHOICE (IRE)**, b c Kheleyf (USA)—Aphorism **Dragon Gate Development Limited**
43 **DASHING DAVID (IRE)**, b c Lemon Drop Kid (USA)—Nyarhini **Sir David Seale**
44 **DOMINATE**, b c Assertive—Blue Goddess (IRE) **G. A. Wilson**
45 **DOUGLAS PASHA (IRE)**, b g Compton Place—Lake Nayasa **Middleham Park Racing II**
46 **EMELL**, ch c Medicean—Londonnetdotcom (IRE) **Mr & Mrs D. D. Clee**
47 **EMULATING (IRE)**, ch c Duke of Marmalade (IRE)—Ascendancy **Mr B. C. M. Wong**
48 **ENDORSING (IRE)**, b c Dylan Thomas (IRE)—Gently (IRE) **Mr B. C. M. Wong**
49 **ENTRAPPING**, b c Tiger Hill (IRE)—Meddle **Mr B. C. M. Wong**
50 **EQUITISSA (IRE)**, b f Chevalier (IRE)—Westcote (USA) **Mrs J. I. Snow**
51 **ERODIUM**, b c Kyllachy—Alovera (IRE) **Rockcliffe Stud**
52 **FLEETING SMILE (USA)**, b f Distorted Humor (USA)—Fleet Indian (USA) **Hamdan Al Maktoum**
53 **FOLLOWEVERYRAINBOW**, b f Oasis Dream—Absolute Precision **Mrs J. Wood**
54 **FOXY DANCER (IRE)**, b f Jeremy (USA)—Date Mate (USA) **Fox Inn Syndicate 4**
55 **GERRARDS CROSS (IRE)**, b c Cape Cross (IRE)—Shin Feign (USA) **Mrs J. Wood**
56 **GLEAN**, ch c Raven's Pass (USA)—Harvest Queen (IRE) **Lady Rothschild**
57 **GOLD MEDAL (IRE)**, b c Dylan Thomas (IRE)—Sogno Verde (IRE) **Mrs J. Wood**
58 **GOLD NUGGET (IRE)**, b c Elusive City (USA)—Glamadour (IRE) **Mrs J. Wood**
59 **HANDS OF TIME**, b c Pivotal—Virtuous **S. H. Altayer**
60 **HAVANA GOLD (IRE)**, b c Teofilo (IRE)—Jessica's Dream (IRE) **Qatar Racing Limited & CSH**
61 **INTRIGO**, b c Medicean—A Thousand Smiles (IRE) **Lady G. De Walden**
62 **JALAA (IRE)**, b c Street Cry (IRE)—Daneleta (IRE) **Hamdan Al Maktoum**
63 **JANOUB NIBRAS (IRE)**, b c Acclamation—Wildsplash (USA) **S. H. Altayer**
64 **KEEP CALM**, b c War Chant (USA)—Mayaar (USA) **Richard Hitchcock Alan King**
65 **LAW ENFORCEMENT (IRE)**, b c Lawman (FR)—Broken Spectre **Mr M. S. Al Shahi**
66 **LIGHT UP MY LIFE (IRE)**, b f Zamindar (USA)—Shine Like A Star **Mr D Boocock & Mr K T Ivory**
67 **LIONS ARCH (IRE)**, b c Rock of Gibraltar (IRE)—Swynford Lady (IRE) **Mr A. T. J. Russell**
68 **MAUREEN (IRE)**, b f Holy Roman Emperor (IRE)—Exotic Mix (IRE) **Mr A. A. Alkhallafi**
69 **MILLERS WHARF (IRE)**, b c Acclamation—Applaud (USA) **Mrs J. M. Heffer**
70 **MONTIRIDGE (IRE)**, b c Ramonti (FR)—Elegant Ridge (IRE) **M Clarke, J Jeffries, R Ambrose, B Reilly**
71 **MOORTAHAN**, b c Dutch Art—Rotunda **Hamdan Al Maktoum**
72 **MUTAZAMEN**, ch c Sakhee's Secret—Disco Lights **Hamdan Al Maktoum**
73 **NINJAGO**, b c Mount Nelson—Fidelio's Miracle (USA) **J Palmer-Brown & Potensis Ltd**
74 **OLYMPIC GLORY (IRE)**, b c Choisir (AUS)—Acidanthera **H.E. Sheikh J. B. H. B. K. Al Thani**
75 **PETHER'S MOON (IRE)**, b c Dylan Thomas (IRE)—Softly Tread (IRE) **J. D. Manley**
76 **PIVOTAL MOVEMENT**, ch c Pivotal—Selinka **Sir A Ferguson, G Mason, R Wood & P Done**
77 **POLISH RIDER**, b g Dutch Art—Lady Darayna **De La Warr Racing**
78 **PRINCE'S TRUST**, b g Invincible Spirit (IRE)—Lost In Wonder (USA) **Her Majesty The Queen**
79 **RAGING BEAR (USA)**, b c Leroidesanimaux (BRZ)—
Gliding Light (USA) **Hughes, Morecombe, Anderson, Netherthorpe**
80 **RAYAHEEN**, b f Nayef (USA)—Natagora (FR) **Hamdan Al Maktoum**
81 **RED REFRACTION (IRE)**, b c Red Clubs (IRE)—Dreamalot **Middleham Park Racing IV & James Pak**
82 **RHAMNUS**, b c Sakhee's Secret—Happy Lady (FR) **Rockcliffe Stud**
83 **RONALDINHO (IRE)**, b c Jeremy (USA)—Spring Glory **Macdonald, Wright, Creed, Smith & Jiggins**
84 **RUNDELL**, b c Notnowcato—Shardette (IRE) **Mrs A. Wigan**
85 **SEA SHANTY (USA)**, b g Elusive Quality (USA)—Medley **Her Majesty The Queen**
86 **SEASIDE ROCK (IRE)**, b c Oratorio (IRE)—Miss Sacha (IRE) **The Heffer Syndicate**
87 **SHAMAHEART**, b c Shamardal (USA)—Encouragement **Dragon Gate Development Limited**
88 **SKY LANTERN (IRE)**, gr ro f Red Clubs (IRE)—Shawanni **Mr B. W. Keswick**

MR RICHARD HANNON - Continued

89 STIFF UPPER LIP (IRE), b c Sakhee's Secret—Just In Love (FR) **Richard Hitchcock Alan King**
90 SUBLIMATION (IRE), ch c Manduro (GER)—Meon Mix **J. Palmer-Brown**
91 SWEET AS HONEY, b f Duke of Marmalade (IRE)—Tempting Prospect **Her Majesty The Queen**
92 TAMAYUZ STAR (IRE), ch c Tamayuz—Magical Peace (IRE) **Mr A. Al Mansoori**
93 TASSEL, b f Kyllachy—Xtrasensory **Highclere Thoroughbred Racing - Herbert Jones**
94 TAWTHEEQ (IRE), b c Acclamation—Grand Slam Maria (FR) **Hamdan Al Maktoum**
95 THE TAJ (USA), ch c Street Cry (IRE)—India (USA) **Hamdan Al Maktoum**
96 TORONADO (IRE), b c High Chaparral (IRE)—Wana Doo (USA) **Carmichael Humber**
97 VAN DER NEER, b c Dutch Art—Lalectra **S. Manana**
98 VICTRIX LUDORUM (IRE), b f Invincible Spirit (IRE)—Matikanehamatidori (JPN) **Mrs J. Wood**
99 WENTWORTH (IRE), b c Acclamation—Miss Corinne **Mrs J Magnier, Mr M Tabor & Mr D Smith**
100 WHATEVER YOU DO (IRE), ch f Barathea (IRE)—Petite Spectre **Mrs J. Wood**
101 WOODSTOCK (IRE), b c High Chaparral (IRE)—Woodwin (IRE) **Mrs J. Wood**
102 WORLD RECORD (IRE), b c Choisir (AUS)—Dancing Debut **Mrs J. Wood**
103 ZURIGHA (IRE), b f Cape Cross (IRE)—Noyelles (IRE) **S. H. Altayer**

TWO-YEAR-OLDS

104 ACQUAINT (IRE), gr f 20/2 Verglas (IRE)—
    Azia (IRE) (Desert Story (IRE)) (82000) **Highclere Thoroughbred Racing - Alcove**
105 ADAPTABILITY, ch f 26/2 Mastercraftsman (IRE)—Sierra (Dr Fong (USA)) **Longview Stud & Bloodstock Ltd**
106 AFTER THE GOLDRUSH, b c 20/4 Kyllachy—Fine Lady (Selkirk (USA)) (85000) **The Gold Rush Partnership**
107 B f 31/3 Pivotal—Ailette (Second Set (IRE)) (111111) **Carmichael Simmons Humber**
108 Ch c 15/3 Exceed And Excel (AUS)—Aljafliyah (Halling (USA)) **Mrs J. Wood**
109 Ch f 19/3 Exceed And Excel (AUS)—Amazon Beauty (IRE) (Wolfhound (USA)) (60000) **S. Manana**
110 ANJAAL, ch c 4/4 Bahamian Bounty—
    Ballymore Celebre (IRE) (Peintre Celebre (USA)) (105000) **Hamdan Al Maktoum**
111 B c 22/3 Cape Cross (IRE)—Anna's Rock (IRE) (Rock of Gibraltar (IRE)) (145000) **S. H. Altayer**
112 ANTICIPATED (IRE), b c 13/4 Whipper (USA)—
    Foreplay (IRE) (Lujain (USA)) (23809) **Woodcock, Bull, Ivory, Hannon**
113 ARRANGER (IRE), b f 10/3 Bushranger (IRE)—El Morocco (USA) (El Prado (IRE)) (26666) **Mrs J. Wood**
114 ASCENDING ANGEL (IRE), b f 6/2 Sea The Stars (IRE)—
    Maskaya (IRE) (Machiavellian (USA)) (63491) **Mrs A. Turner**
115 AUTUMN SUNRISE (IRE), ch f 16/3 Camacho—Convenience (IRE) (Ela-Mana-Mou) (23809) **Mr M. Daniels**
116 BANAADEER (IRE), ch c 19/2 Tamayuz—Loose Julie (IRE) (Cape Cross (IRE)) **Hamdan Al Maktoum**
117 BEAU NASH (IRE), b c 2/3 Dandy Man (IRE)—
    Dathuil (IRE) (Royal Academy (USA)) (23809) **The Best Turned Out Partnership**
118 BIOGRAPHY, ch c 23/3 Assertive—Dahshah (Mujtahid (USA)) (24761) **Mrs V Hubbard & Mrs J K Powell**
119 BIRD OF LIGHT (IRE), b f 23/2 Elnadim (USA)—Lady Docker (IRE) (Docksider (USA)) (24761) **Rockcliffe Stud**
120 BISHOP WULSTAN (IRE), b c 9/4 Oratorio (IRE)—Laurentine (USA) (Private Account (USA)) (40000)
121 B c 7/4 Thousand Words—Blue Bamboo (Green Desert (USA)) (18000) **The Sydney Arms, Chelsea**
122 BOLD SPIRIT, b c 9/3 Invincible Spirit (IRE)—Far Shores (Distant View (USA)) **Her Majesty The Queen**
123 B c 9/2 Jeremy (USA)—Bon Ton Roulet (Hawk Wing (USA)) (30000) **Mr G. Moss**
124 B f 7/5 Exceed And Excel (AUS)—Broadway Hit (Sadler's Wells (USA)) (65000) **Saif Ali & Saeed H. Altayer**
125 BUNKER (IRE), br c 24/1 Hurricane Run (IRE)—
    Endure (IRE) (Green Desert (USA)) (50000) **Morecombe, Anderson, Hughes**
126 B f 23/3 Bahamian Bounty—Cake (IRE) (Acclamation) **Mr D. J. Anderson**
127 Ch c 5/4 Art Connoisseur (IRE)—
    Capetown Girl (Danzero (AUS)) (47619) **Potensis Ltd, Chris Giles, J Palmer-Brown**
128 CARTHAGE (IRE), b c 5/3 Mastercraftsman (IRE)—Pitrizzia (Lando (GER)) (79364) **M. Pescod**
129 CAY DANCER, gr f 29/4 Danehill Dancer (IRE)—White Cay (Dalakhani (IRE)) (40000) **R. Barnett**
130 B c 23/3 Holy Roman Emperor (IRE)—Chanrossa (IRE) (Galileo (IRE)) (190000) **Carmichael Humber**
131 CHIEF BARKER (IRE), b c 23/3 Azamour (IRE)—Millay (Polish Precedent (USA)) **Middleham Park Racing XXIII**
132 B f 17/3 Teofilo (IRE)—Chrysalis (Soviet Star (USA)) (85000) **S. H. Altayer**
133 B c 10/2 Kyllachy—Coming Home (Vettori (IRE)) (45000) **Sheikh J. Al Dalmook Maktoum**
134 CONFLICTING, b c 27/4 Kyllachy—Piper's Ash (USA) (Royal Academy (USA)) (67460) **Mrs F. H. Hay**
135 CONSTANTINE, b c 26/3 Holy Roman Emperor (IRE)—
    Whatami (Daylami (IRE)) (75000) **The Royal Ascot Racing Club**
136 CORNCOCKLE, b f 28/3 Invincible Spirit (IRE)—Alovera (IRE) (King's Best (USA)) **Rockcliffe Stud**
137 COULSTY (IRE), b c 22/3 Kodiac—Hazium (IRE) (In The Wings) (57000) **Lord Vestey**
138 COUNTESS LEMONADE (IRE), b f 14/4 Duke of Marmalade (IRE)—
    Kelly Nicole (IRE) (Rainbow Quest (USA)) (50000) **Cheveley Park Stud Limited**
139 Ch c 28/2 Compton Place—Crowd Pleaser (IRE) (Royal Applause) (62000) **M. A. C. Buckley**
140 CRYSTAL NYMPH (IRE), b f 8/3 Rock of Gibraltar (IRE)—
    Flower of Kent (USA) (Diesis) (25000) **Mrs E. C. Roberts**
141 B c 19/2 Excellent Art—Dama'a (IRE) (Green Desert (USA)) (34285) **Chris Giles, Potensis Ltd, J Palmer-Brown**

MR RICHARD HANNON - Continued

142 B c 4/4 Kyllachy—Danceatdusk (Desert Prince (IRE)) (85000) **M Hughes & M Kerr-Dineen**
143 Ch c 14/2 Major Cadeaux—Dayville (USA) (Dayjur (USA)) (32380) **Mr M. Sultan**
144 **DIME DANCER (IRE),** b f 2/3 Azamour (IRE)—
                                  Happy Land (IRE) (Refuse To Bend (IRE) (31000) **Mr Michael Pescod & Mr Justin Dowley**
145 **DIZZY MISS LIZZY (IRE),** gr f 11/3 Verglas (IRE)—Maramba (USA) (Hussonet (USA)) **P. Newton**
146 **DOVER THE MOON (IRE),** b c 13/4 Bushranger (IRE)—
                                  Gold Script (FR) (Script Ohio (USA)) (100000) **The Arts Club (London) Limited**
147 **DOWNTON,** b c 18/3 Invincible Spirit (IRE)—Jouet (Reprimand) (115000) **Mrs J. Wood**
148 B f 28/3 Invincible Spirit (IRE)—Dundel (IRE) (Machiavellian (USA)) **C. F. Harrington**
149 B f 5/3 War Front (USA)—Easy To Cope (USA) (Copelan (USA)) (92165) **Qatar Racing Limited**
150 Ch c 10/3 Dubawi (IRE)—Eclaircie (IRE) (Thunder Gulch (USA)) **Sheikh J. Al Dalmook Maktoum**
151 **EDGE (IRE),** b c 17/2 Acclamation—Chanter (Lomitas) (55000) **Hughes, Morecombe, Anderson**
152 B c 20/4 Bushranger (IRE)—Evictress (IRE) (Sharp Victor (USA)) (47619) **Carmichael Humber**
153 **EXCEED AND EXCEED,** b c 6/4 Exceed And Excel (AUS)—
                                  Gandini (Night Shift (USA)) (53333) **Mr A. Al Mansoori**
154 **EXCHEQUER (IRE),** ch c 19/4 Exceed And Excel (AUS)—
                                  Tara's Force (IRE) (Acclamation) (67460) **Highclere Thoroughbred Racing - Lake Coniston**
155 **EXPERT (IRE),** gr c 12/3 Mastercraftsman (IRE)—Raphimix (FR) (Linamix (FR)) **Mrs J. Wood**
156 B c 30/3 Bushranger (IRE)—Fairmont (IRE) (Kingmambo (USA)) (23809) **D. W. Barker**
157 **FAST (IRE),** b f 7/4 Kodiac—Gypsy Royal (IRE) (Desert Prince (IRE)) (9523) **Mrs J. Wood**
158 B c 27/2 Tamayuz—Flanders (IRE) (Common Grounds) (70000) **Qatar Racing Limited**
159 Ch c 12/3 Dubawi (IRE)—Forest Storm (Galileo (IRE)) (32000) **S. Manana**
160 B f 12/3 Selkirk (USA)—Forgotten Dreams (Olden Times) (52000) **S. Manana**
161 B c 15/3 Acclamation—Glitter Baby (IRE) (Danehill Dancer (IRE)) **Mrs J. Wood**
162 B c 14/2 Kyllachy—Gold And Blue (IRE) (Bluebird (USA)) (57142) **Mr A. T. J. Russell**
163 **GOLD TOP (IRE),** ch f 6/2 Teofilo (IRE)—Top Row (Observatory (USA)) (32380) **D. Boocock**
164 **GREEN RUN,** b f 24/2 Compton Place—Gee Kel (Danehill Dancer (IRE)) (70000) **Qatar Racing Limited**
165 **HEDGE END (IRE),** gr f 10/3 Verglas (IRE)—Trilemma (Slip Anchor) (11000) **Grimes, Ivory, Bull, Hannon**
166 B f 23/1 Exceed And Excel (AUS)—Holamo (IRE) (Montjeu (IRE)) **Mrs J. Wood**
167 Ch f 26/2 Duke of Marmalade (IRE)—
                                  Honey Gold (IRE) (Indian Ridge) (14285) **Chris Giles, Simon Brown, Potensis Ltd**
168 **HOUSE CAPTAIN,** ch c 10/2 Captain Gerrard (IRE)—Dalmunzie (IRE) (Choisir (AUS)) (18095) **Mrs J. Wood**
169 **JANA,** ch f 2/2 Compton Place—Hasten (USA) (Lear Fan (USA)) (7619) **B. Bull**
170 **JIVE,** b f 24/3 Major Cadeaux—Lindy Hop (IRE) (Danehill Dancer (IRE)) (12000) **T. G. Holdcroft**
171 **KANTARA CASTLE (IRE),** b c 4/4 Baltic King—Arbitration (IRE) (Bigstone (IRE)) (26983) **R. Hannon**
172 **KARRAAR,** b c 10/2 Dubawi (IRE)—Maghya (IRE) (Mujahid (USA)) **Hamdan Al Maktoum**
173 **KINLOSS,** ch f 6/2 Kheleyf (USA)—Celtic Cross (Selkirk (USA)) **Her Majesty The Queen**
174 **LADY DAY,** b f 2/2 Selkirk (USA)—Lady Links (Bahamian Bounty) (80000) **M. Pescod**
175 B c 19/3 Tamayuz—Lady Livius (IRE) (Titus Livius (FR)) (37698) **De La Warr Racing**
176 **LAHUROOB,** b c 26/3 Kyllachy—Complimentary Pass (Danehill (USA)) (110000) **Hamdan Al Maktoum**
177 **LANGAVAT (IRE),** b c 21/2 Bushranger (IRE)—
                                  Bishop's Lake (Lake Coniston (IRE)) (50000) **Kennet Valley Thoroughbreds II**
178 **LAW APPEAL,** b c 14/4 Lawman (FR)—Demi Voix (Halling (USA)) **Longview Stud & Bloodstock Ltd**
179 **LEGEND RISING (IRE),** ch c 19/4 Tamayuz—Encouragement (Royal Applause) (63491) **Mr M. S. Al Shahi**
180 B c 17/3 Invincible Spirit (IRE)—Lia (IRE) (Desert King (IRE)) (87300) **H.E. Sheikh J. B. H. B. K. Al Thani**
181 **LIGEIA,** b c 24/3 Rail Link—Elegant Beauty (Olden Times) (2000) **The Pineapple Stud**
182 B f 1/3 Acclamation—Light It Up (IRE) (Elusive City (USA)) **Mrs J. Wood**
183 **LILBOURNE LASS,** ch f 15/1 Pastoral Pursuits—Talampaya (USA) (Elusive Quality (USA)) (15238) **Mrs S. Ensor**
184 **LINDART (ITY),** ch c 4/5 Dutch Art—
                                  Linda Surena (ARG) (Southern Halo (USA)) (45238) **Potensis Limited & Mr Chris Giles**
185 **LORD LEXINGTON,** ch c 15/4 Dutch Art—Spiralling (Pivotal) (62000) **Middleham Park Racing XXIII**
186 Ch f 18/5 Rock of Gibraltar (IRE)—
                                  Magnificent Bell (IRE) (Octagonal (NZ)) (30158) **Bull, Ivory, Woodcock, Hannon**
187 B c 10/3 Acclamation—Maid To Order (IRE) (Zafonic (USA)) (49523) **Mrs J Magnier, Mr M Tabor & Mr D Smith**
188 **MALACHIM MIST (IRE),** gr c 28/3 Dark Angel (IRE)—
                                  Sixfields Flyer (IRE) (Desert Style (IRE)) (42857) **Mr M. Daniels**
189 **MALORY TOWERS,** b f 2/2 Giant's Causeway (USA)—Dalisay (IRE) (Sadler's Wells (USA)) **P. Newton**
190 **MANDERLEY (IRE),** gr f 28/4 Clodovil (IRE)—Three Days In May (Cadeaux Genereux) (150000) **Mrs J. Wood**
191 **MANOR WAY (IRE),** b c 26/2 Holy Roman Emperor (IRE)—Cannikin (IRE) (Lahib (USA)) (50000) **Mrs A. Williams**
192 B f 28/1 Sir Percy—Medicea Sidera (Medicean) (55555) **Thurloe Thoroughbreds XXXI**
193 B f 19/4 Dylan Thomas (IRE)—Meseta (Lion Cavern (USA)) (13095) **Mr A. T. J. Russell**
194 **MIDNITE ANGEL (IRE),** gr f 14/2 Dark Angel (IRE)—
                                  Two Sets To Love (IRE) (Cadeaux Genereux) (24761) **Elaine Chivers & Richard Kidner**
195 **MIGHTY FORCE (IRE),** b c 21/4 Acclamation—Ikan (IRE) (Sri Pekan (USA)) (38095) **Mr M. S. Al Shahi**
196 **MILDENHALL,** ch f 14/2 Compton Place—Night Kiss (FR) (Night Shift (USA)) (22857) **B. Bull**

MR RICHARD HANNON - Continued

197 B f 24/1 Raven's Pass (USA)—Miss Anabaa (Anabaa (USA)) (130000) **S. Manana**
198 B c 13/3 Royal Applause—Mountain Law (USA) (Mountain Cat (USA)) (45000) **Malih L. Al Basti**
199 B f 19/3 Teofilo (IRE)—Mpumalanga (Observatory (USA)) (40000) **Sheikh J. Al Dalmook Maktoum**
200 MUHEED (IRE), b c 31/1 Raven's Pass (USA)—
Wolf Cleugh (IRE) (Last Tycoon) (130000) **H.E. Sheikh J. B. H. B. K. Al Thani**
201 MUMTAZA, b f 31/3 Nayef (USA)—Natagora (FR) (Divine Light (JPN)) **Hamdan Al Maktoum**
202 MUNFALLET (IRE), b c 26/2 Royal Applause—
Princess Mood (GER) (Muhtarram (USA)) (220000) **Hamdan Al Maktoum**
203 MUNJALLY, b c 15/3 Acclamation—Parabola (Galileo (IRE)) (71428) **Hamdan Al Maktoum**
204 MUSICAL COMEDY, b c 3/3 Royal Applause—Spinning Top (Alzao (USA)) **Her Majesty The Queen**
205 MUSICORA, b f 17/3 Acclamation—Belladera (IRE) (Alzao (USA)) (91269) **The Three Points Partnership**
206 MUTAMAKKIN (IRE), b c 20/3 Shamardal (USA)—
Princess Speedfit (FR) (Desert Prince (IRE)) (245000) **Hamdan Al Maktoum**
207 MUTAWATHEA, b c 26/2 Exceed And Excel (AUS)—
Esteemed Lady (IRE) (Mark of Esteem (IRE)) **Hamdan Al Maktoum**
208 B c 29/3 Exceed And Excel (AUS)—Mystery Ocean (Dr Fong (USA)) (80000) **S. H. Altayer**
209 B f 24/2 Holy Roman Emperor (IRE)—Nadwah (Shadeed (USA)) (16190) **P. A. Byrne**
210 NOS GALAN (IRE), b c 27/3 Dylan Thomas (IRE)—Chalice Wells (Sadler's Wells (USA)) **Mrs J. Wood**
211 B c 26/3 Kodiac—Olympia Theatre (Galileo (IRE)) (43809) **Carmichael Humber**
212 B f 1/4 Fastnet Rock (AUS)—On The Nile (IRE) (Sadler's Wells (USA)) (119047) **Carmichael Humber**
213 ORIEL, b f 21/2 Fastnet Rock (AUS)—
Labisa (IRE) (High Chaparral (IRE)) (60000) **Highclere Thoroughbred Racing -Petrushka**
214 OXLIP, b f 17/2 Three Valleys (USA)—Age of Chivalry (IRE) (Invincible Spirit (IRE)) **Rockcliffe Stud**
215 B c 23/3 Royal Applause—
Peaceful Kingdom (USA) (King of Kings (IRE)) (100000) **H.E. Sheikh J. B. H. B. K. Al Thani**
216 B f 3/2 Acclamation—Pina Colada (Sabrehill (USA)) **Mrs J. Wood**
217 B c 28/4 Exceed And Excel (AUS)—Pink Stone (FR) (Bigstone (IRE)) (50000) **S. Ali**
218 B f 9/2 Dubawi (IRE)—Portmeirion (Polish Precedent (USA)) (65000) **S. Ali**
219 PRISCA, b f 23/1 Holy Roman Emperor (IRE)—Ainia (Alhaarth (IRE)) **Mrs J. Wood**
220 PUPIL (IRE), b c 29/3 Mastercraftsman (IRE)—Blue Iris (Petong) (103174) **Mr W. A. Tinkler**
221 RAAJIS (IRE), gr f 4/1 Dark Angel (IRE)—Rumline (Royal Applause) (71428) **Hamdan Al Maktoum**
222 B f 23/2 Duke of Marmalade (IRE)—Rekindled Cross (IRE) (Cape Cross (IRE)) **Middleham Park Racing VI**
223 RISING DAWN (IRE), gr c 26/2 Dark Angel (IRE)—Irish Design (IRE) (Alhaarth (IRE)) (28571) **Mr M. S. Al Shahi**
224 B c 11/3 Royal Applause—Rolexa (Pursuit of Love) (160000) **Carmichael Humber**
225 Ch c 23/4 Iffraaj—Sagaing (Machiavellian) (USA)) **Mrs J. Wood**
226 B c 31/3 Teofilo (IRE)—
Saint Ann (USA) (Geiger Counter (USA)) (49523) **J Palmer-Brown, Potensis Ltd, Chris Giles**
227 Ch c 24/2 Winker Watson—Sakaka (Tobougg (IRE)) (20952) **Mr M. S. Al Shahi**
228 SAND DANCER (IRE), b f 15/2 Footstepsinthesand—
Annacloy Pearl (Mull of Kintyre (USA)) (40000) **Mr Michael Pescod & Mr Justin Dowley**
229 Gr c 30/3 Manduro (GER)—Sea Drift (FR) (Warning) (42000) **S. Manana**
230 SEBASTIAN BEACH (IRE), b c 22/4 Yeats (IRE)—
Night Club (Mozart (IRE)) (58000) **Mr Justin Dowley & Mr Michael Pescod**
231 SHAFRAH (IRE), b c 5/4 Acclamation—Rosy Dudley (IRE) (Grand Lodge (USA)) (240000) **Hamdan Al Maktoum**
232 SHAMSHON (IRE), b c 29/3 Invincible Spirit (IRE)—
Greenisland (IRE) (Fasliyev (USA)) (420000) **H.E. Sheikh J. B. H. B. K. Al Thani**
233 SHIFTING POWER, ch c 30/1 Compton Place—
Profit Alert (IRE) (Alzao (USA)) (28000) **Ms Elaine Chivers & Potensis Ltd**
234 SHOWPIECE, b c 12/2 Kyllachy—Striving (IRE) (Danehill Dancer (IRE)) (50000) **Cheveley Park Stud Limited**
235 B f 24/1 Royal Applause—Singitta (Singspiel (IRE)) (95000) **Sheikh R. D. Al Maktoum**
236 Ch c 26/4 Special Touch (IRE)—Spinning World (USA) (17000) **The Sydney Arms, Chelsea**
237 B c 24/4 Invincible Spirit (IRE)—Starry Messenger (Galileo (IRE)) **D. J. Barry**
238 STEVENTON STAR, b c 11/4 Pastoral Pursuits—
Premiere Dance (IRE) (Loup Solitaire (USA)) (55000) **Mr R. W. Tyrrell**
239 STRAIT RUN (IRE), ch c 1/3 Rock of Gibraltar (IRE)—
Gentlemen's Guest (USA) (Gentlemen (ARG)) (36190) **Noodles Racing**
240 SUITE (IRE), b f 21/2 Invincible Spirit (IRE)—Rakiza (IRE) (Elnadim (USA)) (62000) **Mrs J. Wood**
241 SWANWICK SHORE (IRE), b c 26/1 Tagula (IRE)—Cinzia Vegas (IRE) (Dr Fong (USA)) (66666) **Mrs J. Wood**
242 TABREEK (USA), ch c 24/2 Distorted Humor (USA)—
Blushing (GER) (Maria's Mon (USA)) (208909) **Hamdan Al Maktoum**
243 Br f 15/5 Cape Cross (IRE)—Tadkiyra (IRE) (Darshaan) (214285) **P. A. Byrne**
244 TANQEYA (IRE), b c 8/3 Intense Focus (USA)—Spinning Well (IRE) (Pivotal) (70000) **Hamdan Al Maktoum**
245 THE ALAMO (IRE), b c 27/4 High Chaparral (IRE)—
Inner Strength (FR) (Take Risks (FR)) (36507) **Ivory, Woodcock, Bull, Hannon**
246 B br c 30/3 Teofilo (IRE)—Think (FR) (Marchand de Sable (USA)) (62000) **Mr P. W. Reglar**

MR RICHARD HANNON - Continued

247 **THUNDER STRIKE**, ch c 16/2 Sakhee's Secret—Trump Street (First Trump) (38095) **Mr M. S. Al Shahi**
248 **TOORMORE (IRE)**, b c 19/3 Arakan (USA)—Danetime Out (IRE) (Danetime (IRE)) (34285)
249 **UNDER MY WING (IRE)**, ch c 12/3 Raven's Pass (USA)—Ra Hydee (USA) (Rahy (USA)) **Mrs J. Wood**
250 B f 11/2 Bushranger (IRE)—Undulation (Alhaarth (IRE)) (39681) **Mr A. Al Mansoori**
251 B c 11/2 Invincible Spirit (IRE)—Unreachable Star (Halling (USA)) **Carmel Stud**
252 B f 7/3 Holy Roman Emperor (IRE)—Valiantly (Anabaa (USA)) (30000) **Carmel Stud**
253 **VALUE (IRE)**, br f 9/3 Clodovil (IRE)—Shalev (GER) (Java Gold (USA)) **Mrs J. Wood**
254 B c 28/4 Acclamation—Venoge (IRE) (Green Desert (USA)) (140000) **Mrs J Magnier, Mr M Tabor & Mr D Smith**
255 **VENTURA ICE (IRE)**, gr f 1/4 Oratorio (IRE)—Tipperary Honor (FR) (Highest Honor (FR)) (43650)
256 Br c 18/4 Mastercraftsman (IRE)—Vingt Et Une (FR) (Sadler's Wells (USA)) (95238)
257 Ch f 6/3 New Approach (IRE)—Wadaat (Diktat) (400000) **H.E. Sheikh J. B. H. B. K. Al Thani**
258 B c 21/2 Mount Nelson—War Shanty (Warrshan (USA)) (1000) **R. Hannon**
259 **WAR SPIRIT**, b c 30/4 Exceed And Excel (AUS)—Alybgood (USA) (Alydeed (CAN)) (59523) **Mr M. S. Al Shahi**
260 **WASHAAR (IRE)**, b c 5/4 Kodiac—Dabtiyra (IRE) (Dr Devious (IRE)) (75000) **Hamdan Al Maktoum**
261 Ch c 27/3 Danehill Dancer (IRE)—
       Wedding Morn (IRE) (Sadler's Wells (USA)) (174603) **H.H. Sheikh Mohammed bin Khalifa Al-Thani**
262 Ch c 2/3 Exceed And Excel (AUS)—Winding·(USA) (Irish River (FR)) **Mrs J. Wood**
263 **WINDSHEAR**, b c 14/2 Hurricane Run (IRE)—Portal (Hernando (FR)) (75396) **Mr M. Daniels**
264 B c 16/2 Bushranger (IRE)—Wings of Fame (IRE) (Namid) **Mrs J. Wood**

Other Owners: Mrs R. Ablett, Mr J. Ablett, Mr R.D. Ambrose, Mr R.J. Blunt, Mr D. P.N. Brown, S. J. Brown, Mrs F. J. Carmichael, Ms E. C. Chivers, Miss C. I. Chivers, Ms L. D. Chivers, Mr M. Clarke, D. D. Clee, Mrs J. P. Clee, Lord De La Warr, Countess De La Warr, Mr D. L. Dixon, Mr P. E. Done, Mr L. J. Dowley, Sir A. Ferguson, Mr J. Fiyaz, Mr R. J. Fowler, Mr C. M. Giles, J. K. Grimes, P. W. Haddock, Mrs F. M. Hallett, S. Hassiakos, Mr R. P. Heffer, Mr H. R. Heffer, The Hon H. M. Herbert, Highclere Thoroughbred Racing Ltd, R. G. Hitchcock, Mrs V. Hubbard, Mr M. B. Hughes, Mr C. M. Humber, K. T. Ivory, Mr J. Jeffries, Mr M. J. Jooste, Mr B. Kantor, Mr. Kerr-Dineen, Mr M. J. Kershaw, Mr S. L. Keswick, Mr R. A. Kidner, A. E. King, Mr S. G. Lake, Mr A. T. Macdonald, Mrs S. Magnier, G. A. Mason, R. H. W. Morecombe, P. H. Morgan, Mrs M. E. Morgan, Mrs K. J. Morton, Lord James Netherthorpe, Mrs M. O'Sullivan, Mr J. Pak, T. S. Palin, O. J. W. Pawle, Potensis Limited, Mrs J. K. Powell, M. Prince, Mr T. J. Ramsden, Mr J. J. Reddington, Mr W. J. Reilly, Mr R. Renwick, Mr N. M. S. Rich, N. J. F. Robinson, Mr M. E. Sangster, R. A. Simmons, D. Smith, Mr A. G. Smith, Miss B. A. Snow, Mr J. A. B. Stafford, Mr J. R. F. Stunt, Mr J. J. Sullivan, M. Tabor, Mr R. J. Wood, N. A. Woodcock, C. N. Wright.

Assistant Trainer: Richard Hannon Jnr

Jockey (flat): Richard Hughes, Pat Dobbs, Ryan Moore, Dane O'Neill, Kieran O'Neill. **Apprentice:** Stephen King, Rufus Vergette, Megan Whitehead.

---

288 MR GEOFFREY HARKER, Thirsk
Postal: **Stockhill Green, York Rd, Thirkelby, Thirsk, North Yorkshire, YO7 3AS**
Contacts: **PHONE (01845) 501117 FAX (01845) 501614 MOBILE (07803) 116412/(07930) 125544**
E-MAIL gandjhome@aol.com

1 **BLING KING**, 4, b g Haafhd—Bling Bling (IRE) **P. I. Harker**
2 **BREEZOLINI**, 5, b m Bertolini (USA)—African Breeze **Northumbria Leisure Ltd**
3 **CONJOLA**, 6, b m Grape Tree Road—Conchita **Miss R. Brewis**
4 **DIALOGUE**, 7, b g Singspiel (IRE)—Zonda **P. I. Harker**
5 4, B f Courteous—Diamond Orchid (IRE) **A. S. Ward**
6 **EIJAAZ (IRE)**, 12, b g Green Desert (USA)—Kismah **A. S. Ward**
7 **EN FUEGO**, 6, b g Firebreak—Yanomami (USA) **P. I. Harker**
8 **FIRESIDE DREAMS**, 4, b g Boogie Street—Champagne N Dreams **J. L. Harker**
9 **FREE ART**, 5, b g Iffraaj—Possessive Artiste **A. S. Ward**
10 **GALA CASINO STAR (IRE)**, 8, ch g Dr Fong (USA)—Abir **Mrs T. Nason**
11 **GAP PRINCESS (IRE)**, 9, b m Noverre (USA)—Safe Care (IRE) **Northumbria Leisure Ltd & J.L Harker**
12 **GINGER JACK**, 6, ch g Refuse To Bend (IRE)—Coretta (IRE) **C. H. McGhie**
13 **I CONFESS**, 8, br g Fantastic Light (USA)—Vadsagreya (FR) **Mr B. Harker**
14 **JIMSNEVERRIGHT**, 5, b g Iktibas—Lady Lexie **Mr James Binks**
15 **MISTY EYES**, 4, b f Byron—Wax Eloquent **Haven Stud**
16 **MOCCASIN (FR)**, 4, b g Green Tune (USA)—Museum Piece **Mr & Mrs H Nensey, Saif Nensey**
17 **PRECIOUS LASS (IRE)**, 5, b m Gold Well—Ardrina **Roger Eddleston & David Cunningham**
18 **SCARLET GEM**, 5, ch m Grape Tree Road—Scarlet Memory
19 **SINAI (IRE)**, 4, b f Moss Vale (IRE)—Ten Commandments (IRE) **Mr & Mrs H Nensey, Saif Nensey**
20 **TARTAN GIGHA (IRE)**, 8, b g Green Desert (USA)—High Standard **A. S. Ward**
21 **TIMEFORTEE (IRE)**, 4, b g Teofilo (IRE)—Begueule (FR) **G. A. Harker**
22 **WANNABE KING**, 7, b g King's Best (USA)—Wannabe Grand (IRE) **Mr & Mrs H Nensey, Saif Nensey**

MR GEOFFREY HARKER - Continued

23 **WHITE DEER (USA)**, 9, b g Stravinsky (USA)—Brookshield Baby (IRE) **A. S. Ward**
24 **YKIKAMOOCOW**, 7, b m Cape Town (IRE)—Pigeon **P. Benson**

THREE-YEAR-OLDS

25 **BRANSTON JUBILEE**, ch f Assertive—Branston Jewel (IRE) **G. A. Harker**

TWO-YEAR-OLDS

26 B f 3/4 Phoenix Reach (IRE)—Comtesse Noire (CAN) (Woodman (USA)) (4761) **GB Racing Club**
27 B f 9/4 Phoenix Reach (IRE)—Rasmalai (Sadler's Wells (USA)) (3809) **GB Racing Club**

Other Owners: Mr David Cunningham, Mr Roger Eddleston, Mrs J. L. Harker, Mr Husain Nensey, Mrs Nissa Nensey, Mr Saif Nensey, Northumbria Leisure Ltd..

Assistant Trainer: Jenny Harker

Jockey (NH): W. T. Kennedy. **Apprentice:** Jordan Nason.

289

MR RICHARD HARPER, Banbury
Postal: Home Farm, Kings Sutton, Banbury, Oxfordshire, OX17 3RS
Contacts: PHONE (01295) 810997 FAX (01295) 812787 MOBILE (07970) 223481
E-MAIL rharper@freeuk.com

1 **CHAPEL HOUSE**, 10, b g Beneficial—My Moona **R. C. Harper**
2 **MASTERPOINT**, 13, ch g Mark of Esteem (IRE)—Baize **R. C. Harper**
3 **TOP BENEFIT (IRE)**, 11, gr g Beneficial—Cottage Lass (IRE) **R. C. Harper**

Assistant Trainer: C. Harper

290

MRS JESSICA HARRINGTON, Kildare
Postal: Commonstown Racing Stables Ltd., Moone, Co. Kildare, Ireland
Contacts: PHONE (00353) 5986 24153 FAX (00353) 5986 24292 MOBILE (00353) 8725 66129
E-MAIL jessica@jessicaharringtonracing.com WEBSITE www.jessicaharringtonracing.com

1 **ANNIE OAKLEY (IRE)**, 5, br b m Westerner—Gaye Artiste (IRE) **Mrs Gina Galvin**
2 **BEACHDALE LAD (IRE)**, 6, ch g Carroll House—Morning Clare (IRE) **Mr Geoffrey Ruddock**
3 **BENDZOLDAN (IRE)**, 5, b m Refuse To Bend (IRE)—Zoldan **Mr Jarlath Smyth**
4 **BEYOND BERLIN (IRE)**, 4, b g Big Bad Bob (IRE)—Soviet Belle (IRE) **Anamoine Ltd**
5 **BIBLE BELT (IRE)**, 5, br m Big Bad Bob (IRE)—Shine Silently (IRE) **Anamoine Ltd**
6 **BOB LE BEAU (IRE)**, 6, br g Big Bad Bob (IRE)—Shine Silently (IRE) **Anamoine Ltd**
7 **BOSTONS ANGEL (IRE)**, 9, b g Winged Love (IRE)—Lady Boston (FR) **Mr Elder Scouller**
8 **BULLOCK HARBOUR (IRE)**, 9, b g Second Empire (IRE)—Coteri Run **Mr Barry Connell**
9 **BURN AND TURN (IRE)**, 7, b m Flemensfirth (USA)—Pescetto Lady (IRE) **Mr Joe O'Flaherty**
10 **CAILIN ANNAMH (IRE)**, 5, b m Definite Article—Prairie Bell (IRE) **Flyers Syndicate**
11 **CELTIC CAILIN (IRE)**, 7, b m Beneficial—Distant Dreams (IRE) **MJK Syndicate**
12 **CHINO VALDES (IRE)**, 8, b g Craigsteel—Marovia (IRE) **Mr Stephen McCormack**
13 **CITIZENSHIP**, 7, b g Beat Hollow—Three More (USA) **Fresh By Nature Syndicate**
14 **DANE STREET (USA)**, 4, br f Street Cry (IRE)—Daneleta (IRE) **Mrs Sonia Rogers**
15 **DIRECTOR'S FORUM (IRE)**, 5, ch g Pivotal—Stage Struck (IRE) **Mr Barry Connell**
16 **EMPRESS OF TARA (IRE)**, 4, br f Holy Roman Emperor (IRE)—Colour Coordinated (IRE) **Mr Joe Keappock**
17 **GIMLI'S ROCK (IRE)**, 7, b g Rock of Gibraltar (IRE)—Beltisaal (FR) **Mr Geoffrey Ruddock**
18 **HURRICANE RIDGE (IRE)**, 4, b g Hurricane Run (IRE)—Warrior Wings **Lakeside Syndicate**
19 **IMPERIAL CASCADE (IRE)**, 8, b g Imperial Ballet (IRE)—Shawiya (IRE) **Mrs Judy Wilson**
20 **JETSON (IRE)**, 8, b g Oscar (IRE)—La Noire (IRE) **Mr Gerard McGrath**
21 **JEZKI (IRE)**, 5, b g Milan—La Noire (IRE) **Mr Gerard McGrath**
22 **KNIGHTSONE (IRE)**, 4, b g Chevalier (IRE)—Delivered (IRE) **Louise Baker**
23 **LADY TEMPTRESS (IRE)**, 5, b m High Chaparral (IRE)—Causeway Song (USA) **Mrs Marie Browne**
24 **MACNICHOLSON (IRE)**, 4, b g Definite Article—Heroic Performer (IRE) **Mr Joe O'Flaherty**
25 **MADAM BOVARY (IRE)**, 7, b m Old Vic—Saraemma **Mr Dermot Cox**
26 **MALLER TREE**, 6, b g Karinga Bay—Annaberg (IRE) **Favourites Racing Ltd**
27 **MASTEROFDECEPTION (IRE)**, 5, b g Darsi (FR)—Sherberry (IRE) **Mr John Harrington**
28 **MISS MACNAMARA (IRE)**, 4, b f Dylan Thomas (IRE)—
Kincob (USA) **Mrs Sonia Rogers & Hot to Trot Racing Club**

MRS JESSICA HARRINGTON - Continued

29 **MOSCOW MAGIC (IRE)**, 5, b g Moscow Society (USA)—
See More Tricks **Mr Hugh Williams & Mr William Jenks**
30 **MR FIFTYONE (IRE)**, 4, b g Jeremy (USA)—Maka (USA) **Mr David Bobbett**
31 **ONE FINE DAY (IRE)**, 4, b f Choisir (AUS)—Night Eyes (IRE) **Mr John Harrington**
32 **OPERATING (IRE)**, 6, b g Milan—Seymourswift **Mr Michael Buckley**
33 **OSCARS WELL (IRE)**, 8, b br g Oscar (IRE)—Placid Willow (IRE) **Molly Malone Syndicate**
34 **OVERCALL (IRE)**, 4, b g Choisir (AUS)—My Darling Dodo (IRE) **Mr Barry Connell**
35 **PAINTED LADY (IRE)**, 4, b f Presenting—Amathea (FR) **Mr Steve Hemstock, Mr John Harrington**
36 **PARADIS DE THAIX (FR)**, 10, ch g April Night (FR)—Etoile de Thaix (FR) **Hard To Get Syndicate**
37 **PARRAMATTA (IRE)**, 5, gr m Aussie Rules (USA)—Aspasias Tizzy (USA) **Mr Gittins**
38 **PASSAGERE (FR)**, 4, b f Great Journey (JPN)—Passing Lady (FR) **Pegasus Farms Ltd**
39 **PENNY OPERA (IRE)**, 5, b m Presenting—
Opera Hat (IRE) **Mrs Caroline Waters, Mrs Diana Cooper & Mrs Valerie Cooper**
40 **PLAY THE MARKET (IRE)**, 6, b g King's Theatre (IRE)—Market Lass (IRE) **Mrs Judy Wilson**
41 **POSH FROCK (IRE)**, 4, b f Oratorio (IRE)—Opera Ridge (FR) **Lord Richard Wellesley**
42 **REEN RINCEOIR (IRE)**, 4, gr f Aussie Rules (USA)—Early Fin (IRE) **Mr Jerry Harrington**
43 **RUN 'N' JUMP (IRE)**, 5, b m Flemensfirth (USA)—Cut 'n' Run (IRE) **Mr Elder Scoulier**
44 **SALUTING (IRE)**, 7, b g Presenting—Seymourswift **Mr George Hartigan**
45 5, B m Flemensfirth (USA)—Serenique **Mr Steve Hemstock**
46 **SMITHFIELD (IRE)**, 5, b g Cape Cross (IRE)—Daraliya (IRE) **A Blessing In Disguise Partnership**
47 **SOMETHINGDIFFERENT (IRE)**, 7, b g Distant Music (USA)—Valleya (FR) **Mr Geoffrey Ruddock**
48 **STEPS TO FREEDOM (IRE)**, 7, b g Statue of Liberty (USA)—Dhakhirah (IRE) **Mrs Elizabeth Hussey**
49 **STOP ROAD LAD (IRE)**, 7, ch g Definite Article—Masriyna (IRE) **Sevens Racing Syndicate**
50 **TAKEYOURCAPOFF (IRE)**, 8, b m King's Theatre (IRE)—Masriyna's Article (IRE) **Sport Racing Club**
51 **THE BIG EASY (IRE)**, 5, b g Hurricane Run (IRE)—
Flaming Song **Mrs P. K. Cooper, Mrs Adam Gurney, Ronchalon Ireland Partnership**
52 **THE ENGINEER (IRE)**, 7, b g Old Vic—Mother Superior (IRE) **Mr Howard Spooner**
53 **TRACK THE PLAGUE (IRE)**, 5, b g Oscar (IRE)—Madmoiselle Eloile (IRE) **Mr David Bobbett**
54 **WHY BUT WHY (USA)**, 5, b g Whywhywhy (USA)—Miss Orah **Mr John Harrington**

THREE-YEAR-OLDS

55 **BANKER BURKE (IRE)**, br g Big Bad Bob (IRE)—Ski For Gold **Anamoine Ltd**
56 **COMEAROUNDSUNDOWN (IRE)**, ch f Shirocco (GER)—Yandina (IRE) **Mr Joe Throsby**
57 **DAVANTI (IRE)**, b f Danehill Dancer (IRE)—Lace (IRE) **Mr Robert Scarborough, Chelston & Orpendale**
58 **FLIGHT OFTHE SAKER (USA)**, b br c Dynaformer (USA)—Ask Me No Secrets (USA) **Dr Kai Chah Tan**
59 **IKE'S POND**, b c Royal Applause—Umlilo **Mr J. P. McManus**
60 B f Kyllachy—Inchberry **Mr J. P. McManus**
61 Ro f Dalakhani (IRE)—Kalagold (IRE) **Mr Noel Carter**
62 **LIBERATING**, b f Iffraaj—Ros The Boss (IRE) **Peter Barnett, Mrs Yvonne Nicoll, Mr Joe Throsby**
63 **MAGICAL STEPS (USA)**, ch f Giant's Causeway (USA)—Mayville's Magic (USA) **McElroy Racing Syndicate**
64 **MOUNT VENUS**, b f Mount Nelson—Honorlina (FR) **Mr Hugh Williams**
65 **NEWBERRY HILL (IRE)**, ch g Kheleyf (USA)—Zonic **Mr Noel Carter**
66 **PEGGY'S LEG (USA)**, b f Henrythenavigator (USA)—Audit (USA) **Mr J. P. McManus**
67 **POLISHED ROCK (IRE)**, ch g Rock of Gibraltar (IRE)—Where We Left Off **Mr Robert Ryan**
68 **PROTESTANT (IRE)**, b g Papal Bull—Vintage Escape (IRE) **Mrs P. K. Cooper**
69 **RUPA (IRE)**, b f Acclamation—Claustra (FR) **Niarchos Family**
70 **TRI NA CEILE (IRE)**, ch f Galileo (IRE)—Pescia (IRE) **Mr J. P. McManus**
71 B g Ramonti (FR)—Triple Green **Mr Frank O'Donnell**
72 **WEATHER WATCH (IRE)**, b c Hurricane Run (IRE)—Caravan of Dreams (IRE) **Mrs P. K. Cooper**
73 B c Azamour (IRE)—Zapping (IRE) **Mr Richard Roche, Mr David Cox & Mr Dermot Cox**

TWO-YEAR-OLDS

74 B c 11/3 Intense Focus (USA)—Aminata (Glenstal (USA)) (8729) **Mr John Harrington**
75 B f 12/3 Shamardal (USA)—Athlumney Lady (Lycius (USA)) (25396) **Mr John Harrington**
76 B f 20/2 Teofilo (IRE)—Azzila (Cadeaux Genereux) **Mr John Harrington**
77 B f 30/3 Big Bad Bob (IRE)—Desert Trail (IRE) (Desert Style (IRE)) (2062) **Mr John Harrington**
78 B f 4/2 Jeremy (USA)—Krynica (USA) (Danzig (USA)) (15079) **Mr John Harrington**
79 **LAKE SUPERIOR (IRE)**, b c 4/5 Dalakhani (IRE)—Lakatoi (Saddlers' Hall (IRE)) **Mr Mark Dixon**
80 B f 16/4 Big Bad Bob (IRE)—Little Miss Diva (IRE) (Diktat) (4/6) **Mr John Harrington**
81 B c 5/5 Azamour (IRE)—Little Whisper (IRE) (Be My Guest (USA)) (20000) **Mr Peter Winkworth**
82 Ch f 10/4 Kheleyf (USA)—Luceball (IRE) (Bluebird (USA)) **Mr Gerry Byrne**
83 B f 25/3 Intikhab (USA)—Lunar Love (IRE) (In The Wings) (33333) **Favourites Racing Ltd**
84 B f 2/2 Acclamation—Mary Arnold (IRE) (Hernando (FR)) (15873) **Niarchos Family**
85 **ODE TO PSYCHE (IRE)**, b f 1/3 Dansili—Quan Yin (IRE) (Sadler's Wells (USA)) **Niarchos Family**

MRS JESSICA HARRINGTON - Continued

Assistant Trainers: Mrs Emma Galway, Mr Eamonn Leigh

Jockey (flat): Fran Berry. **Jockey (NH):** Robert Power, Andrew Leigh, Mark Bolger, Tommy Treacy. **Conditional:** Kevin Sexton. **Apprentice:** Charlie Elliott. **Amateur:** Mr Mark Fahey, Miss Kate Harrington.

 MR RONALD HARRIS, Chepstow
Postal: Ridge House Stables, Earlswood, Chepstow, Monmouthshire, NP16 6AN
Contacts: **PHONE** (01291) 641689 **FAX** (01291) 641258 **MOBILE** (07831) 770899
E-MAIL ridgehousestables.ltd@btinternet.com **WEBSITE** www.ronharrisracing.co.uk

1 **ABHAATH (USA)**, 4, b g Hard Spun (USA)—Above Perfection (USA) **Ridge House Stables Ltd**
2 **APRIL FOOL**, 9, ch g Pivotal—Palace Affair **S. & A. Mares**
3 **ATHAAKEEL (IRE)**, 7, b m Almutawakel—Asaafeer (USA) **Drag Star On Swan**
4 **BELLE BAYARDO (IRE)**, 5, b g Le Vie Dei Colori—Heres The Plan (IRE) **William Jones Lisa Harrington**
5 **COMMON CENTS**, 4, ch g Pivotal—Small Change (IRE) **S & A Mares & M Saunders**
6 **DIAMOND VINE (IRE)**, 5, b h Diamond Green (FR)—Glasnas Giant **T. Reffell**
7 **FAITHFUL RULER (USA)**, 9, b br g Elusive Quality (USA)—Fancy Ruler (USA) **Ridge House Stables Ltd**
8 **FANTASY FIGHTER (IRE)**, 8, b g Danetime (IRE)—Lady Montekin **The Fantasy Fellowship F**
9 **FICELLE (IRE)**, 4, b f Chineur (FR)—Petite Boulangere (IRE) **B. G. Hicks**
10 **ITALIAN TOM (IRE)**, 6, b h Le Vie Dei Colori—Brave Cat (IRE) **S. & A. Mares**
11 **JALORS (IRE)**, 5, b g Invincible Spirit (IRE)—Julie Jalouse (USA) **David & Gwyn Joseph**
12 **KEPT**, 4, ch g Pivotal—Possessed **Robert & Nina Bailey**
13 **LADY MANGO (IRE)**, 5, ch m Bahamian Bounty—Opera **Mr L. Scadding**
14 **LIGHT FROM MARS**, 8, gr g Fantastic Light (USA)—Hylandra (USA) **Mrs N. J. Macauley**
15 **NIGER (IRE)**, 4, ch c Pivotal—Tithcar **Mrs R. M. Serrell**
16 **NIGHT TRADE (IRE)**, 6, b m Trade Fair—Compton Girl **Alan & Adam Darlow, A Darlow Productions**
17 **NOVERRE TO GO (IRE)**, 7, ch g Noverre (USA)—Ukraine Venture **Robert & Nina Bailey**
18 **OFFBEAT SAFARIS (IRE)**, 5, b g Le Vie Dei Colori—Baywood **Mrs J. E. F. Adams**
19 **PERLACHY**, 9, b g Kyllachy—Perfect Dream **Mrs N. J. Macauley**
20 **SILENT ENERGY (IRE)**, 4, b g Le Vie Dei Colori—Ghada (USA) **Ridge House Stables Ltd**
21 **SIR DYLAN**, 4, b g Dylan Thomas (IRE)—Monteleone (IRE) **Ridge House Stables Ltd**
22 **SIR MOZART (IRE)**, 10, b g Mozart (IRE)—Lady Silver Hawk (USA) **Ridge House Stables Ltd**
23 **SPIC 'N SPAN**, 8, b g Piccolo—Sally Slade **P. Nurcombe**
24 **SPINNING RIDGE (IRE)**, 8, ch g Spinning World (USA)—Summer Style (IRE) **Ridge House Stables Ltd**
25 **WATCH THE BIRDIE (IRE)**, 5, b m Kodiac—Silk Point (IRE) **The Yes No Wait Sorries**

THREE-YEAR-OLDS

26 **AL SULAIMI (IRE)**, br c Jeremy (USA)—Capital Gain (FR) **Mr A. N. Mubarak**
27 **CHELSEA GREY (IRE)**, gr f Verglas (IRE)—Kapera (FR) **Mr L. Scadding**
28 **HIDDEN LINK**, b g Rail Link—Gloved Hand **Ridge House Stables Ltd**
29 **HYPNOTISM**, ch g Pivotal—Hypnotize **Ridge House Stables Ltd**
30 **KHEFYN (IRE)**, br g Kheleyf (USA)—Highly Respected (IRE) **Robert & Nina Bailey**
31 **KODATISH (IRE)**, b c Kodiac—Atishoo (IRE) **Mr J Hatherell & Ridge House Stables**
32 **LUCKY SUIT (IRE)**, b f Red Clubs (IRE)—Alexander Family (USA) **S. & A. Mares**
33 **MELODEE PRINCESS (IRE)**, b f Acclamation—Pitrizzia **S & A Mares & M Benton**
34 **VERGALITY RIDGE (IRE)**, gr g Verglas (IRE)—Phoenix Factor (IRE) **Ridge House Stables Ltd**
35 **WINDFORPOWER (IRE)**, b g Red Clubs (IRE)—Dubai Princess (IRE) **Mr A. D. Cooke**
36 **XCLUSIVE**, b g Pivotal—Dance A Daydream **Ridge House Stables Ltd**

TWO-YEAR-OLDS

37 B f 27/2 Bushranger (IRE)—Brave Cat (IRE) (Catrail (USA)) (14000) **Ridge House Stables Ltd**
38 **GO GLAMOROUS (IRE)**, b f 22/5 Elnadim (USA)—
Glamorous Air (IRE) (Air Express (IRE)) (15873) **Robert & Nina Bailey**
39 B c 20/4 Arakan (USA)—Grandel (Owington) (15872) **Ridge House Stables Ltd**
40 **M'SELLE (IRE)**, b f 21/3 Elnadim (USA)—Key Rose (IRE) (Key of Luck (USA)) (15079) **Robert & Nina Bailey**
41 **MR DANDY MAN (IRE)**, ch c 1/4 Dandy Man (IRE)—Boudica (IRE) (Alhaarth (IRE)) (11904) **S. & A. Mares**
42 **WALTA (IRE)**, b c 4/2 Tagula (IRE)—Hi Katriona (IRE) (Second Empire (USA)) (9523) **Robert & Nina Bailey**

Other Owners: R. M. Bailey, Mrs J. H. Bailey, Mr A. Baker, M. J. Benton, A. M. Blewitt, C. S. J. Coley, P Coll, Mr A. M. Darlow, Mr A. Darlow, Ms L. J. Harrington, Mr R. A. J. Hatherell, D. M. Hussey, Mr W. D. Jones, Mr D. M. Joseph, Mr D. G. Joseph, Mr S. Mares, Mrs A. Mares, Mr L. A. McGuinness, Mr M. Saunders.

Apprentice: Darren Egan, Gary Phillips.

292 MR SHAUN HARRIS, Worksop

Postal: Pinewood Stables, Carburton, Worksop, Nottinghamshire, S80 3BT
Contacts: PHONE (01909) 470936 FAX (01909) 470936 MOBILE (07768) 950460
E-MAIL shaunharris.racing@hotmail.co.uk WEBSITE www.shaunharrisracing.co.uk

1 EL BRAVO, 7, ch g Falbrav (IRE)—Alessandra **Nottinghamshire Racing**
2 FATHER SHINE (IRE), 10, b br g Supreme Leader—Shean Hill (IRE) **Mrs A. Kenny**
3 GUAVA, 4, b f Kyllachy—Spunger **R. Naylor**
4 MEDAM, 4, b f Medicean—Mamounia (IRE) **Burton Agnes Bloodstock**
5 MIEREVELD, 6, b g Red Ransom (USA)—Mythic **Mrs A. Kenny**
6 MUSICAL STRIKE, 4, b g Striking Ambition—Musical Fair **Mr W. Hobson**
7 RAZZLE DAZZLE 'EM, 4, b g Phoenix Reach—Rasmani **Winterbeck Manor Stud Ltd**
8 RICHO, 7, ch g Bertolini (USA)—Noble Water (FR) **Miss G. H. Ward**
9 RISE TO GLORY (IRE), 5, b h King's Best (USA)—Lady At War **The Moorhouse Partnership**
10 ROY'S LEGACY, 4, b c Phoenix Reach (IRE)—Chocolada **Karl Blackwell Steve Mohammed S A Harris**
11 SEDGWICK, 11, b g Nashwan (USA)—Imperial Bailiwick (IRE) **Mr W. Hobson**
12 TENANCY (IRE), 9, b g Rock of Gibraltar (IRE)—Brush Strokes **Nottinghamshire Racing**

THREE-YEAR-OLDS

13 BETTY BOO (IRE), ch f Thousand Words—Poker Dice **Mr A. K. Elton**
14 BLUE CLUMBER, b f Sleeping Indian—Blue Nile (IRE) **Wilf Hobson & Miss H Ward**
15 Ch g Phoenix Reach (IRE)—Rainbows Guest (IRE) **Mr C. Harris**
16 Ch f Phoenix Reach (IRE)—Rasmani
17 RED STAR LADY (IRE), b f Redback—Vigorous (IRE) **Lease Terminated**

TWO-YEAR-OLDS

18 B f 4/2 Pastoral Pursuits—Blue Nile (IRE) (Bluebird (USA)) (1000) **Nottinghamshire Racing**
19 COME ON LULU, ch f 2/6 Calcutta—Flashing Floozie (Muhtarram (USA)) **Mrs A. Kenny**
20 B f 13/2 Firebreak—Manila Selection (USA) (Manila (USA)) (2380) **Mr C. Harris**
21 Gr f 23/4 Clodovil (IRE)—Masakira (IRE) (Royal Academy (USA)) (5714) **Mr W. Hobson**
22 B f 17/4 Phoenix Reach (IRE)—Shosolosa (IRE) (Dansili)

Other Owners: Mr K. Blackwell, Mrs M. C. Coltman, The Hon Mrs E. S. Cunliffe-Lister, S. A. Harris, Mrs V. Hobson, Mr S. Mohammed, Mr S. Rowley.

293 MISS LISA HARRISON, Aldoth

Postal: Cobble Hall, Aldoth, Nr Silloth, Cumbria, CA7 4NE
Contacts: PHONE (01697) 361753 FAX (01697) 342250 MOBILE (07725) 535554
E-MAIL lisa@daharrison.co.uk

1 SOLWAY BAY, 11, b g Cloudings (IRE)—No Problem Jac **David A. Harrison**
2 SOLWAY DANDY, 6, b g Danroad (AUS)—Solway Rose **David A. Harrison**
3 SOLWAY DORNAL, 8, b g Alflora (IRE)—Solway Donal (IRE) **David A. Harrison**
4 SOLWAY GENT, 5, b g Gentleman's Deal (IRE)—Solway Rose **David A. Harrison**
5 SOLWAY LEGEND, 6, ch g And Beyond (IRE)—Spicey Cut **David A. Harrison**
6 SOLWAY SAM, 10, b g Double Trigger (IRE)—Some Gale **David A. Harrison**
7 SOLWAY SILVER, 7, gr g Silver Patriarch (IRE)—Solway Rose **David A. Harrison**
8 SOLWAY STAR, 10, ch g Zaha (CAN)—Cuddle Bunny **David A. Harrison**
9 VIVONA HILL, 9, b g Overbury (IRE)—Lets Go Dutch **Mrs F. Crone & Mrs V. Birnie**

Other Owners: Mrs V. A. Birnie, Mrs F. H. Crone.

294 MR BEN HASLAM, Middleham

Postal: Castle Barn Cottage, Castle Hill, Middleham, Leyburn, North Yorkshire, DL8 4QW
Contacts: PHONE (01969) 624351 FAX (01969) 624463 MOBILE (07764) 411660
E-MAIL office@benhaslamracing.com WEBSITE www.benhaslamracing.com

1 AZZURRA DU CAPRIO (IRE), 5, ch m Captain Rio—Dunbrody (FR) **Blue Lion Racing IX**
2 DANCE FOR GEORGIE, 4, ch f Motivator—Chetwynd (IRE) **Mr M. J. James**
3 DREAMING OF RUBIES, 4, b f Oasis Dream—Rubies From Burma (USA) **Middleham Park Racing XXVII**
4 EXECUTIVE'S HALL (IRE), 9, b g Saddlers' Hall (IRE)—Overtime (IRE) **Mrs C. Barclay**
5 HI DANCER, 10, b g Medicean—Sea Music **Mr R. Tocher**

MR BEN HASLAM - Continued

  6 **LILIARGH (IRE)**, 4, b f Acclamation—Discover Roma (IRE) **Middleham Park Racing XXVII**
  7 **OPERATEUR (IRE)**, 5, b g Oratorio (IRE)—Kassariya (IRE) **Mrs Alison Royston & Mrs C Barclay**
  8 **SOUTHAMPTON (IRE)**, 7, b g Sadler's Wells (USA)—Katiyfa **Mrs A. Royston**

THREE-YEAR-OLDS

  9 Br f Ishiguru (USA)—Again Royale (IRE)
10 **DIAKTOROS (IRE)**, b g Red Clubs (IRE)—Rinneen (IRE) **Mr S Hassiakos & Sir Alex Ferguson**
11 **HI CANDY (IRE)**, b f Diamond Green (FR)—Dancing Steps **Go Alfresco Racing**
12 **INDIE BANNED**, b g Indesatchel (IRE)—Day By Day **Middleham Park Racing I**
13 Ch f Sakhee's Secret—May Day Queen (IRE) **Miss Karen Theobald**
14 **PINK CADILLAC (IRE)**, b f Clodovil (IRE)—Green Life **Go Alfresco Racing**
15 **POETIC STAR**, b g Byron—Balwarah (IRE) **Go Alfresco Racing**
16 **SHESNOTFORTURNING (IRE)**, b f Refuse To Bend (IRE)—Diplomats Daughter **Mrs C. Barclay**

Other Owners: Mr M. T. Buckley, Sir A. Ferguson, Mr B. M. R. Haslam, S. Hassiakos, T. S. Palin, M. Prince, R. Young.

Assistant Trainer: Leanne Kershaw

Jockey (NH): Barry Keniry. **Conditional:** Craig Gallagher.

---

295 **MR P. J. HASSETT, Quin**
Postal: **Parkview House, Moyriesk, Quin, Co. Clare, Ireland**
Contacts: **PHONE (00353) 65 6840555 (00353) 65 6825621 FAX (00353) 65 6825621**

  1 **A NEW DAWN (IRE)**, 7, b g Old Vic—Andros Dawn (IRE) **Summer Sun Syndicate**
  2 **BOURGELAT (IRE)**, 6, b g Flemensfirth (USA)—Sister Cinnamon **Look At Me Syndicate**
  3 4, Br g Kaieteur (USA)—Bridgeville Queen (IRE) **P. J. Hassett**
  4 **MIYAJIMA**, 13, b g Polar Prince (IRE)—Patina **BallyC Syndicate**
  5 **STOP N STARE (IRE)**, 7, b g Danetime (IRE)—Ballina Belle **P. M. Hassett**
  6 6, B m Revoque (IRE)—Swing The Lead (IRE) **P. J. Hassett**
  7 **WIN FOR US (IRE)**, 8, ch g Rossini (USA)—Noble Flame (IRE) **BallyC Syndicate**

Assistant Trainer: G. Hassett

Amateur: Mr P. J. O'Neill.

---

296 **MRS FLEUR HAWES, Diss**
Postal: **Hill Farm Barn, High Rd, Bressingham, Diss, Norfolk, IP22 2AT**
Contacts: **MOBILE (07775) 795805**
E-MAIL fleur@fleurhawesracingltd.co.uk WEBSITE www.fleurhawesracing.co.uk

  1 **BERTENBAR**, 9, b g Bertolini (USA)—Ardenbar **Mr T. J. Wyatt**
  2 **CAPPIELOW PARK**, 4, b g Exceed And Excel (AUS)—Barakat **Wing & A Prayer**
  3 **FLAMING GORGE (IRE)**, 8, ch g Alderbrook—Solmus (IRE) **A Fool & His Money**
  4 **FRAUDSTER (UAE)**, 10, b g Jade Robbery (USA)—Anaam **Mrs F. Hawes**
  5 **PLAYED AWAY**, 5, b g Squared Away—Fleet Amour (USA) **Mrs R Smith & Mr George Taylor**
  6 **SCOTLAND YARD (UAE)**, 10, b g Jade Robbery (USA)—Aqraba **Air Hair Lair Partnership**

Other Owners: Mr F. Duffin, Mr J. Edwards, Mrs E. Kenward, Mrs R. Smith, Mr G. Taylor.

---

297 **MR NIGEL HAWKE, Tiverton**
Postal: **Thorne Farm, Stoodleigh, Tiverton, Devon, EX16 9QG**
Contacts: **MOBILE (07899) 922827**
E-MAIL nigel@thornefarmracing.co.uk

  1 **ANAY TURGE (FR)**, 8, b g Turgeon (USA)—Anayette (FR) **Ms K. Mead**
  2 **GOLDEN ACORN (IRE)**, 4, b f Ad Valorem (USA)—Golden Heart **Pearce Bros Partnership**
  3 **LINTON HILL (IRE)**, 4, b g Tiger Hill (IRE)—Klaribel (IRE) **Pearce Bros Partnership**
  4 **MASTER NEO (FR)**, 7, gr g Turgeon (USA)—Really Royale (FR) **W. E. Donohue J. M. Donohue**
  5 **MISTER WISEMAN**, 11, gr g Bal Harbour—Genie Spirit **Ms K. Mead**
  6 **NAIL'M (IRE)**, 5, b h Milan—Honor Kicks (USA) **Junction 24 Ltd**
  7 **NUDGE THE NUGGET**, 5, br h Grape Tree Road—Furry Dance (USA) **D. R. Mead**

MR NIGEL HAWKE - Continued

8 **PAGHAM BELLE**, 5, b m Brian Boru—Sambara (IRE) **John Haste & Michael Fowler**
9 **PIRANS CAR**, 7, b g Sleeping Car (FR)—Karolina (FR) **R. J. & Mrs J. A. Peake**
10 **SAMINGARRY (FR)**, 6, ch g Ballingarry (IRE)—Samansonnienne (FR) **Junction 24 Ltd**
11 **SEDGEMOOR CLASSACT (IRE)**, 5, b m Exit To Nowhere (USA)—Kim Fontenail (FR) **Junction 24 Ltd**
12 **ZIMBABWE (FR)**, 13, b g Turgeon (USA)—Razzamatazz (FR) **R. J. & Mrs J. A. Peake**

Other Owners: Mrs Kate Brain, Mr W. E. Donohue, Mrs J. M. Donohue, Mr M. G. Fowler, Mr J. Haste, Junction 24, Mr Russell J. Peake, Mrs J. A. Peake, Mr Steve Pearce.

Assistant Trainer: David Judd

---

298 **MR RICHARD HAWKER, Frome**
Postal: **Rode Farm, Rode, Bath, Somerset, BA11 6QQ**
Contacts: **PHONE (01373) 831479**

1 **EXEMPLARY**, 6, b g Sulamani (IRE)—Epitome (IRE) **Winning Edge Racing**
2 **MONDERON (FR)**, 6, b br g Laveron—Lomonde (FR) **Winning Edge Racing**
3 **RODE RUNNER**, 5, ch g Nomadic Way (USA)—Pacific Girl (IRE) **Winning Edge Racing**

Other Owners: R. G. B. Hawker, Mrs S. E. Hawker.

---

299 **MR DEREK HAYDN JONES, Pontypridd**
Postal: **Garth Paddocks, Efail Isaf, Pontypridd, Mid-Glamorgan, CF38 1SN**
Contacts: **PHONE (01443) 202515 FAX (01443) 201877 MOBILE (07967) 680012**

1 **ALL RIGHT NOW**, 6, b g Night Shift (USA)—Cookie Cutter (IRE) **Mr J. Hay**
2 **CATFLAP (IRE)**, 4, b f One Cool Cat (USA)—Consignia (IRE) **Llewelyn, Newman & Runeckles**
3 **CHIK'S DREAM**, 6, ch g Dreams End—Chik's Secret **Mr T. L. G. Jenkins**
4 **FIRST POST (IRE)**, 6, b g Celtic Swing—Consignia (IRE) **Llewelyn, Runeckles**
5 **IONWY**, 4, b f Piccolo—Dim Ots **G. I. D. Llewelyn**
6 **MOLLY JONES**, 4, b f Three Valleys (USA)—And Toto Too **North Cheshire Trading & Storage Ltd**
7 **NEED TO BE BOLD**, 4, b f Needwood Blade—Bold Loch **Mrs E. A. Crewe**
8 **TENBRIDGE**, 4, b f Avonbridge—Tenebrae (IRE) **Mrs E. M. Haydn Jones**
9 **TINSHU (IRE)**, 7, ch m Fantastic Light (USA)—Ring of Esteem **Llewelyn, Runeckles**

THREE-YEAR-OLDS

10 **CERYS**, ch f Three Valleys (USA)—Tenebrae (IRE) **G. I. D. Llewelyn**
11 **CHAMTILLE (IRE)**, gr f Verglas (IRE)—Tahtheeb (IRE) **Mr J. Hay**
12 **SCHOTTISCHE**, ch f Pastoral Pursuits—Calligraphy **Mrs E. M. Haydn Jones**
13 **TRISTESSA**, b f Amadeus Wolf—On Point **G. I. D. Llewelyn**

TWO-YEAR-OLDS

14 **JESSY MAE**, b f 2/5 Oratorio (IRE)—Welsh Valley (USA) (Irish River (FR)) (5500) **North Cheshire Trading**
15 **LLYRICAL**, b c 30/3 Firebreak—One of The Family (Alzao (USA)) (5000) **Llewelyn, Runeckles**
16 **VERSIGNIA (IRE)**, gr f 3/5 Verglas (IRE)—Consignia (IRE) (Definite Article) **Llewelyn, Runeckles**

Other Owners: Mr Jon Blencowe, Mr Ian Dodds-Smith, Mr Bobby Gould, Mrs E. M. Haydn Jones, Mrs D. J. Hughes, Mr D. Llewelyn, Mrs M. L. Parry, Mr J. Runeckles, Mr Brian Sheppard, Mr Gordon Vine.

Assistant Trainer: Mrs E. M. Haydn Jones

---

300 **MR JONATHAN HAYNES, Brampton**
Postal: **Cleugh Head, Low Row, Brampton, Cumbria, CA8 2JB**
Contacts: **PHONE (01697) 746253 MOBILE (07771) 511471**

1 **BERTIELICIOUS**, 5, b g And Beyond (IRE)—Pennepoint **J. C. Haynes**
2 **BEYOND THE POINT**, 6, b m And Beyond (IRE)—Pennepoint **J. C. Haynes**
3 **BEYONDTEMPTATION**, 5, ch m And Beyond (IRE)—Tempted (IRE) **J. C. Haynes**

MR JONATHAN HAYNES - Continued

4 **MRS GRASS**, 6, ch m And Beyond (IRE)—Tempted (IRE) **J. C. Haynes**
5 **PANTHERS RUN**, 13, b g Jendali (USA)—Dorado Beach **J. C. Haynes**

 301

MR TED HAYNES, Highworth
Postal: **Red Down Farm, Highworth, Wiltshire, SN6 7SH**
Contacts: **PHONE/FAX (01793) 762437 FAX (01793) 762437 MOBILE (07704) 707728**
E-MAIL reddownracing@aol.com

1 **EBONY STORM**, 6, b g Zafeen (FR)—Stormworthy Miss (IRE) **Miss S. R. Haynes**
2 **MR TED**, 6, b g Kayf Tara—Fly Home **Miss S. R. Haynes**
3 **PRINCESS KIERA**, 5, b m Kier Park (IRE)—Rupert's Princess (IRE)
4 4, B g Kier Park (IRE)—Rupert's Princess (IRE)
5 **STANWELL**, 5, ch g Kier Park (IRE)—Magical Dancer (IRE) **The Reddown High Explosive Partnership**
6 **STORMWOOD**, 8, b g Fleetwood (IRE)—Stormworthy Miss (IRE) **Miss S. R. Haynes**
7 **TARASHAN**, 8, b m Kayf Tara—Rupert's Princess (IRE) **Miss S. R. Haynes**
8 **THE NAMES HARRY**, 8, b g Sir Harry Lewis (USA)—Fly Home **Miss S. R. Haynes**

Other Owners: Mr Sam Beach, H. E. Haynes, Mrs H. E. Haynes, Mr L. J. Manners.

Assistant Trainer: Sally R Haynes (07711) 488341

302

MRS C. HEAD-MAAREK, Chantilly
Postal: **32 Avenue du General Leclerc, 60500 Chantilly, France**
Contacts: **PHONE (0033) 3445 70101 FAX (0033) 3445 85333 MOBILE (0033) 6073 10505**
E-MAIL christiane.head@wanadoo.fr

1 **AMERICAN PICK (FR)**, 4, b g American Post—Pick A Poket (FR)
2 **GOLF JUAN (USA)**, 4, b g Invasor (ARG)—Great Buy (USA)
3 **NICE ASSOCIATION (FR)**, 5, b m High Yield (USA)—Pick A Poket (FR)
4 5, B g Iron Mask (USA)—Padina (GER)
5 **SEA TRIAL (FR)**, 4, b c Panis (USA)—Sea Life (FR)
6 **TARTARIN (IRE)**, 6, b g Statue of Liberty (USA)—Tigresse Africaine (FR)

THREE-YEAR-OLDS
7 **ADMIRALTY ARCH**, ch c Three Valleys (USA)—Marching West (USA)
8 **ASSEZ CLAIR (USA)**, b c Pleasant Tap (USA)—Pretty Clear (USA)
9 **DECISION (FR)**, ch f Kentucky Dynamite (USA)—Dame Blanche (USA)
10 **EXPLOSIVE (FR)**, ch f Kentucky Dynamite (USA)—Ryde (FR)
11 **FILIMBI (USA)**, gr ro f Mizzen Mast (USA)—Flute (USA)
12 **GALVESTON (FR)**, b c Green Tune (USA)—Great News (FR)
13 **HARRISTOWN**, ch c Bering—New Abbey
14 **HOUSEHOLD NAME**, ch f Zamindar (USA)—Coraline
15 **MARTINI (GER)**, b c Rock of Gibraltar (IRE)—Missing Link (IRE)
16 **MINXILINX**, gr f Zamindar (USA)—Lixian
17 **RADIATION (FR)**, b f Anabaa (USA)—Riziere (FR)
18 **ROCAILLE (FR)**, b f Anabaa (USA)—Rose Rose (USA)
19 **SAVOIR (FR)**, b c Anabaa (USA)—Silverware (FR)
20 **SNOW DUST**, b f First Defence (USA)—Etoile Montante (USA)
21 **SQUAMISH**, b c More Than Ready (USA)—Sister Swank (USA)
22 **TECLA (IRE)**, b f Whipper (USA)—Mahalia (IRE)
23 **TREVE (FR)**, b f Motivator—Trevise (FR)
24 **TROYA (IRE)**, b f Jeremy (USA)—Segesta (IRE)
25 **VALMARDAL**, b c Shamardal (USA)—Vanishing River (USA)
26 **VOYAGEUSE (FR)**, b f Kentucky Dynamite (USA)—Villadolide (FR)
27 **WHY AREEB (IRE)**, B C Galileo (IRE)—Piquetnol (USA)
28 **WINTERWELL (USA)**, b f First Defence (USA)—Kinetic Force (USA)

TWO-YEAR-OLDS
29 B f 27/1 Zamindar (USA)—Acquisition (Dansili)
30 B f 5/2 Oasis Dream—African Rose (Observatory) (USA))

MRS C. HEAD-MAAREK - Continued

31 B c 28/1 Successful Appeal (USA)—Chaffinch (USA) (Lear Fan (USA))
32 DIVINITE, b f 1/2 Mr Sidney (USA)—Dissertation (FR) (Sillery (USA)) (83333)
33 DONATRICE (FR), b f 20/3 Mr Sidney (USA)—Dalna (FR) (Anabaa (USA))
34 B f 21/2 Artiste Royal (IRE)—Fantasy Lady (USA) (Grand Slam (USA)) (23809)
35 GLORIEUX (FR), b c 23/3 Dunkerque (FR)—Grenade (FR) (Bering) (23809)
36 GREENSTREET, b c 2/2 Mr Sidney (USA)—Treasure Queen (USA) (Kingmambo (USA)) (63492)
37 HORNBLOWER, b c 30/4 Mr Sidney (USA)—Riziere (FR) (Groom Dancer (USA)) (23809)
38 B f 14/4 Empire Maker (USA)—Jazz Drummer (USA) (Dixieland Band (USA))
39 Gr ro c 22/4 Empire Maker (USA)—Kinetic Force (USA) (Holy Bull (USA))
40 LISTRIA (IRE), b br f 24/3 Footstepsinthesand—Perugina (FR) (Highest Honor (FR))
41 MS MONIQUE (FR), b f 21/2 Mr Sidney (USA)—Ares Choix (Choisir (AUS))
42 B c 25/2 Dubawi (IRE)—Peach Pearl (Invincible Spirit (IRE)) (83333)
43 PIEDRA (IRE), b f 4/1 Lawman (FR)—Albisola (IRE) (Montjeu (IRE))
44 ROYALE MISS (FR), b f 22/1 Mr Sidney (USA)—Royalemixa (FR) (Linamix (FR)) (5555)
45 SEIGNEUR (FR), b c 1/1 Sevres Rose (IRE)—Spenderella (Common Grounds)
46 B f 29/3 Empire Maker (USA)—Shoogle (USA) (A P Indy (USA))
47 SILVAPLANA (FR), b f 8/4 Montmartre (FR)—Silvery Bay (FR) (Numerous (USA)) (19841)
48 SIRIUS (FR), ch c 29/1 Gold Away (FR)—Sylverina (FR) (Numerous (USA))
49 TERRIENNE (FR), ch f 1/1 Henny Hughes (USA)—Gout de Terroir (USA) (Lemon Drop Kid (USA))
50 TROPHEE (FR), b f 9/5 Mr Sidney (USA)—Trevise (FR) (Anabaa (USA))
51 VOYAGER, b c 11/4 Mr Sidney (USA)—Villadolide (FR) (Anabaa (USA))
52 B c 30/3 Rail Link—Zorleni (Zafonic (USA))

Assistant Trainer: Charley Rossi

---

303 | **MR COLIN HEARD, Boscastle**
Postal: **Lower Pennycrocker Farm, Boscastle, Cornwall, PL35 0BY**
Contacts: **PHONE (01840) 250613 MOBILE (07967) 605392**

1 CARHENEY RIVER (IRE), 8, b g Flemensfirth (USA)—Odeeka (IRE) **Mrs S. A. White**
2 LITTLE EAGLET (IRE), 9, br g Dushyantor (USA)—Bagatelle (IRE) **Mrs S. A. White**

Assistant Trainer: Karyn Heard

Jockey (NH): Liam Heard. **Conditional:** Ian Popham.

---

304 | **MR PETER HEDGER, Hook**
Postal: **P C F Racing, Chalkey Lane, Dogmersfield, Hook, Hampshire, RG27 8TG**
Contacts: PHONE **(01243) 543863** FAX **(01243) 543913** MOBILE **(07860) 209448**
E-MAIL **hedgerlaura@hotmail.com**

1 BARNMORE, 5, b g Royal Applause—Veronica Franco **P C F Racing Ltd**
2 FRANCO IS MY NAME, 7, b g Namid—Veronica Franco **P C F Racing Ltd**
3 HARLESTONE WOOD, 4, b c Olden Times—Harlestone Lady **P C F Racing Ltd**
4 HE'SAHIT (FR), 5, b g Strike Out (USA)—Lucky Us (IRE) **P. R. Hedger**
5 KAAFEL (IRE), 4, b c Nayef (USA)—Tafaani (IRE) **P C F Racing Ltd**
6 LISAHANE BOG, 6, b g Royal Applause—Veronica Franco **P C F Racing Ltd**
7 SISTER GURU, 4, b f Ishiguru (USA)—Ulysses Daughter (IRE) **Mr J. F. McHale**
8 SLIP SLIDING AWAY (IRE), 6, b g Whipper (USA)—Sandy Lady (IRE) **Bernard Keay & Partners**
9 TRANQUIL BAY (IRE), 4, ch g Medecis—Tranquil Sky **P C F Racing Ltd**
10 WHIPCRACKAWAY (IRE), 4, b g Whipper (USA)—Former Drama (USA) **P. R. Hedger**

THREE-YEAR-OLDS

11 AFRO, b f Araafa (IRE)—Largo (IRE) **P C F Racing Ltd**
12 BIG DUKE (IRE), b g Duke of Marmalade (IRE)—Liscune (IRE) **P C F Racing Ltd**
13 BRIDGE BUILDER, b c Avonbridge—Amazing Dream (IRE) **P C F Racing Ltd**
14 LUCKY DI, br f Araafa (IRE)—Lucky Date (IRE) **P C F Racing Ltd**
15 PUTMEINTHESWINDLE, ch g Monsieur Bond (IRE)—Birthday Belle **P C F Racing Ltd**
16 ROSE AYR, b f Refuse To Bend (IRE)—Gaelic Swan (IRE) **Mr W. F. N. Davis**
17 VERONICA'S PURSUIT, b f Pastoral Pursuits—Veronica Franco **P C F Racing Ltd**

MR PETER HEDGER - Continued

TWO-YEAR-OLDS

18 **FRANCO'S SECRET,** b c 7/5 Sakhee's Secret—Veronica Franco (Darshaan) **P C F Racing Ltd**

Other Owners: Mrs M. J. Boylan, Mr S. R. Holt, B. J. Keay.

Assistant Trainer: John Swallow

Jockey (flat): Dane O'Neill. **Jockey (NH):** Leighton Aspell.

305	**MR NICKY HENDERSON, Lambourn** Postal: **Seven Barrows, Lambourn, Hungerford, Berkshire, RG17 8UH** Contacts: PHONE **(01488) 72259** FAX **(01488) 72596** MOBILE **(07774) 608168** E-MAIL nj.henderson@virgin.net

 1 **ABBEY COURT (IRE),** 5, b g Wareed (IRE)—North Kerry Rose (IRE) **M. A. C. Buckley**
 2 **ACCORDINGTOJODIE (IRE),** 7, b g Accordion—La Fiamma (FR) **Sir Peter & Lady Gibbings**
 3 **ACT ALONE,** 4, b g Act One—Figlette **S W Group Logistics Limited**
 4 **ACT FOUR (IRE),** 5, b g Old Vic—Quadrennial (IRE) **Triermore Stud**
 5 **ALEXANDRE SIX (FR),** 4, b g Robin des Champs (FR)—Karmiva (FR) **S. E. Munir**
 6 **ALL THE ACES (IRE),** 8, b g Spartacus (IRE)—Lili Cup (FR) **A. D. Spence**
 7 **ANQUETTA (IRE),** 9, b g Anshan—Quetta (IRE) **The Ten From Seven**
 8 **BARENGER (IRE),** 6, b g Indian Danehill (IRE)—Build A Dream (USA) **R. A. Bartlett**
 9 **BEAR'S AFFAIR (IRE),** 7, br g Presenting—Gladtogetit **G. B. Barlow**
10 **BINOCULAR (FR),** 9, b g Enrique—Bleu Ciel Et Blanc (FR) **J. P. McManus**
11 **BLACK SPIRIT (USA),** 6, b g Black Minnaloushe (USA)—L'extra Honor (USA) **A. D. Spence**
12 **BOBS WORTH (IRE),** 8, b g Bob Back (USA)—Fashionista (IRE) **The Not Afraid Partnership**
13 **BRIGADIER MILLER,** 6, gr g Act One—Tread Carefully **W. H. Ponsonby**
14 **BRINGITHOMEMINTY,** 4, gr g Presenting—Rosie Redman (IRE) **Walters Plant Hire Ltd**
15 **BROADBACKBOB (IRE),** 8, b g Broadway Flyer (USA)—Back Home (IRE) **Anthony Speelman**
16 **BUCKIE BOY (IRE),** 7, b g Bahri (USA)—Wooden (USA) **North South Partnership**
17 **BURTON PORT (IRE),** 9, b g Bob Back (USA)—Despute (IRE) **T. J. Hemmings**
18 **CAPE EXPRESS (IRE),** 8, b g Cape Cross (IRE)—Lilissa (IRE) **A. D. Spence**
19 **CAPTAIN CONAN (IRE),** 6, b g Kingsalsa (USA)—Lavandou **Triermore Stud**
20 **CAPTAIN CUTTER (IRE),** 6, b g Westerner—Hollygrove Samba (IRE) **J. P. McManus**
21 **CASH AND GO (IRE),** 6, b g Sulamani (IRE)—Calcida (GER) **Mr R. J. H. Geffen**
22 **CEVARO (IRE),** 5, b m Milan—Jollie Bollie (IRE) **Seven Barrows Limited**
23 **CHARLES ONZE (IRE),** 6, b g Epalo (GER)—Karmiva (FR) **Mrs C. M. Mould**
24 **CHATTERBOX (IRE),** 5, b g Poliglote—Ney Will (FR) **The Not Afraid Partnership 2**
25 **CLOSE TOUCH,** 5, ch g Generous (IRE)—Romantic Dream **Her Majesty The Queen**
26 **COCKTAILS AT DAWN,** 5, b g Fair Mix (IRE)—Fond Farewell (IRE) **R J H Geffen & Sir John Ritblat**
27 **COOL MACAVITY (IRE),** 5, b g One Cool Cat (USA)—Cause Celebre (IRE) **Triermore Stud**
28 **COURTESY CALL (IRE),** 4, br g Manduro (GER)—Three Wrens (IRE) **A. D. Spence**
29 **CUCUMBER RUN (IRE),** 8, b g Oscar (IRE)—Back To Roost (IRE) **The Goblyns**
31 **DEFINITE RUBY (IRE),** 5, b m Definite Article—Sunset Queen (IRE) **Trevor & Linda Marlow**
32 **DUNGARVAN LASS (IRE),** 4, ch f Presenting—Flying Iris (IRE) **Brian, Gwen, Terri & Kelly Griffiths**
33 **EARTH AMBER,** 4, ch f Hurricane Run (IRE)—Too Marvelous (FR) **Pump & Plant Services Ltd**
34 **ELECTROLYSER (IRE),** 8, gr g Daylami (IRE)—Iviza (IRE) **Mr & Mrs P. Hargreaves**
35 **ERICHT (IRE),** 7, b g Alderbrook—Lady Orla (IRE) **Mrs B. A. Hanbury**
36 **FABRIKA,** 5, b m Presenting—Daprika (FR) **Mr & Mrs R. G. Kelvin Hughes**
37 **FINIAN'S RAINBOW (IRE),** 10, b g Tiraaz (USA)—Trinity Gale (IRE) **M. A. C. Buckley**
38 **FIRST IN THE QUEUE (IRE),** 6, b g Azamour (IRE)—Irina (IRE) **L. Breslin**
39 **FOREVER PRESENT (IRE),** 6, br m Presenting—Sidalcea (IRE) **Lets Live Racing (Tinbar)**
40 **FORGOTTEN VOICE (IRE),** 8, b g Danehill Dancer (IRE)—Asnieres (USA) **Mrs S. M. Roy**
41 **FOURTH ESTATE (IRE),** 7, b g Fantastic Light (USA)—Papering (IRE) **Out The Box Racing**
42 **FOXBRIDGE (IRE),** 7, b g King's Theatre (IRE)—Fairy Native (IRE) **Walters Plant Hire Spiers & Hartwell**
43 **FREE THINKING,** 5, b m Hernando (FR)—Liberthine (FR) **R. B. Waley-Cohen**
44 **FRENCH OPERA,** 10, b g Bering—On Fair Stage (IRE) **Mrs Judy Wilson & Martin Landau**
45 **GENERAL MILLER,** 8, b g Karinga Bay—Millers Action **W. H. Ponsonby**
46 **GHIMAAR,** 8, b g Dubai Destination (USA)—Charlecote (IRE) **Mr M. F. George**
47 **GIORGIO QUERCUS (FR),** 8, b g Starborough—Winter Breeze (FR) **Seasons Holidays**
48 **GLORIOUS TWELFTH (IRE),** 6, b m Old Vic—Bilboa (FR) **Mr & Mrs R. G. Kelvin Hughes**
49 **GOLDEN HOOF (IRE),** 5, b g Oscar (IRE)—Nuovo Style (IRE) **The Hoof Partnership**
50 **GRANDOUET (FR),** 6, b br g Al Namix (FR)—Virginia River (FR) **S. E. Munir**

MR NICKY HENDERSON - Continued

51 **HADRIAN'S APPROACH (IRE)**, 6, b g High Chaparral (IRE)—
Gifted Approach (IRE) **Mr & Mrs R. G. Kelvin Hughes**
52 **HAMMERSLY LAKE (FR)**, 5, b g Kapgarde (FR)—Loin de Moi (FR) **M. A. C. Buckley**
53 **HERONRY (IRE)**, 5, b g Heron Island (IRE)—In A Tizzy **The Ten From Seven**
54 **JOKER CHOKER (IRE)**, 8, b g Oscar (IRE)—Stormy Lady **Bradley Partnership**
55 **KAKI DE LA PREE (FR)**, 6, b g Kapgarde (FR)—Kica (FR) **M. A. C. Buckley**
56 **KARAZHAN**, 5, b g Dr Fong (USA)—Karasta (IRE) **Pump & Plant Services Ltd**
57 **KELLS BELLE (IRE)**, 7, b m Alflora (IRE)—Clandestine **Brian,Gwen,Terri & Kelly Griffiths**
58 **KHYBER KIM**, 11, b g Mujahid (USA)—Jungle Rose **Mrs C. M. Mould**
59 **KID CASSIDY (IRE)**, 7, b g Beneficial—Shuil Na Lee (IRE) **J. P. McManus**
60 **KILLIECRANKIE**, 5, b g Kayf Tara—Bella Macrae **Her Majesty The Queen**
61 **KINGS DESTINY**, 7, b g Dubai Destination (USA)—Jalousie (IRE) **Mr D. A. Yardy**
62 **KINGS LODGE**, 7, b g King's Theatre (IRE)—Mardello **W. H. Ponsonby**
63 4, B g Milan—Lady Lamb (IRE) **Seven Barrows Limited**
64 **LADY OF PROVENCE**, 4, gr f Fair Mix (IRE)—Rosa Canina **W. H. Ponsonby**
65 **LAMORNA WINK**, 5, b m Beat Hollow—Wardeh **W. H. Ponsonby**
66 **LAUDATORY**, 7, b g Royal Applause—Copy-Cat **Mr Eric Newnham and Mrs Julia Newnham**
67 **LIEUTENANT MILLER**, 7, b g Beat All (USA)—Still Runs Deep **W. H. Ponsonby**
68 **LITTLE DUTCH GIRL**, 4, ch f Dutch Art—Photographie (USA) **Mrs J. F. Maitland-Jones**
69 **LITTLE FRITZ (FR)**, 6, gr g Turgeon (USA)—Hunorisk (FR) **Mr & Mrs J. D. Cotton**
70 **LONG RUN (FR)**, 8, b g Cadoudal (FR)—Libertina (FR) **R. B. Waley-Cohen**
71 **LOOKING HOPEFUL (IRE)**, 7, b g Heron Island (IRE)—Mahaasin **M. J. & Mrs T. Padfield**
72 **LYVIUS**, 5, b g Paolini (GER)—Lysuna (GER) **T. J. Hemmings**
73 **MA FILLEULE (FR)**, 5, gr m Turgeon (USA)—Kadaina (FR) **S. E. Munir**
74 **MAKARI**, 6, b g Makbul—Seraphim (FR) **Matt & Lauren Morgan**
75 **MALT MASTER (IRE)**, 6, b g Milan—Dantes Profit (IRE) **J. P. McManus**
76 **MASTER OF THE GAME (IRE)**, 7, ch g Bob's Return (IRE)—
Lady Monilousha (IRE) **Mr & Mrs R. G. Kelvin Hughes**
77 **MASTER OF THE HALL (IRE)**, 9, b g Saddlers' Hall (IRE)—
Frankly Native (IRE) **Martin Landau & Jonathan Duffy**
78 **MAYFAIR MUSIC (IRE)**, 4, br f Presenting—Native Bid (IRE) **Mrs E. C. Roberts**
79 **MEGALYPOS (FR)**, 4, b br g Limnos (JPN)—Bourbonnaise (FR) **Mr Simon Munir & Mr Isaac Souede**
80 **MINELLA CLASS (IRE)**, 8, br g Oscar (IRE)—Louisas Dream (IRE) **Deal George Kelvin-Hughes Nicolson**
81 **MINELLA FORFITNESS (IRE)**, 6, b g Westerner—Ring of Water (USA) **M. A. C. Buckley**
82 **MISS BALLANTYNE**, 6, br m Definite Article—Gardana (FR) **Mr & Mrs R. G. Kelvin Hughes**
83 **MISTER CHAIRMAN (IRE)**, 5, b g Shantou (USA)—Out of Trouble (IRE) **Lady Tennant**
84 **MISTER DILLON**, 6, b g Sulamani (IRE)—Kabayil **Elite Racing Club**
85 **MOEL FAMAU**, 4, b f Flemensfirth (USA)—Daprika (FR) **Racegoers Club Owners Group**
86 **MOLOTOF (FR)**, 6, gr g Smadoun (FR)—Memorial (FR) **S. E. Munir**
87 **MONO MAN (IRE)**, 7, b g Old Vic—Quadrennial (IRE) **Mrs B. A. Munir**
88 **MY TENT OR YOURS (IRE)**, 6, b g Desert Prince (IRE)—Spartan Girl (IRE) **J. P. McManus**
89 **MY WIGWAM OR YOURS (IRE)**, 4, b g Beneficial—Midnight Pond (IRE) **The Happy Campers**
90 **NADIYA DE LA VEGA (FR)**, 7, b br m Lost World (IRE)—Shinobie (FR) **J. P. McManus**
91 **NELSON'S BRIDGE (IRE)**, 6, b g Oscar (IRE)—High Park Lady (IRE) **J. P. McManus**
92 **NO PUSHOVER**, 4, b f Scorpion (IRE)—Poussetiere Deux (FR) **The Perfect Day Partnership**
93 **ONE CONEMARA (IRE)**, 5, b g Milan—Rose of Kerry (IRE) **Triermore Stud**
94 **ONE LUCKY LADY**, 5, b m Lucky Story (USA)—One For Philip **S W Group Logistics Limited**
95 **OPEN HEARTED**, 6, b g Generous (IRE)—Romantic Dream **Her Majesty The Queen**
96 **OSCAR HOOF (IRE)**, 5, b g Oscar (IRE)—New Legislation (IRE) **The Hoof Partnership**
97 **OSCAR NOMINEE (IRE)**, 6, b g Old Vic—Native Bid (IRE) **M. A. C. Buckley**
98 **OSCAR WHISKY (IRE)**, 8, b g Oscar (IRE)—Ash Baloo (IRE) **Walters Plant Hire Ltd**
99 **OSCARA DARA (IRE)**, 8, b g Oscar (IRE)—Lisa's Storm (IRE) **BG Racing Partnership**
100 **OTTO THE GREAT (FR)**, 5, gr g Turgeon (USA)—Hunorisk (FR) **Mr & Mrs J. D. Cotton**
101 **OWEN GLENDOWER (IRE)**, 8, br g Anshan—Native Success (IRE) **The Ten From Seven**
102 **PETIT ROBIN (FR)**, 10, b g Robin des Pres—Joie de Cotte (FR) **S W Group Logistics Limited**
103 **PICTURE POST (USA)**, 6, b g Mr Greeley (USA)—Cherokee (USA) **Out The Box Racing**
104 **PIPPA GREENE**, 9, b g Galileo (IRE)—Funny Girl **R. A. H. Evans**
105 **POLLY PEACHUM (IRE)**, 5, b m Shantou (USA)—Miss Denman (IRE) **Lady Tennant**
106 **PRINCE OF PIRATES (IRE)**, 8, b g Milan—Call Kate (IRE) **J. P. McManus**
107 **PRIVATE EQUITY (FR)**, 5, b g High Yield (USA)—Annette Girl (IRE) **Million in Mind Partnership**
108 **PRYDE ROCK**, 6, b g Fair Mix (IRE)—Knight Ryde **Mrs N. S. Tregaskes**
109 **PUNJABI**, 10, b g Komaite (USA)—Competa **R. C. Tooth**
110 **QUANTITATIVEEASING (IRE)**, 8, ch g Anshan—Mazuma (IRE) **J. P. McManus**
111 **RAJDHANI EXPRESS**, 6, br g Presenting—Violet Express (FR) **R. B. Waley-Cohen**
112 **REVERB**, 4, b g Tiger Hill (IRE)—Gemini Gold (IRE) **Elite Racing Club**

MR NICKY HENDERSON - Continued

113 **RIVER MAIGUE (IRE)**, 6, b g Zagreb (USA)—Minor Tantrum (IRE) **M. A. C. Buckley**
114 **RIVERSIDE THEATRE**, 9, b g King's Theatre (IRE)—Disallowed (IRE) **Jimmy Nesbitt Partnership**
115 **ROBERTO GOLDBACK (IRE)**, 11, b g Bob Back (USA)—Mandysway (IRE) **S. E. Munir**
116 **ROLLING STAR (FR)**, 4, b g Smadoun (FR)—Lyli Rose (FR) **Michael Buckley & The Vestey Family**
117 **ROYAL BOY (FR)**, 6, b br g Lavirco (GER)—Quintanilla (FR) **M. A. C. Buckley**
118 **RUN RABBIT RUN**, 5, b g Hurricane Run (IRE)—Triple Gold (IRE) **A. D. Spence**
119 **SEAHAM HALL**, 5, ch m Peintre Celebre (USA)—Freni (GER) **Seasons Holidays**
120 **SENTRY DUTY (FR)**, 11, b g Kahyasi—Standing Around (FR) **Mr R. P. A. Spiller**
121 **SHAKALAKABOOMBOOM (IRE)**, 9, b g Anshan—Tia Maria (IRE) **L. Breslin**
122 **SHERNANDO**, 6, b g Hernando (FR)—Shimmering Sea **Mr & Mrs Sandy Orr**
123 **SIDE STEP**, 4, b f Norse Dancer (IRE)—Magic Score **Her Majesty The Queen**
124 **SIMONSIG**, 7, gr g Fair Mix (IRE)—Dusty Too **R. A. Bartlett**
125 **SNAKE EYES (IRE)**, 5, b g Oscar (IRE)—Be My Belle (IRE) **J. P. McManus**
126 **SPARTAN ANGEL (IRE)**, 5, b m Beneficial—Greek Melody (IRE) **Sir Eric Parker & Mary Anne Parker**
127 **SPEED MASTER (IRE)**, 7, b g King's Theatre (IRE)—Handy Lass **Walters Plant Hire Spiers & Hartwell**
128 **SPEEDY TUNES (IRE)**, 6, b g Heron Island (IRE)—Art Lover (IRE) **Jimmy Hack Racing Partners**
129 **SPIRIT RIVER (FR)**, 8, b g Poliglote—Love River (FR) **M. A. C. Buckley**
130 **SPRINGINHERSTEP (IRE)**, 6, b m Saddlers' Hall (IRE)—Lady Lamb (IRE) **Turf Club 2012**
131 **SPRINTER SACRE (FR)**, 7, b br g Network (GER)—Fatima III (FR) **Mrs C. M. Mould**
132 **STAND TO REASON (IRE)**, 5, ch g Danehill Dancer (IRE)—Ho Hi The Moon (IRE) **Seasons Holidays**
133 **STATE BENEFIT (IRE)**, 8, b g Beneficial—Gifted **M. A. C. Buckley**
134 **SUNGLASSES (IRE)**, 6, b g Fruits of Love (USA)—Penny Haven (IRE) **Bradley Partnership**
135 **TAKE A BOW**, 4, b g Norse Dancer (IRE)—Madame Illusion (FR) **M. A. C. Buckley**
136 **TANKS FOR THAT (IRE)**, 10, br g Beneficial—Lady Jurado (IRE) **Mrs B. A. Hanbury**
137 **TETLAMI (IRE)**, 7, ch g Daylami (IRE)—Tetou (IRE) **Mrs S. M. Roy**
138 **THANKS FOR COMING**, 7, b g Helissio (FR)—Kyle Rhea **Unchartered Waters**
139 **TILLER BELLE**, 5, b m Revoque (IRE)—Farmer's Pet **W. H. Ponsonby**
140 **TISTORY (FR)**, 6, ch g Epalo (GER)—History (FR) **Mrs J. Wilson**
141 **TOM DU LYS (FR)**, 5, b g Enrique—La Floriana (IRE) **S. E. Munir**
142 **TOP OF THE RANGE (IRE)**, 6, br g Presenting—Brenny's Pearl (IRE) **Walters Plant Hire Ltd**
143 **TOUR D'ARGENT (FR)**, 6, b g Martaline—Keep Well (FR) **M. A. C. Buckley**
144 **TRADEWINDS (FR)**, 5, b g Kapgarde (FR)—Royale Floriane (FR) **M. A. C. Buckley**
145 **TRIOLO D'ALENE (FR)**, 6, ch g Epalo (GER)—Joliette d'alene (FR) **Mr & Mrs Sandy Orr**
146 **UNE ARTISTE (FR)**, 5, b m Alberto Giacometti (IRE)—Castagnette III (FR) **S. E. Munir**
147 **UTOPIE DES BORDES (FR)**, 5, b m Antarctique (IRE)—Miss Berry (FR) **Mr Simon Munir & Mr Isaac Souede**
148 **VAGNER (FR)**, 4, b g Voix du Nord (FR)—Evane (FR) **Mrs Robin Birley**
149 **VASCO DU RONCERAY (FR)**, 4, gr g Al Namix (FR)—
　　　　　　　　　　　　　　　　　　　　　Landza de Ronceray (FR) **Mr Simon Munir & Mr Isaac Souede**
150 **VODKA 'N TONIC (IRE)**, 4, b g Presenting—Ballagh Dawn (IRE) **Bradley Partnership**
151 **VODKAONTHEROCKS (IRE)**, 5, b g Oscar (IRE)—My Native (IRE) **Walters Plant Hire Ltd**
152 **WEST WIZARD (FR)**, 4, b br g King's Theatre (IRE)—Queen's Diamond (GER) **Walters Plant Hire Ltd**
153 **WHISPER (FR)**, 5, b g Astarabad (USA)—Belle Yepa (FR) **Walters Plant Hire Ltd**
154 **WHO'S CROSS (IRE)**, 5, b g Runyon (IRE)—Mystery Escort **Mr D. Donohoe**
155 **YOUR TEPEE OR MINE (IRE)**, 7, b g Indian Danehill (IRE)—Kerry Lily (IRE) **The Happy Campers**

Other Owners: S. G. Adams, Mr R. B. Antell, Mrs V. A. P. Antell, Mrs D. E. Austin, M. Ball, Mr D. Bickerton, Mr P. Boyle, Mrs D. C. Broad, A. R. Bromley, B. G. Brown, Mr S. W. Buckley, E. Burke, Miss A. J. Burr, A. Chandler, Mr D. Clegg, A. K. Collins, P. J. Cornell, Mr S. F. Coton, J. D. Cotton, Mrs B. Cotton, R. Cressey, G. M. Davies, P. A. Deal, K. H. M. Doyle, Mr P. J. Dudson, J. B. Duffy, Mrs G. J. Edwards, A. T. Eggleton, J. H. W. Finch, Mr R. Fisher, L. R. Frampton, Mr A. J. Garton, Mr D. A. George, Sir Peter Gibbings, The Hon Lady Gibbings, Mr I. H. Goldsmith, G. F. Goode, Mr M. J. Gould, B. J. Griffiths, Mrs G. E. A. Griffiths, C. O. P Hanbury, R. V. Harding, Mrs R. J. Hargreaves, Mr P. K. Hargreaves, Mr S. Harris, Mr K. A. Harris, N. J. Henderson, A. J. Hill, Mrs J. Hooper, J. Hornsey, Mr E. J. Hughes, D. Humphreys, R. A. Hurst, Hyphen Bloodstock, Mr R. A. Jacobs, Miss Y. M. G. Jacques, J. F. Jarvis, Mr A.C. Joyce, R. G. Kelvin-Hughes, Mrs E. A. Kelvin-Hughes, M. Khan, Mr. Khan, Mr M. B. J. Kimmins, Mrs M. E. Kirk, Miss E. A. Lake, M. R. Landau, The Hon Mrs J. V. Leigh, Mr J. Lomas, D. J. Long, Dr C. V. MacPhail, Mr T. G. Marlow, Mrs L. E. Marlow, Mrs F. Marner, Miss N. Martin, Mr C. W. Matthews, Mr M. J. Mckenna, Mr D. M. Menzies, Mr I. D. Miller, W. D. C. Minton, M. Morgan, Mrs L. K. Morgan, Mr K. R. Munn, Mr W. J. Nesbitt, Mr E. R. Newnham, Mrs J. T. Newnham, Mrs D. C. Nicholson, M. M. Nicolson, Miss M. Noden, Mr J. O'Keefe, Mrs C. R. Orr, Mr J. A. M. Orr, M. A. Osborne, M. J. Padfield, Mrs T. Padfield, Sir Eric Parker, Mrs M. Parker, Mr P. Patel, Mr R. Pathak, S. R. C. Philip, Mrs J. Plumptre, Dr C. E. Ponsonby, Brig C. K. Price, Mr P. Quinn, Mr A. Reid, Mr W. A. Rice, Sir J. H. Ritblat, Paul Robson, Miss P. A. Ross, Mr G. Royal, U. E. Schwarzenbach, W. G. C. Shaw, Mr R. Sheppard, Mr G. A. Sheppard, Mr J. Simpson, Mr R. H. D. Smith, Mr I. Souede, Spiers & Hartwell Ltd, B. T. Stewart-Brown Esq, D. F. Sumpter, Mr R. Thayne, Mrs N. J. G. Thorbek-Hooper, Lord Vestey, The Hon A. G. Vestey, The Hon W. G. Vestey, Mrs C. Wells, Mr. L. J. Westwood, J. Whittle, Miss S. Wilde, Mr S. T. Williams-Thomas, Mr J. R. L. Wilson, Mr M. J. F. T. Wilson, Mrs K. L. Yates.

MR NICKY HENDERSON - Continued

Jockey (NH): Barry Geraghty, A. P. McCoy, Andrew Tinkler, David Bass. **Conditional:** Gary Derwin, Jeremiah McGrath, Peter Carberry, Edmond Linehan, Jack Sherwood. **Amateur:** Mr Nico De Boinville.

---

306 **MR PAUL HENDERSON, Whitsbury**
Postal: **1 Manor Farm Cottage, Whitsbury, Fordingbridge, Hampshire, SP6 3QP**
Contacts: PHONE (01725) 518113 FAX (01725) 518113 MOBILE (07958) 482213
E-MAIL phendersonracing@gmail.com

1 ADMIRAL BOOM (IRE), 7, b g Beneficial—Gleann Na Smaointe (IRE) **The Admiral Boom Partnership**
2 BALLYHILTY BRIDGE, 7, b g Exit To Nowhere (USA)—Gemolly (IRE) **J. H. W. Finch**
3 CHASERS CHANCE (IRE), 10, ch g Shernazar—Lucy Walters (IRE) **D. S. Dennis**
4 DOHENY BAR (IRE), 10, b g Freddie's Star—Old Fontaine (IRE) **John Finch & The Rockbourne Partnership**
5 FUHGEDDABOUDIT, 6, ch g Generous (IRE)—Serraval (FR) **J. T. Brown**
6 GRACE AND BEAUTY (IRE), 5, b m Diamond Green (FR)—Balliamo (IRE) **Antell, Coles & Finch**
7 KASBAN, 9, b g Kingmambo (USA)—Ebaraya (IRE) **J. D. Sells**
8 KYLENOE FAIRY (IRE), 9, ch m Anshan—Supreme Stroke (IRE) **The Rockbourne Partnership**
9 LIFE OF A LUSO (IRE), 9, b g Luso—Life of A Lady (IRE) **Mareildar Racing Part 1**
10 LUCY'S LEGEND (IRE), 7, b m Norwich—Townhall (IRE) **The Rockbourne Partnership**
11 MINELLA RANGER (IRE), 7, ch g Beneficial—Minella Lass (IRE) **Mr R. B. Antell**
12 MINELLA SPECIAL (IRE), 7, b g King's Theatre (IRE)—Della Wee (IRE) **Mr R. B. Antell**
13 NEXT OASIS (IRE), 7, b g Classic Cliche (IRE)—Clearwater Glen **P. F. Henderson**
14 ONLY VINTAGE (USA), 13, b g Diesis—Wild Vintage (USA) **D. S. Dennis**
15 RIOR (IRE), 6, b g King's Theatre (IRE)—Sara's Gold (IRE) **Mr R. B. Antell**
16 RULE OF THUMB, 5, b g Tobougg (IRE)—Carreamia **GLR Racing**
17 STEEL CITY, 5, gr g Act One—Serraval (FR) **J. T. Brown**
18 ZELKOVA ISLAND (IRE), 8, gr g Rashar (USA)—Island Diva (IRE) **Mr R. B. Antell**
Other Owners: Mrs V. A. P. Antell, D. J. Coles, Mr G. Evans, Mr R. J. Galpin, Mr R. B. Griffin.

---

307 **LADY HERRIES, Littlehampton**
Postal: **Angmering Park, Littlehampton, West Sussex, BN16 4EX**
Contacts: YARD (01903) 871605 HOME (01903) 871421 FAX (01903) 871609
MOBILE (07785) 282996
E-MAIL angparkstables@btconnect.com

1 BOUGGATTI, 5, b g Tobougg (IRE)—Western Sal **Lady S. Clutton**
2 COTTON KING, 6, b g Dubawi (IRE)—Spinning The Yarn **Lady Mary Mumford**
3 DUMBFOUNDED (FR), 5, b br g Vettori (IRE)—Take The Light (FR) **Lady S. Clutton**
4 GENEVA GEYSER (GER), 7, b g One Cool Cat (USA)—Genevra (IRE) **Angmering Park**
5 JEWELLED, 7, b m Fantastic Light (USA)—Danemere (IRE) **Seymour Bloodstock (UK) Ltd**
6 JUST ARCHIE (USA), 5, b g Arch (USA)—Copper Rose (USA) **Lady S. Clutton**
7 LADY LAYLA, 4, b f Excellent Art—Tartouche **Angmering Park**
8 SWIFT BLADE (IRE), 5, ch g Exceed And Excel (AUS)—Gold Strike (IRE) **Angmering Park**

THREE-YEAR-OLDS

9 MUSICAL MOON, b g Piccolo—Lunasa (IRE) **Lady Herries**
10 PEARL RANSOM (IRE), b g Intikhab (USA)—Massada **Seymour Bloodstock (UK) Ltd**

---

308 **MR MICHAEL HERRINGTON, Thirsk**
Postal: **Garbutt Farm, Cold Kirby, Thirsk, North Yorkshire, YO7 2HJ**
Contacts: PHONE (01845) 597966 MOBILE (07855) 396858
E-MAIL hlloyd19@gmail.com

1 BAILEYS AGINCOURT, 5, ch g Beat Hollow—Numberonedance (USA) **H. M. Hurst**
2 CHEYENNE RED (IRE), 7, br g Namid—Red Leggings **Mr J. S. Herrington**
3 DUKE OF RAINFORD, 6, gr g Bahamian Bounty—Night Haven **Mr J. S. Herrington**
4 ECHO OF FOOTSTEPS, 4, b f Authorized (IRE)—Opening Ceremony (USA) **H. M. Hurst**
5 PETER'S FRIEND, 4, b g Gentleman's Deal (IRE)—Giffoine **H. M. Hurst**

MR MICHAEL HERRINGTON - Continued

THREE-YEAR-OLDS
6 **TAXIFORMISSBYRON**, b f Byron—Miss Respect **H. M. Hurst**

TWO-YEAR-OLDS
7 B g 9/3 Piccolo—Dolphin Dancer (Dolphin Street (FR)) **D. G. Clayton**

Assistant Trainer: Helen Lloyd-Herrington

---

309 MR PETER HIATT, Banbury
Postal: **Six Ash Farm, Hook Norton, Banbury, Oxfordshire, OX15 5DB**
Contacts: **PHONE (01608) 737255 FAX (01608) 730641 MOBILE (07973) 751115**

1 **ANOTHER SQUEEZE**, 5, gr m Proclamation (IRE)—Tight Squeeze **Burt Gibbs Harrisons**
2 **BARLOWS GLANCE**, 4, b f Passing Glance—Mud Pie **Ivor Potter & Peter Gardner**
3 **CRIMSON MONARCH (USA)**, 9, b g Red Ransom (USA)—Tolltally Light (USA) **P. W. Hiatt**
4 **FLAG OF GLORY**, 6, b g Trade Fair—Rainbow Sky **N. D. Edden**
5 **JOHNS PORRIDGE**, 4, ch f Needwood Blade—Obsessive Secret (IRE) **Mr R. Robinson**
6 **KILLMORE COTTAGE**, 6, b g Tamure (IRE)—Singing Cottage **The Blue Harlequin Racing Club**
7 **MAZIJ**, 5, b m Haafhd—Salim Toto **P. Kelly**
8 **MENADATI (USA)**, 5, b g More Than Ready (USA)—Ramatuelle (CHI) **Mr C. Demczak**
9 **MOONSHINE RUBY**, 7, ch m Minster Son—Over The Moon **Mr E. P. Spain**
10 **PLAY TIGER (FR)**, 4, b g Tiger Hill (IRE)—Shagadelic (USA) **P. W. Hiatt**
11 **SHIRATAKI (IRE)**, 5, b g Cape Cross (IRE)—Noodle Soup (USA) **Mr C. Demczak**
12 **TUXEDO**, 8, ch g Cadeaux Genereux—Serengeti Bride (USA) **P. Kelly**
13 **WAAHEJ**, 7, b g Haafhd—Madam Ninette **Monarch Hose & Hydraulics / P. W. Hiatt**

Other Owners: Mr S. Aspinall, Mr Carl Demczak, Mr P. J. R. Gardner, Mr Anthony Harrison, Mrs C. E. Harrison, Mr P. W. Hiatt, Mr Ivor Potter, Mr T. Shreeve.

Assistant Trainer: Mrs E. Hiatt

Jockey (flat): William Carson, Chris Catlin. **Apprentice:** Ryan Clark. **Amateur:** Miss M. Edden.

---

310 MRS LAWNEY HILL, Aston Rowant
Postal: **Woodway Farm, Aston Rowant, Watlington, Oxford, OX49 5SJ**
Contacts: **PHONE (01844) 353051 FAX (01844) 354751 MOBILE (07769) 862648**
E-MAIL lawney@lawneyhill.co.uk WEBSITE www.lawneyhill.co.uk

1 **AGHILL (IRE)**, 9, ch g Denel (FR)—Hannah's Pet (IRE) **Mr M B Clarke & Mr A Hill**
2 **ALPHA NATIVE**, 9, b g Alflora (IRE)—Cassia **Diana Clark & Alan Hill**
3 **AVISON (IRE)**, 5, b g Diamond Green (FR)—Actoris (USA) **Fortnum Racing & Alan Hill**
4 **BILLY TWYFORD (IRE)**, 6, b g Brian Boru—The Distaff Spy **Mr A. J. Weller**
5 **BROUGH ACADEMY (IRE)**, 7, b g Key of Luck (USA)—Cantaloupe **Mrs D. M. Caudwell**
6 **CARROWBEG (IRE)**, 5, b g Cape Cross (IRE)—Love And Affection (USA) **Mr A. Hill**
7 **CHAMPION VERSIONS (IRE)**, 6, b g Presenting—Kelly Gales (IRE) **Ms J. Matthews**
8 **COME ON LAURIE (IRE)**, 5, b g Oscar (IRE)—Megan's Magic **Mr P. Mellett**
9 **COOL CASCADE**, 7, b m Alderbrook—Miss Pout **Mr John Southwell & Miss Frances Molle**
10 **DOUBLE HANDFUL (GER)**, 7, bl g Pentire—Durania (GER) **Fortnum Racing & Alan Hill**
11 **EASTER DANCER**, 6, ch m Karinga Bay—Easter Comet **Mr & Mrs Willes & Mr & Mrs J Brankin-Frisby**
12 **FONT**, 10, b g Sadler's Wells (USA)—River Saint (USA) **A Hill, S Florey, H Webb**
13 **FREE FALLING**, 7, ch m Selkirk (USA)—Free Flying **A.C. Entertainment Technologies Limited**
14 **FRONTIER DANCER (IRE)**, 9, b g New Frontier (IRE)—All The Gear (IRE) **Jump For Fun Racing**
15 **GIANT O MURCHU (IRE)**, 9, b g Carroll House—Centralspires Best **A. Hill**
16 **I HAVE DREAMED (IRE)**, 11, b g Montjeu (IRE)—Diamond Field (USA) **G. Byard**
17 **KING CARACTACUS**, 8, b g Fleetwood (IRE)—Go Tally-Ho **Mr A. J. Weller**
18 **KING OZZY (IRE)**, 9, b g King Charlemagne—Kingpin Delight **Ace Of Diamonds Partnership**
19 **MINELLA THEATRE (IRE)**, 10, b g King's Theatre (IRE)—
Ring of Water (USA) **Middleham Park Racing XXIV & Dan Gilbert**
20 **MISS MAYFAIR (IRE)**, 6, b m Indian Danehill (IRE)—Cocktail Party (USA) **A. Hill**
21 **MR VALENTINO (IRE)**, 8, b g Dr Massini (IRE)—Miss Ranova **M 2 C Racing Partnership**
22 **OVERLAY**, 9, br m Overbury (IRE)—Lay It Off (IRE) **The Aftertimers**
23 **QUARL EGO (FR)**, 9, b g Ungaro (GER)—Journenuit (FR) **A. L. Cohen**

MRS LAWNEY HILL - Continued

24 **ROYAL ETIQUETTE (IRE)**, 6, b g Royal Applause—Alpine Gold (IRE) **John Bull & Alan Hill**
25 **TURTLETHOMAS (IRE)**, 7, br g Turtle Island (IRE)—Makingyourmindup (IRE) **Mr A. J. Weller**

Other Owners: Mr J. M. Basquill, Mrs Jonathan Brankin-Frisby, Mr John Bull, Exors of the Late Mr Greg Clark, Mrs Diana Clark, Mr M. B. Clarke, Mr Dominic Collier, Mr Simon Florey, Mr Dan Gilbert, Mr Alan Hill, Mr Brian Hiskey, Mr A. R. W. Marsh, Mr T. S. Palin, Mr M. Prince, Mr Ian A. Robinson, Mrs Gillian Robinson, Mr R. I. Sims, Mr Gary James Styles, Mr D. F. Sumpter, Mr H. J. M. Webb, Mr Andy Weller, Mr Simon Willes, Mr G. Wills.

Jockey (flat): Dane O'Neill. Jockey (NH): David Bass, Aidan Coleman, Harry Skelton. Apprentice: Leonna Mayor. Amateur: Mr Joe Hill.

---

311 **MR MARTIN HILL, Totnes**
Postal: **The Barn, Knaves Ash Stables, Nr Redpost, Littlehempston, Totnes, Devon, TQ9 6NG**
Contacts: PHONE (01803) 813102 MOBILE (07980) 490220
E-MAIL info@martinhillracing.co.uk WEBSITE www.martinhillracing.co.uk

1 **BEAT THE BOUNDS**, 4, b g Beat All (USA)—Regally **M. E. Hill**
2 **DETROIT RED**, 7, b m Hamairi (IRE)—Kingston Black **The Detroit Reds**
3 **HIGGSY**, 5, ch g Generous (IRE)—Carmel's Joy (IRE) **M. E. Hill**
4 **KIM TIAN ROAD (IRE)**, 7, b m King's Theatre (IRE)—Shaunies Lady (IRE) **M. E. Hill**
5 **PALMYRA (IRE)**, 4, ch f Haafhd—Tasjeel (USA) **M. E. Hill**
6 **RYDON PYNES**, 5, b g Beat All (USA)—Persian Smoke **The Rydon Pynes Partnership**
7 **SEMI COLON (FR)**, 7, ch m Robin des Champs (FR)—Hi Colon (FR) **The R. C. Partnership**
8 **TZORA**, 8, b g Sakhee (USA)—Lucky Arrow **Tzora Partners**
9 **Y A BON (IRE)**, 5, b g Black Sam Bellamy (IRE)—Tarte Fine (FR) **M. E. Hill**

TWO-YEAR-OLDS
10 **MIKEY MISS DAISY**, ch f 20/2 Champs Elysees—Savoy Street (Vettori (IRE)) **Mr M. Leach**

Other Owners: Mr J. L. Coombs, Mr Jon Hearne, Mr Martin Hill, Mr Neil. C. Matthews, Mr Ian Tharby, Mr R. Thomasson.

Assistant Trainer: Rachel Williams

Jockey (flat): Luke Morris. Jockey (NH): Hadden Frost. Conditional: Jeremiah McGrath.

---

312 **MR CHARLES HILLS, Lambourn**
Postal: **Wetherdown House, Lambourn, Hungerford, Berkshire, RG17 8UB**
Contacts: PHONE (01488) 71548 FAX (01488) 72823
E-MAIL info@charleshills.co.uk WEBSITE www.charleshills.com

1 **ANGELS WILL FALL (IRE)**, 4, b f Acclamation—Coconut Squeak **Mrs E. O'Leary**
2 **BASSETERRE (IRE)**, 4, b c Cape Cross (IRE)—Higher Love (IRE) **Mr H. R. Mould**
3 **CAPTAIN BERTIE (IRE)**, 5, ch g Captain Rio—Sadika (IRE) **Mr A. L. R. Morton**
4 **FORGOTTEN HERO (IRE)**, 4, b g High Chaparral (IRE)—Sundown **Mrs Julie Martin & David R. Martin**
5 **GARRISSON (IRE)**, 4, b g Cape Cross (IRE)—Desertion (IRE) **Mrs J. K. Powell**
6 **GLEN MOSS (IRE)**, 4, b c Moss Vale (IRE)—Sail With The Wind **Mr John C. Grant**
7 **HAZEL LAVERY (IRE)**, 4, b f Excellent Art—Reprise **T. Hyde**
8 **MODEL PUPIL**, 4, b c Sinndar (IRE)—Modesta (IRE) **Mr K. Abdulla**
9 **PERENNIAL**, 4, ch g Motivator—Arum Lily (USA) **Mr K. Abdulla**
10 **RED ART (IRE)**, 4, b c Excellent Art—All Began (IRE) **Mr Des Anderson & Mr R. J. Arculli**
11 **RED JAZZ (USA)**, 6, b h Johannesburg (USA)—Now That's Jazz (USA) **Mr R. J. Arculli**
12 **SHROPSHIRE (IRE)**, 5, gr g Shamardal (USA)—Shawanni **The Hon Mrs J. M. Corbett & Mr C. Wright**
13 **SIR PEDRO**, 4, b g Acclamation—Milly-M **R. Morecombe, J. Netherthorpe, C. Wright**
14 **WEST LEAKE DIMAN (IRE)**, 4, b g Namid—Roselyn **Mr Henry Barton**

THREE-YEAR-OLDS
15 **AFRICAN OIL (FR)**, b c Royal Applause—Ahdaaf (USA) **Mr Ron Bauer**
16 **AJRAAM (USA)**, b g Daaher (CAN)—Abby Road (IRE) **Hamdan Al Maktoum**
17 **ALNAWIYAH**, b f Dalakhani (IRE)—Mokaraba **Hamdan Al Maktoum**
18 **BARBS PRINCESS**, ch f Bahamian Bounty—Halland Park Girl (IRE) **Mrs Barbara James**
19 **BOSSA NOVA BABY (IRE)**, b f High Chaparral (IRE)—Attilia (GER) **Mr Phil Cunningham**
20 **CALLMEAKHAB (IRE)**, b f Intikhab (USA)—Viola Royale (IRE) **AEGIS Partnership**
21 **CAMISOLE (IRE)**, br f Teofilo (IRE)—Sleeveless (USA) **The Hon Mrs J. M. Corbett & Mr C. Wright**

MR CHARLES HILLS - Continued

22 **COMPLEXITY**, b c Multiplex—Asinara (GER) **Mr Robert Ng**
23 **COUNTRY WESTERN**, b c Oasis Dream—Musical Horizon (USA) **Mr K. Abdulla**
24 **DAIRAM (USA)**, b c Jazil (USA)—Tarteel (USA) **Hamdan Al Maktoum**
25 **DALI'S LOVER (IRE)**, b f Excellent Art—Hendrina (IRE) **Triermore Stud**
26 **DESERT IMAGE**, b f Beat Hollow—Western Appeal (USA) **Mr K. Abdulla**
27 **DUBAI APPLAUSE**, b f Royal Applause—Maimoona (IRE) **Sheikh Hamdan Bin Maktoum Al Maktoum**
28 **EBN ARAB (USA)**, b c Dixie Union (USA)—Daffaash (USA) **Hamdan Al Maktoum**
29 **ENGLISHMAN**, b c Royal Applause—Tesary **Qatar Racing Limited & Mr P. Winkworth**
30 **ESTIBDAAD (IRE)**, b c Haafel (USA)—Star of Siligo (USA) **Hamdan Al Maktoum**
31 **ESTIFZAAZ (IRE)**, b c Invincible Spirit (IRE)—Lulua (USA) **Hamdan Al Maktoum**
32 **FIRE FAIRY (USA)**, b br f Henrythenavigator (USA)—Fabulous Fairy (USA) **Mr B. W. Hills**
33 **FUNK SOUL BROTHER**, b g Cockney Rebel (IRE)—Sweet Afton (IRE) **Mr Phil Cunningham**
34 **GLENARD**, b c Arch (USA)—Olaya (USA) **Highclere T'Bred Racing & John C. Grant**
35 **GOLDEN CAUSEWAY**, ch f Giant's Causeway (USA)—Cast In Gold (USA) **Swettenham Stud & Marston Stud**
36 **JUST THE JUDGE (IRE)**, br f Lawman (FR)—Faraday Light (IRE) **Qatar Racing Limited & Sangster Family**
37 **KERBAAJ (USA)**, b br c Dixie Union (USA)—Mabaahej (USA) **Hamdan Al Maktoum**
38 **KING WOOD (TUR)**, ch c Dilum (USA)—Dancingintheclouds (IRE) **Mr Mehmet Kurt**
39 **LOVE EXCEL**, b c Exceed And Excel (AUS)—Navajo Love Song (IRE) **Mr Robert Ng**
40 **LUCKY BEGGAR (IRE)**, gr c Verglas (IRE)—Lucky Clio (IRE) **Hon Mrs Corbett, C. Wright, Mrs B. W. Hills**
41 **MARKET TOWN (USA)**, b c Mizzen Mast (USA)—Geographic (USA) **Mr K. Abdulla**
42 **MAWJ TAMY (USA)**, b c Invasor (ARG)—Plenty of Sugar (CAN) **Hamdan Al Maktoum**
43 **MAYAASEM**, b c Royal Applause—Rolexa **Hamdan Al Maktoum**
44 **MOVEMENTNEVERLIES**, ch f Medicean—Frabjous **Mr Nicholas Roberts & Mrs E. Roberts**
45 **MRS WARREN**, b f Kyllachy—Bold Bunny **Mrs J. K. Powell & Mr David F. Powell**
46 **MY HEARTS RACING (IRE)**, b f Montjeu (IRE)—Nuriva (USA) **Mr Tony Elliott & Mr Jeff King**
47 **NO TRUTH (IRE)**, b f Galileo (IRE)—State Crystal (IRE) **Triermore Stud**
48 **NOBLE BULL**, b g Papal Bull—Fernlawn Hope (IRE) **John C. Grant & Ray Harper**
49 **OGBOURNE DOWNS**, b c Royal Applause—Helen Sharp **S W Group Logistics Limited**
50 **ONE WORD MORE (IRE)**, b c Thousand Words—Somoushe (IRE) **Tony Wechsler & Ann Plummer**
51 **OVERRIDER**, b g Cockney Rebel (IRE)—Fustaan (IRE) **Phil Cunningham & Mr D. Nightingale**
52 **PENANG POWER**, b f Manduro (GER)—Penang Pearl (FR) **Mrs A. K. H. Ooi**
53 **PERMEATE**, b f Rail Link—Quota **Mr K. Abdulla**
54 **PREMIUM**, b f Dansili—Arum Lily (USA) **Mr K. Abdulla**
55 **PULIGNY (IRE)**, b f Holy Roman Emperor (IRE)—Le Montrachet **Mrs E. Roberts**
56 **RED DRAGON (IRE)**, b c Acclamation—Delphie Queen (IRE) **Mr R. J. Arculli & Mr Des Anderson**
57 **RED EXPLORER (IRE)**, b c Henrythenavigator (USA)—Remote (USA) **Mr R. J. Arculli & Mr Robert Ng**
58 **RED INVADER (IRE)**, b c Red Clubs (IRE)—Tifariti (USA) **Mr R. J. Arculli**
59 **RED VALERIAN (IRE)**, b c Royal Applause—Hidden Heart (USA) **Mr B. W. Hills**
60 **REFER**, b c Rail Link—Trellis Bay **Mr K. Abdulla**
61 **REGAL DAN (IRE)**, b c Dark Angel (IRE)—Charlene Lacy (IRE) **N. N. Browne, Paul McNamara, Hon Mrs Napier**
62 **REYAADAH**, b f Tamayuz—Tafaani (IRE) **Hamdan Al Maktoum**
63 **RUFOOF**, b f Zamindar (USA)—Tahrir (IRE) **Hamdan Al Maktoum**
64 **SAND BOY (IRE)**, b c Footstepsinthesand—Farbenspiel (USA) **Sir A. Ferguson, Mr, Mrs J. Cotton, J. Hanson**
65 **SEAMLESS**, b c Beat Hollow—Fashionable **Mr K. Abdulla**
66 **SHAISHEE (USA)**, b br c Indian Charlie (USA)—Hatpin (USA) **Hamdan Al Maktoum**
67 **SINGLE MAST (USA)**, ch f Mizzen Mast (USA)—Single Market (USA) **Mr K. Abdulla**
68 **SOCIETY PEARL (IRE)**, b f Kheleyf (USA)—Mamonta **Pearl Bloodstock Limited**
69 **STORM (IRE)**, b f Excellent Art—Bali Breeze (IRE) **R. Morecombe, J. Netherthorpe, E. O'Leary**
70 **SUNBULA (USA)**, ch f Singspiel (IRE)—Uroobah (USA) **Hamdan Al Maktoum**
71 **TEQUILA SUNRISE**, gr f Dansili—Kenmist **Mr Christopher Wright**
72 **THE WELSH WIZARD (IRE)**, b c Dylan Thomas (IRE)—
                                               Golden Dew (IRE) **Mr, Mrs J. Cotton, Sir A. Ferguson, J. Hanson**
73 **UNMOOTHAJ**, b c Green Desert (USA)—Sundus (USA) **Hamdan Al Maktoum**
74 **WINTER SONG (IRE)**, b f Pivotal—Speed Song **Mrs E. O'Leary**
75 **WOLFS BREATH (TUR)**, b f Montjeu (IRE)—Uva (TUR) **Mr Mehmet Kurt**
76 **ZIPP (IRE)**, b f Excellent Art—Subito **Mr Richard Morecombe & Mr S. E. Sangster**

TWO-YEAR-OLDS

77 B f 14/5 Fastnet Rock (AUS)—Adjalisa (IRE) (Darshaan)
78 **ALMUHALAB**, b br c 15/2 Dansili—Ghanaati (Giant's Causeway (USA))
79 **ALZAMMAAR (USA)**, b c 18/3 Birdstone (USA)—Alma Mater (Sadler's Wells (USA)) (170000)
80 B f 9/2 Holy Roman Emperor (IRE)—Art Work (Zafonic (USA)) (36190)
81 **BEATABOUT THE BUSH (IRE)**, b br c 13/2 Bushranger (IRE)—Queen of Fibres (IRE) (Scenic) (34285)
82 B c 17/4 Dark Angel (IRE)—Birthday Present (Cadeaux Genereux) (63491)
83 B f 6/4 Footstepsinthesand—Blue Crystal (IRE) (Lure (USA)) (26983)

MR CHARLES HILLS - Continued

84 B c 25/1 Bushranger (IRE)—Broadways Millie (IRE) (Imperial Ballet (IRE)) (63491)
85 **CAPE KARLI (IRE)**, br f 26/4 Cape Cross (IRE)—Karliysha (IRE) (Kalanisi (IRE)) (45238)
86 **CHRISELLIAM (IRE)**, b f 2/2 Iffraaj—Danielli (IRE) (Danehill (USA)) (40000)
87 B f 28/3 High Chaparral (IRE)—Civility Cat (USA) (Tale of The Cat (USA)) (69047)
88 B f 26/1 Champs Elysees—Codename (Sadler's Wells (USA))
89 B f 24/4 Montjeu (IRE)—Crystal Curling (IRE) (Peintre Celebre (USA))
90 **CULDAFF (IRE)**, b c 21/2 Aqlaam—Nenuphar (IRE) (Night Shift (USA)) (33333)
91 Ch c 8/3 Three Valleys (USA)—Cut Corn (King's Theatre (IRE))
92 **DESPOT (IRE)**, gr c 24/4 Verglas (IRE)—Ms Bossy Boots (USA) (Grand Slam (USA)) (43809)
93 B f 23/3 High Chaparral (IRE)—En Garde (USA) (Irish River (FR)) (47619)
94 Ch f 5/3 Dutch Art—Endless Love (IRE) (Dubai Destination (USA))
95 **EXCELLENT ROYALE (IRE)**, b c 10/4 Excellent Art—Farbenspiel (IRE) (Desert Prince (IRE)) (33333)
96 B br f 15/2 Mizzen Mast (USA)—Faraway Flower (USA) (Distant View (USA))
97 **FROSTY THE SNOWMAN (IRE)**, gr c 23/3 Mastercraftsman (IRE)—

Sleeveless (USA) (Fusaichi Pegasus (USA)) (80000)

98 **GOWN (IRE)**, b f 20/1 Excellent Art—Chehalis Sunset (Danehill Dancer (USA)) (10000)
99 **GREEB**, b br c 28/1 Oasis Dream—Shamtari (IRE) (Alhaarth (IRE))
100 B f 9/3 Excellent Art—Ibtikar (USA) (Private Account (USA)) (51587)
101 **IFTAAR (IRE)**, b c 21/2 Bushranger (IRE)—Kheleyf's Silver (IRE) (Kheleyf (USA)) (85714)
102 B br f 21/3 Empire Maker (USA)—Introducing (USA) (Deputy Minister (CAN))
103 B c 11/3 Danehill Dancer (IRE)—Jazz Baby (IRE) (Fasliyev (USA)) (31745)
104 B f 16/5 Acclamation—Kahira (IRE) (King's Best (USA)) (55000)
105 **KIYOSHI**, b f 5/3 Dubawi (IRE)—Mocca (IRE) (Sri Pekan (USA)) (80000)
106 **MAAYAAT (USA)**, b f 15/2 Jazil (USA)—Wasnah (USA) (Nijinsky (CAN))
107 **MAHATTA (IRE)**, b f 29/1 Halling (USA)—Tafaani (IRE) (Green Desert (USA))
108 **MARMOOM**, ch c 3/4 Dutch Art—Cosmic Song (Cosmonaut) (80000)
109 **MARTELA (IRE)**, b c 18/4 Marju (IRE)—Khatela (IRE) (Shernazar) (63491)
110 **MAYSVILLE (IRE)**, b br f 22/3 Lawman (FR)—Morality (Elusive Quality (USA)) (8571)
111 **MINNIE HAZEL (IRE)**, ch f 7/3 Excellent Art—Reprise (Darshaan) (11904)
112 **MY PAINTER (IRE)**, b f 9/2 Jeremy (USA)—Last Cry (FR) (Peintre Celebre (USA)) (22221)
113 **NATHR (USA)**, b br c 10/2 Dixie Union (USA)—Sweet Rider (USA) (Seeking The Gold (USA)) (122887)
114 B c 14/3 Lucky Story (USA)—One For Philip (Blushing Flame (USA))
115 B c 2/4 Royal Applause—Passing Hour (USA) (Red Ransom (USA)) (55000)
116 **QAWAASEM (IRE)**, b f 6/2 Shamardal (USA)—Misdaqeya (Red Ransom (USA))
117 B c 18/3 Bushranger (IRE)—Rainbow Lyrics (IRE) (Rainbow Quest (USA)) (47619)
118 **RANDWICK (IRE)**, b c 22/3 High Chaparral (IRE)—Subito (Darshaan) (70000)
119 B f 4/2 Tagula (IRE)—Rebel Aclaim (IRE) (Acclamation) (26666)
120 B f 28/2 Acclamation—Regatta (USA) (Giant's Causeway (USA)) (126983)
121 **ROCK OF DREAMS (IRE)**, b c 21/2 Rock of Gibraltar (IRE)—

Manhattan Dream (USA) (Statue of Liberty (USA)) (32000)

122 **ROMULETTE**, b f 7/1 Holy Roman Emperor (IRE)—Royal Confidence (Royal Applause)
123 B c 2/3 Invincible Spirit (IRE)—Rose de France (IRE) (Diktat) (103174)
124 **ROSEHILL ARTIST (IRE)**, b f 10/5 Excellent Art—Conference (IRE) (Montjeu (IRE)) (35000)
125 B br f 23/2 Aptitude (USA)—Rouwaki (USA) (Miswaki (USA))
126 **SAHRA AL KHADRA**, b c 1/3 Green Desert (USA)—Maimoona (IRE) (Pivotal)
127 **SCILLONIAN SUNSET (IRE)**, ch f 30/1 Teofilo (IRE)—

Hundred Year Flood (USA) (Giant's Causeway (USA)) (35000)

128 **SELLINGALLTHETIME (IRE)**, ch c 12/4 Tamayuz—Anthyllis (GER) (Lycius (USA)) (55555)
129 **SO SATISFIED**, b c 12/5 Aqlaam—Pirouetting (Pivotal) (14000)
130 **SOCIAL RISER (IRE)**, b f 6/4 High Chaparral (IRE)—Parvenue (FR) (Ezzoud (IRE)) (41269)
131 **SOLID JUSTICE (IRE)**, b c 25/2 Rock of Gibraltar (IRE)—Burnin' Memories (USA) (Lit de Justice (USA)) (67460)
132 B br c 6/2 Latent Heat (USA)—Storming On (USA) (Storm Cat (USA))
133 B f 19/2 Marju (IRE)—Talwin (IRE) (Alhaarth (IRE)) (50000)
134 **TAMALUK (USA)**, b c 25/1 Discreet Cat (USA)—Mabaahej (USA) (Belong To Me (USA))
135 **TANZEEL (IRE)**, b c 10/5 Elusive City (USA)—Royal Fizz (IRE) (Royal Academy (USA)) (100000)
136 B c 2/3 Three Valleys (USA)—Tarot Card (Fasliyev (USA))
137 Ch c 27/2 Mizzen Mast (USA)—Tolerance (USA) (Seeking The Gold (USA))
138 Ch f 6/3 Bahamian Bounty—Treasure Trove (USA) (The Minstrel (CAN)) (43650)

Other Owners: Miss E. Asprey, W. H. Carson, Decadent Racing, Mrs G. Galvin, Jeremy Gompertz, Mr Jim Hill, Mrs Susan Hill, Mrs G. W. Hills, Mrs Philippa Hills, Mr D. M. James, Stewart Jones, Mr Arthur Mitchell, P O'Callaghan, David Reid-Scott, Mrs Susan Roy, Mr B. V. Sangster, M. E. Sangster, Mr R. A. Scarborough, Lady Richard Wellesley.

Assistant Trainer: Kevin Mooney

Apprentice: Matthew Lawson.

313 MR J. W. HILLS, Lambourn

Postal: **The Croft, Upper Lambourn, Newbury, Berkshire, RG17 8QH**
Contacts: **PHONE (01488) 73144 FAX (01488) 73099 MOBILE (07836) 283091**
E-MAIL john@johnhills.com TWITTER: @HillsJW WEBSITE www.johnhills.com

1 **B FIFTY TWO (IRE)**, 4, br c Dark Angel (IRE)—Petite Maxine **Gary & Linnet Woodward**
2 **BOOMERANG BOB (IRE)**, 4, b c Aussie Rules (USA)—Cozzene's Pride (USA) **R. J. Tufft**
3 **FEISTY CHAMPION (IRE)**, 4, b g Captain Rio—Deylviyna (IRE) **Mr M. C. E. Wong**
4 **JOHNNO**, 4, br g Excellent Art—Vert Val (USA) **Gary & Linnet Woodward**
5 **PADDYFROMMENLO (IRE)**, 4, ch c Hurricane Run (IRE)—Dolce Dovo **Mr Pat McDonagh**
6 **XINBAMA (IRE)**, 4, b c Baltic King—Persian Empress **Tony Waspe Partnership**

THREE-YEAR-OLDS

7 **A GOOD YEAR (IRE)**, b f Montjeu (IRE)—Noble Pearl (GER) **Corinthian**
8 **AMARILLO STARLIGHT (IRE)**, b br f Dalakhani (IRE)—Briolette (IRE)
9 **ARMS (IRE)**, b c Excellent Art—Enchanting Way **Mr M. H. Lui**
10 **BRIGHT YOUNG THING (IRE)**, b f Danehill Dancer (IRE)—Portentous **J. W. Hills**
11 **CARRERA**, b c Sixties Icon—Aileen's Gift (IRE) **Gary & Linnet Woodward**
12 **DANGEROUS AGE**, br f Sleeping Indian—Rye (IRE) **Ross Hunter & David Klein**
13 **DUCHESS OF HYGROVE**, b f Duke of Marmalade (IRE)—Elegant Pride **Mr D. H. Francis**
14 **ELUSIVE GOLD (IRE)**, b f Elusive City (USA)—Lady Angola (USA) **Gold, Clark, McDonagh, Stopp & Tofts**
15 **EMERALD ART (IRE)**, ch f Excellent Art—Greenvera (USA) **Hills' Angels**
16 **K LIGHTNING**, ch g Danehill Dancer (IRE)—Arosa (IRE) **Mr Y. K. Liu**
17 **KEENE'S POINTE**, br c Avonbridge—Belle's Edge **Mrs D. Abberley**
18 **KIWANI BAY**, b f Nayef (USA)—Isle of Spice (USA) **Mr P. A. Abberley**
19 **MICK DUNDEE (IRE)**, b c Aussie Rules (USA)—Lucky Oakwood (USA) **R. J. Tufft**
20 **NORTH WEALD (IRE)**, b f Hurricane Run (IRE)—Foreign Relation (IRE) **Abbott Racing Partners**
21 **RIOJA DAY (IRE)**, b c Red Clubs (IRE)—Dai E Dai (USA) **Neil Ledger and Gary Woodward**
22 **SOUL INTENT (IRE)**, b c Galileo (IRE)—Flamingo Guitar (USA) **Andy Weller & Gary Styles**
23 **SWEET VINTAGE (IRE)**, b f Singspiel (IRE)—Sauterne **Lord Lloyd Webber**
24 B f Galileo (IRE)—Tea Break
25 **TESTA ROSSA (IRE)**, b c Oratorio (IRE)—Red Rita (IRE) **Gary & Linnet Woodward**
26 **TOFFEE SHOT**, ch f Dutch Art—Toffee Vodka (IRE) **Gary & Linnet Woodward**
27 **TWO NO BIDS (IRE)**, b br c Footstepsinthesand—Milwaukee (FR) **J. W. Hills**
28 **WATCHEROFTHESKIES**, b g Dutch Art—Red Heaven **R. J. Tufft**

TWO-YEAR-OLDS

29 B c 15/3 High Chaparral (IRE)—Cabo (FR) (Sagamix (FR)) (35000) **Prolinx Limited**
30 B f 14/3 Excellent Art—Course de Diamante (IRE) (Galileo (IRE)) (24000)
31 **SEAT OF MARS (IRE)**, b c 30/4 Yeats (IRE)—Haraplata (GER) (Platini (GER)) (14000) **Mr P. A. Abberley**
32 B f 3/3 Sleeping Indian—Toffee Vodka (IRE) (Danehill Dancer (IRE)) (13809) **Gary & Linnet Woodward**

Other Owners: Mr Daniel Abbott, Mr N. N. Browne, Mr Nick Clark, Mr D. Fulford, Mr Paul Gold, Mrs S. Heinemann, Mrs F. Hills, Mr J. W. Hills, Mr R. Hunter, Mrs M. Kingham, Mr David Klein, Mr Neil Ledger, Mr Pat McDonagh, Mr Peter Stopp, Mr Gary James Styles, Mr Luke Tofts, Mr T. Waspe, Mr Andy Weller, Mr Gary Woodward, Mrs Linnet Woodward.

Assistant Trainer: Henry Tett

Jockey (flat): Seb Sanders. **Apprentice:** Leah-Anne Avery.

314 MR MARK HOAD, Lewes

Postal: **Windmill Lodge Stables, Spital Road, Lewes, East Sussex, BN7 1LS**
Contacts: **PHONE (01273) 477124/(01273) 480691 FAX (01273) 477124 MOBILE (07742) 446168**
E-MAIL markhoad@aol.com

1 **ALFIE ALEXANDER (IRE)**, 5, b g Indian Danehill (IRE)—Bella Galiana (ITY) **Mrs L. Bangs**
2 **DOCTOR HILARY**, 11, b g Mujahid (USA)—Agony Aunt **J. Baden White**
3 **MAFI (IRE)**, 5, b g Modigliani (USA)—Yulara (IRE) **Mrs J. E. Taylor**
4 **TOTAL OBSESSION**, 6, b m Mujahid (USA)—Buon Amici **Miss H. S. Matthews**

THREE-YEAR-OLDS

5 **WE'RE IN THE RED (IRE)**, br g Daaher (CAN)—Elaflaak (USA) **Gee Ceffyl Bach Club**

Other Owners: D. M. I. Simcock, Mrs A. Simcock.

315 MR ANDY HOBBS, Hanley Swan
Postal: 2 The Old Dairy, Tyre Hill Stables, Hanley Swan, Worcestershire, WR8 0EQ
Contacts: PHONE (01684) 311760 MOBILE (07717) 664115
E-MAIL teamhobbs@btinternet.com WEBSITE www.andyhobbsracing.co.uk

1 BENNYS QUEST (IRE), 10, ch g Beneficial—Wonder Winnie (IRE) **John Hobbs & Dave Harris**
2 DIAMOND TAMMY (IRE), 7, b g Tamayaz (CAN)—
    Mary Dont Be Long (IRE) **Three Counties Racing 2 & A G Hobbs**
3 GARYRICKEN (IRE), 8, b g Oscar (IRE)—Tamed **Mr R. S. Williams**
4 GOT ATTITUDE (IRE), 10, ch g Beneficial—Ilderton Road
5 JOKER OF THE PACK (IRE), 8, b g Craigsteel—Callmartel (IRE) **Tyre Hill Racing**
6 JOMADE (IRE), 7, b g Definite Article—Culmore Native (IRE) **Tyre Hill Racing**
7 LORD LANDEN (IRE), 8, br g Beneficial—Agua Caliente (IRE) **The B Lucky Partnership**
8 NETHER STREAM (IRE), 9, b g Blueprint (IRE)—Shuil Ub **Tyre Hill Racing**
9 SIR PITT, 6, b g Tiger Hill (IRE)—Rebecca Sharp **G. D. Kendrick**
10 TRUCKERS PRINCESS (IRE), 9, b m Beneficial—Lady Jurado (IRE) **P. J. Jones**
11 UNWANTED GIFT (IRE), 8, b g Tendulkar (USA)—Slieverue (IRE)
12 VITAL MERLIN, 4, b g Vital Equine—Claradotnet **G. D. Kendrick**
13 WALTZING TORNADO (IRE), 9, ch g Golden Tornado (IRE)—Lady Dante (IRE) **John Hobbs & Andy Hobbs**
14 ZAKAROO, 5, b g Auction House (USA)—Claradotnet **G. D. Kendrick**

Other Owners: M. A. Blackford, Mr S. W. Bowers, N. A. Brimble, Mr D. B. Harris, Mrs R. M. Hobbs, Mr J. Hobbs, Mr A. G. Hobbs, N. Scanlan.

316 MR PHILIP HOBBS, Minehead
Postal: Sandhill, Bilbrook, Minehead, Somerset, TA24 6HA
Contacts: PHONE (01984) 640366 FAX (01984) 641124 MOBILE (07860) 729795
E-MAIL pjhobbs@pjhobbs.com WEBSITE www.pjhobbs.com

1 AL ALFA, 6, ch g Alflora (IRE)—Two For Joy (IRE) **The Hon J. R. Drummond**
2 ALLONS ZEE (IRE), 4, ch g Zerpour (IRE)—Bu Hagab (IRE) **A. P. Staple**
3 ALLTHEKINGSHORSES (IRE), 7, b g King's Theatre (IRE)—Penny Brae (IRE) **R Triple H**
4 ARTHURIAN LEGEND, 8, b g Alflora (IRE)—Be My Adelina (IRE) **Mr R. T. Kanter & Mr A. J. Scrimgeour**
5 AUGUST HILL (IRE), 5, b m Presenting—Nuit des Chartreux (FR) **Mrs Caren Walsh & Mrs Kathleen Quinn**
6 BALLYGARVEY (FR), 7, b g Laveron—Vollore (FR) **The Dark Horse Syndicate**
7 BALLYTOBER, 7, b g Kahyasi—Full of Birds (FR) **Mrs D. L. Whateley**
8 BALTHAZAR KING (IRE), 9, b g King's Theatre (IRE)—Aldala (IRE) **The Brushmakers**
9 BERKELEY BARRON (IRE), 5, b g Subtle Power (IRE)—Roseabel (IRE) **Mrs E. A. Prowting**
10 BERTIE BORU (IRE), 6, b g Brian Boru—Sleeven Lady **Unity Farm Holiday Centre Ltd**
11 BEST TIME EVER, 5, b g Tobougg (IRE)—Lucky Arrow **A. L. Cohen**
12 BIG EASY (GER), 6, b g Ransom O'war (USA)—Basilea Gold (GER) **J. T. Warner**
13 BILLESLEY ROAD, 5, ch g Zafeen (FR)—Doubletta (IRE) **James & Jean Potter**
14 BINCOMBE, 5, gr g Indian Danehill (USA)—Siroyalta (FR) **M. Short**
15 BOLD HENRY, 7, b g Kayf Tara—Madam Min **J. P. McManus**
16 BRIGHT ABBEY, 5, ch g Halling (USA)—Bright Hope (IRE) **Mrs C. J. Walsh**
17 CALUSA COMET (IRE), 5, b g Alamshar (IRE)—Erins Love (IRE) **P. Luff**
18 CALUSA STAR, 4, b g Multiplex—Pugnacious Lady **P. Luff**
19 CALUSA STORM (IRE), 5, b g Millenary—Well Composed (IRE) **P. Luff**
20 CAPTAIN CHRIS (IRE), 9, b g King's Theatre (IRE)—Function Dream (IRE) **Mrs D. L. Whateley**
21 CARRIGMORNA KING (IRE), 7, b g King's Theatre (IRE)—Carrigmorna Flyer (IRE) **R. & Mrs J. E. Gibbs**
22 CELTIC ABBEY, 6, br g Overbury (IRE)—Celtic Native (IRE) **A. Stennett**
23 CHAMPAGNE WEST (IRE), 5, b g Westerner—Wyndham Sweetmarie (IRE) **R. S. Brookhouse**
24 CHANCE DU ROY (FR), 9, ch g Morespeed—La Chance Au Roy (FR) **Miss I. D. Du Pre**
25 CHELTENIAN (FR), 7, b g Astarabad (USA)—Salamaite (FR) **R. S. Brookhouse**
26 COCKNEY TRUCKER (IRE), 11, b g Presenting—Kiltiernan Easter (IRE) **P. J. Hobbs**
27 CODDINGTON BOY, 5, br g Fair Mix (IRE)—Coddington Girl **Outhart, Trembath, Hyde, Fletcher, Hill**
28 COLOUR SQUADRON (IRE), 7, b g Old Vic—That's The Goose (IRE) **J. P. McManus**
29 DANANDY (IRE), 6, b g Cloudings (IRE)—Tower Princess (IRE) **Mrs C. J. Walsh**
30 DE LA BECH, 6, ch g Karinga Bay—Vallis Vale **B. K. Peppiatt**
31 DREAMS AND SONGS, 5, ch m Presenting—Vianne (IRE) **D. J. Burke**
32 DUKE OF LUCCA (IRE), 8, b g Milan—Derravaragh Native (IRE) **Mrs L. H. Field**
33 FAIR ALONG (GER), 11, b g Alkalde (GER)—Fairy Tango (FR) **A. E. Peterson**
34 FIGHTING FLYNN, 8, b g Old Vic—Innovate (IRE) **J. P. McManus**
35 FILBERT (IRE), 7, b g Oscar (IRE)—Coca's Well (IRE) **R Triple H**

MR PHILIP HOBBS - Continued

36 **FINGAL BAY (IRE)**, 7, b g King's Theatre (IRE)—Lady Marguerrite **Mrs C. Skan**
37 **GARDE LA VICTOIRE (FR)**, 4, b g Kapgarde (FR)—Next Victory (FR) **Mrs D. L. Whateley**
38 **GAS LINE BOY (IRE)**, 7, b g Blueprint (IRE)—Jervia **Mick Fitzgerald Racing Club**
39 **GAUVAIN (GER)**, 11, b g Sternkoenig (IRE)—Gamina (GER) **The Spoofers**
40 **HORIZONTAL SPEED (IRE)**, 5, b g Vertical Speed (FR)—Rockababy (IRE) **Favourites Racing Ltd**
41 **IF IN DOUBT (IRE)**, 5, b g Heron Island (IRE)—Catchers Day (IRE) **J. P. McManus**
42 **IMPERIAL CIRCUS (IRE)**, 7, b g Beneficial—Aunty Dawn (IRE) **R. A. S. Offer**
43 **IRISH BUCCANEER (IRE)**, 6, b g Milan—Supreme Serenade (IRE) **J. P. McManus**
44 **JAYANDBEE (IRE)**, 6, b g Presenting—Christines Gale (IRE) **J & B Gibbs & Sons Ltd**
45 **JOSEPH MERCER (IRE)**, 6, b g Court Cave (IRE)—Vikki's Dream (IRE) **R. Green**
46 **KAP GUN (FR)**, 5, br g Kapgarde (FR)—Aubisquinette (FR) **M. J. Tuckey**
47 **KARTANIAN (IRE)**, 7, br g Kalanisi (IRE)—Katiykha (IRE) **Louisville Syndicate III**
48 **KEKI BUKU (FR)**, 10, b g Kadalko (FR)—Bigouden **Mrs D. L. Whateley**
49 **LADY CHARISMA**, 4, b f Presenting—Lady Cad (FR)
50 **LAMB OR COD (IRE)**, 6, ch g Old Vic—Princess Lizzie (IRE) **J. T. Warner**
51 **LORD PROTECTOR (IRE)**, 6, b g Oscar (IRE)—Warts And All (IRE) **Louisville Syndicate**
52 **MARUFO (IRE)**, 11, b g Presenting—Bucks Cregg (IRE) **N. R. A. Sutton**
53 **MEIRIG'S DREAM (IRE)**, 7, b g Golan (IRE)—Women In Love (IRE) **Miss V. Dunn & Mr H. Davies**
54 **MENORAH (IRE)**, 8, b g King's Theatre (IRE)—Maid For Adventure (IRE) **Mrs D. L. Whateley**
55 **MIGHTY MOBB (IRE)**, 6, b g Accordion—Dusty Lane (IRE) **T. J. Hemmings**
56 **MILLIE O'BRIEN**, 5, b m Milan—Mrs Philip **Mrs S. Hobbs**
57 **MILOSAM (IRE)**, 6, b g Milan—Lady Sam (IRE) **R. J. Croker**
58 **MISS POLI**, 4, b f Ballingarry (IRE)—Polivalente (FR) **M. J. Tuckey**
59 **MISTER BRICOLAGE (IRE)**, 6, br g Oscar (IRE)—Almost Trumps **Mrs C. Skan**
60 **NO LIKEY (IRE)**, 6, b g Helissio (FR)—Money Galore (IRE) **Touchwood Racing**
61 **NUTIN FANCY (IRE)**, 7, br g Oscar (IRE)—Ennel Lady (IRE) **Julie & Tony Phillips**
62 **OLDRIK (GER)**, 10, b g Tannenkonig (IRE)—Onestep (GER) **D. J. Jones**
63 **ORABORA**, 7, b g Alflora (IRE)—Magic Orb **Dr V. M. G. Ferguson**
64 **OSCAR DAVY (IRE)**, 7, b g Oscar (IRE)—Galtee Castle (IRE) **Mr A. R. E. Ash**
65 **OSCAR ZULU (IRE)**, 6, b g Oscar (IRE)—The Gullett (IRE) **Mr T Syder & Mr M St Quinton**
66 **PATEESE (FR)**, 8, b g Priolo (USA)—Flyer (FR) **The Test Valley Partnership**
67 **PERSIAN SNOW (IRE)**, 7, b g Anshan—Alpine Message **D. R. Peppiatt**
68 **PISTOL (IRE)**, 4, b g High Chaparral (IRE)—Alinea (USA) **Clark, Devlin, Knox & Wells & Monroe**
69 **PLANET OF SOUND**, 11, b g Kayf Tara—Herald The Dawn **Mr C. G. M. Lloyd-Baker**
70 **PRINCELY PLAYER (IRE)**, 6, b g King's Theatre (IRE)—Temptation (FR) **Thurloe 52**
71 **QUADRILLER (FR)**, 6, b g Lando (GER)—Tabachines (FR) **P. E. Atkinson**
72 **QUICK DECISSON (IRE)**, 5, b g Azamour (IRE)—Fleet River (USA) **Owners For Owners: Quick Decisson**
73 **RETURN SPRING (IRE)**, 6, b g Vinnie Roe (IRE)—Bettys Daughter (IRE) **D. J. Jones**
74 **ROALCO DE FARGES (FR)**, 8, gr g Dom Alco (FR)—Vonaria (FR) **The Brushmakers**
75 **ROB CONTI (FR)**, 8, b br g Network (GER)—Initiale Royale (FR) **P. J. Hobbs**
76 **ROLL THE DICE (IRE)**, 7, b g Oscar (IRE)—Sallowglen Gale (IRE) **The Kingpins**
77 **ROYAL REGATTA (IRE)**, 5, b g King's Theatre (IRE)—Friendly Craic (IRE) **Mr J C Murphy & Mrs L Field**
78 **SADLER'S RISK (IRE)**, 5, b g Sadler's Wells (USA)—Riskaverse (USA) **R. S. Brookhouse**
79 **SALFORD LADY**, 4, b f Zafeen (FR)—She's The Lady **R. S. Brookhouse**
80 **SAMMYS GONE (IRE)**, 7, ch g Flemensfirth (USA)—Gaelic Million (IRE) **R. S. Brookhouse**
81 **SATOU (FR)**, 7, gr g Fragrant Mix (IRE)—Jonquiere (FR) **P. J. Hobbs**
82 **SAUSALITO SUNRISE (IRE)**, 5, b g Gold Well—Villaflor (IRE) **Mrs D. L. Whateley**
83 **SHINROCK HILL**, 9, b g Turtle Island (IRE)—Clashdermot Lass **R. S. Brookhouse**
84 **SNAP TIE (IRE)**, 11, b g Pistolet Bleu (IRE)—Aries Girl **Mrs D. L. Whateley**
85 **SO FINE (IRE)**, 7, b br g Definite Article—Not So Green (IRE) **Mrs L. R. Lovell**
86 **SOFTSONG (FR)**, 5, b g Singspiel (IRE)—Soft Gold (USA) **A. L. Cohen**
87 **SONOFTHEKING (IRE)**, 5, b g King's Theatre (IRE)—Nikadora (FR) **Bradley Partnership**
88 **TALKONTHESTREET (IRE)**, 6, b g Milan—Super Size (IRE) **Mrs D. L. Whateley**
89 **TAMIRA**, 6, b m Tamure (IRE)—Welsh Lustre (IRE) **Mrs L. R. Lovell**
90 **THE DISENGAGER (IRE)**, 9, b g Snurge—The Doctors Wife (IRE) **Govier & Brown**
91 **THE SKYFARMER**, 5, br g Presenting—Koral Bay (FR) **Mrs J. J. Peppiatt**
92 **THOMAS WILD**, 8, ch g Muhtarram (USA)—Bisque **C L T**
93 **THUNDERSTORM (IRE)**, 8, b g Milan—Elizabeth Tudor (IRE) **J. P. McManus**
94 **TIQRIS**, 5, ch g Midnight Legend—Calaminta **R. S. Brookhouse**
95 **TONY STAR (FR)**, 6, b g Lone Bid (FR)—Effet de Star (FR) **Thurloe 51**
96 **TOOWOOMBA (IRE)**, 5, b g Milan—Lillies Bordello (IRE) **Michael Watt, J A McGrath, The Anzacs**
97 **TRIGGERMAN**, 11, b g Double Trigger (IRE)—Carrikins **M. G. St Quinton**
98 **UNCLE JIMMY (IRE)**, 6, b br g Alderbrook—Carrabawn **Mr A. R. E. Ash**
99 **VILLAGE VIC (IRE)**, 6, b g Old Vic—Etoile Margot (FR) **A. E. Peterson**
100 **VOLADOR (IRE)**, 9, b g Old Vic—She's The One (IRE) **Louisville Syndicate II**

MR PHILIP HOBBS - Continued

101 **WEIGH IT UP (IRE)**, 5, ch g Flemensfirth (USA)—Uppermost **James & Jean Potter**
102 **WESTERN JO (IRE)**, 5, b g Westerner—Jenny's Jewel (IRE) **T. J. Hemmings**
103 **WHO'S JEFF (IRE)**, 5, b g Westerner—Kitty Maher (IRE) **Coalville Glass & Glazing Ltd**
104 **WISHFULL THINKING**, 10, ch g Alflora (IRE)—Poussetiere Deux (FR) **Mrs D. L. Whateley**
105 **WOODFORD COUNTY**, 6, b g Sonus (IRE)—Moylena **P. J. Hobbs**

Other Owners: Mr R. B. Antell, Mr D. J. Baker, Mr J. A. Barnes, G. S. Brown, C. J. Butler, Mr G. P. A. Clark, H. J. Davies, R. W. Devlin, Miss V. C. Dunn, Mr N. Fletcher, H. R. Gibbs, Mrs J. E. Gibbs, Mrs C. F. Godsall, Mr P. Govier, Mr P. F. Govier, Mr R. H. M. Grant, Mr T. M. Hailstone, J. R. Hall, S. R. Harman, Mr J. R. Holmes, Mr E. J. Hughes, Mr B. R. Ingram, R. T. Kanter, Mr S. Kidston, Knox & Wells Limited, Mr A. P. Maddox, Miss N. Martin, J. A. McGrath, Mr J. R. Monroe, C. Murphy, H. A. Murphy, Mrs A. L. M. Murphy, Mr I. A. Nunn, Mr T. E. Olver, A. J. Outhart, O. J. W. Pawle, N. D. Peppiatt, Mr A. C. Phillips, Mr A. K. Phillips, Mrs J. A. Phillips, Miss J. Pimblett, J. E. Potter, Mrs M. J. Potter, Mrs K. Quinn, D. A. Rees, Mr M. C. Sargent, A. J. Scrimgeour, Mr J. Simpson, Mr J. A. B. Stafford, T. D. J. Syder, M. H. Watt, T. C. Wheeler, Mrs T. S. Wheeler, Mr R. M. E. Wright.

Assistant Trainer: Richard White

Jockey (NH): Richard Johnson, Tom O'Brien. **Conditional:** James Best, Chris Davies, Jonathan Moore, Micheal Nolan. **Amateur:** Mr Tom Cheesman, Mr Ciaran Gethings, Mr Conor Smith.

---

317   MR RON HODGES, Somerton
Postal: **Bull Brook Stables, West Charlton, Charlton Mackrell, Somerton, Somerset, TA11 7AL**
Contacts: PHONE (01458) 223922 FAX (01458) 223969 MOBILE (07770) 625846
E-MAIL mandyhodges@btconnect.com

1 **BUTE STREET**, 8, b g Superior Premium—Hard To Follow **J. W. Mursell**
2 **DREAMS OF GLORY**, 5, ch h Resplendent Glory (IRE)—Pip's Dream **P. E. Axon**
3 **MAY BOY**, 7, br g Bandmaster (USA)—Kathies Pet **R. J. Hodges**
4 **MISS TENACIOUS**, 6, b m Refuse To Bend (IRE)—Very Speed (USA) **John Frampton & Paul Frampton**
5 **MISTER MUSICMASTER**, 4, b g Amadeus Wolf—Misty Eyed (IRE) **Mrs L. Sharpe & Mrs S. G. Clapp**
6 **MORPET**, 4, b g Morpeth—Kathies Pet **Mrs S. Hutchings**
7 **OH DEAR OH DEAR**, 5, b m Pasternak—Post It **Mr J. M. Dare**
8 **ONE LAST DREAM**, 4, ch g Resplendent Glory (IRE)—Pip's Dream **P. E. Axon**
9 **POSH EMILY**, 10, b m Rakaposhi King—Persistent Gunner **Racing Demons Partnership**
10 **SETTER'S PRINCESS**, 7, ch m Generous (IRE)—Setter Country **Mrs L. Sharpe & Mrs S. G. Clapp**
11 **THE QUARTERJACK**, 4, b g Haafhd—Caressed **P. E. Axon**
12 **UNDERLAY UNDERLAY**, 5, b g Namid—Rainbow Nation **K. J. Corcoran**

THREE-YEAR-OLDS

13 **BARNEY ROYAL**, b g Royal Storm (IRE)—The Grey Bam Bam **Mrs C. P. Taylor**
14 **TAMMIS**, b f Whipper (USA)—Tamise (USA) **Miss R. J. Dobson**

Other Owners: Mrs S. G. Clapp, Mr K. J. Corcoran, Mr J. L. Frampton, Mr Paul S. Frampton, Mr R. J. Hodges, Mr Andrew Midgley, Mrs L. Sharpe.

---

318   MR SIMON HODGSON, Yeovil
Postal: **28 The Glebe, Queen Camel, Yeovil, Somerset, BA22 7PR**

1 **ARBEEJAY**, 4, b f Iceman—Diliza **Jim Heal, Miss B Duffin, Mrs L Clarke**
2 **DUN SEE DEE (IRE)**, 9, b m Flemensfirth (USA)—Crafty Classy (IRE) **J. Heaney**
3 6, B gr g Baryshnikov (AUS)—Jessinca

TWO-YEAR-OLDS

4 B f 17/3 Crosspeace (IRE)—Jessinca (Minshaanshu Amad (USA))

Other Owners: Mrs L. M. Clarke, Miss B. Duffin, Mr J. Heal.

319 MR HENRY HOGARTH, Stillington

Postal: **New Grange Farm, Stillington, York, YO61 1LR**
Contacts: **PHONE (01347) 811168 FAX (01347) 811168 MOBILE (07788) 777044**

1 **AITCH FACTOR**, 7, b g Beat All (USA)—Farmers Girl **Hogarth Racing**
2 **DENY**, 5, ch g Mr Greeley (USA)—Sulk (IRE) **Hogarth Racing**
3 **IFANDBUTWHY (IRE)**, 11, b g Raise A Grand (IRE)—Cockney Ground (IRE) **Hogarth Racing**
4 **LAKEFIELD REBEL (IRE)**, 7, b br g Presenting—River Mousa (IRE) **Hogarth Racing**
5 **MASTER CONOR (IRE)**, 7, b g Classic Cliche (IRE)—Shuil Iontach (IRE) **Hogarth Racing**
6 **MURRELL (IRE)**, 8, b g Dushyantor (USA)—Lady Mayday (IRE) **Hogarth Racing**
7 **MYSTERIOUS WORLD (IRE)**, 9, ch g Desert Prince (IRE)—Salligram **Hogarth Racing**
8 **NICKY TAM (IRE)**, 11, b br g Presenting—Wigmore **Hogarth Racing**
9 **OVER AND ABOVE (IRE)**, 7, b g Overbury (IRE)—Rose Gold (IRE) **Hogarth Racing**
10 **PAMAK D'AIRY (FR)**, 10, b'g Cadoubel (FR)—Gamaska d'airy (FR) **Hogarth Racing**
11 **ROJO VIVO**, 7, b g Deploy—Shareef Walk **Hogarth Racing**

Other Owners: Mr H. P. Hogarth, Mr P. H. Hogarth, Mr J. Hogarth, Mr J. L. Hogarth.

Jockey (NH): Fearghal Davis.

320 MR ALAN HOLLINGSWORTH, Feckenham

Postal: **Lanket House, Crofts Lane, Feckenham, Redditch, Worcestershire, B96 6PU**
Contacts: **PHONE (01527) 68644/892054 FAX (01527) 60310 MOBILE (07775) 670644**
E-MAIL kombined@btconnect.com

1 **AGITATION**, 9, b g Cloudings (IRE)—Shadowgraff **A. F. Hollingsworth**
2 **BRAGABOUT**, 6, b g Alflora (IRE)—Gemmabel **A. F. Hollingsworth**
3 **CLEETONS TURN**, 6, b g Alflora (IRE)—Indyana Run **A. F. Hollingsworth**
4 **EXACTLY**, 10, br g Terimon—Emmabella **A. F. Hollingsworth**
5 **GEMMALOCK**, 7, ch m Grape Tree Road—Gemmabel **A. F. Hollingsworth**
6 **GEMMASON**, 9, ch g Alflora (IRE)—Gemmabel **A. F. Hollingsworth**
7 **RIN TIN TIN**, 6, br g Alflora (IRE)—Celtic Tore (IRE) **A. F. Hollingsworth**

Assistant Trainer: Sharon Smith

Jockey (NH): James Davies, Nick Scholfield.

321 MR REG HOLLINSHEAD, Upper Longdon

Postal: **Lodge Farm, Upper Longdon, Rugeley, Staffordshire, WS15 1QF**
Contacts: **PHONE (01543) 490298 FAX (01543) 490490**

1 **AMBITIOUS BOY**, 4, bl g Striking Ambition—Cherished Love (IRE) **Mr C. W. Wardle & Mrs J. E. Wardle**
2 **ASTONISHED HARRY (GER)**, 4, b g Dubai Destination (USA)—Aijala (FR) **D. Coppenhall**
3 **AUREOLIN GULF**, 4, b g Proclamation (IRE)—Vermilion Creek **M. A. N. Johnson**
4 **BILASH**, 6, gr g Choisir (AUS)—Goldeva **Mr M. Pyle & Mrs T. Pyle**
5 **BOA**, 8, b m Mtoto—Maradata (IRE) **Mr G. Lloyd**
6 **CADMIUM LOCH**, 5, b g Needwood Blade—Vermilion Creek **M. A. N. Johnson**
7 **CLOUDY SPIRIT**, 8, gr m Silver Patriarch (IRE)—Miss Lacroix **Mrs N. S. Harris**
8 **DANGER IN THE PARK**, 4, ch g Central Park (IRE)—Danger Bird (IRE) **Miss S. Sharratt**
9 **EASTERN MAGIC**, 6, b g Observatory (USA)—Inchtina **Mrs C. A. Stevenson**
10 **FOURSQUARE FUNTIME**, 4, b g Common World (USA)—Farina (IRE) **T. Kelly**
11 **HYSON**, 4, ch g Hernando (FR)—Be Decisive
12 **LACEY**, 4, b g Rail Link—Shamana (USA) **Mr N. S. Sweeney**
13 **LANDOWN LITTLEROCK**, 4, b g Sakhee (USA)—Maraha **R. Hollinshead**
14 **LETS GO PRIMO**, 4, b c Primo Valentino (IRE)—Weet By Far **Lease Terminated**
15 **LORD PAGET**, 4, b g Three Valleys (USA)—Appelone **The Giddy Gang**
16 **MOUNT HOLLOW**, 8, b g Beat Hollow—Lady Lindsay (IRE) **Lease Terminated**
17 **NOUAILHAS**, 5, b g Mark of Esteem (IRE)—Barachois Princess (USA) **Mr C. W. Wardle & Mrs J. E. Wardle**
18 **ONE SCOOP OR TWO**, 7, b g Needwood Blade—Rebel County (IRE) **Showtime Ice Cream Concessionaire**
19 **OUR EM**, 7, gr m Fair Mix (IRE)—Andy Coin **Mr R. J. R. Moseley**
20 **RAPID HEAT LAD (IRE)**, 4, b c Aussie Rules (USA)—Alwiyda (USA) **Graham Brothers Racing Partnership**
21 **SPANISH PLUME**, 5, b g Ishiguru (USA)—Miss Up N Go **The Three R's**

MR REG HOLLINSHEAD - Continued

22 STRAVERSJOY, 6, b m Kayf Tara—Stravsea Miss S. A. Hollinshead
23 TOO AMBITIOUS, 4, b f Striking Ambition—Ticcatoo (IRE) The Giddy Gang
24 ZENAFIRE, 4, b c Firebreak—Zen Garden E Coquelin R Moseley

THREE-YEAR-OLDS

25 DHA CHARA (IRE), b g Ramonti (FR)—Campiglia (IRE) Mr N. S. Sweeney
26 DIVINE REWARD (USA), b g Divine Park (USA)—World of Thanks (USA) N. Chapman
27 EYELINE, b g Needwood Blade—Waterline Twenty (IRE) X8 Racing Partnership 1
28 B g Vitus—Farina (IRE) R. Hollinshead
29 LADY JEAN, b f Striking Ambition—Parkside Prospect J. M. Graham
30 MOORWAY (IRE), b c Dylan Thomas (IRE)—Cordelia Moores Metals Ltd
31 REFUSE TO MAMBO, ch g Refuse To Bend (IRE)—Sovereign's Honour (USA) J. L. Marriott
32 SCARLET STRAND, b f Pastoral Pursuits—Vermilion Creek M. A. N. Johnson
33 SEWN UP, ch c Compton Place—Broughton Bounty J. L. Marriott
34 SNOWY DAWN, gr g Notnowcato—Tereyna Mrs C. A. Stevenson
35 STRIKING ECHO, b g Striking Ambition—Sunderland Echo (IRE) Mr G. Lloyd
36 UNCLE BERNIE (IRE), gr g Aussie Rules (USA)—Alwiyda (USA) Graham Brothers Racing Partnership

Other Owners: Mrs H. Bellingham, Mrs E. M. Coquelin, Mr P. Edwards, Mr A. M. Graham, Mr M. P. Graham, D. R. Horne, Mr E. T. D. Leadbeater, D. J. Lockwood, A. L. Marriott, M. J. F. Pyle, Mrs T. P. Pyle, R. Robinson, C. W. Wardle, Mrs J. E. Wardle.

Assistant Trainer: A N Hollinshead

Jockey (flat): Russ Kennemore. Apprentice: Jack Duern.

---

322   MR PATRICK HOLMES, Brandsby
Postal: The Bungalow, Foulrice Farm, Brandsby, York, North Yorkshire, YO61 4SB
Contacts: PHONE (01347) 889008 MOBILE (07740) 589857
E-MAIL patrick@foulriceparkracing.com WEBSITE www.foulriceparkracing.com

1 BOW FIDDLE (IRE), 7, br m Anshan—Elite Racing Mrs A. M. Stirling
2 DOBERDAN (USA), 8, b g Street Cry (IRE)—Sophonisbe Mrs C M Clarke, Foulrice Park Racing Ltd
3 DORLESH WAY (IRE), 6, ch g Rakti—Patalavaca (GER) Di Midwinter Foulrice Park Racing Ltd
4 FOOT THE BILL, 8, b g Generous (IRE)—Proudfoot (IRE) Mr C. R. Stirling
5 HURRY ON LIL (IRE), 4, ch f Hurricane Run (IRE)—Foreign Relation (IRE) Foulrice Park Racing Limited
6 LIL SOPHELLA (IRE), 4, ch f Indian Haven—Discotheque (USA) Foulrice Park Racing Limited
7 PIRATE CHEST (IRE), 5, b g Montjeu (IRE)—Cash Run (USA) Foulrice Park Racing Limited
8 REX ROMANORUM (IRE), 5, b g Holy Roman Emperor (IRE)—Willowbridge (IRE) Foulrice Park Racing Limited
9 SUMMERLEA (IRE), 7, ch g Alhaarth (IRE)—Verbania (IRE) Foulrice Park Racing Limited
10 TIME OF MY LIFE (IRE), 4, b g Galileo (IRE)—In My Life (IRE) Foulrice Park Racing Limited
11 VOICE FROM ABOVE (IRE), 4, b f Strategic Prince—Basin Street Blues (IRE) Foulrice Park Racing Limited
12 YOURHOLIDAYISOVER (IRE), 6, ch g Sulamani—Whitehaven Foulrice Park Racing Limited

THREE-YEAR-OLDS

13 SLIP OF A GIRL (IRE), b f Strategic Prince—Fig Leaf (FR) Foulrice Park Racing Limited

Other Owners: Mrs C. M. Clarke, Miss D. Midwinter.

---

323   MR JOHN HOLT, Peckleton
Postal: Hall Farm, Church Road, Peckleton, Leicester
Contacts: PHONE/FAX (01455) 821972 MOBILE (07850) 321059
E-MAIL hallfarmracing@btconnect.com WEBSITE www.hallfarmracing.co.uk

1 AVE SOFIA, 4, b f Byron—Snoozy New Kids On The Trot
2 CHIPPY, 5, b g Diktat—French Mannequin (IRE) Mr G. F. Archer
3 DAYLAMI DREAMS, 9, gr g Daylami (IRE)—Kite Mark Cleartherm Glass Sealed Units Ltd
4 HERES ACTION MAN, 5, b g Nomadic Way (USA)—Jesmund Ms C. A. Lacey
5 IZZA DIVA, 5, b m Nomadic Way (USA)—Pebbles Moonlight (IRE) Mr P. R. Burgess
6 6, B h Winged Love (IRE)—Keady
7 LHOTSE SHERPA, 4, b g Byron—Soyalang (FR) J. R. Holt
8 MARINA BAY, 8, b m Karinga Bay—Marina Bird Mr K. & Mr A. K. Smith
9 MINI'S DESTINATION, 5, b m Dubai Destination (USA)—Heather Mix J. R. Holt

MR JOHN HOLT - Continued

10 **NOMADIC WARRIOR**, 8, b g Nomadic Way (USA)—Jesmund **Ms C. A. Lacey**
11 **NUMBER THEORY**, 5, b g Halling (USA)—Numanthia (IRE) **Mr M. S. Fonseka**
12 **SOLERA TIME**, 4, b f Librettist (USA)—Sophie'jo **Mr E. Boumans**

THREE-YEAR-OLDS

13 **DUTCH GAL**, b f Dutch Art—Spangle **Mr E. Boumans**
14 **EMPERATRIZ**, b f Holy Roman Emperor (IRE)—Fairmont (IRE) **Mr E. Boumans**
15 **JAMNEAN**, b f Byron—Dazzling View (USA) **Clive Giles & Phil Thomas**
16 **LOCH FYNE LADY**, b f Holy Roman Emperor (IRE)—Inveraray **Hall Farm Four Partnership**
17 **RAPID RABBIT FOOT**, ch f Three Valleys (USA)—Rabshih (IRE) **Mr E. Boumans**

TWO-YEAR-OLDS

18 **DUTCH LADY**, ch f 29/4 Dutch Art—Tattling (Warning) (7619) **Mr J. J. Guest**
19 Gr f 14/4 Kodiac—Gone Sailing (Mizzen Mast (USA)) (3809) **D. R. Botterill**
20 **MISHNAH**, b f 12/2 Orpen (USA)—Minshar (Noverre (USA)) (761)
21 B c 31/1 Rail Link—Nippy (FR) (Anabaa (USA)) (9523) **Mr E. Boumans**
22 B f 26/4 Champs Elysees—Phi Phi (IRE) (Fasliyev (USA)) (3000)
23 Ch f 27/3 Sakhee (USA)—Sweet Reply (Opening Verse (USA))

Other Owners: Mr V. H. Coleman, Mr D. R. Gardner, Mr C. Giles, Mr S. Jones, Mr J. N. Lucas, Mr K. Smith, A. K. Smith, Mr P. V. Thomas.

Assistant Trainer: Jessica Holt

---

324 | **MR ANTHONY HONEYBALL, Beaminster**
Postal: **Potwell Farm, Mosterton, Beaminster, Dorset, DT8 3HG**
Contacts: **PHONE** (01308) 867452 **MOBILE** (07815) 898569
E-MAIL a.honeyballracing@btinternet.com **WEBSITE** www.ajhoneyballracing.co.uk

1 **ALPANCHO**, 7, ch g Alflora (IRE)—Run Tiger (IRE) **Apple Pie Partnership**
2 **AS DE FER (FR)**, 7, b g Passing Sale (FR)—Miss Hollywood (FR) **Midd Shire Racing**
3 **BALLYBOUGH PAT (IRE)**, 6, b g Waky Nao—Princess Ruth (IRE) **Favourites Racing Ltd**
4 **CHANTARA ROSE**, 4, br f Kayf Tara—Fragrant Rose **Steve & Jackie Fleetham**
5 **CHILL FACTOR (IRE)**, 4, b g Oscar (IRE)—Glacial Princess (IRE) **A. Honeyball**
6 **DOUBLE SPARKLE**, 4, ch f Double Trigger (IRE)—Encore du Cristal (USA) **R. W. Huggins**
7 **ELEVEN FIFTY NINE**, 7, b m Midnight Legend—Essex Bird **M. Rowe & B. Wright**
8 **FOUNTAINS MARY**, 5, gr m Midnight Legend—Carswell Mayfly VII **The Fountains Partnership**
9 **HELL'S SPRITE**, 5, b g Oscar (IRE)—Last Century (IRE) **Favourites Racing Ltd**
10 **HES OUR LAD (IRE)**, 7, b g Rudimentary (USA)—Polyzar (IRE) **A. Smith S. E. Wall A. J. Forde**
11 **JACKIES SOLITAIRE**, 5, ch m Generous (IRE)—Bond Solitaire **Steve & Jackie Fleetham**
12 **JAJA DE JAU**, 4, br f Sakhee (USA)—Jadidh **Anthony Honeyball Racing Club Ltd**
13 **KALANI KING (IRE)**, 6, b g Ashkalani (IRE)—
    Supreme Kellycarra (IRE) **S. Brimble, A. J. Forde, S Honeyball, T. Harris**
14 4, Br f Act One—Lady Turk (FR)
15 **MARIE DES ANGES (FR)**, 5, b m Ballingarry (IRE)—No Coincidence (IRE) **Atlantic Racing & R. W. Huggins**
16 **MIDNIGHT MINX**, 6, b m Midnight Legend—Phar Breeze (IRE) **Mrs J. M. E. Mann**
17 **MISTER HENDRE**, 5, gr g Fair Mix (IRE)—Bonne Anniversaire **Steve & Jackie Fleetham**
18 **ON THE MOVE**, 5, b m Sir Harry Lewis (USA)—What A Mover **J. M. Dare, T. Hamlin, J. W. Snook**
19 **OSCARTEEA (IRE)**, 4, b g Oscar (IRE)—Miss Arteea (IRE) **Steve & Jackie Fleetham**
20 **REGAL ENCORE (IRE)**, 5, b g King's Theatre (IRE)—Go On Eileen (IRE) **J. P. McManus**
21 **ROUQUINE SAUVAGE**, 5, ch m Loup Sauvage (USA)—No Need For Alarm **Anthony Honeyball Racing Club Ltd**
22 **ROYAL ANNOUNCEMENT**, 6, b g Flemensfirth (USA)—Made For A King **Anthony Honeyball Racing Club Ltd**
23 **ROYAL NATIVE (IRE)**, 5, b g King's Theatre (IRE)—Hollygrove Native (IRE) **Michael & Angela Bone**
24 **ROYAL SWAIN (IRE)**, 7, b g Val Royal (FR)—Targhyb (IRE) **Steve & Jackie Fleetham**
25 **SIR TOBY TYLER (IRE)**, 4, b g Kayf Tara—Corrieann (IRE) **Steve & Jackie Fleetham**
26 **SOLSTICE SON**, 4, b g Haafhd—Karasta (USA) **J. Pike & G. Pike**
27 **SWINCOMBE STONE**, 6, ch g Best of The Bests (IRE)—Soloism **Yeo Racing Partnership**
28 **TARADREWE**, 6, b m Kayf Tara—Karearn **Frosties Friends II**
29 **UNCLE JOHNNY**, 8, b g Alflora (IRE)—Lady Speckles (IRE) **Mr D. Billington**
30 **VELATOR**, 6, b g Old Vic—Jupiter's Message **Steve & Jackie Fleetham**
31 **VICATOR**, 5, b g Old Vic—Jupiter's Message **Favourites Racing Ltd**
32 **VICTORS SERENADE (IRE)**, 8, b g Old Vic—Dantes Serenade (IRE) **Michael & Angela Bone**

MR ANTHONY HONEYBALL - Continued

Other Owners: Atlantic Racing Limited, Mr George T. Birks, Mrs A. P. Bone, Mr Michael Bone, Mrs Marion Bowden, Mrs Susan Brimble, Mr J. M. Dare, Mrs George Eyre, Mr Steve Fleetham, Mrs Jacqueline Fleetham, Mr D. Flynn, Miss Emma Foley, Mrs A. J. Forde, Mr A. R. Franklin, Mr Matthew Franklin, Mr T. C. Frost, Mr T. Hamlin, Mr R. W. Huggins, Mr B. G. Middleton, Mr K. B. W. Parkhouse, Mr M. Rowe, Mr A. J. Shire, Mr Andy Smith, Mr J. Snook, Mrs S. E. Wall, Mr B. J. C. Wright, Mrs K. D. Yeo.

Assistant Trainer: Rachael Green

Jockey (NH): Aidan Coleman, Rachael Green, Sam Thomas.

---

325 MR MICHAEL HOURIGAN, Limerick
Postal: **Lisaleen Stables, Patrickswell, Co. Limerick, Ireland**
Contacts: PHONE (00353) 6139 6603 FAX (00353) 6139 6812 MOBILE (00353) 8682 26655
E-MAIL info@mhourigan.ie WEBSITE www.mhourigan.ie

1 A FINE YOUNG MAN (IRE), 8, b g Snurge—Miss Platinum (IRE) **Doran Bros (London) Ltd**
2 A NEW STORY (IRE), 15, b g Fourstars Allstar (USA)—Diyala (FR) **Storey's Over Syndicate**
3 ADAMS WOOD (IRE), 6, b g Waky Nao—Hurada (IRE) **Michael P. Hourigan**
4 AERLITE SUPREME (IRE), 6, b g Gold Well—Supreme Evening (IRE) **J. Murphy & G. Walsh**
5 ALLEE GARDE (FR), 8, b g Kapgarde (FR)—Allee Du Port (FR) **Doran Bros (London) Ltd**
6 4, Ch f Old Vic—Ashnaya (FR) **Mrs A. Hourigan**
7 BALLYSTEEN (IRE), 7, b g Elnadim (USA)—Winning Jenny (IRE) **Gigginstown House Stud**
8 BEST SERVED COLD, 7, b g King's Theatre (IRE)—Mirana (IRE) **Gigginstown House Stud**
9 CARRAMORE BOY (IRE), 5, b g Dr Massini (IRE)—Carramore Lass (IRE) **J. McDonnell**
10 5, Ch g Where Or When (IRE)—Chelsea (USA) **M. Hourigan**
11 CLEAR HILLS (IRE), 6, b g Marju (IRE)—Rainbows For All (IRE) **Doran Bros (London) Ltd**
12 CRAIGS DREAM (IRE), 7, b g Craigsteel—Sinead's Dream (IRE) **Donal O'Connor**
13 CRASH (IRE), 8, b g Milan—Mary Connors (IRE) **Gigginstown House Stud**
14 5, Gr m Oscar (IRE)—Dalkey Pride **Michael Hourigan**
15 DANCING TORNADO (IRE), 12, ch g Golden Tornado (IRE)—Lady Dante (IRE) **J. P. McManus**
16 DAWERANN (IRE), 4, b g Medicean—Dawera (IRE) **T. Morrisson**
17 DEBT TO SOCIETY (IRE), 6, ch g Moscow Society (USA)—Nobody's Darling (IRE) **H. Williams**
18 DINGALING (IRE), 7, b g Milan—Keralba (USA) **J. P. McManus**
19 DOESHEEVERSTOP (IRE), 5, b g Turtle Island (IRE)—Mary Connors (IRE) **Cairde Chiarrai Syndicate**
20 DUSHYBEAG (IRE), 6, b g Dushyantor (USA)—Bula Beag (IRE) **Donal O'Connor**
21 4, B g Elnadim (USA)—Ecco Mi (IRE) **M. Hourigan**
22 ENCHANTED FOREST (IRE), 5, b h Galileo (IRE)—Halland Park Lass (IRE) **Francis Campbell**
23 FALSE ECONOMY (IRE), 8, b g Orpen (USA)—Ashanti Dancer (IRE) **Mrs Miriam Murphy**
24 FINE PRESENTATION (IRE), 6, ch g Presenting—Time To Ask (IRE) **John Carey**
25 FRIENDLY SOCIETY (IRE), 8, ch g Moscow Society (USA)—Friendly Breeze **Virginia Lady Petersham**
26 GATE PLEASE (IRE), 8, b g Rashar (USA)—Linda Babe (IRE) **Storey's Over Syndicate**
27 HANS CRESCENT (FR), 8, b g Dansili—Embroider (USA) **S.Lucey / Mrs Mary Curtin**
28 HOLEINTHEWALL BAR (IRE), 5, b g Westerner—Cockpit Lady (IRE) **S. Fahy**
29 JENNYS SURPRISE (IRE), 5, b m Hawk Wing (USA)—Winning Jenny (IRE) **D. Redden**
30 KILBEGGAN KNIGHT (IRE), 6, b g Wizard King—Adare Princess **Golf At Ballyneety Syndicate**
31 4, B g Westerner—Kitty Maher (IRE) **M. Hourigan**
32 MAGICAL MOON, 4, b g Dansili—Sheppard's Watch **Burrow Syndicate**
33 MR CRACKER (IRE), 8, ch g Anshan—Sesame Cracker **Gigginstown House Stud**
34 OUR MAN ZEBO (IRE), 6, gr g Cloudings (IRE)—Main Suspect (USA) **John B. O'Hagan**
35 PAY YOUR HUNT SUB, 7, ch g Redback—Particular Friend **Mrs A. Hourigan**
36 RUN WITH THE WIND (IRE), 7, b g Sadler's Wells (USA)—Race The Wild Wind (USA) **John B. O'Hagan**
37 SHERCO SPORTS (IRE), 6, b br m Fruits of Love (USA)—Vintage Classic (IRE) **Tuffy Ten Syndicate**
38 5, B g Kier Park (IRE)—Sylphide **M. Hourigan**
39 THE CRAFTY BUTCHER (IRE), 6, b g Vinnie Roe (IRE)—Ivy Queen (IRE) **Cairde Chiarrai Syndicate**
40 THE JOB IS RIGHT, 5, gr g With Approval (CAN)—Common Request (USA) **Mrs Mary Devine**
41 TROPICAL THREE (IRE), 5, gr m Portrait Gallery (IRE)—
                                        Tropical Ocean (IRE) **Mary Curtin / S. Lucey / M. Hourigan**
42 4, B g Zerpour (IRE)—Two T'three Weeks **Mrs Mary Devine**
43 WHATS HAPPENING (IRE), 6, b g Lahib (USA)—Rebeccas Star (IRE) **Karen Hourigan**

Assistant Trainer: Kay Hourigan

Jockey (NH): A. P. Heskin.

326 MR STUART HOWE, Tiverton
Postal: **Ringstone Stables, Oakford, Tiverton, Devon, EX16 9EU**
Contacts: **PHONE (01398) 351224 MOBILE (07802) 506344**
E-MAIL hshowe@stuarthoweracing.co.uk

1 ASHKALARA, 6, b m Footstepsinthesand—Asheyana (IRE) **C R Hollands Cutting Tools Company Ltd**
2 MIXED MEANING (IRE), 5, gr g Fair Mix (IRE)—Connotation **Horses Away Ltd**
3 MY LEGAL LADY, 8, b m Sir Harry Lewis (USA)—Clifton Mist **H. S. Howe**
4 5, B m Beat All (USA)—Nunsdream
5 PARTY PALACE, 9, b m Auction House (USA)—Lady-Love **Horses Away Ltd**
6 4, Gr f Tamure (IRE)—Pems Gift

327 MR PAUL HOWLING, Bramshill
Postal: **57 David Newberry Drive, Lee-On-The-Solent, Hampshire, PO13 8FG**
Contacts: **MOBILE (07866) 674469**
E-MAIL billichang@aol.com

1 DVINSKY (USA), 12, b g Stravinsky (USA)—Festive Season (USA) **Mr D. A. Hardaker**
2 GALLANTRY, 11, b g Green Desert (USA)—Gay Gallanta (USA) **Mr J Wright Mr D Patrick Mr P D Woodward**
3 HUZZAH (IRE), 8, b g Acclamation—Borders Belle (IRE) **Mr J. M. J. Esau**
4 MR OPTIMISTIC, 5, b g Kyllachy—Noble Desert (FR) **Eclipse Horse Racing**
5 NOT MY CHOICE (IRE), 8, ch g Choisir (AUS)—Northgate Raver **Mr E. W. Gordon**
6 ROYAL ENVOY (IRE), 10, b g Royal Applause—Seven Notes **P. Howling**
7 THE KERNIGAL (IRE), 4, b g Red Clubs (IRE)—Ellens Princess (IRE) **Mr M. G. McCaffrey**

THREE-YEAR-OLDS
8 ALSHAN FAJER, ch g Lemon Drop Kid (USA)—Illuminise (IRE) **Mr F. Al Dabbous**
9 LUCILLA, b f Holy Roman Emperor (IRE)—Lady In Waiting **Eclipse Horse Racing**
10 MILL I AM (USA), b f Henny Hughes (USA)—Courageous (USA) **Eclipse Horse Racing**

Other Owners: Mr N. J. Funnell, Mrs J. P. Howling, Mr M. Montague, Mr R. Morris, D. C. Patrick, P. D. Woodward, Mr J. Wright.

Assistant Trainer: Mrs J. Howling

Jockey (flat): Ian Mongan, Michael Stainton.

328 MR D. T. HUGHES, Kildare
Postal: **Osborne Lodge, Kildare, Co. Kildare, Ireland**
Contacts: **PHONE (00353) 4552 1490 FAX (00353) 4552 1643 MOBILE (00353) 8625 34098**
E-MAIL dthughes1@eircom.net

1 ACTION MASTER, 7, b g Domedriver (IRE)—All Is Fair **All Gone West Syndicate**
2 APACHE JACK (IRE), 5, b g Oscar (IRE)—Cailin Supreme (IRE) **Mrs P. Sloane**
3 ART OF LOGISTICS (IRE), 5, b g Exit To Nowhere (USA)—Sanadja (IRE) **Munnelly Support Services Ltd.**
4 BRIGHT LIGHT CITY (IRE), 7, b g Elusive City (USA)—Alajyal (IRE) **D. T. Hughes**
5 BRIGHT NEW DAWN (IRE), 6, br g Presenting—Shuil Dorcha (IRE) **Gigginstown House Stud**
6 CAHERONAUN (IRE), 7, b m Milan—Fair Present (IRE) **Dan Corry**
7 CANALY (IRE), 8, b g Bob Back (USA)—Starry Lady (IRE) **Michael Moore**
8 CAPTAIN ARCEUS (IRE), 7, b g Captain Rio—Siana Springs (IRE) **T. O'Driscoll**
9 CAPTAIN LOB (IRE), 6, b g Luso—Jemima Jay (IRE) **U. S. Of Pieland Syndicate**
10 CHASING SHADOWS (IRE), 7, b m Presenting—Chancy Lass (IRE) **Michael Moore**
11 CLAUDIA AUGUSTA (IRE), 7, b m Oscar (IRE)—Latin Mistress **Mrs E. Reilly**
12 DEAL DONE (FR), 9, b g Vertical Speed (FR)—Five Rivers (FR) **Mrs A. N. Durkan**
13 DISTANT SOUND (IRE), 6, b g Luso—Distant Dreams (IRE) **D. T. Hughes**
14 EARLSON GRAY (FR), 8, gr g Take Risks (FR)—Euadne (GER) **J. P. Dunne**
15 EL FONTAN (IRE), 8, gr g Verglas (FR)—Valeriane (FR) **Mrs P. Sloane**
16 ERRITT LAKE (IRE), 10, b g Bob Back (USA)—Bramdean **D. T. Hughes**
17 HUNTING PARTY (IRE), 7, b g City Honours (USA)—Highland May (IRE) **D. T. Hughes**
18 JULIE PRINCE (IRE), 7, b g Desert Prince (IRE)—Daniella Ridge (IRE) **Mr Con Harrington**
19 KILAVALLEY (IRE), 6, b g City Honours (USA)—Cry In The Dark **A. M. Ryan**
20 LADY OF GLENCOE (IRE), 5, b m Marju (USA)—Nabadhaat (USA) **T. O'Driscoll**
21 LITTLE ROCKY, 5, b h Cadeaux Genereux—Tahirah **Barry Connell**

MR D. T. HUGHES - Continued

22 **LYREEN LEGEND (IRE)**, 6, b g Saint des Saints (FR)—Bint Bladi (FR) **Lyreen Syndicate**
23 **MACKEYS FORGE (IRE)**, 9, b g Mr Combustible (IRE)—Lucy Walters (IRE) **Seven To Eleven Syndicate**
24 **MAGNANIMITY (IRE)**, 9, b br g Winged Love (IRE)—Mossy Mistress (IRE) **Gigginstown House Stud**
25 **MINSK (IRE)**, 5, b g Dalakhani (IRE)—Penza **Barry Connell**
26 **MISS ACCURATE (IRE)**, 6, ch m Presenting—Elphis (IRE) **D. T. Hughes**
27 **NASHVILLE SWING (IRE)**, 7, b g Presenting—Portobello Lady (IRE) **Patrick F. Kehoe**
28 **NEW RIVER (IRE)**, 5, b m Montjeu (IRE)—Quiet Waters (USA) **Martin Clarke**
29 **OUR CONOR (IRE)**, 4, b g Jeremy (USA)—Flamands (IRE) **Man About Town Syndicate**
30 **RARE BOB (IRE)**, 11, b br g Bob Back (USA)—Cut Ahead **D. A. Syndicate**
31 **RATHFEIGH (IRE)**, 7, b m Pilsudski (IRE)—Sweet Rocket (IRE) **John Purfield**
32 **RAZ DE MAREE (FR)**, 8, ch g Shaanmer (IRE)—Diyala III (FR) **J. J. Swan**
33 **REDUNDANT MAN**, 5, b g Kayf Tara—Lady Emily **Mrs A. N. Durkan**
34 **RUDOLF (IRE)**, 5, b g Oscar (IRE)—Stormweather Girl (IRE) **Horseplay Syndicate**
35 **SARTEANO (FR)**, 10, gr g Kaldounevees (FR)—Sovereign Touch (IRE) **More Busted Sofa's Syndicate**
36 **SCHINKEL (IRE)**, 8, ch g Subtle Power (IRE)—Last Sprite **Mr Jerome Sheehan**
37 **SEEFOOD (IRE)**, 6, b g Kahyasi—Anne Theatre **Lyreen Syndicate**
38 **SI C'ETAIT VRAI (FR)**, 7, b g Robin des Champs (FR)—Bleu Perle (FR) **Gigginstown House Stud**
39 **SOMETHINGWONDERFUL (IRE)**, 5, b br g Viking Ruler (AUS)—Innishmore (IRE) **Gigginstown House Stud**
40 **STONEMASTER (IRE)**, 8, br g Old Vic—Rose of Stradbally (IRE) **Gigginstown House Stud**
41 **STONEY**, 6, b g Stowaway—Classical Rachel (IRE) **Slaneyville Syndicate**
42 **TALES OF MILAN (IRE)**, 6, b g Milan—The Millers Tale (IRE) **Down To Four Syndicate**
43 **THUNDER AND ROSES (IRE)**, 5, b br g Presenting—Glen Empress (IRE) **Gigginstown House Stud**
44 **TOFINO BAY (IRE)**, 10, br g Bishop of Cashel—Boyne View (IRE) **Gigginstown House Stud**
45 **TROUBLED (IRE)**, 6, b g Vinnie Roe (IRE)—Tart of Tipp (IRE) **Gigginstown House Stud**
46 **WHISPERING HILLS (IRE)**, 8, b g Tiger Hill (IRE)—Wells Whisper (FR) **P. Aspell**
47 **WHITE STAR LINE (IRE)**, 9, b g Saddlers' Hall (IRE)—Fairly Deep **Patsy Byrnes**
48 **WISE OSCAR (IRE)**, 9, b g Oscar (IRE)—Mona Curra Gale (IRE) **P. G. Wyse**

Other Owners: Laurance Byrne, Patsy Byrne, Joseph Doyle, Michael Gannon, F. Kenny, P. Kenny, London Calling Syndicate, J. P. McManus, Phil Munnelly, Three Locks Syndicate.

Jockey (NH): Bryan J. Cooper, Roger Loughran. **Conditional:** Mark Enright, Ian McCarthy. **Amateur:** Mr Johnny King.

---

329 MR J. S. HUGHES, Gilfach Goch
Postal: 4 Pontrhondda Road, Tonypandy, Mid-Glamorgan, CF40 2SZ

1 **TIGER MAROON**, 5, b g Westerner—Priolaine (FR) **J. S. Hughes**

---

330 MRS JO HUGHES, Lambourn
Postal: Hill House Stables, Folly Road, Lambourn, Hungerford, Berkshire, RG17 8QE
Contacts: PHONE (01488) 71444 FAX (01488) 71103 MOBILE (07900) 680189
E-MAIL johughes3@aol.co.uk WEBSITE www.johughesracing.co.uk

1 **ASTERALES**, 6, b m Royal Applause—Shalimar (IRE) **Mr G. Sheehy**
2 **BEACHWOOD BAY**, 5, b g Tobougg (IRE)—The Terrier **Mrs L. Hayward**
3 **CALEDONIA LADY**, 4, b f Firebreak—Granuaile O'malley (IRE) **Isla & Colin Cage**
4 **CALEDONIA PRINCE**, 5, b g Needwood Blade—Granuaile O'malley (IRE) **Isla & Colin Cage**
5 **CALLISTO MOON**, 9, b g Mujahid (USA)—Nursling (IRE) **Mr B. Bedford & Mrs Gill White**
6 **CANDELITA**, 6, b m Trade Fair—Gramada (IRE) **Paul & David Bedford**
7 **DAZEEN**, 6, b g Zafeen (FR)—Bond Finesse (IRE) **Mr & Mrs D. Yates**
8 **GENTLEMAN JON**, 5, b g Beat All—Sudden Spirit (FR)
9 **I SEE YOU**, 4, ch f Sleeping Indian—Pikaboo **Mrs C. C. Regalado-Gonzalez**
10 **ICELANDER (USA)**, 4, b g Stormy Atlantic (USA)—Painted Lady (USA) **Mrs J. F. Hughes**
11 **JAT PUNJABI**, 9, b g Karinga Bay—Balmoral Princess **Mr H. S. Maan**
12 **JOSIE'S DREAM (IRE)**, 5, b g Tau Ceti—Gallery Breeze **J. Smith**
13 **LA ROSIERE (USA)**, 4, b f Mr Greeley (USA)—Snowtime (IRE) **Mrs C. C. Regalado-Gonzalez**
14 **LIGHTS OF BROADWAY (IRE)**, 7, b m Broadway Flyer (USA)—Supreme Call (IRE) **B Parren & Jo Hughes**
15 **MAYFORDE JACK**, 4, b g Septieme Ciel—Jessinca **P. T. Newell**
16 **MULLINS WAY (USA)**, 5, ch g Mr Greeley (USA)—Aljawza (USA) **Mrs J. F. Hughes**
17 **NOBLE JACK (IRE)**, 7, b g Elusive City (USA)—Begine (IRE) **Mr & Mrs D. Yates**
18 **OSCAR TANNER (IRE)**, 5, br g Oscar (IRE)—Rose Tanner (IRE) **Mrs J. F. Hughes**

MRS JO HUGHES - Continued

19 **PARADISE SEA (USA)**, 4, b f Stormy Atlantic (USA)—
Paradise River (USA) **Eastwind Racing Ltd & Martha Trussell**
20 **PENSNETT BAY**, 8, ch g Karinga Bay—Balmoral Princess **Mr H. S. Maan**
21 **REGAL BROOK**, 7, br m Alderbrook—Cadal Queen (FR) **Mrs K. M. C. Lundberg-Young**
22 **SOLL**, 8, ch g Presenting—Montelfolene (IRE) **D. Mossop**
23 **SON OF MAY**, 4, b g Royal Applause—Second of May **Sterling Racing, Don Bird & Jo Hughes**
24 **SPEIGHTOWNS KID (USA)**, 5, gr ro g Speightstown (USA)—Seize the Wind (USA) **Mr R. P. Phillips**
25 **SUPERMIGHTYFINE**, 6, b g Slip Anchor—Wordy's Wonder **Ms M. J. Hughes**
26 **SUPREME SPIRIT (IRE)**, 6, b m Invincible Spirit (IRE)—Asseverate (USA) **Mrs C. C. Regalado-Gonzalez**
27 **THEWINNINGMACHINE**, 4, b f Kheleyf (USA)—Spinning Reel **J. A. Rattigan**
28 **WICKED WENCH**, 4, b f Kyllachy—Effervescent **Mr J. M. H. Hearne**
29 **ZAFISIO (IRE)**, 7, b g Efisio—Goldthroat (IRE) **Mr D. A. Looney**

THREE-YEAR-OLDS

30 **ALPINE MIST**, b f Elusive Quality (USA)—Snowtime (IRE) **Mrs C. C. Regalado-Gonzalez**
31 **ANNALEY MY DARLING (IRE)**, b f Shamardal (USA)—Unreal **Mr & Mrs D. Yates**
32 **CHIEF EXECUTIVE (IRE)**, gr c Dalakhani (IRE)—Lucky (IRE) **Eastwind Racing Ltd & Martha Trussell**
33 **ETERNAL VIEW (IRE)**, b f Pivotal—Alstemeria (IRE)
34 **EXZACHARY**, b g Multiplex—Icky Woo **J. Smith**
35 **FLYING GIANT (IRE)**, ch c Danroad (AUS)—Our Emmy Lou **Champion Bloodstock Limited**
36 **FOCAL POINT**, ch g Pivotal—Centreofattention (AUS) **Mrs C. C. Regalado-Gonzalez**
37 **GLACIAL AGE (IRE)**, gr c Verglas (IRE)—Lady's Secret **James Henderson, Hugh Downs, Jo Hughes**
38 **HARBOUR CAPTAIN (IRE)**, ch g Captain Rio—English Harbour **Mr J. M. H. Hearne**
39 **INTERIOR MINISTER**, b c Nayef (USA)—Sister Maria (USA) **Eastwind Racing Ltd & Martha Trussell**
40 **JUST A POUND (IRE)**, b g Ad Valorem (USA)—Gallery Breeze **J. Smith**
41 **LONDON BRIDGE (USA)**, b c Arch (USA)—Kindness **Eastwind Racing Ltd & Martha Trussell**
42 **LUV U WHATEVER**, b g Needwood Blade—Lady Suesanne (IRE) **21C Telecom.co.uk**
43 **MRS MANN (USA)**, gr ro f Mizzen Mast (USA)—Dixiana Delight (USA)
44 Ch g Central Park (IRE)—Non Disclosure (IRE) **Mrs J. F. Hughes**
45 **RED DIESEL (IRE)**, ch g Captain Rio—With Finesse **Mr J. Hearne**
46 **SHES ELLIE**, ch f Lucky Story (USA)—Shes Minnie **S. G. Martin**
47 **SHINING CROSS (IRE)**, b g Cape Cross (IRE)—Shining Debut (IRE) **Mrs C. C. Regalado-Gonzalez**
48 **SMALL FURY (IRE)**, b f Windsor Knot (IRE)—Sisal (IRE) **Joseph Hearne, D Bird, H Downs, J Hughes**
49 **SMART FOOTSTEP (IRE)**, br g Footstepsinthesand—Easy Going **Champion Bloodstock Limited**
50 **SMART SPENDER (IRE)**, b g Chineur (FR)—Smart Starprincess **Brooklands Racing**
51 **SO LYRICAL**, b f Pivotal—Caro George (USA) **Mrs C. C. Regalado-Gonzalez**
52 **VOL FREAK**, b g Kyllachy—Sister Moonshine
53 B g Johannesburg (USA)—Whatcameoverme (USA)

TWO-YEAR-OLDS

54 B f 24/4 Pivotal—Alstemeria (IRE) (Danehill (USA))
55 B f 17/5 Myboycharlie (IRE)—Belle Annie (USA) (Aptitude (USA)) (800) **Mrs J. F. Hughes**
56 **CALEDONIA LAIRD**, b c 17/2 Firebreak—Granuaile O'malley (IRE) (Mark of Esteem (IRE)) **Isla & Colin Cage**
57 Br c 21/4 Teofilo (IRE)—Castle Quest (IRE) (Grand Lodge (USA)) (15000)
58 B c 29/4 Camacho—Consultant Stylist (IRE) (Desert Style (IRE)) (2857)
59 B f 11/3 Sakhee's Secret—Dictatrix (Diktat) (3809)
60 B f 14/4 Multiplex—Ellen Mooney (Efisio)
61 Ch f 24/3 Captain Gerrard (IRE)—Elusive Deal (USA) (Elusive Quality (USA)) (4761)
62 **HEAVENS EYES (IRE)**, b f 5/5 Oasis Dream—Snowtime (IRE) (Galileo (IRE))
63 B f 17/4 Captain Gerrard (IRE)—Lady Suesanne (IRE) (Cape Cross (IRE))
64 B c 24/4 Multiplex—Littlemisstutti (IRE) (Noverre (USA))
65 B c 18/3 Piccolo—Past 'n' Present (Cadeaux Genereux) (3047)
66 B c 10/5 Dylan Thomas (IRE)—Renowned (IRE) (Darshaan) (5000)
67 B c 6/5 Shamardal (USA)—Silversword (FR) (Highest Honor (FR)) (23809)
68 **SWEET CHERRY (IRE)**, b f 18/3 Mastercraftsman (IRE)—Dear Gracie (IRE) (In The Wings)
69 B f 22/4 Multiplex—Tacinja (GER) (Acatenango (GER)) **T. J. Wardle**
70 B f 6/3 Tobougg (IRE)—Take The Plunge (Benny The Dip (USA)) (523)
71 B c 11/3 Multiplex—Vita Mia (Central Park (IRE)) (4761)
72 B c 25/4 Sleeping Indian—Voice (Zamindar (USA)) (2857)
73 B c 18/3 Bahri (USA)—Wana Doo (USA) (Grand Slam (USA)) **Mrs J. F. Hughes**

MRS JO HUGHES - Continued

Other Owners: M. H. Bates, Mr D. N. Bedford, Mr P. N. Bedford, B. W. Bedford, D. G. Bird, Mrs I. Cage, C. J. Cage, B. H. Downs, East Wind Racing Ltd, Mr J. Henderson, Mr R. A. Hunt, Mrs N. Hunt, D. S. Lovatt, Mrs A. M. Mercs, J. E. Mottram, B. W. Parren, Mr J. F. Simpson, Mrs M. Trussell, Mrs G. A. White, Mr D. Yates, Mrs A. V. Yates.

Assistant Trainer: Paul Blockley

Jockey (flat): Paul Hanagan, Tony Culhane. **Jockey (NH):** Mark Grant. **Apprentice:** Josh Baudains.

---

331 MR STEPHEN HUGHES, Gilfach Goch
Postal: **Dusty Forge, 2 Oak Street, Gilfach Goch, Porth, Mid-Glamorgan, CF39 8UG**
Contacts: **PHONE** 07823334300 (01443) 672110 **FAX** (01443) 672110 **MOBILE** 07823334282
E-MAIL dustyforge@aol.com

1 NOT YET HARTLEY, 7, b g Relief Pitcher—Beinn Mohr
2 POUR CHANGER (FR), 8, b g Daliapour (IRE)—Chop And Change (FR)

Assistant Trainer: Maggie Kidner Hughes

---

332 MS N. M. HUGO, Malpas
Postal: **Yewtree House, 1 Brasseys Contract Road, Edge, Malpas, Cheshire, SY14 8LB**
Contacts: **PHONE** (01829) 782020 (01948) 820649 **FAX** (01829) 782020 **MOBILE** (07736) 360550
E-MAIL nicky.hugo@btconnect.com

1 HIDDEN SPRINGS, 8, b g Kayf Tara—Meole Brace **Magnate Racing**
2 MY MATE PADDY, 6, b g Deploy—City Times (IRE) **Mr J. R. Barnett**
3 WHATS GOIN ON (IRE), 4, b g Trade Fair—Beckerson (IRE) **Mr A. T. Murphy**

Other Owners: J. Tomlinson, Mrs L. E. Tomlinson.

---

333 MRS SARAH HUMPHREY, West Wratting
Postal: **Yen Hall Farm, West Wratting, Cambridge, Cambridgeshire, CB21 5LP**
Contacts: **PHONE** (01223) 291445 **FAX** (01223) 291451 **MOBILE** (07798) 702484
E-MAIL sarah.yenhallfarm@btinternet.com **WEBSITE** www.sarahhumphrey.co.uk

1 ARFUR DIDIT (IRE), 5, b g Blueprint (IRE)—Authentic Creature (IRE) **Yen Hall Farm Racing**
2 BEDOUIN BAY, 6, b g Dubai Destination (USA)—Sahara Sonnet (USA) **Mrs Z. Wentworth**
3 BRASS MONKEY (IRE), 6, b g Craigsteel—Saltee Great (IRE) **The Cheeky Monkeys**
4 BURLINGTON BERTIE (IRE), 5, ch g Old Vic—Clara's Dream (IRE) **D. N. Green**
5 CALL AT MIDNIGHT, 8, b m Midnight Legend—Second Call **Yen Hall Farm Racing**
6 CARPINCHO (FR), 9, b br g Jimble (FR)—La Rapaille (IRE) **Mr J. B. Waterfall**
7 CHAIN OF EVENTS, 6, ch g Nayef (USA)—Ermine (IRE) **Mr P. J. Edwards**
8 CHENDIYR (FR), 4, gr g Red Ransom (USA)—Cherryxma (IRE) **Mrs S. Humphrey**
9 FLEMI TWO TOES (IRE), 7, b g Flemensfirth (USA)—Silva Venture (IRE) **A Whyte, J Custerson, D Nott**
10 I NEED A HERO (IRE), 8, b g Oscar Schindler (IRE)—Old Fontaine (IRE) **The Bonnie Tyler Partnership**
11 KICKING TIME (IRE), 7, b g Luso—Fairy Dawn (IRE) **P & C Chapman, D. Nott & S. Humphrey**
12 LITTLE BIT LIVELY (IRE), 4, br g Flemensfirth (USA)—Goldenswift (IRE) **Cooper Cahill & Robert Burdett**
13 MINELLA HERO (IRE), 5, b g Old Vic—Shannon Rose (IRE) **P. Chapman**
14 MOYALIFF (IRE), 6, b g King's Theatre (IRE)—Instant Queen (IRE) **P. Chapman**
15 PRESENTING PADDY (IRE), 5, b g Presenting—Bula Beag (IRE) **Mrs S. Humphrey**
16 REVE DE NUIT (USA), 7, ch g Giant's Causeway (USA)—My Dream Castles (USA) **Mrs Z. Wentworth**
17 THE ROYAL BROMPTON, 7, b g Kayf Tara—Goldenswift (IRE) **Cooper Cahill & Robert Burdett**
18 TORNADE D'ESTRUVAL (FR), 6, b m Network (GER)—Onde d'estruval (FR) **Mrs J. A. Bowen**
19 UNO D'ESTRUVAL (FR), 5, b g Nononito (FR)—Dune d'estruval (FR) **Mrs Z. Wentworth**
20 VASCO D'YCY (FR), 4, b g Equerry (USA)—Ingrid des Mottes (FR) **P. Chapman**

Other Owners: Mr K. B. Bailey, Mr & Mrs C. Bearman, Dr R. Britton, Mr R. J. Burdett, Mr Brett Cahill, Mr P. Chapman, Miss J. M. Custerson, Miss M. Folley, Mrs L. Gregson, Mrs S. J. Humphrey, Mr A. R. Humphrey, Mrs S. Lintott, Mr D. F. Nott, Mr T. Passfield, S. C. B. Limited, Mr G. Thomas, Mr A. A. Whyte.

Assistant Trainer: Mr A. Humphrey

Jockey (NH): Aidan Coleman, Jack Doyle, Charlie Huxley. **Amateur:** Mr M. Ennis.

334   MR KEVIN HUNTER, Natland
Postal: **Larkrigg, Natland, Cumbria, LA9 7QS**
Contacts: **PHONE (01539) 560245**

1 **LAUNCHPAD**, 6, ch g Starcraft (NZ)—Revival **J. K. Hunter**
2 4, B g Dutch Art—Mac Rhapsody **J. K. Hunter**

335   MISS LAURA HURLEY, Kineton
Postal: **Kineton Grange Farm, Kineton, Warwick, Warwickshire, CV35 0EE**
Contacts: **PHONE (01926) 640380**

1 **BEST LOVER (FR)**, 11, ch g Great Palm (USA)—Droid (FR) **Mrs R. Hurley**
2 **GAME DORABELLA**, 5, ch m Avonbridge—Ground Game **Mrs R. Hurley**
3 **LAUGHING GAME**, 9, b m Classic Cliche (IRE)—Ground Game **Mrs R. Hurley**
4 **MOSCOW MULE**, 10, b g Moscow Society (USA)—Madam Advocate **Mrs R. Hurley**
5 **ORANG OUTAN (FR)**, 11, b g Baby Turk—Ellapampa (FR) **Mrs R. Hurley**

336   MISS ALISON HUTCHINSON, Exning
Postal: **116 Parkers Walk, Studlands, Newmarket, Suffolk, CB8 7AP**
Contacts: **PHONE (01638) 482180 MOBILE (07960) 630204**
E-MAIL alison.hutchinson1@hotmail.co.uk
WEBSITE www.alisonhutchinsonhorseracing.weebly.com

1 **BIG WAVE (IRE)**, 5, b m Choisir (AUS)—Mystery Solved (USA) **Mr P. Carney**
2 **MUCKY MOLLY**, 5, ch m Bahamian Bounty—Indian Flag (IRE) **Miss A. L. Hutchinson**
3 **MY OH MOUNT BROWN (IRE)**, 6, b g Millenary—My O Mio (IRE) **Miss A. L. Hutchinson**
4 **STRIKE FORCE**, 9, b g Dansili—Miswaki Belle (USA) **Miss A. L. Hutchinson**

337   MR ROGER INGRAM, Epsom
Postal: **Wendover Stables, Burgh Heath Road, Epsom, Surrey, KT17 4LX**
Contacts: **PHONE (01372) 748505 or (01372) 749157 FAX (01372) 748505**
MOBILE (0777) 3665980
E-MAIL roger.ingram.racing@virgin.net WEBSITE www.rogeringramracing.com

1 **BRIDGE THAT GAP**, 5, b h Avonbridge—Figura **The Stargazers**
2 **BUXTON**, 9, b g Auction House (USA)—Dam Certain (IRE) **Mr P. J. Burton**
3 **DILYS MAUD**, 6, b m Auction House (USA)—Dam Certain (IRE) **The Stargazers**
4 **FLUTER PHIL**, 6, b g Piccolo—Figura **The Stargazers & Mr G E Ley**
5 **FONTERUTOLI (IRE)**, 6, gr g Verglas (IRE)—Goldendale (IRE) **Mrs Cathy Hallam & Mr Martyn Cruse**
6 **IT AIN'T TO GRAND**, 4, ch g Auction House (USA)—Charlottevalentina (IRE) **The Smugglers**
7 4, Ch f Joe Bear (IRE)—Its All Too Much **Rhiain Ingram**
8 **MADE OF MORE**, 4, ch c Auction House (USA)—Dam Certain (IRE) **The Smugglers**
9 **MRS BRIDGES**, 4, b f Avonbridge—Figura **The Stargazers**
10 **NADIA NAES (IRE)**, 4, b f Strategic Prince—Tread The Boards **Mr James Coyne**
11 **POSE (IRE)**, 6, b m Acclamation—Lyca Ballerina **Mrs E. N. Nield**
12 **SILVER MARIZAH (IRE)**, 4, b f Manduro (GER)—Maharani (USA) **Mr Z. Malik**

TWO-YEAR-OLDS

13 B f 23/3 Byron—Sea Jade (IRE) (Mujadil (USA)) **Hanif Barma**
14 B f 18/3 Byron—Sunny Times (IRE) (Raise A Grand (IRE)) **Hanif Barma**

Other Owners: Mr Stephen Andrews, Mr Stephen Appleyard, Mr R. J. Clark, Mr Martyn Cruse, Mrs C. Hallam, Mr Michael Joy, Mr Andrew Lane-Joynt, Mr G. E. Ley, Mr Ade McLoughlin, Mr Kevin McMorrow, Mr John Rogan, Mr D. Ross-Watt, Mr Shaun Steele, Mr Henry Watson.

Assistant Trainer: Sharon Ingram

Apprentice: Tommy Harrigan. **Amateur:** Miss Rhiain Ingram.

338 MR DEAN IVORY, Radlett

Postal: Harper Lodge Farm, Harper Lane, Radlett, Hertfordshire, WD7 7HU
Contacts: PHONE (01923) 855337 FAX (01923) 852470 MOBILE (07785) 118658
E-MAIL dean.ivory@virgin.net WEBSITE www.deanivoryracing.co.uk

1 BATCHWORTH FIREFLY, 5, b m Piccolo—Batchworth Belle **Mrs D. T. M. S. Price**
2 ECECHEIRA, 4, ch f Three Valleys (USA)—Evening Guest (FR) **Mrs A. R. Ruggles**
3 ELEGANT OPHELIA, 4, ch f Osorio (GER)—Ela's Giant **World Freight Consultants Ltd**
4 ESPRIT DE MIDAS, 7, b g Namid—Spritzeria **Mr G. M. Copp**
5 GUARDI (IRE), 4, gr g Dalakhani (IRE)—Grizel **Heather Yarrow & Lesley Ivory**
6 HEREFORD BOY, 9, ch g Tomba—Grown At Rowan **Recycled Products Limited**
7 HILL OF DREAMS (IRE), 4, b f Indian Danehill (IRE)—Shaunas Vision (IRE) **Mr I Gethin & Mr R Gethin**
8 KINGS 'N DREAMS, 6, b g Royal Applause—Last Dream (IRE) **Mr Ian Gethin & Mr Richard Gethin**
9 LAUGH OR CRY, 5, br g Firebreak—Turkish Delight **Non Racing Agreement**
10 LINKS DRIVE LADY, 5, br m Striking Ambition—Miskina **It's Your Lucky Day**
11 LUJEANIE, 7, br g Lujain (USA)—Ivory's Joy **K. T. Ivory**
12 MACK'S SISTER, 6, ch m Pastoral Pursuits—Linda's Schoolgirl (IRE) **Recycled Products Limited**
13 MIDNIGHT BAHIA (IRE), 4, b f Refuse To Bend (IRE)—Midnight Partner (IRE) **Mr K. B. Taylor**
14 RUSSIAN ICE, 5, ch m Iceman—Dark Eyed Lady (IRE) **Mr R. Beadle**
15 SHAUNAS SPIRIT (IRE), 5, b m Antonius Pius (USA)—Shaunas Vision (IRE) **Cynthia Smith & Dean Ivory**
16 SIRIUS PROSPECT (USA), 5, b br g Gone West (USA)—Stella Blue (FR) **Miss N. I. Yarrow**
17 SNOW TROOPER, 5, ch g Iceman—Snow Shoes **Mr K. B. Taylor**
18 TAGULA NIGHT (IRE), 7, ch g Tagula (IRE)—Carpet Lady (IRE) **Hufford & Papworth**
19 TROPICS (USA), 5, ch g Speightstown (USA)—Taj Aire (USA) **D. K. Ivory**
20 VALID REASON, 6, b g Observatory (USA)—Real Trust (USA) **Mr M. J. Yarrow**

THREE-YEAR-OLDS

21 ADA LOVELACE, b f Byron—Satin Braid **Mr D. A. Clark**
22 AYE AYE SKIPPER (IRE), b g Captain Marvelous (IRE)—Queenfisher **Heather Yarrow & Lesley Ivory**
23 BATCHWORTH LADY, b f Pastoral Pursuits—Batchworth Belle **Mrs D. T. M. S. Price**
24 EL MIRAGE (IRE), b f Elusive Quality (USA)—Hucking Hot **Mrs H. Yarrow**
25 FOSSA, b g Dubai Destination (USA)—Gayanula (USA) **Mr G. M. Copp**
26 HIGH TONE, b f Bertolini (USA)—High Finale **K. T. Ivory**
27 JOYOUS, b f Assertive—Ivory's Joy **K. T. Ivory**
28 LANCELOT DU LAC (ITY), b c Shamardal (USA)—Dodie Mae (USA) **Mr M. J. Yarrow**
29 ROYAL GUINEVERE, b f Invincible Spirit (IRE)—Elegant Beauty **Mr M. J. Yarrow**
30 VISUAL ASPECT, b g Assertive—Enclave (USA) **K. T. Ivory**
31 WORLD FREIGHT GIRL, ch f Tumbleweed Ridge—Bens Georgie (IRE) **World Freight Consultants Ltd**

TWO-YEAR-OLDS

32 GREY ODYSSEY, gr c 9/2 Verglas (IRE)—Reading Habit (USA) (Half a Year (USA)) (60000) **Miss N. I. Yarrow**

Assistant Trainer: Chris Scally

339 MISS TINA JACKSON, Loftus

Postal: Tick Hill Farm, Liverton, Loftus, Saltburn, Cleveland, TS13 4TG
Contacts: PHONE (01287) 644952 MOBILE (07774) 106906

1 BORIS THE BLADE, 11, gr g Cloudings (IRE)—Cherry Lane **Mrs P A Cowey & Panther Racing**
2 HITMAN HARRY, 5, b g Sir Harry Lewis (USA)—Bonnie Buttons **Mrs P A Cowey & Panther Racing**
3 MANYSHADESOFBLACK (IRE), 5, b m Tikkanen (USA)—Wynyard Dancer **Mrs P A Cowey & Panther Racing**
4 NO LADY, 6, b m Exit To Nowhere (USA)—Bonnie Buttons **Mrs P A Cowey & Panther Racing**
5 SORY, 6, b g Sakhee (USA)—Rule Britannia **H. L. Thompson**

Other Owners: Mrs P. A. Cowey, Panther Racing Limited.

340 MRS VALERIE JACKSON, Newcastle Upon Tyne

Postal: Edge House, Belsay, Newcastle Upon Tyne, Tyne and Wear, NE20 0HH
Contacts: PHONE (01830) 530218 MOBILE (07808) 812213

1 CAST IRON CASEY (IRE), 11, ch g Carroll House—Ashie's Friend (IRE) **Mrs V. S. Jackson**
2 SPORTS MODEL (IRE), 7, ch g Presenting—Belmirata (IRE) **Mrs V. S. Jackson**

MRS VALERIE JACKSON - Continued

3 **WAVE POWER (IRE)**, 9, ch g Definite Article—Romany Rose (IRE) **Mrs V. S. Jackson**
4 **WHEYAYE**, 11, ch m Midnight Legend—Sayin Nowt **Mrs V. S. Jackson**

341	**MR LEE JAMES, Malton**

Postal: **Cheesecake Hill Stables, Norton, Malton, North Yorkshire, YO17 9PJ**
Contacts: **PHONE (01653) 699466 FAX (01653) 691455 MOBILE (07732) 556322**

1 **BASHURE**, 4, b g Tillerman—Blackburn Meadows
2 **FREEDOM FLYING**, 10, b m Kalanisi (IRE)—Free Spirit (IRE)
3 **REVOLVING WORLD (IRE)**, 10, b g Spinning World (USA)—Mannakea (USA)
4 **SHADOW OF THE DAY**, 6, b g Sugarfoot—She Who Dares Wins
5 **STRIKEMASTER (IRE)**, 7, b g Xaar—Mas A Fuera (IRE)
6 **TOBY MAC**, 11, b g Presidium—Ski Path
7 **ZOOM IN**, 5, b g Indesatchel (IRE)—Korolieva (IRE)

THREE-YEAR-OLDS

8 B c Echo of Light—Alisdanza
9 B f Dubai Destination (USA)—Palisandra (USA)

Assistant Trainer: Carol James

Conditional: Kyle James. **Amateur:** Mr Aaron James.

342	**MR IAIN JARDINE, Hawick**

Postal: **Paradise Cottage, Gatehousecote, Bonchester Bridge, Hawick, Roxburghshire, TD9 8JD**
Contacts: **PHONE (01450) 860718**

1 **AZERODEGREE (IRE)**, 4, b g Azamour (IRE)—Fairy (USA) **Fortune Favours The Brave Racing**
2 **BUYWISE (IRE)**, 6, b g Tikkanen (USA)—Greenogue Princess (IRE) **Mr I. Jardine**
3 **ROWAN ROAD**, 9, gr m Minster Son—Yemaail (IRE) **Mr A. Dawson & Mrs K. Campbell**
4 **STAFF SERGEANT**, 6, b g Dubawi (IRE)—Miss Particular (IRE) **Derek Walpole & Iain Jardine**
5 **ULTRA SPECIAL**, 6, b m Reset (AUS)—Exclusive Davis (USA) **The Gold Cup In Mind**

Other Owners: Mrs S. M. Barker, Mrs K. Campbell, A. Dawson, Mr I. McAllan, Mrs S Monteith, Mr A. G. Short, Mr D. S. Walpole.

343	**MR ALAN JARVIS, Twyford**

Postal: **Twyford Mill, Mill Lane, Twyford, Buckingham, Buckinghamshire, MK18 4HA**
Contacts: **PHONE (01296) 730707 FAX (01296) 733572 MOBILE (07770) 785551**
E-MAIL alan@alanjarvis.co.uk WEBSITE www.alanjarvis.co.uk

1 **BOW TO NO ONE (IRE)**, 7, b m Refuse To Bend (IRE)—Deadly Buzz (IRE) **A. L. R. Morton**
2 **DICEY VOWS (USA)**, 5, b g Broken Vow (USA)—Pretty Dicey (USA) **A. L. R. Morton**
3 **KING VAHE (IRE)**, 4, b g One Cool Cat (USA)—Tethkar **Cedars Partnership**
4 **NAVAJO CHARM**, 4, b f Authorized (IRE)—Navajo Love Song (IRE) **Mr G. S. Bishop**
5 **RIGHT STEP**, 6, b g Xaar—Maid To Dance **Allen B. Pope & Jarvis Associates**
6 **TURNED TO GOLD (IRE)**, 4, ch g Teofilo (IRE)—Silver Bracelet **Nesbitt Emery**

THREE-YEAR-OLDS

7 **POETIC BELLE**, b f Byron—Sahariri (IRE) **Christopher Shankland & Ann Jarvis**
8 **SECRET WOMAN (IRE)**, b f Manduro (GER)—Coveted **Cedars Partnership**

TWO-YEAR-OLDS

9 B c 11/4 Excellent Art—Aspasias Tizzy (USA) (Tiznow (USA))
10 Ch f 10/3 Intense Focus (USA)—Barbera (GER) (Night Shift (USA)) (7936)
11 B f 10/3 Bushranger (IRE)—Brogan's Well (IRE) (Caerleon (USA)) (22221)
12 B f 15/1 Mastercraftsman (IRE)—Cover Look (SAF) (Fort Wood (USA))
13 Ch f 26/4 Peintre Celebre (USA)—Cream Tease (Pursuit of Love)
14 Ch c 11/4 Lando (GER)—Dallaah (Green Desert (USA))
15 **DIAMOND SOLITAIRE (IRE)**, br f 15/3 Diamond Green (FR)—
Eastern Blue (IRE) (Be My Guest (USA)) **Market Avenue Racing Club Ltd**

MR ALAN JARVIS - Continued

16 Gr c 6/4 Verglas (IRE)—Fury Dance (USA) (Cryptoclearance (USA)) (11904)
17 B f 22/2 High Chaparral (IRE)—Gassal (Oasis Dream) (23809)
18 Gr f 12/5 Mastercraftsman (IRE)—Joyful (IRE) (Green Desert (USA))
19 B c 16/3 Iffraaj—Lady Naomi (USA) (Distant View (USA))
20 B c 12/3 High Chaparral (IRE)—Lady of Talent (USA) (Siphon (BRZ))
21 B c 1/5 Refuse To Bend (IRE)—Mad Annie (USA) (Anabaa (USA)) **Jarvis Associates**
22 B c 3/5 Major Cadeaux—Mancunian Way (Green Desert (USA))
23 MIDFIELD DIAMOND (IRE), b c 17/3 Diamond Green (FR)—Jacquelin Jag (IRE) (Fayruz)
24 Ch f 13/4 Virtual—Moon Crystal (Fasliyev (USA)) **Mr G. S. Bishop**
25 B c 12/4 Firebreak—My Sweet Georgia (IRE) (Royal Applause) (13333) **Jarvis Associates**
26 B c 2/5 Amadeus Wolf—Newgate Lodge (IRE) (Namid)
27 B f 10/2 High Chaparral (IRE)—Rose Parade (Machiavellian (USA))
28 B f 26/1 Excellent Art—Shanty (Selkirk (USA))
29 B f 31/3 Refuse To Bend (IRE)—Spring Goddess (IRE) (Daggers Drawn (USA)) **Grant & Bowman Limited**
30 Ch c 19/4 Iffraaj—Sweet Myrtle (USA) (Mutakddim (USA))
31 B c 14/4 Holy Roman Emperor (IRE)—Web of Intrigue (Machiavellian (USA))

Other Owners: Mrs Ann Jarvis, A. P. Jarvis, A. B. Pope, C. H. Shankland.

Assistant Trainer: M. A. Jarvis, S. E. Simmons, T. O. Jarvis

Apprentice: Jordan Uys.

---

344 MR WILLIAM JARVIS, Newmarket
Postal: **Phantom House, Fordham Road, Newmarket, Suffolk, CB8 7AA**
Contacts: **OFFICE (01638) 669873 HOME (01638) 662677 FAX (01638) 667328**
E-MAIL mail@williamjarvis.com WEBSITE www.williamjarvis.com

1 ASHDOWN LAD, 4, ch g Sir Percy—Antibes (IRE) **The Fops**
2 BEAUFORT TWELVE, 4, b g Hurricane Run (IRE)—Violette **Tony Foster & John Kelsey-Fry**
3 CARAZAM (IRE), 6, b g Azamour (IRE)—Carallia (IRE) **Dr Jim Walker**
4 CHEVIOT QUEST (IRE), 4, ch g Sir Percy—Cushat Law (IRE) **Mr Anthony Reed**
5 EMBANKMENT, 4, b c Zamindar (USA)—Esplanade **Canisbay Bloodstock**
6 KATY'S SECRET, 6, b m Mind Games—Katy O'hara **Miss S. E. Hall**
7 LOKI'S REVENGE, 5, b g Kyllachy—Amira **Dr Jim Walker**
8 5, B g Cadeaux Genereux—Orlena (USA) **Mrs Susan Davis**
9 PRIVATE EQUITY (IRE), 7, b m Haafhd—Profit Alert (IRE) **Mrs Susan Davis**

THREE-YEAR-OLDS

10 ARGENT KNIGHT, gr g Sir Percy—Tussah **Dr Jim Walker**
11 BOSHAM, b c Shamardal (USA)—Awwal Malika (USA) **The Bosham Partnership**
12 CAVALIERI (IRE), b c Oratorio (IRE)—Always Attractive (IRE) **The Cavalieri Partnership**
13 CRAVE, b f Sakhee's Secret—Bolsena (USA) **St Albans Bloodstock LLP**
14 DUMBARTON ROCK, b g Kyllachy—Ellablue **Dr Jim Walker**
15 EL MASSIVO (IRE), b c Authorized (IRE)—Umthoulah (IRE) **The B A D D Partnership**
16 JODIES JEM, br g Kheleyf (USA)—First Approval **Mrs M. C. Banks**
17 LAUDATION, b c Royal Applause—Calamanco **The Laudation Partnership**
18 NIGHT'S WATCH, b c Authorized (IRE)—Nachtigall (GER) **Dr Jim Walker**
19 PERSIAN PATRIOT, ch f Bahamian Bounty—Persian Lass (IRE) **Miss Jo Margossian**
20 RASKOVA (USA), b f Henrythenavigator (USA)—Diamond Necklace (USA) **Mr Kevin Hickman**

TWO-YEAR-OLDS

21 B f 28/3 Fastnet Rock (AUS)—Amethyst (IRE) (Sadler's Wells (USA)) (51586) **Mr Kevin Hickman**
22 BEAKERS N NUM NUMS (IRE), b c 25/2 Iffraaj—
        Ivy League Star (IRE) (Sadler's Wells (USA)) (10000) **A Partnership**
23 BISHAN BEDI (IRE), b c 6/4 Intikhab (USA)—Knockatotaun (Spectrum (IRE)) (27000) **Dr Jim Walker**
24 B f 10/5 Dubawi (IRE)—Bronwen (IRE) (King's Best (USA)) (35000) **Mr A. S. Belhab**
25 NEW ROW, b f 4/2 Teofilo (IRE)—Memo (Groom Dancer (USA)) (16000) **A Partnership**
26 SILVER MOUNTAIN, gr c 19/3 Sir Percy—Pearl Bright (FR) (Kaldoun (FR)) (20000) **Ms Wendy Dio**
27 B c 23/4 Royal Applause—Sparkling Eyes (Lujain (USA)) (25000) **A Partnership**

MR WILLIAM JARVIS - Continued

Other Owners: Mr D. Brooks, Mrs Victoria Donald, Mrs Victoria Donald, Pauline Etkin, A. Foster, G. B. Turnbull Ltd, Mr J. R. B. George, Mrs P. J. George, Mr Richard Griffiths, Mr Giles Hargreave, Mr Kevin Hickman, Mr William Jarvis, J. Kelsey-Fry, R. F. Kilby, Mr D. G. Marshall, Mr Patrick McSwinney, A. M. Mitchell, Mr D. Morgan, Mr David Murrell, Ms Liz Newton, A. E. Pakenham, Mrs V. H. Pakenham, Mr E. Randall, Mr Max Robertson, Mr Patrick Savage, Mrs J. A. Slogrove, Mr Bradley St Pierre, A. J. Stone, Mrs M. F. Stone, Miss M. E. Stopher, Dr J. Walker, Mr Neil Warnock, Mr Alex Wood, Mr S. J. Wyatt.

---

345 MR MALCOLM JEFFERSON, Malton
Postal: Newstead Cottage Stables, Norton, Malton, North Yorkshire, YO17 9PJ
Contacts: **PHONE** (01653) 697225 **MOBILE** (07710) 502044
E-MAIL newsteadracing@btconnect.com **WEBSITE** www.malcolmjefferson.co.uk

1 4, Gr f Grape Tree Road—Altogether Now (IRE)
2 4, B f Revoque (IRE)—Anabranch **Mrs S. Jefferson**
3 **ANEYEFORANEYE (IRE),** 7, ch m Definite Article—Resolute Approach (IRE) **Mrs J. U. Hales & Mrs L. M. Joicey**
4 **ATTAGLANCE,** 7, b g Passing Glance—Our Ethel **H Young, G Eifert, R Snyder**
5 **BEAMAZED,** 9, ch g Silver Patriarch (IRE)—Gotogeton **Mr T. A. Pearcy**
6 **CAPE TRIBULATION,** 9, b g Hernando (FR)—Gay Fantastic **J. D. Abell**
7 **CAPE YORK,** 5, ch g Revoque (IRE)—Altogether Now (IRE) **J. D. Abell**
8 **CROXTON KERRIAL,** 4, b g Doyen (IRE)—Julatten (IRE) **J. D. Abell**
9 **CRUSHED ICE,** 7, gr g Silver Patriarch (IRE)—Altogether Now (IRE) **Mrs M. M. Jagger**
10 **DREAMERS OF DREAMS (IRE),** 8, b g Flemensfirth (USA)—
Cushogan (IRE) **Dean Bostock & Raymond Bostock**
11 **ENCHANTED GARDEN,** 5, ch g Sulamani (IRE)—Calachuchi **Mrs D. W. Davenport**
12 **FIRTH OF THE CLYDE,** 8, b g Flemensfirth (USA)—Miss Nel **R. H. Goldie**
13 **GLOBAL FELLA (IRE),** 8, b g Chevalier (IRE)—Antaporua (IRE) **T. J. Hemmings**
14 **HENRY JENKINS,** 6, gr g Fair Mix (IRE)—Altogether Now (IRE) **Mrs K. M. Richardson**
15 **HI GEORGE,** 5, b g Doyen (IRE)—Our Ethel **Mr & Mrs H Young**
16 **KING FONTAINE (IRE),** 10, b g King's Theatre (IRE)—Kerfontaine **T. J. Hemmings**
17 **KING OF THE WOLDS (IRE),** 6, b g Presenting—Azaban (IRE) **J. M. Jefferson**
18 **KNOCKTURNAL (IRE),** 5, ch m Refuse To Bend (IRE)—Knocktartan (IRE) **Racegoers Club Owners Group**
19 **MAC AEDA,** 9, gr g Kayf Tara—Altogether Now (IRE) **Mrs D. W. Davenport**
20 **MAGIC PRESENT,** 6, b g Presenting—Magic Bloom **P. Nelson**
21 **MARY MILAN (IRE),** 6, b m Milan—Pristina (IRE) **C. R. Clark**
22 **MCMURROUGH (IRE),** 9, b g Spectrum (IRE)—Sensitive (IRE) **Mrs D. W. Davenport**
23 **MILAN ROYALE,** 8, b g Milan—Siroyalta (FR) **T. J. Hemmings**
24 **OUR BOY BEN,** 4, b c Revoque (IRE)—Magic Bloom **P. Nelson**
25 **PAIR OF JACKS (IRE),** 5, ch g Presenting—Halona **Mrs R. Williams**
26 **QUITE THE MAN (IRE),** 8, b g Zagreb (USA)—Ballinard Lizzie (IRE) **Boundary Garage (Bury) Limited**
27 **RENOYR (FR),** 8, b g Kalmoss (FR)—Idee de Valeur (FR) **Mr Michael Harvey**
28 **SCHINKEN OTTO (IRE),** 12, ch g Shinko Forest (IRE)—Athassel Rose (IRE) **J. Donald**
29 **SECRETE STREAM (IRE),** 4, ch g Fruits of Love (USA)—Bonny River (IRE) **Mrs M. E. Dixon**
30 **SHE WILL ROCK YOU (IRE),** 6, b m Milan—Me Grannys Endoors (IRE) **Mr A. Barclay**
31 **SUN CLOUD (IRE),** 6, b g Cloudings (IRE)—Miss Melrose **Boundary Garage (Bury) Limited**
32 **THE MAGIC BISHOP,** 8, b g Bishop of Cashel—Magic Bloom **P. Nelson**
33 **THE PANAMA KID (IRE),** 9, b g Presenting—Mrs Jodi **Mrs D. W. Davenport**
34 **UNCLE BRIT,** 7, b g Efisio—Tarneem (USA) **J. M. Jefferson**
35 **UPPINGHAM,** 4, ch g Doyen (IRE)—Karakul (IRE) **J. D. Abell**

THREE-YEAR-OLDS

36 Gr f Proclamation (IRE)—Altogether Now (IRE)
37 B f Primo Valentino (IRE)—Annie's Gift (IRE) **Mrs A. Nelson & Partners**
38 **NAUTICAL TWILIGHT,** gr f Proclamation (IRE)—Anabranch **Capt M. S. Bagley**
39 B g Kayf Tara—Shuildante (IRE) **Mrs K. S. Gaffney & Mrs A. Stevenson**

Other Owners: Mr G. Eifert, Mrs J. U. Hales, Mrs L. M. Joicey, Mr R. Synder Jnr, Mrs E. A. Young, Mr H. Young.

Assistant Trainer: Ruth Jefferson

Jockey (NH): Harry Haynes, Brian Hughes. **Conditional:** Jack Jordan. **Amateur:** Mr J. Teal.

346 MR J. R. JENKINS, Royston

Postal: Kings Ride, Baldock Road, Royston, Hertfordshire, SG8 9NN
Contacts: PHONE (01763) 241141 HOME (01763) 246611 FAX (01763) 248223
MOBILE Car: (07802) 750855
E-MAIL john@johnjenkinsracing.co.uk WEBSITE www.johnjenkinsracing.co.uk

1 **ABADEJO**, 5, b g Acclamation—Silvereine (FR) **Mrs I. C. Hampson**
2 **AMOSITE**, 7, b m Central Park (IRE)—Waterline Dancer (IRE) **Mrs C. Goddard**
3 **BILLY RED**, 9, ch g Dr Fong (USA)—Liberty Bound **Mrs I. C. Hampson**
4 **BINT ALAKAABER (IRE)**, 5, b m Elusive City (USA)—Lady of Pleasure (IRE) **R. Bradbury**
5 **BLADEWOOD GIRL**, 5, b m Needwood Blade—Willmar (IRE) **Byron Boys**
6 **BOOKIESINDEX BOY**, 9, b br g Piccolo—United Passion **Mr R. Stevens**
7 **BOOKIESINDEXDOTNET**, 4, b f Piccolo—United Passion **Bookmakers Index Ltd**
8 **CARAMELITA**, 6, b m Deportivo—Apple of My Eye **La Senoritas**
9 **D'URBERVILLE**, 6, b g Auction House (USA)—Laser Crystal (IRE) **Mrs W. A. Jenkins**
10 **DORCEUS**, 6, b g Doyen (IRE)—Jawwala (USA) **P. J. Kirkpatrick**
11 **FROSTY FRIDAY**, 5, b m Storming Home—Seasonal Blossom (IRE) **R. Bradbury**
12 **GO AMWELL**, 10, b g Kayt Tara—Daarat Alayaam (IRE) **Mr R. Stevens**
13 **GREAT EXPECTATIONS**, 5, b g Storming Home—Fresh Fruit Daily **The Great Expectations Partnership**
14 **GROUP LEADER (IRE)**, 7, ch g Noverre (USA)—Stem The Tide (USA) **Mr & Mrs J. Sales**
15 **HANDSOME KING**, 6, ch g Lucky Story (USA)—Samar Qand **R. Bradbury**
16 **HI TIDE (IRE)**, 9, br g Idris (IRE)—High Glider **Mrs W. A. Jenkins**
17 **JERMATT**, 4, b g Kyllachy—Miss Ippolita **David Bryans & Philippa Casey**
18 **KARAM ALBAARI (IRE)**, 5, b h King's Best (USA)—Lilakiya (IRE) **R. Bradbury**
19 **LAURA'S BAIRN**, 4, ch g Piccolo—Primula Bairn **Mr M. D. Goldstein**
20 **LOUPHOLE**, 11, ch g Loup Sauvage (USA)—Goodwood Lass (IRE) **Byron Boys**
21 **LOVE YOU LOUIS**, 7, b g Mark of Esteem (IRE)—Maddie's A Jem **J. Pepper**
22 **MAWAAKEF (IRE)**, 5, b g Azamour (IRE)—Al Euro (FR) **The Three Honest Men**
23 **MEDITERRANEAN SEA (IRE)**, 7, b m Medecis—High Glider **Mrs W. A. Jenkins**
24 **MINSTRELS GALLERY (IRE)**, 4, ch g Refuse To Bend (IRE)—Lilakiya (IRE) **The Three Honest Men**
25 **MISHRIF (USA)**, 7, b br g Arch (USA)—Peppy Priscilla (USA) **Mrs W. A. Jenkins**
26 **MONSIEUR JAMIE**, 5, b g Monsieur Bond (IRE)—Primula Bairn **Mark Goldstein & Stephen Pettman**
27 **MY MANEKINEKO**, 4, b g Authorized (IRE)—Echo River (USA) **Bond Street General Services Ltd**
28 **MYBOYALFIE (USA)**, 6, b g Johannesburg (USA)—Scotchbonnetpepper (USA) **D. Badham**
29 **NOT TIL MONDAY (IRE)**, 7, b g Spartacus (IRE)—Halomix **The Three Honest Men**
30 **ONLY TEN PER CENT (IRE)**, 5, b g Kheleyf (USA)—Cory Everson (IRE) **B. Silkman**
31 **PINK LIPS**, 5, b m Noverre (USA)—Primrose Queen **Mr & Mrs J. Sales**
32 **QUEEN CASSIOPEIA**, 4, b f Echo of Light—Fresh Fruit Daily **R. B. Hill**
33 **RAMBO WILL**, 5, b g Danbird (AUS)—Opera Belle **Mr & Mrs T H Bambridge**
34 **RAY OF JOY**, 7, b m Tobougg (IRE)—Once Removed **Mr R. Stevens**
35 **SANTORINI SUNSET**, 4, ch f Haafhd—Fantasy Ridge **D. R. Tucker**
36 **SHARE THE DOSH**, 5, ch m Doyen (IRE)—Lady Starlight (IRE) **The Speech Partnership**
37 **SPITFIRE**, 8, b g Mujahid (USA)—Fresh Fruit Daily **Mrs W. A. Jenkins**
38 **SWEET SUGAR (FR)**, 7, ch g Loup Solitaire (USA)—Violette d'avril (FR) **Sweet Sugar Racing Club**
39 **THANK YOU JOY**, 5, b m Iceman—Once Removed **Mr R. Stevens**
40 **TIRADIA (FR)**, 6, b br g Without Connexion (IRE)—Jimanji (FR) **B. S. P. Dowling**
41 **WILLOW BEAUTY**, 4, br f Val Royal (FR)—Opera Belle **Susan Bambridge & Wendy Jenkins**

THREE-YEAR-OLDS

42 **I NEED A DOLLAR**, b c Phoenix Reach (IRE)—Lady Starlight (IRE) **The Speech Partnership**
43 **LADY CAVALLO**, b f Tiger Hill (IRE)—Cavallo da Corsa **Byron Boys**
44 **LITTLE INDIAN**, b c Sleeping Indian—Once Removed **Two Little Indians**
45 **OSCARS JOURNEY**, ch g Dubai Destination (USA)—Fruit of Glory **R. B. Hill**
46 **SAKASH**, b c Sakhee (USA)—Ashwell Rose **Mr & Mrs C. Schwick**
47 **SOMOUD (IRE)**, ch c Kheleyf (USA)—Harmonist (USA) **Sheik Ahmad Yousuf Al Sabah**

TWO-YEAR-OLDS

48 **TEMPLAR BOY**, br c 6/4 Myboycharlie (IRE)—Zagala (Polar Falcon (USA)) (2857) **Mrs C. Goddard**

Other Owners: D. Abrey, Mrs S. Bambridge, S. J. Brewer, D. J. P. Bryans, Mr S. M. Bullock, Mr G. J. Burchell, Mr I. J. Callaway, Miss P. Casey, Mrs C. A. Hill, Mr T H Bambridge T/As The Willow Stud, G. J. Pascoe, Mr S. P. Pettman, Mr A. M. Phillips, Mr P. Pooley, Mr J. Sales, Mrs K. Sales, Miss C. A. Salmon, Miss K. Salmon, C. Schwick, Mrs C. V. Schwick, Mr P. Trotter.

Apprentice: Danny Brock. **Amateur:** Mr Ray Barrett.

347 MR ALAN JESSOP, Chelmsford
Postal: **Flemings Farm, Warren Road, South Hanningfield, Chelmsford, Essex, CM3 8HU**
Contacts: **PHONE (01268) 710210 MOBILE (07718) 736482**

1 CHORAL BEE, 4, b f Oratorio (IRE)—Chief Bee **Mrs G. Jessop**
2 MAJY D'AUTEUIL (FR), 11, b g Discover d'auteuil (FR)—Majestic Dancer (FR) **Mrs G. Jessop**
3 MAX MILANO (IRE), 8, b g Milan—Stellissima (IRE) **Mrs G. Jessop**
4 STEEPLEOFCOPPER (IRE), 7, ch g Classic Cliche (IRE)—Tanya Thyne (IRE) **Mrs G. Jessop**

348 MRS LINDA JEWELL, Sutton Valence
Postal: **Southfield Stables, South Lane, Sutton Valence, Maidstone, Kent, ME17 3AZ**
Contacts: **PHONE (01622) 842788 FAX (01622) 842943 MOBILE (07856) 686657**
E-MAIL **lindajewell@hotmail.com** WEBSITE **www.lindajewellracing.co.uk**

1 BOYZEE, 5, b g Resplendent Glory (IRE)—Busy (IRE) **Miss V. Pratt**
2 BYRESTEADS FARM, 6, b m Beat All (USA)—Kinnahalla (IRE) **Mrs L. C. Jewell**
3 CLONUSKER (IRE), 5, b g Fasliyev (USA)—Tamburello (IRE) **Mrs L. C. Jewell**
4 FIFI L'AMOUR (IRE), 7, ch m Flemensfirth (USA)—Supreme Adventure (IRE) **P. A. Oppenheimer**
5 FLEETING INDIAN (IRE), 4, b g Sleeping Indian—Glebe Garden **Mr M. J. Boutcher**
6 INDISPENSABELLE, 4, b f Passing Glance—Belle Largesse **Mr R. Churcher**
7 ITOLDYOU (IRE), 7, ch g Salford Express (IRE)—Adisadel (IRE) **Mr G. Robinson**
8 KAYFLIN (FR), 5, b m Kayf Tara—Flinders **Leith Hill Chasers**
9 KINGSCOMBE (USA), 4, gr ro g Mizzen Mast (USA)—Gombeen (USA) **P. A. Oppenheimer**
10 RED ANCHOR (IRE), 9, ch g Snurge—Clonartic (IRE) **Mrs S. M. Stanier**
11 REDINGA, 7, ch m Karinga Bay—Medway Queen **Mrs S. M. Stanier**
12 ROE VALLEY (IRE), 6, ch g Arakan (USA)—Waaedah (USA) **R. B. Morton**
13 ROWE PARK, 10, b g Dancing Spree (USA)—Magic Legs **Mrs S. M. Ashdown**
14 SHE'S HUMBLE (IRE), 11, ch m Humbel (USA)—She's No Tourist (IRE) **Valence Racing Too**
15 SHE'S JOLLY (IRE), 8, b m Jolly Jake (NZ)—She's No Tourist (IRE) **Mrs R. V. Watson**
16 SPIRIT OF XAAR (IRE), 7, b g Xaar—Jet Cat (IRE) **K. Johnson, K. Jessup**
17 STRATEGIC ACTION (IRE), 4, ch g Strategic Prince—Ruby Cairo (IRE) **Mr M. J. Boutcher**

THREE-YEAR-OLDS

18 RUNNING BULL (IRE), b c Papal Bull—Miss Barbados (IRE) **Mr G. Robinson**

Other Owners: Mr K. P. Jessup, Mr K. W. Johnson, Mrs J. Maltby, Mr N. F. Maltby, Mrs A. May, R. I. B. Young.

Assistant Trainer: Karen Jewell

Jockey (flat): Steve Drowne. **Jockey (NH):** Richard Johnson, Jamie Moore, Andrew Thornton. **Amateur:** Mr T. Cheesman.

349 MR BRETT JOHNSON, Epsom
Postal: **The Durdans Stables, Chalk Lane, Epsom, Surrey, KT18 7AX**
Contacts: **MOBILE (07768) 697141**
E-MAIL **thedurdansstables@googlemail.com** WEBSITE **www.brjohnsonracing.co.uk**

1 ABIGAILS ANGEL, 6, br m Olden Times—Make Ready **B. R. Johnson**
2 CAYUGA, 4, b c Montjeu (IRE)—Ithaca (USA) **J. Daniels**
3 EAGLE NEBULA, 9, ch g Observatory (USA)—Tarocchi (USA) **Tann Racing**
4 KING'S COLOUR, 8, b g King's Best (USA)—Red Garland **Tann Racing**
5 MINORITY INTEREST, 4, ch g Galileo (IRE)—Minority **J. Daniels**
6 MUMBAI MILLIONAIRE (IRE), 4, ch c Indian Haven—Almaviva (IRE) **B. R. Johnson**
7 MY SCAT DADDY (USA), 4, b g Scat Daddy (USA)—Will Be A Bates (USA) **J. Daniels**
8 ONEIRIC, 5, gr m Act One—Ecstasy **Mr S. Sivagnanam**
9 TORRES DEL PAINE, 6, b h Compton Place—Noble Story **J. Daniels**
10 VALENTINO ROCKS, 4, b c Arkadian Hero (USA)—Orpen Annie (IRE) **Exors of the Late Mr G. W. Chambers**

THREE-YEAR-OLDS

11 BOBBY TWO SHOES, b g Byron—Taminoula (IRE) **Mrs A. M. Upsdell**
12 FIRMDECISIONS (IRE), b c Captain Rio—Luna Crescente (IRE) **White Bear Racing**
13 JUBILINI, ch f Bertolini (USA)—Days of Grace **Omni Colour Presentations & Lee Liddle**
14 XANDERS SECRET, br f Sakhee's Secret—Point Perfect **Tann Racing**

MR BRETT JOHNSON - Continued

Other Owners: Mr S. T. J. Broderick, Miss N. J. Hood, Mr L. Liddle, M. G. Mackenzie, Omni Colour Presentations Ltd, G. Tann, Mrs E. Tann.

Assistant Trainer: Vanessa Johnson

---

350 MISS EVE JOHNSON HOUGHTON, Blewbury
Postal: **Woodway, Blewbury, Didcot, Oxfordshire, OX11 9EZ**
Contacts: **PHONE (01235) 850480 (01235) 850500 (Home) FAX (01235) 851045**
MOBILE (07721) 622700
E-MAIL Eve@JohnsonHoughton.com WEBSITE www.JohnsonHoughton.com

1 **ARABIAN CORAL (IRE)**, 9, b m Intikhab (USA)—Tropical Dance (USA) **Exors of the Late Mr G. Ward**
2 **CATCHANOVA (IRE)**, 6, b g Catcher In The Rye (IRE)—Head For The Stars (IRE) **Miss E. A. Johnson Houghton**
3 **JUDD STREET**, 11, b g Compton Place—Pudding Lane (IRE) **R. F. Johnson Houghton**
4 **LUNAR DEITY**, 4, b g Medicean—Luminda (IRE) **Eden Racing (III) & P. A. Deal**
5 **ORDERS FROM ROME (IRE)**, 4, b g Holy Roman Emperor (IRE)—Fatat Alarab (USA) **G. C. Stevens**
6 **PHLUKE**, 12, b g Most Welcome—Phlirty **Mrs F. M. Johnson Houghton**
7 **RUN OF THE DAY**, 4, b f Three Valleys (USA)—Shall We Run **Mrs F. M. Johnson Houghton**
8 **THE CHEKA (IRE)**, 7, b g Xaar—Veiled Beauty (USA) **Anthony Pye-Jeary & Mel Smith**
9 **UNCLE ROGER (IRE)**, 4, b g Camacho—Felin Gruvy (IRE) **Mrs J. E. O'Halloran**
10 **YURITUNI**, 6, b m Bahamian Bounty—Vax Star **The Ascot Colts & Fillies Club**

THREE-YEAR-OLDS
11 **CARDMASTER (IRE)**, gr g Red Clubs (IRE)—El Morocco (USA) **H Marsh, C Crossley Cooke & R Maynard**
12 **CLEMENT (IRE)**, b c Clodovil (IRE)—Winnifred **Mrs F. M. Johnson Houghton**
13 **HAND GRENADE (IRE)**, b f Majestic Missile (IRE)—Felin Gruvy (IRE) **Mrs J. E. O'Halloran**
14 **KNIGHT CHARM**, b g Haafhd—Enchanted Princess **Fairweather Friends**
15 **PANTHER PATROL (IRE)**, b c Tagula (IRE)—Quivala (USA) **G. C. Stevens**
16 **PEACE TREATY**, b c Lucky Story (USA)—Peace Lily **Eden Racing Club**
17 **RECTORY LANE**, ch f Compton Place—Pudding Lane (IRE) **R. F. Johnson Houghton**
18 **ROCK GOD (IRE)**, br c Shirocco (GER)—Melatonina (IRE) **J. R. Wallis**
19 **ROYAL BARGE (IRE)**, b f Shirocco (GER)—Sahara Lady (IRE) **P. L. Winkworth**
20 **SPILLWAY**, b c Rail Link—Flower Market **Mrs V. D. Neale**
21 **STARLIGHT SYMPHONY (IRE)**, b f Oratorio (IRE)—Phillippa (IRE) **Brian & Liam McNamee, Les & Ian Dawson**
22 **TAGALAKA (IRE)**, b g Tagula (IRE)—Queeny's Princess (IRE) **Eden Racing IV**

TWO-YEAR-OLDS
23 **AJIG**, ch f 27/2 Bahamian Bounty—Atwirl (Pivotal) (9000) **Eden Racing Club**
24 **BOCCADOIR (FR)**, b c 1/3 Creachadoir (IRE)—
             Boccatenera (GER) (Artan (IRE)) (23000) **Anthony Pye-Jeary & Mel Smith**
25 **KAITAKI (GER)**, b c 27/3 Duke of Marmalade (IRE)—Kalahari Dancer (Dalakhani (IRE)) (19000) **Miss E. A. Johnson Houghton**
26 B c 11/3 Bahamian Bounty—Keritana (FR) (One Cool Cat (USA)) (14285)
27 B f 18/3 Kodiac—Marasem (Cadeaux Genereux) (12300) **Miss E. A. Johnson Houghton**
28 B c 8/4 High Chaparral (IRE)—Numbers Game (Rainbow Quest (USA)) (15000)
29 **PEACEMAKER (IRE)**, b f 17/4 High Chaparral (IRE)—
             Sauterne (Rainbow Quest (USA)) (8000) **Mr R L Maynard & Mr B McNamee**
30 **PERSIAN BOLT (USA)**, b f 15/4 U S Ranger (USA)—
             Silent Cat (USA) (Rahy (USA)) (53174) **B Larizadeh P Wollaston**
31 B c 4/3 Henrythenavigator (USA)—
             Princess Desire (IRE) (Danehill (USA)) (38095) **Anthony Pye-Jeary & Mel Smith**
32 **SATIN WATERS**, b f 21/2 Halling (USA)—Velvet Waters (Unfuwain (USA)) **Mr R. E. Crutchley**
33 **SPARKLING ICE (IRE)**, gr f 8/3 Verglas (IRE)—
             Sand Crystal (IRE) (Singspiel (IRE)) (8333) **Miss E. A. Johnson Houghton**
34 B f 30/3 Oratorio (IRE)—Starlit Sky (Galileo (IRE)) **Mrs H. B. Raw**

Other Owners: Mr C. K. Crossley Cooke, Mr L. W. Dawson, Mr I. W. Dawson, Mrs P. A. Deal, P. A. Deal, T. F. Harris, Mrs E. A. Harris, Mr B. Larizadeh, Mr P. H. Marsh, R. L. Maynard, B. P. McNamee, Mr L. P. McNamee, Mrs J. A. McWilliam, A. J. Pye-Jeary, M. K. Smith, Mr P. R. Wollaston.

Assistant Trainer: R. F. Johnson Houghton

351 MR ROBERT JOHNSON, Newcastle Upon Tyne
Postal: Johnson Racing Ltd, Grange Farm, Newburn, Newcastle Upon Tyne, NE15 8QA
Contacts: PHONE (01912) 674464 FAX (01912) 674464 MOBILE (07774) 131133
E-MAIL rwjohnsonracing@talktalk.net WEBSITE www.rwjohnsonracing.co.uk

1 ALMOND COURT (IRE), 10, ch m Accordion—Glencairn Fox (IRE) R. W. Johnson & A. V. W. Kidd
2 BALLYBANKS (IRE), 9, b g Exit To Nowhere (USA)—Incharder (IRE) Mrs A. E. Speke
3 BUNRATTY (IRE), 7, b g Rudimentary (USA)—Miss Huff N Puff (IRE) A. Slack & E. G. Tunstall
4 BYGONES FOR COINS (IRE), 5, ch m Danroad (USA)—Reservation (IRE) Do Well Racing
5 DOLLY ROYAL (IRE), 8, b m Val Royal (FR)—Roos Rose (IRE) Mr M. Saunders
6 I'LL BE GOOD, 4, b c Red Clubs (IRE)—Willisa Do Well Racing
7 LORD BRENDY, 5, gr g Portrait Gallery (IRE)—Hervey Bay T. L. A. Robson
8 MOHEEBB (IRE), 9, b g Machiavellian (USA)—Rockerlong Sterling Racing
9 NAPOLETANO (ITY), 7, b g Kyllachy—Nationality R. W. Johnson
10 SUNRISE DANCE, 4, ch f Monsieur Bond (IRE)—Wachiwi (IRE) Mr M. Saunders

Other Owners: Mr Graham D. Brown, Mr Robert Johnson, Mr B. Maxted, Mr Jim Mottram, Mr J. Simpson.

Jockey (NH): Kenny Johnson. Amateur: Mr P. Johnson, Mr T. Speke.

352 MRS SUSAN JOHNSON, Madley
Postal: Carwardine Farm, Madley, Hereford, HR2 9JQ
Contacts: PHONE (01981) 250214 FAX (01981) 251538

1 THE LAST BRIDGE, 6, b g Milan—Celtic Bridge I. K. Johnson

Jockey (NH): Richard Johnson.

353 MR MARK JOHNSTON, Middleham
Postal: Kingsley House Racing Stables, Middleham, Leyburn, North Yorkshire, DL8 4PH
Contacts: PHONE (01969) 622237 FAX (01969) 622484
E-MAIL mark@markjohnstonracing.com WEBSITE www.markjohnstonracing.com

1 ASSIZES, 4, b gr c Teofilo (IRE)—Requesting Sheikh Hamdan Bin Mohammed Al Maktoum
2 AUTHENTICATION, 4, b c Authorized (IRE)—Valley of Gold (FR) Sheikh Hamdan Bin Mohammed Al Maktoum
3 BOUNTY SEEKER (USA), 4, b g A P Indy (USA)—Plenty of Light (USA) A. D. Spence
4 BROXBOURNE (IRE), 4, b f Refuse To Bend (IRE)—Rafting (IRE) Ready To Run Partnership
5 BUTE HALL, 4, ch g Halling (USA)—Les Hurlants (IRE) Always Trying Partnership X
6 COPPERWOOD, 8, ch g Bahamian Bounty—Sophielu Ready To Run Partnership
7 DISCAY, 4, b g Distant Music (USA)—Caysue C. H. Greensit & W. A. Greensit
8 ES QUE LOVE (IRE), 4, br c Clodovil (IRE)—Es Que Crone Stud Farms Ltd
9 FENNELL BAY (IRE), 4, b g Dubawi (IRE)—Woodrising Sheikh Hamdan Bin Mohammed Al Maktoum
10 GALICIAN, 4, gr f Redoute's Choice (AUS)—Gweneira Sheikh Hamdan Bin Mohammed Al Maktoum
11 HAJRAS (IRE), 4, b g Dubai Destination (USA)—Nufoos Hamdan Al Maktoum
12 HURRICANE HIGGINS (IRE), 5, br g Hurricane Run (IRE)—Mare Aux Fees A. D. Spence
13 ITHOUGHTITWASOVER (IRE), 5, b h Hurricane Run (IRE)—Green Castle (IRE) Crone Stud Farms Ltd
14 LADY MACDUFF (IRE), 4, b f Iffraaj—Tamora Sheikh Hamdan Bin Mohammed Al Maktoum
15 LICENCE TO TILL (USA), 6, b g War Chant (USA)—With A Wink (USA) The Vine Accord
16 ORIENTAL FOX (GER), 5, ch g Lomitas—Oriental Pearl (GER) M. W. Graff
17 PARTY LINE, 4, b f Montjeu (IRE)—Party (IRE) S. R. Counsell
18 QUEEN'S ESTATE (GER), 4, b g Hurricane Run (IRE)—Questabelle Mr J. C. Daley
19 RED ORATOR, 4, ch g Osorio (GER)—Red Roses Story (FR) Newsells Park Stud Limited
20 SCATTER DICE (IRE), 4, ch f Manduro (GER)—Sensation Sheikh Hamdan Bin Mohammed Al Maktoum
21 SIR GRAHAM WADE (IRE), 4, gr c Dalakhani (IRE)—Needwood Epic P. Dean
22 STAR LAHIB (IRE), 4, b f Cape Cross (USA)—Cannikin (IRE) J. Abdullah
23 TARTAN JURA, 5, b g Green Desert (USA)—On A Soapbox (USA) Mr F. Bird
24 UNIVERSAL (IRE), 4, ch c Dubawi (IRE)—Winesong (IRE) Mr A. Al Mansoori
25 WILLPOWER (IRE), 4, b g Montjeu (IRE)—Noble Pearl (GER) A. D. Spence

THREE-YEAR-OLDS

26 ALTA LILEA (IRE), b f Galileo (IRE)—In My Life (IRE) Mrs S Bianco & Ms J Bianco
27 ALWAYS FABULOUS, b f Mount Nelson—Really Polish (USA) Always Trying Partnership IX
28 AMBLESIDE, b c Cape Cross (IRE)—Zarara (USA) Sheikh Hamdan Bin Mohammed Al Maktoum

MR MARK JOHNSTON - Continued

29 **ARYAL,** b c Singspiel (IRE)—Majoune (FR) **Sheikh Hamdan Bin Mohammed Al Maktoum**
30 **BAILEYS JUBILEE,** b f Bahamian Bounty—Missisipi Star (IRE) **G. R. Bailey Ltd**
31 **BELL'ARTE (IRE),** b f Zamindar (USA)—Art Eyes (USA) **Ms J. F. Bianco**
32 **BETZYOUCAN,** b f Royal Applause—Mint Royale (IRE) **D. C. Livingston**
33 **BIRDY BOY (USA),** ch g Elusive Quality (USA)—Flip Flop (FR) **Mr F. Bird**
34 **BLUE IS THE COLOUR (IRE),** b c Dalakhani (IRE)—Coyote **A. D. Spence**
35 **BLUE WAVE (IRE),** b c Raven's Pass (USA)—Million Waves (IRE) **Sheikh Hamdan Bin Mohammed Al Maktoum**
36 **BROUGHTON (GER),** b c Teofilo (IRE)—Boccassini (GER) **Sheikh Hamdan Bin Mohammed Al Maktoum**
37 B g Rob Roy (USA)—Caysue **C. H. Greensit**
38 **CHARM CRY (USA),** b f Street Cry (IRE)—Nasheej (USA) **Malih L. Al Basti**
39 **CONVERSING (USA),** ch c Raven's Pass (USA)—
                              Mini Chat (USA) **Sheikh Hamdan Bin Mohammed Al Maktoum**
40 **CORN SNOW (USA),** b c Raven's Pass (USA)—Zofzig (USA) **Sheikh Hamdan Bin Mohammed Al Maktoum**
41 **DAME NELLIE MELBA,** gr f Aussie Rules (USA)—Scandalette **Miss K. Rausing**
42 **DECLAMATION (IRE),** ch c Shamardal (USA)—Dignify (IRE) **Sheikh Hamdan Bin Mohammed Al Maktoum**
43 **DISCERNABLE,** ch f Elusive Quality (USA)—
                              Louve Mysterieuse (USA) **Sheikh Hamdan Bin Mohammed Al Maktoum**
44 **DORFMAN,** b g Halling (USA)—Cercle d'amour (USA) **Sheikh Hamdan Bin Mohammed Al Maktoum**
45 **DOUBLE YOUR MONEY (IRE),** b g Shamardal (USA)—Zeiting (IRE) **A. D. Spence**
46 **DREAMILY (IRE),** b br f New Approach (IRE)—Idilic Calm (IRE) **Sheikh Hamdan Bin Mohammed Al Maktoum**
47 **ENZAAL (USA),** b c Invasor (ARG)—Ekleel (IRE) **Hamdan Al Maktoum**
48 **FEDERAL BLUE (USA),** b c Elusive Quality (USA)—
                              Blue Duster (USA) **Sheikh Hamdan Bin Mohammed Al Maktoum**
49 **FLASHLIGHT (IRE),** b c Shamardal (USA)—Jazzy Jan (IRE) **Sheikh Hamdan Bin Mohammed Al Maktoum**
50 **FRASERBURGH (IRE),** b g Shamardal (USA)—Nova Cyngi (USA) **Sheikh Hamdan Bin Mohammed Al Maktoum**
51 **GREELEYS LOVE (USA),** ch c Mr Greeley (USA)—Aunt Winnie (IRE) **Crone Stud Farms Ltd**
52 **GREY BLUE (IRE),** gr g Verglas (IRE)—Zut Alors (IRE) **A. D. Spence**
53 **HAMLA,** b f Cape Cross (IRE)—High Days (IRE) **Sheikh Hamdan Bin Mohammed Al Maktoum**
54 **HAVERSTOCK,** b g New Approach (IRE)—Endorsement **Sheikh Hamdan Bin Mohammed Al Maktoum**
55 **HEAVY METAL,** b c Exceed And Excel (AUS)—Rock Opera (SAF) **Sheikh Hamdan Bin Mohammed Al Maktoum**
56 **HENRY THE AVIATOR (USA),** b c Henrythenavigator (USA)—Fashion Star (USA) **Crone Stud Farms Ltd**
57 **HOUSE OF ORANGE (IRE),** b g Kheleyf (USA)—
                              Cox Orange (IRE) **Sheikh Hamdan Bin Mohammed Al Maktoum**
58 **HUNTING RIGHTS (USA),** ch g E Dubai (USA)—
                              Possession (USA) **Sheikh Hamdan Bin Mohammed Al Maktoum**
59 **IRISH DREAM (IRE),** b br f Oasis Dream—Royal Blue **Mr T. J. Monaghan**
60 **IZZY BOY (USA),** b g Elusive Quality (USA)—Michele Royale (USA) **Mr F. Bird**
61 **KING OF THE DANES,** b c Dansili—Our Queen of Kings **Newsells Park Stud Limited**
62 **LEVEL BEST,** b g Oasis Dream—Utmost (IRE) **Sheikh Hamdan Bin Mohammed Al Maktoum**
63 **LIGHT ROSE (IRE),** b f Cape Cross (IRE)—Laureldean Lady (IRE) **J. Abdullah**
64 **LIMIT UP,** b g Shamardal (USA)—Love Me Tender **Sheikh Hamdan Bin Mohammed Al Maktoum**
65 **LOVE MARMALADE (IRE),** ch c Duke of Marmalade (IRE)—Green Castle (IRE) **Crone Stud Farms Ltd**
66 **MAPUTO,** b c Cape Cross (IRE)—Insijaam (USA) **Sheikh Hamdan Bin Mohammed Al Maktoum**
67 **MARSHLAND,** b g Kheleyf (USA)—Neptune's Bride (USA) **Sheikh Hamdan Bin Mohammed Al Maktoum**
68 **MIRTH,** ch f Teofilo (IRE)—Birthstone **Sheikh Hamdan Bin Mohammed Al Maktoum**
69 **MISTER IMPATIENCE,** b c Hernando (FR)—Katy Nowaitee **The Originals**
70 **MOANING BUTCHER,** b c Lucarno (USA)—Musical Chimes **J. Jones Racing Ltd**
71 **MOJAVE DESERT (IRE),** b f Shamardal (USA)—Innclassic (USA) **Sheikh Hamdan Bin Mohammed Al Maktoum**
72 **MOSCOW CIRCUS (IRE),** b c Hurricane Run (IRE)—Zalama (FR) **Christopher Wright & Miss Emily Asprey**
73 **MUDAAWEM (USA),** ch g Exchange Rate (USA)—Raajiya (USA) **Ready To Run Partnership**
74 **MUSHAAKIS (IRE),** b c Shamardal (USA)—Shamayel **Hamdan Al Maktoum**
75 **NELLIE BLY,** b f Exceed And Excel (AUS)—La Presse (USA) **Sheikh Hamdan Bin Mohammed Al Maktoum**
76 **OFCOURSEWECAN (USA),** b c Elusive Quality (USA)—Valid Warning (USA) **D. C. Livingston**
77 **OMOTESANDO,** b g Street Cry (IRE)—Punctilious **Sheikh Hamdan Bin Mohammed Al Maktoum**
78 **OPEN LETTER (IRE),** b f New Approach (IRE)—Deveron (USA) **Sheikh Hamdan Bin Mohammed Al Maktoum**
79 **OPT OUT,** ch g Pivotal—Easy Option (IRE) **Sheikh Hamdan Bin Mohammed Al Maktoum**
80 **OUTSET (USA),** ch c Street Boss (USA)—Now It Begins (USA) **Sheikh Hamdan Bin Mohammed Al Maktoum**
81 **PARTY ROYAL,** b c Royal Applause—Voliere **D & G Mercer 1**
82 **PENNY ROSE,** b f Danehill Dancer (IRE)—Love Everlasting **Greenland Park Stud**
83 **POLISH CROWN,** b f Royal Applause—Czarna Roza **Sheikh Hamdan Bin Mohammed Al Maktoum**
84 **PURE EXCELLENCE,** b f Exceed And Excel (AUS)—Albavilla **Excellence Racing**
85 **RAVEN'S TOWER (USA),** b c Raven's Pass (USA)—
                              Tizdubai (USA) **Sheikh Hamdan Bin Mohammed Al Maktoum**
86 **REGGAE STAR,** b f Cape Cross (IRE)—Caribbean Dancer (USA) **Mr H. C. Hart**
87 **ROSE RANSOM (IRE),** b f Oasis Dream—Rapid Ransom (USA)

MR MARK JOHNSTON - Continued

88 **ROYAL SKIES (IRE)**, b c Dubawi (IRE)—Kalana (FR) **Sheikh Hamdan Bin Mohammed Al Maktoum**
89 **SALUTATION (IRE)**, b g Iffraaj—Totally Yours (IRE) **Sheikh Hamdan Bin Mohammed Al Maktoum**
90 **SANDY'S ROW (IRE)**, b f Street Cry (IRE)—
Carry On Katie (USA) **Sheikh Hamdan Bin Mohammed Al Maktoum**
91 **SCEPTICISM (USA)**, b g Elusive Quality (USA)—
Never Is a Promise (USA) **Sheikh Hamdan Bin Mohammed Al Maktoum**
92 **SENNOCKIAN STAR**, ch g Rock of Gibraltar (IRE)—Chorist **The Vine Accord**
93 **SHABABEEK (IRE)**, b c Shirocco (GER)—Tanaghum **Hamdan Al Maktoum**
94 **SHAGWA (IRE)**, b f Clodovil (IRE)—Hedera (USA) **Mr A. Jaber**
95 **SKYTRAIN**, ch g Exceed And Excel (AUS)—Viola da Braccio (IRE) **A. D. Spence**
96 **SPECIAL MEANING**, b f Mount Nelson—Specifically (USA) **Newsells Park Stud Limited**
97 **STAFFHOSS**, b c Lucky Story (USA)—Jerre Jo Glanville (USA) **Emjayaarrghh Syndicate**
98 **STEER BY THE STARS (IRE)**, b f Pivotal—Mundus Novus (USA) **Capt Alasdair & Mrs Eliza Ross**
99 **STORM MOON (USA)**, b g Invincible Spirit (IRE)—
Storm Lily (USA) **Sheikh Hamdan Bin Mohammed Al Maktoum**
100 **STREET ARTIST (IRE)**, ch c Street Cry (IRE)—Portrayal (USA) **Sheikh Hamdan Bin Mohammed Al Maktoum**
101 **STRICTLY BALLROOM (IRE)**, b f Choisir (AUS)—Desert Alchemy (IRE) **Mr Gerry Ryan**
102 **SUCCESSFUL YEAR**, b c Distorted Humor (USA)—
Emotion Parade (ARG) **Sheikh Hamdan Bin Mohammed Al Maktoum**
103 **SUPEROO (IRE)**, ch g Bahamian Bounty—Roo **M. J. Pilkington**
104 **TALLAAY (IRE)**, b c Cape Cross (IRE)—Ghizlaan (USA) **Hamdan Al Maktoum**
105 **THOROUGHFARE (IRE)**, b c Teofilo (IRE)—Passageway (USA) **Sheikh Hamdan Bin Mohammed Al Maktoum**
106 **TORNADO BATTLE**, b c War Chant (USA)—Child Bride (USA) **J. Abdullah**
107 **TRAIN HARD**, b g Rail Link—Melpomene **Mrs C. E. Budden**
108 **TRIBAL PATH (IRE)**, b c Giant's Causeway (USA)—Navajo Moon (IRE) **Racegoers Club Owners Group**
109 **TUSSIE MUSSIE**, b f Royal Applause—Loveleaves **Inner Circle Thoroughbreds - Carpe Diem**
110 **UPPER ECHELON**, ch f Danehill Dancer (IRE)—Lady High Havens (USA) **Mr N N Browne & Mr S Richards**
111 **WADACRE SARKO**, b c Oratorio (IRE)—Saxon Maid **Tom Heywood & Jeanette Matthew-Griffiths**
112 **WELLINGROVE (IRE)**, b g Cape Cross (IRE)—Isla Azul (IRE) **Sheikh Hamdan Bin Mohammed Al Maktoum**
113 **WINDHOEK**, b c Cape Cross (IRE)—Kahlua Kiss **Sheikh Hamdan Bin Mohammed Al Maktoum**
114 **WORLD MAP (IRE)**, b f Pivotal—Danse Arabe (IRE) **Sheikh Hamdan Bin Mohammed Al Maktoum**
115 B g Josr Algarhoud (IRE)—Young Sue **C. H. Greensit**

TWO-YEAR-OLDS

116 Ch c 19/3 Shamardal (USA)—
Adonesque (IRE) (Sadler's Wells (USA)) **Sheikh Hamdan Bin Mohammed Al Maktoum**
117 Gr f 6/3 Clodovil (IRE)—Adultress (IRE) (Ela-Mana-Mou) (8333) **Atlantic Racing Limited**
118 **ALEX MY BOY (IRE)**, b c 2/2 Dalakhani (IRE)—Alexandrova (IRE) (Sadler's Wells (USA)) (59523) **J. Abdullah**
119 B c 26/3 Invincible Spirit (IRE)—Alizes (NZ) (Rory's Jester (AUS)) **Sheikh Hamdan Bin Mohammed Al Maktoum**
120 B c 10/3 Cape Cross (IRE)—Amenixa (FR) (Linamix (FR)) (70000) **Sheikh Hamdan Bin Mohammed Al Maktoum**
121 B c 21/2 Tamayuz—Anne Tudor (IRE) (Anabaa (USA)) (23809) **Mr A. Al Mansoori**
122 **ARABDA**, b br f 19/3 Elnadim (USA)—Ghizlaan (USA) (Seeking The Gold (USA)) **Hamdan Al Maktoum**
123 B c 4/4 Shamardal (USA)—Arctic Air (Polar Falcon (USA)) (75000) **Mark Johnston Racing Ltd**
124 **ATHEERA (IRE)**, ch f 8/5 Shamardal (USA)—Alshamatry (USA) (Seeking The Gold (USA)) **Hamdan Al Maktoum**
125 B c 27/4 Shamardal (USA)—
Beneventa (Most Welcome) (130000) **Sheikh Hamdan Bin Mohammed Al Maktoum**
126 B c 6/5 Stormy Atlantic (USA)—Bluemamba (USA) (Kingmambo (USA)) (49155) **R. S. Brookhouse**
127 B f 24/2 Three Valleys (USA)—Boa Estrela (IRE) (Intikhab (USA)) (20000) **Mark Johnston Racing Ltd**
128 **BROWNSVILLE (USA)**, b c 10/2 Bernstein (USA)—
Net Worth (USA) (Forty Niner (USA)) (30721) **Sheikh Majid Bin Mohammed Al Maktoum**
129 **BY THE LIGHT (IRE)**, gr c 19/2 Verglas (IRE)—Margarita (IRE) (Marju (IRE)) **Elite Racing Club**
130 B c 10/2 Pivotal—Calista (Caerleon (USA)) **Sheikh Hamdan Bin Mohammed Al Maktoum**
131 B c 14/3 Authorized (IRE)—Caribbean Dancer (USA) (Theatrical) **Mr H. C. Hart**
132 B f 16/2 Cape Cross (IRE)—Charita (IRE) (Lycius (USA)) (95238) **Sheikh Hamdan Bin Mohammed Al Maktoum**
133 B c 8/2 Dubawi (IRE)—Come What May (Selkirk (USA)) **Sheikh Hamdan Bin Mohammed Al Maktoum**
134 Ch c 4/4 Tamayuz—Cradle Brief (IRE) (Brief Truce (USA)) (27777) **Mr A. Al Mansoori**
135 B c 15/4 Exceed And Excel (AUS)—Crossover (Cape Cross (IRE)) **Sheikh Hamdan Bin Mohammed Al Maktoum**
136 B f 22/2 Selkirk (USA)—Crystany (IRE) (Green Desert (USA)) (32000) **Haras d'Etreham**
137 **DAMAAH (USA)**, b f 27/3 Lemon Drop Kid (USA)—Ekleel (IRE) (Danehill (USA)) **Hamdan Al Maktoum**
138 B c 3/5 Azamour (IRE)—Damask Rose (IRE) (Dr Devious (IRE)) (6348) **R. W. Huggins**
139 B c 4/4 Authorized (IRE)—Debonnaire (Anabaa (USA)) (45000) **Sheikh Hamdan Bin Mohammed Al Maktoum**
140 Br c 28/4 Shamardal (USA)—Desertion (IRE) (Danehill (USA)) (13888) **The New Fairyhouse Partnership**
141 B c 11/2 Shamardal (USA)—Designed (Zaminder (USA)) **Sheikh Hamdan Bin Mohammed Al Maktoum**
142 B c 8/3 Tiznow (USA)—Dianehill (IRE) (Danehill (USA)) (92165) **Crone Stud Farms Ltd**
143 **DRIPPING (FR)**, b f 23/2 Dubawi (IRE)—Brianza (USA) (Thunder Gulch (USA)) (25396) **J. Abdullah**

MR MARK JOHNSTON - Continued

144 Ch c 19/2 Mount Nelson—Dusty Moon (Dr Fong (USA)) (28000) **Newsells Park Stud Limited**
145 B c 27/3 Dubawi (IRE)—Easy To Love (USA) (Diesis) (40000) **Sheikh Hamdan Bin Mohammed Al Maktoum**
146 **EMAAD (USA)**, b c 4/4 Arch (USA)—Red Dot (USA) (Diesis) (73732) **Hamdan Al Maktoum**
147 Ch f 25/3 Halling (USA)—Embassy (Cadeaux Genereux) **Sheikh Hamdan Bin Mohammed Al Maktoum**
148 Ch c 11/4 Shamardal (USA)—Ever Love (BRZ) (Nedawi) **Sheikh Hamdan Bin Mohammed Al Maktoum**
149 B c 20/4 Sea The Stars (IRE)—Exciting Times (FR) (Jeune Homme (USA)) **R. S. Brookhouse**
150 Ch f 24/2 Tamayuz—Fearn Royal (IRE) (Ali-Royal (IRE)) (11904) **The New Fairyhouse Partnership**
151 **FIRE FIGHTING (IRE)**, b c 21/2 Soldier of Fortune (IRE)—Savoie (Anabaa (USA)) (55555) **A. D. Spence**
152 B c 16/5 Shamardal (USA)—Flamelet (USA) (Theatrical) **Sheikh Hamdan Bin Mohammed Al Maktoum**
153 B f 16/5 High Chaparral (IRE)—Fortunately (Forzando) (15000) **Mr Gerry Ryan**
154 B f 19/4 Acclamation—Fritta Mista (IRE) (Linamix (FR)) (8000) **Mark Johnston Racing Ltd**
155 B c 12/2 Mount Nelson—Glen Rosie (IRE) (Mujtahid (USA)) (20000) **Newsells Park Stud Limited**
156 Ch c 5/3 New Approach (IRE)—
                   Hallowed Park (IRE) (Barathea (IRE)) **Sheikh Hamdan Bin Mohammed Al Maktoum**
157 **HASTA LA VISTA**, b f 12/3 Hernando (FR)—Sterling Sound (USA) (Street Cry (IRE)) **Miss K. Rausing**
158 B c 13/4 Mount Nelson—Helter Helter (USA) (Seeking The Gold (USA)) (3000) **The New Fairyhouse Partnership**
159 **IBECKE**, b f 21/4 Exceed And Excel (AUS)—Granted (FR) (Cadeaux Genereux) (60000) **J. Abdullah**
160 **IFWECAN**, b c 17/4 Exceed And Excel (AUS)—Kirk (Selkirk (USA)) (32000) **D. C. Livingston**
161 B c 27/4 Shamardal (USA)—Ile Rousse (Danehill (USA)) (43650) **Mr A. Al Mansoori**
162 **INSAANY**, b c 22/4 Shamardal (USA)—
                   Mother of Pearl (IRE) (Sadler's Wells (USA)) (65000) **Hamdan Al Maktoum**
163 B c 14/5 Bahamian Bounty—Intellibet One (Compton Place) **Mark Johnston Racing Ltd**
164 B f 26/2 Mastercraftsman (IRE)—
                   Isle of Flame (Shirley Heights) (5500) **Mr S Richards, Mr N Browne, Mrs R Frossell**
165 B c 6/4 Halling (USA)—Jomana (IRE) (Darshaan) **Sheikh Hamdan Bin Mohammed Al Maktoum**
166 B c 4/4 Cape Cross (IRE)—
                   Just Special (Cadeaux Genereux) (120000) **Sheikh Hamdan Bin Mohammed Al Maktoum**
167 Ch f 8/5 Mount Nelson—Key Academy (Royal Academy (USA)) (11904) **Mark Johnston Racing Ltd**
168 B f 23/4 Shamardal (USA)—Kindling (Dr Fong (USA)) (25000) **Mark Johnston Racing Ltd**
169 B f 4/3 Exceed And Excel (AUS)—Lady Catherine (Bering) **Sheikh Hamdan Bin Mohammed Al Maktoum**
170 **LAMORAK (FR)**, b c 16/3 King's Best (USA)—
                   Indian Jewel (GER) (Local Suitor (USA)) (20634) **Mr A. Al Mansoori**
171 **LAWMAN'S LADY (IRE)**, b f 8/1 Lawman (FR)—Hasanat (Night Shift (USA)) (14285) **J. Abdullah**
172 **LEADERENE**, b f 16/4 Selkirk (USA)—La Felicita (Shareef Dancer (USA)) **Miss K. Rausing**
173 Ch f 19/4 Tamayuz—Livius Lady (IRE) (Titus Livius (FR)) (15000) **Mr T. J. Monaghan**
174 B c 1/3 Art Connoisseur (IRE)—Luck Will Come (IRE) (Desert Style (IRE)) **Steven Gay**
175 **LYN VALLEY**, b c 28/1 Shamardal (USA)—Demisemiquaver (Singspiel (IRE)) (42000) **Mr J. A. Barson**
176 B c 19/5 Cape Cross (IRE)—
                   Ma Paloma (FR) (Highest Honor (FR)) (95238) **Sheikh Hamdan Bin Mohammed Al Maktoum**
177 **MAMBO RHYTHM**, b f 28/2 Authorized (IRE)—
                   Mambo Halo (USA) (Southern Halo (USA)) (10000) **Around The World Partnership**
178 **MASTER OF FINANCE (IRE)**, ch c 13/3 Mastercraftsman (IRE)—
                   Cheal Rose (IRE) (Dr Devious (IRE)) (30000) **Mr J David Abell & Mr Markus Graff**
179 **MAXIE T**, b c 16/2 Dalakhani (IRE)—Ballet Ballon (USA) (Rahy (USA)) (25000) **Mr C. Johnston**
180 Ch f 8/4 Shamardal (USA)—Meiosis (USA) (Danzig (USA)) **Sheikh Hamdan Bin Mohammed Al Maktoum**
181 B f 19/3 Rail Link—Melpomene (Peintre Celebre (USA)) **Martin Budden**
182 **MOONSTEP**, ch f 16/3 Halling (USA)—Step This Way (USA) (Giant's Causeway (USA)) (15238) **S. R. Counsell**
183 **MUKHTAZEL (IRE)**, ch c 4/5 Nayef (USA)—Tomoohat (USA) (Danzig (USA)) **Hamdan Al Maktoum**
184 **MUSIC STOP**, b f 21/2 Iffraaj—Tan Tan (King's Best (USA)) (6348) **J. Abdullah**
185 **MUTALABA**, b f 26/1 Aqlaam—Zaaqya (Nayef (USA)) **Hamdan Al Maktoum**
186 **MUTEELA**, b f 19/2 Dansili—Nufoos (Zafonic (USA)) **Hamdan Al Maktoum**
187 B f 26/2 Aussie Rules (USA)—Naomh Geileis (USA) (Grand Slam (USA)) **Martin Budden**
188 **NOVAYA GAZETA**, b f 8/3 Archipenko (USA)—Nadeszhda (Nashwan (USA)) **Miss K. Rausing**
189 Br f 20/4 Footstepsinthesand—Palm Cove (UAE) (Jade Robbery (USA)) (4761) **Mark Johnston Racing Ltd**
190 B f 24/4 Cape Cross (IRE)—Persian Belle (Machiavellian (USA)) (55555) **Sheikh M. B. M. Al Maktoum**
191 **PIGEON PIE**, b f 12/3 Bahamian Bounty—Pixie Ring (Pivotal) **Hot To Trot Racing Club**
192 Ch c 1/3 Shirocco (GER)—Pivotal Drive (IRE) (Pivotal) (40000) **Sheikh Majid Bin Mohammed Al Maktoum**
193 B c 3/4 Cape Cross (IRE)—
                   Questina (FR) (Rainbow Quest (USA)) (34000) **Sheikh Hamdan Bin Mohammed Al Maktoum**
194 **RAINBOW'S END (IRE)**, gr c 10/3 Verglas (USA)—
                   Rainbows For All (IRE) (Rainbows For Life (CAN)) (18095) **Mr Isaac Katz & Mrs Margaret Katz**
195 Ch c 30/1 Shamardal (USA)—
                   Riotous Applause (Royal Applause) (115000) **Sheikh Hamdan Bin Mohammed Al Maktoum**
196 B c 5/3 Archipenko (USA)—Scandalette (Niniski (USA)) (9000) **T T Bloodstocks**

MR MARK JOHNSTON - Continued

197 B c 13/3 Shamardal (USA)—
　　　　Seamstress (IRE) (Barathea (IRE)) (30158) **Sheikh Hamdan Bin Mohammed Al Maktoum**
198 B c 6/2 Cape Cross (IRE)—
　　　　Shell Garland (USA) (Sadler's Wells (USA)) (52000) **Sheikh Hamdan Bin Mohammed Al Maktoum**
199 B c 5/5 Shamardal (USA)—Shersha (IRE) (Priolo (USA)) (60000) **Sheikh Hamdan Bin Mohammed Al Maktoum**
200 Ch f 25/4 Captain Rio—Silver Whale (FR) (Highest Honor (FR)) (7142) **The New Fairyhouse Partnership**
201 B f 24/3 Duke of Marmalade (IRE)—Sina Cova (IRE) (Barathea (IRE)) (17460) **Mr Gerry Ryan**
202 SIR CHARLIE KUNZ, ch gr c 8/4 Dalakhani (IRE)—Darrfonah (Singspiel (IRE)) (47000) **P. Dean**
203 SIR GUY PORTEOUS (IRE), ch c 2/2 Shamardal (USA)—Ermine And Velvet (Nayef (USA)) (67000) **P. Dean**
204 SIR PAUL DEAN, b c 25/2 Byron—
　　　　Hunter's Fortune (USA) (Charismatic (USA)) (8000) **Mark Johnston Racing Ltd**
205 B c 2/2 Shamardal (USA)—Solva (Singspiel (IRE)) (130000) **Sheikh Hamdan Bin Mohammed Al Maktoum**
206 B c 27/3 Dynaformer (USA)—
　　　　Sometime (IRE) (Royal Academy (USA)) **Sheikh Majid Bin Mohammed Al Maktoum**
207 B f 5/4 Royal Applause—Southern Psychic (USA) (Alwasmi (USA)) (30000) **G. R. Bailey Ltd**
208 B c 4/4 Art Connoisseur (IRE)—Suzi Spends (IRE) (Royal Applause) **Steven Gay**
209 TANSEEB, b c 4/2 Royal Applause—Perfect Story (IRE) (Desert Story (IRE)) (90000) **Hamdan Al Maktoum**
210 Ro f 23/3 New Approach (IRE)—Testama (IRE) (Testa Rossa (AUS)) (51587) **A. D. Spence**
211 B f 25/4 Aqlaam—Third Party (Terimon) **G. R. Bailey Ltd**
212 B c 28/3 Shamardal (USA)—
　　　　Three Wrens (IRE) (Second Empire (IRE)) **Sheikh Hamdan Bin Mohammed Al Maktoum**
213 TORNADO CHALLENGE (USA), b c 30/4 War Chant (USA)—Princess Kris (Kris) (28571) **J. Abdullah**
214 B c 2/3 Montjeu (IRE)—Viking's Cove (USA) (Miswaki (USA)) (75396) **A. D. Spence**
215 VINE DE NADA, b c 25/3 Bahamian Bounty—Hip (Pivotal) (13000) **Inner Circle Thoroughbreds - New World**
216 WATERSMEET, gr c 6/2 Dansili—Under The Rainbow (Fantastic Light (USA)) (75000) **Mr J. A. Barson**
217 B c 9/2 Raven's Pass (USA)—
　　　　Zacheta (Polish Precedent (USA)) (80000) **Sheikh Hamdan Bin Mohammed Al Maktoum**
218 B f 24/1 Bernardini (USA)—Zanoubia (USA) (Our Emblem (USA)) **N. Mourad**
219 B c 16/4 Hernando (FR)—Zooming (IRE) (Indian Ridge) (9523) **Mark Johnston Racing Ltd**

Other Owners: J. D. Abell, Miss E. Asprey, Mr A. J. Bell, Mr B. Bennett, Mrs S. Bianco, E. Brierley, N. N. Browne, M. Budden, M. Budden, Mr A. J. Burke, Mrs S. P. B. Frosell, A. Greenhalgh, W. A. Greensit, Mr I. Harland, A. J. Hill, Mr R. B. Huckerby, Inner Circle Thoroughbreds Limited, Mrs D. Johnston, Mr I. Katz, Mrs M. J. Katz, J. R. Kennedy, Exors of the Late Mrs Y. J. Kennedy, Mrs J. E. Knight, Mr A. A. Larnach, Mr R. M. Lightbody, M. W. Lightbody, Mrs J. G. Lightbody, Mr M. R. Lonsdorfer, Mr J. C. McGrath, Mr D. C. Mercer, G. Mercer, Miss M. Noden, Mr C. Norton, Mr S. J. Richards, Capt A. Ross, Mrs E. M. Y. Ross, C. Wachter, J. Wachter, D. F. White, C. N. Wright.

Assistant Trainers: Deirdre Johnston & Jock Bennett

Jockey (flat): Silvestre De Sousa, Joe Fanning.

---

354 MR ALAN JONES, Minehead
Postal: **East Harwood Farm, Timberscombe, Minehead, Somerset, TA24 7UE**
Contacts: **FAX 01633 680232 MOBILE (07901) 505064**
E-MAIL **heritageracing@btconnect.com** WEBSITE **www.alanjonesracing.co.uk**

1 ASK SCOTTY, 10, b g Kayf Tara—Minnie Bloo Min (IRE) **Mr T. S. M. S. Riley-Smith**
2 BOBBITS WAY, 8, b g Overbury (IRE)—Bit of A Chick **Mr S. H. Spence**
3 BULL MARKET, 10, b bl g Danehill (USA)—Paper Moon (IRE) **Mr S. H. Spence**
4 EMERALD GLADE (IRE), 6, b m Azamour (IRE)—Woodland Glade **Mr J. E. Parsons**
5 FANJOS LUCK (IRE), 6, b g Oscar (IRE)—Dr Bernish Lass (IRE) **Mrs B. Blair**
6 HIDDENSEE (USA), 11, b g Cozzene (USA)—Zarani Sidi Anna (USA) **Mr T. S. M. S. Riley-Smith**
7 HUMBEL BEN (IRE), 10, br g Humbel (USA)—Donegans Daughter **Mr S. H. Spence**
8 KORALSDARLING (IRE), 9, b g Witness Box (USA)—Jenny's Jewel (IRE) **Mr S. H. Spence**
9 LETS GET CRACKING (FR), 9, b g Anabaa Blue—Queenhood (FR) **Mr T. S. M. S. Riley-Smith**
10 NORISAN, 9, ch g Inchinor—Dream On Deya (IRE) **Mr S. H. Spence**
11 QUINCY DES PICTONS (FR), 9, b g Kadalko (FR)—Izabel des Pictons (FR) **Mr S. H. Spence**
12 REST AND BE (IRE), 6, b br m Vinnie Roe (IRE)—Bobs Star (IRE) **Mr S. H. Spence**
13 SECRET DANCER (IRE), 8, b g Sadler's Wells (USA)—Discreet Brief (IRE) **Mr S. H. Spence**
14 TIQUER (FR), 5, b g Equerry (USA)—Tirenna (FR) **Mr S. H. Spence**

Assistant Trainer: Miss A. Bartelink

Jockey (NH): Christian Williams, Richard Johnson, Paddy Brennan, Tom O' Brien. **Amateur:** Mr O. Greenall.

355 **MR GEORGE JONES, Tenbury Wells**
Postal: **13 Market Square, Tenbury Wells, Worcestershire, WR15 8BL**

1 ALMOWJ, 10, b g Fasliyev (USA)—Tiriana **Mrs A. M. McCartney**
2 MI MAN SAM (IRE), 8, ch g Exit To Nowhere (USA)—Brinawa (IRE) **Tom Mulkeen, Mick Mifflin & George Jones**
Other Owners: G. H. Jones, T. M. Mifflin, Mr T. G. Mulkeen.

356 **MS LUCY JONES, Kilgetty**
Postal: **2 South Row, Cresselly, Kilgetty, Pembrokeshire, SA68 0SR**

1 CALL ME FRANKIE (IRE), 7, b g Indian Danehill (IRE)—Violets Wild (IRE) **S. Jones**
2 GENTLEMAN JEFF (IRE), 9, ch g Mr Greeley (USA)—Wooing (USA) **Mr H. D. R. Harrison-Allen**
3 GENUINE ART, 6, b m Generosity—Impulsive Bid (IRE) **Mr A. A. Palmer**
4 LADY KARINGA, 8, ch m Karinga Bay—Tachometer (IRE) **Terry Harman & Jan Johnson**
5 RAVING RENEE, 5, b m Overbury (IRE)—Chartridge Hill **S. Jones**
6 SHANKS A LOT, 6, b g Beat All (USA)—Florida Fact **BW & RE Mansell**
7 5, B g Overbury (IRE)—Tachometer (IRE)
8 THISTLE STIKK, 6, b g Selkirk (USA)—Tamso (USA) **Palms Landscaping Limited**
Other Owners: Mr T. A. Harman, Mrs J. M. Johnson, Mrs R. E. Mansell, Mr B. W. Mansell.

357 **MRS VIOLET M. JORDAN, Moreton Morrell**
Postal: **Far Westfields Farm, Moreton Morrell, Warwick, Warwickshire, CV35 9DB**
Contacts: **MOBILE (07831) 101632**
E-MAIL jordyracer29@hotmail.co.uk

1 AL KHAN (IRE), 4, b g Elnadim (USA)—Popolo (IRE) **Rakebackmypoker.com**
2 ALACCORDION, 8, br g Alflora (IRE)—Song For Jess (IRE) **Farmers & Cricketers Partnership**
3 ALDERLEY STAR (IRE), 8, b g Alderbrook—Cherry Avenue **Mrs Violet M. Jordan**
4 ALL THE FASHION (IRE), 9, br m Alflora (IRE)—Fashion Day **Mrs Violet M. Jordan**
5 AMBA, 7, ch m Hold That Tiger (USA)—Gal Gloria (PR) **Mrs J. A. Cornwell**
6 AMENABLE (IRE), 6, b g Bertolini (USA)—Graceful Air (IRE) **Rakebackmypoker.com**
7 BAZRON (IRE), 5, b m Byron—Bazelle **Mrs J. A. Cornwell**
8 BROWN PETE (IRE), 5, b br g Aussie Rules (USA)—Banba (IRE) **Rakebackmypoker.com**
9 CHAPELLERIE (IRE), 4, b f Acclamation—Castellane (FR) **Rakebackmypoker.com**
10 CLOUDY START, 7, b g Oasis Dream—Set Fair (USA) **A. Cocum**
11 CONCORDIA NOTTE (IRE), 4, b f Elusive City (USA)—Laylati (IRE) **Rakebackmypoker.com**
12 CUT THE CACKLE (IRE), 7, b m Danetime (IRE)—Alexander Anapolis (IRE) **Rakebackmypoker.com**
13 DANCING FREDDY (IRE), 6, b g Chineur (FR)—Majesty's Dancer (IRE) **Rakebackmypoker.com**
14 DANIEL THOMAS (IRE), 11, b g Dansili—Last Look **Rakebackmypoker.com**
15 DECENT FELLA (IRE), 7, b g Marju (IRE)—Mac Melody (IRE) **Rakebackmypoker.com**
16 EMERALD GIRL (IRE), 6, b m Chineur (FR)—Faypool (IRE) **Rakebackmypoker.com**
17 FAIRY WING (IRE), 6, b g Hawk Wing (USA)—Mintaka (IRE) **Rakebackmypoker.com**
18 FORMEDABLE (IRE), 11, ch g Moonax (USA)—Castle Flame (IRE) **Farmers & Cricketers Partnership**
19 FROGNAL (IRE), 7, b g Kheleyf (USA)—Shannon Dore (USA) **Rakebackmypoker.com**
20 HARTING HILL, 8, b g Mujahid (USA)—Mossy Rose **Farmers & Cricketers Partnership**
21 HIDDEN FOX, 5, ch g Kadastrof (FR)—Hidden Smile (USA) **Mr T. Powell**
22 JERRY LEE (IRE), 10, b g Orpen (USA)—Vinicky (USA) **Mrs Violet M. Jordan**
23 JOYOUSLY, 5, ch m Needwood Blade—Lambadora **Rakebackmypoker.com**
24 LITTLE CARMELA, 9, gr m Beat Hollow—Carmela Owen **Near & Far Racing**
25 LORD GOLAN, 5, b g Singspiel (IRE)—Lady Golan (IRE) **Mrs J. A. Cornwell**
26 MAJURO (IRE), 9, b g Danetime (IRE)—First Fling (IRE) **Rakebackmypoker.com**
27 MCCONNELL (USA), 8, ch g Petionville (USA)—Warsaw Girl (IRE) **Rakebackmypoker.com**
28 MON REVE, 5, br m Fair Mix (USA)—Song For Jess (IRE) **Mrs Violet M. Jordan**
29 MONSIEUR GEORGES (FR), 13, b g Kadalko (FR)—Djoumi (FR) **Near & Far Racing**
30 ON THE CUSP (IRE), 6, b g Footstepsinthesand—Roman Love (FR) **Rakebackmypoker.com**
31 SLATEY HEN (IRE), 5, b m Acclamation—Silver Arrow (USA) **Rakebackmypoker.com**
32 THE WHICH DOCTOR, 8, b g Medicean—Oomph **Rakebackmypoker.com**
33 UNBREAK MY HEART (IRE), 8, ch g Bahamian Bounty—Golden Heart **Rakebackmypoker.com**

MRS VIOLET M. JORDAN - Continued

34 **WAABEL**, 6, b br g Green Desert (USA)—Najah (IRE) **Rakebackmypoker.com**
35 **WOLF HALL (IRE)**, 6, br g Presenting—Water Rock **Mrs Violet M. Jordan**

THREE-YEAR-OLDS

36 **TRUTH HURTS**, br g Cockney Rebel (IRE)—Vino Veritas (USA) **Mrs J. A. Cornwell**

Other Owners: Mr S. Arnold, R. K. Betts, Mrs E. Lucey-Butler, Mr D. J. Pearson, D. M. Thornton, Mrs J. G. Williams.

Assistant Trainer: Gaye Williams

---

358   **MR TOM KEDDY, Newmarket**
Postal: **246 Exning Road, Newmarket, Suffolk, CB8 0AN**
Contacts: **PHONE (01638) 561498 FAX (01638) 561498 MOBILE (07542) 036544/(07745) 238018**
E-MAIL **tkracing1@hotmail.co.uk**

1 **ARCHIE RICE (USA)**, 7, b g Arch (USA)—Gold Bowl (USA) **Hayley Keddy**
2 **BIG SUR**, 7, ch g Selkirk (USA)—Bombazine (IRE) **A. J. Duffield**
3 **CAIRANNE**, 5, b m High Chaparral (IRE)—Celestial Choir **J. H. Fielding**
4 **DESERT ICON (IRE)**, 7, b g Desert Style (IRE)—Gilded Vanity (IRE) **Evergreen Racing Newmarket**
5 **EVERGREEN FOREST (IRE)**, 5, ch g Haafhd—Inaaq **Evergreen Racing Newmarket**
6 **GREYFRIARSCHORISTA**, 6, ch g King's Best (USA)—Misty Heights **Evergreen Racing Newmarket**
7 **KARISTAR (IRE)**, 4, b f Montjeu (IRE)—Showcall (USA) **A. J. Duffield**
8 **PISCEAN (USA)**, 8, b br g Stravinsky (USA)—Navasha (USA) **A. J. Duffield**
9 **RASTEAU (IRE)**, 5, b g Barathea (IRE)—Mistra (IRE) **J. H. Fielding**
10 **SASSI SIOUX**, 4, b f Sleeping Indian—Dhurwah (IRE) **A. J. Duffield**
11 **ZIP LOCK (IRE)**, 7, b g Invincible Spirit (IRE)—Buckle (IRE) **Evergreen Racing Newmarket**

THREE-YEAR-OLDS

12 **DOWNRIGHT DIZZIE**, ch f Notnowcato—Italian Goddess **Evergreen Racing Newmarket**
13 **MY PEGGY SUE**, b f Cockney Rebel (IRE)—Groom Landing (PR) **Evergreen Racing Newmarket**

Assistant Trainer: Hayley Keddy

Jockey (NH): Jack Quinlan. **Apprentice:** Ryan Clark. **Amateur:** Miss Jessica Westgate.

---

359   **MRS CAROLINE KEEVIL, Motcombe**
Postal: **Larkinglass Farm, Motcombe, Shaftesbury, Dorset, SP7 9HY**
Contacts: **PHONE (07768) 867424 FAX (01761) 463927 MOBILE (07768) 867424**
E-MAIL **carolinekeevil@yahoo.co.uk**

1 **ARCTIC FLOW**, 9, b m Alflora (IRE)—Flow **Mrs H. R. Dunn**
2 **BALLY LEGEND**, 8, b g Midnight Legend—Bally Lira **B. A. Derrick**
3 **BLUE BLOODED**, 7, b g Nayef (USA)—Aristocratique **Mrs Angela Yeoman & Mr Peter Hart**
4 **CINEVATOR (IRE)**, 6, b g Dr Massini (IRE)—Hurricane Bella (IRE) **The Optimist & Pessimist Partnership**
5 **DARKESTBEFOREDAWN (IRE)**, 6, br g Dr Massini (IRE)—Camden Dolphin (IRE) **The Jago Family Partnership**
6 **DINER AU PARC**, 4, b f Central Park (IRE)—Gourmet (IRE) **Mr S. Potter**
7 **GYPSY MOTH (IRE)**, 7, gr m Zagreb (USA)—Hurst Flyer **Gypsy Moth Partnership**
8 **JACK BY THE HEDGE**, 4, b g Overbury (IRE)—Bluebell Path **Mrs E J Heathcote & The Hon Mrs Pease**
9 **LARKS WING (IRE)**, 5, b g Desert King (IRE)—Thyne Square (IRE) **The Optimist & Pessimist Partnership**
10 **MARSHAL ZHUKOV (IRE)**, 7, b g Morozov (USA)—Artic Brush (IRE) **Mrs Sara Biggins & Mrs Celia Djivanovic**
11 **MATAKO (FR)**, 10, b g Nikos—Verabatim (FR) **P. M. Bryant**
12 **MIDNIGHT LIRA**, 6, ch m Midnight Legend—Bally Lira **B. A. Derrick**
13 **MOORLAND SUNSET**, 6, b g Pasternak—Lady Harriet Luis **P. F. Popham**
14 **MRS WINCHESTER (IRE)**, 4, b f Scorpion (IRE)—Supreme Nova **Mrs H. R. Dunn**
15 **POD**, 5, b g Tikkanen—Opal'Iou (FR) **Mrs H. R. Dunn**
16 **PUSH TO EXIT**, 5, b g Exit To Nowhere (USA)—Shiny Thing (USA) **Mrs C. Keevil**
17 **RIGHTONTHYME**, 6, b m Milan—Four Thyme **Miss S. C. C. R. Jenks**
18 **SHADDAII (FR)**, 7, gr g April Night (FR)—Gypsie d'artois (FR) **Mrs C. E. Davies**
19 **SOUTHFIELD BELLE (IRE)**, 4, b f Presenting—Laureldean Belle (IRE) **Mrs A. B. Yeoman**
20 **STRAWBERRY HILL (IRE)**, 7, b g Winged Love—Icydora (IRE) **K S B Bloodstock**
21 **SYLVAN LEGEND**, 5, b g Midnight Legend—Sylvan Warbler (USA) **B. A. Derrick**
22 **THE OMEN**, 7, b g Sir Harry Lewis (USA)—High Sturt **J. Myerscough-Walker**
23 **TIME DO (FR)**, 6, ch g Grand Tresor (FR)—Demoiselle Do (FR) **Mrs L. R. Lovell**

MRS CAROLINE KEEVIL - Continued

Other Owners: Mr S. R. Belasco, Mrs S. J. Biggins, Mr K. W. Biggins, Mrs C. J. Djivanovic, Mr M. Doughty, Mr S. R. Dyer, Mrs J. N. Edwards-Heathcote, P L. Hart, Mr P J. A. Jago, Mrs J. L. Jago, Miss M. L. A. Jago, Mr F. C. A. Jago, Mr T. H. B. Nicholson, The Hon Mrs R. Pease.

Jockey (NH): Tom O'Brien, Will Kennedy. Conditional: Ian Popham.

---

360 **MR MARTIN KEIGHLEY, Cheltenham**
Postal: Condicote Stables, Luckley, Moreton-In-Marsh, Gloucestershire, GL56 0RD
Contacts: MOBILE (07767) 472547
E-MAIL info@martinkeighleyracing.com WEBSITE www.martinkeighleyracing.com

1 ALWAYS BOLD (IRE), 8, ch g King's Best (USA)—Tarakana (USA) **Mrs B. J. Keighley**
2 ANNACOTTY (IRE), 5, b g Beneficial—Mini Moo Min **Mrs Peter Prowting**
3 ANY CURRENCY (IRE), 10, b g Moscow Society (USA)—Native Bavard (IRE) **Cash Is King**
4 BENBANE HEAD (USA), 9, ch g Giant's Causeway (USA)—Prospectress (USA) **Mrs L. Jones**
5 BOBBLE EMERALD (IRE), 5, ch g Rudimentary (USA)—Aunt Emeralds (IRE) **Mr D. A. Thorpe**
6 BRUKIRK LASS, 8, ch m Kirkwall—Bruley **Mrs Anne Lee-Warner**
7 BUDDY LOVE, 6, gr m Silver Patriarch (IRE)—O My Love **Mr S. Cottrill**
8 CHAMPION COURT (IRE), 8, b g Court Cave (IRE)—Mooneys Hill (IRE) **M. Boothright**
9 COURT IN SESSION (IRE), 8, b g Court Cave (IRE)—Dangerous Dolly (IRE) **The Figjam Partnership**
10 CREEPY (IRE), 5, b g Westerner—Prowler (IRE) **M. Boothright, T. Hanlon, S. Harman**
11 FAULTLESS FEELINGS (IRE), 7, b g Milan—Duchess of Cork (IRE) **Mrs E. A. Prowting**
12 FLEMENTIME (IRE), 5, ch m Flemensfirth (USA)—Funny Times **Figjam II**
13 GOLBELINN (IRE), 8, ch m Bertolini (USA)—Final Faze **D. Bishop, C. Bowkley, M. Parker & M. Thornton**
14 HAIL TIBERIUS, 6, b g Iktibas—Untidy Daughter **Mr T. J. F. Exell**
15 HAVINGOTASCOOBYDO (IRE), 8, b g Witness Box (USA)—
                                      In Blue (IRE) **D. Bishop, C. Bowkley, M. Parker, M. Thornton**
16 HEELS OVERHEAD, 7, ch m Karinga Bay—Killatty Player (IRE) **Miss J. E. Balmer**
17 4, B f Milan—Indian Mask **Mr R. T. Crellin**
18 JOHNNY OG, 4, b g Flemensfirth (USA)—Mrs Roberts **T. Hanlon, M. Boothright, S. Henlon & N. Martin**
19 KYLES FAITH (IRE), 5, b g Court Cave (IRE)—Littleton Liberty
20 MAURICETHEATHLETE (IRE), 10, b g Sayarshan (FR)—Ardagh Princess **Mr A. G. Slatter**
21 MERLIN'S WISH, 8, gr g Terimon—Sendai **Miss R. Toppin**
22 MIDNIGHT MYTH, 6, b m Midnight Legend—Little Dish **Mr Bryan Eccles**
23 MIDNIGHT THOMAS, 4, b g Midnight Legend—Vivacious Lass (IRE) **Close Partnership**
24 MONTY'S REVENGE (IRE), 8, b g Bob's Return (IRE)—Native Bavard (IRE) **The Red Socks**
25 ONE MORE COOKIE (IRE), 7, b m Old Vic—Lady Bellingham (IRE) **Mr R. T. Crellin**
26 POLLYSTONE (IRE), 7, b m High-Rise (IRE)—Miss Polferton (IRE) **Mr R. T. Crellin**
27 SEYMOUR ERIC, 8, b g Bollin Eric—Seymour Chance **Mrs C. J. Black & Ten Out Of Ten Racing**
28 SKY CALLING, 10, b m Bal Harbour—Curlew Calling (IRE) **Nicholson Racing Syndicates A**
29 THE FOX'S DECREE, 9, br g Diktat—Foxie Lady **Mrs B. J. Keighley**
30 THE WICKED KIPPER, 5, b m King's Theatre (IRE)—Wicked Crack (IRE) **Mr R. T. Crellin**
31 TYPHON DE GUYE (FR), 6, ch g Dom Alco (FR)—Mascotte de Guye (FR) **Daydream Believers**
32 UKRAINIAN STAR (IRE), 10, ch g Carrowkeel (IRE)—Gemmasdelemma (IRE) **The Class Act Partnership**
33 UP IN FLAMES (IRE), 4, b g Red Clubs (IRE)—Flames
34 5, B g Fair Mix (IRE)—Wannaplantatree

Other Owners: Mr M. J. Allen, Mr Neil Bannister, Mr Shaun Bannister, Mr Alain Felder, Mr S. R. Harman, Mr Mark Johnson, Mr M. Keighley, Mrs D. Nicholson, Mr A. Saffrin, Mr G. M. Thornton, Mr E. M. Thornton.

Assistant Trainer: Mrs Belinda Keighley

Jockey (NH): Alain Cawley. Conditional: Ian Popham, Daniel Hiskett.

---

361 **MR CHRISTOPHER KELLETT, Swadlincote**
Postal: Jubilee Racing Stables, Snarestone Road, Appleby Magna, Swadlincote, Derbyshire, DE12 7AJ
Contacts: PHONE (01530) 515395 FAX (01530) 515395 MOBILE (07966) 097989
E-MAIL christopherkellett@btinternet.com WEBSITE www.chriskellettracing.co.uk

1 BEHTARINI (IRE), 6, b g Dalakhani (IRE)—Behkyira (IRE) **Mr P. L. Norchi**
2 CELTS ESPERE, 10, ch g Samraan (USA)—Celtic Dream **Ricochet Management Limited**
3 FEMME D'ESPERE, 7, b m Celts Espere—Drummer's Dream (IRE) **Ricochet Management Limited**

MR CHRISTOPHER KELLETT - Continued

4 **GEORGE BENJAMIN**, 6, b g Trade Fair—Unchain My Heart **The Edwardsons**
5 **LADIES BEST**, 9, b g King's Best (USA)—Lady of The Lake **Mr P. L. Norchi**
6 **MR SQUIRREL (IRE)**, 6, gr g Great Palm (USA)—
                                        Patsy Donnellan (IRE) **D. H. Muir & Exors of the Late Mrs R. E. Muir**
7 4, B f Afflora (IRE)—Precious Island **Mr T. J. Ellis**
8 **SPANISH TRAIL**, 4, b f Rail Link—La Coruna **The Haynes Family**
9 **SPLENDID BLUE (IRE)**, 7, br m Blueprint (IRE)—
                                        Splendid Choice (IRE) **D. H. Muir & Exors of the Late Mrs R. E. Muir**
10 **TANJUNG AGAS (IRE)**, 5, b g Montjeu (IRE)—Najmati **J. E. Titley**
11 **UPPER LAMBOURN (IRE)**, 5, ch g Exceed And Excel (AUS)—In The Fashion (IRE) **Mr K. W. Edwardson**

THREE-YEAR-OLDS

12 **BRYTER LAYTER**, b g Deportivo—Bahhmirage (IRE) **Miss S. L. Walley**

TWO-YEAR-OLDS

13 Ch c 28/4 Resplendent Glory (IRE)—Bahhmirage (IRE) (Bahhare (USA)) **Miss S. L. Walley**

Other Owners: Mr Kevin Edwardson, Mrs Julia Edwardson, Mr J. R. Haynes, Mrs J. S. Haynes, Mr Drew Muir, Exors of the late Mrs R. E. Muir.

362	**MISS GAY KELLEWAY, Newmarket**

Postal: **Queen Alexandra Stables, 2 Chapel Street, Exning, Newmarket, Suffolk, CB8 7HA**
Contacts: **PHONE (01638) 577778 MOBILE (07974) 948768**
E-MAIL gaykellewayracing@hotmail.co.uk WEBSITE www.gaykellewayracing.com

1 **AVON SUPREME**, 5, ch m Avonbridge—Fredora **B. C. Oakley**
2 **CONDUCTING**, 5, b g Oratorio (IRE)—Aiming **J Farley, M Brunner & M Whatley**
3 **CROWNING STAR (IRE)**, 4, b g Royal Applause—Dossier **Countrywide Classics Ltd**
4 **LAYLINE (IRE)**, 6, b g King's Best (USA)—Belle Reine **M Bartram, R Smith & N Scandrett**
5 **THE NEW BLACK (IRE)**, 4, gr f Oratorio (IRE)—Zarawa (IRE) **P Kerridge, G Kelleway & R Edwards**
6 **UPHOLD**, 6, b g Oasis Dream—Allegro Viva (USA) **Miss G. M. Kelleway**
7 **YOJOJO (IRE)**, 4, ch f Windsor Knot (IRE)—Belle of The Blues (IRE) **Winterbeck Manor Stud Ltd**

THREE-YEAR-OLDS

8 **PIXILATED**, b g Phoenix Reach (IRE)—Chocolada **Patricia Crook & Francis Aspin**
9 **SMILESWITHHISEYES (IRE)**, b g Marju (IRE)—Amoureux (USA) **Mr R. Ng**
10 **SPANISH ART**, b g Byron—Spanish Gold **Gay Kelleway & Robbie Doe**
11 **WOZA MOYA (USA)**, b c Mizzen Mast (USA)—Mrs Marcos (USA) **Mr I. Collier**

TWO-YEAR-OLDS

12 **LUCKY SURPRISE**, b f 22/3 Lucky Story (USA)—Bella Bertolini (Bertolini (USA)) (5000) **R. V. Young**
13 **LUCKY VISIONE**, b c 15/3 Lucky Story (USA)—Maid For Running (Namaqualand (USA)) (6000)

Other Owners: Mr F. E. Aspin, Mr M. Bartram, Mr M. J. Brunner, Miss P.F. Crook, Mr R. Doe, Mrs R. A. Edwards, Mr J. W. Farley, Mr P. B. Kerridge, N. S. Scandrett, R. W. Smith, M. C. Whatley.

Head Girl: Liz Mullin

Jockey (NH): Jamie Moore. **Apprentice:** Lauren Hunter.

363	**MR G. P. KELLY, Sheriff Hutton**

Postal: **3 Church End Cottages, Sheriff Hutton, North Yorkshire, YO60 6SY**
Contacts: **HOME (01347) 878770/878994 MOBILE (07866) 285187**

1 **AZYGOUS**, 10, ch g Foxhound (USA)—Flag **G. P. Kelly**
2 **BIGALO'S LAURA B (IRE)**, 5, ch m Needwood Blade—Rash **Mr J. R. Swift**
3 **HIGH WINDOW (IRE)**, 13, b g King's Theatre (IRE)—Kayradja (IRE) **G. P. Kelly**
4 **KEEN'S TOKEN**, 7, b g Keen—Bella Mary **C. I. Ratcliffe**
5 **TEALS DEAL**, 6, b m Gentleman's Deal (IRE)—Morcat **C. I. Ratcliffe**

Assistant Trainer: Ian Ratcliffe

Jockey (flat): James Sullivan, Paddy Aspell. **Apprentice:** David Simmonson. **Amateur:** Miss S. Brotherton.

364 MISS LYNSEY KENDALL, Carlisle
Postal: **The Stables, Lambley Bank, Scotby, Carlisle, Cumbria, CA4 8BX**
Contacts: **PHONE (01228) 513069 MOBILE (07818) 487227**
E-MAIL lynseykendall@hotmail.co.uk

1 GRIMWITH, 6, b g Doyen (IRE)—Poyle Caitlin (IRE) **Mr & Mrs R. S. Kendall**
2 WALTHAM ABBEY, 12, b g Relief Pitcher—Flash-By **Mr & Mrs R. S. Kendall**

Other Owners: Mr R. S. Kendall, Mrs M. E. Kendall.

365 MR NICK KENT, Brigg
Postal: **Newstead House, Cadney Road, Brigg, Lincolnshire, DN20 9HP**
Contacts: **PHONE (01652) 650628 FAX (01652) 650065 MOBILE (07710) 644428**
E-MAIL nick@nickkentracing.com WEBSITE www.nickkentracing.co.uk

1 AROUND A POUND (IRE), 8, b g Old Vic—Mary Ellen Best (IRE) **Nick Kent Racing Club**
2 ARWEN, 5, gr m Silver Patriarch (IRE)—Sally Smith **J. N. Kent**
3 BOWIE (IRE), 6, br g Pelder (IRE)—La Fenice (IRE) **Cynthia Commons,Marina Kent,Nick Kent**
4 CIAN BOY (IRE), 7, b br g Indian Danehill (IRE)—Dotty Dee (IRE) **Newstead Priory Racing Club**
5 COMBUSTIBLE KATE (IRE), 7, b m Mr Combustible (IRE)—Aussie Hope **Nick Kent Racing Club II**
6 CONSIGLIORI (IRE), 8, b g Bob's Return (IRE)—Eurocurrency (IRE) **Newstead Priory Racing Club**
7 DOTING, 4, b g Pursuit of Love—Star Sign **G. N. Parker**
8 5, B m Turtle Island (IRE)—Eye Vision (IRE) **J. N. Kent**
9 IVANS BACK (IRE), 8, b g Soviet Star (USA)—Better Back Off (IRE) **Mrs V. M. Branson**
10 LOST IN NEWYORK (IRE), 6, b g Arakan (USA)—Lace Flower **Timbercare Racing Partnership**
11 OUR CHOICE (IRE), 11, b g Indian Danehill (IRE)—Spring Daffodil **R. H. Lee**
12 SKYFIRE, 6, ch g Storm Cat (USA)—Sunray Superstar **Cynthia Commons, Nick Kent**
13 THE BLACK LION (IRE), 12, b g Un Desperado (FR)—Satrouse (IRE) **R. H. Lee**
14 WHISTLE WE GO (GER), 5, ch m Kalatos (GER)—Whoopie (GER) **Whistle & Flute**

Other Owners: Mr R. F. Boot, Mr K. R. Boot, Miss C. Commons, R. J. Jackson, Mrs M. Kent, Ms V. Mitchell, Mrs E. K. Styles, Mrs W. M. Wesley.

366 MISS SARAH KERSWELL, Kingsbridge
Postal: **Bearscombe Farm, Kingsbridge, Devon, TQ7 2DW**

1 MAGICAL ISLAND, 10, gr g Thowra (FR)—Alice's Mirror **R. H. Kerswell**
2 MAGICAL LEGEND, 12, gr m Midnight Legend—Alice's Mirror **R. H. Kerswell**
3 MAGICAL TREASURE, 9, gr g Riverwise (USA)—Alice's Mirror **R. H. Kerswell**
4 ROMANCE DANCE, 10, b m Terimon—Run On Stirling **Miss S. L. Kerswell**

367 MR ALAN KING, Wroughton
Postal: **Barbury Castle Stables, Wroughton, Wiltshire, SN4 0QZ**
Contacts: **PHONE (01793) 815009 FAX (01793) 845080 MOBILE (07973) 461233**
E-MAIL alanking.racing@virgin.net WEBSITE www.alankingracing.co.uk

1 ALI BABA, 7, ch g Nayef (USA)—Alligram (USA) **Alan King**
2 ANOTHER LAUGH, 5, ch g Where Or When (IRE)—Jane Jubilee (IRE) **Alan King**
3 ARABIAN HEIGHTS, 5, gr g Araafa (IRE)—Makhsusah (IRE) **McNeill Family Ltd**
4 ARALDUR (FR), 9, ch g Spadoun (FR)—Aimessa (FR) **Mr D. J. S. Sewell**
5 ARDLUI (IRE), 5, b g Galileo (IRE)—Epping **T. Barr**
6 AWESOME BELLA, 6, b m Karinga Bay—Awesome Aunt (IRE) **Mrs G. Meacham**
7 BAKBENSCHER, 10, gr g Bob Back (USA)—Jessolle **Three Line Whip**
8 BALDER SUCCES (FR), 5, b g Goldneyev (USA)—Frija Eria (FR) **Masterson Holdings Limited**
9 BENSALEM (IRE), 10, b g Turtle Island (IRE)—Peace Time Girl (IRE) **Alan Marsh & John D. Duggan**
10 BLESS THE WINGS (IRE), 8, b g Winged Love (IRE)—Silva Venture (IRE) **Mrs L. H. Field**
11 BOBBYJACK (IRE), 4, b g Scorpion (IRE)—Kates Choice (IRE) **Mr D. J. S. Sewell**
12 CALL ME A STAR, 6, b m Midnight Legend—Second Call **Mrs K. Holmes**
13 CALYPSO PRINCESS, 6, b m Helissio (FR)—Marathea (FR) **The Wildmoor Racing Partnership**
14 CHAMPAGNE N CAVIAR (IRE), 5, b g Tiger Hill (IRE)—Leukippids (IRE) **Atlantic Equine**

MR ALAN KING - Continued

15 **COLD KNIGHT**, 7, b g Sir Harry Lewis (USA)—Arctic Chick **Winter Madness**
16 **CUSTER OF THE WEST (IRE)**, 8, ch g Shernazar—Karlybelle (FR) **Mrs E. A. Prowting**
17 **DALAVAR (IRE)**, 5, b g Dalakhani (IRE)—Giant's Way (IRE) **Incipe Partnership**
18 **DESERT ROBE**, 5, b g Desert King (IRE)—Hot 'n Saucy **M. R. Brooks**
19 **DEVIL TO PAY**, 7, b g Red Ransom (USA)—My Way (IRE) **Horace 5**
20 **DUNDEE**, 5, ch g Definite Article—Gardana (FR) **T. J. Hemmings**
21 **FAIR TRADE**, 6, ch g Trade Fair—Ballet **R. C. Tooth**
22 **FIGHTER JET**, 5, b g Oasis Dream—Totality **Ladas**
23 **FINE WORDS**, 5, b g Alflora (IRE)—Gospel (IRE) **Mrs S. C. Welch**
24 **FORRESTERS FOLLY**, 7, b g Bollin Eric—Miss Wyandotte **Mr E. T. D. Leadbeater**
25 **FRANKLINO (IRE)**, 6, ch g Gold Away (IRE)—Amour Fatal (IRE) **McNeill Family Ltd**
26 **FRED LE MACON (FR)**, 4, b g Passing Sale (FR)—Princess Leyla **Alan King & Niall Farrell**
27 **GENSTONE TRAIL**, 7, b m Generous (IRE)—Stoney Path **Mickleton Racing Club**
28 **GODSMEJUDGE (IRE)**, 7, b g Witness Box (USA)—Eliza Everett (IRE) **Favourites Racing Ltd**
29 **GOLD INGOT**, 6, ch g Best of The Bests (IRE)—Realms of Gold (USA) **Mrs Sue Welch & Ms Caroline Rowland**
30 **GONE TOO FAR**, 5, b g Kayf Tara—Major Hoolihan **J. P. McManus**
31 **GRUMETI**, 5, b g Sakhee (USA)—Tetravella (IRE) **McNeill Family Ltd**
32 **HANDAZAN (IRE)**, 4, b g Nayef (USA)—Handaza (IRE) **McNeill Family Ltd**
33 **HENRY SAN (IRE)**, 6, ch g Exceed And Excel (AUS)—Esclava (USA) **Mrs J. A. Watts**
34 **HINDON ROAD (IRE)**, 6, b g Antonius Pius (USA)—Filoli Gardens **A. J. Viall**
35 **HOLD ON JULIO (IRE)**, 10, br g Blueprint (IRE)—Eileens Native (IRE) **Mr & Mrs F Bell, N Farrell, A Marsh**
36 **HOLLOW PENNY**, 5, b g Beat Hollow—Lomapamar **Mr D. J. S. Sewell**
37 **HOT WHISKEY (IRE)**, 5, ch g Flemensfirth (USA)—Fair Gina (IRE) **H. Redknapp**
38 **HUNG PARLIAMENT (FR)**, 5, b g Numerous (USA)—Sensational Mover (USA) **The Tipperary Partners**
39 **IOLITH (GER)**, 8, b g Monsun (GER)—Indian Jewel (GER) **Favourites Racing Ltd**
40 **IRON CHANCELLOR (IRE)**, 8, b g Alderbrook—Masriyna (IRE) **Mrs Lesley Field, J Sigler & D Anderson**
41 **ISHIKAWA (IRE)**, 5, b g Chineur (FR)—Nautical Light **ROA Racing Partnership V**
42 **JETNOVA (IRE)**, 8, b g Luso—Yamashina (IRE) **Mr D. J. S. Sewell**
43 **JOJABEAN (IRE)**, 6, b g Milan—Garden City (IRE) **The Dunkley & Reilly Partnership**
44 **KAUTO THE ROC (FR)**, 9, ch g With The Flow (USA)—
    Kauto of Realm (FR) **Davies, Horton, King, Lake, Powell & West**
45 **KENAI PENINSULA**, 5, gr g Tikkanen (USA)—Realms of Gold (USA) **Ian Payne & Kim Franklin**
46 **KING OF DUDES**, 4, b g Dansili—Leto (USA) **Masterson Holdings Limited**
47 **KUDA HURAA (IRE)**, 5, b g Montjeu (IRE)—Healing Music (FR) **Thurloe 53**
48 **KUMBESHWAR**, 6, b g Doyen (IRE)—Camp Fire (IRE) **McNeill Family & Mr Nigel Bunter**
49 **L'UNIQUE (FR)**, 4, b f Reefscape—Sans Tune (FR) **D. J. Barry**
50 **LA BELLE DOYENNE**, 5, ch m Doyen (IRE)—Tarabela (CHI) **Mrs C. Skan**
51 **LETSBY AVENUE**, 5, b g Tikkanen (USA)—Peel Me A Grape **Mrs E. A. Prowting**
52 **LIDAR (FR)**, 8, ch g Take Risks (FR)—Light Wave (FR) **High 5**
53 **LOTUS POND (IRE)**, 8, b g Beneficial—Capard Lady (IRE) **T. J. Hemmings**
54 **LOVCEN (GER)**, 8, b g Tiger Hill (IRE)—Lady Hawk (GER) **The Barbury Apes**
55 **MANYRIVERSTOCROSS (IRE)**, 8, b g Cape Cross (IRE)—Alexandra S (IRE) **Mrs M. C. Sweeney**
56 5, B m Double Trigger (IRE)—Marathea (FR) **The Wildmoor Racing Partnership**
57 **MCVICAR**, 4, b g Tobougg (IRE)—Aries (GER) **Mr & Mrs R. Scott**
58 **MEDERMIT (FR)**, 9, gr g Medaaly—Miss d'hermite (IRE) **The Dunkley & Reilly Partnership**
59 **MEDINAS (FR)**, 6, b br g Malinas (GER)—Medicis (FR) **Mr & Mrs F. D. Bell**
60 **MIDNIGHT APPEAL**, 8, b g Midnight Legend—Lac Marmot (FR) **Mr D. J. S. Sewell**
61 **MIDNIGHT CATARIA**, 4, b f Midnight Legend—Calamintha **Mrs K. Holmes**
62 **MIDNIGHT PRAYER**, 8, b g Midnight Legend—Onawing Andaprayer **The Legends Partnership**
63 **MIDNIGHT SAIL**, 10, b g Midnight Legend—Mayina **M 2 C Racing Partnership**
64 **MISS EXHIBITIONIST**, 5, b m Trade Fair—Miss McGuire **The Trouble Partnership**
65 5, B h Fair Mix (IRE)—Miss Wyandotte **Alan King**
66 **MONEY FOR NOTHING**, 4, b g Kayf Tara—Top of The Dee **Mrs M. C. Sweeney**
67 **NELSON'S BAY**, 4, b g Needwood Blade—In Good Faith (USA) **R. C. Tooth**
68 **OH CRICK (FR)**, 10, ch g Nikos—Other Crik (FR) **Mr D. J. S. Sewell**
69 **OUR PHYLLI VERA (IRE)**, 4, b f Motivator—With Colour **Let's Live Racing**
70 **PANTXOA (FR)**, 6, b g Daliapour (IRE)—Palmeria (FR) **Mrs J. A. Watts**
71 **PATSY FINNEGAN**, 11, b g Sir Harry Lewis (USA)—Bampton Fair **The Wasp Partnership**
72 4, Ch g Bach (IRE)—Peace Time Beauty (IRE) **Alan King**
73 **RAYA STAR (IRE)**, 7, b g Milan—Garden City (IRE) **S. E. Munir**
74 **RAYADOUR (IRE)**, 4, b g Azamour (IRE)—Rayyana (IRE) **S. E. Munir**
75 **REDDY TOBOUGGIE**, 5, b g Tobougg (IRE)—Waraqa (USA) **Nigel Bunter & Tim Leadbeater**
76 **ROBERTO PEGASUS (USA)**, 7, b br g Fusaichi Pegasus (USA)—
    Louju (USA) **Mrs P Andrews, I Payne & Ms K Franklin**
77 **RUM EXPECTATIONS (IRE)**, 5, b g Darsi (FR)—Jennypenney **A. P. Racing**

MR ALAN KING - Continued

78 **SALMANAZAR**, 5, b g Classic Cliche (IRE)—Leroy's Sister (FR) **Top Brass Partnership**
79 **SECRET EDGE**, 5, b g Tobougg (IRE)—Burton Ash **Nigel Bunter & David Anderson**
80 **SEVENTH SIGN**, 4, b g Pivotal—Rahayeb **Masterson Holdings Limited**
81 **SHADY LANE**, 6, b m Alflora (IRE)—Stoney Path **Mrs C Rowland,Mrs Welch & R Fitzgerald**
82 **SIMPLY A LEGEND**, 4, b g Midnight Legend—Disco Danehill (IRE) **Mrs E. A. Prowting**
83 **SMAD PLACE (FR)**, 6, gr g Smadoun (FR)—Bienna Star (FR) **Mrs P. Andrews**
84 **SOIXANTE SIX**, 5, gr g Fair Mix (IRE)—Pennant Princess **S. E. Munir**
85 **STAR HILL**, 6, b m Starcraft (NZ)—Mistress Bankes (IRE) **Alan King**
86 **STONEY'S TREASURE**, 9, ch g Silver Patriarch (IRE)—Stoney Path **Mrs S. C. Welch**
87 **TAFFY DARE (IRE)**, 4, b f Court Cave (IRE)—Three More (USA) **A. P. Racing**
88 **TANTE SISSI (FR)**, 6, b m Lesotho (USA)—Kadjara (FR) **Thurloe 51**
89 **THE MUMPER (IRE)**, 6, br g Craigsteel—Na Moilltear (IRE) **The Weighed In Partnership**
90 **THE PIRATE'S QUEEN (IRE)**, 4, b f King's Theatre (IRE)—Shivermetimber (IRE) **Mr & Mrs C. Harris**
91 **TRIGGER THE LIGHT**, 12, ch g Double Trigger (IRE)—Lamper's Light **Mrs D. Shutes**
92 **TURN OVER SIVOLA (FR)**, 6, b g Assessor (IRE)—Notting Hill (FR) **International Plywood (Importers) Ltd**
93 **TWO ROCKERS (IRE)**, 6, b g Milan—Foxhall Blue (IRE) **Masterson Holdings Limited**
94 **ULYS DU CHARMIL (FR)**, 5, b g Malinas (GER)—Jest In Ball (FR) **S. E. Munir**
95 **URGENCE D'ESTRUVAL (FR)**, 5, b m Enrique—Perle d'estruval (FR) **S. E. Munir**
96 **URIAH HEEP (FR)**, 4, b g Danehill Dancer (IRE)—Canasita **Alan King**
97 **UXIZANDRE (FR)**, 5, ch g Fragrant Mix (IRE)—Jolisandre (FR) **Million in Mind Partnership**
98 **VALDEZ**, 6, ch g Doyen (IRE)—Skew **Riverdee Stable**
99 **VENDOR (FR)**, 5, gr g Kendor (FR)—Village Rainbow (FR) **Thurloe 52**
100 **VOLCAN SURPRISE (FR)**, 5, b g Dom Alco (FR)—Invitee Surprise (FR) **Lady Bamford & Tim Leadbeater**
101 **WALKON (FR)**, 8, gr g Take Risks (FR)—La Tirana (FR) **McNeill Family Ltd**
102 **WEST END ROCKER (IRE)**, 11, b br g Grand Plaisir (IRE)—
    Slyguff Lord (IRE) **Mr Barry Winfield & Mr Tim Leadbeater**
103 **WILDE BLUE YONDER (IRE)**, 4, b g Oscar (IRE)—Blue Gallery (IRE) **Maybe Only Fools Have Horses**
104 **WILLOUGHBY HEDGE**, 6, b g King's Theatre (IRE)—Mini Mandy **J. W. Haydon**

THREE-YEAR-OLDS

105 **CHOCALA (IRE)**, b g Rock of Gibraltar (IRE)—Arbella **High 5**
106 **HEROD THE GREAT**, ch c Sakhee's Secret—Pella **Mr S M Smith & Mr D Minton**
107 **LEVICHE**, ch g Shirocco (GER)—Alla Prima (IRE) **N. S. G. Bunter**

Other Owners: Mr D. J. Anderson, M. Ball, Lady Bamford, Mrs H. L. Bell, Mr F. D. Bell, R. J. Benton, Mrs A. Blackwell, A. R. Bromley, Mrs C. E. Caddick, Mr R. J. Caddick, Mr N. J. Carter, Mr S. Clancy, Exors of the Late Mr G. J. Clark, Mr N. Clyne, Mr D. E. Collier, Mrs A. L. Davies, J. D. Duggan, P. J. Dunkley, Mrs S. Evans, N. Farrell, Mr R. J. N. Fitzgerald, L. R. Frampton, Miss K. M. Franklin, G. F. Goode, Mr M. Grier, Mr C. I. K. Harris, Mrs C. A. Harris, Mr P. S. Hayward, Mr D. A. Heffer, D. F. Hill, J. Holmes, Mr A. Horne, Mr A. Humphreys, Mr S. R. Kapoor, Mrs R. J. King, Mr W. P. Ledward, Ms M. Machin-Jefferies, Mr A. R. W. Marsh, W. D. C. Minton, Mr C. Mullin, Mrs M. T. Mullin, Mr J. J. Murray, Mr G. Nicholas, Mrs D. C. Nicholson, Mr P. J. O'Neill, Mrs L. H. Oakley, O. J. W. Pawle, Mr I. T. Payne, Mr R. M. Potter, Mr S. P. Price, Mr C. R. Pugh, D. F. Reilly, J. P. L. Reynolds, Ms C. C. Rowland, R. F. Sayer, R. Scott, Mrs P. M. Scott, J. Sigler, Prof D. B. A. Silk, S. M. Smith, Mr J. A. B. Stafford, J. A. Thompson, Mrs C. Townroe, Mrs K. J. Tudor, Mr M. Warren, Mrs S. J. Warren, B. Winfield.

Assistant Trainers: Noel Williams, Oliver Wardle

Jockey (NH): Robert Thornton, Wayne Hutchinson, Charlie Huxley, Gerard Tumelty. **Conditional:** Peter Hatton. **Amateur:** Mr Dan Horsford, Mr Josh Newman.

---

368   MR NEIL KING, Newmarket
Postal: St Gatien Racing Ltd, St Gatien Cottage, Vicarage Road, Newmarket, Suffolk, CB8 8HP
Contacts: **PHONE/FAX** (01638) 666150 **FAX** (01638) 666150 **MOBILE** (07880) 702325
E-MAIL neil@neil-king.co.uk **WEBSITE** www.neil-king.co.uk

1 **A LITTLE SWIFTER (IRE)**, 7, ch m Noverre (USA)—Swiftur **Dr Clive Layton & Ken Lawrence**
2 **ATTWAAL (IRE)**, 4, b g Teofilo (IRE)—Qasirah (IRE) **Dr C. A. Layton**
3 **BALLYVONEEN (IRE)**, 8, b g Stowaway—Miss Ira Zarad (IRE) **Across The Pond Partnership**
4 **BOLLIN TAHINI**, 7, b m Bollin Eric—Cinnamon Club **A. W. K. Merriam**
5 **CERIUM (FR)**, 12, b g Vaguely Pleasant (FR)—Tantatura (FR) **Mr R. N. Bothway**
6 **DELGANY DEMON**, 5, b g Kayf Tara—Little Twig (IRE) **C. M. Wilson**
7 **DELGANY GUNNER**, 9, b g Commanche Run—No Grandad **Charles Wilson & Charles Garside**
8 **EVELLA (IRE)**, 9, ch m Beneficial—Drimadrian **The St Gatien Racing For Fun Partnership**
9 **GET READY TO GO (IRE)**, 9, b g Turtle Island (IRE)—Buckalong (IRE) **Mr R. N. Bothway**

MR NEIL KING - Continued

10 **IRONICALLY (IRE)**, 4, b f Refuse To Bend (IRE)—Dutch Auction (USA) **Mr B. Bell**
11 **KAYSERSBERG (FR)**, 6, b g Khalkevi (IRE)—Alliance Royale (FR) **Mrs Julien Turner & Mr Andrew Merriam**
12 **MILANSBAR (IRE)**, 6, b g Milan—Ardenbar **Mr R. N. Bothway**
13 **NAFAATH (IRE)**, 7, ch g Nayef (USA)—Alshakr **Sarah & Wayne Dale**
14 **NATIVE COLONY**, 5, b g St Jovite (USA)—Self Esteem **didjabringabeeralong, Three Lions Pub**
15 **ONTHESLATE (IRE)**, 7, b g Beneficial—Florida (IRE) **Merriam Tolhurst Spurrier Bazeley**
16 **OUTBACK (IRE)**, 4, b g Kodiac—Florida City (IRE) **Mr D. Nott, Mr & Mrs M. Harrod, P. Beadles**
17 **PAIRC NA GCAPALL (IRE)**, 11, b g Taipan (IRE)—Ballindante (IRE) **The St Gatien Racing For Fun Partnership**
18 **PEINTRE STER (IRE)**, 6, ch g Peintre Celebre (USA)—Goldster (IRE) **Mrs H. M. Buckle**
19 **PERSIAN HERALD**, 5, gr g Proclamation (IRE)—Persian Fortune **The St Gatien Racing For Fun Partnership**
20 **RUSSIAN FLAG (FR)**, 10, b g Kingsalsa (USA)—Nousa Nousa (FR) **N. King**
21 **SAMARKAND (IRE)**, 5, b g Sadler's Wells (USA)—Romantic Venture (IRE) **Mark & Tracy Harrod**
22 **TENDER SURPRISE**, 4, b f Doyen (IRE)—Spring Surprise **Mr D. A. Howes & Mr R. Johnston**
23 **WOM**, 5, b g Tiger Hill (IRE)—Vayavaig **Mr Mark Harrod & Mr John Hitchin**
24 **ZEPNOVE (IRE)**, 7, b m Noverre (USA)—Royal Zephyr (USA) **Stephen Lower Insurance Services Limited**

Other Owners: Mrs C. Bazeley, Mr P. M. H. Beadles, Mr N. J. Catterwell, Mrs S. J. Dale, Mr Wayne Dale, Mr Charles A. Garside, Mr Mark Harrod, Mrs Tracy Harrod, Mr John Hitchin, Mr David Howes, Mr R. S. Johnston, Mr Neil King, Mr Ken Lawrence, Dr Clive Layton, Mrs A. W. K. Merriam, Mr A. W. K. Merriam, Mr Gareth Milburn, Mr D. F. Nott, Mr J. H. Smith, Miss Caroline Spurrier, Mrs E. A. Tolhurst, Mrs Julien Turner, Mr B. M. V. Williams, Mr C. M. Wilson.

Assistant Trainer: Marie Parker

Jockey (flat): Adam Kirby, Hayley Turner. **Jockey (NH):** Dougie Costello, Richard Johnson, Alex Merriam, Jamie Moore. **Conditional:** Trevor Whelan. **Amateur:** Miss Clare Twemlow.

369	**MR RICHARD KING, Dorchester**

Postal: **The Lanches, East Farm, Tolpuddle, Dorchester, Dorset, DT2 7EP**
Contacts: **PHONE (01305) 848592 FAX (01305) 849134 MOBILE (07779) 991356**
E-MAIL sherilyn.king@yahoo.co.uk

1 **MADAM NOSO**, 9, ch m Riverwise (USA)—Lady Noso **Mrs S. King**

370	**MR WILLIAM KINSEY, Ashton**

Postal: **R Kinsey Partnership, Peel Hall, Gongar Lane, Ashton, Chester**
Contacts: **PHONE (01829) 751230 MOBILE (07803) 753719**
E-MAIL kinsey.peelhall@tiscali.co.uk

1 **ALPHA VICTOR (IRE)**, 8, b g Old Vic—Harvest View (IRE) **Denton, Kinsey, Osborne Hse, Wesley-Yates**
2 **AMBER CLOUD**, 6, ch m Lomitas—Diamant Noir **Mr W. R. Kinsey**
3 **BLAZING DESERT**, 9, b g Beat All (USA)—Kingsfold Blaze **The Deeside Partnership**
4 **FIDDLEESTICKS (IRE)**, 5, b g Heron Island (IRE)—Dawn Native (IRE) **Manley Steeplechasing**
5 **GREATOWN (IRE)**, 6, gr g Great Palm (USA)—Townhall (IRE) **Mr W. R. Kinsey**
6 **GWLADYS STREET (IRE)**, 6, b g Portrait Gallery (USA)—Native Ocean (IRE) **The Missing Link**
7 **HARRIS (IRE)**, 6, b g Beneficial—Porter Tastes Nice (IRE) **Mr W. R. Kinsey**
8 **KYKATE**, 7, b m Hamas (IRE)—Coleham **David Bithell Racing**
9 **MAC STEAMY (IRE)**, 7, ch g Bienamado (USA)—Aroseforclare **The Steam Powered Syndicate**
10 **MATCHLOCK (IRE)**, 6, b g Heron Island (IRE)—Katies Gun (IRE) **Mr W. R. Kinsey**
11 **MISS DUFFY**, 5, ch m Sir Harry Lewis (USA)—Dolly Duff **Mr W. R. Kinsey**
12 **SHOULDAVBOUGHTGOLD (IRE)**, 6, b g Classic Cliche (IRE)—Sancta Miria (IRE) **The Missing Link**

Other Owners: D. P. Bithell, Mr C. B. Denton, Mr T. B. Denton, R. B. Francis, Mrs J. Kinsey, Osborne House Ltd, Mr M. C. Plumridge, J. M. Tomlinson, D. Wesley-Yates.

371	**MR PHILIP KIRBY, Middleham**

Postal: **Sharp Hill Farm, Middleham, Leyburn, North Yorkshire, DL8 4QY**
Contacts: **PHONE (01969) 624400 MOBILE (07984) 403558**
E-MAIL wakingned1@hotmail.com WEBSITE www.philipkirbyracing.co.uk

1 **ACKNOWLEDGEMENT**, 11, b g Josr Algarhoud (IRE)—On Request (IRE) **Mr P. Kirby**
2 **AGGLESTONE ROCK**, 8, b g Josr Algarhoud (IRE)—Royalty (IRE) **Geoff Kirby & Pam Kirby & Brian Cobbett**

MR PHILIP KIRBY - Continued

3 **ALICESAM**, 4, b f Revoque (IRE)—Hinton Grace **Preesall Garage**
4 **ANCIENT TIMES (USA)**, 6, b br g Smart Strike (CAN)—Histoire Sainte (FR) **Mr R. Hadfield**
5 **ANDORN (GER)**, 9, b h Monsun (GER)—Anthyllis (GER) **Preesall Garage**
6 **AVANOS (FR)**, 8, b g Kaldounevees (FR)—Annee de La Femme (IRE) **C B Construction (Cleveland) Limited**
7 **AVIDITY**, 4, b g Passing Glance—Epicurean **Keep The Faith Partnership**
8 **BARNEY RUBBLE**, 4, b g Medicean—Jade Chequer **W. A. Bethell**
9 **BOB'S TICKET (IRE)**, 8, ch g Bob's Return (IRE)—Some Ticket (IRE) **The Kwick Syndicate**
10 **BRIGADOON**, 6, b g Compton Place—Briggsmaid **Mr R. Oliver**
11 **CALL IT ON (IRE)**, 7, ch g Raise A Grand (IRE)—Birthday Present **The Wiggins Family**
12 **CLEVE COTTAGE**, 5, ch g Presenting—Reverse Swing **G Fawcett & D Phillips**
13 **COOL OPERATOR**, 10, b g Kahyasi—Gardana (FR) **The Gathering & Alderclad**
14 **ELSPETH'S BOY (USA)**, 6, b br g Tiznow (USA)—Miss Waki Club (USA) **Preesall Garage**
15 **EMBSAY CRAG**, 7, b g Elmaamul (USA)—Wigman Lady (IRE) **Grange Park Racing IV**
16 **EVERAARD (USA)**, 7, ch g Lion Heart (USA)—Via Gras (USA) **Tennant, Sharpe & Boston**
17 **FAIRYNUFF**, 9, gr g Terimon—Hand Inn Glove **New Roc**
18 **FOXY GILLIAN**, 6, b m Alflora (IRE)—Supreme Lass (IRE) **Ean Muller Associates**
19 **FULL SPEED (GER)**, 8, b g Sholokhov (IRE)—Flagny (FR) **Mr R. Hadfield**
20 **GOLD RULES**, 6, ch g Gold Away (IRE)—Raphaela (FR) **The Dibble Bridge Partnership**
21 **GOLDAN JESS (IRE)**, 9, b g Golan (IRE)—Bendis (GER) **The Jessies, Colin Fletcher, Philip Kirby**
22 **GREY COMMAND (USA)**, 8, gr g Daylami (IRE)—Shmoose (IRE) **The Shades of Grey Partnership**
23 **IKTIVIEW**, 5, ch g Iktibas—Eastview Princess **Eastview Thoroughbreds**
24 **INCH MANOR (IRE)**, 5, b g Fruits of Love (USA)—Erald-de-Mo (IRE) **Ingham Racing Syndicate**
25 **JASPER MASSINI (IRE)**, 8, b g Dr Massini (IRE)—Graigue Lass (IRE) **Billy & Philip Platts**
26 **JUST CAMERON**, 6, b g Kayf Tara—Miss Fencote **Mr & Mrs P. Chapman**
27 **KETTLEWELL**, 4, ch g Auction House (USA)—Angel Chimes **Mr S. E. Kettlewell**
28 4, B g Golan (IRE)—Leave Me Be (IRE) **Mrs L. M. Hannity**
29 **LITTLE POPPET**, 4, b f Kayf Tara—Mini Mandy
30 **MAC TIERNAN (IRE)**, 6, b g Minashki (IRE)—Softly Softly (IRE) **Mr P. Kirby**
31 **MANGAS COLORADES (IRE)**, 5, b g Kalanisi (IRE)—Al Cairo (IRE) **G. R. Orchard**
32 **MATTHEW RILEY (IRE)**, 6, b g Dr Massini (IRE)—Helorhiwater (IRE) **Mr & Mrs P. Chapman**
33 **MORGAN BE**, 13, b g Alderbrook—Vicie **Mr S. Breakspeare**
34 **MRS EFF**, 7, b m Tamure (IRE)—Roman Uproar **Mrs K. Walton**
35 **NOBLE SCHOLAR (IRE)**, 8, b g Anabaa (USA)—Lisieux Rose (IRE) **The Kwick Syndicate**
36 **OSCAR O'SCAR (IRE)**, 5, b g Oscar (IRE)—Shining Lights (IRE) **G. R. Orchard**
37 **PASS MUSTER**, 6, b g Theatrical—Morning Pride (IRE) **C B Construction (Cleveland) Limited**
38 **PEN GWEN (FR)**, 10, b g Le Balafre (FR)—Dans Dro (FR) **Mrs K. Walton**
39 **PICKS MILAN (IRE)**, 7, b g Milan—Butchies Girl (IRE) **Mr H. J. Pickersgill**
40 **PICKWORTH (IRE)**, 8, b m Milan—Loshian (IRE) **C B Construction (Cleveland) Limited**
41 **PLATINUM (IRE)**, 6, b g Azamour (IRE)—Dazzling Park (IRE) **Mrs P. R. Kirby**
42 **PREACHERS PET**, 5, ch g Courteous—Moonshine Malt **L. Waugh**
43 **RUMBLE OF THUNDER (IRE)**, 7, b g Fath (USA)—Honey Storm (IRE) **The Well Oiled Partnership**
44 **STOPPED OUT**, 8, gr g Montjoy (USA)—Kiomi **The Well Oiled Partnership**
45 **STORMY MORNING**, 7, ch g Nayef (USA)—Sokoa (USA) **Colin Fletcher & Ownaracehorse**
46 **TAXI DES OBEAUX (FR)**, 6, b br g Maresca Sorrento (FR)—Madrilene (FR) **Sharp Hill 2**
47 **VICTOR LYNCH (IRE)**, 7, b g Old Vic—Jmember (IRE) **I. M. Lynch**
48 **WESTERN TRIGGER (IRE)**, 4, b g Westerner—Single Trigger (IRE) **Yarm Racing Partnership**
49 **WORTH A KING'S**, 7, b g Red Ransom (USA)—Top Romance (IRE) **Mr G. S. Kirby**

THREE-YEAR-OLDS

50 **DANEHILL FLYER (IRE)**, b c Danehill Dancer (IRE)—Zagreb Flyer **Mr P. Kirby**

TWO-YEAR-OLDS

51 **BACK BABY PARIS (IRE)**, b f 27/1 Flemensfirth (USA)—Babygotback (IRE) (Amilynx (FR)) **Mrs J. Haughton**
52 **WARRIOR JACK (IRE)**, b g 22/4 Coroner (IRE)—On The Up (IRE) (Luso) (952) **Mrs J. Haughton**

Other Owners: Alderclad Ltd, Mr J. K. Bell, Mr A. D. Bingham, R. A. Brown, Mr P. W. Chapman, Mrs J. Chapman, Mr E. L. Coates, Mr B. A. G. Cobbett, Mr D. G. Colledge, A. D. Crombie, Mr A. C. Davies, Mr G. Fawcett, Mr C. Fletcher, K. D. Hague, Mr R. Hamilton, Mr W. Hayler, Mr P. A. Helm, Mr M. P. Helm, Mr G. K. Henderson, Mr T. S. Ingham, Mrs P. S. Kirby, J. H. Madden, Mr P McMartin, E. A. C. Muller, T. I. Nicol, Mr A. Norrington, Ownaracehorse Ltd, Mr M. D. Parker, Mr D. J. Phillips, Mr W. N. Platts, Mr P. Platts, Mr A. J. Roberts, C. M. Sharpe, Mr J. G. R. Stent, J. M. Swinglehurst, Mrs G. M. Swinglehurst, J. E. Tennant, Mr L. C. Wiggins, Mr S. A. Wiggins, Mrs C. Wiggins.

Assistant Trainer: Simon Olley

Jockey (NH): James Reveley, Richie McGrath. **Conditional:** Kyle James.

372 MR SYLVESTER KIRK, Upper Lambourn

Postal: **Cedar Lodge Stables, Upper Lambourn, Hungerford, Berkshire, RG17 8QT**
Contacts: **PHONE (01488) 73215 FAX (01488) 670012 MOBILE (07768) 855261**
E-MAIL info@sylvesterkirkracing.co.uk WEBSITE www.sylvesterkirkracing.co.uk

1 **BERWIN (IRE)**, 4, b f Lawman (FR)—Topiary (IRE) **Mr & Mrs R Kelvin-Hughes**
2 **CELESTIAL BAY**, 4, b f Septieme Ciel (USA)—Snowy Mantle **Homebred Racing**
3 **CHARLES CAMOIN (IRE)**, 5, b g Peintre Celebre (USA)—
Birthday (IRE) **Mr C. Wright & The Hon Mrs J. M. Corbett**
4 **CHASIN' RAINBOWS**, 5, b m Piccolo—Tamara **J. B. J. Richards**
5 **DELAGOA BAY (IRE)**, 5, b m Encosta de Lago (AUS)—Amory (GER) **Homebred Racing**
6 **FROCK (IRE)**, 4, b f Excellent Art—Maimana (IRE) **S. A. Kirk**
7 **GLENNTEN**, 4, b g Ishiguru (USA)—Uplifting **Mr S. H. Glenn**
8 **GOODIE GOODIE**, 4, b f Shirocco (GER)—Goodie Twosues **Lady Davis**
9 **ORATORIAN (IRE)**, 4, b g Oratorio (IRE)—Raindancing (IRE) **S. A. Kirk**
10 **PURLEY QUEEN (IRE)**, 4, b f Piccolo—Queenie **S. A. Kirk**
11 **THE GIVING TREE (IRE)**, 4, b f Rock of Gibraltar (IRE)—Starry Messenger **Knockainey Stud Limited**
12 **THE NOBLE ORD**, 4, b g Indesatchel (IRE)—Four Legs Good (IRE) **Verano Quartet I**
13 **VEYEPEA**, 4, ch f Dutch Art—Endear **S. A. Kirk**

THREE-YEAR-OLDS

14 **ADMIRALS WALK (IRE)**, b g Tagula (IRE)—Very Racy (USA) **N. Pickett**
15 **BANOVALLUM**, b c Invincible Spirit (IRE)—Sinduda **Mr C. Wright & The Hon Mrs J. M. Corbett**
16 **BURMA DAYS (USA)**, b g Medaglia d'oro (USA)—Becky In Pink (USA) **Mr H. Balasuriya**
17 **CAPETOWN KID**, gr g Cape Town (IRE)—Doris Souter (IRE) **Mr P. D. Merritt**
18 **EXOTIC LADY (IRE)**, b br f Excellent Art—Princess Sabaah (IRE) **D. Boocock**
19 **HURRICANE EMMA (USA)**, b br f Mr Greeley (USA)—Victorica (USA) **Ms C. Cleary**
20 **LANDAU (IRE)**, gr g Aussie Rules (USA)—Before The Storm **Mrs Barbara Facchino**
21 Ch c Ad Valorem (USA)—Lapis Lazuli **S. A. Kirk**
22 **LITTLE MISS ZURI (IRE)**, ch f Choisir (AUS)—Miss Kinabalu **I. A. N. Wight**
23 **MOJO BEAR**, b f Indesatchel (IRE)—Four Legs Good (IRE) **S. A. Kirk**
24 **ROCK DIAMOND (IRE)**, b f Rock of Gibraltar (IRE)—Yaky Romani (IRE) **Ron Gander & Barbara Matalon**
25 **SECRET REBEL**, ch c Sakhee's Secret—Indiana Blues **J. C. Smith**
26 **SEE AND BE SEEN**, b g Sakhee's Secret—Anthea **T. K. Pearson**
27 **SHOW MORE FAITH**, b g Pastoral Pursuits—Lalina (GER) **I. A. N. Wight**
28 **SOMETHING MAGIC**, b gr f Proud Citizen (USA)—Comeback Queen **Mr & Mrs Christopher Wright**
29 **TERPSICHORE**, ch f Beat Hollow—Effie **Effie Beat**

TWO-YEAR-OLDS

30 Ch f 20/3 Danehill Dancer (IRE)—A P Easy (USA) (A P Indy (USA)) (20000) **M. Nicolson, G. Doran, A. Wilson**
31 B c 14/3 Dandy Man (IRE)—Anne Bonney (Jade Robbery (USA)) (18000) **Mr R. Hannon & Mr P. Rogers**
32 **BELLETRISTE (FR)**, gr f 3/3 Literato (FR)—
Mulled Wine (FR) (Night Shift (USA)) (25396) **The Hon Mrs J. M. Corbett & Mr C. Wright**
33 Gr ro c 28/1 Henrythenavigator (USA)—C'est La Cat (USA) (Mountain Cat (USA)) (30000) **Verano Quartet**
34 Gr c 10/2 Archipenko (USA)—Cherrycombe-Row (Classic Cliche (IRE)) (11000) **T. K. Pearson**
35 B c 17/4 Sleeping Indian—Doris Souter (IRE) (Desert Story (IRE)) **Mr P. Merritt**
36 B f 9/2 Zamindar (USA)—Duty Paid (IRE) (Barathea (IRE)) **Mr J. C. Smith**
37 **FOREST GLEN (IRE)**, b f 16/4 Camacho—Lisfannon (Bahamian Bounty) (15238) **Sapphire Racing Partnership**
38 Ch f 28/3 Tagula (IRE)—Full of Nature (Monsieur Bond (IRE)) **S. A. Kirk**
39 B f 29/3 Amadeus Wolf—Glencoe Solas (IRE) (Night Shift (USA)) (7142) **S. A. Kirk**
40 B c 22/2 Duke of Marmalade (IRE)—Green Room (FR) (In The Wings) (15000) **S. A. Kirk**
41 B f 14/4 Footstepsinthesand—Inis Boffin (Danehill Dancer (IRE)) **Ms C. Cleary & Mr D. O'Loughlin**
42 **INSPECTOR NORSE**, b c 22/2 Norse Dancer (IRE)—Indiana Blues (Indian Ridge) **Mr J. C. Smith**
43 B c 5/5 Invincible Spirit (IRE)—Lady Windermere (IRE) (Lake Coniston (IRE)) (50000) **Mr H. Balasuriya**
44 B f 28/3 Archipenko (USA)—Mennetou (USA) (Entrepreneur) (37000) **Mr T. Cummins**
45 **NORSE STAR**, b c 14/3 Norse Dancer (IRE)—Spot Prize (USA) (Seattle Dancer (USA)) **Mr J. C. Smith**
46 B c 24/4 Tagula (IRE)—Notepad (King's Best (USA)) (10317) **S. A. Kirk**
47 B f 17/4 Mastercraftsman (IRE)—Sheba Five (USA) (Five Star Day (USA)) (22000) **Mr Nelius Hayes**
48 **SIMMA (IRE)**, gr f 21/2 Dark Angel (IRE)—Staylily (IRE) (Grand Lodge (USA)) (12500) **Mr N. Simpson**

Other Owners: Miss J. A. Challen, The Hon Mrs C. Corbett, Mr M. Crow, R. A. Gander, R. Hannon, R. G. Kelvin-Hughes, Mrs E. A. Kelvin-Hughes, Mr Sylvester Kirk, Dr B. A. Matalon, Mr D. P. Moss, Mr Timothy Pearson, Mr Robert Pocock, J. S. Threadwell, C. M. Wall, Mrs S. Wall, C. N. Wright, Mrs Chris Wright.

Assistant Trainer: Fanny Kirk

Jockey (flat): James Doyle, Liam Keniry. **Amateur:** Miss C. Boxall.

373 MR ALAN KIRTLEY, West Auckland

Postal: **Acrum Lodge, Staindrop Road, West Auckland, Durham**
Contacts: **PHONE (07802) 614931**
E-MAIL alankirtleyracing@yahoo.co.uk

1 6, Ch g Prince Daniel (USA)—Good Morning
2 **MISS MATIZ**, 6, b m Rock City—Doodle Wood **Mrs D. Wood**

THREE-YEAR-OLDS

3 **KALANI'S DIAMOND**, ch f Kalani Bay (IRE)—Cryptonite Diamond (USA)

374 MR STUART KITTOW, Cullompton

Postal: **Haynefield Farm, Blackborough, Cullompton, Devon, EX15 2JD**
Contacts: **HOME (01823) 680183 FAX (01823) 680601 MOBILE (07714) 218921**
E-MAIL stuartkittowracing@hotmail.com WEBSITE stuartkittowracing.com

1 **FROZEN OVER**, 5, b g Iceman—Pearly River **P. A. & M. J. Reditt**
2 **KLEITOMACHOS (IRE)**, 5, b g Barathea (IRE)—Theben (GER) **E. J. S. Gadsden**
3 **MACDILLON**, 7, b g Acclamation—Dilys **Boswell, Pillans, Harris ,Urquhart & Kittow**
4 **MAY BE SOME TIME**, 5, ch g Iceman—Let Alone **Dr G. S. Plastow**
5 **ON STAGE**, 4, ch f Act One—In The Stocks **E. J. S. Gadsden**
6 **OUR FOLLY**, 5, b g Sakhee (USA)—Regent's Folly (IRE) **Midd Shire Racing**
7 **RESURGE (IRE)**, 8, b g Danehill Dancer (USA)—Resurgence **Chris & David Stam**
8 **ROYAL REYAH**, 4, b g Royal Applause—Dilys **B Hopkins, M Harris & R Perry**
9 **SIGNIFICANT MOVE**, 6, b g Motivator—Strike Lightly **Midd Shire Racing**
10 **UPPERCUT**, 5, ch g Needwood Blade—Uplifting **H. A. Cushing**
11 **WEAPON OF CHOICE (IRE)**, 5, b g Iffraaj—Tullawadgeen (IRE) **Chris & David Stam**

THREE-YEAR-OLDS

12 B f Haafhd—All Glory **The Black Type Partnership III**
13 **DILGURA**, b f Ishiguru (USA)—Dilys **S. Kittow, R. Perry, B. Hopkins**
14 **GUILDED SPIRIT**, b c Ishiguru (USA)—Soft Touch (IRE) **The Racing Guild**
15 **PADDY BURKE**, b g Bertolini (USA)—Feathergrass (IRE) **P. J. Green**
16 **RUSSIAN ROYALE**, b f Royal Applause—Russian Ruby (FR) **P. A. & M. J. Reditt**

TWO-YEAR-OLDS

17 B c 6/5 Muhtathir—Capefly (Cape Cross (IRE)) (5000) **R. S. E. Gifford**
18 B f 8/3 Iffraaj—Fashion Guide (IRE) (Bluebird (USA)) (11000)
19 Ch f 3/3 Tobougg (IRE)—Let Alone (Warning) (5238) **Dr G. S. Plastow**
20 B c 28/4 Piccolo—Mrs Snaffles (IRE) (Indian Danehill (IRE)) (11428)
21 **PLAUSEABELLA**, b f 21/3 Royal Applause—Ellablue (Bahamian Bounty) (16000) **Midd Shire Racing**

Other Owners: Mrs S. G. Arnesen, D. W. Arnesen, John Boswell, Andrew Bull, M. E. Harris, Mr B. S. Hopkins, W. S. Kittow, B. G. Middleton, Mr R. N. Olsen, Mrs R. J. M. Perry, Mr M. D. Pillans, Mrs P. A. Reditt, M. J. Reditt, A. J. Shire, Mr D. B. Stam, Dr C. Stam, Ms W. A. Stoker, R. A. Stoker, Mr J. R. Urquhart.

Assistant Trainer: Mrs Judy Kittow

Jockey (flat): Fergus Sweeney. **Jockey (NH):** Tom Scudamore.

375 MR WILLIAM KNIGHT, Angmering

Postal: **Lower Coombe Racing Stables, Angmering Park, Littlehampton, West Sussex, BN16 4EX**
Contacts: **PHONE (01903) 871188 FAX (01903) 871184 MOBILE (07770) 720828**
E-MAIL william@wknightracing.co.uk WEBSITE www.wknightracing.co.uk

1 **BEACON LADY**, 4, ch f Haafhd—Oriental Lady (IRE) **The Pro-Claimers**
2 **BLOODSWEATANDTEARS**, 5, b g Barathea (IRE)—Celestial Princess **Canisbay Bloodstock**
3 **CAPHIRA**, 4, ch f Singspiel (IRE)—Dream Quest **Bluehills Racing Limited**
4 **COOL SKY**, 4, b g Millkom—Intersky High (USA) **No Quarter Partnership**
5 **DUSTY RED**, 4, ch f Teofilo (IRE)—Dust Dancer **Mr & Mrs John Kelsey-Fry**
6 **FIRE SHIP**, 4, b g Firebreak—Mays Dream **IGP Partnership & P. Winkworth**
7 **FLY HAAF (IRE)**, 4, b g Haafhd—Rose Indien (FR) **The Pheasant Rew Partnership**

MR CARLOS LAFFON-PARIAS - Continued

86 **RAREMENT (IRE)**, ch f 11/2 Monsun (GER)—Fidelite (IRE) (In The Wings) **Wertheimer Et Frere**
87 **REDING (FR)**, b c 6/3 Pivotal—Alfaguara (USA) (Red Ransom (USA)) (15873) **Sarl Darpat France**
88 B g 17/3 Elusive City (USA)—Reverie Solitaire (IRE) (Nashwan (USA)) **Stilvi Compania Financiera**
89 **SOSIA (GER)**, b f 1/1 Shamardal (USA)—Sahel (GER) (Monsun (GER)) **Wertheimer Et Frere**
90 **SPIRITUEUX (IRE)**, b c 9/3 Invincible Spirit (IRE)—Stormina (USA) (Gulch (USA)) **Wertheimer Et Frere**
91 **TARISIOS (GR)**, b c 18/1 Kavafi (IRE)—Lyssodis (GR) (So Factual (USA)) **Stilvi Compania Financiera**
92 **TAXILOS (FR)**, b c 5/2 Kavafi (IRE)—Vraona (Fantastic Light (USA)) **Stilvi Compania Financiera**
93 **TELMIOS (IRE)**, gr c 19/3 Mastercraftsman (IRE)—
                Drosia (IRE) (King's Best (USA)) (17460) **Stilvi Compania Financiera**
94 **VESTA (GR)**, gr f 16/4 Ialysos (GR)—Thymodis (GR) (Evippos (GR)) **Stilvi Compania Financiera**
95 **VILLANUEVA (IRE)**, b f 6/3 Whipper (USA)—Mabalane (IRE) (Danehill (USA)) (31746) **Sarl Darpat France**
96 **VRISSA (FR)**, gr f 20/4 Duke of Marmalade (IRE)—
                Pearl Earrine (FR) (Kaldounevees (FR)) **Stilvi Compania Financiera**
97 **WADIRUM (IRE)**, b c 26/1 Dashing Blade—Dubai (IRE) (Galileo (USA)) **Wertheimer Et Frere**
98 **WISIGO (GER)**, b c 2/2 Tiger Hill (IRE)—Wild Star (USA) (Sternkoenig (IRE)) **Wertheimer Et Frere**
99 B f 6/2 Aqlaam—Zarkavean (Medicean) (126984) **Mr P. Fudge**

Assistant Trainer: Charles Peck

Jockey (flat): Olivier Peslier. **Conditional:** Jerome Claudic. **Apprentice:** Rudy Pimbonnet.

---

378 MR NICK LAMPARD, Marlborough
Postal: **South Cottage, 2 The Crossroads, Clatford, Marlborough, Wiltshire, SN8 4EA**
Contacts: **PHONE (01672) 861420**

1 **GOOCHYPOOCHYPRADER**, 6, ch m Karinga Bay—Mrs Ritchie **The Outside Chance Racing Club**
2 **HEATHYARDS FLYER**, 10, b g Beat All (USA)—Heathyards Gem **Mr I. M. Scaramanga**
3 **JUST SATISFACTION**, 4, b f Trade Fair—Bathwick Fancy (IRE) **The Outside Chance Racing Club**
4 **PINNACLE OFPASSION (IRE)**, 5, b m Presenting—Olives Idol (IRE) **Mr H Spooner & Mr M Jonas**
5 **PODIUM DANCER**, 6, b m Revoque (IRE)—Mille Et Une Nuits (FR) **The Outside Chance Racing Club**

Other Owners: Mr M. Jonas, Miss A. E. A. Solomon, Mr H. Spooner.

---

379 MR RICARDO LANFRANCO, Leyburn
Postal: **Bolton Hall Racing Stables, Bolton Hall, Wensley, Leyburn, North Yorkshire, DL8 4UF**
Contacts: **PHONE (01969) 621180 MOBILE (07946) 017115**
E-MAIL admin@boltonhallstables.co.uk WEBSITE www.boltonhallstables.co.uk

1 4, B g Misu Bond (IRE)—Chasetown Cailin
2 **HURRICANE SPEAR**, 5, ch g Hurricane Run (IRE)—Sarissa (USA) **Field & Country Racing**
3 **IMPERIAL BOND**, 4, b g Misu Bond (IRE)—Liability (IRE) **Mr S. J. Matheson**
4 **LITTLEMOOR LASS**, 4, b f Motivator—Frazzled (USA)

Other Owners: Lamont Racing, Mrs S. Matheson.

Assistant Trainer: Stuart Matheson

---

380 MR DAVID LANIGAN, Upper Lambourn
Postal: **Kingsdown Stables, Upper Lambourn, Hungerford, Berkshire, RG17 8QX**
Contacts: **PHONE (01488) 71786 FAX (01488) 674148**
E-MAIL david@laniganracing.co.uk WEBSITE www.laniganracing.co.uk

1 **BIOGRAPHER**, 4, b c Montjeu (IRE)—Reflective (USA)
2 **DAWN SKY**, 9, b g Fantastic Light (USA)—Zacheta
3 **FOR WHAT (USA)**, 5, ch h Mingun (USA)—Cuanto Es (USA)
4 **HANDSOME RANSOM**, 4, b g Red Ransom (USA)—Maid For The Hills
5 **MAIN SEQUENCE (USA)**, 4, ch g Aldebaran (USA)—Ikat (IRE)
6 **PERFECT HEART**, 4, gr g Dalakhani (IRE)—Maid To Perfection
7 **TROPICAL BEAT**, 5, b g Beat Hollow—Tropical Heights (FR)

MR WILLIAM KNIGHT - Continued

8 **NASSAU STORM**, 4, b g Bahamian Bounty—Got To Go **The Oil Men Partnership**
9 **OBLITEREIGHT (IRE)**, 4, ch g Bertolini (USA)—Doctrine **The Oil Men Partnership**
10 **PALACE MOON**, 8, b g Fantastic Light (USA)—Palace Street (USA) **Canisbay Bloodstock**
11 **PROPER CHARLIE**, 5, b g Cadeaux Genereux—Ring of Love **Mr Peter Oakley & Mr Charles Whittaker**
12 **ROWAN RIDGE**, 5, ch g Compton Place—Lemon Tree (USA) **Mr & Mrs N. Welby**
13 **SAOI (USA)**, 6, ch g Wiseman's Ferry (USA)—Careyes (IRE) **Surrey Horseracing Limited**
14 **SIGNOR SASSI**, 4, b g Acclamation—Fairy Contessa (IRE) **Mr A. L. Brooks**
15 **STORY WRITER**, 4, b g Sakhee (USA)—Celestial Princess **Mr J. B. Henderson**
16 **TITAN TRIUMPH**, 9, b g Zamindar (USA)—Triple Green **Canisbay Bloodstock**
17 **VIOLA DA GAMBA (IRE)**, 4, b f Alhaarth (IRE)—Addaya (IRE) **Mrs S. M. Mitchell**

THREE-YEAR-OLDS
18 **AEOLIAN BLUE**, ch f Bahamian Bounty—Blue Mistral (IRE) **Mrs S. M. Mitchell**
19 **AUSSIE REIGNS (IRE)**, b c Aussie Rules (USA)—Rohain (IRE) **The Old Brokers**
20 **EXCLUSIVE WATERS (IRE)**, b g Elusive City (USA)—Pelican Waters (IRE) **The Old Brokers**
21 **GOODWOOD MIRAGE (IRE)**, b c Jeremy (USA)—
                Phantom Waters **Goodwood Racehorse Owners Group (19) Ltd**
22 Br f Superior Premium—Hinton Pearl **Miss S. Bannatyne**
23 **KEEP THE SECRET**, ch f Sakhee's Secret—Starfleet **Mr & Mrs N. Welby**
24 **MODERNSTONE**, b f Duke of Marmalade (IRE)—Post Modern (USA) **Biddestone Stud**
25 **NOBLE GIFT**, ch c Cadeaux Genereux—Noble Penny **Gail Brown Racing (V)**
26 **PIRA PALACE (IRE)**, b f Acclamation—Takrice **Miss T. K. Walters**
27 **SCALA ROMANA (IRE)**, b f Holy Roman Emperor (IRE)—Sliding Scale **Mr & Mrs John Kelsey-Fry**
28 **SPORTING CLUB GIRL**, b f Kyllachy—Validate **The National Sporting Club**
29 **SWEET MARTONI**, b f Dubawi (IRE)—Sweetness Herself **Grainger Lavell**
30 **WHIPPER SNAPPER (IRE)**, b g Whipper (USA)—Topiary (IRE) **The Oil Merchants**

TWO-YEAR-OLDS
31 **ALLERGIC REACTION (IRE)**, b c 12/3 Kyllachy—
                Wood Chorus (Singspiel (IRE)) (35000) **Four Men & A Dream Partnership**
32 **BEACH BAR (IRE)**, b c 1/3 Azamour (IRE)—
                Toasted Special (USA) (Johannesburg (USA)) (22000) **Mr P. Winkworth & Mrs Bex Seabrook**
33 **CAPMONDE (IRE)**, b f 15/4 Cape Cross (IRE)—Esclarmonde (IRE) (In The Wings) (20634) **Mrs F. Ashfield**
34 B f 12/2 Bushranger (IRE)—Corps de Ballet (IRE) (Fasliyev (USA)) (32000) **G. Roddick**
35 B f 15/4 Duke of Marmalade (IRE)—Crinolette (IRE) (Sadler's Wells (USA)) (18000) **Mr & Mrs N. Welby**
36 Gr c 31/1 Mastercraftsman (IRE)—Demerger (USA) (Distant View (USA)) (48000) **Brooks, Cavanagh, Tracey**
37 **EXALTED (IRE)**, b c 8/4 Acclamation—Eman's Joy (Lion Cavern (USA)) (83333) **The Old Brokers**
38 **GOODWOOD STORM**, ch f 13/4 Shamardal (USA)—
                Artifice (Green Desert (USA)) (27000) **Goodwood Racehorse Owners Group (20) Ltd**
39 **HANDS UP (IRE)**, b c 25/3 Bushranger (IRE)—Christa Maria (Alhaarth (IRE)) (31428) **Richoux Partnership**
40 B f 18/3 Dancing Spree (USA)—Hinton Pearl (Loch Pearl) **Miss S. Bannatyne**
41 Ch c 31/3 Duke of Marmalade (IRE)—Kylemore (IRE) (Sadler's Wells (USA)) (25000) **Mrs Melba Bryce**
42 **ONE PIXEL**, b f 20/1 Primo Valentino (IRE)—
                Mays Dream (Josr Algarhoud (IRE)) (19047) **Hot To Trot Racing Club**
43 **PERCYBELLE**, ch f 5/3 Sir Percy—Chelsea (USA) (Miswaki (USA)) (11000) **Jon and Julia Aisbitt**
44 B c 19/4 Gentlewave (IRE)—Shawhill (Dr Fong (USA)) **Chasemore Farm**
45 B f 10/5 Holy Roman Emperor (IRE)—Sliding Scale (Sadler's Wells (USA)) (12000) **Mr & Mrs John Kelsey-Fry**
46 **SOUNDTRACK (IRE)**, br c 28/3 Excellent Art—Umthoulah (IRE) (Unfuwain (USA)) (12000) **Wardley Bloodstock**
47 B c 24/3 Royal Applause—Stormy Weather (Nashwan (USA)) (52000) **Brooks, Cavanagh, Tracey**
48 Gr f 18/2 Verglas (IRE)—Totally Yours (IRE) (Desert Sun) (24000) **Merton Place Stud**
49 B f 11/5 Footstepsinthesand—Whipped Queen (USA) (Kingmambo (USA)) (15000) **Merton Place Stud**

Other Owners: Mr Tareq Al-Mazeedi, Mr A. Black, Mrs M. M. Boyd, Mr A. Brooks, Mr R. G. W. Brown, Mr G. J. Burchell, Mr I. J. Callaway, Mr J. Cavanagh, Mrs H. G. Clinch, Mr D. A. Docherty, Mr Matthew Duncan, Mr D. Ellis, Mr G. H. Fry, Mr R. F. Kilby, Mr W. J. Knight, Mrs Margaret Lavell, Mr I. G. Martin, Mr Peter Oakley, Mr Nick Peacock, Mr N. J. Galazka, Mr Laurence Grainger, Mrs Susan Hearn, Mr Barry Hearn, Miss K. J. Keir, Mr John Kelsey-Fry, Mrs Sally Kelsey-Roach, Mr Mike Rudd, Mr M. Stone, Miss Maureen Stopher, Mr Mark Tracey, Mr N. Welby, Mrs N. Welby, Mr Charles Whittaker, Mr B. Willis, Mrs D. A. Willis, Mr P. Winkworth.

Assistant Trainer: Matthew Darling

Jockey (flat): Jim Crowley.

376 MR DANIEL KUBLER, Whitsbury
Postal: 2 Warditch Cottages, Whitsbury, Fordingbridge, Hampshire, SP6 3QH
Contacts: PHONE (01725) 518690 MOBILE (07984) 287254
E-MAIL daniel@kublerracing.com WEBSITE www.kublerracing.com

1 FIREBACK, 6, b g Firebreak—So Discreet **Ignite Partnership**
2 MONOPOLI, 4, ch f Cadeaux Genereux—Jump Ship **The Villains**
3 SHERMAN MCCOY, 7, ch g Reset (AUS)—Naomi Wildman (USA) **Ignite Partnership**
4 SPECIAL BRANCH, 5, b g Red Ransom (USA)—Love Everlasting **Mr & Mrs G. Middlebrook**

THREE-YEAR-OLDS
5 CHANDELLE CELESTE, ch f Septieme Ciel (USA)—First Candlelight **Skeltools Ltd**
6 GHETTO DIVA, b f Compton Place—Like A Virgin (IRE) **Mrs C. E. Kubler**
7 LALINDE, b f Tiger Hill (IRE)—Ciboure **Mr & Mrs G. Middlebrook**
8 LISA'S LEGACY, b g Kyllachy—Lisathedaddy **Mrs P Wilson & Mr C Wilson**
9 MONT SIGNAL, ch g Pivotal—Anse Victorin (USA) **Mr & Mrs G. Middlebrook**
10 MULTI FOURS, ch f Medicean—Spiralling **Mr M Grayson & Mr I P O'Brien**
11 ORREST HEAD, b g Sakhee (USA)—Saint Ann (USA) **Mr & Mrs G. Middlebrook**
12 ROSACEOUS, ch f Duke of Marmalade (IRE)—Briery (IRE) **Mr & Mrs G. Middlebrook**

TWO-YEAR-OLDS
13 B f 4/2 Bertolini (USA)—Carollan (IRE) (Marju (IRE)) (12500) **Whitsbury Hopefuls II**
14 DISKO (IRE), b f 2/4 Kodiac—Dissonance (Rossini (USA)) (5714)
15 IL PAPARAZZI, b c 19/3 Royal Applause—Birdie (Alhaarth (IRE)) (32000) **Capture The Moment**
16 B c 27/4 Oratorio (IRE)—Imperial Bailiwick (IRE) (Imperial Frontier (USA)) **Mr & Mrs G. Middlebrook**
17 B c 1/4 Kheleyf (USA)—Montcalm (IRE) (Montjeu (USA)) **Mrs C. E. Kubler**
18 NORSE LEGEND, b c 13/4 Norse Dancer (IRE)—Methodical (Lujain (USA)) (952) **Woodhaven Racing Syndicate**
19 POETIC JUSTICE, b c 14/4 Byron—Toleration (Petong) (2380) **Woodhaven Racing Syndicate**
20 TRINITY RIVER, b f 1/2 Three Valleys (USA)—Blane Water (USA) (Lomond (USA)) **Mr P. Whitten**

Assistant Trainer: Claire Kubler

Jockey (flat): Mickael Barzalona, Martin Dwyer, Richard Kingscote.

377 MR CARLOS LAFFON-PARIAS, Chantilly
Postal: 38, Avenue du General Leclerc, 60500 Chantilly, France
Contacts: PHONE (0033) 344 575375 FAX (0033) 680 182909
E-MAIL ecuries.laffon.parias@wanadoo.fr

1 ACTIVISTE (IRE), 4, b c Giant's Causeway (USA)—Occupandiste (IRE) **Wertheimer Et Frere**
2 ASAGAYA (FR), 4, ch c Medicean—Akhla (USA) **Stilvi Compania Financiera**
3 CHINCHON (FR), 8, b h Marju (IRE)—Jarama (IRE) **Sarl Darpat France**
4 ESLES (FR), 5, b h Motivator—Resquilleuse **Bering S.L.**
5 FOREIGN TUNE, 4, b f Invincible Spirit (IRE)—Gwenseb (FR) **Wertheimer Et Frere**
6 GRAFFITO (FR), 4, b c Aussie Rules—Diotima **Stilvi Compania Financiera**
7 INCROYABLE (USA), 4, b f Singspiel (IRE)—Soft Pleasure (USA) **Wertheimer Et Frere**
8 LOUSSIA (FR), 4, b f Footstepsinthesand—Obsidianne (FR) **Stilvi Compania Financiera**
9 MENYLLOS (GR), 4, b g Kavafi (USA)—Ipeiros (GR) **Stilvi Compania Financiera**
10 NUTELLO (USA), 4, b c Lemon Drop Kid (USA)—Nutcase (USA) **Wertheimer Et Frere**
11 SOFT LIPS, 4, b f Rahy (USA)—Iron Lips **Wertheimer Et Frere**
12 TREVIERES (FR), 5, ch h Gold Away (IRE)—Castilly **Stilvi Compania Financiera**
13 VASIAS, 5, b h Motivator—Vivacity **Stilvi Compania Financiera**
14 VICTORINNA (FR), 5, ch m Gentlewave (IRE)—Marcela Howard (IRE) **Stilvi Compania Financiera**

THREE-YEAR-OLDS
15 ACCALMIE (FR), b f Invincible Spirit (USA)—Underwater (USA) **Wertheimer Et Frere**
16 AGUAFRIA (USA), b f More Than Ready (USA)—Briviesca **Sarl Darpat France**
17 ALAJAR (IRE), b f Galileo (IRE)—Arazena (USA) **Sarl Darpat France**
18 ALIGATO, ch c Monsun (GER)—Acago (USA) **Wertheimer Et Frere**
19 AMARYSIA (FR), ch f Medicean—Light Quest (USA) **Stilvi Compania Financiera**
20 ARNOLFINI (IRE), b c Peintre Celebre (USA)—Wandering Spirit (GER) **Wertheimer Et Frere**
21 BAYAKA (FR), b f Nayef (USA)—Senkaya (USA) **Wertheimer Et Frere**
22 CANTABRICO, ch c Sakhee (USA)—Sakha **Felipe Hinojosa**
23 CHURADA (IRE), b f Green Tune (USA)—Agiel (FR) **Stilvi Compania Financiera**

MR CARLOS LAFFON-PARIAS - Continued
24 COALIS, b c Oasis Dream—Gwenseb (FR) **Wertheimer Et Frere**
25 CROSSTOWN, b c Cape Cross (IRE)—Esneh (IRE) **Wertheimer Et Frere**
26 DISTORTION, b f Distorted Humor (USA)—Icelips (USA) **Wertheimer Et Frere**
27 DIVISME (USA), b f Elusive Quality (USA)—Toppisme (USA) **Wertheimer Et Frere**
28 EFTEOS (FR), b c Teofilo—Efesos **Stilvi Compania Financiera**
29 ERASMIOS (FR), ch c King's Best—Eriza **Stilvi Compania Financiera**
30 EURATO (FR), c Medicean—Double Green (IRE) **Wertheimer Et Frere**
31 EXAMOS (FR), ch c Green Tune—Delfinia **Stilvi Compania Financiera**
32 FEREVIA (IRE), b f Motivator—Frynia (USA) **Stilvi Compania Financiera**
33 GOLDATOR (FR), b c Cape Cross (IRE)—Soft Gold (USA) **Wertheimer Et Frere**
34 IZNATE, ch c Pivotal—Trylko (USA) **Sarl Darpat France**
35 KHE SE VA, b f Kheleyf (USA)—Se Me Va (USA) **Mme Africa Cuadra-Lores**
36 KRYMKA (IRE), ch f Medicean—La Seine (USA) **Stilvi Compania Financiera**
37 LYKASTOS (IRE), b c Holy Roman Emperor (IRE)—Granadilla **Stilvi Compania Financiera**
38 LYKEA (IRE), b f Oasis Dream—Alyzea (USA) **Stilvi Compania Financiera**
39 MANIKARAA (FR), b f Anabaa—Zaragoza Girl (BRZ) **Wertheimer et Frere**
40 MELIVEA (FR), b f Green Tune (USA)—Cerita (USA) **Stilvi Compania Financiera**
41 MELODIQUE (FR), b f Falco (USA)—Elodie des Charmes (FR) **Wertheimer et Frere**
42 MENEAS (FR), b c American Post—Okalea (IRE) **Stilvi Compania Financiera**
43 MODESTIE (FR), ch f Nayef (USA)—Gold Round (IRE) **Wertheimer Et Frere**
44 NIKODAMOS (GR), b c Clodovil (IRE)—Shikasta (IRE) **Stilvi Compania Financiera**
45 SEAHORSE (FR), b c Falco—Sea Paint **Wertheimer et Frere**
46 SEVROS (FR), b c Falco (USA)—Betwixt (USA) **Stilvi Compania Financiera**
47 SILASOL (IRE), b f Monsun (GER)—Stormina (USA) **Wertheimer Et Frere**
48 SINGING (FR), b c Singspiel (IRE)—Ring Beaune (USA) **Stilvi Compania Financiera**
49 SINGLE (FR), b f Singspiel (IRE)—Tender Morn (USA) **Wertheimer et Frere**
50 SNOWDAY (FR), b c Falco—Oceanique (USA) **Wertheimer et Frere**
51 SOJO (USA), b c Smart Strike (CAN)—Arme Ancienne **Wertheimer Et Frere**
52 SPILIADA (FR), b f Falco (USA)—Vivacity **Stilvi Compania Financiera**
53 THARSIS (IRE), b f Gold Away (IRE)—Highphar (FR) **Sarl Darpat France**
54 TOP CHILL (FR), b c Falco—Top Order **Wertheimer et Frere**
55 TOPAZE BLANCHE (IRE), b f Zamindar (USA)—Pearl Earrine (FR) **H.H. Sheikh Mohammed Bin Khalifa Al Thani**
56 UTOPIQUE (USA), b f Falco (USA)—Ydillique (IRE) **Wertheimer Et Frere**
57 VARDARIS (FR), b c Beat Hollow—Drosia (IRE) **Stilvi Compania Financiera**
58 VENGA VENGA (IRE), b f Montjeu (USA)—Betilla (IRE) **C. Laffon-Parias**

TWO-YEAR-OLDS
59 Ch c 2/3 Dubawi (IRE)—Antioquia (Singspiel (IRE)) (49206) **Felipe Hinojosa**
60 BAWINA (FR), b f 9/2 Dubawi (IRE)—Esneh (IRE) (Sadler's Wells (USA)) **Wertheimer Et Frere**
61 B c 27/4 Arch (USA)—Briviesca (Peintre Celebre (USA)) **Sarl Darpat France**
62 CHANT DE SABLE (FR), b f 31/3 Oasis Dream—Akhla (USA) (Nashwan (USA)) **Stilvi Compania Financiera**
63 B c 3/3 Manduro (GER)—Chill (FR) (Verglas (IRE)) (39682) **Bering S.L.**
64 COSCA (FR), b b 15/3 Kavafi (FR)—Vytinna (FR) (Victory Note (USA)) **Stilvi Compania Financiera**
65 DHUMA, b br f 5/2 Falco (USA)—Tender Morn (USA) (Dayjur (USA)) **Wertheimer Et Frere**
66 DREAM GIRL, b f 23/3 Oasis Dream—Iron Lips (Iron Mask (USA)) **Wertheimer Et Frere**
67 EMPREINTE (USA), ch f 29/3 Footstepsinthesand—Zagzig (Selkirk (USA)) **Stilvi Compania Financiera**
68 ERIAS (FR), ch c 14/4 Gold Away (IRE)—Betwixt (USA) (Sinndar (IRE)) **Stilvi Compania Financiera**
69 FARADAN (FR), ch f 23/4 King's Best (USA)—Eriza (Distant Relative) **Stilvi Compania Financiera**
70 FLAMBEUSE, b f 18/1 Cape Cross (IRE)—Flamenba (USA) (Kingmambo (USA)) **Wertheimer Et Frere**
71 GALINEA (IRE), b f 4/3 Excellent Art—Galkatea (Statue of Liberty (USA)) **Stilvi Compania Financiera**
72 ICARIUM (FR), ch c 28/4 Medicean—Delfinia (FR) (Drastikos (GER)) **Stilvi Compania Financiera**
73 KARACTERIEL, b c 12/3 Dalakhani (IRE)—Spring Star (Danehill (USA)) **Wertheimer Et Frere**
74 KILAVA (FR), b f 25/5 Invincible Spirit (IRE)—Agiel (FR) (Bering) (35714) **Stilvi Compania Financiera**
75 KYRINI (GR), b f 28/1 Pythios (IRE)—Dafnea (FR) (Hawk Wing (USA)) **Mr P. Fudge**
76 B f 9/4 Medaglia d'oro (USA)—Lindelaan (Rahy (USA)) **Wertheimer Et Frere**
77 MEDEO (FR), b c 17/2 Elusive City (USA)—Oceanique (USA) (Forest Wildcat (USA)) **Wertheimer Et Frere**
78 MENANDORE (FR), b f 30/4 Invincible Spirit (IRE)—Kezia (IRE) (Spectrum (IRE)) **Stilvi Compania Financier**
79 MONAWAY (FR), ch c 23/1 Gold Away (IRE)—Red Stella (FR) (Rainbow Quest (USA)) **Wertheimer et Frer**
80 NO MOOD, ch c 15/4 Monsun (GER)—Impressionnable (Danehill (USA)) **Wertheimer Et Frere**
81 ORSOVIA, ch f 24/2 Shamardal (USA)—Alyzea (IRE) (King Charlemagne (USA)) (51587) **Stilvi Compania Financi**
82 PLANETAIRE, b c 26/3 Galileo (IRE)—Occupandiste (IRE) (Kaldoun (FR)) **Wertheimer Et Frere**
83 PRIVATE, b c 4/4 Pivotal—Icelips (USA) (Unbridled (USA)) (43650) **Wertheimer Et Frere**
84 QUALIDA (FR), b f 2/5 Falco (USA)—Queen's Conquer (King's Best (USA)) (43650) **Stilvi Compania Financiera**
85 RAEST (FR), b f 30/3 Kavafi (IRE)—Dexandra (GR) (Evippos (GR)) **Stilvi Compania Financiera**

MR DAVID LANIGAN - Continued

THREE-YEAR-OLDS

8 **BELLA BELLISSIMA (USA)**, b br f Street Cry (IRE)—Meribel (USA)
9 **BLACKBALL (USA)**, b br g Speightstown (USA)—Wild Decision (USA)
10 **BRAVESTAR (IRE)**, b g Lawman (FR)—High Fidelity (GER)
11 **BRIGHT GLOW**, ch f Exceed And Excel (AUS)—Lighthouse
12 B c Dalakhani (IRE)—Clear Vision
13 **DANCE KING**, ch c Danehill Dancer (IRE)—One So Wonderful
14 **DUKES DELIGHT (IRE)**, b f Duke of Marmalade (IRE)—Fashion Model
15 **FOOTSTEPSINTHERAIN (IRE)**, b g Footstepsinthesand—Champagne Toni (IRE)
16 **FURIBONDO**, br g Monsun (GER)—Geminiani (IRE)
17 **GASPARD**, b c Sakhee (USA)—Photogenic
18 **INTERCEPTION (IRE)**, ch f Raven's Pass (USA)—Badee'a (IRE)
19 **KNIGHT OF CUPS**, b c Sakhee (USA)—Maid To Perfection
20 **LABIENUS**, b c Compton Place—Guermantes
21 **LEONARD THOMAS**, b c Singspiel (IRE)—Monawara (IRE)
22 **MASQUERADING (IRE)**, b g Singspiel (IRE)—Moonlight Dance (USA)
23 **NO JET LAG (USA)**, b g Johar (USA)—Desert Sky (IRE)
24 **NOS DA**, b f Cape Cross (IRE)—Nantyglo
25 **NUR JAHAN (IRE)**, b f Selkirk (USA)—Have Faith (IRE)
26 **PINK ANEMONE**, b f Dansili—Crystal Reef
27 **PLENUM (GER)**, b c Shamardal (USA)—Prima Luce (IRE)
28 **PLUTOCRACY (IRE)**, b c Dansili—Private Life (FR)
29 **PORTMONARCH (IRE)**, b c Galileo (IRE)—Egyptian Queen (USA)
30 **PROGENITOR (IRE)**, b g Mujadil (USA)—Bradamante
31 **PURE MISCHIEF (IRE)**, ch f Rock of Gibraltar (IRE)—Fig Tree Drive (USA)
32 **SCOTIA GIRL (IRE)**, ch f Hurricane Run (IRE)—Rose Parade
33 **SPIN A SPELL (USA)**, b f Empire Maker (USA)—Arabian Spell (IRE)
34 **STREAK**, b f Marju (IRE)—Eliza Gilbert
35 **TENUTO (IRE)**, b g Montjeu (IRE)—Musical Note
36 **THE MECHANIC (IRE)**, b c Monsun (GER)—Melodramatic (IRE)
37 **TINGHIR**, b c Dansili—Palmeraie (USA)
38 **TYPHON (USA)**, b c Proud Citizen (USA)—Seven Moons (JPN)
39 **WANNABE YOUR MAN**, b c Halling (USA)—Wannabe Posh (IRE)

TWO-YEAR-OLDS

40 **ALLEGATION (FR)**, b f 29/4 Lawman (FR)—Anja (IRE) (Indian Ridge) (65079)
41 B c 13/5 Sea The Stars (IRE)—Ange Bleu (USA) (Alleged (USA))
42 Ch c 6/4 Pivotal—Bright Morning (USA) (Storm Cat (USA)) (200000)
43 **DON OTTAVIO**, b c 9/4 Amadeus Wolf—Lyric Art (USA) (Red Ransom (USA)) (8000)
44 B f 23/2 Duke of Marmalade (IRE)—Fille de Joie (IRE) (Royal Academy (USA)) (24000)
45 **HIGHPLAINS DRIFTER (IRE)**, b c 9/5 High Chaparral (IRE)—Qhazeenah (Marju (IRE)) (123015)
46 **HOIST THE COLOURS (IRE)**, b c 14/3 Sea The Stars (IRE)—
                                        Multicolour Wave (IRE) (Rainbow Quest (USA)) (475000)
47 Ch c 27/2 Speightstown (USA)—Ikat (IRE) (Pivotal)
48 **ILE FLOTTANTE**, b f 2/3 Duke of Marmalade (IRE)—Aqaarid (USA) (Nashwan (USA))
49 B f 9/4 Sea The Stars (IRE)—My Branch (Distant Relative)
50 B f 27/3 Sea The Stars (IRE)—Palmeraie (USA) (Lear Fan (USA))
51 **POLYBIUS**, b c 16/4 Oasis Dream—Freedonia (Selkirk (USA))
52 **PRETZEL**, ch c 13/3 New Approach (IRE)—Foodbroker Fancy (IRE) (Halling (USA))
53 **RAINBOW LOLLIPOP**, b f 2/3 Dubawi (IRE)—Cross Section (USA) (Cape Cross (IRE))
54 **REMBRANDT VAN RIJN (IRE)**, b c 13/5 Peintre Celebre (USA)—Private Life (FR) (Bering)
55 **SALMON SUSHI**, ch c 8/2 Dalakhani (IRE)—Salsa Steps (USA) (Giant's Causeway (USA))
56 **SEQUESTER**, ch f 18/5 Selkirk (USA)—Al Theraab (USA) (Roberto (USA))
57 **SHOTGUN WEDDING**, b f 20/2 Champs Elysees—Ransomed Bride (Cape Cross (IRE))
58 **ST VINCENT (IRE)**, b c 6/3 Danehill Dancer (IRE)—Lace (IRE) (Sadler's Wells (USA)) (125000)
59 **WANNABE YOURS (IRE)**, b c 15/2 Dubawi (IRE)—Wannabe Posh (IRE) (Grand Lodge (USA))
60 **WARRIOR OF LIGHT (IRE)**, b c 10/3 High Chaparral (IRE)—
                                        Strawberry Fledge (USA) (Kingmambo (USA)) (320000)

Owners: Mr Ben Arbib, Sir Martyn Arbib, Mr Paul Brosnan, Mr Catesby Clay, Favourites Racing, The Greyston Partnership, Liza Judd, The Kathryn Stud, Mrs David Lanigan, Mr Bob Lanigan, Mr Robert Lapenta, Lord Lloyd-Webber, Mrs John Magnier, Mr Mick Mariscotti, Mrs Janice Mariscotti, Mr and Mrs Bill McAlpin, Niarchos Family, Mr B. E. Nielsen, Normandie Stud, Mr Ben Sangster, Usk Valley Stud, Wedgewood Estates, Mr Christopher Wright.

Jockey (flat): Ted Durcan.

381 MISS EMMA LAVELLE, Andover

Postal: Cottage Stables, Hatherden, Andover, Hampshire, SP11 0HY
Contacts: PHONE (01264) 735509 OFFICE (01264) 735412 FAX (01264) 735529
MOBILE (07774) 993998
E-MAIL emma@elavelle.freeserve.co.uk WEBSITE www.emmalavelle.com

1 AFRICAN EAGLE (IRE), 6, b g Trade Fair—Trushan **Frisky Fillies 6**
2 BLUES AND TWOS, 7, b g Presenting—Blue Gallery (IRE) **N. Mustoe & T. Syder**
3 BOUGGLER, 8, b g Tobougg (IRE)—Rush Hour (IRE) **Axom (XXI)**
4 BRANTINGHAM BREEZE, 5, gr m Tamure (IRE)—Absalom's Lady **Cottage Stables Racing Club**
5 CAMAS BRIDGE, 7, ch g Alflora (IRE)—Bobupandown **The High Altitude Partnership**
6 CAPTAIN SUNSHINE, 7, b g Oscar (IRE)—Gaye Fame **Mrs N. C. Turner**
7 4, B g King's Theatre (IRE)—Chevet Girl (IRE) **T. Syder & M. St Quintin**
8 CLARET CLOAK (IRE), 6, b g Vinnie Roe (IRE)—Bewildered (IRE) **Hawksmoor Partnership**
9 CLOSING CEREMONY (IRE), 4, b g Flemensfirth (USA)—
      Supreme Von Pres (IRE) **The High Altitude Partnership**
10 CLYFFE DANCER, 5, b m Grape Tree Road—Chandni (IRE) **Mrs C. F. E. Hall**
11 COMPASSION, 5, b m Tiger Hill (IRE)—Windmill **Mrs S. Metcalfe**
12 COOLE RIVER (IRE), 9, ch g Carroll House—Kyle Cailin **Queens' Prices Syndicate**
13 COURT BY SURPRISE (IRE), 8, b g Beneficial—Garryduff Princess (IRE) **N. Mustoe**
14 COURT IN MOTION (IRE), 8, br g Fruits of Love (USA)—Peace Time Girl (IRE) **N. Mustoe**
15 COURT VICTORY (IRE), 8, b g Old Vic—Sarah's Smile **N. Mustoe**
16 4, B g Kayf Tara—Cullen Bay (IRE) **Colin Bothway & Roger Hetherington**
17 DANCING TEASEL, 6, ch m Snurge—Cajole (IRE) **Mrs S. H. West**
18 DAYMAR BAY (IRE), 7, b g Oscar (IRE)—Sunset View (IRE) **The Second Fox Inn Syndicate**
19 DAYS GONE BY, 5, b g Kayf Tara—Nuzzle **Swanbridge Bloodstock Limited**
20 DEMOGRAPHIC (USA), 4, b g Aptitude (USA)—Private Line (USA) **Mrs A. C. Lavelle**
21 EASTER METEOR, 7, b g Midnight Legend—Easter Comet **Mr S. C. Willes**
22 FIRE AND RAIN (FR), 10, b g Galileo (IRE)—Quatre Saisons (FR) **Fraser Miller Racing**
23 FIREY KING (IRE), 6, b g Flemensfirth (USA)—Chapel Queen (IRE) **The Rams Syndicate**
24 FIX IT RIGHT (IRE), 5, br g Vinnie Roe (IRE)—Rock Cottage Lady (IRE) **The Fox Inn Syndicate**
25 FONTANO (FR), 7, gr g Astarabad (USA)—Little Bud (FR) **Mrs Julien Turner & Mr Andrew Merriam**
26 FOX APPEAL (IRE), 6, b g Brian Boru—Lady Appeal (IRE) **Fox Inn Syndicate 3**
27 FURTHER MORE (IRE), 6, gr g Hasten To Add (USA)—Cottage Lass (IRE) **Frisky Fillies 4**
28 GLEANN EAGAS (IRE), 6, b g Gold Well—Glen Princess (IRE) **R. J. Lavelle**
29 GLOBAL WARMING (IRE), 9, b g King's Theatre (IRE)—Croi Na Greine (IRE) **The Older But No Wiser Syndicate**
30 GOOD BOY JACKSON, 5, b g Firebreak—Fisher Island (IRE) **The C H F Partnership**
31 GREY WULFF (IRE), 8, gr g Oscar (IRE)—Only A Rose **Mrs S. V. M. Stevens**
32 GULLINBURSTI (IRE), 7, b g Milan—D'ygrande (IRE) **N. Mustoe**
33 HATTON BANK, 4, ch f Flemensfirth (USA)—Persian Walk (FR) **Mr G. P. MacIntosh**
34 HIGHLAND LODGE (IRE), 7, b g Flemensfirth (USA)—Supreme Von Pres (IRE) **The Unusual Suspects**
35 HURRICANE HENRY (IRE), 6, b g Highest Honor (FR)—Make Rings **T. D. J. Syder**
36 JUST GOT LUCKY, 5, ch m Definite Article—Single Handed **Swanbridge Bloodstock Limited**
37 KANGAROO COURT (IRE), 9, b g Lahib (USA)—Tombazaan (IRE) **N. Mustoe**
38 KENTFORD GREY LADY, 7, gr m Silver Patriarch (IRE)—Kentford Grebe **D. I. Bare**
39 KILLYGLASS (IRE), 6, b g Heron Island (IRE)—Grande Solitaire (FR) **Mr T. D. J. Syder & Mr N. Mustoe**
40 KIND OF EASY (IRE), 7, b g Kalanisi (IRE)—Specifiedrisk (IRE) **Mr T. D. J. Syder & Mr N. Mustoe**
41 KINDLY NOTE, 6, ch m Generous (IRE)—Vent d'aout (IRE) **Elite Racing Club**
42 KING BORU (IRE), 5, b g Brian Boru—Final Instalment **Lavelle Wallis Farrington**
43 KUSADIKI (IRE), 7, b g Tobougg (IRE)—Mother Molly (USA) **The Optimists**
44 LE BEC (FR), 5, ch g Smadoun (FR)—La Pelode (FR) **T. D. J. Syder**
45 MILANESE (IRE), 5, b g Milan—Elma Joyce (IRE) **The C H F Partnership**
46 MOSSPARK (IRE), 5, b g Flemensfirth (USA)—Patio Rose **N. Mustoe & T. Syder**
47 OCEANA GOLD, 9, ch g Primo Valentino (IRE)—Silken Dalliance **The C H F Partnership**
48 OFF THE GROUND (IRE), 7, b g Oscar (IRE)—Kaysel (IRE) **Axom (XXVI)**
49 OUZBECK (FR), 11, b br g Denham Red (FR)—Volodia (FR) **Axom VII**
50 PASKALIS, 4, b c Kayf Tara—Easter Comet **Mr S. C. Willes**
51 PAUSE AND CLAUSE (IRE), 9, b g Saddlers' Hall (IRE)—Silver Glen (IRE) **Mr R. D. P. Cohen**
52 QIANSHAN LEADER (IRE), 9, b g Anshan—Gaelic Leader (IRE) **The Pick 'N' Mix Partnership**
53 RECHERCHE, 4, b f Sirillio (GER)—Rattina (GER) **The Hon Mrs F. P. Guinness**
54 RED MILE (FR), 8, ch g Kapgarde (FR)—Katespeed (FR) **T. D. J. Syder**
55 RED ROCK (FR), 8, b g Saint Cyrien (FR)—Ariloba de Brize (FR) **Mrs S. V. M. Stevens**
56 ROYAL COMMISSION (IRE), 6, b g Orpen (USA)—Princess of Iona (IRE) **Cakey Bundles**
57 SHOTGUN PADDY (IRE), 6, b g Brian Boru—Awesome Miracle (IRE) **Axom (XXXVI)**
58 SILVER FOOTNOTE, 8, gr g Silver Patriarch (IRE)—
      Mavourneen (IRE) **James Thorburn-Muirhead&John Kevin Lomax**

MISS EMMA LAVELLE - Continued

59 STAIGUE FORT, 5, b g Kirkwall—Mulberry Wine **Lady Bland**
60 THE LAST NIGHT (FR), 6, ch g April Night (FR)—La Pelode (FR) **T. D. J. Syder**
61 THE POTTING SHED (IRE), 6, br g Presenting—Barracree Rose (IRE) **N. Mustoe & T. Syder**
62 TIDAL DANCE (IRE), 6, b g Craigsteel—Musical Waves (IRE) **Pinks Gym & Leisure Wear Ltd**
63 TIM THE CHAIR (IRE), 8, b g Pierre—Dinah B (IRE) **Frisky Fillies 5**
64 TOCCA FERRO (FR), 8, gr g April Night (FR)—La Pelode (FR)
65 VAGRANT EMPEROR (IRE), 10, b g Oscar (IRE)—Dragonmist (IRE) **Mrs A. C. Lavelle**
66 VENDREDI TROIS (FR), 4, b g Shaanmer (IRE)—Legende Sacree (FR) **Awdry, Gemmell, Pomford & Williams**
67 WATER WAGTAIL, 6, b g Kahyasi—Kentford Grebe **D. I. Bare**
68 WELL REGARDED (IRE), 8, b g Dr Massini (IRE)—Glenelly Valley (IRE) **The Unusual Suspects**
69 WOODLAND WALK, 5, ch m Generous (IRE)—Duchess of Kinsale (IRE) **Cottage Stables Racing Club**
70 YABADABADOO, 5, b g Doyen (IRE)—Kabayil **Elite Racing Club**
71 ZARRAFAKT (IRE), 9, b g Rudimentary (USA)—Carrick Glen (IRE) **Mr G. P. MacIntosh**

THREE-YEAR-OLDS

72 STARLIGHT SONATA, b f Tagula (IRE)—Starlight Express (FR) **D. M. Bell**

Other Owners: C. V. Awdry, Axom Ltd, R. A. Beach, C. H. Bothway, R. M. Cathery, G. C. Clifford, K. J. Clifford, I. W. Dale, D. Downie, W. T. Farrington, K. H. Fischer, C. H. Fischer, Mrs J. R. Foster, R. J. Fowler, A. Gemmell, C. G. Hellyer, Mrs S. C. Hepworth, R. R. Hetherington, A. J. Hill, J. R. Hulme, J. R. Lavelle, K. J. Lomax, J. J. P. McNeile, A. W. K. Merriam, P. B. Mitford-Slade, P. Nicholls, Miss M. Noden, B. G. Pomford, K. P. Ryan, O. F. Ryan, Sir David Sieff, B. G. Slade, J. Thorburn-Muirhead, J. W. Turner, Mrs J. C. Verity, J. R. Wallis, M. T. Ward, P. R. Weston, A. G. Weston, Mrs P. H. Williams.

Assistant Trainer: Barry Fenton

---

382 JOAN L. LE BROCQ, Jersey
Postal: Greystones, La Rue Coentyn, St Ouens, Jersey, Channel Islands, JE3 2GY
Contacts: PHONE/FAX (01534) 481461 MOBILE (07797) 750823
E-MAIL joanlebrocq@gmail.com

1 BOLLIN FERGUS, 9, br g Vettori (IRE)—Bollin Harriet **Joan Le Brocq & Angie Richardson**
2 HIGH VOLTAGE, 12, ch g Wolfhound (USA)—Real Emotion (USA) **Joan Le Brocq**
3 LANDOLINO (FR), 8, b g Trempolino (USA)—Champagne Sorbet (FR) **Lavender Racing**
4 LORD OF THE WING, 8, b g Daggers Drawn (USA)—Brangane (IRE) **Frank & Annette Brady**
5 MOOSE MORAN (USA), 6, gr ro g Lemon Drop Kid (USA)—After All (IRE) **Joan Le Brocq**
6 ROBBMAA (FR), 8, bl g Cape Cross (IRE)—Native Twine **Joan Le Brocq**
7 RUNAROUND RITA (FR), 5, ch m Protektor (GER)—Wild Rita **Joan Le Brocq**
8 SCULASTIC, 10, b g Galileo (IRE)—Mutual Consent (IRE) **Joan Le Brocq**
9 SECRET ASSASSIN (IRE), 10, b g Daggers Drawn (USA)—Lypharden (IRE) **The Name's Bond Partnership**
10 WILD IN WOOLLY (FR), 6, gr g Al Namix (FR)—Wild Rita **Joan Le Brocq**

Other Owners: D. Barrons, Mr Allan Butler, J. Davies, Seamus Gallagher, Advocate R. Michel, Caroline Michel, Mike Quenault, Joe Quinn, Lesley Norton, David Fish, Mr M. & Mrs J. Chambers, Jannine Davies, Lavender Racing.

Assistant Trainer: Martin Edwards

Jockey (NH): Mattie Batchelor, Jamie Goldstein.

---

383 MR BARRY LEAVY, Stoke-on-Trent
Postal: Cash Heath Farm, Cash Heath, Forsbrook, Stoke-on-Trent, ST11 9DE
Contacts: HOME/FAX (01782) 398591 MOBILE (07540) 806915
E-MAIL lauraleavy@hotmail.co.uk

1 ALFIE MOONE, 5, b g Deploy—Capricorn Princess **Mrs Laura Leavy**
2 BRIDAL MEDIC, 4, ch g Medicean—Bridal Path **Mr J. A. Ashley**
3 DANCING DUDE (IRE), 6, ch g Danehill Dancer (IRE)—Wadud **Cops & Robbers**
4 EL CAMINO REAL (IRE), 5, b g Dansili—Soviet Artic (FR) **Mr Barry Leavy**
5 FLOBURY, 5, b m Overbury (IRE)—Miss Flora **Mr J. K. Cresswell**
6 HYDE LEA FLYER, 8, b g Hernando (FR)—Sea Ridge **Mr Barry Leavy**
7 KING ZEAL (IRE), 9, b g King's Best (USA)—Manureva (USA) **Deborah Hart & Alan Jackson**
8 KIRKHAMMERTON (IRE), 11, ch g Grand Lodge (USA)—Nawara **Valentino Racing**
9 LEAN BURN (USA), 7, b g Johannesburg (USA)—Anthelion (USA) **Mr N. Heath**
10 MOHI RAHRERE (IRE), 10, b g New Frontier (IRE)—Collinstown Lady (IRE) **Mrs S D Ashford & Mr J G Williams**

MR BARRY LEAVY - Continued

11 **NOT BAD FOR A BOY (IRE)**, 4, b g Elusive City (USA)—Reign of Fire (IRE) **Mr Brendan Jones**
12 **ON THE RIGHT PATH**, 6, b g Pursuit of Love—Glen Falls **Mr N. Heath**
13 **WESTLIN' WINDS (IRE)**, 7, b g Montjeu (IRE)—Uliana (USA) **Mrs AD Snaith & Mrs SD Williams-Ashford**
14 **WHENHARRYMETDEBBIE**, 4, b f Sir Harry Lewis (USA)—Debbie **Mrs D. Hart & Mr A. Jackson**

Other Owners: Mr Frank Dronzek, Mrs Deborah Hart, Mr Alan Jackson, Mr Barry Leavy, Mr Chris Nightingale, Mr D. Rowlinson, Mrs A. D. Snaith, Mr J. G. Williams, Mrs S. D. Ashford.

Assistant Trainer: Mrs L Leavy

384

MR RICHARD LEE, Presteigne
Postal: **The Bell House, Byton, Presteigne, LD8 2HS**
Contacts: PHONE **(01544) 267672** FAX **(01544) 260247** MOBILE **(07836) 537145**
E-MAIL **rleeracing@btinternet.com** WEBSITE **www.rleeracing.com**

1 **BACKFROMTHECONGO (IRE)**, 12, b br g Bob Back (USA)—
  Market Lass (IRE) **D. Cound, J. Jackson & A. Compton**
2 **BACKSTREET BILLY (IRE)**, 9, br g Presenting—Basically (IRE) **P. A. Bonner**
3 **BIG NEWS**, 7, ch g Karinga Bay—Welcome News **Mrs Caroline Shaw & Mrs Christine Graves**
4 **BLACK IS BEAUTIFUL (FR)**, 5, b g Black Sam Bellamy (IRE)—Queen's Theatre (FR) **B Bailey & K Edwards**
5 **CADOUDALAS (FR)**, 10, b g Cadoudal (FR)—Popie D'ecorcei (FR) **Six To Five Against G D Thorp, R L Baker**
6 **CHIQUILLINE (FR)**, 7, b br g Kapgarde (FR)—Sheyrinca (FR) **Miss T. O. Blazey**
7 **DROPZONE (USA)**, 4, b g Smart Strike (CAN)—Dalisay (IRE) **R. A. Lee**
8 **GASSIN GOLF**, 4, b g Montjeu (IRE)—Miss Riviera Golf **W. Roseff**
9 **GOODTOKNOW**, 5, b g Presenting—Atlantic Jane **Burling Daresbury MacEchern Nolan Potter**
10 **GREY GOLD (IRE)**, 8, gr g Strategic Choice (USA)—Grouse-N-Heather **Mrs M. A. Boden**
11 **HECTOR'S CHOICE (FR)**, 9, b br g Grey Risk (FR)—The Voice (FR) **James & Jean Potter**
12 **HIGHWAY CODE (USA)**, 7, b g Street Cry (IRE)—Fairy Heights (IRE) **D. E. Edwards**
13 **INCENTIVISE (IRE)**, 10, ch g Snurge—Festive Isle (IRE) **Ron Bartlett, F J Ayres & Jeff Hulston**
14 **KNOCK A HAND (IRE)**, 8, br g Lend A Hand—Knockcross (IRE) **D. A. Halsall**
15 **MILO MILAN (IRE)**, 8, b g Milan—Simply Divine (IRE) **Mrs Caroline Shaw & Mrs Christine Graves**
16 **MOUNTAINOUS (IRE)**, 8, b g Milan—Mullaghcloga (IRE) **Walters Plant Hire & James & Jean Potter**
17 **RAVENS BROOK (IRE)**, 7, br g Alderbrook—Triple Triumph (IRE) **R. A. Lee**
18 **RIFLEMAN (IRE)**, 13, ch g Starborough—En Garde (USA) **J. M. Jackson**
19 **RUSSE BLANC (FR)**, 6, wh g Machiavellian Tsar (FR)—Fleur de Mad (FR) **Mr M. R. H. Jackson**
20 **SARRACO (IRE)**, 7, ch g Old Vic—Harelda **George Brookes & Family II**
21 **SCALES (IRE)**, 7, b g Bob Back (USA)—Mrs Avery (IRE) **A Beard B Beard S Ripley**
22 **SIMPLY WINGS (IRE)**, 9, b g Winged Love (IRE)—Simply Deep (IRE) **G. D. Thorp**
23 **THE CHAZER (IRE)**, 8, gr g Witness Box (USA)—Saffron Holly (IRE) **Mr & Mrs C. R. Elliott**
24 **TRESOR DE BONTEE (FR)**, 6, b g Grand Seigneur (FR)—Bontee (FR) **Willow National Hunt Racing Club**
25 **VICTORY GUNNER (IRE)**, 15, ch g Old Vic—Gunner B Sharp **Ron Bartlett & F. J. Ayres**
26 **WALCOT LATHYRUS**, 8, b g Alflora (IRE)—Strong Cloth (IRE) **D. Pugh**

Other Owners: Mrs S. Archdale, F. J. Ayres, B. J. Bailey, Mr R. L Baker, R. Bartlett, A. C. Beard, B. M. Beard, G. E. Brookes, Mr P. R. Burling, Mrs R. L. Burling, A. J. Compton, J. D. Cound, Lord Daresbury, K. Edwards, C. R. Elliott, Mrs J. A. Elliott, Mrs C. M. Graves, R. L. C. Hartley, J. P Hulston, Mrs C. J. Lee, G. M. MacEchern, Mr P Nolan, J. E. Potter, Mrs M. J. Potter, Lady H. S. Ripley, Mrs C. L. Shaw, Mr D. J. Smith, Walters Plant Hire Ltd, Mr M. Wilson.

Assistant Trainer: Kerry Lewis

Jockey (NH): Charlie Poste, Richard Johnson. **Conditional:** James Jeavons, Micheal Nolan.

385

MRS SOPHIE LEECH, Westbury-on-Severn
Postal: **Tudor Racing Stables, Elton Road, Elton, Newnham, Gloucestershire, GL14 1JN**
Contacts: PHONE **(01452) 760691** MOBILE **(07775) 874630**
E-MAIL **info@leechracing.co.uk** WEBSITE **www.leechracing.co.uk**

1 **BANYAN TREE (IRE)**, 6, b g Danehill Dancer (IRE)—User Friendly **C. J. Leech**
2 **BLOWING A HOOLIE (IRE)**, 5, b m Val Royal (FR)—Moly **C J Leech & S Bryan**
3 **EASTWELL SMILES**, 9, gr g Erhaab (USA)—Miss University (USA) **C. J. Leech**
4 **GOD'S COUNTY (FR)**, 8, gr g Verglas (IRE)—Toujours Elle (USA) **G. Doel & C. J. Leech**
5 **GREY SOLDIER (IRE)**, 8, gr g Galileo (IRE)—Crusch Alva (FR) **J. O'Brien & C. J. Leech**
6 **GTAAB**, 7, b g Cape Cross (IRE)—Nabadhaat (USA) **Cheltenham Racing Club**
7 **HELIUM (FR)**, 8, b g Dream Well (FR)—Sure Harbour (SWI) **G Thompson, C J Leech, P Stock**

MRS SOPHIE LEECH - Continued

```
 8  IS IT ME (USA), 10, ch g Sky Classic (CAN)—Thea (GER) Cheltenham Racing Club
 9  KEENES DAY (FR), 8, gr g Daylami (IRE)—Key Academy J. O'Brien & C. J. Leech
10  LE GRAND CHENE (FR), 7, b g Turgeon (USA)—Faitiche d'aubry (FR) T. Westmacott & C. J. Leech
11  NICENE CREED, 8, b g Hernando (FR)—First Fantasy C. J. Leech
12  OLD MAGIC (IRE), 8, b g Old Vic—Maeve's Magic (IRE) Cheltenham Racing Club
13  OLYMPIAN BOY (IRE), 9, b g Flemensfirth (USA)—Notanissue (IRE) J Cocks, P Stock & CJ Leech
14  PETARA BAY (IRE), 9, b g Peintre Celebre (USA)—Magnificient Style (USA) C. J. Leech
15  PRINCE PIPPIN (IRE), 7, b g King Charlemagne (USA)—Staploy J Cocks, P Stock & CJ Leech
16  REFERENT (FR), 8, b g Ultimately Lucky (IRE)—Haida IV (FR) Cheltenham Racing Club
17  RIVER D'OR (FR), 8, b g Saint Preuil (FR)—Une Pomme d'or (FR) G. Doel & C. J. Leech
18  SHOUDA (IRE), 7, b g Tiger Hill (IRE)—Sommernacht (GER) C. J. Leech
19  SOUTH O'THE BORDER, 11, b g Wolfhound (USA)—Abbey's Gal C. J. Leech
20  TAKE OF SHOC'S (IRE), 9, ch g Beneficial—Dear Dunleer (IRE) C. J. Leech
21  TASHEBA, 8, ch g Dubai Destination (USA)—Tatanka (IRE) C. J. Leech
22  WINSTON CHURCHILL (IRE), 7, b g Presenting—Star Councel (IRE) G. D. Thompson
```

Other Owners: S. J. Bryan, Mr J. J. Cocks, G. Doel, Mr C J Hodgson, J. O'Brien, Mr C. Parkin, Mr T. Westmacott.

Assistant Trainer: Charlotte Leech (07880) 788464

Jockey (NH): Paul Moloney

---

386 **MR DAVID LEWIS, Tewkesbury**
Postal: **Broadfields Farm, Longdon, Tewkesbury, Gloucestershire, GL20 6AN**
Contacts: **PHONE (01684) 830185**

```
1  CASTLE LEGEND, 8, ch g Midnight Legend—Morstoncastle Rose Mr D. T. Lewis
2  DR ANUBIS (IRE), 8, ch g Beneficial—Gaelic (IRE) Mr D. T. Lewis
3  OSCAR RAINBOW, 7, b g Oscar (IRE)—Fionnula's Rainbow (IRE) Mr D. T. Lewis
4  PASSONATE BLEU (IRE), 5, b m Classic Cliche (IRE)—Blue Passion (IRE) Mr J. T. Cleaver
5  SMILEY MILEY (IRE), 5, ch m Danroad (AUS)—Music Teacher Mr D. T. Lewis
6  TOTAL VICTORY (IRE), 10, br g Titus Livius (FR)—Snipe Victory (IRE) Mr D. T. Lewis
```

---

387 **MR ALASTAIR LIDDERDALE, Lambourn**
Postal: **Lidderdale Racing LLP, High View Stables, Folly Road, Lambourn, Hungerford, Berkshire, RG17 8QE**
Contacts: **PHONE (01488) 670443 (01488) 73694 FAX (01488) 670443 MOBILE (07785) 785375**
E-MAIL alastair@lidderdaleracing.co.uk WEBSITE www.lidderdaleracing.co.uk

```
 1  ABSENT AMY (IRE), 4, b f Redback—Twitcher's Delight The Strawberries To A Donkey Partnership
 2  ADDAZERO, 4, b g Putra Sas (IRE)—Poker Queen Red Hot Partnership
 3  ASIAN PRINCE (IRE), 4, b g Strategic Prince—Asian Alliance (IRE) Lidderdale Racing LLP
 4  AVERTIS, 8, b g Averti (IRE)—Double Stake (USA) Mrs S. J. Doyle
 5  BLACK OR RED (IRE), 8, b g Cape Cross (USA)—Gentle Thoughts Mr G. Bradbury
 6  BUBBLINA, 6, b m Pastoral Pursuits—Streccia Mrs S. J. Doyle
 7  CAMROCK STAR, 4, b f Rock of Gibraltar (IRE)—Night Cam (USA) Lidderdale Racing LLP
 8  CELTIC SULTAN (IRE), 9, b g Celtic Swing—Farjah (IRE) Trinity TT Racing Partnerships
 9  CHELLA THRILLER (SPA), 4, b f Chevalier (IRE)—Arundhati (IRE) The Saucy Horse Partnership
10  DUBAI STORY, 4, b f Dubai Destination (USA)—Madrigale Mr C. S. J. Beek
11  GRAPESHOT VERSE, 4, ch f Grape Tree Road—Caballe (USA) B. S. Hicks
12  KIJIVU, 8, gr m Erhaab (USA)—Alsiba KMC Partnership Three
13  KILBURN, 9, b g Grand Lodge (USA)—Lady Lahar Royal Windsor Racing Club
14  4, B f Multiplex—Kingsfold Blaze Gary Gillies
15  KINGSWINFORD (IRE), 7, b g Noverre (USA)—Berenica (IRE) Mr C. S. J. Beek
16  MAJESTIC ZAFEEN, 4, b f Zafeen (FR)—Arasong Lambourn Valley Racing II
17  MAJOR ERADICATOR (USA), 6, b g Purge (USA)—Pontook (USA) Mr C. S. J. Beek
18  MICHAEL'S NOOK, 6, b g Intikhab (USA)—Mysterious Plans (IRE) Mr C. S. J. Beek
19  NORTH CAPE (USA), 7, b g Action This Day (USA)—Cape (USA) Mr A. McIver
20  OGARITMO, 4, ch f Manduro (GER)—Querida Dr Ornella Carlini Cozzi
21  OSTENTATION, 6, ch g Dubawi (IRE)—Oshiponga Mr C. S. J. Beek
22  PEACHEZ, 5, ch m Observatory (USA)—Streccia Mrs S. J. Doyle
23  PHANTOM RANCH, 4, b g Act One—Highbrook (USA) The Diamond White Partnership
24  POCKETWOOD, 11, b g Fleetwood (IRE)—Pocket Venus (IRE) The sw1ft Buck Partnership
```

MR ALASTAIR LIDDERDALE - Continued

25 **POTENTIALE (IRE),** 9, ch g Singspiel (IRE)—No Frills (IRE) **Trinity TT Partnership**
26 **PYTHEAS (USA),** 6, b g Seeking The Gold (USA)—Neptune's Bride (USA) **Mr C. S. J. Beek**
27 **RHOSSILI BAY,** 4, b f Beat Hollow—Welsh Dawn **Jackie Gittins Steve McAvoy Stuart Hawtin**
28 **ROYAL ALCOR (IRE),** 6, b g Chevalier (IRE)—Arundhati (IRE) **Royal Windsor Racing Club**
29 **SCARLETTE D'OR,** 4, ch f Iceman—Double Stake (USA) **Mrs S. J. Doyle**
30 **SSAFA,** 5, b m Motivator—Orange Sunset (IRE) **Ssafa Partnership**
31 **TOOGOOD (IRE),** 4, ch g Pivotal—Woodland Orchid (IRE) **Team Toogood**
32 **WHERE'S REILEY (USA),** 7, b br g Doneraile Court (USA)—Plateau (USA) **Chris Beek & Steve Jakes**

THREE-YEAR-OLDS

33 **CANDY KITTEN,** b f Assertive—Birthday Venture **Lady Whent**
34 **HERBALIST,** ch g Haafhd—Puya **Trinity TT Partnership**
35 **ISHISOBA,** ch f Ishiguru (USA)—Bundle Up (USA) **Mr M. M. Cox**
36 **MARMOT BAY (IRE),** b f Kodiac—Tides **Mr C. S. J. Beek**
37 **ROYAL MIZAR (SPA),** b g What A Caper (IRE)—Zahaadid (FR) **Royal Windsor Racing Club**

TWO-YEAR-OLDS

38 B f 5/4 Byron—Kathy's Rocket (USA) (Gold Legend (USA)) (380) **Trinity TT Partnership**

Other Owners: Mr C. S. J. Beek, Mr Tom Castle, Mr Peter Chilton, Mr Anthony Crampton, Mrs Sally Doyle, Mr J. Duffy, Mr Bill Evans, Mr Stefan Fellows, Mr M. J. Foxton-Duffy, Mrs Jackie Gittins, Mrs Lola Grogan, Mr Ray Grogan, Mr Dave Hadley, Mr Mark Hallesey, Mr Stuart Hawtin, Mr W. R. Hinge, Mrs C. Houghton, Mr Steve Jakes, Mrs C. Jordan, Mr M. Jordan, Mr A. J. D. Lidderdale, Mr Stephen McAvoy, Mr K. P. McCarthy, Mrs Grace Moir, Mr David J. Muir, Mr M. M. Peel, Mrs C. Potter, Mr John Searchfield, Ms J. M. Smith, Ms L. Stoten, Mr John Tackley, Mr Anthony Taylor, Mr Kevin Thompson, Mrs Joanne Thompson, Mr D. Woodhead.

Assistant Trainer: Clark Judd

Apprentice: Leonna Mayor, Semira Pashai. **Amateur:** Miss Zoe Lilly, Miss Jennifer Pahlman.

---

388 MR NICK LITTMODEN, Newmarket
Postal: **Brook Farm, Dullingham Ley, Dullingham, Newmarket, Suffolk, CB8 9XG**
Contacts: **PHONE (01638) 508491 FAX (01638) 508491 MOBILE (07770) 964865**
E-MAIL nicklittmoden@btinternet.com WEBSITE www.nicklittmoden.com

1 **CUT ACROSS (IRE),** 5, b g Cape Cross (IRE)—Incise **N. R. Shields**
2 **LIVING LEADER,** 4, b g Oasis Dream—Royal Jade **N. R. Shields**
3 **MILLIBAR,** 4, b f Manduro (GER)—Iktidar **Mrs L. M. Francis**
4 **MUHANDIS (IRE),** 5, b g Muhtathir—Ahdaaf (USA) **A. A. Goodman**
5 **PENBRYN (USA),** 6, b g Pivotal—Brocatelle **Mrs K Graham, N Littmoden, A Highfield**

THREE-YEAR-OLDS

6 **BARNABY BROOK (CAN),** b c North Light (IRE)—Mascara (USA) **A. A. Goodman**
7 B g Cape Cross (IRE)—Brazilian Samba (IRE)
8 B g Pivotal—Gracefully (IRE)
9 Br g Anabaa (USA)—Lanciana (IRE)
10 B g Medicean—Lilli Marlene
11 B g Shamardal (USA)—Mania (IRE)
12 B g Stormy Atlantic (USA)—Rose of Zollern (IRE)
13 Ch g Dubawi (IRE)—Salee (IRE) **N. P. Littmoden**
14 B g Oasis Dream—Singed
15 B g Danehill Dancer (IRE)—Spinola (FR)

TWO-YEAR-OLDS

16 B g 26/4 Bahamian Bounty—Copy-Cat (Lion Cavern (USA)) (85000)
17 B br g 29/1 Elusive City (USA)—Rock Harmonie (FR) (Rock of Gibraltar (IRE)) (103174)

Other Owners: Ms P. Ferguson, Mrs K. B. Graham, Mr A. J. Highfield.

389 MR BERNARD LLEWELLYN, Bargoed
Postal: Ffynonau Duon Farm, Pentwyn, Fochriw, Bargoed, Mid-Glamorgan, CF81 9NP
Contacts: PHONE (01685) 841259 FAX (01685) 843838 MOBILE (07971) 233473/(07971) 283262
E-MAIL bernard.llewellyn@btopenworld.com

1 ARCH EVENT, 8, ch m Umistim—Arch Angel (IRE) **Mr D. P. Maddocks**
2 CAPTAIN SHARPE, 5, ch g Tobougg (IRE)—Helen Sharp **Bluebirds Racing & Co**
3 COME ON ANNIE, 7, b m Karinga Bay—Irish Ferry **Mrs E. V. A. Trotman**
4 DRUMMOND, 4, b g Zamindar (USA)—Alrisha (IRE) **B. J. Llewellyn**
5 FILATORE (IRE), 4, ch g Teofilo (IRE)—Dragnet (IRE) **Bluebirds Racing & Co**
6 FUZZY LOGIC (IRE), 4, b g Dylan Thomas (IRE)—Gates of Eden (USA) **G. Mills**
7 JUST BASIL, 6, b g Kayf Tara—Anagrammatic **Mr J. Griffiths**
8 KASHGAR, 4, b g Hernando (FR)—Miss Katmandu (IRE) **B. J. Llewellyn**
9 KOZMINA BAY, 4, b f Notnowcato—Kozmina (IRE) **B. J. Llewellyn**
10 LISSELAN PLEASURE (USA), 6, gr m Macho Uno (USA)—Cute Connie (USA) **B. W. Parren**
11 PANCAKE (FR), 10, ch g Cyborg (FR)—Six Fois Sept (FR) **R. C. Hambleton**
12 SHARAGEN, 6, br m Generous (USA)—Sharadiya (IRE) **The Futures Bright Partnership**
13 STAG HILL (IRE), 4, ch g Redback—Counting Blessings **B. J. Llewellyn**
14 TIMETORING, 11, ch g Karinga Bay—Little Time **B. J. Llewellyn**
15 TURBULANCE (IRE), 11, gr g Snurge—Full Deck (IRE) **A. J. Williams**

Other Owners: Mr G. Bryan, S. J. Bryan, B. H. Downs, Mr A. James, Mrs Beth Williams.

Assistant Trainer: J L Llewellyn

Jockey (flat): David Probert, Robert Havlin. **Jockey (NH):** Christian Williams, Donal Fahy. **Conditional:** Robert Williams. **Apprentice:** Robert Williams.

390 MISS NATALIE LLOYD-BEAVIS, East Garston
Postal: 2 Parsonage Cottages, Newbury Road, East Garston, Hungerford, Berkshire, RG17 7ER
Contacts: PHONE (07768) 117656 MOBILE (07768) 117656
E-MAIL nlbracing@gmail.com

1 JOHNCAN (IRE), 7, ch g Beneficial—Mary's View (IRE) **Caloona Racing**
2 PEINTRE DU ROI (USA), 9, ch g El Prado (IRE)—Peinture Bleue (USA) **Mr S. Lloyd-Beavis**

THREE-YEAR-OLDS
3 IMMACULATE HEART (IRE), b f Papal Bull—Caipirinia (IRE) **Mr S. Lloyd-Beavis**

TWO-YEAR-OLDS
4 DOUNEEDAHAND, b f 15/4 Royal Applause—Our Sheila (Bahamian Bounty) (3500) **Caloona Racing**
5 B f 1/2 Three Valleys (USA)—Salim Toto (Mtoto) (4500) **Caloona Racing**

Other Owners: P. R. Attwater, Mr H. R. Attwater.

Assistant Trainer: Hywel Davies

Jockey (NH): James Davies. **Apprentice:** Ryan Clark.

391 MR ALAN LOCKWOOD, Malton
Postal: Fleet Cross Farm, Brawby, Malton, North Yorkshire, YO17 6QA
Contacts: PHONE (01751) 431796 MOBILE (07747) 002535

1 BOLLIN FREDDIE, 9, ch g Golden Snake (USA)—Bollin Roberta **Highgreen Partnership**
2 PORT VIEW (IRE), 7, b g Classic Cliche (IRE)—Francie's Treble **A. J. Lockwood**
3 SAXBY (IRE), 6, ch g Pastoral Pursuits—Madam Waajib (IRE) **A. J. Lockwood**

Other Owners: J. Richardson, J. Stubbs, D. Wilson.

392 MR JOHN E. LONG, Woldingham
Postal: **Main Yard, Tillingdowns, Woldingham, Caterham, Surrey, CR3 7JA**
Contacts: **PHONE** (01883) 340730 **MOBILE** (07958) 296945/(07815) 186085
E-MAIL winalot@aol.com

1 **AMARONI**, 5, b g Sulamani (IRE)—Fortunes Favourite **Advani Family**
2 **BERMACHA**, 8, ch m Bertolini (USA)—Machaera **M. J. Gibbs**
3 **CATIVO CAVALLINO**, 10, ch g Bertolini (USA)—Sea Isle **M. J. Gibbs**
4 **CHANDRAYAAN**, 6, ch g Bertolini (USA)—Muffled (USA) **R. D. John**
5 **CUSTOM HOUSE (IRE)**, 5, b g Tale of The Cat (USA)—L'acajou (CAN) **Mr B C Oakley & Mr H Robin Heffer**
6 **FOR LIFE (IRE)**, 11, b g Bachir (IRE)—Zest (USA) **B. C. Oakley**
7 **ICE APPLE**, 5, b m Iceman—Star Apple **Mr & Mrs K. G. Newland**
8 **MICROLIGHT**, 5, b g Sleeping Indian—Skytrial (USA) **R. D. John**
9 **PRINCESS WILLOW**, 5, b m Phoenix Reach (IRE)—Highland Hannah (IRE) **Mr & Mrs T H Bambridge**
10 **RED WILLOW**, 7, ch m Noverre (USA)—Chelsea Blue (ITY) **J. King**
11 **TINKERBELL WILL**, 6, ch m Where Or When (IRE)—Highland Hannah (IRE) **Mr & Mrs T H Bambridge**
12 **TRUST ME BOY**, 5, gr g Avonbridge—Eastern Lyric **R. Pearson & J. Pearson**

THREE-YEAR-OLDS

13 **GURU BABY**, b f Ishiguru (USA)—Lefty's Dollbaby (USA) **Downlands Racing**

Other Owners: V. V. Advani, A. Advani, Mrs S. Bambridge, Mr H. R. Heffer, Mr T H Bambridge T/As The Willow Stud, Mr K. G. Newland, Mrs J. E. Newland, Mr R. J. Pearson, Miss J. L. Pearson, Mrs A. M. Sturges, Mr R. W. Sturges.

Assistant Trainer: Miss S Cassidy

Jockey (flat): Natalia Gemelova, Richard Thomas.

393 MR CHARLIE LONGSDON, Chipping Norton
Postal: **Hull Farm Stables, Stratford Road, Chipping Norton, Oxfordshire, OX7 5QF**
Contacts: **PHONE** (08450) 525264 **FAX** (08450) 525265 **MOBILE** (07775) 993263
E-MAIL charlie@charlielongsdonracing.com **WEBSITE** www.charlielongsdonracing.com

1 **BALLINCURRIG (IRE)**, 7, b g Craigsteel—Flora Rambler **H. B. Hodge**
2 **BE MY LIGHT (IRE)**, 7, b m Oscar (IRE)—Simply Divine (IRE) **Foxtrot NH Racing Partnership IV**
3 **BE MY PRESENT (IRE)**, 6, b m Presenting—Simply Divine (IRE) **Mrs L. Suenson-Taylor**
4 **BRASSICK**, 6, b g Presenting—No More Money **P. Murphy**
5 **BRIEF MARK (IRE)**, 8, b g Revoque (IRE)—Queens Mark (IRE) **R. Jenner & J. Green**
6 **CASTLETOWN BRIDGE (IRE)**, 6, ch g Bienamado (USA)—Midnight Orchid (IRE) **Mr T. Hanlon**
7 **CATCH THE RHYTHM (IRE)**, 5, b g Bandari (IRE)—Christys Wish (IRE) **R. D. J. Swinburne**
8 **CONSTANT CONTACT**, 6, b g Passing Glance—Floriana **R. Drye**
9 **COURT APPEAL (IRE)**, 6, b g Court Cave (IRE)—Lady Braid (IRE) **Fly Like The Wind Partnership**
10 **CREDIT FOR LIFE (IRE)**, 6, b g Zagreb (USA)—Nero's Gem **Hopeful Half Dozen**
11 **CROSS OF HONOUR (IRE)**, 6, ch g Publisher (USA)—
          Threecrossmammies (IRE) **C. Booth, J. Hughes, M. Ogilvy, R. Perkins**
12 **DAWN COMMANDER (GER)**, 6, gr g Mamool (IRE)—Dark Lady (GER) **D. A. Halsall**
13 **DOM LUKKA (FR)**, 5, b br g Dom Alco (FR)—Orlamonde Queen (FR) **R. D. J. Swinburne**
14 **DONT TAKE ME ALIVE**, 4, b g Araafa (IRE)—Up At Dawn **T. P. Bostwick**
15 **DROP OUT JOE**, 5, ch g Generous (USA)—La Feuillarde (FR) **The Jesters**
16 **ELY BROWN (IRE)**, 8, b g Sunshine Street (USA)—
          Browneyed Daughter (IRE) **Countrywide Vehicle Rentals Limited**
17 **FENNIS BOY (IRE)**, 9, ch g Scribano—Beeches Princess (IRE) **Mr C. F. White**
18 **FRISCO DEPOT**, 9, b g King's Theatre (IRE)—Gardana (FR) **Waley-Cohen, Burke, Broughton, Broughton**
19 **GLENFORD DORIE**, 6, ch g Alflora (IRE)—Dancing Pearl **R. D. J. Swinburne**
20 **GRANDADS HORSE**, 7, b br g Bollin Eric—Solid Land (FR) **Mr J. White**
21 **GREEN HACKLE (IRE)**, 8, b g Stowaway—Honey Mustard (IRE) **Mrs C. G. Watson**
22 **GREENLAW**, 7, b g Helissio (FR)—Juris Prudence (IRE) **Mr & Mrs Simon and June Cadzow**
23 **HANNIBAL THE GREAT (IRE)**, 5, b g Milan—Town Gossip (IRE) **The Pantechnicons**
24 **HAYJACK**, 8, b g Karinga Bay—Celtic Native (IRE) **James Hayman-Joyce**
25 **HAZY TOM (IRE)**, 7, b g Heron Island (IRE)—The Wounded Cook (IRE) **D. A. Halsall**
26 **HUMPHREY BEE (IRE)**, 10, br g Oscar Schindler (IRE)—Gladriels Jem (IRE) **A. H. B. Hodge**
27 **JAVA ROSE**, 4, b f Ishiguru (USA)—Mighty Splash **Mrs Mary Low**
28 **JOSEPH LISTER**, 6, b g Nayef (USA)—Logic **C. Longsdon**
29 **KAUTO RELKO (FR)**, 9, b g With The Flow (USA)—Kauto Relka (FR) **Countrywide Vehicle Rentals Limited**
30 **KELLYS BROW (IRE)**, 6, b g Golan (IRE)—Eyebright (IRE) **R. Drye**

MR CHARLIE LONGSDON - Continued

31 **KEY TO THE WEST (IRE)**, 6, b g Westerner—Monte Solaro (IRE) **Favourites Racing Ltd**
32 **LIARS POKER (IRE)**, 6, b g Beneficial—Strong Willed **Mick Fitzgerald Racing Club**
33 **LITTLE CHIP (IRE)**, 6, b g Dushyantor (USA)—Aunt Chris (IRE) **L. Dens (Shipbrokers) Limited**
34 **LONG LUNCH**, 4, b g Kayf Tara—Royal Keel **Battersby, Birchall, Halsall & Vestey**
35 **LONG WAVE (IRE)**, 6, b g Milan—Mrs Avery (IRE) **Neysauteur Partnership**
36 **LOOSE CHIPS**, 7, b g Sir Harry Lewis (USA)—Worlaby Rose **Barrels Of Courage**
37 **LOUDMOUTH (IRE)**, 6, br g Milan—Grandy Invader (IRE) **Andrew Macdonald**
38 **NEWTON THISTLE**, 6, b g Erhaab (USA)—Newton Venture **J. H. & N. J. Foxon**
39 **NEWTON TONIC**, 8, b g Sir Harry Lewis (USA)—Wedidthat (IRE) **J. H. & N. J. Foxon**
40 **NO NO BINGO (IRE)**, 7, b g Craigsteel—Little Anna (IRE) **R. Jenner & J. Green**
41 **NO NO CHARLIE (IRE)**, 6, b g Croco Rouge (IRE)—Dianeme **R. Jenner & J. Green**
42 **NO NO MAC (IRE)**, 4, b g Oscar (IRE)—Whatdoyouthinkmac (IRE) **R. Jenner & J. Green**
43 **ORANGE NASSAU (FR)**, 7, gr g Martaline—Vilaya (FR) **The Ferandlin Peaches**
44 **OSTLAND (GER)**, 8, b g Lando (GER)—Ost Tycoon (GER) **Mr Richard & Mrs Susan Perkins**
45 **PAINTBALL (IRE)**, 6, b g Le Vie Dei Colori—Camassina (USA) **D. A. Halsall**
46 **PAMPELONNE (IRE)**, 7, b m Oscar (IRE)—Bondi Storm (IRE) **The Stewkley Shindiggers Partnership**
47 **PENDRA (IRE)**, 5, ch g Old Vic—Mariah Rollins (IRE) **J. P. McManus**
48 **PETE THE FEAT (IRE)**, 9, b g King's Theatre (IRE)—Tourist Attraction (IRE) **Mr G. J. Larby & Mr P. J. Smith**
49 **PURE STYLE (IRE)**, 5, b g Desert Style (IRE)—Pure Fiction **Mr P. J. Curtin**
50 **PUSH THE TRIGGER**, 6, b g Double Trigger (IRE)—Pushing Gold **Mrs L. Suenson-Taylor**
51 **REBLIS (FR)**, 8, b g Assessor (IRE)—Silbere (FR) **Kingsley, Avery, Farr, Glover, Humphreys**
52 **REY NACARADO (IRE)**, 8, b g Posidonas—Ice Pearl **Runthatbymeagainagain**
53 **ROSSMORE LAD (IRE)**, 8, b br g Beneficial—Celestial Rose (IRE) **T. P. Bostwick**
54 **SERGEANT MATTIE (IRE)**, 5, b g Naheez (USA)—Glyde Lady (IRE) **Fly Like the Wind Partnership**
55 **SHANTOU MAGIC (IRE)**, 6, b g Shantou (USA)—Supreme Magical **Owners For Owners**
56 **SKINT**, 7, b g King's Theatre (IRE)—No More Money **Favourites Racing Ltd**
57 **SPANISH ARCH (IRE)**, 6, b g Westerner—Piepowder **James Hayman-Joyce & HJ Racing**
58 **SPIRIT OF SHANKLY**, 5, ch g Sulamani (IRE)—Lago d'oro **D. A. Halsall**
59 **STRONGBOWS LEGEND**, 8, ch g Midnight Legend—Miss Crabapple **Box A45**
60 **SUPERIOR QUALITY (IRE)**, 8, br g Winged Love (IRE)—
                                        Unknown Quality **The Stewkley Shindiggers Partnership**
61 **TARBECK**, 9, b g Kayf Tara—Ellerbeck **C. Longsdon**
62 **TIDAL WAY (IRE)**, 4, gr g Red Clubs (IRE)—Taatof (IRE) **C. Longsdon**
63 **TIME FOR SPRING (IRE)**, 9, b g Snurge—Burksie (IRE) **G. MacEchern, P. Pottinger, C. Badcock**
64 **TOPAZE COLLONGES (FR)**, 6, gr g Dom Alco (FR)—Flicka Collonges (FR) **No Boys Allowed**
65 **UNIVERSAL SOLDIER (IRE)**, 8, b g Winged Love (IRE)—Waterland Gale (IRE) **Lindie Donaldson & Regan King**
66 **UP TO SOMETHING (FR)**, 5, b g Brier Creek (USA)—Evane (FR) **E. M. G. Roberts**
67 **VENCEREMOS**, 6, b m Generous (IRE)—Miss Orchestra (IRE) **D. M. Huglin**
68 **VINCITORE (FR)**, 7, b g Starborough—Viva Vodka (IRE) **The Veni, Vidi, Vici Partnership**
69 **VULCANITE (IRE)**, 6, b g Dubawi (IRE)—Daraliya (IRE) **J. P. McManus**
70 **WADSWICK COURT (IRE)**, 5, b g Court Cave (IRE)—Tarasandy (IRE) **The Chosen Few**
71 **WILLOW'S SAVIOUR**, 6, ch g Septieme Ciel (USA)—Willow Gale **Triple F Partnership**
72 **YES I WILL**, 4, b g Kahyasi—Flinders **Leith Hill Chasers**

Other Owners: Mr D. Abraham, Mr Clive Badcock, Mr C. J. Booth, Sir Martin Broughton, Mr Stephen Broughton, Mrs Valda Burke, Mr S. Cadzow, Mrs J. Cadzow, Mr A. E. Connor, Mrs Margaret Cuff, Miss L. M. Donaldson, Mr H. Fentum, Mr J. H. Foxon, Mrs N. J. Foxon, Mrs J. Green, Mr M. W. Gregory, Mr Jonathan Halsall, Mr B. R. Halsall, Mr James Hayman-Joyce, Mrs Lottie Hayman-Joyce, Mr W. John Henderson, Mrs H. J. Hoffman, Mr J. R. Holmes, Mr Jon Hughes, Mr Rob Jackson, Ms R. Jenner, Mr Regan King, Mr P. Kingsley, Mr G. J. Larby, Mr Charles Liverton, Mr Gavin MacEchern, Mrs N. F. Maltby, Mr N. F. Maltby, Mr C. Marriott, Mrs A. May, Mr R. D. Nicholas, Dr M. M. Ogilvy, Mr R. A. H. Perkins, Mr P. J. D. Pottinger, Mr Peter J. Smith, Mr S. Spencer-Jones, Mrs S. Spencer-Jones, Mrs S. Spencer-Jones, Mr Robert Waley-Cohen.

Jockey (NH): Noel Fehily. **Conditional:** Kielan Woods. **Amateur:** Miss Claire Hart.

---

394   MR DANIEL MARK LOUGHNANE, Butterton
Postal: **10 Appleton Drive, Whitmore, Newcastle-under-Lyme, Staffordshire, ST5 5BT**

1 **FIRST IN COMMAND (IRE)**, 8, b g Captain Rio—Queen Sigi (IRE) **Mrs C. M. Loughnane**
2 **FOR SHIA AND LULA (IRE)**, 4, b g Majestic Missile (IRE)—
                            Jack-N-Jilly (IRE) **Loughnane, Fletcher, Ward & Ebanks-Blake**
3 **HONEST STRIKE (USA)**, 6, b g Smart Strike (CAN)—Honest Lady (USA) **K Kilbane, J O'Shea & S Hunt**
4 **JOHNSTOWN LAD (IRE)**, 9, b g Invincible Spirit (IRE)—Pretext **Mrs C. M. Loughnane**
5 **JUMBO PRADO (USA)**, 4, gr ro g El Prado (IRE)—Sant Elena **Mrs C. M. Loughnane**

MR DANIEL MARK LOUGHNANE - Continued

6 LOWPARKLAD (IRE), 7, b g Traditionally (USA)—Shaigino (IRE) **Mr G. McGuinness**
7 MA TOOLAN (IRE), 6, b m Presenting—Killoughey Fairy (IRE) **Mrs C. M. Loughnane**
8 NAFA (IRE), 5, br m Shamardal (USA)—Champs Elysees (USA) **Mr Ian O'Connor**
9 PRIME EXHIBIT, 8, b g Selkirk (USA)—First Exhibit **D Fower & N J Titterton**
10 SAHARIA (IRE), 6, b g Oratorio (IRE)—Inchiri **Brooklands Racing**
11 VERUS DELICIA (IRE), 4, b f Chineur (FR)—Ribbon Glade (UAE) **Mr R. M. Brilley**
12 YOURINTHEWILL (USA), 5, ch g Aragorn (IRE)—Lenarue (USA) **Mrs C. M. Loughnane**

THREE-YEAR-OLDS

13 COMBUSTIBLE (IRE), b f Halling (USA)—Jazz Baby (IRE) **Mrs C. M. Loughnane**
14 LUCKY MORGAN, ch c Pastoral Pursuits—Basbousate Nadia **Mrs C. M. Loughnane**
15 SCOOBYS GIRL (IRE), b f Holy Roman Emperor (IRE)—Mystiara (IRE) **Mr Ian O'Connor**

TWO-YEAR-OLDS

16 B c 15/2 Myboycharlie (IRE)—Akhira (Emperor Jones (USA)) (4000) **Mr Ian O'Connor**
17 Br c 4/3 Excellent Art—Atienza (USA) (Chief's Crown (USA)) (5555) **D. S. Lovatt**
18 Gr c 3/3 Misu Bond (IRE)—Kilmovee (Inchinor) (2380) **Mr P. Moran**

Other Owners: M. H. Bates, Mr S. Ebanks-Blake, Mr S. Fletcher, D. Fower, Mr S. Hunt, Mr K. D. Kilbane, Mrs A. M. Mercs, Mr J. O'Shea, N. J. Titterton, Mr S. Ward.

---

395 MR SHAUN LYCETT, Bourton-On-The-Water
Postal: **Bourton Hill Farm, Bourton Hill, Bourton-On-The-Water, Cheltenham, Gloucestershire, GL54 2LF**
Contacts: PHONE **(01451) 824143 MOBILE (07788) 100894**
E-MAIL **trainer@bourtonhillracing.co.uk** WEBSITE **www.bourtonhillracing.co.uk**

1 ALL THE WINDS (GER), 8, ch g Samum (GER)—All Our Luck (GER) **Nicholls Family**
2 ASTRAGAL, 5, b m Shamardal (USA)—Landinium (ITY) **Lord J. Blyth**
3 HACKETT (IRE), 5, b h Hawk Wing (USA)—Khudud **S. Lycett**
4 HARVEST MIST (IRE), 5, ch m Captain Rio—Thaw **Mr C. C. Buckingham**
5 KALAMILL (IRE), 6, b g Kalanisi (IRE)—Desert Pageant (IRE) **R. Davies**
6 MALLUSK (IRE), 8, b g Exit To Nowhere (USA)—Saucy Nun (IRE) **Worcester Racing Club**
7 SCOTSBROOK LEGEND, 5, b m Midnight Legend—Scots Brook Terror **A. E. J. Price**
8 THE WINGED ASSASIN (USA), 7, b g Fusaichi Pegasus (USA)—Gran Dama (USA) **Mr A. R. James**
9 TINELYRA (IRE), 7, b g Mr Combustible (IRE)—Ladyogan (IRE) **Mr M. Costello**
10 TRAM EXPRESS (FR), 9, ch g Trempolino (USA)—Molly Dance (FR) **S. Lycett**
11 WELLFORTH (IRE), 9, b g New Frontier (IRE)—Faitch's Lady (IRE) **Miss Clare L. Ellam**

Other Owners: M. P. Hill, Mr R. Nicholls, Mrs E. Nicholls.

---

396 MR GER LYONS, Dunsany
Postal: **Glenburnie Stables, Kiltale, Dunsany, Co. Meath, Ireland**
Contacts: PHONE **(00353) 46 9025666 FAX (00353) 46 9026364 MOBILE (00353) 86 8502439**
E-MAIL **office@gerlyons.ie** WEBSITE **www.gerlyons.ie**

1 BIBLE BLACK (IRE), 4, br g Big Bad Bob (IRE)—Convent Girl (IRE) **Anamoine Ltd**
2 BRENDAN BRACKAN (IRE), 4, b g Big Bad Bob (IRE)—Abeyr **Anamoine Ltd**
3 BURN THE BOATS (IRE), 4, br g Big Bad Bob (IRE)—Forever Phoenix **Mrs Lynne Lyons**
4 GREEK CANYON (IRE), 4, gr g Moss Vale (IRE)—Lazaretta (IRE) **Mr Sean Jones**
5 JAMMING (IRE), 4, b g Jeremy (USA)—Perfect Sound (FR) **Mrs Lynne Lyons**
6 JOE EILE (IRE), 5, b g Iffraaj—Encouragement **HB Partnership**
7 LILY'S ANGEL (IRE), 4, b f Dark Angel (IRE)—Noyelles (IRE) **Mrs Clodagh Mitchell**
8 MOUNT MERU (IRE), 4, b g Red Clubs (IRE)—Shangazi (USA) **Mr Sean Jones**
9 PC HENRY, 4, b g Ishiguru (USA)—Elhida (IRE) **Mrs Lynne Lyons**
10 PIRI WANGO (IRE), 4, ch g Choisir (AUS)—Zoldan **Mr David Spratt**
11 SHUKHOV (IRE), 4, b g Ivan Denisovich (IRE)—Just One Smile (IRE) **Mr Sean Jones**
12 THE REAPER (IRE), 5, b g Footstepsinthesand—Lady Gregory (IRE) **Mr Sean Jones**

MR GER LYONS - Continued

THREE-YEAR-OLDS

13 **ABBEY VALE (IRE)**, b g Moss Vale (IRE)—Cloonkeary **Mr Vincent Gaul**
14 **ANGELA'S DREAM (IRE)**, b f Chineur (FR)—Church Mice (IRE) **R M S Racing Syndicate**
15 **ARCH PEARL (USA)**, b br g Arch (USA)—Reem Al Barari (USA) **Pearl Bloodstock**
16 **BEATBOXING (USA)**, b c Street Sense (USA)—Make My Heart Sing (USA) **Sheikh Mohammed**
17 **BUMBLE BEE SLIM**, ch g Bertolini (USA)—Questama **Mr Sean Jones**
18 **CAMPESTRAL SCENE**, ch c Pastoral Pursuits—Raindrop **Mr Vincent Gaul**
19 **DAFT DAVE (IRE)**, b g Excellent Art—Chameleon **Mr Chris Dineen**
20 **DR FUNKENSTEIN (IRE)**, ch g Excellent Art—Romancing **Mr Sean Jones**
21 B g King's Best (USA)—Gamma (FR) **Mr Sean Jones**
22 **HARMONIC NOTE**, b f Nayef (USA)—Musical Key **Qatar Racing Ltd**
23 **HIGHEST OFFICE**, ch g Papal Bull—Catspraddle (USA) **Mr Damian Nolan**
24 **HOUND DOG TAYLOR**, b g Sir Percy—Mrs Brown **Mr Sean Jones**
25 **KEEPING (IRE)**, b f Teofilo (IRE)—My **Sheikh Mohammed**
26 **LIGHTNIN HOPKINS (IRE)**, b g Kodiac—Bundle of Joy (IRE) **Mr Sean Jones**
27 **MACHETE MARK (IRE)**, b g Indian Haven—Beziers (IRE) **Mr David Spratt**
28 **MARVELOUS JAMES (IRE)**, b g Captain Marvelous (IRE)—Answer Do **Mr Chris Dineen**
29 **MAXIMAL CRAZY**, b g Notnowcato—Marias Magic **Mr Sean Jones**
30 **MEMPHIS RED (IRE)**, ch c Danehill Dancer (IRE)—Rain Flower (IRE) **Mr Sean Jones**
31 **MINISTER OF MAYHEM**, ch g Sakhee's Secret—First Fantasy **Mr Damian Nolan**
32 **MISSISSIPPI JOHN (IRE)**, b g Lawman (FR)—Requested Pleasure (IRE) **Mr Sean Jones**
33 **MORDANMIJOBSWORTH (IRE)**, b g Clodovil (IRE)—Alta Petens **R M S Syndicate**
34 B c Henrythenavigator (USA)—Mythical Echo (USA) **Mr Damian Nolan**
35 **NOMONEYNOHONEY (IRE)**, ch f Ad Valorem (USA)—Tawaafud **Mr Charles Harvey**
36 **PEARL CAUSEWAY (USA)**, ch c Giant's Causeway (USA)—Northern Mischief (USA) **Pearl Bloodstock**
37 **PEARL TURN (USA)**, b f Bernardini (USA)—Turn Me Loose (USA) **Pearl Bloodstock**
38 **PRIVATE ALEXANDER (IRE)**, b f Footstepsinthesand—Private Seductress (USA) **Mr Noel O'Callaghan**
39 **QUEEN OF THE SAND (IRE)**, br f Footstepsinthesand—Lough Mewin (IRE) **Mr Declan Landy**
40 **ROCKABILLY RIOT (IRE)**, b br g Footstepsinthesand—Zawariq (IRE) **Mr Sean Jones**
41 **TENNESSEE WILDCAT (IRE)**, b g Kheleyf (USA)—Windbeneathmywings (IRE) **Mr Sean Jones**
42 **WYOYO (IRE)**, b g Moss Vale (IRE)—Jersey Lillie (IRE) **Mr Damian Nolan**

TWO-YEAR-OLDS

43 B c 28/3 Dubawi (IRE)—Anayid (A P Indy (USA)) **Qatar Racing Ltd**
44 Ch c 29/4 Piccolo—Antonia's Choice (Music Boy) (24761) **Mr Sean Jones**
45 B c 22/4 Oratorio (IRE)—Bluebell Park (USA) (Gulch (USA)) (17000) **Mr Sean Jones**
46 Gr c 21/4 Verglas (IRE)—Candelabra (Grand Lodge (USA)) (26190) **Mr Sean Jones**
47 **CRISTAL FASHION (IRE)**, b f 16/2 Jeremy (USA)—Mango Groove (IRE) (Unfuwain (USA)) **Jim McDonald**
48 B c 12/5 Kodiac—Dancing Debut (Polar Falcon (USA)) (26000) **Mr Vincent Gaul**
49 B c 19/3 Azamour (IRE)—Fez (Mujtahid (USA)) (21428) **Mr Sean Jones**
50 **FOG OF WAR**, b c 18/4 Azamour (IRE)—Cut Short (USA) (Diesis) (120000) **Qatar Racing Ltd**
51 B c 8/4 Azamour (IRE)—High Lite (Observatory (USA)) (12000) **Mr Sean Jones**
52 **KAMINARI (IRE)**, b f 30/3 Sea The Stars (IRE)—Karmifira (FR) (Always Fair (USA)) (222221) **Qatar Racing Ltd**
53 B c 15/2 Moss Vale (IRE)—Ladylishandra (IRE) (Mujadil (USA)) (20952) **Mr Sean Jones**
54 B c 26/4 Oratorio (IRE)—Mandaraka (FR) (Ashkalani (IRE)) (19840) **Mr Sean Jones**
55 Gr ro c 20/3 Henrythenavigator (USA)—Minicolony (USA) (Pleasant Colony (USA)) (42000) **Mr Sean Jones**
56 Ch f 6/4 Camacho—Miss Orah (Unfuwain (USA)) (3967) **Muppet Syndicate**
57 B f 12/4 Cape Cross (IRE)—Mount Elbrus (Barathea (IRE)) **Sheikh Mohammed**
58 Gr c 23/3 Dark Angel (IRE)—Moy Joy (IRE) (Orpen (USA)) **Mr John Quinn**
59 Ch c 28/3 Iffraaj—Nasharaat (IRE) (Green Desert (USA)) (30000) **Mr Sean Jones**
60 B c 25/3 Exceed And Excel (AUS)—Noodle Soup (USA) (Alphabet Soup (USA)) (30000) **Mr Sean Jones**
61 **OBLITERATOR (IRE)**, br c 28/4 Oratorio (IRE)—
        Faraday Light (IRE) (Rainbow Quest (USA)) (55555) **Qatar Racing Ltd**
62 B c 20/4 Teofilo (IRE)—Posterity (IRE) (Indian Ridge) **Mr Sean Jones**
63 **ROHERYN (IRE)**, b f 23/2 Galileo (IRE)—La Chunga (USA) (More Than Ready (USA)) (245775) **Qatar Racing Ltd**
64 B c 5/5 Dubawi (IRE)—Round The Cape (Cape Cross (IRE)) (38000) **Mr Sean Jones**
65 B c 25/4 Dark Angel (IRE)—Secret Key (IRE) (Key of Luck (USA)) (19047) **Mr Sean Jones**
66 B c 29/1 Compton Place—Small Fortune (Anabaa (USA)) (35000) **Mr Sean Jones**
67 **SNOWMANE (IRE)**, b c 3/5 Galileo (IRE)—Tree Tops (Grand Lodge (USA)) (190000) **Qatar Racing Ltd**
68 B c 19/5 Dutch Art—Valley of The Moon (IRE) (Monashee Mountain (USA)) (28571) **Mr Sean Jones**
69 B f 26/2 Alhaarth (IRE)—Za Aamah (USA) (Mr Prospector (USA)) **Ennistown Stud**

Assistant Trainer: Shane Lyons

Jockey (flat): Gary Carroll, Emmet McNamara.

397 MR GUILLAUME MACAIRE, Les Mathes

Postal: **Hippodrome de la Palmyre, 17570 Les Mathes, France**
Contacts: **PHONE (0033) 5462 36254 FAX (0033) 5462 25438 MOBILE (0033) 6076 54992**
E-MAIL entrainement-g.macaire@wanadoo.fr

1 AMOUR DU PUY NOIR (FR), 4, b g Ballingarry (IRE)—Virosa (FR) **Mr Jacques Detre**
2 ANALANDIA (GER), 4, b f Sholokhov (IRE)—Arganta (GER) **Mr Robert Fougedoire**
3 ANNAKOV (GER), 4, b g Sholokhov (IRE)—Anna Diana (GER) **Ecurie Jaeckin**
4 ASTARABAS (FR), 4, b g Astarabad (USA)—Dindouna (FR) **Mme Patrick Papot**
5 BIEN FAIT, 4, b g Doyen (IRE)—Dardshi (IRE) **Mr Simon Munir**
6 BROTHER BADGER, 5, b g Doyen (IRE)—Persistent Memory (USA) **Mr Gerard Laboureau**
7 CLASSIC DIVA (GER), 4, b f Sholokhov (IRE)—Classic Cara (GER) **Ecurie Jaeckin**
8 COELHO (FR), 5, ch g Kapgarde (FR)—Exela (FR) **Mr David Powell**
9 GORVELLO (FR), 4, b g Poliglote—Rolandale (FR) **Mme Patrick Papot**
10 HORIZONT, 4, b g Shirocco (GER)—Hollywood Love (GER) **Mr Bernd Glutsch**
11 IRISH BAY (FR), 4, b g Irish Wells (FR)—Mary Bay (FR) **Mr Jacques Detre**
12 LADY CORALINE (FR), 4, gr f Martaline—Lady Dancer (FR) **Mr Gilbert Morosini**
13 LARTETA (FR), 4, b g Enrique—Ariel (FR) **Mr Simon Munir**
14 LE ROUTIER SYMPA (FR), 4, b g Sagamix (FR)—The Voice (FR) **Mme Maurice Prod'homme**
15 LOFTE PLACE (FR), 4, b f Poliglote—Queen Place (FR) **Mme Marie-Claire Tyssandier**
16 MILLION (FR), 4, br g Motivator—Miss Alabama (FR) **Mr Gerard Laboureau**
17 MISTER MARTLIM (FR), 4, gr g Martaline—Miss Manson (FR) **Mr Xavier Papot**
18 NOTARIO HAS (FR), 4, gr g Turgeon (USA)—Noria des Bordes (FR) **Mr Simon Munir**
19 OTTOSTAR (GER), 4, b g Sholokhov (IRE)—Omicenta (IRE) **Ecurie Jaeckin**
20 PEPITO DE LUNE (FR), 4, b g Irish Wells (FR)—Pepite de Lune (FR) **Mr Francis Picoulet**
21 QUEL PLAISIR, 4, b g Act One—Pleasuring **Mr Simon Munir**
22 ROCKBURN (FR), 4, b f Saint des Saints (FR)—Segre (FR) **Mme Patrick Papot**
23 ROYAL PASCAL (FR), 4, b g Arvico (FR)—Forget Me Knot (FR) **Mr Gilbert Morosini**
24 STORM OF SAINTLY (FR), 4, b g Saint des Saints (FR)—The Storm (FR) **Mr Jeannot Andt**
25 SUERTE PARA TODOS (FR), 4, ch g Kapgarde (FR)—Hever Rose (GER) **Mr Pierre de Maleissye**
26 ULM DES PLAGES (FR), 5, b g Passing Sale (FR)—Lady des Plages (FR) **Mr Terry Amos**
27 UNITED PARK (FR), 5, b g Antarctique (IRE)—Goldoulyssa (FR) **Mr Terry Amos**
28 USTAN (FR), 5, gr g Persian Ruler—Milved Baby (FR) **Mr Dominique Lemesle**
29 VAGUE D'ESTRUVAL (FR), 4, b f Khalkevi (IRE)—Kob d'estruval (FR) **Mme Bernard Le Gentil**
30 VALLON D'ESTRUVAL (FR), 4, b g Network (GER)—Haie d'estruval (FR) **Mme Bernard Le Gentil**
31 VANILLA CRUSH (FR), 4, b g Martaline—Latitude (FR) **Mme Patrick Papot**
32 VATULELE (FR), 4, b g Lavirco (GER)—Nouvelle Zelande (FR) **Mr Jacques Detre**
33 VAUDAIRE (FR), 4, b f Astarabad (USA)—Miss Academy (FR) **Mme Joseph Shalam**
34 VAUTOUR (FR), 4, b g Robin des Champs (FR)—Gazelle de Mai (FR) **Haras de St Voir**
35 VELEHA (FR), 4, b f Saint des Saints (FR)—Ellapampa (FR) **Mme Magalen Bryant**
36 VENT D'ESTRUVAL (FR), 4, b g Voix du Nord (FR)—Onde d'estruval (FR) **Mme Bernard Le Gentil**
37 VERY TIEP (FR), 4, b g Apple Tree (FR)—Unetiepy (FR) **Mr Jean-Claude Zentz**
38 VIF ARGENT (FR), 4, b g Dom Alco (FR)—Formosa (FR) **Haras de Saint Voir**
39 VINGT DIEUX (FR), 4, b g Robin des Champs (FR)—Ribalina (FR) **Mr Jean-Paul Moutafian**
40 VIRKELLE (FR), 4, b f Lavirco (GER)—Saone Et Loire (FR) **Gold And Blue Ltd**
41 VISION DES CHAMPS (FR), 4, b g Saint des Saints (FR)—Manita Des Champs (FR) **Mr Jacques Detre**
42 VISTA D'ESTRUVAL (FR), 4, b f Network (GER)—Nouvelle d'estruval (FR) **Mme Bernard Le Gentil**
43 VIZIR D'ESTRUVAL (FR), 4, b g Cachet Noir (USA)—Heure d'estruval (FR) **Mme Bernard Le Gentil**
44 VOEUX D'ESTRUVAL (FR), 4, b g Daliapour (IRE)—Perle d'estruval (FR) **Mr Simon Munir**
45 VOIX DU PERE (FR), 4, b g Shirocco (GER)—Behariya (IRE) **Haras De St Voir**
46 VOLCAN D'ESTRUVAL (FR), 4, b g Forestier (FR)—Grotte d'estruval (FR) **Mme Bernard Le Gentil**
47 VOLCANIC D'ALBAIN (FR), 4, b g Dom Alco (FR)—Kandy de Vonnas (FR) **Mr Simon Munir**
48 VOTEZ POUR MOI (FR), 4, gr g Sacro Saint (FR)—Biblique (FR) **Haras De St Voir**
49 VUE D'ESTRUVAL (FR), 4, b f Subotica (FR)—Aluette (FR) **Mme Bernard Le Gentil**
50 WALK ON THE BEACH (FR), 4, b g Walk In The Park (IRE)—Beach Madrague (FR) **Mme Maurice Prod'homme**

THREE-YEAR-OLDS

51 AINSI FIDELES (FR), ch g Dream Well (FR)—Loya Lescribaa (FR) **Mr Terry Amos**
52 AINSIQUE DE L'ISLE (FR), b g Lavirco (GER)—Naiade de Lisle (FR) **Mr Terry Amos**
53 ALAPARO (FR), b c Saint des Saints (FR)—Messine (FR) **Mr Francois Parreau**
54 ALTO DE LA ROQUE (FR), b g Kapgarde (FR)—Louve de La Roque (FR) **Mr Robert Mongin**
55 AMOUR DE LA ROQUE (FR), b c Laveron—La Orotava (FR) **Mr Robert Mongin**
56 ANCOLIE DE COTTE (FR), ch f Dom Alco (FR)—Pensee de Cotte (FR) **Mr Terry Amos**
57 ANGE DE LA ROQUE (FR), b g Kapgarde (FR)—Nacelle de La Roque (FR) **Mr Robert Mongin**
58 ARAMSEL (FR), b g Daramsar (FR)—Saone Et Loire (FR) **Gold and Blue Ltd**

MR GUILLAUME MACAIRE - Continued

59 **ARIANE NOPOLIS (FR)**, b f Saint des Saints (FR)—Okawanga Royale (FR) **Mme Benoit Gabeur**
60 **ART MAJEUR (FR)**, b g Panoramic—Magenta (FR) **Mr Jacques Detre**
61 **ART MAURESQUE (FR)**, b g Policy Maker (IRE)—Modeva (FR) **Mr Robert Fougedoire**
62 **ART SACRE (FR)**, b g Saint des Saints (FR)—Sixtees (FR) **Mr Jacques Detre**
63 **ASTARTE (FR)**, b f Apsis—Ellapampa (FR) **Mr Pierre de Maleissye**
64 **AUPALIM (FR)**, b g Martaline—Mayence (FR) **Ecurie Sagara**
65 **BAIKAL RIVER (FR)**, b f Chichi Creasy (FR)—Naharia (FR) **Mr Robert Fougedoire**
66 **BASQUIAT (SPA)**, b g Leadership—La Catedral **Mr Claude Uzan**
67 **BEBE STAR (FR)**, b g Poliglote—Benefique (FR) **Mr Denys Audouard**
68 **BEUVRON (FR)**, b g Martaline—Virginia River (FR) **Mr Robert Fougedoire**
69 **COEUR EN JOIE (IRE)**, b g Presenting—Bolas **Mme Patrick Papot**
70 **CRAP SHOOT (FR)**, b g Linda's Lad—In Tune (FR) **Mme Benoit Gabeur**
71 **FAUTINA (FR)**, b f Poliglote—Fautine (FR) **Mme Patrick Papot**
72 **FLOGASORTE (FR)**, b g Marshall (FR)—Rosala (FR) **Mr Francis Fernandes**
73 **GABO (FR)**, ch g Forestier—Merciki (FR) **Mme Patrick Papot**
74 **GILLO (FR)**, b g Balko (FR)—Syva (FR) **Mr Gilles Baratoux**
75 **GRANDISSIME (FR)**, b c Saint des Saints (FR)—Vie de Reine (FR) **Mr Jean-Claude Audry**
76 **GUERLINA (FR)**, gr f Martaline—Incorrigible (FR) **Ecurie de L'Hegagone**
77 **HOLY VIRGIN (FR)**, bl f Saint des Saints (FR)—Topira (FR) **Mme Patrick Papot**
78 **HOTLINE (FR)**, b f Poliglote—Haute Tension (FR) **Mme Patrick Papot**
79 **KATGARY (FR)**, b g Ballingarry (IRE)—Kotkira (FR) **Haras Du Saubouas**
80 **KITCHAPOLY (FR)**, b g Poliglote—Kotkicha (FR) **Mousquetaire Investissement**
81 **KITKALINO (FR)**, b g Martaline—Kitka (FR) **Mr Denys Audouard**
82 **LADY KOKO**, b f Kapgarde (FR)—Aconit (FR) **Mr Francis Picoulet**
83 **LAMEIRO (FR)**, b g Lawman (FR)—Esclarmonde (IRE) **Mousquetaire Investissement**
84 **MARKETING (FR)**, b g Martaline—Kitara (GER) **Mme Patrick Papot**
85 **MARRONNIER (FR)**, b g Forestier (FR)—Notabilite (FR) **Mr Robert Fougedoire**
86 **MIAM MIAM (FR)**, ch g Martaline—La Faena (FR) **Mme Patrick Papot**
87 **MON NICKSON (FR)**, b c Nickname (FR)—Linaving (FR) **Mr Edouard Coirre**
88 **MOUNTYFIRTH (FR)**, b g Flemensfirth (USA)—Valleyofthedolls **Mr Denys Audouard**
89 **MY ALCO (FR)**, ch f Dom Alco (FR)—My Asadore (FR) **Mr Jacques Detre**
90 **POLID'AJONC (FR)**, b f Poliglote—Fleur d'ajonc (FR) **Mme Magalen Bryant**
91 **POLLINIE (FR)**, b f Poliglote—Darae (FR) **Mr Francis Picoulet**
92 **PUR FLY (FR)**, b f Passing Sale (FR)—Bright Idea (FR) **Mme Patrick Papot**
93 **QUEEN'S GUARD (FR)**, ch g Kapgarde (FR)—Queen's Theatre (FR) **Mme Benoit Gabeur**
94 **REINE DES VALOIS (FR)**, b f Kapgarde (FR)—Bara Bahau (FR) **Ecurie Des Valois**
95 **SAINTE NATION (FR)**, b f Saint des Saints (FR)—Damnation (FR) **Mr Jeannot Andt**
96 **SANTA GIRL (FR)**, b f Saint des Saints (FR)—Bumble (FR) **Mr Jacques Detre**
97 **SCORPIO IMPERATOR (FR)**, b c Scorpion (IRE)—Aubane (FR) **Miss Murielle Legriffon**
98 **SKELLIG MICHAEL (FR)**, b g Saint des Saints (FR)—Skellig Mist (FR) **Mr John Cotton**
99 **SUNDRIVER (FR)**, b g Poliglote—Myrthe (GER) **Ecurie Sagara**
100 **SYSTEMIQUE (FR)**, b g Saint des Saints (FR)—Gavotte de Brejoux (FR) **Mr Jacques Detre**
101 **TIDAL RIVER (GER)**, b g Sholokhov (IRE)—The Beauty (FR) **Mme Patrick Papot**
102 **URZEIT**, b f Sholokhov (IRE)—Ustilla (GER) **Mr Jeannot Andt**
103 **VERKAP (FR)**, b g Kapgarde (FR)—Hever Rose (GER) **Mr Pierre de Maleissye**
104 **VESTIDO (GER)**, b g Sholokhov (IRE)—Vumanji (GER) **Mr Daniel Chabassier**

---

398 **MR R. MACDONALD, Hawick**
Postal: **Midburn Farm Cottage, Hawick, Roxburghshire, TD9 9SD**
Contacts: **PHONE (01450) 860724 MOBILE (07921) 317692**
E-MAIL midburnracingstables@hotmail.co.uk

1 **GOLDEN EMPEROR (IRE)**, 6, ro gr g Antonius Pius (USA)—Lily Shing Shang **R. MacDonald**
2 **KIT CARSON (IRE)**, 13, b g Dr Massini (IRE)—Roses Niece (IRE) **Mrs M. A. MacDonald**
3 **THE DUNION**, 10, br g Beckett (IRE)—Dacian (USA) **Mrs M. A. MacDonald**
4 **WOR LASS**, 5, br m And Beyond (IRE)—Patience Please **Mrs M. A. MacDonald**

Assistant Trainer: Les Dodds

Jockey (NH): Brian Hughes. **Conditional:** Gary Rutherford.

399 MR JOHN MACKIE, Church Broughton
Postal: **The Bungalow, Barton Blount, Church Broughton, Derby, Derbyshire, DE65 5AN**
Contacts: **PHONE (01283) 585604/585603 FAX (01283) 585603 MOBILE (07799) 145283**
E-MAIL jmackie@bartonblount.freeserve.co.uk WEBSITE www.johnmackieracing.co.uk

1 AEGEAN DESTINY, 6, b m Beat Hollow—Starlist **Derbyshire Racing III**
2 ARIZONA JOHN (IRE), 8, b g Rahy (USA)—Preseli (IRE) **Derbyshire Racing**
3 AVAILABLE (IRE), 4, b f Moss Vale (IRE)—Divert (IRE) **Derbyshire Racing V**
4 BOSAMCLIFF (IRE), 8, b m Daylami (IRE)—L'animee **R. Kent**
5 FARMER'S FRIEND, 4, b g Passing Glance—Flawspar **Mr N. J. Sessions**
6 FLASH HARRIET, 9, ch m Classic Cliche (IRE)—Harry's Bride **A. J. Wall**
7 GLASS MOUNTAIN (IRE), 5, gr g Verglas (IRE)—Exotic Mix (FR) **Derbyshire Racing VI**
8 HALLSTATT (IRE), 7, ch g Halling (USA)—Last Resort **Mr A. B. Hill**
9 ILLUSTRIOUS FOREST, 5, ch g Shinko Forest (IRE)—Illustre Inconnue (USA) **Derbyshire Racing VII**
10 INANDOVER, 8, b g Dover Patrol (IRE)—Inspirational (IRE) **Mrs K. L. Oliver**
11 KNIGHT IN PURPLE, 9, b g Sir Harry Lewis (USA)—Cerise Bleue (FR) **A. J. Wall, G. Hicks & N. Hooper**
12 LAYLA'S BOY, 6, ch g Sakhee (USA)—Gay Romance **RJM Racing**
13 LUCKY EMILY, 4, b f Central Park (IRE)—Father's Pride **G. A. Greaves**
14 MARMAS, 4, ch c Sir Percy—Kitabaat (IRE) **Mr G. R. Shelton**
15 PEARL WAR (USA), 4, b f War Front (USA)—B W Chargit (USA) **Mrs E. M. Mackie**
16 RIVER PURPLE, 6, b g Bollin Eric—Cerise Bleue (FR) **Sotby Farming Company Limited**
17 ROCK SONG, 4, b c Rock of Gibraltar (IRE)—Jackie's Opera (FR) **Sotby Farming Company Limited**
18 SAINT THOMAS (IRE), 6, b g Alhaarth (IRE)—Aguilas Perla (IRE) **P. Riley**
19 SONNY JIM, 5, b g Needwood Blade—Sonderborg **Mr G. R. Shelton**

THREE-YEAR-OLDS

20 MIXED MESSAGE (IRE), b f Kodiac—Berenica (IRE) **W. I. Bloomfield**
21 OFF THE PULSE, b c Araafa (IRE)—Off By Heart **G. B. Maher**

Other Owners: Mr M. A. Bates, Mr Gary Hicks, Mr Neil Hooper, Mrs J. Mackie, Mr Roger Milner, Mr David Penman, Mr Gary Shelton, Mr A. J. Wall.

400 MR ALAN MACTAGGART, Hawick
Postal: **Wells, Denholm, Hawick, Roxburghshire, TD9 8TD**
Contacts: **PHONE (01450) 870060 MOBILE (07711) 200445**

1 OLIVE GROVE, 7, ch m Central Park (IRE)—Olive Branch **A. H. Mactaggart**
2 ROYAL MACKINTOSH, 12, b g Sovereign Water (FR)—Quick Quote **Mrs A. H. Mactaggart**

Assistant Trainer: Mrs M A Mactaggart

401 MR BRUCE MACTAGGART, Hawick
Postal: **Greendale, Hawick, Roxburghshire, TD9 7LH**
Contacts: **PHONE/FAX (01450) 372086 MOBILE (07764) 159852/(07718) 920072**
E-MAIL brucemct@btinternet.co.uk

1 CRAICNEASY (IRE), 10, br g Anshan—Craic Go Leor **Harlequin Racing**
2 4, B f King's Theatre (IRE)—Friendly Craic (IRE)
3 RED TANBER (IRE), 10, ch g Karinga Bay—Dreamy Desire **Hugh T. Redhead**

THREE-YEAR-OLDS

4 B f Flemensfirth (USA)—Water Stratford (IRE) **W. B. Mactaggart**

Other Owners: Mr J. R. Elgin, Mrs Frances Godson, Mr J. B. Jeffrey, Mr B. Mactaggart, Mrs Hilary Mactaggart, Mr. K. Rennie.

Assistant Trainer: Mrs H. Mactaggart

402 MR PETER MADDISON, Skewsby
Postal: **5 West End Cottages, Skewsby, York, YO61 4SG**
Contacts: **PHONE (01347) 888385**

1 BATTLEDANCER, 7, b g Baryshnikov (AUS)—Cede Nullis **P. Maddison**

403 MR MICHAEL MADGWICK, Denmead
Postal: **Forest Farm, Forest Road, Denmead, Waterlooville, Hampshire, PO7 6UA**
Contacts: **PHONE/FAX (02392) 258313 MOBILE (07835) 964969**

1 COMEDY HOUSE, 5, b g Auction House (USA)—Kyle Akin **Los Leader**
2 CRACKER MILL, 4, b g Act One—Linda's Schoolgirl (IRE) **Recycled Products Limited**
3 DICHOH, 10, b g Diktat—Hoh Dancer **M. J. Madgwick**
4 DOYLE'S DREAM, 4, gr f Cape Town (IRE)—Think It Over (IRE) **Recycled Products Limited**
5 HERE COMES JEANIE, 4, b f Act One—Full English **Recycled Products Limited**
6 RAY DIAMOND, 8, ch g Medicean—Musical Twist (USA) **Mrs L. N. Harmes**
7 SHANTOU BREEZE (IRE), 6, b m Shantou (USA)—Homersmare (IRE) **I. M. McGready**
8 SUPERSTICION, 4, b f Red Ransom (USA)—Go Supersonic **Supersticion Partnership**
9 WARBOND, 5, ch g Monsieur Bond (IRE)—Pick A Nice Name **M. J. Madgwick**
10 WHERE'S SUSIE, 8, ch m Where Or When (IRE)—Linda's Schoolgirl (IRE) **Recycled Products Limited**

THREE-YEAR-OLDS
11 GOLD WEIGHT, ch g Denounce—Jewel (IRE) **Mrs L. N. Harmes**
12 MONEY TALKS, b g Motivator—Movie Mogul **Recycled Products Limited**
13 MULTITASK, b g Multiplex—Attlongglast **Mrs L. N. Harmes**
14 TOUGH QUESTION, ch c Needwood Blade—Quiz Time **Mrs L. N. Harmes**

Other Owners: Mr M. Madgwick, Mr Robert Oliver, Mr T. Smith.

Assistant Trainer: David Madgwick

Jockey (flat): George Baker, Adam Kirby. **Jockey (NH):** Marc Goldstein.

404 MRS HEATHER MAIN, Wantage
Postal: **Kingston Common Farm, Kingston Lisle, Wantage, Oxfordshire, OX12 9QT**
Contacts: **PHONE (01367) 820124 FAX (01367) 820125**
E-MAIL heather.main@hotmail.com WEBSITE www.heathermainracing.com

1 ACHALAS (IRE), 5, b g Statue of Liberty (USA)—Princess of Iona (IRE) **Mr & Mrs D. R. Guest**
2 BEAUTIFUL LANDO (FR), 5, b br g Lando (GER)—Beautiful Baroness (USA) **Les Chevaliers**
3 HECTOR'S CHANCE, 4, ch g Byron—Fleur A Lay (USA) **Mr M. Scott Russell**
4 JUST POPSY, 7, gr m Turgeon (USA)—Festival Day (FR) **Highnote Thoroughbreds**
5 PRINCESS SIX, 4, b m Generous (IRE)—Segsbury Belle **Highnote Thoroughbreds**
6 SOUTH KENTER (USA), 4, ch c Silver Deputy (CAN)—Crystal Downs (USA) **Les Chevaliers**
7 TOKYO BROWN (USA), 4, b g Marquetry (USA)—Miasma (USA) **Wetumpka Racing**

THREE-YEAR-OLDS
8 BYRONESS, b f Byron—Parting Gift **Les Chevaliers**
9 HAPPY FAMILIES, b f Singspiel (IRE)—One of The Family **K Mercer & Wetumpka Racing**
10 B f Henny Hughes (USA)—Heart Lake (CAN) **Mrs H. S. Main**
11 ROARING ROCKS (FR), gr g Stormy River (FR)—Saulace (FR) **R P Foden & Les Chevaliers**
12 SOLVANNA, b f Haafhd—Solva **Wetumpka Racing & Andrew Knott**

TWO-YEAR-OLDS
13 Ch f 16/3 Byron—Parting Gift (Cadeaux Genereux)
14 POKER GOLD (FR), b c 21/2 Gold Away (IRE)—
  Becquarette (FR) (Nombre Premier) (22222) **Unregistered Partnership**

Other Owners: R. P. Foden, Mr D. R. Guest, Mr A. Knott, J. P. M. Main, K. J. Mercer.

405 MR PETER MAKIN, Marlborough

Postal: **Bonita Racing Stables, Ogbourne Maisey, Marlborough, Wiltshire, SN8 1RY**
Contacts: **PHONE (01672) 512973 FAX (01672) 514166**
E-MAIL hq@petermakin-racing.com WEBSITE www.petermakin-racing.com

1 **BLANC DE CHINE (IRE)**, 4, gr f Dark Angel (IRE)—Nullarbor **R. P. Marchant & Mrs E. Lee**
2 **KNAVE OF CLUBS (IRE)**, 4, b g Red Clubs (IRE)—Royal Bounty (IRE) **Mr J. P. Carrington**
3 **LUNAR LIMELIGHT**, 8, b g Royal Applause—Moon Magic **Mrs P. J. Makin**
4 **MORACHE MUSIC**, 5, b g Sleeping Indian—Enchanted Princess **R P Marchant D M Ahier Mrs E Lee**
5 **SAINT BONIFACE**, 4, ch g Bahamian Bounty—Nursling (IRE) **Mrs P. J. Makin**
6 **WORDISMYBOND**, 4, b g Monsieur Bond (IRE)—La Gessa **T. W. Wellard & Partners**

THREE-YEAR-OLDS

7 **JUST ISLA**, ch f Halling (USA)—Island Rapture **D. A. Poole**
8 **KOHARU**, b gr f Ishiguru (USA)—Vellena **Keith & Brian Brackpool**
9 **UNISON (IRE)**, b c Jeremy (USA)—Easter Song **Mr J. P. Carrington**

TWO-YEAR-OLDS

10 B f 27/2 Halling (USA)—Amarullah (FR) (Daylami (IRE)) (25000) **R. P. Marchant & J. P. Carrington**
11 B f 11/4 Sholokhov (IRE)—Chaguaramas (IRE) (Mujadil (USA)) (6000) **B. Mortimer & Partners**
12 B f 23/4 Kyllachy—Enchanted Princess (Royal Applause) (28000) **R. P. Marchant & J. P. Carrington**
13 B c 4/4 Virtual—Point Perfect (Dansili) (14000) **M. H. Holland & Partners**
14 B f 13/3 Iffraaj—Romea (Muhtarram (USA)) (9000) **Mrs J. N. Humphreys**
15 B c 5/4 Captain Gerrard (IRE)—Ryan's Quest (IRE) (Mukaddamah (USA)) (6000) **OG Racing Partnership**
16 B f 5/3 Sleeping Indian—Scarlett Ribbon (Most Welcome) (6000) **Ten Of Hearts**
17 B c 4/4 Alhaarth (IRE)—Wassendale (Erhaab (USA)) (7000) **Unregistered Partnership**

Other Owners: D. M. Ahier, D. Allen, B. A. W. Brackpool, K. Brackpool, Mr K. A. Carter, H. J. W. Davies, F. J. Everleigh, Mr R. A. Henley, R. Kent, Mr P. A. Lee, The Countess Of Lonsdale, Mrs Nicky Lyon, Mrs P. J. Makin, Mr P. J. Makin, Mr R. P. Marchant, Miss L. McGrath, Mr B. Mortimer, W. H. Simpson, T. W. Wellard, Mr & Mrs S. Woods.

406 MRS ALYSON MALZARD, Jersey

Postal: **Les Etabl'yes, Grosnez Farm, St Ouen, Jersey, JE3 2AD**
Contacts: **MOBILE (07797) 738128**
E-MAIL themalzards@localdial.com

1 **AZARIA (FR)**, 7, b m Miesque's Son (USA)—Polar Return (FR) **Macwin Racing**
2 **COUNTRY BLUE (FR)**, 4, b g Country Reel (USA)—Exica (FR) **Mr A. Taylor**
3 **DEEPIKA (IRE)**, 5, b rm Key of Luck (USA)—Soul Society (IRE) **Mr A. Taylor**
4 **KERSIVAY**, 7, ch g Royal Applause—Lochmaddy **Malzard Racing**
5 **LA VERTE RUE (USA)**, 7, b m Johannesburg (USA)—Settling In (USA) **Mr A. Taylor**
6 **LANG SHINING (IRE)**, 9, ch g Dr Fong (USA)—Dragnet (IRE) **Mr A. Taylor**
7 **NEUILLY**, 6, b m Nayef (USA)—Narasimha (USA) **Bob & Helene Bonney**
8 **NORDIC LIGHT**, 9, b br g Belong To Me (USA)—Midriff (USA) **Phil Banfield & John Hackett**
9 **PAS D'ACTION**, 5, ch g Noverre (USA)—Bright Vision **Jim Jamouneau**
10 **REACH OUT**, 5, ch g Phoenix Reach (IRE)—Cocorica (IRE) **Malzard Racing**
11 **ROCQUAINE (IRE)**, 4, b f Oratorio (IRE)—Watch The Clock **Trevor & Pat Gallienne**
12 **SISSI GUIHEN (FR)**, 7, ch m Lord of Men—Assermara (FR) **P. A. Guiton & Y. Stead**
13 **SPANISH BOUNTY**, 8, b g Bahamian Bounty—Spanish Gold **Malzard Racing**
14 **UNIFORM RUBY**, 5, b m Iceman—Winter Moon **The Unwin Family**
15 **VAMOS (IRE)**, 7, b g Royal Applause—Feather Boa (IRE) **Bob & Helene Bonney**

Jockey (flat): Jemma Marshall. **Jockey (NH):** Mattie Batchelor. **Amateur:** Miss Caroline Hurley.

407 MR JAMES JOSEPH MANGAN, Mallow

Postal: **Curraheen, Conna, Mallow, Co. Cork, Ireland**
Contacts: **PHONE (00353) 585 9116 FAX (00353) 585 9116 MOBILE (00353) 8726 84611**

1 **ANNACARTON (IRE)**, 9, b g Oscar (IRE)—Gallica (IRE) **Mrs Mary Mangan**
2 **CARRIES DARLING**, 6, b m Flemensfirth (USA)—Knock Down (IRE) **Mr W. M. Mangan**
3 **CASTLE WINGS (IRE)**, 8, b g Winged Love (IRE)—Mrs Hegarty **The Kings Syndicate**
4 **CYPRUSORMILAN**, 6, b g Milan—Persrolla **Handford Chemists Ltd**

MR JAMES JOSEPH MANGAN - Continued

5 **DONT TELL PA (IRE)**, 6, b g Oscar (IRE)—Glacial Snowboard (IRE) **Mrs Mary Mangan**
6 **FAIR DILEMMA (IRE)**, 8, b g Dr Massini (IRE)—Midnight Dilemma (IRE) **Patrick Furey**
7 **KILCREA (IRE)**, 6, b g Definite Article—Lightly Dreaming (FR) **Mr M. I. O'Driscoll**
8 **MONTYS MEADOW (IRE)**, 5, b g Oscar (IRE)—Montys Miss (IRE) **Hanford's Chemist Ltd**
9 **NORAS FANCY (IRE)**, 7, b m Brian Boru—Verney Bird (IRE) **Mr M. I. Dixon**
10 **OSCAR DELTA (IRE)**, 10, b g Oscar (IRE)—Timerry (IRE) **Miss Karen O'Driscoll**
11 **OSCAR TOWN (IRE)**, 6, b m Oscar (IRE)—Meadstown Miss (IRE) **John J. Bermingham**
12 **QUARRYVALE (IRE)**, 9, b m Beneficial—Miss McCormick (IRE) **Thomas O'Flynn**
13 **SMALL IS BEAUTIFUL (IRE)**, 5, b m Beneficial—Cherry Black (IRE) **Mrs Mary Mangan**
14 **THE FLYING DOC (IRE)**, 5, b m Dr Massini (IRE)—Meadstown Miss (IRE) **Mrs Rita Keating**
15 **TIPP ON AIR (IRE)**, 5, b m Indian River (FR)—Air Affair **After Ten Syndicate**
16 **WHATSTHECRACK JACK (IRE)**, 6, b g Croco Rouge (IRE)—Glebe Melody (IRE) **Conor Lannen**

Assistant Trainer: Mary Mangan

---

408 MR CHARLIE MANN, Upper Lambourn
Postal: **Neardown, Upper Lambourn, Hungerford, Berkshire, RG17 8QP**
Contacts: **PHONE (01488) 71717 / 73118 FAX (01488) 73223 MOBILE (07721) 888333**
E-MAIL charlie@charliemann.info WEBSITE www.charliemann.com

1 **ATTIMO (GER)**, 4, ch g Nayef (USA)—Alanda (GER) **The Neardown VI**
2 **BALLYMURRY (IRE)**, 7, b g Publisher (USA)—Little Nibbler (IRE) **C Hunter, D Batten, S Beccle, T Stapleton**
3 **BIG JER**, 6, b g Flemensfirth (USA)—Roses of Picardy (IRE) **Mrs J. M. Mayo**
4 **DUKE OF MONMOUTH (IRE)**, 6, b g Presenting—Hayley Cometh (IRE) **Bryan & Philippa Burrough**
5 **ENTER PARADISE (IRE)**, 9, ch g Moscow Society (USA)—
                                                Cappamore Girl (IRE) **The Four Minutes Of Madness Partnership**
6 **FEISTY LASS (IRE)**, 7, ch m Flemensfirth (USA)—Back The Queen (IRE) **The Icy Fire Partnership**
7 **FINE PARCHMENT (IRE)**, 10, b g Presenting—Run For Cover (IRE) **N. W. A. Bannister**
8 4, B g Wareed (IRE)—Katie Buckers (IRE) **C. J. Mann**
9 **KING ARTHUR (GER)**, 4, ch g Elnadim (USA)—Konigin Shuttle (GER) **The Neardown VI**
10 **LORD OF HOUSE (GER)**, 5, ch g Lord of England (GER)—Lake House (IRE) **Good Lord Partnership**
11 **MARINGO BAY (IRE)**, 8, b g Old Vic—Waterland Lady **John & Peter Heron**
12 **MASKED MAN (IRE)**, 10, ch g Alhaarth (IRE)—Misbegotten (IRE) **Major J. G. Thorneloe**
13 **PROLINX (IRE)**, 8, b g Oscar (IRE)—Winter Break (IRE) **Prolinx Limited**
14 **SEVENTH SKY (GER)**, 6, b g King's Best (USA)—Sacarina **John & Peter Heron**
15 **STONEY SILENCE**, 5, b g Generous (IRE)—Stoney Path **C. J. Mann**
16 **VAN DIEMENS LAND (USA)**, 6, b g Arch (USA)—Trylko (USA) **Mr A. J. Weller**
17 **VICTOR LEUDORUM (IRE)**, 6, b g Wareed (IRE)—Rock Garden (IRE) **R. Curry, C. Leuchars & R. Tompkins**
18 **WESTERN KING (IRE)**, 6, b g Definite Article—Western Road (GER) **The Western King Partnership**
19 **WHO OWNS ME (IRE)**, 7, b g Milan—Top Lassie (IRE) **Fromthestables.Com Racing**
20 **YAZDI (IRE)**, 4, b g Galileo (IRE)—Lucky Spin **The Neardown VI**

Other Owners: Amity Finance Ltd, Mr D. H. Batten, Mr B. Beacham, Mr S. E. Beccle, B. R. H. Burrough, Mrs P. J. Burrough, Mr N. A. Coster, Mr R. Curry, R. N. Frosell, R. E. Good, Mr R. C. Heginbotham, Mr J. Heron, Mr P. Heron, Mrs C. J. Hill, Mr S. J. Hind, Mrs C. H. C. Hunter, Ms D. E. Jones, Mr N. J. Kempner, Mr I. G. Martin, R. P. B. Michaelson, C. R. Nugent, Mr T. A. Simmons, A. W. Stapleton, Mrs L. C. Taylor, R. J. Tompkins, Mrs P. J. Zarbafi.

Assistant Trainer: D J Jeffreys

Jockey (NH): Noel Fehily. **Conditional:** Gavin Sheehan.

---

409 MR GEORGE MARGARSON, Newmarket
Postal: **Graham Lodge, Birdcage Walk, Newmarket, Suffolk, CB8 0NE**
Contacts: **HOME/FAX (01638) 668043 MOBILE (07860) 198303**
E-MAIL george@georgemargarson.co.uk WEBSITE www.georgemargason.co.uk

1 **ARTFUL LADY (IRE)**, 4, br f Excellent Art—Fear And Greed (IRE) **Mrs E. L. Hook**
2 **EXCELLENT AIM**, 6, b g Exceed And Excel (AUS)—Snugfit Annie **Graham Lodge Partnership**
3 **EXCELLENT GUEST**, 6, b g Exceed And Excel (AUS)—Princess Speedfit (FR) **John Guest Racing**
4 **IMAGINARY DIVA**, 7, b m Lend A Hand—Distant Diva **Graham Lodge Partnership**
5 **MAGICAL SPEEDFIT (IRE)**, 8, ch g Bold Fact (USA)—Magical Peace (IRE) **Graham Lodge Partnership**
6 **REBELLIOUS GUEST**, 4, b g Cockney Rebel (IRE)—Marisa (GER) **John Guest Racing**
7 **STORM RUNNER (IRE)**, 5, b g Rakti—Saibhreas (IRE) **Pitfield Partnership**

MR GEORGE MARGARSON - Continued

8 **UPRISE**, 4, b g Pivotal—Soar **Pitfield Partnership**
9 **WOOFALL SOVEREIGN (IRE)**, 7, b g Noverre (USA)—Mandragore (USA) **Wildcard Racing**
10 **YOUNG JACKIE**, 5, b m Doyen (IRE)—Just Warning **Exors of the Late Mr M. F. Kentish**
11 **YOUNG LISA**, 4, b f Echo of Light—Just Warning **Exors of the Late Mr M. F. Kentish**

THREE-YEAR-OLDS

12 **EXOTIC GUEST**, ch g Bahamian Bounty—Mamoura (IRE) **John Guest Racing**
13 **JAMMY GUEST (IRE)**, b c Duke of Marmalade (IRE)—Ardbrae Lady **John Guest Racing**
14 **RED CATKIN**, b f Notnowcato—Red Salvia **Mrs E. L. Hook**
15 **SHINING CROSS (IRE)**, b g Cape Cross (IRE)—Shining Debut (IRE) **Mrs C. C. Regalado-Gonzalez**
16 **SOUBRETTE**, ch f Zafeen (FR)—Nihal (IRE) **Stableside Racing Partnership**
17 **SPEEDFIT BOY (IRE)**, b g Red Clubs (IRE)—Princess Speedfit (FR) **John Guest Racing**

TWO-YEAR-OLDS

18 **BOUNTIFUL SIN**, ch c 23/4 Sinndar (IRE)—
    Tropical Barth (IRE) (Peintre Celebre (USA)) (12500) **Maxwell Morrison**
19 **ELUSIVE GUEST (FR)**, b c 3/4 Elusive City (USA)—Mansoura (IRE) (Kalanisi (IRE)) (150793) **John Guest Racing**
20 **LUCKY KRISTALE**, b f 6/3 Lucky Story (USA)—Pikaboo (Pivotal) (22000) **Graham Lodge Partnership**
21 B c 26/1 Bushranger (IRE)—Prodigal Daughter (Alhaarth (IRE)) (80000) **John Guest Racing**
22 **SHYRON**, b c 21/4 Byron—Coconut Shy (Bahamian Bounty) **Mr & Mrs F. Butler**

Other Owners: Mr J. Donnison, Mr P. J. Donnison, Mrs E. L. Hook, Mr G. G. Margarson.

Assistant Trainer: Katie Margarson

Jockey (flat): Ian Mongan, Tom Queally. **Apprentice:** Jordan Vaughan. **Amateur:** Miss Katie Margarson.

---

410 MR A. J. MARTIN, Summerhill

Postal: Arodstown, Moynalvey, Summerhill, Co. Meath, Ireland
Contacts: PHONE (00353) 46 955 8633 FAX (00353) 46 955 8632 MOBILE (00353) 86 276 0835
E-MAIL arodstown@eircom.net

1 **BANK GUARANTEE (IRE)**, 8, br g Bob's Return (IRE)—Rosy Rockford (IRE) **Mrs Marie Martin**
2 **BENEFFICIENT (IRE)**, 7, ch g Beneficial—Supreme Breda (IRE) **Aidan Shiels/Nial Reilly Partnership**
3 **BLACKMAIL (FR)**, 5, b g Black Sam Bellamy (IRE)—Same To You (FR) **John Breslin**
4 **BOG WARRIOR (IRE)**, 9, b g Strategic Choice (USA)—Kilmac Princess (IRE) **Gigginstown House Stud**
5 **BUNSEN BURNER (USA)**, 8, b g Langfuhr (CAN)—Navarene (USA) **Out All Night Syndicate (Des McCaffrey)**
6 **CNOCAN DIVA (IRE)**, 5, b m Danehill Dancer (IRE)—Dancing Diva (FR) **John Breslin**
7 **DEDIGOUT (IRE)**, 7, b g Bob Back (USA)—Dainty Daisy (IRE) **Gigginstown House Stud**
8 **EDEYMI (IRE)**, 5, b g Barathea (IRE)—Edabiya (IRE) **Gigginstown House Stud**
9 **EIGHT CHIMES (FR)**, 5, gr g Kaldounevees (FR)—Octet (FR) **Sheila Moffett**
10 **GALLOPING GANDER (IRE)**, 7, b g Danehill Dancer (IRE)—Silly Goose (IRE) **John Breslin**
11 **GENTLE AUSSIE (IRE)**, 4, b br g Aussie Rules (IRE)—Gintilgalla (IRE) **Mulvanys Bar Syndicate**
12 **GOLANTILLA (IRE)**, 5, b g Golan (IRE)—Scintilla **Barry Connell**
13 **GUNNS ISLAND (IRE)**, 6, br g Heron Island (IRE)—Il Porto (IRE) **Adrian Collins**
14 **HAVING NIGHTMARES (IRE)**, 9, b br g King's Theatre (IRE)—Quare Dream's (IRE) **Mrs Marie Martin**
15 **KING OF THE REFS (IRE)**, 8, b g Zagreb (USA)—Regal Pursuit (IRE) **Eamon Waters**
16 **LIVING NEXT DOOR (IRE)**, 7, b g Beneficial—Except Alice (IRE) **John Breslin**
17 **MATSUKAZE (IRE)**, 6, b g Norwich—The Bowlers Boreen **Tom McGoldrick**
18 **MILITARY BOWL (USA)**, 5, b g Mr Greeley (USA)—
    Turtle Bow (FR) **Bowled Over Syndicate (Mrs Sheila Moffett)**
19 **MIRIAM'S DREAM (IRE)**, 7, b g Lord Americo—Butlers Meadow (IRE) **Ultimate Dreams Syndicate**
20 **PIRES**, 9, br g Generous (IRE)—Kaydee Queen (IRE) **Lily Lawlor**
21 **QUICK JACK (IRE)**, 4, ch g Footstepsinthesand—Miss Polaris **John Breslin**
22 **QUICKPICK VIC (IRE)**, 6, b g Old Vic—Anotherlling (IRE) **Joseph Duff**
23 **RACEVIEWS DIAMOND (IRE)**, 5, b g Diamond Green (FR)—Mitsubishi Trium (IRE) **Robert Donaldson**
24 **REDERA (IRE)**, 7, b g Chevalier (IRE)—Lady Redera (IRE) **Peter William Partnership - D. Fields/J. W. Touhy**
25 **REGUSCI (IRE)**, 5, b g Lord of Appeal—Sarahs Choice (IRE) **John Breslin**
26 **SAVELLO (IRE)**, 7, ch g Anshan—Fragrant Frances (IRE) **Gigginstown House Stud**
27 **SENSATIONAL SEMA (IRE)**, 9, br g Witness Box (USA)—Shuil Ar Sproai (IRE) **Pats Bar Syndicate**
28 **SHEMSHAL (FR)**, 5, b g Dalakhani (IRE)—Shemala (IRE) **Tony Martin/Mrs Sheila Moffett**
29 **SRAID PADRAIG (IRE)**, 7, b g Revoque (IRE)—Loughaneala (IRE) **Barry Connell**
30 **TED VEALE (IRE)**, 6, b g Revoque (IRE)—Rose Tanner (IRE) **John Breslin**
31 **THOMAS EDISON (IRE)**, 6, b g Danehill Dancer (IRE)—Bright Bank (IRE) **J. P. McManus**

MR A. J. MARTIN - Continued

32 **TOP FOUR (IRE)**, 8, ch g Karinga Bay—Rash-Gale (IRE) **J. R. Shaw**
33 **UMPACT (FR)**, 5, b g Voix du Nord (FR)—Niponne (FR) **Gigginstown House Stud**
34 **UNBREAKABLE (IRE)**, 5, b g King's Theatre (IRE)—Sejour (IRE) **Gigginstown House Stud**
35 **WINGTIPS (FR)**, 5, gr g High Chaparral (IRE)—Without Shoes (FR) **Mrs Sheila Moffett**

Other Owners: Badger Syndicate, P. A. Byrne, Byrne Bros (Formwork) Ltd, Timothy Fitzgerald, Seamus D. Fitzpatrick, Dominick Glennane, Hard Hat Syndicate, Independent Syndicate, Irish Rover Syndicate, R. Jordan, Lyreen Syndicate, P. J. McGee, Alan Murray, Joseph Brendan Quin, Sox Syndicate, Two K's Syndicate, V. R. Walsh.

Jockey (flat): F. Berry, J. P. Murtagh. **Jockey (NH):** P. Carberry, D. J. Casey, N. P. Madden, R. Moran, R. M. Power, D. N. Russell, P. Townend, R. Walsh. **Conditional:** Shane Shortall. **Apprentice:** Luke Dempsey, Colin Keane. **Amateur:** Mr Simon Craig, Mr M. J. P. O'Connor.

---

411   **MR ANDREW J. MARTIN, Chipping Norton**
Postal: **Yew Tree Barn, Hook Norton Road, Swerford, Chipping Norton, Oxfordshire, OX7 4BF**

1 **DIGGER TIME**, 10, b m Exit To Nowhere (USA)—Making Time **A. J. Martin**
2 **FITZ VOLONTE**, 6, br g Passing Glance—Swordella **A. J. Martin**
3 **ORANGER (FR)**, 11, b g Antarctique (IRE)—True Beauty **A. J. Martin**
4 **SUNNY LEDGEND**, 8, b g Midnight Legend—Swordella **A. J. Martin**
5 **TRACKING TIME**, 6, b g Central Park (IRE)—E Minor (IRE) **A. J. Martin**
6 **TRIFOLLET**, 8, b m Kirkwall—St Doughla's (IRE) **A. J. Martin**

---

412   **MR CHRISTOPHER MASON, Caerwent**
Postal: **Whitehall Barn, Five Lanes, Caerwent, Monmouthshire, NP26 5PE**
Contacts: **PHONE (01291) 422172 FAX (01633) 666690 MOBILE (07767) 808082**
E-MAIL cjmason@tiscali.co.uk

1 **ARTHUR'S EDGE**, 9, b g Diktat—Bright Edge **Christopher & Annabelle Mason**
2 **SUPERIOR EDGE**, 6, b m Exceed And Excel (AUS)—Beveled Edge **Christopher & Annabelle Mason**

THREE-YEAR-OLDS

3 **EDGED OUT**, b f Piccolo—Edge of Light **Christopher & Annabelle Mason**

TWO-YEAR-OLDS

4 **HEAVENS EDGE**, b f 20/4 Royal Applause—Elidore (Danetime (IRE)) (30000) **Christopher & Annabelle Mason**

Assistant Trainer: Annabelle Mason

---

413   **MRS JENNIFER MASON, Cirencester**
Postal: **Manor Farm, Ablington, Bibury, Cirencester, Gloucestershire, GL7 5NY**
Contacts: **PHONE (01285) 740445 MOBILE (07974) 262438**
E-MAIL pwmason2002@yahoo.co.uk WEBSITE www.jennifermasonracing.com

1 **LANARKSHIRE (IRE)**, 4, ch g Iffraaj—Voyage of Dreams (USA) **The If At First Partnership**
2 **LOVE OF TARA**, 11, b m Kayf Tara—O My Love **North Park Farm Racing**
3 **MONKSGOLD (IRE)**, 5, b g Gold Well—Opium **The Dreamers**
4 **PRETTY PENNY**, 9, b m Alflora (IRE)—Mrs Moneypenny **Mr C. C. B. Mathew**

Other Owners: Mr J. A. Cover, Mrs R. D. Greenwood, Mr N. G. Jackson, Mr R. E. Pullen, Mrs M. E. Slocock, Mr B. Wallis.

Assistant Trainer: Mr Peter W. Mason

Jockey (NH): Felix De Giles, Timmy Murphy. **Amateur:** Mr Peter Mason, Mr Lewis Gordon.

414 MR ROBIN MATHEW, Burford
Postal: **Church Farm, Little Barrington, Burford, Oxfordshire, OX18 4TE**
Contacts: **PHONE (01451) 844311**

1 BALLY SANDS (IRE), 9, b g Luso—Sandwell Old Rose (IRE) **R. Mathew**
2 BRAVO RIQUET (FR), 7, br g Laveron—Jeroline (FR) **R. Mathew**
3 EMPEROR COMMODOS, 6, b g Midnight Legend—Theme Arena **R. Mathew**
4 ERGO SUM, 6, bl g Fair Mix (IRE)—Idiot's Lady **R. Mathew**

Jockey (NH): Dave Crosse, Lee Edwards.

415 MISS OLIVIA MAYLAM, Epsom
Postal: **Chalk Pit Stables, Headley Road, Epsom, Surrey, KT18 6BW**
Contacts: **MOBILE (07776) 303422**
E-MAIL olivia_maylam@hotmail.co.uk **WEBSITE** www.oliviamaylamracing.com

1 ARTFUL DODGER, 6, b g Josr Algarhoud (IRE)—Artistic Belle (IRE) **Mr K. Tyre**
2 CALYPSO MAGIC (IRE), 5, gr g Aussie Rules (USA)—Calypso Dancer (FR) **Mr A. C. D. Main**
3 CHARMING (IRE), 4, b f Invincible Spirit (IRE)—Nofa's Magic (IRE) **Mrs V. A. Ward**
4 JACKIE LOVE (IRE), 5, b m Tobougg (IRE)—Gutter Press (IRE) **Miss O. Maylam**
5 JUST BREATHE (IRE), 4, b f Choisir (AUS)—Opium Creek (IRE) **Mr A. C. D. Main**
6 LLAMADAS, 11, b g Josr Algarhoud (IRE)—Primulette **Mr K. Tyre**
7 MAD GINGER ALICE, 5, ch m Beat Hollow—Peryllys **B. Neaves**
8 SCOTTISH LAKE, 5, b g Bertolini (USA)—Diabaig **A. C. Maylam**

THREE-YEAR-OLDS
9 B c Modigliani (USA)—Bom Chicka Wah Wah (USA) **B. Neaves**
10 MARGUERITE ST JUST, b f Sir Percy—Ships Watch (IRE) **Mr J. Pearce**

416 MR KEVIN MCAULIFFE, Faringdon
Postal: **Fernham Farm, Fernham, Faringdon, Oxfordshire, SN7 7NX**

THREE-YEAR-OLDS
1 B f Royal Applause—Ribbonwood (USA)

417 MR CHARLIE MCBRIDE, Newmarket
Postal: **Exeter House Stables, 33 Exeter Road, Newmarket, Suffolk, CB8 0NY**
Contacts: **PHONE/FAX (01638) 667841 MOBILE (07929) 265711**

1 GHOST OPERA, 5, b m Librettist (USA)—Materialize (USA) **P. J. McBride**
2 HARRY BUCKLE, 4, ch c Byron—Native Ring (FR) **Four Winds Racing Partnership**

THREE-YEAR-OLDS
3 NAPINDA, b f Sleeping Indian—Aptina (USA) **Mr P. H. Wagstaffe**

Other Owners: S. J. Mear, Mrs E. A. Mear.

418 MR ALAN MCCABE, Averham
Postal: **Cheveral Barn, Averham, Newark, Nottinghamshire, NG23 5RU**
Contacts: **PHONE (01636) 701668 FAX (01636) 706579 MOBILE (07766) 302092**
E-MAIL ajmacc@tiscali.co.uk

1 AMETHYST DAWN (IRE), 7, gr m Act One—A L'aube (IRE) **A. S. Reid**
2 ASCENDANT, 7, ch g Medicean—Ascendancy **A. S. Reid**
3 ATHLETIC, 4, b g Doyen (IRE)—Gentle Irony **A. S. Reid**
4 AUBRIETIA, 4, b f Dutch Art—Petong's Pet **Mrs M. J. McCabe**

MR ALAN MCCABE - Continued

5 **AZRAEL**, 5, b g Makbul—Fontaine Lady **The Cor Blimey Partnership**
6 **CHAMBLES**, 4, b f Shamardal (USA)—Pants **A. S. Reid**
7 **CORNUS**, 11, ch g Inchinor—Demerger (USA) **Triple A Partnership**
8 **DOCTOR DAVID**, 10, gr g Zilzal (USA)—Arantxa **Dr D. S. Myers & Mr A. S. Reid**
9 **ELUSIVE WARRIOR (USA)**, 10, b g Elusive Quality (USA)—Love To Fight (CAN) **Mrs M. J. McCabe**
10 **ENJOYMENT**, 6, b m Dansili—Have Fun **A. J. McCabe**
11 **FLYING PICKETS (IRE)**, 4, b g Piccolo—Burn **Mr T. Al Nisf**
12 **FOLLOW THE FLAG (IRE)**, 9, ch g Traditionally (USA)—Iktidar **Mr S. Gillen**
13 **FRATELLINO**, 6, ch h Auction House (USA)—Vida (IRE) **Sale Of The Century**
14 **KAI**, 4, b g Kyllachy—Belle Ile (USA) **Mr J. R. Atherton**
15 **MALTEASE AH**, 4, br f Librettist (USA)—Manic **A. S. Reid**
16 **MASTERFUL ACT (USA)**, 6, ch g Pleasantly Perfect (USA)—Catnip (USA) **Universal Recycling Company**
17 **MOUSIE**, 4, b f Auction House (USA)—Goes A Treat (IRE) **Lucky Heather**
18 **MR PLOD**, 8, ch g Silver Patriarch (IRE)—Emily-Mou (IRE) **A. S. Reid**
19 **OVERWHELM**, 5, ch m Bahamian Bounty—Depressed **A. S. Reid**
20 **PULLMEN**, 5, gr g Silver Patriarch (IRE)—Moon Spinner **A. S. Reid**
21 **SEXTONS HOUSE (IRE)**, 5, b g King's Best (USA)—Lolita's Gold (USA) **Mrs M. J. McCabe**
22 **SHOWBOATING (IRE)**, 5, b g Shamardal (USA)—
                                    Sadinga (IRE) **Mr M & Mrs L Cooke Mr A Pierce Mr A McCabe**
23 **SILVER WIND**, 8, b g Ishiguru (USA)—My Bonus **Shoot The Breeze Partners**
24 **SOVENTO (GER)**, 9, ch g Kornado—Second Game (GER) **Mrs M. J. McCabe**
25 **SPARTIC**, 5, gr g Needwood Blade—Celtic Spa (IRE) **D. J. Buckley**
26 **SPIRIT OF DIXIE**, 6, ch m Kheleyf (USA)—Decatur **Ms Sara Hattersley**

THREE-YEAR-OLDS

27 **BOUGALOO**, b g Tobougg (IRE)—Benjarong **The Michaelmas Daisy Partnership**
28 Ch g Compton Place—Cugina
29 **DARAKTI (IRE)**, b g Rakti—Mitawa (IRE) **Mrs D. E. Sharp**
30 **DOLLY BANTRY**, ch f Pastoral Pursuits—Seeker **Lucky Heather**
31 **LINCOLNROSE (IRE)**, gr f Verglas (IRE)—Imelda (USA) **P C Coaches of Lincoln Limited**
32 **LITTLE DOLLY**, b f Nayef (USA)—Tahirah **C. J. Murfitt**
33 **PROVENTI**, b g Auction House (USA)—Miss Poppy **Sale Of The Century**
34 B f Firebreak—Reel Cool **Ms Sara Hattersley**
35 **TAMING THE TWEET**, b f Act One—Pants **A. S. Reid**
36 **UNA BELLA COSA**, b f Dubai Destination (USA)—Blinding Mission (IRE) **Averham Racing Syndicates 1**
37 **UNDERWHELM**, ch f Bahamian Bounty—Depressed **A. S. Reid**
38 **WHATWEHAVEWEHOLD**, b c Avonbridge—Dancing Loma (FR) **Ms Sara Hattersley**

TWO-YEAR-OLDS

39 B c 26/4 Auction House (USA)—Amwell Star (USA) (Silver Buck (USA))
40 B f 3/3 Mount Nelson—Clever Millie (USA) (Cape Canaveral (USA)) (12000) **Mr K. Dasmal**
41 **LOMA MOR**, b f 10/4 Auction House (USA)—Dancing Loma (FR) (Danehill Dancer (IRE)) (4952) **Lucky Heather**
42 B c 24/4 Byron—Loose Caboose (IRE) (Tagula (IRE))
43 **PACKET STATION**, ch f 1/4 Compton Place—Jump Ship (Night Shift (USA)) **Mr M. Dixon**
44 B c 13/3 Royal Applause—Tiana (Diktat) (8000) **Premspace Ltd**
45 Ch f 1/4 Iffraaj—Timewee (USA) (Romanov (IRE)) (2285) **Mr D. Emsley**
46 Ch c 25/4 Auction House (USA)—Vida (IRE) (Wolfhound (USA))
47 B c 1/1 Sleeping Indian—Well of Echoes (Diktat)
48 Ch f 4/4 Soviet Star (USA)—Why Now (Dansili) (9523)
49 **WOTNOWDOCTOR**, b g 29/4 Notnowcato—Arantxa (Sharpo) **Dr D. S. Myers & Mr A. S. Reid**

Other Owners: Mr J. Babb, Mr A. D. Baker, Miss H. P. Chellingworth, Mr Paul Collins, Mr M. Cooke, Mr John Cooke, Mr M. W. Lawrence, Mrs M. J. McCabe, Mr A. J. McCabe, Dr D. S. Myers, Mr A. S. Reid, Mr Peter Smith, Mr A. C. Timms, Mr Charles Wentworth.

Jockey (flat): Shane Kelly, Seb Sanders, Robert Winston.

419 **MR DONALD MCCAIN, Cholmondeley**
Postal: **Bankhouse, Cholmondeley, Malpas, Cheshire, SY14 8AL**
Contacts: **PHONE (01829) 720352/720351 FAX (01829) 720475 MOBILE (07903) 066194**
E-MAIL bankhouse.racing@virgin.net WEBSITE www.donaldmccain.co.uk

1 **A BRIDGE TOO FAR (IRE)**, 7, b g Oscar (IRE)—Private Rose (IRE) **Glen's Fools**
2 **AAZIF (IRE)**, 4, ch g Nayef (USA)—Ayun (USA) **Askew Dick Hernon Reynard**

MR DONALD MCCAIN - Continued

3 **ABBEY STORM (IRE)**, 7, br g Presenting—Bobbies Storm (IRE) **Mr & Mrs Paul Rooney**
4 **ABSINTHE (IRE)**, 7, b g King's Best (USA)—Triple Try (IRE) **Mr & Mrs Paul Rooney**
5 **ACROSS THE BAY (IRE)**, 9, b g Bob's Return (IRE)—The Southern (IRE) **Scotch Piper Syndicate**
6 **AGENT ARCHIE (USA)**, 6, b g Smart Strike (CAN)—Dans La Ville (CHI) **D. M. Gorton**
7 **AL QEDDAAF (IRE)**, 7, b g Alhaarth (IRE)—Just Special **T. G. Leslie**
8 **ALDERLEY ROVER (IRE)**, 9, gr g Beneficial—St Anne's Lady (IRE) **A. Craig & A. Dick**
9 **AN CAPALL MOR (IRE)**, 7, b g Flemensfirth (USA)—Corravilla (IRE) **Boretech & Tony Sadler**
10 **ANY GIVEN DAY (IRE)**, 8, gr g Clodovil (IRE)—Five of Wands **T. G. Leslie**
11 **AVENGING ACE (IRE)**, 7, b g Heron Island (IRE)—How Provincial (IRE) **T. G. Leslie**
12 4, B g Shantou (USA)—Back Log (IRE) **Mr & Mrs Paul Rooney**
13 **BALLABRIGGS (IRE)**, 12, b g Presenting—Papoose (IRE) **T. J. Hemmings**
14 **BALLYBRIGGAN (IRE)**, 9, b g Flemensfirth (USA)—Shean Hill (IRE) **Stewart Andrew & Jim Shaw**
15 **BARDELI (IRE)**, 6, br g Overbury (IRE)—Miss Denman (IRE) **T. G. Leslie**
16 **BEEVES (IRE)**, 6, b g Portrait Gallery (IRE)—Camas North (IRE) **Mr & Mrs Paul Rooney**
17 **BENJAMIN BITTERN (IRE)**, 6, b g Heron Island (IRE)—Reasoning **Passant Williams Tipton**
18 **BHALTAIR (IRE)**, 7, gr g Great Palm (USA)—Gypsy Kelly (IRE) **Boretech Limited**
19 **BILLIE HALE (IRE)**, 6, b g Vinnie Roe (IRE)—Charnwood Song **Mr J. M. Glews**
20 **BIT OF A JIG (IRE)**, 6, ch g Alderbrook—Ardower (IRE) **Let's Live Racing**
21 **BLACKWATER KING (IRE)**, 5, b br g Beneficial—Accordian Lady (IRE) **Mr & Mrs Paul Rooney**
22 **BOUND FOR GLORY (IRE)**, 7, b g Witness Box (USA)—Musical View (IRE) **T Meehan & D J Burke**
23 **BOURNE**, 7, gr g Linamix (FR)—L'affaire Monique **Timeform Betfair Racing Club & M Taylor**
24 **BRADBURY (IRE)**, 5, ch g Redback—Simonaventura (IRE) **Mr D. Charlesworth**
25 **BRADY (IRE)**, 7, ch g Albano (IRE)—Quiet Sovereign **Luxham Racing**
26 **CALL BACK**, 5, b g Beat Hollow—Payphone **Mr D. Hanafin**
27 **CINDERS AND ASHES**, 6, b g Beat Hollow—Moon Search **Dermot Hanafin & Phil Cunningham**
28 **CLONDAW DRAFT (IRE)**, 5, b g Shantou (USA)—Glen Ten (IRE) **T. G. Leslie**
29 **CLONDAW KAEMPFER (IRE)**, 5, b g Oscar (IRE)—Gra-Bri (IRE) **T Leslie & D Gorton**
30 **CLOUD CREEPER (IRE)**, 6, b g Cloudings (IRE)—First of April (IRE) **Mick Fitzgerald Racing Club**
31 **CORRIN WOOD (IRE)**, 6, gr g Garuda (IRE)—Allstar Rose (IRE) **Mr D. Hanafin**
32 **COUNSEL (IRE)**, 4, b g Dansili—Kitty O'shea **T. G. Leslie**
33 **CRABBIE'S CLOUDY (IRE)**, 6, b g Cloudings (IRE)—Santavino (IRE) **Halewood International Ltd**
34 **DANNANCEYS HILL (IRE)**, 6, b g Revoque (IRE)—Some Orchestra (IRE) **T. G. Leslie**
35 **DARLINGTON COUNTY (IRE)**, 5, b g Oscar (IRE)—Laura's Native (IRE) **Brendan Richardson & Jon Glews**
36 **DEISE DYNAMO (IRE)**, 5, br g Zagreb (USA)—Magical Mist (IRE) **Mr D. Hanafin**
37 **DESERT CRY (IRE)**, 7, b br g Desert Prince (IRE)—Hataana (USA) **N.Y.P.D Racing**
38 **DIAMOND KING (IRE)**, 5, b g King's Theatre (IRE)—Georgia On My Mind (FR) **Mrs D. L. Whateley**
39 **DILIGENT**, 5, b m Generous (IRE)—Diletia **Chasing Gold Limited**
40 **DIOCLES (IRE)**, 7, b g Bob Back (USA)—Ardrina **L. G. M. Racing**
41 **DJ MILAN (IRE)**, 7, b g Milan—Cafe Matisse (IRE) **Boretech Limited**
42 **DOYLY CARTE**, 5, b m Doyen (IRE)—Generous Diana **Elite Racing Club**
43 **DREAM DESTINY**, 4, b f King's Theatre (IRE)—Queen's Banquet **T Meehan & D J Burke**
44 **DREAMS OF MILAN (IRE)**, 5, b g Milan—Joe's Dream Catch (IRE) **Axom XXXVII**
45 **DRILL SERGEANT**, 8, br g Rock of Gibraltar (IRE)—Dolydille (IRE) **T. G. Leslie**
46 **DUNGEEL (IRE)**, 7, b g Moscow Society (USA)—Mis Fortune (IRE) **Mr M. R. Kemp**
47 **DUNOWEN POINT (IRE)**, 7, b g Old Vic—Esbeggi **T. G. Leslie**
48 **EMRANI (USA)**, 6, b g Rahy (USA)—Ebaza (IRE) **T. G. Leslie**
49 **FABALU (IRE)**, 11, b g Oscar (IRE)—Lizes Birthday (IRE) **T. G. Leslie**
50 **FINLAY**, 10, gr g Parthian Springs—Grey Scally **D. Lockwood, P. Edwards, J. Koumas**
51 **FLICKA WILLIAMS (IRE)**, 6, b g Broadway Flyer (USA)—
　　　　　　　　　　　Millies Girl (IRE) **Twenty Four Seven Recruitment Services Ltd**
52 **FRECKLETON (IRE)**, 5, b g Milan—Chancy Lass (IRE) **David Barlow & John A Raybone**
53 **FRED WILLETTS (IRE)**, 5, b g Noverre (USA)—Intaglia (GER) **24 - 7 Recruitment/ Mr Allan Jones**
54 **GOODACRES GARDEN (IRE)**, 6, b g Oscar (IRE)—Living A Dream (IRE) **J Basquill, A Barr, M Basquill, G Wills**
55 **GRANDILOQUENT**, 4, b g Rail Link—High Praise (USA) **Mrs J. Bownes**
56 **GREAT BOSS (IRE)**, 7, b g Great Palm (USA)—Rezoned (IRE) **Mr J. M. Glews**
57 **GREENSALT (IRE)**, 5, b g Milan—Garden City (IRE) **T. J. Hemmings**
58 **GROUSE LODGE (IRE)**, 7, b g Well Chosen—Arctic Jane (IRE) **Mr F. McAleavy**
59 **GULF PUNCH (IRE)**, 8, b m Dubawi (IRE)—Fruit Punch (IRE) **Mr R. J. Gwynne**
60 **GULFPORT**, 4, b f Three Valleys (USA)—Biloxi **D. R. McCain**
61 **HALO MOON**, 5, br g Kayf Tara—Fragrant Rose **Mr P. A. Cafferty**
62 **HALOGEN**, 4, b g Halling (USA)—Trompette (USA) **Elite Racing Club**
63 **HELLORBOSTON (IRE)**, 5, b g Court Cave (IRE)—Helorhiwater (IRE) **Thomson & Fyffe Racing**
64 **HIE MOSSY (IRE)**, 6, ch g Moscow Society (USA)—Sarah's Smile **D. McCain Jnr**
65 **HOLLOW TREE**, 5, b g Beat Hollow—Hesperia **Brannon Dick Holden**
66 **HOWABOUTNEVER (IRE)**, 5, b g Shantou (USA)—Sarah's Cottage (IRE) **Brannon, Dick, Hernon & Holden**

MR DONALD MCCAIN - Continued

67 HOWABOUTNOW (IRE), 6, ch g Shantou (USA)—Sarah's Cottage (IRE) **Brannon, Dick, Hernon & Holden**
68 HURRABORU (IRE), 6, b g Brian Boru—Fastlass **Deva Racing Brian Boru Partnership**
69 IFYOUSAYSO (IRE), 6, ch g Definite Article—Rosato (IRE) **The Joaly Partnership**
70 ILE DE RE (FR), 7, gr g Linamix (FR)—Ile Mamou (IRE) **Mr D. Mead**
71 INDEPUB, 4, b g Indesatchel (IRE)—Champenoise **D. W. Barker**
72 INDIAN CASTLE (IRE), 5, b g Dr Massini (IRE)—Indian Legend (IRE) **Askew Dick Hernon Reynard**
73 IT'S OSCAR (IRE), 6, b g Oscar (IRE)—Lady Bramble (IRE) **Leach, Viney & Wilson**
74 JACKSON CAGE (IRE), 8, b g Oscar (IRE)—Phenics Allstar (IRE) **Penketh & Sankey Jech Racing Club**
75 JE T'AIME (IRE), 4, b f Heron Island (IRE)—J'y Reste (FR) **Mr K. Cotter**
76 JUMBO SUPREME (IRE), 7, gr g Portrait Gallery (IRE)—Supreme Caution (IRE) **Lucky Bin Racing**
77 KEENELAND (IRE), 6, b g Westerner—Delphinium (IRE) **Mr & Mrs Paul Rooney**
78 KIE (IRE), 5, b g Old Vic—Asura (GER) **A. Stennett**
79 KING'S GRACE, 7, b g King's Theatre (IRE)—Beauchamp Grace **T. G. Leslie**
80 KINGS BANDIT (IRE), 5, b g King's Theatre (IRE)—Gentle Lady (IRE) **Mrs D. L. Whateley**
81 KOUP DE KANON (FR), 7, b g Robin des Pres (FR)—
    Coup de Sabre (FR) **Timeform Betfair Racing Club & M Taylor**
82 KRUZHLININ (GER), 6, ch g Sholokhov (USA)—Karuma (GER) **Mr & Mrs Paul Rooney**
83 LEXI'S BOY (IRE), 5, gr g Verglas—Jazan (IRE) **T. G. Leslie**
84 LIFE AND SOUL (IRE), 6, b g Azamour (IRE)—Way For Life (GER) **M. J. Taylor**
85 LIVELY BARON (IRE), 8, b g Presenting—Greavesfind **T. J. Hemmings**
86 LORD NAVITS (IRE), 5, b g Golan (IRE)—Nanavits (IRE) **Jobarry Partnership**
87 MARL THE SNARL (IRE), 4, b f Definite Article—Calendula **Twenty Four Seven Recruitment Services Ltd**
88 MASTER RED (IRE), 4, b g Red Clubs (IRE)—Glory Days (IRE) **Mr P. A. Rooney**
89   4, B g Scorpion (IRE)—Melodic Tune (IRE) **Mr T. Perkins**
90 MOSCOW PRESENTS (IRE), 5, b g Presenting—Moscow Madame (IRE) **Boretech & Tony Sadler**
91 MOUNT HOPE (IRE), 6, ch g Albano (IRE)—Quiet Sovereign **Roger O'Byrne**
92 MR HOPEFUL (IRE), 4, b g Helissio (FR)—Lisadian Lady (IRE) **Essential Racing 2**
93 MR PEPPERPOT, 4, b g Sir Harry Lewis (USA)—Parslin **The Trevor-McDonald Partnership**
94   5, B g Darsi (FR)—Mrs McClintock (IRE) **Twenty Four Seven Recruitment Services Ltd**
95   4, B g Fair Mix (IRE)—Mrs Moneypenny **Deva Racing Fair Mix Partnership**
96 MULLIGAN'S MAN (IRE), 6, b g Morozov (USA)—Rashmulligan (IRE) **Crowe Partnership 1**
97 MY FLORA, 9, b m Afflora (IRE)—Bishop's Folly **Mr W D Edwards & Mr J Whitfield**
98 NEFYN BAY, 4, b g Overbury (IRE)—So Cloudy **Tim & Miranda Johnson**
99 NODFORM RICHARD, 7, b g Groom Dancer (USA)—Shayzara (IRE) **D. M. Gorton**
100 NOTIMETOWASTE (IRE), 6, b m Revoque (IRE)—Supreme Blend (IRE) **Boretech & Tony Sadler**
101 NOWURHURLIN (IRE), 6, b g Saddlers' Hall (IRE)—Pint Taken (IRE) **The Ground Hurlers**
102 OFALLTHESTARS (IRE), 6, b g Oscar (IRE)—Just Stars (IRE) **Mr M. R. Kemp**
103 ORLITTLEBYLITTLE, 7, b g Bollin Eric—Davana Blue (IRE) **Deva Racing Bollin Eric Partnership**
104 OSCATARA (IRE), 6, b br g Oscar (IRE)—Nethertara **T. G. Leslie**
105 OUR MICK, 7, gr g Karinga Bay—Dawn's Della **K. Benson & Mrs E. Benson**
106 OVERAFRICA (IRE), 7, b g Overbury (IRE)—Siberiansdaughter (IRE) **T. J. Hemmings**
107 OVERTURN (IRE), 9, b g Barathea (IRE)—Kristal Bridge **T. G. Leslie**
108 PEDDLERS CROSS (IRE), 8, b g Oscar (IRE)—Patscilla **T. G. Leslie**
109 PLAN AGAIN (IRE), 6, b g Gamut (IRE)—Niamh's Leader (IRE) **Mr P. A. Rooney**
110 POLARBROOK (IRE), 6, br g Alderbrook—Frozen Cello (IRE) **Lucky Bin Racing**
111 PRETTYASAPICTURE, 4, b f King's Theatre (IRE)—Fortune's Girl **Goldford Stud & R Haggas**
112 RADIO NOWHERE (IRE), 5, b g Beneficial—Creidim (IRE) **Mr J. M. Glews**
113 RAILWAY DILLON (IRE), 8, b g Witness Box (USA)—Laura's Native (IRE) **T W Johnson & G Maxwell**
114 RAIN MAC, 5, b h Beat Hollow—Quenched **Mr A. G. Bloom**
115 REAL MILAN (IRE), 8, b g Milan—The Real Athlete (IRE) **Mrs D. L. Whateley**
116 RECORD BREAKER (IRE), 6, b g In The Wings—Overruled (IRE) **The Generals Men Racing Club 1**
117 RED MERLIN (IRE), 8, ch g Soviet Star (USA)—
    Truly Bewitched (USA) **Timeform Betfair Racing Club & M Taylor**
118 RED ROCCO (IRE), 6, ch g Croco Rouge (IRE)—Youbetido (IRE) **Glen's Fools 2**
119 RIFLE SHOT (IRE), 6, b br g Indian River (FR)—Ravaleen (IRE) **K. S. Pratt, J. P. F. Dixon, A. Mallen**
120 RIGHT TO RULE (IRE), 4, b g Rock of Gibraltar (IRE)—Epistoliere (IRE) **Mr F. McAleavy**
121 RUBRICS (IRE), 4, gr g High Chaparral (IRE)—Inner Strength (FR) **Mr D. Mead**
122 SAGA DE TERCEY (FR), 8, b g Sagacity (FR)—Fanciulla Del West (USA) **Mr P. Holden**
123 SALTO CHISCO (IRE), 5, b g Presenting—Dato Fairy (IRE) **Mrs D. L. Whateley**
124 SEALOUS SCOUT (IRE), 5, b g Old Vic—Hirayna **T. G. Leslie**
125 SEPARATE SHADOWS (FR), 5, ch g Bernebeau (FR)—Chagrin d'amour (IRE) **Mr H. Q. Spooner**
126 SHANTOU TIGER (IRE), 4, b g Shantou (USA)—Opus One **Deva Racing Shantou Partnership**
127 SHE RANKS ME (IRE), 6, gr m Golan (IRE)—Rosealainn (IRE) **Roger O'Byrne**
128 SHORT TAKES (USA), 5, ch g Lemon Drop Kid (USA)—Gabriellina Giof **Mr T. P. McMahon & Mr D. McMahon**
129 SILVER GYPSY (IRE), 8, b m Luso—Your Life **Mrs T. D. Yeomans**

MR DONALD MCCAIN - Continued

130 SMADYNIUM (FR), 5, gr g Smadoun (FR)—Sea Music (FR) **The Vacuum Pouch Company Limited**
131 SMART ACT (IRE), 7, b g Oscar (IRE)—La Luna (IRE) **T. J. Hemmings**
132 SON OF FLICKA, 9, b g Groom Dancer (USA)—Calendula **Twenty Four Seven Recruitment Services Ltd**
133 SPITFIRE ACE (IRE), 5, b g Zagreb (USA)—Coolafancy (IRE) **D & G Mercer 1**
134 STAR IN FLIGHT, 6, b g Mtoto—Star Entry **Lucky Bin Racing**
135 STORMIN EXIT (IRE), 10, b g Exit To Nowhere (USA)—Stormin Norma (IRE) **Fyffees & Robinson**
136 STORMING GALE (IRE), 7, b g Revoque (IRE)—Dikler Gale (IRE) **T. G. Leslie**
137 SUD PACIFIQUE (IRE), 5, b g Montjeu (IRE)—Anestasia (IRE) **Mr A. G. Bloom**
138 SUPER DUTY (IRE), 7, b g Shantou (USA)—Sarah's Cottage (IRE) **Brannon, Dick, Hernon & Holden**
139 SUPREME ASSET (IRE), 5, b g Beneficial—Hollygrove Supreme (IRE) **Lucky Bin Racing**
140 SWATOW TYPHOON (IRE), 6, b g Shantou (USA)—Oscar Leader (IRE) **Mr G. Fitzpatrick**
141 SWIFT ARROW (IRE), 7, b g Overbury (IRE)—Clover Run (IRE) **Mrs A. E. Strang Steel**
142 SWITCHED OFF, 8, b g Catcher In The Rye (IRE)—Button Hole Flower (IRE) **Mr P Nicholls & Mr D Mead**
143 SYDNEY PAGET (IRE), 6, b g Flemensfirth (USA)—Shuil Aoibhinn (IRE) **Roger O'Byrne**
144 TARA ROYAL, 8, b g Kayf Tara—Poussetiere Deux (FR) **T. G. Leslie**
145 TARLAN (IRE), 7, b g Milan—Nethertara **T. G. Leslie**
146 THE BELLS O PEOVER, 5, b g Selkirk (USA)—Bay Tree (IRE) **D & G Mercer**
147 THE FLYING COLUMN (IRE), 7, b g Dr Massini (IRE)—Annie Cares (IRE) **Brannon, Dick, Hernon & Holden**
148 THE WEATHERMAN (IRE), 6, b g Definite Article—Stateable Case (IRE) **Clwydian Connections**
149 THIMAAR (USA), 5, b br g Dynaformer (USA)—Jinaan (USA) **Jon Glews, 24-7, D Lockwood, Fred Lockwood**
150 THUNDERCRACK (IRE), 8, b g Oscar (IRE)—Champagne Warrior (IRE) **Mrs A. D. Bassington**
151 TICK TOCKER (IRE), 5, b g Beat Hollow—Cortona (IRE) **T. G. Leslie**
152 TONVADOSA, 5, b m Flemensfirth (USA)—Sleepless Eye **T Meehan & D J Burke**
153 TORNADO BOB (IRE), 8, b br g Bob Back (USA)—Double Glazed (IRE) **Mrs D. L. Whateley**
154 TREND IS MY FRIEND (USA), 4, b br g Lemon Drop Kid (USA)—Silva (FR) **T Leslie & D Gorton**
155 UBALTIQUE (FR), 5, b g Balko (FR)—Ode Antique (FR) **T. G. Leslie**
156 UNDERWRITTEN, 4, b g Authorized (IRE)—Grain of Gold **Mr M. W. Sanders**
157 UNKNOWN REBEL (IRE), 5, b g Night Shift (USA)—Crystalline Stream (FR) **D. Reilly & Mrs C. Reilly**
158 UP AND GO (FR), 5, ch g Martaline—Santoria (FR) **T. G. Leslie**
159 VALLEYOFMILAN (IRE), 6, b g Milan—Ikdam Valley (IRE) **Tim & Miranda Johnson**
160 VELOCE (IRE), 5, b g Hurricane Run (IRE)—Kiftsgate Rose (FR) **Axom XL**
161 VERDASCO (FR), 4, b g Sassanian (USA)—Babolna (FR) **Deva Racing Festival Partnership**
162 VINSTAR (FR), 4, b g Charming Groom (FR)—Kali Star (FR) **T. G. Leslie**
163 WEIRD AL (IRE), 10, b g Accordion—Bucks Gift (IRE) **Brannon Dick Holden**
164 WELSH BARD (IRE), 4, ch g Dylan Thomas (IRE)—Delphinium (IRE) **George Tobitt & Richard Gurney**
165 WHISKEY CHASER (IRE), 5, br g Flemensfirth (USA)—
Cregane Lass (IRE) **Deva Racing Flemensfirth Partnership**
166 WITNESS IN COURT (IRE), 6, b g Witness Box (USA)—Inter Alia (IRE) **T. G. Leslie**
167 WOODPOLE ACADEMY (IRE), 6, b g Beneficial—Midday Caller (IRE) **Boretech Limited**
168 WYMOTT (IRE), 9, b g Witness Box (USA)—Tanya Thyne (IRE) **T. J. Hemmings**

Other Owners: Mr B. A. Adams, S. Andrew, Mr N. P. Armstrong, Axom Ltd, M. Ball, Mr D. Barlow, K. Benson, Mrs E. Benson, Boretech, Mr Andrew Brown, D. J. Burke, Mr Mick Burrowes, Mr N. Caddy, Mr M. J. Campbell, Mr A. P. Coyne, Mr K. Coyne, P. M. Cunningham, Mr A. D. Dick, Mr Jonathan Dixon, Mr D. Downie, W. D. Edwards, Mr J. C. Evans, M. D. Foster, Mrs J. Foster, L. R. Frampton, Mr J. Fyffe, Mr S. Fyffe, Mr J. Fyffe Snr, Mr Jon Glews, Mr D. Gorton, Mr R. Griffiths, R. Gurney, Mr T. M. Hailstone, Mr Dermot Hanafin, Mr Tony Hill, Mr Philip Holden, Mr J. R. Holmes, Mr T. Johnson, Mrs M. Johnson, Mr S. A. Kaznowski, Mr P. J. Leach, Mr T. G. Leslie, Mr B. Madden, A. Mallen, Mrs J. Massey, C. D. Massey, Mr G. Maxwell, Mr I. McAleavy, Mr R. J. McAlpine, Mrs B. McCain, Mr D. McCain Jnr, Mr D. Mead, Mr T. F. Meagher, Mr M. G. Meagher, Mr A. E. Meehan, Mr D. C. Mercer, G. Mercer, Mr D. Moyes, Mr K. A. J. Mulville, Mr P. R. Nicholls, Miss M. Noden, Mr D. R. Passant, Mr Ray Pattison, Mr J. E. Potter, Mrs J. E. Potter, Mrs K. S. Pratt, Mr J. A. Raybone, D. P. Reilly, Mrs C. J. Reilly, Mr B. J. Richardson, Mr B. Robbins, Mr W. Robinson, Mrs C. Rooney, Mr P. A. Rooney, Mr P. Ryan, Mr A. Sadler, Mrs Angela Sommerville, Mrs A. J. Sproson, Mr P. Sproson, Mr Matthew Taylor, Timeform Betfair Racing Club Ltd, C. J. Tipton, G. E. Tobitt, Mr K. Viney, Mr E. C. Watson, Mr N. Watt, Miss H. L. Webster, Mr Andy White, Mr E. J. Whitfield, Mr H. Williams, Mr S. Wilson, Mr G. W. Worsley.

Assistant Trainers: Darren O'Dwyer, Mrs B. McCain

Jockey (NH): Jason Maguire, John Kington, Adrian Lane. **Conditional:** Callum Whillans, Henry Brooke, Paul O'Brien. **Amateur:** Mr N. Slatter.

420 MR TIM MCCARTHY, Godstone
Postal: **Nags Hall Farm, Oxted Road, Godstone, Surrey, RH9 8DB**
Contacts: **PHONE (01883) 740379 FAX (01883) 740381 MOBILE (07887) 763062**

1 **CAVALRY GUARD (USA)**, 9, ch g Officer (USA)—Leeward City (USA) **Surrey Racing Club**
2 **GHOST TRAIN (IRE)**, 4, b g Holy Roman Emperor (IRE)—Adrastea (IRE) **T. D. McCarthy**
3 **JIMMY RYAN (IRE)**, 12, b g Orpen (USA)—Kaysama (FR) **Mrs C. V. McCarthy**
4 **MA FILLE SAUVAGE**, 5, ch m Loup Sauvage (USA)—Ma Barnicle (IRE) **Mrs C. V. McCarthy**
5 **UNDERSTORY (USA)**, 6, b g Forestry (USA)—Sha Tha (USA) **The Bordeaux Fine Wines Racing Club**
6 **VINCES**, 9, gr g Lomitas—Vadinaxa (FR)
7 **ZIEFHD**, 4, b f Haafhd—Zietory **Living Sports**

Other Owners: Mr J. A. Collins, Mr K. J. P. Gundlach, Mr N. P. Horsfall, S. J. Piper.

Assistant Trainer: Mrs C.V. McCarthy

421 MISS DANIELLE MCCORMICK, Westhead
Postal: **Brookfields, Charity Lane, Westhead, Ormskirk, Lancashire, L40 6LG**
Contacts: **PHONE (01695) 579334 MOBILE (07590) 513752**
E-MAIL danielle-mccormick@hotmail.co.uk

1 **BALLINARGH GIRL (IRE)**, 5, b m Footstepsinthesand—Rack And Ruin (IRE) **M. R. Johnson & J. Kenny**
2 **JACKS LAST HOPE**, 4, b g King's Theatre (IRE)—Ninna Nanna (FR) **Mr J. Kenny**
3 **JAQUES VERT (FR)**, 7, ch g Dr Fong (USA)—Sayuri (USA) **Mr M. R. Johnson & Mr A. Draper**
4 **JAY KAY**, 4, b g Librettist (USA)—Turn Back **Mr J. Kenny**
5 **LORD WESTHEAD (IRE)**, 4, b g Bach (IRE)—Dawning Day (IRE) **M. R. Johnson**
6 **MIND SHOWER (IRE)**, 7, b g Bach (IRE)—Knockacool Breeze **M. R. Johnson & J. Kenny**
7 **SPLENDID SENORITA (IRE)**, 6, b m Helissio (FR)—Friendly Craic (IRE) **M. R. Johnson**

THREE-YEAR-OLDS
8 **AMELIA JAY**, b f Avonbridge—Rainbow Spectrum (FR) **M. R. Johnson**
9 **MILLIE N AIRE**, b f Multiplex—Hillside Girl (IRE) **M. R. Johnson**

Other Owners: Mr Alan Draper, Mr M. R. Johnson, Mr John Kenny.

Amateur: Miss A. McCormick.

422 MR PHIL MCENTEE, Newmarket
Postal: **Racefield Stables, Carriageway, Hamilton Road, Newmarket, Suffolk, CB8 7JQ**
Contacts: **PHONE (01638) 662092 FAX (01638) 662092 MOBILE (07802) 663256**

1 **ACTIVATE**, 6, b g Motivator—Princess Manila (CAN) **Mr S. Jakes**
2 **BACK FOR TEA (IRE)**, 5, b g Redback—Jasmine Pearl (IRE) **Mr R. Favarulo**
3 **BEACH CANDY (IRE)**, 4, ch f Footstepsinthesand—Endure (IRE) **Mr S. Jakes**
4 **BIRD DOG**, 7, ch g Compton Place—Form At Last **S. P. Shore**
5 **BONBON BONNIE**, 5, b m Storming Home—Form At Last **S. P. Shore**
6 **DARSAN (IRE)**, 5, ch m Iffraaj—Coolrain Lady (IRE) **Eventmaker Racehorses**
7 **DESERT RED (IRE)**, 4, b f Green Desert (USA)—Penicuik (USA) **Mrs R. L. McEntee**
8 **ISHIAMIRACLE**, 4, ch f Ishiguru (USA)—Sukuma (IRE) **Mr S. Jakes**
9 **JONNIE SKULL (IRE)**, 7, b g Pyrus (USA)—Sovereign Touch (IRE) **Eventmaker Racehorses**
10 **PUTIN (IRE)**, 5, b g Fasliyev (USA)—Consignia (IRE) **Mr S. Jakes**
11 **SILK SKY**, 7, ch m Shahrastani (USA)—Insulate **Mr S. J. March**
12 **SUMMER SUN**, 4, b f Oratorio (IRE)—Woodland Glade **Mr S. Jakes**
13 **SWISS CROSS**, 6, b g Cape Cross (IRE)—Swiss Lake (USA) **Mr S. Jakes**

THREE-YEAR-OLDS
14 **DIVINE ANGEL (IRE)**, gr f Dark Angel (IRE)—Downland (USA) **Mr S. Jakes**

Other Owners: Mr M. A. Humphris, T. D. Johnson.

Jockey (NH): Jimmy McCarthy.

423 MR MURTY MCGRATH, Maidstone
Postal: **Spicketts House, Kiln Barn Road, East Malling, Kent, ME19 6BG**
Contacts: **PHONE (01732) 840173 FAX (01732) 873774 MOBILE (07818) 098073**
E-MAIL mjmcgrath@hotmail.com

1 **AMERICAN BLING (USA)**, 4, b g Johannesburg (USA)—American Jewel (USA) **Gallagher Equine Ltd**
2 **FINLODEX**, 6, ch g Pastoral Pursuits—Ela Aphrodite **Mr R. P. Gallagher**
3 **REZWAAN**, 6, b g Alhaarth (IRE)—Nasij (USA) **Gallagher Equine Ltd**

THREE-YEAR-OLDS
4 **CULTURE TRIP**, b g Royal Applause—Spanish Springs (IRE) **Gallagher Equine Ltd**
5 **GREAT CRESTED (IRE)**, br gr c Clodovil (IRE)—Roskeen (IRE) **Gallagher Equine Ltd**

Assistant Trainer: Heidi Harris (07795) 178178

Jockey (flat): Shane Kelly. **Jockey (NH):** Timmy Murphy.

424 MRS JEAN MCGREGOR, Milnathort
Postal: **Matale, Tillyrie, Milnathort, Kinross, KY13 0RW**
Contacts: **PHONE (01577) 862519 MOBILE (07764) 464299**
E-MAIL purebred68@hotmail.co.uk

1 **ASKALOTT (IRE)**, 8, b g Ashkalani (IRE)—Alottalady (IRE) **Miss A. L. McGregor**
2 4, B g Desideratum—Blue Morning
3 **CIGALAS**, 8, ch g Selkirk (USA)—Langoustine (AUS) **Tillyrie Racing Club**
4 **JACKOFHEARTS**, 5, b g Beat Hollow—Boutique **Mr S. Taylor**
5 5, B g Rambling Bear—Lingham Bridesmaid **Mrs D. Thomson**
6 **NELSON DU RONCERAY (FR)**, 12, b g Lute Antique (FR)—Trieste (FR) **Miss A. L. McGregor**
7 **SNOOZE N YOU LOSE**, 8, b g Helissio (FR)—Utmost (IRE) **The Good To Soft Firm**
8 **THEHOODLUM**, 6, b g Fraam—Trilby **Tillyrie Racing Club**
9 **WATERSKI**, 12, b g Petoski—Celtic Waters **Miss A. L. McGregor**

TWO-YEAR-OLDS
10 Gr c 13/4 Paris House—Gemini Lady (Emperor Fountain)

Other Owners: Mr. S. Burnett, Mrs Jean McGregor, Mr. G. Newstead, Mr. M. O'Conner, Mrs Dorothy Thomson, Mr. John Thomson.

Jockey (flat): Andrew Mullen. **Jockey (NH):** Adrian Lane. **Amateur:** Miss A.L. McGregor.

425 MR IAN MCINNES, Catwick
Postal: **Ivy House, Main Street, Catwick, Beverley, North Humberside, HU17 5PJ**
Contacts: **HOME/FAX (01964) 542115 FAX (01964) 542115 MOBILE (07720) 451233**

1 **BLUE CHARM**, 9, b g Averti (IRE)—Exotic Forest **J. Morris**
2 **BONNIE PRINCE BLUE**, 10, ch g Tipsy Creek (USA)—Heart So Blue **Mr M. Hardcastle**
3 **BYTON**, 4, b f Byron—Arculinge **S. P. Hudson**
4 **DREAM WALKER (FR)**, 4, gr g Gold Away (IRE)—Minnie's Mystery (FR) **Mr K. Brown**
5 **INGLEBY STAR (IRE)**, 8, b g Fath (USA)—Rosy Scintilla (IRE) **S. P. Hackney**
6 **KEY GOLD**, 4, b f Cape Cross (IRE)—Key Academy **T. Elsey**
7 **MAJOR MUSCARI (IRE)**, 5, ch g Exceed And Excel (AUS)—Muscari **J. Morris**
8 **MORAL ISSUE**, 5, b g Ishiguru (USA)—Morale **B. Valentine**
9 **NORTHERN BOLT**, 8, b g Cadeaux Genereux—Shafir (IRE) **Mr K. Brown**
10 **ONEOFAPEAR (IRE)**, 7, b g Pyrus (USA)—Whitegate Way **Mr B. W. Gibson**
11 **PERFECT BLOSSOM**, 6, b m One Cool Cat (USA)—Perfect Peach **Mrs A. Morris**
12 **POWERFUL PIERRE**, 6, ch g Compton Place—Alzianah **T. Elsey**
13 **ROCKGOAT (IRE)**, 4, b g Rock of Gibraltar (IRE)—Queveda (IRE) **B. Kirby**
14 **STRIKER TORRES (IRE)**, 7, ch g Danehill Dancer (IRE)—Silver Skates (IRE) **B. Kirby**

THREE-YEAR-OLDS
15 **BALTIC ROSE (IRE)**, b f Baltic King—Rosy Scintilla (IRE) **Mr K. Brown**
16 B br g Chineur (FR)—Desert Design **Mr K. Brown**
17 **GRAND JIPECK (IRE)**, b g Soviet Star (USA)—Inourthoughts (IRE) **Mrs I. Woolfitt**

MR IAN MCINNES - Continued

18 **MISSIE SNAFFLES**, b f Compton Place—Mrs Snaffles (IRE) **B. Valentine**
19 **NOBLE MAXIMUS**, b c Oratorio (IRE)—Perfect Peach **Mrs A. Morris**
20 **SPITHEAD**, b g Tiger Hill (IRE)—Cyclone Connie **B. Valentine**
21 **TOP NOTCH TONTO (IRE)**, ch g Thousand Words—Elite Hope (USA) **Mr K. Brown**
22 **WITCH WAY WENT**, b f Royal Applause—Celestial Princess **Mr K. Brown**

TWO-YEAR-OLDS

23 B f 31/3 Haatef (USA)—Fee Faw Fum (IRE) (Great Commotion (USA)) (3333) **Mr K. Brown**
24 B f 27/4 Captain Gerrard (IRE)—Hillside Heather (IRE) (Tagula (IRE)) (761) **Mr K. Brown**
25 B f 9/4 Sakhee's Secret—Julia Domna (Dominion) (1904) **Mr K. Brown**
26 B f 26/4 Byron—Local Fancy (Bahamian Bounty) (4000) **Mr K. Brown**

Assistant Trainer: Mr Ian McInnes (Senior)

MS KAREN MCLINTOCK, Newcastle Upon Tyne
Postal: **The Byerley Stud, Ingoe, Newcastle-Upon-Tyne, NE20 0SZ**
Contacts: **PHONE (01661) 886356 FAX (01661) 886356 MOBILE (07966) 776710**
E-MAIL karen.mclintock@equiname.co.uk WEBSITE www.karenmclintock.co.uk

1 **ANOTHER BYGONES (IRE)**, 4, b g High-Rise (IRE)—Little Chartridge **Mr A. C. Lamont**
2 **BRIDLINGTONBYGONES (IRE)**, 8, br g Bob's Return (IRE)—Slaney Athlete (IRE) **Mr A. C. Lamont**
3 **CADDELLS ROW**, 5, b g Lahib (USA)—Tartan Belle **Mr A. C. Lamont**
4 **DUKEOFCHESTERWOOD**, 11, ch g Missed Flight—Gale Storm **Mrs C. J. Todd**
5 **FUNCTION TIMES**, 6, ch m Central Park (IRE)—Function Dreamer **Mrs Alurie O'Sullivan**
6 **GOLDEN VIEW (IRE)**, 8, b g Goldmark (USA)—In Grace's View (IRE) **Mr J. Callow**
7 **GURKHA BRAVE (IRE)**, 5, b g Old Vic—Honeyed (IRE) **Mr A. C. Lamont**
8 **LUCKY BYGONES**, 6, b m Lucky Owners (NZ)—Particular Friend **Mr A. C. Lamont**
9 **MADAME BLAVATSKY (FR)**, 5, gr m Super Celebre (FR)—Lovarisk (FR) **Ms D. Young**
10 **MASON DAVID BROWN (IRE)**, 6, b g Luso—Hindi (FR) **Mr A. C. Lamont**
11 **MASON HINDMARSH**, 6, ch g Dr Fong (USA)—Sierra Virgen (USA) **B. Chicken**
12 **NODFORMS VIOLET (IRE)**, 9, ch g Rashar (USA)—Whose Yer Wan (IRE) **Mr A. C. Lamont**
13 **NORTHERN EXECUTIVE (IRE)**, 5, b g Milan—Letterwoman (IRE) **Mr C. A. Kerr**
14 **OMANI REBEL**, 5, b g Runyon—Forgotten Flowers (IRE) **Mr A. C. Lamont**
15 **ULTIEP (FR)**, 5, gr g Ragmar (FR)—Naltiepy (FR) **Mr A. C. Lamont**

Other Owners: Equiname Ltd.

Assistant Trainer: Donald Eddy

MR ED MCMAHON, Lichfield
Postal: **Horsley Brook Farm, Tamworth Road, Lichfield, Staffordshire, WS14 9PT**
Contacts: **PHONE (01543) 481224 FAX (01543) 651100 MOBILE (07787) 951630**
E-MAIL comeracing@horsleybrook.fsnet.co.uk WEBSITE www.edmcmahonracing.co.uk

1 **ANGELITO**, 4, ch g Primo Valentino (IRE)—Supreme Angel **Least Moved Partners**
2 **ARTISTIC JEWEL (IRE)**, 4, ch f Excellent Art—Danish Gem **R. L. Bedding**
3 **EASY OVER (IRE)**, 5, ch g Dr Fong (USA)—Desert Alchemy (IRE) **D. J. Allen. S. E. Allen/ G. A. Weetman**
4 **NOBLE STORM (USA)**, 7, b h Yankee Gentleman (USA)—Changed Tune (USA) **R. L. Bedding**
5 **OCEANA DREAMER (IRE)**, 4, b g Oasis Dream—Arbella **The C H F Partnership**
6 **PASSIONADA**, 4, b br f Avonbridge—Lark In The Park (IRE) **Mia Racing**
7 **RACY**, 6, b g Medicean—Soar **The C H F Partnership**
8 **RADIO GAGA**, 4, b f Multiplex—Gagajulu **Lease Terminated**
9 **TARTIFLETTE**, 4, b f Dr Fong (USA)—Bright Moll **A. R. F. Buxton**

THREE-YEAR-OLDS

10 **ARLECCHINO (IRE)**, b c Hernando (FR)—Trullitti (IRE) **The LAM Partnership**
11 **AVEC SOLEIL**, gr g With Approval (CAN)—Rosy Sunset (IRE) **Major W. R. Paton-Smith**
12 **COLOUR MY WORLD**, gr c With Approval (CAN)—Nadeszhda **Mr P. A. Wilkins**
13 **DUSTY STORM (IRE)**, ch f Kyllachy—Halliwell House **R. L. Bedding**
14 **EMJAYEM**, ch g Needwood Blade—Distant Stars (IRE) **Mrs J. McMahon**
15 Ch f Three Valleys (USA)—Fireburst **B. N. Toye**
16 **FLIRTINASKIRT**, b f Avonbridge—Talampaya (USA) **Mr P. A. Wilkins**

MR ED MCMAHON - Continued

17 **MISS METICULOUS**, ch f Bahamian Bounty—Umniya (IRE) **The LAM Partnership**
18 **PUCKER UP**, b f Royal Applause—Smooch **J. C. Fretwell**
19 Ch g Byron—Rosapenna (IRE) **J. C. Sillett**
20 **SAKHEE'S ROSE**, b f Sakhee's Secret—Isobel Rose (IRE) **Mr J. R. Dwyer**
21 **SECRET LOOK**, ch g Sakhee's Secret—Look Here's Carol (IRE) **S. L. Edwards**
22 **SECRETINTHEPARK**, ch c Sakhee's Secret—Lark In The Park (IRE) **Mia Racing**
23 **SILKEN BEAUTY**, b f Piccolo—Silken Dalliance **The C H F Partnership**
24 **WINNING EXPRESS (IRE)**, gr f Camacho—Lady Fabiola (IRE) **Milton Express Limited**

TWO-YEAR-OLDS

25 B c 3/3 Compton Place—Athboy Nights (IRE) (Night Shift (USA)) (11428)
26 **EXPRESS HIMSELF (IRE)**, b c 20/4 Dylan Thomas (IRE)—
Lightwood Lady (IRE) (Anabaa (USA)) (28000) **Milton Express Limited**
27 B f 13/1 Dark Angel (IRE)—First Lady (IRE) (Indian Ridge) (12380)
28 **INCITING INCIDENT (IRE)**, b c 20/4 Camacho—Halliwell House (Selkirk (USA)) (13333) **The W.H.O. Society**
29 **KOPKAP**, ch c 21/3 Captain Gerrard (IRE)—Sharoura (Inchinor) (3809)
30 Ch c 1/4 Kyllachy—Look Here's Carol (IRE) (Safawan) **S. L. Edwards**
31 Gr c 2/2 Alhaarth (IRE)—Look Here's Dee (Dansili) **S. L. Edwards**
32 B c 28/4 Nayef (USA)—Magic Tree (UAE) (Timber Country (USA)) (32000) **The LAM Partnership**
33 B c 27/2 Excellent Art—Miss Informed (IRE) (Danehill (USA)) (30476)
34 B c 25/2 Multiplex—Oceana Blue (Reel Buddy (USA)) (2095) **The C H F Partnership**
35 **RENAISSANCE RIO (IRE)**, b f 21/3 Captain Rio—Danish Gem (Danehill (USA))
36 B c 6/4 Jeremy (USA)—River Abouali (Bluebird (USA)) (37142)
37 Ch c 6/3 Firebreak—Silken Dalliance (Rambo Dancer (CAN)) (5714) **The C H F Partnership**
38 B c 23/4 Avonbridge—Succumb (Pursuit of Love) (17142)
39 Ch c 22/3 Compton Place—Tinnarinka (Observatory) (40000)
40 **WHERE THE BOYS ARE (IRE)**, b f 29/3 Dylan Thomas (IRE)—
Promise of Love (Royal Applause) (12380) **Mr P. A. Wilkins**
41 Br c 16/2 Duke of Marmalade (IRE)—Winged Harriet (IRE) (Hawk Wing (USA)) (30000) **E. S. A. McMahon**

Other Owners: D. J. Allen, Mrs S. E. Allen, L. F. Chamberlain, K. H. Fischer, C. H. Fischer, Dr M. F. Ford, Ms L. M. Mulcahy, F. G. Poingdestre, Mr D. Thomas, M. A. Tickle, A. Tickle, Mrs I. M. Tickle, Mrs G. A. Weetman.

Assistant Trainer: Bryan Arthur McMahon

---

428 **MR GRAEME McPHERSON, Stow-On-The-Wold**
Postal: **Martins Hill, Bledington Road, Stow-on-the-Wold, Gloucestershire, GL54 1JH**
Contacts: **PHONE** (01451) 830769 **MOBILE** (07815) 887360
WEBSITE www.mcphersonracing.co.uk

1 4, B f Kayf Tara—Alina Rheinberg (GER) **Mr M. Paul**
2 **ARTIC NIGHT (FR)**, 7, gr g Take Risks (FR)—Just Win (FR) **Mr P. A. Randall**
3 **BAKARI**, 5, bl g Trade Fair—Wathbat Mtoto **Cheltenham & Three Counties Race Club**
4 **BOBBIE MAGERN**, 8, b g Alderbrook—Outfield **Exors of the Late Mr R. Nicholls**
5 **CANADIAN DREAMER (IRE)**, 6, b g Westerner—Ride The Tide (IRE)
6 **CLAN GATHERING**, 5, b g Diktat—Perfect Dream **Mr J. M. Snellings**
7 **CLEEVE HILL LAD**, 5, b g Overbury (IRE)—Lady Prunella (IRE) **The High Roost Partnership**
8 **DANCING EMILY (IRE)**, 7, ch m Anshan—Goodthyne Lady (IRE) **Mr S. H. Spence**
9 **DO BE DASHING**, 5, b m Doyen (IRE)—Be Brave (FR) **Mr J. Fildes**
10 **EARTH PLANET (IRE)**, 11, b g Kayf Tara—Arctic Rose (IRE) **Mr P. A. Randall**
11 **GETTING READY (IRE)**, 6, b g Westerner—Last Campaign (IRE) **The I.O.U. Partnership**
12 **GLACIAL ROCK (IRE)**, 7, b g Sonus (IRE)—Glacial Princess (IRE) **G. McPherson**
13 **GREAT VALUE (IRE)**, 8, b g Revoque (IRE)—Dame de L'oise (USA) **The Martins Hill Racing Partnership**
14 **HARRY HUNT**, 6, b g Bertolini (USA)—Qasirah (USA) **Arion Racing**
15 **KILCREA ASLA (IRE)**, 12, b g Oscar (IRE)—Alottalady (IRE) **Mrs L. Day**
16 7, Br gr m Silver Patriarch (IRE)—Lady Prunella (IRE) **Mrs V. Williams**
17 **MISS BROWNES FANCY (IRE)**, 5, b m Encosta de Lago (AUS)—
Be Dignified (IRE) **The Martins Hill Racing Partnership**
18 **NOMADIC STORM**, 5, b g Nomadic Way (USA)—Cateel Bay (IRE) **Arion Racing**
19 **PALUS SAN MARCO (IRE)**, 4, b g Holy Roman Emperor (IRE)—Kylemore (IRE) **4 Left Footers & A Blewnose**
20 **PERFECT REWARD**, 9, b g Cadeaux Genereux—Maid To Perfection **C. A. Bosley**
21 **PRESENTED (IRE)**, 6, ch g Presenting—Rustic Court (IRE) **The Presented Out Of Court Partnership**
22 **SANNIBEL**, 5, ch m Needwood Blade—Socialise **Mrs V. Williams**
23 **SOCIETY SHARES (IRE)**, 8, ch g Moscow Society (USA)—Presenting Shares (IRE)

MR GRAEME MCPHERSON - Continued

24 4, B f Erhaab (USA)—Solid Land (FR) **G. McPherson**
25 4, B g Royal Anthem (USA)—Supreme Baloo (IRE)
26 4, B f Exit To Nowhere (USA)—Sweet Empire (IRE) **G. McPherson**
27 **THE GOOD GUY (IRE)**, 10, b g Lord Americo—Lady Farnham (IRE) **The Martins Hill Racing Partnership**
28 **TICKATACK (IRE)**, 8, gr g Tikkanen (USA)—Theflyingcannister (IRE) **Andy Weller & The Drummers**
29 **TIMESISHARD (IRE)**, 6, b g Misternando—Smokey Flavour (IRE) **Mr J. Chamberlain**
30 **WERENEARLYOUTOFIT (IRE)**, 5, b g Asian Heights—Ballerina Laura (IRE) **The Ladies Of Martins Hill**
31 **WYCHWOODS BROOK**, 7, b g Midnight Legend—Miss Millbrook **Kevin & Anne Glastonbury**
32 **ZANIR (FR)**, 9, b g Munir—Shamhy (USA) **Mrs L. Day**

Other Owners: Mr M. Ball, Mr Samuel Barnes, Mr Howard Burdett, Mr L. R. Frampton, Mr Kevin Glastonbury, Mrs Anne Glastonbury, Mr D. A. Jervis, Mr Chris Jordan, Mr H. J. Kelly, Mr S. P. Lamberton, Mrs S. Mattle, Mr Graeme P. McPherson, Mrs S. M. McPherson, Mr Peter Randall, Mr Gary James Styles, Mr Andy Weller, Mr Jim White, Mr P. Williams.

Assistant Trainer: Mick Finn, Jodie Mogford

Jockey (NH): Wayne Hutchinson. Conditional: Ollie Garner, Tom Molloy, Killian Moore.

---

429 MR HUGH MCWILLIAMS, Pilling
Postal: **Moss Side Farm, Lancaster Road, Pilling, Preston, Lancashire, PR3 6SR**
Contacts: **PHONE (01995) 606276**

1 **CARNIVAL DREAM**, 8, b m Carnival Dancer—Reach The Wind (USA) **J. D. Riches**
2 **COLAMANDIS**, 6, b m Lucky Story (USA)—Merry Mary **J. D. Riches**
3 **FORZARZI (IRE)**, 9, b g Forzando—Zarzi (IRE) **J. D. Riches**
4 **IDAROSE (IRE)**, 4, b f Scorpion (IRE)—Garra Princess (IRE) **J. D. Riches**
5 **SPOKEN WORDS**, 4, b f Fruits of Love (USA)—Jerre Jo Glanville (USA) **Mrs L. Wohlers**

---

430 MR MARTYN MEADE, Malmesbury
Postal: **Ladyswood Stud, Sherston, Malmesbury, Wiltshire, SN16 0JL**
Contacts: **PHONE (01666) 840880 FAX (01666) 840073**

1 **DEIRE NA SLI (IRE)**, 5, b m Aussie Rules (USA)—Malignia (IRE) **Ladyswood Stud Ltd**
2 **FARLEAZE**, 4, b f Rail Link—Monkshill **Ladyswood Stud Ltd**
3 **TRUE TO FORM (IRE)**, 6, b g Rock of Gibraltar (IRE)—Truly Yours (IRE) **Ladyswood Stud Ltd**

TWO-YEAR-OLDS
4 B f 17/2 Three Valleys (USA)—Doctor's Note (Pursuit of Love) **Ladyswood Stud Ltd**
5 Ch f 9/5 Refuse To Bend (IRE)—Mika's Fable (FR) (Muhtathir) **Ladyswood Stud Ltd**

---

431 MR NOEL MEADE, Navan
Postal: **Tu Va Stables, Castletown-Kilpatrick, Navan, Co. Meath, Ireland**
Contacts: **PHONE (00 353) 46 905 4197 FAX (00 353) 46 905 4459 MOBILE (00 353) 87 256 6039**
E-MAIL tuvastables@eircom.net

1 **ALLY CASCADE (IRE)**, 5, b g Golan (IRE)—Nikkis Alstar (IRE)
2 **ANGE BALAFRE (FR)**, 4, b g Ange Gabriel (FR)—Balafre Rose (FR)
3 **ANOTHER PALM (IRE)**, 8, gr g Great Palm (USA)—Park Rose (IRE)
4 **APACHE STRONGHOLD (IRE)**, 5, b g Milan—First Battle (IRE)
5 **AVIDIUS CASSIUS (IRE)**, 5, b g Flemensfirth (USA)—Rixdale (FR)
6 **BAT MASTERSON (IRE)**, 5, b g Alhaarth (IRE)—Desert Grouse (USA)
7 **BENEMEADE (IRE)**, 5, b g Beneficial—Millicent Bridge (IRE)
8 **BENEVOLENT (IRE)**, 6, ch g Beneficial—Bobs Lass (IRE)
9 **BLACK BART (IRE)**, 5, b g High-Rise (IRE)—Kasakov Park
10 **BLISSFUL MOMENT (USA)**, 6, b br g Dynaformer (USA)—Arabian Spell (IRE)
11 **BLUE CANNON (IRE)**, 5, B G High Chaparral (IRE)—Blushing Barada (USA)
12 **BOSE IKARD (IRE)**, 5, b g Brian Boru—Dolldyedee (IRE)
13 **BUSTY BROWN (IRE)**, 7, b g Mr Combustible (IRE)—Misty Brown (IRE)
14 **CAMLIN FLOW (IRE)**, 6, b g Oscar (IRE)—Shannon Foam
15 **CHANCOL (FR)**, 4, b br g Vangelis (USA)—Boreade (FR)

MR NOEL MEADE - Continued

16 **CLOUDGAZER (IRE)**, 5, b g Dalakhani (IRE)—City Zone (IRE)
17 **COPS AND ROBBERS**, 5, ch g Pivotal—Threefold (USA)
18 **CORBALLY GHOST (IRE)**, 6, gr g Central Park (IRE)—Classic Lin (FR)
19 **CORSKEAGH ROYALE (IRE)**, 10, ch g Beneficial—Rubys Shadow (IRE)
20 **COULEUR FRANCE (IRE)**, 5, b g Flemensfirth (USA)—Gaye Mercy
21 **CROSS APPEAL (IRE)**, 7, b g Cape Cross (IRE)—Hadeb
22 **CURLEY BILL (IRE)**, 5, b g Heron Island (IRE)—In Excelsis (GER)
23 **DAN BOGAN (IRE)**, 4, b g Windsor Knot (IRE)—Housekeeping
24 **DARING DECOY (IRE)**, 5, gr g Great Palm (USA)—Blue Pool
25 **DARK PROSPECT**, 8, b g Nayef (USA)—Miss Mirasol
26 **DEVILS PAINTBRUSH (IRE)**, 5, b g Shantou (USA)—Back Log (IRE)
27 **DYLAN ROSS (IRE)**, 7, b g Shantou (USA)—Quit The Noise (IRE)
28 **ELIGIBLE (FR)**, 5, b g Martaline—Incorrigible (FR)
29 **ELIJAH GARDNER (IRE)**, 4, b g Refuse To Bend (IRE)—Anna Kareena (IRE)
30 **EVERY WHICH WAY**, 4, b g Kayf Tara—Simply Divine (IRE)
31 **FERMOYLE FLYER (IRE)**, 6, b br g Presenting—Fille d'argent (IRE)
32 **FICKLE FORTUNE (IRE)**, 5, b m Heron Island (IRE)—That's The Bonus (IRE)
33 **FISHER BRIDGE (IRE)**, 10, ch g Singspiel (IRE)—Kristal Bridge
34 **FULLY FUNDED (USA)**, 8, b g Aptitude (USA)—Fully Invested (USA)
35 **GAIUS MARIUS (IRE)**, 5, b g Tiger Hill (IRE)—Russian Muse (FR)
36 **GOLD TURTLE (FR)**, 4, b c Turtle Bowl (IRE)—Trasimene
37 **HARCHIE (IRE)**, 5, gr g Oscar (IRE)—Dame d'harvard (USA)
38 **HARTSIDE (GER)**, 4, b g Montjeu (IRE)—Helvellyn (USA)
39 **HARVEY LOGAN (IRE)**, 4, b g Saffron Walden (FR)—Baie Barbara (IRE)
40 **HE'S A DELIGHT (IRE)**, 9, b g Craigsteel—Maori's Delight
41 **HECK THOMAS (IRE)**, 5, b g Oscar (IRE)—Good Heighway (IRE)
42 **HONOURABLE EMPEROR (IRE)**, 4, b c Holy Roman Emperor (IRE)—Belle of Honour (USA)
43 **IKE CLANTON (IRE)**, 4, b g Heron Island (IRE)—Shbrook (IRE)
44 **IL FENOMENO (ITY)**, 7, b g Denon (USA)—Fabulous Charm (ITY)
45 **IPSOS DU BERLAIS (FR)**, 7, gr g Poliglote—Isis Du Berlais (FR)
46 **JAKROS (IRE)**, 8, b g Beneficial—Parkdota (IRE)
47 **JAMIES BENEFIT (IRE)**, 6, b g Beneficial—Torus Or You (IRE)
48 **JAZZ CONCERTO (IRE)**, 6, b g Ransom O'war (USA)—In The Saltmine (FR)
49 **JIM BOWIE (IRE)**, 8, b g Dushyantor (USA)—Delibonne (IRE)
50 **JOHANNISBERGER (IRE)**, 6, b g Arakan (USA)—Housekeeping
51 **JOSIE BASSETT (IRE)**, 4, b f Hurricane Run (IRE)—Showering
52 **KILLEENMORE (IRE)**, 10, b g Flemensfirth (USA)—Clever Move (IRE)
53 **KNOCKGRAFFON KING (IRE)**, 8, ch g Beneficial—Kilternan Gale (IRE)
54 **LEROY PARKER (IRE)**, 5, ch g Titus Livius (FR)—Jameela (IRE)
55 **LONDON BRIDGE**, 7, br g Beat Hollow—Cantanta
56 **MAXIM GORKY (IRE)**, 6, b g Montjeu (IRE)—Altruiste (USA)
57 **MEDICAL CARD (IRE)**, 9, b g Flemensfirth (USA)—Me Grannys Endoors (IRE)
58 **MILT YARBERRY**, 4, b g Librettist (USA)—Polar Storm (IRE)
59 4, B g Flemensfirth (USA)—Miss Brandywell (IRE)
60 **MONKSLAND (IRE)**, 6, b g Beneficial—Cush Jewel (IRE)
61 **MUIRHEAD (IRE)**, 10, b g Flemensfirth (USA)—Silaoce (FR)
62 **MULLAGHANOE RIVER (IRE)**, 5, b g Beneficial—Wahiba Hall (IRE)
63 **NED BUNTLINE**, 5, b g Refuse To Bend (IRE)—Intrum Morshaan (IRE)
64 **ORIGINAL OPTION (IRE)**, 8, br g Anshan—Deepest Thoughts (IRE)
65 **OUTLAWED TUNES (IRE)**, 6, br g Lord Americo—Thousand Springs (IRE)
66 **OWEN MC (IRE)**, 5, b g Oscar (IRE)—They Call Me Molly (CAN)
67 **PANDORAMA (IRE)**, 10, b g Flemensfirth (USA)—Gretchen's Castle (IRE)
68 **PAT GARRETT (IRE)**, 6, b g Fruits of Love (USA)—Junga Connection
69 **PERFECT SMILE (IRE)**, 8, b br g Anshan—Mambo Music (FR)
70 **PLEASE TALK (IRE)**, 7, b g Beneficial—Fresh Partner (IRE)
71 **PRIMA VISTA**, 8, b g Singspiel (IRE)—Papering (IRE)
72 **PROTARAS (USA)**, 6, b br g Lemon Drop Kid (USA)—Seven Moons (JPN)
73 **RAISE THE RANSOM (IRE)**, 5, b g Red Ransom (USA)—Dawn Surprise (USA)
74 **REALT DUBH (IRE)**, 9, b g Beneficial—Suez Canal (FR)
75 **ROAD TO RICHES (IRE)**, 6, b g Gamut (IRE)—Bellora (IRE)
76 **RORY MAC (IRE)**, 4, b g Flemensfirth (USA)—Wild Fuchsia (IRE)
77 **RUBE BURROW (IRE)**, 4, b g Presenting—Sarah Massini (IRE)
78 4, B f Flemensfirth (USA)—Seeds of Doubt (IRE)
79 **SILVER TASSIE (IRE)**, 5, b g Shantou (USA)—Silver Castor (IRE)
80 **SILVERHAND (IRE)**, 9, gr g Lend A Hand—Karmisymixa (FR)

MR NOEL MEADE - Continued

81 4, B g Scorpion (IRE)—Sister Swing
82 **SIX STONE NED (IRE)**, 7, gr g Great Palm (USA)—Ashfield Rosie (IRE)
83 **SLEMISHFIRTH (IRE)**, 6, b g Flemensfirth (USA)—She's No Tourist (IRE)
84 **SUE AND ISI (IRE)**, 4, b f Kalanisi (IRE)—Susy In The Summer (IRE)
85 **SWORD OF DESTINY (IRE)**, 7, gr g Shantou (USA)—Sparkling Sword
86 **TEXAS JACK (IRE)**, 7, b g Curtain Time (IRE)—Sailors Run (IRE)
87 **THE CONTENDER (IRE)**, 4, b g Scorpion (IRE)—Welsh Rhapsody (IRE)
88 **THEGREATJOHNBROWNE (IRE)**, 9, ch g Beneficial—Alltoplayfor (IRE)
89 **THOMOND (IRE)**, 5, b g Definite Article—Hushaby (IRE)
90 **THOUVA (FR)**, 6, b g Ragmar (FR)—Lady Thou (FR)
91 **TONTO MURPHY (IRE)**, 9, b g Oscar (IRE)—Brown Willows (IRE)
92 **TOP O'TULLY (IRE)**, 5, b g Flemensfirth (USA)—Polly's Joy (IRE)
93 4, Ch g Flemensfirth (USA)—Tricky Present (IRE)
94 **TULSA JACK (IRE)**, 4, b g Urban Ocean (IRE)—Jessica's Pet (IRE)
95 **WES HARDIN (IRE)**, 4, b g Beneficial—Luas Luso (IRE)
96 **WESTHAVEN (IRE)**, 5, b g Alhaarth (IRE)—Dashiba
97 **WILDEBEEST (IRE)**, 4, b g Oscar (IRE)—Cailin's Princess (IRE)

THREE-YEAR-OLDS

98   **CHAMPOLEON (FR)**, gr g Turtle Bowl (IRE)—Trasimene
99   **NATIVE REALM (IRE)**, ch g Fracas (IRE)—Gift of Grace (FR)
100 **ROCK OF GLENSTAL**, b g Mount Nelson—Amandian (IRE)

TWO-YEAR-OLDS

101 B g 28/3 Robin des Champs (FR)—Daizinni (Dr Massini (IRE)) (9126)
102 B g 28/5 Scorpion (IRE)—Kilmington Breeze (IRE) (Roselier (FR)) (7936)
103 Ch c 23/2 Refuse To Bend (IRE)—Paradise Dancer (IRE) (Danehill Dancer (IRE)) (5000)
104 B g 17/4 Scorpion (IRE)—Silvestre (ITY) (Unfuwain (USA)) (4920)

Assistant Trainer: Damien McGillick

Jockey (NH): Davy Condon, Paul Carberry. **Amateur:** Miss Nina Carberry, Mr Jason McKeown.

---

432 **MR BRIAN MEEHAN, Manton**
Postal: The Racing Office, Manton House Estate, Manton, Marlborough, Wiltshire, SN8 1PN
Contacts: **PHONE** (01672) 517191 **FAX** (01672) 517192 **MOBILE** (07836) 754254
E-MAIL info@brianmeehan.com **WEBSITE** www.brianmeehan.com

1   **AAIM TO PROSPER (IRE)**, 9, br g Val Royal (FR)—Bint Al Balad (IRE) **CGA Racing Partnership 2**
2   **ANGELIC NOTE (IRE)**, 4, b f Excellent Art—Evangeline **Mrs L. O. Sangster**
3   **ARCHBISHOP (USA)**, 4, b c Arch (USA)—Avaricity (USA) **Mr C. W. Clay**
4   **BALLESTEROS**, 4, ch g Tomba—Flamenco Dancer **Mrs P. Good**
5   **BURANO (IRE)**, 4, ch c Dalakhani (IRE)—Kalimanta (IRE) **Mr J. R. Harvey**
6   **CAPITOL GAIN (IRE)**, 4, b g Bahamian Bounty—Emmas Princess (IRE) **B. V. Sangster**
7   **CRIMSON KNIGHT**, 5, ch h Zafeen (FR)—Kaylianni **W. A. Harrison-Allan**
8   **ELUSIVITY (IRE)**, 5, b g Elusive City (USA)—Tough Chic (IRE) **Mrs P. Good**
9   **HOMETOWN GLORY**, 4, b c Compton Place—Pomponette (USA) **Mascalls Stud**
10 **SAMOAN (IRE)**, 4, b g Danehill Dancer (IRE)—Rain Flower (IRE) **Sangster Family & Mrs J. Magnier**
11 **SIR BEDIVERE (IRE)**, 4, b g Dansili—Miss Ivanhoe (USA) **Trelawny II**

THREE-YEAR-OLDS

12 **ARBAAH (USA)**, b f Invasor (ARG)—Alshadiyah (USA) **Hamdan Al Maktoum**
13 **ASBAAB (USA)**, ch g Jazil (USA)—Alsaabeqa (USA) **Hamdan Al Maktoum**
14 **CALLING**, b f Dalakhani (IRE)—Almatinka (IRE) **D. J. Burke**
15 **CORRESPONDENT**, ch c Exceed And Excel (AUS)—Indian Love Bird **Mrs P. Good**
16 **DA DO RUN RUN**, b g Sixties Icon—Fascinatin Rhythm **W. A. Harrison-Allan**
17 **DISCO INFERNO (IRE)**, b c Lawman (FR)—Pink Sovietstaia (FR) **Bayardo**
18 **DOWNHILL DANCER (IRE)**, b f Montjeu (IRE)—Wiener Wald (USA) **Car Colston Hall Stud Syndicate**
19 **ESHTIAAL (USA)**, b c Dynaformer (USA)—Enfiraaj (USA) **Hamdan Al Maktoum**
20 **ETIJAAH (USA)**, b c Daaher (CAN)—Hasheema (IRE) **Hamdan Al Maktoum**
21 **FANTACISE**, ch f Pivotal—My First Romance **Mr T. G. & Mrs M. E. Holdcroft**
22 **FREEPORT**, b c Bahamian Bounty—Perdicula (IRE) **R. C. Tooth**
23 **GIVE WAY NELSON (IRE)**, b f Mount Nelson—Give A Whistle (IRE) **Newsells Park Stud Limited**

MR BRIAN MEEHAN - Continued

24 **GRANELL (IRE)**, ch c Excellent Art—Granny Kelly (USA) **Native Colony Partnership**
25 **GREAT HALL**, b c Halling (USA)—L'affaire Monique **R. C. Tooth**
26 **GREGORI (IRE)**, b c Invincible Spirit (IRE)—Three Wrens (IRE) **S. P. Tucker**
27 **HARRY BOSCH**, b g Kyllachy—Fen Guest **M. A. C. Buckley**
28 **HASAAD (USA)**, b c Kheleyf (USA)—Maha Dubai (USA) **Hamdan Al Maktoum**
29 **INDEX WAITER**, ch g Exceed And Excel (AUS)—Snowy Indian **R. P. Foden**
30 **INTIBAAH**, b g Elnadim (USA)—Mawaared **Hamdan Al Maktoum**
31 **LAZARUS BELL**, ch c Bahamian Bounty—Snake's Head **Lanesborough**
32 **LEGAL WAVES (IRE)**, b c Lawman (FR)—Surf The Web (IRE) **Orwell Partnership**
33 **MASTER MING (IRE)**, b c Excellent Art—China Pink **Mr Michael Wilmshurst & Mr N. B. Attenborough**
34 **MEETING IN PARIS (IRE)**, b f Dutch Art—Sharplaw Star **Sir R. Ogden C.B.E., LLD**
35 **MOSS STREET**, b g Moss Vale (IRE)—Street Style (IRE) **Bayardo**
36 **MUJAZIF (IRE)**, br c Shamardal (USA)—Red Bandanna (IRE) **F. Nass**
37 **MUTASHABEK (USA)**, b g Arch (USA)—Siyadah (USA) **Hamdan Al Maktoum**
38 **NUMBER ONE LONDON (IRE)**, b c Invincible Spirit (IRE)—Vadorga **Mr S. Jones**
39 **PATENTLY (IRE)**, b c Moss Vale (IRE)—Trader Secret (IRE) **Lanesborough**
40 **PEARL BELL (IRE)**, b f Camacho—Magnificent Bell (IRE) **Pearl Bloodstock Limited**
41 **PINARIUS (IRE)**, b c Amadeus Wolf—Cantaloupe **KSB Bloodstock & Sam Sangster**
42 **RED ROCKER (IRE)**, ch c Redback—Feet of Flame (USA) **Lanesborough**
43 **ROMAN ORDER (IRE)**, b c Holy Roman Emperor (IRE)—Web of Intrigue **Decadent Racing**
44 Gr c Duke of Marmalade (IRE)—Santa Sophia (IRE) **Bayardo**
45 **SAVED BY THE BELL (IRE)**, b c Teofilo (IRE)—Eyrecourt (USA) **M. A. C. Buckley**
46 **SECULAR SOCIETY**, b g Royal Applause—Fantastic Santanyi **Orwell Partnership**
47 **STABLEFORD**, ch c Smart Strike (CAN)—Paris Winds (IRE) **Sangster Family**
48 **SUPERNOVA HEIGHTS (IRE)**, b f Oasis Dream—Athene (IRE) **Ballymacoll Stud Farm Ltd**
49 **THANKSGIVING DAY (USA)**, b g Harlan's Holiday (USA)—Frappay (USA) **M. A. C. Buckley**
50 **TIPPOTINA**, b f Indesatchel (IRE)—Ballerina Suprema (IRE) **Mrs M. Buckley**
51 **WHIPPER'S BOY (IRE)**, b g Whipper (USA)—Glympse (IRE) **Trelawny II**
52 **WRECKING BALL (IRE)**, b c Royal Applause—Shatarah **Clipper Group Holdings Ltd**

TWO-YEAR-OLDS

53 B c 31/3 Acclamation—Abington Angel (Machiavellian (USA)) (38095) **Trelawny II**
54 **AHD (USA)**, b f 5/3 Elusive Quality (USA)—Abby Road (IRE) (Danehill (USA)) **Hamdan Al Maktoum**
55 **ALFAAYZA (IRE)**, b f 6/3 Dansili—Ayun (USA) (Swain (IRE)) **Hamdan Al Maktoum**
56 **ARCHIPELIGO**, b c 23/4 Archipenko (USA)—Red Slew (Red Ransom (USA)) (26000) **R. C. Tooth**
57 B c 2/2 Holy Roman Emperor (IRE)—Bankeress (IRE) (Barathea (IRE)) (65000)
58 B f 19/3 Footstepsinthesand—Canterbury Lace (USA) (Danehill (USA)) **Mr A. Rosen**
59 B c 23/5 Henrythenavigator (USA)—Chalamont (IRE) (Kris) (20000) **Sangster Family**
60 B c 17/2 Empire Maker (USA)—Deaconess Bonnie (USA) (Pulpit (USA)) (153609) **Reddam Racing LLC**
61 B c 17/2 Archipenko (USA)—Diablerette (Green Desert (USA)) (42000)
62 **EMERALD SWELL (IRE)**, gr f 8/2 Dalakhani (IRE)—
                                    Dance of The Sea (IRE) (Sinndar (IRE)) **Ballymacoll Stud Farm Ltd**
63 **EMTINAAN (IRE)**, ch f 3/3 Tamayuz—Almass (IRE) (Elnadim (USA)) **Hamdan Al Maktoum**
64 B c 20/2 Exceed And Excel (AUS)—Fair Sailing (IRE) (Docksider (USA)) (30000) **Trelawny II**
65 Ch f 14/4 Dutch Art—Felucca (Green Desert (USA)) (48000)
66 B f 11/2 High Chaparral (IRE)—Fin (Groom Dancer (USA)) (40000)
67 **GHASAQ (IRE)**, b c 1/3 Invincible Spirit (IRE)—
                                    Manuka Magic (Key of Luck (USA)) (71428) **Hamdan Al Maktoum**
68 B c 26/4 Iffraaj—Graceful Air (IRE) (Danzero (AUS)) (38000)
69 Ch c 4/5 Camacho—Grand Baie (IRE) (Grand Lodge (USA)) (19047) **Decadent Racing**
70 Br c 22/4 Captain Rio—Grannys Reluctance (IRE) (Anita's Prince) (28571)
71 B c 24/2 Kyllachy—Have Fun (Indian Ridge) (38095)
72 **HEWAYAAT**, b f 27/1 Cape Cross (IRE)—Wink (Salse (USA)) (90000) **Hamdan Al Maktoum**
73 B c 4/3 Kyllachy—Khyber Knight (Night Shift (USA)) (25000)
74 B c 18/4 Dylan Thomas (IRE)—Kournikova (SAF) (Sportsworld (USA)) (32000)
75 Ch c 19/3 Smart Strike (CAN)—L'ile Aux Loups (IRE) (Rock of Gibraltar (IRE)) (55000)
76 B gr c 18/3 Mount Nelson—La Gandilie (FR) (Highest Honor (FR)) (77000)
77 **LOVE TANGLE (IRE)**, b c 12/2 Azamour (IRE)—Dragnet (IRE) (Rainbow Quest (USA)) **Ballymacoll Stud Farm Ltd**
78 **MADEED**, b c 5/3 Nayef (USA)—Danehill Dreamer (USA) (Danehill (USA)) (40000) **Hamdan Al Maktoum**
79 **MAWFOOR (IRE)**, b c 25/2 Iffraaj—Miss Odlum (IRE) (Mtoto) (78095) **Hamdan Al Maktoum**
80 **MUSTADAAM (IRE)**, b c 15/4 Dansili—Sundus (USA) (Sadler's Wells (USA)) **Hamdan Al Maktoum**
81 Ch f 2/2 Street Cry (IRE)—On A Cloud (USA) (Silver Hawk (USA)) (122887) **Reddam Racing LLC**
82 B c 22/2 Firebreak—On The Brink (Mind Games) (14000)
83 **PIPE DREAM**, ch c 15/4 Piccolo—Bold Love (Bold Edge) (19047) **Mr M. Wilmshurst**
84 B c 25/1 Cape Cross (IRE)—Raskutani (Dansili) (7000) **W. A. Harrison-Allan**

MR BRIAN MEEHAN - Continued

85 Ch f 21/4 Distorted Humor (USA)—Rolling Sea (USA) (Sefapiano (USA)) (147465) **Reddam Racing LLC**
86 Gr ro c 11/4 Mastercraftsman (IRE)—Rose Briar (IRE) (Grand Lodge (USA)) (55000)
87 B c 16/3 Lawman (FR)—Royal Alchemist (Kingsinger (IRE)) (58000)
88 **SAALIB (USA)**, b c 21/2 War Front (USA)—
　　　　　　　　　　　　　Dixie Quest (USA) (Coronado's Quest (USA)) (150000) **Hamdan Al Maktoum**
89 B c 19/4 Clodovil (IRE)—Salonga (IRE) (Shinko Forest (IRE)) (35000)
90 **SEFAAT**, b br f 9/2 Haatef (USA)—Thamara (USA) (Street Cry (IRE)) **Hamdan Al Maktoum**
91 B f 28/2 Arch (USA)—Shootha (IRE) (Bluebird (USA)) (153609) **Mr A. Rosen**
92 B f 28/3 Oasis Dream—So Silk (Rainbow Quest (USA)) (155000) **Mr A. Rosen**
93 Ch f 2/4 Mount Nelson—Statua (IRE) (Statoblest) (40000) **Newsells Park Stud Limited**
94 B c 26/3 Excellent Art—Stormy Larissa (IRE) (Royal Applause) (19047) **Decadent Racing**
95 **TAGHREEB**, b c 25/3 Dubawi (IRE)—Ghaneema (USA) (Forestry (USA)) **Hamdan Al Maktoum**
96 **TASAABOQ**, b c 30/3 Aqlaam—Seldemosa (Selkirk (USA)) (55000) **Hamdan Al Maktoum**
97 B c 26/3 Iffraaj—There's Two (IRE) (Ashkalani (IRE)) (20000)
98 Gr c 3/5 Aussie Rules (USA)—Trois Graces (USA) (Alysheba (USA)) (60000)
99 B br c 25/5 Awesome Again (CAN)—
　　　　　　　　　　　　　Unbridled Ambiance (USA) (Unbridled Time (USA)) (92165) **Reddam Racing LLC**
100 B br f 23/3 Marju (IRE)—Urgele (FR) (Zafonic (USA)) (140000)
101 **VASILIOS**, ch c 30/3 Sixties Icon—Kaylianni (Kalanisi (IRE)) **W. A. Harrison-Allan**
102 **WINTRY LIGHT**, gr f 1/5 Archipenko (USA)—Frosty Welcome (USA) (With Approval (CAN))
103 B c 14/4 Lawman (FR)—Woodland Orchid (IRE) (Woodman (USA)) (50793)
104 **ZIEBAWI**, b f 31/3 Dubawi (IRE)—Zietory (Zieten (USA)) (50000)

Other Owners: N. B. Attenborough, Mrs S. J. Biggins, Mr K. W. Biggins, Mr J. M. Carroll, Mrs S. J. Hearn, B. M. W. Hearn, Mr Stewart Jones, Mrs S. Magnier, Mr D. R. Mann, Mr D. A. Mccormick, B. J. Meehan, Mr N. P. Nunn, G. E. Sangster, Mr S. E. Sangster, Mr B. V. Sangster, Mrs L. M. Shanahan, Mr M. Tabor, Mr Michael Wilmshurst.

Assistant Trainer: R. O'Dowd

Amateur: Miss Jade Muggeridge.

433　MR ANTHONY MIDDLETON, Banbury
Postal: Culworth Grounds Stables, Culworth, Banbury, Oxfordshire, OX17 2ND
Contacts: PHONE (01844) 292463 **FAX** (01844) 292463 **MOBILE** (07894) 909542
E-MAIL tony@granboroughracing.co.uk **WEBSITE** www.granboroughracing.co.uk

1 **AMERICAN LIFE (FR)**, b, 6, b br g American Post—Poplife (FR) **Racing Roses Partnership**
2 **ANEYEFORASELLER**, 6, b g Alflora (IRE)—Severn Gale **N. J. Allen**
3 **BELURA (IRE)**, 5, gr m High-Rise (IRE)—Full Deck (IRE) **Mrs D. Dewbery**
4 **BETWEEN THE LINES (IRE)**, 4, gr g Dalakhani (IRE)—Stage Struck (IRE) **Mrs S. E. Brown**
5 **BOB LEWIS**, 7, b g Sir Harry Lewis (USA)—Teelyna **Mrs L. M. Edwards**
6 **BRUNSTON**, 7, gr g High Chaparral (IRE)—Molly Mello (GER) **Mr P. F. Barry**
7 **CAUGHT BY WITNESS (IRE)**, 8, b g Witness Box (USA)—Donegans Daughter **Mrs D. Dewbery**
8 **CHANINBAR (FR)**, 10, b g Milford Track (IRE)—Logicia (FR)
9 **DONTGOEASY**, 5, b g Dubai Destination (USA)—Talkasha (IRE) **Mr S. J. Corcoran**
10 **ESCORT'MEN (FR)**, 7, ch g Robin des Champs (FR)—Escortee (FR) **Macable Partnership**
11 **FITANDPROPERJOB**, 7, b g Helissio (FR)—Talkasha (IRE) **S.E.D Racing Partnership**
12 **FLYING FORTRESS**, 16, b g Petoski—Misty Fort
13 **GRAFITE**, 8, gr g Act One—Silver Gyre (IRE) **J Dalton C Shankland P Fitzgerald**
14 **JAYA BELLA (IRE)**, 8, gr m Tikkanen (USA)—Maxis Girl (IRE) **C. H. Shankland**
15 **KID SUITOR (IRE)**, 4, ch g Choisir (AUS)—Fancy Intense **Byerley Racing Limited**
16 **LOUGH COI (IRE)**, 7, b g Insatiable (IRE)—Roisin Dove (IRE) **Mrs R. Wenman**
17 **MAISEY MILAN (IRE)**, 7, b m Milan—Scead (IRE) **Mr T. Donnelly**
18 **MARLENO (GER)**, 7, b g Lecroix (GER)—Mondalita (GER) **Pet Necessities Partnership**
19 4, B g Norse Dancer (IRE)—Miss Lewis
20 **MISS OVERBURY (IRE)**, 7, br m Overbury (IRE)—Chickabiddy **Mrs D. Dewbery**
21 **PAXFORD JUNIOR**, 7, b g Bollin Eric—Paxford Lady **Mrs D. Dewbery**
22 **PERCY LEWIS**, 6, b g Erhaab (USA)—Miss Lewis **Mrs J. May**
23 **PILGRIMS LANE (IRE)**, 9, b g Dr Massini (IRE)—Miss Mylette (IRE) **Mrs S. E. Brown**
24 **PIPE BANNER**, 9, b g Silver Patriarch (IRE)—Bella Macrae **Miss C. Elks**
25 **SALTAGIOO (ITY)**, 9, b g Dr Devious (IRE)—Sces **Mrs D. Dewbery**
26 **SHAMELESS MAN (IRE)**, 6, b g Atraf—Fleetfoot (IRE) **Mrs R. Wenman**
27 **SNAKE CHARMER**, 10, b g Golden Snake (USA)—Moly **Racing Roses Partnership**
28 **TESHALI (IRE)**, 7, br gr g Anabaa (USA)—Tashiriya (IRE) **Mrs S. E. Brown**

MR ANTHONY MIDDLETON - Continued

29 **THE BOOGEYMAN (IRE)**, 7, br g King's Theatre (IRE)—Market Lass (IRE) **Nic Allen & Paul Frank Barry**
30 **TOUGHNESS DANON**, 7, b g Tiger Hill (IRE)—Templerin (GER) **Mr P. F. Barry**
31 **VA'VITE (IRE)**, 6, b m Vinnie Roe (IRE)—Presenting Shares (IRE) **Ms B Woodcock & Mrs D Dewbery**
32 **WHEAT FREE**, 4, b f Midnight Legend—Talkasha (IRE) **N. J. Allen**

Other Owners: Dr J. D. Dalton, Mr S. Darvill, Mr P. Fitzgerald, Mrs D. Hopkins, Mr S. Mackintosh, Mr F. W. Mackintosh, Mr J.P. Naylor, Mr J. Peavoy, Ms B. Woodcock.

Jockey (NH): James Banks, Dave Crosse, Charlie Poste. **Conditional:** Mark Marris.

434
MR PHILIP MIDDLETON, Aylesbury
Postal: **The Stables, Dorton Park Farm, Dorton, Aylesbury, Buckinghamshire, HP18 9NR**
Contacts: **PHONE (01844) 237503 FAX (01844) 237503 MOBILE (07860) 426607**

1 **ALWAYSTHEOPTIMIST**, 10, b g Muhtarram (USA)—Miss Optimist **P. W. Middleton**
2 **SAIL AND RETURN**, 9, b g Kayf Tara—Maidwell **P. W. Middleton**
3 **TRIP THE LIGHT**, 8, b g Fantastic Light (USA)—Jumaireyah **P. W. Middleton**

Assistant Trainer: Helen Day

435
MR PAUL MIDGLEY, Westow
Postal: **Sandfield Farm, Westow, York, YO60 7LS**
Contacts: **Office (01653) 658790 FAX (01653) 658790 MOBILE (07976) 965220**
E-MAIL ptmidgley@aol.com **WEBSITE** www.ptmidgley.com

1 **ANOTHER WISE KID (IRE)**, 5, b g Whipper (USA)—Romancing **M. Ng**
2 **CHOC'A'MOCA (IRE)**, 6, b g Camacho—Dear Catch (IRE) **John Milburn - Andrew Stephenson**
3 **DOLLY DIVA**, 4, b f Iffraaj—Charlie Girl **Mr Mrs S Turton & Mrs D Blackburn**
4 **HAAJES**, 9, ch g Indian Ridge—Imelda (USA) **Sandfield Racing**
5 **MAD FOR FUN (IRE)**, 4, b f Ivan Denisovich (IRE)—Franny **Mad 4 Fun**
6 **MAID OF MEFT**, 6, b m Auction House (USA)—Lady Margaret **D. Mann**
7 **NO MEAN TRICK (USA)**, 7, b g Grand Slam (USA)—Ruby's Reception (USA) **J. A. Milburn**
8 **OLDJOESAID**, 9, b g Royal Applause—Border Minstral (IRE) **Pee Dee Tee Syndicate & T W Midgley**
9 **PHOENIX CLUBS (IRE)**, 4, b f Red Clubs (IRE)—Hollow Haze (USA) **Williams, Lindley, Turton, Bate**
10 **QUAROMA**, 8, ch m Pivotal—Quiz Time **The Legend's Syndicate II**
11 **SILVANUS (IRE)**, 8, b g Danehill Dancer (IRE)—Mala Mala (IRE) **C. Alton**
12 **SUNRAIDER (IRE)**, 6, b g Namid—Doctrine **Gap Personnel Franchises Limited**

THREE-YEAR-OLDS

13 **EDITH ANNE**, b f Sakhee's Secret—Accusation (IRE) **D. Mann**
14 **MOSS THE BOSS (IRE)**, b g Moss Vale (IRE)—Lady of Bilston (IRE) **21st Century Racing & P T Midgley**
15 **RED STYLE (IRE)**, b g Red Clubs (IRE)—In The Fashion (IRE) **R. Wardlaw**

TWO-YEAR-OLDS

16 Ch c 1/3 Pastoral Pursuits—Smart Hostess (Most Welcome) (10952) **Mrs M. Verity**

Other Owners: Mr G. Bate, Mr P. Bateson, Mr J. Batty, J. N. Blackburn, A. W. Catterall, Mrs B. Catterall, E. Jagger, Mr C. Jagger, Mr P. N. Lindley, Mr T. W. Midgley, P. T. Midgley, T. A. Stephenson, Mr A. Turton, Mr A. D. Ward, A. Williams.

Assistant Trainer: Miss W. Gibson

Jockey (flat): Micky Fenton. **Amateur:** Miss H. Dukes, Miss W. Gibson.

436
MR ROD MILLMAN, Cullompton
Postal: **The Paddocks, Kentisbeare, Cullompton, Devon, EX15 2DX**
Contacts: **PHONE/FAX (01884) 266620 MOBILE (07885) 168447**
E-MAIL rod.millman@ic24.net

1 **DANCE**, 4, b f Erhaab (USA)—Shi Shi **Mrs C. Knowles**
2 **GAELIC ICE**, 4, b f Iceman—Gaelic Lime **The Jack High Racing Partnership**
3 **GALATIAN**, 6, ch g Traditionally (USA)—Easy To Imagine (USA) **Tarka Racing**

MR ROD MILLMAN - Continued

4 **GEORGE THISBY**, 7, b g Royal Applause—Warning Belle **Mr R. G. Thisby**
5 **GLADIATRIX**, 4, b f Compton Place—Lady Dominatrix (IRE) **Harry Dutfield & Partners**
6 **ICE TRES**, 4, br f Iceman—Tup Tim **P. G. Gibbins**
7 **ICEBUSTER**, 5, ch g Iceman—Radiate **The Links Partnership**
8 **INTO THE WIND**, 6, ch m Piccolo—In The Stocks **E. J. S. Gadsden**
9 **ISHI**, 4, b f Ishiguru (USA)—Chorus **Kintyre Racing**
10 **IVOR'S PRINCESS**, 4, b f Atraf—Rosina May (IRE) **Mr P.G. Gibbins & Mr W. I. M. Perry**
11 **MADAME KINTYRE**, 5, b m Trade Fair—Chorus **Rod Millman Racing Club**
12 **MASAI MOON**, 9, b g Lujain (USA)—Easy To Imagine (USA) **Rod Millman Racing Club**
13 **PRINCESS ANNABELLE**, 4, ch f Sworn In (USA)—Marybelle **C. J. T. Payne**
14 **SHAVANSKY**, 9, b g Rock of Gibraltar (IRE)—Limelighting (USA) **The Links Partnership**
15 **STARVING MARVIN**, 5, b g Hawk Wing (USA)—Oleana (IRE) **Seasons Holidays**
16 **WYNDHAM WAVE**, 4, gr g Dr Fong (USA)—Atlantic Light **Kentisbeare Racing**

THREE-YEAR-OLDS

17 **ASTRUM**, gr g Haafhd—Vax Star **The Links Partnership**
18 **BURNT FINGERS (IRE)**, b f Kheleyf (USA)—Play With Fire (FR) **Miss G. J. Abbey**
19 **ISIS BLUE**, b g Cockney Rebel (IRE)—Bramaputra (IRE) **Cantay Racing**
20 **PERCY'S PLEASURE**, b f Sir Percy—Danalia (IRE) **P. Webb**
21 **POETIC VERSE**, gr f Byron—Nina Fontenail (FR) **The Links Partnership**
22 **SHAHDAROBA (IRE)**, b g Haatef (USA)—Gold Script (FR) **The Links Partnership**
23 **SWEET ALABAMA**, gr f Johannesburg (USA)—Alybgood (CAN) **The Links Partnership**
24 **WINNIE PERRY**, ch g Assertive—Hayley's Flower (IRE) **Mr G. Thompson**

TWO-YEAR-OLDS

25 B c 25/3 Myboycharlie (IRE)—Be Decisive (Diesis) (19047) **Seasons Holidays**
26 B c 10/2 Azamour (IRE)—Best Side (IRE) (King's Best (USA)) (11000) **Mustajed Partnership**
27 **BLUE ANCHOR BAY (IRE)**, b c 15/2 Ad Valorem (USA)—
New Foundation (IRE) (College Chapel) (8729) **Crowcombe Racing**
28 B c 8/2 Aqlaam—Bramaputra (IRE) (Choisir (AUS)) **Mrs M. Campbell-Andenaes**
29 **COTTON CLUB (IRE)**, b c 26/3 Amadeus Wolf—
Slow Jazz (USA) (Chief's Crown (USA)) (17142) **The Links Partnership**
30 **DOVIL'S DUEL (IRE)**, b c 21/4 Clodovil (IRE)—Duelling (Diesis) (4761) **Always Hopeful Partnership**
31 **GRAPHENE**, b c 10/2 Nayef (USA)—Annapurna (IRE) (Brief Truce (USA)) (22000)
32 **MASTER CARPENTER (IRE)**, ch c 27/2 Mastercraftsman (IRE)—
Fringe (In The Wings) (23809) **The Links Partnership**
33 Br g 27/4 Pastoral Pursuits—Nina Fontenail (FR) (Kaldounevees (FR)) **The Links Partnership**
34 B c 21/2 Kyllachy—Sheka (Ishiguru (USA)) (23809) **Seasons Holidays**
35 Gr c 31/3 Intense Focus (USA)—Sioduil (IRE) (Oasis Dream) (19047) **Mustajed Partnership**

Other Owners: P. Bartlam, J. Burley, A. J. Conway, K. L. Dare, Mrs A. C. Dominy, Mr H. Dutfield, S. J. Dutfield, Mrs J. Elliott, Mr N. D. Elliott, Mr R. D. Gamlin, Mr D. J. Hornby, Mr E. J. Hughes, V. B. Lewer, D. A. Little, Mrs L. S. Millman, B. R. Millman, Mr A. M. Nolan, G. G. Payne, S. M. Perry, W. I. M. Perry, Mr T. Tompkins.

Assistant Trainers: Louise Millman, James Millman

Jockey (flat): Andrea Atzeni. **Conditional:** Pat Millman. **Apprentice:** Pat Millman.

437
MR ROBERT MILLS, Epsom
Postal: **Loretta Lodge Racing Stables, Tilley Lane, Headley, Surrey, KT18 6EP**
Contacts: **PHONE** (01372) 377209 **FAX** (01372) 386578
E-MAIL lorettalodge@aol.com

1 **CHARLTON**, 10, b g Inchinor—Sabina **Mrs B. B. Mills**
2 **JACOBS SON**, 5, ch g Refuse To Bend (IRE)—Woodwin (IRE) **Jacobs Construction (Holdings) Limited**
3 **PAPERETTO**, 5, b g Selkirk (USA)—Song of Hope **Mrs B. B. Mills**

THREE-YEAR-OLDS

4 **CANADIAN RUN (IRE)**, ch g Hurricane Run (IRE)—Vale View (FR) **Mr B. Kerr**
5 **CLOSE TOGETHER (IRE)**, b f Dylan Thomas (IRE)—Maritana (USA) **Miss J A Leighs & Mrs B B Mills**
6 **CLUB HOUSE (IRE)**, b g Marju (IRE)—Idesia (IRE) **Mr Trevor Jacobs & Mrs B B Mills**
7 **DREAM ABOUT YOU (IRE)**, b f Amadeus Wolf—Peshawar **Mrs B. B. Mills**
8 **JACKAMIA**, ch g Kyllachy—Sheila's Secret (IRE) **Sherwoods Transport Ltd**
9 **LITTLE BUXTED (USA)**, b br c Mr Greeley (USA)—Mo Cheoil Thu (IRE) **Buxted Partnership**

MR ROBERT MILLS - Continued

10 **RAVENS NEST**, b g Piccolo—Emouna **Jacobs Construction & Mrs B B Mills**
11 **SWING EASY**, b c Zamindar (USA)—Shahmina (IRE) **Mrs B B Mills, Mr J Harley, Mr T Jacobs**

Other Owners: P. A. Byrne, J. P. Hanifin, J. E. Harley, T. Jacobs, Miss J. A. Leighs, Mrs J. Ruthven.

Assistant Trainer: Richard Ryan

---

438 MR NICK MITCHELL, Dorchester
Postal: **Brick House, Piddletrenthide, Dorchester, Dorset, DT2 7QP**
Contacts: **PHONE (01300) 348049 MOBILE (07770) 892085**
E-MAIL nick.mitch@tiscali.co.uk WEBSITE www.nickmitchellracing.com

1 **BAND OF THUNDER**, 5, ch g Shirocco (GER)—Black Opal **J. R. Boughey**
2 **BOLLIN PIPER**, 5, b g Bollin Terry—Astraliser **The Happy Days Partnership**
3 **COLIN'S DESIRE**, 7, gr g Pasternak—Sarah's Destiny **C. W. Mitchell**
4 **ELECTRIC MAYHEM**, 6, b g Alflora (IRE)—She's No Muppet **Mr & Mrs Andrew May**
5 **GIVE US THE WINK**, 5, br m Loup Sauvage (USA)—Wink And Whisper
6 **KAYFROU**, 8, b g Kayf Tara—Roufontaine **Mr Nick Mitchell**
7 **MISS FLEUR**, 10, b m Bandmaster (USA)—Floral Park **Milcombe Racing**
8 **OVER THE RUBICON (IRE)**, 6, gr g Overbury—Brasya (FR) **The Rubicon Club**
9 **PHONE HOME (IRE)**, 6, b br g Heron Island (IRE)—Ancestral Voices (IRE) **Mr & Mrs Andrew May & Nick Elliott**
10 **PLUG IN BABY**, 5, b m Xaar—Medinaceli (IRE) **Mr Nick Mitchell**
11 **RICKETYROCK**, 7, b g Riverwise (USA)—Apatura Cherry **Mrs E. Mitchell**
12 **SIMPLY BEN (IRE)**, 7, b g Pilsudski (IRE)—Peace Time Girl (IRE) **Guy and Sophie Henderson**

TWO-YEAR-OLDS

13 B f 2/5 Alflora (IRE)—She's No Muppet (Teenoso (USA)) **Nick Mitchell & Bob Frosell**

Other Owners: Mrs P. Elliot, Mr Nick Elliott, Mr Michael Green, Mr Guy Henderson, Mrs Sophie Henderson, Mrs Andrew May, Mr Andrew May, Mr Nick Mitchell, Mrs D. Peck, Mr L. R. Pinkawa, Mr Anthony Shead.

Jockey (NH): Daryl Jacob. **Amateur:** Mr R. G. Henderson.

---

439 MR RICHARD MITCHELL, Dorchester
Postal: **East Hill Stables, Piddletrenthide, Dorchester, Dorset, DT2 7QY**
Contacts: **PHONE/FAX (01300) 348739 MOBILE (07775) 843136**

1 **BEDIBYES**, 5, b m Sleeping Indian—Aunt Sadie **J. R. Boughey**
2 **BETHEHOLYGOBBS (IRE)**, 11, ch g Insan (USA)—Parverb (IRE) **Mrs E. Mitchell**
3 **MASSINI SUNSET (IRE)**, 13, b g Dr Massini (IRE)—Burgundy Sunset (IRE) **Mr & Mrs Andrew May**
4 **REILLYS DAUGHTER**, 5, b m Diktat—Compose **Piddle Valley Racing Club & N R Mitchell**
5 **THUNDERING HOME**, 6, gr g Storming Home—Citrine Spirit (IRE) **Mrs K. M. Boughey**

Other Owners: Mrs S. H. May, A. J. May, N. R. Mitchell.

Assistant Trainer: Mrs E. Mitchell

---

440 MR JAMES MOFFATT, Grange-Over-Sands
Postal: **Pit Farm Racing Stables, Cartmel, Grange-Over-Sands, Cumbria, LA11 6PJ**
Contacts: **PHONE (01539) 536689 FAX (01539) 536236 MOBILE (07767) 367282**
E-MAIL james@jamesmoffatt.co.uk WEBSITE www.jamesmoffatt.co.uk

1 **BLUE LODGE (IRE)**, 7, b g Wareed (IRE)—Glacial Air (IRE) **Mr V. R. Vyner-Brooks**
2 **BOLLIN DOLLY**, 10, ch m Bien Bien (USA)—Bollin Roberta **D. J. Moffatt**
3 **BORDER TALE**, 13, b g Selkirk (USA)—Likely Story (IRE) **D. J. Moffatt**
4 **CAPTAIN RHYRIC**, 4, ch g Dylan Thomas (IRE)—Nuts In May (USA) **Coachmans Cottagers**
5 **DUN MASC (IRE)**, 8, b g Right Win (IRE)—Timber Toes (IRE) **Mr V. R. Vyner-Brooks**
6 **HAMPSFELL**, 5, gr g Distant Music (USA)—Schatzi **Mrs J. A. Moffatt**
7 **ITSTOOEARLY**, 10, br m Overbury (IRE)—Deb's Ball **Kernow Bloodstock**
8 **MAYBE I WONT**, 8, b g Kyllachy—Surprise Surprise **The Sheroot Partnership**
9 **MORNING ROYALTY (IRE)**, 6, b g King's Theatre (IRE)—Portryan Native (IRE) **Mrs E. M. Milligan**
10 **QUEL ELITE (FR)**, 9, b g Subotica (FR)—Jeenly (FR) **Mr M. W. Chapman**

MR JAMES MOFFATT - Continued

11 **SAM LORD**, 9, ch g Observatory (USA)—My Mariam **Coachmans Cottagers**
12 **SEIZE**, 11, gr g Silver Patriarch (IRE)—Sleepline Princess **Mr V. R. Vyner-Brooks**
13 **SMART RULER (IRE)**, 7, ch g Viking Ruler (AUS)—Celebrated Smile (IRE) **The Vilprano Partnership**
14 **TONGALOOMA**, 7, ch m Shinko Forest (IRE)—Schatzi **Mrs J. A. Moffatt**
15 **TROPENFEUER (FR)**, 6, b m Banyumanik (IRE)—Tropensonne (GER) **Walton, Bushell, Moffatt**

THREE-YEAR-OLDS

16 **HANDA ISLAND**, b g Misu Bond (IRE)—Schatzi **Mrs J. A. Moffatt**

Other Owners: K. Bowron, Mr P. E. Bushell, Mrs A. L. Heayns, T. O. Heayns, A. R. Mills, Mr B. Walton, Mr S. Wilson, Mrs J. C. Wilson.

Assistant Trainer: Jennie Moffatt

Jockey (flat): Royston Ffrench, P. J. McDonald, Darren Moffatt. **Jockey (NH):** Brian Harding, Brian Hughes, Wilson Renwick. **Amateur:** Miss Rebecca Sparkes.

---

441 **MR ISMAIL MOHAMMED, Newmarket**
Postal: **Revida Place Stables, Hamilton Road, Newmarket, Suffolk, CB8 7JQ**
Contacts: **PHONE (01638) 669074 MOBILE (07771) 777121**
E-MAIL **diane.carter@dubairacingclub.com**

1 **ADMIRALTY**, 4, b c Iffraaj—Camp Riverside (USA) **A. Al Shaikh**
2 **AUTUMNUS (IRE)**, 4, b c Manduro (GER)—Turning Light (GER) **Mr A. Ali**
3 **CAPE SAMBA**, 4, b c Cape Cross (IRE)—Dancing Feather **Mr I. Mohammed**
4 **COMETOGRAPHY (IRE)**, 4, b c Teofilo (IRE)—Halle Bop **Mr A. Menahi**
5 **EDUCATE**, 4, b g Echo of Light—Pasithea (IRE) **S. Ali**
6 **LIGHT BURST (USA)**, 4, b c Hard Spun (USA)—Kew Garden (USA) **S. H. Altayer**
7 **MUBTADI**, 5, b g Dr Fong (USA)—Noble Peregrine **Mr A. Al Mansoori**

THREE-YEAR-OLDS

8 **ALHAARTH BEAUTY (IRE)**, b f Alhaarth (IRE)—Endis (IRE) **Mr A. Al Mansoori**
9 **ALL DRESSED UP**, b f Pivotal—Satin Finish (IRE) **Mr I. Mohammed**
10 **ANA SHABABIYA (IRE)**, ch f Teofilo (IRE)—Call Later (USA) **A. Al Shaikh**
11 **COURT LIFE (IRE)**, ch c New Approach (IRE)—Tudor Court (IRE) **S. Ali**
12 **MAGIC LANDO (FR)**, b c Lando (GER)—Blackberry Pie **Mr A. Al Mansoori**
13 **RED WARRIOR (IRE)**, ch c Iffraaj—Wiolante (GER) **Mr I. Mohammed**

TWO-YEAR-OLDS

14 B c 11/4 New Approach (IRE)—Al Hasnaa (Zafonic (USA)) (85000) **S. Ali**
15 **MOTAMAYEZAH**, ch f 13/2 Tamayuz—
Classical Dancer (Dr Fong (USA)) (50000) **Sheikh Juma Delmook Al Maktoum**
16 B c 29/4 Iffraaj—Tortue (IRE) (Turtle Island (IRE)) (28000) **S. H. Altayer**
17 B c 15/4 Nayef (USA)—Voile (IRE) (Barathea (IRE)) (20000) **Mr A. Al Mansoori**

---

442 **MRS LAURA MONGAN, Epsom**
Postal: **Condover Stables, Langley Vale Road, Epsom, Surrey, KT18 6AP**
Contacts: **PHONE (01372) 271494 FAX (01372) 271494 MOBILE (07788) 122942**
E-MAIL **ljmongan@hotmail.co.uk WEBSITE www.lauramongan.co.uk**

1 **CASINO STAR**, 4, ch g Norse Dancer (IRE)—Royal Roulette **Mrs P. J. Sheen**
2 **CINEMATIQUE (IRE)**, 5, br g King's Theatre (IRE)—Chantoue Royale (FR) **Mrs P. J. Sheen**
3 **COSSACK PRINCE**, 8, b g Dubai Destination (USA)—Danemere (IRE) **Mrs P. J. Sheen**
4 **DIVINE RULE (IRE)**, 5, br g Cacique (IRE)—Island Destiny **Mrs L. J. Mongan**
5 **FIRST AVENUE**, 8, b g Montjeu (IRE)—Marciala (IRE) **Mrs L. J. Mongan**
6 **KEPPEL ISLE (IRE)**, 4, b g Heron Island (IRE)—Wadi Khaled (FR) **Mrs P. J. Sheen**
7 **MOUNT ABORA (IRE)**, 6, br m Rock of Gibraltar (IRE)—Ragtime Blues (IRE) **Condover Racing**
8 **NORFOLK SKY**, 4, ch f Haafhd—Cayman Sound **Condover Racing**
9 **ORSM**, 6, b g Erhaab (USA)—Royal Roulette **Mrs P. J. Sheen**
10 **PEPITO COLLONGES (FR)**, 10, b g Brier Creek (USA)—Berceuse Collonges (FR) **Mrs P. J. Sheen**
11 **ROSOFF**, 11, b g New Frontier (USA)—Annida (IRE) **Mrs P. J. Sheen**
12 **SEA CADET**, 11, gr g Slip Anchor—Stormy Gal (IRE) **Mrs P. J. Sheen**

MRS LAURA MONGAN - Continued

13 **SHINE IN TIME (IRE)**, 5, b m Definite Article—Time To Shine **Mrs P. J. Sheen**
14 **SYNTHE DAVIS (FR)**, 8, b m Saint des Saints (FR)—Trumpet Davis (FR) **Mrs P. J. Sheen**
15 **TUSCAN GOLD**, 6, ch g Medicean—Louella (USA) **Mrs P. J. Sheen**

Other Owners: Condover Racing, Mrs L. J. Mongan, Mrs P. J. Sheen.

Jockey (flat): Ian Mongan. **Conditional:** Nathan Adams.

---

443 MR ARTHUR MOORE, Naas

Postal: **Dereens, Naas, Co. Kildare, Ireland**
Contacts: PHONE (00353) 4587 6292 FAX (00353) 4589 9247 MOBILE (00353) 8725 52535
E-MAIL arthurlmoore@eircom.net WEBSITE www.arthurmooreracing.com

1 **AUTHINGER (IRE)**, 5, b g Sadler's Wells (USA)—Ange Bleu (USA) **Irish Shamrock Syndicate**
2 **BACK OFF MATE (IRE)**, 5, b g Old Vic—Flyhalf (IRE) **M. Beresford**
3 **BY DESIGN (IRE)**, 7, b g Snurge—Designer Lady (IRE) **Mr J. P. McManus**
4 **CLARAGH NATIVE (IRE)**, 8, ch g Beneficial—Susy In The Summer (IRE) **Not For Friend Partnership**
5 4, B g Milan—Cool Summer (IRE) **J. Byrne**
6 **DANDRIDGE**, 4, ch g Doyen (IRE)—Arantxa **R. Bartlett**
7 **DEAR BOSS (IRE)**, 7, ch g Flemensfirth (USA)—Banderole (IRE) **Mr J. P. McManus**
8 **DRUMLISTER (IRE)**, 7, b g Luso—Murrurundi (IRE) **P. Hale**
9 **EL SORO (FR)**, 5, b g Malinas (GER)—La Esplendida (FR) **P. McCarthy**
10 **GENTLEMAN DUKE (IRE)**, 5, b g Bachelor Duke (USA)—Housekeeping **Mr J. P. McManus**
11 **GOLDEN HERON (IRE)**, 5, b g Heron Island (IRE)—Dear As Gold (IRE) **S. Haughey**
12 **GOWITHDFLO (IRE)**, 6, b m Flemensfirth (USA)—Lady Zephyr (IRE) **Mr M. Jonas**
13 **HIGH DESERT (GER)**, 8, b g Next Desert (IRE)—Helsinki (GER) **T. J. Murray**
14 **HOME FARM (IRE)**, 6, b g Presenting—Tynelucy (IRE) **C. Jones**
15 **HOP IN (IRE)**, 6, b g Flemensfirth (USA)—Prowler (IRE) **C. Hanbury**
16 4, Gr g Stormy River (FR)—In Tune (FR) **Mrs A. L. T. Moore**
17 **LASTOFTHELEADERS (IRE)**, 10, b g Supreme Leader—Heather Breeze (IRE) **Desmond Doherty/Declan Gannon**
18 **MERRYDOWN BLACK**, 5, b g Kayf Tara—Right On Target (IRE) **Mrs P. Sloan**
19 **MIRACLE AT MEDINAH**, 4, b g Kayf Tara—Noisetine (FR) **Mrs A. L. T. Moore**
20 **MITEBEALL FORLUCK**, 5, b g Westerner—Iborga (FR) **C. Hanbury**
21 **ORGANISEDCONFUSION (IRE)**, 8, b g Laveron—Histologie (FR) **Mrs A. Dunlop**
22 **PASS THE HAT**, 6, ch g Karinga Bay—Moor Spring **M. Beresford**
23 4, B g Muhtathir—Pink Topaz (USA) **Mrs A. L. T. Moore**
24 **POSITIVE VIBES**, 4, ch g Nayef (USA)—Steeple **F. Jones**
25 **SIPING (FR)**, 6, b g Sleeping Car (FR)—Maille Sissi (FR) **Mrs A. Dunlop**
26 **TALBOT ROAD (IRE)**, 5, b g Old Vic—Over The Glen (IRE) **J. P. Byrne**
27 **TREAT YOURSELF (IRE)**, 6, b g Beat Hollow—Cartesian **L. Breslin**
28 **WHAT A CHARM (IRE)**, 6, b m Key of Luck (USA)—Atalina (FR) **C. Jones**

THREE-YEAR-OLDS

29 **HARLEY'S HARLEY (IRE)**, b f Cockney Rebel (IRE)—Signella **L. Flood**
30 **QUININE**, b f Dark Angel (IRE)—Quadri **Lady Legard**

TWO-YEAR-OLDS

31 Ch f 13/2 Lomitas—Cool Storm (IRE) (Rainbow Quest (USA)) (4761) **L. Flood**

Assistant Trainer: M. O'Sullivan

Jockey (flat): F. M. Berry, S. Foley. **Jockey (NH):** D. J. Casey, B. Cash, D. Russell. **Conditional:** G. Malone. **Amateur:** Mr N. M. Kelly.

---

444 MR GARY MOORE, Horsham

Postal: **Cisswood Racing Stables, Sandygate Lane, Lower Beeding, Horsham, West Sussex, RH13 6LR**
Contacts: HOME (01403) 891997 YARD (01403) 891912 FAX (01403) 891924
MOBILE (07753) 863123
E-MAIL garyjayne.moore@virgin.net WEBSITE www.garymooreracing.com

1 **ACCESS**, 5, b g Diktat—All About Love (GER) **Mr J. C. Hingston**
2 **AL AMAAN**, 8, b g Nayef (USA)—Siobhan **Mr Mark Waters**

MR GARY MOORE - Continued

3 **ALLTERRAIN (IRE)**, 10, b g Almutawakel—
Queen of Art (IRE) **Mr Raymond Petchey & Mr & Mrs David Newland**
4 **AMAURY DE LUSIGNAN (IRE)**, 7, b g Dushyantor (USA)—Celtic Sails (IRE) **Mr A. E. Dean**
5 **AMEN (IRE)**, 5, b g Galileo (IRE)—Kitza (IRE) **Heart Of The South Racing**
6 **ANNESBROOK (IRE)**, 7, b g Needle Gun (IRE)—Stefphonic (IRE) **Lady Forwood**
7 **AROUND THE WORLD (GER)**, 4, br f Samum (GER)—Arpista (GER) **Stiftung Gestut Fahrhof**
8 **ASKER (IRE)**, 5, b g High Chaparral (IRE)—Pay The Bank **Mr Nurlan Bizakov**
9 **BALLYHEIGUE (IRE)**, 4, b g High Chaparral (IRE)—Lypharden (IRE) **Mr Tony Head**
10 **BE ALL MAN (IRE)**, 6, b g Dubawi (IRE)—Belle Allemande (CAN) **Mr A. Head, Mr R. Lockwood & Mr M. Burne**
11 5, B g High-Rise (IRE)—Beardie's Dream (IRE)
12 **BERGO (GER)**, 10, b g Silvano (GER)—Bella Figura (USA) **Mrs A. Burrows**
13 **BERT THE ALERT**, 5, b g Proclamation (IRE)—Megalex **Herbert, Curwen, Hinds & Waddington**
14 **BOBBYSCOT (IRE)**, 6, b g Alhaarth (IRE)—Sogno Verde (IRE) **Mr Ramzan Kadyrov**
15 **BOW QUEST**, 6, b m Rainbow High—Fair Kai (IRE) **Mr E. A. Condon**
16 **BRAVE VIC (IRE)**, 5, b g Old Vic—Baliya (IRE) **R. Henderson**
17 **CABIMAS**, 6, b g King's Best (USA)—Casanga (IRE) **Stiftung Gestut Fahrhof**
18 **CANDLEFORT LADY (IRE)**, 8, b m Beneficial—Lady Blayney (IRE) **Mr E. A. Condon**
19 **CHARITABLE ACT (FR)**, 4, b g Cadeaux Genereux—Acatama (USA) **G. A. Jackman**
20 **CHARLIE CHEESECAKE (IRE)**, 7, br g Kayf Tara—Darabaka (IRE) **Mr Graham Gillespie**
21 **CHECKPOINT**, 4, ch g Zamindar (USA)—Kalima **Mr Ben Hayes**
22 **CHIEFY (IRE)**, 5, b g Milan—Womenofninetyeight (IRE) **Mr A. E. Dean**
23 **CHRIS PEA GREEN**, 4, b g Proclamation (IRE)—
Another Secret **C. Green & Galloping On The South Downs Partnership**
24 **CRUZ ON TED**, 6, b g Helissio (FR)—Dublivia **Mr Tony Head**
25 **DALAYIR (FR)**, 6, gr g Tiger Hill (GER)—Dalataya (IRE) **C. E. Stedman**
26 **DE BLACKSMITH (IRE)**, 5, b g Brian Boru—Gift of the Gab (IRE) **Mrs Elizabeth Kiernan**
27 **DEUX ETOILES (IRE)**, 6, b g Montjeu (IRE)—Onereuse **Heart Of The South Racing**
28 **DOROTHY'S DANCING (IRE)**, 5, b m Acclamation—Segoria (IRE) **Mr T. Glynn**
29 **DR THISTLE (IRE)**, 6, b g Dr Massini (IRE)—Thistle Thyme (IRE) **Mr D. Leon**
30 **DUTCH OLD MASTER**, 4, b g Jeremy (USA)—Wicken Wonder **Mr R. A. Green**
31 **DYNAMIC IDOL (USA)**, 6, b g Dynaformer (USA)—El Nafis (USA) **Heart Of The South Racing**
32 **FATHOM FIVE (IRE)**, 9, b g Fath (USA)—Ambria (ITY) **Win, Drooze Or Law Partnership**
33 **FORGET IT**, 8, b g Galileo (IRE)—Queens Way (FR) **The Cockpit Crew**
34 **FRUITY O'ROONEY**, 10, b g Kahyasi—Recipe **Heart Of The South Racing**
35 **GAELIC SILVER (FR)**, 7, b g Lando (GER)—Galatza (FR) **The Winning Hand**
36 **GALIOTTO (IRE)**, 7, b g Galileo (IRE)—Welsh Motto (USA) **Mr A. D. Bradmore**
37 **GEE DEE NEN**, 10, b g Mister Baileys—Special Beat **Mr C. Duggan & Mr B. Gilligan**
38 **GIGONDAS**, 4, ch g Grape Tree Road—Queen's Dancer **C. E. Stedman**
39 **GOLANOVA**, 5, b g Golan (IRE)—Larkbarrow **Galloping On The South Downs Partnership**
40 **GOOD LUCK CHARM**, 4, b g Doyen (IRE)—Lucky Dice **Heart Of The South Racing**
41 **GRABTHEGLORY (IRE)**, 7, b g Accordion—Full of Surprises (IRE) **Mr Stanley J. Cohen**
42 **GUARDS CHAPEL**, 5, b g Motivator—Intaaj (IRE) **Mr A. D. Bradmore**
43 **HARRY TRICKER**, 9, b g Hernando (FR)—Katy Nowaitee **Mr R. A. Green**
44 **HERSCHEL (IRE)**, 7, br g Dr Fong (USA)—Rafting (IRE) **Mr G. L. Moore**
45 4, B g Gold Well—Hillside Native (IRE)
46 **JODAWES (USA)**, 6, b br g Burning Roma (USA)—Venetian Peach (USA) **Stephen Fisher & Pat Wilkins**
47 **JOLLY'S CRACKED IT (FR)**, 4, b g Astarabad (USA)—Jolly Harbour **GDM Partnership**
48 **JUPITER STORM**, 4, ch g Galileo (IRE)—Exciting Times (FR) **Heart Of The South Racing**
49 **KAMBIS**, 5, b g Tobougg (IRE)—Queen Tomyra (IRE) **Mr & Mrs Leslie Vine**
50 **KAYLEE**, 4, b f Selkirk (USA)—Mrs Brown **Mr D. Phelan**
51 **KINGSFOLD FLARE**, 6, ch m Central Park (IRE)—Kingsfold Blaze **8 Wealth Management**
52 **KNIGHT OF PLEASURE**, 4, ch g Exit To Nowhere (USA)—Kim Fontenail (FR) **The Knights Of Pleasure**
53 **LAJIDAAL (USA)**, 6, b g Dynaformer (USA)—Tayibah (IRE) **Dedman Properties**
54 **LEO LUNA**, 4, b g Galileo (IRE)—Eva Luna (USA) **Mr P. B. Moorhead**
55 **LIGHT WELL (IRE)**, 5, b g Sadler's Wells (USA)—L'ancresse (IRE) **Mr B. D. Siddle, Mr B. D. Haynes**
56 **LIGHTNING SPIRIT**, 5, b m Storming Home—Lucky Dice **Heart Of The South Racing**
57 **LOMBOK**, 7, b g Hernando (FR)—Miss Rinjani **Pink Punters & Partners**
58 **LORD SINGER (FR)**, 8, b g Secret Singer (FR)—Cricale (FR) **The Winning Hand**
59 **MEGASTAR**, 8, b g Kayf Tara—Megalex **Galloping On The South Downs Partnership**
60 **MINISTRY**, 5, b g Iceman—Choirgirl **Mr Phil Collins**
61 **MODERATOR**, 4, b g Motivator—Alessandra **Mr D. J. Deer**
62 **MOUNTAINEER (FR)**, 4, b g Saint des Saints (FR)—Mistica (FR) **C. E. Stedman**
63 **MR FICKLE (IRE)**, 4, b g Jeremy (USA)—Mamara Reef **Mr Tony Perkins**
64 **NEBULA STORM (IRE)**, 6, b g Galileo (IRE)—Epping **Mr R. H. MacNabb**
65 **NETHERBY**, 7, b g Fair Mix (IRE)—Lissadell (IRE) **Mr R. A. Green**

MR GARY MOORE - Continued

66 **NEW CODE**, 6, ch g Reset (AUS)—Illeana (GER) **Mrs Elizabeth Kiernan**
67 **PETIT ECUYER (FR)**, 7, b g Equerry (USA)—Petite Majeste (FR) **A. Jee, F. Ledger, J. Bateman**
68 **PICTURE DEALER**, 4, b g Royal Applause—Tychy **Mr R. A. Green**
69 **PORTRAIT EMOTION (IRE)**, 6, ch g Portrait Gallery (IRE)—Gleann Present (IRE) **Heart Of The South Racing**
70 **PSI (USA)**, 8, b g Hernando (FR)—Visions of Clarity (IRE) **Mr Nick Peacock**
71 **QUAILS HOLLOW (IRE)**, 5, b g Beat Hollow—Bloemfontain (IRE) **Mr A. Head, Mr R. Lockwood & Mr M. Burne**
72 **RAJAMAND (FR)**, 7, gr g Linamix (FR)—Ridafa (IRE) **GDM Partnership**
73 **REGAL PARK (IRE)**, 6, b g Montjeu (IRE)—Classic Park **Mrs A. Gloag**
74 **REZWAAN**, 6, b g Alhaarth (IRE)—Nasij (USA) **Gallagher Equine Limited**
75 **RIDGEWAY KEZIA**, 5, b m Tobougg (IRE)—Al Kahina **Mr Albert Neaves**
76 **RIGHT STUFF (FR)**, 10, b br g Dansili—Specificity (USA) **The Ashden Partnership & Partners**
77 4, Ch g Generous (IRE)—Saffron Pride (IRE) **Mr Philip Herbert**
78 **SANTADELACRUZE**, 4, b c Pastoral Pursuits—Jupiters Princess **Mr D. M. & Mrs M. A. Newland**
79 **SAWAGO (FR)**, 7, b br g Gold Away (FR)—Maikawa (FR) **Mr M. D. Ogburn**
80 **SHADARPOUR (IRE)**, 4, b c Dr Fong (USA)—Shamadara (IRE) **G. L. Porter**
81 **SHAMAHAN**, 4, b c Shamardal (USA)—Hanella (IRE) **Heart Of The South Racing**
82 **SILVER BULLITT**, 5, gr g Proclamation (IRE)—Eurolinka (IRE) **Dahab Racing**
83 **SIRCOZY (IRE)**, 7, b g Celtic Swing—Furnish **Mr G. L. Moore**
84 **SIRE DE GRUGY (FR)**, 7, ch g My Risk (FR)—Hirlish (FR) **The Preston Family & Friends**
85 **SOUTH CAPE**, 10, b g Cape Cross (IRE)—Aunt Ruby (USA) **Heart Of The South Racing & Friends**
86 **STEELY**, 5, b g Librettist (USA)—No Comebacks **Mr E. A. Condon**
87 **STENTORIAN (IRE)**, 5, ch g Street Cry (IRE)—Nomistakeaboutit (CAN) **B. G. Homewood**
88 **TENURE**, 4, b g Dansili—Alumni **Mr R. A. Green**
89 **THE GAME IS A FOOT (IRE)**, 6, b g Oscar (IRE)—Cooksgrove Rosie (IRE) **Mr G. L. Moore**
90 **TOTHEMOONANDBACK (IRE)**, 5, gr g Dr Massini (IRE)—Mrs Jones (FR) **David & Jane George**
91 **UBAK (FR)**, 5, b g Kapgarde (FR)—Gesse Parade (FR) **Mr N. J. Peacock**
92 **VINO GRIEGO (FR)**, 8, b g Kahyasi—Vie de Reine (FR) **C. E. Stedman**
93 **WAARID**, 8, b g Alhaarth (IRE)—Nibbs Point (IRE) **Mr G. L. Moore**
94 **WELL REFRESHED**, 9, b g Nikos—Cool Spring (IRE) **P. J. Wilmott**
95 **WHILE YOU WAIT (IRE)**, 4, b g Whipper (USA)—Azra (IRE) **Galloping On The South Downs Partnership**
96 **WHINGING WILLIE (IRE)**, 4, b g Cape Cross (IRE)—Pacific Grove **Mr P. B. Moorhead**
97 **WHITBY JACK**, 6, b g Bering—Sablonne (USA) **C. E. Stedman**
98 **WINNING SPARK (USA)**, 6, b g Theatrical—Spark Sept (FR) **Mrs Elizabeth Kiernan Paul Chapman**
99 **WOOLFALL TREASURE**, 8, gr g Daylami (IRE)—Treasure Trove (USA) **Mr A. D. Bradmore**
100 **ZOUTI (FR)**, 5, b g Kahyasi—Reine de Sabot (FR) **Mr David Miles & Mr M. G. Rogers**

THREE-YEAR-OLDS

101 **ANJUNA BEACH (USA)**, b c Artie Schiller (USA)—Hidden Temper (USA) **C. E. Stedman**
102 **BALTIC BLADE (IRE)**, b c Baltic King—Anita's Contessa (IRE) **Mr J. R. Craik-White**
103 **BUILDING ZIET**, b g Dubai Destination (USA)—Zietunzeen (IRE) **Mrs M. Shenkin & Dr I. Shenkin**
104 **BUY ART**, b c Acclamation—Kondakova (USA) **Mr R. A. Green**
105 **CHOCOLATE CAVIAR (IRE)**, ch f Tamayuz—Jazz Up **Dahab Racing**
106 **COULOIR EXTREME (IRE)**, gr c Verglas (IRE)—Chica Roca (USA) **C. E. Stedman**
107 **DELPHICA (IRE)**, b f Acclamation—Expectation (IRE) **Dahab Racing**
108 **DUTCH MASTERPIECE**, b g Dutch Art—The Terrier **Mr R. A. Green**
109 **FREDDY WITH A Y (IRE)**, b g Amadeus Wolf—Mataji (IRE) **Mrs M. J. George**
110 **GREAT CRESTED (IRE)**, br gr c Clodovil (IRE)—Roskeen (IRE) **Gallagher Equine Limited**
111 **HANGA ROA (IRE)**, b g Hannouma (IRE)—Fine And Mellow (FR) **C. E. Stedman**
112 **JUBILEE BRIG**, b g Kheleyf (USA)—Voile (IRE) **Lookout Partnership**
113 **LYBICA (IRE)**, b f Galileo (IRE)—Tingling (USA) **Ms Sylvia Vrska**
114 **MARMALADY (IRE)**, ch f Duke of Marmalade (IRE)—Grecian Glory (IRE) **Heart Of The South Racing**
115 **MY GIGI**, b f Medicean—Choirgirl **Mrs H. J. Moorhead**
116 **ONE DARK NIGHT**, b g Proclamation (IRE)—Night Storm **Mr W. Thornton & Mr R. E. Anderson**
117 **OUR THREE GRACES (IRE)**, b f Red Clubs (IRE)—Villa Nova (IRE) **Mr P. B. Moorhead**
118 **OVETT**, b c Exceed And Excel (AUS)—Stormy Weather **8 Wealth Management**
119 B f Black Sam Bellamy (IRE)—Queen's Dancer **C. E. Stedman**
120 **SAND AND DELIVER**, b f Royal Applause—Alhufoof (USA) **P. D. Crate**
121 B g Dubai Destination (USA)—Takegawa **Leydans Farm Stud**
122 **VIOLET DANCER**, b g Bertolini (USA)—Another Secret **Galloping On The South Downs Partnership**

TWO-YEAR-OLDS

123 B c 24/2 Dutch Art—Censored (Pivotal) (50000) **Mr R. A. Green**
124 B f 6/4 Duke of Marmalade (IRE)—Empress Anna (IRE) (Imperial Ballet (IRE)) (20000) **Sir Eric Parker**
125 B f 6/4 Proclamation (IRE)—Night Storm (Night Shift (USA)) **Mr R. E. Anderson**

MR GARY MOORE - Continued

Other Owners: Mr A. J. Allright, Dr C. A. Barnett, Mr Wayne Barr, Mr J. Bateman, Mr T. Bates, Mr C. Bird, Mr R. Brown, Rev L. M. Brown, Mr M. Burne, Mr A. M. Carding, Mr Paul Chapman, Mr Gregory Charlesworth, Mr Daniel Charlesworth, Mr Chris Duggan, Mr S. Fisher, Mr Bryan Fry, Mr D. W. George, Mrs Jane George, Mr Bill Gibson, Mr Brendan Gilligan, Mr M. Goodrum, Mr I. Gould, Mr Chris Green, Mr B. D. Haynes, Mr Ashley Head, Mr Philip Herbert, Mr R. W. Hills, Mrs Elizabeth Kiernan, Mrs F. Ledger, Mr S. C. Lee, Mr Richard Lockwood, Mr D. Miles, Mr G. L. Moore, Mr D. Newland, Mrs M. A. Newland, Mr John Penny, Miss Eloise Penny, Mr Terence Pollock, Mr S. Preston, Mr John Ripley, Mr M. G. Rogers, www.Select-Racing-Club.co.uk, Mr D. Sheldon, Mr R. K. Simmons, Mr Michael Smith, Mr L. R. Vine, Mrs S. J. Vine, Ms Sylvia Vrska, Mr M. C. Waddingham, Mrs P. A. Wilkins, Mr David J. Wood.

Assistant Trainer: David Wilson

Jockey (flat): George Baker, Ryan Moore, Fergus Sweeney. **Jockey (NH):** Andrew Glassonbury, Jamie Moore. **Conditional:** Joshua Moore, Lee Oswin. **Apprentice:** Ned Curtis. **Amateur:** Miss Hayley Moore.

MR GEORGE MOORE, Middleham
Postal: **Warwick Lodge Stables, Middleham, Leyburn, North Yorkshire, DL8 4PB**
Contacts: **PHONE (01969) 623823 FAX (01969) 623823 MOBILE (07711) 321117**
E-MAIL georgeandcarolmoore@hotmail.co.uk WEBSITE www.george-moore-racing.co.uk

1 **ALFAPOINT,** 5, ch g Alflora (IRE)—Rascella **Barrow Brook Racing**
2 **ARIZONA RIVER,** 7, b m Fair Mix (IRE)—Halo Flora **Miss S. R. Robertson**
3 **BIJOU DAN,** 12, ch g Bijou d'inde—Cal Norma's Lady (IRE) **Mrs I. I. Plumb**
4 **BRASINGAMAN ERIC,** 6, b g Bollin Eric—Serene Pearl (IRE) **Mr R. J. Morgan**
5 **BRASINGAMAN ESPEE,** 4, b g Silver Patriarch (IRE)—Serene Pearl (IRE) **Mr R. J. Morgan**
6 **CHARLES DE MILLE,** 5, b g Tiger Hill (IRE)—Apple Town **Mrs Liz Ingham**
7 **COWSLIP,** 4, b f Tobougg (IRE)—Forsythia
8 **DANBIRD'S FORTUNE,** 6, b g Danbird (AUS)—Fortune's Filly **Mrs G. A. Kendall**
9 **EXCLUSIVE DANCER,** 4, gr f Notnowcato—Exclusive Approval (USA) **Mr D. Parker**
10 **FINELLAS FORTUNE,** 8, b m Elmaamul (USA)—Fortune's Filly **Mrs G. A. Kendall**
11 **HI BOB,** 5, b g Bollin Eric—Leading Line **J. B. Wallwin**
12 **ISOLDE'S RETURN,** 4, b f Avonbridge—Up And About **Mrs Liz Ingham**
13 **JACK THE GENT (IRE),** 9, b g Anshan—Asidewager (IRE) **J. B. Wallwin**
14 **JUST FABULOUS,** 4, b f Sakhee (USA)—Tipsy Me **Mr S. Graham**
15 **KEALSHORE,** 6, ch g Alflora (IRE)—Top of The Dee **Mr J. Pickavance**
16 **KEALSHORE AGAIN (IRE),** 4, br g Exit To Nowhere (USA)—Sinnaja **Mr J. Pickavance**
17 **LADY AMAKHALA,** 5, b m Val Royal (FR)—Isla Negra (IRE) **Mrs D. N. B. Pearson**
18 **MASKA PONY (IRE),** 9, gr g Celtic Swing—Clotted Cream (USA) **Diane Russell & Paul Blair**
19 **NEVER FOREVER,** 4, ch g Sir Percy—Codename **Northern Premier Partnership**
20 **PETELLA,** 7, b m Tamure (IRE)—Miss Petronella **A. Crute & Partners**
21 **PUY D'ARNAC (FR),** 10, b g Acteur Francais (USA)—Chaumeil (FR) **Barrow Brook Racing**
22 **SILVER TIGRESS,** 5, gr m Tiger Hill (IRE)—Cinnamon Tree (IRE) **A. Crute & Partners**
23 **STARS LEGACY,** 4, b f Presidium—Pagan Star **Mr R. Phizacklea**
24 **TARANTELLA LADY,** 5, b m Noverre (USA)—Shortfall **Mr D. Parker**
25 **THE SHY MAN (IRE),** 10, b g Grand Plaisir (IRE)—Black Betty **Mr S. P. Graham**
26 **TOURTIERE,** 5, b g Act One—Kindle **Mr J. Andrews**
27 **TURF TRIVIA,** 6, gr g Alhaarth (IRE)—Exclusive Approval (USA) **Mrs M. Hatfield & Mrs S. Kramer**
28 **WOLF SHIELD (IRE),** 6, b g King's Theatre (IRE)—Garlucy (IRE) **G. R. Orchard**

THREE-YEAR-OLDS

29 **BELLA CINDERELLA,** b f Tiger Hill (IRE)—Design Perfection (USA) **A. Crute & Partners**
30 **DON'T TELL,** ch f Sakhee's Secret—Starry Sky **Evelyn, Duchess of Sutherland**
31 **ERICA STARPRINCESS,** b f Bollin Eric—Presidium Star **Mr R. Phizacklea**
32 **LADY POPPY,** b f Kyllachy—Poppets Sweetlove **Ingham Racing Syndicate**

TWO-YEAR-OLDS

33 **BENTONS LAD,** b g 21/4 Bollin Eric—Spirit of Ecstacy (Val Royal (FR)) **Mrs D. N. B. Pearson**
34 B g 26/4 Multiplex—Blushing Heart (Observatory (USA)) **Mrs D. N. B. Pearson**
35 B c 8/2 Pastoral Pursuits—Extreme Pleasure (IRE) (High Chaparral (IRE)) (761)
36 **LADY YEATS,** b f 13/2 Yeats (IRE)—Oblique (IRE) (Giant's Causeway (USA)) (8000) **A. Crute & Partners**
37 **ROKEBY,** b c 7/4 Byron—Scarlet Royal (Red Ransom (USA)) **Mrs Liz Ingham**
38 B f 9/1 Byron—Sister Rose (FR) (One Cool Cat (USA)) (4761) **Mrs Liz Ingham**

MR GEORGE MOORE - Continued

Other Owners: Mrs J. M. Gray, Mrs Mary Hatfield, Mrs Susan Kramer, Mr Peter Thompson, Mr J. Townson.

Assistant Trainer: Mrs Susan Moore

Jockey (flat): P. J. McDonald, Andrew Mullen. **Jockey (NH):** Barry Keniry. **Conditional:** Joseph Palmowski. **Amateur:** Mr Mathew Garnett.

446

MR J. S. MOORE, Upper Lambourn
Postal: **Berkeley House Stables, Upper Lambourn, Hungerford, Berkshire, RG17 8QP**
Contacts: **PHONE (01488) 73887 FAX (01488) 73997 MOBILE (07860) 811127 / (07900) 402856**
E-MAIL jsmoore.racing@btopenworld.com WEBSITE www.stanmooreracing.co.uk

1 EVERVESCENT (IRE), 4, b g Elnadim (USA)—Purepleasureseeker (IRE) **Ever Equine**
2 LOYAL MASTER (IRE), 4, b g Modigliani (USA)—Santa Gertrudis (IRE) **Mr R. Hull**
3 ROSEWOOD LAD, 6, ch g Needwood Blade—Meandering Rose (USA) **Miss D L Wisbey & Mr R J Viney**
4 SHEILA'S BUDDY, 4, ch g Reel Buddy (USA)—Loreto Rose **R. J. Styles**

THREE-YEAR-OLDS
5 ALFAISALIAH (IRE), b f Red Clubs (IRE)—Falcolnry (IRE) **Sheikh A. H. F. M. A. Al Sabah**
6 ALMALEKIAH (IRE), gr f Clodovil (IRE)—Majestic Night (IRE) **Sheikh A. H. F. M. A. Al Sabah**
7 AMELIA HULL, b f Byron—Sweetypie (IRE) **Mr R. Hull**
8 BLACK EYED GIRL (IRE), br f Jeremy—Holda (IRE) **Mr Mrs Evelyn Yates Mr T Yates and J S Moore**
9 DON EDUARDO, b c Byron—Angie And Liz (IRE) **Mr Mrs Evelyn Yates Mr T Yates and J S Moore**
10 ELUSIVE THOUGHT (IRE), b g Elusive City (USA)—Thought Is Free **Mrs F. H. Hay**
11 EVERREADYNEDDY, ch g Ad Valorem (USA)—Maugwenna **Ever Equine 2**
12 FIACHRA (IRE), b g Elnadim (USA)—Nesaah's Princess **Mr Peter Grimes**
13 GRACE HULL, gr f Piccolo—Smart Hostess **Mr R. Hull**
14 INESSA ARMAND (IRE), ch f Shamardal (USA)—Shakti **Norton Common Farm Racing Ltd**
15 LADY LUNCHALOT (USA), b f More Than Ready (USA)—Betty Johanne (USA) **Mr M. A. Briddon & J. S. Moore**
16 MYZAMOUR, b f Azamour (IRE)—Lady Ragazza (IRE) **R. J. Styles**
17 PADDY'S SALTANTES (IRE), b c Redback—Shall We Tell **Wall To Wall Partnership**
18 PIXIE CUT (IRE), b f Chineur (FR)—Fantastic Cee (IRE) **Mr G V March & J S Moore**
19 PRINCESS SHEILA (IRE), b f Jeremy (USA)—Princess Atoosa (USA) **Mr Ray Styles & J. S. Moore**
20 RAKTICATE (IRE), b f Rakti—Authenticate **Mr G V March & J S Moore**
21 SALUTE TO SEVILLE (IRE), b f Duke of Marmalade (IRE)—Vingt Et Une (FR) **Dr Dean Harron & J S Moore**
22 STAR OF NAMIBIA (IRE), b c Cape Cross (IRE)—Sparkle of Stones (FR) **Mr Ray Styles & J. S. Moore**
23 TEOLAGI (IRE), ch c Teofilo (IRE)—Satulagi (USA) **Mrs F. H. Hay**
24 THE BLACK JACOBIN, b g Piccolo—Greenfly **Norton Common Farm Racing Ltd**
25 TILLY T (IRE), b f Thousand Words—Pippi (IRE) **J. S. Moore**

TWO-YEAR-OLDS
26 Br c 14/4 Footstepsinthesand—Animalu (IRE) (Dalakhani (IRE)) (9047)
27 B c 20/4 Bahamian Bounty—Anthea (Tobougg (IRE)) (4000) **Paul Mendoza & J. S. Moore**
28 AWEEBITOWINKER, ch g 28/2 Winker Watson—
                                        French Connexion (IRE) (Chineur (FR)) (1428) **Mr & Mrs Yates & Mr M Fisher**
29 B f 17/4 Acclamation—Cloonkeary (In The Wings) (1428) **Mr Peter Grimes & J. S. Moore**
30 COCKNEY BOB, b g 19/4 Cockney Rebel (IRE)—Wizby (Wizard King) (476) **Miss D L Wisbey & Mr R Viney**
31 B f 13/5 Excellent Art—Colour And Spice (IRE) (Machiavellian (USA)) (7936) **Eventmasters Ltd.**
32 B f 26/3 Sakhee's Secret—Diliza (Dilum (USA)) (4200)
33 B f 9/4 Multiplex—Ella Y Rossa (Bertolini (USA)) (1904) **Miss D L Wisbey & Mr R J Viney**
34 B g 3/3 Elnadim (USA)—Endis (IRE) (Distant Relative) (3967) **Mr K Kirkup & J S Moore**
35 B c 25/4 Diamond Green (FR)—Florista Gg (URU) (Gulpha Gorge (USA)) **Mrs F. H. Hay**
36 B f 9/4 Sakhee's Secret—Forest Girl (IRE) (Shinko Forest (IRE)) (1190)
37 ISLAND KINGDOM (IRE), ch c 2/4 Duke of Marmalade (IRE)—
                                        Tohama (In The Wings) (1904) **Mr D Kerr & J S Moore**
38 B c 17/4 Thousand Words—Lady Piste (IRE) (Ali-Royal (IRE)) (3333)
39 B f 14/3 Bushranger (IRE)—Lady Thyne (IRE) (Mujadil (USA)) (476)
40 B f 11/4 Byron—Last Romance (IRE) (Last Tycoon) (952)
41 B f 19/2 Ad Valorem (USA)—Monsusu (IRE) (Montjeu (USA)) (4761)
42 B c 3/3 Balmont (USA)—Novosibirsk (USA) (Distant View (USA)) (1586) **The Moore The Merrier**
43 B g 3/3 Ad Valorem (USA)—Peps (IRE) (Val Royal (FR)) (3809) **Mr G B Watts & J S Moore**
44 B g 11/2 Oratorio (IRE)—Personal Design (IRE) (Traditionally (USA)) (5238)
45 SHEILA'S FOOTSTEPS, b g 19/4 Footstepsinthesand—
                                        Marmaga (IRE) (Shernazar) (4761) **Mr Ray Styles & J. S. Moore**

MR J. S. MOORE - Continued

46 Ch f 17/3 Firebreak—Smooth As Silk (IRE) (Danehill Dancer (IRE)) (2200) **Mr Paul Mendoza & J. S. Moore**
47 B c 21/4 Diamond Green (FR)—Soul Society (IRE) (Inchinor) (6666) **Mrs A G Kavanagh & J S Moore**
48 B g 21/4 Art Connoisseur (IRE)—Tomanivi (Caerleon (USA)) (9523)
49 **VODKA CHASER (IRE),** b f 25/1 Baltic King—
          Suffer Her (IRE) (Whipper (USA)) (6190) **Mr N Attenborough, Mrs L Mann, J S Moore**
50 B f 24/2 Lawman (FR)—Zingari (Groom Dancer (USA)) (3571) **Mr G V March & J S Moore**

Other Owners: Mr N. B. Attenborough, Mr Gerry Connor, Mr Kevin Elliott, Mr M. Feehan, Mr Ian J. Gray, Dr Dean Harron, Mrs A. Jones, Mrs Lyndsey Mann, Mr G. V. March, Marchwood Aggregates, Mr J. S. Moore, Mr Sean O'Sullivan, Mr S. Sheehan, Mr Ray Styles, Mr R. J. Viney, Miss D. L. Wisbey, Mr T. Yates, Mrs Evelyn Yates.

Assistant Trainer: Mrs S. Moore

Jockey (flat): Liam Keniry, Luke Morris. **Apprentice:** Ryan Powell, Charlotte Jenner.

---

447 **MR KEVIN MORGAN, Newmarket**
Postal: Gazeley Park Stables, 13 - 15 Moulton Road, Gazeley, Newmarket, Suffolk, CB8 8RA
Contacts: **PHONE (01638) 551888 FAX (01638) 551888 MOBILE (07768) 996103**
E-MAIL morgan.k@btconnect.com

1 ANAN, 7, br g Cape Cross (IRE)—Hawafiz **Roemex Ltd**
2 EZDIYAAD (IRE), 9, b g Galileo (IRE)—Wijdan (USA) **Roemex Ltd**
3 ISDAAL, 6, ch m Dubawi (IRE)—Faydah (USA) **Roemex Ltd**
4 7, Ch m Karinga Bay—Nessfield **Mr J. Duckworth**
5 RAAMZ (IRE), 6, ch m Haafhd—Tarbiyah **Roemex Ltd**
6 TAARESH (IRE), 8, b g Sakhee (USA)—Tanaghum **Roemex Ltd**

Head Lad: S. Rathore

Jockey (flat): Jimmy Quinn. **Jockey (NH):** Leighton Aspell.

---

448 **MR DAVE MORRIS, Newmarket**
Postal: Mokefield, Baxters Green, Wickhambrook, Newmarket, Suffolk, CB8 8UY
Contacts: **PHONE (01284) 850248 FAX (01284) 850248 MOBILE (07711) 010268**

1 CHEZ VRONY, 7, b g Lujain (USA)—Polish Abbey **Stag & Huntsman**
2 DARWINIAN, 4, b f Three Valleys (USA)—Force of Nature (USA) **D. P. Fremel**
3 ZAHEEB, 5, b g Haafhd—Gay Music (FR) **Mr S. C. Wood**

Other Owners: Ms C. C. Fagerstrom, The Hon W. H. Smith.

Jockey (flat): Franny Norton.

---

449 **MR M. F. MORRIS, Fethard**
Postal: Everardsgrange, Fethard, Co. Tipperary, Ireland
Contacts: **PHONE (00353) 52 6131474 FAX (00353) 52 6131654**
E-MAIL mouse@eircom.net

1 BAILY DUSK (IRE), 7, br g Dushyantor (USA)—Gentle Lady (IRE) **A. R. Scott**
2 BAILY GREEN (IRE), 7, b g King's Theatre (IRE)—Dream On Boys (IRE) **A. R. Scott**
3 BORN IN FIRE (FR), 5, b g Limnos (JPN)—Maranta (FR) **Gigginstown Stud**
4 BRUFF (IRE), 6, b g Presenting—Aniston (IRE) **J. P. McManus**
5 CALL ROG (IRE), 5, b g Beneficial—Lady Fancy (IRE) **J. P. McManus**
6 CARRY EACH OTHER (IRE), 7, b g Milan—Jennys Supreme (IRE) **Gigginstown Stud**
7 CHINA ROCK (IRE), 10, ch g Presenting—Kigali (IRE) **Mr M. O'Flynn**
8 DROMNEA (IRE), 6, b br g Presenting—Fifth Imp (IRE) **Mrs A. Daly**
9 ELYSIAN ROCK (IRE), 9, b g King's Theatre (IRE)—Elaine Tully (IRE) **Mr M. O'Flynn**
10 FIRST LIEUTENANT (IRE), 8, ch g Presenting—Fourstargale (IRE) **Gigginstown Stud**
11 MIRADANE, 6, b g Kayf Tara—Coolvawn Lady (IRE) **B. Maloney**
12 PRESENT POTENTIAL (IRE), 6, b g Presenting—Calbrooke (IRE) **B. Maloney**
13 RATHLIN, 8, b g Kayf Tara—Princess Timon **Gigginstown Stud**
14 RAVISHED (IRE), 5, b g Oscar (IRE)—Fair Present (IRE) **Gigginstown Stud**
15 ROGUE ANGEL (IRE), 5, b g Presenting—Carrigeen Kohleria (IRE) **Gigginstown Stud**

MR M. F. MORRIS - Continued

16 **RULE THE WORLD**, 6, b g Sulamani (IRE)—Elaine Tully (IRE) **Gigginstown Stud**
17 **SPOT FINE**, 7, b g Kayf Tara—Lily The Lark **M. & J. O'Flynn**
18 **TILLAHOW (IRE)**, 6, b g Tillerman—Ale' Ale' (USA) **Gigginstown Stud**
19 **TINAKELLYLAD (IRE)**, 9, b g Witness Box (USA)—Iora (IRE) **Mrs B. Twomey**
20 **WAR CORRESPONDENT (IRE)**, 6, b g Westerner—Una Juna (IRE) **Gigginstown Stud**

450	**MR PAT MORRIS, Prescot**

Postal: **Avenue House, George Hale Avenue, Knowsley Park, Prescot, Merseyside, L34 4AJ**
Contacts: **MOBILE (07545) 425235**
E-MAIL info@patmorrisracing.co.uk WEBSITE www.patmorrisracing.co.uk

THREE-YEAR-OLDS

1 **CLAUDE GREENWOOD**, b g Lucky Story (USA)—Greenmeadow **Dr M. B. Q. S. Koukash**
2 **GABRIAL THE DUKE (IRE)**, ch g Duke of Marmalade (IRE)—Literacy (USA) **Dr M. B. Q. S. Koukash**
3 **LAYLA'S OASIS**, b f Oasis Dream—Kirk **Dr M. B. Q. S. Koukash**
4 **LEXI'S BEAUTY (IRE)**, br f Kheleyf (USA)—Voyage of Dreams (USA) **Dr M. B. Q. S. Koukash**
5 **RAINFORD GLORY (IRE)**, ch g Rock of Gibraltar (IRE)—My Dolly Madison **Dr M. B. Q. S. Koukash**

TWO-YEAR-OLDS

6 B f 2/5 Dalakhani (IRE)—Brazilian Samba (IRE) (Sadler's Wells (USA)) (31745) **Dr M. B. Q. S. Koukash**
7 Br c 7/4 Manduro (GER)—Causeway Song (USA) (Giant's Causeway (USA)) (29364) **Dr M. B. Q. S. Koukash**
8 B c 18/4 Rock of Gibraltar (IRE)—Jojeema (Barathea (IRE)) (52000) **Dr M. B. Q. S. Koukash**
9 Br c 21/5 Rock of Gibraltar (IRE)—Royal Reprieve (FR) (Celtic Swing) (8729) **Dr M. B. Q. S. Koukash**
10 B f 15/3 High Chaparral (IRE)—Shakti (Indian Ridge) (23809) **Dr M. B. Q. S. Koukash**

451	**MR HUGHIE MORRISON, East Ilsley**

Postal: **Summerdown, East Ilsley, Newbury, Berkshire, RG20 7LB**
Contacts: **PHONE (01635) 281678 FAX (01635) 281746 MOBILE (07836) 687799**
E-MAIL hughie@hughiemorrison.co.uk WEBSITE www.hughiemorrison.co.uk

1 **ABI SCARLET (IRE)**, 4, b f Baltic King—Petarga **H. Morrison**
2 **ABUNDANTLY**, 4, b f Sakhee (USA)—Composing (IRE) **J. Repard & S. Dibb**
3 **BROTHER BRIAN (IRE)**, 5, b g Millenary—Miner Detail (IRE) **L. A. Garfield**
4 **BURNHAM**, 4, b g Nayef (USA)—Salim Toto **The Hill Stud**
5 **CAPTAIN BELLAMY (USA)**, 5, ch g Bellamy Road (USA)—Thesky'sthelimit (USA) **H. Morrison**
6 **CECILY PARSLEY**, 7, b m Fantastic Light (USA)—Salim Toto **L. A. Garfield**
7 **CHIL THE KITE**, 4, b c Notnowcato—Copy-Cat **Hazel Lawrence & Graham Doyle**
8 **COQUET**, 4, b f Sir Percy—One So Marvellous **Hon Mary Morrison & Partners**
9 **COSIMO DE MEDICI**, 6, b g Medicean—Wish **Bevan, Doyle & Lawrence**
10 **COUSIN KHEE**, 6, b g Sakhee (USA)—Cugina **R. C. Tooth**
11 **DECANA**, 5, ch m Doyen (IRE)—Sahara Belle (USA) **R. M., S. R. & P. J. Payne**
12 **FLEXIBLE FLYER**, 4, b g Exceed And Excel (AUS)—Windermere Island **A. J. Struthers, J. F. Dean & Mrs J. Scott**
13 **HALLING'S QUEST**, 4, b g Halling (USA)—Capriolla **The Fairy Story Partnership**
14 **MILLER'S MAVERICK**, 5, b g Millkom—Gables Girl **P. J. Cave**
15 **MILLERS PUDSEY**, 7, b g Pasternak—Gables Girl **P. J. Cave**
16 **NAZREEF**, 6, b g Zafeen (FR)—Roofer (IRE) **Deborah Collett & M. J. Watson**
17 **PASTORAL PLAYER**, 6, b g Pastoral Pursuits—Copy-Cat **The Pursuits Partnership**
18 **PETE THE PASTOR**, 5, b g Pastoral Pursuits—Franciscaine (FR) **Mrs M. D. W. Morrison**
19 **QUIZ MISTRESS**, 5, ch m Doyen (IRE)—Seren Quest **The Fairy Story Partnership**
20 **SHIROCCO STAR**, 4, b f Shirocco (GER)—Spectral Star **Helena Springfield Ltd**

THREE-YEAR-OLDS

21 **ANOTHER COCKTAIL**, b c Dalakhani (IRE)—Yummy Mummy **M. Kerr-Dineen**
22 **BANOFFEE (IRE)**, b f Hurricane Run (IRE)—Nanabanana (IRE) **M. Kerr-Dineen, Hon. W. H. Smith & Partners**
23 **BURGOYNE (USA)**, b g Officer (USA)—Married for Money (USA) **Lord Margadale H. ScottBarrett & Partners**
24 **CODEBREAKER**, ch g Sakhee's Secret—Folly Lodge **Thurloe Thoroughbreds XXX**
25 **CONQUESTADIM**, b c Elnadim (USA)—Conquestadora **The Fairy Story Partnership**
26 **COUNTRYMAN**, b c Pastoral Pursuits—Baileys Silver (USA) **H. Scott-Barrett, S. de Zoete & A. Pickford**
27 Ch f Indian Haven—Coventina (IRE) **The Lavington Stud**

MR HUGHIE MORRISON - Continued

28 **DAVID'S SECRET,** ch c Sakhee's Secret—Mozie Cat (IRE) **David Cliff, Philippa Clunes & C. Mather**
29 **DUSKY LARK,** b g Nayef (USA)—Snow Goose **Sir Thomas Pilkington**
30 **FANZINE,** ch f Medicean—Dash To The Front **Helena Springfield Ltd**
31 B g Pastoral Pursuits—Fealeview Lady (USA) **Pangfield Pursuits**
32 **FELIX FABULLA,** b c Lucky Story (USA)—Laser Crystal (IRE) **Mrs I. Eavis**
33 **GET GOING,** b g Motivator—Good Girl (IRE) **L. A. Garfield**
34 **JOSEFA GOYA,** b f Sakhee's Secret—Maria Theresa **Lord Margadale**
35 **JUBILANTE,** b f Royal Applause—
⠀⠀⠀⠀Lavinia's Grace (USA) **Mr S. de Zoete, Mr A. Pickford & Mr R. C. A. Hammond**
36 **LE TIGRE DE BRONZE,** b c Tiger Hill (IRE)—Papillon de Bronze (IRE) **Lord Blyth**
37 **LYRIC BALLAD,** b f Byron—Skies Are Blue **Mr T. D. Rootes & Mr O. F. Waller**
38 **MAISIE'S MOON (USA),** b f Curlin (USA)—Reverently (CAN) **Simply Racing Limited**
39 **MIDAZ,** br g Zamindar (USA)—Schlague (FR) **Mrs M. T. Bevan, Mr S. De Zoete**
40 **MINT CRISP,** gr f Dalakhani (IRE)—Peppermint Green **Helena Springfield Ltd**
41 **NEARLY CAUGHT (IRE),** b c New Approach (IRE)—Katch Me Katie **A. N. Solomons**
42 **REALIZE,** b g Zafeen (FR)—Relkida **Deborah Collett & M. J. Watson**
43 B g Beat Hollow—Riverine **Pangfield Partners**
44 **SECRET TALENT,** b g Sakhee's Secret—Aqaba **Wood Street Syndicate IV**
45 **SPERONELLA,** ch f Raven's Pass (USA)—Rosinka (IRE) **Capt J. Macdonald-Buchanan**
46 **SPICY DAL,** ch f Dalakhani (IRE)—Salsa Steps (USA) **Ben & Sir Martyn Arbib**
47 **SUSPENSION,** b f Avonbridge—Summertime Parkes **Mr S. D. Malcolm**
48 **TOWN MOUSE,** ch g Sakhee (USA)—Megdale (IRE) **Justin Dowley & Mouse Hamilton-Fairley**
49 **WILD ANTHEM,** b f Manduro (GER)—Wild Gardenia **Lofts Hall Stud & Mrs C. R. Philipson**
50 **ZIEKHANI,** ch gr c Dalakhani (IRE)—Zietory **The Fairy Story Partnership**

TWO-YEAR-OLDS

51 B f 14/4 Teofilo (IRE)—Angel Falls (Kingmambo (USA)) (60000) **Thurloe Thoroughbreds**
52 **BACKSTAGE GOSSIP,** b f 4/2 Sakhee's Secret—Theatre Royal (Royal Applause) **Runs In The Family**
53 B f 15/2 Cape Cross (IRE)—Balalaika (Sadler's Wells (USA)) **Helena Springfield Ltd**
54 **BALTIC BRAVE (IRE),** b c 30/3 Baltic King—Negria (IRE) (Al Hareb (USA)) (11904) **The Brave Partnership**
55 **CONCRETE MAC,** b c 5/2 Mastercraftsman (IRE)—
⠀⠀⠀⠀Merry Diva (Bahamian Bounty) (25000) **Adrian McAlpine & Partners**
56 **FUN MAC (GER),** ch c 1/3 Shirocco (GER)—
⠀⠀⠀⠀Favorite (GER) (Montjeu (IRE)) (22000) **Mrs A. McAlpine & Partners**
57 Ch f 14/2 Pivotal—Keladora (USA) (Crafty Prospector (USA)) (30000) **M. E. Wates**
58 **MARSH DAISY,** ch f 26/4 Pivotal—
⠀⠀⠀⠀Bella Lambada (Lammtarra (USA)) (80000) **Sir Thomas Pilkington & Mrs S. Rogers**
59 B f 19/2 Major Cadeaux—Miss Poppy (Averti (IRE)) (13333) **A. C. Pickford**
60 **NISSAKI KASTA,** ch f 4/3 Sakhee's Secret—Casterossa (Rossini (USA)) **Mr D. Barrie**
61 Ch f 19/3 Bahamian Bounty—
⠀⠀⠀⠀Palace Affair (Pursuit of Love) (55000) **Mr M. Kerr-Dineen, Mr M. Pallett, Mrs L. Tullett**
62 Ch c 14/4 Black Sam Bellamy (IRE)—Riverine (Risk Me (FR)) **Pangfield Racing**
63 B c 16/4 Dansili—Rosinka (IRE) (Soviet Star (USA)) **Capt J. MacDonald-Buchanan**
64 B f 26/3 Nayef (USA)—So Blissful (IRE) (Cape Cross (IRE)) **L. A. Garfield**
65 **SOUTHERN CROSS,** ch f 5/3 Mount Nelson—
⠀⠀⠀⠀Bread of Heaven (Machiavellian (USA)) (22000) **Major D. Chappell, Mr R. Lloyd & Partners**
66 Br c 19/3 High Chaparral (IRE)—Supamova (USA) (Seattle Slew (USA)) **Sir Martyn Arbib**
67 **SWEEPING UP,** b f 14/4 Sea The Stars (IRE)—Farfala (FR) (Linamix (FR)) **Ben & Sir Martyn Arbib**
68 B f 2/4 Royal Applause—Triple Sharp (Selkirk (USA)) **Lady Hardy**
69 **VENT DE FORCE,** b c 25/2 Hurricane Run (IRE)—Capriolla (In The Wings) **The Fairy Story Partnership**
70 Gr c 25/4 Dalakhani (IRE)—
⠀⠀⠀⠀Victoire Celebre (USA) (Stravinsky (USA)) (62000) **Eason, Kerr-Dineen, Hughes, Edward-Jones**
71 B f 7/4 Sakhee (USA)—You Too (Monsun (GER)) (5238) **Helena Springfield Ltd**

Other Owners: Mr B. G. Arbib, Mr C. E. M. Benson, M. T. Bevan, Mrs P G. Billington, T. M. Bird, Major D. N. Chappell, D. Cliff, Mrs P K. Clunes, Miss D. Collett, Mr S. M. De Zoete, J. F. Dean, Mr S. M. Dibb, Mr L. J. Dowley, Mr G. J. Doyle, W. D. Eason, Mr M. E. S. Edwards-Jones, Mrs H. S. Ellingsen, R. E. Goodwin, Mrs A. J. Hamilton-Fairley, Mr R. C. A. Hammond, Mr M. B. Hughes, Miss H. M. Lawrence, Mrs S. A. Lloyd, R. E. Lloyd, Lady Margadale, Mrs Satu Marks, Mr C. Mather, The Hon Miss M. A. Morrison, Mrs P J. Payne, Mr S. R. Payne, Mrs A. B. Plummer, J. P Repard, T. D. Rootes, Mr A. H. Scott, Mrs B. M. Scott, Mrs J. M. M. Scott, Miss C. S. Scott-Balls, H. Y. Scott-Barrett, The Hon W. H. Smith, Mr M. R. Stokes, Mr A. J. Struthers, G. D. W. Swire, J. D. N. Tillyard, O. F. Waller, M. J. Watson, Mr J. A. M. Wechsler, M. Weinfeld, S. G. West.

Pupil Assistant: Nicola Dumelow

Apprentice: Alice White. **Amateur:** Miss Nicola Dumelow, Mr Robert Pooles.

452 MR GARRY MOSS, Tickhill
Postal: Ron Hull Group, PO BOX 590, Rotherham, South Yorkshire, S62 6WT
Contacts: PHONE (01524) 791514 MOBILE (07962) 021526

1 CAPONE (IRE), 8, b g Daggers Drawn (USA)—Order of The Day (USA) **Brooklands Racing**
2 KEY AMBITION, 4, ch g Auction House (USA)—Love Thing **Mr R. Hull**
3 LENNY BEE, 7, gr ro g Kyllachy—Smart Hostess **Mr R. Hull**
4 LUCKY MARK (IRE), 4, b g Moss Vale (IRE)—Vracca **Mr R. Hull**
5 MOORHOUSE LAD, 10, b g Bertolini (USA)—Record Time **Mr R. Hull**
6 RONINSKI (IRE), 5, b g Cadeaux Genereux—Ruby Affair (IRE) **Mr R. Hull**

THREE-YEAR-OLDS
7 BROTHER DUKE, b g Bachelor Duke (USA)—Kathy's Rocket (USA) **Mr R. Hull**

TWO-YEAR-OLDS
8 ARROWZONE, b c 20/2 Iffraaj—Donna Giovanna (Mozart (IRE)) (22857) **Mr R. Hull**
9 BOOLOO (IRE), b c 26/3 Bushranger (IRE)—Ink Pot (USA) (Green Dancer (USA)) (19047) **Mr R. Hull**
10 RUBY HULL (IRE), b f 14/2 Bushranger (IRE)—Zuzu (IRE) (Acclamation) (14285) **Mr R. Hull**
11 SLINKY MCVELVET, ch f 2/2 Refuse To Bend (IRE)—Rania (GER) (Paolini (GER)) **Mr R. Hull**

Other Owners: M. H. Bates, D. S. Lovatt, Mrs A. M. Mercs.

453 MR WILLIAM MUIR, Lambourn
Postal: Linkslade, Wantage Road, Lambourn, Hungerford, Berkshire, RG17 8UG
Contacts: OFFICE (01488) 73098 HOME (01488) 73748 FAX (01488) 73490
MOBILE (07831) 457074
E-MAIL william@williammuir.com WEBSITE www.williammuir.com

1 ALICE'S DANCER (IRE), 4, br f Clodovil (IRE)—Islandagore (IRE) **Perspicacious Punters Racing Club**
2 BREAKING THE BANK, 4, ch g Medicean—Russian Dance (USA) **R. Devlin**
3 CRUISER, 5, b g Oasis Dream—Good Girl (IRE) **C. L. A. Edginton**
4 GRIFFIN POINT (IRE), 6, b m Tagula (IRE)—Lady Corduff (IRE) **F. P. Hope**
5 HILDEN, 4, b f Dansili—Singleton **Mrs J. M. Muir**
6 HOLLYWOOD ALL STAR (IRE), 4, b g Kheleyf (USA)—Camassina (IRE) **The Lavelle Family**
7 KITTENS, 4, b f Marju (IRE)—Purring (USA) **Muir Racing Partnership - Chester**
8 LITTLE CHINA, 4, b f Kyllachy—China Beads **Mr S. Lamb**
9 LOWTHERWOOD, 4, b g Green Desert (USA)—
Imperial Bailiwick (IRE) **Mr & Mrs Middlebrook/Mr & Mrs Nicholson**
10 MAGIC SECRET, 5, b g Trade Fair—Just Devine (IRE) **Carmel Stud**
11 SAINT HILARY, 4, b f Authorized (IRE)—Bright Halo (IRE) **Usk Valley Stud**
12 SANGRAIL, 4, b f Singspiel (IRE)—Wars (IRE) **Muir Racing Partnership - London**
13 SIOUXPERHERO (IRE), 4, b g Sleeping Indian—Tintern **Muir Racing Partnership - Bath**
14 STEPPER POINT, 4, b c Kyllachy—Sacre Coeur **Mr C. L. A. Edginton**
15 THE GURU OF GLOOM (IRE), 5, b g Dubai Destination (USA)—Gabriella **R. Haim**
16 TYPOGRAPHY, 4, br g Byron—Bold Byzantium **North Farm Partnership**
17 WE HAVE A DREAM, 8, b br g Oasis Dream—Final Shot **The Dreaming Squires**

THREE-YEAR-OLDS
18 BELLA MICHELLE, b f Sakhee's Secret—Michelle Ma Belle (IRE) **Mrs M. Cousins**
19 CALIFANTE, b f Kyllachy—Call Mariah (USA) **Foursome Thoroughbreds**
20 FOIE GRAS, b g Kyllachy—Bint Zamayem (IRE) **Mrs G. E. Rowland-Clark**
21 GRAYSWOOD, gr c Dalakhani (IRE)—Argent du Bois (USA) **C. L. A. Edginton**
22 HEAVENLY PROSPECT, b f Authorized (IRE)—Bread of Heaven **Usk Valley Stud**
23 KALAHARI BREEZE (IRE), b f Jeremy (USA)—Staceymac (IRE) **Muir Racing Partnership - Newbury**
24 KENNY'S GIRL (IRE), b f Manduro (GER)—Tanz (IRE) **Mr David White**
25 PURR ALONG, b f Mount Nelson—Purring (USA) **H.E. Sheikh J. B. H. B. K. Al Thani**
26 SECRET MISSILE, b c Sakhee's Secret—Malelane (IRE) **Muir Racing Partnership - Manchester**
27 SECRET WEAPON, b g Choisir (AUS)—Just Devine (IRE) **Mr Peter Morgan**
28 SONG OF SNOWDON, b f Singspiel (IRE)—Portmeirion **Usk Valley Stud**
29 SUNBLAZER (IRE), gr c Dark Angel (IRE)—Damask Rose (IRE) **Mrs D. L. Edginton**

MR WILLIAM MUIR - Continued

TWO-YEAR-OLDS

30 B f 6/2 Acclamation—Amistad (GER) (Winged Love (IRE)) (45000) **M. J. Caddy**
31 **ARMOURER (IRE),** b c 30/4 Azamour (IRE)—
Engraving (Sadler's Wells (USA)) (30000) **D. G. Clarke & C. L. A. Edginton**
32 **CHILLY IN RIO (IRE),** gr f 29/1 Verglas (IRE)—
Brazilian Spirit (IRE) (Invincible Spirit (IRE)) (9523) **Muir Racing Partnership - Manchester**
33 B c 15/4 Acclamation—Daqtora (Dr Devious (IRE)) (40000)
34 **DIVISION BELLE,** gr f 12/2 Dalakhani (IRE)—Multiplication (Marju (IRE)) (65000) **Foursome Thoroughbreds**
35 B c 2/4 Nayef (USA)—Ermine (IRE) (Cadeaux Genereux) (28000) **Mr J. M. O'Mulloy**
36 **GULLAND ROCK,** b c 26/4 Exceed And Excel (AUS)—
Sacre Coeur (Compton Place) (60000) **C. L. A. Edginton & K. Mercer**
37 **IMPROVIZED,** b f 16/3 Authorized (IRE)—Rhapsodize (Halling (USA)) (13000) **Foursome Thoroughbreds**
38 **JAMMY MOMENT,** ch f 31/1 Duke of Marmalade (IRE)—
Special Moment (IRE) (Sadler's Wells (USA)) **Foursome Thoroughbreds**
39 Gr f 4/2 Mount Nelson—Lady Xara (IRE) (Xaar) (14000)
40 **LOVE SPICE,** b f 19/3 Cape Cross (IRE)—Zanzibar (IRE) (In The Wings) **Usk Valley Stud**
41 Ch c 24/2 Halling (USA)—Oatey (Master Willie) (14000) **Mr R. Haim**
42 **ORACLE BOY,** b c 6/3 Mount Nelson—Snow Princess (IRE) (Ela-Mana-Mou) (10000)
43 B c 20/4 Manduro (GER)—Ornellaia (IRE) (Mujadil (USA)) (15000)
44 **PINK AND BLACK (IRE),** b f 5/4 Yeats (IRE)—Raysiza (IRE) (Alzao (USA)) (31746) **Mrs D. L. Edginton**
45 **SEVERN CROSSING,** b c 17/2 Authorized (IRE)—Croeso Cariad (Most Welcome) **Usk Valley Stud**
46 Ch f 6/3 Mount Nelson—Strawberry Lolly (Lomitas) (10000)
47 Gr f 18/2 Dark Angel (IRE)—Tintern (Diktat) (17000)
48 B f 7/3 Manduro (GER)—Welsh Cake (Fantastic Light (USA)) (25000) **M. J. Caddy**

Other Owners: Mr D. G. Clarke, Mr G. Cox, Mr Mike Dawson, Mr C. L. A. Edginton, Mr John H. W. Finch, Mr Melvyn Ford, Mr R. Haim, Mr John Hobson, Mr Stewart Jones, Mr D. P. Knox, Mr K. J. Mercer, Mrs S. Mercer, Mr G. Middlebrook, Mrs L. Middlebrook, Mr Stephen Moss, Mrs J. M. Muir, Mr Graham Stacey, Mr David F. White, Mr Geoffrey E. Wood.

Jockey (flat): Martin Dwyer.

---

454 **MR CLIVE MULHALL, Scarcroft**
Postal: **Scarcroft Hall Farm, Thorner Lane, Scarcroft, Leeds, LS14 3AQ**
Contacts: **PHONE** (0113) 2893095 **FAX** (0113) 2893095 **MOBILE** (07979) 527675
E-MAIL clive@scarcrofthallracing.co.uk **WEBSITE** www.scarcrofthallracing.co.uk

1 **ALFINSKI,** 8, b g Alflora (IRE)—Auntie Alice **Carl Chapman & Mrs C M Mulhall**
2 **ALIMURE,** 7, b m Tamure (IRE)—Auntie Alice **Carl Chapman & Mrs C M Mulhall**
3 **CHEEKY CHEROKEE,** 4, b g Sleeping Indian—Berkeley Note (IRE)
4 **IFONLYWECUD,** 4, b g Celtic Swing—Mrs Dalloway (IRE) **Carl Chapman & Mrs C M Mulhall**
5 **SHARADIYN,** 10, b g Generous (IRE)—Sharadiya (IRE) **Simon Ballance & Mrs C M Mulhall**
6 **SIMHAL,** 9, b g Minster Son—Busky Girl **Josttigo Racing**
7 **THINK,** 6, ch g Sulamani (IRE)—Natalie Jay **Mrs C M Mulhall & Over The Rainbow**
8 **TUKITINYASOK (IRE),** 6, b g Fath (USA)—Mevlana (IRE) **Carl Chapman & Mrs C M Mulhall**

THREE-YEAR-OLDS

9 B f Moss Vale (IRE)—Mimic **Carl Chapman & Mrs C M Mulhall**

Other Owners: Mr S. T. Ballance, Mr M. Bisogno, Mr C. Chapman, G. Halsall, Mrs C. M. Mulhall, Mr C. Sim, Mr T. D. Wooldridge.

Assistant Trainer: Mrs Martina Mulhall

---

455 **MR NEIL MULHOLLAND, Limpley Stoke**
Postal: **Conkwell Grange, Conkwell, Limpley Stoke, Bath, Avon, BA2 7FD**
Contacts: **MOBILE** (07739) 258607
E-MAIL neil@neilmulhollandracing.com **WEBSITE** www.neilmulhollandracing.com

1 **ADIYNARA (IRE),** 5, b m Halling (USA)—Adirika (IRE) **J & S Baigent D Smith & I Woodward**
2 **AGAPANTHUS (GER),** 8, b g Tiger Hill (IRE)—Astilbe (GER) **Neil Mulholland Racing Ltd**
3 **ASHCOTT BOY,** 5, ch g Lahib (USA)—Last Ambition (IRE) **Mr J. Hobbs**
4 **BARTON JUBILEE,** 5, ch g Midnight Legend—Home From The Hill (IRE) **Lady H. J. Clarke**
5 **BENEATH,** 6, b g Dansili—Neath **Wellcroomed Ltd**

MR NEIL MULHOLLAND - Continued

6 **BUCK MAGIC (IRE)**, 7, b g Albano (IRE)—Green Sea **B. A. Derrick**
7 **CAROLE'S DESTRIER**, 5, b g Kayf Tara—Barton May **Mrs C. Skipworth**
8 **CAUNAY**, 6, ch g Generous (IRE)—Chantilly Lady **Mr R. Moore**
9 **CHANCEALOT**, 5, b g Reel Buddy (USA)—Party Charmer **Mr P. A. Brewer**
10 5, B m Oscar (IRE)—Fashions Monty (IRE) **Mr B. F. Mulholland**
11 4, B f Oscar (IRE)—Fashions Monty (IRE) **Mr B. F. Mulholland**
12 **FRAN'S FOLLY**, 7, b m Baryshnikov (AUS)—Lansdowne Park **Neil Mulholland Racing Club**
13 **HOBB'S DREAM (IRE)**, 9, br m Winged Love (IRE)—La-Greine **John & Jeanette Hobbs & Mr P J Proudley**
14 **HOLMWOOD LEGEND**, 12, b g Midnight Legend—West-Hatch-Spirit **B. A. Derrick**
15 **HOPATINA (IRE)**, 7, b m Flemensfirth (USA)—Bonny Lass **J & S Baigent**
16 **ISTHEREADIFFERENCE (IRE)**, 6, gr g Amilynx (FR)—Jennys Grove (IRE) **Colony Stable Llc**
17 **JIM JOB JONES**, 9, b g Tipsy Creek (USA)—Sulapuff **Dajam Ltd**
18 **KING HELISSIO (IRE)**, 5, b g Helissio (FR)—Banner Buzz (IRE) **Mrs J. Gerard-Pearse**
19 **MABEL TASMAN**, 7, ch m Midnight Legend—West Coast **Mabels Ladies Partnership**
20 **MAD MAX (IRE)**, 11, b g Kayf Tara—Carole's Crusader **Mrs C. Skipworth**
21 **MATROW'S LADY (IRE)**, 6, b m Cloudings (IRE)—I'm Maggy (NZ) **Matrow Properties Limited**
22 **MEET ME AT DAWN**, 9, ch m Alflora (IRE)—Quiet Dawn **Dajam Ltd**
23 **MIDNIGHT CHASE**, 11, b g Midnight Legend—Yamrah **Lady H. J. Clarke**
24 **MINELLA DEFINITELY (IRE)**, 6, br g Definite Article—West Along **Wellcroomed Ltd**
25 **MR BURBIDGE**, 5, b g Midnight Legend—Twin Time **Dajam Ltd**
26 **NEWMANS BOY**, 6, ch g Loup Sauvage (USA)—Newman's Conquest **P. C. Tory**
27 **NORMANDY LANDINGS**, 10, gr g Alflora (IRE)—Hinemoa (IRE) **Mrs H. R. Cross**
28 **NOVABRIDGE**, 5, ch g Avonbridge—Petrovna (IRE) **Dajam Ltd**
29 **PASS THE TIME**, 4, b f Passing Glance—Twin Time **Dajam Ltd**
30 **PINDAR (GER)**, 9, b g Tertullian (USA)—Pierette (GER) **Wellcroomed Ltd**
31 **REALTA MO CROI (IRE)**, 5, b m Westerner—Solar Quest (IRE) **Neil Mulholland Racing Ltd**
32 **STERLING BILL (IRE)**, 5, gr m Cloudings (IRE)—Coolgarry Girl (IRE) **Neil Mulholland Racing Ltd**
33 **THE YOUNG MASTER**, 4, b g Echo of Light—Fine Frenzy (IRE) **Dajam Ltd**
34 **TOONEY MALOONEY**, 8, gr m Silver Patriarch (IRE)—Sulapuff **Dajam Ltd**
35 **UIMHIR A SEACHT (IRE)**, 6, br m Millenary—Benefit Ball (IRE) **Neil Mulholland Racing Club**

Other Owners: Mrs J. A. V. Allen, J. R. Baigent, Exors of the Late Mrs S. J. Baigent, B. D. Makepeace, Mr N. P. Mulholland, Mrs M. F. Poole, Mr P. J. Proudley, David H. Smith, Mrs A. G. L. Walker, Mr I. S. Woodward.

Conditional: Andrias Guerin.

---

456 **MR LAWRENCE MULLANEY, Malton**
Postal: Raikes Farm, Great Habton, Malton, North Yorkshire, YO17 6RX
Contacts: PHONE (01653) 668208 MOBILE (07899) 902565

1 **DENISON FLYER**, 6, b g Tobougg (IRE)—Bollin Victoria **L. A. Mullaney**
2 **FILE AND PAINT (IRE)**, 5, b m Chevalier (IRE)—Have A Heart (IRE) **Ontoawinner 3**
3 **POPPANELLA (IRE)**, 4, b f Namid—Bobanlyn (IRE) **L. A. Mullaney**
4 **SHAMO HILL THEATRE**, 6, b g Millkom—Hannalou (FR) **Mr R. M. Heatherill**

Other Owners: N. J. O'Brien.

---

457 **MR MICHAEL MULLINEAUX, Tarporley**
Postal: Southley Farm, Alpraham, Tarporley, Cheshire, CW6 9JD
Contacts: PHONE (01829) 261440 FAX (01829) 261440 MOBILE (07753) 650263
E-MAIL southleararacing@btinternet.com WEBSITE www.southleyfarm.co.uk

1 **BLODWEN ABBEY**, 4, b f Firebreak—Miss Mirasol **J. M. Davies**
2 **CHICAMIA**, 9, b m Kyllachy—Inflation **Abbey Racing**
3 **FAST RUBY**, 6, ch m Fleetwood (IRE)—Tinoforty (FR) **Mr A. Johnstone**
4 **FRANCIS ALBERT**, 7, b g Mind Games—Via Dolorosa **Southley Racing Partnership**
5 **LORD OF THE DANCE (IRE)**, 7, ch g Indian Haven—Maine Lobster (USA) **H. Clewlow**
6 **LULU'S GIFT (IRE)**, 7, gr m Lahib (USA)—She's A Gift **The Weaver Group**
7 **METHAALY (IRE)**, 10, b g Red Ransom (USA)—Santorini (USA) **S. A. Pritchard**
8 **MINTY JONES**, 4, b c Primo Valentino (IRE)—Reveur **P. Clacher**
9 **MOLKO JACK (FR)**, 9, b br g Lavirco (GER)—Line As (FR) **D. Ashbrook**
10 **MUZEY'S PRINCESS**, 7, b m Grape Tree Road—Premier Princess **D. M. Drury**
11 **MY TIME**, 4, b g Mind Games—Tick Tock **M. Mullineaux**

MR MICHAEL MULLINEAUX - Continued

12 OLYNARD (IRE), 7, b g Exceed And Excel (AUS)—Reddening **Mr G. Cornes**
13 ORPEN BID (IRE), 8, b m Orpen (USA)—Glorious Bid (IRE) **Miss L. S. Young**
14 PRIMO BLANCA, 4, b g Primo Valentino (IRE)—Quay Four (IRE) **C. A. Oats**
15 ROYAL SEA (IRE), 4, b g Refuse To Bend (IRE)—Janayen (USA) **P. Currey**
16 SACCO D'ORO, 7, b m Rainbow High—Speedy Native (IRE) **Mr P. R. D'Amato**
17 SIR BOSS (IRE), 8, b g Tagula (IRE)—Good Thought (IRE) **Miss M Mullineaux, Mr P Lawton, Mr I Ross**
18 SMIRFY'S SILVER, 9, b g Desert Prince (IRE)—Goodwood Blizzard **Mrs D. Plant**
19 TWO TURTLE DOVES (IRE), 7, b m Night Shift (USA)—Purple Rain (IRE) **Mr G. Cornes**
20 WYMESWOLD, 6, b m Alflora (IRE)—Dominie Breeze **The Hon Mrs S. Pakenham**
21 ZORRO'S BLADE, 5, b g Needwood Blade—Beechy Bank (IRE) **Miss L. S. Young**

THREE-YEAR-OLDS

22 B c Vita Rosa (JPN)—Common Request (USA)
23 B c Starcraft (NZ)—Jig Time
24 Ch c Primo Valentino (IRE)—Sunny Parkes **S. A. Pritchard**

Other Owners: Mr E. A. Griffiths, Mr G. C. Horner, P. J. Lawton, Miss V. C. Lawton, Miss M. Mullineaux, Mr P. Murray, Mr I. S. Ross.

Assistant Trainer: Stuart Ross & Susan Mullineaux

Amateur: Miss M. J. L. Mullineaux.

---

458 **MR SEAMUS MULLINS, Amesbury**
Postal: **Wilsford Stables, Wilsford-Cum-Lake, Amesbury, Salisbury, Wiltshire, SP4 7BL**
Contacts: **PHONE/FAX (01980) 626344 MOBILE (07702) 559634**
E-MAIL **info@jwmullins.co.uk** WEBSITE **www.seamusmullins.co.uk**

1 ALDER MAIRI (IRE), 6, ch m Alderbrook—Amari Queen **F. G. Matthews**
2 ANNIMATION (IRE), 9, b m Accordion—Euro Breeze (IRE) **Dr R. Jowett**
3 ANTEROS (IRE), 5, b g Milan—Sovereign Star (IRE)
4 BRUNETTE'SONLY (IRE), 8, ch m Flemensfirth (USA)—Pride of St Gallen (IRE) **Mrs M. M. Rayner**
5 CHAMBRAY DANCER (IRE), 5, b m Darsi (FR)—Cotton Gale **First Impressions Racing Group**
6 FERGALL (IRE), 6, br g Norwich—Gaybrook Girl (IRE) **Andrew Cocks & Tara Johnson**
7 FLUGZEUG, 5, gr g Silver Patriarch (IRE)—Telmar Flyer **New Forest Racing Partnership**
8 HEAD SPIN (IRE), 5, b g Beneficial—Who Tells Jan **Mr M. Adams**
9 HIGH SAMANA, 5, b g High Chaparral—Kirkby Belle **Chimera Racing**
10 MARMALADE MAN, 7, ch g Karinga Bay—Kentford Duchess **D. I. Bare**
11 MIGHT AS WELL, 8, b g Terimon—Might Be **Dr & Mrs John Millar**
12 OR SING ABOUT (FR), 11, b g Le Balafre (FR)—Grande Folie (FR) **A. M. Day**
13 ORION STAR (IRE), 11, ch g Fourstars Allstar (USA)—Rosies Sister (IRE) **C. A. Green**
14 ROMEO AMERICO (IRE), 6, b g Lord Americo—Crazy Falcon (IRE) **Mr M. Adams**
15 RUBY GLOW, 5, b m Septieme Ciel (USA)—Ruby Too **Dr R. Jowett**
16 SAPPHIRE ROUGE (IRE), 7, ch m Alderbrook—Emerald Express **Lake Racing**
17 SHARP SUIT (IRE), 6, b br g Milan—True Blade **Andrew Cocks & Tara Johnson**
18 SOMCHINE, 5, b g Volochine (IRE)—Seem of Gold **Mr C. R. Dunning**
19 TIME TO THINK, 8, b m Alflora (IRE)—Shuil Do (IRE) **Mrs V. F. Hewett**
20 TOP SMART, 7, b g Karinga Bay—Clover Dove **The Calvera Partnership No. 2**
21 TWILIGHT LEGEND (IRE), 4, b f Chevalier (IRE)—Almost Twilight (USA) **Church Racing Partnership**
22 WILDE RUBY (IRE), 6, b m Oscar (IRE)—Ruby Thewes (IRE) **J. W. Mullins**

THREE-YEAR-OLDS

23 RUFF LUCK, b f Lucarno (USA)—Ruffie (IRE) **D and C Bloodstock**

Other Owners: Mr J. E. Bone, Mr Andrew Cocks, Mr C. R. Dunning, Mr T. Green, Mr R. Hatchard, Mr P. Hickey, Mr Alan K. Horsman, Miss Tara Johnson, Dr Roger Jowett, Mr John Kavanagh, Mr D. A. Lucie-Smith, Dr John Millar, Mrs John Millar, Mr Seamus Mullins, Mr J. Oakey, Mr D. D. Sutherland, Miss Lynda Whitehorn, Mr Charles Wilson.

Assistant Trainer: Miss Charlotte Brown

Jockey (NH): Wayne Kavanagh, Andrew Thornton. **Amateur:** Mr K. Jones.

459 MR WILLIAM P. MULLINS, Carlow

Postal: **Closutton, Bagenalstown, Co. Carlow, Ireland**
Contacts: PHONE **(00353) 5997 21786** FAX **(00353) 5997 22709** MOBILE **(00353) 8725 64940**
E-MAIL **wpmullins@eircom.net** WEBSITE **www.wpmullins.com**

1 **ABBEY LANE (IRE)**, 8, b g Flemensfirth (USA)—Hazel Sylph (IRE) **Martin Lynch**
2 **ALFRED JAMES**, 7, b g Old Vic—Jupiter's Message **Mrs Rose Boyd**
3 **ALLURE OF ILLUSION (IRE)**, 7, ch g Captain Rio—Sixhills (FR) **Mrs S. Ricci**
4 **ALONSO (SPA)**, 4, ch g Green Tune (USA)—Lady Cree (IRE) **Andrea & Graham Wylie**
5 **ANDIAMOS (IRE)**, 6, b g Beneficial—Iron Mariner (IRE) **Roderick Ryan**
6 **ANNIE POWER (IRE)**, 5, ch m Shirocco (GER)—Anno Luce **Mrs S. Ricci**
7 **APT APPROACH (IRE)**, 10, ch g Bob Back (USA)—Imminent Approach (IRE) **Greenstar Syndicate**
8 **ARE YA RIGHT CHIEF (IRE)**, 8, b g Flemensfirth (USA)—River Clyde (IRE) **Mrs M McMahon**
9 **ARVIKA LIGEONNIERE (FR)**, 8, b g Arvico (FR)—Daraka (FR) **Mrs S. Ricci**
10 **AUPCHARLIE (IRE)**, 7, b g Daliapour (IRE)—Lirfa (USA) **Ann & Alan Potts Partnership**
11 **AWAY WE GO (IRE)**, 10, ch g Stowaway—Margurites Pet (IRE) **Michael A. O'Gorman**
12 **BACK IN FOCUS (IRE)**, 8, ch g Bob Back (USA)—Dun Belle (IRE) **Andrea & Graham Wylie**
13 **BALLY LONGFORD (IRE)**, 5, b g Gold Well—Stay On Line (IRE) **Ann & Alan Potts**
14 **BALLYCASEY (IRE)**, 6, gr g Presenting—Pink Mist (IRE) **Mrs S. Ricci**
15 **BALNASLOW (IRE)**, 6, b g Presenting—Noble Choice **Gigginstown House Stud**
16 **BELUCKYAGAIN (IRE)**, 5, b m Old Vic—Whizz **Supreme Horses Racing Club**
17 **BISHOPSFURZE (IRE)**, 8, b g Broadway Flyer (USA)—Supreme Dipper (IRE) **Mrs C. M. Hurley**
18 **BLACKSTAIRMOUNTAIN (IRE)**, 8, b g Imperial Ballet (IRE)—Sixhills (FR) **Mrs S. Ricci**
19 **BLAZING TEMPO (IRE)**, 9, b m Accordion—Leading Duke (IRE) **Mrs S. Ricci**
20 **BLOOD COTIL (FR)**, 4, b g Enrique—Move Along (FR) **Mrs S. Ricci**
21 **BOSTON BOB (IRE)**, 8, b g Bob Back (USA)—Bavaway **Andrea & Graham Wylie**
22 **BOWFINGER (IRE)**, 10, ch g Anshan—Galley Flash (IRE) **Mrs J. M. Mullins**
23 **BOXER GEORG (IRE)**, 11, b g Taipan (IRE)—Country Course (IRE) **Mr W. Murray**
24 **BRIAR HILL (IRE)**, 5, b g Shantou—Backaway (IRE) **Andrea & Graham Wylie**
25 **BUNDLE OF FUN (IRE)**, 10, ch g Topanoora—Leaden Sky (IRE) **Shanakiel Racing Syndicate**
26 **CADSPEED (FR)**, 10, b g Vertical Speed (FR)—Cadmina (FR) **Carra Ethos Syndicate**
27 **CALL ME BUBBLES (IRE)**, 4, gr g Stormy River (FR)—Tempete Tropicale (FR) **Mrs S. Ricci**
28 **CALL THE POLICE (IRE)**, 10, b g Accordion—Evangelica (USA) **DD Racing Syndicate**
29 **CELTIC WISH (IRE)**, 10, b g Beneficial—Balda Girl (IRE) **P. W. Mullins**
30 **CHAMPAGNE AGENT (IRE)**, 7, b g Smadoun (FR)—Madame Jean (FR) **John J. Fallon**
31 **CHAMPAGNE FEVER (IRE)**, 6, gr g Stowaway—Forever Bubbles (IRE) **Mrs S. Ricci**
32 **CHILTERN HILLS (IRE)**, 6, ch m Beneficial—Mirazur (IRE) **Supreme Horse Racing Club**
33 **CITY SLICKER (IRE)**, 5, b g King's Theatre (IRE)—Donna's Princess (IRE) **John P. McManus**
34 **CLONDAW COURT (IRE)**, 6, br g Court Cave (IRE)—Secret Can't Say (IRE) **Mrs S. Ricci**
35 **DANEKING**, 4, b g Dylan Thomas (IRE)—Sadie Thompson (IRE) **Mrs S. Ricci**
36 **DANI CATALONIA (IRE)**, 7, b m Daggers Drawn (USA)—Tryphaena (FR) **W. K. McCarthy**
37 **DARROUN (IRE)**, 5, gr g Dalakhani (IRE)—Darayka (FR) **Mrs S. Ricci**
38 **DEUTSCHLAND (USA)**, 10, b g Red Ransom (USA)—Rhine Valley (USA) **A. McLuckie**
39 **DEVILS BRIDE (IRE)**, 6, b g Helissio (FR)—Rigorous **Gigginsstown House Stud**
40 **DIAKALI (FR)**, 4, gr g Sinndar (IRE)—Diasilixa (FR) **Wicklow Bloodstock Limited**
41 **DIGEANTA (IRE)**, 6, b g Helissio (FR)—
                    Scolboa Gold (IRE) **Dr I. M. P. Moran, Colland Sand & Gravel Syndicate**
42 **DJAKADAM (IRE)**, 4, b g Saint des Saints (FR)—Rainbow Crest (FR) **Mrs S. Ricci**
43 **DOGORA (FR)**, 4, gr g Robin des Pres (FR)—Garde de Nuit (FR) **Mrs S. Ricci**
44 **DOUGAL PHILPS**, 4, b g Echo of Light—Bella Bertolini **Mrs S Ricci**
45 **DRIVE ON REGARDLES (IRE)**, 10, ch g Shernazar—Wayward Queen **S. Ahern**
46 **DRIVE TIME (USA)**, 8, b g King Cugat (USA)—Arbusha (USA) **Andrea & Graham Wylie**
47 **EARLS QUARTER (IRE)**, 7, b g Shantou—Par Street (IRE) **B. Doyle**
48 **EQUITY SWAP (IRE)**, 4, ch g Strategic Prince—Medicean Star (IRE) **Ann & Alan Potts**
49 **EQUUS MAXIMUS (IRE)**, 13, b g Flemensfirth (USA)—Sambara (IRE) **Greenstar Syndicate**
50 **FATCATINTHEHAT**, 4, b g Authorized (IRE)—Fin **Mrs S. Ricci**
51 **FAUGHEEN (IRE)**, 5, b g Germany (USA)—Miss Pickering (IRE) **Mrs S. Ricci**
52 **FELIX YONGER (IRE)**, 7, b g Oscar (IRE)—Marble Sound (IRE) **Andrea & Graham Wylie**
53 **FINAL APPROACH**, 7, b g Pivotal—College Fund Girl (IRE) **Mr D. Taylor**
54 **FIVEFORTHREE (IRE)**, 11, gr g Arzanni—What A Queen **Olde Crowbars Syndicate**
55 **FLASH OF GENIUS, 7**, b g Definite Article—Fortune's Girl **Gigginstown House Stud**
56 **FLAT OUT (FR)**, 8, gr g Sagamix (FR)—Divine Rodney (FR) **M. O'Riordan**
57 **GLENS MELODY (IRE)**, 5, b m King's Theatre (IRE)—Glens Music (IRE) **Ms Fiona McStay**
58 **GOLDBOY (IRE)**, 5, b g Gold Well—Woodbinesandroses (IRE) **CCR Racing Syndicate**
59 **GORGEOUS SIXTY (FR)**, 5, b m Touch of The Blues (FR)—Sixty Six (IRE) **Mrs S. Ricci**
60 **HURRICANE FLY (IRE)**, 9, b g Montjeu (IRE)—Scandisk (IRE) **George Creighton**

MR WILLIAM P. MULLINS - Continued

61 **IMMEDIATE RESPONSE (IRE)**, 10, b g Strategic Choice (USA)—Rosies All The Way **Kates Monkeys Syndicate**
62 **INISH ISLAND (IRE)**, 7, ch g Trans Island—Ish (IRE) **Susan Flanagan**
63 **KERB APPEAL (IRE)**, 8, b g Needle Gun (IRE)—Great Days (IRE) **Olde Crowbars Syndicate**
64 **LAGANBANK (IRE)**, 7, b g Norwich—Listen Up **Mrs Rose Boyd**
65 **LAMBRO (IRE)**, 8, b g Milan—Beautiful Tune (IRE) **Byerly Thoroughbred Racing**
66 **LEGAL LYRIC (IRE)**, 4, b f Lawman (FR)—Flaming Song (IRE) **JPM O'Connor**
67 **LETHERBELUCKY (IRE)**, 6, b m Luso—Silaoce (FR) **Supreme Horse Racing Club**
68 **LOCH ARD (IRE)**, 5, b g Pivotal—My Giddy Aunt (IRE) **Wicklow Bloodstock Ltd**
69 **LUCKY BRIDLE (IRE)**, 4, b c Dylan Thomas (IRE)—Auction Room (USA) **Andrea & Graham Wylie**
70 **MADE IN GERMANY (IRE)**, 5, ch g Germany (USA)—Black Dot Com (IRE) **Gigginstown House Stud**
71 **MAID FROM MILAN (IRE)**, 8, b m Milan—Raishah (GER) **Brian Keenan**
72 **MAKE YOUR MARK (IRE)**, 6, b g Beneficial—Bell Star (IRE) **Gigginstown House Stud**
73 **MARASONNIEN (FR)**, 7, b g Mansonnien (FR)—Maracay (FR) **Mrs S. Ricci**
74 **MARITO (GER)**, 7, b g Alkalde (GER)—Maratea (USA) **Mrs S. Ricci**
75 **MIDNIGHT GAME (IRE)**, 6, b g Montjeu (IRE)—Midnight Angel (GER) **Gigginstown House Stud**
76 **MIDNIGHT OIL (IRE)**, 5, b g Motivator—One So Marvellous **Gigginstown House Stud**
77 **MIKAEL D'HAGUENET (FR)**, 9, b g Lavirco (GER)—Fleur d'haguenet (FR) **Mrs S. Ricci**
78 **MOURAD (IRE)**, 8, ch g Sinndar (IRE)—Mouramara (IRE) **Teahon Consulting Limited**
79 **MOVEABLE ASSET (IRE)**, 5, b g Trans Island—Mica Male (ITY) **Mrs T. Burns**
80 **MOZOLTOV (IRE)**, 7, b g Kayf Tara—Fairmead Princess **Martin Lynch**
81 **MR GROOCOCK (IRE)**, 8, b g Dolpour—Steel Typhoon **Howard Johnstone**
82 **ON HIS OWN (IRE)**, 9, b g Presenting—Shuil Na Mhuire (IRE) **Andrea & Graham Wylie**
83 **OUTLANDER (IRE)**, 5, b g Stowaway—Western Whisper (IRE) **Gigginstown House Stud**
84 **PASSAGE VENDOME (FR)**, 7, b g Polish Summer—Herodiade (FR) **Mr G. Mullins**
85 **PATANNE (IRE)**, 5, b g Golan (IRE)—Best Wait (IRE) **Shanakiel Racing Syndicate**
86 **PERFECT GENTLEMAN (IRE)**, 8, b g King's Theatre (IRE)—Millennium Lilly (IRE) **Mrs J. M. Mullins**
87 **PICKAPOCKETORTWO (IRE)**, 9, b g Fruits of Love (USA)—Lamp of Phoebus (USA) **YITBA Racing Club**
88 **PIQUE SOUS (FR)**, 6, gr g Martaline—Six Fois Sept (FR) **Not Just Any Racing Club**
89 **PONT ALEXANDRE (GER)**, 5, b g Dai Jin—Panzella (FR) **Mrs S. Ricci**
90 **POPCORN (FR)**, 10, b g Roakarad—Baie de Chalamont (FR) **Mrs J. M. Mullins**
91 **PRIDE OFTHE PARISH (IRE)**, 9, b g Flemensfirth (USA)—Rose Island **Mrs V. O'Leary**
92 **PRIMROSEANDBLUE (IRE)**, 9, b g Shernazar—Karlybelle (FR) **Mrs J. M. Mullins**
93 **PRINCE DE BEAUCHENE (FR)**, 10, b g French Glory—Chipie d'angron (FR) **Andrea & Graham Wylie**
94 **QUEL ESPRIT (FR)**, 9, gr g Saint des Saints (FR)—Jeune d'esprit (FR) **Red Barn Syndicate**
95 **QUEVEGA (FR)**, 9, b m Robin des Champs (FR)—Vega IV (FR) **Hammer & Trowel Syndicate**
96 **QUISCOVER FONTAINE (FR)**, 9, b g Antarctique (IRE)—Blanche Fontaine (FR) **J. P. McManus**
97 **RAISE HELL (IRE)**, 6, b g Presenting—Markiza (IRE) **Gigginstown House Stud**
98 **RAPTOR (FR)**, 8, gr g Caballo Raptor (CAN)—Tiwa (FR) **Aiden Devawey**
99 **RATTAN (USA)**, 8, ch g Royal Anthem (USA)—Rouwaki (USA) **J. A. Coleman**
100 **REINE ANGEVINE (FR)**, 5, b m Poliglote—Alliance Royale (FR) **Supreme Horse Racing Club**
101 **ROCKYABOYA (IRE)**, 9, ch g Rock Hopper—Motility **P. W. Mullins**
102 **ROLLY BABY (FR)**, 8, b g Funny Baby (FR)—Vancia (FR) **Teahon Consulting**
103 **ROUGH JUSTICE (IRE)**, 5, b g Beneficial—Ringzar (IRE) **Gigginstown House Stud**
104 **RUPERT LAMB (IRE)**, 7, gr g Central Park (IRE)—Charlotte Lamb **Andrea & Graham Wylie**
105 **SAMAIN (GER)**, 7, b g Black Sam Bellamy (IRE)—Selva (IRE) **Gigginstown House Stud**
106 **SARABAD (FR)**, 5, b g Astarabad (USA)—Saraphine (FR) **Mrs S. Ricci**
107 **SECURITY BREACH (IRE)**, 5, b g Red Clubs (IRE)—Lear's Crown (USA) **Gigginstown House Stud**
108 **SERGENT GUIB'S (FR)**, 7, b br g Califet (FR)—Miss Quessie (FR) **Mrs S. Ricci**
109 **SHAKE THE TREE (IRE)**, 6, b m Shantou (USA)—Back Log (IRE) **J. P. M. O'Connor**
110 **SHAKERVILZ (FR)**, 10, b g Villez (USA)—Zamsara (FR) **Mrs J. M. Mullins**
111 **SHAMAR (FR)**, 5, b h Dr Fong (USA)—Shamalana (IRE) **Mrs S. Ricci**
112 **SHAMSIKHAN (IRE)**, 4, ch g Dr Fong (USA)—Shamdala (IRE) **Mrs Audrey Turley**
113 **SICILIAN SECRET (IRE)**, 10, b g Flemensfirth (USA)—Kala Supreme (IRE) **Mrs S. Ricci**
114 **SIMENON (IRE)**, 6, b g Marju (IRE)—Epistoliere (IRE) **Wicklow Bloodstock Ltd**
115 **SIN PALO (IRE)**, 9, b g Dushyantor (USA)—Platinum Gold **Downthehatch Syndicate**
116 **SIR DES CHAMPS (FR)**, 7, b br g Robin des Champs (FR)—Liste En Tete (FR) **Gigginstown House Stud**
117 **SIZING BRISBANE (IRE)**, 5, b g Nayef (USA)—Elaine Tully (IRE) **Ann & Alan Potts**
118 **SIZING CHILE (IRE)**, 5, b g Flemensfirth (USA)—Smooching (IRE) **Ann & Alan Potts**
119 **SIZING SAHARA (IRE)**, 5, gr g Shirocco (GER)—Aristocratique **Ann & Alan Potts Partnership**
120 **SIZING TENNESSEE (IRE)**, 5, ch g Robin des Champs (FR)—Jolivia (FR) **Ann & Alan Potts**
121 **SO YOUNG (FR)**, 7, b g Lavirco (GER)—Honey (FR) **Mrs McMahon**
122 **SUNTIEP (FR)**, 7, b g Ungaro (GER)—Galostiepy (FR) **J. T. Ennis**
123 **SUPER MIX (FR)**, 7, b g Fragrant Mix (FR)—Fhilida (FR) **Philip J. Reynolds**
124 **SUPREME CAROLINA (IRE)**, 6, b m Traditionally (USA)—Carolina (FR) **Supreme Horse Racing Club**
125 **SWEET MY LORD (FR)**, 7, b g Johann Quatz (FR)—Hasta Manana (FR) **Mr A. Devaney**

MR WILLIAM P. MULLINS - Continued

126 **TANGO LOUVO (FR)**, 6, ch g Kapgarde (FR)—La Pipriataine (FR) **Supreme Horse Racing Club**
127 **TARLA (FR)**, 7, b m Lavirco (GER)—Targerine (FR) **Mrs S. Ricci**
128 **TASITIOCHT (IRE)**, 6, b m Oscar (IRE)—Victorine (IRE) **CCr Racing Syndicate**
129 **TENNIS CAP (FR)**, 6, b g Snow Cap (FR)—Jijie (FR) **Mrs Violet O'Leary**
130 **TERMINAL (FR)**, 6, b g Passing Sale (FR)—Durendal (FR) **Favourites Racing Syndicate**
131 **THE BOSSES COUSIN (IRE)**, 8, b g King's Theatre (IRE)—Seductive Dance **Mrs J. M. Mullins**
132 **THE MIDNIGHT CLUB (IRE)**, 12, ch g Flemensfirth (USA)—Larry's Peach **Mrs S. Ricci**
133 **THE PAPARRAZI KID (IRE)**, 6, b g Milan—Banbury Cross (IRE) **Byerley Thoroughbred Racing**
134 **THELEZE (FR)**, 6, b m Lavirco (GER)—Divette (FR) **Ann & Alan Potts Partnership**
135 **THOUSAND STARS (FR)**, 9, gr g Grey Risk (FR)—Livaniana (FR) **Hammer & Trowel Syndicate**
136 **TOOSTRONG (FR)**, 6, ch g Network (GER)—Fleurissa (FR) **Gigginstown House Stud**
137 **TURBAN (FR)**, 6, b g Dom Alco (FR)—Indianabelle (FR) **Edward O'Connell**
138 **TURNANDGO (IRE)**, 5, b g Morozov (USA)—Crazy Alice (IRE) **Gigginstown House Stud**
139 **TWIGLINE (FR)**, 6, gr m Martaline—Natty Twigy (FR) **Hammer & Trowel Syndicate**
140 **TWINLIGHT (FR)**, 6, b g Muhtathir—Fairlight (GER) **M L Bloodstock Limited**
141 **UN ATOUT (FR)**, 5, b g Robin des Champs (FR)—Badrapette (FR) **Gigginstown House Stud**
142 **UN BEAU ROMAN (FR)**, 5, bl g Roman Saddle (IRE)—Koukie (FR) **Aiden Devaney**
143 **UNCLE JUNIOR (IRE)**, 12, b g Saddlers' Hall (IRE)—Caslain Nua **Mrs M. McMahon**
144 **UNION DUES (FR)**, 5, b br g Malinas (GER)—Royale Dorothy (FR) **Allan McLuckie**
145 **UP THE BEAT**, 8, b br g Beat All (USA)—Everything's Rosy **Mrs A. M. Varmen**
146 **UPAZO (FR)**, 5, b g Enrique—Honey (FR) **Philip J Reynolds**
147 **UPSIE (FR)**, 5, b m Le Balafre (FR)—Medjie (FR) **John P. McManus**
148 **URANNA (FR)**, 5, gr m Panoramic—Irresistible Anna (FR) **Supreme Horse Racing Club**
149 **URANO (FR)**, 5, b g Enrique—Neiland (FR) **Mrs M. Mahon**
150 **VERY VITE (IRE)**, 8, b g Presenting—Lonizera (IRE) **Mrs J. M. Mullins**
151 **VESPER BELL (IRE)**, 7, b g Beneficial—Fair Choice (IRE) **Mrs S. Ricci**
152 **WELL READ MAN (IRE)**, 6, b g Presenting—Silent Orders (IRE) **Mrs M McMahon**
153 **WICKLOW GOLD (FR)**, 5, b g Robin des Champs (FR)—Gamine d'ici (FR) **Wicklow Bloodstock Limited**
154 **ZADARSKA (IRE)**, 8, b g Zagreb (USA)—Betterbebob (IRE) **Festival Syndicate**
155 **ZAIDPOUR (FR)**, 7, b g Red Ransom (USA)—Zainta (FR) **Mrs S. Ricci**
156 **ZUZKA (IRE)**, 6, b m Flemensfirth (USA)—Downtown Train (IRE) **Supreme Horse Racing Club**

---

460   MRS ANABEL MURPHY, Stratford-upon-Avon
Postal: **Ridgeway House, Billesley Road, Wilmcote, Stratford-upon-Avon, Warwickshire, CV37 9XG**
Contacts: **OFFICE (01789) 205087 HOME (01789) 298346 FAX (01789) 263260**
MOBILE (07774) 117777
E-MAIL **anabelking.racing@virgin.net** WEBSITE **www.anabelmurphy.co.uk**

1 **AMALRIC (FR)**, 6, b g Laveron—Aimessa du Berlais (FR) **Touchwood Racing**
2 **ASTON CANTLOW**, 5, b g Hurricane Run (IRE)—Princess Caraboo (IRE) **H. A. Murphy**
3 **BLACK CACHE (IRE)**, 7, b g Cachet Noir (USA)—Hindi (FR) **Mr Roger Outhwaite & Mrs Annabel Murphy**
4 **BOYCHUK (IRE)**, 12, b g Insan (USA)—Golden Flower (GER) **H. A. Murphy**
5 **CAP FALCO (IRE)**, 8, gr g Beneficial—Banderole (IRE) **H. A. Murphy**
6 **DORMOUSE**, 8, b g Medicean—Black Fighter (USA) **H. A. Murphy**
7 **KAKAPUKA**, 6, br g Shinko Forest (IRE)—No Rehearsal (FR) **Mrs E Mills & Mr A Murphy**
8 **KING'S ROAD**, 8, ch g King's Best (USA)—Saphire **Mrs A. L. M. Murphy**
9 **KORNATI KID**, 11, b g Kayf Tara—Hiltonstown Lass (IRE) **H. A. Murphy**
10 **LIBERATE**, 10, ch g Lomitas—Eversince (USA) **Mrs A. L. M. Murphy**
11 **LIFE LONG**, 9, b g Old Vic—Be My Rainbow (IRE) **Mr Roger Outhwaite & Mrs Annabel Murphy**
12 **PRINCE OF DENIAL (IRE)**, 9, b g Old Vic—Lerichi (IRE) **Vendman Systems Limited**
13 **RIGOLLETO (IRE)**, 5, b g Ad Valorem (USA)—Jallaissine (IRE) **All The Kings Horses**
14 **WALTER DE LA MARE (IRE)**, 6, b g Barathea (IRE)—Banutan (IRE) **The Early Boys**
15 **WARREN CHASE**, 8, b g Oscar (IRE)—Kilcash Cross (IRE) **Touchwood Racing**
16 **WHATSABILLION (IRE)**, 11, b br g Lahib (USA)—Outstanding Order (IRE) **Touchwood Racing**

Other Owners: Mr C. Logan, Mrs E. A. Mills, Mr R. Outhwaite, Mr Z. Whitbread.

Assistant Trainer: Aiden Murphy

Amateur: Mr O. J. Murphy.

461 MR COLM MURPHY, Gorey
Postal: **Ballinadrummin, Killena, Gorey, Co. Wexford, Ireland**
Contacts: PHONE **(00353) 53 9482690** FAX **(00353) 53 9482690** MOBILE **(00353) 862 629538**
E-MAIL **murphycolma@hotmail.com** WEBSITE **www.colmmurphyracing.ie**

1 ALADDINS CAVE, 9, b g Rainbow Quest (USA)—Flight of Fancy **Treasure Hunters Syndicate**
2 BOUILLABAISSE (IRE), 7, b m Beat Hollow—Cattermole (USA) **Barry Connell**
3 CARA'S OSCAR (IRE), 7, b g Oscar (IRE)—Distant Gale (IRE) **A. T. Battersby**
4 CORR POINT (IRE), 6, b g Azamour (IRE)—Naazeq **Declan Hogan**
5 DANGAN DAYLIGHT (IRE), 7, ch m Old Vic—Nobull (IRE) **Michael Hoare**
6 DREAM FUNCTION (IRE), 8, b m King's Theatre (IRE)—Function Dream (IRE) **Bernard Cloney**
7 EASY MATE (IRE), 7, ch m Monsun (GER)—All To Easy **John Doyle**
8 GATES OF ROME (IRE), 9, b g Luso—Express Mail (IRE) **Gigginstown House Stud**
9 GLAM GERRY (IRE), 9, b g Dr Massini (IRE)—Daraheen Diamond (IRE) **Barry Connell**
10 GROVE FIELD (IRE), 6, ch g Moscow Society (USA)—Wall-Nut Grove (IRE) **E. Nolan**
11 JAROB, 6, br g Beat All (USA)—Wishy (IRE) **C. Jones**
12 MAGIC SPEAR (IRE), 7, b g Dr Massini (IRE)—Charming Present (IRE) **Barry Connell**
13 MISTER HOTELIER (IRE), 6, b g Beneficial—Accordian Lady (IRE) **Mark McDonagh**
14 PRESENTING BEARA (IRE), 5, b g Presenting—Ginger Bar (IRE) **Winning Ways Solar Syndicate**
15 QUITO DE LA ROQUE (FR), 9, b g Saint des Saints (FR)—Moody Cloud (FR) **Gigginstown House Stud**
16 RAISE THE BEAT, 8, b g Beat All (USA)—Autumn Leaf **Winning Ways Enigma Syndicate**
17 RYE MARTINI (IRE), 6, b g Catcher In The Rye (IRE)—Nocturne In March (IRE) **Gigginstown House Stud**
18 SHARIYAN (IRE), 7, b g Kahyasi—Sharesha (IRE) **Mrs Teresa Murphy**
19 THE HARD HAT (IRE), 9, b g Beneficial—Three Hats (IRE) **Shane J. Harrington**
20 THE WESTENER BOY (IRE), 6, b g Westerner—Designer Lady (IRE) **J. P. McManus**
21 VOLER LA VEDETTE (IRE), 9, b m King's Theatre (IRE)—Steel Grey Lady (IRE) **Mrs M. Brophy**

Other Owners: Owen Cloney, S. Delaney, Maura Doyle, Sean Hoare.

Assistant Trainer: Patrick Murphy

Amateur: Mr C. Motherway, Mr A. J. Walsh.

462 MR FERDY MURPHY, West Witton
Postal: **Wynbury Stables, West Witton, Leyburn, North Yorkshire, DL8 4LR**
Contacts: PHONE **(01969) 622289** FAX **(01969) 625278**
MOBILE **(07703) 444398** & **(07747) 017960**
E-MAIL **office@wynburystables.fsnet.co.uk** WEBSITE **www.ferdymurphyracing.co.uk**

1 ALCO BABA (IRE), 5, ch m Dom Alco (FR)—Aintree Baba (FR) **F. Murphy**
2 ALMADAN (IRE), 5, b g Azamour (IRE)—Alamouna (IRE) **A & S Enterprises Ltd**
3 ANGEL SUN (FR), 7, b g Astarabad (USA)—Five Rivers (FR) **Outhart, Trembath, Hyde, Fletcher, Hill**
4 ANTIRRHINUM, 6, b g Bollin Eric—Artemesia **Beautifully Bred Partnership**
5 BADGERS DEN, 5, ch g Tobougg (IRE)—Lumpini Park **F. Murphy**
6 BADGERS RETREAT, 7, b g Elusive City (USA)—Heuston Station (IRE) **F. Murphy**
7 BALDING BANKER (IRE), 7, b g Accordion—What A Breeze (IRE) **Club Racing Banker Partnership**
8 BORDERHOPPER, 9, ch g Zaha (CAN)—Tom's Influence **Mr P. Cranney**
9 BRANDON THOMAS (IRE), 7, br g Norwich—Last Sunrise (IRE) **Mr S Hubbard Rodwell & Mr Ferdy Murphy**
10 5, B m Heron Island (IRE)—Caracool (FR) **F. Murphy**
11 CHARINGWORTH (IRE), 10, b g Supreme Leader—Quinnsboro Guest (IRE) **A & S Enterprises Ltd**
12 CHAVOY (FR), 8, br g Saint des Saints (FR)—Dictania (FR) **Miss R. E. A. Menzies**
13 COCCINELLE (FR), 5, b m Caballo Raptor (CAN)—Pierrebrune (FR) **D. Parry**
14 DE BOITRON (FR), 9, b g Sassanian (USA)—Pondiki (FR) **Mrs J. Morgan & Mrs Lindsey J. Shaw**
15 DE VOUS A MOI (FR), 5, b g Sinndar (IRE)—Dzinigane (FR) **Mrs J. Morgan**
16 DIVERS (FR), 9, gr g Highest Honor—Divination (USA) **Let's Live Racing**
17 DOMOLY (FR), 10, b g Varese (FR)—Queen d'ouilly (FR) **The Extra Time Partnership**
18 ELIADES RUN (IRE), 7, b g Turtle Island (IRE)—Chancy Gal **Mr C. T. Eliades**
19 ERIN DANCER (IRE), 8, b g Chevalier (IRE)—Negria (IRE) **J. & A. Millar**
20 EWE ARE JOKING, 5, b g Midnight Legend—Ewe Beauty (FR) **Mr & Mrs Neil Iveson & Mr R G Capstick**
21 FORMULATION (IRE), 6, b g Danehill Dancer (IRE)—
Formal Approval (USA) **Poppies Europe Ltd, Clinton, Gale, Murphy**
22 GAVROCHE GAUGAIN (FR), 9, b g Varese (FR)—Jobereine (FR) **Universal Recycling Company**
23 GEORGE ANTON (FR), 5, ch g Croco Rouge (IRE)—Belmarita (IRE) **Mr S Hubbard Rodwell & Mr Ferdy Murphy**
24 GLASSON LAD (IRE), 6, b g Quws—Glasson House (IRE) **M. F. Bourke**
25 GOING WRONG, 10, b g Bob Back (USA)—Lucy Glitters **Universal Recycling Company**

MR FERDY MURPHY - Continued

26 HEL TARA, 4, b f Kayf Tara—Heltornic (IRE) **S. L. Rodwell**
27 HOLLO LADIES (IRE), 8, ch g Captain Rio—Lace Flower **M. F. Bourke**
28 IBN HIYYAN (USA), 6, gr ro g El Prado—Lovely Later (USA) **Mr C. Eliades & Mr C. McHugh**
29 4, B g Generous (IRE)—Indian Empress
30 LAP OF HONOUR (IRE), 9, b g Danehill Dancer (IRE)—Kingsridge (IRE) **D. Clinton, S. Gale, M. Milns**
31 LORD VILLEZ (FR), 9, b g Villez (USA)—Samina (FR) **A. G. Chappell**
32 LOXENDOR (FR), 7, b g Loxias (FR)—Tronevenne (FR) **F. Murphy**
33 MANSONIEN L'AS (FR), 7, b g Mansonnien (FR)—Star des As (FR) **Let's Live Racing**
34 MCNULTY WRAY (IRE), 5, b g Westerner—Lyphard Abu (USA) **Poppies Europe Limited**
35 MISTER WALL STREET (FR), 8, b br g Take Risks (FR)—Miss Breezy (FR) **Gay & Peter Hartley**
36 5, B g Midnight Legend—Obligee de Sivola (FR) **F. Murphy**
37 OCKEY DE NEULLIAC (FR), 11, ch g Cyborg (FR)—Graine de Neulliac (FR) **F. Murphy**
38 ON GOSSAMER WINGS (IRE), 9, b g Winged Love (IRE)—Katie Parson **Premier Racing Partnerships**
39 OR D'OUDAIRIES (FR), 11, b g April Night (FR)—Belle Truval (FR) **Gay & Peter Hartley**
40 OUEST ECLAIR (FR), 8, b g Sagacity (FR)—Kalistina (FR) **Premier Racing Partnerships**
41 OZIER HILL (IRE), 4, br g Arcadio (GER)—Lady Clara (IRE) **Mrs R. D. Cairns**
42 POKER DE SIVOLA (FR), 10, b g Discover d'auteuil (FR)—Legal Union **D. A. Johnson**
43 POPPIES MILAN (IRE), 4, b g Milan—Second Best (IRE) **Poppies Europe Limited**
44 RECKLESS ROMEO (IRE), 4, b g Heliostatic (IRE)—Ballerina Babe (IRE) **E. Banville**
45 RICH LORD, 9, b g Zamindar (USA)—Al Corniche (IRE) **Let's Live Racing**
46 RIGUEZ DANCER, 9, b g Dansili—Tricoteuse **Let's Live Racing**
47 SAMSON COLLONGES (FR), 7, gr g Fragrant Mix (IRE)—Idole Collonges (FR) **Premier Racing Partnerships**
48 SAN CASSIANO (IRE), 6, b g Bertolini (USA)—
                                              Celtic Silhouette (FR) **Mitchell, Jackson, Shaw, Joseph & Martin**
49 SECRET DESERT, 7, b g Dubai Destination (USA)—Lady Bankes (IRE) **The Extra Time Partnership**
50 SMART MISTRESS, 11, b gr m Silver Patriarch (IRE)—Smart Rhythm **Helen Harvey Robert Woodward**
51 STAND CLEAR, 8, b m Sir Harry Lewis (USA)—Clair Valley **Premier Racing Partnerships**
52 6, B g Bienamado (USA)—Starshade (IRE) **F. Murphy**
53 THE HOLLINWELL, 10, b g Classic Cliche (IRE)—Action de Balle (FR) **Mr & Mrs N. Iveson**
54 UTE ANTIQUE (FR), 5, b m Robin des Pres (FR)—
                                              Joie de Cotte (FR) **Mr S Hubbard Rodwell & Mr Ferdy Murphy**
55 VUVUZELA, 7, ch g Sir Harry Lewis (USA)—Clair Valley **Premier Racing Partnerships**
56 WADNAAN, 6, ch g Shamardal (USA)—Australian Dreams **Mrs J. Morgan**
57 ZACANA (FR), 5, b m Robin des Champs (FR)—Cohiba (FR) **F. Murphy**

Other Owners: M. Ball, J. Berry, R. G. Capstick, Miss D. M. Clinton, Mrs M. Feely, Mr N. Fletcher, L. R. Frampton, Mrs S. V. Gale, P. A. H. Hartley, Mrs R. C. Hartley, Mrs H. M. Harvey, D. N. Iveson, Mrs J. E. Iveson, Mr S. R. Jackson, R. C. Joseph, Mr J. S. Martin, C. J. McHugh, Mr A. R. Millar, Mrs J. Millar, Mrs M. Milns, Dr J. C. Mitchell, A. J. Outhart, Mr G. W. Peacock, Mr L. D. Shaw, Mrs L. J. Shaw, Major P. H. K. Steveney, Ms J. S. Storrow, Miss C. B. Storrow, R. H. Woodward.

Assistant Trainer: Rebecca Menzies

Jockey (NH): James Reveley. **Conditional:** Lucy Alexander, Tony Kelly, Dylan McDonagh, John Winston. **Amateur:** Mr Rees Morgan Murphy, Miss Catherine Walton.

---

463 **MR M. P. F. MURPHY, Newmarket**
Postal: 76 Weston Way, Newmarket, Suffolk, CB8 7SF
Contacts: PHONE (01638) 561099 MOBILE (07951) 766035
E-MAIL mpfequine@hotmail.co.uk

1 CELTIC LEGACY, 6, ch m Where Or When (IRE)—An Cailin Rua **Mr M. P. F. Murphy**
2 ENTHUSIASTIC, 5, b h Galileo (IRE)—Que Puntual (ARG) **Mr M. Keller**
3 IMPRESS ME, 5, ch m Sulamani (IRE)—An Cailin Rua **Michael P Murphy & Marie Wymer**
4 JACK FIREFLY, 4, b g Echo of Light—Charlottebutterfly **Future Electrical Services Ltd**
5 NOGUCHI (IRE), 8, ch g Pivotal—Tuscania (USA) **Mr M. P. F. Murphy**
6 ROCK OF AGES, 4, ch g Pivotal—Magic Peak (IRE) **R. W. Smith**

TWO-YEAR-OLDS

7 B c 30/1 Sakhee (USA)—Lake Diva (Docksider (USA))

Other Owners: Mrs M. Wymer.

464 MR MIKE MURPHY, Westoning

Postal: **Broadlands, Manor Park Stud, Westoning, Bedfordshire, MK45 5LA**
Contacts: PHONE **(01525) 717305** FAX **(01525) 717305** MOBILE **(07770) 496103**
E-MAIL **mmurphy@globalnet.co.uk** WEBSITE **www.mikemurphyracing.co.uk**

1 **ANGEL WAY (IRE)**, 4, br f Trans Island—Zilayah (USA) **Mr D. Ellis**
2 **AVONMORE STAR**, 5, b g Avonbridge—
    Pooka's Daughter (IRE) **Goff, Hoskins, Hyde, Lobo & Smith x 2 & Partner**
3 **CHAPTER AND VERSE (IRE)**, 7, gr g One Cool Cat (USA)—Beautiful Hill (IRE) **Mr D. J. Ellis**
4 **DUCAL**, 5, b g Iceman—Noble Lady **The Icebreakers**
5 **GREENSWARD**, 7, b g Green Desert (USA)—Frizzante **The Furlong Friends**
6 **HURRICANE LADY (IRE)**, 5, b m Hurricane Run (IRE)—Yaria (IRE) **Mr Borgatti & Mr Moir**
7 **IF YOU WHISPER (IRE)**, 5, b g Iffraaj—Little Whisper (IRE) **Mr P. J. A. Woods**
8 **IL PAZZO**, 4, b g Multiplex—Nut (IRE) **Borgatti Moir and Murphy**
9 **KAKATOSI**, 6, br g Pastoral Pursuits—Ladywell Blaise (IRE) **Robert E. Tillett**
10 **LA FORTUNATA**, 6, b m Lucky Story (USA)—Phantasmagoria **James Patton**
11 **LOVE YOUR LOOKS**, 5, b m Iffraaj—Play Around (IRE) **M. Murphy**
12 **LUTINE BELL**, 6, ch g Starcraft (NZ)—Satin Bell **Rogerson, Carr & Murphy**
13 **MUHDIQ (USA)**, 4, b c Hard Spun (USA)—Enfiraaj (USA) **Ms A. D. Tibbett**
14 **RED SOMERSET (USA)**, 10, b g Red Ransom (USA)—Bielska (USA) **M. Murphy**
15 **REGALO ROSADO**, 4, ch f Cadeaux Genereux—Pinkai (IRE) **Goff, Hoskins, Hyde, Lobo & Smith x 2**
16 **ROCK ANTHEM (IRE)**, 9, ch g Rock of Gibraltar (IRE)—Regal Portrait (IRE) **R. Bright**

THREE-YEAR-OLDS

17 **CAPTAIN CAROLINE**, b f Multiplex—Nut (IRE) **Mrs C. J. Barr**
18 **CHORAL PRINCE (IRE)**, b c Oratorio (IRE)—Princess of Iona (IRE) **The Oratorios**
19 **DANEGLOW (IRE)**, ch f Thousand Words—Valluga (IRE) **Mrs J. E. A. Thompson**
20 **DIVIDEND DAN (IRE)**, ch g Danroad (AUS)—Pip'n Judy (IRE) **Mr N. C. F. McLeod-Clarke**
21 **ETON MISS (IRE)**, ch f Windsor Knot (IRE)—Miss Barcelona (IRE) **Basing, Jennings, Murphy & Murphy**
22 **PRINCESS CAMMIE (IRE)**, b f Camacho—Hawattef (IRE) **Mr N. C. F. McLeod-Clarke**
23 **UP TIPP**, ch g Medicean—Jetbeeah (IRE) **Cobby, Williams, O'Connell, Murphy**

TWO-YEAR-OLDS

24 **LOSTINTHECLOUDS**, b f 29/1 Firebreak—Day By Day (Kyllachy) (18000) **Borgatti & Moir**
25 B f 14/4 Myboycharlie (IRE)—Play Around (IRE) (Niniski (USA)) **A Partnership**
26 **SHEER POETRY (IRE)**, b f 1/3 Yeats (IRE)—Sassari (IRE) (Darshaan) (10000) **Borgatti & Moir**

Other Owners: Mr A. M. Basing, Mr Mario Borgatti, Mrs Milly Bright, Mr R. S. Hoskins, Mr Stuart Moir, Mr M. Murphy, Mr Bill Rogerson, Mr A. C. Smith.

Assistant Trainer: J.P. Cullinan

465 MR PAT MURPHY, Hungerford

Postal: **Glebe House Stables, School Lane, East Garston, Nr Hungerford, Berkshire, RG17 7HR**
Contacts: OFFICE **(01488) 648473** FAX **(01488) 649775** MOBILE **(07831) 410409**
E-MAIL **pat@mabberleys.freeserve.co.uk** WEBSITE **www.patmurphyracing.com**

1 **CATALINAS DIAMOND (IRE)**, 5, b m One Cool Cat (USA)—Diamondiferous (USA) **Briton International**
2 **CLOUDY BOB (IRE)**, 6, gr g Cloudings (IRE)—Keen Supreme (IRE) **Men Of Stone**
3 **MOSCOW IN APRIL (IRE)**, 6, ch m Moscow Society (USA)—Muharib Lady (IRE) **P. G. Murphy**
4 **WESTERN DIVA (IRE)**, 4, b f Westerner—Duck 'n' Dive (IRE) **Mrs D. E. Murphy**

Other Owners: B. H. Goldswain, Mrs J. B. H. Goldswain, Mr R. Guest, Mr P. D. Lloyd.

Assistant Trainer: Mrs Dianne Murphy

Jockey (flat): Steve Drowne, Robert Havlin. Jockey (NH): Leighton Aspell, Colin Bolger.

466 MR BARRY MURTAGH, Carlisle

Postal: **Hurst Farm, Ivegill, Carlisle, Cumbria, CA4 0NL**
Contacts: PHONE **(01768) 484649** FAX **(01768) 484744** MOBILE **(07714) 026741**
E-MAIL **sue@suemurtagh.wanadoo.co.uk**

1 **CARRIETAU**, 10, b g Key of Luck (USA)—Carreamia **A. R. White**

MR BARRY MURTAGH - Continued

2 **DAY DREAM GIRL**, 5, b m Overbury (IRE)—Globe Dream (IRE) **G. & P. Barker Ltd**
3 **HORTON**, 5, b g Beat All (USA)—Fen Terrier **Mrs S. Murtagh**
4 **ILLUSTRATION (IRE)**, 5, b g Pivotal—In Anticipation (IRE) **R & K Carter**
5 **KEALIGOLANE (IRE)**, 9, gr g Beneficial—Leone Des Pres (FR) **J. R. Callow**
6 **KING'S CHORISTER**, 7, ch g King's Best (USA)—Chorist **Woodgate Partnership**
7 **LUCKY MELLOR**, 6, b g Lucky Story (USA)—Lady Natilda **Mr Don O'Connor & Mr Derek Wilson**
8 **PATRIOT (IRE)**, 9, b g Sadler's Wells (USA)—Sweeten Up **Mrs S. Murtagh**
9 **PETE**, 10, b g Overbury (IRE)—Fen Terrier **Mrs S. Murtagh**
10 **RAGGIOS BOY**, 7, ch g Karinga Bay—Fen Terrier **Mrs S. Murtagh**
11 **SHAKER STYLE (USA)**, 7, ch g Gulch (USA)—Carr Shaker (USA) **Mr K. Fitzsimons & Mr G. Fell**
12 **STANLEY BRIDGE**, 6, b g Avonbridge—Antonia's Folly **The Early Doors Partnership**
13 **TORREDELAROCA (IRE)**, 5, b m Flemensfirth (USA)—Gortbofearna (IRE) **Affordable Fun**
14 **TROUBLE IN PARIS (IRE)**, 6, ch g Great Palm (USA)—Ten Dollar Bill (IRE) **Hurst Farm Racing**
15 **UNEX PICASSO**, 5, b g Galileo (IRE)—Ruff Shod (USA) **Mrs S. Murtagh**

THREE-YEAR-OLDS

16 **BARABOY (IRE)**, b c Barathea (IRE)—Irina (IRE) **A. R. White**

Other Owners: Mr Robert Carter, Mrs F. K. Carter, Mr G. Fell, Mr K. Fitzsimons, Mrs Ann Holt-Thomas, Mrs M. Hutt, Mr James Murtagh, Mr F. P. Murtagh, Mr Trevor Noble, Mr D. O'Connor, Mr Michael A. Proudfoot, Mr David J. Swindlehurst, Mr Dave Teasdale, Mr Keith Thomas, Mr Derek Wilson.

Assistant Trainer: S A Murtagh

---

467   **MR WILLIE MUSSON, Newmarket**
Postal: **Saville House, St Mary's Square, Newmarket, Suffolk, CB8 0HZ**
Contacts: PHONE **(01638) 663371** FAX **(01638) 667979**
E-MAIL willie@williemusson.co.uk WEBSITE www.williemusson.co.uk

1 **ABSOLUTELY ME (IRE)**, 4, ch f Barathea (IRE)—Attymon Lill (IRE) **Miss Alison Jones**
2 **AKARANA (IRE)**, 6, b g Danehill Dancer (IRE)—Castle Quest (IRE) **W. J. Musson**
3 **BOLD ADVENTURE**, 9, ch g Arkadian Hero (USA)—Impatiente (USA) **W. J. Musson**
4 **BROUGHTON PLACE**, 5, b m Compton Place—Classic Millennium **Broughton Thermal Insulations**
5 **BROUGHTONS BANDIT**, 6, b g Kyllachy—Broughton Bounty **Broughton Thermal Insulations**
6 **BROUGHTONS STAR**, 6, ch g Starcraft (NZ)—Marrakech (IRE) **Broughton Thermal Insulations**
7 **CAPRISKA**, 4, b f Bahri (USA)—Guignol (IRE) **Mr L. J. Mann**
8 **COMMON TOUCH (IRE)**, 5, ch g Compton Place—Flying Finish (FR) **Broughton Thermal Insulations**
9 **COZY TIGER (USA)**, 8, gr g Hold That Tiger (USA)—Cozelia (USA) **McHugh & Partners**
10 **EMEEBEE**, 7, b g Medicean—Broughtons Motto **Broughton Thermal Insulations**
11 **ENSNARE**, 8, b g Pivotal—Entrap (USA) **Mr C. Owen**
12 **HURRICANE HYMNBOOK (USA)**, 8, b g Pulpit (USA)—April Squall (USA) **W. J. Musson**
13 **LIFE OF LAUGHTER (USA)**, 5, b g Elusive Quality (USA)—Country Garden **W. J. Musson**
14 **MAC'S POWER (IRE)**, 7, b g Exceed And Excel (AUS)—Easter Girl **Broughton Thermal Insulations**
15 **MADAME ALLSORTS**, 8, b m Double Trigger (IRE)—Always A Pleasure **Mr R Musson & Mr P Thompson**
16 **MAGICALMYSTERYTOUR (IRE)**, 10, b g Sadler's Wells (USA)—Jude **Broughton Thermal Insulations**
17 **MOUNTAIN RANGE (IRE)**, 5, b g High Chaparral (IRE)—Tuscany Lady (IRE) **W. J. Musson**
18 **NOVELLEN LAD (IRE)**, 8, b g Noverre (USA)—Lady Ellen **Johnson & Broughton**
19 **ROCKET ROB (IRE)**, 7, b g Danetime (IRE)—Queen of Fibres (IRE) **W. J. Musson**
20 **RUSTIC DEACON**, 6, ch g Pastoral Pursuits—Anne-Lise **Mrs R. H. Brown**
21 **SAFWAAN**, 6, b g Selkirk (USA)—Kawn **W. J. Musson**
22 5, B g Where Or When (IRE)—Sleave Silk (IRE) **Broughton Thermal Insulations**

THREE-YEAR-OLDS

23 **BROUGHTONS CHARM (IRE)**, b f Invincible Spirit (IRE)—Parisian Elegance **Broughton Thermal Insulations**
24 **LADY COOPER**, b f Ishiguru (USA)—Mistress Cooper **Mrs R. H. Brown**
25 B f Bahri (USA)—Yaqootah (USA) **Broughton Thermal Insulations**

TWO-YEAR-OLDS

26 B f 24/2 Aqlaam—Hidden Meaning (Cadeaux Genereux) (57000) **Broughton Thermal Insulations**
27 B c 4/3 Medicean—
              Lifetime Romance (IRE) (Mozart (IRE)) (25000) **Broughton Thermal Insulation & B. N. Fulton**
28 B f 16/2 Mount Nelson—Motif (Observatory (USA)) (5000) **W. J. Musson**

MR WILLIE MUSSON - Continued

Other Owners: Miss A. Abdullah, Mr C. Eliades, Mr Fergus Falk, Mrs M. Graham-Campbell, Mr Chris McHugh, Mr R. D. Musson, Mr W J Musson, Mr John Scrider, Mr Patrick Thompson, K. L. West.

Jockey (flat): Stevie Donohoe, Jamie Mackay. **Jockey (NH):** Leighton Aspell.

---

468 **MR DAVID NAGLE, Fethard**
Postal: Kilconnell Stables, Mocklers Hill, Fethard, Co Tipperary, Ireland
Contacts: **MOBILE (00353) 87 2664390**
E-MAIL kilconnellstables@gmail.com

1 ACCLAIMED ANGEL (IRE), 4, gr g Dark Angel (IRE)—There With Me (USA) **Lisbunny Syndicate**
2 AQUA REGIA (IRE), 4, ch g Pivotal—Aquarist **Lisatunny Syndicate**
3 BATU (IRE), 4, b g Lawman (FR)—Expectation (IRE) **Lisatunny Syndicate**
4 4, B f Presenting—Berkeley House (IRE) **John Quinn**
5 CHALET GIRL, 4, b f Oasis Dream—Sauterne **Lisduff Syndicate**
6 CHINA REIGN (IRE), 5, ch m Golan (IRE)—Supreme Baloo (IRE) **Caroline Haney**
7 CLORAN CHARLIE (IRE), 5, b g Millenary—Joyful Music (IRE) **John Power**
8 DARK DANGER (IRE), 4, b f Amadeus Wolf—Danzelline **Lisbunny Syndicate**
9 DOOKS LAD (IRE), 6, b g Rudimentary—Deverells Tina (IRE) **David Meredith**
10 FANTASTIC MYSTERY (IRE), 4, b f Chapel Royal (USA)—You're Fantastic (USA) **Mrs P. Nagle**
11 LIGHT ZABEEL (USA), 4, b f Invasor (ARG)—Ashraakat (USA) **Lisduff Syndicate**
12 LONG STRAND (IRE), 9, b g Saddlers' Hall (IRE)—Oh So Breezy (IRE) **Evanna McCutcheon**
13 LORD NELLERIE (FR), 14, b g Panoramic—Epsom Nellerie (FR) **Evanna McCutcheon**
14 MAAREK, 6, b g Pivotal—Ruby Rocket (IRE) **Lisbunny Syndicate**
15 OSUS (USA), 4, b g Street Sense (USA)—Aurelia (USA) **Lisatunny Syndicate**
16 PENNY LAFARGE (IRE), 5, ch m Classic Cliche (IRE)—Gymslip (IRE) **John Kenrick**
17 TINCAN TOM (IRE), 4, b g Moss Vale (IRE)—Brave Dance (IRE) **Thomas A. Keating**

TWO-YEAR-OLDS

18 B f 17/4 Captain Rio—Positano Princess (Tobougg (IRE)) (1586)
19 Ch f 4/3 Fracas (IRE)—Rajani (IRE) (Johannesburg (USA)) (8333)
20 B c 7/2 Jeremy (USA)—Sonic Night (IRE) (Night Shift (USA)) (3174)

Other Owners: M. Fogarty, P. M. Guerin.

Assistant Trainer: Evanna McCutcheon

Jockey (flat): R. P. Cleary, J. A. Heffernan, M. Hussey, W. J. Lee, W. M. Lordan, J. P. O'Brien. **Jockey (NH):** J. R. Barry, J. Cullen. **Conditional:** M. Ferris. **Apprentice:** M. A. Cleere. **Amateur:** Mr Ben Crawford, Miss E. McCutcheon.

---

469 **DR JEREMY NAYLOR, Shrewton**
Postal: The Cleeve, Elston Lane, Shrewton, Wiltshire, SP3 4HL
Contacts: PHONE (01980) 620804 MOBILE (07771) 740126
E-MAIL info@jeremynaylor.com WEBSITE www.jeremynaylor.com

1 ACOSTA, 9, b g Foxhound (USA)—Dancing Heights (IRE) **The Acosta Partnership**
2 4, B f Striking Ambition—Daphne's Doll (IRE) **The Acosta Partnership**
3 4, B f Double Trigger (IRE)—Hilarious (IRE) **Miles Electronics Ltd**
4 ILDIKO (USA), 6, b m Yes It's True (USA)—Eternity **Dr J. R. J. Naylor**
5 PADOVA, 7, b g Shahrastani (USA)—My Song of Songs **Mr A. Brown**
6 POPPY GREGG, 8, b m Tamure (IRE)—Opalette **The Acosta Partnership**
7 TOUS LES DEUX, 10, b g Efisio—Caerosa **Dr J. R. J. Naylor**
8 WASPY, 4, ch f King's Best (USA)—Gib (IRE) **Cleeve Stables Racing Partnership**

TWO-YEAR-OLDS

9 B f 22/4 Striking Ambition—Sweet Request (Best of The Bests (IRE)) **Mrs S. P. Elphick**

Other Owners: Mr T. Bougourd, Mrs S. P. Elphick.

Jockey (NH): Wayne Kavanagh, Robert Kirk.

470 MR JOHN NEEDHAM, Ludlow
Postal: **Gorsty Farm, Mary Knoll, Ludlow, Shropshire, SY8 2HD**
Contacts: **PHONE (01584) 872112/874826 FAX (01584) 873256 MOBILE (07811) 451137**

1 BRINGEWOOD BELLE, 10, b m Kayf Tara—Carlingford Belle **J. L. Needham**
2 ELTON FOX, 8, br g Bob Back (USA)—Leinthall Fox **Miss J. C. L. Needham**
3 7, B h Bob Back (USA)—Leinthall Fox **Miss J. C. L. Needham**
4 MORTIMERS CROSS, 12, b g Cloudings (IRE)—Leinthall Doe **J. L. Needham**

Assistant Trainer: P. Hanly

Jockey (NH): Jason Maguire, Paul Moloney. **Amateur:** Mr Paul John.

471 MRS HELEN NELMES, Dorchester
Postal: **Warmwell Stables, 2 Church Cottages, Warmwell, Dorchester, Dorset, DT2 8HQ**
Contacts: **PHONE/FAX (01305) 852254 MOBILE (07977) 510318**
E-MAIL warmwellstud@tiscali.co.uk WEBSITE www.warmwellracing.co.uk

1 CRANKY CORNER, 9, b g Classic Cliche (IRE)—Pondimari (FR) **K. A. Nelmes**
2 HIGH BALL ROLLER, 5, ch g Selkirk (USA)—Minerva (IRE) **K. A. Nelmes**
3 KALMBEFORETHESTORM, 5, ch g Storming Home—Miss Honeypenny (IRE) **Warmwellcome Partnership**
4 4, B f Amrak Ajeeb (IRE)—Larry's Law (IRE) **K. A. Nelmes**
5 MANICS MAN, 8, ch g Double Trigger (IRE)—No Near Miss **Mrs Kim House & Mrs Heather Heal**
6 ORVITA (FR), 11, b g Lute Antique (FR)—Ulvita (FR) **K. A. Nelmes**
7 THE CLYDA ROVER (IRE), 9, ch g Moonax (IRE)—Pampered Molly (IRE) **K. A. Nelmes**
8 UNOWHATIMEANHARRY, 5, b g Sir Harry Lewis (USA)—Red Nose Lady **Miss S. J. Hartley**
9 WEST BAY HOOLIE, 7, b g Nomadic Way (USA)—West Bay Breeze **C. T. & A. Samways**
10 WITCHESINTUNE, 6, b m Beat Hollow—Music Park (IRE) **Miss S. J. Hartley**
11 ZULU PRINCIPLE, 6, b g Tiger Hill (IRE)—Tu Eres Mi Amore (IRE) **K. A. Nelmes**

Other Owners: Mrs H. A. Heal, Mrs K. M. House, Miss V. O. Kardas, C. T. Samways, Mrs A. Samways.

Assistant Trainer: K Nelmes

Amateur: Mr James Legg.

472 MR CHRIS NENADICH, Sutton
Postal: **Lakes Farm, Sutton, Herefordshire, HR1 3NS**
Contacts: **PHONE (01432) 880278 MOBILE (07860) 484400**

1 HADRON COLLIDER (FR), 8, ch g Dubai Destination (USA)—Liver De Saron (USA) **Chris & Nick Nenadich**
Other Owners: Mr N. Nenadich, C. Nenadich.

Assistant Trainer: Marion Collins

473 MR TONY NEWCOMBE, Barnstaple
Postal: **Lower Delworthy, Yarnscombe, Barnstaple, Devon, EX31 3LT**
Contacts: **PHONE/FAX (01271) 858554 MOBILE (07785) 297210**
E-MAIL huntshawequineforest@talktalk.net

1 BITTER LEMON, 4, b f Indesatchel (IRE)—Citron **Joli Racing**
2 BRANNOC (IRE), 8, b g Pilsudski (IRE)—Ned's Choice (IRE) **D. G. Staddon**
3 DUNHOY (IRE), 5, ch g Goodricke—Belle of The Blues (IRE) **D. M. J. Gilbert**
4 EVER THE OPTIMIST (IRE), 5, b g Cape Cross (IRE)—Have Faith (IRE) **D. M. J. Gilbert**
5 HANOVERIAN BARON, 8, b g Green Desert (USA)—Josh's Pearl (IRE) **P. Moulton**
6 HOLDEN EAGLE, 8, b g Catcher In The Rye (IRE)—Bird of Prey (IRE) **The About A Fortnight Partnership**
7 JOLLY RANCH, 7, gr m Compton Place—How Do I Know **Joli Racing**
8 KAY SERA, 5, b g Kayf Tara—Inflation **N. P. Hardy**
9 LUNDY SKY, 8, b g Zaha (CAN)—Rosina Mae **The Devonian Partnership**
10 MAMBO SPIRIT (IRE), 9, b g Invincible Spirit (IRE)—Mambodorga (USA) **N. P. Hardy**
11 MY METEOR, 6, b g Bahamian Bounty—Emerald Peace (IRE) **A. G. Newcombe**
12 SIGNORA FRASI (IRE), 8, b m Indian Ridge—Sheba (IRE) **Mr K. Eastup**

MR TONY NEWCOMBE - Continued

13 **SPELLMAKER**, 4, b g Kheleyf (USA)—Midnight Spell **Joli Racing**
14 **TEUTONIC KNIGHT (IRE)**, 6, ch g Daggers Drawn (USA)—Azyaa **R. J. Turton**
15 **VICTORIAN BOUNTY**, 8, b g Bahamian Bounty—Baby Bunting **D. M. J. Gilbert**
16 **WITCHRY**, 11, gr g Green Desert (USA)—Indian Skimmer (USA) **Joli Racing**

THREE-YEAR-OLDS

17 B c King's Theatre (IRE)—Talinas Rose (IRE) **Reefer Distribution Services Ltd**

Other Owners: Mr S. R. Baker, M. Blagg, C. J. Buckerfield, A. G. Craig, Mr J. W. Heal, Mr G. Milsom, Mr C. S. Pike.

Assistant Trainer: John Lovejoy

Jockey (flat): Dane O'Neill, Fergus Sweeney, Tom Queally. **Jockey (NH):** Liam Treadwell, Andrew Thornton.

---

474 **DR RICHARD NEWLAND, Claines**
Postal: **Newland Associates Ltd, Linacres Farm, Egg Lane, Claines, Worcester, WR3 7SB**
Contacts: **PHONE (07956) 196535**
E-MAIL richard.newland1@btopenworld.com

1 **ACT OF KALANISI (IRE)**, 7, b g Kalanisi (IRE)—
　　　　　　　　　　Act of The Pace (IRE) **Mr C. E. Stedman, Dr & Mrs R. D. P. Newland**
2 **AHYAKNOWYERSELF (IRE)**, 7, b g Milan—Summer Break (IRE) **G Carstairs & R Marker**
3 **ANGELOT DU BERLAIS (FR)**, 4, b g Poliglote—Afragha (IRE) **C. E. Stedman**
4 **ANTON DOLIN (IRE)**, 5, ch g Danehill Dancer (IRE)—Ski For Gold **Mrs M L Trow, Barwell & Newland**
5 **ARDKILLY WITNESS (IRE)**, 7, b g Witness Box (USA)—Ardkilly Angel (IRE) **C E Stedman & Dr R D P Newland**
6 **BELLFLOWER BOY**, 10, b g Old Vic—Dante's Arrow (IRE) **The Five Nations Partnership**
7 **BOBOWEN (IRE)**, 7, b g Bob Back (USA)—Opus One **Mr J. Stewart**
8 **CALLHIMWHATYOUWANT (IRE)**, 8, b g Old Vic—
　　　　　　　　　　Jaynes Supreme (IRE) **Prof D.E.Newland & Mr R.J.L.Newland**
9 **CHANGING THE GUARD**, 7, b g King's Best (USA)—Our Queen of Kings **BetterTipster.co.uk**
10 **CONNECTIVITY (IRE)**, 9, b g Flemensfirth (USA)—Garden Town (IRE) **Mr P. Drinkwater**
11 **DASHING GEORGE (IRE)**, 11, ch g Beneficial—Here It Is **Dr R. D. P. Newland**
12 **REGAL D'ESTRUVAL (FR)**, 8, b g Panoramic—Haie d'estruval (FR) **Mr P. Jenkins**
13 **RENEGOTIATE**, 4, ch g Trade Fair—L'extra Honor (USA) **BetterTipster.co.uk**
14 **YOUNG HURRICANE (IRE)**, 7, b g Oscar (IRE)—Georgia On My Mind (FR) **Mr P. Jenkins**

Other Owners: A. P Barwell, Mr T. J. Baynham, G. N. Carstairs, Mr J. R. Couldwell, R. J. T. Marker, Prof D. E. Newland, Mr R. J. L. Newland, Mrs L. J. Newland, S. R. Trow, Mrs M. L. Trow.

Assistant Trainer: S. R. Trow

Amateur: Mr T. Weston.

---

475 **MISS ANNA NEWTON-SMITH, Polegate**
Postal: **Bull Pen Cottage, Jevington, Polegate, East Sussex, BN26 5QB**
Contacts: **PHONE (01323) 488354 FAX (01323) 488354 MOBILE (07970) 914124**
E-MAIL anna_newtonsmith@o2.co.uk WEBSITE www.annanewtonsmith.co.uk

1 **BUDDSON**, 7, b g Alflora (IRE)—Little Bud **Mrs S. B. S. Grist**
2 **GORING ONE (IRE)**, 8, b g Broadway Flyer (USA)—Brigette's Secret **Mr G. E. Goring**
3 **GORING TWO (IRE)**, 8, br g Needle Gun (IRE)—Kam Slave **Mr G. E. Goring**
4 **LITTLE ROXY (IRE)**, 8, b m Dilshaan—Brunswick **The Ash Tree Inn Racing Club**
5 **SHERREB (IRE)**, 7, b g Zagreb (USA)—Sherberry (IRE) **PPS Racing**
6 **TWIN BUD**, 8, b m Double Trigger (IRE)—Little Bud **Mrs S. B. S. Grist**

Other Owners: Mr M. Baker, His Honour Judge A. Patience, His Honour Judge Peppitt, Mr A. K. Walker.

Assistant Trainer: Sally Harler

Jockey (flat): Hayley Turner. **Jockey (NH):** Mattie Batchelor, Marc Goldstein, Nick Scholfield, Andrew Thornton.
Conditional: Tom Cannon, Adam Wedge.

476 MR DAVID NICHOLLS, Thirsk

Postal: **Tall Trees Racing Ltd, Tall Trees, Sessay, Thirsk, North Yorkshire, YO7 3ND**
Contacts: **PHONE (01845) 501470 FAX (01845) 501666 MOBILE (07971) 555105**
E-MAIL david.nicholls@btconnect.com WEBSITE www.davidnichollsracing.com

1 **ADDICTIVE DREAM (IRE)**, 6, ch g Kheleyf (USA)—
Nottambula (IRE) **Brian Morton & Pinnacle Dream Partnership**
2 **ALBERT TATLOCK (IRE)**, 4, b g Antonius Pius (USA)—Double Precedent **D. Nicholls**
3 **BEACON LODGE (IRE)**, 8, b g Clodovil (IRE)—Royal House (FR) **McManus Devaney Harrington Flood**
4 **BONNIE CHARLIE**, 7, ch g Intikhab (USA)—Scottish Exile (IRE) **Ann-Marie McManus & Finola Devaney**
5 **BOWDLER'S MAGIC**, 6, b g Hernando (FR)—Slew The Moon (ARG) **D. Nicholls**
6 **COME ON DAVE (IRE)**, 4, b g Red Clubs (IRE)—Desert Sprite (IRE) **Middleham Park Racing XLIV**
7 **DADDY WARBUCKS (IRE)**, 4, b g Multiplex—Skerries (IRE) **Mr M. Love**
8 **DECENT FELLA (IRE)**, 7, b g Marju (IRE)—Mac Melody (IRE) **Dr M. B. Q. S. Koukash**
9 **DESERT CREEK (IRE)**, 7, ch g Refuse To Bend (IRE)—Flagship **D W Barker & D Nicholls**
10 **DON'T CALL ME (IRE)**, 6, ch g Haafhd—Just Call Me (NZ) **Matt & Lauren Morgan**
11 **DORBACK**, 6, ch g Kyllachy—Pink Supreme **Ms S. V. Hattersley**
12 **DUNN'O (IRE)**, 4, b g Cape Cross (IRE)—Indian Express **D Nicholls M Morgan & Mrs M C Jacobs**
13 **EWELL PLACE (IRE)**, 4, br g Namid—Miss Gibraltar **Dr M. B. Q. S. Koukash**
14 **FITZ FLYER (IRE)**, 7, b g Acclamation—Starry Night **Mr Mike Browne**
15 **GREENHEAD HIGH**, 5, b g Statue of Liberty (USA)—Artistry **Mr C. Castle**
16 **HAMOODY (USA)**, 9, ch g Johannesburg (USA)—Northern Gulch (USA) **Hart Inn I**
17 **IMPERIAL LEGEND (IRE)**, 4, b g Mujadil (USA)—Titian Saga (IRE) **Pinnacle Mujadil Partnership**
18 **INDEGO BLUES**, 4, b g Indesatchel (IRE)—Yanomami (USA) **Pinnacle Indesatchel Partnership**
19 **INDIAN TRAIL**, 13, ch g Indian Ridge—Take Heart **Mr M. Love**
20 **INXILE (IRE)**, 8, b g Fayruz—Grandel **Mr D. Nicholls & Mrs J. Love**
21 **JACK DAWKINS (USA)**, 8, b g Fantastic Light (USA)—Do The Mambo (USA) **The Three K's**
22 **JOHN COFFEY (IRE)**, 4, b g Acclamation—Appleblossom Pearl (IRE) **D. Nicholls**
23 **KARAKA JACK**, 6, ch g Pivotal—Mauri Moon **M. Mackay & S. Bruce**
24 **KEYS OF CYPRUS**, 11, ch g Deploy—Krisia **The Beasley Gees**
25 **KUANYAO (IRE)**, 5, b g American Post—Nullarbor **D. Nicholls**
26 **LLEWELLYN**, 5, b g Shamardal (USA)—Ffestiniog (IRE) **D. Nicholls**
27 **MAJESTIC MANANNAN (IRE)**, 4, b g Majestic Missile (IRE)—Miraculous (IRE) **Mark & Maureen Schofield**
28 **MISTER MANANNAN (IRE)**, 6, b g Desert Style (IRE)—Cover Girl (IRE) **Mrs M. C. Schofield**
29 **MUJAADEL (USA)**, 8, ch g Street Cry (IRE)—Quiet Rumour (USA) **W R B Racing 49**
30 **RASSELAS (IRE)**, 6, b g Danehill Dancer (USA)—Regal Darcey (IRE) **Mr J. P. Honeyman**
31 **REX IMPERATOR**, 4, b g Royal Applause—Elidore **Clipper Group Holdings Ltd**
32 **RIO COBOLO (IRE)**, 7, b g Captain Rio—Sofistication (IRE) **The Grech Family & The Quinn Family**
33 **RODRIGO DE TORRES**, 6, ch g Bahamian Bounty—Leonica **B. Morton**
34 **ST MORITZ (IRE)**, 7, b g Medicean—Statua (IRE) **Mr Billy Hughes**
35 **SUMMERINTHECITY (IRE)**, 6, ch g Indian Ridge—Miss Assertive **Dr M. B. Q. S. Koukash**
36 **SWILLY FERRY (USA)**, 6, b g Wiseman's Ferry (USA)—Keepers Hill (IRE) **Mr J. A. Law**
37 **TAJNEED (IRE)**, 10, b g Alhaarth (IRE)—Indian Express **Mrs A. Nicholls**
38 **TAKEALOOKATMENOW (IRE)**, 4, b f Moss Vale (IRE)—Batool (USA) **Mr D Nicholls & Mrs S J Barker**
39 **TANGO SKY (IRE)**, 4, b g Namid—Sky Galaxy (USA) **Dr M. B. Q. S. Koukash**
40 **TAX FREE (IRE)**, 11, b g Tagula (IRE)—Grandel **Mr D. Nicholls & Mrs J. Love**
41 **WEST LEAKE HARE (IRE)**, 4, b c Choisir (AUS)—March Hare **D. Nicholls**
42 **XILERATOR (IRE)**, 6, b g Arakan (USA)—Grandel **Mr J. A. Law**

THREE-YEAR-OLDS

43 **ARCSY (IRE)**, b g Antonius Pius (USA)—Nouvelle Nova (IRE) **D. Nicholls**
44 B g Elusive City (USA)—Cat Whistle
45 **CAZZA**, b f Indesatchel (IRE)—Yanomami (USA) **D. Nicholls**
46 B g Royal Applause—Dash of Lime **Pinnacle Royal Applause Partnership**
47 **DOODLES**, b f Pastoral Pursuits—Burton Ash **D. Nicholls**
48 **LADY NIRAMAX**, b f Indesatchel (IRE)—Just A Gem **Niramax Solutions**
49 **MR SNOOKS**, b g Bertolini (USA)—Meadow Floss **Mr C. J. Titcomb**
50 **NO REPLY**, gr g Avonbridge—En Grisaille **The Friar Tuck Racing Club & Partner**
51 **QUEEN FLUSH (IRE)**, b f Red Clubs (IRE)—Alexander Nitelady (IRE) **T Marnane & C Mills A Fallon G Purchase**
52 **ROCKET RONNIE (IRE)**, b g Antonius Pius (USA)—Ctesiphon (USA) **Mills, Fallon, Purchase & Love**
53 Ch f Peintre Celebre (USA)—Shellin (IRE)
54 **TRUE THAT (IRE)**, b c Captain Marvelous (IRE)—Bratislava **Ann-Marie McManus & Finola Devaney**

MR DAVID NICHOLLS - Continued

Other Owners: Mrs S. J. Barker, Mr D. W. Barker, Mr S. Baynes, Mrs S. Beasley, Ms Finola Devaney, Mr Claudio Michael Grech, Mrs Caroline Harrington, Mrs Marie C. Jacobs, Mrs Jackie Love, Mrs A. McManus, Mr Matthew Morgan, Mrs Lauren Morgan, Mr Brian Morton, Mr T. Murray, Mr D. Nicholls, Mrs Alex Nicholls, Mr T. S. Palin, Mr M. Prince, Mr K. Robinson, Mr A. L. Roche, Mr M. A. Scaife, Mr A. Scaife, Mr J. R. F. Stunt, Mrs S. Thomson, Mr Andrew Turton, Mr L. Vettraino, Mr A. Williams.

Assistant Trainer: Ben Beasley

Jockey (flat): Andrew Mullen, Adrian Nicholls, Paul Quinn. **Apprentice:** Shirley Teasdale. **Amateur:** Mrs Adele Mulrennan.

477

MR PAUL NICHOLLS, Ditcheat
Postal: **Manor Farm Stables, Ditcheat, Shepton Mallet, Somerset, BA4 6RD**
Contacts: PHONE (01749) 860656 FAX (01749) 860523 MOBILE (07977) 270706
E-MAIL info@paulnichollsracing.com WEBSITE www.paulnichollsracing.com

1 **AAIM TO PROSPER (IRE)**, 9, br g Val Royal (FR)—Bint Al Balad (IRE) **CGA Racing Partnership 2**
2 **AERIAL (FR)**, 7, b g Turgeon (USA)—Fille Formidable (USA) **Tony Hayward & Barry Fulton**
3 **AIKIDEAU (FR)**, 6, b g Le Balafre (FR)—Kizitso (FR) **The Stewart Family**
4 **AL FEROF (FR)**, 8, gr g Dom Alco (FR)—Maralta (FR) **Mr J. R. Hales**
5 **AMERICAN TRILOGY (IRE)**, 9, gr g Sendawar (IRE)—
　　　　　　　　　　　　　　　　Affaire Classee (FR) **Fulton, Donlon, Kilduff & Scott-MacDonald**
6 **BAR A MINE (FR)**, 4, b g Martaline—Treekle Toffee (FR) **Walters Plant Hire Ltd**
7 **BENVOLIO (IRE)**, 6, b g Beneficial—Coumeenoole Lady **Dobson, Sutton & Woodhouse**
8 **BIG BUCK'S (FR)**, 10, b br g Cadoudal (FR)—Buck's (FR) **The Stewart Family**
9 **BLACK COW (IRE)**, 5, br g Presenting—Back Market Lass (IRE) **P. F. Nicholls**
10 **BLACK THUNDER (FR)**, 6, bl g Malinas (GER)—Blackmika (FR) **Donlon, Macdonald, Fulton & Webb**
11 **BRAMPOUR (IRE)**, 6, b g Daylami (IRE)—Brusca (USA) **Arron & Katya Banks**
12 **BRINESTINE (USA)**, 4, b g Bernstein (USA)—Miss Zafonic (FR) **The Johnson & Stewart Families**
13 **BUCK'S BOND (FR)**, 7, gr g Turgeon (USA)—Buck's Beauty (FR) **Mrs C. E. Penny**
14 **BURY PARADE (IRE)**, 7, br g Overbury (IRE)—
　　　　　　　　　　　　　Alexandra Parade (IRE) **HighclereThoroughbredRacing- Bury Parade**
15 **CAID DU BERLAIS (FR)**, 4, b g Westerner—Kenza du Berlais (FR) **Donlon, MacDonald, C Barber & P Nicholls**
16 **CAPTAIN KELLY (IRE)**, 6, b g Oscar (IRE)—Tri Folene (FR) **Donlon, Doyle, MacDonald & Webb**
17 **CEDRE BLEU (FR)**, 6, b g Le Fou (IRE)—Arvoire (FR) **Mr Paul K. Barber & Mr D. A. Johnson**
18 **CELESTIAL HALO (IRE)**, 9, b g Galileo (IRE)—Pay The Bank **The Stewart Family**
19 **COMEONGINGER (IRE)**, 6, b g King's Theatre (IRE)—Miss Poutine (FR) **Chris Giles,Potensis Ltd & P K Barber**
20 **COWARDS CLOSE (IRE)**, 6, br g Presenting—Parsee (IRE) **Mr Paul K Barber & Mr Barry Fulton**
21 **CRIQTONIC (FR)**, 6, ch g Green Tune (USA)—Criquetot (FR) **Axom XXXIII**
22 **CURRENT EVENT (FR)**, 6, b g Muhtathir—La Curamalal (IRE) **Mrs A. M. Millard**
23 **CURTAIN RAZER (IRE)**, 7, b g Old Vic—Echo Creek (IRE) **C. G. Roach**
24 **DARK LOVER (GER)**, 8, b g Zinaad—Dark Lady (GER) **Mr Des Nichols & Mr Peter Hart**
25 **DEFINITY (IRE)**, 10, br g Definite Article—Ebony Jane **C. G. Roach**
26 **DEIREADH RE (IRE)**, 7, b g Old Vic—Donaghmore Lady (IRE) **Mr Ian J. Fogg & Mrs Wendy Fogg**
27 **DILDAR (IRE)**, 5, b g Red Ransom (USA)—Diamond Tango (FR) **Mrs S. De La Hey**
28 **DODGING BULLETS**, 5, b g Dubawi (IRE)—Nova Cyngi (USA) **Martin Broughton & Friends**
29 **DOESLESSTHANME (IRE)**, 9, ch g Definite Article—Damemill (IRE) **Andrea & Graham Wylie**
30 **DOMTALINE (FR)**, 6, gr g Martaline—Domna Noune (FR) **Mr & Mrs J. D. Cotton**
31 **EASTER DAY (FR)**, 5, b g Malinas (GER)—Sainte Lea (FR) **B. Fulton, Broughton Thermal Insulation**
32 **EDGARDO SOL (FR)**, 6, ch g Kapgarde (FR)—Tikiti Dancer (FR) **Axom XXXII**
33 **ELENIKA (FR)**, 5, gr g Martaline—Nika Glitters (FR) **Million in Mind Partnership**
34 **EMPIRE LEVANT (USA)**, 6, gr ro g Empire Maker (USA)—
　　　　　　　　　　　　　　　　Orellana **Sir A Ferguson, G Mason, R Wood & P Done**
35 **EURYSTHEUS (IRE)**, 4, b g Acclamation—Dust Flicker **Sir A Ferguson, G Mason, S Hassiakos, P Nicholls**
36 **FAGO (FR)**, 5, b br g Balko (FR)—Merciki (FR) **Andrea & Graham Wylie**
37 **FAR WEST (FR)**, 4, b g Poliglote—Far Away Girl (FR) **Axom XXXIX**
38 **FASCINO RUSTICO**, 5, b g Milan—Rustic Charm (IRE) **Mr J. R. Hales**
39 **FIVE DREAM (FR)**, 9, b g Take Risks (FR)—Jenny Pous (FR) **Scott-MacDonald, Kilduff, Donlon & Doyle**
40 **FOGGY'S WALL (FR)**, 5, b g Golan (IRE)—Mrs Masters (IRE) **Mr & Mrs Mark Woodhouse**
41 **FOR TWO (FR)**, 4, gr g Act One—Forcat (FR) **Andrea & Graham Wylie**
42 **FOX RUN (IRE)**, 5, b g Shantou (USA)—Viola Crown (IRE) **C. G. Roach**
43 **FUNNY STAR (FR)**, 5, ch g Tot Ou Tard (IRE)—Funny Miss (FR) **Mr & Mrs J. D. Cotton**
44 **GHIZAO (GER)**, 9, b g Tiger Hill (IRE)—Glorosia (FR) **The Johnson & Stewart Families**
45 **GRANDIOSO (IRE)**, 6, b g Westerner—Champagne Warrior (IRE) **Andrea & Graham Wylie**

MR PAUL NICHOLLS - Continued

46 **GWANAKO (FR)**, 10, b br g Sin Kiang (FR)—Vaubecourt (FR) **The Stewart Family**
47 **THEY THE VIKING**, 8, ch g Sir Harry Lewis (USA)—Viking Flame **Sir A Ferguson, G Mason, R Wood & P Done**
48 **HAWKES POINT**, 8, b g Kayf Tara—Mandys Native (FR) **C. G. Roach**
49 **HINTERLAND (FR)**, 5, b g Poliglote—Queen Place (FR) **Mr Chris Giles & Potensis Limited**
50 **IRISH SAINT (FR)**, 4, b br g Saint des Saints (FR)—Minirose (FR) **Mrs S. De La Hey**
51 **ITALIAN MASTER (IRE)**, 7, b br g Milan—Augusta Brook (IRE) **Mr J. R. Hales**
52 **JOIN TOGETHER (IRE)**, 8, b g Old Vic—Opan Cry (IRE) **Mr Ian J. Fogg & Mr Paul K. Barber**
53 **JUMP CITY (FR)**, 7, b g Muhtathir—Just Fizzy **Mrs Angela Tincknell & Mr W. Tincknell**
54 **JUST A PAR (IRE)**, 6, b g Island House (IRE)—Thebrownhen (IRE)
55 **KAUTO D'ALOES (FR)**, 4, ch g Byzantium (FR)—Kauto Karolyna (FR)
56 **KAUTO STONE (FR)**, 7, ch g With The Flow (USA)—Kauto Relka (FR) **Mr R. J. H. Geffen**
57 **KEPPOLS HILL (IRE)**, 7, b g Indian Danehill (IRE)—
                                   Keppols Princess (FR) **Timeform Betfair Racing & Mr Paul K Barber**
58 **LAC FONTANA (FR)**, 4, b g Shirocco (GER)—Fontaine Riant (FR) **Potensis Limited & Mr Chris Giles**
59 **LANDSCAPE (FR)**, 5, b g Lando (GER)—
                                   Universelle (USA) **Betfair & Ambassadors Dixon Greenwood Vaughan**
60 **LIGHTENTERTAINMENT (IRE)**, 5, b g King's Theatre (IRE)—
                                   Dochas Supreme (IRE) **P K Barber, I J Fogg & P F Nicholls**
61 **MAC'S RETURN (IRE)**, 6, b g Flemensfirth (USA)—Dark Mist (IRE) **Mr J. R. Hales**
62 **MAXI CHOP (FR)**, 5, b g Muhaymin (USA)—Scotch Mockery (FR) **The Stewart Family**
63 **MCLLHATTON (IRE)**, 5, b g Fruits of Love (USA)—Penny Haven (FR) **Donlon, MacDonald & Giles**
64 **MERRION SQUARE (IRE)**, 7, b g Kotashaan (FR)—Parverb (IRE) **The Stewart Family**
65 **MICHEL LE BON (FR)**, 10, b g Villez (USA)—Rosacotte (FR) **C. G. Roach**
66 **MINELLAHALFCENTURY (IRE)**, 5, b g Westerner—Shanakill River (IRE) **Mr Jeffrey Hordle & Mr Peter Hart**
67 **MORITO DU BERLAIS (FR)**, 4, b g Turgeon (USA)—Chica du Berlais (FR) **C. G. Roach**
68 **MR HUDSON (IRE)**, 8, b g Old Vic—Esbeggi **Mrs Angela Tincknell & Mr W. Tincknell**
69 **MR MOLE (IRE)**, 5, br g Great Pretender (IRE)—Emmylou du Berlais (FR) **J. P. McManus**
70 **NO LOOSE CHANGE (IRE)**, 8, b g Bob Back (USA)—Quit The Noise (IRE) **Donlon, Doyle, MacDonald & Webb**
71 **NOBLE FRIEND (IRE)**, 5, b g Presenting—Laragh (IRE) **Mr Ian J. Fogg & Mr Paul K. Barber**
72 **OSCAR AMY (IRE)**, 6, b m Oscar (IRE)—Penny Farthing **Mr R. J. H. Geffen**
73 **OSCARGO (IRE)**, 9, b g Oscar (IRE)—Broken Rein (IRE) **Hordle, Evans & Nicholls**
74 **PACHA DU POLDER (FR)**, 6, b g Muhtathir—Ambri Piotta (FR) **The Stewart & Wylie Families**
75 **PAY THE KING (IRE)**, 6, b g King's Theatre (IRE)—Knocktartan (IRE) **Mr R. J. H. Geffen**
76 **PEARL SWAN (FR)**, 5, b g Gentlewave (IRE)—Swanson (USA) **Mr R. J. H. Geffen**
77 **POLISKY (FR)**, 6, b g Poliglote—Dusky Royale (FR) **Mrs S. De La Hey**
78 **POQUELIN (FR)**, 10, b g Lahint (USA)—Babolna (FR) **The Stewart Family**
79 **POUNGACH (FR)**, 7, b g Daliapour (IRE)—Shalaine (FR) **Donlon, Doyle, MacDonald & Webb**
80 **PRINCE TOM**, 9, b g King's Theatre (IRE)—Cresswell Native (IRE) **Mrs Angela Tincknell & Mr W. Tincknell**
81 **PROSPECT WELLS (FR)**, 8, b g Sadler's Wells (USA)—Brooklyn's Dance (FR) **Andrea & Graham Wylie**
82 **PROVO (IRE)**, 6, br g Presenting—Pairtree **Hilton & Lyn Ramseyer**
83 **PTIT ZIG (FR)**, 4, b g Great Pretender (IRE)—Red Rym (FR)
84 **PURE OXYGEN (IRE)**, 5, br g Presenting—Katday (FR) **C. G. Roach**
85 **RANGITOTO (IRE)**, 8, b g Old Vic—Kendos Dream (IRE) **Charles Whittaker & P. K. Barber**
86 **RANJAAN (FR)**, 5, b g Dubai Destination (USA)—Ridafa (IRE) **Highclere Thoroughbred Racing - Ranjaan**
87 **REBEL DU MAQUIS (FR)**, 8, b g Brier Creek (USA)—Jade de Chalamont (FR) **Mrs Kathy Stuart & P F Nicholls**
88 **REBEL REBELLION (IRE)**, 8, b g Lord Americo—Tourmaline Girl (IRE) **Potensis Limited & Mr Chris Giles**
89 **ROCKY CREEK (IRE)**, 7, b g Dr Massini (IRE)—Kissantell (IRE) **The Johnson & Stewart Families**
90 **ROGER BEANTOWN (IRE)**, 8, b g Indian Danehill (IRE)—Best Wait (IRE) **Andrea & Graham Wylie**
91 **ROLLING ACES (IRE)**, 7, b g Whitmore's Conn (USA)—Pay Roll (IRE) **David Martin, Ian Fogg & Paul Barber**
92 **ROYAL CHARM (FR)**, 8, bl g Cadoudal (FR)—Victoria Royale (FR) **Mrs Angela Tincknell & Mr W. Tincknell**
93 **RUBEN COTTER (IRE)**, 7, b g Beneficial—Bonnie Thynes (IRE) **C. G. Roach**
94 **SAINT ROQUE (FR)**, 7, b g Lavirco (GER)—Moody Cloud (FR) **Potensis Limited & Mr Chris Giles**
95 **SALUBRIOUS (IRE)**, 6, b g Beneficial—Who Tells Jan **The Johnson & Stewart Families**
96 **SAM WINNER (FR)**, 6, b g Okawango (USA)—Noche (IRE) **Mrs A. B. Yeoman**
97 **SAMETEGAL (FR)**, 4, b g Saint des Saints (FR)—Loya Lescribaa (FR) **Mr & Mrs J. D. Cotton**
98 **SANCTUAIRE (FR)**, 7, b br g Kendor (FR)—Biblique (FR) **Potensis Limited & Mr Chris Giles**
99 **SAPHIR DU RHEU (FR)**, 4, gr g Al Namix (FR)—Dona du Rheu (FR) **The Stewart Family**
100 **SHARENI (IRE)**, 4, b g Azamour (IRE)—Sharesha (FR) **Highclere Thoroughbred Racing - Shareni**
101 **SHOOTERS WOOD (IRE)**, 9, b g Needle Gun (IRE)—Talbot's Hollow (IRE) **W. A. Harrison-Allan**
102 **SIDNEY MELBOURNE (USA)**, 6, ch g Lemon Drop Kid (USA)—Tolltally Light (USA) **Cga Racing Partnership 5**
103 **SILSOL (GER)**, 4, b g Soldier Hollow—Silveria (GER) **Michelle And Dan Macdonald**
104 **SILVINIACO CONTI (FR)**, 7, ch g Dom Alco (FR)—Gazelle Lulu (FR) **Mr Chris Giles & Potensis Limited**
105 **SIN BIN (IRE)**, 7, b g Presenting—Navaro (IRE) **T. J. Hemmings**
106 **SIRE COLLONGES (FR)**, 7, gr g Dom Alco (FR)—Idylle Collonges (FR) **Mrs Angela Tincknell & Mr W. Tincknell**
107 **SKY WATCH (IRE)**, 6, b g Flemensfirth (USA)—The Shining Force (IRE) **Potensis Limited & Mr Chris Giles**

MR PAUL NICHOLLS - Continued

108 **SOUND INVESTMENT (IRE)**, 5, b g Dr Massini (IRE)—Drumcay Polly (IRE) **Andrea & Graham Wylie**
109 **SOUTHFIELD THEATRE (IRE)**, 5, b g King's Theatre (IRE)—Chamoss Royale (FR) **Mrs A. B. Yeoman**
110 **SPOCK (FR)**, 8, b g Lost World (IRE)—Quark Top (FR) **J. G. Hordle**
111 **SUERTE AL SALTO (IRE)**, 6, b g Old Vic—The Great O'malley (IRE) **Mr Paul K. Barber & Mr Chris Giles**
112 **TED SPREAD**, 6, b g Beat Hollow—Highbrook (USA) **False Nose 'n Glasses Partnership**
113 **THE KNOXS (IRE)**, 10, b g Close Conflict (USA)—Nicola Marie (IRE) **Andrea & Graham Wylie**
114 **THE MOBB (IRE)**, 5, b g Westerner—Marlogan (IRE) **T. J. Hemmings**
115 **THEMILANHORSE (IRE)**, 7, b g Milan—Sports Leader (IRE) **Mr J. R. Hales**
116 **THERE'S NO PANIC (IRE)**, 8, ch g Presenting—Out Ranking (FR) **The Stewart Family**
117 **TIDAL BAY (IRE)**, 12, b g Flemensfirth (USA)—June's Bride (IRE) **Andrea & Graham Wylie**
118 **TOBY LERONE (IRE)**, 6, b g Old Vic—Dawn's Double (IRE) **Regan, Dunning, Pettey, Morgan & Gibbs**
119 **TOUBAB (FR)**, 7, gr g Martaline—Tabachines (FR) **Hills of Ledbury Ltd**
120 **TRICKY TRICKSTER (IRE)**, 10, b g Oscar (IRE)—Pavlova (IRE) **Mr C. M. Giles**
121 **ULCK DU LIN (FR)**, 5, b g Sassanian (USA)—Miss Fast (FR) **Mrs S. De La Hey**
122 **UNIONISTE (FR)**, 5, gr g Dom Alco (FR)—Gleep Will (FR) **Mr J. R. Hales**
123 **URUBU D'IRLANDE (FR)**, 5, b g Sleeping Car (FR)—Noceane (FR) **Mr C R Whittaker & Mr P F Nicholls**
124 **VAGO COLLONGES (FR)**, 4, b g Voix du Nord (FR)—Kapucine Collonges (FR) **Andrea & Graham Wylie**
125 **VALCO DE TOUZAINE (FR)**, 4, gr g Dom Alco (FR)—Narcisse de Touzaine (FR) **The Gi Gi Syndicate**
126 **VAROM (FR)**, 4, gr g Charming Groom (FR)—Morava (FR) **Mr John & Jordan Lund**
127 **VERY NOBLE (FR)**, 4, b g Martaline—Isati's (FR) **Mr Ian J. Fogg & Mr Paul K. Barber**
128 **VIBRATO VALTAT (FR)**, 4, gr g Voix du Nord (FR)—La Tosca Valtat (FR) **Axom XLIII**
129 **WHAT A FRIEND**, 10, b g Alflora (IRE)—Friendly Lady **Mr Ged Mason & Sir Alex Ferguson**
130 **WHISKY YANKEE (IRE)**, 6, b g Presenting—Southcoast Gale (IRE) **Walters Plant Hire Ltd**
131 **WIFFY CHATSBY (IRE)**, 6, br g Presenting—Star Child (GER) **Inch Bloodstock**
132 **WILTON MILAN (IRE)**, 5, b g Milan—Biondo (IRE) **J. T. Warner**
133 **WONDERFUL CHARM (FR)**, 5, b g Poliglote—Victoria Royale (FR) **Mr R. J. H. Geffen**
134 **WORKBENCH (FR)**, 9, b g Network (GER)—Danhelis (FR) **N. W. Lake**
135 **ZARKANDAR (IRE)**, 6, b g Azamour (IRE)—Zarkasha (IRE) **Mr Chris Giles & Potensis Limited**

Other Owners: Mr S. A. Ashley, Axom Ltd, Mr A. F. A. Banks, Mrs E. Banks, P. K. Barber, Mr C. L. Barber, Mr G. Barrett, A. R. Bromley, Sir M. F. Broughton, S. W. Broughton, Broughton Thermal Insulations, Mr A. P. Brown, D. J. Coles, J. D. Cotton, Mrs B. Cotton, Miss R. J. Dobson, Mr P. E. Done, Mr C. A. Donlon, Mr D. Downie, Mr A. Doyle, Mr C. W. Evans, Sir A. Ferguson, Mr I. J. Fogg, Mrs W. Fogg, B. N. Fulton, G. F. Goode, Miss L. J. Hales, Mrs C. A. Harrison-Allan, P. L. Hart, S. Hassiakos, A. A. Hayward, The Hon H. M. Herbert, Highclere Thoroughbred Racing Ltd, A. J. Hill, Mr M. J. Holman, Mr P. J. Inch, Mrs L. Inch, D. A. Johnson, T. Kilduff, Mr J. E. Lund, Mr J. E. Lund, Mrs M. Macdonald, Mr W. D. Macdonald, Mr D. J. Martin, G. A. Mason, W. D. C. Minton, Mrs M. E. Moody, Mr S. Morgan, Mr D. J. Nichols, Mrs D. C. Nicholson, Mr G. Pettit, Potensis Limited, Mr H. Ramseyer, Mrs L. Ramseyer, G. J. P. Regan, Mrs L. Scott-MacDonald, Miss Claire Simmonds, Mr D. D. Stevenson, Mr A. Stewart, Mrs J. A. Stewart, Mrs K. A. Stuart, Ms C. Sutton, Timeform Betfair Racing Club Ltd, Mrs A. Tincknell, W. C. Tincknell, S. L. Walker, Mr R. A. Webb, C. R. Whittaker, Mr R. J. Wood, Mrs T. A. Woodhouse, M. J. M. Woodhouse, A. W. G. Wylie, Mrs A. Wylie.

Assistant Trainers: Daniel Skelton, Tom Jonason

Jockey (NH): Ruby Walsh, Daryl Jacob, Nick Scholfield, Harry Skelton. **Conditional:** James Cowley, Harry Derham, Ryan Mahon. **Amateur:** Mr Steven Clements, Mr Andrew Doyle, Mr Will Potter.

---

478   MR PETER NIVEN, Malton
Postal: Clovafield, Barton-Le-Street, Malton, North Yorkshire, YO17 6PN
Contacts: PHONE (01653) 628176 FAX (01653) 627295 MOBILE (07860) 260999
E-MAIL pruniven@btinternet.com

1 **ALIKING**, 6, b g Alflora (IRE)—Kingennie **Mrs J. A. Niven**
2 **BARTON BOUNTY**, 6, b g Bahamian Bounty—Tenebrae (IRE) **Francis Green Racing Ltd**
3 **BLADES LAD**, 4, ch g Haafhd—Blades Girl **Crown Select**
4 **CLEVER COOKIE**, 5, b g Primo Valentino (IRE)—Mystic Memory **Francis Green Racing Ltd**
5 **DESGREY**, 5, gr g Desideratum—Briden **Mr S. W. Knowles**
6 **GOLDEN FUTURE**, 10, b g Muhtarram (USA)—Nazca **The Little Ice Club**
7 **INDIAN EMPEROR (IRE)**, 5, b g Araafa (IRE)—Soft (USA) **Francis Green Racing Ltd**
8 **LUKIE**, 5, ch g Revoque (IRE)—Subtle Blush **Vanessa Frith & Stuart Barker**
9 4, Gr f Fair Mix (IRE)—Mille Et Une Nuits (FR) **David Bamber**
10 **POSH BIRD (IRE)**, 10, b m Winged Love (IRE)—Lady Oakwell (IRE) **David Bamber**
11 **REV UP RUBY**, 5, b m Revoque (IRE)—Kingennie **Mrs K. J. Young**
12 **UNCUT STONE (IRE)**, 5, b g Awesome Again (CAN)—Suitably Discreet (USA) **Francis Green Racing Ltd**

Other Owners: S. V. Barker, M. J. Feneron, Miss V. C. Frith, D. Holgate, Mrs J. Iceton, Mr K. J. Little, Ms L. P. Tomkins.

479   MR RAYSON NIXON, Selkirk
Postal: **Oakwood Farm, Ettrickbridge, Selkirk, Selkirkshire, TD7 5HJ**
Contacts: PHONE (01750) 52245 FAX (01750) 52313

1 GYMDOLI, 6, br g Endoli (USA)—Split The Wind **Rayson & Susan Nixon**
2 JUST MADDIE, 9, gr m Supreme Sound—Delightfool **Rayson & Susan Nixon**
3 POLITICAL PADDY, 11, b g Vitus—Political Mill **Rayson & Susan Nixon**
4 5, Br g Supreme Sound—Split The Wind **Rayson & Susan Nixon**

Other Owners: G. R. S. Nixon, Mrs S. Nixon.

Assistant Trainer: Mrs S. Nixon

Jockey (NH): Ryan Mania, Fearghal Davis.

480   MRS SUSAN NOCK, Stow-on-the-Wold
Postal: **Smenham Farm, Icomb, Stow-On-The-Wold, Cheltenham, Gloucestershire, GL54 1JQ**
Contacts: PHONE (01451) 831688 FAX (01451) 831404 MOBILE (07816) 889500

1 HATTERS RIVER (IRE), 6, b g Milan—Curzon Ridge (IRE) **G. Nock**
2 MYLORD COLLONGES (FR), 13, bl g Video Rock (FR)—Diane Collonges (FR) **Camilla & Rosie Nock**
3 ROYAL GUARDSMAN (IRE), 6, b g King's Theatre (IRE)—Lisa du Chenet (FR) **Camilla & Rosie Nock**

Other Owners: Miss R. C. Nock, Miss C. D. Nock.

481   MR S. T. NOLAN, Kilcock
Postal: **Damastown Stables, Ballybrack, Kilcock, Co. Kildare, Ireland**
Contacts: PHONE (00353) 1651 9654 FAX (00353) 1628 7423 MOBILE (00353) 8585 11883
E-MAIL stephennolanracing@gmail.com

1 CARLOWSANTANA (IRE), 10, b g Blue Ocean (USA)—Lees First Step **Santana Syndicate**
2 7, B m Old Vic—Country Store **Sandra Nolan**
3 4, B f Kalanisi (IRE)—Country Store **Sandra Nolan**
4 DUSHLAIN (IRE), 9, b g Dushyantor (USA)—Pharavo (IRE) **John P. Prunty**
5 LADY BOWOOD (IRE), 9, b m Sunshine Street (USA)—Rechime **Myriam Rhode-Joyce**
6 LITTLE BING BANG (IRE), 5, br g Acclamation—Foreign Love (USA) **Mr S. T. Nolan**
7 MILL MOSS (IRE), 7, b g Tagula (IRE)—Lady Flyer (IRE) **Patrick O'Reilly**
8 6, B m Catcher In The Rye (IRE)—Peruke (IRE) **John P. Prunty**
9 PRINCE RUDI (IRE), 11, b g Rudimentary (USA)—Ware Princess **J & C Industrial Holding**
10 4, B f Kalanisi (IRE)—Rose Whisper (IRE) **John P. Prunty**
11 SHAMIRAN (IRE), 8, b g Polish Precedent (USA)—Sharemata (IRE) **McNally Syndicate**
12 TEN CEATHAIR DEAG (IRE), 7, b g Brian Boru—Lemonfield Lady (IRE) **John P. Prunty**
13 WONDERFUL MEMORIES (IRE), 5, b g Antonius Pius (USA)—Winter Dolphin (USA) **Mr S. T. Nolan**

Jockey (flat): Mark Enright, Conor Hoban, Niall McCullagh. **Jockey (NH):** Ian McCarthy. **Conditional:** Mark Enright.
Amateur: Mr J. J. King.

482   MRS LUCY NORMILE, Glenfarg
Postal: **Duncrievie, Glenfarg, Perthshire, PH2 9PD**
Contacts: PHONE (01577) 830330 FAX (01577) 830658 MOBILE (07721) 454818
E-MAIL lucy@normileracing.co.uk WEBSITE www.normileracing.co.uk

1 AGRICULTURAL, 7, b g Daylami (IRE)—Rustic (IRE) **Mrs J. Carnaby**
2 BADGED, 4, b g High Chaparral (IRE)—Meshhed (USA) **Mrs L. B. Normile**
3 BALLYCARBERY, 7, b g Bollin Eric—Carbery Spirit (IRE) **Mrs F. M. Whitaker**
4 BARR HEAD (IRE), 9, b g Anshan—Doolin Lake (IRE) **Mrs L. B. Normile**
5 BLACK VELVET BELLE (IRE), 6, br m Spadoun (FR)—Shimla (IRE) **L B N Racing Club**
6 CADORE (IRE), 5, b g Hurricane Run (IRE)—Mansiya **Mr S. Townshend**
7 5, B m Revoque (IRE)—Carbery Spirit (IRE) **Mrs F. M. Whitaker**
8 CRUACHAN (IRE), 4, b g Authorized (IRE)—Calico Moon (USA) **Oatridge Ltd**
9 DICKIE HENDERHOOP (IRE), 8, b g Milan—Merry Breeze **L B N Racing Club**
10 DIDDLEY DEE, 9, b g Riverhead (USA)—Ballydiddle **The Fiddlers**

MRS LUCY NORMILE - Continued

11 **ENGLISH CITY (IRE)**, 10, ch h City On A Hill (USA)—Toledana (IRE) **Mr P. Carnaby**
12 **FLOGAROSE (FR)**, 4, ch f Bonbon Rose (FR)—Rosala (FR) **Tulloch Family Syndicate**
13 **FRITH (IRE)**, 11, b g Benny The Dip (USA)—Melodist (USA) **L B N Racing Club**
14 **KARINGO**, 6, ch g Karinga Bay—Wild Happening (GER) **Douglas Black, P A Carnaby, P J Carnaby**
15 **LAGO VERDE (SWI)**, 8, ch g Generous (IRE)—La Venta (USA) **Mrs L. B. Normile**
16 **LORD REDSGIRTH (IRE)**, 8, ch g Flemensfirth (USA)—Wisebuy (IRE) **Mr S. Townshend**
17 **MISS DEEFIANT**, 7, b m Muhtarram (USA)—Hiding Place **Mrs L. B. Normile**
18 **MR MANSSON (IRE)**, 6, b g Millenary—Supreme Dare (IRE) **Mr K. N. R. MacNicol**
19 **PARSON'S PUNCH**, 8, b g Beat Hollow—Ordained **Mr K. N. R. MacNicol**
20 **PRIMROSE TIME**, 10, gr m Alflora (IRE)—The Whirlie Weevil **The Explorers**
21 **REMEMBER ROCKY**, 4, ch g Haafhd—Flower Market **Byrne Racing**
22 **RHYTON (IRE)**, 6, b g Rainbow Quest (USA)—Sea Picture (IRE) **Mrs J. M. Fraser**
23 **RINNAGREE ROSIE**, 7, gr m Silver Patriarch (IRE)—Gretton **The Silver Tops**
24 **SILVERTON**, 6, gr m Silver Patriarch (IRE)—Gretton **Twentys Plenty**
25 **STROBE**, 9, ch g Fantastic Light (USA)—Sadaka (USA) **Miss P. A. & Mr P. J. Carnaby**
26 **WOLF HEART (IRE)**, 5, b g Dalakhani (IRE)—Lisieux Orchid (IRE) **Mr S. Townshend**
27 **YASIR (USA)**, 5, b g Dynaformer (USA)—Khazayin (USA) **Mr S. Townshend**

THREE-YEAR-OLDS

28 **BERKSHIRE DOWNS**, b f Tiger Hill (IRE)—Cut Corn **Mr S. Townshend**
29 **HAIDEES REFLECTION**, b f Byron—Exchanging Glances **Mr A. Doig**
30 **ROYAL DUCHESS**, b f Dutch Art—Royal Citadel (IRE) **Mr S. W. Dick**

Other Owners: Mr D. M. Black, P. Byrne, Miss P. A. Carnaby, Mr P. J. Carnaby, Miss F. M. Fletcher, Mr A. C. Rodger, Mr K. F. Tulloch, Mrs S. M. Tulloch, D. A. Whitaker.

Assistant Trainer: Libby Brodie (07947) 592438

Jockey (NH): Jimmy McCarthy, Dougie Costello. **Conditional:** Lucy Alexander, Alexander Voy. **Amateur:** Mr R. Wilson.

---

483 | **MR JOHN NORTON, Barnsley**
Postal: Globe Farm, High Hoyland, Barnsley, South Yorkshire, S75 4BE
Contacts: **PHONE/FAX** (01226) 387633 **MOBILE** (07970) 212707
E-MAIL johnrnorton@hotmail.com **WEBSITE** www.johnrnortonracehorsetrainer.co.uk

1 **BARTERED BRIDE**, 5, b m Gentleman's Deal (IRE)—Stolen Glance **J. R. Norton Ltd**
2 **CAPTIVE MOMENT**, 7, b m Almaty (IRE)—Captive Heart **J. Norton**
3 7, B g Convinced—Carole's Dove **J. Norton**
4 **DEPORTATION**, 6, b g Deportivo—Kyle Rhea **Mr William M. Brown**
5 **DR VICTORIA**, 4, ch f Three Valleys (USA)—Spielbound **Mrs H. Tattersall**
6 **FLYING POWER**, 5, b g Dubai Destination (USA)—Rah Wa (USA) **Jaffa Racing Syndicate**
7 **GOREY LANE (IRE)**, 7, b g Oscar (IRE)—Supremely Deep (IRE) **Jaffa Racing Syndicate**
8 5, Gr m Act One—Huwaidah **Andy Middleton**
9 **NIPPY NIKKI**, 5, b m Needwood Blade—Spielbound **J. Norton**
10 4, B f Danbird (AUS)—Rapturous **J. R. Norton Ltd**
11 **SNOW ALERT**, 7, ch g Where Or When (IRE)—Ela Aphrodite **Fellowship Of The Rose Partnership**

THREE-YEAR-OLDS

12 **FINN MAC**, ch g Norse Dancer (IRE)—Strictly Elsie (IRE) **M. R. & T. Simcox**
13 B g Tiger Hill (IRE)—Ma-Arif (IRE) **Mrs P. Cockerill**

TWO-YEAR-OLDS

14 **SKYE HIGH**, b f 1/3 Rainbow High—Celinda (FR) (Bering) **A M Racing Syndicate**

Other Owners: Mr R. M. Firth, Mr P. J. Marshall, Mr Tim Simcox.

---

484 | **MR JEREMY NOSEDA, Newmarket**
Postal: Shalfleet, 17 Bury Road, Newmarket, Suffolk, CB8 7BX
Contacts: **PHONE** (01638) 664010 **FAX** (01638) 664100 **MOBILE** (07710) 294093
E-MAIL jeremy@jeremynoseda.com **WEBSITE** www.jeremynoseda.com

1 **BURKE'S ROCK**, 4, br f Cape Cross (IRE)—Miss Lacey (IRE)

MR JEREMY NOSEDA - Continued

2 **DELFT,** 4, b f Dutch Art—Plucky
3 **GRANDEUR (IRE),** 4, gr ro g Verglas (IRE)—Misskinta (IRE)
4 **HARVARD N YALE (USA),** 4, ch c Smart Strike (CAN)—Compete (USA)
5 **INSTANCE,** 5, b m Invincible Spirit (IRE)—Hannda (IRE)
6 **NET WHIZZ (USA),** 4, b br c Mr Greeley (USA)—Reboot (USA)
7 **NOCTURN,** 4, b g Oasis Dream—Pizzicato
8 **PETER MARTINS (USA),** 5, ch g Johannesburg (USA)—Pretty Meadow (USA)
9 **RECKONING (IRE),** 4, b f Danehill Dancer (IRE)—Great Hope (IRE)
10 **SHIRAZZ,** 4, b f Shirocco (GER)—Streccia
11 **VALBCHEK (IRE),** 4, b c Acclamation—Spectacular Show (IRE)

THREE-YEAR-OLDS

12 **ACHTUNG,** b c Montjeu (IRE)—Funsie (FR)
13 **BELLE ISLE,** br f Pastoral Pursuits—Bowness
14 **COCONELL,** b f Rock of Gibraltar (IRE)—Marula (IRE)
15 **CONSIGN,** b c Dutch Art—Maid To Dance
16 **COUNTESS ANNA (USA),** ch f More Than Ready (USA)—Awesome Lady (USA)
17 **DUTIFUL SON (IRE),** b c Invincible Spirit (IRE)—Grecian Dancer
18 **ELAS LAW,** gr f Lawman (FR)—Ela Athena
19 **ENDLESS LIGHT,** ch f Pivotal—Celeste
20 **EVIDENT (IRE),** b c Excellent Art—Vestavia (IRE)
21 **EXCUSE TO LINGER,** ch c Compton Place—Lady Le Quesne (IRE)
22 **EXEMPT,** gr f Exceed And Excel (AUS)—Miss University (USA)
23 **FANTASTIC MOON,** ch c Dalakhani (IRE)—Rhadegunda
24 B f Invincible Spirit (IRE)—Greek Symphony (IRE)
25 **HAVELOVEWILLTRAVEL (IRE),** b f Holy Roman Emperor (IRE)—Strategy
26 **HENRIETTA ROSE (USA),** b f Henrythenavigator (USA)—Shermeen (IRE)
27 **HI FILWAH (USA),** b c Medaglia d'oro (USA)—Star Landing (USA)
28 **HOMAGE (IRE),** b c Acclamation—Night Sphere (IRE)
29 **HORNBOY,** b c Medicean—Soar
30 **IAN'S DREAM (USA),** ch c Speightstown (USA)—She's Loaded (USA)
31 **INFINITE MAGIC (USA),** b c More Than Ready (USA)—Truly Enchanting (IRE)
32 **INTIMIDATE,** b c Royal Applause—Crystal Power (USA)
33 **INTREPID (IRE),** b g Invincible Spirit (IRE)—Imiloa (USA)
34 **INVESTMENT EXPERT (IRE),** b c Tamayuz—Kindling
35 **IRIDESCENCE,** b f Dutch Art—Radiate
36 **JOE PALOOKA (IRE),** b c Galileo (IRE)—Glinting Desert (IRE)
37 **KAJOKSEE (IRE),** gr c Verglas (IRE)—Dazzling Dancer
38 **KEPT WELL (USA),** b f Scat Daddy (USA)—Prosperous Move (USA)
39 **MAGIQUE (IRE),** b f Jeremy (USA)—Misskinta (IRE)
40 **MARIA LOMBARDI,** b f Medicean—Fabulously Fast (USA)
41 **MESSILA STAR,** ch c Pivotal—Jamboretta (IRE)
42 B f Van Nistelrooy (USA)—Miss Zafonic (FR)
43 **MORE THAN AMAZING (USA),** b f More Than Ready (USA)—Baffled (USA)
44 **OCEAN SECRET (IRE),** ch c Shirocco (GER)—Shell Garland (USA)
45 **PROPHETS PRIDE,** b c Sakhee (USA)—Winner's Call
46 **RED BATON,** b f Exceed And Excel (AUS)—Ruby Rocket (IRE)
47 **RED TURBAN,** b f Kyllachy—Red Tiara (USA)
48 **REGAL SILK,** b f Pivotal—Regal Velvet
49 B br c Mr Greeley (USA)—Sand Pirate (CAN)
50 **SAVVY CHIC (USA),** ch f Street Boss (USA)—Special Grayce (USA)
51 **SILVER DIXIE (USA),** b c Dixie Union (USA)—More Silver (USA)
52 **SWEET DEAL (IRE),** gr g Verglas (IRE)—Compromise (FR)
53 **THE BEST DOCTOR (IRE),** ch c Pivotal—Strawberry Fledge (USA)
54 **THE GOLD CHEONGSAM (IRE),** b f Red Clubs (IRE)—Fuerta Ventura (IRE)
55 **WARRIGAL (IRE),** ch c Mount Nelson—Waldblume (GER)
56 **WILD OCEAN,** b f Pivotal—Mystery Ocean
57 **YEAGER (USA),** b br c Medaglia d'oro (USA)—Lucky Flyer (USA)
58 **ZAMOYSKI,** ch g Dutch Art—Speech

TWO-YEAR-OLDS

59 **BIJOU BLANCHE,** b f 24/2 Azamour (IRE)—Shanghai Lily (IRE) (King's Best (USA))
60 **BISHOPS AVENUE,** b c 7/4 Lawman (FR)—Shesasmartlady (IRE) (Dolphin Street (FR)) (360000)
61 B c 30/4 Henrythenavigator (USA)—Bosset (Stravinsky (USA))
62 B c 13/5 High Chaparral (IRE)—Caona (USA) (Miswaki (USA)) (3967)

MR JEREMY NOSEDA - Continued

63 DESCENT OF KINGS, b c 15/3 Shamardal (USA)—Winners Chant (IRE) (Dalakhani (IRE))
64 DRACO'S CODE, b c 8/4 Galileo (IRE)—Lady Karr (Mark of Esteem (IRE)) (260000)
65 DREAMING BEAUTY, b f 16/3 Oasis Dream—Independence (Selkirk (USA)) (200000)
66 B gr c 10/4 Duke of Marmalade (IRE)—Exotic Mix (FR) (Linamix (FR)) (95000)
67 B c 16/2 Acclamation—Fathoming (USA) (Gulch (USA)) (120000)
68 GONE WITH THE WIND (GER), b c 14/3 Dutch Art—Gallivant (Danehill (USA)) (115000)
69 HEAVENLY, b f 11/2 Pivotal—Celeste (Green Desert (USA))
70 B c 30/3 Danehill Dancer (IRE)—Helena Molony (IRE) (Sadler's Wells (USA)) (130000)
71 Br f 7/3 More Than Ready (USA)—High Heel Sneakers (Dansili) (100000)
72 B f 30/4 Invincible Spirit (IRE)—House In Wood (FR) (Woodman (USA)) (130000)
73 B br c 11/4 Cape Cross (IRE)—Imiloa (USA) (Kingmambo (USA))
74 KING'S PROSPECT, b c 12/2 Authorized (IRE)—Sovereign's Honour (USA) (Kingmambo (USA))
75 MARGARET'S MISSION (IRE), b f 27/2 Shamardal (USA)—Wimple (USA) (Kingmambo (USA)) (310000)
76 MERLETTA, b f 17/2 Raven's Pass (USA)—Light Hearted (Green Desert (USA))
77 B f 7/3 Rock of Gibraltar (IRE)—Music House (IRE) (Singspiel (IRE)) (68000)
78 NIGHTLIGHT, b f 11/2 Pivotal—Floodlit (Fantastic Light (USA))
79 OUTBACK TRAVELLER (IRE), b c 6/4 Bushranger (IRE)—Blue Holly (IRE) (Blues Traveller (IRE)) (92000)
80 B c 27/3 Bushranger (IRE)—Polish Belle (Polish Precedent (USA)) (220000)
81 RED VELOUR, ch f 18/2 Pivotal—Regal Velvet (Halling (USA))
82 REGAL SASH, br c 4/4 Pivotal—Regal Riband (Fantastic Light (USA))
83 B c 19/3 Pastoral Pursuits—Rhapsilian (Dansili) (35238)
84 B br c 23/2 Smart Strike (CAN)—Rite Moment (USA) (Vicar (USA)) (144393)
85 SHAMA'S CROWN (IRE), ch f 18/2 New Approach (IRE)—Classic Park (Robellino (USA)) (206348)
86 Ch c 18/4 Teofilo (IRE)—Sky Wonder (Observatory (USA)) (115000)
87 Gr f 27/3 Acclamation—Step Too Far (USA) (Cozzene (USA)) (120000)
88 B c 19/3 Holy Roman Emperor (IRE)—Taking Liberties (IRE) (Royal Academy (USA)) (63492)
89 B c 25/2 Giant's Causeway (USA)—Ticket to Seattle (USA) (Capote (USA)) (92165)
90 VIRTUALLY, b f 10/4 Virtual—Red Tiara (USA) (Mr Prospector (USA))
91 YOU'VE GOT IT, b f 10/4 Sea The Stars (IRE)—Song (IRE) (Sadler's Wells (USA))

Assistant Trainers: Dave Bradley, Harry Eustace

 485

MR A. P. O'BRIEN, Ballydoyle

The following list has not been supplied by the trainer and has been compiled from information in the public domain.

1 CAMELOT, 4, b c Montjeu (IRE)—Tarfah (USA)
2 MOST IMPROVED (IRE), 4, b c Lawman (FR)—Tonnara (IRE)
3 ST NICHOLAS ABBEY (IRE), 6, b h Montjeu (IRE)—Leaping Water

THREE-YEAR-OLDS

4 A STAR IS BORN (IRE), b f Galileo (IRE)—Looking Back (IRE)
5 AFONSO DE SOUSA (USA), b c Henrythenavigator (USA)—Mien (USA)
6 AGREEMENT (IRE), b c Galileo (IRE)—Cozzene's Angel (USA)
7 ARMY RANGER (IRE), b c Galileo (IRE)—D'articleshore (USA)
8 AU REVOIR (IRE), b c Singspiel (IRE)—First
9 BALLYGLASHEEN (IRE), ch c Galileo (IRE)—Luas Line (IRE)
10 BATTLE OF MARENGO (IRE), b c Galileo (IRE)—Anna Karenina (IRE)
11 CAILLEBOTTE (IRE), b c Montjeu (IRE)—Catherine Linton (IRE)
12 COUNT OF LIMONADE (IRE), b c Duke of Marmalade (IRE)—Hoity Toity
13 CRISTOFORO COLOMBO (USA), b c Henrythenavigator (USA)—La Traviata (USA)
14 EMBELLISHED (IRE), b c Galileo (IRE)—Moments of Joy
15 EVERGLADES ISLAND (IRE), b c Montjeu (IRE)—Hula Angel (USA)
16 EXOTIC (IRE), ch f Galileo (IRE)—Ice Queen (IRE)
17 EYE OF THE STORM (IRE), ch c Galileo (IRE)—Mohican Princess
18 FARE THEE WELL (IRE), b c Duke of Marmalade (IRE)—Bowstring (IRE)
19 FESTIVE CHEER (FR), b c Montjeu (IRE)—Bold Classic (USA)
20 FLYING THE FLAG (IRE), ch c Galileo (IRE)—Halfway To Heaven (IRE)
21 FORESTER (IRE), gr c Danehill Dancer (IRE)—Amenixa (FR)
22 FORTIFY (IRE), b c Danehill Dancer (IRE)—Shaanara (IRE)
23 FOUNDRY (IRE), b c Galileo (IRE)—Sharp Lisa (IRE)
24 FRANCIS OF ASSISI (IRE), b c Danehill Dancer (IRE)—Queen Cleopatra (IRE)

MR A. P. O'BRIEN - Continued

25 **FREEDOM FIGHTER (IRE)**, b c Danehill Dancer (IRE)—Rose of Petra (IRE)
26 **FREEWHEEL (IRE)**, b c Galileo (IRE)—La Chunga (USA)
27 **GALE FORCE TEN**, b c Oasis Dream—Ronaldsay
28 **GEORGE VANCOUVER (USA)**, b c Henrythenavigator (USA)—Versailles Treaty (USA)
29 **GREAT EXPLORER (IRE)**, b c Galileo (IRE)—Starchy
30 **HALF MOON (IRE)**, b f Duke of Marmalade (IRE)—Quarter Moon (IRE)
31 **HALL OF MIRRORS (IRE)**, ch c Duke of Marmalade (IRE)—Apache Dream (IRE)
32 **HANKY PANKY (IRE)**, ch f Galileo (IRE)—Mariah's Storm (USA)
33 **HEIRLOOM**, b c Dansili—Flawly
34 **HIS EMINENCE (IRE)**, ch c Galileo (IRE)—Mona Lisa
35 **IL PALAZZO (USA)**, ch f Giant's Causeway (USA)—Starlight Night (USA)
36 **ILLUSTRATE (IRE)**, b c Oasis Dream—Kassiopeia (IRE)
37 **INDIAN CHIEF (IRE)**, b c Montjeu (IRE)—Buck Aspen (USA)
38 **INFANTA BRANCA (USA)**, b f Henrythenavigator (USA)—Totemic (USA)
39 **INSTRUCTION (IRE)**, b c Danehill Dancer (IRE)—Chenchikova (IRE)
40 **JUST PRETENDING (USA)**, b f Giant's Causeway (USA)—Moon Safari (USA)
41 **KING OF THE ROMANS (IRE)**, b c Holy Roman Emperor (IRE)—Queen Titi (IRE)
42 **KINGDOM (IRE)**, b c Montjeu (IRE)—Shadow Song (IRE)
43 **KINGSBARNS (IRE)**, b c Galileo (IRE)—Beltisaal (FR)
44 **KINGSTON JAMAICA (IRE)**, b c Galileo (IRE)—Aleagueoftheirown (IRE)
45 **LAKE MICHIGAN (IRE)**, b c Montjeu (IRE)—Cherry Hinton
46 **LAKE NOVA (IRE)**, b c Montjeu (IRE)—Metaphor (USA)
47 **LEADING LIGHT (IRE)**, b c Montjeu (IRE)—Dance Parade (USA)
48 **LEAGUE OF NATIONS (IRE)**, b c Galileo (IRE)—Last Love (IRE)
49 **LINE DRUMMER (FR)**, b c Galileo (IRE)—Miss Bio (FR)
50 **LINES OF BATTLE (USA)**, b br c War Front (USA)—Black Speck (USA)
51 **LOS CABOS**, b c Montjeu (IRE)—Beyond The Dream (USA)
52 **MAGIC SPELL (IRE)**, b c Galileo (IRE)—Mora Bai (IRE)
53 **MAGICAL DREAM (IRE)**, b f Galileo (IRE)—Red Evie (IRE)
54 **MAGICIAN (IRE)**, b c Galileo (IRE)—Absolutelyfabulous (IRE)
55 **MARS (IRE)**, ch c Galileo (IRE)—Massarra
56 **MASTER SPEAKER (IRE)**, b c Danehill Dancer (IRE)—First Breeze (USA)
57 **MILESTONE (IRE)**, b c Galileo (IRE)—Cassydora
58 **MONTCLAIR (IRE)**, b c Montjeu (IRE)—Minaccia (GER)
59 **MOTH (IRE)**, b f Galileo (IRE)—Pieds de Plume (FR)
60 **NEVIS (IRE)**, b c Dansili—Moonstone
61 **NORTH DAKOTA (IRE)**, b c Galileo (IRE)—Rafina (USA)
62 **NYMPH (IRE)**, b f Galileo (IRE)—Myth (USA)
63 **PARLIAMENT SQUARE (IRE)**, b c Acclamation—Bold Desire
64 **PEDRO THE GREAT (USA)**, b c Henrythenavigator (USA)—Glatisant
65 **PERFORMANCE (IRE)**, b c Danehill Dancer (IRE)—Ahdaab (USA)
66 **PIET MONDRIAN**, gr c Danehill Dancer (IRE)—Last Second (IRE)
67 **PLINTH (IRE)**, b c Montjeu (IRE)—Crazy Volume (IRE)
68 **POINT PIPER (USA)**, b c Giant's Causeway (USA)—Imagine (IRE)
69 **RAIN GOD (USA)**, b c Henrythenavigator (USA)—Lotta Dancing (USA)
70 **RENEW (IRE)**, b c Dansili—Hold Me Love Me (IRE)
71 **RULER OF THE WORLD (IRE)**, ch c Galileo (IRE)—Love Me True (USA)
72 **SARDINIA (IRE)**, b c Galileo (IRE)—Shouk
73 **SAY (IRE)**, b f Galileo (IRE)—Riskaverse (USA)
74 **SIR WALTER SCOTT (IRE)**, b c Galileo (IRE)—Flamingo Sea (USA)
75 **SMASHING (IRE)**, b f Galileo (IRE)—Adalya (IRE)
76 **SMOKE SCREEN**, b c Montjeu (IRE)—Time Over
77 **SNOW QUEEN (IRE)**, b f Danehill Dancer (IRE)—Bonheur (IRE)
78 **TABLEAUX (USA)**, ch c Giant's Causeway (USA)—Golden Antigua (USA)
79 **TERESCHENKO (USA)**, b c Giant's Causeway (USA)—Mr P's Princess (USA)
80 **THE FERRYMAN (IRE)**, b c Galileo (IRE)—Dietrich (USA)
81 **THE GRAND DUKE**, b c Duke of Marmalade (IRE)—Night Frolic
82 **THE UNITED STATES (IRE)**, ch c Galileo (IRE)—Beauty Is Truth (IRE)
83 **THE VATICAN (IRE)**, b c Galileo (IRE)—Play Misty For Me (IRE)
84 **THEATRE (IRE)**, b c Galileo (IRE)—Rumplestiltskin (IRE)
85 **THOUGH (IRE)**, b f Dansili—Listen (IRE)
86 **TRAVERTINE (IRE)**, b c Danehill Dancer (IRE)—Mer de Corail (IRE)
87 **TWILIGHT ZONE (IRE)**, b c Danehill Dancer (IRE)—All My Loving (IRE)
88 **VELVET RIBBON (IRE)**, b f Duke of Marmalade (IRE)—Superfonic (FR)
89 **VENUS DE MILO (IRE)**, br f Duke of Marmalade (IRE)—Inchmahome

MR A. P. O'BRIEN - Continued

90 **VESTIGE,** b c Montjeu (IRE)—Llia
91 **VICTORY SONG (IRE),** b c Dansili—All Too Beautiful (IRE)
92 **VINSON MASSIF (USA),** ch c Giant's Causeway (USA)—Swan Nebula (USA)
93 **WAVER (IRE),** ch c Galileo (IRE)—Nell Gwyn (IRE)

TWO-YEAR-OLDS

94 B c 9/3 Galileo (IRE)—Again (IRE) (Danehill Dancer (IRE))
95 B c 28/1 Galileo (IRE)—Alexander Goldrun (IRE) (Gold Away (IRE)) (950000)
96 B c 11/2 Galileo (IRE)—Beauty Is Truth (IRE) (Pivotal)
97 B c 6/3 Montjeu (IRE)—Belesta (Xaar)
98 B c 2/3 Montjeu (IRE)—Birmanie (USA) (Aldebaran (USA)) (515873)
99 B c 1/3 Galileo (IRE)—Bywayofthestars (Danehill (USA))
100 Ch c 8/2 Galileo (IRE)—Chintz (IRE) (Danehill Dancer (IRE))
101 B c 27/3 Montjeu (IRE)—Crazy Volume (IRE) (Machiavellian (USA))
102 B c 13/2 Galileo (IRE)—Crystal Valkyrie (IRE) (Danehill (USA))
103 B c 20/3 Montjeu (IRE)—Dance Parade (USA) (Gone West (USA))
104 B c 25/3 Galileo (IRE)—Dancing Shoes (IRE) (Danehill (USA))
105 Gr c 24/3 Montjeu (IRE)—Dibenoise (FR) (Kendor (FR)) (412698)
106 B c 9/4 Galileo (IRE)—Dietrich (USA) (Storm Cat (USA))
107 B c 19/2 Galileo (IRE)—Elletelle (IRE) (Elnadim (USA))
108 **FOUR CARAT (GER),** b c 24/3 Montjeu (IRE)—Four Roses (IRE) (Darshaan) (119047)
109 B c 8/4 Oasis Dream—Galaxy Highflyer (Galileo (IRE)) (675000)
110 Ch c 19/3 Giant's Causeway (USA)—Galleon of Gold (USA) (Gone West (USA)) (129032)
111 B c 27/3 Galileo (IRE)—Guaranda (Acatenango (GER))
112 B c 18/2 Montjeu (IRE)—Helsinki (Machiavellian (USA))
113 B c 26/2 Montjeu (IRE)—Honorlina (FR) (Linamix (FR)) (450000)
114 B c 24/2 Montjeu (IRE)—Hula Angel (USA) (Woodman (USA))
115 B c 7/2 Galileo (IRE)—Ice Queen (IRE) (Danehill Dancer (IRE))
116 B c 7/2 High Chaparral (IRE)—Inchmina (Cape Cross (IRE)) (110000)
117 B c 4/4 Montjeu (IRE)—Jewel In The Sand (IRE) (Bluebird (USA)) (396824)
118 B c 12/4 Galileo (IRE)—Khoruna (GER) (Lagunas)
119 B c 21/4 Montjeu (IRE)—Lasting Chance (USA) (American Chance (USA))
120 B c 4/1 Galileo (IRE)—Looking Back (IRE) (Stravinsky (USA))
121 B c 8/4 Montjeu (IRE)—Love Me True (USA) (Kingmambo (USA))
122 B c 24/3 Montjeu (IRE)—Lucina (Machiavellian (USA)) (700000)
123 B c 4/3 High Chaparral (IRE)—Lure of The Moon (USA) (Lure (USA)) (130000)
124 B c 10/3 Oasis Dream—Masskana (IRE) (Darshaan)
125 B c 26/2 Montjeu (IRE)—Metaphor (USA) (Woodman (USA))
126 B c 28/4 Montjeu (IRE)—Mixed Blessing (Lujain (USA))
127 B c 4/4 Fastnet Rock (AUS)—My Emma (Marju (IRE))
128 B c 25/3 Galileo (IRE)—Mystical Lady (IRE) (Halling (USA))
129 B c 18/4 Galileo (IRE)—Mythical Echo (USA) (Stravinsky (USA))
130 B c 17/3 High Chaparral (IRE)—Night Teeny (Platini (GER)) (174603)
131 Ch c 20/2 Galileo (IRE)—One Moment In Time (IRE) (Danehill (USA))
132 Ch c 8/4 Galileo (IRE)—Ouija Board (Cape Cross (IRE)) (525000)
133 B c 17/5 Montjeu (IRE)—Penny's Gold (USA) (Kingmambo (USA))
134 B c 5/4 Galileo (IRE)—Pieds de Plume (FR) (Seattle Slew (USA))
135 B c 3/4 Galileo (IRE)—Queen of France (USA) (Danehill (USA))
136 B c 12/2 High Chaparral (IRE)—Rainbow Queen (FR) (Spectrum (USA)) (125000)
137 B c 6/2 Galileo (IRE)—Ramruma (USA) (Diesis)
138 B c 18/2 Galileo (IRE)—Red Evie (IRE) (Intikhab (USA))
139 B c 29/3 Montjeu (IRE)—Reina Blanca (Darshaan)
140 B c 2/5 Montjeu (IRE)—Simaat (USA) (Mr Prospector (USA))
141 B c 10/1 Galileo (IRE)—Simply Perfect (Danehill (USA))
142 Ch c 8/1 Galileo (IRE)—Squeak (Selkirk (USA))
143 B c 18/4 Galileo (IRE)—Trading Places (Dansili)
144 B c 4/4 Galileo (IRE)—Withorwithoutyou (IRE) (Danehill (USA))

---

486 **MR DANIEL O'BRIEN, Tonbridge**
Postal: **Knowles Bank, Capel, Tonbridge, Kent, TN11 0PU**
Contacts: **PHONE (01892) 824072**

1 **ACHIEVED,** 10, b g Lahib (USA)—Equity's Darling (IRE) **D. C. O'Brien**

MR DANIEL O'BRIEN - Continued

2 **INTHEJUNGLE (IRE)**, 10, ch g Bob Back (USA)—Whizz **A Achilleous, C Attrell, D C O'Brien**
3 **NEMO SPIRIT (IRE)**, 8, gr g Daylami (IRE)—La Bayadere **A Achilleous, C Attrell, D C O'Brien**
4 **SACRILEGE**, 8, ch g Sakhee (USA)—Idolize **D. C. O'Brien**
5 **SPARTILLA**, 4, b c Teofilo (IRE)—Wunders Dream (IRE) **D. C. O'Brien**
6 **THE SAUCY SNIPE**, 7, b m Josr Algarhoud (IRE)—The Dark Eider **D. C. O'Brien**

Other Owners: Mr A. Achilleous, Mr C. Attrell.

Assistant Trainer: Christopher O'Bryan

Jockey (NH): M. Batchelor, Sam Twiston-Davies.

---

487 MR FERGAL O'BRIEN, Cheltenham
Postal: Cilldara Stud, Coln St. Dennis, Cheltenham, Gloucestershire, GL54 3AR
Contacts: **PHONE** (01285) 721150 **MOBILE** (07771) 702829
E-MAIL fergaljelly@aol.com

1 **ACHILLES HARE (IRE)**, 5, b g Alderbrook—Easter Day (IRE) **Only A Fool Partnership**
2 **ALLERTON (IRE)**, 6, b g Flemensfirth (USA)—Bonny Hall (IRE) **T. M. Evans**
3 **ALVARADO (IRE)**, 8, ch g Goldmark (USA)—Mrs Jones (IRE) **Mr & Mrs William Rucker**
4 **BALLYGROOBY BERTIE (IRE)**, 5, b g King's Theatre (IRE)—Vigna Maggio (FR) **Mr H. J. Millar**
5 **BRADLEY**, 9, ch g Karinga Bay—Good Taste **J. C. Collett**
6 **CHASE THE SPUD**, 5, b g Alflora (IRE)—Trial Trip **Mrs C. J. Banks**
7 **DAMMAM**, 8, b g Josr Algarhoud (IRE)—Vanessa Bell (IRE) **The New Club Partnership**
8 **DARK ENERGY**, 9, br g Observatory (USA)—Waterfowl Creek (IRE) **The Yes No Wait Sorries**
9 **DOUBLE SILVER**, 6, gr m Silver Patriarch (IRE)—Shadows of Silver **Mr R. C. Mayall**
10 **DOUBLETOILNTROUBLE (IRE)**, 7, b g Hubbly Bubbly (USA)—Boolindrum Lady (IRE) **Peter & Lisa Hall**
11 **EMILY'S FLYER (IRE)**, 6, b m Oscar (IRE)—Lady Rolfe (IRE) **Mr F. M. O'Brien**
12 **FARMER MATT (IRE)**, 7, b br g Zagreb (USA)—Ashville Native (IRE) **S. D. Hemstock**
13 **FIDDLERS BID**, 6, b g Sulamani (IRE)—Charitini (GER) **The Yes No Wait Sorries**
14 **GALLIC WARRIOR (FR)**, 6, b g Nononito (FR)—Rosa Gallica **Mrs J. Hodgkiss**
15 **GEMINI AHHS (IRE)**, 10, b g Broken Hearted—Madam Madcap **Mrs C. E. M. R. Mackness**
16 **GUD DAY (IRE)**, 5, gr g Aussie Rules (USA)—Queen Al Andalous (IRE) **The People's Horse**
17 **HURRICANE EMILY (IRE)**, 6, b m Hubbly Bubbly (USA)—Boolindrum Lady (IRE) **Peter & Lisa Hall**
18 **JACKS GREY**, 8, gr g Karinga Bay—Arctic Chick **The Yes No Wait Sorries**
19 **KILMACOWEN (IRE)**, 7, b g Flemensfirth (USA)—Baunfaun Run (IRE) **The Kilmacowens**
20 **LOUXOR DES MOTTES (FR)**, 5, ch g High Yield (USA)—

Thebes Eria (FR) **Jilly Scott Jane Tufnell Scilla Phillips**
21 **MANBALLANDALL (IRE)**, 5, b g Flemensfirth (USA)—Omas Lady (IRE)
22 **MYSTIFIABLE**, 5, gr g Kayf Tara—Royal Keel **Graham & Alison Jelley**
23 **NURSE RATCHED (IRE)**, 4, b f Presenting—Mascareigne (FR) **Mr F. M. O'Brien**
24 **PERFECT CANDIDATE (IRE)**, 6, b g Winged Love (IRE)—Dansana (IRE) **ISL Recruitment**
25 **QUEEN OF MANTUA (IRE)**, 7, b m Old Vic—Papoose (IRE) **Mr R. J. Rexton**
26 **ROCKCHASEBULLETT (IRE)**, 5, b g Catcher In The Rye (IRE)—Last Chance Lady (IRE) **The Yes No Wait Sorries**
27 **SAMTHEMAN**, 8, b g Dancing Spree (USA)—Sisterly **Mr F. M. O'Brien**
28 **SILVER ROQUE (FR)**, 7, b g Laveron—Bible Bun (USA) **Lord Vestey**
29 **SUPER COLLIDER**, 6, b g Montjeu (IRE)—Astorg (USA) **Mr F. M. O'Brien**
30 **THUNDER SHINE (IRE)**, 5, b h Green Tune (USA)—Realy Queen (USA) **Mr R. J. Rexton**
31 **WELL METT (IRE)**, 6, b g Gold Well—Beit Millat (USA) **The Yes No Wait Sorries**

Other Owners: N. B. Attenborough, J. S. Cantrill, C. S. J. Coley, J. S. Dale, P.A. Deal, I. Dunbar, Mrs L. Hall, Mr P. Hall, D. M. Hussey, G. S. Jelley, Mrs A. D. Jelley, G. F. Keeys, Mrs C. M. Keeys, Mr C. Levan, D. M. Mason, C. McFadden, Mr D. V. Owen, Mrs P. M. Phillips, W. J. Rucker, Mrs A. Rucker, Mrs J. Scott, M. J. Silver, C. R. Trembath, Mrs R. J. Tufnell.

---

488 MR JEDD O'KEEFFE, Leyburn
Postal: Highbeck, Brecongill, Coverham, Leyburn, North Yorkshire, DL8 4TJ
Contacts: **PHONE** (01969) 640330 **FAX** (01969) 640397 **MOBILE** (07710) 476705
E-MAIL jedd@jeddokeefferacing.co.uk **WEBSITE** www.jeddokeefferacing.co.uk

1 **BID FOR GOLD**, 9, b g Auction House (USA)—Gold And Blue (IRE) **Richard Johnson**
2 **HIGHLAND LOVE**, 8, b g Fruits of Love (USA)—Diabaig **John & Susan Robertson**
3 **KIAN'S JOY**, 4, b g Mind Games—Lunasa (IRE) **Jenny & Ray Butler**

MR JEDD O'KEEFFE - Continued

4 **LADY KILDARE (IRE)**, 5, br m Bachelor Duke (USA)—Teodora (IRE) **The Fatalists**
5 **SATANIC BEAT (IRE)**, 4, br g Dark Angel (IRE)—Slow Jazz (USA) **Caron & Paul Chapman**

THREE-YEAR-OLDS

6 **BYRON'S DREAM**, b g Byron—Fresher **Highbeck Racing**
7 **CAPTAIN'S DREAM (IRE)**, b g Kheleyf (USA)—Somaggia (IRE) **Mr & Mrs Bruce McAllister**
8 **CAUSEWAY FOOT (USA)**, ch c Giant's Causeway (USA)—Flat Fleet Feet (USA) **Caron & Paul Chapman**
9 **DARK OCEAN (IRE)**, b g Dylan Thomas (IRE)—Neutral **Miss Sharon Long**
10 **DREAM ALLY (IRE)**, b c Oasis Dream—Alexander Alliance (IRE) **Caron & Paul Chapman**
11 **FRENCH REVOLUTION**, gr g Paris House—Hula Ballew **Highbeck Racing**
12 **ROYAL JENRAY**, gr g Royal Applause—In The Highlands **Jenny & Ray Butler**

TWO-YEAR-OLDS

13 B c 1/2 Excellent Art—Atlas Silk (Dansili) (28571) **Arthur Walker**
14 B c 10/2 Auction House (USA)—Noble Nova (Fraam) (11428) **Highbeck Racing**
15 B br f 8/3 Authorized (IRE)—Wannabe Free (Red Ransom (USA)) (7000) **Mr & Mrs Bruce McAllister**
16 B c 20/2 Tiger Hill (IRE)—Where's Broughton (Cadeaux Genereux) (8571) **Arthur Walker**

Other Owners: Mr R. Berry, Mrs Jennifer Butler, Mr P. Chapman, Mrs C. A. Chapman, Mr & Mrs P. Griffiths, Mr A. Henderson, Miss D. Lacey, David & Louise Louden, Mr & Mrs J. McGhee, Colin & Melanie Moore, Mr & Mrs J. Murphy, Mr Jedd O'Keeffe, Mr R. P. Ord, Mr & Mrs R. Rhumann, Mr & Mrs E. Rider, Mr John Robertson, Mrs Susan Robertson, Mr H. M. Sadler, Mr & Mrs K. Shaw, Mr A. Walker.

Assistant Trainer: Andrea O'Keeffe

Jockey (NH): Brian Harding.

489	**MR DAVID O'MEARA**, Nawton

Postal: **Arthington Barn, Highfield Lane, Nawton, York, North Yorkshire, YO62 7TU**
Contacts: **PHONE (01439) 771400 FAX (01439) 771775**
WEBSITE **www.davidomeara.co.uk**

1 **ABLE MASTER (IRE)**, 7, b g Elusive City (USA)—Foresta Verde (USA) **Direct Racing Club**
2 **ANDERIEGO (IRE)**, 5, b g Invincible Spirit (IRE)—Anna Frid (GER) **Ebor Racing Club**
3 **ART HISTORY (IRE)**, 5, gr g Dalakhani (IRE)—What A Picture (FR) **Claire Hollowood & Henry Dean**
4 **BALLYHOULIHAN (IRE)**, 5, b g Golan (IRE)—Dun Ar Aill (IRE) **Mr D. J. G. O'Keeffe**
5 **BEDLOE'S ISLAND (IRE)**, 8, b g Statue of Liberty (USA)—Scenaria (USA) **Mr J. G. Lumsden & Mr M. F. Hogan**
6 **BERLUSCA (IRE)**, 4, b g Holy Roman Emperor (IRE)—Shemanikha (FR) **Mr Peter Ball**
7 **BLUE BAJAN (IRE)**, 11, b g Montjeu (IRE)—Gentle Thoughts **Dr J. Hollowood**
8 **BRUNELLO (IRE)**, 5, b g Leporello (IRE)—Lydia Maria **Mrs L. Lumley**
9 **BUNCE (IRE)**, 5, b g Good Reward (USA)—Bold Desire **Wildcard Racing Syndicate X1 & Partners**
10 **CELTIC AGENT (IRE)**, 5, b g Kayf Tara—Poor Celt **Mrs S. Johnson**
11 **CHANCERY (USA)**, 5, b g Street Cry (IRE)—Follow That Dream **Hollowdean**
12 **CLASSIC COLORI (IRE)**, 6, b g Le Vie Dei Colori—Beryl **The Classic Strollers Partnership**
13 **CLASSICAL MIST**, 9, ch m Classic Cliche (IRE)—Mademist Jaz **The Cuckoo Partnership**
14 **CREEK FALCON (IRE)**, 4, b g Elnadim (USA)—Jewaar (USA)
15 **CROSS THE BOSS (IRE)**, 6, b g Cape Cross (IRE)—Lady Salsa (IRE) **Widdop Wanderers**
16 **DICK BOS**, 4, ch g Dutch Art—Cosmic Countess (IRE) **Middleham Park Racing III & Partners**
17 **DOC HAY (USA)**, 6, b br g Elusive Quality (USA)—Coherent (USA) **Mr S. Laffan**
18 **ELTHEEB**, 6, gr g Red Ransom (USA)—Snowdrops **Geoff & Sandra Turnbull**
19 **ELUSIVE BONUS (IRE)**, 4, b f Elusive City (USA)—Over Rating **The Three County Partnership**
20 **ESTEMAALA (IRE)**, 4, b f Cape Cross (IRE)—Elutrah **Middleham Park Racing**
21 **FIDDLER ONTHE HOOF (IRE)**, 4, b c Librettist (USA)—Venus Rising **Mr George Leggott & Mr John Haydock**
22 **FREDERICKTHEGREAT**, 4, b g Exceed And Excel (AUS)—
                                                      Torgau (IRE) **Middleham Park Racing XXI & Partners 2**
23 **FRONTIER FIGHTER**, 5, b g Invincible Spirit (IRE)—Rawabi **Mr A. Nichol**
24 **GRAN CANARIA QUEEN**, 4, b br f Compton Place—Ex Mill Lady **Mr M. Gillies**
25 **HEROSTATUS**, 6, ch g Dalakhani (IRE)—Desired **R. Naylor**
26 **HIT THE JACKPOT (IRE)**, 4, ch g Pivotal—Token Gesture (IRE) **Hambleton Racing Ltd**
27 **ICY QUIET**, 5, br m Shirocco (GER)—Winter Silence **P. Bamford**
28 **IFANDBUTWHYNOT (IRE)**, 7, b g Raise A Grand (IRE)—Cockney Ground (IRE) **Claire Hollowood & Henry Dean**
29 **INGLEBY ANGEL (IRE)**, 4, br g Dark Angel (IRE)—Mistress Twister **Mr D. Scott**
30 **LEGAL BOND**, 4, b g Misu Bond (IRE)—Lawless Bridget **Mr G. Forrest & Mrs S. O'Meara**
31 **LOOSE PREFORMER (IRE)**, 7, b g Luso—Out Performer (IRE) **Middleham Park Racing**

MR DAVID O'MEARA - Continued

32 **LOUIS THE PIOUS**, 5, b br g Holy Roman Emperor (IRE)—Whole Grain **F. Gillespie**
33 **LUCKY NUMBERS (IRE)**, 7, b g Key of Luck (USA)—Pure Folly (IRE) **Tom Tuohy & Tony Jafrate**
34 **MAISON DE VILLE (GER)**, 5, b m Sholokhov (IRE)—Morbidezza (GER) **Mr G. Schoeningh**
35 **MAYOMAN (IRE)**, 8, b g Namid—America Lontana (FR) **Mr T. J. Tuohy**
36 **MISS BUNTER**, 4, b f Bahamian Bounty—The Terrier **D. Fravigar Miss K. Dixon & Mrs R. Mitchell**
37 **MONKEY MILAN (IRE)**, 7, b g Milan—Beech Lodge (IRE) **S. C. B. Limited & Kevin Bailey**
38 **MONT RAS (IRE)**, 6, ch g Indian Ridge—Khayrat (IRE) **Colne Valley Racing**
39 **MOROCCO**, 4, b g Rock of Gibraltar (IRE)—Shanghai Lily (IRE) **Equality Racing**
40 **PARAMOUR**, 6, b g Selkirk (USA)—Embraced **Mr R. Jeffrey & Partners**
41 **PEEDEEQUE**, 7, b g Kayf Tara—Sister Kit (IRE) **Mrs C. Hollowood**
42 **PENANG PEGASUS**, 4, ch g Zamindar (USA)—Pulau Pinang (IRE) **Mrs A. K. H. Ooi**
43 **PENITENT**, 7, b g Kyllachy—Pious **Middleham Park Racing XVII**
44 **PEPPER LANE**, 6, ch m Exceed And Excel (AUS)—Maid To Matter **Mr K. Nicholson**
45 **PETROL**, 4, ch g Danehill Dancer (IRE)—Pongee **Mrs S. O'Meara & Mr R. G. Fell**
46 **PITTODRIE STAR**, 6, ch g Choisir (AUS)—Jupiter Inlet (IRE) **Mr Evan M. Sutherland**
47 **POWERFUL PRESENCE (IRE)**, 7, ch g Refuse To Bend (IRE)—
Miss a Note (USA) **The Lawton Bamforth Partnership**
48 **ROBERT THE PAINTER (IRE)**, 5, b g Whipper (USA)—Lidanna **Mr S. Humphreys**
49 **ROC DE PRINCE**, 4, b g Shirocco (GER)—Louella (USA) **Favourites Racing Ltd**
50 **ROKER PARK (IRE)**, 8, b g Choisir (AUS)—Joyful (IRE) **Mr Trevor Alderson & Partners**
51 **ROMAN FLIGHT (IRE)**, 5, b g Antonius Pius (USA)—Flight Sequence **Favourites Racing Syndicate**
52 **ROSE OF THE MOON (IRE)**, 8, gr g Moonax (IRE)—
Little Rose (IRE) **Middleham Park Racing XXXIII & Partners**
53 **ROSIE'S LADY (IRE)**, 4, b f Elusive City (USA)—Blushing Libra **Postracing Ltd The Charity Horse**
54 **SAREEAH (IRE)**, 4, b f Cadeaux Genereux—Jules (IRE)
55 **SET THE TREND**, 7, b br g Reset (AUS)—Masrora (USA) **Corbett Stud**
56 **SIMPLE JIM (FR)**, 9, b g Jimble (FR)—Stop The Wedding (USA) **Direct Racing Club**
57 **SMARTY SOCKS (IRE)**, 9, ch g Elnadim (USA)—Unicamp **Direct Racing Club**
58 **SPIEKEROOG**, 7, ch g Lomitas—Special **Mr G. Schoeningh**
59 **SWITCHER (IRE)**, 4, b f Whipper (USA)—Bahamamia
60 **TWO FOR TWO (IRE)**, 5, b g Danehill Dancer (IRE)—D'articleshore (IRE)
61 **WAR POET**, 6, b g Singspiel (IRE)—Summer Sonnet **Mr M. Kirby**
62 **WHITE FUSION**, 5, gr g Oratorio (IRE)—Divine Grace (IRE) **G. Clarkson, D. Dodsworth, K. Looney**

THREE-YEAR-OLDS

63 **ARCH EBONY (USA)**, b br g Arch (USA)—Dot C C (USA) **Geoff & Sandra Turnbull**
64 **BONDESIRE**, b f Misu Bond (IRE)—Lawless Bridget **Geoff & Sandra Turnbull**
65 **EXCELLENT ADDITION (IRE)**, ch g Excellent Art—Race The Wild Wind (USA) **The Roses Partnership**
66 **GOLDEN FLOWER**, b f Royal Applause—Silver Kestrel (USA) **Middleham Park Racing XLII**
67 **GRANDORIO (IRE)**, b g Oratorio (IRE)—Grand Splendour **Hambleton Racing Ltd - Three In One**
68 **HIDDON COIN (IRE)**, b g Red Clubs (IRE)—Dianella (IRE) **Hambleton Racing Ltd - Three In One**
69 **JEBULANI**, b g Jelani (IRE)—Susan's Dowry **Mrs C. Hollowood**
70 **LADY MARGAEUX (IRE)**, b f Redback—Storm Lady (IRE) **Mrs Margaret Pett & Partners**
71 **LEXINGTON BLUE**, b g Bertolini (USA)—Jasmine Breeze **Middleham Park Racing XLIX**
72 **NURPUR (IRE)**, b f Dark Angel (IRE)—The Good Life (IRE) **Middleham Park Racing**
73 **OUR DIANE (IRE)**, b f Exceed And Excel (AUS)—Medalha Milagrosa (USA) **Middleham Park Racing XII**
74 **PHILOSOFY**, ch f Barathea (IRE)—Idealistic (IRE)
75 **ROSE OF MAY (IRE)**, b f Chineur (FR)—Flower Bowl (IRE)
76 **SHARAARAH (IRE)**, b f Oasis Dream—Nidhaal (IRE) **Middleham Park Racing**
77 **SILKELLY**, b f Medicean—Sleave Silk (IRE) **Middleham Park Racing XLVIII**
78 **SILVIO DANTE (USA)**, ch g Street Boss (USA)—Merit (USA) **F. Gillespie**
79 **SMOOTHTALKINRASCAL (IRE)**, b g Kodiac—Cool Tarifa (IRE) **Middleham Park Racing**
80 **SPIDER HOUSE**, b br g Araafa (IRE)—Golden Flyer (FR)
81 **THE CODGER**, bl g Observatory (USA)—Berry Baby (IRE) **Middleham Park Racing XXVI**
82 **VITAL EDITION (IRE)**, b g Pivotal—Triple Edition (USA) **Hambleton Racing Ltd - Three In One**
83 **WAR LORD (IRE)**, b g Aussie Rules (USA)—Carn Lady (USA) **Geoff & Sandra Turnbull**

TWO-YEAR-OLDS

84 Ch f 11/4 Intense Focus (USA)—Aqualina (IRE) (King's Theatre (IRE)) (2777)
85 B f 8/3 Amadeus Wolf—Carranza (IRE) (Lead On Time (USA)) (5714)
86 Ch f 28/3 Layman (USA)—Dream Rose (IRE) (Anabaa (USA)) (5158) **Top Flight Horse**
87 **EMRYS**, ch g 26/4 Shirocco (GER)—Movie Star (IRE) (Barathea (IRE)) **Mr Richard Walker**

MR DAVID O'MEARA - Continued

88 **FROST IN MAY (IRE)**, gr f 20/3 Verglas (IRE)—
    Venus Rising (Observatory (USA)) (15238) **R. S. Cockerill (Farms) Ltd**
89 Ch f 24/2 Turtle Bowl (IRE)—Karawan (Kris) (2380)
90 B f 27/2 Indian Haven—Kathy Sun (IRE) (Intikhab (USA)) (2857)
91 **MADAGASCAR MOLL (IRE)**, b br f 18/4 Captain Gerrard (IRE)—Fontanally Springs (IRE) (Namid) (6666)
92 **MAUPITI EXPRESS (FR)**, b g 26/1 Chineur (FR)—Azucar (FR) (Marathon (USA)) (9523)
93 B f 25/4 Duke of Marmalade (IRE)—Pride of My Heart (Lion Cavern (USA)) (30000) **Hambleton Racing Ltd**
94 B f 24/2 Pastoral Pursuits—Queens Jubilee (Cayman Kai (IRE)) (11428) **Hambleton Racing Ltd**
95 B f 20/4 Footstepsinthesand—Saffron Crocus (Shareef Dancer (USA)) (11507)
96 B f 7/3 Bushranger (IRE)—Telesina (ITY) (Marju (IRE))
97 **THORNABY NASH**, br c 18/4 Kheleyf (USA)—Mistress Twister (Pivotal) **Mr Dave Scott**

Other Owners: Mr K. B. Bailey, Mr Mark Bates, Mr J. M. Binns, Mr Lee Bolingbroke, Mr Andy Bonarius, Mr N. J. Bonarius, Mr C. Charlton, Mr Geoffrey Clarkson, Lord Daresbury, Mr H. T. H. Dean, Miss Kathy Dixon, Mr David Dodsworth, Mr K. M. Everitt, Mr R. G. Fell, Mr Graham Forrest, Mr David Fravigar, Ms R. Galbraith, Mr D. P Grundy, Hambleton Racing Ltd, Mr M. J. Hill, Mrs Claire Hollowood, Mr R. Hull, Mr D. Humphries, Mr Richard Jeffrey, Dr Kieran Looney, Mrs Lynne Lumley, McMahon Thoroughbreds Ltd, Mrs R. J. Mitchell, Mr K. Nicholson, Mr Mark Norcliffe, Mrs S. O'Meara, Mr T. S. Palin, Mr M. Prince, S. C. B. Limited, Mr Evan M. Sutherland, Mr S. R. H. Turner, Mr N. C. White, Mr Ian White, Mrs C. E. White.

Assistant Trainer: R. G. Fell

Jockey (flat): Silvestre De Sousa, Daniel Tudhope. **Jockey (NH):** Denis O'Regan. **Conditional:** Jake Greenall. **Apprentice:** David Bergin. **Amateur:** Miss J. Gillam, Miss R. Heptonstall.

490 **MR JOHN O'NEILL, Bicester**
Postal: Hall Farm, Stratton Audley, Nr Bicester, Oxfordshire, OX27 9BT
Contacts: PHONE (01869) 277202 MOBILE (07785) 394128
E-MAIL jgoneill4@gmail.com

1 CABARET GIRL, 6, ch m Karinga Bay—Little Miss Prim **Ms D. Keane**
2 IRISH GUARD, 12, b g Infantry—Sharp Practice **J. G. O'Neill**

491 **MR JONJO O'NEILL, Cheltenham**
Postal: Jackdaws Castle, Temple Guiting, Cheltenham, Gloucestershire, GL54 5XU
Contacts: PHONE (01386) 584209 FAX (01386) 584219
E-MAIL reception@jonjooneillracing.com WEBSITE www.jonjooneillracing.com

1 ABNAKI (IRE), 8, b g Milan—Laboc **Masterson Holdings Limited**
2 ACCORDION EXHIBIT (IRE), 7, ch g Accordion—Curraghmeela (IRE) **Masterson Holdings Limited**
3 ALBERTAS RUN (IRE), 12, b g Accordion—Holly Grove Lass **T. J. Hemmings**
4 ALFIE SHERRIN, 10, b g Kayf Tara—Mandys Native (IRE) **J. P. McManus**
5 AMERICAN LEGEND (IRE), 5, b g Presenting—Coole Eile (IRE) **J. P. McManus**
6 AN TAILLIUR (IRE), 4, b g Milan—Tavildara (IRE) **P. Hickey**
7 ANOTHER SENSATION (FR), 4, b g Martaline—Powder Card (FR) **J. P. McManus**
8 ANOTHER TRUMP (NZ), 9, b g Montjeu (IRE)—She's A Trump (NZ) **J. P. McManus**
9 ARBOR SUPREME (IRE), 11, b g Supreme Leader—Peter's Well (IRE) **J. P. McManus**
10 ATRIPTOMILAN (IRE), 5, b g Milan—Lady of Sonas (IRE) **Mrs A. F. Bond**
11 BALINROAB (IRE), 6, b g Milan—Gentle Eyre (IRE) **T. J. Hemmings**
12 BANKROLL, 6, b g Pivotal—Lady Bountiful **Mrs A. F. Bond**
13 BECKHANI, 6, b g Flemensfirth (USA)—Nicklup **Mrs G. K. Smith**
14 BILLING (IRE), 5, b g Milan—Melodic Tune (IRE) **T. J. Hemmings**
15 BLACKWELL SYNERGY (FR), 7, b g Antarctique (IRE)—Pyu (GER) **John Joseph Byrne**
16 BOLD RAIDER (IRE), 6, b g Presenting—Dato Fairy (IRE) **J. P. McManus**
17 CARLTON JACK, 5, b g Erhaab (USA)—Harry's Bride **J. P. McManus**
18 CATCHING ON (IRE), 5, b g Milan—Miracle Lady **Mrs G. K. Smith**
19 CHOSEN DREAM (IRE), 5, b g Well Chosen—Peoples Dream (IRE) **J. C. & S. R. Hitchins**
20 CLASSICAL TWIST (IRE), 5, br g Oscar (IRE)—Basically Supreme (IRE) **Mrs G. K. Smith**
21 CLOUDY COPPER (IRE), 6, gr g Cloudings (IRE)—Copper Supreme (IRE) **Mrs G. K. Smith**
22 COFFEE (IRE), 6, b br g Beneficial—Boro Cruise (IRE) **J. P. McManus**
23 CUT THE CARDS (IRE), 6, ch g Vinnie Roe (IRE)—Mansonienne (FR) **J. P. McManus**
24 DON'T BE LATE (IRE), 5, b g Court Cave (IRE)—Sylvella **J. P. McManus**

MR JONJO O'NEILL - Continued

25 **DRAMATIC DUKE (IRE)**, 7, b g Old Vic—Dramatic Dame (IRE) **Favourites Racing Ltd**
26 **DREAM AGAIN BOYS (IRE)**, 6, ch g Presenting—The Silver Dyer (IRE) **Crutched Flyers**
27 **DREAMSOFTHEATRE (IRE)**, 5, gr g King's Theatre (IRE)—Caroline Fontenail (IRE) **J. P. McManus**
28 **DURSEY SOUND (IRE)**, 5, b g Milan—Glendante (IRE) **J. P. McManus**
29 **EASTLAKE (IRE)**, 7, b g Beneficial—Guigone (FR) **J. P. McManus**
30 **EDMAAJ (IRE)**, 5, ch g Intikhab (USA)—Lady Angola (USA) **J. P. McManus**
31 **EVEN IF**, 5, b g King's Theatre (IRE)—Melody Maid **J. P. McManus**
32 **FEAST OF FIRE (IRE)**, 6, ch g St Jovite (USA)—Bellagrana (USA) **J. C. & S. R. Hitchins**
33 **FINGER ONTHE PULSE (IRE)**, 12, b g Accordion—Quinnsboro Ice (IRE) **J. P. McManus**
34 **FOUNDATION MAN (IRE)**, 6, b g Presenting—Function Dream (IRE) **P. Hickey**
35 **FULL OF JOY (IRE)**, 8, b g King's Theatre (IRE)—Penny Brae (IRE) **J. P. McManus**
36 **GALAXY ROCK (IRE)**, 9, b g Heron Island (IRE)—Blue Pool **Michael & John O'Flynn**
37 **GET BACK IN LINE (IRE)**, 5, b g Milan—Daraheen Diamond (IRE) **J. P. McManus**
38 **GET ME OUT OF HERE (IRE)**, 9, b g Accordion—Home At Last (IRE) **J. P. McManus**
39 **HAWAII FIVE NIL (IRE)**, 5, b g Gold Well—Polish Rhythm (IRE) **Regulatory Finance Solutions Limited**
40 **HIRED HAND (IRE)**, 7, b g High Chaparral (IRE)—Piffle **J. P. McManus**
41 **HOLYWELL (IRE)**, 6, b g Gold Well—Hillcrest (IRE) **Mrs G. K. Smith**
42 **I CAN RUN CAN YOU (IRE)**, 7, ch g Old Vic—Merry Batim (IRE) **Mrs G. K. Smith**
43 **IN THE BINYANIS (IRE)**, 6, b g Waky Nao—Black Ouzel (IRE) **Bond, Bond & Bond**
44 **IT IS WHAT IT IS (IRE)**, 6, b g Presenting—Valley (IRE) **J. P. McManus**
45 **IT'S A GIMME (IRE)**, 6, b g Beneficial—Sorcera (GER) **J. P. McManus**
46 **IT'S A NEW DAY**, 5, br g Kayf Tara—One of Those Days **J. P. McManus**
47 **IT'S LIKE THAT (IRE)**, 13, b g Accordion—Hollygrove Cezanne (IRE) **J. P. McManus**
48 **JOHNS SPIRIT (IRE)**, 6, b g Gold Well—Gilt Ridden (IRE) **Mr C. Johnston**
49 **KANDARI (FR)**, 9, b g Kahyasi—Nee Brune (FR) **J. P. McManus**
50 **KEEP KICKING (IRE)**, 6, b g Tiger Hill—Dalannda (IRE) **P. McCarthy**
51 **KNOCKRAHEEN (IRE)**, 5, b g Heron Island (IRE)—Nancy's Stile (IRE)
52 **LARKS LAD (IRE)**, 9, b g Bob Back (USA)—Higher Again (IRE) **Pitman Gold Syndicate IV**
53 **LAST SHADOW**, 4, b g Notnowcato—Fairy Queen (IRE) **J. P. McManus**
54 **LISTEN AND LEARN (IRE)**, 5, b g Presenting—Loyal Gesture (IRE) **J. P. McManus**
55 **LOOKOUT MOUNTAIN (IRE)**, 5, b g Flemensfirth (USA)—
    Thegoodwans Sister (IRE) **Mr D Smith, Mr M Tabor & Mrs J Magnier**
56 **LOST LEGEND (IRE)**, 6, b g Winged Love (IRE)—Well Orchestrated (IRE) **Mrs G. K. Smith**
57 **MADEIRA GIRL (IRE)**, 4, b f Bachelor Duke (USA)—Last Cry (FR) **Jonjo O'Neill Racing Club**
58 **MASTER MALT**, 5, b g Milan—Mrs Malt (IRE) **J. P. McManus**
59 **MASTER MILAN (IRE)**, 7, b g Milan—English Clover **J. P. McManus**
60 **MATRIPAJO (IRE)**, 4, br g Westerner—Una Juna (IRE) **P. Hickey**
61 **MEET THE CRITICS (IRE)**, 10, b g Rashar (USA)—Rose Basket (IRE) **The Roysun Syndicate**
62 **MERRY KING (IRE)**, 6, ch g Old Vic—Merry Queen (IRE) **F. Gillespie**
63 **MICKELSON (IRE)**, 7, b g Old Vic—Life Support (IRE) **Phil Tufnell Racing**
64 **MINELLA FIFTY (IRE)**, 5, b g King's Theatre (IRE)—Burnt Out (IRE) **Mrs G. K. Smith**
65 **MINELLA FOR STEAK (IRE)**, 6, b g King's Theatre (IRE)—
    Preview Days (IRE) **Mrs Gay Smith & Mrs John Magnier**
66 **MISSION COMPLETE (IRE)**, 7, b g Milan—Kilmington Breeze (IRE) **J. P. McManus**
67 **MISSISSIPPI BLUES (IRE)**, 5, b g Poliglote—Allee Sarthoise (FR) **Mrs E. A. M. W. Bellamy**
68 **MISTER HYDE (IRE)**, 8, b g Beneficial—Solar Quest (IRE) **Bensaranat Club & Mr W McLuskey**
69 **MOONLIGHT DRIVE (IRE)**, 7, b g Oscar (IRE)—Perspex Queen (IRE) **Maxilead Limited**
70 **MORE OF THAT (IRE)**, 5, b g Beneficial—Guigone (FR) **J. P. McManus**
71 **MR BELLAMY (IRE)**, 5, b g Fasliyev (USA)—Egoli (USA) **The Knights Templar Partnership**
72 **MR WATSON (IRE)**, 6, b g Gold Well—Risk And Reward (IRE) **Mrs G. K. Smith**
73 **O'CALLAGHAN STRAND (AUS)**, 7, ch g Galileo (IRE)—New Gold Dream (AUS) **J. P. McManus**
74 **OLD PALS ACT (IRE)**, 5, ch g Presenting—Golden Bay **J. P. McManus**
75 **ON THE OFF CHANCE**, 5, b m Presenting—Winnowing (IRE) **J. P. McManus**
76 **ON THE RECORD (IRE)**, 5, br g Presenting—Diva Antonia (IRE) **J. P. McManus**
77 **OPEN DAY (IRE)**, 7, b g Oscar (IRE)—Shaping **J. P. McManus**
78 **OSCAR FORTUNE (IRE)**, 5, b g Oscar (IRE)—Platin Run (IRE) **The Jackdaws Strangers**
79 **PORTOFINO WASP (IRE)**, 4, b g Milan—Kiniohio (FR) **Mrs A. F. Bond**
80 **PRESENCE FELT (IRE)**, 5, br g Heron Island (IRE)—Faeroe Isle (IRE) **Mrs A. F. Bond**
81 **PUMPKIN PUZZLE (IRE)**, 5, b g Shantou (USA)—Erintante (IRE) **Ids Fzco**
82 **REDISCOVER (IRE)**, 5, ch m Golan (IRE)—Chidsicove (IRE) **Mrs E. A. M. W. Bellamy**
83 **RON**, 5, ch g Dubai Destination (USA)—Trew Class **Local Parking Security Limited**
84 **RUM AND BUTTER (IRE)**, 5, b g Milan—Silent Valley **J. P. McManus**
85 **SALPIERRE (IRE)**, 8, b g Pierre—Promalady (IRE) **F. Gillespie**
86 **SCORER (IRE)**, 5, b g Oscar (IRE)—Mandysway (IRE) **Mrs G. K. Smith**
87 **SEE U BOB (IRE)**, 10, b g Bob Back (USA)—Hidden Ability (IRE) **J. P. McManus**

MR JONJO O'NEILL - Continued

88 **SENTIMENTALJOURNEY (IRE)**, 6, ch g Portrait Gallery (IRE)—Hazy Rose (IRE) **J. P. McManus**
89 **SERANWEN (IRE)**, 6, b g Old Vic—Glenarb Molly (IRE) **Walters Plant Hire Ltd Egan Waste Ltd**
90 **SHUTTHEFRONTDOOR (IRE)**, 6, b br g Accordion—Hurricane Girl (IRE) **J. P. McManus**
91 **SOCIAL REALISM (IRE)**, 5, b m Pivotal—Russian Revolution **Mrs D. Carr**
92 **SPOIL ME (IRE)**, 6, b g Presenting—Akayid **Mrs A. F. Bond**
93 **SPOT THE BALL (IRE)**, 8, b g Oscar (IRE)—Sudden Inspiration (IRE) **J. P. McManus**
94 **STORM SURVIVOR (IRE)**, 7, b g Milan—Lindas Present (IRE) **J. P. McManus**
95 **STRONGLY SUGGESTED (IRE)**, 6, b g Kayf Tara—Branston Lily **J. P. McManus**
96 **SUNNYHILLBOY (IRE)**, 10, b g Old Vic—Sizzle **J. P. McManus**
97 **SWEET PRINCE (IRE)**, 6, b g Court Cave (IRE)—Simply Sweep (IRE) **Mrs S. M. Farmer**
98 **TACKLER (IRE)**, 5, b g Presenting—Merry Queen (IRE) **T. J. Hemmings**
99 **TAQUIN DU SEUIL (FR)**, 6, b br g Voix du Nord (FR)—Sweet Laly (FR) **Martin Broughton & Friends 1**
100 **TARVINI (IRE)**, 8, b g Kalanisi (IRE)—Tarwila (IRE) **J. P. McManus**
101 **TELL ME Y (IRE)**, 6, ch g Kris Kin (USA)—Ebony Jane **T. J. Hemmings**
102 **TEMPLE LORD (FR)**, 7, gr g Califet (FR)—Temple Queen (GER) **J. P. McManus**
103 **TENMOKU**, 4, b f Westerner—Blast Freeze (IRE) **Mrs V. F. Burke**
104 **THE NEPHEW (IRE)**, 5, b g Indian River (FR)—Charlottine (IRE) **Mrs G. K. Smith**
105 **THEATRE EVENING (IRE)**, 5, b g King's Theatre (IRE)—Waydale Hill **Masterson Holdings Limited**
106 **TIGRESSE BLEUE**, 5, b m Bachelor Duke (USA)—Tigresse Africaine (FR) **Mr J. Loudon**
107 **TITCHWOOD (IRE)**, 5, b g Flemensfirth (USA)—Aker Wood **Mrs G. K. Smith**
108 **TOMINATOR**, 6, gr g Generous (IRE)—Jucinda **P. A. Byrne**
109 **TULLY ROE (IRE)**, 5, b g Vinnie Roe (IRE)—Kay Tully **Mrs E. A. M. W. Bellamy**
110 **TWIRLING MAGNET (IRE)**, 7, b g Imperial Ballet (IRE)—Molly Maguire (IRE) **Mrs G. K. Smith**
111 **UPSWING (IRE)**, 5, b g Beneficial—Native Country (IRE) **J. P. McManus**
112 **VALLEY VIEW (IRE)**, 7, b g Anshan—Sweet Valley High (IRE) **J. P. McManus**
113 **VERY STYLISH (IRE)**, 9, b g Winged Love (IRE)—Native Craft (IRE) **Mrs G. K. Smith**
114 **VIMIERO (USA)**, 6, b br g Dynaformer (USA)—Merrymaker (ARG) **Trinity Racing**
115 **WELL HELLO THERE (IRE)**, 7, b g Oscar (IRE)—Bird of Passage **J. P. McManus**
116 **WHERES THE HARE (IRE)**, 6, b g Flemensfirth (USA)—Knocknabrogue (IRE) **Mrs A. F. Bond**
117 **WHISTLING SENATOR (IRE)**, 6, b g Presenting—Merry Batim (IRE) **J. P. McManus**
118 **WILD RHUBARB**, 8, ch m Hernando (FR)—Diamant Noir **D. J. Burke**

Other Owners: Mr P. J. Bond, Mr G. D. Bond, Mr M. H. Bond, Mrs K. F. Bourdon, Mr L. H. Brewin, Sir M. F. Broughton, Mrs J. M. Broughton, S. W. Broughton, Mr A. P. Brown, Mr J. Cockcroft, Egan Waste Services Ltd, Mrs Noel Harwerth, J. C. Hitchins, S. R. Killalea, Mrs S. Magnier, Mr W. McLuskey, Mr T. H. Milvain, Mr M. O'Flynn, Mr J. O'Flynn, Mrs J. S. T. O'Neill, Mr J. O'Neill, Mr S. L. A. Perry, M. A. Pitman, Mr J. J. Powell, G. E. Powell, Mr R. Seed, D. Smith, M. Tabor, Mr P. Tufnell, Walters Plant Hire Ltd, Mr M. Warren, Mrs S. J. Warren.

---

492 MR JOHN O'SHEA, Newnham

Postal: **The Stables, Bell House, Lumbars Lane, Newnham, Gloucestershire, GL14 1LH**
Contacts: **(01452) 760835 FAX (01452) 760233 MOBILE (07917) 124717**
WEBSITE **www.johnoshearacing.co.uk**

1 **BROWN VOLCANO (IRE)**, 4, b g Waky Nao—Lavish Spirit (USA) **Acousta Foam Limited**
2 **CITYAR (FR)**, 9, b g Sagacity (FR)—Starry Dust (FR) **Quality Pipe Supports (Q.P.S.) Ltd**
3 **LITTLEDEAN JIMMY (IRE)**, 8, b g Indian Danehill (IRE)—Gold Stamp **K. W. Bell**
4 **MY VIKING BAY (IRE)**, 9, b m Saddlers' Hall (IRE)—So Supreme (IRE) **Mrs R. E. Nelmes**
5 **NICKY NUTJOB (GER)**, 7, b g Fasliyev (USA)—Natalie Too (USA) **Quality Pipe Supports (Q.P.S.) Ltd**
6 **PEAK STORM**, 4, b g Sleeping Indian—Jitterbug (IRE) **The Cross Racing Club**
7 **PHARAON DE TOUZAINE (FR)**, 10, b g Subotica (FR)—Diana de Vonnas (FR) **K. W. Bell & Son Ltd**
8 **RADMORES EXPRESS**, 4, b g Primo Valentino (IRE)—Emma Lilley (USA) **J. R. Salter**
9 **RADMORES RETURN**, 5, b m Overbury (IRE)—Harvey's Sister **J. R. Salter**
10 **RADMORES REVENGE**, 6, b g Overbury (IRE)—Harvey's Sister **J. R. Salter**
11 **RED SKIPPER (IRE)**, 8, ch g Captain Rio—Speed To Lead (IRE) **The Cross Racing Club**
12 **STACCATO VALTAT (FR)**, 7, gr g Fragrant Mix (IRE)—Harmonie de Valtat (FR) **Mrs R. E. Nelmes**
13 **SWENDAB (IRE)**, 5, b g Trans Island—Lavish Spirit (USA) **The Cross Racing Club & Patrick Brady**
14 **TAKE TWO**, 4, b g Act One—Lac Marmot (FR) **S. P. Bloodstock**
15 **THE JAILER**, 10, b m Mujahid (USA)—Once Removed **Quality Pipe Supports (Q.P.S.) Ltd**
16 **THOMAS BELL (IRE)**, 9, b g Moscow Society (USA)—Cottage Girl (IRE) **K. W. Bell**
17 **TRIBAL DANCE**, 7, br g Flemensfirth (USA)—Native Sparkle (IRE) **Mr L. Herbert**

Other Owners: N. G. H. Ayliffe, P. Brady, C. L. Dubois, Mr S. T. Wallace, Mrs P. S. Wallace.

Jockey (flat): Robert Havlin, Luke Morris, Fergus Sweeney. **Jockey (NH):** Charlie Wallis. **Amateur:** Miss S. Randell.

493 MR JIM OLD, Wroughton

Postal: **Upper Herdswick Farm, Rackpen, Burderop, Wroughton, Swindon, Wiltshire, SN4 0QH**
Contacts: **PHONE** (01793) 845200 **CAR** (07836) 721459 **OFFICE** (01793) 845200
FAX (01793) 845201 **MOBILE** (07836) 721459
E-MAIL racing@jimold.co.uk **WEBSITE** www.jimoldracing.co.uk

1 ALDEBURGH, 4, b g Oasis Dream—Orford Ness **W. E. Sturt**
2 COUNTING HOUSE (IRE), 10, ch g King's Best (USA)—Inforapenny **W. E. Sturt**
3 OKAFRANCA (IRE), 8, b g Okawango (USA)—Villafranca (IRE) **W. E. Sturt**
4 PINK GIN, 5, ch g Alflora (IRE)—Miss Mailmit **Mrs J Fowler & Mr C Jenkins**
5 ROUND THE HORN (IRE), 13, ch g Master Willie—Gaye Fame **Old Fools Partnership**
6 THEDREAMSTILLALIVE (IRE), 13, ch g Houmayoun (FR)—State of Dream (IRE) **J. A. B. Old**
7 TODAREISTODO, 7, gr g Fair Mix (IRE)—Its Meant To Be **Mrs J. A. Fowler**
8 VAL D'ALLIER (FR), 4, b g Special Kaldoun (IRE)—Exlilie (FR) **W. E. Sturt**
9 VALID POINT (IRE), 7, b g Val Royal (FR)—Ricadonna **W. E. Sturt**
10 WITCH'S HAT (IRE), 10, br g Hubbly Bubbly (IRE)—Bold Shilling (IRE) **Old Fools Partnership**

Other Owners: Mrs P. V. Antrobus, C. J. Jenkins, C. C. Walker.

Assistant Trainer: Emma Grierson

Jockey (NH): Jason Maguire, Mark Grant, Timmy Murphy.

494 MR GEOFFREY OLDROYD, Malton

Postal: **Flint Hall Farm, Morr Lane, Brawby, Malton, North Yorkshire, YO17 6PZ**
Contacts: **PHONE** (01653) 668279 **MOBILE** (07730) 642620

1 ALFRED HUTCHINSON, 5, ch g Monsieur Bond (IRE)—Chez Cherie **R. C. Bond**
2 BOND ARTIST (IRE), 4, b f Excellent Art—Pitrizza (IRE) **R. C. Bond**
3 BOND FASTRAC, 6, b g Monsieur Bond (IRE)—Kanisfluh **R. C. Bond**
4 CHARMEL'S DELIGHT, 4, b f Monsieur Bond (IRE)—Jane's Delight (IRE) **Mr R S Marshall & Mr R C Bond**
5 CHOSEN FOREVER, 8, b g Choisir (AUS)—Forever Bond **R. C. Bond**
6 CROSSLEY, 4, ch g Monsieur Bond (IRE)—Dispol Diamond **P. Drewery**
7 EXCLUSIVE PREDATOR, 4, b g Misu Bond (IRE)—Triple Tricks (IRE) **R. C. Bond**
8 JAMAICAN BOLT (IRE), 5, b g Pivotal—Chiming (IRE) **R. C. Bond**
9 JUST BOND (IRE), 11, b g Namid—Give Warning (IRE) **R. C. Bond**
10 LADIES ARE FOREVER, 5, b m Monsieur Bond (IRE)—Forever Bond **R. C. Bond**
11 LADY ROYALE, 5, ch m Monsieur Bond (IRE)—Bond Royale **R. C. Bond**
12 PRINCESS KHELEYF, 4, b f Kheleyf (USA)—Jugendliebe (IRE) **G. Oldroyd**

THREE-YEAR-OLDS

13 ANGEL GRIGIO, gr f Dark Angel (IRE)—Owdbetts (IRE) **R. C. Bond**
14 BOND CLUB, b g Misu Bond (IRE)—Bond Platinum Club **R. C. Bond**
15 BOND EMPIRE, b g Misu Bond (IRE)—At Amal (IRE) **R. C. Bond**
16 BOND'S GIFT, ch f Monsieur Bond (IRE)—Bond Shakira **South Yorkshire Racing**
17 JUBILEE DANCER, b f Misu Bond (IRE)—Bond Babe **Moneypenny Racing**
18 MONSIEUR ROYALE, ch c Monsieur Bond (IRE)—Bond Royale **Casino Royale Racing**
19 REGGIE BOND, ch g Monsieur Bond (IRE)—Triple Tricks (IRE) **R. C. Bond**

TWO-YEAR-OLDS

20 Ch g 6/3 Monsieur Bond (IRE)—Bond Babe (Forzando) **R. C. Bond**
21 Ch f 13/3 Captain Gerrard (IRE)—Kanisfluh (Pivotal) (9523) **R. C. Bond**
22 Ch f 18/5 Monsieur Bond (IRE)—Triple Tricks (IRE) (Royal Academy (USA)) (8571) **R. C. Bond**

Other Owners: Mr J. N. Blackburn, Mr C. S. Bond, Mr R. C. Bond, Mr R. S. Marshall, Mr Andrew Turton.

Amateur: Mr Aaron James.

495 MR JAMIE OSBORNE, Upper Lambourn

Postal: **The Old Malthouse, Upper Lambourn, Hungerford, Berkshire, RG17 8RG**
Contacts: **PHONE** (01488) 73139 **FAX** (01488) 73084 **MOBILE** (07860) 533422
E-MAIL info@jamieosborne.com **WEBSITE** www.jamieosborne.com

1 ALMAIL (USA), 7, b g Swain (IRE)—Khassah **A. Taylor**

MR JAMIE OSBORNE - Continued

2 **AMADEUS WOLFE TONE (IRE)**, 4, b g Amadeus Wolf—Slieve **B. T. McDonald**
3 **ANEGADA DREAM**, 4, b f Shirocco (GER)—Last Dream (IRE) **William Harris Mrs Elaine White P Blows**
4 **APOSTLE (IRE)**, 4, gr g Dark Angel (IRE)—Rosy Dudley (IRE) **Dr M. B. Q. S. Koukash**
5 **BALTY BOYS (IRE)**, 4, b c Cape Cross (IRE)—Chatham Islands (USA) **Dr M. B. Q. S. Koukash**
6 **COMMERCIAL (IRE)**, 5, br g Kodiac—Call Collect (IRE) **Mrs F. Walwyn**
7 **COMMUNITY (USA)**, 5, b m Proud Citizen (USA)—Rimini Road (USA) **Mr S. Jakes**
8 **DRAWNFROMTHEPAST (IRE)**, 8, ch g Tagula (IRE)—Ball Cat (FR) **MCSD Racing, Mark Benton, Neil Benton**
9 **EASTBURY**, 5, ch gr g Pivotal—Sita (IRE) **Mrs F. Walwyn**
10 **FIELD OF DREAM**, 6, b g Oasis Dream—Field of Hope (IRE) **Mr K. J. P. Gundlach**
11 **GUNNER WILL (IRE)**, 4, b g Le Vie Dei Colori—Ros The Boss (IRE) **J. A. Osborne**
12 4, Ro f Fair Mix (IRE)—Heron Marsh (IRE) **P. W. Beck**
13 **JERICHO (IRE)**, 4, br g Manduro (GER)—Jinsiyah (USA) **Morsethehorse Syndicate**
14 **KING TORUS (IRE)**, 5, b g Oratorio (IRE)—Dipterous (IRE) **Dr M. B. Q. S. Koukash**
15 **MITCH RAPP (USA)**, 4, b g Yankee Gentleman (USA)—Foolish Party (USA) **M. A. C. Buckley**
16 **MR DAVID (USA)**, 6, b g Sky Mesa (USA)—Dancewiththebride (USA) **Mr K. J. P. Gundlach**
17 **PABUSAR**, 5, b g Oasis Dream—Autumn Pearl **Mr K. J. P. Gundlach**
18 **RAKAAN (IRE)**, 6, ch g Bahamian Bounty—Petite Spectre **J. A. Osborne**
19 **RESPLENDENT ALPHA**, 9, ch g Best of The Bests (IRE)—Sunley Scent **Mr L. Marshall**
20 **RUSSIAN BULLET**, 4, b g Royal Applause—Gandini **Mr S. Jakes**
21 **SONDEDURO**, 4, br g Manduro (GER)—Madame Cerito (USA) **Lady Blyth**
22 **TREADWELL (IRE)**, 6, b h Footstepsinthesand—Lady Wells (IRE) **Mrs F Walwyn & A Taylor**

THREE-YEAR-OLDS

23 **BE ON THE BELL**, br f Byron—Bella Beguine **Mr M. Turner**
24 **BEAM OF LIGHT**, b f Bertolini (USA)—Lighted Way **The Beam Of Light Partnership**
25 **CARINA PALACE**, b f Dutch Art—Ellcon (IRE) **Mr M. Turner**
26 **CASH RICH**, ch g Assertive—Dahshah **K J P Gundlach, Lady Whent & Partners**
27 B c First Samurai (USA)—Conquestress (USA) **M M Racing**
28 **CONTINENTAL DIVIDE (IRE)**, ch g Kheleyf (USA)—Leenane (IRE) **M. A. C. Buckley**
29 **DALGIG**, b c New Approach (IRE)—Bright Halo (IRE) **Mr K. J. P. Gundlach**
30 **DARKEST NIGHT (IRE)**, b g Dark Angel (IRE)—Vadarousse (GER) **Miss E. Asprey**
31 **DEVOUT (IRE)**, b f Holy Roman Emperor (IRE)—Raphimix (FR) **Dean Margolis, Paul Hearn & Partners**
32 **ELEANOR ROOSEVELT (IRE)**, b f Dalakhani (IRE)—
                                        Shesasmartlady (IRE) **Dean Margolis, Paul Hearn & Partners**
33 **EXCELLENT PUCK (IRE)**, b c Excellent Art—Puck's Castle **Mr K. J. P. Gundlach**
34 **HARDY RED (IRE)**, b g Mujadil (USA)—Salonga (IRE) **Tony Taylor & Patrick Gage**
35 **IS THIS LOVE (IRE)**, b f Danehill Dancer (IRE)—Glamour (IRE)
36 **LAYLA'S OASIS**, b f Oasis Dream—Kirk **Dr M. B. Q. S. Koukash**
37 **LIVING THE LIFE (IRE)**, b f Footstepsinthesand—Colour And Spice (IRE) **M. A. C. Buckley**
38 **LORAINE**, b f Sir Percy—Emirates First (IRE) **Mrs F Walwyn Mr & Mrs A Pakenham A Taylor**
39 **MOSMAN**, b c Haafhd—Last Dream (IRE) **Mrs Elaine White William Harris P Blows**
40 **ORATORIO'S JOY (IRE)**, b f Oratorio (IRE)—Seeking The Fun (USA) **Mr D. G. Christian**
41 **OUTBID**, ch f Auction House (USA)—Thicket **Paul Hearn, Dean Margolis & Partners**
42 **POOR DUKE (IRE)**, b g Bachelor Duke—Graze On Too (IRE) **The Duke's Partnership**
43 **SAINT JEROME (IRE)**, b g Jeremy—Eminence Gift
44 **SYCOPHANTIC (IRE)**, b g Cape Cross (IRE)—Amarice **Lady Blyth**
45 **WHISKEY N STOUT (IRE)**, b g Amadeus Wolf—Yasmin Satine (IRE) **B. T. McDonald**

TWO-YEAR-OLDS

46 **ALMOST FAMOUS (IRE)**, b c 1/3 Acclamation—Array of Stars (IRE) (Barathea (IRE)) (29364) **M. A. C. Buckley**
47 Br f 5/2 High Chaparral (IRE)—Birthday (IRE) (Singspiel (IRE)) (22221)
48 B c 4/5 Dandy Man (IRE)—
                        Bronze Queen (IRE) (Invincible Spirit (IRE)) (22221) **Chris Watkins & David N. Reynolds**
49 B f 7/4 Royal Applause—Child Bride (USA) (Coronado's Quest (USA)) (25000)
50 B c 5/4 Thewayyouare (USA)—Claire Soleil (USA) (Syncline (USA)) (47619)
51 B g 15/3 Avonbridge—Coup de Torchon (FR) (Namid) **Homecroft Wealth Racing**
52 **FEISTY DRAGON (IRE)**, b f 12/3 Camacho—Ejder (IRE) (Indian Ridge) (9523) **Cavendish Star Racing**
53 B c 18/2 Lawman (FR)—Flaming Song (IRE) (Darshaan) (20634) **Dean Margolis & J. O'Connor**
54 **NICE ARTY (IRE)**, b c 30/4 Amadeus Wolf—Fritillary (Vettori (IRE)) (14000) **B. T. McDonald**
55 B f 30/4 Clodovil (IRE)—Secret Circle (Magic Ring (IRE)) (35000) **Tony Taylor & Patrick Gage**
56 B c 21/4 Papal Bull—Sharadja (IRE) (Doyoun) **P. W. Beck**
57 **SUMMERSAULT (IRE)**, b c 4/5 Footstepsinthesand—Sumingasefa (Danehill (USA)) (17460)
58 Ro f 21/3 Clodovil (IRE)—Sweet Times (Riverman (USA)) (16000) **From The Stables Partnership**

MR JAMIE OSBORNE - Continued

59 Gr f 29/3 Captain Gerrard (IRE)—Ultimate Court (IRE) (Kendor (FR)) (7809) **Mrs F. Walwyn**
60 B c 14/2 Pastoral Pursuits—Wondrous Story (USA) (Royal Academy (USA)) (50000) **Patrick Gage & Tony Taylor**

Other Owners: Lady Aitken, Mrs Z. C. Campbell-Harris, Miss J. M. Driver, Mr P. J. Gage, Mr K. J. P Gundlach, Mr W. H. Harris, Mr P. J. Hearn, B. D. Heath, Dr J. A. E. Hobby, Mr J. R. Hobby, Mr S. Johnson, D. Margolis, Mr J. A. Osborne, A. E. Pakenham, Mrs V. H. Pakenham, Brig A. H. Parker Bowles, S. J. Piper, D. M. I. Simcock, Mr M. A. Stone, Mr A. Taylor, Mrs F. Walwyn, Lady Whent, Mrs E. M. White.

---

496 **MR JOHN M. OXX, Kildare**
Postal: Creeve, Currabeg, Kildare, Co. Kildare, Ireland
Contacts: **PHONE (00353) 455 21310 FAX (00353) 455 22236**

1 **CALL TO BATTLE (IRE)**, 4, b g King's Best (USA)—Dance The Classics (IRE) **Mr N. Jones**
2 **KATIOLA (IRE)**, 4, b f Oratorio (IRE)—Katiykha (IRE) **H. H. Aga Khan**
3 **SADDLER'S ROCK (IRE)**, 5, b h Sadler's Wells (USA)—Grecian Bride (IRE) **Mr M. O'Flynn**
4 **SINDJARA (USA)**, 4, br f Include (USA)—Sindirana (IRE) **H. H. Aga Khan**
5 **SOMEWHERE (IRE)**, 4, gr f Dalakhani (IRE)—Quest For Eternity (IRE) **Mr N. Jones**

THREE-YEAR-OLDS

6 **ABU NAYEF (IRE)**, ch g Nayef (USA)—Queen's Logic (IRE) **Jaber Abdullah**
7 **AL DESTOOR**, ch g Teofilo (IRE)—In A Silent Way (IRE) **Sultan Ali**
8 **ALAZEYA (IRE)**, b f Shirocco (GER)—Alasha (IRE) **H. H. Aga Khan**
9 **AWESOME D'ORO (IRE)**, b f Medaglia d'oro (USA)—Always Awesome (USA) **Mr C. Fipke**
10 **CASTLE OF ARGH (USA)**, b br c Arch (USA)—Xinji (IRE) **Mr F. Fabre**
11 **DALUKA (IRE)**, b f Dylan Thomas (IRE)—Daliya (IRE) **H. H. Aga Khan**
12 **FLASHY APPROACH**, ch c New Approach (IRE)—Flashy Wings **Jaber Abdullah**
13 **HARASIYA (IRE)**, br f Pivotal—Hazariya (IRE) **H. H. Aga Khan**
14 **HASANOUR (USA)**, b c Giant's Causeway (USA)—Hasanka (IRE) **H. H. Aga Khan**
15 **HEJAZ (IRE)**, ch c Manduro (GER)—Halawanda (IRE) **H. H. Aga Khan**
16 **HERMIA (IRE)**, b f Cape Cross (IRE)—Twinkling (NZ) **Mr J. R. Ancell**
17 **JUMAIRA TOWER (IRE)**, b g Dubawi (IRE)—Jumaireyah **Sheikh Mohammed Obaid Al Maktoum**
18 **KARAMAYA (IRE)**, b f Invincible Spirit (IRE)—Karawana (IRE) **H. H. Aga Khan**
19 **KERISA (IRE)**, b f Azamour (IRE)—Kerania (IRE) **H. H. Aga Khan**
20 **LITTLE WHITE CLOUD (IRE)**, gr c Dalakhani (IRE)—Quest For Eternity (IRE) **Mr N. Jones**
21 **MAJESTIC JASMINE (IRE)**, ch f New Approach (IRE)—Majestic Roi (USA) **Jaber Abdullah**
22 **MOURANI (IRE)**, b c Dalakhani (IRE)—Mouramara (IRE) **H. H. Aga Khan**
23 **PALACE OF WINDS (IRE)**, b f Monsun (GER)—Exciting Times (FR) **Mrs B. Keller**
24 **PAPAYA (IRE)**, ch f Teofilo (IRE)—Janaat **Sheikh Mohammed**
25 **QEWY (IRE)**, b c Street Cry (USA)—Princess Nada **Sheikh Mohammed Obaid Al Maktoum**
26 **RIYABA (IRE)**, b f Dalakhani (IRE)—Riyafa (IRE) **H. H. Aga Khan**
27 **ROCKTIQUE (USA)**, b f Rock Hard Ten (USA)—High Maintenance **Mr P. Garvey**
28 **ROMAN ROMANCE (IRE)**, ch f Peintre Celebre (USA)—Romandie (GER) **Dr Rolf Schmid**
29 **SHADAGANN (IRE)**, b c Invincible Spirit (IRE)—Shamadara (IRE) **H. H. Aga Khan**
30 **SHARKAYLA (IRE)**, b f Zamindar (USA)—Sharleez (IRE) **H. H. Aga Khan**
31 **SHEER DELIGHT (IRE)**, b f Marju (IRE)—Sheer Bliss (IRE) **Mr M. Morris/Dundalk Racing Club**
32 **SHELINA (IRE)**, b f Dalakhani (IRE)—Shemaka (IRE) **H. H. Aga Khan**
33 **SHOURANOUR (IRE)**, b c Lawman (FR)—Sharesha (IRE) **H. H. Aga Khan**
34 **SINANIYA (IRE)**, b br f More Than Ready (USA)—Sindirana (IRE) **H. H. Aga Khan**
35 **SIXPENNY SWEETS (IRE)**, gr f Dalakhani (IRE)—Angel of The Gwaun (IRE) **Mr N. Jones**
36 **SMOLENSK (IRE)**, b f Rock of Gibraltar (IRE)—Penza **Mrs S. Rogers**
37 **STEPWISE (IRE)**, b c Azamour (IRE)—Cadence **CDA Bloodstock**
38 **SWIFT ACTION (IRE)**, b f Invincible Spirit (IRE)—Littlefeather (IRE) **Sir E. Loder**
39 **TARANA (IRE)**, b f Cape Cross (IRE)—Tarakala (IRE) **H. H. Aga Khan**
40 **TETRANEMA (IRE)**, b f Montjeu (IRE)—Veneration **Mr L. Walshe**
41 **TIMIKAR (USA)**, b c Dynaformer (USA)—Timarwa (IRE) **H. H. Aga Khan**
42 **WAAHY (IRE)**, b c Manduro (GER)—Wonder Why (GER) **Jaber Abdullah**
43 **WHAT STYLE (IRE)**, ch f Teofilo (IRE)—Out of Time (IRE) **Mr C. Jones**
44 **WINTER LION (IRE)**, ch c Galileo (IRE)—Hill of Snow **Mr N. Jones**
45 **ZAND (IRE)**, b c Zamindar (USA)—Zanara (USA) **H. H. Aga Khan**

TWO-YEAR-OLDS

46 B c 22/3 Sea The Stars (IRE)—Affianced (IRE) (Erins Isle) **Mr C. Tsui**
47 B f 11/4 Holy Roman Emperor (IRE)—Akdara (IRE) (Sadler's Wells (USA)) **H. H. Aga Khan**

MR JOHN M. OXX - Continued

48 B f 4/2 Cape Cross (IRE)—Alaiyma (IRE) (Refuse To Bend (IRE)) **H. H. Aga Khan**
49 B f 31/3 Sea The Stars (IRE)—Alizaya (IRE) (Highest Honor (FR)) **Mr C. Tsui**
50 **ALYASAN (IRE)**, ch c 1/4 Sea The Stars (IRE)—Alaya (Ela-Mana-Mou) **H. H. Aga Khan**
51 B c 19/4 Sea The Stars (IRE)—Approach (Darshaan) (250000) **Mr C. Tsui**
52 **AWESOME STAR (IRE)**, b c 19/4 Sea The Stars (IRE)—
Always Awesome (USA) (Awesome Again (CAN)) **Mr C. E. Fipke**
53 **AZAMA (IRE)**, b f 5/2 Sea The Stars (IRE)—Asmara (USA) (Lear Fan (USA)) **H. H. Aga Khan**
54 Ch f 11/4 Shamardal (USA)—Bal de La Rose (IRE) (Cadeaux Genereux) (158730) **Mr C. Tsui**
55 B f 11/2 Shamardal (USA)—Baliyana (IRE) (Dalakhani (IRE)) **H. H. Aga Khan**
56 B c 5/5 Sea The Stars (IRE)—Bitooh (Diktat) **Mr C. Tsui**
57 Ch c 14/4 Sea The Stars (IRE)—Coyote (Indian Ridge) **Mr C. Tsui**
58 **DUNURE HARBOUR**, ch c 19/2 Dubawi (IRE)—Hobby (Robellino (USA)) (85000) **T. Barr**
59 B c 13/3 Oasis Dream—Ebadiyla (IRE) (Sadler's Wells (USA)) **H. H. Aga Khan**
60 B f 1/3 Oasis Dream—Ebalista (IRE) (Selkirk (USA)) **H. H. Aga Khan**
61 Gr f 28/4 Mizzen Mast (USA)—Ebaza (IRE) (Sinndar (IRE)) **H. H. Aga Khan**
62 Ch c 19/4 Nayef (USA)—Elegant Way (IRE) (Cape Cross (IRE)) **Sheikh Mohammed**
63 **EMERALD PRINCE (IRE)**, b c 20/3 Teofilo (IRE)—Nofa's Magic (IRE) (Rainbow Quest (USA)) **Jaber Abdullah**
64 B br f 24/4 Sea The Stars (IRE)—Epping (Charnwood Forest (IRE)) **Mr C. Tsui**
65 B f 24/2 Acclamation—Erdiyna (IRE) (Selkirk (USA)) **H. H. Aga Khan**
66 B f 12/3 Sea The Stars (IRE)—Fairy of The Night (IRE) (Danehill (USA)) **Mr C. Tsui**
67 B f 21/2 Sea The Stars (IRE)—Girouette (IRE) (Pivotal) **Mr C. Tsui**
68 B f 19/2 Oasis Dream—Hazariya (IRE) (Xaar) **H. H. Aga Khan**
69 **HOOF BEAT (IRE)**, b c 22/3 Azamour (IRE)—Cadence (Cadeaux Genereux) **CDA Bloodstock**
70 **JUPITER AND MARS (IRE)**, b c 3/6 Sea The Stars (IRE)—Hill of Snow (Reference Point) (75000) **Ms Pinar Araci**
71 B f 9/2 Oratorio (IRE)—Kadayna (IRE) (Dalakhani (IRE)) **H. H. Aga Khan**
72 **KAREZAK (IRE)**, b c 7/3 Azamour (IRE)—Karawana (IRE) (King's Best (USA)) **H. H. Aga Khan**
73 B c 5/2 Cape Cross (IRE)—Katiyra (IRE) (Peintre Celebre (USA)) **H. H. Aga Khan**
74 B c 27/2 Manduro (GER)—Kerania (IRE) (Daylami (IRE)) **H. H. Aga Khan**
75 B f 7/2 Dansili—Kiyra Wells (IRE) (Sadler's Wells (USA)) (310000) **Mr C. Tsui**
76 Ch c 18/2 Mr Greeley (USA)—Lidakiya (IRE) (Kahyasi) **H. H. Aga Khan**
77 **MARAKOUSH (IRE)**, b c 12/3 Danehill Dancer (IRE)—Mouramara (IRE) (Kahyasi) **H. H. Aga Khan**
78 Ch f 3/3 Selkirk (USA)—Masiyma (IRE) (Dalakhani (IRE)) **H. H. Aga Khan**
79 B f 9/4 Sea The Stars (IRE)—Night Fairy (IRE) (Danehill (USA)) **H. H. Aga Khan**
80 **PONFEIGH (IRE)**, gr c 23/4 Teofilo (IRE)—Water Fountain (Mark of Esteem (IRE)) (150000) **T. Barr**
81 **PRIMOGENITURE (IRE)**, b c 18/4 Glory of Dancer—
Jacqueline (IND) (King Charlemagne (USA)) **Mr K. Dhunjibhoy**
82 **PRINCESS YOUMZAIN**, b f 7/3 Dalakhani (IRE)—Wonder Why (GER) (Tiger Hill (IRE)) **Jaber Abdullah**
83 B c 2/3 Sea The Stars (IRE)—Ripples Maid (Dansili) **Mr C. Tsui**
84 **ROMANICO (IRE)**, gr c 25/4 Clodovil (IRE)—Romandie (GER) (Monsun (GER)) **Dr Rolf Schmid**
85 B c 14/3 Invincible Spirit (IRE)—Rose Quartz (Lammtarra (USA)) **H. H. Aga Khan**
86 B c 19/3 Kheleyf (USA)—Royal Crescent (IRE) (Spectrum (IRE)) **Sheikh Mohammed**
87 B f 18/4 Azamour (IRE)—Sarima (IRE) (Sinndar (IRE)) **H. H. Aga Khan**
88 B c 27/2 Galileo (IRE)—Sassenach (IRE) (Night Shift (USA)) **Mr C. Tsui**
89 B f 15/2 Pivotal—Seraya (FR) (Danehill (USA)) **H. H. Aga Khan**
90 B f 9/5 Holy Roman Emperor (IRE)—Sharesta (IRE) (Ashkalani (USA)) **H. H. Aga Khan**
91 **SHE'S MINE (IRE)**, b f 17/5 Sea The Stars (IRE)—Scribonia (IRE) (Danehill (USA)) **Mr V. I. Araci**
92 B f 15/3 Acclamation—Shehira (FR) (Sendawar (IRE)) **H. H. Aga Khan**
93 B c 9/5 Smart Strike (CAN)—Sindirana (IRE) (Kalanisi (IRE)) **H. H. Aga Khan**
94 B c 12/4 Sea The Stars (IRE)—Speed Song (Fasliyev (USA)) **Mr C. Tsui**
95 **TARABYIN (IRE)**, br gr c 9/2 Sinndar (IRE)—Timabiyra (IRE) (Linamix (FR)) **H. H. Aga Khan**
96 B c 11/5 Ghostzapper (USA)—Timarwa (IRE) (Daylami (IRE)) **H. H. Aga Khan**
97 **TITHONUS (IRE)**, b c 27/4 Glory of Dancer—Aurora Aurealis (IND) (Indictment (IND)) **Mr K. Dhunjibhoy**
98 B c 11/3 Acclamation—Zafayra (IRE) (Nayef (USA)) **H. H. Aga Khan**
99 B c 11/4 Marju (IRE)—Zarwala (IRE) (Polish Precedent (USA)) **H. H. Aga Khan**

Jockey (flat): N. G. McCullagh, B. A. Curtis, D. P. McDonogh.

497	**MR BRYN PALLING, Cowbridge**
	Trainer did not wish details of his string to appear.

498 MR HUGO PALMER, Newmarket
Postal: **Kremlin Cottage Stables, Snailwell Road, Newmarket, Suffolk, CB8 7DP**
Contacts: **PHONE (01638) 669880 FAX (01638) 666383 MOBILE (07824) 887886**
E-MAIL info@hugopalmer.com WEBSITE www.hugopalmer.com

1 ASCRIPTION (IRE), 4, b c Dansili—Lady Elgar (IRE) **Mr V. I. Araci**
2 GAME ALL (IRE), 4, b f Acclamation—Love Thirty **Astor, Brudenell, Deal, Fellowes, Palmer & 2JC**
3 KHUBALA (IRE), 4, b c Acclamation—Raghida (IRE) **Miss P. Araci**
4 MAKING EYES (IRE), 5, b m Dansili—Lady's View (USA) **Starter For Ten Partnership**
5 ZERO MONEY (IRE), 7, ch g Bachelor Duke (USA)—Dawn Chorus (IRE) **Kremlin Cottage III**

THREE-YEAR-OLDS

6 AUDACIA (IRE), b f Sixties Icon—Indiannie Moon **Carmichael Simmons Humber**
7 BORN TO RUN, b f Ishiguro (USA)—Maid For Running **Born To Run Racing**
8 EARLY ONE MORNING, b f Medicean—Still Small Voice **Mrs M. Bryce**
9 FLAWLESS BEAUTY, b f Excellent Art—Desert Classic **Decadent Racing**
10 HEROES WELCOME (IRE), b f Ramonti (FR)—Sagaing **Mrs P. A. Hancock**
11 HIGH TIME TOO (IRE), b f High Chaparral (IRE)—Dane Thyme (IRE) **Mrs S. C. Magnier**
12 OMBRELLINO (IRE), b g New Approach (IRE)—Dame's Violet (IRE) **De La Warr Racing**
13 QUEENOFTHENORTH (IRE), b f Halling (USA)—Polska (USA) **Mrs M. Bryce**
14 RED RED WINE, b c Dutch Art—Atnab (USA) **Mr K. J. P. Gundlach**
15 SHORT SQUEEZE (IRE), b g Cape Cross (IRE)—Sunsetter (USA) **W. A. L. Duff Gordon**
16 STAR SEQUENCE (IRE), b f Tagula (IRE)—Sonic Night (IRE) **RJWP Partnership**
17 TIPPING OVER (IRE), gr f Aussie Rules (USA)—Precipice **Anglia Bloodstock Syndicate**
18 TWO IN THE PINK (IRE), b f Clodovil (IRE)—Secret Circle **Mr K. J. P. Gundlach**
19 WOTABOOTY, b f Black Sam Bellamy (IRE)—Exexel **Pirate Racing**

TWO-YEAR-OLDS

20 Ch c 6/3 Pivotal—Alvee (IRE) (Key of Luck (USA)) (150000) **Mr V. I. Araci**
21 Ch c 30/3 Exceed And Excel (AUS)—Chanterelle (IRE) (Indian Ridge) (30000) **Kremlin Cottage II**
22 B f 2/4 Dylan Thomas (IRE)—Classical Flair (Distant Music (USA)) (38000) **Anglia Bloodstock II**
23 KNIFE POINT (GER), b c 6/4 High Chaparral (IRE)—Knightsbridge (BRZ) (Yagli (USA)) (12698) **Decadent Racing**
24 B f 28/1 Royal Applause—Miss Otis (Danetime (IRE)) (8000)
25 Br f 29/5 Notnowcato—Navajo Love Song (IRE) (Dancing Brave (USA)) (11000) **H. Palmer**
26 B f 31/3 Rock of Gibraltar (IRE)—Rubileo (Galileo (IRE)) (25396) **Kremlin Cottage I**
27 B c 1/4 Haafet (USA)—Sierva (GER) (Darshaan) (20000) **Weybridge Mafia**
28 THREE HEART'S, b f 29/1 Three Valleys—Heart's Harmony (Blushing Groom (FR)) **Mrs D. M. Haynes**
29 B f 11/4 Azamour (IRE)—Vittoria Vetra (Danehill Dancer (IRE)) **Mr V. I. Araci**

Other Owners: Lady Ampthill, Anglia Bloodstock Syndicate II, Gordon Angus, The Angus Family, The Hon. Jake Astor, Peter Bickmore, David Bowes-Lyon, Tom Brideoake, Amanda Brudenell, Lady Henrietta Spencer Churchill, Peter Deal, Alexander Fellows, Eddie Fitzpatrick, Anthea Gibson Fleming, Miss Kate Grimwade, Mr & Mrs Grimwade, Violet Henderson, Francis Hicks, Craig Hillier, Chris Humber, Jill Hunter, Ian Hunter, Time Hyde Jnr, Lord Kimball, Kremlin Cottate I, M V Magnier, Tom Magnier, Lady Manton, John Oakes, Fleur Ovr-Ewing, Lady Laura Palmer, Lady Palmer, Mrs Basil Phillips, David Ruck-Keene, Julie Sampson, Sam Sangster, Sam Sangster, Max Sangster, Paul Shanahan, Pete Shemilt, Mr Stanley, Mrs Becky Steel, Calie Stone, Julie Stone, Lady Tidbury, The Hon Arthur Vestey.

Apprentice: Noel Garbutt.

499 MR JOHN PANVERT, Tiverton
Postal: **Steart Farm Racing Stables, Stoodleigh, Tiverton, Devon, EX16 9QA**
Contacts: **MOBILE (07590) 120314**

1 CHOISIREZ (IRE), 4, b f Choisir (AUS)—Filimeala (IRE) **J. F. Panvert**
2 CLADDING, 7, b g Deploy—Sharway Lady **J. F. Panvert**
3 4, Ch f Trans Island—Cool Merenda (IRE) **I. W. Moss**
4 GLADSTONE (IRE), 5, b g Dansili—Rockerlong **J. F. Panvert**
5 4, B g Exit To Nowhere (USA)—Sharway Lady **J. F. Panvert**
6 SOVEREIGNS LEGACY, 6, b g Helissio (FR)—Sovereign **J. F. Panvert**
7 TITCH STRIDER, 8, b m Milan—Just Little **J. F. Panvert**

Jockey (flat): Jim Crowley, Luke Morris. **Jockey (NH):** David England, Conor O'Farrell.

500 MRS HILARY PARROTT, Redmarley
Postal: **Chapel Farm, Chapel Lane, Redmarley, Gloucester, Gloucestershire, GL19 3JF**
Contacts: **PHONE (01452) 840139 FAX (01452) 840139 MOBILE (07972) 125030**
E-MAIL hkparrott@btinternet.com

1 BERTIES COIN, 4, b g Sakhee (USA)—Spinning Coin **Mr T. J. & Mrs H. Parrott**
2 BIT OF A SCRUFF (IRE), 6, b g Westerner—Collage **Mr T. J. & Mrs H. Parrott**
3 BOB 'N' YOU (IRE), 10, b g Bob Back (USA)—Hue 'n' Cry (IRE) **Mr T. J. & Mrs H. Parrott**
4 5, B g Heron Island (IRE)—Clare Hogan (IRE) **Unregistered Partnership**
5 4, B c Presenting—Parsee (IRE) **Unregistered Partnership**
6 SIMPLY CHARLES (IRE), 6, ch g Blueprint (IRE)—Stormy Sea (IRE) **Mr T. J. & Mrs H. Parrott**
7 4, B g Flemensfirth (USA)—Tinopasa (FR) **Unregistered Partnership**
8 WAYWARD PRINCE, 9, b g Alflora (IRE)—Bellino Spirit (IRE) **Mr T. J. & Mrs H. Parrott**

THREE-YEAR-OLDS

9 B g Kayt Tara—Dalriath **Mr T. J. & Mrs H. Parrott**
10 B c Kalanisi (IRE)—Grangeclare Star (IRE) **Mr T. J. & Mrs H. Parrott**

Other Owners: Mr T. J. Parrott, Mrs H. Parrott.

Jockey (NH): Jack Doyle. **Amateur:** Mr Sam Drinkwater.

501 MR JAMES PAYNE, Dulverton
Postal: **Lower Holworthy Farm, Brompton Regis, Dulverton, Somerset, TA22 9NY**
Contacts: **HOME/FAX (01398) 371244**
E-MAIL holworthyfarm@aol.co.uk WEBSITE www.holworthyfarm.com

1 DOWN THE STRETCH, 13, b g Rakaposhi King—Si-Gaoith **J. R. Payne**
2 KNAPP BRIDGE BOY, 13, b g Wimbleball—Toll Bridge **R. J. Payne**

502 MR RAY PEACOCK, Tenbury Wells
Postal: **Elliott House Farm, Vine Lane, Kyre, Tenbury Wells, Worcestershire, WR15 8RL**
Contacts: **PHONE (01885) 410772 MOBILE (07748) 565574/ 07881440135**

1 GIFTED HEIR (IRE), 9, b g Princely Heir (IRE)—Inzar Lady (IRE) **R. E. Peacock**
2 INTERCHOICE STAR, 8, b g Josr Algarhoud (USA)—Blakeshall Girl **Mr J. P. Evitt**
3 KOMREYEV STAR, 11, b g Komaite (USA)—L'ancressaan **R. E. Peacock**
4 PORTRUSH STORM, 8, ch m Observatory (USA)—Overcast (IRE) **Mr J. P. Evitt**
5 RICH HARVEST (USA), 8, b br g High Yield (USA)—Mangano (USA) **R. E. Peacock**
6 SWORDS, 11, b g Vettori (IRE)—Pomorie (IRE) **R. E. Peacock**

Assistant Trainer: Mrs C Peacock

Jockey (flat): David Probert. **Apprentice:** Charles Bishop. **Amateur:** Miss S. Peacock.

503 MRS LYDIA PEARCE, Newmarket
Postal: **Wroughton House, 37 Old Station Road, Newmarket, Suffolk, CB8 8DT**
Contacts: **PHONE (01638) 664669 MOBILE (07787) 517864**
E-MAIL lsp_8@live.co.uk

1 COUNT CEPRANO (IRE), 9, b g Desert Prince (IRE)—Camerlata **Mrs L. J. Marsh**
2 DAZZLING BEGUM, 8, b m Okawango (USA)—Dream On Me **Mr J. T. Mangan**
3 DR FINLEY (IRE), 6, ch g Dr Fong (USA)—Farrfesheena (USA) **Killarney Glen**
4 DUKE OF ARICABEAU (IRE), 4, ch g Modigliani (USA)—Essential Fear (IRE) **A Partnership**
5 GHUFA (IRE), 9, b g Sakhee (USA)—Hawriyah (USA) **A Partnership**
6 HATTA STREAM (IRE), 7, b g Oasis Dream—Rubies From Burma (USA) **S & M Supplies (Aylsham) Ltd**
7 ICEMAN GEORGE, 9, b g Beat Hollow—Diebiedale **Mr J. T. Mangan**
8 MERCHANTS RETURN, 4, b c Byron—Molly Pitcher (IRE) **S & M Supplies (Aylsham) Ltd**
9 NEWINGTON, 4, b f Iceman—Almunia (IRE) **Mr A. R. Old**
10 OLNEY LASS, 6, b m Lucky Story (USA)—Zalebe **Mr P. J. Stephenson**

MRS LYDIA PEARCE - Continued

11 SALBATORE, 5, ch g Chineur (FR)—Au Contraire **Mr J. T. Mangan**
12 TINY THOMPSON, 4, b f Tobougg (IRE)—Mon Petit Diamant **Mr R. Devereux**

THREE-YEAR-OLDS

13 DAISIE CUTTER, b f Tobougg (IRE)—Bowled Out (GER) **Wroughton House Partnership**
14 SHAMALAD, b c Shamardal (USA)—Steam Cuisine **Killarney Glen**
15 SWEET TALKING GUY (IRE), b g Oratorio (IRE)—Sweet Namibia (IRE) **Killarney Glen**

Other Owners: Mr Stuart Andrews, Mr N. Grevette, Mr N. M. Hanger, Mr Geoff Jewitt, Mr Eric Jones, Mr Eric Jones, Mrs Jennifer Marsh, Mr K. A. Mullins, Mrs Lydia Pearce, Mr A. B. Puddick, Mr P. J. Stephenson, Mr R. G. Thurston.

Jockey (flat): Simon Pearce.

---

504 **MR OLLIE PEARS, Malton**
Postal: **The Office, Old Farmhouse, Beverley Road, Norton, Malton, North Yorkshire, YO17 9PJ**
Contacts: PHONE (01653) 690746 MOBILE (07760) 197103
E-MAIL info@olliepearsracing.co.uk WEBSITE www.olliepearsracing.co.uk

1 BOY THE BELL, 6, b g Choisir (AUS)—Bella Beguine **K. C. West**
2 LEAN ON PETE (IRE), 4, b g Oasis Dream—Superfonic (FR) **C. V. Wentworth**
3 MR FREDDY (IRE), 7, b g Intikhab (USA)—Bubble N Squeak (IRE) **Mr R. F. White**
4 MY ARCH, 11, b g Silver Patriarch (IRE)—My Desire **Mr J. D. Spensley & Mrs M. A. Spensley**
5 PRIORS GOLD, 6, ch g Sakhee (USA)—Complimentary Pass **O. J. Pears**
6 SOUND AMIGO (IRE), 5, b g Iceman—Holly Hayes (IRE) **Mr T. J. McManus**
7 VILLAGE GREEN, 4, b g Green Desert (USA)—Avessia **Ownaracehorse Ltd**

THREE-YEAR-OLDS

8 HIT THE LIGHTS (IRE), b g Lawman (FR)—Dawn Chorus (IRE) **C. V. Wentworth**
9 NAUGHTYBYCHOICE, gr g Dubai Destination (USA)—Gracia **Mrs V. A. Pears**
10 ZAITSEV (IRE), ch g Refuse To Bend (IRE)—Zuniga's Date (USA) **Mrs Z. Wentworth**

TWO-YEAR-OLDS

11 B c 19/4 Kodiac—Rajmahal (UAE) (Indian Ridge) (51586) **C. V. Wentworth**
12 STARLITE JEWEL, b f 16/2 Virtual—Celestial Empire (USA) (Empire Maker (USA)) **Mr J. M. Worrall**

Other Owners: Mrs M. A. Spensley, Mr J. D. Spensley.

Assistant Trainer: Vicky Pears

Jockey (NH): Brian Hughes.

---

505 **MR DAVID PEARSON, High Peak**
Postal: **Lower Fold Farm, Rowarth, High Peak, Derbyshire, SK22 1ED**
Contacts: PHONE (01663) 741471 MOBILE (07775) 842009

1 BALLYCRACKEN (IRE), 9, b g Flemensfirth (USA)—Cons Dual Sale (IRE) **D. Pearson**
2 HEVER ROAD (IRE), 14, ch g Anshan—The Little Bag **D. Pearson**

Assistant Trainer: Eileen Pearson

---

506 **MISS LINDA PERRATT, East Kilbride**
Postal: **North Allerton Farm, East Kilbride, Glasgow, Lanarkshire, G75 8RR**
Contacts: PHONE (01355) 303425 MOBILE (07931) 306147
E-MAIL linda.perratt@btinternet.com

1 ANITOPIA, 8, gr g Alflora (IRE)—The Whirlie Weevil **Mrs A. Hay**
2 BERBICE (IRE), 8, gr g Acclamation—Pearl Bright (FR) **J. K. McGarrity**
3 CAFE EXPRESS (IRE), 4, ch f Bertolini (USA)—Cafe Creme (IRE) **Mrs S. Burns**
4 CAYMAN FOX, 8, ch m Cayman Kai (IRE)—Kalarram **Mr R. R. Whitton**
5 DISTANT SUN (USA), 9, b g Distant View (USA)—The Great Flora (USA) **Jackton Racing Club**
6 DYNAMIC DRIVE (IRE), 6, b g Motivator—Biriyani (IRE) **Ring Of Fire**

MISS LINDA PERRATT - Continued

7 **EBONY CLARETS**, 4, b f Kyllachy—Pachanga **Mrs H. F. Perratt**
8 **GEANIE MAC (IRE)**, 4, ch f Needwood Blade—Dixie Evans **J. K. McGarrity**
9 **HIGH RESOLUTION**, 6, ch g Haafhd—Individual Talents (USA) **Mrs H. F. Perratt**
10 **JINKY**, 5, b g Noverre (USA)—Aries (GER) **Mr J. Murphy**
11 **LOLLYPOP LADY**, 4, b f Misu Bond (IRE)—Frabrofen **Mr R. R. Whitton**
12 **MR KHAN**, 5, ch g Rambling Bear—Frabrofen **Mrs H. F. Perratt**
13 **PITT RIVERS**, 4, br g Vital Equine (IRE)—Silca Boo
14 **RETREAT CONTENT (IRE)**, 5, b g Dubai Destination (USA)—Sharp Point (IRE) **Jackton Racing Club**
15 **ROCK CANYON (IRE)**, 4, b g Rock of Gibraltar (IRE)—Tuesday Morning **Mrs H. F. Perratt**
16 **ROYAL STRAIGHT**, 8, ch g Halling (USA)—High Straits **J. K. McGarrity**
17 **SABRATHA (IRE)**, 5, b m Hawk Wing (USA)—Aitch (IRE) **Helen Perratt & John Murphy**
18 **SAXONETTE**, 5, b m Piccolo—Solmorin **Mr J. Murphy**
19 **SCHMOOZE (IRE)**, 4, b f One Cool Cat (USA)—If Dubai (USA) **Jackton Racing Club**
20 **SILVER RIME (FR)**, 8, gr g Verglas (IRE)—Severina **J. K. McGarrity**

THREE-YEAR-OLDS

21 **FINDOG**, b g Pastoral Pursuits—Night Home (ITY) **J. K. McGarrity**
22 **NORTHSIDE ACE (IRE)**, b g Red Clubs (IRE)—Baltic Belle (IRE) **Miss L. A. Perratt**
23 **PRINCESS CAYAN (IRE)**, b f Kodiac—Silk Point (IRE) **Mrs H. F. Perratt**

Other Owners: I. Burns, Mr S. J. Houliston, Mr D. W. McIntyre, Mr N. North, M. Sawers.

Jockey (flat): Tom Eaves, Tony Hamilton, Paul Hanagan, Graham Lee, Phillip Makin. **Jockey (NH):** Brian Hughes, Wilson Renwick. **Conditional:** Callum Whillans. **Apprentice:** Paul Norton, Ross Smith.

MRS AMANDA PERRETT, Pulborough
Postal: **Coombelands Racing Stables LLP, Pulborough, West Sussex, RH20 1BP**
Contacts: **OFFICE** (01798) 873011 **HOME** (01798) 874894 **FAX** (01798) 875163
MOBILE (07803) 088713
E-MAIL aperrett@coombelands-stables.com **WEBSITE** www.amandaperrett.com

1 **ARCH VILLAIN (IRE)**, 4, b g Arch (USA)—Barzah (IRE) **Mr & Mrs F Cotton, Mr & Mrs P Conway**
2 **BLANK CZECH (IRE)**, 4, b g Clodovil (IRE)—Shamboda (IRE) **G. D. P. Materna**
3 **BLUE SURF**, 4, ch g Excellent Art—Wavy Up (IRE) **John Connolly And Partners**
4 **BRAMSHILL LASS**, 4, ch f Notnowcato—Disco Ball **Mrs K. J. L. Hancock**
5 **HEAD OF STEAM (USA)**, 6, ch g Mizzen Mast (USA)—Summer Mist (USA) **G. D. P. Materna**
6 **JOHNNY CASTLE**, 5, b g Shamardal (USA)—Photogenic **George Materna & John McInerney**
7 **LADY BARASTAR (IRE)**, 5, b m Barathea (IRE)—Stariya (IRE) **Mrs K. J. L. Hancock**
8 **PENCHESCO (IRE)**, 8, b g Orpen (USA)—Francesca (IRE) **Mrs K. J. L. Hancock**
9 **PRESTO VOLANTE (IRE)**, 5, b g Oratorio (IRE)—
    Very Racy (USA) **Mrs S Conway, Mr & Mrs M Swayne, Mr A Brooke, Mrs R Doel**
10 **RIO ROYALE (IRE)**, 7, b g Captain Rio—Lady Nasrana (FR) **Mrs A. J. Perrett**
11 **ROXY FLYER (IRE)**, 6, b m Rock of Gibraltar (IRE)—Dyna Flyer (USA) **Mr & Mrs F. Cotton Mrs S. Conway**
12 **SABORIDO (USA)**, 7, gr g Dixie Union (USA)—Alexine (ARG) **Cotton, James, Slade**
13 **SIGNED UP**, 4, b c Rail Link—Sing For Fame (USA) **K. Abdulla**
14 **SIR MIKE**, 4, ch g Haafhd—Tara Moon **M. H. and Mrs G. Tourle**

THREE-YEAR-OLDS

15 **ANNUNCIATE (USA)**, b br c Arch (USA)—Valentine Band (USA) **K. Abdulla**
16 **CZECH IT OUT (IRE)**, b c Oratorio (IRE)—Naval Affair (IRE) **G. D. P. Materna**
17 **EBONY ROC (IRE)**, br g Shirocco (GER)—Chia Laguna (IRE) **The To-Agori-Mou Partnership**
18 **ELVIN**, br c Rock of Gibraltar (IRE)—Petite Nymphe **Woodcote Stud Ltd**
19 **EMPIRICIST (IRE)**, b g Holy Roman Emperor (IRE)—Charaig **John Connolly & Odile Griffith**
20 **EXTRASOLAR**, b g Exceed And Excel (AUS)—Amicable Terms **Odile Griffith & John Connolly**
21 **FAST PACE**, ch f Observatory (USA)—Market Forces **K. Abdulla**
22 **FIRST WARNING**, b g Rail Link—Tricked **K. Abdulla**
23 **HARWOODS STAR (IRE)**, b c Danehill Dancer (IRE)—Showbiz (IRE) **Harwoods Racing Club Limited**
24 **HERO'S STORY**, b c Mount Nelson—Red Roses Story (FR) **The Recitation Partnership**
25 **KNIGHT'S PARADE (IRE)**, b g Dark Angel (IRE)—Toy Show (IRE) **The Recitation Partnership**
26 **LION BEACON**, ch g Beat Hollow—Second of May **Mrs A. J. Chandris**
27 **OVATORY**, b c Acclamation—Millsini **John Connolly & Odile Griffith**
28 **PIVOTAL SILENCE**, ch f Vita Rosa (JPN)—Tara Moon **M. H. and Mrs G. Tourle**
29 **ROYAL SIGNALLER**, b c Dylan Thomas (IRE)—Whirly Bird **Woodcote Stud Ltd**
30 **SAUCY MINX (IRE)**, b f Dylan Thomas (IRE)—Market Day **Mr & Mrs F Cotton, Mr & Mrs P Conway**

MRS AMANDA PERRETT - Continued

31 SUBLIMATE (USA), gr ro f Mizzen Mast (USA)—Complex (USA) **K. Abdulla**
32 TIGERISH, b g Tiger Hill (IRE)—Dimakya (USA) **Sir Eric Parker**

TWO-YEAR-OLDS

33 A LEGACY OF LOVE (IRE), b f 30/1 Sea The Stars (IRE)—
Nashmiah (IRE) (Elusive City (USA)) (200000) **Mrs B. A. Karn-Smith**
34 APPROACHING (IRE), ch c 15/4 New Approach (IRE)—
Dust Dancer (Suave Dancer (USA)) **Bluehills Racing Limited**
35 ARTFUL ROGUE (IRE), b c 5/5 Excellent Art—
Szabo (IRE) (Anabaa (USA)) (55000) **Mr & Mrs F Cotton,Mr & Mrs P Conway**
36 ARTISTIC FLAME, b c 8/5 Archipenko (USA)—Umlilo (Mtoto) (25000) **Coombelands Racing Syndicate**
37 ASTRONEREUS (IRE), ch c 17/2 Sea The Stars (IRE)—
Marie Rheinberg (GER) (Surako (GER)) **John Connolly & Odile Griffith**
38 BEST KEPT, ch c 7/5 Sakhee's Secret—
Ashlinn (IRE) (Ashkalani (IRE)) (30000) **Coombelands Racing Syndicate 3**
39 DOUBLE CZECH (IRE), b c 23/2 Bushranger (IRE)—
Night of Joy (IRE) (King's Best (USA)) (55000) **G. D. P. Materna**
40 DREAMING BRAVE, b c 20/2 Sleeping Indian—
Beechnut (IRE) (Mujadil (USA)) (35000) **Coombelands Racing Syndicate 2**
41 EXCEDO PRAECEDO, b c 3/2 Exceed And Excel (AUS)—
Merle (Selkirk (USA)) (150000) **John Connolly & Odile Griffith**
42 B c 19/4 Champs Elysees—Fairy Steps (Rainbow Quest (USA)) **K. Abdulla**
43 HARWOODS VOLANTE (IRE), ch c 11/2 Kheleyf (USA)—
Semiquaver (IRE) (Mark of Esteem (IRE)) (45000) **Harwoods Racing Club Limited**
44 B br f 4/3 First Defence (USA)—Out of Reach (Warning) **K. Abdulla**
45 PACK LEADER (IRE), b c 2/2 Hurricane Run (IRE)—
Bright Enough (Fantastic Light (USA)) (65000) **G. D. P. Materna**
46 B f 2/3 Arch (USA)—Proud Fact (USA) (Known Fact (USA)) **K. Abdulla**
47 B c 18/2 New Approach (IRE)—Shadow Dancing (Unfuwain (USA)) (55000) **A. D. Spence**
48 Ch f 13/2 Shirocco (GER)—Spotlight (Dr Fong (USA)) (10000) **Bluehills Racing Limited**
49 B c 11/2 Kitten's Joy (USA)—Tinge (USA) (Kingmambo (USA)) **K. Abdulla**
50 Ch c 18/2 Three Valleys (USA)—Western Appeal (USA) (Gone West (USA)) **K. Abdulla**

Other Owners: Mr S. W. Barnett, A. W. Brooke, J. P. Connolly, Mrs S. M. Conway, F. G. Cotton, Mrs S. H. Cotton, Mrs R. J. Doel, Mrs J. M. V. Freeman, Ms O. L. Griffith, Guy Harwood, D. M. James, Dr J. P. McInerney, D. M. Slade, Mrs V. J. M. Slade, Mr M. B. Swayne, Mrs A. J. Swayne, Mr M. H. Tourle, Mrs G. O. Tourle.

Assistant Trainer: Mark Perrett

---

508 **MR PAT PHELAN, Epsom**
Postal: **Ermyn Lodge, Shepherds Walk, Epsom, Surrey, KT18 6DF**
Contacts: PHONE **(01372) 229014** FAX **(01372) 229001** MOBILE **(07917) 762781**
E-MAIL **pat.phelan@ermynlodge.com** WEBSITE **www.ermynlodge.com**

1 BABY DOTTIE, 6, ch m Dr Fong (USA)—Auntie Dot Com **Mr A. J. Smith**
2 BUBBLY BRAVEHEART (IRE), 6, b g Cape Cross (IRE)—Infinity (FR) **The Only Pub In The World**
3 CELTIC CHARLIE (FR), 8, ch g Until Sundown (USA)—India Regalona (USA) **Celtic Contractors Limited**
4 COUP DE GRACE (IRE), 4, b g Elusive City (USA)—No Way (IRE) **Mr J. F. Lang**
5 DOUBLE U DOT EDE'S, 4, b g Rock of Gibraltar (IRE)—Reveuse de Jour (IRE) **Ede's (UK) Ltd**
6 EDE'S, 13, ch g Bijou d'inde—Ballagarrow Girl **Ede's (UK) Ltd**
7 ELLIE IN THE PINK (IRE), 5, ch m Johannesburg (USA)—Stravinia (USA) **A. B. Pope**
8 ERMYNTRUDE, 6, b br m Rock of Gibraltar (IRE)—Ruthie **Epsom Racegoers No.2**
9 JAKEYS GIRL, 6, b m Dubai Destination (USA)—Rosewood Belle (USA) **K. S. Thomas**
10 REGGIE PERRIN, 5, ch g Storming Home—Tecktal (FR) **Ermyn Lodge Stud Limited**
11 REPRESENTINGCELTIC (IRE), 8, ch g Presenting—Nobull (IRE) **Celtic Contractors Limited**
12 ROCK WITH YOU, 6, b m Rock of Gibraltar (IRE)—Karsiyaka (IRE) **Maginn & Harfitt**
13 RULBIN REALTA, 6, b m Jendali (USA)—Paulines Gem (IRE) **The Red Filly**
14 SILLY BILLY (IRE), 5, b g Noverre (USA)—Rock Dove (IRE) **The Only Pub In The World**
15 SUPER DUPLEX, 6, b g Footstepsinthesand—Penelope Tree (IRE) **Special Piping Materials Ltd**

THREE-YEAR-OLDS

16 COUNTESS LOVELACE, b f Byron—Muwasim (USA) **Mr W. Bocking**
17 JAKEY (IRE), b c Cape Cross (IRE)—Off Message (IRE) **A. B. Pope**
18 LADY BONANOVA (IRE), b f Haatef (USA)—Lady Express (IRE) **The Pooley Stevens Partnership**

MR PAT PHELAN - Continued

TWO-YEAR-OLDS

19 **SOFTLY SHE TREADS (IRE)**, b f 6/2 Azamour (IRE)—Lady Lucre (IRE) (Last Tycoon) (11000) **Mr B. P. Donovan**

Other Owners: I. W. Harfitt, Mr G. Maginn, Mr R. G. Mappley, J. Mcgrath, Mr J. O'Sullivan, Mr P. Pooley, Mr R. Stevens, Mr P. J. Wheatley, T. Zachariades.

Assistant Trainer: Mr Gareth Thomas

Jockey (flat): Ian Mongan. **Jockey (NH):** Colin Bolger. **Amateur:** Mr. Freddie Mitchell.

---

509 **MR RICHARD PHILLIPS, Moreton-in-Marsh**
Postal: **Adlestrop Stables, Adlestrop, Moreton-in-Marsh, Gloucestershire, GL56 0YN**
Contacts: **PHONE (01608) 658710 FAX (01608) 658713 MOBILE (07774) 832715**
E-MAIL **info@richardphillipsracing.com** WEBSITE **www.richardphillipsracing.com**

1 **ANDHAAR**, 7, b g Bahri (USA)—Deraasaat **Bissett Racing**
2 **BLUEGRASS BID (USA)**, 6, b g During (USA)—Call Cleta (USA) **The Someday's Here Racing Partnership**
3 **BRIGHT LIGHT**, 6, ch m Exit To Nowhere (USA)—Lamp's Return **Mrs S. C. Welch**
4 **CAPTAIN TIDDS (IRE)**, 12, b g Presenting—Kilmana (IRE) **C. Pocock**
5 **CASH FOR STEEL (IRE)**, 6, b m Craigsteel—Neiges Eternelles (FR) **M. D. Coulson**
6 **CRYSTAL SWING**, 6, b g Trade Fair—Due West **Enjoy The Journey**
7 **DEVIL'S PROVINCE (USA)**, 6, b g Saarland (USA)—
                                       Devilish Amour (USA) **The Someday's Here Racing Partnership**
8 **FAIR BREEZE**, 6, b m Trade Fair—Soft Touch (IRE) **Ellangowan Racing Partners**
9 **FANTASTIC SMARTIE**, 4, b f Fantastic Spain (USA)—Smart Cassie **RAMPS**
10 **GREAT HERO**, 8, ch g Arkadian Hero (USA)—Great Tern **The Adlestrop Club**
11 **IFITS A FIDDLE**, 4, b f Kalanisi (IRE)—Fiddling Again **Mrs E. C. Roberts**
12 **JUST BENNY (IRE)**, 8, b g Beneficial—Artic Squaw (IRE) **Upthorpe Racing**
13 **KING JACK**, 11, b g Classic Cliche (IRE)—Hack On **Gryffindor I (www.vendeeevents.com)**
14 **LIGHT THE WORLD (FR)**, 5, b g Layman (USA)—Lignite (IRE) **The Pink Ladies**
15 **LISHEEN HILL (IRE)**, 7, b g Witness Box (USA)—Lady Lamb (IRE) **The Aspirationals**
16 **LOCHAN (IRE)**, 6, b g Millenary—Petit Roilelet (IRE) **W. D. S. Murdoch**
17 **LUCKY THIRTEEN**, 5, b g Passing Glance—Lingua Franca **Mr D. Stockdale**
18 5, B m Flemensfirth (USA)—Mandys Native (IRE) **R. T. Phillips**
19 **MASTER VINTAGE**, 5, b g Kayf Tara—What A Vintage (IRE) **The Someday's Here Racing Partnership**
20 **MISTER NEWBY (IRE)**, 7, b g Oscar (IRE)—Sallie's Girl (IRE) **C. Pocock**
21 **MOTOU (FR)**, 8, b g Astarabad (USA)—Picoletta (FR) **G. Lansbury**
22 **MR TINGLE**, 9, br g Beat All (USA)—Dianthus (IRE) **Mr & Mrs W. Brogan-Higgins & Gryffindor**
23 **MY MANIKATO**, 6, ch g Starcraft (NZ)—Rainbow Queen (FR) **Mr & Mrs R. Scott**
24 **NO COMPROMISE**, 4, b f Avonbridge—Highly Liquid **Mrs S. J. Harvey**
25 **RAFAAF (IRE)**, 5, b g Royal Applause—Sciunfona (IRE) **J. A. Gent**
26 **RICH BUDDY**, 7, b g Kayf Tara—Silver Gyre (IRE) **Mrs E. A. Prowting**
27 **SALTO D'ALBAIN (FR)**, 7, b g Dark Moondancer—Emeraude du Moulin (FR) **The Squashed Club**
28 **STOP THE SHOW (IRE)**, 12, b g King's Theatre (IRE)—Rathsallagh Tartan **The Adlestrop Club**
29 **THORNTON ALICE**, 8, b m Kayf Tara—Lindrick Lady (IRE) **The Listeners**
30 **UPPER DECK (IRE)**, 8, b g Beckett (IRE)—Princess Accord (USA) **Mr C. A. J. Allan**
31 **WHENEVER**, 9, ch g Medicean—Alessandra **Dozen Dreamers Partnership**
32 **WHICHEVER**, 7, ch m Where Or When (IRE)—Pips Way (IRE) **Upthorpe Racing**

THREE-YEAR-OLDS

33 **OCEAN POWER (IRE)**, b g Papal Bull—Petticoat Power (IRE) **Mr W. McLuskey**

Other Owners: Ms K. M. Anderson, J. E. Barnes, A. A. Bissett, Mrs J. Bissett, Mr J. R. Brown, Mr E. G. Brown, Mrs E. J. Clarke, Mr J. E. S. Colling, B. J. Duckett, Mrs H. M. Nixseaman, M. T. Phillips, R. Scott, Mrs P. M. Scott, Dr E. D. Theodore, Mrs L. A. Wright, A. W. D. Wright.

Jockey (NH): Sean Quinlan, Richard Johnson, Sam Twiston-Davies.

510 MR DAVID PIPE, Wellington

Postal: **Pond House, Nicholashayne, Wellington, Somerset, TA21 9QY**
Contacts: **PHONE (01884) 840715 FAX (01884) 841343**
E-MAIL david@davidpipe.com WEBSITE www.davidpipe.com

1 AFRICAN BROADWAY (IRE), 7, b g Broadway Flyer (USA)—African Lily (IRE) A. E. Frost
2 ALDERLUCK (IRE), 10, ch g Alderbrook—Cecelia's Charm (IRE) Mrs C. J. Rayner
3 AMIGO (FR), 6, b g Ballingarry (IRE)—Allez Y (FR) Willsford Racing & Andrew L Cohen
4 ASHKAZAR (FR), 9, b g Sadler's Wells (USA)—Asharna (IRE) D. A. Johnson
5 BAD GIRLS (FR), 4, b f Astarabad (USA)—Canadiane (FR) The Blackdown Three
6 BALTIMORE ROCK (IRE), 4, b g Tiger Hill (IRE)—La Vita E Bella (IRE) R. S. Brookhouse
7 BAMBOLEO (IRE), 6, b g Old Vic—Sorivera M. C. Denmark
8 BARNEY COOL, 6, b g Bollin Eric—Laurel Diver N. G. Mills
9 BASIL FAWLTY (IRE), 8, b g Balakheri (IRE)—Laughing Lesa (IRE) M. C. Denmark
10 BATTLE GROUP, 8, b g Beat Hollow—Cantanta Jolly Boys Outing
11 BEYOND (IRE), 6, ch g Galileo (IRE)—Run To Jane (IRE) Mr R. J. H. Geffen
12 BIG OCCASION (FR), 6, b g Sadler's Wells (USA)—Asnieres (USA) The Old Betfairians
13 BLADOUN (FR), 5, gr g Smadoun (FR)—Blabliramic (FR) H. M. W. Clifford
14 BOIS DES AIGLES (FR), 4, gr g Stormy River (FR)—Silver Fun (FR) Prof C. Tisdall
15 BROADWAY BUFFALO (IRE), 5, ch g Broadway Flyer (USA)—Benbradagh Vard (IRE) The Broadway Partnership
16 BUDDY BOLERO (IRE), 7, b g Accordion—Quinnsboro Ice (IRE) M. C. Denmark
17 BYGONES SOVEREIGN (IRE), 7, b g Old Vic—Miss Hollygrove (IRE) Arnie & Alan Kaplan
18 CENTASIA, 6, b m Presenting—Cent Prime R. S. Brookhouse
19 CLOSE HOUSE, 6, b g Generous (IRE)—Not Now Nellie R. S. Brookhouse
20 CONSIGLIERE (FR), 10, ch g Trempolino (USA)—Gianna Nannini (ITY) Mr E. A. P. Scouller
21 DAN BREEN (IRE), 8, b g Mull of Kintyre (USA)—Kunuz Mr Stuart & Simon Mercer
22 DECOY (FR), 7, b g Della Francesca (USA)—Vagualame (FR) Stefanos Stefanou
23 DOCTOR HARPER (IRE), 5, b g Presenting—Supreme Dreamer (IRE) D. A. Johnson
24 DYNASTE (FR), 7, gr g Martaline—Bellissima de Mai (FR) A. J. White
25 E STREET BOY, 7, b g Kayf Tara—Eau de Vie Roger Stanley & Yvonne Reynolds
26 EDMUND KEAN (IRE), 6, b g Old Vic—Baliya (IRE) Walters Plant Hire & James & Jean Potter
27 EL LOBO (FR), 6, b g Loup Solitaire (USA)—Mirage du Simbeu (FR) James & Jean Potter
28 FAMOUSANDFEARLESS (IRE), 5, b g Presenting—Clandestine The Bravo Partnership
29 FLYING CROSS (IRE), 6, b h Sadler's Wells (USA)—Ramruma (USA) Mr R. J. H. Geffen
30 FRANKLIN ROOSEVELT (IRE), 7, b g Beneficial—Glen's Gale (IRE) M. C. Denmark
31 GARRYLEIGH (IRE), 6, b g Statue of Liberty (USA)—Hunter's Valley Brocade Racing
32 GARYNELLA (IRE), 6, b g Ballingarry (IRE)—Pimpinella (FR) T. Neill
33 GEVREY CHAMBERTIN (FR), 5, gr g Dom Alco (FR)—Fee Magic (FR) Roger Stanley & Yvonne Reynolds III
34 GOULANES (IRE), 7, b g Mr Combustible (IRE)—Rebolgiane (IRE) R. S. Brookhouse
35 GRAND EXIT, 7, b m Exit To Nowhere (USA)—Little Feat J. L. Rowsell
36 GRANDS CRUS (FR), 8, gr g Dom Alco (FR)—Fee Magic (FR) Roger Stanley & Yvonne Reynolds III
37 GUESS AGAIN (IRE), 8, b g Milan—Guess Twice M. C. Denmark
38 HEATH HUNTER (IRE), 6, b g Shantou (USA)—Deep Supreme (IRE) The Heath Hunter Partnership
39 HENOK (FR), 7, ch g Kapgarde (FR)—Harkosa (FR) Walters Plant Hire Ltd
40 HIDDEN DISCOUNTS, 4, b g Echo of Light—Deep Ravine (USA) Stefanos Stefanou
41 HIGH VILLE (IRE), 7, b g Beneficial—Brenny's Pearl (IRE) G. D. Thompson
42 HIS EXCELLENCY (IRE), 5, ch g King's Best (USA)—Road Harbour (USA) Mrs J. Tracey
43 HOME RUN (GER), 5, ch g Motivator—Hold Off (IRE) W. F. Frewen
44 HUGO DRAX (IRE), 6, b g Bienamado (USA)—Young Love (FR) M. C. Denmark
45 HUNTERVIEW, 7, ch g Reset (AUS)—Mount Elbrus Mrs J. Tracey
46 I SHOT THE SHERIFF (IRE), 6, b g Westerner—Sherin (GER) M. C. Denmark
47 INVESTISSEMENT, 7, b g Singspiel (IRE)—Underwater (USA) Mr R. J. H. Geffen
48 JUNIOR, 10, ch g Singspiel (IRE)—For More (FR) Middleham Park Racing LI
49 KATKEAU (FR), 6, b g Kotky Bleu (FR)—Levine (FR) Prof C Tisdall, Mr J A Gent, Mr R Wilkin
50 KAZLIAN (FR), 5, b g Sinndar (IRE)—Quiet Splendor (USA) Twelve Pipers Piping
51 KEEP THE CASH (IRE), 5, b g Oscar (IRE)—Waterloo Ball (IRE) Kelly, Pipe & Fawkhandles
52 KILRYE (IRE), 6, b g Catcher In The Rye (IRE)—Kiladante (IRE) A. J. White & Mrs A. Underhill
53 KINGS PALACE (IRE), 6, b g King's Theatre (IRE)—Sarahs Quay (IRE) Drew, George, Johnson Partnership
54 KNIGHT PASS (IRE), 7, b g Accordion—Toulon Pass (IRE) M. C. Denmark
55 LAFLAMMEDEGLORIE, 7, b g Fair Mix (IRE)—Swazi Princess (IRE) D. R. Mead
56 LEADER OF THE GANG, 7, b g Karinga Bay—Material Girl M. C. Denmark
57 LOLA GALLI, 5, br m Old Vic—Tahoe (IRE) R. J. McCreery
58 MASTER OVERSEER (IRE), 10, b g Old Vic—Crogeen Lass Brocade Racing
59 MATUHI, 10, b g Dansili—Montserrat Willsford Racing Ltd
60 MIDNIGHT TUESDAY (FR), 8, b g Kapgarde (FR)—Deat Heat (FR) A. C. Eaves
61 MILITARY PRECISION (IRE), 7, b g Exit To Nowhere (USA)—Devil Leader (USA) M. C. Denmark

MR DAVID PIPE - Continued

62 **MILOR DE LA BORIE (FR),** 4, gr g Turgeon (USA)—Trop Tard (FR) **Prof C. Tisdall**
63 **NO SECRETS (IRE),** 9, b g King's Theatre (IRE)—Happy Native (IRE) **M. C. Denmark**
64 **NOTUS DE LA TOUR (FR),** 7, b g Kutub (IRE)—Ridiyla (IRE) **D Bradshaw, J Dale, P Deal, J Smee, W Walsh**
65 **ODDJOB (IRE),** 9, b g Bob's Return (IRE)—Bettyhill **M. C. Denmark**
66 **OFF THE WALL (IRE),** 6, ch g Presenting—Ginger Bar (IRE) **M. C. Denmark**
67 **ON KHEE,** 6, b m Sakhee (USA)—Star Precision **Palatinate Thoroughbred Racing Limited**
68 **OTTERBURN (IRE),** 7, b g Flemensfirth (USA)—Mrs Battle (IRE) **James & Jean Potter**
69 **OUR FATHER (IRE),** 7, gr g Shantou (USA)—Rosepan (IRE) **The Ives & Johnson Families**
70 **PALACE JESTER,** 8, b g King's Theatre (IRE)—Jessolle **M. C. Pipe**
71 **POOLE MASTER,** 8, ch g Fleetwood (IRE)—Juste Belle (FR) **G. D. Thompson**
72 **PRIME LOCATION,** 7, b g Generous (IRE)—Sovereignsflagship (IRE) **M. C. Denmark**
73 **PROBLEMA TIC (FR),** 7, b g Kapgarde (FR)—Atreide (FR) **Mrs J. Tracey**
74 **PURPLE 'N GOLD (IRE),** 4, b g Strategic Prince—Golden Dew (IRE) **Mrs L. Webb**
75 **QALINAS (FR),** 6, gr g Malinas (GER)—Tabletiere (FR) **Middleham Park Racing XX & M C Pipe**
76 **QUINTE DU CHATELET (FR),** 9, b g Lavirco (GER)—Grandeur Royale (FR) **Brocade Racing**
77 **RED SHERLOCK,** 4, ch g Shirocco (GER)—Lady Cricket (FR) **D. A. Johnson**
78 **RONALDO DES MOTTES (FR),** 8, b g Rifapour (IRE)—Gemma (IRE) **K & D Ives**
79 **ROYAL MILE (IRE),** 9, br g Bob's Return (IRE)—Country Style **M. C. Denmark**
80 **ROYAL PEAK (IRE),** 6, b g Bach (IRE)—Dante's Ville (IRE) **M. C. Pipe**
81 **ROYAL RATIONALE (IRE),** 9, b g Desert Prince (IRE)—Logic **Pond House Racing**
82 **RUBY BROOK,** 5, b g Sakhee (USA)—Highbrook (USA) **Mr A. E. Frost & Mr A. R. Adams**
83 **SHAKING HANDS (IRE),** 9, b g Bach (IRE)—Picton Lass **Brocade Racing**
84 **SHOEGAZER (IRE),** 8, b g Bach (IRE)—American Native (IRE) **H. M. W. Clifford**
85 **SHOTAVODKA (IRE),** 7, ch g Alderbrook—Another Vodka (IRE) **Mrs J. Gerard-Pearse**
86 **SIR FRANK (IRE),** 8, b g Old Vic—Leave Me Be (IRE) **R. Wilkin And The Frankophiles**
87 **SMOOTH CLASSIC (IRE),** 9, b g Luso—Noan Rose (IRE) **Mr Malcolm Denmark & Mr Callum Denmark**
88 **SOLIWERY (FR),** 5, b g Equerry (USA)—Solimade (FR) **Prof C. Tisdall**
89 **SONA SASTA (IRE),** 10, b g Sonus (IRE)—Derry Lark (IRE) **R. S. Brookhouse**
90 **STANDING OVATION (IRE),** 6, b g Presenting—Glittering Star (IRE) **The Bravo Partnership**
91 **STAR OF ANGELS,** 9, b g Diktat—City of Angels **R. S. Brookhouse**
92 **STARLIFE (FR),** 4, b f Saint des Saints (FR)—Presidence (FR) **Mrs J. D. Brown**
93 **STORM LANTERN,** 4, b g King's Theatre (IRE)—Katoune (FR) **R. B. Waley-Cohen**
94 **STREET ENTERTAINER (IRE),** 6, br g Danehill Dancer (IRE)—Opera Ridge (FR) **Barnett, Manasseh & Partners**
95 **SWING BILL (FR),** 12, gr g Grey Risk (FR)—Melodie Royale (FR) **D. A. Johnson**
96 **SWING BOWLER,** 6, b m Galileo (IRE)—Lady Cricket (FR) **D. A. Johnson**
97 **TAKE OVER SIVOLA (FR),** 6, b g Assessor (IRE)—Maya Rock (FR) **G. D. Thompson**
99 **TANERKO EMERY (FR),** 7, b g Lavirco (GER)—Frequence (FR) **Walters Plant Hire Ltd Egan Waste Ltd**
100 **THE LIQUIDATOR,** 5, b g Overbury (IRE)—Alikat (IRE) **R. S. Brookhouse**
101 **THE PACKAGE,** 10, br g Kayf Tara—Ardent Bride **D. A. Johnson**
102 **THE PIER (IRE),** 7, ch g Alhaarth (IRE)—Cois Cuain (IRE) **A. Stennett**
103 **THE TRACEY SHUFFLE,** 7, br g Kapgarde (FR)—Gaspaisie (FR) **Mrs J. Tracey**
104 **TOO GENEROUS,** 5, b g Generous (IRE)—Little Feat **A. E. Frost**
105 **TOP GAMBLE (IRE),** 5, ch g Presenting—Zeferina (IRE) **Walters Plant Hire & James & Jean Potter**
106 **TOP WOOD (FR),** 6, ch g Kotky Bleu (FR)—Heure Bleu (FR) **Lady H. J. Clarke**
107 **UNIQUE DE COTTE (FR),** 5, b g Voix du Nord (FR)—Kadalka de Cotte (FR) **J. P. McManus**
108 **VERGRIGIO (IRE),** 4, gr g Verglas (IRE)—Roystonea **Axiomatic Partnership**
109 **VIEUX LION ROUGE (FR),** 4, ch g Sabiango (GER)—Indecise (FR) **Prof Caroline Tisdall & Mr John Gent**
110 **WAR SINGER (USA),** 6, b g War Chant (USA)—Sister Marilyn (USA) **The War Cabinet**
111 **WATER GARDEN (FR),** 7, gr g Turgeon (USA)—Queenstown (FR) **D. A. Johnson**
112 **WATERUNDER (IRE),** 6, br g Vinnie Roe (IRE)—Be My Katie (IRE) **Mrs S. Clifford**
113 **WEATHER BABE,** 5, b m Storming Home—Bathwick Babe (IRE) **H. M. W. Clifford**
114 **WEEKEND MILLIONAIR (IRE),** 6, ch g Arakan (USA)—Almi Ad (USA) **H. M. W. Clifford**
115 **WINGS OF ICARUS (IRE),** 6, ch g Cut Quartz (FR)—Moody Cloud (FR) **Shirl & The Girls**
116 **ZAYNAR (FR),** 8, gr g Daylami (IRE)—Zainta (IRE) **Men In Our Position**

Other Owners: Mr A. R. Adams, J. Apiafi, Mr J. Barnett, Miss A. Barrie, Miss H. M. Bonner, Mr D. M. Bradshaw, Mr G. R. Broom, Mrs A. E. M. Broom, Mr M. Caine, Mr J. T. Chalmers, V. W. Chandler, A. L. Cohen, Mr M. J. Cruddace, Mr M. A. J. Cueto, J. S. Dale, P. A. Deal, Mr C. N. C. Denmark, Mr B. J. C. Drew, Egan Waste Services Ltd, J. T. Ennis, Mrs L. A. Farquhar, Mr M. J. Fitzpatrick, J. A. Gent, Mr P. George, Mr J. Gwyther, J. J. Hathorn, Mrs F. K. Hathorn, Mr D. L. Ives, Mr K. R. Ives, Mrs D. A. Johnson, Mrs C. Johnson, M. B. Jones, Mr R. Jones, Alan Kaplan, N. R. Kelly, Mrs S. J. Ling, Mr D. C. Manasseh, S. M. Mercer, Mr S. S. Mercer, Mr C. G. Paletta, T. S. Palin, Mr D. J. Peel, Mr M. Peterlechner, Mrs M. C. Pipe, J. E. Potter, Mrs M. J. Potter, Mr A. T. Powell, Mr M. Prince, D. J. Reid, Mrs Y. J. Reynolds, D. G. Robinson, Mr L. R. Rolfe, Mr P. S. Russell, Mr J. Smee, R. K. Stanley, Mrs A. Underhill, W. T. Walsh, Mr J. Webb, Mr R. C. Wilkin, Mr M. K. Williams.

Assistant Trainer: Mr M. C. Pipe C.B.E.

MR DAVID PIPE - Continued

Jockey (NH): Hadden Frost, Timmy Murphy, Conor O'Farrell, Tom Scudamore. **Conditional:** Tom Bellamy, Kieron Edgar, Anthony Fox, Francis Hayes, Sam Welton. **Amateur:** Mr Jamie Bargary, Mr Michael Ennis, Mr Michael Heard.

---

511 MR TIM PITT, Newmarket
Postal: **Frankland Lodge, Hamilton Road, Newmarket, Suffolk, CB8 7JQ**
Contacts: **PHONE (01638) 666344 FAX (01638) 666344 MOBILE (07917) 541341**
E-MAIL timjoelpitt@aol.com WEBSITE www.timpittracing.com

1 DARK RANGER, 7, br g Where Or When (IRE)—Dark Raider (IRE) **Recycled Products Limited**
2 ELECTRICIAN, 4, b g Echo of Light—Primrose Lane (JPN) **Saintly Racing**
3 MR RED CLUBS (IRE), 4, b g Red Clubs (IRE)—Queen Cobra (IRE) **Ferrybank Properties Limited**
4 OUR JONATHAN, 6, b g Invincible Spirit (IRE)—Sheik'n Swing **Dr Marwan Koukash**
5 QUEEN OF SKIES (IRE), 4, b f Shamardal (USA)—Attractive Crown (USA) **Ferrybank Properties Limited**

THREE-YEAR-OLDS
6 CHEROKEE PRINCESS (IRE), ch f Iffraaj—Radiancy (IRE) **Ferrbank Properties Limited**
7 DARK JUSTICE (IRE), b f Lawman (FR)—Dark Raider (IRE) **Recycled Products Limited**
8 KATIE GALE, b f Shirocco (GER)—Karla June **Ferrybank Properties Limited**
9 LAVENDER BAY, b f Needwood Blade—In Good Faith (USA) **Invictus**
10 LIVELY LITTLE LADY, b f Beat All (USA)—Ever So Lonely **Saintly Racing**
11 PEARL SPICE, ch g Dalakhani (IRE)—Cinnamon Rose (USA) **Decadent Racing**
12 SERGIO'S SON, b g Zamindar (USA)—Mail Express (IRE) **Saintly Racing**
13 SIOUX CHIEFTAIN (IRE), b g Mount Nelson—Lady Gin (USA) **Ferrybank Properties Limited**
14 SOMETHINGBOUTMARY, ch f Sleeping Indian—Lochleven **Wildcard Racing Syndicate**

TWO-YEAR-OLDS
15 DARK TSARINA (IRE), b f 8/4 Soviet Star (USA)—
    Dark Raider (IRE) (Definite Article) (6348) **Recycled Products Limited**
16 B f 14/5 Tobougg (IRE)—Maidenhair (IRE) (Darshaan) **Drinkmore Stud**
17 ONE CHANCE (IRE), b f 22/2 Invincible Spirit (IRE)—
    Towards (USA) (Fusaichi Pegasus (USA)) (120000) **Recycled Products Limited**
18 B c 23/3 Art Connoisseur (IRE)—Paix Royale (Royal Academy (USA)) (6000) **Only Fools Buy Horses**
19 Ch f 9/3 Selkirk (USA)—Rubies From Burma (USA) (Forty Niner (USA)) (33000) **Ferrybank Properties Limited**

Jockey (flat): Shane Kelly. **Apprentice:** George Buckell.

---

512 MR CHARLES POGSON, Farnsfield
Postal: **Allamoor Farm, Mansfield Road, Farnsfield, Nottinghamshire, NG22 8HZ**
Contacts: **PHONE (01623) 882275 MOBILE (07977) 016155**

1 HOPEAND, 8, b m King's Theatre (IRE)—Land of Glory **C. T. Pogson**
2 MILAN OF HOPE (IRE), 6, b g Milan—Miss Bertaine (IRE) **C. T. Pogson**
3 MONDO CANE (IRE), 6, b g Beneficial—La Vita E Bella (FR) **C. T. Pogson**
4 NOBLE WITNESS (IRE), 10, b g Witness Box (USA)—Jennas Pride (IRE) **Wordingham Plant Hire & Partner**
5 YELLOW DUKE (FR), 6, ch g Robin des Champs (FR)—Miss Cadouline (FR) **Wordingham Plant Hire & Partner**

Other Owners: P. L. Wordingham, Mrs P. A. Wordingham.

Assistant Trainer: Adam Pogson

Jockey (NH): Adam Pogson.

---

513 MR NICHOLAS POMFRET, Tilton-on-the-Hill
Postal: **Red Lodge Farm, Marefield Lane, Tilton-on-the-Hill, Leicester, Leicestershire, LE7 9LJ**
Contacts: **PHONE (01162) 597537 MOBILE (07885) 598810**

1 ARROWMINT, 7, b m Executive Perk—Araminta **R. P. Brett**
2 EXECUTIVE STRIKE, 7, b g Executive Perk—Double Chimes **Mr I. P. Crane**

514 MR JONATHAN PORTMAN, Upper Lambourn

Postal: Whitcoombe House Stables, Upper Lambourn, Hungerford, Berkshire, RG17 8RA
Contacts: PHONE **(01488) 73894** FAX **(01488) 72952** MOBILE **(07798) 824513**
E-MAIL jonathan@jonathanportmanracing.com WEBSITE www.jonathanportmanracing.com

1 **ADAEZE (IRE)**, 5, b m Footstepsinthesand—Ringmoor Down **Prof C. D. Green**
2 **BALMORAL CASTLE**, 4, b g Royal Applause—Mimiteh (USA) **Out To Grass Partnership**
3 **COURTLAND AVENUE (IRE)**, 4, b g Kodiac—Chingford (IRE) **Prof C. D. Green**
4 **CUCKOO ROCK (IRE)**, 6, b g Refuse To Bend (IRE)—Ringmoor Down **Prof C. D. Green**
5 **CUNNING ACT**, 5, ch g Act One—Saffron Fox **M. J. Vandenberghe**
6 **INDIAN SHUFFLE (IRE)**, 5, b g Sleeping Indian—Hufflepuff (IRE) **J. G. B. Portman**
7 **ISOLA BELLA**, 4, ch f Sleeping Indian—Tetravella (IRE) **Berkeley Racing**
8 **JOE PACKET**, 6, ch g Joe Bear (IRE)—Costa Packet (IRE) **P. Moulton**
9 **LILY IN PINK**, 5, b m Sakhee (USA)—In Luck **Mrs S. L. Morley**
10 **MOLL FLANDERS**, 4, b f Hawk Wing (USA)—Sokoa (USA) **Berkeley Racing**
11 **NOW WHAT**, 6, ch m Where Or When (IRE)—Vallauris **Mrs S. J. Portman**
12 **OBSCURITY (IRE)**, 5, ch g Exit To Nowhere (USA)—Lady Cadia (FR) **M. J. Vandenberghe**
13 **PLAY STREET**, 4, ch f Tobougg (IRE)—Zoena **Anthony Boswood**
14 **QUITE A CATCH (IRE)**, 5, b g Camacho—Dear Catch (IRE) **J. G. B. Portman**
15 **ROYAL AWARD**, 4, b f Cadeaux Genereux—Red Sovereign **Miss J. Goodearl**
16 **SHESHA BEAR**, 8, b m Tobougg (IRE)—Sunny Davis (USA) **RWH Partnership**
17 **UNCLE PETTIT (IRE)**, 5, b br g Heron Island (IRE)—Special Ballot (IRE) **A. R. Boswood**
18 **WILDE AT HEART (IRE)**, 6, b m Oscar (IRE)—Back To Bavaria (IRE) **Mr P. R. Wales**
19 **ZEN FACTOR**, 8, b g Josr Algarhoud (IRE)—Zabelina (USA) **Mr J. T. Habershon-Butcher**

THREE-YEAR-OLDS

20 **ANNECDOTE**, b f Lucky Story (USA)—May Fox **Tom Edwards & Partners**
21 **DOUBLE STAR**, b f Elusive City (USA)—Tease (IRE) **The Hon Mrs D. Joly**
22 **HALLINGHAM**, b g Halling (USA)—In Luck **The Ladies Of The Manor Syndicate**
23 **IMPERTINENT**, b f Halling (USA)—Incarnation (IRE) **P. Moulton**
24 **JACOBELLA**, b f Rob Roy (USA)—Veni Bidi Vici **Stuart McPhee & Mike Webley**
25 **JEBRIL (FR)**, b g Astronomer Royal (USA)—Happy Clapper **Mr L. Raissi**
26 **LEAD THE WAY**, b f Indian Haven—Way To The Stars **Tom Edwards & Partners**
27 **MONSIEUR RIEUSSEC**, bl c Halling (USA)—Muscovado (USA) **Mr J. T. Habershon-Butcher**
28 **PASAKA BOY**, ch c Haafhd—Shesha Bear **RWH Partnership**
29 B c High Chaparral (IRE)—Renowned (IRE) **Mrs June Watts**
30 **RISKY RIZKOVA**, b g Sleeping Indian—Tri Pac (IRE) **Mr J. R. Walton**
31 **THREE CROWNS**, b f Three Valleys (USA)—Red Sovereign **Miss J. Goodearl**
32 **TREGERETH (IRE)**, b f Footstepsinthesand—Ringmoor Down **Prof C. D. Green**
33 **ZINNOBAR**, gr f Ishiguru (USA)—Demolition Jo **Prof C. D. Green**

TWO-YEAR-OLDS

34 B f 22/3 Azamour (IRE)—Akarita (IRE) (Akarad (FR)) (5714)
35 B f 24/2 Mount Nelson—Apple Blossom (IRE) (Danehill Dancer (IRE)) (7619) **Dr Anne Gillespie**
36 B c 26/3 Aussie Rules (USA)—Chingford (IRE) (Redback) **Prof C. D. Green**
37 **CUECA (FR)**, b f 14/3 Country Reel (USA)—Costa Packet (IRE) (Hussonet) (9523)
38 Ch gr f 21/2 Verglas (IRE)—Deira (USA) (Green Desert (USA)) (8333)
39 **FENELLA FOGHORN**, b f 24/4 Elnadim (USA)—Bundle Up (USA) (Miner's Mark (USA)) (16190) **Mr D. Redvers**
40 **FERNGROVE (USA)**, gr c 26/2 Rockport Harbor (USA)—
                Lucky Pipit (Key of Luck (USA)) (38000) **Mr J. T. Habershon-Butcher**
41 B c 3/5 Holy Roman Emperor (IRE)—Gambling Spirit (Mister Baileys) (9523) **Port Or Brandy Syndicate**
42 B c 12/4 Assertive—High Bird (IRE) (Polar Falcon (USA)) **Lady Whent**
43 **MOLLASSES**, b f 13/4 Authorized (IRE)—Muscovado (USA) (Mr Greeley) (24000) **Mrs J. Wigan**
44 Ch c 12/4 Sakhee's Secret—Polar Dawn (Polar Falcon (USA)) (7539) **Whitcoombe Park Racing**
45 **RUSSIAN REMARQUE**, b c 20/2 Archipenko (USA)—Accede (Acclamation) (13333) **The Traditionalists**
46 Gr f 1/3 Mastercraftsman (IRE)—Second Act (Sadler's Wells (USA)) (7619)
47 Gr c 19/1 Archipenko (USA)—Si Belle (IRE) (Dalakhani (IRE))
48 **SUMMERLING (IRE)**, br f 19/2 Excellent Art—Seven Seasons (IRE) (Salse (USA)) (7000) **A. H. Robinson**
49 Br c 21/4 Footstepsinthesand—Tara Too (IRE) (Danetime (IRE)) **Prof C. D. Green**

Other Owners: Mrs M. Atkinson, J. W. M. Brownlee, Mr D. Cadger, G. F. Clark, Mr S. Dawes, Mr Tony Edwards, Mr A. Frost, Mr P. Hibbard, Mrs L. Hobson, Mr J. Homan, Mrs J. Laurie, Mr D. Milton, Mrs L. Pritchard, Mr S. Ransom, Mrs E. Scaddan, Mrs S. Symonds, Mr G. C. Wickens.

Assistant Trainer: Sophie Portman

515 MR JAMIE POULTON, Lewes

Postal: White Cottage, Telscombe, Lewes, East Sussex, BN7 3HZ
Contacts: YARD (01273) 300515 HOME (01273) 300127 FAX (01273) 300915
MOBILE (07980) 596952
E-MAIL jamie@poulton8.orangehome.co.uk

1 5, B g Tagula (IRE)—Alouchier (FR) **J. R. Poulton**
2 FARBREAGA (IRE), 7, b g Shernazar—Gleann Alainn **Miss V. Markowiak**
3 FORMIDABLE GUEST, 9, b m Dilshaan—Fizzy Treat **Oceana Racing**
4 GORHAMS GIFT, 5, b g Double Trigger (IRE)—Linden Grace (USA) **The Never Dropped Partnership**
5 MIGHTY FLIGHTY (IRE), 5, b m Majestic Missile (IRE)—Bridelina (FR) **Telscombe Racing**
6 PUSH ME (IRE), 6, gr m Verglas (IRE)—Gilda Lilly (USA) **Alex & Janet Card**
7 RIVER SAVA (IRE), 6, b g Zagreb (USA)—Running Board (IRE) **Miss V. Markowiak**

THREE-YEAR-OLDS

8 DOUBLE DEALITES, b f Double Trigger (IRE)—Linden Grace (USA) **Alex & Janet Card**
9 FEATHER DANCER, b f Norse Dancer (IRE)—Featherlight **Oceana Racing**

TWO-YEAR-OLDS

10 B c 22/4 Sakhee (USA)—Featherlight (Fantastic Light (USA)) **J. R. Poulton**
11 B f 25/5 Josr Algarhoud (IRE)—Linden Lime (Double Trigger (IRE)) **J. R. Poulton**

Other Owners: Mr A. Baker, Mr A. M. Card, Mrs J. A. Card, Mr I. C. Cusselle, Mr K. Farmer, J. Harrison, Mr G. Mercer, Mr B. Pearce.

Assistant Trainer: Mrs C D Poulton

Jockey (flat): Ian Mongan. **Jockey (NH):** Mattie Batchelor.

516 MR BRENDAN POWELL, Upper Lambourn

Postal: Newlands Stables, Upper Lambourn, Hungerford, Berkshire, RG17 8QX
Contacts: PHONE (01488) 73650 FAX (01488) 73650 MOBILE (07785) 390737
E-MAIL brendan.powell@btconnect.com WEBSITE www.brendanpowellracing.com

1 ACIANO (IRE), 5, b g Kheleyf (USA)—Blue Crystal (IRE) **Mrs S. M. Tucker**
2 ALLTHEROADRUNNING (IRE), 6, b g Oscar (IRE)—Another Crack **B. G. Powell**
3 AMAZING SCENES (IRE), 4, b br g Desert King (IRE)—Lady Leila (IRE) **Let's Get Ready To Rumble Partnership**
4 AWARD WINNER, 10, b g Alflora (IRE)—Blackwater Bay (IRE) **J. P. McManus**
5 BEFORE BRUCE, 6, b g Danbird (AUS)—Bisque **Accountable Racing**
6 BENNYS WELL (IRE), 7, b g Beneficial—Alure (IRE) **Mrs A. Ellis**
7 BOB TUCKER (IRE), 6, b g Brian Boru—Acumen (IRE) **Mr N. Davies**
8 BOHEMIAN RHAPSODY (IRE), 4, b c Galileo (IRE)—Quiet Mouse (USA) **Mr A. A. Byrne**
9 CANADIAN DIAMOND (IRE), 6, ch g Halling (USA)—Six Nations (USA) **Nicholls Family**
10 CATCH ME UP (IRE), 5, b g Brian Boru—Hartwell Lake (IRE) **Mr N. Davies**
11 CONIGRE, 6, b g Selkirk (USA)—Mystify **Delamere Racing & Ian Kidger**
12 COPPER FALLS, 4, b f Trade Fair—Strat's Quest **P. Banfield**
13 DARK AND DANGEROUS (IRE), 5, b g Cacique (IRE)—Gilah (IRE) **North South Alliance**
14 FROMTHESTABLES COM (IRE), 4, b c Strategic Prince—Kathy Tolfa (IRE) **Fromthestables.com Racing**
15 FULGORA, 5, b m Desert King (IRE)—Lightning Princess **Vino Veritas**
16 GLEN COUNTESS (IRE), 6, b m Pilsudski (IRE)—Countessdee (IRE) **The Naughty Partnership**
17 GUANCIALE, 6, b g Exit To Nowhere (USA)—Thenford Lass (IRE) **The Beefeaters**
18 KING SPIRIT (IRE), 5, b g Fruits of Love (USA)—Tariana (IRE) **Mr J. J. King**
19 KNOCKGRAFFON LAD (USA), 6, b g Forestry (USA)—Miss Dahlia (USA) **Mr N. Davies**
20 LADY FROM GENEVA, 6, ch m Generous (IRE)—Schizo-Phonic **Geneva Finance PLC**
21 LADY ROMANZA (IRE), 4, b f Holy Roman Emperor—Sharakawa (IRE) **Mr P. Morris**
22 LINKABLE, 4, b c Rail Link—Fashionable **Jonathan Ross**
23 MAY CONTAIN NUTS, 5, b g Auction House (USA)—Sweet Coincidence **I. S. Smith**
24 MERCHANT OF MILAN, 5, b g Milan—Repunzel **Mr & Mrs A. J. Mutch**
25 MILANS WELL (IRE), 7, b g Milan—Panoora Queen (IRE) **A. Head**
26 MORESTEAD (IRE), 8, ch g Traditionally (USA)—Itsy Bitsy Betsy (USA) **L. Gilbert**
27 NEWFORGE HOUSE (IRE), 5, b g High-Rise (IRE)—Treasure Island **The Beefeaters**
28 NIGHT FORCE, 10, b g Sovereign Water (FR)—Oatis Rose **Balios Racing**
29 ONE FOR THE BOSS (IRE), 6, b g Garuda (IRE)—Tell Nothing (IRE) **J. E. Mutch**
30 ONLY WITNESS (IRE), 8, b g Witness Box (USA)—Shiny Button **Arkle Bar Partnership & Mr R Stanley**
31 PHANTOM PRINCE (IRE), 4, b g Jeremy (USA)—Phantom Waters **C. F. Harrington**

MR BRENDAN POWELL - Continued

32 **RATIFY**, 9, br g Rakaposhi King—Sea Sky **Mr J. J. King**
33 **REACH THE BEACH**, 4, ch f Phoenix Reach (IRE)—Comtesse Noire (CAN) **Winterbeck Manor Stud Ltd**
34 **SCOTTISH BOOGIE (IRE)**, 6, b g Tobougg (IRE)—Scottish Spice **Mr A. A. Byrne**
35 **SHIPTON**, 4, b g Nayef (USA)—Silk Road **Mr N. Davies**
36 **SHOREACRES (IRE)**, 10, b g Turtle Island (IRE)—Call Me Dara (IRE) **D. P. Nash**
37 **SIR FREDLOT (IRE)**, 4, b g Choisir (AUS)—Wurfklinge (GER) **Rupert Williams & P Winkworth**
38 **SONORAN SANDS (IRE)**, 5, b g Footstepsinthesand—Atishoo (IRE) **C. F. Harrington**
39 **STOCK HILL FAIR**, 5, b g Sakhee (USA)—April Stock **Mrs M. Fairbairn, E. Gadsden & P. Dean**
40 **SUN AND STARS**, 5, ch h Haafhd—Leading Role **J. H. Widdows**
41 4, B f Oscar (IRE)—Sunshine Rays **Mr H. Redknapp**
42 **TEN FIRES (GER)**, 11, b br g Acambaro (GER)—Tosca Dona (GER) **Mr Ian Kidger & Miss Ann Sturgis**
43 **THEATRELANDS**, 5, ch g Beat Hollow—Dance Dress (USA) **Mr N Davies & Mr S Crowley**
44 **UNCLE DERMOT (IRE)**, 5, b g Arakan (USA)—Cappadoce (IRE) **Mr K. R. E. Rhatigan**
45 **VIOLETS BOY (IRE)**, 6, br g King's Theatre (IRE)—Sunshine Rays **H. Redknapp**
46 **YACHT LONDON LADY**, 7, b m Beat All (USA)—Country Choice (IRE) **Yacht London Racing**

THREE-YEAR-OLDS

47 **CHARLIE EM**, b f Kheleyf (USA)—Miss Meggy **Mr M. Foley**
48 **DARK EMERALD (IRE)**, gr c Dark Angel (IRE)—Xema **Mr K. Rhatigan**
49 **INSTINCTUAL**, ch g Observatory (USA)—Be Glad **Mr N. Davies**
50 **QUELLE AFFAIRE**, b f Bahamian Bounty—Qui Moi (CAN) **Mr A. A. Byrne**
51 **SILVER ARNY**, b f Footstepsinthesand—Medici Gold **Dr E. Semple & Russ Pendleton**

TWO-YEAR-OLDS

52 **BROCKHOLES FLYER (IRE)**, b g 9/2 Balmont (USA)—Condilessa (IRE) (Key of Luck (USA)) (2857) **Mrs A. Ellis**
53 Ch g 2/4 Rock of Gibraltar (IRE)—Toolentidhaar (USA) (Swain (IRE)) (11428) **I. S. Smith**

Other Owners: Mr P. Burgoyne, Mrs Lynn Chapman, Mr N. A. Coster, Mr S. Crowley, Mr Nigel M. Davies, Mrs A. Ellis, Mr Gary Flood, Mr Les Guest, Mr Ian Kidger, Mr D. Leon, Mr I. G. Martin, Mr B. P. McNamee, Mr P. Morris, Mr J. Morris, Mr A. J. Mutch, Mrs S. Mutch, Mr Royston Nicholls, Mrs Eileen Nicholls, Mr A. D. Peachey, Mr Jonathan Peppiatt, Mr B. G. Powell, Ms Jane Smith, Mrs L. Smith, Mr R. Stanley, Miss Ann Sturgis, Miss Tor Sturgis, Mr A. J. Viall, Mr J. B. Williams, Mrs T. L. Williams, Mr Rupert Williams, Mr P. Winkworth.

Jockey (flat): Kirsty Milczarek, Seb Sanders. **Jockey (NH):** A P McCoy, Andrew Tinkler. **Conditional:** Brendan Powell. **Apprentice:** Matthew Lawson. **Amateur:** Miss Jenny Powell.

---

517 | **MR TED POWELL, Reigate**
Postal: **Nutwood Farm, Gatton Park Road, Reigate, Surrey, RH2 0SX**
Contacts: **PHONE (01737) 765612**

1 **AJJAADD (USA)**, 7, b g Elusive Quality (USA)—Millstream (USA) **Katy & Lol Pratt**
2 **CORMORANT WHARF (IRE)**, 13, b g Alzao (USA)—Mercy Bien (IRE) **Miss J. Powell**

Other Owners: Mrs K. J. Pratt, L. C. Pratt.

---

518 | **SIR MARK PRESCOTT BT, Newmarket**
Postal: **Heath House, Newmarket, Suffolk, CB8 8DU**
Contacts: **PHONE (01638) 662117 FAX (01638) 666572**

1 **ALBAMARA**, 4, b f Galileo (IRE)—Albanova **Miss K. Rausing**
2 **ATHENIAN (IRE)**, 4, b f Acclamation—Ziria (IRE) **AXOM (XXXI)**
3 **BETWEEN US**, 4, b f Galileo (IRE)—Confidante (USA) **Cheveley Park Stud**
4 **CELESTIAL RAY**, 4, ch c Pivotal—Heavenly Ray (USA) **Cheveley Park Stud**
5 **FRESA**, 4, b f Selkirk (USA)—Flor Y Nata (USA) **Miss K. Rausing**
6 **ITALIAN RIVIERA**, 4, b g Galileo (IRE)—Miss Corniche **J. L. C. Pearce**
7 **MUTUAL REGARD (IRE)**, 4, b g Hernando (FR)—Hidden Charm (IRE) **Moyglare Stud Farms Ltd**
8 **PALLASATOR**, 4, b g Motivator—Ela Athena **Baxter, Gregson, Jenkins & Warman**
9 **REPEATER**, 4, b g Montjeu (IRE)—Time Over **Cheveley Park Stud**
10 **SOLAR VIEW (IRE)**, 4, ch g Galileo (IRE)—Ellen (IRE) **Neil Greig - Osborne House**

SIR MARK PRESCOTT BT - Continued

THREE-YEAR-OLDS

11 ALCAEUS, b c Hernando (FR)—Alvarita **Ne'er Do Wells IV**
12 ALWILDA, gr f Hernando (FR)—Albanova **Miss K. Rausing**
13 ALZAVOLA, gr f With Approval (CAN)—Alizadora **Miss K. Rausing**
14 BIG THUNDER, gr g Dalakhani (IRE)—Charlotte O Fraise (IRE) **John Brown & Megan Dennis**
15 CURIOUS MIND, b f Dansili—Intrigued **Denford Stud**
16 INHERITED, b g Selkirk (USA)—Akdariya (IRE) **P. J. McSwiney - Osborne House**
17 KHOTAN, b c Hernando (FR)—Miss Katmandu (IRE) **J. L. C. Pearce**
18 LYRIC PIECE, ch f Dutch Art—Humouresque **Cheveley Park Stud**
19 MAN FROM SEVILLE, ch g Duke of Marmalade (IRE)—Basanti (USA) **Mr & Mrs William Rucker**
20 NORTH POLE, b g Compton Place—Cool Question **Lady Fairhaven & The Hon C & H Broughton**
21 PIGEON POWER, b f Byron—Making Waves (IRE) **P. Bamford**
22 PORTRAIT, ch f Peintre Celebre (USA)—Annalina (USA) **Denford Stud**
23 SAGESSE, ch f Smart Strike (CAN)—Summer Night **Miss K. Rausing**
24 SAVANNA LA MAR (USA), ch f Curlin (USA)—Soft Morning **Miss K. Rausing**
25 SCALA ROMANA (IRE), b f Holy Roman Emperor (IRE)—Sliding Scale **Mr & Mrs John Kelsey-Fry**
26 SECRET SONG, b g Singspiel (IRE)—Confidante (USA) **W. E. Sturt - Osborne House II**
27 SLIP OF THE TONGUE, ch g Zamindar (USA)—Kiswahili **J. E. Fishpool - Osborne House**
28 SZABO'S ART, br f Excellent Art—Violette **C. G. Rowles-Nicholson**

TWO-YEAR-OLDS

29 ABOODY, b c 27/3 Dutch Art—Rabshih (IRE) (Green Desert (USA)) (70000) **Fawzi Abdulla Nass**
30 ALBA VERDE, gr f 3/2 Verglas (IRE)—Algarade (Green Desert (USA)) **Miss K. Rausing**
31 ANJIN (IRE), b c 18/3 Danehill Dancer (IRE)—
    Twyla Tharp (IRE) (Sadler's Wells (USA)) (110000) **Syndicate 2012**
32 BEWITCHMENT, b f 6/4 Pivotal—Hypnotize (Machiavellian (USA)) **Cheveley Park Stud**
33 CANNES MOUGINS, b c 7/2 Galileo (IRE)—Miss Riviera Golf (Hernando (FR)) **J. L. C. Pearce**
34 B f 8/3 Dalakhani (IRE)—Charlotte O Fraise (IRE) (Beat Hollow) **Lord Derby**
35 Gr c 25/3 Cape Cross (IRE)—Chinese White (IRE) (Dalakhani (IRE)) **Lady O'Reilly**
36 CLARICE, b f 15/4 Cape Cross (IRE)—Phillipina (Medicean) **Cheveley Park Stud**
37 FLORA MEDICI, b f 13/3 Sir Percy—Florentia (Medicean) **Neil Greig**
38 FOREMOST, b c 18/3 Hernando (FR)—
    Flor Y Nata (IRE) (Fusaichi Pegasus (USA)) (48000) **W. E. Sturt - Osborne House**
39 B f 24/2 Rockport Harbor (USA)—Gulch Girl (USA) (Gulch (USA)) (34285) **Axom XLI**
40 HIGH SECRET (IRE), b c 16/2 High Chaparral (IRE)—
    Secret Question (Rahy (USA)) (60000) **Charles C. Walker - Osborne House**
41 HOT REPLY, br f 3/4 Notnowcato—
    Cool Question (Polar Falcon (USA)) **Lady Fairhaven & The Hon C & H Broughton**
42 JOLIE BLONDE, ch f 8/3 Sir Percy—Affaire d'Amour (Hernando (FR)) **Miss K. Rausing**
43 LADY BINGO (IRE), b f 3/5 Galileo (IRE)—Sharp Lisa (USA) (Dixieland Band (USA)) (153609) **Qatar Racing Ltd**
44 LEGAL SHARK (IRE), b c 28/4 Lawman (FR)—
    Sea Searcher (USA) (Theatrical) (68000) **Tim Bunting - Osborne House II**
45 MISS VERDOYANTE, b f 23/2 Montjeu (IRE)—Miss Provence (Hernando (FR)) **J. L. C. Pearce**
46 MOSCATO, gr c 30/3 Hernando (FR)—Alba Stella (Nashwan (USA)) (33333) **The Green Door Partnership**
47 MOUNTAIN KINGDOM (IRE), b c 28/2 Montjeu (IRE)—
    Althea Rose (IRE) (Green Desert (USA)) (95000) **Tim Bunting - Osborne House II**
48 NAMELY (IRE), b f 14/2 Rock of Gibraltar (IRE)—Viz (IRE) (Darshaan) (47619) **Mrs Sonia Rogers**
49 REAL JAZZ (IRE), b f 21/3 Marju (IRE)—Sedna (IRE) (Priolo (USA)) (55000) **T. J. Rooney**
50 RED PASSIFLORA, b f 25/4 Danehill Dancer (IRE)—Red Peony (Montjeu (IRE)) **Cheveley Park Stud**
51 ROHESIA, b f 7/3 High Chaparral (IRE)—Common Knowledge (Rainbow Quest (USA)) **Qatar Racing Ltd**
52 SANCUS, ch c 16/4 Compton Place—Blue Echo (Kyllachy) (37000) **William Charnley & Richard Pegum**
53 SARPECH (IRE), b c 6/3 Sea The Stars (IRE)—Sadima (IRE) (Sadler's Wells (USA)) (430000) **Qatar Racing Ltd**
54 SECRET KEEPER, ch f 23/4 New Approach (IRE)—Confidante (USA) (Dayjur (USA)) **Cheveley Park Stud**
55 SHAFT OF LIGHT, b c 11/3 Exceed And Excel (AUS)—Injaaz (Sheikh Albadou) (42000) **B. Haggas**
56 B f 10/5 Holy Roman Emperor (IRE)—Sliding Scale (Sadler's Wells (USA)) **Mr & Mrs John Kelsey-Fry**
57 SOIREE D'ETE, b f 20/2 Selkirk (USA)—Souvenance (Hernando (FR)) **Miss K. Rausing**
58 SUNSET SHORE, b f 23/2 Oasis Dream—Summer Night (Nashwan (USA)) **Miss K. Rausing**
59 THREETIMESALADY, b f 27/4 Royal Applause—Triple Joy (Most Welcome) (37000) **Bluehills Racing Ltd**
60 TIMELY, gr f 17/3 Pivotal—Last Second (IRE) (Alzao (USA)) **Denford Stud**
61 UPSHOT, b f 4/4 Pivotal—Soar (Danzero (AUS)) **Cheveley Park Stud**
62 WILLIAM OF ORANGE, b c 4/5 Duke of Marmalade (IRE)—
    Critical Acclaim (Peintre Celebre (USA)) **Nicholas Jones**
63 WINDSHIELD, b f 26/3 Montjeu (IRE)—Westerly Air (USA) (Gone West (USA)) **Cheveley Park Stud**

SIR MARK PRESCOTT BT - Continued

Other Owners: Mr E. A. Baxter, Mr B. D. Burnet, Mr Terry Corden, Mr Joe Donnelly, Mr Darren Ellis, Mr Phil Fry, The Hon Mrs G. Greenwood, Mrs Caroline Gregson, Mr P. G. Goulandris, Mr Chris Jenkins, Mr L. A. Larratt, Mr David Lowrey, Mr E. B. Rimmer, Mr Mike Rudd, Mr & Mrs Dennis Russell, Prince Faisal Salman, Mr Ian Spearing, Mr Barry Taylor, Mrs J. Taylor, Mr Roger Tindall, Mr Mark Tracey, The Hon. Lady Troubridge, Mrs S. L. Warman, Mr E. J. Williams.

Assistant Trainer: William Butler, **Pupil Assistant:** James Ferguson

Jockey (flat): L. Morris, C. Catlin. **Apprentice:** R. Jessop, T. Clark.

---

519 **MR ANDREW PRICE, Leominster**
Postal: **Eaton Hall Farm, Leominster, Herefordshire, HR6 0NA**
Contacts: **PHONE (01568) 611137 FAX (01568) 611137 MOBILE (07729) 838660**
E-MAIL helen@aepriceracing.plus.com

1 BOBBY DOVE, 6, b g Fraam—Flakey Dove **A. E. Price**
2 5, B g Beat All (USA)—Flakey Dove **A. E. Price**
3 FLORA LEA, 6, b m Alflora (IRE)—Castanet **Mrs C. Davis**
4 MIDNIGHT DOVE, 8, ch g Karinga Bay—Flighty Dove **M. G. Racing**
5 MISS BEATTIE, 6, b m Beat All (USA)—Scratch The Dove **Mrs H. L. Price**
6 MISS TILLY DOVE, 5, b m Overbury (IRE)—Scratch The Dove **A. E. Price**
7 SPENCER LEA, 5, b g Overbury (IRE)—Castanet **Mrs C. Davis**

Other Owners: A. G. Bathurst, Mr M. Jones, Mrs E. R. Kitt.

Assistant Trainer: Mrs H L Price

---

520 **MR JOHN PRICE, Ebbw Vale**
Postal: **41 Beaufort Terrace, Ebbw Vale, Gwent, NP23 5NW**
Contacts: **PHONE (01495) 306113 MOBILE (07870) 475156**

1 DESCARO (USA), 7, gr g Dr Fong (USA)—Miarixa (FR) **J. K. Price**

Assistant Trainer: A J Price

---

521 **MR RICHARD PRICE, Hereford**
Postal: **Criftage Farm, Ullingswick, Hereford, Herefordshire, HR1 3JG**
Contacts: **PHONE (01432) 820263 FAX (01432) 820785 MOBILE (07929) 200598**

1 IN THE CROWD (IRE), 4, ch g Haafhd—Eliza Gilbert **K. Reece**
2 K ISLAND (IRE), 5, b m Fruits of Love (USA)—Indiana Princess **H. B. McGahon**
3 LOYAL N TRUSTED, 5, b g Motivator—Baby Don't Cry (USA) **The Net Partnership & G. Robinson**
4 NALEDI, 9, b g Indian Ridge—Red Carnation (IRE) **Mrs J. Thompson**
5 OAKDOWN, 5, ch g Selkirk—Miss Katmandu (IRE) **Hugh B McGahon & Richard Price**
6 RILEYS LEGEND, 5, b m Midnight Legend—Rileys Dream **Mr G. Robinson**
7 TAURUS TWINS, 7, b g Deportivo—Intellibet One **G. E. Amey & G. D. Bailey**

Other Owners: G. E. Amey, Mr G. D. Bailey, S. Martin, R. J. Price, Mr J. S. Williams.

Assistant Trainer: Jane Price

Amateur: Mr M. Price.

---

522 **MR PETER PRITCHARD, Shipston-on-Stour**
Postal: **The Gate House, Whatcote, Shipston-On-Stour, Warwickshire, CV36 5EF**
Contacts: **PHONE (01295) 680689**

1 COWBRIDGE (IRE), 7, b g Pilsudski (IRE)—Clyde Goddess (IRE) **Trustmark**
2 EARCOMESTHEDREAM (IRE), 10, b g Marignan (USA)—
Play It By Ear (IRE) **Woodland Generators & Mr D R Pritchard**
3 JUBILEE JOY (IRE), 7, b m Windsor Castle—Icy Allstar (IRE) **Mr R. W. Stowe**
4 OVERTON LAD, 12, gr g Overbury (IRE)—Safe Arrival (USA) **D. R. Pritchard**

MR PETER PRITCHARD - Continued

5 SAFARI SUNBEAM, 5, br g Primo Valentino (IRE)—Bathwick Finesse (IRE) **D. R. Pritchard**
6 5, B g Tikkanen (USA)—Safe Arrival (USA) **D. R. Pritchard**
7 SHADESOFNAVY, 7, ch g Fleetwood (IRE)—Safe Arrival (USA) **Whittington Racing Club**
8 TISFREETDREAM (IRE), 12, b g Oscar (IRE)—Gayley Gale (IRE) **Woodland Generators & Mr D R Pritchard**

Other Owners: Mr W. R. Evans, Mr R. A. Evans, Mrs V. L. Pryor, Mr C. S. White, Woodlands (Worcestershire) Ltd.

Assistant Trainer: Mrs. E. Gardner

Jockey (NH): Jack Doyle, Jamie Moore.

---

523 MR PETER PURDY, Bridgwater

Postal: Fyne Court Farm, Broomfield, Bridgwater, Somerset, TA5 2EQ
Contacts: PHONE (01823) 451632 FAX (01823) 451632 MOBILE (07860) 392786
E-MAIL purdy844@btinternet.com

1 BOWMANS WELL (IRE), 8, b m Cadeaux Genereux—Guignol (IRE) **P. D. Purdy**
2 COURT FINALE, 12, ch g One Voice (USA)—Tudor Sunset **P. D. Purdy**
3 COURT HUMOUR, 10, b g Joligeneration—Tudor Sunset **P. D. Purdy**
4 JOLI'S DAUGHTER, 8, b m Joligeneration—Tudor Sunset **P. D. Purdy**
5 MAY COURT, 6, b g Groomsbridge May I—Tudor Sunset **P. D. Purdy**
6 THE BLONDE EMPEROR, 8, ch g Emperor Fountain—Tudor Blonde **P. D. Purdy**

Jockey (flat): Neil Chambers. Jockey (NH): Wayne Kavanagh.

---

524 MR NOEL QUINLAN, Newmarket

Postal: Harratan Stables, Chapel Street, Exning, Newmarket, CB8 7HA
Contacts: PHONE (01638) 660464 FAX (01638) 663282 MOBILE (07815) 072946
E-MAIL noelquinlanracing@hotmail.co.uk

1 BAHRAIN STORM (IRE), 10, b g Bahhare (USA)—Dance Up A Storm (USA) **The Festival Partnership**
2 BURNS NIGHT, 7, ch g Selkirk (USA)—Night Frolic **The Unique Partnership**
3 CHISWICK BEY (IRE), 5, b g Elusive City (USA)—Victoria Lodge (IRE) **The Unique Partnership**
4 FIRE IN BABYLON, 5, b g Montjeu (USA)—Three Owls (IRE) **Mrs F. A. Shaw**
5 IOANNOU, 4, b c Excellent Art—Sandtime (IRE) **A & P Skips Limited**
6 KHAWATIM, 5, b g Intikhab (USA)—Don't Tell Mum (IRE) **The Unique Partnership**
7 MONASTEREVIN (IRE), 5, ch g Danroad (AUS)—Alpathar (IRE) **Miss M. A. Quinlan**
8 SCARLETT FEVER, 4, b f Haafhd—Scarlet Buttons (IRE) **T. Cummins**
9 SKY KHAN, 4, b g Cape Cross (IRE)—Starlit Sky **The Unique Partnership**
10 TWEEDLE DEE, 4, b f Araafa (IRE)—Sismique **Mr G. Wilding**

THREE-YEAR-OLDS

11 BLAZEOFENCHANTMENT (USA), b c Officer (USA)—Willow Rush (USA) **The Unique Partnership**
12 FINAZ, b c Bertolini (USA)—Newkeylets **The Unique Partnership**
13 LOUCAL, b c Lucky Story (USA)—Penny Ha'penny **Mr B. Dick**
14 SHENVAL, b c Celtic Swing—Cape Finisterre (IRE) **Mr T. Mann**
15 VITRUVIAN LADY, b f Manduro (GER)—Vas Y Carla (USA) **Mr I. P. O'Rourke**

TWO-YEAR-OLDS

16 B c 6/4 Pastoral Pursuits—Nine Red (Royal Applause) **R. C. Tooth**
17 Ch c 20/4 Kyllachy—Penmayne (Inchinor) (130000) **Newtown Anner Stud Farm Ltd**
18 B f 19/3 Halling (USA)—White Turf (GER) (Tiger Hill (IRE)) (7000) **Burns Farm Racing**

Other Owners: Mr W. R. Asquith, M. Fahy, Mr A. R. Findlay, Mrs G. Findlay, Mr B. F. Payne, Mrs C. G. Scott.

---

525 MR JOHN QUINN, Malton

Trainer did not wish details of his string to appear.

526   MR MICHAEL QUINN, Newmarket
Postal: Southgate Barn, Hamilton Road, Newmarket, Suffolk, CB8 0WY
Contacts: PHONE (01638) 660017 FAX (01638) 660017 MOBILE (07973) 260054
E-MAIL mick@quinn2562.fsnet.co.uk

1 GAY GALLIVANTER, 5, b m Iceman—Gallivant **A. Viner**
2 MIAKORA, 5, ch m Compton Place—Hickleton Lady (IRE) **M. Quinn**
3 ROYAL DEFENCE (IRE), 7, b g Refuse To Bend—Alessia (GER) **M. Quinn**
4 WATERLOO DOCK, 8, b g Hunting Lion (IRE)—Scenic Air **Mr M. J. Quinn**
5 WHISKEY JUNCTION, 9, b g Bold Edge—Victoria Mill **S. Astaire**

THREE-YEAR-OLDS

6 PAIGE FLYER, b f Multiplex—Captain Margaret **Mr K. F. C. Bruce**

Other Owners: Mr A. Newby, J. E. Quorn.

Assistant Trainer: Miss Karen Davies

Jockey (flat): Franny Norton.

527   MR C. I. RATCLIFFE, Welburn
Postal: Teal Cottage Stud, Greets House Road, Welburn, York, YO6 7EP
Contacts: PHONE (01653) 68884
E-MAIL ci.ratcliffe@btinternet.com

1 BILLY TEAL, 8, ch g Keen—Morcat **C. I. Ratcliffe**
2 TEALS STAR, 9, b g Gods Solution—Morcat **C. I. Ratcliffe**

Amateur: Mr John Willey.

528   MR WILLIAM REED, Umberleigh
Postal: Stowford Farm, East Stowford, Chittlehampton, Umberleigh, Devon, EX37 9RU
Contacts: PHONE (01769) 540292 MOBILE (07967) 130991

1 J R HAWK (IRE), 5, b br g Hawk Wing (USA)—Miss Shivvy (IRE) **W. J. Reed**
2 SAN BELLINO, 5, ch g Galileo (IRE)—Canda (USA) **W. J. Reed**
3 WADHAM HILL, 11, b m Bandmaster (USA)—Sport of Fools (IRE) **W. J. Reed**

529   MR DAVID REES, Haverfordwest
Postal: The Grove Yard, Clarbeston Road, Haverfordwest, Pembrokeshire, SA63 4SP
Contacts: PHONE (01437) 731308 FAX (01437) 731551 MOBILE (07775) 662463
E-MAIL davidreesfencing@lineone.net

1 ACCORDINGTOPALM (IRE), 7, ch g Great Palm (USA)—Supreme Accord (IRE) **D. A. Rees**
2 AHEAD AHEAD (IRE), 8, b g Heron Island (IRE)—Lady Tenby (IRE) **Mrs P. J. Lewis**
3 ARGUIDOS (IRE), 9, b g Winged Love (IRE)—Open Meeting (IRE) **Mr J. Rees**
4 4, B g Kayf Tara—Benny's Marble (IRE) **D. A. Rees**
5 CAWDOR HOUSE BERT, 6, b g Kayf Tara—Lady Shanan (IRE) **A. J. & Dai Rees**
6 CHANGING LANES, 10, b g Overbury (IRE)—Snowdon Lily **Mr J. F. Mathias & Mr E. Morris**
7 COMEHOMEQUIETLY (IRE), 9, b g King's Theatre (IRE)—Windswept Lady (IRE) **IWEC International Ltd**
8 FISHING BRIDGE (IRE), 8, ch g Definite Article—Rith Ar Aghaidh (IRE) **D. A. Rees**
9 LYDSTEP HILLS, 9, b g Beat All (USA)—Firechick **Mrs J. Mathias**
10 LYDSTEP POINT, 6, b g Beat All (USA)—Compton Chick (IRE) **Mrs J. Mathias**
11 MACRA NA FEIRME (IRE), 10, br g Exit To Nowhere (USA)—De Derri (IRE) **IWEC International Ltd**
12 RIMINI (FR), 8, b g Bedawin (FR)—Ma'am (FR) **Pixie Go Racing**
13 SIR MATTIE (IRE), 8, b br g Moscow Society (USA)—Manhattan Catch (IRE) **Mr R. J. C. Lewis/Mr P. A. T. Rice**
14 SMILING LADY (IRE), 7, ch m Kris Kin (USA)—Band of Colour (IRE) **D. A. Rees**
15 SUPERMAN DE LA RUE (FR), 7, b g Akhdari (USA)—Impala de La Rue (FR) **Crew Racing**
16 TWO SHOOK MEN (IRE), 9, b g Posidonas—Birthday Honours (IRE) **D. A. Rees**
17 WARWICKSHIRE (IRE), 6, b g Westerner—Emeranna (IRE) **Mr R. J. C. Lewis/Mr P. A. T. Rice**

MR DAVID REES - Continued

Other Owners: Mr M. Cole, Mr W. J. Evans, Mr R. J. C. Lewis, Mr J. F. Mathias, Mr E. W. Morris, Mr J. Rees, Mr A. J. Rees, Mr D. Rees, Mr P. Rice, Mr Mark Williams.

Assistant Trainer: Mr John Mathias

---

530 **MRS HELEN REES, Dorchester**
Postal: **Distant Hills, Chalmington, Dorchester, Dorset, DT2 0HB**
Contacts: **PHONE (01300) 320683 MOBILE (07715) 558289**
E-MAIL helen-rees@live.co.uk

1 CNOC MOY (IRE), 9, b g Mull of Kintyre (USA)—Ewar Sunrise **Mrs H. E. Rees**
2 RESIDENCE AND SPA (IRE), 5, b g Dubai Destination (USA)—Toffee Nosed **Mrs H. E. Rees**

Assistant Trainer: Mr Rupert Rees

---

531 **MR SEAN REGAN, Middleham**
Postal: **Low Beck, Coverham, Middleham, Leyburn, North Yorkshire, DL8 4TJ**
Contacts: **MOBILE (07866) 437476**
E-MAIL sean@seanreganracing.com WEBSITE www.seanreganracing.com

1 4, B f Danbird (AUS)—Nikita Sunrise (IRE)
2 PTOLOMEOS, 10, b g Kayf Tara—Lucy Tufty **Mrs C. D. Taylor**
3 RIDLEY TAYLOR, 10, b m Karinga Bay—Saxon Gift **S. Regan**
4 SHEILA'S CASTLE, 9, b m Karinga Bay—Candarela **S. Regan**

---

532 **MR ANDREW REID, Mill Hill, London**
Postal: **Highwood Lodge, Highwood Hill, Mill Hill, London, NW7 4HB**
Contacts: **PHONE (07836) 214617 FAX (02089) 061255 MOBILE (07747) 751603**

1 4, B f Doyen (IRE)—Emily-Mou (IRE) **A. S. Reid**
2 MALTEASE AH, 4, br f Librettist (USA)—Manic **A. S. Reid**
3 4, B br f Doyen (IRE)—Moon Spinner

THREE-YEAR-OLDS
4 MODERN SOCIETY, pt c I Was Framed (USA)—Artzola (IRE) **A. S. Reid**
5 UNDERWHELM, ch f Bahamian Bounty—Depressed **A. S. Reid**

Jockey (flat): Jim Crowley.

---

533 **MRS JACQUELINE RETTER, Cullompton**
Postal: **Dulford Cottage, Dulford, Cullompton, Devon, EX15 2DX**
Contacts: **PHONE/FAX (01884) 266078 MOBILE (07912) 889655**

1 EXILES RETURN (IRE), 11, b g Needle Gun (IRE)—Moores Girl (IRE) **Mrs J. G. Retter**

---

534 **MR KEITH REVELEY, Saltburn**
Postal: **Groundhill Farm, Lingdale, Saltburn-by-the-Sea, Cleveland, TS12 3HD**
Contacts: **OFFICE (01287) 650456 FAX (01287) 653095 MOBILE (07971) 784539**
E-MAIL reveleyracing@yahoo.co.uk

1 BENNY BE GOOD, 10, b g Benny The Dip (USA)—Hembane (FR) **J. Wade**
2 BRAVE SPARTACUS (IRE), 7, b g Spartacus (IRE)—Peaches Polly **R. Collins**
3 BROCTUNE PAPA GIO, 6, b g Tobougg (IRE)—Fairlie **Broctune Partners I**
4 CATEGORICAL, 10, b g Diktat—Zibet **Rug, Grub & Pub Partnership**
5 COLUMBUS SECRET (IRE), 8, b g Luso—Bid For Fun (USA) **R. Collins**
6 CORKAGE (IRE), 10, b g Second Empire (IRE)—Maslam (IRE) **The Scarth Racing Partnership**

MR KEITH REVELEY - Continued

7 **CROWNING JEWEL**, 7, b g Sulamani (IRE)—Pennys Pride (IRE) **Sir Ian Good**
8 **CUE TO CUE**, 7, b m King's Theatre (IRE)—Marello **Mr & Mrs W. J. Williams**
9 **D'GIGI**, 7, ch m Beat Hollow—Strictly Cool (USA) **Sunking Partnership**
10 **DANCE OF TIME**, 6, b g Presenting—Northern Native (IRE) **Mrs S. A. Smith**
11 **DANCING ART (IRE)**, 7, b g Definite Article—Seductive Dance **R. Collins**
12 **DELTA FORTY**, 5, b m Alflora (IRE)—Northern Native (IRE) **Mrs S. A. Smith**
13 **FLEMENS PRIDE**, 5, b m Flemensfirth (USA)—Pennys Pride (IRE) **J. M. & Mrs M. R. Edwardson**
14 **FLORA'S PRIDE**, 9, b m Alflora (IRE)—Pennys Pride (IRE) **Reveley Farms**
15 **GIVEITAGO**, 4, b g Tobougg (IRE)—Trevorsninepoints **Mrs M. E. Child**
16 **GO TEESCOMPONENTS**, 6, b g Septieme Ciel (USA)—Linea-G **Tees Components Ltd**
17 **HARVEY'S HOPE**, 7, b g Sinndar (IRE)—Ancara **The Home & Away Partnership**
18 4, Ch g Grape Tree Road—I Got Rhythm **Thomson-Fyffe Racing**
19 **IRISH CHAPERONE (IRE)**, 6, b g High Chaparral (IRE)—Harry's Irish Rose (USA) **R. Collins**
20 **IVAN BORU (IRE)**, 5, b g Brian Boru—Miranda's Lace (IRE) **Furness Thwaites & Lord Zetland**
21 **JESSICA VALENTINE (IRE)**, 6, b m King's Theatre (IRE)—Jessica One (IRE) **Mr I. Valentine**
22 **KINGS GREY (IRE)**, 9, gr g King's Theatre (IRE)—Grey Mo (IRE) **J. Wade**
23 **LA CALINDA**, 6, b m Presenting—Bayrouge (IRE) **Mac & Lingdale Optimists Partnership**
24 **MADRASA (IRE)**, 5, b g High Chaparral (IRE)—Shir Dar (FR) **Mr M. W. Joyce**
25 **MR PUCK (IRE)**, 6, gr g Tikkanen (USA)—Vicky's Music (IRE) **Major & Mrs P. Arkwright & Mrs I. C. Sellars**
26 **MR SUPREME (IRE)**, 8, b g Beneficial—Ardfallon (IRE) **Mrs S. P. Granger**
27 **NIGHT IN MILAN (IRE)**, 7, b g Milan—Chione (IRE) **R. Collins**
28 4, B g Grape Tree Road—Our Tees Component (IRE) **Tees Components Ltd**
29 4, B f Beat All (USA)—Pennys Pride (IRE) **Reveley Farms**
30 **REASONABLE FORCE**, 7, b g Forzando—Noreasonatall **Cristiana's Crew & A. G. Knowles**
31 **ROBBIE**, 9, b g Robellino (USA)—Corn Lily **Mrs S. McDonald**
32 **SAMBELUCKY (IRE)**, 8, b g Barathea (IRE)—Kalimar (IRE) **M. Foxton, JBP & DAG Partnership**
33 **SEREN GRIS**, 7, gr m Fair Mix (IRE)—Bayrouge (IRE) **Phoenix Racing & Mr Jeremy Mitchell**
34 **SEREN ROUGE**, 8, b g Old Vic—Bayrouge (IRE) **Phoenix Racing & Mr Jeremy Mitchell**
35 **SHADRACK (IRE)**, 9, gr g Tamayaz (CAN)—Alba Dancer **Mrs S. Granger**
36 **SPECIAL CATCH (IRE)**, 6, b g Catcher In The Rye (USA)—Top Quality **Mr Mike Browne & Mr William McKeown**
37 **SWINGING SULTAN**, 5, b g Sulamani (IRE)—Nobratinetta (FR) **Reveley Racing I**
38 **TEKTHELOT (IRE)**, 7, b g Shantou (USA)—Bryna (IRE) **Mrs A. Trevaskis**
39 **THURNHAM**, 7, b g Tobougg (IRE)—Nobratinetta (FR) **J. M. & Mrs M. R. Edmondson**
40 **VICTOR HEWGO**, 8, b g Old Vic—Pennys Pride (IRE) **Sir Ian Good**
41 **VINETTA**, 5, b m Grape Tree Road—Nobratinetta (FR) **The Thoughtful Partnership**
42 **WALTZ DARLING (IRE)**, 5, b g Iffraaj—Aljafliyah **M. F. Browne**
43 **WHICHWAYTOBOUGIE**, 4, b g Tobougg (IRE)—Whichway Girl **The Supreme Partnership**

THREE-YEAR-OLDS

44 B g Black Sam Bellamy (IRE)—Nobratinetta (FR) **Supreme Alliance**

Other Owners: Mr. R. J. Ainscough, Mr C. Alessi, Mr C. Anderson, Mr Philip Arkwright, Mrs Philip Arkwright, Mrs Marilyn Bauckham, Mr Doug Bauckham, Mr D. E. Baxter, Mrs C. M. Baxter, Mr J. P. Bladen, Mr D. Bowen, Mr M. Bradley, Mr A. E. Brown, Mr Mike Browne, Mrs M. Clark-Wright, Mr J. W. Coates, Mr E. Coll, Mr A. E. Corbett, Mr M. Cressey, Mrs P. E. Drinkall, Mr Bernard Drinkall, Mr J. M. Edwardson, Mrs M. R. Edwardson, Mrs J. W. Furness, Mr Brian W. Goodall, Mr Jeff Goodall, Mr David A. Green, Mrs D. Greenhalgh, Mr Roger Hart, Mr Anthony Iceton, Mr Ernest Johnson, Mr M. W. Joyce, Mr A. G. Knowles, Mr P. Longstaff, Mr D. Lovell, Mr Ron MacDonald, Mr W. McKeown, Mr T. M. McKain, Miss J. Mitchell, Mrs Lynn Morrison, Mr D. A. Oliver, Mr D. Playforth, Mr Douglas Renton, Mr Graeme Renton, Exors of the Late Mr John Renton, Mrs M. A. Renton, Reveley Farms, Mr D. M. D. Robinson, Mr J. Rodgers, Mrs A. Rodgers, Mr J. Scarth, Mrs Ian Sellars, Mr Richard V. Smith, Mrs Elizabeth Stephens, Mr Jim Struth, Mr J. Thoroughgood, Mrs M. B. Thwaites, Mr David Wild, Mr W. J. Williams, Mrs M. Williams, Mrs C. M. Yates, Mr D. Young, Lord Zetland.

Assistant Trainer: Fiona Reveley

Jockey (NH): James Reveley. **Amateur:** Mr Colm McCormack, Mr Russell Lindsay.

<table>
<tr><td>535</td><td>

MR PAUL RICH, Newport
Postal: Cwrt-y-Mwnws Farmhouse, Allt-yr-Yn, Newport, Gwent, NP20 5EL
Contacts: PHONE (01633) 262791 MOBILE (07971) 218286
E-MAIL paul@m-rich.freeserve.co.uk

</td></tr>
</table>

1 **BOOM TO BUST (IRE)**, 5, br g Big Bad Bob (IRE)—Forever Phoenix **P. M. Rich**
2 **LADY ANNE BOLEYN**, 8, bl gr m Karinga Bay—Zambran Calypso **Miss D. T. Hamblin**
3 **OFFICER IN COMMAND (USA)**, 7, b br g Officer (USA)—Luv to Stay n Chat (USA) **P. M. Rich**

536 MR DAVID RICHARDS, Abergavenny
Postal: **White House, Llantilio Crossenny, Abergavenny, Gwent, NP7 8SU**
Contacts: **PHONE (01600) 780235**

1 **ANOTHER KATE (IRE)**, 9, gr m Norwich—Cracking Kate (IRE) **D. M. Richards**
2 5, Gr g Vertical Speed (FR)—Cracking Kate (IRE) **D. M. Richards**

Jockey (NH): Sam Thomas.

537 MRS LYDIA RICHARDS, Chichester
Postal: **Lynch Farm, Hares Lane, Funtington, Chichester, West Sussex, PO18 9LW**
Contacts: **YARD (01243) 574379 HOME (01243) 574882 MOBILE (07803) 199061**
E-MAIL lydia.richards@sky.com

1 **AALY**, 6, b g Milan—Leyaaly **Mrs Lydia Richards**
2 **BAYTOWN BERTIE**, 4, b g Orientor—Baytown Flyer **Mrs Lydia Richards**
3 **DEMOISELLE BOND**, 5, ch m Monsieur Bond (IRE)—Baytown Flyer **The Demoiselle Bond Partnership**
4 **INNER STEEL (IRE)**, 8, b g Zagreb (USA)—Mrs McClintock (IRE) **The Inner Steel Partnership**
5 **MYETTA**, 5, gr m Silver Patriarch (IRE)—Henrietta Holmes (IRE) **Mrs E. F. J. Seal**
6 **NOVEL DANCER**, 5, b g Dansili—Fictitious **Mrs Lydia Richards**
7 **OUR PLAY (IRE)**, 5, b g Oratorio (IRE)—Red Shoe **Mrs Lydia Richards**
8 **VENETIAN LAD**, 8, ro g Midnight Legend—Henrietta Holmes (IRE) **The Venetian Lad Partnership**
9 **ZIGZAGA (IRE)**, 7, b g Zagreb (USA)—Mrs McClintock (IRE) **Mrs Lydia Richards**

Other Owners: Exors of the Late Mr L. Howard, Mr H. B. Kinmond, Mr G. H. R. Musker, E. T. Wright.

538 MR NICKY RICHARDS, Greystoke
Postal: **Rectory Farm, Greystoke, Penrith, Cumbria, CA11 0UJ**
Contacts: **OFFICE (01768) 483392 HOME (01768) 483160 FAX (01768) 483933**
MOBILE (07771) 906609
E-MAIL n.g.richards@virgin.net

1 **ABBEY GARTH (IRE)**, 6, b g Dr Massini (IRE)—Elegant Gale (IRE) **J. P. McManus**
2 4, B g Old Vic—Afdala (IRE) **Mrs Pat Sloan**
3 **AND THE MAN**, 7, ch g Generous (IRE)—Retro's Lady (IRE) **The Little Green Syndicate**
4 4, B g Brian Boru—Ballyknock Present (IRE) **Miss J. R. Richards**
5 **BENMADIGAN (IRE)**, 11, ch g Presenting—Dont Tell Nell (IRE) **Charlie & Nick Fortescue**
6 **BERNARDELLI (IRE)**, 5, b g Golan (IRE)—Beautiful Blue (IRE) **Mark Barnard & Richard Helliwell**
7 **BISHOPS GATE (IRE)**, 7, b g Bishop of Cashel—
Lischelle Star (IRE) **Mrs T. H. Barclay & Mrs F. D. McInnes Skinner**
8 **BRIJOMI QUEEN (IRE)**, 6, b m King's Theatre (IRE)—Tempest Belle (IRE) **M S Borders Racing Club & Partners**
9 **CHIDSWELL (IRE)**, 4, b g Gold Well—Manacured (IRE) **Langdale Bloodstock**
10 **DUKE OF NAVAN (IRE)**, 5, b br g Presenting—Greenfieldflyer (IRE) **David & Nicky Robinson**
11 **EARLY APPLAUSE**, 5, b g Royal Applause—Early Evening **C. W. Jenkins**
12 **EDUARD (IRE)**, 5, b g Morozov (USA)—Dinny Kenn (IRE) **Kingdom Taverns Ltd**
13 **FLIPPING**, 6, br g Kheleyf (USA)—Felona **Mr Reg Gifford**
14 **GLINGERBURN (IRE)**, 5, b g King's Theatre (IRE)—Wychnor Dawn (IRE) **James Westoll**
15 **GOLD FUTURES (IRE)**, 4, b g Gold Well—Don't Discount Her (IRE) **Mrs C. A. Torkington**
16 **HANNAH JACQUES (IRE)**, 8, b m Flemensfirth (USA)—
Richs Mermaid (IRE) **M S Borders Racing Club & Partners**
17 **HOUSTON DYNIMO (IRE)**, 8, b g Rock of Gibraltar (IRE)—Quiet Mouse (USA) **Miss J. R. Richards**
18 **ITZACLICHE (IRE)**, 13, b g Classic Cliche (IRE)—Ower (IRE) **Miss J. R. Richards**
19 **MALIN BAY (IRE)**, 8, b g Milan—Mirror of Flowers **David & Nicky Robinson**
20 **MERRYDOWN (IRE)**, 10, b g Oscar (IRE)—Euro Coin Lady (IRE) **Mrs E. E. R. Sloan**
21 **MISTER MARKER (IRE)**, 9, ch g Beneficial—Bavards Girl (IRE) **J. A. Dudgeon**
22 **MOUFATANGO (FR)**, 7, b br g Sagacity (FR)—Bold-E-Be **Miss J. R. Richards**
23 **NEW VIC (IRE)**, 7, ch g Old Vic—Innovate (IRE) **Mr Peter Dale**
24 **NOBLE ALAN (GER)**, 10, gr g King's Theatre (IRE)—Nirvavita (FR) **C. Bennett**
25 **ONE FOR HARRY (IRE)**, 5, b g Generous (IRE)—Strawberry Fool (FR) **The Fife Boys + 1**
26 **ONE FOR HOCKY (IRE)**, 5, b g Brian Boru—Wire Lady (IRE) **Kingdom Taverns Ltd**
27 **PARC DES PRINCES (USA)**, 7, b br g Ten Most Wanted (USA)—Miss Orah **Bob Bennett & Bill Graham**
28 **PEACHEY MOMENT (USA)**, 8, b br g Stormin Fever (USA)—
Given Moment (USA) **Peachey Moment Partnership**

MR NICKY RICHARDS - Continued

29 **PREMIER SAGAS (FR)**, 9, b g Sagacity (FR)—Estampe (FR) **D. Wesley-Yates**
30 **RAIN STOPS PLAY (IRE)**, 11, b g Desert Prince (IRE)—Pinta (IRE) **P. Montgomery**
31 **SCARLET FIRE (IRE)**, 6, b g Helissio (FR)—Ross Dana (IRE) **Mrs T. H. Barclay & Mrs F. D. McInnes Skinner**
32 **SHIVALRIC (IRE)**, 5, b g Fruits of Love (USA)—Shamaiyla (FR) **Mrs J. Fortescue, E. Gifford & D. McGawn**
33 **SIMPLY NED (IRE)**, 6, ch g Fruits of Love (USA)—Bishops Lass (IRE) **David & Nicky Robinson**
34 **SIR VINSKI (IRE)**, 4, ch g Vinnie Roe (IRE)—Mill Emerald **Langdale Bloodstock**
35 **ST GREGORY (IRE)**, 5, ch m Presenting—Ardrom **Mrs S. Johnson**
36 **STREAMS OF WHISKEY (IRE)**, 6, br g Spadoun (FR)—Cherry Tops (IRE) **Mr & Mrs R. G. Kelvin Hughes**
37 **SUNDOWN TRAIL (IRE)**, 8, ch g Old Vic—Mary's View (IRE) **Stilvi Compania Financiera**
38 **TALKIN THOMAS (IRE)**, 7, b g Talkin Man (CAN)—Keerou Lady (IRE) **Henriques & Lloyd-Bakers**
39 **TCHATCHACO YA YA**, 6, b g Equerry (USA)—Tchatchacoya (FR) **C. P. Norbury**
40 **TEDDY TEE (IRE)**, 4, b g Mountain High (IRE)—Knocksouna Lady (IRE) **David & Nicky Robinson**
41 **THAT'LL DO NICELY (IRE)**, 10, b g Bahhare (USA)—Return Again (IRE) **Miss J. R. Richards**
42 **TOP BILLING**, 4, br g Monsun (GER)—La Gandilie (FR) **Mr J. Dudgeon & Partners**
43 **TUTCHEC (FR)**, 6, gr g Turgeon (USA)—Pocahontas (FR) **Club 4 Racing**
44 **WARRIORS TALE**, 4, b g Midnight Legend—Samandara (FR) **Langdale Bloodstock**
45 **WINTER ALCHEMY (IRE)**, 8, b g Fruits of Love (USA)—Native Land **The Alchemy Partnership**

Other Owners: Mr A. Clark, Mr G. Dowd, Mr G. Dowling, Mrs R. L. Elliot, Mrs Judy Fortescue, Mr Andrew Hamilton, Mr M. Henriques, Mr P. Laverty, Mr C. G. M. Lloyd-Baker, Mr H. M. A. Lloyd-Baker, Mr Edward Melville, Mr Walter Morris, Mr A. T. Murphy.

Assistant Trainer: Miss Joey Richards

Jockey (NH): Brian Harding, Davy Russell. **Conditional:** Brian Treanor. **Amateur:** Miss J. R. Richards.

---

539 | **MR MARK RIMELL, Witney**
Postal: **Fairspear Racing Stables, Fairspear Road, Leafield, Witney, Oxfordshire, OX29 9NT**
Contacts: **PHONE (01993) 878551 MOBILE (07778) 648303/(07973) 627054**
E-MAIL rimell@rimellracing.com WEBSITE www.rimellracing.com

1 **BHAKTI (IRE)**, 6, b g Rakti—Royal Bossi (IRE) **M. G. Rimell**
2 **CAPTAIN WILSON**, 6, b g Olden Times—Competa **Mr P. Balding**
3 **DEFINITE LADY (IRE)**, 7, b m Definite Article—Phillis Hill **M. G. Rimell**
4 **JAZZ MAN (IRE)**, 6, ch g Beneficial—Slaney Jazz **M. G. Rimell**
5 **JUST BLUE**, 7, gr g Silver Patriarch (IRE)—Miss Millie **W. W. Stroud**
6 **MON HOMME**, 6, br g Loup Sauvage (USA)—Mistinguett (IRE) **Kevin Wright, Mark Rimell**
7 **NOMADIC DREAMER**, 10, ch g Nomadic Way (USA)—Nunsdream **Mr J. D. Stallard**
8 **PONCHO**, 4, b f Cape Cross (IRE)—Pixie Ring
9 4, B f Overbury (IRE)—Royal Roxy (IRE) **Annie Rimell**
10 4, B f Needwood Blade—Sudden Spirit (FR)
11 **SUPER SAY (IRE)**, 7, ch g Intikhab (USA)—Again Royale (IRE) **Castle Racing**
12 **TOP CHIEF**, 5, b g Doyen—For More (IRE) **M. G. Rimell**
13 **TWOWAYS (IRE)**, 7, br g Bob's Return (IRE)—Braw Lass **M. G. Rimell**

THREE-YEAR-OLDS

14 B f Black Sam Bellamy (IRE)—Royal Roxy (IRE) **Mark Rimell**
15 **SPIRAEA**, ch f Bahamian Bounty—Salvia

Other Owners: Mr C. Beek, Mr M. Glover, Mr N. Hoare, Mr S. Nightingale, Mr D. Pratt, Mr Mark Rimell, Mr J. Wetherald, Mr K. Wright.

Assistant Trainer: Anne Rimell

---

540 | **MR MARK RIMMER, Newmarket**
Postal: **2 Pinetree Bungalows, Philipps Close, Newmarket, Suffolk, CB8 0PB**
Contacts: **PHONE (01638) 577498 MOBILE (07913) 111205**

1 **CORN MAIDEN**, 4, b f Refuse To Bend (IRE)—Namat (IRE) **Ms J. McHugh**
2 **EMERALD WILDERNESS (IRE)**, 9, b g Green Desert (USA)—Simla Bibi **Mr F. J. Perry**
3 **SATWA BALLERINA**, 5, b m Barathea (IRE)—Ballerina Rosa (FR) **M. E. Rimmer**

MR MARK RIMMER - Continued

THREE-YEAR-OLDS

4 GRAPES HILL, b f Kingsalsa (USA)—Red Blossom **C. Dennett**

Amateur: Mr J. Pearce.

---

541 **MISS BETH ROBERTS, Bridgend**
Postal: **14 Pwllcarn Terrace, Pontycymmer, Bridgend, Mid-Glamorgan, CF32 8AS**
Contacts: **PHONE (01656) 870076**

1 CHESNUT ANNIE (IRE), 12, ch m Weld—Leaden Sky (IRE) **Miss H. E. Roberts**
2 KIMS QUEST (IRE), 5, b m Needle Gun (IRE)—Flyingagain (IRE) **Miss H. E. Roberts**

---

542 **MRS RENEE ROBESON, Newport Pagnell**
Postal: **Fences Farm, Tyringham, Newport Pagnell, Buckinghamshire, MK16 9EN**
Contacts: **PHONE/FAX (01908) 611255 MOBILE (07831) 579898**
E-MAIL robesons@attglobal.net

1 AMISTRESS, 5, b m Kalanisi (IRE)—Atwirl **Mrs R. L. M. Robeson**
2 BENEFIT CUT (IRE), 7, b g Beneficial—I'm Maggy (NZ) **Howard Cooke & Terence Jenner**
3 COLEBROOKE, 5, b g Shamardal (USA)—Shimna **TMT Grand**
4 E MAJOR, 8, ch g Singspiel (IRE)—Crystal Cavern (USA) **Sir E. de Rothschild**
5 GENNY WREN, 7, ch m Generous (IRE)—Wren Warbler **Mrs R. L. M. Robeson**
6 GRASSFINCH, 7, ch m Generous (IRE)—Stock Dove **Mrs R. L. M. Robeson**
7 JUSTAZIPPY, 6, b m Where Or When (IRE)—Theatre Lady (IRE) **M. W. Lawrence**
8 NORSE WREN, 5, ch g Norse Dancer (IRE)—Wren Warbler **Mrs R. L. M. Robeson**
9 OGEE, 10, ch g Generous (IRE)—Aethra (USA) **Sir E. de Rothschild**
10 REYNO, 5, b g Sleeping Indian—Tereyna **Mrs R. L. M. Robeson**
11 SAN TELM (IRE), 8, b g Oscar (IRE)—Magical Mist (IRE) **The Tyringham Partnership**
12 SMART EXIT (IRE), 6, b g Exit To Nowhere (USA)—Navaro (IRE) **The Ravenstone Partnership**
13 TANNERMAN (IRE), 7, br g Presenting—Coolsilver (IRE) **Nick Brown Racing**
14 THE FONZ, 7, b g Oasis Dream—Crystal Cavern (USA) **Anthony & David De Rothschild**
15 WILLOW WREN, 8, ch m Afflora (IRE)—Wren Warbler **Mrs R. L. M. Robeson**

Other Owners: Mr N. J. Brown, Mr H. J. Cooke, Mr T. A. Jenner, Mr B. H. Turner, D. Yates, Mr A. J. de Rothschild, Mr D. M. de Rothschild.

---

543 **MISS SARAH ROBINSON, Bridgwater**
Postal: **Newnham Farm, Shurton, Stogursey, Bridgwater, Somerset, TA5 1QG**
Contacts: **PHONE (01278) 732357 FAX (01278) 732357 MOBILE (07866) 435197**
E-MAIL info@sarahrobinsonracing.co.uk WEBSITE www.sarahrobinsonracing.co.uk

1 COUNTRYWIDE CITY (IRE), 7, b g Elusive City (USA)—Handy Station (IRE) **Mr B. Robinson**
2 FIRST SPIRIT, 7, ch m First Trump—Flaming Spirt **Mr B. Robinson**
3 NEWNHAM FLYER (IRE), 11, gr m Exit To Nowhere (USA)—Paper Flight **Mr B. Robinson**
4 THEROADTOGOREY (IRE), 7, b g Revoque (IRE)—Shannon Mor (IRE) **Mr B. Robinson**

Assistant Trainer: Mr B. Robinson

---

544 **MISS PAULINE ROBSON, Capheaton**
Postal: **Kidlaw Farm, Capheaton, Newcastle Upon Tyne, NE19 2AW**
Contacts: **PHONE (01830) 530241 MOBILE (07721) 887489 or (07814) 708725 (David)**
E-MAIL pauline.robson@virgin.net

1 6, B g Rashar (USA)—Crossgales Flutter (IRE)
2 GET THE PAPERS, 6, b g Kayf Tara—Smart Topsy **S. P. Graham**
3 HUMBIE (IRE), 9, b g Karinga Bay—South Queen Lady (IRE) **Mr & Mrs Raymond Anderson Green**
4 LOCKED INTHEPOCKET (IRE), 9, b g Beneficial—Ruby Rubenstein (IRE) **Mr & Mrs Raymond Anderson Green**

MISS PAULINE ROBSON - Continued

5 **RIVAL D'ESTRUVAL (FR)**, 8, b g Khalkevi (IRE)—
　　　　　Kermesse d'estruval (FR) **Mr & Mrs Raymond Anderson Green**
6 **SHANEN (IRE)**, 7, b g Tikkanen (USA)—Ursha (IRE) **Mr & Mrs Raymond Anderson Green**
7 **UPSILON BLEU (FR)**, 5, b g Panoramic—Glycine Bleue (FR) **Mr & Mrs Raymond Anderson Green**
8 **YOUNG SPARKY (IRE)**, 6, b br g Oscar (IRE)—Our Dream (IRE) **Mr & Mrs Raymond Anderson Green**

Other Owners: R. A. Green, Mrs A. Green.

Assistant Trainer: David Parker

Jockey (NH): Timmy Murphy, Richie McGrath.

---

545 | **MR FRANCOIS ROHAUT, Sauvagnon**
Postal: **26, Rue Du Bearn, 64230 Sauvagnon, France**
Contacts: **PHONE (0033) 5593 32486 FAX (0033) 5596 24652 MOBILE (0033) 6727 75619**
E-MAIL ecurie.rohaut@wanadoo.fr

1 **AGENT SECRET (IRE)**, 7, br h Pyrus (USA)—Ron's Secret **Mr R. Tema**
2 **ASYL (IRE)**, 4, b f Peintre Celebre (USA)—Coup d'eclat (IRE) **Mr Saeed Nasser Al Romaithi**
3 **BLITZ (FR)**, 5, b g Country Reel (USA)—Benzolina (IRE) **Mme M. Rohaut-Leger**
4 **BORGO**, 5, b g Poliglote—Bengalie (FR) **Mr F. Rohaut**
5 **BRAVIA**, 4, ch f Shamardal (USA)—Albahaca (USA) **Mme A. Cuadra-Lores**
6 **BROOKLYN THOMAS (IRE)**, 4, b g Dylan Thomas (IRE)—Brooklyn Academy (USA) **S. Boucheron**
7 **CANNES TO CAPRI (IRE)**, 4, b f Galileo (IRE)—Croisiere (USA) **Skymarc Farm**
8 **COMMON DENOMINATOR**, 4, b c Royal Applause—Lalectra **J. Calva**
9 **FORTUNE HUNTER (FR)**, 4, b f High Chaparral (IRE)—King's Folly (FR) **Skymarc Farm**
10 **INNER BEAUTY (FR)**, 4, ch f Pivotal—Indian Maiden (IRE) **Haras de Saint Pair**
11 **KALAHARI GOLD (IRE)**, 8, ch g Trans Island—Neat Shilling (IRE) **Hamdan Al Maktoum**
12 **LHENY (FR)**, 4, b g Le Triton (USA)—Besca Nueva (FR) **M. Cordero**
13 **LUCRECE**, 4, ch f Pivotal—Sun Bittern (USA) **SARL Ecurie Tagada**
14 **MARONI (IRE)**, 8, b g Oasis Dream—Miss Chryss (IRE) **Mr M. Perret**
15 **MISS POST OFFICE (FR)**, 4, b f American Post—Miss Prism (USA) **Mr J. J. Taieb**
16 **MRS DUBAWI (IRE)**, 4, b f Dubawi (IRE)—Lucky Lune (USA) **G. Laboureau**
17 **NOVA KEDIET (USA)**, 5, b g Speightstown (USA)—Dynamous (USA) **Mr A. Mouknass**
18 **OMINOUS**, 4, b c Oasis Dream—Merle **J. Wigan**
19 **ORMEL**, 4, b g Observatory (USA)—Eiszeit (GER) **Mr G. Augustin-Normand**
20 **PATH OF HOPE (USA)**, 4, gr ro g Bernstein (USA)—Kenbu (FR) **Michel Cordero**
21 **PEARLS OR PASSION**, 4, b f Monsun (GER)—Pearly Shells **Haras de Saint Pair**
22 **RJWA (IRE)**, 4, ch f Muhtathir—Minallon (ARG) **Sheikh Joaan Bin Hamad Al Thani**
23 **ROERO (FR)**, 4, b g Acclamation—Ricine (IRE) **Haras de Saint Pair**
24 **SEBIA**, 4, b f American Post—Silver Silence (FR) **Mr F. Rohaut**
25 **SINNKOSAKO**, 4, b c Anabaa—Reinamixa **Mme L. Samoun**
26 **TURTLE GREEN (FR)**, 4, b g Turtle Bowl (IRE)—Love Green (FR) **Mr J. Strauss**
27 **ZACK HALL (FR)**, 6, b g Muhtathir—Halawa (IRE) **Mr M. Offenstadt**

THREE-YEAR-OLDS

28 **ALWAYS ROYAL (FR)**, b f King's Best (USA)—Abime (USA) **Lady O'Reilly**
29 **BAKI (FR)**, b f Turtle Bowl—Benzolina **Mr F. Rohaut**
30 **BROOKLYN BOWL (USA)**, b c Henrythenavigator (USA)—Turtle Bow (FR) **B. Van Dalfsen**
31 **CALL ME MAYBE**, ch f Dubai Destination (USA)—Reaf **Mr A. Mouknass**
32 **CASA TUA (FR)**, b f Oasis Dream—Cattiva Generosa **Haras de Saint Pair**
33 **ENCORE MERCI (IRE)**, ch f Danehill Dancer (IRE)—Thanks Again (IRE) **Haras de Saint Pair**
34 **EYJAFJOLL (FR)**, b g Slickly (FR)—Efisia (FR) **Georges Duca**
35 **FACE SURFACE (GER)**, ch c Turtle Bowl (IRE)—Flower Bowl (FR) **B. Van Dulfsen**
36 **FAITHFILLY (IRE)**, b f Red Clubs (IRE)—Bauci (IRE) **Haras de Saint Pair**
37 **FULL METAL JACK (FR)**, b c Stormy River (FR)—Touch of Pink (FR) **Pandora Stud LLC**
38 **HELOISE (FR)**, b f American Post—Hijaziyah **P. Chedeville**
39 **HOH MY ESTELLE (FR)**, b f Sakhee (USA)—Hoh My Darling **Team Hogdala A. B.**
40 **IDEAL STEP (IRE)**, b f Footstepsinthesand—Ideal World (IRE) **Mme Francis Teboul**
41 **IFTIKAAR (IRE)**, b c Cape Cross (IRE)—Anbella (FR) **Hamdan Al Maktoum**
42 **INTERNALRUNNER**, b c Manduro (GER)—Iphianassa (GER) **Mr G. Augustin-Normand**
43 **IRON LADY (FR)**, b f Irish Wells (FR)—Lady Zorreghuietta (FR) **B. Van Dalfsen**
44 **KAPOUR (IRE)**, b c Toylsome—Kitcat (GER) **Haras de Saint Pair**
45 **KAWAAKIB (USA)**, b f Nayef (USA)—Muthabara (IRE) **Hamdan Al Maktoum**

MR FRANCOIS ROHAUT - Continued

46 **KEEN GLANCE (IRE)**, ch f Sakhee (USA)—Glint of Green (USA) **James Wigan**
47 **LAPONIE BOREALE (IRE)**, b f Orpen (USA)—Labour of Love (USA) **Mme Robert G. Ehrnrooth**
48 **LE THOLONEY (FR)**, b c Great Journey (JPN)—Reinamixa (FR) **Mme L. Samoun**
49 **LICTUS (FR)**, b c Literato (IRE)—Lunaba (FR) **Raphael Verspieren**
50 **LITANIBREAK JUNIOR (FR)**, ch f Sunday Break (JPN)—Litani Queen **Bernard Jeffroy**
51 **MANDURA (FR)**, b f Manduro (GER)—Sign of The Vine (FR) **B. Van Dalfsen**
52 **MLLE AGAPEE (IRE)**, b f Whipper (USA)—Ziria (IRE) **Ecurie Tagada SAS**
53 **MLLE TOSCA (IRE)**, ch f Iffraaj—Tallassee **Jean-Jacques Taieb**
54 **MOOSIR (USA)**, b c Daaher (CAN)—Torrestrella (IRE) **Hamdan Al Maktoum**
55 **MUTABASER (FR)**, b c Muhtathir—Tuiga (FR) **Hamdan Al Maktoum**
56 **OSADA (FR)**, b f Authorized (IRE)—Albahaca (USA) **Mme A. Cuadra-Lores**
57 **OSRATTY (IRE)**, b f Invincible Spirit (IRE)—Moon's Whisper (USA) **Hamdan Al Maktoum**
58 **PEARLY AVENUE (FR)**, b f Anabaa (USA)—Pearly Shells **Haras de Saint Pair**
59 **PRETTY PANTHER (FR)**, ch f Hurricane Run—Princesse Jasmine **P. Sabban**
60 **PRINCE SUHAIL (IRE)**, b c Marju (IRE)—Larme (IRE) **Khalifa Dasmal**
61 **QUATORZE (FR)**, b c Elusive City (USA)—Queseraisjesanstoi (FR) **Haras D'Etreham**
62 **RASHFA (FR)**, b f Cape Cross (IRE)—Ayun (USA) **Hamdan Al Maktoum**
63 **RIME A RIEN (FR)**, b f Amadeus Wolf—Rainbow Crossing **Skymarc Farm**
64 **RISAS (FR)**, b c Tiger Hill (IRE)—Atiza (IRE) **Mme A. Cuadra-Lores**
65 **SAYRAH (FR)**, b f Sakhee (USA)—Tomoohat (USA) **Hamdan Al Maktoum**
66 **SEVEN EVEN (FR)**, b f Turtle Bowl (IRE)—Ejina (FR) **Mr A. Mouknass**
67 **SHAGRA (IRE)**, ch f Pivotal—Noelani (IRE) **Sheikh Joaan Bin Hamad Al Thani**
68 **SHINING LIFE**, b f American Post—Ask For Rain **Mr A. Mouknass**
69 **SIESTA TIME**, b f Oasis Dream—In The Light **James Wigan**
70 **STAR OF SUNDAY (FR)**, b c Sunday Break (JPN)—Lilli Star (FR) **G. Juppe**
71 **SUSHI TUNA**, ch f Halling (USA)—Sleeping Storm (IRE) **Haras de Saint Pair**
72 **TERRA SIENA (FR)**, ch f Medicean—Sayoko (IRE) **Jean-Jacques Taieb**
73 **TESTOSTEROSSA (FR)**, b f Astronomer Royal (USA)—Epopee (IRE) **B. Van Dalfsen**
74 **TUNA PAPITA (USA)**, b f Henrythenavigator (USA)—Viapervita (IRE) **Sheikh Joaan Bin Hamad Al Thani**
75 **TURTLE INN (FR)**, b f Turtle Bowl (IRE)—Irish Source **B. Van Dalfsen**
76 **VERNITA GREEN (FR)**, b f Turtle Bowl (IRE)—Loving Smile (FR) **Mr A. Mouknass**
77 **XYNTHIA (FR)**, b f Keltos (FR)—Love And Kiss (FR) **Mme Michel Daugreilh**
78 **ZAMAAM**, b br c Muhtathir—Nasheed (USA) **Hamdan Al Maktoum**

TWO-YEAR-OLDS

79 **AMY ERIA (IRE)**, b f 27/2 Shamardal (USA)—
    Berroscoberro (FR) (Octagonal (NZ)) (67460) **Sheikh Joaan Bin Hamad Al Thani**
80 **ANNOVILLE (FR)**, ch f 1/3 Le Havre (IRE)—Absolute Lady (IRE) (Galileo (IRE)) **Mr G. Augustin-Normand**
81 B c 7/2 Invincible Spirit (IRE)—Apperella (Rainbow Quest (USA)) (35714) **Sheikh Joaan Bin Hamad Al Thani**
82 B f 23/3 Galileo (IRE)—Arkadina (IRE) (Danehill (USA)) (700000) **Sheikh Joaan Bin Hamad Al Thani**
83 **BEST EXIT (FR)**, b f 9/4 King's Best (USA)—No Exit (FR) (Exit To Nowhere (USA)) (27777) **Mr A. Mouknass**
84 **DAHER SAFRA (FR)**, ch f 15/4 Soldier of Fortune (IRE)—
    Killgra (IRE) (Grand Lodge (USA)) (23809) **Mr A. Mouknass**
85 **HANDASY**, b c 20/3 Hard Spun (USA)—Atayeb (USA) (Rahy (USA)) **Hamdan Al Maktoum**
86 Ch c 5/2 New Approach (IRE)—Hexane (FR) (Kendor (FR)) (75396) **Sheikh Joaan Bin Hamad Al Thani**
87 **JUFOOL (FR)**, b f 13/2 Rail Link—
    Flying Millie (IRE) (Flying Spur (AUS)) (39682) **Sheikh Joaan Bin Hamad Al Thani**
88 **JUFOON**, gr f 5/3 Dubawi (IRE)—Symba's Dream (USA) (Vindication (USA)) (158730) **Hamdan Al Maktoum**
89 **LA GOHANNIERE (FR)**, b f 1/1 Le Havre (IRE)—Landskia (FR) (Lando (GER)) **Mr G. Augustin-Normand**
90 **LAJUMOOD (IRE)**, ch c 3/3 Pivotal—Bahja (USA) (Seeking The Gold (USA)) **Hamdan Al Maktoum**
91 **MAFILLE (FR)**, ch f 14/4 Stormy River (FR)—Mamitador (Anabaa (USA)) (36507) **Mr A. Mouknass**
92 **MITLAA (FR)**, b f 13/3 Naaqoos—Djayapura (FR) (Fabulous Dancer (USA)) (59523) **Hamdan Al Maktoum**
93 **MOOBTY (IRE)**, b c 5/5 Dalakhani (IRE)—Esloob (USA) (Diesis) **Hamdan Al Maktoum**
94 **MU GAMARA**, b f 2/2 Muhtathir—Mooteeah (USA) (Sakhee (USA)) **Hamdan Al Maktoum**
95 **MULAMASA**, br f 11/2 Medicean—Nasheed (USA) (Riverman (USA)) **Hamdan Al Maktoum**
96 **MUNGAMIS**, ch c 19/3 Medicean—Cadenza (FR) (Dansili) **Hamdan Al Maktoum**
97 **PLAISANCIERE (FR)**, ch f 18/1 Astronomer Royal (USA)—Princesse Jasmine (FR) (Gold Away (IRE)) **P. Sabban**
98 **PROPORTION DIVINE (FR)**, b f 11/4 Malinas (GER)—
    Beccaria (USA) (Hold That Tiger (USA)) (8730) **Mr A. Mouknass**
99 **SCALAMBRA**, ch f 15/3 Nayef (USA)—Seal Bay (IRE) (Hernando (FR)) (11904) **Maurice Lagasse**
100 **SIGNS OF BLESSING (IRE)**, b c 25/2 Invincible Spirit (IRE)—
    Sun Bittern (USA) (Seeking The Gold (USA)) (80952) **Pandora Stud LLC**
101 **STOLEN FILLY (FR)**, b f 3/3 Green Tune (USA)—Diamond Laly (Observatory (USA)) (9523) **Mr A. Mouknass**
102 B f 27/2 Street Boss (USA)—Super Nana (FR) (Anabaa (USA)) (71428) **Haras de Saint Pair**
103 B f 1/1 Speightstown (USA)—Torrestrella (IRE) (Orpen (USA)) **Hamdan Al Maktoum**

MR FRANCOIS ROHAUT - Continued

104 B c 29/1 Lawman (FR)—Via Milano (FR) (Singspiel (IRE)) **Haras de Saint Pair**
105 **VODKA REDBULLA (FR),** b f 23/3 Turtle Bowl (IRE)—Melanzane (Arazi (USA)) (11111) **Mr F. Rohaut**
106 B f 8/4 Lawman (FR)—Winning Family (IRE) (Fasliyev (USA)) (67460) **Sheikh Joaan Bin Hamad Al Thani**

Assistant Trainer: G. Lemoigne

546	**MISS JOSIE ROSS, Dalkeith**
	Postal: **Lothian Recycling, Cousland, Dalkeith, Midlothian, EH22 2PJ**

1 **DAVY BOY LEGEND (IRE),** 10, gr g Saint Preuil (FR)—Samarinnda (IRE) **Miss J. M. Ross**
2 **JACK KANE,** 6, ch g Ishiguru (USA)—Armada Grove
3 **LILLY GROVE,** 8, b m Mtoto—Armada Grove
4 **MALGURU,** 9, b g Ishiguru (USA)—Vento Del Oreno (FR)
5 **QUICK GOURMET,** 7, b m Lend A Hand—Rhiann

547	**MR BRIAN ROTHWELL, Malton**
	Postal: **Old Post Office, Oswaldkirk, York, YO62 5XT**
	Contacts: **PHONE (01439) 788859 MOBILE (07969) 968241**
	E-MAIL brian.rothwell1@googlemail.com

1 **BONNIE BURNETT (IRE),** 6, b br m Hawk Wing (USA)—Chameleon **Mrs G. Sparks**
2 **DORRY K (IRE),** 4, b f Ad Valorem (USA)—Ashtaroute (USA)
3 **INIS BEAG (IRE),** 7, b m Heron Island (IRE)—Forest Imp (IRE) **B. S. Rothwell**
4 **MAJESTIC ANGEL (IRE),** 4, b f Majestic Missile (IRE)—Free Angel (USA) **B. S. Rothwell**
5 **PRECENTORS COURT (IRE),** 6, b g Bienamado (USA)—Buck On **Mrs G. Sparks**
6 **QUEEN OF EPIRUS,** 5, ch m Kirkwall—Andromache **J. T. Brown**
7 **ROLEN SLY,** 4, b g Tillerman—Feiticeira (USA) **Mrs June Jackson**
8 **TINSELTOWN,** 7, b g Sadler's Wells (USA)—Peony **Mr A. F. Arnott**
9 6, B m Gold Well—Vulcan Belle **B. S. Rothwell**

THREE-YEAR-OLDS
10 **DOUBLE HAPPINESS,** ch f Sakhee (USA)—Fu Wa (USA) **B. S. Rothwell**

TWO-YEAR-OLDS
11 **TAWAN,** b c 20/3 Tiger Hill (IRE)—Lady Netbetsports (IRE) (In The Wings) **Paul Moorhouse**

Other Owners: Mr B. S. Rothwell, Mr A. J. Sparks.

548	**MR P. J. ROTHWELL, Tinahely**
	Postal: **Fairwood Stables, Tinahely, Co Wicklow, Ireland**
	Contacts: **PHONE (00 353) 402 38663 FAX (00 353) 402 28812 MOBILE (00 353) 8683 15484**
	E-MAIL fairwoodstables@gmail.com WEBSITE www.pjrothwell.com

1 **AMPLE APPEAL (IRE),** 7, b g Craigsteel—Wake Me Gently (IRE) **J. S. O'Neill, Paul H O'Neill**
2 **BALLYBURKE (IRE),** 8, b g Tikkanen (USA)—Moonshee (IRE) **J. P. McManus**
3 **BARNEYS HONOUR (IRE),** 9, b g City Honours (USA)—
Ballyburn Lady (IRE) **Anthony Deegan, E. Joseph Logan, P. J. Rothwell**
4 **CELTIC CAROL (IRE),** 8, b m Milan—Celtic Angel (IRE) **Herewegonow Syndicate**
5 **CURRENT RESESSION (IRE),** 8, b g Jimble (FR)—Victoria Theatre (IRE) **Mrs J. Lambert**
6 **DONT TELL THE BOYS,** 7, gr g Silver Patriarch (IRE)—Deep C Diva (IRE) **Germaines Top Lounge Syndicate**
7 **FAIRWOOD MASSINI (IRE),** 8, b g Dr Massini (IRE)—
Supreme Sirene (IRE) **Thisiswhenthetroublestarts Syndicate**
8 **GLENBANE GENT (IRE),** 10, ch g Anshan—Sparky Mary (IRE) **Mrs M. O'Keeffe**
9 **GROVE DALE (IRE),** 9, b g Dushyantor (USA)—Tramorekaska (IRE) **William John Hamilton**
10 **JACKS ISLAND (IRE),** 10, br g Turtle Island (IRE)—Good Thyne Mary (IRE) **Butlersgrange Racing Syndicate**
11 **JAK DREAM,** 12, ch g Dreams End—Jaki's Roulette **J. Hillard**
12 **LANNIGANS TOWER (IRE),** 8, b g Craigsteel—Delias Fancy (IRE) **G. Berkery**
13 **LUDDSDENENE (IRE),** 8, b g Beneficial—Kilcowan (IRE) **Brian Redmond**
14 **MANGER HANAGMENT (IRE),** 8, br g Heron Island (IRE)—Island Religion (IRE) **Robert Rafferty/S. McAuley**

MR P. J. ROTHWELL - Continued

15 **PACO JACK (IRE)**, 9, b g Soviet Star (USA)—Tocade (IRE) **C. Beirne**
16 **PADDY O DEE**, 8, b g Kasakov—Baladiya **O. Barden**
17 **ROCKERS FIELD (IRE)**, 11, b br g Insatiable (IRE)—Princess Douglas **P. J. Rothwell**
18 **TRUMPH CARD (IRE)**, 9, b g House of Cards—Le Agio **Five O Syndicate**
19 **VARDAS PARTNER (IRE)**, 8, b g Anshan—O Kay Partner (IRE) **Carol Hogan**
20 **VIA MANTUA**, 9, b m Halling (USA)—Isabella Gonzaga **Mrs J. Lambert**

---

549 | **MR J. C. ROUGET, Pau**
Postal: **Chemin de la Foret Bastard, Domaine de l'Aragnon, 64000 Pau, France**
Contacts: **PHONE (0033) 5593 32790 FAX (0033) 5593 32930 MOBILE (0033) 6102 70335**

1 **APHELIE**, 4, b f Street Sense (USA)—Anja (IRE) **Haras d'Etreham**
2 **BABY CROSS**, 4, b c Cape Cross (IRE)—Priere **G. Laboureau**
3 **BAINO ROCK (FR)**, 4, b f Rock of Gibraltar (IRE)—Baino Ridge (FR) **Ecurie I. M. Fares**
4 **CAIRON (IRE)**, 4, br g Clodovil (IRE)—Gold Blended (IRE) **Franklin Finance**
5 **ESPERO (FR)**, 4, gr c Verglas (IRE)—Queen's Conquer **Franklin Finance**
6 **GAILY GAME**, 5, b h Montjeu (IRE)—Gaily Tiara (FR) **Ecurie I. M. Fares**
7 **HECTOMARE (IRE)**, 4, b g Hurricane Run (IRE)—Overruled (IRE) **Franklin Finance**
8 **HIGH STAR (FR)**, 6, ch g High Yield (USA)—Etoile d'or (FR) **Simone Brogi**
9 **KEIRA (FR)**, 4, gr f Turtle Bowl (IRE)—Nazlia (FR) **Bernard Benaych**
10 **LAUGH OUT LOUD**, 4, gr f Clodovil (IRE)—Funny Girl (IRE) **Martin S Schwartz**
11 **MISTER GIBRALTAR (IRE)**, 7, ch g Rock of Gibraltar (IRE)—Carisheba (USA) **Raymond Leca**
12 **OPEN EAGLE (IRE)**, 4, b g Montjeu (IRE)—Princesse de Viane (FR) **D. Treves**
13 **OURI (IRE)**, 4, gr c Dansili—Clodora (FR) **Joel Seche**
14 **PICTURE BOOK (FR)**, 5, b g Kaldounevees (FR)—Tendre Pensee (FR) **Jean-Pierre Rios**
15 **RIVERKAYE (FR)**, 4, b f Orpen (USA)—River Ballade (USA) **Gerard Laboureau**
16 **ROCKY ROULETTE (IRE)**, 4, b f Holy Roman Emperor (IRE)—Allegro Vivace (FR) **J. L. Tepper**
17 **SAN MARTIN**, 6, b g Oasis Dream—Suedoise **Bertrand Belinguier**
18 **SILAS MARNER (FR)**, 6, b h Muhtathir—Street Kendra (FR) **Cuadra Montalban**
19 **SOCRATE (IRE)**, 5, b h Shamardal (USA)—Quest For Ladies **Bertrand Belinguier**
20 **SUNNY (FR)**, 4, b c Muhtathir—Vol Sauvage (FR) **B. Magrez**
21 **SYNDIC (FR)**, 4, b c Sinndar (IRE)—Kalatuna (FR) **A. Caro**
22 **TWO DAYS IN PARIS (FR)**, 4, b f Authorized (IRE)—Isalou (FR) **J. L. Tepper**
23 **YARUBO (FR)**, 5, ch h Muhtathir—Miss Mission (IRE) **A. Caro**

THREE-YEAR-OLDS

24 **AFRICAN WATERS (USA)**, b c Henrythenavigator (USA)—Louve des Reves (IRE) **J. Allen**
25 **AGY (IRE)**, b c Dylan Thomas (IRE)—Diamond Star (IRE) **Franklin Finance**
26 **AKHLAAQ (USA)**, b f Dayjur (USA)—Aljariah (USA) **Hamdan Al Maktoum**
27 **ALMOONQITH (USA)**, b c Dynaformer (USA)—Bohemian Lady (USA) **Hamdan Al Maktoum**
28 **ALTERITE (FR)**, b f Literato (FR)—Ana Luna **M. S. Schwartz**
29 **ANTHARES (FR)**, b g Zamindar (USA)—Spring of Pearls (IRE)
30 **ARSHEEF (USA)**, b f Hard Spun (USA)—Atayeb (USA) **Hamdan Al Maktoum**
31 **BALASHKOVA (FR)**, b f Montjeu (IRE)—Ecume du Jour (FR) **Cuadra Montalban**
32 **BARADARI (IRE)**, b c Manduro (GER)—Behra (FR) **H. H. Aga Khan**
33 **BELLE DE FRANCE (FR)**, ch f Muhtathir—Life On The Road (IRE) **L. Dassault**
34 **BLAST ECHO (IRE)**, ch f Falco (USA)—Breath of Love (USA) **Janus Bloodstock**
35 **BLISSFUL THINKING**, b c Oasis Dream—Sky Wonder **Millenium Horses SRL**
36 **BRIYANAK (FR)**, b c Acclamation—Brofalya (FR) **H. H. Aga Khan**
37 **CAMARETZ (USA)**, ch c Mr Greeley (USA)—Drums of Freedom (USA) **Ecurie Tagada**
38 **CHANCELIER (FR)**, b c Peer Gynt (JPN)—Particuliere **Franklin Finance**
39 **CHEEKY (USA)**, b f Lemon Drop Kid (USA)—Derrianne (USA) **Mousquetaire Investissement**
40 **CHEF CHAUDARD (FR)**, ch c Turtle Bowl (IRE)—Scottish Diva **A. Caro**
41 **CHRYSOS (GER)**, b g Big Shuffle (USA)—Centre Point **Franklin Finance**
42 **COURCY (FR)**, b c Mizzen Mast (USA)—Insan Mala (USA) **Franklin Finance**
43 **CRICKEL WOOD (FR)**, b c Muhtathir—Tanguista (FR) **A. Caro**
44 **DALWARI (USA)**, b c More Than Ready (USA)—Dalmiya (IRE) **H. H. Aga Khan**
45 **ELISHPOUR (IRE)**, b c Oasis Dream—Elbasana (IRE) **H. H. Aga Khan**
46 **ETALONDES (FR)**, b c Royal Applause—Fancy Dance **Franklin Finance**
47 **EVA LUNA (FR)**, ch f Peintre Celebre (USA)—Honorable Love **A. Caro**
48 **FAIZIYA (FR)**, gr f Rock of Gibraltar (IRE)—Fragrancia (FR) **H. H. Aga Khan**
49 **FAUGUERON (FR)**, b c Elusive City (USA)—Shakeyourbody (USA) **Franklin Finance**
50 **FOLIE DOUCE**, b f Tiger Hill (IRE)—Vastanya (USA) **D. Treves**

MR J. C. ROUGET - Continued

51 **GOING IN THE NIGHT (FR)**, b f Archange d'or (IRE)—Wedding Night (FR) **G. Forien**
52 **GOTHAM NEWS (USA)**, ch c Awesome Again (CAN)—Teammate (USA) **J. Allen**
53 **GOTTINGEN (FR)**, b c Holy Roman Emperor (IRE)—Ring Ring (FR) **D. Treves**
54 **GRACIE SQUARE (USA)**, gr f Awesome Again (CAN)—Starry Dreamer (USA) **J. Allen**
55 **GROOVIN HIGH (USA)**, b f Elusive Quality (USA)—Tiz the Hour (USA) **D. Treves**
56 **GUAJARAZ (FR)**, b c Rashbag—Rahyna (USA) **A. Caro**
57 **HIGH SHOES (FR)**, gr g High Chaparral (USA)—Without Shoes (FR) **A. Caro**
58 **JILNAAR (IRE)**, b f Dansili—Cerulean Sky (IRE) **Hamdan Al Maktoum**
59 **KALIMANTAN (IRE)**, b c Azamour (IRE)—Kalamba (IRE) **H. H. Aga Khan**
60 **KHADIMA (FR)**, b f Zamindar (USA)—Khalasha (FR) **H. H. Aga Khan**
61 **KILIMANDJARO (FR)**, b c Elusive City (USA)—Relais d'aumale
62 **LA ROCQUE (FR)**, b f War Chant (USA)—Polysheba (FR) **Franklin Finance**
63 **LAMORLAYE (IRE)**, b f Danehill Dancer (IRE)—Love To Dance (IRE) **Franklin Finance**
64 **LANDING IN HEAVEN (FR)**, b f Lando (GER)—Zalida (IRE) **Jean-Francois Gribomont**
65 **LARAFALE (FR)**, b f Lion Heart (USA)—Dix Huit (USA) **Laurent Dassault**
66 **LIDIYANA (FR)**, gr f Motivator—Laxlova (USA) **H. H. Aga Khan**
67 **LILLEBONNE (FR)**, b f Danehill Dancer (IRE)—Lidana (IRE) **Franklin Finance**
68 **MAUPERTUS**, b c Montjeu (IRE)—Brooklyn Academy (USA) **Franklin Finance**
69 **MEDICAL KISS (FR)**, ch f Medicean—Katelyns Kiss (USA) **Ecurie I. M. Fares**
70 **MONTEILLE (FR)**, b f Oasis Dream—Lady Calido (USA) **Franklin Finance**
71 **MORANDI (FR)**, gr c Holy Roman Emperor (IRE)—Vezina (FR) **D. Treves**
72 **MUTIN (FR)**, b c Kentucky Dynamite (USA)—Mytographie (FR) **Hamdan Al Maktoum**
73 **NERON (FR)**, b c Holy Roman Emperor (IRE)—Armanda (GER) **D. Treves**
74 **NIDINA (IRE)**, b f Hurricane Run (IRE)—Secrete Marina (IRE) **Giovanni Di Falduto**
75 **ORIENTAL WIND, b f Zamindar (USA)—Orion Girl (GER) **Haras des Monceaux**
76 **PANDANA (FR)**, b f Desert Style (IRE)—Pink And Red (USA) **H. H. Aga Khan**
77 **PAPRIFORMER (FR)**, b c Dynaformer (USA)—Louve Royale (IRE) **J. Allen**
78 **PEACE BURG (FR)**, b f Sageburg (IRE)—Peace Talk (FR) **Cuadra Montalban**
79 **POLICEWOMAN (IRE)**, b f Lawman (FR)—Lupa Romana (IRE) **Ecurie I. M. Fares**
80 **PURELY PRICELESS (IRE)**, b f Galileo (IRE)—Peeping Fawn (USA) **Haras d'Etreham**
81 **QUANAH PARKER (FR)**, b c Authorized (IRE)—Marie Laurencin **Haras de Saint Pair**
82 **RIVIERE DU LOUP (USA)**, b c Ghostzapper (USA)—Volga (FR) **J. Allen**
83 **ROSE MEMORY (IRE)**, b f Elusive City (USA)—Rose Melody (IRE) **Haras des Monceaux**
84 **SAINT AGNAN (FR)**, gr c Verglas (IRE)—Scapegrace (IRE) **Franklin Finance**
85 **SAINT CREPIN (FR)**, b c Cape Cross (IRE)—Aldeburgh Music (IRE) **Franklin Finance**
86 **SALAALEM (IRE)**, gr c Slickly (FR)—Macotte (FR) **Hamdan Al Maktoum**
87 **SALUBERLIN (FR)**, b g Layman (USA)—Sohaila (GER)
88 **SANGO (IRE)**, gr c Dalakhani (IRE)—Home You Stroll (IRE) **Jean-Claude Weill**
89 **SEFRI (USA)**, b g Jazil (USA)—Taseel (USA) **Hamdan Al Maktoum**
90 **SHENLIYKA (FR)**, b f Danehill Dancer (IRE)—Shemissa (IRE) **H. H. Aga Khan**
91 **SIAN KAAN (FR)**, ch c Literato (FR)—Birdy Namnam (USA) **Franklin Finance**
92 **SILKA GLAZ (FR)**, gr f Literato (FR)—Super Crusty (IRE) **Pierre Beziat**
93 **SNAP CALL**, ch c Tamayuz—Sister Agnes (IRE) **D. Treves**
94 **SOUL SACRIFICE**, ch c Indian Haven—Dream Dance (USA) **D. Treves**
95 **SPOONFUL (FR)**, b c Della Francesca (USA)—Magic Date (FR) **Bertrand Belinguier**
96 **STAR PRINCE (FR)**, b c Green Tune (USA)—Princess Love (FR) **A. Caro**
97 **TABAAYUN (IRE)**, b c Nayef (USA)—Garden City (FR) **Hamdan Al Maktoum**
98 **TABLE RONDE (IRE)**, br f Astronomer Royal (USA)—Tanzania (IRE) **Eric Puerari**
99 **TAKARIYZA (FR)**, b f Anabaa (USA)—Takaniya (IRE) **H. H. Aga Khan**
100 **TASHINI (FR)**, gr c Dylan Thomas (IRE)—Tashiriya (FR) **H. H. Aga Khan**
101 **THE BROTHERS WAR (USA)**, b c War Front (USA)—Moon Queen (IRE) **J. Allen**
102 **VAREGA (FR)**, b f Danehill Dancer (IRE)—Mimalia (USA) **Jean-Claude Weill**
103 **VAUNOISE (IRE)**, b f Teofilo (IRE)—Tipperary Honor (FR) **Franklin Finance**
104 **VILLEQUIER (FR)**, b c Footstepsinthesand—Interior (USA) **Franklin Finance**
105 **VISOMIYA (FR)**, gr f Rock of Gibraltar (IRE)—Visorama (IRE) **H. H. Aga Khan**
106 **WAR CORRESPONDENT (FR)**, b c War Front (USA)—Tempo West (USA) **J. Allen**
107 **WEDGE TRUST (IRE)**, ch f Zamindar (USA)—Wedge (USA) **Ecurie I. M. Fares**
108 **WIGHT IS WIGHT (IRE)**, b c Peintre Celebre (USA)—Alenteja (IRE) **D. Treves**
109 **WILD HORSE (IRE)**, b c Kheleyf (USA)—Life Rely (USA) **D. Treves**
110 **WIRE TO WIRE (FR)**, b c Observatory (USA)—Sachet (USA) **Ecurie I. M. Fares**
111 **WUNDERBAR (GER)**, b c Silvano (GER)—Wonderful World (GER) **Franklin Finance**
112 **ZAFARANI (FR)**, b c Cape Cross (IRE)—Zalafira (FR) **H. H. Aga Khan**

MR J. C. ROUGET - Continued

TWO-YEAR-OLDS

113 AFTER MATH (FR), b c 17/1 Sunday Break (JPN)—Ducere (IRE) (Lando (GER)) (22222)
114 Ch f 16/4 Sunday Break (JPN)—Algoa (FR) (Common Grounds) (38095) **J-C Weill**
115 B f 13/2 Le Havre (IRE)—Alyousufeya (IRE) (Kingmambo (USA)) (22222) **Franklin Finance**
116 ANAHITA (FR), b f 18/2 Turtle Bowl (IRE)—Nazlia (FR) (Polish Precedent (USA)) (33333)
117 ANNALULU (IRE), b f 30/1 Hurricane Run (IRE)—Louve de Saron (FR) (Loup Solitaire (USA)) (23809)
118 APUS (FR), b f 2/2 Kentucky Dynamite (USA)—Teatime (FR) (Loup Solitaire (USA)) (19841) **Haras de Saubouas**
119 AR POULGWENN (IRE), b c 5/4 Nayef (USA)—Ballerina Blue (IRE) (High Chaparral (USA)) (39682) **J. Seche**
120 AREOS (USA), b br c 1/2 Henrythenavigator (USA)—Momix (Selkirk (USA)) (25000)
121 B f 1/2 Elusive City (USA)—Artistica (IRE) (Spectrum (IRE)) **H. H. Aga Khan**
122 B c 24/3 Sinndar (IRE)—Ashalina (FR) (Linamix (FR)) **H. H. Aga Khan**
123 AVALON SUNSET (FR), b c 12/4 Orpen (USA)—Top Over (IRE) (One Cool Cat (USA)) (13492) **D. Treves**
124 AVENIR CERTAIN (FR), b f 30/4 Le Havre (IRE)—Puggy (FR) (Mark of Esteem (IRE)) (35714) **A. Caro**
125 B c 4/4 Soldier of Fortune (USA)—Back The Winner (IRE) (Entrepreneur) (37301)
126 BAINO HOPE (FR), b f 28/2 Jeremy (USA)—Baino Ridge (FR) (Highest Honor (USA)) **Ecurie I. M. Fares**
127 BATTLEFRONT (USA), b c 1/1 War Front (USA)—Baroness Richter (IRE) (Montjeu (IRE)) **J. Allen**
128 BEAUTY PARLOR (USA), b f 1/1 Elusive Quality (USA)—Moon Queen (IRE) (Sadler's Wells (USA)) **J. Allen**
129 BRIGHT SMILE (FR), b f 22/2 Elusive City (USA)—Bright Style (FR) (Fasliyev (USA)) (33333)
130 BRIONES (FR), gr f 26/4 Green Tune (USA)—Golden Glare (FR) (Verglas (IRE)) **M. S. Schwartz**
131 B c 10/2 Sinndar (IRE)—Caribena (FR) (Linamix (FR)) **H. H. Aga Khan**
132 CASTING IN PARIS (FR), b c 24/3 Lawman (FR)—Last Cast (FR) (Marju (IRE)) (27777) **J. L. Tepper**
133 CHORISTE (FR), b c 26/4 Panis (USA)—Luna Jolie (FR) (Septieme Ciel (USA))
134 B f 1/3 Zamindar (USA)—Clodovina (IRE) (Rock of Gibraltar (IRE)) **H. H. Aga Khan**
135 B f 8/4 Oasis Dream—Coquerelle (IRE) (Zamindar (USA)) **Haras des Monceaux**
136 CRISOLLES (FR), b f 22/2 Le Havre (IRE)—Sandsnow (IRE) (Verglas (IRE)) **Franklin Finance**
137 B c 28/1 Elusive City (USA)—Diasilixa (FR) (Linamix (FR)) **H. H. Aga Khan**
138 DNIEPER (USA), b c 1/1 Giant's Causeway (USA)—Volga (IRE) (Caerleon (USA)) **J. Allen**
139 ELUSIVE KAY (FR), b f 14/4 Elusive City (USA)—Lunashkaya (Muhtathir)
140 B f 4/4 Nayef (USA)—Elva (IRE) (King's Best (USA)) **H. H. Aga Khan**
141 EN CONFIANCE (FR), b f 19/2 Selkirk (USA)—Ommadawn (IRE) (Montjeu (IRE)) (31000)
142 FLAMBOYANT (FR), b c 18/2 Peer Gynt (JPN)—Relicia Bere (FR) (Until Sundown (USA)) (22222)
143 FLAVIN (FR), ch c 23/3 Pomellato (GER)—Some Other Spring (FR) (Majorien) **G. Laboureau**
144 FOURDRINIER (FR), b c 8/4 Dynaformer (USA)—Grande Melody (IRE) (Grand Lodge (USA)) **J. Allen**
145 FRIARDEL (FR), ch c 18/3 Le Havre (IRE)—Fancy Dance (Rainbow Quest (USA)) **J. Allen**
146 GLADSTONE (FR), b c 22/3 Mizzen Mast (USA)—Bahia Gold (Woodman (USA)) (25396) **D. Treves**
147 GONNA RUN (FR), b c 27/2 Hurricane Cat (USA)—Realdad (ARG) (Victory Speech (USA)) (39682) **D. Treves**
148 GRACE OF LOVE (IRE), b f 11/1 Lawman (FR)—Rampaldina (Montjeu (IRE)) (22222) **P. Augier**
149 Ch c 27/1 Pivotal—Grenadia (USA) (Thunder Gulch (USA)) **Janus Bloodstock**
150 HAWAAJIB (FR), b f 13/3 Elusive City (USA)—

    Marie Laurencin (Peintre Celebre (USA)) (119047) **Hamdan Al Maktoum**
151 HONEYMOON COCKTAIL (FR), gr c 1/1 Martaline—Caipirinia (FR) (Hawk Wing (USA)) (31746) **D. Treves**
152 IKER CHOP (FR), b c 7/2 Soave (GER)—Moon Serenade (Key of Luck (USA)) **G. Laboureau**
153 B c 16/3 Green Tune (USA)—Ishi Adiva (Ishiguru (USA)) (24603) **G. Laboureau**
154 JALLY (IRE), ch c 13/3 Tamayuz—Miss Beatrix (IRE) (Danehill Dancer (IRE)) (63491) **Hamdan Al Maktoum**
155 KAIA (FR), b f 29/3 Deportivo—Kadance Blue (FR) (Anabaa Blue) **D. Treves**
156 B f 15/3 Acclamation—Kerasha (FR) (Daylami (IRE)) **H. H. Aga Khan**
157 KIFAAH (FR), b c 17/4 Dubawi (IRE)—Mokaraba (Unfuwain (USA)) **Hamdan Al Maktoum**
158 B c 12/4 Elusive City (USA)—King Luna (FR) (King's Best (USA)) **H. H. Aga Khan**
159 KOLIAKHOVA (FR), b f 19/2 Literato (FR)—Lia Waltz (FR) (Linamix (FR))
160 L'ARDENT (FR), b c 16/5 Soldier of Fortune (USA)—Princesse de Viane (FR) (Kaldoun (FR)) (63492) **B. Magrez**
161 LA HOGUETTE (FR), b f 17/4 Le Havre (IRE)—Isanous (FR) (Zamindar (USA)) **Franklin Finance**
162 LA TEMPERANTE (IRE), gr f 15/4 Naaqoos—Magical Hawk (USA) (Silver Hawk (USA)) (59523) **B. Magrez**
163 LAUNETTE (FR), b c 9/3 Le Havre (IRE)—Langrune (IRE) (Fasliyev (USA)) **Franklin Finance**
164 B c 8/4 Zamindar (USA)—Laxlova (FR) (Linamix (FR)) **H. H. Aga Khan**
165 LAYOS (IRE), gr c 4/3 Verglas (IRE)—Towanda (USA) (Dynaformer (USA)) (15873) **A. Caro**
166 LE SCRIBE (FR), b c 25/3 Orpen (USA)—Rhodagna (IRE) (Mark of Esteem (IRE)) (17460) **Joel Seche**
167 LEGAZPI (IRE), ch c 23/4 Mastercraftsman (IRE)—Japan (GER) (Key Royal (IRE)) (30158) **A. Caro**
168 LESSTALK IN PARIS (IRE), b f 11/2 Cape Cross (IRE)—Top Toss (IRE) (Linamix (FR)) (99206) **J. L. Tepper**
169 LIDNER (FR), b c 5/4 Pastoral Pursuits—Picolette (Piccolo) (35000) **Mr D. Treves**
170 LOVE STRIKE (IRE), b c 24/4 Zamindar (USA)—Sculpted (FR) (Orpen (USA)) (5555)
171 B f 25/4 Walk In The Park (IRE)—Lucena (FR) (Marathon (USA)) **G. Laboureau**
172 MAJRAA (FR), b f 15/2 Invincible Spirit (IRE)—

    Santa Louisia (Highest Honor (FR)) (134920) **Hamdan Al Maktoum**
173 MARSOUD (USA), b br c 6/3 Dixie Union (USA)—

    Paris Rose (USA) (Accelerator (USA)) (141321) **Hamdan Al Maktoum**

MR J. C. ROUGET - Continued

174 Ch f 16/2 Dutch Art—Masakala (IRE) (Cadeaux Genereux) (17460) **G. Laboureau**
175 **MEANS OF ASSENT (FR),** b f 25/2 Empire Maker (USA)—Louve des Reves (IRE) (Sadler's Wells (USA)) **J. Allen**
176 **MUSAADAQA (IRE),** b f 25/2 Tamayuz—Million Waves (IRE) (Mull of Kintyre (USA)) **Hamdan Al Maktoum**
177 **PAN DI STELLE (FR),** b f 8/4 Panis (USA)—Orion Queen (FR) (Speedmaster (GER)) (17460)
178 **PASSION BLANCHE,** b f 20/3 Dutch Art—Siren Sound (Singspiel (IRE)) (30000) **B. Magrez**
179 B c 21/4 Mybycharlie (IRE)—Phone the Diva (USA) (Phone Trick (USA)) (51587) **D. Treves**
180 **PINKAS,** b c 12/4 Dutch Art—Peachy Pear (Mark of Esteem (IRE)) (24000) **D. Treves**
181 **PURPLE GRAPES (FR),** b c 6/4 Orpen (USA)—Purple Prose (GER) (Law Society (USA)) (9523) **Phillipe Augier**
182 **RANEK (IRE),** ch c 3/4 Medicean—Spirit of South (AUS) (Giant's Causeway (USA)) (71428) **D. Treves**
183 **RUN IN PARIS (IRE),** b f 29/3 Hurricane Run (IRE)—Epistole (IRE) (Alzao (USA)) (31746) **D. Treves**
184 **SAANE (FR),** b c 27/3 Le Havre (IRE)—Salamon (Montjeu (IRE)) **Franklin Finance**
185 **SAINT GREGOIRE (FR),** b c 29/3 Le Havre (IRE)—Scapegrace (IRE) (Cape Cross (IRE)) **Franklin Finance**
186 **SAINT POIS (FR),** b c 14/3 Le Havre (IRE)—Our Dream Queen (Oasis Dream) **Franklin Finance**
187 **SALAI (FR),** b c 26/3 Mybycharlie (IRE)—Mabadi (USA) (Sahm (USA)) (43650)
188 **SANABOWL (FR),** b c 8/5 Turtle Bowl (FR)—Sanagora (IRE) (Mujadil (USA)) (38095) **D. Treves**
189 **SANTE CROIX (FR),** b f 21/2 Le Havre (IRE)—Sainte Adresse (Elusive City (USA)) **Franklin Finance**
190 Ch f 15/4 Creachadoir (IRE)—Save Me The Waltz (FR) (Halling (USA)) (33333) **J. F. Gribomont**
191 B c 4/4 Alhaarth (IRE)—Serasana (Red Ransom (USA)) **H. H. Aga Khan**
192 **SEUL ARTISTE (FR),** b c 2/5 Artiste Royal (FR)—Pas Seule (FR) (Iron Mask (USA)) (19841) **A. Caro**
193 B f 7/4 Turtle Bowl (FR)—Sky Spark (USA) (Septieme Ciel (USA)) **G. Laboureau**
194 **SPEED ROAD (FR),** ch c 10/4 King's Best (USA)—
   Life On The Road (IRE) (Persian Heights) (39682) **Laurent Dassault**
195 **STEP AND GO (IRE),** b c 29/1 Footstepsinthesand—Fresh Laurels (IRE) (Rock of Gibraltar (IRE)) (42857)
196 **STONE ME (FR),** ch f 9/4 Muhaymin (USA)—Jennhill (FR) (Sabrehill (USA)) **D. Treves**
197 **TALIE (FR),** ch f 24/3 Medicean—Sister Agnes (IRE) (Dr Fong (USA)) (15873) **D. Treves**
198 **TCHEKOV (FR),** b c 2/3 King's Best (USA)—From This Day On (USA) (El Prado (IRE))
199 **TEEN ANGEL (USA),** ch f 1/1 Smart Strike (CAN)—Wonder Woman (USA) (Storm Cat (USA)) **J. Allen**
200 B c 11/5 Slickly (FR)—Tossup (USA) (Gone West (USA)) (30158)
201 **TRIPTYKA (IRE),** br gr f 28/3 Mastercraftsman (IRE)—Acatama (USA) (Efisio) (17460)
202 B f 2/2 Dansili—Visorama (IRE) (Linamix (FR)) **H. H. Aga Khan**
203 **VITA (FR),** gr f 12/3 Elusive City (USA)—Vezina (FR) (Bering) (51587) **D. Treves**
204 **VOLKOVKHA,** b f 15/4 Holy Roman Emperor (IRE)—Armanda (GER) (Acatenango (GER)) (39682)
205 **WAKINA LUTA (IRE),** b f 9/5 King's Best (USA)—Top Crystal (IRE) (Sadler's Wells (USA)) (11904)
206 **WAR EFFORT (USA),** b f 3/5 War Front (USA)—Louve Royale (IRE) (Peintre Celebre (USA)) **J. Allen**
207 **WIRELESS (FR),** ch c 30/4 Kentucky Dynamite (USA)—Sachet (USA) (Royal Academy (USA)) **I. M. Fares**
208 **YOLA (FR),** b c 7/4 Vespone (IRE)—Mille Etoiles (USA) (Malibu Moon (USA)) (11904) **A. Caro**
209 **ZABROV (IRE),** b c 3/5 Mastercraftsman (IRE)—Fine And Mellow (FR) (Lando (GER)) (39682) **Cuadra Montalban**
210 **ZVAROV (IRE),** b c 21/2 Elusive City (USA)—Marie Rossa (Testa Rossa (AUS)) (55555) **Cuadra Montalban**

Assistant Trainers: Jean Bernard Roth, Jean Rene Dubosq, Simone Brogi

Jockey (flat): Christophe Soumillon, Jean-Bernard Eyquem, Thomas Henderson, Ioritz Mendizabal. **Apprentice:** Jefferson Smith, Sofiane Saadi

---

550 | **MR RICHARD ROWE, Pulborough**
Postal: **Ashleigh House Stables, Sullington Lane, Storrington, Pulborough, West Sussex, RH20 4AE**
Contacts: **PHONE (01903) 742871 MOBILE (07831) 345636**
E-MAIL r.rowe.racing@virgin.net WEBSITE www.richardrowe-racing.co.uk

1 **ALTERANTHELA (IRE),** 9, br g Alderbrook—Anthela (GER) **T. L. Clowes**
2 **AMIRICO (IRE),** 8, b g Lord Americo—Maori's Delight **Mr A. D. Didlick**
3 **ARCHELAO (IRE),** 5, br g Cape Cross (IRE)—Brindisi **Miss V. J. Baalham**
4 **BENNELONG,** 7, b g Bahamian Bounty—Bundle Up (USA) **Miss V. J. Baalham**
5 **BURNBRAKE,** 8, b g Mujahid (USA)—Duena **B. H. Page**
6 **COLLYNS AVENUE,** 10, ch g Bal Harbour—Flower of Dunblane **Mr S. J. McDougall**
7 **CURRENT CLIMATE (IRE),** 9, b g Luso—Kambaya (IRE) **The Encore Partnership IV**
8 **FATHER ARTHUR,** 5, gr g Silver Patriarch (IRE)—Amber Starlight **Winterfields Farm Ltd**
9 **GRACE AND FORTUNE,** 6, b m Grape Tree Road—Nouveau Cheval **Fortune Racing**
10 **HALF COCKED,** 11, b g Double Trigger (IRE)—Half Asleep **Richard Rowe Racing Partnership**
11 **I NO UNDERSTAND (IRE),** 7, b g Overbury (IRE)—Falika (FR) **Richard Rowe Racing Partnership**
12 **LEGAL LEGACY,** 7, ch g Beat Hollow—Dan's Delight **Miss V. J. Baalham**
13 **MARBLE WALK (IRE),** 8, b g Oscar (IRE)—Clowater Lassie (IRE) **Winterfields Farm Ltd**
14 **MUNSARIM (IRE),** 6, b g Shamardal (USA)—Etizaaz (USA) **Miss V. J. Baalham**
15 **PASTORAL JET,** 5, b br h Pastoral Pursuits—Genteel (IRE) **Mr A. J. Taylor**

MR RICHARD ROWE - Continued

16 **TANG ROYAL (FR)**, 6, ch g Epalo (GER)—Bea de Forme (FR) **R. Rowe**
17 **TATANIANO (FR)**, 9, b g Sassanian (USA)—Rosa Carola (FR) **The Stewart Family**
18 **TATENEN (FR)**, 9, b g Lost World (IRE)—Tamaziya (IRE) **The Stewart Family**
19 **THE BISHOPS BABY (IRE)**, 10, b m Bishop of Cashel—Mystical Treat (IRE) **Richard Rowe Racing Partnership**
20 **WATERGATE (FR)**, 7, gr g Verglas (IRE)—Moy Water (IRE) **The Stewart Family**
21 **WHATAGOA (IRE)**, 6, b m Bishop of Cashel—Gotta Goa (IRE) **Richard Rowe Racing Partnership**

Other Owners: Mr R. Rowe, M. W. Barber, A. Blades, Mr D. M. Bradshaw, Mrs H. C. G. Butcher, Mr N. S. Campbell, M. D. P. Fortune, Miss L. Gemmell, Mrs F. M. Gordon, Lady Neville, Capt A. Pratt, Mr A. Stewart, Mrs J. A. Stewart, T. W. Wellard.

---

551 **MISS MANDY ROWLAND, Lower Blidworth**
Postal: Kirkfields, Calverton Road, Lower Blidworth, Nottingham, Nottinghamshire, NG21 0NW
Contacts: PHONE (01623) 794831 MOBILE (07768) 224666
E-MAIL kirkfieldsriding@hotmail.co.uk

1 **ANNIES IDEA**, 4, ch f Yoshka—Danum Diva (IRE) **Miss M. E. Rowland**
2 **FOOLS CREST**, 4, b g Generous (IRE)—Watercress **Miss M. E. Rowland**
3 **HIGHLAND BRAVE (IRE)**, 7, b g High Chaparral (IRE)—Princessa (GER) **Miss M. E. Rowland**
4 **MISS CHARDONAY**, 6, b m Helissio (FR)—Up The Creek (IRE) **Miss M. E. Rowland**
5 **MR CHOCOLATE DROP (IRE)**, 9, b g Danetime (IRE)—Forest Blade (IRE) **Miss M. E. Rowland**
6 **ROXY MADAM**, 4, br f Generous (IRE)—Masouri Sana (IRE) **Miss M. E. Rowland**
7 **SKY DIAMOND (IRE)**, 5, b g Diamond Green (FR)—Jewell In The Sky (IRE) **Miss M. E. Rowland**

THREE-YEAR-OLDS

8 **SARAHS PAL**, b f No Time (IRE)—Danum Diva (IRE) **Miss M. E. Rowland**
9 **UNTIL IT SLEEPS**, b f Sleeping Indian—Cape Dancer (IRE) **Miss M. E. Rowland**

Assistant Trainer: Sarah Mitchel

Jockey (flat): Adam Kirby, Jimmy Quinn. **Jockey (NH):** Adam Pogson. **Apprentice:** Nathan Alison.

---

552 **MR A. DE ROYER-DUPRE, Chantilly**
Postal: 3 Chemin des Aigles, 60500 Chantilly, France
Contacts: PHONE (0033) 34458 0303 FAX (0033) 34457 3538 MOBILE (0033) 6702 32901
E-MAIL de-royer-dupre@wanadoo.fr

1 **ALMALYK (FR)**, 4, gr g Oratorio (IRE)—Alnamara (FR) **H. H. Aga Khan**
2 **BARAAN (FR)**, 5, gr g Dalakhani (IRE)—Brusca (USA) **H. H. Aga Khan**
3 **BAYRIR (FR)**, 4, b c Medicean—Balankiya (IRE)
4 **BRICMATE (IRE)**, 4, b c Montjeu (IRE)—Spirit of South (AUS) **Finn Blichfeldt**
5 **CATERINA DE MEDICI (FR)**, 4, b f Redoute's Choice (AUS)—Night Dhu **Peter Maher**
6 **FAIRLY FAIR (FR)**, 4, gr f Sinndar (IRE)—Fairly Grey (FR) **SCEA Haras de Saint Pair**
7 **FATE (FR)**, 4, b f Teofilo (IRE)—Specificity (USA) **Salinity Stables**
8 **GIOFRA**, 5, b m Dansili—Gracefully (IRE) **Haras De La Perelle**
9 **I'M YOUR MAN (FR)**, 4, b br c Cape Cross (IRE)—Via Saleria (IRE) **Salinity Stables**
10 **LAGO MINTO**, 4, ch g Galileo (IRE)—Maroussie (FR) **Mise de Moratalla**
11 **LIL'WING (IRE)**, 4, b f Galileo (IRE)—Louve (USA) **Ecurie Wildenstein**
12 **MANDOUR (USA)**, 4, ch c Smart Strike (CAN)—Mandesha (FR) **Princess Z. P. Aga Khan**
13 **NOW'S THE TIME (IRE)**, 4, b g Dansili—Pride (GER) **Salinity Stables**
14 **PIRACICABA (IRE)**, 4, b f Dansili—Montaria (GER) **Julio Gerin Almeida Camargo**
15 **PLEINE FORME (USA)**, 5, b br m Grand Slam (USA)—Why Worry (FR) **Salinity Stables**
16 **SANO DI PIETRO**, 5, gr g Dalakhani (IRE)—Special Delivery (IRE) **Ecurie Wildenstein**
17 **SARKIYLA (IRE)**, 4, b f Oasis Dream—Sarlisa (FR) **S. A. Aga Khan**
18 **SHARETA (IRE)**, 5, b br m Sinndar (IRE)—Shawara (IRE) **S. A. Aga Khan**
19 **SINDAJAN (IRE)**, 8, b h Medicean—Sinndiya (IRE) **S. A. Aga Khan**
20 **STARLET'S SISTER (IRE)**, 4, ch f Galileo (IRE)—Premiere Creation (FR) **William J. Preston**
21 **VALIYR (IRE)**, 5, b g Alhaarth (IRE)—Valima (FR) **H. H. Aga Khan**
22 **VEREMA (FR)**, 4, b f Barathea (IRE)—Vermentina (USA) **S. A. Aga Khan**
23 **ZELAMAR (FR)**, 4, b g Zamindar (USA)—Zewara (IRE) **S. A. Aga Khan**

MR A. DE ROYER-DUPRE - Continued

THREE-YEAR-OLDS

24 **ANIYSA (FR)**, gr f Dalakhani (IRE)—Alnamara (FR) **H. H. Aga Khan**
25 **ANTICIPATION (FR)**, ch f Muhtathir—Specificity (USA) **Salinity Stables**
26 **ARBELAN (FR)**, b c Montjeu (IRE)—Artistique (IRE) **H. H. Aga Khan**
27 **ARCH DUCHESS (FR)**, b f Arch (USA)—Jacira (FR) **Mme Magalen Bryant**
28 **ARGANNZA (FR)**, b f Sinndar (IRE)—Artistica (IRE) **H. H. Aga Khan**
29 **ASHJAR (FR)**, b c Oasis Dream—Asharna (IRE) **S. A. Aga Khan**
30 **ASHKA (FR)**, b f Tiger Hill (IRE)—Ashalina (FR) **H. H. Aga Khan**
31 **ASKANIA NOVA (IRE)**, ch f New Approach (IRE)—Bal de La Rose (IRE) **Viktor Timoshenko**
32 **BALANKIYLA (FR)**, b f Montjeu (IRE)—Balankiya (IRE) **S. A. Aga Khan**
33 **BASIRA (FR)**, b f Azamour (IRE)—Behkara (FR) **S. A. Aga Khan**
34 **BELLA QATARA (IRE)**, b f Dansili—Alexandrova (IRE) **H. H. Cheik Mohammed bin Khalifa**
35 **BERRIYMA (FR)**, b f Authorized (IRE)—Bernimixa (FR) **H. H. Aga Khan**
36 **CAMINIYA (FR)**, b f Sinndar (IRE)—Clodovina (IRE) **H. H. Aga Khan**
37 **CHERANA (FR)**, b f Sinndar (IRE)—Cherryxma (FR) **H. H. Aga Khan**
38 **CHICQUITA (IRE)**, b f Montjeu (IRE)—Prudenzia (IRE) **Paul Makin**
39 **DAANA QATAR**, b f Galileo (IRE)—Evita **H. H. Cheik Mohammed bin Khalifa**
40 **DALAYNA (FR)**, b f Anabaa (USA)—Daltaiyma (IRE) **S. A. Aga Khan**
41 **DALDENA (IRE)**, b f Anabaa (USA)—Daltama (IRE) **S. A. Aga Khan**
42 **DALILAR (USA)**, b br c Dynaformer (USA)—Daltaya (FR) **S. A. Aga Khan**
43 **DANOYA (FR)**, ch f Raven's Pass (USA)—Damoiselle (USA) **Haras De La Perelle**
44 **DANSILITO**, b c Dansili—Caesarine (FR) **Mme Chantal Sanglier**
45 **DARDAWAN (FR)**, gr g Anabaa (USA)—Dardania (IRE) **S. A. Aga Khan**
46 **DARYSINA (USA)**, b f Smart Strike (CAN)—Daryaba (FR) **S. A. Aga Khan**
47 **DAWALAN (FR)**, b c Azamour (IRE)—Daltawa (IRE) **S. A. Aga Khan**
48 **DERCIA (FR)**, b f Raven's Pass (USA)—Diamond Tango (FR) **H. H. Aga Khan**
49 **DOUTZEN (IRE)**, b f Shirocco (GER)—Dacca **Mme Sandra Debernardi**
50 **EBIYZA (IRE)**, ch f Rock of Gibraltar (IRE)—Ebalista (IRE) **S. A. Aga Khan**
51 **FARZAD (FR)**, b c Dansili—Fraloga (IRE) **H. H. Aga Khan**
52 **GALATEIA (IRE)**, b f Dansili—Gagnoa (IRE) **Ecurie Wildenstein**
53 **GHAZALI (FR)**, ch c Dalakhani (IRE)—Grand Vadla (FR) **H. H. Aga Khan**
54 **GYRELLA (IRE)**, b f Oasis Dream—Ysoldina (FR) **Mme Gilles Forien**
55 **HANDANA (IRE)**, b f Desert Style (IRE)—Handaza (IRE) **S. A. Aga Khan**
56 **HIDDEN COVE (IRE)**, b f Nayef (USA)—Pas d'heure (IRE) **Mise de Moratalla**
57 **INANYA (IRE)**, gr f Sinndar (IRE)—Windya (IRE) **H. H. Aga Khan**
58 **IPSWICH (IRE)**, ch f Danehill Dancer (IRE)—Imperial Beauty (USA) **Ecurie Wildenstein**
59 **JAMBOREE (IRE)**, b f Peintre Celebre (USA)—Logjam (IRE) **William J. Preston**
60 **JONA (FR)**, ch f Dylan Thomas (IRE)—Jade Jewel (USA) **Haras De La Perelle**
61 **KADESHA (FR)**, b f Azamour (IRE)—Kadiana (IRE) **S. A. Aga Khan**
62 **KARKIYRA (FR)**, b f Cape Cross (IRE)—Karkiyla (IRE) **S. A. Aga Khan**
63 **KING OF ENGLAND (IRE)**, ch c Galileo (IRE)—Royal Highness (GER) **Waratah Thoroughbreds Pty Ltd**
64 **LA ROQUETTE (IRE)**, ch f Dylan Thomas (IRE)—She Is Zen (FR) **Malcolm Parrish**
65 **LORALAI (FR)**, b f High Chaparral (IRE)—Luna Gulch (FR) **H. H. Aga Khan**
66 **LUNE ORIENTALE (FR)**, b f Dalakhani (IRE)—Lune d'or (FR) **Ecurie Wildenstein**
67 **MANNDAWI (FR)**, gr c Dalakhani (IRE)—Mintly Fresh (USA) **H. H. Aga Khan**
68 **MARYEF**, br gr f Nayef (USA)—Martines (FR) **Zaro Srl**
69 **MASIYANN (FR)**, b c Anabaa (USA)—Marasima (FR) **S. A. Aga Khan**
70 **MILA (FR)**, b f Cape Cross (IRE)—Minatlya (FR) **H. H. Aga Khan**
71 **MODERN EAGLE (GER)**, b f Montjeu (IRE)—Millionaia (IRE) **Ecurie Wildenstein**
72 **NARNIYN (IRE)**, b f Dubawi (IRE)—Narmina (IRE) **S. A. Aga Khan**
73 **OTTIMA (FR)**, gr f Dalakhani (IRE)—Attima **SCEA Haras de Saint Pair**
74 **PIONEER GIRL (IRE)**, b f Anabaa (USA)—Porlezza (FR) **Ecurie Wildenstein**
75 **PORTLAND RIVER (FR)**, b f Stormy River (FR)—Porza (FR) **Ecurie Wildenstein**
76 **RAYAK (IRE)**, b c Invincible Spirit (IRE)—Rayyana (IRE) **S. A. Aga Khan**
77 **ROSASPERA (IRE)**, b f Azamour (IRE)—Rose Story (FR) **Edoardo Balbo di Vinadio**
78 **RUSTAMABAD (FR)**, ch c Dylan Thomas (IRE)—Rosawa (FR) **H. H. Aga Khan**
79 **SAGHANIYA (IRE)**, b f Rock of Gibraltar (IRE)—Saga d'ouilly (FR) **H. H. Aga Khan**
80 **SALADINE (IRE)**, b f Dalakhani (IRE)—Delicieuse Lady **Ecurie Serval**
81 **SELINA (FR)**, gr f Samum (GER)—Saudade (GER) **Haras De La Perelle**
82 **SHALIANZI (IRE)**, b c Azamour (IRE)—Shalama (IRE) **S. A. Aga Khan**
83 **SHAMARINA (FR)**, b f Dalakhani (IRE)—Shamalana (IRE) **S. A. Aga Khan**
84 **SHAZOUD (FR)**, b c Manduro (GER)—Shamdara (IRE) **S. A. Aga Khan**
85 **SHEHILA (IRE)**, b f Zamindar (USA)—Shehira (FR) **S. A. Aga Khan**
86 **SHIKARPOUR (IRE)**, ch c Dr Fong (USA)—Shibina (IRE) **S. A. Aga Khan**
87 **SINDARIYA (IRE)**, b f Azamour (IRE)—Sinndiya (IRE) **S. A. Aga Khan**

MR A. DE ROYER-DUPRE - Continued

88 **SIYENICA (FR)**, b f Azamour (IRE)—Sichilla (IRE) **H. H. Aga Khan**
89 **VADAIYMA (FR)**, b f Dansili—Vadawina (IRE) **H. H. Aga Khan**
90 **VADAPOUR (FR)**, b c Cape Cross (IRE)—Vadapolina (FR) **H. H. Aga Khan**
91 **VALIRANN (FR)**, b c Nayef (USA)—Valima (FR) **H. H. Aga Khan**
92 **VAYAKHAN (FR)**, b c Dalakhani (IRE)—Vadaza (FR) **H. H. Aga Khan**
93 **VISIYANI (FR)**, gr c Rock of Gibraltar (IRE)—Visionnaire (FR) **H. H. Aga Khan**
94 **VISIYNA (FR)**, b f Manduro (GER)—Visanilla (FR) **H. H. Aga Khan**
95 **ZAFERI (IRE)**, b c Raven's Pass (USA)—Zafaraniya (FR) **S. A. Aga Khan**
96 **ZARDAKA (IRE)**, b f Zamindar (USA)—Zarafsha (FR) **S. A. Aga Khan**
97 **ZAYAM (FR)**, b c Shamardal (USA)—Zayanida (IRE) **S. A. Aga Khan**
98 **ZERDABI (FR)**, b c Tiger Hill (GER)—Zewara (IRE) **S. A. Aga Khan**

TWO-YEAR-OLDS

99 B c 1/4 Sinndar (IRE)—Ashalanda (FR) (Linamix (FR)) **H. H. Aga Khan**
100 **BARENIA (FR)**, b f 2/2 Zamindar (USA)—
　　　　　　　Bargouzine (USA) (Stravinsky (USA)) (158730) **Cheik Joaan bin Hamad Al Thani**
101 B c 4/3 Sea The Stars (IRE)—Bekhara (IRE) (Kris) **S. A. Aga Khan**
102 **BLARNEY STONE (IRE)**, ch f 16/4 Peintre Celebre (USA)—
　　　　　　　Bastet (IRE) (Giant's Causeway (USA)) **Ecurie Wildenstein**
103 **CAREFUL CHARLIE (IRE)**, ch f 7/3 Tapit (USA)—
　　　　　　　Careless Charlie (USA) (Johannesburg (USA)) (142857) **Charles E. Fipke**
104 B f 19/2 Dalakhani (IRE)—Classira (IRE) (Danehill (USA)) (115079) **Julio Gerin Almeida Camargo**
105 B c 15/5 Sinndar (IRE)—Daltaiyma (IRE) (Doyoun) **S. A. Aga Khan**
106 B f 5/4 Azamour (IRE)—Daltama (IRE) (Indian Ridge) **S. A. Aga Khan**
107 B f 8/5 Gold Away (IRE)—Danedrop (IRE) (Danehill (USA)) **Ecurie des Monceaux**
108 B f 19/3 Invincible Spirit (IRE)—Dardania (Dalakhani (IRE)) **S. A. Aga Khan**
109 B f 11/5 Sea The Stars (IRE)—Darinska (IRE) (Zilzal (USA)) **Princess Z. P. Aga Khan**
110 Gr c 26/3 Dalakhani (IRE)—Darjina (FR) (Zamindar (USA)) **Princess Z. P. Aga Khan**
111 B c 16/5 Street Cry (IRE)—Daryaba (IRE) (Night Shift (USA)) **S. A. Aga Khan**
112 **DELORGUES (IRE)**, ch f 11/2 Rock of Gibraltar (IRE)—Dacca (Deploy)
113 B c 20/2 Authorized (IRE)—Diamond Tango (FR) (Acatenango (GER)) **H. H. Aga Khan**
114 **DONCELLA (IRE)**, b f 24/1 High Chaparral (IRE)—
　　　　　　　Onereuse (Sanglamore (USA)) (230000) **Waratah Thoroughbreds Pty Ltd**
115 **EDKHAN (IRE)**, gr c 3/2 Sea The Stars (IRE)—
　　　　　　　Alpine Rose (FR) (Linamix (FR)) (952380) **Cheik Joaan bin Hamad Al Thani**
116 B c 1/5 Montjeu (IRE)—Fraloga (IRE) (Grand Lodge (USA)) **H. H. Aga Khan**
117 Gr c 16/2 Sinndar (IRE)—Horasana (FR) (Galileo (IRE)) **H. H. Aga Khan**
118 **LBREGA (FR)**, b f 13/3 Elusive City (USA)—Fee du Nord (Inchinor) (35714) **Cheikh Joaan bin Hamad Al Thani**
119 B f 15/3 Zamindar (USA)—Louvain (IRE) (Sinndar (IRE)) (75396) **Finn Blichfeldt**
120 B f 18/4 Dubawi (IRE)—Marasima (FR) (Barathea (IRE)) **S. A. Aga Khan**
121 Gr f 23/2 Zamindar (USA)—Minatlya (FR) (Linamix (FR)) **H. H. Aga Khan**
122 **OAK HARBOR**, b c 18/2 Sinndar (IRE)—Onega Lake (IRE) (Peintre Celebre (USA)) **Ecurie Wildenstein**
123 **PRAIRIE DALE (FR)**, b br c 3/6 Dalakhani (IRE)—Prairie Runner (Arazi (USA)) **Ecurie Wildenstein**
124 B f 23/4 Azamour (IRE)—Sarlisa (FR) (Rainbow Quest (USA)) **S. A. Aga Khan**
125 B f 14/1 Pivotal—Shamakiya (IRE) (Intikhab (USA)) **S. A. Aga Khan**
126 B c 18/4 Sea The Stars (IRE)—Shemaya (FR) (Darshaan) **S. A. Aga Khan**
127 Gr f 15/3 Dansili—Shemima (Dalakhani (IRE)) **S. A. Aga Khan**
128 **SORIANO**, ch c 7/5 Halling (USA)—Sureyya (GER) (Monsun (GER)) **Ecurie Wildenstein**
129 B c 4/4 Dubawi (IRE)—Tashiriya (IRE) (Kenmare (FR)) **S. A. Aga Khan**
130 B f 3/4 Dansili—Vadapolina (FR) (Trempolino (USA)) **H. H. Aga Khan**
131 B f 19/3 Sea The Stars (IRE)—Vadaza (FR) (Zafonic (USA)) **H. H. Aga Khan**
132 Ch f 20/2 Selkirk (USA)—Vadiya (FR) (Peintre Celebre (USA)) **H. H. Aga Khan**
133 **VICTOR HARBOR (FR)**, ch c 7/2 Green Tune (USA)—Verveine (USA) (Lear Fan (USA)) **Ecurie Wildenstein**
134 Gr f 2/4 Zamindar (USA)—Visionnaire (FR) (Linamix (FR)) **H. H. Aga Khan**
135 B f 20/1 Muhtathir—Wadjeka (USA) (Oasis Dream) (71428) **Julio Gerin Almeida Camargo**
136 B c 21/4 Dalakhani (IRE)—Zakania (IRE) (Indian Ridge) (35714) **Cheikh Joaan bin Hamad Al Thani**
137 B c 11/2 Sea The Stars (IRE)—Zarkava (IRE) (Zamindar (USA)) **S. A. Aga Khan**
138 B f 14/3 Elusive City (USA)—Zewara (IRE) (Alhaarth (IRE)) **S. A. Aga Khan**

Assistant Trainer: Laurent Metais

Jockey (flat): Antoine Hamelin, Christophe Patrice Lemaire. **Apprentice:** Mickael Berto.

553 MS LUCINDA RUSSELL, Kinross

Postal: Arlary House Stables, Milnathort, Kinross, Tayside, KY13 9SJ
Contacts: PHONE (01577) 862482 YARD (01577) 865512 OFFICE (01577) 865512
FAX (01577) 861171 MOBILE (07970) 645261
E-MAIL lucinda@arlary.fsnet.co.uk WEBSITE www.lucindarussell.com

1 BALLYBEN (IRE), 5, ch g Beneficial—I'm Maggy (NZ) **Drew & Ailsa Russell**
2 BALLYCOOL (IRE), 6, b g Helissio (FR)—Carnoustie (USA) **Mr & Mrs T. P. Winnell**
3 BARLIFFEY (IRE), 8, b g Bahri (USA)—Kildare Lady (IRE) **P. J. S. Russell**
4 BEN AKRAM (IRE), 5, b g Beneficial—Ring Four (IRE) **Mrs M. Gleeson**
5 BESCOT SPRINGS (IRE), 8, b g Saddlers' Hall (IRE)—Silver Glen (IRE) **Mrs J. Tracey**
6 BLENHEIM BROOK (IRE), 8, br g Alderbrook—Blenheim Blinder (IRE) **The County Set Three**
7 BOBBLE HAT BOB (FR), 8, b g Lost World (IRE)—Bisette (FR) **Mrs C. Innes**
8 BOLD SIR BRIAN (IRE), 7, b g Brian Boru—Black Queen (IRE) **Major A. R. Trotter**
9 CASTLELAWN (IRE), 6, b g Runyon (IRE)—Pure Magic (IRE) **J. R. Adam**
10 CATCHTHEMOONLIGHT, 5, b m Generous (IRE)—Moon Catcher **Dig In Racing**
11 CLONDAW FLICKA (IRE), 5, ch g Stowaway—Bealaha Essie (IRE) **Dan & Michelle Macdonald, Mackie, Levein**
12 CLONDAW KNIGHT (IRE), 5, b g Heron Island (IRE)—Sarah Supreme (IRE) **Mr A. N. Seymour**
13 COPPER'S GOLD (IRE), 9, b g Presenting—West Hill Rose (IRE) **J. R. Adam**
14 CRACKERJACK LAD (IRE), 10, br g Exit To Nowhere (USA)—Crowther Homes **Mr I. D. Miller**
15 DE BEE KEEPER (IRE), 5, b g Milan—Festival Leader (IRE) **Mr J. Henderson**
16 DEGAS ART (IRE), 10, b g Danehill Dancer (IRE)—Answer **Bruce Barber Levein Russell**
17 DELIGHTFULLY (FR), 9, br m Sagacity (FR)—Green House (FR) **Mr R. M. Boyd**
18 DEVOTION TO DUTY (IRE), 7, b g Montjeu (IRE)—Charmante (USA) **Racing Management & Training Ltd**
19 DO IT FOR DALKEY, 11, b g Silver Patriarch (IRE)—Dalkey Sound **G. S. Brown**
20 DOTTIES DILEMA (IRE), 5, b g Pierre—Tellarue (IRE) **Stewart Dempster Mitchell**
21 ET MAINTENANT (FR), 11, ch g Johann Quatz (FR)—Dunlora **Mr K. Alexander**
22 ETXALAR (FR), 10, b g Kingsalsa (USA)—Tender To Love **Mrs E. B. Ferguson**
23 EYRE APPARENT (IRE), 8, ch g Turgeon (USA)—Miss Poutine (FR) **Mr A. N. Seymour**
24 FIGHTSTAR (FR), 9, b g Lord of Men—Parla (GER) **Mr D. J. Petterson**
25 FOG PATCHES (IRE), 7, br g Oscar (IRE)—Flash Parade **Sunny Days**
26 GARTH (IRE), 5, b g Sayadaw (FR)—Zaffaran Express (IRE) **Mr A. M. Russell**
27 GREEN FLAG (IRE), 6, b g Milan—Erin Go Brea (IRE) **J. R. Adam**
28 GREYHOPE, 4, gr g Pastoral Pursuits—Espana **Mrs S. C. Russell**
29 HALLMARK STAR, 4, b g Nayef (USA)—Spring **The County Set (Two)**
30 IMJOEKING (IRE), 6, b g Amilynx (FR)—Go Franky **Mr K. Alexander**
31 INNOCENT GIRL (IRE), 4, b f King's Theatre (IRE)—Belle Innocence (FR) **John J. Murray & Niall Farrell**
32 ISLAND CONFUSION (IRE), 5, b g Heron Island (IRE)—Anshan Gail (IRE) **Mrs A. E. Giles**
33 KINGSWELL THEATRE, 4, b g King's Theatre (IRE)—Cresswell Native (IRE) **Mr J. J. Murray**
34 KRIS CROSS (IRE), 6, ch g Kris Kin (USA)—Perfidia **Ms D. Thomson**
35 LADY OF VERONA (IRE), 6, b m Old Vic—Innovate (IRE) **Peter K. Dale Ltd**
36 LONE FOOT LADDIE (IRE), 4, b g Red Clubs (IRE)—Alexander Phantom (IRE) **Dr J. Wilson**
37 LONG DISTANCE (IRE), 8, b br g Storming Home—Lovers Luck (IRE) **P. J. S. Russell**
38 LORD OF DRUMS (IRE), 7, b g Beat of Drums—Treat A Lady (IRE) **The Ormello Way**
39 LUCKY SUNNY (IRE), 10, b g Pasternak—Flying Fur (IRE) **Suzanne & Nigel Williams**
40 MASTER SEBASTIAN, 14, ch g Kasakov—Anchor Inn **P. J. S. Russell**
41 MOMKINZAIN (USA), 6, b g Rahy (USA)—Fait Accompli (USA) **John R. Adam & Sons Ltd**
42 MONSOON MUSIC (IRE), 9, b g Dushyantor (USA)—Stormey Tune (IRE) **Peter K. Dale Ltd**
43 MORNING TIME (IRE), 7, b g Hawk Wing (USA)—Desert Trail (USA) **Mr W. G. H. Forrester**
44 MR OPULENCE, 4, ch g Generous (IRE)—Miss Opulence (IRE) **S. M. Smith**
45 NUTS N BOLTS, 7, b g Marju (IRE)—Anniversary **The County Set**
46 ON BROADWAY (IRE), 7, b g Broadway Flyer (USA)—Snap Out of It (IRE) **Mr G. Truscott**
47 PENA DORADA (IRE), 6, b g Key of Luck (USA)—Uluwatu (IRE) **Mr J. J. Murray**
48 PRESENTING REBEL (IRE), 7, ch g Presenting—Random Bless (IRE) **Mr W. T. Scott**
49 PROSECCO (IRE), 11, b g Perpendicular—Bay Gale (IRE) **Tay Valley Chasers Racing Club**
50 QUACITY (FR), 9, b g Sagacity (FR)—Desert Show (IRE) **J. R. Adam**
51 QUINDER SPRING (FR), 9, gr g Chef de Clan (FR)—Virginia Spring (FR) **Kelso Members Lowflyers Club**
52 QUITO DU TRESOR (FR), 9, b g Jeune Homme (USA)—Itiga (FR) **P. J. S. Russell**
53 RHYMERS HA', 6, br g Kasakov—Salu **Mr G. F. Adam**
54 RHYMERS STONE, 5, b g Desideratum—Salu **Mr G. F. Adam**
55 ROWDY ROCHER (IRE), 7, br g Winged Love (IRE)—Madam Rocher (IRE) **Michelle And Dan Macdonald**
56 SAPHIR RIVER (FR), 7, gr g Slickly (FR)—Miss Bio (FR) **Mr A. N. Seymour**
57 SHOOTING TIMES, 8, b g Commanche Run—Rainbow Times (IRE) **Mrs J. M. R. Lancaster**
58 SILVER BY NATURE, 11, gr g Silver Patriarch (IRE)—Gale **G. S. Brown**
59 SIMARTHUR, 6, gr g Erhaab (USA)—Dusty Too
60 STORMION (IRE), 8, b g Flemensfirth (USA)—El Moss (IRE) **Maclennan Stewart Russell**

MS LUCINDA RUSSELL - Continued

61 **TANTAMOUNT**, 4, b g Observatory (USA)—Cantanta **Wildcard Racing**
62 **TAP NIGHT (USA)**, 6, ch g Pleasant Tap (USA)—Day Mate (USA) **J. P. McManus**
63 **THE FRIARY (IRE)**, 6, b g Kris Kin (USA)—Native Design (IRE) **Mrs S Russell & A M Russell**
64 **TITO BUSTILLO (FR)**, 8, b g Kahyasi—Litani Queen **Mrs A. Yeoman & Mrs S. Larson**
65 **UISGE BEATHA (IRE)**, 5, b g Alderbrook—Me Grannys Endoors (IRE) **Last Alders**
66 **URBAN KODE (IRE)**, 5, b g Kodiac—Urbanize (USA) **Suzy Brown, John Baird, Tony Evans**
67 **VALLANI (IRE)**, 8, ch m Vettori (IRE)—Hecuba **Mr R. M. Boyd**
68 **VAMIZI (IRE)**, 10, b g Supreme Leader—Cuilin Bui (IRE) **Remenham Racing**
69 **VENITZIA (IRE)**, 7, b br g Presenting—Bloom Berry **Hadrian's Warriors**
70 **WAYNE MANOR (IRE)**, 4, br g Cape Cross (IRE)—Inchmahome
71 **WILD GEESE (IRE)**, 6, br g Cape Cross (IRE)—Intrepidity **Tay Valley Chasers Racing Club**
72 **WIND SHUFFLE (GER)**, 10, b g Big Shuffle (USA)—Wiesensturmerin (GER) **Mrs S. Bruce & Mrs L. Mackay**
73 **YON DORA (IRE)**, 5, b m And Beyond (IRE)—Senora d'or **Mrs J. Millar**

Other Owners: Mr G. G. Adamson, R. D. Anderson, Mr J. B. Baird, Mr D. Bamlet, R. H. T. Barber, G. F. Bear, Mr A. J. Bonarius, Mrs S. Brown, Mr P. R. Brown, Mr C. G. W. Bruce, Mrs S. E. Bruce, H. A. Brydon, A. Cadger, Mr K. Carruthers, Mr J. T. Dawson, Mr E. W. Dempster, Mr Gary Etheridge, Mr A. Evans, Mrs B. V. Evans, N. Farrell, G. Godsman, Mrs I. M. Grant, P. N. Gray, E. D. Haggart, Mrs M. Hamilton, Mr A. W. Henderson, Mrs D. Jeromson, Mrs M Kennedy, Mrs S. K. Larson, Mr J. S. Lessells, Mr C. W. Levein, Mrs M. Macdonald, Mr W. D. Macdonald, Mrs L. P. Mackay, Mr K. J. Mackie, Mr A. Maclennan, Mrs L. Maclennan, Mr J. M. Mcintyre, Mr M. G. Mellor, Mr J. Mitchell, Mr J. M. Murphy, Mr G. G. Ritchie, A. J. R. Russell, Ms L. V. Russell, Mrs A. Russell, Mr A. Savage, Mr A. B. Shepherd, Mr B. T. E. Shrubsall, A. W. Sinclair, A. D. Stewart, Mrs M. E. Stewart, Mrs C. A. Todd, Mrs S. E. Williams, N. Williams, Mr T. P. Winnell, Mrs M. Winnell, Mrs A. B. Yeoman.

Assistant Trainers: Jaimie Duff, Peter Scudamore

Jockey (NH): Peter Buchanan. **Conditional:** Craig Nichol, Graham Watters, Steven Fox, Grant Cockburn. **Amateur:** Mr Jamie Lyttle, Miss Rachael Macdonald, Mr Hamish McNeil, Mr Nick Orpwood.

---

554   MR JOHN RYALL, Yeovil
Postal: **Higher Farm, Rimpton, Yeovil, Somerset, BA22 8AD**
Contacts: **PHONE/FAX (01935) 850222 MOBILE (07592) 738848**
E-MAIL bjmryall@btconnect.com

1 **CHIPLESS (IRE)**, 10, b g Tel Quel (FR)—Emerald Forest **Mr I. & Mrs K. G. Fawcett**
2 **CYPRESS GROVE (IRE)**, 10, b g Windsor Castle—Grecian Queen **Mr P. J. O'Donovan**
3 **MICHIGAN D'ISOP (FR)**, 13, b g Cadoudal (FR)—Julie Du Berlais (FR) **B. J. M. Ryall**
4 5, Br g Loup Sauvage (USA)—Spring Grass **B. J. M. Ryall**
5 6, B g Emperor Fountain—Win A Hand **B. J. M. Ryall**

Other Owners: Mr I. Fawcett, Mrs K. G. Fawcett, Mr B. J. M. Ryall.

Assistant Trainer: Mrs R C Ryall

---

555   MR JOHN RYAN, Newmarket
Postal: **Cadland Stables, Moulton Road, Newmarket, Suffolk, CB8 8DU**
Contacts: **PHONE (01638) 664172 MOBILE (07739) 801235**
E-MAIL john.ryan@jryanracing.com WEBSITE www.jryanracing.com

1 **FOCAIL MAITH**, 5, b g Oratorio (IRE)—Glittering Image (IRE) **Mr C. Fegan**
2 **IF WHAT AND MAYBE**, 5, ch g Needwood Blade—Pink Champagne **John Ryan Racing**
3 **IVER BRIDGE LAD**, 6, b h Avonbridge—Fittonia (FR) **The Iver Lads**
4 **MASTERS BLAZING**, 4, ch g Iceman—Loquacity **Mr G. R. McGladery**
5 **OCEAN TEMPEST**, 4, gr g Act One—Ipsa Loquitur **Mr W McCluskey & Mr C Little**
6 **OCEAN'S MINSTREL**, 7, b g Pivotal—Minstrel's Dance (CAN) **Mr W. McCluskey**
7 **SOMEMOTHERSDOHAVEM**, 4, ch g Avonbridge—Show Off **The Somemothers Partnership**
8 **SPIN AGAIN (IRE)**, 8, b g Intikhab (USA)—Queen of The May (IRE) **M. M. Foulger**
9 **THECORNISHCOCKNEY**, 4, bl g Cockney Rebel (IRE)—Glittering Image (IRE) **Mr C Letcher & Mr J Ryan**
10 **THECORNISHCOWBOY**, 4, b g Haafhd—Oriental Dance **Mr C Letcher & Mr J Ryan**
11 **THECORNISHWREN (IRE)**, 4, ch f Medecis—Coulisse (IRE) **Chris Letcher & Partners**
12 **WILDOMAR**, 4, b g Kyllachy—Murrieta **Mr W. McCluskey**

MR JOHN RYAN - Continued

THREE-YEAR-OLDS

13 OCEAN APPLAUSE, b c Royal Applause—Aldora **Mr W. McLuskey**
14 ROYAL CAPER, b g Royal Applause—Ukraine (IRE) **Kilco (International) Ltd**

TWO-YEAR-OLDS

15 Ch c 7/4 Three Valleys (USA)—Fittonia (FR) (Ashkalani (IRE)) (10000) **Mr G. R. McGladery**
16 Ch f 5/4 Avonbridge—Snow Shoes (Sri Pekan (USA)) (5500)

Other Owners: Dr R. A. Dixon, Mrs J. L. Dixon, Mr M. Foulger, Mr Neil Hooper, Mr Christopher Letcher, Mr McGladery, Mr W. McLuskey, Mr J. Ryan, Mrs J. Williams.

Apprentice: Bradley Bosley, Caroline Kelly.

---

556 **MR KEVIN RYAN, Hambleton**
Postal: **Hambleton Lodge, Hambleton, Thirsk, North Yorkshire, YO7 2HA**
Contacts: **PHONE Office (01845) 597010 / (01845)597622 FAX (01845) 597622**
MOBILE (07768) 016930
E-MAIL kevin.hambleton@virgin.net

1 ADVANCED, 10, b g Night Shift (USA)—Wonderful World (GER) **Mrs J. H. Ryan**
2 ARAKU VALLEY (IRE), 6, b g Indian Danehill (IRE)—Bobazure (IRE) **Mr P. Beirne**
3 ARDMAY (IRE), 4, b g Strategic Prince—Right After Moyne (IRE) **A. C. Henson**
4 BAJAN TRYST (USA), 7, b br g Speightstown (USA)—
Garden Secrets (USA) **Mrs Margaret Forsyth & Mrs R G Hillen**
5 BAPAK CHINTA (USA), 4, gr ro c Speightstown (USA)—Suena Cay (USA) **Mr T. A. Rahman**
6 BEAUTIFUL DAY, 5, b g Piccolo—Evening **G. Reed**
7 BOGART, 4, ch c Bahamian Bounty—Lauren Louise **Mrs A. Bailey**
8 CAPAILL LIATH (IRE), 5, gr g Iffraaj—Bethesda **Mr T. A. Rahman**
9 CAPTAIN RAMIUS (IRE), 7, b g Kheleyf (USA)—Princess Mood (GER) **Mrs C. McStay**
10 CHEVIOT (USA), 7, b g Rahy (USA)—Camlet **Mrs J. Penman, G. Robertson, W. Robinson**
11 CHOOSEDAY (IRE), 4, b g Choisir (AUS)—Break of Day (USA) **Mrs S. J. Barker**
12 CLAYTON, 4, b g Peintre Celebre (USA)—Blossom **G. Reed**
13 DAM BEAUTIFUL, 4, b f Sleeping Indian—Nellie Melba **Mrs J. H. Ryan**
14 DISCRESSION, 4, b c Indesatchel (IRE)—Night Gypsy **Mr T. G. & Mrs M. E. Holdcroft, Mr K. MacPherson**
15 FLAMING ARROW (IRE), 5, b g Sadler's Wells (USA)—Pescia (IRE) **Mrs R. G. Hillen**
16 FORGET ME NOT LANE (IRE), 4, b g Holy Roman Emperor (IRE)—
Mrs Arkada (FR) **Mr J. Hanson & Sir Alex Ferguson**
17 HAMZA (IRE), 4, b g Amadeus Wolf—Lady Shanghai (IRE) **Mr Mubarak Al Naemi**
18 HAYWAIN, 4, b g Peintre Celebre (USA)—Shall We Dance **G. Reed**
19 HITTIN'THE SKIDS (IRE), 5, ch m Fruits of Love (USA)—Hush Deal **D. J. Emsley**
20 HOPES N DREAMS (IRE), 5, b m Elusive City (USA)—Hope of Pekan (IRE) **J. C. G. Chua & C. K. Ong**
21 INDEPUB, 4, b g Indesatchel (IRE)—Champenoise **Mr D. W. Barker**
22 JEDWARD (IRE), 6, ch m Namid—Input **Mr M. Beaumont**
23 KING KURT (IRE), 5, b g Holy Roman Emperor (IRE)—Rutledge (IRE) **M. J. Taylor**
24 LAFFAN (IRE), 4, b g Dark Angel (IRE)—Lady Corduff (IRE) **Mr Mubarak Al Naemi**
25 LE TOREADOR, 8, ch g Piccolo—Peggy Spencer **G. Reed**
26 LIGHTNING CLOUD (IRE), 5, gr g Sleeping Indian—Spree (IRE) **Hambleton Racing Ltd XVIII**
27 NASHARRA (IRE), 5, ch g Iffraaj—There With Me (USA) **Mr & Mrs Julian & Rosie Richer**
28 OASIS DANCER, 6, br gr g Oasis Dream—Good Enough (FR) **A. D. Dale**
29 PEA SHOOTER, 4, b g Piccolo—Sparkling Eyes **Mrs M. Forsyth**
30 PINTURA, 6, ch g Efisio—Picolette **Mr M. Beaumont**
31 RALPHY BOY (IRE), 4, b g Acclamation—Silcasue **Frank Lowe**
32 SARDANAPALUS, 4, b g Byron—Crinkle (IRE) **J. Nixon**
33 TIDDLIWINKS, 7, b g Piccolo—Card Games **G. Reed**
34 TORERO, 4, b g Hernando (FR)—After You **G. Reed**
35 TRAIL BLAZE (IRE), 4, b g Tagula (IRE)—Kingpin Delight **Mr & Mrs Julian & Rosie Richer**
36 TRIBAL MYTH (IRE), 6, b g Johannesburg (USA)—Shadow Play (USA) **Mr & Mrs K. S. Hughes & Dr J. Gozzard**
37 WAKING WARRIOR, 5, b g Sleeping Indian—Scented Garden **Hambleton Racing Ltd XVII**
38 WARFARE, 4, b g Soviet Star (USA)—Fluffy **G. Reed**
39 YAIR HILL (IRE), 5, b g Selkirk (USA)—Conspiracy **D. J. Emsley**
40 YES DADDY (IRE), 5, b g Golan (IRE)—Hollygrove Samba (IRE) **Matt & Lauren Morgan**
41 YORK GLORY (USA), 5, gr ro h Five Star Day (USA)—Minicolony (USA) **Salman Rashed & Mohamed Khalifa**

MR KEVIN RYAN - Continued

THREE-YEAR-OLDS

42 A STAR IN MY EYE (IRE), b f Authorized (IRE)—Vyatka **Sultan Ali**
43 AL UDEID (IRE), gr g Verglas (IRE)—Gold Strike (IRE) **Mr Mubarak Al Naemi**
44 ANGILINA, b f Teofilo (IRE)—Finnmark **Sultan Ali**
45 AU RENOIR, ch f Peintre Celebre (USA)—Goodbye **G. Reed**
46 AYR MISSILE, b f Cadeaux Genereux—Venoge (IRE) **Middleham Park Racing XLV**
47 BAIN'S PASS (IRE), ch g Johannesburg (USA)—Rose Bourbon (USA) **Mrs M. Forsyth**
48 BAPAK BANGSAWAN, b c Pastoral Pursuits—Nsx **H.R.H. Sultan Ahmad Shah**
49 BAPAK BESAR (CAN), b c Speightstown (USA)—Valid Move (USA) **Mr T. A. Rahman**
50 BAPAK MUDA (USA), ch c Distorted Humor (USA)—Shiva (JPN) **Mr T. A. Rahman**
51 BAPAK PESTA (IRE), b c Haatef (USA)—Penny Fan **Mr T. A. Rahman**
52 BAPAK SAYANG (USA), b c Medaglia d'oro (USA)—Emily Ring (USA) **Mr T. A. Rahman**
53 BLACK RIDER (IRE), b c Elnadim (USA)—Barracade (IRE) **Mrs J. H. Ryan**
54 BLAINE, ch c Avonbridge—Lauren Louise **Matt & Lauren Morgan**
55 B f Oratorio (IRE)—Blue Indigo (FR) **Mrs J. H. Ryan**
56 BOUSATET (FR), b f Muhtathir—Miss Mission (IRE) **Highbank Stud**
57 BURNING BLAZE, b c Danroad (AUS)—Demeter (USA) **Qatar Racing Ltd**
58 CAN YOU CONGA, b c Piccolo—Takes Two To Tango **G. Reed**
59 CARDS, b f Tobougg (IRE)—Card Games **G. Reed**
60 CHASING DREAMS, ch f Pastoral Pursuits—Welanga **Hambleton Racing Ltd XXIV**
61 COMPLICATOR, br c Pastoral Pursuits—Thara'a (IRE) **Mrs J. Bownes**
62 CUPERTINO, b c Sakhee (USA)—Arantxa **S. C. B. Limited**
63 DELORES ROCKET, b f Firebreak—Artistic (IRE) **J. Nixon**
64 DERBY TO DUBAI, ch g Dubai Destination (USA)—Bukhoor (IRE) **Matt & Lauren Morgan**
65 DEWI CHINTA (IRE), b f Tagula (IRE)—Damjanich (IRE) **Mr T. A. Rahman**
66 EQUITY RISK (USA), b c Henrythenavigator (USA)—Moon's Tune (USA) **Clipper Logistics**
67 GEORGE ROOKE (IRE), b c Rock of Gibraltar (IRE)—Double Fantasy (GER) **Kenneth MacPherson**
68 GLORY AWAITS (IRE), ch c Choisir (AUS)—Sandbox Two (IRE) **A & A**
69 HALF TO YOU, b f Haafhd—After You **G. Reed**
70 JORDANSTOWN, ch g Piccolo—Pigment **Mrs Margaret Forsyth & Mrs D. McAllister**
71 LADY OF THE HOUSE (IRE), b f Holy Roman Emperor (IRE)—Miss Delila (USA) **Matt & Lauren Morgan**
72 MARHABA MALAYEEN (IRE), b c Dutch Art—Poyle Caitlin (IRE) **A. Al Shaikh**
73 MOE'S PLACE (IRE), b g Acclamation—Sahara Sky (IRE) **C. S. Ryan**
74 NORDIKHAB (IRE), b g Intikhab (USA)—Pourquoi Pas (IRE) **Hambleton Racing Ltd XXIII**
75 PANAMA CAT (USA), b f Tale of The Cat (USA)—Oceans Apart **Elite Racing Club**
76 PLUNDER, ch c Zamindar (USA)—Reaching Ahead (USA) **Graham Hillen & Fitzpatrick**
77 RAPSCALLION DEEP (IRE), b c Danehill Dancer (IRE)—Lucina **Mr P. Brosnan**
78 RED PALADIN (IRE), b g Red Clubs (IRE)—Alexander Goldmine **Hambleton Racing Ltd XXII**
79 REPETITION, b c Royal Applause—Uno **G. Reed**
80 SIGNING (IRE), b g Byron—Muja Farewell **Mrs A. Bailey**
81 STAR UP IN THE SKY (USA), gr ro f Speightstown (USA)—Prenuptial Plans (USA) **Matt & Lauren Morgan**
82 SWEHAN (IRE), b g Diamond Green (FR)—Golden (FR) **Mr Mubarak Al Naemi**
83 UNASSAILABLE, ch g Bahamian Bounty—Reeling N' Rocking (IRE) **J. Nixon**
84 VICKY VALENTINE, b f Rock of Gibraltar (IRE)—Silcasue **Frank Lowe**

TWO-YEAR-OLDS

85 ALASKAN NIGHT (IRE), b c 27/4 Kodiac—
Fingal Nights (IRE) (Night Shift (USA)) (34285) **Michael Beaumont & Brian Dunn**
86 Ch f 23/3 Captain Rio—Alexander Goldmine (Dansili) (12380) **Mr N. I. O'Callaghan**
87 B c 10/4 Sleeping Indian—Aptina (USA) (Aptitude (USA)) (9523) **Mrs J. H. Ryan**
88 ARA DUBAI (IRE), gr c 20/5 Verglas (IRE)—Intaglia (GER) (Lomitas) (25000) **Mr A. A. Al Shaikh**
89 B c 29/3 Exceed And Excel (AUS)—Awwal Malika (USA) (Kingmambo (USA) (54000) **Saeed Manana**
90 B f 2/2 Mount Nelson—Bandnana (Bandmaster (USA)) (20952) **Hambleton Racing Ltd**
91 B c 18/3 Sleeping Indian—Bijan (IRE) (Mukaddamah (USA)) (13333) **Mrs J. H. Ryan**
92 B f 20/3 Beat Hollow—Cadeau Speciale (Cadeaux Genereux) **Hambleton Racing Ltd**
93 B c 10/1 Bushranger (IRE)—Choice House (USA) (Chester House (USA)) (35000) **Saeed Manana**
94 B f 22/3 Sleeping Indian—Confidentiality (IRE) (Desert Style (IRE)) (24761) **Mrs J. H. Ryan**
95 B f 31/3 Dutch Art—Dance Card (Cape Cross (IRE))
96 DISTANT PAST, b c 20/3 Pastoral Pursuits—Faraway Lass (Distant Relative) (4761) **Mr M. Wynne**
97 B c 22/3 Bushranger (IRE)—Geht Fasteur (IRE) (Chineur (FR)) (14284) **J. M. Birkett**
98 GEORGE THE FIRST, gr c 2/5 Aqlaam—Mrs Gray (Red Sunset) (9523) **Wildcard Racing**
99 B c 18/4 Bushranger (IRE)—Hawk Eyed Lady (IRE) (Hawk Wing (USA)) (25714) **Kenneth MacPherson**
100 B c 21/2 Myboycharlie (IRE)—However (IRE) (Hector Protector (USA)) (28571) **Mr D. Cork**
101 HOYAM THE SECOND, ch f 21/2 Sleeping Indian—Elhida (IRE) (Mujtahid (USA)) (9523) **A & A**
102 B c 22/3 Sleeping Indian—Impetuous (Inchinor) (20000) **Hambleton Racing Ltd**

MR KEVIN RYAN - Continued

103 B c 17/2 Tagula (IRE)—Malta (USA) (Gone West (USA)) (29523) **D. W. Barker**
104 MINDBLOWING, b c 17/2 Mind Games—
Musical Day (Singspiel (IRE)) (23809) **Mr T. G. & Mrs M. E. Holdcroft, Mr K. MacPherson**
105 B c 14/4 Amadeus Wolf—Nawaji (USA) (Trempolino (USA)) (23809) **Mrs J. H. Ryan**
106 OASIS TOWN, br f 5/2 Sleeping Indian—
Town And Gown (Oasis Dream) (7619) **M & S Beaumont, North, O'Farrell & Saunders**
107 ONLINE ALEXANDER (IRE), b f 21/2 Acclamation—Dance Club (IRE) (Fasliyev (USA)) **Mr N. I. O'Callaghan**
108 PATIENCE'S ROCK (IRE), b c 9/4 Rock of Gibraltar (IRE)—
Shakeeba (IRE) (Sendawar (IRE)) (14285) **Mr M. Beaumont**
109 PINEROLO (ITY), b c 18/3 Red Rocks (IRE)—American Beauty (GER) (Goofalik (USA)) (33333) **A. Al Shaikh**
110 Ch f 13/2 Duke of Marmalade (IRE)—Pitrizza (IRE) (Machiavellian (USA)) (16000) **Racegoers Owners Club**
111 B c 17/3 Sleeping Indian—Plausabelle (Royal Applause) (13333) **Mrs J. H. Ryan**
112 PROCLAMATIONOFWAR, b c 3/3 Proclamation (IRE)—Rockburst (Xaar) (30476) **Mr M. Beaumont**
113 B c 13/3 Sleeping Indian—Silvereine (FR) (Bering) (20952) **Middleham Park Racing XIX**
114 B c 9/4 Whipper—Stella Del Mattino (USA) (Golden Gear (USA)) (5952) **Mrs J. H. Ryan**
115 B f 6/3 Kodiac—Storm Lady (IRE) (Alhaarth (IRE)) (23809) **Mrs J. H. Ryan**
116 B c 28/5 Distorted Humor (USA)—Sweet Hope (USA) (Lemon Drop Kid (USA)) **Highbank Stud**
117 B c 29/3 Acclamation—Thankful (Diesis) (38095) **Matt & Lauren Morgan**
118 THE BOSS OF ME, ch c 26/2 Bahamian Bounty—Orange Pip (Bold Edge) (29523) **B. T. McDonald**
119 UPLIFTED (IRE), b c 4/4 Jeremy (USA)—
Misty Peak (IRE) (Sri Pekan (USA)) (19047) **Mr Michael & Jacqueline Beaumont**
120 B c 3/2 Bahamian Bounty—Xtrasensory (Royal Applause) (66666) **Matt & Lauren Morgan**
121 YORKSHIRE RELISH (IRE), b c 6/3 Amadeus Wolf—Patroller (USA) (Grand Slam (USA)) (7142) **J. Berry**

Other Owners: Sheikh S. R. Al Khalifa, Mr S. M. Alkhalifa, Mrs J. Beaumont, Mr A. J. Bonarius, C. G. J. Chua, B. Dunn, Sir A. Ferguson, Mr M. Fitzpatrick, Dr J. G. Gozzard, S. P. Graham, J. Hanson, A. J. Hill, Mr T. G. & Mrs M. E. Holdcroft, K. S. Hughes, Mrs D. Hughes, Mrs D. Jeromson, Mrs D. M. McAllister, M. Morgan, Mrs L. K. Morgan, Miss M. Noden, Mr F. Ong, T. S. Palin, Mrs J. Penman, M. Prince, Mrs R. L. Richer, J. Richer, Mr G. J. Robertson, Mr W. Robinson, Mr S. R. H. Turner, Mrs I. M. Wainwright, Mr M. A. Wainwright.

Assistant Trainer: Joe O'Gorman

Jockey (flat): Philip Makin, Amy Ryan. **Conditional:** Brian Toomey. **Apprentice:** Julie Burke, Paul McGiff, Kevin Stott.

---

557 MR AYTACH SADIK, Kidderminster
Postal: **Wolverley Court Coach House, Wolverley, Kidderminster, Worcestershire, DY10 3RP**
Contacts: **PHONE (01562) 852362 MOBILE (07803) 040344**

1 APACHE DAWN, 9, ch g Pursuit of Love—Taza **A. M. Sadik**
2 BLIZZARD BLUES (USA), 7, ch g Mr Greeley (USA)—Blush Damask (USA) **A. M. Sadik**
3 FINCH FLYER (IRE), 6, ch g Indian Ridge—Imelda (USA) **A. M. Sadik**
4 HOW'S D STRAWBOSS (IRE), 8, gr g Environment Friend—Taken For A Ride (IRE) **A. M. Sadik**
5 SILVER PANTHER, 5, gr g Proclamation (IRE)—Sydney Star **A. M. Sadik**

---

558 MR MATTHEW SALAMAN, Lambourn
Postal: **16 Larksfield, Swindon, Wiltshire, SN3 5AD**
Contacts: **PHONE (01488) 73646 (Office) MOBILE (07912) 039015**
E-MAIL matthewsalaman@hotmail.com

1 FRED KENNET, 8, ch g Kadastrof (FR)—Evaporate **The New Kennet Connection**
2 MOTORHEAD, 4, ch c Motivator—Duchcov **Withyslade**

Other Owners: Mr David Bond, Mr J. M. Duncan, Miss H. Pease, Miss A. E. A. Solomon.

Assistant Trainer: S. Keighley

559 MR PETER SALMON, Wetherby
Postal: **Ingmanthorpe Racing Stables, Loshpot Lane, Kirk Deighton, Wetherby, West Yorkshire, LS22 5HL**
Contacts: **PHONE (01937) 587552 FAX (01937) 587552 MOBILE (07828) 958820**
E-MAIL **psalmon@ingmanthorperacing.co.uk**

1 ALASKAN PRINCE (IRE), 8, b g Exit To Nowhere (USA)—Alaskan Princess (IRE) **Mrs W. M. Crump**
2 CALYPSO CAY, 5, b g Tiger Hill (IRE)—Tessa Reef (IRE) **Mr R. Durkin**
3 CELTIC SIXPENCE (IRE), 5, b m Celtic Swing—Penny Ha'penny **Keiron Smith**
4 CHANGE THE SUBJECT (USA), 5, gr ro g Maria's Mon (USA)—Victory Lap (USA) **The Three D's**
5 EL MCGLYNN (IRE), 4, b f Elnadim (USA)—Evelyn One **Leeds Contracts Limited**
6 HALF A CROWN (IRE), 8, b g Compton Place—Penny Ha'penny **Viscount Environmental**
7 HYDRANT, 7, b g Haafhd—Spring **Mr C. Hatch**
8 SO CHEEKY, 4, ch f Fantastic View (USA)—Fallujah **Mr M. J. Buck**
9 SOUTER POINT (USA), 7, b br g Giant's Causeway (USA)—Wires Crossed (USA) **Leeds Contracts Limited**

THREE-YEAR-OLDS
10 BEAUTIFULWILDTHING, b f Mount Nelson—Euro Empire (USA) **Leeds Contracts Limited**
11 SPEEDY UTMOST MEG, b f Medicean—Al Joudha (FR) **Leeds Contracts Limited**

TWO-YEAR-OLDS
12 GOOD OLD BOY LUKEY, ch c 24/4 Selkirk (USA)—Pivotting (Pivotal) (12000) **Leeds Contracts Limited**

Other Owners: Mr Graham Davies, Mr D. R. Garthwaite, Mr I. Hartley, Mr S. H. Lamb, Mrs Ann Lumley, K. Smith.

Assistant Trainer: Jack M. Salmon

Jockey (flat): Paul Hanagan, Adam Beschizza, Frankie Dettori, Andrew Mullen. **Jockey (NH):** Andrew Thornton.
Conditional: Adam Nicol. **Amateur:** Mr Jack Salmon.

---

560 MRS MARY SANDERSON, Tiverton
Postal: **New Cottage, Rackenford Road, Calverleigh, Tiverton, Devon, EX16 8BE**
Contacts: **PHONE (01884) 254217**
E-MAIL **h9bas@live.co.uk**

1 APPLAUSE FOR AMY (IRE), 6, b m King's Theatre (IRE)—Amathea (FR) **Mrs Mary Sanderson**
2 CALVERLEIGH COURT (IRE), 6, b m Presenting—Alexandra Parade (IRE) **Mrs Mary Sanderson**
3 ECLIPSE AWARD (IRE), 7, br g Definite Article—Aries Girl **Mrs Mary Sanderson**

Conditional: Micheal Nolan. **Amateur:** Mr Matthew Hampton.

---

561 MR MALCOLM SAUNDERS, Wells
Postal: **Blue Mountain Farm, Wells Hill Bottom, Haydon, Wells, Somerset, BA5 3EZ**
Contacts: **OFFICE/FAX (01749) 841011 MOBILE (07771) 601035**
E-MAIL **malcolm@malcolmsaunders.co.uk WEBSITE www.malcolmsaunders.co.uk**

1 CAPTAIN CAREY, 7, b g Fraam—Brigadiers Bird (IRE) **M. S. Saunders**
2 FANROUGE (IRE), 4, b f Red Clubs (IRE)—Silk Fan (IRE) **B. C. Scott**
3 GINZAN, 5, b m Desert Style (IRE)—Zyzania **Mr P. S. G. Nicholas**
4 JAWIM, 4, br f Piccolo—Craic Sa Ceili (IRE) **B. C. Scott**
5 SARANGOO, 5, b m Piccolo—Craic Sa Ceili (IRE) **B. C. Scott**
6 SUNNY FUTURE (IRE), 7, b g Masterful (IRE)—Be Magic **M. S. Saunders**

THREE-YEAR-OLDS
7 BALTIC GIN (IRE), b f Baltic King—Deeday Bay (IRE) **M. S. Saunders**
8 KWANTO, b f Piccolo—Craic Sa Ceili (IRE) **B. C. Scott**
9 MAJESTIC RED (IRE), b f Red Clubs (IRE)—Majestic Eviction (IRE) **The New Foursome Partnership 1**
10 SILVERRICA (IRE), gr f Ad Valorem (USA)—Allegorica (IRE) **Mrs V. L. Nicholas**

TWO-YEAR-OLDS
11 B g 27/4 Amadeus Wolf—Allegorica (IRE) (Alzao (USA)) (3571) **M. S. Saunders**
12 Ch g 10/4 Ad Valorem (USA)—Await (IRE) (Peintre Celebre (USA)) (10317) **Mr P. S. G. Nicholas**

MR MALCOLM SAUNDERS - Continued

13 CAMELEY DAWN, b f 14/4 Alhaarth (IRE)—Apply Dapply (Pursuit of Love) (15000) **Mr & Mrs J Harris**
14 Br g 30/3 Piccolo—Craic Sa Ceili (IRE) (Danehill Dancer (IRE))
15 B f 31/3 Ad Valorem (USA)—Swiss Roll (IRE) (Entrepreneur) (2777)
16 Ch f 9/3 Lucky Story (USA)—Willisa (Polar Falcon (USA))

Other Owners: G. P. Cowell, J. A. Gent, Mr J. E. Harris, Mrs P. A. Harris.

562	**MRS DIANNE SAYER, Penrith**

Postal: **Town End Farm, Hackthorpe, Penrith, Cumbria, CA10 2HX**
Contacts: **PHONE (01931) 712245 MOBILE (07980) 295316**

1 AUBERGE (IRE), 9, ch m Blueprint (IRE)—Castlegrace (IRE) **R. H. Affleck**
2 COOL BARANCA (GER), 7, b m Beat Hollow—Cool Storm (IRE) **Mr D. J. Coppola**
3 DISCOVERIE, 5, b g Runyon (IRE)—Sri (IRE) **Mr D. J. Coppola**
4 ENDEAVOR, 8, ch g Selkirk (USA)—Midnight Mambo (USA) **Mrs M. Coppola**
5 GOODLUKIN LUCY, 6, ch m Supreme Sound—Suka Ramai **Evergreen Racing**
6 JACK ALBERT (IRE), 6, gr g Cloudings (IRE)—Lisdoylelady (IRE) **E F Sporting**
7 MARKADAM, 7, b g Mark of Esteem (IRE)—Elucidate **Mr R. A. Harrison**
8 MORE EQUITY, 11, b m Classic Cliche (IRE)—Sillymore **Mrs M. Coppola**
9 MY FRIEND GEORGE, 7, ch g Afflora (IRE)—Snowgirl (IRE) **J. A. Sayer**
10 NEWDANE DANCER (IRE), 6, b m Golan (IRE)—Flagofconvienience (IRE) **A. R. White**
11 SENDIYM (FR), 6, b g Rainbow Quest (USA)—Seraya (FR) **Mr A. S. Ambler**
12 SERGEANT PINK (IRE), 7, b g Fasliyev (USA)—Ring Pink (USA) **J. A. Sayer**
13 SHOAL BAY DREAMER, 7, b m Central Park (IRE)—Ninfa (IRE) **The Transatlantics**
14 SOLIS (GER), 10, ch g In The Wings—Seringa (GER) **Mr D. J. Coppola**
15 STAGS LEAP (IRE), 6, b g Refuse To Bend (IRE)—Swingsky (IRE) **Mr D. J. Coppola**
16 THATCHERITE (IRE), 5, gr g Verglas (IRE)—Damiana (IRE) **United Five Racing**

Other Owners: Mr S. J. Baird, Mr K. J. Burrow, Mr A. J. Burrow, Mrs J. D. Howard, Mr D. Hunter, R. Kent, J. Millican, Mr P. Moorby, Mr K. E. Moorby, Mrs H. D. Sayer, E. G. Tunstall, Mrs C. Tunstall.

Assistant Trainer: Miss Joanna Sayer

Amateur: Miss Emma Sayer, Miss Natalie Sayer, Miss Robyn Gray.

563	**DR JON SCARGILL, Newmarket**

Postal: **Red House Stables, Hamilton Road, Newmarket, Suffolk, CB8 0TE**
Contacts: **PHONE (01638) 663254 MOBILE (07785) 350705**
E-MAIL scargill@redhousestables.freeserve.co.uk WEBSITE www.drjonscargill.co.uk

1 ASIA MINOR (IRE), 4, ch f Pivotal—Anka Britannia (USA) **Strawberry Fields Stud**
2 CARPENTRAS, 5, b m Val Royal (FR)—Molly Brown **D. Meilton**
3 JUNKET, 6, b m Medicean—Gallivant **Silent Partners**

THREE-YEAR-OLDS

4 DOUBLE JEOPARDY, b g Tobougg (IRE)—Four-Legged Friend **J P T Partnership & R. W. Huggins**
5 MAN IN THE ARENA, b g Bertolini (USA)—Torver **Mrs S. M. Scargill**
6 B f Proclamation (IRE)—Ribh **J P T Partnership**
7 THE GINGER BERRY, ch g First Trump—Dolly Coughdrop (IRE) **Strawberry Fields Stud**

TWO-YEAR-OLDS

8 B c 25/4 Bertolini (USA)—Torver (Lake Coniston (IRE)) **J P T Partnership**

Other Owners: G. A. Brigford, P. Darlington, J. Dutton, P. J. Edwards, A. Holness, S. Howard, L. Meadows, Mr Andrew Millar, Mr G. F. L. Robinson, P. J. Scargill, S. E. Scargill, B. Watson, R. Watson, Mr Basil White.

564 MR DERRICK SCOTT, Minehead
Postal: **East Lynch, Minehead, Somerset, TA24 8SS**
Contacts: **PHONE** (01643) 702430 **FAX** (01643) 702430

1 LUPITA (IRE), 9, ch m Intikhab (USA)—Sarah (IRE) **Mrs R. Scott**
2 ROYBUOY, 6, b g Royal Applause—Wavy Up (IRE) **Mrs R. Scott**

565 MRS ELIZABETH SCOTT, Axbridge
Postal: **Moorland Farm, Axbridge, Somerset, BS26 2BA**

1 DIAMOND DAVE, 7, ch g Thornberry (USA)—Queens Curate **Mrs E. B. Scott**
2 PORTMEADE, 11, b g Thowra (FR)—Oneninefive **Mrs E. B. Scott**

566 MR JEREMY SCOTT, Dulverton
Postal: **Higher Holworthy Farm, Brompton Regis, Dulverton, Somerset, TA22 9NY**
Contacts: **PHONE** (01398) 371414 **MOBILE** (07709) 279483
E-MAIL holworthyfarm@yahoo.com

1 ADDICTION, 8, b m Alflora (IRE)—Premier Princess **Gale Force Four**
2 ALBEROBELLO (IRE), 5, b g Old Vic—Tourist Attraction (IRE) **Bradley Partnership**
3 BALLINAHOW STAR (IRE), 7, b m Definite Article—Ballinahowliss (IRE) **Pillhead House Partners**
4 BENEFITOFHINDSIGHT, 4, ch g Sir Harry Lewis (USA)—Aoninch **Mr G. J. Wilson**
5 BEST BOY BARNEY (IRE), 7, b g Rashar (USA)—Graigue Lass (IRE) **G. T. Lever**
6 BROCKWELL PARK, 6, ch m Central Park (IRE)—Little Brockwell (IRE) **D. R. Churches**
7 DECIMUS (IRE), 6, b g Bienamado (USA)—Catch Me Dreaming (IRE) **The Ten 2 One Gang**
8 DREAM DEAL, 5, b g Presenting—Rowlands Dream (IRE) **Messer Bennetts, Clarke Hall & Gilbert**
9 DREAMBROOK LADY (IRE), 7, b m Alderbrook—Easter Day (IRE) **Ms M. Miles**
10 DUKE'S AFFAIR, 5, b g Fair Mix (IRE)—Dunsfold Duchess (IRE) **Mrs H. L. Stoneman**
11 EMPIRACLE (IRE), 6, ch g Kris Kin (USA)—Mogul Shine (IRE) **The Town & Country Partnership**
12 FLORIDA QUAYS (IRE), 5, b g Craigsteel—Florida Bay (IRE) **Favourites Racing Ltd**
13 GLENWOOD PRINCE (IRE), 7, b g King's Theatre (IRE)—Moll Rawn (IRE) **Gale Force Seven**
14 GREY MISSILE, 8, gr g Terimon—Bonne Anniversaire **I. R. Murray**
15 JOSH'S DREAMWAY (IRE), 7, b m Deploy—Midway (IRE) **Ms M. Miles**
16 KILMURVY (IRE), 5, b g Shantou (USA)—Spagna (IRE) **I. R. Murray**
17 MASTER BENJAMIN, 6, b g Fair Mix (IRE)—Morning Flight (IRE) **The Master Partners 2**
18 MASTER FLIGHT, 9, ch g Alflora (IRE)—Morning Flight (IRE) **Master Partners 1**
19 MELODIC RENDEZVOUS, 7, ch g Where Or When (IRE)—Vic Melody (FR) **Cash For Honours**
20 MOORLANDS MIST, 6, gr g Fair Mix (IRE)—Sandford Springs (USA) **Mrs L. M. Williams**
21 MYSTIC APPEAL (IRE), 7, br g Alderbrook—Piseog (IRE) **Gale Force Two**
22 ON THE BRIDGE (IRE), 8, b g Milan—Bay Dove **Mr C. J. James**
23 PALFREY BOY, 7, b g Tamure (IRE)—Fresh Gale **Pot Black Racing**
24 PAUPERS PRESENT (IRE), 5, b m Presenting—Paumafi (IRE) **A. G. Selway**
25 PERICOLOSO (IRE), 7, b g Heron Island (IRE)—Phills Serenade (IRE) **The Wild Bunch**
26 PORTERS WAR (IRE), 11, ch g Flemensfirth (USA)—Grainne Geal **Sarah Waugh & Paul Porter**
27 PYLEIGH LASS, 7, gr m Silver Patriarch (IRE)—Lady Callernish **F. D. Popham**
28 QUADDICK LAKE (IRE), 10, br g Blueprint (IRE)—Wondermac (IRE) **The Exmoor Pack**
29 RISK (IRE), 10, ch g Acatenango (GER)—Belua (GER) **Fuzzy Logic Racing Partnership**
30 SIR KEZBAAH (IRE), 9, b g Oscar (IRE)—Madam Chloe **Andrew & Vanessa Maddox**
31 SPRING STEEL (IRE), 4, b g Dushyantor (USA)—Fieldtown (IRE) **Mr S. M. Cook**
32 TINY TENOR (IRE), 7, b g Indian Danehill (IRE)—Blue Infanta **Favourites Racing Ltd**
33 WEBBERYS DREAM, 10, b g Bandmaster (USA)—Sheilas Dream **S. G. Searle**
34 WHAT ER SAY, 8, b g Karinga Bay—Spread The Word **Mrs P. J. Pengelly**

Other Owners: Mr M. P. Ansell, Mr J. F. C. Atkins, Mr J. Bagwell-Purefoy, Mr P. W. Brockman, Mrs C. Clarke-Hall, R. Coates, Mr C. Cole, Mr R. J. L. Flood, Mr A. P. Gale, Mrs A. G. Gale, Mrs K. Gilbert, Mrs G. D. Giles, Mr P. Govier, Mr P. F. Govier, M. D. Greatorex, Mr C. F. Hayes, R. W. S. Jevon, Mr S. J. Loosemore, A. Loze, Mrs C. Loze, Mr A. P. Maddox, Mrs V. Maddox, P. T. Maggs, Miss N. Martin, Mrs S. D. Messer-Bennetts, Dr M. M. Ogilvy, P. Porter, Mrs S. M. Ragg, Mr J. Simpson, Mr M. J. Swallow, Miss S. M. Waugh, Mr A. Westwood.

Assistant Trainer: Camilla Scott

Jockey (NH): Nick Scholfield. **Amateur:** Miss V. Wade.

567 MR MICHAEL SCUDAMORE, Bromsash

Postal: **Eccleswall Court, Bromsash, Nr. Ross-on-Wye, Herefordshire, HR9 7PP**
Contacts: **PHONE** (01989) 750844 **FAX** (01989) 750281 **MOBILE** (07901) 853520
E-MAIL michael.scu@btconnect.com **WEBSITE** www.scudamoreracing.co.uk

1 ADDIKT (IRE), 8, b h Diktat—Frond **Good Breed Limited**
2 BOUNDS AND LEAPS, 8, b m Laveron—Geisha **Mason Scudamore Racing**
3 CHURCH MUSIC (IRE), 4, b c Amadeus Wolf—Cappella (IRE) **JCG Chua & CK Ong**
4 DA PONTE, 5, b g Librettist (USA)—Naharnook **Mrs B. V. Evans**
5 FAIR GUN LADY, 5, gr m Fair Mix (IRE)—Persistent Gunner **Mrs J. J. Fenn & Mr W. J. Fenn**
6 FROMTHETOP (IRE), 7, b g Windsor Castle—Rose of Solway **Mr M. R. Blandford**
7 GUEST BOOK (IRE), 6, b g Green Desert (USA)—Your Welcome **M. Scudamore**
8 I'LLDOIT, 6, br g Tamayuz (CAN)—Club Oasis **Good Breed Limited**
9 KAYEF (GER), 6, ch h Nayef (USA)—Kassna (IRE) **Chua, Katriya, Hunter & Ong**
10 MONBEG DUDE (IRE), 8, b g Witness Box (USA)—Ten Dollar Bill (IRE) **Oydunow**
11 NEXT SENSATION (IRE), 6, b g Brian Boru—Road Trip (IRE) **Mr M. R. Blandford**
12 NO THROUGH ROAD, 6, b g Grape Tree Road—Pendil's Delight **Mr A. P. Barwell**
13 PRINCESSE FLEUR, 5, b m Grape Tree Road—Princesse Grec (FR) **The Honfleur Syndicate**
14 RASH MOMENT (FR), 14, b g Rudimentary (USA)—Ashura (FR) **Simpson-Daniel & Scudamore Racing**
15 RED CURRENT, 9, b m Soviet Star (USA)—Fleet Amour (USA) **Simpson-Daniel & Scudamore Racing**
16 RIPTIDE, 7, b g Val Royal (FR)—Glittering Image (IRE) **Middletons**
17 SANKYOUPLEASE (IRE), 5, b g Golan (IRE)—Special Case (IRE) **Mr M. R. Blandford**
18 SEVEN IRON SID, 7, b g Lahib (USA)—Geisha **Mason Scudamore Racing**
19 UNE DES BIEFFES (FR), 5, b m Le Fou (IRE)—Belle D'ecajeul (FR) **Michael Fitzpatrick & Mark Blandford**
20 VON GALEN (IRE), 12, b g Germany (USA)—Castle Carrig (IRE) **Mrs B. V. Evans**
21 WITH HINDSIGHT (IRE), 5, ch g Ad Valorem (USA)—Lady From Limerick (IRE) **M. Scudamore**

THREE-YEAR-OLDS

22 EASTERN DRAGON (IRE), b c Elnadim (USA)—Shulammite Woman (IRE) **Chua Ong Salthouse**

Other Owners: Mr Sydney Baker, Mr Mark Blandford, Mr J. C. G. Chua, Mr Michael Fitzpatrick, Mr Keith Hunter, Mr A. Mason, Mr G. D. Middleton, Mr A. D. Middleton, Mr C. K. Ong, Dr S. M. Readings, Mr W. J. Salthouse, Mr M. Scudamore, Mrs Marilyn Scudamore, Mr J. D. Simpson-Daniel, Mr S. M. Smith.

568 MR DEREK SHAW, Sproxton

Postal: **The Sidings, Saltby Road, Sproxton, Melton Mowbray, Leicestershire, LE14 4RA**
Contacts: **PHONE** (01476) 860578 **FAX** (01476) 860578 **MOBILE** (07721) 039645
E-MAIL mail@derekshawracing.com **WEBSITE** www.derekshawracing.com

1 ARASHI, 7, b g Fantastic Light (USA)—Arriving **Mr P. Derbyshire**
2 AVONROSE, 6, b m Avonbridge—Loveleaves **Sunny Dubai Racing**
3 BLACKSTONE VEGAS, 7, ch g Nayef (USA)—Waqood (USA) **Shakespeare Racing**
4 CHATEAU LOLA, 4, b f Byron—Glensara **Basingstoke Commercials & Ownaracehorse**
5 CLIMAXFORTACKLE (IRE), 5, b m Refuse To Bend (IRE)—Miss Asia Quest **Shakespeare Racing**
6 CONAS ATA TU, 4, b f Medicean—Sociable **Mr D. Shaw**
7 DANCING ELLIE MAE, 4, b f Proclamation (IRE)—Park Star **Mrs L. J. Shaw**
8 LOYALTY, 6, b g Medicean—Ecoutia (USA) **Mr B. Johnson**
9 MATAAJIR (USA), 5, b g Redoute's Choice (AUS)—Hamasah (USA) **Mr B. Johnson**
10 OUR PRINCESS ELLIE (USA), 5, ch m Borrego (USA)—Dear Abigail (USA) **Mrs L. J. Shaw**
11 PRINCE OF PASSION (CAN), 5, ch g Roman Ruler (USA)—Rare Passion (CAN) **Mr C. B. Hamilton**
12 REFLECT (IRE), 5, b g Hurricane Run (IRE)—Raphimix (FR) **Mr C. B. Hamilton**
13 SHAWKANTANGO, 6, b g Piccolo—Kitty Kitty Cancan **Shawthing Racing Partnership**
14 SIX SILVER LANE, 5, gr g Aussie Rules (USA)—Aurelia **Mr D. Shaw**
15 TEENAGE DREAM (IRE), 5, b g Antonius Pius (USA)—Lucayan Star (IRE) **Market Avenue Racing Club Ltd**
16 THORNCLIFFER, 9, ch g Generous (IRE)—Recipe **Moorland Racing & Mr P R Whilock**

THREE-YEAR-OLDS

17 LAST CHANCE RANCH, b c Manduro (GER)—Rakata (USA) **Mr D. Shaw**
18 B f Authorized (IRE)—Nice Tune **Mrs L. J. Shaw**
19 TWIST AND TWIRL, b f Cockney Rebel (IRE)—Silent Miracle (IRE) **Mr D. Shaw**
20 WHITEFLATS, b c Mind Games—Chertsey (IRE) **Houghton Bloodstock**

MR DEREK SHAW - Continued

TWO-YEAR-OLDS

21 B c 28/1 Excellent Art—Amaryllis (IRE) (Sadler's Wells (USA)) (15238) **Mr B. Johnson**
22 B c 14/4 Acclamation—Cambara (Dancing Brave (USA)) (50000) **Mr B. Johnson**
23 B f 17/2 Major Cadeaux—Charlie Girl (Puissance) (13333) **Mr B. Johnson**
24 B f 29/3 Dandy Man (IRE)—Colourpoint (USA) (Forest Wildcat (USA)) (6000) **Mr D. Shaw**
25 B c 2/3 Bahamian Bounty—Eastern Appeal (IRE) (Shinko Forest (IRE)) (30000) **Mr B. Johnson**
26 B c 12/2 Holy Roman Emperor (IRE)—Final Opinion (IRE) (King's Theatre (IRE)) (59047) **Mr B. Johnson**
27 B c 20/3 Holy Roman Emperor (IRE)—Jazz Up (Cadeaux Genereux) (38000) **Mr B. Johnson**
28 B c 16/3 Piccolo—Kitty Kitty Cancan (Warrshan (USA)) **Mrs L. J. Shaw**
29 Ch c 15/4 Piccolo—Madrasee (Beveled (USA)) **Mrs L. J. Shaw**
30 B c 3/3 New Approach (IRE)—Obsessive (USA) (Seeking The Gold (USA)) (42000) **Mr B. Johnson**
31 B c 6/2 Footstepsinthesand—Ruthie (Pursuit of Love) (15000) **Mr B. Johnson**
32 Gr c 1/5 Elnadim (USA)—The Manx Touch (IRE) (Petardia) (40000) **Mr B. Johnson**
33 Ch c 24/4 Pivotal—Visualize (Medicean) (20952) **Mr B. Johnson**

Other Owners: Mr P. Bridges, Mr P. Derbyshire, Mr B. Goodyear, Mr N. Higginson, Mr Bryan Johnson, Mr T. Lively, S. A. Mace, D. N. McLeish, Ownaracehorse Ltd, Mr D. Shaw, Mrs L. J. Shaw, Mr A. P. Simmill, Mrs C. M. Simmill, Mr S. Warren, Mr P. R. Whilock, Mr S. A. Whiteman.

Yard Sponsor - Grosvenor Contracts Leasing Ltd

Jockey (flat): Martin Dwyer. **Apprentice:** Adam McLean.

---

569 MRS PATRICIA SHAW, Looe
Postal: Kilminorth Park, Looe, Cornwall, PL13 2NE

1 FIREWELD, 6, b m Weld—Bella Astra **Mr D. C. Odgers**
2 JOAACI (IRE), 13, b g Presenting—Miss Sarajevo (IRE) **Mr D. C. Odgers**
3 MOBAASHER (USA), 10, ch g Rahy (USA)—Balistroika (USA) **Mr D. C. Odgers**

---

570 MR MATT SHEPPARD, Ledbury
Postal: Home Farm Cottage, Eastnor, Ledbury, Herefordshire, HR8 1RD
Contacts: FAX (01531) 634846 MOBILE (07770) 625061
E-MAIL matthew.sheppard@cmail.co.uk WEBSITE www.mattsheppardracing.co.uk

1 ACHIMOTA (IRE), 7, b g Double Eclipse (IRE)—Tullyfoyle (IRE) **W. J. Odell**
2 BIG ROBERT, 9, b g Medicean—Top Flight Queen **S. J. D. Gegg**
3 DANEVA (IRE), 9, b m Turtle Island (IRE)—Testaway (IRE) **Matt Sheppard Racing Club**
4 HAZEYMM (IRE), 10, b g Marju (IRE)—Shimna **Mrs N. Sheppard**
5 IKORODU ROAD, 10, b g Double Trigger (IRE)—Cerisier (IRE) **W. J. Odell**
6 LOUGHALDER (IRE), 7, ch g Alderbrook—Lough Lein Leader (IRE) **Mr Simon Gegg & Mr Tony Scrivin**
7 SEYMOUR ALFIE, 7, b g Afflora (IRE)—Seymour Chance **Mrs C. J. Black**
8 WITNESS THAT (IRE), 7, b g Witness Box (USA)—Mabrooka (USA) **Lost In The Summer Wine**

Other Owners: Mr C. M. Brookes, R. A. Kujawa, Mr A. J. Scrivin, Mr P. R. W. Smith.

Amateur: Mr J. M. Ridley.

---

571 MR FRANK SHERIDAN, Wolverhampton
Postal: 3 The Mews, Gorsebrook Road, Dunstall Park, Wolverhampton, West Midlands, WV6 0PE
Contacts: MOBILE (07889) 962218
E-MAIL sheridanfrank@libero.it

1 GREEN KING (ITY), 4, b g King's Theatre (IRE)—Asura (GER) **F. Sheridan**
2 GREEN MITAS (ITY), 4, ch c Denon (USA)—Sequita (GER) **Mr C. Beek**
3 JAWKING, 4, b g Compton Place—Just Down The Road (IRE) **J A & S Wilcox**
4 NEEDWOOD RIDGE, 6, ch g Needwood Blade—Aspen Ridge (IRE) **T. Maud-Powell**
5 OZZ, 4, gr f Aussie Rules (USA)—Spicey **F. Sheridan**
6 PRIGSNOV DANCER (IRE), 8, ch g Namid—Brave Dance (IRE) **J. M. Lacey**
7 TYRUR TED, 8, b g Val Royal (FR)—Spanish Serenade **Mr F. Sheridan**

MR FRANK SHERIDAN - Continued

THREE-YEAR-OLDS

  8 **ALPINE JERRY (IRE),** b f Jeremy (USA)—Champoluc (IRE)
  9 **FIREY SALLY (IRE),** b f Strategic Prince—Serious Rock (IRE)
 10 **GREEN AND WHITE (ITY),** b c Denon (USA)—Sequita (GER) **F. Sheridan**
 11 **GREEN SPECIAL (ITY),** ch g Denon (USA)—Groove (ITY) **F. Sheridan**

Other Owners: Mr Martin Fisher, Mr T. J. Maud-Powell, Mr J. A. Wilcox, Mrs S. Wilcox.

572	**MR OLIVER SHERWOOD, Upper Lambourn** Postal: Rhonehurst House, Upper Lambourn, Hungerford, Berkshire, RG17 8RG Contacts: PHONE (01488) 71411 FAX (01488) 72786 MOBILE (07979) 591867 E-MAIL oliver.sherwood@virgin.net WEBSITE www.oliversherwood.com

  1 **ARKOSE (IRE),** 9, b g Luso—Endless Patience (IRE) **D. P. Barrie & Partners 'A'**
  2 **BEFOREALL (IRE),** 5, b g Spadoun (FR)—Maggie Howard (IRE) **Beforeall Partnership**
  3 **BEN CEE PEE M (IRE),** 8, ch g Beneficial—Supreme Magical **CPM Group Limited**
  4 **BERTIE'S DESIRE,** 5, b g King's Theatre (IRE)—Temptation (FR) **T. D. J. Syder**
  5 **CAMDEN (IRE),** 7, b g Old Vic—Electric View (IRE) **T. D. J. Syder**
  6 **CIRCUS OF DREAMS,** 10, b g Kayf Tara—Foehn Gale (IRE) **D. B. Knox**
  7 **D'ARGENT CLOUD,** 5, gr g Tikkanen (USA)—Sounds Familiar (IRE) **CPM Group Limited**
  8 **DEPUTY DAN (IRE),** 5, b g Westerner—Louisas Dream (IRE) **T. D. J. Syder**
  9 **DRUM VALLEY,** 5, b g Beat Hollow—Euippe **Mr D. J. Burke & Mr T. Meehan**
 10 **EXITAS (IRE),** 5, b g Exit To Nowhere (USA)—Suntas (IRE) **Fawley House Stud**
 11 **FAIR BRAMBLE,** 7, b m Fair Mix (IRE)—Briery Ann **P. A. Deal**
 12 **FIFTYONEFIFTYONE (IRE),** 9, b g Oscar (IRE)—Great Dante (IRE) **A. Taylor**
 13 **FINANCIAL CLIMATE (IRE),** 6, b g Exit To Nowhere (USA)—Claudia's Pearl **Mrs S. C. Fillery**
 14 **FLING ME (IRE),** 6, b g Definite Article—Seductive Dance **T. J. Hemmings**
 15 **FLORAFERN,** 8, b m Alflora (IRE)—Mossy Fern **G. R. Waters**
 16 **FURROWS,** 8, b g Alflora (IRE)—See More Furrows **Furrows Ltd**
 17 **GLOBAL POWER (IRE),** 7, b g Subtle Power (IRE)—Bartelko (IRE) **It Wasn't Us**
 18   5, B g Alflora (IRE)—Ivy Edith **Furrows Ltd**
 19 **JEANO DE TOULOUSE (FR),** 6, b g Lavirco (GER)—Indecidable (FR) **D. P. Barrie & D. Redhead**
 20 **KAITUNA (IRE),** 7, b m Flemensfirth (USA)—Southern Skies (IRE) **P. Deal & N. Chamberlain**
 21 **KASBADALI (FR),** 8, b g Kahyasi—Nikalie (FR) **T. D. J. Syder**
 22 **KNOCKALONGI,** 7, b g Fair Mix (IRE)—Understudy **The St Joseph Partnership**
 23   4, B f Kayf Tara—L'ultima (FR) **T. D. J. Syder**
 24 **LADY SINATRA,** 5, b m Where Or When (IRE)—Kythia (IRE) **The Pretty Hopeful Syndicate**
 25 **LEMONY BAY,** 4, b g Overbury (IRE)—Lemon's Mill (USA) **R. Waters**
 26 **LUCI DI MEZZANOTTE,** 5, ch m Sulamani (IRE)—Dissolve **P. K. Gardner T/A Springcombe Park Stud**
 27 **MAJORICA KING (FR),** 7, b g Kahyasi—Majorica Queen (FR) **Mrs S. Griffiths**
 28 **MANY CLOUDS (IRE),** 6, br g Cloudings (IRE)—Bobbing Back (IRE) **T. J. Hemmings**
 29 **MILGEN BAY,** 7, br g Generous (IRE)—Lemon's Mill (USA) **G. R. Waters**
 30 **MISCHIEVOUS MILLY (IRE),** 5, b m Old Vic—Jennifers Diary (IRE) **A. Stewart & A. Taylor**
 31 **MISS OVERDRIVE,** 9, b m Overbury (IRE)—Free Travel **Partners In Wine**
 32 **MORNING REGGIE,** 4, gr g Turgeon (USA)—Nile Cristale (FR) **T. D. J. Syder**
 33 **MOULIN DE LA CROIX,** 9, b m Muhtarram (USA)—Brambly Hedge **Luksonwood Partnership**
 34 **PUFFIN BILLY (IRE),** 5, b g Heron Island (IRE)—Downtown Train (IRE) **T. D. J. Syder**
 35 **RAYVIN BLACK,** 4, b c Halling (USA)—Optimistic **V. J. Walsh**
 36 **UBALDO DES MENHIES (FR),** 5, b br g Network (GER)—Ker Marie (FR) **Million in Mind Partnership**
 37 **WHATSUPJACK (IRE),** 6, b g Catcher In The Rye (IRE)—Riverstown Girl (IRE) **Mr M. G. St Quinton**

Other Owners: Mr D. P. Barrie, Mr A. R. Bromley, Mr D. J. Burke, Mr Nigel Chamberlain, Ms Liz Clark, Mr P. A. Deal, Mrs J. G. Donald, Mr Graham Goode, Mr Richard Jenkins, Mrs Michael Lambert, Mrs Julia Lukas, Mrs S. McGrath, Mr R. McGrath, Mr Tony Meehan, Mr D. Minton, Mrs D. Nicholson, Mr M. E. O'Hara, Mr Julian Palfreyman, Mr H. M. J. Pope, Mr D. Redhead, Mr O. M. C. Sherwood, The Hon Mrs S. Sherwood, Mr Adrian Stewart, Mr A. Taylor, Lady Thompson, Mr D. P. Walsh, Mr V. J. Walsh, Mr W. S. Watt.

Assistant Trainer: Tom Fillery **Head Lad:** Stefan Namesansky

Jockey (NH): Sam Jones, Leighton Aspell, Dominic Elsworth. **Amateur:** Mr J. Sherwood.

573 MR SIMON SHIRLEY-BEAVAN, Hawick
Postal: **Gatehousecote, Bonchester Bridge, Hawick, Roxburghshire, TD9 8JD**
Contacts: **PHONE (01450) 860210**

1 **QOLLIOURE (FR)**, 9, b g Bulington (FR)—Bonne Bibine (FR) **Mrs P. M. Shirley-Beavan**
2 **RAPIDOLYTE DE LADALKA (FR)**, 8, b g Network (GER)—Emeraude du Moulin (FR) **Mrs P. M. Shirley-Beavan**
3 **SHOW PUBLIC (FR)**, 7, b g Network (GER)—Grageline (FR) **Mrs P. M. Shirley-Beavan**
4 **SORCIER (FR)**, 7, b g Shaanmer (IRE)—Donitille (FR) **Mrs P. M. Shirley-Beavan**
5 **TAMBOUR MAJOR (FR)**, 6, b g Myrakalu (FR)—Joaillere (FR) **Mrs P. M. Shirley-Beavan**

574 MISS LYNN SIDDALL, Tadcaster
Postal: **Stonebridge Farm, Colton, Tadcaster, North Yorkshire, LS24 8EP**
Contacts: **PHONE (01904) 744291 FAX (01904) 744291 MOBILE (07778) 216692/4**

1 **ALFIE'S BOW**, 6, ch g Alflora (IRE)—Long Shot **Mr G. Kennington**
2 **ANNIE'S DAUGHTER**, 6, b m Danbird (AUS)—Moondance **Podso Racing**
3 **BACH STREET GIRL (IRE)**, 9, ch m Bach (IRE)—Millmount (IRE) **Mr G. Kennington**
4 **BLUE COVE**, 8, ch g Karinga Bay—Meadow Blue **Mr G. Kennington**
5 **CADGERS HOLE**, 6, b g Helissio (FR)—Not So Prim **Mrs D. Ibbotson**
6 **DIRECT APPROACH (IRE)**, 9, b g Tel Quel (FR)—Miss Telimar (IRE) **Mr G. Kennington**
7 **I KNOW THE CODE (IRE)**, 8, b g Viking Ruler (AUS)—Gentle Papoose **Lynn Siddall Racing II**
8 **LISDONAGH HOUSE (IRE)**, 11, b g Little Bighorn—Lifinsa Barina (IRE) **J. P. G. Cooke**
9 **PRIZE FIGHTER (IRE)**, 11, b g Desert Sun—Papal **Pennine Racing Associates**
10 **WESTWIRE TOBY (IRE)**, 11, ch g Anshan—Ware It Well (IRE) **Stonebridge Racing II**

Other Owners: Mr C. W. Abbott, Mrs P. J. Clark, Mrs E. W. Cooper, Mr B. Donkin, Mrs V. Ellison, Mr I. Grice, Mr P. M. Hornby, Mrs D. Ibbotson, Mrs K. M. Kennington, Miss S. Lythe, Miss J. M. Slater, Miss Sue Vinden.

Assistant Trainer: Stephen Hackney

Jockey (NH): Tom Siddall.

575 MR DAVID SIMCOCK, Newmarket
Postal: **The Office, Trillium Place, Birdcage Walk, Newmarket, Suffolk, CB8 0NE**
Contacts: **PHONE (01638) 662968 FAX (01638) 663888 MOBILE (07808) 954109**
E-MAIL david@davidsimcock.co.uk WEBSITE www.davidsimcock.co.uk

1 **AL KHAWANEEJ**, 5, br h Arch (USA)—Fraulein
2 **ANY GIVEN DREAM (IRE)**, 4, b g Bahri (USA)—Anazara (USA)
3 **ATTRACTION TICKET**, 4, b g Selkirk (USA)—Trick (IRE)
4 **CARDINAL WALTER (IRE)**, 4, br b g Cape Cross (IRE)—Sheer Spirit (IRE)
5 **CASTILO DEL DIABLO (IRE)**, 4, br g Teofilo (IRE)—Hundred Year Flood (USA)
6 **ENGLISH SUMMER**, 6, b g Montjeu (IRE)—Hunt The Sun
7 **GUCCI D'ORO (USA)**, 4, b br c Medaglia d'oro (USA)—Ninette (USA)
8 **HIERARCH (IRE)**, 6, b g Dansili—Danse Classique (IRE)
9 **I'M A DREAMER (IRE)**, 6, b m Noverre (USA)—Summer Dreams (IRE)
10 **MALEKAT JAMAL (IRE)**, 4, b f Dutch Art—Haretha (IRE)
11 **MARTIN CHUZZLEWIT (IRE)**, 4, ch g Galileo (IRE)—Alta Anna (FR)
12 **MEAN IT (IRE)**, 4, b g Danehill Dancer (IRE)—Lilissa (IRE)
13 **MOMENT IN TIME (IRE)**, 4, b f Tiger Hill (IRE)—Horatia (IRE)
14 **NAVE (USA)**, 6, b g Pulpit (USA)—Lakabi (USA)
15 **NO HERETIC**, 5, b g Galileo (IRE)—Intrigued
16 **OTTOMAN EMPIRE (FR)**, 7, ch g Pivotal—Chesnut Bird (IRE)
17 **RED DUKE (USA)**, 4, ch g Hard Spun (USA)—Saudia (USA)
18 **SAUNTA**, 4, b f Invincible Spirit (IRE)—Baize
19 **SHEIKHZAYEDROAD**, 4, b g Dubawi (IRE)—Royal Secrets (IRE)
20 **TRADE STORM**, 5, b h Trade Fair—Frisson
21 **VAINGLORY (USA)**, 9, ch g Swain (IRE)—Infinite Spirit (USA)
22 **WAVEGUIDE (IRE)**, 4, b f Dubawi (IRE)—Million Waves (IRE)
23 **WHISPERING WARRIOR (IRE)**, 4, b c Oasis Dream—Varenka (IRE)
24 **WHITE NILE (IRE)**, 4, b c Galileo (IRE)—Super Gift (IRE)

MR DAVID SIMCOCK - Continued

THREE-YEAR-OLDS

25 **AL ENBESS (IRE)**, b c Kyllachy—Taghreed (IRE)
26 **AL MEEZAN**, ch c Nayef (USA)—Festivale (IRE)
27 **BEAUTIFUL LIFE**, b f Footstepsinthesand—My Heart's Deelite (USA)
28 **BIRDMAN (IRE)**, b g Danehill Dancer (IRE)—Gilded Vanity (IRE)
29 **BRAZEN**, b c Kyllachy—Molly Brown
30 **BRETON ROCK (IRE)**, b c Bahamian Bounty—Anna's Rock (IRE)
31 **BRIGH (IRE)**, ch f Galileo (IRE)—La Vida Loca (IRE)
32 **COULD BE (IRE)**, b c Sakhee (USA)—Catch Us (FR)
33 **DEIRA PHANTOM (IRE)**, b c Cape Cross (IRE)—Ammo (IRE)
34 **DREAM CAST (IRE)**, b c Refuse To Bend (IRE)—Star Studded
35 **EDWYN RALPH**, b c Sir Percy—Edwardian Era
36 **EVERLASTING DREAM**, b f Oasis Dream—Magdalene
37 **EXCELLENT HIT**, b c Exceed And Excel (AUS)—Broadway Hit
38 **FATIMA'S GIFT**, b f Dalakhani (IRE)—Heavenly Whisper (IRE)
39 **GABRIAL THE BOSS (USA)**, ch g Street Boss (USA)—Bacinella (IRE)
40 **GLASS OFFICE**, br gr c Verglas (IRE)—Oval Office
41 **GO ANGELLICA (IRE)**, ch f Kheleyf (USA)—Areyaam (USA)
42 **GREAT ORMOND (IRE)**, b g Zamindar (USA)—Paint The Town (IRE)
43 **HERFUL SCHNERFUL**, b f Jeremy (USA)—Valandraud (IRE)
44 **INDIA'S SONG**, b f Zamindar (USA)—Sea Chorus
45 **KELADIVA**, b f Dixie Union (USA)—Keladora (USA)
46 **LINE OF REASON (IRE)**, br c Kheleyf (USA)—Miss Party Line (USA)
47 **MAJEED**, b c Mount Nelson—Clever Millie (USA)
48 **MIDNIGHT FLOWER (IRE)**, b f Haafhd—Takawiri (IRE)
49 **MISS YOU TOO**, b f Montjeu (IRE)—Portrait of A Lady (IRE)
50 **NEAMOUR**, b f Oasis Dream—Ever Rigg
51 **PENCOMBE (FR)**, b c Teofilo (IRE)—Barbuda
52 **POSTE RESTANTE**, b f Halling (USA)—Postage Stampe
53 **RAY WARD (IRE)**, b c Galileo (IRE)—Kentucky Warbler (IRE)
54 **STASIO (USA)**, b c Street Boss (USA)—Believe (USA)
55 **VULCAN (IRE)**, b g Tiger Hill (IRE)—Messias da Silva (USA)
56 **WHISPERING LADY (IRE)**, b f Pivotal—Bon Nuit (IRE)
57 **ZEVA**, b f Zamindar (USA)—Mennetou (IRE)

TWO-YEAR-OLDS

58 **AFFAIRE DE COEUR**, b f 10/2 Dalakhani (IRE)—Divergence (USA) (Red Ransom (USA)) (19047)
59 **ANYA'S ANGEL**, b f 9/3 Holy Roman Emperor (IRE)—Someone's Angel (USA) (Runaway Groom (CAN)) (13333)
60 B f 6/3 Kheleyf (USA)—Areyaam (USA) (Elusive Quality (USA))
61 B f 31/1 Nayef (USA)—Bakhoor (USA) (Royal Applause)
62 Ch c 28/1 Galileo (IRE)—Baraka (IRE) (Danehill (USA)) (50000)
63 B c 8/2 Duke of Marmalade (IRE)—Blessing (USA) (Pulpit (USA))
64 **BORISOCRACY (IRE)**, b c 5/3 Acclamation—River Mountain (Reset (AUS)) (150793)
65 **BRETON COMMANDER**, b c 1/4 Zamindar (USA)—Lady Donatella (Last Tycoon) (30000)
66 **BREUGHEL (GER)**, b c 27/2 Dutch Art—Bezzaaf (Machiavellian (USA)) (95238)
67 **CAN'T CHANGE IT (IRE)**, gr c 8/3 Verglas (IRE)—All Tied Up (IRE) (Desert Prince (IRE)) (28571)
68 B c 15/3 High Chaparral (IRE)—Clincher Club (Polish Patriot (USA)) (72000)
69 **COLONEL ALI**, b c 30/3 Kyllachy—Night Premiere (IRE) (Night Shift (USA)) (55238)
70 B c 12/2 New Approach (IRE)—Dance Lively (USA) (Kingmambo (USA)) (78000)
71 B g 26/4 Rock of Gibraltar (IRE)—Delisha (Salse (USA)) (25000)
72 B f 3/5 Shamardal (USA)—Divisa (GER) (Lomitas) (15000)
73 **DOCTOR SARDONICUS**, ch c 5/3 Medicean—Never A Doubt (Night Shift (USA)) (95238)
74 B c 22/2 Kyllachy—Dream Dance (Diesis) (32000)
75 B br f 26/4 War Front (USA)—Eclisse (FR) (Ski Chief (USA)) (25806)
76 B f 3/4 High Chaparral (IRE)—English Ballet (USA) (Danehill Dancer (IRE)) (30000)
77 **ERRONEOUS (IRE)**, br c 10/2 Footstepsinthesand—Atir Love (USA) (Green Dancer (USA)) (40000)
78 B c 29/4 Kheleyf (USA)—Komena (Komaite (USA)) (27619)
79 **MADAME CHIANG**, b f 20/4 Archipenko (USA)—Robe Chinoise (Robellino (USA))
80 B c 28/1 Iffraaj—Miss Gibraltar (Rock of Gibraltar (IRE)) (85714)
81 C c 9/3 Street Cry (IRE)—Modesty Blaise (USA) (A P Indy (USA)) (61443)
82 B f 10/5 Danehill Dancer (IRE)—Mountain Chain (USA) (Royal Academy (USA))
83 Br f 12/5 Dylan Thomas (IRE)—Niner's Home (USA) (Forty Niner (USA))
84 B c 18/3 Archipenko (USA)—Oblige (Robellino (USA)) (45238)
85 **PURPLE LANE (IRE)**, ch c 4/5 Danehill Dancer (IRE)—Big Heart (Mr Greeley (USA))
86 B f 6/4 Montjeu (IRE)—Race For The Stars (USA) (Fusaichi Pegasus (USA)) (65079)

MR DAVID SIMCOCK - Continued

87 Gr f 14/4 Dalakhani (IRE)—Rock Salt (Selkirk (USA)) (280000)
88 B f 11/4 Duke of Marmalade (IRE)—Rosamixa (FR) (Linamix (FR))
89 B f 6/2 Shirocco (GER)—Sakhya (IRE) (Barathea (IRE))
90 B f 22/2 Giant's Causeway (USA)—Swan Nebula (USA) (Seeking the Gold (USA)) (190476)
91 ULTRAVIOLET (IRE), b f 9/4 Tamayuz—Aphorism (Halling (USA))
92 B f 25/3 Fastnet Rock (AUS)—Uriah (GER) (Acatenango (GER)) (42000)

Owners: A & A, A. Al Shaikh, Mrs J. M. Annable, HE Sheikh Sultan Bin Khalifa Al Nahyan, A. W. Black, O. Brendon, Malcolm Caine, J. M. Cook, K. A. Dasmal, Z. A. Galadari, Gee Ceffyl Bach Club, Mrs F. H. Hay, A. G. D. Hogarth, M. Jaber, Mr A. Jaber, Dr Marwan Koukash, S. Manana, Maxilead Limited, Bob Michaelson, New Dreamers, Sir Robert Ogden, Mr D. Pittack, Miss K. Rausing, Rutland Park Racing, D. M. I. Simcock, St Albans Bloodstock, S. Suhail, Tick Tock Partnership, Universal Racing, Mrs C. J. Wates, C. V. Wentworth, Mr A. P. C. Whitlock, Major M. G. Wyatt.

Assistant Trainer: Tom Clover

Jockey (flat): Martin Lane, William Buick, Jamie Spencer. **Apprentice:** Alice Haynes, Siobhan Miller.

---

576 | MRS EVELYN SLACK, Appleby
Postal: **Stoneriggs, Hilton, Appleby, Cumbria, CA16 6LS**
Contacts: PHONE **(01768) 351354** MOBILE **(07503) 161240**

1 GRAND VINTAGE (IRE), 7, gr g Basanta (IRE)—Rivers Town Rosie (IRE) **A. Slack**
2 SCRIPTWRITER, 11, b g Sadler's Wells (USA)—Dayanata **A. Slack**
3 VAN MILDERT (IRE), 4, b f Observatory (USA)—Vanilla Delight (IRE) **Mrs D. E. Slack**

Assistant Trainer: K. A. A. Slack (01768) 351922 Or (07931) 137413

Amateur: Miss Natalie Sayer.

---

577 | MRS PAM SLY, Peterborough
Postal: **Singlecote, Thorney, Peterborough, Cambridgeshire, PE6 0PB**
Contacts: PHONE **(01733) 270212** MOBILE **(07850) 511267**

1 ARKAIM, 5, b g Oasis Dream—Habariya (IRE) **G.A.Libson D.L.Bayliss G.Taylor P.M.Sly**
2 BOUNTIFUL CATCH, 4, ch g Bahamian Bounty—Saida Lenasera (FR) **Mrs P. M. Sly**
3 CHICKLEMIX, 7, gr m Fair Mix (IRE)—Chichell's Hurst **M. H. Sly, Dr T. Davies & Mrs P. Sly**
4 CIRCUS STAR (USA), 5, b g Borrego (USA)—Picadilly Circus (USA) **G.A.Libson D.L.Bayliss G.Taylor P.M.Sly**
5 HELPSTON, 9, b g Sir Harry Lewis (USA)—Chichell's Hurst **Mrs P. M. Sly**
6 HOOKED ON LINE (IRE), 8, b g Catcher In The Rye (IRE)—Pohutakawa (FR) **P. J. Turner**
7 KAYAAN, 6, br g Marju (IRE)—Raheefa (USA) **D. L. Bayliss**
8 PHEIDIAS (IRE), 9, ch g Spectrum (IRE)—Danse Grecque (IRE) **G.A.Libson D.L.Bayliss G.Taylor P.M.Sly**
9 SAN ANTONIO, 13, b g Efisio—Winnebago **Mrs P. M. Sly**
10 SCARLET WHISPERS, 4, b f Sir Percy—Hieroglyph **Mr G. A. Libson**
11 SCARVA, 5, br m King's Theatre (IRE)—Dara's Pride (IRE) **Mrs V. M. Edmonson**
12 SYNCOPATE, 4, b g Oratorio (IRE)—Millistar **Unregistered Partnership**
13 TRICKY TREE (IRE), 7, b g Montjeu (IRE)—Ruissec (USA) **Mrs V. M. Edmonson**
14 VERMUYDEN, 4, b g Oasis Dream—Speciosa (IRE) **M. H. Sly, Dr T. Davies & Mrs P. Sly**

THREE-YEAR-OLDS

15 BOUNTIFUL BESS, ch f Bahamian Bounty—Saida Lenasera (FR) **Mrs P. M. Sly**
16 SPECIALTY (IRE), b f Oasis Dream—Speciosa (IRE) **M. H. Sly, Dr T. Davies & Mrs P. Sly**
17 TRYMYLUCK, b f Royal Applause—Borders Belle (IRE) **Mrs P. M. Sly**

TWO-YEAR-OLDS

18 Br c 24/3 Pastoral Pursuits—Black Salix (USA) (More Than Ready (USA)) **Mrs P. M. Sly**
19 B f 29/3 Sea The Stars (IRE)—Speciosa (IRE) (Danehill Dancer (IRE)) **M. H. Sly, Dr T. Davies & Mrs P. Sly**

Other Owners: Mr David L. Bayliss, Dr T. J. W. Davies, Mr G. A. Libson, Mrs P. M. Sly, Mr Michael H. Sly, Mr G. Taylor.

Jockey (NH): Sean Quinlan. **Amateur:** Miss Gina Andrews.

578 MR DAVID SMAGA, Lamorlaye

Postal: **17 Voie de la Grange des Pres, 60260 Lamorlaye, France**
Contacts: PHONE **(0033) 3442 15005** FAX **(0033) 3442 15356** MOBILE **(0033) 6078 37287**
E-MAIL david-smaga@wanadoo.fr

1 BOOKEND, 9, b g Dansili—Roupala (USA) **Mr D Smaga**
2 BROWN TIGER (IRE), 4, b c Galileo (IRE)—Guarded **Mr R. Nahas**
3 CHEAM KSAH (IRE), 4, b f Hurricane Run (IRE)—Mawhiba (USA) **Mr D. Smaga**
4 DON BOSCO (FR), 6, ch h Barathea (IRE)—Perfidie (IRE) **Mr O. El Sharif**
5 DORADE ROSE (FR), 5, b m Marchand de Sable (USA)—Shadai Stone (JPN) **Mr R Bellaiche**
6 FRED LALLOUPET, 6, b h Elusive City (USA)—Firm Friend (IRE) **Mr M. Lagasse**
7 HAREM LADY (FR), 4, b f Teofilo (IRE)—Luminosity **Mr R. Nahas**
8 HIDDEN RAINBOW (IRE), 10, ch g Spectrum (IRE)—Grecian Urn **Mr D. Smaga**
9 KATCHAGUA (FR), 4, b f Anabaa (USA)—Pats Martini (USA) **Mr A. Louis-Dreyfus**
10 MOONDAY SUN (USA), 4, gr ro c Mizzen Mast (USA)—Storm Dove (USA) **K. Abdulla**
11 MR DOYEN, 5, b br h Doyen (IRE)—Masrora (USA) **Mr G. Augustin-Normand**
12 SAINT ELIER (FR), 4, b c Stormy River (FR)—Basse Besogne (IRE) **Mr G. Augustin-Normand**
13 SAPHIRSIDE (IRE), 4, b g Elusive City (USA)—Silirisa (FR) **Mr G. Augustin-Normand**

THREE-YEAR-OLDS

14 BONNEVILLE (FR), ch f Anabaa Blue—Maya de La Luz **Mr G. Augustin-Normand**
15 CANDESTA (USA), b c First Defence (USA)—Wandesta **K. Abdulla**
16 CLARA LUNA (IRE), b f Muhtathir—Perfidie (IRE) **Mr A. M. Haddad**
17 DELANTERA (FR), b f Lawman (FR)—Dirigeante (USA) **Haras D'Etreham**
18 EGADE (FR), ch f Royal Assault (USA)—Flavignana (FR) **Mme K. Bokobsa**
19 FOXTROT YANKEE (USA), b f First Defence (USA)—Birthplace (USA) **K. Abdulla**
20 GONAWIN (FR), b f Anabaa (USA)—Funny Feerie (FR) **Mr W. Said**
21 LUCKY LOOK (FR), b f Teofilo (IRE)—Victoria College (FR) **Mr A. M. Haddad**
22 MILEDOUSHE (USA), b f Dylan Thomas (IRE)—Khamsin (USA) **Mr A. Louis-Dreyfus**
23 MIZZENWAY (USA), b f Mizzen Mast (USA)—Gateway (USA) **K. Abdulla**
24 OMY, b c Zamindar (USA)—Galipette **Mr O. El Sharif**
25 PARATY DREAM (FR), b f Elusive Quality (USA)—Sur Ma Vie (USA) **Mr R. Nahas**
26 ROYAL MANIFICO (IRE), b c Hannouma (IRE)—Poltava (FR) **Mr D. Smaga**
27 SANIMA (IRE), b f Galileo (IRE)—Sophisticat (USA) **Haras D'Etreham**
28 SUGAR TRAIN, b c Rail Link—Plum Fairy **K. Abdulla**
29 TINGLE TANGLE (USA), b br c Mizzen Mast (USA)—Tinge (USA) **K. Abdulla**
30 VAL DE SAANE (IRE), b c Rock of Gibraltar (IRE)—Mahendra (GER) **Mr G. Augustin-Normand**

TWO-YEAR-OLDS

31 ALMERIA, b f 17/5 Shamardal (USA)—Suedoise (Kris) (63492) **Mr A. M. Haddad**
32 Ch f 6/2 Hurricane Run (IRE)—Arrow of Desire (Danehill Dancer (IRE)) **Mr R. Nahas**
33 Ch c 14/2 Mastercraftsman (IRE)—Chaibia (IRE) (Peintre Celebre (USA)) (91269) **Mr A. M. Haddad**
34 B f 24/2 Elusive City (USA)—Firm Friend (IRE) (Affirmed (USA)) **Mr M. Lagasse**
35 B f 6/5 Zamindar (USA)—Fully Invested (USA) (Irish River (FR)) **K. Abdulla**
36 B br c 4/2 Mizzen Mast (USA)—Gainful (USA) (Gone West (USA)) **K. Abdulla**
37 Gr ro f 20/2 Mizzen Mast (USA)—Gateway (USA) (A P Indy (USA)) **K. Abdulla**
38 B f 6/5 High Chaparral (IRE)—Larme (IRE) (Soviet Star (USA)) **Mr R. Nahas**
39 B c 1/1 Cape Cross (IRE)—Luminosity (Sillery (USA)) (39682) **Haras D'Etreham**
40 MISTER GINO, ch c 12/2 Teofilo (IRE)—Ginostra (Oasis Dream) (43650) **Mr F. Amar**
41 NOLLEVAL (FR), b c 29/4 Gold Away (IRE)—
                        Amazing Story (FR) (Cricket Ball (USA)) (14285) **Mr G. Augustin-Normand**
42 B c 16/2 Rail Link—Plum Fairy (Sadler's Wells (USA)) **K. Abdulla**
43 B f 8/4 Mastercraftsman (IRE)—Poltava (FR) (Victory Note (USA)) (59523) **Mr M. Parrish**
44 B f 17/3 Champs Elysees—Posteritas (USA) (Lear Fan (USA)) **K. Abdulla**
45 B f 24/2 First Defence (USA)—Privity (USA) (Private Account (USA)) **K. Abdulla**
46 RAFFINEE (FR), b f 22/4 Air Eminem (IRE)—Gioconda Umbra (ITY) (Sicyos (USA)) **Mme M. Fougy**
47 ROCALISA (FR), b f 1/6 Gentlewave (IRE)—Flavignana (FR) (Anabaa Blue) **Mme K Bokobsa**
48 B c 4/5 New Approach (IRE)—Sasanuma (USA) (Kingmambo (USA)) **Mr R. Nahas**
49 Br c 16/3 Three Valleys (USA)—Silver Yen (USA) (Silver Hawk (USA)) **K. Abdulla**
50 SKIPPY, b f 25/3 Gold Away (IRE)—Zghorta (USA) (Gone West (USA)) (10317) **Mr A. Louis-Dreyfus**
51 Ch f 12/3 Gentlewave (IRE)—Sometime (FR) (Anabaa (USA)) **Mr R. Nahas**
52 C c 31/1 Falco (USA)—Spring Fun (FR) (Kingmambo (USA)) **Mr R. Nahas**
53 B br c 19/2 Mizzen Mast (USA)—Storm Dove (USA) (Storm Bird (CAN)) **K. Abdulla**
54 B f 10/2 Slickly (FR)—Vezara (IRE) (Grand Lodge (USA)) **Mr R. Nahas**
55 B c 15/4 Whipper (USA)—Whisper To Dream (USA) (Gone West (USA)) **Mr R. Nahas**

579 MR BRYAN SMART, Hambleton

Postal: Hambleton House, Sutton Bank, Thirsk, North Yorkshire, YO7 2HA
Contacts: PHONE (01845) 597481 FAX (01845) 597480 MOBILE (07748) 634797
E-MAIL office@bryansmart.plus.com WEBSITE www.bryansmart-racing.com

1 BANDSTAND, 7, b g Royal Applause—Incise **Crossfields Racing**
2 BARTLEY, 4, ch g Monsieur Bond (IRE)—Annie Harvey **Mrs V. Smart**
3 BOP IT, 4, b g Misu Bond (IRE)—Forever Bond **A. Turton, J. Blackburn & R. Bond**
4 CODE SIX (IRE), 4, gr f Kodiac—Grey Pursuit (IRE) **Woodcock Electrical Limited**
5 DA'QUONDE (IRE), 5, br m Pivotal—Bobcat Greeley (USA) **The Barber Girls**
6 DUBAI HILLS, 7, b g Dubai Destination (USA)—Hill Welcome **Mrs F. Denniff**
7 EMILY HALL, 4, ch f Paris House—Raven (IRE) **R & E Hall & Son**
8 ENDERBY SPIRIT (GR), 7, gr g Invincible Spirit (IRE)—Arctic Ice (IRE) **Mrs P. M. Brown**
9 EXCEL BOLT, 5, ch g Exceed And Excel (AUS)—Dearest Daisy **Elders, Turton, Rhodes & Smart**
10 EXCELETTE (IRE), 4, b f Exceed And Excel (AUS)—Madam Ninette **Crossfields Racing**
11 FEEL THE HEAT, 6, ch g Firebreak—Spindara (IRE) **B. Smart**
12 FLASH CITY (ITY), 5, b g Elusive City (USA)—Furnish **Ceffyl Racing**
13 FREE ZONE, 4, b g Kyllachy—Aldora **Fromthestables.com Racing**
14 MASTER BOND, 4, b g Misu Bond (IRE)—Bond Royale **Bonded Twentyten Partnership**
15 MONTE CASSINO (IRE), 8, ch g Choisir (AUS)—Saucy Maid (IRE) **Woodcock Electrical Limited**
16 ORWELLIAN, 4, b g Bahamian Bounty—Trinny **B. Smart**
17 RONINSKI (IRE), 5, b g Cadeaux Genereux—Ruby Affair (IRE) **R. Hull**
18 SMALLJOHN, 7, ch g Needwood Blade—My Bonus **B. Smart**
19 TANGERINE TREES, 8, b g Mind Games—Easy To Imagine (USA) **Tangerine Trees Partnership**
20 VERINCO, 7, b g Bahamian Bounty—Dark Eyed Lady (IRE) **B. Smart**
21 WELLS LYRICAL (IRE), 8, b g Sadler's Wells (USA)—Lyrical **M. Barber**
22 WILD SAUCE, 4, b f Exceed And Excel (AUS)—Salsa Brava (AUS) **R. A. Page**

THREE-YEAR-OLDS

23 APACHE RISING, ch g Sleeping Indian—Distant Music **The Smart Distant Music Partnership**
24 ARMADA BAY (IRE), b g Tamayuz—Yara (IRE) **Fromthestables.com Racing**
25 AYASHA, b f Indesatchel (IRE)—Nizhoni (USA) **Crossfields Racing**
26 BOXING SHADOWS, b g Camacho—Prima Ballerina **Clipper Group Holdings Ltd**
27 CHESSFIELD PARK, ch g Byron—Annie Harvey **Mrs V. Smart**
28 DIFFERENT, ch f Bahamian Bounty—Hill Welcome **Mrs F. Denniff**
29 EQUINOX, b f Medicean—Plucky **Crossfields Racing**
30 ICHIMOKU, b c Indesatchel (IRE)—Mythicism **Crossfields Racing**
31 LUCY MINAJ, b f Dylan Thomas—Keyaki (IRE) **M. Barber**
32 MANDY LAYLA (IRE), ch f Excellent Art—Chervil **B. Smart**
33 MISS HYGROVE (IRE), b f Exceed And Excel (AUS)—Durrah Green **Mr D. H. Francis**
34 MOVIESTA (USA), b g Hard Spun (USA)—Miss Brickyard (USA) **H. Redknapp**
35 B g Footstepsinthesand—Nan Scurry (FR)
36 NOS DA, b f Cape Cross (IRE)—Nantyglo **Usk Valley Stud**
37 RHAGORI AUR, ch f Exceed And Excel (AUS)—Aberdovey **Ceffyl Racing**
38 ROSIE HALL (IRE), ch f Lion Heart (USA)—Baltic Dip (IRE) **R & E Hall & Son**
39 SECRET EMPRESS, b f Sakhee's Secret—Empress Jain **The Smart Empress Jain Partnership**
40 SPACE ARTIST (IRE), b g Captain Marvelous (IRE)—Dame Laura (IRE) **The Smart Dame Laura Partnership**

TWO-YEAR-OLDS

41 B f 24/2 Captain Gerrard (IRE)—Annellis (UAE) (Diesis) (5238) **The Smart Annellis Partnership**
42 B f 28/4 Captain Gerrard (IRE)—Annie Harvey (Fleetwood) (761) **Mrs V. Smart**
43 APPLICATION, ch c 25/3 Major Cadeaux—Choisette (Choisir (AUS)) **Crossfields Racing**
44 B c 22/4 Misu Bond (IRE)—Bond Royale (Piccolo) **R. C. Bond**
45 B f 28/4 Captain Gerrard (IRE)—Dazzling Quintet (Superlative) (7619) **B. Smart**
46 B f 12/4 Bushranger (IRE)—Desert d'argent (IRE) (Desert Story (IRE)) (14285) **Woodcock Electrical Limited**
47 DISCLOSURE, b c 3/3 Indesatchel (IRE)—Gemini Gold (King's Best (USA)) (7619) **T. Holdcroft**
48 B c 7/5 Captain Gerrard (IRE)—Easy To Imagine (USA) (Cozzene (USA)) (20000)
49 Ch c 20/4 Kheleyf (USA)—Fancy Feathers (IRE) (Redback) (38095) **Sir Alex Ferguson, Peter Deal & Gerry Lowe**
50 Ch f 17/4 New Approach (IRE)—Hill Welcome (Most Welcome) (65000) **Mrs F. Denniff**
51 B c 28/3 Dylan Thomas (IRE)—Keyaki (IRE) (Shinko Forest (IRE)) (761) **M. Barber**
52 KINKOHYO, b f 16/4 Indesatchel (IRE)—Mythicism (Oasis Dream) **Crossfields Racing**
53 MAJOR ROWAN, b g 12/4 Captain Gerrard (IRE)—Julie's Gift (Presidium) (1904) **David H. Cox**
54 Ch f 11/2 Kyllachy—Mary Read (Bahamian Bounty) (9523) **Just For Girls Partnership**
55 NZHOO, ch c 7/2 Major Cadeaux—Nizhoni (USA) (Mineshaft (USA)) **Crossfields Racing**
56 B c 12/1 Sakhee's Secret—Prima Ballerina (Pivotal) (9523) **Mr S. Tolley**

MR BRYAN SMART - Continued

57 B f 30/3 Captain Gerrard (IRE)—
Silca Destination (Dubai Destination (USA)) (14285) **Middleham Park Racing VIII & Partners**
58 B c 14/4 Captain Marvelous (IRE)—
Stoneacre Sarah (Cadeaux Genereux) (10476) **The Smart Stoneacre Sarah Partnership**
59 B c 2/4 Captain Gerrard (IRE)—Tibesti (Machiavellian (USA)) (14285) **Mr Michael Moses & Mr Terry Moses**

Other Owners: Mr M. Barber, Mr J. N. Blackburn, Mr R. C. Bond, Mr C. S. Bond, Mr M. G. Bullock, Mrs T. Bullock, Mr N. A. Coster, Mrs F. Denniff, Mr R. Hall, Mr R. C. Hall, Mrs A. C. Hudson, Mr I. G. Martin, Mr Richard Page, Mr B. Smart, Mrs V. R. Smart, Mr Andrew Turton, Mrs Judy Youdan.

Assistant Trainers: Mrs V. R. Smart, Mr K. Edmunds.

Jockey (flat): Tom Eaves. **Apprentice:** Justin Newman.

---

580 MR CHARLES SMITH, Bawtry
Postal: **Martin Grange Lodge, Martin Common, Bawtry, Doncaster, South Yorkshire, DN10 6DD**
Contacts: **PHONE/FAX (01526) 833245 MOBILE (07778) 149188**

1 CATALYZE, 5, b g Tumblebrutus (USA)—Clarita Dear (CHI) **W. McKay**
2 COASTAL PASSAGE, 5, b g Ishiguru (USA)—Ellcon (IRE) **W. McKay**
3 EL DECECY (USA), 9, b g Seeking The Gold (USA)—Ashraakat (USA) **W. McKay**
4 FATHEY (IRE), 7, ch g Fath (USA)—Christoph's Girl **R. J. Lewin**
5 GENERAL TUFTO, 8, b g Fantastic Light (USA)—Miss Pinkerton **Mr J. R. Theaker**
6 MUNAAWIB, 5, b g Haafhd—Mouwadh **Mrs J. C. Lumb**
7 NINE BEFORE TEN (IRE), 5, ch m Captain Rio—Sagaing **W. McKay**
8 PENDERYN, 6, b m Sakhee (USA)—Brecon **Mr N. J. Baines**
9 SAIRAAM (IRE), 7, b m Marju (IRE)—Sayedati Eljamilah (USA) **J. Martin-Hoyes**
10 5, Br m Kayf Tara—Santa Ana **C. Smith**
11 VISIONS OF JOHANNA (USA), 8, b g Johannesburg (USA)—Belle Turquoise (FR)

THREE-YEAR-OLDS

12 ROVERS TILL I DIE (IRE), b g Captain Marvelous (IRE)—Foolish Gift (FR) **W. McKay**
13 Ch c Notnowcato—Salanka (IRE) **W. McKay**

TWO-YEAR-OLDS

14 B c 14/4 Excellent Art—My Lass (Elmaamul (USA)) (75396) **W. McKay**

---

581 MR JULIAN SMITH, Tirley
Postal: **Tirley Court, Tirley, Gloucester**
Contacts: **PHONE (01452) 780461 FAX (01452) 780461 MOBILE (07748) 901175**
E-MAIL nicola.smith9156@o2.co.uk

1 EMERALD ROSE, 6, b m Sir Harry Lewis (USA)—Swiss Rose **Grand Jury Partnership**
2 FORTUNA ROSE, 7, b m Sir Harry Lewis (USA)—Swiss Rose **Grand Jury Partnership**
3 HARRIET'S ARK, 6, ch m Sir Harry Lewis (USA)—Brush The Ark **Exors of the Late Mr D. E. S. Smith**
4 HERO'S CALL, 8, b m Arkadian Hero (USA)—Sense of Value **Exors of the Late Mr D. E. S. Smith**
5 IONA DAYS (IRE), 8, br g Epistolaire (IRE)—Miss Best (FR) **Mrs J.A. Benson & Miss S.N. Benson**
6 MIDNIGHT GOLD, 13, ch g Midnight Legend—Yamrah **Blue Skyes**
7 NO PRINCIPLES, 10, b g Overbury (IRE)—Selective Rose **Exors of the Late Mr D. E. S. Smith**
8 PETIT FLEUR, 11, b m Nomadic Way (USA)—Sense of Value **Exors of the Late Mr D. E. S. Smith**
9 SAILOR'S SOVEREIGN, 12, b g Sovereign Water (FR)—Tirley Pop Eye **Exors of the Late Mr D. E. S. Smith**

Other Owners: P. F. D. Badham, Mrs J. A. Benson, Miss S. N. Benson, A. W. Brookes, R. Brookes, Ms G. E. Morgan.

Assistant Trainer: Mrs Nicky Smith

Jockey (NH): Charles Greene, Timmy Murphy, Sam Twiston-Davies. **Amateur:** Mr J. M. Ridley.

582 MR MICHAEL SMITH, Kirkheaton
Postal: **Toft Hall Farm, Kirkheaton, Newcastle Upon Tyne, Tyne and Wear, NE19 2DH**
Contacts: **PHONE (01830) 530044 MOBILE (07976) 903233**
E-MAIL sandy.smith01@btinternet.com

1 AMISFIELD LAD, 4, b g Zafeen (FR)—Flying Wind **J. W. Stephenson**
2 BOP ALONG (IRE), 6, b g Double Eclipse (IRE)—Bob Girl (IRE) **East-West Partnership**
3 DANTE'S FROLIC, 5, b m Overbury (IRE)—Dusky Dante (IRE) **East-West Partnership**
4 IMPERIAL VIC (IRE), 8, b br g Old Vic—Satco Rose (IRE) **J. W. Stephenson**
5 LEES ANTHEM, 6, b g Mujahid (USA)—Lady Rock **Mr P. J. McMahon**
6 MAKBULLET, 6, gr g Makbul—Gold Belt (IRE) **Mr D. Armstrong**
7 NADEEN (IRE), 6, b g Bahamian Bounty—Janayen (USA) **Miss R. J. Smith**
8 ORSIPPUS (USA), 7, b br g Sunday Break (JPN)—Mirror Dancing (USA) **Mrs S. Smith**
9 PRINCE OF VASA (IRE), 6, b g Kheleyf (USA)—Suzy Street (IRE) **Mrs S. Smith**
10 REGAL RAMIREZ, 5, bl gr g Needwood Blade—Beverley Hills (IRE) **Mr D. Armstrong**
11 4, B g Subtle Power (IRE)—Satco Rose (IRE)
12 SOMERSET ISLAND (IRE), 5, b g Barathea (IRE)—Art Work **Mr D. Armstrong**
13 VITO VOLTERRA (IRE), 6, b g Antonius Pius (USA)—River Abouali **Ace Racing**
14 WAR ON (IRE), 6, br g Presenting—Alannico **Mr D. Armstrong**

Other Owners: Mr C. Davidson, Mr W. J. Muir, M. Smith.

Assistant Trainer: Sandra Smith

583 MR RALPH SMITH, Chipstead
Postal: **Stud Managers Cottage, Cheval Court Stud, High Road, Chipstead, Surrey, CR5 3SD**
Contacts: **PHONE (01737) 851368**
E-MAIL rjsmith.racing@hotmail.com

1 4, B g Night Shift (USA)—Call Me Roxane (GER)
2 EMPERORS WALTZ (IRE), 4, b f Antonius Pius (USA)—Gavotte **T. Hirschfeld**
3 LIBERAL LADY, 5, b m Statue of Liberty (USA)—Noble Story **Mr N. Tozer**
4 ROOKNRASBRYRIPPLE, 4, b f Piccolo—Here To Me **Cavendish Star Racing & Tony Hirschfeld**
5 SINCHIROKA (FR), 7, b g Della Francesca (USA)—Great Care (USA) **K. Old**
6 THE CASH GENERATOR (IRE), 5, b g Peintre Celebre (USA)—
                                    Majestic Launch **The Cash Generator Racing Corporation**
7 WHO'S THAT CHICK (IRE), 4, ch f Footstepsinthesand—Poule de Luxe (IRE) **Piper, Harris, Churchill, Hirschfeld**

Other Owners: Mr S. P. Churchill, R. Frost, Mrs C. Harris, S. J. Piper, Mrs J. C. Smith, Mr S. Wilkinson.

584 MR ROBERT SMITH, Galston
Postal: **West Loudoun Farm, Galston, Ayrshire, KA4 8PB**
Contacts: **PHONE (01563) 822062**

1 HAWTHORNE BAY, 10, b g Karinga Bay—Teeton Bubbley **Mrs Angela Matheson & Mr Michael Smith**
2 JOVIAL (IRE), 6, b g Sakhee (USA)—Baalbek **R. M. Smith**
3 KNIGHT WOODSMAN, 9, ch g Sir Harry Lewis (USA)—Jowoody **Smith & Lawson**
4 ONLY CLINT, 5, b g Kayf Tara—Princess Ermyn **Smith & Spittal**
5 OSCAR DALLAS (IRE), 6, b g Oscar (IRE)—Ring Mam (IRE) **Ms A. D. Matheson**
6 5, Gr g Croco Rouge—Rosetown Girl (IRE)
7 SCOTCH WARRIOR, 9, ch g Karinga Bay—Tarda **R. M. Smith**
8 SULLIVANS HILL (IRE), 7, b g Catcher In The Rye (IRE)—Fairwood Euro (IRE) **R. M. Smith**

Other Owners: Mr R. Lawson, Miss B. Spittal.

585 MRS SUE SMITH, Bingley
Postal: **Craiglands Farm, High Eldwick, Bingley, West Yorkshire, BD16 3BE**
Contacts: **PHONE (01274) 564930 FAX (01274) 560626**
E-MAIL craiglandsracing@yahoo.co.uk

1 ALBA KING (IRE), 7, b g Beauchamp King—Alba Dancer **Mrs S. J. Smith**
2 ALF THE AUDACIOUS, 7, gr g Alflora (IRE)—Rua Ros (IRE) **Mr R. Preston**

MRS SUE SMITH - Continued

3 **ALTA ROCK (IRE)**, 8, b g Luso—Princess Lulu (IRE) **Mrs S. J. Smith**
4 **AURORAS ENCORE (IRE)**, 11, b g Second Empire (IRE)—
Sama Veda (IRE) **D. Pryde, J. Beaumont & D. P. van der Hoeven**
5 **BOLD SLASHER (IRE)**, 5, b g Millenary—Witney Girl **Widdop Wanderers**
6 **BROADWAY LIGHTS (IRE)**, 7, b g Broadway Flyer (USA)—Soggy Bottom Girl (IRE) **Mrs S. J. Smith**
7 **BROTHER SCOTT (IRE)**, 6, b g Kirkwall—Crimson Shower **Mrs S. J. Smith**
8 **CAMDEN GEORGE (IRE)**, 12, b g Pasternak—Triple Town Lass (IRE) **M. B. Scholey & R. H. Scholey**
9 **CLAN WILLIAM (IRE)**, 5, b g Antonius Pius (USA)—Celebrated Smile (IRE) **Mrs S. J. Smith**
10 **CLOUDY TOO (IRE)**, 7, b g Cloudings (IRE)—Curra Citizen (IRE) **Formulated Polymer Products Ltd**
11 **COVERHOLDER (IRE)**, 6, b g Oscar (IRE)—Lasado (IRE) **Mrs S. J. Smith**
12 **CRAFTI BOOKIE (IRE)**, 7, b g Winged Love—Cerise de Totes (FR) **Mrs S. J. Smith**
13 **DARTFORD WARBLER (IRE)**, 6, b br g Overbury (IRE)—Stony View (IRE) **Mrs S. J. Smith**
14 **DOUGLAS JULIAN**, 11, br g Overbury (IRE)—Swing Quartet (IRE) **Mrs S. J. Smith**
15 **EXECUTIVE BENEFIT (IRE)**, 6, b m Beneficial—Executive Dream (IRE) **Mrs A. E. Astall**
16 **FILL THE POWER (IRE)**, 7, b g Subtle Power (IRE)—Our Alma (IRE) **McGoldrick Racing Syndicates**
17 **FURIUS**, 7, b g Montjeu (IRE)—Frottola **Mrs S. J. Smith**
18 **GANSEY (IRE)**, 11, br g Anshan—Ebony Jane **T. J. Hemmings**
19 **GREEN WIZARD (IRE)**, 7, b g Wizard King—Ajo Green (IRE) **Mrs S. J. Smith**
20 **HERDSMAN (IRE)**, 8, b g Flemensfirth (USA)—My Sunny South **T. J. Hemmings**
21 **HIGHRATE (IRE)**, 7, b g Presenting—Hollygrove Cliche **T. J. Hemmings**
22 **KARINGA DANDY (IRE)**, 7, b g Karinga Bay—Well Then Now Then (IRE) **Mrs M B Scholey & Mrs S J Smith**
23 **KENT STREET (IRE)**, 8, ch g Flemensfirth (USA)—Fernhill (IRE) **K. Nicholson**
24 **KILKENNY ALL STAR (IRE)**, 12, b g Alderbrook—Borris Bounty (IRE) **Mrs S. J. Smith**
25 **LACKAMON**, 8, b g Fleetwood (IRE)—Pearlossa **Mrs S. J. Smith**
26 **MR MOONSHINE (IRE)**, 9, b g Double Eclipse (IRE)—Kinross **Mrs S. J. Smith**
27 **MWALESHI**, 8, b g Oscar (IRE)—Roxy River **Mrs S. J. Smith**
28 **NEXT HIGHT (IRE)**, 6, b g High Chaparral (IRE)—Night Petticoat (GER) **Mrs S. J. Smith**
29 **PAPA CARUSO**, 9, b g Kayf Tara—Madonna da Rossi **Mrs S. J. Smith**
30 **PINEROLO**, 7, b g Milan—Hollybush (IRE) **Mrs S. J. Smith**
31 **RATTLIN**, 5, b m Bollin Eric—Parslin **Broadband Partnership**
32 **REBEL SWING**, 7, b g Robellino (USA)—Ninia (USA) **Broadway Racing Club 15**
33 **STAGECOACH HARRY**, 7, b g Sir Harry Lewis (USA)—Linwood **Mrs S. J. Smith**
34 **STAGECOACH JASPER**, 7, b g Sir Harry Lewis (USA)—Flintwood **Mrs J. Conroy**
35 **STAGECOACH PEARL**, 9, gr g Classic Cliche (IRE)—Linwood **John Conroy Jaqueline Conroy**
36 **SWISS ART (IRE)**, 8, ch g One Cool Cat (USA)—Alpine Park (IRE) **The Cartmel Syndicate**
37 **TAHITI PEARL (IRE)**, 9, b g Winged Love—Clara's Dream (IRE) **M. B. Scholey & R. H. Scholey**
38 **TWICE LUCKY**, 6, b g Mtoto—Foehn Gale (IRE) **Mrs S. J. Smith**
39 **VINTAGE STAR (IRE)**, 7, b g Presenting—Rare Vintage (IRE) **T. J. Hemmings**
40 **WHATDOIDOWITHTHAT**, 10, ch g Minster Son—Wynyard Lady **M. F. Spence**
41 **WHISKEY RIDGE (IRE)**, 7, b g High-Rise (IRE)—Little Chartridge **Widdop Wanderers**
42 **WILLY C**, 7, b g Zamindar (USA)—Rosa Canina **M. F. Spence**
43 **YOU KNOW YOURSELF (IRE)**, 10, b g Dr Massini (IRE)—Gift of The Gab (IRE) **Mrs S. J. Smith**
44 **YUROK (IRE)**, 9, b g Alflora (IRE)—Wigwam Mam (IRE) **T. J. Hemmings**

Other Owners: J. J. Beaumont, Mr R. S. Bebb, R. F. Broad, J. Conroy, A. D. Hollinrake, W. S. D. Lamb, R. J. Longley, C. C. S. MacMillan, D. Musgrave, Mr M. Norcliffe, Mr A. M. Phillips, D. G. Pryde, Mrs J. B. Pye, Mrs M. B. Scholey, R. H. Scholey, Mr D. P. van der Hoeven.

Jockey (NH): Ryan Mania. **Conditional:** Shane Byrne, Zachery-James Gaughan, Darryl Horner Jnr, Jonathan England.

586	**MISS SUZY SMITH, Lewes**

Postal: **County Stables, The Old Racecourse, Lewes, East Sussex, BN7 1UR**
Contacts: **PHONE (01273) 477173 FAX (01273) 477173 MOBILE (07970) 550828**
E-MAIL suzy@suzysmithracing.co.uk WEBSITE www.suzysmithracing.co.uk

1 **BEAU LAKE (IRE)**, 9, b br g Heron Island (IRE)—Brennan For Audits (IRE)
2 **BRAVE DECISION**, 6, gr g With Approval (CAN)—Brave Vanessa (USA) **Mr R. I. Knight**
3 **EMMASLEGEND**, 8, b m Midnight Legend—Cherrygayle (IRE) **Mrs E. C. Stewart**
4 **INVICTA LAKE (IRE)**, 6, b g Dr Massini (IRE)—Classic Material **Bernard & Jan Wolford**
5 **LAUGHTON PARK**, 8, ch g Karinga Bay—Brass Castle (IRE) **A. G. C. Russell**
6 **MADAME JASMINE**, 8, gr m Karinga Bay—Roslin **Mrs Y. E. Allsop**
7 **MARIET**, 4, ch f Dr Fong (USA)—Medway (IRE) **Pollards Bloodstock**
8 **MATERIAL STAR**, 4, b g Kayf Tara—Material World **Material World Racing Club**
9 **NATURAL SPRING**, 8, b m Generous (IRE)—Highbrook (USA) **The Natural Spring Partnership**

MISS SUZY SMITH - Continued

10 O MALLEY'S OSCAR (IRE), 8, b g Oscar (IRE)—Notre Dame (IRE) **Exors of the Late Mr M. J. Weaver**
11 OURMANMASSINI (IRE), 5, b g Dr Massini (IRE)—Aunty Dawn (IRE) **The Seagull Partnership**
12 QUIPE ME POSTED (FR), 9, b g Discover d'auteuil (FR)—Harlem (FR) **Mrs V. Palmer**
13 ROYAL KICKS (FR), 12, b g Garde Royale—Al Kicks (FR) **Four J's Partnership**
14 SAMURAI LEGEND, 5, b g Midnight Legend—Cherrygayle (IRE)
15 SHE'S NOBLE, 6, b m Karinga Bay—Alta **Mr N. L. Crawford-Smith**

Other Owners: Mrs D. J. Arstall, Mr L. Arstall, Exors of the Late Mr G. J. Bush, J. H. Bush, Mr D. J. Harrison, Mr M. Hess, J. A. A. S. Logan, Mr A. J. McDonald, Mr M. J. Sechiari, R. F. Smith, Miss S. Smith, B. Wolford, Mrs J. Wolford, Mrs H. M. T. Woods.

Assistant Trainer: Mr S E Gordon-Watson

Jockey (flat): Sam Hitchcott. **Jockey (NH):** Colin Bolger.

---

587 **MR GILES SMYLY, Broadway**
Postal: Garden Cottage, Wormington Grange, Broadway, Worcestershire, WR12 7NJ
Contacts: PHONE (01386) 584085 FAX (01386) 584085 MOBILE (07747) 035169
E-MAIL gilessmiler@aol.com WEBSITE www.smylyracing.co.uk

1 BUFFALO CREEK (FR), 9, b g Indian River (FR)—Mealasta (FR) **M. Burford**
2 FERGAL MAEL DUIN, 5, gr g Tikkanen (USA)—Fad Amach (IRE) **Messenger Family Et Al**
3 FREDDIE MAEL DUIN, 4, gr g Fair Mix (IRE)—Fad Amach (IRE) **Messenger Family Et Al**
4 LETEMGO (IRE), 5, b g Brian Boru—Leteminletemout (IRE) **A. C. Ward-Thomas**
5 LIEUTENANT GEORGE (IRE), 5, b g Broadway Flyer (USA)—Kept In The Dark **D. Maxwell**
6 PINGARO DE LA VIRE (FR), 10, br g Ungaro (GER)—Kina de La Vire (FR) **D. Maxwell**
7 PLUM PUDDING (FR), 10, b g Fado (FR)—Tale (FR) **Messenger Family Et Al**

Other Owners: Mr J. P. R. Buob-Aldorf, J. M. Messenger, Mrs K. Smyly.

Assistant Trainer: Kim Smyly

Jockey (NH): David England, Liam Treadwell. **Conditional:** Ed Cookson.

---

588 **MR JAMIE SNOWDEN, Lambourn**
Postal: Folly House, Upper Lambourn Road, Lambourn, Hungerford, Berkshire, RG17 8QG
Contacts: PHONE (01488) 72800 (office) Twitter: @jamiesnowden MOBILE (07779) 497563
E-MAIL info@jamiesnowdenracing.co.uk WEBSITE www.jamiesnowdenracing.co.uk

1 BALLYBOKER BOY (IRE), 9, b g Snurge—Ballyboker Lady (IRE) **The Ballyboker Boy Partnership**
2 BREAKING BITS (IRE), 6, b br g Oscar (IRE)—Lantern Lark (IRE) **Colin Peake & John H W Finch Partnership**
3 BUXOM (IRE), 6, b m Milan—Bermuda Bay (IRE) **Ward, Smith & Harper Families**
4 FOUR SHUCK MEN (IRE), 5, b g Spartacus (IRE)—Shed **Tom Malone**
5 GRADUATION NIGHT, 7, br g Kayf Tara—Jadidh **Martin Broughton Racing Partners**
6 HOUNDSCOURT (IRE), 6, b g Court Cave (IRE)—Broken Rein (IRE) **Owners For Owners: Houndscourt**
7 IXORA (IRE), 7, gr m Milan—Tucacas (FR) **The Ixora Racing Partnership**
8 JAMESSON (IRE), 8, b g Bishop of Cashel—Native Belle (IRE) **The Sandylini Racing Partnership**
9 JAMMY (IRE), 4, b g Oscar (IRE)—Tabachines (FR) **Mrs W. P. Cohen**
10 JEAN FLEMING (IRE), 6, b m Flemensfirth (USA)—Dromhale Lady (IRE) **Mrs K B Gunn**
11 JOANNE ONE (IRE), 5, ch m Vinnie Roe (IRE)—Bobs Star (IRE) **Sir Chippendale Keswick**
12 KNIGHTON COMBE, 13, b g Midnight Legend—Cindercombe **Mr I. R. Snowden**
13 LEMONS GROUND, 4, ch c Generous (IRE)—Misty Move (IRE) **William Wallace**
14 LOUGH DERG WAY (IRE), 7, b g Dushyantor (USA)—Lotschberg Express **The Folly Partnership**
15 LUCYS GIRL (IRE), 6, b m Portrait Gallery (IRE)—Bubbleover (IRE) **Mr John H. W. Finch**
16 MAGIC VIXEN (IRE), 6, b m Old Vic—Magic Park (IRE) **Sir Chippendale Keswick**
17 MAJOR MILBORNE, 5, ch g Exit To Nowhere (USA)—Motown Melody (IRE) **Nowhere To Run Friends**
18 MARODIMA (FR), 10, b g Robin des Pres (FR)—Balbeyssac (FR) **Mareildar Racing Part 2**
19 MISS MILBORNE, 7, b m Tamure (IRE)—Motown Melody (IRE) **Adrian Brown and Friends**
20 NIKI ROYAL (FR), 8, b m Nikos—Balgarde (FR) **The Mirror Punters Club**
21 PRESENT VIEW, 5, b g Presenting—Carry Me (IRE) **Sir Chippendale Keswick**
22 QUEEN OF THE WEST (IRE), 6, b m Vinnie Roe (IRE)—Slow Starter (IRE) **Mareildar Racing Part 3**
23 ROYAL MACNAB (IRE), 5, b g Beneficial—Tina McBride (IRE) **Jeremy Sykes & Jamie Snowden**
24 SANDY'S DOUBLE, 7, ch g Double Trigger (IRE)—Skipcarl (IRE) **Ms Linda Agran**
25 SCUDERIA (IRE), 6, b g Kris Kin (USA)—Class Society (IRE) **Whites 'n Oops**

MR JAMIE SNOWDEN - Continued

26 **SHINKO MOON**, 6, b g Shinko Forest (IRE)—Silver Moon **Mr Colin Roberts**
27 **SIR GALE**, 5, b g Tamure (IRE)—Whatagale **Ann & Tony Gale**
28 5, b m Milan—Skipcarl (IRE) **Ms Linda Agran**
29 **SOUTINE (IRE)**, 7, b g Flemensfirth (USA)—Bells Chance (IRE) **A. L. Cohen**
30 5, Ch g Alflora (IRE)—Spot The Dot **David Gandolfo**
31 **STORMY OSCAR (IRE)**, 6, b g Oscar (IRE)—So Proper (IRE) **Jamie Snowden Racing Club**
32 **SUTTON WHO (FR)**, 7, b g Dark Moondancer—Magik (FR) **The Franks Family**
33 **TEA CADDY**, 7, b m Kadastrof (IRE)—Little Tern (IRE) **Mr R Matthews**
34 **TOM SANG (FR)**, 6, b g Dom Alco (FR)—Idee (FR) **Pat & Tony Bath**
35 **TURNSTONE**, 5, b g Kadastrof (IRE)—Little Tern (IRE) **Mr R Matthews**
36 **ULTRA KLASS (FR)**, 5, b g Ungaro (GER)—Leathou (FR) **Ultra Klass Racing**
37 **WYFIELD ROSE**, 4, b f Kayf Tara—Miniature Rose **Mrs Nicholas Jones & Friends**
38 **ZAVA RIVER (IRE)**, 6, b g Zagreb (USA)—Great Accord (IRE) **Chalke Valley Racing Partnership**

Other Owners: Mr R. B. Antell, Mr A. C. T. Bath, Mrs P. I. Bath, S. W. Broughton, Mr A. P. Brown, Mrs M. L. Carter, D. J. Coles, Mr N. G. P. Donaldson, Mr A. P. Gale, Mrs A. G. Gale, Mr R. J. Galpin, C. G. Hellyer, Mr M. J. Holman, Mr E. J. Hughes, Mr A. J. Huntly, Mrs N. Jones, Mr R. Kilford, Mr C. Peake, Mr C. Ricketts, Mr M. Shenfield, J. E. Snowden, Mr J. R. Sykes, Mr A. Watson.

Assistant Trainer: Kate Robinson

Jockey (NH): Tom O'Brien, Harry Skelton. **Conditional:** Brendan Powell, Matthew Stanley.

589
MR MIKE SOWERSBY, York
Postal: **Southwold Farm, Goodmanham Wold, Market Weighton, York, East Yorkshire, YO43 3NA**
Contacts: **PHONE (01430) 810534 MOBILE (07855) 551056**

1 **BUGBUG N BOOBOO**, 4, b g Tobougg (IRE)—Cryptogam **R. D. Seldon**
2 **CARMELA MARIA**, 8, b m Medicean—Carmela Owen **Mrs Janet Cooper & Mr M. E. Sowersby**
3 **HALJAFERIA (UAE)**, 7, ch g Halling (USA)—Melisendra (FR) **Mr P. W. Clifton**
4 **ICING SUGAR**, 5, ch m Doyen (IRE)—Cryptogam **R. D. Seldon**
5 **KITRIDGE LANE**, 5, b m Tikkanen (USA)—Tinoforty **Mrs E. A. Verity**
6 **MOON MELODY (GER)**, 10, b g Montjeu (IRE)—Midnight Fever (IRE) **Mrs J. H. Cooper**
7 **QUITE SPARKY**, 6, b g Lucky Story (USA)—Imperialistic (IRE) **R. D. Seldon**
8 **SYCHO FRED (IRE)**, 12, b g Buster King—Rebecca Steel (IRE) **Mrs E. A. Verity**
9 **TEEIYGEE**, 5, b g Bollin Eric—Paxford Lady **Mrs M. J. F. Gourley & Exors of the Late Mr T. I. Gourley**
10 **TENNESSEE BIRD**, 5, b g Danbird (AUS)—Tennessee Star **Queens Head Racing Club**
11 **TREGARO (FR)**, 7, b g Phantom Breeze—Touques (FR) **A. Lyons**

Other Owners: Mrs Janet Cooper, Mr J. Deno, Exors of the Late Mr T. I. Gourley, Mrs M. Gourley, Mr M. E. Sowersby, Mrs J. Wiltschinsky.

Assistant Trainer: Mary Sowersby

Jockey (flat): Tom Eaves. **Jockey (NH):** Keith Mercer. **Conditional:** Edmond Linehan.

590
MR JOHN SPEARING, Kinnersley
Postal: **Kinnersley Racing Stables, Kinnersley, Severn Stoke, Worcestershire, WR8 9JR**
Contacts: **PHONE (01905) 371054 FAX (01905) 371054 MOBILE (07801) 552922**
E-MAIL jlspearing@aol.com

1 **AMANTIUS**, 4, b g Multiplex—Ghana (GER) **H. M. W. Clifford**
2 **ASHPAN SAM**, 4, b c Firebreak—Sweet Patoopie **Advantage Chemicals Holdings Ltd**
3 **BARTON GIFT**, 6, b g Alflora (IRE)—Marina Rima **Mercy Rimell & Kate Ive**
4 **BERMONDSEY BOB (IRE)**, 7, b g Trans Island—Tread Softly (IRE) **A. A. Campbell**
5 **CLEAR SPRING (IRE)**, 5, b h Chineur (FR)—Holly Springs **Mr H. James**
6 **CROESO MAWR**, 7, ch m Bertolini (USA)—Croeso-I-Cymru **Mrs S. A. Evans**
7 **EQUULEUS PICTOR**, 9, b g Piccolo—Vax Rapide **J. L. Spearing**
8 **FULL SHILLING (IRE)**, 5, b m Intikhab (USA)—Full Cream (USA) **Not The Full Shilling Syndicate**
9 **HAWK MOTH (IRE)**, 5, b g Hawk Wing (USA)—Sasimoto (USA) **Kinnersley Partnership**
10 **IDOLSE (IRE)**, 4, b g Elusive Quality (USA)—Victoria Star (IRE)
11 **MISS CONDUCT**, 4, b f Overbury (IRE)—Risky Valentine **Miss C. J. Ive**
12 **PEARLS LEGEND**, 6, b g Midnight Legend—Pearl's Choice (IRE) **The Corsairs**
13 **RING OF FIRE**, 6, b g Firebreak—Sweet Patoopie

MR JOHN SPEARING - Continued

14 RITA SPEAK, 6, ch m Central Park (IRE)—Hopbine Mr J. Tucker
15 ROCK ON CANDY, 4, b f Excellent Art—Rock Candy (IRE) T. M. Hayes
16 STARLIGHT AIR, 10, ch m Karinga Bay—Moonlight Air Mrs W. M. Badger
17 TABLE BLUFF (IRE), 4, ch g Indian Haven—Double Deal
18 WHITECREST, 5, ch m Ishiguru (USA)—Risky Valentine G. M. Eales

THREE-YEAR-OLDS

19 BLACK EIDER, b f Piccolo—The Dark Eider Kinnersley Partnership II
20 CASHEL'S MISSILE (IRE), b g Majestic Missile (IRE)—Cashel Mead Masonaires
21 CLEAR LOCH, gr g Proclamation (IRE)—Loch Shiel (IRE) Mr H. James
22 FROSTED OFF, gr g Verglas (IRE)—Dispol Veleta Advantage Chemicals Holdings Ltd
23 B f Piccolo—The Lady Mandarin

TWO-YEAR-OLDS

24 Gr f 23/2 Proclamation (IRE)—Loch Shiel (IRE) (Selkirk (USA)) (4285)
25 Ch f 13/3 Sleeping Indian—Penrice Castle (Averti (IRE)) (2857)

Other Owners: Mr S. J. Court, Mr G. J. Daly, Mr Eddie Devereaux, Mr J. Eccleson, Mr W. J. Goddard, Miss C. Ive, Mr Andrew O'Brien, Major H. R. M. Porter, Mrs Mercy Rimell, Mr J. Spearing.

Assistant Trainer: Miss C Ive

---

591 **MR MICHAEL SQUANCE, Newmarket**
Postal: 36 Golden Miller Close, Newmarket, Suffolk, CB8 7RT
Contacts: PHONE (01638) 661824 MOBILE (07532) 372557
WEBSITE www.michaelsquanceracing.co.uk

1 CAMERA SHY (IRE), 9, ch g Pivotal—Shy Danceuse (FR) Mr M. D. Ogburn
2 DIPLOMATIC (IRE), 8, b g Cape Cross (IRE)—Embassy Miss K. L. Squance
3 ONCEAPONATIME (IRE), 8, b g Invincible Spirit (IRE)—Lake Nyasa (IRE) Miss K. L. Squance

THREE-YEAR-OLDS

4 HARROGATE FAIR, b g Trade Fair—Starbeck (IRE) K. D. Crabb
5 TAVISTOCK FAIR, b g Proclamation (IRE)—Music Maid (IRE) K. D. Crabb

TWO-YEAR-OLDS

6 Ch f 7/4 King's Best (USA)—Winner's Call (Indian Ridge) (3000)

---

592 **MR TOMMY STACK, Cashel**
Postal: Thomastown Castle, Golden, Cashel, Co. Tipperary, Ireland
Contacts: PHONE (00353) 62 54129
E-MAIL tommystack@eircom.net WEBSITE www.stackracing.ie

1 ANGELS GUARD THEE (IRE), 4, ch f Dylan Thomas (IRE)—State Crystal (IRE)
2 BIRD'S EYE VIEW, 4, b f Royal Applause—Opopmil (IRE)
3 BUSTED TYCOON (IRE), 4, b f Marju (IRE)—Khatela (IRE)
4 CAPE OF APPROVAL (IRE), 4, b g Cape Cross (IRE)—Wyola (USA)
5 CROI AN OR (IRE), 4, b g Windsor Knot (IRE)—Exponent (USA)
6 LORD LUCA (IRE), 4, b g Dylan Thomas (IRE)—Chanterelle (IRE)
7 MISTER CARTER (IRE), 6, b g Antonius Pius (USA)—Kotdiji
8 NERO EMPEROR (IRE), 4, b c Holy Roman Emperor (IRE)—Blue Iris
9 PIVOTAL ROCK (IRE), 6, b g Pivotal—Kitza (IRE)
10 QUEENS VISIT, 4, b f Authorized (IRE)—Royale Rose (FR)
11 STRADATER (IRE), 4, b g Catcher In The Rye (IRE)—Starring Role (IRE)

THREE-YEAR-OLDS

12 ADDICTEDTOPROGRESS (IRE), b f Holy Roman Emperor (IRE)—Farthingale (IRE)
13 ALIVE ALIVE OH, b f Duke of Marmalade (IRE)—Higher Love (IRE)
14 ALMANACK, b c Haafet (USA)—Openness
15 BARBEQUE (IRE), b f Elusive City (USA)—Babberina (IRE)
16 CLANCY AVENUE (USA), b c Henrythenavigator (USA)—Saintly Speech (USA)

MR TOMMY STACK - Continued

17 GMAC (IRE), b br c Excellent Art—Kafayef (USA)
18 GREAT MINDS (IRE), ch g Bahamian Bounty—Raja (IRE)
19 KENTUCKY WOMAN (IRE), b f Galileo (IRE)—Banquise (IRE)
20 LIGHT STORM CASS (IRE), b f Dylan Thomas (IRE)—Fand (USA)
21 MISCHIEF N MAYHEM, b f Nayef (USA)—Mail The Desert (IRE)
22 MUIZENBERG NIGHTS (IRE), b f Shamardal (USA)—Nassma (IRE)
23 OVERLAND EXPRESS (IRE), b f Dylan Thomas (IRE)—No Way (IRE)
24 PECTIN (IRE), b f Duke of Marmalade (IRE)—On Air (FR)
25 SCREAM BLUE MURDER (IRE), b f Oratorio (IRE)—Holly Blue
26 SNAKES AND LADDERS (IRE), br c Rock of Gibraltar (IRE)—Jalisco (IRE)
27 SPEEDWAY CASS (IRE), ch c Shamardal (USA)—Golden Mask (USA)
28 WANNABE BETTER (IRE), b f Duke of Marmalade (IRE)—Wannabe
29 YOUR PAL TAL, b g Dark Angel (IRE)—Good Health

TWO-YEAR-OLDS

30 B f 4/4 Daaher (CAN)—Alabaq (USA) (Riverman (USA))
31 B br f 4/5 Galileo (IRE)—Alpha Lupi (IRE) (Rahy (USA)) (373015)
32 B f 18/4 Mastercraftsman (IRE)—Amazing Krisken (USA) (Kris S (USA))
33 B f 3/3 Royal Applause (IRE)—Asheyana (IRE) (Soviet Star (USA)) (32000)
34 B f 1/5 Sea The Stars (IRE)—Blas Ceoil (IRE) (Mr Greeley (USA))
35 Ch f 31/1 Danehill Dancer (IRE)—Challow Hills (USA) (Woodman (USA)) (82000)
36 B f 28/4 Oratorio (IRE)—Chantarella (IRE) (Royal Academy (USA))
37 B c 5/3 Duke of Marmalade (IRE)—Embark (Soviet Star (USA))
38 Gr f 21/2 Mastercraftsman (IRE)—Fand (Kingmambo (USA))
39 B c 26/4 Bushranger (IRE)—Fantastic Cee (IRE) (Noverre (USA)) (30000)
40 B g 19/3 High Chaparral (IRE)—Fear And Greed (USA) (Brief Truce (USA))
41 B c 23/5 Galileo (IRE)—Flames (Blushing Flame (USA)) (634920)
42 B f 16/4 Kheleyf (USA)—Harmonist (USA) (Hennessy (USA)) (31428)
43 B f 30/3 Cape Cross (IRE)—Idilic Calm (IRE) (Indian Ridge) (79364)
44 B c 13/3 Bushranger (IRE)—Lady Precise (IRE) (Hawk Wing (USA)) (9523)
45 B c 22/3 Oratorio (IRE)—Mala Mala (IRE) (Brief Truce (USA))
46 B f 14/4 Fastnet Rock (AUS)—Mer de Corail (IRE) (Sadler's Wells (USA)) (142857)
47 B c 13/1 Montjeu (IRE)—Miss Khaya (IRE) (Danehill Dancer (IRE))
48 B f 13/2 Royal Applause—Miss Smilla (Red Ransom (USA)) (66666)
49 Gr f 16/2 Myboycharlie (IRE)—Misty Eyed (IRE) (Paris House) (65000)
50 B c 17/4 Rock of Gibraltar (IRE)—Moojeh (IRE) (King's Best (USA)) (45000)
51 B c 6/5 Danehill Dancer (IRE)—Mowaadah (IRE) (Alzao (USA)) (79365)
52 Gr c 14/5 Dark Angel (IRE)—Non Dimenticar Me (IRE) (Don't Forget Me) (21428)
53 Ch c 24/2 Footstepsinthesand—Pivotalia (IRE) (Pivotal) (24000)
54 B f 22/2 Myboycharlie (IRE)—Prithee (Barathea (IRE)) (952)
55 ROBIN'S CHOICE (IRE), b f 14/4 Bushranger (IRE)—Creekhaven (IRE) (Definite Article) (55555)
56 B f 13/5 Danehill Dancer (IRE)—Simadartha (USA) (Gone West (USA)) (70000)
57 B f 11/3 Royal Applause—Starry Sky (Oasis Dream) (13500)
58 TREADSTONE, b c 17/2 Myboycharlie (IRE)—Lilli Marlane (Sri Pekan (USA)) (49523)
59 B f 20/2 Oratorio (IRE)—Willowbridge (IRE) (Entrepreneur)

Owners: Mr Michael Begley, Mr John Byrne, Mr Justin Caffrey, Mr John Connaughton, Mr Terry Corden, Mr T. Hyde Jnr, JSC Kasandros Grupe, Mr D. Keoghan, Lady Laidlaw, Mrs J. Magnier, Mr Casey McKliney, Mr J. P. McManus, Eimear Mulhearne, Newtownanner Stud, Mr Gerard O'Brien, Mr M. J. O'Flynn, Mr Peter Piller, Mr David Slater, Mr Derrick Smith, Mr Alfred Sweetnam, Mr Michael Tabor, The Pension Fund Syndicate, The Tallyho Kiddo Syndicate, Ms Kinvara Vaughan, Wilgerbosdrift.

Jockey (flat): Wayne Lordan. **Jockey (NH):** W. J. Lee. **Apprentice:** S. A. Gray, P. C. O'Donnell.

---

593 **MR DANIEL STEELE, Henfield**
Postal: **Blacklands House, Wheatsheaf Road, Wineham, nr Henfield, West Sussex, BN5 9BE**
Contacts: **MOBILE (07500) 556398**
E-MAIL danielsteele14@hotmail.co.uk

1 HUDIBRAS (IRE), 9, b g Bluebird (USA)—Mannequin (IRE) **Mr D. R. Steele**
2 WHITCOMBE SPIRIT, 8, b g Diktat—L'evangile **Mr D. R. Steele**

594   MRS JACKIE STEPHEN, Inverurie
Postal: Conglass Farmhouse, Inverurie, Aberdeenshire, AB51 5DN

1 MO ROUGE (IRE), 5, b g Croco Rouge (IRE)—Just A Mo (IRE) Mrs J. S. Stephen
2 RELAND (FR), 8, ch g Shaanmer (IRE)—Falkland III (FR) Mr P. G. Stephen
3 SAFARI ADVENTURES (IRE), 11, b g King's Theatre (IRE)—Persian Walk (FR) Mr P. G. Stephen

595   MR OLLY STEVENS, Chiddingfold
Postal: Robins Farm Stables, Fisher Lane, Chiddingfold, Godalming, Surrey, GU8 4TB
Contacts: PHONE (01428) 682059 FAX (01428) 682466 MOBILE (07585) 123178
E-MAIL ostevens@robinsfarmracing.com WEBSITE www.robinsfarmracing.com

1 JACOB CATS, 4, b c Dutch Art—Ballet Pearl Bloodstock Limited
2 SAFARI MISCHIEF, 10, b g Primo Valentino (IRE)—Night Gypsy P. L. Winkworth
3 SCHOOL FEES, 4, b f Royal Applause—Cankara (IRE) Elias, Mitchell & Newton

THREE-YEAR-OLDS
4 BOLEYN, b f Sir Percy—Moody Margaret Ms Y. Ferguson
5 B br c Hat Trick (JPN)—Cotton Club Ballet (USA) Pearl Bloodstock Limited
6 HARD WALNUT (IRE), b f Cape Cross (IRE)—Yaria (IRE) Qatar Racing Limited
7 THE ART OF RACING (IRE), b g Acclamation—Divert (IRE) Qatar Racing Limited
8 UNCLE MUF (USA), b c Curlin (USA)—Peak Maria's Way (USA) Pearl Bloodstock Limited

TWO-YEAR-OLDS
9 B f 8/4 Azamour (IRE)—Aladiyna (IRE) (Indian Danehill (IRE)) (17500) Pearl Bloodstock Limited
10 Ch f 28/2 Sleeping Indian—Eforetta (GER) (Dr Fong (USA)) Pearl Bloodstock Limited
11 B c 29/3 Kyllachy—Ellens Princess (IRE) (Desert Prince (IRE)) (34285) Pearl Bloodstock Limited
12 EXTORTIONIST (IRE), b c 4/2 Dandy Man (IRE)—
                                Dream Date (IRE) (Oasis Dream) (28571) Sheikh S. A. K. H. Al Thani
13 Ch c 13/3 Dandy Man (IRE)—First Bank (FR) (Anabaa (USA)) (17460) Pearl Bloodstock Limited
14 B f 23/1 Kyllachy—Forest Prize (Charnwood Forest (IRE)) (15238) P. L. Winkworth
15 FRACKING (IRE), b c 30/3 Intikhab (USA)—Carson Dancer (USA) (Carson City (USA)) (24761) P. L. Winkworth
16 HASUFEL (IRE), b c 19/3 Amadeus Wolf—
                                Gemini Diamond (IRE) (Desert King (IRE)) (23809) Sheikh S. A. K. H. Al Thani
17 HOKU (IRE), b f 19/2 Holy Roman Emperor (IRE)—
                                Scylla Cadeaux (IRE) (Cadeaux Genereux) (13333) Sheikh S. A. K. H. Al Thani
18 B c 10/5 Camacho—Inourhearts (IRE) (Pips Pride) (18095) Pearl Bloodstock Limited
19 B f 3/5 Jeremy (USA)—Interpose (Indian Ridge) Mr D. Redvers
20 B f 29/4 Thousand Words—Islandagore (IRE) (Indian Ridge) (14000) Pearl Bloodstock Limited
21 B c 17/2 Medicean—Light Impact (IRE) (Fantastic Light (USA)) (40000) Pearl Bloodstock Limited
22 B f 10/2 Bushranger (IRE)—Lilakiya (IRE) (Dr Fong (USA)) (25396) Pearl Bloodstock Limited
23 B f 15/2 Echo of Light—Lovely Dream (IRE) (Elnadim (USA)) (1904) Unregistered Partnership
24 B f 7/2 Bushranger (IRE)—Nightbird (IRE) (Night Shift (USA)) (9523) Pearl Bloodstock Limited
25 B f 2/3 Bahamian Bounty—Nina Blini (Bertolini (USA)) (15000) Pearl Bloodstock Limited
26 QUEEN OF THE TARTS, b f 26/2 Royal Applause—Tart And A Half (Distant Relative) (30476) Pearl Bloodstock Limited
27 B g 19/4 Intense Focus—Saoodah (IRE) (Green Desert (USA)) (16666) Pearl Bloodstock Limited
28 B f 14/4 Intikhab (USA)—Saramacca (IRE) (Kahyasi) (15872) Pearl Bloodstock Limited
29 B c 26/2 Captain Gerrard (IRE)—Seren Teg (Timeless Times (USA)) (11428) Pearl Bloodstock Limited
30 B f 8/4 Orpen (USA)—Summer Show (IRE) (Singspiel (IRE)) Mr R. S. Hoskins
31 B c 14/2 Hurricane Run (IRE)—Trick (IRE) (Shirley Heights) (28000) Pearl Bloodstock Limited
32 B c 27/2 Moss Vale—Walnut Lady (Forzando) (7539) Pearl Bloodstock Limited

Other Owners: Sir Thomas Lea.

Assistant Trainer: Hetta Stevens

596 **MR JOHN STIMPSON, Newcastle-under-Lyme**
Postal: **Trainers Lodge, Butterton Racing Stables, Off Park Road, Butterton, Newcastle-Under-Lyme, Staffordshire, ST5 4DZ**
Contacts: **PHONE (01782) 636020 FAX (01782) 633533 MOBILE (07768) 213531**
E-MAIL info@jtsintltd.co.uk

1 APACHE GLORY (USA), 5, b br m Cherokee Run (USA)—Jumeirah Glory (USA) **J. Stimpson**
2 FLUMPS, 4, ch f Auction House (USA)—Demolition Jo **Marshmallows International S. L.**
3 HAWAIIAN FREEZE, 4, b f Avonbridge—Autumn Affair **J. T. S. (International) Ltd**
4 JAWBREAKER (IRE), 8, b g Catcher In The Rye (IRE)—Alpine Lady (IRE) **J. T. S. (International) Ltd**
5 LION COURT (IRE), 5, ch g Iffraaj—Spanish Falls **J. Stimpson**
6 MR MALLO, 4, b g Bertolini (USA)—Londonnet (IRE) **Marshmallows International S. L.**

THREE-YEAR-OLDS

7 CANDY HOUSE GIRL (USA), b f Hard Spun (USA)—Princess Mitterand (USA) **J. T. S. (International) Ltd**
8 DILETTA TOMMASA (IRE), ch f Dylan Thomas (IRE)—Chronicle **J. Stimpson**
9 ZED CANDY GIRL, ch f Sakhee's Secret—Musical Twist **J. T. S. (International) Ltd**

Assistant Trainer: Mandy Bradley (07850) 775349

597 **MISS ANN STOKELL, Southwell**
Postal: **2 Chippendale Road, Lincoln, Lincolnshire, LN6 3PP**
Contacts: **MOBILE (07814) 579982**
E-MAIL ann.stokell@gmail.com

1 AMBER MOON, 8, ch m Singspiel (IRE)—Merewood (USA) **Ms C. Stokell**
2 BERRYMEAD, 8, br m Killer Instinct—Mill End Quest **Ms C. Stokell**
3 CENN FUAIT (IRE), 7, b m Imperial Ballet (IRE)—Confey Lass (IRE) **Ms C. Stokell**
4 ELUSIVE, 7, b m Reel Buddy (USA)—Love Is All (IRE) **Ms C. Stokell**
5 GYPSY JAZZ (IRE), 6, b m Antonius Pius (USA)—Dawn's Folly (IRE) **Ms C. Stokell**
6 HOLD THE STAR, 7, b m Red Ransom (USA)—Sydney Star **Ms C. Stokell**
7 ISLAND EXPRESS (IRE), 6, b g Chineur (FR)—Cayman Expresso (IRE) **Ms C. Stokell**
8 KNEESY EARSY NOSEY, 7, ch m Compton Place—Evie Hone (IRE) **Ms C. Stokell**
9 PAWAN (IRE), 13, ch g Cadeaux Genereux—Born To Glamour **Ms C. Stokell**

Other Owners: Mr G. B. Pacey.

Assistant Trainer: Caron Stokell

598 **MR WILLIAM STONE, West Wickham**
Postal: **The Meadow, Streetly End, West Wickham, Cambridge, Cambridgeshire, CB21 4RP**
Contacts: **PHONE (01223) 894617 MOBILE (07788) 971094**
E-MAIL williamstone1@hotmail.co.uk

1 DELORAIN (IRE), 10, b g Kalanisi (IRE)—Lady Nasrana (FR) **Miss C. M. Scott**
2 IMJIN RIVER (IRE), 6, b g Namid—Lady Nasrana (FR) **Miss C. M. Scott**
3 LACONICOS (IRE), 11, ch g Foxhound (USA)—Thermopylae **Miss C. M. Scott**
4 PLACE THAT FACE, 4, b f Compton Place—Notjustaprettyface (IRE) **Miss C. M. Scott**
5 ROEDEAN (IRE), 4, b f Oratorio (IRE)—Exotic Mix (FR) **Mr S. A. Fairweather**
6 WARDEN BOND, 5, ch g Monsieur Bond (IRE)—Warden Rose **Mr J. A. Ross & Miss C. M. Scott**

THREE-YEAR-OLDS

7 THREE CHOIRS (IRE), br f Rock of Gibraltar (IRE)—Three Owls (IRE) **The Plenipo Partnership**

599 **MR BRIAN STOREY, Kirklinton**
Postal: **Low Dubwath, Kirklinton, Carlisle, Cumbria, CA6 6EF**
Contacts: **PHONE (01228) 675376 FAX (01228) 675977 MOBILE (07950) 925576/ (07912) 898740**
E-MAIL jackie@brianstoreyracing.co.uk WEBSITE www.brianstoreyracing.co.uk

1 BIRNIES BOY, 9, b g Thowra (FR)—Drumkilly Lilly (IRE) **Mrs V. Birnie & Mr G. Wilkinson**
2 HURRYONHARRY, 7, b g Erhaab (USA)—Gypsy Race (IRE) **Mr & Mrs J. Hutchinson**

MR BRIAN STOREY - Continued

3 KNOCKAVILLA (IRE), 10, b g Saddlers' Hall (IRE)—Native Singer (IRE) **Mr & Mrs J. Hutchinson**
4 5, Gr m Overbury (IRE)—Ladylliat (FR) **Mrs V. A. Birnie**
5 PEGASUS PRINCE (USA), 9, b g Fusaichi Pegasus (USA)—Avian Eden (USA) **Mr G. Wilkinson**
6 QUO VISTA (IRE), 8, b g Anshan—Miss Cooline (IRE) **F. S. Storey**
7 4, Br g Court Cave (IRE)—Raise A Flag (IRE) **Mr & Mrs J. Hutchinson**
8 RUNSWICK DAYS (IRE), 6, b g Presenting—Miss Lauren Dee (IRE) **J. Wade**
9 THATWASTHEPENSION (IRE), 7, b g Milan—Biondo (IRE) **Stepol Stud**
10 WOODYS BROTHER (IRE), 10, b g Flemensfirth—Woodram Delight **Mr J. T. Hutchinson**

Other Owners: Mr J. Hutchinson (Hexham), Mrs V. A. Hutchinson.

Assistant Trainer: Mrs Jackie Storey

Jockey (flat): P. J. McDonald. **Jockey (NH):** Brian Hughes, Richie McGrath. **Amateur:** Miss Jackie Coward.

600

MR WILF STOREY, Consett
Postal: **Grange Farm & Stud, Muggleswick, Consett, Co. Durham, DH8 9DW**
Contacts: **PHONE (01207) 255259 FAX (01207) 255259 MOBILE (07860) 510441**
E-MAIL **wlstorey@metronet.co.uk WEBSITE www.wilfstorey.com**

1 BLOWN, 4, b g Shirocco (GER)—Lawyers Choice **W. L. Storey**
2 DAN'S HEIR, 11, b g Dansili—Million Heiress **P. Tomlinson**
3 JAN SMUTS (IRE), 5, b g Johannesburg (USA)—Choice House (USA) **H. S. Hutchinson & W. Storey**
4 KID WIZZARD (USA), 4, b g Lemon Drop Kid (USA)—Dear Daughter **D. M. Partnership**
5 MONTHLY MEDAL, 10, b g Danehill Dancer (IRE)—Sovereign Abbey (IRE) **Gremlin Racing**
6 TRISKAIDEKAPHOBIA, 10, b g Bertolini (USA)—Seren Teg **W. Storey & Steve Gilbey**

THREE-YEAR-OLDS

7 CARD HIGH (IRE), b g Red Clubs (IRE)—Think (FR) **W. L. Storey**

Other Owners: Mr Steve Gilbey, Mr D. D. Gillies, Mr H. S. Hutchinson, Mr W. Storey.

Assistant Trainer: Miss S. Storey

Amateur: Miss S. M. Doolan.

601

SIR MICHAEL STOUTE, Newmarket
Postal: **Freemason Lodge, Bury Road, Newmarket, Suffolk, CB8 7BY**
Contacts: **PHONE (01638) 663801 FAX (01638) 667276**

1 COMMEND, 4, ch g Pivotal—Reputable
2 DANK, 4, b f Dansili—Masskana (IRE)
3 DUKE OF FIRENZE, 4, ch c Pivotal—Nannina
4 EAGLES PEAK, 5, b h Galileo (IRE)—High Praise (USA)
5 ELYSIAN, 4, b f Galileo (IRE)—Echelon
6 ENROL, 4, b f Pivotal—Constitute (USA)
7 ESTIMATE (IRE), 4, b f Monsun (GER)—Ebaziya (IRE)
8 GOSPEL CHOIR, 4, ch c Galileo (IRE)—Chorist
9 LABARINTO, 5, b g Dansili—Tarocchi (USA)
10 LADYSHIP, 4, b f Oasis Dream—Peeress
11 LUCANIN, 4, b g Galileo (IRE)—Teggiano (IRE)
12 MARIA'S CHOICE (IRE), 4, b g Oratorio (IRE)—Amathusia
13 MAWAQEET (USA), 4, b g Dynaformer (USA)—Lady Ilsley (USA)
14 MODERN TUTOR, 4, b c Selkirk (USA)—Magical Romance (IRE)
15 MR MAYNARD, 4, ch c Notnowcato—Crystal Cavern (USA)
16 OPINION (IRE), 4, b c Oasis Dream—Kiltubber (IRE)
17 RUSSELLIANA, 4, ch f Medicean—Rosacara
18 RYE HOUSE, 4, b c Dansili—Threefold (USA)
19 SIR JOHN HAWKWOOD (IRE), 4, b g Sir Percy—Athene (IRE)
20 TALES OF GRIMM (USA), 4, b c Distorted Humor (USA)—Stupendous Miss (USA)
21 TAZAHUM (USA), 5, b h Redoute's Choice (AUS)—Huja (USA)
22 ULTRASONIC (USA), 4, b f Mizzen Mast (USA)—Quickfire

SIR MICHAEL STOUTE - Continued

THREE-YEAR-OLDS

23 **ABSEIL (USA)**, b c First Defence (USA)—Intercontinental
24 **ALTHAROOS (IRE)**, br g Sakhee (USA)—Thamara (USA)
25 **ARAB SPRING (IRE)**, b c Monsun (GER)—Spring Symphony (IRE)
26 **ASTONISHING (IRE)**, b f Galileo (IRE)—Amazing Krisken (USA)
27 **ASTORGS GALAXY**, b f Galileo (IRE)—Astorg (USA)
28 **AULD ALLIANCE (IRE)**, b f Montjeu (IRE)—Highland Gift (IRE)
29 **AVIETTA (IRE)**, gr f Dalakhani (IRE)—Alabastrine
30 **BAIHAS**, b c Nayef (USA)—Allegretto (IRE)
31 **BEDOUIN INVADER (IRE)**, b g Oasis Dream—Hovering (IRE)
32 **BEEP**, b f Beat Hollow—Dialing Tone (USA)
33 **BERKELEY STREET (USA)**, b g Street Cry (IRE)—Dream Ticket (USA)
34 **BOHEMIAN DANCE (IRE)**, br f Dansili—Islington (IRE)
35 **BOLD SNIPER**, b c New Approach (IRE)—Daring Aim
36 **CALL AHEAD**, ch f Three Valleys (USA)—Payphone
37 **CENTRED (IRE)**, gr f Dalakhani (IRE)—Drama Class (IRE)
38 **CHENGHO (USA)**, b g Henrythenavigator (USA)—Christmas In Aiken (USA)
39 **CIRCUS TURN (USA)**, b g Street Cry (IRE)—Showlady (USA)
40 **CLAIM (IRE)**, b g Acclamation—Raysiza (IRE)
41 **COULD IT BE (IRE)**, b f Galileo (IRE)—Butterfly Cove (USA)
42 **DAMBUSTER (IRE)**, b c Dalakhani (IRE)—Threefold (USA)
43 **DEFENDANT**, b c Medicean—Razzle (USA)
44 **DREAM WILD**, b f Oasis Dream—Wince
45 **DUKE COSIMO**, ch g Pivotal—Nannina
46 **ECONOMY**, gr c Dalakhani (IRE)—Quiff
47 **ELIK (IRE)**, b f Dalakhani (IRE)—Elopa (GER)
48 **ENOBLED**, b c Dansili—Peeress
49 **EVANGELIST**, b c Oasis Dream—Hi Calypso (IRE)
50 **FANTASY IN BLUE**, b f Galileo (IRE)—Blue Symphony
51 **GOLDEN TOUCH**, b c Galileo (IRE)—Approach
52 **HILLSTAR**, b c Danehill Dancer (IRE)—Crystal Star
53 **INFATUATE**, gr f Dalakhani (IRE)—Fantasize
54 **INTEGRAL**, b f Dalakhani (IRE)—Echelon
55 **INTRINSIC**, b c Oasis Dream—Infallible
56 **JAREEDA (USA)**, b br f First Samurai (USA)—Manaal (USA)
57 **JUST DARCY**, b f Danehill Dancer (IRE)—Jane Austen (IRE)
58 **KING'S REQUEST (IRE)**, ch g New Approach (IRE)—Palace Weekend (USA)
59 **LEGENDS (IRE)**, b c Medaglia d'oro (USA)—Elusive Legend (USA)
60 **LIBER NAUTICUS (IRE)**, b f Azamour (IRE)—Serres (IRE)
61 **LOVE MAGIC**, b f Dansili—Magical Romance (IRE)
62 **MADAME VESTRIS (IRE)**, ch f Galileo (IRE)—Mrs Lindsay (USA)
63 **MANGO DIVA**, b f Holy Roman Emperor (IRE)—Mango Mischief (IRE)
64 **MAYPOLE LASS**, ch f Halling (USA)—Maigold Lass
65 **MEDDLING**, ch f Halling (USA)—Piffling
66 **MISSION APPROVED**, b c Dansili—Moon Search
67 **MUTAJALLY**, b c Teofilo (IRE)—Dhelaal
68 **NAZYM (IRE)**, ch f Galileo (IRE)—Brigid (USA)
69 **NORTHERN MEETING (IRE)**, b f Dylan Thomas (IRE)—Scottish Stage (IRE)
70 **OMNIPRESENT**, b c Rail Link—Protectress
71 **OTROOHA (IRE)**, b f Oasis Dream—Mumayeza
72 **PAVLOSK (USA)**, b f Arch (USA)—Tsar's Pride
73 **PERSEPOLIS (IRE)**, b c Dansili—La Persiana
74 **PLAYBILL**, b f Medicean—Set The Scene (IRE)
75 **PLOVER**, b f Oasis Dream—Short Dance (USA)
76 **PRESSURE POINT**, b c Oasis Dream—Arrive
77 **PROXIMATE**, b c Nayef (USA)—Contiguous (USA)
78 **QAREENAH (USA)**, b f Arch (USA)—Princess Kris
79 **RAUSHAN (IRE)**, gr f Dalakhani (IRE)—Chiang Mai (IRE)
80 **RUN WITH PRIDE (IRE)**, b g Invincible Spirit (IRE)—Zibilene
81 **RUSSIAN REALM**, b c Dansili—Russian Rhythm (USA)
82 **SHADES OF SILVER**, b g Dansili—Silver Pivotal (USA)
83 B f Dynaformer (USA)—Sometime (IRE)
84 **STOMACHION (IRE)**, b c Duke of Marmalade (IRE)—Insight (FR)
85 **STRENGTH AND HONOR (IRE)**, b c Galileo (IRE)—Kasora (IRE)
86 **TAFAASEEL (USA)**, b f Mr Greeley (USA)—Wasseema (USA)

SIR MICHAEL STOUTE - Continued

87 **TELESCOPE (IRE)**, b c Galileo (IRE)—Velouette
88 **THEODORE GERICAULT (IRE)**, b g Sir Percy—Tableau Vivant (IRE)
89 **VITAL EVIDENCE (USA)**, b c Empire Maker (USA)—Promising Lead
90 **VOTE EARLY**, br f Dansili—Reel Style
91 **WAILA**, ch f Notnowcato—Crystal Cavern (USA)
92 **WANNAAN (IRE)**, b g Pivotal—Hathrah (IRE)
93 **WATCHABLE**, ch c Pivotal—Irresistible
94 **WEST OF THE MOON**, ch f Pivotal—Canda (USA)

TWO-YEAR-OLDS

95 **ADORE**, b f 19/2 Oasis Dream—Fantasize (Groom Dancer (USA))
96 **ALEX VINO (IRE)**, b c 3/3 High Chaparral (IRE)—Rare Ransom (Oasis Dream)
97 **ALMUHEET**, b c 22/4 Dansili—Arwaah (IRE) (Dalakhani (IRE))
98 **ALTAAYIL (IRE)**, br c 19/2 Sea The Stars (IRE)—Alleluia (Caerleon (USA)) (550000)
99 **ARBAAB**, br c 26/2 Dynaformer (USA)—Kaseema (USA) (Storm Cat (USA))
100 **ASYAD (IRE)**, b f 30/3 New Approach (IRE)—Elle Danzig (GER) (Roi Danzig (USA))
101 Br f 30/1 Exchange Rate (USA)—Boasting (USA) (Kris S (USA))
102 B c 17/4 Cape Cross (IRE)—Candy Mountain (Selkirk (USA)) (150000)
103 **CANNOCK CHASE (USA)**, b c 20/3 Lemon Drop Kid (USA)—
                                             Lynnwood Chase (USA) (Horse Chestnut (SAF)) (310000)
104 Ch c 31/1 Champs Elysees—Change Course (Sadler's Wells (USA))
105 **DIANORA**, b f 8/5 New Approach (IRE)—Nannina (Medicean)
106 Gr ro c 14/3 Mizzen Mast (USA)—Discuss (USA) (Danzig (USA))
107 B f 26/2 Shamardal (USA)—Eva Luna (USA) (Alleged (USA))
108 **EXECUTRIX**, b f 18/5 Oasis Dream—Exclusive (Polar Falcon (USA))
109 **EXTENT**, ch f 11/3 Exceed And Excel (AUS)—Selkirk Sky (Selkirk (USA)) (150000)
110 **JUVENILE THEATRE (IRE)**, ch c 21/2 Danehill Dancer (IRE)—Scottish Stage (IRE) (Selkirk (USA))
111 B c 24/2 Montjeu (IRE)—Festoso (IRE) (Diesis)
112 **FITNAH (IRE)**, b f 5/2 Sea The Stars (IRE)—Ecoutila (USA) (Rahy (USA))
113 **GHAAWY**, b c 19/4 Teofilo (IRE)—Asawer (IRE) (Darshaan)
114 B f 23/5 Dubawi (IRE)—Heat Haze (Green Desert (USA))
115 **HEHO**, b f 3/3 Dansili—Nitya (FR) (Indian Ridge)
116 **INHERITANCE**, b f 5/5 Oasis Dream—Peeress (Pivotal)
117 **JONE DES CHAMPS (IRE)**, b c 20/4 Montjeu (IRE)—Desert Bloom (IRE) (Pilsudski (IRE))
118 **JUVENILE LEAD (IRE)**, ch c 3/4 Sea The Stars (IRE)—Drama Class (IRE) (Caerleon (USA))
119 **LONG VIEW (IRE)**, b f 24/4 Galileo (IRE)—Highland Light (IRE) (Generous (IRE))
120 **MAIRISE**, b c 13/3 Authorized (IRE)—Maigold Lass (Mark of Esteem (IRE))
121 B c 27/4 Kyllachy—Maugwenna (Danehill (USA)) (150000)
122 **MEZEL**, b c 20/3 Tamayuz—Mumayeza (Indian Ridge)
123 Ch f 11/3 Galileo (IRE)—Midnight Angel (GER) (Acatenango (GER))
124 **MONTONE (IRE)**, ch c 9/2 Danehill Dancer (IRE)—Leocorno (IRE) (Pivotal)
125 **MUNAASER**, b c 17/2 New Approach (IRE)—Safwa (IRE) (Green Desert (USA))
126 **NOBLE DESCENT**, ch f 9/2 Pivotal—Noble Lady (Primo Dominie)
127 **NOWREYNA**, gr f 20/4 Notnowcato—Kryena (Kris)
128 B c 7/3 Oasis Dream—Orford Ness (Selkirk (USA))
129 **PAS DE CHEVAL (IRE)**, ch c 21/1 Pivotal—Olympienne (IRE) (Sadler's Wells (USA))
130 **PIVOTAL BRIDE**, ch f 14/4 Dubawi (IRE)—Brazilian Bride (IRE) (Pivotal) (174602)
131 B f 16/3 Empire Maker (USA)—Promising Lead (Danehill (USA))
132 **PROVENANCE**, b f 23/3 Galileo (IRE)—Echelon (Danehill (USA))
133 **PSYCHOMETRY (FR)**, b f 23/1 Danehill Dancer (IRE)—Seven Magicians (USA) (Silver Hawk (USA))
134 **QAFFAAL (USA)**, b c 8/2 Street Cry (IRE)—Wasseema (USA) (Danzig (USA))
135 B f 18/1 Oasis Dream—Quiff (Sadler's Wells (USA))
136 B c 16/2 Danehill Dancer (IRE)—Riberac (Efisio) (135000)
137 **ROCHAMBEAU (IRE)**, b c 3/4 Sir Percy—Tableau Vivant (IRE) (Pivotal)
138 **ROYAL SEAL**, b f 3/3 Dansili—Queen's Best (King's Best (USA))
139 **SAINT'S VICTORY**, b f 14/3 Oasis Dream—Hi Calypso (IRE) (In The Wings)
140 B f 15/2 Champs Elysees—Sandglass (Zafonic (USA))
141 **SEA THE BLOOM**, b f 7/3 Sea The Stars (IRE)—Red Bloom (Selkirk (USA))
142 **SHAMA'S SONG (IRE)**, b f 2/2 Teofilo (IRE)—Green Dollar (IRE) (Kingmambo (USA))
143 Gr c 8/4 Oasis Dream—Shreyas (IRE) (Dalakhani (IRE))
144 **SIR ROSCO**, b c 6/3 Sir Percy—Rosacara (Green Desert (USA))
145 **SONG OF NAMIBIA (IRE)**, br c 21/2 Cape Cross (IRE)—Spring Symphony (IRE) (Darshaan)
146 B f 4/5 Dansili—Summer Breeze (Rainbow Quest (USA))
147 B c 16/4 High Chaparral (IRE)—Summerhill Parkes (Zafonic (USA)) (100000)
148 **TALL SHIP (IRE)**, b c 30/3 Sea The Stars (IRE)—Magical Romance (IRE) (Barathea (IRE))

SIR MICHAEL STOUTE - Continued

149 **TAMASHA**, ch f 5/3 Sea The Stars (IRE)—Tamarind (IRE) (Sadler's Wells (USA))
150 **TERCEL (IRE)**, b c 24/1 Monsun (GER)—Kitty Hawk (Danehill Dancer (IRE))
151 **TOP TUG (IRE)**, ch c 30/4 Halling (USA)—Top Romance (IRE) (Entrepreneur)
152 **UPPER STREET (IRE)**, b f 17/1 Dansili—Islington (IRE) (Sadler's Wells (USA))
153 B c 29/3 King's Best (USA)—Village Fete (Singspiel (IRE))
154 B c 5/2 Nayef (USA)—Winter Silence (Dansili)

Owners: HM The Queen, Mr K. Abdulla, HE Sheikh Joaan Bin Hamad Al Thani, HH Sheikh Mohammed bin Khalifa Al Thani, Antoniades Family, Ballymacoll Stud, Mr Nurlan Bizakov, Cheveley Park Stud, Mr Athos Christodoulou, Sir Evelyn de Rothschild, Prince A A Faisal, Mr Hamdan al Maktoum, Mrs E. A. Haynes, Highclere Thoroughbred Racing, Mrs John Magnier, Miss A. H. Marshall, Newsells Park Stud, Mr Philip Newton, Mr Robert Ng, Niarchos Family, Sir Robert Ogden, Lady Rothschild, Mr Derrick Smith, Mr George Strawbridge, Mr Saeed Suhail, Mr Michael Tabor, Mr James Wigan.

602

MISS KRISTIN STUBBS, Malton
Postal: **Beverley House Stables, Beverley Road, Malton, North Yorkshire, YO17 9PJ**
Contacts: **PHONE (01653) 698731 FAX (01653) 698724 MOBILE (07932) 977279 / (07801) 167707**
E-MAIL l.stubbs@btconnect.com

1 **BRONZE BEAU**, 6, ch g Compton Place—Bella Cantata **D. G. Arundale**
2 **ICE TROOPER**, 5, b g Iceman—Out Like Magic **J. P. Hames**
3 **SILVERWARE (USA)**, 5, b br g Eurosilver (USA)—Playing Footsie (USA) **Paul & Linda Dixon**
4 **TARQUIN (IRE)**, 4, b g Excellent Art—Umlani (IRE) **D. G. Arundale**

THREE-YEAR-OLDS

5 **ANTONIUS**, b g Antonius Pius (USA)—Queen of Poland (FR) **The B.P.J. Partnership**
6 **BOGSNOG (IRE)**, b g Moss Vale (IRE)—Lovers Kiss **Facts & Figures**
7 **GOLD BEAU (FR)**, b g Gold Away (IRE)—Theorie (FR) **D. G. Arundale**
8 **MASTER MOON (IRE)**, b g Excellent Art—Moon On A Spoon **P & L Partners**
9 **MEGAMUNCH (IRE)**, b g Camacho—Liscoa (IRE) **P & L Partners**
10 **MIDNIGHT DREAM (FR)**, b br g Country Reel (USA)—Tatante (IRE) **O. J. Williams**
11 **POLAR CHIEF**, b g Motivator—Polar Storm **P & L Partners**
12 **SOUTHERN SAPPHIRE**, ch g Compton Place—Brecon **D. M. Smith**

TWO-YEAR-OLDS

13 **DANFAZI (IRE)**, ch g 6/4 Dandy Man (IRE)—Distant Shore (IRE) (Jareer (USA)) (12000) **Facts & Figures**
14 **IDAMANTE**, b g 14/4 Amadeus Wolf—
    Gower Valentine (Primo Valentino (IRE)) (10000) **O. J. Williams & P. G. Shorrock**
15 **RIO YUMA (ITY)**, b f 25/3 Gold Sphinx (USA)—Selsey (Selkirk (USA)) (2500) **D. Grieve**
16 **TOO ELUSIVE**, b g 4/2 Major Cadeaux—Elusive Kitty (USA) (Elusive Quality (USA)) (14000) **Paul & Linda Dixon**

Other Owners: Mr D. Arundale, Paul W. H. Dixon, Mrs L. J. Dixon, Mr D. Grieve, Mr J. P. Hames, Mr A. Larkin, Mr N. Lyons, Mr Barry Midgley, G. Pickering, Mrs Valerie Pittman, P. A. Saxton, P. G. Shorrock, Mr John Wright.

Jockey (flat): Tony Hamilton, Tom Eaves, Graham Lee.

603

MR ROB SUMMERS, Solihull
Postal: **Summerhill Cottage, Danzey Green, Tanworth-in-Arden, Solihull, West Midlands, B94 5BJ**
Contacts: **PHONE (01564) 742667 MOBILE (07775) 898327**

1 **ARCTIC ECHO**, 14, b g Alderbrook—Arctic Oats **R. P. D. T. Dineen**
2 5, Ch m Desideratum—Arctic Oats **R. P. D. T. Dineen**
3 **FINTAN**, 10, ch g Generous (IRE)—Seeker **Mr S. W. Dunn**
4 **MASSACHUSETTS**, 6, ch g Singspiel (IRE)—Royal Passion
5 **MONTJUIC (FR)**, 9, b h Montjeu (IRE)—Apparentee (USA) **K. W. Bradley**
6 **OSCAR HILL (FR)**, 7, b g Oscar (FR)—Elizabeth Tudor (IRE) **K. W. Bradley**
7 **PHOTOGENIQUE (FR)**, 10, b m Cyborg (FR)—Colombia (IRE) **Solihull Racing Club**
8 **RED ROSSO**, 8, ch g Executive Perk—Secret Whisper **Solihull Racing Club**
9 **RED WHISPER**, 9, ch g Midnight Legend—Secret Whisper **Solihull Racing Club**
10 **ROSE RED**, 6, ch m Weld—Secret Whisper **Mrs G. M. Summers**

Other Owners: Mr S. J. Wood.

Assistant Trainer: Mrs G. M. Summers

604 MR JOHN A. SUPPLE, Abbeyfeale
Postal: **Feale View Stud, Coolaneelig, Abbeyfeale P.O., Co. Limerick, Ireland**
Contacts: **PHONE (00353) 68 45890 FAX (00353) 68 45890 MOBILE (00353) 86 7390841**
E-MAIL j.supple@fealeviewstud.com

1 KNOCKANAR (IRE), 5, b g Kalanisi (IRE)—Fairy Dawn (IRE) **Mr Johnny Byrne**
2 ROADTOABBEYFEALE (IRE), 8, b g Milan—Lady Bramble (IRE) **Mr Johnny Byrne**
3 THELIFEOF (IRE), 7, b g Brian Boru—Dream Adventure (IRE) **Mr Johnny Byrne**

THREE-YEAR-OLDS
4 B g Catcher In The Rye (IRE)—Dangerous Business (IRE) **Mr William Byrne**
5 B g Milan—Kashmir Lady (FR) **Mr Johnny Byrne**

Other Owners: Mr Nolan Byrne, Miss Julianna Byrne, Miss Lorna Preston.

Assistant Trainer: Lorna Preston

Jockey (NH): E. J. O'Conell.

605 MR ALAN SWINBANK, Richmond
Postal: **Western House Stables, East Road, Melsonby, Richmond, North Yorkshire, DL10 5NJ**
Contacts: **PHONE (01325) 339964 FAX (01325) 377113 MOBILE (07860) 368365 / (07711) 488341**
E-MAIL info@alanswinbank.com WEBSITE www.alanswinbank.com

1 AD VALUE (IRE), 5, b g Ad Valorem (USA)—Sopran Marida (IRE) **Mrs V. McGee**
2 ANNA'S ARCH (IRE), 6, b g Arch (USA)—Lady Angharad (IRE) **C. Tremewan**
3 BANDANAMAN (IRE), 7, b g Danehill Dancer (USA)—Band of Angels (IRE) **Miss J. S. Peat**
4 BIG WATER (IRE), 5, ch g Saffron Walden (FR)—Magic Feeling (IRE) **T. B. Tarn**
5 BIGGINS BOY (IRE), 4, b g Motivator—Optimal (IRE) **Mr G. H. Bell**
6 BOB'S LADY TARA, 5, b m Kayf Tara—Bob Back's Lady (IRE) **J. R. Wills**
7 BORN TO PERFORM, 8, b g Theatrical—My Hansel (USA) **Panther Racing Limited**
8 BORN TO SHINE (IRE), 5, b g Suave (USA)—Sentimental Keep (USA) **Mrs J. M. Perratt**
9 CHERRY TREE HILL (IRE), 5, b g Ivan Denisovich (IRE)—Ring Pink (USA) **N. Shutts**
10 CORAL SANDS (IRE), 5, bl g Footstepsinthesand—Daziyra (IRE) **Mrs J. M. Penney**
11 DANCING PADDY (IRE), 5, b g Azamour (IRE)—Moucha (FR) **Mr M. Robson**
12 DARK RULER (IRE), 4, b g Dark Angel (IRE)—Gino Lady (IRE) **Mrs E. Walters**
13 DUBAI SONNET, 4, b g Dubai Destination (USA)—Twilight Sonnet **Solway Stayers**
14 EBONY EXPRESS, 4, bl g Superior Premium—Coffee Ice **Mrs T. Blackett**
15 ENTIHAA, 5, b g Tiger Hill (IRE)—Magic Tree (UAE) **Elsa Crankshaw & G. Allan**
16 EUTROPIUS (IRE), 4, b g Ad Valorem (USA)—Peps (IRE) **Ontoawinner 2**
17 4, B g Teofilo (IRE)—Fidelio's Miracle (USA)
18 FLY SOLO, 4, b g Soviet Star (USA)—Vino **G. Reed**
19 FLYDAYNIGHT GIRL (IRE), 4, b f Red Ransom (USA)—Miss Amanpuri **Mr & Mrs M. Miller**
20 GOGEO (IRE), 6, b g Val Royal (FR)—Steal 'em **Mrs J. Porter**
21 HONEST DEAL, 5, b g Trade Fair—Sincerely **G. Reed**
22 I'M SUPER TOO (IRE), 6, b g Fasliyev (USA)—Congress (IRE) **Mr D. C. Young**
23 LADY KASHAAN (IRE), 4, b f Manduro (GER)—Lady's Secret (IRE) **Mr G. Brogan**
24 LINROYALE BOY (USA), 5, ch g Giant's Causeway (USA)—Welcometotheworld (USA) **Spiral Bracken**
25 LOTHAIR (IRE), 5, b g Holy Roman Emperor (IRE)—Crafty Example (USA) **Mrs J. Porter**
26 LUCKY WINDMILL, 6, b g Lucky Story (USA)—Windmill Princess **Mrs J. Porter**
27 MAJOR BUCKLEY (IRE), 4, ch g Haafhd—Woodwin (IRE) **Shropshire Wolves II**
28 MITCHELL'S WAY, 6, ch g Needwood Blade—Ghana (GER) **Ontoawinner 2**
29 NABURN, 5, b g Cape Cross (IRE)—Allespagne (USA) **Elsa Crankshaw & G. Allan**
30 NORTHSIDE PRINCE (IRE), 7, b g Desert Prince (IRE)—Spartan Girl (IRE) **Mrs J. M. Penney**
31 PAINTED TAIL (IRE), 6, b m Mark of Esteem (IRE)—Bronwen (IRE) **Ms A. L. I. Winbergh**
32 PERSIAN PERIL, 9, br g Erhaab (USA)—Brush Away **Mrs J. Porter**
33 PHOENIX RETURNS (IRE), 5, br g Phoenix Reach (IRE)—Oscar's Lady (IRE) **Mrs J. Porter**
34 POWDERONTHEBONNET (IRE), 5, b g Definite Article—Zuhal **J. P. Jones**
35 QUAN (IRE), 4, b g Shamardal (USA)—Assumption **S. P. C. Woods**
36 REGAL SWAIN (IRE), 5, b g Ivan Denisovich (IRE)—Targhyb (IRE) **Mr A. J. Sparks**
37 SAFFRON TOWN (IRE), 4, ch g Saffron Walden (FR)—Magic Feeling (IRE) **B. Boanson & M. Wane**
38 SARTINGO (IRE), 6, b g Encosta de Lago (AUS)—Alicia (IRE) **Mr M. Robson**
39 SAVEIRO (FR), 9, b g Raintrap—Branceilles (FR) **Anthea Findlay**
40 SELDOM INN, 5, ch g Double Trigger (IRE)—Portland Row (IRE) **W. A. Walker**
41 SYGNATURE, 4, b g Authorized (IRE)—Perfect Story (IRE) **Ontoawinner 2**

MR ALAN SWINBANK - Continued

42 **THE BOLD LORD (IRE)**, 5, ch g Bachelor Duke (USA)—Bold Nora (IRE) **T. B. Tarn**
43 **THE FERICK (IRE)**, 7, b g Kris Kin (USA)—Minaun Heights **Mr A. Wright**
44 **URBONITE (IRE)**, 4, b g Proud Citizen (USA)—Bronze Baby (USA) **Mr A. J. Sparks**

THREE-YEAR-OLDS

45 **ARAMIST (IRE)**, gr g Aussie Rules (USA)—Mistic Sun **Pam & Richard Ellis**
46 **BITUSA (USA)**, b g Roman Ruler (USA)—Richen (USA) **Mrs J. Porter**
47 **CHEVALGRIS**, gr g Verglas (IRE)—Danzelline **Mr D. C. Young**
48 **LADY ARTISTE (IRE)**, ch f Excellent Art—Elauyun (IRE)
49 **RED JOKER (IRE)**, br g Red Clubs (IRE)—Lady Singspiel (IRE) **C. Tremewan**

TWO-YEAR-OLDS

50 B c 24/2 Halling (USA)—Anamilina (IRE) (Anabaa (USA)) (32000) **Mr G. McGann**
51 B g 13/3 Piccolo—Harlestone Lady (Shaamit (IRE)) (8500) **Mr I. Tweddall**
52 B g 21/3 Iffraaj—Hawatref (IRE) (Mujtahid (USA)) (12000) **Mr G. McGann**
53 B g 19/3 Intense Focus (USA)—I'll Be Waiting (Vettori (IRE)) (35714) **Mr G. McGann**
54 B f 11/4 Manduro (GER)—La Vita E Bella (IRE) (Definite Article) (14285)
55 B g 26/4 Tiger Hill (IRE)—Mamoura (IRE) (Lomond (USA)) (23809) **Mr G. McGann**
56 Ch g 6/3 Bahamian Bounty—Phoebe Woodstock (IRE) (Grand Lodge (USA)) (31000) **Mr G. McGann**
57 Ch c 24/4 Intense Focus (USA)—Reine de Neige (Kris) (28571) **Mr G. McGann**
58 Ch c 14/3 Elnadim (USA)—Sagrada (GER) (Primo Dominie) (22857) **Mr G. McGann**
59 B c 13/4 Mastercraftsman (IRE)—Shining Hour (USA) (Red Ransom (USA)) (33333) **Mrs I. Gibson**
60 B c 6/4 Lawman (FR)—True Crystal (IRE) (Sadler's Wells (USA)) (35000)

Other Owners: Mr J. Babb, Mrs B. Boanson, Mr D. Bracken, Mr Mac Creedon, Mrs P. Ellis, Mrs I. Gibson, Mr Matthew Green, Miss Sally R. Haynes, Mr G. McGann, Mr M. Miller, Mrs C. Miller, Mr N. J. O'Brien, Dr Roy Palmer, Mr Richard Simpson, Miss M. Swinbank, Mr I. Tweddall, Mrs E. Walters, Mr Martyn Wane, Miss S. A. Ward, Mr D. C. Young.

Assistant Trainer: Mr W.W. Haigh & Miss Sally Haynes

Jockey (flat): Garry Whillans, Robert Winston. **Jockey (NH):** Fearghal Davis, Rachael Green. **Conditional:** Jake Greenall.

---

606 **MR TOM SYMONDS, Ross-On-Wye**
Postal: **Dason Court Cottage, Hentland, Ross-on-Wye, Herefordshire, HR9 6LW**
Contacts: **PHONE (01989) 730869 MOBILE (07823) 324649**
E-MAIL dasoncourt@gmail.com WEBSITE www.thomassymonds.co.uk

1 **ABRUZZI**, 5, b g Milan—Shannon Native (IRE) **G & M Roberts, Churchward, Frost, Green, W-Williams**
2 **AMBER FLUSH**, 4, b f Sir Harry Lewis (USA)—Sari Rose (FR) **Mr T. R. Symonds**
3 **ANY PEARL**, 5, b m Alflora (IRE)—Posh Pearl **Shade Oak Stud & D Jenks**
4 **BAR BOY (IRE)**, 4, gr g Acambaro (GER)—Carminda Thyne (IRE) **Sir Peter & Lady Gibbings**
5 **FOXCUB (IRE)**, 5, b g Bahri (USA)—Foxglove **Celia & Michael Baker**
6 **GARRETT**, 5, br g Westerner—Like Manner **Mr D. Ford**
7 **GENERAL ROSS (IRE)**, 6, b g Generous (IRE)—Rossmore Girl (IRE) **Mrs S. Tainton**
8 **IVEBEENTHINKING**, 5, b m One More Tiger—Moonlight Saunter (USA) **Mrs V. J. Norbury**
9 **KING KILLER (IRE)**, 5, b g Classic Cliche (IRE)—River Puttens (IRE)
10 **LIQUEUR ROSE**, 6, b m Alflora (IRE)—Teenero **The Mumbo Jumbos**
11 **MALIBU ROCK**, 5, b g Tiger Hill (IRE)—High Straits
12 **MARICO (FR)**, 5, b br g Lavirco (GER)—Mary Bay (FR) **Thomas Symonds Racing Syndicate**
13 **MIDNIGHT BELLE**, 6, b m Midnight Legend—Cherry Alley (IRE) **Mrs P. E. Holtorp**
14 **MIDNIGHT REQUEST**, 4, b g Midnight Legend—Friendly Request **W E Donohue J M Donohue**
15 **MIRIFIC (FR)**, 7, gr g Linamix (FR)—Matanilla (FR) **The Vin de Roy Racing Syndicate**
16 **NUISANCE**, 5, b m Overbury (IRE)—Mothers Help **Mr T. R. Symonds**
17 **OSCAR'S PET (IRE)**, 5, b m Oscar (IRE)—Kilcoleman Lady (IRE) **J. Palmer-Brown**
18 **PRINCE BUSTER (FR)**, 10, b g Sinjar (FR)—Eliflo (FR) **The Unusual Racegoers Partnership**
19 **SCHOLASTICA**, 6, b m Old Vic—La Perrotine (FR) **Mr D. Redvers**
20 **STRAITS OF MESSINA (IRE)**, 4, b g Mountain High (IRE)—Scylla **Mr T. R. Symonds**
21 **STRATHCAL**, 7, b g Beat Hollow—Shall We Run **Shenkman, Foster, Tinsley, Coe, Stagg**
22 **SUMMER SOUNDS (IRE)**, 4, b br g Definite Article—Marble Sound (FR) **Sir Peter & Lady Gibbings**
23 **THE WESTERN HILL (IRE)**, 4, b g Westerner—Marie The (FR) **Sir Peter & Lady Gibbings**
24 **TROJAN SUN**, 7, b br g Kayf Tara—Sun Dante (IRE) **I. A. Low**
25 **TWEEDLEDRUM**, 6, b m Beat Hollow—Tweed Mill **Wainwright, Hill, Atkin, Cheshire & Rowlinson**

MR TOM SYMONDS - Continued

26 **VALMARI (IRE)**, 10, b m Kalanisi (IRE)—Penza **Leonard Jay Ltd**
27 **WHEN BEN WHEN (IRE)**, 4, b g Beneficial—Almnadia (IRE) **Mrs S. Tainton**

Other Owners: Mr C. Adams, Mrs Celia Baker, Mr Michael Baker, Mrs P. J. Buckler, Mr W. E. Donohue, Mrs J. M. Donohue, Mr J. R. Driscoll, Sir Peter Gibbings, Lady Gibbings, Mr F. M. Green, Mrs Emma Hockenhull, Mr P. D. Hockenhull, Mr David Jenks, Mr Jeremy Mason, Mr G. A. Roberts, Mrs Jane Rowlinson, Mr M. S. Scott, Mrs Jane Symonds, Mr Thomas R. Symonds, Mr Denis Tinsley, Mr Michael Wainwright.

607
MR PATRICK TALLIS, Freshford
Postal: **Clontubrid, Freshford, Co. Kilkenny, Ireland**
Contacts: **PHONE (00353) 56 883 2216 FAX (00353) 56 883 2350 MOBILE (00353) 86 256 0968**
E-MAIL **info@tallis.ie**

1 **BATTLE FOR GLORY (IRE)**, 5, b g Ivan Denisovich (IRE)—Hever Golf Lover (IRE) **C. Holohan**
2 **KNIGHTLIFE (IRE)**, 5, b g Hawk Wing (USA)—Homegrown (IRE) **P. Tallis**
3 **KNOCKOWN (IRE)**, 5, b g Alamshar (IRE)—Trebles (IRE) **B. Wall**

THREE-YEAR-OLDS

4 B f Cape Cross (IRE)—Begin The Beguine (IRE) **C. Holohan**
5 **TRENDY GENT (IRE)**, b g Bachelor Duke (USA)—Trendy Celt (IRE) **P. Tallis**

TWO-YEAR-OLDS

6 Gr f 15/4 Peintre Celebre (USA)—Bysshe (Linamix (FR)) (5555) **P. Tallis**
7 B g 21/2 Kheleyf (USA)—Homegrown (IRE) (Mujadil (USA)) **C. Holohan**
8 B f 22/2 Rock of Gibraltar (IRE)—Lady Gregory (IRE) (In The Wings) **P. Tallis**

Assistant Trainer: D. Bergin

Jockey (flat): Seamus Heffernan.

608
MR JAMES TATE, Newmarket
Postal: **Jamesfield Place, Hamilton Road, Newmarket, Suffolk, CB8 7JQ**
Contacts: PHONE (01638) 669861 FAX (01638) 676634 MOBILE (07703) 601283
E-MAIL james@jamestateracing.com WEBSITE www.jamestateracing.com

1 **DUBAWI ISLAND (FR)**, 4, b g Dubawi (IRE)—Housa Dancer (FR) **S. Ali**
2 **IPTISAM**, ch g Rahy (USA)—Grain of Truth **S. Manana**
3 **TROIS VALLEES (USA)**, 4, b br g Elusive Quality (USA)—Chamrousse (USA) **S. Ali**

THREE-YEAR-OLDS

4 **ARAAJMH (USA)**, b f Street Cry (IRE)—Rajeem **S. Manana**
5 **ASHAMALY**, br c Shamardal (USA)—Tullynally **S. Ali**
6 **BIN MANDURO**, b c Manduro (GER)—Dust Dancer **S. Ali**
7 **BIN SINGSPIEL**, br c Singspiel (IRE)—Mexican Hawk (USA) **S. Ali**
8 **EL MANATI (IRE)**, b f Iffraaj—Limit (IRE) **Sheikh R. D. Al Maktoum**
9 **FREE ISLAND**, b f Kheleyf (USA)—Island Race **Sheikh J. Al Dalmook Maktoum**
10 **GEBAYL**, b f Compton Place—Glimpse **S. Manana**
11 **GRILLETTO (USA)**, b c Exchange Rate (USA)—Casuarina (USA) **Sheikh J. Al Dalmook Maktoum**
12 **GWAEL (USA)**, b f A P Indy (USA)—Maskunah (IRE) **S. Manana**
13 **LEAD ROLE**, b f Exceed And Excel (AUS)—Fanny's Fancy **S. Manana**
14 **LEBRESEM**, b c Elusive City (USA)—Laheen (IRE) **S. Manana**
15 **MACAABRA (IRE)**, b f Exceed And Excel (AUS)—Al Cobra (IRE) **S. Ali**
16 **MASAADR**, br c Manduro (GER)—Masandra (IRE) **S. Manana**
17 **MIRSAALE**, ch c Sir Percy—String Quartet (IRE) **S. Ali**
18 **MIZYEN (IRE)**, b g Teofilo (IRE)—Housekeeper (IRE) **Sheikh J. Al Dalmook Maktoum**
19 **MOUNT TIGER**, b c Tiger Hill (IRE)—Fly Me To The Moon (GER) **S. Ali**
20 **MYSTICAL MAN**, br c Sakhee's Secret—Dancing Nelly **S. Manana**
21 **NARU (IRE)**, b c Authorized (IRE)—Jabbara (IRE) **S. Manana**
22 **NASIJAH**, b f Authorized (IRE)—Nasij (USA) **S. Ali**
23 **NEW FALCON (IRE)**, b f New Approach (IRE)—Wimple (USA) **S. Manana**
24 **REGAL HAWK**, br f Singspiel (IRE)—Elegant Hawk **S. Manana**
25 **SHEEMA**, ch f Teofilo (IRE)—Shimna **S. Manana**

MR JAMES TATE - Continued

26 **TIGHT KNIT (USA)**, b c Hard Spun (USA)—Tamdiid (USA) **S. Manana**
27 **WADAA (USA)**, b f Dynaformer (USA)—Cloud Castle **S. Manana**
28 **YAHILWA (USA)**, br f Medaglia d'oro (USA)—Verbanella (USA) **Sheikh J. Al Dalmook Maktoum**

TWO-YEAR-OLDS

29 B c 3/4 Sixties Icon—Aileen's Gift (IRE) (Rainbow Quest (USA)) (65000) **S. Ali**
30 B f 28/4 Firebreak—Alexander Ballet (Mind Games) (60000) **S. Ali**
31 Ch f 24/1 Art Connoisseur (IRE)—Aquatint (Dansili) (23809) **S. Manana**
32 B f 21/4 Exceed And Excel (AUS)—Areeda (IRE) (Refuse To Bend (IRE)) (46031) **S. Ali**
33 Br f 4/3 Kheleyf (USA)—Barracade (IRE) (Barathea (IRE)) (11428) **S. Manana**
34 Ch f 22/3 Shamardal (USA)—Benedicte (IRE) (Galileo (IRE)) (35000) **S. Ali**
35 **BLACK VALE (IRE)**, b c 10/4 Moss Vale (IRE)—Limit (IRE) (Barathea (IRE)) (30000) **Sheikh R. D. Al Maktoum**
36 **BLHADAWA (IRE)**, b f 6/2 Iffraaj—
                         Trois Heures Apres (Soviet Star (USA)) (37000) **Sheikh J. Al Dalmook Maktoum**
37 B c 10/5 Myboycharlie (IRE)—Calico Moon (USA) (Seeking The Gold (USA)) (9523) **S. Manana**
38 B c 17/2 Royal Applause—Cedar Sea (IRE) (Persian Bold) (76190) **S. Manana**
39 B f 13/2 Royal Applause—Choosey Girl (IRE) (Choisir (AUS)) (19047) **S. Manana**
40 B c 4/3 Authorized (IRE)—Circle of Love (Sakhee (USA)) (20000) **S. Manana**
41 B f 20/4 Royal Applause—Clinet (IRE) (Docksider (USA)) (24000) **S. Manana**
42 B f 27/3 Street Cry (IRE)—Cloud Castle (In The Wings) **S. Manana**
43 B f 23/4 Azamour (IRE)—Deauville Vision (Danehill Dancer (IRE)) (49205) **S. Ali**
44 **DESERT RANGER (IRE)**, b c 21/3 Bushranger (IRE)—
                         Maleha (IRE) (Cape Cross (IRE)) (25000) **Sheikh J. Al Dalmook Maktoum**
45 B f 3/4 Cape Cross (IRE)—Deveron (USA) (Cozzene (USA)) (40000) **S. Ali**
46 B f 17/3 Dutch Art—Ellway Queen (USA) (Bahri (USA)) (41904) **S. Ali**
47 Ch f 26/1 Elusive Quality (USA)—Elrehaan (Sadler's Wells (USA)) (13000) **S. Manana**
48 **EXCEL BEST**, b c 17/3 Exceed And Excel (AUS)—
                         Hannah's Dream (King's Best (USA)) (30000) **Sheikh J. Al Dalmook Maktoum**
49 **EXCEL'S BEAUTY**, b f 30/1 Exceed And Excel (AUS)—
                         Continua (USA) (Elusive Quality (USA)) (56000) **Sheikh J. Al Dalmook Maktoum**
50 Ch c 10/4 Shamardal (USA)—Fortress (Generous (IRE)) (36190) **S. Ali**
51 **HADYA (IRE)**, b f 12/2 Teofilo (IRE)—Lafleur (IRE) (Grand Lodge (USA)) (28000) **Sheikh R. D. Al Maktoum**
52 B f 16/4 Tobougg (IRE)—Happy Lady (IRE) (Cadeaux Genereux) (29523) **S. Ali**
53 Ch c 8/2 Sir Percy—Hermanita (Hernando (FR)) (26000) **S. Manana**
54 Ch f 22/1 Sakhee's Secret—Jasmick (IRE) (Definite Article) (25000) **S. Manana**
55 Gr f 29/1 Verglas (IRE)—Katimont (IRE) (Montjeu (IRE)) (25000) **S. Manana**
56 Ch f 4/4 Halling (USA)—Louella (USA) (El Gran Senor (USA)) (48000) **S. Ali**
57 B c 7/4 Dandy Man (IRE)—Lucky Flirt (USA) (Gulch (USA)) (25000) **S. Manana**
58 B f 9/2 Bahamian Bounty—Malyana (Mtoto) (43650) **S. Ali**
59 B c 30/3 Cape Cross (IRE)—Marine City (JPN) (Carnegie (IRE)) (20000) **S. Ali**
60 Ch f 13/3 Shamardal (USA)—Miss Hepburn (IRE) (Gone West (USA)) (11000) **S. Manana**
61 B f 3/4 Champs Elysees—Mrs Seek (Unfuwain (USA)) (75000) **S. Manana**
62 **SORRY SAEED**, b f 19/2 Raven's Pass (USA)—Clear Impression (IRE) (Danehill (USA)) (65000) **S. Ali**
63 B f 13/3 Shamardal (USA)—State Secret (Green Desert (USA)) (26000) **S. Ali**
64 Gr f 14/2 Authorized (IRE)—Swift Dispersal (Shareef Dancer (USA)) (22000) **S. Ali**
65 **UMNEYATI**, b f 28/3 Iffraaj—Honky Tonk Sally (Dansili) (30000) **Sheikh R. D. Al Maktoum**
66 **YAJAMILA**, b f 6/3 Royal Applause—Yatir (FR) (Red Ransom (USA)) (38095) **Sheikh R. D. Al Maktoum**
67 **ZALZILAH**, b c 23/3 Kheleyf (USA)—Tarneem (USA) (Zilzal (USA)) (42857) **Sheikh J. Al Dalmook Maktoum**

---

609 **MR TOM TATE, Tadcaster**
Postal: **Castle Farm, Hazelwood, Tadcaster, North Yorkshire, LS24 9NJ**
Contacts: **PHONE (01937) 836036 FAX (01937) 530011 MOBILE (07970) 122818**
E-MAIL tomtate@castlefarmstables.fsnet.co.uk WEBSITE www.tomtate.co.uk

1 **EAGLE ROCK (IRE)**, 5, b g High Chaparral (IRE)—Silk Fan (IRE) **The Ivy Syndicate**
2 **ELAND ALLY**, 5, b g Striking Ambition—Dream Rose (IRE) **The Ivy Syndicate**
3 **JOYFUL MOTIVE**, 4, ch g Motivator—Triple Joy **T T Racing**
4 **KUDU COUNTRY (IRE)**, 7, gr g Captain Rio—Nirvavita (FR) **The Flat Cap Syndicate**
5 **PRINCE OF JOHANNE (IRE)**, 7, gr g Johannesburg (USA)—Paiute Princess (FR) **Mr D. Storey**
6 **RED SEAL**, 4, ch g Haafhd—Seal Indigo (IRE) **T T Racing**
7 **SKY CROSSING**, 4, b g Cape Cross (IRE)—Sky Wonder **T T Racing**

MR TOM TATE - Continued

THREE-YEAR-OLDS

8 FLYING NELLIE, b f Mount Nelson—Ares Vallis (IRE) **T T Racing**
9 GOOD SPEECH (IRE), ch f Haatef (USA)—Privileged Speech (USA) **T T Racing**
10 B g Bahamian Bounty—Hagwah (USA)
11 SABRINA'S SECRET, b f Sakhee's Secret—Sabrina Brown **T T Racing**

TWO-YEAR-OLDS

12 Ch f 12/4 Shamardal (USA)—Excellent (Grand Lodge (USA)) (30476)
13 Ch g 24/2 Captain Rio—Festivite (IRE) (Fasliyev (USA)) (9523) **Ms M. F. Cassidy**
14 Ch g 3/3 Majestic Missile (IRE)—Magdalene (FR) (College Chapel) (13333)
15 B g 12/4 Sir Percy—Temple of Thebes (IRE) (Bahri (USA)) (36000) **The Ivy Syndicate**

Other Owners: Mr D. M. W. Hodgkiss, Mrs S. Hodgkiss, Mr T. P. Tate, Mrs Hazel Tate.

Assistant Trainer: Hazel Tate

Jockey (flat): Micky Fenton, Graham Lee, Jamie Spencer.

---

610 MRS SUSAN TAYLOR, Alnwick
Postal: **The Lookout, Lesbury, Alnwick, Northumberland, NE66 3PQ**

1 CHAMPERTY (IRE), 7, b m Saffron Walden (FR)—Nashville Skyline **Mrs S. Taylor**
2 CHESTER LEGEND, 6, ch g Pasternak—Sally Smith **Mrs S. Taylor**
3 HIGH INTEREST, 7, b g Milieu—Witness of Truth **Mrs S. Taylor**

---

611 MR COLIN TEAGUE, Wingate
Postal: **Bridgefield Farm, Trimdon Lane, Station Town, Wingate, Co. Durham, TS28 5NE**
Contacts: **PHONE (01429) 837087 MOBILE (07967) 330929**
E-MAIL colin.teague@btopenworld.com

1 5, Ch m Millkom—Habla Me (IRE)
2 MICKY MAC (IRE), 9, b g Lend A Hand—Gazette It Tonight **Collins Chauffeur Driven Executive Cars**
3 MONTE PATTINO (USA), 9, ch g Rahy (USA)—Jood (USA) **Collins Chauffeur Driven Executive Cars**
4 MUJAHOPE, 8, b g Mujahid (USA)—Speak **Collins Chauffeur Driven Executive Cars**
5 ON THE HIGH TOPS (IRE), 5, b g Kheleyf (USA)—Diplomats Daughter **Collins Chauffeur Driven Executive Cars**
6 PETERON, 5, b g Danbird (AUS)—Lady Rock **A. Rice**
7 RUBICON BAY (IRE), 6, b m One Cool Cat (USA)—Mrs Moonlight **Collins Chauffeur Driven Executive Cars**
8 5, Ch h Where Or When (IRE)—Sovereign Seal
9 STAR BETA, 4, b g Danbird (AUS)—Lady Rock **Mr J. R. Bowman**
10 5, B m Garrison Savannah (NZ)—Transylvania

---

612 MR ROGER TEAL, Epsom
Postal: **Thirty Acre Barn Stables, Shepherds Walk, Epsom, Surrey, KT18 6BX**
Contacts: **PHONE (01372) 279535 FAX (01372) 271981 MOBILE (07710) 325521**
E-MAIL rteal@thirtyacre.co.uk WEBSITE www.thirtyacrestables.co.uk

1 CHARLOTTE ROSINA, 4, b f Choisir (AUS)—Intriguing Glimpse **Homecroft Wealth Racing**
2 CHRISSYCROSS (IRE), 4, b f Cape Cross (IRE)—Penang (IRE) **A. J. Morton**
3 FREDDY Q (IRE), 4, ch g Iffraaj—Barnabas (ITY) **H. Hunt**
4 JACK OF DIAMONDS (IRE), 4, b g Red Clubs (IRE)—Sakkara Star (IRE) **Inside Track Racing Club**
5 JOHNNY SPLASH (IRE), 4, b g Dark Angel (IRE)—Ja Ganhou **Epping Racing**
6 LANGLEY VALE, 4, b g Piccolo—Running Glimpse (IRE) **Dr G F Forward & Mr F C Taylor**
7 PUCON, 4, b f Kyllachy—The Fugative **Mr J. A. Redmond**
8 RACHAEL'S RUBY, 6, b m Joe Bear (IRE)—Fajjoura (IRE) **Ms R. Bezuidenhout**
9 RED LARKSPUR (IRE), 4, b f Red Clubs (IRE)—Holda (IRE) **The Gracenote Partnership**
10 THE TICHBORNE (IRE), 5, b g Shinko Forest (IRE)—Brunswick **Mr Chris Simpson & Mick Waghorn**
11 TIGERS TALE (IRE), 4, b g Tiger Hill (IRE)—Vayenga (FR) **Mr B Kitcherside & Big Cat Partnership**

MR ROGER TEAL - Continued

THREE-YEAR-OLDS

  12 **CLASSIC ART**, ch g Excellent Art—Sensibility **John Morton & Andrew Sharpe**
  13 **HAWAIIAN DREAM (IRE)**, b f Catcher In The Rye (IRE)—Polynesian Goddess (IRE) **A. J. Morton**
  14 **TILSTARR (IRE)**, b f Shamardal (USA)—Vampire Queen (IRE) **H. Hunt**
  15 B c Authorized (IRE)—Yazmin (IRE) **Mr M. Vickers**

TWO-YEAR-OLDS

  16 **BERKELEY VALE**, b c 7/3 Three Valleys (USA)—
                                  Intriguing Glimpse (Piccolo) **Mrs Muriel Forward & Dr G C Forward**
  17 Ch c 4/4 Nayef (USA)—Miss Penton (Primo Dominie) **The Rat Racers**
  18 B f 11/2 Exceed And Excel (AUS)—Never Lose (Diktat) (52000) **Mr M. Vickers**

Other Owners: A. J. Chambers, Mrs E. Curley, Mr S. Fisher, Dr G. C. Forward, Mrs M. E. Forward, R. Frost, B. Kitcherside, R. B. Kolien, Mr P. O. Mooney, S. J. Piper, Mrs R. Pott, Mr C. Roase, E. Sames, Miss B. Sanders, Mr A. M. Sharpe, A. C. Simpson, Mr F. C. Taylor, M. F. Waghorn, Mr D. G. Waterer, Mr S. Wylde, Mr M. S. Wynn.

613	**MRS D. THOMAS, Bridgend** Postal: Pen-Y-Lan Farm, Aberkenfig, Bridgend, Mid Glam Contacts: PHONE (01656) 720254 FAX (01656) 720254 MOBILE (07989) 462130 E-MAIL beccania@hotmail.com

  1 **AM I BLUE**, 7, b m Dubai Destination (USA)—Seal Indigo (IRE) **Mrs D. Thomas**

Assistant Trainer: Brett Norris

Jockey (NH): Richard Johnson. **Amateur:** Mr Simon Walker.

614	**MR DAVID THOMPSON, Darlington** Postal: South View Racing, Ashley Cottage, South View, Bolam, Darlington, Co. Durham, DL2 2UP Contacts: PHONE (01388) 835806 (01388) 832658 FAX (01325) 835806 MOBILE (07795) 161657 E-MAIL dwthompson61@hotmail.co.uk WEBSITE www.dwthompson.co.uk

  1 **ANTIHERO**, 6, b g Motivator—Damsel **Mr N. Park**
  2 **CRACKERJAC BOY (USA)**, 8, b g Catienus (USA)—Julie Apple (USA) **J. A. Moore**
  3 **CRISPO (IRE)**, 5, b g Byron—Titania **J. A. Moore**
  4 **ESCAPE ARTIST**, 6, gr g Act One—Free At Last **Mr T. J. A. Thompson**
  5 **EVERDON BROOK (IRE)**, 8, br g Laveron—Shean Rose (IRE) **J. A. Moore**
  6 **GREAT OCEAN ROAD (IRE)**, 10, ch g Shernazar—Princess Breda (IRE) **Mrs H. E. Thompson**
  7 **LOGICAL APPROACH (IRE)**, 6, b g Tikkanen (USA)—Anntella (IRE) **A. J. Duffield**
  8 **MANGO MUSIC**, 10, ch m Distant Music—Eurolink Sundance **Mr T. J. A. Thompson**
  9 **ROYAL AND ANCIENT (IRE)**, 6, b g Danehill Dancer (IRE)—Champaka (IRE) **A. J. Duffield**
  10 **RUFF DIAMOND (USA)**, 8, b br g Stormin Fever (USA)—Whalah (USA) **A. J. Duffield**
  11 **SAVANNAH'S CHOICE**, 5, b m Garrison Savannah (NZ)—Barbara Frietchie (IRE) **Mr A. Sayers**
  12 **SHANNINA**, 8, b g Shaanmer (IRE)—Jannina (FR) **J. A. Moore**
  13 **SILVER SPEECH**, 5, gr m Proclamation (IRE)—Sophies Symphony **A. J. Duffield**
  14 **THE DIAL HOUSE**, 7, b g Tagula (IRE)—Marliana (IRE) **A. J. Duffield**
  15 **THE THIRSTY BRICKY (IRE)**, 11, b g Saddlers' Hall (IRE)—Splendid Choice (IRE) **Mr T. J. A. Thompson**
  16 **VIVARINI**, 9, b g Hernando (FR)—Venetian Red (USA) **Mr T. J. A. Thompson**
  17 **WILLIE WHISTLE**, 4, b g Supreme Sound—Zahara Joy **A. B. Graham**

Assistant Trainer: A Dickman

Jockey (flat): Andrew Elliott, Tony Hamilton. **Amateur:** Mr G. R. Smith.

615	**MR VICTOR THOMPSON, Alnwick** Postal: Link House Farm, Newton By The Sea, Embleton, Alnwick, Northumberland, NE66 3ED Contacts: PHONE (01665) 576272

  1 **ANZINGER (IRE)**, 7, b g Milan—Tarmons Duchess (IRE) **V. Thompson**
  2 **CHANCEOFA LIFETIME (IRE)**, 6, ch g Beneficial—Bounty Queen (IRE) **V. Thompson**
  3 **CHOSEN KEYS (IRE)**, 7, b m Well Chosen—Lost Keys (IRE) **V. Thompson**

MR VICTOR THOMPSON - Continued

4 GIN COBBLER, 7, b g Beneficial—Cassia **V. Thompson**
5 HAVE ONE FOR ME (IRE), 6, b g Sonus (IRE)—Dunmanogue (IRE) **V. Thompson**
6 HEATHER GLEN (IRE), 7, b m Luso—Kadara (IRE) **Mr Mark Thompson**
7 INDIAN PRINT (IRE), 9, ch g Blueprint (IRE)—Commanche Glen (IRE) **V. Thompson**
8 KILLEANEY PRINCESS (IRE), 10, b m Flemensfirth (USA)—Niamh's Song (IRE) **V. Thompson**
9 KNACKY LAD (IRE), 7, b g Bach (IRE)—Sin Ceist Eile (IRE) **V. Thompson**
10 LASTING MEMORYS (IRE), 8, b g Sonus (IRE)—Collinstown Queen (IRE) **V. Thompson**
11 MAFTEN (IRE), 10, b g City Honours (USA)—Mafiosa **V. Thompson**
12 MISSING YOU (IRE), 7, b g Witness Box (USA)—Mega Drama (IRE) **V. Thompson**
13 MONOGRAM, 9, ch g Karinga Bay—Dusky Dante (IRE) **V. Thompson**
14 MR SHAHADY (IRE), 8, b g Xaar—Shunaire (USA) **V. Thompson**
15 MR STINT (IRE), 6, b g Jammaal—Shamrock's Pet **V. Thompson**
16 PATS PREFERENCE (IRE), 7, b br g Tamayaz (CAN)—Kissangel (IRE) **V. Thompson**
17 RED MYST (IRE), 8, ch g Beneficial—That's Not Fair (IRE) **V. Thompson**
18 SENOR ALCO (FR), 7, gr g Dom Alco (FR)—Alconea (FR) **V. Thompson**
19 SIR TAMBURLANE (IRE), 8, b g Tamayaz (CAN)—Lady Lupin **Mr Mark Thompson**
20 TOM'S PRIDE (IRE), 10, br g Witness Box (USA)—Proverb's Way **V. Thompson**
21 TOMMYS LAD (IRE), 7, br g Luso—Monalee Dream (IRE) **V. Thompson**
22 TOMMYSTEEL (IRE), 8, br g Craigsteel—Sarahs Music (IRE) **V. Thompson**
23 TWO STROKE (IRE), 7, b br g Turtle Island (IRE)—Bannockburn (IRE) **V. Thompson**

Assistant Trainer: M Thompson

616
MR SANDY THOMSON, Greenlaw
Postal: **Lambden, Greenlaw, Duns, Berwickshire, TD10 6UN**
Contacts: PHONE **(01361) 810211** MOBILE **(07876) 142787**
E-MAIL **sandy@lambdenfarm.co.uk** WEBSITE **www.lambdenracing.co.uk**

1 5, B g Alflora (IRE)—An Bothar Dubh **Mr James R. Adam**
2 ANY GIVEN MOMENT (IRE), 7, b g Alhaarth (IRE)—Shastri (USA) **Mr & Mrs A. M. Thomson**
3 4, B g Oscar (IRE)—Biddy Earley (IRE) **Mr James R. Adam**
4 BLAZING DIVA (IRE), 10, gr m Blueprint (IRE)—Irene's Call (IRE) **Mr & Mrs A. M. Thomson**
5 BLUE KASCADE (IRE), 6, ch g Kaieteur (USA)—Lydia Blue (IRE) **Mrs Q. R. Thomson**
6 CHANDOS (IRE), 5, b g Heron Island (IRE)—Park Belle (IRE) **Mr James R. Adam**
7 JUST AWAKE, 6, b g Prince Daniel (USA)—Katinka **Mr & Mrs A. M. Thomson**
8 NETMINDER (IRE), 7, b g Insatiable (IRE)—
                                         Princess Douglas **Quona Thomson, David Spratt, Kevin McMunigal**
9 5, B g Oscar (IRE)—Storm Call **Mr James R. Adam**
10 THE SHRIMP (IRE), 6, gr g Indian Danehill (IRE)—Rheban Lass (IRE) **Mrs Q. R. Thomson**

Other Owners: Mr James R. Adam, Mr Kevin McMunigal, Mr D. Spratt, Mrs A. M. Thomson, Mr A. M. Thomson.

Assistant Trainer: Mrs A. M. Thomson

617
MR RUAIDHRI J. TIERNEY, Kinsale
Postal: **Ardkilly Stables, Sandycove, Kinsale, Co. Cork, Ireland**
Contacts: PHONE **(00353) 86 0424763**
E-MAIL **r.j.tierney@hotmail.com** WEBSITE **www.rjtierneyracing.com**

1 BOLAND'S CORNER (GER), 8, br g Fraam—Bravo Gorl (GER) **De Courcey Syndicate**

618
MR NIGEL TINKLER, Malton
Trainer did not wish details of his string to appear.

619 MR COLIN TIZZARD, Sherborne

Postal: **Venn Farm, Milborne Port, Sherborne, Dorset, DT9 5RA**
Contacts: **PHONE** (01963) 250598 **FAX** (01963) 250598 **MOBILE** (07976) 778656
E-MAIL info@colintizzard.co.uk **WEBSITE** www.colintizzard.co.uk

1 4, B g Kayf Tara—Ardent Bride **Mrs H. A. Snook**
2 **AVEC MOI CE SOIR (IRE)**, 10, b g Marignan (USA)—Claregary (IRE) **Blackmore Vale Syndicate**
3 **BE MARVELLOUS (IRE)**, 5, gr g Old Vic—Kalamix (IRE) **The Park Homes Syndicate**
4 **BESIDE THE FIRE**, 8, b g Cois Na Tine (IRE)—Champagne N Dreams **The Con Club**
5 **BILLY NO NAME (IRE)**, 5, b g Westerner—Just Little **Mrs J. R. Bishop**
6 **BOLD CUFFS**, 4, b g Dutch Art—Chambray (IRE) **Mr J. P. Romans**
7 **BUCKHORN TOM**, 5, b g Tamure (IRE)—Waimea Bay **The Buckhorn Racing Team**
8 **CANNINGTON BROOK (IRE)**, 9, b g Winged Love (IRE)—
                                        Rosie Brook (IRE) **Mrs Sara Biggins & Mrs Celia Djivanovic**
9 **CEEPEEGEE (IRE)**, 8, b g Karinga Bay—That's Holly **Mrs W. M. Hezel**
10 **CUE CARD**, 7, b g King's Theatre (IRE)—Wicked Crack (IRE) **Mrs J. R. Bishop**
11 **DARK DESIRE**, 4, b g Generous (IRE)—Diletia **Chasing Gold Limited**
12 **DIMPSY TIME**, 7, b m Kayf Tara—Cool Shuil (IRE) **Mrs J. E. Purdie**
13 **FALCON ISLAND**, 8, b g Turtle Island (IRE)—Dolly Sparks (IRE) **The Butterwick Syndicate**
14 **FLAMING CHARMER (IRE)**, 5, ch g Flemensfirth (USA)—Kates Charm (IRE) **T. H. Chadney**
15 **FOURTH ACT (IRE)**, 4, b g King's Theatre (IRE)—Erintante (IRE) **Mrs J. R. Bishop**
16 **GOLDEN CHIEFTAIN (IRE)**, 8, b g Tikkanen (USA)—Golden Flower (GER) **Brocade Racing**
17 **HANDY ANDY (IRE)**, 7, b g Beneficial—Maslam (IRE) **Brocade Racing**
18 **HEY BIG SPENDER (IRE)**, 10, b g Rudimentary (USA)—Jims Monkey **Brocade Racing**
19 **INSIDE DEALER (IRE)**, 9, b g Presenting—Sea Gale (IRE) **J. M. Dare, T. Hamlin, J. W. Snook**
20 **IVOR'S KING (IRE)**, 6, b g King's Theatre (IRE)—Christelle (IRE) **W. I. M. Perry**
21 **JUMPS ROAD**, 6, b g Clerkenwell (USA)—Diletia **Chasing Gold Limited**
22 5, Ch g Old Vic—Katty Barry (IRE)
23 **KINGS LAD (IRE)**, 6, b g King's Theatre (IRE)—Festival Leader (IRE) **G. F. Gingell**
24 **LORD OF THE DUNES**, 5, b g Desert King (IRE)—Dame Fonteyn **Barrow Hill**
25 **MASTERS HILL (IRE)**, 7, gr g Tikkanen (USA)—Leitrim Bridge (IRE) **K S B, Mr M Doughty & Mrs Sarah Tizzard**
26 **MIBLEU (FR)**, 13, b g Agent Bleu (FR)—Eauseille (FR) **Chasing Gold Limited**
27 **MILARROW (IRE)**, 6, b g Milan—Fleeting Arrow (IRE) **P. M. Warren**
28 **MR BINGLEY**, 5, b g Generous (IRE)—Fiancee (FR) **K S B Bloodstock**
29 **MULTITUDE OF SINS**, 6, b g Lucky Owners (NZ)—Lady Turk (FR) **Barrow Hill**
30 **NAMPOUR (FR)**, 8, gr g Daylami (IRE)—Nadira (FR) **J. T. Warner**
31 **NO WOMAN NO CRY**, 8, b g Kayf Tara—Motown Melody (IRE) **Mr & Mrs R. Tizzard**
32 **OHIO GOLD (IRE)**, 7, b g Flemensfirth (USA)—Kiniohio (FR) **P. M. Warren**
33 **OISEAU DE NUIT (FR)**, 11, b g Evening World (FR)—Idylle du Marais (FR) **J. T. Warner**
34 **OLD TRICKS (IRE)**, 6, b g Flemensfirth (USA)—Cabin Glory **Mrs K. Harvey**
35 4, B g Flemensfirth (USA)—Phardester (IRE)
36 **QUEENS BAY**, 7, b m Karinga Bay—Minibelle **Mrs L. Dickinson**
37 **QUITE BY CHANCE**, 4, b g Midnight Legend—Hop Fair **T Hamlin, J M Dare, J W Snook, J T Warner**
38 **RUSSIAN SONG (IRE)**, 9, b g Moscow Society (USA)—Sweet Charm (IRE) **John & Heather Snook**
39 **SEW ON TARGET (IRE)**, 8, b g Needle Gun (IRE)—Ballykea (IRE) **A. G. Selway**
40 **SONG SUNG BLUE (IRE)**, 10, b g Supreme Leader—Greenflag Princess (IRE) **Singing & Dancing Racing**
41 **SPENDING TIME**, 4, b g King's Theatre (IRE)—Karello Bay **Brocade Racing**
42 **THEATRE GUIDE (IRE)**, 6, b g King's Theatre (IRE)—Erintante (IRE) **Mrs J. R. Bishop**
43 **THEATRICAL STAR**, 7, b g King's Theatre (IRE)—Lucy Glitters **Brocade Racing**
44 **THIRD ACT (IRE)**, 4, b g King's Theatre (IRE)—Starry Lady (IRE) **Mrs J. R. Bishop**
45 **THIRD INTENTION (IRE)**, 6, b g Azamour (IRE)—Third Dimension (FR) **Mr & Mrs R. Tizzard**
46 **TIME BOOK (IRE)**, 7, b g Galileo (IRE)—Pocket Book (IRE) **D. V. Stevens**
47 **VIRGINIA ASH (IRE)**, 5, ch g Definite Article—Peace Time Girl (IRE) **Mr J. P. Romans**
48 **XAARCET (IRE)**, 6, b g Xaar—Anoukit **T. H. Chadney**

Other Owners: Mrs S. J. Biggins, Mr K. W. Biggins, Mr Garth Broom, Mrs Anne Broom, Mr J. M. Dare, Mrs L. Dickinson, Mrs Celia Djivanovic, Mr M. Doughty, Mr R. M. Fear, Mr R. Goodfellow, Mr T. Hamlin, Mr M. McD. Hooker, Mr Eric Jones, Mr Derrick Mayes, Mr J. P. Romans, Mr J. Snook, Mrs H. A. Snook, Mr R. G. Tizzard, Mrs Sarah Tizzard, Mr E. Vickery, Mr Terry Warner.

Assistant Trainer: Mrs K. Gingell

Jockey (NH): Joe Tizzard. **Conditional:** Brendan Powell. **Amateur:** Mr M. Legg.

620 MR MARTIN TODHUNTER, Penrith
Postal: **The Park, Orton, Penrith, Cumbria, CA10 3SD**
Contacts: PHONE **(01539) 624314** FAX **(01539) 624811** MOBILE **(07976) 440082**
WEBSITE www.martintodhunter.co.uk

1 ACORDINGTOSCRIPT (IRE), 7, ch g Accordion—Jane Jones (IRE) **The Surf & Turf Partnership**
2 ADIOS SAFFRON (IRE), 6, ch g Saffron Walden (FR)—Play A Tune (IRE) **P. G. Airey**
3 ALLANARD (IRE), 9, b g Oscar (IRE)—Allatrim (IRE) **Mr E. R. Madden**
4 ALMUTAHAM (USA), 6, b br g Dynaformer (USA)—Forest Lady (USA) **David & Nicky Robinson**
5 AUTHENTIC ACT (IRE), 9, ch g Pivotal—All In All **Mr & Mrs Ian Hall**
6 CAVITE ETA (IRE), 6, br g Spadoun (FR)—Samarinnda (IRE) **Don't Tell Henry**
7 COTTIERS DEN (IRE), 6, b g Snurge—Silvretta (IRE) **Leeds Plywood & Doors Ltd**
8 DEFINITE MAYBE (IRE), 5, b g Definite Article—Nahla **J. D. Gordon**
9 EL CABALLO, 4, b g Sir Harry Lewis (USA)—Woodwind Down **Park Farms Racing Syndicate II**
10 FORZY ORIGNY (FR), 11, gr g Sleeping Car (FR)—Forza Malta (FR) **Charles Broome & Partners**
11 FRANKY SPEC (IRE), 5, ch g Golan (IRE)—Sieglindes Threat (USA) **Park Farms Racing Syndicate I**
12 GRANNY BLACKWOOD, 5, b m Nayef (USA)—Aunt Rita (IRE) **Mrs S. J. Matthews**
13 JUST TYN (IRE), 6, b g Westerner—Christian Cullen (IRE) **Mr E. R. Madden**
14 OLD DEVEREUX (IRE), 5, b g Pierre—Wrong In Okanagan (IRE) **www.freebetting.co.uk**
15 PRESENTING JUNIOR (IRE), 6, b g Presenting—Dr Alice (IRE) **Mr W. & Mrs J. Garnett**
16 PRESENTING JUNO (IRE), 6, ch m Presenting—Elegant City **Murphy's Law Partnership**
17 QUETZAL (IRE), 8, b g Mr Combustible (IRE)—Auction Piece (IRE) **Gill & Bill Hazeldean**
18 SEE WHAT HAPPENS (IRE), 7, b g Tikkanen (USA)—Fontanalia (FR) **J. D. Gordon**
19 THE LODGE ROAD (IRE), 5, b g Holy Roman Emperor (IRE)—Golden Coral (USA) **Mr & Mrs Ian Hall**
20 THE MONGOLIAN (IRE), 5, b m Presenting—Elegant City **Murphy's Law Partnership**
21 TRANSACT (IRE), 8, ch g Trans Island—Khrisma **J D Racing**
22 WESTERN GALE (IRE), 10, br g Presenting—Kate Gale (IRE) **Mr & Mrs Ian Hall**
23 5, B g Sulamani (IRE)—Woodwind Down **Foremost Racing**
24 WORD OF WARNING, 9, gr g War Chant (USA)—Frosty Welcome (USA) **Twelve Go Racing**

Other Owners: Mr P. G. Airey, Mr Andrew G. Bell, Mr C. M. Broome, Mr James Callow, Mr P Clement, Mr I. Conroy, Mr Micheal Croan, Mr W. Downs, Mr W. Garnett, Mrs J. Garnett, Mr J. W. Hazeldean, Mrs Gill Hazeldean, Mr J. D. Hornsby, Mr J. McGahon, Mrs Anna Noble, Mr J. B. Pattinson, Mr David Robinson (Little Langdale), Mrs N. G. Robinson, Mr Colin G Snoddy, Mr M. Todhunter, Mr Thomas Uprichard.

Jockey (NH): Henry Brooke, Denis O'Regan, James Reveley. **Conditional:** Lucy Alexander.

621 MR JAMES TOLLER, Newmarket
Postal: **Eve Lodge Stables, Hamilton Road, Newmarket, Suffolk, CB8 0NY**
Contacts: PHONE **(01638) 668918** FAX **(01638) 669384** MOBILE **(07887) 942234**
E-MAIL james.toller@btconnect.com

1 ALEZANNA, 4, ch f Halling (USA)—Denica (IRE) **Skeltools Ltd**
2 LOVING SPIRIT, 5, b g Azamour (IRE)—Lolla's Spirit (IRE) **P. C. J. Dalby & R. D. Schuster**
3 REWARDED, 4, b g Motivator—Granted (FR) **P. C. J. Dalby & R. D. Schuster**
4 SOHAR, 5, b m Iceman—Desert Joy **G. B. Partnership**
5 SOHO SUSIE (IRE), 4, br f Montjeu—Lucina **G. B. Partnership**

THREE-YEAR-OLDS

6 CHANDELLE CELESTE, ch f Septieme Ciel (USA)—First Candlelight **Skeltools Ltd**
7 CHERRY TIGER, b c Tiger Hill (IRE)—Lolla's Spirit (IRE) **Buckingham Thoroughbreds I**
8 CHESTER ROW, ch c Compton Place—Sophie's Girl **P. C. J. Dalby & R. D. Schuster**
9 LIVING DESERT, gr g Oasis Dream—Sell Out **G. B. Partnership**
10 RED PILGRIM (IRE), b c Authorized (IRE)—Plenty of Action (USA) **Mr James C Cummings**
11 SHORT SHRIFT (IRE), ch f Nayef (USA)—Dusty Answer **J. A. R. Toller**
12 SMOKETHATTHUNDERS (IRE), gr g Elusive City (USA)—Zinstar (IRE) **M. E. Wates**
13 SOHO DANCER, b f Galileo (IRE)—River Belle **G. B. Partnership**
14 SUNNY HOLLOW, b f Beat Hollow—Corndavon (USA) **Mr S. A. Herbert**

TWO-YEAR-OLDS

15 MAJESTIC SONG, b f 4/3 Royal Applause—Sakhee's Song (IRE) (Sakhee (USA)) (50000)

Other Owners: P. C. J. Dalby, M. G. H. Heald, Mr A. M. H. Heald, Mrs J. E. Lee-Smith, R. D. Schuster, L. G. Straszewski.

Jockey (flat): Robert Havlin.

622 MR MARK TOMPKINS, Newmarket

Postal: **Flint Cottage Stables, Rayes Lane, Newmarket, Suffolk, CB8 7AB**
Contacts: **PHONE (01638) 661434 FAX (01638) 668107 MOBILE (07799) 663339**
E-MAIL mht@marktompkins.co.uk WEBSITE www.marktompkins.co.uk

1 **AKULA (IRE)**, 6, ch g Soviet Star (USA)—Danielli (IRE) **Jay Three Racing**
2 **ASTROGOLD**, 4, ch f Motivator—Mega (IRE) **Mystic Meg Limited**
3 **ASTROMAGICK**, 5, b m Rainbow Quest (USA)—Astrocharm (IRE) **Mystic Meg Limited**
4 **ASTROSCARLET**, 4, ch f Carnival Dancer—Astrolove (IRE) **Mystic Meg Limited**
5 **BARWICK**, 5, b g Beat Hollow—Tenpence **Mr S. A. Ashley**
6 **CHANKILLO**, 4, ch g Observatory (USA)—Seasonal Blossom (IRE) **H. Squared Electronics**
7 **COMRADE BOND**, 5, ch g Monsieur Bond (IRE)—Eurolink Cafe **Raceworld**
8 **DAZINSKI**, 7, ch g Sulamani (IRE)—Shuheb **Mrs B. M. Lockey**
9 **EANANS BAY (IRE)**, 4, b g Tiger Hill (IRE)—Gold Hush (USA) **Mr D. Sinclair**
10 **FIVE HEARTS**, 5, b m Bertolini (USA)—Light Hand **TCWS Ltd**
11 **JOE THE COAT**, 4, ch g Act One—Torcross **Roalco Ltd**
12 **LIKE CLOCKWORK**, 4, b g Rail Link—Tenpence **Mrs J. I. Simpson**
13 **LOCUM**, 8, ch g Dr Fong (USA)—Exhibitor (USA) **Ray Smith & Partners**
14 **MY GUARDIAN ANGEL**, 4, b g Araafa (IRE)—Angels Guard You **Sarabex**
15 **SMOKEY OAKEY (IRE)**, 9, b g Tendulkar (USA)—Veronica **Judi Dench & Bryan Agar**
16 **STAR COMMANDER**, 5, b g Desert Style (IRE)—Barakat **J. Brenchley**
17 **TOPTEMPO**, 4, ch f Halling (USA)—Topatoo **Roalco Ltd**
18 **ZENARINDA**, 6, b m Zamindar (USA)—Tenpence **Dullingham Park**

THREE-YEAR-OLDS

19 **ASTRODREAMS**, b f Rail Link—Nutmeg (IRE) **Mystic Meg Limited**
20 **ASTROSAPPHIRE**, b f Manduro (GER)—Astromancer (USA) **Mystic Meg Limited**
21 **BARBSIZ (IRE)**, ch f Elnadim (USA)—Bianca Cappello (IRE) **Mr G. J. Megson**
22 **FREDERICK ALFRED**, ch c Halling (USA)—Trew Class **Russell Trew Ltd**
23 **LIKELIKELIKELIKEIT**, b f Avonbridge—Rutland Water (IRE) **Michael Harvey & Partners**
24 **MARSH DRAGON**, b f Beat Hollow—Qilin (IRE) **Mr K. Lawrence**
25 **SILK SCARF (IRE)**, br f Windsor Knot (IRE)—Tarziyma (IRE) **TCWS Ltd**
26 **STAR OF MISSOURI**, ch g Namid—Missouri **J. Brenchley**
27 **TOPAMICHI**, b g Beat Hollow—Topatori (IRE) **Roalco Ltd**

TWO-YEAR-OLDS

28 **ASTROCAT**, b f 27/2 Zamindar (USA)—Mega (IRE) (Petardia) **Mystic Meg Limited**
29 **ASTRODIAMOND**, b f 14/2 Black Sam Bellamy (IRE)—
      Astromancer (USA) (Silver Hawk (USA)) **Mystic Meg Limited**
30 B c 20/4 Virtual—Astrolove (IRE) (Bigstone (IRE))
31 **ASTROWOLF**, b c 18/2 Halling (USA)—Optimistic (Reprimand) **Mystic Meg Limited**
32 **BLUE BOUNTY**, ch c 18/4 Bahamian Bounty—Laheen (IRE) (Bluebird (USA)) **Raceworld**
33 **LITTLE TINKA**, b f 5/3 Three Valleys (USA)—Tenpence (Bob Back (USA)) **Dullingham Park**
34 B f 19/4 Beat Hollow—Missouri (Charnwood Forest (IRE))
35 **NANCY**, b f 9/4 Rail Link—Feabhas (IRE) (Spectrum (IRE)) **J. Brenchley**
36 **SEE ME SOMETIME**, ch c 12/3 Observatory (USA)—
      Nice Time (IRE) (Tagula (IRE)) **H-Squared Electronics Limited**
37 Ch c 10/3 Pastoral Pursuits—Sosumi (Be My Chief (USA))
38 **SWILKEN**, ch c 2/3 Halling (USA)—Azure Mist (Bahamian Bounty) **Mr D. Noblett**
39 **TOPALING**, ch f 29/4 Halling (USA)—Topatori (IRE) (Topanoora) **M. P. Bowring**
40 Ch c 23/2 Sakhee (USA)—Topatoo (Bahamian Bounty) **Roalco Ltd**
41 **TRAIN SET**, b c 4/3 Sakhee (USA)—Dolls House (Dancing Spree (USA)) **Dullingham Park**

Other Owners: Mr N. M. Hanger, Mr Eric Jones, Mr Conrad Lockey, Mr R. D. E. Marriott, Mrs P. M. Rickett, Mr W. H. Simpson, Mr D. Tompkins.

Assistant Trainers: Steven Avery & Iain Williams

Jockey (NH): Colin Bolger. **Apprentice:** Jordon McMurray. **Amateur:** Miss Nikki McCaffrey.

623 MR KEVIN TORK, Leigh

Postal: **Westcoats Farm, Clayhill Road, Leigh, Reigate, Surrey, RH2 8PB**
Contacts: **PHONE (01306) 611616 MOBILE (07988) 206544**

1 6, B g Dushyantor (USA)—Minstrel Hall **K. Tork**

MR KEVIN TORK - Continued

2 4, Ch g Alflora (IRE)—Miss O'grady (IRE) **K. Tork**
3 UPTON MEAD (IRE), 6, b g Jimble (FR)—Inchinnan **K. Tork**
4 ZHUKOV (IRE), 11, b g Saddlers' Hall (IRE)—Tamasriya (IRE) **K. Tork**

THREE-YEAR-OLDS

5 Ch g Mount Nelson—Franglais (GER) **K. Tork**

Assistant Trainer: Ms Daisy Tork (07977) 769316

---

624 **MR EDWIN TUER, Northallerton**
Postal: **Granary Barn, Birkby, Northallerton, North Yorkshire, DL7 0EF**
Contacts: **PHONE (01609) 881798 FAX (01609) 881798 MOBILE (07808) 330306**

1 AILSA CRAIG (IRE), 7, b m Chevalier (IRE)—Sharplaw Destiny (IRE) **E. Tuer**
2 BIG BENJIE, 5, ch g Lahib (USA)—Bula Rose (IRE) **E. Tuer**
3 BLUE MAISEY, 5, b m Monsieur Bond (IRE)—Blue Nile (IRE) **E. Tuer**
4 DORA'S GIFT, 4, b f Cadeaux Genereux—Conquestadora **E. Tuer**
5 EASY TERMS, 6, b m Trade Fair—Effie **E. Tuer**
6 FAZZA, 6, ch g Sulamani (IRE)—Markievicz (IRE) **E. Tuer**
7 GOLD SHOW, 4, gr f Sir Percy—Pearl Bright (FR) **E. Tuer**
8 PATAVIUM (IRE), 10, b g Titus Livius (FR)—Arcevia (IRE) **Mr J. A. Nixon**
9 SALLY FRIDAY (IRE), 5, b m Footstepsinthesand—Salee (IRE) **E. Tuer**
10 SPHINX (FR), 15, b g Snurge—Egyptale **E. Tuer**
11 SUPER TRUPER, 4, b g Winged Love (IRE)—Bula Rose (IRE) **E. Tuer**
12 THE BLUE BANANA (IRE), 4, b g Red Clubs (IRE)—Rinneen (IRE) **Mr E Tuer & Mr & Mrs C Tompkins**

Other Owners: A. C. Tompkins, Mrs A. R. Tompkins.

---

625 **MR JOSEPH TUITE, Hungerford**
Postal: **Tailswins, Abingdon Road, East Ilsley, Newbury, Berkshire, RG20 7LZ**
Contacts: **MOBILE (07769) 977351**
E-MAIL joe.tuite@tuiteracing.com WEBSITE www.tuiteracing.com

1 CAMACHE QUEEN (IRE), 5, b m Camacho—Alinda (IRE) **Mr A. Liddiard**
2 COME ON SAFARI (IRE), 6, b g Antonius Pius (USA)—Calypso Dancer (FR) **Montagu Racing**
3 INTERAKT, 6, b m Rakti—Amelie Pouliche (FR) **Heart Of The South Racing**
4 LADY SYLVIA, 4, ch f Haafhd—Abide (FR) **Mr D. J. Keast**
5 MR SPIGGOTT (IRE), 4, b g Intikhab (USA)—Green Green Grass **Heart Of The South Racing**
6 ONERTOTHER, 4, b g Nomadic Way (USA)—Ceilidh Band **Penny/Adrian Burton, Bob/Angela Lampard**
7 PRESBURG (IRE), 4, b g Balmont (USA)—Eschasse (USA) **Ise Language**
8 THANE OF CAWDOR (IRE), 4, b g Danehill Dancer (IRE)—Holy Nola (USA) **Alan & Christine Bright**
9 TIME TO DANCE, 4, b g Silent Times (IRE)—Bravo Dancer **Miss S. Watkins**
10 WHITSTABLE NATIVE, 5, b g Bertolini (USA)—Break of Dawn (USA) **Mr B. Woodward**

THREE-YEAR-OLDS

11 BE EXCELLENT, b f Oratorio (IRE)—Saphila (IRE) **Mr D. J. Keast**
12 BHELEYF (IRE), b f Kheleyf (USA)—Carraigoona (IRE) **Heart Of The South Racing**
13 IWILSAYZISONLYONCE, ch g Kyllachy—Resistance Heroine **Mr J. M. Tuite**
14 PICC OF BURGAU, b f Piccolo—Rosein **The Outta Lunch Partnership**

TWO-YEAR-OLDS

15 FLASHY QUEEN (IRE), ch f 6/2 Bahamian Bounty—Somersault (Pivotal) (15000) **J. Abdullah**
16 LADY KATHIAN (IRE), gr f 17/3 Verglas (IRE)—Nurama (Daylami (IRE)) (14285) **I & K Prince**
17 B c 17/4 Camacho—Nortolixa (FR) (Linamix (FR)) (6666)
18 Ch c 25/1 Footstepsinthesand—Sweet Nicole (Okawango (USA)) (18000)

Other Owners: Mr R. Grogan, Mrs L. Grogan.

Apprentice: Nora Looby.

626 MR ANDREW TURNELL, Swindon

Postal: **Elmcross House, Broad Hinton, Swindon, Wiltshire, SN4 9PF**
Contacts: **PHONE** (01793) 731481 **FAX** (01793) 739001 **MOBILE** (07973) 933450
E-MAIL info@andyturnellracing.com **WEBSITE** andyturnellracing.com

1 CAULFIELDS VENTURE (IRE), 7, b g Catcher In The Rye (IRE)—Saddlers' Venture (IRE) **C. F. Colquhoun**
2 DAN'S WEE MAN, 4, b g Kayf Tara—Hazel Bank Lass (IRE) **Mr M. J. Tedham**
3 FAHA (IRE), 7, b m Catcher In The Rye (IRE)—Tarayib **Mr V Askew & CCC Partnership**
4 HAAR, 9, ch g Selkirk (USA)—Chilly Start (IRE) **Mrs R. M. Hill**
5 MICHEAL FLIPS (IRE), 9, b g Kayf Tara—Pianissimo (IRE) **Mr M. J. Tedham**
6 PIANO CONCERTO (IRE), 6, b g Red Ransom (USA)—
                                Storm Song (USA) **Buckle, Deal, Garner, Inverdale, Thorner**
7 RIVER DANCING (IRE), 6, b g Muhtarram (USA)—Peacefull River (IRE) **John & Heather Snook**
8 ROUGH FIGHTER (USA), 4, b g Mizzen Mast (USA)—Louis d'or (USA) **Maori Partnership**
9 SABLAZO (FR), 7, b g Ragmar (FR)—Daytona II (FR) **Miss S. Douglas-Pennant**
10 SPANISH TREASURE (GER), 7, b g Black Sam Bellamy (IRE)—Santa Zinaada (GER) **Mr M. J. Tedham**
11 SUBORDINATE (GER), 4, b g Echo of Light—Suborneuse (USA) **The Jumping Stars**
12 THE DRUIDS NEPHEW (IRE), 6, b g King's Theatre (IRE)—Gifted **The Stonehenge Druids**
13 TOUJOURS L'ATTAQUE (IRE), 6, b g Craigsteel—Dempseys Luck (IRE) **Andrew Turnell**
14 ULLSWATER (IRE), 5, b g Singspiel (IRE)—Uluwatu (IRE) **The Jumping Stars**
15 WHILEAWAY (USA), 4, b g Mizzen Mast (USA)—Routine (USA) **Maori Partnership**

Other Owners: V. Askew, Mrs L. S. Atwell, Mr S. M. Brown, C. R. Buckle, Mr D. C. Codling, Mrs A. C. Crofts, P. A. Deal, Mr L. P. Dunne, Mrs A. M. Dunne, Mr R. F. Garner, M. P. Hill, J. B. Inverdale, Mr L. G. Kimber, Mr S. T. Merry, Mrs D. J. Merry, Mrs C. A. Moysey, J. W. Snook, Mrs H. A. Snook, Mrs M. R. Taylor, Mr G. E. Thorner, Mr G. J. Villis.

Jockey (NH): James Banks, Nick Scholfield, Gerard Tumelty.

627 MR BILL TURNER, Sherborne

Postal: **Sigwells Farm, Sigwells, Corton Denham, Sherborne, Dorset, DT9 4LN**
Contacts: **PHONE** (01963) 220523 **FAX** (01963) 220046 **MOBILE** (07932) 100173
E-MAIL billturnerracing@gmail.com

1 CONCRETE JUNGLE (IRE), 5, b g Chineur (FR)—Finty (IRE) **Miss C. J. Overton**
2 EDEIFF'S LAD, 6, ch g Loup Sauvage (USA)—Ede'iff **Hawks & Doves Racing Syndicate**
3 EDLOMOND (IRE), 7, gr g Great Palm (USA)—Samardana (IRE) **Mrs Tracy Turner**
4 FLORAL SPINNER, 6, b m Alflora (IRE)—Dawn Spinner **The Floral Farmers**
5 FRECKLE FACE, 6, br g Septieme Ciel (USA)—Wavet **Mrs C. M. Goldsmith**
6 HARD TO TELL (IRE), 7, b g Presenting—Superior Dawn (IRE) **P. P. Thorman**
7 LADY PRODEE, 5, b m Proclamation (IRE)—Dee-Lady **Mrs M. S. Teversham**
8 LORD DEEVERT, 8, br g Averti (IRE)—Dee-Lady **Mrs M. S. Teversham**
9 LUCKY DIVA, 6, ch m Lucky Story (USA)—Cosmic Countess (IRE) **D. Coombes**
10 SING ALANA SING, 5, b m Singspiel (IRE)—Choralist **Mrs I. T. Horsington**
11 SIX OF CLUBS, 7, ch g Bertolini (USA)—Windmill Princess **Gongolfin**
12 THE DANCING LORD, 4, br g Imperial Dancer—Miss Brookie **Mrs M. S. Teversham**

THREE-YEAR-OLDS

13 BLUE GEM, b f Diamond Green (FR)—Oh So Rosie (IRE) **Miss Karen Theobald**
14 BLUE MISSILE, b g Majestic Missile (IRE)—Secret Combe (IRE) **Miss Karen Theobald**
15 CAPTAIN BLUE, b g Captain Marvelous (IRE)—Amoras (IRE) **Miss Karen Theobald**
16 CARBAS (ITY), b c Acclamation—Carya (IRE) **Mr Patrick Moyles**
17 COCONUT KISSES, ch f Bahamian Bounty—Royal Mistress **Mr P. Venner**
18 FARAWAY STAR (IRE), gr f Slickly (IRE)—Princess Bankes **Mrs P. A. Turner**
19 HILLBILLY BOY (IRE), b g Haafhd—Erreur (IRE) **E. A. Brook**
20 IT'S ONLY BUSINESS, ch c Haafhd—Noble Plum (IRE) **Ansells Of Watford**
21 JUST PAST ANDOVER (IRE), b g Amadeus Wolf—Fancy Feathers (IRE) **Wackey Racers Harefield**
22 MISTERAY, ch c Singspiel (IRE)—Hannda (IRE) **Ansells Of Watford**
23 Ch gr g Zafeen (FR)—Molly Malone **G. S. Tuck**
24 MOSSBOW (IRE), b f Moss Vale (IRE)—Delicia (IRE) **Mr R. Jeffries**
25 SQUAWK, ch f Sleeping Indian—Easy Mover (IRE) **P. P. Thorman**

TWO-YEAR-OLDS

26 B c 28/4 Captain Marvelous (IRE)—Amoras (IRE) (Hamas (IRE)) **Miss Karen Theobald**
27 B f 6/3 Bertolini (USA)—Bahawir Pour (USA) (Green Dancer (USA)) **Mrs D. du Feu**

MR BILL TURNER - Continued

28 B c 15/2 Moss Vale (IRE)—Clodova (IRE) (Clodovil (IRE)) **E. A. Brook**
29 B f 5/4 Champs Elysees—Drastic Measure (Pivotal) (2857) **Mrs Tracy Turner**
30 Ch f 17/4 Proclamation (IRE)—Dusty Bankes (Greensmith) **Mrs Tracy Turner**
31 EL DUQUE, b c 27/2 Byron—Royal Tavira Girl (IRE) (Orpen (USA)) (3500) **Mrs B. Ansell**
32 Ch f 14/4 Proclamation (IRE)—Grace Bankes (Elisio) **Mr T. Lightbowne**
33 Ch f 25/5 Distant Peak (IRE)—Hispaniola (IRE) (Barathea (IRE)) **Miss Tracey Turner**
34 LADY TEE, b f 5/4 Proclamation (IRE)—Wavet (Pursuit of Love) **Mr B. J. Goldsmith**
35 B c 15/4 Art Connoisseur (IRE)—Loch Fyne (Ardkinglass) **Mr. Nicholson**
36 Ch c 1/4 Captain Gerrard (IRE)—Miss Dunwoody (Classic Cliche (IRE)) (1047) **Mrs Tracy Turner**
37 B c 30/3 Captain Marvelous (IRE)—Oh So Rosie (IRE) (Danehill Dancer (IRE)) **Miss Karen Theobald**
38 B c 6/4 Oratorio (IRE)—Poilane (Kris) (2857) **E. A. Brook**
39 Ch f 22/2 Compton Place—Repetischa (IRE) (Peintre Celebre (USA)) **Mr D. Bell**
40 B f 7/5 Pastoral Pursuits—Rouge Dancer (Elusive City (USA)) (2857)
41 B c 30/4 Arakan (USA)—Secret Combe (IRE) (Mujadil (USA)) **Miss Karen Theobald**
42 B c 12/3 Bahamian Bounty—Sheer Indulgence (FR) (Pivotal) (20000) **Mrs Tracy Turner**
43 B f 15/4 Acclamation—Sheik'n Swing (Celtic Swing) **P. P. Thorman**
44 B f 28/3 Byron—Slightly Foxed (Royal Applause) **Mrs Tracy Turner**
45 B f 12/3 Firebreak—Upton Seas (Josr Algarhoud (IRE)) **Mrs Tracy Turner**
46 B c 16/5 Dubawi (IRE)—With Fascination (USA) (Dayjur (USA)) (16000) **E. A. Brook**

Other Owners: Mr B. C. Ansell, Mrs B. C. Ansell, Mr R. L. Ansell, Mrs Natasha Ansell, Mr R. A. Bracken, Mr Nick Conduit, Mr A. Morrish, Mr J. P. Rawlins, Mr John Sunnucks, Mr E. Vickery.

Jockey (NH): Tom O'Connor. **Apprentice:** Jake Payne, Ryan While.

---

628 | **MR JAMES TURNER, Helperby**
Postal: **Mayfield Farm, Norton-le-Clay, Helperby, York, North Yorkshire, YO61 2RS**
Contacts: **PHONE (01423) 322239 FAX (01423) 322239**

1 LUKEY LUKE, 10, b g Kayf Tara—Skiddaw Samba **Mr D. M. Wordsworth**
2 SQUEALY KEELY, 5, b m Kahyasi—Granny Shona (IRE) **J. R. Turner**

Assistant Trainer: Oliver J. Turner

Jockey (flat): Paddy Aspell, Paul Hanagan.

---

629 | **MRS KAREN TUTTY, Northallerton**
Postal: **Trenholme House Farm, Osmotherley, Northallerton, North Yorkshire, DL6 3QA**
Contacts: **PHONE (01609) 883624 FAX 01609 883624 MOBILE (07967) 837406**
E-MAIL **karentutty@btinternet.com** WEBSITE **www.karentuttyracing.co.uk**

1 BALLYAGRAN (IRE), 13, b g Pierre—Promalady (IRE) **Ivor Fox**
2 GRACEFUL DESCENT (FR), 8, b m Hawk Wing (USA)—Itab (USA) **Thoroughbred Homes Ltd**
3 HARARE, 12, b g Bahhare (USA)—Springs Eternal **Grange Park Racing**
4 HOAR FROST, 8, b m Fraam—Natalie Jay **Thoroughbred Homes Ltd**
5 JUPITER FIDIUS, 6, b g Haafhd—Kyda (USA) **Grange Park Racing**
6 KILCASKIN STAR (IRE), 7, b g Zagreb (USA)—Kentucky Key (IRE)
7 LADY NICKANDY (IRE), 4, b f Kheleyf (USA)—Tanzie (IRE) **Thoroughbred Homes Ltd**
8 MERCERS ROW, 6, b g Bahamian Bounty—Invincible **K. Fitzsimons**
9 5, B g Pierre—Promalady (IRE) **Ivor Fox**
10 SADDLERS MOT, 9, b m Saddlers' Hall (IRE)—Be My Mot (IRE) **Grange Park Racing**
11 5, Ch g Generous (IRE)—Seems So Easy (USA)
12 TALENT SCOUT (IRE), 7, b g Exceed And Excel (AUS)—Taalluf (USA) **Thoroughbred Homes Ltd**
13 TONY HOLLIS, 5, b g Antonius Pius (USA)—Seasons Parks **Thoroughbred Homes Ltd**

THREE-YEAR-OLDS

14 WHINCHAT, b g Shirocco (GER)—Cushat Law (IRE) **Ivor Fox**

TWO-YEAR-OLDS

15 Ch f 4/2 Proclamation (IRE)—Anapola (GER) (Polish Precedent (USA)) (1904)
16 Ch f 31/3 Sir Percy—Galette (Caerleon (USA)) (5000) **Arrand & Tutty**
17 JACBEQUICK, b c 7/6 Calcutta—Toking N' Joken (IRE) (Mukaddamah (USA)) (761) **Cherry Garth Racing**

MRS KAREN TUTTY - Continued

Other Owners: Mr C. G. Arrand, Cherry Garth Racing, Mr Alan D. Crombie, Ivor Fox, Grange Park Racing, Mr E. Surr, Thoroughbred Homes Ltd, N. D. Tutty.

Conditional: Brian Toomey. **Apprentice:** Gemma Tutty. **Amateur:** Miss Phillipa Tutty.

630

MR NIGEL TWISTON-DAVIES, Cheltenham
Postal: T/a Grange Hill Farm Limited, Grange Hill Farm, Naunton, Cheltenham, Gloucestershire, GL54 3AY
Contacts: **PHONE** (01451) 850278 **FAX** (01451) 850101 **MOBILE** (07836) 664440
E-MAIL nigel@nigeltwistondavies.co.uk **WEBSITE** www.nigeltwistondavies.co.uk

1 **ACCORDING TO TREV (IRE)**, 7, ch g Accordion—Autumn Sky (IRE) **Mr F. J. Mills & Mr W. Mills**
2 **ACKERTAC (IRE)**, 8, ch g Anshan—Clonsingle Native (IRE) **Mark Aspey & Steve Catton**
3 **AFRICAN GOLD (IRE)**, 5, b g King's Theatre (IRE)—Mrs Dempsey (IRE) **Mr R. Bauer**
4 **AMMUNITION (IRE)**, 13, b g Needle Gun (IRE)—Flapping Freda (IRE) **Miss K. J. Holland**
5 **ASTRACAD (FR)**, 7, br g Cadoudal (FR)—Astre Eria (FR) **H. R. Mould**
6 **BALLYCASSEL (IRE)**, 8, ch g Presenting—Sara's Gold (IRE) **Celia & Michael Baker**
7 **BALLYFITZ**, 13, b g Overbury (IRE)—Running For Gold **Mr F. J. Mills & Mr W. Mills**
8 **BATTLECRY**, 12, b br g Accordion—Miss Orchestra (IRE) **N. A. Twiston-Davies**
9 **BENBENS (IRE)**, 8, ch g Beneficial—Millicent Bridge (IRE) **Mrs S. E. Such**
10 **BILLIE MAGERN**, 9, b g Alderbrook—Outfield Exors of the Late **Mr R. Nicholls**
11 **BROUSSE EN FEUX (FR)**, 10, ch m April Night (FR)—Antoniola (FR) **N. A. Twiston-Davies**
12 **CAUSING CHAOS (IRE)**, 7, b g Alderbrook—Sue's Song **Mr R. J. Rexton**
13 **CHANGING TIMES (IRE)**, 7, b g Dr Massini (IRE)—Pharenna (IRE) **Mr C. J. Haughey**
14 **COOL TOUCH (IRE)**, 10, b g Marju (IRE)—Feather Star **N. A. Twiston-Davies**
15 **COOTEHILL (IRE)**, 9, b g Alflora (IRE)—Dancing Dove (IRE) **Mrs F. E. Griffin**
16 **DEFINITELY LOVELY**, 8, b m Definite Article—Fair Maid Marion (IRE) **C. B. Brookes**
17 **DIAMOND CRESCENT (IRE)**, 6, b g Marignan (USA)—Shaunies Nora (IRE) **The Crescent Partnership**
18 **DOLLY PENROSE**, 8, b m Hernando (FR)—Mistinguett (IRE) **G. M. Rowe**
19 **DOUBLE ROSS (IRE)**, 7, ch g Double Eclipse (IRE)—Kinross **Options O Syndicate**
20 **ELLNANDO QUEEN**, 5, b m Hernando (FR)—Queen of Spades (IRE) **Rita Vaughan**
21 **ELYSIAN HEIGHTS (IRE)**, 5, b g Galileo (IRE)—Ziffany **I. Robinson**
22 **EURO TRASH (IRE)**, 7, b g Anshan—Euroblend (IRE) **Mr D. T. Gardiner**
23 **FLEMISH INVADER (IRE)**, 10, b g Flemensfirth (USA)—Lite 'n Easy (IRE) **A. M. Armitage**
24 **FRONTIER SPIRIT (IRE)**, 9, b g New Frontier (IRE)—Psalmist **Jump For Fun Racing**
25 **GO ON ARCH (IRE)**, 7, b g Oscar (IRE)—Good Aim (IRE) **Walters Plant Hire P T Civil Engineering**
26 **GOAT CASTLE (IRE)**, 9, b g Goldmark (USA)—Rolands Girl **N. A. Twiston-Davies**
27 **GOLDEN JUBILEE (USA)**, 4, b br g Zavata (USA)—Love Play (USA) **Mrs J. K. Powell**
28 **HAVE YOU SEEN ME (IRE)**, 10, b g Beneficial—Silent Supreme (IRE) **The Maple Hurst Partnership**
29 **HE'S THE DADDY**, 6, b g Generous (IRE)—Brambly Hedge **Mr A. Gillman**
30 **HUNTERS LODGE (IRE)**, 7, ch g Subtle Power (IRE)—Native Orchid (IRE) **Exors of the Late Mr R. Nicholls**
31 **IMPERIAL COMMANDER (IRE)**, 12, b g Flemensfirth (USA)—Ballinlovane **Our Friends in the North**
32 **IMPERIAL LEADER (IRE)**, 5, b g Flemensfirth (USA)—
   Glamorous Leader (IRE) **Imperial Racing Partnership No.2**
33 **JASPERITO**, 7, b g Bollin Eric—Tamergale (IRE) **Mrs R. I. Vaughan**
34 **JAUNTY JOURNEY**, 10, ch g Karinga Bay—Jaunty June **Mr C. Roberts**
35 **JEAN DE FLORETTE (IRE)**, 6, b g Helissio (FR)—Ismene (FR) **Alan Parker**
36 **JIMMY THE HAT (IRE)**, 7, b g Accordion—Pride 'n' Joy (IRE) **T. J. Atkin**
37 **KAYBEEW, 8**, b g Alflora (IRE)—Lunareva (USA) **Roberts Green Whittall-Williams Savidge**
38 **KAYF ARAMIS**, 11, b g Kayf Tara—Ara **Kayf Aramis Racing**
39 **KAYLIF ARAMIS**, 6, b g Kayf Tara—Ara **N. A. Twiston-Davies**
40 **KILVERGAN BOY (IRE)**, 9, br g Zagreb (USA)—Brigante (IRE) **The Yes No Wait Sorries**
41 **LILLYBROOK (IRE)**, 7, br m Alderbrook—Lilly Bolero **N. A. Twiston-Davies**
42 **LISTEN BOY (IRE)**, 7, ch g Presenting—Buckalong (IRE) **Bryan & Philippa Burrough**
43 **LITTLE POP**, 5, b g Pasternak—Flagship Daisy May (IRE) **Mrs S. E. Such**
44 **LODGICIAN (IRE)**, 11, b g Grand Lodge (USA)—Dundel (IRE) **The Yes No Wait Sorries**
45 **LOVELY MUCK**, 8, b m Alflora (IRE)—Madam Muck **N. A. Twiston-Davies**
46 **MAD MOOSE (IRE)**, 9, ch g Presenting—Sheshollystar (IRE) **Middleham Park Racing XXXV & Partner**
47 **MAHOGANY BLAZE (FR)**, 11, b g Kahyasi—Mahogany River **Mrs L. M. Berryman**
48 **MAJOR MALARKEY (IRE)**, 10, b g Supreme Leader—Valley (IRE) **Mr J. Baker, Mr J. Dodd & Mr D. Cooke**
49 **MASTER OF THE SEA (IRE)**, 6, b g Misternando—Sea Gale (IRE) **N. A. Twiston-Davies**
50 **MAVALENTA (IRE)**, 6, b m Montjeu (IRE)—Velouette **The Yes No Wait Sorries**
51 **MISS TILLY OSCAR (IRE)**, 7, b m Oscar (IRE)—Whisky Chaser **Mr B. J. Mould**
52 **MY BOY PADDY (IRE)**, 9, ch g Accordion—Securon Rose (IRE) **Miss K. J. Holland**

MR NIGEL TWISTON-DAVIES - Continued

53 **NEZ ROUGE (FR)**, 12, gr g April Night (FR)—Gracieuse des Bois (FR) **N. A. Twiston-Davies**
54 **NIGHT SAFE (IRE)**, 12, b g Safety Catch (USA)—Rock All Night (IRE) **Ian & Ann Dimmer**
55 **NUDGE AND NURDLE (IRE)**, 12, b g Shernazar—Firey Comet (IRE) **The Yes No Wait Sorries**
56 **OSCAR MAGIC (IRE)**, 6, b br g Oscar (IRE)—Just An Illusion (IRE) **Mrs L. M. Berryman**
57 **PAPRADON**, 9, b g Tobougg (IRE)—Salvezza (IRE) **A. J. Cresser**
58 **PETTIFOUR (IRE)**, 11, b g Supreme Leader—Queen of Natives (IRE) **Mr J. B. Pettifer**
59 **PIGEON ISLAND (IRE)**, 10, gr g Daylami (IRE)—Morina (USA) **H. R. Mould**
60 **POWER PACK JACK (IRE)**, 10, b g Rudimentary (USA)—Monas Jem (IRE) **N. A. Twiston-Davies**
61 **POWERMAKER (IRE)**, 5, b g Oscar (IRE)—Torduff Storm (IRE) **Walters Plant Hire & N A Twiston-Davies**
62 **PURE SCIENCE (IRE)**, 5, ch g Galileo (IRE)—Rebelline (IRE) **H. R. Mould**
63 **QUAPRILAND (FR)**, 9, br m Dark Moondancer—Falkland III (FR) **Mrs A. Barclay**
64 **RANSOM NOTE**, 6, b g Red Ransom (USA)—Zacheta **H. R. Mould**
65 **RED HOT POKER**, 11, b g Emarati (USA)—Red Hot Hebe **Mr J. Goodman**
66 **RED RIVERMAN**, 5, b g Haahd—Mocca (IRE) **N. A. Twiston-Davies**
67 **RED ROUBLE (IRE)**, 8, ch g Moscow Society (USA)—Chirouble (IRE) **The Double Octagon Partnership**
68 **RHUM (IRE)**, 8, ch g Dark Moondancer—Ireland (IRE) **N. A. Twiston-Davies**
69 **RIVER EXIT (IRE)**, 6, b g Exit To Nowhere (USA)—Kilbricken Sunset (IRE) **Mrs A. Barclay**
70 **SAME DIFFERENCE (IRE)**, 7, b g Mr Combustible (IRE)—Sarahs Reprive (IRE) **Mrs R. I. Vaughan**
71 **SAMENERVE (FR)**, 6, br g Protektor (GER)—Sweetberry (FR) **Million in Mind Partnership**
72 **SPECIAL MATE**, 7, br g Generous (IRE)—Flying Iris (IRE) **Walters Plant Hire & James & Jean Potter**
73 **SPLASH OF GINGE**, 5, b g Oscar (IRE)—Land of Honour **Mr J. Neild**
74 **STARLET MANDY (IRE)**, 10, br m Presenting—Actress Mandy (IRE) **N. A. Twiston-Davies**
75 **SUSQUEHANNA RIVER (IRE)**, 6, b g Indian River (FR)—Calistoga (IRE) **Martin Maxted**
76 **TARA ROSE**, 8, br m Kayf Tara—True Rose (IRE) **Mr B. J. Mould**
77 **THE COCKNEY MACKEM (IRE)**, 7, b g Milan—Divine Prospect (IRE) **Mills & Mason Partnership**
78 **THE MUSICAL GUY (IRE)**, 7, b g Lahib (USA)—Orchestral Sport (IRE) **The Musical Guy's Girls**
79 **THE NEW ONE (IRE)**, 5, b g King's Theatre (IRE)—Thuringe (FR) **Mrs S. E. Such**
80 **TOUR DES CHAMPS (FR)**, 6, b br g Robin des Champs (FR)—Massada (FR) **H. R. Mould**
81 **TULLYRAINE (IRE)**, 9, b g Winged Love (IRE)—Struell Princess **Geoffrey & Donna Keeys**
82 **VIKING BLOND (FR)**, 8, ch g Varese (FR)—Sweet Jaune (FR) **Mrs C. M. Mould**
83 **WHAT A GOOD NIGHT (IRE)**, 5, br g Westerner—Southern Skies (IRE) **Mr & Mrs Gordon Pink**
84 **WHAT A WARRIOR (IRE)**, 6, b g Westerner—Be Right (IRE) **Mr & Mrs Gordon Pink**
85 **WHAT AN OSCAR (IRE)**, 8, b g Oscar (IRE)—Katie Buckers (IRE) **Mr & Mrs Gordon Pink**
86 **WINGED CRUSADER (IRE)**, 5, b g Winged Love (IRE)—Reine Berengere (FR) **Imperial Racing**
87 **WOOD YER (IRE)**, 7, ch g Anshan—Glenasheen (IRE) **Miss K. J. Holland**
88 **ZAYFIRE ARAMIS**, 4, ch g Zafeen (FR)—Kaylia Aramis **Isobel Phipps-Coltman**

Other Owners: M. R. Aspey, Mrs C. A. M. Baker, Mr M. J. Baker, Mrs E. M. Bathurst, Mr B. R. H. Burrough, Mrs Philippa Burrough, Mr S. P Catton, C. S. J. Coley, Mrs Judy England, F. M. Green, Mrs F. V. C. Gregory, Mr Graham Jelley, Mrs Alison Jelley, G. F. Keeys, Mrs D. Keeys, Mr H. J. Kelly, Mrs S. A. MacEchern, F. J. Mills, W. R. Mills, W. D. C. Minton, P T Civil Engineering Ltd, Mrs Scilla Phillips, Mrs I. Phipps Coltman, Mr G. K. G. Pink, Mrs K. M. Pink, J. E. Potter, Mrs J. E. Potter, G. M. Powell, M. Prince, G. A. Roberts, Mrs G. C. Robinson, Mr Ian A. Robinson, G. W. Sanders, Mr M. G. Savidge, Mrs C. M. Scott, R. I. Sims, N. A. Twiston-Davies, Walters Plant Hire Ltd, Mr E. B. Whittal-Williams, Mr S. G. Wignall.

Assistant Trainer: Carl Llewellyn

Jockey (NH): Sam Twiston-Davies, David England. **Conditional:** William Twiston-Davies. **Amateur:** Mr Ryan Hatch.

---

631 **MR JAMES UNETT, Oswestry**
Postal: **Garden Cottage, Tedsmore, West Felton, Oswestry, Shropshire, SY11 4HD**
Contacts: PHONE **(01691) 610001** FAX **(01691) 610001** MOBILE **(07887) 534753**
E-MAIL **jamesunett1327@yahoo.co.uk** WEBSITE **www.jamesunettracing.com**

1 **BIG SYLV (IRE)**, 4, gr f Clodovil (IRE)—Casual Remark (IRE) **Miss C. Doyle**
2 **CAPE KIMBERLEY**, 6, b g Arakan (USA)—Etoile Volant (USA) **J. R. Salter**
3 **CHES JICARO (IRE)**, 5, ch g Majestic Missile (IRE)—Kelso Magic (USA) **G. D. Kendrick**
4 **DUTCH MISTRESS**, 4, b f Dutch Art—Royal Mistress **G. D. Kendrick**
5 **KNOWE HEAD (NZ)**, 6, b g High Chaparral (IRE)—Royal Errant (NZ) **Lord S. J. Stone**
6 **MCCOOL BANNANAS**, 5, b g Firebreak—Dances With Angels (IRE) **Mark Sheehy & Malcolm Hall**
7 **MONUMENTAL MAN**, 4, b g Vital Equine (IRE)—Spark Up **P. Fetherston-Godley**

THREE-YEAR-OLDS

8 **DALHOUSIE LASSIE**, b f Indesatchel (IRE)—Miss Mirasol **Guyzance Hall Ltd**
9 **HER ROYAL EMPRESS**, b f Holy Roman Emperor (IRE)—Aurelia **Lord S. J. Stone**

MR JAMES UNETT - Continued

10 B f Clodovil (IRE)—Kibarague **P. Fetherston-Godley**
11 **MIGHT SURPRISE (IRE)**, b f Mujadil (USA)—Ambria (ITY) **Lord S. J. Stone**
12 **SERENDIPPIDY**, b f Indesatchel (IRE)—Dipple **G. D. Kendrick**
13 **TONKALILI**, b f Firebreak—Amber Mill **Mr N. Rowlands**

TWO-YEAR-OLDS

14 B c 21/3 Cockney Rebel (IRE)—Dances With Angels (IRE) (Mukaddamah (USA)) **Mr M. Sheehy**
15 B c 24/4 Multiplex—Lady Castanea (Superlative) **Mrs S. Downes**
16 **PIXMIESTER**, b c 15/3 Piccolo—Rare Cross (IRE) (Cape Cross (IRE)) **Mr W. Hennessey**
17 B c 28/3 Rob Roy (USA)—Spark Up (Lahib (USA)) **Mr J. Unett**

Other Owners: Mr M. Hall, Mr M. A. Sheehy.

Assistant Trainer: Miss C. H. Jones

---

632 **MR JOHN UPSON, Towcester**
Postal: **Glebe Stables, Blakesley Heath, Maidford, Towcester, Northamptonshire, NN12 8HN**
Contacts: **PHONE (01327) 860043 FAX (01327) 860238**

1 **CURSUM PERFICIO**, 11, b g Tagula (IRE)—Simply Sooty **The Nap Hand Partnership**
2 **DRAMATIC VICTORY (IRE)**, 6, b g Old Vic—Pinky The Nose (IRE) **The Peter Partnership**
3 **GIDAM GIDAM (IRE)**, 11, b g King's Best (USA)—Flamands (IRE) **A. C. Kemp**
4 **GRITTI PALACE (IRE)**, 13, b g Duky—Glittering Grit (IRE) **Miss Tracey Leeson**
5 **HALIANA**, 4, ch f Sakhee (USA)—Boojum **Mr N. A. Price**
6 **ISAAC'S WARRIOR (IRE)**, 7, b g Pushkin (IRE)—Point The Finger (IRE) **Lord Nicholas Wilson**
7 **KEVIN FANCY (IRE)**, 7, b m Zagreb (USA)—Top Flight Travel (IRE) **The Nap Hand Partnership**
8 **ROSE OF MARRON (IRE)**, 6, b g Dilshaan—Sunset Park (IRE) **The Marron Partnership**
9 **SAMIZDAT (FR)**, 10, b g Soviet Star (USA)—Secret Account (FR) **Honorvell Partnership**
10 **THEFRIENDLYGREMLIN**, 5, b g Vinnie Roe (IRE)—Queens Fantasy **The Nap Hand Partnership**
11 **WISHES OR WATCHES (IRE)**, 13, br g Bravefoot—Shadya's Amal **The Peter Partnership**

Other Owners: M. H. Beesley, D. Deveney, G. G. Fowler, Mr R. W. George, Mrs K. Hopewell, Mrs J. M. Letts, Miss K. J. Letts, M. E. White.

---

633 **MR MARK USHER, Upper Lambourn**
Postal: **Saxon House Stables, Upper Lambourn, Hungerford, Berkshire, RG17 8QH**
Contacts: **PHONE (01488) 72598 FAX (01488) 73630 MOBILE (07831) 873531**
E-MAIL markusherracing@btconnect.com WEBSITE www.markusherracing.co.uk

1 **BEST BE CAREFUL (IRE)**, 5, b m Exceed And Excel (AUS)—Precautionary **Mrs J. F. Pellett**
2 **BLING IT GIRL (IRE)**, 6, b m Old Vic—Afarka (IRE) **Ms A. Greaves**
3 **BOBLINI**, 5, b m Bertolini (USA)—Boojum **Itchen Valley Stud**
4 **CALCULATING (IRE)**, 9, b g Machiavellian (USA)—Zaheemah (USA) **B. C. Rogan**
5 4, B c Old Vic—East Rose **The Ridgeway Partnership**
6 **ELSIE BAY**, 4, b f Sakhee (USA)—Mary Sea (FR) **Janet Gawthorpe & Ron Goddard**
7 **HONOURABLE KNIGHT (IRE)**, 5, b g Celtic Swing—Deemeh (IRE) **Mr B. Fry**
8 **HOPE POINT**, 5, b m Overbury (IRE)—East Rose **The Ridgeway Partnership**
9 **IDOL DEPUTY (FR)**, 7, gr g Silver Deputy (CAN)—Runaway Venus (USA) **Miss J. C. Blackwell**
10 **KATMAI RIVER (IRE)**, 6, b g Choisir (AUS)—Katavi (USA) **M. D. I. Usher**
11 **LADY OF BURGUNDY**, 7, b m Montjeu (IRE)—Helena's Paris (IRE) **B. C. Rogan**
12 **LADY PERCY (IRE)**, 4, b f Sir Percy—Genuinely (IRE) **Ushers Court**
13 **LENNOXWOOD (IRE)**, 5, gr ro g Verglas (IRE)—Sigonella (IRE) **Midweek Racing**
14 **LITTLECOTE LADY**, 4, b f Byron—Barefooted Flyer (USA) **Littlecote House Racing**
15 **MAY'S BOY**, 5, gr h Proclamation (IRE)—Sweet Portia (IRE) **High Five Racing**
16 **MY SISTER**, 6, b m Royal Applause—Mysistra (FR) **Itchen Valley Stud & Partners**
17 **REGINALD CLAUDE**, 5, b g Monsieur Bond (IRE)—Miller's Melody **High Five Racing**
18 **RIDGEWAY HAWK**, 5, ch g Monsieur Bond (IRE)—Barefooted Flyer (USA) **Goodracing Partnership**
19 **RIDGEWAY SAPPHIRE**, 6, b m Zafeen (FR)—Barefooted Flyer (USA) **Goodracing Partnership**
20 **SONGBIRD BLUES**, 4, b f Beat All (USA)—Billie Holiday **Goodracing Partnership**
21 **SPICE FAIR**, 6, ch g Trade Fair—Focosa (ITY) **Saxon House Racing**
22 **SWEET OVATION**, 4, b f Royal Applause—Sweetest Revenge (IRE) **The Ridgeway Bloodstock Company Ltd**

MR MARK USHER - Continued

23 **THE BENDY FELLA (IRE)**, 5, ch g Choisir (AUS)—Missish **M. D. I. Usher**
24 **TITAN DIAMOND (IRE)**, 5, b g Diamond Green (FR)—Ditton Dancer **The Swell Racing Partnership**

THREE-YEAR-OLDS

25 **BLACK TRUFFLE (FR)**, b c Kyllachy—Some Diva **Ushers Court**
26 **BULLSEYE BABE**, ch f Notnowcato—Mary Sea (FR) **Mr A. C. Fortune**
27 **COPPER RAG**, ch g Kirkwall—Pajada **Ron Goddard & Partners**
28 **DIRECT TRADE**, ch f Trade Fair—Bold Love **Saxon House Racing**
29 **HAATEFINA**, b f Haatef (USA)—Felona **Ushers Court**
30 **ISHI HONEST**, b f Ishiguru (USA)—Honesty Pays **High Five Racing**
31 **IT'S TABOO**, b f Tobougg (IRE)—Faraway Moon **Mrs T. J. Channing-Williams**
32 **JINKS AND CO**, ch f Ishiguru (USA)—Crofters Ceilidh **The High Jinks Partnership**
33 **MIGHTY MATA**, b c Lucky Story (USA)—Dudleys Delight **R. H. Brookes**
34 **MY SWEET LORD**, b g Byron—Sweetest Revenge (IRE) **The Ridgeway Alchemist's**
35 **NOOR AL HAYA (IRE)**, b f Tamayuz—Hariya (IRE) **Imran Butt & High Five Racing**

TWO-YEAR-OLDS

36 B c 6/3 Piccolo—Alvarinho Lady (Royal Applause) **M. D. I. Usher**
37 **HARLEQUIN JINKS**, b f 23/2 Lucky Story (USA)—
                                    Crofters Ceilidh (Scottish Reel) (14285) **The High Jinks Partnership**
38 B f 12/3 Bertolini (USA)—Just Down The Road (IRE) (Night Shift (USA)) **M. D. I. Usher**
39 B f 19/4 Kheleyf (USA)—Knockenduff (Oratorio (IRE)) (7000) **High Five Racing**
40 B f 9/3 Compton Place—Queen of Havana (USA) (King of Kings (IRE)) (3000) **Ushers Court**
41 Ch c 12/4 Milk It Mick—Smart Ass (IRE) (Shinko Forest (IRE)) (2857) **Ushers Court**
42 Ch f 26/2 Compton Place—Splicing (Sharpo) (7142) **Ushers Court**
43 Ch c 29/4 Compton Place—Time Clash (Timeless Times (USA)) **Mark & Debbie Hughes**
44 B f 14/4 Manduro (GER)—Tuscania (USA) (Woodman (USA)) (15000) **High Five Racing**

Other Owners: Mrs A. D. Bourne, Mr R. H. Brookes, Mr Imran Butt, Mr T. Channing-Williams, Mrs J. A. Gawthorpe, R. A. Goddard, Mrs Jean Johnson, Mr M. D. I. Usher.

Jockey (flat): David Probert, Liam Keniry, Lee Newnes. **Jockey (NH):** David Crosse. **Apprentice:** Racheal Kneller, Emily Melbourn.

---

634 **MR ROGER VARIAN, Newmarket**
Postal: Kremlin House Stables, Fordham Road, Newmarket, Suffolk, CB8 7AQ
Contacts: **PHONE** (01638) 661702 **FAX** (01638) 667018 **MOBILE** (07879) 414664
E-MAIL info@varianstable.com WEBSITE www.varianstable.com

1 **ALJAMAAHEER (IRE)**, 4, ch c Dubawi (IRE)—Kelly Nicole (IRE) **Hamdan Al Maktoum**
2 **AMBIVALENT (IRE)**, 4, b f Authorized (IRE)—Darrery **Mr A. S. Belhab**
3 **CAMERON HIGHLAND (IRE)**, 4, b c Galileo (IRE)—Landmark (USA) **H.R.H. Sultan Ahmad Shah**
4 **DANCEWITHTHEDEVIL (SAF)**, 7, b m Modus Vivendi—Emperor's Dance (SAF)
5 **EKTIHAAM (IRE)**, 4, b g Invincible Spirit (IRE)—Liscune (IRE) **Hamdan Al Maktoum**
6 **ETON FOREVER (IRE)**, 6, b g Oratorio (IRE)—True Joy (IRE) **H.R.H. Sultan Ahmad Shah**
7 **FARRAAJ (IRE)**, 4, b g Dubai Destination (USA)—Pastorale **Sheikh Ahmed Al Maktoum**
8 **FRASERS HILL**, 4, ch c Selkirk (USA)—Shemriyna (IRE) **H.R.H. Sultan Ahmad Shah**
9 **FULL SWING**, 4, br g Manduro (GER)—Glorosia (FR) **A. D. Spence**
10 **GLADYS' GAL**, 5, b m Tobougg (IRE)—Charming Lotte **Fishlake Commercial Motors Ltd**
11 **JUSTINEO**, 4, b c Oasis Dream—Loulwa (IRE) **Saleh Al Homaizi & Imad Al Sagar**
12 **MIJHAAR**, 5, b g Shirocco (GER)—Jathaabeh **Sheikh Ahmed Al Maktoum**
13 **OOJOOBA**, 4, b f Monsun (GER)—Ameerat **Sheikh Ahmed Al Maktoum**
14 **PANETTONE (IRE)**, 4, b f Montjeu (IRE)—Tea Break **Mr Duncan Jones & Dr Sosie Kassab**
15 **PERFECT STEP (IRE)**, 4, b f Iffraaj—Spiritual Air **Clipper Group Holdings Ltd**
16 **PINK DAMSEL (IRE)**, 4, b f Galileo (IRE)—Riskaverse (USA) **Mrs F. H. Hay**
17 **SOUND HEARTS (USA)**, 4, b br f Sir Percy—Crystal Seas **Mr Y. Masuda**
18 **SPORTING GOLD (IRE)**, 4, b g Shirocco (GER)—Pink Stone (FR) **A. D. Spence**
19 **SRI PUTRA**, 7, b h Oasis Dream—Wendylina (IRE) **H.R.H. Sultan Ahmad Shah**
20 **STEPS (IRE)**, 5, br g Verglas (IRE)—Killinallan **Michael Hill**
21 **TAFAWUK (USA)**, 4, b g Nayef (USA)—Yaqeen **Michael Hill**
22 **TIOMAN PEARL**, 4, b c Royal Applause—Mazarine Blue **H.R.H. Sultan Ahmad Shah**
23 **UPPER GROSVENOR**, 4, b c Notnowcato—Nsx **H.R.H. Sultan Ahmad Shah**
24 **ZANOTTI**, 4, b g Authorized (IRE)—Majestic Sakeena (IRE) **Saleh Al Homaizi & Imad Al Sagar**

MR ROGER VARIAN - Continued

THREE-YEAR-OLDS

25 **AGERZAM**, b c Holy Roman Emperor (IRE)—Epiphany **Saleh Al Homaizi & Imad Al Sagar**
26 **AGLAOPHONOS**, ch g Dutch Art—Lasting Image **Sir Alex Ferguson & Sotirios Hassiakos**
27 **AL BAAHI (IRE)**, b g Shamardal (USA)—Lanzana (IRE) **Sheikh Ahmed Al Maktoum**
28 **ALOHA**, b f With Approval (CAN)—Almamia **Miss K. Rausing**
29 **ARDINGLY (IRE)**, b f Danehill Dancer (IRE)—Asnieres (USA) **Mrs F. H. Hay**
30 **ASHAADD (IRE)**, b g Dansili—Vital Statistics **Sheikh Ahmed Al Maktoum**
31 **AZENZAR (IRE)**, b f Danehill Dancer (IRE)—Dashing (IRE) **Saleh Al Homaizi & Imad Al Sagar**
32 **BASTION (USA)**, b c Giant's Causeway (USA)—Marital Spook (USA) **Highclere Thoroughbred Racing - Regime**
33 **BIT OF A GIFT (FR)**, gr c Dark Angel (IRE)—Dilag (IRE) **S. Suhail**
34 **CHELWOOD GATE (IRE)**, b gr c Aussie Rules (USA)—Jusoor (USA) **Mrs F. H. Hay**
35 **DEGLET NOOR**, br f New Approach (IRE)—Almoutezah (USA) **Hamdan Al Maktoum**
36 Gr f Excellent Art—Divine Grace (IRE) **A. D. Spence**
37 **DUCAB (IRE)**, b c Dansili—Twyla Tharp (IRE) **S. Ali**
38 **DUROBLE MAN**, b c Manduro (GER)—Jalousie (IRE) **Mr D. A. Yardy**
39 **ELKAAYED (USA)**, ch c Distorted Humor (USA)—Habibti (USA) **Hamdan Al Maktoum**
40 **ELSINIAAR**, bl c New Approach (IRE)—Comic (USA) **Hamdan Al Maktoum**
41 **ERSAAL**, b c Dubawi (IRE)—Makaaseb (USA) **Hamdan Al Maktoum**
42 **EXCEPTIONELLE**, br f Exceed And Excel (AUS)—Turning Leaf (IRE) **Thurloe Thoroughbreds XXX**
43 **FAMILLIARITY**, ch f Nayef (USA)—Millistar **Helena Springfield Ltd**
44 **HASHEEM**, ch c New Approach (IRE)—Masaafat **Hamdan Al Maktoum**
45 **HAZZAAT (IRE)**, ch g Iffraaj—Hurricane Irene (IRE) **Sheikh Ahmed Al Maktoum**
46 **HEKAAYAAT (USA)**, ch f Mr Greeley (USA)—Mostaqeleh (USA) **Hamdan Al Maktoum**
47 **HORSTED KEYNES (FR)**, ch c Giant's Causeway (USA)—Viking's Cove (USA) **Mrs F. H. Hay**
48 **HUFFOOF (IRE)**, b f Dalakhani (IRE)—Albahja **Sheikh Ahmed Al Maktoum**
49 **IFFRAAJ PINK (IRE)**, b f Iffraaj—Red Vale (IRE) **Mrs F. H. Hay**
50 **JALADEE**, b c Cape Cross (IRE)—Atamana (IRE) **Sheikh Ahmed Al Maktoum**
51 **KABBAAS (IRE)**, ch g Pivotal—Dorrati (USA) **Sheikh Ahmed Al Maktoum**
52 B g Authorized (IRE)—Kartuzy (JPN) **S. Ali**
53 **KOHLAAN (IRE)**, b g Elusive City (USA)—Rock Salt **Sheikh Ahmed Al Maktoum**
54 **LANANSAAK (IRE)**, ch f Zamindar (USA)—Bunood (IRE) **Hamdan Al Maktoum**
55 **MISHAAL (IRE)**, ch g Kheleyf (USA)—My Dubai (IRE) **Sheikh Ahmed Al Maktoum**
56 **MORAWIJ**, ch c Exceed And Excel (AUS)—Sister Moonshine (FR) **Sheikh Ahmed Al Maktoum**
57 **MUDAWALA (USA)**, b f Haafhd—Reefaljamal (USA) **Hamdan Al Maktoum**
58 **MUTASHADED (USA)**, b c Raven's Pass (USA)—Sortita (GER) **Hamdan Al Maktoum**
59 **MUTHMERA (USA)**, b f Dynaformer (USA)—Burooz (IRE) **Hamdan Al Maktoum**
60 **ONE PEKAN (IRE)**, b c Hard Spun (USA)—Stormy Blessing (USA) **H.R.H. Sultan Ahmad Shah**
61 **ORBISON (IRE)**, b c Azamour (IRE)—Glenmara (USA) **A. D. Spence**
62 **PRINCESS LOULOU (IRE)**, ch f Pivotal—Aiming **Saleh Al Homaizi & Imad Al Sagar**
63 **PUTRA ETON (IRE)**, b c Danehill Dancer (IRE)—Anna Pallida (IRE) **H.R.H. Sultan Ahmad Shah**
64 **PYREXIA**, br c Singspiel (IRE)—Street Fire (IRE) **Mr A.D. Spence & Mr & Mrs P.Hargreaves**
65 **QAWAARY (IRE)**, b f Street Cry (IRE)—Eswarah **Hamdan Al Maktoum**
66 **RAVEN'S ROCK (IRE)**, b g Raven's Pass (USA)—Delphinus **A. D. Spence**
67 **RIBAAT (IRE)**, b c Invincible Spirit (IRE)—Fonda (USA) **Hamdan Al Maktoum**
68 **ROCKY GROUND (IRE)**, b c Acclamation—Keriyka (IRE) **Clipper Logistics & Cheveley Park Stud**
69 **SAADATT**, b f New Approach (IRE)—Ameerat **Sheikh Ahmed Al Maktoum**
70 **SENSIZ (IRE)**, b f Marju (IRE)—Much Faster (USA) **Saleh Al Homaizi & Imad Al Sagar**
71 **SEVERIANO (USA)**, b g Danehill Dancer (IRE)—Time Control **Merry Fox Stud Limited**
72 **SHEMAAL (IRE)**, b c Monsun (GER)—Zahrat Dubai **Sheikh Ahmed Al Maktoum**
73 **SINISTER (IRE)**, b c Sinndar (IRE)—Shamsada (IRE) **Clanbrooke Racing International**
74 **SOARING SPIRITS (IRE)**, ch g Tamayuz—Follow My Lead **J Collins, N Horsfall & N O'Sullivan**
75 **STAR PEARL (USA)**, b f Tapit (USA)—Lexi Star (USA) **Pearl Bloodstock Limited**
76 **TAJHEEZ (IRE)**, b c Raven's Pass (USA)—Ghaidaa (IRE) **Hamdan Al Maktoum**
77 **TANTSHI (IRE)**, b f Invincible Spirit (IRE)—Qasirah (USA) **Sheikh Ahmed Al Maktoum**
78 **TEFFLAH**, b f Teofilo (IRE)—Anaamil (IRE) **Sheikh Ahmed Al Maktoum**
79 **TENOR (IRE)**, b c Oratorio (IRE)—Cedar Sea (IRE) **Highclere Thoroughbred Racing-JohnPorter**
80 B c Green Desert (USA)—Thorntoun Piccolo **Mr P. D. Smith**
81 **TOUCH A MILLION (IRE)**, b c Green Tune (USA)—Janistra (USA) **S. Suhail**
82 **TUSCAN FUN**, ch g Medicean—Elfin Laughter **K Allen, R Marchant & G Jarvis**
83 **TWARY (USA)**, b c Indian Charlie (USA)—Street Sounds (CAN) **Hamdan Al Maktoum**
84 **WILHANA (IRE)**, b f Singspiel (IRE)—Jathaabeh **Sheikh Ahmed Al Maktoum**
85 **YARROOM (IRE)**, b c Cape Cross (IRE)—Aryaamm (IRE) **Sheikh Ahmed Al Maktoum**

MR ROGER VARIAN - Continued

TWO-YEAR-OLDS

86 B f 13/4 Cape Cross (IRE)—Albahja (Sinndar (IRE)) **Sheikh Ahmed Al Maktoum**
87 **ALJAAZIAH,** b br f 23/2 Medaglia d'oro (USA)—Eswarah (Unfuwain (USA)) **Hamdan Al Maktoum**
88 **ALMASHOOQA (USA),** b br f 7/2 Dubawi (IRE)—Almoutezah (USA) (Storm Cat (USA)) **Hamdan Al Maktoum**
89 B f 7/4 Invincible Spirit (IRE)—Alsace (King's Best (USA)) (80000) **Sheikh Juma Al Dalmook Maktoum**
90 B f 26/3 Halling (USA)—Anaamil (IRE) (Darshaan) **Sheikh Ahmed Al Maktoum**
91 B f 2/3 Cape Cross (IRE)—Aryaamm (IRE) (Galileo (IRE)) **Sheikh Ahmed Al Maktoum**
92 Gr ro c 15/1 Mastercraftsman (IRE)—Audacieuse (Rainbow Quest (USA)) (70000) **Mr P. D. Smith**
93 **BAAREZ (USA),** ch c 20/1 Hard Spun (USA)—Sortita (GER) (Monsun (GER)) **Hamdan Al Maktoum**
94 **BAROQUE,** b f 10/3 Black Sam Bellamy (IRE)—Moody Margaret (Bahamian Bounty) (619) **Ms Y. Ferguson**
95 Br f 31/3 Oasis Dream—Blessing (Dubai Millennium) **Lordship Stud**
96 **CERTIFICATE,** ch c 5/3 Pivotal—Graduation (Lomitas) (100000) **Cheveley Park Stud Limited**
97 Ch f 7/2 New Approach (IRE)—Dance Treat (Nureyev (USA)) (30000) **S. Ali**
98 B f 26/2 Shirocco (GER)—Danzelline (Danzero (AUS)) (22221) **Sheikh Juma Al Dalmook Maktoum**
99 B c 21/2 Sea The Stars (IRE)—Dashing (IRE) (Sadler's Wells (USA)) **Saleh Al Homaizi & Imad Al Sagar**
100 B c 1/3 Lawman (FR)—Dawn Raid (IRE) (Docksider (USA)) (70000) **Sheikh Ahmed Al Maktoum**
101 B f 10/4 Shamardal (USA)—Dorrati (USA) (Dubai Millennium) **Sheikh Ahmed Al Maktoum**
102 **EJADAH (IRE),** b f 20/4 Clodovil (IRE)—Bintalreef (USA) (Diesis) (170000) **Hamdan Al Maktoum**
103 **ELSHAADIN,** gr f 7/2 Dalakhani (IRE)—Distinctive Look (IRE) (Danehill (USA)) (550000) **Hamdan Al Maktoum**
104 **EMARATIYA ANA (IRE),** b f 28/4 Excellent Art—Tina Heights (Shirley Heights) (22000) **A. Al Shaikh**
105 B c 4/5 Dutch Art—Embraced (Pursuit of Love) (60000) **Sheikh Ahmed Al Maktoum**
106 Br c 8/3 Authorized (IRE)—Epiphany (Zafonic (USA)) **Saleh Al Homaizi & Imad Al Sagar**
107 B f 29/1 Holy Roman Emperor (IRE)—Gentle Night (Zafonic (USA)) (114285) **Saleh Al Homaizi & Imad Al Sagar**
108 B c 6/4 Galileo (IRE)—Gino's Spirits (Perugino (USA)) (200000) **H.R.H. Sultan Ahmad Shah**
109 **GO SAKHEE,** br c 16/4 Sakhee's Secret—
          Bling Bling (IRE) (Indian Ridge) (32000) **K Allen G Moss R & S Marchant & G Jarvis**
110 B c 20/3 Exceed And Excel (AUS)—Gower Song (Singspiel (IRE)) (200000) **H.R.H. Sultan Ahmad Shah**
111 **HADAATHA (IRE),** gr f 24/4 Sea The Stars (IRE)—Hathrah (Linamix (FR)) **Hamdan Al Maktoum**
112 B c 7/2 Captain Rio—Harvest Joy (IRE) (Daggers Drawn (USA)) (32380) **Mr K. J. P. Gundlach**
113 **HERBAH,** b f 15/2 Dansili—Khulood (USA) (Storm Cat (USA)) **Hamdan Al Maktoum**
114 **HIGH ACCOLADE,** ch f 13/2 Medicean—
          Hightime Heroine (IRE) (Danetime (IRE)) (26000) **Cheveley Park Stud Limited**
115 Ch c 7/3 Compton Place—Highly Liquid (Entrepreneur) (38095) **Mrs F. H. Hay**
116 **HUMOUR (IRE),** b c 26/4 Invincible Spirit (IRE)—
          Hucking Hot (Desert Prince (IRE)) (170000) **Highclere Thoroughbred Racing - Heritage**
117 B c 4/4 Dubawi (IRE)—Idonea (CAN) (Swain (IRE)) (70000) **Sheikh Juma Al Dalmook Maktoum**
118 Ch c 16/3 Dutch Art—Interlace (Pivotal) (65000) **Sheikh Ahmed Al Maktoum**
119 **KAFEEL (USA),** b c 11/2 First Samurai (USA)—Ishraak (USA) (Sahm (USA)) **Hamdan Al Maktoum**
120 **KEEPER'S RING (USA),** b f 31/1 Street Cry (IRE)—
          Liffey Dancer (IRE) (Sadler's Wells (USA)) **Merry Fox Stud Limited**
121 **KING'S PROCESSION (IRE),** ch c 12/3 Teofilo—Sateen (Barathea (IRE)) (110000) **S. Suhail**
122 **LADY SPARKLER (IRE),** b f 28/4 Tamayuz—
          Capote West (USA) (Capote (USA)) (42000) **Sotirios Hassiakos & Maurice Manasseh**
123 **LAFTAH (IRE),** b f 18/4 Invincible Spirit (IRE)—Liscune (IRE) (King's Best (USA)) **Hamdan Al Maktoum**
124 B c 4/4 Montjeu (IRE)—Madame Cerito (IRE) (Diesis) (125000) **A. D. Spence**
125 **MAHAABA (IRE),** b f 8/3 Oasis Dream—Masaafat (Act One) **Hamdan Al Maktoum**
126 **MASTER OF ALKMAAR,** ch c 1/4 Dutch Art—Lalina (GER) (Trempolino (USA)) (47619) **Mrs F. H. Hay**
127 B c 5/3 Shamardal (USA)—Mazzaya (USA) (Cozzene (USA)) (60000) **S. Ali**
128 B f 11/5 Cape Cross (IRE)—Miss Champagne (FR) (Bering) (90000) **Sheikh R. D. Al Maktoum**
129 Ch c 1/5 Exchange Rate (USA)—Miss Delta Dawn (USA) (Thirty Six Red (USA)) (100000) **Mrs F. H. Hay**
130 **MUHAWALAH (IRE),** ch f 5/3 Nayef (USA)—Al Ishq (FR) (Nureyev (USA)) **Hamdan Al Maktoum**
131 **MUSHIR,** b c 24/3 Oasis Dream—Shimah (USA) (Storm Cat (USA)) **Hamdan Al Maktoum**
132 **MUSTAJJID,** b c 27/3 Byron—Skara Brae (Inchinor) (71428) **Hamdan Al Maktoum**
133 **MUTARAADIF (USA),** b c 3/4 Dynaformer—Dawla (Alhaarth (IRE)) **Hamdan Al Maktoum**
134 Ch c 6/5 Sea The Stars (IRE)—My Dubai (IRE) (Dubai Millennium) **Sheikh Ahmed Al Maktoum**
135 B c 20/4 Exceed And Excel (AUS)—My Love Thomas (IRE) (Cadeaux Genereux) (90000) **A. D. Spence**
136 B c 1/5 More Than Ready (USA)—Nasmatt (Danehill (USA)) **Sheikh Ahmed Al Maktoum**
137 B f 9/2 Mastercraftsman (IRE)—Perfect Star (Act One) (120000) **Qatar Racing Limited**
138 B f 27/4 Teofilo (IRE)—Qasirah (IRE) (Machiavellian) (USA)) **Sheikh Ahmed Al Maktoum**
139 **QUASQAZAH,** ch c 11/4 Bahamian Bounty—Rock Lily (Rock of Gibraltar) (150000) **Hamdan Al Maktoum**
140 Ch c 17/2 New Approach (IRE)—Rafting (IRE) (Darshaan) (80000) **Mrs F. H. Hay**
141 **RAINBEAM,** b f 20/2 Rock of Gibraltar (IRE)—
          Rainbow Queen (Rainbow Quest (USA)) **Cheveley Park Stud Limited**
142 **RAPID ADVANCE,** b c 25/2 Medicean—Snow Gretel (IRE) (Green Desert (USA)) (100000) **S. Suhail**
143 **REESHA,** b f 25/3 Teofilo (IRE)—Sana Abel (IRE) (Alhaarth (IRE)) **Hamdan Al Maktoum**

MR ROGER VARIAN - Continued

144 B br f 26/3 Dynaformer (USA)—Shelly River (USA) (Irish River (FR)) **S. Ali**
145 **SHERIFF'S STAR (IRE),** gr c 17/4 Lawman (FR)—Silver Bandana (USA) (Silver Buck (USA)) (50000) **S. Suhail**
146 B c 9/4 Clodovil (IRE)—Somoushe (IRE) (Black Minnaloushe (USA)) (150000) **Sheikh Ahmed Al Maktoum**
147 Ch c 17/2 Danehill Dancer (IRE)—Splashdown (Falbrav (IRE)) (100000) **Mr K. J. P. Gundlach**
148 **STAR JET (IRE),** br gr f 9/3 Teofilo (IRE)—Silver Shoon (IRE) (Fasliyev (USA)) (126983) **Mr C. Mullin**
149 Ch c 9/4 Dalakhani (IRE)—
                       Sweet Firebird (IRE) (Sadler's Wells (USA)) (70000) **Saleh Al Homaizi & Imad Al Sagar**
150 B br f 6/2 Shamardal (USA)—Taarkod (IRE) (Singspiel (IRE)) **Sheikh Ahmed Al Maktoum**
151 B f 22/1 Kheleyf (USA)—Tempete (Dubai Millennium) **Sheikh Ahmed Al Maktoum**
152 **THURAYAAT,** b f 8/3 Tamayuz—Ghaidaa (IRE) (Cape Cross (IRE)) **Hamdan Al Maktoum**
153 **TOOFI (FR),** b c 15/2 Henrythenavigator (USA)—
                       Silver Bark (Royal Applause) (220000) **Saleh Al Homaizi & Imad Al Sagar**
154 **TOUCH THE SKY,** b f 16/4 Authorized (IRE)—La Sky (IRE) (Law Society (USA)) **Sheikh Ahmed Al Maktoum**
155 B c 10/3 Cape Cross (IRE)—Whatizzit (Galileo (IRE)) (40000) **Sheikh Juma Al Dalmook Maktoum**

Other Owners: Mr Imad Al-Sagar, Mr K. Allen, Mr J. A. Collins, Mr D. Dicarra, Mrs H. S. Ellingsen, Sir Alex Ferguson, Mr F. Guerra, Mr P. K. Hargreaves, Mrs R. J. Hargreaves, T. F. Harris, Mrs E. A. Harris, Mr S. Hassiakos, The Hon H. Herbert, Highclere Thoroughbred Racing Ltd, Mr Saleh Al Homaizi, Mr N. P. Horsfall, Mr D. Humphries, Mrs Gay Jarvis, Mr Duncan Jones, Mr Sosie Kassab, Mr M. Manasseh, Mr R. P. Marchant, Mr S. Marchant, Mr G. Moss, Mr Nigel O'Sullivan, O. J. W. Pawle, Mr J. A. B. Stafford, Mr M. Weinfeld.

Assistant Trainers: Gay Jarvis, David Eustace

Jockey (flat): Andrea Atzeni, Neil Callan, Dominic Fox. **Apprentice:** Jean Van Overmeire.

MR ED VAUGHAN, Newmarket

635

Postal: **Machell Place Cottage, Old Station Road, Newmarket, Suffolk, CB8 8DW**
Contacts: **PHONE** (01638) 667411 **FAX** (01638) 667452 **MOBILE** (07799) 144901
E-MAIL ed@efvaughan.com WEBSITE www.efvaughan.com

1 **DANCE AND DANCE (IRE),** 7, b g Royal Applause—Caldy Dancer (IRE)
2 **LEGENDARY,** 4, b g Exceed And Excel (AUS)—Red Carnation (IRE)
3 **REDVERS (IRE),** 5, br g Ishiguru (USA)—Cradle Brief (IRE)
4 **ROBIN HOODS BAY,** 5, b g Motivator—Bijou A Moi
5 **WHITBY JET (IRE),** 5, b g Mujadil (USA)—Anazah (USA)

THREE-YEAR-OLDS

6 **AWATTAN,** b f Singspiel (IRE)—Mureefa (USA)
7 **CLEAR PEARL (USA),** ch f Giant's Causeway (USA)—Clear In The West (USA)
8 **CLOUDWALKER (USA),** b br f Tale of The Cat (USA)—Angel Flying (USA)
9 **DARK TEMPLAR,** ch g Starcraft (NZ)—Shuaily (PER)
10 **KELVINGROVE (IRE),** b g Hurricane Run (IRE)—Silversword (FR)
11 **MINI BOSS (IRE),** b c Street Boss (USA)—Mini Brush (USA)
12 **ON WITH THE DANCE (IRE),** ch g Byron—Caldy Dancer (IRE)

TWO-YEAR-OLDS

13 Gr c 22/2 Dalakhani (IRE)—Adventure (USA) (Unbridled's Song (USA)) (85000)
14 B c 7/4 Royal Applause—Alhufoof (USA) (Dayjur (USA)) (45000)
15 B f 12/2 Kheleyf (USA)—Caldy Dancer (IRE) (Soviet Star (USA)) (30000)
16 **COSTA FILEY,** b c 10/2 Pastoral Pursuits—Cosmic Destiny (IRE) (Soviet Star (USA))
17 B c 30/3 Authorized (IRE)—Eternity Ring (Alzao (USA)) (40000)
18 **GENUINE QUALITY (USA),** b f 25/1 Elusive Quality (USA)—
                       Genuine Devotion (IRE) (Rock of Gibraltar (IRE)) (86021)
19 Ch c 31/3 Mount Nelson—Lacework (Pivotal) (41000)
20 Gr f 24/2 Oratorio (IRE)—Miss Sazanica (FR) (Zafonic (USA)) (50000)
21 **QUAINTRELLE (IRE),** b f 30/4 Dandy Man (IRE)—Extravagance (IRE) (King's Best (USA)) (10000)
22 Ch c 15/2 Pivotal—Quiet Protest (USA) (Kingmambo (USA)) (100000)
23 B br c 7/2 Speightstown (USA)—Reboot (USA) (Rubiano (USA)) (120000)
24 **SI SENOR (IRE),** b c 23/4 Dansili—Kotsi (IRE) (Nayef (USA))
25 B c 20/3 Rock Hard Ten (USA)—To The Brim (CAN) (Ascot Knight (CAN)) (60000)

Owners: Mr P. Anastasio, Mr K. E. Biddick, Mr R. G. W. Brown, Mr John Fleming, Mr C. M. Hamer, Mr M. M. Hawkes, Mr E. J. C. Hawkes, Mr P. Moroney, Mr R. Ng, Mr A. E. Oppenheimer, Pearl Bloodstock Limited, Mr G. Peterson, Mr A. M. Pickering, Mr M. Rashid, Mrs S. Rashid, Mrs Doreen M. Swinburn, Mr E. F. Vaughan, Mr Thomas Whitehead.

636 MR TIM VAUGHAN, Cowbridge

Postal: **Pant Wilkin Stables, Llanquian Road, Aberthin, Cowbridge, South Glamorgan, CF71 7HE**
Contacts: **PHONE (01446) 771626 FAX (01446) 774371 MOBILE (07841) 800081**
E-MAIL tim@timvaughanracing.com WEBSITE www.timvaughanracing.com

1 **ALBORZ (IRE)**, 4, b g Dubai Destination (USA)—Mount Elbrus **Diamond Racing Ltd**
2 **ALPHABETICAL ORDER**, 5, b g Alflora (IRE)—Lady Turk (FR) **Great Northern Partnership**
3 **AMOK (GER)**, 5, b g Shirocco (GER)—Alharmina **Mr D. R. Passant**
4 **AWBEG MASSINI (IRE)**, 7, b g Dr Massini (IRE)—
                Awbeg Flower (IRE) **www.Select-Racing-Club.co.uk & Partners**
5 **BALLYMOAT**, 6, b g Grape Tree Road—Frosty Mistress **Cleeve Hill Racing**
6 **BALLYROCK (IRE)**, 7, b g Milan—Ardent Love (IRE) **Pearn's Pharmacies Ltd**
7 **BALOTTI (IRE)**, 5, b g Oscar (IRE)—Have At It (IRE) **The Balotti Partnership**
8 **BE BOP BORU (IRE)**, 6, b g Brian Boru—Henrietta Howard (IRE) **The Oak Syndicate**
9 **BESHABAR (IRE)**, 11, ch g Flemensfirth (USA)—In Our Intrest (IRE) **Middleham Park Racing X & Ann Burrows**
10 **BILLYBO**, 10, b g Kayf Tara—Pollys Perk (IRE) **Oceans Racing**
11 **BUCKING THE TREND**, 5, b g Kayf Tara—Macklette (IRE) **The Marinades**
12 **CAPTAIN MOONMAN (IRE)**, 8, b g Milan—Bridgeofallen (IRE) **Diamond Racing Ltd**
13 **CARAVEL (IRE)**, 9, ch g Medicean—Caraiyma (IRE) **Oceans Racing**
14 **CHILBURY HILL**, 10, b g Bahhare (USA)—Fire Goddess **Mr B. M. Jones**
15 **CHRISTMAS CRACKER (IRE)**, 5, b m Flemensfirth (USA)—
                Laughing Lesa (IRE) **The Select Racing Club Limited**
16 **DESTROYER DEPLOYED**, 7, b g Deploy—Supreme Cove **The Craftsmen**
17 **DISTANT MEMORIES (IRE)**, 7, b g Falbrav (IRE)—Amathia (IRE) **Oceans Racing**
18 **DOVILS DATE**, 4, gr g Clodovil (IRE)—Lucky Date (IRE) **Smith & Wright**
19 **DUNEEN POINT (IRE)**, 9, b g Saddlers' Hall (IRE)—Miss Ogan (IRE) **The Mirror Punters Club**
20 **EARTH TREMOR (IRE)**, 7, b g Definite Article—Arctic Rose (IRE) **Mrs G. M. Owens**
21 **EXPERIMENTALIST**, 5, b g Monsieur Bond (IRE)—Floppie (FR) **Two Gents & An Orange Bloke Racing**
22 **EXPLAINED (IRE)**, 6, b g Exit To Nowhere (USA)—All Told (IRE) **D N V Churton & Mrs C Wilson**
23 **FIGARO**, 5, ch g Medicean—Chorist **Pearn's Pharmacies Ltd**
24 **FINNEGAN PADDY (IRE)**, 7, ch g Moscow Society (USA)—Holy Easter (IRE) **Mr J. P. M. Bowtell**
25 **FIRST FANDANGO**, 6, b g Hernando (FR)—First Fantasy **WRB Racing 40 & Premier Chance Racing**
26 **FREE WORLD (FR)**, 9, b g Lost World (IRE)—Fautine (FR) **Miss M. Gut**
27 **GALLOX BRIDGE**, 8, b g Kayf Tara—Explorer **Mr D. W. Fox**
28 **GROOMED (IRE)**, 5, b g Acclamation—Enamoured **Mr N. W. Wright**
29 **HIDDEN IDENTITY (IRE)**, 7, b m Beneficial—Swanbrook Leader (IRE) **Mr J. P. M. Bowtell**
30 **IFAN (IRE)**, 5, b g Ivan Denisovich (IRE)—Montana Miss (IRE) **Mr Bryn Palling & Mr Derek Clee**
31 **IN THE DOCK (IRE)**, 7, b g Witness Box (USA)—Company Credit (IRE) **R. M. Kirkland**
32 **IVAN VASILEVICH (IRE)**, 5, b g Ivan Denisovich (IRE)—Delisha **Mr C. S. Hinchy**
33 **J'ADHERE (FR)**, 8, b g Nikos—Lettre de Lune (FR) **David & Susan Luke**
34 **JIMBILL (IRE)**, 7, br g Flying Legend—Ah Gowan (IRE) **Mr M. E. Moore & Mr B. Ead**
35 **JUDICIARY (IRE)**, 6, b g Invincible Spirit (IRE)—Theory of Law **Diamond Racing Ltd**
36 **JUNO THE MUFFINMAN (IRE)**, 4, b g Holy Roman Emperor (IRE)—
                Mackenzie's Friend **Mr A. Black & Owen Promotions Limited**
37 **KING ROLFE (IRE)**, 5, b g King's Theatre (IRE)—Lady Rolfe (IRE) **F. J. Brennan**
38 **KING'S SUNSET (IRE)**, 8, br g Old Vic—Dysart Lady **Brook Farm Bloodstock**
39 **KOULTAS KING (IRE)**, 6, b g Exit To Nowhere (USA)—Carrigmoorna Style (IRE) **Pearn's Pharmacies Ltd**
40 **LANDENSTOWN STAR (IRE)**, 8, ch g Bob's Return (IRE)—Slieve Bernagh (IRE) **Mr W. Jones**
41 **LATEST TREND (IRE)**, 7, b g Moscow Society (IRE)—Wall-Nut Grove (IRE) **Mr D. W. Fox**
42 **LECALE LAD (IRE)**, 6, b g Revoque (IRE)—Thyngreesa **R. M. Kirkland**
43 **LIBERTY COURT (IRE)**, 6, b g Court Cave (IRE)—Miss Vikki (IRE) **Passant & Butt**
44 **MILANEEN**, 7, b m Milan—Kosheen (IRE) **Mr A. Roberts**
45 **MINELLA FOR PARTY (IRE)**, 6, b g Flemensfirth (USA)—Dame Foraine (FR) **Brook Farm Bloodstock**
46 **MON DESIR (FR)**, 5, b g Le Fou (IRE)—Tribal Art (IRE) **Pearn's Pharmacies Ltd**
47 **MULTI MAX**, 4, br f Librettist (USA)—Maxilla (IRE) **Mr K. B. Hodges**
48 **NEXT EXIT (IRE)**, 8, b g Exit To Nowhere (USA)—Pilgrim Star (IRE) **R. M. Kirkland**
49 4, B g Golan (IRE)—Opera Lover (IRE) **T. E. Vaughan**
50 **OSCARS DEN (IRE)**, 5, b g Oscar (IRE)—Lyre Hill (IRE) **T. E. Vaughan**
51 **OUR ISLAND (IRE)**, 8, b g Turtle Island (IRE)—Linda's Leader (IRE) **Oceans Racing**
52 **PADDY PARTRIDGE**, 7, b g Pivotal—Treble Heights (IRE) **Owen Promotions Limited**
53 **PETROUPETROV (FR)**, 10, br g Ungaro—Harlem (FR) **Mike Harris Racing Club**
54 **PIMENT D'ESTRUVAL (FR)**, 10, b br g Sheyrann—Gabika de Keroger (FR) **Mrs M. J. Worgan**
55 **POLAR ANNIE**, 8, b m Fraam—Willisa **Miss H. A. Cross**
56 **POWER OF GOD (IRE)**, 5, b g Heron Island (IRE)—Aruba Dam (IRE) **Mr J. H. Frost**
57 **PURE ANTICIPATION (IRE)**, 8, gr m Old Vic—Lady of Gortmerron (IRE) **Cloud Nine**
58 **QOUBILAI (FR)**, 9, b g Passing Sale (FR)—Varcady (FR) **Mr J. H. Frost**

MR TIM VAUGHAN - Continued

59 **QUADRATO (GER)**, 6, br g Sholokhov (IRE)—Quadrata (GER) **Pearn's Pharmacies Ltd**
60 **QUALVIRO (FR)**, 9, b g Lavirco (GER)—French County (FR) **Double Trouble Partnership**
61 **RIGIDITY**, 6, b g Indian Ridge—Alakananda **Pearn's Pharmacies Ltd**
62 **ROBBERS ROOST (IRE)**, 5, b g Flemensfirth (USA)—Chapel Queen (IRE) **T. E. Vaughan**
63 **SAFFERANO (IRE)**, 7, b g Saffron Walden (FR)—Paryiana (IRE) **Mr R. H. D. Smith**
64 **SAINT ARE (FR)**, 7, b br g Network (GER)—Fortanea (FR) **Mr D. W. Fox**
65 **SASH OF HONOUR (IRE)**, 4, ch c Galileo (IRE)—Adoration (USA) **Mr R. H. D. Smith**
66 **SAVED BY JOHN (IRE)**, 8, b g Revoque (IRE)—Lady Appeal (IRE) **M & S Clarke**
67 **SCORCHED SON (IRE)**, 10, b g Norwich—Scorched Air **Diamond Racing Ltd**
68 **SHADOW CRUISE (IRE)**, 4, b g Touch of Land (FR)—Rosafi (IRE) **G. Mills**
69 **SILENTPLAN**, 5, b g Blueprint (IRE)—Sprig Muslin **Mr T. J. Malone**
70 **SILKY BOB (IRE)**, 7, b br g Bob Back (USA)—Harir **Mr R. I. Clay**
71 **SKI SUNDAY**, 8, b g King's Best (USA)—Lille Hammer **Scarlet Pimpernel**
72 **SOLARAS EXHIBITION (IRE)**, 5, b g Great Exhibition (USA)—Solara (GER) **Mr C. Davies**
73 **SPEED STEED (IRE)**, 5, b g One Cool Cat (USA)—Dhakhirah (IRE) **Mr J. H. Frost**
74 **SPIRIT OF ADJISA (IRE)**, 9, br g Invincible Spirit (IRE)—Adjisa (IRE) **Darr, Johnson, Weston & Whitaker**
75 **SWAMPFIRE (IRE)**, 5, b g Anabaa (USA)—Moonfire **Smith & Beach**
76 **SWIFT ESCAPE**, 6, b g Exit To Nowhere (USA)—Vivre Aimer Rire (FR) **Diamond Racing Ltd**
77 **SWNYMOR (IRE)**, 4, b g Dylan Thomas (IRE)—Propaganda (IRE) **Mr C. S. Hinchy**
78 **TARTAK (FR)**, 10, b g Akhdari (USA)—Tartamuda (FR) **Power Panels Electrical Systems Ltd**
79 **THE BIG FREEZE (IRE)**, 7, b g Beneficial—Kilfane (IRE) **Pearn's Pharmacies Ltd**
80 **THELOBSTERCATCHER**, 9, gr g Silver Patriarch (IRE)—Everything's Rosy **G. A. Moore**
81 **THIRD HALF**, 4, b g Haafhd—Treble Heights (IRE) **Owen Promotions Limited**
82 **TIPSY GYPSY (IRE)**, 6, b g Milan—Montanara (IRE) **Mr J. P. M. Bowtell**
83 **TITUS MILLS (IRE)**, 5, ch g Dubawi (IRE)—Anayid **Mrs A. Burrows**
84 **TROP FORT (FR)**, 6, b g Bernebeau (FR)—Violeta (FR) **A. E. Peterson**
85 **TRUCKERS BENEFIT (IRE)**, 8, b g Beneficial—Lady Jurado (IRE) **Prince, Reuter, Wadley, Williams**
86 **UT MAJEUR AULMES (FR)**, 5, ch g Northern Park (USA)—My Wish Aulmes (FR) **Mr D. W. Fox**
87 **VINTAGE KID (IRE)**, 7, b g Flemensfirth (USA)—Lios Supreme (IRE) **Mr C. S. Hinchy**
88 **VINTAGE VIXEN (IRE)**, 6, b m Moscow Society (USA)—Bar Un'que (IRE) **Mr R. H. D. Smith**
89 **WINDS OF WAR (IRE)**, 9, ch g Presenting—Shining Willow **T. E. Vaughan**
90 **WINGS OF SMOKE (IRE)**, 8, gr g King's Theatre (IRE)—Grey Mo (IRE) **Pearn's Pharmacies Ltd**

Other Owners: A. W. A. Bates, Mr I. Beach, A. W. Black, Mr P. A. Brannan, Mr G. W. T. Butt, Mr D. N. V. Churton, Mr S. A. Clarke, Mr M. S. Clarke, D. D. Clee, Mr P. Coates, Mr B. Ead, Mr S. H. Easterby, Mr P. C. Etty, K. H. Foster, Mr I. S. Gallacher, Mr M. Gear, Mr J. Goodrick, Mr J. A. Goodrick, Mr A. L. Gregg, Mr M. E. Harris, A. D. I. Harris, Ms S. J. Johnson, T. E. Kerfoot, Mrs S. Luke, Mr D. A. Luke, Mr F. L. McKenna, Mr G. McKenzie, Mr R. Middleton, Mr S. Middleton, Mr M. E. Moore, Mr J. M. Mordecai, Mr G. P. O'Shea, T. S. Palin, Bryn Palling, Mr J. C. Peak, Mr J. T. Phillips, Mr A. J. Pigott, D. Prince, M. Prince, Mr N. S. C. Proctor, Mr P. Pyatt, Mr J. W. Reuter, A. Robinson, Mr J. Sanders, Mr A. Smallman, Mr J. J. R. Wadley, D. J. Wallis, Mr K. H. Weston, Wetherby Racing Bureau Ltd, Mr N. D. Whitham, Mrs P. H. Williams, Mrs C. S. Wilson.

Assistant Trainer: Rhys Hughes

Jockey (flat): Fergus Sweeney. **Jockey (NH):** Richard Johnson. **Conditional:** Michael Byrne. **Amateur:** Mr Matthew Barber, Mr Tom David, Mr Bradley Gibbs.

637　**MR CHRISTIAN VON DER RECKE, Weilerswist**
Postal: Rennstall Recke, Hovener Hof, D-53919, Weilerswist, Germany
Contacts: **PHONE** (0049) 2254 84 53 14 **FAX** (0049) 2254 845315 **MOBILE** (0049) 171 542 50 50
E-MAIL recke@t-online.de **WEBSITE** www.rennstall-recke.de

1 **AL MAMZAR (IRE)**, 4, b c Teofilo (IRE)—Avila **Frau R & A Hacker**
2 **AUENDANCER (GER)**, 6, b g Seattle Dancer (USA)—Auenburg (GER) **Stall Hasfeld**
3 **BAITSILEIR (IRE)**, 5, b g Bachelor Duke (USA)—Alamanta (IRE) **Stall Walcheren**
4 **BE MY LION (GER)**, 4, b c Areion (GER)—Boucheron (GER) **C. F. von der Recke**
5 **BIRTHDAY GUEST (GER)**, 4, ch c Areion (GER)—Birthday Spectrum (GER) **Stall Waldhaus**
6 **CAPE VIOLET (IRE)**, 4, b f Cape Cross (IRE)—Violet Ballerina (IRE) **C. F. von der Recke**
7 **CAPRICORNUS (USA)**, 6, ch g Rahy (USA)—Silent Partner (USA) **Frau L. Seiffert**
8 **CARA MIA (GER)**, 4, ch f Toylsome—Cordona (GER) **G. Schmitz**
9 **CHINK OF LIGHT**, 6, ch g Dr Fong (USA)—Isle of Flame **P. Vogt**
10 **CIOCCO SAM (GER)**, 5, b g Samum (GER)—Cioccolata (GER) **Stall Blankenese**
11 **CIOCCOMIA (GER)**, 4, bl f Samum (GER)—Cioccolata (GER) **Stall Blankenese**
12 **DANCING ALL NIGHT**, 5, b m Iceman—Sociable **A. Mulder**
13 **DARING RUDOLPH (GER)**, 6, b g Soviet Star (USA)—Delightful Sofie (GER) **Frau R & A Hacker**

MR CHRISTIAN VON DER RECKE - Continued

14 **DREAMSPEED (IRE)**, 6, b g Barathea (IRE)—Kapria (FR) **BMK Racing**
15 **DUBBURG (USA)**, 8, ch g Johannesburg (USA)—Plaisir Des Yeux (FR) **Stall Karlshorst**
16 **EARLSALSA (GER)**, 9, b g Kingsalsa (USA)—Earthly Paradise (GER) **Stall Blankenese**
17 **FASCINATING (IRE)**, 5, b g Cape Cross (IRE)—Something Exciting **Stall Chevalex**
18 **FIRST STREAM (GER)**, 9, ch g Lomitas—First Class (GER) **Stall Saarbrucken**
19 **GHAAYER (GER)**, 7, ch g Nayef (USA)—Valthea (FR) **Galopp Club Deutschland**
20 **HELGA (GER)**, 4, b f Lateral—Helgalill (IRE) **Stall Klosters-Serneus**
21 **INIKA (GER)**, 6, b m Dashing Blade—Ishika (GER) **Frau R & A Hacker**
22 **ISHAN (GER)**, 7, b g Sholokhov (IRE)—Ishika (GER) **Frau R & A Hacker**
23 **KONIGIN CONCORDIA (GER)**, 4, b f Big Shuffle (USA)—Konigin Set (GER) **Gestut Elsetal**
24 **LA NEXT (GER)**, 5, b m Next Desert (IRE)—La Constancia **Gestut Elsetal**
25 **LEMON DROP**, 4, b f Kallisto—Lam Love **G. Neu**
26 **LENNDORMANIK**, 5, b g Banyumanik—Lavinia **R. Reutershan**
27 **MECCA'S TEAM**, 5, ch m Ishiguru (USA)—Clancassie **Stall Fly Baby Fly**
28 **MISTOFFELEES**, 7, b g Tiger Hill (IRE)—Auenlust (GER) **EAR Racing**
29 **OASIS KNIGHT (IRE)**, 7, b g Oasis Dream—Generous Lady **Stall Chevalex**
30 **ODIT (GER)**, 4, br c Kallisto (GER)—Ordura (GER) **Stall Seeheim**
31 **ONE DAY SHADOW (GER)**, 4, b c Dai Jin—One Day Star (GER) **Stall Vier Pfoten**
32 **PEGASUS AGAIN (GER)**, 8, b g Fusaichi Pegasus (USA)—Chit Chatter (USA) **BMK Racing**
33 **PICCOLA (GER)**, 4, b f Mamool (IRE)—Pawella (GER) **Stall Seeheim**
34 **RED AVALANCHE (IRE)**, 6, gr g Verglas (IRE)—Maura's Guest (IRE) **R. J. Turton**
35 **SPARK (GER)**, 4, b g Nicaron (GER)—Song of Night (GER) **Stall Nizza**
36 **STORMY GLAZ (FR)**, 4, b g Stormy River (FR)—South Island (IRE) **Stall Karlshorst**
37 **TABLE MOUNTAIN (GER)**, 4, b f Nicaron (GER)—Templemore (GER) **Gestut Romerhof**
38 **TINLEY LODGE**, 4, b c Montjeu (IRE)—Shining Bright **Frau U & H Alck**

THREE-YEAR-OLDS

39 **ANIMA (GER)**, ch f Mamool (IRE)—Api Sa (IRE) **Stall Seeheim**
40 **CAFE AU LAIT (GER)**, b c Nicaron (GER)—Cariera (GER) **Stall Nizza**
41 **DOUBLE TROUBLE (GER)**, b f Liquido (GER)—Double Dagger Lady (USA) **Frau A. Lammertz**
42 **FEUERFUCHS (GER)**, b c Lord of England (GER)—Flair Sensation (GER) **Stall Blau-Weiss**
43 **I'M ON FIRE (GER)**, b f Shirocco (GER)—In My Heart (GER) **Stall Nizza**
44 **MAGIC DASH (GER)**, ch c Call Me Big—Magic Love **R. Reutershan**
45 **MANDARIN BAR**, b f Kyllachy—Lady Donatella **BMK Racing**
46 **PANESIDORA (GER)**, b f Soviet Star (USA)—Paradise Search (IRE) **M. E. Veeck**
47 **PICANTA (GER)**, b f Mamool (IRE)—Pawella (GER) **Stall Seeheim**
48 **RAVAISCH**, b c Kalatos—Rajputana **H F v.Hodenberg**
49 **RIBBERY (GER)**, b c Areion (GER)—Rosaly (GER) **Stall Lydien**
50 **TERRA BIG**, b c Call Me Big—Terra Novalis **R. Reutershan**

TWO-YEAR-OLDS

51 Ch c 1/1 Mamool—Api Sa **M. Buchner**
52 **BAVARIAN BEAUTY (GER)**, b f 29/4 Desert Prince (IRE)—Best Moving (GER) (Reset (AUS)) (4365) **M. E. Veeck**
53 **IGNAZ**, ch c 1/1 Peppercorn—Isi Going **P. Vogt**
54 **LADY KATE (GER)**, b f 2/4 Liquido (GER)—Lady Di (GER) (Samum (GER)) (2142) **Home Farm Racing**
55 B c 1/1 Mamool—Pawella **M. Buchner**
56 **PERFECT CARE (SWI)**, b c 16/2 Captain Rio—Perfectly Chilled (IRE) (Dalakhani (IRE)) **Stall Klosters-Serneus**
57 B f 1/1 Literato—Queen's Diamond **Quadriga**

---

638 MR JOHN WADE, Sedgefield
Postal: **Howe Hills, Mordon, Sedgefield, Cleveland, TS21 2HG**
Contacts: **PHONE (01740) 630310 FAX (01740) 630310 MOBILE (07831) 686968**

1 **AIAAM AL NAMOOS**, 4, b g Teofilo (IRE)—Deveron (USA) **J. Wade**
2 **ALWAYS RIGHT (IRE)**, 11, ch g Right Win (IRE)—Kemal Brave (IRE) **J. Wade**
3 **APACHE BLUE (IRE)**, 9, b g Presenting—La Eile (IRE) **J. Wade**
4 **ARROW BARROW (IRE)**, 8, b g Moscow Society (USA)—Miss Nee (IRE) **J. Wade**
5 **BEANEY TUNES**, 7, b g Central Park (IRE)—Fun While It Lasts **J. Wade**
6 **BEAU DANDY (IRE)**, 8, b br g Exit To Nowhere (USA)—Northern Dandy **J. Wade**
7 **BLAZING BULL (IRE)**, 9, b g Winged Love (IRE)—Our Buttons (IRE) **J. Wade**
8 **BOLT FROM THE BLUE**, 8, gr g Terimon—Den Is Over (IRE) **J. Wade**
9 **BOW BADGER**, 7, b g Sadler's Wells (USA)—Biloxi **J. Wade**
10 **CALL ME MULLIGAN (IRE)**, 9, ch g Bach (IRE)—They Call Me Molly (CAN) **J. Wade**

MR JOHN WADE - Continued

11 **CASUAL CAVALIER (IRE)**, 5, br g Presenting—Asklynn (IRE) **J. Wade**
12 **COLLEGE GREEN**, 6, b g Beat All (USA)—Velvet Leaf **J. Wade**
13 **COURT RED (IRE)**, 7, b g Court Cave (IRE)—An Bonnan Bui (IRE) **J. Wade**
14 **DESPERANTO (IRE)**, 7, b g Dushyantor (USA)—Desperado Dawn (IRE) **J. Wade**
15 **DIAMOND FRONTIER (IRE)**, 10, gr g Sadler's Wells (USA)—Diamond Line (FR) **J. Wade**
16 **DIAMOND NATIVE (IRE)**, 5, b g Alderbrook—Native Sylph (IRE) **J. Wade**
17 **DIGG WHITAKER (IRE)**, 4, b g Mounting Spendent—Function Dreamer **J. Wade**
18 **DINGO BAY**, 7, b g Karinga Bay—Do It On Dani **Miss M. D. Myco**
19 **DISSIDANCER (IRE)**, 5, b g Bishop of Cashel—Dancing At Lunasa (IRE) **J. Wade**
20 **DOOR BOY (IRE)**, 10, b br g Dr Massini (IRE)—Door Stopper (IRE) **J. Wade**
21 **EXOTIC MAN (FR)**, 8, ch g Arvico (FR)—Northine (FR) **J. Wade**
22 **FORTY CROWN (IRE)**, 7, b g Court Cave (IRE)—Forty Quid (IRE) **Miss M. D. Myco**
23 **GENERAL HARDI**, 12, b g In Command (IRE)—Hardiprincess **J. Wade**
24 **GLENCREE (IRE)**, 9, b g Presenting—Hidden Ability (IRE) **J. Wade**
25 **GRAND UNION (IRE)**, 9, b g Bob Back (USA)—Queens Mark (IRE) **J. Wade**
26 **HARRIS HAWK**, 8, b g Karinga Bay—Harristown Lady **J. Wade**
27 **INDIAN GROOM (IRE)**, 8, gr g High Chaparral (IRE)—Taatof (IRE) **J. Wade**
28 **IRISH BY NAME (IRE)**, 7, ch g Definite Article—Rosies All The Way **J. Wade**
29 **JAGO RIVER (IRE)**, 7, b g Milan—Light And Airy **J. Wade**
30 **JOKERS AND ROGUES (IRE)**, 5, b g Beneficial—Ashfield Girl (IRE) **J. Wade**
31 **JUKEBOX MELODY (IRE)**, 7, b g Brian Boru—Carmels Cottage (IRE) **J. Wade**
32 **LETTERPRESS (IRE)**, 9, b g King's Theatre—Empress of Light **J. Wade**
33 **MANNERED**, 8, b g Afflora (IRE)—Manettia (IRE) **J. Wade**
34 **MOMOTARO (IRE)**, 8, ch g Alderbrook—Gaye Diane **J. Wade**
35 **NEWSPAGE (IRE)**, 7, b g Blueprint (IRE)—Newlineview (IRE) **J. Wade**
36 **NO WAY HOZAY**, 7, b g Nomadic Way (USA)—Sweet Sensation **J. Wade**
37 **NOIR ANGELIS**, 6, b g Needle Gun (IRE)—Bubbling **J. Wade**
38 **NORTHERN CROSS (IRE)**, 9, br g Accordion—Gale Johnston (IRE) **J. Wade**
39 **OTTO QUERCUS (FR)**, 8, b g Saint Cyrien (FR)—La Haie Blanche (FR) **J. Wade**
40 **PUDSEY HOUSE**, 6, b g Double Trigger (IRE)—Dara's Pride (IRE) **J. Wade**
41 **QUEL BALLISTIC**, 9, b g Kayf Tara—Herballistic **J. Wade**
42 **RISKIER**, 8, gr g Kier Park (IRE)—Risky Girl **J. Wade**
43 **RIVER MUSIC (IRE)**, 8, b g Flemensfirth—Shean Bracken (IRE) **J. Wade**
44 **ROMANY RYME**, 7, ch g Nomadic Way (USA)—Rakaposhi Ryme (IRE) **J. Wade**
45 **ROSEVILLE COTTAGE (IRE)**, 6, b g Kris Kin (USA)—Johnny's Idea (IRE) **J. Wade**
46 **RUNSWICK RELAX**, 7, ch g Generous (IRE)—Zany Lady **J. Wade**
47 **SAGLIERE**, 8, gr g Sagamix (FR)—D'egliere (FR) **J. Wade**
48 **SITTING TENNANT**, 10, b g Erhaab (USA)—Aeolina (FR) **J. Wade**
49 **TAKAATUF (IRE)**, 7, b g Dubai Destination (USA)—Karlaka (IRE) **J. Wade**
50 **TARAS JOY (IRE)**, 8, b g Kayf Tara—Native Sylph (IRE) **J. Wade**
51 **TOPLANDER (IRE)**, 9, ch g Topanoora—Okeemo Hall (IRE) **J. Wade**
52 **TRIGGERS SUN**, 8, ch g Double Trigger (IRE)—Four Leaf Clover **J. Wade**
53 **TYRONE HOUSE (IRE)**, 9, b g Strategic Choice (USA)—Naughty Marietta (IRE) **J. Wade**
54 **VIKING CHIEF (IRE)**, 6, b g Westerner—Diamond Sal **J. Wade**
55 **WALSER (IRE)**, 6, b g Milan—Brass Neck (IRE) **J. Wade**
56 **WHATS UP WOODY (IRE)**, 8, b g Beneficial—Lady Noellel (IRE) **J. Wade**
57 **WOODY WALLER**, 8, ch g Lomitas—Reamzafonic **J. Wade**

Assistant Trainer: Miss Maria Myco (07798) 775932

Jockey (NH): Brian Hughes, Wilson Renwick, James Reveley. **Conditional:** John Dawson.

MRS LUCY WADHAM, Newmarket
Postal: **The Trainer's House, Moulton Paddocks, Newmarket, Suffolk, CB8 7PJ**
Contacts: **PHONE (01638) 662411 FAX (01638) 668821 MOBILE (07980) 545776**
E-MAIL lucy.wadham@virgin.net WEBSITE www.lucywadhamracing.co.uk

1 **ALL ANNALENA (IRE)**, 7, b m Dubai Destination (USA)—Alla Prima (IRE) **Mr & Mrs A. E. Pakenham**
2 **BABY SHINE (IRE)**, 7, b m King's Theatre (IRE)—
Brambleshine (IRE) **P.A. Philipps, T.S. Redman & Mrs L. Redman**
3 **BOLIVIA (GER)**, 7, ch m Monsun (GER)—Be My Lady (GER) **Mr & Mrs A. E. Pakenham**
4 **BRUNTON BLUE**, 8, b m Compton Place—Persian Blue **Mark Law**
5 **DALIANCE (IRE)**, 4, ch g Dalakhani (IRE)—Everlasting Love **Black Eyed Mara**
6 **DAWN TWISTER (GER)**, 6, br g Monsun (GER)—Dawn Side (CAN) **Mr R. Davies**

MRS LUCY WADHAM - Continued

7 **EL DANCER (GER)**, 9, b g Seattle Dancer (USA)—Elea (GER) **Mr R. Davies**
8 **ELEAZAR (GER)**, 12, b br g Alkalde (GER)—Eicidora (GER) **J. J. W. Wadham**
9 **EMPEROR CONCERTO**, 10, ch g Emperor Fountain—Busy Mittens **Ms K. J. Austin, J. J. W. Wadham**
10 **GENERAL TING (IRE)**, 8, b g Daylami (IRE)—Luana **The A. T. Partnership**
11 **HERON REEF (IRE)**, 7, b g Heron Island (IRE)—Catherinestown **J. J. W. Wadham**
12 **HORTENSE MANCINI**, 4, ch f King's Best (USA)—Have Fun **The Woughton Partnership**
13 **LE REVE (IRE)**, 5, b g Milan—Open Cry (IRE) **P. H. Betts**
14 **MANSHOOR (IRE)**, 8, gr g Linamix (FR)—Lady Wells (IRE) **Mr T. R. Wood**
15 **MIDNIGHT MACARENA**, 8, ch m Midnight Legend—Royal Tango **The Bees**
16 **MISTRAL REINE**, 4, b f King's Theatre (IRE)—Classic Gale (USA) **Mrs Sara Dennis, Dominic and Sarah Reilly**
17 **NOBLE SILK**, 4, gr g Sir Percy—Tussah **The Fops**
18 **PETERBROWN (IRE)**, 5, b g Shantou (USA)—Grove Juliet (IRE) **P. H. Betts**
19 **QUEEN AVALON**, 4, b f Overbury (IRE)—Newton Mo **Mr R. S. Keeley**
20 **RASHEED**, 5, b g Oasis Dream—Alexandrine (IRE) **Peter Howell & Richard S Keeley**
21 **RISING TEAL**, 4, b f Phoenix Reach (IRE)—Tealby **The Dyball Partnership**
22 **SONGSMITH**, 5, b g Librettist (USA)—Venus Rising **Team Supreme**
23 **SPYDER**, 5, b g Resplendent Glory (IRE)—Collect **Miss Christina Blockley**
24 **TEALISSIO**, 7, b g Helissio (FR)—Tealby **The Dyball Partnership**
25 **THE BLACK BARON (IRE)**, 11, br g Lord Americo—Royal Nora (IRE) **The Bees**
26 **TUSCANIA**, 5, b m King's Best (USA)—Contiguous (USA) **Mr & Mrs A. E. Pakenham**
27 **WATERED SILK**, 5, gr g Encosta de Lago (AUS)—Tussah **Mr & Mrs A. E. Pakenham**
28 **WIESENTRAUM (GER)**, 7, ch g Next Desert (IRE)—Wiesenblute (GER) **G. Pascoe & S. Brewer**

THREE-YEAR-OLDS

29 **NULLARBOR SKY (IRE)**, gr f Aussie Rules (USA)—Grenouillere (USA) **Mr T. R. Wood**
30 **PERNICA**, b f Sir Percy—Nicola Bella (IRE) **Mr & Mrs A. E. Pakenham**
31 **ZIGGY'S SECRET**, b f Sakhee's Secret—Ziggy Zaggy **Mr & Mrs A. E. Pakenham**

TWO-YEAR-OLDS

32 B f 25/2 Sir Percy—Bermondsey Girl (Bertolini (USA)) **The Fops**
33 B f 14/1 Sir Percy—Cartoon (Danehill Dancer (IRE)) **The Fops**
34 B f 7/3 Cape Cross (IRE)—Genoa (Zafonic (USA)) (6000)

Other Owners: Ms K. J. Austin, Mr S. J. Brewer, Mr D. J. S. Dyball, Mrs C. A. Dyball, Mrs Victoria Pakenham, Mr A. E. Pakenham, Mr G. J. Pascoe, Mr P. A. Philipps, Mr T. S. Redman, Mrs L. E. Redman, Mr Chris Smith, Mrs Lucy Wadham, Mr J. J. W. Wadham.

Jockey (NH): Leighton Aspell, Dominic Elsworth. **Amateur:** Mr Sam Davis.

---

640   MISS TRACY WAGGOTT, Spennymoor
Postal: **Awakening Stables, Merrington Lane, Spennymoor, Co. Durham, DL16 7HB**
Contacts: **PHONE (01388) 819012 MOBILE (07979) 434498**

1 **BORDER BANDIT (USA)**, 5, b g Selkirk (USA)—Coretta (IRE) **Elsa Crankshaw Gordon Allan**
2 **COPT HILL**, 5, b g Avonbridge—Lalique (IRE) **H. Conlon**
3 **DEAN IARRACHT (IRE)**, 7, b g Danetime (IRE)—Sirdhana **Mr M. J. Howarth**
4 **KING PIN**, 8, b g Pivotal—Danehurst **H. Conlon**
5 **MISS BOSSY BOOTS**, 4, b f Ishiguru (USA)—Mighty Flyer (IRE) **Mr D. Tate**
6 **MISSION IMPOSSIBLE**, 8, gr g Kyllachy—Eastern Lyric **H. Conlon**
7 **NO QUARTER (IRE)**, 6, b g Refuse To Bend (IRE)—Moonlight Wish (IRE) **Miss T. Waggott**
8 **PIVOTAL PROSPECT**, 5, b m Nayef (USA)—Buon Amici **Mr C. J. Allan**
9 **RIVER ARDECHE**, 8, b g Elnadim (USA)—Overcome **Littlethorpe Park Racing**
10 **RUNNING REEF (IRE)**, 4, b g Hurricane Run (IRE)—Half-Hitch (USA) **Elsa Crankshaw Gordon Allan**
11 **SHADOWTIME**, 8, b g Singspiel (IRE)—Massomah (USA) **H. Conlon**
12 **SINATRAMANIA**, 6, b g Dansili—Come Fly With Me **Miss T. Waggott**
13 **SOLAR SPIRIT (IRE)**, 8, b g Invincible Spirit (IRE)—Misaayef (USA) **Mr C. J. Allan**
14 **THRUST CONTROL (IRE)**, 6, ch g Fath—Anazah (USA) **Mr D. Tate**
15 **TUIBAMA (IRE)**, 4, ch g Bertolini (USA)—Supportive (IRE) **H. Conlon**
16 **WHISPERED TIMES (USA)**, 6, b br g More Than Ready (USA)—Lightning Show (USA) **Miss T. Waggott**

THREE-YEAR-OLDS

17 **DARKSIDE**, b g Indesatchel (IRE)—Romantic Destiny **Mr D. Tate**
18 **ONLINE**, b g Rail Link—Fairy Steps **Elsa Crankshaw Gordon Allan**

641 MR JOHN WAINWRIGHT, Malton
Postal: **Hanging Hill Farm, Kennythorpe, Malton, North Yorkshire, YO17 9LA**
Contacts: PHONE **(01653) 658537** FAX **(01653) 658658** MOBILE **(07798) 778070**
E-MAIL **jswainwright@googlemail.com**

1 AMERICAN LOVER (FR), 6, b m American Post—Lovarisk (FR) **P. W. Cooper**
2 BENIDORM, 5, b g Bahamian Bounty—Famcred **Miss J. M. Slater**
3 BLUE NOODLES, 7, b g Reset (AUS)—Gleam of Light (IRE) **drawn2win.co.uk Partnership**
4 BOUNTIFUL GIRL, 4, b f Bahamian Bounty—Cheeky Girl **Ms J. A. French**
5 EXIT TO FREEDOM, 7, ch g Exit To Nowhere (USA)—Bobanvi **Mrs F. J. Wainwright**
6 FROSTY BERRY, 4, gr f Proclamation (IRE)—Star Entry **Ms J. A. French**
7 KING OF WINDSOR (IRE), 6, b g Intikhab (USA)—Kismah **drawn2win.co.uk Partnership**
8 KURAANDA, 4, b f Kyllachy—Palm Cove (UAE) **drawn2win.co.uk Partnership**
9 MEDECIS MOUNTAIN, 4, b g Medecis—Moon Cat (IRE) **S. Enwright**
10 MEDIA JURY, 6, b g Lucky Owners (NZ)—Landofheartsdesire (IRE) **S. Enwright**
11 MERRJANAH, 5, b m Diktat—Aberdovey **Ms J. A. French**
12 ONIZ TIPTOES (IRE), 12, ch g Russian Revival (USA)—Edionda (IRE) **drawn2win.co.uk Partnership**
13 QUEEN'S PRINCESS, 5, b m Danbird (AUS)—Queen's Lodge (IRE) **Mr W. Bavill & Mr D. Bavill**

THREE-YEAR-OLDS
14 FOREST PHILLY (IRE), b f Moss Vale (IRE)—Red Beach (IRE) **P. Cooper**
15 KNOCKAMANY BENDS (IRE), b c Majestic Missile (IRE)—Sweet Compliance **D. R. & E. E. Brown**

TWO-YEAR-OLDS
16 B f 17/2 Misu Bond (IRE)—Morristown Music (IRE) (Distant Music (USA))

Other Owners: D. R. Brown, Mrs E. E. Brown, J. S. Wainwright, Mrs Fiona Wainwright, Mr P. R. Walker.

Assistant Trainer: Mrs Fiona Wainwright

Jockey (flat): Paddy Aspell, Tom Eaves, Tony Hamilton.

642 MR ROBERT WALEY-COHEN, Banbury
Postal: **Upton Viva, Banbury, Oxfordshire, OX15 6HT**
Contacts: PHONE **(02072) 446022** MOBILE **(07831) 888778**
E-MAIL **rwc@uptonviva.co.uk** WEBSITE **www.uptonestate.co.uk**

1 ASHTOWN BOY (IRE), 7, ch g Trans Island—Provacatrice (USA) **R. B. Waley-Cohen**
2 KATNAPPING, 5, br m Sleeping Car (FR)—Karolina (FR) **R. B. Waley-Cohen**
3 MANTON, 6, b br g Milan—Rachel C (IRE) **R. B. Waley-Cohen**
4 ROULEZ COOL, 10, b g Classic Cliche (IRE)—Makounji (FR) **R. B. Waley-Cohen**
5 RUMBAVU (IRE), 7, br g Overbury (IRE)—Strong Swimmer (IRE) **R. B. Waley-Cohen**

Assistant Trainer: Kate Mawle

Amateur: Mr S. Waley-Cohen.

643 MR ROBERT WALFORD, Blandford
Postal: **Heart of Oak Stables, Okeford Fitzpane, Blandford, Dorset, DT11 0LW**
Contacts: MOBILE **(07815) 116209**
E-MAIL **robert.walford@tesco.net**

1 AEGEAN DAWN, 8, b g Alflora (IRE)—Wychnor Dawn (IRE) **P. Murphy**
2 BRODY BLEU (FR), 6, b g Kotky Bleu (FR)—Brodie Blue (FR) **Mr R. J. Brown**
3 CAROLE'S SPIRIT, 5, b m Hernando (FR)—Carole's Crusader **P. Murphy**
4 EBBOR GORGE, 5, b g Septieme Ciel (USA)—Danse Slave (FR) **Mr E. W. White**
5 ITS APRIL, 5, b m Pasternak—Lorgnette **A. J. M. Trowbridge**
6 JOHNNY RED (IRE), 7, b g Anshan—Miss Faithlegg (IRE) **The White Hart Company**
7 JUST CLOUDY, 9, b g Cloudings (IRE)—Tycoon Tina **A. J. M. Trowbridge**
8 MOUNT GUNNERY, 5, b g Kayf Tara—Bobs Bay (IRE) **Clipper Group Holdings Ltd**
9 ROSA IMPERIALIS, 4, ch f Imperial Dancer—Motcombe **Lady N. F. Cobham**
10 UMBERTO D'OLIVATE (FR), 5, b g Alberto Giacometti (IRE)—Komunion (FR) **Mrs S. De Wilde**

Other Owners: Mr A. G. Ham.

644 MR TIM WALFORD, Sheriff Hutton
Postal: **Cornborough Manor, Sheriff Hutton, York, YO60 6QN**
Contacts: **PHONE (01347) 878382 FAX (01347) 878547 MOBILE (07904) 237676**
E-MAIL g_walford@hotmail.com WEBSITE www.timwalford.co.uk

1 BIG SOUND, 6, b g Supreme Sound—Tarbolton Moss **Mrs G. B. Walford**
2 BLUE TOP, 4, b g Millkom—Pompey Blue **Mr Brown, Evans, Lister, Cowley**
3 BRIGHT CLOUD (IRE), 8, gr m Cloudings (IRE)—Barton Gale (IRE) **Mrs M. Cooper**
4 FENTARA, 8, b m Kayf Tara—Miss Fencote **Chasing Gold Limited**
5 FLY BY KNIGHT, 4, b g Desert King (IRE)—Lox Lane (IRE) **Townroe & Mitchell**
6 FRANK'S FOLLY (IRE), 4, b g Tiger Hill (IRE)—Pocket Book (IRE) **Mrs F Horsfield, D Dickson & J Walford**
7 GRANWOOD, 7, ch m Midnight Legend—Half Each **Mrs C. A. Watson**
8 HIGHLANDER TED, 5, b g Midnight Legend—Half Each **Mrs C. A. Watson**
9 HONEYPOT LANE, 6, b g Slip Anchor—Lyra **Richard Adcock Joe Grindal & Nigel Skinner**
10 KEYHOLE KATE, 4, b f Kheleyf (USA)—Striking Pose (IRE) **Walford, Agran, Ellis & Silver**
11 KING OF STRINGS (IRE), 4, b g Desert King (IRE)—Lemon Cello (IRE) **Mrs E. Holmes**
12 LETS BE ON, 6, ch m Silver Patriarch (IRE)—Gotogeton **Mrs G. B. Walford**
13 MEDIEVAL BISHOP (IRE), 4, b g Bachelor Duke (USA)—
                          On The Backfoot (IRE) **K Hamilton, D Dickson, N Skinner**
14 MIGHTAVAGO, 4, b g Sir Harry Lewis (USA)—Cashel Dancer **Mr K. Hanson**
15 MR SNOOZY, 4, b g Pursuit of Love—Hard To Follow **T. W. Heseltine**
16 NORTHERN OSCAR (IRE), 5, b g Oscar (IRE)—Cailin's Princess (IRE) **Allott Bowler Roberts Stanser Gittus**
17 SHIMLA DAWN (IRE), 5, b g Indian Danehill (IRE)—Tina Thyne (IRE) **Mrs M. Cooper**
18 TAMANACO (IRE), 6, b g Catcher In The Rye (IRE)—Right After Moyne (IRE) **Mr A. J. Hulme**
19 UNO VALOROSO (FR), 5, b g Voix du Nord (FR)—Danse d'avril (FR) **Mr C. N. Herman**
20 ZEFOOHA (FR), 9, ch m Lomitas—Bezzaaf **Mr S. Conway**

THREE-YEAR-OLDS
21 HOLLOW BEAT, b f Beat Hollow—Sing For Fame (USA) **Mr A. K. Quirke**
22 THE MIGHTY PEG, b g Mujadil (USA)—Messina (IRE) **Mr A. J. Hulme**

TWO-YEAR-OLDS
23 Ch f 29/4 Camacho—Alwyda (USA) (Trempolino (USA)) (1586) **Mrs G. B. Walford**
24 CRAGGAKNOCK, b c 1/3 Authorized (IRE)—Goodie Twosies (Fraam) (32000) **Mrs M. Longstaff**
25 SIRPERTAN, b c 22/1 Sir Percy—Tanwir (Unfuwain (USA)) (28000) **Mr S. Woodall**

Other Owners: R. J. Adcock, N. N. Agran, Mr J. Allott, Mr J. Bowler, Mr M. D. Brown, Lady N. F. Cobham, Mr E. J. Cowley, D. J. Dickson, Mr C. F. J. Ellis, Mr C. E. Evans, Miss J. L. Gittus, C. J. Grindal, Mrs J. Hamilton, Mr K. Hamilton, Mrs F. Horsfield, Miss R. Lister, P. McMahon, Dr J. C. Mitchell, Mr A. Pegler, M. G. Roberts, P. Scholes, M. J. Silver, N. Skinner, Mr M. T. Stanser, Mrs C. Townroe, Mr J. Walford.

Assistant Trainer: Mark Walford

Jockey (flat): Graham Gibbons.

645 MR ED WALKER, Newmarket
Postal: **Grange House Stables, Hamilton Road, Newmarket, CB8 0TE**
Contacts: **MOBILE (07787) 534145**
E-MAIL ed@edwalkerracing.com WEBSITE www.edwalkerracing.com

1 ANYA, 4, b f Monsieur Bond (IRE)—Dyanita **Mrs Linda Alexander**
2 AXIOM, 9, ch g Pivotal—Exhibitor (USA) **S. Al Ansari**
3 DUKE OF DESTINY (IRE), 4, br g Bachelor Duke (USA)—Marghelan (FR) **Dubai Thoroughbred Racing**
4 EIGHTY EIGHT RED, 4, ch g Dubawi (IRE)—Half Past Twelve (USA) **Mrs M. Campbell-Andenaes**
5 HIGH NET WORTH, 4, b c Oasis Dream—Return (USA) **P S Racing**
6 INDIAN JACK (IRE), 5, ch g Indian Haven—Almaviva (GER) **Forza Azzurri**
7 LIVIA'S DREAM (IRE), 4, b f Teofilo (IRE)—Brindisi **Mrs O. Hoare**
8 MORINDA, 4, b f Selkirk (USA)—Morning Queen (GER) **Mrs M. Campbell-Andenaes**
9 NICHOLASCOPERNICUS (IRE), 4, ch g Medicean—Ascendancy **Greenwood, Halsall and Pegum**
10 RUSCELLO (IRE), 4, b g Cape Cross (IRE)—Sea Picture (IRE) **L. A. Bellman**
11 WILLIE WAG TAIL (USA), 4, b g Theatrical—Night Risk (USA) **Qatar Racing Limited**

MR ED WALKER - Continued

THREE-YEAR-OLDS

12 **ABLE DASH**, ch g Dutch Art—Evasive Quality (FR) **Dr Cornel Li**
13 **CARNEADES (IRE)**, b c Exceed And Excel (AUS)—Ivy League Star (IRE) **S. Manana**
14 **DARING DRAGON**, gr g Intikhab (USA)—The Manx Touch (IRE) **Ms A. A. Yap**
15 **GLORIOUS PROTECTOR (IRE)**, b c Azamour (IRE)—Hasaiyda (IRE) **Ms A. A.Yap**
16 **GLORIOUS STAR (IRE)**, ch g Soviet Star (USA)—Caerlonore (IRE) **Ms A. A. Yap**
17 **HARD RUN (USA)**, b c Cherokee Run (USA)—Meniatarra (USA) **K. A. Dasmal**
18 **INDIAN TRIFONE (IRE)**, ch c Indian Haven—Almaviva (IRE) **Forza Azzurri**
19 **LIGHT ECHO**, b f Echo of Light—Inishdalla (IRE) **Sheikh J. Al Dalmook Maktoum**
20 **MEMORIZE (IRE)**, b g Dark Angel (IRE)—Cape Cod (IRE) **L. A. Bellman**
21 **MEMPHIS MAGIC (GER)**, b g Tertullian (USA)—Maltage (USA) **One Carat Partnership**
22 **PAELLA (IRE)**, b f Oasis Dream—Chibola (ARG) **Mrs James Wigan**
23 **SAN GABRIEL (IRE)**, b c Soviet Star (USA)—Rancho Cucamonga (IRE) **S. Manana**
24 **SOUND OF GUNS**, b f Acclamation—Eastern Lily (USA) **Mr Howard. J. A. Russell**
25 **SURGE AHEAD (IRE)**, b c Danehill Dancer (USA)—Croisiere (USA) **K. A. Dasmal**
26 **YOU'RE THE BOSS**, b c Royal Applause—Trinny **L. A. Bellman**

TWO-YEAR-OLDS

27 Gr f 7/4 Mastercraftsman (IRE)—Amathia (IRE) (Darshaan) (160000) **Chasemore Stud**
28 **AYA'S GIFT**, ch c 2/2 Compton Place—Ringarooma (Erhaab (USA)) (40000) **K. A. Dasmal**
29 B c 9/3 Tamayuz—Beat The Rain (Beat Hollow) (22857) **De La Warr Racing**
30 B c 3/2 Notnowcato—Blaenavon (Cadeaux Genereux) (34000) **Sheikh J. Al Dalmook Maktoum**
31 B c 5/4 Oratorio (IRE)—Bronze Star (Mark of Esteem (IRE)) (20000) **Benatom Racing 2**
32 **FRESH AND FRESH**, b c 5/3 Medicean—Red Blossom (Green Desert (USA)) (40000) **Mr W. T. Cheng**
33 **FRESH KINGDOM (IRE)**, ch c 17/4 Dubawi (IRE)—Polyquest (IRE) (Poliglote) (75000) **Mr W. T. Cheng**
34 **FULL MOON FEVER (IRE)**, b f 8/3 Azamour (IRE)—
    Hasaiyda (IRE) (Hector Protector (USA)) (9523) **Bellman, Donald, Walker & Walker**
35 **GLORIOUS EMPIRE (IRE)**, br c 5/2 Holy Roman Emperor (IRE)—
    Humble And Proud (IRE) (Pivotal) (90000) **Ms A. A. Yap**
36 Ch c 17/2 Giant's Causeway (USA)—Gossamer (USA) (Seattle Slew (USA)) (126983) **Marc Keller**
37 **GRACEFILLY**, b f 27/4 Invincible Spirit (IRE)—
    Marula (IRE) (Sadler's Wells (USA)) (60000) **Mr Laurence Bellman**
38 **HOPEFILLY (IRE)**, b f 25/3 Compton Place—Kondakova (IRE) (Soviet Star (USA)) (9523) **L. A. Bellman**
39 **INCREDIBLE FRESH (IRE)**, b c 12/4 Bushranger (IRE)—Red Fox (Spectrum (IRE)) (70000) **Mr W. T. Cheng**
40 **INVINCIBLE FRESH (IRE)**, b c 23/2 Footstepsinthesand—
    Princess Serena (USA) (Unbridled's Song (USA)) (80000) **Mr W. T. Cheng**
41 B c 15/3 Bushranger (IRE)—Lady Lucia (IRE) (Royal Applause) (60000) **L. A. Bellman**
42 B f 18/3 Bahamian Bounty—Loveleaves (Polar Falcon (USA)) (24000) **Mr Brandon Lui**
43 B c 4/3 Myboycharlie (IRE)—Madam President (Royal Applause) (42000) **Saeed Manana**
44 B f 6/2 Invincible Spirit (IRE)—Madura (GER) (Dashing Blade) (50000) **Saeed Manana**
45 B c 5/3 Notnowcato—Meredith (Medicean) (30000) **Al Ansari, Greenwood, Pegum**
46 B c 4/5 Pastoral Pursuits—Messelina (Noverre (USA)) (38000) **Saeed Manana**
47 B c 16/2 Royal Applause—Naizak (Medicean) (55000) **Mr Brandon Lui**
48 **OUTLAWED**, b c 24/2 Kyllachy—Regent's Park (Green Desert (USA)) (52000) **L. A. Bellman**
49 B c 12/4 Selkirk (USA)—Starlit Sands (Oasis Dream) (70000) **Saif Ali**
50 Ch c 7/3 Dutch Art—Stravie (IRE) (Stravinsky (USA)) (85000) **Mr Ching Fat Ma**
51 B c 11/4 Medicean—Sweet Cando (IRE) (Royal Applause) (50000) **Ms A. A. Yap**
52 **TWENTY ROSES (IRE)**, b f 5/2 Mastercraftsman (IRE)—
    Stunning Rose (IRE) (Sadler's Wells (USA)) (107142) **Highland Yard LLC**
53 B c 19/1 Tiger Hill (IRE)—Valoria (Hernando (FR)) **Mt Stuart Stuckey**
54 Ch c 16/2 Mount Nelson—White Dress (IRE) (Pivotal) (40000) **John Nicholls (Trading) Ltd**
55 **XANTHOS**, ch c 12/3 Medicean—My Girl Jode (Haafhd) (19047) **Mr M. J. Cottis**

Other Owners: Mr Philip Corbisiero, Mr Alastair Donald, Mr P Gleeson, Mr B. Greenwood, Mr Alan Halsall, Mr J. G. Moore, Mr R. Pegum, Mr Onofrio Tona, Mr E. C. D. Walker, Mrs T. Walker.

---

646 **MR CHRIS WALL, Newmarket**
Postal: **Induna Stables, Fordham Road, Newmarket, Suffolk, CB8 7AQ**
Contacts: **OFFICE (01638) 661999 HOME (01638) 668896 FAX (01638) 667279**
MOBILE (07764) 940255
E-MAIL christianwall@btconnect.com WEBSITE www.chriswallracing.co.uk

1 **ALECO**, 4, b g Sakhee (USA)—Vanishing Point (USA) **Ms Aida Fustoq**

MR CHRIS WALL - Continued

2 **BASSARA (IRE)**, 4, b f Oasis Dream—Sauvage (FR) **Ms Aida Fustoq**
3 **CHARITY BOX**, 4, b f Haafhd—Bible Box (IRE) **Mr John E. Sims & Mr M. Sinclair**
4 **CITRUS STAR (USA)**, 6, b g Broken Vow (USA)—Twist a Lime (USA) **Induna Racing Partners (Two)**
5 **CURLY COME HOME**, 4, b f Notnowcato—Cuyamaca (IRE) **The Hut Partnership**
6 **FOOT TAPPER**, 4, b c Invincible Spirit (IRE)—Jazz Princess (IRE) **Howlett, Norden & Westley**
7 **INTENSE PINK**, 4, b f Pivotal—Clincher Club **Mr D. S. Lee**
8 **LANGHAM LILY (USA)**, 4, b br f Badge of Silver (USA)—Silver Frau (USA) **P. J. W. Botham**
9 **MIDNIGHT RIDER (IRE)**, 5, b g Red Ransom (USA)—Foreplay (IRE) **The Leap Year Partnership**
10 **NO JUSTICE**, 5, b g Authorized (IRE)—Regrette Rien (USA) **Ms Aida Fustoq**
11 **OH SO SPICY**, 6, ch m Pastoral Pursuits—Almasi (IRE) **The Eight of Diamonds**
12 **PEARL BLUE (IRE)**, 5, b m Exceed And Excel (AUS)—Sanfrancullinan (IRE) **Archangels 2**
13 **PREMIO LOCO (USA)**, 9, ch g Prized (USA)—Crazee Mental **Mr Bernard Westley**
14 **QANAN**, 4, b g Green Desert (USA)—Strings **Alan & Jill Smith**
15 **ROYAL ROCK**, 9, b g Sakhee (USA)—Vanishing Point (USA) **Ms Aida Fustoq**
16 **SILVER LACE (IRE)**, 4, br gr f Clodovil (IRE)—Rockahoolababy (IRE) **The Equema Partnership**
17 **SNOW HILL**, 5, gr g Halling (USA)—Swift Dispersal **Mollers Racing**
18 **ZE KING**, 4, b g Manduro (GER)—Top Flight Queen **Ms Aida Fustoq**

THREE-YEAR-OLDS

19 **BALLYSHONAGH**, b f Tiger Hill (IRE)—Shamara (IRE) **Lady Juliet Tadgell**
20 **BLESSING BOX**, b f Bahamian Bounty—Bible Box (IRE) **M. Sinclair**
21 **EMERALD SEA**, b f Green Desert (USA)—Wind Surf (USA) **Lady Juliet Tadgell & Major M. G. Wyatt**
22 **FIRST PENINSULAR**, ch c Excellent Art—Sarah's First **Mollers Racing**
23 **GOOD AS NEW**, b f Araafa (IRE)—New Design (IRE) **Lady Juliet Tadgell**
24 **GRAVITATIONAL (IRE)**, b g Invincible Spirit (IRE)—Flower of Kent (USA) **Mr D. Gilbert**
25 **MEET ME HALFWAY**, b f Exceed And Excel (AUS)—Pivotal Drive (IRE) **Mr Des Thurlby**
26 **NEVER TOO MUCH (IRE)**, b c Johannesburg (USA)—Muskoka Dawn (USA) **Mr D. S. Lee**
27 **OH SO SASSY**, b f Pastoral Pursuits—Almasi (IRE) **The Eight of Diamonds**
28 **PEARL QUEEN (USA)**, b br f Street Sense (USA)—Island Queen (USA) **Pearl Bloodstock Limited**
29 **POSH BOY (IRE)**, b g Duke of Marmalade (IRE)—Sauvage (FR) **Mr D. M. Thurlby**
30 **RAINBOWS AND ROSES**, ch f Beat Hollow—Rainbow Sky **Follow The Flag Partnership**
31 **RAVENSBURG**, ch f Raven's Pass (USA)—Generous Lady **Ms Aida Fustoq**
32 **ROCKSILLA**, b f Rock of Gibraltar (IRE)—Hope Island (IRE) **Moyns Park Estate and Stud Ltd**
33 **RUNNINGLIKETHEWIND (IRE)**, b g Hurricane Run (IRE)—Virgin Hawk (USA) **Mr D. M. Thurlby**
34 **SILVALA DANCE**, b f Kyllachy—Bride of The Sea **Mrs D. Lochhead**
35 **SMART ALICE**, b f Soviet Star (USA)—Ailincala (IRE) **Racingeight Partners**
36 **SWITCH ON**, b c Oasis Dream—Noodle Soup (USA) **Ms Aida Fustoq**
37 **THOUSAND KISSES**, b f Authorized (IRE)—Trinkila (USA) **Mr D. S. Lee**
38 **TIGER JIM**, b g Tiger Hill (IRE)—Quintrell **Follow The Flag Partnership**
39 **TRUCANINI**, b f Mount Nelson—Jalissa (USA) **Dolly's Dream Syndicate**
40 **VANDROSS (IRE)**, b g Iffraaj—Mrs Kanning **Mr D. S. Lee**

TWO-YEAR-OLDS

41 **BURMESE BREEZE**, b g 2/4 Shirocco (GER)—Crimson Topaz (Hernando (FR)) (30000) **Mr Des Thurlby**
42 **ELEUSIS**, b f 20/4 Elnadim (USA)—Demeter (USA) (Diesis) **Lady Juliet Tadgell**
43 **JOHARA (IRE)**, b f 11/4 Iffraaj—Hurricane Irene (IRE) (Green Desert (USA)) (22000) **Mrs Claude Lilley**
44 B c 17/4 Teofilo (IRE)—Kalagold (IRE) (Magical Strike (USA)) (38000) **Mr D. S. Lee**
45 **MAY QUEEN**, ch f 21/4 Shamardal (USA)—Mango Lady (Dalakhani (IRE)) **Ms Aida Fustoq**
46 **QUEEN OF THE NILE**, b f 4/5 Sakhee (USA)—Vanishing Point (USA) (Cailer I D (USA)) **Ms Aida Fustok**
47 **SYRIAN PEARL**, b gr f 29/3 Clodovil (IRE)—Syrian Queen (Slip Anchor) (15000) **The Clodhoppers**
48 **THE NEW PHARAOH (IRE)**, b c 8/3 Montjeu (IRE)—Out West (USA) (Gone West (USA)) **Ms Aida Fustoq**

Other Owners: Mr T. J. Bater, Mr David Cherry, Mrs J. E. Dobie, Mr S. Feast, Mr R. Fraiser, Mr P Hitchcock, Mr Don Howlett, Mrs E. J. Kerr-Smiley, Mr Roger Nash, Mr Richard Norden, Mr D. Popely, Mr R. A. Popely, Mr Ian Radford, Mr A. Reeve, Mr Ray Rice, Prudence, Lady Salt, Mrs M. Shawsmith, Mr John E. Sims, Lady Stuttaford, Mrs C. A. Wall, Mr R. J. Wayman, Mrs P. Williams.

Assistant Trainer: Richard Freeman

Jockey (flat): George Baker, Ted Durcan.

647 **MRS SARAH WALL, Dallington**
Postal: **Little Pines, Bakers Lane, Dallington, Heathfield, East Sussex, TN21 9JS**
Contacts: **PHONE/FAX (01435) 831048 MOBILE (07783) 370856**
E-MAIL sarah55french@btinternet.com

1 BACH TO FRONT (IRE), 8, b m Bach (IRE)—Celtic Leader (IRE) **J. P. C. Wall**
2 BALLINHASSIG (IRE), 8, ch g Beneficial—Dear Polly (IRE) **Mrs S. Wall**
3 TIGRIDIA (IRE), 6, br m Brian Boru—Indian Legend (IRE) **Mrs S. Wall**

Assistant Trainer: Jeremy Wall

648 **MR TREVOR WALL, Church Stretton**
Postal: **Harton Manor, Harton, Church Stretton, Shropshire, SY6 7DL**
Contacts: **PHONE (01694) 724144 FAX (01694) 724144 MOBILE (07972) 732080**

1 DESERT FAIRY, 7, b m Tobougg (IRE)—Regal Fairy (IRE) **A. H. Bennett**
2 ECHO DANCER, 7, br g Danehill Dancer (IRE)—Entail (USA) **The Wenlock Edge Optimists**
3 FAIRY ALISHA, 5, ch m Doyen (IRE)—Regal Fairy (IRE) **Moorland Racing**
4 4, Ch f Needwood Blade—Lola Lola (IRE) **T. R. Wall**
5 5, B g Sulamani (IRE)—Margarets Wish **A. H. Bennett**
6 NGINA, 5, b m Iceman—Nairobi (FR)

Other Owners: J. D. Evans, S. A. Mace, Mrs A. M. Mace.

Assistant Trainer: Mrs J. A. Wall

Conditional: Josh Wall.

649 **MR JAMES WALTON, Morpeth**
Postal: **Flotterton Hall, Thropton, Morpeth, Northumberland, NE65 7LF**
Contacts: **PHONE (01669) 640253 FAX (01669) 640288 MOBILE (07808) 592701**

1 CENTRAL FLAME, 5, ch g Central Park (IRE)—More Flair **Messrs F. T. Walton**
2 COQUET HEAD, 7, br g Alflora (IRE)—Coquet Gold **Messrs F. T. Walton**
3 HIGHLAND CATHEDRAL, 9, ch g Minster Son—Celtic Waters **Messrs F. T. Walton**
4 JOB FOR ERIC, 6, b g Bollin Eric—Gone Astray **Messrs F. T. Walton**
5 MERRY MIX, 5, br m Fair Mix (IRE)—Merry Tina **Messrs F. T. Walton**
6 RETRACE YOUR STEPS, 6, b m Danroad (AUS)—Candida Casa **Messrs F. T. Walton**
7 RUPERT BEAR, 7, b g Rambling Bear—Glittering Stone **Messrs F. T. Walton**
8 SACRED MOUNTAIN, 12, b g Primitive Rising (USA)—Gone Astray **Messrs F. T. Walton**
9 SADDLE PACK (IRE), 10, b g Saddlers' Hall (IRE)—Zuhal **Messrs F. T. Walton**

Other Owners: J. B. Walton, F. A. Walton.

650 **MRS JANE WALTON, Otterburn**
Postal: **Dunns Houses, Otterburn, Newcastle Upon Tyne, Tyne and Wear, NE19 1LB**
Contacts: **PHONE (01830) 520677 FAX (01830) 520677 MOBILE (07808) 592701**
E-MAIL dunnshouses@hotmail.com WEBSITE www.janewaltonhorseracing.co.uk

1 CHARMING KNIGHT (IRE), 12, b g Mohaajir (USA)—Arctic Laura **Mrs J. M. Walton**
2 HAVE YOU HAD YOURS (IRE), 7, br g Whitmore's Conn (USA)—
Mandys Moynavely (IRE) **Highly Recommended Partnership**
3 MASTER MURPHY (IRE), 8, b g Flemensfirth (USA)—Awbeg Beauty (IRE) **Mrs J. M. Walton**
4 SUN LADY (FR), 7, b m Rifapour (FR)—Vousseliere (FR) **Mr G. A. Smith**
5 SUNARRI (IRE), 9, b g Sonus (IRE)—Rosearro (IRE) **Fresh Start Partnership**

Other Owners: Mrs L. Duncan, Mr John McCreanor, Mrs M. Ridley, Miss J. Rutherford, Mr G. Smith, Mrs J. M. Walton.

Assistant Trainer: Mrs Patricia Robson

Jockey (NH): Alistair Findlay.

651 MRS SHEENA WALTON, Hexham
Postal: **Linacres, Wark, Hexham, Northumberland, NE48 3DP**
Contacts: **PHONE (01434) 230656 MOBILE (07752) 755184**
E-MAIL rchrdwltn@aol.com

1 DYSTONIA'S REVENGE (IRE), 8, b g Woods of Windsor (USA)—Lady Isaac (IRE) **Mr J. L. Blacklock**
2 KANE RIVER (IRE), 7, gr g Tikkanen (USA)—Barnish River (IRE) **Linacres Racing Partnership**
3 NATIVE OPTIMIST (IRE), 6, b g Broadway Flyer (USA)—Native Orchid (IRE) **Rede Tyne Racing**

Other Owners: Mr T. Rand, Mrs M. Rogerson, R. H. Walton.

Assistant Trainer: Mr R. H. Walton

652 MR JASON WARD, Middleham
Postal: **The Dante Yard, Manor House Stables, Middleham, Leyburn, North Yorkshire, DL8 4QL**
Contacts: **PHONE (01969) 622730 MOBILE (07967) 357595**
E-MAIL info@jasonwardracing.co.uk WEBSITE www.jasonwardracing.co.uk

1 BRIDGE VALLEY, 6, ch g Avonbridge—Go Between **Pear Tree Partnership**
2 CLOUDS OF GLORY, 4, b f Resplendent Glory (IRE)—Rosewings **Miss V. Pratt**
3 EASTWARD HO, 5, ch g Resplendent Glory (IRE)—Mofeyda (IRE) **Miss V. Pratt**
4 GLADSOME, 5, b m Resplendent Glory (IRE)—Christening (IRE) **Miss V. Pratt**
5 HEROSTATUS, 6, ch g Dalakhani (IRE)—Desired **Mr R. Naylor**
6 HOPE FOR GLORY, 4, b g Proclamation (IRE)—Aissa **Mr C. Tateson**
7 KUWAIT STAR, 4, ch g Resplendent Glory (IRE)—Mofeyda (IRE) **Miss V. Pratt**
8 MORNA'S GLORY, 4, b f Resplendent Glory (IRE)—Tipsy Cake **Miss V. Pratt**
9 ROMANTICIZE, 7, b m Kyllachy—Romancing **Miss V. Pratt**
10 SWEETNESSANDLIGHT, 4, b f Aussie Rules—Taschlynn (IRE) **Mrs Jill Ward**
11 TREASON TRIAL, 12, b g Peintre Celebre (USA)—Pampabella (IRE) **Mr & Mrs W. H. Woods**
12 YPRES, 4, b g Byron—Esligier (IRE) **Pear Tree Partnership**

TWO-YEAR-OLDS
13 BAHAMA DANCER, ch f 21/5 Bahamian Bounty—
Arlene Phillips (Groom Dancer (USA)) (1800) **Mr A. Catterall & Mr B. Harker**
14 HELLO SWEETNESS, b f 16/3 Aqlaam—Atnab (USA) (Riverman (USA)) (952)
15 PACARAMA, b f 20/4 Avonbridge—Skirt Around (Deploy) (952) **Mr Geoff Holgate**

Other Owners: Mr P. Adams, Mr R. Briggs, Mr & Mrs McDonald, Mr M. Smith, Mr C. J. Teal, Mr J. Teal, Mr C. Teal, Mr M. Walmsley, Mrs Jill Ward.

Assistant Trainer: Tim Ward

Jockey (flat): Kieren Fallon, Tony Hamilton. **Apprentice:** Kieran Schofield.

653 MR FREDERICK WATSON, Sedgefield
Postal: **Beacon Hill, Sedgefield, Stockton-On-Tees, Cleveland, TS21 3HN**
Contacts: **PHONE (01740) 620582 MOBILE (07773) 321472**
E-MAIL fredwatson@talktalk.net

1 BILLY REDPATH, 5, b g Distant Music (USA)—Shardda **Mr B. Emery**
2 CARA'S DELIGHT (AUS), 6, b m Fusaichi Pegasus (USA)—Carahill (AUS) **Mr B. Emery**
3 CONJUROR'S BLUFF, 5, b h Tiger Hill (IRE)—Portmeirion **F. Watson**
4 DESTINATION AIM, 6, b g Dubai Destination (USA)—Tessa Reef (IRE) **F. Watson**
5 SPOKESPERSON (USA), 5, b h Henny Hughes (USA)—Verbal (USA) **F. Watson**
6 UNDER AMBITION, 5, b m Striking Ambition—Understudy **F. Watson**

654 MRS SHARON WATT, Richmond
Postal: **Rosey Hill Farm, Scorton Road, Brompton on Swale, Richmond, North Yorkshire, DL10 7EQ**
Contacts: **PHONE (01748) 812064 FAX (01748) 812064 MOBILE (07970) 826046**
E-MAIL wattfences@aol.com

1 ALLORA FLORA, 5, b m Alflora (IRE)—Pequenita **J. A. & M. A. Knox & C. Scollay**

MRS SHARON WATT - Continued

2 **JEWELLED DAGGER (IRE)**, 9, b g Daggers Drawn (USA)—Cappadoce (IRE) **Major E.J. Watt**
3 **LERIDA**, 11, ch g Groom Dancer (USA)—Catalonia (IRE) **Famous Five Racing**
4 **MADAM LILIBET (IRE)**, 4, b f Authorized (IRE)—Foxilla (IRE) **D. H. Montgomerie**
5 **VODKA MOON**, 4, gr g Beat All (USA)—Auntie Kathleen **Mrs S. A. Watt & Mrs G. Handley**

TWO-YEAR-OLDS

6 Gr c 24/2 Aussie Rules (USA)—Garabelle (IRE) (Galileo (IRE)) (4761)
7 B f 23/4 Virtual—Maidford (IRE) (Singspiel (IRE))
8 B f 27/3 Jeremy (USA)—Passionforfashion (IRE) (Fasliyev (USA)) (9523)

Jockey (NH): Keith Mercer. **Conditional:** Joseph Palmowski.

---

655 MR SIMON WAUGH, Morpeth
Postal: **Molesden House, Molesden, Morpeth, Northumberland, NE61 3QF**
Contacts: **MOBILE (07860) 561445**
E-MAIL swaugh@dircon.co.uk

1 **AW RIPE CHINA (IRE)**, 5, b g Bach (IRE)—Karolena Bay **S. G. Waugh**
2 **NEWYEARSRESOLUTION (IRE)**, 9, b g Mr Combustible (IRE)—That's Magic (IRE) **S. G. Waugh**
3 **REAR VIEW (IRE)**, 6, b g Alhaarth (IRE)—Sadinga (IRE) **S. G. Waugh**
4 **TOTAL ASSETS**, 5, b m Alflora (IRE)—Maid Equal **S. G. Waugh**

---

656 MISS AMY WEAVER, Newmarket
Postal: **Green Lodge, Severals, Newmarket, Suffolk, CB8 7BS**
Contacts: **MOBILE (07947) 442083**
E-MAIL amy@amyweaverracing.com WEBSITE www.amyweaverracing.com

1 **CARINYA (IRE)**, 5, br m Iffraaj—Ma N'ieme Biche (USA) **Mr R. M. Boyd**
2 **CHAIN REACTOR**, 7, b g Hamas (IRE)—Rose Tina **M. C. Denmark**
3 **DEN OF INIQUITY**, 12, b g Supreme Leader—Divine Comedy (IRE) **M. C. Denmark**
4 **JULIUS GEEZER (IRE)**, 5, b g Antonius Pius (USA)—Victoria's Secret (IRE) **Wildcard Racing Syndicate**
5 **MARFORD MISSILE (IRE)**, 4, b g Majestic Missile (IRE)—Khawafi **Wildcard Racing Syndicate**
6 **PACIFIC RIDGE (USA)**, 4, b br c Gone West (USA)—National Pastime (USA) **Mr Michael Bringloe**
7 **SANDY LANE (IRE)**, 4, b g Elusive City (USA)—Ipanema Beach **Mr C. P. White**
8 **YOU'RE SO VAIN**, 10, b g Silver Patriarch (IRE)—Gaye Mercy **M. C. Denmark**

THREE-YEAR-OLDS

9 **HAMMER SHAFT (IRE)**, b g Excellent Art—Delicacy (IRE) **Mr R. Davison**
10 **MARCHWOOD**, b g Assertive—Reeli Silli **Wildcard Racing Syndicate**
11 **PRINCE RAKAN (USA)**, b c Proud Citizen (USA)—Yousefia (USA) **Mr D. Al Ajmi**

TWO-YEAR-OLDS

12 B f 16/4 Lucky Story (USA)—Applesnap (IRE) (Clodovil (IRE)) **Mr Michael Bringloe**

---

657 MR PAUL WEBBER, Banbury
Postal: **Cropredy Lawn, Mollington Road, Cropredy, Banbury, Oxfordshire, OX17 1DR**
Contacts: **PHONE (01295) 750226 FAX (01295) 758482 MOBILE (07836) 232465**
E-MAIL paul@paulwebberracing.com WEBSITE www.paulwebberracing.com

1 **ALASI**, 9, b m Alflora (IRE)—Anamasi **Mrs S. Liebermann**
2 **ANTONIUS LAD (IRE)**, 6, b g Antonius Pius (USA)—Fey Lady (IRE) **Mr S. Liebermann**
3 **AUSTRALIA DAY (IRE)**, 10, gr g Key of Luck (USA)—Atalina (FR) **Skippy & The Partners**
4 **BAYLEY'S DREAM**, 4, b g Presenting—Swaythe (USA) **The Sweep Stakes Partnership**
5 4, B g Darsi (FR)—Beechberry (IRE) **Paul Webber Racing**
6 **CANTLOW (IRE)**, 8, b g Kayf Tara—Winnowing (IRE) **J. P. McManus**
7 **CITRUS MARK**, 8, b g Mark of Esteem (IRE)—Lemon's Mill (USA) **Economic Security**
8 **COCOA MINNIE (IRE)**, 7, ch m Presenting—Native Lucy **Jolly Wolf Racing**
9 **COLONEL ALF**, 8, b g Alflora (IRE)—Re-Spin **D. R. Stoddart**
10 **COULDHAVEHADITALL (IRE)**, 5, b g Milan—Night Leader (IRE) **R. C. Moody**

MR PAUL WEBBER - Continued

11 **CRIME DONT PAY (IRE)**, 9, b g Saddlers' Hall (IRE)—Maddy's Supreme (IRE) **R. W. Barnett**
12 **DANVILLA**, 6, b m Dansili—Newtown Villa **Mr S. Liebermann**
13 **DECEPTIVE**, 5, b m Red Ransom (USA)—Fleeting Memory **The Not-So Secret Seven**
14 **DEFINITELY GLAD (IRE)**, 6, b m Definite Article—Gladys May (IRE) **Mr S. Liebermann**
15 **DEIA SUNRISE (IRE)**, 4, gr g Clodovil (IRE)—Hedera (USA) **M Hughes & M Kerr-Dineen**
16 **DUNLOUGH BAY (IRE)**, 7, ch g Flemensfirth (USA)—Loch Lomond (IRE) **The Horwoods Partnership**
17 4, B g Scorpion (IRE)—Emesions Lady (IRE) **Paul Webber Racing**
18 **ENDOFDISCUSION (IRE)**, 6, b g Flemensfirth (USA)—Fake Tan (IRE) **D. C. R. Allen**
19 **ETOILE TANTUM (FR)**, 7, b m Ballingarry (IRE)—Eoline (FR) **Mr D. Carrington**
20 **FIRM ORDER (IRE)**, 8, b g Winged Love (IRE)—Fairylodge Scarlet (IRE) **The Syndicators**
21 **FORTYSCORE (IRE)**, 6, b g Zagreb (USA)—Minnie O'grady (IRE) **Fawley House Stud**
22 **GRAVITATE**, 4, ch g Pivotal—Spacecraft (USA) **Mrs P. V. E. Morrell**
23 **GUEST OF HONOUR (FR)**, 5, b g Hurricane Run (IRE)—Pats Martini (USA) **M. Tabor**
24 **HALUCHA (IRE)**, 8, b g Luso—Rose Basket (FR) **R. W. Barnett**
25 **HARRIS GARDEN (IRE)**, 6, b g Pilsudski (IRE)—Bay Pearl (FR) **C. W. Booth**
26 **HONOUR A PROMISE**, 5, b m Norse Dancer (IRE)—Motcombe (USA) **Honour A Promise**
27 **KEY CUTTER (FR)**, 9, b g Alderbrook—Two Roads **Mrs A. W. Timpson**
28 **KNOCKDOLIAN (IRE)**, 6, b g Montjeu (IRE)—Doula (USA) **Lady Wellesley**
29 **KOOLALA (IRE)**, 5, b m Kayf Tara—Squaw Talk (USA) **Lady Wellesley**
30 **LADY KATHLEEN**, 6, b m Hernando (FR)—Lady of Fortune (IRE) **Mr S. Liebermann**
31 **LEMON DROP RED (USA)**, 5, b g Lemon Drop Kid (USA)—Skipper's Mate (USA) **John Nicholls (Trading) Ltd**
32 **LEMON'S GENT**, 6, br g Generous (USA)—Lemon's Mill (USA) **G. R. Waters**
33 **LIGHTNING STRIKE (GER)**, 10, ch g Danehill Dancer (USA)—La Capilla **John Nicholls (Trading) Ltd**
34 **LLAMA FARMER**, 8, br gr g Sagamix (FR)—Quick Quick Sloe **Mrs A. W. Timpson**
35 **LUCANOR (IRE)**, 5, b g Indian Danehill (IRE)—Persian Avenue (IRE) **The Spaniards Partnership**
36 **MARLEY ROCA (IRE)**, 9, b br g Tamayaz (CAN)—Gaye Gordon **Mr D. Carrington**
37 **MISS HOLBECK GHYLL**, 3, b m Alflora (IRE)—Dominie Breeze **Miss A. M. Dobie**
38 **MONEYMIX**, 6, gr g Fair Mix (IRE)—Sticky Money **D. C. R. Allen**
39 **ORCHARD BOY (IRE)**, 5, b g Oscar (IRE)—Beech Lodge (IRE) **R. M. Kirkland**
40 **RAJNAGAN (IRE)**, 9, ch g Muhtarram (USA)—Rajnagara (IRE) **Mrs P. V. E. Morrell**
41 **REPEAT BUSINESS (IRE)**, 5, b g Croco Rouge (IRE)—Bay Pearl (FR) **R. M. Kirkland**
42 **RESOURCEFUL MISS**, 4, b f Dubai Destination (USA)—Resourceful (IRE) **The Resourceful Partnership**
43 **RHAPANDO**, 4, b g Hernando (FR)—Rhapsody Rose (USA) **D. C. R. Allen**
44 5, B m Flemensfirth (USA)—Rith Ar Aghaidh (IRE) **Paul Webber Racing**
45 **ROYALRACKET (IRE)**, 5, b g Royal Anthem (USA)—Allaracket (IRE) **D. C. R. Allen**
46 **RUN ON STERLING**, 4, b g Dr Fong (USA)—Dansara **Andrew Rowland**
47 **RYSBRACK (USA)**, 7, ch g Selkirk (USA)—Super Tassa (IRE) **C. Humphris / The Hon. David Howard**
48 **SARANDO**, 8, b g Hernando (FR)—Dansara **Eight Men & A Hoss**
49 **SCAMPI BOY (IRE)**, 9, b g Flemensfirth (USA)—Loch Lomond (IRE) **Mr D. Carrington**
50 **SEPTEMBER BLAZE**, 6, b m Exit To Nowhere (USA)—Mid Day Chaser (IRE) **The Blaze Partnership**
51 **SIKSIKA (IRE)**, 5, b m Golan (IRE)—Native Delight (IRE) **Mrs Diane Bowley**
52 **SIX ONE AWAY (IRE)**, 4, gr g Tikkanen (USA)—Surfing France (FR) **Mrs A. W. Timpson**
53 **SIXTY SOMETHING (FR)**, 7, gr g Dom Alco (FR)—Jaunas (FR) **Mrs A. W. Timpson**
54 **STAR PRESENTER (IRE)**, 5, b g Presenting—Star Councel (IRE) **Archie's Partnership**
55 **STRUANMORE**, 6, ch g Doyen (IRE)—Burghmuir (IRE) **Mr I. R. Watters**
56 **SUSSEX SUNSET**, 7, b m Milan—Deep Sunset (IRE) **Neil Grover, Family & Friends**
57 **TAFIKA**, 9, b g Kayf Tara—Shiwa **The Tafika Partnership**
58 **THEODORE LAMB**, 8, b g Lahib (USA)—Our Leader (IRE) **Peter Charter & Mobley Homes**
59 **THISGUNSFORHIRE (IRE)**, 5, b g Flemensfirth (USA)—Midnight Lover **Mrs L. M. Shanahan**
60 **TINDARO (FR)**, 6, gr g Kingsalsa (USA)—Star's Mixa (FR) **The Tindaro Partnership**
61 5, B g Kayf Tara—Tisho **Mrs A. Scott-Dunn**
62 **TOO MUCH TOO SOON (IRE)**, 4, b g Craigsteel—Zara Rose (IRE) **Dunton Racing Partnership**

THREE-YEAR-OLDS
63 **PINAMAR**, ch f Shirocco (GER)—Highland Ceilidh (IRE) **Cyril Humphris**

Other Owners: Mr N. M. Birch, Mr P. Bowden, Mr H. F. Bowley, Mr D. G. Carrington, Mr W. H. Carson, P.F. Charter, Mr J. F. Clay, Mrs Sarah Drysdale, R. N. Frosell, Mrs M. F. Gardiner, N. A. Grover, Mr P. J. Hewett, D. W. Higgins, The Hon David F. Howard, Mr P. S. Lewis, Sir I. Magee, Mr M. V. Magnier, Mr A. Massey, Prof D. H. Metcalf, Mobley Homes, Mr S. R. G. Packer, M. L. Pepper, Mr J. Phelan, A. Roche, R. P. Rocher, Mr N. Sercombe, A. G. Sim, Mr J. Southan, Mrs D. J. Webber, Paul Webber.

Jockey (flat): Jimmy Fortune. **Jockey (NH):** Dominic Elsworth, Denis O'Regan.

658 MR D. K. WELD, The Curragh

Postal: **Rosewell House, The Curragh, Co. Kildare, Irish Republic**
Contacts: **PHONE (00353) 4544 1273 / 441 476 FAX (00353) 4544 1119**
E-MAIL dkweld@eircom.net

1 **CAPONATA (USA)**, 4, b f Selkirk (USA)—Daring Diva **Mr K Abdulla**
2 **CASUAL CONQUEST (IRE)**, 8, b g Hernando (FR)—Lady Luck (IRE) **Moyglare Stud Farm**
3 **DIPLOMAT (USA)**, 4, b g Kitten's Joy (USA)—Waki Affair (USA) **Dr Ronan Lambe**
4 **EXHORTATION**, 4, b g Zamindar (USA)—Winter Silence **Mr K Abdulla**
5 **GRECIAN TIGER (IRE)**, 4, b g Tiger Hill (IRE)—Allexina **Mr J Higgins**
6 **HISAABAAT (IRE)**, 5, b g Dubawi (IRE)—Phariseek (IRE) **Dr Ronan Lambe**
7 **INSTRUCT (USA)**, 4, b g Empire Maker (USA)—Etoile Montante (USA) **Mr K Abdulla**
8 **NOTABLE GRADUATE (IRE)**, 5, b g Galileo (IRE)—Market Slide (USA) **Dr Ronan Lambe**
9 **OLYMPIAD (IRE)**, 5, b g Galileo (IRE)—Caumshinaun (IRE) **Sir Robert Ogden**
10 **PACELLI ROAD (IRE)**, 4, b g Oratorio (IRE)—Lexy May (USA) **Mr J P McManus**
11 **PALE MIMOSA (IRE)**, 4, b f Singspiel (USA)—Katch Me Katie **Dr Ronan Lambe**
12 **PRINCESS HIGHWAY (USA)**, 4, b f Street Cry (IRE)—Irresistible Jewel (IRE) **Moyglare Stud Farm**
13 **RITE OF PASSAGE**, 9, ch g Giant's Causeway (USA)—Dahlia's Krissy (USA) **Dr Ronan Lambe**
14 **ROCK CRITIC (IRE)**, 8, b g Pivotal—Diamond Trim (IRE) **Moyglare Stud Farm**
15 **SAPPHIRE (IRE)**, 5, b m Medicean—Polished Gem (IRE) **Moyglare Stud Farm**
16 **SHOW COURT (IRE)**, 4, b g Vinnie Roe (IRE)—Sparkling Gem (IRE) **Mr Kris Weld**
17 **TANDEM**, 4, b g Dansili—Light Ballet **Mr K Abdulla**
18 **TREASURE THE RIDGE (IRE)**, 4, b g Galileo (IRE)—Treasure The Lady (IRE) **Mrs Anne Coughlan**
19 **TROON**, 5, b g Kitten's Joy (USA)—Sunday Sport (USA) **Mr Kris Weld**
20 **UNACCOMPANIED (IRE)**, 6, b m Danehill Dancer (IRE)—Legend Has It (IRE) **Moyglare Stud Farm**
21 **VOLEUSE DE COEURS (IRE)**, 4, b f Teofilo (IRE)—Vadorga **Lady O'Reilly**
22 **WAAHEB (USA)**, 6, b br g Elusive Quality (USA)—Nafisah (USA) **Mr. J P McManus**
23 **YELLOW ROSEBUD (IRE)**, 4, b f Jeremy (USA)—Nebraas **Mrs C C Regalado Gonzalez**

THREE-YEAR-OLDS

24 **ACTING TALENT (USA)**, b f Bernstein (USA)—Soaring Emotions (USA) **Moyglare Stud Farm**
25 B f Teofilo (IRE)—Agnetha (GER) **Mr Pat Fleming**
26 **ALKALI (IRE)**, gr f Dalakhani (IRE)—Alambic **Lady O'Reilly**
27 **AMBER ROMANCE (IRE)**, ch f Bahamian Bounty—Polished Gem (IRE) **Moyglare Stud Farm**
28 **AWE STRUCK**, b f Rail Link—Aspiring Diva (USA) **Mr K Abdulla**
29 **BIG BREAK**, b f Dansili—Fame At Last (USA) **Mr K Abdulla**
30 **BOOM TIME**, gr c Empire Maker (USA)—Jibboom (USA) **Mr K Abdulla**
31 **BRACING BREEZE**, b f Dansili—Nebraska Tornado (USA) **Mr K Abdulla**
32 **COCKTAIL HOUR (IRE)**, b f Notnowcato—Out of Thanks (IRE) **Moyglare Stud Farm**
33 **CONVOCATE (USA)**, ro f Exchange Rate (USA)—Private Line (USA) **Mr K Abdulla**
34 **DIESEL TEN (IRE)**, b g Refuse To Bend (IRE)—Zoudie **Deus Bros Syndicate**
35 **DIVINE PORT (USA)**, b c Arch (USA)—Out of Reach **Mr K Abdulla**
36 **FORGOTTEN RULES (IRE)**, b c Nayef (USA)—Utterly Heaven (IRE) **Moyglare Stud Farm**
37 **GHAAMER (USA)**, b c Hard Spun (USA)—Teeba (USA) **Sheikh Hamdan Al Maktoum**
38 **HAMMERED SILVER (IRE)**, gr c Dalakhani (IRE)—Desert Ease (IRE) **Moyglare Stud Farm**
39 **HAZY GLOW (IRE)**, b f Invincible Spirit (IRE)—Genuine Charm (IRE) **Moyglare Stud Farm**
40 **HIGHEST PRAISE**, b f Acclamation—Yarastar **Lady O'Reilly**
41 **IMPERIAL CONCORDE (IRE)**, b c High Chaparral (IRE)—Irish Style (IRE) **Dr Ronan Lambe**
42 **INSTANT UPDATE (IRE)**, b c Pivotal—Instant Sparkle (IRE) **Moyglare Stud Farm**
43 **JAYED JIDAN (IRE)**, gr c Teofilo (IRE)—Cassandra Go (IRE) **Sheikh Hamdan Al Maktoum**
44 **KHOTHRY (IRE)**, b f Marju (IRE)—Esterlina (IRE) **Sheikh Hamdan Al Maktoum**
45 **LAKE DISTRICT (IRE)**, b f Raven's Pass (USA)—Vista Bella **Sheikh Mohammed**
46 **LAPIS BLUE (IRE)**, b f Invincible Spirit (IRE)—Triple Try (USA) **Moyglare Stud Farm**
47 **LATE ROSEBUD (IRE)**, b f Jeremy (USA)—Nebraas **Lady O'Reilly**
48 **LINEMAN**, b c Rail Link—Shamana (USA) **Mr K Abdulla**
49 **MAGNOLIA RIDGE (IRE)**, b c Galileo (IRE)—Treasure The Lady (IRE) **Mrs Anne Coughlan**
50 **MAKE THE NEWS (IRE)**, b c Montjeu (IRE)—Market Slide (USA) **Moyglare Stud Farm**
51 **MANHATTAN SWING (IRE)**, b g Invincible Spirit (IRE)—Bluebell Park (USA) **Mr Joseph Higgins**
52 **MILITARY DEVICE (IRE)**, b c Shirocco (GER)—Sharp Point (IRE) **Mr Steven Lo**
53 **MOUTEAB (IRE)**, b g Marju (IRE)—Katoom (IRE) **Sheikh Hamdan Al Maktoum**
54 **MUAANID**, ch c Kheleyf (USA)—Rifqah (USA) **Sheikh Hamdan Al Maktoum**
55 **NABAT ALI**, b f Haatef (USA)—Laywaan (USA) **Sheikh Hamdan Al Maktoum**
56 **PARK PLACE**, b c Beat Hollow—Blend **Mr K Abdulla**
57 **PAY DAY KITTEN (USA)**, b br f Kitten's Joy (USA)—Annual Dues (USA) **Mr Kenneth & Mrs Sarah Ramsey**
58 **PEACE ACCORD**, ch g Pivotal—Embassy **Sheikh Mohammed**

MR D. K. WELD - Continued

59 **RASMEYAA (IRE)**, ch f New Approach (IRE)—Posterity (IRE) **Sheikh Hamdan Al Maktoum**
60 **RAWAAQ**, b f Invincible Spirit (IRE)—Zaqrah (USA) **Sheikh Hamdan Al Maktoum**
61 **REGAL CONCORDE (IRE)**, b g Lawman (FR)—Fernanda **Dr Ronan Lambe**
62 **RESOLUTE RESPONSE (IRE)**, b c Dansili—Lady Luck (IRE) **Moyglare Stud Farm**
63 **SALHOODA (IRE)**, b f Nayef (USA)—Alshakr **Sheikh Hamdan Al Maktoum**
64 **SHARP CRISP AIR (IRE)**, ch f Danehill Dancer (IRE)—Token Gesture (IRE) **Moyglare Stud Farm**
65 **SHUNNED**, b f Three Valleys (USA)—Avoidance (USA) **Mr K Abdulla**
66 **SLEEPING BEAUTY (IRE)**, b f Oasis Dream—Nightime (IRE) **Mrs C L Weld**
67 **SUNSHINE KITTEN (USA)**, ch f Kitten's Joy (USA)—La Coruna (USA) **Mr Kenneth & Mrs Sarah Ramsey**
68 **TABAARY (USA)**, b br c Street Cry (IRE)—Commodities (USA) **Sheikh Hamdan Al Maktoum**
69 **TAMAAH (IRE)**, gr c Dalakhani (IRE)—Sahool **Sheikh Hamdan Al Maktoum**
70 **TUSCAN LIGHT**, b f Medicean—Bright And Clear **Mr K Abdulla**

TWO-YEAR-OLDS

71 **AFTERNOON SUNLIGHT (IRE)**, ch f 10/4 Sea The Stars (IRE)—Lady Luck (IRE) (Kris) **Moyglare Stud Farm**
72 **ALKASSER (IRE)**, b c 7/4 Shamardal (USA)—
    Alexander Queen (IRE) (King's Best (USA)) (206348) **Sheikh Hamdan Al Maktoum**
73 **ANTIQUE PLATINUM (IRE)**, b f 17/5 Holy Roman Emperor (IRE)—
    Summer Trysting (USA) (Alleged (USA)) **Moyglare Stud Farm**
74 B c 18/4 Dansili—Aspiring Diva (USA) (Distant View (USA)) **Mr K Abdulla**
75 B f 1/4 Galileo (IRE)—Banquise (Last Tycoon) **Sir Robert Ogden**
76 B c 14/4 Shamardal (USA)—Bee Eater (IRE) (Green Desert (USA)) (174602) **Sheikh Mohammed**
77 **CARLA BIANCA (IRE)**, gr f 7/3 Dansili—Majestic Silver (IRE) (Linamix (FR)) **Moyglare Stud Farm**
78 Ch c 1/3 Dandy Man (IRE)—Cecilia's Pearl (Woodman) (31745) **Dr Ronan Lambe**
79 B f 1/2 Bushranger (IRE)—Chamela Bay (IRE) (Sadler's Wells (USA)) (47619) **Dr Ronan Lambe**
80 Gr c 19/3 Oasis Dream—Comeback Queen (Nayef (USA)) (130000) **Mr K Abdulla**
81 Br c 27/4 Bushranger (IRE)—Dame Noir (IRE) (Alzao (USA)) (42000) **Dr Ronan Lambe**
82 B f 4/3 Empire Maker (USA)—Daring Diva (Dansili) **Mr K Abdulla**
83 **EALAIN AIBREAN (IRE)**, b f 10/2 Excellent Art—
    April (IRE) (Rock of Gibraltar (IRE)) (14285) **Brunabonne Syndicate**
84 **ENTIQAAM**, b br c 11/2 Sea The Stars (IRE)—Cuis Ghaire (IRE) (Galileo (IRE)) **Hamdan Al Maktoum**
85 Ch c 23/5 Champs Elysees—Fame At Last (USA) (Quest For Fame) **Mr K Abdulla**
86 **FREE EAGLE (IRE)**, b c 4/5 High Chaparral—Polished Gem (Danehill (USA)) **Moyglare Stud Farm**
87 B g 4/4 Amadeus Wolf—Fully Fashioned (IRE) (Brief Truce (USA)) (23809) **Mr Glen Devlin**
88 Gr ro f 5/2 Mizzen Mast (USA)—Geographic (USA) (Empire Maker (USA)) **Mr K Abdulla**
89 B c 26/4 Kyllachy—Gloved Hand (Royal Applause) (57142) **Dr Ronan Lambe**
90 **GO FOR GOAL (IRE)**, gr c 23/4 Verglas (USA)—Triple Try (IRE) (Sadler's Wells (USA)) **Moyglare Stud Farm**
91 **GOOD TRADITION (IRE)**, b c 1/4 Pivotal—Token Gesture (IRE) (Alzao (USA)) **Moyglare Stud Farm**
92 B f 15/3 First Defence (USA)—Hasardeuse (USA) (Distant View (USA)) **Mr K Abdulla**
93 B f 12/3 Authorized (IRE)—Historian (IRE) (Pennekamp (USA)) **Sheikh Mohammed**
94 **I'M YOURS**, b f 21/4 Invincible Spirit (IRE)—Rebelline (IRE) (Robellino (USA)) (333333) **Moyglare Stud Farm**
95 B f 11/3 Dansili—Indication (Sadler's Wells (USA)) **Mr K Abdulla**
96 **INTISAAB**, b c 4/3 Elnadim (USA)—Katoom (IRE) (Soviet Star (USA)) **Sheikh Hamdan Al Maktoum**
97 B gr f 29/3 Oasis Dream—Jibboom (USA) (Mizzen Mast (USA)) **Mr K Abdulla**
98 Gr c 21/3 Verglas (USA)—Katch Me Katie (Danehill (USA)) (31745) **Dr Ronan Lambe**
99 **KATIMAVIK (IRE)**, b br c 3/2 Invincible Spirit (IRE)—Nunavik (IRE) (Indian Ridge) **Moyglare Stud Farm**
100 B c 22/3 Bushranger (IRE)—Lady Meagan (IRE) (Val Royal (FR)) (61904) **Dr Ronan Lambe**
101 **MADAKHEEL (USA)**, b f 15/3 Mr Greeley (USA)—Manaal (USA) (Bahri (USA)) **Sheikh Hamdan Al Maktoum**
102 Ch c 2/2 Galileo (IRE)—Magic Carpet (IRE) (Danehill (USA)) **Sir Robert Ogden**
103 **MAWRED (IRE)**, b c 6/2 Tamayuz—Roscoff (IRE) (Daylami (IRE)) (67460) **Sheikh Hamdan Al Maktoum**
104 **MUMARASAAT (USA)**, b f 14/3 Elusive Quality (USA)—
    Reefaljamal (USA) (Dixieland Band (USA)) **Sheikh Hamdan Al Maktoum**
105 **MUSTAJEEB**, ch c 18/3 Nayef (USA)—Rifqah (USA) (Elusive Quality (USA)) **Sheikh Hamdan Al Maktoum**
106 **NEXT BEND (IRE)**, b c 21/4 Azamour (IRE)—Polite Reply (IRE) (Be My Guest (USA)) **Moyglare Stud Farm**
107 **NIDHAAM**, ch f 18/2 Nayef (USA)—Malakaat (Danzig (USA)) **Sheikh Hamdan Al Maktoum**
108 B f 7/4 High Chaparral (IRE)—Perfect Touch (Miswaki (USA)) **Mrs C L Weld**
109 **PIRITA (IRE)**, b f 28/3 Invincible Spirit (IRE)—Spinamix (Spinning World (USA)) (261904) **Moyglare Stud Farm**
110 B f 2/2 Selkirk (USA)—Prove (Danehill (USA)) **Mr K Abdulla**
111 **RED DOOR (IRE)**, ch c 23/4 Medicean—Out of Thanks (IRE) (Sadler's Wells (USA)) **Moyglare Stud Farm**
112 **SAILORS SWAN (USA)**, b c 28/4 Henrythenavigator (USA)—
    Society Hostess (USA) (Seeking The Gold (USA)) **Moyglare Stud Farm**
113 Ch f 29/4 Dandy Man (IRE)—Saphire (College Chapel) (52000) **Mrs C L Weld**
114 **SEEKING TRUTH (IRE)**, b c 24/5 Acclamation—
    Suitably Discreet (USA) (Mr Prospector (USA)) **Moyglare Stud Farm**

MR D. K. WELD - Continued

115 SIMPLE LOVE (USA), b f 4/4 Proud Citizen (USA)—
Offbeat Fashion (IRE) (Rock of Gibraltar (IRE)) **Moyglare Stud Farm**
116 B f 21/3 Danehill Dancer (IRE)—Snowy Day In La (IRE) (Sadler's Wells (USA)) (49205) **Dr Ronan Lambe**
117 B f 6/4 Galileo (IRE)—Sophisticat (USA) (Storm Cat (USA)) **Mrs J Magnier**
118 SPARKLE FACTOR (IRE), b f 6/3 Arch (USA)—Thoughtless Moment (IRE) (Pivotal) **Moyglare Stud Farm**
119 Br c 22/3 Myboycharlie (IRE)—Spring Glory (Dr Fong (USA)) (115079) **Dr Ronan Lambe**
120 STAY DE NIGHT (IRE), b c 18/5 Shamardal (USA)—Where We Left Off (Dr Devious (IRE)) **Moyglare Stud Farm**
121 B br c 16/2 Empire Maker (USA)—Supposition (Dansili) **Mr K Abdulla**
122 TAHAANY (IRE), b f 9/2 Raven's Pass (USA)—
Photophore (IRE) (Clodovil (IRE)) (190476) **Sheikh Hamdan Al Maktoum**
123 TARFASHA (IRE), ch f 26/4 Teofilo (IRE)—
Grecian Bride (IRE) (Groom Dancer (USA)) **Sheikh Hamdan Al Maktoum**
124 B f 8/4 Sea The Stars (IRE)—Treasure The Lady (IRE) (Indian Ridge) **Mrs C L Weld**
125 TWO IN ONE (USA), b c 26/3 Bernstein (USA)—Unique Pose (IRE) (Sadler's Wells (USA)) **Moyglare Stud Farm**
126 VINTAGE NOUVEAU (IRE), b f 27/3 Montjeu (IRE)—Utterly Heaven (IRE) (Danehill (USA)) **Moyglare Stud Farm**
127 WATEED (IRE), b c 1/2 Iffraaj—Miss Adelaide (IRE) (Alzao (USA)) (68000) **Sheikh Hamdan Al Maktoum**
128 WELD ARAB (IRE), b c 29/1 Shamardal (USA)—Itqaan (USA) (Danzig (USA)) **Sheikh Hamdan Al Maktoum**
129 WHITEY O' GWAUN (IRE), gr c 15/2 Dalakhani (IRE)—
Angel of The Gwaun (IRE) (Sadler's Wells (USA)) (110000) **Sheikh Mohammed**
130 Gr c 25/3 Verglas (IRE)—Wrong Key (IRE) (Key of Luck (USA)) (111110) **Dr Ronan Lambe**

Jockey (flat): P. J. Smullen. **Apprentice:** S. M. Gorey, L. F. Roche.

---

659 **MR DEREK WELLICOME, Llandeilo**
Postal: Beili Llwyd Farm, Manordeilo, Llandeilo, Carmarthenshire, SA19 7BL
Contacts: PHONE (01550) 779061 MOBILE (07976) 426421
E-MAIL d.wellicome@btinternet.com

1 CHANDLER JACK, 6, b g Lujain (USA)—Moonlight Seas **Mr D. R. Wellicome**
2 MASEFIELD, 5, b g Cacique (IRE)—Becalmed **Mr D. R. Wellicome**

---

660 **MISS SHEENA WEST, Lewes**
Postal: 5 Balmer Farm Cottages, Brighton Road, Lewes, East Sussex, BN7 3JN
Contacts: PHONE (01273) 621303 FAX (01273) 622189 MOBILE (07748) 181804
E-MAIL sheenawest11@aol.com WEBSITE www.sheenawest.com

1 ALFRAAMSEY, 5, b g Fraam—Evanesce **Tapestry Partnership**
2 ARDMADDY (IRE), 9, b g Generous (IRE)—Yazmin (IRE)
3 BRILLIANT BARCA, 5, b g Imperial Dancer—Fading Away **The Affordable Partnership**
4 CANNON FODDER, 6, b m Nomadic Way (USA)—Grace Dieu **The Cheapskates**
5 CAPTAIN CARDINGTON (IRE), 4, b g Strategic Prince—Alkaffeyeh (IRE) **Tapestry Partnership**
6 COOLAGAD STAR (IRE), 5, b m Dr Massini (IRE)—Trinity Flyer (IRE) **Stephen Monks & Niall Coakley**
7 DUBAI GLORY, 5, b m Dubai Destination (USA)—Rosse **The Affordable (2) Partnership**
8 FEB THIRTYFIRST, 4, ch g Shirocco (GER)—My Mariam **M. Moriarty**
9 FLASHY STAR, 4, ch f Mr Greeley (USA)—Galileo's Star (IRE) **The Affordable (3) Partnership**
10 GEORDIE BOY, 4, b br g Araafa (IRE)—Entail (USA) **The Affordable (3) Partnership**
11 GOLAN WAY, 9, b g Golan (IRE)—Silk Daisy **W R B Racing 58**
12 HI NOTE, 5, b m Acclamation—Top Tune **G. West**
13 IMPERIAL ELEGANCE, 4, b f Imperial Dancer—Canadian Capers **G. L. Flight**
14 IMPERIAL STARGAZER, 4, gr g Imperial Dancer—Sky Light Dreams **P. Taplin**
15 JUST JOSIE, 7, b m Josr Algarhoud (IRE)—Spatham Rose **Saloop**
16 LEG IRON (IRE), 8, b g Snurge—Southern Skies (IRE) **M. Moriarty**
17 LENNY THE GREAT, 4, b g Beat All (USA)—Hamadeenah **Sandbanks Racing Partnership**
18 MR MUDDLE, 6, gr g Imperial Dancer—Spatham Rose **Saloop**
19 SCREAMING BRAVE, 7, br g Hunting Lion (IRE)—Hana Dee **Tracey Walsom & Alex Woodger**
20 SHIVSINGH, 4, b g Montjeu (IRE)—Vistaria (USA) **Nick & Olga Dhandsa & John & Zoe Webster**
21 SILVER SIX, 4, gr g Aussie Rules (USA)—Bahara **The Affordable (3) Partnership**
22, 4, B f Grape Tree Road—Sister Dee **Mr S. J. Antram**
23, 4, Gr g Kayf Tara—Spatham Rose **Saloop**
24 YA HAFED, 5, ch g Haafhd—Rule Britannia **Mr A. J. Head**

MISS SHEENA WEST - Continued

Other Owners: Mr J. A. Barnes, A. W. A. Bates, M. R. Channon, Mr S. Clegg, Mr N. Coakley, Dr N. Dhandsa, Mr R. C. G. Dodds, Mrs L. Dyett, Mrs S. Finch, Mr P. Holian-Dyett, Mr D. L. Lacey, Mr S. Monks, Mr L. T. Morris, Mrs C. S. Muddle, R. A. Muddle, Mrs E. Turner, Miss T. Walsom, Mr J. Webster, Miss S. West, Wetherby Racing Bureau Ltd, Mr A. G. R. Woodger, D. M. Woodward.

Assistant Trainer: Jamie Goldstein

Jockey (flat): J. Goldstein. **Jockey (NH):** J. Goldstein. **Conditional:** M. Goldstein.

---

661 MR SIMON WEST, Middleham
Postal: **14A St Alkeldas Road, Middleham, Leyburn, North Yorkshire, DL8 4PW**
Contacts: **MOBILE (07855) 924529**
E-MAIL simonwest21@hotmail.co.uk **WEBSITE** www.mkmracing.co.uk

1 **CAPTAIN CLAYTON (IRE)**, 6, b g Subtle Power (IRE)—Dont Hurry (IRE) **Wild West Racing**
2 **FEV ROVER (IRE)**, 6, br g Zagreb (USA)—Mrs Pharback (IRE) **Mr S. G. West**
3 **KUKURUDU (IRE)**, 6, b g Tikkanen (USA)—Tullyfoyle (IRE) **Mr P. Hothersall**
4 **MURAAFIQ (USA)**, 4, b br g Jazil (USA)—Reem Al Barari (USA) **Mr C. R. Hirst**
5 **SPRINGANA**, 14, ch g Minster Son—Galway Gal **Mrs J. M. L. Milligan**
6 **WESLEYDALE (IRE)**, 6, b g Westerner—Fully Focused (IRE) **Wild West Racing**
7 **WOODMORE (IRE)**, 9, b g Luso—Supreme Stream (IRE) **Mr P. Hothersall**

Other Owners: Mr K. Flint.

Apprentice: Paul Pickard. **Amateur:** Miss L. Stead.

---

662 MR MARTIN WESTON, Hindlip
Postal: **Offerton Farm, Hindlip, Worcestershire, WR3 8SX**

1 **ADVISOR (FR)**, 7, gr g Anabaa (USA)—Armilina (FR) **M. H. Weston**
2 **GREEN LIGHTNING (IRE)**, 6, b g Montjeu (IRE)—Angelic Song (CAN) **M. H. Weston**
3 **MOUNT WELCOME (IRE)**, 9, b g Bach (IRE)—Be My Vixen (IRE) **M. H. Weston**

---

663 MISS JESSICA WESTWOOD, Minehead
Postal: **Monkham House, Exford, Minehead, Somerset, TA24 7NA**
Contacts: **MOBILE (07536) 021449**
E-MAIL JessWestwoodracing@gmail.com

1 **MONKERTY TUNKERTY**, 10, b g Silver Patriarch (IRE)—Orphan Annie **Miss J. J. Westwood**

Other Owners: Mr A. Westwood.

---

664 MR JOHN WEYMES, Middleham
Postal: **Ashgill, Coverham, Leyburn, North Yorkshire, DL8 4TJ**
Contacts: **PHONE (01969) 640420 FAX (01969) 640505 MOBILE (07753) 792516**
E-MAIL johnweymes@johnweymes.co.uk **WEBSITE** www.johnweymesracing.co.uk

1 **ALMATY EXPRESS**, 11, b g Almaty (IRE)—Express Girl **Highmoor Racing 4 & Tag Racing**
2 **ARTISTIC DAWN (IRE)**, 4, b f Excellent Art—Midnight Mist (IRE) **T. A. Scothern**
3 **BRIAN SPROUT**, 5, ch g Zafeen (FR)—Ducal Diva **Thoroughbred Partners**
4 **ELIZABETH COFFEE (IRE)**, 5, b m Byron—Queens Wharf (IRE) **T. A. Scothern**
5 **FIREFLY**, 4, b g Firebreak—Quick Flight **High Moor Racing 2**
6 **HARRYS WHIM**, 8, b m Sir Harry Lewis (USA)—Whimbrel **J. R. Wills**
7 **IMTITHAL (IRE)**, 4, b f Invincible Spirit (IRE)—Dream Time **Thoroughbred Partners**
8 **JUST FIVE (IRE)**, 7, b g Olmodavor (USA)—Wildsplash (USA) **Thoroughbred Racing Club**
9 **SKIDDAW VIEW**, 5, b m Goodricke—Skiddaw Wolf **J. R. Wills**
10 **TOMASINI**, 4, b g Misu Bond (IRE)—Bond Stasia (IRE) **Mr P. M. Boland**
11 **VALDEMAR**, 7, ch g Tobougg (IRE)—Stealthy Times **Thoroughbred Racing Club**

MR JOHN WEYMES - Continued

THREE-YEAR-OLDS

12 **CROMWELL ROSE (IRE)**, ch f Haafhd—Bonny Rose **Grange Park Racing 1 & Thoroughbred Partners**
13 **FALCON'S GINGER**, ch f Grape Tree Road—Sheriff's Falcon (IRE)
14 Ch c Indian Haven—Graceful Air (IRE) **Thoroughbred Racing Club**
15 **GREENFORDGIRL (IRE)**, b f Diamond Green (FR)—Cappadoce (IRE) **Mrs B. Hardiman**
16 **HIGHWAY UNITED (IRE)**, ch f Arakan (USA)—Luscinia **Mr P. M. Mannion**
17 **LILYOFTHEVALLEY**, b f Avonbridge—Linden's Lady **E Kingsley, T Scothern & K Buckle**
18 **MJAAL (IRE)**, ch f Haatef (USA)—Tawaajud (USA) **Leadbetter, Scothern, Jackson**
19 **SHESTHECAPTAIN (IRE)**, br f Captain Marvelous (IRE)—
                            Shewillishewants (IRE) **Speedlic Racing & Thoroughbred Partners**
20 **SILVER FAWN (IRE)**, gr g Clodovil (IRE)—Tinareena (IRE) **Thoroughbred Partners**
21 **SILVER FOREST (IRE)**, b f Mujadil (USA)—Forest Storm (USA) **Thoroughbred Partners**
22 **SYNPHONIC AIR (IRE)**, b f Amadeus Wolf—Summer Crush (USA) **Scothern, Leadbetter, T'bred Partners**
23 **TWINWOOD STAR (IRE)**, b f Moss Vale (IRE)—Bonkers **High Moor Racing 1**

TWO-YEAR-OLDS

24 B f 10/3 Myboycharlie (IRE)—Crossed Wire (Lycius (USA))

Other Owners: Mr Federico Barberini, Mr P. D. Bickley, Miss K. Buckle, A. D. Crombie, Mr R. Gayton, Mr A. J. Jackson, Mr E. P. Kingsley, Mr M. J. Leadbetter, Mr A. Norrington, Mr G. Quintale, J. R. Weymes.

Assistant Trainer: Kirsty Buckle (Kirsty@Johnweymes.co.uk)

Jockey (flat): Darryll Holland, Philip Makin. **Jockey (NH):** Keith Mercer, Dougie Costello.

---

665 MR ERIC WHEELER, Pangbourne
Postal: **15 St Michaels Close, Lambourn, Hungerford, Berkshire, RG17 8FA**
Contacts: **PHONE (07795) 844185 FAX (01189) 841924 MOBILE (07795) 844185**

1 **BATCHWORTH BLAISE**, 10, b g Little Jim—Batchworth Dancer **E. A. Wheeler**
2 **BEGGERS BELIEF**, 5, ch g Bertolini (USA)—Dropitlikeit's Hot (IRE) **Mr G. W. Witheford**
3 **CLIFFORDS REPRIEVE**, 5, b g Kheleyf (USA)—Bijan (IRE) **Mr G. W. Witheford**
4 **EL LIBERTADOR (USA)**, 7, b br g Giant's Causeway (USA)—Istikbal (USA) **Mr J. L. Day**
5 **EVEN BOLDER**, 10, ch g Bold Edge—Level Pegging (IRE) **E. A. Wheeler**
6 **KISS MY HEART**, 4, br f Byron—Kisses **Wedgewood Estates**

THREE-YEAR-OLDS

7 **BEGGERS LUCK**, b f Lucky Story (USA)—Dropitlikeit's Hot (IRE) **Mr G. W. Witheford**

Assistant Trainer: Miss C Nosworthy

Apprentice: Joey Haynes.

---

666 MR ALISTAIR WHILLANS, Hawick
Postal: **Esker House, Newmill-On-Slitrig, Hawick, Roxburghshire, TD9 9UQ**
Contacts: **PHONE (01450) 376642 FAX (01450) 376082 MOBILE (07771) 550555**
E-MAIL acwracing@hotmail.com

1 **AHHDEHKEN**, 8, b g Cloudings (IRE)—Swazi Princess (IRE) **A. C. Whillans**
2 **APACHEE PRINCE (IRE)**, 4, br g Indian Danehill (IRE)—Wheredidthemoneygo (IRE) **J. D. Wright**
3 **CLAUDE CARTER**, 9, b g Elmaamul (USA)—Cruz Santa **Mrs L. M. Whillans**
4 **DALLAS BELL**, 11, ch g Minster Son—Eleanor May **A. C. Whillans**
5 **DANCING GIZMO**, 8, b g Where Or When (IRE)—Tactile **A. C. Whillans**
6 **DUNDOCK**, 12, gr g Cloudings (IRE)—Rakajack **A. C. Whillans**
7 **EUSTON SQUARE**, 7, b g Oasis Dream—Krisia **Granite City Racing & Mr John Waugh**
8 **FLYING DOCTOR**, 10, b g Mark of Esteem (IRE)—Vice Vixen (CAN) **Mr T. McNicholas**
9 **FUNKY MUNKY**, 8, b g Talaash (IRE)—Chilibang Bang **The Twelve Munkys**
10 **GALILEE CHAPEL (IRE)**, 4, b g Baltic King—Triple Zero (IRE) **The Blues Gang**
11 **GLEANN NA NDOCHAIS (IRE)**, 7, b g Zagreb (USA)—Nissereen (USA) **Mr W J E Scott & Mrs M A Scott**
12 **HEART O' THE WEST (IRE)**, 9, b g Tamayaz (USA)—She's All Heart **K. Milligan Partnership**
13 **JON (IRE)**, 5, ch g Refuse To Bend—Calgarth (IRE) **Mr F. Lowe**
14 **LADY BLUESKY**, 10, gr m Cloudings (IRE)—M N L Lady **Mrs S. Harrow Mrs L. M. Whillans**
15 **MEADOWCROFT BOY**, 4, b g Kayf Tara—Blackbriery Thyne (IRE) **W. J. E. Scott**

MR ALISTAIR WHILLANS - Continued

16 ONE IN A ROW (IRE), 6, ch g Saffron Walden (FR)—Rostarr (IRE) **Wildcard Racing**
17 RAVI RIVER (IRE), 9, ch g Barathea (IRE)—Echo River (USA) **Gold Tooth Racing**
18 SAMMY SPIDERMAN, 10, b g Karinga Bay—Thorterdykes Lass (IRE) **John & Liz Elliot, P Copeland**
19 SCRAPPER SMITH (IRE), 7, b g Choisir (AUS)—Lady Ounavarra (IRE) **A. C. Whillans**
20 VITTACHI, 6, b g Bertolini (USA)—Miss Lorilaw (FR) **Sutherland Five**

THREE-YEAR-OLDS

21 ALEXANDRAKOLLONTAI (IRE), b f Amadeus Wolf—Story **R Cabrey W Orr C Spark**

Other Owners: W. M. Ballantyne, Mr A. J. Bonarius, Mr R. Cabrey, J. J. Elliot, Mrs E. J. Elliot, Mr S. R. Fraser, Mr R. J. Goodfellow, T. D. Griffiths, Mr J. S. B. Harrold, Mrs S. Harrow, Mrs D. Jeromson, Mr B. Melrose, K. J. Milligan, Mr W. Orr, Mrs M. A. Scott, Mr C. Spark, Mr G. J. Vallely, Mr J. Waugh, Mr N. Yeoman.

---

667 MR DONALD WHILLANS, Hawick
Postal: **Dodlands Steading, Hawick, Roxburghshire, TD9 8LG**
Contacts: BUSINESS **(01450) 373128** HOME **(01450) 379810** FAX **(01450) 376082**
MOBILE **(07771) 550556**
E-MAIL **donaldwhillans@aol.com** WEBSITE **www.donaldwhillansracing.com**

1 ALLEGHENY VALLEY (IRE), 5, br g Indian Danehill (IRE)—Polyanthus Jones **Mr A. J. M. Duncan**
2 BOLLIN FIONA, 9, ch m Silver Patriarch (IRE)—Bollin Nellie **C. N. Whillans**
3 BOLLIN JULIE, 6, b m Bollin Eric—Bollin Nellie **C. N. Whillans**
4 CHARLIE BUCKET, 10, ch g Sugarfoot—Stoproveritate **Milsey Bay Racing**
5 ELLISTRIN BELLE, 5, b m Helissio (FR)—Hannah Park (IRE) **The Potassium Partnership**
6 HAWAII KLASS, 8, ch g Classic Cliche (IRE)—Youandi **Star Racing**
7 KING KALIUM (IRE), 7, b g Kayf Tara—Hannah Park (IRE) **The Potassium Partnership**
8 LEITH WALK (IRE), 10, ch m Posidonas—Gothic Shadow (IRE) **D. McComb**
9 4, Ch g Courteous—Meda's Song
10 MIA MATRIARCH, 7, ch m Silver Patriarch (IRE)—Youandi **Allan Gilchrist & Peter Wylie**
11 MINI THE MINX (IRE), 7, br m Accordion—Gypsy Run **D. W. Whillans**
12 NODDA HIGH KID, 7, ch g Sir Harry Lewis (USA)—Lindajane (IRE) **D. W. Whillans**
13 SAM PATCH, 10, ch g Weldnaas (USA)—Youandi **Star Racing**
14 SHADOW BOXER, 8, gr g Makbul—Shadows of Silver **The Peeskie Partnership**
15 SNAPPING TURTLE (IRE), 8, b g Turtle Island (IRE)—Rachael's Dawn **D. W. Whillans**
16 TEXAS TILLY, 8, ch m Sir Harry Lewis (USA)—Lindajane (IRE) **Mrs H. M. Whillans**
17 7, B m Meadowbrook—Wee Willow **D. W. Whillans**
18 YINFORTHEROAD (IRE), 6, b g Cloudings (IRE)—Another Whiskey (IRE) **D. W. Whillans**
19 YO LA TENGO (IRE), 6, b g Classic Cliche (IRE)—Strong Edition (IRE) **Mr A. J. M. Duncan**

Other Owners: Mr J. Anderson, Mr R. Bannerman, H. G. Beeby, Mr G. Fairgrieve, A. Gilchrist, Mrs A.M. Rhind, Mr S. A. Taylor, P. A. Wylie.

Jockey (flat): Garry Whillans. **Jockey (NH):** Wilson Renwick. **Conditional:** Ryan Nichol, Callum Whillans.

---

668 MR RICHARD WHITAKER, Scarcroft
Postal: **Hellwood Racing Stables, Hellwood Lane, Scarcroft, Leeds, West Yorkshire, LS14 3BP**
Contacts: PHONE **(01132) 892265** FAX **(01132) 893680** MOBILE **(07831) 870454**
E-MAIL **rmwhitaker@btconnect.com** WEBSITE **www.richardwhitaker.org**

1 AVON BREEZE, 4, b f Avonbridge—African Breeze **Grange Park Racing II & Partner**
2 BAVARIAN NORDIC (USA), 8, b g Barathea (USA)—Dubai Diamond **Six Iron Partnership**
3 DIAMOND BLUE, 5, ch m Namid—Petra Nova **Mrs J. E. Newett**
4 ENDLESS APPLAUSE, 4, b f Royal Applause—Petra Nova **Mrs J. E. Newett**
5 ICY BLUE, 5, b g Iceman—Bridal Path **Country Lane Partnership**
6 LOVE ISLAND, 4, b f Acclamation—Sally Traffic **J. B. Pemberton**
7 MEY BLOSSOM, 8, ch m Captain Rio—Petra Nova **Waz Developments Ltd**
8 MISS ELLA JADE, 4, b f Danbird (AUS)—Keen Melody (USA) **R. M. Whitaker**
9 RIO SANDS, 8, b g Captain Rio—Sally Traffic **The Barflys**
10 RIO'S ROSANNA (IRE), 6, b m Captain Rio—Ling Lane **J. R. Marshall**
11 SAM NOMBULIST, 5, ch g Sleeping Indian—Owdbetts (IRE) **Robert Macgregor**
12 SHALOO DIAMOND, 8, b g Captain Rio—Alacrity **The Barflys**
13 SPIN A WISH, 5, b m Captain Rio—Be My Wish **R. M. Whitaker**

MR RICHARD WHITAKER - Continued

14 **WHATS FOR PUDDING (IRE)**, 5, ch m Kheleyf (USA)—Margaret's Dream (IRE) **Mr R. J. Ball**
15 **WOODACRE**, 6, b g Pyrus (USA)—Fairy Ring (IRE) **Mrs R. M. Whitaker**

THREE-YEAR-OLDS

16 **HAARMONIC**, ch g Haafhd—Abundant **Mr D. A. Walker**
17 **LICHEN ANGEL**, gr f Dark Angel (IRE)—Moss Likely (IRE) **David Horner & David Walker**
18 **PIPERS NOTE**, ch g Piccolo—Madam Valentine **Six Iron Partnership & Partner**
19 **THREEPENCE**, b c Three Valleys (USA)—The Jotter **Nice Day Out Partnership**
20 **TUMBLEWIND**, ch f Captain Rio—African Breeze **Nice Day Out Partnership**
21 **WOTALAD**, b g Bertolini (USA)—Cosmic Song **Mrs J. M. Willows**

TWO-YEAR-OLDS

22 Ch f 2/4 Three Valleys (USA)—Petra Nova (First Trump) (7619)
23 Ch c 20/2 Avonbridge—Scooby Dooby Do (Atraf) (8571)

Other Owners: T. Adams, M. Allen, K. M. Brown, C. Clague, Mrs M. Clayton, A. D. Crombie, Paul Davies (H/gate), J. C. Holmes, Mr D. A. Horner, Exors of the Late Mrs S. Marshall, Mr A. Norrington, G. Pemberton, G. Sanderson, Mr R. M. Whitaker, Mrs R. M. Whitaker, Mrs L. Ziegler.

Assistant Trainer: Simon R Whitaker

MR ARTHUR WHITEHEAD, Craven Arms
Postal: **Lawn Farm, Beambridge, Aston on Clun, Craven Arms, Shropshire, SY7 0HA**
Contacts: **PHONE (01588) 660424**

1 **DELLA SUN (FR)**, 7, b g Della Francesca (USA)—Algarve Sunrise (IRE) **A. J. Whitehead**
2 **JAWAHAL DU MATHAN (FR)**, 5, b g Smadoun (FR)—Stone's Glow (USA) **A. J. Whitehead**
3 **JEANRY (FR)**, 10, b g Marathon (USA)—Envergure **A. J. Whitehead**
4 **ZALGARRY (FR)**, 6, b g Ballingarry (IRE)—Spleen (FR) **A. J. Whitehead**

Jockey (NH): Will Kennedy. **Conditional:** Josh Wall.

MR ARTHUR WHITING, Dursley
Postal: **38 Barrs Lane, North Nibley, Dursley, Gloucestershire, GL11 6DT**
Contacts: **PHONE (01453) 546375 MOBILE (07786) 152539**

1 5, B m Sir Harry Lewis (USA)—Cashel Dancer **A. J. Whiting**
2 **CHARLIE RUFFLES (IRE)**, 5, b g Milan—Rosie Ruffles (IRE) **A. J. Whiting**
3 **INDIAN CITIZEN (IRE)**, 6, ch m Indian River (FR)—Curra Citizen (IRE) **A. J. Whiting**
4 **THE WEE LASS**, 6, b m Act One—Fragrant Rose **A. J. Whiting**
5 **THE WEE MIDGET**, 8, b g Mtoto—Fragrant Rose **A. J. Whiting**

MR HARRY WHITTINGTON, Sparsholt Firs
Postal: **Hill Barn Stables, Sparsholt Firs, Wantage, Oxfordshire, OX12 9XB**
Contacts: **MOBILE (07734) 388357**
E-MAIL harry@harrywhittington.co.uk WEBSITE www.harrywhittington.co.uk

1 **CUBAN PIECE (IRE)**, 5, b g Azamour (IRE)—Naazeq **Lead The Way Syndicate**
2 **DUBAI KISS**, 4, b g Dubai Destination (USA)—Smooch **Lead The Way Syndicate**
3 **FOUROVAKIND**, 8, b g Sir Harry Lewis (USA)—
Four M's **Mr M. G. Hazell, Mr G. Hazell, Mr Andrew F. Sawyer, Mr C. Bosley**
4 **TOMIBOLA (IRE)**, 5, b g Definite Article—Cebola (FR) **Laurence Bellman & Harry Whittington**
5 **VENIR ROUGE**, 9, ch g Dancing Spree (USA)—Al Awaalah **Leading Edge Racing Club**

672 **MR MICHAEL WIGHAM, Newmarket**
Postal: Hamilton Stables, Hamilton Road, Newmarket, Suffolk, CB8 7JQ
Contacts: PHONE (01638) 668806 FAX (01638) 668806 MOBILE (07831) 456426
E-MAIL michaelwigham@hotmail.co.uk

1 AEGEAN KING, 7, b g Falbrav (IRE)—Aegean Dream (IRE) **D. Hassan**
2 BRYANT PARK (USA), 4, ch g Street Cry (IRE)—Cala (FR) **Mr M. Bartram**
3 CATHEDRAL, 4, b c Invincible Spirit (IRE)—Capades Dancer (USA) **Mr C. Bowles**
4 FAIRWAY TO HEAVEN (IRE), 4, b c Jeremy (USA)—Luggala (IRE) **Palatinate Thoroughbred Racing Limited**
5 NORWEGIAN REWARD (IRE), 5, ch g Hernando (FR)—Stay Behind **Tapas Partnership**
6 STEPTURN, 4, b g Invincible Spirit (IRE)—Gay Gallanta (USA) **R. J. Lorenz**
7 SWEET LAVENDER (IRE), 5, b m Dalakhani (IRE)—Dievotchkina (IRE) **Mr M. Bartram**
8 TEE IT UP TO TOMMO (IRE), 4, gr g Clodovil (IRE)—Lamh Eile (IRE) **Palatinate Thoroughbred Racing Limited**
9 THE BLUE DOG (IRE), 6, b m High Chaparral (IRE)—Jules (IRE) **Mr R. W. Carson**
10 YANKEE STORM, 8, b g Yankee Gentleman (USA)—Yes Virginia (USA) **R. L. Maynard**

THREE-YEAR-OLDS

11 CHARTER (IRE), b c Elusive City (USA)—Lucky Norwegian (IRE) **Healwayswantstopullthetrigger**
12 ST GEORGES HILL (IRE), b c Marju (IRE)—Lyrical Dance (USA) **Palatinate Thoroughbred Racing Limited**
13 SUPERBOOT (IRE), b c Holy Roman Emperor (IRE)—
Balting Lass (IRE) **Palatinate Thoroughbred Racing Limited**

Other Owners: H. J. Collingridge, W. R. Hinge, Mr A. T. Murphy, A. Walmsley, M. Wigham.

Assistant Trainer: Sharon Kenyon

673 **MR MARTIN WILESMITH, Dymock**
Postal: Bellamys Farm, Dymock, Gloucestershire, GL18 2DX
Contacts: PHONE (01531) 890410 (01684) 561238 FAX (01684) 893428 MOBILE (07970) 411638
E-MAIL martin@mswilesmith.co.uk

1 LORD BELLAMY (IRE), 11, b g Lord Americo—Paean Express (IRE) **M. S. Wilesmith**
2 SHE'SOLOVELY, 9, b m Alflora (IRE)—Cashmere Lady **M. S. Wilesmith**
3 7, Ch m Alflora (IRE)—Silk Oats **M. S. Wilesmith**
4 SILK ROSE, 9, gr m Terimon—Silk Oats **M. S. Wilesmith**

Assistant Trainer: Ms E. C. Wilesmith (07976 926906)

674 **MR DAI WILLIAMS, Abberley**
Postal: Stable End, Worsley Stables, Bank Lane, Abberley, Worcester, Worcestershire, WR6 6BQ
Contacts: HOME (01488) 638636 FAX (01488) 638121 MOBILE (07879) 403160 (07879) 403595

1 DARK OASIS, 7, b g Dubai Destination (USA)—Silent Waters **Mrs P. S. Yardley**
2 MUSTGO MAN (IRE), 8, b g Karinga Bay—Sister Clyde (IRE) **D. L. Williams**
3 TURN THE TIDE, 5, b m Footstepsinthesand—Syrian Dancer (IRE) **P. V. Charlesworth**

Assistant Trainer: Miss Lucy Horner

Amateur: Miss L. Horner.

675 **MR EVAN WILLIAMS, Llancarfan**
Postal: Aberogwrn Farm, Llancarfan, Nr Barry, Vale of Glamorgan, CF62 3AD
Contacts: PHONE (01446) 754069 (01446) 754045 FAX (01446) 754069 MOBILE (07950) 381227
E-MAIL evanwilliamsracing@hotmail.co.uk

1 A HIT IS A HIT (FR), 8, b g Kahyasi—Highness Lady (GER) **Mrs C. A. Williams**
2 ADAJARAD (IRE), 6, b g Tiger Hill (IRE)—Adirika (IRE) **R. E. R. Williams**
3 AGREE TO DIFFER (IRE), 7, b g Orpen (USA)—Compton Fair **Mr E. O'Sullivan**
4 AJMAN (IRE), 8, b g Orpen (USA)—Grand Madam **Mr R. P. O'Neil**
5 AKARSHAN (IRE), 8, b g Intikhab (USA)—Akdara (IRE) **Mr A. Turton & Mr P. Langford**
6 ARGAUM (IRE), 6, ch g Medicean—Poppy Carew (IRE) **G. Houghton**
7 BALLYMACAHILLCROSS (IRE), 5, br g Presenting—Topanberry (IRE) **Mr & Mrs William Rucker**

MR EVAN WILLIAMS - Continued

8 **BARIZAN (IRE)**, 7, b g Kalanisi (IRE)—Behra (IRE) **Mr P Conway & Mr John Lee Jones**
9 **BARRAKILLA (IRE)**, 6, b g Milan—Kigali (IRE) **Mr & Mrs William Rucker**
10 **BAY CENTRAL (IRE)**, 9, b g Exit To Nowhere (USA)—Pretty Beau (IRE) **R. E. R. Williams**
11 **BILLY BLADE**, 6, b g Generous (IRE)—Lady Blade (IRE) **R. E. R. Williams**
12 **BONOMAN (IRE)**, 10, b g Aboo Hom—Toreva (IRE) **R. E. R. Williams**
13 **BUCK MULLIGAN**, 8, b g Robellino (USA)—Music Park (IRE) **Mr T. L. Fell**
14 **BULLET STREET (IRE)**, 5, ch g Arakan (USA)—Play A Tune (IRE) **Mrs Janet Davies & Mrs C Williams**
15 **CAPITAINE COURAGE (IRE)**, 8, ch g Bering—Four Green (FR) **T. H. Jones**
16 **CAPPA BLEU (IRE)**, 11, b g Pistolet Bleu (IRE)—Cappagale (IRE) **Mr & Mrs William Rucker**
17 **CAPTAIN BROWN**, 5, b g Lomitas—Nicola Bella (IRE) **Mr & Mrs William Rucker**
18 **CAPTAIN PAULIE (IRE)**, 10, b g Lahib (USA)—Garvivonne **R. E. R. Williams**
19 **CLARION CALL**, 5, b g Beat Hollow—Fanfare **M. D. Jones**
20 **COPPER BIRCH (IRE)**, 5, ch g Beneficial—Givehertime (IRE) **Mrs J. Davies**
21 **COURT MINSTREL (IRE)**, 6, b g Court Cave (IRE)—Theatral **Mrs J. Davies**
22 **DANTARI (IRE)**, 8, b g Alhaarth (IRE)—Daniysha (IRE) **Mr D. J. Burchell**
23 **DARCEYS DANCER (IRE)**, 10, b g Lear Spear (USA)—Dun Oengus (IRE) **Mrs C. A. Williams**
24 **DARK SPIRIT (IRE)**, 5, b m Whipper (USA)—Dark Raider (IRE) **Richard Abbott & Mario Stavrou**
25 **DASHING DOC (IRE)**, 6, ch g Dr Fong (USA)—Dashiba **W. R. Thomas**
26 **DE FAOITHESDREAM (IRE)**, 7, br g Balakheri (IRE)—Cutteen Lass (IRE) **Mr R Abbott & Mr M Stavrou**
27 **DEFINITE DREAM (IRE)**, 6, b g Definite Article—Brooks Chariot (IRE) **Mr R. J. H. Geffen**
28 **DEVIL'S DYKE (USA)**, 5, b br g Redoute's Choice (AUS)—Kotuku **R. E. R. Williams**
29 **DI KAPRIO (FR)**, 7, b g Kapgarde (FR)—Miss Nousha (FR) **Mr & Mrs William Rucker**
30 **EMERGING ARTIST (FR)**, 7, b g Dubai Destination (USA)—Picture Princess **R. E. R. Williams**
31 **FIREBIRD FLYER (IRE)**, 6, b g Winged Love (IRE)—Kiora Lady (IRE) **R. E. R. Williams**
32 **FIVE OUT OF FIVE (IRE)**, 9, b g Saddlers' Hall (IRE)—Grangemills **Mr D. J. Burchell**
33 **GAMBO (IRE)**, 7, b g Oscar (IRE)—River Thyne (IRE) **Mr R. J. Gambarini**
34 **GAP OF DUNLOE (IRE)**, 5, b g Hurricane Run (IRE)—Karri Valley (USA) **Einsley & Angela Harries**
35 **GET IT ON (IRE)**, 8, b g King's Theatre (IRE)—Keshia **Mr J. L. Jones**
36 **GOING CONCERN (IRE)**, 6, b g Overbury (IRE)—Scorpio Girl
37 **GRAN TORINO (IRE)**, 8, b g Milan—Miss Greinton (GER) **W. J. Evans**
38 **GURTACRUE (IRE)**, 8, ch g Deploy—Biddy Early (IRE) **Mr & Mrs William Rucker**
39 **HOLD COURT (IRE)**, 6, br g Court Cave (IRE)—Tipsy Miss (IRE) **Edwards & Howell**
40 **INEEDANAME**, 5, ch m Generous (IRE)—Absalom's Girl **Mrs C. A. Williams**
41 **ISLANDMAGEE (IRE)**, 6, b g Heron Island (IRE)—Sakanda (IRE) **Mr & Mrs William Rucker**
42 **JACKY LE CHATELAIN (FR)**, 5, b g Kapgarde (FR)—Nabucca (FR) **Mrs C. A. Waters**
43 **KAYALAR (IRE)**, 5, b g Noverre (USA)—Katiykha (IRE) **Mrs J. Davies**
44 **KING MASSINI (IRE)**, 7, b g Dr Massini (IRE)—King's Linnet (IRE) **R. E. R. Williams**
45 **KING OF WING (IRE)**, 4, b g Hawk Wing (USA)—Miss Shivvy (IRE) **Chris Watkins & David N. Reynolds**
46 **LANCETTO (IRE)**, 8, b g Dubai Destination (USA)—Lanciana (IRE) **Mr R. J. Gambarini**
47 **LAUBERHORN**, 6, b g Dubai Destination (USA)—Ski Run **Border Pointers**
48 **LAVA LAMP (GER)**, 6, b g Shamardal (USA)—La Felicita **Mrs J. Davies**
49 **LIENOSUS (IRE)**, 7, b g Old Vic—Red Supporter **Mr & Mrs William Rucker**
50 **LUCAINDUBAI (IRE)**, 7, b br g Orpen (USA)—Singhana (USA) **Mr R. J. Gambarini**
51 **MAKETHE MOSTOFNOW (IRE)**, 8, b g Milan—Pass The Leader (IRE) **Mrs J. Davies**
52 **MEGABILL (IRE)**, 9, b g King's Theatre (IRE)—Dawn Bid (IRE) **Mrs J. Davies**
53 **MERCURY BAY (IRE)**, 8, ch g Karinga Bay—Jolie Landaise (FR) **Mr E. C. Jones**
54 **MILO MAN (IRE)**, 5, b g Milan—Rilmount (IRE) **Mr & Mrs William Rucker**
55 **MR MOSS (IRE)**, 8, b g Moscow Society (USA)—Yesterdays Gorby (IRE) **Mr & Mrs William Rucker**
56 **NODIVIDENDSAGAIN**, 5, b g Kayf Tara—Catherine's Run (IRE) **POS Partnership**
57 **ONE IN A MILAN (IRE)**, 8, b g Milan—Kitty Star (IRE) **Mr P. M. Langford**
58 **OSCAR GOGO (IRE)**, 11, b g Oscar (IRE)—Ceolbridgequeen (IRE) **Mrs D. Mccabe**
59 **OSCAR SUNSET (IRE)**, 6, b g Oscar (IRE)—Derravarra Sunset (IRE) **Geoff & Anne Price**
60 **PRIMA PORTA**, 7, b m American Post—Porta Marzia (CHI) **D.P.Barrie & H.A.F. Parshall**
61 **SAKHEE BOB**, 4, ch g Sakhee (USA)—Absolve (USA) **R. E. R. Williams**
62 **SEREN CWMTUDU (IRE)**, 9, b m Glacial Storm (USA)—Keel Row **T. H. Jones**
63 **SHAYS RIVER (IRE)**, 8, b g Heron Island (IRE)—Miss Flic **R. E. R. Williams**
64 **SIBERIAN TIGER (IRE)**, 8, b g Xaar—Flying Millie (IRE) **Mrs J. Davies**
65 **SILVERBURN (IRE)**, 12, b g Presenting—Polly Puttens **Mrs C. A. Williams**
66 **SIMARIAN (IRE)**, 8, b g Kalanisi (IRE)—Sinnariya (IRE) **Mr P. Conway**
67 **STILL BELIEVING (IRE)**, 5, ch m Blueprint (IRE)—Im A Believer (IRE) **R. E. R. Williams**
68 **STORMYISLAND AHEAD**, 8, b g Turtle Island (IRE)—Queen's Banquet **Mr D. M. Williams**
69 **SUBLIME TALENT (IRE)**, 8, b g Sadler's Wells (USA)—Summer Trysting (USA) **Itsfuninit**
70 **TARKARI (IRE)**, 8, ch g Fantastic Light (USA)—Taraza (IRE) **Clive Cook & Irving Struel**
71 **TEDNEY EXPRESS (IRE)**, 6, b g Presenting—Persian Argument (IRE) **Mr & Mrs William Rucker**
72 **TEMPTING PARADISE (IRE)**, 10, ch g Grand Lodge (USA)—Summer Trysting (USA) **Norwester Racing Club**

MR EVAN WILLIAMS - Continued

73 **THE ROCKIES (IRE)**, 6, b g Oscar (IRE)—Calling Classy (IRE) **Mr D. M. Williams**
74 **THEGAYGARDENER**, 5, b g Sulamani (IRE)—Lady Blade (IRE) **Mrs D. E. Cheshire**
75 **THINK ITS ALL OVER (USA)**, 6, b g Tiznow (USA)—A P Petal (USA) **J. T. Warner**
76 **TIGER O'TOOLE (IRE)**, 8, gr g King's Theatre (IRE)—Memsahib Ofesteem **Ms S. A. Howell**
77 **TIMESAWASTIN (IRE)**, 5, b g Curtain Time (IRE)—Innocent Approach (IRE) **Mrs C. A. Waters**
78 **TIN POT MAN (IRE)**, 7, br g Tillerman—White-Wash **Oaks**
79 **TORNADO IN MILAN (IRE)**, 7, b g Milan—Julika (GER) **Mr & Mrs William Rucker**
80 **TORNANT (IRE)**, 7, b g Milan—Graffogue (IRE) **Mrs C. A. Williams**
81 **TRADITIONAL BOB (IRE)**, 8, b g Saddlers' Hall (IRE)—Portia's Delight (IRE) **Mr W. J. Eddy-Williams**
82 **TRIPTICO (FR)**, 7, gr g Turgeon (USA)—Al Kicks (FR) **Mr & Mrs William Rucker**
83 **TROOPER CLARENCE**, 9, b g Trempolino (USA)—Ten To Six **Mrs S. De Wilde**
84 **UGO (USA)**, 5, b g Street Cry (IRE)—Min Elreeh (USA) **Mrs C. A. Williams**
85 **WEST WITH THE WIND**, 8, b g Fasliyev (USA)—Midnight Angel (GER) **Mrs J. Davies**
86 **WESTER ROSS (IRE)**, 9, b g Fruits of Love (USA)—Diabaig **T. H. Jones**
87 **WILLIAM'S WISHES (IRE)**, 8, b g Oscar (IRE)—Strong Wishes (IRE) **Mrs D. E. Cheshire**
88 **ZAMA ZAMA**, 6, b g Sakhee (USA)—Insinuation (IRE) **ARC**
89 **ZARZAL (IRE)**, 5, b g Dr Fong (USA)—Zarwala (IRE) **Mrs J. Davies**

Other Owners: R. J. Abbott, D. P. Barrie, Mr C. Cook, M. V. Dawson, J. R. Edwards, Mr P. Griffiths, Mr W. E. V. Harries, Mrs A. Harries, Mrs N. P. Lloyd, D. G. Long, W. J. G. Morse, Mr H. A. F. Parshall, Mr M. Prendergast, Mr G. Price, Mrs A. C. Price, Mr P. Pyatt, Mr D. N. Reynolds, W. J. Rucker, Mrs A. Rucker, Mr P. Sevenoaks, Mr D. G. Sevenoaks, Mr A. Smallman, M. Stavrou, I. Struel, Mr C. Trigg, Mr A. Turton, C. D. Watkins, Mr S. Williams.

Assistant Trainers: James Tudor, Cath Williams

Jockey (NH): Paul Moloney, Christian Williams.

676
MR IAN WILLIAMS, Alvechurch
Postal: **Dominion Racing Stables, Seafield Lane, Alvechurch, Birmingham, B48 7HL**
Contacts: **PHONE (01564) 822392 FAX (01564) 829475 MOBILE (07976) 645384**
E-MAIL info@ianwilliamsracing.com WEBSITE www.ianwilliamsracing.com

1 **AMPLEFORTH**, 5, ch g Pivotal—Anna Amalia (IRE) **Macable Partnership**
2 **AN CAT DUBH (IRE)**, 4, b g One Cool Cat (USA)—Bella Estella (GER) **Mr P. E. Wildes**
3 **BAILE ANRAI (IRE)**, 9, b g Norwich—Rose Ana (IRE) **Massive**
4 **BALLYALTON (IRE)**, 6, b g Pierre—Almilto (IRE) **Mr J. Westwood**
5 **BARBATOS (FR)**, 7, gr g Martaline—Peace Bay (FR) **Power Panels Electrical Systems Ltd**
6 **BOBCATBILLY (IRE)**, 7, b g Overbury (IRE)—Cush Jewel (IRE) **P. J. Vogt**
7 **CARTER**, 7, b g Reset (AUS)—Cameo Role (GER) **Stratford Bards Racing No 2**
8 **CLASSIC CASE (IRE)**, 6, b g Classic Cliche (IRE)—Rashie (IRE) **The Three Graces**
9 **COMMISSAR**, 4, b g Soviet Star (USA)—Sari **S. Hassiakos**
10 **CONRY (IRE)**, 7, ch g Captain Rio—Altizaf **Mr T. Birchall**
11 **COOL HAND LUKE (IRE)**, 4, br g Le Vie Dei Colori—Thelma Louise (IRE) **Mr P. L. Mousley**
12 **COTILLION**, 7, b g Sadler's Wells (USA)—Riberac **P. J. Vogt**
13 **CRUISE TOTHELIMIT (IRE)**, 5, b g Le Vie Dei Colori—Kiva **Odysian Limited**
14 **DRUMLANG (IRE)**, 7, b g Soviet Star (USA)—Sherekiya (IRE) **M. Roberts J. O'Shea S. Hunt R. Stearman**
15 **ETANIA**, 5, b m King's Theatre (IRE)—Linnet (GER) **Denarius Consulting Ltd**
16 **FINE MOMENT**, 5, b m Pivotal—Evasive Quality (IRE) **The Ferandlin Peaches**
17 **FREDO (IRE)**, 9, ch g Lomitas—Felina (GER) **Mrs J. S. Allen**
18 **GABRIAL'S GIFT (IRE)**, 4, gr g Verglas (IRE)—Sahara Lady (IRE) **Dr M. B. Q. S. Koukash**
19 **GABRIAL'S HOPE (FR)**, 4, b g Teofilo (IRE)—Wedding Night (IRE) **Dr M. B. Q. S. Koukash**
20 **GABRIAL'S KING (IRE)**, 4, b g Hurricane Run (IRE)—Danella (IRE) **Dr M. B. Q. S. Koukash**
21 **GENZY (FR)**, 5, b g Gentlewave (IRE)—Zycia (IRE) **Michael H. Watt & Chris N. Wright**
22 **GHOST OF A SMILE (IRE)**, 5, b g Oscar (IRE)—Dix Huit Brumaire (FR) **Mr S. Cox**
23 **GLASSAWINE**, 6, gr g Verglas (IRE)—Persian Ruby (IRE) **R. S. Brookhouse**
24 **GRAND GIGOLO (FR)**, 4, b g Enrique—Belle D'ecajeul (FR) **Mr P. A. Downing**
25 **HAWKESHEAD**, 6, b g Rainbow Quest (USA)—Ciboure **Mr & Mrs G. Middlebrook**
26 **EL PRESIDENTE (GER)**, 6, ch g Royal Dragon (USA)—Independent Miss (GER) **P. J. Vogt**
27 **INCENDO**, 7, ch g King's Best (USA)—Kindle **I. P. Williams**
28 **JUNE FRENCH (FR)**, 5, b m Jimble (FR)—Sunbelt Broker **Brigadier Racing**
29 **KIWAYU**, 4, b g Medicean—Kibara **Mr P. E. Wildes**
30 **LAYLA'S HERO (IRE)**, 6, b g One Cool Cat (USA)—Capua (USA) **Dr M. B. Q. S. Koukash**
31 **MANADAM (FR)**, 10, b g Mansonnien (FR)—Cadoudane (FR) **Macable Partnership**
32 **MISS LUCKY PENNY (IRE)**, 7, ch m Karinga Bay—Singing Cottage **S. G. Adams**
33 **MORANT BAY (IRE)**, 4, b f Montjeu—Quad's Melody (IRE) **Mr N. Martin**

MR IAN WILLIAMS - Continued

34 **MR DREAM MAKER (IRE)**, 5, b g Araafa (IRE)—Paola Maria **The Blue Celery Racing Partnership**
35 **NASHVILLE (IRE)**, 4, b g Galileo (IRE)—Brown Eyes **Dr M. B. Q. S. Koukash**
36 **NEWNTON LODGE**, 4, b g Rail Link—Widescreen (USA) **Mr P. E. Wildes**
37 **NUBAR BOY**, 6, ch g Compton Place—Out Like Magic **Mr P. Slater**
38 **ORTEA**, 4, b g Vital Equine (IRE)—Artistic (IRE) **Mr P. Slater**
39 **PARISIAN PYRAMID (IRE)**, 7, gr g Verglas (IRE)—Sharadja (IRE) **Dr M. B. Q. S. Koukash**
40 **POETIC POWER (IRE)**, 4, b g Dylan Thomas (IRE)—Chalice Wells **Stratford Bards Racing**
41 **PORTWAY FLYER (IRE)**, 5, br g King's Theatre (IRE)—Next Best Thing (IRE) **P. Kelly**
42 **RICHMOND (FR)**, 8, b g Assessor (IRE)—Hirondel de Serley (FR) **Hills of Ledbury Ltd**
43 **ROSSETTI**, 5, gr g Dansili—Snowdrops **Mr P. E. Wildes**
44 **SAM SHARP (USA)**, 7, b br g Johannesburg (USA)—Caffe (USA) **Mr N. Martin**
45 **SEE THE STORM**, 5, b br g Statue of Liberty (USA)—Khafayif (USA) **Keating Bradley Fold Limited**
46 **SIR MAXIMILIAN (IRE)**, 4, b g Royal Applause—Nebraska Lady (IRE) **Mr P. E. Wildes**
47 **SOLIX (FR)**, 7, b br g Al Namix (FR)—Solimade (FR) **P. J. Vogt**
48 **SONOFAGUN (FR)**, 7, b g Turgeon—Detonante (FR) **The Piranha Partnership**
49 **STAR OF SALFORD**, 4, b f Hernando (FR)—City of Angels **R. S. Brookhouse**
50 **STETSON**, 7, b g Groom Dancer (USA)—Mindomica **Mr B. Brookhouse**
51 **SWINGING HAWK (IRE)**, 7, ch g Hawk Wing (USA)—Saldenschwinge (GER) **Jamie Roberts & Jack Turton**
52 **TADABEER**, 5, b g Green Desert (USA)—Perfect Plum (IRE) **Sir Alex Ferguson & Sotirios Hassiakos**
53 **TEAK (IRE)**, 6, b g Barathea (IRE)—Szabo (IRE) **Farranamanagh**
54 **TYRANA (GER)**, 10, ch m Acatenango (GER)—Tascalina (GER) **The Piranha Partnership**
55 **WATT BRODERICK (IRE)**, 4, ch g Hawk Wing (USA)—Kingsridge (IRE) **P. Kelly**
56 **WESTERN APPROACHES**, 6, b m Westerner—Bayariyka (IRE) **M. H. Watt**

THREE-YEAR-OLDS

57 **MR VENDMAN (IRE)**, b g Whipper (USA)—So Precious (IRE) **Vendman Systems Limited**

Other Owners: Mr Sam Allardyce, Mrs M. C. Antrobus, Mr Stephen Bell, Mr Ian Bennett, Mr T. J. Boniface, Ms Karen Bourdon, Mr Phil Brown, Mr M. Burford, Mr D. J. Bussell, Sir Alex Ferguson, Mr P. J. Hall, Mr P. V. Harris, Ms R. J. Harris, Mr T. Hart, Mr S. Hassiakos, Mr S. Hunt, Mr A. Killoran, Mr Peter James Legros, Mr S. Mackintosh, Mr F. Mackintosh, Mr G. Middlebrook, Mrs L. Middlebrook, Mr A. Miles, Mr A. J. Moore, Mr Michael Morrissey, Mrs Anne Morrissey, Mr Paul R. Nodder, Mr John F. O'Shea, Mr S. D. Petty, Mr M. J. Petty, Mr M. M. Pitman, Mr M. M. Roberts, Mr Jamie Robert Roberts, Mr Mark J. Savage, Mr T. Spraggett, Mr R. Stearman, Mr R. J. Swinbourne, Mrs Lucy Thomas, Mr P. Thwaites, Mr R. J. Turton, Mr J. Tyrrell, Mr R. J. Tyrrell, Mr Michael H. Watt, Mr Christopher Wright.

Assistant Trainer: Kevin Frost

Jockey (NH): Dougie Costello, Harry Skelton. **Conditional:** Robbie McCarth.

---

677 **MR NICK WILLIAMS, South Molton**
Postal: **Culverhill Farm, George Nympton, South Molton, Devon, EX36 4JE**
Contacts: **HOME (01769) 574174 FAX (01769) 573661 MOBILE (07855) 450379**

1 **ALFIE SPINNER (IRE)**, 8, b g Alflora (IRE)—Little Red Spider **Alan Beard & Brian Beard**
2 **BENEFIQUE ROYALE**, 5, ch m Beneficial—Royale De Vassy (FR) **Jakeman, Davies, Downes, Hewlett & Booth**
3 **BLACKSTAFF (IRE)**, 8, b g Needle Gun (IRE)—Sister Swing **Mrs J. R. Williams**
4 **COMTE D'ANJOU**, 4, b g Desert King (IRE)—Delayed (FR) **Mrs S. J. Faulks**
5 **CORNAS (NZ)**, 11, b g Prized (USA)—Duvessa (NZ) **The Gascoigne Brookes Partnership**
6 **DIAMOND ECLIPSE (IRE)**, 7, b g Double Eclipse (IRE)—Glory-Glory (IRE) **Larkhills Racing Partnership**
7 **DIAMOND HARRY**, 10, b g Sir Harry Lewis (USA)—Swift Conveyance (IRE) **Paul Duffy Diamond Partnership**
8 **FATHER PROBUS**, 7, ch g Fleetwood (IRE)—Nearly At Sea **Mr E. G. M. Beard**
9 **FOR NON STOP (IRE)**, 8, b g Alderbrook—Lost Link (IRE) **Potensis Limited & Mr Chris Giles**
10 **GEORGE NYMPTON (IRE)**, 7, br g Alderbrook—Countess Camilla **The Bacchanalians**
11 **GREYWELL BOY**, 6, gr g Fair Mix (IRE)—Rakajack **Chasing Gold Limited**
12 **HORATIO HORNBLOWER (IRE)**, 5, b br g Presenting—Countess Camilla **Huw & Richard Davies**
13 **KATEAL**, 10, b m Supreme Leader—Quiet City **Yeo Racing Partnership**
14 **MALJIMAR (IRE)**, 13, b g Un Desperado (FR)—Marble Miller (IRE) **Mrs J. R. Williams**
15 **MATERIAL BOY**, 6, b g Karinga Bay—Material Girl **You Can Be Sure**
16 **PINKNEYS PRINCE**, 6, b g Fair Mix (IRE)—Cool Run **Mr M. F. Stenning**
17 **POLITEO (FR)**, 7, ch g Lando (GER)—Italienne (USA) **Mr M. F. Stenning**
18 4, B f Milan—Rachel C (IRE) **Mrs S. A. Noott**
19 **REVE DE SIVOLA (FR)**, 8, b g Assessor (IRE)—Eva de Chalamont (FR) **Paul Duffy Diamond Partnership**
20 **RIO DE SIVOLA (FR)**, 4, bl g Caballo Raptor (CAN)—Pierrebrune (FR) **Forty Winks Syndicate**

MR NICK WILLIAMS - Continued

21 **ROYALE'S CHARTER,** 7, ch g Karinga Bay—
Royale De Vassy (FR) **Jakeman, Davies, Downes, Booth & Birchenough**
22 **RUMPLETEAZER (IRE),** 5, b g Oscar (IRE)—Fleeting Arrow (IRE) **S. J. Brown**
23 4, B g Winged Love (IRE)—Sardagna (FR) **Mrs S. J. Faulks**
24 **SARIKA (FR),** 7, b g Grand Tresor (FR)—Arika (FR) **Mrs J. R. Williams**
25 **SHALIMAR FROMENTRO (FR),** 7, gr g Martaline—Miss des Ormeaux (FR) **Mrs J. R. Williams**
26 **SWINCOMBE FLAME,** 7, b m Exit To Nowhere (USA)—Lady Felix **Yeo Racing Partnership**
27 **TEA FOR TWO,** 4, b g Kayf Tara—One For Me **Mrs J. R. Williams**
28 **THE ITALIAN YOB (IRE),** 5, b g Milan—The Rebel Lady (IRE) **The Macaroni Beach Society**
29 **ULIS DE VASSY (FR),** 5, b g Voix du Nord (FR)—
Helathou (FR) **Len & White, Hewlett, Robinson, Banyard & Booth**
30 **UN AMI (FR),** 5, gr g Dom Alco (FR)—Immage (FR) **Mrs J. R. Williams**
31 **UN BON P'TIT GARS (FR),** 5, b g Robin des Champs (FR)—Nee A Saint Voir (FR) **K Alexander/ R Watts**
32 **URBAIN DE SIVOLA (FR),** 5, ch g Le Fou (IRE)—Neva de Sivola (FR) **Potensis Limited & Mr Chris Giles**
33 **VEAUCE DE SIVOLA (FR),** 4, b g Assessor (IRE)—Eva de Chalamont (FR) **D. P. Duffy**
34 **WAYWARD FROLIC,** 7, br g Fair Mix (IRE)—Mighty Frolic **Mrs J. R. Williams**

THREE-YEAR-OLDS

35 **ABRACADABRA SIVOLA (FR),** b g Le Fou (IRE)—Pierrebrune (FR) **White, Underhill & Ling**
36 **AFTER EIGHT SIVOLA (FR),** b g Shaanmer (IRE)—Eva de Chalamont (FR) **Larkhills Racing Partnership III**
37 B g Saint des Saints (FR)—Belle du Roi (FR) **White, Underhill & Ling**
38 **DOLORES DELIGHTFUL (FR),** b f Saint des Saints (FR)—Us Et Coutumes (FR) **Mrs E. Hutton**
39 **FOX NORTON (FR),** b g Lando (GER)—Natt Musik (FR) **B. Dunn**

Other Owners: Mrs Celia Djivanovic, Mr K. Alexander, Mr Kerry Barker, B. M. Barrett, A. C. Beard, B. M. Beard, Dr M. Booth, Mr N. Brookes, Mr T. H. Chadney, Mr K. Conlan, Dr C. Cowell, H. G. Davies, Mr R. L. Davies, Mr A. S. P. Drake, Mr Paul Duffy, Mrs Sarah Faulks, Mr N. Ferrand, Mr A. P. Gale, Mr C. J. Garner, Mr D. A. Gascoigne, Mr C. M. Giles, Mr Peter Green, Mr A. Holt, Mrs Ellissa Hutton, L. J. Jakeman, Mr J. E. Lawrence, D. Morgan, K. B. W. Parkhouse, Mr I. Paye, M. L. Pepper, Potensis Limited, Mr G. C. Pratt, Mr J. D. Robinson, Ms C. A. Sawer, Miss Alice Simmons, Mr R. C. Watts, Mrs K. D. Yeo.

Assistant Trainer: Mrs Jane Williams

Amateur: Miss Lizzie Kelly.

---

678 **MR STUART WILLIAMS, Newmarket**
Postal: Diomed Stables, Hamilton Road, Newmarket, Suffolk, CB8 0PD
Contacts: STABLES/OFFICE (01638) 663984 HOME (01638) 560143 MOBILE (07730) 314102
E-MAIL stuart@stuartwilliamsracing.co.uk WEBSITE www.stuartwilliamsracing.co.uk

1 **ALDERMOOR (USA),** 7, b g Tale of The Cat (USA)—Notting Hill (BRZ) **Mr D. Hudson-Wood**
2 **AQUILONIUS (IRE),** 4, b c Soviet Star (USA)—Via Verbano (IRE) **T W Morley & Mrs J Morley**
3 **BLUE JACK,** 8, b g Cadeaux Genereux—Fairy Flight (IRE) **Mr D. Hudson-Wood**
4 **CHAPTER SEVEN,** 4, ch g Excellent Art—My First Romance **Pearl Bloodstock Limited**
5 **ETON RIFLES (IRE),** 8, b g Pivotal—Maritsa (IRE) **The Eton Riflemen**
6 **EX ORIENTE (IRE),** 4, b g Azamour (IRE)—Little Whisper (IRE) **Mrs J Morley**
7 **MY KINGDOM (IRE),** 7, b g King's Best (USA)—Nebraas **My Kingdom For A Horse**
8 **PETTOCHSIDE,** 4, b g Refuse To Bend (IRE)—Clear Impression (IRE) **J. G. Thom**
9 **PRINCELY SUM (IRE),** 4, b c Refuse To Bend (IRE)—Green Dollar (IRE) **Essex Racing Club et al**
10 **RESONARE,** 4, b g Echo of Light—Pretty Kool **G. D. Thompson**
11 **SIM SALA BIM,** 5, gr ro h Act One—Francia **Mr A. B. Atkins**
12 **TAROOQ (USA),** 7, b g War Chant (USA)—Rose of Zollern (IRE) **H Chamberlain, I Pearce**
13 **THE STRIG,** 6, b g Mujahid (USA)—Pretty Kool **Brian Piper & David Cobill**
14 **VENETIAS DREAM (IRE),** 4, b f Librettist (USA)—Machaera **Essex Racing Club**
15 **WELEASE BWIAN (IRE),** 4, b g Kheleyf (USA)—Urbanize (USA) **W. E. Enticknap**

THREE-YEAR-OLDS

16 **CHARLOTTE RHODES,** b f Halling (USA)—Kunda (IRE) **Mr D. Hudson-Wood**
17 **CHERRY PRINCESS,** ch gr f Act One—Francia **Mr B Piper & Mr D Shekells**
18 **HELAMIS,** b f Shirocco (GER)—Alnoor (USA) **Mr D. Shekells**
19 **HOLLEY SHIFTWELL,** ch f Bahamian Bounty—Persario **J. W. Parry**
20 **JIMMY THE SNOOZE (IRE),** b c Moss Vale (IRE)—Mrs Kepple **Eclipse Horse Racing**
21 **LITTLE ALICE,** ch f Haafhd—Allespagne (USA) **Alasdair Simpson**
22 **LUCK (IRE),** b g Red Clubs (IRE)—Pure Fiction **L. Sheridan**

MR STUART WILLIAMS - Continued

23 **POSITIVE PARENTING (IRE)**, b f Malibu Moon (USA)—Real Cat (USA) **S. C. Williams**
24 **PRINCE OF PROPHETS (IRE)**, b g Antonius Pius (USA)—
Chifney Rush (IRE) **Miss Emily Stevens & Mr Paul Stevens**
25 **TYCHAIOS**, b g Green Desert (USA)—Tychy **Mr P. Ellinas**

TWO-YEAR-OLDS

26 **CHAINSAW**, b c 1/4 Pastoral Pursuits—Roodeye (Inchinor) (50000) **Qatar Racing Limited**
27 B c 7/4 Araafa (IRE)—Evening Charm (IRE) (Bering) **S. C. Williams**
28 Ch f 25/3 Pastoral Pursuits—Imperialistic (IRE) (Imperial Ballet (IRE)) (50000) **J. W. Parry**
29 B f 4/3 Tiger Hill (IRE)—Ipsa Loquitur (Unfuwain (USA)) (6000) **Alasdair Simpson**
30 **NOVA CHAMP (IRE)**, ch c 22/3 Intikhab (USA)—Baby Bunting (Wolfhound (USA)) (63491) **Qatar Racing Limited**
31 Gr c 31/3 Verglas (IRE)—Russian Empress (IRE) (Trans Island) (15000) **S. C. Williams**
32 B f 19/4 Royal Applause—Tora Bora (Grand Lodge (USA)) (20000) **J. W. Parry**
33 Br f 21/1 Dixie Union (USA)—Witten (USA) (Fusaichi Pegasus (USA)) (17000) **J. W. Parry**

Other Owners: Mr D. L. Cobill, Mr M. Montague, T. W. Morley, Mrs M. J. Morley, Mr R. Morris, Mr B. V. Piper, R. B. Root, Mrs J. P. Root, D. A. Shekells, P. W. Stevens, Mr Stuart C. Williams.

Assistant Trainer: Kirstine Wright

Apprentice: Nanna Hansen. **Amateur:** Miss Natalie Hambling.

---

679 **MISS VENETIA WILLIAMS, Hereford**
Postal: Aramstone, Kings Caple, Hereford, Herefordshire, HR1 4TU
Contacts: PHONE (01432) 840646 MOBILE (07770) 627108
E-MAIL venetia.williams@virgin.net WEBSITE www.venetiawilliams.com

1 **ADELAR (GER)**, 8, b g Samum (GER)—Arpista (GER) **Mr B Dice & Mr D Jinks**
2 **ART PROFESSOR (IRE)**, 9, b g In The Wings—Itab (USA) **J. P. Hancock**
3 **BAILEYS CONCERTO (IRE)**, 7, b g Bach (IRE)—None The Wiser (IRE) **G. R. Bailey Ltd**
4 **BALLYOLIVER**, 9, b g Kayf Tara—Macklette (IRE) **Mr R. M. Britten-Long**
5 **BENNYS MIST (IRE)**, 7, b g Beneficial—Dark Mist (IRE) **Mezzone Family**
6 **BOBBLE BORU (IRE)**, 5, b m Brian Boru—Balreask Lady (IRE) **Mrs B. B. Grainger**
7 **BRICK RED**, 6, ch g Dubawi (IRE)—Duchcov **Julian Taylor & Andrew Brooks**
8 **BROWNS BROOK (IRE)**, 7, b g Bob Back (USA)—All Over Now (IRE) **Mrs V. A. Bingham**
9 **CARRICKBOY (IRE)**, 9, b g Silver Patriarch (IRE)—Alaskan Princess (IRE) **T. J. Hemmings**
10 **CICERON (IRE)**, 7, b g Pivotal—Aiglonne (USA) **Verrier, Bowditch, Secretan**
11 **CLOUDED THOUGHTS (IRE)**, 7, br g Definite Article—Native Design (IRE) **Howard Spooner & N Wellington**
12 **DARE ME (IRE)**, 9, b g Bob Back (USA)—Gaye Chatelaine (IRE) **Shire Birds**
13 **DRUMSHAMBO (USA)**, 7, b g Dynaformer (USA)—Gossamer (USA) **The Grouse Partnership**
14 **DUAISEOIR (IRE)**, 7, b g Bachelor Duke (USA)—Masnada (IRE) **Mezzone Family**
15 **DUNGENESS**, 5, b g Beat All (USA)—Maydoo (IRE) **The Bellamy Partnership**
16 **EMPEROR'S CHOICE (IRE)**, 6, b g Flemensfirth (USA)—House-of-Hearts (IRE) **The Bellamy Partnership**
17 **FALCON'S PRESENT**, 5, br m Presenting—Mini Mandy **Falcons Line Ltd**
18 **FANNYTHEWUNDAHORSE (IRE)**, 6, b m Alderbrook—Woodford Beauty (IRE) **Suzanne & Nigel Williams**
19 **FINE LILY**, 4, gr f Fair Mix (IRE)—Lily Grey (FR) **Allen & Monica Powley**
20 **GENERALISE**, 7, br g Generous (IRE)—Polarise **R. J. Cadoret**
21 **GORGEHOUS LLIEGE (FR)**, 7, b g Lavirco (GER)—Charme d'estruval (FR) **Mr A. L. Brooks**
22 **GUYDUS (IRE)**, 9, b m Old Vic—Lady Mayday (IRE) **Zara & John Johnstone, & Nicky Coe**
23 **HADA MEN (USA)**, 8, b g Dynaformer (USA)—Catchy (USA) **Gay & Peter Hartley**
24 **HOUBLON DES OBEAUX (FR)**, 6, b g Panoramic—Harkosa (FR) **Mrs J. Blackwell**
25 **HOWARD'S LEGACY (IRE)**, 7, b g Generous (IRE)—Ismene (FR) **A. G. Parker**
26 **HUFF AND PUFF**, 6, b g Azamour (IRE)—Coyote **Gay & Peter Hartley**
27 **IDARAH (USA)**, 10, gr g Aljabr (USA)—Fatina **The Shedding Greys**
28 **JUPITER REX (FR)**, 6, ch g Dano-Mast—Creme Pralinee (FR) **Mr P. G. Nathan & Mrs J. Young**
29 **KAHSABELLE (FR)**, 8, b m Kahyasi—Lysabelle (FR) **Miss V. M. Williams**
30 **KAPGA DE CERISY (FR)**, 5, ch g Kapgarde (FR)—Non Liquet **Mr A. L. Brooks**
31 **KATENKO (FR)**, 7, b g Laveron—Katiana (FR) **Mr A. L. Brooks**
32 **KING OF GLORY**, 5, b g Kayf Tara—Glory Be **Mrs B. M. Willcocks**
33 **KINGCORA (FR)**, 5, b g King's Theatre (IRE)—Coralisse Royale (FR) **Mrs J. Blackwell**
34 **KINGS RIVER (FR)**, 4, b br g Lost World (IRE)—Si Parfaite (FR) **Mrs J. Blackwell**
35 **LAST SHOT (FR)**, 6, b g Le Fou (IRE)—Lucky Shot (FR) **Mr Basil Richards**
36 **LEGEND ERRY (IRE)**, 9, b g Act One—Azure Lake (USA) **The Legend's Syndicate 1**
37 **LEVIATHAN**, 6, b g Dubawi (IRE)—Gipsy Moth **H. E. Ansell**

MISS VENETIA WILLIAMS - Continued

38 **LONE RANGER (FR)**, 5, b h Muhtathir—L'etoile de Mer (FR) **Mr A. L. Brooks**
39 **LOOKING ON**, 5, b g Observatory (USA)—Dove Tree (FR) **Mr Irvin S. Naylor**
40 **LOWER HOPE DANDY**, 6, gr g Karinga Bay—Cheeky Mare **Mr W. S. C. Richards**
41 **MARKET OPTION (IRE)**, 7, b g Lord Americo—Ticklepenny (IRE) **The Gambling Cousins**
42 **MENTALIST (FR)**, 5, b g Westerner—Lady Carole (FR) **Brooks, Burke & Cunningham**
43 **MIKO DE BEAUCHENE (FR)**, 13, b g Nashamaa—Chipie d'angron (FR) **Mr A. O. Wiles**
44 **MON MOME (FR)**, 13, b g Passing Sale (FR)—Etoile du Lion (FR) **Mrs V. A. Bingham**
45 **MONETARY FUND (USA)**, 7, b g Montjeu (IRE)—Maddie G (USA) **Mr A. L. Brooks**
46 **MOUJIK BORGET (FR)**, 5, ch g Layman (USA)—Fancy Tune (FR) **Sunday Lunch Partnership**
47 **MRS JORDAN (IRE)**, 5, b m King's Theatre (IRE)—Regents Dancer (IRE) **The Hon J. R. Drummond**
48 **NAGPUR (FR)**, 7, b g Byzantium (FR)—Bel'cris (FR) **Miss S. Douglas-Pennant**
49 **NICEONEFRANKIE**, 7, b g Ishiguru (USA)—Chesnut Ripple **Old Carthusian Racing Society**
50 **NOBUNAGA**, 8, ch g Beat Hollow—Absolute Precision (USA) **The Risky Partnership**
51 **OLD WAY (IRE)**, 7, b g Gold Away (IRE)—Brooklyn's Dance (FR) **B. C. Dice**
52 **ONEDIN LINE**, 5, ch g Pivotal—One So Wonderful **EPDS Racing Partnership 4**
53 **OPERA OG (IRE)**, 7, b g Oscar (IRE)—Maspaloma (IRE) **Craig, Dick, Duckworth & Matthewman**
54 **PANAMA PETRUS (IRE)**, 5, b g Alflora (IRE)—Pride 'n' Joy (IRE) **Andrew Brooks & Julian Taylor**
55 **PENTIFFIC (NZ)**, 10, br g Pentire—Sailing High (NZ) **P Sinn, P Lawrence, L Sutcliffe & M Smith**
56 **PEPITE ROSE (FR)**, 6, b br m Bonbon Rose (FR)—Sambre (FR) **Falcons Line Ltd**
57 **PLEIN POUVOIR (FR)**, 10, b g Maresca Sorrento (FR)—Dellerie (FR) **Dr M. A. Hamlin**
58 **QUARTZ DE THAIX (FR)**, 9, b g Ragmar (FR)—Une Amie (FR) **ROA Arkle Partnership**
59 **RADICAL IMPACT (IRE)**, 5, ch g Beneficial—Shean Alainn (IRE) **Mr C. A. J. Drury**
60 **RED COURTIER**, 6, b g Red Ransom (USA)—Lady In Waiting **Richard Manley & John Williams**
61 **REGINALDINHO (UAE)**, 7, b g Galileo (IRE)—River Patrol **The Neighbours Partnership**
62 **RELAX (FR)**, 8, b g Fragrant Mix (IRE)—Magik (FR) **The Bellamy Partnership**
63 **RENARD (FR)**, 8, b br g Discover d'auteuil (FR)—Kirmelia (FR) **ROA Arkle Partnership**
64 **RENARD D'IRLANDE (FR)**, 8, gr g April Night (FR)—Isati's (FR) **Hills of Ledbury Ltd**
65 **RIGADIN DE BEAUCHENE (FR)**, 8, b br g Visionary (FR)—Chipie d'angron (FR) **Mr A. O. Wiles**
66 **ROCKY BENDER (IRE)**, 8, b g Saddlers' Hall (IRE)—Silver Spirit (IRE) **Miss S. Douglas-Pennant**
67 **ROSA FLEET (IRE)**, 5, b m Alflora (IRE)—Crimond (IRE) **Mezzone Family**
68 **ROYAL PALLADIUM (FR)**, 5, gr g King's Theatre (IRE)—Dent Sucree (FR) **Mrs A. W. Timpson**
69 **RUNAWAY GREEN (FR)**, 7, gr g Balleroy (USA)—Dora Dante (IRE) **The Runaway Green Partnership**
70 **RYDALIS (FR)**, 8, b m Kapgarde (FR)—Fleurissa (FR) **Mrs V. A. Bingham**
71 **SAROQUE (IRE)**, 6, b g Revoque (IRE)—Sarakin (IRE) **Connect Racing**
72 **SAWPIT SECRET**, 6, b m Westerner—Rustic Charm (IRE) **D. A. Hunt**
73 **SENDINPOST**, 10, b m Dansili—Colleville **Miss V. M. Williams**
74 **SHANGANI (USA)**, 7, b g Giant's Causeway (USA)—Tanzania (IRE) **The Bellamy Partnership**
75 **SPECIAL ROBON (FR)**, 5, b g Robin des Champs (FR)—Spinage (FR) **Dr M. A. Hamlin**
76 **STONE LIGHT (FR)**, 5, ch m Ballingarry (IRE)—Yellow Light (FR) **Mr A. L. Brooks**
77 **SUMMERY JUSTICE (IRE)**, 9, b g Witness Box (USA)—Kinsellas Rose (IRE) **Mrs P. Brown**
78 **SUSTAINABILITY (IRE)**, 8, ch g Old Vic—Over The Glen (IRE) **The Silver Cod Partnership**
79 **TAKE THE MICK**, 6, b g Ishiguru (USA)—Michaelmas Daizy **Sir Geoffrey & Lady Vos**
80 **TANGO DE JUILLEY (FR)**, 5, b g Lesotho (USA)—Lasalsa de Juilley (FR) **Mr M. N. Khan**
81 **TARRACO (FR)**, 6, b g Sassanian (USA)—Marie Esther (FR) **Mrs V. A. Bingham**
82 **TENOR NIVERNAIS (FR)**, 6, b g Shaanmer (IRE)—Hosanna II (FR) **Mr M. N. Khan**
83 **TORGAMAH LAD (IRE)**, 5, b g High-Rise (IRE)—Brook Forte **Miss Mandy D Coughlan & Mr T. B. James**
84 **TOUBEERA**, 7, b m Tobougg (IRE)—Efizia **Mr R. M. Britten-Long**
85 **UHLAN BUTE (FR)**, 5, ch g Brier Creek (USA)—Jonquiere (FR) **Lady N. S. Coe**
86 **UPEPITO (FR)**, 5, b g Khalkevi (IRE)—Friandise II (FR) **Mr A. L. Brooks**
87 **VINNIESLITTLE LAMB (IRE)**, 5, b m Vinnie Roe (IRE)—Polar Lamb (IRE) **D. A. Hunt**
88 **WALDORF SALAD**, 5, b g Millenary—Ismene (FR) **A. G. Parker**
89 **WING MIRA (IRE)**, 5, b g Winged Love (FR)—Miraflores (IRE) **You Can Be Sure**
90 **ZAMDY MAN**, 4, b g Authorized (IRE)—Lauderdale (GER) **Mr M. N. Khan**

Other Owners: Mrs Peter Andrews, Mrs C. Belloc Lowndes, Dr Martin Booth, Mr James Bowditch, Mr Robert Boyce, Mr D. J. Burke, Mr T. H. G. Cooper, Dr Chris Cowell, Mr Phil Cunningham, Mr O. P. Dakin, Mr J. S. Dale, Mr P. Davies, Mr P. A. Davies, Mr Michael J. Davies, Mr P. A. Deal, Mr Andrew Dick, Mr R. W. E. Dimsey, Mr Andrew Duckworth, Mrs Lisa Fellows, Mrs J. E. Gorton, Mr Ted Jagger, Mr Christopher James, Mr D. Jinks, John Nicholls (Trading) Ltd, Miss G. Magee, Mrs Rosemary Mason, Mr M. Secretan, Sir John Becher.

Jockey (NH): Aidan Coleman, Liam Treadwell, Robert Dunne, Sam Thomas. **Conditional:** Harry Challoner.

680 MRS LISA WILLIAMSON, Chester
Postal: Saighton Hall, Saighton, Chester, Cheshire, CH3 6EE
Contacts: PHONE (01244) 314254 FAX (01244) 314254 (please ring before sending)
MOBILE (07970) 437679
E-MAIL info@lisawilliamson.co.uk WEBSITE www.lisawilliamson.co.uk

1 ALL GOOD NEWS (IRE), 4, gr g Moss Vale (IRE)—Blanche Neige (USA) **Bluegrass Racing Ltd**
2 ANOTHER JOURNEY, 4, b g Rail Link—Singasongosixpence **Chester Racing Club Ltd**
3 BABUSHKA'S GIRL, 4, b f Central Park (IRE)—Shaymee's Girl **B & B Hygiene Limited**
4 BERTIE BLU BOY, 5, b g Central Park (IRE)—Shaymee's Girl **B & B Hygiene Limited**
5 CHESTER DEELYTE (IRE), 5, b m Desert Style (IRE)—Bakewell Tart (IRE) **Hindford Oak Racing**
6 CHESTER'SLITTLEGEM (IRE), 4, b f Atraf—Ceylon Round (FR) **Chester Racing Club Ltd**
7 5, B g Pursuit of Love—Classic Quartet **Mrs L. V. Williamson**
8 4, B f Fraam—Classic Quartet **Mrs L. V. Williamson**
9 CRABBIES GOLD (IRE), 5, ch g Sleeping Indian—Sharpe's Lady **Halewood International Ltd**
10 ELAMMATO (IRE), 4, b g Strategic Prince—Boadicea **Tony Sykes**
11 HAL OF A LOVER, 5, b g Halling (USA)—Latent Lover (IRE) **Glen Briers**
12 JOHN CRABBIES (FR), 6, b g Super Celebre (FR)—Clelia La Belle (FR) **Halewood International Ltd**
13 MUSICAL BRIDGE, 4, b g Night Shift (USA)—Carrie Pooter **Trevor Conway**
14 ODD BALL (IRE), 6, b g Redback—Luceball (IRE) **Mr A. T. Sykes**
15 PUYOL (IRE), 11, b br g Zaffaran (USA)—Star Mover **Halewood International Ltd**
16 ROUGHLYN, 4, ch g Haafhd—Dime Bag **Chester Racing Club Ltd**
17 RYAN STYLE (IRE), 7, b g Desert Style (IRE)—Westlife (IRE) **Bluegrass Racing Ltd**
18 SCHOOLBOY CHAMP, 6, ch g Trade Fair—Aswhatilldois (IRE) **Opolski Racing**
19 5, Ch g Alflora (IRE)—Top of The Dee **Halewood International Ltd**

THREE-YEAR-OLDS

20 B g Auction House (USA)—Amwell Star (USA) **Chester Racing Club Ltd**
21 B g Vitus—Danehill Princess (IRE) **John Levenson**
22 B g Kheleyf (USA)—Danehill's Dream (IRE) **Chester Racing Club Ltd**
23 B g Assertive—Not So Generous (IRE) **Chester Racing Club Ltd**
24 Ch g Cockney Rebel (IRE)—Para Siempre **Hazel Roberts**
25 SENORA LOBO (IRE), b f Amadeus Wolf—Valencia (FR) **Mr G. H. Briers**
26 THE BAY TIGRESS, b f Tiger Hill (IRE)—Singasongosixpence **Chester Racing Club Ltd**
27 TIME FOR LAMBRINI (IRE), b f Amadeus Wolf—Princess Madaen (IRE) **Halewood International Ltd**
28 B g Moss Vale (IRE)—Westlife (IRE) **Halewood International Ltd**

TWO-YEAR-OLDS

29 B f 18/3 Amadeus Wolf—Papaha (FR) (Green Desert (USA)) (4761) **Chester Racing Club Ltd**
30 Ch f 25/4 Three Valleys (USA)—Poly Blue (IRE) (Thatching) (3047) **Chester Racing Club Ltd**

Other Owners: Mr J. H. Martin, Mr M. L. Rush, Mrs Lisa Williamson, Mr S. C. Wundke.

Assistant Trainer: Mark Williamson

Jockey (flat): Tom Eaves. Jockey (NH): Brian Hughes. Conditional: Harry Challoner. Amateur: Mr C. Ellingham.

681 MR CHRISTOPHER WILSON, Darlington
Postal: Manor Farm, Manfield, Darlington, Co. Durham, DL2 2RW
Contacts: PHONE (01325) 374595 FAX (01325) 374595 MOBILE (07815) 952306/(07721) 379277
E-MAIL wilsonracing@aol.com

1 ESME RIDES A GAINE, 11, gr m Doubletour (USA)—Silver Penny **Mrs J. Wilson**
2 INGENTI, 5, ch m Blue Dakota (IRE)—Kungfu Kerry **D. A. J. Bartlett**
3 LATEST FASHION (IRE), 7, ch m Ashkalani (IRE)—Musical Bramble (IRE) **Mrs J. Wilson**
4 NICEONEMYSON, 4, b g Misu Bond (IRE)—Kungfu Kerry **D. A. J. Bartlett**
5 NO TIME TO CRY, 4, b f Josr Algarhoud (IRE)—Autumn Bloom (IRE) **Mrs J. Wilson**
6 ORMUS, 10, b g Rambling Bear—Adar Jane **Mrs J. Wilson**
7 SHARP SHOES, 6, br g Needwood Blade—Mary Jane **Mrs J. Wilson**
8 STELLA MARRIS, 6, b rm Danroad (AUS)—Riyoom (USA) **D. A. J. Bartlett**
9 URSUS, 8, ch g Rambling Bear—Adar Jane **Mrs J. Wilson**
10 VALSESIA (IRE), 6, b m Milan—Ballinapierce Lady (IRE) **Mrs J. Wilson**

MR CHRISTOPHER WILSON - Continued

Assistant Trainer: Julie Wilson

Jockey (flat): Paddy Aspell, Silvestre De Sousa. **Jockey (NH):** Keith Mercer. **Conditional:** Ewan Whillans. **Apprentice:** Julie Burke.

---

682 MR JIM WILSON, Cheltenham
Postal: **Glenfall Stables, Ham, Charlton Kings, Cheltenham, Gloucestershire, GL52 6NH**
Contacts: **PHONE (01242) 244713 FAX (01242) 226319 MOBILE (07932) 157243**
E-MAIL ajwglenfall@aol.com

1 CAPTAIN SULLY (IRE), 8, b g Pairumani Star (IRE)—Ginger Lily (IRE) **The Cotswold Partnership**
2 RUBY VALENTINE (FR), 10, b m Kayf Tara—A Ma Valentine (FR) **The Winbledon Partnership**
3 SEYMOUR LEGEND, 7, b g Midnight Legend—Rosehall **Exors of the Late Mrs T. D. Pilkington**

Other Owners: H. H. J. Fentum, J. W. Griffin, B. J. Hughes, D. B. O'Beirne, Mrs M. J. Wilson.

---

683 MISS MAIRI WILSON, Bawtry
Postal: **Martin Common Farm, Bawtry, Doncaster, South Yorkshire, DN10 6DB**

1 BUSTANINCH, 9, ch g Arkadian Hero (USA)—Inchmore **Mrs M. F. and Miss M. C. Wilson**
2 COFFEE KING (IRE), 4, b g King's Best (USA)—Passarelle (USA) **Mrs M. F. and Miss M. C. Wilson**
3 6, Ch m Lucky Story (USA)—Inchmore **Mrs M. F. and Miss M. C. Wilson**
4 RHYME ROYAL, 4, b f Byron—Burton Ash **Mrs M. F. and Miss M. C. Wilson**

Other Owners: Mrs M. F. Wilson, Miss M. C. Wilson.

---

684 MR NOEL WILSON, Middleham
Postal: **Caphall Lodge, Coverham, Middleham, Leyburn, North Yorkshire, DL8 4TL**
Contacts: **PHONE (01969) 622780 FAX (01969) 622780 MOBILE (07718) 613206**
E-MAIL nlwilson69@live.com

1 DEMOLITION, 9, ch g Starborough—Movie Star (IRE) **M. Wormald**
2 DIAMOND SUNRISE (IRE), 5, b m Diamond Green (FR)—Sunrise (IRE) **B. Hoyle**
3 DRIVE HOME (USA), 6, b br g Mr Greeley (USA)—Unique Pose (IRE) **Downes Kennedy Tobin Pallister**
4 GRAND ART (IRE), 9, b g Raise A Grand (IRE)—Mulberry River (IRE) **P. Tsim**
5 GREAT ROAR (USA), 5, b g Thunder Gulch (USA)—Boasting (USA) **N. Wilson**
6 KINGARRICK, 5, ch g Selkirk (USA)—Rosacara **Hurn Racing Club**
7 KOOLGREYCAT (IRE), 4, gr f One Cool Cat (USA)—Brooks Masquerade **N. Wilson**
8 MYJESTIC MELODY (IRE), 5, b m Majestic Missile (IRE)—Bucaramanga (IRE) **Hurn Racing Club & Partners**
9 PARTNER (IRE), 7, b g Indian Ridge—Oregon Trail (USA) **G. J. Paver**
10 PAVERS STAR, 4, ch g Pastoral Pursuits—Pride of Kinloch **Mrs C. K. Paver**

THREE-YEAR-OLDS
11 MAPSTONE, b c Echo of Light—Classic Lass **Mrs J. Bartley**
12 RIDGEBLADE, ch f Bahamian Bounty—Verasina (USA) **Ridgeblade Partnership**
13 SAKHEES ROMANCE, b f Sakhee (USA)—Chance For Romance **RedHotGardogs**
14 SHATIN SECRET, b c Sakhee's Secret—Al Corniche (IRE) **P. Tsim**

TWO-YEAR-OLDS
15 PAVERS BOUNTY, ch c 7/4 Bahamian Bounty—Pride of Kinloch (Dr Devious (IRE)) **Mrs C. K. Paver**

Other Owners: Mr T. Alderson, Mr J. Beamson, Mr P. A. Burgess, Mr R. G. Capstick, Mr P. A. P. Clays, Mr J. Devlin, Mr Steven Downes, Mrs I. M. Jessop, Mr Gary Kennedy, Mr Michael McNellis, Mr Matthew Morgan, Mr John R. Owen, Mr Ian B. Pallister, Mr David Percival, Mr Hugh T. Redhead, Mr F. Tobin, Mr Simon Twiggs, Mr N. Wilson, Mr M. Wormald.

Assistant Trainer: Miss Alex Porritt

Jockey (flat): Jimmy Quinn, Barry McHugh, Daniel Tudhope. **Jockey (NH):** Wilson Renwick. **Conditional:** Brian Toomey. **Apprentice:** Neil Farley. **Amateur:** Miss K. Bannon.

685 **MR KEN WINGROVE, Bridgnorth**
Postal: **6 Netherton Farm Barns, Netherton Lane, Highley, Bridgnorth, Shropshire, WV16 6NJ**
Contacts: **HOME (01746) 861534 MOBILE (07974) 411267**

1 **ANTOELLA (IRE)**, 6, gr m Antonius Pius (USA)—Bella Estella (GER)
2 **ARTY FARMER**, 9, b g Karinga Bay—One of Those Days **Mr N. J. Morris**
3 **BRUNDON**, 4, ch f Refuse To Bend (IRE)—Anna of Brunswick **F. L. Matthews**
4 **GRAND FELLA (IRE)**, 8, ch g Raise A Grand (IRE)—Mummys Best **F. L. Matthews**
5 **LEAHNESS (IRE)**, 6, br m Arakan (USA)—En Retard (IRE) **F. L. Matthews**
6 **WEET IN NERJA**, 7, b g Captain Rio—Persian Fortune **F. L. Matthews**
7 **WINROB**, 7, b g Exceed And Excel (AUS)—High Standard **Mr N. J. Morris**
8 **WOR JOSIE (IRE)**, 5, br m Zagreb (USA)—Garw Valley **F. L. Matthews**

Assistant Trainer: Isobel Willer

686 **MR ADRIAN WINTLE, Westbury-On-Severn**
Postal: **29 Colchester Close, Westbury-On-Severn, Gloucestershire, GL14 1PU**

1 **NOBLE PERK**, 8, ch g Executive Perk—Far From Perfect (IRE) **A. A. Wintle**
2 **SHALONE**, 9, ch g Tobougg (IRE)—Let Alone **A. A. Wintle**
3 **THE TWO OF US**, 7, ch g Killer Instinct—Lady Busted **A. A. Wintle**

687 **MR STEVE WOODMAN, Chichester**
Postal: **Parkers Barn Stables, 8 Pook Lane, East Lavant, Chichester, West Sussex, PO18 0AU**
Contacts: **OFFICE (01243) 527136 FAX (01243) 527136 MOBILE (07889) 188519**
E-MAIL **stevewoodman83@msn.com**

1 **CHEVISE (IRE)**, 5, b m Holy Roman Emperor (IRE)—Lipica (IRE) **The Chevise Partnership**
2 **GOING TWICE**, 8, b g Josr Algarhoud (IRE)—Its Your Bid **Mrs S. B. Woodman**
3 **HIGHLY LIKELY (IRE)**, 4, b g Elnadim (USA)—Height of Fantasy (IRE) **Mrs S. B. Woodman**
4 **LORD ALDERVALE (IRE)**, 6, br g Alderbrook—Monavale (IRE) **The Sir Kenneth Partnership**

Other Owners: Mr D. N. Boxall, Mrs P. M. Tyler.

688 **MR GARRY WOODWARD, Retford**
Postal: **21 Camden Grove, Maltby, Rotherham, South Yorkshire, S66 8GE**
Contacts: **HOME (01709) 813431 MOBILE (07739) 382052**
E-MAIL **gwoodwardracing@aol.com** WEBSITE **www.garrywoodward.co.uk**

1 **DOUBLE CARPET (IRE)**, 10, b g Lahib (USA)—Cupid Miss **G. Woodward**
2 **ERRIGAL LAD**, 8, ch g Bertolini (USA)—La Belle Vie **Mrs E. Cash**
3 **INSIDE KNOWLEDGE (USA)**, 7, gr ro g Mizzen Mast (USA)—Kithira **Mrs E. Cash**
4 **KINGAROO (IRE)**, 7, b g King Charlemagne (USA)—Lady Naomi (USA) **J. Pownall**
5 **PRINCEOFTHEDESERT**, 7, b g Nayef (USA)—Twilight Sonnet **G. Woodward**
6 **RUNNING ON FAITH**, 5, b g Phoenix Reach (IRE)—Amazing Grace Mary **Mrs E. Cash**
7 **SELF EMPLOYED**, 6, b g Sakhee (USA)—Twilight Sonnet **G. Woodward**
8 **TOOTHACHE**, 5, gr m Proclamation (IRE)—Zilkha **G. Woodward**

689 **MR RICHARD WOOLLACOTT, South Molton**
Postal: **Nethercott Manor, Rose Ash, South Molton, Devon, EX36 4RE**
Contacts: **PHONE (01769) 550483**
WEBSITE **www.richardwoollacottracing.co.uk**

1 **ANGLES HILL (IRE)**, 6, b g Heron Island (IRE)—No Tails Told (IRE) **R. G. Westacott**
2 **BLACK COFFEE**, 8, br g Vettori (IRE)—In The Woods **Mr N. Piper**
3 **CIVIL DISOBEDIENCE**, 9, b g Roi de Rome (USA)—Biddies **R. C. Mitford-Slade**
4 **CRIDDA BOY**, 7, ch g Mark of Esteem (IRE)—Second Affair (IRE) **D. G. Staddon**
5 **FOLLY FARM (IRE)**, 5, gr g Definite Article—West Hill Rose (IRE) **D. G. Staddon**

MR RICHARD WOOLLACOTT - Continued

6 **GAY SLOANE (IRE)**, 9, b g Anabaa (USA)—Seattle's Wood (USA) **The Spoofers**
7 **GREAT KICKER (IRE)**, 8, b g Great Palm (USA)—Keep The Change (IRE) **John & Greer Norman**
8 **HAZY DAWN**, 8, b m Cloudings (IRE)—Quiet Dawn **The King's Men**
9 **KRUSEMAN**, 6, b g Doyen (IRE)—Polar Charge **R. J. Weeks**
10 **MIDNIGHT WHISPER**, 7, ch g Midnight Legend—Spread The Word **Mrs E. M. Roberts**
11 **NOTHINGBUTTHETRUTH (IRE)**, 9, b g Witness Box (USA)—Named And Shamed (IRE) **Mr J. Pike & Mr G. Pike**
12 **PETIE MCSWEETIE (IRE)**, 6, b g Accordion—Crafty Rule (IRE) **Eight Ball Partnership**
13 **PICKLEGEND**, 7, b g Midnight Legend—Miss Pickle VII **Mr D. Newton**
14 **PRICKLES**, 8, ch m Karinga Bay—Squeaky
15 **VALOROSO**, 8, b g Laveron—Millennium Rose (IRE) **Mrs A. E. R. Goodwin**
16 **VICTORIA ROSE (IRE)**, 8, b m Old Vic—West Hill Rose (IRE) **D. G. Staddon**
17 **WAK A TURTLE (IRE)**, 5, b g Turtle Island (IRE)—Playwaki (USA) **R. Woollacott**

Other Owners: M. J. Bevan, G. S. Brown, R. B. Denny, Mr G. J. Evans, Mrs L. Fielding-Johnson, Mr P. Govier, Mr P. F. Govier, Mr S. Kidston, Mr A. P. Maddox, John Norman, Mrs G. O. Norman, Mr J. M. Pike, Mr G. E. Pike, E. J. Saunders.

---

690   MR RAYMOND YORK, Cobham
Postal: Newmarsh Farm, Horsley Road, Cobham, Surrey, KT11 3JX
Contacts: PHONE (01932) 863594 FAX (01932) 860703 MOBILE (07808) 344131
E-MAIL ray.york@virgin.net

1 **CUNNING PLAN (IRE)**, 6, ch g Bachelor Duke (USA)—Madamaa (IRE) **Mrs K. H. York**
2 **MURFREESBORO**, 10, b g Bahamian Bounty—Merry Rous **Dukes Head Racing**
3 **RINGA BAY**, 8, ch g Karinga Bay—Redgrave Wolf **M. Kehoe**
4 **SORSE**, 7, b g Central Park (IRE)—Tachelle (IRE) **R. H. York**
5 5, B g Sir Harry Lewis (USA)—Veredus **R. H. York**

Other Owners: M. H. D. Barlow, J. L. Collins, Mr P. G. Dalton, Miss R. Dorrell.

Amateur: Mr P. York.

---

691   MRS LAURA YOUNG, Bridgwater
Postal: Rooks Castle Stables, Broomfield, Bridgwater, Somerset, TA5 2EW
Contacts: PHONE (01278) 661555 FAX (01278) 661555 MOBILE (07766) 514414
E-MAIL ljyracing@hotmail.com

1 **ADMIRAL BLAKE**, 6, b g Witness Box (USA)—Brenda Bella (FR) **Mrs L. J. Young**
2 4, B f Doyen (IRE)—Ballyquintet (IRE) **Mrs L. J. Young**
3 **BANDOL (IRE)**, 5, b g Zagreb (USA)—Formal Affair **J. J. Boulter**
4 5, B m Brian Boru—Buckland Filleigh (IRE) **Mrs L. J. Young**
5 **BY COMMAND**, 8, b g Red Ransom (USA)—Rafha **Total Plumbing Supporters Club**
6 **CASTLEBOY WARRIOR (IRE)**, 7, b g Tikkanen (USA)—Spring Beauty (IRE) **The Isle Of Frogs Partnership**
7 **COURTING WHITNEY**, 8, b m Witness Box (USA)—Lady Lamb (IRE) **Total Plumbing Supporters Club**
8 **JIGSAW FINANCIAL (IRE)**, 7, b g Brian Boru—Ardcolm Cailin (IRE) **Mrs L. J. Young**
9 **KAP WEST (FR)**, 8, b g Kapgarde (FR)—Themis Eria (FR) **Mrs S. A. White**
10 **MAID OF MIGHT (IRE)**, 5, b m Flemensfirth (USA)—Kestral Heights (IRE) **Mrs L. J. Young**
11 **TAIL OF THE BANK (IRE)**, 10, b g Flemensfirth (USA)—Dear Money (IRE) **Total Plumbing Supporters Club**

Other Owners: C. E. Handford, Mr I. D. Moses, Mr G. C. Vining, Mr C. V. Vining.

Assistant Trainer: James Young

---

692   MR WILLIAM YOUNG, Carluke
Postal: Watchknowe Lodge, Crossford, Carluke, Lanarkshire, ML8 5QT
Contacts: PHONE (01555) 860856 (01555) 860226 FAX (01555) 860137 MOBILE (07900) 408210
E-MAIL watchknowe@talktalk.net

1 **LEWLAUR SUPREME (IRE)**, 10, b g Supreme Leader—Dark Dame (IRE) **W. G. Young**
2 **SIXTIES ROCK**, 6, ch g Rock of Gibraltar (IRE)—Scene (IRE) **W. G. Young**

Assistant Trainer: William G Young Snr

INDEX TO HORSES

The Figure before the name of the horse refers to the number of the team in which it appears and **The Figure after** the horse supplies a ready reference to each animal. Horses are indexed strictly alphabetically, e.g. THE FUGUE appears in the T's, MR PUCK in the MR's, ST ELMO'S FIRE in the ST's etc.

455 **BARTON JUBILEE** (GB) 4
622 **BARWICK** (GB) 5
58 **BASEBALL TED** (IRE) 3
95 **BASFORD BEN** (GB) 3
209 **BASHAMA** (GB) 2
341 **BASHURE** (GB) 1
510 **BASIL FAWLTY** (IRE) 9
149 **BASINGSTOKE** (IRE) 3
552 **BASIRA** (FR) 33
48 **BASLE** (GB) 2
14 **BASODA** (GB) 9
397 **BASQUIAT** (SPA) 66
646 **BASSARA** (IRE) 2
312 **BASSETERRE** (IRE) 2
149 **BASSETT ROAD** (IRE) 4
31 **BASSINET** (USA) F 67
634 **BASTION** (USA) 32
431 **BAT MASTERSON** (IRE) 6
665 **BATCHWORTH BLAISE** (GB) 1
338 **BATCHWORTH FIREFLY** (GB) 1
338 **BATCHWORTH LADY** (GB) 23
109 **BATELEUR** (GB) 7
118 **BATGIRL** (GB) 2
62 **BATHCOUNTY** (IRE) 1
2 **BATHRAT AMAL** (JPN) 67
45 **BATHWICK BRAVE** (IRE) 1
48 **BATHWICK JUNIOR** (GB) 3
206 **BATHWICK STREET** (GB) 4
275 **BATTALION** (IRE) 24
607 **BATTLE FOR GLORY** (IRE) 1
510 **BATTLE GROUP** (GB) 10
485 **BATTLE OF MARENGO** (IRE) 10
630 **BATTLECRY** (GB) 8
402 **BATTLEDANCER** (GB) 1
549 **BATTLEFRONT** (USA) 127
468 **BATU** (IRE) 3
637 **BAVARIAN BEAUTY** (GER) 52
668 **BAVARIAN NORDIC** (USA) 2
66 **BAWDEN ROCKS** (GB) 9
377 **BAWINA** (IRE) 60
675 **BAY CENTRAL** (IRE) 9
211 **BAY STREET BELLE** (GB) 111
377 **BAYAKA** (FR) 21
211 **BAYAN KASIRGA** (IRE) 63
24 **BAYBSHAMBLES** (IRE) 2
657 **BAYLEY'S DREAM** (GB) 4
38 **BAYLEYF** (IRE) 2
552 **BAYRIR** (FR) 3
537 **BAYTOWN BERTIE** (GB) 2
357 **BAZRON** (IRE) 7
444 **BE ALL MAN** (IRE) 10
636 **BE BOP BORU** (IRE) 8
436 **BE DECISIVE** (GB) C 25
243 **BE DEFINITE** (IRE) 7
625 **BE EXCELLENT** (GB) 11
619 **BE MARVELLOUS** (IRE) 3
273 **BE MY DEPUTY** (IRE) 3
393 **BE MY LIGHT** (IRE) 2
637 **BE MY LION** (GER) 4
393 **BE MY PRESENT** (GB) 3
272 **BE MY ROCK** (GB) 2
495 **BE ON THE BELL** (GB) 23
53 **BE PERFECT** (USA) 1
375 **BEACH BAR** (IRE) 32
53 **BEACH BUNNY** (IRE) C 76
422 **BEACH CANDY** (IRE) 3
75 **BEACH CLUB** (GB) 6
4 **BEACH RHYTHM** (USA) 1

290 **BEACHDALE LAD** (IRE) 2
330 **BEACHWOOD BAY** (GB) 2
375 **BEACON LADY** (GB) 1
476 **BEACON LODGE** (IRE) 3
344 **BEAKERS N NUM NUMS** (IRE) 22
495 **BEAM OF LIGHT** (GB) 24
345 **BEAMAZED** (GB) 5
638 **BEANEY TUNES** (GB) 5
154 **BEAR BEHIND** (IRE) 5
305 **BEAR'S AFFAIR** (IRE) 9
444 **BEARDIE'S DREAM** (IRE) G 11
287 **BEAT OF THE DRUM** (IRE) 31
10 **BEAT ROUTE** (GB) 1
311 **BEAT THE BOUNDS** (GB) 1
645 **BEAT THE RAIN** (GB) C 29
173 **BEAT THE TIDE** (IRE) 23
312 **BEATABOUT THE BUSH** (IRE) 81
396 **BEATBOXING** (USA) 16
134 **BEATRIX POTTER** (IRE) C 51
638 **BEAU DANDY** (IRE) 6
586 **BEAU LIE** (IRE) 1
263 **BEAU MISTRAL** (IRE) 1
287 **BEAU NASH** (IRE) 117
198 **BEAU SELECT** (IRE) 4
95 **BEAUBOREEN** (IRE) 4
1 **BEAUCHAMP AMBER** (GB) 14
1 **BEAUCHAMP ASTRA** (GB) 8
1 **BEAUCHAMP BELLA** (GB) 9
1 **BEAUCHAMP GEM** (GB) 15
1 **BEAUCHAMP KITE** (GB) 16
1 **BEAUCHAMP MELBA** (GB) 17
1 **BEAUCHAMP ROCK** (GB) 18
1 **BEAUCHAMP SUNSET** (GB) 1
1 **BEAUCHAMP XERXES** (GB) 1
344 **BEAUFORT TWELVE** (GB) 2
216 **BEAUJOLAIS** (IRE) 4
556 **BEAUTIFUL DAY** (GB) 14
404 **BEAUTIFUL LANDO** (FR) 2
575 **BEAUTIFUL LIFE** (GB) 27
109 **BEAUTIFUL STORY** (IRE) 41
559 **BEAUTIFULWILDTHING** (GB) 10
275 **BEAUTY BRIGHT** (IRE) F 83
485 **BEAUTY IS TRUTH** (IRE) C 96
206 **BEAUTY PAGEANT** (IRE) 5
549 **BEAUTY PARLOR** (USA) 128
106 **BEAUTY PARLOUR** (GB) 2
397 **BEBE STAR** (FR) 67
105 **BEBINN** (IRE) 1
201 **BECAUSEWECAN** (USA) 9
100 **BECKERMET** (IRE) 3
491 **BECKHANI** (GB) 13
117 **BECQUANIS** (FR) 1
32 **BEDARA** (GB) F 75
8 **BEDARRA BOY** (GB) 2
50 **BEDECKED** (IRE) 16
439 **BEDIBYES** (GB) 1
489 **BEDLOE'S ISLAND** (IRE) 5
333 **BEDOUIN BAY** (GB) 2
217 **BEDOUIN BLUE** (IRE) 5
601 **BEDOUIN INVADER** (IRE) 31
658 **BEE EATER** (IRE) C 76
109 **BEE JAY KAY** (GB) 42
657 **BEECHBERRY** (IRE) G 5
287 **BEEDEE** (GB) 32
601 **BEEP** (GB) 32
419 **BEEVES** (IRE) 16
516 **BEFORE BRUCE** (GB) 5
572 **BEFOREALL** (IRE) 2

37 **BEGGAR'S OPERA** (IRE) 2
665 **BEGGERS BELIEF** (GB) 2
665 **BEGGERS LUCK** (GB) 7
607 **BEGIN THE BEGUINE** (GB) F 4
552 **BEHKARA** (IRE) C 101
277 **BEHLAYAN** (IRE) 32
361 **BEHTARINI** (IRE) 1
106 **BEJEWELED** (IRE) 37
485 **BELESTA** (GB) C 97
17 **BELFILO** (IRE) 103
16 **BELGIAN BILL** (GB) 4
214 **BELIEVE IN ME** (GB) 21
93 **BELINSKY** (IRE) 1
353 **BELL'ARTE** (IRE) 31
380 **BELLA BELLISSIMA** (USA) 8
445 **BELLA CINDERELLA** (GB) 29
453 **BELLA MICHELLE** (GB) 18
552 **BELLA QATARA** (IRE) 34
330 **BELLE ANNIE** (USA) F 55
291 **BELLE BAYARDO** (IRE) 4
16 **BELLE DE FONTENAY** (FR) 5
549 **BELLE DE FRANCE** (FR) 33
31 **BELLE DES AIRS** (IRE) C 68
677 **BELLE DU ROI** (FR) G 37
484 **BELLE ISLE** (GB) 13
89 **BELLE NOVERRE** (IRE) 2
372 **BELLETRISTE** (FR) 32
474 **BELLFLOWER BOY** (IRE) 6
210 **BELLGROVE** (IRE) 1
52 **BELLINDA** (GB) 3
136 **BELLINGO** (GB) 1
53 **BELLITUDO** (IRE) 30
80 **BELLOSGUARDO** (GB) 2
31 **BELROG** (GB) 69
459 **BELUCKYAGAIN** (IRE) 16
118 **BELUGA BISCUIT** (GB) 3
433 **BELURA** (IRE) 3
553 **BEN AKRAM** (IRE) 4
572 **BEN CEE PEE M** (IRE) 3
222 **BEN CYFELACH** (GB) 2
90 **BENANDONNER** (USA) 1
360 **BENBANE HEAD** (USA) 4
630 **BENBENS** (IRE) 9
280 **BENDANT** (GB) 1
265 **BENDIGO CREEK** (USA) 1
290 **BENDZOLDAN** (IRE) 3
249 **BENE LAD** (IRE) 3
455 **BENEATH** (GB) 5
608 **BENEDICTE** (IRE) F 34
410 **BENEFFICIENT** (IRE) 2
210 **BENEFICIAL REFORM** (IRE) 2
677 **BENEFIQUE ROYALE** (GB) 2
542 **BENEFIT CUT** (IRE) 2
566 **BENEFITOFHINDSIGHT** (GB) 4
431 **BENEMEADE** (IRE) 7
353 **BENEVENTA** (GB) C 125
431 **BENEVOLENT** (IRE) 8
169 **BENGALINE** (GB) 4
144 **BENHIER** (IRE) 3
641 **BENIDORM** (GB) 2
419 **BENJAMIN BITTERN** (IRE) 17
538 **BENMADIGAN** (IRE) 5
550 **BENNELONG** (GB) 4
534 **BENNY BE GOOD** (GB) 1
253 **BENNY THE SWINGER** (IRE) 2
529 **BENNY'S MARBLE** (IRE) G 4
679 **BENNYS MIST** (IRE) 5
315 **BENNYS QUEST** (IRE) 1

273 **CAPTAIN SCOOBY** (GB) 4
389 **CAPTAIN SHARPE** (GB) 2
139 **CAPTAIN STARLIGHT** (IRE) 17
682 **CAPTAIN SULLY** (IRE) 1
381 **CAPTAIN SUNSHINE** (GB) 6
509 **CAPTAIN TIDDS** (IRE) 4
539 **CAPTAIN WILSON** (GB) 2
488 **CAPTAIN'S DREAM** (IRE) 7
483 **CAPTIVE MOMENT** (GB) 2
275 **CARA GINA** (GB) 27
637 **CARA MIA** (GER) 8
35 **CARA VIC** (IRE) 4
653 **CARA'S DELIGHT** (AUS) 2
461 **CARA'S OSCAR** (IRE) 3
462 **CARACOOL** (FR) F 10
287 **CARAMACK** (GB) 37
198 **CARAMEL SUNDAE** (GB) 5
346 **CARAMELITA** (GB) 8
112 **CARAVAN ROLLS ON** (GB) 2
636 **CARAVEL** (IRE) 13
344 **CARAZAM** (IRE) 3
627 **CARBAS** (ITY) 16
482 **CARBERY SPIRIT** (IRE) F 7
159 **CARBIS BAY** (GB) 3
600 **CARD HIGH** (IRE) 7
207 **CARD LOVER** (GB) 4
132 **CARDINAL** (GB) 2
575 **CARDINAL WALTER** (IRE) 4
350 **CARDMASTER** (IRE) 11
556 **CARDS** (GB) 59
552 **CAREFUL CHARLIE** (IRE) 103
206 **CARELESS FREEDOM** (GB) F 48
303 **CARHENEY RIVER** (IRE) 1
353 **CARIBBEAN DANCER** (USA) C 131
213 **CARIBBEAN PEARL** (USA) C 53
549 **CARIBENA** (FR) C 131
245 **CARIFLORA** (GB) 2
495 **CARINA PALACE** (GB) 25
656 **CARINYA** (IRE) 1
658 **CARLA BIANCA** (IRE) 77
32 **CARLARAJAH** (GB) 26
481 **CARLOWSANTANA** (IRE) 1
491 **CARLTON JACK** (GB) 17
90 **CARLTON SCROOP** (FR) 3
203 **CARLY BAY** (GB) F 6
589 **CARMELA MARIA** (GB) 2
645 **CARNEADES** (IRE) 13
429 **CARNIVAL DREAM** (GB) 1
52 **CAROBELLO** (IRE) 6
455 **CAROLE'S DESTRIER** (GB) 7
483 **CAROLE'S DOVE** (GB) G 3
643 **CAROLE'S SPIRIT** (GB) 3
49 **CAROLINGIAN** (USA) 3
376 **CAROLLAN** (IRE) F 13
563 **CARPENTRAS** (GB) 2
263 **CARPET LOVER** (IRE) F 13
262 **CARPIES BOY** (GB) 4
333 **CARPINCHO** (FR) 6
69 **CARRAGOLD** (GB) 3
325 **CARRAMORE BOY** (IRE) 9
489 **CARRANZA** (IRE) F 85
313 **CARRERA** (GB) 11
200 **CARRIBS LEAP** (IRE) 3
679 **CARRICKBOY** (GB) 9
407 **CARRIES DARLING** (GB) 2
466 **CARRIETAU** (GB) 1
22 **CARRIGDHOUN** (IRE) 5
316 **CARRIGMORNA KING** (IRE) 21

310 **CARROWBEG** (IRE) 6
60 **CARRUTHERS** (GB) 2
449 **CARRY EACH OTHER** (IRE) 6
287 **CARRY ON SYDNEY** (GB) 38
676 **CARTER** (GB) 7
287 **CARTHAGE** (IRE) 128
109 **CARTIMANDUA** (GB) F 100
639 **CARTOON** (GB) F 33
545 **CASA TUA** (FR) 32
305 **CASH AND GO** (IRE) 21
509 **CASH FOR STEEL** (IRE) 5
242 **CASH INJECTION** (GB) 3
211 **CASH IS KING** (GB) 66
495 **CASH RICH** (GB) 26
670 **CASHEL DANCER** (GB) F 1
590 **CASHEL'S MISSILE** (IRE) 20
259 **CASIMIR ROAD** (IRE) 2
31 **CASINO DANCER** (GB) 73
215 **CASINO MARKETS** (IRE) 4
442 **CASINO STAR** (GB) 1
251 **CASPER'S SHADOW** (IRE) 2
26 **CASSELLS ROCK** (IRE) 22
114 **CASSIQUE LADY** (IRE) C 53
340 **CAST IRON CASEY** (IRE) 1
121 **CASTAGNA GIRL** (GB) 14
26 **CASTAGNOU** (IRE) 71
31 **CASTARA BEACH** (IRE) F 74
575 **CASTILO DEL DIABLO** (IRE) 5
549 **CASTING IN PARIS** (FR) 132
144 **CASTLE BEACH** (IRE) 6
151 **CASTLE CONFLICT** (IRE) 6
215 **CASTLE CONNELL** (IRE) 5
277 **CASTLE GUEST** (IRE) 4
386 **CASTLE LEGEND** (GB) 1
37 **CASTLE MYTH** (USA) 7
496 **CASTLE OF ARGH** (USA) 10
330 **CASTLE QUEST** (IRE) C 57
407 **CASTLE WINGS** (IRE) 3
691 **CASTLEBOY WARRIOR** (IRE) 6
553 **CASTLELAWN** (IRE) 9
23 **CASTLEMORRIS KING** (GB) 1
393 **CASTLETOWN BRIDGE** (IRE) 6
215 **CASTLETOWN WARRIOR** (IRE) 6
638 **CASUAL CAVALIER** (IRE) 11
658 **CASUAL CONQUEST** (IRE) 2
17 **CASUAL GLANCE** (GB) F 107
38 **CASUAL MOVER** (IRE) 4
2 **CAT O'MOUNTAIN** (USA) 70
476 **CAT WHISTLE** (GB) G 44
114 **CATADUPA** (GB) 54
465 **CATALINAS DIAMOND** (IRE) 1
580 **CATALYZE** (GB) 1
273 **CATAWOLLOW** (GB) 5
516 **CATCH ME UP** (IRE) 10
1 **CATCH THE CIDER** (GB) 11
54 **CATCH THE FIRE** (GB) 8
393 **CATCH THE RHYTHM** (IRE) 7
134 **CATCH US** (FR) F 55
350 **CATCHANOVA** (IRE) 2
245 **CATCHER STAR** (IRE) 3
491 **CATCHING ON** (IRE) 18
207 **CATCHING STARDUST** (GB) 3
553 **CATCHTHEMOONLIGHT** (GB) 10
534 **CATEGORICAL** (GB) 4
552 **CATERINA DE MEDICI** (FR) 5
299 **CATFLAP** (GB) 3
672 **CATHEDRAL** (GB) 3
392 **CATIVO CAVALLINO** (GB) 3

117 **CATNISS** (USA) 20
17 **CATRIONA'S BOY** (GB) 108
132 **CATS EYES** (GB) 3
255 **CAUCUS** (GB) 3
433 **CAUGHT BY WITNESS** (IRE) 7
3 **CAUGHT IN THE ACT** (IRE) 6
626 **CAULFIELDS VENTURE** (IRE) 1
455 **CAUNAY** (GB) 8
135 **CAUSEWAY CHARM** (USA) F 28
488 **CAUSEWAY FOOT** (USA) 3
276 **CAUSEWAY KING** (USA) 4
450 **CAUSEWAY SONG** (USA) C 7
630 **CAUSING CHAOS** (IRE) 12
344 **CAVALIERI** (IRE) 12
25 **CAVALLO BELLA** (GB) 51
420 **CAVALRY GUARD** (USA) 1
44 **CAVALRYMAN** (GB) 2
627 **CAVITE ETA** (IRE) 6
529 **CAWDOR HOUSE BERT** (GB) 5
287 **CAY DANCER** (GB) 129
506 **CAYMAN FOX** (GB) 4
216 **CAYMAN ISLANDS** (GB) 9
44 **CAYMANS** (AUS) 13
353 **CAYSUE** (GB) G 37
349 **CAYUGA** (GB) 2
476 **CAZZA** (GB) 45
277 **CEBUANO** (GB) 5
658 **CECILIA'S PEARL** (USA) C 78
124 **CECILY** (GB) F 15
451 **CECILY PARSLEY** (GB) 6
608 **CEDAR SEA** (IRE) C 38
477 **CEDRE BLEU** (FR) 17
85 **CEEKAY'S GIRL** (GB) 25
619 **CEEPEEGEE** (IRE) 9
50 **CEISTEACH** (IRE) 72
57 **CELEB STYLE** (IRE) G 24
372 **CELESTIAL BAY** (GB) 2
477 **CELESTIAL HALO** (IRE) 18
235 **CELESTIAL ISLAND** (GB) 2
518 **CELESTIAL RAY** (GB) 4
316 **CELTIC ABBEY** (GB) 22
489 **CELTIC AGENT** (GB) 10
150 **CELTIC BALLAD** (IRE) 1
290 **CELTIC CAILIN** (IRE) 11
548 **CELTIC CAROL** (IRE) 4
175 **CELTIC CELEB** (IRE) 3
508 **CELTIC CHARLIE** (FR) 3
243 **CELTIC INTRIGUE** (IRE) 10
463 **CELTIC LEGACY** (GB) 1
559 **CELTIC SIXPENCE** (IRE) 3
387 **CELTIC SULTAN** (IRE) 8
459 **CELTIC WISH** (IRE) 29
361 **CELTS ESPERE** (GB) 2
597 **CENN FUAIT** (IRE) 3
444 **CENSORED** (GB) C 123
510 **CENTASIA** (GB) 18
649 **CENTRAL FLAME** (GB) 1
275 **CENTRAL FORCE** (GB) F 88
50 **CENTRE OF INTEREST** (USA) 73
601 **CENTRED** (IRE) 37
57 **CEOL COIS TINE** (IRE) 74
175 **CERAMICK** (FR) 40
53 **CEREMONIAL JADE** (UAE) 4
368 **CERIUM** (FR) 5
202 **CERTAINLY BRAVE** (GB) C 221
277 **CERTERACH** (IRE) 6
634 **CERTIFICATE** (GB) 96
2 **CERTIFY** (USA) 71

575 **DOCTOR SARDONICUS** (GB) 73
58 **DOCTOR TOM** (IRE) 5
430 **DOCTOR'S NOTE** (GB) F 4
255 **DOCTRINE** (GB) F 111
183 **DODGEY DREAM** (GB) 1
477 **DODGING BULLETS** (GB) 28
112 **DODINA** (IRE) 12
325 **DOESHEEVERSTOP** (IRE) 19
477 **DOESLESSTHANME** (IRE) 29
112 **DOGARESSA** (IRE) 31
459 **DOGORA** (FR) 43
306 **DOHENY BAR** (IRE) 4
262 **DOLATULO** (FR) 7
2 **DOLDRUMS** (USA) 75
245 **DOLLAR BILL** (GB) 6
418 **DOLLY BANTRY** (GB) 30
159 **DOLLY COLMAN** (GB) 4
191 **DOLLY COUGHDROP** (IRE) C 16
435 **DOLLY DIVA** (GB) 3
630 **DOLLY PENROSE** (GB) 18
351 **DOLLY ROYAL** (IRE) 5
677 **DOLORES DELIGHTFUL** (FR) 38
308 **DOLPHIN DANCER** (GB) G 7
201 **DOLPHIN ROCK** (GB) 20
211 **DOLPHIN VILLAGE** (IRE) 68
393 **DOM LUKKA** (FR) 13
287 **DOMINATE** (GB) 44
238 **DOMINIUM** (USA) 6
462 **DOMOLY** (FR) 17
477 **DOMTALINE** (FR) 30
578 **DON BOSCO** (FR) 4
446 **DON EDUARDO** (GB) 9
123 **DON LIBRE** (GB) 2
114 **DON MARCO** (GB) 24
380 **DON OTTAVIO** (GB) 4
140 **DON PADEJA** (GB) 28
8 **DON POOLEONI** (IRE) 3
140 **DON'T** (GB) 72
491 **DON'T BE LATE** (IRE) 24
476 **DON'T CALL ME** (IRE) 10
23 **DON'T LOOK BACH** (IRE) 2
213 **DON'T STARE** (IRE) 8
445 **DON'T TELL** (GB) 30
302 **DONATRICE** (FR) 3
552 **DONCELLA** (IRE) 114
246 **DONT CALL ME OSCAR** (IRE) 7
66 **DONT DO MONDAYS** (IRE) 6
393 **DONT TAKE ME ALIVE** (GB) 14
407 **DONT TELL PA** (FR) 5
95 **DONT TELL SAILOR** (IRE) 12
548 **DONT TELL THE BOYS** (GB) 4
433 **DONTGOEASY** (GB) 9
201 **DONTPAYTHEFERRYMAN** (USA) 21
476 **DOODLES** (GB) 47
468 **DOOKS LAD** (IRE) 9
638 **DOOR BOY** (IRE) 20
81 **DORA CANINA** (GB) 4
624 **DORA'S GIFT** (GB) 4
578 **DORADE ROSE** (FR) 5
476 **DORBACK** (GB) 11
346 **DORCEUS** (GB) 10
353 **DORFMAN** (GB) 44
259 **DORIAN BAY** (IRE) 5
372 **DORIS SOUTER** (IRE) C 35
322 **DORLESH WAY** (FR) 3
460 **DORMOUSE** (GB) 6
444 **DOROTHY'S DANCING** (IRE) 28
634 **DORRATI** (USA) F 101

547 **DORRY K** (IRE) 2
22 **DORSET DORA** (GB) 6
173 **DOS AMIGOS** (IRE) 6
365 **DOTING** (GB) 7
553 **DOTTIES DILEMA** (IRE) 20
688 **DOUBLE CARPET** (IRE) 1
262 **DOUBLE CEE** (GB) 8
66 **DOUBLE CHOCOLATE** (GB) 7
507 **DOUBLE CZECH** (IRE) 39
16 **DOUBLE DASH** (GB) 11
2 **DOUBLE DEALER** (GB) 13
515 **DOUBLE DEALITES** (GB) 8
154 **DOUBLE DISCOUNT** (IRE) 23
81 **DOUBLE DIZZY** (GB) 5
50 **DOUBLE FOCUS** (GB) 80
310 **DOUBLE HANDFUL** (GER) 10
547 **DOUBLE HAPPINESS** (GB) 3
563 **DOUBLE JEOPARDY** (GB) 4
187 **DOUBLE MEAD** (GB) 2
81 **DOUBLE OR QUITZ** (GB) 6
630 **DOUBLE ROSS** (IRE) 19
487 **DOUBLE SILVER** (GB) 9
324 **DOUBLE SPARKLE** (GB) 6
514 **DOUBLE STAR** (GB) 21
637 **DOUBLE TROUBLE** (GER) 41
508 **DOUBLE U DOT EDE'S** (GB) 5
17 **DOUBLE VIE** (IRE) C 115
353 **DOUBLE YOUR MONEY** (IRE) 45
487 **DOUBLETOILNTROUBLE** (IRE) 10
36 **DOUCHKIRK** (FR) 2
459 **DOUGAL PHILPS** (GB) 44
585 **DOUGLAS JULIAN** (GB) 14
287 **DOUGLAS PASHA** (IRE) 45
390 **DOUNEEDAHAND** (GB) 4
552 **DOUTZEN** (IRE) 49
2 **DOVE** (IRE) C 137
287 **DOVER THE MOON** (IRE) 146
279 **DOVER'S HILL** (GB) 1
436 **DOVIL'S DUEL** (IRE) 30
636 **DOVILS DATE** (GB) 18
501 **DOWN THE STRETCH** (GB) 1
432 **DOWNHILL DANCER** (IRE) 18
358 **DOWNRIGHT DIZZIE** (GB) 12
287 **DOWNTON** (GB) 147
136 **DOWNTOWN BOY** (IRE) 2
155 **DOYENTHEDECENTHING** (GB) 3
403 **DOYLE'S DREAM** (GB) 4
419 **DOYLY CARTE** (GB) 42
386 **DR ANUBIS** (IRE) 2
192 **DR DREAMY** (IRE) 4
503 **DR FINLEY** (IRE) 3
282 **DR FLYNN** (IRE) 1
396 **DR FUNKENSTEIN** (IRE) 20
200 **DR LIVINGSTONE** (IRE) 4
444 **DR THISTLE** (IRE) 29
483 **DR VICTORIA** (GB) 5
106 **DR YES** (FR) 6
484 **DRACO'S CODE** (GB) 64
186 **DRAGON CITY** (GB) 7
177 **DRAGON'S DEN** (IRE) 5
213 **DRAHEM** (GB) 26
491 **DRAMATIC DUKE** (IRE) 25
632 **DRAMATIC VICTORY** (IRE) 2
627 **DRASTIC MEASURE** (GB) F 29
495 **DRAWNFROMTHEPAST** (IRE) 8
437 **DREAM ABOUT YOU** (IRE) 1
491 **DREAM AGAIN BOYS** (IRE) 26
488 **DREAM ALLY** (IRE) 10

575 **DREAM CAST** (IRE) 34
96 **DREAM CATCHER** (FR) 3
575 **DREAM DANCE** (GB) C 74
69 **DREAM DAY** (FR) C 28
26 **DREAM DAY** (FR) F 76
566 **DREAM DEAL** (GB) 8
419 **DREAM DESTINY** (GB) 43
461 **DREAM FUNCTION** (IRE) 6
377 **DREAM GIRL** (GB) 66
255 **DREAM MELODY** (GB) 112
207 **DREAM PROSPECTOR** (GB) 4
201 **DREAM RISK** (FR) 22
489 **DREAM ROSE** (IRE) F 86
139 **DREAM RULER** (GB) 23
69 **DREAM SCENARIO** (GB) 16
134 **DREAM SIKA** (IRE) 57
134 **DREAM TUNE** (GB) 3
195 **DREAM VALE** (IRE) 84
275 **DREAM VALLEY** (IRE) C 94
68 **DREAM VISION** (USA) F 38
425 **DREAM WALKER** (FR) 4
601 **DREAM WILD** (GB) 44
201 **DREAM WIN** (GB) 23
566 **DREAMBROOK LADY** (IRE) 9
345 **DREAMERS OF DREAMS** (IRE) 10
353 **DREAMILY** (IRE) 46
484 **DREAMING BEAUTY** (GB) 65
507 **DREAMING BRAVE** (GB) 40
294 **DREAMING OF RUBIES** (GB) 3
316 **DREAMS AND SONGS** (GB) 31
317 **DREAMS OF GLORY** (GB) 5
419 **DREAMS OF MILAN** (IRE) 44
491 **DREAMSOFTHEATRE** (IRE) 27
637 **DREAMSPEED** (IRE) 14
157 **DRESDEN** (IRE) 7
275 **DRESS UNIFORM** (USA) F 95
139 **DRESSED IN LACE** (GB) 40
277 **DRIFTING MIST** (GB) 37
419 **DRILL SERGEANT** (GB) 45
353 **DRIPPING** (FR) 143
265 **DRISHOGUE LAD** (IRE) 3
684 **DRIVE HOME** (USA) 3
215 **DRIVE ON LOCKY** (IRE) 8
459 **DRIVE ON REGARDLES** (IRE) 45
459 **DRIVE TIME** (USA) 46
449 **DROMNEA** (IRE) 8
192 **DROMORE HILL** (IRE) 5
393 **DROP OUT JOE** (GB) 15
384 **DROPZONE** (GB) 7
572 **DRUM VALLEY** (GB) 9
130 **DRUMADOON** (IRE) 3
676 **DRUMLANG** (IRE) 14
443 **DRUMLISTER** (IRE) 8
389 **DRUMMOND** (GB) 4
679 **DRUMSHAMBO** (USA) 13
52 **DRUSSELL** (IRE) 7
679 **DUAISEOIR** (IRE) 14
92 **DUAL MAC** (GB) 3
312 **DUBAI APPLAUSE** (GB) 27
93 **DUBAI CELEBRATION** (GB) 4
195 **DUBAI DESTINY** (GB) 21
100 **DUBAI DYNAMO** (GB) 4
191 **DUBAI EMERALD** (USA) 1
660 **DUBAI GLORY** (GB) 6
579 **DUBAI HILLS** (GB) 6
611 **DUBAI KISS** (GB) 2
673 **DUBAI POST** (IRE) 55
7 **DUBAI RYTHM** (GB) 9

427 **FLIRTINASKIRT** (GB) 16
262 **FLITE** (IRE) 14
210 **FLIXX** (GB) 31
275 **FLOATING ALONG** (IRE) 41
383 **FLOBURY** (GB) 5
482 **FLOGAROSE** (FR) 12
397 **FLOGASORTE** (FR) 72
519 **FLORA LEA** (GB) 3
518 **FLORA MEDICI** (GB) 37
30 **FLORA SKY** (GB) 6
534 **FLORA'S PRIDE** (GB) 14
572 **FLORAFERN** (GB) 15
181 **FLORAL SPARK** (GB) F 34
627 **FLORAL SPINNER** (GB) 4
89 **FLORALYS** (USA) 5
17 **FLORIANA** (GB) C 119
17 **FLORIDA BEAT** (GB) 51
566 **FLORIDA QUAYS** (GB) 12
446 **FLORISTA GG** (URU) C 35
106 **FLOW** (USA) 52
261 **FLOW CHART** (IRE) 5
69 **FLOWER BREEZE** (USA) F 7
57 **FLOWING AIR** (IRE) 6
458 **FLUGZEUG** (GB) 7
596 **FLUMPS** (GB) 2
337 **FLUTER PHIL** (GB) 4
644 **FLY BY KNIGHT** (GB) 5
375 **FLY HAAF** (IRE) 7
605 **FLY SOLO** (GB) 18
55 **FLYING APPLAUSE** (GB) 5
237 **FLYING AWARD** (IRE) 3
510 **FLYING CROSS** (IRE) 29
666 **FLYING DOCTOR** (GB) 8
213 **FLYING FINISH** (FR) C 60
433 **FLYING FORTRESS** (GB) 12
330 **FLYING GIANT** (GB) 35
186 **FLYING HIGHEST** (GB) F 28
65 **FLYING KITTY** (GB) 5
609 **FLYING NELLIE** (GB) 8
255 **FLYING OFFICER** (USA) 42
83 **FLYING PHOENIX** (GB) 6
418 **FLYING PICKETS** (IRE) 11
483 **FLYING POWER** (GB) 6
46 **FLYING QUEST** (GB) 2
171 **FLYING SQUAD** (UAE) 2
185 **FLYING TEMPO** (GB) 3
485 **FLYING THE FLAG** (IRE) 20
111 **FLYING TRADER** (USA) 7
149 **FLYLOWFLYLONG** (IRE) C 40
211 **FLYMAN** (GB) 72
272 **FLYNN'S BOY** (GB) 6
555 **FOCAIL MAITH** (GB) 1
330 **FOCAL POINT** (GB) 36
50 **FOCAS MOR** (IRE) 85
50 **FOCUS ON VENICE** (IRE) 86
181 **FOCUSOFOURTHOUGHTS** (IRE) 35
10 **FOCUSSED** (IRE) 87
396 **FOG OF WAR** (GB) 50
553 **FOG PATCHES** (IRE) 25
477 **FOGGY'S WALL** (IRE) 40
453 **FOIE GRAS** (GB) 20
173 **FOLGA** (GB) F 39
549 **FOLIE DOUCE** (GB) 50
418 **FOLLOW THE FLAG** (IRE) 12
226 **FOLLOW THE MASTER** (GB) 3
287 **FOLLOWEVERYRAINBOW** (GB) 53
689 **FOLLY FARM** (IRE) 5
132 **FONDLED** (GB) C 38

17 **FONSECA** (IRE) 52
310 **FONT** (GB) 12
381 **FONTANO** (FR) 25
337 **FONTERUTOLI** (IRE) 5
149 **FOOLBYTHEPOOL** (GB) 30
551 **FOOLS CREST** (GB) 2
646 **FOOT TAPPER** (GB) 6
322 **FOOT THE BILL** (GB) 4
286 **FOOTSTEPS** (IRE) G 3
380 **FOOTSTEPSINTHERAIN** (IRE) 15
392 **FOR LIFE** (IRE) 6
677 **FOR NON STOP** (IRE) 9
2 **FOR POSTERITY** (GB) 81
284 **FOR SAHKEY MOONY** (IRE) 1
394 **FOR SHIA AND LULA** (GB) 2
180 **FOR THE STAFF** (IRE) 5
477 **FOR TWO** (FR) 41
380 **FOR WHAT** (USA) 3
32 **FORCED FAMILY FUN** (GB) 36
3 **FORCEFIELD** (GB) 12
176 **FORCEFUL APPEAL** (USA) 7
198 **FORCEFUL FLAME** (GB) 4
24 **FOREIGN RHYTHM** (IRE) 3
377 **FOREIGN TUNE** (GB) 5
518 **FOREMOST** (GB) 38
206 **FOREST EDGE** (IRE) 16
446 **FOREST GIRL** (IRE) F 36
372 **FOREST GLEN** (IRE) 37
641 **FOREST PHILLY** (IRE) 14
595 **FOREST PRIZE** (GB) F 14
26 **FOREST RAIN** (FR) F 82
134 **FOREST ROW** (GB) 7
287 **FOREST STORM** (GB) C 159
485 **FORESTER** (IRE) 21
248 **FOREVER FINE** (USA) F 27
263 **FOREVER JANEY** (GB) 4
36 **FOREVER LOVED** (GB) F 18
54 **FOREVER MY FRIEND** (IRE) 14
305 **FOREVER PRESENT** (IRE) 39
213 **FORFEIT** (USA) 61
444 **FORGET IT** (GB) 33
556 **FORGET ME NOT LANE** (IRE) 16
211 **FORGING THE PATH** (USA) 73
287 **FORGIVE** (GB) 7
287 **FORGOTTEN DREAMS** (IRE) F 160
243 **FORGOTTEN GOLD** (IRE) 19
312 **FORGOTTEN HERO** (IRE) 4
23 **FORGOTTEN PROMISE** (GB) 3
658 **FORGOTTEN RULES** (IRE) 36
305 **FORGOTTEN VOICE** (IRE) 40
357 **FORMEDABLE** (IRE) 18
515 **FORMIDABLE GUEST** (GB) 3
462 **FORMULATION** (IRE) 21
367 **FORRESTERS FOLLY** (GB) 24
195 **FORSTER STREET** (IRE) 28
185 **FORT BASTION** (IRE) 3
149 **FORT BELVEDERE** (GB) 13
32 **FORTIETH AND FIFTH** (IRE) 9
86 **FORTIFICATION** (USA) 3
485 **FORTIFY** (IRE) 22
31 **FORTINBRASS** (IRE) 31
608 **FORTRESS** (GB) C 50
17 **FORTROSE ACADEMY** (IRE) 13
581 **FORTUNA ROSE** (GB) 2
353 **FORTUNATELY** (GB) F 153
545 **FORTUNE HUNTER** (FR) 9
638 **FORTY CROWN** (IRE) 22
657 **FORTYSCORE** (IRE) 21

138 **FORTYSECOND STREET** (IRE) 9
429 **FORZARZI** (IRE) 3
620 **FORZY ORIGNY** (FR) 10
338 **FOSSA** (GB) 25
109 **FOSTER'S ROAD** (GB) 12
491 **FOUNDATION MAN** (IRE) 34
485 **FOUNDRY** (IRE) 23
324 **FOUNTAINS MARY** (GB) 8
485 **FOUR CARAT** (GER) 108
53 **FOUR LEAVES** (IRE) 9
16 **FOUR NATIONS** (USA) 12
588 **FOUR SHUCK MEN** (IRE) 4
132 **FOUR WINDS** (GB) 7
549 **FOURDRINIER** (USA) 144
195 **FOURJACKS** (GB) 29
671 **FOUROVAKIND** (GB) 3
321 **FOURSQUARE FUNTIME** (GB) 10
619 **FOURTH ACT** (IRE) 15
305 **FOURTH ESTATE** (IRE) 41
381 **FOX APPEAL** (IRE) 26
677 **FOX NORTON** (FR) 39
477 **FOX RUN** (IRE) 42
305 **FOXBRIDGE** (IRE) 42
606 **FOXCUB** (IRE) 5
107 **FOXHAVEN** (GB) 9
238 **FOXTROT INDIA** (IRE) 8
31 **FOXTROT JUBILEE** (IRE) 32
578 **FOXTROT YANKEE** (USA) 19
287 **FOXY DANCER** (IRE) 54
371 **FOXY GILLIAN** (GB) 18
125 **FOZY MOSS** (GB) 1
595 **FRACKING** (IRE) 15
106 **FRAGONARD** (GB) 8
53 **FRAGRANCY** (IRE) F 80
552 **FRALOGA** (IRE) C 115
455 **FRAN'S FOLLY** (GB) 12
149 **FRANCESCADARIMINI** (GB) 41
457 **FRANCIS ALBERT** (GB) 4
130 **FRANCIS DU MESNIL** (FR) 4
485 **FRANCIS OF ASSISI** (IRE) 24
248 **FRANCISCA** (GB) 28
140 **FRANCISCAN** (GB) 4
304 **FRANCO IS MY NAME** (GB) 2
304 **FRANCO'S SECRET** (GB) 18
114 **FRANGIPANNI** (IRE) 63
623 **FRANGLAIS** (GER) G 5
182 **FRANK LLOYD WRIGHT** (IRE) 15
285 **FRANK THE SLINK** (GB) 9
644 **FRANK'S FOLLY** (IRE) 6
218 **FRANKIE FALCO** (GB) 1
3 **FRANKIE'S PROMISE** (IRE) 13
510 **FRANKLIN ROOSEVELT** (IRE) 30
367 **FRANKLINO** (IRE) 25
620 **FRANKY SPEC** (IRE) 11
217 **FRANS HALS** (GB) 13
353 **FRASERBURGH** (IRE) 50
634 **FRASERS HILL** (GB) 8
418 **FRATELLINO** (GB) 13
296 **FRAUDSTER** (UAE) 4
627 **FRECKLE FACE** (GB) 5
419 **FRECKLETON** (IRE) 52
91 **FRED BOJANGALS** (IRE) 1
558 **FRED KENNET** (GB) 1
578 **FRED LALLOUPET** (GB) 6
367 **FRED LE MACON** (FR) 26
45 **FRED THE SHRED** (IRE) 5
419 **FRED WILLETTS** (IRE) 53
113 **FREDDIE BROWN** (GB) 4

320 **GEMMASON** (GB) 6
638 **GENERAL HARDI** (GB) 23
305 **GENERAL MILLER** (GB) 45
606 **GENERAL ROSS** (IRE) 7
30 **GENERAL SAMARSKI** (GB) 7
639 **GENERAL TING** (IRE) 10
580 **GENERAL TUFTO** (GB) 5
286 **GENERAL VILLEGAS** (IRE) 4
679 **GENERALISE** (GB) 20
164 **GENERALYSE** (GB) 4
69 **GENEROUS DREAM** (GB) 8
186 **GENEROUS HEART** (GB) 31
37 **GENEROUS JUNE** (IRE) 8
245 **GENEROUS RANSOM** (IRE) 8
122 **GENEROUS SPENDER** (GB) 2
7 **GENES QUEST** (GB) 16
307 **GENEVA GEYSER** (GER) 4
2 **GENIUS BEAST** (USA) 20
2 **GENIUS STEP** (IRE) 21
542 **GENNY WREN** (GB) 5
639 **GENOA** (GB) F 34
367 **GENSTONE TRAIL** (GB) 27
410 **GENTLE AUSSIE** (IRE) 11
634 **GENTLE NIGHT** (GB) F 107
239 **GENTLEMAN ANSHAN** (IRE) 4
443 **GENTLEMAN DUKE** (IRE) 10
162 **GENTLEMAN IS BACK** (USA) 7
356 **GENTLEMAN JEFF** (USA) 2
330 **GENTLEMAN JON** (GB) 8
356 **GENUINE ART** (GB) 3
635 **GENUINE QUALITY** (USA) 18
676 **GENZY** (FR) 21
658 **GEOGRAPHIC** (USA) F 88
660 **GEORDIE BOY** (GB) 10
197 **GEORDIE MAN** (GB) 10
22 **GEORGE ALMIGHTY** (GB) 10
462 **GEORGE ARTHUR** (GB) 23
16 **GEORGE BAKER** (IRE) 13
361 **GEORGE BENJAMIN** (GB) 4
32 **GEORGE CINQ** (GB) 38
273 **GEORGE FENTON** (GB) 8
10 **GEORGE GURU** (GB) 6
255 **GEORGE HERBERT** (GB) 117
677 **GEORGE NYMPTON** (IRE) 10
556 **GEORGE ROOKE** (IRE) 67
556 **GEORGE THE FIRST** (GB) 98
436 **GEORGE THISBY** (GB) 4
485 **GEORGE VANCOUVER** (USA) 4
273 **GEORGEBERNARDSHAW** (IRE) 9
85 **GEORGIAN BAY** (IRE) 9
138 **GERONIMO CHIEF** (IRE) 10
287 **GERRARDS CROSS** (IRE) 55
30 **GERS BENEFIT** (IRE) 8
106 **GERTRUDE GRAY** (IRE) 53
491 **GET BACK IN LINE** (IRE) 37
193 **GET BACK TO ME** (IRE) 3
451 **GET GOING** (GB) 33
675 **GET IT ON** (IRE) 35
491 **GET ME OUT OF HERE** (IRE) 38
368 **GET READY TO GO** (IRE) 9
544 **GET THE PAPERS** (GB) 4
195 **GETABUZZ** (GB) 30
428 **GETTING READY** (IRE) 11
510 **GEVREY CHAMBERTIN** (FR) 33
658 **GHAAMER** (USA) 37
601 **GHAAWY** (GB) 113
637 **GHAAYER** (GB) 19
2 **GHANAIAN** (FR) 82

275 **GHANY** (IRE) 103
432 **GHASAQ** (IRE) 67
552 **GHAZALI** (FR) 53
53 **GHENWAH** (FR) C 81
376 **GHETTO DIVA** (GB) 6
305 **GHIMAAR** (GB) 46
94 **GHITA** (IRE) G 4
477 **GHIZAO** (GB) 44
676 **GHOST OF A SMILE** (IRE) 22
417 **GHOST OPERA** (GB) 1
106 **GHOST RUNNER** (IRE) 54
420 **GHOST TRAIN** (IRE) 2
2 **GHOSTFLOWER** (GB) F 83
148 **GHOSTWING** (GB) 4
503 **GHUFA** (IRE) 5
255 **GHURAIR** (USA) 44
310 **GIANT O MURCHU** (IRE) 15
118 **GIANTSTEPSAHEAD** (IRE) 5
632 **GIDAM GIDAM** (IRE) 3
205 **GIFT OF MUSIC** (IRE) 13
36 **GIFT OF SILENCE** (GB) 4
123 **GIFTED GIRL** (IRE) 3
502 **GIFTED HEIR** (IRE) 1
444 **GIGONDAS** (GB) 38
253 **GILDED AGE** (GB) 5
153 **GILES CROSS** (IRE) 4
52 **GILES DREAM** (IRE) 8
397 **GILLO** (FR) 74
210 **GILNOCKIE** (GB) 8
276 **GILZEAN** (IRE) 9
112 **GIMASHA** (GB) F 36
290 **GIMLI'S ROCK** (IRE) 17
615 **GIN COBBLER** (GB) 4
169 **GINGER COOKIE** (GB) F 27
105 **GINGER FIZZ** (GB) 6
288 **GINGER JACK** (GB) 12
194 **GINGER'S LAD** (IRE) 16
634 **GINO'S SPIRITS** (GB) C 108
561 **GINZAN** (GB) 3
552 **GIOFRA** (GB) 8
53 **GIOIA DI VITA** (GB) 36
305 **GIORGIO QUERCUS** (FR) 47
248 **GIRL AT THE SANDS** (IRE) 17
496 **GIROUETTE** (IRE) F 67
17 **GIVE HIM A GLANCE** (GB) 121
188 **GIVE IT A WHIRL** (GB) 16
188 **GIVE US A BELLE** (IRE) 5
35 **GIVE US A HAND** (IRE) 9
438 **GIVE US THE WINK** (GB) 5
432 **GIVE WAY NELSON** (IRE) 23
192 **GIVEITACHANCE** (IRE) 7
534 **GIVEITAGO** (GB) 15
242 **GIZZIT** (GB) 4
330 **GLACIAL AGE** (IRE) 37
428 **GLACIAL ROCK** (IRE) 12
169 **GLAD EYE GLADYS** (GB) 10
436 **GLADIATRIX** (GB) 5
652 **GLADSOME** (GB) 4
549 **GLADSTONE** (FR) 146
499 **GLADSTONE** (GB) 4
274 **GLADSTONE** (IRE) 3
634 **GLADYS' GAL** (GB) 10
257 **GLAISDALE** (GB) 8
461 **GLAM GERRY** (IRE) 9
213 **GLANELY** (GB) 7
399 **GLASS MOUNTAIN** (IRE) 7
575 **GLASS OFFICE** (GB) 40
676 **GLASSAWINE** (GB) 23

462 **GLASSON LAD** (IRE) 24
165 **GLASTONBERRY** (GB) 5
287 **GLEAN** (GB) 56
381 **GLEANN EAGAS** (IRE) 28
666 **GLEANN NA NDOCHAIS** (IRE) 11
260 **GLEANNACREIM** (IRE) 2
516 **GLEN COUNTESS** (IRE) 16
312 **GLEN MOSS** (IRE) 6
353 **GLEN ROSIE** (IRE) C 155
211 **GLEN'S DIAMOND** (GB) 27
312 **GLENARD** (GB) 34
548 **GLENBANE GENT** (IRE) 8
248 **GLENCAL** (GB) F 29
372 **GLENCOE SOLAS** (IRE) F 39
638 **GLENCREE** (IRE) 24
393 **GLENFORD DORIE** (GB) 19
372 **GLENNTEN** (GB) 2
147 **GLENREEF** (GB) 8
248 **GLENRIDDING** (GB) 4
459 **GLENS MELODY** (IRE) 57
81 **GLENWOOD PRESENT** (IRE) 7
566 **GLENWOOD PRINCE** (IRE) 13
150 **GLIDEWELL** (GB) 2
538 **GLINGERBURN** (IRE) 14
287 **GLITTER BABY** (IRE) C 161
235 **GLITZ** (IRE) F 14
44 **GLOBAL CITY** (IRE) 25
13 **GLOBAL DOMINATION** (GB) 6
345 **GLOBAL FELLA** (IRE) 13
13 **GLOBAL FLYER** (GB) 7
572 **GLOBAL POWER** (IRE) 17
50 **GLOBAL REACH** (IRE) 27
381 **GLOBAL WARMING** (IRE) 29
100 **GLORIAM** (USA) 10
302 **GLORIEUX** (FR) 35
645 **GLORIOUS EMPIRE** (IRE) 35
645 **GLORIOUS PROTECTOR** (IRE) 15
645 **GLORIOUS STAR** (IRE) 16
305 **GLORIOUS TWELFTH** (IRE) 48
556 **GLORY AWAITS** (IRE) 68
53 **GLORY CITY** (IRE) 37
50 **GLOVE SMITH** (IRE) 28
658 **GLOVED HAND** (GB) C 89
255 **GM HOPKINS** (GB) 118
592 **GMAC** (IRE) 17
346 **GO AMWELL** (GB) 12
575 **GO ANGELLICA** (IRE) 41
158 **GO ANNIE** (GB) 3
12 **GO FAR** (GB) 19
658 **GO FOR GOAL** (IRE) 90
291 **GO GLAMOROUS** (IRE) 38
162 **GO NANI GO** (GB) 8
630 **GO ON ARCH** (IRE) 25
634 **GO SAKHEE** (GB) 109
205 **GO SET GO** (GB) 3
534 **GO TEESCOMPONENTS** (GB) 16
151 **GO WEST YOUNG MAN** (IRE) 11
630 **GOAT CASTLE** (IRE) 26
144 **GOD OF THE KOP** (IRE) 9
385 **GOD'S COUNTY** (FR) 4
243 **GOD'S OWN** (IRE) 20
272 **GODS GIFT** (IRE) 23
367 **GODSMEJUDGE** (IRE) 28
198 **GOES A TREAT** (IRE) C 16
605 **GOGEO** (IRE) 20
675 **GOING CONCERN** (IRE) 36
83 **GOING FRENCH** (IRE) 7
211 **GOING GREY** (IRE) 28

370 **GREATOWN** (IRE) 5
140 **GREATWOOD** (GB) 33
123 **GRECIAN** (IRE) 33
658 **GRECIAN TIGER** (IRE) 5
312 **GREEB** (GB) 99
396 **GREEK CANYON** (IRE) 4
134 **GREEK EASTER** (IRE) C 61
162 **GREEK ISLANDS** (IRE) 9
484 **GREEK SYMPHONY** (IRE) F 24
2 **GREEK WAR** (IRE) 23
353 **GREELEYS LOVE** (USA) 51
571 **GREEN AND WHITE** (ITY) 10
175 **GREEN BANANAS** (FR) 10
553 **GREEN FLAG** (IRE) 27
393 **GREEN HACKLE** (IRE) 21
27 **GREEN HOWARD** (GB) 2
571 **GREEN KING** (ITY) 1
662 **GREEN LIGHTNING** (IRE) 2
117 **GREEN MAN** (FR) 27
238 **GREEN MILLIONAIRE** (GB) 27
571 **GREEN MITAS** (ITY) 2
213 **GREEN MONKEY** (GB) 29
205 **GREEN MUSIC** (GB) 17
101 **GREEN PARK** (IRE) 4
372 **GREEN ROOM** (FR) C 40
287 **GREEN RUN** (GB) 164
571 **GREEN SPECIAL** (ITY) 11
51 **GREEN SPEED** (FR) 21
98 **GREEN TO GOLD** (IRE) 4
585 **GREEN WIZARD** (IRE) 19
181 **GREENBURY** (IRE) 37
114 **GREENERY** (IRE) 27
664 **GREENFORDGIRL** (IRE) 15
476 **GREENHEAD HIGH** (GB) 15
393 **GREENLAW** (GB) 22
419 **GREENSALT** (IRE) 57
96 **GREENSIDE** (GB) 41
302 **GREENSTREET** 36
464 **GREENSWARD** (GB) 5
432 **GREGORI** (IRE) 26
255 **GREGORIAN** (IRE) 9
549 **GRENADIA** (USA) C 149
53 **GRENDISAR** (IRE) 38
131 **GRENOLI** (FR) 3
34 **GRETHEL** (IRE) 7
109 **GREVILLEA** (IRE) 107
353 **GREY BLUE** (IRE) 52
371 **GREY COMMAND** (USA) 22
69 **GREY DESTINY** (GB) 17
109 **GREY GAZELLE** (GB) 57
384 **GREY GOLD** (IRE) 10
53 **GREY MIRAGE** (GB) 11
566 **GREY MISSILE** (GB) 14
264 **GREY MISTRAL** (GB) F 6
338 **GREY ODYSSEY** (GB) 32
197 **GREY PEARL** (GB) F 11
385 **GREY SOLDIER** (IRE) 5
211 **GREY STREET** (GB) 79
381 **GREY WULFF** (IRE) 31
96 **GREY'S ELEGY** (GB) 20
358 **GREYFRIARSCHORISTA** (GB) 6
553 **GREYHOPE** (GB) 28
134 **GREYLAMI** (IRE) 8
677 **GREYWELL BOY** (GB) 11
453 **GRIFFIN POINT** (IRE) 4
608 **GRILLETTO** (USA) 11
157 **GRIMLEY GIRL** (GB) 3
117 **GRIMOD** (FR) 6

364 **GRIMWITH** (GB) 1
195 **GRISSOM** (IRE) 31
632 **GRITTI PALACE** (IRE) 4
636 **GROOMED** (IRE) 28
53 **GROOVE ON** (IRE) 39
549 **GROOVIN HIGH** (USA) 55
222 **GROUCH ONTHE COUCH** (IRE) 10
346 **GROUP LEADER** (IRE) 14
419 **GROUSE LODGE** (IRE) 58
548 **GROVE DALE** (IRE) 9
461 **GROVE FIELD** (IRE) 10
151 **GROVE PRIDE** (GB) 13
280 **GROVEMERE** (IRE) 2
367 **GRUMETI** (GB) 31
385 **GTAAB** (GB) 6
549 **GUAJARAZ** (FR) 56
516 **GUANCIALE** (GB) 17
485 **GUARANDA** (GB) C 111
275 **GUARANTEE** (GB) 7
68 **GUARANTIA** (GB) C 42
338 **GUARDI** (IRE) 5
444 **GUARDS CHAPEL** (GB) 42
292 **GUAVA** (GB) 3
575 **GUCCI D'ORO** (USA) 7
487 **GUD DAY** (IRE) 16
397 **GUERLINA** (FR) 76
510 **GUESS AGAIN** (IRE) 37
567 **GUEST BOOK** (IRE) 3
657 **GUEST OF HONOUR** (FR) 23
53 **GUEST OF HONOUR** (IRE) 12
374 **GUILDED SPIRIT** (GB) 14
90 **GUILDED WARRIOR** (GB) 5
222 **GUILETTA** (IRE) 11
272 **GUILIA** (GB) C 41
197 **GUILTY SECRET** (IRE) G 12
75 **GUISING** (GB) 3
518 **GULCH GIRL** (USA) F 39
419 **GULF PUNCH** (GB) 59
419 **GULFPORT** (GB) 60
453 **GULLAND ROCK** (GB) 36
54 **GULLIBLE GORDON** (IRE) 15
381 **GULLINBURSTI** (IRE) 32
276 **GUMBRILLS'S GEORGE** (GB) 10
257 **GUMND** (IRE) 10
38 **GUNG HO JACK** (GB) 6
495 **GUNNER WILL** (IRE) 11
52 **GUNNING FOR GLORY** (GB) 18
410 **GUNNS ISLAND** (IRE) 13
167 **GUNS OF LOVE** (IRE) 16
284 **GUNSHIP** (IRE) 2
426 **GURKHA BRAVE** (IRE) 7
675 **GURTACRUE** (IRE) 38
392 **GURU BABY** (GB) 13
144 **GUS MACRAE** (IRE) 10
679 **GUYDUS** (IRE) 22
608 **GWAEL** (USA) 12
477 **GWANAKO** (FR) 46
54 **GWILI SPAR** (GB) 16
370 **GWLADYS STREET** (IRE) 6
185 **GWORN** (GB) 34
479 **GYMDOLI** (GB) 1
597 **GYPSY JAZZ** (IRE) 5
359 **GYPSY MOTH** (IRE) 7
552 **GYRELLA** (IRE) 54
206 **HAADEETH** (GB) 17
31 **HAAF A SIXPENCE** (GB) 7
134 **HAAFAGUINEA** (GB) 33
435 **HAAJES** (GB) 4

626 **HAAR** (GB) 4
668 **HAARMONIC** (GB) 16
633 **HAATEFINA** (GB) 29
100 **HAB REEH** (GB) 12
611 **HABLA ME** (IRE) F 1
395 **HACKETT** (GB) 3
634 **HADAATHA** (IRE) 111
679 **HADA MEN** (USA) 23
68 **HADAJ** (GB) 6
68 **HADEEYA** (GB) 19
305 **HADRIAN'S APPROACH** (IRE) 51
472 **HADRON COLLIDER** (FR) 1
608 **HADYA** (IRE) 51
53 **HAFTOHAF** (GB) 13
609 **HAGWAH** (USA) G 10
482 **HAIDEES REFLECTION** (GB) 29
103 **HAIL PROMENADER** (IRE) 6
360 **HAIL TIBERIUS** (GB) 14
107 **HAIL TO PRINCESS** (GB) 18
275 **HAIRY ROCKET** (GB) 45
353 **HAJRAS** (IRE) 11
173 **HAKUNA MATATA** (GB) 9
680 **HAL OF A LOVER** (GB) 11
173 **HALF A BILLION** (IRE) 10
559 **HALF A CROWN** (IRE) 6
550 **HALF COCKED** (GB) 10
26 **HALF GLANCE** (GB) F 83
105 **HALF INCH** (GB) G 7
485 **HALF MOON** (IRE) 30
556 **HALF TO YOU** (GB) 69
632 **HALIANA** (GB) 5
216 **HALIFAX** (IRE) 17
589 **HALJAFERIA** (UAE) 3
485 **HALL OF MIRRORS** (IRE) 31
50 **HALLA NA SAOIRE** (IRE) 30
96 **HALLBECK** (GB) 42
213 **HALLELUJAH** (GB) 6
243 **HALLEY** (FR) 22
104 **HALLING DANCER** (GB) 2
451 **HALLING'S QUEST** (GB) 13
17 **HALLING'S TREASURE** (GB) 53
38 **HALLING'S WISH** (GB) 20
514 **HALLINGHAM** (GB) 22
17 **HALLINGS COMET** (GB) 14
194 **HALLMARK HARRY** (GB) 17
553 **HALLMARK STAR** (GB) 29
353 **HALLOWED PARK** (IRE) C 156
399 **HALLSTATT** (IRE) 8
419 **HALO MOON** (GB) 61
419 **HALOGEN** (GB) 62
657 **HALUCHA** (IRE) 24
106 **HALUL** (GB) 56
106 **HAMELIN** (IRE) 57
59 **HAMIS AL BIN** (IRE) 15
195 **HAMISH MCGONAGALL** (GB) 32
353 **HAMLA** (GB) 53
656 **HAMMER SHAFT** (IRE) 9
658 **HAMMERED SILVER** (IRE) 38
305 **HAMMERSLY LAKE** (FR) 52
476 **HAMOODY** (USA) 16
440 **HAMPSFELL** (GB) 6
556 **HAMZA** (IRE) 17
149 **HANALEI BAY** (IRE) 31
350 **HAND GRENADE** (IRE) 13
132 **HAND IN GLOVE** (GB) 23
262 **HAND ON BACH** (IRE) 15
440 **HANDA ISLAND** (GB) 16
552 **HANDANA** (IRE) 55

44 IBTAHAJ (GB) 29
312 IBTIKAR (USA) F 100
242 ICANBOOGIE (GB) 7
192 ICANMOTOR (GB) 9
108 ICANSEECLEARLYNOW (GB) 8
377 ICARIUM (FR) 72
246 ICE 'N' EASY (IRE) 10
392 ICE APPLE (GB) 7
154 ICE PIE (GB) 29
485 ICE QUEEN (IRE) C 115
436 ICE TRES (GB) 6
602 ICE TROOPER (GB) 2
194 ICEBLAST (GB) 20
436 ICEBUSTER (GB) 7
330 ICELANDER (USA) 10
503 ICEMAN GEORGE (GB) 7
579 ICHIMOKU (GB) 30
589 ICING SUGAR (GB) 1
164 ICON DANCE (GB) 14
276 ICONOCLAST (IRE) 11
668 ICY BLUE (GB) 5
489 ICY QUIET (GB) 27
602 IDAMANTE (GB) 14
679 IDARAH (USA) 27
429 IDAROSE (IRE) 4
234 IDE NO IDEA (IRE) 3
545 IDEAL STEP (IRE) 40
592 IDILIC CALM (IRE) F 43
633 IDOL DEPUTY (FR) 9
590 IDOLISE (IRE) 10
634 IDONEA (CAN) C 117
17 IF (GER) 125
16 IF I HAD HIM (IRE) 7
217 IF I WERE A BOY (IRE) 9
316 IF IN DOUBT (IRE) 41
213 IF SO (GB) 3
555 IF WHAT AND MAYBE (GB) 2
464 IF YOU WHISPER (IRE) 7
195 IF YOU WISH (IRE) 37
636 IFAN (IRE) 30
319 IFANDBUTWHY (IRE) 3
489 IFANDBUTWHYNOT (IRE) 28
634 IFFRAAJ PINK (IRE) 49
509 IFITS A FIDDLE (GB) 11
30 IFONLYALFIE (GB) 9
454 IFONLYWECUD 4
312 IFTAAR (IRE) 101
545 IFTIKAAR (IRE) 41
353 IFWECAN (GB) 160
419 IFYOUSAYSO (IRE) 69
257 IFYOUTHINKSO (GB) 11
637 IGNAZ 53
185 IHTIKAR (USA) 38
380 IKAT (IRE) C 47
431 IKE CLANTON (IRE) 43
290 IKE'S POND (GB) 59
549 IKER CHOP (FR) 152
44 IKHTISAS (USA) 87
570 IKORODU ROAD (GB) 5
371 IKTIVIEW (GB) 23
431 IL FENOMENO (ITY) 44
485 IL PALAZZO (USA) 35
376 IL PAPARAZZI (GB) 15
464 IL PAZZO (GB) 8
676 IL PRESIDENTE (GER) 26
469 ILDIKO (USA) 4
419 ILE DE RE (FR) 70
380 ILE FLOTTANTE (GB) 48

353 ILE ROUSSE (GB) C 161
152 ILLEGALE (IRE) 2
75 ILLUMINATING DREAM (IRE) 26
485 ILLUSTRATE (IRE) 36
466 ILLUSTRATION (IRE) 4
399 ILLUSTRIOUS FOREST (GB) 9
101 ILLUSTRIOUS PRINCE (IRE) 5
409 IMAGINARY DIVA (GB) 4
18 IMAGINARY WORLD (IRE) 1
17 IMELDA (GB) G 126
484 IMILOA (USA) C 73
598 IMJIN RIVER (IRE) 2
553 IMJOEKING (IRE) 30
390 IMMACULATE HEART (IRE) 3
459 IMMEDIATE RESPONSE (IRE) 61
132 IMMEDIATELY (GB) 24
114 IMPASSE (GB) 28
26 IMPATIENTE (FR) 34
376 IMPERIAL BAILIWICK (IRE) C 16
379 IMPERIAL BOND (GB) 3
290 IMPERIAL CASCADE (IRE) 19
316 IMPERIAL CIRCUS (IRE) 42
630 IMPERIAL COMMANDER (IRE) 31
658 IMPERIAL CONCORDE (IRE) 41
100 IMPERIAL DJAY (IRE) 14
660 IMPERIAL ELEGANCE (GB) 13
17 IMPERIAL GLANCE (GB) 58
240 IMPERIAL LAIDY (IRE) 4
630 IMPERIAL LEADER (IRE) 32
476 IMPERIAL LEGEND (IRE) 17
119 IMPERIAL ROYALE (IRE) 1
109 IMPERIAL SPIRIT (GB) 60
660 IMPERIAL STARGAZER (GB) 14
582 IMPERIAL VIC (IRE) 4
678 IMPERIALISTIC (IRE) F 28
514 IMPERTINENT (GB) 23
556 IMPETIOUS (GB) C 102
463 IMPRESS ME (IRE) 3
12 IMPRIMIS TAGULA (IRE) 6
2 IMPROVISATION (IRE) 86
453 IMPROVIZED (GB) 37
17 IMPULSIVE MOMENT (IRE) 127
664 IMTITHAL (IRE) 7
243 IN BY MIDNIGHT (GB) 26
491 IN THE BINYANIS (IRE) 43
521 IN THE CROWD (IRE) 1
636 IN THE DOCK (IRE) 31
144 IN THE POST (IRE) 12
443 IN TUNE (FR) G 16
181 IN VINO VERITAS (IRE) 40
44 INAAD (IRE) 88
399 INANDOVER (GB) 10
552 INANYA (FR) 57
114 INAUGURAL (GB) 29
265 INCA KOLA (GB) 4
4 INCANTARE (GB) 2
149 INCENDIO (GB) C 42
676 INCENDO (GB) 27
384 INCENTIVISE (IRE) 13
371 INCH MANOR (IRE) 4
290 INCHBERRY (GB) F 60
112 INCHILA (GB) 40
2 INCHMAHOME (GB) C 141
485 INCHMINA (GB) C 116
683 INCHMORE (GB) F 3
427 INCITING INCIDENT (IRE) 28
177 INCOGNITA (GB) 26
197 INCORPORATE (GB) 13

645 INCREDIBLE FRESH (IRE) 39
377 INCROYABLE (USA) 7
49 INDABA (IRE) F 15
476 INDEGO BLUES (GB) 18
556 INDEPUB (GB) 21
419 INDEPUB (GB) 71
432 INDEX WAITER (GB) 29
575 INDIA'S SONG (GB) 44
59 INDIAN AFFAIR (GB) 33
205 INDIAN ANGEL (GB) F 18
221 INDIAN BILLIONAIRE (IRE) 7
419 INDIAN CASTLE (IRE) 72
485 INDIAN CHIEF (IRE) 37
670 INDIAN CITIZEN (IRE) 3
478 INDIAN EMPEROR (IRE) 7
462 INDIAN EMPRESS (GB) G 29
638 INDIAN GROOM (IRE) 27
645 INDIAN JACK (IRE) 6
360 INDIAN MISS (GB) F 17
615 INDIAN PRINT (IRE) 7
58 INDIAN RIFLE (GB) 6
514 INDIAN SHUFFLE (IRE) 6
132 INDIAN TINKER (GB) 9
476 INDIAN TRAIL (GB) 19
645 INDIAN TRIFONE (IRE) 18
159 INDIAN VIOLET (IRE) 8
658 INDICATION (GB) F 95
112 INDIGO LADY (GB) 17
121 INDIGO MOON (GB) 9
348 INDISPENSABELLE (GB) 6
255 INDOLENTE (IRE) F 121
44 INDUNA (AUS) 30
675 INEEDANAME (GB) 40
446 INESSA ARMAND (IRE) 14
255 INFAMOUS ANGEL (GB) C 122
485 INFANTA BRANCA (USA) 38
601 INFATUATE (GB) 53
109 INFFIRAAJ (IRE) 17
484 INFINITE MAGIC (USA) 31
154 INFINITELY (GB) F 60
681 INGENTI (GB) 2
489 INGLEBY ANGEL (IRE) 29
211 INGLEBY ROYALE (GB) 81
211 INGLEBY SPIRIT (GB) 31
425 INGLEBY STAR (IRE) 5
211 INGLEBY SYMPHONY (IRE) 82
31 INGOT OF GOLD (GB) 37
601 INHERITANCE (GB) 116
518 INHERITED (GB) 16
17 INHIBITION (GB) C 128
637 INIKA (GER) 21
547 INIS BEAG (IRE) 3
372 INIS BOFFIN (GB) F 41
459 INISH ISLAND (IRE) 62
111 INJUN SANDS (GB) 22
31 INKA SURPRISE (IRE) 38
2 INLER (IRE) 24
2 INNCLASSIC (IRE) C 142
545 INNER BEAUTY (FR) 10
537 INNER STEEL (IRE) 4
249 INNISCASTLE BOY (GB) 12
255 INNOCENT AIR (GB) F 123
553 INNOCENT GIRL (IRE) 31
42 INOOGOO (IRE) 5
595 INOURHEARTS (IRE) C 18
195 INOVATE (IRE) 89

638 **JAGO RIVER** (IRE) 29
324 **JAJA DE JAU** (GB) 12
548 **JAK DREAM** (GB) 11
102 **JAKE THE SNAKE** (IRE) 14
16 **JAKE'S DESTINY** (IRE) 19
508 **JAKEY** (IRE) 17
508 **JAKEYS GIRL** (GB) 9
53 **JAKKALBERRY** (IRE) 14
431 **JAKROS** (IRE) 46
287 **JALAA** (IRE) 62
634 **JALADEE** (GB) 50
109 **JALLOTA** (GB) 112
549 **JALLY** (IRE) 154
291 **JALORS** (IRE) 11
42 **JAMADDJI** (GB) 6
494 **JAMAICAN BOLT** (IRE) 8
252 **JAMARJO** (IRE) 9
177 **JAMBOBO** (GB) 7
552 **JAMBOREE** (IRE) 59
185 **JAMBORETTA** (IRE) C 72
216 **JAMEEL** (USA) 19
211 **JAMESBO'S GIRL** (GB) 83
588 **JAMESSON** (IRE) 8
431 **JAMIES BENEFIT** (IRE) 47
396 **JAMMING** (IRE) 5
588 **JAMMY** (IRE) 9
409 **JAMMY GUEST** (IRE) 13
453 **JAMMY MOMENT** (GB) 38
323 **JAMNEAN** (GB) 15
31 **JAN DE HEEM** (GB) 39
6 **JAN JANDURA** (IRE) 11
600 **JAN SMUTS** (IRE) 3
287 **JANA** (GB) 169
186 **JANET'S LEGACY** (GB) 32
287 **JANOUB NIBRAS** (IRE) 63
130 **JANUARY** (GB) 6
421 **JAQUES VERT** (FR) 3
601 **JAREEDA** (USA) 56
461 **JAROB** (GB) 11
59 **JARROW** (IRE) 19
74 **JASANI** (GB) 3
608 **JASMICK** (IRE) F 54
371 **JASPER MASSINI** (IRE) 25
630 **JASPERITO** (GB) 33
330 **JAT PUNJABI** (GB) 11
68 **JATHABAH** (IRE) 7
630 **JAUNTY JOURNEY** (GB) 34
196 **JAUNTY WALK** (GB) G 2
393 **JAVA ROSE** (GB) 27
96 **JAVA ROSE** (GB) 4
669 **JAWAHAL DU MATHAN** (FR) 2
596 **JAWBREAKER** (IRE) 4
561 **JAWIM** (GB) 4
206 **JAWINSKI** (IRE) 40
571 **JAWKING** (GB) 3
264 **JAXELLE** (FR) G 7
421 **JAY KAY** (GB) 4
433 **JAYA BELLA** (IRE) 14
316 **JAYANDBEE** (IRE) 44
658 **JAYED JIDAN** (IRE) 43
312 **JAZZ BABY** (IRE) C 103
431 **JAZZ CONCERTO** (IRE) 48
302 **JAZZ DRUMMER** (USA) F 38
539 **JAZZ MAN** (IRE) 4
140 **JAZZ MASTER** (GB) 35
568 **JAZZ UP** (GB) C 27
206 **JAZZY LADY** (IRE) 50
245 **JAZZY REFRAIN** (IRE) G 11

245 **JAZZY REFRAIN** (IRE) F 10
245 **JAZZY REFRAIN** (IRE) G 9
147 **JD ROCKEFELLER** (GB) 9
419 **JE T'AIME** (IRE) 75
630 **JEAN DE FLORETTE** (IRE) 35
588 **JEAN FLEMING** (IRE) 10
149 **JEANNIE GALLOWAY** (IRE) 16
572 **JEANO DE TOULOUSE** (FR) 19
669 **JEANRY** (FR) 3
514 **JEBRIL** (FR) 25
489 **JEBULANI** (GB) 69
556 **JEDWARD** (IRE) 22
154 **JEED** (IRE) C 62
185 **JEERAAN** (USA) 41
61 **JEMIMAVILLE** (IRE) 2
98 **JENNYLEE** (IRE) G 5
325 **JENNYS SURPRISE** (IRE) 29
495 **JERICHO** (IRE) 13
346 **JERMATT** (GB) 17
357 **JERRY LEE** (IRE) 22
534 **JESSICA VALENTINE** (IRE) 21
106 **JESSICA'S DREAM** (IRE) F 102
188 **JESSICA'S GOLD** (GB) 7
195 **JESSIE K** (GB) 126
181 **JESSIE'S SPIRIT** (IRE) 5
318 **JESSINCA** (GB) G 3
318 **JESSINCA** (GB) F 4
299 **JESSY MAE** (GB) 14
3 **JET MASTER** (IRE) 19
96 **JETHOU ISLAND** (GB) 43
367 **JETNOVA** (IRE) 42
290 **JETSON** (IRE) 20
485 **JEWEL IN THE SAND** (IRE) C 117
307 **JEWELLED** (GB) 5
654 **JEWELLED DAGGER** (IRE) 2
153 **JEWELLERY** (IRE) 9
290 **JEZKI** (IRE) 21
242 **JEZZA** (GB) 5
658 **JIBBOOM** (USA) F 97
457 **JIG TIME** (GB) C 23
691 **JIGSAW FINANCIAL** (IRE) 8
109 **JILLNEXTDOOR** (IRE) 61
263 **JILLY WHY** (IRE) F 15
549 **JILNAAR** (IRE) 58
431 **JIM BOWIE** (IRE) 49
455 **JIM JOB JONES** (GB) 17
636 **JIMBILL** (IRE) 34
138 **JIMMIE BROWN** (USA) 11
420 **JIMMY RYAN** (IRE) 3
7 **JIMMY SEWELL** (IRE) 22
134 **JIMMY STYLES** (GB) 12
203 **JIMMY THE BRAVE** (GB) 2
630 **JIMMY THE HAT** (IRE) 36
678 **JIMMY THE SNOOZE** (IRE) 20
288 **JIMSNEVERRIGHT** (GB) 14
162 **JINKER NOBLE** (GB) 10
633 **JINKS AND CO** (GB) 32
506 **JINKY** (GB) 10
154 **JINSKYS GIFT** (IRE) F 63
132 **JIROFT** (ITY) 10
287 **JIVE** (GB) 170
569 **JOAACI** (IRE) 2
588 **JOANNE ONE** (IRE) 11
649 **JOB FOR ERIC** (GB) 4
96 **JOCASTA DAWN** (GB) 5
444 **JODAWES** (USA) 46
344 **JODIES JEM** (GB) 16
396 **JOE EILE** (IRE) 6

514 **JOE PACKET** (GB) 8
484 **JOE PALOOKA** (IRE) 36
622 **JOE THE COAT** (GB) 11
16 **JOEY'S DESTINY** (IRE) 36
211 **JOHANNES** (IRE) 32
431 **JOHANNISBERGER** (IRE) 50
646 **JOHARA** (IRE) 43
17 **JOHN BISCUIT** (IRE) 18
476 **JOHN COFFEY** (IRE) 22
680 **JOHN CRABBIES** (FR) 12
200 **JOHN GULLY** (IRE) 7
29 **JOHN POTTS** (GB) 10
206 **JOHN REEL** (FR) 21
159 **JOHN'S GEM** (GB) 9
390 **JOHNCAN** (IRE) 1
313 **JOHNNO** (GB) 4
507 **JOHNNY CASTLE** (GB) 6
273 **JOHNNY CAVAGIN** (GB) 10
360 **JOHNNY OG** (IRE) 18
643 **JOHNNY RED** (IRE) 6
612 **JOHNNY SPLASH** (IRE) 5
283 **JOHNNYOFCOURSE** (IRE) 4
309 **JOHNS PORRIDGE** (GB) 5
491 **JOHNS SPIRIT** (IRE) 48
394 **JOHNSTOWN LAD** (IRE) 4
80 **JOIN THE NAVY** (GB) 3
477 **JOIN TOGETHER** (IRE) 52
67 **JOIN UP** (GB) 7
367 **JOJABEAN** (IRE) 43
450 **JOJEEMA** (GB) C 8
305 **JOKER CHOKER** (GB) 54
315 **JOKER OF THE PACK** (IRE) 5
638 **JOKERS AND ROGUES** (IRE) 30
31 **JOLAINE** (GB) 6
102 **JOLI SOLEIL** (GB) 15
523 **JOLI'S DAUGHTER** (GB) 4
518 **JOLIE BLONDE** (GB) 42
175 **JOLIE NOCE** (FR) 11
16 **JOLLIFICATION** (IRE) 37
239 **JOLLY BOYS OUTING** (IRE) 5
473 **JOLLY RANCH** (GB) 7
444 **JOLLY'S CRACKED IT** (FR) 47
315 **JOMADE** (IRE) 6
353 **JOMANA** (IRE) C 165
101 **JOMARI** (GB) 22
666 **JON** (IRE) 13
552 **JONA** (FR) 60
601 **JONE DES CHAMPS** (IRE) 117
422 **JONNIE SKULL** (IRE) 9
249 **JONNY DELTA** (GB) 13
195 **JONNY LESTERS HAIR** (IRE) 38
7 **JONNY RYE** (IRE) 23
224 **JONNY WOMBAT** (GB) 33
129 **JONSFELLA** (GB) 6
109 **JONTLEMAN** (IRE) 4
556 **JORDANSTOWN** (GB) 70
34 **JORDAURA** (GB) 8
451 **JOSEFA GOYA** (GB) 34
393 **JOSEPH LISTER** (GB) 28
316 **JOSEPH MERCER** (IRE) 45
566 **JOSH'S DREAMWAY** (IRE) 15
149 **JOSHUA THE FIRST** (IRE) 17
185 **JOSHUA TREE** (IRE) 7
431 **JOSIE BASSETT** (IRE) 51
330 **JOSIE'S DREAM** (IRE) 12
277 **JOURNEY'S END** (IRE) C 63
584 **JOVIAL** (IRE) 4
124 **JOY FOR LIFE** (GB) 3

477 **KAUTO D'ALOES** (FR) 55
393 **KAUTO RELKO** (FR) 29
243 **KAUTO SHINY** (FR) 28
477 **KAUTO STONE** (FR) 56
367 **KAUTO THE ROC** (FR) 44
261 **KAVERI** (USA) C 7
167 **KAWA** (FR) 17
545 **KAWAAKIB** (USA) 45
34 **KAY GEE BE** (IRE) 9
473 **KAY SERA** (GB) 8
577 **KAYAAN** (GB) 7
675 **KAYALAR** (IRE) 43
630 **KAYBEEW** (GB) 37
145 **KAYCEE** (IRE) 6
567 **KAYEF** (GB) 9
630 **KAYF ARAMIS** (GB) 38
151 **KAYFLEUR** (GB) 16
348 **KAYFLIN** (GB) 8
438 **KAYFROU** (GB) 6
444 **KAYLEE** (GB) 50
630 **KAYLIF ARAMIS** (GB) 39
176 **KAYPEA** (GB) 10
368 **KAYSERSBERG** (FR) 11
224 **KAZBOW** (IRE) 12
114 **KAZEEM** (GB) C 30
510 **KAZLIAN** (FR) 50
44 **KAZZIA** (GER) C 126
323 **KEADY** (GB) C 6
466 **KEALIGOLANE** (IRE) 5
445 **KEALSHORE** (GB) 15
445 **KEALSHORE AGAIN** (IRE) 16
545 **KEEN GLANCE** (IRE) 46
363 **KEEN'S TOKEN** (GB) 4
313 **KEENE'S POINTE** (GB) 17
419 **KEENELAND** (IRE) 77
385 **KEENES DAY** (FR) 9
203 **KEEP A WELCOME** (GB) 3
287 **KEEP CALM** (GB) 64
109 **KEEP CLOSE** (GB) 113
135 **KEEP IT DARK** (GB) 5
491 **KEEP KICKING** (IRE) 50
510 **KEEP THE CASH** (IRE) 51
123 **KEEP THE DREAM** (GB) 16
375 **KEEP THE SECRET** (GB) 23
634 **KEEPER'S RING** (USA) 120
396 **KEEPING** (IRE) 25
228 **KEEVERFIELD** (IRE) 2
549 **KEIRA** (FR) 9
316 **KEKI BUKU** (FR) 48
575 **KELADIVA** (GB) 49
451 **KELADORA** (USA) F 57
305 **KELLS BELLE** (IRE) 57
393 **KELLYS BROW** (IRE) 30
159 **KELLYS EYE** (IRE) 5
243 **KELLYSTOWN LAD** (IRE) 29
195 **KELSO MAGIC** (USA) C 127
635 **KELVINGROVE** (IRE) 10
367 **KENAI PENINSULA** (GB) 45
20 **KENALECK** (GER) 3
154 **KENNY POWERS** (GB) 13
453 **KENNY'S GIRL** (FR) 24
32 **KENSINGTON GARDENS** (GB) 46
585 **KENT STREET** (IRE) 23
381 **KENTFORD GREY LADY** (GB) 38
592 **KENTUCKY WOMAN** (IRE) 19
442 **KEPPEL ISLE** (IRE) 6
477 **KEPPOLS HILL** (IRE) 57
291 **KEPT** (GB) 12

484 **KEPT WELL** (USA) 38
496 **KERANIA** (IRE) C 74
549 **KERASHA** (FR) F 156
459 **KERB APPEAL** (IRE) 63
312 **KERBAAJ** (USA) 37
201 **KERCHAK** (USA) 31
176 **KERFUFFLE** (IRE) 11
496 **KERISA** (IRE) 19
350 **KERITANA** (FR) C 26
105 **KERNEL VICTOR** (GB) 10
195 **KERRY'S DREAM** (GB) F 128
406 **KERSIVAY** (GB) 4
151 **KESHI PEARL** (GB) 17
371 **KETTLEWELL** (GB) 27
632 **KEVIN FANCY** (IRE) 7
353 **KEY ACADEMY** (GB) F 167
452 **KEY AMBITION** (GB) 2
123 **KEY APPOINTMENT** (GB) 4
657 **KEY CUTTER** (FR) 27
425 **KEY GOLD** (GB) 6
177 **KEY TO MILAN** (GB) 8
393 **KEY TO THE WEST** (IRE) 31
177 **KEY WEST** (FR) G 9
579 **KEYAKI** (IRE) C 51
644 **KEYHOLE KATE** (GB) 10
476 **KEYS OF CYPRUS** (GB) 24
275 **KHAAWY** (USA) 107
549 **KHADIMA** (FR) 60
181 **KHAFAYIF** (USA) F 41
214 **KHAJAALY** (IRE) 10
175 **KHASMA** (IRE) 14
524 **KHAWATIM** (GB) 6
25 **KHAYRAT** (IRE) F 59
192 **KHAZIUM** (IRE) 10
377 **KHE SE VA** (GB) 35
291 **KHEFYN** (IRE) 30
211 **KHELMAN** (IRE) 85
110 **KHESKIANTO** (IRE) 6
140 **KHIONE** (GB) 7
49 **KHLOE** (GB) 17
255 **KHOBARAA** (GB) 47
485 **KHORANA** (GER) C 118
518 **KHOTAN** (GB) 17
658 **KHOTHRY** (IRE) 44
498 **KHUBALA** (IRE) 3
255 **KHUDOUA** (GB) 48
305 **KHYBER KIM** (GB) 58
432 **KHYBER KNIGHT** (IRE) C 73
488 **KIAN'S JOY** (GB) 3
631 **KIBARAGUE** (GB) F 10
333 **KICKING TIME** (IRE) 11
272 **KICKINGTHELILLY** (GB) 8
102 **KICKS MILAN** (IRE) 16
305 **KID CASSIDY** (FR) 59
433 **KID SUITOR** (IRE) 15
600 **KID WIZZARD** (USA) 4
114 **KIDDING APART** (USA) 66
419 **KIE** (IRE) 78
29 **KIELTY'S FOLLY** (GB) 12
549 **KIFAAH** (GB) 157
265 **KIGALI** (IRE) F 5
387 **KIJIVU** (GB) 12
140 **KIKONGA** (GB) 36
377 **KILAVA** (FR) 74
328 **KILAVALLEY** (IRE) 14
325 **KILBEGGAN KNIGHT** (IRE) 30
387 **KILBURN** (GB) 13
239 **KILCASCAN** (GB) 6

629 **KILCASKIN STAR** (IRE) 6
145 **KILCOMMON PRIDE** (IRE) 7
407 **KILCREA** (IRE) 7
428 **KILCREA ASLA** (IRE) 15
232 **KILDERRY DEAN** (IRE) 4
549 **KILIMANDJARO** (FR) 61
585 **KILKENNY ALL STAR** (IRE) 24
615 **KILLEANEY PRINCESS** (IRE) 8
431 **KILLEENMORE** (IRE) 52
305 **KILLIECRANKIE** (GB) 60
309 **KILLIMORE COTTAGE** (GB) 6
381 **KILLYGLASS** (IRE) 39
487 **KILMACOWEN** (IRE) 19
431 **KILMINGTON BREEZE** (IRE) G 102
394 **KILMOVEE** (GB) C 18
566 **KILMURVY** (IRE) 16
510 **KILRYE** (IRE) 52
630 **KILVERGAN BOY** (IRE) 40
311 **KIM TIAN ROAD** (IRE) 4
32 **KIMBERELLA** (GB) 47
149 **KIMONO** (IRE) C 43
20 **KIMORA** (FR) 4
541 **KIMS QUEST** (IRE) 2
106 **KIND** (FR) F 103
381 **KIND OF EASY** (IRE) 40
109 **KINDALLACHAN** (GB) C 114
10 **KINDIA** (IRE) 8
353 **KINDLING** (GB) F 168
381 **KINDLY NOTE** (GB) 41
140 **KINDU** (GB) 37
185 **KINEMA** (IRE) 74
302 **KINETIC FORCE** (USA) C 39
408 **KING ARTHUR** (GER) 9
112 **KING BERTIE** (IRE) 18
381 **KING BORU** (IRE) 42
3 **KING BREX** (DEN) 20
121 **KING CALYPSO** (GB) 15
310 **KING CARACTACUS** (GB) 17
253 **KING EDMUND** (GB) 6
345 **KING FONTAINE** (IRE) 16
12 **KING GEORGE RIVER** (IRE) 21
455 **KING HELISSIO** (IRE) 18
509 **KING JACK** (GB) 13
667 **KING KALIUM** (IRE) 7
606 **KING KILLER** (IRE) 9
556 **KING KURT** (IRE) 23
549 **KING LUNA** (FR) C 158
219 **KING MAK** (GB) 1
675 **KING MASSINI** (IRE) 44
17 **KING MURO** (GB) 60
259 **KING OF ARAN** (IRE) 7
367 **KING OF DUDES** (GB) 46
5 **KING OF EDEN** (IRE) 5
552 **KING OF ENGLAND** (GB) 63
679 **KING OF GLORY** (GB) 32
32 **KING OF JAZZ** (IRE) 10
169 **KING OF KUDOS** (IRE) 22
5 **KING OF PARADISE** (IRE) 6
644 **KING OF STRINGS** (IRE) 11
195 **KING OF THE CELTS** (IRE) 40
353 **KING OF THE DANES** (GB) 61
83 **KING OF THE MOORS** (USA) 8
233 **KING OF THE NIGHT** (GB) 10
410 **KING OF THE REFS** (IRE) 15
485 **KING OF THE ROMANS** (IRE) 41
345 **KING OF THE WOLDS** (IRE) 17
641 **KING OF WINDSOR** (IRE) 7
675 **KING OF WING** (IRE) 45

185 **LA SYLVIA** (IRE) F 75
549 **LA TEMPERANTE** (IRE) 162
406 **LA VERTE RUE** (USA) 5
605 **LA VITA E BELLA** (IRE) F 54
2 **LAAJOOJ** (IRE) 26
44 **LAATAFREET** (IRE) 35
601 **LABARINTO** (GB) 9
380 **LABIENUS** (GB) 20
477 **LAC FONTANA** (FR) 58
49 **LACANDONA** (USA) F 18
635 **LACEWORK** (GB) C 19
321 **LACEY** (GB) 12
585 **LACKAMON** (GB) 25
96 **LACOCK** (GB) 44
598 **LACONICOS** (IRE) 3
494 **LADIES ARE FOREVER** (GB) 10
361 **LADIES BEST** (GB) 5
177 **LADIES DANCING** (GB) 11
235 **LADWEB** (GB) 12
445 **LADY AMAKHALA** (GB) 17
117 **LADY ANA** (FR) 9
535 **LADY ANNE BOLEYN** (GB) 2
605 **LADY ARTISTE** (IRE) 48
507 **LADY BARASTAR** (IRE) 7
34 **LADY BENTINCK** (IRE) 10
518 **LADY BINGO** (IRE) 43
666 **LADY BLUESKY** (GB) 14
508 **LADY BONANOVA** (IRE) 18
481 **LADY BOWOOD** (IRE) 5
246 **LADY BRIDGET** (GB) 11
17 **LADY BRORA** (GB) C 131
181 **LADY BY RED** (IRE) 7
34 **LADY CALANTHA** (GB) 21
631 **LADY CASTANEA** (GB) C 15
353 **LADY CATHERINE** (GB) F 169
346 **LADY CAVALLO** (GB) 43
173 **LADY CHAPARRAL** (GB) 12
316 **LADY CHARISMA** (GB) 49
467 **LADY COOPER** (GB) 24
397 **LADY CORALINE** (FR) 12
198 **LADY CORDUFF** (IRE) C 18
252 **LADY DARAYNA** (GB) C 22
287 **LADY DAY** (IRE) 174
132 **LADY FARAH** (GB) 25
516 **LADY FROM GENEVA** (GB) 20
249 **LADY GARGOYLE** (GB) 5
215 **LADY GERONIMO** (IRE) 16
607 **LADY GREGORY** (IRE) F 8
275 **LADY IN BLUE** (IRE) 109
123 **LADY IN PINK** (IRE) 18
181 **LADY JAMESWAY** (IRE) 42
26 **LADY JANE** (FR) 36
321 **LADY JEAN** (GB) 29
356 **LADY KARINGA** (GB) 4
605 **LADY KASHAAN** (IRE) 23
637 **LADY KATE** (GER) 54
625 **LADY KATHIAN** (IRE) 16
657 **LADY KATHLEEN** (GB) 30
488 **LADY KILDARE** (IRE) 4
397 **LADY KOKO** (GB) 82
305 **LADY LAMB** (IRE) G 63
307 **LADY LAYLA** (GB) 7
222 **LADY LECTRA** (GB) 14
266 **LADY LIBBY LAMB** (GB) 7
287 **LADY LIVIUS** (IRE) C 175
211 **LADY LOCH** (GB) 35
645 **LADY LUCIA** (IRE) C 41
446 **LADY LUNCHALOT** (USA) 15

353 **LADY MACDUFF** (IRE) 14
291 **LADY MANGO** (IRE) 13
489 **LADY MARGAEUX** (IRE) 70
109 **LADY MARMELO** (IRE) 64
85 **LADY MCBETH** (IRE) F 58
658 **LADY MEAGAN** (IRE) C 100
343 **LADY NAOMI** (USA) C 19
629 **LADY NICKANDY** (IRE) 7
476 **LADY NIRAMAX** (GB) 48
275 **LADY NOUF** (GB) 48
633 **LADY OF BURGUNDY** (GB) 11
149 **LADY OF EDGE** (GB) 18
328 **LADY OF GLENCOE** (IRE) 20
305 **LADY OF PROVENCE** (GB) 64
343 **LADY OF TALENT** (USA) C 20
556 **LADY OF THE HOUSE** (IRE) 71
17 **LADY OF THE VINE** (USA) 61
553 **LADY OF VERONA** (IRE) 35
149 **LADY OF WINDSOR** (IRE) F 44
633 **LADY PERCY** (IRE) 12
96 **LADY PIMPERNEL** (GB) 22
446 **LADY PISTE** (IRE) C 38
445 **LADY POPPY** (GB) 32
592 **LADY PRECISE** (IRE) C 44
627 **LADY PRODEE** (GB) 7
428 **LADY PRUNELLA** (FR) F 16
173 **LADY RAFFA** (GB) 28
154 **LADY RAJ** (USA) C 64
516 **LADY ROMANZA** (IRE) 21
494 **LADY ROYALE** (GB) 11
572 **LADY SINATRA** (GB) 24
634 **LADY SPARKLER** (IRE) 122
330 **LADY SUESANNE** (IRE) F 63
625 **LADY SYLVIA** (GB) 4
139 **LADY TABITHA** (IRE) 19
627 **LADY TEE** (GB) 34
290 **LADY TEMPTRESS** (GB) 24
446 **LADY THYNE** (IRE) F 39
324 **LADY TURK** (FR) F 14
67 **LADY TYCOON** (GB) 8
31 **LADY VERMEER** (GB) 40
31 **LADY WHO** (GB) 41
246 **LADY WILLA** (IRE) 12
372 **LADY WINDERMERE** (IRE) C 43
453 **LADY XARA** (IRE) F 39
445 **LADY YEATS** (GB) 36
85 **LADY-LOVE** (GB) F 34
73 **LADYDOLLY** (GB) 6
396 **LADYLISHANDRA** (IRE) C 53
599 **LADYLLIAT** (FR) F 4
211 **LADYS FIRST** (GB) 36
601 **LADYSHIP** (GB) 10
556 **LAFFAN** (IRE) 24
510 **LAFLAMMEDEGLORIE** (GB) 55
634 **LAFTAH** (IRE) 123
459 **LAGANBANK** (IRE) 64
206 **LAGER TIME** (IRE) 41
552 **LAGO MINTO** (GB) 10
482 **LAGO VERDE** (SWI) 15
255 **LAHAAG** (GB) 12
287 **LAHUROOB** (GB) 176
167 **LAIDBACK LEO** (GB) 19
444 **LAJIDAAL** (USA) 12
545 **LAJUMOOD** (IRE) 90
26 **LAKA** (IRE) 85
658 **LAKE DISTRICT** (GB) 45
463 **LAKE DIVA** (GB) C 7
167 **LAKE LEGEND** (GB) 20

485 **LAKE MICHIGAN** (IRE) 45
485 **LAKE NOVA** (IRE) 46
290 **LAKE SUPERIOR** (IRE) 79
319 **LAKEFIELD REBEL** (IRE) 4
201 **LAKEMAN** (IRE) 34
379 **LAKOTA GHOST** (USA) 4
376 **LALINDE** (GB) 7
316 **LAMB OR COD** (IRE) 50
109 **LAMBERT PEN** (USA) 65
459 **LAMBRO** (GB) 65
397 **LAMEIRO** (GB) 83
353 **LAMORAK** (FR) 170
305 **LAMORLAYE** (IRE) 63
305 **LAMORNA WINK** (GB) 65
48 **LAMPS** (GB) 9
185 **LAMUSAWAMA** (GB) 43
634 **LANANSAAK** (IRE) 54
413 **LANARKSHIRE** (IRE) 1
338 **LANCELOT DU LAC** (ITY) 28
675 **LANCETTO** (IRE) 46
388 **LANCIANA** (IRE) G 9
44 **LANDAMAN** (IRE) 36
372 **LANDAU** (IRE) 20
636 **LANDENSTOWN STAR** (IRE) 40
252 **LANDESHERR** (GER) 11
549 **LANDING IN HEAVEN** (FR) 64
382 **LANDOLINO** (FR) 3
321 **LANDOWN LITTLEROCK** (GB) 13
477 **LANDSCAPE** (FR) 59
180 **LANDULPH LASS** (GB) 6
406 **LANG SHINING** (IRE) 6
287 **LANGAVAT** (IRE) 177
646 **LANGHAM LILY** (USA) 8
612 **LANGLEY VALE** (GB) 6
548 **LANNIGANS TOWER** (IRE) 12
462 **LAP OF HONOUR** (IRE) 30
658 **LAPIS BLUE** (IRE) 46
372 **LAPIS LAZULI** (GB) C 21
545 **LAPONIE BOREALE** (IRE) 47
7 **LAPWORTH** (IRE) 24
549 **LARAFALE** (FR) 65
491 **LARKS LAD** (IRE) 52
359 **LARKS WING** (IRE) 9
578 **LARME** (IRE) F 38
471 **LARRY'S LAW** (IRE) F 4
1 **LARS KRISTER** (USA) 13
397 **LARTETA** (FR) 13
211 **LAS VERGLAS STAR** (IRE) 37
211 **LASARALEEN** (IRE) 87
148 **LASCAUX** (GB) 6
238 **LASER BLAZER** (GB) 12
195 **LAST BID** (GB) 41
568 **LAST CHANCE RANCH** (GB) 17
44 **LAST FIGHTER** (IRE) 37
202 **LAST HOORAY** (GB) 13
215 **LAST INSTALMENT** (IRE) 17
446 **LAST ROMANCE** (IRE) F 40
491 **LAST SHADOW** (GB) 53
679 **LAST SHOT** (FR) 35
101 **LASTCHANCELUCAS** (GB) 23
485 **LASTING CHANCE** (USA) C 119
615 **LASTING MEMORYS** (IRE) 10
174 **LASTKINGOFSCOTLAND** (IRE) 8
443 **LASTOFTHELEADERS** (IRE) 17
258 **LATE REG** (GB) 3
658 **LATE ROSEBUD** (IRE) 47
188 **LATER IN LIFE** (GB) 8
252 **LATERLY** (IRE) 12

117 **MA JOIE** (IRE) 32
285 **MA KELLYS** (IRE) 16
353 **MA PALOMA** (FR) C 176
394 **MA TOOLAN** (IRE) 7
194 **MA-ARIF** (IRE) F 66
483 **MA-ARIF** (GB) G 13
55 **MAAKIRR** (IRE) 7
468 **MAAREK** (GB) 14
312 **MAAYAAT** (USA) 106
455 **MABEL TASMAN** (GB) 19
345 **MAC AEDA** (GB) 19
50 **MAC LIR** (USA) 35
334 **MAC RHAPSODY** (GB) G 2
370 **MAC STEAMY** (IRE) 9
371 **MAC TIERNAN** (IRE) 30
159 **MAC'S GREY** (IRE) 14
467 **MAC'S POWER** (IRE) 14
477 **MAC'S RETURN** (IRE) 61
213 **MAC'S SUPERSTAR** (FR) 33
608 **MACAABRA** (IRE) 15
145 **MACCABEES** (GB) 8
272 **MACCHIARA** (GB) 9
374 **MACDILLON** (GB) 3
256 **MACGILLYCUDDY** (IRE) 2
396 **MACHETE MARK** (IRE) 27
338 **MACK'S SISTER** (GB) 12
328 **MACKEYS FORGE** (IRE) 23
290 **MACNICHOLSON** (IRE) 24
529 **MACRA NA FEIRME** (IRE) 11
38 **MAD ABOUT HARRY** (IRE) 23
343 **MAD ANNIE** (USA) C 21
435 **MAD FOR FUN** (IRE) 5
415 **MAD GINGER ALICE** (GB) 7
135 **MAD JAZZ** (GB) 20
455 **MAD MAX** (IRE) 20
630 **MAD MOOSE** (IRE) 46
131 **MAD PROFESSOR** (IRE) 4
109 **MADAEN** (USA) F 117
489 **MADAGASCAR MOLL** (IRE) 91
658 **MADAKHEEL** (USA) 101
290 **MADAM BOVARY** (GB) 54
654 **MADAM LILIBET** (IRE) 4
369 **MADAM NOSO** (GB) 1
645 **MADAM PRESIDENT** (GB) C 43
467 **MADAME ALLSORTS** (GB) 17
426 **MADAME BLAVATSKY** (FR) 9
154 **MADAME BOULANGERE** (GB) F 67
634 **MADAME CERITO** (GB) C 124
575 **MADAME CHIANG** (GB) 79
140 **MADAME CLOUSEAU** (FR) 80
32 **MADAME DEFARGE** (IRE) 49
586 **MADAME JASMINE** (GB) 6
436 **MADAME KINTYRE** (GB) 11
601 **MADAME VESTRIS** (IRE) 62
177 **MADE FOR A KING** (GB) F 15
459 **MADE IN GERMANY** (IRE) 70
103 **MADE IT** (IRE) 13
337 **MADE OF MORE** (GB) 8
432 **MADEED** (GB) 78
491 **MADEIRA GIRL** (IRE) 57
534 **MADRASA** (IRE) 24
568 **MADRASEE** (GB) C 29
645 **MADURA** (GER) F 44
49 **MAE CIGAN** (FR) 6
114 **MAFETENG** (GB) 10
314 **MAFI** (IRE) 3
545 **MAFILLE** (FR) 91
615 **MAFTEN** (IRE) 11

609 **MAGDALENE** (FR) G 14
272 **MAGDALENE** (GB) G 44
7 **MAGGIE PINK** (GB) 28
265 **MAGGIO** (FR) 7
185 **MAGHAANEM** (IRE) 77
658 **MAGIC CARPET** (IRE) C 102
287 **MAGIC CITY** (IRE) 10
637 **MAGIC DASH** 44
278 **MAGIC HAZE** (GB) 2
213 **MAGIC HURRICANE** (IRE) 34
36 **MAGIC ICE** (GB) 11
441 **MAGIC LANDO** (FR) 12
14 **MAGIC MONEY** (GB) 23
85 **MAGIC MUSIC** (IRE) C 59
106 **MAGIC OF REALITY** (FR) 63
224 **MAGIC PEAK** (IRE) F 34
345 **MAGIC PRESENT** (GB) 20
453 **MAGIC SECRET** (GB) 10
461 **MAGIC SPEAR** (IRE) 12
485 **MAGIC SPELL** (IRE) 52
427 **MAGIC TREE** (UAE) C 32
53 **MAGIC TREND** (IRE) 43
588 **MAGIC VIXEN** (IRE) 16
485 **MAGICAL DREAM** (IRE) 53
55 **MAGICAL FLUTE** (GB) F 16
366 **MAGICAL ISLAND** (GB) 1
53 **MAGICAL KINGDOM** (IRE) 44
366 **MAGICAL LEGEND** (GB) 2
25 **MAGICAL MACEY** (USA) 16
325 **MAGICAL MOON** (GB) 32
147 **MAGICAL ROSE** (IRE) 11
409 **MAGICAL SPEEDFIT** (IRE) 5
290 **MAGICAL STEPS** (GB) 63
366 **MAGICAL TREASURE** (GB) 3
467 **MAGICALMYSTERYTOUR** (IRE) 16
485 **MAGICIAN** (IRE) 54
53 **MAGIKA** (GB) 45
484 **MAGIQUE** (IRE) 39
255 **MAGISTRAL** (GB) 49
17 **MAGMA** (IRE) 19
328 **MAGNANIMITY** (IRE) 24
287 **MAGNIFICENT BELL** (IRE) F 186
658 **MAGNOLIA RIDGE** (IRE) 49
114 **MAGOG** (GB) 32
634 **MAHAABA** (IRE) 125
162 **MAHADEE** (IRE) 14
312 **MAHATTA** (IRE) 107
630 **MAHOGANY BLAZE** (FR) 47
202 **MAID A MILLION** (GB) 15
213 **MAID FOR WINNING** (USA) C 69
459 **MAID FROM MILAN** (IRE) 71
435 **MAID OF MEFT** (GB) 2
691 **MAID OF MIGHT** (IRE) 10
60 **MAID OF OAKSEY** (GB) 7
287 **MAID TO ORDER** (IRE) C 187
511 **MAIDENHAIR** (IRE) F 16
654 **MAIDFORD** (IRE) F 7
243 **MAIL DE BRAYE** (FR) 32
106 **MAIL THE DESERT** (FR) F 105
380 **MAIN SEQUENCE** (USA) 5
26 **MAINSAIL** (FR) 7
601 **MAIRISE** (GB) 120
433 **MAISEY MILAN** (IRE) 17
451 **MAISIE'S MOON** (USA) 38
179 **MAISON BRILLET** (IRE) 1
489 **MAISON DE VILLE** (GER) 34
208 **MAIZY MISSILE** (IRE) 1
243 **MAJALA** (FR) 33

575 **MAJEED** (GB) 47
547 **MAJESTIC ANGEL** (IRE) 4
237 **MAJESTIC BULL** (USA) 6
194 **MAJESTIC DREAM** (IRE) 25
496 **MAJESTIC JASMINE** (IRE) 21
148 **MAJESTIC JESS** (IRE) 15
476 **MAJESTIC MANANNAN** (IRE) 27
211 **MAJESTIC MOON** (IRE) 92
211 **MAJESTIC MYLES** (IRE) 40
561 **MAJESTIC RED** (IRE) 9
275 **MAJESTIC SAKEENA** (IRE) C 114
621 **MAJESTIC SONG** (GB) 15
387 **MAJESTIC ZAFEEN** (GB) 16
106 **MAJESTY** (IRE) 64
605 **MAJOR BUCKLEY** (IRE) 27
205 **MAJOR CRISPIES** (GB) 19
285 **MAJOR DOMO** (FR) 17
387 **MAJOR ERADICATOR** (USA) 17
630 **MAJOR MALARKEY** (IRE) 48
588 **MAJOR MILBORNE** (GB) 17
425 **MAJOR MUSCARI** (IRE) 7
579 **MAJOR ROWAN** (GB) 53
572 **MAJORICA KING** (FR) 27
549 **MAJRAA** (IRE) 172
357 **MAJURO** (IRE) 26
347 **MAJY D'AUTEUIL** (FR) 2
140 **MAKAFEH** (GB) 39
305 **MAKARI** (GB) 74
582 **MAKBULLET** (GB) 6
31 **MAKE ME BLUSH** (USA) C 91
658 **MAKE THE NEWS** (IRE) 50
459 **MAKE YOUR MARK** (IRE) 72
285 **MAKELLYS BLACKPOOL** (GB) 18
675 **MAKETHE MOSTOFNOW** (IRE) 51
3 **MAKHZOON** (USA) 22
53 **MAKIN** (IRE) 46
498 **MAKING EYES** (IRE) 4
215 **MAKING HEADLINES** (IRE) 20
211 **MAKINSON LANE** (IRE) 93
592 **MALA MALA** (IRE) C 45
287 **MALACHIM MIST** (IRE) 188
102 **MALANOS** (IRE) 23
13 **MALAPIE** (IRE) 8
176 **MALAYSIAN BOLEH** (GB) 20
575 **MALEKAT JAMAL** (IRE) 10
106 **MALEKOV** (IRE) 9
546 **MALGURU** (GB) 4
606 **MALIBU ROCK** (GB) 11
164 **MALIH** (GB) 7
134 **MALILLA** (IRE) 37
538 **MALIN BAY** (IRE) 19
81 **MALIN HEAD** (IRE) 9
248 **MALINDI** (GB) 6
677 **MALJIMAR** (IRE) 14
290 **MALLER TREE** (GB) 26
140 **MALLERY HEIGHTS** (IRE) 40
395 **MALLUSK** (IRE) 6
287 **MALORY TOWERS** (GB) 189
305 **MALT MASTER** (IRE) 75
556 **MALTA** (USA) C 103
532 **MALTEASE AH** (GB) 2
418 **MALTEASE AH** (GB) 15
197 **MALVADILLA** (IRE) F 21
608 **MALYANA** (GB) F 58
275 **MAMA ANGELA** (IRE) C 115
353 **MAMBO RHYTHM** (GB) 177
473 **MAMBO SPIRIT** (IRE) 10
605 **MAMOURA** (IRE) G 55

650 **MASTER MURPHY** (IRE) 3
52 **MASTER MYLO** (IRE) 11
297 **MASTER NEO** (FR) 4
MASTER OF ALKMAAR (GB) 126
29 **MASTER OF DISGUISE** (GB) 15
353 **MASTER OF FINANCE** (IRE) 178
55 **MASTER OF SONG** (GB) 10
305 **MASTER OF THE GAME** (GB) 76
305 **MASTER OF THE HALL** (IRE) 77
630 **MASTER OF THE SEA** (IRE) 49
510 **MASTER OVERSEER** (IRE) 58
419 **MASTER RED** (GB) 88
553 **MASTER SEBASTIAN** (GB) 40
485 **MASTER SPEAKER** (IRE) 56
509 **MASTER VINTAGE** (GB) 19
232 **MASTER WELLS** (IRE) 5
111 **MASTER WIZARD** (GB) 17
38 **MASTERED** (IRE) 24
418 **MASTERFUL ACT** (USA) 16
178 **MASTERLEADERMAN** (IRE) 2
290 **MASTEROFDECEPTION** (IRE) 27
44 **MASTEROFTHEROLLS** (IRE) 43
289 **MASTERPOINT** (GB) 2
555 **MASTERS BLAZING** (GB) 4
619 **MASTERS HILL** (IRE) 25
2 **MASTERSTROKE** (USA) 30
7 **MATA HARI BLUE** (GB) 29
568 **MATAAJIR** (USA) 9
359 **MATAKO** (FR) 11
255 **MATALLEB** (USA) 130
370 **MATCHLOCK** (IRE) 10
677 **MATERIAL BOY** (GB) 9
586 **MATERIAL STAR** (GB) 8
253 **MATERIALITY** (GB) 6
202 **MATILDA PEACE** (GB) F 24
182 **MATILDA PLUM** (IRE) 16
138 **MATMATA DE TENDRON** (FR) 12
491 **MATRIPAJO** (IRE) 60
275 **MATROOH** (USA) 51
455 **MATROW'S LADY** (IRE) 21
410 **MATSUKAZE** (IRE) 17
371 **MATTHEW RILEY** (IRE) 32
510 **MATUHI** (GB) 59
601 **MAUGWENNA** (GB) C 121
549 **MAUPERTUS** (GB) 68
489 **MAUPITI EXPRESS** (FR) 92
287 **MAUREEN** (IRE) 68
360 **MAURICETHEATHLETE** (IRE) 20
630 **MAVALENTA** (IRE) 50
195 **MAVEN** (GB) 48
255 **MAVERICK WAVE** (USA) 131
31 **MAVERIK** (GB) 10
346 **MAWAAKEF** (IRE) 22
601 **MAWAQEET** (USA) 13
432 **MAWFOOR** (IRE) 79
44 **MAWHUB** (GB) 44
312 **MAWJ TAMY** (USA) 42
658 **MAWRED** (IRE) 103
114 **MAWSON** (GB) 33
19 **MAX LAURIE** (FR) 3
8 **MAX MILAN** (IRE) 8
347 **MAX MILANO** (IRE) 3
154 **MAX ONE TWO THREE** (GB) F 68
73 **MAXDELAS** (FR) 7
112 **MAXENTIUS** (IRE) 19
477 **MAXI CHOP** (FR) 62
255 **MAXI DRESS** (IRE) 50
353 **MAXIE T** (GB) 179

431 **MAXIM GORKY** (IRE) 56
396 **MAXIMAL CRAZY** (GB) 29
53 **MAXIMITO** (GB) 47
182 **MAXIMUM FEAT** (IRE) 6
154 **MAY** (GB) F 69
374 **MAY BE SOME TIME** (GB) 4
317 **MAY BOY** (GB) 3
516 **MAY CONTAIN NUTS** (GB) 23
523 **MAY COURT** (GB) 5
294 **MAY DAY QUEEN** (IRE) F 13
646 **MAY QUEEN** (GB) 45
633 **MAY'S BOY** (GB) 15
312 **MAYAASEM** (GB) 43
102 **MAYAN FLIGHT** (IRE) 24
134 **MAYBE I WILL** (IRE) C 68
440 **MAYBE I WONT** (GB) 8
195 **MAYBEAGREY** (GB) 49
229 **MAYDREAM** (GB) 5
305 **MAYFAIR MUSIC** (IRE) 78
69 **MAYFIELD GIRL** (IRE) 21
330 **MAYFORDE JACK** (GB) 15
489 **MAYOMAN** (IRE) 35
206 **MAYPOLE JOE** (IRE) 42
601 **MAYPOLE LASS** (GB) 64
312 **MAYSVILLE** (IRE) 110
2 **MAYWOOD** (GB) 31
12 **MAZ** (GB) 7
634 **MAZAAYA** (USA) C 127
277 **MAZANDARAN** (IRE) 40
309 **MAZIJ** (GB) 7
110 **MAZOVIAN** (USA) 8
105 **MAZUMA** (IRE) G 12
147 **MCBIRNEY** (IRE) 5
357 **MCCONNELL** (USA) 27
631 **MCCOOL BANNANAS** (GB) 6
477 **MCLLHATTON** (IRE) 63
345 **MCMURROUGH** (IRE) 22
462 **MCNULTY WRAY** (IRE) 34
367 **MCVICAR** (GB) 57
277 **MEA PARVITAS** (IRE) 16
666 **MEADOWCROFT BOY** (GB) 15
575 **MEAN IT** (GB) 12
549 **MEANS OF ASSENT** (FR) 175
2 **MEASURING TIME** (GB) 32
637 **MECCA'S TEAM** (GB) 27
95 **MECOX BAY** (IRE) 23
667 **MEDA'S SONG** (GB) G 9
292 **MEDAM** (GB) 4
601 **MEDDLING** (GB) 65
641 **MEDECIS MOUNTAIN** (GB) 9
377 **MEDEO** (FR) 77
85 **MEDERMIT** (FR) 58
85 **MEDIA HYPE** (GB) 11
641 **MEDIA JURY** (GB) 13
431 **MEDICAL CARD** (IRE) 57
549 **MEDICAL KISS** (IRE) 69
287 **MEDICEA SIDERA** (GB) F 192
238 **MEDICEAN MAN** (GB) 14
195 **MEDICI DANCER** (GB) 93
195 **MEDICI TIME** (GB) 50
644 **MEDIEVAL BISHOP** (IRE) 59
96 **MEDISKA** (GB) 23
346 **MEDITERRANEAN SEA** (IRE) 23
455 **MEET ME AT DAWN** (GB) 22
646 **MEET ME HALFWAY** (GB) 25
491 **MEET THE CRITICS** (IRE) 61
432 **MEETING IN PARIS** (IRE) 34

275 **MEETING WATERS** (GB) 117
285 **MEETINGS MAN** (IRE) 20
675 **MEGABILL** (IRE) 52
212 **MEGALEKA** (GB) 9
305 **MEGALYPOS** (FR) 79
602 **MEGAMUNCH** (GB) 9
17 **MEGAN'S MOTIVATOR** (GB) 20
144 **MEGANISI** (IRE) 14
444 **MEGASTAR** (GB) 59
60 **MEGASTYLE** (GB) 8
224 **MEGLIO ANCORA** (GB) 15
353 **MEIOSIS** (USA) F 180
316 **MEIRIG'S DREAM** (IRE) 53
69 **MELANDRE** (GB) F 31
134 **MELBOURNE MEMORIES** (GB) 38
377 **MELIVEA** (FR) 40
291 **MELODEE PRINCESS** (IRE) 33
566 **MELODIC RENDEZVOUS** (GB) 19
419 **MELODIC TUNE** (IRE) G 89
377 **MELODIQUE** (FR) 41
181 **MELODY OF LOVE** (GB) 20
353 **MELPOMENE** (GB) F 181
31 **MELROSE ABBEY** (IRE) 92
17 **MELVIN THE GRATE** (IRE) 66
645 **MEMORIZE** (IRE) 20
645 **MEMPHIS MAGIC** (GER) 21
396 **MEMPHIS RED** (IRE) 30
162 **MEN DON'T CRY** (IRE) 15
309 **MENADATI** (USA) 8
377 **MENANDORE** (FR) 78
26 **MENARDAIS** (FR) 8
44 **MENDIP** (USA) 45
377 **MENEAS** (FR) 42
154 **MENELIK** (IRE) 14
372 **MENNETOU** (IRE) F 44
316 **MENORAH** (IRE) 54
2 **MENTAL** (AUS) 31
679 **MENTALIST** (FR) 42
377 **MENYLLOS** (GB) 9
592 **MER DE CORAIL** (IRE) F 46
629 **MERCERS ROW** (GB) 8
285 **MERCHANT OF MEDICI** (GB) 21
516 **MERCHANT OF MILAN** (GB) 24
503 **MERCHANTS RETURN** (GB) 8
675 **MERCURY BAY** (IRE) 53
645 **MEREDITH** (GB) C 45
7 **MEREVALE** (GB) 30
234 **MERIDIEM** (GB) 4
123 **MERITOCRACY** (IRE) 34
484 **MERLETTA** (GB) 76
360 **MERLIN'S WISH** (GB) 21
477 **MERRION SQUARE** (IRE) 64
641 **MERRJANAH** (GB) 11
491 **MERRY KING** (IRE) 62
17 **MERRY ME** (IRE) 136
649 **MERRY MIX** (GB) 5
538 **MERRYDOWN** (IRE) 20
443 **MERRYDOWN BLACK** (GB) 18
287 **MESETA** (GB) F 193
53 **MESMERIZED** (IRE) 48
32 **MESSAGEINABOTTLE** (USA) 50
645 **MESSELINA** (GB) C 46
484 **MESSILA STAR** (GB) 41
485 **METAPHOR** (USA) C 125
106 **METEOROID** (USA) 106
457 **METHAALY** (IRE) 7
84 **METROPOLITAN CHIEF** (GB) 3
186 **MEXICAN HAWK** (USA) F 33

611 **ON THE HIGH TOPS** (IRE) 5
194 **ON THE HOOF** (GB) 29
324 **ON THE MOVE** (GB) 18
287 **ON THE NILE** (IRE) C 212
491 **ON THE OFF CHANCE** (GB) 75
35 **ON THE RADAR** (IRE) 10
491 **ON THE RECORD** (IRE) 19
383 **ON THE RIGHT PATH** (GB) 12
245 **ON TREND** (IRE) 16
635 **ON WITH THE DANCE** (IRE) 12
216 **ONCE MORE DUBAI** (USA) 24
591 **ONCEAPONATIME** (IRE) 3
277 **ONDEAFEARS** (IRE) 18
173 **ONE BOY** (IRE) 42
511 **ONE CHANCE** (IRE) 17
305 **ONE CONEMARA** (IRE) 93
444 **ONE DARK NIGHT** (GB) 116
637 **ONE DAY SHADOW** (GER) 31
290 **ONE FINE DAY** (IRE) 31
538 **ONE FOR HARRY** (IRE) 25
538 **ONE FOR HOCKY** (IRE) 26
222 **ONE FOR JOULES** (IRE) 17
195 **ONE FOR LUCK** (GB) 56
312 **ONE FOR PHILIP** (GB) C 124
516 **ONE FOR THE BOSS** (IRE) 29
109 **ONE GIANT LEAP** (IRE) F 123
675 **ONE IN A MILAN** (IRE) 57
666 **ONE IN A ROW** (IRE) 16
32 **ONE KOOL DUDE** (GB) 11
317 **ONE LAST DREAM** (GB) 8
305 **ONE LUCKY LADY** (GB) 94
171 **ONE MILLION** (GB) 7
485 **ONE MOMENT IN TIME** (IRE) C 131
360 **ONE MORE COOKIE** (IRE) 25
270 **ONE MORE DINAR** (GB) 1
194 **ONE OF TWINS** (GB) 30
634 **ONE PEKAN** (IRE) 60
375 **ONE PIXEL** (GB) 42
321 **ONE SCOOP OR TWO** (GB) 18
144 **ONE TERM** (IRE) 19
206 **ONE WAY OR ANOTHER** (AUS) 27
312 **ONE WORD MORE** (IRE) 50
679 **ONEDIN LINE** (GB) 52
349 **ONEIRIC** (GB) 8
75 **ONELADYOWNER** (GB) 4
425 **ONEOFAPEAR** (IRE) 10
625 **ONERTOTHER** (GB) 6
641 **ONIZ TIPTOES** (IRE) 5
640 **ONLINE** (GB) 18
556 **ONLINE ALEXANDER** (IRE) 107
584 **ONLY CLINT** (GB) 4
259 **ONLY EXCEPTION** (IRE) 9
285 **ONLY ORSENFOOLSIES** (GB) 25
346 **ONLY TEN PER CENT** (IRE) 30
306 **ONLY VINTAGE** (USA) 14
516 **ONLY WITNESS** (IRE) 30
368 **ONTHESLATE** (IRE) 15
188 **ONWARDS'N'UPWARDS** (GB) 11
634 **OOJOOBA** (GB) 13
491 **OPEN DAY** (IRE) 77
549 **OPEN EAGLE** (IRE) 12
305 **OPEN HEARTED** (IRE) 95
353 **OPEN LETTER** (IRE) 78
17 **OPEN WATER** (FR) 25
233 **OPENING BATSMAN** (IRE) 11
17 **OPERA DUKE** (IRE) 146
277 **OPERA GLOVES** (IRE) 42
636 **OPERA LOVER** (IRE) G 49

679 **OPERA OG** (IRE) 53
294 **OPERATEUR** (IRE) 7
290 **OPERATING** (IRE) 32
17 **OPERATION CHARIOT** (IRE) 75
102 **OPERETTIST** (GB) 30
154 **OPERISSIMO** (GB) C 71
601 **OPINION** (IRE) 16
2 **OPINION POLL** (IRE) 41
103 **OPT OUT** (GB) 79
106 **OPTICAL** (GB) 69
53 **OPUS CACTUS** (USA) 50
214 **OPUS TOO** (IRE) 29
462 **OR D'OUDAIRIES** (FR) 39
3 **OR DE GRUGY** (FR) 27
458 **OR SING ABOUT** (FR) 12
316 **ORABORA** (GB) 63
453 **ORACLE BOY** (GB) 42
335 **ORANG OUTAN** (FR) 5
393 **ORANGE NASSAU** (FR) 43
105 **ORANGEADAY** (GB) 16
411 **ORANGER** (FR) 3
372 **ORATORIAN** (IRE) 9
495 **ORATORIO'S JOY** (IRE) 40
634 **ORBISON** (IRE) 61
173 **ORBIT THE MOON** (IRE) 17
657 **ORCHARD BOY** (IRE) 39
177 **ORDENSRITTER** (GER) 18
75 **ORDER OF SERVICE** (GB) 13
350 **ORDERS FROM ROME** (IRE) 5
601 **ORFORD NESS** (GB) C 128
443 **ORGANISEDCONFUSION** (IRE) 21
287 **ORIEL** (GB) 213
353 **ORIENTAL FOX** (GER) 16
549 **ORIENTAL WIND** (GB) 75
431 **ORIGINAL OPTION** (IRE) 64
231 **ORIGINAL STAR** (IRE) 2
106 **ORIGINATE** (GB) 70
327 **ORION EXPRESS** (GB) 7
458 **ORION STAR** (IRE) 13
211 **ORIONS HERO** (IRE) 97
235 **ORLA** (IRE) 5
36 **ORLA'S RAINBOW** (IRE) 13
344 **ORLENA** (USA) G 8
419 **ORLITTLEBYLITTLE** (GB) 103
545 **ORMEL** (GB) 19
681 **ORMUS** (GB) 6
453 **ORNELLAIA** (IRE) C 43
457 **ORPEN BID** (IRE) 13
110 **ORPEN WIDE** (IRE) 10
229 **ORPEN'ARRY** (IRE) 6
109 **ORPHA** (IRE) 71
100 **ORPSIE BOY** (IRE) 21
376 **ORREST HEAD** (GB) 11
582 **ORSIPPUS** (USA) 8
442 **ORSM** (GB) 9
377 **ORSOVIA** (GB) 81
676 **ORTEA** (GB) 38
471 **ORVITA** (FR) 6
579 **ORWELLIAN** (IRE) 16
545 **OSADA** (GB) 56
26 **OSAGE** (FR) 90
477 **OSCAR AMY** (FR) 72
269 **OSCAR BABY** (IRE) 5
36 **OSCAR BERNADOTTE** (GB) 6
584 **OSCAR DALLAS** (IRE) 5
316 **OSCAR DAVY** (IRE) 64
407 **OSCAR DELTA** (IRE) 10
102 **OSCAR FLYER** (IRE) 31

491 **OSCAR FORTUNE** (IRE) 78
675 **OSCAR GOGO** (IRE) 58
603 **OSCAR HILL** (IRE) 6
305 **OSCAR HOOF** (IRE) 96
630 **OSCAR MAGIC** (IRE) 56
305 **OSCAR NOMINEE** (IRE) 97
371 **OSCAR O'SCAR** (IRE) 36
245 **OSCAR PAPA** (GB) 17
262 **OSCAR PRAIRIE** (IRE) 23
386 **OSCAR RAINBOW** (GB) 3
233 **OSCAR ROCK** (IRE) 12
195 **OSCAR ROMEO** (IRE) 57
171 **OSCAR STANLEY** (IRE) 8
675 **OSCAR SUNSET** (IRE) 59
330 **OSCAR TANNER** (IRE) 18
407 **OSCAR TOWN** (IRE) 11
305 **OSCAR WHISKY** (IRE) 98
316 **OSCAR ZULU** (IRE) 65
606 **OSCAR'S PET** (IRE) 17
14 **OSCAR'S SECRET** (IRE) 31
305 **OSCARA DARA** (IRE) 99
477 **OSCARGO** (IRE) 73
636 **OSCARS DEN** (IRE) 50
346 **OSCARS JOURNEY** (GB) 45
98 **OSCARS WAY** (IRE) 8
290 **OSCARS WELL** (IRE) 33
324 **OSCARTEEA** (IRE) 9
419 **OSCATARRA** (IRE) 104
112 **OSCILATE WILDLY** (IRE) 22
114 **OSHIPONGA** (GB) C 70
253 **OSMOSIA** (FR) 11
245 **OSO SPECIAL** (GB) F 18
245 **OSO SPECIAL** (GB) G 19
57 **OSRATTY** (IRE) 57
44 **OSTAAD** (IRE) 98
387 **OSTENTATION** (GB) 21
393 **OSTLAND** (GER) 44
211 **OSTRALEGUS** (GB) 98
468 **OSUS** (USA) 15
601 **OTROOHA** (IRE) 71
510 **OTTERBURN** (IRE) 68
552 **OTTIMA** (FR) 73
638 **OTTO QUERCUS** (FR) 39
38 **OTTO THE FIRST** (GB) 26
305 **OTTO THE GREAT** (FR) 100
575 **OTTOMAN EMPIRE** (FR) 16
397 **OTTOSTAR** (GER) 19
462 **OUEST ECLAIR** (FR) 40
485 **OUIJA BOARD** (GB) C 132
233 **OUR BOMBER HARRIS** (GB) 13
345 **OUR BOY BEN** (GB) 24
307 **OUR CHOICE** (IRE) 11
328 **OUR CONOR** (IRE) 29
194 **OUR CRUSADE** (GB) 31
489 **OUR DIANE** (IRE) 73
321 **OUR EM** (GB) 19
510 **OUR FATHER** (IRE) 69
374 **OUR FOLLY** (GB) 6
74 **OUR GOLDEN BOY** (IRE) 5
636 **OUR ISLAND** (IRE) 51
7 **OUR IVOR** (GB) 34
42 **OUR JOEY** (IRE) 7
511 **OUR JONATHAN** (GB) 4
23 **OUR JOSEPH** (IRE) 4
325 **OUR MAN ZEBO** (IRE) 34
419 **OUR MICK** (GB) 105
275 **OUR OBSESSION** (IRE) 57
367 **OUR PHYLLI VERA** (IRE) 69

75 **SATSUMA** (GB) 15
32 **SATURN GIRL** (IRE) F 96
540 **SATWA BALLERINA** (GB) 3
174 **SATWA LAIRD** (GB) 10
132 **SATWA'S SISTER** (GB) 32
134 **SAUCY BARON** (GB) 21
507 **SAUCY MINX** (IRE) 30
575 **SAUNTA** (GB) 18
316 **SAUSALITO SUNRISE** (IRE) 82
109 **SAVANNA DAYS** (IRE) 24
518 **SAVANNA LA MAR** (USA) 24
614 **SAVANNAH'S CHOICE** (GB) 11
14 **SAVANT BLEU** (FR) 37
549 **SAVE ME THE WALTZ** (FR) F 190
101 **SAVE THE BEES** (GB) 14
636 **SAVED BY JOHN** (IRE) 66
432 **SAVED BY THE BELL** (IRE) 45
605 **SAVEIRO** (FR) 39
410 **SAVELLO** (IRE) 26
138 **SAVILLE ROW** (IRE) 18
302 **SAVOIR** (FR) 19
484 **SAVVY CHIC** (USA) 50
444 **SAWAGO** (GB) 79
66 **SAWPIT SAMBA** (IRE) 22
679 **SAWPIT SECRET** (GB) 72
66 **SAWPIT SUPREME** (GB) 23
391 **SAXBY** (IRE) 3
185 **SAXON SOLDIER** (GB) 56
506 **SAXONETTE** (GB) 18
485 **SAY** (IRE) 73
32 **SAY NO NOW** (IRE) C 97
53 **SAYED YOUMZAIN** (GB) 87
545 **SAYRAH** (GB) 65
44 **SAYTARA** (IRE) 63
518 **SCALA ROMANA** (IRE) 25
375 **SCALA ROMANA** (IRE) 27
545 **SCALAMBRA** (GB) 99
384 **SCALES** (IRE) 21
255 **SCALLYWAG** (IRE) 70
29 **SCAMPERDALE** (GB) 18
657 **SCAMPI BOY** (IRE) 49
353 **SCANDALETTE** (GB) C 196
44 **SCARF** (AUS) 64
538 **SCARLET FIRE** (IRE) 31
288 **SCARLET GEM** (GB) 18
114 **SCARLET PLUM** (GB) 74
24 **SCARLET ROCKS** (IRE) 8
96 **SCARLET SASH** (GB) 51
181 **SCARLET SPIRIT** (IRE) 25
321 **SCARLET STRAND** (GB) 32
577 **SCARLET WHISPERS** (GB) 10
524 **SCARLETT FEVER** (GB) 8
167 **SCARLETT O'TARA** (GB) 28
405 **SCARLETT RIBBON** (GB) F 16
387 **SCARLETTE D'OR** (GB) 29
577 **SCARVA** (GB) 11
50 **SCATINA** (IRE) C 121
353 **SCATTER DICE** (IRE) 20
134 **SCENT OF ROSES** (IRE) 47
181 **SCENTPASTPARADISE** (GB) 26
353 **SCEPTICISM** (USA) 91
95 **SCHEHERAZADESDREAM** (GB) 28
328 **SCHINKEL** (IRE) 36
345 **SCHINKEN OTTO** (IRE) 28
506 **SCHMOOZE** (IRE) 19
606 **SCHOLASTICA** (GB) 19
595 **SCHOOL FEES** (GB) 3
37 **SCHOOL FOR SCANDAL** (IRE) 19

680 **SCHOOLBOY CHAMP** (GB) 18
61 **SCHOOLMASTER** (GB) 3
299 **SCHOTTISCHE** (GB) 12
312 **SCILLONIAN SUNSET** (IRE) 127
50 **SCINTILLULA** (IRE) 48
668 **SCOOBY DOOBY DO** (GB) C 23
394 **SCOOBYS GIRL** (IRE) 15
17 **SCOPPIO DEL CARRO** (GB) 154
636 **SCORCHED SON** (IRE) 67
491 **SCORER** (GB) 86
397 **SCORPIO IMPERATOR** (FR) 97
210 **SCORPIONS STING** (IRE) 17
68 **SCOTCH BONNET** (IRE) C 61
584 **SCOTCH WARRIOR** (GB) 7
144 **SCOTER FONTAINE** (FR) 24
380 **SCOTIA GIRL** (IRE) 32
296 **SCOTLAND YARD** (UAE) 6
149 **SCOTS LAW** (IRE) 49
206 **SCOTSBROOK CLOUD** (GB) 28
395 **SCOTSBROOK LEGEND** (GB) 7
256 **SCOTSWELL** (GB) 4
68 **SCOTTENDALE** (IRE) F 62
516 **SCOTTISH BOOGIE** (IRE) 34
107 **SCOTTISH GLEN** (GB) 13
415 **SCOTTISH LAKE** (GB) 6
205 **SCOTTISH STAR** (GB) 7
666 **SCRAPPER SMITH** (IRE) 19
592 **SCREAM BLUE MURDER** (IRE) 25
660 **SCREAMING BRAVE** (GB) 19
206 **SCRIBE** (IRE) 29
34 **SCRIPT** (GB) 15
576 **SCRIPTWRITER** (IRE) 2
169 **SCROOBY DOO** (GB) 14
275 **SCRUTINY** (GB) 133
588 **SCUDERIA** (IRE) 25
114 **SCUFFLE** (GB) F 75
382 **SCULASTIC** (GB) 8
442 **SEA CADET** (GB) 12
138 **SEA CLIFF** (IRE) 19
287 **SEA DRIFT** (FR) C 229
117 **SEA FIGHT** (USA) 12
31 **SEA HERE** (GB) 100
337 **SEA JADE** (IRE) F 13
216 **SEA LORD** (IRE) 32
106 **SEA MEETS SKY** (FR) 83
287 **SEA SHANTY** (USA) 85
17 **SEA SOLDIER** (IRE) 32
601 **SEA THE BLOOM** (GB) 141
302 **SEA TRIAL** (FR) 5
205 **SEABOUGG** (GB) 8
17 **SEAFLOWER REEF** (IRE) F 155
255 **SEAGULL** (IRE) 146
305 **SEAHAM HALL** (IRE) 119
477 **SEAHORSE** (FR) 45
213 **SEAL OF APPROVAL** (IRE) 15
419 **SEALOUS SCOUT** (IRE) 124
312 **SEAMLESS** (GB) 65
224 **SEAMSTER** (GB) 22
353 **SEAMSTRESS** (IRE) C 197
102 **SEAQUEL** (GB) 37
133 **SEAS OF GREEN** (GB) 3
287 **SEASIDE ROCK** (IRE) 86
31 **SEASIDE SIZZLER** (GB) 17
198 **SEASONAL STYLE** (IRE) C 21
313 **SEAT OF MARS** (IRE) 31
201 **SEATTLE DRIVE** (IRE) 55
55 **SEAWOOD** (GB) 11
287 **SEBASTIAN BEACH** (IRE) 230

545 **SEBIA** 24
514 **SECOND ACT** (GB) F 46
26 **SECOND HAPPINESS** (USA) F 94
146 **SECOND REEF** (GB) 3
140 **SECOND STEP** (IRE) 93
114 **SECONDO** (FR) 41
149 **SECRET ADVICE** (GB) 36
173 **SECRET APPLAUSE** (GB) 43
31 **SECRET ART** (IRE) 56
382 **SECRET ASSASSIN** (IRE) 9
111 **SECRET ASSET** (IRE) 13
31 **SECRET BEAU** (GB) 57
495 **SECRET CIRCLE** (GB) F 55
27 **SECRET CITY** (IRE) 9
627 **SECRET COMBE** (IRE) C 41
354 **SECRET DANCER** (IRE) 13
462 **SECRET DESERT** (GB) 49
367 **SECRET EDGE** (GB) 79
579 **SECRET EMPRESS** (GB) 39
31 **SECRET GESTURE** (GB) 58
17 **SECRET HINT** (GB) 156
53 **SECRET JUSTICE** (USA) C 88
518 **SECRET KEEPER** (GB) 54
396 **SECRET KEY** (GB) C 65
427 **SECRET LOOK** (GB) 21
102 **SECRET MILLIONAIRE** (IRE) 38
453 **SECRET MISSILE** (GB) 26
44 **SECRET NUMBER** (GB) 100
272 **SECRET OF SUCCESS** (GB) 31
372 **SECRET REBEL** (GB) 25
53 **SECRET SESSION** (USA) 56
518 **SECRET SONG** (GB) 26
123 **SECRET SUCCESS** (GB) 21
451 **SECRET TALENT** (GB) 44
453 **SECRET WEAPON** (GB) 27
343 **SECRET WOMAN** (IRE) 8
163 **SECRET WORLD** (IRE) 2
345 **SECRETE STREAM** (IRE) 29
427 **SECRETINTHEPARK** (GB) 22
96 **SECRETLY** (GB) 28
432 **SECULAR SOCIETY** (GB) 46
459 **SECURITY BREACH** (IRE) 107
53 **SEDENOO** (GB) 57
297 **SEDGEMOOR CLASSACT** (IRE) 11
292 **SEDGWICK** (GB) 11
372 **SEE AND BE SEEN** (GB) 26
195 **SEE CLEARLY** (GB) 64
35 **SEE IT AS IT IS** (IRE) 12
622 **SEE ME SOMETIME** (GB) 36
227 **SEE THE LEGEND** (GB) 7
676 **SEE THE STORM** (GB) 45
491 **SEE U BOB** (IRE) 87
27 **SEE VERMONT** (GB) 10
620 **SEE WHAT HAPPENS** (IRE) 18
13 **SEE YOU JACK** (GB) 15
153 **SEEBRIGHT** (GB) 22
200 **SEEDLING** (GB) 9
431 **SEEDS OF DOUBT** (IRE) F 78
200 **SEEDSMAN** (GB) 10
328 **SEEFOOD** (IRE) 37
255 **SEEK AGAIN** (USA) 71
134 **SEEKING MAGIC** (GB) 22
658 **SEEKING TRUTH** (IRE) 114
261 **SEEKING UTOPIA** (GB) F 13
32 **SEEMENOMORE** (GB) 58
629 **SEEMS SO EASY** (USA) G 11
69 **SEEMS SO EASY** (USA) F 10
432 **SEFAAT** (GB) 90

538 **THAT'LL DO NICELY** (IRE) 41
131 **THAT'S THE DEAL** (IRE) 7
32 **THATCHEREEN** (IRE) 104
562 **THATCHERITE** (IRE) 16
2 **THATCHMASTER** (USA) 118
257 **THATILDEE** (IRE) 31
599 **THATWASTHEPENSION** (IRE) 9
167 **THE ABSENT MARE** (GB) 31
287 **THE ALAMO** (IRE) 245
595 **THE ART OF RACING** (IRE) 7
680 **THE BAY TIGRESS** (GB) 26
144 **THE BEAR TRAP** (IRE) 27
419 **THE BELLS O PEOVER** (GB) 146
633 **THE BENDY FELLA** (IRE) 23
484 **THE BEST DOCTOR** (IRE) 53
32 **THE BETCHWORTH KID** (GB) 18
290 **THE BIG EASY** (IRE) 51
636 **THE BIG FREEZE** (IRE) 79
550 **THE BISHOPS BABY** (IRE) 19
639 **THE BLACK BARON** (IRE) 25
446 **THE BLACK JACOBIN** (GB) 24
365 **THE BLACK LION** (IRE) 13
523 **THE BLONDE EMPEROR** (GB) 6
624 **THE BLUE BANANA** (IRE) 12
672 **THE BLUE DOG** (IRE) 9
605 **THE BOLD LORD** (IRE) 42
433 **THE BOOGEYMAN** (IRE) 29
35 **THE BOOSHY MAN** (IRE) 16
556 **THE BOSS OF ME** (GB) 118
459 **THE BOSSES COUSIN** (IRE) 131
549 **THE BROTHERS WAR** (USA) 101
135 **THE BULL HAYES** (IRE) 13
583 **THE CASH GENERATOR** (IRE) 6
384 **THE CHAZER** (IRE) 23
350 **THE CHEKA** (IRE) 8
471 **THE CLYDA ROVER** (IRE) 7
630 **THE COCKNEY MACKEM** (IRE) 77
489 **THE CODGER** (GB) 81
49 **THE COMPOSER** (GB) 10
96 **THE CONFESSOR** (GB) 9
431 **THE CONTENDER** (IRE) 87
325 **THE CRAFTY BUTCHER** (IRE) 39
627 **THE DANCING LORD** (GB) 12
114 **THE DARK WIZARD** (IRE) 47
167 **THE DE THAIX** (FR) 32
614 **THE DIAL HOUSE** (GB) 14
316 **THE DISENGAGER** (IRE) 90
626 **THE DRUIDS NEPHEW** (IRE) 12
214 **THE DUCKING STOOL** (GB) 18
398 **THE DUNION** (GB) 3
290 **THE ENGINEER** (IRE) 52
151 **THE FALKLANDER** (GB) 34
286 **THE FERBANE MAN** (IRE) 5
605 **THE FERICK** (IRE) 43
485 **THE FERRYMAN** (IRE) 80
419 **THE FLYING COLUMN** (IRE) 147
407 **THE FLYING DOC** (IRE) 14
542 **THE FONZ** (GB) 14
360 **THE FOX'S DECREE** (GB) 29
553 **THE FRIARY** (IRE) 63
255 **THE FUGUE** (IRE) 19
195 **THE FUN CRUSHER** (GB) 66
444 **THE GAME IS A FOOT** (IRE) 89
66 **THE GIANT BOLSTER** (GB) 28
563 **THE GINGER BERRY** (GB) 7
372 **THE GIVING TREE** (IRE) 11
484 **THE GOLD CHEONGSAM** (IRE) 54
428 **THE GOOD GUY** (IRE) 27

130 **THE GOSSMOOR YANK** (IRE) 13
485 **THE GRAND DUKE** (GB) 81
185 **THE GREAT GABRIAL** (GB) 16
59 **THE GREY ONE** (IRE) 30
453 **THE GURU OF GLOOM** (IRE) 15
81 **THE HAPPY WARRIOR** (GB) 14
461 **THE HARD HAT** (IRE) 19
462 **THE HOLLINWELL** (GB) 53
139 **THE HOLYMAN** (IRE) 13
158 **THE IRON MAIDEN** (GB) 14
677 **THE ITALIAN YOB** (IRE) 28
492 **THE JAILER** (GB) 15
325 **THE JOB IS RIGHT** (GB) 40
144 **THE JUGOPOLIST** (IRE) 28
327 **THE KERNIGAL** (IRE) 7
67 **THE KICKING LORD** (GB) 21
253 **THE KINGS ASSASSIN** (IRE) 19
477 **THE KNOXS** (IRE) 13
590 **THE LADY MANDARIN** (GB) F 23
32 **THE LARK** (GB) 67
352 **THE LAST BRIDGE** (GB) 1
381 **THE LAST NIGHT** (FR) 60
510 **THE LIQUIDATOR** (GB) 100
7 **THE LOCK MASTER** (IRE) 42
620 **THE LODGE ROAD** (IRE) 9
345 **THE MAGIC BISHOP** (GB) 32
32 **THE MANX MISSILE** (GB) 68
568 **THE MANX TOUCH** (IRE) C 32
182 **THE MASIE** (IRE) 13
253 **THE MASTER REMOVER** (IRE) 20
380 **THE MECHANIC** (IRE) 36
459 **THE MIDNIGHT CLUB** (IRE) 132
644 **THE MIGHTY PEG** (IRE) 22
477 **THE MOBB** (IRE) 114
620 **THE MONGOLIAN** (IRE) 20
206 **THE MONGOOSE** (IRE) 34
367 **THE MUMPER** (IRE) 89
630 **THE MUSICAL GUY** (IRE) 78
301 **THE NAMES HARRY** (GB) 8
491 **THE NEPHEW** (IRE) 104
362 **THE NEW BLACK** (IRE) 5
630 **THE NEW ONE** (IRE) 79
646 **THE NEW PHARAOH** (IRE) 48
195 **THE NIFTY BLAZE** (IRE) 109
372 **THE NOBLE ORD** (IRE) 12
359 **THE OMEN** (GB) 22
155 **THE OSTEOPATH** (IRE) 3
510 **THE PACKAGE** (GB) 101
345 **THE PANAMA KID** (IRE) 33
459 **THE PAPARRAZI KID** (IRE) 133
510 **THE PIER** (IRE) 102
367 **THE PIRATE'S QUEEN** (IRE) 90
381 **THE POTTING SHED** (IRE) 14
248 **THE POWER OF ONE** (IRE) 21
235 **THE PUNDIT** (GB) 8
30 **THE PURCHASER** (IRE) 21
317 **THE QUARTERJACK** (GB) 11
14 **THE RAINBOW HUNTER** (GB) 46
396 **THE REAPER** (GB) 12
73 **THE RINKY DINK** (GB) 15
54 **THE ROAD AHEAD** (GB) 38
675 **THE ROCKIES** (GB) 73
144 **THE ROMFORD PELE** (IRE) 29
333 **THE ROYAL BROMPTON** (GB) 17
486 **THE SAUCY SNIPE** (GB) 6
81 **THE SAWYER** (BEL) 15
109 **THE SCUTTLER** (IRE) 88
616 **THE SHRIMP** (IRE) 10

445 **THE SHY MAN** (IRE) 25
316 **THE SKYFARMER** (GB) 91
109 **THE SMART ONE** (IRE) 134
164 **THE STOUT ITALIAN** (IRE) 12
678 **THE STRIG** (GB) 13
287 **THE TAJ** (USA) 95
255 **THE THIRD MAN** (IRE) 157
614 **THE THIRSTY BRICKY** (IRE) 15
612 **THE TICHBORNE** (IRE) 10
185 **THE TIGER** (GB) 17
510 **THE TRACEY SHUFFLE** (IRE) 103
215 **THE TULLOW TANK** (IRE) 30
686 **THE TWO OF US** (GB) 3
485 **THE UNITED STATES** (IRE) 82
485 **THE VATICAN** (IRE) 83
258 **THE WALNUT TREE** (IRE) 4
419 **THE WEATHERMAN** (IRE) 148
229 **THE WEE CHIEF** (IRE) 7
670 **THE WEE LASS** (GB) 4
670 **THE WEE MIDGET** (GB) 5
312 **THE WELSH WIZARD** (IRE) 72
461 **THE WESTENER BOY** (IRE) 20
606 **THE WESTERN HILL** (IRE) 23
357 **THE WHICH DOCTOR** (GB) 32
360 **THE WICKED KIPPER** (GB) 30
395 **THE WINGED ASSASIN** (USA) 8
17 **THE WIZARD OF AUS** (IRE) 91
102 **THE YANK** (GB) 46
455 **THE YOUNG MASTER** (GB) 33
241 **THEA'S DANCE** (GB) 12
163 **THEAIMANS GIRL** (GB) 3
485 **THEATRE** (IRE) 84
491 **THEATRE EVENING** (IRE) 105
619 **THEATRE GUIDE** (IRE) 42
516 **THEATRELANDS** (GB) 43
619 **THEATRICAL STAR** (GB) 43
555 **THECORNISHCOCKNEY** (GB) 9
555 **THECORNISHCOWBOY** (GB) 10
555 **THECORNISHWREN** (GB) 11
177 **THEDEBOFTHEYEAR** (GB) 23
493 **THEDREAMSTILLALIVE** (IRE) 6
632 **THEFRIENDLYGREMLIN** (GB) 10
675 **THEGAYGARDENER** (GB) 74
431 **THEGREATJOHNBROWNE** (IRE) 88
424 **THEHOODLUM** (GB) 8
459 **THELEZE** (FR) 134
604 **THELIFEOF** (IRE) 3
636 **THELOBSTERCATCHER** (GB) 80
159 **THELORDBEWITHYOU** (IRE) 23
477 **THEMILANHORSE** (IRE) 115
601 **THEODORE GERICAULT** (IRE) 88
657 **THEODORE LAMB** (GB) 58
252 **THEOLOGY** (GB) 19
50 **THEOPHILUS** (IRE) 130
245 **THEOPHRASTUS** (IRE) 27
477 **THERE'S NO PANIC** (IRE) 116
273 **THERE'S NO RULES** (GB) 23
432 **THERE'S TWO** (IRE) C 97
53 **THEREABOUTS** (USA) 22
7 **THEREABOUTS** (USA) 43
248 **THERMOPYLAE** (GB) F 35
543 **THEROADTOGOREY** (IRE) 4
251 **THEWESTWALIAN** (USA) 9
330 **THEWINNINGMACHINE** (GB) 27
195 **THIANG** (GB) 139
419 **THIMAAR** (USA) 149
287 **THINK** (FR) C 246
454 **THINK** (GB) 7

130 **VOTE FOR DOODLE** (IRE) 16
397 **VOTEZ POUR MOI** (FR) 48
175 **VOUS MEME** (FR) 24
275 **VOW** (GB) 15
302 **VOYAGER** 51
302 **VOYAGEUSE** (FR) 26
377 **VRISSA** (FR) 96
397 **VUE D'ESTRUVAL** (FR) 49
575 **VULCAN** (IRE) 55
547 **VULCAN BELLE** F 9
393 **VULCANITE** (IRE) 69
462 **VUVUZELA** (GB) 55
357 **WAABEL** (GB) 34
658 **WAAHEB** (USA) 22
309 **WAAHEJ** (GB) 13
496 **WAAHY** (IRE) 42
444 **WAARID** (GB) 93
608 **WADAA** (USA) 27
287 **WADAAT** (GB) F 257
353 **WADACRE SARKO** (GB) 111
528 **WADHAM HILL** (GB) 3
 44 **WADI AL HATTAWI** (IRE) 110
 32 **WADI ALAMARDI** (GB) 105
377 **WADIRUM** (GB) 97
552 **WADJEKA** (USA) F 135
462 **WADNAAN** (GB) 56
393 **WADSWICK COURT** (IRE) 70
 25 **WAFFLE** (GB) 31
 66 **WAH WAH TAYSEE** (IRE) 30
601 **WAILA** (GB) 91
 32 **WAIT IT OUT** (USA) C 106
689 **WAK A TURTLE** (IRE) 17
266 **WAKE UP SIOUX** (IRE) 10
 95 **WAKE YOUR DREAMS** (IRE) 31
 53 **WAKEUP LITTLE SUZY** (IRE) 69
549 **WAKINA LUTA** (IRE) 205
556 **WAKING WARRIOR** (GB) 37
 17 **WAKYTARA** (GB) C 170
384 **WALCOT LATHYRUS** (GB) 26
102 **WALDEN PRINCE** (IRE) 55
679 **WALDORF SALAD** (GB) 88
143 **WALDSEE** (GER) 8
173 **WALK IN MY SHADOW** (IRE) G 35
397 **WALK ON THE BEACH** (FR) 50
252 **WALKABOUT CREEK** (IRE) 21
367 **WALKON** (FR) 101
154 **WALL OF SOUND** (GB) 44
213 **WALL STREET BOSS** (USA) 46
255 **WALLENBERG** (GB) 87
595 **WALNUT LADY** (GB) C 32
638 **WALSER** (IRE) 55
291 **WALTA** (IRE) 42
460 **WALTER DE LA MARE** (IRE) 14
364 **WALTHAM ABBEY** (GB) 2
534 **WALTZ DARLING** (IRE) 42
315 **WALTZING TORNADO** (IRE) 13
330 **WANA DOO** (USA) C 73
601 **WANNAAN** (IRE) 92
592 **WANNABE BETTER** (IRE) 28
488 **WANNABE FREE** (GB) F 15
288 **WANNABE KING** (GB) 22
255 **WANNABE LOVED** (GB) 21
380 **WANNABE YOUR MAN** (GB) 39
380 **WANNABE YOURS** (IRE) 59
360 **WANNAPLANTATREE** (GB) G 34
549 **WAR CORRESPONDENT** (FR) 106
449 **WAR CORRESPONDENT** (IRE) 20
549 **WAR EFFORT** (USA) 206

185 **WAR HORSE** (FR) 60
489 **WAR LORD** (IRE) 83
582 **WAR ON** (IRE) 14
489 **WAR POET** (GB) 61
287 **WAR SHANTY** (GB) C 258
510 **WAR SINGER** (USA) 110
287 **WAR SPIRIT** (GB) 259
403 **WARBOND** (GB) 9
211 **WARCROWN** (IRE) 55
598 **WARDEN BOND** (GB) 6
109 **WARDEN HILL** (IRE) 35
556 **WARFARE** (GB) 38
283 **WARNE** (IRE) 6
109 **WARRANT OFFICER** (GB) 93
460 **WARREN CHASE** (IRE) 15
 96 **WARRENDALE** (GB) 56
484 **WARRIGAL** (IRE) 55
371 **WARRIOR JACK** (IRE) 52
380 **WARRIOR OF LIGHT** (IRE) 60
538 **WARRIORS TALE** (GB) 44
170 **WARSAW PACT** (IRE) 5
529 **WARWICKSHIRE** (IRE) 17
158 **WAS MY VALENTINE** (IRE) 15
 36 **WASABI** (IRE) 8
109 **WASEEM FARIS** (IRE) 36
287 **WASHAAR** (IRE) 260
469 **WASPY** (GB) 8
405 **WASSENDALE** (GB) C 17
240 **WATCH HOUSE** (IRE) 7
291 **WATCH THE BIRDIE** (IRE) 25
601 **WATCHABLE** (GB) 93
313 **WATCHEROFTHESKIES** (GB) 28
 22 **WATCHMEGO** (GB) 24
658 **WATEED** (IRE) 127
510 **WATER GARDEN** (FR) 111
193 **WATER RAIL** (GB) 13
401 **WATER STRATFORD** (IRE) F 4
381 **WATER WAGTAIL** (GB) 67
114 **WATERCLOCK** (IRE) 18
639 **WATERED SILK** (GB) 27
550 **WATERGATE** (IRE) 20
254 **WATERHOUSE** (IRE) 13
526 **WATERLOO DOCK** (GB) 4
424 **WATERSKI** (GB) 9
353 **WATERSMEET** (GB) 216
510 **WATERUNDER** (IRE) 112
 31 **WATERWAY RUN** (USA) 64
243 **WATLEDGE** (FR) 61
676 **WATT BRODERICK** (IRE) 55
101 **WATTS UP SON** (IRE) 17
340 **WAVE POWER** (IRE) 3
575 **WAVEGUIDE** (IRE) 22
485 **WAVER** (GB) 93
  2 **WAVERUNNER** (GB) 124
108 **WAVES AND WIND** (IRE) 10
102 **WAVING** (GB) 56
246 **WAYLON** (GB) 18
553 **WAYNE MANOR** (IRE) 70
677 **WAYWARD FROLIC** (GB) 34
 37 **WAYWARD GLANCE** (GB) 25
500 **WAYWARD PRINCE** (GB) 8
270 **WAYWOOD PRINCESS** (GB) 3
 32 **WE ARE CITY** (GB) 69
453 **WE HAVE A DREAM** (GB) 17
194 **WE'LL DEAL AGAIN** (GB) 47
 50 **WE'LL GO WALKING** (IRE) 61
314 **WE'RE IN THE RED** (IRE) 5
374 **WEAPON OF CHOICE** (IRE) 11

510 **WEATHER BABE** (GB) 113
290 **WEATHER WATCH** (IRE) 72
343 **WEB OF INTRIGUE** (GB) C 31
566 **WEBBERYS DREAM** (IRE) 33
 93 **WEBBOW** (IRE) 11
287 **WEDDING MORN** (IRE) C 261
213 **WEDDING SPEECH** (IRE) 47
549 **WEDGE TRUST** (IRE) 107
 14 **WEDGER PARDY** (IRE) 50
155 **WEDGEWOOD STAR** (GB) C 8
135 **WEE GIANT** (USA) 17
667 **WEE WILLOW** (GB) F 17
 68 **WEEK END** (GB) F 72
510 **WEEKEND MILLIONAIR** (IRE) 114
685 **WEET IN NERJA** (GB) 6
 22 **WEETFROMTHECHAFF** (GB) 25
316 **WEIGH IT UP** (IRE) 101
419 **WEIRD AL** (IRE) 163
 31 **WEISSE SOCKEN** (IRE) 106
658 **WELD ARAB** (IRE) 128
678 **WELEASE BWIAN** (IRE) 15
134 **WELL ACQUAINTED** (IRE) 49
491 **WELL HELLO THERE** (IRE) 115
487 **WELL METT** (IRE) 31
418 **WELL OF ECHOES** (GB) C 47
227 **WELL OILED** (IRE) 9
275 **WELL PAINTED** (IRE) 16
459 **WELL READ MAN** (IRE) 152
444 **WELL REFRESHED** (GB) 94
381 **WELL REGARDED** (IRE) 68
148 **WELL SPRUNG** (IRE) 12
395 **WELLFORTH** (IRE) 11
353 **WELLINGROVE** (IRE) 112
579 **WELLS LYRICAL** (IRE) 21
419 **WELSH BARD** (IRE) 164
453 **WELSH CAKE** (GB) F 48
 17 **WELSH DIVA** (GB) F 171
 65 **WELSH INLET** (IRE) 12
182 **WELSH NAYBER** (GB) 14
106 **WEMYSS BAY** (GB) F 125
 14 **WENLOCKS BOXER** (GB) 51
287 **WENTWORTH** (IRE) 99
428 **WERENEARLYOUTOFIT** (IRE) 30
431 **WES HARDIN** (IRE) 95
661 **WESLEYDALE** (IRE) 6
151 **WESSEX KING** (IRE) 43
471 **WEST BAY HOOLIE** (GB) 9
 26 **WEST DAKOTA** (USA) C 102
 55 **WEST END LAD** (GB) 14
367 **WEST END ROCKER** (IRE) 102
 84 **WEST LEAKE** (IRE) 5
312 **WEST LEAKE DIMAN** (IRE) 14
476 **WEST LEAKE HARE** (IRE) 41
601 **WEST OF THE MOON** (GB) 94
675 **WEST WITH THE WIND** (GB) 85
305 **WEST WIZARD** (FR) 152
  8 **WESTAWAY** (IRE) 19
675 **WESTER ROSS** (IRE) 86
167 **WESTERLY BREEZE** (IRE) 39
507 **WESTERN APPEAL** (USA) C 50
676 **WESTERN APPROACHES** (GB) 56
 91 **WESTERN BOUND** (IRE) 3
144 **WESTERN COMMANDER** (IRE) 30
465 **WESTERN DIVA** (IRE) 4
620 **WESTERN GALE** (IRE) 22
 37 **WESTERN HIGH** (GB) 26
316 **WESTERN JO** (IRE) 102
408 **WESTERN KING** (IRE) 18

LATE ENTRIES

MR ANDREW LYNCH, Dunsany
Postal: Killeen, Dunsany, Co. Meath, Ireland
Contacts: PHONE (00353) 46 9025525   MOBILE (00353) 86 8144447

1 **AHORSECALLEDMOLLY (IRE)**, 12, b g Arzanni—Leonora (IRE) **Andrew Lynch**
2 **ANTIPODE (GER)**, 10, b g Zinaad—Avellquina (IRE) **Andrew Lynch**
3 **DUSHY PRIDE (IRE)**, 4, b g Dushyantor (USA)—Mid West Girl (IRE) **Brendan Smyth**
4 **FUTURAMIC (IRE)**, 6, b g Shantou (USA)—Backaway (IRE) **Andrew Lynch**
5 **LAPSE OF REASON (IRE)**, 9, b g Presenting—Sarcastic (IRE)
6 **SIX SENSES (IRE)**, 7, b g Milan—One More Dash (IRE) **Andrew Lynch**
7 **WHATS IN THE BOX (IRE)**, 5, b m Gamut (IRE)—Go Onyeahgoodthing (IRE) **Andrew Lynch**
8 **WILDE REBEL (IRE)**, 8, b g Oscar (IRE)—The Rebel Lady (IRE) **Andrew Lynch**
9 **YEATS LODGE (IRE)**, 5, b g Sleeping Car (FR)—Reine Josephine (FR) **Aiden Murray**
10 **ZABANA (IRE)**, 4, ch g Halling (USA)—Gandia (IRE)

MR THOMAS GIBNEY, Kells
Postal: Ballyhist, Carnaross, Kells, Co Meath, Ireland
Contacts: MOBILE (00353) 87 7499778
E-MAIL gibneyracing@gmail.com WEBSITE www.gibneyracing.com

1 **BALNAGON BOY (IRE)**, 5, ch g Hernando (FR)—Taormina (IRE) **Tom, Mick & Pat Syndicate**
2 5, B g Norwich—Beglawella **Anne Keane**
3 **BETWEEN ME AND YOU (IRE)**, 9, br g Norwich—Sealthedeal **Heidi Gibney**
4 **CHICKEN CHASER (IRE)**, 7, b g Mull of Kintyre (USA)—Sweet Lass **Fergus Grimes**
5 **CROCON SI (IRE)**, 9, gr g Great Palm (USA)—Belle Dame (IRE) **Heidi Gibney**
6 4, Gr f Zagreb (USA)—Curracloe Rose (IRE) **Noeleen Gaughran**
7 5, B g Kutub (IRE)—Devon Cherry (IRE) **Frank Daly**
8 **FURZE FLYER (IRE)**, 6, b g Dr Massini (IRE)—Dereenavurrig (IRE)
9 **GRANNYS GARDEN (IRE)**, 7, b m Sayarshan (FR)—The Top Road (IRE) **Lorna Groarke**
10 **IVANOR BOY (IRE)**, 8, b g Craigsteel—Legal Lady (IRE) **Ivan Maxwell**
11 **LION NA BEARNAI (IRE)**, 11, b g New Frontier (IRE)—Polly Plum (IRE) **The Lock Syndicate**
12 **MAISIE MC (IRE)**, 6, ch m Exit To Nowhere (USA)—Lerichi (IRE) **Daniel McCarten**
13 **NATIVE PALM (IRE)**, 7, gr g Great Palm (USA)—Neath Native Sky (IRE) **Palm Tree Syndicate**
14 4, Ch f Raintrap—Ninevah (IRE) **Larry Green**
15 **ORPHEUS VALLEY (IRE)**, 10, ch g Beneficial—Native Mo (IRE) **No Horse Box Syndicate**
16 6, B h Expelled (USA)—Passion Killer (IRE) **Nicholas Brown**
17 **SHAHRAFI (IRE)**, 7, b g Barathea (IRE)—Sharamana (IRE) **Shahrafi Syndicate**
18 **TO CHOOSE (IRE)**, 4, b g Choisir (AUS)—Jannadav (IRE) **Lennard Kinsella**

THREE-YEAR-OLDS

19 **CIRCE'S ISLAND (IRE)**, b f Kodiac—Circe's Melody (IRE) **Meath & Co Syndicate**

STOP PRESS Additional horses

211	**MR RICHARD FAHEY, Malton**

Postal: RF Racing Ltd, Mews House, Musley Bank, Malton, North Yorkshire, YO17 6TD
Contacts: PHONE (01653) 698915   FAX (01653) 699735 MOBILE (07713) 478079
E-MAIL enquiries@richardfahey.com WEBSITE www.richardfahey.com

TWO-YEAR-OLDS

111 **ABBEY VILLAGE (IRE)**, ch c 18/3 Aqlaam—Balladonia (Primo Dominie) (80000)
112 B c 16/3 Bushranger (IRE)—Alexander Anapolis (IRE) (Spectrum (IRE)) (49205)
113 B c 18/2 Selkirk (USA)—Alizadora (Zilzal (USA)) (38000)

MR RICHARD FAHEY—continued

114 BACK LANE, Gr c 15/4 Verglas (IRE)—Artisia (IRE) (Peintre Celebre (USA)) (40000)
115 BACK LANE, b c 2/2 Invincible Spirit (IRE)—Rivalry (Medicean) (1428)
116 BAHAMIAN C, b c 17/4 Bahamian Bounty—Amandian (IRE) (Indian Ridge) (36000)
117 BALLYHURST (IRE), b c 23/3 High Chaparral (IRE)—Billet (IRE) (Danehill (USA)) (134920)
118 BAY STREET BELLE, ch f 15/3 Bahamian Bounty—Donna Anna (Be My Chief (USA)) (25000)
119 Ch c 6/3 Winker Watson—Blades Baby (Bertolini (USA)) (4761)
120 BRUNI HEINKE (IRE), ch f 3/4 Dutch Art—Penchant (Kyllachy) (71428)
121 CANYARI (IRE), b c 4/3 Dandy Man (IRE)—Morna's Fan (FR) (Lear Fan (USA)) (47619)
122 B f 25/2 Tagula (IRE)—Carmona (Rainbow Quest (USA)) (5714)
123 B f 6/3 Invincible Spirit (IRE)—Chatline (IRE) (One Cool Cat (USA))
124 COCOA'S PRINCESS, b f 19/3 Kyllachy—Princess Cocoa (IRE) (Desert Sun)
125 Ch c 7/3 Authorized (IRE)—Collette's Choice (Royal Applause)
126 DOLPHIN CLUB (IRE), ch c 21/2 Duke of Marmalade (IRE)—Meon Mix (Kayf Tara) (17460)
127 DRINKS FOR LOSERS (IRE), b c 27/3 Mastercraftsman (IRE)—Heart's Desire (IRE) (Royal Applause) (25396)
128 DUTCH COURAGE, b f 19/3 Dutch Art—Poldhu (Cape Cross (IRE)) (100000)
129 ECCLESTON, b c 28/3 Acclamation—Miss Meggy (Pivotal) (9523)
130 EMERAHLDZ (IRE), b f 29/3 Excellent Art—Sancia (IRE) (Docksider (USA)) (15872)
131 FLYCATCHER (IRE), ro f 22/2 Medicean—Night Haven (Night Shift (USA)) (45000)
132 FOXY CLARETS (IRE), ch c 26/2 Camacho—Muscari (Indian Ridge) (17142)
133 B c 1/3 Mastercraftsman (IRE)—Golden Legacy (IRE) (Rossini (USA))
134 Br c 21/4 Intense Focus (USA)—Guajira (FR) (Mtoto) (55000)
135 HESKETH BANK, b c 2/3 Aqlaam—Wendylina (IRE) (In The Wings) (36000)
136 HESKIN (IRE), b f 19/3 Acclamation—Carpet Lady (IRE) (Night Shift (USA)) (83333)
137 IMSHIVALLA (IRE), b f 19/3 Acclamation—Subtle Affair (IRE) (Barathea (IRE)) (10000)
138 JAN VAN HOOF (IRE), b c 14/2 Dutch Art—Cosenza (Bahri (USA)) (80000)
139 KALAHARI KINGDOM (IRE), b c 1/2 Footstepsinthesand—Visite Royale (USA) (Danehill Dancer (IRE))
140 B c 27/2 Bahamian Bounty—Kate The Great (Xaar) (23809)
141 KHALICE (IRE), b f 15/3 Bahamian Bounty—Siena Gold (Key of Luck (USA)) (12380)
142 KINDANYCE (IRE), b f 7/3 Bushranger (IRE)—Rublevka Star (USA) (Elusive Quality (USA)) (20634)
143 Ch c 15/4 Exceed And Excel (AUS)—Kristal Bridge (Kris)
144 LADIES IN WAITING, b f 29/4 Piccolo—Rose Siog (Bahamian Bounty) (952)
145 B c 19/2 Iffraaj—Lafontaine Bleu (Piccolo)
146 B c 4/4 Royal Applause—Little Greenbird (Ardkinglass) (19840)
147 Ch f 29/3 Kyllachy—Locharia (Wolfhound) (21000)
148 LONGTON, b c 26/3 Myboycharlie (IRE)—Lauren Louise (Tagula (IRE)) (135000)
149 LORD CLYDE, ch c 30/4 Sakhee's Secret—Sabina (Prince Sabo) (15000)
150 B f 16/2 Major Cadeaux—Love Quest (Pursuit of Love) (6666)
151 MENDELITA, ch f 1/2 Archipenko—Dame de Noche (Lion Cavern (USA))
152 MIAPLACIDUS (IRE), b c 4/4 Shamardal (USA)—Nandy's Cavern (Lion Cavern (USA)) (47619)
153 MISS LUCY JANE, ch f 24/4 Aqlaam—Ocean View (USA) (Gone West (USA)) (15000)
154 MOSSY LEA, ch f 21/2 Bahamian Bounty—Dea Caelestis (FR) (Dream Well (FR)) (3809)
155 MR CARBONFOOTPRINT, ch c 17/3 Footstepsinthesand—Diamond Lass (IRE) (Rock of Gibraltar (IRE))
156 MRS PAT, b f 8/2 With Approval (CAN)—Miss Prism (Niniski (USA))
157 NEIGHBOTHER, b c 20/2 Invincible Spirit (IRE)—Aravonian (Night Shift (USA)) (95238)
158 NEW STREET (IRE), gr c 13/4 Acclamation—New Deal (Rainbow Quest (USA)) (100000)
159 OVERDRIVE, b f 2/3 Sakhee's Secret—La Fija (USA) (Dixieland Band (USA)) (5714)
160 PARBOLD (IRE), b c 16/4 Dandy Man (IRE)—Gala Style (IRE) (Elnadim (USA)) (42000)
161 B f 19/1 Authorized (IRE)—Parsonagehotelyork (IRE) (Danehill (USA))
162 PENIAPHOBIA (IRE), b c 8/4 Dandy Man (IRE)—Umlani (IRE) (Great Commotion (USA)) (19047)
163 B c 15/3 Manduro (GER)—Polish Affair (IRE) (Polish Patriot (USA)) (28000)
164 B f 1/3 Virtual—Quadrophenia (College Chapel) (10000)
165 QUEEN OF ARTS, ch f 23/2 Dutch Art—Grande Terre (IRE) (Grand Lodge (USA)) (4952)
166 B f 11/5 Tiger Hill (IRE)—Quest For Freedom (Falbrav (IRE)) (15872)
167 QUEST OF COLOUR (IRE), b f 13/3 Iffraaj—With Colour (Rainbow Quest (USA)) (14000)
168 REFLECTION, ch f 12/2 Major Cadeaux—River Song (USA) (Siphon (BRZ)) (16000)
169 REGIMENT, ch c 22/4 Major Cadeaux—My First Romance (Danehill (USA)) (34000)
170 RIBBLETON, b c 28/4 Bushranger (IRE)—Bayleaf (Efisio) (1904)
171 RUFFORD (IRE), b f 19/2 Invincible Spirit (IRE)—Speedy Sonata (USA) (Stravinsky (USA)) (47619)
172 B c 14/4 Excellent Art—Run To Jane (IRE) (Doyoun) (22857)
173 SANDIVA (IRE), ch f 21/2 Footstepsinthesand—Miss Corinne (Mark of Esteem (IRE)) (17142)
174 SEDGE WARBLER, b f 5/5 High Chaparral (IRE)—Salamanca (Pivotal) (8000)
175 SHORE PATROL (IRE), br c 10/4 Footstepsinthesand—Fatwa (IRE) (Lahib (USA)) (79364)
176 Br f 12/4 Diamond Green (FR)—Silk Point (Barathea (IRE)) (9523)
177 Gr c 16/2 Royal Applause—Silver Dip (Gulch (USA)) (28000)
178 B c 3/2 Pastoral Pursuits—Slave To The Rythm (IRE) (Hamas (IRE)) (14000)
179 Ch c 3/3 Pastoral Pursuits—Sound of Sleat (Primo Dominie) (32000)

MR RICHARD FAHEY—continued

180 **SPICEUPYOURLIFE (IRE),** b f 4/3 Sakhee's Secret—Tiger Spice (Royal Applause)
181 **SUPPLICANT,** b c 10/3 Kyllachy—Pious (Bishop of Cashel) (65000)
182 B c 30/3 Authorized (IRE)—Tagula Sunrise (IRE) (Tagula (IRE))
183 Ch c 9/3 Compton Place—Tender (IRE) (Zieten (USA)) (9523)
184 **THE GRUMPY GNOME (IRE),** b c 25/4 Dandy Man (IRE)—Certain Charm (USA) (Thunder Gulch (USA)) (28000)
185 Ch f 5/3 Bahamian Bounty—Through The Forest (USA) (Forestry (USA)) (21000)
186 B c 25/4 Bahamian Bounty—Todber (Cape Cross (IRE))
187 Ch f 20/2 Footstepsinthesand—West One (Gone West (USA))
188 **WITHERNSEA (IRE),** b c 10/4 Dark Angel (IRE)—Charlene Lacy (IRE) (Pips Pride) (38000)

---

392 MR JOHN E. LONG, Woldingham

DR DANCE, 4, ch f Dr Fong (USA)—Star Apple **Mr & Mrs K. G. Newland**
ICEBREAKER TWO, 4, b c Iceman—Mintlaw **Mr & Mrs K. G. Newland**

THREE-YEAR-OLDS

B f Sakhee (USA)—Be Decisive **Mr & Mrs K. G. Newland**
GRACEFUL WILLOW, b f Phoenix Reach (IRE)—Opera Belle **Mr & Mrs T. H. Bambridge**

TWO-YEAR-OLDS

BYRONEGETONEFREE, b g 29/4 Byron—Lefty's Dollbaby (USA) (Brocco (USA)) **Downlands Racing**

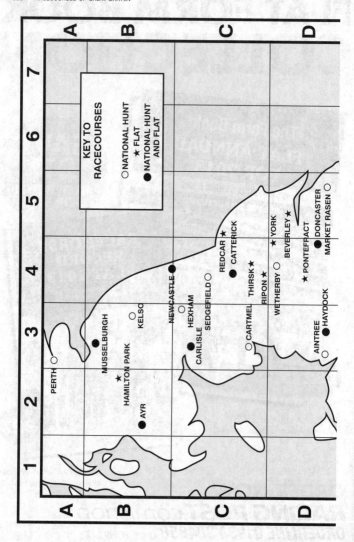

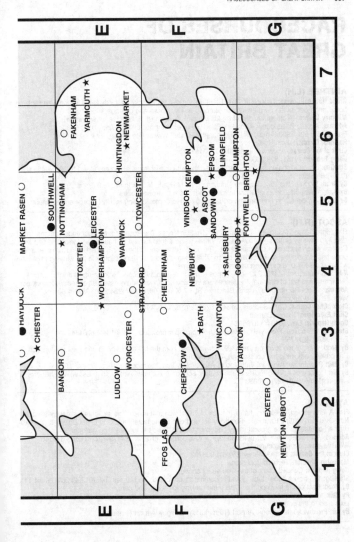

RACECOURSES OF GREAT BRITAIN

AINTREE (L.H)
Grand National Course: Triangular, 2m 2f (16) 494y run-in with elbow. Perfectly flat. A severe test for both horse and rider, putting a premium on jumping ability, fitness and courage.
Mildmay Course: Rectangular, 1m 4f (8) 260y run-in. A very fast, flat course with sharp bends.
Address: Aintree Racecourse, Ormskirk Road, Aintree, Liverpool, L9 5AS Tel: (0151) 523 2600
Fax: (0151) 522 2920 E-mail: aintree@rht.net Website: www.aintree.co.uk
Regional Director: John Baker
Clerk of the Course: Andrew Tulloch (07831) 315104
Going Reports: (0151) 523 2600.
Stabling: Boxes allocated in strict rotation. Facilities are available on the course for up to 100 stable staff.
(0151) 522 2937.
By Road: North of the City, near the junction of the M57 and M58 with the A59 (Preston).
By Rail: Aintree Station is adjacent to the Stands, from Liverpool Central.
By Air: Liverpool (John Lennon) Airport is 10 miles. Helicopter landing facility by prior arrangement.

ASCOT (R.H)
Flat: Right-handed triangular track just under 1m 6f in length. The Round course descends from the 1m 4f start into Swinley Bottom, the lowest part of the track. It then turns right-handed and joins the Old Mile Course, which starts on a separate course. The course then rises to the right-handed home turn over a new underpass to join the straight mile course. The run-in is about 3f, rising slightly to the winning post. The whole course is of a galloping nature with easy turns.
N.H. Triangular, 1m 6f (10) 240y run-in mostly uphill. A galloping course with an uphill finish, Ascot provides a real test of stamina. The fences are stiff and sound jumping is essential, especially for novices.
Address: Ascot Racecourse, Ascot, Berkshire SL5 7JX Tel: (08707) 271234 Fax: (08704) 601250
Website: www.ascot.co.uk
Clerk of the Course: Chris Stickels (01344) 878502/(07970) 621440
Chief Executive: Charles Barnett
Going Reports: Day: (01344) 878502
Stabling: 175 boxes. Free, with shavings, straw or paper provided. Tel: (01344) 878454
Fax: (0870) 4214755
By Road: West of the town on the A329. Easy access from the M3 (Junction 3) and the M4 (Junction 6).
Car parking adjoining the course and Ascot Heath.
By Rail: Regular service from Waterloo to Ascot (500y from the racecourse).
By Air: Helicopter landing facility at the course. London (Heathrow) Airport 15 miles, White Waltham
Airfield 12 miles (01427) 718800.

AYR (L.H)
Flat: A left-handed, galloping, flat oval track of 1m 4f with a 4f run-in. The straight 6f is essentially flat.
N.H. Oval, 1m 4f (9) 210y run-in. Relatively flat and one of the fastest tracks in Great Britain. It is a well-drained course and the ground rarely becomes testing. Suits the long-striding galloper.
Address: Ayr Racecourse, Whitletts Road, Ayr KA8 0JE Tel: (01292) 264179 Fax: (01292) 610140
Website: www.ayr-racecourse.co.uk
Clerk of the Course: Emma Marley (07881) 908702
Managing Director: Richard Johnstone
Going Reports: Contact Clerk of the Course as above.
Stabling: 175 boxes. Free stabling and accommodation for lads and lasses. Tel: (01292) 264179 ext 141.
By Road: East of the town on the A758. Free parking for buses and cars.
By Rail: Ayr Station (trains on the half hour from Glasgow Central). Journey time 55 minutes. Buses and taxis also to the course.
By Air: Prestwick International Airport (10 minutes), Glasgow Airport (1 hour).

BANGOR-ON-DEE (L.H)

N.H. Circular, 1m 4f (9) 325y run-in. Apart from some 'ridge and furrow', this is a flat course notable for three sharp bends, especially the paddock turn. Suits handy, speedy sorts.
Address: Bangor-on-Dee Racecourse, Overton Road, Bangor-On-Dee, Wrexham. LL13 0DA
Tel: (01978) 782081, Fax: (01978) 780985 Website: www.bangorondeeraces.co.uk
Racecourse Manager & Clerk of the Course: Andrew Morris
Chief Executive: Richard Thomas
General Manager: Jeannie Chantler
Going Reports: Contact Clerk of the Course as above.
Stabling: 85 stables, allotted on arrival. Shavings (straw on request). Applications to the Manager.
Tel: (01978) 782081.
By Road: 5 miles southeast of Wrexham, off the B5069.
By Rail: Wrexham Station (bus or taxi to the course).
By Air: Helicopters may land by prior arrangement with Clerk of the Course at entirely their own risk.

BATH (L.H)

Flat: Galloping, left-handed, level oval of 1m 4f 25y, with long, stiff run-in of about 4f which bends to the left. An extended chute provides for races over 5f 11y and 5f 161y.
Address: The Racecourse, Lansdown, Bath BA1 9BU. Tel: (01225) 424609 Fax: (01225) 444415.
Website: www.bath-racecourse.co.uk
Clerk of the Course: Keith Ottesen (07813) 043453
General Manager: Katie Stephens
Going Reports: Contact Clerk of the Course as above.
Stabling: 120 boxes. Free stabling and accommodation for lads and lasses. Tel: (01225) 424609
By Road: 2 miles northwest of the City (M4 Junction 18) at Lansdown. Unlimited free car and coach parking space immediately behind the stands. Special bus services operate from Bath to the racecourse.
By Rail: Bath Station (from Paddington).
By Air: Bristol or Colerne Airports. Helicopter landing facilities available by prior arrangement.

BEVERLEY (R.H)

Flat: A right-handed oval of 1m 3f, generally galloping, with an uphill run-in of two and a half furlongs. The 5f course is very stiff.
Address: Beverley Race Co. Ltd., York Road, Beverley, Yorkshire HU17 9QZ
Tel: (01482) 867488 / 882645. Website: www.beverley-racecourse.co.uk
General Manager & Clerk of the Course: Sally Iggulden (07850) 458605
Going Reports: Tel: (01482) 867488 / 882645 or Head Groundsman (John Morley) (07885) 678186
Stabling: 111 boxes. Free stabling. Accommodation available for lads and lasses
Tel: (01482) 867488 / 882645.
By Road: 7 miles from the M62 (Junction 38) off the A1035. Free car parking opposite the course. Owners and Trainers use a separate enclosure.
By Rail: Beverley Station (Hull-Scarborough line). Occasional bus service to the course (1 mile).

BRIGHTON (L.H)

Flat: Left-handed, 1m 4f horseshoe with easy turns and a run-in of three and a half furlongs. Undulating and sharp, the track suits handy types.
Address: Brighton Racecourse, Brighton, East Sussex BN2 2XZ Tel: (01273) 603580 Fax: (01273) 673267
Website: www.brighton-racecourse.co.uk
Clerk of the Course: Edward Arkell (07977) 587713
General Manager: Stuart Dorn
Going Reports: Available on www.brighton-racecourse.co.uk or contact main office/Clerk of the Course as above
Stabling: 102 boxes. Stabling & accommodation: Tel: (01273) 603580, available on request.
By Road: East of the city on the A27 (Lewes Road). There is a car park adjoining the course.
By Rail: Brighton Station (from Victoria on the hour, London Bridge or Portsmouth). Special bus service to the course from the station (approx 2 miles).
By Air: Helicopters may land by prior arrangement.

CARLISLE (R.H)

Flat: Right-handed, 1m 4f pear-shaped track. Galloping and undulating with easy turns and a stiff uphill run-in of three and a half furlongs. The 6f course begins on an extended chute.

N.H. Pear-shaped, 1m 5f (9) 300y run-in uphill. Undulating and a stiff test of stamina, ideally suited to the long-striding thorough stayer. Three-mile chases start on a chute, and the first fence is only jumped once.

Address: Carlisle Racecourse, Durdar Road, Carlisle CA2 4TS Tel: (01228) 554700 Fax: (01228) 554747 Website: www.carlisle-races.co.uk

Regional Director: John Baker

Clerk of the Course: Andrew Tulloch (07831) 315104

General Manager: Richard Clements

Going Reports: (01228) 554700 recorded or contact Clerk of the Course above

Stabling: 98 boxes. Stabling and accommodation available on request. Please phone Head Groundsman on (07889) 987542, or Fax Stable Office on (01228) 554747 by 1pm day before racing.

By Road: 2 miles south of the city (Durdar Road). Easy access from the M6 (Junction 42). The car park is free (adjacent to the course).

By Rail: Carlisle Station (2 miles from the course).

By Air: Helicopter landing facility by prior arrangement.

CARTMEL (L.H)

N.H. Oval, 1m 1f (6) 800y run-in. Almost perfectly flat but very sharp, with the longest run-in in the country, approximately half a mile. The fences are stiff but fair.

Address: Cartmel Racecourse, Cartmel, nr Grange-Over-Sands, Cumbria LA11 6QF Tel: (01539) 536340. Out of season: (01539) 533335 Fax: (01539) 536004 Website: www.cartmel-racecourse.co.uk

Managing Director: Jonathan Garratt

Clerk of the Course: Anthea Morshead (07837) 559861

Going Reports: (01539) 536340 or contact Clerk of the Course as above.

Stabling: 75 boxes. Boxes and accommodation for lads and lasses is limited. Prior booking is required by 12 noon the day before racing (01539) 534609.

By Road: 1 mile west of the town, 2 miles off the B5277 (Grange-Haverthwaite road). M6 (Junction 36).

By Rail: Cark-in-Cartmel Station (2½ miles) (Carnforth-Barrow line). Raceday bus service.

By Air: Light aircraft facilities available at Cark Airport (4 miles from the course). Helicopter landing facility at the course, by prior arrangement only.

CATTERICK (L.H)

Flat: A sharp, left-handed, undulating oval of 1m 180y with a downhill run-in of 3f.

N.H. Oval, 1m 1f (9) 240y run-in. Undulating, sharp track that favours the handy, front-running sort, rather than the long-striding galloper.

Address: The Racecourse, Catterick Bridge, Richmond, North Yorkshire DL10 7PE Tel: (01748) 811478 Fax: (01748) 811082 Website: www.catterickbridge.co.uk

General Manager & Clerk of the Course: Fiona Needham (07831) 688625

Going Reports: Contact Clerk of the Course as above

Stabling: 116 Boxes. Allotted on arrival.

By Road: The course is adjacent to the A1, 1 mile northwest of the town on the A6136. There is a free car park.

By Rail: Darlington Station (special buses to course - 14 mile journey).

By Air: Helicopters can land by prior arrangement. Fixed wing planes contact RAF Leeming Tel: (01677) 423041

CHELTENHAM (L.H)

Old Course: Oval, 1m 4f (9) 350y run-in. A testing, undulating track with stiff fences. The ability to stay is essential.

New Course: Oval, 1m 5f (10) 220y run-in. Undulating, stiff fences, testing course, uphill for the final half-mile.

Address: Cheltenham Racecourse, Prestbury Park, Cheltenham, Gloucestershire GL50 4SH Tel: (01242) 513014 Fax: (01242) 224227 Website: www.cheltenham.co.uk

Regional Director: Ian Renton

Director of Racing & Clerk of the Course: Simon Claisse (07785) 293966

Going Reports: Available from six days before racing (01242) 513014 (option 2, then 6)

Stabling: 299 boxes. Ample stabling and accommodation for lads.

Apply to the Stable Manager (01242) 537602 or 521950.

By Road: 1.5 miles north of the town on the A435. M5 (Junction 10 or 11).
By Rail: Cheltenham Spa Station. Buses and taxis to course.
By Air: Helicopter landing site to the northeast of the stands.

CHEPSTOW (L.H)

Flat: A left-handed, undulating oval of about 2m, with easy turns, and a straight run-in of 5f. There is a straight track of 1m 14y.
N.H. Oval, 2m (11) 240y run-in. Many changing gradients, five fences in the home straight. Favours the long-striding front-runner, but stamina is important.
Address: Chepstow Racecourse, Chepstow, Monmouthshire NP16 6BE Tel: (01291) 622260
Fax: (01291) 627061 Website: www.chepstow-racecourse.co.uk
Clerk of the Course: Keith Ottesen (07813) 043453
Acting General Manager: Rebecca Joy
Going Reports: Contact Clerk of the Course as above.
Stabling: 106 boxes, allotted on arrival. Limited accommodation for lads and lasses.
Apply: (01291) 622260.
By Road: 1 mile North-West of the town on the A466. (1 mile from Junction 22 of the M4 (Severn Bridge) or M48 Junction 2. There is a free public car park opposite the entrance.
By Rail: Chepstow Station (from Paddington, change at Gloucester or Newport). The course is a mile from the station.
By Air: Helicopter landing facility in the centre of the course.

CHESTER (L.H)

Flat: A level, sharp, left-handed, circular course of 1m 73y, with a short run-in of 230y.
Chester is a specialists' track which generally suits the sharp-actioned horse.
Address: The Racecourse, Chester CH1 2LY Tel: (01244) 304600 Fax: (01244) 304648
Website: www.chester-races.co.uk
Racecourse Manager & Clerk of the Course: Andrew Morris
Chief Executive: Richard Thomas
Going Reports: Contact Main Office (01244) 304600
Stabling: 138 boxes and accommodation. Tel: (01244) 324880 or (01244) 304610
By Road: The course is near the centre of the city on the A548 (Queensferry Road). The Owners' and Trainers' car park is adjacent to the Leverhulme Stand. There is a public car park in the centre of the course.
By Rail: Chester Station (¾ mile from the course). Services from Euston, Paddington and Northgate.
By Air: Hawarden Airport (2 miles). Helicopters are allowed to land on the racecourse by prior arrangement only.

DONCASTER (L.H)

Flat: A left-handed, flat, galloping course of 1m 7f 110y, with a long run-in which extends to a straight mile.
N.H. Conical, 2m (11) 247y run-in. A very fair, flat track ideally suited to the long-striding galloper.
Address: Doncaster Racecourse, Leger Way, Doncaster DN2 6BB Tel: (01302) 304200,
Fax: (01302) 323271 Email: info@doncaster-racecourse.co.uk
Website: www.doncaster-racecourse.co.uk
Clerk of the Course: Jon Pullin (01302) 304200 or (07775) 943341
Managing Director: Mark Spincer
Going Reports: Contact Clerk of the Course as above or Estate Manager (07831) 260373.
Stabling: 147 boxes. Free stabling and accommodation. Tel: (01302) 304200
By Road: East of the town, off the A638 (M18 Junctions 3 & 4). Club members' car park reserved. Large public car park free and adjacent to the course.
By Rail: Doncaster Central Station (from King's Cross). Special bus service from the station (1 mile).
By Air: Helicopter landing facility by prior arrangement only. Doncaster Robin Hood Airport is 15 minutes from the racecourse.

EPSOM (L.H)

Flat: Left-handed and undulating with easy turns, and a run-in of just under 4f. The straight 5f course is also undulating and downhill all the way, making it the fastest 5f in the world.
Address: The Racecourse, Epsom Downs, Surrey, KT18 5LQ. Tel: (01372) 726311, Fax: (01372) 748253
Website: www.epsomderby.co.uk
Regional Director: Rupert Trevelyan
Clerk of the Course: Andrew Cooper. Tel: (01372) 726311, Mobile: (07774) 230850.

Going Reports: Contact Clerk of the Course as above.
Stabling: 108 boxes. Free stabling and accommodation. Tel: (01372) 460454
By Road: Two miles south of the town on the B290 (M25 Junctions 8 & 9). For full car park particulars apply to: The Club Secretary, Epsom Grandstand, Epsom Downs, Surrey KT18 5LQ. Tel: (01372) 726311.
By Rail: Epsom, Epsom Downs or Tattenham Corner Stations (trains from London Bridge, Waterloo, Victoria). Regular bus services run to the course from Epsom and Morden Underground Station.
By Air: London (Heathrow) and London (Gatwick) are both within 30 miles of the course. Heliport (Derby Meeting only) apply to Hascombe Aviation. Tel: (01279) 680291.

EXETER (R.H)

N.H.: Oval, 2m (11) 300y run-in uphill. Undulating with a home straight of half a mile. A good test of stamina, suiting the handy, well-balanced sort.
Address: Exeter Racecourse, Kennford, Exeter, Devon EX6 7XS Tel: (01392) 832599
Fax: (01392) 833454 Email: Exeter@thejockeyclub.co.uk Website: www.exeter-racecourse.co.uk
Regional Director: Ian Renton
Clerk of the Course: Barry Johnson (07976) 791578
General Manager: Tim Darby
Going Reports: Contact Clerk of the Course as above.
Stabling: 90 loose boxes at the course. Sleeping accommodation and canteen for both lads and lasses by prior arrangement. Apply to Racecourse Office. Tel: (01392) 832599 by 12 noon on day before racing.
By Road: The course is at Haldon, 5 miles southwest of Exeter on the A38 (Plymouth) road, 2 miles east of Chudleigh.
By Rail: Exeter (St Davids) Station. Free bus service to course.
By Air: Helicopters can land by prior arrangement.

FAKENHAM (L.H)

N.H. Square, 1m (6) 200y run-in. On the turn almost throughout and undulating, suiting the handy front-runner. The going rarely becomes heavy.
Address: The Racecourse, Fakenham, Norfolk NR21 7NY Tel: (01328) 862388 Fax: (01328) 855908
email: info@fakenhamracecourse.co.uk Website: www.fakenhamracecourse.co.uk
Clerk of the Course & Chief Executive: David Hunter Tel: (01328) 862388 Mobile: (07767) 802206.
Going Reports: Contact Clerk of the Course as above.
Stabling: 70 boxes available. Tel: (01328) 862388 Fax: (01328) 855908.
By Road: A mile south of the town on the B1146 (East Dereham) road.
By Rail: Norwich Station (26 miles) (Liverpool Street line), King's Lynn (22 miles) (Liverpool Street/Kings Cross).
By Air: Helicopter landing facility in the centre of the course by prior arrangement only.

FFOS LAS (L.H)

Flat & N.H. : The track is a 60m wide, basically flat, 1m4f oval with sweeping bends. Races over 5f and 6f start on a chute.
Address: Ffos Las Racecourse, Trimsaran, Carmarthenshire, SA17 4DE Tel: (01554) 811092
Fax: (01554) 811037 Website: www.ffoslasracecourse.com
Clerk of the Course & General Manager: Tim Long (07966) 893531
Going Reports: Contact Clerk of the Course as above.
Stabling: 120 box stable yard.
By Road: From the east take J48 from the M4 and join the A4138 to Llanelli, then follow the brown tourist signs to the racecourse. From the west take the A48 to Carmarthen then the A484 to Kidwelly before following the brown signs.
By Air: The course has the facilities to land helicopters on race days.

FOLKESTONE

No fixtures scheduled for 2013.

FONTWELL PARK (Fig. 8)

N.H. 2m (7) 230y run-in with left-hand bend close home. The figure-of-eight chase course suits handy types and is something of a specialists' track. The left-handed hurdle course is oval, one mile round with nine hurdles per two and a quarter miles.
Address: Fontwell Park Racecourse, nr Arundel, West Sussex BN18 0SX Tel: (01243) 543335
Fax: (01243) 543904 Website: www.fontwellpark.co.uk

Clerk of the Course: Edward Arkell (07977) 587713
General Manager: Tracy Skinner
Executive Director: Phil Bell
Going Reports: (01243) 543335 during office hours.
Stabling: 90 boxes. Limited accommodation. If arriving the day before the meeting, contact:
Tel: (01243) 543335.
By Road: South of village at the junction of the A29 (Bognor) and A27 (Brighton-Chichester) roads.
By Rail: Barnham Station (2 miles). Brighton-Portsmouth line (access via London Victoria).
By Air: Helicopter landing facility by prior arrangement with the Clerk of the Course.

GOODWOOD (R.H)

Flat: A sharp, undulating, essentially right-handed track with a long run-in. There is also a straight 6f course.
Address: Goodwood Racecourse Ltd., Goodwood, Chichester, West Sussex PO18 0PX
Tel: (01243) 755022, Fax: (01243) 755025 Website: www.goodwood.co.uk
Managing Director: Adam Waterworth
Clerk of the Course: Seamus Buckley (07774) 100223
Going Reports: (01243) 755022 (recorded message) or Clerk of the Course.
Stabling: Free stabling and accommodation for runners (130 well equipped boxes at Goodwood House). Please book in advance. Subsidised canteen and recreational facilities. Tel: (01243) 755022 / 755036.
By Road: 6 miles north of Chichester between the A286 & A285. There is a car park adjacent to the course. Ample free car and coach parking.
By Rail: Chichester Station (from Victoria or London Bridge). Regular bus service to the course (6 miles).
By Air: Helicopter landing facility by prior arrangement (01243) 755030. Goodwood Airport 2 miles (taxi to the course).

HAMILTON PARK (R.H)

Flat: Sharp, undulating, right-handed course of 1m 5f with a five and a half-furlong, uphill run-in. There is a straight track of 6f.
Address: Hamilton Park Racecourse, Bothwell Road, Hamilton, Lanarkshire ML3 0DW
Tel: (01698) 283806 Fax: (01698) 286621 Website: www.hamilton-park.co.uk
Racing Manager & Clerk of the Course: Hazel Peplinski (01698) 283806 (raceday). Mobile: (07774) 116733. Fax: (01698) 286621
Chief Executive: Vivien Kyles (01698) 283806
Going Reports: Track Manager: (07736) 101130 or Clerk of the Course.
Stabling: Free stabling (102 boxes) and accommodation on request. Tel: (01698) 284892 or Office.
By Road: Off the A72 on the B7071 (Hamilton-Bothwell road). (M74 Junction 5). Free parking for cars and buses.
By Rail: Hamilton West Station (1 mile).
By Air: Glasgow Airport (20 miles).

HAYDOCK PARK (L.H)

Flat: A galloping, almost flat, oval track, 1m 5f round, with a run-in of four and a half furlongs and a straight six-furlong course.
N.H. Oval, 1m 5f (10) 440y run-in. Flat, galloping chase course. The hurdle track, which is sharp, is inside the chase course and has some tight bends.
Address: Haydock Park Racecourse, Newton-le-Willows, Merseyside WA12 0HQ Tel: (01942) 402609
Fax: (01942) 270879 Website: www.haydock-park.co.uk
Regional Director: John Baker
General Manager: Garry Fortune
Clerk of the Course: Kirkland Tellwright (01942) 725963 or (07748) 181595
Going Reports: Contact Clerk of the Course as above or Head Groundsman (07831) 849298
Stabling: 124 boxes. Applications to be made to the Racecourse for stabling and accommodation.
Tel: (01942) 725963 or (01942) 402615 (racedays).
By Road: The course is on the A49 near Junction 23 of the M6.
By Rail: Newton-le-Willows Station (Manchester-Liverpool line) is 2.5 miles from the course. Earlstown 3 miles from the course. Warrington Bank Quay and Wigan are on the London to Carlisle/Glasgow line.
By Air: Landing facilities in the centre of the course for helicopters and planes not exceeding 10,000lbs laden weight. Apply to the Sales Office.

HEREFORD
No fixtures scheduled for 2013.

HEXHAM (L.H)
N.H. Oval, 1m 4f (10) 220y run-in. An undulating course that becomes very testing when the ground is soft, it has easy fences and a stiff uphill climb to the finishing straight, which is on a separate spur.
Address: Hexham Racecourse, The Riding, Hexham, Northumberland NE46 2JP Tel: (01434) 606881
Fax: (01434) 605814, Racedays: (01434) 603738. Email: admin@hexham-racecourse.co.uk
Website: www.hexham-racecourse.co.uk
Chief Executive: Charles Enderby
Clerk of the Course: James Armstrong (01434) 606881 or (07801) 166820
Going Reports: Contact Clerk of the Course as above
Stabling: 93 Boxes allocated in rotation. Please book stabling and accommodation the day before by Fax: (01434) 605814.
By Road: 1.5 miles southwest of the town off the B6305.
By Rail: Hexham Station (Newcastle-Carlisle line). Free bus to the course.
By Air: Helicopter landing facility in centre of course (by special arrangement only).

HUNTINGDON (R.H)
N.H. Oval, 1m 4f (9) 200y run-in. Perfectly flat, galloping track with a tricky open ditch in front of the stands. The two fences in the home straight can cause problems for novice chasers. Suits front runners.
Address: The Racecourse, Brampton, Huntingdon, Cambridgeshire PE28 4NL Tel: (01480) 453373
Fax: (01480) 455275 Website: www.huntingdon-racecourse.co.uk
Regional Director: Amy Starkey
Clerk of the Course: Sulekha Varma
Managing Director: Sophie Able
Going Reports: Tel: (01480) 453373 or (07990) 774295
Stabling: 100 boxes available. Allotted on arrival. Telephone Racecourse Office.
By Road: The course is situated at Brampton, 2 miles west of Huntingdon on the A14. Easy access from the A1 (½ mile from the course).
By Rail: Huntingdon Station. Buses and taxis to course.
By Air: Helicopter landing facility by prior arrangement.

KELSO (L.H)
N.H. Oval, 1m 3f (8), uphill run-in reduced to just over a furlong for the 2012-13 season. Rather undulating with two downhill fences opposite the stands, it suits the nippy, front-running sort, though the uphill finish helps the true stayer. The hurdle course is smaller and very sharp with a tight turn away from the stands.
Address: Kelso Racecourse, Kelso, Roxburghshire TD5 7SX Tel: (01668) 280800
Website: www.kelso-races.co.uk
Clerk of the Course: Hazel Peplinski (07774) 116733
Managing Director: Richard Landale
Going Reports: Racecourse: (01573) 224822 Groundsman Tel: (07774) 172527
Stabling: 94 boxes allotted in rotation. Reservations for stabling and accommodation for lads and lasses at the racecourse, please phone Head Groundsman Tel: (01573) 224767 or Racecourse stables: (01573) 224822 from 3pm the day before racing.
By Road: 1 mile north of the town, off the B6461.
By Rail: Berwick-upon-Tweed Station. 23-mile bus journey to Kelso.
By Air: Helicopters can land at course by arrangement, fixed wing aircraft Winfield, regular aircraft Edinburgh.

KEMPTON PARK (R.H)
Flat: A floodlit Polytrack circuit. A 1m 2f outer track accommodates races over 6f, 7f, 1m, 1m 3f, 1m 4f and 2m. The 1m inner track caters for races over 5f and 1m 2f.
N.H. Triangular, 1m 5f (10) 175y run-in. Practically flat; sharp course where the long run between the last obstacle on the far side and the first in the home straight switches the emphasis from jumping to speed. The hurdles track is on the outside of the chase track. The course crosses the Polytrack at two points on each circuit.
Address: Kempton Park Racecourse, Sunbury-on-Thames, Middlesex TW16 5AQ Tel: (01932) 782292
Fax: (01932) 782044 Raceday Fax: (01932) 779525 Website: www.kempton.co.uk
Email: kempton@rht.net

Regional Director: Rupert Trevelyan
Clerk of the Course & Director of Racing: Brian Clifford (07880) 784484
General Manager: Phil White
Going Reports: (01932) 782292 if unavailable contact Clerk of the Course as above
Stabling: 117 boxes. Allocated on arrival. Prior booking required for overnight stay. Tel: (01932) 782292
By Road: On the A308 near Junction 1 of the M3.
By Rail: Kempton Park Station (from Waterloo).
By Air: London (Heathrow) Airport 6 miles.

LEICESTER (R.H)

Flat: Stiff, galloping, right-handed oval of 1m 5f, with a 5f run-in. There is a straight course of seven furlongs.
N.H. Rectangular, 1m 6f (10) 250y run-in uphill. An undulating course with an elbow 150y from the finish, it can demand a high degree of stamina, for the going can become extremely heavy and the last three furlongs are uphill.
Address: Leicester Racecourse, Oadby, Leicester LE2 4AL. Tel: (0116) 2716515 Fax: (0116) 2711746
Website:www.leicester-racecourse.co.uk
Clerk of the Course: Jimmy Stevenson (0116) 2712115 or (07774) 497281
General Manager: David Maykels (0116) 2716515
Going Reports: Recorded message (0116) 2710875 or contact Clerk of the Course as above.
Stabling: 108 boxes. Allocated on arrival. Canteen opens at 7.30a.m. Tel: (0116) 271 2115.
By Road: The course is 2.5 miles southeast of the City on the A6 (M1, Junction 21). The car park is free.
By Rail: Leicester Station (from St Pancras) is 2.5 miles.
By Air: Helicopter landing facility in the centre of the course.

LINGFIELD PARK (L.H)

Flat, Turf: A sharp, undulating left-handed circuit, with a 7f 140y straight course.
Flat, Polytrack: The left-handed Polytrack is 1m 2f round, with an extended chute to provide a 1m 5f start. It is a sharp, level track with a short run-in.
N.H. Conical, 1m 5f (10) 200y run-in. Severely undulating with a tight downhill turn into the straight, the chase course suits front runners and those of doubtful resolution.
Address: Lingfield Park Racecourse, Lingfield, Surrey RH7 6PQ Tel: (01342) 834800 Fax: (01342) 832833
Website: www.lingfield-racecourse.co.uk
Clerk of the Course: Neil Mackenzie Ross (01342) 831720 Mobile: (07917) 326977
Managing Director: Paul Shrimpton
Going Reports: Contact Clerk of the Course as above.
Stabling: 106 boxes. For details of accommodation Tel: (01342) 831718. Advance notice for overnight accommodation required before 12 noon on the day before racing.
By Road: Southeast of the town off the A22 (M25 Junction 6). Ample free parking.
By Rail: Lingfield Station (regular services from London Bridge and Victoria). ½m walk to the course.
By Air: London (Gatwick) Airport 10 miles. Helicopter landing facility south of wind-sock.

LUDLOW (R.H)

N.H. Oval, 1m 4f (9) 185y run-in. The chase course is flat and has quite sharp bends into and out of the home straight, although long-striding horses never seem to have any difficulties. The hurdle course is on the outside of the chase track and is not so sharp.
Address: Ludlow Race Club Ltd, The Racecourse, Bromfield, Ludlow, Shropshire SY8 2BT
Tel: (01584) 856221 (Racedays) or see below. Website:www.ludlowracecourse.co.uk
Manager & Clerk of the Course: Bob Davies. Tel: (01584) 856221, Mobile (07970) 861533,
Fax: (01584) 856217 Email: bobdavies@ludlowracecourse.co.uk
Going Reports: Contact Clerk of the Course as above or Groundsman Tel: (01584) 856289 or
(07970) 668353
Stabling: Free and allocated on arrival. 100 stables, mainly cardboard with a limited number of shavings and straw. Tel: (01584) 856221.
By Road: The course is situated at Bromfield, 2 miles north of Ludlow on the A49.
By Rail: Ludlow Station (Hereford-Shrewsbury line) 2 miles.
By Air: Helicopter landing facility in the centre of the course by arrangement with the Clerk of the Course and entirely at own risk.

MARKET RASEN (R.H)

N.H. Oval, 1m 2f (8) 250y run-in. A sharp, undulating course with a long run to the straight, it favours the handy, front-running type.

Address: Market Rasen Racecourse, Legsby Road, Market Rasen, Lincolnshire LN8 3EA

Tel: (01673) 843434 Fax: (01673) 844532 Website: www.marketrasenraces.co.uk

Regional Director: Amy Starkey

Clerk of the Course: Robert Bellamy

Managing Director: Pip Kirkby

Going Reports: Contact Clerk of the Course as above.

Stabling: 86 boxes at the course, allocated on arrival. Accommodation for lads and lasses is by reservation only. Tel: (01673) 842307 (racedays only)

By Road: The town is just off the A46, and the racecourse is one mile east of the town on the A631. Free car parks.

By Rail: Market Rasen Station 1 mile (King's Cross - Cleethorpes line).

By Air: Helicopter landing facility by prior arrangement only.

MUSSELBURGH (R.H)

Flat: A sharp, level, right-handed oval of 1m 2f, with a run-in of 4f. There is an additional 5f straight course.

N.H. Rectangular, 1m 3f (8) 150y run-in (variable). A virtually flat track with sharp turns, suiting the handy, front-running sort. Drains well.

Address: Musselburgh Racecourse, Linkfield Road, Musselburgh, East Lothian EH21 7RG

Tel: (0131) 665 2859 (Racecourse) Fax: (0131) 653 2083 Website:www.musselburgh-racecourse.co.uk

Clerk of the Course: Harriet Graham (07843) 380401

General Manager: Bill Farnsworth (07710) 536134

Going Reports: Contact main office as above or Clerk of the Course.

Stabling: 101 boxes. Free stabling. Accommodation provided. Tel: (07773) 048638, Stables (racedays): (0131) 665 2796.

By Road: The course is situated at Musselburgh, 5 miles east of Edinburgh on the A1. Car park, adjoining course, free for buses and cars.

By Rail: Waverley Station (Edinburgh). Local Rail service to Musselburgh.

By Air: Edinburgh (Turnhouse) Airport 30 minutes

NEWBURY (L.H)

Flat: Left-handed, oval track of about 1m 7f, with a slightly undulating straight mile. The round course is level and galloping with a four and a half furlong run-in. Races over the round mile start on the adjoining chute.

N.H. Oval, 1m 6f (11) 255y run-in. Slightly undulating, wide and galloping in nature. The fences are stiff and sound jumping is essential. One of the fairest tracks in the country.

Address: The Racecourse, Newbury, Berkshire RG14 7NZ Tel: (01635) 40015 Fax: (01635) 528354 Website: www.newbury-racecourse.co.uk

Managing Directors: Stephen Higgins & Sarah Hordern.

Raceday Clerk: Richard Osgood (07977) 426947

Going Reports: Clerk of the Course as above.

Stabling: 164 boxes. Free stabling and accommodation for lads and lasses. Tel: (01635) 40015.

By Road: East of the town off the A34 (M4, Junction 12 or 13). Car park, adjoining enclosures, free.

By Rail: Newbury Racecourse Station adjoins the course.

By Air: Light Aircraft landing strip East/West. 830 metres by 30 metres wide. Helicopter landing facilities.

NEWCASTLE (L.H)

Flat: Galloping, easy, left-handed oval of 1m 6f, with an uphill 4f run-in. There is a straight course of 1m 3y.

N.H. Oval, 1m 6f (11) 220y run-in. A gradually rising home straight of four furlongs makes this galloping track a true test of stamina, especially as the ground can become very heavy.

Address: High Gosforth Park, Newcastle-Upon-Tyne NE3 5HP Tel: (0191) 236 2020 Fax: (0191) 236 7761 Website: www.newcastle-racecourse.co.uk

Clerk of the Course: James Armstrong (07801) 166820

Executive Director: David Williamson

Stabling: 135 boxes. Stabling Free. It is essential to book accommodation in advance. Apply via the Racecourse Office.

Going Reports: Contact Clerk of the Course as above or Head Groundsman (07860) 274289.

By Road: 4 miles north of the city on the A6125 (near the A1). Car and coach park free.
By Rail: Newcastle Central Station (from King's Cross). A free bus service operates from South Gosforth and Regent Centre Metro Station.
By Air: Helicopter landing facility by prior arrangement. The Airport is 4 miles from the course.

NEWMARKET (R.H)

Rowley Mile Course: There is a straight ten-furlong course, which is wide and galloping. Races over 1m 4f or more are right-handed. The Rowley Mile course has a long run-in and a stiff finish.
July Course: Races up to a mile are run on the Bunbury course, which is straight. Races over 1m 2f or more are right-handed, with a 7f run-in. Like the Rowley Mile course, the July Course track is stiff.
Address: Newmarket Racecourse, Newmarket, Suffolk CB8 0TG Tel: (01638) 663482 (Main Office), (01638) 663762 (Rowley), (01638) 675416 (July) Fax: Rowley (01638) 675340. Fax: July (01638) 675410 Website: www.newmarketracecourses.co.uk
Clerk of the Course: Michael Prosser, Westfield House, The Links, Newmarket. Tel: (01638) 675504 or (07802) 844578
Regional Director: Amy Starkey
Going Reports: Contact main office or Clerk of the Course as above
Stabling: 100 boxes. Free accommodation available at the Links Stables. Tel: (01638) 662200 or (07747) 766614
By Road: Southwest of the town on the A1304 London Road (M11 Junction 9). Free car parking at the rear of the enclosure. Annual Badge Holders' car park free all days. Free courtesy bus service from Newmarket Station, Bus Station and High Street, commencing 90 minutes prior to the first race, and return trips up to 60 minutes after the last race.
By Rail: Infrequent rail service to Newmarket Station from Cambridge (Liverpool Street) or direct bus service from Cambridge (13-mile journey).
By Air: Landing facilities for light aircraft and helicopters on racedays at both racecourses. See Flight Guide. Cambridge Airport 11 miles.

NEWTON ABBOT (L.H)

N.H. Oval, 1m 2f (7) 300y run-in. Flat with two tight bends and a water jump situated three fences from home. The nippy, agile sort is favoured. The run-in can be very short on the hurdle course.
Address: Newton Abbot Races Ltd., Kingsteignton Road, Newton Abbot, Devon TQ12 3AF
Tel: (01626) 353235 Fax: (01626) 336972 Website: www.newtonabbotracing.com
Clerk of the Course: Jason Loosemore (07766) 228109
Managing Director: Pat Masterson. Tel: (01626) 353235 Fax: (01626) 336972 Mobile: (07917) 830144.
Going reports: Clerk of the Course as above.
Stabling: 80 boxes, allocated on arrival. Tel: (07766) 202938
By Road: North of the town on the A380. Torquay 6 miles, Exeter 17 miles.
By Rail: Newton Abbot Station (from Paddington) ¾ mile. Buses and taxis operate to and from the course.
By Air: Helicopter landing pad in the centre of the course.

NOTTINGHAM (L.H)

Flat: Left-handed, galloping, oval of about 1m 4f, and a run-in of four and a half furlongs. Flat with easy turns.
Address: Nottingham Racecourse, Colwick Park, Nottingham NG2 4BE Tel: (0870) 8507634
Fax: (0115) 958 4515 Website: www.nottinghamracecourse.co.uk
Regional Director: Amy Starkey
Clerk of the Course: Robert Bellamy
Managing Director: Pip Kirkby
Going Reports: Contact main office as above or Clerk of the Course.
Stabling: 122 boxes allotted on arrival. Hostel for lads and lasses. Tel: (0870) 850 7634
By Road: 2 miles east of the city on the B686.
By Rail: Nottingham (Midland) Station. Regular bus service to course (2 miles).
By Air: Helicopter landing facility in the centre of the course.

PERTH (R.H)

N.H. Rectangular, 1m 2f (8) 283y run-in. A flat, easy track with sweeping turns. Not a course for the long-striding galloper. An efficient watering system ensures that the ground rarely gets hard.
Address: Perth Racecourse, Scone Palace Park, Perth PH2 6BB Tel: (01738) 551597 Fax: (01738) 553021
Website: www.perth-races.co.uk
Clerk of the Course: Harriet Graham (07843) 380401

General Manager: Sam Morshead Tel: (01738) 551597 Mobile: (07768) 868848
Going Reports: Groundsman: (07899) 034012 or contact Clerk of the Course as above.
Stabling: 96 boxes and accommodation for lads and lasses Tel: (01738) 551597.
Stables Tel: (01738) 621604 (racedays only).
By Road: 4 miles north of the town off the A93.
By Rail: Perth Station (from Dundee) 4 miles. There are buses to the course.
By Air: Scone Airport (3.75 miles). Edinburgh Airport 45 minutes.

PLUMPTON (L.H)

N.H. Oval, 1m 1f (7) 200y run-in uphill. A tight, undulating circuit with an uphill finish, Plumpton favours the handy, fast jumper. The ground often gets heavy, as the course is based on clay soil.
Address: Plumpton Racecourse, Plumpton, East Sussex, BN7 3AL Tel: (01273) 890383
Fax: (01273) 891557 Website: www.plumptonracecourse.co.uk
Clerk of the Course: Mark Cornford (07759) 151617
Chief Executive: Claire Sheppard
Going Reports: Tel: (01273) 890383, or (07759) 151617.
Stabling: 76 boxes. Advance notice required for overnight arrival. Tel: (07759) 151617
By Road: 2 miles north of the village off the B2116.
By Rail: Plumpton Station (from Victoria) adjoins course.
By Air: Helicopter landing facility by prior arrangement with the Clerk of the Course.

PONTEFRACT (L.H)

Flat: Left-handed oval, undulating course of 2m 133y, with a short run-in of 2f. It is a particularly stiff track with the last 3f uphill.
Address: Pontefract Park Race Co. Ltd., The Park, Pontefract, West Yorkshire Tel: (01977) 781307
(Racedays) Fax: (01977) 781850 Website: www.pontefract-races.co.uk
Managing Director & Clerk of the Course: Norman Gundill (01977) 781307
Assistant Manager & Clerk of the Course: Richard Hamill
Going Reports: Contact Office as above, or Clerk of the Course
Stabling: 113 boxes. Stabling and accommodation must be reserved. They will be allocated on a first come-first served basis. Tel: (01977) 702323
By Road: 1 mile north of the town on the A639. Junction 32 of M62. Free car park adjacent to the course.
By Rail: Pontefract Station (Tanshelf, every hour to Wakefield), 1½ miles from the course. Regular bus service from Leeds.
By Air: Helicopters by arrangement only. (Nearest Airfields: Robin Hood (Doncaster), Sherburn-in-Elmet, Yeadon (Leeds Bradford).

REDCAR (L.H)

Flat: Left-handed, level, galloping, oval course of 1m 6f with a straight run-in of 5f. There is also a straight mile.
Address: Redcar Racecourse, Redcar, Cleveland TS10 2BY Tel: (01642) 484068 Fax: (01642) 488272
Website: www.redcarracing.com
Clerk of the Course: Jonjo Sanderson Tel: 01642 484068 Mobile: 07766 022893
General Manager: Amy Fair
Going Reports: Contact main office as above or Clerk of the Course.
Stabling: 144 Boxes available. Tel: Stables (01642) 484068 or racedays only (01642) 484254).
By Road: In town off the A1085. Free parking adjoining the course for buses and cars.
By Rail: Redcar Station (¼ mile from the course).
By Air: Landing facilities at Turners Arms Farm (600yds runway) Yearby, Cleveland. Two miles south of the racecourse - transport available. Durham Tees Valley airport (18 miles west of Redcar).

RIPON (R.H)

Flat: A sharp, undulating, right-handed oval of 1m 5f, with a 5f run-in. There is also a 6f straight course.
Address: Ripon Racecourse, Boroughbridge Road, Ripon, North Yorkshire HG4 1UG Tel: (01765) 530530
Fax: (01765) 698900 E-mail: info@ripon-races.co.uk Website: www.ripon-races.co.uk
Clerk of the Course & Managing Director: James Hutchinson
Going Reports: Tel: 01765 603696 or Head Groundsman (07976) 960177
Stabling: Trainers requiring stabling (103 boxes available) are requested to contact the Stable Manager prior to 12 noon the day before racing. Tel: (01765) 604135

By Road: The course is situated 2 miles southeast of the city, on the B6265. There is ample free parking for cars and coaches. For reservations apply to the Secretary.
By Rail: Harrogate Station (11 miles), or Thirsk (15 miles). Bus services to Ripon.
By Air: Helicopters only on the course. Otherwise Leeds/Bradford airport.

SALISBURY (R.H)

Flat: Right-handed and level, with a run-in of 4f. There is a straight mile track. The last half-mile is uphill, providing a stiff test of stamina.
Address: Salisbury Racecourse, Netherhampton, Salisbury, Wiltshire SP2 8PN Tel: (01722) 326461
Fax: (01722) 412710 Website: www.salisburyracecourse.co.uk
Clerk of the Course & General Manager: Jeremy Martin (07880) 744999
Going Reports: Contact Clerk of the Course as above
Stabling: Free stabling (114 boxes) and accommodation for lads and lasses, apply to the Stabling Manager (01722) 327327.
By Road: 3 miles southwest of the city on the A3094 at Netherhampton. Free car park adjoins the course.
By Rail: Salisbury Station is 3.5 miles (from London Waterloo). Bus service to the course.
By Air: Helicopter landing facility near the 1m 2f start.

SANDOWN PARK (R.H)

Flat: An easy right-handed oval course of 1m 5f with a stiff straight uphill run-in of 4f. Separate straight 5f track is also uphill. Galloping.
N.H. Oval, 1m 5f (11) 220y run-in uphill. Features seven fences on the back straight; the last three (the Railway Fences) are very close together and can often decide the outcome of races. The stiff climb to the finish puts the emphasis very much on stamina, but accurate-jumping, free-running sorts are also favoured. Hurdle races are run on the Flat course.
Address: Sandown Park Racecourse, Esher, Surrey KT10 9AJ Tel: (01372) 464348 Fax: (01372) 470427
www.sandown.co.uk
Regional Director: Rupert Trevelyan
Clerk of the Course: Andrew Cooper, Sandown Park, Esher, Surrey. Tel: (01372) 461213
Mobile: (07774) 230850.
Going Reports: (01372) 461212.
Stabling: 110 boxes. Free stabling and accommodation for lads and lasses. Tel: (01372) 463511.
By Road: Four miles southwest of Kingston-on-Thames, on the A307 (M25 Junction 10).
By Rail: Esher Station (from Waterloo) adjoins the course.
By Air: London (Heathrow) Airport 12 miles.

SEDGEFIELD (L.H)

N.H. Oval, 1m 2f (8) 200y run-in: Hurdles 200y run-in. Undulating with fairly tight turns, it doesn't suit big, long-striding horses.
Address: Sedgefield Racecourse, Sedgefield, Stockton-on-Tees, Cleveland TS21 2HW
Tel: (01740) 621925 Office Fax: (01740) 620663 Website: www.sedgefield-racecourse.co.uk
Clerk of the Course: Phil Tuck
General Manager: Jill Williamson
Going Reports: Tel: (01740) 621925 or contact Clerk of the Course as above
Stabling: 116 boxes filled in rotation. No forage. Accommodation for horse attendants:
Tel: (01740) 621925
By Road: ¾ mile southwest of the town, near the junction of the A689 (Bishop Auckland) and the A177 (Durham) roads. The car park is free.
By Rail: Darlington Station (9 miles). Durham Station (12 miles).
By Air: Helicopter landing facility in car park area by prior arrangement only.

SOUTHWELL (L.H)

Flat, Turf: Tight left-handed track.
Flat, Fibresand: Left-handed oval, Fibresand course of 1m 2f with a 3f run-in. There is a straight 5f. Sharp and level, Southwell suits front-runners.
N.H. Oval, 1m 1f (7) 220y run-in. A tight, flat track with a short run-in, suits front-runners.
Address: Southwell Racecourse, Rolleston, Newark, Nottinghamshire NG25 0TS Tel: (01636) 814481
Fax: (01636) 812271 Website: www.southwell-racecourse.co.uk
Clerk of the Course: Roderick Duncan (07772) 958685
General Manager: Amanda Boby

Going Reports: Contact Clerk of the Course as above.
Stabling: 113 boxes at the course. Applications for staff and horse accommodation to be booked by noon the day before racing on (01636) 814481.
By Road: The course is situated at Rolleston, 3 miles south of Southwell, 5 miles from Newark.
By Rail: Rolleston Station (Nottingham-Newark line) adjoins the course.
By Air: Helicopters can land by prior arrangement.

STRATFORD-ON-AVON (L.H)

N.H. Triangular, 1m 2f (8) 200y run-in. Virtually flat with two tight bends, and quite a short home straight. A sharp and turning course, Stratford-on-Avon suits the well-balanced, handy sort.
Address: Stratford Racecourse, Luddington Road, Stratford-upon-Avon, Warwickshire CV37 9SE
Tel: (01789) 267949 Fax: (01789) 415850 Website: www.stratfordracecourse.net
Clerk of the Course & Managing Director: Stephen Lambert. Mobile (07836) 384932.
Assistant to Managing Director: Ilona Barnett
Going reports: Contact main office as above or Head Groundsman Tel: (07770) 623366.
Stabling: 89 boxes allotted on arrival. Advance notice must be given for overnight stays.
Tel: (01789) 267949.
By Road: A mile from the town centre, off the A429 (Evesham road).
By Rail: Stratford-on-Avon Station (from Birmingham New Street or Leamington Spa) 1 mile.
By Air: Helicopter landing facility by prior arrangement.

TAUNTON (R.H)

N.H. Elongated oval, 1m 2f (8) 150y run-in uphill. Sharp turns, especially after the winning post, with a steady climb from the home bend. Suits the handy sort.
Address: Taunton Racecourse, Orchard Portman, Taunton, Somerset TA3 7BL Tel: (01823) 337172
(Office) Fax: (01823) 325881 Website: www.tauntonracecourse.co.uk
Clerk of the Course: Michael Trickey, The Racecourse, Taunton, Somerset TA3 7BL. Tel: (01823) 337172
General Manager: Bob Young
Going reports: Contact Clerk of the Course as above, or Head Groundsman (after 4.30pm) (07971) 695132.
Stabling: 90 boxes allotted on arrival. Advance bookings for long journeys. Apply to the Stable Manager, (01823) 337172
By Road: Two miles south of the town on the B3170 (Honiton) road (M5 Junction 25).
By Rail: Taunton Station 2½ miles. There are buses and taxis to course.
By Air: Helicopter landing facility by prior arrangement.

THIRSK (L.H)

Flat: Left-handed, oval of 1m 2f with sharp turns and an undulating run-in of 4f. There is a straight 6f track.
Address: The Racecourse, Station Road, Thirsk, North Yorkshire YO7 1QL Tel: (01845) 522276
Fax: (01845) 525353. Website: www.thirskracecourse.net
Clerk of the Course & Managing Director: James Sanderson
Going reports: Contact main office or Clerk of the Course as above
Stabling: 110 boxes. For stabling and accommodation apply to the Racecourse Tel: (01845) 522096
By Road: West of the town on the A61. Free car park adjacent to the course for buses and cars.
By Rail: Thirsk Station (from King's Cross). ½ mile from the course.
By Air: Helicopters can land by prior arrangement. Tel: Racecourse (01845) 522276. Fixed wing aircraft can land at RAF Leeming. Tel: (01677) 423041. Light aircraft at Bagby. Tel: (01845) 597385 or (01845) 537555.

TOWCESTER (R.H)

N.H. Square, 1m 6f (10) 200y run-in uphill. The final six furlongs are uphill. One of the most testing tracks in the country with the emphasis purely on stamina.
Address: The Racecourse, Easton Neston, Towcester, Northants NN12 7HS Tel: (01327) 353414
Fax: (01327) 358534 Website: www.towcester-racecourse.co.uk
Clerk of the Course: Robert Bellamy (07836) 241458
General Manager: Kevin Ackerman.
Going Reports: Tel: (01327) 353414 or contact Clerk of the Course as above.
Stabling: 101 stables in a new block. Allocated on arrival. Please contact racecourse in advance for overnight stabling / accommodation (01327) 350200.
By Road: 1 mile southeast of the town on the A5 (Milton Keynes road). M1 (Junction 15a).

By Rail: Northampton Station (Euston) 9 miles, buses to Towcester; or Milton Keynes (Euston) 12 miles, taxis available.
By Air: Helicopters can land by prior arrangement with the Racecourse Manager.

UTTOXETER (L.H)

N.H. Oval, 1m 2f (8) 170y run-in. A few undulations, easy bends and fences and a flat home straight of over half a mile. Suits front-runners, especially on the 2m hurdle course.
Address: The Racecourse, Wood Lane, Uttoxeter, Staffordshire ST14 8BD Tel: (01889) 562561
Fax: (01889) 562786 Website: www.uttoxeter-racecourse.co.uk
Clerk of the Course: Charlie Moore (07764) 255500
General Manager: David MacDonald
Going Reports: Contact main office or Clerk of the Course as above.
Stabling: 102 boxes, allotted on arrival. Tel: (01889) 562561. Overnight and Accommodation requirements must be notified in advance as no hostel at course.
By Road: South-East of the town off the B5017 (Marchington Road).
By Rail: Uttoxeter Station (Crewe-Derby line) adjoins the course.
By Air: Helicopters can land by prior arrangement with the raceday office.

WARWICK (L.H)

Flat: Left-handed, sharp, level track of 1m 6f 32y in circumference, with a run-in of two and a half furlongs.
N.H. Circular, 1m 6f (10) 240y run-in. Undulating with tight bends, five quick fences in the back straight and a short home straight, Warwick favours handiness and speed rather than stamina.
Address: Warwick Racecourse, Hampton Street, Warwick CV34 6HN Tel: (01926) 491553
Fax: (01926) 403223 Website: www.warwickracecourse.co.uk
Regional Director: Ian Renton
Clerk of the Course: Sulekha Varma
Managing Director: Huw Williams
Going Reports: Contact main office or Clerk of the Course as above.
Stabling: 117 boxes allocated on arrival or by reservation (01926) 491553.
By Road: West of the town on the B4095 adjacent to Junction 15 of the M40.
By Rail: Warwick or Warwick Parkway Stations.
By Air: Helicopters can land by prior arrangement with the Clerk of the Course.

WETHERBY (L.H)

N.H. Oval, 1m 4f (9) 200y run-in slightly uphill. A flat, very fair course which suits the long-striding galloper.
Address: The Racecourse, York Road, Wetherby, LS22 5EJ Tel: (01937) 582035 Fax: (01937) 588021
Website: www.wetherbyracing.co.uk
Clerk of the Course & Chief Executive: Jonjo Sanderson (07831) 437453
Going reports: Tel: 01937 582035, or Head Groundsman: (07880) 722586
Stabling: 91 boxes allocated on arrival. Accommodation available. Tel: (01937) 582035 or from 2pm the day before racing (01937) 582074.
By Road: East of the town off the B1224 (York Road). Adjacent to the A1. Excellent bus and coach facilities. Car park free.
By Rail: Leeds Station 12 miles. Buses to Wetherby.
By Air: Helicopters can land by prior arrangement

WINCANTON (R.H)

N.H. Rectangular, 1m 3f (9) 200y run-in. Good galloping course where the going rarely becomes heavy. The home straight is mainly downhill.
Address: Wincanton Racecourse, Wincanton, Somerset BA9 8BJ Tel: (01963) 32344 Fax: (01963) 34668
Website: www.wincantonracecourse.co.uk
Regional Director: Ian Renton
Clerk of the Course: Barry Johnson (07976) 791578
General Manager: Steve Parlett
Going Reports: Contact Racecourse Office as above.
Stabling: 94 boxes allocated on arrival, overnight accommodation must be booked in advance. Apply to the Stable Manager, Wincanton Racecourse. Tel: (01963) 32344.
By Road: 1 mile north of the town on the B3081.

By Rail: Gillingham Station (from Waterloo) or Castle Cary Station (from Paddington). Buses and taxis to the course.
By Air: Helicopter landing area is situated in the centre of the course.

WINDSOR (Fig. 8)

Flat: Figure of eight track of 1m 4f 110y. The course is level and sharp with a long run-in. The 6f course is essentially straight.
Address: Royal Windsor Racecourse, Maidenhead Road, Windsor, Berkshire SL4 5JJ Tel: (01753) 498400
Fax: (01753) 830156. Website: www.windsor-racecourse.co.uk
Clerk of the Course: Jeff Green
Managing Director: Daniel Clark
Going Reports: Contact Clerk of the Course as above.
Stabling: 114 boxes available. Reservation required for overnight stay and accommodation only.
Tel: (07825) 603236 or (01753) 498405 (racedays).
By Road: North of the town on the A308 (M4 Junction 6).
By Rail: Windsor Central Station (from Paddington) or Windsor & Eton Riverside Station (from Waterloo).
By Air: London (Heathrow) Airport 15 minutes. Also White Waltham Airport (West London Aero Club) 15 minutes.
River Bus: Seven minutes from Barry Avenue promenade at Windsor.

WOLVERHAMPTON (L.H)

Flat: Left-handed oval Polytrack of 1m, with a run-in of 380y. A level track with sharp bends.
Address: Wolverhampton Racecourse, Dunstall Park, Gorsebrook Road, Wolverhampton WV6 0PE
Tel: (01902) 390000 Fax: (01902) 421621 Website: www.wolverhampton-racecourse.co.uk
Clerk of the Course: Fergus Cameron (07971) 531162
General Manager: Dave Roberts
Going Reports: Contact Main Office as above
Stabling: 103 boxes allotted on arrival. Applications for lads and lasses, and overnight stables must be made to Racecourse by noon on the day before racing. Tel: (07971) 531162. Fax: (01902) 421621.
By Road: 1 mile north of the city on the A449 (M54 Junction 2 or M6 Junction 12). Car parking free of charge.
By Rail: Wolverhampton Station (from Euston) 1 mile.
By Air: Halfpenny Green Airport 8 miles.

WORCESTER (L.H)

N.H. Elongated oval, 1m 5f (9) 220y run-in. Flat with easy turns, Worcester is a very fair, galloping track.
Address: Worcester Racecourse, Pitchcroft, Worcester WR1 3EJ Tel: (01905) 25364 Fax: (01905) 617563
Website: www.worcester-racecourse.co.uk
Clerk of the Course: Fergus Cameron (07971) 531162.
Managing Director: Dave Roberts (01905) 25364.
Going Reports: Contact Clerk of the Course as above, or (01905) 25364 (racedays).
Stabling: 97 boxes allotted on arrival. Overnight accommodation for lads and lasses in Worcester.
Tel: (01905) 25364 Fax: (01905) 617563.
By road: West of the city off the A449 (Kidderminster road) (M5 Junction 8).
By Rail: Foregate Street Station, Worcester (from Paddington) ¾ mile.
By Air: Helicopter landing facility in the centre of the course, by prior arrangement only.

YARMOUTH (L.H)

Flat: Left-handed, level circuit of 1m 4f, with a run-in of 5f. The straight course is 1m long.
Address: The Racecourse, Jellicoe Road, Great Yarmouth, Norfolk NR30 4AU Tel: (01493) 842527
Fax: (01493) 843254 Website: www.greatyarmouth-racecourse.co.uk
Clerk of the Course: Richard Aldous (07738) 507643
General Manager: Glenn Tubby
Going Reports: Contact Main Office or Clerk of the Course as above
Stabling: 127 boxes available. Allocated on arrival. Tel: (01493) 855651 (racedays only) or racecourse office.
By Road: 1 mile east of town centre (well signposted from A47 & A12).
By Rail: Great Yarmouth Station (1 mile). Bus service to the course.
By Air: Helicopter landing available by prior arrangement with Racecourse Office

YORK (L.H)

Flat: Left-handed, level, galloping track, with a straight 6f. There is also an adjoining course of 6f 214y.
Address: The Racecourse, York YO23 1EX Tel: (01904) 683932 Fax: (01904) 611071
Website: www.yorkracecourse.co.uk
Clerk of the Course & Chief Executive: William Derby (07812) 961176
Assistant Clerk of the Course: Anthea Morshead
Going Reports: Contact (01904) 683932 or Clerk of the Course as above.
Stabling: 177 boxes available Tel: (01904) 706317 (Racedays) or (07712) 676434.
By Road: 1 mile southeast of the city on the A1036.
By Rail: 1½ miles York Station (from King's Cross). Special bus service from station to the course.
By Air: Light aircraft and helicopter landing facilities available at Rufforth aerodrome (5,000ft tarmac runway). £20 landing fee - transport arranged to course. Leeds Bradford airport (25 miles).

THE INVESTEC DERBY STAKES (GROUP 1), EPSOM DOWNS SATURDAY 1ST JUNE 2013

SECOND ENTRIES BY APRIL 9TH; SUPPLEMENTARY ENTRIES BY MAY 27TH.

HORSE	TRAINER	HORSE	TRAINER
ABQARI (IRE)	Saeed bin Suroor	DARE TO ACHIEVE	William Haggas
ACHERNAR (USA)	P. Bary, France	DAWALAN (FR)	A. de Royer Dupre, France
AGREEMENT (IRE)	Aidan O'Brien, Ireland	DAWN CALLING (IRE)	Mahmood Al Zarooni
AJLAAN (USA)	J. E. Hammond, France	DEFICIT (IRE)	Michael Bell
ALANSARI (IRE)	David Wachman, Ireland	DEIRA PHANTOM (IRE)	David Simcock
ALAYAZ (IRE)	M. Delzangles, France	DEMONIC	Sir Henry Cecil
ALCAEUS	Sir Mark Prescott	DENOTE	Paul Cole
ALGORITHMIC (IRE)	Michael Bell	DESERVING HONOUR	Mahmood Al Zarooni
ALMOONQITH (USA)	Jean Claude Rouget, France	DESTRUCT	A. Fabre, France
ALPINIST	J. S. Bolger, Ireland	DISPOUR (IRE)	M. Delzangles, France
AMIRR (IRE)	Saeed bin Suroor	DUKE OF DANCE (IRE)	David Wachman, Ireland
AMRALAH (IRE)	Mick Channon	EDERAN (IRE)	M. Delzangles, France
ANOTHER COCKTAIL	Hughie Morrison	EL CORDOBES (IRE)	Ed Dunlop
APPARENTLY	Mahmood Al Zarooni	ELIDOR	Mick Channon
AQALIM	Saeed bin Suroor	ELISHPOUR (IRE)	Jean Claude Rouget, France
ARABIAN SKIES (IRE)	Saeed bin Suroor	ELKAAYED (USA)	Roger Varian
ARBELAN (FR)	A. de Royer Dupre, France	ELSINIAAR	Roger Varian
ARISTOTELES (FR)	M. Delzangles, France	ELVIN	Amanda Perrett
ARKHIP	M. Delzangles, France	EMAZAR (USA)	John M. Oxx, Ireland
ARMY RANGER (IRE)	Aidan O'Brien, Ireland	EMBELLISHED (IRE)	Aidan O'Brien, Ireland
ASHDAN	John Gosden	ENDLESS CREDIT (IRE)	Luca Cumani
ASK DAD		ESHARAAT (IRE)	J. E. Hammond, France
ATARAXIS (FR)	Sir Henry Cecil	ETERNAL RAY	F. Head, France
AU REVOIR (IRE)	Aidan O'Brien, Ireland	EVERGLADES ISLAND (IRE)	Aidan O'Brien, Ireland
AUTUN (IRE)	Sir Henry Cecil	EXCELLENT RESULT (IRE)	Saeed bin Suroor
AZIKI (IRE)	William Haggas	EXCESS KNOWLEDGE	John Gosden
AZRUR (IRE)	Michael Bell	EXPERT ANSWER	Saeed bin Suroor
BAIHAS	Sir Michael Stoute	EXPLORATORY (USA)	Mahmood Al Zarooni
BALLYGLASHEEN (IRE)	Aidan O'Brien, Ireland	EYE OF THE STORM (IRE)	Aidan O'Brien, Ireland
BALMORAL MILLS (IRE)	E. Lellouche, France	FAR AFIELD	A. Fabre, France
BARADARI (IRE)	Jean Claude Rouget, France	FARE THEE WELL (IRE)	Aidan O'Brien, Ireland
BARAWEEZ (IRE)	F. Head, France	FARZAD (FR)	A. de Royer Dupre, France
BATTLE OF MARENGO (IRE)	Aidan O'Brien, Ireland	FEEL LIKE DANCING	John Gosden
BOMBER THORN	Tom Dascombe	FESTIVE CHEER (IRE)	Aidan O'Brien, Ireland
BOOKTHEBAND (IRE)	Clive Brittain	FIGHTER SQUADRON (USA)	David Wachman, Ireland
BRAVODINO (USA)	J. E. Pease, France	FIRST MOVE	Mahmood Al Zarooni
BREDEN (IRE)	John Gosden	FLASHHEART (IRE)	Marcus Tregoning
BRETON BLUES	Mahmood Al Zarooni	FLEDGED	John Gosden
BUCHANAN	Sir Henry Cecil	FLOW (USA)	Sir Henry Cecil
BUSHEL (USA)		FLYING OFFICER (USA)	John Gosden
CAILLEBOTTE (IRE)	Aidan O'Brien, Ireland	FLYING THE FLAG (IRE)	Aidan O'Brien, Ireland
CAPE OF HOPE (IRE)	Peter Chapple-Hyam	FORTIFY (IRE)	Aidan O'Brien, Ireland
CAP O'RUSHES	Mahmood Al Zarooni	FOUNDRY (IRE)	Aidan O'Brien, Ireland
CARRERA	J. W. Hills	FRANCIS OF ASSISI (IRE)	Aidan O'Brien, Ireland
CAT O'MOUNTAIN (USA)	Mahmood Al Zarooni	FREEDOM FIGHTER (IRE)	Aidan O'Brien, Ireland
CHANCE TO DANCE (IRE)	J. S. Bolger, Ireland	FREEWHEEL (IRE)	Aidan O'Brien, Ireland
CHERRY TIGER	James Toller	GALEB WARRIOR	William Haggas
CHEYENNE HOME	P. Bary, France	GALILEO ROCK (IRE)	David Wachman, Ireland
CHIEF EXECUTIVE (IRE)	Mikael Magnusson	GAMBOL (FR)	J. E. Hammond, France
COLOUR MY WORLD	Ed McMahon	GENIUS BOY	Mahmood Al Zarooni
COOL RUNNINGS (IRE)	Tom Dascombe	GHAZALI (FR)	A. de Royer Dupre, France
CORYCIAN (IRE)	P. Bary, France	GIANT WAVE (USA)	Roger Varian
COSMIC CURIOUS (GER)	Sir Henry Cecil	GLENARD	Charles Hills
COUNT OF LIMONADE (IRE)	Aidan O'Brien, Ireland	GODS GIFT (IRE)	Rae Guest
CYCLONE		GOLD BAND (IRE)	J. S. Bolger, Ireland
DAAREE (IRE)	Saeed bin Suroor	GOLDEN TOUCH	Sir Michael Stoute
DALGIG	Jamie Osborne	GOLD MEDAL (IRE)	Richard Hannon
DAMBUSTER (IRE)	Sir Michael Stoute	GRAYSWOOD	William Muir
DANCE KING	David Lanigan	GREAT EXPLORER (IRE)	Aidan O'Brien, Ireland

HORSE	TRAINER
GREAT FIGHTER	Saeed bin Suroor
GREATWOOD	Luca Cumani
GROUNDBREAKING	Mahmood Al Zarooni
HACHITA VALLEY (USA)	A. Fabre, France
HAMELIN (IRE)	Sir Henry Cecil
HASANOUR (USA)	John M. Oxx, Ireland
HASHEEM	Roger Varian
HAWKER	Mahmood Al Zarooni
HEIRLOOM	Aidan O'Brien, Ireland
HEJAZ (IRE)	John M. Oxx, Ireland
HERO'S STORY	Amanda Perrett
HILLSTAR	Sir Michael Stoute
HIPPOKRATES (FR)	M. Delzangles, France
HIS EMINENCE (IRE)	Aidan O'Brien, Ireland
HOME FRONT (IRE)	John Gosden
HONEST BOY	
HORSTED KEYNES (FR)	Roger Varian
HUNTING GROUND (USA)	Mahmood Al Zarooni
I'TILAF	Saeed bin Suroor
IKHTISAS (USA)	Saeed bin Suroor
ILLUSTRATE (IRE)	Aidan O'Brien, Ireland
IMPERIAL CONCORDE (IRE)	D. K. Weld, Ireland
IMPROVISATION (IRE)	Mahmood Al Zarooni
INAAD (IRE)	Saeed bin Suroor
INDIAN CHIEF (IRE)	Aidan O'Brien, Ireland
INSTRUCTION (IRE)	Aidan O'Brien, Ireland
JAMMY GUEST (IRE)	George Margarson
JAZZ MASTER	Luca Cumani
JEERAAN (USA)	Ed Dunlop
KAJOKSEE (IRE)	Jeremy Noseda
KALIMANTAN (IRE)	Jean Claude Rouget, France
KARLIDI (USA)	John M. Oxx, Ireland
KINGDOM (IRE)	Aidan O'Brien, Ireland
KING GEORGE RIVER (IRE)	Alan Bailey
KING OF ENGLAND	A. de Royer Dupre, France
KINGSBARNS (IRE)	Aidan O'Brien, Ireland
KINGSTON JAMAICA (IRE)	Aidan O'Brien, Ireland
LAKE MICHIGAN (IRE)	Aidan O'Brien, Ireland
LAKE NOVA (IRE)	Aidan O'Brien, Ireland
LAURENTIDES	D. Sepulchre, France
LAYL (USA)	Mahmood Al Zarooni
LEADING LIGHT (IRE)	Aidan O'Brien, Ireland
LEAGUE OF NATIONS (IRE)	Aidan O'Brien, Ireland
LE COEUR DE LA MER (GER)	M. Delzangles, France
LEGENDS (IRE)	Sir Michael Stoute
LEITIR MOR (IRE)	J. S. Bolger, Ireland
LIFE PARTNER (IRE)	Mahmood Al Zarooni
LINE DRUMMER (FR)	Aidan O'Brien, Ireland
LINFORD	in U.S.A.
LLAREGYB (IRE)	David Elsworth
LORD PROVOST (IRE)	Mahmood Al Zarooni
LOS CABOS	Aidan O'Brien, Ireland
MAC LIR (USA)	J. S. Bolger, Ireland
MAGIC HURRICANE (IRE)	James Fanshawe
MAGICIAN (IRE)	Aidan O'Brien, Ireland
MAGIC SPELL (IRE)	Aidan O'Brien, Ireland
MAJEED	David Simcock
MAJESTY (IRE)	Sir Henry Cecil
MALLORY HEIGHTS (IRE)	Luca Cumani
MANNDAWI (FR)	A. de Royer Dupre, France
MANSOREEN	Saeed bin Suroor
MARKTTAG	Luca Cumani
MARS (IRE)	Aidan O'Brien, Ireland
MARTIAN (IRE)	William Haggas
MASTER SPEAKER (IRE)	Aidan O'Brien, Ireland
MAWJ TAMY (USA)	Charles Hills
MAXIMUM VELOCITY (FR)	J. E. Hammond, France

HORSE	TRAINER
MEINER ETERNEL	in Japan
MERCHANT'S QUAY (USA)	David Wachman, Ireland
MIGHTY THOR	Simon Dow
MIGHTY YAR (IRE)	Sir Henry Cecil
MILESTONE (IRE)	Aidan O'Brien, Ireland
MISSION APPROVED	Sir Michael Stoute
MOMBASA	Ralph Beckett
MONSIEUR RIEUSSEC	Jonathan Portman
MONTCLAIR (IRE)	Aidan O'Brien, Ireland
MONTJEU MINDER (IRE)	David Wachman, Ireland
MOURANI (IRE)	John M. Oxx, Ireland
MUHTARIS (IRE)	Saeed bin Suroor
MURPHY'S DELIGHT (IRE)	David Wachman, Ireland
MUSICIANSHIP (IRE)	
MUTAJALLY	Sir Michael Stoute
MUTASHADED (USA)	Roger Varian
MUTHABIR (IRE)	Saeed bin Suroor
MUTHAFAR (IRE)	William Haggas
MY HISTORY (IRE)	Saeed bin Suroor
NELSON'S VICTORY	
NEVIS (IRE)	Aidan O'Brien, Ireland
NEW LOOK (IRE)	
NEWS AT SIX (IRE)	J. S. Bolger, Ireland
NEWSREADER (USA)	Mahmood Al Zarooni
NICHOLS CANYON	John Gosden
NORPHIN	Denis Coakley
NORTH DAKOTA (IRE)	Aidan O'Brien, Ireland
OCEAN APPLAUSE	John Ryan
OCOVANGO	A. Fabre, France
ORATOR (IRE)	David Wachman, Ireland
ORBISON (IRE)	Roger Varian
OSTAAD (IRE)	Saeed bin Suroor
OUR GOLDEN GIRL	Shaun Lycett
PACK THE PUNCH (IRE)	J. S. Bolger, Ireland
PARALLAX (IRE)	Sir Henry Cecil
PARKER RIDGE (FR)	Luca Cumani
PASAKA BOY	Jonathan Portman
PEDRO THE GREAT (USA)	Aidan O'Brien, Ireland
PEGASUS BRIDGE	K. Borgel, France
PENCOMBE (FR)	David Simcock
PERFECT SPELL	Andrew Balding
PERFORMANCE (IRE)	Aidan O'Brien, Ireland
PERSEPOLIS (IRE)	Sir Michael Stoute
PETRANI (IRE)	
PHOSPHORESCENCE (IRE)	Sir Henry Cecil
PIET MONDRIAN	Aidan O'Brien, Ireland
PLEASURE BENT	Luca Cumani
PLINTH (IRE)	Aidan O'Brien, Ireland
PLUTOCRACY (IRE)	David Lanigan
POINT PIPER (USA)	Aidan O'Brien, Ireland
POLHEM	Jessica Long, Sweden
PORTMONARCH (IRE)	David Lanigan
PRAIRIE RANGER	Andrew Balding
PRESSURE POINT	Sir Michael Stoute
PROBABLY (IRE)	David Wachman, Ireland
PROUD DANCER (IRE)	Sir Mark Prescott Bt
PUBLICATION (IRE)	Mahmood Al Zarooni
PUTRA ETON (IRE)	Roger Varian
QAHIR (IRE)	F. Head, France
QUEL AVANTAGE	F. H. Graffard, France
QUEST FOR MORE (IRE)	Roger Charlton
RACE AND STATUS (IRE)	Andrew Balding
RANGI	John Gosden
RAZERA (IRE)	
REFECTORY (IRE)	Andrew Balding
RENEW (IRE)	Aidan O'Brien, Ireland
RESPONSE	William Haggas

HORSE	TRAINER
RESTRAINT OF TRADE (IRE)	Mahmood Al Zarooni
RETIREMENT PLAN	Sir Henry Cecil
RICHARD SENIOR	
RI NA SI	Pat Phelan
ROYAL BALLET	Luca Cumani
ROYAL FLAG	Saeed bin Suroor
ROYAL SIGNALLER	Amanda Perrett
RULER OF THE WORLD (IRE)	Aidan O'Brien, Ireland
RUNAIOCHT (IRE)	J. S. Bolger, Ireland
RUSSIAN REALM	Sir Michael Stoute
RUST	Mrs Ann Duffield
RUSTAMABAD (FR)	A. de Royer Dupre, France
SACRED SQUARE (GER)	William Haggas
SAINT AND SINNER (GER)	A. Wohler, Germany
SAKASH	J. R. Jenkins
SAMOSET	Alan Swinbank
SARDINIA (IRE)	Aidan O'Brien, Ireland
SARWISTAN (IRE)	Jean Claude Rouget, France
SASKATCHEWAN	Luca Cumani
SATWA STORY	Mahmood Al Zarooni
SECRET NUMBER	Saeed bin Suroor
SEUSSICAL (IRE)	David Wachman, Ireland
SHALIANZI (IRE)	A. de Royer Dupre, France
SHANTI	Michael Bell
SHAZOUD (FR)	A. de Royer Dupre, France
SHIKARPOUR (IRE)	A. de Royer Dupre, France
SILVER TRAIL	M. Delzangles, France
SINISTER (IRE)	Roger Varian
SIR WALTER SCOTT (IRE)	Aidan O'Brien, Ireland
SLEEPING GIANT (GER)	Luca Cumani
SMOKE SCREEN	Aidan O'Brien, Ireland
SOUL INTENT (IRE)	J. W. Hills
SOVIET ROCK (IRE)	Andrew Balding
SPACE SHIP	John Gosden
SPESSARTINE (IRE)	Robert Eddery
SPIRIT RIDER (USA)	John Gosden
STOMACHION (IRE)	Sir Michael Stoute
STREET ARTIST (IRE)	Mark Johnston
STRENGTH AND HONOR (IRE)	Sir Michael Stoute
STRING THEORY (IRE)	Marco Botti
SUCCESSFUL YEAR	Mark Johnston
SUGAR TRAIN	D. Smaga, France
SUMMERFREE (USA)	
SUPERFECTION	in U.S.A.
SUPERPLEX (FR)	Michael Figge, Germany
SURREALIST (IRE)	Aidan O'Brien, Ireland
SWEEPING ROCK (IRE)	Marcus Tregoning
SWING EASY	Robert Mills
TABLEAUX (USA)	Aidan O'Brien, Ireland
TAKAATHUR (USA)	Saeed bin Suroor
TARIKHI (USA)	Saeed bin Suroor
TATISCHEV (FR)	M. Delzangles, France
TEKTITE	J. E. Pease, France
TELESCOPE (IRE)	Sir Michael Stoute
TENOR (IRE)	Roger Varian
THA'IR (IRE)	Saeed bin Suroor
THATCHMASTER (USA)	Mahmood Al Zarooni
THEATRE (IRE)	Aidan O'Brien, Ireland
THE FERRYMAN (IRE)	Aidan O'Brien, Ireland
THE GRAND DUKE	Aidan O'Brien, Ireland
THE MECHANIC (IRE)	David Lanigan
THE UNITED STATES (IRE)	Aidan O'Brien, Ireland
THE VATICAN (IRE)	Aidan O'Brien, Ireland
THE WELSH WIZARD (IRE)	Charles Hills
THOMAS HOBSON	John Gosden
THOROUGHFARE (IRE)	Mark Johnston
THOUGHT AND MEMORY (IRE)	Mick Channon

HORSE	TRAINER
TIME FOR ACTION (IRE)	David Wachman, Ireland
TIMIKAR (USA)	John M. Oxx, Ireland
TINGHIR (IRE)	David Lanigan
TORONADO (IRE)	Richard Hannon
TRADING LEATHER (IRE)	J. S. Bolger, Ireland
TRAVERTINE (IRE)	Aidan O'Brien, Ireland
TURNBUCKLE	
TWILIGHT ZONE (IRE)	Aidan O'Brien, Ireland
URBAN TALK	in U.S.A.
VAYAKHAN (FR)	A. de Royer Dupre, France
VESTIGE	Aidan O'Brien, Ireland
VICTORY SONG (IRE)	Aidan O'Brien, Ireland
VINSON MASSIF (USA)	Aidan O'Brien, Ireland
VITAL EVIDENCE (USA)	Sir Michael Stoute
WADI AL HATTAWI (IRE)	Saeed bin Suroor
WALLENBERG	John Gosden
WANNABE YOUR MAN	David Lanigan
WARRIGAL (IRE)	Jeremy Noseda
WAVER (IRE)	Aidan O'Brien, Ireland
WEATHER WATCH (IRE)	Mrs J. Harrington, Ireland
WELL'S DANCER (IRE)	David Wachman, Ireland
WHY AREEB	Mme C. Head-Maarek, France
WILDHEART (IRE)	Michael Figge, Germany
WINGED FOOT (IRE)	E. Lellouche, France
WINTER LION (IRE)	John M. Oxx, Ireland
WINTERLUDE (IRE)	Mahmood Al Zarooni
WOODSTOCK (IRE)	Richard Hannon
ZAFERI (IRE)	A. de Royer Dupre, France
ZAIN EAGLE	Gerard Butler
ZAIN HONOUR	Gerard Butler
ZARLIMAN (IRE)	M. Delzangles, France
ZAYAM (FR)	A. de Royer Dupre, France
ZHIYI (USA)	P Bary, France
ZIEKHANI	Hughie Morrison
EX HENTIES BAY (IRE)	Roger Varian
EX TALINAS ROSE (IRE)	Tony Newcombe

THE BET AT BLUESQUARE.COM
EUROPEAN FREE HANDICAP
NEWMARKET CRAVEN MEETING 2013
(ON THE ROWLEY MILE COURSE)
WEDNESDAY APRIL 17TH

The Bet at Bluesq.com European Free Handicap (Class 1) (Listed race) with total prize fund of £37,000 for two-year-olds only of 2012 which are included in the European 2-y-o Thoroughbred Rankings or which, in 2012, either ran in Great Britain or ran for a trainer who at the time was licensed by the British Horseracing Authority, and are Rated 100 or above; lowest weight 8st; highest weight 9st 7lbs. Penalty for a winner after December 31st 2012, 5 lbs. Seven furlongs.

Rating		st	lb
124	DAWN APPROACH (IRE)	9	7
118	KINGSBARNS (IRE)	9	1
117	GEORGE VANCOUVER (USA)	9	0
117	LEITIR MOR (IRE)	9	0
117	OLYMPIC GLORY (IRE)	9	0
117	RECKLESS ABANDON (GB)	9	0
116	MOOHAAJIM (IRE)	8	13
115	GALE FORCE TEN (GB)	8	12
114	CERTIFY (USA)	8	11
114	DESIGNS ON ROME (IRE)	8	11
114	LOCH GARMAN (IRE)	8	11
114	MORANDI (FR)	8	11
114	PARLIAMENT SQUARE (IRE)	8	11
114	PENNY'S PICNIC (IRE)	8	11
114	STEELER (IRE)	8	11
114	TORONADO (IRE)	8	11
114	VAN DER NEER (GB)	8	11
113	ANNA'S PEARL (GB)	8	10
113	DUNDONNELL (USA)	8	10
112	INDIAN JADE (GB)	8	10
112	CRISTOFORO COLOMBO (USA)	8	9
112	PEDRO THE GREAT (USA)	8	9
112	SIR PRANCEALOT (IRE)	8	9
111	BATTLE OF MARENGO (IRE)	8	8
111	FIRST CORNERSTONE (IRE)	8	8
111	FLOTILLA (FR)	8	8
111	GHURAIR (USA)	8	8
111	PURR ALONG (GB)	8	8
111	SILASOL (IRE)	8	8
111	SKY LANTERN (IRE)	8	8
111	TAWHID (GB)	8	8
111	US LAW (IRE)	8	8
111	VIZTORIA (IRE)	8	8
111	WHAT A NAME (IRE)	8	8
110	ALTERITE (FR)	8	7
110	ARTIGIANO (USA)	8	7
110	BUNGLE INTHEJUNGLE (GB)	8	7
110	HAVANA GOLD (IRE)	8	7
110	HEAVY METAL (GB)	8	7
110	LAW ENFORCEMENT (IRE)	8	7
110	ROSDHU QUEEN (IRE)	8	7
110	TOPAZE BLANCHE (IRE)	8	7
109	CAY VERDE (GB)	8	6
109	FANTASTIC MOON (GB)	8	6
108	BLAINE (GB)	8	5
108	BOOMSHACKERLACKER (IRE)	8	5
108	GLASS OFFICE (GB)	8	5

Rating		st	lb
108	MASTER OF WAR (GB)	8	5
108	TAAYEL (IRE)	8	5
108	THA'IR (IRE)	8	5
107	AFONSO DE SOUSA (USA)	8	4
107	ALHEBAYEB (IRE)	8	4
107	ASHDAN (GB)	8	4
107	BAILEYS JUBILEE (GB)	8	4
107	JUST THE JUDGE (IRE)	8	4
107	SENDMYLOVETOROSE (GB)	8	4
107	WINNING EXPRESS (IRE)	8	4
106	CEILING KITTY (GB)	8	3
106	GARSWOOD (GB)	8	3
106	HAJAM (GB)	8	3
106	IAN'S DREAM (USA)	8	3
106	LINES OF BATTLE (USA)	8	3
106	MAUREEN (IRE)	8	3
106	TRADING LEATHER (IRE)	8	3
105	BIRDMAN (IRE)	8	2
105	COUR VALANT (GB)	8	2
105	DEAUVILLE PRINCE (FR)	8	2
105	MORAWIJ (GB)	8	2
105	SOUND OF GUNS (GB)	8	2
105	THE GOLD CHEONGSAM (IRE)	8	2
104	HOTOTO (GB)	8	1
104	INDIGO LADY (GB)	8	1
104	MAXENTIUS (IRE)	8	1
104	MOCENIGO (IRE)	8	1
104	MONTIRIDGE (IRE)	8	1
104	OLLIE OLGA (USA)	8	1
104	ROZ (GB)	8	1
104	SORELLA BELLA (IRE)	8	1
103	AHERN (GB)	8	0
103	AL WAAB (GB)	8	0
103	CHILWORTH ICON (GB)	8	0
103	GINGER GOOSE (GB)	8	0
103	HOYAM (GB)	8	0
103	JADANNA (IRE)	8	0
103	NARGYS (IRE)	8	0
103	PEARL ACCLAIM (IRE)	8	0
103	UPWARD SPIRAL (GB)	8	0
103	WATERWAY RUN (USA)	8	0
103	WELL ACQUAINTED (IRE)	8	0
102	AMAZONAS (IRE)	7	13
102	AYAAR (IRE)	7	13
102	COCKTAIL QUEEN (IRE)	7	13
102	EL MANATI (IRE)	7	13

Rating		st	lb
102	**EXCESS KNOWLEDGE** (GB)	7	13
102	**GLEAN** (GB)	7	13
102	**INVINCIBLE WARRIOR** (IRE)	7	13
102	**LIGHT UP MY LIFE** (IRE)	7	13
102	**RACE AND STATUS** (IRE)	7	13
102	**THE FERRYMAN** (IRE)	7	13
101	**AGENT ALLISON** (GB)	7	12
101	**DESERT BLOSSOM** (IRE)	7	12
101	**FIRE EYES** (GB)	7	12
101	**LUCKY BEGGAR** (IRE)	7	12
101	**PURE EXCELLENCE** (GB)	7	12
101	**ROYAL RASCAL** (GB)	7	12

Rating		st	lb
101	**SANDREAMER** (IRE)	7	12
101	**TAMAYUZ STAR** (IRE)	7	12
101	**WILLIE THE WHIPPER** (GB)	7	12
100	**CITY IMAGE** (IRE)	7	11
100	**EMELL** (GB)	7	11
100	**EUXTON HALL** (IRE)	7	11
100	**ODOOJ** (IRE)	7	11
100	**PREMIER STEPS** (IRE)	7	11
100	**REYAADAH** (GB)	7	11
100	**SAVANNA LA MAR** (USA)	7	11
100	**SIR PATRICK MOORE** (FR)	7	11
100	**WHIPPER'S BOY** (IRE)	7	11

WORLD THOROUGHBRED RANKINGS

for three-year-olds rated 115 or greater by the IFHA World Thoroughbred Rankings Conference. Horses rated 114-110 by the European Thoroughbred Rankings Conference do not constitute a part of the World Thoroughbred Rankings. Those ratings were compiled on behalf of the European Pattern Committee

Rating		Trained
125	I'LL HAVE ANOTHER (USA)	USA
124	BODEMEISTER (USA)	USA
124	CAMELOT (GB)	IRE
124	GOLD SHIP (JPN)	JPN
123	DULLAHAN (USA)	USA
122	GENTILDONNA (JPN)	JPN
122	PASTORIUS (GER)	GER
121	ALL TOO HARD (AUS)	AUS
121	PAYNTER (USA)	USA
120	ENCKE (USA)	GB
120	FENOMENO (JPN)	JPN
120	RIDASIYNA (FR)	FR
120	VALYRA (GB)	FR
119	GOING SOMEWHERE (BRZ)	BRZ
119	QUESTING (GB)	USA
119	UNION RAGS (USA)	USA
118	BEAUTY PARLOUR (GB)	FR
118	DEEP BRILLANTE (JPN)	JPN
118	FRENCH FIFTEEN (FR)	FR
118	INDY POINT (ARG)	ARG
118	NOVELLIST (GB)	GER
118	PIERRO (AUS)	AUS
118	TRINNIBERG (USA)	USA
118	UNBRIDLED COMMAND (USA)	USA
118	WENT THE DAY WELL (USA)	USA
117	BELIEVE YOU CAN (USA)	USA
117	CREATIVE CAUSE (USA)	USA
117	CURREN BLACK HILL (JPN)	JPN
117	GRANDEUR (IRE)	USA
117	GREAT HEAVENS (GB)	GB
117	IMPERIAL MONARCH (IRE)	IRE
117	MY MISS AURELIA (USA)	USA
117	PRINCESS HIGHWAY (USA)	IRE
116	SAONOIS (FR)	FR
116	AESOP'S FABLES (USA)	FR
116	ALPHA (USA)	USA
116	CASPAR NETSCHER (GB)	GB
116	DAYATTHESPA (USA)	USA
116	ELUSIVE KATE (USA)	GB
116	FALLEN FOR YOU (GB)	GB
116	GIROLAMO (GER)	GER
116	GOLDEN TICKET (USA)	USA
116	HOMECOMING QUEEN (IRE)	IRE
116	JUST A WAY (JPN)	JPN
116	LAST TRAIN (GB)	FR
116	MOST IMPROVED (IRE)	GB
116	MOUNT SHASTA (JPN)	JPN
116	SILVER MAX (USA)	USA
116	THE FUGUE (GB)	GB
116	THE LUMBER GUY (USA)	USA
116	TOSEN HOMAREBOSHI (JPN)	JPN
116	WORLD ACE (JPN)	JPN
115	ASTROLOGY (IRE)	IRE
115	ATIGUN (USA)	USA
115	BAYRIR (FR)	FR
115	BORN TO SEA (IRE)	IRE

Rating		Trained
115	BOURBON COURAGE (USA)	USA
115	BROADWAY'S ALIBI (USA)	USA
115	CONTESTED (USA)	USA
115	DUNDEEL (NZ)	NZ
115	EDEN'S MOON (USA)	USA
115	FAST FALCON (USA)	USA
115	FEUERBLITZ (GER)	GER
115	GRACE HALL (USA)	USA
115	HAKASSAN (CHI)	CHI
115	JIMMY CREED (USA)	USA
115	LES BEAUFS (FR)	FR
115	MAIN SEQUENCE (USA)	GB
115	NECK 'N NECK (USA)	USA
115	NOBLE MISSION (GB)	GB
115	SAINT BAUDOLINO (IRE)	FR
115	SKY DIGNITY (JPN)	JPN
115	SPEAKING OF WHICH (IRE)	IRE
115	TAKE CHARGE INDY (USA)	USA
115	THOUGHT WORTHY (USA)	GB
115	THUNDER MOCCASIN (USA)	USA
115	UNBRIDLED'S NOTE (USA)	USA
115	WINNING PRIZE (ARG)	ARG
114	BALTIC ROCK (IRE)	GER
114	BONFIRE (GB)	GB
114	CANTICUM (GB)	FR
114	GREGORIAN (IRE)	GB
114	HERMIVAL (IRE)	FR
114	KESAMPOUR (FR)	FR
114	MASTERSTROKE (USA)	FR
114	MICHELANGELO (GB)	GB
114	NUTELLO (USA)	FR
114	SO BEAUTIFUL (FR)	FR
114	TOP TRIP (GB)	FR
114	TRUMPET MAJOR (IRE)	GB
113	ARCHBISHOP (USA)	GB
113	DADDY LONG LEGS (USA)	IRE
113	DALKALA (USA)	FR
113	DRAGON PULSE (IRE)	IRE
113	DUNTLE (IRE)	IRE
113	LIGHT HEAVY (IRE)	IRE
113	LUCAYAN (FR)	FR
113	MINCE (GB)	GB
113	POWER (GB)	IRE
113	RJWA (IRE)	FR
113	STARBOARD (GB)	GB
113	WAS (IRE)	IRE
112	ABTAAL (USA)	FR
112	ALL SHAMAR (GB)	GER
112	AMARON (GB)	GER
112	BLACK ARROW (IRE)	GER
112	DABIRSIM (FR)	FR
112	DECLARATION OF WAR (USA)	IRE
112	EKTIHAAM (IRE)	GB
112	ENERGIZER (GER)	GER
112	FULBRIGHT (GB)	GB
112	FURNER'S GREEN (IRE)	IRE

Rating	Trained
112 **HARTANI** (IRE)	IRE
112 **REMUS DE LA TOUR** (FR)	FR
112 **RESTIADARGENT** (FR)	FR
112 **ROMANTICA** (GB)	FR
112 **SALOMINA** (GER)	GER
112 **SAMITAR** (GB)	GB/USA
112 **SHIROCCO STAR** (GB)	GB
112 **UP** (IRE)	IRE
112 **URSA MAJOR** (IRE)	IRE
112 **VENETO** (FR)	FR
112 **YELLOW AND GREEN** (GB)	FR
111 **AMARILLO** (IRE)	GER
111 **COUPE DE VILLE** (IRE)	GB
111 **KENDAM** (FR)	FR
111 **LAUGH OUT LOUD** (GB)	GB
111 **LETHAL FORCE** (IRE)	GB
111 **LIL'WING** (IRE)	FR
111 **MAINSAIL** (GB)	GB
111 **MASSIYN** (IRE)	IRE
111 **SOVEREIGN DEBT** (IRE)	IRE
111 **TANNERY** (IRE)	IRE
111 **THOMAS CHIPPENDALE** (IRE)	GB
110 **AKLAN** (IRE)	IRE
110 **ALBION** (GB)	FR
110 **ALJAMAAHEER** (IRE)	GB

Rating	Trained
110 **ASHKIYR** (FR)	FR
110 **AUENTURM** (GER)	GER
110 **CAPONATA** (USA)	IRE
110 **CHAMONIX** (IRE)	IRE
110 **CHERRY COLLECT** (IRE)	ITY
110 **COUP DE THEATRE** (FR)	FR
110 **FIRE LILY** (IRE)	IRE
110 **FORCES OF DARKNESS** (IRE)	FR
110 **FOXTROT ROMEO** (IRE)	GB
110 **FRACTIONAL** (IRE)	FR
110 **GALVAUN** (IRE)	FR
110 **GUSTO** (GB)	GB
110 **KISSED** (IRE)	IRE
110 **LA CONQUERANTE** (GB)	FR
110 **MASHOORA** (IRE)	FR
110 **PRODUCER** (GB)	GB
110 **SAGAWARA** (GB)	FR
110 **SEDICIOSA** (IRE)	FR
110 **SIR JADE** (FR)	FR
110 **SMOKING SUN** (USA)	FR
110 **STIPULATE** (GB)	GB
110 **TENENBAUM** (GB)	FR
110 **XANADOU** (IRE)	FR
110 **YANG TSE KIANG** (FR)	FR

OLDER HORSES 2012

For four-year-olds and up rated 115 or greater by the IFHA World Thoroughbred Rankings Conference. Horses rated 114-110 by the European Thoroughbred Rankings Conference do not constitute a part of the World Thoroughbred Rankings. Those ratings were compiled on behalf of the European Pattern Committee

Rating	Age	Trained
140 **FRANKEL** (GB)	4	GB
131 **CIRRUS DES AIGLES** (FR)	6	FR
130 **BLACK CAVIAR** (AUS)	6	AUS
130 **EXCELEBRATION** (IRE)	4	IRE
129 **WISE DAN** (USA)	5	USA
127 **ORFEVRE** (JPN)	4	JPN
126 **MONTEROSSO** (GB)	5	GB
126 **NATHANIEL** (IRE)	4	GB
126 **SO YOU THINK** (NZ)	6	IRE
125 **FORT LARNED** (USA)	4	USA
125 **HAY LIST** (AUS)	7	AUS
124 **AMBITIOUS DRAGON** (NZ)	6	HK
124 **ANIMAL KINGDOM** (USA)	4	USA
124 **CITYSCAPE** (GB)	6	GB
124 **DANEDREAM** (GER)	4	GER
124 **FARHH** (GB)	4	GB
124 **KRYPTON FACTOR** (GB)	4	UAE
124 **MUCHO MACHO MAN** (USA)	4	USA
124 **SNOW FAIRY** (IRE)	5	GB
124 **ST NICHOLAS ABBEY** (IRE)	5	IRE
123 **GAME ON DUDE** (USA)	5	USA
123 **LITTLE MIKE** (USA)	5	USA
123 **POINT OF ENTRY** (USA)	4	USA
123 **RULERSHIP** (JPN)	5	JPN
123 **SEA MOON** (GB)	4	GB
122 **ACCLAMATION** (USA)	6	USA
122 **ATLANTIC JEWEL** (AUS)	4	AUS
122 **CALEB'S POSSE** (USA)	4	USA
122 **DUNADEN** (FR)	6	FR
122 **MEANDRE** (FR)	4	FR

Rating	Age	Trained
122 **MORE JOYOUS** (NZ)	6	AUS
122 **OBVIOUSLY** (IRE)	4	USA
122 **OCEAN PARK** (NZ)	4	
122 **PORTUS BLENDIUM** (USA)	6	HK
122 **RELIABLE MAN** (GB)	4	FR
122 **ROCKET MAN** (AUS)	7	SIN
122 **SEPOY** (AUS)	4	AUS
122 **SOLEMIA** (FR)	4	FR
121 **CAPPONI** (IRE)	5	UAE
121 **DARK SHADOW** (JPN)	5	JPN
121 **EISHIN FLASH** (JPN)	5	JPN
121 **FOXWEDGE** (AUS)	4	AUS
121 **GROUPIE DOLL** (USA)	4	USA
121 **MENTAL** (AUS)	4	AUS
121 **MOONLIGHT CLOUD** (GB)	4	FR
121 **ROYAL DELTA** (USA)	4	USA
121 **SHACKLEFORD** (USA)	4	USA
120 **AFRICAN STORY** (GB)	5	UAE
120 **AMAZOMBIE** (USA)	6	USA
120 **AMERICAIN** (USA)	7	FR
120 **GLORIOUS DAYS** (AUS)	5	HK
120 **LORD KANALOA** (JPN)	4	JPN
120 **MUFHASA** (NZ)	8	NZ
120 **NO RISK AT ALL** (FR)	5	FR
120 **PLANTEUR** (IRE)	5	GB
120 **RON THE GREEK** (USA)	5	USA
120 **STAY THIRSTY** (USA)	4	USA
120 **TO THE GLORY** (JPN)	5	JPN
120 **WHAT A WINTER** (SAF)	5	SAF
120 **XTENSION** (IRE)	5	HK

Rating	Age	Trained
119 **ABLE ONE** (NZ)	10	HK
119 **CARLTON HOUSE** (USA)	4	GB
119 **FAMOUS NAME** (GB)	7	IRE
119 **FLAT OUT** (USA)	6	USA
119 **MANIGHAR** (FR)	6	AUS
119 **MR COMMONS** (USA)	4	USA
119 **OCEAN BLUE** (JPN)	4	JPN
119 **SHEA SHEA** (SAF)	5	SAF
119 **SHONAN MIGHTY** (JPN)	4	JPN
119 **TRAILBLAZER** (JPN)	5	JPN
119 **TWICE OVER** (GB)	7	GB
119 **VARIETY CLUB** (SAF)	4	SAF
118 **CHINCHON** (IRE)	7	FR
118 **CRACKERJACK KING** (IRE)	4	ITY
118 **EARL OF TINSDAL** (GER)	4	GER
118 **GIMMETHEGREENLIGHT** (AUS)	4	SAF
118 **GOLDEN LILAC** (IRE)	4	FR
118 **GORDON LORD BYRON** (IRE)	4	IRE
118 **GREEN MOON** (IRE)	5	AUS
118 **JACKSON** (SAF)	4	SAF
118 **JACKSON BEND** (USA)	5	USA
118 **JAKKALBERRY** (IRE)	6	GB
118 **JERANIMO** (USA)	6	USA
118 **LITTLE BRIDGE** (NZ)	6	HK
118 **LUCK OR DESIGN** (IRE)	5	HK
118 **RAIN AFFAIR** (AUS)	5	AUS
118 **SADAMU PATEK** (JPN)	4	JPN
118 **SHARETA** (IRE)	4	FR
118 **SHOOT OUT** (AUS)	6	AUS
118 **SMART FALCON** (JPN)	7	JPN
118 **STRONG RETURN** (JPN)	6	JPN
118 **SUCCESSFUL DAN** (USA)	6	USA
118 **SUPER EASY** (NZ)	4	SIN
118 **TO HONOR AND SERVE** (USA)	4	USA
118 **VEYRON** (NZ)	7	NZ
118 **WINTER MEMORIES** (USA)	4	USA
118 **ZAGORA** (FR)	5	USA
117 **AL KAZEEM** (GB)	4	GB
117 **ALTERNATION** (USA)	4	USA
117 **AWESOME MARIA** (USA)	5	USA
117 **BEAT BLACK** (JPN)	5	JPN
117 **BRAVURA** (SAF)	6	SAF
117 **BUFFERING** (AUS)	5	AUS
117 **CAMP VICTORY** (USA)	5	USA
117 **COIL** (USA)	4	USA
117 **COLOUR VISION** (FR)	4	GB
117 **DUBAWI GOLD** (GB)	4	GB
117 **EFFICIENT** (NZ)	9	AUS
117 **ETHIOPIA** (AUS)	4	AUS
117 **FIORENTE** (IRE)	4	GB
117 **FOX HUNT** (IRE)	5	UAE
117 **GIOFRA** (GB)	4	FR
117 **GOLD BLITZ** (JPN)	5	JPN
117 **GRAND PRIX BOSS** (JPN)	4	JPN
117 **HUNTER'S LIGHT** (IRE)	4	GB
117 **IT'S TRICKY** (USA)	4	USA
117 **JOY AND FUN** (NZ)	9	HK
117 **LASER HAWK** (AUS)	4	AUS
117 **MAYSON** (GB)	4	GB
117 **METAL BENDER** (NZ)	7	AUS
117 **MOSHEEN** (AUS)	4	AUS
117 **MOUNT ATHOS** (IRE)	5	GB
117 **MUSIR** (AUS)	6	UAE
117 **NATES MINESHAFT** (USA)	5	USA
117 **NIHONPIRO OURS** (JPN)	5	JPN
117 **PACKING COMMANDER** (AUS)	6	HK
117 **RANGIRANGDOO** (NZ)	8	AUS

Rating	Age	Trained
117 **RICHARD'S KID** (USA)	7	USA
117 **SIYOUMA** (IRE)	4	FR
117 **SOCIETY ROCK** (IRE)	5	GB
117 **STEINBECK** (IRE)	5	HK
117 **TAPIZAR** (USA)	4	USA
117 **THE FACTOR** (USA)	4	USA
117 **TOSEN JORDAN** (JPN)	6	JPN
117 **TREASURE BEACH** (GB)	4	IRE
116 **ADMIRATION** (AUS)	5	HK
116 **AFSARE** (IRE)	5	GB
116 **ALCOPOP** (AUS)	8	AUS
116 **ATO** (SAF)	5	SIN
116 **BATED BREATH** (GB)	5	GB
116 **BROWN PANTHER** (GB)	4	GB/GB
116 **CAPITAL ACCOUNT** (USA)	5	USA
116 **CAPTAIN OBVIOUS** (AUS)	7	SIN
116 **CHASE ME** (NZ)	5	SIN
116 **DANLEIGH** (AUS)	9	AUS
116 **DATA LINK** (USA)	4	USA
116 **DECEMBER DRAW** (IRE)	6	AUS
116 **DRUNKEN SAILOR** (IRE)	7	AUS
116 **EMCEE** (USA)	4	USA
116 **EXPRESSIVE HALO** (ARG)	5	ARG
116 **GLENCADAM GOLD** (IRE)	4	AUS
116 **HAPPY TRAILS** (AUS)	5	AUS
116 **I'M A DREAMER** (IRE)	5	GB
116 **IZZI TOP** (GB)	4	GB
116 **JOSHUA TREE** (IRE)	5	GB
116 **LUCAS CRANACH** (GER)	5	AUS
116 **MARKETING MIX** (CAN)	4	USA
116 **MAWINGO** (GER)	4	AUS
116 **MONTON** (AUS)	6	AUS
116 **MR BIG** (AUS)	5	SIN
116 **NAHRAIN** (GB)	4	GB/GB
116 **OPINION POLL** (IRE)	6	GB
116 **OVAMBO QUEEN** (GER)	5	GER
116 **PLENTY OF KICKS** (BRZ)	4	BRZ
116 **POLISH KNIGHT** (NZ)	4	AUS
116 **QUICK CASABLANCA** (CHI)	4	CHI
116 **RED CADEAUX** (GB)	6	GB
116 **REDEEMED** (USA)	4	USA
116 **REKINDLED INTEREST** (AUS)	5	AUS
116 **ROMAN LEGEND** (JPN)	4	JPN
116 **SAPPHIRE** (IRE)	4	IRE
116 **SINCERO** (AUS)	5	AUS
116 **TAPITSFLY** (USA)	5	USA
116 **TESTA MATTA** (USA)	6	JPN
116 **THUMBS UP** (NZ)	8	HK
116 **TURBO COMPRESSOR** (USA)	4	USA
116 **ULTIMATE EAGLE** (USA)	4	USA
116 **VOILA ICI** (IRE)	7	AUS
116 **WARNING FLAG** (USA)	4	HK
116 **WILLCOX INN** (USA)	4	USA
116 **WIN VARIATION** (JPN)	4	JPN
116 **WORTHADD** (IRE)	5	GB
116 **ZINABAA** (FR)	7	FR
115 **AL QASR** (USA)	4	PER
115 **AL REP** (IRE)	4	HK
115 **ALIANTHUS** (GER)	7	GER
115 **AMBIDEXTER** (AUS)	4	AUS
115 **ARALDO** (AUS)	4	GER
115 **ATOMIC FORCE** (AUS)	7	AUS
115 **BARAKEY** (AUS)	5	AUS
115 **BETTER LIFE** (AUS)	4	SIN
115 **BETTER THAN EVER** (AUS)	6	SIN
115 **BRAMBLES** (NZ)	4	AUS
115 **CARACORTADO** (USA)	5	USA

Rating		Age	Trained	Rating		Age	Trained
115	CITY STYLE (USA)	6	UAE	115	WOORIM (AUS)	7	AUS
115	COLOMBIAN (IRE)	4	GB	115	ZAZOU (GER)	5	GER
115	DAISY DEVINE (USA)	4	USA	114	BASCHAR (GB)	5	GER
115	DIDIMO (BRZ)	4	BRZ	114	DANDINO (GB)	5	GB
115	DON BOSCO (FR)	5	FR	114	DUBAI PRINCE (IRE)	4	GB
115	ESPOIR CITY (JPN)	7	JPN	114	GALIKOVA (FR)	4	FR
115	FAME AND GLORY (GB)	6	IRE	114	MAAREK (GB)	5	IRE
115	FAT AL (AUS)	4	AUS	114	MOLLY MALONE (FR)	4	FR
115	FLYING FULTON (AUS)	6	SIN	114	PIRIKA (IRE)	4	FR
115	FORCE FREEZE (USA)	7	USA	114	SAAMIDD (GB)	4	GB
115	GET STORMY (USA)	6	USA	114	SIR LANDO (GB)	5	NOR
115	GLASS HARMONIUM (IRE)	6	AUS	114	TEMIDA (IRE)	4	GER
115	GREAT ATTACK (USA)	5	USA	114	TIMEPIECE (GB)	5	GB
115	GUSTAVE CRY (JPN)	4	JPN	114	WALDPARK (GER)	4	GER
115	HARRIS TWEED (GB)	5	GB	113	AIKEN (GB)	4	GB
115	HIGHLAND KNIGHT (IRE)	5	GB	113	AIZAVOSKI (IRE)	6	FR
115	HIRUNO D'AMOUR (JPN)	5	JPN	113	BEATEN UP (GB)	4	GB
115	HUNTERS BAY (USA)	5	CAN	113	CAVALRYMAN (GB)	6	GB
115	HYMN BOOK (USA)	6	USA	113	CHACHAMAIDEE (IRE)	5	GB
115	INCLUDE ME OUT (USA)	4	USA	113	DREAM PEACE (IRE)	4	FR/USA
115	IOYA BIGTIME (USA)	5	USA	113	GALILEO'S CHOICE (IRE)	6	IRE
115	IVORY LAND (FR)	5	FR	113	HAMISH MCGONAGALL (GB)	7	GB
115	JAGUAR MAIL (JPN)	8	JPN	113	HIGH JINX (IRE)	4	GB
115	JERSEY TOWN (USA)	6	USA	113	HITCHENS (IRE)	7	GB
115	JIMMY CHOUX (NZ)	5	NZ	113	LA POMME D'AMOUR (GB)	4	FR
115	KINDERGARDEN KID (USA)	5	USA	113	MAXIOS (GB)	4	FR
115	LIGHTS OF HEAVEN (NZ)	5	AUS	113	MOONWALK IN PARIS (FR)	4	FR
115	LOVE AND PRIDE (USA)	4	USA	113	MULL OF KILLOUGH (GB)	6	GB
115	LOVE CONQUERS ALL (AUS)	6	AUS	113	PAGERA (FR)	4	FR
115	LUCKYGRAY (AUS)	5	AUS	113	QUESTIONING (IRE)	4	GB
115	MASTER OF DESIGN (AUS)	7	AUS	113	RITE OF PASSAGE (GB)	8	IRE
115	MASTER OF HOUNDS (USA)	4	UAE	113	TAC DE BOISTRON (FR)	5	FR
115	MIKHAIL GLINKA (IRE)	5	UAE	113	WIZZ KID (IRE)	4	FR
115	MUSICAL ROMANCE (USA)	5	USA	112	ALTANO (GB)	6	GER
115	MUSKETIER (GER)	10	CAN	112	ANDROMEDA GALAXY (FR)	4	FR
115	MUTAHADEE (IRE)	4	UAE	112	ATEMPO (GER)	4	GER
115	ORTENSIA (AUS)	7	AUS	112	BULLET TRAIN (GB)	5	GB
115	PENITENT (GB)	6	GB	112	DUX SCHOLAR (GB)	4	CHR
115	PINWHEEL (AUS)	7	AUS	112	EMULOUS (GB)	5	IRE
115	PLUM PRETTY (USA)	4	USA	112	FANUNALTER (GB)	6	GB
115	PRINCE BISHOP (IRE)	5	UAE	112	GATEWOOD (GB)	4	GB
115	PUISSANCE DE LUNE (IRE)	4	AUS	112	GLEN'S DIAMOND (GB)	4	GB
115	RAIL TRIP (USA)	7	USA	112	GULF OF NAPLES (IRE)	4	GB
115	SADDLER'S ROCK (IRE)	4	IRE	112	HAWKEYETHENOO (GB)	6	GB
115	SEA SIREN (AUS)	4	AUS	112	INDOMITO (GER)	6	GER
115	SECRET ADMIRER (AUS)	5	AUS	112	JET AWAY (GB)	5	GB
115	SHEZ SINSATIONAL (NZ)	5	NZ	112	JOVIALITY (GB)	4	GB
115	SHIMRAAN (FR)	5	UAE	112	LIBRANNO (GB)	4	GB
115	SICHUAN SUCCESS (AUS)	6	HK	112	OVERTURN (IRE)	8	GB
115	SIDE GLANCE (GB)	5	GB	112	PRAIRIE STAR (GB)	4	FR/AUS
115	SLIM SHADEY (GB)	5	USA	112	ROYAL DIAMOND (IRE)	6	IRE
115	SOLE POWER (GB)	5	IRE	112	SAGA DREAM (FR)	6	FR
115	SOUL (AUS)	5	GB	112	SAGRAMOR (GB)	4	GB
115	SPIRIT QUARTZ (IRE)	4	GB	112	SAJJHAA (GB)	5	GB
115	SRI PUTRA (GB)	6	GB	112	SARATOGA BLACK (IRE)	5	ITY
115	STREAMA (AUS)	4	AUS	112	SHAHWARDI (FR)	6	FR
115	SUGGESTIVE BOY (ARG)	4	USA	112	TIDDLIWINKS (IRE)	6	GB
115	SUNNY KING (IRE)	9	HK	112	TULLIUS (IRE)	4	GB
115	TALES OF BRAVERY (SAF)	6	SAF	112	USUELO (FR)	4	FR
115	TEMPLE OF BOOM (AUS)	6	AUS	112	VITA NOVA (IRE)	5	GB
115	THE APACHE (SAF)	5	SAF	111	AAIM TO PROSPER (IRE)	8	GB
115	TIMES UP (GB)	6	GB	111	ASKAR TAU (FR)	7	GB
115	TIN HORSE (IRE)	4	FR	111	BRIGANTIN (USA)	5	FR
115	VADAMAR (FR)	4	FR	111	COMBAT ZONE (IRE)	6	GER
115	WAIKATO (NZ)	9	SIN	111	DANDY BOY (ITY)	6	IRE
115	WIGMORE HALL (IRE)	5	GB	111	DONN HALLING (IRE)	4	CHR
115	WONDER ACUTE (JPN)	6	JPN	111	ETON FOREVER (IRE)	5	GB

Rating		Age	Trained
111	KASBAH BLISS (FR)	10	FR
111	KING AIR (FR)	5	FR
111	LOST IN THE MOMENT (IRE)	5	GB
111	MASKED MARVEL (GB)	4	GB
111	MEMPHIS TENNESSEE (IRE)	4	IRE
111	MONSIEUR JOE (IRE)	5	GB
111	NOCTURNAL AFFAIR (SAF)	6	IRE
111	OK CORAL (FR)	5	FR
111	PASTORAL PLAYER (GB)	5	GB
111	PREMIO LOCO (USA)	8	GB
111	QUEST FOR PEACE (IRE)	4	GB
111	RED JAZZ (USA)	5	GB
111	RHYTHM OF LIGHT (GB)	4	GB
111	SCALO (GB)	5	GER
111	SHAMALGAN (FR)	5	FR
111	SHARESTAN (IRE)	4	IRE
111	SIR OSCAR (GER)	5	GER
111	SORTILEGE (IRE)	4	GER
111	TRES ROCK DANON (FR)	6	GER
111	VAGABOND SHOES (IRE)	5	FR
110	ALLIED POWERS (IRE)	7	GB
110	AQUAMARINE (JPN)	4	FR
110	DANCE AND DANCE (IRE)	6	GB
110	DURBAN THUNDER (GER)	6	GER
110	ELECTROLYSER (IRE)	7	GB

Rating		Age	Trained
110	EMPIRE STORM (GER)	5	GER
110	FERRO SENSATION (GER)	6	HOL
110	GEREON (GER)	4	GER
110	HAWAAFEZ (GB)	4	GB
110	HAYA LANDA (FR)	4	FR
110	INXILE (IRE)	7	GB
110	MAC LOVE (GB)	11	GB
110	MYASUN (FR)	5	FR
110	NOVA HAWK (GB)	4	FR
110	OCCHIO DELLA MENTE (IRE)	5	ITY
110	ORSINO (GER)	5	GER
110	POET (GB)	7	GB
110	PRINCE D'ALIENOR (IRE)	4	FR
110	QUIZA QUIZA QUIZA (GB)	6	ITY
110	RETRIEVE (AUS)	5	GB
110	SEISMOS (IRE)	4	GER
110	SILVANER (GER)	4	GER
110	SILVER VALNY (FR)	6	FR
110	SKILFUL (GB)	4	GB
110	SPRING OF FAME (USA)	6	GB
110	STRONG SUIT (USA)	4	GB
110	TAZAHUM (USA)	4	GB
110	THE REAPER (IRE)	4	IRE
110	WILD COCO (GER)	4	GB

RACEFORM CHAMPIONS 2012
THREE-YEAR-OLDS AND UP

5f-6f

7f-1m1f

1m2f-1m4f

1m5f+

RACEFORM CHAMPIONS 2012
TWO-YEAR-OLDS

5f-6f

MOOHAJIM	117	PARLIAMENT SQUARE	112
RECKLESS ABANDON	117	PEDRO THE GREAT	112
GALE FORCE TEN	116	PENNY'S PICNIC	112
DAWN APPROACH	114	VITZTORIA	112
GEORGE VANCOUVER	113		

7f-1m1f

DAWN APPROACH	123	LEITIR MOR	116
KINGSBARNS	120	MORANDI	116
GEORGE VANCOUVER	117	STEELER	116
OLYMPIC GLORY	117	VAN DE NEER	116

MEDIAN TIMES 2012

The following Raceform median times are used in the calculation of the Split Second speed figures. They represent a true average time for the distance, which has been arrived at after looking at the winning times for all races over each distance within the past five years, except for those restricted to two or three-year-olds.

Some current race distances have been omitted as they have not yet had a sufficient number of races run over them to produce a reliable average time.

ASCOT
5f 1m 0.50	7f 1m 27.60	1m 4f 2m 32.50
5f 110y 1m 8.30	1m Round 1m 40.70	2m 3m 29.00
6f 1m 14.50	1m Straight 1m 40.80	2m 4f 4m 24.80
6f 110y 1m 21.0	1m 2f 2m 7.40	2m 5f 159y 4m 49.40

AYR
5f 59.40	1m 1m 43.80	1m 5f 13y 2m 54.00
6f 1m 12.40	1m 1f 20y 1m 57.50	1m 7f 3m 20.40
7f 50y 1m 33.40	1m 2f 2m 12.00	2m 1f 105y 3m 59.70

BATH
5f 11y 1m 2.50	1m 2f 46y 2m 11.00	1m 5f 22y 2m 52.00
5f 161y 1m 11.20	1m 3f 144y 2m 30.60	2m 1f 34y 3m 51.90
1m 5y 1m 40.80		

BEVERLEY
5f 1m 3.50	1m 100y 1m 47.60	1m 4f 16y 2m 39.80
7f 100y 1m 33.80	1m 1f 207y 2m 7.00	2m 35y 3m 39.80

BRIGHTON
5f 59y 1m 2.30	6f 209y 1m 23.10	1m 1f 209y 2m 3.60
5f 213y 1m 10.20	7f 214y 1m 36.00	1m 3f 196y 2m 32.70

CARLISLE
5f 1m 0.80	7f 200y 1m 40.00	1m 6f 32y 3m 7.50
5f 193y 1m 13.70	1m 1f 61y 1m 57.60	2m 1f 52y 3m 53.00
6f 192y 1m 27.10	1m 3f 107y 2m 23.10	

CATTERICK
5f 59.80	7f 1m 27.00	1m 5f 175y 3m 3.60
5f 212y 1m 13.60	1m 3f 214y 2m 38.90	1m 7f 177y 3m 32.00

CHEPSTOW
5f 16y 59.30	1m 14y 1m 36.20	2m 49y 3m 38.90
6f 16y 1m 12.00	1m 2f 36y 2m 10.60	2m 2f 4m 3.60
7f 16y 1m 23.20	1m 4f 23y 2m 39.00	

CHESTER
5f 16y 1m 1.00	7f 122y 1m 33.80	1m 5f 89y 2m 52.70
5f 110y 1m 6.20	1m 2f 75y 2m 11.20	1m 7f 195y 3m 28.00
6f 18y 1m 13.80	1m 3f 79y 2m 24.80	2m 2f 147y 4m 4.80
7f 2y 1m 26.50	1m 4f 66y 2m 38.50	

DONCASTER
5f 1m 0.50	7f 1m 26.30	1m 4f 2m 34.90
5f 140y 1m 8.80	1m Straight 1m 39.30	1m 6f 132y 3m 7.40
6f 1m 13.60	1m Round 1m 39.70	2m 110y 3m 40.40
6f 110y 1m 19.90	1m 2f 60y 2m 9.40	2m 2f 3m 55.00

EPSOM

5f 55.70	7f 1m 23.30	1m 2f 18y 2m 9.70
6f 1m 9.40	1m 114y 1m 46.10	1m 4f 10y 2m 38.90

FFOS LAS

5f 58.30	1m 2f 2m 9.40	1m 6f 3m 3.80
6f 1m 10.00	1m 4f 2m 37.40	2m 3m 30.00
1m 1m 41.00		

GOODWOOD

5f 1m 0.20	1m 1f 1m 56.30	1m 6f 3m 3.60
6f 1m 12.20	1m 1f 192y 2m 8.10	2m 3m 29.00
7f 1m 27.00	1m 3f 2m 26.50	2m 5f 4m 31.00
1m 1m 39.90	1m 4f 2m 38.40	

HAMILTON

5f 4y 1m 0.0	1m 1f 36y 1m 59.70	1m 4f 17y 2m 38.60
6f 5y 1m 12.20	1m 3f 16y 2m 25.60	1m 5f 9y 2m 53.90
1m 65y 1m 48.40		

HAYDOCK

5f (inner) 1m 0.80	7f 1m 30.70	1m 3f 200y 2m 33.80
5f (outer) 1m 0.80	1m 1m 43.70	1m 6f 3m 2.00
6f (inner) 1m 13.80	2m 2f 95y 2m 15.50	2m 45y 3m 34.30
6f (outer) 1m 13.80		

KEMPTON (A.W)

5f 1m 0.50	1m 1m 39.80	1m 4f 2m 34.50
6f 1m 13.10	1m 2f 2m 8.00	2m 3m 30.10
7f 1m 26.00	1m 3f 2m 21.90	

LEICESTER

5f 2y 1m 0.0	1m 3m 30.10	1m 1f 218y 2m 7.90
5f 218y 1m 13.00	1m 60y 1m 45.10	1m 3f 183y 2m 33.90
7f 9y 1m 26.20		

LINGFIELD

5f 58.20	7f 140y 1m 32.30	1m 3f 106y 2m 31.50
6f 1m 11.20	1m 1f 1m 56.60	1m 6f 3m 10.00
7f 1m 23.30	1m 2f 2m 10.50	2m 3m 34.80

LINGFIELD (A.W)

5f 58.80	1m 1m 38.20	1m 5f 2m 46.00
6f 1m 11.90	1m 2f 2m 6.60	2m 3m 25.70
7f 1m 24.80	1m 4f 2m 33.00	

MUSSELBURGH

5f 1m 0.40	1m 1f 1m 53.90	1m 5f 2m 52.00
7f 30y 1m 29.00	1m 4f 2m 39.70	1m 6f 3m 5.30
1m 1m 41.20	1m 4f 100y 2m 42.00	2m 3m 33.50

NEWBURY

5f 34y 1m 1.40	1m Straight 1m 39.70	1m 3f 5y 2m 21.20
6f 8y 1m 13.00	1m Round 1m 38.70	1m 4f 5y 2m 35.50
6f 110y 1m 19.30	1m 1f 1m 55.50	1m 5f 61y 2m 52.00
7f Straight 1m 25.70	1m 2f 6y 2m 8.80	2m 3m 32.00

NEWCASTLE

5f 1m 1.10	1m 3y Straight 1m 43.40	1m 4f 93y 2m 45.60
6f 1m 14.60	1m 1f 9y 1m 58.10	1m 6f 97y 3m 11.30
7f 1m 27.80	1m 2f 32y 2m 11.90	2m 19y 3m 39.40
1m Round 1m 45.30		

NEWMARKET (ROWLEY MILE)

5f 59.10	1m 1f 1m 51.70	1m 6f 2m 57.00
6f 1m 12.20	1m 2f 2m 5.80	2m 3m 30.50
7f 1m 25.40	1m 4f 2m 32.00	2m 2f 3m 52.00
1m 1m 38.60		

NEWMARKET (JULY COURSE)

5f 59.10	1m 1m 40.00	2m 5f 2m 44.00
6f 1m 12.50	1m 2f 2m 5.50	1m 6f 175y 3m 8.40
7f 1m 25.70	1m 4f 2m 32.90	2m 24y 3m 27.00

NOTTINGHAM

5f 13y 1m 1.50	1m 75y 1m 49.00	1m 6f 15y 3m 7.00
6f 15y 1m 14.70	1m 2f 50y 2m 14.30	2m 9y 3m 34.50

PONTEFRACT

5f 1m 3.30	1m 2f 6y 2m 13.70	2m 1f 216y 3m 56.20
6f 1m 16.90	1m 4f 8y 2m 40.80	2m 5f 122y 4m 51.00
1m 4y 1m 45.90	2m 1f 22y 3m 44.60	

REDCAR

5f 58.60	1m 1m 38.00	1m 3f 2m 21.70
6f 1m 11.80	1m 1f 1m 53.00	1m 6f 19y 3m 4.70
7f 1m 24.50	1m 2f 2m 7.10	2m 4y 3m 31.40

RIPON

5f 1m 0.70	1m 1f 1m 54.70	1m 4f 10y 2m 36.70
6f 1m 13.00	1m 1f 170y 2m 5.40	2m 3m 31.80
1m 1m 41.40		

SALISBURY

5f 1m 1.00	1m 1m 43.50	1m 4f 2m 38.00
6f 1m 14.80	1m 1f 198y 2m 9.90	1m 6f 21y 3m 7.40
6f 212y 1m 28.60		

SANDOWN

5f 6y 1m 1.60	1m 1f 1m 55.70	1m 6f 3m 4.50
7f 16y 1m 29.50	1m 2f 7y 2m 10.50	2m 78y 3m 38.70
1m 14y 1m 43.30		

SOUTHWELL (A.W)

5f 59.70	1m 1m 43.70	1m 6f 3m 8.30
6f 1m 16.50	1m 3f 2m 28.00	2m 3m 45.50
7f 1m 30.30	1m 4f 2m 41.00	

THIRSK

5f 59.60	7f 1m 27.20	1m 4f 2m 36.20
6f 1m 12.70	1m 1m 40.10	2m 3m 28.30

WARWICK

5f 59.60	7f 26y 1m 24.60	1m 4f 134y 2m 44.60
5f 110y 1m 5.90	1m 22y 1m 41.00	1m 6f 213y 3m 19.00
6f 1m 11.80	1m 2f 188y 2m 21.10	2m 39y 3m 33.80

WINDSOR

5f 10y................................. 1m 0.30	1m 67y................................. 1m 44.70	1m 3f 135y........................ 2m 29.50
6f................................. 1m 13.00	1m 2f 7y................................. 2m 8.70	

WOLVERHAMPTON (A.W)

5f 20y................................. 1m 2.30	1m 141y................................. 1m 50.50	1m 5f 194y........................ 3m 6.00
5f 216y................................. 1m 15.00	1m 1f 103y................................. 2m 1.70	2m 119y........................ 3m 41.80
7f 32y................................. 1m 29.60	1m 4f 50y................................. 2m 41.10	

YARMOUTH

5f 43y................................. 1m 2.70	1m 3y................................. 1m 40.60	1m 3f 101y........................ 2m 28.70
6f 3y................................. 1m 14.40	1m 1f................................. 1m 55.80	1m 6f 17y........................ 3m 7.60
7f 3y................................. 1m 26.60	1m 2f 21y................................. 2m 10.50	2m........................ 3m 32.40

YORK

5f................................. 59.30	1m................................. 1m 39.00	1m 6f........................ 3m 0.20
5f 89y................................. 1m 4.10	1m 208y................................. 1m 52.00	2m 88y........................ 3m 34.50
6f................................. 1m 11.90	1m 2f 88y................................. 2m 12.50	2m 2f........................ 3m 55.40
7f................................. 1m 25.30	1m 4f................................. 2m 33.20	

RACEFORM RECORD TIMES (FLAT)

ASCOT

DISTANCE	TIME	AGE	WEIGHT	GOING	HORSE	DATE		
5f	59.17 secs	2	8-12	Good To Firm	MAQAASID	Jun	16	2010
5f	57.44 secs	6	9-1	Good To Firm	MISS ANDRETTI	Jun	19	2007
6f	1m 12.46	2	9-1	Good To Firm	HENRYTHENAVIGATOR	Jun	19	2007
6f	1m 11.50	3	9-10	Good To Firm	MINCE	Aug	11	2012
7f	1m 27.9	2	7-12	Good To Firm	RELATIVE ORDER	Aug	11	2007
7f	1m 24.94	3	8-12	Good To Firm	RAINFALL	July	16	2010
7f	1m 25.89	6	8-12	Good	ADVANCED	Sep	26	2009
1m (Rnd)	1m 39.55	2	8-12	Good	JOSHUA TREE	Sep	26	2009
1m (Rnd)	1m 38.32	3	9-0	Good To Firm	GHANAATI	Jun	19	2009
1m (Str)	1m 37.16	5	9-0	Good To Firm	INVISIBLE MAN	Jun	16	2010
1m 2f	2m 02.52	5	9-3	Good	CIRRUS DES AIGLES	Oct	15	2011
1m 4f	2m 26.78	4	9-7	Good	HARBINGER	July	24	2010
2m	3m 24.13	3	9-1	Good To Firm	HOLBERG	May	2	2007
2m 4f	4m 16.92	6	9-2	Good To Firm	RITE OF PASSAGE	Jun	17	2010
2m 5f 159y	4m 47.79	7	9-2	Good To Firm	BERGO	Jun	19	2010

AYR

DISTANCE	TIME	AGE	WEIGHT	GOING	HORSE	DATE		
5f	56.9 secs	2	8-11	Good	BOOGIE STREET	Sep	18	2003
5f	55.68 secs	3	8-11	Good To Firm	LOOK BUSY	Jun	21	2008
6f	1m 09.7	2	7-10	Good	SIR BERT	Sep	17	1969
6f	1m 08.37	5	8-6	Good To Firm	MAISON DIEU	Jun	21	2008
7f 50y	1m 28.9	2	9-0	Good	TAFAAHUM	Sep	19	2003
7f 50y	1m 28.07	5	9-0	Good To Firm	GINGER TRACK	May	30	2012
1m	1m 39.2	2	9-0	Good To Firm	KRIBENSIS	Sep	17	1986
1m	1m 36.0	4	7-13	Firm	SUFI	Sep	16	1959
1m 1f 20y	1m 50.3	4	9-3	Good	RETIREMENT	Sep	19	2003
1m 2f	2m 04.0	4	9-9	Good To Firm	ENDLESS HALL	July	17	2000
1m 5f 13y	2m 45.8	4	9-7	Good To Firm	EDEN'S CLOSE	Sep	18	1991
1m 7f	3m 13.1	3	9-4	Good	ROMANY RYE	Sep	19	1991
2m 1f 105y	3m 45.0	4	6-13	Good	CURRY	Sep	16	1955

BATH

DISTANCE	TIME	AGE	WEIGHT	GOING	HORSE	DATE		
5f 11y	59.50 secs	2	9-2	Firm	AMOUR PROPRE	July	24	2008
5f 11y	58.75 secs	3	8-12	Firm	ENTICING	May	1	2007
5f 161y	1m 08.7	2	8-12	Firm	QALAHARI	July	24	2008
5f 161y	1m 08.1	6	9-0	Firm	MADRACO	May	22	1989
1m 5y	1m 40.3	2	8-12	Good To Firm	KHASSAH	Sep	9	1999
1m 5y	1m 37.2	5	8-12	Good To Firm	ADOBE	Jun	17	2000
1m 2f 46y	2m 05.6	3	9-0	Good To Firm	CONNOISSEUR BAY	May	29	1998
1m 3f 144y	2m 25.74	3	9-0	Hard	TOP OF THE CHARTS	Sep	8	2005
1m 5f 22y	2m 47.2	4	10-0	Firm	FLOWN	Aug	13	1991
2m 1f 34y	3m 43.4	6	7-9	Firm	YAHESKA	Jun	14	2003

BEVERLEY

DISTANCE	TIME	AGE	WEIGHT	GOING	HORSE	DATE	
5f	1m 01.0	2	8-2	Good To Firm	ADDO	July 17	2001
5f	1m 00.1	4	9-5	Firm	PIC UP STICKS	Apr 16	2003
7f 100y	1m 31.1	2	9-0	Firm	MAJAL	July 30	1991
7f 100y	1m 29.5	3	7-8	Firm	WHO'S TEF	July 30	1991
1m 100y	1m 43.3	2	9-0	Firm	ARDEN	Sep 24	1986
1m 100y	1m 42.2	3	8-4	Firm	LEGAL CASE	Jun 14	1989
1m 1f 207y	2m 01.00	3	9-7	Good To Firm	EASTERN ARIA	Aug 29	2009
1m 4f 16y	2m 34.88	6	10-0	Firm	WEE CHARLIE CASTLE	Aug 30	2009
2m 35y	3m 29.5	4	9-2	Good To Firm	RUSHEN RAIDER	Aug 14	1996

BRIGHTON

DISTANCE	TIME	AGE	WEIGHT	GOING	HORSE	DATE	
5f 59y	1m.00.1	2	9-0	Firm	BID FOR BLUE	May 6	1993
5f 59y	59.3 secs	3	8-9	Firm	PLAY HEVER GOLF	May 26	1993
5f 213y	1m 08.1	2	8-9	Firm	SONG MIST	July 16	1996
5f 213y	1m 07.3	3	8-9	Firm	THIRD PARTY	Jun 3	1997
5f 213y	1m 07.3	5	9-1	Good To Firm	BLUNDELL LANE	May 4	2000
7f 214y	1m 32.8	2	9-7	Firm	ASIAN PETE	Oct 3	1989
7f 214y	1m 30.5	5	8-11	Firm	MYSTIC RIDGE	May 27	1999
1m 1f 209y	2m 04.7	2	9-0	Good To Soft	ESTEEMED MASTER	Nov 2	2001
1m 1f 209y	1m 57.2	3	9-0	Firm	GET THE MESSAGE	Apr 30	1984
1m 3f 196y	2m 25.8	4	8-2	Firm	NEW ZEALAND	July 4	1985

CARLISLE

DISTANCE	TIME	AGE	WEIGHT	GOING	HORSE	DATE	
5f	1m 00.1	2	8-5	Firm	LA TORTUGA	Aug 2	1999
5f	59.3 secs	3	8-12	Firm	FRIAR TUCK	July 21	2000
5f 193y	1m 12.45	2	9-6	Good To Firm	MUSICAL GUEST	Sep 11	2005
5f 193y	1m 10.83	4	9-0	Good To Firm	BO MCGINTY	Sep 11	2005
6f 192y	1m 24.3	3	8-9	Good To Firm	MARJURITA	Aug 21	2002
7f 200y	1m 37.34	5	9-7	Good To Firm	HULA BALLEW	Aug 17	2005
1m 1f 61y	1m 53.8	3	9-0	Firm	LITTLE JIMBOB	Jun 14	2004
1m 3f 107y	2m 22.00	7	9-5	Good To Firm	TARTAN GIGHA	Jun 4	2012
1m 3f 206y	2m 29.13	5	9-8	Good To Firm	TEMPSFORD	Sep 19	2005
1m 6f 32y	3m 02.2	6	8-10	Firm	EXPLOSIVE SPEED	May 26	1994

CATTERICK

DISTANCE	TIME	AGE	WEIGHT	GOING	HORSE	DATE	
5f	57.7 secs	2	9-0	Good To Firm	VERDE ALITALIA	Sep 21	1991
5f	57.1 secs	4	8-7	Firm	KABCAST	July 7	1989
5f 212y	1m 11.4	2	9-4	Firm	CAPTAIN NICK	July 11	1978
5f 212y	1m 09.8	9	8-13	Good To Firm	SHARP HAT	May 30	2003
7f	1m 24.1	2	8-11	Firm	LINDA'S FANTASY	Sep 18	1982
7f	1m 22.5	6	8-7	Firm	DIFFERENTIAL	May 31	2003
1m 3f 214y	2m 30.5	3	8-8	Good To Firm	RAHAF	May 30	2003
1m 5f 175y	2m 54.8	3	8-5	Firm	GERYON	May 31	1984
1m 7f 177y	3m 20.8	4	7-11	Firm	BEAN BOY	July 8	1982

CHEPSTOW

DISTANCE	TIME	AGE	WEIGHT	GOING	HORSE	DATE		
5f 16y	57.6 secs	2	8-11	Firm	MICRO LOVE	July	8	1986
5f 16y	56.8 secs	3	8-4	Firm	TORBAY EXPRESS	Sep	15	1979
6f 16y	1m 08.5	2	9-2	Firm	NINJAGO	July	27	2012
6f 16y	1m 08.1	3	9-7	Firm	AMERICA CALLING	Sep	18	2001
7f 16y	1m 20.8	2	9-0	Good To Firm	ROYAL AMARETTO	Sep	12	1996
7f 16y	1m 19.3	3	9-0	Firm	TARANAKI	Sep	18	2001
1m 14y	1m 33.1	2	8-11	Good To Firm	SKI ACADEMY	Aug	28	1995
1m 14y	1m 31.6	3	8-13	Firm	STOLI	Sep	18	2001
1m 2f 36y	2m 04.1	5	8-9	Hard	LEONIDAS	July	5	1983
1m 2f 36y	2m 04.1	5	7-8	Good To Firm	IT'S VARADAN	Sep	9	1989
1m 2f 36y	2m 04.1	3	8-5	Good To Firm	ELA ATHENA	July	23	1999
1m 4f 23y	2m 31.0	3	8-9	Good To Firm	SPRITSAIL	July	13	1989
1m 4f 23y	2m 31.0	7	9-6	Hard	MAINTOP	Aug	27	1984
2m 49y	3m 27.7	4	9-0	Good To Firm	WIZZARD ARTIST	July	1	1989
2m 2f	3m 56.4	5	8-7	Good To Firm	LAFFAH	July	8	2000

CHESTER

DISTANCE	TIME	AGE	WEIGHT	GOING	HORSE	DATE		
5f 16y	59.94 secs	2	9-2	Good To Firm	LEIBA LEIBA	June	26	2010
5f 16y	59.2 secs	3	10-0	Firm	ALTHREY DON	July	10	1964
6f 18y	1m 13.2	2	8-11	Good To Firm	ACE OF PARKES	July	11	1998
6f 18y	1m 12.7	3	8-3	Good To Firm	PLAY HEVER GOLF	May	4	1993
6f 18y	1m 12.7	6	9-2	Good	STACK ROCK	Jun	23	1993
7f 2y	1m 26.2	2	8-4	Good To Firm	BY HAND	Aug	31	1991
7f 2y	1m 23.75	5	8-13	Good To Firm	THREE GRACES	July	9	2005
7f 122y	1m 35.0	2	9-0	Firm	DOUBLE VALUE	Sep	1	1972
7f 122y	1m 30.91	3	8-12	Good To Firm	CUPID'S GLORY	Aug	18	2005
1m 2f 75y	2m 7.15	3	8-8	Good To Firm	STOTSFOLD	Sep	23	2006
1m 3f 79y	2m 22.17	3	8-12	Good To Firm	PERFECT TRUTH	May	6	2009
1m 4f 66y	2m 34.2	3	8-11	Good To Firm	OLD VIC	May	9	1989
1m 5f 89y	2m 45.4	5	8-11	Firm	RAKAPOSHI KING	May	7	1987
1m 7f 195y	3m 24.5	7	7-11	Good To Firm	MOONLIGHT QUEST	July	30	1995
2m 2f 147y	3m 58.59	7	9-2	Good To Firm	GREENWICH MEANTIME	May	9	2007

DONCASTER

DISTANCE	TIME	AGE	WEIGHT	GOING	HORSE	DATE		
5f	58.1 secs	2	9-5	Good To Firm	SAND VIXEN	Sep	11	2009
5f	57.2 secs	6	9-12	Good To Firm	CELTIC MILL	Sep	9	2004
5f 140y	1m 07.2	2	9-0	Good To Firm	CARTOGRAPHY	Jun	29	2003
5f 140y	1m 05.6	9	9-10	Good	HALMAHERA	Sep	8	2004
6f	1m 09.6	2	8-11	Good	CAESAR BEWARE	Sep	8	2004
6f	1m 09.56	3	8-10	Good To Firm	PROCLAIM	May	30	2009
6f 110y	1m 17.22	2	8-3	Good To Firm	SWILLY FERRY	Sep	10	2009
7f	1m 22.6	2	9-1	Good To Firm	LIBRETTIST	Sep	8	2004
7f	1m 21.6	3	9-4	Good To Firm	PASTORAL PURSUITS	Sep	9	2004
1m Str	1m 36.5	2	8-6	Good To Firm	SINGHALESE	Sep	9	2004
1m Rnd	1m 35.4	2	9-0	Good To Firm	PLAYFUL ACT	Sep	9	2004
1m Str	1m 35.52	4	8-9	Good To Firm	DREAM LODGE	July	24	2008
1m Rnd	1m 34.46	4	8-12	Good To Firm	STAYING ON	April	18	2003
1m 2f 60y	2m 13.4	2	8-8	Good	YARD BIRD	Nov	6	1981
1m 2f 60y	2m 04.81	4	8-13	Good To Firm	RED GALA	Sep	12	2007
1m 4f	2m 27.48	3	8-4	Good To Firm	SWIFT ALHAARTH	Sep	10	2011
1m 6f 132y	3m 00.44	3	9-0	Good To Firm	MASKED MARVEL	Sep	10	2011
2m 110y	3m 34.4	4	9-12	Good To Firm	FARSI	Jun	12	1992
2m 2f	3m 48.41	4	9-4	Good To Firm	SEPTIMUS	Sep	14	2007

EPSOM

DISTANCE	TIME	AGE	WEIGHT	GOING	HORSE	DATE		
5f	55.0 secs	2	8-9	Good To Firm	**PRINCE ASLIA**	Jun	9	1995
5f	53.6 secs	4	9-5	Firm	**INDIGENOUS**	Jun	1	1960
6f	1m 07.8	2	8-11	Good To Firm	**SHOWBROOK**	Jun	5	1991
6f	1m 07.21	5	9-13	Good To Firm	**MAC GILLE EOIN**	July	2	2009
7f	1m 21.3	2	8-9	Good To Firm	**RED PEONY**	July	29	2004
7f	1m 20.1	4	8-7	Firm	**CAPISTRANO**	Jun	7	1972
1m 114y	1m 42.8	2	8-5	Good To Firm	**NIGHTSTALKER**	Aug	30	1988
1m 114y	1m 40.7	3	8-6	Good To Firm	**SYLVA HONDA**	Jun	5	1991
1m 2f 18y	2m 03.5	5	7-13	Good	**CROSSBOW**	Jun	7	1967
1m 4f 10y	2m 32.3	3	9-0	Good To Firm	**WORKFORCE**	Jun	5	2010

FFOS LAS

DISTANCE	TIME	AGE	WEIGHT	GOING	HORSE	DATE		
5f	57.06 secs	2	9-3	Good To Firm	**MR MAJEIKA**	May	5	2011
5f	56.35 secs	5	8-8	Good	**HAAJES**	Sep	12	2009
6f	1m 9.93	2	9-0	Good To Firm	**LUNAR DEITY**	May	26	2010
6f	1m 7.80	8	8-4	Good To Firm	**THE JAILER**	May	5	2011
1m	1m 40.61	2	9-0	Good To Firm	**SHARAAYEEN**	Sep	13	2009
1m	1m 37.12	5	9-0	Good To Firm	**ZEBRANO**	May	5	2011
1m 2f	2m 04.85	8	8-12	Good To Firm	**PELHAM CRESCENT**	May	5	2011
1m 4f	2m 32.61	5	9-8	Good To Firm	**LADY OF BURGUNDY**	July	11	2011
1m 6f	2m 58.61	4	9-7	Good To Firm	**LADY ECLAIR**	July	12	2010
2m	3m 29.86	4	9-7	Good	**BLACK OR RED**	July	21	2009

GOODWOOD

DISTANCE	TIME	AGE	WEIGHT	GOING	HORSE	DATE		
5f	57.51 secs	2	9-0	Good	**REQUINTO**	July	26	2011
5f	56.0 secs	5	9-0	Good To Firm	**RUDI'S PET**	July	27	1999
6f	1m 09.8	2	8-11	Good To Firm	**BACHIR**	July	28	1999
6f	1m 09.1	6	9-0	Good To Firm	**TAMAGIN**	Sep	12	2009
7f	1m 24.9	2	8-11	Good To Firm	**EKRAAR**	July	29	1999
7f	1m 23.8	3	8-7	Firm	**BRIEF GLIMPSE**	July	25	1995
1m	1m 37.21	2	9-0	Good	**CALDRA**	Sep	9	2006
1m	1m 35.61	4	8-9	Good To Firm	**SPECTAIT**	Aug	4	2006
1m 1f	1m 52.8	3	9-6	Good	**VENA**	July	27	1995
1m 1f 192y	2m 02.81	3	9-3	Good To Firm	**ROAD TO LOVE**	Aug	3	2006
1m 3f	2m 23.0	3	8-8	Good To Firm	**ASIAN HEIGHTS**	May	22	2001
1m 4f	2m 31.5	3	8-10	Firm	**PRESENTING**	July	25	1995
1m 6f	2m 58.05	4	9-6	Good To Firm	**EASTERN ARIA**	July	29	2010
2m	3m 21.55	5	9-10	Good To Firm	**YEATS**	Aug	3	2006
2m 4f	4m 11.7	3	7-10	Firm	**LUCKY MOON**	Sep	2	1990

HAMILTON

DISTANCE	TIME	AGE	WEIGHT	GOING	HORSE	DATE		
5f 4y	57.95 secs	2	8-8	Good To Firm	**ROSE BLOSSOM**	May	29	2009
6f 5y	1m 10.0	2	8-12	Good To Firm	**BREAK THE CODE**	Aug	24	1999
6f 5y	1m 09.3	4	8-7	Firm	**MARCUS GAME**	July	11	1974
1m 65y	1m 45.8	2	8-11	Firm	**HOPEFUL SUBJECT**	Sep	24	1973
1m 65y	1m 42.7	6	7-7	Firm	**CRANLEY**	Sep	25	1972
1m 1f 36y	1m 53.6	5	9-6	Good To Firm	**REGENT'S SECRET**	Aug	10	2005
1m 3f 16y	2m 19.32	3	8-1	Good To Firm	**CAPTAIN WEBB**	May	16	2008
1m 4f 17y	2m 30.52	5	9-10	Good To Firm	**RECORD BREAKER**	Jun	10	2009
1m 5f 9y	2m 45.1	6	9-6	Firm	**MENTALASANYTHIN**	Jun	14	1995

HAYDOCK

DISTANCE	TIME	AGE	WEIGHT	GOING	HORSE	DATE		
5f (Inner)	56.39 secs	5	9-4	Firm	BATED BREATH	May	26	2012
5f	58.56 secs	2	8-2	Good To Firm	BARRACUDA BOY	Aug	11	2012
5f	57.15 secs	3	8-11	Good To Firm	FLEETING SPIRIT	Sep	3	2005
6f	1m 09.9	4	9-0	Good To Firm	IKTAMAL	Sep	7	1996
7f	1m 27.62	2	9-4	Good	TICKLE TIME	Aug	10	2012
7f	1m 26.27	4	9-1	Good To Firm	ZACYNTHUS	Sept	7	2012
1m 30y	1m 40.6	2	8-12	Good	BESIEGE	Sep	7	1996
1m	1m 39.02	3	8-11	Good	LADY MACDUFF	Aug	10	2012
1m 2f 95y	2m 08.25	3	9-0	Good To Firm	PRUSSIAN	Sept	7	2012
1m 3f 200y	2m 25.53	4	8-12	Good To Firm	NUMBER THEORY	May	24	2012
1m 6f	2m 55.20	5	9-9	Good To Firm	HUFF AND PUFF	Sep	7	2012
2m 45y	3m 27.0	4	8-13	Firm	PRINCE OF PEACE	May	26	1984

KEMPTON (A.W)

DISTANCE	TIME	AGE	WEIGHT	GOING	HORSE	DATE		
5f	58.96	2	8-6	Standard	GLAMOROUS SPIRIT	Nov	28	2008
5f	58.33	3	9-1	Standard	EXCEEDANCE	May	7	2012
6f	1m 11.44	2	9-5	Standard	SIGNS IN THE SAND	Oct	6	2010
6f	1m 10.77	7	9-7	Standard	CAPONE	Nov	1	2012
7f	1m 23.95	2	8-10	Standard	TAMARKUZ	Oct	10	2012
7f	1m 23.29	5	8-11	Standard	PRIMAEVAL	Nov	16	2011
1m	1m 37.50	2	9-4	Standard	I'M BACK	Oct	3	2012
1m	1m 35.73	3	8-9	Standard	WESTERN ARISTOCRAT	Sep	5	2011
1m	1m 36.58	6	9-2	Standard	RIGGINS	Nov	27	2010
1m 2f	2m 3.77	6	8-13	Standard	KANDIDATE	Mar	29	2008
1m 3f	2m 16.98	5	9-6	Standard	IRISH FLAME	Nov	10	2011
1m 4f	2m 28.99	6	9-3	Standard	SPRING OF FAME	Nov	7	2012
2m	3m 21.50	4	8-12	Standard	COLOUR VISION	May	2	2012

LEICESTER

DISTANCE	TIME	AGE	WEIGHT	GOING	HORSE	DATE		
5f 2y	58.4 secs	2	9-0	Firm	CUTTING BLADE	Jun	9	1986
5f 2y	57.85 secs	5	9-5	Good To Firm	THE JOBBER	Sep	18	2006
5f 218y	1m 09.99	2	9-0	Good	EL MANATI	Aug	1	2012
5f 218y	1m 09.12	6	8-12	Good To Firm	PETER ISLAND	Apr	25	2009
7f 9y	1m 22.6	2	9-0	Good To Firm	MARIE DE MEDICI	Oct	6	2009
7f 9y	1m 20.8	3	8-7	Firm	FLOWER BOWL	Jun	9	1986
1m 60y	1m 44.05	2	8-11	Good To Firm	CONGRESSIONAL	Sep	6	2005
1m 60y	1m 41.89	5	9-7	Good To Firm	VAINGLORY	Jun	18	2009
1m 1f 218y	2m 05.3	2	9-1	Good To Firm	WINDSOR CASTLE	Oct	14	1996
1m 1f 218y	2m 02.4	3	8-11	Firm	EFFIGY	Nov	4	1985
1m 1f 218y	2m 02.4	4	9-6	Good To Firm	LADY ANGHARAD	Jun	18	2000
1m 3f 183y	2m 27.1	5	8-12	Good To Firm	MURGHEM	Jun	18	2000

LINGFIELD (TURF)

DISTANCE	TIME	AGE	WEIGHT	GOING	HORSE	DATE		
5f	57.07 secs	2	9-0	Good To Firm	QUITE A THING	June	11	2011
5f	56.09 secs	3	9-4	Good To Firm	PERFECT TRIBUTE	May	7	2011
6f	1m 08.36	2	8-12	Good To Firm	FOLLY BRIDGE	Sep	8	2009
6f	1m 08.2	6	9-10	Firm	AL AMEAD	July	2	1986
7f	1m 21.3	2	7-6	Firm	MANDAV	Oct	3	1980
7f	1m 20.1	3	8-7	Good To Firm	ZELAH	May	13	1998
7f 140y	1m 29.32	2	9-3	Good To Firm	DUNDONNELL	Aug	4	2012
7f 140y	1m 26.7	3	8-6	Good To Firm	HIAAM	Jul	11	1987
1m 1f	1m 52.4	4	9-2	Good To Firm	QUANDARY	July	15	1995
1m 2f	2m 04.6	3	9-3	Firm	USRAN	July	15	1989
1m 3f 106y	2m 23.9	3	8-5	Firm	NIGHT-SHIRT	July	14	1990
1m 6f	2m 59.1	5	9-5	Firm	IBN BEY	July	1	1989
2m	3m 23.7	3	9-5	Good To Firm	LAURIES CRUSADOR	Aug	13	1988

LINGFIELD (A.W)

DISTANCE	TIME	AGE	WEIGHT	GOING	HORSE	DATE		
5f	58.29 secs	2	8-8	Standard	SMOKEY RYDER	Dec	14	2008
5f	57.26 secs	8	8-12	Standard	MAGIC GLADE	Feb	27	2007
6f	1m 09.99	2	8-12	Standard	SWISS DIVA	Nov	19	2008
6f	1m 09.61	6	9-0	Standard	EXCUSEZ MOI	Feb	23	2008
6f	1m 09.61	4	9-5	Standard	JACONET	Sep	4	2009
7f	1m 23.68	2	8-4	Standard	YOUNG DOTTIE	Oct	21	2008
7f	1m 22.7	6	9-12	Standard	VORTEX	Apr	9	2005
1m	1m 36.33	2	9-7	Standard	YARROOM	Dec	5	2012
1m	1m 34.77	4	9-3	Standard	BAHARAH	Oct	30	2008
1m 2f	2m 01.79	5	9-0	Standard	CUSOON	Feb	24	2007
1m 4f	2m 27.97	4	9-3	Standard	MIDSUMMER SUN	Apr	14	2012
1m 5f	2m 41.08	3	8-8	Standard	MISCHIEF MAKER	Oct	30	2008
2m	3m 20.07	4	9-0	Standard	NIGHT CRUISE	Aug	8	1992

MUSSELBURGH

DISTANCE	TIME	AGE	WEIGHT	GOING	HORSE	DATE		
5f	57.7 secs	2	8-2	Firm	ARASONG	May	16	1994
5f	57.3 secs	3	8-12	Firm	CORUNNA	Jun	3	2000
7f 30y	1m 27.46	2	8-8	Good	DURHAM REFLECTION	Sep	14	2009
7f 30y	1m 27.1	5	8-12	Good	DIAMOND DECORUM	Jun	18	2001
1m	1m 40.3	2	8-12	Good To Firm	SUCCESSION	Sep	26	2004
1m	1m 36.83	3	9-5	Good To Firm	GINGER JACK	July	13	2010
1m 1f	1m 50.42	8	8-11	Good To Firm	DHAULAR DHAR	Sep	3	2010
1m 4f	2m 33.7	3	9-11	Firm	ALEXANDRINE	Jun	26	2000
1m 4f 100y	2m 36.80	3	8-3	Good To Firm	HARRIS TWEED	Jun	5	2010
1m 5f	2m 47.51	6	9-11	Good To Firm	DIMASHQ	July	31	2008
1m 6f	2m 59.2	3	9-7	Firm	FORUM CHRIS	July	3	2000
2m	3m 28.1	3	8-1	Good To Firm	WARRING KINGDOM	Sep	13	1999

NEWBURY

DISTANCE	TIME	AGE	WEIGHT	GOING	HORSE	DATE		
5f 34y	59.1 secs	2	8-6	Good To Firm	SUPERSTAR LEO	July	22	2000
5f 34y	59.2 secs	3	9-5	Good To Firm	THE TRADER	Aug	18	2001
6f 8y	1m 11.07	2	8-4	Good To Firm	BAHATI	May	30	2009
6f 8y	1m 09.42	3	8-11	Good To Firm	NOTA BENE	May	13	2005
7f	1m 24.1	2	8-11	Good To Firm	HAAFHD	Aug	15	2003
7f	1m 21.5	3	8-4	Good To Firm	THREE POINTS	July	21	2000
1m	1m 37.5	2	9-1	Good To Firm	WINGED CUPID	Sep	16	2005
1m	1m 33.59	6	9-0	Firm	RAKTI	May	14	2005
1m 1f	1m 49.6	3	8-0	Good To Firm	HOLTYE	May	21	1995
1m 2f 6y	2m 1.2	3	8-7	Good To Firm	WALL STREET	July	20	1996
1m 3f 5y	2m 16.5	3	8-9	Good To Firm	GRANDERA	Sep	22	2001
1m 4f 5y	2m 28.26	4	9-7	Good To Firm	AZAMOUR	Jul	23	2005
1m 5f 61y	2m 44.9	5	10-0	Good To Firm	MYSTIC HILL	July	20	1996
2m	3m 25.4	8	9-12	Good To Firm	MOONLIGHT QUEST	July	19	1996

NEWCASTLE

DISTANCE	TIME	AGE	WEIGHT	GOING	HORSE	DATE		
5f	58.8 secs	2	9-0	Firm	ATLANTIC VIKING	Jun	4	1997
5f	58.0 secs	4	9-2	Firm	PRINCESS OBERON	July	23	1994
6f	1m 11.98	2	9-3	Good	PEARL ARCH	Sep	6	2010
6f	1m 10.58	4	9-9	Good To Firm	JONNY MUDBALL	June	26	2010
7f	1m 24.2	2	9-0	Good To Firm	ISCAN	Aug	31	1998
7f	1m 23.3	4	9-2	Good To Firm	QUIET VENTURE	Aug	31	1998
1m 3y	1m 37.1	2	8-3	Good To Firm	HOH STEAMER	Aug	31	1998
1m 3y	1m 37.3	3	8-8	Good To Firm	IT'S MAGIC	May	27	1999
1m 1f 9y	2m 03.2	2	8-13	Soft	RESPONSE	Oct	30	1993
1m 1f 9y	1m 58.4	3	8-8	Good To Firm	INTRODUCING	Aug	6	2003
1m 2f 32y	2m 06.5	3	8-11	Firm	MISSIONARY RIDGE	July	29	1990
1m 4f 93y	2m 37.3	5	8-12	Firm	RETENDER	Jun	25	1994
1m 6f 97y	3m 06.4	3	9-6	Good To Firm	ONE OFF	Aug	6	2003
2m 19y	3m 24.3	4	8-10	Good	FAR CRY	Jun	26	1999

NEWMARKET (ROWLEY MILE)

DISTANCE	TIME	AGE	WEIGHT	GOING	HORSE	DATE		
5f	58.76 secs	2	8-5	Good To Firm	VALIANT ROMEO	Oct	3	2002
5f	56.8 secs	6	9-2	Good To Firm	LOCHSONG	Apr	30	1994
6f	1m 09.56	2	8-12	Good To Firm	BUSHRANGER	Oct	3	2008
7f	1m 22.39	2	8-12	Good To Firm	ASHRAM	Oct	2	2008
7f	1m 22.18	3	9-0	Good To Firm	CODEMASTER	May	14	2011
1m	1m 35.67	2	8-12	Good	STEELER	Sep	29	2012
1m	1m 34.07	4	9-0	Good To Firm	EAGLE MOUNTAIN	Oct	3	2008
1m 1f	1m 47.26	5	8-12	Good To Firm	MANDURO	Apr	19	2007
1m 2f	2m 04.6	2	9-4	Good	HIGHLAND CHIEFTAIN	Nov	2	1985
1m 2f	2m 00.13	3	8-12	Good	NEW APPROACH	Oct	18	2008
1m 4f	2m 26.07	3	8-9	Good To Firm	MOHEDIAN LADY	Sept	22	2011
1m 6f	2m 51.59	3	8-7	Good	ART EYES	Sep	29	2005
2m	3m 18.64	5	9-6	Good To Firm	TIMES UP	Sept	22	2011
2m 2f	3m 47.5	3	7-12	Hard	WHITEWAY	Oct	15	1947

NEWMARKET (JULY COURSE)

DISTANCE	TIME	AGE	WEIGHT	GOING	HORSE	DATE		
5f	58.5 secs	2	8-10	Good	SEDUCTRESS	July	10	1990
5f	56.09 secs	6	9-11	Good	BORDERLESCOTT	Aug	22	2008
6f	1m 10.35	2	8-11	Good	ELNAWIN	Aug	22	2008
6f	1m 09.5	3	8-13	Good To Firm	STRAVINSKY	July	8	1999
7f	1m 23.57	2	9-5	Good To Firm	LIGHT UP MY LIFE	Aug	18	2012
7f	1m 22.5	3	9-7	Firm	HO LENG	July	9	1998
1m	1m 37.47	2	8-13	Good	WHIPPERS LOVE	Aug	28	2009
1m	1m 35.5	3	8-6	Good To Firm	LOVERS KNOT	July	8	1998
1m 2f	2m 00.9	4	9-3	Good To Firm	ELHAYQ	May	1	1999
1m 4f	2m 25.11	3	8-11	Good	LUSH LASHES	Aug	22	2008
1m 6f 175y	3m 04.2	3	8-5	Good	ARRIVE	July	11	2001
2m 24y	3m 20.2	7	9-10	Good	YORKSHIRE	July	11	2001

NOTTINGHAM

DISTANCE	TIME	AGE	WEIGHT	GOING	HORSE	DATE		
5f 13y	57.9 secs	2	8-9	Firm	HOH MAGIC	May	13	1994
5f 13y	57.6 secs	6	9-2	Good To Firm	CATCH THE CAT	May	14	2005
6f 15y	1m 11.4	2	8-11	Firm	JAMEELAPI	Aug	8	1983
6f 15y	1m 10.0	4	9-2	Firm	AJANAC	Aug	8	1988
1m 75y	1m 45.23	2	9-0	Good	TACTFULLY	Sept	28	2011
1m 75y	1m 42.25	5	9-1	Good To Firm	RIO DE LA PLATA	June	2	2010
1m 2f 50y	2m 9.54	4	9-12	Good To Firm	GENEVA GEYSER	July	3	2010
1m 2f 50y (I)	2m 10.61	6	8-13	Firm	SHAVANSKY	April	27	2010
1m 6f 15y	2m 57.8	3	8-10	Firm	BUSTER JO	Oct	1	1985
2m 9y	3m 25.25	3	9-5	Good	BULWARK	Sep	27	2005

PONTEFRACT

DISTANCE	TIME	AGE	WEIGHT	GOING	HORSE	DATE		
5f	1m 01.1	2	9-0	Firm	GOLDEN BOUNTY	Sep	20	2001
5f	1m 00.8	4	8-9	Firm	BLUE MAEVE	Sep	29	2004
6f	1m 14.0	2	9-3	Firm	FAWZI	Sep	6	1983
6f	1m 12.6	2	7-13	Firm	MERRY ONE	Aug	29	1970
1m 4y	1m 42.8	2	9-13	Firm	STAR SPRAY	Sep	6	1970
1m 4y	1m 41.3	7	8-9	Firm	NIGRASINE	Sep	20	2001
1m 2f 6y	2m 12.8	2	9-0	Good To Firm	WARBROOK	Oct	2	1995
1m 2f 6y	2m 08.2	4	7-8	Hard	HAPPY HECTOR	July	9	1979
1m 4f 8y	2m 33.72	3	8-7	Firm	AJAAN	Aug	8	2007
2m 1f 22y	3m 40.67	4	8-7	Good To Firm	PARADISE FLIGHT	Jun	6	2005
2m 1f 216y	3m 51.1	3	8-8	Firm	KUDZ	Sep	9	1986
2m 5f 122y	4m 47.8	4	8-4	Firm	PHYSICAL	May	14	1984

REDCAR

DISTANCE	TIME	AGE	WEIGHT	GOING	HORSE	DATE		
5f	56.9 secs	2	9-0	Firm	MISTER JOEL	Oct	24	1995
5f	56.01 secs	10	9-3	Firm	HENRY HALL	Sep	20	2006
6f	1m 08.8	2	8-3	Good To Firm	OBE GOLD	Oct	2	2004
6f	1m 08.6	3	9-2	Good To Firm	SIZZLING SAGA	Jun	21	1991
7f	1m 21.28	2	9-3	Firm	KAROO BLUE	Sep	20	2006
7f	1m 21.0	3	9-1	Firm	EMPTY QUARTER	Oct	3	1995
1m	1m 34.37	2	9-0	Firm	MASTERSHIP	Sep	20	2006
1m	1m 32.42	4	10-0	Firm	NANTON	Sep	20	2006
1m 1f	1m 52.4	2	9-0	Firm	SPEAR	Sep	13	2004
1m 1f	1m 48.5	5	8-12	Firm	MELLOTTIE	July	25	1990
1m 2f	2m 10.1	2	8-11	Good	ADDING	Nov	10	1989
1m 2f	2m 01.4	5	9-2	Firm	ERADICATE	May	28	1990
1m 3f	2m 17.2	3	8-9	Firm	PHOTO CALL	Aug	7	1990
1m 6f 19y	2m 59.81	4	9-1	Good To Firm	ESPRIT DE CORPS	Sep	11	2006
2m 4y	3m 24.9	3	9-3	Good To Firm	SUBSONIC	Oct	8	1991

RIPON

DISTANCE	TIME	AGE	WEIGHT	GOING	HORSE	DATE		
5f	57.8 secs	2	8-8	Firm	SUPER ROCKY	July	5	1991
5f	57.6 secs	5	8-5	Good	BROADSTAIRS BEAUTY	May	21	1995
6f	1m 10.9	2	8-11	Good	KAHIR ALMAYDAN	Aug	28	1995
6f	1m 09.8	4	9-8	Good To Firm	TADEO	Aug	16	1997
6f	1m 09.8	5	7-10	Firm	QUOIT	July	23	1966
1m	1m 39.79	2	8-6	Good	TOP JARO	Sep	24	2005
1m	1m 36.62	4	8-11	Good To Firm	GRANSTON	Aug	29	2005
1m 1f	1m 50.4	3	9-2	Good To Firm	BOLD WORDS	Apr	9	1997
1m 2f	2m 02.6	3	9-4	Firm	SWIFT SWORD	July	20	1990
1m 4f 10y	2m 31.40	4	8-8	Good To Firm	DANDINO	Apr	16	2011
2m	3m 27.07	5	9-12	Good To Firm	GREENWICH MEANTIME	Aug	30	2005

SALISBURY

DISTANCE	TIME	AGE	WEIGHT	GOING	HORSE	DATE		
5f	59.3 secs	2	9-0	Good To Firm	AJIGOLO	May	12	2005
5f	59.4 secs	3	8-11	Firm	BELLSABANGING	May	5	1993
6f	1m 12.1	2	8-0	Good To Firm	PARISIAN LADY	Jun	10	1997
6f	1m 11.09	3	9-0	Firm	L'AMI LOUIS	May	1	2011
6f 212y	1m 25.9	2	9-0	Firm	MORE ROYAL	Jun	29	1995
6f 212y	1m 24.91	3	9-4	Firm	CHILWORTH LAD	May	1	2011
1m	1m 40.48	2	8-13	Firm	CHOIR MASTER	Sep	17	2002
1m	1m 38.29	3	8-7	Good To Firm	LAYMAN	Aug	11	2005
1m 1f 198y	2m 04.81	3	8-5	Good To Firm	PRIMEVERE	Aug	10	2011
1m 4f	2m 31.6	3	9-5	Good To Firm	ARRIVE	Jun	27	2001
1m 6f 21y	3m 0.84	8	8-12	Firm	KANGAROO COURT	May	24	2012

SANDOWN

DISTANCE	TIME	AGE	WEIGHT	GOING	HORSE	DATE		
5f 6y	59.4 secs	2	9-3	Firm	TIMES TIME	July	22	1982
5f 6y	58.8 secs	6	8-9	Good To Firm	PALACEGATE TOUCH	Sep	17	1996
7f 16y	1m 26.56	2	9-0	Good To Firm	RAVEN'S PASS	Sep	1	2007
7f 16y	1m 26.3	3	9-0	Firm	MAWSUFF	Jun	14	1983
1m 14y	1m 41.1	2	8-11	Firm	REFERENCE POINT	Sep	23	1986
1m 14y	1m 39.0	3	8-8	Firm	LINDA'S FANTASY	Aug	19	1983
1m 1f	1m 54.6	2	8-8	Good To Firm	FRENCH PRETENDER	Sep	20	1988
1m 1f	1m 52.4	7	9-3	Good To Firm	BOURGAINVILLE	Aug	11	2005
1m 2f 7y	2m 02.1	4	8-11	Firm	KALAGLOW	May	31	1982
1m 6f	2m 56.9	4	8-7	Good To Firm	LADY ROSANNA	July	19	1989
2m 78y	3m 29.86	4	9-0	Good To Firm	KING OF WANDS	July	3	2010

SOUTHWELL (TURF)

DISTANCE	TIME	AGE	WEIGHT	GOING	HORSE	DATE		
6f	1m 15.03	2	9-3	Good	TREPA	Sep	6	2006
6f	1m 13.48	4	8-10	Good	PARIS BELL	Sep	6	2006
7f	1m 27.56	2	9-7	Good	HART OF GOLD	Sep	6	2006
7f	1m 25.95	3	9-0	Good	AEROPLANE	Sep	6	2006
1m 2f	2m 7.47	3	8-11	Good To Firm	DESERT AUTHORITY	Sep	7	2006
1m 3f	2m 20.13	4	9-12	Good	SANCHI	Sep	6	2006
1m 4f	2m 34.4	5	9-3	Good To Firm	CORN LILY	Aug	10	1991
2m	3m 34.1	5	9-1	Good To Firm	TRIPLICATE	Sep	20	1991

SOUTHWELL (A.W)

DISTANCE	TIME	AGE	WEIGHT	GOING	HORSE	DATE		
5f	57.85 secs	2	9-3	Standard	ARCTIC FEELING	Mar	31	2010
5f	56.80 secs	5	9-7	Standard	GHOSTWING	Jan	3	2012
6f	1m 14.0	2	8-5	Standard	PANALO	Nov	8	1989
6f	1m 13.3	3	9-2	Standard	RAMBO EXPRESS	Dec	18	1990
7f	1m 27.1	2	8-12	Standard	WINGED ICARUS	Aug	28	2012
7f	1m 26.8	5	8-4	Standard	AMENABLE	Dec	13	1990
1m	1m 38.0	2	8-9	Standard	ALPHA RASCAL	Nov	13	1990
1m	1m 38.0	2	8-10	Standard	ANDREW'S FIRST	Dec	30	1989
1m	1m 37.2	3	8-6	Standard	VALIRA	Nov	3	1990
1m 3f	2m 21.5	4	9-7	Standard	TEMPERING	Dec	5	1990
1m 4f	2m 33.9	4	9-12	Standard	FAST CHICK	Nov	8	1989
1m 6f	3m 01.6	3	7-7	Standard	QUALITAIR AVIATOR	Dec	1	1989
1m 6f	3m 01.6	3	7-8	Standard	EREVNON	Dec	29	1990
2m	3m 37.6	9	8-12	Standard	OLD HUBERT	Dec	5	1990

THIRSK

DISTANCE	TIME	AGE	WEIGHT	GOING	HORSE	DATE		
5f	57.2 secs	2	9-7	Good To Firm	PROUD BOAST	Aug	5	2000
5f	56.1 secs	7	8-0	Firm	SIR SANDROVITCH	Jun	26	2003
6f	1m 09.2	2	9-6	Good To Firm	WESTCOURT MAGIC	Aug	25	1995
6f	1m 08.8	6	9-4	Firm	JOHAYRO	July	23	1999
7f	1m 23.7	2	8-9	Firm	COURTING	July	23	1999
7f	1m 22.8	4	8-5	Firm	SILVER HAZE	May	21	1988
1m	1m 37.9	2	9-0	Good To Firm	SUNDAY SYMPHONY	Sep	4	2004
1m	1m 34.8	4	8-13	Firm	YEARSLEY	May	5	1990
1m 4f	2m 29.9	5	9-12	Firm	GALLERY GOD	Jun	4	2001
2m	3m 22.3	3	8-10	Firm	TOMASCHEK	Aug	1	1964

WARWICK

DISTANCE	TIME	AGE	WEIGHT	GOING	HORSE	DATE		
5f	57.95 secs	2	8-9	Good To Firm	**AMOUR PROPRE**	Jun	26	2008
5f	57.8 secs	5	9-4	Good To Firm	**ANOTHER EPISODE**	Aug	29	1994
5f 110y	1m 03.6	5	8-6	Good To Firm	**DIZZY IN THE HEAD**	Jun	27	2004
6f	1m 11.22	2	9-3	Good To Firm	**HURRICANE HYMNBOOK**	Sep	15	2007
6f	1m 09.44	5	8-12	Good To Firm	**PETER ISLAND**	Jun	26	2008
7f 26y	1m 22.9	2	9-3	Good To Firm	**COUNTRY RAMBLER**	Jun	20	2004
7f 26y	1m 21.2	3	8-11	Good To Firm	**LUCKY SPIN**	Jun	19	2004
1m 22y	1m 37.1	3	8-11	Firm	**ORINOCOVSKY**	Jun	26	2002
1m 2f 188y	2m 14.98	4	8-12	Good To Firm	**RONALDSAY**	Jun	16	2008
1m 4f 134y	2m 39.5	3	8-13	Good To Firm	**MAIMANA**	Jun	22	2002
1m 6f 135y	3m 07.5	3	9-7	Good To Firm	**BURMA BAY**	July	2	1999
2m 39y	3m 30.6	5	8-1	Good To Firm	**RENAISSANCE LADY**	Jun	27	2001

WINDSOR

DISTANCE	TIME	AGE	WEIGHT	GOING	HORSE	DATE		
5f 10y	58.69 secs	2	9-0	Good To Firm	**CHARLES THE GREAT**	May	23	2011
5f 10y	58.08 secs	5	8-13	Good To Firm	**TAURUS TWINS**	April	4	2011
6f	1m 10.5	2	9-5	Good To Firm	**CUBISM**	Aug	17	1998
6f	1m 09.89	4	9-0	Good To Firm	**BATED BREATH**	May	23	2011
1m 67y	1m 42.46	2	8-9	Good To Firm	**TIGER CUB**	Oct	10	2011
1m 67y	1m 40.19	4	9-4	Good	**NATIONALISM**	June	25	2011
1m 2f 7y	2m 03.0	3	9-1	Firm	**MOOMBA MASQUERADE**	May	19	1990
1m 3f 135y	2m 21.5	3	9-2	Firm	**DOUBLE FLORIN**	May	19	1980

WOLVERHAMPTON (A.W)

DISTANCE	TIME	AGE	WEIGHT	GOING	HORSE	DATE		
5f 20y	1m 00.96	2	9-3	Standard	**MOVIESTA**	Sept	17	2012
5f 20y	59.79 secs	7	9-7	Standard	**WOOLFALL SOVEREIGN**	Jan	1	2013
5f 216y	1m 12.61	2	9-0	Standard To Fast	**PRIME DEFENDER**	Nov	8	2006
7f 32y	1m 27.7	2	9-5	Standard	**BILLY DANE**	Aug	14	2006
7f 32y	1m 26.42	7	8-12	Standard	**PRIME EXHIBIT**	Sept	8	2012
1m 141y	1m 47.68	2	9-3	Standard	**GLORY CITY**	Dec	26	2012
1m 141y	1m 46.48	3	8-9	Standard	**GITANO HERNANDO**	Sep	17	2009
1m 1f 103y	2m 00.74	2	8-4	Standard	**LUCY BEE**	Dec	3	2012
1m 1f 103y	1m 57.34	4	8-13	Standard	**BAHAR SHUMAAL**	Oct	28	2006
1m 4f 50y	2m 34.75	5	8-13	Standard To Fast	**FANTOCHE**	May	3	2007
1m 5f 194y	2m 58.68	3	9-2	Standard	**INSTRUMENTALIST**	Oct	9	2012
2m 119y	3m 35.85	5	8-11	Standard To Fast	**MARKET WATCHER**	Nov	21	2006

YARMOUTH

DISTANCE	TIME	AGE	WEIGHT	GOING	HORSE	DATE		
5f 43y	1m 00.4	2	8-6	Good To Firm	EBBA	July	26	1999
5f 43y	1m 00.2	3	8-11	Firm	CHARM BIRD	Sep	15	1988
6f 3y	1m 10.4	2	9-0	Firm	LANCHESTER	Aug	15	1988
6f 3y	1m 10.0	3	8-10	Good To Firm	TIPSY CREEK	Aug	10	1997
7f 3y	1m 22.2	2	9-0	Good To Firm	WARRSHAN	Sep	14	1988
7f 3y	1m 22.12	4	9-4	Good To Firm	GLENBUCK	Apr	26	2007
1m 3y	1m 36.3	2	8-2	Good To Firm	OUTRUN	Sep	15	1988
1m 3y	1m 33.9	3	8-8	Firm	BONNE ETOILE	Jun	27	1995
1m 1f	1m 52.00	3	9-5	Good To Firm	TOUCH GOLD	July	5	2012
1m 2f 21y	2m 02.83	3	8-9	Firm	REUNITE	July	18	2006
1m 3f 101y	2m 23.1	3	8-9	Firm	RAHIL	July	1	1993
1m 6f 17y	2m 57.8	3	8-2	Good To Firm	BARAKAT	July	24	1990
2m	3m 26.7	4	8-2	Good To Firm	ALHESN	July	26	1999

YORK

DISTANCE	TIME	AGE	WEIGHT	GOING	HORSE	DATE		
5f 3y	57.33 secs	2	9-0	Good To Firm	STAR ROVER	Aug	19	2009
5f 3y	56.2 secs	3	9-9	Good To Firm	OASIS DREAM	Aug	21	2003
5f 89y	1m 2.31	3	9-3	Good To Firm	EL VIENTO	Sept	5	2010
5f 89y	1m 2.31	6	9-5	Good To Firm	BARNEY MCGREW	Aug	19	2009
6f	1m 9.28	2	8-12	Good To Firm	SHOWCASING	Aug	19	2009
6f	1m 08.23	3	8-11	Good To Firm	MINCE	Sept	9	2012
7f	1m 22.45	2	9-0	Good To Firm	ELUSIVE PIMPERNEL	Aug	18	2009
7f	1m 21.83	4	9-8	Good To Firm	DIMENSION	July	28	2012
1m	1m 36.24	3	9-2	Good To Firm	CAPPONI	Jul	10	2010
1m 205y	1m 52.4	2	8-1	Good To Firm	ORAL EVIDENCE	Oct	6	1988
1m 208y	1m 46.76	5	9-8	Good To Firm	ECHO OF LIGHT	Sep	5	2007
1m 2f 88y	2m 05.29	3	8-11	Good To Firm	SEA THE STARS	Aug	18	2009
1m 3f 198y	2m 27.4	4	9-4	Good To Firm	ISLINGTON	Aug	20	2003
1m 6f	2m 54.96	4	9-0	Good To Firm	TACTIC	May	22	2010
1m 7f 195y	3m 18.4	3	8-0	Good To Firm	DAM BUSTERS	Aug	16	1988
2m 88y	3m 30.55	5	9-0	Good To Firm	HEROSTATUS	July	28	2012

Raceform
I N T E R A C T I V E

Compile your own horse comments, ratings and lists to follow and form your OWN opinion.

TOP FLAT JOCKEYS IN BRITAIN 2012

(JANUARY 1ST - DECEMBER 31ST)

W-R	%	JOCKEY	2ND	3RD	TOTAL PRIZE	WIN PRIZE
188-1138	17%	JOE FANNING	150	118	1,146,427	806,790
177-859	21%	RICHARD HUGHES	142	92	2,137,991	1,411,480
159-1531	10%	LUKE MORRIS	188	175	915,459	530,000
148-848	17%	JIM CROWLEY	102	81	1,215,114	869,531
145-982	15%	SILVESTRE DE SOUSA	118	125	1,231,978	774,103
130-696	19%	WILLIAM BUICK	85	99	3,514,962	2,093,267
122-801	15%	PAUL HANAGAN	92	101	1,853,871	1,247,934
119-747	16%	ADAM KIRBY	112	91	834,817	525,542
116-603	19%	RYAN MOORE	87	81	2,461,588	1,455,553
108-893	12%	GRAHAM LEE	111	87	918,456	502,818
103-691	15%	JAMIE SPENCER	98	98	1,338,452	786,979
98-751	13%	ROBERT WINSTON	94	73	617,567	401,789
93-553	17%	RICHARD KINGSCOTE	70	61	650,164	399,796
92-785	12%	HAYLEY TURNER	88	100	704,460	346,743
87-651	13%	KIEREN FALLON	72	75	1,698,312	1,136,234
85-628	14%	GEORGE BAKER	78	69	714,015	469,059
80-580	14%	JAMES DOYLE	61	64	1,074,382	503,641
78-558	14%	FRANNY NORTON	58	74	838,827	619,707
76-488	16%	DANIEL TUDHOPE	67	56	700,842	528,293
76-618	12%	TOM QUEALLY	58	55	2,718,782	2,267,141
76-654	12%	NEIL CALLAN	92	79	867,515	511,430
76-940	8%	TOM EAVES	62	103	415,354	229,660
74-656	11%	MARTIN HARLEY	66	78	719,530	371,881
71-665	11%	CHRIS CATLIN	56	63	327,323	200,801
71-665	11%	PAUL MULRENNAN	67	79	501,445	293,965
70-733	10%	SHANE KELLY	73	80	463,108	231,229
69-704	10%	DAVID PROBERT	89	67	496,690	307,579
68-545	12%	IAN MONGAN	48	58	530,467	252,446
67-471	14%	FREDERIK TYLICKI	57	49	419,042	289,409
66-414	16%	MICKAEL BARZALONA	49	51	1,234,635	887,861
66-620	11%	JIMMY FORTUNE	87	73	1,221,923	468,039
64-749	9%	WILLIAM CARSON	78	83	437,156	245,082
63-539	12%	GRAHAM GIBBONS	50	54	399,245	245,077
63-633	10%	DANE O'NEILL	74	55	429,990	254,106
60-539	11%	PHILLIP MAKIN	47	50	653,351	517,152
59-558	11%	TONY HAMILTON	65	48	567,479	350,895
56-503	11%	TED DURCAN	63	50	710,447	215,625
54-425	13%	ANDREA ATZENI	46	33	325,850	214,181
54-625	9%	MARTIN LANE	63	79	340,389	191,095
52-605	9%	FERGUS SWEENEY	53	56	245,728	142,022
51-377	14%	PAT DOBBS	33	52	733,708	572,746
51-398	13%	FRANKIE DETTORI	63	54	1,876,687	818,307
50-729	7%	LIAM KENIRY	75	67	353,462	195,256
48-472	10%	RAUL DA SILVA	48	56	225,665	156,196
47-481	10%	DARREN EGAN	51	54	316,766	217,955
46-426	11%	AMY RYAN	43	49	341,607	194,009
45-458	10%	EDDIE AHERN	42	52	548,339	322,103
43-423	10%	CATHY GANNON	33	47	232,220	140,534
42-483	9%	BARRY MCHUGH	47	61	291,423	167,566
42-535	8%	MARTIN DWYER	47	53	355,976	143,674

TOP FLAT TRAINERS IN BRITAIN 2012

TRAINER	LEADING HORSE	W-R	2ND	3RD	4TH	TOTAL PRIZE	WIN PRIZE
JOHN GOSDEN	Nathaniel	119-629	101	101	74	3,739,407	2,150,284
A P O'BRIEN	Camelot	13-73	7	12	6	3,554,170	2,677,793
RICHARD HANNON	Victrix Ludorum	218-1367	194	153	131	2,821,469	1,767,369
SIR HENRY CECIL	Frankel	56-289	37	30	37	2,676,863	2,233,666
MARK JOHNSTON	Fulbright	215-1344	161	152	113	2,284,275	1,545,130
RICHARD FAHEY	Mayson	142-1294	159	136	123	1,982,267	1,213,826
SAEED BIN SUROOR	Farhh	85-436	71	66	42	1,817,649	1,020,127
ANDREW BALDING	Side Glance	93-712	96	83	62	1,365,377	779,847
WILLIAM HAGGAS	Rosdhu Queen	83-448	69	56	44	1,257,840	748,501
KEVIN RYAN	Hototo	95-789	74	79	72	1,228,983	853,827
MAHMOOD AL ZAROONI	Encke	65-393	53	49	33	1,211,199	831,715
TIM EASTERBY	Body And Soul	88-972	106	98	78	1,042,964	687,967
MICK CHANNON	Bungle Inthejungle	109-944	112	135	91	1,032,576	527,168
SIR MICHAEL STOUTE	Carlton House	69-363	66	48	33	1,022,421	609,776
ROGER CHARLTON	Cityscape	40-249	28	29	22	993,473	440,564
ROGER VARIAN	Sri Putra	72-398	55	60	46	877,983	532,154
CLIVE COX	Reckless Abandon	36-383	49	43	46	717,908	381,333
DAVID O'MEARA	Penitent	69-542	64	64	39	709,691	517,115
JEREMY NOSEDA	The Gold Cheongsam	47-259	35	36	21	686,459	546,985
DAVID SIMCOCK	Miss You Too	68-467	62	75	51	655,046	307,858
CHARLES HILLS	Hazel Lavery	55-456	59	47	41	641,356	366,206
BRIAN MEEHAN	Most Improved	50-406	30	66	29	615,486	485,327
JAMES FANSHAWE	Society Rock	34-222	35	34	24	607,936	336,865
TOM DASCOMBE	Ceiling Kitty	79-465	62	47	48	604,502	407,213
RALPH BECKETT	Moone's My Name	64-381	59	42	42	582,999	350,313
P SCHIERGEN	Danedream	1-3	0	0	2	573,264	567,100
HUGHIE MORRISON	Shirocco Star	35-353	42	41	39	563,400	196,323
LUCA CUMANI	My Quest For Peace	46-285	37	35	28	549,764	358,382
MARCO BOTTI	Moohaajim	52-372	48	45	36	502,760	289,755
DAVID LANIGAN	Main Sequence	22-128	23	9	10	500,820	111,409
MICHAEL BELL	Sovereign Debt	52-428	48	52	25	486,532	263,549
ED DUNLOP	Red Cadeaux	43-304	30	45	30	475,602	226,179
DAVID BARRON	Pearl Secret	50-358	34	32	47	450,888	286,729
MARCUS TREGONING	Bronze Angel	29-191	21	20	24	429,718	271,166
JIM GOLDIE	Hawkeyethenoo	28-375	25	27	35	397,045	238,221
D K WELD	Sapphire	5-9	0	1	0	389,678	381,070
SIR MARK PRESCOTT BT	Liber	51-255	39	27	22	380,226	196,302
A DE ROYER-DUPRE	Shareta	2-9	2	0	3	378,113	266,537
DAVID NICHOLLS	Don't Call Me	50-488	35	46	31	373,922	218,891
BRIAN ELLISON	Global Village	61-442	51	47	26	358,537	242,118
DAVID EVANS	Verse Of Love	82-784	65	81	64	346,748	237,871
PETER CHAPPLE-HYAM	King's Warrior	29-183	15	22	18	328,066	261,336
J S BOLGER	Dawn Approach	3-10	1	0	1	319,358	241,017
RONALD HARRIS	Secret Witness	63-602	61	63	44	313,012	201,100
JAMIE OSBORNE	Field Of Dream	52-343	49	40	27	303,586	207,475
RICHARD GUEST	Barnet Fair	61-719	66	78	50	300,807	213,494
JOHN DUNLOP	Times Up	19-236	23	32	23	296,681	198,315
MICHAEL DODS	Mass Rally	40-351	40	52	28	295,135	177,860
PETER G MOODY	Black Caviar	1-1	0	0	0	283,550	283,550
MRS K BURKE	Media Hype	43-312	39	36	37	282,990	161,356

TOP FLAT OWNERS IN BRITAIN IN 2012

OWNER	LEADING HORSE	W-R	2ND	3RD	4TH	TOTAL PRIZE	WIN PRIZE
GODOLPHIN	FARHH	149-805	122	110	75	3,180,679	2,011,074
K ABDULLA	FRANKEL	65-354	53	45	41	3,091,329	2,200,161
DERRICK SMITH & MRS JOHN MAGNIER & MICHAEL TABOR	CAMELOT	5-29	4	7	4	2,579,043	1,909,992
SHEIKH HAMDAN BIN MOHAMMED AL MAKTOUM	FULBRIGHT	112-674	90	78	47	1,306,680	907,210
HAMDAN AL MAKTOUM	GHURAIR	93-562	69	90	65	1,202,091	823,376
DR MARWAN KOUKASH	GABRIAL	101-714	106	79	66	1,026,386	624,093
GEORGE STRAWBRIDGE	THOUGHT WORTHY	18-71	9	12	7	622,141	287,816
LADY ROTHSCHILD & NEWSELLS PARK STUD	NATHANIEL	1-3	1	1	0	596,464	241,584
GESTUT BURG EBERSTEIN & TERUYA YOSHIDA	DANEDREAM	1-1	0	0	0	567,100	567,100
MRS J WOOD	VICTRIX LUDORUM	12-90	13	11	4	532,192	448,580
MRS JOHN MAGNIER & MICHAEL TABOR & DERRICK SMITH	HOMECOMING QUEEN	7-24	1	2	1	504,690	438,873
CHEVELEY PARK STUD	STARSCOPE	31-209	45	31	18	482,794	210,449
LADY ROTHSCHILD	MINCE	27-83	6	13	7	472,473	393,542
NIARCHOS FAMILY	MAIN SEQUENCE	9-48	7	7	8	452,731	106,728
H R H PRINCESS HAYA OF JORDAN	JOVIALITY	25-130	24	17	14	434,472	281,271
C H STEVENS	BODY AND SOUL	9-65	10	9	3	402,786	310,642
DAVID W ARMSTRONG	MAYSON	9-70	12	6	9	401,583	352,028
THE QUEEN	CARLTON HOUSE	15-98	16	14	10	400,725	155,332
PEARL BLOODSTOCK LTD	SIDE GLANCE	18-111	18	12	15	364,767	175,544
ANDREW TINKLER	SIR PRANCEALOT	29-235	21	27	30	346,441	161,909
LORD LLOYD-WEBBER	THE FUGUE	2-9	2	3	1	298,023	141,775
HELENA SPRINGFIELD LTD	SHIROCCO STAR	6-30	6	1	1	290,013	108,601
B E NIELSEN	MICHELANGELO	10-72	10	6	2	287,800	144,634
G J WILKIE, MRS K J WILKIE ET AL	BLACK CAVIAR	1-1	0	0	0	283,550	283,550
SMITH/MAGNIER/TABOR/DATOTAN/TUNKUYAHAYA	SO YOU THINK	1-1	0	0	0	283,550	283,550
JEAN-CLAUDE-ALAIN DUPOUY	CIRRUS DES AIGLES	0-1	1	0	0	279,500	0
QATAR RACING LIMITED	SPIRIT QUARTZ	6-65	9	9	8	276,548	36,594
KENNETH MACPHERSON	HOTOTO	5-17	3	3	1	268,906	192,447
R J ARCULLI	RED CADEAUX	9-54	9	4	4	268,756	123,653
ARASHAN ALI	THE GOLD CHEONGSAM	3-7	0	2	0	268,705	236,010
SHEIKH MOHAMMED BIN KHALIFA AL MAKTOUM	MICKDAAM	6-29	4	7	5	262,167	86,722
SHEIKH AHMED AL MAKTOUM	SHOLAAN	21-123	19	22	19	257,244	160,554
J C SMITH	HIGHLAND KNIGHT	20-148	17	15	18	257,082	171,063
H R H SULTAN AHMAD SHAH	SRI PUTRA	11-77	7	11	7	255,124	172,147
CLIPPER LOGISTICS	ROSDHU QUEEN	11-48	9	8	1	243,979	207,550
MOYGLARE STUD FARM	SAPPHIRE	6-19	1	1	1	240,326	237,242
MATT & LAUREN MORGAN	BLAINE	10-30	4	3	1	226,509	180,783
A D SPENCE	BLACK SPIRIT	21-136	23	15	8	225,082	140,456
A D N FRASER, MISS A C N FRASER & MS E J H RIDLEY	ORTENSIA	2-5	0	0	1	222,712	198,485
LISBUNNY SYNDICATE	MAAREK	3-7	0	3	0	219,160	200,355
NORMANDIE STUD LTD	FALLEN FOR YOU	8-42	6	6	2	217,117	193,250
SIR ROBERT OGDEN	THOMAS CHIPPENDALE	15-98	10	12	7	213,404	155,561
SIMON GIBSON	SOCIETY ROCK	1-16	2	5	2	210,978	127,597
KO KAM PIU	LITTLE BRIDGE	1-1	0	0	0	198,485	198,485
SAIF ALI	HAJAM	17-128	20	16	11	193,072	64,236
MRS H STEEL	LADYS FIRST	10-119	15	11	15	191,148	100,791
IRAJ PARVIZI	MOST IMPROVED	3-31	6	4	2	187,722	173,116

TOP FLAT HORSES
IN BRITAIN 2012

HORSE (AGE)	WIN & PLACE £	W-R	TRAINER	OWNER	BREEDER
FRANKEL (4)	1,625,592	5-5	Sir Henry Cecil	K Abdulla	Juddmonte Farms Ltd
CAMELOT (3)	1,083,170	2-3	A P O'Brien	Derrick Smith & Mrs John Magnier & Michael Tabor	Sheikh Abdulla Bin Isa Al-Khalifa
EXCELEBRATION (4)	679,975	1-3	A P O'Brien	Derrick Smith & Mrs John Magnier & Michael Tabor	Owenstown Stud
NATHANIEL (4)	596,464	1-3	John Gosden	Lady Rothschild & Newsells Park Stud	Kincorth Investments Inc
DANEDREAM (4)	567,100	1-1	P Schiergen	Gestut Burg Eberstein & Teruya Yoshida	Gestut Brummerhof
FARHH (4)	382,412	1-5	Saeed Bin Suroor	Godolphin	Darley
MAIN SEQUENCE (3)	377,389	2-5	David Lanigan	Niarchos Family	Flaxman Holdings Ltd
ST NICHOLAS ABBEY (5)	355,740	1-3	A P O'Brien	Derrick Smith & Mrs John Magnier & Michael Tabor	Barton Bloodstock & Villiers Synd
ENCKE (3)	348,584	2-4	Mahmood Al Zarooni	Godolphin	Darley
MAYSON (4)	311,264	3-6	Richard Fahey	D W Armstrong & Cheveley Park Stud	Highfield Farm Llp
THE FUGUE (3)	297,267	2-6	John Gosden	Watership Down Stud	Watership Down Stud
BODY AND SOUL (2)	285,956	4-6	Tim Easterby	C H Stevens	Michael Downey & Roalso Ltd
GHURAIR (2)	285,604	2-3	John Gosden	Hamdan Al Maktoum	Kirsten Rausing
BLACK CAVIAR (6)	283,550	1-1	Peter G Moody	G J Wilkie, Mrs K J Wilkie et al	R Jamieson
SO YOU THINK (6)	283,550	1-1	A P O'Brien	Smith/Magnier/Tabor/DatoTan /TunkuYahaya	M J Moran & Piper Farm Ltd
CIRRUS DES AIGLES (6)	279,500	0-1	Mme C Barande-Barbe	Jean-Claude-Alain Dupouy & Xavier Niel	M Yvon Lelimouzin & M Benoit Deschamps
THE GOLD CHEONGSAM (2)	268,705	3-7	Jeremy Noseda	Arashan Ali	Tally-Ho Stud
WAS (3)	261,104	1-4	A P O'Brien	Derrick Smith & Mrs John Magnier & Michael Tabor	Lodge Park Stud
HOTOTO (2)	258,060	3-10	Kevin Ryan	Kenneth Macpherson	B P Hammond
FULBRIGHT (3)	249,377	6-12	Mark Johnston	Sheikh Hamdan Bin Mohammed Al Maktoum	R F And S D Knipe
CITYSCAPE (6)	237,833	0-2	Roger Charlton	K Abdulla	Juddmonte Farms Ltd
COLOUR VISION (4)	231,929	2-5	Saeed Bin Suroor	Godolphin	Capricorn Stud
ORTENSIA (7)	222,712	2-5	Paul Messara	A D N Fraser, Miss A C N Fraser & Ms E J H Ridley	L D Rhodes
VICTRIX LUDORUM (2)	222,317	2-4	Richard Hannon	Mrs J Wood	Yukiko Hosokawa
MAAREK (5)	218,920	3-6	David Peter Nagle	Lisbunny Syndicate	New England Stud & P J & P M Vela
DAWN APPROACH (2)	218,333	2-2	J S Bolger	Godolphin	J S Bolger
THOUGHT WORTHY (3)	214,995	2-6	John Gosden	George Strawbridge	George Strawbridge
HOMECOMING QUEEN (3)	213,513	1-2	A P O'Brien	Mrs John Magnier & Michael Tabor & Derrick Smith	Tower Bloodstock
SOCIETY ROCK (5)	207,883	1-5	James Fanshawe	Simon Gibson	San Gabriel Investments
LITTLE BRIDGE (6)	198,485	1-1	C S Shum	Ko Kam Piu	Llanhennock Trust
CARLTON HOUSE (4)	196,315	1-4	Sir Michael Stoute	The Queen	Darley
RED CADEAUX (6)	185,758	1-5	Ed Dunlop	R J Arculli	Foursome Thoroughbreds
ASTROLOGY (3)	181,800	1-3	A P O'Brien	Derrick Smith	A-Mark Racing Et Al
ELUSIVE KATE (3)	176,400	0-3	John Gosden	Teruya Yoshida	Clovelly Farms
SHARETA (4)	175,801	1-1	A De Royer-Dupre	H H Aga Khan	His Highness The Aga Khan's Studs S C
SHIROCCO STAR (3)	174,649	0-5	Hughie Morrison	Helena Springfield Ltd	Meon Valley Stud
ROSDHU QUEEN (2)	173,320	4-4	William Haggas	Clipper Logistics	Old Carhue & Graeng Bloodstock
MICHELANGELO (3)	170,938	2-5	John Gosden	B E Nielsen	Denford Stud And Balmerino Bloodstock

TOP NH JOCKEYS IN BRITAIN 2011/12

W-R	%	JOCKEY	2ND	3RD	TOTAL PRIZE
199-727	27%	A P MCCOY	128	77	1,468,131
153-834	18%	RICHARD JOHNSON	152	115	1,292,711
144-625	23%	JASON MAGUIRE	115	69	1,095,247
83-455	18%	DARYL JACOB	77	48	1,391,365
83-536	15%	TOM O'BRIEN	57	51	575,404
82-477	17%	PADDY BRENNAN	74	53	568,806
81-598	14%	SAM TWISTON-DAVIES	91	68	629,021
70-547	13%	PAUL MOLONEY	65	56	471,716
65-450	14%	TOM SCUDAMORE	53	53	701,409
63-220	29%	BARRY GERAGHTY	37	17	1,735,426
58-381	15%	AIDAN COLEMAN	53	39	455,518
55-221	25%	R WALSH	30	24	1,497,668
55-428	13%	DENIS O'REGAN	46	40	509,502
53-414	13%	JAMES REVELEY	62	59	419,645
53-492	11%	BRIAN HUGHES	50	60	314,864
51-353	14%	ROBERT THORNTON	49	47	683,902
49-351	14%	NOEL FEHILY	56	46	710,592
48-287	17%	ANDREW TINKLER	46	18	290,601
48-381	13%	NICK SCHOLFIELD	39	43	333,072
44-299	15%	FELIX DE GILES	38	27	259,363
43-316	14%	WAYNE HUTCHINSON	55	39	511,979
42-302	14%	TIMMY MURPHY	45	30	562,154
42-355	12%	HENRY BROOKE	40	36	232,249
42-378	11%	DOUGIE COSTELLO	56	51	438,607
42-460	9%	JAMIE MOORE	53	50	366,349
41-377	11%	LEIGHTON ASPELL	47	48	223,930
39-449	9%	ANDREW THORNTON	38	53	224,798
38-300	13%	CAMPBELL GILLIES	38	34	253,040
38-307	12%	PETER BUCHANAN	46	39	229,626
38-332	11%	LUCY ALEXANDER	32	37	188,779
36-292	12%	DOMINIC ELSWORTH	38	43	403,940
35-258	14%	CONOR O'FARRELL	38	39	271,553
32-220	15%	DAVID BASS	28	25	198,296
32-239	13%	ADAM WEDGE	20	35	158,819
32-281	11%	TOM CANNON	35	38	167,481
32-327	10%	RICHIE MCGRATH	35	35	189,905
31-299	10%	GRAHAM LEE	40	38	206,675
30-306	10%	SAM THOMAS	24	26	142,130
29-222	13%	BRENDAN POWELL	22	30	123,254
27-133	20%	JACK QUINLAN	19	12	117,267
26-139	19%	RICHARD KILLORAN	11	17	94,033
26-215	12%	JOE TIZZARD	25	30	259,778
25-207	12%	JACK DOYLE	21	26	158,245
25-212	12%	LEE EDWARDS	24	19	109,933
25-274	9%	WILL KENNEDY	20	30	177,126
24-309	8%	WILSON RENWICK	30	41	136,093
23-132	17%	KIELAN WOODS	15	14	79,521
22-133	17%	JEREMIAH MCGRATH	16	19	159,921
21-80	26%	RACHAEL GREEN	9	11	90,152
21-168	13%	RYAN MANIA	28	25	199,350

TOP NH TRAINERS IN BRITAIN 2011/12

TRAINER	LEADING HORSE	W-R	2ND	3RD	4TH	TOTAL PRIZE	WIN PRIZE
PAUL NICHOLLS	NEPTUNE COLLONGES	138-598	97	75	47	3,297,804	2,577,194
NICKY HENDERSON	FINIAN'S RAINBOW	165-621	108	49	56	2,736,256	2,068,712
DONALD MCCAIN	OVERTURN	153-712	118	87	54	1,246,544	849,027
JONJO O'NEILL	SYNCHRONISED	97-649	81	53	50	1,144,901	685,164
ALAN KING	RAYA STAR	81-516	80	70	53	1,132,081	724,961
DAVID PIPE	GREAT ENDEAVOUR	101-631	74	70	63	996,492	686,358
PHILIP HOBBS	MENORAH	73-512	74	57	47	959,802	492,420
NIGEL TWISTON-DAVIES	ASTRACAD	70-578	96	67	49	666,757	324,111
EVAN WILLIAMS	CAPPA BLEU	88-579	74	78	54	588,367	342,144
TIM VAUGHAN	STEWARTS HOUSE	102-591	104	72	51	547,816	341,775
COLIN TIZZARD	HEY BIG SPENDER	46-320	38	45	33	413,389	240,385
LUCINDA RUSSELL	BRINDISI BREEZE	57-454	69	66	47	397,826	270,174
CHARLIE LONGSDON	PAINTBALL	68-346	50	31	23	380,162	275,505
TOM GEORGE	NACARAT	40-247	43	29	18	356,574	216,540
SUE SMITH	AURORAS ENCORE	45-337	37	49	32	356,412	220,503
VENETIA WILLIAMS	PEPITE ROSE	52-401	46	29	32	344,273	220,610
NICK WILLIAMS	GAUVAIN	20-132	20	21	9	342,707	167,191
PETER BOWEN	ALWAYS WAINING	53-412	47	38	35	340,139	219,332
W P MULLINS	SIR DES CHAMPS	5-52	3	4	4	327,672	149,967
BRIAN ELLISON	SOUND ACCORD	36-223	33	40	13	323,881	208,663
VICTOR DARTNALL	GILES CROSS	24-154	25	19	9	307,346	223,617
MALCOLM JEFFERSON	CAPE TRIBULATION	26-178	13	27	21	304,944	241,759
EMMA LAVELLE	KENTFORD GREY LADY	41-216	26	28	18	274,218	177,524
MARTIN KEIGHLEY	CHAMPION COURT	34-248	39	34	21	270,357	121,192
GARY MOORE	FRUITY O'ROONEY	29-311	39	43	20	253,494	102,832
PAUL WEBBER	TIME FOR RUPERT	31-209	19	21	22	246,661	137,551
KEITH REVELEY	BENNY BE GOOD	31-199	37	26	27	229,404	139,683
HENRIETTA KNIGHT	SOMERSBY	9-122	17	14	11	227,338	152,083
REBECCA CURTIS	TEAFORTHREE	39-180	25	22	15	217,485	164,038
RICHARD LEE	LE BEAU BAI	17-150	13	15	21	215,218	142,227
DAVID BRIDGWATER	THE GIANT BOLSTER	13-70	10	2	8	186,464	61,658
JOHN QUINN	COUNTRYWIDE FLAME	17-74	17	9	7	180,782	131,217
FERDY MURPHY	DIVER	22-331	31	48	34	177,794	73,165
HENRY DALY	ARCTIC BEN	26-186	26	31	17	174,503	111,157
KIM BAILEY	BUFFALO BOB	32-211	30	26	17	171,075	111,983
IAN WILLIAMS	BAILE ANRAI	29-228	26	25	18	166,755	97,623
GORDON ELLIOTT	MANGER HANAGMENT	32-149	28	15	5	162,762	99,680
JAMES EWART	QUICUYO	23-153	22	21	19	160,597	104,647
HENRY DE BROMHEAD	SIZING EUROPE	3-18	1	1	3	159,889	80,520
BRENDAN POWELL	ONLY WITNESS	30-264	27	30	23	138,600	87,356
ANDREW PARKER	MERIGO	9-60	11	4	2	138,196	126,339
NICKY RICHARDS	PEACHEY MOMENT	29-170	28	23	14	136,404	85,717
CHARLIE MANN	HOW'S BUSINESS	22-203	25	23	22	136,290	78,076
NEIL MULHOLLAND	MIDNIGHT CHASE	16-181	20	27	11	130,614	97,333
JAMIE SNOWDEN	KNIGHTON COMBE	19-120	19	16	11	127,015	93,465
JEREMY SCOTT	COOL FRIEND	24-138	18	15	16	125,356	86,703
DR RICHARD NEWLAND	THEOLOGIST	21-139	14	24	16	119,929	74,518
JIM GOLDIE	LOS NADIS	16-150	25	19	9	118,482	63,041
TONY CARROLL	MALANOS	23-237	29	23	27	113,753	62,017
CHRIS GRANT	MICRO MISSION	23-235	25	25	17	112,490	66,695

TOP NH OWNERS IN BRITAIN IN 2011/12

OWNER	LEADING HORSE	W-R	2ND	3RD	4TH	TOTAL PRIZE	WIN PRIZE
JOHN P MCMANUS	Synchronised	99-534	75	38	46	1,393,421	911,138
J HALES	Neptune Collonges	3-21	4	3	2	639,044	581,722
THE STEWART FAMILY	Big Buck's	16-59	8	6	3	525,282	460,872
MICHAEL BUCKLEY	Finian's Rainbow	17-59	10	5	7	423,966	358,773
T G LESLIE	Overturn	25-96	21	8	6	410,231	257,816
ANDREA & GRAHAM WYLIE	Tidal Bay	18-76	15	8	8	345,553	217,437
TREVOR HEMMINGS	Albertas Run	22-183	24	23	20	337,127	115,262
SIMON MUNIR	Raya Star	12-49	7	4	3	334,543	299,672
THE FESTIVAL GOERS	Rock On Ruby	3-8	1	1	0	256,741	224,811
CLIVE D SMITH	Kauto Star	3-8	0	1	0	250,023	244,673
JIMMY NESBITT PARTNERSHIP	Riverside Theatre	2-3	0	0	0	232,547	232,547
JOHN WADE	Benny Be Good	20-224	37	28	20	216,720	120,977
MRS DIANA L WHATELEY	Menorah	9-56	6	8	9	205,788	83,934
MRS T P RADFORD	Somersby	6-35	7	4	2	202,415	142,759
WALTERS PLANT HIRE LTD	Oscar Whisky	16-75	9	9	9	189,565	164,200
POTENSIS LIMITED & CHRIS GILES	Zarkandar	4-15	4	1	1	188,415	161,898
MR & MRS RAYMOND ANDERSON GREEN	Merigo	14-88	16	7	7	183,424	150,959
MRS CAROLINE MOULD	Sprinter Sacre	7-28	3	2	3	181,372	171,275
ROBERT WALEY-COHEN	Long Run	1-22	3	5	1	163,393	17,085
D A JOHNSON	Great Endeavour	11-42	7	3	5	155,136	126,813
MRS S SMITH	Mr Moonshine	27-156	16	17	14	153,982	118,861
GIGGINSTOWN HOUSE STUD	Sir Des Champs	2-27	5	2	4	140,876	53,854
ANN & ALAN POTTS PARTNERSHIP	Sizing Europe	1-7	1	0	1	140,582	68,340
SIMON HUNT	The Giant Bolster	1-7	2	0	2	136,777	22,780
THE DUNKLEY & REILLY PARTNERSHIP	Medermit	1-13	4	4	2	135,707	34,170
MR & MRS WILLIAM RUCKER	Cappa Bleu	10-53	9	11	4	135,707	54,347
BROCADE RACING	Hey Big Spender	11-48	3	7	6	129,070	113,421
TERRY WARNER	Featherbed Lane	10-70	5	12	8	126,364	64,109
MRS JO TRACEY	I'msingingtheblues	7-35	4	5	6	124,806	74,590
MCNEILL FAMILY	Grumeti	5-16	1	3	1	119,132	96,920
R A BARTLETT	Simonsig	5-10	2	0	1	116,057	102,126
BRANNON DENNIS DICK HOLDEN	Weird Al	4-13	1	2	0	109,311	80,289
C G ROACH	The Minack	7-29	4	4	1	104,601	83,734
JARED SULLIVAN & SIMON BROWN	Gauvain	2-10	3	3	1	104,219	59,734
GUNNERS SYNDICATE	Seabass	0-1	0	1	0	102,862	0
JARED SULLIVAN	Sanctuaire	4-11	3	0	0	102,151	67,413
BANKS, BLACKSHAW & GANNON	Brampour	2-6	0	1	0	98,995	85,085
ESTIO PINNACLE RACING	Countrywide Flame	4-7	3	0	0	98,418	67,281
THE NOT AFRAID PARTNERSHIP	Bobs Worth	2-4	1	1	0	97,489	87,703
SIMON W CLARKE	Nacarat	3-18	4	2	1	97,324	73,197
H R MOULD	Astracad	8-51	10	4	6	90,844	54,520
THE BRUSHMAKERS	Roalco De Farges	4-14	2	1	0	90,775	52,152
THE OAKSEY PARTNERSHIP	Carruthers	1-5	0	1	0	89,705	85,425
HAMMER & TROWEL SYNDICATE	Thousand Stars	1-3	1	0	1	88,231	39,389
REDGAP PARTNERSHIP	Follow The Plan	1-1	0	0	0	84,405	84,405
BLOOMFIELDS	Cotton Mill	14-51	9	3	4	80,501	46,527
MRS R J SKAN	Fingal Bay	5-14	2	0	1	80,094	57,069
DERMOT HANAFIN & PHIL CUNNINGHAM	Cinders And Ashes	4-5	1	0	0	78,853	76,821
R S BROOKHOUSE	Sadler's Risk	8-68	6	7	9	78,285	36,887
JAMES AND JEAN POTTER	Hector's Choice	5-27	2	4	1	78,262	38,068

TOP NH HORSES
IN BRITAIN 2011/12

HORSE (AGE)	WIN & PLACE £	W-R	TRAINER	OWNER	BREEDER
NEPTUNE COLLONGES (11)	574,674	1-5	Paul Nicholls	J Hales	G A E C Delorme Freres
FININAN'S RAINBOW (9)	328,736	3-4	Nicky Henderson	Michael Buckley	J O'Keeffe
SYNCHRONISED (9)	292,775	1-4	Jonjo O'Neill	John P McManus	Mrs Noreen McManus
BIG BUCK'S (9)	292,648	5-5	Paul Nicholls	The Stewart Family	Henri Poulat
ROCK ON RUBY (7)	254,035	2-4	Paul Nicholls	The Festival Goers	John O'Dwyer
OVERTURN (8)	248,087	3-6	Donald McCain	T G Leslie	Pendley Farm
SUNNYHILLBOY (9)	235,802	1-5	Jonjo O'Neill	John P McManus	J P N Parker
RIVERSIDE THEATRE (8)	232,547	2-3	Nicky Henderson	Jimmy Nesbitt Partnership	Goldford Stud
KAUTO STAR (12)	216,064	2-3	Paul Nicholls	Clive D Smith	Mme Henri Aubert
SPRINTER SACRE (6)	164,160	5-5	Nicky Henderson	Mrs Caroline Mould	Christophe Masle
LONG RUN (7)	152,465	1-4	Nicky Henderson	Robert Waley-Cohen	Mrs Marie-Christine Gabeur
THE GIANT BOLSTER (7)	136,777	1-7	David Bridgwater	Simon Hunt	Gestut Fahrhof
SIZING EUROPE (10)	136,724	1-2	Henry De Bromhead	Ann & Alan Potts Prtship	Mrs Angela Bracken
RAYA STAR (9)	131,298	3-7	Alan King	Simon Munir	Patrick Fennessy
MEDERMIT (8)	128,666	1-6	Alan King	The Dunkley & Reilly Prtship	Philippe Gasdoue
OSCAR WHISKY (7)	127,661	3-5	Nicky Henderson	Walters Plant Hire Ltd	Stephanie Hanly
SOMERSBY (8)	120,322	2-7	Henrietta Knight	Mrs T P Radford	Miss Nicola Ann Adams
TIDAL BAY (11)	115,213	1-5	Paul Nicholls	Andrea & Graham Wylie	John Dorgan
BINOCULAR (8)	112,956	2-4	Nicky Henderson	John P McManus	Elie Lellouche
CELESTIAL HALO (8)	112,421	3-6	Paul Nicholls	The Stewart Family	Roncon Churchtown Bloodstock & Lane Ltd
MERIGO (11)	108,163	2-6	Andrew Parker	Mr & Mrs Raymond Anderson Green	Noel Pelat
SIMONSIG (6)	104,707	4-5	Nicky Henderson	R A Bartlett	Simon Tindall
SEABASS (9)	102,862	0-1	T M Walsh	Gunners Syndicate	John F Costigan
ALBERTAS RUN (11)	102,689	1-3	Jonjo O'Neill	Trevor Hemmings	Oliver and Salome Brennan
GRANDOUET (5)	99,059	2-3	Nicky Henderson	Simon Munir	Dominique Le Baron
BRAMPOUR (5)	98,995	2-6	Paul Nicholls	Banks, Blackshaw & Gannon	Haras De Son Altesse L'Aga Khan Scea
COUNTRYWIDE FLAME (4)	98,418	4-7	John Quinn	Estio Pinnacle Racing	Michael Clarke
BOBS WORTH (7)	97,489	2-4	Nicky Henderson	The Not Afraid Partnership	Mrs L Eadie
ZARKANDAR (5)	96,764	1-3	Paul Nicholls	Potensis Limited & Chris Giles	His Highness The Aga Khan's Studs S C
GRUMETI (4)	96,759	4-6	Alan King	McNeill Family	Catridge Farm Stud Ltd
GREAT ENDEAVOUR (8)	93,420	1-4	David Pipe	D A Johnson	Kevin Roche
GAUVAIN (10)	92,778	2-6	Nick Williams	Jared Sullivan & Simon Brown	Stall Epona
CARRUTHERS (9)	89,705	1-5	Mark Bradstock	The Oaksey Partnership	Lord Oaksey
QUANTITATIVEEASING (7)	89,005	1-3	Nicky Henderson	John P McManus	Mrs C A Moore
FOLLOW THE PLAN (9)	84,405	1-1	Oliver McKiernan	Redgap Partnership	Patrick Sheehan
CAPPA BLEU (10)	84,167	1-4	Evan Williams	Mr & Mrs William Rucker	Thomas O'Connor
MENORAH (7)	80,751	3-7	Philip Hobbs	Mrs Diana L Whateley	Mrs E Grant And Miss Anna Brislane
CINDERS AND ASHES (5)	78,853	4-5	Donald McCain	Dermot Hanafin & Phil Cunningham	Juddmonte Farms Ltd
WEIRD AL (9)	78,702	1-4	Donald McCain	Brannon Dick Holden	C Ronaldson
FINGAL BAY (6)	76,840	4-5	Philip Hobbs	Mrs R J Skan	James Kinsella
NACARAT (11)	75,943	1-5	Tom George	Simon W Clarke	Francis Maze
BRINDISI BREEZE (6)	74,633	4-5	Lucinda Russell	Sandy Seymour	Miss Annette McMahon
SILVINIACO CONTI (6)	73,934	2-5	Paul Nicholls	Potensis Limited & Chris Giles	Patrick Joubert
HUNT BALL (7)	73,146	7-9	Keiran Burke	Anthony Knott	Michael Slevin
AURORAS ENCORE (10)	72,005	1-5	Sue Smith	Mrs Alicia Skene & W S Skene	Mountarmstrong Stud
LOVCEN (7)	71,031	3-6	Alan King	The Barbury Apes	G Baron Von Ullmann
GILES CROSS (10)	70,078	2-4	Victor Dartnall	Mrs Kay Birchenhough	Mrs Kay Birchenough

LEADING SIRES OF 2012 IN GREAT BRITAIN AND IRELAND

STALLION	BREEDING	RNRS	WNRS	WINS	WIN MONEY	PLACES	PLACE MONEY	TOTAL
GALILEO (IRE)	by Sadler's Wells (USA)	226	104	154	4135932	334	1638626	5774558
MONTJEU (IRE)	by Sadler's Wells (USA)	111	43	67	2347981	186	807225	3155206
INVINCIBLE SPIRIT (IRE)	by Green Desert (USA)	194	76	118	1359546	350	922310	2281856
EXCEED AND EXCEL (AUS)	by Danehill (USA)	170	70	117	1453990	309	624857	2078847
DANSILI (GB)	by Danehill (USA)	152	68	98	1339225	236	641373	1980598
PIVOTAL (GB)	by Polar Falcon (USA)	159	74	120	1017390	330	873467	1890857
OASIS DREAM (GB)	by Green Desert (USA)	184	86	134	949333	357	449729	1399062
DANEHILL DANCER (IRE)	by Danehill (USA)	166	58	85	717446	293	611403	1328849
DUBAWI (IRE)	by Dubai Millennium (GB)	109	51	82	685569	191	618528	1304097
HOLY ROMAN EMPEROR (IRE)	by Danehill (USA)	144	63	84	705186	271	476941	1182127
CAPE CROSS (IRE)	by Green Desert (USA)	183	73	116	579281	303	418397	997679
SELKIRK (USA)	by Sharpen Up	75	32	46	366743	116	627724	994467
ACCLAMATION (GB)	by Royal Applause (GB)	180	75	116	617615	324	370262	987877
DARK ANGEL (IRE)	by Acclamation (GB)	96	48	75	623168	211	355370	978538
ELUSIVE QUALITY (USA)	by Gone West (USA)	52	26	37	636486	83	293707	930193
MEDICEAN (USA)	by Machiavellian (USA)	115	38	53	672247	173	254167	926414
TEOFILO (IRE)	by Galileo (IRE)	105	45	71	466751	154	441681	908432
ROCK OF GIBRALTAR (IRE)	by Danehill (USA)	134	48	71	620094	203	260436	880530
HIGH CHAPARRAL (IRE)	by Sadler's Wells (USA)	93	31	43	654866	135	196873	851740
RED CLUBS (IRE)	by Red Ransom (USA)	117	43	66	621822	237	212168	833990
KYLLACHY (GB)	by Pivotal (GB)	156	63	100	506421	279	320685	827105
SHAMARDAL (USA)	by Giant's Causeway (USA)	123	48	84	517381	194	274348	791730
FOOTSTEPSINTHESAND (GB)	by Giant's Causeway (USA)	103	35	51	478683	201	305913	784596
INTIKHAB (USA)	by Red Ransom (USA)	62	22	38	552856	103	134848	687704
CHOISIR (AUS)	by Danehill Dancer (IRE)	107	46	77	477066	216	201033	678099

LEADING SIRES OF 2012
(GREAT BRITAIN, IRELAND AND OVERSEAS)

STALLION	BREEDING	DOMESTIC WNRS	WINS	WIN MONEY	OVERSEAS WNRS	WINS	WIN MONEY	TOTAL
MONTJEU (IRE)	by Sadler's Wells (USA)	43	67	2347981	33	50	3829063	6177044
DUBAWI (IRE)	by Dubai Millennium (GB)	51	82	685569	42	66	5362824	6048393
GALILEO (IRE)	by Sadler's Wells (USA)	104	154	4135932	37	57	1389646	5525577
PIVOTAL (GB)	by Polar Falcon (USA)	74	120	1017390	58	96	1910632	2928023
SELKIRK (USA)	by Sharpen Up	32	46	366743	19	26	2548456	2915199
OASIS DREAM (GB)	by Green Desert (USA)	86	134	949333	79	164	1688703	2638036
INVINCIBLE SPIRIT (IRE)	by Green Desert (USA)	76	118	1359546	64	99	1208028	2567574
DANSILI (GB)	by Danehill (USA)	68	98	1339225	54	86	1127571	2466796
KING'S BEST (USA)	by Kingmambo (USA)	28	40	353392	47	70	2012852	2366244
SHAMARDAL (USA)	by Giant's Causeway (USA)	48	84	517381	58	101	1817000	2334381
EXCEED AND EXCEL (AUS)	by Danehill (USA)	70	117	1453990	40	76	864387	2318377
HOLY ROMAN EMPEROR (IRE)	by Danehill (USA)	63	84	705186	60	105	1564815	2270001
MEDICEAN (GB)	by Machiavellian (USA)	38	53	672247	63	93	1467056	2139303
KYLLACHY (GB)	by Pivotal (GB)	63	100	506421	48	75	1624113	2130534
POLIGLOTE (GB)	by Sadler's Wells (USA)	0	0		3	5	2004333	2004333
ROCK OF GIBRALTAR (IRE)	by Danehill (USA)	48	71	620094	71	109	1274961	1895055
ORATORIO (IRE)	by Danehill (USA)	51	76	463851	78	141	1323006	1786857
FOOTSTEPSINTHESAND (GB)	by Giant's Causeway (USA)	35	51	478683	54	85	1272634	1751317
SINGSPIEL (IRE)	by In The Wings	28	39	199085	59	108	1451341	1650426
MARJU (IRE)	by Last Tycoon	25	45	203843	28	45	1380856	1584699
CHOISIR (AUS)	by Danehill Dancer (IRE)	46	77	477066	38	75	1083476	1560542
DANEHILL DANCER (IRE)	by Danehill (USA)	58	85	717446	40	57	775104	1492550
REFUSE TO BEND (IRE)	by Sadler's Wells (USA)	35	56	222898	73	144	1256984	1479881
HIGH CHAPARRAL (IRE)	by Sadler's Wells (USA)	31	43	654866	45	75	730325	1385191
MOTIVATOR (GB)	by Montjeu (IRE)	39	51	316092	48	77	1023556	1339648

LEADING TWO-YEAR-OLD SIRES OF 2012 IN GREAT BRITAIN AND IRELAND

STALLION	BREEDING	RNRS	WNRS	WINS	WIN MONEY	PLACES	PLACE MONEY	TOTAL
RED CLUBS (IRE)	by Red Ransom (USA)	54	22	36	527528	99	114074	641603
INVINCIBLE SPIRIT (IRE)	by Green Desert (USA)	58	24	32	523647	80	93534	617181
ELUSIVE QUALITY (USA)	by Gone West (USA)	19	11	16	484779	31	37514	522293
GALILEO (IRE)	by Sadler's Wells (USA)	51	19	23	377155	36	102219	479374
EXCEED AND EXCEL (AUS)	by Danehill (USA)	50	19	35	223702	77	241168	464869
HOLY ROMAN EMPEROR (IRE)	by Danehill (USA)	55	21	25	163858	83	237329	401187
TEOFILO (IRE)	by Galileo (IRE)	46	20	26	164853	36	204530	369383
SLEEPING INDIAN (GB)	by Indian Ridge	30	8	15	236402	44	132388	368790
ACCLAMATION (GB)	by Royal Applause (GB)	54	26	33	170820	96	184993	355813
DANEHILL DANCER (IRE)	by Danehill (USA)	49	17	22	192602	62	139052	331655
BAHAMIAN BOUNTY (GB)	by Cadeaux Genereux	46	16	26	191070	77	131754	322824
CAPTAIN RIO (GB)	by Pivotal (GB)	10	4	7	261983	15	47649	309632
DUTCH ART (GB)	by Medicean (GB)	42	18	23	112275	64	145792	258067
KHELEYF (USA)	by Green Desert (USA)	58	27	36	158883	104	87230	246113
CHOISIR (AUS)	by Danehill Dancer (IRE)	20	9	13	170712	41	50697	221410
CAPE CROSS (IRE)	by Green Desert (USA)	45	12	16	103603	54	116971	220574
VERGLAS (IRE)	by Highest Honor (FR)	34	16	23	155261	59	57766	213027
PIVOTAL (GB)	by Polar Falcon (USA)	34	13	17	85162	44	123236	208398
ROYAL APPLAUSE (GB)	by Waajib	62	17	20	95681	101	105554	201236
DARK ANGEL (IRE)	by Acclamation (GB)	40	17	19	107905	74	76874	184779
OASIS DREAM (GB)	by Green Desert (USA)	47	16	18	66501	78	117276	183776
LAWMAN (FR)	by Invincible Spirit (IRE)	27	10	14	101398	29	70804	172202
DANSILI (GB)	by Danehill (USA)	35	13	15	98485	33	46539	145024
MONTJEU (IRE)	by Sadler's Wells (USA)	20	6	6	41293	25	103160	144453
KYLLACHY (GB)	by Pivotal (GB)	45	16	20	76097	67	65645	141742

(Not including First Crop Sires)

LEADING FIRST CROP SIRES OF 2012 IN GREAT BRITAIN AND IRELAND

STALLION	BREEDING	RNRS	WNRS	WINS	WIN MONEY	PLACES	PLACE MONEY	TOTAL
NEW APPROACH (IRE)	by Galileo (IRE)	30	10	18	482052	34	55846	537898
HENRYTHENAVIGATOR (USA)	by Kingmambo (USA)	24	11	12	156414	31	105149	261563
RAVEN'S PASS (USA)	by Elusive Quality (USA)	34	12	17	137676	34	113856	251532
TAMAYUZ (GB)	by Nayef (USA)	26	8	11	134669	30	54058	188727
SAKHEE'S SECRET (GB)	by Sakhee (USA)	61	22	27	92867	80	47436	140304
SIXTIES ICON (GB)	by Galileo (IRE)	17	8	14	64422	50	56443	120865
DUKE OF MARMALADE (IRE)	by Danehill (USA)	37	5	6	46478	35	42340	88818
HAATEF (USA)	by Danzig (USA)	21	7	9	41596	40	35938	77534
HANNOUMA (IRE)	by Anabaa (USA)	2	1	3	62233	0	0	62233
MOUNT NELSON (GB)	by Rock Of Gibraltar (IRE)	22	6	8	28155	19	29308	57463
THOUSAND WORDS (GB)	by Dansili (GB)	18	4	6	24835	33	30647	55482
FIRST DEFENCE (USA)	by Unbridled's Song (USA)	2	1	2	33372	3	18854	52226
CAPTAIN MARVELOUS (IRE)	by Invincible Spirit (IRE)	19	6	12	27823	30	12702	40526
RAMONTI (FR)	by Martino Alonso (IRE)	6	4	6	27418	6	11444	38862
ASSERTIVE (GB)	by Bold Edge (GB)	14	5	6	13707	22	11026	24733
CURLIN (USA)	by Smart Strike (CAN)	4	1	1	4528	4	8993	13522
LINNGARI (IRE)	by Indian Ridge	1	1	2	8992	3	2767	11759
FRACAS (IRE)	by In The Wings	2	1	2	11500	0	0	11500
STREET BOSS (USA)	by Street Cry (IRE)	5	2	3	7807	7	3279	11086
ASTRONOMER ROYAL (USA)	by Danzig (USA)	4	2	2	7051	3	4006	11058
HEATSEEKER (IRE)	by Giant's Causeway (USA)	1	1	1	8338	1	1933	10271
PAPAL BULL (GB)	by Montjeu (IRE)	14	1	1	2264	4	1985	4249
MIDNIGHT LUTE (USA)	by Real Quiet (USA)	1	0	0	0	2	3333	3333
VITA ROSA (JPN)	by Sunday Silence (USA)	3	0	0	0	4	1655	1655
WHAT A CAPER (IRE)	by Cape Cross (IRE)	1	0	0	0	1	1398	1398

LEADING MATERNAL GRANDSIRES OF 2012 IN GREAT BRITAIN AND IRELAND

STALLION	BREEDING	RNRS	WNRS	WINS	WIN MONEY	PLACES	PLACE MONEY	TOTAL
DANEHILL (USA)	by Danzig (USA)	246	110	150	3811914	398	808975	4620889
SADLER'S WELLS (USA)	by Northern Dancer	371	139	207	1821938	569	1230244	3052182
KINGMAMBO (USA)	by Mr Prospector (USA)	83	24	37	1861919	94	269052	2130972
INDIAN RIDGE	by Ahonoora	169	66	105	1305723	259	650802	1956525
DARSHAAN	by Shirley Heights	185	72	111	1184759	295	543474	1728233
RAINBOW QUEST (USA)	by Blushing Groom (FR)	196	71	109	769072	366	750034	1519106
GREEN DESERT (USA)	by Danzig (USA)	209	69	105	869120	371	531680	1400800
PIVOTAL (GB)	by Polar Falcon (USA)	128	56	80	788492	217	523879	1312371
SILVER HAWK (USA)	by Roberto (USA)	44	14	18	560405	66	563714	1124119
BARATHEA (IRE)	by Sadler's Wells (USA)	146	52	78	732895	202	202679	935574
SPECTRUM (IRE)	by Rainbow Quest (USA)	69	30	46	545450	116	274269	819719
DIESIS	by Sharpen Up	88	32	49	589594	112	224898	814493
SELKIRK (USA)	by Sharpen Up	154	66	90	516360	261	275162	791522
CADEAUX GENEREUX	by Young Generation	129	54	91	452274	209	271065	723340
NIGHT SHIFT (USA)	by Northern Dancer	160	56	75	413711	291	307313	721024
DISTANT VIEW (USA)	by Mr Prospector (USA)	43	17	24	211229	89	462679	673907
DESERT SUN (GB)	by Green Desert (USA)	21	11	17	594447	41	72673	667120
ROYAL ACADEMY (USA)	by Nijinsky (CAN)	128	42	68	333067	180	288674	621742
QUEST FOR FAME	by Rainbow Quest (USA)	21	11	24	406031	32	181379	587410
UNFUWAIN (USA)	by Northern Dancer	85	26	40	183357	143	396542	579899
MACHIAVELLIAN (USA)	by Mr Prospector (USA)	122	48	79	392148	219	184148	576296
ZAFONIC (USA)	by Gone West (USA)	96	36	54	406375	150	153110	559485
MARK OF ESTEEM (IRE)	by Darshaan	78	36	64	358845	149	200052	558897
DANEHILL DANCER (IRE)	by Danehill (USA)	78	31	57	396496	151	143458	539954
DR DEVIOUS (IRE)	by Ahonoora	39	15	27	358389	67	180636	539025

FLAT STALLIONS' EARNINGS FOR 2012

(includes every stallion who sired a winner on the Flat in Great Britain and Ireland in 2012)

STALLIONS	RNRS	STARTS	WNRS	WINS	PLACES	TOTAL (£)
ACATENANGO (GER)	2	20	1	2	6	5399.05
ACCLAMATION (GB)	180	1034	75	116	324	987876.81
ACCORDION	7	27	1	1	11	15515.00
ACT ONE (GB)	26	135	8	12	37	54485.51
AD VALOREM (USA)	36	177	11	15	51	85366.50
AFLEET ALEX (USA)	2	12	1	3	2	22236.86
AGENT BLEU (FR)	1	1	1	1	0	4025.00
ALAMSHAR (IRE)	3	14	2	4	4	36925.00
ALDEBARAN (USA)	5	34	5	6	11	395238.09
ALHAARTH (IRE)	46	203	13	21	62	145671.25
ALJABR (USA)	6	28	2	6	7	13996.45
ALKAADHEM (GB)	2	12	1	1	1	6333.33
ALMATY (IRE)	2	23	1	2	2	4163.50
ALMUTAWAKEL (GB)	6	30	1	1	7	4852.66
AMADEUS WOLF (GB)	59	385	26	40	117	252124.72
ANABAA (USA)	16	102	6	7	34	40474.50
ANTONIUS PIUS (USA)	64	328	19	33	80	198274.94
ANY GIVEN SATURDAY (USA)	3	17	1	1	6	4570.42
ARAAFA (IRE)	29	141	9	12	31	53798.17
ARAGORN (IRE)	3	24	2	4	9	18126.62
ARAKAN (USA)	14	73	5	9	21	123080.18
ARCH (USA)	30	114	13	22	31	144226.68
ARKADIAN HERO (USA)	5	30	1	1	5	3314.05
ASHKALANI (IRE)	3	16	1	3	6	18049.99
ASSERTIVE (GB)	14	61	5	6	22	24732.80
ASTRONOMER ROYAL (USA)	4	10	2	2	3	11057.63
ATRAF (GB)	10	47	2	5	9	14548.00
AUCTION HOUSE (USA)	33	175	5	6	40	66002.06
AUSSIE RULES (USA)	52	299	25	44	95	277210.78
AUTHORIZED (IRE)	78	306	37	49	104	361628.23
AVERTI (IRE)	8	41	1	1	8	5253.83
AVONBRIDGE (GB)	84	472	27	47	128	297424.86
AWESOME AGAIN (CAN)	3	12	1	1	3	3488.90
AZAMOUR (IRE)	48	207	17	25	80	234819.01
BACHELOR DUKE (USA)	33	154	8	11	44	92422.96
BACHIR (IRE)	2	5	1	1	0	1704.25
BADGE OF SILVER (USA)	2	11	2	2	6	11507.51
BAGO (FR)	2	7	1	3	1	9724.01
BAHAMIAN BOUNTY (GB)	132	814	49	81	243	625334.89
BAHHARE (USA)	6	59	2	4	20	16390.46
BAHRI (USA)	17	80	4	5	29	27200.82
BALLA COVE	1	15	1	3	9	23160.41
BALLET MASTER (USA)	5	33	2	2	5	5693.95
BALMONT (USA)	9	60	4	7	18	73948.40
BALTIC KING (GB)	22	136	10	19	29	88372.90
BARATHEA (IRE)	51	276	14	20	65	113742.18
BEAT ALL (USA)	12	63	5	8	20	37196.07
BEAT HOLLOW (GB)	63	297	23	28	84	344419.51
BEL ESPRIT (AUS)	1	1	1	1	0	283550.00
BELLAMY ROAD (USA)	1	5	1	2	1	4920.75
BENEFICIAL (GB)	8	34	4	5	10	40742.68
BERNARDINI (USA)	20	57	6	8	14	61252.92
BERNSTEIN (USA)	9	60	4	10	16	103762.10
BERTOLINI (USA)	117	728	37	59	184	349861.76
BEST OF THE BESTS (IRE)	7	55	2	5	15	15635.61
BIEN BIEN (USA)	1	2	1	1	0	2045.10
BIG BAD BOB (IRE)	27	125	6	9	44	156282.26
BIG SHUFFLE (USA)	6	31	1	1	10	10222.68

STALLIONS	RNRS	STARTS	WNRS	WINS	PLACES	TOTAL (£)
BISHOP OF CASHEL (GB)	3	14	1	1	3	17561.15
BLACK MINNALOUSHE (USA)	1	7	1	2	4	67140.60
BLACK SAM BELLAMY (IRE)	5	19	1	1	6	7654.44
BLUE DAKOTA (IRE)	3	11	1	1	2	2633.55
BOB BACK (USA)	3	4	1	1	1	5091.67
BOB'S RETURN (IRE)	3	7	1	2	3	12399.99
BOLD EDGE (GB)	10	81	2	2	30	21538.15
BOLD FACT (USA)	6	50	1	2	10	11400.58
BYRON (GB)	103	565	32	46	140	331493.10
CACIQUE (IRE)	5	31	2	2	10	7642.57
CADEAUX GENEREUX	55	311	22	27	98	381068.80
CAMACHO (GB)	41	251	14	17	75	158755.28
CAPE CROSS (IRE)	183	940	73	116	303	997678.69
CAPTAIN MARVELOUS (IRE)	19	96	6	12	30	40525.58
CAPTAIN RIO (GB)	71	471	29	46	134	564977.18
CARNEGIE (IRE)	1	20	1	1	7	5059.31
CARNIVAL DANCER (GB)	4	22	1	1	5	3382.99
CARROLL HOUSE	1	6	1	1	2	6291.66
CATCHER IN THE RYE (IRE)	19	81	4	7	20	24735.82
CATIENUS (USA)	1	10	1	1	2	1978.00
CAYMAN KAI (IRE)	4	21	1	1	3	8443.25
CELTIC SWING (GB)	36	175	8	13	37	158968.66
CENTRAL PARK (IRE)	3	21	2	2	3	5205.81
CHEVALIER (IRE)	23	135	5	8	34	61926.49
CHINEUR (FR)	43	310	26	43	97	267236.06
CHOISIR (AUS)	107	682	46	77	216	678098.89
CITY ON A HILL (USA)	5	25	2	2	6	12214.17
CLODOVIL (IRE)	78	423	32	55	160	557260.39
CLOUDINGS (IRE)	2	10	1	2	2	5052.67
COCKNEY REBEL (IRE)	37	190	16	20	52	102065.99
COMMANDS (AUS)	1	6	1	1	4	75695.28
COMMON WORLD (USA)	3	14	1	1	3	4076.25
COMPTON PLACE (GB)	100	683	40	66	204	559757.81
CONSOLIDATOR (USA)	2	16	2	2	4	15299.99
COUNTRY REEL (USA)	5	33	2	2	9	9429.36
CRAFTY PROSPECTOR (USA)	1	17	1	1	8	6795.34
CURLIN (USA)	4	10	1	1	4	13521.55
CYRANO DE BERGERAC	1	8	1	1	4	4093.50
DAAHER (CAN)	2	5	2	2	2	6861.85
DAGGERS DRAWN (USA)	10	26	1	2	7	18196.10
DALAKHANI (IRE)	94	368	30	41	131	529201.64
DANBIRD (AUS)	21	144	7	9	50	46903.40
DANCING SPREE (USA)	2	9	1	1	2	7157.55
DANEHILL (USA)	5	28	1	4	4	10638.41
DANEHILL DANCER (IRE)	166	810	58	85	293	1328848.87
DANETIME (IRE)	24	227	12	23	67	255401.63
DANROAD (AUS)	15	82	3	4	13	19238.44
DANSILI (GB)	152	650	68	98	236	1980597.89
DANZERO (AUS)	2	16	1	2	3	10787.31
DANZIG (USA)	2	19	2	2	3	9904.82
DARK ANGEL (IRE)	96	611	48	75	211	978538.41
DARNAY (GB)	2	12	1	1	3	3081.85
DAYLAMI (IRE)	14	61	6	6	19	77691.78
DEEP IMPACT (JPN)	3	6	1	1	1	4026.35
DEFINITE ARTICLE (GB)	10	28	2	2	8	12862.50
DELLA FRANCESCA (USA)	5	21	2	3	4	9453.00
DELTA DANCER (GB)	1	9	1	2	1	3696.20
DEPLOY	5	19	1	2	2	11558.82
DEPORTIVO (GB)	10	78	5	8	18	43041.87
DESERT MILLENNIUM (IRE)	2	18	1	1	7	5114.34
DESERT PRINCE (IRE)	13	97	5	9	21	55520.04
DESERT STYLE (IRE)	22	110	6	10	33	70180.14
DESERT SUN (GB)	7	61	1	2	24	33599.67

STALLIONS	RNRS	STARTS	WNRS	WINS	PLACES	TOTAL (£)
DIAMOND GREEN (FR)	49	284	16	22	72	116943.17
DIESIS	7	43	3	6	10	24954.28
DIKTAT (GB)	40	254	12	15	75	157465.34
DILSHAAN (GB)	6	48	3	5	16	63721.67
DISTANT MUSIC (USA)	11	68	3	4	14	24290.49
DISTANT VIEW (USA)	1	22	1	1	9	5741.59
DISTORTED HUMOR (USA)	19	76	9	9	38	117104.87
DIXIE UNION (USA)	10	44	3	4	11	24214.30
DOCKSIDER (USA)	2	27	1	2	9	19956.70
DOMEDRIVER (IRE)	5	27	2	4	8	45679.33
DONERAILE COURT (USA)	2	25	2	3	2	6344.69
DOUBLE ECLIPSE (IRE)	1	2	1	1	1	9091.67
DOYEN (IRE)	35	258	16	28	82	238088.55
DR FONG (USA)	51	283	18	24	90	137645.87
DR MASSINI (IRE)	5	13	2	2	3	12849.99
DUBAI DESTINATION (USA)	108	594	38	62	193	589833.47
DUBAWI (IRE)	109	514	51	82	191	1304096.53
DUKE OF MARMALADE (IRE)	37	108	5	6	35	88817.64
DUSHYANTOR (USA)	3	6	2	3	0	15812.50
DUTCH ART (GB)	88	418	43	66	149	677164.42
DYLAN THOMAS (IRE)	84	363	28	39	125	499139.66
DYNAFORMER (USA)	30	103	14	18	38	482918.65
ECHO OF LIGHT (GB)	39	208	13	20	62	97058.51
ECTON PARK (USA)	2	13	1	1	5	8636.91
EDDINGTON (USA)	2	8	1	2	1	12046.99
E DUBAI (USA)	4	32	2	5	6	14235.08
EFISIO	8	79	4	11	22	112831.39
EL CORREDOR (USA)	6	20	1	2	3	5932.20
ELNADIM (USA)	43	230	16	24	77	202062.26
EL PRADO (IRE)	10	49	1	1	8	5994.03
ELUSIVE CITY (USA)	111	574	42	65	165	463300.27
ELUSIVE QUALITY (USA)	52	240	26	37	83	930192.58
EMPEROR FOUNTAIN	1	10	1	1	6	5501.70
EMPIRE MAKER (USA)	9	17	3	3	2	9569.34
ENCOSTA DE LAGO (AUS)	10	70	4	5	18	68011.55
ENGLISH CHANNEL (USA)	2	9	1	1	3	5218.93
ERHAAB (USA)	5	36	1	1	12	15602.77
EUROSILVER (USA)	1	12	1	3	2	8655.90
EXCEED AND EXCEL (AUS)	170	956	70	117	309	2078847.03
EXCELLENT ART (GB)	79	404	32	46	141	488081.81
EXCHANGE RATE (USA)	9	32	5	8	10	155825.19
EXPELLED (USA)	2	10	2	2	1	6544.75
FAIR MIX (IRE)	4	22	2	2	9	7554.64
FALBRAV (IRE)	7	49	6	7	10	80224.41
FALTAAT (USA)	1	1	1	1	0	198485.00
FANTASTIC LIGHT (USA)	32	165	11	17	44	142251.41
FASLIYEV (USA)	40	290	13	23	80	108997.10
FATH (USA)	25	211	8	19	39	128235.10
FAYRUZ	5	35	2	3	19	40625.58
FIREBREAK (GB)	30	177	6	11	65	116690.41
FIRST DEFENCE (USA)	2	6	1	2	3	52225.94
FIRST SAMURAI (USA)	5	19	2	4	4	34585.32
FIRST TRUMP (GB)	4	25	1	2	7	5497.59
FIVE STAR DAY (USA)	2	16	1	2	4	18722.98
FOOTSTEPSINTHESAND (GB)	103	568	35	51	201	784595.94
FOREST CAMP (USA)	2	15	1	2	1	3912.00
FOREST DANGER (USA)	1	9	1	1	2	5191.66
FORESTRY (USA)	4	21	1	1	4	4528.55
FOREST WILDCAT (USA)	5	18	1	1	2	6501.68
FORZANDO	3	23	1	1	8	4531.89
FOXHOUND (USA)	4	39	2	3	14	26078.80
FRAAM (GB)	18	130	9	15	34	53528.95
FRACAS (IRE)	2	7	1	2	0	11500.00

STALLIONS	RNRS	STARTS	WNRS	WINS	PLACES	TOTAL (£)
FRENCHMANS BAY (FR)	2	16	1	2	5	8256.40
FRUITS OF LOVE (USA)	7	29	1	1	2	2375.07
FUSAICHI PEGASUS (USA)	8	21	1	1	3	7656.40
GALILEO (IRE)	227	838	104	154	335	5774558.10
GENEROUS (IRE)	16	65	7	8	16	107598.29
GENTLEMAN'S DEAL (IRE)	10	71	4	7	16	21629.74
GERMANY (USA)	1	1	1	1	0	13270.83
GHOSTZAPPER (USA)	3	12	1	1	5	6699.95
GIANT'S CAUSEWAY (USA)	47	192	10	15	43	214657.87
GOLAN (IRE)	13	51	4	7	15	53742.77
GOLD AWAY (IRE)	7	45	3	3	18	16299.33
GOLDEN SNAKE (USA)	4	22	2	2	5	9065.43
GONE WEST (USA)	6	36	3	3	11	60317.85
GOOD REWARD (USA)	1	10	1	1	4	3561.53
GOODRICKE (GB)	3	20	1	1	4	8299.93
GOTHENBERG (IRE)	1	5	1	1	2	4608.33
GRAND LODGE (USA)	6	24	1	1	3	6085.08
GRAND SLAM (USA)	5	26	3	3	5	24701.31
GREAT COMMOTION (USA)	1	4	1	1	0	2385.95
GREAT EXHIBITION (USA)	8	16	1	1	2	5658.53
GREAT PALM (USA)	2	7	1	1	0	3208.33
GREEN DESERT (USA)	66	422	27	36	132	293143.00
GREEN TUNE (USA)	3	10	1	1	3	13697.55
GROOM DANCER (USA)	7	33	1	2	11	8538.27
GULCH (USA)	4	29	1	1	4	3063.40
HAAFHD (GB)	101	605	48	69	183	557365.39
HAATEF (USA)	21	107	7	9	40	77533.90
HALLING (USA)	72	324	25	35	105	426009.29
HAMAIRI (IRE)	1	9	1	1	2	2218.75
HANNOUMA (IRE)	2	9	1	3	0	62233.34
HARD SPUN (USA)	31	114	13	17	45	82092.82
HARLAN'S HOLIDAY (USA)	4	12	1	1	4	62210.52
HAWK WING (USA)	68	340	19	28	85	356893.56
HEATSEEKER (IRE)	1	3	1	1	1	10270.83
HELIOSTATIC (IRE)	7	32	1	1	9	16214.88
HENNESSY (USA)	3	11	1	1	1	2571.99
HENRYTHENAVIGATOR (USA)	24	80	11	12	31	261562.60
HERNANDO (FR)	38	174	15	21	62	209857.16
HIGH CHAPARRAL (IRE)	93	426	31	43	135	851739.86
HIGHEST HONOR (FR)	3	17	2	2	6	9179.10
HIGH YIELD (USA)	3	23	1	1	3	3567.35
HOLD THAT TIGER (USA)	5	33	2	3	7	13802.47
HOLY ROMAN EMPEROR (IRE)	144	757	63	84	271	1182126.89
HUNTING LION (IRE)	2	14	1	2	3	5991.25
HURRICANE RUN (IRE)	70	362	28	48	123	492613.57
ICEMAN (GB)	67	446	24	37	130	244376.21
IFFRAAJ (GB)	101	616	41	56	195	413803.80
IMPERIAL BALLET (IRE)	7	45	3	4	15	24560.00
IMPERIAL DANCER (GB)	19	125	6	9	28	136275.43
INCHINOR (GB)	6	30	1	2	9	53935.69
INCLUDE (USA)	2	6	1	1	1	15750.00
INDESATCHEL (IRE)	45	214	13	18	52	74637.68
INDIAN DANEHILL (IRE)	10	61	2	3	9	12606.42
INDIAN HAVEN (GB)	26	100	3	3	28	25971.58
INDIAN RIDGE	18	124	6	7	35	55540.57
IN THE WINGS	10	27	1	2	7	11122.05
INTIKHAB (USA)	62	347	22	38	103	687704.25
INVASOR (ARG)	10	30	1	1	10	14218.50
INVINCIBLE SPIRIT (IRE)	194	1013	76	118	350	2281856.01
IRON MASK (USA)	6	53	2	4	12	18783.01
ISHIGURU (USA)	69	447	28	45	119	283047.37
IVAN DENISOVICH (IRE)	23	108	3	4	25	20720.31
JAZIL (USA)	5	11	1	1	6	7463.63

STALLIONS	RNRS	STARTS	WNRS	WINS	PLACES	TOTAL (£)
JEREMY (USA)	56	303	25	37	78	280272.82
JOHANNESBURG (USA)	40	251	16	25	81	304579.76
JOHAR (USA)	3	21	2	4	6	31603.96
JOSR ALGARHOUD (IRE)	14	72	4	5	16	17664.79
KAHYASI	4	19	1	1	5	3458.10
KALANISI (IRE)	20	98	2	4	30	68478.56
KALDOUNEVEES (FR)	2	7	1	1	2	2261.25
KAYF TARA (GB)	8	26	2	2	2	4029.75
KEY OF LUCK (USA)	19	91	3	6	26	44602.82
KHELEYF (USA)	141	867	52	79	266	624754.44
KING CHARLEMAGNE (USA)	10	70	5	8	15	29612.50
KING CUGAT (USA)	1	2	1	1	1	5558.33
KINGMAMBO (USA)	13	53	5	7	18	436164.75
KINGSALSA (USA)	4	31	3	5	12	30334.29
KING'S BEST (USA)	75	418	28	40	136	588569.77
KING'S THEATRE (IRE)	9	38	2	2	13	19734.67
KIRKWALL (GB)	5	15	1	1	5	5112.30
KITTEN'S JOY (USA)	11	42	3	5	9	49261.41
KODIAC (GB)	69	443	29	41	169	336020.43
KOMAITE (USA)	4	16	1	1	3	3014.00
KRIS KIN (USA)	6	33	1	2	10	17821.15
KYLLACHY (GB)	156	996	63	100	279	827105.47
LAHIB (USA)	8	41	2	4	10	16710.32
LANDO (GER)	9	27	2	5	7	30966.23
LANGFUHR (CAN)	6	35	2	3	7	19976.45
LAPIERRE	1	6	1	1	1	4720.83
LAVIRCO (GER)	1	2	1	1	0	4600.00
LAWMAN (FR)	63	260	18	27	81	519413.68
LAYMAN (USA)	3	9	1	1	3	2810.80
LEMON DROP KID (USA)	20	77	8	10	27	73158.63
LEND A HAND (GB)	6	24	1	1	6	3240.10
LEPORELLO (IRE)	2	6	1	1	3	2797.45
LEROIDESANIMAUX (BRZ)	4	28	1	1	9	32236.05
LE VIE DEI COLORI (GB)	19	155	10	26	49	263420.98
LIBRETTIST (USA)	35	206	11	18	52	209477.78
LIL'S BOY (USA)	1	12	1	2	6	19920.83
LINAMIX (FR)	8	30	3	4	6	158040.72
LINNGARI (IRE)	1	7	1	2	3	11759.31
LION HEART (USA)	6	17	1	1	7	7058.69
LITTLETOWN BOY (USA)	2	8	1	1	3	2717.62
LOMITAS (GB)	12	42	4	7	17	610275.48
LONHRO (AUS)	2	12	2	3	6	44382.70
LUCKY OWNERS (NZ)	9	45	2	3	10	35616.61
LUCKY STORY (USA)	46	231	15	24	47	157717.81
LUJAIN (USA)	16	117	7	12	34	50248.33
MACHIAVELLIAN (USA)	10	106	4	6	26	51506.61
MAJESTIC MISSILE (IRE)	35	215	14	27	65	257500.41
MAKBUL	8	60	3	6	18	53606.91
MANDURO (GER)	66	262	21	33	98	341686.07
MARIA'S MON (USA)	5	26	2	4	4	17838.70
MARJU (IRE)	55	306	25	45	99	277986.98
MARK OF ESTEEM (IRE)	22	144	9	14	44	57900.50
MARTINO ALONSO (IRE)	1	3	1	1	1	32670.00
MASTERFUL (USA)	3	11	1	1	6	8882.63
MEDAGLIA D'ORO (USA)	19	52	7	7	15	41615.88
MEDECIS (GB)	18	106	7	10	23	77504.53
MEDICEAN (GB)	115	574	38	53	173	926413.67
MERDON MELODY	1	8	1	1	3	3736.75
MIDNIGHT LEGEND (GB)	3	7	1	1	2	2026.09
MIESQUE'S SON (USA)	1	9	1	3	2	10903.55
MILK IT MICK (GB)	16	79	2	2	25	19992.92
MILLKOM (GB)	4	29	2	3	11	9967.72
MINASHKI (IRE)	1	3	1	1	1	2207.50

STALLIONS	RNRS	STARTS	WNRS	WINS	PLACES	TOTAL (£)
MIND GAMES (GB)	15	83	4	6	14	19865.51
MINGUN (USA)	2	13	2	2	5	10542.21
MISU BOND (IRE)	29	130	7	9	33	35682.40
MIZZEN MAST (USA)	22	137	14	16	48	115652.92
MODIGLIANI (USA)	19	120	5	7	30	40660.92
MONASHEE MOUNTAIN (USA)	8	34	2	4	9	17860.19
MONSIEUR BOND (IRE)	53	326	19	35	87	153579.39
MONSUN (GER)	33	134	18	23	43	349633.76
MONTJEU (IRE)	111	502	43	67	186	3155205.74
MORE THAN READY (USA)	11	74	6	7	17	30864.47
MOSS VALE (IRE)	62	324	17	25	87	142551.39
MOST WELCOME	4	27	2	3	6	15063.92
MOTIVATOR (GB)	88	395	39	51	127	500859.13
MOUNT NELSON (GB)	22	59	6	8	19	57462.81
MOZART (IRE)	5	45	2	3	9	30089.44
MR GREELEY (USA)	47	201	13	15	51	82438.23
MTOTO	8	40	2	3	10	20464.95
MUHTARRAM	6	18	1	1	5	6728.51
MUHTATHIR (GB)	11	45	3	4	12	26232.41
MUJADIL (USA)	31	248	14	24	79	143765.71
MUJAHID (USA)	21	150	8	12	33	95041.58
MULL OF KINTYRE (USA)	16	86	8	19	18	253659.97
MULTIPLEX (GB)	47	229	14	19	65	116708.95
NAMID (GB)	50	349	21	28	77	235474.41
NASHWAN (USA)	1	15	1	2	5	6591.40
NAYEF (USA)	98	424	37	50	139	398206.72
NEEDWOOD BLADE (GB)	51	284	15	25	71	105669.77
NEW APPROACH (IRE)	30	87	10	18	34	537897.72
NIGHT SHIFT (USA)	15	137	8	11	32	130747.66
NOMADIC WAY (USA)	2	16	1	1	2	2327.75
NORSE DANCER (IRE)	11	65	4	6	15	59887.80
NORTHERN AFLEET (USA)	1	11	1	3	5	6621.96
NORTH LIGHT (IRE)	6	20	1	1	5	21991.38
NOTNOWCATO (GB)	47	196	14	27	44	235473.67
NOVERRE (USA)	45	324	22	36	82	231649.42
NUMEROUS (USA)	3	23	1	1	5	7958.54
OASIS DREAM (GB)	184	1036	86	134	357	1399062.31
OBSERVATORY (USA)	30	144	7	10	41	150816.45
OFFICER (USA)	5	25	2	2	7	6789.37
OLDEN TIMES (GB)	4	25	2	5	13	165357.57
OLMODAVOR (USA)	1	16	1	2	2	4163.50
ONE COOL CAT (USA)	65	391	24	32	117	232625.62
ORATORIO (IRE)	114	652	51	76	198	613424.15
ORIENTATE (USA)	5	33	2	2	12	87532.42
ORIENTOR (GB)	7	40	2	6	15	100406.41
ORPEN (USA)	20	107	6	8	21	102459.14
OSORIO (GER)	5	32	2	6	12	23801.81
PAIRUMANI STAR (IRE)	2	16	1	2	6	27375.00
PAPAL BULL (GB)	14	31	1	1	4	4248.70
PARIS HOUSE (GB)	6	24	1	2	5	15011.95
PASSING GLANCE (GB)	9	36	4	4	8	143087.07
PASTORAL PURSUITS (GB)	101	493	35	49	154	338976.13
PEARL OF LOVE (IRE)	4	19	2	3	2	5459.66
PEINTRE CELEBRE (USA)	30	119	9	12	30	103789.23
PELDER (IRE)	1	7	1	1	3	5716.66
PENTIRE (GB)	4	10	1	1	2	4893.42
PERRYSTON VIEW (GB)	2	18	1	3	9	11115.10
PETARDIA (GB)	1	13	1	2	3	9231.20
PETIONVILLE (USA)	2	16	1	3	5	6783.84
PHOENIX REACH (IRE)	24	110	4	6	23	37847.51
PICCOLO (GB)	86	596	30	47	154	285675.22
PIVOTAL (GB)	159	891	74	120	330	1890857.41
POLISH PRECEDENT (USA)	5	11	1	1	1	20875.00

STALLIONS	RNRS	STARTS	WNRS	WINS	PLACES	TOTAL (£)
POMEROY (USA)	1	11	1	1	6	6224.25
PRESENTING (GB)	3	8	1	1	2	6566.66
PRIMARY (USA)	3	9	1	3	3	7696.04
PRIMO VALENTINO (IRE)	19	109	5	10	31	35718.23
PRINCELY HEIR (IRE)	7	42	1	1	7	3076.73
PRIZED (USA)	1	5	1	2	1	124180.00
PROCLAMATION (IRE)	39	206	11	17	43	81552.76
PROUD CITIZEN (USA)	21	116	7	9	33	37058.08
PURSUIT OF LOVE (GB)	7	31	2	2	11	7836.75
PYRUS (USA)	14	125	7	12	50	136916.28
QUIET AMERICAN (USA)	2	11	1	1	1	4408.80
RAHY (USA)	18	86	7	9	28	118536.09
RAIL LINK (GB)	33	117	9	13	34	93622.13
RAINBOW QUEST (USA)	14	51	5	7	17	264833.12
RAISE A GRAND (IRE)	7	41	2	3	7	9937.51
RAKTI (GB)	16	96	3	5	28	24586.12
RAMBLING BEAR (GB)	5	24	1	1	7	3985.79
RAMONTI (FR)	6	22	4	6	6	38861.54
RAVEN'S PASS (USA)	34	82	12	17	34	251532.38
REDBACK (GB)	51	308	19	32	92	153823.42
RED CLUBS (IRE)	117	711	43	66	237	833990.16
REDOUTE'S CHOICE (AUS)	6	48	4	5	19	62058.29
RED RANSOM (USA)	39	206	10	16	64	111205.48
REEL BUDDY (USA)	7	30	2	5	6	16171.77
REFUSE TO BEND (IRE)	111	595	35	56	172	339388.26
REINALDO (FR)	1	11	1	3	5	42814.50
REPENT (USA)	1	6	1	1	3	8841.66
RESET (AUS)	19	123	5	7	29	36164.26
RESPLENDENT GLORY (IRE)	10	63	3	5	20	22622.16
REVOQUE (IRE)	4	16	1	1	9	16161.12
ROCK HARD TEN (USA)	6	23	2	2	9	11029.35
ROCK OF GIBRALTAR (IRE)	134	654	48	71	203	880530.19
ROMAN RULER (USA)	4	23	1	2	5	6800.77
ROSSINI (USA)	5	23	1	2	3	17188.81
ROUVRES (FR)	1	7	1	1	1	2347.20
ROYAL APPLAUSE (GB)	175	1004	55	80	323	556333.86
ROYAL DRAGON (USA)	1	11	1	2	3	14327.02
SADDLERS' HALL (IRE)	4	10	1	1	4	7204.16
SADLER'S WELLS (USA)	46	158	6	10	45	259890.85
SAFFRON WALDEN (FR)	7	19	2	3	9	14090.00
SAHM (USA)	3	17	1	1	10	9691.64
SAKHEE (USA)	66	310	24	32	110	215226.44
SAKHEE'S SECRET (GB)	61	228	22	27	80	140303.57
SAMPOWER STAR (GB)	3	37	1	1	10	9694.04
SAMUM (GER)	4	13	1	1	3	4340.80
SCORPION (IRE)	3	13	1	1	3	7674.99
SEA FREEDOM (GB)	1	6	1	2	1	5513.45
SECOND EMPIRE (IRE)	2	23	2	2	12	18087.63
SEEKING THE GOLD (USA)	7	36	1	1	9	5898.47
SELKIRK (USA)	75	381	32	46	116	994466.91
SEPTIEME CIEL (USA)	4	20	1	2	3	7725.65
SESARO (USA)	2	11	1	1	4	5772.70
SHAMARDAL (USA)	123	563	48	84	194	791729.56
SHERNAZAR	3	6	1	1	0	8050.00
SHINKO FOREST (IRE)	11	84	4	5	23	40433.79
SHIROCCO (GER)	58	228	12	16	85	571888.66
SILVER DEPUTY (CAN)	3	20	1	3	1	6207.52
SILVER PATRIARCH (IRE)	8	36	3	5	7	17729.10
SINGSPIEL (IRE)	94	431	28	39	131	378666.06
SINNDAR (IRE)	12	49	6	7	13	230958.27
SIR PERCY (GB)	48	254	25	36	117	289106.97
SIXTIES ICON (GB)	17	107	8	14	50	120865.15
SKI CHIEF (USA)	1	4	1	1	1	2506.20

STALLIONS	RNRS	STARTS	WNRS	WINS	PLACES	TOTAL (£)
SKY MESA (USA)	2	14	1	1	3	8228.85
SLEEPING INDIAN (GB)	79	480	23	37	144	549483.29
SMART STRIKE (CAN)	13	62	6	8	21	40836.28
SOLDIER HOLLOW (GB)	2	3	1	1	2	76013.33
SONGANDAPRAYER (USA)	2	18	1	2	7	14754.76
SOVIET STAR (USA)	27	138	8	13	37	66716.07
SPARTACUS (IRE)	10	43	1	2	8	8333.35
SPECTRUM (IRE)	5	57	2	5	10	13231.22
SPEIGHTSTOWN (USA)	31	144	13	17	48	151748.14
SPINNING WORLD (USA)	10	58	4	7	16	45765.59
STARCRAFT (NZ)	18	105	6	8	32	37846.45
STATUE OF LIBERTY (USA)	35	222	16	24	68	162138.25
STORMING HOME (GB)	21	121	8	11	32	53060.87
STORMY ATLANTIC (USA)	11	58	5	9	16	63848.62
STORMY RIVER (FR)	4	15	1	2	4	19014.63
STRATEGIC PRINCE (GB)	56	316	16	25	81	175769.53
STRAVINSKY (USA)	3	52	2	6	22	41375.53
STREET BOSS (USA)	5	23	2	3	7	11086.01
STREET CRY (IRE)	80	345	31	42	100	651551.53
STREET SENSE (USA)	13	53	5	10	21	58548.47
STRIKING AMBITION (GB)	16	87	4	9	18	32680.08
SUAVE (USA)	1	2	1	1	0	3169.81
SUCCESSFUL APPEAL (USA)	3	14	2	4	2	16394.05
SULAMANI (IRE)	21	108	4	7	39	45921.48
SUNDAY BREAK (JPN)	2	12	2	2	5	11389.71
SUPERIOR PREMIUM (GB)	7	54	4	9	10	28464.65
TAGULA (IRE)	54	374	19	38	110	281584.49
TAJRAASI (USA)	1	5	1	1	1	4883.33
TALE OF THE CAT (USA)	13	123	7	10	40	109138.65
TAMAYUZ (GB)	26	78	8	11	30	188727.26
TAPIT (USA)	5	18	2	2	3	6882.17
TAU CETI (GB)	2	23	1	2	9	7196.37
TEOFILIO (IRE)	1	6	1	1	1	2207.50
TEOFILO (IRE)	105	428	45	71	154	908431.66
TERTULLIAN (USA)	6	22	2	4	2	8627.08
TESTA ROSSA (AUS)	1	5	1	2	1	222712.00
THEATRICAL	6	28	2	6	11	21998.07
THOUSAND WORDS (GB)	18	83	4	6	33	55482.32
THREE VALLEYS (USA)	50	233	9	14	53	90000.34
THUNDER GULCH (USA)	5	25	1	1	8	7166.40
TIGER HILL (GB)	90	413	27	44	109	279517.55
TIPSY CREEK (USA)	5	30	2	2	8	6135.65
TITUS LIVIUS (FR)	31	224	9	10	53	72619.66
TIZNOW (USA)	3	7	1	1	2	2870.21
TOBOUGG (IRE)	67	339	20	36	93	207538.30
TOMBA (GB)	9	68	4	5	25	62772.61
TRADE FAIR (GB)	43	300	21	32	85	261786.73
TRADITIONALLY (USA)	4	53	2	2	17	19801.80
TRANS ISLAND (GB)	23	145	8	12	35	53695.52
TREMPOLINO (USA)	3	13	2	2	1	4290.64
TUMBLEBRUTUS (USA)	1	14	1	1	0	1704.25
TUMBLEWEED RIDGE (GB)	5	27	1	1	4	5900.38
UMISTIM (GB)	2	8	1	1	4	3152.03
UNTIL SUNDOWN (USA)	1	14	1	2	7	5070.57
VAL ROYAL (FR)	31	166	11	14	45	180773.52
VAN NISTELROOY (USA)	7	28	3	4	5	17126.10
VERGLAS (IRE)	96	549	41	63	180	599571.60
VETTORI (IRE)	7	47	1	1	14	20797.75
VIKING RULER (AUS)	8	34	2	2	6	8442.93
VINDICATION (USA)	3	16	2	2	1	8283.33
VINNIE ROE (IRE)	3	10	2	2	4	15916.68
VISION OF NIGHT (GB)	1	13	1	3	4	9399.70
VITAL EQUINE (IRE)	9	39	3	4	10	23745.89

STALLIONS	RNRS	STARTS	WNRS	WINS	PLACES	TOTAL (£)
WAKY NAO (GB)	3	16	1	3	5	18789.85
WAR CHANT (USA)	10	66	3	5	26	85145.80
WAR FRONT (USA)	5	22	4	7	11	113647.62
WESTERNER (GB)	10	28	2	2	11	13926.54
WHERE OR WHEN (IRE)	18	107	7	9	35	61905.11
WHIPPER (USA)	57	322	24	37	110	310545.18
WHITE MUZZLE (GB)	1	2	1	1	0	8625.00
WHYWHYWHY (USA)	2	6	1	1	0	4025.00
WINDSOR KNOT (IRE)	19	95	7	12	26	80787.21
WINGED LOVE (IRE)	3	5	1	1	0	0.00
WISEMAN'S FERRY (USA)	4	21	2	2	6	7287.31
WITH APPROVAL (CAN)	12	56	6	6	18	26408.64
WOODMAN (USA)	2	17	2	4	5	15841.05
XAAR (GB)	13	80	4	5	20	199606.53
YANKEE GENTLEMAN (USA)	4	33	1	1	12	10205.99
YES IT'S TRUE (USA)	7	28	3	3	4	6912.59
ZAFEEN (FR)	36	165	8	12	41	80463.36
ZAHA (CAN)	6	22	1	1	4	5130.70
ZAMINDAR (USA)	57	214	19	24	64	281962.00
ZAVATA (USA)	1	8	1	1	0	2264.15

BY KIND PERMISSION OF WEATHERBYS

NH STALLIONS' EARNINGS FOR 2011/12

(includes every stallion who sired a winner over jumps in Great Britain and Ireland in 2011/12)

STALLIONS	RNRS	STARTS	WNRS	WINS	PLACES	TOTAL (£)
AAHSAYLAD	4	15	2	3	4	23152.60
ABOO HOM (GB)	4	16	1	1	5	8178.95
ACATENANGO (GER)	8	30	2	5	9	51986.44
ACCESS SKI	5	19	1	1	6	6607.88
ACCLAMATION (GB)	13	57	4	5	31	32814.59
ACCONDY (IRE)	1	6	1	2	1	5784.79
ACCORDION	104	404	35	47	139	914014.31
ACTEUR FRANCAIS (USA)	1	2	1	1	1	2623.65
ACTION THIS DAY (USA)	3	11	1	1	3	8010.90
ACT ONE (GB)	18	55	5	5	16	23223.64
AD VALOREM (USA)	4	12	1	1	2	6910.46
AGENT BLEU (FR)	3	21	3	6	11	51927.23
AGNES WORLD (USA)	4	14	1	2	5	8420.23
AKBAR (IRE)	3	12	1	1	7	8108.18
ALAMO BAY (USA)	3	13	1	1	4	22584.39
ALBERTO GIACOMETTI (IRE)	4	17	2	5	4	69695.38
ALDEBARAN (USA)	1	10	1	2	4	10449.94
ALDERBROOK (GB)	117	442	30	43	152	558781.73
ALEXIUS (IRE)	3	9	1	1	1	2664.29
ALFLORA (IRE)	168	564	40	58	170	413773.11
ALHAARTH (IRE)	43	182	16	24	67	226381.68
ALJABR (USA)	5	27	3	4	11	32089.67
ALKALDE (GER)	3	12	1	1	8	44742.61
ALL MY DREAMS (IRE)	4	13	1	4	3	106466.24
ALMUTAWAKEL (GB)	6	26	1	2	13	17057.14
AL NAMIX (FR)	4	13	4	7	4	156242.40
ALWUHUSH (USA)	2	18	1	2	13	15991.10
AMERICAN POST (GB)	3	8	1	2	2	6416.94
AMILYNX (FR)	15	44	1	2	8	15331.05
ANABAA (USA)	12	59	4	7	21	44713.67
ANABAA BLUE (GB)	3	16	1	1	9	12993.24
ANSHAN	138	510	37	59	173	766211.45
ANTARCTIQUE (IRE)	5	18	2	3	4	26310.60
ANTONIUS PIUS (USA)	22	91	1	2	17	19573.15
ANZILLERO (GER)	3	10	2	2	1	11369.24
APPLE TREE (FR)	3	11	1	2	4	17770.74
APRIL NIGHT (FR)	13	54	3	4	18	47352.08
ARAAFA (IRE)	4	10	1	2	2	3834.62
ARAKAN (USA)	11	31	4	7	12	55718.77
ARCH (USA)	7	33	4	5	11	21664.76
ARCTIC LORD	13	55	3	4	15	29607.70
AREION (GER)	1	17	1	4	2	10732.33
ARKADIAN HERO (USA)	9	26	2	2	9	8427.32
ARZANNI	1	7	1	3	2	19379.31
ASHKALANI (IRE)	16	47	3	5	8	30236.58
ASSESSOR (IRE)	7	23	2	4	12	23626.74
ASTAIR (FR)	1	6	1	1	2	3161.71
ASTARABAD (USA)	14	46	2	2	11	21298.12
ATRAF (GB)	11	50	3	6	18	44733.02
AUCTION HOUSE (USA)	8	24	1	1	5	3620.17
AUENADLER (GER)	2	6	1	1	1	2778.08
AUSSIE RULES (USA)	5	22	1	1	9	10672.25
AVERTI (IRE)	3	9	1	1	2	3048.50
AVONBRIDGE (GB)	13	48	4	8	12	23678.22
AZAMOUR (IRE)	22	96	8	9	28	168908.24
BABY TURK	4	17	1	1	6	4213.65
BACH (IRE)	72	267	12	23	79	175719.93
BACHELOR DUKE (USA)	8	28	1	1	9	12954.92
BACHIR (IRE)	2	13	2	4	3	35456.89
BAHAMIAN BOUNTY (GB)	13	27	1	1	6	5243.98

STALLIONS	RNRS	STARTS	WNRS	WINS	PLACES	TOTAL (£)
BAHHARE (USA)	11	69	4	6	20	46704.62
BAHRI (USA)	19	72	4	5	12	20031.74
BAL HARBOUR (GB)	5	19	2	4	3	12449.11
BALKO (FR)	1	2	1	1	1	4053.00
BALLEROY (USA)	3	18	1	1	7	5558.78
BALLINGARRY (IRE)	12	47	3	3	8	19611.29
BANDMASTER (USA)	10	26	2	2	8	14037.02
BANYUMANIK (IRE)	2	15	1	2	7	22285.84
BARATHEA (IRE)	36	177	10	15	62	375953.71
BARYSHNIKOV (AUS)	21	63	3	6	17	25538.22
BASANTA (IRE)	9	40	3	6	9	64200.07
BEAT ALL (USA)	82	263	10	13	64	96612.72
BEAT HOLLOW (GB)	41	187	16	31	67	297416.83
BEAUCHAMP KING (GB)	6	27	2	3	10	13410.63
BEAU VENTURE (USA)	1	3	1	1	0	8327.59
BECKETT (IRE)	8	28	2	4	7	10943.38
BENEFICIAL (GB)	315	1324	102	154	395	1350039.95
BENNY THE DIP (USA)	3	16	3	3	9	68110.63
BERNSTEIN (USA)	2	10	2	2	4	8818.86
BERTOLINI (USA)	26	73	6	6	14	23469.62
BEST OF THE BESTS (IRE)	11	29	2	2	5	5878.19
BIENAMADO (USA)	11	48	3	4	7	11059.18
BIG BAD BOB (IRE)	8	31	1	2	9	18020.26
BIJOU D'INDE (GB)	3	6	1	1	2	2682.18
BISHOP OF CASHEL (GB)	27	90	5	6	22	63010.78
BLACK SAM BELLAMY (IRE)	10	29	1	1	11	138956.55
BLUE OCEAN (USA)	4	22	2	3	13	50936.88
BLUEPRINT (IRE)	29	122	8	12	31	87599.71
BLUSHING FLAME (USA)	6	18	1	1	6	4421.95
BOB BACK (USA)	122	469	37	55	161	765056.51
BOB'S RETURN (IRE)	72	285	14	19	97	241099.59
BOLLIN ERIC (GB)	22	74	6	9	17	33266.43
BONBON ROSE (FR)	4	17	3	7	6	43617.67
BRAVE ACT (GB)	1	6	1	3	0	27655.18
BRIAN BORU (IRE)	57	177	10	18	44	123887.96
BRIER CREEK (USA)	8	34	3	5	9	48489.80
BRIGHT LAUNCH (USA)	1	8	1	1	3	3596.72
BROADWAY FLYER (USA)	29	78	8	11	21	68057.13
BROKEN HEARTED	15	74	6	8	20	66116.13
BULINGTON (FR)	3	17	1	2	2	35203.70
BUSTER KING	1	12	1	2	4	6729.84
BUSY FLIGHT (GB)	8	22	1	1	6	3050.53
BYRON (GB)	5	12	1	1	4	4280.25
BYZANTIUM (FR)	2	13	1	3	4	12622.13
CABALLO RAPTOR (CAN)	5	21	1	1	4	11636.46
CACHET NOIR (USA)	1	7	1	1	1	2187.90
CACIQUE (IRE)	3	9	1	2	3	8806.66
CADEAUX GENEREUX	10	28	2	2	5	7721.75
CADOUDAL (FR)	19	77	6	14	26	632758.60
CALIFET (FR)	4	24	2	3	8	22646.83
CAPE CROSS (IRE)	32	126	10	15	50	193974.65
CAPE TOWN (IRE)	4	20	2	5	5	14036.97
CAPTAIN RIO (GB)	22	77	7	10	23	91421.34
CARNIVAL DANCER (GB)	6	20	2	2	4	5072.95
CARROLL HOUSE	31	128	8	8	25	69419.18
CARROWKEEL (IRE)	3	12	1	3	5	7560.95
CATCHER IN THE RYE (IRE)	54	187	16	24	37	162173.76
CATIENUS (USA)	2	5	1	1	0	1809.31
CELTIC SWING (GB)	23	69	6	7	19	42275.84
CENTRAL PARK (IRE)	19	66	2	4	16	34230.10
CHARENTE RIVER (IRE)	4	19	2	2	5	12591.53
CHARMER	2	14	1	1	6	20926.34
CHEVALIER (IRE)	23	67	6	9	19	51719.97
CHICHICASTENANGO (FR)	1	6	1	1	2	2690.28

STALLIONS	RNRS	STARTS	WNRS	WINS	PLACES	TOTAL (£)
CHOISIR (AUS)	12	37	1	3	13	23592.32
CHRISTOPHENE (USA)	2	4	1	1	2	6491.37
CHURLISH CHARM (GB)	2	6	2	2	2	6099.08
CITY HONOURS (IRE)	28	58	1	1	14	12805.73
CLACKSON (BRZ)	1	6	1	1	1	3048.30
CLASSIC CLICHE (IRE)	68	253	16	19	81	139141.67
CLERKENWELL (USA)	6	28	1	1	5	5216.95
CLODOVIL (IRE)	4	9	1	1	2	24532.80
CLOSE CONFLICT (USA)	22	100	4	6	23	60899.61
CLOUDINGS (IRE)	60	228	17	22	63	129104.30
COIS NA TINE (IRE)	3	15	2	2	3	5777.89
COLONEL COLLINS (USA)	4	15	2	2	5	6464.66
COLONIAL AFFAIR (USA)	1	4	1	1	2	7344.40
COMMANCHE RUN	7	39	3	5	11	19718.25
COMMANDER COLLINS (IRE)	12	44	1	2	17	9794.74
COMPTON PLACE (GB)	8	19	2	2	4	10149.88
COURT CAVE (IRE)	34	124	9	13	39	133792.43
COURTEOUS (GB)	4	10	1	1	2	2914.56
COZZENE (USA)	4	18	2	2	3	9500.48
CRAIGSTEEL (GB)	50	186	12	14	46	123123.66
CROCO ROUGE (IRE)	18	64	2	2	19	25140.36
CUPIDON (FR)	1	3	1	1	2	2507.89
CURTAIN TIME (IRE)	5	17	2	4	5	30389.45
CUT QUARTZ (FR)	1	4	1	1	2	1985.79
CYBORG (FR)	10	38	3	5	9	14418.71
CYRANO DE BERGERAC	1	1	1	1	0	4163.79
DADARISSIME (FR)	2	6	1	1	1	2970.98
DALAKHANI (IRE)	29	79	6	8	22	43946.40
DALIAPOUR (IRE)	6	29	3	3	13	37902.95
DANEHILL (USA)	7	23	1	4	5	10118.54
DANEHILL DANCER (IRE)	40	158	14	21	47	166132.05
DANROAD (AUS)	7	24	1	1	6	7001.50
DANSILI (GB)	35	167	13	25	59	151280.45
DANZIG (USA)	2	3	1	1	0	2053.20
DARAZARI (IRE)	4	12	1	1	7	28337.40
DARK MOONDANCER (GB)	13	46	1	1	14	14897.03
DARNAY (GB)	12	37	2	2	10	19659.94
DARSI (FR)	4	8	1	1	2	1802.68
DASHING BLADE	8	21	2	3	6	15665.72
DAYLAMI (IRE)	44	206	12	18	74	249840.40
DEFINITE ARTICLE (GB)	155	551	42	63	172	595116.88
DELLA FRANCESCA (USA)	5	19	3	4	5	48259.40
DENEL (FR)	5	29	2	3	8	25451.87
DENON (USA)	1	5	1	2	1	27357.76
DEPLOY	40	134	7	12	33	70419.01
DESERT KING (IRE)	9	24	1	2	4	5493.27
DESERT PRINCE (IRE)	29	125	8	11	35	81927.59
DESERT STYLE (IRE)	13	41	2	2	12	20012.76
DESERT SUN (GB)	10	27	1	1	5	14116.77
DIABLENEYEV (USA)	1	2	1	1	1	1837.92
DIAMOND GREEN (FR)	5	15	1	1	3	10233.74
DIESIS	13	44	4	5	14	30460.11
DIKTAT (GB)	35	120	8	10	27	42651.24
DILSHAAN (GB)	15	54	3	4	13	22218.56
DISCOVER D'AUTEUIL (FR)	10	49	5	9	17	53978.39
DISTANT MUSIC (USA)	6	33	3	4	10	23046.34
DOLPOUR	8	27	1	1	12	17308.12
DOM ALCO (FR)	23	90	11	16	44	860649.13
DOMEDRIVER (IRE)	13	38	2	4	4	23661.87
DOUBLE BED (FR)	2	4	1	2	1	19337.85
DOUBLE ECLIPSE (IRE)	9	29	3	4	11	54377.94
DOUBLETOUR (USA)	3	13	1	2	4	9407.42
DOUBLE TRIGGER (IRE)	37	132	9	12	37	134337.81
DOYEN (IRE)	28	96	7	8	28	63774.91

STALLIONS	RNRS	STARTS	WNRS	WINS	PLACES	TOTAL (£)
DREAM WELL (FR)	4	27	1	1	11	7449.75
DR FONG (USA)	30	103	5	6	26	41260.49
DR MASSINI (IRE)	113	469	36	44	128	394876.85
DUBAI DESTINATION (USA)	44	172	12	20	67	151256.59
DUBAWI (IRE)	14	57	8	11	23	177420.11
DUSHYANTOR (USA)	65	230	19	26	68	181664.65
D'WILDCAT (USA)	1	5	1	2	1	7925.85
DYNAFORMER (USA)	18	81	8	9	21	81209.64
EAST OF HEAVEN (IRE)	2	5	1	1	3	9965.57
EDDINGTON (USA)	1	6	1	2	3	8096.64
EFISIO	4	15	1	1	3	5453.90
ELMAAMUL (USA)	7	50	4	4	24	19049.97
ELNADIM (USA)	4	12	1	2	3	18293.39
EL PRADO (IRE)	3	11	1	1	3	3738.85
ELUSIVE CITY (USA)	7	23	1	1	4	3473.01
ELUSIVE QUALITY (USA)	3	6	1	1	0	2053.20
EMPEROR FOUNTAIN	8	33	3	3	9	9386.77
EMPIRE MAKER (USA)	6	14	2	3	1	19381.37
ENCOSTA DE LAGO (AUS)	3	14	1	1	6	7875.53
ENDOLI (USA)	5	24	1	4	5	14133.44
ENRIQUE (GB)	4	19	3	5	4	119585.83
ENVIRONMENT FRIEND (GB)	17	53	3	4	12	101880.57
EPALO (GER)	6	11	2	2	0	11444.40
EPERVIER BLEU	2	7	1	1	3	26409.13
EPISTOLAIRE (IRE)	2	11	1	1	4	8997.87
EQUERRY (USA)	3	10	1	1	3	3485.34
ERHAAB (USA)	22	62	1	1	18	9832.54
EXCEED AND EXCEL (AUS)	8	16	1	1	1	3447.21
EXECUTIVE PERK	7	30	2	6	8	26949.36
EXIT TO NOWHERE (USA)	90	290	19	28	83	157429.63
FADO (FR)	3	13	2	2	6	12568.30
FAIR MIX (IRE)	32	95	5	8	31	124529.82
FALBRAV (IRE)	3	5	2	2	1	9133.46
FANTASTIC LIGHT (USA)	30	116	7	11	31	77465.00
FASLIYEV (USA)	11	39	3	6	8	54362.68
FATH (USA)	15	77	6	12	19	65010.00
FIRST TRUMP (GB)	7	22	1	2	5	28761.22
FLEETWOOD (IRE)	16	57	4	9	17	53913.44
FLEMENSFIRTH (USA)	281	1088	92	139	346	1250715.86
FLYING LEGEND (USA)	17	80	5	8	20	97383.08
FOOTSTEPSINTHESAND (GB)	11	32	2	3	9	16213.50
FOREST CAMP (USA)	1	4	1	1	2	7760.92
FOREST WILDCAT (USA)	1	13	1	1	6	5488.98
FORT MORGAN (USA)	2	14	1	1	3	2623.14
FORZANDO	4	14	1	1	2	2853.24
FOURSTARS ALLSTAR (USA)	17	77	6	10	24	73559.14
FRAAM (GB)	27	94	7	11	27	52804.05
FRAGRANT MIX (IRE)	10	39	4	6	12	32713.89
FRENCH GLORY	1	2	1	1	0	21666.67
FRUITS OF LOVE (USA)	23	91	7	12	28	84672.83
FUSAICHI PEGASUS (USA)	6	30	2	2	7	8045.25
GALILEO (IRE)	64	249	21	36	77	326972.90
GARDE ROYALE	5	19	2	2	5	26459.33
GENEROUS (USA)	67	244	24	32	79	159985.68
GENTLEWAVE (IRE)	1	3	1	1	1	11190.70
GERMANY (USA)	9	43	1	1	17	44088.79
GIANT'S CAUSEWAY (USA)	23	87	8	12	31	71565.18
GILDORAN	1	10	1	2	3	5115.69
GLACIAL STORM (USA)	20	68	3	3	22	22650.12
GOLAN (IRE)	35	94	7	11	22	98107.14
GOLD AWAY (IRE)	6	26	1	1	10	30180.72
GOLDEN SNAKE (USA)	8	29	1	1	9	11599.60
GOLDEN TORNADO (IRE)	18	76	4	6	13	39014.88
GOLDMARK (USA)	20	85	2	6	25	37915.28

STALLIONS	RNRS	STARTS	WNRS	WINS	PLACES	TOTAL (£)
GOLDNEYEV (USA)	5	26	3	7	11	118203.58
GOLD WELL (GB)	14	49	6	9	19	56204.99
GONE WEST (USA)	2	18	1	2	8	6704.89
GOOD THYNE (USA)	8	30	2	3	9	21845.28
GOOFALIK (USA)	1	3	1	2	1	2227.06
GOTHLAND (FR)	4	13	1	3	1	7468.07
GOVERNOR BROWN (USA)	4	22	1	1	8	15470.58
GRAND LODGE (USA)	13	52	2	2	18	14500.53
GRAND PLAISIR (IRE)	5	23	4	4	10	126683.02
GRAND TRESOR (FR)	6	22	2	4	5	16655.84
GRAPE TREE ROAD (GB)	45	108	2	3	20	11947.53
GREAT EXHIBITION (USA)	2	11	1	1	6	6089.30
GREAT PALM (USA)	77	260	14	21	61	253275.92
GREAT PRETENDER (IRE)	3	9	1	1	3	2792.88
GREEN TUNE (FR)	5	21	2	2	9	12454.32
GREY RISK (FR)	3	21	3	4	13	210487.72
GROOM DANCER (USA)	15	58	6	7	21	72053.82
GULLAND (GB)	6	32	1	2	8	19473.27
GUNNER B	6	24	1	2	13	10619.83
HAAFHD (GB)	15	55	4	7	23	133971.60
HALLING (USA)	27	104	8	9	25	79121.33
HAMAS (IRE)	5	12	2	2	2	5567.18
HAWKEYE (IRE)	8	28	1	1	8	7048.84
HAWK WING (USA)	43	150	8	12	51	65098.65
HAZAAF (USA)	4	17	1	2	7	6683.74
HELISSIO (FR)	20	57	3	3	10	10155.48
HERNANDO (FR)	43	171	17	22	60	198728.22
HERON ISLAND (IRE)	69	220	14	21	67	150274.07
HERO'S TRIBUTE (USA)	1	4	1	1	3	4348.66
HIGH CHAPARRAL (IRE)	57	206	15	18	72	127126.32
HIGHEST HONOR (FR)	14	51	3	5	16	62182.61
HIGH ROLLER (IRE)	9	31	1	1	5	6142.91
HONOR GLIDE (USA)	1	12	1	2	4	9384.94
HUBBLY BUBBLY (USA)	22	79	2	4	31	28393.73
HUMBEL (USA)	17	60	4	4	19	18796.42
HURRICANE RUN (IRE)	10	24	3	3	12	28735.44
HUSSONET (USA)	1	12	1	1	6	4900.04
ICEMAN (GB)	11	39	3	5	10	19393.15
IDRIS (IRE)	2	11	2	4	4	20244.82
IMPERIAL BALLET (IRE)	15	80	4	5	29	60316.02
IMPERIAL DANCER (GB)	9	24	2	2	5	8421.18
INCHINOR (GB)	7	23	1	2	7	14040.92
INDESATCHEL (IRE)	4	13	1	1	5	3642.94
INDIAN CREEK (GB)	2	9	1	1	1	2261.88
INDIAN DANEHILL (IRE)	43	137	5	7	24	42172.95
INDIAN HAVEN (GB)	9	18	1	1	4	3732.28
INDIAN RIDGE	16	86	5	8	31	72590.87
INDIAN RIVER (FR)	7	15	1	1	2	2723.61
INDIAN ROCKET (GB)	2	5	2	3	1	8985.40
INSAN (USA)	10	41	3	6	13	28409.67
INSATIABLE (IRE)	12	42	2	3	11	18904.63
IN THE WINGS	20	80	2	3	27	38316.34
INTIKHAB (USA)	23	62	2	3	19	29894.87
INVINCIBLE SPIRIT (IRE)	21	75	5	5	22	33016.69
IRON MASK (USA)	5	12	1	1	3	3409.78
ISHIGURU (USA)	7	26	1	4	4	17801.46
IVAN DENISOVICH (IRE)	8	25	1	4	6	52732.62
JACKSON'S DRIFT (USA)	1	7	1	3	3	31961.21
JADE ROBBERY (USA)	6	12	1	1	3	4917.96
JAMMAAL (GB)	1	2	1	1	1	3429.18
JENDALI (USA)	2	19	1	2	2	4530.24
JEUNE HOMME (USA)	1	8	1	2	2	16660.20
JIMBLE (FR)	9	41	2	4	8	16466.03
JOHANNESBURG (USA)	13	43	1	1	9	8955.70

STALLIONS	RNRS	STARTS	WNRS	WINS	PLACES	TOTAL (£)
JOHANN QUATZ (FR)	3	14	2	2	8	29864.00
JOHN FRENCH	2	10	1	3	4	14896.84
JOLLY JAKE (NZ)	4	18	1	1	2	7535.96
JOSR ALGARHOUD (IRE)	15	43	2	5	12	30002.37
KADALKO (FR)	5	17	1	3	7	24931.25
KADASTROF (FR)	13	53	3	6	11	22354.63
KADEED (IRE)	3	12	1	2	0	11004.31
KAHYASI	39	160	9	13	57	128787.03
KALANISI (IRE)	30	104	11	14	29	78470.06
KALDOUNEVEES (FR)	7	16	1	1	5	17736.94
KAPGARDE (FR)	23	103	13	17	35	142012.11
KARINGA BAY	136	548	40	64	165	382268.50
KASAKOV (GB)	2	19	1	1	11	11248.72
KAYF TARA (GB)	144	594	54	80	209	698426.32
KELTOS (FR)	2	4	1	1	1	6227.20
KENDOR (FR)	6	23	3	8	6	82821.20
KEY OF LUCK (USA)	20	92	7	16	30	111933.20
KHALKEVI (IRE)	3	18	2	5	7	28973.66
KHELEYF (USA)	8	23	2	2	7	13797.20
KIDDER (FR)	1	7	1	2	1	5433.48
KILLER INSTINCT (GB)	8	22	2	4	3	19012.60
KING CHARLEMAGNE (USA)	9	30	2	2	8	8407.32
KING CUGAT (USA)	1	1	1	1	0	41333.33
KINGMAMBO (USA)	7	41	4	4	8	15302.03
KINGSALSA (USA)	7	37	3	3	15	52182.02
KING'S BEST (USA)	56	217	14	20	70	156125.94
KING'S THEATRE (IRE)	201	843	78	117	286	1676426.19
KIRKWALL (GB)	11	32	3	5	9	18755.19
KIZITCA (FR)	2	8	1	1	4	9527.42
KODIAC (GB)	4	16	2	2	4	8466.60
KOMAITE (USA)	3	7	1	1	1	6691.03
KOTASHAAN (FR)	10	22	1	1	1	2677.30
KOTKY BLEU (FR)	1	2	1	1	0	2014.38
KRIS	4	24	4	4	6	10878.05
KRIS KIN (USA)	19	42	2	2	4	6914.43
KUTUB (IRE)	5	18	2	3	4	20919.84
KYLLACHY (GB)	14	44	1	1	19	11446.78
LAHIB (USA)	41	147	7	9	31	49144.19
LANDO (GER)	13	65	3	6	20	47538.71
LASTING APPROVAL (USA)	1	3	1	1	1	3026.60
LAVERON (GB)	19	69	7	7	23	33975.81
LAVIRCO (GER)	18	71	7	11	21	137205.77
LEAR FAN (USA)	1	12	1	2	9	14207.64
LE BALAFRE (FR)	4	20	2	4	6	20788.08
LE FOU (IRE)	5	15	2	3	3	14490.95
LEMON DROP KID (USA)	8	30	5	5	8	25946.78
LEND A HAND (GB)	9	42	2	5	9	31944.37
LESOTHO (USA)	4	12	2	3	6	29441.63
LE VIE DEI COLORI (GB)	7	29	4	5	10	70187.65
LIBRETTIST (USA)	4	16	1	2	5	9134.93
LIL'S BOY (USA)	5	30	1	1	4	3344.95
LIMNOS (JPN)	3	14	1	1	1	5034.48
LINAMIX (FR)	19	85	7	11	32	69350.25
LION HEART (USA)	5	17	1	3	4	20340.72
LOMITAS (GER)	22	104	10	13	39	108229.66
LORD AMERICO	61	232	12	15	79	114617.58
LORD OF APPEAL (GB)	15	47	3	3	11	35452.77
LORD OF ENGLAND (GER)	1	7	1	2	3	9073.80
LORD OF MEN (GB)	2	9	1	2	4	7471.86
LOST WORLD (IRE)	15	64	6	9	15	106642.03
LOUP SAUVAGE (USA)	22	64	2	4	12	19784.45
LUCKY DREAM (FR)	2	6	1	1	1	5922.32
LUCKY STORY (USA)	7	20	2	3	5	10211.22
LUJAIN (USA)	2	9	1	1	3	2653.02

STALLIONS	RNRS	STARTS	WNRS	WINS	PLACES	TOTAL (£)
LUSO (GB)	118	438	28	41	113	317831.07
LUTE ANTIQUE (FR)	5	28	3	3	6	14874.04
MACHIAVELLIAN (USA)	10	34	1	1	8	21068.95
MAILLE PISTOL (FR)	4	17	1	1	7	4153.32
MAJESTIC MISSILE (IRE)	5	15	1	1	8	4566.35
MAKBUL	11	51	3	4	21	20291.80
MALINAS (GER)	6	24	3	6	9	17745.93
MAMOOL (IRE)	1	6	1	2	2	8998.83
MANSONNIEN (FR)	13	53	5	8	19	93006.87
MARATHON (USA)	6	22	1	2	10	14046.85
MARCHAND DE SABLE (USA)	3	14	1	2	4	9955.80
MARESCA SORRENTO (FR)	8	30	2	2	8	16093.79
MARIGNAN (USA)	19	54	2	4	11	12339.45
MARJU (IRE)	27	106	9	11	43	79150.58
MARK OF ESTEEM (IRE)	27	114	9	12	43	95111.41
MARTALINE (GB)	14	58	10	16	18	185233.19
MEDAALY (GB)	1	6	1	1	5	128666.85
MEDICEAN (GB)	43	198	18	27	68	134643.47
MIDNIGHT LEGEND (GB)	85	337	29	42	91	316343.44
MIESQUE'S SON (USA)	3	16	1	1	8	9663.43
MILAN (GB)	236	891	81	127	278	937594.61
MINSTER SON	20	83	3	3	28	25060.51
MISSED FLIGHT (GB)	7	23	2	3	9	16519.00
MISTER LORD (USA)	9	21	2	3	4	8996.25
MOHAAJIR (USA)	7	39	3	5	9	36001.76
MONASHEE MOUNTAIN (USA)	12	41	1	1	5	7088.12
MONSIEUR BOND (IRE)	8	16	1	1	6	6456.66
MONSUN (GER)	12	40	4	4	17	30433.59
MONTJEU (IRE)	87	314	30	41	96	490071.72
MOONAX (IRE)	13	39	2	2	13	12103.35
MORESPEED	1	6	1	2	4	56619.76
MORE THAN READY (USA)	3	15	1	1	3	13875.00
MOROZOV (USA)	8	26	3	4	10	15651.93
MORPETH (GB)	7	23	1	3	3	6011.79
MOSCOW SOCIETY (USA)	77	303	18	27	89	244769.55
MOTIVATOR (GB)	17	40	4	5	5	28356.10
MR COMBUSTIBLE (IRE)	23	93	6	10	30	49931.35
MR GREELEY (USA)	14	52	3	3	13	38396.85
MTOTO	11	54	4	7	19	24032.42
MUHTARRAM (USA)	19	71	6	12	22	61967.06
MUHTATHIR (GB)	9	32	4	9	13	60746.06
MUJAHID (USA)	17	69	2	6	15	27319.69
MULL OF KINTYRE (USA)	25	87	3	4	23	44148.91
MUROTO	3	18	2	2	8	70111.84
MY RISK (FR)	1	5	1	1	2	27208.25
NAHEEZ (USA)	15	38	2	2	5	9690.87
NAYEF (USA)	30	94	5	6	27	33228.95
NEEDLE GUN (IRE)	33	111	4	5	27	32761.08
NEEDWOOD BLADE (GB)	21	72	6	8	24	34207.01
NETWORK (GER)	15	52	5	10	20	321509.10
NEW FRONTIER (IRE)	24	119	11	17	34	233176.67
NEXT DESERT (IRE)	4	19	2	2	8	13738.55
NIGHT SHIFT (USA)	7	27	2	2	8	7648.85
NIKOS	14	65	3	3	34	82743.52
NO EXCUSE NEEDED (GB)	4	10	1	2	4	5832.22
NOMADIC WAY (USA)	17	55	5	5	13	31994.45
NORTH BRITON	1	5	1	3	1	6961.86
NORWICH	50	178	10	15	44	252461.75
NOVERRE (USA)	28	115	9	14	38	68408.83
OASIS DREAM (GB)	10	30	2	2	6	6665.52
OBSERVATORY (USA)	16	61	4	5	22	34170.37
OLD VIC	227	826	85	126	260	1190599.32
ONE COOL CAT (USA)	11	57	4	8	22	64359.83
ORATORIO (IRE)	7	26	2	2	4	6604.02

STALLIONS	RNRS	STARTS	WNRS	WINS	PLACES	TOTAL (£)
ORPEN (USA)	26	80	3	4	25	44587.39
OSCAR (IRE)	348	1158	79	122	320	1622193.57
OSCAR SCHINDLER (IRE)	24	71	4	7	15	39773.74
OUTOFTHEBOX (USA)	1	6	1	1	4	7104.28
OVERBURY (IRE)	98	383	29	46	125	343359.85
PANORAMIC	4	23	3	3	7	44969.96
PAOLINI (GER)	3	9	1	2	2	6327.12
PARTHIAN SPRINGS (GB)	9	39	2	3	9	15731.62
PASSING GLANCE (GB)	8	40	2	6	10	73920.44
PASSING SALE (FR)	14	57	5	5	16	35286.51
PASTERNAK (GB)	18	73	4	4	20	30767.79
PASTORAL PURSUITS (GB)	4	11	1	1	2	2597.44
PEINTRE CELEBRE (USA)	14	43	4	5	11	44918.71
PELDER (IRE)	4	19	2	3	5	23219.24
PENTIRE (GB)	4	24	3	4	11	33641.55
PERUGINO (USA)	5	23	1	3	2	30215.51
PETRIZZO	1	2	1	1	0	874.44
PHANTOM BREEZE	2	16	1	1	9	5819.28
PHARDANTE (FR)	2	2	1	1	0	988.95
PHOENIX REACH (IRE)	7	31	2	5	13	26592.25
PIERRE (GB)	15	68	5	7	20	34949.36
PILSUDSKI (IRE)	33	87	3	3	28	21340.76
PISTOLET BLEU (IRE)	31	130	10	12	45	341748.21
PIVOTAL (GB)	31	113	11	13	32	72802.78
PLEASANT TAP (USA)	2	8	1	3	5	25054.45
POLIGLOTE (GB)	11	43	4	6	13	63086.54
POLISH PRECEDENT (USA)	9	38	2	3	14	20089.73
POLISH SUMMER (GB)	4	20	2	2	5	34953.93
PORT LYAUTEY (FR)	5	15	2	2	4	8768.28
PORTRAIT GALLERY (IRE)	27	123	9	13	32	97737.03
POSIDONAS (GB)	9	23	2	2	8	16312.55
PRESENTING (GB)	336	1180	77	104	346	1084157.11
PRIMATICO (USA)	1	9	1	1	3	4530.70
PRIMO VALENTINO (IRE)	7	16	1	2	5	15181.07
PRINCE DANIEL (USA)	6	16	1	1	2	3216.80
PRINCE KIRK (FR)	1	5	1	1	3	2493.89
PRIOLO (USA)	7	18	2	3	2	21709.33
PROCLAMATION (IRE)	7	13	1	1	3	2843.49
PROTEKTOR (GER)	2	6	1	1	3	4565.59
PUBLISHER (GB)	10	29	2	4	7	27336.87
PURSUIT OF LOVE (GB)	10	56	4	6	20	20167.53
PUT IT BACK (USA)	1	7	1	1	2	5491.37
PUTRA SANDHURST (IRE)	2	5	1	1	0	4600.00
PYRAMUS (USA)	1	7	1	1	2	6232.76
PYRUS (USA)	16	35	1	2	10	23612.21
QUIET AMERICAN (USA)	1	8	1	2	3	8585.19
QUWS (GB)	29	99	4	5	22	46272.49
RAGMAR (FR)	14	48	4	4	10	31803.05
RAINBOW HIGH (GB)	12	50	2	2	12	12240.42
RAINBOW QUEST (USA)	18	63	5	7	18	28185.85
RAINTRAP (GB)	2	7	1	1	2	4125.60
RAISE A GRAND (IRE)	13	62	4	5	14	14291.59
RAKAPOSHI KING	9	35	2	2	10	9875.47
RAKTI (GB)	10	30	1	1	11	7555.35
RANSOM O'WAR (USA)	1	8	1	2	3	17164.80
RASHAR (USA)	31	125	3	4	25	38793.78
REDBACK (GB)	17	57	4	4	18	53881.04
RED RANSOM (USA)	29	114	4	7	35	135814.35
RED SUNSET	1	4	1	1	1	2593.70
REFUSE TO BEND (IRE)	30	101	8	12	34	55301.28
RELIGIOUSLY (USA)	5	33	4	4	20	26463.29
RESET (AUS)	10	39	3	4	12	18082.17
RESTLESS CARL (IRE)	1	3	1	1	1	1441.40
REVOQUE (IRE)	52	163	11	18	36	110498.80

STALLIONS	RNRS	STARTS	WNRS	WINS	PLACES	TOTAL (£)
RIDGEWOOD BEN (GB)	2	6	1	2	1	4360.32
RIGHT WIN (IRE)	6	22	2	2	3	18090.86
RIVERHEAD (USA)	2	6	1	1	3	3915.95
RIVERWISE (USA)	4	15	1	1	3	4690.82
ROAKARAD	3	8	2	3	1	8825.66
ROBELLINO (USA)	8	30	2	2	12	27652.82
ROBERTICO (GB)	4	21	1	1	9	8855.13
ROBIN DES CHAMPS (FR)	27	87	8	15	26	407629.51
ROBIN DES PRES (FR)	14	49	2	5	11	26302.44
ROCHESSON (FR)	3	15	1	2	4	10579.48
ROCK CITY	6	27	1	1	10	8104.92
ROCK HOPPER	14	35	2	3	8	16660.27
ROCK OF GIBRALTAR (IRE)	39	155	10	12	48	75796.03
ROI DE ROME (USA)	6	35	3	3	14	51654.28
ROSELIER (FR)	2	2	1	1	0	15005.00
ROSSINI (USA)	6	30	3	4	12	23380.33
ROYAL ANTHEM (USA)	10	31	1	1	5	12837.32
ROYAL APPLAUSE (GB)	33	139	11	18	37	75547.48
ROYAL CANAL (USA)	1	9	1	1	3	4870.68
ROYAL DRAGON (USA)	1	2	1	1	0	1437.24
RUDIMENTARY (USA)	51	196	14	20	57	227966.53
RUSSIAN REVIVAL (USA)	1	15	1	1	8	7567.93
SADDLERS' HALL (IRE)	111	504	29	53	149	478090.99
SADLER'S WELLS (USA)	79	349	28	43	129	697454.03
SAFETY CATCH (USA)	7	31	2	4	8	31557.22
SAFFRON WALDEN (FR)	12	43	4	7	7	45399.21
SAGACITY (FR)	15	64	4	7	19	31406.30
SAGAMIX (FR)	5	16	1	1	5	5692.32
SAINT CYRIEN (FR)	4	15	1	1	9	7028.93
SAINT DES SAINTS (FR)	12	40	6	11	15	335748.57
SAINT PREUIL (FR)	5	35	2	2	14	25254.19
SAKHEE (USA)	29	126	12	21	35	165579.32
SAMUM (GER)	2	9	1	1	4	5901.48
SASSANIAN (USA)	15	67	5	5	25	80065.63
SAUMAREZ	2	4	1	1	2	4125.60
SAYARSHAN (FR)	13	35	2	3	6	13506.71
SCRIBANO (GB)	9	40	3	6	12	29936.94
SCRIBE (IRE)	1	2	1	1	0	1916.32
SEA RAVEN (IRE)	6	28	2	4	8	66382.01
SECOND EMPIRE (IRE)	8	39	6	11	11	247875.20
SEEKING THE GOLD (USA)	2	6	1	1	2	2511.12
SELKIRK (USA)	38	113	5	11	32	39747.66
SENDAWAR (IRE)	5	16	2	4	6	21311.13
SESARO (USA)	3	15	1	2	2	8635.50
SHAANMER (IRE)	7	23	1	2	2	14276.90
SHAHRASTANI (USA)	8	36	1	2	7	12531.07
SHAMARDAL (USA)	7	36	2	4	20	28058.49
SHAMBO	6	28	2	6	7	17353.64
SHANTOU (USA)	39	153	14	22	44	200483.61
SHEER DANZIG (IRE)	1	10	1	1	0	4758.62
SHERNAZAR	40	173	8	13	50	126443.49
SHEYRANN	4	12	1	1	5	6030.85
SHIROCCO (GER)	5	20	1	2	4	6539.30
SHOLOKHOV (IRE)	4	27	3	6	10	65934.05
SILVANO (GER)	3	14	1	2	4	52872.21
SILVER PATRIARCH (IRE)	85	297	15	22	81	174827.79
SIMPLY GREAT (FR)	8	43	3	4	16	15069.95
SINGSPIEL (IRE)	19	81	4	6	33	54490.43
SIN KIANG (FR)	1	3	1	2	0	4719.33
SINNDAR (IRE)	14	52	4	5	17	92663.23
SIR HARRY LEWIS (USA)	66	259	18	30	87	231815.63
SLEEPING CAR (FR)	22	76	5	6	24	29277.97
SLICKLY (FR)	4	14	1	1	4	30078.34
SMADOUN (FR)	13	52	6	8	27	189458.28

STALLIONS	RNRS	STARTS	WNRS	WINS	PLACES	TOTAL (£)
SMART STRIKE (CAN)	3	16	2	3	3	8863.32
SNURGE	48	170	7	9	59	64613.61
SONUS (IRE)	18	61	2	3	16	37274.14
SOVEREIGN WATER (FR)	9	24	1	1	13	31586.77
SOVIET STAR (USA)	27	111	7	8	25	42360.23
SPADOUN (FR)	12	47	4	4	19	33578.18
SPARTACUS (IRE)	19	76	4	6	14	28960.96
SPECTRUM (IRE)	15	68	2	2	25	37868.25
SPINNING WORLD (USA)	5	13	1	3	3	18916.86
SPLENDID SENOR (USA)	1	1	1	1	0	1844.05
STARBOROUGH (GB)	6	25	3	4	11	29570.08
STATUE OF LIBERTY (USA)	22	64	3	8	13	56662.77
STERNKOENIG (IRE)	1	7	1	2	2	92778.24
STORMIN FEVER (USA)	2	12	2	3	3	12824.82
STORMING HOME (GB)	18	51	4	5	21	25142.08
STOWAWAY (GB)	25	86	9	13	28	148326.32
STRATEGIC CHOICE (USA)	12	46	5	9	12	96620.13
STRAVINSKY (USA)	2	8	1	1	3	6155.17
STREET CRY (IRE)	18	66	6	6	23	33745.20
SUBOTICA (FR)	10	36	2	3	13	15429.04
SUBTLE POWER (IRE)	18	80	3	4	24	47030.23
SULAMANI (IRE)	24	76	9	15	22	117214.78
SUNDAY SILENCE (USA)	2	10	1	2	3	11416.12
SUNSHINE STREET (USA)	11	45	2	3	9	18763.42
SUPER CELEBRE (FR)	2	6	1	1	3	5380.25
SUPERIOR PREMIUM (GB)	4	10	1	2	1	5601.42
SUPREME LEADER	55	207	15	17	55	161744.72
SUPREME SOUND (GB)	10	43	1	1	11	10058.51
SURE BLADE (USA)	5	19	1	1	9	5678.03
SYLVAN EXPRESS	3	5	1	1	2	3485.40
SYNEFOS (USA)	1	6	1	1	2	7633.33
SYSTEMATIC (GB)	4	10	1	1	6	3921.33
TAGULA (IRE)	11	41	5	9	7	81317.02
TAIPAN (IRE)	26	116	9	14	28	149633.31
TAKE RISKS (FR)	7	38	4	6	20	90964.69
TALAASH (IRE)	1	11	1	1	5	4589.64
TALE OF THE CAT (USA)	2	5	1	1	3	5121.21
TALKIN MAN (CAN)	14	40	1	1	12	10345.73
TAMAYAZ (CAN)	28	91	5	6	21	50388.57
TAMURE (IRE)	18	69	2	4	23	22687.69
TANNENKONIG (IRE)	1	5	1	2	0	11306.52
TEENOSO (USA)	1	7	1	2	2	5531.76
TEL QUEL (FR)	8	29	1	1	9	17670.09
TENDULKAR (USA)	5	34	3	3	17	20575.83
TEN MOST WANTED (USA)	1	5	1	2	2	6930.52
TERIMON	31	117	9	10	39	53500.26
TERTULLIAN (USA)	5	21	1	2	6	5403.64
THEATRICAL	6	31	1	1	10	9939.46
THEN AGAIN	1	7	1	2	0	6952.86
THUNDER GULCH (USA)	3	22	2	5	8	21414.77
TIDARO (USA)	2	18	1	1	5	9957.75
TIGER HILL (IRE)	42	121	8	13	32	143992.70
TIKKANEN (USA)	44	128	14	16	31	77446.43
TILLERMAN (GB)	11	42	4	4	6	17655.95
TIMBER COUNTRY (USA)	1	4	1	1	0	1788.87
TIMBOROA (GB)	1	7	1	1	3	3044.11
TIPSY CREEK (USA)	4	18	2	3	5	9248.89
TIRAAZ (USA)	8	25	3	5	7	362914.57
TITUS LIVIUS (FR)	7	28	2	2	9	14033.95
TOBOUGG (IRE)	57	221	11	14	54	91237.50
TOMBA (GB)	9	33	2	2	15	35999.05
TOPANOORA	18	70	6	7	19	66257.11
TOP OF THE WORLD	1	2	1	1	0	7757.44
TOULON (GB)	1	12	1	1	4	4051.80

STALLIONS	RNRS	STARTS	WNRS	WINS	PLACES	TOTAL (£)
TRADE FAIR (GB)	17	70	4	8	21	23900.30
TRADITIONALLY (USA)	15	68	5	8	20	73670.89
TRAGIC ROLE (USA)	9	48	2	3	23	31877.45
TRANS ISLAND (GB)	28	83	5	7	18	32345.66
TREMPOLINO (USA)	18	93	8	12	36	121177.45
TURBO SPEED	2	10	1	1	5	7329.57
TURGEON (USA)	33	139	13	17	57	194803.76
TURTLE ISLAND (IRE)	61	270	11	19	84	332268.27
TZAR RODNEY (FR)	1	6	1	1	4	5632.92
ULTIMATELY LUCKY (IRE)	3	16	1	1	6	4626.80
UMISTIM (GB)	5	33	1	1	9	4836.08
UNFUWAIN (USA)	8	27	3	3	11	86155.92
UNGARO (GER)	9	30	2	3	20	16669.37
UNTIL SUNDOWN (USA)	3	8	1	1	2	8416.93
URBAN OCEAN (FR)	3	10	1	1	7	6641.59
USEFUL (FR)	7	34	1	1	9	6496.29
VAGUELY PLEASANT (FR)	2	15	1	1	4	17458.56
VAL ROYAL (FR)	28	89	5	8	19	47965.84
VALSEUR (USA)	1	6	1	1	1	8917.80
VARESE (FR)	5	20	1	1	7	14374.90
VERGLAS (IRE)	24	86	3	3	7	75262.57
VERTICAL SPEED (FR)	4	9	1	1	5	8068.45
VETTORI (IRE)	17	62	3	5	17	25334.50
VICTORY NOTE (USA)	5	10	2	2	3	11762.08
VIC TOTO (FR)	1	9	1	1	4	4734.56
VIDEO ROCK (FR)	12	51	3	4	17	25571.13
VIKING RULER (AUS)	10	51	1	1	10	13337.51
VILLAGE STAR (FR)	1	3	1	2	0	216064.40
VILLEZ (USA)	5	19	2	2	6	20995.33
VINNIE ROE (IRE)	30	83	4	7	28	42746.85
VISIONARY (FR)	2	14	2	2	4	15459.55
VOIX DU NORD (FR)	3	6	1	1	0	1949.40
WAKY NAO (GB)	9	24	3	3	2	15115.18
WAR CHANT (USA)	10	42	1	1	17	10935.36
WAREED (IRE)	7	27	2	3	10	14719.86
WEET-A-MINUTE (IRE)	1	7	1	2	2	6755.30
WELD	6	18	1	1	3	3128.33
WELL CHOSEN (GB)	6	24	3	4	4	19338.47
WESTERNER (GB)	51	166	17	20	46	102300.12
WHERE OR WHEN (IRE)	22	81	3	5	22	35690.44
WHIPPER (USA)	10	22	2	2	6	6825.64
WHITMORE'S CONN (USA)	14	30	2	2	6	11748.41
WIMBLEBALL	1	6	1	1	4	4392.57
WINDSOR CASTLE (GB)	8	35	2	2	12	12536.31
WINGED LOVE (IRE)	69	313	22	36	96	314820.20
WINNING SMILE (FR)	2	3	2	2	1	20262.50
WISEMAN'S FERRY (USA)	1	9	1	3	3	17498.10
WITH APPROVAL (CAN)	4	11	1	2	4	13430.94
WITH THE FLOW (USA)	3	17	2	2	11	65031.19
WITNESS BOX (USA)	76	369	27	40	115	319714.11
WIZARD KING (GB)	18	52	3	4	9	21039.03
WOODS OF WINDSOR (USA)	8	35	2	4	12	88692.82
XAAR (GB)	18	79	4	5	25	34982.60
ZAFFARAN (USA)	20	70	3	4	28	103748.02
ZAGREB (USA)	49	175	10	14	52	76842.62
ZAHA (CAN)	8	17	2	2	2	5088.14
ZAMINDAR (USA)	8	36	2	3	9	21151.23
ZINDABAD (FR)	4	16	1	2	5	6026.79

BY KIND PERMISSION OF WEATHERBYS

IT'S SHOWTIME

BONUS WINNERS
TAKE A BOW

HIGH-PRICED YEARLINGS OF 2012 AT TATTERSALLS SALES
The following yearlings realised 72,000 Guineas and over at Tattersalls Sales in 2012:-

Name and Breeding	Purchaser	Guineas
HYDROGEN (GB) B C GALILEO (IRE) - FUNSIE (FR)	DAVID REDVERS BS	2500000
AL JASSASIYAH (IRE) B F GALILEO (IRE) - ALLURING PARK (IRE)	MANDORE INTERNATIONAL	1500000
B F GALILEO (IRE) - SHADOW SONG (IRE)	DEMI O'BYRNE	1300000
B C GALILEO (IRE) - ALEXANDER GOLDRUN (IRE)	DEMI O'BYRNE	950000
B F GALILEO (IRE) - SECRET GARDEN (IRE)	BLANDFORD BS	925000
GALAYA (IRE) B F GALILEO (IRE) - WITCH OF FIFE (USA)	WARATAH THOROUGHBREDS	900000
CH C RAVEN'S PASS (USA) - NIGHTIME (IRE)	JOHN FERGUSON BS	800000
DANJEU (IRE) B C MONTJEU (IRE) - WANNA (IRE)	WARATAH THOROUGHBREDS	725000
B F GALILEO (IRE) - ARKADINA (IRE)	MANDORE INTERNATIONAL	700000
B C MONTJEU (IRE) - LUCINA (GB)	DEMI O'BYRNE	700000
B C OASIS DREAM (GB) - GALAXY HIGHFLYER (GB)	DEMI O'BYRNE	700000
MIHANY (IRE) B C TEOFILO (IRE) - LOVE EXCELLING (FR)	SHADWELL ESTATE COMPANY	600000
ROYAL BATTALION (GB) B C SEA THE STARS (IRE) - YUMMY MUMMY (GB)	DAVID REDVERS BS	575000
B F GALILEO (IRE) - LA SYLVIA (IRE)	BADGERS BS	570000
B F DANSILI (GB) - NEARTICA (FR)	HUGO LASCELLES BS	550000
ELSHAADIN (GB) GR F DALAKHANI (IRE) - DISTINCTIVE LOOK (IRE)	SHADWELL ESTATE COMPANY	550000
ALTAAYIL (IRE) BR C SEA THE STARS (IRE) - ALLELUIA (GB)	SHADWELL ESTATE COMPANY	550000
CRITERIA (IRE) B F GALILEO (IRE) - ALEAGUEOFTHEIROWN (IRE)	CHEVELEY PARK STUD	535000
B F OASIS DREAM (GB) - AROSA (IRE)	WARATAH THOROUGHBREDS	525000
B F INVINCIBLE SPIRIT (IRE) - LANDMARK (USA)	DEMI O'BYRNE	525000
CH C GALILEO (IRE) - OUIJA BOARD (GB)	DEMI O'BYRNE	525000
B C SEA THE STARS (IRE) - MUSICAL TREAT (IRE)	MCCALMONT BS	500000
B F PIVOTAL (GB) - KITTY MATCHAM (IRE)	JOHN FERGUSON BS	485000
HOIST THE COLOURS (IRE) B C SEA THE STARS (IRE) - MULTICOLOUR WAVE (IRE)	C GORDON-WATSON BS	475000
B C DUBAWI (IRE) - MANOEUVRE (IRE)	FORM BS	470000
B C MONTJEU (IRE) - HONORLINA (FR)	DEMI O'BYRNE	450000
B C GALILEO (IRE) - HVEGER (AUS)	STEPHEN HILLEN BS	450000
B F OASIS DREAM (GB) - ARTY CRAFTY (USA)	HUGO LASCELLES BS	450000
SARPECH (IRE) B C SEA THE STARS (IRE) - SADIMA (IRE)	DAVID REDVERS BS	430000
B F MANDURO (GER) - WALDMARK (GER)	JOHN FERGUSON BS	430000
B C OASIS DREAM (GB) - BEACH BUNNY (IRE)	MARCO BOTTI	425000
B C OASIS DREAM (GB) - ATTRACTION (GB)	DEMI O'BYRNE	420000
B C INVINCIBLE SPIRIT (IRE) - GREENISLAND (IRE)	MANDORE INTERNATIONAL	420000
B F GALILEO (IRE) - JESSICA'S DREAM (IRE)	ROB SPEERS	400000
B C MONSUN (GER) - PONGEE (GB)	JOHN FERGUSON BS	400000
CH F SEA THE STARS (IRE) - MRS LINDSAY (USA)	RABBAH BS	400000
CH F NEW APPROACH (IRE) - WADAAT (GB)	MANDORE INTERNATIONAL	400000
BISHOPS AVENUE (IRE) B C LAWMAN (FR) - SHESASMARTLADY (IRE)	SACKVILLEDONALD	360000
B C DUBAWI (IRE) - EVER RIGG (GB)	WARREN / GORDON-WATSON	360000
B C INVINCIBLE SPIRIT (IRE) - ALEXANDER YOUTH (IRE)	JOHN FERGUSON BS	350000
B C DUBAWI (IRE) - SAVANNAH BELLE (GB)	JOHN FERGUSON BS	350000
GHARAANEEJ (IRE) BR F PIVOTAL (GB) - NEVERLETME GO (IRE)	SHADWELL ESTATE COMPANY	340000
B F GALILEO (IRE) - MAURALAKANA (FR)	HARUYA YOSHIDA	340000
CH C PIVOTAL (GB) - NOBLE ONE (GB)	HONG KONG JOCKEY CLUB	340000
B F MONSUN (GER) - SHEMISSA (IRE)	NICOLAS CLEMENT	320000
B C DANSILI (GB) - QUELLE VITESSE (GB)	MCCALMONT BS	320000
WARRIOR OF LIGHT (IRE) B C HIGH CHAPARRAL (IRE) - STRAWBERRY FLEDGE (USA)	COURSE INVESTMENT CORP	320000
GR C NEW APPROACH (IRE) - SCARLET EMPIRE (IRE)	JOHN FERGUSON BS	320000
B F INVINCIBLE SPIRIT (IRE) - SONACHAN (IRE)	C GORDON-WATSON BS	320000
B C DUBAWI (IRE) - MISS DELILA (USA)	JOHN FERGUSON BS	320000
B C INVINCIBLE SPIRIT (IRE) - MADEIRA MIST (IRE)	JS COMPANY	320000
MARGARET'S MISSION (IRE) B F SHAMARDAL (USA) - WIMPLE (USA)	SACKVILLEDONALD	310000
B F DANSILI (GB) - KIYRA WELLS (IRE)	SUNDERLAND HOLDINGS INC	310000
B C LEMON DROP KID (USA) - LYNNWOOD CHASE (USA)	C GORDON-WATSON BS	310000
B F OASIS DREAM (GB) - CAST IN GOLD (USA)	JOHN FERGUSON BS	310000
B F INVINCIBLE SPIRIT (IRE) - MISS DELA (IRE)	DEMI O'BYRNE	300000
B C DUBAWI (IRE) - ONE SO MARVELLOUS (GB)	YES/AL SHAHANIA STUD	300000
B F INVINCIBLE SPIRIT (IRE) - HOITY TOITY (GB)	JOHN FERGUSON BS	290000
CH C NEW APPROACH (IRE) - DUBAI SURPRISE (GB)	JOHN FERGUSON BS	280000
GR F DALAKHANI (IRE) - ROCK SALT (GB)	BLANDFORD BS	280000
B F SEA THE STARS (IRE) - LOVE TO DANCE (IRE)	MANDORE INTERNATIONAL	280000
B F OASIS DREAM (GB) - ALL FOR LAURA (GB)	JOHN GOSDEN RACING LLP	280000
B F ACCLAMATION (GB) - RED BLOSSOM (USA)	JOHN FERGUSON BS	280000
MR SMITH (GB) GR C GALILEO (IRE) - INTRIGUED (GB)	BLANDFORD BS	280000
B C GALILEO (IRE) - MOMENTS OF JOY (GB)	MCCALMONT BS	275000
B C DUBAWI (IRE) - LION FOREST (USA)	JOHN FERGUSON BS	260000
LIGHTNING SPEAR (GB) CH C PIVOTAL (GB) - ATLANTIC DESTINY (IRE)	DAVID REDVERS BS	260000
B C DUBAWI (IRE) - VALLOTA (GB)	JOHN WARREN BS	260000

Name and Breeding	Purchaser	Guineas
VIVA VALARIA (GB) B F OASIS DREAM (GB) - ON A SOAPBOX (USA)	WARATAH THOROUGHBREDS	260000
MUTAKAYYEF (GB) CH C SEA THE STARS (IRE) - INFALLIBLE (GB)	SHADWELL ESTATE COMPANY	260000
DRACO'S CODE (GB) B C GALILEO (IRE) - LADY KARR (GB)	VENDOR	260000
B C GALILEO (IRE) - NIGHT WOMAN (GER)	MARC KELLER	260000
B C NEW APPROACH (IRE) - CRIMSON RIBBON (USA)	WARATAH THOROUGHBREDS	260000
B C SEA THE STARS (IRE) - APPROACH (GB)	SUNDERLAND HOLDING INC	250000
MUTAMAKKIN (IRE) B C SHAMARDAL (USA) - PRINCESS SPEEDFIT (FR)	PETER & ROSS DOYLE BS	245000
TAQNEEN (IRE) B C CAPE CROSS (IRE) - BADEE'A (IRE)	SHADWELL ESTATE COMPANY	240000
B F MEDICEAN (GB) - TIME SAVED (GB)	DAVID REDVERS BS	240000
B F TAMAYUZ (GB) - FANTASTIC ACCOUNT (GB)	BLANDFORD BS	240000
BR C MONSUN (GER) - MIRACLE SEEKER (GB)	VENDOR	240000
SHAFRAH (IRE) B C ACCLAMATION (GB) - ROSY DUDLEY (IRE)	SHADWELL ESTATE COMPANY	240000
B F DUBAWI (IRE) - SIGNORINA CATTIVA (USA)	NORTH HILLS CO	240000
NICTATE (IRE) BR F TEOFILO (IRE) - WOODMAVEN (USA)	COURSE INVESTMENT CORP	240000
B C MONTJEU (IRE) - THINKING POSITIVE (GB)	BBA IRELAND	240000
DONCELLA (IRE) B F HIGH CHAPARRAL (IRE) - ONEREUSE (GB)	WARATAH THOROUGHBREDS	230000
SEA THE MOON (GER) B C SEA THE STARS (IRE) - SANWA (GER)	VENDOR	230000
B C SHAMARDAL (USA) - FRAPPE (IRE)	VENDOR	230000
B C BUSHRANGER (IRE) - POLISH BELLE (GB)	JEREMY NOSEDA RACING	220000
TOOFI (FR) B C HENRYTHENAVIGATOR (USA) - SILVER BARK (GB)	TONY NERSES	220000
B C TEOFILO (IRE) - POPPETS SWEETLOVE (GB)	TONY NERSES	220000
MUNFALLET (IRE) B C ROYAL APPLAUSE (GB) - PRINCESS MOOD (GER)	SHADWELL ESTATE COMPANY	220000
B C SHAMARDAL (USA) - AMAZED (GB)	JUDDMONTE FARMS	220000
B F INVINCIBLE SPIRIT (IRE) - VENTURI (GB)	JOHN McCORMACK BS	210000
CH/GR F GALILEO (IRE) - HOTELGENIE DOT COM (GB)	HUGO LASCELLES BS	210000
VOICE OF A LEADER (IRE) B C DANEHILL DANCER (IRE) - THEWAYTOSANJOSE (USA)	STEPHEN HILLEN BS	210000
CH C DUBAWI (IRE) - BEAUTIFUL FILLY (GB)	JOHN FERGUSON BS	210000
B F GALILEO (IRE) - REDSTONE DANCER (IRE)	BBA IRELAND	205000
B C MONTJEU (IRE) - FLEETING AFFAIR (USA)	DWAYNE WOODS	205000
DREAMING BEAUTY (GB) B F OASIS DREAM (GB) - INDEPENDENCE (GB)	JEREMY NOSEDA RACING	200000
CH C PIVOTAL (GB) - BRIGHT MORNING (USA)	C GORDON-WATSON BS	200000
B C EXCEED AND EXCEL (AUS) - GOWER SONG (GB)	C GORDON-WATSON BS	200000
GR C DARK ANGEL (IRE) - WIN CASH (IRE)	JOHN FERGUSON BS	200000
B F MEDAGLIA D'ORO (USA) - EMPRESS OF FRANCE (USA)	VENDOR	200000
A LEGACY OF LOVE (IRE) B F SEA THE STARS (IRE) - NASHMIAH (IRE)	BRENDA KARN-SMITH	200000
STAR CHART (IRE) B F DUBAWI (IRE) - STAR EXPRESS (GB)	CHEVELEY PARK STUD	200000
B C DANSILI (GB) - HEAVEN SENT (GB)	HONG KONG JOCKEY CLUB	200000
B C HENRYTHENAVIGATOR (USA) - SHERMEEN (IRE)	JOHN WARREN BS	200000
B/BR C ARCH (USA) - ZAPPEUSE (USA)	WARATAH THOROUGHBREDS	200000
B F INVINCIBLE SPIRIT (IRE) - CROSSMOLINA (IRE)	RABBAH BS	200000
CH F GALILEO (IRE) - CASTARA BEACH (IRE)	VENDOR	200000
B C GALILEO (IRE) - GINO'S SPIRITS (GB)	C GORDON-WATSON BS	200000
CH C EXCEED AND EXCEL (AUS) - ARIAN DA (GB)	HONG KONG JOCKEY CLUB	200000
CH C GALILEO (IRE) - PARTY (IRE)	SEASONS HOLIDAYS	200000
MEKHBAT (IRE) B C GALILEO (IRE) - KENTUCKY WARBLER (IRE)	MANDORE INTERNATIONAL	200000
BR C SEA THE STARS (IRE) - LOVE DIVINE (GB)	VENDOR	200000
B F DANSILI (GB) - HYPNOLOGY (USA)	VENDOR	195000
B C GALILEO (IRE) - TREE TOPS (GB)	DAVID REDVERS BS	190000
B C DUTCH ART (GB) - REGENCY ROSE (GB)	HUGO MERRY BS	190000
B C CAPE CROSS (IRE) - MISCHIEF MAKING (USA)	JOHN FERGUSON BS	190000
B C HOLY ROMAN EMPEROR (IRE) - CHANROSSA (IRE)	MRS A SKIFFINGTON	190000
B F ACCLAMATION (GB) - SOMERSET FALLS (UAE)	TONY NERSES	190000
CH F NEW APPROACH (IRE) - RIVER BELLE (GB)	JOHN FERGUSON BS	190000
B C SEA THE STARS (IRE) - DASH TO THE TOP (GB)	JILL LAMB BS	190000
B F GALILEO (IRE) - MORA BAI (GB)	J O'BYRNE	185000
B C TEOFILO (IRE) - CHANGEABLE (GB)	TONY NERSES	180000
B F PIVOTAL (GB) - BRIGITTA (IRE)	JOHN WARREN BS	180000
B F AUTHORIZED (IRE) - WELSH DIVA (GB)	JOHN WARREN BS	180000
B C SAKHEE'S SECRET (GB) - COFFEE TIME (IRE)	HONG KONG JOCKEY CLUB	180000
B C MONTJEU (IRE) - GHURRA (USA)	DWAYNE WOODS	180000
B F INVINCIBLE SPIRIT (IRE) - APPLAUDED (IRE)	WILLIAM HAGGAS	180000
B F GALILEO (IRE) - DOULA (USA)	BLANDFORD BS	175000
B F SELKIRK (USA) - SISTER MARIA (USA)	HUGO LASCELLES BS	170000
B C DUBAWI (IRE) - TANGO TONIC (IRE)	JOHN FERGUSON BS	170000
B F CHAMPS ELYSEES (GB) - SHEMRIYNA (IRE)	VENDOR	170000
B C NEW APPROACH (GB) - PARISIAN ELEGANCE (GB)	JOHN FERGUSON BS	170000
B C SEA THE STARS (IRE) - MODEL QUEEN (GB)	GERARD BUTLER	170000
ALZAMMAAR (USA) B C BIRDSTONE (USA) - ALMA MATER (GB)	SHADWELL ESTATE COMPANY	170000
EJADAH (IRE) B F CLODOVIL (IRE) - BINTALREEF (USA)	SHADWELL ESTATE COMPANY	170000
B C HOLY ROMAN EMPEROR (IRE) - SYVILLA (GB)	DEMI O'BYRNE	170000
B C DALAKHANI (IRE) - ALLEGRETTO (IRE)	DATO HAN CHUN ONG	170000

Name and Breeding	Purchaser	Guineas
GR F MASTERCRAFTSMAN (IRE) - AMATHIA (IRE)	BLANDFORD BS	160000
B C MYBOYCHARLIE (IRE) - TIME WILL SHOW (FR)	DEMI O'BYRNE	160000
B F INVINCIBLE SPIRIT (IRE) - CABRIOLE (GB)	JOHN FERGUSON BS	160000
B C ROYAL APPLAUSE (GB) - ROLEXA (GB)	MRS A SKIFFINGTON	160000
B C DANEHILL DANCER (IRE) - SHARPLAW STAR (GB)	MCCALMONT BS	160000
B F DUBAWI (IRE) - PAST THE POST (USA)	JOHN FERGUSON BS	160000
B F ROYAL APPLAUSE (GB) - SILCA CHIAVE (GB)	AGENCE FIPS	160000
B C SHAMARDAL (USA) - KAPRIA (FR)	JOHN FERGUSON BS	155000
B G ROCK OF GIBRALTAR (IRE) - SOUTHERN HOUSE (IRE)	MARK CROSSMAN	155000
B F DUBAWI (IRE) - SAABIQ (USA)	JOHN FERGUSON BS	155000
B F OASIS DREAM (GB) - SO SILK (GB)	HUGO MERRY BS	155000
EXCEDO PRAECEDO (GB) B C EXCEED AND EXCEL (AUS) - MERLE (GB)	PETER & ROSS DOYLE BS	150000
CH C PIVOTAL (GB) - ALVEE (IRE)	ROB SPEERS	150000
B C WAR FRONT (USA) - DIXIE QUEST (USA)	SHADWELL ESTATE COMPANY	150000
SEA LION (GB) CH C SEA THE STARS (IRE) - BOURBONELLA (GB)	JOHN FERGUSON BS	150000
B C SEA THE STARS (IRE) - RAMONA (GB)	VENDOR	150000
EXTENT (GB) CH F EXCEED AND EXCEL (AUS) - SELKIRK SKY (GB)	CHEVELEY PARK STUD	150000
B C CLODOVIL (IRE) - SOMOUSHE (IRE)	SHADWELL ESTATE COMPANY	150000
CH F GALILEO (IRE) - MUBKERA (IRE)	BADGERS BS (P.S.)	150000
B F HIGH CHAPARRAL (IRE) - TWYLA (AUS)	PAUL MORONEY BS	150000
B C SEA THE STARS (IRE) - ZIBILENE (GB)	BBA IRELAND	150000
B F GALILEO (IRE) - SMALL CHANGE (IRE)	VENDOR	150000
B C SHAMARDAL (USA) - MIN ALHAWA (USA)	JOHN FERGUSON BS	150000
B C CAPE CROSS (IRE) - CANDY MOUNTAIN (GB)	JOHN WARREN BS	150000
QUASQAZAH (GB) CH C BAHAMIAN BOUNTY (GB) - ROCK LILY (GB)	SHADWELL ESTATE COMPANY	150000
PONFEIGH (IRE) GR C TEOFILO (IRE) - WATER FOUNTAIN (GB)	BBA IRELAND	150000
B C SHAMARDAL (USA) - MIRACOLIA (IRE)	JOHN FERGUSON BS	150000
GR F CLODOVIL (IRE) - THREE DAYS IN MAY (GB)	PETER & ROSS DOYLE BS	150000
B F INVINCIBLE SPIRIT (IRE) - ENTRE NOUS (IRE)	ROB SPEERS	150000
B C KYLLACHY (GB) - MAUGWENNA (GB)	C GORDON-WATSON BS	150000
B C GALILEO (IRE) - KITE MARK (GB)	VENDOR	150000
B C ORATORIO (IRE) - CAPE COLUMBINE (GB)	HONG KONG JOCKEY CLUB	145000
B C ACCLAMATION (GB) - COEUR DE LA MER (IRE)	JOHN FERGUSON BS	145000
B C CAPE CROSS (IRE) - ANNA'S ROCK (IRE)	PETER & ROSS DOYLE BS	145000
B C SEA THE STARS (IRE) - DANELETA (IRE)	VENDOR	145000
GR C INVINCIBLE SPIRIT (IRE) - SELL OUT (GB)	HONG KONG JOCKEY CLUB	140000
B C INVINCIBLE SPIRIT (IRE) - QUAD'S MELODY (IRE)	VENDOR	140000
GR F SEA THE STARS (IRE) - NORDHOCK (USA)	JS COMPANY	140000
B C ACCLAMATION (GB) - VENOGE (IRE)	DEMI O'BYRNE	140000
B F DANEHILL DANCER (IRE) - MAIL THE DESERT (IRE)	C DE MOUBRAY	140000
B C GALILEO (IRE) - SOMETHING MON (USA)	VENDOR	140000
B F GALILEO (IRE) - THERMOPYLAE (GB)	VENDOR	140000
B/BR F MARJU (IRE) - URGELE (FR)	VENDOR	140000
B F SHAMARDAL (USA) - DOLLAR BIRD (IRE)	FORM BS	140000
B C ACCLAMATION (GB) - MUSICAL BAR (IRE)	JOHN FERGUSON BS	140000
B F DANSILI (GB) - MUSICAL NOTE (GB)	J O'BYRNE	135000
B C OASIS DREAM (GB) - I'M IN LOVE (USA)	VENDOR	135000
B C MYBOYCHARLIE (IRE) - LAUREN LOUISE (GB)	HIGHFIELD FARM LLP	135000
B C STORMY ATLANTIC (USA) - WATCHFUL (IRE)	HARRY DUNLOP RACING	135000
B C MANDURO (GER) - CHILI DIP (GB)	BLANDFORD BS	135000
B C DANEHILL DANCER (IRE) - RIBERAC (GB)	JOHN WARREN BS	135000
B C FASTNET ROCK (AUS) - STREETCAR (IRE)	DATO HAN CHUN ONG	135000
B C OASIS DREAM (GB) - I'M IN LOVE (USA)	DEMI O'BYRNE	135000
GR C OASIS DREAM (GB) - COMEBACK QUEEN (GB)	JUDDMONTE FARMS	130000
B F DANSILI (GB) - TU ERES MI AMORE (IRE)	HARUYA YOSHIDA	130000
CATRIONA'S BOY (GB) CH C EXCEED AND EXCEL (AUS) - MISS CHAUSSINI (IRE)	STEPHEN HILLEN BS	130000
CH F TAMAYUZ (GB) - LAURELDEAN EXPRESS (IRE)	HARUYA YOSHIDA	130000
B F RAVEN'S PASS (USA) - MISS ANABAA (GB)	RABBAH BS	130000
B F INVINCIBLE SPIRIT (IRE) - HOUSE IN WOOD (FR)	SACKVILLEDONALD	130000
B C HIGH CHAPARRAL (IRE) - LURE OF THE MOON (USA)	DEMI O'BYRNE	130000
B F FASTNET ROCK (AUS) - ZAGREB FLYER (GB)	MARGARET O'TOOLE (IRE)	130000
B C SHAMARDAL (USA) - BENEVENTA (GB)	JOHN FERGUSON BS	130000
B C RAVEN'S PASS (USA) - WOLF CLEUGH (IRE)	MANDORE INTERNATIONAL	130000
CH C KYLLACHY (GB) - PENMAYNE (GB)	BBA IRELAND	130000
B C SHAMARDAL (USA) - MOURIYANA (IRE)	VENDOR	130000
B F ACCLAMATION (GB) - HAVE FAITH (IRE)	TONY NERSES	130000
B F FASTNET ROCK (AUS) - SLOW SAND (USA)	CHARLES LIVERTON	130000
B F LEMON DROP KID (USA) - NAFISAH (GB)	ANDREW BALDING	130000
B C SHAMARDAL (USA) - SOLVA (GB)	JOHN FERGUSON BS	130000
B C DANEHILL DANCER (IRE) - HELENA MOLONY (IRE)	HUGO MERRY BS	130000
B F DANSILI (GB) - SO SQUALLY (GER)	ANTHONY STROUD BS	130000

Name and Breeding	Purchaser	Guineas
CH C GALILEO (IRE) - ALTESSE IMPERIALE (IRE)	JOHN MURTAGH	130000
B C HIGH CHAPARRAL (IRE) - RAINBOW QUEEN (FR)	MV MAGNIER	125000
B C SEA THE STARS (IRE) - TIME ON (GB)	JOHN FERGUSON BS	125000
ST VINCENT (IRE) B C DANEHILL DANCER (IRE) - LACE (IRE)	C GORDON-WATSON BS	125000
B C TEOFILO (IRE) - BEZANT (IRE)	JOHN FERGUSON BS	125000
B C MONTJEU (IRE) - MADAME CERITO (USA)	ROGER P VARIAN	125000
B C SEA THE STARS (IRE) - VIRTUOSITY (GB)	JOHN FERGUSON BS	125000
TAANIF (GB) B C AQLAAM (GB) - FIREBELLY (GB)	SHADWELL ESTATE COMPANY	125000
ONE CHANCE (IRE) B F INVINCIBLE SPIRIT (IRE) - TOWARDS (USA)	RECYCLED PRODUCTS LTD.	120000
GR F ACCLAMATION (GB) - STEP TOO FAR (USA)	SACKVILLEDONALD	120000
B C ROCK OF GIBRALTAR (IRE) - IWUNDER (IRE)	STEPHEN HILLEN BS	120000
B C PIVOTAL (GB) - INFAMOUS ANGEL (GB)	JOHN FERGUSON BS	120000
B C DUTCH ART (GB) - BLITHE (GB)	SHADWELL ESTATE COMPANY	120000
B C CAPE CROSS (IRE) - ADA RIVER (GB)	ANTHONY STROUD BS	120000
CH C BAHAMIAN BOUNTY (GB) - HOH CHI MIN (GB)	HONG KONG JOCKEY CLUB	120000
B C CAPE CROSS (IRE) - JUST SPECIAL (GB)	MARK JOHNSTON RACING	120000
B C ACCLAMATION (GB) - FATHOMING (USA)	JEREMY NOSEDA RACING	120000
B F MASTERCRAFTSMAN (IRE) - PERFECT STAR (GB)	DAVID REDVERS BS	120000
B C AZAMOUR (IRE) - CUT SHORT (USA)	DAVID REDVERS BS	120000
B F CAPE CROSS (IRE) - BRISEIDA (GB)	FRANCE TURF INTERNATIONAL	120000
B/BR C SPEIGHTSTOWN (USA) - REBOOT (USA)	OLIVER ST LAWRENCE BS	120000
B C CAPE CROSS (IRE) - MOON SISTER (IRE)	JOHN WARREN BS	115000
GONE WITH THE WIND (GER) B C DUTCH ART (GB) - GALLIVANT (GB)	HUGO MERRY BS	115000
CH C TEOFILO (IRE) - SKY WONDER (GB)	HUGO MERRY BS	115000
CH C SHAMARDAL (USA) - RIOTOUS APPLAUSE (GB)	MARK JOHNSTON RACING	115000
B C INVINCIBLE SPIRIT (IRE) - JOUET (GB)	PETER & ROSS DOYLE BS	115000
B C ACCLAMATION (GB) - CHARAIG (GB)	C GORDON-WATSON BS	110000
ANJIN (IRE) B C DANEHILL DANCER (IRE) - TWYLA THARP (USA)	HIGHFLYER BS	110000
B C NEW APPROACH (IRE) - CRAIGMILL (GB)	C GORDON-WATSON BS	110000
B C GALILEO (IRE) - INCHENI (IRE)	DWAYNE WOODS	110000
CH C NEW APPROACH (IRE) - MILLENNIUM DASH (GB)	DAVID REDVERS BS	110000
LAHUROOB (GB) B C KYLLACHY (GB) - COMPLIMENTARY PASS (GB)	PETER & ROSS DOYLE BS	110000
CH F PIVOTAL (GB) - MOON DAZZLE (USA)	VENDOR	110000
B C INVINCIBLE SPIRIT (IRE) - LOVE EVERLASTING (GB)	JOHN WARREN BS (P.S.)	110000
CH F PIVOTAL (GB) - ENTENTE CORDIALE (IRE)	VENDOR	110000
WHITEY O' GWAUN (IRE) GR C DALAKHANI (IRE) - ANGEL OF THE GWAUN (IRE)	JOHN FERGUSON BS	110000
B C BUSHRANGER (IRE) - CHAMPION TIPSTER (GB)	JOHN FERGUSON BS	110000
B C HOLY ROMAN EMPEROR (IRE) - AUNT NICOLA (GB)	LAKIN BS/GEOFFREY HOWSON	110000
B C HENRYTHENAVIGATOR (USA) - INDIA HALO (ARG)	D WACHMAN	110000
B C HIGH CHAPARRAL (IRE) - INCHMINA (GB)	DEMI O'BYRNE	110000
B C ACCLAMATION (GB) - VINTAGE ESCAPE (IRE)	ANTHONY STROUD BS	110000
KING'S PROCESSION (IRE) CH C TEOFILO (IRE) - SATEEN (GB)	C GORDON-WATSON BS	110000
ENSURING (GB) BR C NEW APPROACH (IRE) - DYNACAM (USA)	D ELSWORTH	110000
B F FASTNET ROCK (AUS) - DABAWIYAH (IRE)	FORM BS	110000
CH C NEW APPROACH (IRE) - MISS MARVELLOUS (USA)	ROGER P VARIAN	110000
MAGIC ARTIST (IRE) BR C IFFRAAJ (GB) - ARTISTI (GB)	MANFRED HOFER	105000
ANJAAL (GB) CH C BAHAMIAN BOUNTY (GB) - BALLYMORE CELEBRE (IRE)	PETER & ROSS DOYLE BS	105000
CH C MEDICEAN (GB) - AMBER QUEEN (IRE)	C GORDON-WATSON BS	105000
BR C INVINCIBLE SPIRIT (IRE) - GEMINI JOAN (GB)	JOHN GOSDEN RACING LLP	105000
B C BUSHRANGER (IRE) - GOLD SCRIPT (FR)	JOHN WARREN BS	100000
ZUMARI (IRE) B C INVINCIBLE SPIRIT (IRE) - MISS INTIMATE (USA)	WARATAH THOROUGHBREDS	100000
B F DUBAWI (IRE) - LOCH JIPP (USA)	JOHN FERGUSON BS	100000
B F OASIS DREAM (GB) - FRONT HOUSE (IRE)	CORMAC MCCORMACK BS	100000
B C MEDICEAN (GB) - SNOW GRETEL (IRE)	C GORDON-WATSON BS	100000
CH C EXCEED AND EXCEL (AUS) - LA HERMANA (GB)	MANFRED HOFER	100000
BR F MORE THAN READY (USA) - HIGH HEEL SNEAKERS (GB)	BADGERS BS	100000
TAQARROB (IRE) B C BUSHRANGER (IRE) - LUCKY DATE (IRE)	SHADWELL ESTATE COMPANY	100000
B C HIGH CHAPARRAL (IRE) - SUMMERHILL PARKES (GB)	JOHN WARREN BS	100000
B F DANEHILL DANCER (IRE) - KUSHNARENKOVO (GB)	HARUYA YOSHIDA	100000
CH C SHIROCCO (GER) - PELAGIA (IRE)	JOHN WARREN BS	100000
RO C DUBAWI (IRE) - BELLE REINE (GB)	JOHN WARREN BS	100000
CH C TEOFILO (IRE) - BELSAY (GB)	HUGO MERRY BS	100000
TANZEEL (IRE) B C ELUSIVE CITY (USA) - ROYAL FIZZ (IRE)	SHADWELL ESTATE COMPANY	100000
CH C DANEHILL DANCER (IRE) - SPLASHDOWN (GB)	ARMANDO DUARTE	100000
GEORGE HERBERT (GB) B C YEATS (IRE) - COLORADO DAWN (GB)	CHARLES LIVERTON	100000
CH C EXCHANGE RATE (USA) - MISS DELTA DAWN (USA)	STEPHEN HILLEN BS	100000
CH F NEW APPROACH (IRE) - BLUE ROCKET (IRE)	VENDOR	100000
B F ACCLAMATION (GB) - WILDSPLASH (USA)	VENDOR	100000
B C ROYAL APPLAUSE (GB) - NEVE LIEVE (IRE)	LAKIN BS/GEOFFREY HOWSON	100000
B C ROCK OF GIBRALTAR (IRE) - LADY LAHAR (GB)	GILL RICHARDSON BS	100000
B C ACCLAMATION (GB) - GALAPAGAR (USA)	JOHN FERGUSON BS	100000

Name and Breeding	Purchaser	Guineas
B C INVINCIBLE SPIRIT (IRE) - HUCKING HOT (GB)	JOHN WARREN BS	100000
B C ROYAL APPLAUSE (GB) - PEACEFUL KINGDOM (USA)	MANDORE INTERNATIONAL	100000
CH F TEOFILO (IRE) - OUT OF TIME (IRE)	PETER & ROSS DOYLE BS	100000
CERTIFICATE (GB) CH C PIVOTAL (GB) - GRADUATION (GB)	OLIVER ST LAWRENCE BS	100000
GR F SHAMARDAL (USA) - INDIAN BELLE (IRE)	FEDERICO BARBERINI, AGENT	100000
B C ORATORIO (IRE) - SHOWCALL (USA)	HONG KONG JOCKEY CLUB	100000
B C ORATORIO (IRE) - LUCY CAVENDISH (USA)	C GORDON-WATSON BS	100000
CH C PIVOTAL (GB) - QUIET PROTEST (USA)	PAUL MORONEY BS	100000
B C CAPE CROSS (IRE) - TRICK OR TREAT (GB)	BLANDFORD BS	100000
B F DUTCH ART (GB) - POLDHU (GB)	CHEVELEY PARK STUD	100000
B F PIVOTAL (GB) - LADY LINDA (USA)	VENDOR	100000
CH C MASTERCRAFTSMAN (IRE) - EUROCELEB (IRE)	D WACHMAN	100000
CH F GALILEO (IRE) - BEAUTY BRIGHT (IRE)	JILL LAMB BS	100000
B C ACCLAMATION (GB) - FATAL ATTRACTION (GB)	VENDOR	95000
B C DANEHILL DANCER (IRE) - MAGNOLIA LANE (IRE)	ANTHONY STROUD BS	95000
B/GR C DUKE OF MARMALADE (IRE) - EXOTIC MIX (FR)	KERRI RADCLIFFE BS	95000
MOUNTAIN KINGDOM (IRE) B C MONTJEU (IRE) - ALTHEA ROSE (IRE).	AMANDA SKIFFINGTON	95000
B C MASTERCRAFTSMAN (IRE) - MOORE'S MELODY (IRE)	CORMAC MCCORMACK BS	95000
B C BUSHRANGER (IRE) - COURTIER (GB)	ARMANDO DUARTE	95000
B F ROYAL APPLAUSE (GB) - SINGITTA (GB)	PETER & ROSS DOYLE BS	95000
B C GALILEO (IRE) - NOELANI (IRE)	MARCO BOTTI	95000
OUTBACK TRAVELLER (IRE) B C BUSHRANGER (IRE) - BLUE HOLLY (IRE)	JEREMY NOSEDA RACING	92000
CH C PIVOTAL (GB) - DOCTOR'S GLORY (USA)	FRIARSTOWN STUD	90000
B F CAPE CROSS (IRE) - MISS CHAMPAGNE (FR)	RABBAH BS	90000
B C BUSHRANGER (IRE) - FUERTA VENTURA (IRE)	NIGEL TINKLER BS LLP	90000
HEWAYAAT (GB) B F CAPE CROSS (IRE) - WINK (GB)	SHADWELL ESTATE COMPANY	90000
ENCOUNTERING (IRE) B C DUKE OF MARMALADE (IRE) - NAVAL AFFAIR (IRE)	D ELSWORTH	90000
BATUTA (IRE) B F NEW APPROACH (IRE) - NANTYGLO (GB)	WOOD HALL STUD	90000
B C CAPE CROSS (IRE) - PINACOTHEQUE (IRE)	PETER & ROSS DOYLE BS	90000
MUZAAHIM (IRE) CH C TAMAYUZ (GB) - ELIZABETH SWANN (GB)	SHADWELL ESTATE COMPANY	90000
B F INVINCIBLE SPIRIT (IRE) - MARIKA (GB)	STUART STUCKEY	90000
B C ROYAL APPLAUSE (GB) - PERFECT STORY (IRE)	SHADWELL ESTATE COMPANY	90000
GHANY (IRE) B F LAWMAN (FR) - BROKEN SPECTRE (GB)	SHADWELL ESTATE COMPANY	90000
B C ACCLAMATION (GB) - ADORN (GB)	SHADWELL ESTATE COMPANY	90000
B C DALAKHANI (IRE) - JAMBORETTA (IRE)	C GORDON-WATSON BS	90000
B/BR C DANSILI (IRE) - COMIC (IRE)	JOHN WARREN BS	90000
B C EXCEED AND EXCEL (AUS) - MY LOVE THOMAS (IRE)	ROGER P VARIAN	90000
CH F GALILEO (IRE) - DELICIEUSE LADY (IRE)	MERIDIAN INT. (P.S.)	90000
BR C HOLY ROMAN EMPEROR (IRE) - HUMBLE AND PROUD (IRE)	SACKVILLEDONALD	90000
GR F OASIS DREAM (GB) - IN THE MIST (GB)	VENDOR	90000
B C ELUSIVE QUALITY (USA) - NORTHERN KRAZE (CAN)	GERARD BUTLER	88000
HESBAAN (IRE) B C ACCLAMATION (GB) - CELESTIAL DREAM (IRE)	SHADWELL ESTATE CO (P.S.)	87000
B F ARTIE SCHILLER (USA) - SIEMPRE ASI (USA)	KERN/LILLINGSTON ASSOCIATION	87000
DUNURE HARBOUR (GB) CH C DUBAWI (IRE) - HOBBY (GB)	BBA IRELAND	85000
CH C TEOFILO (IRE) - ARCTIC CHAR (GB)	WILLIAM HAGGAS	85000
B F DUBAWI (IRE) - GRASSHOPPERGREEN (IRE)	WILLIAM HAGGAS	85000
B C AQLAAM (GB) - AUNTY MARY (GB)	JOHN WARREN BS	85000
RO C INVINCIBLE SPIRIT (IRE) - EXCLUSIVE APPROVAL (USA)	SACKVILLEDONALD	85000
GR C DALAKHANI (IRE) - ADVENTURE (USA)	OLIVER ST LAWRENCE BS	85000
B C NEW APPROACH (IRE) - SHIMNA (GB)	BLANDFORD BS	85000
B/BR F NEW APPROACH (IRE) - RAINBOW DESERT (USA)	BBA IRELAND	85000
B C KYLLACHY (GB) - DANCEATDUSK (GB)	PETER & ROSS DOYLE BS	85000
KINSHASA (GB) B C PIVOTAL (GB) - KIBARA (GB)	VENDOR	85000
AFTER THE GOLDRUSH (GB) B C KYLLACHY (GB) - FINE LADY (GB)	PETER & ROSS DOYLE BS	85000
B F CAPE CROSS (IRE) - AVILA (GB)	BLANDFORD BS	85000
B F TAMAYUZ (GB) - FRENCH FERN (IRE)	VENDOR	85000
B C CAPE CROSS (IRE) - REFORM ACT (USA)	JOHN FERGUSON BS	85000
B G BAHAMIAN BOUNTY (GB) - COPY-CAT (GB)	HONG KONG JOCKEY CLUB	85000
B F AQLAAM (GB) - HIDDEN MEANING (GB)	VENDOR	85000
B C CAMACHO (GB) - CATCH THE SEA (IRE)	SHADWELL ESTATE COMPANY	85000
B C NEW APPROACH (IRE) - AL HASNAA (GB)	RABBAH BS	85000
CH C DUTCH ART (GB) - STRAVIE (IRE)	SACKVILLEDONALD	85000
B F TEOFILO (IRE) - CHRYSALIS (GB)	PETER & ROSS DOYLE BS	85000
BR C PASTORAL PURSUITS (GB) - DANSA QUEEN (GB)	WILLIAM HAGGAS	85000
B C SEA THE STARS (IRE) - DANASKAYA (IRE)	DAVID REDVERS BS	85000
CH F DANEHILL DANCER (IRE) - CHALLOW HILLS (USA)	CORMAC MCCORMACK BS	82000
B C FASTNET ROCK (AUS) - BOWSTRING (IRE)	KERN/LILLINGSTON ASSOCIATION	82000
GR F MASTERCRAFTSMAN (IRE) - REFLECTED IMAGE (IRE)	PETER & ROSS DOYLE BS	82000
GR F VERGLAS (IRE) - AZIA (IRE)	JOHN WARREN BS	82000
B F DUBAWI (IRE) - BLAISE CASTLE (USA)	FEDERICO BARBERINI, AGENT	82000
B C EXCEED AND EXCEL (AUS) - EXTREME BEAUTY (USA)	BLANDFORD BS	80000

Name and Breeding	Purchaser	Guineas
ROSSO CORSA (GB) B C FOOTSTEPSINTHESAND (GB) - LADY SCARLETT (GB)	GILL RICHARDSON BS	80000
B C HIGH CHAPARRAL (IRE) - TIPSY ME (GB)	JOHN WARREN BS	80000
HIGHLAND ACCLAIM (IRE) B C ACCLAMATION (GB) - EMMA'S STAR (ITY)	VENDOR	80000
B C EXCEED AND EXCEL (AUS) - MYSTERY OCEAN (GB)	RABBAH BS	80000
CH C AQLAAM (GB) - BALLADONIA (GB)	HIGHFIELD FARM LLP	80000
B F INVINCIBLE SPIRIT (IRE) - ALSACE (GB)	RABBAH BS	80000
B C DUBAWI (IRE) - DIXEY (GB)	JOHN FERGUSON BS	80000
B C MONTJEU (IRE) - HIGH RESERVE (GB)	VENDOR	80000
B F INVINCIBLE SPIRIT (IRE) - LULUA (USA)	JEREMY BRUMMITT	80000
GR C CLODOVIL (IRE) - SHAMBODIA (IRE)	RABBAH BS	80000
INVINCIBLE FRESH (IRE) B C FOOTSTEPSINTHESAND (GB) - PRINCESS SERENA (USA)	SACKVILLEDONALD	80000
CHINOTTO (IRE) B C DUKE OF MARMALADE (IRE) - MUSKOKA DAWN (USA)	ANDREW BALDING	80000
B C CAPE CROSS (IRE) - CINNAMON ROSE (GB)	BLANDFORD BS	80000
B C EXCEED AND EXCEL (AUS) - PASSE PASSE (USA)	WILLIE BROWNE	80000
MARMOOM (GB) CH C DUTCH ART (GB) - COSMIC SONG (GB)	SHADWELL ESTATE COMPANY	80000
B C DUTCH ART (GB) - COSENZA (GB)	R O'RYAN	80000
B F DUBAWI (IRE) - MOCCA (IRE)	DAVID REDVERS BS	80000
B C GALILEO (IRE) - MAROOCHYDORE (IRE)	AMANDA PERRETT	80000
B C BUSHRANGER (IRE) - PRODIGAL DAUGHTER (GB)	GEORGE MARGARSON RACING	80000
B F CAPE CROSS (IRE) - FANN (USA)	GEOFFREY HOWSON BS	80000
CH C NEW APPROACH (IRE) - RAFTING (IRE)	HUGO MERRY BS	80000
B C RAVEN'S PASS (USA) - ZACHETA (GB)	JOHN FERGUSON BS	80000
LADY DAY (GB) B F SELKIRK (USA) - LADY LINKS (GB)	VENDOR	80000
MUSALAHA (IRE) B F NAYEF (USA) - GILDED (IRE)	SHADWELL ESTATE COMPANY	80000
FROSTY THE SNOWMAN (IRE) GR C MASTERCRAFTSMAN (IRE) - SLEEVELESS (USA)	BBA IRELAND	80000
B/BR F EXCHANGE RATE (USA) - BALL GOWN (USA)	VENDOR	80000
B C INVINCIBLE SPIRIT (IRE) - PORT PROVIDENCE (GB)	VENDOR	80000
MARSH DAISY (GB) CH F PIVOTAL (GB) - BELLA LAMBADA (GB)	HUGH MORRISON	80000
B C NEW APPROACH (IRE) - DANCE LIVELY (GB)	A & A	78000
B/GR C MOUNT NELSON (GB) - LA GANDILIE (FR)	MCKEEVER BS	77000
B C HOLY ROMAN EMPEROR (IRE) - GREEK EASTER (IRE)	ANTHONY STROUD BS	77000
B F NAYEF (USA) - POST MODERN (USA)	BROADHURST AGENCY	77000
FRESH KINGDOM (IRE) CH C DUBAWI (IRE) - POLYQUEST (IRE)	SACKVILLEDONALD	75000
B C SHAMARDAL (USA) - ARCTIC AIR (GB)	MARK JOHNSTON RACING	75000
JUPITER AND MARS (IRE) B C SEA THE STARS (IRE) - HILL OF SNOW (IRE)	ROB SPEERS	75000
B F CHAMPS ELYSEES (GB) - MRS SEEK (IRE)	RABBAH BS	75000
WATERSMEET (GB) GR C DANSILI (GB) - UNDER THE RAINBOW (GB)	MARK JOHNSTON RACING	75000
B C AUTHORIZED (IRE) - AUDAZ (GB)	RABBAH BS	75000
BR F NAYEF (USA) - WHAZZIS (GB)	JOHN WARREN BS	75000
CH C DANEHILL DANCER (IRE) - BALLYMORE LADY (USA)	VENDOR	75000
B C HIGH CHAPARRAL (IRE) - AL IHSAS (IRE)	MCCALMONT BS	75000
WASHAAR (IRE) B C KODIAC (GB) - DABTIYRA (IRE)	PETER & ROSS DOYLE BS	75000
B F FASTNET ROCK (AUS) - REGAL DARCEY (IRE)	JOHN WARREN BS	75000
B C HOLY ROMAN EMPEROR (IRE) - WHATAMI (GB)	JOHN WARREN BS	75000
VECHEKA (IRE) B C LAWMAN (FR) - LIDANSKI (IRE)	ANDREW BALDING	75000
B F CAPE CROSS (IRE) - SMARTEST (IRE)	BBA IRELAND	75000
B C ROYAL APPLAUSE (GB) - FAME GAME (IRE)	CHIKA RACING	75000
GR/RO C ARCH (USA) - MYSTIC MIRACLE (GB)	WILL EDMEADES BS	75000
CH C CHAMPS ELYSEES (GB) - ZEE ZEE GEE (GB)	ANTHONY STROUD BS	75000
B F SEA THE STARS (IRE) - QUILANGA (GER)	LILY CORPORATION LP	75000
B C SMART STRIKE (CAN) - GREEN ROOM (USA)	VENDOR	75000
B C NEW APPROACH (IRE) - HOPE ISLAND (IRE)	HONG KONG JOCKEY CLUB	75000
CH C PIVOTAL (GB) - CHOIR MISTRESS (GB)	COSMO VIEW FARM	75000
B C SAKHEE'S SECRET (GB) - SINDUDA (GB)	C GORDON-WATSON BS	75000
CH F AQLAAM (GB) - PIVOTAL'S PRINCESS (IRE)	BBA IRELAND	74000
CH C TAMAYUZ (GB) - SQUANDER (GB)	JOHN FERGUSON BS	72000
RO F MASTERCRAFTSMAN (IRE) - QUALITY LOVE (USA)	MARGARET O'TOOLE (IRE)	72000
BACK TO BUXTED (IRE) B C AQLAAM (GB) - INCOMING CALL (USA)	C GORDON-WATSON BS	72000
B C TEOFILO (IRE) - QUITE ELUSIVE (USA)	C GORDON-WATSON BS	72000
B C HIGH CHAPARRAL (IRE) - CLINCHER CLUB (GB)	BLANDFORD BS	72000

HIGH-PRICED YEARLINGS OF 2012 AT GOFFS
The following yearlings realised 43,000 euros and over at Goffs Sales in 2012:-

Name and Breeding	Purchaser	Euros
B C GALILEO (IRE) - FLAMES (GB)	FORM BS	800000
PRUDENT APPROACH (IRE) B F NEW APPROACH (IRE) - HYMN OF THE DAWN (USA)	PETER & ROSS DOYLE BS	775000
B C MONTJEU (IRE) - JEWEL IN THE SAND (IRE)	D O'BYRNE	500000
CH C PIVOTAL (GB) - SUMORA (IRE)	MANDORE INTERNATIONAL	500000
B C MONTJEU (IRE) - ALLEVIATE (IRE)	MANDORE INTERNATIONAL	500000
B/BR F GALILEO (IRE) - ALPHA LUPI (IRE)	FORM BS	470000
I'M YOURS (GB) B F INVINCIBLE SPIRIT (IRE) - REBELLINE (IRE)	MOYGLARE STUD FARM	420000
AERIALIST (IRE) CH C SEA THE STARS (IRE) - MAOINEACH (USA)	B O'RYAN	400000
B F INVINCIBLE SPIRIT (IRE) - ALSHAKR (GB)	J FERGUSON	380000
GR F GALILEO (IRE) - ALABASTRINE (GB)	HUGO MERRY BS	340000
PIRITA (IRE) BR F INVINCIBLE SPIRIT (IRE) - SPINAMIX (GB)	MOYGLARE STUD FARM	330000
B C CAPE CROSS (IRE) - ALTRUISTE (USA)	J WARREN	320000
CRAIC AGUS SPRAOI (IRE) B F INTENSE FOCUS (USA) - HALLA SIAMSA (IRE)	BBA (IRELAND)	300000
B F SEA THE STARS (IRE) - KARMIFIRA (FR)	DAVID REDVERS BS	280000
B C OASIS DREAM (GB) - LITTLEFEATHER (IRE)	D O'BYRNE	280000
CH C TEOFILO (IRE) - GOLDTHROAT (IRE)	J FERGUSON	280000
BR F CAPE CROSS (IRE) - TADKIYRA (IRE)	PETER & ROSS DOYLE BS	270000
OBSTINATE (IRE) B C FASTNET ROCK (AUS) - SANGITA (GB)	S HILLEN	260000
SHAMA'S CROWN (IRE) CH F NEW APPROACH (IRE) - CLASSIC PARK (GB)	C GORDON-WATSON BS	260000
ALKASSER (IRE) B C SHAMARDAL (USA) - ALEXANDER QUEEN (IRE)	SHADWELL ESTATE CO.	260000
KINEMA (IRE) B C GALILEO (IRE) - BON NUIT (IRE)	M KELLER	250000
TAHAANY (IRE) B F RAVEN'S PASS (USA) - PHOTOPHORE (IRE)	SHADWELL ESTATE CO.	240000
GR C GALILEO (IRE) - ST ROCH (IRE)	BBA (IRELAND)	235000
B C SHAMARDAL (USA) - BEE EATER (IRE)	JOHN FERGUSON BS	220000
PIVOTAL BRIDE (GB) CH F DUBAWI (IRE) - BRAZILIAN BRIDE (IRE)	C GORDON-WATSON BS	220000
B C MONTJEU (IRE) - CAWETT (IRE)	TEAM VALOR	200000
B C MONSUN (GER) - SQILLO (IRE)	HUGO MERRY BS	200000
B F MASTERCRAFTSMAN (IRE) - SOGNO VERDE (IRE)	T HYDE	200000
BORISOCRACY (IRE) B C ACCLAMATION (GB) - RIVER MOUNTAIN (GB)	HUGO MERRY BS	190000
B C HOLY ROMAN EMPEROR (IRE) - TARASCON (IRE)	BIG RED FARM	180000
B C TEOFILO (IRE) - QUEEN OF LYONS (USA)	GILL RICHARDSON BS	170000
BALLYHURST (IRE) B C HIGH CHAPARRAL (IRE) - BILLET (IRE)	N STEEL	170000
BR/GR F DALAKHANI (IRE) - NOYELLES (IRE)	J MCCORMACK	170000
B C TEOFILO (IRE) - MY PERSONAL SPACE (USA)	DAVID REDVERS BS	170000
STAR JET (IRE) BR/GR F TEOFILO (IRE) - SILVER SHOON (IRE)	C & M MULLEN	160000
CH C GIANT'S CAUSEWAY (USA) - GOSSAMER (USA)	M KELLER	160000
B F NEW APPROACH (IRE) - ROUGE NOIR (USA)	BLANDFORD BS	160000
B F ACCLAMATION (GB) - REGATTA (USA)	BBA (IRELAND)	160000
HIGHPLAINS DRIFTER (IRE) B C HIGH CHAPARRAL (IRE) - QHAZEENAH (GB)	J BRUMMITT	155000
B/BR C FOOTSTEPSINTHESAND (GB) - ANNOUNCING PEACE (GB)	DAVID REDVERS BS	150000
B C EXCELLENT ART (GB) - MAGIC SISTER (GB)	TEAM VALOR	150000
CH F SEA THE STARS (IRE) - UIMHIR A HAON (IRE)	B O'RYAN	150000
B C FASTNET ROCK (AUS) - ON THE NILE (IRE)	A SKIFFINGTON	150000
FOUR CARAT (GER) B C MONTJEU (IRE) - FOUR ROSES (IRE)	D O'BYRNE	150000
B C GALILEO (IRE) - VELOUETTE (GB)	S HILLEN	150000
B F DANEHILL DANCER (IRE) - FOOFARAW (USA)	D REDVERS	145000
BR C MYBOYCHARLIE (IRE) - SPRING GLORY (GB)	B O'RYAN	145000
B C HOLY ROMAN EMPEROR (IRE) - DANCE AVENUE (IRE)	HONG KONG JOCKEY CLUB	140000
GR C VERGLAS (IRE) - WRONG KEY (IRE)	B O'RYAN	140000
B C DANEHILL DANCER (IRE) - RIVER FLOW (USA)	S HILLEN	140000
STARCHITECT (IRE) B C SEA THE STARS (IRE) - HUMILIS (IRE)	BBA (IRELAND)	140000
TWENTY ROSES (IRE) B F MASTERCRAFTSMAN (IRE) - STUNNING ROSE (IRE)	A STROUD	135000
CH C NEW APPROACH (IRE) - VISTARIA (USA)	C GORDON-WATSON BS	135000
PUPIL (IRE) B C MASTERCRAFTSMAN (IRE) - BLUE IRIS (GB)	PETER & ROSS DOYLE BS	130000
B C IFFRAAJ (GB) - LUXIE (IRE)	GILL RICHARDSON BS	130000
B C ROYAL APPLAUSE (GB) - RICE MOTHER (IRE)	W J HAGGAS	130000
B C INVINCIBLE SPIRIT (IRE) - ROSE DE FRANCE (IRE)	BBA (IRELAND)	130000
B C FOOTSTEPSINTHESAND (GB) - CLAUSTRA (FR)	HONG KONG JOCKEY CLUB	130000
B C HOLY ROMAN EMPEROR (IRE) - TYRANNY (GB)	D O'BYRNE	130000
B F FASTNET ROCK (AUS) - CHRISALICE (GB)	DAVID REDVERS BS	130000
B C BUSHRANGER (IRE) - LILIUM (GB)	J FERGUSON	125000
B C EXCEED AND EXCEL (AUS) - QUINZEY'S BEST (IRE)	K RADCLIFFE	125000
CH F ELNADIM (USA) - GIVE A WHISTLE (IRE)	BBA (IRELAND)	120000
NEIGHBOTHER (GB) B C INVINCIBLE SPIRIT (IRE) - ARAVONIAN (GB)	N STEEL	120000
DOCTOR SARDONICUS (GB) CH C MEDICEAN (GB) - NEVER A DOUBT (GB)	T MALONE	120000
CORRECT APPROACH (IRE) CH C NEW APPROACH (IRE) - GLEIGEAL (USA)	BBA (IRELAND)	120000
BREUGHEL (GER) B C DUTCH ART (GB) - BEZZAAF (GB)	T MALONE	120000
B F CAPE CROSS (IRE) - CHARITA (IRE)	J FERGUSON	120000

Name and Breeding	Purchaser	Euros
B C CAPE CROSS (IRE) - MA PALOMA (FR)	J FERGUSON	120000
BR C MASTERCRAFTSMAN (IRE) - VINGT ET UNE (FR)	PETER & ROSS DOYLE BS	120000
B C NEW APPROACH (IRE) - TARBELA (IRE)	DARLEY STUD	120000
CH C EXCEED AND EXCEL (AUS) - POLICY SETTER (USA)	D DENNIS	115000
B C DANEHILL DANCER (IRE) - PERIHELION (IRE)	J WARREN	115000
B F KHELEYF (USA) - ATISHOO (IRE)	GILL RICHARDSON BS	110000
GR/RO C MASTERCRAFTSMAN (IRE) - SPARKLE OF STONES (FR)	D WACHMAN	110000
B C INVINCIBLE SPIRIT (IRE) - LIA (IRE)	MANDORE INTERNATIONAL	110000
B F MONTJEU (IRE) - BUCK ASPEN (USA)	NARVICK INT.	108000
EXALTED (IRE) B C ACCLAMATION (GB) - EMAN'S JOY (GB)	RICHARD KNIGHT BS	105000
B F ACCLAMATION (GB) - CARPET LADY (IRE)	HIGHFIELD FARM	105000
B C DUKE OF MARMALADE (IRE) - CLASSIC LEGEND (GB)	MAB AGENCY	105000
CH F MASTERCRAFTSMAN (IRE) - WYOLA (USA)	NARVICK INT.	105000
B C NEW APPROACH (IRE) - MARION (IRE)	J S BOLGER	105000
B F CAPE CROSS (IRE) - IDILIC CALM (IRE)	FORM BS	100000
B F DANEHILL DANCER (IRE) - ROYAL SHYNESS (GB)	GILL RICHARDSON BS	100000
SHORE PATROL (IRE) BR C FOOTSTEPSINTHESAND - FATWA (IRE)	N STEEL	100000
CARTHAGE (IRE) B C MASTERCRAFTSMAN (IRE) - PITRIZZIA (GB)	PETER & ROSS DOYLE BS	95000
B C EXCELLENT ART (GB) - MY LASS (GB)	A O'RYAN	95000
B C ROYAL APPLAUSE (GB) - AIR BISCUIT (IRE)	J FERGUSON	95000
B C INVINCIBLE SPIRIT (IRE) - CHICA ROCA (IRE)	VENDOR	92000
CH F SEA THE STARS (IRE) - LUMINARIA (IRE)	NARVICK INT.	90000
GHASAQ (IRE) B C INVINCIBLE SPIRIT (IRE) - MANUKA MAGIC (IRE)	SHADWELL ESTATE CO.	90000
B C KYLLACHY (GB) - VIKING FAIR (GB)	J MURTAGH	90000
GR F VERGLAS (IRE) - IVE GOTA BAD LIVER (USA)	H LASCELLES	87000
B F HIGH CHAPARRAL (IRE) - CIVILITY CAT (USA)	BBA (IRELAND)	85000
B C AUTHORIZED (IRE) - SO ADMIRABLE (GB)	J FERGUSON	85000
CH C EXCELLENT ART (GB) - ASK CAROL (IRE)	HUGO MERRY BS	85000
CONFLICTING (GB) B C KYLLACHY (GB) - PIPER'S ASH (USA)	HUGO MERRY BS	85000
CH C EXCEED AND EXCEL (AUS) - TARA'S FORCE (IRE)	J WARREN	85000
MAWRED (IRE) B C TAMAYUZ (GB) - ROSCOFF (IRE)	SHADWELL ESTATE CO.	85000
B C ROCK OF GIBRALTAR (IRE) - BURNIN' MEMORIES (USA)	J & S HILL	85000
B C FOOTSTEPSINTHESAND (GB) - BRIGHT BANK (IRE)	SACKVILLEDONALD	82000
B F MONTJEU (IRE) - RACE FOR THE STARS (USA)	BLANDFORD BS	80000
B C DARK ANGEL (IRE) - BIRTHDAY PRESENT (GB)	BBA (IRELAND)	80000
B F NAYEF (USA) - FROND (GB)	TEAM VALOR	80000
B F MONTJEU (IRE) - LADY ROCKFIELD (IRE)	BBA (IRELAND)	80000
B C BUSHRANGER (IRE) - BROADWAYS MILLIE (IRE)	SHADWELL ESTATE CO.	80000
JALLY (IRE) CH C TAMAYUZ (GB) - MISS BEATRIX (IRE)	J & S HILL	80000
B C MARJU (IRE) - KHATELA (IRE)	DAVID REDVERS BS	80000
CH C INTIKHAB (USA) - BABY BUNTING (GB)	PETER & ROSS DOYLE BS	80000
IONSAI NUA (IRE) B F NEW APPROACH (IRE) - TOIRNEACH (USA)	A BALDING	80000
KNOCKROON (GB) B C ROYAL APPLAUSE (GB) - SPRING TOUCH (USA)	PETER & ROSS DOYLE BS	80000
ASCENDING ANGEL (IRE) B F SEA THE STARS (IRE) - MASKAYA (IRE)	PETER & ROSS DOYLE BS	80000
LEGEND RISING (IRE) CH C TAMAYUZ (GB) - ENCOURAGEMENT (GB)	BBA (IRELAND)	75000
B C MARJU (IRE) - KHATELA (IRE)	S HILLEN	75000
B C HERNANDO (FR) - OVAL OFFICE (IRE)	GROVE STUD	75000
B C FOOTSTEPSINTHESAND (GB) - MISSKINTA (IRE)	PETER & ROSS DOYLE BS	75000
WAR SPIRIT (GB) B C EXCEED AND EXCEL (AUS) - ALYBGOOD (CAN)	J WARREN	75000
B C DANEHILL DANCER (IRE) - BEYOND BELIEF (IRE)	NARVICK INT.	75000
B F INVINCIBLE SPIRIT (IRE) - VADORGA (GB)	B O'RYAN	75000
COUNTY WEXFORD (IRE) B C TEOFILO (IRE) - TIFFED (USA)	R ALLCOCK	75000
BR C DUKE OF MARMALADE (IRE) - WINGED HARRIET (IRE)	RANGEFIELD BS	73000
B C SHAMARDAL (USA) - ORIENTAL MELODY (USA)	B O'RYAN	72000
B C KYLLACHY (GB) - GLOVED HAND (GB)	C MARNANE	72000
B C NEW APPROACH (IRE) - GRECIAN DANCER (GB)	TINA RAU BS	72000
B F TAMAYUZ (GB) - RADA (IRE)	DARLEY STUD	72000
B C SHAMARDAL (USA) - INCHMAHOME (GB)	GILL RICHARDSON BS	70000
B F FASTNET ROCK (AUS) - MADAEN (USA)	BLANDFORD BS	70000
GR C INVINCIBLE SPIRIT (IRE) - POETRY IN MOTION (IRE)	SHADWELL ESTATE CO.	70000
SAAKHEN (IRE) B C INVINCIBLE SPIRIT (IRE) - UPPERVILLE (IRE)	BBA (IRELAND)	70000
B C DARK ANGEL (IRE) - ANOTHER VALENTINE (IRE)	BBA (IRELAND)	70000
B C FASTNET ROCK (AUS) - HOLLY BLUE (GB)	D REDVERS	70000
BR C ORATORIO (IRE) - FARADAY LIGHT (IRE)	PETER & ROSS DOYLE BS	70000
B F SIR PERCY (GB) - MEDICEA SIDERA (IRE)	CORMAC MCCORMACK BS	70000
ROBIN'S CHOICE (IRE) B F BUSHRANGER (IRE) - CREEKHAVEN (IRE)	C COX	70000
CH C NAYEF (USA) - BEATRIX POTTER (IRE)	J & S HILL	70000
CH C TAMAYUZ (GB) - ANTHYLLIS (GER)	MAB AGENCY	70000
B C INVINCIBLE SPIRIT (IRE) - RAPID RANSOM (USA)	A BALDING	68000
MYMATECHRIS (IRE) B C HIGH CHAPARRAL (IRE) - SPLENDEUR (FR)	J MURTAGH	67000
B C ARAKAN (USA) - BRATISLAVA (GB)		

Name and Breeding	Purchaser	Euros
CH F DANEHILL DANCER (IRE) - NANCY SPAIN (IRE)	NARVICK INT.	66000
CH C HURRICANE RUN (IRE) - HAUTE VOLTA (FR)	LONGFIELD RACING	65000
CH F DANEHILL DANCER (IRE) - FIRST BREEZE (USA)	BBA (IRELAND)	65000
B F CAPE CROSS (IRE) - MISS SALLY (IRE)	GILL RICHARDSON BS	65000
B C KODIAC (GB) - RAJMAHAL (UAE)	MALONE/PEARS	65000
B F AZAMOUR (IRE) - ANGELIC SOUNDS (IRE)	VENDOR	65000
B F FASTNET ROCK (AUS) - AMETHYST (IRE)	RIC WYLIE BS	65000
B C LAWMAN (FR) - WOODLAND ORCHID (IRE)	MCKEEVER BS	65000
B C BUSHRANGER (IRE) - ALEXANDER ANAPOLIS (IRE)	R O'RYAN	64000
B F AZAMOUR (IRE) - DEAUVILLE VISION (IRE)	ANTHONY STROUD BS	62000
B F DANEHILL DANCER (IRE) - SNOWY DAY IN LA (USA)	D WELD	62000
CH C EXCEED AND EXCEL (AUS) - RIDOTTO (GB)	GROVE STUD	62000
NAMELY (IRE) B F ROCK OF GIBRALTAR (IRE) - VIZ (IRE)	VENDOR	62000
GR C ACCLAMATION (GB) - KAPERA (FR)	LONGFIELD RACING	60000
B C THEWAYYOUARE (USA) - CLAIRE SOLEIL (IRE)	VENDOR	60000
CH F RAVEN'S PASS (USA) - MOWAZANA (IRE)	SKYMARC FARM	60000
B F TEOFILO (IRE) - MAYENNE (USA)	VENDOR	60000
B F BUSHRANGER (IRE) - CHAMELA BAY (IRE)	B O'RYAN	60000
B F HIGH CHAPARRAL (IRE) - EN GARDE (USA)	BBA (IRELAND)	60000
MIAPLACIDUS (IRE) B F SHAMARDAL (USA) - NANDY'S CAVERN (GB)	N STEEL	60000
HIGHLY TOXIC (IRE) GR C DALAKHANI (IRE) - CHIANG MAI (IRE)	P FLYNN	60000
B F RAVEN'S PASS (USA) - VERONICA COOPER (IRE)	J FERGUSON	60000
B C INTENSE FOCUS (USA) - NOVELINA (IRE)	A STROUD	60000
B C BUSHRANGER (IRE) - EVICTRESS (IRE)	A SKIFFINGTON	60000
B C ACCLAMATION (GB) - DAQTORA (GB)	YEOMANSTOWN STUD	60000
CH C IFFRAAJ (GB) - SILICON STAR (FR)	PETER & ROSS DOYLE BS	58000
B C CAPE CROSS (IRE) - SKIPHALL (GB)	BROWN ISLAND STABLES	58000
B F EXCEED AND EXCEL (AUS) - AREEDA (IRE)	ANTHONY STROUD BS	58000
BR F CAPE CROSS (IRE) - KARLIYSHA (IRE)	J & S HILL	57000
B C ARCHIPENKO (USA) - OBLIGE (GB)	BLANDFORD BS	57000
CH C MEDICEAN (GB) - STREET STYLE (IRE)	TEAM VALOR	55000
B F EXCELLENT ART (GB) - TRIPLE AXEL (IRE)	BBA (IRELAND)	55000
CH F DUKE OF MARMALADE (IRE) - REAL CAT (USA)	J RYAN	55000
B F BAHAMIAN BOUNTY (GB) - MALYANA (GB)	ANTHONY STROUD BS	55000
B G IFFRAAJ (GB) - YIN (GB)	SIR M PRESCOTT	55000
CH F TEOFILO (IRE) - IN SAFE HANDS (IRE)	TEAM VALOR	55000
CH F BAHAMIAN BOUNTY (GB) - TREASURE TROVE (USA)	BBA (IRELAND)	55000
B F MYBOYCHARLIE (IRE) - JUST DREAMS (GB)	A SKIFFINGTON	55000
B F AZAMOUR (IRE) - GRAND OIR (IRE)	A O'RYAN	54000
THATCHEREEN (IRE) B F MASTERCRAFTSMAN (IRE) - ROOF FIDDLE (USA)	RICHARD FRISBY BS	54000
B F HIGH CHAPARRAL (IRE) - PARVENUE (FR)	J & S HILL	52000
B/BR C BIRDSTONE (USA) - SONGERIE (GB)	J MURTAGH	52000
GR C HIGH CHAPARRAL (IRE) - ALAMBIC (GB)	ANTHONY STROUD BS	52000
B C GREEN DESERT (USA) - HAWAS (IRE)	SACKVILLEDONALD	50000
B C TEOFILO (IRE) - CHEYENNE STAR (IRE)	J MCCONNELL	50000
B C ACCLAMATION (GB) - SILVERDREAMMACHINE (IRE)	VENDOR	50000
B F HIGH CHAPARRAL (IRE) - MASSADA (GB)	DAVID REDVERS BS	50000
B C IFFRAAJ (GB) - JOURNEY'S END (IRE)	J FERGUSON	50000
SHUSHU SUGARTOWN (IRE) B F INVINCIBLE SPIRIT (IRE) - LANDELA (GB)	MCKEEVER BS	50000
B C THOUSAND WORDS (GB) - ATHLUMNEY DANCER (IRE)	C MARNANE	50000
GRECIAN (IRE) GR C DARK ANGEL (GB) - LAW REVIEW (IRE)	S HILLEN	50000
B C TEOFILO (IRE) - ORIENTAL DANCE (GB)	BELIAR BS	50000
B F FASTNET ROCK (AUS) - APPLEBLOSSOM PEARL (IRE)	M V MAGNIER	50000
B C U S RANGER (USA) - DYNAMOUS (USA)	S MURPHY	50000
B F BUSHRANGER (IRE) - UNDULATION (USA)	PETER & ROSS DOYLE BS	50000
B F DUKE OF MARMALADE (IRE) - PRIDE OF MY HEART (GB)	GLENVALE STUD	50000
CH C TAMAYUZ (GB) - RAYDANIYA (IRE)	C GORDON-WATSON BS	48000
B C HENRYTHENAVIGATOR (USA) - PRINCESS DESIRE (IRE)	E JOHNSON HOUGHTON	48000
B C TAMAYUZ (GB) - LADY LIVIUS (IRE)	SACKVILLEDONALD (P.S.)	47500
BR F SHAMARDAL (USA) - TROPICAL GLAMOUR (IRE)	HORSE FRANCE	47000
B C HIGH CHAPARRAL (IRE) - INNER STRENGTH (FR)	PETER & ROSS DOYLE BS	46000
GR F MASTERCRAFTSMAN (IRE) - KINCOB (USA)	NARVICK INT.	45000
B C FOOTSTEPSINTHESAND (GB) - CLOSE REGARDS (IRE)	NEW RACING FACTORY	45000
B F DANEHILL DANCER (IRE) - KICKING BIRD (IRE)	VENDOR	45000
B C INTENSE FOCUS (USA) - I'LL BE WAITING (GB)	MGANN	45000
BR C BUSHRANGER (IRE) - SHINING DESERT (IRE)	D DENNIS	45000
ZILBER (GER) B C HIGH CHAPARRAL (IRE) - ZEPHYRINE (IRE)	S HILLEN	45000
B F FASTNET ROCK (AUS) - DELPHINIUM (IRE)	F BARRY	43000
BR C BUSHRANGER (IRE) - SHINING DESERT (IRE)	BARODA & COLBINSTOWN	43000

HIGH-PRICED YEARLINGS OF 2012 AT DONCASTER
The following yearlings realised 27,619 Guineas and over at Doncaster Sales in 2012:-

Name and Breeding	Purchaser	Guineas
B C MASTERCRAFTSMAN (IRE) - WEEKEND FLING (USA)	E FITZPATRICK	176190
GR C DUBAWI (IRE) - RONALDSAY (GB)	J FERGUSON	171428
MAGHAANEM (IRE) B C ACCLAMATION (GB) - SHISHANGAAN (IRE)	E DUNLOP	123809
CH F NEW APPROACH (IRE) - MONTURANI (IRE)	J FERGUSON	123809
B F HOLY ROMAN EMPEROR (IRE) - GENTLE NIGHT (GB)	T NERSES	114285
B F INVINCIBLE SPIRIT (IRE) - ALSHARQ (IRE)	J FERGUSON	109523
CH F DUTCH ART (GB) - PETONG'S PET (GB)	T NERSES	104761
GR C ACCLAMATION (GB) - NEW DEAL (GB)	HIGHFIELD FARM	100000
IFTAAR (IRE) B C BUSHRANGER (IRE) - KHELEYF'S SILVER (IRE)	SHADWELL ESTATE CO	85714
B C IFFRAAJ (GB) - MISS GIBRALTAR (IRE)	BLANDFORD BS	85714
MOOWFAD (IRE) B C BUSHRANGER (IRE) - MIST AND STONE (IRE)	SHADWELL ESTATE CO	85714
MAWFOOR (IRE) B C IFFRAAJ (GB) - MISS ODLUM (IRE)	SHADWELL ESTATE CO	78095
B C ROYAL APPLAUSE (GB) - CEDAR SEA (IRE)	RABBAH BS	76190
AYERS ROCK (IRE) B C BUSHRANGER (IRE) - RED FUSCHIA (GB)	PETER & ROSS DOYLE BS	73333
MUNJALLY (GB) B C ACCLAMATION (GB) - PARABOLA (GB)	PETER & ROSS DOYLE BS	71428
MUSTAJJID (GB) B C BYRON (GB) - SKARA BRAE (IRE)	SHADWELL ESTATE CO	71428
RAAJIS (IRE) GR F DARK ANGEL (IRE) - RUMLINE (GB)	PETER & ROSS DOYLE BS	71428
CH C DANDY MAN (IRE) - NOBLE VIEW (USA)	BLANDFORD BS	71428
CH F DUTCH ART (GB) - PENCHANT (GB)	HIGHFIELD FARM	71428
CH C KYLLACHY (GB) - ANNELIINA (GB)	OLIVER ST LAWRENCE BS	71428
AMBIANCE (IRE) B C CAMACHO (GB) - THAWRAH (IRE)	GILL RICHARDSON BS	66666
B F ROYAL APPLAUSE (GB) - MISS SMILLA (GB)	J O'BYRNE	66666
B C BAHAMIAN BOUNTY (GB) - XTRASENSORY (IRE)	HILLEN & RYAN	66666
B C TAGULA (IRE) - CINZIA VEGAS (IRE)	PETER & ROSS DOYLE BS	66666
CH C MASTERCRAFTSMAN (IRE) - TEDDY BEARS PICNIC (GB)	T NERSES	61904
B C BUSHRANGER (IRE) - LADY MEAGAN (IRE)	B O'RYAN	61904
CH C DUTCH ART (GB) - OASIS BREEZE (GB)	T EASTERBY	59047
B C HOLY ROMAN EMPEROR (IRE) - FINAL OPINION (IRE)	D SHAW	59047
B F PIVOTAL (GB) - HEAVENLY BAY (USA)	BLANDFORD BS	57142
B C KYLLACHY (GB) - GOLD AND BLUE (IRE)	PETER & ROSS DOYLE BS	57142
B C MEDICEAN (GB) - PHILLIPPA (IRE)	BLANDFORD BS	55238
B C KYLLACHY (GB) - NIGHT PREMIERE (IRE)	M CROSSMAN	55238
B C EXCEED AND EXCEL (AUS) - GANDINI (GB)	PETER & ROSS DOYLE BS	53333
B F JEREMY (USA) - STARTARETTE (USA)	MCKEEVER BS	52380
VIVA VERGLAS (IRE) GR C VERGLAS (IRE) - YELLOW TRUMPET (GB)	HARROWGATE BS	52380
B C INVINCIBLE SPIRIT (IRE) - LOVELY THOUGHT (GB)	BLANDFORD BS	52380
B C ACCLAMATION (GB) - MAID TO ORDER (IRE)	PETER & ROSS DOYLE BS	49523
TREADSTONE (GB) B C MYBOYCHARLIE (IRE) - LILLI MARLANE (GB)	CORMAC MCCORMACK	49523
B C TEOFILO (IRE) - SAINT DAY (USA)	PETER & ROSS DOYLE BS	49523
MASTER OF ALKMAAR (IRE) CH C DUTCH ART (GB) - LALINA (GER)	HUGO MERRY BS	47619
SONG OF ROWLAND (IRE) B C HOLY ROMAN EMPEROR (IRE) - MAKAROVA (IRE)	HUGO MERRY BS	47619
CANYARI (IRE) B C DANDY MAN (IRE) - MORNA'S FAN (FR)	R O'RYAN	47619
CH C ART CONNOISSEUR (IRE) - CAPETOWN GIRL (GB)	PETER & ROSS DOYLE BS	47619
B C INVINCIBLE SPIRIT (IRE) - SPEEDY SONATA (USA)	HIGHFIELD FARM	47619
B C BUSHRANGER (IRE) - RAINBOW LYRICS (IRE)	BBA (IRELAND)	47619
CH F EXCELLENT ART (GB) - ROYAL BOUNTY (GB)	D REDVERS	47619
B F INVINCIBLE SPIRIT (IRE) - LA REINE MAMBO (USA)	POWERSTOWN STUD	47619
CH C PIVOTAL (GB) - FIRST BLOOM (USA)	HUGO MERRY BS	47619
B C ORATORIO (IRE) - PRIMISSIMA (GER)	WILL EDMEADES BS	47619
B F AUTHORIZED (IRE) - UMNIYA (IRE)	GILL RICHARDSON BS	45714
DESPOT (IRE) GR C VERGLAS (IRE) - MS BOSSY BOOTS (USA)	BBA (IRELAND)	43809
CH C EXCEED AND EXCEL (AUS) - CLICHE (GB)	W BROWNE	43809
B C KODIAC (GB) - OLYMPIA THEATRE (GB)	A SKIFFINGTON	43809
B F ACCLAMATION (GB) - DANCE SET (GB)	N GILCHRIST	42857
MALACHIM MIST (IRE) GR C DARK ANGEL (IRE) - SIXFIELDS FLYER (IRE)	PETER & ROSS DOYLE BS	42857
ZALZILAH (GB) B C KHELEYF (USA) - TARNEEM (USA)	RABBAH BS	42857
B F ROCK OF GIBRALTAR (IRE) - FINAL DYNASTY (GB)	GILL RICHARDSON BS	41904
B F DUTCH ART (GB) - ELLWAY QUEEN (GB)	RABBAH BS	41904
CH C COMPTON PLACE (GB) - RAPHAELA (FR)	SACKVILLEDONALD	41904
ERRONEOUS (IRE) BR C FOOTSTEPSINTHESAND (GB) - ATIR LOVE (USA)	HUGO MERRY BS	40000
BISHOP WULSTAN (IRE) B C ORATORIO (IRE) - LAURENTINE (USA)	PETER & ROSS DOYLE BS	40000
WEISSE SOCKEN (IRE) B F ACCLAMATION (GB) - PLAYFUL (GB)	R FRISBY	40000
B C ART CONNOISSEUR (IRE) - NARMEEN (GB)	T NERSES	40000
CH C COMPTON PLACE (GB) - TINNARINKA (GB)	J FRETWELL	40000
MIGHTY FORCE (IRE) B C ACCLAMATION (GB) - IKAN (IRE)	PETER & ROSS DOYLE BS	38095
B C KYLLACHY (GB) - HAVE FUN (GB)	MCKEEVER BS	38095
B C ACCLAMATION (GB) - ABINGTON ANGEL (GB)	MCKEEVER BS	38095

THUNDER STRIKE (GB) CH C SAKHEE'S SECRET (GB) - TRUMP STREET (GB)	PETER & ROSS DOYLE BS	38095
B C KODIAC (GB) - GEROBIES GIRL (USA)	VENDOR	38095
CH C COMPTON PLACE (GB) - HIGHLY LIQUID (GB)	HUGO MERRY BS	38095
B C ACCLAMATION (GB) - THANKFUL (GB)	HILLEN & RYAN	38095
FEMALE STRATEGY (IRE) B F HOLY ROMAN EMPEROR (IRE) - STRATEGY (GB)	BLANDFORD BS	38095
B C HAATEF (USA) - SYMBOL OF PEACE (IRE)	W BROWNE	38095
CH C KHELEYF (USA) - FANCY FEATHERS (IRE)	B O'RYAN	38095
MERITOCRACY (IRE) B C KHELEYF (USA) - CHIOSINA (IRE)	VENDOR	38095
B C BUSHRANGER (IRE) - ZAYNABA (IRE)	SACKVILLEDONALD	38095
YAJAMILA (GB) B F ROYAL APPLAUSE (GB) - YATIR (FR)	RABBAH BS	38095
B C JEREMY (USA) - RIVER ABOUALI (GB)	J FRETWELL	37142
CH C SHAMARDAL (USA) - FORTRESS (GB)	RABBAH BS	36190
SOUL BROTHER (IRE) B C CAPTAIN RIO (GB) - GOODWOOD MARCH (GB)	T EASTERBY	36190
STRAIT RUN (IRE) CH C ROCK OF GIBRALTAR (IRE) - GENTLEMEN'S GUEST (USA)	PETER & ROSS DOYLE BS	36190
CH C DUTCH ART (GB) - LIPSIA (IRE)	BLANDFORD BS	36190
B F HOLY ROMAN EMPEROR (IRE) - ART WORK (GB)	BBA (IRELAND)	36190
B C PASTORAL PURSUITS (GB) - RHAPSILIAN (GB)	HUGO MERRY BS	35238
B C HOLY ROMAN EMPEROR (IRE) - CALYPSO DANCER (FR)	SACKVILLEDONALD	34285
BOWSERS BOLD (GB) B C FIREBREAK (GB) - CRISTAL CLEAR (IRE)	M TREGONING	34285
BEATABOUT THE BUSH (IRE) B/BR C BUSHRANGER (IRE) - QUEEN OF FIBRES (IRE)	GEOFFREY HOWSON BS	34285
B F KODIAC (GB) - TIDES (GB)	JOHN WARREN BS	34285
B F ROCKPORT HARBOR (USA) - GULCH GIRL (USA)	VENDOR	34285
B C KYLLACHY (GB) - ELLENS PRINCESS (IRE)	D REDVERS	34285
ALASKAN NIGHT (IRE) B C KODIAC (GB) - FINGAL NIGHTS (IRE)	HILLEN & RYAN	34285
B C EXCELLENT ART (GB) - DAMA'A (IRE)	PETER & ROSS DOYLE BS	34285
TOORMORE (IRE) B C ARAKAN (USA) - DANETIME OUT (IRE)	PETER & ROSS DOYLE BS	34285
DINNERATMIDNIGHT (GB) B C KYLLACHY (GB) - THE TERRIER (GB)	GLOBAL EQUINE	33333
CRAZY CHIC (IRE) GR C EXCEED AND EXCEL (AUS) - MARTINES (FR)	BLANDFORD BS	33333
CH C MAJOR CADEAUX (GB) - DAYVILLE (USA)	ANTHONY STROUD BS	32380
B C CAPTAIN RIO (GB) - HARVEST JOY (IRE)	A DUARTE	32380
B F ORATORIO (IRE) - MACKENZIE'S FRIEND (GB)	D WACHMAN	32380
GOLD TOP (IRE) CH F TEOFILO (IRE) - TOP ROW (GB)	PETER & ROSS DOYLE BS	32380
B C KODIAC (GB) - MIRA (IRE)	W BROWNE	32380
SHADES OF SILK (GB) B F BAHAMIAN BOUNTY (GB) - TERENTIA (GB)	ANTHONY STROUD BS	31428
HANDS UP (IRE) B C BUSHRANGER (IRE) - CHRISTA MARIA (GB)	N GILCHRIST	31428
B F KHELEYF (USA) - HARMONIST (USA)	CORMAC MCCORMACK	31428
B F DUTCH ART (GB) - SWEET COINCIDENCE (GB)	GAYBROOK LODGE	31428
PRINCESS ROSE (GB) B F ROYAL APPLAUSE (GB) - MYSTICAL SPIRIT (IRE)	A SKIFFINGTON	30476
B F ROYAL APPLAUSE (GB) - FABINE (GB)	SACKVILLEDONALD	30476
B C HOLY ROMAN EMPEROR (IRE) - CAPPAGH STRAND (USA)	BLANDFORD BS	30476
B C EXCELLENT ART (GB) - MISS INFORMED (IRE)	J FRETWELL	30476
B C KODIAC (GB) - SILK FAN (IRE)	RABBAH BS	30476
PROCLAMATIONOFWAR (GB) B C PROCLAMATION (IRE) - ROCKBURST (GB)	HILLEN & RYAN	30476
QUEEN OF THE TARTS (GB) B F ROYAL APPLAUSE (GB) - TART AND A HALF (GB)	D REDVERS	30476
CH F SHAMARDAL (USA) - EXCELLENT (GB)	T TATE	29523
B C TAGULA (IRE) - MALTA (USA)	HILLEN & RYAN	29523
B F TOBOUGG (IRE) - HAPPY LADY (FR)	RABBAH BS	29523
THE BOSS OF ME (GB) CH C BAHAMIAN BOUNTY (GB) - ORANGE PIP (GB)	HILLEN & RYAN	28571
B C MYBOYCHARLIE (IRE) - HOWEVER (IRE)	HILLEN & RYAN	28571
B F CHAMPS ELYSEES (GB) - INTERVENE (GB)	VENDOR	28571
BR C CAPTAIN RIO (GB) - GRANNYS RELUCTANCE (IRE)	MCKEEVER BS	28571
WADI ALAMARDI (GB) CH C LUCKY STORY (USA) - THICKET (GB)	R FRISBY	28571
B F TAGULA (IRE) - TEODORA (IRE)	SACKVILLEDONALD	28571
B C EXCELLENT ART (GB) - ATLAS SILK (GB)	A WALKER	28571
B C DUTCH ART (GB) - VALLEY OF THE MOON (IRE)	BBA (IRELAND)	28571
MIMI LUKE (USA) B F U S RANGER (USA) - HARD AS NAILS (USA)	A BAILEY	28571
ROYAL CONNECTION (GB) B F BAHAMIAN BOUNTY (GB) - FISADARA (GB)	PETER & ROSS DOYLE BS	28571
CH C KHELEYF (USA) - SPIRIT OF HOPE (IRE)	S M HILLEN	28571
B F ACCLAMATION (GB) - DIVERT (IRE)	BLANDFORD BS	28571
CAN'T CHANGE IT (IRE) GR C VERGLAS (IRE) - ALL TIED UP (IRE)	S M HILLEN	28571
CH C DANDY MAN (IRE) - PEARLY BROOKS (GB)	SACKVILLEDONALD	28571
B C DANDY MAN (IRE) - DREAM DATE (IRE)	D REDVERS (PS.)	28571
B C IFFRAAJ (GB) - MONARCHY (IRE)	O'RYAN	28571
B C DUKE OF MARMALADE (IRE) - CELTIC HEROINE (IRE)	E LYNAM	28571
CH C PASTORAL PURSUITS (GB) - PRINCESS MILETRIAN (IRE)	O'RYAN	28571
B F ELUSIVE CITY (USA) - COACHHOUSE LADY (IRE)	J FRETWELL	28571
B F LAWMAN (FR) - SVEVA (IRE)	MARCO BOTTI	28571
B C DANDY MAN (IRE) - MRS MOONLIGHT (GB)	T MALONE	28571
B/GR C TAMAYUZ (GB) - RECTIFY (IRE)	VENDOR	27619
B C KHELEYF (USA) - KOMENA (GB)	A & A	27619

HIGH-PRICED YEARLINGS OF 2012 AT TATTERSALLS IRELAND SALES

The following yearlings realised 17,500 euros and over at Tattersalls Ireland Sales in 2012:-

Name and Breeding	Purchaser	Euros
B C YEATS (IRE) - BLEU CIEL ET BLANC (FR)	ORMOND BS	100000
ELEVENTWENTYEIGHT (IRE) B C BUSHRANGER (IRE) - CLEVER DAY (USA)	U SUTER	75000
CH C PASTORAL PURSUITS (GB) - RIGHT AFTER MOYNE (IRE)	H BUTLER	64000
B G YEATS (IRE) - STRICTLY COOL (USA)	J O'BYRNE	62000
LINDART (ITY) CH C DUTCH ART (GB) - LINDA SURENA (ARG)	PETER & ROSS DOYLE BS	57000
INTENSICAL (IRE) B C INTENSE FOCUS (USA) - CHRISTMAS LETTER (IRE)	J T GORMAN	55000
CH C MASTERCRAFTSMAN (IRE) - AWANI (GB)	A DUARTE	55000
B C TAMAYUZ (GB) - LUCKY CLIO (IRE)	A DUARTE	55000
BIG BANG ALLEN (FR) BR/B G NETWORK (GER) - ETOILE D'OR II (FR)	HIGHFLYER BS	55000
B G ROBIN DES CHAMPS (FR) - KOKO ROSE (IRE)	J O'BYRNE	50000
BR G ROBIN DES CHAMPS (FR) - CHERRY BLACK (IRE)	WOOD HALL STUD	47000
B C EXCEED AND EXCEL (AUS) - EMIRATES HILLS (GB)	A BOTTI	44000
B F ART CONNOISSEUR (IRE) - MADAME BOULANGERE (GB)	SACKVILLEDONALD	43000
B C BAHAMIAN BOUNTY (GB) - LINDESBERG (GB)	SACKVILLEDONALD	42000
B C HOLY ROMAN EMPEROR (IRE) - PAINT THE TOWN (IRE)	BANSHA HOUSE STABLES	40000
B F BUSHRANGER (IRE) - RIBBON GLADE (UAE)	LONGFIELD RACING	40000
B G KING'S THEATRE (IRE) - MISS ARTEEA (IRE)	A MURPHY	40000
B G ROBIN DES CHAMPS (FR) - SARAH PRINCESS (IRE)	K ROSS BS	40000
CH F ROCK OF GIBRALTAR (IRE) - MAGNIFICENT BELL (IRE)	PETER & ROSS DOYLE BS	38000
KAP AU LARGE (FR) CH G KAPGARDE (FR) - CYBERTINA (FR)	WOOD HALL STUD LTD	38000
B C ACCLAMATION (GB) - ARRAY OF STARS (IRE)	J OSBORNE	37000
CH C INTIKHAB (USA) - LAQATAAT (IRE)	MILLTOWN STUD	36000
B F SHIROCCO (GER) - SENSIBILITY (GB)	A BOTTI	36000
GR F VERGLAS (IRE) - JAMRAH (IRE)	MILLTOWN STUD	35000
STRATEGIC FORCE (IRE) B C STRATEGIC PRINCE (GB) - MOOCHING ALONG (IRE)	C COX	35000
B/BR C PRESENTING (GB) - SUPREME DREAMER (IRE)	J O'BYRNE	35000
KANTARA CASTLE (IRE) B C BALTIC KING (GB) - ARBITRATION (IRE)	PETER & ROSS DOYLE BS	34000
GR F CLODOVIL (IRE) - FIVE OF WANDS (GB)	BELIAR BS	33000
B F PASTORAL PURSUITS (GB) - ALMOST AMBER (USA)	PETER & ROSS DOYLE BS	33000
B F HIGH CHAPARRAL (IRE) - ALL EMBRACING (IRE)	SACKVILLEDONALD	33000
B G FLEMENSFIRTH (USA) - LEADING LADY (IRE)	FABRICATED PRODUCTS LTD	33000
B C PRESENTING (GB) - PROWLER (IRE)	J O'BYRNE	33000
CH C HELIOSTATIC (IRE) - PUREPLEASURESEEKER (IRE)	J J QUINN	32000
B F BUSHRANGER (IRE) - LILAKIYA (IRE)	D REDVERS	32000
B F ROCK OF GIBRALTAR (IRE) - RUBILEO (GB)	A SKIFFINGTON	32000
CH F ROCK OF GIBRALTAR (IRE) - SIGHTSEER (USA)	SACKVILLEDONALD	32000
B F SHAMARDAL (USA) - ATHLUMNEY LADY (IRE)	BBA (IRELAND)	32000
B C FLEMENSFIRTH (USA) - ALLEYGROVE LASS (IRE)	LANDSCAPE STUD	32000
BR C DIAMOND GREEN (FR) - STRAIGHT MISS (IRE)	C DE MOUBRAY	31000
BR F PRESENTING (GB) - MOLLY MAGUIRE (IRE)	J O'BYRNE	31000
B C PRESENTING (GB) - UNCERTAIN AFFAIR (IRE)	G MERRIGAN	30000
HEART FOCUS (IRE) B F INTENSE FOCUS (USA) - HAVE A HEART (IRE)	BBA (IRELAND)	30000
B G FLEMENSFIRTH (USA) - ROYALE LAGUNA (FR)	HIGHFLYER BS	30000
B C AMADEUS WOLF (GB) - NAWAJI (USA)	HILLEN & RYAN	30000
CH F TAMAYUZ (GB) - LIVIUS LADY (IRE)	VENDOR	30000
B F KODIAC (GB) - STORM LADY (IRE)	HILLEN & RYAN	30000
B C YEATS (IRE) - HIDDEN RESERVE (IRE)	VENDOR	30000
B C DANDY MAN (IRE) - BRONZE QUEEN (IRE)	J OSBORNE	28000
B G KING'S THEATRE (IRE) - CINCENTA (IRE)	FABRICATED PRODUCTS LTD	28000
CH F INTENSE FOCUS (USA) - RYALAHINA (IRE)	C COX	27000
GR C DARK ANGEL (IRE) - NON DIMENTICAR ME (IRE)	J O'BYRNE	27000
B C YEATS (IRE) - CLINGING VINE (USA)	B O'RYAN	27000
B C AZAMOUR (IRE) - FEZ (GB)	G LYONS	27000
B C LAWMAN (FR) - CUTE CAIT (GB)	C MARNANE	27000
CH C SHIROCCO (GER) - ADEES DANCER (GB)	A MURPHY	27000
B G GOLD WELL (GB) - FOREIGN ESTATES (IRE)	J MERNAGH	27000
B C INDIAN HAVEN (GB) - MADDIE'S PEARL (IRE)	T MALONE	26000
B F ACCLAMATION (GB) - UNLOCK (IRE)	C COX	26000
B F KYLLACHY (GB) - AUTHORITATIVE (GB)	W M WANLESS	26000
B C KODIAC (GB) - NELLY'S GLEN (GB)	W BROWNE	26000
GR C CLODOVIL (IRE) - AJIG DANCER (GB)	GILL RICHARDSON BS	26000
GR F ACCLAMATION (GB) - LEGAL STEPS (IRE)	BERTRAND LE METAYER BS	25000
B C BENEFICIAL (GB) - SUPREME BREDA (IRE)	T COOPER	25000
B C ORATORIO (IRE) - MANDARAKA (FR)	G LYONS	25000
B F DARK ANGEL (IRE) - DALAL (GB)	D GEARY	25000
B F TEOFILO (IRE) - ROSE BOURBON (USA)	B ELLISON	25000
BR G PRESENTING (GB) - FORGOTTEN STAR (IRE)	WOOD HALL STUD	25000

Name and Breeding	Purchaser	Euros
B C WESTERNER (GB) - NOSTRA (FR)	I FERGUSON	25000
B G SCORPION (IRE) - SHAMEENA (GB)	J BLEAHEN	25000
BR/B C AL NAMIX (FR) - LALY LIGHT (FR)	I FERGUSON	25000
CH F THOUSAND WORDS (GB) - INDIANNIE MOON (GB)	GILL RICHARDSON BS	25000
B C PRESENTING (GB) - BAY PEARL (FR)	R E ROHAN	25000
B G KAYF TARA (GB) - DANCING DASI (IRE)	VENDOR	24000
BR C BIG BAD BOB (IRE) - LANASARA (GB)	F BARBERINI	24000
B/BR G PRESENTING (GB) - DAME FORAINE (FR)	J MERNAGH	24000
GR F CLODOVIL (IRE) - KNAPTON HILL (GB)	E LYNAM	24000
B C IFFRAAJ (GB) - ROYAL ESTEEM (GB)	KEVIN ROSS BS	24000
BACCARA SACREE (FR) B F FRAGRANT MIX (IRE) - FATIMA III (FR)	J KENNY	24000
CH C CAPTAIN RIO (GB) - QUIZZICAL LADY (GB)	KEVIN ROSS BS	23000
B G YEATS (IRE) - PETRALONA (USA)	M CONNAIRE	23000
B C MYBOYCHARLIE (IRE) - FOREST EXPRESS (AUS)	JANDA BS	23000
B G PRESENTING (GB) - KNEELAND LASS (IRE)	HIGHFLYER BS	23000
CH C DANDY MAN (IRE) - FIRST BANK (FR)	D REDVERS	22000
B C FOOTSTEPSINTHESAND (GB) - SUMINGASEFA (GB)	BBA (IRELAND)	22000
CH G ROBIN DES CHAMPS (FR) - CULLEEN LADY (IRE)	ANA BS	22000
B F MASTERCRAFTSMAN (IRE) - HIGH SPOT (GB)	VENDOR	21000
GR F VERGLAS (IRE) - BARATHIKI (GB)	SACKVILLEDONALD	21000
CH C FIREBREAK (GB) - MANDERINA (GB)	A BALDING	21000
B G INTENSE FOCUS (USA) - SAOODAH (IRE)	D REDVERS	21000
B F SHAMARDAL (USA) - BUNOOD (IRE)	J COOGAN	21000
BELLATOR (FR) B C NETWORK (GB) - ONYSIA (FR)	J KENNY	20000
B F TIGER HILL (IRE) - QUEST FOR FREEDOM (GB)	S HILLEN	20000
B G PRESENTING (GB) - WATER ROCK (GB)	FUTURERATE LIMITED	20000
B/BR C KODIAC (GB) - TEEM (IRE)	SACKVILLEDONALD	20000
GR C INTENSE FOCUS (USA) - WICKED MARIA (IRE)	EMERALD BS	20000
B F INTIKHAB (USA) - SARAMACCA (IRE)	D REDVERS	20000
SHREWD BOB (IRE) B C WHIPPER (USA) - CHEYENNE SPIRIT (GB)	R EDDERY	20000
B F JEREMY (USA) - ALL BEGAN (IRE)	KEVIN ROSS BS	20000
B C TAGULA (IRE) - WESTLIFE (IRE)	NIGEL TINKLER BS	20000
B F HAATEF (USA) - CAFE CREME (IRE)	E SACKVILLE	20000
CRAFTY CODGER (IRE) CH C MASTERCRAFTSMAN (IRE) - RAINBOW MELODY (IRE)	F BARRY	20000
B C ORATORIO (IRE) - WARRIOR WINGS (GB)	RICHARD KNIGHT BS	20000
B C KODIAC (GB) - KRIS'S BANK (GB)	KEVIN ROSS BS	20000
BR F BERNSTEIN (USA) - PRONGHORN (USA)	M JOHNSTON	20000
B C DYLAN THOMAS (IRE) - NELLIE NOLAN (USA)	OHS SLOVAKIA	20000
CH F ORIENTATE (USA) - SINGING FIELD (IRE)	B O'RYAN	20000
B G GOLD WELL (GB) - SITE MISTRESS (IRE)	R FRISBY	20000
B C ROYAL APPLAUSE (GB) - TATBEEQ (IRE)	W BROWNE	20000
B C BENEFICIAL (GB) - MILLICENT BRIDGE (IRE)	K O'BRIEN	20000
CH C ART CONNOISSEUR (IRE) - KAFAYEF (USA)	SACKVILLEDONALD	20000
B C INDIAN HAVEN (GB) - CAPPUCCINO (IRE)	W M WANLESS	20000
B C KING'S THEATRE (IRE) - NINNA NANNA (FR)	I FERGUSON	20000
PIXIE HOLLOW (IRE) GR F VERGLAS (IRE) - HIGH FUN (FR)	F BARRY	19000
B C INTIKHAB (USA) - MIDNIGHT OASIS (USA)	BANSHA HOUSE STABLES	19000
B F JEREMY (USA) - KRYNICA (USA)	BBA (IRELAND)	19000
B C KAYF TARA (GB) - VIA FERRATA (FR)	T MURPHY	19000
B G PRESENTING (GB) - ALDER FLOWER (IRE)	LIME STUD	18500
B G BENEFICIAL (GB) - BOBBIES STORM (IRE)	FABRICATED PRODUCTS LTD	18000
GR F MIZZEN MAST (USA) - ZEN DIVA (USA)	A BOTTI	18000
GR C KODIAC (GB) - PETIT GRISE (IRE)	MARCO BOZZI BS	18000
GR C AUSSIE RULES (USA) - GOODWOOD BLIZZARD (GB)	VENDOR	18000
B C MYBOYCHARLIE (IRE) - MONDOVI (FR)	E LYNAM	18000
PATIENCE'S ROCK (IRE) B C ROCK OF GIBRALTAR (IRE) - SHAKEEBA (IRE)	HILLEN & RYAN	18000
CH C ELNADIM (USA) - START THE MUSIC (IRE)	HILLEN & RYAN	18000
RO C MASTERCRAFTSMAN (IRE) - MOST-SAUCY (GB)	VENDOR	18000
BR G PRESENTING (GB) - REGLE D'OR (FR)	VENDOR	18000
B G MILAN (GB) - SPORTS LEADER (IRE)	T O'SULLIVAN	18000
B G KAYF TARA (GB) - SUAVE SHOT (GB)	H BLEAHEN	17500
KOKOVOKO (IRE) BR C TRANS ISLAND (GB) - KHAZARIA (FR)	A BALDING	17500
BR C SHAMARDAL (USA) - DESERTION (IRE)	M JOHNSTON	17500
B F AUSSIE RULES (USA) - ARDENT LADY (GB)	MARCO BOZZI BS	17500
B C YEATS (IRE) - MIDNIGHT FLIRT (IRE)	BRENDAN BASHFORD BS	17500

2000 GUINEAS STAKES (3y) Newmarket-1 mile

Year	Owner	Winner and Price	Jockey	Trainer	Second	Third	Ran	Time
1971	Mrs J Hislop's	BRIGADIER GERARD (11/2)	J Mercer	R Hern	Mill Reef	My Swallow	6	39.20
1972	Sir J Thorn's	HIGH TOP (85/40)	W Carson	B Van Cutsem	Roberto	Sun Prince	12	40.82
1973	Sir B Davis's	MON FILS (50/1)	F Durr	R Hannon	Noble Decree	Sharp Edge	18	42.97
1974	Mme M Berger's	NONOALCO (19/2)	Y Saint Martin	F Boutin	Giacometti	Apalachee	18	39.53
1975	C d'Alessio's	BOLKONSKI (33/1)	G Dettori	H Cecil	Grundy	Dominion	24	39.53
1976	C d'Alessio's	WOLLOW (evens)	G Dettori	H Cecil	Vitiges	Thieving Demon	17	38.09
1977	N Schibbye's	NEBBIOLO (20/1)	G Curran	K Prendergast	Tachypous	The Minstrel	19	38.54
1978	J Hayter's	ROLAND GARDENS (28/1)	F Durr	D Sasse	Remainder Man	Wetth Nan	18	47.33
1979	A Shead's	TAP ON WOOD (20/1)	S Cauthen	B Hills	Kris	Young Generation	20	43.60
1980	K Abdulla's	KNOWN FACT (14/1)	W Carson	J Tree	Posse	Night Alert	14	40.46

Nureyev finished first but was disqualified

Year	Owner	Winner and Price	Jockey	Trainer	Second	Third	Ran	Time
1981	Mrs A Muinos's	TO-AGORI-MOU (5/2)	G Starkey	G Harwood	Mattaboy	Bel Bolide	19	41.43
1982	G Oldham's	ZINO (8/1)	F Head	F Boutin	Wind and Wuthering	Tender King	26	37.13
1983	R Sangster's	LOMOND (9/1)	Pat Eddery	V O'Brien	Tolomeo	Muscatite	16	43.87
1984	R Sangster's	EL GRAN SENOR (15/8)	Pat Eddery	V O'Brien	Chief Singer	Lear Fan	16	37.41
1985	Maktoum Al Maktoum's	SHADEED (4/5)	L Piggott	M Stoute	Bairn	Supreme Leader	14	37.41
1986	K Abdulla's	DANCING BRAVE (15/8)	G Starkey	G Harwood	Green Desert	Huntingdale	15	40.00
1987	J Horgan's	DON'T FORGET ME (9/1)	W Carson	R Hannon	Bellotto	Midyan	13	36.74
1988	H H Aga Khan's	DOYOUN (4/5)	W R Swinburn	M Stoute	Charmer	Bellefella	9	41.73
1989	Hamdan Al-Maktoum's	NASHWAN (3/1)	W Carson	R Hern	Exbourne	Danehill	14	36.44
1990	John Horgan's	TIROL (9/1)	M Kinane	R Hannon	Machiavellian	Anshan	14	35.64
1991	Lady Beaverbrook's	MYSTIKO (13/2)	M Roberts	C Brittain	Lycius	Ganges	14	37.83
1992	R Sangster's	RODRIGO DE TRIANO (6/1)	L Piggott	P Chapple-Hyam	Lucky Lindy	Pursuit of Love	16	38.37
1993	K Abdulla's	ZAFONIC (5/6)	Pat Eddery	A Fabre	Barathea	Bin Alwaad	14	35.32
1994	G R Bailey Ltd's	MISTER BAILEYS (16/1)	J Weaver	M Johnston	Grand Lodge	Colonel Collins	23	35.08
1995	Godolphin's	PENNEKAMP (9/2)	T Jarnet	A Fabre	Celtic Swing	Bahri	11	35.16
1996	Godolphin's	MARK OF ESTEEM (8/1)	L Dettori	S bin Suroor	Even Top	Bijou D'Inde	13	37.59
1997	M Tabor & Mrs J Magnier's	ENTREPRENEUR (11/2)	M Kinane	M Stoute	Revoque	Poteen	16	35.64
1998	M Tabor & Mrs J Magnier's	KING OF KINGS (7/2)	M Kinane	A O'Brien	Lend A Hand	Border Arrow	18	39.25
1999	Godolphin's	ISLAND SANDS (10/1)	L Dettori	S bin Suroor	Enrique	Mujahid	16	37.14

(Run on July Course)

Year	Owner	Winner and Price	Jockey	Trainer	Second	Third	Ran	Time
2000	Saeed Suhail's	KING'S BEST (13/2)	K Fallon	Sir M Stoute	Giant's Causeway	Barathea Guest	27	37.77
2001	Lord Weinstock's	GOLAN (11/1)	K Fallon	Sir M Stoute	Tamburlaine	Frenchmans Bay	18	37.48
2002	Sir A Ferguson & Mrs J Magnier's	ROCK OF GIBRALTAR (9/1)	J Murtagh	A O'Brien	Hawk Wing	Redback	22	36.50
2003	Moyglare Stud Farm's	REFUSE TO BEND (9/1)	P J Smullen	D Weld	Zafeen	Norse Dancer	20	37.98
2004	Hamdan Al Maktoum's	HAAFHD (11/2)	R Hills	B Hills	Snow Ridge	Azamour	14	36.60
2005	Mr M Tabor & Mrs John Magnier's	FOOTSTEPSINTHESAND (13/2)	K Fallon	A O'Brien	Rebel Rebel	Kandidate	19	36.10
2006	Mrs J Magnier, Mr M Tabor & Mr D Smith's	GEORGE WASHINGTON (6/4)	K Fallon	A O'Brien	Sir Percy	Olympian Odyssey	14	36.80
2007	P Cunningham's	COCKNEY REBEL (25/1)	O Peslier	G Huffer	Vital Equine	Dutch Art	24	35.28
2008	Mrs J Magnier's	HENRYTHENAVIGATOR (11/1)	J Murtagh	A O'Brien	New Approach	Stubbs Art	15	39.14
2009	C Tsui's	SEA THE STARS (8/1)	M Kinane	J Oxx	Delegator	Gan Amhras	19	35.88
2010	M Offenstadt's	MAKFI (33/1)	C Lemaire	M Delzangles	Dick Turpin	Canford Cliffs	19	36.35
2011	K Abdulla's	FRANKEL (1/2)	T Queally	H Cecil	Dubawi Gold	Native Khan	13	37.30
2012	D Smith, Mrs J Magnier & M Tabor's	CAMELOT (15/8)	J O'Brien	A O'Brien	French Fifteen	Hermival	18	42.46

1000 GUINEAS STAKES (3y fillies) Newmarket-1 mile

Year	Owner	Winner and Price	Jockey	Trainer	Second	Third	Ran	Time
1971	F Hue-Williams's	ALTESSE ROYALE (25/1)	Y Saint Martin	N Murless	Super Honey	Catherine Wheel	10	40.90
1972	Mrs R Stanley's	WATERLOO (8/1)	E Hide	N Murless	Mariscal	Rose Dubarry	18	39.49
1973	G Pope's	MYSTERIOUS (11/1)	G Lewis	J W Watts	Jacinth	Shellshock	14	40.45
1974	The Queen's	HIGHCLERE (12/1)	J Mercer	R Hern	Polygamy	Mrs Twiggywinkle	15	40.32
1975	Mrs D O'Kelly's	NOCTURNAL SPREE (14/1)	J Roe	S Murless	Girl Friend	Mrs Twiggywinkle	16	41.07
1976	D Wildenstein's	FLYING WATER (2/1)	Y Saint Martin	A Penna	Konafa	Joking Apart	25	37.83
1977	Mrs E Kettlewell's	MRS McARDY (16/1)	E Hide	M W Easterby	Freeze the Secret	Kessar Queen	18	37.03
1978	R Bonnycastle's	ENSTONE SPARK (35/1)	E Johnson	B Hills	Fair Salinia	Sandiki	16	41.08
1979	Helena Springfield Ltd's	ONE IN A MILLION (evens)	J Mercer	H Cecil	Abbeydale	Seraphina	17	41.56
1980	O Phipps's	QUICK AS LIGHTNING (12/1)	B Rouse	J Dunlop	Our Home	Yanuka	23	43.06
1981	H Joel's	FAIRY FOOTSTEPS (6/4)	L Piggott	H Cecil	Tolmi	Go Leasing	14	41.99
1982	Sir P Oppenheimer's	ON THE HOUSE (33/1)	J Reid	H Wragg	Time Charter	Dione	15	40.43
1983	Maktoum Al-Maktoum's	MA BICHE (5/2)	F Head	Mme C Head	Favoridge	Habibti	18	40.45
1984	M Lemos's	PEBBLES (8/1)	P Robinson	C Brittain	Meis El-Reem	Desirable	15	41.71
1985	Sheikh Mohammed's	OH SO SHARP (2/1)	S Cauthen	H Cecil	Al Bahathri	Bella Colora	17	38.18
1986	H Ranier's	MIDWAY LADY (10/1)	R Cochrane	B Hanbury	Maysoon	Sonic Lady	15	38.85
1987	S Niarchos's	MIESQUE (15/8)	F Head	F Boutin	Milligram	Interval	14	41.54
1988	E Aland's	RAVINELLA (4/5)	G W Moore	Mme C Head	Dabaweyaa	Diminuendo	12	38.48
1989	Sheikh Mohammed's	MUSICAL BLISS (7/2)	W Swinburn	M Stoute	Kerrera	Aldhourne	7	40.88
1990	Hamdan Al-Maktoum's	SALSABIL (6/4)	W Carson	J Dunlop	Heart of Joy	Negligent	10	42.69
1991	Hamdan Al-Maktoum's	SHADAYID (4/6)	W Carson	J Dunlop	Kooyonga	Crystal Gazing	14	38.06
1992	Maktoum Al-Maktoum's	HATOOF (5/1)	W R Swinburn	Mme C Head	Marling	Kenbu	14	38.18
1993	Mohamed Obaid's	SAYYEDATI (4/1)	W R Swinburn	C Brittain	Niche	Alfian	12	39.45
1994	R Sangster's	LAS MENINAS (12/1)	J Reid	T Stack	Balanchine	Coup de Genie	15	37.34
1995	Hamdan Al-Maktoum's	HARAYIR (5/1)	R Hills	Major W R Hern	Aqaarid	Moonshell	14	36.71
1996	Wafic Said's	BOSRA SHAM (10/11)	Pat Eddery	H Cecil	Matya	Bint Shadayid	13	37.75
1997	Greenbay Stables Ltd's	SLEEPYTIME (5/1)	L Dettori	H Cecil	Oh Nellie	Dazzle	15	37.66
1998	Godolphin's	CAPE VERDI (100/30)	L Dettori	S Bin Suroor	Shahtoush	Exclusive	16	37.86
1999	K Abdulla's	WINCE (4/1)	K Fallon	H Cecil	Wannabe Grand	Valentine Waltz	22	37.91

(Run on July Course)

Year	Owner	Winner and Price	Jockey	Trainer	Second	Third	Ran	Time
2000	Hamdan Al-Maktoum's	LAHAN (14/1)	R Hills	J Gosden	Princess Ellen	Petrushka	18	1 38.38
2001	Sheikh Ahmed Al Maktoum's	AMEERAT (11/1)	P Robinson	M Jarvis	Muwakleh	Toroca	15	1 38.36
2002	Godolphin's	KAZZIA (14/1)	L Dettori	S Bin Suroor	Snowfire	Alasha	17	1 37.85
2003	Cheveley Park Stud's	RUSSIAN RHYTHM (12/1)	K Darley	Sir M Stoute	Six Perfections	Intercontinental	19	1 38.43
2004	Duke of Roxburghe's	ATTRACTION (11/2)	K Fallon	M Johnston	Sundrop	Hathrah	16	1 36.70
2005	Mrs John Magnier & M M Tabor's	VIRGINIA WATERS (12/1)	K Fallon	A O'Brien	Maids Causeway	Vista Bella	20	1 36.50
2006	Mr Sly, Dr Davies & Mrs P Sly's	SPECIOSA (10/1)	M Fenton	Mrs P Sly	Confidential Lady	Nashejj	13	1 40.50
2007	M Ryan's	FINSCEAL BEO (5/4)	K Manning	J Bary	Arch Swing	Simply Perfect	21	1 34.94
2008	S Friborg's	NATAGORA (11/4)	C Lemaire	P Bary	Spacious	Saoirse Abu	15	1 38.99
2009	Hamdan Al-Maktoum's	GHANAATI (20/1)	R Hills	B Hills	Cuis Ghaire	Super Sleuth	14	1 34.22
2010	K Abdulla's	SPECIAL DUTY (9/2)	S Pasquier	Mme C Head-Maarek	Jacqueline Quest	Gile Na Greine	17	1 39.66

(The first two placings were reversed by the Stewards)

Year	Owner	Winner and Price	Jockey	Trainer	Second	Third	Ran	Time
2011	Godolphin's	BLUE BUNTING (16/1)	L Dettori	M Al Zarooni	Maqaasid		18	1 39.27
2012	Mrs John Magnier, M Tabor & D Smith's	HOMECOMING QUEEN (25/1)	R Moore	A O'Brien	Starscope	Maybe	17	1 40.45

OAKS STAKES (3y fillies) Epsom-1 mile 4 furlongs 10 yards

Year	Owner	Winner and Price	Jockey	Trainer	Second	Third	Ran	Time
1976	D Wildenstein's	PAWNEESE (6/5)	Y Saint Martin	A Penna	Roses for the Star	African Dancer	14	2 35.25
1977	The Queen's	DUNFERMLINE (6/1)	W Carson	R Hern	Freeze the Secret	Vaguely Deb	13	2 36.53
1978	S Hanson's	FAIR SALINIA (8/1)	G Starkey	M Stoute	Dancing Maid	Suni	15	2 36.82
1979	J Morrison's	SCINTILLATE (20/1)	Pat Eddery	J Tree	Bonnie Isle	Britannia's Rule	14	2 43.74
1980	Mrs B Firestone's	BIREME (9/2)	W Carson	R Hern	Vielle	The Dancer	12	2 34.33
1981	R's	BLUE WIND (3/1)	L Piggott	D Weld	Madam Gay	Leap Lively	12	2 40.93
1982	Sir M Sobell's	TIME CHARTER (12/1)	W Newnes	H Candy	Slightly Dangerous	Last Feather	15	2 34.21
1983	Sir R McAlpine's	SUN PRINCESS (6/1)	W Carson	J Hern	Acclimatise	New Coins	15	2 40.98
1984	H Ranier's	CIRCUS PLUME (4/1)	L Piggott	J Dunlop	Media Luna	Poquito Queen	15	2 38.97
1985	Sheikh Mohammed's	OH SO SHARP (6/4)	S Cauthen	H Cecil	Triptych	Dubian	12	2 41.37
1986	H Ranier's	MIDWAY LADY (15/8)	R Cochrane	B Hanbury	Untold	Maysoon	15	2 35.60
1987	Sheikh Mohammed's	UNITE (11/1)	W R Swinburn	M Stoute	Bourbon Girl	Three Tails	11	2 38.17
1988	Sheikh Mohammed's	DIMINUENDO (7/4)	S Cauthen	H Cecil	Sudden Love	Animatrice	11	2 35.02
1989	Saeed Maktoum Al Maktoum's	SNOW BRIDE (13/2)	S Cauthen	H Cecil	Roseate Tern	Mamaluna	9	2 34.22
	(Aliysa finished first but was disqualified)							
1990	Hamdan Al-Maktoum's	SALSABIL (2/1)	W Carson	J Dunlop	Game Plan	Knight's Baroness	8	2 38.70
1991	Maktoum Al-Maktoum's	JET SKI LADY (50/1)	C Roche	J Bolger	Shamshir	Shadayid	9	2 37.30
1992	W J Gredley's	USER FRIENDLY (5/1)	G Duffield	C Brittain	All At Sea	Pearl Angel	7	2 39.77
1993	Sheikh Mohammed's	INTREPIDITY (5/1)	M Roberts	A Fabre	Royal Ballerina	Oakmead	14	2 34.19
1994	Godolphin's	BALANCHINE (6/1)	L Dettori	H Ibrahim	Wind in Her Hair	Hawajiss	10	2 40.37
1995	Maktoum Al Maktoum/Godolphin's	MOONSHELL (3/1)	L Dettori	S bin Suroor	Dance A Dream	Pure Grain	10	2 35.44
1996	Watic Said's	LADY CARLA (100/30)	Pat Eddery	H Cecil	Prickel	Mezzogiorno	11	2 35.55
1997	K Abdulla's	REAMS OF VERSE (5/6)	K Fallon	H Cecil	Gazelle Royale	Crown of Light	12	2 35.59
1998	Mrs D Nagle & Mrs J Magnier's	SHAHTOUSH (12/1)	M Kinane	A O'Brien	Bahr	Midnight Line	8	2 38.23
1999	F Salman's	RAMRUMA (3/1)	K Fallon	H Cecil	Noushkey	Zahrat Dubai	10	2 38.72
2000	Lordship Stud's	LOVE DIVINE (9/4)	T Quinn	H Cecil	Kalypso Katie	Melikah	16	2 43.11
2001	Mrs D Nagle & Mrs J Magnier's	IMAGINE (3/1)	M Kinane	A O'Brien	Flight Of Fancy	Relish The Thought	14	2 36.70
2002	Godolphin's	KAZZIA (100/30)	L Dettori	S bin Suroor	Quarter Moon	Shadow Dancing	14	2 44.52
2003	W S Farish III's	CASUAL LOOK (10/1)	M Dwyer	A Balding	Yesterday	Summitville	15	2 38.07
2004	Lord Derby's	OUIJA BOARD (7/2)	K Fallon	E Dunlop	All Too Beautiful	Punctilious	15	2 35.40
2005	Hamdan Al Maktoum's	ESWARAH (11/4)	R Hills	M Jarvis	Something Exciting	Pictavia	12	2 39.00
2006	Mrs J Magnier, Mr M Tabor & Mr D Smith's	ALEXANDROVA (9/4)	K Fallon	A O'Brien	Rising Cross	Short Skirt	10	2 37.70
2007	Niarchos Family's	LIGHT SHIFT (13/2)	T Durcan	H Cecil	Peeping Fawn	All My Loving	14	2 40.38
2008	J H Richmond-Watson's	LOOK HERE (33/1)	S Sanders	R Beckett	Moonstone	Kalyra	16	2 36.89
2009	Lady Bamford's	SARISKA (9/4)	J Spencer	R Bell	Midday	High Heeled	10	2 35.28
2010	Aramone Ltd's	SNOW FAIRY (9/1)	R Moore	E Dunlop	Remember When	Rumoush	15	2 35.77
	(Meghah finished second but was disqualified)							
2011	M J & L A Taylor's	DANCING RAIN (20/1)	J Murtagh	W Haggas	Wonder of Wonders	Izzi Top	13	2 41.73
2012	D Smith, Mrs J Magnier & M Tabor's	WAS (20/1)	S Heffernan	A O'Brien	Shirocco Star	The Fugue	12	2 38.68

DERBY STAKES (3y) Epsom-1 mile 4 furlongs 10 yards

Year	Owner	Winner and Price	Jockey	Trainer	Second	Third	Ran	Time
1973	A Budgett's	MORSTON (25/1)	E Hide	A Budgett	Cavo Doro	Freefoot	25	2 35.92
1974	Mrs N Phillips's	SNOW KNIGHT (50/1)	B Taylor	P Nelson	Imperial Prince	Giacometti	18	2 35.04
1975	Dr C Vittadini's	GRUNDY (5/1)	Pat Eddery	P Walwyn	Nobiliary	Hunza Dancer	18	2 35.35
1976	N B Hunt's	EMPERY (10/1)	L Piggott	M Zilber	Relkino	Oats	23	2 35.69
1977	R Sangster's	THE MINSTREL (5/1)	L Piggott	V O'Brien	Hot Grove	Blushing Groom	22	2 36.44
1978	Lord Halifax's	SHIRLEY HEIGHTS (8/1)	G Starkey	J Dunlop	Hawaiian Sound	Remainder Man	25	2 35.30
1979	Sir M Sobell's	TROY (6/1)	W Carson	R Hern	Dickens Hill	Northern Baby	23	2 36.59
1980	Mrs A Plesch's	HENBIT (7/1)	W Carson	R Hern	Master Willie	Rankin	24	2 34.77
1981	H H Aga Khan's	SHERGAR (10/11)	W Swinburn	M Stoute	Glint of Gold	Scintillating Air	18	2 44.21
1982	R Sangster's	GOLDEN FLEECE (3/1)	Pat Eddery	V O'Brien	Touching Wood	Silver Hawk	18	2 34.27
1983	E Moller's	TEENOSO (9/2)	L Piggott	G Wragg	Carlingford Castle	Shearwalk	21	2 49.07
1984	L Miglitti's	SECRETO (14/1)	C Roche	D O'Brien	El Gran Senor	Mighty Flutter	17	2 39.12
1985	Lord H. de Walden's	SLIP ANCHOR (9/4)	S Cauthen	H Cecil	Law Society	Damister	14	2 36.23
1986	H H Aga Khan's	SHAHRASTANI (11/2)	W Swinburn	M Stoute	Dancing Brave	Mashkour	17	2 37.13
1987	H H Aga Khan's	REFERENCE POINT (6/4)	S Cauthen	H Cecil	Most Welcome	Bellotto	19	2 33.90
1988	L Freedman's	KAHYASI (11/1)	R Cochrane	L Cumani	Glacial Storm	Doyoun	14	2 33.84
1989	Hamdan Al-Maktoum's	NASHWAN (5/4)	W Carson	R Hern	Terimon	Cacoethes	12	2 34.90
1990	K Abdulla's	QUEST FOR FAME (7/1)	Pat Eddery	R Charlton	Blue Stag	Elmaamul	18	2 37.26
1991	F Salman's	GENEROUS (9/1)	A Munro	P Cole	Marju	Star of Gdansk	13	2 34.00
1992	Sidney H Craig's	DR DEVIOUS (8/1)	J Reid	P Chapple-Hyam	St Jovite	Silver Wisp	18	2 36.19
1993	K Abdulla's	COMMANDER IN CHIEF (15/2)	M Kinane	H Cecil	Blue Judge	Blues Traveller	16	2 34.51
1994	Hamdan Al-Maktoum's	ERHAAB (7/2)	W Carson	J Dunlop	King's Theatre	Colonel Collins	25	2 34.16
1995	Saeed Maktoum Al Maktoum's	LAMMTARRA (14/1)	W Swinburn	S Bin Suroor	Tamure	Presenting	15	2 32.31
1996	K Dasmal's	SHAAMIT (12/1)	M Hills	W Haggas	Dushyantor	Shantou	20	2 35.05
1997	L Knight's	BENNY THE DIP (11/1)	W Ryan	J Gosden	Silver Patriarch	Romanov	20	2 35.77
1998	Sheikh Mohammed	HIGH-RISE (20/1)	O Peslier	L Cumani	City Honours	Border Arrow	15	2 33.88
1999	Thoroughbred Corporation's	OATH (13/2)	K Fallon	H Cecil	Daliapour	Beat All	16	2 37.43
2000	H H Aga Khan's	SINNDAR (7/1)	J Murtagh	J Oxx	Sakhee	Beat Hollow	15	2 36.75
2001	M Tabor & Mrs J Magnier's	GALILEO (11/4)	M Kinane	A O'Brien	Golan	Tobougg	12	2 33.27
2002	M Tabor & Mrs J Magnier's	HIGH CHAPARRAL (7/2)	J Murtagh	A O'Brien	Hawk Wing	Moon Ballad	12	2 39.45
2003	Saeed Suhail's	KRIS KIN (6/1)	K Fallon	Sir M Stoute	The Great Gatsby	Alamshar	20	2 33.35
2004	Ballymacoll Stud's	NORTH LIGHT (7/2)	K Fallon	Sir M Stoute	Rule of Law	Let The Lion Roar	14	2 33.70
2005	The Royal Ascot Racing Club's	MOTIVATOR (3/1)	J Murtagh	M Bell	Walk In The Park	Dubawi	13	2 35.60
2006	A E Pakenham's	SIR PERCY (6/1)	M Dwyer	M Tregoning	Dragon Dancer	Dylan Thomas	18	2 35.20
2007	Saleh Al Homaizi & Imad Al Sagar's	AUTHORIZED (5/4)	L Dettori	P Chapple-Hyam	Eagle Mountain	Aqaleem	17	2 34.77
2008	HRH Princess Haya of Jordan's	NEW APPROACH (5/1)	K Manning	J Bolger	Tartan Bearer	Casual Conquest	16	2 36.50
2009	C Tsui's	SEA THE STARS (11/4)	M Kinane	J Oxx	Fame And Glory	Masterofthehorse	12	2 36.74
2010	K Abdulla's	WORKFORCE (6/1)	R Moore	Sir M Stoute	At First Sight	Rewilding	12	2 31.33
2011	Mrs John Magnier, M Tabor & M Tabor's	POUR MOI (4/1)	M Barzalona	A Fabre	Treasure Beach	Carlton House	13	2 34.54
2012	D Smith, Mrs J Magnier & M Tabor's	CAMELOT (8/13)	J O'Brien	A O'Brien	Main Sequence	Astrology	9	2 33.90

ST LEGER STAKES (3y) Doncaster–1 mile 6 furlongs 132 yards

Year	Owner	Winner and Price	Jockey	Trainer	Second	Third	Ran	Time
1970	C Engelhard's	NIJINSKY (2/7)	L Piggott	V O'Brien	Meadowville	Politico	9	3 6.40
1971	Mrs J Rogerson's	ATHENS WOOD (7/2)	L Piggott	H T Jones	Homeric	Falkland	8	3 14.90
1972	O Phipps's	BOUCHER (5/2)	L Piggott	V O'Brien	Our Mirage	Ginevra	7	3 28.71
1973	W Behrens's	PELEID (28/1)	F Durr	W Elsey	Bury	Duke of Ragusa	13	3 8.21
1974	Lady Beaverbrook's	BUSTINO (11/10)	J Mercer	R Hern	Giacometti	Ribocco	10	3 9.02
1975	C St George's	BRUNI (9/1)	A Murray	R Price	King Pellinore	Libra's Rib	12	3 9.02
1976	D Wildenstein's	CROW (6/1)	Y Saint-Martin	A Penna	Secret Man	Scallywag	15	3 13.17
1977	The Queen's	DUNFERMLINE (10/1)	W Carson	R Hern	Alleged	Classic Example	13	3 5.17
1978	M Lemos's	JULIO MARINER (28/1)	E Hide	C Brittain	Le Moss	M-Lolshan	14	3 4.94
1979	A Rolland's	SON OF LOVE (20/1)	A Lequeux	R Collet	Soleil Noir	Niniski	17	3 9.02
1980	H Joel's	LIGHT CAVALRY (3/1)	J Mercer	H Cecil	Water Mill	World Leader	7	3 11.48
1981	Sir J Astor's	CUT ABOVE (28/1)	J Mercer	R Hern	Glint of Gold	Bustomi	7	3 11.60
1982	Maktoum Al Maktoum's	TOUCHING WOOD (7/1)	P Cook	H T Jones	Zilos	Diamond Shoal	15	3 3.53
1983	Sir M Sobell's	SUN PRINCESS (11/8)	W Carson	R Hern	Esprit du Nord	Carlingford Castle	10	3 16.65
1984	I Allan's	COMMANCHE RUN (7/4)	L Piggott	L Cumani	Baynoun	Alphabatim	11	3 9.93
1985	Sheikh Mohammed's	OH SO SHARP (8/11)	S Cauthen	H Cecil	Phardante	Lanfranco	6	3 7.13
1986	Duchess of Norfolk's	MOON MADNESS (9/2)	Pat Eddery	J Dunlop	Celestial Storm	Untold	8	3 5.03
1987	L Freedman's	REFERENCE POINT (4/11)	S Cauthen	H Cecil	Mountain Kingdom	Dry Dock	7	3 5.91
1988	Lady Beaverbrook's	MINSTER SON (15/2)	W Carson	N A Graham	Diminuendo	Sheriff's Star	6	3 6.80
1989	C St George's	MICHELOZZO (6/4)	S Cauthen	H Cecil	Sapience	Roseate Tern	8	3 20.72
		(Run at Ayr)						
1990	M Arbib's	SNURGE (7/2)	T Quinn	P Cole	Hellenic	River God	8	3 8.78
1991	K Abdulla's	TOULON (5/2)	Pat Eddery	A Fabre	Saddlers' Hall	Micheletti	10	3 3.12
1992	W J Gredley's	USER FRIENDLY (7/4)	G Duffield	C Brittain	Sonus	Bonny Scot	7	3 5.48
1993	Mrs G A E Smith's	BOB'S RETURN (3/1)	P Robinson	B Hills	Armiger	Edbaysaan	9	3 5.85
1994	Sheikh Mohammed's	MOONAX (40/1)	Pat Eddery	B Hills	Broadway Flyer	Double Trigger	8	3 4.19
1995	Godolphin's	CLASSIC CLICHE (100/30)	L Dettori	S Bin Suroor	Minds Music	Istidad	10	3 9.74
1996	Sheikh Mohammed's	SHANTOU (8/1)	L Dettori	J Gosden	Dushyantor	Samraan	11	3 5.10
1997	P Winfield's	SILVER PATRIARCH (5/4)	Pat Eddery	J Dunlop	Vertical Speed	The Fly	10	3 6.92
1998	Godolphin's	NEDAWI (5/2)	J Reid	S Bin Suroor	High and Low	Sunshine Street	9	3 5.61
1999	Godolphin's	MUTAFAWEQ (11/2)	R Hills	S Bin Suroor	Ramruma	Adair	9	3 2.75
2000	N Jones's	MILLENARY (11/4)	T Quinn	J Dunlop	Air Marshall	Chimes At Midnight	11	3 2.58
2001	M Tabor & Mrs J Magnier's	MILAN (13/8)	M Kinane	A O'Brien	Demophilos	Mr Combustible	10	3 5.16
2002	Sir Neil Westbrook's	BOLLIN ERIC (7/1)	K Darley	T Easterby	Highest	Bandari	8	3 2.92
2003	Mrs J Magnier's	BRIAN BORU (5/4)	J P Spencer	A O'Brien	High Accolade	Phoenix Reach	12	3 4.64
2004	Godolphin's	RULE OF LAW (3/1)	K McEvoy	S Bin Suroor	Quiff	Tycoon	9	3 9.20
2005	Mrs J Magnier & M Tabor's	SCORPION (10/11)	L Dettori	A O'Brien	The Geezer	Tawqeet	6	3 19.20
2006	Mrs S Roy's	SIXTIES ICON (11/8)	L Dettori	J Noseda	The Last Drop	Red Rocks	11	3 57.20
		(Run at York)						
2007	G Strawbridge's	LUCARNO (7/2)	J Fortune	J Gosden	Mahler	Honolulu	10	3 1.90
2008	Ballymacoll Stud's	CONDUIT (8/1)	L Dettori	Sir M Stoute	Unsung Heroine	Look Here	14	3 7.92
2009	Godolphin's	MASTERY (14/1)	T Durcan	S Bin Suroor	Kite Wood	Monitor Closely	8	3 4.81
2010	Ms R Hood & R Geffen's	ARCTIC COSMOS (12/1)	W Buick	J Gosden	Midas Touch	Corsica	10	3 3.12
2011	B Nielsen's	MASKED MARVEL (15/2)	W Buick	J Gosden	Brown Panther	Sea Moon	9	3 0.44
2012	Godolphin's	ENCKE (25/1)	M Barzalona	M Al Zarooni	Camelot	Michelangelo	9	3 3.81

KING GEORGE VI AND QUEEN ELIZABETH STAKES Ascot-1 mile 4 furlongs

Year	Owner	Winner and Price	Jockey	Trainer	Second	Third	Ran	Time
1974	N B Hunt's	DAHLIA 4-9-4 (15/8)	L Piggott	M Zilber	Highclere	Dankaro	10	2 33.03
1975	Dr C Vittadini's	GRUNDY 3-8-7 (4/5)	P Eddery	P Walwyn	Bustino	Dahlia	11	2 26.98
1976	D Wildenstein's	PAWNEESE 3-8-5 (9/4)	Y Saint Martin	A Penna	Bruni	Orange Bay	11	2 29.36
1977	R Sangster's	THE MINSTREL 3-8-8 (7/4)	L Piggott	V O'Brien	Orange Bay	Exceller	11	2 30.48
1978	D McCall's	ILE DE BOURBON 3-8-8 (12/1)	J Reid	F Houghton	Hawaiian Sound	Montcontour	14	2 30.53
1979	Sir M Sobell's	TROY 3-8-8 (2/5)	W Carson	R Hern	Gay Mecene	Ela-Mana-Mou	7	2 33.75
1980	S Weinstock's	ELA-MANA-MOU 4-9-7 (11/4)	W Carson	R Hern	Mrs Penny	Gregorian	10	2 35.39
1981	H H Aga Khan's	SHERGAR 3-8-8 (2/5)	W Swinburn	M Stoute	Madam Gay	Fingals Cave	7	2 35.40
1982	A Ward's	KALAGLOW 4-9-7 (13-2)	G Starkey	G Harwood	Assert	Glint of Gold	7	2 31.58
1983	R Barnett's	TIME CHARTER 4-9-4 (5/1)	J Mercer	H Candy	Diamond Shoal	Sun Princess	9	2 30.78
1984	E Moller's	TEENOSO 4-9-7 (13/2)	L Piggott	G Wragg	Sadler's Wells	Tolomeo	13	2 27.95
1985	Lady Beaverbrook's	PETOSKI 3-8-8 (12/1)	W Carson	G Harwood	Oh So Sharp	Rainbow Quest	12	2 27.61
1986	K Abdulla's	DANCING BRAVE 3-8-8 (6/4)	Pat Eddery	G Harwood	Shardari	Triplych	9	2 29.49
1987	L Freedman's	REFERENCE POINT 3-8-8 (11/10)	S Cauthen	H Cecil	Celestial Storm	Triplych	9	2 34.63
1988	Sheikh Ahmed Al Maktoum	MTOTO 5-9-7 (4/1)	M Roberts	A C Stewart	Unfuwain	Tony Bin	10	2 27.33
1989	Hamdan Al-Maktoum's	NASHWAN 3-8-8 (2/9)	W Carson	R Hern	Cacoethes	Top Class	7	2 32.27
1990	Sheikh Mohammed's	BELMEZ 3-8-9 (15/2)	M Kinane	H Cecil	Old Vic	Assatis	11	2 30.76
1991	F Salman's	GENEROUS 3-8-9 (4/6)	A Munro	P Cole	Sanglamore	Rock Hopper	9	2 28.99
1992	Mrs V K Payson's	ST JOVITE 3-8-9 (4/5)	S Craine	J Bolger	Saddlers' Hall	Opera House	8	2 30.85
1993	Sheikh Mohammed's	OPERA HOUSE 5-9-7 (8/1)	M Roberts	M Stoute	White Muzzle	Commander in Chief	10	2 33.94
1994	Sheikh Mohammed's	KING'S THEATRE 3-8-9 (12/1)	M Kinane	H Cecil	White Muzzle	Wagon Master	12	2 28.92
1995	Saeed Maktoum's	LAMMTARRA 3-8-9 (9/4)	L Dettori	S Bin Suroor	Pentire	Strategic Choice	7	2 31.01
1996	Mollers Racing's	PENTIRE 4-9-2 (100/30)	M Hills	G Wragg	Classic Cliche	Shaamit	8	2 28.11
1997	Godolphin's	SWAIN 5-9-7 (16/1)	J Reid	S Bin Suroor	Pilsudski	Helissio	8	2 36.45
1998	Godolphin's	SWAIN 6-9-7 (11/2)	L Dettori	S Bin Suroor	High-Rise	Royal Anthem	8	2 29.06
1999	Godolphin's	DAYLAMI 5-9-7 (3/1)	L Dettori	S Bin Suroor	Nedawi	Fruits Of Love	8	2 29.35
2000	M Tabor's	MONTJEU 4-9-7 (1/3)	M Kinane	A O'Brien	Fantastic Light	Daliapour	7	2 29.98
2001	Mrs J Magnier & M Tabor's	GALILEO 3-8-9 (1/2)	M Kinane	A O'Brien	Fantastic Light	Hightori	12	2 27.71
2002	Exors of the late Lord Weinstock's	GOLAN 4-9-7 (1/2)	K Fallon	Sir M Stoute	Nayef	Zindabad	9	2 29.70
2003	H H Aga Khan	ALAMSHAR 3-8-9 (13/2)	J Murtagh	J Oxx	Sulamani	Kris Kin	12	2 33.26
2004	Godolphin's	DOYEN 4-9-7 (11/2)	L Dettori	S Bin Suroor	Hard Buck	Sulamani	11	2 33.10
2005	H H Aga Khan's (Run at Newbury)	AZAMOUR 4-9-7 (5/2)	M Kinane	J Oxx	Norse Dancer	Bago	12	2 28.20
2006	M Tabor's	HURRICANE RUN 4-9-7 (5/6)	C Soumillon	A Fabre	Electrocutionist	Heart's Cry	6	2 30.20
2007	Mrs J Magnier & M Tabor's	DYLAN THOMAS 4-9-7 (5/4)	J Murtagh	A O'Brien	Youmzain	Marahel	8	2 31.10
2008	Mrs J Magnier & M Tabor's	DUKE OF MARMALADE 4-9-7 (4/6)	J Murtagh	A O'Brien	Papal Bull	Youmzain	8	2 27.91
2009	Ballymacoll Stud's	CONDUIT 4-9-7 (13/8)	R Moore	Sir M Stoute	Tartan Bearer	Ask	8	2 28.73
2010	Highclere Thoroughbred Racing (Adm Rous)'s	HARBINGER 4-9-7 (4/1)	O Peslier	Sir M Stoute	Cape Blanco	Youmzain	6	2 26.78
2011	Lady Rothschild's	NATHANIEL 3-8-9 (11/2)	W Buick	J Gosden	Workforce	St Nicholas Abbey	5	2 35.07
2012	Gestut Burg Eberstein & Teruya Yoshida's	DANEDREAM 4-9-4 (9/1)	A Starke	P Schiergen	Nathaniel	St Nicholas Abbey	10	2 31.62

PRIX DE L'ARC DE TRIOMPHE Longchamp-1 mile 4 furlongs

Year	Owner	Winner and Price	Jockey	Trainer	Second	Third	Ran	Time
1971	P Mellon's	MILL REEF 3-8-10 (7/10)	G Lewis	I Balding	Pistol Packer	Cambrizzia	18	2 28.30
1972	Countess M Batthyany's	SAN SAN 3-8-7 (3/2)	F Head	A Penna	Rescousse	Homeric	19	2 28.30
1973	H Zeisel's	RHEINGOLD 4-9-6 (7/10)	L Piggott	B Hills	Allez France	Hard to Beat	27	2 35.80
1974	D Wildenstein's	ALLEZ FRANCE 4-9-3 (1/2)	Y Saint Martin	A Penna	Comtesse de Loir	Margouillat	20	2 36.90
1975	W Zeilebach's	STAR APPEAL 5-9-6 (119/1)	G Starkey	T Grieper	On My Way	Comtesse de Loir	24	2 33.60
1976	J Wertheimer's	IVANJICA 4-9-1 (71/10)	F Head	A Head	Crow	Youth	20	2 39.40
1977	R Sangster's	ALLEGED 3-8-11 (38/10)	L Piggott	V O'Brien	Balmerino	Crystal Palace	26	2 30.60
1978	R Sangster's	ALLEGED 4-9-4 (7/5)	L Piggott	V O'Brien	Trillon	Dancing Maid	18	2 36.10
1979	Mme G Head's	THREE TROIKAS 3-8-8 (88/10)	F Head	Mme C Head	Le Marmot	Troy	22	2 28.50
1980	R Sangster's	DETROIT 3-8-8 (67/10)	Pat Eddery	O Douieb	Argument	Ela-Mana-Mou	20	2 28.00
1981	J Wertheimer's	GOLD RIVER 4-9-1 (53/1)	G W Moore	A Head	Bikala	April Run	24	2 35.20
1982	H H Aga Khan's	AKIYDA 3-8-8 (43/4)	Y Saint Martin	F. Mathet	Ardross	Awaasil	17	2 37.00
1983	D Wildenstein's	ALL ALONG 4-9-1 (173/10)	W Swinburn	P. Biancone	Sun Princess	Luth Enchantee	26	2 28.10
1984	D Wildenstein's	SAGACE 4-9-4 (29/10)	Y Saint Martin	P. Biancone	Northern Trick	All Along	25	2 39.10
1985	K Abdulla's	RAINBOW QUEST 4-9-4 (71/10)	Pat Eddery	J Tree	Sagace	Kozana	15	2 29.50

(The first two placings were reversed by the Stewards)

Year	Owner	Winner and Price	Jockey	Trainer	Second	Third	Ran	Time
1986	K Abdulla's	DANCING BRAVE 3-8-11 (11/10)	Pat Eddery	G Harwood	Bering	Triptych	15	2 27.70
1987	P. de Moussac's	TREMPOLINO 3-8-11 (20/1)	Pat Eddery	C Head	Tony Bin	Triptych	11	2 26.30
1988	Mrs V Gaucci del Bono's	TONY BIN 5-9-4 (14/1)	J Reid	L Camici	Mtoto	Boyatino	24	2 27.30
1989	A Balzarini's	CARROLL HOUSE 4-9-4 (19/1)	M Kinane	M Jarvis	Behera	Saint Andrews	19	2 30.80
1990	B McKall's	SAUMAREZ 3-8-11 (15/1)	G Mosse	N Clement	Epervier Bleu	Snurge	21	2 29.80
1991	H Chalhoub's	SUAVE DANCER 3-8-11 (37/10)	C Asmussen	J Hammond	Magic Night	Pistolet Bleu	14	2 29.40
1992	D Tsui's	SUBOTICA 4-9-4 (88/10)	T Jarnet	A Fabre	User Friendly	Vert Amande	18	2 39.00
1993	D Tsui's	URBAN SEA 4-9-1 (37/1)	E Saint Martin	J Lesbordes	White Muzzle	Opera House	23	3 11.10
1994	Sheikh Mohammed's	CARNEGIE 3-8-11 (3/1)	T Jarnet	A Fabre	Hernando	Apple Tree	20	3 11.80
1995	Saeed Maktoum Al Maktoum's	LAMMTARRA 3-8-11 (2/1)	L Dettori	Sin Suroor	Freedom Cry	Swain	16	2 30.00
1996	E Sarasola's	HELISSIO 3-8-11 (18/10)	O Peslier	E Lellouche	Pilsudski	Oscar Schindler	16	2 29.90
1997	D Wildenstein's	PEINTRE CELEBRE 3-8-11 (2210)	O Peslier	A Fabre	Pilsudski	Borgia	18	2 24.60
1998	J-L Lagardère's	SAGAMIX 3-8-11 (5/2)	O Peslier	A Fabre	Leggera	Tiger Hill	14	2 34.50
1999	H H Aga Khan's	MONTJEU 3-8-11 (6/4)	M Kinane	J Hammond	El Condor Pasa	Croco Rouge	14	2 38.50
2000	H H Aga Khan's	SINNDAR 3-8-11 (6/4)	L Dettori	Dox	Egyptband	Volvoreta	10	2 25.80
2001	Godolphin's	SAKHEE 4-9-5 (22/10)	L Dettori	Sin Suroor	Aquarelliste	Sagacity	17	2 36.10
2002	Godolphin's	MARIENBARD 5-9-5 (158/10)	L Dettori	Sin Suroor	Sulamani	High Chaparral	16	2 26.70
2003	H H Aga Khan's	DALAKHANI 3-8-11 (9/4)	C Soumillon	A De Royer-Dupre	Mubtaker	High Chaparral	13	2 32.30
2004	Niarchos Family's	BAGO 3-8-11 (10/1)	T Gillet	J E Pease	Cherry Mix	Ouija Board	13	2 25.00
2005	M Tabor's	HURRICANE RUN 3-8-11 (11/4)	K Fallon	A Fabre	Westerner	Bago	15	2 27.40
2006	K Abdulla's	RAIL LINK 3-8-11 (8/1)	S Pasquier	A Fabre	Pride	Hurricane Run	8	2 26.30

(Deep Impact disqualified from third place)

Year	Owner	Winner and Price	Jockey	Trainer	Second	Third	Ran	Time
2007	Mrs J Magnier & M Tabor's	DYLAN THOMAS 4-9-5 (11/2)	K Fallon	A O'Brien	Youmzain	Sagara	12	2 28.50
2008	H H Aga Khan's	ZARKAVA 3-8-8 (13/8)	C Soumillon	A De Royer-Dupre.	Youmzain	Soldier of Fortune/It's Gino	16	2 28.80
2009	C Abdulla's	SEA THE STARS 3-8-11 (4/6)	M Kinane	J Oxx	Youmzain	Cavalryman	19	2 26.30
2010	K Abdulla's	WORKFORCE 3-8-11 (6/1)	R Moore	Sir M Stoute	Nakayama Festa	Sarafina	18	2 35.30
2011	Gestut Burg Eberstein & T Yoshida's	DANEDREAM 3-8-8 (20/1)	A Stoke	P Schiergen	Shareta	Snow Fairy	16	2 24.49
2012	Wertheimer & Frere's	SOLEMIA 4-9-2 (33/1)	O Peslier	C Laffon-Parias	Orfevre	Masterstroke	18	2 37.68

GRAND NATIONAL STEEPLECHASE Aintree-4m 4f

Year	Winner and Price	Age & Weight	Jockey	Second	Third	Ran	Time
1968	RED ALLIGATOR (100/7)	8 10 0	B Fletcher	Moidore's Token	Different Class	45	9 28.60
1969	HIGHLAND WEDDING (100/9)	12 10 4	E Harty	Steel Bridge	Rondetto	30	9 30.90
1970	GAY TRIP (15/1)	8 11 5	P Taaffe	Vulture	Miss Hunter	28	9 38.00
1971	SPECIFY (28/1)	9 10 1	J Cook	Black Secret	Astbury	38	9 34.20
1972	WELL TO DO (14/1)	9 10 1	G Thorner	Gay Trip	Black Secret/General Symons	42	10 08.40
1973	RED RUM (9/1)	8 10 5	B Fletcher	Crisp	L'Escargot	38	9 01.90
1974	RED RUM (11/1)	9 12 0	B Fletcher	L'Escargot	Charles Dickens	42	9 20.30
1975	L'ESCARGOT (13/2)	12 11 3	T Carberry	Red Rum	Spanish Steps	31	9 31.10
1976	RAG TRADE (14/1)	10 10 12	J Burke	Red Rum	Eyecatcher	32	9 20.90
1977	RED RUM (9/1)	12 11 8	T Stack	Churchtown Boy	Eyecatcher	42	9 30.30
1978	LUCIUS (14/1)	9 10 9	B R Davies	Sebastian V	Drumroll	37	9 33.90
1979	RUBSTIC (25/1)	10 10 0	M Barnes	Zongalero	Rough and Tumble	34	9 52.90
1980	BEN NEVIS (40/1)	12 10 12	Mr C Fenwick	Rough and Tumble	The Pilgarlic	30	10 17.40
1981	ALDANITI (10/1)	11 10 13	R Champion	Spartan Missile	Royal Mail	39	9 47.20
1982	GRITTAR (7/1)	9 11 5	Mr C Saunders	Hard Outlook	Loving Words	39	9 12.60
1983	CORBIERE (13/1)	8 11 4	B de Haan	Greasepaint	Yer Man	41	9 47.04
1984	HALLO DANDY (13/1)	10 10 2	N Doughty	Greasepaint	Corbiere	40	9 21.04
1985	LAST SUSPECT (50/1)	11 10 5	H Davies	Mr Snugfit	Corbiere	40	9 42.70
1986	WEST TIP (15/2)	9 10 11	R Dunwoody	Young Driver	Classified	40	9 33.00
1987	MAORI VENTURE (28/1)	11 10 13	S C Knight	The Tsarevich	Lean Ar Aghaidh	40	9 19.30
1988	RHYME 'N' REASON (10/1)	9 11 0	B Powell	Durham Edition	Monanore	40	9 53.50
1989	LITTLE POLVEIR (28/1)	12 10 3	J Frost	West Tip	The Thinker	40	10 06.80
1990	MR FRISK (16/1)	11 10 6	Mr M Armytage	Durham Edition	Rinus	38	8 47.80
1991	SEAGRAM (12/1)	11 10 6	N Hawke	Garrison Savannah	Auntie Dot	40	9 29.90
1992	PARTY POLITICS (14/1)	8 10 7	C Llewellyn	Romany King	Laura's Beau	40	9 06.30
1993	Race void - false start						
1994	MIINNEHOMA (16/1)	11 10 8	R Dunwoody	Just So	Moorcroft Boy	36	10 18.80
1995	ROYAL ATHLETE (40/1)	12 10 6	J Titley	Party Politics	Over The Deel	35	9 04.00
1996	ROUGH QUEST (7/1)	10 10 7	M Fitzgerald	Encore Un Peu	Superior Finish	27	9 00.80
1997	LORD GYLLENE (14/1)	9 10 0	A Dobbin	Suny Bay	Camelot Knight	36	9 05.80
1998	EARTH SUMMIT (7/1)	10 10 5	C Llewellyn	Suny Bay	Samlee	37	10 51.40
1999	BOBBYJO (10/1)	9 10 0	P Carberry	Blue Charm	Call It A Day	32	9 14.00
2000	PAPILLON (10/1)	9 10 12	R Walsh	Mely Moss	Niki Dee	40	9 09.70
2001	RED MARAUDER (33/1)	11 10 11	R Guest	Smarty	Blowing Wind	40	11 00.10
2002	BINDAREE (20/1)	8 10 4	J Culloty	What's Up Boys	Blowing Wind	40	9 07.00
2003	MONTY'S PASS (16/1)	10 10 7	B J Geraghty	Supreme Glory	Amberleigh House	40	9 21.70
2004	AMBERLEIGH HOUSE (16/1)	12 10 10	G Lee	Clan Royal	Lord Atterbury	39	9 20.30
2005	HEDGEHUNTER (7/1)	9 11 1	R Walsh	Royal Auclair	Simply Gifted	40	9 20.90
2006	NUMBERSIXVALVERDE (11/1)	10 10 8	N Madden	Hedgehunter	Clan Royal	40	9 41.00
2007	SILVER BIRCH (33/1)	10 10 6	R Power	McKelvey	Slim Pickings	40	9 13.60
2008	COMPLY OR DIE (7/1)	9 10 9	T Murphy	King Johns Castle	Snowy Morning	40	9 16.60
2009	MON MOME (100/1)	9 11 0	L Treadwell	Comply Or Die	My Will	40	9 32.90
2010	DON'T PUSH IT (10/1)	10 11 5	A P McCoy	Black Apalachi	State Of Play	40	9 04.60
2011	BALLABRIGGS (14/1)	10 11 0	J Maguire	Oscar Time	Don't Push It	40	9 01.20
2012	NEPTUNE COLLONGES (33/1)	11 11 6	D Jacob	Sunnyhillboy	Seabass	40	9 05.10

WINNERS OF GREAT RACES

LINCOLN HANDICAP
Doncaster-1m
2003	PABLO 4-8-11	24
2004	BABODANA 4-9-10	24
2005	STREAM OF GOLD 4-9-10	22
*2006	BLYTHE KNIGHT 6-8-10	30
**2007	VERY WISE 5-8-11	21
2008	SMOKEY OAKEY 4-8-9	21
2009	EXPRESSO STAR 4-8-12	20
2010	PENITENT 4-9-2	21
2011	SWEET LIGHTNING 6-9-4	21
2012	BRAE HILL 6-9-1	22

*Run at Redcar
**Run at Newcastle

GREENHAM STAKES (3y)
Newbury-7f
2003	MUQBIL 9-0	8
2004	SALFORD CITY 9-0	10
2005	INDESATCHEL 9-0	9
2006	RED CLUBS 9-0	5
2007	MAJOR CADEAUX 9-0	6
2008	PACO BOY 9-0	8
2009	VOCALISED 9-0	8
2010	DICK TURPIN 9-0	5
2011	FRANKEL 9-0	6
2012	CASPAR NETSCHER 9-0	5

EUROPEAN FREE HANDICAP (3y)
Newmarket-7f
2003	INDIAN HAVEN 9-1	6
2004	BRUNEL 8-13	11
2005	KAMAKIRI 8-10	8
2006	MISU BOND 8-13	8
2007	PRIME DEFENDER 9-5	7
2008	STIMULATION 9-3	11
2009	OUQBA 8-9	10
2010	RED JAZZ 9-6	7
2011	PAUSANIAS 8-12	6
2012	TELWAAR 8-11	7

CRAVEN STAKES (3y)
Newmarket-1m
2003	HURRICANE ALAN 8-9	6
2004	HAAFHD 8-9	5
2005	DEMOCRATIC DEFICIT 8-12	8
2006	KILLYBEGS 8-12	9
2007	ADAGIO 8-12	7
2008	TWICE OVER 8-12	10
2009	DELEGATOR 8-12	7
2010	ELUSIVE PIMPERNEL 8-12	9
2011	NATIVE KHAN 8-12	6
2012	TRUMPET MAJOR 9-1	12

JOCKEY CLUB STAKES
Newmarket-1m 4f
2003	WARRSAN 5-8-9	7
2004	GAMUT 5-8-9	6
2005	ALKAASED 5-8-9	5
2006	SHIROCCO 5-9-3	7
2007	SIXTIES ICON 4-9-3	5
2008	GETAWAY 5-9-1	10
2009	BRONZE CANNON 4-8-12	3

CHESTER VASE (3y)
Chester-1m 4f 66yds
2003	DUTCH GOLD 8-10	4
2004	RED LANCER 8-10	6
2005	HATTAN 8-10	5
2006	PAPAL BULL 8-12	5
2007	SOLDIER OF FORTUNE 9-2	4
2008	DOCTOR FREMANTLE 8-12	8
2009	GOLDEN SWORD 8-12	8
2010	TED SPREAD 8-12	7
2011	TREASURE BEACH 8-12	5
2012	MICKDAAM 8-12	5

CHESTER CUP
Chester-2m 2f 147yds
2003	HUGS DANCER 6-8-11	16
2004	ANAK PEKAN 4-8-2	17
2005	ANAK PEKAN 5-9-6	17
2006	ADMIRAL 5-8-1	17
2007	GREENWICH MEANTIME 7-9-2	17
2008	BULWARK 6-9-4	17
2009	DARAAHEM 4-9-0	17
2010	MAMLOOK 6-8-12	17
2011	OVERTURN 7-8-13	17
2012	ILE DE RE 6-8-11	16

OAKS TRIAL (3y fillies)
Lingfield-1m 3f 106yds
2003	SANTA SOPHIA 8-8	8
2004	BARAKA 8-8	5
2005	CASSYDORA 8-10	6
2006	SINDIRANA 8-10	10
2007	KAYAH 8-12	7
2008	MIRACLE SEEKER 8-12	6
2009	MIDDAY 8-12	4
2010	DYNA WALTZ 8-12	5
2011	ZAIN AL BOLDAN 8-12	9
*2012	VOW 8-12	8

*Run over 1m4f on Polytrack

DERBY TRIAL (3y)
Lingfield-1m 3f 106yds
2003	FRANKLINS GARDENS 8-7	6
2004	PERCUSSIONIST 8-7	4
2005	KONG 8-10	6
2006	LINDA'S LAD 9-3	5
2007	AQALEEM 8-12	7
2008	ALESSANDRO VOLTA 8-12	5
2009	AGE OF AQUARIUS 8-12	5
2010	BULLET TRAIN 8-12	7
2011	DORDOGNE 8-12	6
*2012	MAIN SEQUENCE 8-12	8

*Run over 1m4f on Polytrack

MUSIDORA STAKES (3y fillies)
York-1m 2f 88yds
2003	CASSIS 8-8	8
2004	PUNCTILIOUS 8-8	6
2005	SECRET HISTORY 8-10	6
2006	SHORT SKIRT 8-12	6

2007 **PASSAGE OF TIME** 9-1.................5
2008 **LUSH LASHES** 8-12...................8
2009 **SARISKA** 8-12.........................6
2010 **AVIATE** 8-12...........................8
2011 **JOVIALITY** 8-12.......................5
2012 **THE FUGUE** 8-12......................6

DANTE STAKES (3y)
York-1m 2f 88yds
2003 **MAGISTRETTI** 8-11...................10
2004 **NORTH LIGHT** 8-11..................10
2005 **MOTIVATOR** 8-11.....................6
2006 **SEPTIMUS** 9-0.........................6
2007 **AUTHORIZED** 9-0......................6
2008 **TARTAN BEARER** 9-0.................6
2009 **BLACK BEAR ISLAND** 9-0...........10
2010 **CAPE BLANCO** 9-0....................5
2011 **CARLTON HOUSE** 9-0................6
2012 **BONFIRE** 9-0...........................7

YORKSHIRE CUP
York-1m 6f (1m 5f 194yds before 2007)
2003 **MAMOOL** 4-8-9.........................8
2004 **MILLENARY** 7-8-13....................10
2005 **FRANKLINS GARDENS** 5-8-10.......9
2006 **PERCUSSIONIST** 5-8-12.............7
2007 **SERGEANT CECIL** 8-9-3............10
2008 **GEORDIELAND** 7-8-12................5
2009 **ASK** 6-8-13.............................8
2010 **MANIFEST** 4-8-12.....................5
2011 **DUNCAN** 6-9-2.........................8
2012 **RED CADEAUX** 6-9-0..................8

DUKE OF YORK STAKES
York-6f
2003 **TWILIGHT BLUES** 4-9-2.............15
2004 **MONSIEUR BOND** 4-9-2.............15
2005 **THE KIDDYKID** 5-9-2................11
2006 **STEENBERG** 7-9-2....................16
2007 **AMADEUS WOLF** 4-9-2..............17
2008 **ASSERTIVE** 5-9-7.....................17
2009 **UTMOST RESPECT** 5-9-7...........16
2010 **PRIME DEFENDER** 6-9-7............12
2011 **DELEGATOR** 5-9-7....................14
2012 **TIDDLIWINKS** 6-9-7..................13

LOCKINGE STAKES
Newbury-1m
2003 **HAWK WING** 4-9-0.....................6
2004 **RUSSIAN RHYTHM** 4-8-11..........15
2005 **RAKTI** 6-9-0............................8
2006 **PEERESS** 5-8-11.......................9
2007 **RED EVIE** 4-8-11......................8
2008 **CREACHADOIR** 4-9-0................11
2009 **VIRTUAL** 4-9-0........................11
2010 **PACO BOY** 5-9-0.......................9
2011 **CANFORD CLIFFS** 4-9-0.............7
2012 **FRANKEL** 4-9-0........................6

HENRY II STAKES
Sandown-2m 78yds
2003 **MR DINOS** 4-9-3......................10
2004 **PAPINEAU** 4-8-12......................9
2005 **FIGHT YOUR CORNER** 6-9-0.......16
2006 **TUNGSTEN STRIKE** 5-9-2...........7
2007 **ALLEGRETTO** 4-9-0....................7
2008 **FINALMENTE** 6-9-2....................8
2009 **GEORDIELAND** 8-9-2..................7
2010 **AKMAL** 4-9-0............................9

2011 **BLUE BAJAN** 9-9-2.....................8
2012 **OPINION POLL** 6-9-4.................10

TEMPLE STAKES
Haydock-5f
(Run at Sandown before 2008)
2003 **AIRWAVE** 3-9-0.........................7
*2004 **NIGHT PROSPECTOR** 4-9-4........12
2005 **CELTIC MILL** 7-9-4....................13
2006 **REVERENCE** 5-9-4.....................12
2007 **SIERRA VISTA** 7-9-1..................12
2008 **FLEETING SPIRIT** 3-8-11............12
2009 **LOOK BUSY** 4-9-1......................9
2010 **KINGSGATE NATIVE** 5-9-4...........9
2011 **SOLE POWER** 4-9-4...................12
2012 **BATED BREATH** 5-9-4................12
*Run at Epsom

BRIGADIER GERARD STAKES
Sandown-1m 2f 7yds
2003 **SIGHTS ON GOLD** 4-8-10...........8
2004 **BANDARI** 5-8-10.......................9
2005 **NEW MORNING** 4-8-7.................5
2006 **NOTNOWCATO** 4-9-3..................6
2007 **TAKE A BOW** 6-9-0....................7
2008 **SMOKEY OAKEY** 4-9-0..............14
2009 **CIMA DE TRIOMPHE** 4-9-0.........12
2010 **STOTSFOLD** 7-9-0.....................8
2011 **WORKFORCE** 4-9-7....................8
2012 **CARLTON HOUSE** 4-9-0..............6

CORONATION CUP
Epsom-1m 4f 10yds
2003 **WARRSAN** 5-9-0........................9
2004 **WARRSAN** 6-9-0......................11
2005 **YEATS** 4-9-0............................7
2006 **SHIROCCO** 5-9-0.......................6
2007 **SCORPION** 5-9-0.......................7
2008 **SOLDIER OF FORTUNE** 4-9-0......11
2009 **ASK** 6-9-0...............................8
2010 **FAME AND GLORY** 4-9-0..............7
2011 **ST NICHOLAS ABBEY** 4-9-0.........5
2012 **ST NICHOLAS ABBEY** 5-9-0.........6

BOND TYRES TROPHY
(2009-10 Reg Griffin Memorial Trophy)
(2008 Betfair Sprint)
(William Hill Trophy before 2008)
York-6f
2003 **DAZZLING BAY** 8-2...................19
2004 **TWO STEP KID** 8-9..................20
2005 **TAX FREE** 8-9.........................20
2006 **PRINCE TAMINO** 8-13...............18
2007 ABANDONED
2008 **BRAVE PROSPECTOR** 9-0..........19
2009 **SWISS DIVA** 9-1.......................20
2010 **VICTOIRE DE LYPHAR** 8-7..........20
2011 **LEXI'S HERO** 8-11....................20
2012 **SHOLAAN** 8-9..........................17

QUEEN ANNE STAKES
Ascot-1m
2003 **DUBAI DESTINATION** 4-9-0........10
2004 **REFUSE TO BEND** 4-9-0............16
*2005 **VALIXIR** 4-9-0..........................7
2006 **AD VALOREM** 4-9-0...................7
2007 **RAMONTI** 5-9-0........................8
2008 **HARADASUN** 5-9-0...................11
2009 **PACO BOY** 4-9-0.......................9

2010   **GOLDIKOVA** 5-8-11 10
2011   **CANFORD CLIFFS** 4-9-0 7
2012   **FRANKEL** 4-9-0 11
*Run at York

PRINCE OF WALES'S STAKES
Ascot-1m 2f
2003   **NAYEF** 5-9-0 10
2004   **RAKTI** 5-9-0 10
*2005 **AZAMOUR** 4-9-0 8
2006   **OUIJA BOARD** 5-8-11 7
2007   **MANDURO** 5-9-0 6
2008   **DUKE OF MARMALADE** 4-9-0 12
2009   **VISION D'ETAT** 4-9-0 8
2010   **BYWORD** 4-9-0 12
2011   **REWILDING** 4-9-0 7
2012   **SO YOU THINK** 6-9-0 11
*Run at York

ST JAMES'S PALACE STAKES (3y)
Ascot-1m
2003   **ZAFEEN** 9-0 11
2004   **AZAMOUR** 9-0 11
*2005 **SHAMARDAL** 9-0 8
2006   **ARAAFA** 9-0 11
2007   **EXCELLENT ART** 9-0 8
2008   **HENRYTHENAVIGATOR** 9-0 8
2009   **MASTERCRAFTSMAN** 9-0 10
2010   **CANFORD CLIFFS** 9-0 9
2011   **FRANKEL** 9-0 9
2012   **MOST IMPROVED** 9-0 16
*Run at York

COVENTRY STAKES (2y)
Ascot-6f
2003   **THREE VALLEYS** 8-12 13
2004   **ICEMAN** 8-12 13
*2005 **RED CLUBS** 8-12 14
2006   **HELLVELYN** 9-1 21
2007   **HENRYTHENAVIGATOR** 9-1 20
2008   **ART CONNOISSEUR** 9-1 18
2009   **CANFORD CLIFFS** 9-1 13
2010   **STRONG SUIT** 9-1 13
2011   **POWER** 9-1 23
2012   **DAWN APPROACH** 9-1 22
*Run at York

KING EDWARD VII STAKES (3y)
Ascot-1m 4f
2003   **HIGH ACCOLADE** 8-11 8
2004   **FIVE DYNASTIES** 8-11 5
*2005 **PLEA BARGAIN** 8-11 5
2006   **PAPAL BULL** 8-12 9
2007   **BOSCOBEL** 8-12 9
2008   **CAMPANOLOGIST** 8-12 9
2009   **FATHER TIME** 8-12 12
2010   **MONTEROSSO** 8-12 8
2011   **NATHANIEL** 8-12 10
2012   **THOMAS CHIPPENDALE** 8-12 5
*Run at York

JERSEY STAKES (3y)
Ascot-7f
2003   **MEMBERSHIP** 8-10 14
2004   **KHELEYF** 8-10 15
*2005 **PROCLAMATION** 8-13 21
2006   **JEREMY** 9-1 14
2007   **TARIQ** 9-1 15
2008   **AQLAAM** 9-1 16

2009   **OUQBA** 9-1 16
2010   **RAINFALL** 8-12 13
2011   **STRONG SUIT** 9-6 9
2012   **ISHVANA** 8-12 22
*Run at York

WINDSOR FOREST STAKES
(fillies & mares)
Ascot-1m
2004   **FAVOURABLE TERMS** 4-8-12 10
*2005 **PEERESS** 4-8-9 8
2006   **SOVIET SONG** 6-8-12 10
2007   **NANNINA** 4-8-12 9
2008   **SABANA PERDIDA** 5-8-12 13
2009   **SPACIOUS** 4-8-12 9
2010   **STRAWBERRYDAIQUIRI** 4-8-12 10
2011   **LOLLY FOR DOLLY** 4-8-12 13
2012   **JOVIALITY** 4-8-12 13
*Run at York

QUEEN MARY STAKES (2y fillies)
Ascot-5f
2003   **ATTRACTION** 8-10 14
2004   **DAMSON** 8-10 17
*2005 **FLASHY WINGS** 8-10 17
2006   **GILDED** 8-12 15
2007   **ELLETELLE** 8-12 21
2008   **LANGS LASH** 8-12 17
2009   **JEALOUS AGAIN** 8-12 13
2010   **MAQAASID** 8-12 18
2011   **BEST TERMS** 8-12 14
2012   **CEILING KITTY** 8-12 27
*Run at York

CORONATION STAKES (3y fillies)
Ascot-1m
2003   **RUSSIAN RHYTHM** 9-0 9
2004   **ATTRACTION** 9-0 11
*2005 **MAIDS CAUSEWAY** 9-0 10
2006   **NANNINA** 9-0 15
2007   **INDIAN INK** 9-0 13
2008   **LUSH LASHES** 9-0 11
2009   **GHANAATI** 9-0 10
2010   **LILLIE LANGTRY** 9-0 13
2011   **IMMORTAL VERSE** 9-0 12
2012   **FALLEN FOR YOU** 9-0 10
*Run at York

ROYAL HUNT CUP
Ascot-1m
2003   **MACADAMIA** 4-8-13 32
2004   **MINE** 6-9-5 31
*2005 **NEW SEEKER** 5-9-0 22
2006   **CESARE** 5-8-8 30
2007   **ROYAL OATH** 4-9-0 26
2008   **MR AVIATOR** 4-9-5 29
2009   **FORGOTTEN VOICE** 4-9-1 25
2010   **INVISIBLE MAN** 4-8-9 29
2011   **JULIENAS** 4-8-8 28
2012   **PRINCE OF JOHANNE** 6-9-3 30
*Run at York

QUEEN'S VASE (3y)
Ascot-2m
2003   **SHANTY STAR** 8-11 12
2004   **DUKE OF VENICE** 8-11 10
*2005 **MELROSE AVENUE** 8-11 10
2006   **SOAPY DANGER** 9-1 11

2007	**MAHLER** 9-1	15
2008	**PATKAI** 9-1	12
2009	**HOLBERG** 9-1	14
2010	**MIKHAIL GLINKA** 9-1	12
2011	**NAMIBIAN** 9-1	11
2012	**ESTIMATE** 8-12	10

*Run at York

DIAMOND JUBILEE STAKES
Ascot-6f
(Run as Golden Jubilee Stakes before 2012)

2003	**CHOISIR** 4-9-4	17
2004	**FAYR JAG** 5-9-4	14
*2005	**CAPE OF GOOD HOPE** 7-9-4	15
2006	**LES ARCS** 6-9-4	18
2007	**SOLDIER'S TALE** 6-9-4	21
2008	**KINGSGATE NATIVE** 3-8-11	17
2009	**ART CONNOISSEUR** 3-8-11	14
2010	**STARSPANGLEDBANNER** 4-9-4	24
2011	**SOCIETY ROCK** 4-9-4	16
2012	**BLACK CAVIAR** 6-9-1	14

*Run at York

NORFOLK STAKES (2y)
Ascot-5f

2003	**RUSSIAN VALOUR** 8-12	8
2004	**BLUE DAKOTA** 8-12	9
*2005	**MASTA PLASTA** 8-12	12
2006	**DUTCH ART** 9-1	11
2007	**WINKER WATSON** 9-1	11
2008	**SOUTH CENTRAL** 9-1	11
2009	**RADIOHEAD** 9-1	11
2010	**APPROVE** 9-1	12
2011	**BAPAK CHINTA** 9-1	15
2012	**RECKLESS ABANDON** 9-1	11

*Run at York

GOLD CUP
Ascot-2m 4f

2003	**MR DINOS** 4-9-0	12
2004	**PAPINEAU** 4-9-0	13
*2005	**WESTERNER** 6-9-2	17
2006	**YEATS** 5-9-2	12
2007	**YEATS** 6-9-2	14
2008	**YEATS** 7-9-2	10
2009	**YEATS** 8-9-2	9
2010	**RITE OF PASSAGE** 6-9-2	12
2011	**FAME AND GLORY** 5-9-2	15
2012	**COLOUR VISION** 4-9-0	9

*Run at York

RIBBLESDALE STAKES (3y fillies)
Ascot-1m 4f

2003	**SPANISH SUN** 8-11	9
2004	**PUNCTILIOUS** 8-11	9
*2005	**THAKAFAAT** 8-11	9
2006	**MONT ETOILE** 8-12	11
2007	**SILKWOOD** 8-12	12
2008	**MICHITA** 8-12	9
2009	**FLYING CLOUD** 8-12	10
2010	**HIBAAYEB** 8-12	11
2011	**BANIMPIRE** 8-12	12
2012	**PRINCESS HIGHWAY** 8-12	14

*Run at York

HARDWICKE STAKES
Ascot-1m 4f

2003	**INDIAN CREEK** 5-8-9	9
2004	**DOYEN** 4-8-9	6

*2005	**BANDARI** 6-8-9	6
2006	**MARAAHEL** 5-9-0	8
2007	**MARAAHEL** 6-9-0	7
2008	**MACARTHUR** 4-9-0	9
2009	**BRONZE CANNON** 4-9-3	9
2010	**HARBINGER** 4-9-0	11
2011	**AWAIT THE DAWN** 4-9-0	9
2012	**SEA MOON** 4-9-0	12

*Run at York

WOKINGHAM STAKES
Ascot-6f

2003	**RATIO** 5-9-3 dead heated with	
	FAYR JAG 4-9-6	29
2004	**LAFI** 5-8-13	29
*2005	**IFFRAAJ** 4-9-6	17
2006	**BALTIC KING** 6-9-10	28
2007	**DARK MISSILE** 4-8-6	26
2008	**BIG TIMER** 4-9-2	27
2009	**HIGH STANDING** 4-8-12	26
2010	**LADDIES POKER TWO** 5-8-11	27
2011	**DEACON BLUES** 4-8-13	25
2012	**DANDY BOY** 6-9-8	28

*Run at York

KING'S STAND STAKES
Ascot-5f

2003	**CHOISIR** 4-9-7	20
2004	**THE TATLING** 7-9-2	19
*2005	**CHINEUR** 4-9-2	16
2006	**TAKEOVER TARGET** 7-9-7	28
2007	**MISS ANDRETTI** 6-9-1	20
2008	**EQUIANO** 3-8-12	13
2009	**SCENIC BLAST** 5-9-4	19
2010	**EQUIANO** 5-9-4	12
2011	**PROHIBIT** 6-9-4	19
2012	**LITTLE BRIDGE** 6-9-4	22

*Run at York

NORTHUMBERLAND PLATE
Newcastle-2m 19yds

2003	**UNLEASH** 4-8-11	20
2004	**MIRJAN** 8-8-3	19
2005	**SERGEANT CECIL** 6-8-8	20
2006	**TOLDO** 4-8-2	20
2007	**JUNIPER GIRL** 4-8-11	20
2008	**ARC BLEU** 7-8-2	18
2009	**SOM TALA** 6-8-8	17
2010	**OVERTURN** 6-8-7	19
2011	**TOMINATOR** 4-8-5	19
2012	**ILE DE RE** 6-9-3	16

ECLIPSE STAKES
Sandown-1m 2f 7yds

2003	**FALBRAV** 5-9-7	15
2004	**REFUSE TO BEND** 4-9-7	12
2005	**ORATORIO** 3-8-10	7
2006	**DAVID JUNIOR** 4-9-7	9
2007	**NOTNOWCATO** 5-9-7	8
2008	**MOUNT NELSON** 4-9-7	8
2009	**SEA THE STARS** 3-8-10	10
2010	**TWICE OVER** 5-9-7	5
2011	**SO YOU THINK** 5-9-7	5
2012	**NATHANIEL** 4-9-7	9

LANCASHIRE OAKS (fillies and mares)
Haydock-1m 3f 200yds

2003	**PLACE ROUGE** 4-9-3	12
2004	**PONGEE** 4-9-3	8

2005	**PLAYFUL ACT** 3-8-5	8
2006	**ALLEGRETTO** 3-8-6	8
*2007	**TURBO LINN** 4-9-5	12
2008	**ANNA PAVLOVA** 5-9-8	9
2009	**BARSHIBA** 5-9-5	8
2010	**BARSHIBA** 6-9-5	10
2011	**GERTRUDE BELL** 4-9-5	7
2012	**GREAT HEAVENS** 3-8-6	9

*Run at Newmarket

CHERRY HINTON STAKES (2y fillies)
Newmarket-6f

2003	**ATTRACTION** 8-12	8
2004	**JEWEL IN THE SAND** 8-9	10
2005	**DONNA BLINI** 8-9	8
2006	**SANDER CAMILLO** 8-12	10
2007	**YOU'RESOTHRILLING** 8-12	14
2008	**PLEASE SING** 8-12	8
2009	**MISHEER** 8-12	10
2010	**MEMORY** 8-12	7
2011	**GAMILATI** 8-12	11
2012	**SENDMYLOVETOROSE** 8-12	10

BUNBURY CUP
(Run as 32Red Trophy in 2010)
Newmarket-7f

2003	**PATAVELLIAN** 5-9-1	20
2004	**MATERIAL WITNESS** 7-9-3	19
2005	**MINE** 7-9-9	18
2006	**MINE** 8-9-10	19
2007	**GIGANTICUS** 4-8-8	18
2008	**LITTLE WHITE LIE** 4-9-0	18
2009	**PLUM PUDDING** 6-9-10	19
2010	**ST MORITZ** 4-9-1	19
2011	**BRAE HILL** 5-9-1	20
2012	**BONNIE BRAE** 5-9-9	15

PRINCESS OF WALES'S STAKES
Newmarket-1m 4f

2003	**MILLENARY** 6-9-2	6
2004	**BANDARI** 5-9-2	8
2005	**GAMUT** 6-9-2	5
2006	**SOAPY DANGER** 3-8-3	4
2007	**PAPAL BULL** 4-9-2	12
2008	**LUCARNO** 4-9-7	6
2009	**DOCTOR FREMANTLE** 4-9-2	9
2010	**SANS FRONTIERES** 4-9-2	8
2011	**CRYSTAL CAPELLA** 6-8-13	8
2012	**FIORENTE** 4-9-2	7

JULY STAKES (2y)
Newmarket-6f

2003	**NEVISIAN LAD** 8-10	8
2004	**CAPTAIN HURRICANE** 8-10	11
2005	**IVAN DENISOVICH** 8-10	7
2006	**STRATEGIC PRINCE** 8-12	9
2007	**WINKER WATSON** 9-1	13
2008	**CLASSIC BLADE** 8-12	7
2009	**ARCANO** 8-12	11
2010	**LIBRANNO** 8-12	5
2011	**FREDERICK ENGELS** 8-12	7
2012	**ALHEBAYEB** 8-12	7

FALMOUTH STAKES (fillies & mares)
Newmarket-1m

2003	**MACADAMIA** 4-9-1	8
2004	**SOVIET SONG** 4-9-1	7
2005	**SOVIET SONG** 5-9-1	7
2006	**RAJEEM** 3-8-10	7

2007	**SIMPLY PERFECT** 3-8-10	7
2008	**NAHOODH** 3-8-10	11
2009	**GOLDIKOVA** 4-9-5	8
2010	**MUSIC SHOW** 3-8-10	8
2011	**TIMEPIECE** 4-9-5	11
2012	**GIOFRA** 4-9-5	10

JULY CUP
Newmarket-6f

2003	**OASIS DREAM** 3-8-13	16
2004	**FRIZZANTE** 5-9-2	20
2005	**PASTORAL PURSUITS** 4-9-5	19
2006	**LES ARCS** 6-9-5	15
2007	**SAKHEE'S SECRET** 3-8-13	18
2008	**MARCHAND D'OR** 5-9-5	13
2009	**FLEETING SPIRIT** 4-9-2	13
2010	**STARSPANGLEDBANNER** 4-9-5	14
2011	**DREAM AHEAD** 3-8-13	16
2012	**MAYSON** 4-9-5	12

PRINCESS MARGARET STAKES (2y fillies)
Ascot-6f

2003	**RIVER BELLE** 8-9	9
2004	**SOAR** 8-9	6
*2005	**MIXED BLESSING** 8-9	12
2006	**SCARLET RUNNER** 8-12	10
2007	**VISIT** 8-12	13
2008	**AFRICAN SKIES** 8-12	16
2009	**LADY OF THE DESERT** 8-12	9
2010	**SORAAYA** 8-12	11
2011	**ANGELS WILL FALL** 8-12	7
2012	**MAUREEN** 8-12	6

*Run at Newbury

STEWARDS' CUP
Goodwood-6f

2003	**PATAVELLIAN** 5-8-11	29
2004	**PIVOTAL POINT** 4-8-11	28
2005	**GIFT HORSE** 5-9-7	27
2006	**BORDERLESCOTT** 4-9-5	27
2007	**ZIDANE** 5-9-1	27
2008	**CONQUEST** 4-8-9	27
2009	**GENKI** 5-9-1	26
2010	**EVENS AND ODDS** 6-8-10	28
2011	**HOOF IT** 4-10-0	27
2012	**HAWKEYETHENOO** 6-9-9	27

GORDON STAKES (3y)
Goodwood-1m 4f

2003	**PHOENIX REACH** 8-10	10
2004	**MARAAHEL** 8-10	8
2005	**THE GEEZER** 8-10	5
2006	**SIXTIES ICON** 9-0	7
2007	**YELLOWSTONE** 9-0	9
2008	**CONDUIT** 9-0	6
2009	**HARBINGER** 9-0	9
2010	**REBEL SOLDIER** 9-0	10
2011	**NAMIBIAN** 9-3	10
2012	**NOBLE MISSION** 9-0	7

SUSSEX STAKES
Goodwood-1m

2003	**REEL BUDDY** 5-9-7	9
2004	**SOVIET SONG** 4-9-4	11
2005	**PROCLAMATION** 3-8-13	12
2006	**COURT MASTERPIECE** 6-9-7	7
2007	**RAMONTI** 5-9-7	8

2008 **HENRYTHENAVIGATOR** 3-8-13 6
2009 **RIP VAN WINKLE** 3-8-13 8
2010 **CANFORD CLIFFS** 3-8-13 7
2011 **FRANKEL** 3-8-13 4
2012 **FRANKEL** 4-9-7 4

RICHMOND STAKES (2y)
Goodwood-6f
2003 **CARRIZO CREEK** 8-11 7
2004 **MONTGOMERY'S ARCH** 8-11 8
2005 **ALWAYS HOPEFUL** 8-11 6
2006 **HAMOODY** 9-0 7
2007 **STRIKE THE DEAL** 9-0 9
2008 **PROLIFIC** 9-0 12
2009 **DICK TURPIN** 9-0 9
2010 **LIBRANNO** 9-3 6
2011 **HARBOUR WATCH** 9-0 10
2012 **HEAVY METAL** 9-0 8

KING GEORGE STAKES
Goodwood-5f
2003 **THE TATLING** 6-9-0 9
2004 **RINGMOOR DOWN** 5-8-11 13
2005 **FIRE UP THE BAND** 6-9-0 12
2006 **LA CUCARACHA** 5-8-11 18
2007 **MOORHOUSE LAD** 4-9-0 17
2008 **ENTICING** 4-8-11 12
2009 **KINGSGATE NATIVE** 4-9-0 17
2010 **BORDERLESCOTT** 8-9-0 15
2011 **MASAMAH** 5-9-0 11
2012 **ORTENSIA** 7-9-5 17

GOODWOOD CUP
Goodwood-2m
2003 **PERSIAN PUNCH** 10-9-4 9
2004 **DARASIM** 6-9-4 9
2005 **DISTINCTION** 6-9-5 10
2006 **YEATS** 5-9-10 15
2007 **ALLEGRETTO** 4-9-5 15
2008 **YEATS** 7-9-12 8
2009 **SCHIAPARELLI** 6-9-7 10
2010 **ILLUSTRIOUS BLUE** 7-9-7 10
2011 **OPINION POLL** 5-9-7 15
2012 **SADDLER'S ROCK** 4-9-7 10

MOLECOMB STAKES (2y)
Goodwood-5f
2003 **MAJESTIC MISSILE** 8-12 9
2004 **TOURNEDOS** 8-12 13
2005 **STRIKE UP THE BAND** 9-1 15
2006 **ENTICING** 8-11 13
2007 **FLEETING SPIRIT** 8-11 16
2008 **FINJAAN** 9-0 11
2009 **MONSIEUR CHEVALIER** 9-0 11
2010 **ZEBEDEE** 9-0 12
2011 **REQUINTO** 9-0 13
2012 **BUNGLE INTHEJUNGLE** 9-0 10

NASSAU STAKES (fillies and mares)
Goodwood-1m 1f 192yds
2003 **RUSSIAN RHYTHM** 3-8-6 8
2004 **FAVOURABLE TERMS** 4-9-2 6
2005 **ALEXANDER GOLDRUN** 4-9-3 11
2006 **OUIJA BOARD** 5-9-5 7
2007 **PEEPING FAWN** 3-8-10 8
2008 **HALFWAY TO HEAVEN** 3-8-10 9
2009 **MIDDAY** 3-8-10 10
2010 **MIDDAY** 4-9-6 7

2011 **MIDDAY** 5-9-6 6
2012 **THE FUGUE** 3-8-11 8

HUNGERFORD STAKES
Newbury-7f
2003 **WITH REASON** 5-8-13 11
2004 **CHIC** 4-8-11 13
2005 **SLEEPING INDIAN** 4-9-0 9
2006 **WELSH EMPEROR** 7-9-3 7
2007 **RED EVIE** 4-9-4 10
2008 **PACO BOY** 3-9-0 9
2009 **BALTHAZAAR'S GIFT** 6-9-3 9
2010 **SHAKESPEAREAN** 3-8-11 7
2011 **EXCELEBRATION** 3-8-13 8
2012 **LETHAL FORCE** 3-8-12 9

GEOFFREY FREER STAKES
Newbury-1m 5f 61yds
2003 **MUBTAKER** 6-9-3 5
2004 **MUBTAKER** 7-9-3 4
2005 **LOCHBUIE** 4-9-3 5
2006 **ADMIRAL'S CRUISE** 4-9-3 5
2007 **PAPAL BULL** 4-9-7 5
2008 **SIXTIES ICON** 5-9-5 8
2009 **KITE WOOD** 3-8-8 8
2010 **SANS FRONTIERES** 4-9-8 8
2011 **CENSUS** 3-8-6 10
2012 **MOUNT ATHOS** 5-9-4 6

INTERNATIONAL STAKES
York-1m 2f 88yds
2003 **FALBRAV** 5-9-5 8
2004 **SULAMANI** 5-9-5 9
2005 **ELECTROCUTIONIST** 4-9-5 7
2006 **NOTNOWCATO** 4-9-5 7
2007 **AUTHORIZED** 3-8-11 7
*2008 **DUKE OF MARMALADE** 4-9-5 9
2009 **SEA THE STARS** 3-8-11 4
2010 **RIP VAN WINKLE** 4-9-5 9
2011 **TWICE OVER** 6-9-5 5
2012 **FRANKEL** 4-9-5 9
*Run at Newmarket over 1m 2f

GREAT VOLTIGEUR STAKES (3y)
York-1m 4f
2003 **POWERSCOURT** 8-9 9
2004 **RULE OF LAW** 8-9 7
2005 **HARD TOP** 8-9 6
2006 **YOUMZAIN** 8-12 10
2007 **LUCARNO** 8-12 9
*2008 **CENTENNIAL** 8-12 5
2009 **MONITOR CLOSELY** 8-12 7
2010 **REWILDING** 8-12 10
2011 **SEA MOON** 8-12 8
2012 **THOUGHT WORTHY** 8-12 6
*Run at Goodwood

YORKSHIRE OAKS (fillies and mares)
York-1m 4f
2003 **ISLINGTON** 4-9-4 8
2004 **QUIFF** 3-8-8 8
2005 **PUNCTILIOUS** 4-9-4 11
2006 **ALEXANDROVA** 3-8-11 6
2007 **PEEPING FAWN** 3-8-11 7
*2008 **LUSH LASHES** 3-8-11 6
2009 **DAR RE MI** 4-9-7 6
2010 **MIDDAY** 4-9-7 8

2011 **BLUE BUNTING** 3-8-11..................8
2012 **SHARETA** 4-9-7.....................6
*Run at Newmarket

EBOR HANDICAP
York-1m 6f (1m 5f 194yds before 2007)
2003 **SAINT ALEBE** 4-8-8.................22
2004 **MEPHISTO** 5-9-4...................19
2005 **SERGEANT CECIL** 6-8-12.............20
2006 **MUDAWIN** 5-8-4....................19
2007 **PURPLE MOON** 4-9-4................19
*2008 **ALL THE GOOD** 5-9-0..............20
2009 **SESENTA** 5-8-8....................19
2010 **DIRAR** 5-9-1......................20
2011 **MOYENNE CORNICHE** 6-8-10...........20
2012 **WILLING FOE** 5-9-2................19
*Run as Newburgh Handicap at Newbury over 1m 5f 61 yds

GIMCRACK STAKES (2y)
York-6f
2003 **BALMONT** 8-11......................9
2004 **TONY JAMES** 8-11..................11
2005 **AMADEUS WOLF** 8-11................13
2006 **CONQUEST** 8-12.....................6
2007 **SIR GERRY** 8-12....................8
*2008 **SHAWEEL** 8-12....................12
2009 **SHOWCASING** 8-12...................6
2010 **APPROVE** 9-1......................11
2011 **CASPAR NETSCHER** 8-12..............9
2012 **BLAINE** 8-12.......................8
*Run at Newbury

NUNTHORPE STAKES
York-5f
2003 **OASIS DREAM** 3-9-9.................8
2004 **BAHAMIAN PIRATE** 9-9-11............12
2005 **LA CUCARACHA** 4-9-8...............16
2006 **REVERENCE** 5-9-11.................14
2007 **KINGSGATE NATIVE** 2-8-1...........16
*2008 **BORDERLESCOTT** 6-9-11.............14
2009 **BORDERLESCOTT** 7-9-11.............16
2010 **SOLE POWER** 3-9-9.................12
2011 **MARGOT DID** 3-9-6.................15
2012 **ORTENSIA** 7-9-8...................19
*Run at Newmarket

PRESTIGE STAKES (2y fillies)
Goodwood-7f
2003 **GRACEFULLY** 8-9.....................6
2004 **DUBAI SURPRISE** 8-9................12
2005 **NANNINA** 8-9.......................9
2006 **SESMEN** 9-0.......................10
2007 **SENSE OF JOY** 9-0..................7
2008 **FANTASIA** 9-0.....................10
2009 **SENT FROM HEAVEN** 9-0..............8
2010 **THEYSKENS' THEORY** 9-0.............7
2011 **REGAL REALM** 9-0...................6
2012 **OLLIE OLGA** 9-0....................8

CELEBRATION MILE
Goodwood-1m
2003 **PRIORS LODGE** 5-9-1.................6
2004 **CHIC** 4-8-12.......................7
2005 **CHIC** 5-8-12.......................8
2006 **CARADAK** 5-9-1.....................6
2007 **ECHELON** 5-8-12....................8
2008 **RAVEN'S PASS** 3-8-9................5
2009 **DELEGATOR** 3-8-9...................7
2010 **POET'S VOICE** 3-8-9................4

2011 **DUBAWI GOLD** 3-8-9..................7
2012 **PREMIO LOCO** 8-9-1.................5

SOLARIO STAKES (2y)
Sandown-7f 16yds
2003 **BARBAJUAN** 8-11....................8
2004 **WINDSOR KNOT** 8-11.................8
2005 **OPERA CAPE** 8-11...................8
2006 **DRUMFIRE** 9-0......................8
2007 **RAVEN'S PASS** 9-0..................9
2008 **SRI PUTRA** 9-0....................11
2009 **SHAKESPEAREAN** 9-0.................8
2010 **NATIVE KHAN** 9-0...................6
2011 **TALWAR** 9-0........................4
2012 **FANTASTIC MOON** 9-0................7

SPRINT CUP
Haydock-6f
2003 **SOMNUS** 3-8-11....................10
2004 **TANTE ROSE** 4-8-11................19
2005 **GOODRICKE** 3-8-12.................17
2006 **REVERENCE** 5-9-3..................11
2007 **RED CLUBS** 4-9-3..................14
*2008 **AFRICAN ROSE** 3-8-12..............15
2009 **REGAL PARADE** 5-9-3...............14
2010 **MARKAB** 7-9-3.....................13
2011 **DREAM AHEAD** 3-9-1................16
2012 **SOCIETY ROCK** 5-9-3...............13
*Run at Doncaster

SEPTEMBER STAKES
Kempton-1m 4f Polytrack
(run on turf before 2006)
2003 **MUBTAKER** 6-9-8....................5
2004 **MAMOOL** 5-9-3......................4
*2005 **IMPERIAL STRIDE** 4-9-8............6
2006 **KANDIDATE** 4-9-8...................6
2007 **STEPPE DANCER** 4-9-4..............7
2008 **HATTAN** 6-9-7.....................12
2009 **KIRKLEES** 5-9-9...................10
2010 **LAAHEB** 4-9-4......................7
2011 **MODUN** 4-9-4.......................7
2012 **DANDINO** 5-9-4.....................9
*Run at Newmarket

MAY HILL STAKES (2y fillies)
Doncaster-1m
2003 **KINNAIRD** 8-10....................10
2004 **PLAYFUL ACT** 8-10..................8
2005 **NASHEEJ** 8-13......................8
*2006 **SIMPLY PERFECT** 8-12..............9
2007 **SPACIOUS** 8-12....................12
2008 **RAINBOW VIEW** 9-1..................7
2009 **POLLENATOR** 8-12...................7
2010 **WHITE MOONSTONE** 8-12..............7
2011 **LYRIC OF LIGHT** 8-12...............8
2012 **CERTIFY** 8-12......................7
*Run at York

PORTLAND HANDICAP
Doncaster-5f 140yds
2003 **HALMAHERA** 8-9-4..................22
2004 **HALMAHERA** 9-9-10.................22
2005 **OUT AFTER DARK** 4-8-12............21
*2006 **FANTASY BELIEVER** 8-8-13.........19
2007 **FULLANDBY** 5-8-13.................21

2008	HOGMANEIGH 5-9-6	21
2009	SANTO PADRE 5-9-1	22
2010	POET'S PLACE 5-9-4	22
2011	NOCTURNAL AFFAIR 5-9-5	21
2012	DOC HAY 5-8-11	20

*Run at York over 5f 89yds

PARK HILL STAKES (fillies and mares)
Doncaster-1m 6f 132yds

2003	DISCREET BRIEF 3-8-5	8
2004	ECHOES IN ETERNITY 4-9-3	10
2005	SWEET STREAM 5-9-3	11
*2006	RISING CROSS 3-8-7	7
2007	HI CALYPSO 3-8-7	14
2008	ALLEGRETTO 5-9-4	8
2009	THE MINIVER ROSE 3-8-6	9
2010	EASTERN ARIA 4-9-4	12
2011	MEEZNAH 4-9-4	7
2012	WILD COCO 4-9-4	9

*Run at York

DONCASTER CUP
Doncaster-2m 2f

2003	PERSIAN PUNCH 10-9-4	6
2004	MILLENARY 7-9-4 dead heated with	
	KASTHARI 5-9-1	8
2005	MILLENARY 8-9-4	7
*2006	SERGEANT CECIL 7-9-4	8
2007	SEPTIMUS 4-9-4	8
2008	HONOLULU 4-9-1	9
2009	ASKAR TAU 4-9-4	5
2010	SAMUEL 6-9-1	10
2011	SADDLER'S ROCK 3-8-1	7
2012	TIMES UP 6-9-1	10

*Run at York

CHAMPAGNE STAKES (2y)
Doncaster-7f

2003	LUCKY STORY 9-0	6
2004	ETLAALA 8-10	10
2005	CLOSE TO YOU 8-10 dead heated with	
	SILENT TIMES 8-10	7
*2006	VITAL EQUINE 8-12	8
2007	MCCARTNEY 8-12	10
2008	WESTPHALIA 8-12	7
2009	POET'S VOICE 8-12	7
2010	SAAMIDD 8-12	6
2011	TRUMPET MAJOR 8-12	5
2012	TORONADO 8-12	5

*Run at York

FLYING CHILDERS STAKES (2y)
Doncaster-5f

2003	HOWICK FALLS 8-12	13
2004	CHATEAU ISTANA 8-12	11
2005	GODFREY STREET 8-12	9
*2006	WI DUD 9-0	9
2007	FLEETING SPIRIT 8-11	8
2008	MADAME TROP VITE 8-11	12
2009	SAND VIXEN 8-11	10
2010	ZEBEDEE 9-0	12
2011	REQUINTO 9-0	10
2012	SIR PRANCEALOT 9-0	9

*Run at York

AYR GOLD CUP
Ayr-6f

2003	QUITO 6-8-6	26
2004	FUNFAIR WANE 5-8-6	24

2005	PRESTO SHINKO 4-9-2	27
2006	FONTHILL ROAD 6-9-2	23
2007	ADVANCED 4-9-9	28
2008	REGAL PARADE 4-8-10	27
2009	JIMMY STYLES 5-9-2	26
2010	REDFORD 5-9-2	26
2011	OUR JONATHAN 4-9-6	26
2012	CAPTAIN RAMIUS 6-9-0	26

MILL REEF STAKES (2y)
Newbury-6f 8yds

2003	BYRON 8-12	10
2004	GALEOTA 8-12	9
2005	COOL CREEK 8-12	13
2006	EXCELLENT ART 9-1	6
2007	DARK ANGEL 9-1	6
2008	LORD SHANAKILL 9-1	9
2009	AWZAAN 9-1	7
2010	TEMPLE MEADS 9-1	7
2011	CASPAR NETSCHER 9-4	9
2012	MOOHAAJIM 9-1	8

ROYAL LODGE STAKES (2y)
Newmarket-1m (run at Ascot before 2011)

2003	SNOW RIDGE 8-11	10
2004	PERFECTPERFORMANCE 8-11	8
*2005	LEO 8-11	8
2006	ADMIRALOFTHEFLEET 8-12	8
2007	CITY LEADER 8-12	11
2008	JUKEBOX JURY 8-12	8
2009	JOSHUA TREE 8-12	10
2010	FRANKEL 8-12	5
2011	DADDY LONG LEGS 8-12	6
2012	STEELER 8-12	8

*Run at Newmarket

CHEVELEY PARK STAKES (2y fillies)
Newmarket-6f

2003	CARRY ON KATIE 8-11	10
2004	MAGICAL ROMANCE 8-11	7
2005	DONNA BLINI 8-11	10
2006	INDIAN INK 8-12	11
2007	NATAGORA 8-12	14
2008	SERIOUS ATTITUDE 8-12	16
2009	SPECIAL DUTY 8-12	7
2010	HOORAY 8-12	11
2011	LIGHTENING PEARL 8-12	9
2012	ROSDHU QUEEN 8-12	11

SUN CHARIOT STAKES
(fillies and mares)
Newmarket-1m

2003	ECHOES IN ETERNITY 3-8-10	10
2004	ATTRACTION 3-8-11	5
2005	PEERESS 4-9-0	10
2006	SPINNING QUEEN 3-8-12	5
2007	MAJESTIC ROI 3-8-13	10
2008	HALFWAY TO HEAVEN 3-8-13	10
2009	SAHPRESA 4-9-2	8
2010	SAHPRESA 5-9-2	11
2011	SAPHRESA 6-9-3	8
2012	SIYOUMA 4-9-3	8

CAMBRIDGESHIRE
Newmarket-1m 1f

2003	CHIVALRY 4-8-1	34
2004	SPANISH DON 6-8-7	32
2005	BLUE MONDAY 4-9-3	30
2006	FORMAL DECREE 3-8-9	33

2007	PIPEDREAMER 3-8-12	34
2008	TAZEEZ 4-9-2	28
2009	SUPASEUS 6-9-1	32
2010	CREDIT SWAP 5-8-7	35
2011	PRINCE OF JOHANNE 5-8-9	32
2012	BRONZE ANGEL 3-8-8	33

CUMBERLAND LODGE STAKES
Ascot-1m 4f

2003	HIGH ACCOLADE 3-8-11	5
2004	HIGH ACCOLADE 4-9-0	9
*2005	MUBTAKER 8-9-0	6
2006	YOUNG MICK 4-9-0	8
2007	ASK 4-9-3	8
2008	SIXTIES ICON 5-9-3	5
2009	MAWATHEEQ 4-9-0	12
2010	LAAHEB 4-9-3	6
2011	QUEST FOR PEACE 3-8-7	7
2012	HAWAAFEZ 4-8-11	6

*Run at Newmarket

FILLIES' MILE (2y fillies)
Newmarket-1m (run as Ascot before 2011)

2003	RED BLOOM 8-10	7
2004	PLAYFUL ACT 8-10	9
*2005	NANNINA 8-10	6
2006	SIMPLY PERFECT 8-12	8
2007	LISTEN 8-12	7
2008	RAINBOW VIEW 8-12	8
2009	HIBAAYEB 8-12	9
2010	WHITE MOONSTONE 8-12	5
2011	LYRIC OF LIGHT 8-12	8
2012	CERTIFY 8-12	6

*Run at Newmarket

MIDDLE PARK STAKES (2y)
Newmarket-6f

*2003	BALMONT 8-11	13
2004	AD VALOREM 8-11	9
2005	AMADEUS WOLF 8-11	6
2006	DUTCH ART 8-12	6
2007	DARK ANGEL 8-12	9
2008	BUSHRANGER 8-12	9
2009	AWZAAN 8-12	5
2010	DREAM AHEAD 8-12	8
2011	CRUSADE 8-12	16
2012	RECKLESS ABANDON 8-12	10

*Three Valleys disqualified from first place

CHALLENGE STAKES
Newmarket-7f

2003	JUST JAMES 4-9-0	11
2004	FIREBREAK 5-9-4	12
2005	LE VIE DEI COLORI 5-9-0	15
2006	SLEEPING INDIAN 5-9-3	16
2007	MISS LUCIFER 3-8-12	15
2008	STIMULATION 3-9-1	15
2009	ARABIAN GLEAM 5-9-3	9
2010	RED JAZZ 3-9-1	14
2011	STRONG SUIT 3-9-5	8
2012	FULBRIGHT 3-9-1	11

DEWHURST STAKES (2y)
Newmarket-7f

2003	MILK IT MICK 9-0	12
2004	SHAMARDAL 9-0	9
2005	SIR PERCY 9-0	8
2006	TEOFILO 9-1	15

2007	NEW APPROACH 9-1	10
2008	INTENSE FOCUS 9-1	13
2009	BEETHOVEN 9-1	15
2010	FRANKEL 9-1	6
2011	PARISH HALL 9-1	9
2012	DAWN APPROACH 9-1	6

CESAREWITCH
Newmarket-2m 2f

2003	LANDING LIGHT 8-9-4	36
2004	CONTACT DANCER 5-8-2	34
2005	SERGEANT CECIL 6-9-8	34
2006	DETROIT CITY 4-9-1	31
2007	LEG SPINNER 6-8-11	33
2008	CARACCIOLA 11-9-6	32
2009	DARLEY SUN 3-8-6	32
2010	AAIM TO PROSPER 6-7-13	32
2011	NEVER CAN TELL 4-8-11	33
2012	AAIM TO PROSPER 8-9-10	34

ROCKFEL STAKES (2y fillies)
Newmarket-7f

2003	CAIRNS 8-9	10
2004	MAIDS CAUSEWAY 8-12	8
2005	SPECIOSA 8-9	14
2006	FINSCEAL BEO 9-2	14
2007	KITTY MATCHAM 8-12	10
2008	LAHALEEB 8-12	15
2009	MUSIC SHOW 8-12	11
2010	CAPE DOLLAR 8-12	10
2011	WADING 8-12	9
2012	JUST THE JUDGE 8-12	11

QIPCO BRITISH CHAMPIONS SPRINT STAKES
Ascot-6f
(run as Diadem Stakes before 2011)

| 2011 | DEACON BLUES 4-9-0 | 16 |
| 2012 | MAAREK 5-9-0 | 15 |

QUEEN ELIZABETH II STAKES (BRITISH CHAMPIONS MILE)
Ascot-1m

2003	FALBRAV 5-9-1	8
2004	RAKTI 5-9-1	11
*2005	STARCRAFT 5-9-1	6
2006	GEORGE WASHINGTON 3-8-13	8
2007	RAMONTI 5-9-3	7
2008	RAVEN'S PASS 3-8-13	7
2009	RIP VAN WINKLE 3-8-13	4
2010	POET'S VOICE 3-8-13	8
2011	FRANKEL 3-9-0	8
2012	EXCELEBRATION 4-9-3	8

*Run at Newmarket

QIPCO BRITISH CHAMPIONS LONG DISTANCE CUP
(formerly Jockey Club Cup, run at Newmarket before 2011)
Ascot-2m

| 2011 | FAME AND GLORY 5-9-0 | 10 |
| 2012 | RITE OF PASSAGE 8-9-7 | 9 |

QIPCO BRITISH CHAMPIONS FILLIES' AND MARES' STAKES
(formerly Pride Stakes, run at Newmarket before 2011)
Ascot-1m 4f

| 2011 | DANCING RAIN 3-8-10 | 10 |
| 2012 | SAPPHIRE 4-9-3 | 10 |

QIPCO CHAMPION STAKES (BRITISH CHAMPIONS MIDDLE DISTANCE)
Ascot-1m 2f
(run at Newmarket before 2011)
2003 **RAKTI** 4-9-2 12
2004 **HAAFHD** 3-8-11 11
2005 **DAVID JUNIOR** 3-8-11 15
2006 **PRIDE** 6-9-0 8
2007 **LITERATO** 3-8-12 12
2008 **NEW APPROACH** 3-8-12 11
2009 **TWICE OVER** 4-9-3 14
2010 **TWICE OVER** 5-9-3 10
2011 **CIRRUS DES AIGLES** 5-9-3 12
2012 **FRANKEL** 4-9-3 6

CORNWALLIS STAKES (2y)
Ascot-5f
2003 **MAJESTIC MISSILE** 9-1 11
*2004 **CASTELLETTO** 8-9 12
2005 **HUNTER STREET 8-12 12
2006 **ALZERRA** 8-1 12
2007 **CAPTAIN GERRARD** 9-0 12
2008 **AMOUR PROPRE** 9-0 19
2009 **OUR JONATHAN** 9-0 17
2010 **ELECTRIC WAVES** 8-11 14
2011 **PONTY ACCLAIM** 8-11 16
2012 **BUNGLE INTHEJUNGLE** 9-3 6
*Run at Newmarket
**Run at Salisbury

TWO-YEAR-OLD TROPHY (2y)
Redcar-6f
2003 **PEAK TO CREEK** 9-0 23
2004 **OBE GOLD** 8-3 24
2005 **MISU BOND** 9-0 24
2006 **DANUM DANCER** 8-3 24
2007 **DUBAI DYNAMO** 9-2 23
2008 **TOTAL GALLERY** 8-9 22
2009 **LUCKY LIKE** 8-6 22
2010 **LADIES ARE FOREVER** 7-12 22
2011 **BOGART** 8-12 22
2012 **BODY AND SOUL** 8-1 21

HORRIS HILL STAKES (2y)
Newbury-7f
2003 **PEAK TO CREEK** 8-9 9
2004 **CUPID'S GLORY** 8-9 13
2005 **HURRICANE CAT** 8-9 13
2006 **DIJEERR** 8-12 10
2007 **BEACON LODGE** 8-12 11
2008 **EVASIVE** 8-12 13
2009 **CARNABY STREET** 8-12 14
2010 **KLAMMER** 8-12 10
2011 **TELL DAD** 8-12 14
2012 **TAWHID** 8-12 8

RACING POST TROPHY (2y)
Doncaster-1m
2003 **AMERICAN POST** 9-0 4
2004 **MOTIVATOR** 9-0 8
2005 **PALACE EPISODE** 9-0 7
*2006 **AUTHORIZED** 9-0 14
2007 **IBN KHALDUN** 9-0 12
2008 **CROWDED HOUSE** 9-0 15
2009 **ST NICHOLAS ABBEY** 9-0 11
2010 **CASAMENTO** 9-0 10
2011 **CAMELOT** 9-0 5
2012 **KINGSBARNS** 9-0 7
*Run at Newbury

NOVEMBER HANDICAP
Doncaster-1m 4f
2003 **TURBO** 4-9-2 24
2004 **CARTE DIAMOND** 3-9-6 24
2005 **COME ON JONNY** 3-8-0 21
*2006 **GROUP CAPTAIN** 4-9-5 20
2007 **MALT OR MASH** 3-8-10 21
2008 **TROPICAL STRAIT** 5-8-13 21
2009 **CHARM SCHOOL** 4-8-12 23
2010 **TIMES UP** 4-8-13 22
2011 **ZUIDER ZEE** 4-8-13 23
2012 **ART SCHOLAR** 5-8-7 23
*Run at Windsor

WINNERS OF PRINCIPAL RACES IN IRELAND

IRISH 2000 GUINEAS (3y)
The Curragh-1m
2003	INDIAN HAVEN 9-0	16
2004	BACHELOR DUKE 9-0	8
2005	DUBAWI 9-0	8
2006	ARAAFA 9-0	11
2007	COCKNEY REBEL 9-0	12
2008	HENRYTHENAVIGATOR 9-0	5
2009	MASTERCRAFTSMAN 9-0	9
2010	CANFORD CLIFFS 9-0	13
2011	RODERIC O'CONNOR 9-0	8
2012	POWER 9-0	10

TATTERSALLS GOLD CUP
The Curragh-1m 2f 110yds
2003	BLACK SAM BELLAMY 4-9-0	8
2004	POWERSCOURT 4-9-0	6
2005	GREY SWALLOW 4-9-0	6
2006	HURRICANE RUN 4-9-0	3
2007	NOTNOWCATO 5-9-0	9
2008	DUKE OF MARMALADE 4-9-0	6
2009	CASUAL CONQUEST 4-9-0	5
2010	FAME AND GLORY 4-9-0	6
2011	SO YOU THINK 5-9-1	5
2012	SO YOU THINK 6-9-1	5

IRISH 1000 GUINEAS (3y fillies)
The Curragh-1m
2003	YESTERDAY 9-0	8
2004	ATTRACTION 9-0	15
2005	SAOIRE 9-0	18
2006	NIGHTIME 9-0	15
2007	FINSCEAL BEO 9-0	11
2008	HALFWAY TO HEAVEN 9-0	13
2009	AGAIN 9-0	16
2010	BETHRAH 9-0	19
2011	MISTY FOR ME 9-0	15
2012	SAMITAR 9-0	8

IRISH DERBY (3y)
The Curragh-1m 4f
2003	ALAMSHAR 9-0	9
2004	GREY SWALLOW 9-0	10
2005	HURRICANE RUN 9-0	9
2006	DYLAN THOMAS 9-0	8
2007	SOLDIER OF FORTUNE 9-0	11
2008	FROZEN FIRE 9-0	11
2009	FAME AND GLORY 9-0	11
2010	CAPE BLANCO 9-0	10
2011	TREASURE BEACH 9-0	8
2012	CAMELOT 9-0	5

PRETTY POLLY STAKES (fillies and mares)
Curragh-1m 2f
2003	HANAMI 3-8-9	6
2004	CHORIST 5-9-7	6
2005	ALEXANDER GOLDRUN 4-9-7	10
2006	ALEXANDER GOLDRUN 5-9-8	7
2007	PEEPING FAWN 3-8-11	9
2008	PROMISING LEAD 4-9-9	9

2009	DAR RE MI 4-9-9	7
2010	CHINESE WHITE 5-9-9	9
2011	MISTY FOR ME 3-8-12	7
2012	IZZI TOP 4-9-9	4

IRISH OAKS (3y fillies)
The Curragh-1m 4f
2003	VINTAGE TIPPLE 9-0	11
2004	OUIJA BOARD 9-0	7
2005	SHAWANDA 9-0	13
2006	ALEXANDROVA 9-0	6
2007	PEEPING FAWN 9-0	12
2008	MOONSTONE 9-0	14
2009	SARISKA 9-0	10
2010	SNOW FAIRY 9-0	15
2011	BLUE BUNTING 9-0	9
2012	GREAT HEAVENS 9-0	7

PHOENIX STAKES (2y)
The Curragh-6f
2003	ONE COOL CAT 9-0	7
2004	DAMSON 8-11	6
2005	GEORGE WASHINGTON 9-0	7
2006	HOLY ROMAN EMPEROR 9-1	7
2007	SAOIRSE ABU 8-12	6
2008	MASTERCRAFTSMAN 9-1	5
2009	ALFRED NOBEL 9-1	8
2010	ZOFFANY 9-1	7
2011	LA COLLINA 8-12	9
2012	PEDRO THE GREAT 9-3	6

MATRON STAKES (fillies and mares)
Leopardstown-1m
2003	FAVOURABLE TERMS 3-8-11	9
2004	SOVIET SONG 4-9-2	6
2005	ATTRACTION 4-9-2	9
2006	RED EVIE 3-8-12	8
2007	ECHELON 5-9-3	9
2008	LUSH LASHES 3-8-12	10
2009	RAINBOW VIEW 3-8-12	7
2010	LILLIE LANGTRY 3-8-12	6
2011	EMULOUS 4-9-5	8
*2012	CHACHAMAIDEE 5-9-5	11

*Duntle disqualified from first place

IRISH CHAMPION STAKES
Leopardstown-1m 2f
2003	HIGH CHAPARRAL 4-9-4	7
2004	AZAMOUR 3-8-11	8
2005	ORATORIO 3-8-11	10
2006	DYLAN THOMAS 3-9-0	5
2007	DYLAN THOMAS 4-9-7	6
2008	NEW APPROACH 3-9-0	8
2009	SEA THE STARS 3-9-0	9
2010	CAPE BLANCO 3-9-0	6
2011	SO YOU THINK 5-9-7	6
2012	SNOW FAIRY 5-9-4	6

IRISH CAMBRIDGESHIRE
The Curragh-1m

2003	DEFINITE BEST 5-8-5	15
2004	DUE RESPECT 4-8-10	18
2005	KESTREL CROSS 3-9-1	20
2006	QUINMASTER 4-10-1	22
2007	JALMIRA 6-8-13	24
2008	TIS MIGHTY 5-8-1	21
2009	POET 4-9-9	27
2010	HUJAYLEA 7-8-3	25
2011	CASTLE BAR SLING 6-8-11	21
2012	PUNCH YOUR WEIGHT 3-8-6	18

MOYGLARE STUD STAKES (2y fillies)
The Curragh-7f

2003	NECKLACE 8-11	11
2004	CHELSEA ROSE 8-11	12
2005	RUMPLESTILTSKIN 8-11	9
2006	MISS BEATRIX 8-12	12
2007	SAOIRSE ABU 8-12	9
2008	AGAIN 8-12	12
2009	TERMAGANT 8-12	7
2010	MISTY FOR ME 8-12	12
2011	MAYBE 9-1	8
2012	SKY LANTERN 9-0	13

VINCENT O'BRIEN (NATIONAL) STAKES (2y)
The Curragh-7f

2003	ONE COOL CAT 9-0	9
2004	DUBAWI 9-0	7
2005	GEORGE WASHINGTON 9-0	7
2006	TEOFILO 9-1	6
2007	NEW APPROACH 9-1	9
2008	MASTERCRAFTSMAN 9-1	7
2009	KINGSFORT 9-1	6
2010	PATHFORK 9-1	9
2011	POWER 9-1	9
2012	DAWN APPROACH 9-3	7

IRISH ST LEGER
The Curragh-1m 6f

2003	VINNIE ROE 5-9-9	6
2004	VINNIE ROE 6-9-8	13
2005	COLLIER HILL 7-9-8	9
2006	KASTORIA 5-9-7	8
2007	YEATS 6-9-11	9
2008	SEPTIMUS 5-9-11	9
2009	ALANDI 4-9-11	8
2010	SANS FRONTIERES 4-9-11	8
2011	DUNCAN 6-9-11 dead heated with	6
	JUKEBOX JURY 5-9-11	6
2012	ROYAL DIAMOND 6-9-11	9

IRISH CESAREWITCH
The Curragh-2m

2003	ZIMBABWE 3-8-0	17
2004	ESSEX 4-7-9	20
2005	CLARA ALLEN 7-8-0	17
2006	IKTITAF 5-8-8	16
2007	SANDYMOUNT EARL 4-9-3	21
2008	SUAILCE 3-8-1	28
2009	DANI CALIFORNIA 5-8-0	29
2010	BRIGHT HORIZON 3-8-7	23
2011	MINSK 3-8-9	19
2012	VOLEUSE DE COEURS 3-9-1	27

BOYLESPORTS.COM HURDLE
Leopardstown-2m
(Pierse Hurdle before 2010)
(MCR Hurdle in 2011)

2004	DROMLEASE EXPRESS 6-10-4	19
2005	ESSEX 5-10-8	21
2006	STUDMASTER 6-10-3	27
2007	SPRING THE QUE 8-10-3	30
2008	BARKER 7-10-6	28
2009	PENNY'S BILL 7-9-9	29
2010	PUYOL 8-10-10	30
2011	FINAL APPROACH 5-10-9	26
2012	CITIZENSHIP 6-10-3	30
2013	ABBEY LANE 8-10-8	28

IRISH CHAMPION HURDLE
Leopardstown-2m

2004	FOREMAN 6-11-10	8
2005	MACS JOY 6-11-10	6
2006	BRAVE INCA 8-11-10	7
2007	HARDY EUSTACE 10-11-10	8
2008	SIZING EUROPE 6-11-10	9
2009	BRAVE INCA 11-11-10	9
2010	SOLWHIT 6-11-10	7
2011	HURRICANE FLY 7-11-10	5
2012	HURRICANE FLY 8-11-10	5
2013	HURRICANE FLY 9-11-10	5

HENNESSY GOLD CUP
Leopardstown-3m

2004	FLORIDA PEARL 12-11-12	7
2005	RULE SUPREME 9-11-12	7
2006	BEEF OR SALMON 10-11-12	7
2007	BEEF OR SALMON 11-11-12	5
2008	THE LISTENER 9-11-10	8
2009	NEPTUNE COLLONGES 8-11-10	6
2010	JONCOL 7-11-10	7
2011	KEMPES 8-11-10	9
2012	QUEL ESPRIT 8-11-10	7
2013	SIR DES CHAMPS 7-11-10	4

IRISH GRAND NATIONAL
Fairyhouse-3m 5f

2003	TIMBERA 9-10-12	21
2004	GRANIT D'ESTRUVAL 10-10-0	28
2005	NUMBERSIXVALVERDE 9-10-1	26
2006	POINT BARROW 8-10-8	26
2007	BUTLER'S CABIN 7-10-4	29
2008	HEAR THE ECHO 7-10-0	23
2009	NICHE MARKET 8-10-5	30
2010	BLUESEA CRACKER 8-10-4	26
2011	ORGANISEDCONFUSION 6-9-13	25
2012	LION NA BEARNAI 10-10-5	29

WINNERS OF PRINCIPAL RACES IN FRANCE

PRIX GANAY
Longchamp–1m 2f 110yds
2003	**FAIR MIX** 5-9-2	9
2004	**EXECUTE** 7-9-2	8
2005	**BAGO** 4-9-2	9
2006	**CORRE CAMINOS** 4-9-2	7
2007	**DYLAN THOMAS** 4-9-2	8
2008	**DUKE OF MARMALADE** 4-9-2	6
2009	**VISION D'ETAT** 4-9-2	8
2010	**CUTLASS BAY** 4-9-2	9
2011	**PLANTEUR** 4-9-2	7
2012	**CIRRUS DES AIGLES** 6-9-2	6

POULE D'ESSAI DES POULAINS (3y)
Longchamp–1m
2003	**CLODOVIL** 9-2	10
2004	**AMERICAN POST** 9-2	7
2005	**SHAMARDAL** 9-2	15
2006	**AUSSIE RULES** 9-2	11
2007	**ASTRONOMER ROYAL** 9-2	14
2008	**FALCO** 9-2	19
2009	**SILVER FROST** 9-2	6
2010	**LOPE DE VEGA** 9-2	15
2011	**TIN HORSE** 9-2	14
2012	**LUCAYAN** 9-2	12

POULE D'ESSAI DES POULICHES (3y filllies)
Longchamp–1m
2003	**MUSICAL CHIMES** 9-0	12
2004	**TORRESTRELLA** 9-0	13
2005	**DIVINE PROPORTIONS** 9-0	8
*2006	**TIE BLACK** 9-0	13
2007	**DARJINA** 9-0	13
2008	**ZARKAVA** 9-0	14
2009	**ELUSIVE WAVE** 9-0	11
**2010	**SPECIAL DUTY** 9-0	10
2011	**GOLDEN LILAC** 9-0	16
2012	**BEAUTY PARLOUR** 9-0	13

*Price Tag disqualified from first place
**Liliside disqualified from first place

PRIX SAINT-ALARY (3y fillies)
Longchamp–1m 2f
2003	**FIDELITE** 9-0	9
2004	**ASK FOR THE MOON** 9-0	7
2005	**VADAWINA** 9-0	8
2006	**GERMANCE** 9-0	8
2007	**COQUERELLE** 9-0	6
2008	**BELLE ET CELEBRE** 9-0	7
2009	**STACELITA** 9-0	7
2010	**SARAFINA** 9-0	9
2011	**WAVERING** 9-0	12
2012	**SAGAWARA** 9-0	8

PRIX JEAN PRAT (3y)
Chantilly–1m (1m 1f before 2005)
2003	**VESPONE** 9-2	8
2004	**BAGO** 9-2	8
2005	**TURTLE BOWL** 9-2	8
2006	**STORMY RIVER** 9-2	11
2007	**LAWMAN** 9-2	7
2008	**TAMAYUZ** 9-2	16
2009	**LORD SHANAKILL** 9-2	9
2010	**DICK TURPIN** 9-2	8
2011	**MUTUAL TRUST** 9-2	7
2012	**AESOP'S FABLES** 9-2	8

PRIX D'ISPAHAN
Longchamp–1m 1f 55yds
2003	**FALBRAV** 5-9-2	8
2004	**PRINCE KIRK** 4-9-2	5
2005	**VALIXIR** 4-9-2	8
2006	**LAVEROCK** 4-9-2	11
2007	**MANDURO** 5-9-2	5
2008	**SAGEBURG** 4-9-2	6
2009	**NEVER ON SUNDAY** 4-9-2	9
2010	**GOLDIKOVA** 5-8-13	8
2011	**GOLDIKOVA** 6-8-13	9
2012	**GOLDEN LILAC** 4-8-13	8

PRIX DU JOCKEY CLUB (3y)
Chantilly–1m 2f 110yds (1m 4f before 2005)
2003	**DALAKHANI** 9-2	7
2004	**BLUE CANARI** 9-2	15
2005	**SHAMARDAL** 9-2	17
2006	**DARSI** 9-2	15
2007	**LAWMAN** 9-2	20
2008	**VISION D'ETAT** 9-2	20
2009	**LE HAVRE** 9-2	17
2010	**LOPE DE VEGA** 9-2	22
2011	**RELIABLE MAN** 9-2	16
2012	**SAONOIS** 9-2	20

PRIX DE DIANE (3y fillies)
Chantilly–1m 2f 110yds
2003	**NEBRASKA TORNADO** 9-0	10
2004	**LATICE** 9-0	17
2005	**DIVINE PROPORTIONS** 9-0	10
2006	**CONFIDENTIAL LADY** 9-0	16
2007	**WEST WIND** 9-0	14
2008	**ZARKAVA** 9-0	13
2009	**STACELITA** 9-0	12
2010	**SARAFINA** 9-0	9
2011	**GOLDEN LILAC** 9-0	9
2012	**VALYRA** 9-0	12

GRAND PRIX DE PARIS (3y)
Longchamp–1m 4f (1m 2f before 2005)
2003	**VESPONE** 9-2	11
2004	**BAGO** 9-2	4
2005	**SCORPION** 9-2	9
2006	**RAIL LINK** 9-2	9
2007	**ZAMBEZI SUN** 9-2	7
2008	**MONTMARTRE** 9-2	13
2009	**CAVALRYMAN** 9-2	8
2010	**BEHKABAD** 9-2	9
2011	**MEANDRE** 9-2	7
2012	**IMPERIAL MONARCH** 9-2	9

GRAND PRIX DE SAINT-CLOUD
Saint-Cloud-1m 4f
2003	ANGE GABRIEL 5-9-9	10
2004	GAMUT 5-9-9	10
2005	ALKAASED 5-9-2	11
2006	PRIDE 6-8-13	6
2007	MOUNTAIN HIGH 5-9-2	6
2008	YOUMZAIN 5-9-2	9
2009	SPANISH MOON 5-9-2	10
2010	PLUMANIA 4-8-13	7
2011	SARAFINA 4-8-13	5
2012	MEANDRE 4-9-2	4

PRIX MAURICE DE GHEEST
Deauville-6f 110yds
2003	PORLEZZA 4-8-12	12
2004	SOMNUS 4-9-2	18
2005	WHIPPER 4-9-2	13
2006	MARCHAND D'OR 3-8-11	17
2007	MARCHAND D'OR 4-9-2	13
2008	MARCHAND D'OR 5-9-2	16
2009	KING'S APOSTLE 5-9-2	12
2010	REGAL PARADE 6-9-2	15
2011	MOONLIGHT CLOUD 3-8-8	13
2012	MOONLIGHT CLOUD 4-8-13	9

PRIX JACQUES LE MAROIS
Deauville-1m
2003	SIX PERFECTIONS 3-8-9	12
2004	WHIPPER 3-8-11	10
2005	DUBAWI 3-8-11	6
2006	LIBRETTIST 4-9-4	10
2007	MANDURO 5-9-4	9
2008	TAMAYUZ 3-8-11	8
2009	GOLDIKOVA 4-9-0	9
2010	MAKFI 3-8-11	8
2011	IMMORTAL VERSE 3-8-8	12
2012	EXCELEBRATION 4-9-4	11

PRIX MORNY (2y)
Deauville-6f
2003	WHIPPER 9-0	8
2004	DIVINE PROPORTIONS 8-11	9
2005	SILCA'S SISTER 8-11	7
2006	DUTCH ART 9-0	7
2007	MYBOYCHARLIE 8-13	6
2008	BUSHRANGER 9-0	14
2009	ARCANO 9-0	5
2010	DREAM AHEAD 9-0	11
2011	DABIRSIM 9-0	7
2012	RECKLESS ABANDON 9-0	11

PRIX DU MOULIN DE LONGCHAMP
Longchamp-1m
2003	NEBRASKA TORNADO 3-8-8	14
2004	GREY LILAS 3-8-8	11
2005	STARCRAFT 5-9-2	9
2006	LIBRETTIST 4-9-2	8
2007	DARJINA 3-8-8	9
2008	GOLDIKOVA 3-8-8	11
2009	AQLAAM 4-9-2	6
2010	FUISSE 4-9-2	6
2011	EXCELEBRATION 3-8-11	8
2012	MOONLIGHT CLOUD 4-8-13	4

CRITERIUM INTERNATIONAL (2y)
Saint-Cloud-1m
2003	BAGO 9-0	7
2004	HELIOS QUERCUS 9-0	8
2005	CARLOTAMIX 9-0	6
2006	MOUNT NELSON 9-0	10
2007	THEWAYYOUARE 9-0	6
2008	ZAFISIO 9-0	11
2009	JAN VERMEER 9-0	7
2010	RODERIC O'CONNOR 9-0	10
2011	FRENCH FIFTEEN 9-0	11
2012	LOCH GARMAN 9-0	6

PRIX VERMEILLE (fillies and mares)
Longchamp-1m 4f
(for 3yo fillies only prior to 2004)
2003	MEZZO SOPRANO 9-0	11
2004	SWEET STREAM 4-9-2	13
2005	SHAWANDA 3-8-7	6
2006	MANDESHA 3-8-7	11
2007	MRS LINDSAY 3-8-9	10
2008	ZARKAVA 3-8-8	12
*2009	STACELITA 3-8-8	12
2010	MIDDAY 4-9-3	12
2011	GALIKOVA 3-8-8	6
2012	SHARETA 4-9-2	13

*Dar Re Mi disqualified from first place

PRIX DU CADRAN
Longchamp-2m 4f
2003	WESTERNER 4-9-2	10
2004	WESTERNER 5-9-6	8
2005	REEFSCAPE 4-9-2	10
2006	SERGEANT CECIL 7-9-2	7
2007	LE MIRACLE 6-9-2	6
2008	BANNABY 5-9-2	11
2009	ALANDI 4-9-2	12
2010	GENTOO 6-9-2	8
2011	KASBAH BLISS 9-9-2	10
2012	MOLLY MALONE 4-8-13	10

PRIX DE L'ABBAYE DE LONGCHAMP
Longchamp-5f
2003	PATAVELLIAN 5-9-11	19
2004	VAR 5-9-11	15
2005	AVONBRIDGE 5-9-11	17
2006	DESERT LORD 6-9-11	14
2007	BENBAUN 6-9-11	17
*2008	MARCHAND D'OR 5-9-11	17
2009	TOTAL GALLERY 3-9-11	16
2010	GILT EDGE GIRL 4-9-7	21
2011	TANGERINE TREES 6-9-11	15
2012	WIZZ KID 4-9-7	18

* re-run; Overdose won void first running

PRIX MARCEL BOUSSAC (2y fillies)
Longchamp-1m
2003	DENEBOLA 8-11	16
2004	DIVINE PROPORTIONS 8-11	10
2005	RUMPLESTILTSKIN 8-11	15
2006	FINSCEAL BEO 8-11	13
2007	ZARKAVA 8-11	10
2008	PROPORTIONAL 8-11	16
2009	ROSANARA 8-11	11
2010	MISTY FOR ME 8-11	8
2011	ELUSIVE KATE 8-11	5
2012	SILASOL 8-11	9

PRIX JEAN-LUC LAGARDERE (2y)
(Grand Criterium before 2003)
Longchamp-7f
2003	**AMERICAN POST** 9-0	6
2004	**ORATORIO** 9-0	6
2005	**HORATIO NELSON** 9-0	6
2006	**HOLY ROMAN EMPEROR** 9-0	9
2007	**RIO DE LA PLATA** 9-0	8
2008	**NAAQOOS** 9-0	7
2009	**SIYOUNI** 9-0	7
2010	**WOOTTON BASSETT** 9-0	9
2011	**DABIRSIM** 9-0	7
2012	**OLYMPIC GLORY** 9-0	8

PRIX DE LA FORET
Longchamp-7f
2003	**ETOILE MONTANTE** 3-8-11	10
2004	**SOMNUS** 4-9-2	7
2005	**COURT MASTERPIECE** 5-9-2	8
2006	**CARADAK** 5-9-3	14
2007	**TOYLSOME** 8-9-2	13
2008	**PACO BOY** 3-9-0	8
2009	**VARENAR** 3-9-0	14
2010	**GOLDIKOVA** 5-8-13	10
2011	**DREAM AHEAD** 3-9-0	8
2012	**GORDON LORD BYRON** 4-9-2	11

PRIX ROYAL-OAK
Longchamp-1m 7f 110yds
2003	**WESTERNER** 4-9-4	14
2004	**WESTERNER** 5-9-4	8
2005	**ALCAZAR** 10-9-4	11
2006	**MONTARE** 4-9-1	10
2007	**ALLEGRETTO** 4-9-1	11
2008	**YEATS** 7-9-4	11
2009	**ASK** 6-9-4	9
2010	**GENTOO** 6-9-4	10
2011	**BE FABULOUS** 4-9-1	14
2012	**LES BEAUFS** 3-8-9	9

CRITERIUM DE SAINT-CLOUD (2y)
Saint-Cloud-1m 2f
2003	**VOIX DU NORD** 9-0	10
2004	**PAITA** 8-11	7
2005	**LINDA'S LAD** 9-0	5
2006	**PASSAGE OF TIME** 8-11	13
2007	**FULL OF GOLD** 9-0	6
2008	**FAME AND GLORY** 9-0	11
2009	**PASSION FOR GOLD** 9-0	9
2010	**RECITAL** 9-0	10
2011	**MANDAEAN** 9-0	8
2012	**MORANDI** 9-0	8

WINNERS OF OTHER OVERSEAS RACES

DUBAI WORLD CUP
Meydan-1m 2f Tapeta
(Run at Nad Al Sheba over 1m 2f on dirt before 2010)
2003	**MOON BALLAD** 4-9-0	11
2004	**PLEASANTLY PERFECT** 6-9-0	12
2005	**ROSES IN MAY** 5-9-0	12
2006	**ELECTROCUTIONIST** 5-9-0	11
2007	**INVASOR** 5-9-0	7
2008	**CURLIN** 4-9-0	12
2009	**WELL ARMED** 6-9-0	14
2010	**GLORIA DE CAMPEAO** 7-9-0	14
2011	**VICTOIRE PISA** 4-9-0	14
2012	**MONTEROSSO** 5-9-0	13

KENTUCKY DERBY
Churchill Downs-1m 2f dirt
2003	**FUNNY CIDE** 9-0	16
2004	**SMARTY JONES** 9-0	18
2005	**GIACOMO** 9-0	20
2006	**BARBARO** 9-0	20
2007	**STREET SENSE** 9-0	20
2008	**BIG BROWN** 9-0	20
2009	**MINE THAT BIRD** 9-0	19
2010	**SUPER SAVER** 9-0	20
2011	**ANIMAL KINGDOM** 9-0	19
2012	**I'LL HAVE ANOTHER** 9-0	20

BREEDERS' CUP TURF
Various courses-1m 4f
2003	**JOHAR** 4-9-0 dead heated with **HIGH CHAPARRAL** 4-9-0	9
2004	**BETTER TALK NOW** 5-9-0	8
2005	**SHIROCCO** 4-9-0	13

2006	**RED ROCKS** 3-8-10	11
2007	**ENGLISH CHANNEL** 5-9-0	8
2008	**CONDUIT** 3-8-9	11
2009	**CONDUIT** 4-9-0	7
2010	**DANGEROUS MIDGE** 4-9-0	7
2011	**ST NICHOLAS ABBEY** 4-9-0	9
2012	**LITTLE MIKE** 5-9-0	12

BREEDERS' CUP CLASSIC
Various courses-1m 2f dirt/pro-ride
2003	**PLEASANTLY PERFECT** 5-9-0	10
2004	**GHOSTZAPPER** 4-9-0	13
2005	**SAINT LIAM** 5-9-0	13
2006	**INVASOR** 4-9-0	13
2007	**CURLIN** 3-8-9	9
2008	**RAVEN'S PASS** 3-8-9	12
2009	**ZENYATTA** 5-8-11	12
2010	**BLAME** 4-9-0	12
2011	**DROSSELMEYER** 4-9-0	12
2012	**FORT LARNED** 4-9-0	12

MELBOURNE CUP
Flemington-2m
2003	**MAKYBE DIVA** 4-8-0	23
2004	**MAKYBE DIVA** 5-8-11	24
2005	**MAKYBE DIVA** 6-9-2	24
2006	**DELTA BLUES** 5-8-11	23
2007	**EFFICIENT** 4-8-8	21
2008	**VIEWED** 5-8-5	24
2009	**SHOCKING** 4-8-0	23
2010	**AMERICAIN** 5-8-8	23
2011	**DUNADEN** 5-8-8	23
2012	**GREEN MOON** 5-8-6	24

JAPAN CUP
Tokyo-1m 4f
2003 **TAP DANCE CITY** 6-9-0.................................18
2004 **ZENNO ROB ROY** 4-9-0...............................16
2005 **ALKAASED** 5-9-0.......................................18
2006 **DEEP IMPACT** 4-9-0...................................11
2007 **ADMIRE MOON** 4-9-0..................................18

2008 **SCREEN HERO** 4-9-0..................................17
2009 **VODKA** 5-8-10..18
*2010 **ROSE KINGDOM** 3-8-9...............................18
2011 **BUENA VISTA** 5-8-9...................................16
2012 **GENTILDONNA** 3-8-5..................................17
*Buena Vista disqualified from first place

WINNERS OF PRINCIPAL NATIONAL HUNT RACES

PADDY POWER GOLD CUP
(H'cap Chase)
Cheltenham-2m 4f 110yds
2003 **FONDMORT** 7-10-13...................................9
2004 **CELESTIAL GOLD** 6-10-2.............................14
2005 **OUR VIC** 7-11-7.......................................18
2006 **EXOTIC DANCER** 6-11-2.............................16
2007 **L'ANTARTIQUE** 7-10-13.............................20
2008 **IMPERIAL COMMANDER** 7-10-7....................19
2009 **TRANQUIL SEA** 7-10-13.............................16
2010 **LITTLE JOSH** 8-10-5.................................18
2011 **GREAT ENDEAVOUR** 7-10-3.........................20
2012 **AL FEROF** 7-11-8.....................................18

BETFAIR CHASE
Haydock-3m
2005 **KINGSCLIFF** 8-11-8..................................
2006 **KAUTO STAR** 6-11-8.................................6
2007 **KAUTO STAR** 7-11-7.................................6
2008 **SNOOPY LOOPY** 10-11-7............................6
2009 **KAUTO STAR** 9-11-7.................................7
2010 **IMPERIAL COMMANDER** 9-11-7....................7
2011 **KAUTO STAR** 11-11-7...............................6
2012 **SILVINIACO CONTI** 6-11-7..........................5

HENNESSY GOLD CUP
H'CAP CHASE
Newbury-3m 2f 110yds
2003 **STRONG FLOW** 6-11-0...............................21
2004 **CELESTIAL GOLD** 6-10-5............................14
2005 **TRABOLGAN** 7-11-12................................19
2006 **STATE OF PLAY** 6-11-4.............................16
2007 **DENMAN** 7-11-12.....................................18
2008 **MADISON DU BERLAIS** 7-11-4......................15
2009 **DENMAN** 9-11-12.....................................19
2010 **DIAMOND HARRY** 7-10-0............................20
2011 **CARRUTHERS** 8-10-4................................18
2012 **BOBS WORTH** 7-11-6................................19

TINGLE CREEK CHASE
Sandown-2m
2003 **MOSCOW FLYER** 9-11-7.............................7
2004 **MOSCOW FLYER** 10-11-7...........................7
2005 **KAUTO STAR** 5-11-7.................................7
2006 **KAUTO STAR** 6-11-7.................................7
2007 **TWIST MAGIC** 5-11-7...............................8
2008 **MASTER MINDED** 5-11-7............................7
2009 **TWIST MAGIC** 7-11-7...............................7
*2010 **MASTER MINDED** 7-11-7...........................9
2011 **SIZING EUROPE** 9-11-7.............................7
2012 **SPRINTER SACRE** 6-11-7...........................7
*Run at Cheltenham over 2m 110yds

CHRISTMAS HURDLE
Kempton-2m
2003 **INTERSKY FALCON** 6-11-7.........................6
2004 **HARCHIBALD** 5-11-7.................................7
*2005 **FEATHARD LADY** 5-11-0............................7
2006 **JAZZ MESSENGER** 6-11-7..........................7
2007 **STRAW BEAR** 6-11-7................................6
2008 **HARCHIBALD** 9-11-7.................................7
2009 **GO NATIVE** 6-11-7...................................7
2010 **BINOCULAR 7-11-7.................................6
2011 **BINOCULAR** 7-11-7...................................5
2012 **DARLAN** 5-11-7.......................................7
*Run at Sandown
**Run in January 2011

KING GEORGE VI CHASE
Kempton-3m
2003 **EDREDON BLEU** 11-11-10...........................12
2004 **KICKING KING** 6-11-10..............................13
*2005 **KICKING KING** 7-11-10.............................9
2006 **KAUTO STAR** 6-11-10...............................9
2007 **KAUTO STAR** 7-11-10...............................7
2008 **KAUTO STAR** 8-11-10...............................10
2009 **KAUTO STAR** 9-11-10...............................13
2010 **LONG RUN 6-11-10.................................9
2011 **KAUTO STAR** 11-11-10.............................7
2012 **LONG RUN** 7-11-10..................................9
*Run at Sandown
**Run in January 2011

WELSH NATIONAL H'CAP CHASE
Chepstow-3m 5f 110yds
2003 **BINDAREE** 9-10-9....................................14
2004 **SILVER BIRCH** 7-10-5...............................17
2005 **L'AVENTURE** 6-10-4.................................18
2006 **HALCON GENELARDAIS** 6-11-3....................18
2007 **MIKO DE BEAUCHENE** 7-10-5......................18
2008 **NOTRE PERE** 7-11-0.................................20
2009 **DREAM ALLIANCE** 8-10-8...........................18
*2010 **SYNCHRONISED** 8-11-6............................18
2011 **LE BEAU BAI** 8-10-1.................................20
2012 **MONBEG DUDE 8-10-1.............................17
*Run in January 2011
**Run in January 2013

VICTOR CHANDLER CHASE
(Handicap before 2008)
Ascot-2m 1f (2m before 2008)
2004 **ISIO** 8-10-5...13
*2005 **WELL CHIEF** 6-11-10...............................10
*2006 **TYSOU** 9-11-2.......................................10
2007 ABANDONED

2008	**TAMARINBLEU** 8-11-7	7
2009	**MASTER MINDED** 6-11-7	5
2010	**TWIST MAGIC** 8-11-7	7
2011	**MASTER MINDED** 8-11-7	9
2012	**SOMERSBY** 8-11-7	8
*2013	**SPRINTER SACRE** 7-11-7	7

*Run at Cheltenham over 2m 110yds
**Run at Sandown over 2m

BETFAIR H'CAP HURDLE
Newbury-2m 110yds
(Tote Gold Tophy until 2004,
Totesport Trophy 2005-2011)

2004	**GEOS** 9-10-9	25
2005	**ESSEX** 5-11-6	25
2006	ABANDONED	
2007	**HEATHCOTE** 5-10-6	20
2008	**WINGMAN** 6-10-0	24
2009	ABANDONED	
2010	**GET ME OUT OF HERE** 6-10-6	23
2011	**RECESSION PROOF** 5-10-8	15
2012	**ZARKANDAR** 5-11-1	20
2013	**MY TENT OR YOURS** 6-11-2	21

SUPREME NOVICES' HURDLE
Cheltenham-2m 110yds

2003	**BACK IN FRONT** 6-11-8	19
2004	**BRAVE INCA** 6-11-7	19
2005	**ARCALIS** 5-11-7	20
2006	**NOLAND** 5-11-7	20
2007	**EBAZIYAN** 6-11-7	22
2008	**CAPTAIN CEE BEE** 7-11-7	22
2009	**GO NATIVE** 6-11-7	20
2010	**MENORAH** 5-11-7	18
2011	**AL FEROF** 6-11-7	15
2012	**CINDERS AND ASHES** 5-11-7	19

ARKLE CHALLENGE TROPHY (NOVICES' CHASE)
Cheltenham-2m

2003	**AZERTYUIOP** 6-11-8	9
2004	**WELL CHIEF** 5-11-3	16
2005	**CONTRABAND** 8-11-7	19
2006	**VOY POR USTEDES** 5-11-2	14
2007	**MY WAY DE SOLZEN** 7-11-7	13
2008	**TIDAL BAY** 7-11-7	14
2009	**FORPADYDEPLASTERER** 7-11-7	17
2010	**SIZING EUROPE** 8-11-7	12
2011	**CAPTAIN CHRIS** 7-11-7	10
2012	**SPRINTER SACRE** 7-11-7	6

CHAMPION HURDLE
Cheltenham-2m 110yds

2003	**ROOSTER BOOSTER** 9-12-0	17
2004	**HARDY EUSTACE** 7-11-10	14
2005	**HARDY EUSTACE** 8-11-10	14
2006	**BRAVE INCA** 8-11-10	18
2007	**SUBLIMITY** 7-11-10	10
2008	**KATCHIT** 5-11-10	15
2009	**PUNJABI** 6-11-10	23
2010	**BINOCULAR** 6-11-10	12
2011	**HURRICANE FLY** 7-11-10	11
2012	**ROCK ON RUBY** 7-11-10	10

QUEEN MOTHER CHAMPION CHASE
Cheltenham-2m

2003	**MOSCOW FLYER** 9-12-0	11
2004	**AZERTYUIOP** 7-11-10	8
2005	**MOSCOW FLYER** 11-11-10	8
2006	**NEWMILL** 8-11-10	12
2007	**VOY POR USTEDES** 6-11-10	10
2008	**MASTER MINDED** 5-11-10	8
2009	**MASTER MINDED** 6-11-10	12
2010	**BIG ZEB** 9-11-10	9
2011	**SIZING EUROPE** 9-11-10	11
2012	**FINIAN'S RAINBOW** 9-11-10	8

NEPTUNE INVESTMENT MANAGEMENT NOVICES' HURDLE
(Royal & SunAlliance Hurdle until 2007,
Ballymore Hurdle 2008-9)
Cheltenham-2m 5f

2003	**HARDY EUSTACE** 6-11-7	19
2004	**FUNDAMENTALIST** 6-11-7	15
2005	**NO REFUGE** 5-11-7	20
2006	**NICANOR** 5-11-7	17
2007	**MASSINI'S MAGUIRE** 6-11-7	15
2008	**FIVEFORTHREE** 6-11-7	15
2009	**MIKAEL D'HAGUENET** 5-11-7	14
2010	**PEDDLERS CROSS** 5-11-7	17
2011	**FIRST LIEUTENANT** 6-11-7	12
2012	**SIMONSIG** 6-11-7	17

RSA CHASE
(Royal & SunAlliance Chase before 2009)
(Cheltenham-3m

2003	**ONE KNIGHT** 7-11-4	9
2004	**RULE SUPREME** 8-11-4	10
2005	**TRABOLGAN** 7-11-4	9
2006	**STAR DE MOHAISON** 5-10-8	15
2007	**DENMAN** 7-11-4	17
2008	**ALBERTAS RUN** 7-11-4	15
2009	**COOLDINE** 7-11-4	14
2010	**WEAPON'S AMNESTY** 7-11-4	9
2011	**BOSTONS ANGEL** 7-11-4	12
2012	**BOBS WORTH** 7-11-4	9

WORLD HURDLE
(Stayers' Hurdle before 2005)
Cheltenham-3m

2003	**BARACOUDA** 8-11-10	11
2004	**IRIS'S GIFT** 7-11-10	10
2005	**INGLIS DREVER** 6-11-10	12
2006	**MY WAY DE SOLZEN** 6-11-10	20
2007	**INGLIS DREVER** 8-11-10	14
2008	**INGLIS DREVER** 9-11-10	17
2009	**BIG BUCK'S** 6-11-10	14
2010	**BIG BUCK'S** 7-11-10	14
2011	**BIG BUCK'S** 8-11-10	13
2012	**BIG BUCK'S** 9-11-10	11

TRIUMPH HURDLE (4y)
Cheltenham-2m 1f

2003	**SPECTROSCOPE** 11-0	27
2004	**MADE IN JAPAN** 11-0	23
2005	**PENZANCE** 11-0	23
2006	**DETROIT CITY** 11-0	17
2007	**KATCHIT** 11-0	17
2008	**CELESTIAL HALO** 11-0	14
2009	**ZAYNAR** 11-0	18
2010	**SOLDATINO** 11-0	17
2011	**ZARKANDAR** 11-0	23
2012	**COUNTRYWIDE FLAME** 11-0	20

CHELTENHAM GOLD CUP
Cheltenham-3m 2f 110yds
2003	**BEST MATE** 8-12-0	15
2004	**BEST MATE** 9-11-10	10
2005	**KICKING KING** 7-11-10	15
2006	**WAR OF ATTRITION** 7-11-10	22
2007	**KAUTO STAR** 7-11-10	18
2008	**DENMAN** 8-11-10	12
2009	**KAUTO STAR** 9-11-10	16
2010	**IMPERIAL COMMANDER** 9-11-10	11
2011	**LONG RUN** 6-11-0	13
2012	**SYNCHRONISED** 9-11-10	14

RYANAIR CHASE (FESTIVAL TROPHY)
Cheltenham-2m 5f
2005	**THISTHATANDTOTHER** 9-11-3	12
2006	**FONDMORT** 10-11-0	11
2007	**TARANIS** 6-11-0	9
2008	**OUR VIC** 10-11-10	9
2009	**IMPERIAL COMMANDER** 8-11-10	10
2010	**ALBERTAS RUN** 9-11-10	13
2011	**ALBERTAS RUN** 10-11-10	11
2012	**RIVERSIDE THEATRE** 8-11-10	12

BETFRED BOWL CHASE
(Martell Cup Chase before 2005)
(Betfair Bowl Chase 2005-8)
(Totesport Bowl Chase 2009-11)
Aintree-3m 1f
2003	**FIRST GOLD** 10-11-12	7
2004	**TIUTCHEV** 11-11-12	8
2005	**GREY ABBEY** 11-11-12	8
2006	**CELESTIAL GOLD** 8-11-8	9
2007	**EXOTIC DANCER** 7-11-12	5
2008	**OUR VIC** 10-11-10	5
2009	**MADISON DU BERLAIS** 8-11-10	10
2010	**WHAT A FRIEND** 7-11-7	5
2011	**NACARAT** 10-11-7	6
2012	**FOLLOW THE PLAN** 9-11-7	11

MELLING CHASE
Aintree-2m 4f
2003	**NATIVE UPMANSHIP** 10-11-10	6
2004	**MOSCOW FLYER** 10-11-10	7
2005	**MOSCOW FLYER** 11-11-10	6
2006	**HI CLOY** 9-11-10	11
2007	**MONET'S GARDEN** 9-11-10	6
2008	**VOY POR USTEDES** 7-11-10	6
2009	**VOY POR USTEDES** 8-11-10	10
2010	**ALBERTAS RUN** 9-11-10	11

2011	**MASTER MINDED** 8-11-10	10
2012	**FINIAN'S RAINBOW** 9-11-10	8

AINTREE HURDLE
Aintree-2m 4f
2003	**SACUNDAI** 6-11-7	11
2004	**RHINESTONE COWBOY** 8-11-7	11
2005	**AL EILE** 5-11-7	9
2006	**ASIAN MAZE** 7-11-0	9
2007	**AL EILE** 7-11-7	11
2008	**AL EILE** 8-11-7	9
2009	**SOLWHIT** 5-11-7	16
2010	**KHYBER KIM** 8-11-7	7
2011	**OSCAR WHISKY** 6-11-7	8
2012	**OSCAR WHISKY** 7-11-7	5

SCOTTISH GRAND NATIONAL (H'CAP CHASE)
Ayr-4m 110 yds (4m 1f before 2007)
2003	**RYALUX** 10-10-5	19
2004	**GREY ABBEY** 10-11-12	28
2005	**JOES EDGE** 8-9-11	20
2006	**RUN FOR PADDY** 10-10-2	30
2007	**HOT WELD** 8-9-9	23
2008	**IRIS DE BALME** 8-9-7	24
2009	**HELLO BUD** 11-10-9	17
2010	**MERIGO** 9-10-0	30
2011	**BESHABAR** 9-10-4	28
2012	**MERIGO** 11-10-2	24

BET365 GOLD CUP (H'CAP CHASE)
(Attheraces Gold Cup 2002-3,
Betfred Gold Cup 2004-7)
Sandown-3m 5f 110yds
2003	**AD HOC** 9-10-10	16
2004	**PUNTAL** 8-11-4	18
2005	**JACK HIGH** 10-10-0	19
2006	**LACDOUDAL** 7-11-5	18
2007	**HOT WELD** 8-10-0	10
2008	**MONKERHOSTIN** 11-10-13	19
2009	**HENNESSY** 8-10-7	14
2010	**CHURCH ISLAND** 11-10-5	19
2011	**POKER DE SIVOLA** 8-10-12	18
2012	**TIDAL BAY** 11-11-12	19

DISTANCE CONVERSION
5f	1,000m	10f	2,000m	15f	3,000m	20f	4,000m
6f	1,200m	11f	2,200m	16f	3,200m	21f	4,200m
7f	1,400m	12f	2,400m	17f	3,400m	22f	4,400m
8f	1,600m	13f	2,600m	18f	3,600m		
9f	1,800m	14f	2,800m	19f	3,800m		

LEADING TRAINERS ON THE FLAT: 1898-2012

1898 R Marsh	1937 C Boyd-Rochfort	1976 H Cecil
1899 J Porter	1938 C Boyd-Rochfort	1977 M V O'Brien
1900 R Marsh	1939 J L Jarvis	1978 H Cecil
1901 J Huggins	1940 F Darling	1979 H Cecil
1902 R S Sievier	1941 F Darling	1980 W Hern
1903 G Blackwell	1942 F Darling	1981 M Stoute
1904 P P Gilpin	1943 W Nightingall	1982 H Cecil
1905 W T Robinson	1944 Frank Butters	1983 W Hern
1906 Hon G Lambton	1945 W Earl	1984 H Cecil
1907 A Taylor	1946 Frank Butters	1985 H Cecil
1908 C Morton	1947 F Darling	1986 M Stoute
1909 A Taylor	1948 C F N Murless	1987 H Cecil
1910 A Taylor	1949 Frank Butters	1988 H Cecil
1911 Hon G Lambton	1950 C H Semblat	1989 M Stoute
1912 Hon G Lambton	1951 J L Jarvis	1990 H Cecil
1913 R Wootton	1952 M Marsh	1991 P Cole
1914 A Taylor	1953 J L Jarvis	1992 R Hannon
1915 P P Gilpin	1954 C Boyd-Rochfort	1993 H Cecil
1916 R C Dawson	1955 C Boyd-Rochfort	1994 M Stoute
1917 A Taylor	1956 C F Elsey	1995 J Dunlop
1918 A Taylor	1957 C F N Murless	1996 Saeed bin Suroor
1919 A Taylor	1958 C Boyd-Rochfort	1997 M Stoute
1920 A Taylor	1959 C F N Murless	1998 Saeed bin Suroor
1921 A Taylor	1960 C F N Murless	1999 Saeed bin Suroor
1922 A Taylor	1961 C F N Murless	2000 Sir M Stoute
1923 A Taylor	1962 W Hern	2001 A O'Brien
1924 R C Dawson	1963 P Prendergast	2002 A O'Brien
1925 A Taylor	1964 P Prendergast	2003 Sir M Stoute
1926 F Darling	1965 P Prendergast	2004 Saeed bin Suroor
1927 Frank Butters	1966 M V O'Brien	2005 Sir M Stoute
1928 Frank Butters	1967 C F N Murless	2006 Sir M Stoute
1929 R C Dawson	1968 C F N Murless	2007 A O'Brien
1930 H S Persse	1969 A M Budgett	2008 A O'Brien
1931 J Lawson	1970 C F N Murless	2009 Sir M. Stoute
1932 Frank Butters	1971 I Balding	2010 R Hannon
1933 F Darling	1972 W Hern	2011 R Hannon
1934 Frank Butters	1973 C F N Murless	2012 J Gosden
1935 Frank Butters	1974 P Walwyn	
1936 J Lawson	1975 P Walwyn	

CHAMPION JOCKEYS ON THE FLAT: 1896-2012

1896 M Cannon 164	1918 S Donoghue 66	1939 G Richards 155
1897 M Cannon 145	1919 S Donoghue 129	1940 G Richards 68
1898 O Madden 161	1920 S Donoghue 143	1941 H Wragg 71
1899 S Loates 160	1921 S Donoghue 141	1942 G Richards 67
1900 L Reiff 143	1922 S Donoghue 102	1943 G Richards 65
1901 O Madden 130	1923 S Donoghue 89	1944 G Richards 88
1902 W Lane 170	C Elliott 89	1945 G Richards 104
1903 O Madden 154	1924 C Elliott 106	1946 G Richards 212
1904 O Madden 161	1925 G Richards 118	1947 G Richards 269
1905 E Wheatley 124	1926 T Weston 95	1948 G Richards 224
1906 W Higgs 149	1927 G Richards 164	1949 G Richards 261
1907 W Higgs 146	1928 G Richards 148	1950 G Richards 201
1908 D Maher 139	1929 G Richards 135	1951 G Richards 227
1909 F Wootton 165	1930 F Fox 129	1952 G Richards 231
1910 F Wootton 137	1931 G Richards 145	1953 G Richards 191
1911 F Wootton 187	1932 G Richards 190	1954 D Smith 129
1912 F Wootton 118	1933 G Richards 259	1955 D Smith 168
1913 D Maher 115	1934 G Richards 212	1956 D Smith 155
1914 S Donoghue 129	1935 G Richards 217	1957 A Breasley 173
1915 S Donoghue 62	1936 G Richards 174	1958 D Smith 165
1916 S Donoghue 43	1937 G Richards 216	1959 D Smith 157
1917 S Donoghue 42	1938 G Richards 206	1960 L Piggott 170

1961 A Breasley 171	1979 J Mercer 164	1997 K Fallon 196
1962 A Breasley 179	1980 W Carson 166	1998 K Fallon 185
1963 A Breasley 176	1981 L Piggott 179	1999 K Fallon 200
1964 L Piggott 140	1982 L Piggott 188	2000 K Darley 152
1965 L Piggott.......................160	1983 W Carson 159	2001 K Fallon 166
1966 L Piggott.......................191	1984 S Cauthen 130	2002 K Fallon 144
1967 L Piggott.......................117	1985 S Cauthen 195	2003 K Fallon 208
1968 L Piggott.......................139	1986 Pat Eddery 176	2004 L Dettori 192
1969 L Piggott.......................163	1987 S Cauthen 197	2005 J Spencer 163
1970 L Piggott.......................162	1988 Pat Eddery 183	2006 R Moore 180
1971 L Piggott.......................162	1989 Pat Eddery 171	2007 S Sanders 190
1972 W Carson 132	1990 Pat Eddery 209	J Spencer 190
1973 W Carson 164	1991 Pat Eddery 165	2008 R Moore 186
1974 Pat Eddery 148	1992 M Roberts 206	2009 R Moore 174
1975 Pat Eddery 164	1993 Pat Eddery 169	2010 P Hanagan 191
1976 Pat Eddery 162	1994 L Dettori 233	2011 P Hanagan 165
1977 Pat Eddery 176	1995 L Dettori 211	2012 R Hughes 172
1978 W Carson 182	1996 Pat Eddery 186	

LEADING OWNERS ON THE FLAT: 1895-2012

1895 Ld de Rothschild	1935 H.H. Aga Khan	1975 Dr C Vittadini
1896 Ld de Rothschild	1936 Ld Astor	1976 Mr D Wildenstein
1897 Mr J Gubbins	1937 H.H. Aga Khan	1977 Mr R Sangster
1898 Ld de Rothschild	1938 Ld Derby	1978 Mr R Sangster
1899 Duke of Westminster	1939 Ld Rosebery	1979 Sir M Sobell
1900 H.R.H. The Prince of Wales	1940 Lord Rothermere	1980 S Weinstock
1901 Sir G Blundell Maple	1941 Ld Glanely	1981 H.H. Aga Khan
1902 Mr R S Sievier	1942 His Majesty	1982 Mr R Sangster
1903 Sir James Miller	1943 Miss D Paget	1983 Mr R Sangster
1904 Sir James Miller	1944 H.H. Aga Khan	1984 Mr R Sangster
1905 Col W Hall Walker	1945 Ld Derby	1985 Sheikh Mohammed
1906 Ld Derby (late)	1946 H.H. Aga Khan	1986 Sheikh Mohammed
1907 Col W Hall Walker	1947 H.H. Aga Khan	1987 Sheikh Mohammed
1908 Mr J B Joel	1948 H.H. Aga Khan	1988 Sheikh Mohammed
1909 Mr "Fairie"	1949 H.H. Aga Khan	1989 Sheikh Mohammed
1910 Mr "Fairie"	1950 M M Boussac	1990 Mr Hamdan Al-Maktoum
1911 Ld Derby	1951 M M Boussac	1991 Sheikh Mohammed
1912 Mr T Pilkington	1952 H. H. Aga Khan	1992 Sheikh Mohammed
1913 Mr J B Joel	1953 Sir Victor Sassoon	1993 Sheikh Mohammed
1914 Mr J B Joel	1954 Her Majesty	1994 Mr Hamdan Al-Maktoum
1915 Mr L Neumann	1955 Lady Zia Wernner	1995 Mr Hamdan Al-Maktoum
1916 Mr E Hulton	1956 Maj L B Holliday	1996 Godolphin
1917 Mr "Fairie"	1957 Her Majesty	1997 Sheikh Mohammed
1918 Lady James Douglas	1958 Mr J McShain	1998 Godolphin
1919 Ld Glanely	1959 Prince Aly Khan	1999 Godolphin
1920 Sir Robert Jardine	1960 Sir Victor Sassoon	2000 H.H. Aga Khan
1921 Mr S B Joel	1961 Maj L B Holliday	2001 Godolphin
1922 Ld Woolavington	1962 Maj L B Holliday	2002 Mr Hamdan Al-Maktoum
1923 Ld Derby	1963 Mr J R Mullion	2003 K Abdullah
1924 H.H. Aga Khan	1964 Mrs H E Jackson	2004 Godolphin
1925 Ld Astor	1965 M J Ternynck	2005 Mr Hamdan Al-Maktoum
1926 Ld Woolavington	1966 Lady Zia Wernher	2006 Godolphin
1927 Ld Derby	1967 Mr H J Joel	2007 Godolphin
1928 Ld Derby	1968 Mr Raymond R Guest	2008 HRH Princess Haya of Jordan
1929 H.H. Aga Khan	1969 Mr D Robinson	2009 Mr Hamdan Al-Maktoum
1930 H.H. Aga Khan	1970 Mr C Engelhard	2010 K Abdullah
1931 Mr J A Dewar	1971 Mr P Mellon	2011 K Abdullah
1932 H.H. Aga Khan	1972 Mrs J Hislop	2012 Godolphin
1933 Ld Derby	1973 Mr N B Hunt	
1934 H.H. Aga Khan	1974 Mr N B Hunt	

LEADING SIRES ON THE FLAT: 1895-2012

1895 St Simon	1897 Kendal	1899 Orme
1896 St Simon	1898 Galopin	1900 St Simon

1901 St Simon	1939 Fairway	1977 Northern Dancer
1902 Persimmon	1940 Hyperion	1978 Mill Reef (USA)
1903 St Frusquin	1941 Hyperion	1979 Petingo
1904 Gallinule	1942 Hyperion	1980 Pitcairn
1905 Gallinule	1943 Fairway	1981 Great Nephew
1906 Persimmon	1944 Fairway	1982 Be My Guest (USA)
1907 St Frusquin	1945 Hyperion	1983 Northern Dancer
1908 Persimmon	1946 Hyperion	1984 Northern Dancer
1909 Cyllene	1947 Nearco	1985 Kris
1910 Cyllene	1948 Big Game	1986 Nijinsky (CAN)
1911 Sundridge	1949 Nearco	1987 Mill Reef (USA)
1912 Persimmon	1950 Fair Trial	1988 Caerleon (USA)
1913 Desmond	1951 Nasrullah	1989 Blushing Groom (FR)
1914 Polymelus	1952 Tehran	1990 Sadler's Wells (USA)
1915 Polymelus	1953 Chanteur II	1991 Caerleon (USA)
1916 Polymelus	1954 Hyperion	1992 Sadler's Wells (USA)
1917 Bayardo	1955 Alycidon	1993 Sadler's Wells (USA)
1918 Bayardo	1956 Court Martial	1994 Sadler's Wells (USA)
1919 The Tetrarch	1957 Court Martial	1995 Sadler's Wells (USA)
1920 Polymelus	1958 Mossborough	1996 Sadler's Wells (USA)
1921 Polymelus	1959 Petition	1997 Sadler's Wells (USA)
1922 Lemberg	1960 Aureole	1998 Sadler's Wells (USA)
1923 Swynford	1961 Aureole	1999 Sadler's Wells (USA)
1924 Son-in-Law	1962 Never Say Die	2000 Sadler's Wells (USA)
1925 Phalaris	1963 Ribot	2001 Sadler's Wells (USA)
1926 Hurry On	1964 Chamossaire	2002 Sadler's Wells (USA)
1927 Buchan	1965 Court Harwell	2003 Sadler's Wells (USA)
1928 Phalaris	1966 Charlottesville	2004 Sadler's Wells (USA)
1929 Tetratema	1967 Ribot	2005 Danehill (USA)
1930 Son-in-Law	1968 Ribot	2006 Danehill (USA)
1931 Pharos	1969 Crepello	2007 Danehill (USA)
1932 Gainsborough	1970 Northern Dancer	2008 Galileo (IRE)
1933 Gainsborough	1971 Never Bend	2009 Danehill Dancer (IRE)
1934 Blandford	1972 Queen's Hussar	2010 Galileo (IRE)
1935 Blandford	1973 Vaguely Noble	2011 Galileo (IRE)
1936 Fairway	1974 Vaguely Noble	2012 Galileo (IRE)
1937 Solario	1975 Great Nephew	
1938 Blandford	1976 Wolver Hollow	

LEADING BREEDERS ON THE FLAT: 1911-2012

1911 Ld Derby (late)	1937 H.H. Aga Khan	1962 Maj L B Holliday
1912 Col. W Hall Walker	1938 Ld Derby	1963 Mr H F Guggenheim
1913 Mr J B Joel	1939 Ld Rosebery	1964 Bull Run Stud
1914 Mr J B Joel	1940 Mr H E Morriss	1965 Mr J Ternynck
1915 Mr L Neumann	1941 Ld Glanely	1966 Someries Stud
1916 Mr E Hulton	1942 National Stud	1967 Mr H J Joel
1917 Mr "Fairie"	1943 Miss D Paget	1968 Mill Ridge Farm
1918 Lady James Douglas	1944 Ld Rosebery	1969 Lord Rosebery
1919 Ld Derby	1945 Ld Derby	1970 Mr E P Taylor
1920 Ld Derby	1946 Lt- Col H Boyd-Rochfort	1971 Mr P Mellon
1921 Mr S B Joel	1947 H.H. Aga Khan	1972 Mr J Hislop
1922 Ld Derby	1948 H.H. Aga Khan	1973 Claiborne Farm
1923 Ld Derby	1949 H.H. Aga Khan	1974 Mr N B Hunt
1924 Lady Sykes	1950 M M Boussac	1975 Overbury Stud
1925 Ld Astor	1951 M M Boussac	1976 Dayton Ltd
1926 Ld Woolavington	1952 H. H. Aga Khan	1977 Mr E P Taylor
1927 Ld Derby	1953 Mr F Darling	1978 Cragwood Estates Inc
1928 Ld Derby	1954 Maj L B Holliday	1979 Ballymacoll Stud
1929 Ld Derby	1955 Someries Stud	1980 P Clarke
1930 Ld Derby	1956 Maj L B Holliday	1981 H.H. Aga Khan
1931 Ld Dewar	1957 Eve Stud	1982 Someries Stud
1932 H.H. Aga Khan	1958 Mr R Ball	1983 White Lodge Stud
1933 Sir Alec Black	1959 Prince Aly Khan and the late	1984 Mr E P Taylor
1934 H.H. Aga Khan	H.H. Aga Khan	1985 Dalham Stud Farms
1935 H.H. Aga Khan	1960 Eve Stud Ltd	1986 H.H. Aga Khan
1936 Ld Astor	1961 Eve Stud Ltd	1987 Cliveden Stud

1988 H. H. Aga Khan	1997 Sheikh Mohammed	2006 Darley
1989 Mr Hamdan Al- Maktoum	1998 Sheikh Mohammed	2007 Darley
1990 Capt. Macdonald- Buchanan	1999 H. H. The Aga Khan's Studs	2008 Darley
1991 Barronstown Stud	2000 H. H. The Aga Khan's Studs	2009 Darley
1992 Swettenham Stud	2001 Shadwell Farm & Estate Ltd	2010 Juddmonte
1993 Juddmonte Farms	2002 Gainsborough Stud	2011 Juddmonte
1994 Shadwell Farm & Estate Ltd	2003 Juddmonte	2012 Juddmonte
1995 Shadwell Farm & Estate Ltd	2004 Juddmonte	
1996 Sheikh Mohammed	2005 Shadwell Farm & Estate Ltd	

LEADING TRAINERS OVER JUMPS: 1946-2012

1946-47 F T T Walwyn	1969-70 T F Rimell	1992-93 M C Pipe
1947-48 F T T Walwyn	1970-71 F T Winter	1993-94 D Nicholson
1948-49 F T T Walwyn	1971-72 F T Winter	1994-95 D Nicholson
1949-50 P V F Cazalet	1972-73 F T Winter	1995-96 M C Pipe
1950-51 T F Rimell	1973-74 F T Winter	1996-97 M C Pipe
1951-52 N Crump	1974-75 F T Winter	1997-98 M C Pipe
1952-53 M V O'Brien	1975-76 T F Rimell	1998-99 M C Pipe
1953-54 M V O'Brien	1976-77 F T Winter	1999-00 M C Pipe
1954-55 H R Price	1977-78 F T Winter	2000-01 M C Pipe
1955-56 W Hall	1978-79 M H Easterby	2001-02 M C Pipe
1956-57 N Crump	1979-80 M H Easterby	2002-03 M C Pipe
1957-58 F T T Walwyn	1980-81 M H Easterby	2003-04 M C Pipe
1958-59 H R Price	1981-82 M W Dickinson	2004-05 M C Pipe
1959-60 P V F Cazalet	1982-83 M W Dickinson	2005-06 P F Nicholls
1960-61 T F Rimell	1983-84 M W Dickinson	2006-07 P F Nicholls
1961-62 H R Price	1984-85 F T Winter	2007-08 P F Nicholls
1962-63 K Piggott	1985-86 N J Henderson	2008-09 P F Nicholls
1963-64 F T T Walwyn	1986-87 N J Henderson	2009-10 P F Nicholls
1964-65 P V F Cazalet	1987-88 D R C Elsworth	2010-11 P F Nicholls
1965-66 H R Price	1988-89 M C Pipe	2010-11 P F Nicholls
1966-67 H R Price	1989-90 M C Pipe	2011-12 P F Nicholls
1967-68 Denys Smith	1990-91 M C Pipe	
1968-69 T F Rimell	1991-92 M C Pipe	

CHAMPION JOCKEYS OVER JUMPS: 1901-2012

Prior to the 1925-26 season the figure relates to racing between January and December

1901 F Mason 58	1926-27 F B Rees 59	1951-52 T Moloney..................99
1902 F Mason 67	1927-28 W Stott 88	1952-53 F Winter 121
1903 P Woodland 54	1928-29 W Stott 65	1953-54 R Francis................76
1904 F Mason 59	1929-30 W Stott 77	1954-55 T Moloney................67
1905 F Mason 73	1930-31 W Stott 81	1955-56 F Winter 74
1906 F Mason 58	1931-32 W Stott 77	1956-57 F Winter 80
1907 F Mason 59	1932-33 G Wilson 61	1957-58 F Winter 82
1908 P Cowley 65	1933-34 G Wilson 56	1958-59 T Brookshaw............83
1909 R Gordon 45	1934-35 G Wilson 73	1959-60 S Mellor..................68
1910 E Piggott 67	1935-36 G Wilson 57	1960-61 S Mellor................118
1911 W Payne..................76	1936-37 G Wilson 45	1961-62 S Mellor..................80
1912 I Anthony..................78	1937-38 G Wilson 59	1962-63 J Gifford..................70
1913 E Piggott 60	1938-39 T F Rimell 61	1963-64 J Gifford..................94
1914 Mr J R Anthony 60	1939-40 T F Rimell 24	1964-65 T Biddlecombe........114
1915 E Piggott 44	1940-41 G Wilson 22	1965-66 T Biddlecombe........102
1916 C Hawkins 17	1941-42 R Smyth 12	1966-67 J Gifford................122
1917 W Smith..................15	1942-43 No racing	1967-68 J Gifford..................82
1918 G Duller..................17	1943-44 No racing	1968-69 B R Davies..............77
1919 Mr H Brown 48	1944-45 N Nicholson............15	T Biddlecombe..........77
1920 F B Rees..................64	T F Rimell 15	1969-70 B R Davies..............91
1921 F B Rees..................65	1945-46 T F Rimell 54	1970-71 G Thorner................74
1922 J Anthony..................78	1946-47 J Dowdeswell 58	1971-72 B R Davies..............89
1923 F B Rees..................64	1947-48 B Marshall 66	1972-73 R Barry................125
1924 F B Rees................108	1948-49 T Moloney..............60	1973-74 R Barry..................94
1925 E Foster..................76	1949-50 T Moloney..............95	1974-75 T Stack..................82
1925-26 T Leader..............61	1950-51 T Moloney..............83	1975-76 J Francome..............96

1976-77 T Stack	97	1988-89 P Scudamore	221
1977-78 J J O'Neill	149	1989-90 P Scudamore	170
1978-79 J Francome	95	1990-91 P Scudamore	141
1979-80 J J O'Neill	117	1991-92 P Scudamore	175
1980-81 J Francome	105	1992-93 R Dunwoody	173
1981-82 J Francome	120	1993-94 R Dunwoody	197
P Scudamore	120	1994-95 R Dunwoody	160
1982-83 J Francome	106	1995-96 A P McCoy	175
1983-84 J Francome	131	1996-97 A P McCoy	190
1984-85 J Francome	101	1997-98 A P McCoy	253
1985-86 P Scudamore	91	1998-99 A P McCoy	186
1986-87 P Scudamore	123	1999-00 A P McCoy	245
1987-88 P Scudamore	132	2000-01 A P McCoy	191

2001-02 A P McCoy	289
2002-03 A P McCoy	256
2003-04 A P McCoy	209
2004-05 A P McCoy	200
2005-06 A P McCoy	178
2006-07 A P McCoy	184
2007-08 A P McCoy	140
2008-09 A P McCoy	186
2009-10 A P McCoy	195
2010-11 A P McCoy	218
2011-12 A P McCoy	199

LEADING OWNERS OVER JUMPS: 1946-2012

(Please note that prior to the 1994-95 season the leading owner was determined by win prizemoney only)

1946-47 Mr J J McDowell	1969-70 Mr E R Courage	Racing Stables Ltd
1947-48 Mr J Proctor	1970-71 Mr F Pontin	1992-93 Mrs J Mould
1948-49 Mr W F Williamson	1971-72 Capt T A Forster	1993-94 Pell-Mell Partners
1949-50 Mrs L Brotherton	1972-73 Mr N H Le Mare	1994-95 Roach Foods Limited
1950-51 J Royle	1973-74 Mr N H Le Mare	1995-96 Mr A T A Wates
1951-52 Miss D Paget	1974-75 Mr R Guest	1996-97 Mr R Ogden
1952-53 Mr J H Griffin	1975-76 Mr P B Raymond	1997-98 Mr D A Johnson
1953-54 Mr J H Griffin	1976-77 Mr N H Le Mare	1998-99 Mr J P McManus
1954-55 Mrs W H E Welman	1977-78 Mrs O Jackson	1999-00 Mr R Ogden
1955-56 Mrs L Carver	1978-79 Snailwell Stud Co Ltd	2000-01 Sir R Ogden
1956-57 Mrs Geoffrey Kohn	1979-80 Mr H J Joel	2001-02 Mr D A Johnson
1957-58 Mr D J Coughlan	1980-81 Mr R J Wilson	2002-03 Mr D A Johnson
1958-59 Mr J E Bigg	1981-82 Sheikh Ali Abu Khamsin	2003-04 Mr D A Johnson
1959-60 Miss W H Wallace	1982-83 Sheikh Ali Abu Khamsin	2004-05 Mr D A Johnson
1960-61 Mr C Vaughan	1983-84 Sheikh Ali Abu Khamsin	2005-06 Mr J P McManus
1961-62 Mr N Cohen	1984-85 T Kilroe and Son Ltd	2006-07 Mr J P McManus
1962-63 Mr P B Raymond	1985-86 Sheikh Ali Abu Khamsin	2007-08 Mr D A Johnson
1963-64 Mr J K Goodman	1986-87 Mr H J Joel	2008-09 Mr J P McManus
1964-65 Mrs M Stephenson	1987-88 Miss Juliet E Reed	2009-10 Mr J P McManus
1965-66 Duchess of Westminster	1988-89 Mr R Burridge	2010-11 Mr T Hemmings
1966-67 Mr C P T Watkins	1989-90 Mrs Harry J Duffey	2011-12 Mr J P McManus
1967-68 Mr H S Alper	1990-91 Mr P Piller	
1968-69 Mr B P Jenks	1991-92 Whitcombe Manor	

LEADING AMATEUR RIDERS OVER JUMPS: 1947-2012

1947-48 Ld Mildmay	22	
1948-49 Ld Mildmay	30	
1949-50 Ld Mildmay	38	
1950-51 Mr P Chisman	13	
1951-52 Mr C Straker	19	
1952-53 Mr A H Moralee	22	
1953-54 Mr A H Moralee	22	
1954-55 Mr A H Moralee	16	
1955-56 Mr R McCreery	13	
Mr A H Moralee	13	
1956-57 Mr R McCreery	23	
1957-58 Mr J Lawrence	18	
1958-59 Mr J Sutcliffe	18	
1959-60 Mr G Kindersley	22	
1960-61 Sir W Pigott-Brown	28	
1961-62 Mr A Biddlecombe	30	
1962-63 Sir W Pigott-Brown	20	
1963-64 Mr S Davenport	32	
1964-65 Mr M Gifford	15	
1965-66 Mr C Collins	24	
1966-67 Mr C Collins	33	
1967-68 Mr R Tate	30	
1968-69 Mr R Tate	17	

1969-70 Mr M Dickinson	23	
1970-71 Mr J Lawrence	17	
1971-72 Mr W Foulkes	26	
1972-73 Mr R Smith	56	
1973-74 Mr A Webber	21	
1974-75 Mr R Lamb	22	
1975-76 Mr P Greenall	25	
Mr G Jones	25	
1976-77 Mr P Greenall	27	
1977-78 Mr G Sloan	23	
1978-79 Mr T G Dun	26	
1979-80 Mr O Sherwood	29	
1980-81 Mr P Webber	32	
1981-82 Mr D Browne	28	
1982-83 Mr D Browne	33	
1983-84 Mr S Sherwood	28	
1984-85 Mr S Sherwood	30	
1985-86 Mr T Thomson Jones	25	
1986-87 Mr T Thomson Jones	19	
1987-88 Mr T Thomson Jones	15	
1988-89 Mr P Fenton	18	
1989-90 Mr P McMahon	15	
1990-91 Mr K Johnson	24	

1991-92 Mr M P Hourigan	24	
1992-93 Mr A Thornton	26	
1993-94 Mr J Greenall	21	
1994-95 Mr D Parker	16	
1995-96 Mr J Culloty	40	
1996-97 Mr R Thornton	30	
1997-98 Mr S Durack	41	
1998-99 Mr A Dempsey	47	
1999-00 Mr P Flynn	41	
2000-01 Mr T Scudamore	24	
2001-02 Mr D Crosse	19	
2002-03 Mr C Williams	23	
2003-04 Mr O Nelmes	14	
2004-05 Mr T Greenall	31	
2005-06 Mr T O'Brien	32	
2006-07 Mr T Greenall	31	
2007-08 Mr T Greenall	23	
2008-09 Mr O Greenall	23	
2009-10 Mr O Greenall	41	
2010-11 Mr R Mahon	19	
2011-12 Miss E. Sayer	11	

LEADING SIRES OVER JUMPS: 1986-2012

1986 Deep Run	1994-95 Strong Gale	2003-04 Be My Native (USA)
1987 Deep Run	1995-96 Strong Gale	2004-05 Supreme Leader
1988 Deep Run	1996-97 Strong Gale	2005-06 Supreme Leader
1989 Deep Run	1997-98 Strong Gale	2006-07 Presenting
1989-90 Deep Run	1998-99 Strong Gale	2007-08 Old Vic
1990-91 Deep Run	1999-00 Strong Gale	2008-09 Presenting
1991-92 Deep Run	2000-01 Be My Native (USA)	2009-10 Presenting
1992-93 Deep Run	2001-02 Be My Native (USA)	2010-11 Presenting
1993-94 Strong Gale	2002-03 Be My Native (USA)	2011-12 King's Theatre

JOCKEYS' AGENTS

Jockeys' Agents and their Contact Details

Agent	Telephone	Mobile/Email	Fax
NICKY ADAMS	01488 72004/72964	07796 547659 nadams52@yahoo.com	
NEIL ALLAN	01243 543870	07985 311141 aneil@aol.com	
NIGEL BAXTER	01942 269972	07973 561521 nigelbaxter@blueyonder.co.uk	01942 269989
PAUL BRIERLEY	01434 608212	07824 828750 bbjockeys@hotmail.co.uk	
CHRIS BROAD	01452 760482/447	07836 622858 c.j.broad@talk21.com	01452 760394
MR A. BURKE	01638 602208	07825 330392 anyprice2001@yahoo.com	
LIZ BUTTERWORTH	01768 361363	07917 717346 lizb345@hotmail.com	01768 361363
JASON BUTTON		07771 811976 jasonbuttonracing1@gmail.com	
PAUL CLARKE	01638 660804	07885 914306 paul.clarke79@btinternet.com	
RAY COCHRANE	01223 812008	07798 651247 ray@raysagency.co.uk	
DANIEL CREIGHTON		07597 945219 danielcreighton@hotmail.com	
SIMON DODDS	01509 852344/852254	07974 924735 simon.dodds@btinternet.com	

Agent	Telephone	Mobile/Email	Fax
JACQUI DOYLE	01672 871894	07831 880678 doyleracing@yahoo.co.uk	
SHIPPY ELLIS	01638 668484 01638 864864	07860 864864 shippysjockeys@btconnect.com	01638 660946
TONY ELVES	01638 454012	07969 051306 tony.elves@yahoo.co.uk	
JOHN W FORD	01954 261122	07830 294210 john.ford47@btinternet.com	
MARK FURNASS	01347 824633	07988 203831 jockeysagent@gmail.com	
MARK GILCHRIST	01903 883356	07810 821787 shaz.gilly@hotmail.co.uk	01903 883797
JAYNE GOLLINGS	01845 597850	07760 993936 jaynemgollings@aol.com	
PAUL GRUNDY	01845 597850	07760 993936 pg2960@btinternet.com	
MICHAEL HAGGAS	01638 660811	07740 624550 mhaggas@ntlworld.com	
RICHARD HALE	01768 88699	07909 520542 richardhale77@hotmail.co.uk	
SUSAN HARDING	01845 597850	07884 665582 exitplan1980@hotmail.co.uk	
DAVID HARRISON	01614 087888	07592 767206 davidpharrison@hotmail.com	
ALAN HARRISON	01969 625006	07846 187991 ahjockagent60@yahoo.co.uk	0560 2729293
TONY HIND	01638 724997	07807 908599 tonyhind@jockeysagent.com	

Agent	Telephone	Mobile/Email	Fax
GAVIN HORNE	01392 423352	07914 897170 gavin.horne@hotmail.co.uk	
RUSS JAMES	01653 699466	07947 414001 russjames2006@btinternet.com	01653 691455
BRUCE JEFFREY	01750 21521	07747 854684 brucejeffrey@live.co.uk	
GUY JEWELL	01672 861231	07765 248859 guyjewell@btconnect.com	01672 861231
ANDREW LEWIS	01908 365945	07838 506594 andrew.lewis11@sky.com	
DAVID LYONS		07957 595780/07861 500508 lyonsdavid56@gmail.com	
SARA-LOUISE METCALFE	01635 298067	07900 207018 troopersjockeys@hotmail.co.uk	
PHILIP MITCHELL	01367 820299	07836 231462 philip@downshouse.com	01372 278701
LEE NEWTON	01302 376370	07710 422437 newton808@btinternet.com	
GARETH OWEN	01638 428007	07958 335206 willowracing@gmail.com	
SHASHI RIGHTON	01353 688081	07825 318350 slasher74@aol.com	
DAVE ROBERTS	01737 761369	07860 234342 daveroberts.racing@nhworld.com	
WILLIE RYAN	01638 666644	07775 858285 willieryan1@hotmail.com	
MICHELLE SMITH	01638 668509	07860 467220 michelle@safetyrelease.co.uk	

Agent	Telephone	Mobile/Email	Fax
ROBERT STRONGE	01635 248710	07887 521333 robert@stronge4380.freeserve.co.uk	
SAM STRONGE	01488 72818	07775 727778 sam.stronge@virgin.net	01488 670378
GARY THOMSON	01642 873152	07986 607014 garythomson73@yahoo.com	01284 850807
JENNIFER WALSH	00353 45883704	00353 87258025 jennifer@ruby-walsh.com	00353 45871929
IAN WARDLE	01793 688858/688859	07831 865974 ian.wardlex@googlemail.com	
LAURA WAY	01704 834488	07775 777494 lauraway@btconnect.com	

FLAT JOCKEYS

Riding weights and contact details

An index of agents appears on page 682

EDDIE AHERN	8 - 6	Mr G. J. Horne\ Mr S. Stronge 07771 777010	
AHMED AJTEBI	8 - 5	Mrs L. H. Way	
DAVID ALLAN	8 - 6	Mr R. A. Hale	
PADDY ASPELL	8 - 8	Mr Paul Clarke	
ANDREA ATZENI	8 - 0	Mr Paul Clarke	
AMY BAKER	7 - 1	Mr G. D. Jewell	
GEORGE BAKER	9 - 0	07704972285	
GARY BARTLEY	8 - 11	Mr R. Cochrane	
MICKAEL BARZALONA	8 - 4	Mr Dave Roberts	
MATTIE BATCHELOR	9 - 5	Mr G. J. Horne	
PADRAIG BEGGY	8 - 5	Mr G D Jewell	
HARRY BENTLEY	7 - 11	Mr John W. Ford	
ADAM BESCHIZZA	8 - 4	07745 988479	
TRAVIS BLOCK	8 - 8	Mr M. R. Haggas	
WILLIAM BUICK	8 - 6	07989 124949	
ROBERT L. BUTLER	8 - 12	Mr S. T. Dodds	
NEIL CALLAN	8 - 6	Mr Neil Allan	
WILLIAM CARSON	8 - 2	Mr N. M. Adams	
CHRIS CATLIN	8 - 3	07776 237477	
NEIL CHALMERS	8 - 4	01923 855337	
CHRIS D. COGAN	8 - 4	Mr S. M. Righton	
PAT COSGRAVE	8 - 8	Mr Mark Gilchrist	
MARK COUMBE	8 - 5	Mr Mark Gilchrist	
STEPHEN CRAINE	8 - 9	Mr G. D. Jewell	
JIM CROWLEY	8 - 7	Mr Mark Gilchrist	
TONY CULHANE	8 - 7	07500 564169	
DUILIO DA SILVA	8 - 2	Mr G. R. Owen\ Mr L. Newton	
RAUL DA SILVA	7 - 13	Mr G. D. Jewell	
MATTHEW DAVIES	8 - 10	Mr T. Elves	
MIRCO DEMURO	8 - 2	Mr G. R. Owen	
SILVESTRE DE SOUSA	7 - 12	Mr R. Cochrane	
FRANKIE DETTORI	8 - 4	Mr Tony Hind	
PAT DOBBS	8 - 7	Mr S. T. Dodds	
STEVIE DONOHOE	8 - 5	Mr G. D. Jewell	
BRETT DOYLE	8 - 5	Ms J. S. Doyle	
JAMES DOYLE	8 - 7	Ms J. S. Doyle	
SOPHIE DOYLE	8 - 0	Mr I. P. Wardle	
STEVE DROWNE	8 - 6	Mr David Harrison	
TED DURCAN	8 - 5	Mr S. T. Dodds	
MARTIN DWYER	8 - 4	Mr R. A. Hale	
TOM EAVES	8 - 6	Mr N. A. Baxter	
ANDREW ELLIOTT	8 - 4	Mr N. M. Adams	
JOHN FAHY	8 - 2	Mrs L. H. Way	
KIEREN FALLON	8 - 7	Mr W. P Grundy	
JOE FANNING	8 - 1	Mr Alan Harrison	
DURAN FENTIMAN	7 - 12	Mr R. A. Hale	
MICKY FENTON	8 - 9	01622 880767	
JENNIFER FERGUSON	8 - 0	Mr R. A. Hale	
ROYSTON FFRENCH	8 - 4	Mr S. M. Righton	
ROBBIE FITZPATRICK	8 - 7	Mr Tony Hind	
JIMMY FORTUNE	8 - 9	M. Furnass	
DOMINIC FOX	7 - 12	Mr Neil Allan	
CATHY GANNON	7 - 12	M. Furnass	
NATALIA GEMELOVA	7 - 9	Mr G. J. Thomson	
CHRISTOPHER GEOGHEGAN	9 - 11	Mrs L. H. Way	
GRAHAM GIBBONS	8 - 4		
SALEEM GOLAM	8 - 5	Mr Paul Clarke	
JAMIE GOLDSTEIN	8 - 7	Mr Mark Gilchrist	
RACHAEL GREEN	9 - 0	01308 868272	
J-P. GUILLAMBERT	8 - 7	Mr S. T. Dodds	
MARC HALFORD	8 - 6	Mr Daniel Creighton	
TONY HAMILTON	8 - 7	Mr R. A. Hale	
PAUL HANAGAN	8 - 0	Mr R. A. Hale	
MARTIN HARLEY	8 - 7	Miss Susan Harding	
KELLY HARRISON	7 - 13	Mr Alan Harrison	
ROBERT HAVLIN	8 - 6	Mr I. P. Wardle	
SAM HITCHCOTT	8 - 5	Mr N. M. Adams	
DARRYLL HOLLAND	8 - 7	Mr G. R. Owen	
RICHARD HUGHES	8 - 7	Mr Tony Hind	
LIAM JONES	8 - 3	Mr Paul Clarke	
SHANE KELLY	8 - 9	Mr G. J. Horne	
LIAM KENIRY	8 - 6	Mr N. M. Adams	
RUSS KENNEMORE	8 - 7	Mr L. R. James	
RICHARD KINGSCOTE	8 - 4	Mr G. D. Jewell	
ADAM KIRBY	8 - 11	Mr N. M. Adams	
MARTIN LANE	8 - 0	Mr S. T. Dodds	
GRAHAM LEE	8 - 11	Mr R. A. Hale	
SEAN LEVEY	8 - 8	Mr Tony Hind	
JAMIE MACKAY	7 - 12	M. Furnass	
NICKY MACKAY	7 - 12	Mr Paul Clarke	
PHILLIP MAKIN	8 - 9	Mr R. A. Hale	
JEMMA MARSHALL	8 - 3	M. Furnass	
PATRICK MATHERS	8 - 1	Mr R. A. Hale	
FRANKIE MCDONALD	7 - 12	Mr N. M. Adams	
P. J. MCDONALD	8 - 4	Mr R. A. Hale	
BARRY MCHUGH	8 - 4	Mr R. A. Hale	
TOM MCLAUGHLIN	8 - 10	Mr G. J. Horne	
KIRSTY MILCZAREK	8 - 3	M. Furnass	
JACK MITCHELL	8 - 7	Mr Philip Mitchell	
IAN MONGAN	8 - 10	Mr N. M. Adams	
RYAN MOORE	8 - 8	Mr Tony Hind	
LUKE MORRIS	8 - 0	Mr Neil Allan	
ANDREW MULLEN	7 - 13	Mr S. M. Righton	
RICHARD MULLEN	8 - 4	Mr Tony Hind	
PAUL MULRENNAN	8 - 7	Mr R. A. Hale	
LEE NEWMAN	8 - 6	01620 830233	
LEE NEWNES	8 - 9	Mr John W. Ford	
ADRIAN NICHOLLS	8 - 2	Mr S. M. Righton	
DAVID NOLAN	8 - 12	Mr R. A. Hale	
FRANNY NORTON	8 - 0	Mr I. P Wardle	
MICHAEL O'CONNELL	8 - 7	Mrs L. H. Way	
DARAGH O'DONOHOE	8 - 5	Mr W. Ryan	
SLADE O'HARA	8 - 10	0777 3009787	
DANE O'NEILL	8 - 8	Mr N. M. Adams	
KIERAN O'NEILL	7 - 8	Mr Tony Hind	
TADHG O'SHEA	8 - 3	Mrs L. H. Way	
SIMON PEARCE	8 - 0	Mr N. M. Adams	
PAUL PICKARD	8 - 5	Mr N. A. Baxter\ Mr S. M. Righton	
LAURA PIKE	8 - 0	Mr L. R. James	
I. POULLIS	8 - 6	Mr L. Newton	
HARRY POULTON	8 - 9	Mr A. D. Lewis	
DAVID PROBERT	7 - 13	Miss S. L. Metcalfe	
TOM QUEALLY	8 - 6	Mr T. Elves	

SEAN QUINLAN .... 8 - 13	Mr C. D. Broad\	
	Mr Mark Gilchrist	
AMIR QUINN .... 8 - 9	Mr L. R. James	
JIMMY QUINN .... 7 - 12	Mr G. J. Horne	
PAUL QUINN .... 7 - 12	Mr S. M. Righton	
AMY RYAN .... 8 - 4	Mr R. A. Hale	
SEB SANDERS .... 8 - 6	Mr I. P. Wardle	
VICTOR SANTOS .... 7 - 13	079711 82923	
KATIA SCALLAN .... 7 - 7	Mr Daniel Creighton	
AMY SCOTT .... 8 - 0	M. Furnass	
J. D. SMITH .... 8 - 10	Mr D. P. J. Lyons	
RENATO SOUZA .... 8 - 7	Mr L. R. James	
JAMIE SPENCER .... 8 - 7	Mr David Harrison	

MICHAEL STAINTON .... 8 - 8	Mr John W. Ford
ANN STOKELL .... 8 - 7	07814 579982
JAMES SULLIVAN .... 8 - 0	Mr R. A. Hale
FERGUS SWEENEY .... 8 - 8	Mr N. M. Adams
NATHAN SWEENEY .... 8 - 0	Mr I. P Wardle
DALE SWIFT .... 8 - 7	Mr R. A. Hale
RICHARD THOMAS .... 8 - 3	Mr I. P Wardle
DANIEL TUDHOPE .... 8 - 7	Mr Alan Harrison
HAYLEY TURNER .... 8 - 2	Mr G. D. Jewell
FREDERIK TYLICKI .... 8 - 6	Mr R. A. Hale
GARRY WHILLANS .... 8 - 6	Mr R. A. Hale
ROBERT WINSTON .... 8 - 6	Mr S. T. Dodds

Only riders we have contact details for are included
in this section.

Are your details missing or incorrect?
Please update us by email:
richard.lowther@racingpost.co.uk
Or leave a message on 0500 007071

Have you tried Raceform Interactive?
Easy to use and maintain, declarations and entries
together with a List Manager to highlight all your horses.
Never miss an entry or runner again.

Visit the new webtour at www.raceform.co.uk

APPRENTICES

Riding weights and contact details

An index of agents appears on page 682

Name	Trainer	Weight	Contact
LUCY ALEXANDER	(N. W. Alexander)	9 - 0	Mr R. A. Hale
NATHAN ALISON	(Jim Boyle)	7 - 12	M. Furnass
TOBY ATKINSON	(Marco Botti)	8 - 4	Mr Philip Mitchell
LEAH-ANNE AVERY	(J. W. Hills)	8 - 2	c/o 01488 73144
LAURA BARRY	(Richard Fahey)	8 - 0	Mr R. A. Hale
JOSH BAUDAINS	(Dominic Ffrench Davis)	8 - 0	Mr A. D. Lewis
CONNOR BEASLEY	(Michael Dods)	8 - 2	Mr R. A. Hale
CHARLIE BENNETT	(Marcus Tregoning)	7 - 12	c/o 01488 73300
DAVID BERGIN	(David O'Meara)	8 - 2	Mr R. A. Hale
SHELLEY BIRKETT	(Julia Feilden)	7 - 10	Mr John W. Ford
CHARLES BISHOP	(Mick Channon)	8 - 2	Miss Susan Harding\Mr S. M. Righton
AIDEN BLAKEMORE	(Tony Carroll)	8 - 4	c/o 01386 861020
PAIGE BOLTON	(Michael Attwater)	8 - 2	c/o 07725 423633
PAUL BOOTH	(Dean Ivory)	7 - 13	Mr A. D. Lewis
BRADLEY BOSLEY	(John Ryan)	7 - 5	Mr Mark Gilchrist
DANNY BROCK	(Phil McEntee)	7 - 13	M. Furnass
THOMAS BROWN	(Andrew Balding)	8 - 5	Mr Mark Gilchrist
GEORGE BUCKELL	(Tim Pitt)	8 - 2	Mrs Michelle Smith
JULIE BURKE	(Kevin Ryan)	8 - 2	Mr R. A. Hale
HARRY BURNS	(Michael Blanshard)	8 - 0	c/o 07785 370093
IAN BURNS	(Jane Chapple-Hyam)	7 - 9	M. Furnass
JACOB BUTTERFIELD	(Ollie Pears)	8 - 4	Mr R. A. Hale
DARYL BYRNE	(Tim Easterby)	8 - 5	Mr Alan Harrison
EIREANN CAGNEY	(Richard Fahey)	8 - 5	c/o 01653 698915
DECLAN CANNON	(Nigel Tinkler)	8 - 0	Mr R. A. Hale
ADAM CARTER	(Tim Easterby)	8 - 2	Mr Alan Harrison
HARRY CHALLONER	(Venetia Williams)	9 - 2	Mr R. A. Hale
GEORGE CHALONER	(Richard Fahey)	8 - 5	Mr R. A. Hale
AARON CHAVE	(Lee Carter)	8 - 6	c/o 01372 740878
RYAN CLARK	(Stuart Williams)	8 - 4	Mr L. R. James
TIM CLARK	(Sir Mark Prescott Bt)	8 - 6	Miss S. L. Metcalfe
KENNY CORBETT	(Mel Brittain)	8 - 2	c/o 01759 371472
JOSH CRANE	(Chris Dwyer)	9 - 0	Mr Mark Gilchrist
BILLY CRAY	(Scott Dixon)	8 - 2	Mr L. Newton
DANIEL CREMIN	(Mick Channon)	8 - 0	Mr I. P. Wardle
NED CURTIS	(Gary Moore)	8 - 6	Mr R. A. Hale\Mr N. M. Adams
ROBERT DODSWORTH	(Mel Brittain)	7 - 7	c/o 01759 371472
GEORGE DOWNING	(Tony Carroll)	8 - 6	Mr L. R. James
KATIE DOWSON	(Micky Hammond)	7 - 10	c/o 07808 572777
JACK DUERN	(Reg Hollinshead)	7 - 11	Mr L. R. James
NATASHA EATON	(Alan Bailey)	7 - 11	Mr A. D. Lewis
DARREN EGAN	(Ronald Harris)	8 - 0	Mr Neil Allan
JANE ELLIOTT	(Ralph Beckett)	8 - 3	c/o 01264 772278
RICHARD EVANS	(David Evans)	9 - 2	c/o 01873 890837
NEIL FARLEY	(Declan Carroll)	8 - 0	Mr Alan Harrison
GERARD GALLIGAN	(Michael Chapman)	9 - 0	Mr L. R. James
NOEL GARBUTT	(Hugo Palmer)	7 - 0	Mr L. R. James
THOMAS GARNER	(Oliver Sherwood)	9 - 2	Mr Dave Roberts
AMELIA GREEN	(Sir Henry Cecil)	8 - 0	c/o 01638 662192
PAUL HAINEY	(George Margarson)	7 - 12	c/o 07860 198303
NANNA HANSEN	(Stuart Williams)	8 - 0	c/o 01638 663984
CONOR HARRISON	(Mrs K. Burke)	8 - 4	Mr Alan Harrison
JASON HART	(Declan Carroll)	8 - 2	Mr Alan Harrison
ALICE HAYNES	(David Simcock)	8 - 0	Mr L. R. James
JOEY HAYNES	(Andrew Balding)	7 - 5	Mr S. T. Dodds
THOMAS HEMSLEY	(Michael Bell)	8 - 0	c/o 07802 264514
JORDAN HIBBERD	(Alan Berry)	7 - 1	Mr A. D. Lewis
PATRICK HILLS	(Luca Cumani)	8 - 9	Mr S. T. Dodds

MATTHEW HOPKINS (Michael Easterby)	7 - 10	Mr L. Newton
LAUREN HUNTER (Gay Kelleway)	8 - 5	c/o 07974 948768
CHLOE INGRAM (Tim Vaughan)	7 - 8	c/o 01446 771626
KYLE JAMES (Brian Ellison)	8 - 13	Mr L. R. James
CHARLOTTE JENNER (J. S. Moore)	8 - 1	Mr Daniel Creighton
ROSIE JESSOP (Sir Mark Prescott Bt)	7 - 13	Mr G. R. Owen
AARON JONES (George Baker)	7 - 12	Mr L. R. James
JAMIE JONES (Rae Guest)	8 - 7	c/o 01638 661508 Liz
CAROLINE KELLY (John Ryan)	7 - 13	Mr Jason Button
MICHAEL KENNY (Declan Carroll)	8 - 0	c/o 07801 553779
STEPHEN KING (Richard Hannon)	8 - 3	c/o 01264 850254
RACHEAL KNELLER (Mark Usher)	8 - 0	Mr G. J. Thomson
MATTHEW LAWSON (Charles Hills)	8 - 0	Mr G. J. Thomson
LUKE LEADBITTER (Declan Carroll)	8 - 0	Mr Alan Harrison
NORA LOOBY (Joseph Tuite)	7 - 6	Mr John W. Ford
KEVIN LUNDIE (John Quinn)	7 - 5	Mr R. A. Hale
GARY MAHON (Tim Easterby)	7 - 7	c/o 01653 668566
HARVEY MASON (John Best)	8 - 0	c/o 07889 362154
MATTHEW MCGHEE (Lisa Williamson)	8 - 2	Mr R. A. Hale
PAUL MCGIFF (Kevin Ryan)	7 - 9	Mr R. A. Hale
ADAM MCLEAN (Derek Shaw)	7 - 11	c/o 07721 039645
JORDON MCMURRAY (Mark H. Tompkins)	8 - 1	c/o 07799 663339
LUKE MCNIFF (David Barron)	8 - 7	Mr R. A. Hale
EMILY MELBOURN (Mark Usher)	8 - 1	Miss S. L. Metcalfe
MICHAEL METCALFE (Mrs K. Burke)	8 - 9	M. Furnass
SIOBHAN MILLER (David Simcock)	8 - 4	c/o 07808 954109
PAT MILLMAN (Rod Millman)	8 - 12	Mr Mark Gilchrist
DANIELLE MOONEY (Nigel Tinkler)	7 - 11	Mr L. R. James
ASHLEY MORGAN (Ed Dunlop)	8 - 3	Mr Mark Gilchrist
EVA MOSCROP (Philip Kirby)	7 - 7	Mr L. R. James
MICHAEL J. M. MURPHY (Alan Jarvis)	8 - 4	Mr S. T. Dodds
CLAIRE MURRAY (David Simcock)	8 - 4	c/o 07808 954109
DANIEL MUSCUTT (Andrew Balding)	8 - 2	Miss S. L. Metcalfe
JORDAN NASON (Geoffrey Harker)	8 - 3	Mr Alan Harrison
GEMMA NELLIST (Marco Botti)	8 - 0	Mr A. D. Lewis
JUSTIN NEWMAN (Bryan Smart)	8 - 8	M. Furnass
NICOLE NORDBLAD (Hans Adielsson)	7 - 12	Mr Neil Allan
PAUL NORTON (Linda Perratt)	8 - 10	Mr J. B. Jeffrey
HANNAH NUNN (Robert Cowell)	8 - 0	Mr L. Newton
RICHARD OLIVER (Brian Ellison)	8 - 0	c/o 07785 747426
JEAN VAN OVERMEIRE (Roger Varian)	8 - 2	Mr Paul Clarke
DAVID PARKES (Alan Jarvis)	8 - 6	c/o 01296 730707
SEMIRA PASHAI (Alastair Lidderdale)	8 - 0	c/o 07785 785375
JAKE PAYNE (Bill Turner)	8 - 4	Mr S. Stronge
BRENDAN POWELL (Colin Tizzard)	8 - 5	Mr Dave Roberts
RYAN POWELL (J. S. Moore)	7 - 12	Mr N. M. Adams
PHILIP PRINCE (Ron Hodges)	7 - 10	Mr Mark Gilchrist
SOPHIE RALSTON (Pat Phelan)	7 - 8	c/o 07917 762781
RACHEL RICHARDSON (Tim Easterby)	7 - 11	c/o 01653 668566
SOPHIE ROBERTSON (Jim Goldie)	8 - 2	c/o 0411 936989
JAMES ROGERS (Ralph Beckett)	8 - 1	Mr L. R. James
KIERAN SCHOFIELD (Jason Ward)	7 - 7	c/o 07967 357595
ROWAN SCOTT (Ann Duffield)	7 - 7	c/o 07802 496332
KIRSTEN SMITH (Ben De Haan)	7 - 12	c/o 07831 104574
ROSS SMITH (Linda Perratt)	8 - 5	c/o 07931 306147
KEVIN STOTT (Kevin Ryan)	8 - 0	Mr R. A. Hale
ROBERT TART (Alan Bailey)	8 - 0	Mr A. D. Lewis
RYAN TATE (Clive Cox)	7 - 13	Mr G. D. Jewell
SHIRLEY TEASDALE (David Nicholls)	7 - 12	Mr S. M. Righton
LISA TODD (Richard Guest)	8 - 0	c/o 07760 755741
BRIAN TOOMEY (Kevin Ryan)	9 - 2	Mr Dave Roberts
LEE TOPLISS (Richard Fahey)	8 - 7	Mr R. A. Hale
BRIAN TREANOR (Nicky Richards)	8 - 1	Mr R. A. Hale
GEMMA TUTTY (Tim Walford)	7 - 1	M. Furnass
WILLIAM TWISTON-DAVIES (Nigel Twiston-Davies)	8 - 7	Mr C. D. Broad\Mr Tony Hind
JORDAN VAUGHAN (George Margarson)	8 - 1	Mr A. D. Lewis
RUFUS VERGETTE (Richard Hannon)	7 - 12	Mr Tony Hind
R. P. WALSH (Brian Ellison)	7 - 4	c/o 07785 747426

RYAN WHILE (Bill Turner) .... 8 - 0
ALICE WHITE (Hughie Morrison) .... 8 - 3
MEGAN WHITEHEAD (Richard Hannon) .... 7 - 4
JONATHAN WILLETTS (Andrew Balding) .... 7 - 11
ROBERT WILLIAMS (Bernard Llewellyn) .... 8 - 13
DANA ZAMECNIKOVA (Frank Sheridan) .... 7 - 12

Mr Mark Gilchrist
c/o 07836 687799
Mr N. A. Baxter
c/o 01635 298210
Mr C. D. Broad
c/o 0039 339 6519361 ITALY

Only riders we have contact details for are included
in this section.

Are your details missing or incorrect?
Please update us by email:
richard.lowther@racingpost.co.uk
Or leave a message on 0500 007071

JUMP JOCKEYS

Riding weights and contact details

An index of agents appears on page 682

LEIGHTON ASPELL	10 - 0	Mr Dave Roberts
JAMES BANKS	9 - 10	Mr L. R. James
DAVID BASS	10 - 5	Mr Dave Roberts
MATTIE BATCHELOR	9 - 7	Mr Dave Roberts
COLIN BOLGER	10 - 0	Mr C. D. Broad
PADDY BRENNAN	9 - 12	Mr Dave Roberts
PETER BUCHANAN	10 - 0	Mr Paul Brierley
ALAIN CAWLEY	9 - 10	Mr Dave Roberts
AIDAN COLEMAN	10 - 0	Mr S. Stronge
AODHAGAN CONLON	10 - 0	Mr Dave Roberts
DANNY COOK	10 - 0	Mr R. A. Hale
DOUGIE COSTELLO	9 - 7	Mr Dave Roberts
DAVE CROSSE	10 - 0	Mr L. R. James
CHRIS DAVIES	10 - 0	Mr Dave Roberts
JAMES DAVIES	10 - 0	Mr L. R. James
FEARGHAL DAVIS	10 - 4	Mr G. J. Thomson
FELIX DE GILES	10 - 0	Mr Dave Roberts
JACK DOYLE	10 - 4	Mr S. Stronge
ROBERT DUNNE	9 - 11	Mr Daniel Creighton
LEE EDWARDS	10 - 0	Mr C. D. Broad
DOMINIC ELSWORTH	10 - 2	07776 255736
DAVID ENGLAND	10 - 0	Mr S. Stronge
DONAL FAHY	10 - 2	Mr S. Stronge
NOEL FEHILY	10 - 4	Mr C. D. Broad
ALISTAIR FINDLAY	10 - 0	Mr Paul Brierley
RHYS FLINT	10 - 10	Mr Dave Roberts
SEAN FOX	10 - 12	07787 434 759
HADDEN FROST	10 - 0	Mr Dave Roberts
CHRISTOPHER GEOGHEGAN	10 - 0	Mr G. J. Thomson
BARRY GERAGHTY	10 - 1	Mr Dave Roberts
ANDREW GLASSONBURY	10 - 2	Mr L. R. James
JAMIE GOLDSTEIN	8 - 1	Mr Mark Gilchrist
MARC GOLDSTEIN	9 - 9	Mr Dave Roberts
MARK GRANT	10 - 0	Mr C. D. Broad
RACHAEL GREEN	9 - 1	01308 868272
CHARLES GREENE	10 - 4	Mr C. D. Broad
BRIAN HARDING	10 - 0	Mr R. A. Hale
HARRY HAYNES	10 - 0	Mr R. A. Hale
LIAM HEARD	10 - 2	Mr C. D. Broad
BRIAN HUGHES	9 - 10	Mr R. A. Hale
WAYNE HUTCHINSON	10 - 0	Mr C. D. Broad
CHARLIE HUXLEY	9 - 12	Mr S. Stronge
DARYL JACOB	10 - 1	Mr C. D. Broad
KENNY JOHNSON	10 - 0	07774 131121
RICHARD JOHNSON	10 - 0	Mr Dave Roberts
SAM JONES	10 - 0	Mr S. Stronge
WAYNE KAVANAGH	9 - 7	Mr Dave Roberts
BARRY KENIRY	10 - 0	Mr Paul Brierley
WILL KENNEDY	10 - 0	Mr Dave Roberts
RICHARD KILLORAN	10 - 0	Mr Dave Roberts
JOHN KINGTON	9 - 11	Mr Dave Roberts
ADRIAN LANE	10 - 0	Mr G. J. Thomson
GRAHAM LEE	10 - 0	Mr R. A. Hale
JASON MAGUIRE	10 - 5	Mr C. D. Broad
RYAN MANIA	10 - 0	Mr J. B. Jeffrey
MICHAEL MCALISTER	10 - 0	Mr Paul Brierley
JIMMY MCCARTHY	10 - 0	Mr L. R. James
A. P. MCCOY	10 - 4	Mr Dave Roberts
RICHIE MCGRATH	10 - 0	Mr R. A. Hale
RICHIE MCLERNON	9 - 10	Mr S. Stronge
ALEX MERRIAM	10 - 0	Mr Dave Roberts
TOM MESSENGER	10 - 0	Mr L. R. James
PAUL MOLONEY	10 - 0	Mr Dave Roberts
JAMIE MOORE	10 - 0	Mr Robert Stronge
TIMMY MURPHY	10 - 0	Mr C. D. Broad
TOM O'BRIEN	10 - 0	Mr Dave Roberts
TOM O'CONNOR	10 - 0	Mr S. Stronge
STEPHEN O'DONOVAN	10 - 7	Mr S. Stronge
CONOR O'FARRELL	9 - 12	Mr S. Stronge\
ALAN O'KEEFFE	10 - 5	Mr Dave Roberts
DENIS O'REGAN	10 - 2	Mr S. Stronge
HENRY OLIVER	10 - 0	0770 106 8759
TOMMY PHELAN	9 - 13	Mr Dave Roberts
ADAM POGSON	10 - 9	07977016155
CHARLIE POSTE	10 - 0	Mr Dave Roberts
MARK QUINLAN	9 - 8	Mr L. R. James
SEAN QUINLAN	10 - 0	Mr C. D. Broad\
		Mr Mark Gilchrist
WILSON RENWICK	10 - 0	Mr G. J. Thomson\
		Mr R. A. Hale
JAMES REVELEY	10 - 4	Mr R. A. Hale
NICK SCHOLFIELD	10 - 0	Mr Dave Roberts
TOM SCUDAMORE	10 - 0	Mr Dave Roberts
TOM SIDDALL	10 - 0	Mr Dave Roberts
HARRY SKELTON	10 - 0	Mr Dave Roberts
J. W. STEVENSON	9 - 7	07933 440810
SAM THOMAS	10 - 9	Mr S. Stronge
ANDREW THORNTON	10 - 4	Mr Dave Roberts
ROBERT THORNTON	10 - 0	Mr Dave Roberts
ANDREW TINKLER	10 - 0	Mr Dave Roberts
JOE TIZZARD	10 - 4	Mr S. Stronge
LIAM TREADWELL	10 - 0	Mr Dave Roberts
GERARD TUMELTY	10 - 0	Mr L. R. James
SAM TWISTON-DAVIES	9 - 10	Mr C. D. Broad
CHARLIE WALLIS	9 - 9	Mr Dave Roberts
RUBY WALSH	10 - 1	Ms J Walsh
EWAN WHILLANS	9 - 11	Mr Paul Brierley
CHRISTIAN WILLIAMS	10 - 0	Mr Dave Roberts

CONDITIONALS

Their employer and contact details

An index of agents appears on page 682

NATHAN ADAMS (Laura Mongan)	9 - 10	Mr S. Stronge
JOSEPH AKEHURST (John Ferguson)	10 - 0	Mr S. Stronge
LUCY ALEXANDER (N. W. Alexander)	9 - 0	Mr R. A. Hale
TOM BELLAMY (David Pipe)	10 - 0	Mr Dave Roberts
DANIEL BENSON (Jonjo O'Neill)	9 - 7	c/o 01386 584209
JAMES BEST (Philip Hobbs)	10 - 0	Mr Dave Roberts
JONATHON BEWLEY (George Bewley)	9 - 12	Miss E. J. Butterworth
PAUL BOHAN (Steve Gollings)	9 - 12	Mrs Jayne M. Gollings
PADDY BRADLEY (Pat Phelan)	8 - 12	c/o 07917 762781
SCOTT BROCKBANK (Philip Kirby)	9 - 4	Mr Paul Brierley
HENRY BROOKE (Donald McCain)	9 - 7	Mr R. A. Hale
MICHAEL BYRNE (Tim Vaughan)	10 - 0	Mr S. Stronge
SHANE BYRNE (Sue Smith)	10 - 7	Mr J. B. Jeffrey
TOM CANNON (Chris Gordon)	10 - 0	Mr Dave Roberts
PETER CARBERRY (Nicky Henderson)	9 - 8	Mr Dave Roberts
HARRY CHALLONER (Venetia Williams)	9 - 5	Mr R. A. Hale
RYAN D. CLARK (Simon West)	9 - 6	Mr A. D. Lewis
GRANT COCKBURN (Lucinda Russell)	9 - 10	Mr Paul Brierley
JOE COLLIVER (Micky Hammond)	9 - 10	Mr R. A. Hale
ED COOKSON (Kim Bailey)	9 - 11	Mr C. D. Broad
JAMES CORBETT (William Amos)	9 - 4	c/o 07810 738149
PATRICK CORBETT (Rebecca Curtis)	9 - 4	Mr Dave Roberts
JOE CORNWALL (John Cornwall)	9 - 7	c/o 07939 557091
JAMES COWLEY (Paul Nicholls)	9 - 7	Mr S. Stronge\Mr Dave Roberts
JOHN DAWSON (John Wade)	10 - 0	Mr Paul Brierley
HARRY DERHAM (Paul Nicholls)	9 - 7	Mr S. Stronge
GARY DERWIN (Nicky Henderson)	9 - 4	Mr Dave Roberts
DONAL DEVEREUX (Peter Bowen)	9 - 11	Mr Dave Roberts
SHAUN DOBBIN (Rose Dobbin)	9 - 12	c/o 01668 215395
SAMANTHA DRAKE (Joanne Foster)	9 - 4	Mr J. B. Jeffrey
KIERON EDGAR (David Pipe)	9 - 7	Mr Dave Roberts
JONATHAN ENGLAND (Sue Smith)	9 - 7	Mr J. B. Jeffrey
RICHARD EVANS (David Evans)	9 - 7	c/o 01873 890837
THOMAS FLINT (John Flint)	10 - 0	Mr Mark Gilchrist
ANTHONY FOX (David Pipe)	10 - 2	c/o 01884 840715
STEVEN FOX (Lucinda Russell)	10 - 3	Mr Paul Brierley\Mr R. A. Hale
ANTHONY FREEMAN (Fergal O'Brien)	9 - 7	Mr C. D. Broad
CRAIG GALLAGHER (Ben Haslam)	9 - 6	Mr Paul Brierley
GERARD GALLIGAN (Michael Chapman)	9 - 0	Mr L. R. James
OLLIE GARNER (Graeme McPherson)	9 - 7	Mr L. R. James
THOMAS GARNER (Oliver Sherwood)	9 - 2	Mr Dave Roberts
GEMMA GRACEY-DAVISON (Zoe Davison)	9 - 5	c/o 07812 007554
JAKE GREENALL (Henry Daly)	9 - 12	Mr Dave Roberts
MATT GRIFFITHS (Jeremy Scott)	10 - 0	Mr Dave Roberts
ANDRIAS GUERIN (Neil Mulholland)	9 - 4	c/o 07739 258607
JOSH HAMER (Tony Carroll)	9 - 11	Mr C. D. Broad
PETER HATTON (Alan King)	9 - 7	c/o 01793 815009
GILES HAWKINS (Bob Buckler)	10 - 0	Mr Dave Roberts
FRANCIS HAYES (David Pipe)	9 - 2	Mr L. R. James
ALICE HAYNES (David Simcock)	8 - 5	Mr L. R. James
JAKE HODSON (David Bridgwater)	9 - 10	Mr Dave Roberts
JAMES HUXHAM (Jonjo O'Neill)	9 - 7	Mr S. Stronge
DALE IRVING (James Ewart)	9 - 6	c/o 01387 370707
KYLE JAMES (Brian Ellison)	9 - 10	Mr L. R. James
JAMES JEAVONS (Richard Lee)	9 - 7	c/o 07836 537145
JACK JORDAN (Malcolm Jefferson)	10 - 4	c/o 07710 502044
TONY KELLY (Ferdy Murphy)	10 - 0	Mr R. A. Hale
ARRON KENNEDY (Robin Dickin)	10 - 0	c/o 07979 518593

JASON KIELY (Tim Vaughan)	9 - 5	c/o 01446 771626
GARRY LAVERY (Brian Ellison)	9 - 5	Mr L. R. James
EDMOND LINEHAN (Nicky Henderson)	9 - 6	Mr Dave Roberts
MAURICE LINEHAN (Jonjo O'Neill)	9 - 9	c/o 01386 584209
RYAN MAHON (Paul Nicholls)	9 - 13	Mr Dave Roberts
MARK MARRIS (Anthony Middleton)	9 - 12	Mr L. R. James
ROBERT MCCARTH (Ian Williams)	9 - 7	Mr C. D. Broad
DYLAN MCDONAGH (Ferdy Murphy)	9 - 4	c/o 01969 622289
JEREMIAH MCGRATH (Nicky Henderson)	10 - 0	Mr Dave Roberts
CIARAN MCKEE (John O'Shea)	9 - 4	Mr S. Stronge
CHRIS MEEHAN (Neil Mulholland)	9 - 0	c/o 07739 258607
DONAGH MEYLER (Charlie Longsdon)	9 - 7	c/o 07775 993263
PAT MILLMAN (Rod Millman)	9 - 5	Mr Mark Gilchrist
TOM MOLLOY (Graeme McPherson)	10 - 0	Mr Dave Roberts
JONATHAN MOORE (Philip Hobbs)	9 - 1	c/o 01984 640366
JOSHUA MOORE (Gary Moore)	10 - 0	Mr Dave Roberts
KILLIAN MOORE (Graeme McPherson)	9 - 7	Mr Dave Roberts
NATHAN MOSCROP (John Weymes)	10 - 4	Mr Paul Brierley
STEPHEN MULQUEEN (Maurice Barnes)	9 - 7	Mr Paul Brierley
CRAIG NICHOL (Lucinda Russell)	9 - 6	Mr Paul Brierley
RYAN NICHOL (Donald Whillans)	9 - 12	c/o 07771 550556
ADAM NICOL (Philip Kirby)	9 - 7	Mr Paul Brierley
MICHEAL NOLAN (Philip Hobbs)	10 - 0	Mr Dave Roberts
PAUL O'BRIEN (Donald McCain)	9 - 12	c/o 01829 720352
PAUL N. O'BRIEN (Charlie Mann)	9 - 3	Mr C. D. Broad
DIARMUID O'REGAN (Chris Grant)	9 - 4	Mr S. Stronge\Mr R. A. Hale
LEE OSWIN (Gary Moore)	10 - 10	c/o 01403 891912
JOSEPH PALMOWSKI (George Moore)	9 - 4	Mr Paul Brierley
WILL PETTIS (Warren Greatrex)	9 - 8	c/o 07920 039114
IAN POPHAM (Martin Keighley)	9 - 11	Mr Dave Roberts
BEN POSTE (Tom Symonds)	9 - 7	Mr Dave Roberts
BRENDAN POWELL (Colin Tizzard)	8 - 4	Mr Dave Roberts
DEAN PRATT (John Quinn)	10 - 0	Mr R. A. Hale
PHILIP PRINCE (Ron Hodges)	7 - 11	Mr Mark Gilchrist
JACK QUINLAN (John Ferguson)	9 - 7	Mr Dave Roberts
GERALD QUINN (Tom George)	9 - 7	Mr C. D. Broad
CONOR QUISH (Emma Lavelle)	9 - 7	c/o 01264 735412
CONOR RING (Evan Williams)	9 - 5	c/o 07950 381227
GARY RUTHERFORD (Harriet Graham)	9 - 4	Mr J. B. Jeffrey
GAVIN SHEEHAN (Charlie Mann)	9 - 8	Mr C. D. Broad
MATTHEW STANLEY (Jamie Snowden)	9 - 6	Mr Dave Roberts
BRIAN TOOMEY (Kevin Ryan)	9 - 7	Mr Dave Roberts
BRIAN TREANOR (Nicky Richards)	9 - 0	Mr R. A. Hale
GEMMA TUTTY (Tim Walford)	7 - 12	M. Furnass
WILLIAM TWISTON-DAVIES (Nigel Twiston-Davies)	9 - 0	Mr C. D. Broad\Mr Tony Hind
ALEXANDER VOY (Chris Grant)	9 - 11	Mr Paul Brierley
JOSH WALL (Trevor Wall)	9 - 10	Mr L. R. James
CHRISTOPHER WARD (Dr Richard Newland)	9 - 7	Mr Dave Roberts
GRAHAM WATTERS (Lucinda Russell)	9 - 7	Mr R. A. Hale
ADAM WEDGE (Evan Williams)	9 - 11	Mr Dave Roberts
SAMUEL WELTON (David Pipe)	9 - 4	c/o 01884 840715
TREVOR WHELAN (Neil King)	9 - 7	Mr Dave Roberts
CALLUM WHILLANS (Donald McCain)	9 - 7	Mr R. A. Hale
ROBERT WILLIAMS (Bernard Llewellyn)	8 - 13	Mr C. D. Broad
JOHN WINSTON (Ferdy Murphy)	10 - 0	Mr Paul Brierley\Mr J. B. Jeffrey
ROSS WISHART (Mick Channon)	9 - 0	c/o 01635 281166
KIELAN WOODS (Charlie Longsdon)	9 - 9	Mr C. D. Broad

AMATEUR RIDERS

Riding weights and contact details

An index of agents appears on page 682

GOSCHEN, A. 10 - 7 .... 07719 611 301
GOSS, J. R. 10 - 0 .... 07747 514321
GRAY, R. 8 - 6 .... 07919 622519
GREENALL, O. C. 10 - 7 .... 07771 571 000
GREENWAY, T. E. 9 - 7 .... 07747 113864
GREENWOOD, T. O. M. 9 - 7 .... Mr Paul Brierley
GUERRIERO, J. T. 11 - 7 07778541714
GUEST, A. L. 9 - 7 .... 07713 132577
HALL, P. G. 11 - 7 .... 01892 553160
HALLEY, N. 10 - 0 .... 07905 077506
HAMILTON, J. 8 - 7 .... 0766 591640
HAMPSON, B. 8 - 7 .... 07825 585218
HAMPTON, M. L. 10 - 3 .... 07515 269391
HANSON, S. P. 9 - 4 .... 07817 275107
HARBOUR, E. 10 - 0 .... 07814 646 230
HARDING, J. 9 - 2 .... 07858 783909
HARPER, F. 9 - 2 .... Mr John W. Ford
HART, C. V. 9 - 10 .... 07871 812251
HATCH, R. 10 - 0 .... Mr C. D. Broad
HAWKER, R. 10 - 0 .... 07891 960365
HAYDON, C. M. E. 10 - 7 .... 07775 517 129
HAYES, N. M. 8 - 9 .... 07794 761353
HEARD, M. R. 8 - 12 .... 077209 72159
HENDERSON, G. 9 - 13 .... 077659 67086
HENDERSON, R. G. 9 - 4 .... Mr C. D. Broad
HEPTONSTALL, R. 9 - 0 .... 07725 185506
HERMANSSON, P. I. 9 - 2 .... 07706 458450
HESKETH, A. 8 - 6 .... 077914 37969
HICKMAN, W. H. W. 10 - 7 07851828530
HILL, J. P. 11 - 5 .... 07584 373313
HOBBS, K. 9 - 0 .... 07513 904617
HOBSON, C. R. W. 9 - 2 .... 07966 734889
HODGES, R. J. 10 - 5 .... 01885 483951
HOGG, R. C. 10 - 0 .... 07548 934272
HOGG, W. S. 10 - 0 .... 01969 622237
HOLMES, D. T. R. 11 - 7 01912847093
HOOPER, J. 9 - 7 .... 07850 278491
HOWE, B. 10 - 1 .... 01904 479295
HUTCHINSON, A. L. 9 - 3 .... 079606 30204
INGRAM, R. B. 7 - 0 .... 07429 449128
INSOLE, J. J. 10 - 0 .... 07891 775449
JAMES, A. M. 9 - 5 .... 07932 479035
JARRETT, R. N. 10 - 10 .... 07527 034069
JENKINSON, J. 10 - 3 .... 01488 73436
JENNINGS, L. 9 - 6 .... 07817 303835
JOHN, P. 9 - 10 .... 07825 868211
JOHNS, A. V. 10 - 0 .... 07919 440910
JOHNSON, M. 11 - 0 .... 07788 138634
JOHNSON, M. S. 9 - 7 .... 07816 60934
JONES, A. 9 - 5 .... 07950 456397
JONES, C. H. 8 - 7 .... 07887 534753
JONES, D. J. 8 - 7 .... 07815 753373
JONES, E. J. 9 - 3 .... 07775 846925
JONES, K. 9 - 12 .... Mr Robert Stronge
JONES, L. 9 - 7 .... 07973 689040
KEADY, M. 9 - 7 .... 01223 701216
KEEGAN, M. 7 - 10 .... 07791 317483
KELLY, E. 10 - 12 .... 07724 839047
KENDRICK, M. L. J. P. 9 - 0 .... 07798 724268
KERR, M. 9 - 0
KERSWELL, S. L. 9 - 7 .... 07799 235 969
KILGARRIFF, L. 9 - 0 .... 07851 396460
KING, A. M. 9 - 0 .... 07710 406834
KING, R. 8 - 5 .... 07845 700971
KINSEY, W. R. 10 - 10 .... 07803 753719
LAMBERT, J. 9 - 3 .... 07581 514852
LEGG, J. 10 - 0 .... 07825 586282
LEGG, M. D. 9 - 7 .... 07590 690898

LENGE, D. 8 - 10 .... 07902 664443
LEVEY, D. 10 - 0 .... Mr Paul Brierley
LEWIS, H. M. 9 - 3 .... 01451 850182
LEWIS, S. 9 - 3 .... 07790 270392
LEYSHON, R. 8 - 10 .... 07977 545239
LILLY, Z. 9 - 2 0148873311
LINDSAY, R. W. 10 - 4 .... Mr J. B. Jeffrey
LORDAN, D. 9 - 10
LYONS, K. 10 - 0 .... 077601 24147
LYTTLE, J. 10 - 5 07774060675
MABON, K. 8 - 11 .... 07565 331808
MACMAHON, E. E. 9 - 5 .... 07747 857950
MAHOT, J. H. M. 10 - 12 .... 07947 299769
MANN, P. R. 11 - 7 .... 07929 535608
MANSELL, D. 10 - 8 .... 07912 974653
MARGARSON, K. L. 9 - 0 .... Mr Paul Brierley
MARTIN, C. J. 9 - 2 .... Mr L. R. James
MARTIN, J. I. 10 - 3 .... 07807 139763
MASON, J. L. 8 - 10 .... 07816 453613
MASON, P. W. 11 - 0 .... 07921 707292
MASTERSON, L. C. 8 - 7 .... 07747 033969
MCCAFFREY, N. A. 8 - 3 .... 07919 624024
MCCORMACK, C. 10 - 2 .... Mr Paul Brierley
MCCORMICK, A. K. 8 - 4 .... 07703 043516
MCGREGOR, A. L. 9 - 7 .... 0759 6684318
MCINTYRE, M. J. 9 - 10 .... 07557 360664
MCLAUGHLIN, D. S. 9 - 0
MCLERNON, J. 9 - 2 .... 07875 532791
MEEK, N. 9 - 4 .... 0787 6505442
METCALFE, L. J. 9 - 2 .... 07414 676756
MICHAEL, A. H. L. 11 - 5 .... 01980 842537
MILLS, A. 8 - 10 .... 07792 504534
MITCHELL, F. 9 - 7 Mr Philip Mitchell\Mr Dave Roberts
MOORE, H. J. 9 - 0 .... 07736 149669
MUGGERIDGE, J. 9 - 4 .... 07561 430118
MULLINEAUX, M. 8 - 7 .... 01829 261440
MULRENNAN, A. C. 8 - 0 .... 07929 349048
MURPHY, A. L. 9 - 7 .... 07711 992500
MURPHY, O. J. 10 - 12 .... 07774 233222
MURPHY, R. J. 10 - 5 .... 077477 15521
MUSPRATT, L. 10 - 0 .... 07585 779121
NEWMAN, J. 10 - 0 07920464705
NIXON, J. 10 - 7 .... 07837 467167
O'KEEFFE, D. P. 9 - 10 .... Mr L. R. James
O'KEEFFE, S. 9 - 4 .... 079441 65177
ORPWOOD, N. 11 - 0 .... 07831 836626
OWEN, J. P. 11 - 0 .... 07880 700 559
PAINTING, S. W. 10 - 0 .... 07919 454844
PARK, J. 10 - 0 .... 07733 840203
PARKER, N. L. 9 - 7 .... 07846 532143
PEACOCK, S. 9 - 2 .... 07775 791153
PEARCE, J. 9 - 5 .... Mr A. D. Lewis
PILKINGTON, J. N. 10 - 7 .... 07445 876009
PIMLOTT, O. 10 - 0 07969216409
PONTING, J. A. 10 - 2 .... 07545 230356
POOLES, R. L. 10 - 4 .... 0766 244716
POTTER, R. D. 10 - 10 .... 07921 761114
POTTER, W. E. 10 - 2 .... 07872 933534
POWELL, J. M. 8 - 0 .... 07785 113422
PRICE, M. R. 10 - 5 .... 07765 490190
PRICHARD, C. 8 - 7 .... 07928 670424
PRICHARD, D. G. 9 - 4 .... Mr Dave Roberts
RANDELL, S. 9 - 0 .... 07868 728440
RAWLINSON, A. A. 9 - 0 .... 07769 220720
REDDINGTON, J. J. 11 - 2 07766767464
RICHARDS, J. R. 9 - 0 .... Mr G. J. Thomson
RICHARDSON, J. A. 10 - 7 .... 07979 991840
RIDLEY, J. M. 10 - 0 .... 0755 7879646

ROBERTS, M. 9 - 7 .... 01305 782218
ROBINSON, S. C. 12 - 0 .... 01424 204190
ROBINSON, S. J. 11 - 3 .... 07850 640067
ROGERS, J. D. 11 - 2 .... 07977 904350
RUSSELL, W. 10 - 0 .... 01273 274 733
SANDERS, S. 9 - 7 .... 07581 250361
SAUNDERS, L. 9 - 0 .... 07931 711532
SAVAGE, J. A. 9 - 8 .... 07818 555214
SAYER, E. C. 9 - 0 .... 07968 320118
SAYER, N. 10 - 0 .... 07870 192027
SCOTT, C. M. 9 - 3 .... 01638 722100
SESTON, M. 10 - 7 .... 07738 359364
SHAW, S. 8 - 8 .... 07742 446168
SHEA, P. C. 9 - 4 .... 07847 948315
SHERWOOD, J. E. 9 - 7 .... Mr Dave Roberts
SHOEMARK, C. P. 9 - 10 .... 077921 25674
SIBBICK, E. 9 - 5 07964541373
SLATTER, N. I. 9 - 7 .... Mr R. A. Hale
SMITH, C. 10 - 4 .... 07702 034401
SMITH, D. J. 10 - 1 .... 07718 275288
SMITH, D. R. 9 - 7 .... 07826 392286
SMITH, G. R. 10 - 0 .... 07748 064384
SMITH, J. 9 - 10 .... Mr A. D. Lewis
SMITH, M. J. J. 10 - 4 .... 01789 772808
SMITH, M. K. 10 - 5 .... 01638 603005
SMITH, R. 9 - 0 .... 07716 919975
SOLE, J. D. 10 - 3 .... 07968 947091
SPARKES, R. M. 9 - 0 07967643373
SPEKE, T. 10 - 2 .... 07870 813256
SPINKOVA, V. 8 - 12 .... 07707 546019
STEAD, E. 9 - 0 .... 07796 680583
STEARN, R. R. P. 11 - 2 .... 07879 412414
STIRLING, A. E. 10 - 7 .... 07557 952057
SUTCLIFFE, L. 9 - 0 .... 07793 084446
SUTTON, N. R. A. 11 - 6 .... 01189 538610
SWAN, G. 9 - 12 .... 07966 801736
SYDDALL, T. M. 8 - 10 .... 07854 309600
TAYLOR, A. 8 - 2 .... 01638 664700
TETT, F. 9 - 7 .... 077863 14587
TICKLE, L. 9 - 12 .... 07769 183447

TRAINOR, M. 10 - 0 .... 07554 992851
TURNER, L. M. 9 - 4 .... 07984 531836
TUTTY, P. L. 9 - 0 .... 07815 798222
TWEMLOW, C. 10 - 4 07752487203
VORSTER, N. 8 - 0 .... 07915 613852
WADE, V. L. 9 - 10 .... 07772 925721
WAGGOTT, J. J. 9 - 12 .... 07789 465482
WAKEFIELD, N. 12 - 0 .... 07973 768039
WALEY-COHEN, S. B. 10 - 3 .... 07887 848425
WALKER, J. 9 - 0 .... 07969 893918
WALKER, S. A. 9 - 7 .... 07778 061662
WALL, M. J. 10 - 10 .... 07990 995053
WALTON, C. M. 9 - 5 .... Mr Paul Brierley
WALTON, J. 9 - 5 .... 07955 260235
WARD, T. D. 9 - 2 .... 07799 4364078
WATSON, H. 9 - 0 .... 07974 442856
WAUGH, A. 8 - 7 .... 07761 040963
WEST, C. 11 - 0 .... 07826 236919
WESTON, T. H. 10 - 7 .... 07752 313698
WHEELER, G. F. 11 - 7 .... 07778 157245
WHITEHEAD, C. L. 9 - 0 .... 07787 391401
WILKINSON, D. S. 8 - 0 .... 01969 640223
WILLEY, J. P. 9 - 5 .... 01909 475962
WILLIAMS, J. C. 9 - 2 .... 07841 576651
WILLIAMS, L. 8 - 4 .... 07871 448437
WILLIAMS, N. R. P. 11 - 4 .... 01308 868272
WILLIAMS, S. R. 11 - 0 .... 07590 208675
WILLIAMSON, C. L. 9 - 10 .... Mr Robert Stronge
WILLS, C. L. 10 - 2 .... 07791 846383
WILSON, L. J. 8 - 10 .... 07747 615037
WILSON, R. 9 - 10 .... Mr J. B. Jeffrey
WILSON, R. E. 8 - 10 .... 07770 732007
WOOD, K. 9 - 10 .... 07429 0780666
WOOD, V. L. 8 - 2 .... 07985 709609
WOODWARD, M. J. 10 - 6 .... 07724 627766
WRIGLEY, E. G. T. 10 - 0 .... 07870 699659
YORK, P. 10 - 7 .... 07774 962168
YOUNG, E. 9 - 10 .... 07732 380913
ZETTERHOLM, A. 9 - 0 .... 07787 936150

Are your contact details missing or incorrect?
If so please update us by email:
richard.lowther@racingpost.co.uk
or leave a message on 0500 007071

NOTES

NOTES

NOTES

NOTES

NOTES

NOTES